ISBN 978-0-428-64586-1
PIBN 11288578

FB &c Ltd, Dalton House, 60 Windsor Avenue, London, SW19 2RR.
Company number 08720141. Registered in England and Wales.

For support please visit www.forgottenbooks.com

THE LAWYERS REPORTS ANNOTATED

BOOK VIII.

ALL CURRENT CASES OF GENERAL VALUE AND IMPORTANCE WITH FULL ANNOTATION

ROBERT DESTY, EDITOR

BURDETT A. RICH, HENRY P. FARNHAM, ASSISTANTS.

1890.

EXTRA ANNOTATED EDITION

WITH L. R. A. CASES AS AUTHORITIES.

ROCHESTER, N. Y.

THE LAWYERS' CO-OPERATIVE PUBLISHING COMPANY.

1905.

E. R. Andrews Printing Company, Rochester, N. Y.

SUPPLEMENTAL TABLE

OF ALL

CASES REPORTED IN LAWYERS' REPORTS, ANNOTATED,

BOOK 8,

NOT OFFICIALLY REPORTED WHEN THIS BOOK WENT TO PRESS.

(To be "tipped in" in front of regular table, used as a book mark or as data for marking each case. Like tables will be furnished for subsequent volumes as fast as possible.)

TABLE

OF

CASES REPORTED

IN

LAWYERS' REPORTS, ANNOTATED, BOOK VIII.

S.

T.

CITATIONS

IN OPINIONS OF THE JUDGES CONTAINED IN THIS BOOK.

A.

B.

Brooklyn v. Brooklyn City R. Co., 47 N. Y. 475 — 592
Brooklyn City & N. R. Co. v. New York Nat. Bank of the Republic, 102 U. S. 14 (26 L. ed. 61) — 165, 166
Brooklyn Park Comrs. v. Armstrong, 45 N. Y. 234 — 502
Brooks v. Burlington & S. W. R. Co., 101 U. S. 443 (25 L. ed. 1057) — 708
v. Duffell, 28 Ga. 441 — 825
Brookville & M. Hydraulic Co. v. Butler, 91 Ind. 136 — 608
Broome v. New York & N. J. Teleph. Co., 5 Cent. Rep. 814, 42 N J. Eq. 141 — 433
Brown v. Brown, 103 N. C. 213 — 260
v. Byers, 16 Mees. & W. 252 — 679
v. Catlettsburg, 11 Bush, 435 — 466
v. Hamilton First Nat. Bank, 3 West. Rep. 601, 44 Ohio St. 269 — 615
v. Howard, 2 Brod. & B. 73 — 818
v. Metropolitan L. Ins. Co., 8 Cent. Rep. 775, 65 Mich. 306 — 780
v. People's Mut. Ins. Co., 11 Cush. 280 — 835
v. Vandergrift, 80 Pa. 142 — 763
v. Ware, 25 Me. 411 — 449
Brown Chemical Co. v. Myer, 31 Fed. Rep. 453 — 644
Browning v. Harris, 99 Ill. 456 — 817
Brua's App., 55 Pa. 294 — 276
Bruff v. Mali, 36 N. Y. 200, 205 — 750
Buckhannon v. Com., 86 Ky. 110 — 86
Buffalo & N. Y. C. R. Co. v. Dudley, 14 N. Y. 352 — 251
Buffett v. Troy & B. R. Co., 40 N. Y. 168 — 227
Bukup v. Valentine, 19 Wend. 554 — 693
Bulkley v. Marks, 15 Abb. Pr. 454 — 716
Bull v. Conroe, 13 Wis. 234 — 813
Bullard v. Bell, 1 Mason, 299 — 191
v. Briggs, 7 Pick. 533 — 445
Buncombe County v. Tommey, 115 U. S. 122 (29 L. ed. 305) — 705
Bunge v. Koop, 48 N. Y. 225 — 259
Burbank v. Pillsbury, 48 N. H. 475 — 606
Burbank's Will, *Re*, 69 Iowa, 378 — 697
Burke v. Child, 88 U. S. 21 Wall. 441 (22 L. ed. 623) — 506
Burke v. Savage, 13 Allen, 408 — 449
v. Smith, 8 L. R. A. 184, *note*, 69 Mich. 380 — 184
Burkham v. Lawrenceburg (Ind.) not yet reported — 608
Burlington v. Leebrick, 43 Iowa, 252 — 109
Burlington & M. R. R. Co. v. Thompson, 31 Kan. 180, 194 — 388, 390, 391, 392, 414
Burlington Ins. Co. v. Gibbons (Kan.) 22 Pac. Rep. 1010 — 76
Burnham v. Chicago, 24 Ill. 499 — 805
v. Webster, 1 Woodb. & M. 172 — 269
Burns v. Lynde, 6 Allen, 305 — 445
Burrall v. Rice, 5 Gray, 539 — 646
Burrell v. Letson, 1 Strobh. L. 239 — 731
Burton v. Great Northern R. Co., 9 Exch. 507 — 411
v. Stratton, 12 Fed. Rep. 696 — 573
Burwell v. Jackson, 9 N. Y. 535 — 592
Bush v. Com., 80 Ky. 244 — 841
v. Lathrop, 22 N. Y. 535 — 62
v. Sherman, 80 Ill. 160 — 725
Butchers Ben. Asso., 35 Pa. 151, 38 Pa. 298 — 201
Butler v. Butler, 21 Kan. 521 — 818
v. Butler, 4 Litt. (Ky.) 202 — 564, 565
v. Gettysburg & H. R. Co., 126 Pa. 160 — 597
v. Lee, 11 Ala. 885 — 665
v. State, 97 Ind. 378 — 38, 39
v. Taylor, 5 Gray, 455 — 555
v. United States, 88 U. S. 21 Wall. 274 (22 L. ed. 615) — 788
Butman v. Fowler, 17 Ohio, 101 — 57
Butt v. Imperial Gas Co., L. R. 2 Ch. 158 — 187
Buttrick v. Allen, 8 Mass. 273 — 209
Butts v. Wood, 37 N. Y. 317 — 256
Buzick v. Buzick, 44 Iowa, 259 — 445
Byles v. Collier, 54 Mich. 1, 5 — 160
Byne v. Byne, 1 Rich. L. 438 — 731
Byrne v. Sisters of Charity of St. Elizabeth, 45 N. J. L. 213 — 209
Byron v. Emes, 12 Mod. 106, 2 Salk. 694 — 422

C.

Cagwin v. Hancock, 84 N. Y. 542 — 251
Cain v. Davie County, 86 N. C. 8 — 874
Cairo & F. R. Co. v. Hecht, 95 U. S. 168 (24 L. ed. 423) — 868
Calahan v. Babcock, 21 Ohio St. 281, 8 Am. Rep. 63, 65 — 169
Calais v. Dyer, 7 Me. 155 — 833
Calder v. Bull, 3 U. S. 3 Dall. 387, 388 (1 L. ed. 648, 649) — 813
Callaway v. Johnson, 51 Mo. 33 — 443
Calloway v. Laydon, 47 Iowa, 456 — 423
Calye's Case, 8 Coke, 32, 1 Smith, Lead. Cas. *197, *note* — 100, 101
Camberford v. Hall, 3 McCord, L. 345 — 730
Cameron v. Little, 62 Me. 550 — 569
Campau v. Konan, 39 Mich. 362, 365 — 475
v. North, 39 Mich. 606 — 781
Campbell v. Beaumont, 91 N. Y. 465 — 697
v. Bridwell, 5 Or. 312 — 142
Campion v. Kille, 14 N. J. Eq. 229 — 172
Canandaigua Academy v. McKechnie, 90 N. Y. 618 — 622
Canedy v. Jones, 19 S. C. 297 — 697
Cannon, *Re*, 47 Mich. 481 — 399
Capron v. Strout, 11 Nev. 304 — 412, 850
Caraker v. Mathews, 25 Ga. 571 — 851
Carey v. Smith, 11 Ga. 539 — 513
Carle v. Bangor & P. C. & R. Co., 43 Me. 269 — 541
Carlos v. Fancourt, 5 T. R. 485 — 395
Carothers v. Philadelphia Co., 11 Cent. Rep. 48, 118 Pa. 468 — 603
Carpenter v. Soule, 88 N. Y. 251-256 — 259
v. Wall, 4 Dev. & B. L. 144 — 381, 382
Carr v. Lowry, 27 Pa. 257 — 606
Carroll Bank v. Taylor, 67 Iowa, 572 — 396, 397
Carson v. Ury (U. S. C. C. Mo.) 5 L. R. A. 614 — 644
Carson & R. L. Co. v. Holtzclaw, 39 Fed. Rep. 885 — 367
Carter v. Howe Mach. Co., 51 Md. 298 — 847
Carton v. Illinois C. R. Co., 59 Iowa, 148 — 550
Carver v. Coffman, 8 West. Rep. 396, 109 Ind. 547 — 291
v. Peck, 131 Mass. 291 — 309, 310, 313
Castle v. State, 75 Ind. 146 — 38
Castro v. Bailey (Cal.) not reported — 577
Caulkins v. Hellman, 47 N. Y. 452 — 247
Cavalli v. Allen, 57 N. Y. 517 — 214
Cayuga County Nat. Bank v. Purdy, 56 Mich. 6 — 396, 397
Celluloid Mfg. Co. v. Cellonite Mfg. Co., 32 Fed. Rep. 94, 97 — 821
Central Land Co. v. Laidley, 32 W. Va. 134 — 705
Central M. T. R. Co. v. Rockafellow, 17 Ill. 541 — 840
Central Nat. Bank v. Connecticut Mut. L. Ins. Co., 104 U. S. 54 (26 L. ed. 693) — 793
Central Ohio Salt Co. v. Guthrie, 35 Ohio St. 666 — 504, 505
Central R. Co. v. Collins, 40 Ga. 582 — 503, 505, 508
Central R. Co. v. Hearne, 32 Tex. 547 — 327
Chaddock v. Briggs, 13 Mass. 248 — 527
Chadwick v. Covell, 6 L. R. A. 839, 151 Mass. — — 643
Chaffee v. New York Fourth Nat. Bank, 71 Me. 514, 36 Am. Rep. 345 — 64
v. United States, 85 U. S. 18 Wall. 516 (21 L. ed. 908) — 191
Chamberlain v. Sibley, 4 Minn. 312 (Gil. 228) — 189
v. West End & C. P. R. Co., 31 L. J. N. S. Q. B. 201 — 788
Chambers v. Atlas Ins. Co., 51 Conn. 17 — 771
v. Davidson, L. R. 1 P. C. 305, 4 Moore, P. C. N. S. 158 — 157
v. McKee, 1 Hill, L. (S. C.) 229 — 730
v. Satterlee, 40 Cal. 497 — 374
Champion v. Bostwick, 18 Wend. 185 — 661
Champlin v. Champlin, 6 New Eng. Rep. 707, 16 R. I. — — 813
Chandler v. Fulton, 10 Tex. 2, 60 Am. Dec. 188, 199 — 151, 156
v. Hollingsworth, 3 Del. Ch. 99 — 817
v. St. Paul F. & M. Ins. Co., 21 Minn. 85, 50, 771
Chapman v. Banker & T. Pub. Co., 128 Mass. 478 — 309
v. Kimball, 9 Conn. 38 — 560
v. Pickersgill, 2 Wils. 145 — 422
v. Searle, 3 Pick. 38 — 159, 160
Chappel v. Brockway, 21 Wend. 157, 159 — 404, 505
Charles River Bridge v. Warren Bridge, 36 U. S. 11 Pet. 420 (9 L. ed. 773) — 548, 863
Charleston City Council v. Wentworth St. Baptist Church, 4 Strobh. L. 310 — 857
Chase v. Cheney, 58 Ill. 509 — 841
v. Kittredge, 11 Allen, 49, 61 — 825
v. Palmer, 25 Me. 341, 346 — 569
v. Sutton Mfg. Co., 4 Cush. 152 — 434
v. Williams, 74 Mo. 429 — 555
Chasemore v. Richards, 7 H. L. Cas. 387, 338 — 186
Chatfield v. Wilson, 28 Vt. 49 — 186
Chedel v. Mallard, 13 R. I. 451 — 555
Chenot v. Lefevre, 8 Ill. 637 — 236
Chesley v. King, 74 Me. 164 — 186
Chester County v. Malany, 64 Pa. 144 — 464
Chevallier v. Straham, 2 Tex. 122 — 325
Chicago v. Bartee, 100 Ill. 61 — 829
v. Hesing, 83 Ill. 204 — 495
v. Larned, 34 Ill. 203 — 374
v. Starr, 42 Ill. 174 — 495, 496

Chicago & A. R. Co. v. Becker, 76 Ill. 25, 84 Ill. 483 .... 495, 496
v. Gregory, 58 Ill. 226 496
v. Murray, 62 Ill. 326 496
v. Ragland, 84 Ill. 375 823
Chicago & E. I. R. Co. v. Hedges, 118 Ind. 5 598
Chicago & E. R. Co. v. Flexman, 103 Ill. 546 227
Chicago & N. W. R. Co. v. Montfort, 60 Ill. 175 509
Chicago Gas-Light & Coke Co. v. People's Gas-Light & Coke Co., 11 West. Rep. 63, 121 Ill. 530 .... 502, 505, 506
Chicago Lumber Co. v. Ashworth, 26 Kan. 212 616
Chicago M. Nat. Bank v. Chicago R. Equip. Co. 25 Fed. Rep. 809 397
Chicago Nat. Bank v. Armstrong, 25 Minn. 530 397
Chicago, P. & S. W. R. Co. v. Marseilles, 84 Ill. 643 502
Chicago, R. I. & P. R. Co. v. Eninger, 114 Ill. 79 496
Child v. Boston, 4 Allen, 41 244
Chipman v. Morrill, 20 Cal. 136 427
Cholmondeley v. Clinton, 2 Jac. & W. 1, 190 483
Chouteau v. Burlando, 20 Mo. 482 166
Churton v. Douglas, Johns. Eng. Ch. 174 574
Cigar-Makers P. Union v. Conhaim, 3 L. R. A. 125, 40 Minn. 243 .... 642, 644
Cincinnati & L. R. Co. v. Smith, 22 Ohio St. 227. 141
Cincinnati, H. & I. R. Co. v. Butler, 1 West. Rep. 110, 103 Ind. 31 596-598
Cincinnati, I. St. L. & C. R. Co. v. Lang, 118 Ind. 579 637
Cincinnati, W. & M. R. Co. v. Hiltzhauer, 99 Ind. 486 596
Citizens Gas & Min. Co. v. Elwood, 14 West. Rep. 92, 114 Ind. 332 547
Citizens Loan Asso. v. Friedley (Ind.) 7 L. R. A. 669 231
Citizens S. & L. Asso. v. Topeka, 87 U. S. 20 Wall. 655 (22 L. ed. 455) 287
Citizens St. R. Co. v. Jones, 34 Fed. Rep. 579 .. 548, 549
City Nat. Bank v. National Park Bank, 32 Hun, 105 221
City Sav. Bank v. Hopson, 2 New Eng. Rep. 556, 53 Conn. 454 665
Clamageran v. Bucks, 4 Mart. N. S. 487 731
Clark v. Clark, 11 West. Rep. 396, 122 Ill. 388 418
v. Conway, 23 Mo. 438 610
v. Dasso, 34 Mich. 86 475
v. Edgar, 84 Mo. 106 750
v. Harlan, 1 Cin. Super. Ct. Rep. 418 423
v. Jones, 1 Denio, 516 763
v. New England Mut. F. Ins. Co., 6 Cush. 342 836
v. Nixon, 5 Hill, 36 622
Clarke v. Morgan, 38 L. T. N. S. 354 526
v. Postan, 6 Car. & P. 423 47
v. Watson, 18 C. B. N. S. 278, 285 .... 209, 210
Cleveland, C. & C. R. Co. v. Elliott, 4 Ohio St. 475 141
Cline v. State, 1 West. Rep. 81, 43 Ohio St. 332 36
Closson v. Staples, 42 Vt. 209 48
Clough v. Davis, 9 N. H. 500 665
Cluck v. State, 40 Ind. 263 87
Clussman v. Long Island R. Co., 9 Hun, 618, 73 N. Y. 606 227
Clute v. Fisher, 8 West. Rep. 121, 65 Mich. 48 581
Coates v. Campbell, 37 Minn. 498 287
v. Pennsylvania F. Ins. Co., 58 Md. 172 770
Coats v. Merrick Thread Co., 36 Fed. Rep. 324 321
Cobb v. Cowdery, 40 Vt. 25 710
v. Standish, 14 Me. 198 87
Coburn v. Ames, 52 Cal. 385 475
Cochran v. Bartle, 8 West. Rep. 707, 91 Mo. 636 612
v. Ripey, 13 Bush, 495 .... 153, 154
Cocke v. McGinnis, Mart. & Y. 361 481
v. Mobile Branch Bank, 3 Ala. 175 679
Coddington v. Bay, 20 Johns. 637 166
Coe v. Columbus, P. & I. R. Co., 10 Ohio St. 372 861
v. Hobby, 7 Hun, 157, 72 N. Y. 141 258
Coffin v. Adams, 131 Mass. 133 818
Coffman v. Wilson, 2 Met. (Ky.) 542 429
Coggs v. Bernard, 1 Smith, Lead. Cas. *307, *notes* 100
Cohn v. Virginia F. & M. Ins. Co., 3 Hughes, 272 808
v. Wausau Boom Co., 47 Wis. 314 813
Cole v. Cunningham, 133 U. S. 107, 115 (33 L. ed. 539, 54?) 646
v. Hall, 103 Ill. 30 839
v. La Grange, 113 U. S. 1 (28 L. ed. 896) 287
Coleman v. Second Ave. R. Co., 38 N. Y. 201 256
Colrick v. Swinburne, 8 Cent. Rep. 701, 105 N. Y. 503 175
Colton v. Hanchett, 13 Ill. 615 57
Colwell v. May's Landing Water Power Co., 19 N. J. Eq. 245 774
Com[illegible] v. Jolly, 8 N. J. Eq. 625 825
Commercial Mut. Ins. Co. v. Detroit F. & M. Ins. Co., 38 Ohio St. 11-16 770

Commercial Nat. Bank v. Iola, 2 Dill. 353 287
Commonwealth v. Alburger, 1 Whart. 469, 488 831
v. Alger, 7 Cush. 85, 89, 93, 95 .... 94, 856
v. Blaisdell, 107 Mass. 234, 235 832
v. Clue, 3 Rawle, 498 776
v. Dorsey, 103 Mass. 412 36
v. Dowdican, 115 Mass. 136 768
v. Gaming Implements, 119 Mass. 332 439
v. German Society, 15 Pa. 251 202
v. Hill, 5 Gratt. 682 408
v. Hope, 22 Pick. 1 685
v. Jennings, 121 Mass. 47 408
v. Keenan, 67 Pa. 203 195
v. McDonald, 16 Serg. & R. 390 832
v. Mitchell, 1 Phila. 63, 2 Pars. Eq. Cas. 431 .... 521, 523
v. Ober, 12 Cush. 493 329
v. Pike Ben. Society, 8 Watts & S. 247 222
v. Power, 7 Met. 596, 600 .... 227, 521, 523
v. Temple, 14 Gray, 69 435
v. Tuttle, 12 Cush. 502 408
v. Webster, 5 Cush. 295 38
Compton v. Milton, 12 N. J. L. 71 825
v. Wilder, 40 Ohio St. 130 309
Comstock v. Dodge, 43 How. Pr. 97 711
v. Hier, 73 N. Y. 269 254
Concord v. Portsmouth Sav. Bank, 92 U. S. 630 (23 L. ed. 630) 405
Concord R. Co. v. Greely, 17 N. H. 47 60
Conduitt v. Ross, 102 Ind. 166 606
Cone v. Niagara F. Ins. Co., 60 N. Y. 619 770
Cones v. Cincinnati, I. St. L. & C. R. Co., 14 West. Rep. 101, 114 Ind. 328 598
Confrey v. Stark, 73 Ill. 187 423
Conkey v. People, 1 Abb. App. Dec. 418 685
Conklin v. State, 25 Neb. 784 .... 777, 778
Conlee Lumber Co. v. Ripon Lumber & Mfg. Co., 66 Wis. 481 850
Conlin v. Aldrich, 98 Mass. 557 609
Connolly v. Poillon, 41 Barb. 366, 369 821
Connor v. Hanover Ins. Co., 28 Fed. Rep. 549 .... 388, 390, 391
Conrow v. Little, 5 L. R. A. 693, 115 N. Y. 387 .219, 220
Consolidated R. E. & F. Ins. Co. v. Cashow, 41 Md. 59 770
Continental Ins. Co. v. Pearce, 39 Kan. 396 75
Cook v. Charlestown, 13 Allen, 190, *note* 86
v. Chicago, R. & I. R. Co., 40 Iowa, 451 280
v. Cook, 100 Mass. 194 526
v. Moffat, 46 U. S. 5 How. 295, 308, 310 (12 L. ed. 159, 165, 166) 646
v. Walling, 2 L. R. A. 769, 117 Ind. 9 .... 796, 798
v. Woolley, 2 N. J. Eq. 209 653
Cooper v. Bill, 3 Hurlst. & C. 721 162
v. Cooper, 76 Ill. 57 655
Cooper Mfg. Co. v. Ferguson, 113 U. S. 727 (28 L. ed. 1137) 550
Cooter v. Dearborn, 2 West. Rep. 309, 115 Ill. 509 291
Copes v. Charleston, 10 Rich. L. 502 857
Corn Exchange Bank v. Nassau Bank, 91 N. Y. 74 632
Corgan v. Frew, 39 Ill. 31 856
Corning v. Lowerre, 6 Johns. Ch. 439, 2 N. Y. Ch. L. ed. 178 457
Cotton v. Pocasset Mfg. Co., 13 Met. 433 619
Couch v. Steel, 3 El. & Bl. 402 799
Coudert v. Cohn, 118 N. Y. 309, 28 N. Y. S. R. 684 223
Countess of Plymouth v. Throgmorton, 1 Salk. 65 569
Covel v. Hart, 56 Me. 518 447
Covenant Mutual Ben. Asso. v. Hoffman, 110 Ill. 606 119
Cowman v. Hall, 3 Gill & J. 398 818
Cox v. Bent, 5 Bing. 185 223
v. Cox, 6 Rich. Eq. 275 601
v. Louisville, N. A. & C. R. Co., 48 Ind. 178 603
Cox's Will, *Re*, 1 Jones, L. 321 825
Craft v. Boite, 1 Saund. 243, *note* 215
v. McConoughy, 79 Ill. 346 505
Craig v. Andes, 93 N. Y. 405, 410 .... 249, 250, 251, 253
v. Gilbreth, 47 Me. 416 449
v. People, 47 Ill. 487 .... 860, 861
v. Rochester City & B. R. Co., 39 N. Y. 404 455
v. Sibbett, 15 Pa. 238 429
Craker v. Chicago & N. W. R. Co., 36 Wis. 657, 658, 17 Am. Rep. 504 .... 227, 425
Cranston v. Crane, 97 Mass. 459 555
Craske v. Christian U. Pub. Co., 17 Hun, 319 223
Crawford v. Spencer, 92 Mo. 498, 509 167
Crawfordsville & E. Turnp. Co. v. Smith, 89 Ind. 290 548
Creighton v. Piper, 14 Ind. 182 607
Crofoot v. Moore, 4 Vt. 204 318
Croft v. Day, 7 Beav. 84 674
Crolley v. Minneapolis & St. L. R. Co., 30 Minn. 541 159

D.

E.

F.

G.

Gatewood v. Gatewood, 75 Va. 407 555
Gauch v. St. Louis Mut. L. Ins. Co., 88 Ill. 251 .. 735
Gavin v. Chicago, 97 Ill. 66 496
Gavit v. Chambers, 3 Ohio, 496 .... 581, 583
Gaynor v. Old Colony & N. R. Co., 100 Mass. 208 676
Gebb v. Rose, 40 Md. 387 796
Geddes v. Bennett, 6 La. Ann. 516 158
Geismer v. Lake Shore & M. S. R. Co., 3 Cent. Rep. 829, 102 N. Y. 563 825
Genesee Chief, The, v. Fitzhugh, 53 U. S. 12 How. 443 (13 L. ed. 1058) 437, 561
Gerhard v. Seekonk River Bridge Comrs., 2 New Eng. Rep. 619, 15 R. I. 334 98
Getchell v. Benedict, 57 Iowa, 121 636
Gibbons v. Ogden, 22 U. S. 9 Wheat. 1, 188 (6 L. ed. 23, 68) 356, 550
v. United States, 75 U. S. 8 Wall. 269 (19 L. ed. 453) 402
Gibbs v. Baltimore City Consol. Gas Co., 130 U. S. 396 (32 L. ed. 979) 505, 508
Gibson v. Gibson, 43 Wis. 23 .... 422, 425
v. Stevens, 49 U. S. 8 How. 384, 399 (12 L. ed. 1123, 1129) 164
Gifford v. Choate, 100 Mass. 343 697
Gill v. Pavenstedt, 7 Am. Law Reg. N. S. 672, 676 161
Gillett v. Bate, 86 N. Y. 87 310
Gilman v. Lockwood, 71 U. S. 4 Wall. 409 (18 L. ed. 432) 646
v. Sheboygan & F. du L. R. Co., 37 Wis. 317 605
v. Wills, 66 Me. 273 569
Gilmanton v. Sanbornton, 56 N. H. 336 709
Gilmer v. Stone, 120 U. S. 586 (30 L. ed. 734) 558
Gittings v. McDermott, 2 Myl. & K. 69 784
Glasgow v. Rowse, 43 Mo. 479-489 378
Glass v. Gelvin, 80 Mo. 297, 300 156
Glazier v. Bailey, 47 Miss. 396 732
v. Douglass, 32 Conn. 393 666
Glen v. Hope Mut. L. Ins. Co., 56 N. Y. 379 770
Glenn v. York County, 6 S. C. 412 295
Gloucester Ferry Co. v. Pennsylvania, 114 U. S. 196 (29 L. ed. 158) 300, 301
Glover v. Glover, 16 Ala. 440 564
Godard v. Gray, L. R. 6 Q. B. 139 270
Godbold v. Lambert, 8 Rich. Eq. 162-164 691
Goddard v. Grand Trunk R. Co., 57 Me. 202, 2 Am. Rep. 39 227
Godillot v. Harris, 81 N. Y. 263 572
Goldsborough v. United States, Taney, C. C. Dec. 80 782
Goldsworthy v. Chicago, M. & St. P. R. Co., 38 Fed. Rep. 769 367
Goodale v. Lawrence, 88 N. Y. 518 464
Goodman v. Simonds, 19 Mo. 106, 107, 116, 61 U. S. 20 How. 343 (15 L. ed. 934) 166, 167
Goodrich v. Reynolds, 31 Ill. 490 859
v. Winchester & D. Turnp. Co., 26 Ind. 119 374
Goodtitle v. Alker, 1 Burr. 143 431
v. Kibbe, 50 U. S. 9 How. 471 (13 L. ed. 220) 561
Goodwin v. Gilbert, 9 Mass. 510 606
v. Griffis, 88 N. Y. 629 .... 218, 219
Goodyear v. Weymouth and Melcombe Regis, 1 Har. & R. 67 209
Goodyear Dental Vulcanite Co. v. Bacon, 148 Mass. 542 436
Goodyear's India Rubber Glove Mfg. Co. v. Goodyear Rubber Co., 128 U. S. 598 (32 L. ed. 535) 572
Gordon v. Anthony, 16 Blatchf. 234 .... 310, 314
v. Sizer, 39 Miss. 805 732
Gorham v. Dodge, 11 West. Rep. 602, 122 Ill. 528 418
Gorman v. Lowell, 117 Mass. 65 428
v. Pacific R. Co., 26 Mo. 441 142
Goss v. Singleton, 2 Head, 79 482
v. Whitney, 24 Vt. 187 665
Gottsman v. Pennsylvania Ins. Co., 56 Pa. 210. 885
Gould v. Atlanta, 55 Ga. 686 274
Goulstone v. Royal Ins. Co., 1 Fost. & F. 276 ... 808
Gouverneur, v Lynch, 2 Paige, 300, 2 N. Y. Ch. L. ed. 916 218
Gowdy v. Sanders, 10 Ky. L. Rep. 912 558
Grace v. American C. Ins. Co., 16 Blatchf. 433, 109 U. S. 278 (27 L. ed. 932) 722
v. Dempsey, 75 Wis. 323 425
Grafton v. Eastern Counties R. Co., 8 Exch. 699 209
Graham v. Graham, 10 Ired. L. 219 825
Grant v. Holmes, 75 Mo. 109 612
v. Kidwell, 30 Mo. 455 167
Graves v. Graves, 36 Iowa, 310 .... 565, 566
Gray v. Barton, 55 N. Y. 68 259
v. Finch, 23 Conn. 495 663
v. New Jersey C. R. Co., 11 Hun, 70 209
Green v. Button, 2 Cromp. M. & R. 707 527
v. Danby, 12 Vt. 338 87
v. Farmers & C. Bank, 25 Conn. 452 387
Green v. Kennedy, 6 Mo. App. 577 165
v. Neal, 31 U. S. 6 Pet. 291 (8 L. ed. 402) 631
v. New York C. & H. R. R. Co., 12 Abb. N. Cas. 124 175
v. Purnell, 12 Md. 333 405
v. Van Buskirk, 72 U. S. 5 Wall. 310 (18 L. ed. 600), 74 U. S. 7 Wall. 139, 150 (19 L. ed. 109, 113) 64, 65, 388, 516
Green Bay Lumber Co. v. Ireland, 77 Iowa, 636 291
Greenbaum v. Megibben, 10 Bush, 419 153
Greenleaf v. Francis, 18 Pick. 117 186
Greenwood v. Taylor, 1 Russ. & M. 185 .... 460, 461
Gregg v. Massachusetts Medical Society, 111 Mass. 185, 194 .... 180, 321
Gregory v. Derby, 8 Car. & P. 749 47
v. Pierce, 4 Met. 478 682
v. Winston, 23 Gratt. 102 817
Greer v. McCarter, 5 Kan. 18, 22 386
Grice v. Richardson, 3 App. Cas. 319, 323 ..... 158, 159
Griffen v. House, 18 Johns. 397 862
Griffin v. Sheffield, 38 Miss. 359 732
. 60
G . 452
G . 397
G . 523
Gu . 645
Gu . 187
Guetig v. State, 63 Ind. 278 39
Gulf, C. & S. F. R. Co. v. Fuller, 63 Tex. 467 181
Guillander v. Howell, 35 N. Y. 657 64
Gulick v. New, 14 Ind. 93 .... 232, 607
Gulzoni v. Tyler, 64 Cal. 334 379
Gumberts v. Adams Exp. Co., 28 Ind. 181 607
Gunn v. Barry, 82 U. S. 15 Wall. 623 (21 L. ed. 215) 405
Gunson v. Healy, 100 Pa. 42 619
Gurney v. Atlantic & G. W. R. Co., 58 N. Y. 358 851
Guy v. Hermance, 5 Cal. 74 94
Gwathmey v. Pearce, 74 N. C. 303 .... 444, 445

H.

Haas v. Kansas City, Ft. S. & G. R. Co., 81 Ga. 792, 35 Am. & Eng. R. R. Cas. 572 825
Hacker v. Everett, 57 Me. 548 336
Haddock v. Grinnell Mfg. Corp., 1 Cent. Rep. 360, 109 Pa. 375 718
Hadley v. Baxendale, 9 Exch. 341 67
Hafer v. Hafer, 33 Kan. 449 817
Hafford v. New Bedford, 16 Gray, 297 244
Hagar v. Reclamation Dist., 111 U. S. 701-715 (28 L. ed. 569-574) 355
Hager v. Adams, 70 Iowa, 746 515
Haile v. State, 11 Humph. 154 36
Hakes v. Burns, 40 Fed. Rep. 33 367
Haldeman v. Bruckhart, 45 Pa. 514 186
Hall v. De Cuir, 95 U. S. 485 (24 L. ed. 547) 550
v. Toby, 1 Cent. Rep. 54, 110 Pa. 318 397
Hallgarten v. Oldham, 135 Mass. 1 152
Halloran v. New York & H. R. R. Co., 2 E. D. Smith, 257 140
Halpin v. Ætna F. Ins. Co., 30 N. Y. S. R. 259 .. 81
v. Phenix Ins. Co., 118 N. Y. 165 81
Halsa v. Halsa, 8 Mo. 303 166
Ham v. Hill, 29 Mo. 275 318
Hamburger v. Rodman, 9 Daly, 93, 96 ... 159, 160, 169
Hamilton v. Boston, 14 Allen, 475 428
v. Dobbs, 19 N. J. Eq. 227 555
v. Elliott, 5 Serg. & R. 375 763
v. Lubukee, 51 Ill. 415 725
v. Rogers, 10 West. Rep. 908, 67 Mich. 135. 387
v. Smith, 57 Iowa, 15 818
Hamlin v. Pairpoint Mfg. Co., 2 New Eng. Rep. 143, 141 Mass. 57 94
Hammel v. Queen Ins. Co., 50 Wis. 240 770
Hammett v. Philadelphia, 65 Pa. 151 358
Hammock v. Farmers Loan & Trust Co., 105 U. S. 77 (26 L. ed. 1111) 601
Hanney v. Com., 8 Cent. Rep. 184, 116 Pa. 323 .. 302
Hannibal & St. J. R. Co. v. Husen, 95 U. S. 465 (24 L. ed. 527) 550
v. Martin, 111 Ill. 219 766
Hanover v. Turner, 14 Mass. 227 464
Hardin v. Osborne, 94 Ill. 571 568
Hardwick v. Pawlet, 36 Vt. 320 709
Hardy v. Atchison, T. & S. F. R. Co., 32 Kan. 698, 18 Am. & Eng. R. R. Cas. 432 550
Hare v. Kennerly, 83 Ala. 608 373
Hargrave v. Le Breton, 4 Burr. 2422 526
Harkness v. Burton, 39 Iowa, 101 280
Harpending v. Haight, 39 Cal. 189 189
Harrell v. Harrell, 117 Ind. 94 796
Harriman v. Harriman, 12 Gray, 341 259
v. Pittsburgh, C. & St. L. R. Co., 9 West. Rep. 438, 45 Ohio St. 11 465

Harris v. Elliott, 35 U. S. 10 Pet. 25 (9 L. ed. 333) 431
v. Knapp, 21 Pick. 412 697
v. New York Mut. Ins. Co., 50 Pa. 341 808
v. Pratt, 17 N. Y. 249 168
v. Ross, 11 West. Rep. 670, 112 Ind. 314 797
v. Stevens, 31 Vt. 79 522, 523
v. White, 81 N. Y. 532 406
Harrison v. Baltimore, 1 Gill, 264 856, 857
v. Hatcher, 44 Ga. 638 514
v. Parker, 6 East, 154 431
v. Vreeland, 38 N. J. L. 366 603
Hart v. Cleis, 8 Johns. 43 408
Hartfield v. Roper, 21 Wend. 615 495, 844, 845
Hartford & D. Turnp. Corp. v. Baker, 17 Pick. 432 862
Hartford F. Ins. Co. v. Walsh, 54 Ill. 164 836
Hartford, N. L. W. & Turnp. Society v. Hosmer, 12 Conn. 361 862
Hartley v. Herring, 8 T. R. 130 526
Hascall v. Cox, 49 Mich. 440, 441 784
Hatch v. Bayley, 10 Cush. 29 156
v. Cincinnati & I. R. Co., 18 Ohio St. 118 182, 183
Hathaway v. Toledo, W. & W. R. Co., 46 Ind. 25 596, 597
Hatfield v. Central R. Co., 33 N. J. L. 251 175
Hauer's Case, 60 Md. 462, 463 676
Haupt's App., 125 Pa. 222 204
Havens v. Hartford & N. H. R. Co., 28 Conn. 663 90
v. Home Ins. Co., 9 West. Rep. 635, 111 Ind. 90 836
Haviland v. Chace, 39 Barb. 283 716
Hawes v. Humphrey, 9 Pick. 350 43
Hawk v. Evans, 76 Iowa, 593 43
Hawkins v. Governor, 1 Ark. 570 189
v. Pearce, 11 Humph. 45 414
v. Sanders, 45 Mich. 491 187
Hawley v. Farrer, 1 Vt. 420 710
Hawthorn v. People, 109 Ill. 302 839
Hay v. Star F. Ins. Co., 77 N. Y. 241 50
Hayden v. Allyn, 5 New Eng. Rep. 37, 55 Conn. 280 662
v. Atlanta, 70 Ga. 817 374
v. Palmer, 2 Hill, 205 612
Haydock Carriage Co. v. Pier, 74 Wis. 582 797
Hayes v. Michigan C. R. Co., 111 U. S. 228 (28 L. ed. 410) 799
Haynes v. Thomas, 7 Ind. 38 603
Hays v. Millar, 77 Pa. 238 206
v. Pacific M. S. S. Co., 58 U. S. 17 How. 596 (15 L. ed. 254) 301
Hayward v. Davidson, 41 Ind. 214 559
v. Gunn, 82 Ill. 385 653
Haywood v. Miller, 3 Hill, 90 711
Hazard v. Martin, 2 Vt. 77 632
Hazeltine v. Case, 46 Wis. 391 813
Hazlehurst v. Savannah, G. & N. A. R. Co., 43 Ga. 13 503, 505
Hazlett v. Sinclair, 76 Ind. 488 606
Heacock v. Sherman, 14 Wend. 58 54
Head v. Georgia P. R. Co., 79 Ga. 358 192
v. Head, 2 Ga. 191 362
Heck v. McEwen, 12 Lea, 97 504
Heine v. Com., 91 Pa. 145 302
Heinz v. Railroad Transfer Co., 82 Mo. 233, 236 170
Hellreigel v. Manning, 97 N. Y. 56 592
Hench v. State, 72 Ind. 297 231
Henderson v. Thornton, 37 Miss. 448 781
Herkenrath v. Am. Mut. Ins. Co., 3 Barb. Ch. 63, 5 N. Y. Ch. L. ed. 818 770
Hermann v. Niagara F. Ins. Co., 1 Cent. Rep. 707, 100 N. Y. 415 722
Hermanns v. Fanning, 151 Mass. — 819
Herrman v. Merchants Ins. Co., 81 N. Y. 184 80
Hertzog v. Hertzog, 29 Pa. 467, 468 191
Hess v. Clark, 11 Mo. App. 492 167
v. Culver (Mich.) 6 L. R. A. 498 477, 480
Heyward v. Cuthbert, 4 McCord, L. 354 48
Heywood v. Buffalo, 14 N. Y. 540 250
Hibbs, *Ex parte*, 26 Fed. Rep. 421 399
Hibernia Nat. Bank v. Lacombe, 84 N. Y. 367 65
Hickman v. Gaither, 2 Yerg. 200 483
Higgins v. Carlton, 28 Md. 115 42
Hill v. Boston, 122 Mass. 344 402
v. Dunham, 7 Gray, 543 665
v. Higdon, 5 Ohio St. 243 374
v. Jordan, 30 Me. 367 569
v. Mitchell, 5 Ark. 618 735
v. Ressegien, 17 Barb. 162 445
v. Shelbley, 68 Ga. 556 661
v. State, 17 Wis. 676 618
v. Smith, Morr. (Iowa) 70 242
Hill's Estate, 67 Cal. 243 426
Hills v. Richmond & D. R. Co., 33 Fed. Rep. 81 367, 368
Hilton v. Houghton, 35 Me. 143 665

Hinde v. Longworth, 24 U. S. 11 Wheat. 206 (6 L. ed. 455) 612
Hindmarsh v. Carlton, 8 H. L. Cas. 160 325
Hinds v. Harbou, 58 Ind. 121 452
v. Overacker, 66 Ind. 547 452
Hines v. Leavenworth, 3 Kan. 186 374
Hinman v. Hartford F. Ins. Co., 36 Wis. 159 835
Hitchcock v. Buchanan, 105 U. S. 416 (26 L. ed. 1078) 118
v. Galveston, 96 U. S. 349 (24 L. ed. 661) 295
Hix v. Gosling, 1 Lea, 568 482
Hoard v. Chesapeake & O. R. Co., 123 U. S. 222 (31 L. ed. 130) 605
Hobart v. Detroit, 17 Mich. 246 112
Hoboken v. Gear, 27 N. J. L. 265 699
Hodges v. Black, 8 Mo. App. 304, 76 Mo. 537 167
Hodgkins v. Montgomery Co. Mut. Ins. Co., 34 Barb. 213 243
Hodsdon v. Kilgore, 77 Me. 155 449
Hogg v. Beerman, 41 Ohio St. 81 580
Hoghton v. Hoghton, 15 Beav. 278 267
Hoke v. Field, 10 Bush, 144, 19 Am. Rep. 58 235
Holbrook v. Wightman, 31 Minn. 168 817
Holden v. James, 11 Mass. 396 813
Holder v. Lafayette, B. & M. R. Co., 71 Ill. 106 256
Holladay v. Marsh, 3 Wend. 142 475
Holland v. Mobile & O. R. Co., 16 Lea, 418, 419 414
Hollen v. Davis, 59 Iowa, 444, 44 Am. Rep. 688, and *note* 366
Holloway v. Holloway, 5 Ves. Jr. 401 734
Holmes v. Holmes, B. & A. Mfg. Co., 37 Conn. 278 821
v. Manning (Mass.) 19 N. E. Rep. 25 172
Home v. Richards, 4 Call (Va.) 441 431
Home Ins. Co. v. Heck, 65 Ill. 111 722
Honsel v. Conant, 12 Ill. App. 259 187
Hood v. Adams, 124 Mass. 481 318
v. New York & N. H. R. Co., 22 Conn. 1 502, 508
Hopkins v. Kent, 9 Ohio, 13 582
Hopt v. Utah, 104 U. S. 631 (26 L. ed. 873) 38
Hopwood v. Thorn, 8 C. B. 308, 309 526, 527
Horne v. Meakin, 115 Mass. 326 428
Horton v. Taunton, 97 Mass. 266, *note* 87
v. Thompson, 71 N. Y. 513 252
Hot Springs R. Co. v. Maher, 48 Ark. 522 209
Houdlette v. Tallman, 14 Me. 400 156
Houghton v. Chicago, D. & M. R. Co., 47 Iowa, 370 561
v. Kendall, 7 Allen, 77 734
Houser v. Tully, 62 Pa. 92 100
Houston & T. C. R. Co. v. Odum, 53 Tex. 353 181
Hovenden v. Annesley, 2 Sch. & Lef. 632 483
Howard v. Ingersoll, 54 U. S. 13 How. 381 (14 L. ed. 189) 561
v. Reid, 51 Ga. 328 274
v. Sexton, 4 N. Y. 157 612
v. Whetstone Twp., 10 Ohio, 365 464
Howard F. & M. Ins. Co. v. Cornick, 24 Ill. 455 836
Howe v. Peabody, 2 Gray, 556 739
Howell v. Fountain, 3 Ga. 176 513
v. Young, 5 Barn. & C. 259 318
Hoxie v. Chaney, 8 New Eng. Rep. 709, 143 Mass. 592 573
Hoyt v. Pawtucket Sav. Inst., 110 Ill. 392 725
Hubbard v. Callahan, 42 Conn. 528 665
Hudspeth v. Harrison, 6 Ky. L. Rep. 304 552
Huff v. Nickerson, 27 Me. 106 606
v. State, 2 Swan, 279 281
Hughes v. Edwards, 22 U. S. 9 Wheat. 489 (6 L. ed. 142) 616
Hughitt v. Johnson, 28 Fed. Rep. 865 397
Huguenin v. Baseley, 14 Ves. Jr. 273 267
Hine v. McConnell, 2 Jones, L. 455 42
Hulbert v. New York C. R. Co., 40 N. Y. 154 227
Hulett v. Fairbanks, 40 Ohio St. 233 661
Hull v. Richmond, 2 Woodb. & M. 337 88
v. Ruggles, 56 N. Y. 424 672
Hund v. Geier, 72 Ill. 393 495, 496
Hunt v. Bennett, 19 N. Y. 173 215
v. Columbian Ins. Co., 55 Me. 290 64
v. State, 22 Tex. App. 396 327
Huntington v. Allen, 44 Miss. 663 732
Hurd v. Elizabeth, 41 N. J. L. 1 64
v. Robinson, 11 Ohio St. 232 615
Hurry v. Mangles, 1 Camp. 452 159, 160
Hurst v. New York Produce Exchange, 1 Cent. Rep. 260, 100 N. Y. 605 180
Huskins v. Cincinnati, N. O. & T. P. R. Co., 37 Fed. Rep. 504 367
Hussner v. Brooklyn City R. Co., 114 N. Y. 433 457
Huston v. Cincinnati & T. R. Co., 21 Ohio St. 235 606
Hutton v. Camden, 39 N. J. L. 122 818
Hydraulic Press Brick Co. v. Newmeister, 15 Mo. App. 592 169

I.

Iddings v. Bruen, 4 Sandf. Ch. 252 65
Iglehart v. Moore, 21 Tex. 501 323
Illinois & St. L. R. & C. Co. v. St. Louis, 2 Dill. 70 808
Illinois C. R. Co. v. Adams, 42 Ill. 474 509
v. Frankenberg, 54 Ill. 88 509
v. Morrison, 19 Ill. 136 509
v. Read, 37 Ill. 484 509
v. Smyser, 38 Ill. 354 509
Illinois G. T. R. Co. v. Cook, 29 Ill. 237 359
Imlay v. Union Branch R. Co., 26 Conn. 255 433
Indiana v. Milk, 11 Fed. Rep. 389 584
Indiana, B. & W. R. Co. v. Allen, 12 West. Rep. 887, 910, 113 Ind. 308, 581 604
v. Dailey, 8 West. Rep. 516, 110 Ind. 75 687
v. Greene, 3 West. Rep. 883, 106 Ind. 279 .... 596, 597, 598
v. Hammock, 12 West. Rep. 297, 113 Ind. 1 598
Indiana Car Co. v. Parker, 100 Ind. 181 637
Indianapolis v. Cross, 7 Ind. 9 603
v. Kingsbury, 101 Ind. 211 603
Indianapolis & St. L. R. Co. v. Stables, 62 Ill. 313 766
v. Watson, 12 West. Rep. 285, 114 Ind. 275 687
Indianapolis, B. & W. R. Co. v. Hartley, 67 Ill. 439 608
Indianapolis, C. & L. R. Co. v. Harter, 38 Ind. 557 140
Inkster v. Carver, 16 Mich. 484 774
Iowa Homestead Co. v. Webster Co., 21 Iowa, 221 774
Irwin v. Mobile, 57 Ala. 6 .... 373, 375
Isaacson v. New York C. & H. R. R. Co., 94 N. Y. 278 227
Isbell v. New York & N. H. R. Co., 27 Conn. 393 142
Ives v. Farmers Bank, 2 Allen, 236 386

J.

Jackson v. Bellevieu, 30 Wis. 251 87
v. Bull, 10 Johns. 20 697
v. Edwards, 7 Paige, 386, 408, 4 N. Y. Ch. L. ed. 200 445
v. Gumaer, 2 Cow. 552 622
v. Holloway, 7 Johns. 394 384
v. Rutland & B. R. Co., 25 Vt. 161 142
v. State, 8 Cent. Rep. 581, 49 N. J. L. 252 613
Jacobs v. Jacobs, 16 Beav. 457, 560 734
Jaffray v. Davis, 48 Hun, 500 259
Jamison v. Beaubien, 4 Ill. 113 513
Jasper County v. Osborn, 59 Iowa, 208 464
Jaynes v. Jaynes, 39 Hun, 40 428
J. B. Palmer's Trade Mark, Re, L. R. 24 Ch. Div. 504, 517, 521 321
Jencks v. Coleman, 2 Sumn. 224 .... 522, 523, 524
Jenkins v. Jones, 2 Giff. 99 555
v. Pierce, 98 Ill. 648 566
Jenne v. Burt, 121 Ind. 275 410
v. Marble, 37 Mich. 319 796
Jenness v. Cutler, 12 Kan. 500 445
Jersey City v. Morris Canal & Bkg. Co., 12 N. J. Eq. 547 832
"Joannes" v. Burt, 6 Allen, 236 215
Johannes v. Phœnix Ins. Co., 66 Wis. 50 770
Johnson v. Ames, 11 Pick. 173 791
v. Hudson R. R. Co., 49 N. Y. 455, 462 717
v. Humboldt Ins. Co., 91 Ill. 92 771
v. Williams, 4 Minn. 260 (Gil. 183) 51
Johnston's App. (Pa.) 5 Cent. Rep. 564 604
Jones v. Ashburnham, 4 East, 455 710
v. Bacon, 68 Me. 34 697
v. Com., 75 Pa. 403 .... 86, 87
v. Hoar, 5 Pick. 285 219
v. Lees, 1 Hurlst. & N. 189 471
v. Neale, 2 Pat. & H. (Va.) 339 616
v. Pettibone, 2 Wis. 308 812
v. Radatz, 27 Minn. 240 .... 395, 398
v. Soulard, 65 U. S. 24 How. 41 (16 L. ed. 604) 562
v. State, 29 Ga. 594 36
v. Tracy, 75 Pa. 417 322
v. Tuck, 3 Jones, L. 202 825
Jouchert v. Johnson, 6 West. Rep. 380, 108 Ind. 436 797
Judge v. Braswell, 13 Bush, 67 679
Judson v. Reardon, 16 Minn. 431 (Gil. 387) 584, 586
Julia Bldg Asso. v. Bell Teleph. Co., 5 West. Rep. 357, 88 Mo. 258 426
Junction R. Co. v. Ruggles, 7 Ohio St. 1 .... 182, 183
v. Sayers, 28 Ind. 318 605
June v. Purcell, 36 Ohio St. 396 581

K.

Kane v. Bloodgood, 7 Johns. Ch. 120, 2 N.Y. Ch. L. ed. 241 483
Kansas City, St. J. & C. B. R. Co. v. Gough, 35 Kan. 1 .... 386, 392
Kansas P. R. Co. v. Cutter, 16 Kan. 568 386
Kansas Protective Union v. Gardner, 41 Kan. 401 75
v. Whitt, 36 Kan. 760 119
Kastner v. Pibilinski, 96 Ind. 229 62
Kaufman v. Cook, 114 Ill. 18 418
Kayser v. Bremen, 16 Mo. 88 109
Keech v. Hall, 1 Doug. 21, 1 Smith, Lead. Cas. *653, 7th Am. ed. 879 569
Keeler v. Goodwin, 111 Mass. 490, 492 158
Keenan v. Com., 44 Pa. 55 36
Kehn v. State, 93 N. Y. 291 .... 782, 783
Kehrer v. Richmond City, 81 Va. 745 435
Keith v. Miles, 39 Miss. 442 710
Kelley v. Drury, 9 Allen, 27 .... 645, 646
Kellinger v. Forty-Second St. & G. St. F. R. Co., 50 N. Y. 206 455
Kellock's Case, L. R. 3 Ch. App. 769 .... 460, 461
Kelly v. Hannibal & St. J. R. Co., 70 Mo. 604 786
v. Harrison, 2 Johns. Cas. 29 445
v. Humboldt F. Ins. Co. (Pa.) 6 Atl. Rep. 740 835
v. Partington, 5 Barn. & Ad. 648 527
Kelsey v. Glover, 15 Vt. 708 87
v. Sargent, 40 Hun, 150 256
Kelso v. Frye, 4 Bibb, 493 429
Kendall v. United States, 37 U. S. 12 Pet. 524 (9 L. ed. 1181) 189
Kensington v. Keith, 2 Pa. 218 681
Kent v. Rand, 2 New Eng. Rep. 858, 64 N. H. 45 797
Kentucky C. R. Co. v. Lebus, 14 Bush, 518 142
Kerr v. Forgue, 54 Ill. 482 496
Kerrains v. People, 60 N. Y. 221 711
Kerwhaker v. Cleveland, C. & C. R. Co., 3 Ohio St. 172 141
Kewanee v. Depew, 80 Ill. 119 767
Key v. Des Moines Ins. Co., 77 Iowa, 174 78
Keyser v. Rice, 47 Md. 203, 218 .... 515, 724
Kidd v. Johnson, 100 U. S. 617 (25 L. ed. 769) 578
Killips v. Putnam F. Ins. Co., 28 Wis. 472 50
Killmer v. Wuchner, 74 Iowa, 359, 360 .... 290, 291
Kilpatrick v. Com., 31 Pa. 198 .... 302, 303
v. Penrose Ferry Bridge Co., 49 Pa. 118 256
Kimball v. Cocheco R. Co., 27 N. H. 448, 59 Am. Dec. 387 60
v. Hildreth, 8 Allen, 167 152
v. Howard F. Ins. Co., 8 Gray, 33 835
v. Lockwood, 6 R. I. 138, 140 570
Kimbro v. Bullitt, 63 U. S. 22 How. 256 (16 L. ed. 313) 679
Kincaid v. Neall, 3 McCord, L. 201 730
King v. Council Bluffs Ins. Co., 72 Iowa, 310 78
v. Portland, 2 Or. 146 874
v. Savage, 121 Mass. 303 426
Kingsbury v. Bradstreet Co., 116 N. Y. 211, 26 N. Y. S. R. 520 215
v. Dedham, 13 Allen, 186 86
Kinsey v. Kinsey, 37 Ala. 393 564
Kirby v. Johnson, 22 Mo. 354 160
Kirke v. Kirke, 4 Russ. 435 384
Kirkland v. Cox, 94 Ill. 400 512
Kirtland v. Moore, 1 Cent. Rep. 466, 40 N. J. Eq. 106 209
Kisler v. Cameron, 39 Ind. 488 607
Knatchbull v. Hallett, 13 Ch. Div. 696, 710, 713, 723 .... 791, 792
Kneeland v. Spitzka, 42 N. Y. Super. Ct. (10 Jones & S.) 470 48
Knight v. Heaton, 22 Vt. 480 832
v. Norris, 13 Minn. 473 (Gil. 438) 851
v. Thayer, 125 Mass. 25 726
Knowles' Petition, 13 R. I. 90 461
Knowles v. Maynard, 13 Met. 352, 355 .... 569, 570
Knowlton v. Rock County, 9 Wis. 410 353
Knox v. Chalouer, 42 Me. 150 832
Knox County v. Johnson (Ind.) 7 L. R. A. 684 .... 236, 607
Koelle v. Knecht, 99 Ill. 396 861
Koerner v. State, 98 Ind. 7 35
Kohn v. Koehler, 96 N. Y. 362, 21 Hun, 466-470 673
Koontz v. Hannibal Sav. & Ins. Co., 42 Mo. 126 536
Kratzenstein v. Western Assur. Co., 116 N. Y. 54, 59 81
Kugler's App., 55 Pa. 123 863
Kurtz v. Hibner, 55 Ill. 514 417
Kyle v. O'Neil, 10 Ky. L. Rep. 709 558

L.

Labouchere v. Earl of Wharncliffe, L. R. 13 Ch. Div. 346 180

M.

Q.

R.

S.

T.

Thomas v. Owens, 4 Md. 189 ... 404, 405
v. Packer, 1 Hurlst. & N. 672 ... 223
Thomas Jefferson, The, 23 U. S. 10 Wheat. 428 (6 L. ed. 358) ... 437
Thompson, *Re*, 45 Mo. 55 ... 737
v. Baltimore & O. R. Co., 28 Md. 396, 404, 406, 407 ... 157, 158, 159, 160
v. Doliver, 132 Mass. 103 ... 152
v. Kenney (Mont.) Jan. 28, 1890 ... 404
v. Lusk, 2 Watts, 17 ... 195
v. Sloan, 23 Wend. 71 ... 395
v. Union P. R. Co., 76 U. S. 9 Wall. 579 (19 L. ed. 792) ... 800
v. Van Vechten, 27 N. Y. 582 ... 695
Thomson v. Davenport, 9 Barn. & C. 78 ... 662
v. Winchester, 19 Pick. 214 ... 644
Thorn v. Thorn, 14 Iowa, 55 ... 291
Thorndyke v. Bath, 114 Mass. 116 ... 160
Thorne v. First Nat. Bank, 37 Ohio St. 254 ... 152
Thorpe v. New York C. & H. R. R. Co., 76 N.Y. 402, 406 ... 226
Throop v. Hart, 7 Duvall, 512, 521 ... 157
Thurston v. Rosenfield, 42 Mo. 474, 97 Am. Dec. 351 ... 64
Tiffany v. Glover, 2 G. Greene, 387 ... 731
v. Warren, 37 Barb. 571, 24 How. Pr. 293 ... 695
Tillman v. Davis, 95 N. Y. 17 ... 734
v. Jackson, 1 Minn. 183 (Gil. 157) ... 52
Tillotson v. Wolcott, 48 N. Y. 188 ... 468
Timm v. Harrison, 109 Ill. 593 ... 839
Tindley v. Salem, 137 Mass. 171 ... 244
Tingley v. Bateman, 10 Mass. 343 ... 387
Tintagel's Case, Hil. T. 8 Geo. II. K. B. 2 Strange, 1003 ... 698
Titus v. Northbridge, 97 Mass. 265 ... 87
Titusville & P. C. R. Co. v. Warren & V. R. Co., 12 Phila. 642 ... 548
Tobias v. Lissberger, 7 Cent. Rep. 723, 105 N. Y. 404 ... 248
Toledo, W. & W. R. Co. v. Beggs, 85 Ill. 80 ... 509
v. Brannagan, 75 Ind. 490 ... 597
v. Grable, 88 Ill. 441 ... 495, 496
Tomblin v. Callen, 69 Iowa, 229 ... 276
Tonawanda R. Co. v. Munger, 5 Denio, 255 ... 129
Toole v. Clifton, 22 Ohio St. 247 ... 583
... 242
... 709
... 202
... 447
... 227
... 140
... 387
Townley v. Crump, 4 Ad. & El. 58 ... 160
Townsend v. Hargraves, 118 Mass. 325, 333 ... 157
v. Smith, 47 Wis. 623 ... 399
Trade Ins. Co. v. Barracliff, 45 N. J. L. 543 ... 808
Trade-Mark Cases, 100 U. S. 82 (25 L. ed. 550) ... 60
Traders Bank v. Alsop, 64 Iowa, 97 ... 276
Travis v. Continental Ins. Co., 32 Mo. App. 198-206 ... 808
Trecothick v. Austin, 4 Mason, 29 ... 791
Trenton Mut. L. & F. Ins. Co. v. Perrine, 23 N. J. L. 402, 415 ... 526, 527
Trenttell v. Barandon, 8 Taunt. 100 ... 46
Trimmier v. Bomar, 20 S. C. 354 ... 295
Trinity & S. W. R. Co. v. Meadows, 73 Tex. 34 ... 181
Tripe v. Marcy, 39 N. H. 439 ... 606
Trout v. Virginia & T. R. Co., 23 Gratt. 623 ... 142
Trow v. Vermont C. R. Co., 24 Vt. 494 ... 141
Troy & G. R. Co. v. Com., 127 Mass. 43 ... 401
Tucker v. Allen, 47 Mo. 488 ... 612
v. McDonald, 105 Mass. 423 ... 809
v. Tucker, 5 Ired. L. 161 ... 42
Tuff v. Warman, 5 C. B. N. S. 573 ... 143
Turner v. Hadden, 62 Barb. 480 ... 464
Turney v. Wilton, 36 Ill. 393 ... 863
Turnipseed v. Hudson, 50 Miss. 429, 19 Am. Rep. 15 ... 230, 235
Tuttle v. Jackson, 6 Wend. 213 ... 214
Tyler v. Ames, 6 Lans. 280 ... 209
v. Beacher, 44 Vt. 648 ... 60
v. Tyler, 126 Ill. 525 ... 514

U.

Uline v. New York C. & H. R. R. Co., 2 Cent. Rep. 116, 101 N. Y. 98 ... 174
Union College v. Wheeler, 61 N. Y. 88, 98 ... 214
Union Depot S. R. & Transfer Co. v. Brunswick, 31 Minn. 301 ... 92, 94
Union Mut. L. Ins. Co. v. McMillen, 24 Ohio St. 67 ... 242
v. Slee, 10 West. Rep. 154, 123 Ill. 93 ... 725
v. Wilkinson, 80 U. S. 13 Wall. 222 (20 L. ed. 617) ... 70
Union Nat. Bank v. International Bank, 13 West. Rep. 778, 123 Ill. 510 ... 796
Union P. R. Co. v. Fort, 84 U. S. 17 Wall. 553 (21 L. ed. 739) ... 492, 821
v. Peniston, 85 U. S. 18 Wall. 5 (21 L. ed. 787) ... 800
Union Slate Co. v. Tilton, 69 Me. 244 ... 449
United States v. Cook, 84 U. S. 17 Wall. 168 (21 L. ed. 538) ... 408
v. Davis, 6 Blatchf. 464 ... 613
v. Holmes, 1 Wall. Jr. 1 ... 298
v. Kirkpatrick, 22 U. S. 9 Wheat. 720 (6 L. ed. 199) ... 403
v. Rauscher, 119 U. S. 407 (30 L. ed. 425) ... 399
v. Reese, 92 U. S. 214 (23 L. ed. 563) ... 60
Unruh v. State, 2 West. Rep. 682, 105 Ind. 117 ... 38
Uppinghouse v. Mundel, 1 West. Rep. 204, 103 Ind. 238 ... 516
Upton v. Larkin, 7 Mont. 462 ... 442
v. Tribilcock, 91 U. S. 45 (23 L. ed. 203) ... 751
Usener v. State, 8 Tex. App. 177 ... 827
Utsey v. Hiott, 30 S. C. 365 ... 857
Uurns v. Lane, 138 Mass. 350, 354 ... 751

V.

Vail v. Jersey Little Falls Mfg. Co., 32 Barb. 564 ... 411
Valley Nat. Bank v. Frank, 12 Mo. App. 460 ... 152, 153
Van Alen v. Am. Nat. Bank, 52 N. Y. 1 ... 792
Van Arnam v. Ayers, 67 Barb. 544 ... 423
Vandegrift v. Rediker, 22 N. J. L. 185 ... 140
Van Heusen v. Radcliff, 17 N. Y. 580 ... 694
Van Horn v. Great Western Mfg. Co., 37 Kan. 523 ... 399
Van Ingen v. Whitman, 62 N. Y. 513 ... 716
Van Riper v. Poppenhausen, 43 N. Y. 73 ... 718
Van Schaack v. Northern Transp. Co., 3 Biss. 394 ... 509
Vansyckel v. Tryon, 6 Phila. 401 ... 187
Van Valkenburgh v. Lenox F. Ins. Co., 51 N.Y. 465 ... 722
Van Vechten v. Hopkins, 1 Am. Lead. Cas. 135 ... 215
Van Winkle v. American S. B. Ins. Co., 52 N. J. L. — ... 799
Vartie v. Underwood, 18 Barb. 561 ... 445
Vaughan v. Marable, 64 Ala. 60 ... 555
Venice v. Woodruff, 62 N. Y. 462 ... 250, 252
Verdery v. Summerville, 82 Ga. 138 ... 273
Vickery v. McCormick, 117 Ind. 594-597 ... 67
Vicksburg & J. R. Co. v. Patton, 31 Miss. 188 ... 142
Virden v. Allan, 107 Ill. 505 ... 839
Virginia Coupon Cases, 114 U. S. 269 (29 L. ed. 185) ... 60
Virginia F. & M. Ins. Co. v. Wells, 83 Va. 736 ... 771
Vogel v. Leichner, 102 Ind. 55 ... 407, 408, 797
Vollmer's App., 61 Pa. 130 ... 187
Vought v. Williams, 8 L. R. A. 591, 120 N. Y. 253 ... 621

W.

Wabash R. Co. v. Elliott, 98 Ill. 481 ... 767
Wabash, St. L. & P. R. Co. v. Jaggerman, 2 West. Rep. 863, 115 Ill. 407 ... 509
v. McCleave, 108 Ill. 368 ... 308
Wager v. Troy Union R. Co., 25 N. Y. 526 ... 455
Wagner v. Diedrich, 50 Mo. 484 ... 429
Waite, *Re*, 99 N. Y. 433 ... 64
Walker v. Board of Public Works, 16 Ohio, 540 ... 581
v. Cronin, 107 Mass. 555 ... 186, 527
v. Roberts, 4 Rich. L. 561 ... 731
v. Shepardson, 4 Wis. 486 ... 813
v. Staples, 5 Allen, 34 ... 152
v. State, 85 Ala. 7, 7 Am. St. Rep. 17 ... 37
Wallace v. Floyd, 29 Pa. 184 ... 411
v. Long, 3 West. Rep. 870, 105 Ind. 522 ... 418
v. Rappleye, 103 Ill. 231 ... 418
Waller v. Harris, 20 Wend. 555 ... 622
Walsh v. Porterfield, 87 Pa. 376 ... 100, 101
Walters v. Whitlock, 9 Fla. 86, 76 Am. Dec. 607 ... 64
Wandling v. Straw, 25 W. Va. 692 ... 86
Wangler v. Swift, 90 N. Y. 38 ... 209
Wanzer v. Bright, 52 Ill. 35 ... 399
Ward v. Doane (Mich.) 43 N. W. Rep. 982 ... 479
Warfield's Will, *Re*, 22 Cal. 71 ... 682
Warner v. Helden, 28 Wis. 517 ... 566
v. Jaffray, 96 N. Y. 248 ... 64, 65
Warren v. Chambers, 25 Ark. 120 ... 562
v. Union Nat. Bank, 7 Phila. 156 ... 64
Warrington v. Early, 2 El. & Bl. 763 ... 366
Warwick v. Mayo, 15 Gratt. 528 ... 432, 437
Washington v. Baltimore & O. R. Co., 17 W.Va. 190 ... 88
Washington Ave., *Re*, 69 Pa. 363, 364 ... 853
Washington Cemetery v. Prospect Park & C. I. R. Co., 68 N. Y. 591, 593 ... 456

Y.

Z.

STATUTES AND CONSTITUTIONS CITED, CONSTRUED, ETC.

Kansas.

Compiled Laws, 1885.

Pp. 703-706, §§ 23-54. Service of process by publication 891

Civil Code.

§ 72. Service by publication 891
281. Discharge of jury 776

Criminal Code.

§ 207. Jurors, impaneling 777
208. Discharge of jurors 776

Kentucky.

Statutes.

1869, March 6. Warehouse receipts; negotiability of 153

Code.

§ 47. Process defined 553
667. Form of process 553

Louisiana.

Civil Code.

Arts. 3125, 3129. Pledge; delivery of possession necessary 153

Maine.

Statutes.

1852, chap. 257. Blasting; precautions required 451

Revised Statutes, 1841.

Chap. 81, § 21. Railroad companies; penalties for neglect to maintain sign boards and gates 451
119, § 63. Garnishment; exemption of wages 822

Revised Statutes.

Chap. 17, §§ 23, 24. Blasting; precautions required 451
18, § 95. Adverse possession of highway 832
90, § 2. Right of mortgagee 569
94, § 2. Verbal lease; effect 569
124, § 20. Lord's Day Act 428
Vol. 4, chap. 30, § 9. Killing game 450

Maryland.

Bill of Rights.

Art. 23. Due process of law 551

Constitution.

Art. 3, § 20. Drawing money from public treasury 404

Statutes.

1798, chap. 72. Decree for assignment of patent 814
1842, chap. 293. Conjugal rights 681
1880, chap. 460. Police officers 847
1882, chap. 265. Conjugal rights 681
1886, chap. 439. Regulating plumbers 551

Code, 1860.

Art. 45, § 7. Conjugal rights 681

Code.

Art. 24, §§ 288-298. Police officers 847
27, § 172. Prohibition of lottery 671
173. Definition of lottery 671
178. Keeping lottery house, prohibited 671
188. Application of statute 672
Art. 45, § 7. Conjugal rights 681

Massachusetts.

Constitution.

Pt. 2, chap. 1, § 4. Power to provide for public service 488

Statutes.

1851, chap. 206. Creditors' bills 809, 812
1855, chap. 194. Jurisdiction of supreme court 811
1856, chap. 88. Jurisdiction of supreme court .. 811
1857, chap. 85. Directors of public institutions 245
chap. 214. Jurisdiction of supreme court 811
1858, chap. 34. Creditors' bill 812
1870, chap. 224. Benefit associations; form of name 821
1884, chap. 285. Creditors' bills 809
1887, chap. 246. Liability of Commonwealth for tort 401
chap. 348. Closing windows 188
1888, chap. 429. Benefit corporations 820

Revised Statutes.

Chap. 81, § 7. Jurisdiction of supreme court .. 811
90, 98. Creditors' bill 812
118, § 43. Jurisdiction of supreme court 811

General Statutes.

Chap. 22, § 1. Authority to maintain almshouse 244
108, § 3. Power of married woman to buy and sell 726
113, § 2, cl. 11. Creditors' bill 812

Public Statutes.

Chap. 22, § 1. Suffolk County charges; responsibility for 244
83, § 1. Authority to maintain almshouse 244
86, § 26. Expenses of state paper 401
106, § 7. Conclusiveness of certificate ... 821
§ 17. Benefit association; form of name 821
§ 21. Issuance of certificate 821
151, § 2. Attachment; equity jurisdiction 624
cl. 11. Creditors' bills 809
152, § 2, cl. 11. Creditors' bill 812
157, §§ 80, 81. Insolvency; discharge 645
§ 83. Trustee process 624
§ 85. Attachment 625
167. Practice Act 526
168, §§ 3-7. Set-off 818
183, § 1. Trustee process 624
186, § 17. Improper granting of franchise; who may take advantage of ... 821
196. Liability of Commonwealth for tort 401
204, § 29. Misdemeanors; punishment in house of correction 244
220, § 61. Support of inmates in house of correction 244

Michigan.

Constitution.

Art. 6, § 31. Unusual punishments prohibited 685

Statutes.

1887. Bohemian oat notes 478
Feb. 22. Cedar Springs; power to borrow money 852

Revised Statutes, 1846.

Chap. 55, tit. 10. Transfer of certificate of stocks 861

Howell's Statutes.

Chap. 188. Sporting club 858
191. Transfer of certificate of stocks ... 861
7697. Execution; right to attach interest of stockholder 858
§ 9180. Horse stealing 685

Minnesota.

Statutes.

1887, chap. 13. Railroad companies; liability for injuries to servant 419

General Statutes, 1878.

Chap. 81, § 9. Mortgage; property to be sold in parcels 53
Pp. 1024, 1080. Bonds to procure seed grain 297

Mississippi.

Code.

§ 1888. Cloud on title 732
2424. Attachment 730
2426. Return of attachment 730

§ 3630c. Foreign life insurance companies 130
4969. Limitation of actions; debtor absent from State 335
5316. Foreclosure sale 616
5916. Wills; witnesses 42
5919. Signatures to will 42
5925. Will; bequest to witness 41
5991. Validity of verbal will 41
6761. *Quo warranto* 186

Oregon.

Statutes.

1885, Feb. 11. Mechanic's lien 702
1889, Feb. 25. Lien of sub-contractor 703

Session Laws.

1889, p. 75. Lien of sub-contractor 703

Code of General Laws.

§§ 4044, 4045. Railroad companies; killing stock on track 186

Civil Code.

§ 650. Contempt 588
651. Punishment for contempt 589
652. Contempt in presence of court 589
653. Contempt not in presence of court 589
655. Proceedings for contempt 589
916. Power of court to preserve order 589

Compilation, 1887.

§ 3669. Mechanic's lien 703, 705
3673. Filing claim 702
3681. What included in 702

Pennsylvania.

Book of Laws, 1676–1700.

Pp. 93-101. Freeman, who is 840
P. 104. Act of union 841
Pp. 221, 222. Taxes 841
P. 233. Assessment of taxes 841
247. Freeman defined 841

Statutes.

1682, Dec. 7, Body of Laws, chap. 58. Elections 841
chap. 127. Taxes 841
1855, May 7. Hotels; notices to guests 101
1874. Incorporation Act 204

Public Laws.

P. 479. Hotels; notices to guests 101

South Carolina.

Constitution.

Art. 1, § 12. Unlawful restraints 857

Statutes.

1841, Dec. 17. Power of corporate authorities 855

Statutes at Large.

Vol. 19, p. 106, § 12. Charter of Greenville; right to own property 295
§ 19. Power to levy tax 295
31. Power to borrow money 295

Code.

§ 112. Fraud; limitation of actions 686

South Dakota.

Compiled Laws.

§ 2588. Duty of husband to support his wife .. 564
3504. Duress defined 563
3505. Menace defined 563
4456. Negotiable instrument defined 395
4457. Must be payable in money only 395
4462. Must not contain any other contract .. 395

Tennessee.

Constitution.

Art. 1, § 21. Eminent domain; just compensation to be made for property 125

Statutes.

1715. Statute of Limitations 482
1889, April 8. Act to provide revenue 281

Acts.

1885, Extra Session, p. 48. Tax upon pool selling 281
1887, p. 17. Revenue Act; tax upon pool selling 281
p. 48. Assessment Act; license of pool selling 281
1889, p. 168, § 52. Assessment Act; license of pool selling 281
p. 260. Revenue Act; tax upon pool selling 281

Milliken & Vertrees' Code.

§§ 1549-1561. Eminent domain; procedure 128
§ 1562. Eminent domain; incidental damages 127
§§ 1563, 1566. Eminent domain; appeal from finding of jury 128
§ 2702. Instruments which bear interest 128
2755. New suit 482
2931. Exemption of wages 413
4870. Betting, a misdemeanor 281
4881. Horse racing exempt from provisions against gaming 281

Texas.

Constitution, 1869.

Art. 1, § 14. Eminent domain; just compensation 181

Constitution, 1876.

Art. 1, § 17. Eminent domain; adequate compensation 181

Statutes.

1889, April 5. Act for inspection of oils 827

Revised Statutes.

Arts. 188, 189. Garnishment; answer of garnishee 822
Art. 212. Garnishment; defense by principal defendant 822
218. Garnishment, exemption of current wages 822
277. Liability of common carrier 825

Paschal's Digest.

Vol. 2, p. 1101. Eminent domain; just compensation 181

Vermont.

Statutes.

1886, p. 59. Closing windows 183

Revised Laws.

§ 2436. Guardians of insane persons 709
§ 3664, subd. 10. Incorporation of literary and scientific institution 113

Virginia.

Constitution.

Art. 5, § 14. Eminent domain; right to take property 432

Statutes.

1880, Feb. 10. Telegraph companies; right to erect poles 431

Session Acts.

1879-80, pp. 53, 54. Telegraph companies; right to erect poles 431

Code.

§§ 1287-1290. Telegraph companies; right to obstruct highway 432

Washington.

Statutes.

1888, Feb. 2. Incorporation of towns and villages 107

West Virginia.

Constitution.

Art. 8, § 24. Power of county authorites 807
10, § 7. Limit of taxation 305
§ 8. Municipal indebtedness prohibited 306
§ 9. Power of municipal taxation 308
12, § 5. School money 306
§ 6. School districts 306

Statutes.

1881, chap. 35. Alternate Road Law 305

Code, 1887.

Chap. 43, § 7. Duties of road surveyor 88
§ 56 *b*. Alternate Road Law 305
93. Forfeiture for nonpayment of rent 764

Wisconsin.

Constitution.

Art. 1, § 9. Remedy for wrong 818
§ 13. Due process of law 813
7, § 2. Judicial power 818

Laws.

1872, chap. 127. Married woman; right to recover for injuries done by liquors sold to her husband 424
1874, chap. 179. Married woman's action for damages 424
1881, chap. 99. Married woman's action for damages 424
1882, chap. 190. Injunction 812
1887, chap. 428. Obstructions in Rock River 813

Revised Statutes, 1858.

Chap. 119, § 33. Abatement 424

Revised Statutes.

§ 1170. Publication of delinquent taxes 782
1173. Contract for publication of taxes 782
1174. Fee for publishing taxes 782
1516. Married woman's action for damages. 424
2159. Homestead; dower 817
29:2, subd. 8. Exemption of goods of trader. 468
3028. Execution; discharge of debt 468
3180. Injunction 812
4974. Abatement 424

LAWYERS' REPORTS,

ANNOTATED.

INDIANA SUPREME COURT.

Edward ASZMAN, *Appt.*,
v.
STATE OF INDIANA.

(.....Ind.....)

1. One who is intoxicated to the extent of being deprived of the mental capacity to deliberate or premeditate cannot commit a crime of which the statute makes premeditation an essential element, if he had formed no purpose to commit the crime prior to the time he became so intoxicated; hence upon the trial of a person charged with having committed murder in the first degree, of which premeditation is an essential element, the fact that the accused was drunk at the time he committed the crime may be considered for the purpose of determining whether or not there was premeditation.

2. Instructions by the trial court which are designed to cast discredit or suspicion upon a defense which is recognized by the law as legitimate, and which an accused person is making in apparent good faith, are not regarded with favor, even although such defense be that of insanity.

(*Elliott and Coffee, JJ., dissent.*)

3. An instruction as to the individual responsibility of the jurors to be fully satisfied of the guilt of a person accused of crime before concurring in a verdict of guilty should be given if seasonably requested.

4. An accused person is not entitled to a special instruction to the effect that the mere finding of an indictment against him does not raise any presumption of guilt, where that idea is conveyed by the general charge of the court.

(April 22, 1890.)

NOTE.—*Voluntary intoxication in extenuation of crime.*

It is well settled that voluntary drunkenness is no excuse for crime. United States v. Clarke, 2 Cranch, C. C. 158; United States v. Drew, 5 Mason, 28; United States v. McGlue, 1 Curt. 1; Respublica v. Weidle, 2 U. S. 2 Dall. 88 (1 L. ed. 301); 1 Russ. Cr. L. 9th ed. 12; 1 Wharton, Cr. L. 8th ed. § 51; Desty, Cr. L. 26a; Williams v. State, 81 Ala. 1; Ford v. State, 71 Ala. 385; Tidwell v. State, 70 Ala. 33; State v. Bullock, 13 Ala. 413; Mooney v. State, 33 Ala. 419; Casat v. State, 40 Ark. 511; People v. Belencia, 21 Cal. 544; People v. King, 27 Cal. 507; People v. Williams, 43 Cal. 344; 1 Green, Cr. L. Rep. 412; People v. Lewis, 36 Cal. 531; Mercer v. State, 17 Ga. 146; Estes v. State, 55 Ga. 31; Hanvey v. State, 68 Ga. 612; Golden v. State, 25 Ga. 527; Jones v. State, 29 Ga. 594; Marshall v. State, 59 Ga. 154; Henry v. State, 33 Ga. 441; McIntyre v. People, 38 Ill. 514; Rafferty v. People, 66 Ill. 118; Upstone v. People, 109 Ill. 169; Reed v. Harper, 25 Iowa, 87; Smurr v. State, 88 Ind. 504; Gillooley v. State, 58 Ind. 182; Sanders v. State, 94 Ind. 147; Dawson v. State, 16 Ind. 428; State v. White, 14 Kan. 538; State v. Horne, 9 Kan. 119, 1 Green, Cr. L. Rep. 718; Curry v. Com. 2 Bush, 67; Tyra v. Com. 2 Met. (Ky.) 1; Kriel v. Com. 5 Bush, 362; Blimm v. Com. 7 Bush, 320; Shannahan v. Com. 8 Bush, 463, 1 Green, Cr. L. Rep. 373; Smith v. Com. 1 Duv. (Ky.) 224; Golliher v. Com. 2 Duvall, 163; State v. Coleman, 27 La. Ann. 691; Com. v. Malone, 114 Mass. 295; Com. v. Hawkins, 3 Gray, 464; People v. Garbutt, 17 Mich. 19; State v. Welch, 21 Minn. 22; Kelly v. State, 3 Smedes & M. 518; Mix v. McCoy, 4 West. Rep. 894, 22 Mo. App. 488; State v. Dearing, 65 Mo. 530; State v. Sneed, 3 West. Rep. 797, 88 Mo. 138; Schaller v. State, 14 Mo. 502; State v. Harlow, 21 Mo. 446; Whitney v. State, 8 Mo. 165; State v. Lowe, 11 West. Rep. 910, 93 Mo. 547; Smith v. State, 4 Neb. 277; State v. Thompson, 12 Nev. 140; People v. Pine, 2 Barb. 566; People v. Rogers, 18 N. Y. 9; Kenny v. People, 31 N. Y. 330; Flanigan v. People, 86 N. Y. 554; State v. John, 8 Ired. L. 330; State v. Wilson, 104 N. C. 868; Com. v. Hart, 2 Brewst. 546; Pennsylvania v. McFall, Addison, 255; Kelly v. Com. 1 Grant, Cas. 484; McGinnis v. Com. 102 Pa. 66; Jones v. Com. 75 Pa. 403; Keenan v. Com. 44 Pa. 55; State v. Paulk, 18 S. C. 514; State v. McCants, 1 Speers, L. 384; State v. Stark, 1 Strob. L. 479; State v. Bundy, 24 S. C. 439; Lancaster v. State, 2 Lea, 575; Cornwell v. State, Mart. & Y. 147; Clark v. State, 8 Humph. 671; Outlaw v. State, 35 Tex. 481; Scott v. State, 12 Tex. App. 31; Jeffries v. State, 9 Tex. App. 598; Carter v. State, 12 Tex. 500; Com. v. Jones, 1 Leigh, 598; Com. v. Haggerty (Pa.) Lewis, U. S. Cr. L. 402; Burrow's Case, 1 Lewin, Cr. Cas. 75; Rennie's Case, Id. 76; Reg. v. Moore, 3 Car. & K. 319; Rex v. Meakin, 7 Car. & P. 297; Pearson's Case, 2 Lewin, Cr. Cas. 144; Rex v. Thomas, 7 Car. & P. 817; Reg. v. Doody, 6 Cox, Cr. Cas. 463.

Evidence of drunkenness; when admissible.

Intoxication at the time of the act committed by the accused is a fact which may affect both physical ability and mental condition. Ferrell v. State, 43 Tex. 503.

It is admissible to prove the mental status of the accused to determine the degree of the offense, where the offense is divisible into degrees. People v. Odell, 1 Dak. 197; Colbath v. State, 4 Tex. App. 76; Brown v. State, Id. 275; McCarty v. State, Id. 461; Payne v. State, 5 Tex. App. 35; Pocket v. State, Id. 552.

One accused of murder in the first degree may give evidence of facts showing that his state of mind was such as to render him incapable of de-

See also 24 L. R. A. 555.

APPEAL by defendant from a judgment of the Criminal Circuit Court for Marion County entered upon a verdict convicting him of the crime of murder in the first degree. *Reversed.*

The facts sufficiently appear in the opinion.

Messrs. **Duncan & Smith**, for appellants:

The accused was entitled to an instruction that each juror must be satisfied of his guilt beyond a reasonable doubt before there could be a conviction.

Castle v. *State*, 75 Ind. 146.

The accused was entitled to the instruction that the mere return of the indictment by the grand jury did not raise any presumption of guilt.

Ibid.

The court erred in instructing that the defense of insanity should be very carefully scrutinized by the jury.

Unruh v. *State*, 2 West. Rep. 632, 105 Ind. 117.

The defendant could not be rightfully convicted of murder in the first degree if at the time of the commission of the alleged offense his mental condition was such that he was not capable of deliberate thought and rational determination though his mental state was the result of mere intoxication.

Fahnestock v. *State*, 23 Ind. 231; *Hopt* v. *Utah*, 104 U. S. 631 (26 L. ed. 873); *Pigman* v. *State*, 14 Ohio, 555; *Jones* v. *Com.* 75 Pa. 403; *State* v. *Johnson*, 40 Conn. 136; *Dawson* v. *State*, 16 Ind. 428; *Bradley* v. *State*, 31 Ind. 494; *Rogers* v. *State*, 33 Ind. 543; *Cluck* v. *State*, 40 Ind. 275; *Fisher* v. *State*, 64 Ind. 440; *Smurr* v. *State*, 88 Ind. 514; *Robinson* v. *State*, 13 West. Rep. 309, 113 Ind. 510; *Cartwright* v. *State*, 8 Lea (Tenn.) 377; *Tidwell* v. *State*, 70 Ala. 46; *People* v. *Belencia*, 21 Cal. 545.

Messrs. **Louis T. Michener**, *Atty-Gen.*, and **John H. Gillett**, *Asst. Atty-Gen.*, for the State:

If the appellant before the killing was capable of entertaining a purpose to kill, and of deliberating upon it, if only for a moment, his act, if preceded by such purpose and deliberation, was murder in the first degree; the mere fact that by intoxication appellant had deprived his reason of the power to dominate over his will does not excuse.

Roberts v. *People*, 19 Mich. 401.

To constitute premeditation there need be no appreciable space of time between the formation of the intention to kill and the killing; they may be as instantaneous as successive thoughts.

---

liberation in the commission of the act charged. State v. Johnson, 40 Conn. 136; Swan v. State, 4 Humph. 136; Pirtle v. State, 9 Humph. 663; Haile v. State, 11 Humph. 154; Boswell v. Com. 20 Gratt. 860. Compare, however, State v. Sneed, 8 West. Rep. 797, 88 Mo. 138.

It may be admitted to show that the accused was in hot blood at the time; but if the design to kill had been already formed, that he was in hot blood is immaterial as to the degree of the offense. State v. Garrand, 5 Or. 216.

In such case his intoxication furnishes no extenuation. See cases cited in first paragraph of *note*; State v. Johnson, 41 Conn. 584; Malone v. State, 49 Ga. 210; Cluck v. State, 40 Ind. 263; State v. Mullen, 14 La. Ann. 577; State v. Garvey, 11 Minn. 154; State v. Gut, 13 Minn. 341; State v. Cross, 27 Mo. 332; State v. Hundley, 46 Mo. 414; Friery v. People, 54 Barb. 319; People v. Fuller, 2 Park. Cr. Rep. 16; People v. Williams, 43 Cal. 344, 1 Green, Cr. L. Rep. 412; United States v. Cornell, 2 Mason, 91.

It is admissible to prove that the accused was incapable of forming a premeditated design (Cartwright v. State, 8 Lea, 376); and is always admissible to disprove the specific intent which is necessary to constitute the crime. Roberts v. People, 19 Mich. 401; People v. Walker, 38 Mich. 156.

It is admissible to prove that his condition was such that he could not form any intent. People v. Harris, 29 Cal. 678; People v. Eastwood, 14 N. Y. 562; Barber v. State, 39 Ohio St. 660; Cline v. State, 1 West. Rep. 81, 43 Ohio St. 332.

The fact of excessive drunkenness is admissible to reduce the grade of the crime only where the question of intent, malice or premeditation is involved. Engelhardt v. State, 88 Ala. 100.

It is admissible to prove that defendant was so intoxicated that he could not have or form the intent which is a necessary ingredient of the crime charged against him. Cline v. State, 1 West. Rep. 81, 43 Ohio St. 332.

In cases which involve intention as well as act, it may be proper to hear proof of the condition of the accused, at the time of the offense, to test his capacity to decide between right and wrong. Wenz v. State, 1 Tex. App. 36.

Drunkenness at the time of the act is a fact which may be essential in determining the nature and character of the act as well as his purpose and intent. Ferrell v. State, 43 Tex. 503.

For what purposes may be considered by the jury.

Where the very essence of the crime charged is the intention with which the act is done, it may be left to the jury to determine whether defendant was so drunk as to be incapable of forming any intention whatever. Reg. v. Cruse, 8 Car. & P. 541; Reg. v. Monkhouse, 4 Cox, Cr. Cas. 55; Com. v. Hogenlock, 1 New Eng. Rep. 105, 140 Mass. 125.

It can only be considered in cases involving the condition of the defendant's mind when the act was done. State v. Mowry, 37 Kan. 369; State v. Lowe, 11 West. Rep. 910, 93 Mo. 547.

Although the voluntary state of drunkenness cannot excuse the commission of crime, yet where, as upon a charge of murder, the question is whether an act is premeditated or not, or whether done only from sudden heat or impulse, the fact of intoxication is a circumstance proper to be taken into consideration. Rex v. Grindley, cited in 1 Russ. Cr. 2d Am. ed. 8; Rex v. Carroll, 7 Car. & P. 145.

In cases which involve intention as well as act, proof of the condition of the accused as to sobriety at the time of his offense may be considered, to test his capacity to decide between right and wrong. Wenz v. State, 1 Tex. App. 36.

Drunkenness may be considered on the question of malice, and whether his expressions manifested a deliberate purpose or were merely the idle utterances of a drunken man. Rex v. Thomas, 7 Car. & P. 817; Wilkerson v. Com. (Ky.) Sept. 13, 1888; Malone v. State, 49 Ga. 210; cases cited in first paragraph of *note*.

On the charge of murder it may be considered in determining whether there was that deliberation, premeditation and intent to kill necessary to constitute the offense. State v. Mowry, *supra*.

If accused was so drunk as to have been incapable to form a design to kill, it cannot be murder in the first degree. Cartwright v. State, 5 Lea, 376.

If the design to kill had been already formed with deliberation and premeditation, it is not material that the accused was in a passion, at the time of killing, caused by his voluntary intoxication. State v. Garrand, 5 Or. 216.

Binns v. *State*, 66 Ind. 428; *McDermott* v. *State*, 89 Ind. 187; *Koerner* v. *State*, 98 Ind. 7.

Mitchell, *Ch. J.*, delivered the opinion of court:

The Grand Jury of Marion County presented, in an indictment duly returned into the criminal court, that Edward Aszman, on a day named, did feloniously, purposely and with premeditated malice, kill and murder Bertha Elff, a human being. The defendant pleaded generally "not guilty," and specially, in writing, that he was of unsound mind when the offense was committed. He was convicted of murder in the first degree and sentenced to suffer death.

The homicide occurred on the evening of August 24, 1889. There was evidence tending to show that the accused came from Chicago, where he had been at work for some weeks, to Indianapolis, about twelve days before the homicide. There was also evidence tending to show that while at Chicago the accused exhibited some peculiarities of conduct, which indicated that he was laboring under some mental delusion or hallucination, as, for example, that he indulged the unfounded belief that he was being pursued by persons armed with long knives. It also appeared that he was addicted to the use of intoxicating drink.

The State attributed all his peculiar conduct to a condition brought on by excessive indulgence in intoxicating drink, while on his behalf it was claimed that his conduct, coupled with the circumstances under which the homicide was committed, and the attempt by the accused to commit suicide, all indicated such a state of mental disorder as rendered him irresponsible, or at least incapable of deliberate thought or rational determination.

The accused seems to have maintained relations of intimacy with Bertha Elff, the victim of the homicide, to whose society he in some way laid claim, to the exclusion of other men. The evidence tends to show that he had been drinking to excess during the day, and that while walking with the deceased during the evening, the subject of her receiving attentions from another man was under discussion. She denied the right of the accused to question her conduct in the respects mentioned, whereupon he inflicted a mortal wound upon her by cutting her across the throat with his knife, and then attempted to take his own life by inflicting a long deep wound across his own throat with the knife. She was found dead from the wound inflicted, as stated above, in a few moments afterwards, and he was found within fifty feet of her body in an unconscious condition, with a self-inflicted wound, from which the evidence tends to show death would have ensued but for timely surgical aid. It is not claimed that there was any evidence tending to show that the accused had formed the design to take the life of the deceased prior to the evening on which the homicide occurred, and that he voluntarily became intoxicated in order to prepare himself for the execution of his premeditated and previously formed purpose.

There was evidence to which an instruction relating to the mental condition of the accused, as affected by the voluntary intoxication, at the time the homicidal act was committed, was applicable. The only instruction given by the court relating to that feature of the case was the following:

"Frenzy, arising solely from the passions of anger and jealousy, no matter how furious, is not insanity. A man with ordinary will power, which is unimpaired by disease, is required by law to govern and control his passions. If he yields to wicked passions and purposely and maliciously slays another, he cannot escape the penalty prescribed by law on the ground of mental incapacity. That state of mind, caused by wicked and ungovernable passions, resulting, not from mental lesion, but solely from evil passions, constitutes that mental condition which the law abhors, and to which the term "malice" is applied. The condition of mind which usually and immediately follows the excessive use of alcoholic liquors is not the unsoundness of mind meant by our law. Voluntary drunkenness does not even palliate or excuse."

The 13th and 14th instructions asked by the accused are in legal effect the same. The 14th is as follows:

"While voluntary intoxication is no excuse or palliation for any crime actually committed, yet if upon the whole evidence in this cause you shall have such reasonable doubt whether, at the time of the killing,—if you shall find from the evidence accused did kill Bertha Elff, —he had sufficient mental capacity to deliberately think upon and rationally to determine so to kill deceased, then you cannot find him guilty of murder in the first degree, although such inability was the result of intoxication."

The propriety of the ruling of the court in refusing to give the 13th and 14th instructions, or either of them, is now before us for consideration. Section 1904, Rev. Stat. 1881, reads as follows: "Whoever purposely and with premeditated malice, or in the perpetration of, or attempt to perpetrate, any rape, arson, robbery or burglary, or by administering poison, or causing the same to be done, kills any human being, is guilty of murder in the first degree, and upon conviction thereof," etc.

Other sections define murder in the second degree, and declare what shall constitute voluntary and involuntary manslaughter. The distinction between murder in the first degree and murder in the second degree has been so often stated, and is so well understood, that it would be useless repetition to reiterate it here. *Fahnestock* v. *State*, 23 Ind. 231; *Binns* v. *State*, 66 Ind. 428; *McDermott* v. *State*, 89 Ind. 187; *Koerner* v. *State*, 98 Ind. 7.

It is sufficient to say that, in order that there may be such premeditated malice as will make a homicide murder in the first decree, the thought of taking life must have been consciously conceived in the mind, the conception must have been meditated upon and a deliberate determination formed to do the act. Where a homicide has been preceded by a concurrence of will, with an intention to kill, and these are followed by a deliberate thought or premeditation, although they follow as instantaneously as successive thoughts can follow each other, the premeditator may be guilty of murder in the first degree. But as it is of the very essence of the crime that there should have been time and opportunity for deliberation or premeditation, after the mind has consciously formed the design to take life, it follows, as a necessary corollary, that there must have been the mental capacity to think deliberately upon and determine rationally in respect to the nature and consequences of the act which follows. It would be a legal as well as a logical incongruity to hold that the crime of murder in the first degree could only be committed after deliberate thought or premeditated malice, and yet that it might be committed by one who was without mental capacity to think deliberately or determine rationally. As a matter of course, the rule is universal that voluntary intoxication is no excuse for crime, nor does it in any degree mitigate or palliate an offense actually committed. To hold otherwise would unbridle crime and subvert public order. On the contrary, where there is reason to believe that one has conceived the design to commit a crime, and, while harboring the unlawful purpose, voluntarily becomes intoxicated in order to blunt his moral sensibilities and nerve himself up to the execution of his preconceived design, the offense is thereby greatly aggravated. *State* v. *Robinson*, 20 W. Va. 713, 43 Am. Rep. 799.

Where, however, the essence of a crime depends upon the intent with which an act was done, or where an essential ingredient of the crime consists in the doing of an unlawful act with a deliberate and premeditated purpose, the mental condition of the accused, whether that condition is occasioned by voluntary intoxication or otherwise, is an important factor to be considered. *Smith* v. *Com.* 1 Duvall, 227; *State* v. *Garvey*, 11 Minn. 163.

Thus in *Cline* v. *State*, 43 Ohio St. 332, 1 West. Rep. 81, the learned judge, delivering the judgment of the court, said: "Where a person having a desire to do to another an unlawful injury drinks intoxicating liquors to nerve himself to the commission of the crime, intoxication is held, and properly, to aggravate the offense; but at present the rule that intoxication aggravates crime is confined to cases of that class . . . But in many cases, evidence of intoxication is admissible with a view to the question whether a crime has been committed; or where a crime consisting of degrees has been committed, such evidence may be important in determining the degree." *Pigman* v. *State*, 14 Ohio, 555; *Lytle* v. *State*, 31 Ohio St. 196; *Davis* v. *State*, 25 Ohio St. 369; *Roberts* v. *People*, 19 Mich. 401; *State* v. *Welch*, 21 Minn. 22.

In the application of this principle, the Supreme Court of the United States reversed a judgment of conviction of murder in the first degree in *Hopt* v. *Utah*, 104 U. S. 631 [26 L. ed. 873]. The court below instructed the jury to the effect that "a man who voluntarily puts himself in a condition to have no control of his actions must be held to intend the consequences. The safety of the community requires this rule. Intoxication is so easily counterfeited, and when real is so often resorted to as a means of nerving a person up to the commission of some desperate act, and is withal so inexcusable in itself, that the law has never recognized it as an excuse for crime."

The accused requested the court to give an instruction similar to that requested and refused in the present case. After asserting the general rule of the common law, that voluntary intoxication affords no excuse, justification or extenuation of a crime committed under its influence, *Mr. Justice* Gray, delivering the judgment of the court, said: "But when a statute establishing different degrees of murder requires deliberate premeditation in order to constitute murder in the first degree, the question whether the accused is in such a condition of mind, by reason of drunkenness or otherwise, as to be capable of deliberate premeditation, necessarily becomes a material subject of consideration by the jury." *Com.* v. *Dorsey*, 103 Mass. 412; *Pirtle* v. *State*, 9 Humph. (Tenn.) 663; *Haile* v. *State*, 11 Humph. 154; *Jones* v. *Com.* 75 Pa. 403; *Keenan* v. *Com*, 44 Pa. 55; *People* v. *Belencia*, 21 Cal. 544; *State* v. *Johnson*, 40 Conn. 136; Maxwell, Crim. Prac. pp. 227–229.

So in *Buckhannon* v. *Com.* 86 Ky. 110, the court said: "A deliberate intent to take life is an essential element of murder. Drunkenness as a fact may therefore be proven as bearing upon its existence or nonexistence. It is not admissible upon the ground that in and of itself it excuses or mitigates the crime, because one offense cannot justify or palliate another, but because, under the circumstances of the case, it may tend to show that the less and not the greater offense was committed." See also *State* v. *Sopher*, 70 Iowa, 494.

In *State* v. *Johnson*, *supra*, the Supreme Court of Connecticut, in reversing a judgment of conviction of murder in the first degree, the court below having given and refused instructions similar to those involved in the present case, used the following language: "A deliberate intent to take life is an essential element of the offense. The existence of such an intent must be shown as a fact. Implied malice is sufficient, at common law, to make the offense murder, but under our Statute, to make it murder in the first degree, actual malice must be proved. Upon this question, the state of the prisoner's mind is material. In behalf of the defense, insanity, intoxication or any other fact which tends to prove that the prisoner was incapable of deliberation, was competent evidence for the jury to weigh. Intoxication is admissible in such cases, not as an excuse for crime, or in mitigation of punishment, but as tending to show that the less and not the greater offense was in fact committed." *State* v. *Johnson*, 41 Conn. 585; *Jones* v. *State*, 29 Ga. 594.

"In those States," says a learned author, "in which murder has been divided by statute into degrees, it has been held that if the accused was intoxicated to such an extent as to deprive him of the power to form a design, the offense could be no more than murder in the second degree." Lawson, Insanity, p. 74; 1 Wharton, Crim. Law, §§ 51, 52.

"Drunkenness, we have seen, does not incapacitate one to commit either murder or manslaughter at the common law," says Mr. Bishop, "because to constitute either the specific intent to take life need not exist, but general malevolence is sufficient. But where murder is divided by statute into two degrees, and to constitute it in the first degree there must be the specific intent to take life, the specific intent does not in fact exist, and the murder is not in this degree where one, not meaning to commit homicide, becomes so drunk as to be incapable of intending to do it and then kills a man" Bishop, Cr. L. § 404.

This court, although not always enunciating it with entire accuracy, has constantly recognized the rule declared in the above cases. Thus, in *Smurr* v. *State*, 88 Ind. 504, where it appeared that the accused was excited by intoxicating drink at the time of the homicide, an instruction was approved as accurately expressing the law, in which the jury were told that "voluntary intoxication is no excuse for crime as long as the offender is capable of conceiving an intelligent design."

So in *Fisher* v. *State*, 64 Ind. 435, a prosecution for larceny, after stating the general rule that voluntary intoxication is no excuse for crime, unless the habit has been indulged to such an extent as to pervert or destroy the mental faculties, the court said: "There are cases which hold that, in prosecutions for murder, drunkenness at the time may be shown as affecting the question of premeditation." *Dawson* v. *State*, 16 Ind. 428; *Bradley* v. *State*, 31 Ind. 494; *Rogers* v. *State*, 33 Ind. 543; *Cluck* v. *State*, 40 Ind. 263; *Bailey* v. *State*, 26 Ind. 422; *Robinson* v. *State*, 113 Ind. 510, 13 West. Rep. 309.

When a homicide results from the use of a dangerous and deadly weapon, the law implies malice and an intention to kill from the effective use of the weapon, and therefore the crime is presumably murder in the second degree. No degree of mental disturbance produced by voluntary intoxication will of itself, disconnected from sudden heat or other circumstances, avail to reduce the crime to a lower grade, unless such a diseased condition of the mind has followed the habit of intoxication as to render the accused incapable of distinguishing between right and wrong, or of controlling his conduct when free from the influence of intoxicating drink. But in the absence of evidence, either direct or circumstantial, there is no presumption from the mere fact that a homicide was committed, except it be in the perpetration of the offenses mentioned in the statute, that it was done with deliberation or premeditated malice. Hence the conclusion logically follows that murder in the first degree, in which, under our Statute, premeditated malice is the distinguishing ingredient, can only be committed by one possessed of the mental capacity to deliberate and premeditate, and that a homicide committed by one who was at the time for any reason incapacitated to think deliberately or determine rationally as to the quality, character and consequences of the act, cannot be murder in the first degree. *Reg.* v. *Davis*, 14 Cox, Cr. Cas. 563, 28 Eng. Rep. (Moak's *notes*) 657.

In order that there may be no misapprehension and to prevent voluntary intoxication from being used as a cloak to shield those who, from sheer wickedness of heart and regardless of consequences, allow themselves to be driven to the commission of crimes, it should be said that mere intoxication, in the absence of such mental incapacity resulting therefrom as renders one who takes the life of another incapable of thinking deliberately and meditating rationally upon the purpose to take human life, and which leaves him with full power to know the quality of his act and to abstain from doing it, cannot of itself be regarded as sufficient to reduce a homicide from murder in the first to murder in the second degree. *Walker* v. *State*, 85 Ala. 7, 7 Am. St. Rep. 17; 1 Bishop, Cr. L. § 410.

"In other words, there must be the absence of that self-determining power which, in a sane mind, renders it conscious of the real nature of its own purposes and capable of resisting wrong impulses. Where this self-governing power is wanting, whether it is caused by insanity, gross intoxication or other controlling influences, it cannot be said truthfully that the mind is fully conscious of its own purposes and deliberates or premeditates, in the sense of the act describing murder in the first degree." *Jones* v. *Com. supra.*

Drunkenness cannot be considered as an excuse for crime, but may be taken into consideration for the purpose solely of passing on the fact of premeditation, keeping in view the fact that a man may act with premeditation while under the influence of intoxicating liquor, or he may have harbored the design to commit the crime before becoming intoxicated. *People* v. *Williams*, 43 Cal. 345; *State* v. *Robinson*, 20 W. Va. 713, 43 Am. Rep. 799.

It seems scarcely necessary to add that we are not dealing with the question of voluntary intoxication as an excuse for crime, or as rendering the accused criminally irresponsible, but only with intoxication resulting in that degree of mental disturbance or distortion that renders the accused incapable of committing murder in the first degree.

By giving the 12th instruction the court gave full recognition to the fact that the subject of the voluntary intoxication of the accused was before the jury for consideration. The jury were told, correctly enough, with what abhorrence the law looked upon frenzy arising solely from jealousy and anger, and from wicked and ungovernable passions, which did not result from mental lesion. They were also told, with eminent propriety, that the condition of mind which usually and immediately follows the excessive use of alcoholic liquors is not the un soundness of mind meant by our law, and that voluntary drunkenness did not excuse or palliate crime.

These instructions were all well enough as far as they went, but the question back of all that was, whether drunkenness, if it existed to the extent of depriving the accused of the power of deliberation, might be considered by the jury as disproving an essential ingredient in the crime of murder in the first degree, viz., the deliberate intention to take human life.

When the accused asked the court to instruct the jury that voluntary intoxication might, in case a mental condition had resulted therefrom which incapacitated him from deliberate thought or rational determination, reduce the crime from the highest to a lower grade of murder, the court refused. The jury were then left without the means of distinguishing between voluntary intoxication as an excuse for crime and intoxication as affecting that particular condition of mind necessary to constitute the crime of murder in the first degree. After admitting evidence tending to show that the accused was in the habit of drinking alcoholic stimulants, and that he had drank to excess on the day of the homicide, the jury were not only told that drunkenness was not only no excuse or palliation for crime, but without any explanation they were left to infer that if it had any effect, it was to aggravate the offense. Either the jury must have excluded the evidence of intoxication from their minds altogether, or they must have given it an effect prejudicial to the accused. The jury may have believed, as did the court, that although the accused may not have had the mental capacity to think deliberately or determine rationally, if his incapacity resulted from voluntary intoxication, he might be guilty of murder in the first degree nevertheless. In the absence of any claim of preconceived design, it was therefore prejudicial error to refuse the instruction asked, which contains an accurate statement of the law.

The court of its own motion charged the jury as follows: "The defense of insanity is one very frequently made in cases of this kind, and it is one which, I may say to you, should be very carefully scrutinized by the jury. The evidence to this point should be carefully considered and weighed by the jury, for the reason that if the accused was in truth insane at the time of the commission of the alleged acts, then he ought not to be punished for such acts. The evidence on this question of insanity ought to be carefully considered by the jury for another reason, and that is, because a due regard for the ends of justice and the peace and welfare of society demands it, to the end that parties charged with crime may not make use of the plea of insanity to defeat the ends of justice and as a shield to protect them from criminal responsibility in case of violation of law."

This instruction met with unqualified approval in *Sawyer* v. *State*, 35 Ind. 80, and the principle therein enunciated has been referred to approvingly in *Sanders* v. *State*, 94 Ind. 147, and *Butler* v. *State*, 97 Ind. 378.

It can hardly be said to contain the statement of any proposition of law, but is rather in the nature of a general disparagement of the defense of insanity which the accused had pleaded as provided by statute. A case might possibly arise in which such a statement could be appropriately made by the court. As the judgment in the present case must be reversed for other reasons, we do not determine whether or not it constituted reversible error in this case. It is sufficient to say that, as at present constituted, the court does not regard with favor any statements by the trial court which are designed to cast discredit or suspicion upon any defense which is recognized by the law as legitimate, and which an accused person is making in apparent good faith. In this respect we are unable to appreciate any well-grounded distinction between the defense of insanity, self-defense or alibi. *Line* v. *State*, 51 Ind. 172; *Sater* v. *State*, 56 Ind. 378; *Albin* v. *State*, 63 Ind. 599; *Simmons* v. *State*, 61 Miss. 243; *Dawson* v. *State*, 62 Miss. 241; Thompson, Trials, § 2433.

In those jurisdictions where judges are permitted to comment upon the weight and value of evidence, it has been held proper for the court to caution the jury concerning a defense which judicial experience has shown to be often attempted by contrivance and perjury. *Com.* v. *Webster*, 5 Cush. 295; Thompson, Trials, § 2434.

This rule does not prevail in Indiana. *Unruh* v. *State*, 105 Ind. 117, 2 West. Rep. 632.

At the proper time the court was requested to give instructions numbered 10 and 11, which are in the following language:

"10. The court presumes the defendant to be innocent of the commission of any crime. And this presumption continues in his favor throughout the trial of the cause, step by step; and you cannot find the accused guilty of any of the crimes covered by the indictment until the evidence in the cause satisfies you beyond a reasonable doubt of his guilt. And so long as you, or any one of you, have a reasonable doubt as to the existence of any of the several elements necessary to constitute the several crimes above defined, the accused cannot be convicted of such crime.

"11. And here the court instructs you that the mere fact that a grand jury has returned an indictment against the accused does not raise any presumption that the accused has been guilty of any crime, and you must not take the filing of the indictment as raising any such presumption until you, and each of you, are satisfied beyond a reasonable doubt, by the evidence here introduced before you, without reference to the nature of the indictment, that the accused is guilty of some of the grades of homicide covered by this indictment, there can be no conviction."

The court declined to give either of the above, and it is conceded that the subjects embraced therein were not covered by the general charge.

In *Castle* v. *State*, 75 Ind. 146, a judgment of conviction for an assault and battery with intent to commit murder was reversed for no other reason than the refusal of the court to give an instruction substantially like that numbered 10 above. While we might hesitate to reverse a judgment which was correct in all other respects, we can see no good reason why such an instruction should be refused when seasonably requested, unless the subject of the individual responsibility of each juror has been adequately covered in some other charge.

There was no error in refusing the 11th charge. It must be assumed that the jury understood from the general charge of the court that the law surrounded the accused with the presumption of innocence notwithstanding the return of an indictment against him, and that that presumption continued until it was overcome by the evidence. It must be assumed that jurors are men of ordinary intelligence and that they are possessed of the information common to well informed citizens.

After the most careful consideration of the instructions, we are impressed with the conviction that too many doubtful questions were resolved against the accused, and that prejudicial error may have intervened in the failure of the court to give the jury the instructions requested upon the subject of the mental incapacity of the accused, resulting from voluntary intoxication, to commit the crime of murder in the first degree. A judgment of a court which pronounces the extreme penalty of the law upon a human being should be free from any error which may have resulted to the prejudice of the person condemned. Lest the one before us may, for the reasons given, not be, *it is reversed.*

The clerk will make the proper order concerning the appellant.

Elliott, J.:

The 19th instruction disapproved by the court is copied word for word from the instruction given in the case of *Sawyer* v. *State*, 35 Ind. 80. Worden, *J.*, delivering the unanimous opinion of the court in that case said: "The observations of the court in that respect meet our unqualified approval. As stated by the court, where the defense of insanity is interposed to a criminal prosecution, the evidence relating to it should be carefully and intelligently scrutinized and considered for the double reason that a really insane person should not be convicted, and a really sane one should not be acquitted and suffered to go unpunished for his crimes on the false theory of insanity." This is, as I am unalterably convinced, sound sense and sound law. If the decision stood alone I should be heartily for sustaining it, for I believe that it is intrinsically right. But it does not stand alone, for it has been repeatedly approved. *Butler* v. *State*, 97 Ind. 378; *Sanders* v. *State*, 94 Ind. 147; *Guetig* v. *State*, 68 Ind. 278.

Other courts have declared a like doctrine. *People* v. *Bumberger*, 45 Cal. 650; *People* v. *Dennis*, 39 Cal. 625; *Sellick's Case*, 1 City Hall Rec. 185; *McKee* v. *People*, 36 N. Y. 118.

In one of the cases cited the jury were instructed, as to the defense of insanity, that, "from its nature it ought to be received in all cases by jurors with the greatest degree of caution and circumspection." In another case the jury were instructed, concerning the plea of insanity, that "it is a plea sometimes resorted to in cases where aggravated crimes have been committed under circumstances which afford full proof of overt acts, and render hopeless all other means of evading punishment. While, therefore, it ought to be received as a not less full and complete than it is a humane defense, when satisfactorily established, it yet should be examined with great care lest an ingenious counterfeit of the malady furnish protection to guilt."

It is, as is everywhere laid down, the duty of a court to abide by its decisions unless it is demonstrated that they are against reason, and this rule ought of itself to constrain us to adhere to former decisions; but in this instance I am convinced that the court is departing from a decision not only without reason, but against both reason and authority.

The departure is, I deferentially affirm, a step in the wrong direction. Our decisions have already too greatly restricted the rights and duties of trial judges, and I am firmly convinced that it is a mistake to fetter them still more. A trial judge is, as I believe, more than a mere moderator, or a mere rehearser of stereotyped phrases, for it is his right and his duty to give the jury such advice and such cautions as shall assist them in reaching a just conclusion.

That the defense of insanity is one frequently resorted to is a matter of common knowledge, and it is so treated in the text-books and decisions, and yet the instruction before us is condemned simply because the jury are informed that it is a defense that is frequently made. This, as I understand the opinion of the court, is the only infirmity in the instruction. To me it seems an element of strength, not of weakness.

Our Statute makes the defense of insanity a peculiar one. Some of the courts hold that it must be established beyond a reasonable doubt. Other courts hold that it must be established by a preponderance of the evidence, and still others hold that it is enough if the evidence raises a reasonable doubt of the sanity of the accused; but, while the courts differ upon the points mentioned, they agree that the defense of insanity is a peculiar one, subject to be abused and meriting rigid scrutiny.

While I dissent from that part of the opinion which disapproves the 19th instruction, I concur in the conclusion that the judgment should be reversed, for I think that the very able opinion of the court prepared by the chief justice unanswerably proves that where the element of premeditation is essential to create the crime of murder in the first degree, the accused cannot be found guilty of that crime if at the time of the killing he was so completely overcome by intoxication as to be incapable of premeditation.

Coffey, J., concurs with **Elliott, J.**

OHIO SUPREME COURT.

Orris D. VROMAN *et al.*, *Plffs. in Err.*,
v.
George O. POWERS.

(47 Ohio St.....)

1. **Where a verbal will is reduced to writing,** and subscribed by two witnesses, one of whom is a legatee thereunder, and the other is his wife, the husband is not a competent, disinterested witness, within the meaning of section 5991 of the Revised Statutes, and the will is invalid.

2. **The two witnesses to a verbal will must be competent,** disinterested witnesses at the time of their attestation, and their dis-

---

NOTE.—*Will defined.*

A will is a legal declaration of a man's intention which he wills to be performed after his death. Jasper v. Jasper, 17 Or. 590.

It is an instrument whereby a person makes a disposition of his property, to take effect after his death. Cover v. Stem, 9 Cent. Rep. 108, 67 Md. 449.

The more general and popular denomination of a will or testament embracing both real and personal property is "last will and testament." Compton v. McMahan, 2 West. Rep. 189, 19 Mo. App. 494.

Although the statute requires a will to be in writing, yet where a will required certain property

qualification as witnesses, by reason of interest under the will, cannot be removed by a renunciation of such interest at the time the will is admitted to probate, or at the trial of an issue to contest the validity of the will.

3. Section 5925 of the Revised Statutes, as to the effect of a witness being a devisee or legatee under the will, is not applicable to verbal wills.

(March 18, 1890.)

ERROR to the Circuit Court for Cuyahoga County to review a judgment in favor of plaintiff rendered upon appeal from the Court of Common Pleas in an action brought to set aside a certain will upon the ground that the statutory requirements as to subscription were not complied with. *Affirmed.*

The facts are fully stated in the opinion.

Messrs. **Alvord, Alvord & Baptiste,** for plaintiffs in error:

Rev. Stat., § 5925, controls and governs in the case of nuncupative wills, as in that of wills generally, and under its provisions Orris D. Vroman was in the very moment that he signed the will by operation of law stripped of all interest and wholly devested of the same, and thus became a disinterested witness.

The Statute devesting the husband of all interest, at the same instant devested the wife of all interest; so that she was the competent, disinterested witness named in the Statute.

Jackson v. *Woods*, 1 Johns. Cas. 163; *Jackson* v. *Durland*, 2 Johns. Cas. 314; *Winslow* v. *Kimball*, 25 Me. 493; 1 Redf. Wills, p. 258.

If the provisions of that Statute did not so operate the filing of the written renunciation and release did; and thereafter for the purposes of making the will a valid verbal last will as it pertained to the other legatees therein named, they were both competent, disinterested witnesses.

Cook v. *Grant*, 16 Serg. & R. 198, 16 Am. Dec. 564; *Burritt* v. *Silliman*, 13 N. Y. 93, 64 Am. Dec. 532; 1 Redf. Wills, pp. 256, 257; 1 Schouler, Wills, § 351, p. 359.

This is so in the case of a nuncupative will as in that of any other.

Brayfield v. *Brayfield*, 3 Harr. & J. 208.

Messrs. **William C. Rogers** and **William Robison,** with *Mr.* **H. C. White,** for defendant in error:

A bequest to a husband makes a wife incompetent to testify in behalf of the will.

Winslow v. *Kimball*, 25 Me. 493; 1 Redf. Wills, pp. 188, 189, 257, 258; *Holdfast* v. *Dowsing*, 2 Strange, 1254; *Lyon* v. *Hamor*, 73 Me. 56; *Ætna Ins. Co.* v. *Stevens*, 48 Ill. 31; *Ryan* v. *Devereux*, 26 Up. Can. Q. B. 100; 1 Woerner, Administrator, § 41, p. 72; *Pease* v. *Allis*, 110 Mass. 157; *Dickinson* v. *Dickinson*, 61 Pa. 401; Abbott, Law Dict. *Disinterested*; *Sullivan* v. *Sullivan*, 106 Mass. 476.

The release offered in evidence should have been filed in the probate court, and before probate, and not for the first time in the circuit court.

Workman v. *Dominick*, 3 Strobh. L. 591.

Witnesses to wills must be, in every way, competent at the time of signing.

Frink v. *Pond*, 46 N. H. 125; *Patten* v. *Tallman*, 27 Me. 17; *Morton* v. *Ingram*, 11 Ired. L. 368; *Higgins* v. *Carlton*, 28 Md. 117, 140; *Stewart* v. *Harriman*, 56 N. H. 25; 1 Schouler, Wills, § 351; *Pease* v. *Allis*, 110 Mass. 157; *Hawes* v. *Humphrey*, 9 Pick. 350, 20 Am. Dec. 483.

Dickman, *J.*, delivered the opinion of the court:

Mary A. Powers, the wife of the defendant in error, George O. Powers, died on the 13th day of December, 1881, leaving issue one child, Orris Irving Powers, who thereafter, and before this suit was begun, died aged six months. It was claimed that Mary A. Powers, in her last sickness, made a verbal will, which was on the 19th day of December, 1881, reduced to writing, and subscribed by Orris D. Vroman and his wife Emma J. Vroman as witnesses. The alleged verbal will was presented to and admitted to probate by the Probate Court of Cuyahoga County. By the terms of the will, Orris D. Vroman, Joseph Vroman, Albert K. Vroman and Adiram Vroman, the plaintiffs in error, brothers of Mary A. Powers, and Orris Irving Powers are named as the several legatees

---

given to a person named to be distributed by him "according to private instructions I give him;" which instructions were verbal and directed payment of the property, which is in a foreign country, to relatives in that country,—equity will carry out the intention by charging the legatee with a constructive trust in favor of the beneficiaries named in the private instructions to him, as against the other heirs; and he will not be charged with a trust in favor of the latter. Curdy v. Berton, 79 Cal. 420.

Nuncupative will; rule in various States.

A nuncupative will must be strictly proved in all essential points. Scaife v. Emmons (Ga.) March 10, 1890.

To render a nuncupative will valid, it must appear that the deceased was *in extremis* when he made it; and it is invalid where deceased had plenty of time and opportunity to execute a formal written will. *Ibid.*

One of the formalities required by the Louisiana Civil Code in the confection of a testament nuncupative in form and received by public act is that the act must be received by a notary in the presence of three witnesses residing in the parish where the instrument is made. This formality must be observed; otherwise the testament is null and void. Weick v. Henne (La.) Dec. 17, 1888.

Nuncupative testaments are full proof of themselves. They must bear upon their faces the evidence that all the formalities required by law have been complied with. An omission of any formality cannot be supplied by evidence *dehors* the testament. *Ibid.*

If executed before two competent witnesses only it is invalid; and if executed before three witnesses, one of whom did not understand the language in which the will was drawn up and the testator expressed himself, it is invalid. Dauterive's Succession, 39 La. Ann. 1092.

A nuncupative will under private signature need not be shown to have been dictated by the testator when written out of the presence of the witness. Pfarr v. Belmont, 39 La. Ann. 294.

A verbal will, to be valid, must be proved by three witnesses present at the making thereof, and

of Mary A. Powers. Suit was brought by George O. Powers, in the court of common pleas, against the plaintiffs in error, to set aside the will, on the ground, among others, that it was not subscribed by two competent, disinterested witnesses. The case was tried in the court of common pleas in May, 1884, and by verdict and judgment of the court the will was set aside. The defendants appealed, and on February 15, 1887, the case was tried in the circuit court, and it was found by the verdict and judgment rendered therein that the paper purporting to be the last will of Mary A. Powers was not her last will. During the trial in the circuit court, a written renunciation of all interest under the will, made and signed February 13, 1887, by Orris D. Vroman and Emma J. Vroman, the two witnesses to the alleged verbal will, was filed in that court, which renunciation, on being offered in evidence, was ruled out by the court.

The court, among other matters, charged the jury as follows: "That if they should find from the evidence that one of said witnesses to said will, Orris D. Vroman, was the brother of the testatrix and one of the residuary legatees mentioned in said alleged will, and that said Emma J. Vroman was at the time the wife of the said Orris D. Vroman, the said witnesses to said will were not, within the meaning of the Statute of Ohio, competent, disinterested witnesses to said will, and because of that fact said will would not be the valid verbal will of the said Mary A. Powers."

It is contended in behalf of the plaintiffs in error that the circuit court erred, first, in charging the jury that Orris D. Vroman and Emma J. Vroman, under the conditions above stated, would not be competent and disinterested witnesses, within the meaning of the Statute; and second, in refusing to allow the paper containing their renunciation of interest to be put in evidence.

I. It is provided by section 5991, of the Revised Statutes that "a verbal will, made in the last sickness, shall be valid in respect to personal property, if reduced to writing, and subscribed by two competent disinterested witnesses, within ten days after the speaking of the testamentary words; and if it be proved by said witnesses that the testator was of sound mind and memory, and not under any restraint, and called upon some person present, at the time the testamentary words were spoken, to bear testimony to said disposition as his will." The Statute requires that both the witnesses shall be competent and disinterested, and not one only. In our judgment, Orris D. Vroman did not meet the requirement of the Statute as to competency and disinterestedness. He had a sufficiently immediate, beneficial interest in the will to disqualify him from becoming a subscribing witness thereto. The alleged will provided that a certain sum of money in the hands of her brother, Orris D. Vroman, belonging to the testatrix, if not used for her sickness and incident expenses, should be placed where her son could have it on arriving at the age of twenty-one years; and that if he died before the age of twenty-one years, the money should go to her brothers; and that, whatever funds were to come from her mother's estate were to go in the same manner. One of the witnesses, therefore, being incompetent and disqualified by reason of interest, there was not a compliance with the statutory requirement that the two witnesses to the verbal will should be competent and disinterested, and the will, in consequence, cannot be held to be valid. We find no error in the charge of the court.

It is urged, however, that if there was a disqualification of interest in one or both of the witnesses, it was removed by the operation of section 5925 of the Revised Statutes, which provides that "if a devise or bequest is given to a person who is a witness to the will, and

---

be made in the last sickness of the testator. The term "last sickness" means *in extremis*. Carroll v. Bonham, 8 Cent. Rep. 649, 42 N. J. Eq. 625.

If decedent could have made a written will, a nuncupative one will be of no avail, and where he lived nine days after, deliberately selecting the nuncupative method, such will cannot be admitted to probate. *Ibid.*

Under N. C. Code, §2148, a nuncupative will which is put in writing within ten days after it is made, may be proved by the witnesses thereof, either before or after the lapse of six months next after it is made; and where the proofs and examination of the witnesses are taken, and an order of citation and publication of notice made within the six months, the proceeding cannot be dismissed because the will is not admitted to probate within the six months. *Re* Haygood's Will, 101 N. C. 574.

The Texas statute authorizing any person who is competent to make a will, to "dispose of his property by nuncupative will," does not apply to real property. It must be considered as intending to re-enact the former law on the subject. Moffett v. Moffett, 67 Tex. 642.

Qualification of witness.

Where the statute requires "at least two credible witnesses" it means persons not disqualified by mental imbecility, interest or crime. Fuller v. Fuller, 83 Ky. 345.

A statute providing that a bequest shall be void when made to a subscribing witness, or the husband or wife of such, does not make void a charitable bequest for the poor of a religious society to which the subscribing witnesses belong. Goodrich's App. 57 Conn. 275.

A husband is not disqualified, on account of his interest, to act as a subscribing witness to a will, on the ground that his wife is named therein as a devisee of real estate. Bates v. Officer, 70 Iowa, 343.

Prior to Statute of 1884, a will was void when one of three witnesses was the husband of one of the legatees. Giddings v. Turgeon, 2 New Eng. Rep. 466, 58 Vt. 106.

Where the will contains a devise or legacy to a town, in trust, a taxpaying inhabitant of the town is not thereby rendered an incompetent witness to the will. *Re* Marston, 3 New Eng. Rep. 601, 79 Me. 25.

Where the will contains a legacy to an incorporated hall association, "in part to secure a liberal policy in respect to the use of the hall for objects of public interest," a stockholder in that association is not thereby rendered an incompetent witness to the will. *Ibid.*

the will cannot otherwise be proved than by the testimony of such witness, the devise or bequest shall be void, and the witness shall be competent to give testimony of the execution of the will, in like manner as if such devise or bequest had not been made."

This section, when considered in connection with the preceding sections of the chapter, including section 5916, is clearly applicable only to duly executed written wills. Section 5919 requires that "every last will and testament (except nuncupative wills hereinafter provided for) shall be in writing, and signed at the end thereof by the party making the same . . . and shall be attested and subscribed in the presence of such party by two or more competent witnesses," etc.

The sections immediately following, embracing section 5925, are so connected by obvious reference to a will in writing, as to preclude the idea of applying the last-mentioned section to nuncupative wills, which, by the Statute, are assigned to a separate and distinct class, and are subject to different requisites and conditions.

Section 5925 in providing that "the witness shall be competent to give testimony in the execution of the will," evidently refers to the full, legal formalities of a signature by the testator, and an attestation by competent witnesses who subscribe in the testator's presence, and not, as in a nuncupative will, to the testator's speaking testamentary words in his last sickness, which are to be reduced to writing and subscribed by competent and disinterested witnesses, within ten days after the words are spoken.

II. The renouncement and release by Orris D. Vroman of all right and interest was not filed until more than five years after the verbal will is alleged to have been made. Such a release did not remove his disqualification as a witness. The Statute contemplates the verbal will as made in the last sickness. Within ten days after the speaking of the testamentary words, the will must be reduced to writing, and subscribed by two witnesses who are then competent and disinterested.

The rule, it is said, which reason should now pronounce the universal one, is that the competency of witnesses, like that of the testator, is tested by one's status at the time when the will was executed. Schouler, Wills, § 351.

In *Patten* v. *Tallman*, 27 Me. 27, the court says: "The competency of an attesting witness is not to be determined upon the state of facts existing at the time when the will is presented for probate, but upon those existing at the time of the attestation."

In *Morton* v. *Ingram*, 11 Ired. L. 368, it was held, that a person named as executor is not competent as an attesting witness to a will of personalty; and that his subsequent renunciation and release will not make him so; and that he must be disinterested at the time of attestation.

In *Huie* v. *McConnell*, 2 Jones, L. 455, the court remarks: "It is well settled that an attesting witness to a will must be competent at the time of attestation, and that no subsequent release, where the objection is one of interest, can restore competency."

In *Workman* v. *Dominick*, 3 Strobh. L. 589, it was held that "credible" means competent; and the competency of the witness must be referred to the time of attestation. Frost, *J.*, said: "This point is settled. It is affirmed by all the elementary writers. . . . If the witnesses do not possess, at the time of the execution of the will, the quality required, it cannot afterwards be supplied. If any of them be not then credible, by reason of a benefit he may take by the instrument, he cannot be made credible by a future release. . . . The will would be absolutely in the power of the witness. If he consents to release, the will is established; if he refuses, the will is annulled. It is in his power to set up the estate at auction between the legatees and next of kin, and sell it to the highest bidder. And thus, being first bribed by an interest in the will to make it, he is open to another bribe to vacate it."

See *Stewart* v. *Harriman*, 56 N. H. 25; *Hawes* v. *Humphrey*, 9 Pick. 350; *Higgins* v. *Carlton*, 28 Md. 115; *Pease* v. *Allis*, 110 Mass. 157; *Allison* v. *Allison*, 4 Hawks, 141; *Tucker* v. *Tucker*, 5 Ired. L. 161; Greenl. Ev. § 691.

The rule laid down in the above citations acquires additional force and significance when applied to the attestation and establishment of verbal wills. The rule, it is true, in its application to wills in writing, is controlled by section 5925 of the Revised Statutes, but that section, as we have before observed, is not applicable to nuncupative wills.

Judgment affirmed.

MASSACHUSETTS SUPREME JUDICIAL COURT.

FREEMAN'S NATIONAL BANK
v.
NATIONAL TUBE WORKS CO.

(....Mass.....)

1. The owner of drafts, who indorses them in blank and places them with a bank for collection, may avail himself of the benefit of a restrictive indorsement placed thereon by such bank when it transmitted them to its correspondent for the purpose of effecting such collection.

2. The legal title to commercial paper indorsed "For collection" passes only so far as to enable the indorsee to demand, receive

NOTE.—*Indorsement of note or bill deposited for collection.*

A special indorsement "For collection" on a promissory note does not transfer the ownership of the note or its proceeds to the indorsee. Sweeny v. Easter, 68 U. S. 1 Wall. 166 (17 L. ed. 681).

Where a bank on its own proposition enters into an arrangement with another bank, whereby it

See also 9 L. R. A. 553; 13 L. R. A. 241; 15 L. R. A. 102, 498; 17 L. R. A. 291;

and sue for the money to be paid; upon such indorsement the owner may control his paper until it is paid, and may intercept the proceeds thereof in the hands of an intermediate agent.

3. **A bank's indorsement of commercial paper directing payment "for account of itself"** does not imply that it is the owner of the paper, where the indorsement of the bank from which its title was derived was of the same kind.

4. **A bank to which commercial paper has been transmitted** for collection will not be permitted to dispute the right of the owner to stop payment thereof, although it has made credits or advances to an intermediate collecting agent on account of the paper, if the same were made before the paper had been collected; nor can such advances be recovered from the owner as money paid for his use.

(May, 1890.)

REPORT from the Supreme Judicial Court for Suffolk County (C. Allen, *J.*) for the opinion of the full court of an action brought to recover the amount alleged to be due upon certain accepted drafts, the payment of which had been stopped by the owner. *Judgment for defendant.*

The National Tube Works Company operated mills at McKeesport, Pa., and had an office in Boston, where the treasurer was located and the finances of the Company were kept. For the purpose of paying the running expenses of the mills it was in the habit of drawing drafts on the treasurer in Boston, and depositing them with the People's Bank of McKeesport, of which C. R. Stuckslager was cashier, for collection.

This suit was brought upon two of those drafts, which were alike with the exception that the amounts were different. There was also a count upon an account annexed for $7,000 for money paid to defendant's use, and interest thereon, being the amount paid by plaintiff to the Penn Bank, under date May 20, 1884.

The following is a copy of one of the drafts:

$20,000. McKeesport, Pa., May 17, 1884.

At sight for value received, pay to the order of A. Chaudon twenty thousand dollars and charge this office as per margin.

National Tube Works Co.,

by E. C. Converse, *Asst. Mgr. for President.*

To Wm. S. Eaton, Treas., 8 Pemberton Square, Boston, Mass.

---

undertakes to collect all paper sent it by the latter, and to transmit the proceeds at or upon designated dates; and, in addition to such agency and services, all paper transmitted for collection contains a special or restrictive indorsement, the form of which is suggested by the collecting bank, directing payment to the latter for the transmitting bank, and stating that the paper was to be collected at par and the proceeds remitted to the transmitting bank on specified dates, without exchange,—the relation thus created, both as respects the paper and the proceeds thereof after collection, is that of principal and agent, and not of debtor and creditor. Commercial Nat. Bank v. Armstrong, 39 Fed. Rep. 684; Farmer's Bank v. Owen, 5 Cranch, C. C. 504.

Where a banker has received from his correspondent a draft indorsed for collection, which is indorsed in like manner to his correspondent, he cannot appropriate the proceeds collected thereon to the latter's debt to himself, and refuse to pay the owner. City Bank v. Weiss, 67 Tex. 331; Sweeny v. Easter, 68 U. S. 1 Wall. 166 (17 L. ed. 681); White v. Miners Nat. Bank, 102 U. S. 659 (26 L. ed. 251); First Nat. Bank v. Reno County Bank, 1 McCrary, 491, 3 Fed. Rep. 257.

An indorsement by a collecting agent of a check sent to him for collection, without using the word "agent," is, in behalf of his principal, an indorsement merely for the purpose of collection, and is not a guaranty of the genuineness of the check. National City Bank v. Westcott, 118 N. Y. 468.

The indorsement of the words "For collection," on invoices accompanying bills of lading attached as collateral security to drafts discounted, implies no guaranty of the genuineness of the bills. Goetz v. Kansas City Bank, 119 U. S. 551 (30 L. ed. 515).

An indorsee of a promissory note for collection has such a title as will enable him to sue thereon in his own name, though he paid nothing for the note. Roberts v. Parrish, 17 Or. 583; Roberts v. Snow (Neb.) Oct. 8, 1889.

He holds the note subject to the same defenses that could have been made to it in the hands of the original payee. *Ibid.*

Collecting bank as agent of owner.

The bank receiving the paper for collection is the agent of the owner and not of the maker who pays it. The latter cannot recover back from the bank the money paid, on the ground that it has failed to account for it to the owner. Smith v. Essex County Bank, 22 Barb. 627; Ward v. Smith, 74 U. S. 7 Wall. 447 (19 L. ed. 207); Alley v. Rogers, 19 Gratt. 383.

It is liable for the neglect, omission or other misconduct of the bank or agent to whom the note or bill is sent by which the money is lost or other injury sustained. Allen v. Merchants Bank, 22 Wend. 215; West Branch Bank v. Fulmer, 3 Pa. 399; Ivory v. State Bank, 36 Mo. 475; Hoard v. Garner, 3 Sandf. 179; Georgia Nat. Bank v. Henderson, 46 Ga. 493.

Liability for neglect of duty to give notice.

It is liable if it fails to give notice to the indorsers in case of the maker's default, where it is the usage of banks to give such notice. Smedes v. Bank of Utica, 20 Johns. 372; Bank of Utica v. Smedes, 3 Cow. 662; Bank of Utica v. McKinster, 11 Wend. 473; McKinster v. Bank of Utica, 9 Wend. 46; Curtis v. Leavitt, 15 N. Y. 9, 157.

If the bill is payable at the place where the bank conducts its business, it is liable for any neglect of duty as to protest and notice, unless there be some agreement to the contrary, express or implied. Montgomery County Bank v. Albany City Bank, 7 N. Y. 459; Fabens v. Mercantile Bank, 23 Pick. 330; Halls v. State Bank, 3 Rich. L. 366; Caldwell v. Evans, 5 Bush, 380; Balme v. Wambaugh, 16 Minn. 120.

A notice issued by the Chicago bank to its customers, after the receipt of the notes for collection, that it would be compelled to place all funds received in payment of collections to the credit of its correspondents in such currency as was received in Chicago—to wit, bills of Illinois banks, to be drawn for only in like bills—does not change the rights of the parties. Marine Bank v. Fulton County Bank, 69 U. S. 2 Wall. 252 (17 L. ed. 785).

If a bank fails to demand payment of a bill held for collection, it makes the bill its own, and becomes liable for the amount. It is agent for the holder, not of the drawer. Bank of Washington v. Triplett, 26 U. S. 1 Pet. 25 (7 L. ed. 37).

Its failure to give notice to the drawer that the drawee was not found at home when called upon to accept the bill is not such negligence as discharges the drawer from his liability, where it is

[In the margin:] No. 6611 charge to account of ——

[Across the face:] May 19-84. Accepted E. R. Hall, Asst. Treas.

[Indorsements:] Pay to the order of C. R. Stuckslager, Cashier. A. Chaudon.

Pay Penn Bank or order for account of People's Bank, McKeesport, Pa. C. R. Stuckslager, Cashier. T. D. Gardner, As. Cash.

Pay Freeman's Nat'l Bank, Boston, or order for account of Penn Bank, Pittsburgh, Pa. G. L. Reiber, Cashier.

The drafts were deposited in the People's Bank, and on the same day they were sent by the People's Bank to its correspondent, the Penn Bank of Pittsburg, indorsed as above and inclosed in the following letter:

Penn Bank Pittsburg
Dear Sir,—We inclose for collection and credit.
W. S. Eaton, Tr. *St.* $20,000
" $9,900
Very Respectfully,
C. R. Stuckslager, Cashier.

The Penn Bank acknowledged their receipt as follows:

People's Bank
Your account has credit
Letter *17* *723.89*
Item *4*
We charge your account
Exchange
We enter for collection *Eaton* item *20,000.00*
" " " " " *9,900.*
To be used when paid.
Very Respectfully,
G. L. Reiber, Cashier.

May 17 the Penn Bank sent the drafts to its Boston correspondent, the Freeman's Bank, indorsed as above and inclosed in the following letter:

Geo. P. Tenney, Esq. Ca.
Boston, Mass.
Dear Sir,—We inclose for collection
W. S. Eaton, Trs., *No. 6611* *20,000*
" " " " *6612* *9,900*
[Stamp:] Yours Respectfully,
FREEMAN'S NAT'L BANK, G. L. Reiber,
BOSTON, MASS. Cashier.
MAY 19, 1884.
CORRESPONDENCE.
Acknowledged.

The drafts were received by the Freeman's Bank May 19, and were accepted by the defendant the same day.

May 20 the Penn-Bank check for $7,000 reached the Freeman's Bank through the Boston Clearing House and was paid.

The drafts, when received by the Freeman's Bank, were entered upon its collection book, but have never been entered upon its account current or upon any other book or account to the credit of the Penn Bank.

On the 21st or 22d of May the Penn Bank failed, and the defendant's treasurer was notified by the People's Bank and the manager of the National Tube Works at McKeesport not to pay the same. Payment was accordingly refused on presentation on May 22, and this suit was thereupon commenced.

Messrs. **W. G. Russell** and **Jabez Fox,** for plaintiff:

The legal title at least passed by the indorsement "Pay Penn Bank or order for account of the People's Bank."

First Nat. Bank v. *Smith,* 132 Mass. 227; *Murrow* v. *Stuart,* 8 Moore, P. C. 267.

A second restrictive indorsement like that of the Penn Bank in the present case is just as unequivocal an assertion of title in the second indorser as if it stood alone.

Merchants Nat. Bank v. *Hanson,* 33 Minn. 40, cited in *Manufacturers Nat. Bank* v. *Continental Bank,* 2 L. R. A. 699, 148 Mass. 558.

The fact that the indorsement of the Penn Bank was restrictive would not prevent the title from passing to the plaintiff to secure the sum advanced.

---

not the usage of the bank to consider the bill dishonored in such a case. *Ibid.*

A bank receiving for collection drafts drawn against shipments of cattle, on which payment is refused, and which fails to send notice of such refusal for more than twenty-four hours, cannot appropriate the proceeds of the cattle, which it collects for the drawee of such drafts, to his indebtedness to the bank on overdrafts. Gillespie v. Union Stockyards Nat. Bank, 41 Fed. Rep. 231.

The bank is responsible for the amount of the bill in case of its negligence as to notice of presentment and nonpayment. Allen v. Suydam, 20 Wend. 321; Borup v. Nininger, 5 Minn. 523; Chicopee Bank v. Seventh Nat. Bank, 75 U. S. 8 Wall. 641 (19 L. ed. 422); Essex County Nat. Bank v. Bank of Montreal, 15 Am. L. Reg. N. S. 418; Woolen v. New York & E. Bank, 12 Blatchf. 359; Indig v. National City Bank, 80 N. Y. 100; Ayrault v. Pacific Bank, 6 Robt. 337.

Liability of agent of collecting bank.

The bank receiving the note for collection, and not its agent, is liable to the owner. Hyde v. First Nat. Bank, 7 Biss. 156.

Where a person goes to a bank, in the ordinary course of business dealing, and intrusts to it the collection of a draft drawn upon some person residing at a distance, and the home bank, through the failure or dishonesty of another bank selected by itself to make the collection, never receives the money paid on such draft by the drawee, in the absence of any agreement in regard to the matter, the home bank is liable to the customer for the loss of the money. Simpson v. Waldby, 6 West. Rep. 158, 63 Mich. 439.

If a collecting bank surrenders a check to a bank on which it is drawn, and accepts a cashier's check or other obligation in lieu thereof, its liability to its depositor is fixed as much as if it had received the cash. Fifth Nat. Bank v. Ashworth, 2 L. R. A. 491, 123 Pa. 212.

If it employs some other bank or individual to collect the bill the latter becomes the agent of the former bank, and not of the owner, to which it is answerable for neglect of its duty as agent. Commercial Bank v. Union Bank, 11 N. Y. 203; Montgomery County Bank v. Albany City Bank, 7 N. Y. 459; Merchants & M. Bank v. Stafford Nat. Bank, 44 Conn. 564; Reeves v. State Bank, 8 Ohio St. 465; Hoover v. Wise, 91 U. S. 308 (23 L. ed. 392).

If a party sends a bill of exchange to his agent for collection, who remits it to a sub-agent, living in the same place with the drawee, who receives the money, the holder of the bill can recover the money of the sub-agent. If the sub-agent has made no advances and given no new credit to the

A banker who has advanced money to another has a lien upon all the securities in his hands, including paper deposited for collection, to secure the amount of such advance.

Wood v. *Boylston Nat. Bank*, 129 Mass. 358; *Backett* v. *Reynolds*, 5 Cent. Rep. 521, 114 Pa. 328; *Bank of Metropolis* v. *New England Bank*, 42 U. S. 1 How. 234 (11 L. ed. 115); *Cody* v. *City Nat. Bank*, 55 Mich. 379; *Sweeny* v. *Easter*, 68 U. S. 1 Wall. 166 (17 L. ed. 681).

It cannot be said that the People's Bank, by permitting the Penn Bank to make this assertion of its own title and to put upon the drafts this direction to collect for its own account, gave that bank a less extensive authority to deal with them than it would have had under a power of attorney "to sell, indorse and assign" the securities "on behalf" of its principal, and yet it has been held that under such a power the agent could pledge the securities for a loan upon his private account.

Bank of Bengal v. *Fagan*, 7 Moore, P. C. 61.

It could be no departure from the line of agency for the plaintiff to remit to the Penn Bank in advance of collection, and to rely upon the security of these drafts.

Where a person had purchased goods from a broker and had paid for them in part by an advance on his general account before the delivery of the goods, such payments would be allowed as against the principal, "if it was the usual practice for payments to be made from time to time, sometimes to a smaller and sometimes to a larger amount than was actually due at the time."

Catterall v. *Hindle*, L. R. 2 C. P. 368; *Fish* v. *Kempton*, 7 C. B. 692; *Warner* v. *M'Kay*, 1 Mees. & W. 591.

The money was paid to the defendant's use and at its request and we can recover independently of any question of title to the drafts.

Homes v. *Dana*, 12 Mass. 190; *Bryant* v. *Goodnow*, 5 Pick. 228; *Mirick* v. *French*, 2 Gray, 420.

Messrs. **Hutchins & Wheeler,** for defendant:

The ownership of these drafts never passed out of the National Tube Works Company.

Commercial Nat. Bank v. *Armstrong*, 39 Fed. Rep. 684; *First Nat. Bank* v. *Armstrong*, 36 Fed. Rep. 59; *Manufacturers Nat. Bank* v. *Continental Bank*, 2 L. R. A. 699, 148 Mass. 553; *Fifth Nat. Bank* v. *Armstrong*, 40 Fed. Rep. 46.

If a bill be indorsed "For the use of" or "For account of" the indorser, it is a restrictive indorsement, and is not an assignment of the security, but merely an authority to collect. The title to the bill does not pass to the indorsee, and such indorsee cannot indorse the bill so as to pass any interest in it.

White v. *Miners Nat. Bank*, 102 U. S. 658 (26 L. ed. 250); *Rice* v. *Stearns*, 3 Mass. 225, 227; *Wilson* v. *Holmes*, 5 Mass. 543; *Sigourney* v. *Lloyd*, 8 Barn. & C. 622; *Rock County Nat. Bank* v. *Hollister*, 21 Minn. 385; *Third Nat. Bank* v. *Clark*, 23 Minn. 263; *Lawrence* v. *Fussell*, 77 Pa. 460; *Williams* v. *Shadbolt*, 1 Cababé & Ellis, 529; 2 Ames, Bills and Notes, index, p. 837.

The Freeman's Bank had notice from the form of the indorsements that the Penn Bank had no interest in the drafts, and that the authority of the Penn Bank to collect might be revoked at any time before the maturity of the drafts. Therefore, if it paid the $7,000 in reliance on acceptances, it acted at its peril.

Treuttel v. *Barandon*, 8 Taunt. 100.

The People's Bank, having received the drafts simply as agents to collect, indorse them "Pay Penn Bank or order for account of People's Bank." This was a restrictive indorsement, and neither the Penn Bank nor any subsequent indorsee could claim to be holder for value without notice as against the National Tube Works, the real owners of the paper.

Treuttel v. *Barandon*, 8 Taunt. 100; *Wilson* v. *Holmes*, 5 Mass. 543; *White* v. *Miners Nat. Bank*, 102 U. S. 658 (26 L. ed. 250); *Sweeny* v. *Easter*, 68 U. S. 1 Wall. 166 (17 L. ed. 681); *Manufacturers Nat. Bank* v. *Continental Bank*, 2 L. R. A. 699, 148 Mass. 553; *First Nat. Bank* v. *Reno County Bank*, 3 Fed. Rep. 257; *Blaine* v. *Bourne*, 11 R. I. 119; *Leary* v. *Blanchard*, 48 Me. 269.

---

agent on account of the remittance of the bill, he cannot protect himself against such an action by passing the amount of the bill to the general credit of the agent, although the agent may be his debtor. Wilson v. Smith, 44 U. S. 3 How. 763 (11 L. ed. 820).

In New York, a collecting agent to whom paper is sent to be collected at some place remote from his place of business has no implied authority to employ a sub-agent in the locality of the payee, and, without some express understanding to that effect or qualifying his liability, is deemed to make such selection and employment of another on his own account, and is alone chargeable for the conduct of the latter. Naser v. First Nat. Bank, 116 N. Y. 492.

Where, upon a bank's agreement to transmit money to a person in a distant city, plaintiff makes with it a special deposit of the amount for that purpose, and receives a letter of advice directed to a bank in that city, to the effect that the latter's account is credited with the money for the use of the one to whom it is to go, plaintiff may recover back the deposit in case the correspondent bank fails before receiving the letter, which is returned with the amount unpaid; and the fact that the money is credited to the account of the correspondent bank on the books of the bank of deposit is immaterial. See *note* to Cutler v. American Exch. Nat. Bank (N. Y.) 4 L. R. A. 328.

A bank holding an assignment of a policy of insurance to collect it and pay certain claims, including one of its own, therefrom, and pay the balance to the insured or his order, cannot be held liable on an order which it has accepted to be paid out of the balance, if, in the exercise of reasonable diligence and in good faith, it has settled the suit to collect the insurance for the amount merely of its own claim, after notice to the person holding the order who made no move or proposition to prosecute the suit. Meyer v. Farmers & T. Bank, 77 Iowa, 388.

Where a check was sent to a company for collection, of which fact the drawee was advised by the indorsement upon it, and the collecting company received the money from the drawee, and, prior to the time of the discovery of the fraudulent character of the check, gave the money to the company from which it was received for collection, the collecting company is not liable to the drawee as for money paid by mistake. National City Bank v. Westcott, 118 N. Y. 468.

The plaintiff may rely on the restrictive indorsement made by its agent, the People's Bank, although it had indorsed the drafts in blank.

Sweeny v. *Easter*, 68 U. S. 1 Wall. 166 (17 L. ed. 681); *Wilson* v. *Holmes*, 5 Mass. 543; *Bank of Washington* v. *Triplett*, 26 U. S. 1 Pet. 25 (7 L. ed. 37); *Lawrence* v. *Stonington Bank*, 6 Conn. 521; *Ayer* v. *Hutchins*, 4 Mass. 370.

"For the use of" or "For the account of" the indorsee, or equivalent words, is the simplest and most direct way of expressing a restrictive indorsement, and such has universally been their construction.

Snee v. *Prescot*, 1 Atk. 245, 249; *Rice* v. *Stearns*, 3 Mass. 225, 227; *Merchants Nat. Bank* v. *Hanson*, 33 Minn. 40; *Treuttel* v. *Barandon*, 8 Taunt. 100; *Wilson* v. *Holmes*, 5 Mass. 543; *Leary* v. *Blanchard*, 48 Me. 269; *White* v. *Miners Nat. Bank*, 102 U. S. 658 (26 L. ed. 250); *Lawrence* v. *Fussell*, 77 Pa. 460.

Knowlton, *J.*, delivered the opinion of the court:

The indorsement from the defendant to the People's Bank, although in terms unrestricted, was without consideration, and merely for the purpose of collection. The People's Bank became the agent of the defendant, and the defendant, as owner of the drafts, can avail itself of all that its agent did for its protection. The subsequent indorsements through which the drafts came to the plaintiff were both restrictive, giving notice that the ownership had not passed beyond the People's Bank. They purported to be made only for the purpose of collection on account of the owner, and they merely passed the legal title so far as to enable the indorsees to demand, receive and sue for the money to be paid. *First Nat. Bank* v. *Smith*, 132 Mass. 227.

It is well settled that upon such an indorsement the owner may control his negotiable paper until it is paid, and may intercept the proceeds of it in the hands of an intermediate agent. *Manufacturers Nat. Bank* v. *Continental Bank*, 148 Mass. 553, 2 L. R. A. 699, and cases there cited.

The indorsement of the Penn National Bank, taken in connection with the former indorsement of the People's Bank, did not by the words "For account of Penn Bank," imply that the Penn Bank was the owner. It was a request to pay "For account of" the Penn Bank as agent of the People's Bank. An unbroken succession of such indorsements would indicate that each indorsee was acting by the direction of the next preceding indorser who was himself an agent of the owner who had before indorsed and for whom the collection was to be made.

Nothing was shown in the course of business of either of the banks necessarily to conflict with the implication to be derived from the form of the indorsements. The letter of the People's Bank, in which the drafts were sent to the Penn Bank, was simply, "We inclose for collection and credit" the drafts, describing them. The Penn Bank in its reply said, "We enter for collection" the drafts described, "to be used when paid." The drafts when received by the Freeman's Bank were entered upon its collection book, but have never been entered upon its account current, or upon any other book of account to the credit of the Penn Bank.

It has so long been held by the courts that an indorsement of this kind is restrictive, protecting the rights of the owner, that officers of banks must be presumed to have well understood the law, and, when they have honored overdrafts drawn by other banks which had sent paper for collection, must have done it trusting in part to the financial soundness of their correspondent, and in part to the probability that the drafts would be paid, and not to a supposed legal right to control the drafts against the owner. *Rice* v. *Stearns*, 3 Mass. 225, 227; *Wilson* v. *Holmes*, 5 Mass. 543; *Treuttell* v. *Barandon*, 8 Taunt. 100; *Sigourney* v. *Lloyd*, 8 Barn. & C. 622; *Leary* v. *Blanchard*, 48 Me. 269; *Sweeny* v. *Easter*, 68 U. S. 1 Wall. 166 [17 L. ed. 681]; *Bank of Washington* v. *Triplett*, 26 U. S. 1 Pet. 25 [7 L. ed. 37]; *Lawrence* v. *Stonington Bank*, 6 Conn. 521; *Bank of Metropolis* v. *New England Bank*, 42 U. S. 1 How. 234 [11 L. ed. 115], 47 U. S. 6 How. 212 [12 L. ed. 409].

One who collects commercial papers through the agency of banks must be held to impliedly contract that the business may be done according to their well-known usages so far as to permit the money collected to be mingled with the funds of the collecting bank. *Dorchester & M. Bank* v. *New England Bank*, 1 Cush. 177.

When a payment is made to his agent and the money is put with the money of the collecting bank he has a right to receive a corresponding sum, but he loses his right to the specific fund. In the absence of directions to the contrary, the collecting bank may pay it to the bank to which it should regularly be remitted, by setting it off against a debt due from that bank and giving credit for it in the account.

Very likely authority to collect would authorize the receipt of the money from the payor before maturity if he saw fit then to pay, and remittances afterwards made, whether by actual transmissions of money or by a set-off and adjustment of accounts in the usual way, would be good against the owner. In the present case no collection was made, for payment was stopped before the draft became due. The plaintiff had no right to advance the Penn Bank $7,000, or any other sum, on account of the defendant. Its only authority was to transmit or pay by adjustment and set-off money which it received for the defendant.

We are of opinion that upon the facts reported, the action cannot be maintained.

Judgment for the defendant.

UNITED STATES CIRCUIT COURT, NORTHERN DISTRICT OF NEW YORK.

Thomas C. COOPER
v.
Philip D. ARMOUR *et al.*

(....Fed. Rep.....)

1. **An action for malicious prosecution will not lie** in favor of one against whom an accusation has been preferred before a magistrate charging a criminal offense, if he was not apprehended and no process for his arrest was issued.

2. **Although an action for libel or slander may be maintained** in such case if the accusation was made with no bona fide intention of prosecuting it, yet an action brought for malicious prosecution cannot be retained and treated as one for libel and slander if the defamatory words are not set out in the complaint.

(April 16, 1890.)

ACTION to recover damages for an alleged malicious prosecution. On plaintiff's motion for a new trial. *Denied.*

Defendants filed an information against plaintiff before a police justice, and made application for a warrant for plaintiff's arrest, for the alleged crime of forgery in the second degree. The justice subpœnaed witnesses to appear before him and be examined to determine whether or not the warrant should issue. Counsel appeared for the respective parties and the proceedings were conducted with all the formality of a regular trial. The justice finally refused to issue the warrant, and plaintiff thereupon brought this action to recover damages for the alleged malicious prosecution.

The action was brought on for trial before *Judge* Wallace and a jury, and the judge directed a verdict for defendants.

The plaintiff thereupon filed this motion for a new trial.

Messrs. **Ward & Cameron,** for plaintiff, in support of the motion:

Defendants inflicted a great injury on plaintiff and are liable therefor in damages in an action on the case.

See *Smith* v. *Smith*, 20 Hun, 555.

There was an actual and technical prosecution.

McCardle v. *McGinley*, 86 Ind. 538, 44 Am. Rep. 343; *McPherson* v. *Runyon* (Minn.) 40 Alb. L. J. 403; *Smith* v. *Smith*, 20 Hun, 555; *Clarke* v. *Postan*, 6 Car. & P. 423; Stephens, Mal. Pros. Wood's ed. p. 8; Addison, Torts, §§ 852, 856; Townshend, Slander and Libel, p. 700, § 422; *Weston* v. *Beeman*, 27 L. J. N. S. Exch. 57.

"To put the criminal law in force maliciously and without any reasonable or probable cause, is wrongful" for which an action will lie for malicious prosecution.

Addison, Torts, §§ 852, 856; Stephens, Mal. Pros. Wood's ed. p. 5; *Clarke* v. *Postan*, *supra; Dawson* v. *Vansandau*, 11 Week. Rep. 516; Townshend, Slander and Libel, § 422, p. 700.

It is not necessary in order to maintain this action for malicious prosecution, to show there was any interference with the person or property of the plaintiff.

McPherson v. *Runyon*, *supra; McCardle* v. *McGinley*, 86 Ind. 538, 44 Am. Rep. 343.

It is not essential to the maintaining of this action that a warrant, summons or other process should actually have been issued.

Smith v. *Smith*, *supra;* Addison, Torts, § 859; Stephens, Mal. Pros. Wood's ed. p. 8.

Messrs. **Stedman, Thompson & Andrews,** for defendants:

In an action of malicious prosecution the gravamen of the charge is that the plaintiff has improperly been made the subject of legal process to his damage.

Newfield v. *Copperman*, 47 How. Pr. 87; *Lawyer* v. *Loomis*, 3 Thomp. & C. 393; *Stewart* v. *Sonneborn*, 98 U. S. 187 (25 L. ed. 116); *Wetmore* v. *Mellinger*, 64 Iowa, 741, 30 Alb. L. J. 55; *Muldoon* v. *Rickey*, 103 Pa. 110, 29 Alb. L. J. 457; *Heyward* v. *Cuthbert*, 4 McCord, L. (S. C.) 354; *Kneeland* v. *Spitzka*, 10 Jones & S. 470; *O'Driscoll* v. *McBurney*, 2 Nott & McC. 54; *Gregory* v. *Derby*, 8 Car. & P. 749.

Wallace, *J.*, delivered the opinion of the court:

The question in this case is whether an action for malicious prosecution will lie against the defendants who have preferred an accusation before a magistrate charging the plaintiff with a criminal offense, notwithstanding the plaintiff was not apprehended and no process for his arrest was issued by the magistrate.

The gist of the action of malicious prosecution is the putting of legal process in force, regularly, for the mere purpose of vexation or injury; and the inconvenience or harm resulting, naturally or directly, from the suit or prosecution, is the legal damage upon which it is founded. Some of the text-writers state that the action will lie whenever the defendant has made a charge of felony against the plaintiff with a view to induce a magistrate or tribunal to entertain it, whether any warrant or other process was issued or not. Stephens, Mal. Pros. Wood's ed. p. 8; Addison, Torts, § 856.

Actions have been maintained in the nature of conspiracy for procuring a false indictment, and even for preferring a false charge of crime upon which the grand jury refused to indict; but the only decisions cited in support of the proposition that the action of malicious prosecution will lie although a criminal proceeding has not actually been instituted by the issuing of process, where the point actually arose, are in the *Nisi Prius* case of *Clarke* v. *Postan*, 6 Car. & P. 423, and in the case of *Dawson* v. *Vansandau*, 11 Week. Rep. 516, in which, although no process was issued, the plaintiff was taken into custody and held for examination upon the charge. On the other hand it was said by Patterson, *J.*, in *Gregory* v. *Derby*, 8 Car. & P. 749, where there was a charge of stealing upon which a warrant was issued against the plaintiff, "that if the party was never apprehended no action would lie; and in *O'Driscoll* v. *McBurney*, 2 Nott & McC. 54, 55, it was said: "There can be no prosecution without an arrest."

The only injury sustained by the person accused when he is not taken into custody and no process has been issued against him is to his reputation; and for such an injury the action of libel or slander is the appropriate remedy, and would seem to be the only remedy. This is the view adopted by Hare & Wallace in their *notes* to American Leading Cases (vol. 1, p. 178); and the learned commentators state that slander or libel is the only appropriate remedy where a charge of felony has been made and a warrant was not thereupon issued, and that malicious prosecution, and not slander or libel, is the remedy whenever a warrant has been issued. The question was fully considered by the Supreme Court of South Carolina in *Heyward* v. *Cuthbert*, 4 McCord, L. 354, whether an action for malicious prosecution would lie founded on a criminal charge upon which no process was issued against the accused, and it was adjudged that it would not. In that case the charge was in the form of an information laid before the magistrate to procure a warrant for the arrest of the plaintiff. To the same effect is the case of *Kneeland* v. *Spitzka*, 42 N. Y. Super. Ct. [10 Jones & S.] 470, where the question was decided in an appellate court.

In the early case of *Ram* v. *Lamley*, Hutt. 113, it was held that an action of slander could not be maintained for an oral charge of felony made to a justice of the peace upon an application for a warrant against the plaintiff, for the reason that if words so spoken were to be held actionable "no other would come to a justice of the peace to inform him of a felony." A defamatory statement spoken or written in a legal proceeding, civil or criminal, which is pertinent and material, is so unqualifiedly privileged that its truth cannot be drawn into question or malice predicated of it in an action for slander or libel. *Revis* v. *Smith*, 18 C. B. 126; *Lea* v. *White*, 4 Sneed, 111; *Garr* v. *Selden*, 4 N. Y. 91; *Hawk* v. *Evans*, 76 Iowa, 593.

If upon considerations of public policy such an action cannot be maintained, upon the same considerations no other action should lie. Without doubt libel or slander will lie for an accusation to a magistrate when made with no bona fide intention of prosecuting it. Unless such facts can be shown by the person accused, or unless he is subjected to the vexation and expense of process against him, upon principle he ought not to be allowed to recover.

The more generally approved doctrine is that for the prosecution of a civil action maliciously and without probable cause, to the injury of the plaintiff, he may maintain an action for damages although there was no interference with his person or property. *Pangburn* v. *Bull*, 1 Wend. 345; *Whipple* v. *Fuller*, 11 Conn. 582; *Closson* v. *Staples*, 42 Vt. 209; *Eastin* v. *Bank of Stockton*, 66 Cal. 123, 56 Am. Rep. 77; *Allen* v. *Codman*, 139 Mass. 136; *Marbourg* v. *Smith*, 11 Kan. 554; *Woods* v. *Finnell*, 13 Bush, 629; *Pope* v. *Pollock* (Ohio) 4 L. R. A. 255; *McCardle* v. *McGinley*, 86 Ind. 538, 44 Am. Rep. 343; *McPherson* v. *Runyon* (Minn.) 40 Alb. L. J. 403; *Smith* v. *Smith*, 20 Hun, 555.

The cases however which sustain this view do not countenance an action when the vexatious suit has not been actually instituted and prosecuted to such effect that the plaintiff has sustained pecuniary loss.

Inasmuch as the defamatory words, which must be set forth in an action for slander or libel, are not alleged in the present complaint, the case cannot be treated as an action for slander or libel.

The motion for a new trial is denied.

CALIFORNIA SUPREME COURT.

George A. CASE, *Respt.*,
v.
SUN INSURANCE CO., *Appt.*

(....Cal.....)

The time for bringing suit on an insurance policy which provides that no suit or action shall be commenced unless within twelve months next after the fire, and also provides that a claim on the policy shall be due and payable sixty days after full completion by the assured of certain requirements of the policy, does not elapse with the expiration of the twelve months after the fire, where a cause of action has not then accrued by completion of such requirements, if the company has insisted on, and the insured has complied with, them as rapidly as he was able.

(March 26, 1890.)

APPEAL by defendant from a judgment of the Superior Court for the City and County of San Francisco in favor of plaintiff, and from an order denying a motion for a new trial, in an action to recover the amount alleged to

---

NOTE.—*Fire insurance; limitation of action on policy.*

A condition in a policy of insurance, that an action cannot be maintained upon the policy unless commenced within twelve months after the loss, is valid. Riddlesbarger v. Hartford F. Ins. Co. 74 U. S. 7 Wall. 386 (19 L. ed. 257); Ghio v. Western Assur. Co. 65 Miss. 532.

The condition is not fulfilled by a previous action commenced within that period, which was dismissed. Riddlesbarger v. Hartford F. Ins. Co. *supra*.

The statute of a State which allows a party who suffers a nonsuit in an action to bring a new action for the same cause within one year afterwards does not affect the rights of the parties in such case. *Ibid.*

The disability to sue imposed by the war relieves the assured wholly from the consequences of failing to bring suit within twelve months after the loss, as required by his policy. Semmes v. City F. Ins. Co. 80 U. S. 13 Wall. 158 (20 L. ed. 490).

Where a policy provides that no action shall be commenced after a year, and that lapse of time shall be taken as conclusive evidence against the validity of the claim, any statute of limitation to the contrary notwithstanding, the statute relative to the bringing of a second action within a year

be due under a policy of fire insurance. *Affirmed.*

The case sufficiently appears in the opinion.

Messrs. **Rhodes & Barstow** for appellant.

Messrs. **Haggin, Van Ness & Dibble,** for respondent:

Until full compliance with the provision of the policy, and the expiration of sixty days thereafter, right of action upon the policy did not accrue.

May, Ins. § 476; *Doyle* v. *Phœnix Ins. Co.* 44 Cal. 264.

The limitation clause does not apply in those cases in which, without fault on the part of the assured, and by reason of the acts of the Company, the right of action does not accrue within a year subsequent to the fire.

Friezen v. *Allemania F. Ins. Co.* 30 Fed. Rep. 352; *Vette* v. *Clinton F. Ins. Co.* Id. 668; *Ellis* v. *Council Bluffs Ins. Co.* 64 Iowa, 507; *Longhurst* v. *Star Ins. Co.* 19 Iowa, 364; *Stout* v. *City F. Ins. Co.* 12 Iowa, 371; *Barber* v. *Wheeling F. & M. Ins. Co.* 16 W. Va. 675; *Owen* v. *Howard Ins. Co.* 87 Ky. 571; *Killips* v. *Putnam F. Ins. Co.* 28 Wis. 472; *Martin* v. *State Ins. Co.* 44 N. J. L. 485; *Little* v. *Phœnix Ins. Co.* 123 Mass. 389; *Barnum* v. *Merchants F. Ins. Co.* 97 N. Y. 188; May, Ins. §§ 486, 487.

Sharpstein, *J.,* delivered the opinion of the court:

The policy upon which this action is based contains, among others, the following clause: "It is mutually agreed that no suit or action for the recovery of any claim by virtue of this policy shall be sustainable in any court of law or chancery until appraisement shall be had, if demanded by this Company, and in accordance with the printed conditions of this policy, nor unless such suit or action shall be commenced within twelve months next after the fire shall occur." The fire is alleged to have occurred on the 12th day of September, 1884; and this action was commenced on the 22d day of November, 1885, more than twelve months next after the fire occurred.

The contention of appellant is that at the time of the commencement of the action it was barred by the terms of said stipulation. That contention must prevail unless the clause upon which it is based is modified by some other clause or clauses of the policy. One clause reads as follows: "The amount of loss or damage to be estimated according to the actual, cash, marketable value of the property at the time of the loss, which in no case shall exceed what it would then cost to replace the same, deducting therefrom a suitable amount for any depreciation of such property by reason of age, wear and tear, location, change of style, lack of adaptation to profitable use or other causes. The adjusted claim under this policy shall be due and payable at the company's office in San Francisco, Cal., sixty days after the full completion by the assured of all the requirements herein contained."

Among the requirements therein contained were the following: "The assured, his, her and their agents and servants, shall, whenever required, submit to an examination or examinations, under oath, by any person appointed by this Company, and subscribe to such examinations when reduced to writing, and shall also produce their books of account and other vouchers, and exhibit the same for examination at the office of this Company in San Francisco as often as required, and permit extracts and copies thereof to be made. The assured also shall produce certified copies of all bills and invoices the originals of which have been lost, and shall exhibit all that remains of the said property, damaged or not damaged, for examination, to any person or persons named by this Company, and shall also furnish such further particulars, and such certificates of a magistrate or officer charged with the duty of investigating fires, as may be required. The proofs of loss shall be made by the party insured in regular form."

It is alleged and proven that appellant exacted a compliance by the assured with all of these requirements, and that the insured complied therewith as rapidly as he was able to, and that he was unable to fully comply therewith before the 16th day of October, 1885,—more than thirteen months after the fire occurred, and more than one month after the expiration of the time within which an action could be commenced, according to the construction which the appellant's counsel insist should be given to the policy. The adjusted claim under the policy was payable sixty days after the full completion of the assured of all the requirements contained in the policy. No right of action accrued until more than three months after it was barred by the twelve-months' limitation clause, unless that clause is modified by some other clause.

In *Spare* v. *Home Mut. Ins. Co.*, 9 Sawy. 142, 17 Fed. Rep. 568, the court, Deady, *J.*, said: "On the authority of adjudged cases (*Davidson* v. *Phœnix Ins. Co.* 4 Sawy. 594; *Riddlesbarger* v. *Hartford Ins. Co.* 74 U. S 7 Wall. 389 [19 L. ed. 259]; May, Ins. § 478), it is admitted by counsel for the plaintiff that this clause in the policy limiting the time within which a suit may be commenced thereon against the defendant is valid, but they contend that it must be read in connection with that other clause which provides

---

after a reversal of the first is inapplicable. Hocking v. Howard Ins. Co. 130 Pa. 170.

Under the Iowa Statute, which provides that no action on a policy of insurance shall be brought within ninety days after notice of loss, anything in the policy or contract to the contrary notwithstanding, any provision in the policy is controlled by the Statute, and receiving proofs of loss and claiming that the policy is void cannot be regarded as a waiver of the provisions of the Statute. Vore v. Hawkeye Ins. Co. 76 Iowa, 548.

The limitation clause in a policy, followed by a clause against a waiver of any conditions unless expressed in writing signed by the president or secretary of the company, are waived by a course of conduct of the company which induces insured to believe that the loss would be adjusted and paid without suit. Dwelling-House Ins. Co. v. Brodie (Ark.) 4 L. R. A. 458, and cases cited on p. 460.

A condition, in a policy of life insurance, that suit shall be brought within six months from date of death, does not apply where the superintendent of the defendant company, before expiration of the time to sue, has promised to pay the money. Metropolitan L. Ins. Co. v. Dempsey (Md.) April 18, 1890.

that a loss does not become payable until sixty days after the proof of that fact is made; and that, taken together, the reasonable construction of them is that, the right to sue on the policy being postponed until the loss is payable, namely, sixty days after proof thereof, the twelve-months' limitation upon such right does not commence to run until that time. This construction is supported by the decided weight of authority and in my judgment is correct on principle. *New York* v. *Hamilton F. Ins. Co.* 39 N. Y. 45; *Hay* v. *Star F. Ins. Co.* 77 N. Y. 241; *Barber* v. *Wheeling F. & M. Ins. Co.* 16 W. Va. 658; *Chandler* v. *St. Paul F. & M. Ins. Co.* 21 Minn. 85; *Steen* v. *Niagara F. Ins. Co.* 89 N. Y. 315; *Killips* v. *Putnam F. Ins. Co.* 28 Wis. 472; May, Ins. § 479.

"In *Steen* v. *Niagara F. Ins. Co.*, 89 N. Y. 323, the policy contained two similar conditions; and the court, in construing them, said: 'We think the intention of the defendant was to give the insured a full period of twelve months, within any part of which he might commence his action; and having, by postponement of the time of payment, secured itself from suit, it did not intend to embrace that period within the term after the expiration of which it could not be sued. In other words, the parties cannot be presumed to have suspended the remedy and provided for the running of the period of limitation during the same time. Indeed, the actual case is stronger; not only was the remedy postponed, but the liability even did not exist at the time of the fire, nor until it was fixed and ascertained according to the provisions of the policy. Having thus made the doing of certain things, and a fixed lapse of time thereafter, conditions precedent to the bringing of an action, the parties must be deemed to have contracted in reference to a time when the insured, except for that contract, might be in a condition to bring an action. Under any other construction the two conditions are inconsistent with each other.'"

This case is distinguishable from *Garido* v. *Am. Cent. Ins. Co.* (Cal.), 8 Pac. Rep. 512, in which the plaintiff had ample time after his right of action accrued to have commenced it within twelve months after the loss occurred. In this case it was more than twelve months after the fire before an action could be commenced. We must concede, however, that *Garido* v. *Am. Cent. Ins. Co.*, *supra*, is not altogether in harmony with the cases which we follow in this case. Under the construction which we give to the policy, we think the complaint states a cause of action not barred by the provisions of the policy; and the evidence is sufficient to justify the verdict of the jury

Judgment and order affirmed.

We concur: **McFarland, J.; Thornton, J.**

MINNESOTA SUPREME COURT.

Susan B. WILLARD
v.
Andrew J. FINNEGAN.

(....Minn.....)

*1. **A sale, under a power in a mortgage,** in gross as one parcel, of several separate and distinct tracts of land, is not void, but only voidable, for good cause shown, as that it was the result of fraud, or that prejudice resulted to the mortgagor or owner of the equity of redemption.

2. **A. executed a mortgage to M., and subsequently conveyed** to W. M. foreclosed his mortgage, and purchased the property at the sale. Neither A. nor W. redeemed from the sale, but a redemption was made by F., as a judgment creditor of A., who obtained a certificate of redemption. But before F. redeemed A. duly tendered him the amount due on his judgment, which he refused to accept. *Held*, that, as be-

*Head notes by MITCHELL, J.

NOTE.—*Power of sale in mortgage.*

A power of sale coupled with an interest cannot be revoked by a mortgagor, and his death cannot defeat or suspend the right to execute the power. Hudgins v. Morrow, 47 Ark. 515; Way v. Mullett, 3 New Eng. Rep. 200, 143 Mass. 49.

The provision of the Montana statutes, that "a mortgage of real property shall not be deemed a conveyance, whatever its terms, so as to enable an owner of the mortgage to recover possession of the real property without foreclosure and sale," does not prevent giving to the mortgagee a power to sell the premises upon default. First Nat. Bank v. Bell Silver & Copper Min. Co. 8 Mont. 32.

It does not follow from the possession of a power of sale by the grantee in a deed absolute on its face, but in fact a mere security, that the power is to be exercised otherwise than by foreclosure. Pearson v. Sharp, 7 Cent. Rep. 494, 115 Pa. 254.

A power of sale in a mortgage or deed of trust may be so limited that a sale under the power cannot be made, and yet there may be a remedy by foreclosure. Davis v. Bessehl, 4 West. Rep. 61, 88 Mo. 439.

The sale of premises under such power will operate as a foreclosure. Way v. Mullett, 3 New Eng. Rep. 200, 143 Mass. 49.

Such sale cuts off the equity of redemption as effectually as a sale under a decree of foreclosure, leaving in the mortgagor nothing but a statutory right of redemption. Gassenheimer v. Molton, 80 Ala. 521.

The purchaser of a mortgage containing a power of sale cannot foreclose the same by advertisement under the statutes of Dakota, unless a written assignment of such mortgage has been first duly executed, acknowledged and recorded. Hickey v. Richards, 3 Dak. 345.

A purchaser purchases at the peril of the sale being void, if a material condition precedent to the exercise of the power does not exist. Hence a purchaser from a trustee under a deed of trust made to secure the payment of certain notes which had been previously paid, and the deed of trust having by its terms thereby become void, takes no title. Temple v. Whittier, 5 West. Rep. 144, 117 Ill. 282.

A mortgagee who becomes the purchaser at his own sale thereby arms the mortgagor with the option, if seasonably expressed, to disaffirm the sale

tween F. and W. (who had no interest in the property), the redemption was valid; that M., the purchaser at the mortgage sale, alone could raise the question whether the tender discharged the lien of F's judgment, so as to terminate his right to redeem.

(February 7, 1890.)

APPEAL by plaintiff from a judgment of the District Court for Hennepin County dismissing the complaint, and from an order denying a motion for a new trial, in an action brought to determine an adverse claim made by defendant to certain real estate to which plaintiff claimed title. *Affirmed.*

APPEAL by defendant from a judgment of the District Court for Hennepin County determining that he had no right to redeem certain real estate from a mortgage sale thereof, and that he had no valid title thereto. *Reversed.*

The case sufficiently appears in the opinion.

Mr. **L. E. Stetler,** for plaintiff:

The sale of the land under the mortgage as an entire tract was unauthorized and absolutely void and the sheriff's certificate of sale void on its face, and Michael Maloney acquired no title to the premises by reason thereof.

Hull v. *King,* 38 Minn. 349.

Mr. **A. D. Smith,** for defendant:

A mere tender, even if kept good, will not extinguish or pay the debt itself. It merely stops costs; it does not even suspend the remedy against the debtor, or any remedy or legal right which the creditor may have as appurtenant to the debt in the form in which it may happen. *A fortiori* a tender does not discharge a judgment.

Jackson v. *Law,* 5 Cow. 248; *Law* v. *Jackson,* 9 Cow. 641; *People* v. *Beebe,* 1 Barb. 379.

The foreclosure of the property in dispute was regular and legal, and passed the title to Michael Maloney, subject to the right of redemption.

Bottineau v. *Ætna L. Ins. Co.* 31 Minn. 125-128; *Vawter* v. *Crafts* (Minn.) June 4, 1889. See also *Abbott* v. *Peck,* 35 Minn. 499.

Mitchell, *J.,* delivered the opinion of the court:

Action to determine an adverse claim of defendant to real property of which plaintiff alleges she is the owner. The defendant denies plaintiff's title, alleges that he is the owner, and asks that it be so adjudged. Plaintiff's title depends upon the validity of a sale, under a power, on a mortgage executed by her grantor, one Abbott, to the Maloneys. Defendant's title depends upon a redemption by him, as a judgment creditor of Abbott, from the sale on the Maloney mortgage. The facts are that Abbott executed to the Maloneys a mortgage on a piece of land according to government description, then constituting a single tract; but subsequently he platted the land, dividing it into urban lots and blocks, the Maloneys not joining in the plat. Under these facts the Maloneys would doubtless have had the right to sell the entire premises as one tract, as it was described in their mortgage; at least, in the absence of a request that the sale be in separate parcels, by one interested in the property, who had some equitable right to have it sold in that way in order to protect his interests. *Johnson* v. *Williams,* 4 Minn. 260 (Gil. 183); *Paquin* v. *Braley,* 10 Minn. 379 (Gil. 304); *Abbott* v. *Peck,* 35 Minn. 499.

But where the mortgagor, subsequent to the mortgage, divides the premises into separate tracts, as by platting it into lots and blocks, the mortgagee has the right to adopt this division, and sell the property, as the Maloneys did in this case, as lots and blocks, according to the descriptions in the plat. But, if he does so, properly he should sell the different tracts according to the plat separately; whereas, in the present instance, although described in the notice of sale according to the plat as separate lots and blocks, all were sold together for one gross sum. This, it is claimed, rendered the sale absolutely void. The Statute provides

---

without regard to its fairness or adequacy of price; and when the sale is set aside, the decree relates back to the sale, and the parties are in the same position as if no sale had been made. Gassenheimer v. Molton, 80 Ala. 521.

Where a third party purchases for the benefit of the mortgagee, the sale is not absolutely void, but voidable only. Nichols v. Otto (Ill.) Jan. 21, 1890.

Requisites to validity of sale.

A sale under a power contained in a mortgage may be set aside for insufficient notice. Dickerson v. Small, 1 Cent. Rep. 497, 64 Md. 395.

A foreclosure sale under a power in the mortgage is not invalidated by the omission of the names of the mortgagor and mortgagee in the advertisement of sale. Cogan v. McNamara, 16 R. I.——, Index EE, 52.

An advertisement of a sale under a power contained in a mortgage which required publication of notice in some newspaper in the County of Providence, Rhode Island, was not insufficient because it appeared in a newspaper published at a place in the county other than one of two certain cities in which the record of the mortgage erroneously required notice to be published. *Ibid.*

The non-observance of a custom among auctioneers to place notices upon doors or windows of houses for sale, stating the time and place of sale, is not sufficient to set aside a sale made under a power in a mortgage. Chilton v. Brooks, 69 Md. 584.

The provision of the Montana statute for "thirty days' notice" of a sale under a power in a mortgage, by publishing once a week for three weeks successively, does not require that all three publications shall be thirty days before the sale, but only that the first one shall be. First Nat. Bank v. Bell Silver & Copper Min. Co. 8 Mont. 32.

A sale of mortgaged real property under a power is not invalid because the notice of sale does not sufficiently describe certain personal property also covered by the mortgage, especially where such description is as full as that in the mortgage. *Ibid.*

That the record of a mortgage incorrectly states the place of publication of the notice of sale will not avoid the notice, if the publication is made as provided in the mortgage. Cogan v. McNamara, *supra.*

A sale of land, under a power in a mortgage, for $1,000 or more below the market value of the property, will be set aside where it was purchased by the mortgagee, and the sale was made on a day when the weather was so inclement as to prevent purchasers from attending. Chilton v. Brooks, *supra.*

that, "if the mortgaged premises consist of separate and distinct farms or tracts, they shall be sold separately." Gen. Stat. 1878, chap. 81, § 9.

Whether a sale, contrary to the Statute, renders it absolutely void, or only voidable where it is made to appear that there was fraud, or that the disregard of the Statute resulted in actual prejudice to the mortgagor or owner of the equity of redemption, is a question upon which there is some conflict of authority, at least in the case of non-judicial sales. As early as *Tillman* v. *Jackson*, 1 Minn. 183 (Gil. 157), it was held that a similar provision as to sales on execution was only directory, and that a violation of it by the sheriff would not invalidate the sale. This case, having stood apparently unquestioned for twenty-three years, was followed and recognized as having become a rule of property in *Lamberton* v. *Merchants Nat. Bank*, 24 Minn. 281, in which this court held that a sale on execution in gross, as one parcel, of several distinct and separate tracts of land not lying in a body, is not void, but might be vacated for cause shown, as that it was the result of actual fraud, or that prejudice resulted to the owner from it, or that there was no just ground for making the sale that way. This decision was followed by the United States Circuit Court for the District of Minnesota, and the same rule applied in the case of a mortgage sale under a power. *Swenson* v. *Balberg*, 1 McCrary, 96, 1 Fed. Rep. 444.

If this doctrine had become a rule of property thirteen years ago, it certainly is so yet, never having been, in the mean time, either overruled or questioned. There is no room for any distinction between sales on execution and sales under a power. Neither are judicial sales. A sale by a sheriff on an ordinary execution is a mere ministerial one, made by the officer by the naked authority of the writ and the requirements of the Statute. A sale under a power contained in a mortgage is made by the mortgagee or his agent pursuant to the convention of the parties. Viewed from a practical stand-point, we think the better rule is that a sale contrary to the Statute is merely voidable when fraud, prejudice or other good cause for vacating it is shown. The reasons in its favor given in *Cunningham* v. *Cassidy*, 17 N. Y. 276, although used with reference to a judicial sale, are equally applicable to one under a power. The consequences of a contrary rule would be disastrous. A great many titles would be open to question and doubt. The inquiry whether the land sold consisted in fact of separate and distinct tracts would often be attended with great difficulty. The question would be one of fact, dependent upon evidence *dehors* the record, and perhaps often doubtful or conflicting. The validity of titles ought not to be made dependent upon such extraneous facts. Our conclusion is that the mortgage sale was valid, and there having been no redemption from it by either Abbott, the mortgagor, or the plaintiff, his grantee, it follows that the latter has no interest in the property. This disposes of her appeal.

2. Defendant, a judgment creditor of Abbott, duly filed his intention to redeem, and seasonably produced to the sheriff, who made the sale, the proper proof of his right to redeem, paid to such officer the proper amount of money, and received from him a certificate of redemption. The court, however, made what, for present purposes, we may assume was a finding that before defendant made this redemption Abbott made to him a good and legal tender of the amount due on the judgment, which defendant arbitrarily refused to accept. It was on this ground that the learned judge decided adversely to the defendant, holding that this tender operated as a payment of the judgment, or at least as a discharge of its lien, so that he could not afterwards "use it for redemption purposes." Whether, as between defendant and Maloney, the purchaser at the mortgage sale, this proposition is correct or not we need not inquire. It is a question that plaintiff is in no position to raise. Maloney alone can raise it, as he alone is interested in it. Defendant has made a redemption in fact which is good on its face. At most, it is merely voidable, at the election of Maloney, on account of the existence of an extrinsic fact. The redemption is good as against the plaintiff, who has no interest in the property. Maloney is not a party to this action, and consequently his interests cannot be adjudicated or in any way affected. A judgment in this case, adjudging that defendant is the owner of the property, will only determine that he is such as between him and the plaintiff, and to such a judgment he is entitled upon the facts found. Upon his appeal, therefore, the order of the trial judge is reversed, and the cause remanded, with directions to render judgment in his favor as prayed for in his answer.

Affirmed on plaintiff's appeal, and reversed on defendant's appeal.

KANSAS SUPREME COURT.

John WALLACE *et al.*, *Plffs. in Err.*,
v.
Joseph EVANS.

(....Kan.....)

*A **party who built a dam**, causing the back water to fill a ravine across which ran a public highway, made a causeway composed of logs, brush, stone and earth at the place where the public highway ran across the ravine, and made a better way than existed before the construction of the dam. The public used it, and it was for a time maintained and repaired by the overseer of highways of the road district. *Held*, that the owner of the dam was not chargeable with its maintenance and repair, and was not liable for the value of mules whose death was occasioned by the causeway being out of repair.

(April 4, 1890.)

*Head note by SIMPSON, C

ERROR to the District Court for Norton County to review a judgment in favor of plaintiff in an action to recover damages for the loss of certain mules which was alleged to have resulted from the obstruction by defendants of a public highway. *Reversed.*

Commissioner's opinion.

The facts are fully stated in the opinion.

Messrs. **L. H. Thompson** and **C.D. Jones,** for plaintiffs in error:

Although Wallace built the dam in question and caused the water to back up into a natural ravine crossing the highway, yet if he left the highway in as good condition as he found it, he had performed all that law or justice required of him.

Venard v. *Cross*, 8 Kan. 260; *State* v. *Cummerford*, 16 Kan. 507; *State* v. *Raypholtz*, 32 Kan. 454; *Missouri, K. & T. R. Co.* v. *Long*, 27 Kan. 684.

The embankment built across the ravine was a bridge as defined by 1 Bouvier's Law Dictionary, p. 222.

By the common law counties are chargeable with the repair of all public bridges unless they can show that other persons are bound to repair particular bridges.

1 Wait, Act. and Def. § 8, p. 731.

The corporation, for whose exclusive benefit a bridge is made over a highway, must keep it in repair, and is liable for injuries caused to third persons in consequence of its being out of repair.

Dygert v. *Schenck*, 23 Wend. 446; *Heacock* v. *Sherman*, 14 Wend. 58; *Perley* v. *Chandler*, 6 Mass. 451.

A bridge, though erected by individuals, yet if dedicated to the public, used by the public and found to be of public utility, must be repaired by the public.

State v. *Campton*, 2 N. H. 513; *Requa* v. *Rochester*, 45 N. Y. 129, 6 Am. Rep. 52.

Mr. **John R. Hamilton,** for defendant in error:

Where the owner of land over which a public highway passes digs a raceway across the road and builds a bridge across the same, and an injury is sustained by anyone in consequence thereof, such owner is liable to any person so injured for damages.

4 Bl. Com. p. 6; *Dygert* v. *Schenck*, 23 Wend. 443.

Such bridge must be kept in repair by him who built it.

Heacock v. *Sherman*, 14 Wend. 58.

This is not a case where the bridge or crossing was voluntarily built. They created the necessity for such crossing, which makes a different rule applicable. They created and maintained a nuisance by obstructing a highway, and are liable for any damages as a result thereof.

Gen. Stat. chap. 89, § 17; 2 Dillon, Mun. Corp. 3d ed. §§ 710, 1032–1035, 1060.

Plaintiffs in error were the creators and maintainers of the nuisance, and they could not shift the liability for any damage which might occur by reason thereof upon the public, who cannot be made liable.

Eikenberry v. *Bazaar Twp.* 22 Kan. 556; *West Bend* v. *Mann*, 59 Wis. 69.

Simpson, *C.*, delivered the following opinion:

The plaintiff below brought his action to recover the sum of $400, the alleged value of a pair of mules, and $200 as exemplary damages. He alleged that in August, 1882, Wallace constructed a dam across a creek that caused the water to fill up a ravine across which ran a public highway that had been located, opened and traveled long before the construction of the dam; that the water had flowed into the ravine until, at the time complained of, it was ten feet deep, and was a hazardous and dangerous obstruction to travel on said highway; that Wallace had sold said dam to Railsback, who, at the time the injury occurred, owned and maintained said dam; that on the 9th day of September, 1885, the plaintiff, with his team of mules, was traveling on said highway with no knowledge of the dangerous condition thereof at the place it crossed the ravine, and that in attempting to cross said ravine his two mules were drowned in the water flowing into said ravine by reason of the construction of said dam. The defendants demurred to the petition, and their demurrer was overruled. They then answered, alleging, among other things, that, at the time the dam was built they caused a safe and suitable embankment to be made of brush, earth and other material across said ravine, on the line of said highway, thereby making a safe and suitable crossing; that this crossing was turned over to the road district, and accepted by it, and these defendants were released from any further liability, or any obligation to keep up and maintain said crossing. They also plead contributory negligence. Cause tried at April Term, 1887, to the court, who rendered a judgment for $400, a motion for a new trial being overruled. Wallace and Railsback bring the case here. They claim that the trial court erred in overruling their demurrer to the petition and evidence; that the right of action is barred by the Statute of Limitations, as the dam was constructed under § 14, chap. 66, Comp. Laws 1885; that there was a misjoinder of parties defendant; that there was an obligation resting on the road district to maintain the crossing and keep it in repair; that the evidence shows contributory negligence.

1. The petition in this case alleges that the place at which the loss occurred to the plaintiff below was a public highway, and alleges an obstruction thereof that was the cause of the loss of the mules. The erection of a dam caused the water to fill up a ravine across which the public highway ran. The man who built the dam constructed across the ravine an embankment of stone, logs, brush and earth, that made a good, safe and reliable crossing as long as it was maintained in the condition in which it was constructed. It was shown at the trial that the road overseer had caused work to be done thereon, and that for some years it was constantly used and reasonably safe. Wallace, one of the plaintiffs in error, built the dam and the embankment, and after owning the mill property, including the dam, for about one year, sold and conveyed it to one Page, who subsequently sold it to Railsback, the other plaintiff in error, who owned the dam at the time of the loss of the mules. On this state of facts it must be apparent that no liability can possibly attach to

Wallace for the loss. Putting this question in the strongest possible attitude for the defendant in error, and assuming for that purpose that the erection of the dam and the back water in the ravine was a continuing nuisance, yet still Railsback and not Wallace is responsible for the damages occasioned by it. When Wallace sold the dam, and someone else purchased it and assumed all liability, there seems to be no point of view in which Wallace could be held longer responsible. The judgment against him is wrong.

2. To constitute an obstruction to a public highway, it must appear that the public travel by reason thereof is actually hindered and endangered. No private action can be maintained if the obstruction continues and becomes a common nuisance on account of the nuisance *per se;* but if any individual suffers a more special injury than any other, from the continuance of such a nuisance, he has his action therefor. All this is alphabetical law, and affords a sure basis upon which the argument in the case must rest. The controlling question in this case is, Who is responsible for the care and repair of the highway at the point where it crosses the ravine? It is as much a part of the highway as any other portion of its length or breadth. The people at large have the right to the free and uninterrupted use of it, not upon the sufferance of the men who built the embankment, but as a matter of right. It has been held that, if a man builds a bridge that is useful to the public in general, it is the duty of the public authorities to repair it, notwithstanding it may be of benefit to the builder. *Rex* v. *West Riding of Yorkshire,* 5 Burr. 2594; *Heacock* v. *Sherman,* 14 Wend. 58; *Requa* v. *Rochester,* 45 N. Y. 129; Thompson, Highw. 3d ed. 12.

If a bridge is erected over a natural stream by a man for his own benefit, and it is of public utility, and is used by the public, the public is bound to keep it in repair; for in such case, although the bridge is of advantage to the man who built it, he did not create the necessity for it. *Dygert* v. *Schenck,* 23 Wend. 446.

Where a person erected a mill and dam for his own profit, and by so doing deepened the water of a ford, through which there was a public highway, but the passage through which, before the deepening, was very inconvenient, and the miller built a bridge over it, and the public used it, and the miller had repaired it, the court held that the county, and not the miller, was chargeable with the repair. *Rex* v. *Kent Co.* 2 Maule & S. 513.

All public bridges are prima facie reparable by the public. Most, if not all, of the earlier cases that have any bearing on this question make this distinction: If the bridge is built by a private person, and it is manifestly to the interest of the public to use it, and they do use it, and the way is better than it was before the bridge was built, the public are chargeable with its repair; but, if the improved way is not better than it was before, the public receives no benefit. This is certainly a very liberal interpretation of the law, so far as the public are concerned. If the principle of these cases is applied to the facts developed on the trial of this case, there can be no recovery against Railsback, as the duty to keep the crossing in repair is devolved upon the road district. Our statutory enactment, requiring railroad corporations to restore to its former condition any public highway it may cross in the course of its construction, seems to have this principle in view. This court, construing this provision, holds that when a railroad company restores the crossing of a public highway to the condition that existed at the time of the construction of its line across the highway, the railroad company is under no obligation thereafter, under this provision, to maintain it in a safe and sufficient state of repair. *Missouri, K. & T. R. Co.* v. *Long,* 27 Kan. 684.

It can be said that it is the Statute that relieves the railroad company from the liability to maintain the highway after it has been restored to its former condition, and that there is no statute that operates in favor of the defendants in error. While it is true that the courts in this country have almost universally refused to hold the public to a common-law liability to repair public highways, the statutes of every State establish their liability, and this is so universal that prima facie they must be chargeable therewith; but the question in this case is, Has not the public, by its acceptance and use of this road-way, and by its control and repair, assumed the liability? It cannot be successfully contended that this particular fill or causeway across the ravine is not a part of the public highway. The public has the absolute control of it. The man who built it has no right to obstruct it. If he lives in that road district, he can be compelled to contribute money or labor to its maintenance and repair. The moment he finished its construction it became a part of the public highway, and his control ceased for every purpose. It then necessarily became the statutory duty of the road district to keep it in repair. The record discloses that at the place where these plaintiffs in error filled the ravine they made a better and safer road-way than existed before. It is shown that it was used for some years by the public. There is some evidence tending to show that the road overseer of the district caused work to be done on it, and at times repaired it. It is not shown that it was located on the land, or that it was erected for the personal benefit of either of the plaintiffs in error. This case was tried and decided upon the theory that both Wallace and Railsback were chargeable with the maintenance and repair of a public highway, and this was error. We recommend that *the judgment be reversed, and a new trial granted.*

Per Curiam:
It is so ordered.
All the Justices concur.

FLORIDA SUPREME COURT.

L. B. SKINNER *et al.*, *Appts.*,
v.
W. B. HENDERSON *et al.*, Commissioners of Hillsborough County.

(....Fla.....)

*1. **Under the Constitution and laws of this State a county cannot impose taxes** except for county purposes, and the building of a bridge in a county within the corporate limits of a municipality in which the county outside of those limits is in nowise interested, the same being for the sole benefit and advantage of the municipality, is not a county purpose.

2. **Where an injunction is sought against a county** to prevent the appropriation of its revenues to aid in the building of a bridge in a city, and the allegations of the bill are that the bridge is on a city street, and not a county road or highway, and that the county outside of the city is nowise interested in it, and that it is for the sole benefit and advantage of the city, it was error to sustain a demurrer to the bill.

3. **But the Statute authorizing the city to build bridges within its limits does not necessarily revoke** the authority given to the county by General Statute, without restriction as to locality, to build a bridge within those limits. As there may be bridges serving only a city purpose, so there may be others demanded in the same territory for county purposes; and where the circumstances create this demand, and the bridge is for the use and benefit of the people of the county at large or of some considerable portion of them, and intended and needed as well for those outside as for those inside the city, the authority of the county to build it is not annulled by the local city statute.

4. **The circumstances of each case must determine the line of authority,** even where there is assent of the municipal government; but in case of conflict between municipal and county officials, it would seem that the county should give way, in deference to the general policy against one jurisdiction clashing with another.

5. **If a county may build a bridge** within the limits of a municipality when the circumstances suit, it may also aid the municipality in building one under like circumstances, even though it is to be constructed under a contract with the municipality, and is to be under its control.

(May, 1890.)

APPEAL by plaintiffs from a decree of the Circuit Court for Hillsborough County dismissing the bill in a suit brought to enjoin defendants from applying county revenues towards the building of a bridge within the City of Tampa. *Reversed.*

The facts are fully stated in the opinion.

Mr. **William Hunter** for appellants.

Messrs. **Sparkman & Sparkman** for appellees.

Maxwell, *J.*, delivered the opinion of the court:

The City of Tampa, in Hillsborough County, made a contract with a certain bridge company for the construction of a bridge within the corporate limits of the city across Hillsborough River. The cost of construction was to be $13,800. Upon petition to the County Commissioners of the County by the citizens of Tampa, and application in behalf of the city by the president of its council, said Commissioners ordered an appropriation of $4,600 towards the construction of the bridge, to be paid by the County, this amount being one third of the contract price for its construction, and contributed on the understanding that it should be a free bridge. Thereupon appellants filed a bill against the County Commissioners (appellees), praying that they be enjoined from paying out said amount for the construction of the bridge.

Besides the foregoing facts stated in the bill, it alleges, among other things immaterial here, that complainants are citizens and taxpayers of the County of Hillsborough; that the Commissioners levied a tax for the year 1887 for general revenue purposes, which will produce a large surplus, and that they did this for the purpose and with the intent of assisting the City of Tampa "to build a bridge across Hillsborough River on Lafayette Street, which is a city street, and not a county road or highway," and said bridge "is to be entirely and exclusively under the jurisdiction and control" of said city; that the County "outside of said City of Tampa, is in nowise interested in the building of said bridge, and that the same is for the sole benefit and advantage of said city;" that the County "receives no consideration" for said appropriation; that "said bridge, being wholly within the corporate limits of said city, is entirely a municipal improvement, and the expense thereof should be defrayed entirely by said city; that the revenues collected from your orators by county taxation are not levied for the purpose of making such improvements in . . . Tampa, or any other municipality, and cannot be legally expended for such purposes, as the building of said bridge in said city is not a "county purpose" within the meaning of the Constitution.

The defendant demurred to the bill for want of equity, and the demurrer was in effect sustained, though the ruling and order thereon were irregular—the order being "that the injunction be denied and the bill dismissed." Then appellants entered an appeal, but no point has been made here on this irregularity.

It is contended by appellants that the money proposed to be expended by the Commissioners to aid in the building of the bridge is not for a "county purpose," and that they have no authority to appropriate money raised by taxation for the County to any other purpose. As to their authority this is clearly correct. The Constitution (§ 5, art. 9) provides that the "Legislature shall authorize the several counties and incorporated cities or towns in the State to assess and impose taxes for county and municipal purposes, and for no other purposes." What is a county purpose, as distinguished from a municipal purpose, is a question arising here from the fact that the City of Tampa is a part of the County of Hillsborough,

*Head notes by MAXWELL, J.

and from the further fact that the County is authorized by statute to build bridges in the County without restriction as to locality, and that the city is authorized by its charter to build bridges within its corporate limits—both having authority for the same purpose there, if that given to the city does not exclude its territory from the domain within the jurisdiction of the County for such purpose. Confining ourselves to the allegations of the bill, it appears that the building of the bridge is wholly a matter belonging to the City of Tampa. The contract for building was its contract. The highway on opposite sides of the river, to be connected by the bridge, is alleged to be a city street, and not a county highway, and it is further alleged that the County outside of the city is in no wise interested in the building of the bridge, and that the bridge is for the sole benefit and advantage of the city, being wholly within its corporate limits, and entirely a municipal improvement. These facts, taken as true under the demurrer, show that the expenditure on the bridge would be for a city, and not a county, "purpose." They do not present the question, whether the County can build, or aid in building, a bridge in the city under any circumstances; or, in other words, whether the jurisdiction of the city entirely excludes the county from its territory for such work. If the Constitution will permit requirements of the county in its highways and in the interest and convenience of all its citizens to affect this question, so as to allow concurrent authority where the work will serve both a county and city purpose, that cannot determine the case here in its present shape. As there may be bridges in a city altogether for local convenience, for aught that appears before us the one in question may be of that class. The bill avers that it is. We know judicially that Tampa is the county seat of Hillsborough, and that outside of Tampa there is habitable territory on both sides of Hillsborough River; but these relations of the County to the city do not of themselves authorize the former to enter the latter for any work that answers only a city purpose, such as the bill alleges of this bridge. If allowed to enter at all, it must be for work that answers a county purpose—that is, work for the use and benefit of the people of the County at large, or of some considerable portion of them, and intended and needed as well for those outside as for those inside the city. The bill does not show that the bridge is a work of this kind, but on the contrary shows only such facts as bespeak a work for merely city use and benefit. We think the County Commissioners are not authorized to aid in such a work, and that their demurrer to the bill should have been overruled.

While this conclusion decides the case upon the present record, we find in the argument of appellant's counsel, and in that of counsel for appellees, a full discussion of the question, whether the legislative grant of authority to the City of Tampa to build bridges within its corporate limits does not intercept the general authority for that purpose given to the county, so far as the territory of the city is concerned—the counsel for appellants insisting that it does, and the counsel for appellees that it does not. Anticipating that in the further progress of the case below, this question may be more pertinently presented, our views on it now will not be out of place.

The theory of appellants is that the officials empowered to act in the management of county affairs have no authority to expend money they raise by taxation for county purposes in building bridges within the corporate limits of any municipality in the County. Whether they have or not is the question to be solved. It is admitted for appellants that if the County has the right to build the bridge, it would likewise have right to appropriate for a part of the expense, but insisted that if it could not pay in whole, it could not pay in part. Then, the problem is, Can the county officials under their general authority, and notwithstanding the special authority of the city, go into the city to build a bridge, or to act in conjunction with the city for that purpose? The rulings on this question are diverse, but they all agree that it depends on constitutional provision or legislative enactment applicable in the particular case, with general principles of law to interpret or construe these. We have mentioned all there is in the Constitution and laws of this State on the subject. Counties cannot expend money except for county purposes; and where a county and municipality cover the same ground, there is nothing which expressly directs what each may do respectively in the line of its authority. The nearest approach to any decision on the question in this State is in the case of *State* v. *Putnam Co.*, 23 Fla. 632, where it was held that the establishment of a municipality on territory over which passes part of a public road established by the road authorities of the county, does not of itself abolish the road as a public highway, nor revoke or suspend the powers and duties of those authorities in regard to it. The court was careful to go no further. But in this decision it appears that a county may, under some circumstances, have powers and duties touching highways in a city or town, for the proper exercise and enforcement of which it can be held responsible, and the same would be true of a bridge similarly situated.

There may be distinctively municipal purposes in respect to bridges within a corporation, as where a small stream, purely local, and having no connection with county highways, should be bridged for the convenience of citizens of the corporation; and it is conceivable that there may also be county purposes in the same respect therein, as where the bridge connects public highways of the county, and is of use and importance to the citizens of the county, irrespective of residence in the corporation, and especially if the court-house of the county is in the corporation. It would seem but just and reasonable in such case that the county should take or share the burden of furnishing to the public the convenience of the bridge. In this connection it is worthy of observation that all the taxpayers of the county, those in municipalities not excepted, are required to contribute to the revenue of the county for bridge purposes, without reference to residence. If residing in a municipality they must pay a bridge tax for any and every locality inside or outside thereof, if in the county; while if not residing in a municipality, if appellants' view is correct, they cannot be taxed for a bridge therein, though for a county purpose. It should not be assumed, and in the absence of assumption there is no reason to hold, that such inequality of tax burden was intended to be imposed. This involves relieving the county from the burden when a county purpose is to be subserved in a municipality, but holding the municipality liable for both county and municipal burden, whether in or out of the corporate limits. The palpable injustice of this is most striking. It is nothing more nor less than imposing a double burden upon municipal citizens, one of which is a burden for a county purpose within the municipality, and exempting other citizens of the county from any burden for such purpose, although interested in common in the object to be attained.

We hence conclude that the special authority given to any municipality to build bridges within its limits does not necessarily supersede the general authority given to the county. But as there may be a municipal purpose in which the county has no concern, and a county purpose in which all are alike, though perhaps not equally, interested, the circumstances of each case must determine the question of authority. And it seems to us that this would be so even where there is assent of the municipal government. Whether that authority should be exercised in the event of conflict between the two bodies is not involved in this case, as the city and county are in accord in the building of the bridge. In cases where such conflict would arise, we are inclined to the opinion that the County should give way, in deference to the general policy against one jurisdiction clashing with another.

As we have said, the authorities differ on the main question under discussion. But much of this difference grows out of the difference in statutes that govern. We will not undertake a review of the cases, but content ourselves with citing those which sustain the views we have expressed. In Ohio it is held that if there is nothing in the Act incorporating a town which limits the power of the county commissioners to establish a county road through or within its corporate limits, that power still exists. *Wells* v. *McLaughlin*, 17 Ohio, 99; *Butman* v. *Fowler*, Id. 101. In Connecticut (*Norwich* v. *Story*, 25 Conn. 44), it is held that the charter of a city conferring power on its common council to lay out new highways, etc., did not devest the county court of the jurisdiction given by statute for the same purpose. A similar ruling in Iowa is valuable as coming from *Judge* Dillon, one of the most eminent of American jurists and law authors now living, and valuable also as having been announced in an opinion which fully discusses the subject—*Bell* v. *Foutch*, 21 Iowa, 119. See also *Barrett* v. *Brooks*, Id. 144.

There is this difference, however, between our statutes and the statutes of Iowa: that while the authority to the counties to build bridges is the same, our statute gives authority to the City of Tampa to establish and regulate bridges within its limits, while that in Iowa (General Act) gives to cities and towns "care, supervision and control of all public . . . bridges . . . within the city, and shall cause the same to be kept open and in repair," etc. But the reasoning on which it is held that the counties are not devested of authority to build bridges in cities is equally applicable to both, with proper modification, giving due weight here to the authority of counties to act for "county purposes." We think the doctrine of these cases is to be preferred under the system established by our Constitution and statutes.

The cases cited for appellants, and maintaining the position that county revenues cannot be expended under a contract to which the county is not a party, do not seem to us to have the force attributed to them here. *Colton* v. *Hanchett*, 18 Ill. 615, simply decides that where legislative authority is given to an individual to build a toll bridge, the county officials cannot appropriate county funds to aid in its construction, because no law of the State authorizes such appropriation. If the view on which we rest our opinion, that in this State a county may build a bridge in a municipality to meet a county purpose, is correct, there is law here to authorize county appropriation of money therefor, and the authority is none the less existent because the appropriation is in aid of a municipal contract to build the bridge, if a county purpose is thereby advanced. Why should not a county expend money to aid in building a bridge, when it has authority to pay the whole expense of building it. If there is anything in the *Colton-Hanchett Case* that seems to make a distinction, it goes beyond the controversy there, for it was a case where the authority to build the bridge was not in the county officials, and of course, therefore, they could not aid therein. The other case (*Atty-Gen.* v. *Bay Co.* 34 Mich. 46), was one where county supervisors undertook to appropriate money for township roads, leaving to the townships to say to what roads it should be applied. It was held this could not be done, partly because the county board had no occasion to raise money for other than its own roads, and partly because there was no definition of purposes, as the expenditure was to be under the direction of the town officer. As to the first ground, that is fully met in this case, if the bridge answers a county purpose, and, as to the second, there is no indefiniteness of purpose to which the money is to be applied. But the court says in the case that "taxes and loans, when authorized to be raised by any public body, must be raised under the implied condition that they are to be applied to the public uses under the control or care of that body. They cannot be raised for the purposes or uses of others, unless such a power is plainly given." It will be seen, upon scrutinizing the case, that this and other similar language of the opinion applied to the action of county supervisors in respect to roads under the supervision of township supervisors, when by the statute their action was limited to "state and territorial roads."

The distinction between that case and the present is obvious. As in that it was held that county revenues could not be used for township roads, so in this we hold that county revenues cannot be used for city bridges as such, but in that the money was being applied to roads not "state and territorial," and not embraced within any authority of the county supervisors; while in this, if the conditions suit, it will be applied to an authorized "county purpose." It does not seem reasonable that in all cases there is such necessary connection between the expenditure of money for public uses and the control ordinarily resulting from such expenditure, as to prevent the expenditure when made for a lawful purpose, because in accomplishing that purpose it is done in a way to relieve from the control that entails further liability.

It is no objection to our conclusion, as applicable to the case at bar, if it can be shown that the bridge answers a county purpose, as distinguished from a local city purpose, that the bridge was to be constructed under a contract with the city, and that the city will have control of the same, and must bear the responsibilities connected with it. This will be that much better for the County. So far as it is said to be objectionable on the ground that the appropriation by the County is towards the payment of a debt of the city, the bridge being built under a contract with the city, that is met by the fact, if found to exist, that the appropriation is for a county purpose, and would be in effect a payment of its own obligation. And so far as it is said to be objectionable on the ground that the ownership and control of the bridge will be in the city, that is met by the admission, connected with our view as to the authority of the County to build the bridge itself if thereby serving a county purpose, that if "the County would have a right to build the bridge, it would likewise have a right to appropriate for a part of it." As to responsibility for proper care and repair of the bridge, we express no opinion. But if the County discharges a duty in the attainment of a county purpose in such manner as to be relieved from further responsibility in the matter, this furnishes no reason against the validity of its action. We are to understand that in making the appropriation the Commissioners acted, not as aiding the city in a work with which they had no concern, but as performing a primary duty of their own under the power vested in them to build bridges in the County. The reservation they made that the bridge would be a free one, was to guard against restrictions in its use which would not be within the scope of their authority, and was a proper consideration for joining in the work.

Under our conclusion it will be for the defendants to determine, upon existing facts of the situation, whether they will further resist the injunction.

The decree is reversed, with leave to them to answer, if they should deem it advisable.

INDIANA SUPREME COURT.

Mary J. LOGAN, *Appt.*,
v.
Lewis V. STOGDALE.

(......Ind.......)

1. **The condemnation of land for a private way** cannot be authorized by the Legislature; hence the Act of March 9, 1889, which attempts to do so, is void.

2. **The circuit court has jurisdiction of a proceeding to establish a way of necessity** over the land of another, since the Act of March 9, 1889, which attempted to confer jurisdiction of such proceedings upon the board of county commissioners, is unconstitutional.

NOTE.—*Eminent domain; right of.*

It is for the Legislature to determine the necessity which exists for the use of the property proposed to be taken. See *note* to Moore v. Sanford (Mass.) 7 L. R. A. 151.

But when the question arises whether the use for which it is sought to be condemned is really a public one, it must be determined by the courts without any regard to a legislative declaration that the use is public. Kansas City v. Baird, 98 Mo. 215; Sadler v. Langham, 34 Ala. 311; Stockton & V. R. Co. v. Stockton, 41 Cal. 147; Consolidated Channel Co. v. Central Pac. R. Co. 51 Cal. 269; Young v. Harrison, 6 Ga. 130; Parham v. Decatur Co. Justices, 9 Ga. 341; Bankhead v. Brown, 25 Iowa, 540; Loughbridge v. Harris, 42 Ga. 501; New Cent. Coal Co. v. George's Creek Coal & I. Co. 37 Md. 537; Talbott v. Hudson, 16 Gray, 417; *Re* St. Paul & N. P. R. Co. 34 Minn. 227; Savannah v. Hancock, 8 West. Rep. 248, 91 Mo. 54; Dickey v. Tennison, 27 Mo. 373; Dayton G. & S. Min. Co. v. Seawell, 11 Nev. 394; St. Louis Co. Ct. v. Griswold, 58 Mo. 175; Scudder v. Trenton D. F. Co. 1 N. J. Eq. 694; Coster v. Tide Water Co. 18 N. J. Eq. 54; *Re* Deansville Cemetery Asso. 66 N. Y. 569; Harris v. Thompson, 9 Barb. 350; Concord R. Co. v. Greely, 17 N. H. 47; McQuillen v. Hatton, 42 Ohio St. 202; Pittsburgh v. Scott, 1 Pa. 309; Anderson v. Turbeville, 6 Coldw. 150; Tyler v. Beacher, 44 Vt. 648; Varner v. Martin, 21 W. Va. 534.

The question of the necessity for the exercise of the right of eminent domain, and in what cases it shall be exercised, is legislative, and not judicial; the questions whether the use to which it is sought to appropriate property is a public use, and whether the power is delegated to the corporation, are subjects of judicial determination. Chicago & E. I. R. Co. v. Wiltz, 4 West. Rep. 121, 116 Ill. 449.

Although the determination of the Legislature is not conclusive that a purpose for which it directs property to be taken is a public use, yet it is conclusive, if the use is public, that a necessity exists which requires the property to be taken. Moore v. Sanford (Mass.) 7 L. R. A. 151.

Private roads; way of necessity.

There is a way by necessity, where another cannot be got or made without reasonable labor and expense; and, in determining the question, the jury may consider the comparative value of the land and the probable cost of such way, and that the word "necessary" cannot be limited to absolute physical necessity. But yet the way must be necessary, and the facts of each case must determine whether it or any other easement thus claimed is necessary. It must be more than one of mere convenience, or one beneficial and convenient, and is only commensurate with the existence of the necessity upon which the implied grant of it is founded, and ceases when the necessity for it ceases. Marvin v. Brewster Iron Min. Co. 55 N. Y. 558; Screven v. Gregorie,

See also 25 L. R. A. 502; 40 L. R. A. 105; 47 L. R. A. 79.

3. A grantee of land across which a prior grantee from the same grantor has the right to a way by necessity takes it subject to such right, although it had been neither exercised nor claimed before his title was acquired.

(April 28, 1890.)

APPEAL by plaintiff from a judgment of the Circuit Court for Grant County sustaining a demurrer to the complaint in an action brought to establish a way of necessity over defendant's land. *Reversed.*

The facts fully appear in the opinion.

Messrs. **W. H. Carroll** and **G. Dean** for appellant.

Messrs. **H. Brownlee** and **H. J. Paulus** for appellee.

Elliott, *J.*, delivered the opinion of the court:

The appellant, in her complaint, describes a tract of land of which she is the owner, and alleges that the appellee is also the owner of a parcel of land which she particularly describes. In addition to the allegations referred to the complaint contains the following: That in the year 1878, Enos Key was the owner of both parcels of land; that in January of that year he sold to the plaintiff the land she owns; that he subsequently sold and conveyed to the appellee's grantor the land now owned by the appellee; that both of the parties to this action hold under Enos Key; that the land of the plaintiff is surrounded on all sides by the lands of divers persons, including the land of the appellant; that the plaintiff's land is completely shut off from any highway; that it is impossible to go to the plaintiff's land without passing over adjoining land; that the appellant refuses to permit the plaintiff to pass over his land to a highway, and for the purpose of preventing her from passing over his land has erected high and strong fences; that he threatens to sue her if she enters upon his land; that there are improvements on her land and her own home is there; that the best and shortest way to a highway is over the appellee's land and that the distance is sixty rods. The prayer is that the court shall establish for the plaintiff, as a way of necessity, a way to the highway across the land of the appellant. To this complaint a demurrer was sustained.

All that is presented in argument in defense of the ruling of the trial court by the appellee's counsel is that, under the Act of March 9, 1889, the action ought to have been brought in the court of the county commissioners, and that the circuit court has no jurisdiction of the subject. The appellant's counsel contend that the Act of March 9, 1889, is in violation of the Constitution and is therefore void.

The Act in question assumes to provide for the establishment of branch highways, and to give any freeholder who has no outlet to a highway the right to petition the board of county commissioners to establish a way. The Act provides that the owner of the land upon which it is proposed to establish a way may remonstrate on two grounds and no other; "*first*, that another convenient and less injurious route can be established over his said lands, or the lands of another; *second*, that the pro-

---

3 Rich. L. 158; Alley v. Carleton, 29 Tex. 79; Ogden v. Jennings, 62 N. Y. 532; Holmes v. Seely, 19 Wend. 507; Nicholas v. Chamberlain, Cro. Jac. 121; Oakley v. Stanley, 5 Wend. 523; Tabor v. Bradley, 18 N. Y. 109; LeRoy v. Platt, 4 Paige, 77; French v. Carhart, 1 N. Y. 96; Voorhees v. Burchard, 55 N. Y. 98; Warren v. Blake, 54 Me. 276; Pierce v. Selleck, 18 Conn. 321.

Right of way by necessity arises from presumption of law that the parties did not intend that land to which the owner had no access should be retained or conveyed. Prowattain v. Philadelphia (Pa.) 2 Cent. Rep. 332.

This right of way by necessity may arise in favor of a parcel of land, when the same is surrounded by what has been the grantor's other land, or partly by this and partly by that of a stranger. Collins v. Prentice, 15 Conn. 39; Marshall v. Trumbull, 28 Conn. 183; Taylor v. Warnaky, 55 Cal. 350; Kuhlman v. Hecht, 77 Ill. 570; Trask v. Patterson, 29 Me. 499; Brice v. Randall, 7 Gill & J. 349; Bass v. Edwards, 126 Mass. 445; Kimball v. Cocheco R. Co. 27 N. H. 449; Lore v. Stiles, 25 N. J. Eq. 381; Wheeler v. Gilsey, 35 How. Pr. 145; New York L. Ins. & T. Co. v. Milnor, 1 Barb. Ch. 353; Tracy v. Atherton, 35 Vt. 52.

A right of way of necessity may be acquired over the land of another, although the road to which the way leads is not a county road, but a mere byroad open to the public. Cheney v. O'Brien, 69 Cal. 199.

The rule allowing a way of necessity preserves access, but does not give two modes of access and double right of way. Kings Co. F. Ins. Co. v. Stevens, 2 Cent. Rep. 430, 101 N. Y. 411.

Where a party acquires a new way by partition or otherwise the right of way by necessity ceases and becomes extinguished. Carey v. Rae, 58 Cal. 159; Abbott v. Stewartstown, 47 N. H. 230.

If it ceases to be a way of necessity, and becomes merely a way of convenience, it is extinguished. Seeley v. Bishop, 19 Conn. 128; Pierce v. Selleck, 18 Conn. 321; Gayetty v. Bethune, 14 Mass. 49; Viall v. Carpenter, 14 Gray, 126; Nichols v. Luce, 24 Pick. 102; Holmes v. Seely, 19 Wend. 507; Lawton v. Rivers, 2 McCord, L. 445; Screven v. Gregorie, 8 Rich. L. 158; Alley v. Carleton, 29 Tex. 78.

Petition for private road.

The power of locating a private road is entirely of a public nature, and a petitioner therefor having pursued the mode pointed out by the Code is entitled to the road as a matter of right. Douglas Co. v. Clark, 15 Or. 3.

The county has no authority to take a bond to indemnify it against expenses of its location and damages assessed thereon. *Ibid.*

A petition of a person asking for a "cartway leading from his dwelling and lands," stating that it "is the only practical way that petitioner can travel either to church, Sunday school or burying ground by wagon, buggy or cart," although informal, sufficiently alleges that he is "settled upon or cultivating land," and that the way is "necessary, reasonable and just." Warlick v. Lowman, 103 N. C. 122.

Where a person petitioning for a private way already has a private way, or by parol license an unobstructed way, across the land of another, his petition should be denied. Warwick v. Lowman, 104 N. C. 403.

A petitioner is not entitled to have a cartway simply upon the ground that no public road leads to his land, or because it will be more convenient for him to have it, but it must appear that it is necessary, reasonable and just, and that he resides on the land, and has no way to get to and from a public road without it. Burwell v. Sneed, 104 N. C. 118.

ceeding is wrongful, oppressive or malicious." Elliott's Supp. §§ 1539–1542.

It is evident from the provisions to which we have just referred, and from other provisions of the Act, that the Legislature intended to grant a freeholder who is shut off from a highway a right to secure a way across the land of another upon the payment of damages. It is not made essential that the way shall be one required by the public, for the whole scope and tenor of the Act indicate that it was intended to secure a right of way to private property owners. That this was the intention is evident from the introductory part of the first section wherein it is provided "that, whenever any freeholder of this State owning lands surrounded by the lands of others, and over which he must necessarily travel in order to reach his own lands, and there is no other outlet to the public road, shall petition the board of commissioners of the county in which the lands necessary to be traveled are situate for the location of a branch highway thereon, setting forth facts in his petition which shall be verified, such board, if it be satisfied that notice has been served upon the owner of such other lands, at least ten days before the meeting of the board at which such petition is to be presented, shall appoint three disinterested persons to view such highway."

The provision is an influential one, for it declares what the petition shall contain, and it is in harmony with other provisions of the Act, for all the influential provisions indicate and express an intention to authorize the seizure of property for private way. The provision as to what the petition shall show, the rigid and emphatic restriction of the questions that may be presented by the property owner whose land it is proposed to seize, and the provisions declaring what questions shall be tried, all combine to prove that the Act was intended to authorize the seizure of property for a private way, and to compel an unwilling property owner to yield his land for that purpose. It is impossible to construe the Act as one authorizing only the establishment of public roads, for it will bear no such construction. Nor is it possible to effect a separation of its provisions, for they are so blended that severance is impossible; and as the provisions are inseparable, the Act must be taken in its entirety. *Griffin* v. *State*, 119 Ind. 520; *State* v. *Indiana & O. O. G. & Min. Co.* 120 Ind. 575; *Baldwin* v. *Franks*, 120 U. S. 678 [30 L. ed. 766]; *Virginia Coupon Cases*, 114 U. S. 269 [29 L. ed. 185]; *Trade Mark Cases*, 100 U. S. 82 [25 L. ed. 550]; *United States* v. *Reese*, 92 U. S. 214 [23 L. ed. 563].

It is true that in the preamble and in some of the provisions in the body of the Act, there is an indirect assertion that the use for which authority is conferred to seize private property is a public one, but such an assertion, even if made in the clearest terms, cannot rescue the Act from condemnation, for it is not within the power of the Legislature to determine what is a public use within the meaning of the Constitution. Whether the use is a public one is a judicial question and not a legislative one *Sadler* v. *Langham*, 34 Ala. 311; *Re Deansville Cemetery Asso.* 66 N. Y. 569; *Bankhead* v. *Brown*, 25 Iowa, 540; *Tyler* v. *Beacher*, 44 Vt. 648; *Re St. Paul & N. P. R. Co.* 34 Minn. 227, *Savannah* v. *Hancock*, 91 Mo. 54, 8 West. Rep. 248; *Concord R. Co.* v. *Greely*, 17 N. H. 47; *Rensselaer* v. *Leopold*, 106 Ind. 29, 3 West. Rep. 874.

A private use cannot be transformed into a public one by a mere legislative declaration.

As the Act assumes to authorize the seizure of the property of one citizen for the benefit of another, it cannot be upheld. Our own decisions declare that land cannot be seized for a private road, and they are well sustained by the decisions of other courts. *Wild* v. *Deig*, 43 Ind. 455; *Stewart* v. *Hartman*, 46 Ind. 331; *Sanxay* v. *Hunger*, 42 Ind. 44; *Blackman* v. *Halves*, 72 Ind. 515.

The doctrine of our cases is sanctioned by *Judge* Cooley, and many decisions asserting the same rule are cited by him. Cooley, Const. Lim. 5th ed. 657.

We are compelled to sustain the contention of the appellant, and adjudge the Act of March 9, 1889, to be void because it violates the provisions of the Constitution. As that Act is without force, the circuit court had jurisdiction of the subject, and the only question is whether the complaint states facts sufficient to constitute a cause of action.

In the case of *Anderson* v. *Buchanan*, 8 Ind. 132, the court quoted with approval from *Chancellor* Kent the following statement: "Thus, if a man sells land to another which is wholly surrounded by his own land, in this case the purchaser is entitled to a right of way over the other's ground to arrive at his own land." 3 Kent, Com. 420.

This is an apt illustration of the old and familiar doctrine of ways by necessity, and the doctrine has often been given effect by our decisions. *Steel* v. *Grigsby*, 79 Ind. 184; *Sanxay* v. *Hunger*, 42 Ind. 44; *Stewart* v. *Hartman*, 46 Ind. 331.

If the appellant's grantor had remained the owner of the land now owned by the appellee, it is clear that she would be entitled to a way, as of necessity, to the public road. *Kimball* v. *Cocheco R. Co.* 27 N. H. 448, 59 Am. Dec. 387.

A way by necessity exists by grant, and the grant is an implied one. *Nichols* v. *Luce*, 24 Pick. 102, 35 Am. Dec. 302.

The theory is that where land is sold that has no outlet, the vendor grants one over the parcel of which he retains the ownership. It results from this that a way of necessity cannot be successfully claimed over the land of a stranger, and if the appellant were asserting a right of way over a stranger's land she could not succeed. If the appellee occupies the position of a stranger, then the appellant must fail; but if he occupies the position as to her that the common grantor did before he parted with title, then she is entitled to the relief she prays. In our judgment, the appellee is in the position of his grantor in so far as the question before us is concerned, and must yield the appellant a right of way. As the law implied a grant at the time the common grantor conveyed to the appellant, and as that grant was prior to the conveyance to the appellee, the latter must carry into effect his predecessor's implied grant.

In *Taylor* v. *Warnaky*, 55 Cal. 350, both parties claimed, as do the parties before us, through a common grantor, and it was held that the party whose land was surrounded was entitled to a way as of necessity across the land of the other. The decision in the case referred to is sustained by the doctrine, maintained by the ancient and the modern authorities, that the original grantor grants, as appurtenant to the parcel expressly conveyed, a way which will enable his grantee to obtain access to the corporeal property expressly conveyed to him. Both the corporeal property and the incorporeal right pass from the grantor at the same time, one as the inseparable incident of the other, and a subsequent grantee must necessarily take the land conveyed to him subject to the burden created by the implied grant.

Our ultimate conclusion is that the action was properly brought in the circuit court, and that such facts are stated in the complaint as require an answer.

Judgment reversed.

William MERRELL, *Appt.*,
v.
Rebecca A. SPRINGER.

(....Ind.....)

The owner of a note which was, after maturity, surreptitiously taken, without his knowledge or consent, from his possession by its nominal payee and sold to a third party, may recover it from the purchaser although the latter paid value for it and had no notice of the defect in the title of his vendor.

(April 30, 1890.)

APPEAL by defendant from a judgment of the Circuit Court for Fayette County in favor of plaintiff, and from an order denying a motion for a new trial, in an action brought to recover possession of a certain promissory note. *Affirmed.*

The case sufficiently appears in the opinion.

Messrs. **R. Conner** and **H. L. Frost** for appellant.

Messrs. **G. G. Florea** and **J. H. Claypool** for appellee.

Coffey, *J.*, delivered the opinion of the court:

This was an action of replevin to recover the possession of a promissory note alleged to be the property of the appellee, and wrongfully detained from her by the appellant.

The only questions discussed by counsel in their respective briefs relate to the alleged error of the circuit court in overruling the appellant's motion for a new trial.

The evidence in the cause tends to prove that the appellee, in November, 1878, deposited with the maker of the note in controversy the sum of $25, and took a note therefor in the name of her son, Orin Springer, who was then about five years old. The note was taken in the name of her son for the reason that the husband of the appellee was much addicted to becoming intoxicated, and was in the habit of appropriating the appellee's property to his own use. To prevent him from obtaining possession of the money represented by this note it was taken in the name of the son, but was kept in the possession of the appellee. The note was renewed from time to time, covering other small deposits, until the 16th day of December, 1884, when the present note for $160 was executed. All the money represented by the note was the money of the appellee. In August, 1886, the son, without the knowledge or consent of the appellee, took the note from a bureau drawer in her possession, and sold it to the appellant.

The theory of the appellant was that the appellee, by making the note in controversy payable to her son, constituted him her trustee, and that as he assigned the note to the appellant, who had no notice of the secret trust between the appellee and her son, the appellant acquired a good title to the note. Acting upon that theory the appellant, at the proper time, prayed the court to give the jury the following instructions, viz.:

"3. If the plaintiff, Rebecca Springer, furnished all the consideration for the execution of the note in question, but had the same made payable to Orin Springer for the purpose and with the understanding that he should hold the legal title to the same in trust for her, and that he has never since the execution of said note transferred his title to the plaintiff; that the said Orin Springer, before the bringing of this suit, for a valuable consideration, by his indorsement in writing, assigned said note to the defendant, and that the defendant, at the time said note was transferred to him, had no knowledge that anyone except said Orin Springer had any interest in said note; and that he purchased the same in good faith and for a valuable consideration, relying upon the apparent title said Orin Springer had to said note,—then, in such case, you should find for the defendant.

"4. If said Rebecca Springer furnished all the consideration for the execution of the note in question, but had the same made payable to Orin Springer, and he has never since the execution of the same transferred his title to said note to the plaintiff, and the plaintiff took said note into her possession, and kept the same where said Orin had free and ready access to the same, and said Orin, without the knowledge or consent of said plaintiff, took said note into his possession, and the defendant in good faith and for a valuable consideration, and relying upon the apparent title thus conferred upon said Orin Springer, purchased said note of him without any knowledge of the claim of the plaintiff to said note; and the said Orin Springer, in pursuance of said purchase, on the 2d day of August, 1886, indorsed said note to the defendant,—then, in such case, you should find for the defendant."

The court refused to give these instructions, but instructed the jury as follows:

"3. If the jury believe that said Rebecca Springer furnished all the consideration for the note in question; that said note was made payable to her son, Orin Springer, by the direction of the said plaintiff, Rebecca Springer; that at the time of its execution it was placed in her hands, and that she never voluntarily parted

NOTE.—See Baldwin v. Ely, 50 U. S. 9 How. 580 (13 L. ed. 266), and note.

with the possession thereof, and that Orin Springer, the payee, got possession of said note surreptitiously, without the knowledge or consent of said Rebecca Springer, and while so holding the same he indorsed and transferred the same to the defendant Merrell, and the plaintiff, Rebecca Springer, before the commencement of this suit, demanded the possession of said note from the defendant Merrell, —in such case the plaintiff will be entitled to recover, although the defendant may have paid a valuable consideration therefor, and had no notice that said Orin Springer was not the owner of said note."

The note in controversy is not negotiable by the law-merchant, and was sold and assigned to the appellant after maturity. In such case the purchaser must inquire as to the title of his assignor, and as to the defenses against the note in the hands of the assignor. *Kastner* v. *Pibilinski*, 96 Ind. 229; *Sims* v. *Wilson*, 47 Ind. 226; *Robeson* v. *Roberts*, 20 Ind. 155; *Schafer* v. *Reilly*, 50 N. Y. 61; *Bush* v. *Lathrop*, 22 N. Y. 535.

It seems to be settled in this State that a purchaser of such a note can acquire no better title than that held by his vendor.

In *Summer* v. *Huston*, 48 Ind. 228, it was said by this court: "It is a familiar principle that no man can confer a greater interest in, or title to, personal property than he has himself, and this principle is as applicable to choses in action (paper governed by the law-merchant of course excepted) as to any other species of personalty. The principle that the purchaser of the legal title to real estate, without notice of an outstanding equity, takes it discharged of the equity, has no application in the case of the purchase of a chose in action. It is a general and well-settled principle that the assignee of a chose in action takes it subject to the same equity it was subject to in the hands of the assignor."

This was but a repetition of what was said in the case of *Robeson* v. *Roberts*, 20 Ind. 155. It was further said in this case that "an abuse of a trust can confer no rights on the party abusing it, nor on those who claim in privity with him."

To the same effect are *Sims* v. *Wilson*, 47 Ind. 226, and *Payne* v. *June*, 92 Ind. 252.

The doctrine that where one of two innocent parties must suffer, the party who put it in the power of the wrong-doer to perpetrate the wrong must suffer the loss, has no application to this case, for there is no evidence in the cause tending to contradict the evidence of the appellee that Orin Springer took the note from her bureau drawer without her knowledge or consent. See authorities above cited.

Under the rules as established by these cases we are constrained to hold that the court did not err in refusing to give the jury the instructions asked, and that the instruction given upon the subject now under consideration states the true rule.

This case is clearly distinguishable from the case of *Moore* v. *Moore*, 112 Ind. 149, 11 West. Rep. 229. In that case the party claiming title had indorsed and delivered the note then in dispute, with the intention of vesting in the assignee title, and it was correctly held that as the note had passed to an innocent purchaser for value, without notice of any fraud by which the assignment was procured, that the assignor was estopped from reclaiming the note from such innocent purchaser. That case rests upon the principle announced in *Parrish* v. *Thurston*, 87 Ind. 437, and *Ourme* v. *Rauh*, 100 Ind. 247.

The appellant also discusses in his brief other questions appearing in the record relating to the admission and rejection of evidence. We have carefully examined these questions, as well as all others presented and discussed, but are unable to discover any error in the ruling of the circuit court.

Judgment affirmed.

Charles E. CATLIN, Receiver, etc., of Clapp & Davies, *Appt.*,

v.

WILCOX SILVER PLATE CO.

(......Ind.......)

The right of a receiver appointed by a foreign tribunal to wind up an insolvent partnership situated within its jurisdiction, to take possession of money due to such partnership from domestic debtors, will not be recognized as against the claims of nonresident creditors of the insolvent partnership who have attached such money under the domestic laws after the appointment of the receiver but before he obtained actual possession of the money or an enforceable lien thereon, even although he has received a general assignment of the partnership property.

(April 29, 1890.)

APPEAL by intervenor from a judgment of the Circuit Court for La Porte County in favor of plaintiffs in an attachment suit brought to recover a debt due by the concern of which the intervenor was receiver out of money due such concern. *Affirmed.*

The facts are fully stated in the opinion.

Mr. **L. A. Cole,** for appellant:

Where two courts, of substantially concurrent jurisdiction, attempt to assert jurisdiction of the same matter, that court which takes the first step will retain the jurisdiction till the end, and the other cannot lawfully interfere. *Taylor* v. *Carryl*, 61 U. S. 20 How. 583 (15

NOTE.—*Foreign receivers.*

Receivers appointed in one jurisdiction are not entitled as of right to recognition in other jurisdictions. See *note* to Humphreys v. Hopkins (Cal.) 6 L. R. A. 792.

A receiver of partnership assets, appointed by a competent court of another State, may maintain an action in New Jersey to set aside a sale of the assets situate in New Jersey by one partner in fraud of the other, when there are no creditors of the firm and the only one to be benefited is the partner defrauded. Sobernheimer v. Wheeler (N. J.) Aug. 16, 1889.

The possession of a receiver appointed in one jurisdiction, of the personal property of a debtor taken by him under order of court, does not exempt it, when taken into another jurisdiction, from attachment by creditors therein, or give the receiver any right to hold the property against the claims of such attaching creditors. Humphreys v. Hopkins, 6 L. R. A. 792, 81 Cal. 551.

L. ed. 1028); *Freeman* v. *Howe*, 65 U. S. 24 How. 450 (16 L. ed. 749); *Buck* v. *Colbath*, 70 U. S. 3 Wall. 334 (18 L. ed. 257); *Heidritter* v. *Elizabeth Oil Cloth Co.* 112 U. S. 294 (28 L. ed. 729); *Senior* v. *Pierce*, 31 Fed. Rep. 625; *Melvin* v. *Robinson*, Id. 634; *Kohn* v. *Ryan*, Id. 636.

This principle is applicable in every respect to the case at bar. This debt was located in Illinois.

Story, Conf. L. 362 *a*, 363, 399, *note 3*, 400; *Connor* v. *Hanover Ins. Co.* 28 Fed. Rep. 549; *Guillander* v. *Howell*, 35 N. Y. 657, and cases cited; *Gale* v. *Carry*, 10 West. Rep. 838, 112 Ind. 39.

An open account is susceptible of assignment, so as to absolutely vest the title thereto in the assignee.

Patterson v. *Crawford*, 12 Ind. 241; *McFadden* v. *Wilson*, 96 Ind. 253.

The attaching creditor can only hold the garnishee for such interest as defendant had at the time the process was served.

2 Wade, Attachm. § 437; *Williams* v. *Pomeroy*, 27 Minn. 85; *Lewis* v. *Bush*, 30 Minn. 244; *Knisely* v. *Evans*, 34 Ohio St. 158; *Schuler* v. *Israel*, 27 Fed. Rep. 851; *Faulkner* v. *Hyman*, 3 New Eng. Rep. 181, 142 Mass. 53; *Butler* v. *Wendell*, 57 Mich. 62.

A court of chancery, having jurisdiction of the person, may for the benefit of creditors compel a debtor to execute such assignments or conveyances as will vest the title to such property in the assignee.

Mitchell v. *Bunch*, 2 Paige, 606; *Phelps* v. *McDonald*, 99 U. S. 298 (25 L. ed. 473); *Great Falls Mfg. Co.* v. *Worster*, 23 N. H. 462.

Messrs. **John H. Bradley, F. E. Osborne** and **W. B. Biddle**, for appellee:

The receiver acquired the property and effects of Clapp & Davies by operation of law by virtue of his appointment, or by an assignment *in invitum*, and, either way, he took no title or interest to or in any property beyond the limits of the State of his appointment.

Paine v. *Lester*, 44 Conn. 196; *Warner* v. *Jaffray*, 96 N. Y. 248; *Hibernia Nat. Bank* v. *Lacombe*, 84 N. Y. 367; *Rhawn* v. *Pearce*, 110 Ill. 350; *May* v. *First Nat. Bank* (Ill.) 7 West. Rep. 681; *Weider* v. *Maddox*, 66 Tex. 372.

The *situs* of this debt for the purpose of attachment and garnishment is in this State.

Smith's App. 104 Pa. 381; *Wyman* v. *Halstead*, 109 U. S. 654 (27 L. ed. 1068); *Owen* v. *Miller*, 10 Ohio St. 136.

Where creditors intervene the right of the receiver is always denied until such claims are satisfied.

Willitts v. *Waite*, 25 N. Y. 577; *Hurd* v. *Elizabeth*, 41 N. J. L. 1; *Lycoming F. Ins. Co.* v. *Wright*, 55 Vt. 526.

Mitchell, *Ch. J.*, delivered the opinion of the court:

The question for decision arises upon the following facts:

Clapp & Davies, partners doing business in the City of Chicago, were indebted to certain judgment creditors residing in that city. They were also indebted to the Wilcox Silver Plate Company, and others, who were residents of the State of Connecticut. At the same time Bagley & Oberreich, partners, residing and doing business at La Porte, Indiana, were indebted in a considerable sum to Clapp & Davies. One of the judgment creditors instituted proceedings in chancery against the latter firm, by filing a creditor's bill in the Superior Court of Cook County. In aid of its jurisdiction in the proceeding thus instituted, that court appointed the appellant, Catlin, receiver, and by an order made on the 14th day of April, 1887, required Clapp & Davies to execute a general deed of assignment transferring all their partnership property and effects to the receiver. Subsequently, in the month of June, the Wilcox Silver Plate Company instituted a suit in attachment in the La Porte Circuit Court against Clapp & Davies, and summoned Bagley & Oberreich to answer as garnishees. The other Connecticut creditors became parties to this last proceeding under § 943, Rev. Stat. 1881. Thereupon Catlin, as receiver of the Superior Court of Cook County, intervened by leave of the La Porte Circuit Court, and asserted the right, in virtue of his appointment as receiver and the assignment made to him, to take and hold the debt due Clapp & Davies, from Bagley & Oberreich.

The controversy, as will appear, involves the right to the fund in the hands of the garnishee-defendants, and the question presented is, Are the rights of the nonresident attaching creditors paramount, in the courts of this State, to those of the receiver of the Superior Court of Cook County, whose appointment antedates the issuing of the writ of attachment? The solution of the question depends upon the extent of power which a court of general jurisdiction, sitting in one State, can exercise over property whose actual *situs* is within the jurisdiction of the courts of a foreign State.

A receiver is nothing more than an officer or creature of the court that appoints him. His acts are those of the court, whose jurisdiction may be aided, but in no wise enlarged or extended, by his appointment. His power is only co-extensive with that of the court which gives him his official character. While it has been held that a court may appoint a receiver and authorize him to take possession of property in a foreign jurisdiction, the doctrine is universal that the appointment confers no legal authority which the receiver can exert over the property without the aid of the courts in whose jurisdiction it is found. The appointment, of its own force, gives him the right to take possession of the property, but it confers upon him no power to compel the recognition of that right, outside the jurisdiction of the court making the appointment. High, Receivers, § 47, p. 241.

While there are authorities of great weight which seem to hold that a receiver appointed in one jurisdiction will not be permitted to maintain a suit in a foreign State, the generally prevailing doctrine, upon which all the decisions seem to be harmonious, is that, upon the principles of comity, the courts of the jurisdiction in which the property or fund is situate will recognize the rights of the receiver, so far as to aid him in reducing it to possession, unless to do so would in some way violate the local policy or interfere with the rights of resident creditors. *Metzner* v. *Bauer*, 98 Ind. 425, and cases cited; Beach, Receivers, §§ 16, 19, 682;

Merchants Nat. Bank v. *McLeod*, 38 Ohio St. 174.

But the recognition of well-established principles of comity and courtesy between courts of different jurisdiction is one thing, while the rights of resident or other attaching creditors, who are seeking to avail themselves of legal proceedings authorized by statutes of the State, for the appropriation of a fund belonging to a nonresident debtor, must be determined upon altogether different principles. As has in effect been said, courts are prepared to extend comity where there is no reason to the contrary; especially if there is no interest of their own citizens, or of the citizens of another State, who are asking the protection of their laws, injuriously affected by such recognition. *Paine* v. *Lester*, 44 Conn. 196; *Milne* v. *Moreton*, 6 Binn. 361.

The rule may be considered as established that a receiver may invoke the aid of a foreign court, in obtaining possession of property or funds within its jurisdiction, to which he is entitled; but aid will only be extended as against those who were parties, or in some way in privity with the proceedings in the court in which his appointment was made, or who are in possession of the property or fund to which the receiver has a right; and not against creditors of a nonresident debtor, who are seeking to subject the property or fund to the payment of their debts, by proceedings duly instituted for that purpose. Accordingly, in *Hurd* v. *Elizabeth*, 41 N. J. L. 1, the court said: "That the officer of a foreign court should not be permitted, as against the claims of creditors resident here, to remove from this State assets of the debtor, is a proposition that appears to be asserted by all the decisions."

The principle upon which the decisions rest is, that it is the policy of every government to retain within its control the property of a foreign debtor until all domestic claims have been satisfied, and hence the right of the receiver of a foreign court to sue, which is allowed only upon considerations of comity, will be denied when it comes in conflict with the interests of domestic creditors. "We decline," said the court in *Runk* v. *St. John*, 29 Barb. 585, "to extend our wonted courtesy so far as to work detriment to citizens of our own State, who have been induced to give credit to the foreign insolvent." *Bagby* v. *Atlantic, M. & O. R. Co.* 86 Pa. 291; *Lycoming F. Ins. Co.* v. *Wright*, 55 Vt. 526; *Thurston* v. *Rosenfield*, 42 Mo. 474, 97 Am. Dec. 351; *Willitts* v. *Waite*, 25 N. Y. 577.

It follows, hence, that the available legal authority of a receiver is co-extensive only with the jurisdiction of the court by which he was appointed when the right of precedence or priority of creditors is asserted in respect to property or funds of a nonresident debtor, which the receiver has not yet reduced to possession. *Hunt* v. *Columbian Ins. Co.* 55 Me. 290; *Warren* v. *Union Nat. Bank*, 7 Phila. 156; *Booth* v. *Clark*, 58 U. S. 17 How. 322 [15 L. ed. 164]; *State* v. *Jacksonville, P. & M. R. Co.* 15 Fla. 202; *Farmers & M. Ins. Co.* v. *Needles*, 52 Mo. 17; *Taylor* v. *Columbian Ins. Co.* 14 Allen, 353.

It is said, however, that as Clapp & Davies were residents of the State of Illinois at the time the receiver was appointed, the debt due them from Bagley & Oberreich was within the jurisdiction of the Superior Court of Cook County, upon the principle that the domicil draws to it the personal property and choses in action of the owner, wherever they may be situate. Hence, the contention is, that as the appointment of the appellant as receiver was followed by a general deed of assignment, valid in the State of Illinois, it must be regarded as valid here, and as devesting Clapp & Davies of all title or interest in the debt in controversy after the date of the assignment. It is, of course, well settled that personal property is transferable according to the law of the owner's domicil, and that a voluntary assignment or transfer made without compulsion or legal coercion is to be governed everywhere by that law, unless the contract by which the transfer was made is limited or restrained by some policy of positive enactment of the State in which the property is situate, or unless it affects citizens of the latter State injuriously. *Ames Iron Works* v. *Warren*, 76 Ind. 512; *Martin* v. *Potter*, 11 Gray, 37, 71 Am. Dec. 689; *Weider* v. *Maddox*, 66 Tex. 372, 59 Am. Rep. 617; *Warner* v. *Jaffray*, 96 N. Y. 248; *Green* v. *Van Buskirk*, 74 U. S. 7 Wall. 150 [19 L. ed. 118]; *Askew* v. *LaCygne Exch. Bank*, 83 Mo. 366; *Law* v. *Mills*, 18 Pa. 185; Burrill, Assignm. 301; Story, Conf. L. 383-390.

"The voluntary transfer of a chattel by the debtor, if not forbidden in other respects by the law at the place of the *situs*, is to be as much regarded there or elsewhere as it would be at the place of the domicil." *Lowry* v. *Hall*, 2 Watts & S 181; *Smith's App.* 104 Pa. 381; *Chafee* v. *Fourth Nat. Bank*, 71 Me. 514, 36 Am. Rep. 345. See 15 Am. L. Rev. 251.

Such an assignment will not be upheld, however, if it contravenes the policy of the law of the place where the property is situate. *Guillander* v. *Howell*, 35 N. Y. 657; *Faulkner* v. *Hyman*, 142 Mass. 53, 2 New Eng. Rep. 181; *Moore* v. *Church*, 70 Iowa, 208; *Re Waite*, 99 N. Y. 433.

The principles above stated are applicable only to transfers or assignments of property which rest essentially on contract and are voluntary in the sense that they are the product of a will acting without legal compulsion. Property in a foreign State that has passed from an assignor to an assignee by a voluntary deed, and not by proceedings *in invitum*, by process of law is distinguished from like property in the hands of a receiver by operation of law, or by an assignment made under legal compulsion.

Assignments of the latter class are held inoperative upon property not situate within the territory over which the laws that make or compel the debtor to make them have dominion. *Rhawn* v. *Pearce*, 110 Ill. 350; *Smith's App.* and *Weider* v. *Maddox*, *supra*.

Involuntary assignments which are made under foreign Insolvent Laws, have no operation outside of the State under whose laws they were made, while a voluntary assignment is a personal common-law right, possessed by every owner of property, and may operate in one State as well as another. *Walters* v. *Whitlock*, 9 Fla. 86, 76 Am. Dec. 607.

Some conflict or contrariety of opinion may be found in the decisions in respect to what may or may not constitute a voluntary assignment under the statutes of different States, but it is unnecessary to enter upon a discussion of the cases relating to voluntary assignments, as all the authorities agree that where an assignment is made under compulsion of law, or where property is taken *ab invitum*, the transfer will not be regarded as voluntary, nor will it be effectual beyond the jurisdiction in which it was made, when it conflicts with the interests of citizens in a foreign jurisdiction. As we have seen, a court cannot extend its jurisdiction by the appointment of a receiver, so it is equally powerless to do so by coercing an assignment of the property in controversy. An assignment is regarded merely as a matter of convenience in aid of the jurisdiction of the court, the established doctrine being that, as against nonresident creditors, the assignment confers no additional or higher right to the property than the receiver had by virtue of his appointment. *Iddings* v. *Bruen*, 4 Sandf. Ch. 252; High, Receivers, § 443.

While it is true, as has been remarked before, the domicil of the owner, in legal contemplation, draws to it his personal estate, wherever it may be, yet as this is so only by fiction of law, the rule is not of universal application. When, by the law and policy of the State where the property is actually located, it is subject to the process of attachment or garnishment at the suit of a domestic or other creditor, the fiction yields, and the actual *situs* of the property determines whether or not it should be subjected to the process of the court. *Warner* v. *Jaffray* and *Green* v. *Van Buskirk*, *supra*.

In cases of attachment and garnishment, like those for founding administration, the *situs* of a debt is the residence of the debtor. *Wyman* v. *Halstead*, 109 U. S 654 [27 L. ed. 1068]; *Owen* v. *Miller*, 10 Ohio St. 136.

It is said, however, that the principles of comity which control in aid of the receiver of a foreign court, who is seeking to obtain possession of a fund, should only be suspended in their operation in favor of domestic creditors, and that inasmuch as the attaching creditors in the present case are all nonresidents of the State, the aid of the court should have been extended to the receiver and denied the creditors. While this position is not without support, it is not in our view maintainable. Although nonresidents, the attaching creditors are properly in our courts, pursuing a remedy which the Statute confers upon foreign as well as domestic creditors. Until the Legislature shall declare a different policy, the rights of a foreign creditor against the property of a debtor must be regarded by the courts as in all respects the same as those of resident creditors, so far as respects proceedings in attachment and garnishment. The rule which commends itself to our judgment is thus declared: "Once properly in the court and accepted as a suitor, neither the law, nor court administering the law, will admit any distinction between the citizen of its own State and that of another. Before the law and its tribunals, there can be no preference of one over the other." *Hibernia Nat. Bank* v. *Lacombe*, 84 N. Y. 367; *Rhawn* v. *Pearce*, *Warner* v. *Jaffray* and *Paine* v. *Lester*, *supra*.

This rule governs the more recent decisions, The conclusions above stated lead to an affirmance of the judgment.

Judgment affirmed, with costs.

BERKEY & GAY FURNITURE CO., *Appt.*,
v.
Milo S. HASCALL.

......(Ind.)......

In case one, who has sold furniture for a hotel and contracted with the proprietor to deliver it by or on a certain date, knowing the purpose for which it is to be used and that it is necessary for the operation of the hotel, fails to deliver it until long after the appointed time, thereby preventing the renting of the rooms to guests, he is liable for the loss sustained by reason of such failure; and such loss may be determined by finding the difference between the value, for the purpose for which they were intended, of the rooms furnished and unfurnished during the time they could not be used for such purpose.

(May 1, 1890.)

APPEAL by plaintiff from a judgment of the Circuit Court for Elkhart County allowing defendant's claim to a set-off and rendering judgment against it thereon, in an action to recover the contract price for certain furniture sold and delivered. *Affirmed.*

The facts are fully stated in the opinion.

Messrs. **W. H. Vesey, C. W. Miller** and **J. M. Vanfleet** for appellant.

Messrs. **H. D. Wilson** and **W. J. Davis** for appellee.

Olds, *J.*, delivered the opinion of the court:

This is an action by the appellant against the appellee to recover a balance of $374.62 for goods sold and delivered.

The answer is in three paragraphs, setting up a counterclaim:

1. It is alleged in the first paragraph that on August 26, 1881, the appellee had just completed his hotel with fifty rooms, and was in need of new furniture therefor, without which he could not carry on his business, as appellant well knew; that on said day, for the purpose of furnishing said hotel in all its parts with suitable furniture, the appellant agreed with him to furnish said furniture and every part thereof complete, and set it up in proper shape and condition in his hotel rooms ready for use by September 15, 1881; that said rooms were irregular and different in sizes, dimension and construction, and for the purpose of making said furniture suitable for said rooms, appellant measured said rooms, and a list of goods was agreed upon, and at the foot thereof appellant executed a memorandum in writing as follows:

We agree to put these goods all in good order (set up in hotel without charge except freight and cartage), castored, with bracket wood-wheels on all beds. All bureaus and washstands to have good wood-wheels on rubber castors. Goods to be ready the 15th of Sept. Any goods not according to order, or not satisfactory, may be returned free of charge.

Goshen, Aug. 26, 1881.

Berkey & Gay Furniture Co.
T. M. Moseley.

The paragraph then alleges that he was ready, able and willing to comply with his part of said contract, but that appellant, with full knowledge of all the facts, violated said agreement, in this, to wit: It failed to deliver any of said goods prior to September 30, 1881, whereby he lost the daily use of twenty-nine rooms, of the rental value of $2 per day for each room from September 15 to September 30; that appellant failed to deliver said goods prior to January 18, 1882, except as set forth in the complaint; that said furniture was purchased to be delivered in sets and suits for specific rooms and places, as set forth in said foregoing memorandum, but the articles so delivered were not in sets or suits, but in disjointed and unmatched pieces, and were not and could not be properly set up or used until all were delivered; by reason of which he lost the daily rental value and use of twenty of said rooms, worth to defendant $2 each per day from October 1, 1881, to January 18, 1882, inclusive; that because of such failure he was compelled to turn away and did turn away twenty persons each day, who desired to become guests at said hotel, whereby the income and profits of said hotel business were diminished $50 per day.

The second paragraph of the counterclaim alleges that on the 26th day of August, 1881, he had just completed his hotel at a cost of $40,000; that it contained forty rooms (besides dining-room, kitchen, etc.) suitable for the entertainment of guests; that it was then operated and run by him in the business of hotel-keeping, and was so operated for the next two years; that the rental value of said hotel, when furnished, was $5,500 per year; that on said 26th day of August, 1881, he was in great need of furniture to supply and furnish thirty of the aforesaid guest rooms in said hotel, which rooms were then unfurnished and empty, in which condition they were of no rental value to defendant, all of which appellant well knew; that to supply and furnish said rooms and hotel as aforesaid, appellant promised and agreed with him to deliver and set up in good order and condition the furniture mentioned in its complaint by the 15th day of September, 1881, according to written specifications and agreement (copied into first paragraph above); that appellant failed and refused to deliver said goods until January 18, 1882, during which time, from September 15, 1881, to January 18, 1882, he was deprived of the use and rental value of said hotel and the several rooms therein, which use and rental was of the value of $2,000.

3. The third paragraph of the counterclaim alleges all the matters contained in the other two paragraphs, showing a little more minutely the rooms for which the different articles of furniture were designed.

A reply in general denial was filed to the answer. The cause was submitted to a jury for trial, and the jury returned a special verdict in the words and figures following:

SPECIAL VERDICT.

1. We, the jury, find that the plaintiff contracted with the defendant, on the 26th day of August, 1881, to sell and deliver to defendant the several items of property mentioned in plaintiff's complaint at and for the price of each article as stated in plaintiff's complaint, and was to deliver the same and set the same up in defendant's hotel in Goshen, Indiana, and have the same ready for use in defendant's hotel, known as Hotel Hascall, by or on the 15th day of September, 1881. That plaintiff at the time of making such contract knew the purpose for which said furniture was to be used.

2. Plaintiff failed and neglected to deliver any of said furniture until the 30th day of September, 1881, and thereupon and thereafter until the 16th day of January, 1882, plaintiff delivered said furniture at the times, and in the specific articles, as severally set forth by the plaintiff in the complaint herein.

3. Defendant paid plaintiff the sums credited to defendant in plaintiff's complaint and returned to plaintiff the items of furniture, as stated in plaintiff's complaint, to the amount of $121.85, thus leaving unpaid of the purchase price of said furniture the sum of $374.62, March, 1882, as stated by the plaintiff.

4. We further find that defendant, at and just prior to the making of said contract, had reconstructed and built his hotel building in the City of Goshen, Indiana, at a cost of $40,000, and defendant was proprietor and manager thereof, and had within said hotel thirty (30) rooms that were unfurnished, and when so unfurnished were of no use or value to the defendant; that all said rooms remained vacant, and of no use or value to defendant, from the 15th day of September, 1881, to the 30th day of September, 1881, on account and by reason of the failure of plaintiff to comply with its agreement aforesaid; that twenty-three (23) of said rooms remained vacant, and of no use to defendant, from the 30th day of September, 1881, until the 19th day of October, 1881, because of the failure of plaintiff to comply with said contract; that seven (7) of said rooms remained vacant and of no use, from the 19th day of October, 1881, to the 5th day of November, 1881, because of the failure of plaintiff to comply with said contract; that from the 5th day of November, 1881, until December 15, 1881, six (6) rooms of said hotel remained vacant and of no use to defendant, because of the non-fulfillment of said contract by the plaintiff; that the use of each one of said rooms to the defendant was nothing when unfurnished.

5. We further find that the rental value and use of each of said rooms, when furnished with the furniture designated for same in said contract, would have been to the defendant 75 cents per day, during said time.

6. If, upon the foregoing facts, the law be with the plaintiff, then we find for the plaintiff, but if the law be with the defendant, then we find for the defendant.

John A. Smith, Foreman.

The appellant moved for judgment on the special verdict, which motion was overruled and an exception reserved. The appellee moved for judgment on the special verdict and the court sustained said motion, to which the appellant excepted. Final judgment was then entered in favor of appellee for $554.68, and costs.

Appellant filed a motion for new trial, which was overruled and exceptions reserved. The appellant assigns as error:

1. That the court erred in overruling appellant's motion for judgment in its favor upon the special verdict.

2. That the court erred in sustaining appellee's motion for judgment in his favor on the special verdict.

3. That the court erred in overruling appellant's motion for new trial.

It is contended that, under the facts found, the appellee is only entitled to compensatory or general damages, and not for the special damages set up as a counterclaim.

We think the facts found in the special verdict entitled the appellee to recover the special damages claimed.

In *Vickery* v. *McCormick*, 117 Ind. 594–597, the court says: "The general rule is, that a party who fails to comply with his contract to furnish goods is liable for the value of the goods in the open market at the time of the failure. But when similar goods cannot be purchased in the market, the measure of damages is the actual loss sustained by the purchaser in not receiving the goods according to the contract."

See *Rahm* v. *Deig*, 121 Ind. 283, and authorities there cited.

In *Hadley* v. *Baxendale*, 9 Exch. 341—Sedgwick, Leading Cases on the Measure of Damages, pp. 126–136—the court states what we deem to be the true rule governing the assessment of damages in such cases as this. In that case it is said: "When two parties have made a contract which one of them has broken, the damages which the other party ought to receive in respect of such breach of contract should be such as may fairly and reasonably be considered either arising naturally, *i. e.*, according to the usual course of things, from such breach of contract itself, or such as may reasonably be supposed to have been in the contemplation of both parties at the time they made the contract as the probable result of the breach of it."

The facts found by the jury show that the appellee, at and just prior to August 26, 1881, had reconstructed and built his hotel building in the City of Goshen, Indiana, at a cost of $40,000, and that appellee was proprietor and manager thereof, and had within said hotel thirty rooms that were unfurnished, and when so unfurnished were of no use or value to the appellee; that upon said day he contracted with the appellant to sell and deliver to him the several items of property mentioned in the appellant's complaint, which consisted of the necessary furniture to furnish said rooms at and for the price of each article as stated in the complaint, and agreed to deliver the same and set the same up in appellee's hotel, and have the same ready for use in said hotel by or on the 15th day of September, 1881; that the appellant, at the time of making of said contract, knew the purpose for which said furniture was to be used. The contract was to furnish the furniture for thirty rooms in a hotel and set it up in the rooms, and have it ready for use and occupancy by a day named. From these facts it necessarily follows as a conclusion that the party contracting to furnish the same knew that the rooms were valueless as hotel apartments when unfurnished; that the furniture was necessary to enable the purchaser to use and occupy the same, and operate his hotel, and that the appellee would be deprived of the use of such rooms for such purpose until it complied with its contract.

The facts found further show that the appellant commenced furnishing the furniture soon after the date when it was all to have been furnished and put up in the rooms, furnishing part at one time and part at another. The facts show the appellee had reconstructed and rebuilt a valuable hotel, and was operating it himself, and the damages naturally resulting from the breach of the contract, according to the facts found, were what the rooms would have been worth to appellee furnished according to the contract more than they were worth to him unfurnished, during the delay in complying with the contract. Appellee built the house for a particular purpose, and was having it furnished for such purpose; he was not bound to rent out the rooms for another purpose, even if he could have done so. If there had been a breach and a total failure of the appellant to have furnished the whole or any part of the furniture, and the appellee had been notified that he was not intending to furnish it, then the appellant would have been liable for the difference in value of the furniture between the price in the open market and the contract price, as well as the loss of the use of the rooms for the time necessary to have procured the furniture elsewhere; but in this case the appellant furnished the furniture and appellee accepted it, so that the damage was the loss sustained by reason of the delay.

We think the loss of the use of the rooms as they were to be furnished might fairly be considered to have been contemplated by the parties at the time of the making of the contract.

In *Richardson* v. *Chynoweth*, 26 Wis. 656, it was held that a defendant failing to deliver an article, knowing the purpose for which it was purchased, was liable for the profits the purchaser would have made. See 1 Sutherland, Damages, 7th ed. pp. 218–239; Field, Damages, § 250; *Terre Haute* v. *Hudnut*, 112 Ind. 542, 11 West. Rep. 333.

It is contended that the facts found do not state the damages correctly; that if the plaintiff is entitled to recover, the amount he is entitled to recover would be the difference between the rental value of the rooms unfurnished and furnished. This objection we do not think available for a reversal of the judgment. When special damages of this character are recoverable, it is the damage the party himself has sustained that he is entitled to recover.

If A purchase grain of B and at the time A has a previous contract to sell and deliver grain to C, and A purchases the grain of B with a view of filling his previous contract with C, and C is advised of that fact, and the contract is such as that, on failure to deliver, B becomes liable to A for the profit he would have made, the damage recoverable is the profit A would have made; and that amount might be determined by a finding of the facts showing the amount A was to pay B for the grain, and the amount he would have received from C for the same.

So in this case, the amount of damage that the appellee was entitled to recover was the difference in value to the appellee in the rooms furnished and unfurnished, for the time they remained unfurnished by reason of appellant's failure to furnish the furniture; and that amount is determined by finding what the use of the rooms was worth to the appellee unfurnished, and what they were worth furnished, for the time he was deprived of the use of them for the purpose for which they were to be used. The jury has found as facts that the use of the rooms unfurnished was worth nothing to the appellee during that time, and furnished they would have been worth 75 cents per day; and the number of days each room was unfurnished from the date appellant contracted to set up the furniture in the rooms is also stated and found in the verdict, and the gross amount may be determined by a mere computation. The facts found in the special verdict entitle the appellee to a judgment for the amount of the damages found to have been sustained by him. *Fossion* v. *Landry*, not yet reported, this term.

The facts found cover all the issues in the case, and that is all that is required by a special verdict.

It is further contended that the court erred in not sustaining the motion for new trial, for the reason that the judgment rendered upon the verdict is in excess of the amount found due the appellee by the verdict; but this question is not presented by the record. If the judgment does not follow the verdict, or is not such a judgment as the party was entitled to have rendered upon the verdict, to present any question as to the amount or form of the judgment, it was necessary to make a motion to modify the judgment, and properly reserve exceptions in case the motion was overruled.

It follows, therefore, from the conclusion we have reached, that there is no error in the record for which the judgment should be reversed.

Judgment affirmed, with costs.

NEW YORK COURT OF APPEALS (2d Div.)

Oceana A. BANCROFT, *Appt.*,
v.
HOME BENEFIT ASSOCIATION of New York, *Respt.*

(....N. Y.....)

1. A slight blow on the throat while engaged in fencing, which causes a person to raise a little blood in consequence of which he is confined to his bed and attended by a physician for the greater part of three days, with no further hemorrhage from the day he was struck to the date of his death a year and a half thereafter, does not constitute "any wound, hurt or serious bodily injury" within the meaning of a question in an application for life insurance.

2. The words "hurt" and "wound," in a question asked of an applicant for life insurance as to any "wound, hurt or serious bodily injury" received by him, mean an injury to the body causing an impairment of health or strength, or rendering the person more liable to contract disease, or less able to resist its effects.

(March 18, 1890.)

APPEAL by plaintiff from a judgment of General Term of the Superior Court of the City of New York, affirming a judgment of the Special Term dismissing the complaint in an action to recover the amount alleged to be due on certain mutual benefit certificates. *Reversed.*

The facts are fully stated in the opinion.

Mr. **William G. Wilson** for appellant.

Mr. **Francis Lawton,** for respondent:

Where there is a warranty of the truth of the answers contained in the application, the materiality of the questions is eliminated from the consideration of the court or jury.

Ætna L. Ins. Co. v. *France*, 91 U. S. 510 (23 L. ed. 401); *Jeffries* v. *Economical Mut. L. Ins. Co.* 89 U. S. 22 Wall. 47 (22 L. ed. 833); *Foot* v. *Ætna L. Ins. Co.* 61 N. Y. 571; *Edington* v. *Ætna L. Ins. Co.* 77 N. Y. 564; *Edington* v. *Ætna L. Ins. Co.* 1 Cent. Rep. 524, 100 N. Y. 536; *Burritt* v. *Saratoga Co. Mut. F. Ins. Co.* 5 Hill, 188; *Dwight* v. *Germania L. Ins. Co.* 4 Cent. Rep. 529, 103 N. Y. 346.

Follett, *Ch. J.*, delivered the opinion of court:

April 28, 1885, John S. Bancroft became a member of defendant's life department, and received two certificates, by each of which the defendant promised to pay, on proof of his death during the continuance of the certificate, $5,000 to the insured's wife, the plaintiff, from the benefit fund of the life department. Each certificate contains the following provisions:

"In consideration of the representations and agreements made in the application herefor, and which is a part of this contract, and of each of the statements made therein, which . . . every person accepting or acquiring any interest in this contract hereby adopts as his own, admits to be material and warrants to be full and true, and to be the only statements upon which this contract is made."

"I. If this certificate . . . has been or shall be obtained through misrepresentation, fraud or concealment, . . . then the same shall be absolutely void."

The application contained this question and answer: "3. *Q.* Have you received any wound, hurt or serious bodily injury? *A.* No."

The application contained the following declarations: "I do hereby declare that all the particulars and statements made by me in connection with this application are true to the best of my knowledge and belief, and I do hereby acknowledge, consent and agree that any untrue or fraudulent statement made by me, or to any medical examiner for said Association, or any concealment of facts by me, shall forfeit and cancel all rights to any benefit under the above-named contract, and expressly waive all provisions of law forbidding any physician who has attended me from disclosing all information which he thereby acquired."

"I further declare and agree that my answers to the questions put by the medical examiner are correct and true, and that I am the person who signed the application on the opposite side, and was examined as stated."

September 19, 1885, the insured died, and this action was brought to recover the amounts insured by the certificates, and was defended at the trial on the sole ground that the answer to the question above quoted was untrue. The issue was tried before the court without a jury, which found as facts that February 21, 1884, the insured received a "wound" (5th finding), a "hurt" (6th finding), and a "serious bodily injury" (7th finding). The 8th finding of fact described with particularity the wound, hurt and serious bodily injury found in the 5th, 6th and 7th findings, and is as follows:

"*Eighth.* That prior to the making and delivery of the said application, and on or about the 21st day of February, 1884, the said John S. Bancroft, while engaged in fencing, did receive a blow from a foil on the throat in the neighborhood of or upon the Adam's apple; that in a few seconds thereafter he raised a little blood; that said blow produced an extravasation of the sub-mucus membrane just over the cricoid cartilage in the posterior part of the throat, almost opposite or behind, but a little below, the Adam's apple; that the force of said blow produced an abrasion, wound or hurt on the inside of the windpipe; that shortly thereafter the said John S. Bancroft was confined to his bed the whole or the greater part of three days, and during that time was attended by a physician; and was by him treated with the same treatment that he gave persons who have the complaint of spitting of blood; but I find that the treatment was not for the complaint of spitting of blood."

In the 9th finding the court found that the insured concealed from the defendant the injury described in the 5th, 6th, 7th and 8th findings, and as a conclusion of law decided that the plaintiff, by reason of the answer given, was not entitled to recover. The plaintiff excepted to the 5th, 6th, 7th and 9th findings of fact, and to this sentence contained in the 8th finding: "That the force of said blow produced an abrasion, wound or hurt on the inside of the wind-pipe," and now insists that they are without any evidence tending to sustain them, and are reviewable in this court as questions of law.

On the evening of February 21, 1884, the insured took at his own house a lesson in fencing with foils. His body was protected by a thickly padded buckskin jacket, fitting closely and high about his neck, and his face was shielded by a visor, which were specially designed for the protection of persons engaged in this exercise. At the end of the exercise he spat, as found, "a little blood," and immediately called his family physician, who, after an examination, expressed the opinion that his throat had been hit by the button of the foil, though no external mark or evidence of injury could be found. The insured was not conscious of having been hit and was quite confident that he had not been. The physician made a careful examination but found no evidence that the blood came from the throat or lungs. After the examination the patient was put to bed and treated in the manner and for the time described in the 8th finding of fact. No other hemorrhage occurred. March 3, 1884, his throat was examined by Dr. Jarvis, a specialist, who testified that by the use of a powerful light and mirrors he discovered the injury, which he described in the language used in the 8th finding. All the evidence descriptive of the injury and its effects was given by Doctors Wright, the attending physician, and Jarvis, the specialist, who were called by the defendant, and by the plaintiff, called in her own behalf. Dr. Wright testified that he had been the insured's family physician for ten or twelve years prior to May, 1885. After having described the injury and its effects, he testified: "I was his attending physician for some time, after this (the accident) until he moved away from that part of the city in May, 1885. During the time that I attended him as a physician he was not at any time seriously ill with any complaint; he was not, to my knowledge, afflicted with any organic or chronic disease at that time; I do not believe that he was."

Q. After all you had seen of this patient at the time of the injury, immediately after the injury, and during the time you attended him as a physician, would you call that a serious injury?

A. The result seems to justify the supposition that it was not a serious injury, but a man bleeding from the throat or lungs is always regarded as possibly a serious case; physicians always give them the benefit of the doubt under such circumstances; as though it was certainly serious.

Q. On the final result of this, would you call it a serious injury?

A. I would not, for the patient got over it.

Dr. Jarvis testified:

Q. Did you regard this as a serious injury?

A. I cannot say that I took it in that light; it was simply to find out what the trouble was that I examined him.

Q. Was it your opinion he would lose the effects of it?

A. I thought it would disappear.

The plaintiff testified that her husband spat no blood between February 21, 1884, and the date of his death. There is no conflict on the evidence and there is none justifying the inference or finding that the injury was serious, or that it was a hurt or wound within the meaning of the contract.

September 14, 1866, the Connecticut Mutual Life Insurance Company insured the life of a Mrs. Wilkinson. The application, which was a part of the contract, and its statements warranties, contained this question and answer:

Q. Has the party ever met with any accidental or serious personal injury; if so, what was it?

A. No.

The insured died in 1869, and in the action on the policy the jury returned a special finding that in 1862 the insured fell from a tree, was injured in consequence thereof, was sick for some time, but that she recovered, and that the injury had no permanent influence on her health. The fact that the insured had fallen and had been somewhat injured was not disclosed to the insurer. It was held that the injury was not within the meaning of the contract a serious one. *Wilkinson* v. *Connecticut Mut. L. Ins. Co.* 30 Iowa, 119.

At about the same time the Union Mutual Life Insurance Company of Maine insured the same life. This application, which was also a part of the contract, and its statements warranties, contained this question and answer:

Q. Has the party ever had any serious illness, local disease or personal injury; if so, of what nature and at what age?

A. No.

The accident which had happened to the insured was not disclosed to the insurer. On the trial of the issue joined, the jury returned a special finding that in 1862 the insured fell from a tree, was injured, but not seriously, and that its effects passed away without subsequently affecting her health. The fact that the insured had so fallen was not disclosed to the insurer. It was held that the injury described by the evidence and found by the jury was not a serious one, within the meaning of the contract, and that the plaintiff was entitled to recover. *Wilkinson* v. *Union Mut. L. Ins. Co.* 2 Dillon, 570; *Union Mut. L. Ins. Co.* v. *Wilkinson*, 80 U. S. 13 Wall. 222 [20 L. ed. 617].

In discussing the case, the meaning of the term "serious bodily injury" when used in life policies was discussed. The court said: "On the first branch of the case the court said to the jury that, if the effects of the fall were temporary, and had entirely passed away before the application was taken, and if it did not affect Mrs. Wilkinson's health or shorten her life, then the nondisclosure of the fall was no defense to the action. On the other hand, if the effects of the fall were not temporary, and remained when the application was taken, or if the fall affected the general health or was so serious that it might affect the health or shorten life, then the nondisclosure would defeat recovery, although the failure to mention the fall was not intentional or fraudulent.

"It is insisted by the counsel for the defendant that if the injury was considered serious at the time, it is one which must be mentioned in reply to the interrogatory, and that whether any further inquiry is expedient on the subject of its permanent influence on the health, is for the insurer to determine before making insurance. But there are grave and obvious difficulties in this construction. The accidents resulting in personal injuries, which at the moment are considered by the parties serious, are so very numerous that it would be almost impossible for a person engaged in active life to recall them at the age of forty or fifty years; and if the failure to mention all such injuries must invalidate the policy, very few would be sustained where thorough inquiry is made into the history of the party whose life is the subject of insurance. There is, besides, the question of what is to be considered a serious injury at the time. If the party gets over the injury completely, without leaving any ill consequences, in a few days it is clear that the serious aspect of the case was not a true one. Is it necessary to state the injury and explain the mistake to meet the requirements of the policy?

"On the other hand, when the question arises, as in this case, on a trial, the jury, and not the insurer, must decide whether the injury was serious or not. In deciding this, are they to reject the evidence of the ultimate effect of the injury on the party's health, longevity, strength and other similar considerations? This would be to leave out of view the essential purpose of the inquiry, and the very matters which would throw most light on the nature of the injury, with reference to its influence on the insurable character of the life proposed.

"Looking, then, to the purpose for which the information is sought by the question, and to the difficulty of answering when an injury was serious in any other manner than by reference to its permanent or temporary influence on the health, strength and longevity of the party, we are of the opinion that the court did not err in the criterion by which it directed the jury to decide the interrogatory propounded to them." See also *Wilkinson* v. *Connecticut Mut. L. Ins. Co.* 30 Iowa, 119.

The words "hurt" and "wound" as used in the application mean an injury to the body causing an impairment of health or strength or rendering the person more liable to contract disease or less able to resist its effects. No such consequences followed from the hurt sustained by the insured. A cut on the face, finger or on any part of the body from which blood flows, though healing in a few days and leaving no evil consequences, is a hurt or wound, but not within the meaning of the contract under consideration. There being no evidence tending to sustain the findings upon which the conclusion of law is based, *the judgment should be reversed, and a new trial granted, with costs to abide event.*

All concur.

KANSAS SUPREME COURT.

GERMAN INSURANCE CO. of Freeport, Ill., *Piff. in Err.*,
v.
Anderson GRAY.

(....Kan.....)

*1. **In an application for insurance,** where correct answers are given to a general agent of the company respecting incumbrances on the property of the applicant, and such agent fails to mention the incumbrances in the written application, but procures the signature of the applicant, accepts the premium and closes the contract, the company will not be relieved from liability on account of misrepresentations in the application, although it was stipulated therein

*Head notes by JOHNSTON, *J.*

NOTE.—*Fire insurance; insured not affected by wrongful acts of company's agent.*

Where an applicant for a policy answers questions truthfully, but the agent of the company inserts the answers incorrectly in the application, such agent's error cannot be imputed to the appli-

· See also 25 L. R. A. 198; 47 L. R. A. 201, 641.

that it should be considered a part of the policy and a warranty by the insured of the truth of the statements which it contained.

2. **A general agent** of an insurance company can modify the insurance contract, or waive a condition of a written policy by parol.

3. **A provision in an insurance policy respecting incumbrances** on the property insured may be waived by the insurance company or its general agent; and this, although the policy contains a printed stipulation that no agent of the company or any person other than the president or secretary shall have authority to waive any of the terms or conditions of the policy, and all agreements by the president or secretary must be signed by either of them.

4. **Where proofs of loss are taken by a duly authorized adjuster** of the company, who expresses satisfaction with the same, and states that he will forward them to the office of the company, and that the loss will soon be paid, the insured has a right to assume, until notified to the contrary, that no other or different proofs will be required; and the failure of the company to object to them within a reasonable time precludes it from thereafter objecting that they are insufficient.

(April 4, 1890.)

ERROR to the District Court for Sumner County to review a judgment in favor of plaintiff in an action to recover the amount alleged to be due upon a policy of fire insurance. *Affirmed.*

Statement by **Johnston,** *J.:*

This was an action for loss by fire upon a policy of insurance executed December 4, 1885, insuring, among other property, the following, for the amounts named: barn and shed, $200; hay in barn, $200; grain in barn and in stack on cultivated premises, $1,500; farming implements, $300. The fire occurred on May 28, 1886, and the property mentioned, which is alleged to be of the total value of $2,200, was wholly destroyed by the fire. The plaintiff alleged that the contract of insurance was in full force at the time of the fire, and that the property was destroyed without any fault of his, and that he had fully complied with all the requirements and agreements of the contract, but the Insurance Company refused, and still refuses, to pay the amount of the loss. He demanded judgment in the sum of $2,200, with interest from the time of the fire. The answer alleged that in the application for insurance by Gray he warranted that all the answers made by him to questions therein propounded were true; that, in response to a question in regard to what mortgages and incumbrances were upon the property, he failed to disclose a mortgage for $5,749.35, dated March 23, 1885, in favor of John S. Woods; and, further, that Gray, after the issuance of the policy, and without the consent of the Insurance Company indorsed on the policy, and in violation of the terms of the policy, incumbered and mortgaged the property insured un-

---

cant. Bennett v. Agricultural Ins. Co. 8 Cent. Rep. 692, 106 N. Y. 243; Commercial U. Assur. Co. v. Elliott (Pa.) 13 Cent. Rep. 668.

The company cannot avoid payment because of misrepresentations as to value, location, incumbrances, etc., inserted by its agent, who had full knowledge of the facts, the assured being illiterate and placing reliance upon the agent, and having no reliable knowledge of the facts constituting such representations. Phenix Ins. Co. v. Golden, 121 Ind. 524.

And this is so although the application provided that the representations should be regarded as warranties. Stone v. Hawkeye Ins. Co. 68 Iowa, 737.

The act of an agent authorized to solicit and take applications for insurance in such a case is binding upon the company. Phœnix Ins. Co. v. Stark, 120 Ind. 444.

He must be deemed the agent of the company in all he does in preparing the application, and in any representation he may make as to the character or effect of the statements therein contained; and this rule is not changed by a stipulation in the policy subsequently issued, that the acts of such agent in making out the application shall be deemed the acts of the insured. Deitz v. Providence-Washington Ins. Co. 31 W. Va. 851.

The company is estopped from taking advantage of the falsity of an answer in an application, where, at the time of the issue of the policy, it personally or through its agent has knowledge of the facts which the question answered is intended to elicit. Dwelling-House Ins. Co. v. Brodie (Ark.) 4 L. R. A. 458.

Where he fills out the blanks in a policy signed by an applicant in blank, without the latter's instructions or authority, he does not thereby become the agent of the applicant; and misrepresentations of such agent will not avoid the policy, although it was afterwards signed by the applicant, who did not read it or know of such misrepresentations. Rogers v. Phenix Ins. Co. 121 Ind. 570.

Where an insurance agent has examined an applicant and received true answers, but omits certain answers, and the applicant signs the application under the agent's direction, the policy is not rendered null and void by such omissions, although it contains a provision that any false representation or omission in the material facts shall render the application void. Kansas Protective Union v. Gardner, 41 Kan. 397.

Plaintiff is not estopped by the fact that a copy of the application was attached to the policy, and he failed to notify the company that the statements were false. Donnelly v. Cedar Rapids Ins. Co. 70 Iowa, 693.

If the company had knowledge, when it issued the policy, that the statements made in the application as warranties were not true, it must be regarded as having waived said warranties; and it is bound by whatever knowledge its soliciting agent had when he took the application. Stone v. Hawkeye Ins. Co. 68 Iowa, 737; Mullin v. Vermont Mut. F. Ins. Co. 2 New Eng. Rep. 483, 58 Vt. 113.

The insurance agent is presumed to be familiar with the construction of the building insured, as well as its divisions, manner of use and description, and the company is bound by his knowledge. Pettit v. State Ins. Co. (Minn.) July 19, 1889.

Limitations in an insurance policy as to the powers of the agents are not conclusive; and if an act is within the scope of an agent's authority at the time it is done, it binds the corporation, without reference to restrictions in the policy. Niagara Ins. Co. v. Lee, 73 Tex. 641.

A restriction upon his powers in the policy, and not in the application, cannot be construed to refer to any act or knowledge of the agent that occurred before the delivery of the policy. Crouse v. Hartford F. Ins. Co. (Mich.) Jan. 24, 1890.

The assured is not bound by private instructions to the agent, not known to him. Commercial U. Assur. Co. v. State, 19 West. Rep. 47, 113 Ind. 331.

der the policy as follows: On May 15, 1886, he made and delivered a mortgage to A. Brennaman for $3,110, upon the real estate on which the insured buildings stood, and upon 2,000 bushels of wheat in the granary, and about 800 acres of growing wheat; and, further, on December 22, 1885, that he made and delivered to Sumner County Bank a mortgage of $700 on some farming implements and other articles covered by the policy. In his reply Gray admitted the existence and the making of the mortgages mentioned in the answer, but alleged that he gave a full statement of all the incumbrances on the property when the application for insurance was made, and also made known to the defendant that the mortgages would mature during the existence of the policy, and that he would be wholly unable to meet the indebtedness or remove the incumbrances, except by making and giving new mortgages, and renewing the incumbrances on the property; and he alleges that it was expressly stipulated and agreed between himself and the Insurance Company that he should be permitted to incumber his property, and that H. Steinbuschel & Bro., the duly authorized agents of the Company, expressly waived the condition written in the policy against incumbrances, and expressly agreed in behalf of the Company that he should have the right, notwithstanding the printed stipulations, to renew and extend the mortgages and incumbrances upon the property, or any part thereof.

Upon the trial the jury returned special findings of fact with their general verdict, as follows:

Q. Were there any chattel mortgages on the wheat covered by the insurance policy sued on in this action at the time said insurance policy was issued and delivered to Anderson Gray?

A. Yes.

(5) Q. Did the said plaintiff at any time after the issuance and delivery to the said Anderson Gray of the insurance policy sued on in this action, and before the time plaintiff claims that the property covered by said policy was destroyed by fire, give to any person any chattel mortgage upon any of the property covered by said policy?

A. Yes.

(7) Q. Were there any chattel mortgages upon any of the property covered by the insurance policy sued on in this action at the time said plaintiff claims the said property was destroyed by fire?

A. Yes.

(10) Q. What was the value of each item of property insured at the time plaintiff claims the same was destroyed by fire?

A. 2,000 bushels wheat, $1,500; six tons hay, $18; 2 two-horse Bain wagons, $80; 1 piano-box single buggy, $100; 1 ten-foot Hodge header, $100; 1 Buckeye mower, $40; 1 Bradley hay-rake, $15; 1 corn-planter, $45; 1 Wier double cultivator, $15; 1 press wheat drill, $40; 2 one-horse wheat-drills, $30; 1 wheat fanning-mill, $30; barn, $800; harness, $55.

(11) Q. What interest did the plaintiff have in and to each separate item of said property at the time he claims said property was destroyed?

A. Wheat, owner; hay, owner; Bain two

Liability of agents for loss arising from their negligence.

Local insurance agents who depart from their instructions are personally liable for losses arising from their negligent omission. Phœnix Ins. Co. v. Pratt, 36 Minn. 409.

Where a local agent, having received instruction from a state agent desiring him to relieve the company of a certain risk as soon as possible, answered by letter requesting as a personal accommodation that the policy might run until expiration, which would occur a few days later, such letter was sufficient evidence that he understood the instructions of his superior to be a direction to cancel, and a recognition of the authority of the latter to so order. *Ibid.*

An insurance company cannot recover more than nominal damages from its agent who has in good faith taken a risk somewhat different from what the company supposes, but not less valuable. State Ins. Co. v. Richmond, 71 Iowa, 519.

Where an insurance agent undertakes that property should be insured to a certain amount from a certain time, he is only liable for his failure to exercise diligence to procure the insurance by the time agreed upon. Arrott v. Walker, 10 Cent. Rep. 608, 118 Pa. 249.

Such agreement, considered as a contract of insurance against fire, on the part of the agent, is void, under Pa. Act 1870, p. 14. *Ibid.*

Acts of agent bind the company.

Insurance companies are responsible for the acts of their agents within the general scope of the business intrusted to their care. Union Mut. L. Ins. Co. v. Wilkinson, 80 U. S. 13 Wall. 222 (20 L. ed. 617).

The company cannot be allowed to hold out a party as its agent, and then disavow responsibility for his acts. Southern L. Ins. Co. v. McCain, 96 U. S. 84 (24 L. ed. 653).

After his appointment in a particular business parties dealing with him in that business have a right to rely upon the continuance of his authority, until in some way informed of its revocation. *Ibid.*

The silence of a company after receiving from an agent, whose authority had been terminated, a statement that a premium on a policy had been paid to him, is equivalent to the adoption of the act of the agent. *Ibid.*

No limitations of their authority will be binding on parties with whom they deal, which are not brought to the knowledge of those parties. Union Mut. L. Ins. Co. v. Wilkinson, *supra.*

An agent of a fire insurance company has authority to waive the conditions of a policy. Alexander v. Continental Ins. Co. 67 Wis. 422; Cleaver v. Traders Ins. Co. 8 West. Rep. 816, 65 Mich. 527.

So of a general agent authorized to represent it and transact its business at a particular place. Kruger v. Western F. & M. Ins. Co. 72 Cal. 91.

The acts of a general agent of an insurance company, through its sub-agent, bind the company. Lingenfelter v. Phœnix Ins. Co. 1 West. Rep. 895, 19 Mo. App. 252.

If the agent authorizes another, for him and in his name, to solicit applications and collect premiums, the company is bound. *Ibid.*

If the agent receives and accepts a proposition for a policy obtained through his sub-agent, the company is bound by the contract. Bodine v. Exchange F. Ins. Co. 51 N. Y. 123; 4 Whit. Act and Def. 89; Keim v. Home Mut. F. & M. Ins. Co. 42 Mo. 41.

The Iowa Act declares that any person who solicits insurance shall be held to be the agent of the

horse wagons, owner; 1 piano-box single buggy, owner; header, owner; 1 mower, owner; 1 hay-rake, owner; corn-planter, owner; double cultivator, owner; press wheat-drill, owner; 2 one-horse wheat-drills, owner; fanning-mill, owner; barn, owner; harness, owner.

(12) *Q.* What was the value of the plaintiff's interest in each item of said property at the time said plaintiff claims the same was destroyed by fire?

A. Same as No. 10.

(13) *Q.* Did the plaintiff read the written application for insurance which has been offered in evidence in the case before or at the time he signed the same?

A. No.

(14) *Q.* Could plaintiff at that time read writing and printing well enough to read such written application?

A. Yes.

(15) *Q.* Did plaintiff have an opportunity to read said written application before or at the time he signed the same?

A. Yes.

(16) *Q.* Did Anderson Gray, the plaintiff in this action, tell Mr. Steinbuschel, the agent of said defendant, at the time said written application for insurance was being written up, or before that time, of the existence of any mortgages upon any of the property covered by said insurance policy other than the one mentioned in said written application?

A. Yes. . . .

(18) *Q.* If you answer question 16 in the affirmative, then you may state if said agent of the defendant stated to plaintiff at that time that he would not mention such mortgages in said written application?

A. Yes. . . .

(20) *Q.* If all the mortgages that were upon the said property, or any part thereof, so covered by said insurance policy, were not mentioned in said written application, state fully why they were not so mentioned, and all the reasons therefor, so far as you find that they were known to plaintiff at that time?

A. Agent refused to put it in application, saying it was not necessary, because "I issue my own policies and adjust the losses."

(21) *Q.* Was the plaintiff at any time authorized by said defendant to mortgage or remortgage the said property covered by said insurance policy after the said insurance was issued and delivered to said plaintiff?

A. Yes.

(22) *Q.* If you answer question No. 21 in the affirmative, you will then please state at what time said authority was given, and by what officer or agent such authority was given, and whether such authority was given orally or in writing?

A. First, when application was made out; *second,* when policy was returned by Steinbuschel and brother, district agent.

Orally. "We, the jury impaneled and sworn in the above-entitled case, do upon our oaths find for the plaintiff, and assess the amount of his recovery at $2,018, with interest at 7 per cent from July 28, 1886."

A motion for a new trial was made and overruled; and the court thereupon entered judgment in accordance with the verdict for

---

company and not of the insured; and for any mistake occurring in the transaction between him and the other agents the company is liable. St. Paul F. & M. Ins. Co. v. Shaver, 76 Iowa, 282.

That one of the trustees of a building insured agreed with the insurance agent that he should place insurance does not make such agent the agent of the trustee. Commercial U. Assur. Co. v. State, 13 West. Rep. 47, 113 Ind. 331.

Though the agent cannot delegate his agency, he may employ clerks and sub-agents, and their acts will bind his principal. Lingenfelter v. Phœnix Ins. Co. *supra.*

But an agent cannot waive the provisions of a policy in a matter outside the scope of his agency. Imperial F. Ins. Co. v. Dunham, 10 Cent. Rep. 577, 117 Pa. 460.

And a clause in an insurance policy accepted by the assured, prohibiting the waiver of its provisions by the local agent, is binding upon the assured. Hankins v. Rockford Ins. Co. 70 Wis. 1.

A local agent with authority to receive premiums and issue policies has no authority to waive the conditions of the policy, requiring the written or printed assent of the company to any change in circumstances or situation increasing the risk. Kyte v. Commercial U. Assur. Co. 3 New Eng. Rep. 684, 144 Mass. 43.

And although he has the fullest authority, conditions cannot be waived except in the manner provided. *Ibid.*

A provision in an insurance policy that no agent of the company shall be held to have waived any of its conditions unless such waiver is indorsed on the policy, is ineffectual to limit the legal capacity of the company to afterwards bind itself, contrary to the conditions of the policy, by an agent acting within the scope of his general authority. Lamberton v. Connecticut F. Ins. Co. 1 L. R. A. 222, 39 Minn. 129.

Breach of condition as to incumbrances.

A breach of warranty against incumbrances is not established by showing records of several unsatisfied judgments against a former owner. *Ibid.*

A judgment is not an incumbrance against insured property, under a condition in the policy that if the property shall become mortgaged or incumbered it shall be null and void. Phœnix Ins. Co. v. Pickel, 119 Ind. 155. But compare Hench v. Agricultural Ins. Co. 122 Pa. 128.

Where the insurance was for separate amounts, a misrepresentation concerning one piece will not bar a recovery for the loss of other pieces with which it is not connected in any way. *Ibid.*

The fact of additional incumbrances on the property insured is not a breach of a condition against incumbrances, where the total amount of all such incumbrances at no time exceeded the amount represented by the assured. Hister v. Lebanon Mut. Ins. Co. 5 L. R. A. 646, 128 Pa. 553.

But where it is stipulated in a policy that if either the real or personal property, or any part of it, be incumbered, it must be so represented in the application or the policy will be void, a misrepresentation as to one subject will invalidate the whole. Smith v. Agricultural Ins. Co. 118 N. Y. 518.

Where an applicant for insurance, on being asked if there is $1,000 incumbrance on the property, answers "Over $2,000," whereas there is $5,000, there is a material misrepresentation. *Ibid.*

Where an application for insurance requires the amount of a mortgage on the premises to be stated, an answer stating the principal sum due on the mortgage is sufficient. Hosford v. Germania F. Ins. Co. 127 U. S. 399 (32 L. ed. 196).

$2,125.95, with interest thereon from June 4, 1887, at the rate of 7 per cent per annum. The Insurance Company brings the case here, alleging error, and asking a reversal of the judgment.

Messrs. **G. W. Barnett, George & King** and **W. F. Rightmire** for plaintiff in error.

Messrs. **McDonald & Parker,** for defendant in error:

The agent who made the contract in this case was a general agent.

Continental Ins. Co. v. *Ruckman*, 127 Ill. 364.

The Company is liable for his acts and agreements and is infected with notice of all that was known to the agent.

Am. Cent. Ins. Co. v. *McLanathan*, 11 Kan. 549; *Sullivan* v. *Phenix Ins. Co.* 34 Kan. 174; *National Mut. F. Ins. Co.* v. *Barnes*, 41 Kan. 163.

The tendency of the modern decisions is to constantly broaden the powers of the agent and make them co extensive with the business intrusted to his care.

Union Mut. Ins. Co. v. *Wilkinson*, 80 U. S. 13 Wall. 222 (20 L. ed. 617).

Even where a policy in terms provides that agents shall not waive forfeitures, alter or discharge contracts, or strike out or modify any of the provisions of the printed policy of insurance, the words of the policy are not conclusive, because it is within the power of the company to waive this provision.

Wood, Fire Ins. 2d ed. p. 886; *Eclectic L. Ins. Co.* v. *Fahrenkrug*, 68 Ill. 463; *American Ins. Co.* v. *Gallatin*, 48 Wis. 36; *Renier* v. *Dwelling-House Ins. Co.* 74 Wis. 89; *Young* v. *Hartford F. Ins. Co.* 45 Iowa, 377; *Morrison* v. *North America Ins. Co.* 69 Tex. 353; *Continental Ins. Co.* v. *Ruckman*, 127 Ill. 364; *McGurk* v. *Metropolitan L. Ins. Co.* 1 L. R. A. 563, 56 Conn. 528; *Lamberton* v. *Connecticut F. Ins. Co.* 1 L. R. A. 222, 39 Minn. 129; *Carroll* v. *Charter Oak Ins. Co.* 10 Abb. Pr. N. S. 166; *King* v. *Council Bluffs Ins. Co.* 72 Iowa, 310.

Johnston, *J.*, delivered the opinion of the court:

The greater part of the testimony taken in the case was with reference to the extent and value of the property destroyed, and as to whether or not the fire was the result of the action of the insured. But these questions, as well as all others upon which there was a conflict of evidence, have been determined by the jury in favor of the insured. The Insurance Company now seeks to escape liability upon the ground that Gray failed to disclose the existence of incumbrances upon the property when he made the application for insurance, and also because he had incumbered the property after the policy was issued without the consent of the Company indorsed thereon, and in violation of its provisions. The application for insurance was made on December 2, 1885, to Steinbuschel & Bro., of Wichita, who were agents of the Company for that portion of the State in which the property was situated. They wrote the answers to the questions propounded to Gray, and the application contained

---

A mortgage executed within the term of a policy, and before its renewal, is not a breach of a condition in the renewal policy. Lebanon Mut. Ins. Co. v. Leathers (Pa.) 6 Cent. Rep. 901.

An undischarged mortgage which has been paid is not an incumbrance. Smith v. Niagara F. Ins. Co. 7 New Eng. Rep. 82, 1 L. R. A. 216, 60 Vt. 682.

Waiver of conditions, what constitutes.

The execution of a policy with full knowledge of existing facts, which by its conditions render it void, is a waiver of those conditions, because otherwise it would be a fraud. Wheeler v. Traders Ins. Co. (N. H.) 1 New Eng. Rep. 322; Liverpool & L. & G. Ins. Co. v. Ende, 65 Tex. 118.

And so as to knowledge of the agent, of incumbrances on the property insured. Breckinridge v. American Cent. Ins. Co. 4 West. Rep. 565, 87 Mo. 62; Phoenix Ins. Co. v. La Pointe, 5 West. Rep. 512, 118 Ill. 384.

If an insurer has knowledge of the assured's title, it is a waiver of the condition making an inaccurate statement of the title an avoidance of the policy. Wheeler v. Traders Ins. Co. (N. H.) 1 New Eng. Rep. 322; Lamb v. Council Bluffs Ins. Co. 70 Iowa, 238.

A principal is chargeable with all the knowledge possessed by the agent in the transaction of the business which he had in charge. Clark v. Hyatt, 118 N. Y. 563; Slattery v. Schwannecke, 118 N. Y. 543; Little Pittsburgh C. M. Co. v. Little Chief C. M. Co. 11 Colo. 223; Wheeler v. McGuire, 2 L. R. A. 808, 86 Ala. 398.

Where an authorized agent of the company delivers a policy acknowledging the payment of the premium, such acknowledgment concludes the company from assailing the legal existence of the policy. Home Ins. Co. v. Gilman, 10 West. Rep. 642, 112 Ind. 7.

The payment of the premium in cash may be waived by an agent authorized to deliver policies and receive payment, notwithstanding a stipulation in the policy to the contrary. *Ibid.*

Where a company authorized its agent to take insurance, collect the premium, deliver the policy, sign with his own name, and attach to the policy, printed provisions not contained in it,—it is bound by the agent's waiver of requirements in such printed slip. Niagara F. Ins. Co. v. Brown, 12 West. Rep. 815, 123 Ill. 356.

A provision that the use of general terms shall not be construed as a waiver of any condition in the policy may be waived by the company through its agent, and is not a limitation as to the manner of the exercise of his powers by the agent. Goldwater v. Liverpool & L. & G. Ins. Co. 13 Cent. Rep. 49, 109 N. Y. 618.

Waiver by agent's knowledge of incumbrances.

An insurance policy cannot be avoided for failure to state all the facts as to the ownership of the property in the policy, if these facts were fully made known to the agent of the company who issued the policy. Crescent Ins. Co. v. Camp, 71 Tex. 503.

The insurer is estopped from showing a breach of warranty by the insured, when the agent of the insurer who effected the insurance is fully apprised of the existence of incumbrances before making the insurance. Breckinridge v. Am. Cent. Ins. Co. 4 West. Rep. 565, 87 Mo. 62.

Where an answer to a question as to incumbrances is inserted in an application for insurance by the agent of a company, without the authority of the insured, who signs the application without knowledge of such answer, the company cannot avoid the policy for that reason. Dunbar v. Phenix Ins. Co. 72 Wis. 492.

See also 15 L. R. A. 668.

the statement that the answers made were true. The application only mentions one mortgage, but Gray testifies that he stated his indebtedness and the incumbrances on his property to the agents fully and in detail, telling them that it would be necessary for him to mortgage and remortgage his property in the conduct of his business during the time for which the insurance was contracted. This is disputed; but the jury sustain Gray, and find that the Company was fully informed in respect to the existing incumbrances. The policy was not delivered by the agents at the time the application was made, but was sent by them to Gray at Conway Springs, Sumner County, near which place he resided. Soon after it had been so delivered, he discovered that it contained a provision that if the property should thereafter become mortgaged or incumbered, or, in case a change should take place in the title, the policy should be null and void. He immediately went to the agent, called his attention to the provision prohibiting the incumbering of his property, and insisted that it must be changed. After looking at the policy, Steinbuschel said that he would waive the condition relative to incumbrances, stating that he had authority for that purpose, and Gray, acting upon this waiver and agreement, mortgaged the property, as has already been stated. The incumbrances placed on the property, however, were mostly, if not entirely, the renewal and extension of debts and mortgages existing when the contract of insurance was made.

In regard to the misrepresentations in the application, we must assume that Gray gave correct answers to all questions asked. There was no concealment nor deception on his part. Steinbuschel, authorized by and acting for the Company, prepared the application, and purposely omitted a fuller statement concerning incumbrances. It was the fault of Steinbuschel or the Company which he represented, and not of the insured, that the application did not contain a complete statement. Steinbuschel having authority, his act must be treated as the act of the Company, and through him the Company had knowledge of all the incumbrances. With this knowledge, the Company accepted the risk, and the premium therefor, induced Gray to sign the application, which did not state the whole truth, and now, when the loss occurs, they cannot, under our decisions, insist on the breach of warranty or the untruth of the representations. *Sullivan* v. *Phenix Ins. Co.* 34 Kan. 170; *Continental Ins. Co.* v. *Pearce*, 39 Kan. 396; *National Mut. F. Ins. Co.* v. *Barnes*, 41 Kan. 161; *Kansas Protective Union* v. *Gardner*, 41 Kan. 401.

It is next contended that the giving of the subsequent mortgages by the insured avoided the policy; and in that connection it is urged that error was committed in admitting testimony of the verbal agreement modifying the terms of the policy, and waiving its conditions. We think the waiver must be upheld, and the point made by the Company overruled. The agents who made the agreement were more than mere local or soliciting agents. They fully represented the Company within a certain district; were authorized to solicit insurance, receive moneys and premiums, issue and renew

---

An agreement by an insurance agent to note on the application the fact of an incumbrance on the property, upon which agreement the applicant relied, estops the company from setting up the incumbrance to defeat a recovery on the policy. Copeland v. Dwelling-House Ins. Co. (Mich.) Nov. 8, 1889.

But the company is not estopped from claiming the forfeiture where the local agent who issued the policy gave the insured to understand that such incumbrances would not invalidate the policy. Smith v. Continental Ins. Co. (Dak.) Oct. 10, 1889.

Where an insurance agent as a matter of fact was informed of the existence of mortgages on the property insured, and obtained a signature of the insured, who was ignorant in such matters, to an application which he had himself made out, the agent's knowledge of the existence of the mortgages was binding upon the company, and a waiver of the condition of the policy against such incumbrances. Renier v. Dwelling-House Ins. Co. 74 Wis. 89.

The knowledge of an agent, before the issue of an insurance policy, of the truth as to the ownership of the insured property and litigation concerning it, will prevent a defense on the ground of misrepresentations as to those matters in the application. Western Assur. Co. v. Stoddard, 88 Ala. 606.

A warranty, in an application, of undisputed ownership is not broken by the pendency of an action by a judgment creditor of a former owner, but not disputing insurer's ownership. Lang v. Hawkeye Ins. Co. 74 Iowa, 673.

Objections to statement of loss.

An objection made by the company to proofs of loss, that they are "deficient both in form and substance," is too general. Myers v. Council Bluffs Ins. Co. 72 Iowa, 176.

Overestimates of value in proofs of loss, not fraudulently made, will not avoid a policy providing that it shall be void upon an attempt to defraud the company before or after loss. Towne v. Springfield F. & M. Ins. Co. 5 New Eng. Rep. 484, 145 Mass. 582.

Nor will such overestimates render proofs of loss insufficient as a written statement of loss to render the company liable. *Ibid.*

The tender by insured of a particular account of his loss to the duly authorized agent of a foreign company is a compliance with the condition of the policy to render such account to the company. North British & M. Ins. Co. v. Crutchfield, 7 West. Rep. 85, 108 Ind. 518.

A statement in proofs of loss that the cause of the fire is to the assured unknown sufficiently states the origin of the fire. Jones v. Howard Ins. Co. 117 N. Y. 103.

Under the Wisconsin statutes, fixing the measure of the value of the insured property in cases of loss, the fact that the insured knowingly and intentionally stated the loss to be greater than it actually was is no defense in an action on the policy. Cayon v. Dwelling-House Ins. Co. 68 Wis. 510.

Where the loss was disputed by the company it was error to dismiss the complaint on the ground that the proofs of loss were insufficient. Karelsen v. Sun Fire Office, 45 Hun, 144.

It is sufficient to declare that "the said fire did not originate by any act, design or procurement on his [the insured's] part, or in consequence of any fraud or evil practice done or suffered by him." Howard Ins. Co. v. Hocking, 6 Cent. Rep. 918, 115 Pa. 415.

In a suit upon a policy of fire insurance, where the defense is that the plaintiff fraudulently misrepresented its loss, the alleged fraud must arise out of and inhere in representations as to the personal property contained in the proof of loss; and

policies; and the testimony is that they appointed sub-agents and adjusted losses. Only a short time previous to the making of the contract in question, they adjusted a loss under another insurance policy issued by the same Company to Gray, and paid him the amount of the loss. Gray had a right to assume, and we may fairly assume, that they were general agents of the Company.

In this State the courts have taken a liberal view with reference to the power of agents, and especially where they were representing foreign companies, which can only act through their agents, and where the agent is practically the principal in the making of contracts. *Am. Cent. Ins. Co.* v. *McLanathan*, 11 Kan. 549, and cases above cited.

Being general agents, empowered to make and renew contracts, they stood in this respect in the place of the Company, and certainly must be held to have the power to modify the same, or to waive any of the conditions in the contract which they had made. We are referred to *Burlington Ins. Co.* v. *Gibbons* (Kan.), 22 Pac. Rep. 1010, where the power of the agent to waive a condition was denied. In that case the agent had no authority from his company except as a soliciting agent, and it did not appear that he had any authority to issue policies, and he did not even countersign them when issued. In that case, however, it was said that "it has generally been held that where a person in procuring an insurance upon his property acts in good faith, and without any knowledge of any limitations upon the authority of the agent of the insurance company effecting the insurance, such person may assume that the agent is a general agent of the insurance company for that purpose; that he stands in the place of the company; and that the company will be bound by any terms or conditions or any waiver of terms or conditions which the agent may agree to while acting for the company in consummating the insurance."

If it was within the power of the Company, acting through its agents, to waive a condition or change the contract, it surely might do so by a parol contract, and might even waive the provisions stated in the policy with reference to the manner of altering or waiving its terms and conditions.

In *Westchester F. Ins. Co.* v. *Earle*, 33 Mich. 143, the court, in considering the question whether an agent of a company might change the conditions of a policy by parol, wherein it was provided that it could only be done upon the consent of the company written thereon, held that the written policy might be changed by parol, and stated that "a written bargain is of no higher legal degree than a parol one. Either may vary or discharge the other, and there can be no more force in an agreement in writing not to agree by parol than a parol agreement not to agree in writing. Every such agreement is ended by the new one which contradicts it." See also *Eclectic L. Ins. Co.* v. *Fahrenkrug*, 68 Ill. 463.

In the present case, as in some of the cases cited, it was stipulated in the policy that no agent of the Company, or any other person than the president and secretary, should have authority to alter or waive any of the terms of

---

in such representations the plaintiff must have been guilty of designedly attempting to perpetrate a fraud upon the insurance company. Oshkosh Packing & P. Co. v. Mercantile Ins. Co. 31 Fed. Rep. 200.

Where the inventory containing the proofs of loss was made out by the wife of insured, negligence in failing to verify the same will be evidence of intended fraud. Mullin v. Vermont Mut. F. Ins. Co. 2 New Eng. Rep. 481, 58 Vt. 113.

A provision requiring proof of loss "in detail" is satisfied by setting out a copy of the description of the property insured by another policy referred to. Towne v. Springfield F. & M. Ins. Co. *supra*.

Neglect of the insured to furnish a detailed statement of the loss, under the Massachusetts standard fire policy, will not of itself defeat a claim. *Ibid.*

And nothing more is required than a statement of the aggregate value of the property destroyed, unless a more particular account is demanded at the time. Miller v. Hartford F. Ins. Co. 70 Iowa, 704.

A waiver of notice and statement of particulars of a loss cannot be shown by the acts of an insurance agent who took the application, or of an adjuster, without proof of their authority. Barre v. Council Bluffs Ins. Co. 76 Iowa, 609.

Provisions requiring statement and proof of loss. See *note* to Kenton Ins. Co. v. Wiggintou (Ky.) 7 L. R. A. 81.

Waiver of notice and statement of loss.

A general agent of an insurance company—unless restricted in his power, and this is known to the plaintiff—can waive a statement of the loss, but only in the manner provided by the policy, although by the terms of the policy that was a condition precedent to recovery. Smith v. Niagara F. Ins. Co. 7 New Eng. Rep. 82, 1 L. R. A. 216, 60 Vt. 682; North British & M. Ins. Co. v. Crutchfield, 7 West. Rep. 89, 108 Ind. 518.

A local agent having authority only to receive proposals for insurance, fix rates of premium and issue policies, cannot waive the condition of a policy requiring a statement of loss. Smith v. Niagara F. Ins. Co. 7 New Eng. Rep. 82, 1 L. R. A. 216, 60 Vt. 682; Knudson v. Hekla F. Ins. Co. (Wis.) Dec. 3, 1889.

Where a fire insurance policy stipulates that the insured shall give notice of loss forthwith, immediate notice to a local agent is sufficient. Fisher v. Crescent Ins. Co. 33 Fed. Rep. 544.

Where the facts are not in dispute, it becomes a question of law for the court to determine whether, in the given case, the notice was reasonable. What constitutes reasonable diligence depends upon the circumstances of the case. Insurance Co. of North America v. Brim, 9 West. Rep. 830, 111 Ind. 281.

A failure to object to the notice after the right of action has expired will not revive the right. *Ibid.*; Barre v. Council Bluffs Ins. Co. 76 Iowa, 609.

But a mere written notice of loss, not in form required by the policy of fire insurance, is insufficient. German-American Ins. Co. v. Hocking, 6 Cent. Rep. 911; 115 Pa. 398.

Proofs of loss to be furnished.

A provision in a policy of insurance, that agents cannot waive "any condition," does not relate to stipulations about proofs of loss. Loeb v. American C. Ins. Co. (Mo.) Nov. 18, 1889.

A local insurance agent authorized simply to fix rates and countersign and deliver policies, subject to the approval of the company, has no authority to waive a provision made a part of the contract requiring assured to give notice and proof of loss. Bowlin v. Hekla F. Ins. Co. 36 Minn. 433.

conditions of the policy, or make any indorsement thereon, and all agreements of the president or secretary must be signed by either of them. This provision, however, may be modified by the Company to the same extent as any other, and whatever the Company can do may be done by its general agents.

Renier v. Dwelling-House Ins. Co., 74 Wis. 89, was a case somewhat similar to the one we are considering. In that case the policy provided that the application should form a part of the policy and a warranty by the assured. In the application for insurance it was stated that the property insured was not incumbered, but it appeared that the property was mortgaged, and that the insured informed the agent of the company of the existence of the mortgages, and he falsely wrote the answers therein, and the application was signed at the request of the agent. In the policy issued was a provision that "no act or omission of the company, or any act of its officers or agents, shall be deemed, construed or held to be a waiver of a full and strict compliance with the foregoing provisions of the terms and conditions of this policy, except it be a waiver or extension in express terms and in writing, signed by the president or secretary of the company." It was held that the action of the agent, with knowledge of the existence of the mortgage, was binding upon the company, and a waiver of the condition of the policy against incumbrances; and this, notwithstanding the limitation of authority of such agent expressed in the provision quoted on the face of the policy. Speaking of the restriction the court said. "We must hold, however, that such attempted restrictions upon the power of the company or its general officers or agents, acting within the scope of their general authority, to subsequently modify the contract and bind the company in a manner contrary to such previous conditions in the policy are ineffectual. Especially is this true in respect to a foreign insurance company whose officers are practically inaccessible to the assured,"—citing *Gans v. St. Paul F. & M. Ins. Co.* 43 Wis. 108; *American L. Ins. Co. v. Gallatin*, 48 Wis. 36; *Shafer v. Phœnix Ins. Co.* 53 Wis. 361; *Lamberton v. Connecticut F. Ins. Co.* 1 L. R. A. 222, 39 Minn. 129; *Willcuts v. Northwestern Mut. L. Ins. Co.* 81 Ind. 308; *Steen v. Niagara F. Ins. Co.* 89 N. Y. 326; *Richmond v. Niagara F. Ins. Co.* 79 N. Y. 230; *Eastern R. Co. v. Relief F. Ins. Co.* 105 Mass. 570; *American L. Ins. Co. v. Green*, 57 Ga. 469; *Westchester F. Ins. Co. v. Earle*, 33 Mich. 143.

The court, proceeding further, says: "Of course, an insurance company, and especially a foreign insurance company, in making contracts of insurance, and adjusting, settling and paying losses, must act through its agents, if at all. To hold that, in such negotiations between such general agents and the assured, the latter is bound, but that in the same transaction the company, the agent's principal, cannot be bound by reason of having incapacitated itself and them, by previous stipulations, from agreeing to anything contrary to the conditions contained in the original contract, is, under most policies, in effect to hold that there is no mutuality in such contracts, and that the powers of such general agents are limited to the

---

A requirement in an insurance policy, that sworn proofs of loss be furnished to the company, is not complied with by the making of a statement of the property lost and its value, to the adjuster at his request. Knudson v Hekla F. Ins. Co. (Wis.) Dec. 2, 1889.

After the mortgagee of property damaged by fire has given the notice provided by the statute to the underwriter, he may furnish the preliminary proofs of loss. Nickerson v. Nickerson, 5 New Eng. Rep. 796, 80 Me. 100.

The provision of a policy that the assured shall, in his proofs of loss, state the interest and title, etc., means state the title at the time of the loss. Jones v. Howard Ins. Co. 117 N. Y. 103.

Reasonable time after he learned that something more was wanted in which to perfect his proofs of loss must be given. Miller v. Hartford F. Ins. Co. 70 Iowa, 704.

Whether proofs of loss were furnished within a reasonable time is a mixed question of law and fact. Am. F. Ins. Co. v. Hazen, 1 Cent. Rep. 631, 110 Pa. 530.

Where the company receives the proofs of loss without objection, after the time prescribed in the policy, it is a reasonable explanation of the delay. Am. Cent. Ins. Co. v. Haws (Pa.) 9 Cent. Rep. 412.

Provision for payment in sixty days after due notice and proof of loss refers to the proofs required within thirty days, and not to other proof required for establishment of claim. Clover v. Greenwich Ins. Co. 3 Cent. Rep. 673, 101 N. Y. 277.

Where the loss was total and immediate notice thereof was given, a further detailed proof of loss is not requisite to the right of recovery. Am. Cent. Ins. Co. v. Haws (Pa.) 9 Cent. Rep. 412.

Proofs of loss signed and sworn to by one member of a partnership are sufficient. Myers v. Council Bluffs Ins. Co. 72 Iowa, 176.

Where goods in two separate buildings are covered by one policy proof of loss should state the damage done in each building. Towne v. Springfield F. & M. Ins. Co. *supra.*

The failure to refer in the proofs of loss or otherwise to the lien of the lessor for rent on the building does not avoid the policy. Dresser v. United Firemen's Ins. Co. 45 Hun, 298.

An objection to the admission of proofs of loss in evidence, on the ground that they were not signed by the plaintiff, is untenable, where plaintiff's name was signed to the affidavit thereto, by another, in his presence and at his instance, and adopted by him. Breckinridge v. Am. Cent. Ins. Co. 4 West. Rep. 565, 87 Mo. 62.

Waiver of proofs of loss.

Proofs of loss may be waived by the underwriter; and waiver is a question for the jury. Nickerson v. Nickerson, 5 New Eng. Rep. 796, 80 Me. 100.

A provision in a policy requiring insured to give notice and proof of loss is waived if the insurer makes no objection to the absence of the proofs, but joins in arbitration proceedings required by the policy to be taken. Carroll v. Girard F. Ins. Co. 72 Cal. 297.

Objections to preliminary proofs of loss are waived by the failure of the company to disclose the same within a reasonable time. Firemen's Ins. Co. v. Floss, 9 Cent. Rep. 91, 67 Md. 403.

So retaining the proofs without objection is a waiver of objectionable defects. Cayon v. Dwelling-House Ins. Co. 68 Wis. 510; Bennett v. Agricultural Ins. Co. 8 Cent. Rep. 893, 106 N. Y. 243.

And stipulations as to proofs of loss are waived when other proofs are accepted without objection by an authorized agent. Indiana Ins. Co. v. Capehart, 8 West. Rep. 669, 108 Ind. 270; Smith v. Niagara F. Ins. Co. 1 L. R. A. 216, 6 New Eng. Rep. 32, 60 Vt. 682.

obtaining of premiums, and then defeating the enforcement of the policies upon which they were paid."

It is clear that the Company was not so bound but that it might modify any contract which it had made, or waive any of the conditions contained therein; and this may be done through its general agents. The knowledge of Steinbuschel & Bro. in this case was the knowledge of the Company, and their act was its act. When Gray applied for the insurance he informed the Company with reference to the incumbrances, as well as his necessity and purpose to continue them. Knowing these facts, the premium was accepted and the policy issued. Subsequent to the issuance of the policy, there was an express agreement that he might renew his mortgages as he had informed the Company it would be necessary to do, and the renewal of the incumbrances did not in any material degree affect the risk which the Company took. Accepting his statement, as the jury have done, we must assume that he acted in good faith with the Company and its agents, and that he was induced by the agreements and action of the Company to believe that he was warranted in renewing the mortgages. After receiving and retaining the premium, knowing the purpose and necessity of Gray to renew the incumbrances, and after a specific agreement waiving that condition of the policy, and authorizing him to renew the incumbrances, and after remaining silent and allowing him to proceed as though he was insured, until a loss occurs, the Company will not be heard to repudiate its contract or to deny its liability. We are aware that the authorities are not uniform upon the subject of waivers in policies like this one, but forfeitures are not favored in the law, and the view we have taken of the power of a general agent to waive the condition of a policy is more satisfactory to us, and is sufficiently supported. In addition to the authorities already cited, see the following: *Young* v. *Hartford F. Ins. Co.* 45 Iowa, 377; *King* v. *Council Bluffs Ins. Co.* 72 Iowa, 310; *Morrison* v. *North America Ins. Co.* 69 Tex. 353; *McGurk* v. *Metropolitan L. Ins. Co.* 1 L. R. A. 563, 56 Conn. 528; *American Ins. Co.* v. *Gallatin*, 48 Wis. 36; *Bartlett* v. *Fireman's F. Ins. Co.* 77 Iowa, 155; *Key* v. *Des Moines Ins. Co.* 77 Iowa, 174; *Sweetser* v. *Odd Fellows Mut. Aid Asso.* 117 Ind. 97; 2 Wood, Ins. §§ 422, 525.

It is further contended that a forfeiture occurred by reason of the failure of Gray to send proofs of loss to the Company. It is shown that immediately after the fire he notified Steinbuschel & Bro. of the loss, and they stated that they would at once inform the Company. Within a few days an adjuster of the Company, whose authority is not denied, came to Gray's place, and requested him to go before an officer and make proof of loss. The proofs were reduced to writing, signed and sworn to, and delivered to the adjuster; and there is testimony to the effect that he expressed satisfaction with them, and stated that he would forward them to the Company's office, and would return in a few days and settle the loss. This testimony was submitted to the jury under the following directions: "There is evidence tending to show that these statements were taken by said Winne as the agent of said Company, and sent to said Company, and it will be a question for the jury to determine whether such statements and proofs are such as are required by the policy; and, if not, whether the plaintiff was justified under the circumstances in believing, and did believe, that the proofs were satisfactory to the agent of the Company and to the Company, and that no further proofs would be required; and if the jury find from the evidence that the plaintiff was justified in believing, and did believe, that the proofs furnished to said Winne were satisfactory to him and to the Company; and further find that such proofs and statements were sent to the Company by said Winne, and that the Company made no objection thereto, and requested no further proofs to be made by the plaintiff within a reasonable time, and within the sixty days after the fire,—the jury would be justified in finding that defendant had waived the making of further proofs of loss. If, at the time such affidavits and statements were made at the request of said Winne, it was understood between said agent and said plaintiff that such statements and affidavits should not constitute the proofs required by the policy, and should not be considered as a waiver of such proofs, and that by taking such statements and affidavits said Winne should not and did not waive the making of the proofs in accordance with the provisions of the policy, then the jury would not be justified in finding that the taking of such statements and affidavits by said Winne, or that the acts and conduct of said Winne at the time of taking such statements and affidavits, con-

Where the insurer bases his refusal to pay on other grounds, he thereby waives his right to object to their insufficiency. Bennett v. Agricultural Ins. Co. *supra*.

A refusal to pay a policy solely on the ground that the insured has no title to premises is a waiver of objections as to proofs of loss. German Ins. Co. v. Gueck (Ill.) 6 L. R. A. 835; Niagara Ins. Co. v. Lee, 73 Tex. 641.

Where the company denied its liability on the ground of a sale in violation of a condition in the policy, it waived proof of loss under the policy. Commercial U. Assur. Co. v. Scammon, 10 West. Rep. 397, 126 Ill. 364.

Directing the insured to make proofs of loss, without objection to a previous change of occupancy, which is known to the insurer at the time, is a waiver of objection on that ground. Jerdee v. Cottage Grove F. Ins. Co. (Wis.) Jan. 7, 1890.

Where the agent denies the validity of a contract of insurance, objections to proofs of loss furnished are waived. Commercial U. Assur. Co. v. State, 13 West. Rep. 47, 113 Ind. 331.

Proof of loss is waived by examination of premises by the insurer's agent, who refuses to pay the loss. Fisher v. Crescent Ins. Co. 33 Fed. Rep. 544.

Where the insurer adopts the acts of its agents, it cannot deny the authority of the agents to waive the proofs. Carroll v. Girard F. Ins. Co. 72 Cal. 297.

Such a waiver is not prevented by a provision in the submission to arbitration, in case of their election to make the submission. *Ibid.*

Where offer of proofs would be a vain act proof of loss is deemed waived. See *note* to Kenton Ins. Co. v. Wigginton (Ky.) 7 L. R. A. 81; German Ins. Co. v. Gueck (Ill.) 6 L. R. A. 835.

stituted a waiver of the proofs required by the policy."

The testimony was sufficient to sustain the finding of the jury. Neither the adjuster nor anyone representing the Company returned the proofs, or claimed that they were insufficient. The Company recognized the loss, took all the proofs it deemed essential to an adjustment, and, instead of claiming that they were insufficient, expressed satisfaction with them, and stated that the loss would soon be paid. Assuming the existence of the facts stated, we think the assured had a right to assume, until notified to the contrary, that no other or different proofs would be required. There are some criticisms in regard to the refusal of the court to give instructions, but what has already been said in the opinion disposes of the material objections that are made. The charge of the court fairly submitted the questions involved to the jury.

Finding no error, *the judgment of the District Court will be affirmed.*

All the Justices concur.

NEW YORK COURT OF APPEALS (2d Div.).

Thomas HALPIN, *Respt.*,

v.

INSURANCE COMPANY OF NORTH AMERICA, of Philadelphia, *Appt.*

(....N. Y.....)

Machinery and apparatus used in the business of manufacturing leather and morocco, including boiler, engine, etc., being the only property covered by a policy of insurance, do not constitute a mill, or the standing still thereof create a forfeiture under a policy which provides that "if a building covered by this policy shall become vacant or unoccupied, or if a mill or manufactory shall stand idle . . . all liability hereunder shall thereupon cease," where a further provision of the policy as to the falling of a building expressly declares that the policy shall cease as to property therein as well as to the building.

(March 21, 1890.)

APPEAL by defendant from a judgment of the General Term of the Supreme Court,

NOTE.—*Fire insurance; forfeiture in case of vacancy or non-occupancy.*

General agents of an insurance company in the matter of issuing policies may make a valid stipulation for the insertion of a clause in a policy relating to the occupancy of the buildings insured. Continental Ins. Co. v. Ruckman, 127 Ill. 364.

And the insured will be presumed to have had knowledge of a provision in his policy that the policy shall be void in case of the property becoming vacant, unoccupied or uninhabited. Burlington Ins. Co. v. Gibbons (Kan.) Jan. 11, 1890.

The condition against non-occupancy, in an insurance policy, must be construed and applied in reference to the subject matter of the contract and the ordinary incidents attending the use of the insured property. Halpin v. Phœnix Ins. Co. 118 N. Y. 165; Whitney v. Black River Ins. Co. 72 N. Y. 117.

The written agreement on a policy as to the use and occupation of the premises must be construed as an express promissory warranty, in the nature of a condition precedent, and a literal compliance is essential to the right of recovery. Dewees v. Manhattan Ins. Co. 34 N. J. L. 244; Carson v. Jersey City Ins. Co. 43 N. J. L. 300; May, Ins. § 156; Wood, F. Ins. § 165; Flanders, F. Ins. 226.

Such a condition does not render the policy absolutely void upon the happening of the event; and if the insurer waives the forfeiture, neither the insured nor a third person can treat the insurance as void. Germania F. Ins. Co. v. Klewer (Ill.) Oct. 31, 1889.

If the insurer does not exercise the power in case of breach of the condition, to declare the forfeiture while the assured is in default, and the premises are again occupied, its right to do so ceases, and its liability on the policy again attaches. Insurance Co. of N. A. v. Garland, 108 Ill. 220; Schmidt v. Peoria, M. & F. Ins. Co. 41 Ill. 295; Insurance Co. of N. A. v. McDowell, 50 Ill. 120; Westchester F. Ins. Co. v. Foster, 90 Ill. 121.

Clauses avoiding a policy on change of occupancy, or use for trade increasing hazard, are not violated by premises becoming vacant. Somerset Co. Mut. F. Ins. Co. v. Usaw, 2 Cent. Rep. 542, 112 Pa. 80; Cumberland Valley Mut. Protection Co. v. Douglas, 58 Pa. 419.

Terms "vacancy" and "non-occupancy" construed.

The terms "vacancy" and "non-occupancy" are used interchangeably in a policy which specially provides that "in case the premises shall be left unoccupied" (Paine v. Agricultural Ins. Co. 5 Thomp. & C. 619); or "shall remain unoccupied" (Keith v. Quincy Mut. F. Ins. Co. 10 Allen, 228); or shall become "vacant" (Cummins v. Agricultural Ins. Co. 5 Hun, 554, 67 N. Y. 260); or "unoccupied" (Wustum v. City F. Ins. Co. 15 Wis. 138); or shall "be vacated" (Ashworth v. Builders Mut. F. Ins. Co. 112 Mass. 422),—the insurance shall be forfeited.

The questions of vacancy and non-occupancy, and of increase of risk from these and other changes of circumstances, are questions of fact for the jury. Gamwell v. Merchants & F. Mut. F. Ins. Co. 12 Cush. 167; Luce v. Dorchester Mut. F. Ins. Co. 105 Mass. 297; Williams v. People's F. Ins. Co. 57 N. Y. 274; Cummins v. Agricultural Ins. Co. *supra*; Robinson v. Mercer Co. Mut. F. Ins. Co. 27 N. J. L. 134; Wood, Ins. § 439.

Dwelling-house.

A dwelling-house chiefly designed for the abode of mankind is occupied when human beings habitually reside in it and unoccupied when no one dwells in it. North American F. Ins. Co. v. Zaenger, 63 Ill. 464; American Ins. Co. v. Padfield, 78 Ill. 167; Phœnix Ins. Co. v. Tucker, 92 Ill. 64; Imperial F. Ins. Co. v. Kiernan, 83 Ky. 468; Stupetski v. Transatlantic F. Ins. Co. 43 Mich. 373; Cook v. Continental Ins. Co. 70 Mo. 610; Herrman v. Merchants Ins. Co. 81 N. Y. 184; Herrman v. Adriatic F. Ins. Co. 85 N. Y. 162; Alston v. Old North State Ins. Co. 80 N. C. 326; Fitzgerald v. Connecticut F. Ins. Co. 64 Wis. 463.

The phrase "left unoccupied" will not be construed as implying an abandonment or willful vacation of the premises, leaving them uncared for. Sonneborn v. Manufacturers Ins. Co. 44 N. J. L. 220.

Object of stipulation.

The object of the stipulation against vacancy and

See also 11 L. R. A. 771; 23 L. R. A. 99; 26 L. R. A. 313; 33 L. R. A. 712; 48 L. R. A. 49.

(Second Department, affirming a judgment of the Kings Circuit entered upon a verdict directed for plaintiff in an action brought to recover the amount alleged to be due upon a policy of fire insurance. *Affirmed.*

Statement by **Vann, J.:**

This is an action upon an insurance policy issued by the defendant on the 10th of February, 1883, whereby it insured the plaintiff, for the period of one year from that day, "against loss or damage by fire, to an amount not exceeding $2,000, on his boiler, steam-engine and connections, machines, machinery, shafting, belting, pulleys, hangers, tubs, tanks, tables, tools, vats and all machinery and apparatus used in the business of manufacturing leather and morocco, all contained in the frame building and extension situate on the south side of Wallabout Street, about 375 feet westerly from Lee Avenue, Brooklyn, L. I."

The defendant answered, alleging that after the delivery of the policy, and before the loss occurred, the plaintiff permitted "the said building in said policy mentioned to become vacant and unoccupied, and the said mill to remain idle, . . . until and at the time of the fire in" question. It appeared that the property insured was totally destroyed by fire on the 4th of January, 1884, and that for several months prior thereto the morocco factory had "stood idle," although the machinery was not removed from the building.

Mr. **Thomas E. Pearsall** for appellant.
Mr. **Nathaniel C. Moak,** with *Mr.* **John Oakey,** for respondent.

Vann, J., delivered the opinion of the court:

The policy in question is a long instrument, containing some provisions that apply exclusively to insurance upon buildings or real property, others that apply only to personal property, and others, still, that are applicable to property of both kinds. The form was evidently designed for use in insuring both kinds together, or either kind separately; but in the latter case, of course, certain provisions were not intended to be operative, as there would be nothing for them to act upon. The only provision specifically pleaded by the defendant in its answer, as a defense to this action, is the following, viz.: "If a building covered by this policy shall become vacant or unoccupied, or if a mill or manufactory shall stand idle, or be run nights or overtime, without notice to and the consent of the company, clearly stated hereon, all liability hereunder will thereupon cease; and if a building shall fall, except as the result of a fire, this policy, if covering thereon, or on property therein, shall thereupon immediately cease and determine."

It is contended by the defendant that "the machinery covered by the policy constituted a mill, and that its standing idle created a forfeiture." On the other hand, the plaintiff claims that a building is the sole subject of insurance contemplated by the first part of the clause above quoted, and that its true meaning is that if a building covered by the policy shall become vacant or unoccupied, or if, being a mill or manufactory, it shall stand idle, all liability shall at once cease. The plaintiff further claims that the property insured was not a mill or manufactory, and that it was not insured as a mill or manufactory, but simply as personal property.

We think that the plaintiff is right in his contention, because it would not be a natural or ordinary use of language to describe machinery used in milling as a mill, or in manufacturing as a manufactory. *Herrman v. Merchants Ins. Co.* 81 N. Y. 184.

The property insured was neither a mill nor

---

non-occupancy is to guard against the increased risk arising from the absence of everybody whose duty or interest might afford protection from fire. Moore v. Phœnix F. Ins. Co. 3 New Eng. Rep. 57, 64 N. H. 140.

So a house from which the owner or tenant has removed with no definite intention of returning is unoccupied or vacant. Sleeper v. New Hampshire F. Ins. Co. 56 N. H. 401; Hartshorne v. Agricultural Ins. Co. 18 Cent. Rep. 188, 50 N. J. L. 427.

But a temporary absence, or the occasional and necessary absence of the family or servants, will not be so construed. Phœnix Ins. Co. v. Tucker, 92 Ill. 64; Laselle v. Hoboken F. Ins. Co. 43 N. J. L. 468; O'Brien v. Commercial F. Ins. Co. 6 Jones & S. 517; Franklin F. Ins. Co. v. Kepler, 95 Pa. 492.

A building is not vacant, unoccupied or not in use although unoccupied except by a clerk who entered and made repairs, occupied and slept therein. Stensgaard v. National F. Ins. Co. 36 Minn. 181; Imperial F. Ins. Co. v. Kiernan, 83 Ky. 468; Hartford F. Ins. Co. v. Smith, 3 Colo. 422.

But where the tenant with his family removes from the building, merely leaving some furniture therein, and resides elsewhere, the building is deemed unoccupied and vacant. Bennett v. Agricultural Ins. Co. 51 Conn. 504; Sexton v. Hawkeye Ins. Co. 69 Iowa, 99; Feshe v. Council Bluffs Ins. Co. 74 Iowa, 676; Ashworth v. Builders Mut. F. Ins. Co. 112 Mass. 422; Corrigan v. Connecticut F. Ins. Co. 122 Mass. 298; Cook v. Continental Ins. Co. 70 Mo. 610; Watertown F. Ins. Co. v. Cherry, 84 Va. 72.

Insurance on mill and machinery.

In a contract of insurance, made for a period of years upon a mill building and machinery, a description of the property as a "sawmill building" had not the effect to restrict the use to the purpose of a sawmill. Frost's D. L. & W. W. Works v. Millers & M. Mut. Ins. Co. 37 Minn. 300.

Where an engine driving planing-mill machinery twenty-two feet distant, and engine room and mill building were connected merely by a shaft transmitting power from the engine to the mill, and by a spout carrying shavings from mill to engine, while beneath these a roadway separated said buildings, insurance on such "mill building and addition and machinery therein" covers such engine-room and contents. Home Mut. Ins. Co. v. Roe, 71 Wis. 33.

Clauses avoiding policy for non-occupancy and vacancy of premises.

To constitute occupancy of a building used for manufacturing purposes, within a clause in an insurance policy against non-occupancy, there must be some practical use or employment of the property. Halpin v. Phenix Ins. Co. 118 N. Y. 165.

But a building used as a manufactory, which is closed and in the hands of an agent to rent, is unoccupied, within a provision in an insurance policy against non-occupancy, although occasionally visited by the agent and a watchman who resides next door. *Ibid.*

A cotton-mill building is not vacant and unoccupied within a policy, where a number of em-a manufactory, as those words are commonly understood. While the word "mill" is used to describe "a machine for grinding," it is also defined as "a building, with its machinery, where grinding, or some process of manufacturing, is carried on." Webster Dict.

A manufactory is "a house or place where anything is manufactured." *Ibid.*

Neither term would be understood or used by the mass of mankind to describe simply "machinery and apparatus used in the business of manufacturing leather and morocco," which is the description in the written part of the policy that is claimed to mean a mill or manufactory as used in the printed part. If the defendant intended to attach the condition in question to machinery used in a mill, it should have said so. In the condition relating to the fall of a building it is provided that "this policy, if covering thereon, or on property therein, shall thereupon immediately cease." So the clause prohibiting the use of certain inflammable substances provides that if they are "stored, kept or used in any building on which, or on the contents of which, there is any insurance," the policy shall be void.

Thus it appears that in certain instances, by the use of language that no one could mistake, the insurer made its intent clear that a certain condition should apply both to real and personal property. If it intended that the condition under consideration should thus apply, why did it not say so? We think that this condition refers to a mill or manufactory in the sense only of a building used for milling or manufacturing, and that it has no application to the personal property covered by the policy.

Moreover, if there is a reasonable doubt as to the meaning or application of this clause, it should be construed most favorably to the insured, because the insurer prepared and executed the contract, and is responsible for the language used. *Kratzenstein* v. *Western Assur. Co.* 116 N. Y. 54, 59; *Dilleber* v. *Home L. Ins. Co.* 69 N. Y. 256, 263.

As was said by this court in a recent case: "The defendant is claiming a forfeiture. When a clause in a contract is capable of two constructions, one of which will support, and the other defeat, the principal obligation, the former will be preferred. Forfeitures are not favored, and the party claiming a forfeiture will not be permitted, upon equivocal or doubtful clauses or words contained in his own contract, to deprive the other party of the benefit of the right or indemnity for which he contracted." *Baley* v. *Homestead F. Ins. Co.* 80 N. Y. 21, 23.

The learned counsel for the defendant has referred us to a case, recently decided by this court, in which the plaintiff sought to recover for a loss upon the building that contained the personal property involved in this action, and destroyed by the same fire. *Halpin* v. *Phenix Ins. Co.* 118 N. Y. 165.

The policy in that case covered the building only, and provided that if said building should become vacant or unoccupied the insurance should cease. We gave effect to that condition, which was clear and unequivocal, by reversing the judgment that the plaintiff had recovered. In another case arising out of the same fire, and decided during the present term, the policy covered personal property only, described as contained in said building; but it provided that "if the above-mentioned premises," referring to the building, should become vacant or unoccupied, the policy should be void. *Halpin* v. *Ætna F. Ins. Co.* 30 N. Y. St. Rep. 259.

In that case, also, we were required by the clear and unmistakable terms of the contract, and the facts as disclosed by the evidence, to

---

ployés are retained in the service of lessee, and are actually engaged about their usual work in the mill up to and on the day of the fire, and all the plant and some material and manufactured goods are there. American F. Ins. Co. v. Brighton Cotton Mfg. Co. 15 West. Rep. 180, 125 Ill. 131.

Where, during repairs of machinery by a manufacturing company, watchmen were on duty and employés were about the factory from its closing until it burned, it is not unoccupied. Brighton Mfg. Co. v. Reading F. Ins. Co. 33 Fed. Rep. 232; Brighton Mfg. Co. v. Fire Asso. of Phila. Id. 234; Lebanon Mut. Ins. Co. v. Leathers (Pa.) 6 Cent. Rep. 901.

Provisions against ceasing to operate mill or machinery.

Provision against ceasing to operate a tannery will not be violated, if at the time of the fire the use of the premises is the same as at the time of insurance. Lebanon Mut. F. Ins. Co. v. Erb, 2 Cent. Rep. 783, 112 Pa. 149.

The temporary suspension of the operation of a steam engine in a planing mill, materially decreasing the risk, the other business continuing, does not avoid a policy conditioned to be void on suspending operations without a special agreement indorsed on the policy. Allemannia F. Ins. Co. v. White (Pa.) 10 Cent. Rep. 65.

But a building insured as a trip-hammer shop, the business therein suspended for more than thirty days, the machinery and tools remaining there and the plaintiff's son going through the shop nearly every day to see if things were right, did not constitute occupancy. Moore v. Phœnix F. Ins. Co. 8 New Eng. Rep. 57, 64 N. H. 140.

A temporary cessation of the operation of a manufactory, occasioned by the prevalence of an epedemic, is not a ceasing of operation. Poss v. Western Assur. Co. 7 Lea, 704.

A mere temporary suspension of business to make repairs, or for want of materials, is not a cessation of operation. Lebanon Mut. Ins. Co. v. Leathers (Pa.) 6 Cent. Rep. 901.

A sawmill lying idle for several weeks for lack of water or want of logs does not thereby cease to be occupied. Whitney v. Black River Ins. Co. 72 N. Y. 117.

The stoppage of a mill, though for the purpose of necessary repairs, without the required notice, is within the provision of a policy that, if the mill shall be shut down or remain idle from any cause whatever, the policy shall be considered suspended until work resumed. Day v. Mill-Owners Mut. F. Ins. Co. 70 Iowa, 710.

A temporary suspension of the operation of a mill for forty-two days, occasioned solely by the want of logs to manufacture, while the logs were expected daily, does not make the policy void, under a provision that if the mill shall cease to be operated, unless shut down for repairs without notice to and consent of the company, it shall be void. City P. & S. Mill Co. v. Merchants M. & C. Mut. F. Ins. Co. (Mich.) Nov. 23, 1888.

reverse the judgment that had been rendered in favor of the plaintiff. But we are called upon in the case at bar to enforce a contract that differs materially from either of the others named, because it fails to attach any condition that was shown to have been violated, to the property covered by the policy.

The judgment in this case, therefore, should be affirmed.

All concur.

WEST VIRGINIA SUPREME COURT OF APPEALS.

John W. SMITH and Wife

v.

COUNTY COURT OF KANAWHA COUNTY, *Pltf. in Err.*

(.... W. Va.....)

*The plaintiff and a lady friend were driving a single horse, in a spring wagon, along the road leading from the City of Charleston to the Town of Malden, in Kanawha County. At a point in said road where it was from twelve to eighteen feet wide, two calves yoked together came suddenly from the pawpaw bushes, and frightened the horse, which the plaintiff had owned for two years, and regarded as gentle; and he commenced backing, and continued so to do until he backed the wagon and its occupants and himself over the steep river bank, whereby the plaintiff was seriously and permanently injured. In a suit brought by said plaintiff against the County Court of Kanawha County to recover damages for the injuries sustained, it was proven by plaintiff that she could have managed the horse but for the narrowness of the road; that she had traveled the same road two or three times a week for the previous two years without accident,—and by another witness that the road was in good condition, smooth and cindered, and that he had traveled said road two hundred times a year for sixteen years, driving all kinds of horses and teams, and had never met with an accident; that the road at that point was wide enough for two teams to pass, and on one side of the road was a steep mountain which slipped into the road in wet times, and on the other side the river bank. *Held*, that under the circumstances of this case, the defendant was not liable for said injury.

*Head note by English, J.

(March 25, 1890.)

ERROR to the Circuit Court for Kanawha County to review a judgment in favor of plaintiffs in an action to recover damages for personal injuries alleged to have resulted from a defect in a public highway. *Reversed.*

The case sufficiently appears in the opinion.

Messrs. **Okey Johnson** and **S. C. Burdett**, with *Messrs.* **Sylvester Chapman** and **A. B. Littlepage**, for plaintiff in error:

The County is not required to make the traveled part of the highway the whole width of the road as laid out, and will not be liable for defects in that part not usually traveled upon which do not affect the safety of the other part.

NOTE.—*Negligence; liability for injuries produced by. The loss or injury attributed to the proximate cause.*

One who violates a duty owed to others, or who commits a tortious or wrongfully negligent act, is liable not only for those injuries which are the direct and immediate consequences of his act, but for such consequential injuries as, according to common experience, are likely to and do in fact result from his act. McDonald v. Snelling, 14 Allen, 290; Metallic C. C. Co. v. Fitchburg R. Co. 109 Mass. 277; Derry v. Flitner, 118 Mass. 131; Wellington v. Downer Kerosene Oil Co. 104 Mass. 64; Smethurst v. Independent Congregational Church, 2 L. R. A. 695, 148 Mass. 261.

The resulting injury must be the natural and probable consequence of the original tortious or negligent act. See *note* to Louisville, N. A. & C. R. Co. v. Lucas (Ind.) 6 L. R. A. 194.

A carrier's act, from which an injury results, will be deemed the proximate cause, unless the consequences were so unnatural and unusual that they could not have been foreseen and provided against by the highest practicable care, although the precise accident which occurred might not have been anticipated. See Louisville, N. A. & C. R. Co. v. Lucas, 6 L. R. A. 193, 119 Ind. 583.

Negligence is the commission of a lawful act in a careless manner, or the omission to perform a legal duty, to the injury of another. Splittorf v. State, 10 Cent. Rep. 699, 108 N. Y. 205; Lehigh & W. Coal Co. v. Lear (Pa.) 8 Cent. Rep. 109.

The basis of liability in negligence is the violation of some legal duty to exercise care. Cusick v. Adams, 115 N. Y. 55.

The fact that an accident is unusual, unexpected or unheard of will not excuse the negligence which causes it. Doyle v. Chicago, St. P. & K. C. R. Co. 4 L. R. A. 420, 77 Iowa, 607.

There should be such affinity or connection in the relation of the cause and the effect, that the influence of the wrongful act should predominate over other supervening causes. Brown v. Wabash, St. L. & P. R. Co. 2 West. Rep. 559, 20 Mo. App. 222; Gilliland v. Chicago & A. R. Co. 2 West. Rep. 138, 19 Mo. App. 411.

When there is no intermediate efficient cause, the original wrong must be considered as reaching to the effect and proximate to it. Milwaukee & St. P. R. Co. v. Kellogg, 94 U. S. 469 (24 L. ed. 256).

In all cases of loss it is to be attributed to the proximate cause, and not to the remote cause. This maxim governs in cases of insurance. Waters v. Merchants Louisville Ins. Co. 36 U. S. 11 Pet. 213 (9 L. ed. 691); West Mahanoy Twp. v. Watson, 8 Cent. Rep. 543, 116 Pa. 344.

If negligence is the proximate cause of the injury, it is of no consequence whether it be by omission or commission. Harriman v. Pittsburgh, C. & St. L. R. Co. 9 West. Rep. 446, 45 Ohio St. 11.

Negligence is not actionable unless it is the proximate cause of the injury complained of. Mathiason v. Mayer, 7 West. Rep. 739, 90 Mo. 585; Pittsburgh, C. & St. L. R. Co. v. Conn, 1 West. Rep. 904, 104 Ind. 64; Carter v. Chambers, 79 Ala. 223.

Negligence in standing on the step of a car platform while the train is in motion is not the proximate cause of injury from a lever or signal of a switch which scraped the cars as they passed. Bos v. Northern Pac. R. Co. 5 Dak. 308.

The stoppage of a gas pipe is not the proximate cause of an accident, during an experiment made to increase the pressure. Taylor v. Baldwin, 78 Cal. 517.

Where one keeps a magazine of explosives in vio-

See also 12 L. R. A. 237, 482; 14 L. R. A. 743; 16 L. R. A. 106, 545; 17 L. R. A. 217, 310; 19 L. R. A. 365; 20 L. R. A. 582; 21 L. R. A. 316, 721; 35 L. R. A. 199.

Dickey v. *Maine Teleg. Co.* 46 Me. 483; *Phillips* v. *Ritchie Co. Ct.* 31 W. Va. 481.

If the road was dangerous, and the female plaintiff knew it was dangerous, but she was willing to risk it if anybody else was, then the evidence shows no right to recover, because she ought not to have driven over it, and it was negligence in her to do so.

Phillips v. *Ritchie Co. Ct.* 31 W. Va. 477; *Moore* v. *Huntington*, Id. 842; *Hubbard* v. *Concord*, 35 N. H. 52; *Raymond* v. *Lowell*, 6 Cush. 524.

If the road was safe and good to the width of eleven to fifteen feet, and safe to pass, if the horse did not become frightened, and the cause of the injury was, not the narrowness of the road, but "the calves coming down from the hillside out of some pawpaw bushes," which frightened the horse and caused him to back over the bank, then she is not entitled to recover, because the fright to the horse by the calves was the cause of the accident, a cause that could in no sense be attributed to any fault or neglect of the County.

Kingsbury v. *Dedham*, 13 Allen, 189; *Lund* v. *Tyngsboro*, 11 Cush. 563.

A county is not liable for every object which renders a public road unsafe and inconvenient for travelers to pass over it, but only for such as not only render the road unsafe and inconvenient, but also defective or out of repair, and the injury must be attributable to the defect or want of repair.

Cook v. *Charlestown*, 13 Allen, 190, *note*.

The duty of the County to the traveling public does not extend to the degree of keeping its road in such condition that no injury could possibly happen.

Wilson v. *Charlestown*, 8 Allen, 137.

Messrs. **Knight & Couch**, with *Mr.* **Sam D. Littlepage**, for defendant in error:

The complaint is good in that it alleges that that particular road, at that particular point where the injury occurred, was in a bad condition and out of repair in point of narrowness, and that that resulted in the injury complained of.

Stone v. *Hubbardston*, 100 Mass. 49.

The mere fact that a traveler is familiar with the road, and knows of the existence of a defect therein, will not impose upon him the duty to use more than ordinary care in avoiding it.

Shearm. & Redf. Neg. §§ 846, 376; *Lyman* v. *Hampshire Co.* 1 New Eng. Rep. 227, 140 Mass. 311; *Henry Co. Turnp. Co.* v. *Jackson*, 86 Ind. 111; *Bullock* v *New York*, 99 N.Y. 654; *Lyman* v. *Amherst*, 107 Mass. 339; *Humphreys* v. *Armstrong Co.* 56 Pa. 204; *Evans* v. *Utica*, 69 N.Y. 166; *Mahoney* v. *Metropolitan R. Co.* 104 Mass. 73; *Smith* v. *St. Joseph*, 45 Mo. 449; *Kavanaugh* v. *Janesville*, 24 Wis. 618; *Kenworthy* v. *Ironton*, 41 Wis. 647; *Murphy* v. *Indianapolis*, 83 Ind. 76; *Wilson* v. *Trafalgar & B. C. Gr. Road Co.* 83 Ind. 326; *Huntington* v. *Breen*, 77 Ind. 29.

Where two causes combine to produce an injury to a traveler upon a highway, both of which are in their nature proximate, the one being a culpable defect in the highway and the other some occurrence for which neither party is responsible, the municipality is liable, pro-

---

lation of law, he is not liable solely because of such violation, unless the violation is in some degree the cause of the injury. Laflin & R. Powder Co. v. Tearney (Ill.) 7 L. R. A. 262.

Where a person willfully turned a stream from a hose upon horses hitched in front of his premises and they ran away and collided with a wagon, he was liable for the injury. Forney v. Geldmacher, 75 Mo. 113.

In determining the proximity of cause the true rule is that the injury must be the natural and probable consequence of the negligence. West Mahanoy Twp. v. Watson, 8 Cent. Rep. 548, 116 Pa. 344; Southside Pass. R. Co. v. Trich, 10 Cent. Rep. 867, 117 Pa. 390.

The ascertainment of the dividing line between proximate and remote cause, in actions for damages for injuries by negligent use of highways by railroad trains, is so perplexing that to a sound judgment must be left each particular case, upon the special facts belonging to it. Brown v. Wabash, St. L. & P. R. Co. 2 West. Rep. 560, 20 Mo. App. 222.

Slipping on an icy street and falling against a cellar door do not show a case of negligence in maintaining the door. Hunter v. Wanamaker (Pa.) 2 Cent. Rep. 70.

The mere act of shooting a dog, though itself a tort, is not the proximate cause of injury to one startled by the report who, owing to previous delicate health, became ill from the nervous shock. Renner v. Canfield, 36 Minn. 90.

The removal of a fence along a railroad is not the proximate cause of a subsequent injury to cattle. Louisville & N. R. Co. v. Guthrie, 10 Lea, 432.

Failure to signal the starting of a train is not the proximate cause of injury to one who knew it was going to start or that it was in motion. Barkley v. Missouri Pac. R. Co. 96 Mo. 367.

Where cattle stopped on a highway by a standing railroad train are injured by another train, the obstruction caused by the standing train is too remote a cause of injury to make the company liable. Brown v. Wabash, St. L. & P. R. Co. *supra*.

Damages resulting from fright or nervous shock to a person not actually struck, caused by the fall of a bundle of laths through the negligence of another person, are too remote to be recovered. Rock v. Denis (Super. Ct.) 4 Montreal L. Rep. 356.

Proximate and remote cause of injury. See *notes* to Louisville, N. A. & C. R. Co. v. Lucas (Ind.) 6 L. R. A. 194; Erickson v. St. Paul & D. R. Co. (Minn.) 5 L. R. A. 786.

Co-operating causes.

When two causes co-operate to produce damage the proximate cause is the originating and efficient cause which sets the other cause in motion. Lapleine v. Morgan's L. & T. R. & Steamship Co. 1 L. R. A. 378, and *note*, 40 La. Ann. 661.

If there be a concurrence of some other immediate agency, that event must have been the effect of the act complained of or within the range of probable occurrence. Gilliland v. Chicago & A. R. Co. 2 West. Rep. 186, 19 Mo. App. 411.

A railroad lawfully built on a public street, and carefully operated, is not liable for injury to a pedestrian, run over by a passing team, by reason of snow-drifts on the sidewalk. The injury in such case results by failure of the city to keep its sidewalks passable. McCandless v. Chicago & N. W. R. Co. 71 Wis. 41.

Where the united and contemporaneous negligence of two persons causes a collision between them on a street, neither can recover for injuries

vided the injury would not have been sustained but for such defect.

Shearm. & Redf. Neg. § 346, and authorities cited in *note; Ring* v. *Cohoes*, 77 N. Y. 83; *Ehrgott* v. *New York*, 96 N. Y. 264; *Hunt* v. *Pownal*, 9 Vt. 411; *Palmer* v. *Andover*, 2 Cush. 600; *Houfe* v. *Fulton*, 29 Wis. 296; *Hey* v. *Philadelphia*, 81 Pa. 44; *Brookville & C. Turnp. Co.* v. *Pumphrey*, 59 Ind. 78; *Hull* v. *Kansas City*, 54 Mo. 599; *Olson* v. *Chippewa Falls*, 71 Wis. 558; *Burrell Twp.* v. *Uncapher*, 10 Cent. Rep. 828, 117 Pa. 353, 2 Am. St. Rep. 664; *North Manheim Twp.* v. *Arnold*, 11 Cent. Rep. 846, 119 Pa. 380; *Flagg* v. *Hudson*, 2 New Eng. Rep. 652, 142 Mass. 280; *Rushville* v. *Adams*, 5 West. Rep. 682, 107 Ind. 475.

The law requires every road to be thirty feet wide.

Warth's Code, chap. 43, § 34.

The defendant was clearly guilty of negligence, not only by reason of the unlawful narrowness of the road at that point, but also by reason of the total absence of any protection to travelers by fence, railing, barriers or otherwise.

Olson v *Chippewa Falls*, 71 Wis. 558; *Houfe* v. *Fulton*, 29 Wis. 296, 9 Am. Rep. 568; *Baldwin* v. *Greenwood's Turnp. Co.* 40 Conn. 238, 16 Am. Rep. 33; *Page* v. *Bucksport*, 64 Me. 51, 18 Am. Rep. 239; *Hey* v. *Philadelphia*, 81 Pa. 44, 22 Am. Rep. 733; *Lower Macungie Twp.* v. *Merkhoffer*, 71 Pa. 276; *Hays* v. *Gallagher*, 72 Pa. 136; *McKee* v *Bidwell*, 74 Pa. 218; *Burrell Twp.* v. *Uncapher*, 10 Cent. Rep. 828, 117 Pa. 353; *Harris* v. *Clinton Twp.* 64 Mich. 447, 8 Am. St. Rep. 842; *Baltimore & H. Turnp. Co.* v. *Bateman*, 68 Md. 389, 6 Am. St. Rep. 449.

English, *J.*, delivered the opinion of the court:

An action of trespass on the case was brought to the February Rules, 1888, in the Circuit Court of Kanawha County, by John W. Smith and Leonora Smith, his wife, against the County Court of Kanawha County. On the 23d day of March, 1888, on the plaintiff's motion, the case was remanded to rules, with leave to them to amend their declaration, and on the 3d day of January, 1889, the defendant appeared by counsel, and demurred to the plaintiffs' declaration, which demurrer, being argued by counsel, and considered by the court, was overruled, and thereupon the defendant pleaded not guilty, and issue was therein joined; and thereupon a trial was had before a jury, which resulted in a verdict in favor of the plaintiffs for $750. The defendant then moved the court to set aside said verdict of the jury as being contrary to the law and the evidence, and award it a new trial, which motion the court, after consideration, overruled, to which action and ruling of the court the defendant excepted, and the court entered up judgment upon said verdict; and the defendant tendered a bill of exceptions to certain actions and rulings of the court, which was made a part of the record in the case; and the defendant applied for and obtained a writ of error and *supersedeas* to said judgment.

The facts set forth in the bill of exceptions shows that the female plaintiff was driving a horse which she and her husband both regarded as gentle, returning home from Charleston in a spring wagon, accompanied by Miss Emma Jacob, along the road leading to her home in

---

sustained thereby. Evans v. Adams Exp. Co. (Ind.) 7 L. R. A. 678, and *note*.

Intervening agency breaks causal connection.

If a new cause intervenes sufficient of itself to cause the misfortune, the former must be considered too remote. Seale v. Gulf, C. & S. F. R. Co. 65 Tex. 274.

The negligence of a responsible agent intervening between defendant's negligence and the injury suffered, *i. e.* the damage, breaks the causal connection. Mahogany v. Ward, 16 R. I. —, Feb. 23, 1889.

So where horses were frightened by the upsetting of a vehicle in a defective highway, and after running for some distance were killed by a train of cars, the town authorities were held not liable. West Mahanoy Twp. v. Watson, 3 Cent. Rep. 243, 112 Pa. 574.

Where a person traveling by night, driven by a drunken driver, is precipitated down an unfenced bank, the drunkenness of the driver, and not the defective condition of the road, is the proximate cause of the injury. Hershey v. Mill Creek Twp. Road Comrs. (Pa.) 8 Cent. Rep. 252.

One negligent person cannot escape liability for his negligence because the negligence of a third person concurred in producing the injury. Louisville, N. A. & C. R. Co. v. Lucas, 6 L. R. A. 193, and *note*, 119 Ind. 583; Pittsburgh, C. & St. L. R. Co. v. Spencer, 98 Ind. 186; Slater v. Mersereau, 64 N. Y. 138; Barrett v. Third Ave. R. Co. 45 N. Y. 628; Thomp. Neg. 1088.

A village is liable for personal injury caused by a fall from an unguarded sidewalk although the direct cause of the fall is the negligence of a third party pushing him off. Carterville v. Cook (Ill.) 4 L. R. A. 721, and *note*.

Negligently piling lumber, concurring with the negligence of a stranger, is the direct and proximate cause of injury from a fall of the lumber pile. Pastene v. Adams, 49 Cal. 87.

Driving at an unlawful rate in the street is the proximate cause of a collision with another vehicle, although the parties were prevented from quickly turning out by reason of the condition of the street railway. De Camp v. Sioux City, 74 Iowa, 392.

Where the wrong of one party places another in a dilemma, such wrong is to be deemed the proximate cause of the injury which ensues. Louisville, N. A. & C. R. Co. v. Falvey, 2 West. Rep. 637, 104 Ind. 430; Harris v. Clinton Twp. 7 West. Rep. 666, 64 Mich. 447; Cody v. N. Y. & N. E. R. Co. (Mass.) 7 L. R. A. 843.

Where one injured by the negligence of another does all that a prudent person could have done under the circumstances it will absolve him from the charge of contributory negligence. Louisville, N. A. & C. R. Co. v. Lucas, *supra*. See Carterville v. Cook (Ill.) 4 L. R. A. 721.

Effect produced by an intervening cause.

An intervening cause cannot affect the liability of a negligent party. Harriman v. Pittsburgh, C. & St. L. R. Co. 9 West. Rep. 446, 45 Ohio St. 11.

Where the intervening cause and its probable or reasonable consequences could reasonably have been anticipated by the original wrong-doer the causal connection between the original wrongful act and subsequent injury is not broken. Seale v. Gulf, C. & S. F. R. Co. 65 Tex. 274. See *note* to Erickson v. St. Paul & D. R. Co. (Minn.) 5 L. R. A. 787.

The fact that land of a third party intervened between the woodland of the plaintiff and the defendant's road would not alone be decisive, if the destruction of the plaintiff's property was the natural and direct effect of the first firing. O'Neill

the Town of Malden; that she had owned the horse for about two years, and had driven him from Malden to Charleston two or three times a week during that time, and had never known him to frighten; and that two calves came down from the hillside, out of the pawpaw bushes, and her horse became frightened, and commenced backing; that she tried to keep him in the road, but could not do so; that the horse backed until he backed across the road and over the river bank, a distance of about forty feet from the top of the river bank; that at the time her horse became frightened she was driving next to the mountain, on the side of the road furthest from the river; that she tried to keep the horse in the road, but he was so badly frightened she could not do so, although he was a gentle horse, easily managed, and had never become frightened before; that the road at that point was about from eleven to eighteen feet wide; that she received injuries from said accident of a serious and permanent character, and was under the treatment of a physician during the entire summer; that she was keeping a boarding-house in the Town of Malden, but had to give up the business on account of the injuries received, and since the accident had been unable to attend to her household affairs; that there was not room for two wagons to pass at the point where the accident occurred; that the road was in about the same condition it was during the two years she had been driving over it; that it looked dangerous; that said plaintiff had always considered it dangerous, but she was willing to risk it if anyone else was; that there was no other road by which she could return home; that she could have managed her horse had it not been for the narrowness of the road. This was, in substance, the testimony of the female plaintiff.

The testimony of J. W. Smith was, in substance, the same, fixing the width of the road, at the point where the accident occurred, at twelve feet, and stating that his wife is helpless now, unable to do any work; that she had to give up her boarding-house in Malden, and remain with him in Charleston, where his business is; that the road where the accident occurred, as far as it was made, was a good road, and the road was a favorite driving place between Charleston and Malden; that the slip from the mountain was not interfering with the road at the time of the accident, that he knew of.

J. E. Dana, a witness for the plaintiffs, proved that the road at that point was sixteen or eighteen feet wide; that the road was a favorite drive for pleasure; that he had driven along the road two hundred times a year for sixteen years, with all kinds of horses and teams, and had never met with an accident, and had never heard of one happening on said road; that the mountain on the upper side always slipped after a heavy rain, but the slips were always cleared away by parties in charge of the road; that the many slips had forced a curve in the road, throwing the road out close to the river bank; that the road was wide enough for two teams to pass; and that he, in driving, passed other teams at said point, and the road was as smooth as any road he had driven over in the County.

W. A. Bradford, a witness for plaintiffs, proved that he was well acquainted with the road at the point where the accident occurred; saw it next day after the accident; saw marks of the wagon wheel where it went over the bank; that the road was narrow at that point; that it was very difficult for two buggies to pass, but that they might, if they were careful; that he had known the road for forty years; that it had been narrow for five years; that it had been repaired, but not widened, and he

---

v. New York, O. & W. R. Co. 115 N. Y. 584; Vandenburg v. Truax, 4 Denio, 464; Pollett v. Long, 56 N. Y. 200; Webb v. Rome, W. & O. R. Co. 49 N. Y. 420.

But where several buildings in succession take fire, each from another, and burn, the sparks which set the first one being carried past the last one burned, by a strong wind which changed its direction and subsided before the latter buildings took fire, while lack of fire apparatus or ladders prevented extinguishing the fire at the beginning, the burning of the last building is not the proximate result of the setting fire to the first one. Read v. Nichols 7 L. R. A. 130, 118 N. Y. 224.

The falling of a tier of berths in a ship's cabin is the proximate cause of injury to a passenger, who, being dragged from her place of peril by the steward, was dashed on the floor and against a door by the sudden lurch of the vessel. Smith v. British & N. A. R. M. S. Packet Co. 14 Jones & S. 86.

A person who hitched his horses by the lines only is liable for injury caused by their fright and running away. Wagner v. Goldsmith, 78 Ind. 517.

So where a horse, through fright at the fall of ice from a building, started and thereby threw the driver and injured him, the fall of ice is the direct cause of the injury. Smethurst v. Independent Congregational Church, 2 L. R. A. 695, 148 Mass. 261.

The blowing of a steam whistle is the proximate cause of injury to a traveler by a horse frightened by the whistle. Gibbs v. Chicago, M. & St. P. R. Co. 26 Minn. 427.

Where a stringer of a bridge breaks while a person is hauling a steam-boiler and a steam-engine over the bridge, and his horses are injured by the steam escaping from the boiler, the breaking of the bridge is the proximate cause of the escape of the steam and water, and the township is liable for the damage if it has been negligent in respect to the bridge. McKeller v. Monitor Twp. (Mich.) Dec. 28, 1889.

Where by negligence the horses of defendant ran away and collided with a carriage, the occupant of which was killed by being dashed down a depression in the road, there is a direct causal connection between the collision and the killing. Belk v. People, 15 West. Rep. 59, 125 Ill. 584.

The unlawful speed of a train is the proximate cause of a collision at a crossing when, if the train had been going only at lawful speed, the traveler at the crossing would have passed over in safety before it arrived. Winstanley v. Chicago, M. & St. P. R. Co. 72 Wis. 375.

Where the employés of a railroad company placed a torpedo where children were in the habit of passing, and one was injured by its explosion, such negligence was the proximate cause of the injury sustained. Harriman v. Pittsburgh, C. & St. L. R. Co. 9 West. Rep. 438, 45 Ohio St. 11.

An unnecessary act which would probably cause a chain to break, may be regarded as the proximate cause of the injury caused by its breaking. King v. Ohio & M. R. Co. 25 Fed. Rep. 799.

thought it was a very dangerous place, but that there was plenty of room for one vehicle to pass in safety, if the horse did not become frightened; that there was a great deal of pleasure driving on that road.

Dr. Thomas, another witness for the plaintiffs, stated that, a short time before the trial of the cause commenced, he examined the plaintiff Mrs J. W. Smith, and took a measurement of her left arm; that it was three fourths of an inch less in circumference than the right arm,—caused, in his opinion, by an injury.

These, in substance, constitute the facts proven by the plaintiffs; and, under the rulings of this court, we must, in considering the motion for a new trial, reject all of the evidence of the exceptor which is in conflict with that of the plaintiffs, and give full force and effect to the evidence of the plaintiffs. See *Dower* v. *Church*, 21 W. Va. 23.

And the same rule must be applied in considering the propriety of the action of the court upon the motion to exclude the evidence of the plaintiffs. See *Wandling* v. *Straw*, 25 W. Va. 692; *Franklin* v. *Geho*, 30 W. Va. 27.

In determining the question as to whether the court erred in overruling the demurrer filed by the defendant in this case, it is only necessary to call attention to the fact that the demurrer was general; and counsel for the defendant do not insist that there was any defect in the second count. Neither is there any error apparent on the face of said second count, so far as we are able to discover; and, the second count being good, the demurrer, being general, was properly overruled. *Nutter* v. *Sydenstricker*, 11 W. Va. 536.

The serious question, however, which is presented by this case for our consideration and determination, is whether or not the court erred in refusing to exclude the evidence of the plaintiffs from the jury as being insufficient to maintain their suit, or in overruling the motion of the defendant to set aside the verdict of the jury as being contrary to the law and the evidence, and award it a new trial; and, as these rulings involve so nearly the same questions of law and fact, they may be considered together. What was it that caused the damage and injury to the female plaintiff on the day this accident is alleged to have occurred? Her own testimony shows that she had passed over this road two or three times a week for the preceding two years without injury. She was driving a horse that the evidence shows was gentle, and was driving him on the side of the road furthest from the river bank, and no doubt would have passed on as usual if the horse had not become frightened at the calves coming down from the hillside out of some pawpaw bushes, and commenced backing. That she tried to keep her horse in the road; but he was so badly frightened she could not do so, although he was gentle, easily managed and never had become frightened before. The witness Dana fixes the width of the road at that point at eighteen feet, and J. W. Smith at twelve feet. Dividing the difference between these witnesses would make the road fifteen feet. Then the plaintiff, driving at the edge of the road next the hill, was as far from the river bank as she would have been if the road had been thirty feet wide, and she had been driving in the middle of the same; and the horse would have to back the same distance to reach the river bank. In the absence of the calves, then, would the narrowness of the road have injured the plaintiff? This question is answered by the testimony of the witness Dana in detailing his experience for the previous sixteen years in passing over said road two hundred times a year, with all kinds of horses and teams, and without an accident, and also by the experience of the plaintiff herself, in passing over the same road for two years, two or three times a week, with this same horse; she encountered no calves on these many trips, and she met with no accident.

What, then, are we to conclude was the proximate cause of the accident? Was it the narrowness of the road? If such was the case, why had it not occurred many times before?

1 Shearm. & Redf. Neg., § 26, says: "The breach of duty upon which an action is brought must be not only the cause, but the proximate cause, of the damage to the plaintiff. We adhere to this old form of words because while it may not have originally meant what is now intended, it is not immovably identified with any other meaning, and is the form which has been so long in use that its rejection would make nearly all reported cases on the question involved unintelligible. The proximate cause of an event must be understood to be that which, in a natural and continuous sequence, unbroken by any new cause, produces that event, and without which that event would not have occurred." And *note 3:* "If it cannot be said that the result would have inevitably occurred by reason of the defendant's negligence, it cannot be found that it did so occur, and plaintiff has not made out his case."

Applying this law to the facts of this case, can it be said the condition of the road was the proximate cause of the accident or injury complained of? If the use of this road, which had been for years in the same condition, without any accident resulting therefrom, had continued uninterrupted or unbroken by any new cause, such as the calves rushing from the bushes, would we be sanctioned in saying the injury would have resulted? Or can we say that, without the occurrence of that unlooked-for event, the horse would have backed the vehicle over the river bank? The experience of the plaintiff and others for years answers in the negative.

In the case of *Kingsbury* v. *Dedham*, 13 Allen 186, it was held that "an object in a highway with which a traveler does not come in contact or collision, and which is not shown to be an actual incumbrance or obstruction in the way of travel, is not to be deemed a defect for the sole reason that it is of a nature to cause a horse to take fright, in consequence of which he escapes from the control of his driver and causes damage." In this case the horse was frightened by a small pile of gravel in the road.

And in the case of *Cook* v. *Charlestown*, reported in a *note* (p. 190) of the same volume, a horse became frightened at another horse which had dropped dead, and was lying at the side of the street; and the frightened horse started and ran, and the carriage struck a tree and the curbstone at a distance of about 180 feet, throwing the plaintiffs out, and injuring them. There was plenty of room for plaintiffs to pass without coming in contact with the dead horse. Under instructions authorizing them to do so, the jury found damages for the plaintiffs, and the defendant excepted; and the case was reversed upon a writ of error.

In the case of *Titus* v. *Northbridge*, 97 Mass. 265, the court holds "that when a horse, by reason of fright, disease or viciousness, becomes actually uncontrollable, so that his driver cannot stop him, or direct his course, or exercise or regain control over his movements, and in this condition comes upon a defect in a highway, or upon a place which is defective for want of a railing, by which the injury is occasioned, the town is not liable for the injury unless it appears that it would have occurred if the horse had not been so uncontrollable. But a horse is not to be considered uncontrollable that merely shies or starts, or is momentarily not controlled by his driver."

In the case of *Horton* v. *Taunton*, reported in a *note* [p. 266] to *Titus* v. *Northbridge*, *supra*, the facts were somewhat similar to the case under consideration: "A laborer employed by the city had deposited a load of stones within the limits of the highway, and near to, but wholly out of, the traveled portion of it, by the side of a reservoir. . . . The plaintiffs were driving from west to east, and had come within a few feet of these stones when their horse took fright at them, and suddenly began to back, and continued backing until he reached a point beyond the end of the railing west of the brook, and within the thirty-one feet where the bank was unprotected by a railing; and there be backed himself and the wagon over the bank, and the injuries were sustained for which this action was brought. The accident occurred, and all the damage was done, within the limits of the highway. The plaintiffs remained in the wagon, and retained hold of the reins, and used the ordinary means to control the horse and prevent the backing, but without success. Neither the horse nor the wagon came in contact with the stones, . . . nor would the accident have occurred if the horse had not been frightened; and it was agreed that 'the accident would not, probably, have occurred had the railing extended further westward,' and . . . that the want of a railing at the point where the horse backed over the bank was a defect in the highway, and had existed for many months." There was a judgment for plaintiffs in the court below. Chapman, *J.*, delivering the opinion of the court, said: "This case was considered by the court in connection with *Titus* v. *Northbridge*, and the two cases must be governed by the same principle;" and, after briefly reviewing the facts, gave judgment for the defendants.

In the case of *Jackson* v. *Bellevieu*, 30 Wis. 251, the court held as follows: "It is not the duty of towns to provide roads which shall be safe for runaway or unmanageable horses, or such as have escaped from control of their drivers without the fault of the town; and where injuries are sustained under such circumstances, it appearing that otherwise they might not have been sustained, the loss must fall upon the owners. See also *Fogg* v. *Nahant*, 98 Mass. 578, where a carriage was upset by a horse getting his tail over the lines and becoming unmanageable.

The plaintiff, Mrs. Smith, stated that "she tried to keep her horse in the road, but he was so badly frightened she could not do so." She does not, however, state what she did in trying to keep her horse in the road. Jennie Jones, however, the witness for defendant, who swears that she was driving the calves, does tell what Mrs. Smith did, and her evidence cannot be regarded as conflicting with any evidence offered by the plaintiffs, for no other witness tells what Mrs. Smith did. She says: "I was driving two calves, and just as they came up to the horse the horse got scared at the calves, and commenced backing; and Mrs. Smith, who was driving, commenced pulling on the lines, and the horse kept on backing, and the wagon and all went over the bank."

Mrs. Smith was in a situation that would have a tendency to excite a lady. The horse was frightened and backing, and the wagon was near the edge of the bank, which the witnesses speak of as being dangerous; and she may not have preserved that coolness which would enable her to properly manage a horse, although she was accustomed to driving. And pulling on the lines, under all the circumstances, would have a direct tendency to contribute to the result. She, however, says that she could have managed her horse had it not been for the narrowness of the road. This is her opinion; but the horse kept backing, till not only the wagon and occupants, but he, went over the bank after them.

Upon this question, as to the width a county road is required to be maintained and kept in order, it is true our Statute requires that "every road shall be thirty feet wide, unless the county court order it to be of a different width." The order establishing this road does not appear as a part of the record, and it does not appear whether it was ordered to be of a different width or not.

Ang. & D. Highw. § 260, says: "It is not required that towns—at least in the country—should incur the expense of having the whole width of a highway of two or four rods passable safely with wheels on the sides, or even a double track for wheels over all public roads including causeways and bridges. But if the town suffers the traveled part to become widened, or a turnout to exist from the traveled part to a private way over adjoining land with the characteristic marks of a highway, it is bound to keep such places, within the limits of the laying out of the highway, in suitable repair for travel usually passing,"—referring to *Kelsey* v. *Glover*, 15 Vt. 708; *Green* v. *Danby*, 12 Vt. 338; *Cobb* v. *Standish*, 14 Me. 198, and others. He says further: "In many cases, as has been remarked, all the property of the town would be insufficient for that purpose. There may be ledges of rocks, ravines and watercourses in the road; and towns are not expected, in all cases, to bridge the whole width of the road, to fill up ravines or cut down ledges of rock. The most that could be required, in a road so difficult by nature, is that the sides should be in such a state as would admit of the passing of carriages when they meet without unusual delay or trouble. 'If a road,' says Woodbury J., in the case of *Hull* v. *Richmond*, 2 Woodb. & M. 337, 'was on a steep mountain side, or was carried up from the bed of a stream against a steep cliff of rocks, or through a narrow notch or gorge among the hills, a double track would seldom be expected, though places should be made, at no great distance, for persons to turn out entirely, and others where, by each turning out in part, each could safely pass,'" etc.

In the case of *Dickey* v. *Maine Teleg. Co.* 46 Me. 483, the court held that "the law does not require the town, in preparing a highway for travel, ordinarily, to make the traveled path the whole width of the road. Towns are not liable for obstructions on the portions of a highway not constituting the traveled path, and not so connected with it as to affect the traveled portion."

In this case, it is evident the road was a difficult one to keep in proper order. On the one side was the steep river bank, and on the other the hillside, which slipped and encroached upon the road in wet weather; but, notwithstanding these facts, the evidence is that the road was in passable condition, and was wide enough for two teams to pass. All that the road surveyor, under our Statute, is required to do, is that "he shall superintend the county roads and bridges, cause the same to be put in good order and repair, of the proper width, well drained, and to be cleared, and kept clear, of rocks, falling timber, landslides, carcasses of dead animals and other obstructions, and remove all dead timber standing within thirty feet thereof." Code 1887, chap. 43, § 7.

The only one of these requirements which it is claimed was not complied with is the one in regard to the width of the road; and the authorities to which we have referred seem clearly to indicate that this requirement is not always to be complied with, but depends upon the character of the country over which the road is laid out; and, for a road located as this one was, with a steep river bank on one side and a slipping hill-side on the other, we think the evidence shows it was in as good condition as could be expected.

Counsel for the defendant in error quote from 2 Shearm. & Redf. Neg., § 346, as follows: "The general rule is that where two causes combine to produce an injury to a traveler upon a highway, both of which are in their nature proximate,—the one being a culpable defect in the highway and the other some occurrence for which neither party is responsible,—the municipality is liable, provided the injury would not have been sustained but for such defect,"—and quote numerous decisions to sustain said proposition. We do not controvert this proposition; but, under the evidence adduced in this case, we hold that the proximate cause of the plaintiff's injury was the sudden appearance of the calves from the pawpaw bushes, which frightened the horse, and without which the injury to plaintiff would not have resulted; that the narrowness of the road must be regarded as the remote cause, although the plaintiff says "she could have managed the horse had it not been for the narrowness of the road."

There would, however, have been no necessity for managing the horse if the calves had not frightened him. Without that extraneous occurrence, we feel confident the plaintiff would have passed along the road as usual. There was no defect in the road that caused the action of the horse, no hole in the ground left by the supervisor, or pile of stone or lumber placed there by him, that caused the backing, as there was in many of the cases reported. The plaintiff gives it as her opinion that she could have managed the horse but for the narrowness; but can we say, from all the circumstances, the horse would not have backed over the bank if the road had been thirty feet wide? He showed no indication of ceasing to back, but kept on after the wheels went over, and until he went over himself; and I cannot say the result would not have been the same if the road had been thirty feet wide.

In the case of *Phillips* v. *Ritchie County Court*, 31 W. Va. 478, this court held that where the defect or obstruction in the road is merely a remote cause of the injury, and the want of care or negligence of the plaintiff is the direct or proximate cause of the injury, the plaintiff cannot recover.

In the case of *Fawcett* v. *Pittsburg, C. & St. L. R. Co.*, 24 W. Va. 755, this court held that "the cause of an injury, in contemplation of law, is that which immediately produces it as its natural consequence; and therefore, if a party be guilty of a default or act of negligence which would naturally produce an injury to another, but, before such injury actually results, a third person does some act which is the immediate cause of the injury, such third person is alone responsible for the injury." See also the case of *Washington* v. *Baltimore & O. R. Co.* 17 W. Va. 190.

In that case, *Judge* Green, delivering the opinion of the court, quotes from the case of *Louisiana Mut. Ins. Co.* v. *Tweed*, 74 U. S. 7 Wall. 52 [19 L. ed. 67], from the opinion of *Justice* Miller, as follows: "One of the most valuable *criteria* furnished us by these authorities is to ascertain whether any new cause has intervened between the fact accomplished and the alleged cause. If a new force or power has intervened, of itself sufficient to stand as the cause of the misfortune, the other must be considered as too remote."

In my view of the case, neither the instructions asked for by the plaintiff nor defendant were relevant, and they should have been rejected. Disregarding, then, the testimony offered by the defendant, and looking only to the testimony of the plaintiffs for the facts and circumstances of the case, and applying the law thereto, *the judgment of the Circuit Court must be reversed*, and the case remanded; and a new trial is awarded the appellant.

Snyder, *P.*, and **Brannon**, *J.*, concurred; **Lucas**, *J.*, concurred in the syllabus.

MINNESOTA SUPREME COURT.

Andreas M. MILLER, *Appt.*,
v.
Luther MENDENHALL, *Respt.*

(....Minn....)

*1. **The State holds the title to the soil in navigable waters** to low-water mark in trust for the people, and chiefly for the protection of the right of navigation.

2. **The riparian owner is entitled to fill in** and make improvements in the shallow waters in front of his land to the line of navigability, and such improvements in aid of navigation are recognized as a public as well as private benefit. These rights pertain to the use and occupancy of the soil below low-water mark, and are valuable property rights, and the exercise thereof, though subject to state regulation, can only be interfered with by the State for public purposes.

3. **The establishment of a dock** or harbor line in pursuance of legislative authority is to be considered as giving to the owners of the upland the privilege of filling in and building out to such line.

4. **Where the owners of upland, bordering upon the Bay of Superior,** in this State, after the establishment of the dock line, adopted a survey and plan of improvement for the use and occupation to such line of the submerged land abreast of the upland owned by them, in connection with the navigation of the lake,—*Held*, that they might not only possess, occupy and improve the same themselves, in connection with the dry land, but might concede to other parties the same rights within the dock line, and might, by the appropriate covenants and stipulations in the deeds to their grantees of the upland, and of sites used or to be used and improved under low-water mark, obligate each and all to respect and recognize the validity of such grants made in conformity with the general plan of improvement of the premises within the dock line, all such grantees thus becoming a party thereto; and in such case a court of equity will not interpose in favor of a grantee of the upland to set aside prior deeds to grantees of sites in the submerged land.

*Head notes by VANDERBURGH, J.

(April 3, 1890.)

APPEAL by plaintiff from an order of the District Court for St. Louis County sustaining a demurrer to the complaint in an action to have a conveyance of certain land covered by the waters of Duluth Harbor declared of no effect and to remove the alleged cloud thereby cast on plaintiff's title. *Affirmed.*

The facts fully appear in the opinion.

Messrs. **Mahon & Howard,** for appellant:

All lands in the State of Minnesota, lying below low water mark on navigable bays and rivers, belong to the State.

Brisbine v. *St. Paul & S. C. R. Co.* 23 Minn. 114; *Union Depot, S. R. & Transfer Co.* v. *Brunswick*, 31 Minn. 297.

The establishment of a dock line, under au-

NOTE.—*Title to soil below ordinary high-water mark.*

All the soil below high-water mark, within the limits of the State, where the tide ebbs and flows, that is the subject of exclusive property and ownership, belongs to the State, subject only to such lawful grants of such soil as may have heretofore been made. Hess v. Muir, 5 Cent. Rep. 585, 65 Md. 601.

But this soil is held by the State, not only subject to, but in some sense in trust for, the enjoyment of certain public rights, among which is the common liberty of taking fish, as well shell-fish as floating fish. *Ibid.*; Smith v. Maryland, 59 U. S. 18 How. 71 (15 L. ed. 269); Martin v. Waddell, 41 U. S. 16 Pet. 367 (10 L. ed. 997); Den v. Jersey Co. 56 U. S. 15 How. 426 (14 L. ed. 757); Corfield v. Coryell, 4 Wash. C. C. 376; Fleet v. Hegeman, 14 Wend. 42; Arnold v. Mundy, 6 N. J. L. 1; Parker v. Cutler Milldam Co. 20 Me. 353; Peck v. Lockwood, 5 Day, 22; Weston v. Sampson, 8 Cush. 347; 1 Vattel, chap. 20, § 246.

The State succeeds to the ownership of channels, and lands under them, formed by gradual encroachment of the sea, in case of permanent acquisition by the sea; but when the water disappears, the proprietorship returns to the original owner, without reference to the lapse of time. Mulry v. Norton, 1 Cent. Rep. 748, 100 N. Y. 424.

The sovereign succeeds to the ownership of such islands only as are originally created in tideways outside the boundaries of individual ownership. *Ibid.*

Title to land under water, and to the shore below ordinary high-water mark, in navigable rivers and arms of the sea, was, by common law, vested in the sovereign. Barney v. Keokuk, 94 U. S. 324 (24 L. ed. 224); Smith v. Maryland, *supra*; Pollard v. Hagan, 44 U. S. 3 How. 212 (11 L. ed. 565); Goodtitle v. Kibbe, 50 U. S. 9 How. 471 (13 L. ed. 220); Teschemacher v. Thompson, 18 Cal. 11; People v. Davidson, 30 Cal. 379; State v. Sargent, 45 Conn. 358; Com. v. Alger, 7 Cush. 53; Weston v. Sampson, 8 Cush. 347; Com. v. Roxbury, 9 Gray, 451; Gough v. Bell, 22 N. J. L. 441; Bell v. Gough, 23 N. J. L. 624; Stevens v. Paterson & N. R. Co. 34 N. J. L. 532; Providence Steam Engine Co. v. Providence & S. Steamship Co. 12 R. I. 348; Galveston v. Menard, 23 Tex. 349; 3 Kent, Com. 427; 1 Bl. Com. 110, 264; Hale, De Jure Mar. chap. 4.

In England only tide-waters were regarded as navigable. This rule has been adopted in many of the States of this country; and in them the public title to beds and shores of navigable streams is confined to tide-waters. Barney v. Keokuk, *supra*.

Since the decision in The Genesee Chief, in 1851 (53 U.S. 12 How. 443, 13 L. ed. 1058), declaring all the great lakes and rivers of the country navigable that are really such, there is no longer any reason for thus restricting the title of the State except as a change might interfere with vested rights and established rules of property. *Ibid.*

In Iowa the true rule has been adopted, and it is held that the bed of the Mississippi River and its banks to high-water mark belong to the State, and that the title of a riparian proprietor extends only to that line. *Ibid.*; Renwick v. Davenport & N. W. R. R. Co. 49 Iowa, 664.

This rule applies to land bounded upon the river generally. Barney v. Keokuk, *supra*.

Public authorities have the right, in Iowa, to build wharves and levees on the bank of the Mississippi below high-water mark,—the title below that line being in the State,—and make other improvements thereon necessary to navigation or public passage by railways or otherwise, without

See also 8 L. R. A. 550; 13 L. R. A. 411, 590; 18 L. R. A. 668; 21 L. R. A. 62; 22 L. R. A. 736; 29 L. R. A. 539; 30 L. R. A. 497; 34 L. R. A. 184; 38 L. R. A. 606.

thority of the Legislature, cannot be regarded as in any way operating as a conveyance from the State to the riparian proprietor of any title, interest or estate in the space between the shore and the dock line as established. The title to the bank and that to the submerged land remain precisely as they were before the dock line was established.

Gould, Waters, § 188; *Wetmore* v. *Brooklyn Gas Light Co.* 42 N. Y. 384; *Atty-Gen.* v. *Hudson Tunnel R. Co.* 27 N. J. Eq. 176; *Boston & H. Steamboat Co.* v. *Munson*, 117 Mass. 34; *People* v. *Broadway Wharf Co.* 31 Cal. 33; *Dana* v. *Jackson Street Wharf Co.* 31 Cal. 118; *Kisling* v. *Johnson*, 13 Cal. 57; *Schurmeier* v. *St. Paul & P. R. Co.* 10 Minn. 82; *St. Paul & P. R. Co.* v. *Schurmeier*, 74 U. S. 7 Wall. 272, 287 (19 L. ed. 74, 78); *McManus* v. *Carmichael*, 3 Iowa, 1; *Champlain & St. L. R. Co.* v. *Valentine*, 19 Barb. 484.

This case falls within the ruling of this court in *Lake Superior Land Co.* v. *Emerson*, 38 Minn. 406, which holds that the riparian right belonging to the owner of the shore is a mere natural right. It exists *jure naturæ*. It is a right incident to the use of land. It follows the ownership and use of the bank and cannot be severed from the abutting land.

For these reasons a deed of conveyance by the owner of the shore, of the submerged land in front of his premises, is inoperative. It passes no estate or interest in land.

Lake Superior Land Co. v. *Emerson*, 38 Minn. 406; *Hanford* v. *St. Paul & D. R. Co.* (Minn.) June 10, 1889.

It is doubtful whether the covenant for title would bar the Improvement Company itself, should it attempt to assert, as against its grantee, the riparian right incident to other land owned by it.

Bliss v. *Kennedy*, 43 Ill. 67; *Brigham* v. *Smith*, 4 Gray, 297.

Covenants for title in a deed cannot operate against the assigns of the covenantor even when named, excepting in the one case of a lease.

Rawle, Covenants for Title, § 313.

Where the truth appears upon the deed or instrument, a party shall not be estopped from taking advantage of it even to the extent of showing that the grantor had nothing to grant.

Pelletreau v. *Jackson*, 11 Wend. 110, 118; *Wheelock* v. *Henshaw*, 19 Pick. 341; *Sinclair* v. *Jackson*, 8 Cow. 543; 2 Devlin, Deeds, § 1278.

To charge land with the burden of a covenant, there must be some privity of estate between the covenantee and the assignee of the lands so burdened or he will not be charged with the covenant.

Brewer v. *Marshall*, 18 N. J. Eq. 337; *National Union Bank* v. *Segur*, 39 N. J. L. 173, 184; *Van Rensselaer* v. *Smith*, 27 Barb. 104, 146; *Plymouth* v. *Carver*, 16 Pick. 183; *Norcross* v. *James*, 1 New Eng. Rep. 327, 140 Mass. 188; *Hurd* v. *Curtis*, 19 Pick. 459; *Bliss* v. *Kennedy*, 43 Ill. 67; *Corning* v. *Troy Iron & Nail Factory* 40 N. Y. 191.

The benefits of these covenants and agreements will not at law accrue or pass to the defendant. They do not run with the land attempted to be conveyed to him.

Am. *note* to *Spencer's Case*, 1 Smith, Lead.

---

the assent of the adjacent proprietor, and without making him compensation. *Ibid.*

On the admission of a new State into the Union, the "shore" or tide lands therein not disposed of by the United States prior thereto become the property of the State. Case v. Loftus (Or.) 5 L. R. A. 684, 39 Fed. Rep. 730.

Upon admission the State of Illinois became entitled to and possessed of all the rights of dominion which belonged to the original States. Huse v. Glover, 119 U. S. 543 (30 L. ed. 487).

The abutting owner has a right of access from his land to the water, and may, subject to the power of the Legislature, erect and maintain a private wharf for his own convenience, so long as he does not materially interfere with the rights of the general public. Case v. Loftus, *supra.*

The water front on the bay of "Florida Promenade"—a public park in the City of Apalachicola, Florida,—was, at the time of the dedication, vested in the United States, but on the admission of Florida as a State, became vested in her. Ruge v. Apalachicola Oyster Canning & Fish Co. (Fla.) Aug. 21, 1889.

The title to the shores of tide waters in this State has since been devested by statute in favor of littoral owners. Geiger v. Filor, 8 Fla. 325; Alden v. Pinney, 12 Fla. 348.

The submerged lands of a bay, not disposed of by the State, are her property, and are not subject to disposition by the adjoining land owner. Ruge v. Apalachicola Oyster Canning & Fish Co. *supra.*

Under the New Jersey Riparian Laws, lands below the high-water mark of navigable waters belong to the State. Hoboken v. Pennsylvania R. Co. 124 U. S. 656 (31 L. ed. 543).

The Colonial patents to Long Island towns vested in them the title to the soil under the waters of the bays within the bounds of the patents. Roe v. Strong, 10 Cent. Rep. 33, 107 N. Y. 350; Brookhaven v. Strong, 60 N. Y. 56; People v. Schermerhorn, 19 Barb. 540.

Private individuals asserting title to a part of the shore within such bonds must establish the devestiture of the title of the town and its acquisition by them. Roe v. Strong, 10 Cent. Rep. 33, 107 N. Y. 350.

The State may either sell or convey its title to a riparian owner or his assigns, or, in case of their neglect to take from the State its grants on the terms offered them, to a stranger who, succeeding to its title, has no relation to the adjacent riparian owner, except that of common boundary. Hoboken v. Pennsylvania R. Co. *supra.*

Grantees from the State have exclusive possession of the premises against an adverse claim of a municipality to an easement over them by virtue of a dedication of the streets to high-water mark by a former proprietor of the premises to whose rights such grantees have succeeded. *Ibid.*; Com. v. Alger, 7 Cush. 53; Com. v. Roxbury, 9 Gray, 451; Arnold v. Mundy, 6 N. J. L. 1; Bell v. Gough, 23 N. J. L. 624; Atty-Gen. v. Delaware & B. B. R. Co. 27 N. J. Eq. 1, 631; Atty-Gen. v. Hudson Tunnel R. Co. Id. 176.

Littoral owner, right to soil to low-water mark.

The proprietor of land on navigable water has an exclusive right to the soil between high and low water mark, for the purpose of erecting wharves and stores thereon. Ladies Seamen's Friends Society v. Halstead, 58 Conn. 144.

Mud flats on a seashore, between high and low water mark, may be used for any purpose which does not interfere with navigation. *Ibid.*

The owner may build upon and inclose it. But while covered with the sea, the public have the right

Cas. 8th Am. ed. 174; *Martin* v. *Drinan*, 128 Mass. 515.

Mr. **Walter Ayers**, for respondent:

So far as anything but the pure legal title is concerned, lands under water in this State to the point of navigability are absolutely the property of the shore owner.

Tuck v *Olds*, 29 Fed. Rep. 738.

The owner of city lots bounded on navigable streams, like the owner of any other lands thus bounded, may limit his conveyance thereof within specific limits, if he shall so choose.

Watson v. *Peters*, 26 Mich. 508.

The ownership of the land under the water will become severed from the land upon the bank adjacent when such is the manifest intent.

Smith v. *Ford*, 48 Wis. 115; *Barker* v. *Bates*, 13 Pick. 255, 23 Am. Dec. 678.

The covenant entered into by plaintiff runs with his land, even under the strict legal doctrine.

Shaber v. *St. Paul Water Co.* 30 Minn. 179; *Kettle River R. Co.* v. *Eastern R. Co.* (Minn.) Oct. 4, 1889.

Where it distinctly appears in a conveyance, either by a recital, an admission, a covenant or otherwise, that the parties actually intend to convey and to receive reciprocally a certain estate, they are estopped from denying the operation of the deed according to its intent.

Bayley v. *McCoy*, 8 Or. 259; *Clark* v. *Baker*, 14 Cal. 627; 2 Herman, Estoppel, §§ 642, 648, 670.

Vanderburgh, *J.*, delivered the opinion of the court:

This case involves the consideration of the riparian rights of the owners of lands abutting upon the Duluth Harbor or Bay of Superior, in the shoals or land covered by water between low-water mark and the deep or navigable waters, and within the dock or harbor line established by the authority of the Legislature. These waters are within the jurisdiction of the state and federal governments, and the State holds the title to low-water mark in its sovereign capacity, in trust for the people, for the purpose chiefly of protecting the rights of navigation. But, though the title is nominally in the State, the common right of the people is limited to what is of public use for the purposes of navigation and fishery; and the riparian owners are permitted to enjoy the remaining rights and privileges in the soil under water beyond their strict boundary lines, after conceding to the State all the public rights. Gould, Waters, § 168.

The right of access and communication with the navigable waters, which pertain peculiarly to the ownership of the upland, in order to be available and of practical use, necessarily includes the right to fill in and to build wharves and other structures in the shallow water in front of such land, and below low-water mark, and the exercise of such rights, though subject to state regulation, can only be interfered with for public purposes; and such improvements are encouraged, because they are in the general

to use it for purposes of navigation. Boston v. Lecraw, 58 U. S. 17 How. 426 (15 L. ed. 118).

The State also, to prevent encroachments in the harbors, may establish lines, and limit this power of the owner over his own property. *Ibid.*

The riparian owner of land only has the right, under North Carolina Entry Laws, to enter the water front up to deep water, for the purpose of erecting a wharf; and in such case, the title to the land passes. Gregory v. Forbes, 96 N. C. 77.

The State can grant land under navigable water for wharf purposes only; and county commissioners have no power to confer upon a party a right to build a wharf upon such land for the purpose of a public road. *Ibid.*

By N. Y. Laws 1875, chap. 249, the dock department of New York City was given authority not previously possessed to authorize the erection of sheds on East River piers, and previous licenses were legalized. People v. Baltimore & O. R. Co. 117 N. Y. 150.

Riparian owners of land on East River, in Brooklyn, have a superior right to build wharves and collect tolls, and may collect damages for a wrongful interference with their rights. Steers v. Brooklyn, 1 Cent. Rep. 798, 101 N. Y. 51.

A riparian proprietor whose land is bounded by a navigable river has the right of access to the navigable part of the river, and the right to make a landing, wharf or pier for his own use or for the use of the public. Yates v. Milwaukee, 77 U. S. 10 Wall. 497 (19 L. ed. 984); St. Paul & P. R. Co. v. Schurmeier, 74 U. S. 7 Wall. 272 (19 L. ed. 74).

He has the right to use the shore in front of his land for any purpose not inconsistent with the rights of the public. Parker v. West Coast Packing Co. 5 L. R. A. 61, 17 Or. 510; Boston v. Lecraw, *supra.*

He may maintain a dock along the shore and extending the necessary distance into the water; and when thus erected, the dock is an appurtenance of the real estate. Tuck v. Olds, 29 Fed. Rep. 738.

Right to construct piers, wharves, etc.

Piers or landing places, and even wharves, may be private or public, although the property may be in an individual owner. Dutton v. Strong, 66 U. S. 1 Black, 23 (17 L. ed. 29).

The owner may have the right to their exclusive enjoyment, and may construct them for his own exclusive use or benefit. *Ibid.*

His right is property of which the owner can be deprived only if necessary that it be taken for the public good, upon due compensation. Yates v. Milwaukee, 77 U. S. 10 Wall. 497 (19 L. ed. 984).

But if erected without other authority than his mere ownership, the structures are unlawful and he will be liable for damages caused thereby. Atlee v. Northwestern Union Packet Co. 88 U. S. 21 Wall. 389 (22 L. ed. 619).

Wharves and permanent piers constructed by the riparian proprietor on the shores of navigable rivers, bays and arms of the sea, or on the lakes, where they do not extend below low-water mark, are not a nuisance, unless they are an obstruction to navigation. Dutton v. Strong, *supra.*

Such structures differ materially from wharves or piers made to aid navigation, and regulated by city or town ordinances, or by statutes or other competent authority, and from piers built for railroad bridges across navigable streams, which are authorized by Acts of Congress or statutes of the States. Atlee v. Northwestern Union Packet Co. *supra.*

A railroad company under the power of eminent domain, granted by the State, cannot appropriate his pier to its own use without compensating him. Davenport & N. W. R. Co. v. Renwick, 102 U. S. 180 (26 L. ed. 51).

Right subject to control.

The State of California did not, by granting the use of the water front to the City of San Francisco, surrender control of the navigable waters of the

interest of navigation and commerce, and are a public as well as a private benefit.

In *Dutton* v. *Strong*, 66 U. S. 1 Black, 32 [17 L. ed. 32], it is said that, "wherever the water is too shoal to be navigable, there is the same necessity for such erections for lake navigation as in the bays and arms of the sea; and where that necessity exists it is difficult to see any reason for denying to the adjacent owner the right to supply it."

And in *Yates* v. *Milwaukee*, 77 U. S. 10 Wall. 497 [19 L. ed. 984], it is held broadly that these riparian privileges are to be treated as valuable property rights, which cannot be taken or interfered with for public use without compensation. *Union Depot, S. R. & Transfer Co.* v. *Brunswick*, 31 Minn. 301.

And, if a stranger makes a filling or an obstruction in the waters in front of his land, the owner of the adjacent upland may enjoin its continuance, or recover in trespass, if not in ejectment.

In the case before us the complaint shows that a corporation known as the "Duluth Improvement Company" was the owner of a large tract of land bordering upon the waters of Duluth Harbor, which communicates with Lake Superior, and is navigable for large boats and vessels. In front of this land, and for a considerable distance into the bay, the water is shallow, and not navigable; and, in pursuance of legislative authority, a dock or harbor line had been duly established by the City of Duluth, extending in front of, and at a distance of a thousand feet or more from, the low-water mark on the tract of land referred to. Thereafter the Improvement Company caused this land, together with the land in front thereof under water, out to the dock line, to be surveyed and platted into lots and blocks, piers, slips, avenues and streets, and caused a plat thereof to be duly made and recorded under the name of the "Bay Front Division of Duluth," and thereafter proceeded to convey divers lots and parcels of the platted land, as well land under water as the dry land, to divers persons, by reference to the recorded plat, and by conveyances of the form set out in the complaint, and containing special covenants and stipulations, as hereinafter mentioned. The complaint further proceeds as follows: "That on or about the 27th day of June, 1887, the said Duluth Improvement Company sold and conveyed to Luther Mendenhall, defendant herein, by deed duly executed, a copy whereof is hereto annexed and made a part of this complaint, the following described tract or parcel of land, the same being a part of the land hereinabove referred to, to wit: All that part of block twenty-seven (27) in the Bay Front Division of Duluth, first re-arrangement, according to the recorded plat thereof, that lies easterly of a

---

bay and the right to erect proper wharves and use them. Payne v. English, 79 Cal. 540.

By the common law of Massachusetts, the grantee of land on navigable waters where the tide ebbs and flows is owner of the soil between high and low water mark. Boston v. Lecraw, 58 U. S. 17 How. 426 (15 L. ed. 118).

The Act of 1806, chap. 18, operates as a legislative grant of the interest in the soil below low water and confers the right to lot owners on Acushnet River to build wharves. Hamlin v. Pairpoint Mfg. Co. 2 New Eng. Rep. 143, 141 Mass. 51.

The private interest in submerged soil at the bottom of a river, which had been granted to a person by a State, is subject to the paramount right of the public to use the river for navigation, and of the United States, in the regulation of commerce and navigation. Hawkins Point Lighthouse Case, 39 Fed. Rep. 77.

A State Legislature may authorize the building of a bridge or other structure tending to obstruct the navigation of a navigable river which is altogether within its own boundary; and it is only when Congress, by virtue of the constitutional provision, acts as to such obstructions, that its will must be obeyed so far as may be necessary to insure free navigation. Green & B. R. Nav. Co. v. Chesapeake, O. & S. W. R. Co. (Ky.) 2 L. R. A. 540, 2 Inters. Com. Rep. 515.

A license under the New Jersey Wharf Act confers no right on licensee, unless he owns the upland abutting on tide-water. New Jersey Z. & I. Co. v. Morris Canal & Bkg. Co. 13 Cent. Rep. 342, 44 N. J. Eq. 398.

The owner of the land abutting on the stream has a license to fill in and dock out to such extent as does not interfere with public rights. *Ibid.*

Under the California statutes, a title to a lot on the Bay of San Francisco was in subordination to the control, by the City of San Francisco, over the space immediately beyond the line of the water-front, and to the right of the State to regulate the construction of wharves and other improvements; and his erection of a wharf was an encroachment on the soil of the State. *Ibid.*; Weber v. State Harbor Comrs. 85 U. S. 18 Wall. 57 (21 L. ed. 798).

Public authorities have the right, in Iowa, to build wharves and levees on the bank of the Mississippi below high-water mark, and make other improvements thereon necessary to navigation or public passage by railways or otherwise, without the assent of the adjacent proprietor, and without making him compensation. Barney v. Keokuk, 94 U. S. 324 (24 L. ed. 224).

The compact between Virginia and Maryland of 1785 secured to their citizens "the privilege of making and carrying out wharves" on the shores of the Potomac only so far as they were "adjoining their lands." Potomac Steamboat Co. v. Upper Potomac Steamboat Co. 109 U. S. 672 (27 L. ed. 1070).

Subject to the exceptions established by paramount law, the City of New Orleans has the right of building levees and wharves on the banks of the Mississippi River, within its corporate limits, for the public utility. New Orleans, M. & T. R. Co. v. Ellerman, 105 U. S. 166 (26 L. ed. 1015).

Riparian rights, how conferred. See *notes* to Haines v. Hall (Or.) 3 L. R. A. 609; Fulmer v. Williams (Pa.) 1 L. R. A. 603; Brooks v. Cedar Brook & S. C. R. Imp. Co. (Me.) 7 L. R. A. 460.

Alienation of right.

The title to the upland bordering on a seashore, and the appurtenant rights in the shore and the mud flats between high and low water mark, are separable, and either may be conveyed without the other. Ladies Seamen's Friends Society v. Halstead, 58 Conn. 144.

A riparian owner conveying land may reserve to himself the right to build wharves out into the water from such land. Parker v. West Coast Packing Co. 5 L. R. A. 61, 17 Or. 510.

A conveyance of land on a river bank passes all the land between high-water mark and the ordinary stage; and a survey which merely goes to high-water mark is not correct. Hess v. Cheney, 83 Ala. 251.

line through said block, parallel with and at equal distances from the lines dividing said block from block twenty-six (26), and from block twenty-eight (28) in said division. That Said Duluth Improvement Company, on or about the 30th day of July, 1887, sold and conveyed to plaintiff, by deed duly executed, and identical in form with and containing the same covenants as the deed to Luther Mendenhall, hereinabove referred to, the following described tract or parcel of land, being a part of the land hereinabove referred to, to wit: All that part of block twenty-seven (27) in the Bay Front Division of Duluth, first re-arrangement, according to the recorded plat thereof, that lies westerly of a line through said block parallel with and at equal distance from the lines dividing said block from block twenty-six (26), and from block twenty-eight (28), in said division, saving and excepting so much of said tract as lies within one hundred (100) feet of the southerly boundary line thereof, which said property so excepted is hereby dedicated for the perpetual use of a slip or water-way for the use and benefit of the owners and occupants of property abutting thereon. Plaintiff further alleges that the greater part of said block 27, so as aforesaid conveyed to plaintiff by the Duluth Improvement Company, consisted of dry land and shore, and that the same extended to the low-water mark on said bay. That all of that part of said block 27, so as aforesaid conveyed to Luther Mendenhall by said Duluth Improvement Company, lies under the water of the bay, beyond the low-water mark of said bay, and in front of and between that part of said block 27 so as aforesaid conveyed to plaintiff, and said established dock or wharf line upon said Duluth Harbor. That the said Luther Mendenhall claims title to the part of said block 27 so as aforesaid conveyed to him by the Duluth Improvement Company under and by virtue of said deed of conveyance to him, and claims the right to cut off and exclude plaintiff from access to the navigable waters of said bay over and across his part of that block, and denies the right of the plaintiff to dock out or make improvements in front of his part of the block to the established dock line, and claims and asserts that all the riparian rights to which plaintiff would be entitled, as owner of the shore along said harbor, are absolutely cut off and limited by the conveyance so as aforesaid made to him, said Mendenhall, as also by the conveyance made to the plaintiff."

Following the descriptions in the deeds to these parties, and to other grantees of the platted lands above referred to, we find the following clauses, covenants and stipulations, viz.: "Together with all the hereditaments thereunto belonging, or in anywise appertaining, but subject, nevertheless, to the reservations, exceptions and conditions of this instrument. And the said party of the first part, for itself, its successors and assigns, does covenant with the said party of the second part, his heirs and assigns, that it has not made, done, executed or suffered any act or thing whatsoever, whereby the above-described premises, or any part thereof, now are, or at any time hereafter shall or may become, imperiled, charged or incumbered in any manner whatsoever; and the title to the above-granted premises, against all persons lawfully claiming the same from or under it, the said party of the first part will forever warrant and defend. It being the intention hereby to vest in the said party of the second part, his heirs and assigns, forever, the exclusive right to use, occupy and enjoy the space covered by the above-mentioned lots, as laid down upon the said recorded plat of said Bay Front Division of Duluth, first re-arrangement, and to estop the party of the first part, its successors and assigns, from having or claiming the use or occupancy of said space by virtue of riparian ownership or otherwise. This conveyance is and shall be construed as a contract between the parties hereto. The character and extent of the premises, and the rights and privileges thereunto appertaining, whether riparian or other rights, shall be determined solely by reference to the plat of said division, and no rights or privileges of any kind shall pass by this conveyance except such as said plat shows to be appurtenant to the premises herein conveyed. The said party of the second part thereby estops himself, his heirs and assigns, from asserting or claiming that the lots or blocks, if any are shown on said plat, between the premises herein conveyed and the established dock line along the northerly side of the Bay or Harbor of Duluth, are not land, and estops himself from claiming or asserting any rights or privileges under this grant in any part of the territory covered by said plat, except such as would solely by reference to said plat vest in him."

The case comes here upon appeal from an order sustaining a demurrer to the complaint. In connection with the general statement in respect to the rights of riparian owners already made, we are to consider the additional fact of the establishment of the dock or harbor line, and the effect of the restrictive covenants in the deeds to the respective parties. The court will take notice of the extensive commerce and great shipping interests which must be accommodated in the Duluth Harbor, and which will require corresponding facilities in the way of local improvements, which must be made in great measure by private enterprise; and in this case we may assume that the plan adopted by the Duluth Improvement Company, in the survey and plat of the submerged land in connection with the upland, was one which was suitable and proper for the improvement and occupation of the same in the interests of navigation, so as to subserve the public as well as private interests. The action of the State, through the Legislature, in establishing the dock lines, is to be construed in connection with the established doctrine of riparian rights of which we have spoken, and the practical use permitted and necessarily made by riparian owners of land under water in front of the dry or upland.

In *Aborn* v. *Smith*, 12 R. I. 373, it is said by the court that the owners of the upland are in such cases impliedly permitted to carry the upland forward to the harbor line, so that each owner will occupy the part abreast his own land.

In *Gerhard* v. *Seekonk River Bridge Comrs.*, 15 R. I. 334, 2 New Eng. Rep. 619, and in *Engs* v. *Peckham*, 11 R. I. 223, 224, it is held to be a permission and invitation by the State to the riparian owner to fill out and incorporate the flats with his upland to the line. *Eldridge* v. *Cowell*, 4 Cal. 80.

In *Fitchburg R. Co.* v. *Boston & M. R. Co.*, 3 Cush. 71, it appeared that the Legislature had established a harbor line for Boston Harbor, but prohibiting the extension of the existing wharves to the line without legislative permission. Afterwards the Legislature passed an Act authorizing the owners of certain wharves to extend them out to the line. This Act was held to be a grant, and not a mere revocable license (page 87); and in *Hamlin* v. *Pairpoint Mfg. Co.*, 141 Mass. 57, 2 New Eng. Rep. 148, a legislative authority to extend wharves to the channel of a river was held equivalent to a grant of a possessory title, if not an absolute interest in the soil. In *Norfolk* v. *Cooke*, 27 Gratt. 438, the court treats the right to use and occupy the land within such lines with wharves, etc., as a qualified proprietary interest in the soil, sufficient to support an action for the possession. *Guy* v. *Hermance*, 5 Cal. 74; *Power* v. *Tazewell*, 25 Gratt. 786.

But the title of the State is not extinguished by such legislative action merely. In this country the generally accepted doctrine is that the *jus privatum* passes to the owner of the adjacent lands, and in this State extends to low-water mark, with the accompanying riparian rights, while the *jus publicum* belongs to the State, which holds the title to the soil under the water as trustee. "The sovereign is trustee for the public, and the use of navigable waters is inalienable." 3 Kent, Com. 427. See *Com.* v. *Alger*, 7 Cush. 89, 93.

The State is authorized to regulate the exercise of riparian rights in the interests of the public, and may also make concessions to private owners of possessory rights in the soil of navigable waters, the effect of which will be to give them private and exclusive rights equivalent to a grant. Gould, Waters, §§ 138-140.

While the public right of navigation and fishery may not be extinguished until the waters are excluded, yet after the submerged land is filled or occupied the riparian owner will have the exclusive right of possession, and the entire beneficial interest; and whether his dominion would be absolute, and his title indefeasible as against the State, is not necessary to inquire. *Union Depot, S. R. & Transfer Co.* v. *Brunswick*, *supra*.

The action of the Legislature in establishing a harbor line is to be construed as a regulation of the exercise of the riparian right. It settles the line of navigability, above which the State will not interfere; and is an implied concession of the right to build, possess and occupy to the established line, which amounts practically to a qualified possessory title. 141 Mass. 57, *supra*.

The importance and substantial character of these rights are recognized by the courts, and there is a growing tendency in different directions to give effect to contracts and grants in respect to riparian occupancy and improvements. *Norfolk* v. *Cooke*, 27 Gratt. 436; *Parker* v. *West Coast Packing Co.* 17 Or. 515, 5 L. R. A. 61.

It is true the right of access and communication with the navigable waters belongs exclusively to the riparian owner, except with his permission. But if in the case of a railway corporation he may, for a consideration, concede the right to occupy with its road-bed the land under the shore, and obstruct such communication by a valid contract, which we presume will not be questioned, why may he not contract with natural persons to grant to them the right of possession and occupancy of building sites within the dock line for wharves or elevators, for use in connection with navigation, or such other purposes (the State not objecting), as the grantees may be advised, with right of way, if need be, over his land, or, as in this case, impliedly over streets laid over the same as designated in the plat and dedicated to the public use? In many instances, however, such right of entry or easement of passage may be found entirely unnecessary, the occupant having other means of reaching the *locus in quo*. If the riparian owner may make such improvements, and afterwards grant and convey his possessory title, or contract to do so, the courts ought not to stand upon so narrow a distinction as that he may not bind himself by contract that another may have and enjoy the same possessory rights in a particular site or lot which he has in it; for his right is not a mere revocable license, though held in subordination to the public interest, and subject to some restraint for the general good as other property may be, though differently situated. *Com.* v. *Alger*, *supra*, 95.

There can be no doubt, we think, that a lease of such property would be operative between the parties, and a subsequent purchaser of the upland, with notice and expressly subject thereto, would also be bound to respect the lessee's rights.

In reference to a lease of a mill-site in the bed of the Mississippi River (at a place not navigable), this court says in *St. Anthony Falls Water Power Co.* v. *Morrison*, 12 Minn. 254 (Gil. 162): "It is not for a private individual, under a pretense of vindicating the abstract rights of the public, to set up the intrusion, in a private and civil action, for the purpose of repudiating his own solemn contract obligations."

In this case the respondent does not find it necessary to question the correctness of the decision in the case of *Lake Superior Land Co.* v. *Emerson*, 38 Minn. 406, because there the grantor simply undertook to convey a strict legal title, which until the land was reclaimed could not be the subject of transfer, and we are not called on to distinguish that case. But this case is rested upon the contract of the parties, incorporated in the several deeds, in which it will be seen the grantor covenants that "the grantees and their assigns shall have the exclusive right to use, occupy and enjoy the space covered by the lots as described in the deed, and as identified by the plat, and covenants to estop the company and its assigns from having or claiming the use and occupancy of such space by virtue of riparian ownership or otherwise." Here there is an express waiver and concession of the grantor's riparian rights in the premises, and consent to the use and occupancy thereof, so as to cut off its access and communication with deep water, except in accordance with the general plan of improvement indicated by the plat. And this is also made a part of plaintiff's contract, and undoubtedly entered into and affected the consideration of the deed to him. He thereby made himself a party to the general plan and arrangement for the improvement and disposition of the property, in which there was nothing unlawful. He took with notice of defendant's deed. We see no reason why he should be relieved from the legitimate operation of these covenants, or why a court of equity should interpose to cancel or declare null and void the defendant's deed, in order to give the plaintiff rights he has expressly agreed to waive.

Order affirmed.

KENTUCKY COURT OF APPEALS.

James C. MURRAY, *Appt.*,
v.
James A. MURRAY *et al.*, Exrs., etc., of Henry H. Murray, Deceased.

(....Ky.....)

1. **A conveyance on the eve of marriage,** to be regarded in equity as a fraud upon the legal rights of the intended wife, and consequently not binding upon her, must be made without her consent or knowledge.

2. **The fact that a conveyance,** made by a man with the consent of his intended wife, reserved a life estate in himself, is not a matter of which she can complain.

3. **A prima facie case of fraud on a wife's marital rights** in her husband's estate exists where, without her knowledge, he gives, either before or after marriage, all or the greater portion of his property to his children by a former marriage.

(March 8, 1890.)

APPEAL by complainant from a judgment of the Circuit Court for Franklin County settling her rights in her deceased husband's estate in an action brought for the settlement of such estate, and to set aside certain conveyances made by him upon the alleged ground that they were in fraud of her marital rights. *Reversed.*

The facts are sufficiently stated in the opinion.

Messrs. **John W. Rodman** and **George C. Drane,** for appellant:

Voluntary conveyances, or gifts by the husband to his children or others of all or the bulk of his estate pending a marriage treaty or during the marriage without the knowledge or concurrence of the wife, will be presumed to be fraudulent and the *onus* is upon the grantees or donees, in a controversy with the widow, to show that no fraud was intended or practiced against her.

Fennessey v. *Fennessey*, 84 Ky. 519.

When such a gift is made with, and for, the purpose of defrauding the wife, it will be set aside to the extent it may affect her rights as widow.

Manikee v. *Beard*, 85 Ky. 20. See 2 Bishop, Married Women, § 351; *Davis* v. *Davis*, 5 Mo. 189; *Stone* v. *Stone*, 18 Mo. 389; *Tucker* v. *Tucker*, 29 Mo. 350; *Hays* v. *Henry*, 1 Md. Ch. 337; *Smith* v. *Smith*, 6 N. J. Eq. 521; *Dunnock* v. *Dunnock*, 3 Md. Ch. 140; *Thayer* v. *Thayer*, 14 Vt. 122; *Dearmond* v. *Dearmond*, 10 Ind. 194.

Messrs. **William Lindsay** and **John B. Lindsley** for appellees.

Holt, *J.*, delivered the opinion of the court:

In May, 1882, the appellant, Jane C. Murray, then Jane C. Jillson, first met Henry H. Murray. He was then a widower for the second time. During the summer of that year they became engaged to marry, the Christmas following being the time fixed for the consummation of the agreement. It was, however, postponed from time to time, at his instance, and upon one excuse or the other, until February 17, 1884, when they were married. He had three children living, to wit, William H. Murray by his first wife, and James A. and John W. Murray by his second wife. When he and the appellant became engaged, he was a gentleman of considerable fortune, being worth in lands and personalty probably not far from $70,000. This was then known to her. They lived together until December, 1886, when he died. In April, 1887, the appellant brought this action, seeking a settlement of his estate, and the cancellation, as to herself, of certain conveyances and gifts by him to his three sons, upon the ground that they were in fraud of her marital rights. Subsequent to their engagement to marry, and on August 17, 1882, he conveyed to his sons James A. and John W. Murray four houses and lots worth $4,000 or $5,000. It is conceded, however, in argument by appellant's counsel, that the consideration recited in the conveyance, to wit, that this property had come by the mother of the grantees, is true. The testimony so shows, and no recovery is now asked on account of it. It is therefore out of the case, and needs no further mention.

Subsequent, also, to their engagement, he, by a deed dated August 1, 1882, and acknowledged on October 30, and recorded November 28, following, conveyed to his sons James and John, in consideration of love and affection, the homestead where they were living, and another house and lot, the two pieces of property being worth from $15,000 to $25,000. The appellant admits, however, both in pleading and her evidence, that he informed her, before the making of this conveyance, of his intention to execute it, and she made no objection to it. She says, however, that she supposed it was to be an absolute one, by way of advancement to the two sons, and that it was not unreasonable in view of his financial condition as stated to her by him. She also says he then promised to do right by her, and provide well for her. She now claims, however, that the deed was in the nature of a testamentary disposition of the property, and in fraud of her coming marital rights, because it provided: "But there is reserved in said party of the first part [H. H. Murray] a right for life, at his option, to occupy,

See also 27 L. R. A. 790; 34 L. R. A. 49.

use, lease and enjoy the profits of each and all of said property for and during his natural life."

A conveyance upon the eve of marriage, to be regarded in equity as a fraud upon the marital rights of the intended wife, and consequently not binding upon her, must be made without her consent or knowledge. *Leach* v. *Duvall*, 8 Bush, 201.

Here she knew of it, and the fact that it conveyed a less estate than she supposed cannot serve as a ground of complaint for her. It was an advantage to her. She, together with her husband, enjoyed during his life the use of at least the homestead, if not all of the property covered by the deed. The conveyances named appear to have embraced all the real estate owned by H. H. Murray.

April 3, 1884, he, in consideration of love and affection, assigned to his son James A. Murray a judgment against the Blantons, secured by mortgage lien, and amounting to about $7,000. The son says that his father had told him some four or five years before that he was to have this debt; and in this statement he is supported by the evidence of the draughtsman of the assignment of the debt, who says that the father said, when he executed it, that he had heretofore given it to the son. The gift was, however, not perfected until April 3, 1884. At the same time, the father, for the same consideration, assigned to the same son a mortgage debt on one Herrman for about $4,000; also a certificate for thirty shares of bank stock, worth $4,500. In November, 1885, he gave to James A., for John Murray, United States bonds of the value of $13,750. Also, at about the same time, he gave to his son William railroad bonds, payable to bearer, worth $4,800. Thus we see that shortly after his marriage he gave to his three sons about $34,000. With the last of these gifts his fortune was substantially gone. The wife had no knowledge of those made after their marriage. At his death he was worth but about $12,500, consisting altogether of personalty. A few days after his marriage he made a will by which he bequeathed all his estate, without naming his wife. It is contended for her that these gifts were merely colorable, and intended to be effective only in case his wife outlived him. In support of this, it is shown that the bank stock was never transferred upon the bank books until after his death; that the checks for the dividends thereon, and for the interest on the United States and railroad bonds, were issued payable to him until his death; and there is some evidence tending to show that he took some control of the property which was purchased in payment of the Blanton debt. The transfers, however, vested the donees with either the legal or equitable title; and there is rebutting testimony showing that they controlled the property from the date of the gifts, and received the money upon the checks issued in payment of the bank dividends, and the interest upon the bonds.

The question remains, however, whether the gifts of the personalty are, under the circumstances, to be regarded as having been made in fraud of the appellant's marital rights. The sons testify—and they are doubtless honest in the belief—that they were bona fide, and made without any intention to defraud the appellant as to her inchoate rights in the estate of her husband. It is difficult, however, in the face of this record, to believe that there was not a purpose upon the part of the husband to lessen the wife's interest in his estate, in the event she survived him, by giving it to his sons. We do not mean to intimate that a husband cannot make any advances to his children, and must preserve his estate intact to meet the inchoate claims of his wife. If the advancements or gifts be reasonable, when considered with reference to the amount of property owned by the husband, and his purpose be to provide for the children, and not to defraud the wife, then she cannot complain, although they in fact diminish the property to which her inchoate rights have attached by the marriage. It is a question of intention upon the part of the grantor. If the property given away constitute all, or the principal part, of the husband's estate, and be such an advancement as is unreasonable, when compared with his entire property, then, while it should not be conclusively presumed to have been made in fraud of the wife's marital rights, yet prima facie it should be so regarded, and the *onus* of showing otherwise be cast upon the donee. Each case must depend upon its own circumstances. If not done to prevent the wife from enjoying a reasonable portion of the husband's estate, or to deprive her of such an interest in it as she might reasonably expect upon her marriage, then the advancement should be upheld as to her. The court must look to the condition of the parties, and all the attending circumstances, in judging of the transaction. It should take into consideration the amount of the husband's estate, the value of the advancements, the time within which they are made, and all other *indicia* which will serve to determine the intention accompanying the transaction.

If, however, a gift or voluntary conveyance of all or the greater portion of his property be made to his children by a former marriage without the knowledge of the intended wife, or it be advanced to them after marriage without the wife's knowledge, a prima facie case of fraud arises; and it rests upon the beneficiaries to explain away such presumption. If the husband have an ample estate, he may, of course, give to the children of a former marriage a reasonable portion of it, and the wife cannot complain. If this were not the rule, then the hands of the husband would be completely and unreasonably tied, and he could make no advancement to his children by a former marriage, however large his estate, and however needful to them; but he would be compelled to hold it all, except from purchasers for value, to meet the inchoate claims of the wife.

Justice Story says that reasonable provision may be made for the children of a former marriage if done under such circumstances as evidence good faith. 1 Story, Eq. Jur. § 273.

In this instance, however, the husband, by successive gifts, advanced to his children, without the knowledge of his wife, nearly all his large estate. They were not her children, and the transfers deprived her of that reasonable expectation as to the enjoyment of a portion of his property which she had a right to form at their marriage. A prima facie case arises in her favor. It is attempted to overturn it with the claim that the greater portion of the husband's property came by the second wife; but, while it appears that she derived some property from her mother, yet the amount of it is not even approximately shown, and is a matter of conjecture. The husband, within a comparatively short time after his marriage to the appellant, and without her knowledge, gave to his children by his former marriages between $30,000 and $40,000. What he so gave, together with his estate remaining at his death, amounts to about $46,000. Allowing for reasonable advancements to the children, the wife was, in our opinion, entitled to $10,000 as her distributable portion of the estate. This, it seems to us, is the equity of the case. The gifts made to the children subsequent to her marriage must, under the circumstances, be regarded as having been made in fraud of her marital rights; and the amount of them, together with the estate of the husband, remaining at his death, less what would have been reasonable advances to the children must be estimated in determining her rights. The chancellor will allow, as of the date of his decree, the sum above named. Any equities which may exist between the other parties to this action remain open for further settlement, not being now presented for determination.

The judgment below, and which allowed the appellant as her distributable portion but one third of the estate in her husband's possession, at the time of his death, *is reversed*, and the cause is remanded for further proceedings consistent with this opinion.

PENNSYLVANIA SUPREME COURT.

EDWIN SHULTZ

v.

Frederick WALL, *Appt.*

(........Pa........)

1. **The responsibility of an innkeeper** for goods and moneys of his guest extends to moneys stolen from the guest, unless they were stolen by a servant or companion of the guest.

2. **The intoxication of a guest** at an inn is no excuse for his negligence which contributes to the loss of his property by theft.

3. **On evidence that the vest of a guest in a hotel was taken** in the night while the door of his room was locked and bolted, and found in the morning in the dining-room carefully folded and laid between two blankets, but his money which he left in it missing, and that an outer door of the hotel bore marks of violence while his door did not, and other evidence showing that plaintiff had been drinking, to some extent at least, the night before, the question of his negligence should be left to the jury, considering the general uncertainty and mystery of the robbery.

4. **Whether a guest at a hotel should be**

NOTE.—*Innkeeper, responsibility of.*

The relation of guest does not depend on the time the traveler remains, or on the contract to pay. Jalie v. Cardinal, 35 Wis. 118.

The relation of innkeeper and guest is not necessarily and conclusively changed by an agreement as to price or any definite length of sojourn. Ross v. Mellin, 36 Minn. 421.

Innkeepers are responsible for the well and safe keeping and custody of the goods and chattels of their guests, and even the absence of negligence will not exempt them from liability. Shaw v. Berry, 31 Me. 478.

The particular responsibility of an innkeeper does not extend to goods lost or stolen from a room occupied by a guest for a purpose of business distinct from his accommodation as guest, such as the exhibition of samples of merchandise. Fisher v. Kelsey, 121 U. S. 383 (30 L. ed. 930).

He is not responsible under the Missouri statute, unless the guest shall have given written notice of having such merchandise for sale or sample, after entering the inn, or unless such loss shall be caused by fire intentionally produced by the innkeeper or his servants, or by their theft. Express knowledge of the innkeeper is not equivalent to written notice. *Ibid.*

They are liable for the loss of goods of a boarder only where they have been guilty of culpable negligence. Manning v. Wells, 9 Hump. 746.

Liability of innkeeper as insurer.

At common law, innholders, like common carriers, are regarded as insurers of the property committed to their care and are liable for any loss if not caused by the act of God, or by a public enemy, or by the neglect or fault of the guest. Mason v. Thompson, 9 Pick. 280; Berkshire Woollen Co. v. Proctor, 7 Cush. 417; Mateer v. Brown, 1 Cal. 221 231; 2 Kent, Com. 594; Story, Bailm. §465.

But he is not an insurer of the goods of a traveler who is not a guest. Lusk v. Belote, 22 Minn. 468.

Either case or assumpsit lies for the loss of baggage through negligence of the innkeeper. Dickinson v. Winchester, 4 Cush. 114.

To make an innkeeper liable in trover, there must be an actual conversion of goods intrusted to him by the guest. Hallenbake v. Fish, 8 Wend. 547, 24 Am. Dec. 88; Wilkins v. Earle, 44 N. Y. 188; Sager v. Blain, Id. 449; Needles v. Howard, 1 E. D. Smith, 60.

Many cases hold that an innkeeper is liable as an insurer for the goods of his guest, and for losses by theft or fire which occur without the negligence of the innkeeper, and is only excused by the act of God, of the public enemy or of the guest. 2 Parsons, Cont. 146; 2 Story, Cont. § 909; Saunders, Neg. 212; Hulett v. Swift, 33 N. Y. 571; Shaw v. Berry, 31 Me. 478; Norcross v. Norcross, 53 Me. 163; Sasseen v. Clark, 37 Ga. 242; Burrows v. Trieber, 21 Md. 320; Hallenbake v. Fish, 8 Wend. 547; Morgan v. Ravey, 6 Hurlst. & N. 265; Day v. Bather, 2 Hurlst. & C. 14; Sibley v. Aldrich, 33 N. H. 553; Holder v. Soulby, 8 C. B. N. S. 254; Gile v. Libby, 36 Barb. 70; Cashill v. Wright, 6 El. & Bl. 891; Oppenheim v. White Lion Hotel Co. L. R. 6 C. P. 515; Fuller v. Coats, 18 Ohio St. 343; Jalie v. Cardinal, 35 Wis. 118.

In other cases, however, the liability has been restricted, particularly in losses by fire, to cases where there is negligence or default on the part of the innkeeper. Addison, Torts, § 684; 2 Kent, Com. 593; Cutler v. Bonney, 30 Mich. 259; Howth v. Franklin, 20 Tex. 798; Woodworth v. Morse, 18 La. Ann. 156; Kisten v. Hildebrand, 9 B. Mon. 72; Metcalf v. Hess, 14 Ill. 129; Johnson v. Richardson, 17 Ill. 302; McDaniels v. Robinson, 26 Vt. 316; Read v. Amidon, 41

See also 16 L. R. A. 188.

treated as having notice of the existence of a safe is a question for the jury, where he has frequently stopped there and there is evidence that on some visit his attention had been called to the safe by the landlord.

5. **Whether carrying a certain amount of money** to his room instead of placing it in the hotel safe is negligence on the part of the guest, is a question for the jury.

(April 21, 1890.)

APPEAL by defendant from a judgment of the Court of Common Pleas for Chester County in favor of plaintiff in an action to recover from a hotel keeper the value of certain money which had been stolen from plaintiff while a guest in the hotel. *Reversed.*

Wall was the keeper of a hotel in Phœnixville. Shultz was the driver of a beer wagon and came to the hotel of Wall on the evening of July 2, 1888, with his wagon and team, put his team in the hotel stable, and remained as a guest of the hotel during the night of July 2, the day and night of the third, and a part of the fourth. Shultz was assigned to a chamber on the door of which was a lock with key upon the inside, and also an inside sliding bolt. A notice was printed at the head of each sheet of the hotel register, which read as follows: "Money, jewelry and other valuables must be placed in the safe. Otherwise the proprietor will not be responsible for loss." Wall claimed to have called Shultz's attention to this notice.

On the night of July 3, Shultz procured a night key to enable him to enter the hotel after it should be closed for the night. He testified that between eleven o'clock and midnight he entered the house by means of the night key and went to his room and retired, and that upon rising in the morning he discovered that his vest was missing and that he had been robbed of some $180 in cash.

Upon the door by which Shultz had entered

Vt. 15; Laird v. Eichold, 10 Ind. 212; Dessauer v. Baker, 1 Wilson (Ind.) 429.

The liability is in some cases held to extend only to necessary articles. Treiber v. Burrows, 27 Md. 130; Maltby v. Chapman, 25 Md. 310; Sasseen v. Clark, 37 Ga. 242; Myers v. Cottrill, 5 Biss. 465; Simon v. Miller, 7 La. Ann. 360.

But in others it is held that his liability is not limited to articles and money necessary for traveling. Pinkerton v. Woodward, 33 Cal. 557; Sneider v. Geiss, 1 Yeates, 34.

An innkeeper is, however, liable for all losses which could have been prevented by ordinary care (Newson ads. Axon, 1 McCord, L. 509); but the loser must have been a guest at the time of the loss. Towson v. Havre-de-Grace Bank, 6 Har. & J. 47.

To render the innkeeper liable the goods must have been brought within the inn. Kent, Com. 593; Albin v. Presby, 8 N. H. 408; Calye's Case, 8 Coke, 32; Sanders v. Spencer, 3 Dyer, 266 *b*; Farnworth v. Packwood, 1 Stark. 249; Burgess v. Clements, 4 Maule & S. 306; Richmond v. Smith, 8 Barn. & C. 9; Jones v. Tyler, 1 Ad. & El. 522; Bennet v. Mellor, 5 T. R. 273; Packard v. Northcraft, 2 Met. (Ky.) 439; Norcross v. Norcross, 53 Me. 163.

The proprietor of a hotel is liable for the loss of baggage of guests through the negligence of a carrier to whom it has been delivered for transportation to the hotel, and whose apparent duty is, by authority of such proprietor, to transport guests and baggage to such hotel; and any private arrangement between the proprietor and carrier unknown to the guest is immaterial. Coskery v. Nagle (Ga.) 6 L. R. A. 483, and *note*.

Liability as bailee.

An innkeeper is liable for money deposited by a guest in the hotel safe, and stolen from it (Wilkins v. Earle, 44 N. Y. 172); and for money deposited with the barkeeper on the credit of the inn. Houser v. Tully, 62 Pa. 92.

The admission of a servant of an inn that he had stolen the jewelry of a guest is not evidence against the innkeeper. Elcox v. Hill, 98 U. S. 218 (25 L. ed. 103).

He is liable for the loss of baggage of a guest left in his custody. Adams v. Clem, 41 Ga. 65; Giles v. Fauntleroy, 13 Md. 126.

He is liable for goods lost during the temporary absence of the guest although the absence extends over several days. Grinnell v. Cook, 3 Hill, 490; McDonald v. Edgerton, 5 Barb. 560; Day v. Bather, 2 Hurlst. & C. 14; Bather v. Day, 32 L. J. N. S. (Exch.) 171; 1 Comyn, Dig. 421; Gelley v. Clerk, Cro. Jac. 188.

Proof of loss of goods, while in charge of the innkeeper, is sufficient prima facie to charge him with liability. Hill v. Owen, 5 Blackf. 323, 35 Am. Dec. 124; Laird v. Eichold, 10 Ind. 212.

Innkeeper may defend on ground of contributory negligence of guest. Elcox v. Hill, *supra*; Houser v. Tully, 62 Pa. 92; Hawley v. Smith, 25 Wend. 642; Chamberlain v. Masterson, 26 Ala. 371; Hadley v. Upshaw, 27 Tex. 547; Kelsey v. Berry, 42 Ill. 469.

Where a guest, on leaving a hotel without the intention of returning as a guest, but without paying his bill, leaves his valise in the charge of the hotel clerk, and returns within forty-eight hours, the innkeeper is liable as a bailee for want of ordinary care; and the loss of the valise raises a presumption of negligence against him. Murray v. Marshall, 9 Colo. 482.

Innkeepers are not bound to receive and keep property of a person who is neither a traveler nor a guest. Grinnell v. Cook, 3 Hill, 485.

A visit by one not requiring present accommodations, but for the purpose of simply depositing money for safe keeping, does not constitute the visitor a guest. Hence, a gambler depositing his money without registering his name is not a guest. Arcade Hotel Co. v. Wiatt, 2 West. Rep. 868, 44 Ohio St. 32.

In Illinois a hotel keeper is exempt from liability for money, jewels and the like, lost by his guest, where a safe for the keeping of such articles is provided, and notice given as required by the statute, and the guest fails to take the benefit of the protection thus furnished him. Elcox v. Hill, 98 U. S. 218 (25 L. ed. 103).

To this rule the statute makes one exception. If the loss occurs "by the hand or through the negligence of the landlord, or by a clerk or servant employed by him in such hotel or inn," the liability remains; but not if the loss was occasioned by the negligence of the guest himself. *Ibid.*; 2 Story, Cont. § 909.

For a guest at a hotel to retain the sum of about $500 in a belt upon his person while sleeping in a room by himself is not negligence as a matter of law, even though the bolt on the door could be opened from the outside by means of a wire. Smith v. Wilson, 36 Minn. 334.

See *note* to Coskery v. Nagle (Ga.) 6 L. R. A. 483, for a full discussion of this subject. See also Pullman Palace Car Co. v. Lowe (Neb.) 6 L. R. A. 809.

with his night key there was both a lock and a dead latch. He was himself the last person to enter that door upon that night, and the next morning the lock was found to have been broken off.

Shultz testified that he both locked and bolted his bed-room door before retiring, but that the next morning he found it standing partially open. If a thief entered that room it was admitted that he entered through that door, which bore no evidence whatever of the lock or bolt having been forced. The vest was found down stairs carefully folded and laid between two lap blankets on the hat-rack in the dining-room, with the pocket-book and everything intact, but the money gone. Matches of a kind not used in the hotel were found scattered at various points.

Wall's hostler, Rahn, testified that at about 11 o'clock of the night of the robbery some men called at his room seeking Shultz, and Mrs. Wall testified that between 11 and 12 o'clock she heard voices on the porch, one of which she recognized as Shultz's.

The court charged the jury, *inter alia*, as follows:

["As I understand the law of this Commonwealth relating to the liability of an innkeeper, I instruct you that he is answerable for all losses happening to the goods of travelers becoming his guests, except such losses as are caused by the act of God or the public enemy, or by improper conduct of the guest himself, or his servant, or the companion whom he brings with him. Wherever the loss does not occur by reason of any of these excepted causes, then the innkeeper in this Commonwealth, in judgment of this court, is answerable for that loss."] (Fifth assignment of error.)

["Mr. Shultz had no servant and he had no companion, and we say to you that we see no testimony in the case which would warrant the jury in concluding that Mr. Shultz by his conduct contributed to the theft, if that theft was committed. You will therefore see that under our view of the law, if a theft was committed in this house, Mr. Wall is answerable for the amount of the loss. You will also see that under the views of the court you have nothing to consider except the question whether or not there was a theft in this house. If there was, then you will ascertain the measure of damages which Mr. Shultz sustained, and the measure of damages will be the amount of that loss."] (Sixth assignment of error.)

Defendant requested the court to charge, *inter alia:*

(2) If the jury find that there was a sufficient lock and bolt on the door of the room occupied by the plaintiff, if properly used, to insure the safety of his property, and if they believe, from the evidence, that the plaintiff did not make use of safety thus supplied him, it is for the jury to find from all the facts whether, under the circumstances of the case, the plaintiff has not discharged the defendant, and, if they so find, the verdict should be for the defendant. *Answer.* In answer to this point, gentlemen, we say that we see no evidence in the case which would justify the jury in concluding that the plaintiff had not made use of the proper means of safety which were furnished him, and therefore disaffirm the point. (Second assignment of error.)

(3) The fact of the guest having the means of securing himself, and choosing not to use them, is one which, with other circumstances of the case, is for the jury to consider; and if they should find from that fact and other circumstances in the case, that the plaintiff did not exercise the ordinary care of a prudent man under the circumstances, and was thus guilty of contributory negligence, their verdict should be for the defendant. *Answer.* The principles of law, set out in that point, are correct. We say to you that there is no evidence in the case, in the estimation of the court, which would warrant you in applying them to the law as here set out, and we therefore disaffirm the point for the reason given. (Third assignment of error.)

There was a verdict for plaintiff for $186.82 and, a rule for a new trial having been discharged, defendant appealed.

Messrs. **I. N. Wynn, Archibald M. Holding** and **Robert E. Monaghan,** for appellant:

Although the loss in itself raises a presumption of negligence on the part of the innkeeper, or of those for whom he is responsible, it is not irrebuttable, but may be overcome by satisfactory proof that the loss did not occur through the negligence of him, or those for whom he is responsible.

Jones, Bailm. 3d London ed. pp. 94-96; Story, Bailm. 7th ed. §§ 470-472; *Merritt* v. *Claghorn*, 23 Vt. 177.

If the innkeeper was free from negligence he is not responsible for the loss.

Dawson v. *Chamney*, 5 Q. B. 164; *Howe Mach. Co.* v. *Pease*, 49 Vt. 477; Registrum Brevium, 105; Fitzh. N. B. 94; *Calye's Case*, 8 Coke, 32; Jones, Bailm. 3d London ed. 94 *a, note; McDaniels* v. *Robinson*, 26 Vt. 317; *Johnson* v. *Richardson*, 17 Ill. 302; *Kisten* v. *Hildebrande*, 9 B. Mon. 72; *Metcalf* v. *Hess*, 14 Ill. 129; *Laird* v. *Eichold*, 10 Ind. 212; *Hill* v. *Owen*, 5 Blackf. 323; *Dessauer* v. *Baker*, 1 Wilson (Ind.) 429; *Cutler* v. *Bonney*, 30 Mich. 259; *Howth* v. *Franklin*, 20 Tex. 798; *Weisenger* v. *Taylor*, 1 Bush, 275; *Vance* v. *Throckmorton*, 5 Bush, 41; *Norcross* v. *Norcross*, 53 Me. 163; *Read* v. *Amidon*, 42 Vt. 15; *Sasseen* v. *Clark*, 37 Ga. 242; *Metcalf* v. *Hess*, 14 Ill. 129.

There was evidence of contributory negligence for the consideration of the jury.

Herbert v. *Markwell*, 45 L. T. N. S. 649; Weekly Notes (Eng.) 1882, p. 112; *Oppenheim* v. *White Lion Hotel Co.* L. R. 6 C. P. 515, 517; *Bohler* v. *Owens*, 60 Ga. 185; *Walsh* v. *Porterfield*, 87 Pa. 376; Story, Bailm. 472.

The plaintiff was guilty of negligence in not availing himself of the place of safety provided by the defendant for the safe keeping of his money, and he cannot maintain this action.

Purvis v. *Coleman*, 21 N. Y. 112; *Chamberlain* v. *West*, 37 Minn. 54; *Jones* v. *Jackson*, 29 L. T. N. S. 399.

Mr. **H. H. Gilkyson,** for appellee:

The liability of the innkeeper, in cases of loss or theft, does not depend upon the measure of care with which he keeps the goods of a guest, nor the means which he has employed to protect them. His liability is analogous to that of a common carrier, who is held absolutely responsible for all loss of goods while in his control, and under his custody, unless the loss be occasioned by an act of God or the public enemy.

Calye's Case, 8 Coke, 32, 1 Smith, Lead. Cas. *104, 7th Am. ed. 241; *Sibley* v. *Aldrich*, 33 N. H. 553; *Hulett* v. *Swift*, 33 N. Y. 571; *Packard* v. *Northcraft*, 2 Met. (Ky.) 439; *Shaw* v. *Berry*, 31 Me. 478; *Sasseen* v. *Clark*, 37 Ga. 242; *Mason* v. *Thompson*, 9 Pick. 280.

The goods are under the protection of the inn, so as to make the innkeeper liable for a breach of duty, unless the negligence of the guest occasions the loss in such a way that the loss could not have happened if the guest had used the ordinary care that a prudent man may be reasonably expected to have taken under the circumstances.

1 Addison, Torts, p. 615; *Houser* v. *Tully*, 62 Pa. 92; *Walsh* v. *Porterfield*, 87 Pa. 376; *Rommel* v. *Schambacher* (Pa.) 9 Cent. Rep. 742, 20 W. N. C. 262.

Mitchell, *J.*, delivered the opinion of the court:

As long ago as *Chancellor* Kent's day it was said: "The responsibility of an innkeeper for the goods of his guest . . . . has been a point of much discussion in the books." 2 Kent, Com. 592.

The common-law rule, as established in *Calye's Case*, 8 Coke, 32, was that the innkeeper was bound absolutely to keep safe the goods of his guest deposited within the inn, and Kent, after considering the cases, lays it down that "an innkeeper, like a common carrier, is an insurer of the goods of his guest." 2 Kent, Com. 594.

The subject is also learnedly discussed in the *note* to *Calye's Case*, 1 Smith, Lead. Cas. *197, and the *notes* to *Coggs* v. *Bernard*, 1 Smith, Lead. Cas. *307, where the learned American annotators sum up the rule in the following form: "An innkeeper is answerable for all losses happening to the goods of travelers becoming his guests, except such losses as are caused by the Act of God, or the public enemies, or by the conduct of the guest himself, or his servant, or the companion whom he brings with him."

The learned counsel for the appellant has presented us a strong array of authorities to show that the true foundation of the rule as administered in the later cases both in England and many of our sister States is the negligence of the innkeeper, and the only difference between the innkeeper and ordinary bailees is that a loss is prima facie proof of the innkeeper's negligence, and throws upon him the burden of disproving it. If the question were open it might be interesting to examine how far the desire to fix the exact limits of the liability, by resting it on something more definite than public policy, has led to modification of the severity of the common-law rule. Conceding negligence to be the foundation, we must logically concede the desired result, that if the innkeeper shows by satisfactory proof that he took due care, he is absolved from liability. For my own part I apprehend that the liability, like that of a common carrier, rested on the surrender of the owner's possession and control of his goods, and public policy which, for the protection of the owner under such circumstances, precluded every excuse for not restoring the goods to the owner, except such as were the result of *vis major*, the act of God or the public enemies, which would be notorious, and could not be fraudulently pretended.

But the rule, whatever its foundation, is no longer open to question in this State.

In *Houser* v. *Tully*, 62 Pa. 92, the common-law liability was laid down by Williams, *J.*, in the following emphatic terms: "His responsibility extends to all his servants and domestics, and to all the goods and moneys of his guest which are placed within the inn; and he is bound in every event to pay for them if stolen unless they were stolen by a servant or companion of the guest." The learned counsel for appellant has distinguished this case very carefully and accurately upon the facts, and claims that the enunciation of the general rule, above quoted, was not really necessary to the decision of the case actually before the court and that it is therefore only dictum. If the case stood alone there would be good ground for the claim, and we might be required now to re-examine the foundation and merits of the rule announced. But in *Walsh* v. *Porterfield*, 87 Pa. 376, the former case was distinctly affirmed in all the breadth of the opinion. The judge below had charged the jury that "at common law an innkeeper was liable, at all events, for the goods and baggage of his guests, ... and the law is the same to-day . . . . It was, in fact, insuring, as it were, the safety of the property of guests, and it was immaterial (if a loss occurred or property was stolen whilst the guest was in the hotel) by whom it was stolen, unless it was by the guest's own servant or a fellow guest of the party who was robbed, or the negligence of the guest; and however vigilant the landlord might have been, he was responsible to the party losing the property. That was the common-law liability. He was practically an insurer of the safety of the property whilst the guests remained in his house."

It was assigned for error that this charge was too broad, and eminent counsel argued there, as here, that the real foundation of the rule is the negligence of the landlord or his servants; but this court in affirming the judgment said: "We adhere to the statement of the law as laid down by our late brother Williams, in *Houser* v. *Tully*, as to the extent and character of the liability of innkeepers for the goods of their guests. An innkeeper is bound to pay for goods stolen in his house from a guest, unless stolen by the servant or companion of the guest. . . . The learned judge below, in his charge to the jury, evidently adopted this case as his chart, and there is no error in his instructions upon the law."

After this deliberate affirmance of the common-law rule in a case where it was applied and the correctness of the instruction distinctly assigned for error, we must regard the rule as settled.

The learned judge therefore was right in the general instruction he gave the jury as to the foundation of the plaintiff's case. In the press of the trial, however, the defense unfortunately did not receive the same consideration. Neither the question of contributory negligence nor the effect of the Statute of 1855 was presented to the jury as it should have been.

Volenti non fit injuria, and conduct of the plaintiff contributing to the loss, whether voluntary or negligent, is always a defense. This principle, though not very clearly enunciated, was applied to the liability of an innkeeper even in *Calye's Case*, where the first resolution was that if the horse was put to pasture at the guest's request and stolen, the innkeeper was not liable, and the eighth (8 Coke, 32), that if the innkeeper requires his guest to put his goods in such a chamber under lock, and the guest leave them in an outer court and they are stolen, the innkeeper shall not be liable. And however it might have been in the days of good Queen Bess, when *Calye's Case* was decided, and when the length of his wine bill might have been deemed sufficient consideration for the duty of an innkeeper to take care of his guest drunk or sober, it is now held in our own case of *Walsh* v. *Porterfield* that intoxication is no excuse for the negligence of a guest which contributes to his loss.

The evidence in the present case leaves the circumstances of the robbery in some degree of mystery. According to the plaintiff's story, he locked and bolted his chamber door on going to bed, and found it open on waking in the morning. The back outer door of the hotel bore marks of violence with a hammer or other tool, the catch of the dead latch was broken off, and matches of a kind not used in the hotel were found scattered at various points. All this pointed to a burglary by outside parties. Yet the evidence is that the plaintiff's bedroom door bore no marks of violence anywhere, the key was in the lock, and the transom window was but a foot high and swung in the middle leaving only a space of six inches through which no person could possibly climb. How then did the thief get in? There is no theory which does not encounter some difficulties, and the first question that arises in the mind is whether the plaintiff may not be mistaken in supposing he locked and bolted his door. The testimony is, that though a sober man he was not a total abstainer, and had been drinking that evening. Did he get more than he thought and is his recollection thereby beclouded? Or did he lock and bolt the door as he thinks, and did the beer get him up again in a confused condition of mind, and was his open door the result of this? The other circumstances only add to the difficulty of a satisfactory explanation. The evidence in general, as already said, points to a robbery by outside parties. But the vest carefully folded and laid between the two lap blankets on the hat-rack in the dining-room is hard to reconcile with such a theory. Again, the evidence of Mrs. Wall as to the voices on the porch, and of Rahn as to the men asking for plaintiff, suggest the possibility of other parties in company with plaintiff and the loss of the money before he entered his room. As already said, there is no view of the evidence that does not meet with some difficulty, and such difficulty is always for the jury to solve.

Jurors are to exercise the same common sense and judgment in the jury box that they do as men in the affairs of life, only with a strict regard, under the direction of the court, to the nature, relevancy and weight of evidence upon both sides. They cannot base verdicts on surmise or conjecture without evidence, but they are not bound to believe an incredible story because no witness contradicts it. It is for them to survey the whole case and say whether the party having the burden of proof has met it by a satisfactory preponderance of evidence. The learned judge below was of opinion that there was not sufficient evidence of plaintiff's negligence to be considered by the jury, and therefore, though stating the law correctly as to such negligence, he limited the jury to the consideration of the single question, whether or not there was a theft. In this view we are unable to concur. The difficulties in the way of the plaintiff's theory and the general uncertainty of the entire occurrence should have sent the whole case to the jury with an affirmance of defendant's second and third points.

The evidence in regard to the safe and the notice to guests is not as full and satisfactory as it might be, but it was sufficient to go to the jury. The provisions of the Act of the 7th of May, 1855 (Pub. Laws, 479), in regard to the place where notices must be posted, are intended to secure knowledge brought home to the guest. They may be said to be mandatory in the sense that as they amount to constructive notice; they must be strictly complied with if constructive notice is relied on. But if notice in fact is proved, then the provisions for constructive notice become immaterial. Defendant testified positively to having called the plaintiff's attention to the notice at the head of the hotel register, though it was probably not on this particular visit. The defendant denied it. This question should have gone to the jury for them to determine, under all the circumstances, the lapse of time since plaintiff saw the notice, if they find that he did have his attention called to it, the frequency of his visits and his consequent familiarity with the customs of the house, etc., whether he should be treated as having notice of the existence of a safe, and if so, whether his omission to avail himself of that protection, and his carrying such an amount of money to his bedroom, was negligence for which he must himself bear the loss.

Judgment reversed, and venire de novo *awarded.*

KENTUCKY COURT OF APPEALS.

Laura GOSS *et al.*, *Appts.*,
v.
Minnie R. FROMAN *et al.*

(......Ky.......)

1. **Proof of the conduct of husband and wife** toward each other, and of their expressions of hatred and fear of each other, and of their statements, during the time they lived together apparently as husband and wife, as to non-access, may be admitted to show non-access, on the question as to the legitimacy of a child.

2. **The presumption that a child born in wedlock is legitimate,** where the husband and wife had opportunities of access, is not conclusive, but may be overcome by clear proof of the contrary, which may consist of proof that the husband was incompetent to have sexual intercourse with his wife or she with him.

3. **Proof of the wife's adultery** is competent on the question of the legitimacy of a child, to corroborate proof that the husband was not capable of performing the sexual act or that he had abstained from performing it with his wife.

4. **A mother is a competent witness** to prove the legitimacy of her child begotten during wedlock if such legitimacy is attacked; and in case she becomes a witness she will not be permitted to withhold on cross-examination any part of the truth, even although it will disclose acts of adultery.

5. **A woman who, during her abandonment of her husband, admits any man** or men to her periodically or whenever it is convenient or opportunity is afforded, is living in adultery within the meaning of the Kentucky statutes which forfeit her dower or distributable share in her husband's property, when she voluntarily leaves him and lives in adultery.

(November 26, 1889.)

APPEAL by cross-defendants from a judgment of the Louisville Law and Equity Court in favor of cross-petitioners in a suit brought by the executor of Solomon Froman, deceased, to obtain a settlement of his accounts, etc., the cross-petition setting up the birth of an heir after the making of the will, and praying a distribution of the estate to such heir subject to the dower rights of his mother. *Reversed.*

The facts are fully stated in the opinion.

Mr. **Burton Vance** for Laura Goss, appellant.

Messrs. **Brown, Humphrey & Davie, C. B. Seymour** and **W. H. McGee** for other devisees and heirs, appellants.

Messrs. **Thomas H. Hines** and **J. M. Wilkins,** with *Messrs.* **Abbott & Rutledge,** for Elizabeth Wilson, appellant:

The prima facie evidence of legitimacy may always be lawfully rebutted by satisfactory evidence that access did not take place between husband and wife, as by the law of nature is necessary in order for the man, in fact, to be father of the child.

NOTE.—*Presumption of legitimacy of child born in wedlock.*

Bastards are persons begotten and born out of lawful wedlock. Miller v. Anderson, 1 West. Rep. 810, 43 Ohio St. 473; 1 Bl. Com. 454; 2 Kent, Com. 208.

If a woman pregnant at her marriage is delivered after marriage the child is legitimate. Miller v. Anderson, *supra.*

The law presumes a child to have been born in lawful wedlock, and this presumption must prevail until overcome by clear and convincing proof adduced by those alleging illegitimacy. Orthwein v. Thomas, 4 L. R. A. 434, 127 Ill. 554.

Children of a married woman, born during coverture, are presumed to be legitimate. *Re* Romero's Estate, 75 Cal. 379.

The fact that a woman gave birth to a fully developed child so soon after marriage as to render it certain that it was begotten before marriage raises a legal presumption that it was begotten by him who became her husband. McCulloch v. McCulloch, 69 Tex. 682.

The presumption of legitimacy is a presumption *juris et de jure.* Miller v. Anderson, 1 West. Rep. 811, 43 Ohio St. 473.

The burden of proving illegitimacy lies entirely with the person seeking to establish it. Overlock v. Hall, 81 Me. 348; Plowes v. Bossey, 8 Jur. N. S. 352, 31 L. J. N. S. Ch. 681.

But in a later decision in England it has been held that it is not a presumption *juris et de jure,* but may be rebutted by evidence which must be clear and conclusive and not resting merely on a balance of probabilities. So where a child was born 276 days after the last opportunity of the husband's access, and there was evidence in the wife's conduct tending to show that she regarded the child as the offspring of her paramour, the question of its legitimacy was properly submitted to the jury. Bosville v. Atty-Gen. L. R. 12 Prob. Div. 177; Morris v. Davies, 5 Clark & F. 163.

A legal presumption relieves him in whose favor it exists from the necessity of any proof, but may be destroyed by rebutting evidence. Otherwise as to presumptions *juris et de jure,* against which no proof can be admitted. Dugas v. Estiletts, 5 La. Ann. 559; Davenport v. Mason, 15 Mass. 85; Baalam v. State, 17 Ala. 451.

Presumption in favor of the legitimacy of children will not be made where the question is to be determined as one of fact and not of law. Blackburn v. Crawford, 70 U. S. 3 Wall. 175 (18 L. ed. 186).

The presumption of legitimacy may be rebutted.

The presumption of legitimacy may be rebutted both by positive and by presumptive evidence. Wright v. Hicks, 12 Ga. 155, 15 Ga. 160.

In Louisiana this legal presumption can be overcome only in the mode and within the time prescribed by law. Dejol v. Johnson, 12 La. Ann. 853.

Elsewhere it can be overcome only by clear and convincing proof of non-intercourse between the husband and wife. Egbert v. Greenwalt, 44 Mich. 250; Van Aernam v. Van Aernam, 1 Barb. Ch. 378; Patterson v. Gaines, 47 U. S. 6 How. 550 (12 L. ed. 553); Sullivan v. Kelly, 3 Allen, 148; Hemmenway v. Towner, 1 Allen, 209; Flettesham v. Julian, 1 Y. B. 7 Hen. IV. 9, pl. 13; Stegall v. Stegall, 2 Brock. 256; Cannon v. Cannon, 7 Humph. 410.

The presumption of legitimacy of a child born during the period of marriage is not rebutted by circumstances which create only doubt and suspicion, but is wholly removed by showing, first, that the husband was incompetent; second, that he was entirely absent, so as to have had no access to the mother; third, or entirely absent at the period during which the child must, in the course of nature, have been begotten; fourth, and present only

See also 12 L. R. A. 350; 25 L. R. A. 477; 41 L. R. A. 760.

Nicholas, Adulterine Bastardy, p. 182; *Banbury Peerage Case*, 1 Sim. & Stu. 153; *Hawes* v. *Draeger*, L. R. 23 Ch. Div. 178; *Morris* v. *Davies*, 3 Car. & P. 215, 427; *Shuler* v. *Bull*, 15 S. C. 428; *Wilson* v. *Babb*, 18 S. C. 69; *State* v. *Shumpert*, 1 S. C. 85; *State* v. *Pettaway*, 3 Hawks (N. C.) 625; *Com.* v. *Wentz*, 1 Ashmead, 271.

The presumption of sexual intercourse between husband and wife may be rebutted by evidence of the feelings and conduct of the parties.

Wright v. *Hicks*, 12 Ga. 161; *Wright* v. *Hicks*, 15 Ga. 169; *Cannon* v. *Cannon*, 7 Humph. 410; *Strode* v. *Magowan*, 2 Bush, 621; *Remmington* v. *Lewis*, 8 B. Mon. 611.

Mrs. Froman was permitted to testify that she had never been unfaithful to her husband, and had never had intercourse, since her marriage, with anyone but him. This was error under the Civil Code, § 606, which provides: "Neither a husband nor his wife shall testify, even after the cessation of their marriage, concerning any communication between them during marriage."

See also *Boykin* v. *Boykin*, 70 N. C. 262; *Patchett* v. *Holgate*, 3 Eng. L. & Eq. 100; *Rex* v. *Sourton*, 5 Ad. & El. 180; *Hamp* v. *Robinson*, 16 L. T. N. S. 29; *Aylesford Peerage Case*, L. R. 11 App. Cas. 1.

Messrs. **Helm & Bruce** for appellees.

Bennett, *J.*, delivered the opinion of the court:

Minnie R. Froman is the widow of Solomon Froman, deceased. He died testate on the 3d day of June, 1884. Soloman White Froman, son of Minnie R. Froman, was begotten during the wedlock of Soloman Froman and Minnie R. Froman, and was born on the 3d day of January, 1885, about seven months after the death of the putative father, Soloman Froman. Soloman Froman's will made no provision for this after-born child, nor any provision for Minnie R. Froman, the widow. Soloman White Froman claimed the entire estate, under the statute, as an after-born pretermitted child. The widow renounced the provisions of the will, and claimed her dowable and distributable share of the estate. Issue was joined as to the legitimacy of Soloman White Froman, and as to the forfeiture of the widow's dowable and distributable interest by reason of her abandoning her husband, Soloman Froman, and living in adultery. These issues were decided against the devisees under the will, and they have appealed to this court.

It is to be regretted that questions like these should ever arise in the courts of this Commonwealth. Kentucky's matrons are famed for their high sense of virtue and exemplary conduct; and it is to be regretted that the conduct of Mrs. Minnie R. Froman was so radical a departure from this fair fame as to impel us to declare her son, Soloman White Froman, illegitimate. The proof is that Mrs. Froman left the house of her husband, Soloman Froman, on the morning of the 4th of April, 1884, and went direct to Bowling Green, to the house of a Mrs. Wilson, where she remained at least a week, and then returned to Louisville, and took boarding with a certain woman, and

---

under circumstances which afford clear and satisfactory proof that there was no sexual intercourse. Hargrave v. Hargrave, 9 Beav. 552; Com. v. Stricker, 1 Browne (Pa.) Append. XLVII.

Proof of impotency of husband.

It is presumed that a mature male has normal powers of virility, and the burden of proving the contrary is on the party asserting it. Gardner v. State, 81 Ga. 144.

The presumption of legitimacy arising from the sleeping together of husband and wife can be rebutted only by clear and satisfactory evidence that some physical incapacity existed. Legge v. Edmonds, 25 L. J. N. S. Ch. 125.

The evidence must prove beyond all reasonable doubt that the husband could not have been the father. Phillips v. Allen, 2 Allen, 453.

The impotency of the putative father, if true and proven, would be conclusive, and evidence thereof is competent. State v. Broadway, 69 N. C. 411.

Proof of non-access.

Access between man and wife is always presumed until otherwise plainly proved, and nothing is allowed to impugn the legitimacy of a child, short of proofs of facts showing it to be impossible that the husband could have been its father. Gaines v. Hennen, 65 U. S. 24 How. 553 (16 L. ed. 770).

But if a husband went beyond seas two years before the birth of her child, the conclusion is irresistible that it is illegitimate. Rex v. Maidstone, 12 East, 550.

So illegitimacy may be shown by proof of abandonment by the husband, and his continued absence from the State, for a period of four years before the birth of the child. Pittsford v. Chittenden, 2 New Eng. Rep. 191, 58 Vt. 49.

Non-access of the husband need not be proved during the whole period of the wife's pregnancy, if the circumstances show a natural impossibility that he could be the father, as where he had access only a fortnight before the birth. Rex v. Luffe, 8 East, 193.

Where a husband after a long absence did not rejoin his wife until eight months before the birth of a full grown child he could not have been the father. Heathcote's Divorce Bill, 1 Macq. H. L. Cas. 585.

Opportunity of access becomes important to consider, where the wife was notoriously living in adultery. Reg. v. Mansfield, 1 Q. B. 444, 5 Jur. 505.

Where the child was born three months after the marriage, the wife was asked on cross-examination, "When did you first become acquainted with your husband?" and on her answering "Twelve months" the subject was dismissed. Anon. v. Anon. 22 Beav. 481; State v. Romaine, 58 Iowa, 48.

Where husband and wife, although living separate and apart, had been in such a situation that access might have been had, the presumption in favor of legitimacy can be rebutted only by strong evidence; and if the access is proved, no inquiry as to paternity can be made. Morris v. Davies, 5 Clark & F. 163, 1 Jur. 911.

Parties themselves not competent witnesses on the subject of access.

A woman cannot give evidence of the non-access of her husband to bastardize her issue, though the husband be deceased (Rex v. Kea, 11 East, 13[illegible]; Goodright v. Moss, Cowp. 591); but the mother is a competent witness to prove the illegitimacy of her children. Rex v. Bramley, 6 T. R. 330; Standen v. Standen, 6 T. R. 331 *note* (*b.*), Peake, N. P. 3[illegible]; Rex v. Reading, Lee, Cas. t. Hardw. 79; Rex v. Luffe 8 East, 193; Tioga Co. v. South Creek Twp. 75 P[illegible]. 433.

The evidence of the husband is not admissible t[illegible]

there remained as boarder until the death of her husband; never visiting or seeing her husband after she left his house on the 4th of April preceding, although she left him sick of a fatal disease, of which he died on the 3d of June. Mrs. Froman claims that her husband, Soloman Froman, on the morning of the 3d of April,—the day before she left his house,—sent for her to come to his room; that she went, and he then had sexual intercourse with her, getting her with child. If this story is to be believed, the appellee, Soloman White Froman, having been thereafter born within the usual time of gestation, is the child of Soloman Froman. But is the story to be believed? Does not the proof disclose a state of case that utterly repels the truth of this story? Does not the proof show a state of case that repels any presumption of sexual intercourse whatever? We think it does. Let us see. We find that Soloman Froman on the 11th day of November, 1883, was affected with Bright's disease, and dropsy of the bowels, scrotum and thighs. Dr. Griffith attended on him almost daily, and treated him for these diseases, until the 7th day of January, 1884, at which time he turned the case over to Dr. Holloway, and he attended on Froman almost daily, and treated him for these diseases, until his death. Froman continued to grow worse from the time Dr. Griffith commenced attending on him until he died. That his condition may clearly appear, we quote from Dr. Holloway's testimony, which is as follows: "He had œdema of the lungs, or asthmatic breathing, and frequent paroxysms of asthma, excessive bronchiæ. He had general dropsy. This dropsy was more generally displayed by the accumulation in his abdomen; by enlargement of the skin; by the dropsy of the skin of the abdomen, and the loins, back and thighs; of the skin of the thighs and legs, and by the general excessive accumulation of the fluid in the scrotum, and in the skin of the penis,—so much so that the penis proper could not be seen upon an examination, only the orifice. He had frequent attacks of vomiting and obstinate constipation, with loss of appetite. He was mentally dull, unless when aroused by some special cause of excitement. He had what is called 'hebetude.' With or without anodynes, he aroused at my visits in a sleepy way in his bed or chair, and had to be questioned before he would give any answer about his case. When aroused by any special cause of excitement, he was more talkative, but con-

---

prove access, or any collateral fact tending to show that he had opportunities of access. Wright v. Holdgate, 3 Car. & K. 158.

The rule precluding the husband or wife from proving non-access for the purpose of bastardizing the issue applies where, on the day following the marriage, the husband abandoned the wife, and the child was born shortly afterward at the house of her employer, whom she sought to charge with the paternity. Tioga Co. v. South Creek Twp. *supra*; Parker v. Way, 15 N. H. 45; Davis v. Houston, 2 Yeates, 289; Page v. Dennison, 1 Grant, Cas. 377; Dennison v. Page, 29 Pa. 420; State v. Wilson, 10 Ired. L. 131; State v. Herman, 13 Ired. L. 502; 1 Phil. Ev. 87, *note*.

Evidence of intercourse with other men.

Evidence of intercourse with other men must be limited to a period such as to admit of the inference that the child derived its paternity from that intercourse. Bowen v. Reed, 103 Mass. 46. Compare Paull v. Padelford, 16 Gray, 263.

Evidence that another man had connection with the wife at about the proper time for begetting the child is not competent unless coupled with evidence that the husband had no connection with her at that time. State v. Bennett, 75 N. C. 305.

Evidence of acts of intercourse with other men twelve months before the birth is inadmissible. Sabins v. Jones, 119 Mass. 167.

The legal presumption is rebutted by the facts, that the wife led the life of a prostitute, was seen as such in company with other men, that though her husband lived in the same town, he always avoided her, and that the child was born in jail three years after their separation. Sibbet v. Ainsley, 3 L. T. N. S. 583.

So illegitimacy is established by evidence of the mother living in adultery at the time when the child was begotten. Barony of Saye and Sele, 1 H. L. Cas. 507.

Illegitimacy may be established by proof of other facts.

Illegitimacy may be established by any competent evidence, and proof thereof is not restricted to evidence of impotency on the part of the husband, or of impossibility of access, or of intercourse between the wife and a man other than her husband. Wilson v. Babb, 18 S. C. 59.

Hearsay evidence may be sufficient. Goerman's App. (Pa.) 1 Cent. Rep. 228.

Depositions are admissible on the trial of an issue of bastardy, as in other civil actions. State v. Hickerson, 72 N. C. 421.

The fact of paternity may be established by a fair preponderance of evidence as in other civil cases. People v. Cantine, 1 Brown, N. P. (Mich.) 140; Young v. Makepeace, 103 Mass. 50.

Evidence not admissible on question of paternity.

Declarations of parties made after cohabitation has ceased are not evidence to bastardize the issue. *Re* Taylor, 9 Paige, 611.

They are not admissible where no evidence is offered of non-access at the time of conception. Dennison v. Page, 29 Pa. 420.

Neither the mother's declarations nor her husband's, she having since deceased, are admissible on the question of paternity (Cope v. Cope, 5 Car. & P. 604, 1 Moody & R. 269); but a baptismal register describing the child as the illegitimate son of his mother is admissible. *Ibid.*

The father's declarations are insufficient to bastardize the issue of his marriage (Bowles v. Bingham, 2 Munf. 442, 3 Munf. 599); it requires the proof to show it was impossible that the husband could be the child's father. Vernon v. Vernon, 6 La. Ann. 243.

But where non-access has been established by evidence *aliunde*, the declaration of the mother is admissible to prove the paternity of the child. Legge v. Edmonds, 25 L. J. N. S. Ch. 125.

Admissions of the wife cannot be received to establish non-access at the period of conception, to bastardize her issue. Cross v. Cross, 3 Paige, 139.

Evidence of the likeness of a child to its supposed father is not admissible upon the question of paternity. United States v. Collins, 1 Cranch, C. C. 592; Hanawalt v. State, 64 Wis. 84. But consult State v. Bowles, 7 Jones, L. 579.

Nor is evidence of the color of the child's eyes admissible. People v. Carney, 29 Hun, 47.

fined himself to the subject that excited him; and then, when that passed away, he would relapse into his condition of hebetude. His urine was very scant, and when boiled with nitric acid it had the appearance of soiled boiled white of an egg. His case was plainly one of Bright's disease in its advanced stages." "This was his condition when I saw him in January, 1884. The dropsical condition of the penis and scrotum got steadily worse from the first time I saw him; only the orifice of the skin where the penis was could be seen. He could not have had sexual intercourse from the time I saw him in January, 1884. In his physical condition it was not possible for him to have emitted semen into a woman. It was not possible for him to have had connection with a woman at any time during my attendance upon him. The usual period of gestation is from 278 days to 280 days." In his second deposition, he says: "I am satisfied that he was not physically capable of performing the sexual act. I do not think it was possible for him to enter a woman so as to bring the semen in the track in such a manner that the spermatozoa could find their way to the ova. I visited him from the 3d to the 9th of February, excepting the 8th; then from the 10th to the 15th, excepting the 14th. I visited him the 17th, 19th, 20th, 21st, 23d, 25th, 27th and 1st of March; then the 4th and 7th of March, twice that week; then the 11th of March, once that week; then the 16th, 21st, 22d, 23d and 27th of March; then the 31st of March and 8th and 11th of April; then the 16th and 19th of April; then 23d and 27th of April and 3d of May, 6th of May and 10th of May. Then I visited him on the 11th, 13th, 14th, 15th, 16th of May, and the 19th, 20th, 21st, 22d, 23d, and on the 24th; twice on the 25th; to the 31st, inclusive, twice every day; twice on the 1st of June; and twice on the 3d of June, the day of his death."

From what Dr. Holloway says, it was a physical impossibility for Soloman Froman to get his wife with child at the respective dates that he visited him. Is it possible that the swelling could have abated between the 31st of March and the 8th of April enough to enable him to have sexual intercourse at any time during said period? It may be possible, but it seems to us that such a conclusion is wholly irrational. The doctor, in his almost daily visits before and after said time, found him so swollen as to be incapable of performing the sexual act, and growing worse all the time. So it seems that there is no ground whatever for forming any rational conclusion that the swelling so abated within said time as to enable him to have had sexual intercourse. Such a conclusion would be wholly irrational. But we are not left to conjecture about this matter; for the nurse, who was in daily attendance upon Soloman Froman, and slept with him nightly, during said time, says that his swelling did not abate, nor did his condition at all improve. He also says that he knows Soloman Froman did not have sexual intercourse with Mrs. Froman on the morning of the 3d of April, nor at any other time for several months previous. It also appears that Soloman and Mrs. Froman lived like cats and dogs for several months prior to her leaving his house on the 4th of April; that he usually spoke of her as "the damned dirty bitch," and she of him as "the damned old son of a bitch." He accused her of poisoning him, and she said that she had poisoned him in order to get him out of the way. She also said, time and again, he could not, even before he was taken sick, have sexual intercourse; that she and he had ceased, for at least a year before his death, to have intercourse with each other. He said the same thing. It also appears from the proof that she had sexual intercourse with Ed Ward in Bowling Green, on the night of the 4th of April, and several other times during her stay in that city, and afterwards with another. It also appears that during her marriage state, before and after her sojourn in Bowling Green, she wrote this Ed Ward unchaste and lascivious letters. The appellees did introduce proof to the effect that, in April and May, Soloman Froman was seen going about his business, and that no swelling was observed, and, from the way that he handled himself, no unusual swelling existed. These witnesses might be mistaken as to the time. Their recollection may be explained upon the ground of mistake as to time; but these doctors and nurses had reason to fix and recollect the time. There is scarcely any room for an honest mistake. Their story is either true, at least as to the swollen condition of this man, or it is a fabrication. From the high character of the physicians, and the apparent honesty of the nurses, the latter fact is wholly improbable.

But it is contended that the proof of the conduct of Mr. and Mrs. Froman towards each other; their expressions of hatred and fear of each other; their statements during the time that they lived together, apparently, as husband and wife, as to non-access,—are incompetent as tending to show non-access. It is also contended that, where parties have opportunities of access,—sexual intercourse,—the child begotten in wedlock is conclusively presumed to be legitimate. We do not so understand the law as to either proposition. We understand the law to be that where the husband and wife have opportunities of access, there arises a very strong presumption that they did have it; but this presumption may be overcome by clear proof to the contrary, which may consist of proof that the husband was incompetent to have sexual intercourse, or from some cause he had declined to have sexual intercourse with his wife, or she with him. If such proof of conduct, declarations, etc., were not admitted as proof, it would be almost impossible to prove that the husband and wife had declined to have sexual intercourse with each other. It is a fact that husbands and wives, though living in the same house or on the same farm, have often so lived, not as husband and wife, but in fact in a state of separation; so, in the absence of proof of constant watch over them, night and day, it would be impossible to prove non-access, unless the proof of conduct, declarations, etc., were admitted as evidence.

It is also contended that the proof of adultery on the part of the wife was incompetent. Where access is either expressly or impliedly admitted, such proof is ordinarily inadmissible, unless it is such proof as unquestionably establishes the fact of illegitimacy; as that of the adulterous intercourse by a white woman, having a white husband, with a negro, and the child born in the usual course of time thereafter was a negro. But where proof shows that the husband is not capable of performing the sexual act, or that the parties have abstained from performing the sexual act, then it is competent to prove adultery on the part of the wife as corroborating the main fact. If Mrs. Froman was shown to be, in fact, a virtuous woman, such fact would create the belief that there was some mistake or false swearing in reference to the incompetency or non-access of her husband, or else incline the chancellor to adopt the theory of the expert physicians, to the effect that though, from the swollen condition of Froman, he could not enter Mrs. Froman's person, yet in his effort to make the entry, his semen found its way into the vagina, and the appellee Soloman White Froman was the fruit. But the proof of her adultery drives away these conjectures and strained theories, made in behalf of chastity, and corroborates the proof of non-access.

We do not understand that, where the husband's access is either expressly or impliedly admitted or proven about the time the child is begotten, the child's legitimacy is in all such cases conclusive. The presumption, in such cases, is only conclusive where proof may be introduced, *pro* and *con*, as to the question of legitimacy. No probabilities can be weighed and considered. The fact of illegitimacy in such case cannot be established by the weight of evidence. Nothing short of some fact thoroughly established, and which, when established, cannot be explained away, as the case just mentioned of a white woman having a negro child, will be allowed to prevail against the presumption. The proof of the illegitimacy of the child, begotten in wedlock, is a direct attack upon the mother's virtue, and an accusation of a wanton violation of her marriage vows, and is a stigma upon the child, and taints its blood, if the charge be true. Therefore, to hold that the mother, thus assailed, could not support her own innocence and honor, and the purity of the blood of her child, by her oath that she was true to herself and offspring by keeping sacred what is enjoined by both divine and human law, and upon the keeping of which the refinement and elevation of the race depend, would be a harsh rule indeed. But, while she is allowed to do this, and in dubious cases she should do this, she should not, upon cross-examination, be allowed to withhold any part of the truth. The whole truth should come, although she would have to disclose acts of adultery.

The General Statutes provide, in substance, that if the wife voluntarily leaves her husband, and lives in adultery, she shall forfeit her right of dower and distributable share in the husband's real and personal estate. This Statute does not mean that she shall constantly live with one man in adultery during her abandonment of the husband, in order to forfeit her right of dower or distributable share; but if she admits any man or men to her periodically, or whenever it is convenient or opportunity is afforded, during said abandonment, such conduct constitutes a living in adultery, within the meaning of the Statute. It is clear from the proof in the cause, that Mrs. Froman's conduct was as above described, in consequence of which she forfeited her right to dower and distributable share in Soloman Froman's estate.

The judgment is reversed, with directions to deny Soloman White Froman any interest whatever in Soloman Froman's estate, and to deny Mrs. Froman any dower or distributable share in said estate, and for further proceedings consistent with this opinion.

Petition for rehearing overruled.

WASHINGTON SUPREME COURT.

TERRITORY of Washington, *ex rel.* George O. KELLY, *Appt.*,

v.

J. P. STEWART *et al.*

(......Wash.......)

A statute authorizing the creation of a municipal corporation by a judicial court, upon petition of a majority of the inhabitants of the territory to be incorporated, is unconstitutional as delegating legislative functions to the court.

(*Dunbar, J., dissents.*)

(February 13, 1890.)

APPEAL by relator from a judgment of the District Court for Pierce County sustaining a demurrer to the complaint in a proceeding to determine by what authority defendants claimed to exercise the powers of trustees of a certain municipal corporation and to dissolve such corporation. *Reversed.*

The facts are fully stated in the opinion.

Messrs. **Fremont Campbell**, *Pros. Atty.*, **C. H. Hanford** and **Thomas Carroll**, for appellant:

Section 1889 of the Revised Statutes of the United States, together with chap. 168, p. 101, 24 United States Statutes at Large, of Congress, Second Session, conferring upon the Legislature the right to create municipal corporations, does not contemplate or permit the Legislature to delegate such right to courts or judges.

Galesburg v. *Hawkinson*, 75 Ill. 153; *People* v. *Carpenter*, 24 N. Y. 89; *People* v. *Nevada*, 6 Cal. 148.

In States where the right is recognized, the courts have universally held that such statutes do not imply any such power against private consent.

Devore's App. 56 Pa. 163; *Borough of Blooming Valley*, 56 Pa. 66; *People* v. *Bennett*, 29 Mich. 451, 18 Am. Rep. 115, 116.

The order incorporating Town of Puyallup is void. The power to make such an order is not judicial and not vested in said judge by law.

See also 33 L. R. A. 638; 39 L. R. A. 214.

People v. *Bennett*, 29 Mich. 451, 18 Am. Rep. 107; *People* v. *Nevada*, 6 Cal. 143.

Messrs. **B. F. Jacobs** and **Town & Likens**, for appellees:

The legislative function is the predetermination of what the law shall be for the regulation of all future cases falling under its provisions.

Bates v. *Kimball*, 2 D. Chipman (Vt.) 77; Cooley, Const. Lim. 5th ed. pp. 109, 110; *Newland* v. *Marsh*, 19 Ill. 383.

The judicial function or power is "to adjudicate upon and protect the rights and interests of the citizens and to that end to construe and apply the law."

Cincinnati, W. & Z. R. Co. v. *Clinton Co.* 1 Ohio St. 77. Examine also *King* v. *Dedham Bank*, 15 Mass. 447; *Gordon* v. *Inghram*, 1 Grant. Cas. 152; *Beebe* v. *State*, 6 Ind. 501; *Taylor* v. *Place*, 4 R. I. 324.

A statute may be conditional and its taking effect may be made to depend upon some subsequent event.

See *Burlington* v. *Leebrick*, 43 Iowa, 252; *Baltimore* v. *Clunet*, 23 Md. 449; *State* v. *Kirkley*, 29 Md. 85; *Walton* v. *Greenwood*, 60 Me. 356.

Act of Territorial Legislature approved February 2, 1888, does not delegate legislative authority to the courts, as the Legislature by that Act prescribes the liabilities, duties, powers and privileges of said corporations, and the Statute, and not the court, determines the extent and nature of the powers of the corporation.

Morristown v. *Shelton*, 1 Head (Tenn.) 24; *Kayser* v. *Bremen*, 16 Mo. 88; *Burlington* v. *Leebrick*, 43 Iowa, 252.

The Act is not unconstitutional because of certain powers and duties conferred upon the courts in relation to the mode of organizing said towns, as these duties are judicial in their nature, and the Legislature, and not the court, prescribes the powers, duties and liabilities of which the corporation is possessed.

Kayser v. *Bremen*, *Morristown* v. *Shelton* and *Burlington* v. *Leebrick*, *supra*; *Bank of Chenango* v. *Brown*, 26 N. Y. 467; *People* v. *Salomon*, 51 Ill. 37; *Burgess* v. *Pue*, 2 Gill, 11; *Hammond* v. *Haines*, 25 Md. 541; *Com.* v. *Montrose*, 52 Pa. 391.

Anders, *Ch. J.*, delivered the opinion of the court:

This action was brought in the District Court of the Second Judicial District of Washington Territory, holding terms at Tacoma, in and for Pierce County, to inquire and determine by what warrant or authority the appellees claim to exercise the powers of a board of trustees of the Town of Puyallup, in that county, and to oust them from office as such board of trustees, and to dissolve said municipal corporation. The complaint states: "(1) That the above-named defendants, at a place called 'Puyallup,' in Pierce County, Wash. T., do now unlawfully act as a municipal corporation under the name and style of the 'Town of Puyallup,' without being legally incorporated as a board of trustees of said alleged municipal corporation. (2) That said defendants act as such corporation, and exercise the powers of such board of trustees, under color of authority conferred by an order made by the judge of this court, at chambers, in the City of Tacoma, Wash. T., on the 31st day of July, A. D. 1888, and entered upon record in this court. (3) That a certified copy of the record of said order, and of the proceedings in the matter relating to the alleged incorporation of said Town of Puyallup, marked 'Exhibit A,' is hereto annexed for reference, and made a part of this complaint, and a correct plat, showing the boundaries of said alleged incorporated Town of Puyallup, as defined in said order, and the location of the relator's farm, hereinafter mentioned, marked 'Exhibit B,' is hereto annexed for reference, and made a part of this complaint. (4) That said order is void, and of no effect; for the same was made by the judge, aforesaid, upon the *ex parte* application of John Beverly, Esq., without a hearing being granted to the relator, or to any of the inhabitants, or owners of property, within the boundaries of said alleged Town of Puyallup, and without any notice being given of said application; and no opportunity was at any time given to the relator, or any other person whomsoever, to remonstrate against or oppose the incorporation of said town, or to question the validity or sufficiency of the petition upon which said order was made, or to make complaint as to the boundaries of said alleged town; and no legal or good evidence was produced before the judge upon which to base the findings of fact recited in said order; and power to make said order is not judicial, and not vested in said judge by law. (5) That the relator is the owner of real property situated within the boundaries of said alleged town, as defined by said order; and he and many others, owners of property situated within said alleged town, have not consented to the incorporation of said town, and are unwilling to have said town incorporated with boundaries including their said property, for that said property is partly improved and cultivated farming land, and no part thereof is platted into town lots and streets; and they are unwilling to consent to the laying out of and extending streets across their said land, or to taxation of said land, by such alleged municipal corporation."

To this complaint the defendants demurred for the alleged reason that the same did not state facts sufficient to constitute a cause of action. The district court sustained the demurrer, and caused judgment for costs to be entered against the plaintiff.

From this judgment plaintiff appeals to this court; and we are called upon to determine the question of the legal existence of the Town of Puyallup, which also involves the validity of the Act of the Legislature approved February 2, 1888, entitled "An Act for the Incorporation of Towns and Villages," the first section of which, so far as is material to this case, is as follows: "Where a majority of the taxable inhabitants of any town or village within this Territory present a petition to the judge of the district court, having jurisdiction of real actions in such county, setting forth the metes and bounds of such town or village, together with the adjacent bounds, in all not exceeding in area one square mile, which they desire to include therein, and praying that they may be incorporated, and police established for their local government, and the judge of the district court shall be satisfied that a majority of the taxable inhabitants of such town or village, as shown by the last assessment roll of said county, shall have signed such petition, such judge of the district court shall cause such petition to be entered in full on the records of such court, together with the names of the petitioners, and shall thereupon make and record an order declaring such town or village duly incorporated, designating in such order the metes and bounds thereof, and the name of such town or village, and thenceforward the inhabitants within such metes and bounds are a body politic and corporate."

The proceedings for incorporating the town were inaugurated by the presentation to the judge of the district court, by one John Beverly, of a petition signed by sixty-three persons therein, representing themselves to be a majority of the taxable inhabitants of the Town of Puyallup, praying that they might be incorporated under the name of the "Town of Puyallup," and police established for their local government, and that trustees be appointed for the government of said town. The petition also specified and defined the metes and bounds of the proposed territory to be incorporated, and alleged the area thereof to be in all not exceeding one square mile. On the 31st day of July, 1888, the judge of the district court, at chambers, in the City of Tacoma, in Pierce County, in response to the prayer of the petition, made and entered of record an order declaring the Town of Puyallup to be duly incorporated under and by virtue of the laws of Washington Territory, and in said order appointed defendants as a board of trustees of the town, in accordance with section 2 of the Incorporation Act.

It is admitted by the demurrer, and was conceded by counsel on the argument of this case, that the relator is the owner of real property situated within the boundaries of the territory described in the petition, and defined by order of the court; that he did not consent to the incorporation of the town; that he was unwilling to have it incorporated with boundaries including his property; that his said real estate is partly improved and cultivated farming land, not platted into town lots and streets, and that he is unwilling to consent to the laying out of and extending streets across the same; that he is unwilling to submit to taxation of his land by said municipal corporation; that no notice of the presentation of the petition was given; and that the relator had no opportunity to be heard, or to remonstrate against, or oppose the incorporation of the town, or to question the validity of the order of the judge, or to make complaint as to the boundaries of the proposed municipal corporation.

The proceedings are assailed by appellant as not being in accordance with the law relating thereto. He objects that the petition is defective in not stating that the signers thereof were a majority of the taxable inhabitants of the town, according to the last assessment roll of the county, and that the order of the judge was made upon the certificate of the county assessor who is not empowered by any law to so certify; that there was no evidence before the judge or court to warrant the order; and that the order was made without jurisdiction of the subject matter by the court. As the law requires that the petition to be presented to the judge shall be signed by a majority of the taxable inhabitants of the town or village to be incorporated, and that the judge shall be satisfied, in some way not specified by law, that a majority of the taxable inhabitants of the town or village, as shown by the last assessment roll of the county, shall have signed the petition, it is quite doubtful whether an omission to state in the petition that the petitioners are a majority of the taxable inhabitants as shown by the last assessment roll of the county, is not a matter substantially affecting the subsequent proceedings. But, however this may be, we are not disposed to hold the incorporation invalid on that account, but will assume that the law was substantially complied with.

We now come to the consideration of validity of the law itself. The object of the Act of the Legislature was the incorporation of towns and villages, as expressed in the title; and, as the meaning of the expression "towns and villages" is not defined by the law, we must presume that the words were intended to be used in their ordinary acceptation, as meaning an aggregation of houses and inhabitants more or less compact. The word "town" was originally from the Anglo-Saxon word "tun," an inclosure, and meant a collection of houses inclosed by a wall. Anderson, Law Dict. title *Town.*

"The fundamental idea of a municipal corporation proper, both in England and in this country, is to invest compact or dense populations with the power of local self-government. Indeed, the necessity for such corporations springs from the existence of centers or agglomerations of population, having, by reason of density and numbers, local or peculiar interests and wants, not common to adjoining sparsely settled or agricultural regions. It is necessary to draw the line which separates the limits of the place and people to be incorporated. This is, with us, a legislative function." 1 Dillon, Mun. Corp. 3d ed. § 183.

In England, this power was formerly given by a royal grant or charter, presumably at the request of the municipalities themselves, but in this country municipal corporations are purely the creatures of statutes. "They possess no powers or faculties not conferred upon them, either expressly or by fair implication, by the law which creates them, or other statutes applicable to them." Id. § 21.

It being conceded that the power to create municipal corporations is vested exclusively in the Legislature, the question arises, Can this power be delegated; and, if so, to whom, or to what agencies? Counsel on both sides agree that the Legislature may delegate its functions in some measure; but they disagree as to the legislative power to carry the principle to the extent attempted in the Act in question. On the one side, it is contended that the Act approved February 2, 1888, does not in fact delegate legislative authority to the courts; that the Statute, and not the court, determines the extent and nature of the powers of the corporation: that a statute may be valid, though its taking effect may depend on some subsequent event, and that the powers and duties of the courts in relation to the mode of organizing towns are judicial in their nature; that the

Legislature, and not the court, prescribes the powers, duties and liabilities of the corporation,—and, on the other, it is urged that the law of Congress conferring upon the Territorial Legislature the right to create municipal corporations does not permit the Legislature to delegate such right to the courts or judges; that the law is mandatory upon the court, is against public policy and authorizes the taking of property without due process of law, and without notice or opportunity to be heard; and that the including of farming land in incorporated towns is unreasonable and unjust.

The incorporation of towns by general statutory law is a departure from original methods, and is of comparatively modern date; and it would naturally be expected that the procedure for their organization by this means would not be uniform throughout the different States of the Union. It would be practically impossible for the Legislature, by a general law, to fix and define the boundaries of every municipal corporation that might be organized under it; and that question is therefore determined in some other way, designated by the general law of the particular jurisdiction. But the authority to incorporate, with us as in England, has been restricted to cases in which compact communities already exist who desire to assume a corporate character, and have police established for their local government. Id. § 183. But, unless specially restrained by constitutional provisions, the Legislature may delegate the power to determine the territorial limits of the municipal corporation, and thereby settle what property and persons will be subject to municipal control, to appropriate local bodies or boards of officers. 1 Dillon, Mun. Corp. *supra; People* v. *Bennett*, 29 Mich. 451.

It would hardly seem probable that the Legislature, while professing to pass a law for the incorporation of "towns and villages", really intended to include therein rural districts or farming lands not platted or laid out in lots or blocks, especially against the will of the owner of such property; and yet the Statute, by its terms, covers and includes just such cases; and we do not feel at liberty to construe it otherwise.

We entirely agree with the learned judge who decided the case of *People* v. *Bennett*, when he says that "there are few, if any, acts of state, bearing upon individuals, more important than those which determine their liberty to be included in particular municipalities; and the cases are very rare in which they have not been allowed an opportunity of being heard in every step of the proceedings." And, where the individual has not expressly assented, or impliedly done so, by settling and remaining in a dense community needing corporate powers and privileges, it seems too plain for argument that he should at least be accorded a hearing before being compelled to subject himself or his property to the dominion of a municipality with whose interests he has nothing in common. This view of the law was adopted in the case of *People* v. *Bennett*, above cited.

In the case of *Borough of Blooming Valley*, 56 Pa. 66, it was held that farming land might be included in the limits of a municipal corporation by consent of the owner, but not otherwise.

And in *Borough of Little Meadows*, 28 Pa. 256, it was held that the community proposing to be incorporated was too sparse to be called a "village", within the meaning of the law.

On the contrary, it has been held in New Hampshire, with equally good reason, that the selectmen of a town, in defining the boundaries of a village, could not exclude any part of it, but must include the whole within the village limits. *Osgood* v. *Clark*, 26 N. H. 307.

Appellees contend, as before intimated, that a statute may be conditional, and its taking effect made to depend upon some subsequent event; and, to a certain extent, the principle is recognized by the courts. As an illustration, the Legislature may enact a general statute for the formation of private corporations; and its taking effect, as to any particular corporation, may depend upon the assent of the parties interested. They may withhold their assent at pleasure, but cannot be forced to become incorporators. If they accept the terms and provisions of the law they are presumed to be benefited thereby; but, if they reject, they cannot be injured.

While a statute may be conditional, and only take effect upon the happening of a future event, we hold that the place where it is to operate, its "*situs*," must be fixed definitely by the Legislature itself, or delegated to some body or agency capable of exercising legislative functions, and not left to the will or caprice of localities to determine whether it shall be applicable to their particular community or not. Local Option Laws have been sustained by some courts, but the place where they were to take effect has always been defined by law, and not left conditioned upon the discretion of the people of any and every locality in the State.

To sustain the position of appellees, counsel cite the case of *Burlington* v. *Leebrick*, 43 Iowa, 252. The question there was as to the power of the City of Burlington to enlarge its limits by extending its boundaries over contiguous territory; and the court held that the law authorizing a petition for the purpose by the city council, to be presented to, and acted upon by, the circuit judge, and issues to be found and tried as in other proceedings, was not invalid as an unwarranted delegation of legislative power, basing the opinion on the ground that the determination of the issues by the court was a judicial act,—a mere ascertaining of the condition upon which the law might take effect. But in delivering the opinion the court used the following language: "Nor is it proper to designate the thing to be accomplished by this Statute as the creation of a corporation. A corporation is an artificial being clothed with certain powers. In the present case, such a corporation exists, known as the 'City of Burlington.' When the Act sought in this petition is accomplished, no new corporation will have been created." From this language we might infer that, had the question before the court been that of the formation of a municipal corporation, the decision might have been different.

In the case of *Kayser* v. *Bremen*, 16 Mo. 88, the incorporation of a town by the county court, in pursuance of a general statute, was upheld on the ground that the court acted judicially, and had no discretion, and no authority to vest any power in the corporation.

And in the case of *Morristown* v. *Shelton*, 1 Head (Tenn.), 24, a law substantially like the one under consideration in this case was held valid and constitutional for the reason that no legislative power was delegated to or exercised by the court. This last decision, however, was under a Constitution which provided that "the Legislature shall have power to grant such charters of incorporation as they may deem expedient for the public good." We do not feel bound by the decisions in these cases. If the court in either of the cases acted judicially in the matter before it, then, certainly, it should have had a right or "discretion" to exercise its judgment. If its action was not judicial, then, surely, it must have been a delegated legislative power which it exercised. Counsel for appellees also cite the case of *Blanchard* v. *Bissell*, 11 Ohio St. 96. The controversy in that case was as to the validity of the Statute in relation to the annexation of territory to cities; and it was claimed by Bissell, in a proceeding to enjoin the collection of certain taxes levied upon his property by the city council, that the order of the county commissioners for the annexation of the district embracing his property was void because it included his property with that of others, without his consent, and against his remonstrance The court sustained the law on the ground that the county commissioners were properly clothed with power to do the acts objected to. Each party was entitled to a hearing under that Statute, and the commissioners were empowered to order the annexation or not, as they might deem reasonable and proper. We agree with that decision; and, if our Statute were like the one upon which it was based, it would be stripped of its most objectionable features.

In the late case of *People* v. *Fleming*, 10 Colo. 553, the Supreme Court of Colorado held that a law which provides that when the inhabitants of any part of the county not embraced within the limits of any city or incorporated town desire to be organized into a city or incorporated town, they may apply by petition to the county court, and providing, also, for the manner of procedure in the organization of such contemplated town or city, was not in conflict with the Constitution. The decision in that case seems to have been based upon the broad ground that the Legislature, if not expressly prohibited by the Constitution, may delegate the power to form municipal corporations to unorganized private individuals; in other words, to the people themselves. We cannot consent to follow the reasoning in that case, or to concur in the conclusion reached by the learned court. We think the better doctrine is that laid down by *Judge* Cooley in his work on Constitutional Limitations, 4th ed. 145, 146, which is as follows: "The prevailing doctrine in the courts appears to be that, except in those cases where, by the Constitution, the people have expressly reserved to themselves a power of decision, the function of legislation cannot be exercised by them even to the extent of accepting or rejecting a law which has been framed for their consideration." But we would not be understood as holding that the Legislature could not delegate the power to put the machinery of municipal corporations in motion to courts which are not purely legal tribunals. The Courts of Quarter Sessions of Pennsylvania, and the County Courts of Oregon, and perhaps of other States, are vested with administrative, and, in a measure, representative, powers; and they are properly intrusted with the functions attempted by our late Territorial Legislature, by the law in question, to be imposed upon the district judge.

We hold that a judicial court cannot exercise legislative functions, and that the Legislature cannot impose such power upon it. *People* v. *Bennett, supra; People* v. *Nevada*, 6 Cal. 143; *Galesburg* v. *Hawkinson*, 75 Ill. 153; *People* v. *Carpenter*, 24 N. Y. 89.

Owing to the importance of this case, we have given it all the consideration in our power, under the circumstances; and we have been greatly aided in our labors by the learning and diligence of counsel on both sides. And we are constrained to hold that the Statute under which the Town of Puyallup was organized is invalid, and cannot be sustained. The cause will therefore be remanded to the court below, with directions to overrule the demurrer, and to proceed in accordance with this opinion. And it is so ordered.

Stiles, Hoyt and **Scott**, *JJ.*, concur.

Dunbar, *J.*:

I concur in the result, because I do not think that the petition was sufficient; but I cannot concur in the opinion that the Act of the Legislature was unconstitutional.

MISSOURI SUPREME COURT.

BARBER ASPHALT PAVING CO., *Respt.*,

v.

Mary C. HUNT, *Appt.*

(......Mo.......)

1. It will be presumed that an ordinance was properly signed by the Speaker of the House of Delegates, where the journal recites that his signature was affixed in open session, and no objection is noted on the journal although it does not expressly recite that all the matters of detail were complied with, and the charter of the city provides that it shall be signed in open session, and that before the officer's signature is affixed "he shall suspend all other business, declaring that such bill will now be read."

2. The adjournment of the House of Delegates on the day bills are presented to the mayor for his approval will not prevent them from becoming valid ordinances, if duly filed by the mayor, with his approval, in the city register's office, although the charter of the city provides that every bill shall become an ordinance when "returned within ten days to the House in which the same originated, with the approval of the mayor."

3. **The facts that the work of street paving prescribed by an ordinance is covered by letters-patent,** under which the exclusive right is held by one company, and therefore that no competition for the work is possible, will not prevent letting a contract for the work under a charter providing that such contracts shall be let to the lowest responsible bidder.

(February 24, 1890.)

APPEAL by defendant from a judgment of the Circuit Court for the City of St. Louis in favor of plaintiff in an action to enforce payment of certain special tax bills issued to plaintiff by the City of St. Louis in payment for work done upon certain streets. *Affirmed.*

The case sufficiently appears in the opinion.

Mr. **Charles M. Napton,** for appellant:

The journals must actually show, on their face, every fact necessary to make valid the proceedings of the General Assembly, and when they do not show this, no presumption will be made that the fact existed.

Spangler v. *Jacoby*, 14 Ill. 297; *Turley* v. *Logan County*, 17 Ill. 151.

The Legislature must be in session when a bill is presented to the governor, and when it is returned by him to the House.

People v. *Hatch*, 33 Ill. 9.

The governor or mayor forms one branch of the legislative body, and can do no act as a part of it after an adjournment..

Trustees of School Dist. No. 1 v. *Ormsby Co.* 1 Nev. 340; *Fowler* v *Peirce*, 2 Cal. 165.

A sending of the bill to the city register is not a "return to the House."

Opinion of Judges (*Re Soldiers Voting Bill*), 45 N. H. 607.

Where a city is empowered by its charter to improve streets at the expense of the adjoining lot owners, but required to let all such work to the lowest bidder, it cannot contract for laying a pavement at the expense of such lot owners, the right to lay which is patented and owned by one firm.

Dean v. *Charlton*, 23 Wis. 590; *Wells* v. *Burnham*, 20 Wis. 112; *Nicolson Pavement Co.* v. *Painter*, 35 Cal. 699; *Ruggles* v. *Collier*, 43 Mo. 353, 377; *Burgess* v. *Jefferson*, 21 La. Ann. 143; *Dolan* v. *New York*, 4 Abb. Pr. N. S. 397; 1 Dillon, Mun. Corp. § 467. See also *Merritt* v. *Portchester*, 71 N. Y. 309; *O'Byrne* v. *Philadelphia*, 93 Pa. 225; *Re Eager*, 46 N. Y. 100; *Harlem Gaslight Co.* v. *New York*, 33 N. Y. 324; *People* v. *Flagg*, 17 N. Y. 584; *Hastings* v. *Columbus*, 42 Ohio St. 585.

Messrs. **Hitchcock, Madill & Finkelnburg** for respondent.

Sherwood, *J.*, delivered the opinion of the court:

The grounds upon which the defendant resists the payment of the tax bills in suit are two: *first*, that the ordinances in question were not passed and approved as required by the charter; and, *second*, that the work provided for in the ordinances was not let as provided in § 27, art. 6, of the charter.

The charter provisions in respect to passing ordinances (art. 3, § 22) are as follows: "No bill shall become an ordinance until the same shall have been signed by the presiding officer of each of the two Houses, in open session; and, before such officer shall affix his signature to any bill, *he shall suspend all other business, declare that such bill will now be read, and that if no* objections be made, he will sign the same, to the end that it may become an ordinance. The bill shall then be read at length, and, if no objection be made, he shall, in the presence of the House, in open session, and before any other business is entertained, affix his signature, which fact shall be noted on the journal, and the bill immediately sent to the other House." 2 Rev. Stat. 1879, p. 1584.

Defendant put in evidence the journal of the House of Delegates for March 20, 1883, which, after giving in full the report of the proper committee that these two bills were truly enrolled, proceeds, as follows: "The bills, as above, were read at length. No objection being made, Mr. Speaker Marriot, in the presence of the House, in open session, affixed his signature thereto, as required by the charter."

Upon this fact being thus shown by the journal, the defendant contends that the charter provisions marked above in italics were not complied with, and therefore the ordinance passed is null. These provisions of the charter are copied from section 37, art. 4, of our State Constitution; and upon that section it has been ruled that a bill passed by the Legislature became a law where the same was signed by the presiding officer of each of the two Houses in open session; that this provision was mandatory, but the other provisions, relating to mere matters of detail, were but directory; and, as no objection was noted on the journal, the presumption would be indulged that the matters of detail were complied with; that the Legislature proceeded by right, and not by wrong. *State* v. *Mead*, 71 Mo. 266.

Here the journal expressly recites that the signature of the speaker of the House was affixed in open session. On the authority of the case cited, it must be ruled that the bills in question become ordinances, as against the objection already considered.

But it is urged that the bills failed to become laws, because never returned to the House in which they originated. Section 23 of art. 3 of the charter provides: "Every bill presented to the mayor, and returned within ten days to the House in which the same originated, with the approval of the mayor, shall become an ordinance."

The testimony shows the bills, though signed by the mayor, were not thus returned, both Houses having adjourned March 27, 1883, *sine die*,—the day on which the bills were presented to the mayor for his approval. But the testimony also shows that the mayor on the same day filed the bills in the city register's office on the day of their approval.

Section 23 of art. 3 of the charter contemplates that cases will arise where a bill shall not have have been returned to the House where the same originates; and, besides, there is no provision in the charter that "no bill shall become an ordinance," which shall not be returned by the mayor to the House where the same originated. The same considerations, therefore, apply here as were applied in *Mead's Case, supra;* and we hold the ordinance as valid, as against this objection also.

Section 27 of article 6 provides how bids

for work shall be awarded, to wit, that the board of public improvements shall "let out said work by contract to the lowest responsible bidder, subject to the approval of the council." Upon this point it is insisted that such provision was violated, because the work of street paving prescribed by the ordinances was covered by letters-patent, under which plaintiff held the exclusive right, and therefore there was no competition for said work. This point, though adjudicated in other jurisdictions, is a case of first impression in this State. In New York it has been ruled, under a statute requiring all city work to be let "to the lowest bidder," that the common council were not prohibited from letting a contract for paving a street with material or in a manner not admitting competitive bids or proposals. *Re Dugro*, 50 N. Y. 513.

This ruling was approvingly followed in *Baird* v. *New York*, 96 N. Y. 567.

Prior to the time the subject was discussed in New York, a similar ruling had been made in Michigan. *Hobart* v. *Detroit*, 17 Mich. 246.

These cases seem to us to rest upon the correct basis. It certainly was never intended that the city authorities should be unable to make a contract, however necessary to the public welfare such contract might be, if the article desired, or the manner of the performance of the contract required the use of a patented article. Such a construction of the charter we regard as "sticking in the bark," and as subordinating the whole powers conferred on the common council to the meaning of two or three words contained in a single section of the charter. Besides, the rights of those interested are protected by the necessity of obtaining the approval of the council to any contract. A different view of the matter under discussion has been taken in Wisconsin (*Dean* v. *Charlton*, 23 Wis. 590), but by a divided court; and it is noteworthy that the Legislature of that State did not approve the view of the statute taken by the court, and so changed the statute, so as to prevent the continued prevalence of the objectionable ruling. *Mills* v. *Charleton*, 29 Wis. 400; *Dean* v. *Borchsenius*, 30 Wis. 239.

For these reasons *we affirm the judgment.*

All concur, but **Barclay**, *J.*, not sitting.

VERMONT SUPREME COURT.

Mary J. TOWNSHEND
v.
George H. GRAY *et al.*, Censors of the Vermont State Eclectic Medical Society.

(...... Vt. ......)

1. **No power to confer the degree** of M. D., or any other degree, is given to a corporation by the general law of a State authorizing incorporation for the purpose of maintaining a literary and scientific institution.

2. **A diploma from an institution** having no power to give it is not sufficient to entitle a person to demand a license as physician from the censors of a medical society under Rev. Laws, § 3911.

(April 5, 1890.)

PETITION for a writ of mandamus to compel defendants to issue to complainant a certificate authorizing her to practice medicine within the State. *Dismissed.*

The facts are fully stated in the opinion.

Mr. **J. C. Baker** for complainant.

Mr. **A. H. Huse** for defendants.

Powers, *J.*, delivered the opinion of the court:

This is a petition by the complainant, claiming to be a graduate of the Vermont Medical College, and holding a diploma of that college conferring upon her the degree of M. D., against the defendants, who are the censors of the Vermont State Eclectic Medical Society, praying that a writ of mandamus be issued commanding the defendants, as such censors, to issue to the complainant a certificate authorizing her to practice medicine in this State.

Our Statute provides that every medical society chartered by the Legislature "shall issue certificates to physicians and surgeons who furnish evidence by diploma from a medical college or university, or by certificate of examination by an authorized board, which satisfies said censors that the person presenting such credentials has been, after due examination, deemed qualified to practice the branches mentioned in such diploma or certificate." The case shows that the complainant presented to the defendants, as such censors, her diploma aforesaid, and the defendants refused to issue the certificate above referred to on the ground that the Vermont Medical College had no legal power to issue a diploma conferring the degree of M. D., and so the complainant had not shown credentials entitling her to a license to practice medicine.

The main question in issue is whether said medical college has the power to issue diplomas which entitle the holder to the license provided for in the Statute. Without going into the question at length, touching the power conferred by the Statute upon the censors, which has been discussed in argument, it is plain that this board has the power to decide in the first instance whether a diploma presented to it as evidence of the holder's right to a license is a genuine or spurious document. So far, at least, the board may sit in judgment upon a diploma; and in this case the board adjudged that this diploma did not have such legal efficacy, as evidence, as would warrant the issue of a licence.

The Vermont Medical College was organized under the provisions of the 10th subdivision of § 3664, Rev. Laws. That section provides that "persons may associate together and have the powers of a corporation for either of the following purposes: . . . (10) To establish and maintain literary and scientific institutions."

Later sections in the same chapter enumerate the powers which such associations may have, namely: may have a corporate name, a corporate seal; may adopt by-laws; may sue and be sued; purchase and hold real estate; may raise money, and divide their capital stock into shares.

Under this subdivision, it is argued that a medical college may be organized with the power to confer the degree of M. D. It is fundamental that a corporation has such power only as is conferred by its charter, with such incidental powers as are necessary to enable it to exercise its chartered power. No express power to confer degrees can be found in the Statute under which this medical college was organized, and hence the power to confer degrees must be classed as incidental to the general powers of a corporation formed for the purpose of maintaining a literary or scientific institution, if it exists at all. It would hardly do to say that literary or scientific institutions have such power upon any theory that without it they cannot answer the ends of their creation. The degree of M. D. is something more than a mere honorary title. It is a certificate attesting the fact that the person upon whom it has been conferred has successfully mastered the curriculum of study prescribed by the authorities of an institution created by law, and by law authorized to issue such certificate. It thus has a legal sanction and authority. But it has more. In practical affairs, it introduces its possessor to the confidence and patronage of the general public. Its legal character gives it a moral and material credit in the estimation of the world, and makes it thereby a valuable property right of great pecuniary value.

The scope of subdivision 10 of the Statute in question may be discovered by looking at the other subdivisions of the same section. These provide for the organization of library associations; bands of music; associations for breeding fish, for bringing to justice thieves and burglars, building meeting houses, securing burial grounds, etc. The articles of association are to be filed in the town clerk's office, in the town where the association is organized. All this points to association of limited and local scope. The filing of the articles of association, which constitute the charter under which the association proceeds with its work, in the town clerk's office, indicates that the Legislature did not regard such associations as having powers, the exercise of which concerned the general public. The power to confer degrees, not being conferred explicitly by the Statute, and not being necessary to enable a literary or scientific institution to carry forward studies of a literary or scientific character, clearly does not exist at all. *Philadelphia Medical College Case*, 8 Whart. 445.

It is no more appropriate to say that a literary or scientific institution, without special statutory power, can confer the degree of M. D., than to say that it may confer the degree of LL. D. or D. D. or A. B.; for it is plain that law schools, theological schools, universities and colleges can be organized under this subdivision equally well with medical schools. Every State in the Union has chartered these institutions, and it is believed that none of them has ever supposed that, with all the widely enumerated powers delegated to them, it had the power to confer degrees of any kind unless such power was expressly conferred in its charter. In the case of the Castleton Medical School, chartered many years ago, the charter at first granted contained no delegation of power to confer degrees, but at the next session of the Legislature it was amended by an Act giving such power. Such has, manifestly, been the legislative idea respecting the necessity of special authority from the law-making power of the government touching the right to confer degrees; and construing this General Statute, providing for the organization, by voluntary association, of persons for local and comparatively unimportant purposes, in the light of the common usages and common understanding of people respecting the rights, privileges and emoluments universally accorded to persons upon whom degrees have been conferred, we are clearly of the opinion that the Vermont Medical College has no power, under its articles of association, to confer degrees of any kind. To hold that the Legislature, by a general law, intended that any three men in any town of the State, however illiterate or irresponsible, might organize and flood the State with doctors of medicine, doctors of law, doctors of divinity, masters of arts, civil engineers and all the other various titles that everywhere in the civilized world have signified high attainments and special equipment for professional work, is to liken it to the witty French minister who threatened to create so many dukes that it would be no honor to be one, and a burning disgrace not to be one.

The complainant, therefore, in submitting her diploma to the board of censors, did not furnish that board any sufficient evidence of qualification that entitled her to the license asked for.

The petition is dismissed, with costs.

CONNECTICUT SUPREME COURT OF ERRORS.

Mary LAWLER, *Appt.*,
v.
John P. MURPHY *et al.*

(58 Conn. 294)

1. An agreement by an insurance association to pay a sum received from a death assessment, not exceeding $1,000, with a further provision that the death claim shall be payable within sixty days after proof, giving the form of notice and process for collecting death assessments, and containing a promise by insured to pay assessments, imports a promise by the insurance association to make, or cause to be made, the necessary assessment.

2. Whatever is necessary to be done

NOTE.—*Contract of mutual benefit association.*

The contract made between a mutual benefit company and its member by the certificate of membership does not differ in any essential particular from an ordinary policy of mutual life insurance, it having all the characteristics of an insurance

See also 37 L. R. A. 587.

in order to accomplish work specially contracted to be performed is parcel of the contract, though not specified.

3. Whatever may fairly be implied from the terms or nature of an instrument is, in judgment of law, contained in it.

4. A complaint alleging a state of facts from which an agreement to make an assessment upon members of an insurance organization can be implied, and claiming damages for failure to make the assessment, is not insufficient because it does not state in terms an agreement to make the assessment.

5. Individual members of an unincorporated association are liable for contracts made in the name of the association without regard to the question whether they so intended, or so understood the law, and even if the other party contracted in form with the association, and was ignorant of the names of the individual members composing it.

6. An action at law can be sustained for breach of the contract of a mutual benefit society to make an assessment.

7. The measure of damages for breach of an agreement by an insurance organization to make an assessment, and to pay the proceeds thereof, not exceeding $1,000, where each member contracts to pay an assessment of whatever the officials deem necessary, upon the death of any member, is prima facie the sum of $1,000.

(December 30, 1889.)

APPEAL by plaintiff from a judgment of the Superior Court for Hartford County sustaining a demurrer to the complaint in an action brought to recover upon a mutual benefit certificate of life insurance. *Reversed.*

The facts are fully stated in the opinion.

Mr. **C. E. Gross,** for appellant:

This is an agreement to pay $1,000 unless the defendants shall within the sixty days make a death assessment and fail to receive therefrom that sum, in which case the agreement is to pay only the amount so received.

Niblack, Mut. Ben. Societies, § 405; *Freeman* v. *National Ben. Society,* 42 Hun, 252, 254, 257; *O'Brien* v. *Home Ben. Society,* 51 Hun, 495, 499; *Peck* v. *Equitable Accident Asso.* 52 Hun, 255; *Kansas Protective Union* v. *Whitt,* 36 Kan. 764; *Hankinson* v. *Page,* 31 Fed. Rep. 184.

That no assessment was made with reference to this case is some evidence that none was necessary.

Freeman v. *National Ben. Society,* 42 Hun, 257. See also *Bailey* v. *Mutual Ben. Asso.* 71 Iowa, 689, 692.

An averment of demand for an assessment is not necessary.

Niblack, Mut. Ben. Societies, § 396; *Freeman* v. *National Ben. Society,* 42 Hun, 255. See also *Kansas Protective Union* v. *Whitt,* 36 Kan. 760; *Smith* v. *Covenant Mut. Ben. Asso.* 24 Fed. Rep. 685.

When the contract provides that an assessment shall be levied and the proceeds thereof, not exceeding a certain sum named, shall be paid to the beneficiary, it has been held that the insurers are prima facie bound to pay the maximum amount named, and the burden of proof is on them to show that a less amount has been or could only have been collected.

Elkhart Mut. Aid, B. & R. Asso. v *Houghton,*

---

contract. Supreme Commandery K. of G. R. v. Ainsworth, 71 Ala. 443; State v. Bankers & M. Mut. Ben. Asso. 23 Kan. 499; Endowment & B. Asso. v. State, 35 Kan. 253; Bolton v. Bolton, 73 Me. 299; Miner v. Michigan Mut. Ben. Asso. 6 West. Rep. 117, 63 Mich. 338; State v. Merchants Exch. Mut. Benev. Society, 72 Mo. 146; State v. Farmers & M. Mut. Benev. Asso. 18 Neb. 276; Folmer's App. 87 Pa. 133.

An association for the transaction of the business of life and casualty insurance on the co-operative or assessment plan is in effect a mutual benefit society, the members of which must take notice of and are bound by its by-laws and articles of association. Hesinger v. Home Ben. Asso. 41 Minn. 516.

The members are presumed to contract with reference to the charter and by-laws of such associations, though they be not recited in the contract. Holland v. Taylor, 9 West. Rep. 606, 111 Ind. 121; Farmer v. State, 69 Tex. 561.

See, as to distinction between mutual benefit associations and life insurance. Burdon v. Massachusetts Safety Fund Asso. 1 L. R. A. 146, 6 New Eng. Rep. 840, 147 Mass. 360.

As to fraternal associations, see Alexander v. Northwestern Masonic Aid Asso. 2 L. R. A. 161, and *notes,* 126 Ill. 558.

Certificates issued entitling the holder to money, to be paid from assessments upon the surviving members, are in legal effect policies of insurance; and the rules of law governing such policies are applicable. Elkhart Mut. Aid B. & R. Asso. v. Houghton, 103 Ind. 286, 1 West. Rep. 234.

A nominee in the certificate is entitled to receive only the amount actually collected, on an assessment made for his benefit, and not a sum equal to $1 assessed to each member. *Re* La Solidarite Mut. Ben. Asso. 68 Cal. 392.

A beneficiary under a policy in a mutual insurance association operated upon the assessment plan cannot recover on the policy by action against the association, where the assessment to pay the policy has not been made; yet he may, by proper proceedings, compel the association to make the assessment. Bainsbarger v. Union Mut. Aid Asso. 72 Iowa, 191.

No claim can be made against a mutual aid association unless a certificate has been issued designating the person who is to receive payment. Bishop v. Grand Lodge E. O. of Mut. Aid, 43 Hun, 472. See Burdon v. Massachusetts Safety Fund Asso. 1 L. R. A. 146, 6 New Eng. Rep. 840, 147 Mass. 360; Davidson v. Old People's Mut. Ben. Society, 1 L. R. A. 482, 39 Minn. 303; Lorcher v. Supreme Lodge K. of H. (Mich.) 3 L. R. A. 208.

Payment of assessments by insured.

Where assured agreed in the application to pay "one assessment" within thirty days from its date, and the by-laws provide for suspension upon failure to pay assessments within thirty days from their date, the certificate lapses upon the failure to pay any one assessment within the prescribed time. Stanley v. Northwestern L. Asso. 36 Fed. Rep. 75.

But to operate a suspension, notice must have been duly given to the delinquent. *Ibid.*

Where the by-laws provide that the time of suspension is to be fixed by vote of the lodge, a suspension by an officer, without such vote, is illegal. Supreme Lodge K. of H. v. Wickser, 72 Tex. 257.

The thirty days within which an assessment is required to be paid should not be estimated from the date of the notice, unless it was sent within a reasonable time after the date of the assessment. Stanley v. Northwestern L. Asso. *supra.*

Where the member holding the certificate was habitually dilatory in the payment of assessments levied against his share, the fact that the association

1 West. Rep. 284, 108 Ind. 286; *Lueders* v. *Hartford L. & Ann. Ins. Co.* 12 Fed. Rep. 465; *Kansas Protective Union* v. *Whitt, supra; Suppiger* v. *Covenant Mut. Ben. Asso.* 20 Ill. App. 595; *Covenant Mut. Ben. Asso.* v. *Hoffman*, 110 Ill. 606.

There is no need to resort to a chancery court to compel an assessment before a recovery can be had at law.

Niblack, Mut. Ben. Societies, §§ 408, 409; *Hankinson* v. *Page*, 31 Fed. Rep. 184; *Taylor* v. *National Temp. Relief Union*, 12 West. Rep. 92, 94 Mo. 35; *Earnshaw* v. *Sun Mut. Aid Society*, 11 Cent. Rep. 508, 68 Md. 465.

The defendants are liable as individuals.

Davison v. *Holden*, 4 New Eng. Rep. 818, 55 Conn. 103; Niblack, Mut. Ben. Societies, § 105. See also *Fredendall* v. *Taylor*, 26 Wis. 286; *Blakely* v. *Fennecke*, 59 Mo. 193.

Messrs. **Charles E. Perkins** and **A. Perkins**, for appellees:

Defendants could not be made liable personally on a written instrument signed by them only in the capacity of officers of the organization.

Hitchcock v. *Buchanan*, 105 U. S. 416 (26 L. ed. 1078); *Hewitt* v. *Wheeler*, 22 Conn. 557.

Upon such an agreement as this no action lies against anyone for the amount of the insurance, but the remedy is in equity to oblige the proper persons to make an assessment and pay it over.

Smith v. *Covenant Mut. Ben. Asso.* 24 Fed. Rep. 685; *Eggleston* v. *Centennial Mut. L. Asso.* 19 Fed. Rep. 201; *Burdon* v. *Massachusetts Safety Fund Asso* 1 L. R. A. 146, 6 New Eng. Rep. 840, 147 Mass. 360; *U. S. Mut. Accident Asso.* v. *Barry*, 131 U. S. 100 (33 L. ed. 60); *Bailey* v. *Mutual Ben. Asso.* 71 Iowa, 689; *Newman* v. *Covenant Mut. Ben. Asso.* 72 Iowa, 242.

Seymour, *J.*, delivered the opinion of the court:

This is an appeal from the judgment of the superior court sustaining the defendant's demurrer. The cause of demurrer upon which the issue was found for the defendants alleges that it appears from the contract for a breach of which the suit was brought, that the only agreement made therein was to pay such sum as might be received from a death assessment, and that it is not alleged in the complaint that any such sum was ever received.

To understand the force of this objection and the considerations applicable to it, it is necessary to set out the contract in full. It is as follows:

Certificate No. 446. Benefit $1,000.

Connecticut State Insurance Fund of the Ancient Order of Hibernians of the State of Connecticut.

In consideration of one dollar, initiation fee, and assessments levied from time to time by the directory, Thomas Lawler, of Division No. 2 of Hartford, County of Hartford, State of Connecticut, receipt of which is hereby acknowledged, and the agreement on the part of the said Thomas Lawler to accept the following conditions and rules as a part of this contract between said A. O. H. Insurance Fund and himself, hereby constitutes the said Thomas

---

in many instances received assessments from him after they were due, and reinstated him as a member, was a waiver of these several forfeitures, but not of the future prompt payment of assessments as one of the conditions of the contract. Crossman v. Massachusetts Ben. Asso. 3 New Eng. Rep. 517, 143 Mass. 435.

The by-laws may provide that upon the death of a member, each member should pay $1, in order to make up the amount to be paid to the nominee in the certificate of the deceased member. Re La Solidarite Mut. Ben. Asso. 68 Cal. 392.

Under a law of a benevolent society, which makes the nonpayment of assessments for a given period after notice operate as a suspension *ipso facto* of the delinquent member, it is not necessary that the suspension shall be judicially determined by any judicatory of the order. Borgraefe v. Supreme Lodge, K. & L. of H. 5 West. Rep. 98, 22 Mo. App. 127.

The beneficiaries of a member who stands suspended at the time of his death cannot recover on the benefit certificate, upon the ground that the subordinate lodge had continued to treat him as a member, and to treat his unpaid dues to the supreme lodge as dues payable to the subordinate lodge for which it had extended him credit. *Ibid.*

Assessments on death of members.

Where assessments upon the death of members were ordered by the association, they became due only after proper notice thereof was given to the insured; and the objection that the notice given was insufficient, under the provisions of the by-laws, because it failed to give the lists of deaths as required, and that it did not notify the member of the amount due from him to the benefit fund, was properly sustained, where the defense rested upon a forfeiture to defeat plaintiff's claim. Miner v. Michigan Mut. Ben. Asso. 6 West. Rep. 117, 63 Mich. 338.

Where it was the directors' duty under the by-laws to order an assessment, and the chairman was empowered to approve the proofs of death, and at the directors' meeting the notice of death was received, but not the proofs, and they instructed the chairman to examine the proofs upon arrival, and instructed the secretary to issue the notice of assessment if the proofs were found correct, and thereafter the assessment was accordingly made in good faith, it was legal; and a member's failure to pay it barred his beneficiary from recovery on his death. Passenger Conductors L. Ins. Co. v. Birnbaum, 10 Cent. Rep. 63, 116 Pa. 565.

Where, at the time the assessment was laid, the association had money enough in its hands to meet all its obligations, such fact will not render the assessment void. Crossman v. Massachusetts Ben. Asso. 3 New Eng. Rep. 517, 143 Mass. 435.

Where an Act provides that, in an action for the recovery of an assessment, a certificate of a mutual insurance company shall be evidence to prove the claim to the assessment, unless the party sued will make a certain affidavit, if such party makes the affidavit, the company must prove its claim. Susquehanna Mut. F. Ins. Co. v. Gackenbach, 7 Cent. Rep. 586, 115 Pa. 492.

Damages, for neglect to make assessment, recoverable at law.

Damages against a mutual benefit insurance society for refusing to make an assessment are recoverable in an action at law, without resorting to an equitable action to enforce the assessment. O'Brien v. Home Ben. Society, 117 N. Y. 310.

It is so liable where it not only neglects and refuses to make an assessment, but denies all liability. Jackson v. Northwestern Mut. Relief Asso. 2 L. R. A. 786, 73 Wis. 507.

Lawler a benefit member of said A. O. H. Insurance Fund, and agrees to pay Mary Lawler, wife, if living, if not, to the heirs-at-law of said member, in sixty days after due proof of the death of said member, a sum received from a death assessment, but not to exceed one thousand dollars.

CONDITIONS.

The conditions upon which this certificate is issued by the fund and accepted by said member, are the following:

First. That the statements and declarations made by and on behalf of said member in his application to become a benefit member of said fund, which are hereby referred to as a basis of this contract, and are a part thereof, and on the faith of which this certificate is issued, are in all respects true, and that no fact has been suppressed relating to his health and circumstances, affecting the interests of said fund or their inducement to accept the risk.

Second. That the said member must be a member in good standing in the order at the time of his death, otherwise this certificate will be null and void.

Third. Any assignment of this certificate shall be void unless assented to in writing by said fund.

Fourth. The death claim under this contract shall be payable in sixty days after satisfactory proof of death of said member shall have been furnished at the office of the secretary of the fund, by the certificate of the attending physician, if there was any, and the full and particular statement of at least one competent and disinterested member of the order, stating the time, place, cause and circumstances of the death of the party.

Fifth. No officers of divisions are authorized to make, alter or discharge contracts or waive forfeitures, and any such act, to be valid, must be done in writing and signed by the president and secretary of the directory.

Sixth. This contract shall be void if the party shall die in or in consequence of a duel, or by the hands of justice, or in the violation of or attempt to violate any criminal law of the United States or of any State or county in which he may be.

Seventh. A failure to comply with the rules of said fund as to payment of assessments, or falling into gross and confirmed habits of intoxication, shall also render the certificate void.

The measure of damages in such a case is the amount assessable upon all the insured, unless it is shown that the amount would be less because all members did not respond to assessments. Bentz v. Northwestern Aid Asso. 2 L. R. A. 784, 40 Minn. 202.

Action upon the contract.

An action at law can be maintained upon a certificate of membership of a mutual benefit association, and it is not necessary, first, to resort to mandamus to compel an assessment. Doty v. New York State Mut. Ben. Asso. 29 N. Y. S. R. 896; Bacon, Benev. Societies, 685; Excelsior Mut. Aid Asso. v. Riddle, 91 Ind. 84; Burland v. Northwestern Mut. Ben. Asso. 47 Mich. 424; Bentz v. Northwestern Aid Asso. 2 L. R. A. 784, 40 Minn. 202.

The proper remedy upon such refusal is by a proceeding in equity. Burdon v. Massachusetts Safety Fund Asso. 1 L. R. A. 146, 6 New Eng. Rep. 840, 147 Mass. 360. See Elkhart Mut. Aid, B. & R. Asso. v. Houghton, 1 West. Rep. 284, 103 Ind. 286; Taylor v. National Temp. Relief Union, 12 West. Rep. 92, 94 Mo. 35.

In such action plaintiff may recover what upon proof he can show such assessment would have yielded if it had been duly made. Earnshaw v. Sun Mut. Aid Society, 11 Cent. Rep. 508, 68 Md. 465.

Even after judgment, upon which execution is returned unsatisfied, sequestration proceedings in the court of equity, and not mandamus, is the proper remedy. Miner v. Michigan Mut. Ben. Asso. 8 West. Rep. 139, 65 Mich. 84.

On a certificate which provides for an assessment upon policy holders within ninety days from the proof of death, and for payment of the sum collected, less 10 per cent, if it does not exceed $5,000, where, at the death of a member, certificates were in force upon which the full amount named could have been realized, but no assessments were made within the time provided, judgment may be rendered against the company for the maximum amount named. Kaw Valley Life Asso. v. Lemke, 40 Kan. 142.

Lack of sufficient money in the death fund to pay a claim on an insurance certificate is no defense to an action at law, although the promise was to pay from the death fund, where by the same contract the association undertook to make a call upon the members if the fund was then insufficient to meet the claim. Darrow v. Family Fund Society, 6 L. R. A. 495, 116 N. Y. 537.

In a suit by the payee and beneficiary, a complaint averring the death of insured and the refusal to pay or to order an assessment on the members is sufficient on demurrer. That the assessment would not produce the amount is matter of defense, and in the absence of such defense plaintiff is entitled to judgment. Elkhart Mut. Aid, B. & R. Asso. v. Houghton, 1 West. Rep. 284, 103 Ind. 286.

A report of the society to the state insurance department, to prove that an assessment would have produced enough to pay a death claim, is of equal dignity and certainty with the records of the society. Freeman v. National Ben. Society, 42 Hun, 252.

Where a certificate of membership provides that the society, in case of the death of the owner, will pay the amount realized from an assessment upon its members, not exceeding a stated sum, no recovery can be had without proof of the amount which would have been realized upon the assessment, or that some amount would have been thus realized. Martin v. Equitable Accident Asso. 56 Hun, 574, 29 N. Y. S. R. 421.

The corporation cannot resist payment of the death claim upon the ground that the promise to pay within ninety days after proof of death furnished was contingent upon an assessment, as there was an implied obligation on the company to make the necessary assessment, and it could not resist payment by omitting to make it. Freeman v. National Ben. Society, 42 Hun, 252.

The furnishing of proofs of death is a demand for payment and for the company to make the necessary assessment. *Ibid.*

An action instituted in a court having no jurisdiction of the defendant will not suspend the running of a condition of limitation in a policy of insurance. Keystone Mut. Ben. Asso. v. Norris, 7 Cent. Rep. 204, 115 Pa. 446.

Eighth. This certificate is subject to all rules and regulations that the state convention may, from time to time, adopt for the general advancement and interest of the fund.

RULES.

The rules governing this contract, and which form a part of the same, are as follows:

First. There shall be paid by the member under this contract to the secretary of the fund, on the day of the month in which this contract was made, the sum of one dollar, and he shall not be liable for any further sum except as follows:

Second. Upon the death of any member the said Thomas Lawler shall at once pay, if required, to its secretary, an additional assessment of whatever the directory shall deem necessary.

Third. The form of notice to, and process of collection from, each of the members of the assessment above named, shall be as follows: A notice shall be sent announcing such assessment, and the number thereof, to the last post-office address given to the secretary of the fund by each member, and if the assessment is not received within forty days from the mailing of said notice, it shall be accepted and taken as sufficient evidence that the brother has decided to terminate his connection with the fund, which connection shall thereupon terminate, and the brother's contract with the fund shall lapse and be void; but said brother may again renew his connection with the fund by a new contract, made in the same manner as at first, or, for valid reasons to the officers of the fund (such as a failure to receive notice of an assessment), he may be reinstated by paying assessment arrearages.

Fourth. The above rule governing the collection of assessments for death claims shall also apply to the collection of the annual assessment.

Fifth. Each applicant to become such member must sign the fund's form of application, countersigned by the board of directors of the division of which he is a member.

In witness whereof the said A. O. H. State Insurance Fund hath, by its president and secretary, signed and delivered this certificate at its office, this 12th day of July, 1886.

John D. Cunningham,
Secretary Ins. Fund.
P. J. O'Connor,
Treasurer Ins. Fund.
John P. Murphy,
President Ins. Fund.

Is it true, as claimed by the defendants, and in the sense in which they claim it, that the only agreement contained in the above contract is to pay such sum as might be received from a death assessment? Or, to put it in another form, what does the agreement to pay a sum received from a death assessment imply and involve, when taken in connection with the other provisions of the contract?

The contract is a peculiar one. It is very inartificially drawn, and it is undoubtedly difficult to give it a satisfactory construction. Of course it should be so construed as to make its contemplated benefits available, if it can legally be done. And we are, at least, warranted in assuming that the insurers, in accepting the money of the insured, and the insured in paying it, understood that some duty devolved upon the former to secure the promised benefits of the contract to the latter.

In addition to the agreement to pay to Mary Lawler, if living, if not, to the heirs of Thomas, in sixty days after due proof of his death, a sum received from a death assessment, but not to exceed $1,000, the contract further provides that the death claim shall be payable in sixty days after satisfactory proof of such death, except in certain cases not necessary to be stated here, and gives the form of notice and process for collecting the death assessment from each member of the association. Each contract contains, also, a promise by the insured that upon the death of any member he will at once pay, if required, to the secretary, an additional assessment of whatever the directory shall deem necessary—additional as the contract shows to the dollar paid upon becoming a member. This is an agreement by the A. O. H. Insurance Fund to pay the proper person, within sixty days after satisfactory proof of the death of the insured, a sum, not to exceed $1,000, received from a death assessment. The contract contains the agreement of members to pay such assessments and specifies the process by which its collection shall be undertaken—"a notice shall be sent" announcing such assessment, etc. All of which, taken in connection with the other provisions of the contract and the situation and manifest intention of the parties, seems to us to import a promise to make, or cause to be made, the necessary assessment to meet the death claim promised to be paid.

It is well established that whatever is necessary to be done in order to accomplish work specifically contracted to be performed, is parcel of the contract, though not specified. It is also a principle of general application that whatever may be fairly implied from the terms or language of an instrument is, in judgment of law, contained in it. *Currier* v. *Boston & M. R. Co.* 34 N. H. 498; *Rogers* v. *Kneeland,* 13 Wend. 114.

Addison, in his work on Contracts, § 1400, says: "Although the words of a contract under seal do not in themselves import any express covenant, yet the law, in order to promote good faith and make men act up to the spirit as well as to the letter of their engagements, will create and supply, as a necessary result and consequence of the contract, certain covenants and obligations which bind the parties as forcibly and effectually as if they had been expressed in the strongest and most explicit terms in the deed itself."

In *White* v. *Snell,* 5 Pick. 425, an action of assumpsit, the defendant "for value received promised to pay a sum of money, if, and when, he should recover his demands against A." It was held competent for the plaintiff to prove that the defendant had no demands against A, and that so the promise was absolute; or that he had not used due diligence to collect them.

In *Savage* v. *Whitaker,* 15 Me. 24, the court says: "An engagement to do a certain thing involves an undertaking to secure and use effectually all the means necessary to accomplish the object."

Marshall, *Ch. J.*, in *Ogden* v. *Saunders*, 25 U. S. 12 Wheat. 341 [6 L. ed. 650], speaking of the power and policy of the law to supply in contracts what in that case is presumed to have been inadvertently omitted by the parties, says that the parties are supposed to have made those stipulations which as honest, fair and just men they ought to have made.

The contract in *Freeman* v. *National Ben. Society*, 42 Hun, 252, is, in many respects, similar to the one under consideration. Although the stipulation in that case was to pay a sum "equal to the amount received from a death assessment, but not to exceed $3,000," instead of "a sum received from a death assessment," etc., yet the court held that "the provision in the body of the certificate that payment should be made of a sum equal to the amount received from a death assessment, not to exceed the sum specified, in ninety days after due proof of the death of the member was given, implies an obligation upon the company to proceed and make the necessary assessment to raise the fund within the time during which it was provided that the claim should remain in abeyance."

We conclude, then, that, in connection with the express promises contained in the contract in this case, there is an implied promise to make an assessment to pay the death claim agreed to be paid; an implied promise which the law, "in order to promote good faith and make the parties act up to the spirit as well as to the letter of their engagements, will create and supply as a necessary result and consequence of their contract." The contract to pay a sum received from a death assessment, taken in connection with the other express provisions, involves, in the language of one of the decisions above quoted, an undertaking to secure and use effectually all the means necessary to accomplish the result, and require that an assessment should be made.

In this view of the case the allegation of the demurrer, that "it appears by said contract that the only agreement made therein was to pay such sum as might be received from a death assessment," is not sustained. There was a further agreement, namely, to make such assessment. The complaint alleges that it was not made nor the amount of insurance paid. This cause of demurrer therefore must fail.

It is true that the complaint does not state, in terms, that the defendants agreed to make an assessment, but it sets out the contract in full and alleges as a breach of it, for which it claims damages, that "said assessment has never been made by the defendants."

This method is sanctioned by the Practice Act and the forms and rules given under it. Rule III., § 5, states that it is unnecessary to allege any promise or duty which the law implies from the facts pleaded.

Whatever, therefore, may have been the theory of the plaintiff, inasmuch as the agreement to make the assessment to pay the death claim is implied in the contract, we cannot sustain the demurrer upon this point.

This disposes of the only ground for demurrer specifically decided by the superior court. The defendants, however, insisted, in the argument before us, that the real question is, whether the suit can be maintained at all against these defendants; that it would be unreasonable not to dispose of the whole matter now and here; and that a demurrer goes back and searches out all the errors in the pleadings. Perhaps, in order to determine whether the plaintiff was injured by the decision of the court sustaining the cause of demurrer already disposed of, we ought to pass upon the other causes assigned, for, if the action cannot, in any event, be sustained against the defendants as individuals, the plaintiff has sustained no injury from the decision that the complaint fails to set forth a cause of action against anybody.

Then, too, all the causes for demurrer were argued before us, and the conclusions to which we have come will not make it unjust to the plaintiff to accede to the defendants' claim, and we should decide all the points which were argued.

The defendants assign for further cause for demurrer, that it appears from the contract declared on that the defendants made no personal agreement upon which they were personally liable, but that the contract was signed by them only as officers of the organization mentioned therein. This issue is raised, not as a question of fact, but as a question of law upon the pleadings.

As a matter of law does the contract, upon its face, show that the defendants made no personal contract upon which they were personally liable? The complaint alleges that they were jointly engaged in carrying on life insurance business under the name of the "Connecticut State Insurance Fund," and that they entered into the contract sued upon. If the facts are so should they not be held liable? Does the contract, as a matter of law, preclude that state of facts? If they had simply been sued as individuals, upon a contract headed with the name of the association and signed by them respectively as president, secretary and treasurer, as appears to have been the case in *Hitchcock* v. *Buchanan*, 105 U. S. 416 [26 L. ed. 1078], cited by the defendants, and the complaint had contained no allegation that they were carrying on the insurance business under a certain name and made the contract with Thomas Lawler, the question would be a different one, especially if it appeared that the association was incorporated. But under the decision of *Davison* v. *Holden*, 55 Conn. 103, 4 New Eng. Rep. 818, the defendants certainly might be liable on a contract signed by them as officers of an organization. If, as the statute permits, the organization consisted simply of individuals united under a distinguishing associate name for business purposes, they did not thereby acquire either corporate power or immunity from individual liability; consequently it could not appear, as a matter of law, from the contract declared on, that the defendants made no personal contract or agreement upon which they were personally liable.

The case of *Davison* v. *Holden* was a suit against certain individuals who were in fact the president and secretary of an unincorporated association. This court held that "as a matter of law the plaintiff, in giving credit to the associate name, gave credit to the individuals who upon inquiry should be found to stand behind it." It seems clear, without pursuing the subject further, that this cause for demurrer cannot be sustained. Individual members of an unincorporated association are liable for contracts made in the name of the association, without regard to the question whether they so intended or so understood the law, and even if the other party contracted in form with the association and was ignorant of the names of the individual members composing it. And it is also held in the case just cited that the individual members of such an association do not acquire any immunity from individual liability by force of the statutes which provide that any number of persons associated and known by some distinguishing name may sue and be sued, plead and be impleaded, by such name, and that the individual property of the members shall not be liable to attachment or levy of execution in a suit brought against the association.

The remaining causes assigned for the demurrer are that the only breach of the contract alleged in the complaint is that the defendants did not make an assessment, whereas there is no provision in the contract that the defendants or any of them should make any such assessment; and that the complaint alleges that by the contract the death assessment was to be made by the defendants, whereas it appears in the contract that death assessments were to be made by the directory of the association, and it is not alleged that the defendants are members of the directory. The conclusion to which we have already come, that the contract implies a promise that the defendants will make, or cause to be made, an assessment to meet death claims, makes further discussion of these causes unnecessary. We do not concur in the assertion therein made, that death assessments were to be made by the directory. Its duty was the subordinate one of ascertaining the amount necessary to be raised by assessment. This the contract undertakes that it shall do, and that an assessment shall thereupon be made by the insurance fund.

Two other questions were discussed before us, namely, whether, if it should be held that the contract contains an agreement to make an assessment, the plaintiff's remedy is at law, or whether she must first go into a court of equity to compel the defendants to make the assessment; and, If an action at law can be sustained, what is the rule of damages? As to the first, we think an action at law can be sustained. Neither circuity nor multiplication of actions is favored by our practice. If there is a contract to make an assessment, a breach of which is alleged and damages demanded therefor, and a rule of damages can be provided, why should not an action at law be sustained? Both Niblack and Bacon, recent writers upon the subject of Mutual Benefit Societies, after examining a great number of cases, come to the conclusion, with which we fully agree, that the decided weight of authority is to the effect that an action at law will lie for damages for the breach of a contract to make an assessment.

It makes no difference with the questions raised by the demurrer whether substantial or nominal damages can be recovered, for it ought to have been overruled if the plaintiff is entitled to any damages at all. Still the rule of damages applicable to the case was thoroughly argued and both parties invited a decision upon it.

Referring again to the contract, the insurance fund agrees to pay to the proper person, in sixty days after due proof of death, a sum received from a death assessment, but not to exceed $1,000. Each member pays $1 upon joining the association, and agrees, upon the death of any member, to pay at once, if required, an additional assessment of whatever the directory shall deem necessary. Deem necessary for what? Clearly not what it shall deem necessary to pay, leaving the amount discretionary with the directory and to be settled in each individual case as it may deem necessary, but what it shall deem it necessary for the association to raise by assessments in order to pay the $1,000. In short, the contract is to be taken as an agreement to make an assessment which, if duly paid, will raise $1,000, or so much thereof as, in addition to funds on hand, will make that sum. The insured takes the risk of the neglect of members to meet their assessments, and of the consequent reduction of the maximum sum named. One thousand dollars is, prima facie, the value of the policy, and the insurance fund was bound to take all the steps which it contracted to in order to realize that sum. Cases cited by the plaintiff, and other cases which we have examined, fully sustain this conclusion. And the rule is a fair one, because it is always within the power of the association to live up to its contract, and thus fix the sum which a death assessment will bring.

In *Elkhart Mut. Aid, B. & R. Asso.* v. *Houghton*, 103 Ind. 286, 1 West. Rep. 234, the certificate entitled the beneficiary to $1,000, or so much thereof as might be realized from one assessment. The complaint alleged the death of the beneficiary, proof of his death duly given, and the refusal of the defendant to pay the amount named in the certificate or any part thereof, and its refusal to order or make any assessment to raise the required sum or any part of it. The defendant was held liable for the maximum amount, it not being shown in defense that an assessment would not produce the full amount of the certificate. It was assumed that it was the duty of the defendant to make an assessment, though the contract contained no express agreement to that effect. *Earnshaw* v. *Sun Mut. Aid Society*, 68 Md. 467, 11 Cent. Rep. 508; *Lueders* v. *Hartford L. & Ann. Ins. Co.* 12 Fed. Rep. 465; *Kansas Protective Union* v. *Whitt*, 36 Kan. 760; *Covenant Mut. Ben. Asso.* v. *Hoffman*, 110 Ill. 606; *Suppiger* v. *Covenant Mut. Ben. Asso.* 20 Ill. App. 595; Niblack, Mut. Ben. Societies, § 410, commenting on *Newman* v. *Covenant Mut. Ben. Asso.* 72 Iowa, 242.

There is error in the judgment appealed from.

In this opinion the other Judges concurred.

Cornelia M. BENEDICT *et al.*
v.
Augustus S. CHASE *et al.*, Admrs., etc., of Charles Benedict, Deceased, *et al.*

(58 Conn. 196.)

1. **A case will not be remanded** for a more specific finding of facts where the facts necessary are stated in effect, and have been assumed by both parties, and the case heard on its merits without objection.

2. **The superior court has jurisdiction** of a suit to compel an intestate's estate, which has been saved from insolvency by the voluntary act of all the heirs of legal age, to refund the expense incurred thereby before distribution.

3. **Administrators have no power to guarantee the payment of bonds** of a corporation, issued for the purpose of taking up its paper upon which decedent was liable as indorser, although such guaranty would procure an extension of time and save the estate from insolvency; hence they will incur no liability by authorizing third persons to make such guaranty on behalf of the estate.

4. **Infant heirs are not liable** to a contribution at law for the amount of liability voluntarily incurred by other heirs in saving the estate from insolvency.

5. **Where a decedent's estate is saved from insolvency** by the act of all the parties interested who were of age and legally capable of acting, in guaranteeing, to a certain extent, with the approval of the administrator, the bonds of a corporation, for which the intestate was liable as indorser, the amount which they were compelled to pay on such guaranty should be refunded to them before distribution, although objection is made by the other interested parties who were infants at the time, and although no claim against the estate was presented within the time limited therefor by law. Having voluntarily sacrificed their own private funds to save the estate, and having in fact saved it, they are equitably entitled to have the whole estate, and not merely their shares of it, bear the burden.

(October 30, 1889.)

RESERVATION from the Superior Court for New Haven County of an action to recover from a decedent's estate the amount which plaintiffs alleged they had advanced to save the estate from insolvency. *Judgment for plaintiffs advised.*

The plaintiffs are the widow and two of the children of Charles Benedict, deceased. Defendants are the minor heirs of said Benedict and the administrators of his estate.

The complaint alleged that at the time of his death the decedent was liable as indorser upon a large amount of commercial paper of Mitchell, Vance & Co., which notes were then maturing and if presented and allowed against the estate would have rendered it wholly insolvent; and that, for the purpose of relieving the estate, the plaintiffs, being then all the parties interested who were of age and legally capable to act, entered into an agreement with the corporation that they would guarantee its bonds to the amount of $144,000, the proceeds of which should be used in taking up the notes, other bonds being guaranteed by other stockholders, and that the bonds were issued and guaranteed, and the notes paid with the proceeds; that the corporation failed in 1887 while a portion of the bonds guaranteed by the plaintiffs remained unpaid, and that in consequence thereof they had been compelled to pay upon them the sum of $47,699, which the administrators, upon demand made, had refused to pay; and that the estate of Benedict was being settled as a solvent estate, and that the time limited for presenting claims against it had long since expired. Judgment at law was prayed for against the administrators for the amount so paid, and for equitable relief.

The defendants demurred to the complaint on the ground that the superior court had no original jurisdiction in the matter. The demurrer was overruled and the defendants then filed a denial.

Upon the trial the following facts were found:

Charles Benedict died on the 30th of October, 1881, and the defendants A. S. Chase and Gilman C. Hill were appointed administrators of his estate. The estate was represented solvent, and the court limited six months from and after the 14th day of November in which to present claims against it.

Benedict died intestate, leaving a widow, Cornelia M. Benedict, and two daughters, Amelia C. Benedict and Charlotte B. Hill, plaintiffs in this action, and minor children of a deceased daughter, heirs-at-law to his estate.

At the time of his death he was indorser of a large amount of notes and drafts of Mitchell, Vance & Co. The total amount of his liability was $600,000. Mitchell, Vance & Co. at the decease of Benedict were supposed to be solvent, but could not meet these notes when they matured without renewals; and for the purpose of enabling the corporation to renew its paper without such indorsement and guaranty they entered into an agreement with the plaintiffs, by which the plaintiffs were to guarantee bonds to be issued by the corporation to an amount equal to one half the stock which Benedict at the time of his death owned and held in the corporation, which amount of guaranteed bonds was $144,000.

These bonds were used by Mitchell, Vance & Co. in taking up their obligations which Benedict had indorsed or guaranteed, which were paid by them upon maturity. These notes and drafts were paid by the corporation and not by the plaintiffs, nor were they in any manner assigned or conveyed to the plaintiffs, nor were they ever presented against Benedict's estate, nor any claim made upon the estate therefor. The bonds were so guaranteed by the plaintiffs on or before the 1st of December, 1881. In the summer of 1887 Mitchell, Vance & Co. failed in business, and a receiver was appointed to settle the affairs of the corporation, and on the 1st day of January, 1888, the plaintiffs were obliged to pay to the receiver the sum of $47,699, being one half the amount of the bonds so guaranteed by them still outstanding and unpaid by the corporation, the corporation also settling its debts for 50 cents on the dollar. The plaintiffs in guaranteeing the bonds supposed they were acting for the benefit of the estate, and relieving it from its liability by reason of the indorsements and guaranties of Benedict in his lifetime, so that no claim therefor would ever come against the estate, believing that Mitchell, Vance & Co. would fully pay and discharge the bonds so guaranteed by them.

The estate of Benedict is now in process of settlement in the probate court. The plaintiffs have presented their claim and made demand of the administrators for payment thereof.

Benedict at the time of his decease was the largest stockholder in the corporation of Mitchell, Vance & Co., and the plaintiffs in making the guaranty of bonds acted as they supposed for the benefit of the estate, to preserve the stock as an asset of value to the estate, as well as to relieve the estate from liability for the indorsements.

If the notes so indorsed by Benedict had matured as a claim against his estate, and been presented against it, it would have subjected the estate to a much larger liability, and rendered it insolvent if compelled to pay them. The bonds were so guaranteed with the knowledge and approval of the administrators, so far as they had any power to approve it.

Upon these facts the case was reserved for the advice of this court.

Mr. **S. W. Kellogg,** for plaintiffs:

The plaintiffs are entitled to judgment against the administrators. It was their duty to take the necessary steps to relieve the estate from liability.

Griswold v. *Bigelow,* 6 Conn. 258; *Davis* v. *Vansands,* 45 Conn. 600.

This was money paid for their benefit as administrators, and can be recovered back.

Bailey v. *Bussing,* 28 Conn. 455; 2 Greenl. Ev. §§ 108, 113, 114; *Exall* v. *Partridge,* 8 T. R. 308.

If the plaintiffs are not entitled to a judgment at law against the administrators, a court of equity will grant them relief.

Wherever there is a wrong there is a remedy.

Hawley v. *Botsford,* 27 Conn. 80; *Bacon* v. *Thorp,* Id. 251; *Davis* v. *Vansands, supra; Booth* v. *Starr,* 5 Day, 419.

Messrs. **C. W. Gillette** and **G. E. Terry,** for defendants:

The superior court has no original jurisdiction to grant any relief. The estate is still in process of settlement in the probate court, and all questions relating to the settlement of the estate, or to the administration account, are exclusively within the jurisdiction of that court, and can only come to the superior court by way of appeal.

Pitkin v. *Pitkin,* 7 Conn. 315; *Bailey* v. *Strong,* 8 Conn. 278; *Beach* v. *Norton,* 9 Conn. 182.

The plaintiffs are not entitled to a judgment at law against the administrators for the money paid as they had no power to bind the estate for any such purpose.

Rhodes v. *Seymour,* 36 Conn. 1.

Carpenter, *J.,* delivered the opinion of the court:

There are two facts essential to the plaintiffs' right to recover: (1) that Benedict's estate was in peril; (2) that it was relieved of that peril by the plaintiffs. The finding does not state either fact in so many words. Are they in effect stated? If so, we can dispose of the case; if not, we must remand the case for a more specific finding.

There are two considerations which incline us to regard the finding as sufficient: 1. The case has been heard upon its merits without objection from either party, or suggestions from the court. 2. Both parties have assumed that both facts exist, and have argued the case upon that assumption.

A careful consideration of the facts stated leads us to the conclusion, if not as a necessary inference, yet as a reasonable and proper one under the circumstances, that the estate was in peril, and that the plaintiffs at their own expense rescued it from its liability.

Benedict in his lifetime assumed a contingent liability for Mitchell, Vance & Co., a New York corporation, of which he was a stockholder, to the amount of $600,000; which liability was on his estate at the time of his decease. The corporation was unable to meet the paper indorsed by Benedict as it matured, without renewals, and no renewals could be had. That finding seems to exclude the supposition that the corporation could meet its paper, unless aided by the estate or by someone interested in it. In less than six years the corporation failed. That it was on the verge of insolvency, if not actually insolvent, is evident from the fact that it was unable to meet its maturing liabilities. Something must be done, or that paper will inevitably be presented against the estate. It necessarily follows that the estate was in imminent peril. Presentation meant payment, and payment by the estate meant insolvency.

Did the plaintiffs relieve it of its peril? In about one month after Benedict's death the plaintiffs guaranteed bonds of the corporation to the amount of $144,000. That was done, as it is found, "for the purpose of enabling the corporation to renew its paper without such indorsement and guaranty." It is also found that "the bonds were used by said Mitchell, Vance & Co. in taking up their obligations which said Benedict had indorsed or guaranteed." A portion of the bonds were outstanding when Mitchell Vance & Co. failed, and the plaintiffs were obliged to pay thereon $47,699. Had they advanced $144,000 in cash instead of guaranteeing bonds, and the money had been used to take up the indorsed paper as it matured, it would have conclusively appeared that they relieved the estate. Is the fact that they accomplished the same result by loaning their credit any less conclusive? In either case it may be said that time is of some importance; that insolvency may have overtaken the corporation after the death of Benedict; so that it is uncertain whether the plaintiffs in fact benefited the estate. The reply is that there is no presumption to that effect; on the contrary, if insolvency originated subsequently, the presumption is that the defendants by an appropriate plea would have called the attention of the court to that fact. In the absence of any claim on that subject, the court is not bound to take into consideration mere possibilities. It is possible that the property of the corporation may have been destroyed by fire with no insurance; that they met with heavy losses otherwise, and the like; but these are not subjects for conjecture, but are matters to be proved. The court is not bound to inquire whether the defendants have a defense which they have not chosen to interpose. It is proper and according to the usual course for us to take the facts as the parties present them to us; and we can safely interpret them as both parties do, more especially if they are hardly susceptible of any other rational interpretation. We conclude, therefore, that the estate was in great peril and that the plaintiffs rescued it.

The time had come when something must be done. The estate could not legally take the risk. The administrators personally might do so, but they were not bound to, and could not be expected to. Two thirds in interest of the heirs could and did lend their aid; the remaining third, being minors, did not. The plaintiffs did not act officiously or unreasonably. On the contrary, it may be characterized as good business management. The result proved that while there was a loss, yet that it was doubtless much less than the estate would have suffered had nothing been done. This is a suit to reimburse the plaintiffs from the assets of the estate. The minor heirs defend. The case is reserved for the advice of this court.

What is it that the plaintiffs ask? They do not ask, as may be supposed from the defendants' brief, that the defendants may be compelled to pay a part of the expenses of a losing venture; neither do they ask any compensation for the risk assumed. They simply ask that the fund which they have saved by a successful venture may refund to them the expense before distribution.

The first defense interposed is a demurrer, raising the claim that the superior court has no jurisdiction; that it is one of those matters within the jurisdiction of the court of probate. Without saying that the court of probate could not have passed upon this matter, we are inclined to regard it as a disputed claim against the estate, not, it is true, an ordinary claim, but still a claim on which a suit may properly be brought to the superior court, especially as it is claimed that the administrators are liable at law. Whether an estate being settled as a solvent estate is indebted or not, legally or equitably, when it is disputed, is a question for the courts. If an administrator incurs expense in the course of his duty, the question whether he is to be repaid from the estate is a question for the court of probate. If, in this case, the administrators had done what the plaintiffs did, the question whether they should be reimbursed would be a question for the court of probate. Other parties having volunteered, they bring a suit claiming that the administrators are liable at law, and if not, then in equity. The question of legal liability seems clearly to be a question for the superior court. We think that the question of liability in equity is also within the jurisdiction of that court.

The next question is, Are the administrators liable at law? They had no power to bind the estate in a matter of this kind. Any previous request, or subsequent promise, would have been of no avail. What they could not do they could not authorize others to do; and it is not claimed that they have made themselves personally liable.

There can be no remedy at law against the defendant heirs, for they were incapable of contracting, and made no contract in fact. No legal duty rested upon them, so that there is no ground on which a request can be implied. For the same reason they are not liable to a contribution at law.

Have the plaintiffs any equitable remedy? It will be noticed that the defendants' brief deals almost exclusively with a contract liability, or a personal liability on some other ground. An equitable claim upon the fund, as distinguished from a claim against the defendants personally, is hardly alluded to. We agree with them that no judgment against them *in personam* should be rendered; but whether the plaintiffs are not entitled to be reimbursed from the fund which they have saved is quite a different question. No case has been referred to, and we are unable to find any directly in point. A simple statement of the case shows such strong equities that authorities are hardly needed, and little else need be said by way of argument.

There are analogous cases, however, which in principle strongly support the plaintiffs' claim. When a cargo at sea is in peril a portion of it is frequently sacrificed to save the balance. In such cases the doctrine of general average compels the freight that is saved to contribute towards making good the loss. Here the whole estate was in peril. The plaintiffs voluntarily sacrificed their own private funds to save it. They in fact saved it. Why should the defendants share in the whole estate as though it had never been in peril, and compel the plaintiffs to bear the whole burden?

So also with the doctrines of apportionment and contribution. They are often applied, especially in cases of burdens upon real estate, where, *ex æquo et bono*, the party is entitled to relief. See Story, Eq. Jur. §§ 477, 478, 479, 483.

Few cases can be supposed in which the equities are stronger than in the present. Take another class of cases; a fund, in which several persons are interested, is attached, or involved in litigation, requiring a heavy expense to defend it, or settle its status, and the like. Usually the fund is charged with the expenses, and the balance only is distributed. These cases and others that might be mentioned are decided upon principles that are fairly applicable to the present case. We do not believe it will be unjust to apply them to this case.

Once more. Suppose these administrators, as they might, although not bound to, had risked their private fortunes in doing precisely what these plaintiffs did, and had thereby saved the estate at an expense to themselves of $50,000. Would these heirs—plaintiffs and defendants—have been heard to say: "You did it voluntarily, no law required it; therefore you must bear the loss while we will enjoy the estate?" Is it so that an administrator, who, prompted by no duty, but simply by a desire to benefit the estate, incurs an expense whereby it is in fact benefited, may not be reimbursed? The case before us can hardly be distinguished in principle from the case supposed. The administrators did not act, but with their approval the plaintiffs did, and justice requires that they should be reimbursed.

The Superior Court is advised to render judgment for the plaintiffs, to be paid from the estate.

In this opinion **Loomis, Prentice** and **J. M. Hall**, *JJ.*, concurred; **Beardsley**, *J.*, dissented.

TENNESSEE SUPREME COURT.

N. E. ALLOWAY and Wife, *Appts.*,
v.
Mayor, etc., of NASHVILLE.

(......Tenn......)

1. **The value for a reservoir site** of property taken for that purpose cannot be taken as the measure of damages for the taking, but must be considered as one of the elements that make up its market value. The market value, in view of all available uses, is the measure of compensation.

2. **The possibility of unskillful and improper construction of a reservoir** which is not yet completed cannot be considered in estimating damages to adjacent property in proceedings by eminent domain. It must be assumed that the work will be done in a skillful and proper manner.

3. **The burden of proof** as to the right of a corporation to take property in the exercise of the right of eminent domain, and to show that the particular property is necessary for its corporate use, is on the corporation.

4. **Concession by the owner of petitioner's right to condemn land,** and limitation of the contest to the question of damages only, do not relieve the petitioner of the burden of proof, or give the land owner the right to open and close the argument.

5. **Interest should be allowed** on the value of property condemned for public use from the time of its appropriation.

(February 11, 1890.)

APPEAL by defendants from a judgment of the Circuit Court for Davidson County, entered upon a verdict assessing their damages at a less amount than they demanded, in proceedings to condemn their property under the power of eminent domain. *Modified and affirmed.*

The facts are fully stated in the opinion.

Messrs. **Demoss & Malone, East & Fogg** and **J. M. Anderson,** for appellants:

In arriving at a fair compensation for the land taken, the situation of the land, its surroundings, natural advantages, its adaptability for any use, must be considered.

Lewis, Em. Dom. 479.

If the value may be estimated for any use that it might be applied to, its value for any particular use may be estimated; and consequently its use for a reservoir site might be considered, and its value for that purpose estimated.

Mississippi & R. R. Boom Co. v. *Patterson*, 98 U. S. 403 (25 L. ed. 206); *Harrison* v. *Young*, 9 Ga. 364, 365; *Louisville, N. O. & T. R. Co.* v. *Ryan*, 64 Miss. 399; *Chicago, E. & L. S. R. Co.* v. *Catholic Bishop*, 8 West. Rep. 881, 119 Ill. 530; *South Park Comrs.* v. *Dunlevy*, 91 Ill. 49; *Sherman* v. *St. Paul, M. & M. R. Co.* 30 Minn. 229; *San Diego Land & Town Co.* v. *Neale*, 3 L. R. A. 83, 78 Cal. 63; *Johnson* v. *Freeport & M. R. R. Co.* 111 Ill. 420; *Chicago & E. R. Co.* v. *Jacobs*, 110 Ill. 416; *Haslam* v. *Galena & S. W. R. Co.* 64 Ill. 353; *Chicago & N. W. R. Co.* v. *Chicago & E. R. Co.* 112 Ill. 608; *Little Rock Junction R. Co.* v.

NOTE.—*Municipal corporation; condemnation of property for public uses.*

Public corporations may be authorized to exercise the power of eminent domain. 2 Morawetz, Priv. Corp. § 1114.

The New York Statute, providing for the creation and formation of waterworks companies, with power to acquire lands by condemnation, etc., is constitutional. *Re* New Rochelle Water Co. 46 Hun, 525.

A municipal corporation cannot exercise the right of eminent domain without an express grant of power. Butler v. Thomasville, 74 Ga. 570.

Under the West Virginia Constitution, private property can be taken for no other purpose than for public use. Fork Ridge Baptist Cemetery Asso. v. Redd (W. Va.) Nov. 20, 1889.

The condemnation of property for supplying the municipality with water is for a public use. Burden v. Stein, 27 Ala. 104; St. Helena Water Co. v. Forbes, 62 Cal. 182; Cummings v. Peters, 56 Cal. 593; Riche v. Bar Harbor Water Co. 75 Me. 91; Kane v. Baltimore, 15 Md. 240; Reddall v. Bryan, 14 Md. 444; Lumbard v. Stearns, 4 Cush. 60; Wayland v. Middlesex Co. 4 Gray, 500; Ham v. Salem, 100 Mass. 350; State v. Morris Aqueduct Co. 46 N. J. L. 495; Olmsted v. Morris Aqueduct Co. 47 N. J. L. 311; *Re* New Rochelle Water Co. 46 Hun, 525; Stamford Water Co. v. Stanley, 39 Hun, 424; State v. Eau Claire, 40 Wis. 533; *Re* Mayor, etc. of N. Y. 1 Cent. Rep. 149, 99 N. Y. 569; Gardner v. Newburgh, 2 Johns. Ch. 162.

An application to condemn land for public use must distinctly state that the land is needed for and will, when condemned, be devoted to such use. Fork Ridge Baptist Cemetery Asso. v. Redd, *supra.*

The Michigan Statute providing for the taking by cities of private property for public improvements, and making it the duty of the jury to determine "the necessity for taking such private property for the use or benefit of the public for proposed improvements," sufficiently complies with the constitutional requirement that the jury shall ascertain the necessity for using such property. Detroit v. Beecher (Mich.) June 28, 1883.

Compensation to be made.

Property cannot be taken under eminent domain without first making or securing payment of damages. Sterling's App. 2 Cent. Rep. 51, 111 Pa. 35.

A municipal corporation has no right to appropriate private property without making compensation. Seifert v. Brooklyn, 2 Cent. Rep. 185, 101 N. Y. 136; Smith v. Inge, 80 Ala. 283; Faust v. Huntsville, 83 Ala. 279; Kansas City v. Baird, 98 Mo. 215.

A statute which attempts to authorize the use of private property for public uses, without making adequate provision for compensation, is unconstitutional and void. Brickett v. Haverhill Aqueduct Co. 2 New Eng. Rep. 319, 142 Mass. 394.

See also 25 L. R. A. 838, 46 L. R. A. 724.

Woodruff, 49 Ark. 394; *Little Rock & Ft. S. R. Co.* v. *McGehee*, 41 Ark. 207; *Amoskeag Mfg. Co.* v. *Worcester*, 60 N. H. 526; *Low* v. *Concord R. Corp.* 2 New Eng. Rep. 275, 63 N. H. 558; *Goodin* v. *Cincinnati & W. Canal Co.* 18 Ohio St. 181; *St. Louis, K. & A. R. Co.* v. *Chapman*, 38 Kan. 307; *Woodfolk* v. *Nashville & C. R. Co.* 2 Swan, 438.

Messrs. **Vertrees & Vertrees and Lytton Taylor**, for appellees:

The property is to be valued on the same principles and considerations as if both parties had agreed upon the sale, and had referred the single question of the intrinsic value of that particular property to the commissioners.

Woodfolk v. *Nashville & C. R. Co.* 2 Swan, 439: *Memphis* v. *Bolton*, 9 Heisk. 508; Code, 1563, *note;* Lewis, Em. Dom. § 478; Mills, Em. Dom. 2d ed. § 168.

It is the market value which is to be ascertained.

Lewis, Em. Dom. § 478; *Mississippi & R.R. Boom Co.* v. *Patterson*, 98 U. S. 408 (25 L. ed. 208).

While the condition and surroundings of the property, and its availability for valuable purposes, may be shown, the witnesses are not to be asked, or be allowed to state, the value of the property for any particular purpose.

Low v. *Concord R. Corp.* 2 New Eng. Rep. 275, 63 N. H. 557; *Stinson* v. *Chicago, St. P. & M. R. Co.* 27 Minn. 291; *Sullivan* v. *Lafayette Co.* 61 Miss. 271; *Black River & M. R. Co.* v. *Barnard*, 9 Hun, 104; *Virginia & T. R. Co.* v. *Elliott*, 5 Nev. 358; *Re Boston, H. T. & W. R. Co.* 22 Hun, 176; *Union Depot, S. R. & Transfer Co.* v. *Brunswick*, 31 Minn. 299; *Albany Northern R. Co.* v. *Lansing*, 16 Barb. 68; Lewis, Em. Dom. p. 624, § 486; Mills, Em. Dom. pp. 344, 355; *Moulton* v. *Newburyport Water Co.* 137 Mass. 163; *Central Pac. R. Co.* v. *Pearson*, 35 Cal. 262; *Searle* v. *Lackawanna & B. R. Co.* 33 Pa. 57, approved in *Reading & P. R. Co.* v. *Balthaser*, 12 Cent. Rep. 175, 119 Pa. 482; 3 Sutherland, Damages, 441, 442; *Haslam* v. *Galena & S. W. R. Co.* 64 Ill. 353.

It is not competent as independent evidence of what the market value was to show that the city contemplated erecting this reservoir on this hill.

Mills, Em. Dom. p. 354; *Cobb* v. *Boston*, 112 Mass. 181; *Re William & Anthony Streets*, 19 Wend. 678.

The award of the jury of view would not bear interest, because the Statute does not provide for interest.

Freem. Judgm. 3d ed. § 441; Code (M. & V.) § 1564; *Williams* v. *Inman*, 5 Coldw. 269.

The money was paid in while the proceedings were pending. If, therefore, interest ought to have been allowed, it should have been allowed only on the difference between $12,532 and $10,327.51.

Mills, Em. Dom. 2d ed. p. 359; *Shattuck* v. *Wilton R. Co.* 23 N. H. 269.

Damages to the residue are to be assessed on the basis that the work will be constructed and operated skillfully and properly.

Mills, Em. Dom. 2d ed. § 220; Lewis, Em. Dom. § 482; *Jones* v. *Chicago & I. R. Co.* 68 Ill. 380; *Jackson* v. *Portland*, 63 Me. 55; *Fremont, E. & M. V. R. Co.* v. *Whalen*, 11 Neb. 585; *Setzler* v. *Pennsylvania S. V. R. Co.* 2 Cent. Rep. 357, 112 Pa. 56; *Nason* v. *Woonsocket U. R. Co.* 4 R. I. 377; *Neilson* v. *Chicago, M. & N. W. R. Co.* 58 Wis. 516.

Caldwell, J., delivered the opinion of the court:

This proceeding was instituted by the City of Nashville, in August, 1887, to condemn and appropriate what is known as "Kirkpatrick's Hill," for reservoir purposes. The jury of view assessed the damages at $9,686. Alloway and wife, the owners of the property, appealed from that report, and obtained a trial in the

---

A statute authorizing condemnation of lands for municipal uses must provide an adequate, certain and definite source and mode of payment of just compensation to the owner. Re Mayor, etc. of N. Y. 1 Cent. Rep. 149, 99 N. Y. 569.

A municipal corporation acting under legislative authority may be authorized to take private lands for public use without first making compensation to the owner. State v. Perth Amboy (N. J.) Nov. 8, 1889.

Where it takes private lands for public use without first making compensation to the owner there must, at the time of taking, exist a provision by which the owner can have his damages assessed and obtain the compensation on his own motion. *Ibid.*

The compensation to be paid must be fixed by the valuation of the property at the date of the filing of the petition. Hence, rights acquired by third parties after that date are acquired *pendente lite*, and are subordinate to the rights of the petitioner. Schreiber v. Chicago & E. R. Co. 3 West. Rep. 101, 115 Ill. 340.

Measure of damages.

In the assessment of damages for taking private property for public use, it is the duty of courts to exercise their powers with a view of enabling the party whose property is taken to obtain such compensation as is assured to him by the Constitution. Beekman v. Jackson Co. (Or.) Jan. 6, 1890.

In estimating the value of real property the jury may not only look to the land itself and the actual site of it, but also to the use to which it is, or is intended to be, applied by the owner. Meinzer v. Racine, 74 Wis. 166; Haslam v. Galena & S. W. R. Co. 64 Ill. 353; Chicago & E. R. Co. v. Jacobs, 110 Ill. 414; Kankakee Stone & Lime Co. v. Kankakee, 128 Ill. 173.

So far as the adaptability of the land to uses other than that to which it is applied enhances its present market value, such uses may be considered by the jury. Reed v. Ohio & M. R. Co. 126 Ill. 48; Laflin v. Chicago, W. & N. R. Co. 33 Fed. Rep. 415; Calumet River R. Co. v. Moore, 18 West. Rep. 506, 124 Ill. 329.

So the value of land taken for a bridge site for that purpose is an element of damages for the taking, although the owner himself had no authority to build a bridge. Little Rock Junction R. Co. v. Woodruff, 49 Ark. 381.

The present market value of the land taken is the true basis of compensation, to be determined by the jury from evidence of witnesses, or by their personal inspection of the premises. Reed v. Ohio & M. R. Co. *supra;* Atchison, T. & S. F. R. Co. v. Schneider, 2 L. R. A. 422, 127 Ill. 144.

In Michigan a jury is not authorized to fix and determine the award to be made in condemnation proceedings, upon a mere view of the premises, regardless of the evidence. Grand Rapids v. Perkins (Mich.) Nov. 15, 1889.

circuit court, when verdict and judgment were rendered for $12,532. From that judgment Alloway and wife prosecuted an appeal in error to this court.

The assignment of errors presents several important and interesting questions of law and practice, which it is necessary to consider somewhat in detail in order to reach an intelligent decision of the case. It is objected, and assigned as error, that the owners of the land were not permitted to show its particular value as a reservoir site; and, again, that the trial judge, in his charge, instructed the jury that, in determining the value of the property taken, they could not single out from the elements of general value its value for one special purpose. These two objections raise the same legal question, and will for that reason be considered together.

The "just compensation" required by our Constitution (art. 1, § 21) is the fair cash value of the land taken for public use, estimated as if the owner were willing to sell, and the corporation desired to buy, that particular quantity at that place and in that form. *Woodfolk* v. *Nashville & C. R. Co.* 2 Swan, 437; *East Tennessee & V. R. Co.* v. *Love*, 3 Head, 67; *Tennessee & A. R. Co.* v. *Adams*, 3 Head, 600; *Memphis* v. *Bolton*, 9 Heisk. 509.

This value means the market value. Lewis, Em. Dom. § 478; *Mississippi & R. R. Boom Co.* v. *Patterson*, 98 U. S. 403 [25 L. ed. 206]; Cooley, Const. Lim. 5th ed. 699.

It includes every element of usefulness and advantage in the property. If it be useful for agriculture or for residence purposes; if it has adaptability for a reservoir site, or for the operation of machinery; if it contains a quarry of stone, or a mine of precious metals; if it possesses advantage of location, or availability for any useful purpose whatever,—all these belong to the owner, and are to be considered in estimating its value. It matters not that the owner uses the property for the least valuable of all the ends to which it is adapted, or that he puts it to no profitable use at all. All its capabilities are his, and must be taken into the estimate. This does not mean that all the capabilities are to be priced separately, and the aggregate put down as the true value; for they do not exist independently of each other, and cannot all be realized at the same time. Nor will it do to restrict the estimate to any one of them, because in one view that would exclude the other elements altogether, and in the other view it would tend to make the degree of benefit to the party appropriating and condemning for a particular purpose the real measure of value, which is never allowable.

The field of investigation, in the case before us, was a very broad one. The location and elevation of the property were given. Its surface, area and present use were described. The existence and character of stone within its compass, and the fact that the best of the stone was used in the construction of the walls of the reservoir, were disclosed. The City's engineer said that the hill had some value for residence purposes, but was valuable "mostly for a reservoir site," and this view was confirmed by Mr. John Overton, who said that there was only "one or two more good places for a reservoir" in reach of the City. No witness was allowed to put a price upon any single element of usefulness or advantage, but all the foregoing facts and circumstances were stated in detail by one witness and another, and from them all the witnesses gave their opinions as to the market value of the property. The questions calling for such opinions were generally in this form: "Considering the property sought to be condemned in the form it was taken, and as it was taken, and having regard to the entire property, and the uses to which it was put, and also the uses to which it was adapted, and assuming that Mr. Alloway wanted to sell, but was not obliged to sell, this piece or parcel of land, and the City wanted to buy it, but was not obliged to have it, what was the cash market value of the same in August, 1887, and what would be just compensation to Mr. Alloway, and what damages should be allowed him?" Some of the witnesses, especially those put upon the stand by the owners, answered that question as to their acquaintance with the property and its market value.

With respect to the mode of ascertaining the value of the land taken, the circuit judge instructed the jury in these words: "In estimating its value, all the capabilities of the property, and all the uses to which it may be applied, are to be considered, and not merely the condition it is in at the time, and the use to which it is then applied by the owner. It is not a question of the value of the property to the owner, nor can the value be advanced by his unwillingness to sell. On the other hand, the damages cannot be measured by the value of the property to the party condemning it, nor by its need of the particular property. The City is entitled to have the land at its fair, market, cash value, unaffected by the fact that it needs it, or desires it. If it were otherwise, the value of land would not be measured by what it is actually worth in the market, but by the extent to which it might be necessary for public use; and so, when an appropriation of land is made for a city reservoir, the question is not what the land is worth to the City for the special purpose, for that would be to measure the value by the immediate necessities of the public, rather than the actual worth of the land. In determining the market cash value, you cannot single out from the elements of general value the value for an especial purpose, but you are to consider all the constituent elements that make up the market value,—its availability, adaptability and capacity for different uses and purposes. In determining the market cash value, everything which enhances or depreciates its worth should be taken into consideration. If the existence of a rock quarry under the surface of the hill augmented or entered into the market value of the land, that fact should be considered; but the jury could make no separate allowance for the rock, for that would necessitate an inquiry into the cost of excavating and raising it. The cash market value of the land with the rock in it would be the proper consideration." To a great extent, and entirely so, so far as the cases are alike, this charge is sustained by the opinion of this court in *Woodfolk* v. *Nashville & C. R. Co.* 2 Swan, 437; and in that and all other respects it is in accord with the doctrine laid down in Lewis, Em. Dom. §§ 478, 479, 486; 3 Sutherland, Dam. 441, 442; Mills, Em. Dom. 2d ed. § 168; *Moulton* v. *Newburyport Water Co.* 137 Mass. 163; *Searle* v. *Lackawanna & B. R. Co.* 33 Pa. 57, and in other cases not necessary to be cited.

Thus, as we think, every legitimate question on this branch of the case was developed, and properly submitted for the consideration of the jury. The action of the trial judge was right, both in the rejection of evidence of the amount of value for a reservoir site, and in the instruction that the jury could not single out and estimate the value for a special purpose.

We fully agree with the learned counsel of Alloway and wife, that "the particular purpose for which a piece of property is most applicable" must be considered in estimating the value of such property. That was done in this case. It was distinctly proven that "Kirkpatrick's Hill" was applicable, "mostly, for a reservoir site," and the jury was told to consider that, and every other element of value. That they did so cannot be doubted for a moment, in the light of the whole proof, and the amount of the verdict returned. Our holding is that, while adaptability for a reservoir site must be considered, the value for such a purpose exclusively cannot be shown in proof, and made the sole basis of a recovery, especially when the property possesses other capabilities, as in this case.

There is a lack of harmony in the decisions on this subject, some of them permitting the inquiry as to the value of the property for one special use, and others holding, as we do, that the market value in view of all available uses is the measure of compensation. It is not desirable to review all the cases in this opinion, but some of them will be mentioned. The latest one in the former line is that of *San Diego Land & Town Co.* v. *Neale*, decided by the Supreme Court of California in 1888, and published in 78 Cal. 63, 3 L. R. A. 83. In that case it was held, distinctly, that it was competent to prove the value of land for a reservoir site, and to make that value the measure of damages, independent of any other consideration or element of value; and that, too, when the land sought to be condemned was in fact not the real site of the reservoir, but only necessary to contain backwater from the dam below. To reach that conclusion, two former decisions by the same court, holding a contrary rule, were overruled, and other authorities cited in the opinion, were followed. In a case of the other line this language is used: "But, where a condemnation is sought for the purposes of a railroad, to single out from the elements of general value the value for the special purposes of such railroad is, in effect, to put to a jury the question, What is the land worth to the particular railroad company? rather than, What is it worth in general? The practical result would be to make the company's necessity the land owner's opportunity to get more than the real value of his land." *Stinson* v. *Chicago, St. P. & M. R. Co.* 27 Minn. 291.

The case of *Mississippi & R. R. Boom Co.* v. *Patterson*, 98 U. S. 403 [25 L. ed. 206], is cited by the California court, and is relied on as sound authority by counsel on both sides of this controversy. Patterson owned one island, and parts of two others, in the Mississippi River, which the boom company condemned. The value was first appraised by commissioners, and afterwards by a jury in the circuit court of the United States. When the case reached the Supreme Court, *Mr. Justice* Field, delivering the opinion of the court, said: "The jury found a general verdict assessing the value of the land at $9,358.33, but accompanied it with a special verdict assessing its value, aside from any consideration of its value for boom purposes, at $300, and, in view of its adaptability for those purposes, a further and additional value of $9,058.33. . . . In determining the value of land appropriated for public purposes, the same considerations are to be regarded as in a sale of property between private parties. The inquiry in such cases must be, What is the property worth in the market, viewed not merely with reference to the uses to which it is at the time applied, but with reference to the uses to which it is plainly adapted? That is to say, What is it worth from its availability for valuable uses? Property is not to be deemed worthless because the owner allows it to go to waste, or to be regarded as valueless because he is unable to put it to any use. Others may be able to use it, and make it subserve the necessities and conveniences of life. Its capability of being made thus available gives it a market value which can be readily estimated. So many and varied are the circumstances to be taken into the account in determining the value of property condemned for public purposes, that it is perhaps impossible to formulate a rule to govern its appraisement in all cases. Exceptional circumstances will modify the most carefully guarded rule, but, as a general thing, we should say that the compensation to the owner is to be estimated by reference to the uses for which the property is suitable, having regard to the existing business or wants of the community, or such as may be reasonably expected in the immediate future. The position of the three islands in the Mississippi fitting them to form, in connection with the west bank of the river, a boom of immense dimensions, capable of holding in safety over twenty millions of feet of logs, added largely to the value of the land. The boom company would greatly prefer them to more valuable agricultural lands, or to lands situated elsewhere on the river; as, by utilizing them in the manner proposed, they would save heavy expenditures of money in constructing a boom of equal capacity. Their adaptability for boom purposes was a circumstance, therefore, which the owner had a right to insist upon as an element in estimating the value of his lands." 98 U. S. 405, 407, 408 [25 L. ed. 207, 208].

This lengthy extract presents the rule for compensation, and its application to the facts of the case. Both, as we understand them, are in harmony with, and suggest, the views expressed in this opinion. There the adaptability of the islands for boom purposes was held to be an element of value to be considered by the jury; here it is decided that the adaptability of the hill for purposes of a reservoir is an element of value to be taken into the estimate. There it was treated as an element only, to be considered in connection with other elements of value; so it is here. In that case the contention of the condemning party was that the adaptability of the islands for boom purposes should not enter into the estimate at all. The court said it should, in the words quoted. No comment is made in the opinion on the fact that the jury, in a special verdict, assessed the value for boom purposes separably. That method is neither approved nor disapproved, by intimation or otherwise. The general verdict, as reduced by the owner on suggestion of the lower court, was affirmed.

A late author, speaking on this subject, says: "The market value of property includes its value for any use to which it may be put. If, by reason of its surroundings, or its natural advantages, or its artificial improvements, or its intrinsic character, it is peculiarly adapted to some particular use, all the circumstances which make up this adaptability may be shown, and the fact of such adaptation may be taken into consideration in estimating the compensation. Some of the cases held that its value for a particular use may be proved; but the proper inquiry is, What is its market value, in view of any use to which it may be applied, and of all the uses to which it is adapted? . . . The conclusion from the authorities and reason of the matter seems to be that witnesses should not be allowed to give their opinions as to the value of property for a particular purpose, but should state its market value in view of any purpose to which it is adapted. The condition of the property, and all its surroundings, may be shown and its availability for any particular use. If it has a peculiar adaptation for certain uses, this may be shown, and if such peculiar adaptation adds to its value the owner is entitled to the benefit of it. But, when all the facts and circumstances have been shown, the question at last is, What is it worth in the market?" Lewis, Em. Dom. § 479.

By statute the owner is entitled to compensation for land actually appropriated, and, in addition, to incidental damages for injury, if any, to the residue of the tract. Mill. & V. Code, § 1562.

Both were claimed in this case, but only the former was allowed by the jury. As ground for incidental damages, the use, amount and relative position of the residue, and the capacity (50,000,000 of gallons) and dimensions of the reservoir, were shown. It was also proven that the walls of the reservoir were made of stone taken from the hill; that some of the stone was good for such purpose, and some of it was not, the yield, altogether, being largely more than was used in the wall. Upon these and some other circumstances the witnesses express various opinions on the question of depreciation or no depreciation in the market value of the residue.

The general charge with respect to incidental damages is not assailed, but error is assigned upon this paragraph: "Damages are to be assessed on the basis that the work will be constructed and operated in a skillful and proper manner. All damages resulting from the neglect in these respects, or from negligence in the use of the reservoir, may be recovered, by appropriate suits, when such damages occur." The objection to this is "because a reasonable apprehension of danger would impair the whole of the property in the vicinity, and, when it had been shown that the walls were built from the stone taken from the site, and that most of the stone in the hill was of bad quality, this was ground to apprehend danger. And, besides, the present owner is entitled to the incidental damages." It seems to be well settled that damages to the residue are to be estimated on the assumption that the part actually appropriated will be used in a skillful and proper manner. Mills, Em. Dom. § 220; Lewis, Em. Dom. § 482.

Clearly, this must be so when the damages are assessed before the construction and operation are commenced. If it were otherwise, no appraisement could be made until after the work is completed, because it could not sooner be known how defective the work will be, nor the amount of depreciation caused thereby. The rule should be the same when the construction is in progress, and not completed. When the trial below occurred, the work on the reservoir had been going on a long while, and was approaching completion, but it could not be finished for several months to come. The City was under legal obligation to so construct its improvement as to do the least injury to the residue of the land; and the presumption that it would perform that duty faithfully should be indulged until the work was finished, and the presumption rebutted. Even though some defects should, through negligence, occur in the construction, it is fair to assume that it will be detected and cured before putting the reservoir to its ultimate use. In like manner, the law devolves upon the City the duty of operating the reservoir carefully and skillfully; and it would be unjust to assume in advance that it will not do so. A different rule would be impracticable, as well as unjust; for no one could tell the amount to be allowed for improper operation until the fact itself should be ascertained, and the consequences seen and weighed.

The owner is entitled to all his damages, those for the land taken, and those to the residue, so soon as the condemnation is made. Neither he nor the condemning party can await future developments to enhance or diminish the amount of damages. These must be estimated on the assumption that the land appropriated will be properly and in a reasonable time put to the use for which it is condemned. We by no means intend to decide that incidental damages must be estimated upon the assumption that the construction and operation of the improvement will be absolutely safe, and that apprehension of danger therefrom may not be considered by the jury. Our meaning is that such damages cannot be enhanced by the suggestion that the corporation appropriating the land will act negligently. The presumption is that it will act carefully. If it act otherwise, and injury result from its negligence, that affords an independent cause of action; and the liability so incurred forms no part of the incidental damages. There may be reasonable apprehensions of danger from inherent defects and unavoidable accidents, notwithstanding skillful construction and careful operation of the improvement. If so, such apprehension, so far as it depreciates the present market value of the land not taken, is an element of incidental damages, and should be considered by the jury in making up their verdict. Such apprehension was not excluded from the consideration of the jury in this case. Only that resulting from the neglect or negligence of the city was so excluded. At this point, it is well to note the fact that there was no proof that any of the inferior stone had been placed in the wall, or that any of the work had been unskillfully done.

Each side claimed the right to open and close the argument before the jury. The trial judge decided in favor of the City, and that action is assigned as error. This question has been decided in several of the States, some of them holding one way, and some the other. The majority of the cases seem to give the opening and conclusion to the land owner. Lewis, Em. Dom. § 426.

The conflict in the decisions is largely due, no doubt, to difference in local practice, or statutory provisions. In this State the proceeding is inaugurated by the party seeking to appropriate the land. It is done by a petition setting forth the land wanted, the object for which it is to be condemned, the name of the owner, and concluding with appropriate prayers. Notice is to be given the owner, after which a jury, to inquire and assess the damages, is summoned and sworn. Either party may appeal from the finding of this jury, and have a trial anew before a jury in the circuit court. Mill. & V. Code, §§ 1549–1566, inclusive.

Not only is the corporation seeking the condemnation required to take the first steps, and bring the land owner before the court, in the prescribed order, but it must, of necessity, show that it is entitled to exercise the right of eminent domain, and that the particular land is necessary for its corporate use. In all this the petitioner is plaintiff, with the affirmative of its claim and the burden of proof upon it. The question of the amount of damages is then considered, and generally one side seeks to make it as small, and the other as large, as possible. Starting out as plaintiff, with the *onus* upon it, the petitioner should be allowed to open and close the case, even though the burden of proof may be shifted to the other party on some question arising in the progress of the trial. Concession by the owner of petitioner's right to condemn, and to take the particular land, and contesting the question of damages only, cannot change the rule; nor can the fact that the owner alone appealed from the appraisement by the jury of inquest, for on that appeal the trial is *de novo*, and the attitude of the parties is the same as before.

The jury allowed no interest. No instructions on that subject were given or requested; but after the verdict was returned, and before judgment was entered, Alloway and wife moved the court to add interest. This the court refused to do; and his action in that regard is now assigned as error. The Statute authorizing the condemnation of private property for public use, and prescribing the mode of proceeding, is silent on this subject; and the General Statutes (Id. § 2702) which enumerates instruments that bear interest as a matter of law, does not embrace a case like that before us. Nevertheless, we have no hesitation in holding, upon general principles, that interest should have been allowed from the time of the appropriation of the property. From that time the original owner was deprived of the use and possession of the land taken. The liability of the City accrued at that date, though the amount thereof is not determined finally until long thereafter. Damages are properly assessed with reference to the value of the land taken, and the depreciation of the residue at the time of condemnation. The legal rights of both parties, so far as the damages are concerned, are fixed at that time. Subsequent enhancement or diminution of the value, though ever so great, cannot be considered by the jury in estimating damages. Witnesses are examined as to the amount of damages at the time of appropriation, and not at the time of the trial. That method was properly adopted in this case. The City, especially, asked her witnesses the value of the property "in August, 1887."

In the case of *East Tennessee, V. & G. R. Co.* v. *Burnett*, 11 Lea, 526, the jury of inquest, though reporting several years after the land was appropriated, failed to allow interest. The petitioner did not appeal, and have a trial *de novo*, but excepted to the report because it did not include interest. The exception was overruled, and the petitioner prosecuted a writ of error. This court allowed the interest. Id. 527.

A discussion of the subject is found in § 499, Lewis, Em. Dom. Refusal to allow interest was error. In the language of one of the counsel for appellants: "If the party in whose favor there is verdict is, as a matter of law, entitled to something additional, the court may allow it." Inasmuch as the error can be readily corrected here, that will be done, instead of reversing and remanding. This court will render the judgment that should have been rendered below. The land was taken about the 10th of August, 1887; hence judgment will be entered for the amount of the verdict, with interest from that date.

On September 22, 1888, the City paid into court, subject to the order of Alloway and wife, the sum of $10,872.51, that being the amount of damages returned by the jury of view, with interest and costs added. Because of this tender, the City now insists that it can in no event be liable for interest on a larger sum than the difference between the verdict and the amount so paid into court. This contention, though plausible at first view, is not sustained by sound reason. A tender of part of a debt, in satisfaction of the whole of it, is no tender at all in law. The sum paid into court in this case was more than $2 000 less than the amount due Alloway and wife, as has since been demonstrated by the verdict of the jury; hence they were under no obligation to receive it, and cannot have their claim for interest abated on account of their refusal to do so.

The other grounds of error assigned, so far as material, fall within principles already announced, and for that reason they will not be further mentioned.

Let the judgment be modified by adding interest, and affirmed, with costs.

OHIO SUPREME COURT.

STATE OF OHIO, ex rel. ATTORNEY-GENERAL,
v.
WESTERN UNION MUTUAL LIFE & ACCIDENT SOCIETY of the United States.

(47 Ohio St.......)

*1. **Corporations organized under section 3630 of the Revised Statutes,** which do not comply with the laws regulating regular mutual life insurance companies, have no power to issue policies guaranteeing any fixed amount to be paid at the death of the member, "except such fixed amount shall be conditioned upon the same being realized from the assessments made on members to meet it;" and those corporations so organized, which do comply with such laws, are authorized to issue endowment policies "promising to pay to members during life any sum of money or thing of value." Such Ohio corporations are not permitted to do business in another State upon substantially the same basis and limitations as they are in Ohio, when by the laws of such other State they are not permitted to issue such endowment policies, nor any policy of insurance so conditioned, nor any that does not specify the sum of money to be paid, and unconditionally obligate such corporation to pay the amount so specified, to the beneficiaries of such payment; and corporations organized on the assessment plan under the laws of such other State are not entitled to do business in this State.

2. **The business, which corporations of other States organized to insure lives of members on the assessment plan** "shall be permitted to do in this State," under the provisions of § 3630c, Rev. Stat., is that contemplated by section 3630, which does not include the business of insuring the lives of members for the benefit of others than their families and heirs. A corporation of another State, organized for insuring lives upon the plan of assessments upon its members, without other limitation than that the policy holder shall have an insurable interest in the life of the member, is not embraced within either of said sections.

3. **That clause of section 3630 of the Revised Statutes, which provides that "such company or association shall not be subject** to the preceding sections of this chapter," does not apply to corporations of other States organized for insuring the lives of members for the benefit of others than their families and heirs. Corporations of that class are not entitled to transact any business of insurance in this State, until they procure from the superintendent of insurance a certificate of authority so to do; nor can any person act as agent in this State for such company, until a license to do so is procured from the superintendent of insurance, as required by § 3604, Rev. Stat. Such licenses continue in force, unless suspended or revoked, until the first day of April of the year next after the date of their issue, and no longer.

4. **When a foreign corporation doing business in this State is exercising** its franchises in contravention of the laws thereof, it may be ousted therefrom, by proceedings in *quo warranto.*

*Head notes by the Court.

Note.—*Foreign insurance companies; conditions imposed by statute.*

A law of a State requiring insurance companies of other States or countries to file security, or take out a license, or pay a specific tax or certain fees and percentages, before they can issue policies in the State, is constitutional. Ducat v. Chicago, 77 U. S. 10 Wall. 410 (19 L. ed. 972); Liverpool & L. L. & F. Ins. Co. v. Oliver, 77 U. S. 10 Wall. 566 (19 L. ed. 1029); Home Ins. Co. v. Augusta, 93 U. S. 116 (23 L. ed. 825); Paul v. Virginia, 75 U. S. 8 Wall. 168 (19 L. ed. 357). See *note* to Pennypacker v. Capital Ins. Co., *post*, —.

A State may require a deposit from a foreign company as a condition precedent to its right to do business. Phenix Ins. Co. v. Burdett, 11 West. Rep. 239, 112 Ind. 204.

Such a statute is constitutional, whether the moneys are regarded as taxes for revenue or as a license. State v. Ins. Co. of North America, 15 West. Rep. 96, 115 Ind. 257.

Under the laws of Michigan requiring a deposit of securities as a condition for the prosecution of their business, a British company must make such deposit, although it may have made the same in another State to acquire a license to do business there. Employers L. Assur. Co. v. Insurance Comr. 7 West. Rep. 851, 64 Mich. 614.

Under the Statute of Louisiana license is imposed on the business pursued by an insurance company in the State of Louisiana, and not on business done by branches or agencies established in other States, subject to their laws and subject to taxation imposed thereby. Sections 6 and 7 of the same Act provide for rate of taxation. State v. Hibernia Ins. Co. 38 La. Ann. 465.

Act 1872, chap. 24, § 110, relating to incorporation of cities, was repealed by Act 1879, § 30, which declares the tax directed to be levied upon the net receipts of foreign insurance companies to be in lieu of all town and municipal licenses. Chicago v. James, 1 West. Rep. 315, 114 Ill. 479.

Section 30 requires affirmative action by the city entitled to it, in fixing the rate, which may be less, but cannot be more, than 2 per cent upon the gross, and not upon the net, receipts of the agents of foreign corporations. *Ibid.*

A foreign corporation suing in Colorado on an insurance policy cannot be defeated by the fact that it has not complied with the statutes in regard to foreign corporations doing business within the State, where the only business done within the State relates to the insurance policy in suit. Tabor v. Goss & P. Mfg. Co. 11 Colo. 419.

The Act making it unlawful for anyone to aid a foreign insurance company in transacting business within the State renders any person so aiding liable, although acting under a contract with the insured as his agent only. People v. People's Ins. Exchange, 2 L. R. A. 340, 126 Ill. 466.

A condition in a policy of a foreign company doing business in this State, that anyone except the insured who procures insurance to be taken by the company shall be deemed the agent of the insured, is null and void. North British & M. Ins. Co. v. Crutchfield, 7 West. Rep. 85, 108 Ind. 518.

An agent of an insurance company incorporated in the District of Columbia is an agent of a company incorporated by a "State" other than the State of Indiana, within Ind. Rev. Stat. 1881, § 3765, requiring a license from such agent. State v. Briggs, 116 Ind. 55.

A state statute, which provides that insurance companies of other States shall not do business in

See also 16 L. R. A. 611; 23 L. R. A. 86.

(March 4, 1890.)

PETITION for a writ of *quo warranto* to oust defendant from exercising the franchise of transacting the business of a life insurance company within the State. *Judgment of ouster.*

Statement by **Williams**, *J.:*

The petition states that the defendant is a corporation organized under the laws of the State of Michigan for the purpose of carrying on, upon the assessment or co-operative plan, the business of insuring the lives of its members, and of providing to its members indemnity for disability by accident; that since the 1st day of April, 1889, the defendant has exercised and claims the right to exercise, in this State, the privilege and franchise of transacting the business of insuring lives upon the assessment plan, which it is not entitled to do, because neither it nor any of its agents obtained from the superintendent of insurance of this State the necessary certificate of authority or license to do business in this State, and also because, by the statutes of Michigan, corporations organized under the laws of Ohio, for the purpose of insuring the lives of members upon the assessment plan, are not permitted to do business in the State of Michigan upon the same basis and limitations as they are in this State; and, the commissioner of insurance of the State of Michigan has refused, and still refuses, to issue to such Ohio corporations his certificate of authority to transact business in that State. The provisions of the Michigan statutes upon the subject are set out in the petition. Such of them as are deemed material to the decision of the case will be noticed in the opinion.

The petition prays for a judgment of ouster against the defendant.

The answer admits that the defendant was incorporated under the Michigan Statute set forth in the petition; that it has exercised, and claims the right to exercise, in this State, the privilege and franchise referred to in the petition, and alleges that it is entitled to do so, because, it avers that on the 9th day of June, 1886, it made application to the superintendent of insurance of this State for permission to carry on in the State of Ohio the business of life insurance, as contemplated in section 3630*e* of the Revised Statutes of Ohio; and that on the 13th day of September, 1886, the superintendent of insurance duly authorized the defendant to transact business in this State; since which time the defendant has continuously prosecuted its business in this State as contemplated in section 3630 of the Revised Statutes. The answer further alleges that Ohio corporations organized for the purpose of insuring their members upon the assessment plan are not debarred by the laws of Michigan from transacting business in that State, and that the insurance commissioner of that State has not refused to issue certificates of authority to transact business in that State, to such Ohio corporations as can and will comply with the laws of the State of Michigan. It is also alleged in the answer that the petition was filed at the instigation of "The People's Mutual Benefit Association of Westerville, Ohio," which corporation, on or about the 24th of October, 1888, made application to the insurance commissioner of Michigan for authority to do business in that State, but was refused such authority, because, upon examination, it was ascertained its business, in part, was that of endowment insurance, which the laws of Michigan did not permit corporations organized on the assessment plan to do.

---

the State until they shall have designated an agent therein upon whom process may be served, confers jurisdiction upon a circuit court of the United States sitting in such State over an action by a citizen of the State against an insurance company of another State, commenced by service upon an agent therein, designated by it under the statute. *Ex parte* Schollenberger, 96 U. S. 369 (24 L. ed. 853).

No foreign insurance company can take fire risks within the State of Michigan unless authorized by the commissioner of insurance. Hartford F. Ins. Co. v. Insurance Comr. 14 West. Rep. 632, 70 Mich. 485.

The statutes of Missouri make it the duty of a foreign insurance company desiring to transact business in the State to file with the superintendent of the insurance department a written instrument designating someone as agent to receive service of process. A sheriff's return on a writ of garnishment served "on one of the agents" is insufficient. Gates v. Tusten, 4 West. Rep. 862, 89 Mo. 131.

It makes the certified copy of the certificate evidence of authority to do business in the State. American Ins. Co. v. Smith, 2 West. Rep. 149, 19 Mo. App. 627.

Where a foreign company, undertaking to prove the existence of its certificate to carry on business for several years, omits proof of the year in question, the submission of the question to the jury, whether it had authority to do business at that time, is proper. *Ibid.*

The mere absence from a recorder's office of a certificate issued to a foreign corporation, will not warrant the inference that no such certificate exists. *Ibid.*

The Legislature has fixed no limit as to the amount of cash business these companies may do; and if the law is defective in this respect, the remedy must come from the law-making power. State v. Manufacturers Mut. F. Ins. Co. 8 West. Rep. 258, 91 Mo. 311.

In New York the Legislature did not intend to prohibit such adjustments by uncertified agents of fire insurance companies of other States and foreign countries, where there appeared to be nothing unlawful in the contract out of which the indebtedness had arisen. People v. Gilbert, 44 Hun, 522.

Under the Nebraska Statute a foreign insurance company, to be authorized to transact business in Nebraska, must be possessed of at least $200,000 of actual paid-up capital, exclusive of any assets of such company deposited in any other State or Territory. State v. Benton, 25 Neb. 834.

The provision of the Wisconsin Statute which imposes a penalty upon every life or accident insurance company doing business in Wisconsin which fails to file the annual statement thereby prescribed, does not apply to a nonresident corporation which has not been licensed, although doing business within the State in violation of law. State v. United States Mut. Accident Asso. 69 Wis. 76.

The Statute of Wisconsin which enacts that a corporation organized in another State shall not transact business within its limits unless it agrees in advance that it will not remove into the federal courts any suit that may be commenced against it by a citizen of Wisconsin, is repugnant to the Constitution of the United States, and void; and the

The defendant also filed a supplemental answer (so called), which charges that the superintendent of insurance has embodied in the annual report which he is required to make to the General Assembly, relating to the conduct and condition of all insurance companies doing business in this State, a statement to the effect that he has lawfully revoked the authority of the defendant to do business in Ohio after April 1, 1889, since which time it has been doing business in this State without authority of law; and that he has omitted to make any statement in his report showing the condition of the defendant Company.

By this pleading, it is sought to make the superintendent of insurance a party to the action, and enjoin him from making such report.

The case is submitted upon demurrers to the answer, and the supplemental answer.

Messrs. **David K. Watson,** *Atty-Gen.*, and **R. A. Harrison** for plaintiff.

Mr. **C. D. Robertson,** for defendant:

Corporations of the class of this defendant, by the provisions of § 3630, Rev. Stat., are not subject to the laws of this State relating to life insurance companies, and are not required to receive annual renewals of authority.

State v. *Mutual Protection Asso.* 26 Ohio St. 19; *State* v. *Standard Life Asso.* 38 Ohio St. 281.

To be permitted to do business in this State foreign companies are simply required to comply with the laws of this State regulating like companies and organizations in this State, and obtain from the superintendent of insurance a certificate of such compliance.

State v. *Moore*, 38 Ohio St. 10.

Williams, *J.*, delivered the opinion of the court:

It is contended, in behalf of the plaintiff, that the defendant is not entitled to carry on its business of insurance in this State, and that it is therefore exercising its franchises here in contravention of law, because: (1) Ohio corporations organized under section 3630 of the Revised Statutes are not permitted to do business in the State of Michigan on substantially the same basis and limitations as they are in Ohio; (2) the law under which the defendant is organized authorizes it to engage in the business of insuring lives on the plan of assessments upon surviving members, without other restriction than that policy holders shall have an insurable interest in the lives of the members, which companies organized for the mutual protection of its members within this State are not permitted to do; and (3) the defendant has failed to comply with the laws of this State, which require that such corporations shall obtain annually, from the superintendent of insurance, a certificate of authority, and licenses to their agents, to do business in this State.

1. The business of life insurance, and the terms and conditions upon which foreign companies may be admitted to carry on that business, are regulated in this State by statute; and the right of the defendant to transact its business of insurance within the State, if possessed by it, must be derived, it is conceded, from § 3630*e*, Rev. Stat., which is as follows: "Any corporation, company or association organized under the law of any other State to insure lives of members on the assessment plan, and authorized to transact the business contemplated in section 3630, shall be permitted to do such business, to wit: the business contemplated in section 3630, in this State, by first complying with the laws of the State of Ohio, regulating corporations, companies or associations organized for the mutual protection of their members

---

agreement of an insurance company made in conformity to this Statute is also void. Home Ins. Co. v. Morse, 87 U. S. 20 Wall. 445 (22 L. ed. 365).

In Vermont an information under Acts 1884, charging an agent with receiving risks for insurance in behalf of a foreign insurance company which has not complied with the Statute, must allege assured's name. State v. Hover, 2 New Eng. Rep. 201, 58 Vt. 496.

Retaliatory legislation.

Under Iowa Code, § 1154, providing that, where another State imposes prohibitions upon Iowa insurance companies doing business therein, the law of such State shall be the law of Iowa, as against insurance companies from such State doing business in Iowa, there need not be any enforcement in such other State of the prohibition imposed on Iowa insurance companies. The existence of such law is sufficient to warrant enforcement of said section. State v. Fidelity & Casualty Co. 77 Iowa, 648.

The Illinois statutory provision that, whenever any other State shall require Illinois insurance companies doing business therein to deposit and pay a greater amount than the Illinois laws require of such companies, then companies of such State doing business in Illinois shall be required to pay or deposit the same amount of tax or license fee, becomes operative upon the passage of a law laying an additional burden upon Illinois companies, whether any such companies are doing business within the State passing the law or not. Germania Ins. Co. v. Swigert, 128 Ill. 237.

A statute of New York providing that if any State shall require a greater deposit of securities or payment of any kind from a corporation of New York, than from foreign corporations of other States, a corporation of such State in New York shall be required to make the same deposit or payment, does not "deny to any person within its jurisdiction the equal protection of the laws." Philadelphia Fire Asso. v. New York, 119 U. S. 110 (30 L. ed. 342).

Article 4, § 2, U. S. Const., giving citizens of each State all privileges and immunities of citizens in the States, does not apply to corporations. *Ibid.*

In accordance with the policy of Minnesota and of the Interstate Law of Comity, foreign insurance corporations are allowed to carry on business in that State. A foreign corporation which has complied with Minnesota laws should not, as measure of retaliation, by force of the retaliatory Statute (Minn. Gen. Stat. chap. 34, § 269), be excluded from doing business in Minnesota, upon the ground that the laws of the State where such foreign corporation was created would exclude corporations of Minnesota from doing business there, unless it is clearly apparent that such is the effect of the foreign law. The proper effect of the statutes of New York in this particular being considered doubtful, and the manner of their practical administration being undisclosed, a judgment of ouster against the New York corporation was refused. State v. Fidelity & C. Ins. Co. 39 Minn. 538.

Quo warranto is a proper proceeding to try the right of a foreign corporation to carry on its corporate business in Minnesota. *Ibid.*

within this State, upon obtaining from the superintendent of insurance of this State a certificate of such compliance, which certificate shall not be granted until such foreign corporation, company or association shall have appointed an agent or attorney within this State upon whom service of process may be had. Provided, that the superintendent of insurance shall not be required to issue certificates to do business in Ohio to an agent of any such corporation, company or association organized in any State in which such Ohio corporations, companies or associations are not permitted to do business on substantially the same basis and limitations as they are in Ohio."

In view of the proviso contained in this section, it becomes important to determine upon what basis and limitations Ohio corporations are permitted to do business in Ohio. These are ascertained by reference to section 3630 and 3630c of the Revised Statutes. The former section is as follows:

"Sec. 3630. A company or association may be organized to transact the business of life or accident insurance on the assessment plan, for the purpose of mutual protection and relief of its members, and for the payment of stipulated sums of money to the families or heirs of the deceased members of such company or association, and may receive money either by voluntary donation or contribution, or collect the same by assessment on its members, and may accumulate, invest, distribute and appropriate the same in such manner as it may deem proper; that all accumulations and accretions thereon shall be held and used as the property of the members and in the interest of the members, and shall not be loaned to, used, appropriated or invested for the benefit of any officer or manager of such company or association; and, provided, that no company or association shall issue a certificate for a greater amount than such company or association shall be able to pay from the proceeds of one assessment; and such company or association shall not be subject to the preceding sections of this chapter."

It is provided in section 3630c that, "no such corporation, company or association issuing endowments, certificates or policies, or undertaking, or promising to pay to members during life any sum of money, or thing of value, or certificate, or policy guaranteeing any fixed amount to be paid at death, except such fixed amount or endowments shall be conditional upon the same being realized from the assessments made on members to meet them, shall be permitted to do business in this State, until they shall comply with the laws regulating regular mutual life insurance companies."

Whatever powers such companies possess are derived exclusively from the laws of this State, and the limitations and restrictions imposed upon them by those laws, both with respect to the classes of business they may transact, and the mode of doing it, operate upon them as well when doing business outside of the State as within it. Their corporate capacity, in these respects, cannot be enlarged by the laws of any other State in which they may be permitted to do business. By the plain provisions of these Statutes, no company organized under section 3630, unless it complies with the laws regulating regular mutual life insurance companies, can issue any policy guaranteeing any fixed amount to be paid at death, "except such amount shall be conditional upon the same being realized from the assessments made on members to meet them." In other words, the obligation of the policy, and the only one the company can thus contract, is to pay, upon the death of the member, such sum, and only such, as may be realized from the assessments made on members to meet it. The policy does not create an unconditional obligation to pay the amount specified in it, nor has the company corporate power to issue such policy, or contract such obligation, in this State or elsewhere. Then those companies, so organized, which do comply with the laws regulating mutual life insurance companies, are authorized to issue endowment policies, undertaking to pay members "during life, any sum of money or thing of value," and policies guaranteeing a fixed amount to be paid at death. These are the basis and limitations upon which such companies are authorized to do business in Ohio, and the question to be determined here is whether they are permitted by the laws of Michigan to do business there upon substantially the same basis and limitations. It is not enough that they be permitted, there, to exercise some of their franchises, or transact a part only of the business they are authorized to do in Ohio, but they must there be permitted to do substantially the same business upon substantially the same terms and conditions as they are in Ohio. If by the laws of Michigan any substantial limitation or restriction is placed upon such Ohio companies in regard to the character or extent of the business they may transact there, to which they are not subject in Ohio, it cannot be said that they are permitted to do business there upon substantially the same basis and limitations as they are in Ohio.

By section 15 of the Michigan Statute, under which it is admitted by the answer the defendant was reorganized, it is provided that "every policy or certificate issued by any corporation in that State and doing business under that Act, and promising a payment to be made upon a contingency of death, or of disability by accident, shall specify the sum of money it promises to pay upon such contingency insured against, and the number of days after satisfactory proof of the happening of such contingency at which such payment should be made; and that upon the occurrence of such contingency, unless the contract shall have been voided by fraud or by breach of its condition, the corporation shall be obligated to the beneficiaries of such payment, at the time and to the amount specified in the policy or certificate; and that this indebtedness shall have priority over all indebtedness thereafter incurred, except as provided in case of the distribution of assets of an insolvent corporation."

And section 17 of the same Act provides that no corporation or association organized under the laws of any other State for the purpose of insuring lives or furnishing accident indemnity upon the co-operative assessment plan shall be authorized to do business in Michigan until it shall have obtained a certificate of authority from the commissioner of insurance of that State; and that no such certificate of authority shall be issued unless the corporation or association applying therefor "has in force policies of insurance upon which the proceeds of one assessment will pay the highest amount insured upon each of the lives of the members for which the assessment is levied, the full amount agreed to be paid upon the death of any one member, and that it is paying, and for twelve months next preceding has paid, the highest amount named in its policies or certificates in full."

Thus it appears that by the laws of Michigan every policy issued by a corporation in that State "promising a payment to be made upon a contingency of death, . . . shall specify the sum of money it promises to pay, . . . and, upon the occurrence of such contingency, . . . the corporation shall be obligated to the beneficiaries of such payment, . . . to the amount specified in the policy," and no certificate of authority to do business in Michigan shall be issued to any corporation or association organized under the laws of any other State unless for the twelve months next preceding it has paid, and is paying, the full amount named in its policies, nor unless it has in force policies upon which the proceeds of one assessment will pay the highest amount insured upon the lives of the members for which the assessment is levied, the full amount agreed to be paid upon the death of any one member. While, as we have already seen, corporations organized under the Ohio Statute are not obligated to pay the full amount specified in the policy, but only such sum as may be realized from assessments made on its members; and their policies must so provide. They are incapable of making any other contract, or issuing any policy of insurance not so conditioned, unless they comply with the laws regulating mutual life insurance companies; in which event they are permitted in Ohio to issue endowment policies.

It is admitted by the answer that the laws of the State of Michigan do not permit endowment policies to be issued or contracts of that kind to be made by corporations organized to do business on the assessment plan, and for that reason the commissioner of insurance of that State refused to issue his certificate of authority to an Ohio company, organized under section 3630, to do business in that State.

Whether, therefore, the Ohio corporation does or does not comply with the laws regulating regular mutual life insurance companies, it is not, in either event, permitted to do business in the State of Michigan upon substantially the same basis and limitations as it is in Ohio.

2. Does the defendant come within the class of companies which, under the provisions of section 3630, may be admitted to do business in this State? It will be observed that only companies organized under the laws of any other State to insure the lives of members on the assessment plan, and authorized to transact the business contemplated in section 3630, are entitled to do business in this State; and furthermore, that it is only the business contemplated in section 3630 that such companies shall be permitted to transact. The language of the Statute is: "Any corporation, company or association, organized under the laws of any other State to insure lives of members on the assessment plan, and authorized to transact the business contemplated in section 3630, shall be permitted to do such business, to wit: the business contemplated in section 3630, in this State," upon the conditions therein specified. As often as the question has been presented, it has been held by this court that section 3630 does not contemplate or permit the business of insuring the lives of members otherwise than for the benefit of their families and heirs.

In *State* v. *Moore*, 38 Ohio St. 7, it is decided that "a company of another State organized for insuring lives upon the plan of assessment upon surviving members, without limitation, does not come under the class of companies provided for in section 3630. That section does not embrace companies insuring the lives of members for the benefit of others than their families and heirs."

And in *State* v. *Moore*, 39 Ohio St. 486, the relator, a New York corporation, organized on the assessment plan and authorized by the law governing it to issue policies payable to the legal representatives of the member, or to any beneficiary designated by such member, sought to compel, by mandamus, the insurance commissioner of this State to issue to it the necessary certificate entitling it to do business in this State. But the writ was refused. Doyle, *J.*, in the opinion, after quoting the above paragraph of the syllabus in *State* v. *Moore*, 38 Ohio St. 7, says: "The principle thus announced must exclude the relator unless the law has been changed by subsequent legislation."

The legislation has not in this respect been changed. It is admitted by the pleadings that the defendant is authorized by the law of its reorganization to issue policies on the lives of its members for the benefit of any person who has an insurable interest in such life.

By section 15 of the Michigan Statute set out in the petition, it is provided that corporations doing business under the Act shall not issue any policy "upon a life in which the beneficiary has not an insurable interest;" and it is further provided by the same section that any member "shall have the right at any time, with the consent of such corporation or association, and with the consent of the beneficiary, if he be a creditor, to make a change in his beneficiary," within certain specified limits; and further, that "such corporation shall not issue policies or certificates to beneficiaries as a creditor or creditors that do not state that they are for collateral security payable as the interest of such beneficiaries may appear; and in every such case said creditor or creditors shall only be entitled to such portion of the amount insured (not exceeding the face of the policy) as shall cover the indebtedness of the member to said creditor at the date of his death. And section 17 of the same Statute provides that "no corporation or association organized or doing business under or by virtue of the laws of any State or Territory of the United States, or District of Columbia, or foreign country, for the purpose of insuring lives, or furnishing accident indemnity upon the co-operative assessment plan, shall be authorized to do business in the State, until it shall have obtained a certificate of authority from the commissioner of insurance of this State, as hereafter provided; nor unless the State, or Territory of the United States, or District of Columbia, or foreign country under whose laws such corporation or association is organized, shall extend the right to such corporations of this State to do business in such State, Territory of the United States, District of Columbia or foreign country, upon similar conditions to those in this Act prescribed." The defendant is therefore not entitled to carry on its business in this State, and the superintendent of insurance may rightfully withhold from it license and authority to do so.

3. It is alleged in the answer that the superintendent of insurance, on the 13th day of September, 1886, authorized the defendant to transact business in this State; but it is admitted that neither the defendant, nor any agent of the defendant, has received any certificate or license from him since that date, and that it has continued to carry on its business in Ohio without other license or authority than that first granted it.

The claim of the defendant is that, when it obtained from the superintendent of insurance the certificate provided for in section 3630*e*, it was placed in all respects upon the same footing as companies organized under section 3630, and is therefore entitled to the benefit of the last clause of that section, which provides that "such company or association shall not be subject to the preceding sections of this chapter."

We regard the case of *State* v. *Moore*, 38 Ohio St. 7, decisive of this claim, adverse to the defendant. The relator in that case claimed that, by reason of the clause referred to in section 3630, and the provisions of the Supplementary Act of April 12, 1880, which enacted section 3630*e* substantially as it is now, so far as it affects this question, it was exempt from the operation of section 3604, which was then, and is now, in the same chapter with section 3630. The Statute under which the relator in that case was organized, authorized it to engage in the business of insuring lives on the plan of assessments upon its surviving members, without other restrictions than that the policy holders should have an interest in the lives of members; and it was held, as before noticed, that such companies did not come within the provisions of section 3630, and that the relator was subject to the preceding sections of the chapter. In the opinion of the court, White, *J.*, says:

"The character of the company or association authorized to do business under section 3630 is thus described in the section: 'A company or association may be organized for the purpose of mutual protection and relief of its members, and for the payment of stipulated sums of money to the families or heirs of the deceased members of such company or association, and may receive money, either by voluntary donation or contribution, or collect the same by assessment on its members . . . and such association shall not be subject to the preceding sections of this chapter. It is companies and associations of this character alone that are exempt from the operation of the preceding sections of the Act; and this exemption is allowed on account of the limited nature of the life insurance they are authorized to assume, being confined to insurance for the benefit of the families and heirs of members.'"

We have already seen that the defendant is engaged in the business of insuring lives upon the plan of assessments upon surviving members without other restriction than that policy holders shall have an insurable interest in the lives of the members, and is not within the class of companies provided for in section 3630, and therefore not exempt from the operation of the preceding sections of that chapter.

One of these sections, 3604, provides that "no company organized by Act of Congress, or under the laws of any other State of the United States, shall transact any business of insurance in this State until it procures from the superintendent of insurance a certificate of authority so to do;" and it further provides that no "person or corporation shall act as agent for any such company in procuring applications for insurance, taking risks, or in any manner transacting the business of insurance, until such person or corporation procures from the superintendent of insurance a license so to do." And by the provisions of section 3616, all licenses so granted "shall continue in force, unless suspended or revoked, until the first day of April of the year next after the date of their issue." We are of the opinion that the license granted to the defendant and its agents on the 13th day of September, 1886, expired on the first day of April ensuing, and that since that time the defendant has been doing business in this State without authority of law.

4. The defendant, availing itself of the rule that the demurrer searches the record and reaches the first defective pleading, contends that the facts averred in the petition do not entitle the plaintiff to the relief demanded. It appears from the petition that the defendant is a corporation organized under the laws of the State of Michigan, and the contention of the defendant is that *quo warranto* cannot be maintained against it in this State, because it can be ousted of its franchises only by the sovereignty which bestowed them. Undoubtedly, the franchises which a State has conferred upon a corporation cannot be taken from it by the act of another State, or by the judgment of its courts. Morawetz, Priv. Corp. § 659.

The purpose of this action, however, is not to deprive the defendant of the franchises with which it has been invested by the laws of the State creating it, but to inquire into its authority to carry on its business in this State, and, if found to be exercising its franchises in this State in contravention of the laws thereof, to oust it therefrom. It is provided by section 6761 of the Revised Statutes that the civil action of *quo warranto* may be brought in the name of the State against a corporation when it claims or has exercised "a franchise, privilege or right in contravention of law."

There can be no doubt of the power of the Legislature to prescribe the terms and conditions upon which foreign corporations may be admitted to do business in this State.

It was held in *W. U. Teleg. Co.* v. *Mayer*, 28 Ohio St. 521, that "foreign corporations can exercise none of their franchises or powers within this State, except by comity or legislative consent. That consent may be upon such terms and conditions as the General Assembly under its legislative power may impose." It was said by Johnson, *J.*, in the opinion in that case, that foreign corporations "may be excluded from the State altogether, or admitted on such terms as the State may prescribe." Before exercising their franchises in this State, such corporations must, of course, comply with the conditions so imposed. Without such compliance, the exercise of their franchises in the State would be in contravention of the laws of the State, and, as just noticed, § 6761, Rev. Stat., expressly authorizes the action of *quo warranto* to be brought by the State against a corporation which claims or has exercised a franchise or privilege in contravention of law. This Statute is not limited to corporations organized under the laws of Ohio, but applies to corporations generally. If it had been intended to confine the application of the Statute to domestic corporations, apt language for that purpose would doubtless have been employed. We hold that a foreign corporation which is carrying on its business, and making contracts in that behalf, in this State, is exercising therein its corporate franchises, from which, when exercised in contravention of the laws of the State, it may be ousted by proceedings in *quo warranto*.

The proper judgment in such case is not to oust the corporation from the franchise of being a corporation, or from any of the franchises conferred on it by the law of its creation, but from the exercise of its franchises in this State.

Demurrers sustained, and judgment of ouster.

OREGON SUPREME COURT.

MOSES, *Respt.*,
v.
SOUTHERN PACIFIC R. CO., *Appt.*

(....Or.....)

*1. **The provisions of our Statute (§§ 4044, 4045) providing that, if a railroad fails to fence** its road against live stock, it shall be liable for the injuries resulting from such failure, etc., do not extend or apply to depot grounds; and in the absence of negligence, the company is not liable for stock killed thereon.

2. **In this State, the common-law rule** requiring every man to keep his stock within his inclosure is not in force, and from its early settlement all kinds of stock have been allowed to run at large upon uninclosed lands.

3. **In those jurisdictions in which the common-law rule prevails** that the owner of cattle is bound to keep them in his own in-

*Head notes by LORD, *J.*

NOTE—*Liability of railroad company for death or injury to cattle by failure to fence; rules in various States.*

Connecticut.

The duty of a railroad company, under Conn. Gen. Stat., § 3505, to fence the sides of its road "except at such place or places as the railroad commissioners shall adjudge them unnecessary," does not require a company to build a fence between its track and that of another company running nearly parallel therewith, although the latter company fails to build a fence on either side of its track. See *note* to Gallagher v. New York & N. E. R. Co. (Conn.) 5 L. R. A. 737.

Illinois.

The Illinois statute makes it the duty of railroad companies "to erect and maintain fences suitable and sufficient to prevent cattle, horses, sheep and hogs from getting upon their road." Chicago & A. R. Co. v. Umphenour, 69 Ill. 198.

Indiana.

A railroad company is liable for the value of cattle killed by reason of its failure to maintain a fence by keeping gate fastenings secure, which it was bound by contract to do. Chicago & A. R. Co. v. Barnes, 116 Ind. 126.

Where the right of way was conveyed in consideration of a covenant to fence, the company is liable for the value of animals killed through its failure to fence, and for pasturage injured by trespassing animals, and for the loss of the increased value of property which would have resulted if the covenant had been complied with. Louisville, N. A. & C. R. Co. v. Sumner, 2 West. Rep. 663, 106 Ind. 55; Louisville, N. A. & C. R. Co. v. Moore, 2 West. Rep. 666, 106 Ind. 600; Logansport, C. & S. W. R. Co. v. Wray, 52 Ind. 578.

Where the railroad company might have fenced its right of way at the place where the animal went upon the track and was killed, the company was held liable, although negligence was not charged. Pennsylvania Co. v. Dunlap, 11 West. Rep. 87, 112 Ind. 93.

One in possession of sheep, accountable for their return or for any injury to them, with the right to half their increase, is the owner within the intent of the Statute, giving a right of recovery against a railroad for animals killed where the road is not securely fenced. New York, C. & St. L. R. Co. v. Auer, 8 West. Rep. 659, 106 Ind. 219.

So the borrower or tenant of an animal stands in the relation of an owner to the company on whose right of way an injury occurs. *Ibid.*

Where a railroad company maintains a bridge in such condition that animals may enter upon it from a public highway, the railroad is not securely fenced. Cincinnati, H. & I. R. Co. v. Jones, 9 West. Rep. 605, 111 Ind. 259.

Contributory negligence is not a defense to an action based upon a statute imposing the duty on railroad companies to fence their right of way. The disregard of this duty is not simply negligence but a tort. Jeffersonville, M. & I. R. Co. v. Ross, 37 Ind. 545; Louisville, N. A. & C. R. Co. v. Cahill, 63 Ind. 340; Louisville, N. A. & C. R. Co. v. Whitesell, 68 Ind. 297; Welty v. Indianapolis & V. R. Co. 2 West. Rep. 652, 105 Ind. 55. See *note* to Dennis v. Louisville, N. A. & C. R. Co. (Ind.) 1 L. R. A. 448.

Iowa.

A railroad company cannot claim exemption for any time, after it begins the movement of trains, on the ground that it should have a reasonable time after the construction of the road within which to build its fences. Glandon v. Chicago, M. & St. P. R. Co. 68 Iowa, 457.

See also 18 L. R. A. 110.

closure,—*it is generally held*, though with some exceptions, that if he suffers them to go at large, and the cattle stray upon the railroad track, and are injured or killed, the company is not liable, unless the conduct of its agents in the management of the train was wanton or wilful.

4. On the other hand, in those jurisdictions in which the common-law rule as to the duty of the owner of cattle to keep them within his own inclosure is not in force,—*it is held*, that a plaintiff, in allowing his stock to run at large, commits no unlawful act, nor is guilty of an omission of ordinary care: and if such stock stray upon an uninclosed railroad track, and are injured or killed, whether they are rightfully there or not, he is not guilty of contributory negligence, but the company is liable, unless it or its agents exercised ordinary care or skill, in the management of its train, to prevent their injury or destruction.

5. The principle is that a railway company is liable in damages for injuries to stock through its negligence, where the plaintiff contributed to the injury no further than permitting his stock to run at large. Such negligence, if it may be called negligence, is not the proximate cause of the injury, and, in the sense of the law, does not constitute contributory negligence.

(*Thayer*, Ch. J., *dissents*.)

(February 11, 1890.)

APPEAL by defendant from a judgment of the Circuit Court for Linn County in favor of plaintiff in an action to recover damages for the death of plaintiff's horse, which was alleged to have resulted from the negligence of defendant's servants. *Affirmed.*

The facts sufficiently appear in the opinion.

Mr. **E. C. Bronough** for appellant.
Mr. **J. K. Weatherford** for respondent.

Lord, *J.*, delivered the opinion of the court:

This is an action to recover damages for negligence in the management of the defendant's railroad, whereby a horse owned by the plaintiff was killed. The answer, after making the usual denials, sets up separately, as a defense, that the injury and damages were caused by the contributory negligence of the plaintiff, all of which he denied in his reply. There was a trial had, resulting in a verdict and judgment for the plaintiff, from which this appeal is taken.

By his brief, the counsel for the defendant, who is the appellant, says that the appeal involves but one question: "What is the liability of a railroad company for an injury done by a moving train to a horse running at large, and seeking pasturage upon the depot grounds of the company, with the knowledge and permission of the owner?" This question arises out of an exception to a modification of an instruction asked, and is as follows: "If the jury believes from the evidence that the plaintiff voluntarily permitted his horse to run at large, and the horse was accustomed to pasture on the depot grounds of the defendant, and wandered on the railroad track, and was killed, such conduct by the plaintiff would not preclude a recovery in this case by the plaintiff, unless the defendant's servants exercised the ordinary care of prudent men in running the train at the time of the accident. In this case, if you believe from the evidence that the

---

Where defendant could be charged with a knowledge of a gap in the fence, the jury might find that the mules got through the gap and were killed by reason of the want of a fence. Accola v. Chicago, B. & Q. R. Co. 70 Iowa, 185.

But an instruction that where cattle get on a railroad on account of the want of fences, where the right to a fence exists, and are killed by the cars, the company is liable whether the cattle are running at large or not, is erroneous. Brentner v. Chicago, M. & St. P. R. Co. 68 Iowa, 530.

Although a horse may be "crazy," if he gets upon the track of a railroad through the want of a fence, where the right to fence exists, and for want of intelligence runs ahead of the engine on the track, when he might escape on either side, and so runs into a bridge and is killed, without being struck by the engine, the company is liable, notwithstanding the horse's want of intelligence and the manner of his death. Liston v. Central Iowa R. Co. 70 Iowa, 714.

Railroad companies need not, under the Iowa Act, build fences so high that they will never be covered with snow; nor need they remove the snow and drifts from the fences, but only sufficient to keep stock off from the track. Patten v. Chicago, M. & St. P. R. Co. 75 Iowa, 459.

In an action for the value of stock killed on a railroad track by reason of the want of a fence, plaintiff is not entitled to interest on his damages prior to the finding of the verdict. Brentner v. Chicago, M. & St. P. R. Co. 68 Iowa, 530.

Michigan.

Under Comp. Laws, § 1967, the neglect to erect or maintain fences along the line of the road will render the corporation owning the road liable for the consequent damages. Under Laws 1867, p. 221, the injured party has the right to elect against which corporation he will proceed. Bay City & E. S. R. Co. v. Austin, 21 Mich. 390.

A railway company is liable for the damages resulting from the insufficiency or want of repair of its fences, in the absence of any proof showing an extraordinary cause for such condition. *Ibid.*

Where a railroad track crosses a highway diagonally, and the company, in fencing its right of way, leaves a space between the termination of its fence and the fence of the adjacent owner, it violates its duty in fencing its right of way; and where a horse escaped by reason of defective fencing of that space, and went upon the track, where it was killed, the company is liable. Coleman v. Flint & P. M. R. Co. 7 West. Rep. 348, 64 Mich. 160.

Minnesota.

A railway company is liable for damages to an abutting farm, rendering its use less valuable, caused by a failure to fence its road. Nelson v. Minneapolis & St. L. R. Co. 41 Minn. 131.

The measure of damages is the depreciation in the rental value of the farm; and evidence of any fact tending to show how and to what extent the absence of a railway fence injuriously affected the value of such use is competent. *Ibid.*

The owner of animals killed by a railroad train is not chargeable with contributory negligence, where they escape and get upon an unfenced railroad track without his fault. Cox v. Minneapolis, S. S. M. & A. R. Co. 41 Minn. 101.

Where a railroad occupies a public street in a city or village, it is not obliged or entitled to fence its tracks and thereby obstruct the street and interfere with its use. Rippe v. Chicago, M. & St. P. R. Co. (Minn.) 5 L. R. A. 864.

Permitting a fence to become rotten is evidence

plaintiff was guilty of negligence in allowing his horse to be upon the depot grounds, and that such negligence contributed to the accident, still, if you believe that the accident could have been avoided by the exercise of ordinary care and diligence on the part of the defendant, the defendant is liable."

The facts upon which this instruction was based were to this effect: That the evidence tended to show that the horse was, at the time he was struck by the locomotive, running at large on the depot grounds of the defendant in the Town of Tangent, and that the locomotive was attached to one of the regular passenger trains which passed through the town, north to south, at 1 o'clock P. M., and was upon the regular time; that the engineer signaled his approach to the station by sounding the whistle when about 300 yards distant therefrom, etc.; that the horse was, during all of said time, and prior to the first sounding of the whistle for the station, running at large at or near said depot grounds, and had, at different times previously to said day, been seen occasionally pasturing upon said depot grounds; that plaintiff resided in said town, and about 700 feet away from said depot grounds; that there is a conflict of evidence as to what the speed of the train was when said horse was first seen to go upon the track, and said alarm whistle was sounded, or as to whether or not said speed was slacked before the horse was overtaken by the locomotive, and as to whether or not the engineer endeavored to and could have stopped the train after the horse went upon the track, and before he was struck by the locomotive, the speed of the train when the horse went upon the track, and before he was struck by the locomotive, being variously estimated by witnesses at from eight to twenty miles per hour, and some of the witnesses testifying that the speed of the train was constantly lessened before the horse was struck, while other witnesses testified that they could not perceive that the speed of the train was at all diminished between the sounding of the alarm and the striking of the horse. The engineer testified that, immediately upon sounding the alarm whistle, he applied the brakes, reversed the engine and did all that was in his power to do towards stopping the train, which was running about three miles an hour when the horse was struck. Other witnesses testified—who were standing on the platform, some 300 yards distant—that the engineer did, and some that he did not, check the speed of the train before striking the horse.

These facts show (1) that the injury to the horse occurred on the track, on the depot grounds; and (2) that, as the horse had been seen prior to the day of the accident, occasionally, to pasture on the depot grounds, it is presumed that he was suffered to run at large with the consent of his owner, and strayed upon the track under the circumstances indicated; and (3) that there is a conflict of evidence as to whether the engineer endeavored to check the speed of the train before striking the horse, but none that he did not sound the alarm whistle, and turn the steam through the cylinder cocks, to drive the horse from the track. Upon this state of facts, the contention of the appellant

---

of negligence. Hovorka v. Minneapolis & St. L. R. Co. 34 Minn. 281.

Under Gen. Stat. 1878, chap. 34, double costs may be allowed in the district court on appeal from justice's court, in cases of negligence in failing to fence a road. Schimmele v. Chicago, M. & St. P. R. Co. 34 Minn. 216.

The statute does not make railroad companies liable for damages done by cattle trespassing upon their lands and passing thence, by reason of a failure to build fences, to the lands of adjoining owners. The liability in such case is upon the owner of the cattle. Gowan v. St. Paul, S. & T. F. R. Co. 25 Minn. 328.

Missouri.

Rev. Stat., § 809, giving double damages for injury to stock in consequence of the railroad company's failing to fence its line, is constitutional. Mo. Const. art. 2, §§ 20, 30, art. 4, § 53, art. 11, § 8; 14th Amend. U. S. Const. § 1; Hines v. Missouri Pac. R. Co. 1 West. Rep. 754, 86 Mo. 629; Hamilton v. Missouri Pac. R. Co. 1 West. Rep. 754, 87 Mo. 85; Phillips v. Missouri Pac. R. Co. 2 West. Rep. 479, 86 Mo. 540; Davis v. Hannibal & St. J. R. Co. 1 West. Rep. 723, 19 Mo. App. 425; Lepp v. St. Louis, I. M. & S. R. Co. 2 West. Rep. 109, 87 Mo. 139; McBride v. Kansas City, St. J. & C. B. R. Co. 2 West. Rep. 522, 20 Mo. App. 216; Trice v. Hannibal & St. J. R. Co. 49 Mo. 438.

A railroad company not fencing its right of way pursuant to General Statute neglects a public duty, and exposes itself to an action for damages resulting therefrom; and the imputed negligence is established by proving the point of injury and the absence of a fence. The Stock Law of 1883, to restrain domestic animals from running at large, constitutes no defense to the action. Boyle v. Missouri Pac. R. Co. 4 West. Rep. 870, 21 Mo. App. 416.

It is the place where the animal got on the road, and not where it was killed, that fixes the liability of the company. Rev. Stat. § 809; Ehret v. Kansas City, St. J. & C. B. R. Co. 2 West. Rep. 555, 20 Mo. App. 251.

Owners of stock are not required to keep up their cattle, or to keep them off the track. Davis v. Hannibal & St. J. R. Co. *supra.*

The Missouri Statute lays on railroad companies the obligation of fencing their tracks along "enclosed or cultivated fields." Wagn. Stat. 310, 311, § 43; Biggerstaff v. St. Louis, K. C. & N. R. Co. 60 Mo. 567. Compare Shelton v. St. Louis, K. C. & N. R. Co. 60 Mo. 412.

Rev. Stat. 1879, § 809, expressly requires defendant to fence uninclosed lands; and the facts that the mare which was injured by the cars strayed away from plaintiff's premises, got upon the commons, and thence found its way through the gate on the road, constitute no defense. Duncan v. St. Louis, I. M. & S. R. Co. 8 West. Rep. 282, 91 Mo. 67.

A railroad company is liable for neglect to fence, where the injury is inflicted by the cars of another corporation, operated by contractors in constructing the road. Silver v. Kansas City, St. L. & C. R. Co. 3 West. Rep. 284, 21 Mo. App. 5.

Where the issue was whether the animals got on the track at a point where it was required by law to erect and maintain a lawful fence, the question of negligence did not arise; defendant became amenable to the penalties of the statute, whether negligent or not. Smith v. St. Louis, I. M. & S. R. Co. 8 West. Rep. 268, 91 Mo. 58.

The statute gives the right to sue for injury occurring anywhere on the road, except where it was inclosed by a lawful fence, or crossed by any public highway. Radcliffe v. St. Louis, I. M. & S. R. Co. 7 West. Rep. 305, 90 Mo. 127.

It exacts of the railroad company a degree of

is, (1) that the depot grounds are not included within the intention of the law requiring railroads to be fenced; and (2) that the plaintiff, in allowing his horse to run at large, and stray upon the depot grounds and track, where he was killed by a moving train, was guilty of contributory negligence which precludes his right of recovery.

The language of the Statute making railroad companies liable for killing stock "upon or near any unfenced track of any railroad in this State, whenever such killing or injury is caused by any moving train or engine or cars upon such track," is broad enough to include that part of the track which is contiguous to its stations or depots. Or. Code, §§ 4044, 4045.

Taking it literally, the Statute would apply to the entire track of the railroad, which would necessarily include such parts of the track as lie upon its depot or station grounds, thereby rendering the railroad company absolutely liable to the owner of any stock injured for an omission to fence its track upon its depot or station grounds. But such a construction is not consistent with the reason of the Statute, or the intention of this enactment. In view of the business transactions at depot grounds, it is as much for the public convenience that it should be opened and unfenced as public highways, to which, applying the strict letter of the law, the Statute would also extend at the places where the railroad track crosses such highways. The purposes for which these are to be used, and the right of public convenience, are inconsistent with the obligations to fence at such places, or to incur the liability created by the Statute, and cannot, therefore, be held to apply to depot grounds, nor to public road crossings, nor to the streets of cities or villages.

In *Davis* v. *Burlington & M. R. R. Co.*, 26 Iowa, 554, Wright, *J.*, said: "The language is, 'its road,' and we do not believe that this includes depot grounds. True, these grounds, including switches, side tracks, etc., may be a part of the road. This is not denied for many purposes, and, indeed, most purposes. And yet we cannot think that the Legislature contemplated these as a part of the 'road' by the Statute under consideration." Within the principle thus declared, on account of the impracticability of fencing such places, we do not think the Statute applies to depot grounds; and so it has often been held by the courts. 1 Rorer, Railroads, 622, 623, and *note; Atchison, T. & S. F.*

---

care and vigilance in looking after its fences, commensurate with the peril to life and property; and the doctrine of contributory negligence does not apply. Davis v. Hannibal & St. J. R. Co. *supra.*

It is only liable, after fences have once been erected as required by law, for a negligent failure to maintain such fences, and is entitled to a reasonable time in which to make repairs. King v. Chicago, R. I. & P. R. Co. 8 West. Rep. 231, 90 Mo. 520.

Knowledge of defects and failure to repair, by the plaintiff, will not prevent his recovery of damages for hogs killed by reason of defects in a fence which it was the duty of the company to repair, and of whose condition it had notice. Wilson v. St. Louis, I. M. & S. R. Co. 3 West. Rep. 274, 87 Mo. 431.

Where a railroad company erected its fence across the bed of a creek at a time when the creek was full of water, and when the creek dried up a space was left below the lower wire, such facts show a negligent omission to erect, rather than to maintain, a fence. Selders v. Kansas City, F. S. & G. R. Co. 1 West. Rep. 436, 19 Mo. App. 334.

Although the company had built a lawful fence across a hollow or branch, yet where the tension of the wires drew the posts up, leaving a space below, and the defect was shown to have existed more than two weeks, the jury might infer negligence on the part of the company. Davis v. Hannibal & St. J. R. Co. *supra.*

A railroad company is not liable, without proof of negligence, for injury to animals at a point where it is necessary for the transaction of its business that the road should not be fenced. Robinson v. St. Louis, I. M. & S. R. Co. 3 West. Rep. 431, 21 Mo. App. 141.

Statutory provisions for double damages for injuries caused by stock breaking over a fence from the track, and for repair of the fence at the cost of the company, are cumulative. Carpenter v. St. Louis, I. M. & S. R. Co. 3 West. Rep. 190, 20 Mo. App. 644.

Where damage to stock is caused by insufficiency of the fence put up by the owner, the company will not be responsible. Biggerstaff v. St. Louis, K. C. & N. R. Co. 60 Mo. 567.

No liability for double damages ensues for failure to fence in certain localities. Manz v. St. Louis, I. M. & S. R. Co. 2 West. Rep. 473, 87 Mo. 278.

The railroad company is not liable if the fence was prostrated by a storm, or thrown down by malicious persons, or by accident of any kind, unless it had notice of its condition, or it had remained so long out of repair that the want of knowledge was negligence. Townley v. Missouri Pac. R. Co. 6 West. Rep. 400, 89 Mo. 31.

Where it was shown that the fences along the right of way of defendant had been burned, and that there were gaps left in them in consequence, the facts of the case may be shown by circumstances, as well as by direct evidence. Mayfield v. St. Louis & S. F. R. Co. 8 West. Rep. 264, 91 Mo. 296.

For damages to crops caused by failure of defendant to fence its line of road through plaintiff's premises, the court may grant any relief consistent with the case and embraced in the issues. Comings v. Hannibal & C. M. R. Co. 48 Mo. 512.

Nebraska.

The provisions of Neb. Comp. Stat., art. 2, chap. 2, § 18, defining a "lawful fence," apply alone to the inclosing of lands, and do not apply to the fencing of a railway. That matter is governed by Neb. Comp. Stat., chap. 72, art. 1, § 1. Chicago, B. & Q. R. Co. v. James (Neb.) March 20, 1889.

This latter Statute requires every railroad company in the State to maintain fences on the sides of its railway, except at the crossings of public roads and highways, and within the limits of towns, cities and villages, etc. *Ibid.*

The company is not required to fence its tracks within the limits of a city. Chicago, B. & Q. R. Co. v. Hogan (Neb.) Nov. 6, 1889.

Where the parties by their attorneys agree in writing that certain stock escaped without fault of the owner and were killed where the company was not required to fence, there can be no recovery. *Ibid.*

New York.

A railroad company which fails to build and maintain fences on the sides of its road is liable to the owner of an adjoining lot, whose horse is killed by falling into a cut through which the tracks are laid. Graham v. Delaware & H. Canal Co. 46 Hun, 386, 12 N. Y. S. R. 390.

The remedy of a land owner for a failure on the part of the corporation to comply with the provis-

R. Co. v. *Shaft*, 33 Kan. 521, 19 Am. & Eng. R. R. Cas. 539, *note*.

Nor is there anything in the complaint or record to indicate that a recovery in damage is sought, or any liability created by the Statute, or other than the ordinary action to recover damages for negligence.

Upon the next question, namely, that the plaintiff, in allowing his horse to run at large, so that he strayed upon the track, was guilty of contributory negligence, and is precluded from a recovery, the authorities are not agreed. There seems, however, to be a line of distinction between them which accounts for this difference in principle, which, perhaps, would not exist without it; and this is, whether the common law rule, which requires the owner of stock to keep them in his own close, at his peril, prevails in the jurisdiction or not. Of course, in any of them, this relates only to such cases as are not within the statutory obligation to fence, or such places as are excepted from its operation. In those jurisdictions in which the common-law rule prevails, that the owner of cattle is bound to keep them in his own inclosure, it is quite generally held that if he suffers them to go at large, and the cattle stray upon the railroad track, and are injured or killed, the company is not liable unless the conduct of its agents in the management of the train was wanton or willful. In such cases the cattle are regarded as unlawfully at large, and exposed to danger by the fault of the owner, which, in the event of their destruction by collision with the locomotive while on the track of the railroad, is considered as the direct consequences of his negligence, which will preclude a right of recovery in him for their loss, although it may have occurred through the negligence or want of care of the railroad company.

In *Tonawanda R. Co.* v. *Munger*, 5 Denio, 255, which was an action to recover damages for negligence in killing the plaintiff's oxen by running over them by a train while on the track of the defendant, the court, after reaching the conclusion that the oxen, when killed, were trespassing on the land of the defendant, under the common-law rule that the owner of cattle is bound, at his peril, to keep them off the land of other persons, says (Beardsley, *Ch. J.*): "It is not pretended the act was done designedly by the persons in charge, but simply that it occurred through their negligence and want of care. It is a well-settled rule of law that such an action cannot be sustained if the wrongful act of the plaintiff co-operated with the mis-

---

tion of the Railroad Act of 1854, § 8, chap. 282, Laws 1854, is not confined to an action for damages given by said Act; but he may enforce the performance of this duty to fence. Jones v. Seligman, 81 N. Y. 190.

In the New York General Railroad Law.—requiring every corporation formed under it to erect and maintain fences on the sides of its road—no exception is made or permission given for openings or gates for the use of the corporation, or its customers, or the public generally, but only for the use of adjoining proprietors. Spinner v. New York Cent. & H. R. R. Co. 67 N. Y. 153.

The Statute amending the General Railroad Act applies to a foreign corporation, so far as such road is open for use within the State. Purdy v. New York & N. H. R. Co. 61 N. Y. 353.

If a railway company permits a portion of its fence to be broken down, and cattle escape through the same upon the railway lands, the company is liable for damages done by one of its engines. Leyden v. New York Cent. & H. R. R. Co. 55 Hun, 114, 28 N. Y. S. R. 72.

A railroad company is bound to build and keep in repair fences along the sides of its track, with gates or bars for the use of adjoining owners at farm crossings. Hungerford v. Syracuse, B. & N. Y. R. Co. 46 Hun, 339, 12 N. Y. S. R. 204.

Proprietors are bound to keep the gates shut, when not open for use in passing over the railroad. Diamond Brick Co. v. New York Cent. & H. R. R. Co. 28 N. Y. S. R. 95.

A railroad company is not liable for a failure to keep bar-ways at farm crossings in repair, unless it is shown to have had notice that the bars were down. Hungerford v. Syracuse, B. & N. Y. R. Co. *supra*. See Donnegan v. Erhardt, 7 L. R. A. 527, 119 N. Y. 468.

North Carolina.

To put cattle in a forty-acre field through which a railroad runs is not contributory negligence, even though the Stock Law is in force. Horner v. Williams, 100 N. C. 230.

Ohio.

Where damage results from defects occurring, without the fault or neglect of the company, in an otherwise sufficient fence, there is no liability. Baltimore & O. R. Co. v. Schultz, 1 West. Rep. 70, 43 Ohio St. 270.

There is nothing which would charge a railroad company, in the absence of negligence, with the consequences of defects in its fence. *Ibid.*

The fact that stock was kept in a field adjoining the right of way, without escaping through such fence, for some time, is not sufficient excuse for neglect. *Ibid.*

The fact that a board or rail had fallen from the fence without the company's knowledge will not excuse it from liability, where the defect was attributable to a general defective condition of the fence. *Ibid.*

Pennsylvania.

The Pennsylvania statute requiring a new road to be built in as perfect manner as the original road, includes erection of fences. North Manheim Twp's App. (Pa.) 12 Cent. Rep. 485.

An Act requiring all railroads to be fenced, and adding that "all railroad companies shall, before a certain date, construct and keep in repair a sufficient fence;" and a supplementary Act making them liable for failure to fence,—apply, in their general requirements, to a road constructed after the date mentioned, but before the supplementary Act was passed. Shurley v. New York, L. E. & W. R. Co. 121 Pa. 511.

The omission of a fence where the track is parallel to a city street is not evidence of negligence, where it appeared that plaintiff's horse, being frightened by the ordinary ringing of the engine bell, backed into the moving engine. Fouhy v. Pennsylvania R. Co. (Pa.) 2 Cent. Rep. 89.

Wisconsin.

Under the Wisconsin Statute excepting depot grounds from the necessity of fencing, a railroad company need not fence its grounds on the main line of the railroad, on which are situated a water tank, a building containing a telegraph and ticket office, and a place for eating and sleeping, which is occupied by its station men and telegraph and ticket agent, and a platform at which trains stop to receive and discharge passengers and freight. Peters v. Stewart, 72 Wis. 133.

conduct of the defendants or their servants to produce the damage sustained. I do not mean that the co-operating act of the plaintiff must be wrong in intention to call for the application of this principle, for such is not the law. The act may have been one of mere negligence on his part. Still, he cannot recover. . . . But injuries inflicted by design are not thus to be excused. A wrong-doer is not necessarily an outlaw, but may justly complain of wanton and malicious mischief. Negligence, however, even when gross, is but an omission of duty. It is not designed and intentional mischief, although it may be cogent evidence of such an act. Of the latter, a trespasser may complain, although he cannot be allowed to do so in regard to the former."

In *Bowman* v. *Troy & B. R. Co.*, 37 Barb. 519, it is held that one who voluntarily suffers his cow to go at large in the public street, with no one to take charge of her, and to stray upon a railroad track at a time when cars are passing, is guilty of carelessness, and cannot recover for injuries to the cow, happening through the negligence of the railroad company, not amounting to gross negligence, Miller, *J.*, saying: "His own act and negligence contributed to produce the injury complained of, and caused the death of the cow; and there is no evidence of gross negligence on the part of the defendant."

In *Maynard* v. *Boston & M. R. Co.*, 115 Mass. 460, Gray, *Ch. J.*, said: "If the horse had been rightfully upon the defendant's land, it would have been their duty to exercise reasonable care to avoid injuring the horse. But, it being admitted by the plaintiff that his horse was trespassing upon the railroad, they did not owe him that duty, and were not liable to him for anything short of reckless and wanton misconduct of those employed in the management of their train."

As the plaintiff is bound at common law to keep his cattle within his own inclosure, and liable for all damages done by them when they stray upon the lands of others, he is the party in fault; and it results, if he suffers them to stray upon the track of a railroad, they are there without right, and as trespassers, through his wrongful conduct, and, if injured or killed by the negligence of the railroad or its agents, in the management of the train, he must abide the consequences, upon the ground that the defendant Company owes no duty of care to trespassing cattle on their tracks, except not wantonly or willfully to destroy them, and that, in permitting the cattle to be at large wrongfully or by his own fault, he has contributed to produce the injury of which he complains, and is precluded from a recovery. When such a state of facts exists, nothing but willfulness on the part of the agents of the Company, or, as the authorities sometimes put it, such negligence as would amount to willfulness, would make the Company liable in damages for the killing of cattle upon its track, so exposed by the fault of their owner. *Indianapolis, C. & L. R. Co.* v. *Harter*, 38 Ind. 557; *Williams* v. *Michigan Cent. R. Co.* 2 Mich. 265; *Stucke* v. *Milwaukee & M. R. Co.* 9 Wis. 202; *Halloran* v. *New York & H. R. R. Co.* 2 E. D. Smith, 257; *Louisville & F. R Co.* v. *Ballard*, 2 Met. (Ky.) 177; *Bennett* v. *Chicago & N. W. R. Co.* 19 Wis. 145; *Tower* v. *Providence & W. R. Co.* 2 R. I. 404; *Vandegrift* v. *Rediker*, 22 N. J. L. 185; *Perkins* v. *Eastern R. Co.* 29 Me. 307; *Woolson* v. *Northern R. Co.* 19 N. H. 267; *New York & E. R. Co.* v. *Skinner*, 19 Pa. 298; *Spinner* v. *New York Cent. & H. R. R. Co.* 67 N. Y. 153; *Pittsburgh, C. & St. L. R. Co.* v. *Stuart*, 71 Ind. 504.

In some of the cases, and especially the older ones, the term "gross negligence" is used as the equivalent of "willful negligence," as used by the later authorities, which imports act or conduct that is willful or wanton, and to which the doctrine of contributory negligence has no application; for, when the injury done the plaintiff is occasioned by the willful and wanton act of the defendant, the negligence of the plaintiff is no defense; and so it is held by the cases referred to, with perhaps some slight exceptions as to cattle trespassing on the track of railroads. As a result of this class of cases, in the States in which the common-law rule prevails, it is generally considered that allowing cattle to run at large is such negligence as precludes a recovery. On the other hand, in those jurisdictions or States in which the common-law rule as to the duty of the owner of stock to keep them on his own inclosure is abrogated, it is generally held that a plaintiff, in permitting his stock to run at large, commits no unlawful act, nor is guilty of an omission of ordinary care; and if they stray upon the uninclosed track of a railroad, and are injured and killed, although they may be regarded as trespassers, he is not guilty of contributory negligence; but that the company is liable for their loss, unless it exercised ordinary care and skill in the management of its trains to prevent their injury or destruction. It is considered, as the act of the plaintiff in suffering his stock to run at large is not unlawful or negligent, nor likewise the act of the defendant in leaving its track uninclosed, yet, when it is so, as the stock may stray upon it as other uninclosed places, the defendant takes the risk of such intrusion upon its track, and the owner the risk of injury to his stock by unavoidable accident, but not of negligence or want of ordinary care; hence the conclusion that railroad companies are liable for the ordinary negligence of their servants. In all such cases and jurisdictions where the common-law rule is not in force, and the owner of stock may allow them to run at large without violating the law, or being guilty of negligence, if such stock stray on an uninclosed track, and are killed by the train, when, by the exercise of ordinary care, that loss or result might have been avoided, the negligence of the railroad company is regarded as the proximate cause of the injury, and the act of the owner in suffering them to run at large as too remotely connected with the negligence of the defendant to constitute contributory negligence, or be operative as such a defense. Such acts are not the immediate cause of the injury or loss of property, nor do they concur and combine at the time with the negligence of the company, as the natural and probable consequence of it, but at most bear only a remote relation to it, which, when stock is on its track, does not release the company from its obligation of reasonable care to avoid injuring them, at least to the extent that the law requires, and common justice and humanity demand, of others, when stock is trespassing upon their lands, not to injure or kill it, if by ordinary care they could prevent it. When the company is not bound to fence, the measure of liability is ordinary care; and, though stock have no right to be on the track, especially when required for use of its trains, yet the company enjoys no special privileges over other owners of lands, and is under the same obligation to exercise care to avoid injuring them, consistent with its duties in the management of the train.

In *Little Rock & Ft. S. R. Co.* v. *Finley*, 37 Ark. 569, it is held that it is the duty of an engineer of a train to keep a careful and constant lookout for stock upon the track, and, although such be wrongfully there, yet he must use ordinary care and diligence to discover it, and avoid injury to it, or the company will be liable for the injury done. The court says: "A very prudent person might not, perhaps, allow his stock to go at large in the immediate vicinity of a railroad, and one who does so may not be altogether free from negligence; yet he assumes only the risk of an accident which might not be avoided by ordinary care and watchfulness of the agents or employés of the railroad company."

In *Balcom* v. *Dubuque & S. C. R. Co.*, 21 Iowa, 103, where the action was for damages sustained by killing the plaintiff's cattle by running the cars over them at a point where the public highway crossed the defendant's road, it was held that, if the cattle were not on the track by the negligence of the plaintiff, the test of the defendant's liability is whether, at the time of the accident, reasonable and proper care was exercised to avoid the injury.

In *Searles* v. *Milwaukee & St. P. R. Co.*, 35 Iowa, 491, which was an action for negligence in killing the plaintiff's ox by a freight train on a public highway crossing, error was assigned for refusal to give, among others, this instruction: "Railroad trains, when cattle are on the track, are not required to slacken their speed, or to make signals by blowing the whistle or ringing the bell at road crossings, or places where the road has not a right to fence;" and Day, *J.*, said: "It was held, at a very early period in the judicial history of this State, that the mere fact of permitting cattle to go at large is not a ground of imputing negligence to the owner. . . . A railway company is liable for injuries resulting from the careless or negligent management of its trains, where the injured party does not by his own negligence contribute to the injury. It is a corollary of these two propositions that a railway company must respond in damages for injuries to stock through its negligence, where the owner has contributed to the injury no further than merely permitting it to run at large."

In *Cincinnati & Z. R. Co.* v. *Smith*, 22 Ohio St. 227, it was held that the servants of a railroad company in operating its trains are bound to use ordinary care to avoid injury to domestic animals trespassing on the track; and the court says: "If the servants of the company in charge of the train, having due regard to their duties for the safety of the persons and property in their charge, could, by the exercise of ordinary care, have seen and saved the horses, we think they were bound to have done so."

In *Blaine* v. *Chesapeake & O. R. Co.*, 9 W. Va. 253, which was an action for negligence in killing a horse on a railroad track, the court, after remarking that the rule of the common law requiring the owners of animals to keep them on his own land had never been in force in West Virginia, being inconsistent with its legislation, among other things, said: "The remote negligence of the plaintiff will not prevent his recovering for an injury to his property immediately caused by the negligence of the defendant. The negligence of the plaintiff that defeats a recovery must be a proximate cause of the injury. Suffering domestic animals to run at large, by means whereof they stray upon an uninclosed railway track, where they are killed by a train, is not, in general, a proximate cause of the loss; and hence, although there may have been some negligence in the owner's permitting the animals to go at large, such negligence being only a remote cause of the loss, it will not prevent his recovering from the railroad company the value of the animals, if the immediate cause of their death or injury was negligence of the company's servants in conducting the train."

The same language was used in *Cleveland, C. & C. R. Co.* v. *Elliott*, 4 Ohio St. 475; and see also *Kerwhaker* v. *Cleveland, C. & C. R. Co.*, 3 Ohio St. 172, in which the principles of the law under discussion were set forth with great ability, and much force and cogency of reasoning.

In *Baltimore & O. R. Co.* v. *Mulligan*, 45 Md. 493, a State in which it is the duty of owners of cattle to keep them within their inclosure, yet, in an action for damages for the loss of a cow run over by the cars of the defendant, Robinson, *J.*, in delivering the opinion of the court, says: "No one has the right to complain of injury to cattle or other stock which he has permitted to stray upon a railroad track, unless such injury can be avoided consistently with these higher and paramount duties resting upon the company [not to endanger its passengers]. What we mean to say and to decide is this: that it is the duty of the company to exercise reasonable care to avoid injury to cattle or stock found on its road, though such cattle and stock may be there through the negligence of the owner."

So, too, in *Trow* v. *Vermont Cent. R. Co.*, 24 Vt. 494, the court says: "When the negligence of the defendants is proximate, and that of the plaintiff remote, the action can then well be sustained, although the plaintiff is not entirely without fault. This seems now to be settled in England and in this country. Therefore, if there be negligence on the part of the plaintiff, yet if, at the time when the injury was committed, it might have been avoided by the defendant, in the exercise of reasonable care and prudence, an action will lie for the injury. So, in this case, if the plaintiff were guilty of negligence, or even of positive wrong, in placing his horse in the road, the defendants were bound to the exercise of reasonable care and diligence in the use of their road and management of the engine and train; and if, for want of that care, the injury arose, they are liable."

"The railroad," said Redfield, *Ch. J.*, "cannot justify either recklessness, want of common care at the time and after the cattle are discovered or wanton injury." *Jackson* v. *Rutland & B. R. Co.* 25 Vt. 161.

"The negligence," said Baldwin, *J.*, "which disables the owner to sue, must be negligence which directly or by natural consequences conduces to the injury. It is not easy for us to see, therefore, that the mere fact that a party suffers his cows to go at large near the line of a railroad, is such negligence as to excuse the corporation from reasonable diligence and care to avoid injury to them when they happen to be on the track. The suffering them to go at large certainly is not the usual or natural cause of such an injury. Such a result would not probably happen once in a thousand, or perhaps ten thousand, times."

The general conclusion to be deduced from this case is that the fact of merely permitting cattle to run at large near the line of a railway is not enough to excuse the company from the exercise of ordinary care and diligence to avoid injuring them when they may happen to stray upon its track, consistently with a due regard for the safety of its trains and passengers; that such acts upon the part of the owner of cattle are too remotely related to the negligence of the defendant to concur and combine with it as the proximate cause of the injury, and, in the sense of the law, do not constitute contributory negligence; but that the failure of the company to exercise ordinary care and diligence under the circumstances is the immediate or proximate cause of the injury or loss of property, and renders the company liable for its negligence. So manifest is the justice of this requirement, not to injure or kill stock which may happen to stray upon the track, if, by the exercise of ordinary care, it can be prevented, that in some jurisdictions, as we have shown, in which the common-law rule prevails as to the duty of owners to keep their stock within their inclosures, it has been adopted and applied. So that, speaking generally, it may be said that a railroad company is liable in damages for injury to stock caused by its negligence, where the owner has contributed to the injury no further than merely permitting them to run at large. *Vicksburg & J. R. Co.* v. *Patton*, 31 Miss. 188; *Gorman* v. *Pacific R. Co.* 26 Mo. 441; *Trout* v. *Virginia & T. R. Co.* 23 Gratt. 623; *Isbell* v. *New York & N. H. R. Co.* 27 Conn. 393; *South & North Ala. R. Co.* v. *Williams*, 65 Ala. 74; *Rockford, R. I. & St. L. R. Co.* v. *Irish*, 72 Ill. 404; *Kentucky Cent. R. Co.* v. *Lebus*, 14 Bush, 518; *McCoy* v. *California Pac. R. Co.* 40 Cal. 532; 1 Thomp. Neg. 498; Beach, Contrib. Neg. § 73.

Now, upon the facts, within which line of reasoning does the case before us come? It has been held that the common-law rule requiring every man to keep his stock within his inclosure is not in force in this State. *Campbell* v. *Bridwell*, 5 Or. 312.

It is a matter of common knowledge that it is not only the general understanding but the custom of the people to allow their stock to run at large, and from the first settlement of the State until the present time all kinds of stock have been allowed to run at large on uninclosed lands. Besides, our legislation in relation to the inclosures, estrays and the marking and branding of stock are inconsistent with its existence in this State. It is not, then, a violation of law, nor a want of ordinary care, merely to allow stock to run at large in this State; and, unless some special circumstances exist, no one, individual nor corporation, may injure or kill them when they stray upon his uninclosed lands, or its railroad track, without incurring liability in damages therefor, unless ordinary care and diligence was exerted to prevent it.

As applied to the facts in hand, within the reasoning of the authorities, the plaintiff's horse was not a trespasser, in the common-law sense, when he strayed on the track near or on the depot grounds; nor, within the intention of the Statute, as we have shown, was the defendant under any obligation to fence its depot grounds so as to exclude the horse or other stock. It is conceded that the defendant had a right to its track; and while, as it was said in *Smith* v. *Chicago, R. I. & P. R. Co.*, 34 Iowa, 508, "while the plaintiff's cattle had no right there, though, negatively stated, they were not in the wrong for being there," yet that circumstance did not relieve the defendant of the duty to exercise ordinary care; and, if the horse was killed, while thus on the track, by its negligence, the defendant is liable. The original act being neither negligent nor unlawful, when the horse strayed upon the track, and was killed, the act of the plaintiff was not the direct nor proximate cause of the injury, and could not, therefore, be such negligence as would operate as a defense and preclude a recovery. To effect that result, there must have been mutual negligence, in the sense of equivalent acts simultaneously concurring to produce the injury. Before that can happen, the original act of turning loose the cattle or stock must have been done under such circumstances as indicated a want of ordinary care upon the part of the plaintiff that contributed directly to produce the injury. Ordinary care always has relation to the situation of the parties, and necessarily varies according to the particular circumstances under which it is exercised. An owner cannot turn loose his stock regardless of circumstances, or at a place where danger to them is constant and imminent, and, when an injury occurs to them as a consequence of his conduct, though the defendant may not have been free from fault, escape the charge of negligence, or a want of ordinary care. There is a marked difference between suffering stock to run at large upon uninclosed lands along the line of a railroad, or adjoining its depot grounds, from which they may stray upon the track, and turning them loose, uncared for, and directly upon the grounds of a depot or station covered with main and side tracks, switches, turn-outs and turn-tables, more or less constantly in use, with trains coming and going, where danger is known to exist, and where injury to them will probably happen as a consequence of the peril in which they have been voluntarily placed. In the former case, if they are killed by the negligence of the company, the act of the plaintiff is only the remote cause of the injury, while in the latter it is the proximate cause of the injury, co-operating with the negligence of the defendant to produce it. In such case, the act itself is equivalent to deliberately putting the stock in a place of danger, and where injury to them is a probable consequence. The stock do not stray into a place of danger, but they are turned loose into a place where danger is known to exist, or may be foreseen by the exercise of ordinary care; and the party cannot and ought not to recover for injuries which are the direct result of his own negligence. While, therefore, an owner may suffer his stock to run at large, and pasture upon uninclosed lands, if they should stray upon the track of a railway, and be injured or killed by the negligence of the company, it is not considered such negligence as directly conduces to the injury, and does not preclude a right of recovery, yet there may be circumstances under which to turn stock loose, uncared for, would indicate such recklessness or such want of ordinary care as would preclude a recovery.

Now, turning to the record, we have presumed, without any direct evidence of the fact, that the plaintiff suffered his horse to run at large, and that he wandered upon the depot grounds and the track where the accident occurred. The record shows that he was running back and along, and upon the track, and away from the train, when he was struck, on the depot grounds, from forty to sixty feet from the place where he started on the track; that when the train was about 300 yards distant, and signaled its approach to the station by blowing its whistle, the horse then was either upon the depot grounds alongside of the track, or else was upon the public road and soon thereafter was seen upon the track. Within the principles of the authorities where it is not unlawful to allow stock to run at large, "a railroad company must respond in damages for injuries to stock through its negligence when the owner has contributed to the injury no further than merely permitting it to run at large." Nor is there anything in the record to except the case from the operation of this principle. There is no suggestion upon the facts, or any special circumstances, which made the conduct of the plaintiff in the premises negligent, or to charge him with a want of ordinary care. The place where the injury occurred was not a railway station in a thickly-populated community, near to or adjoining some large and thriving town, netted with tracks and switches and turnouts, at which a volume of business was done, requiring the constant use of its depot grounds for its trains passing and repassing, and where danger to roaming stock could be foreseen, and where to turn them loose would be voluntarily putting them where injury to them would be the natural and probable consequence.

We concur in the case of *Smith* v. *Chicago, R. I. & P. R. Co.*, 34 Iowa, 518, to which we have been referred, that "the owner of cattle may not turn them out, and enable them to frequent a place of great peril on the depot grounds or track of a railroad company, and then demand that the railroad company shall stop its trains, and drive off his cattle, or slacken the speed, or change the time-table in order to deliver his cattle from the peril in which he has voluntarily placed them." But it must not be overlooked that the court immediately added that, "if the injury to the cattle was caused by the negligence of those having charge of the train, and which injury might have been avoided by the use of ordinary diligence and care, then of course, the plaintiff might recover." The use of the words in the last clause of the instruction, "and that such negligence contributed to the accident," was not in the sense of such negligence as was the proximate cause of the injury, and operative as a defense, but only as a remote cause of the injury, and would not preclude a recovery. The instruction must be examined by the light of the facts to which it is applied, and the circumstance of allowing the horse to run at large, except under special circumstances not raised by this record, is not an omission of ordinary care; and the law is, when a railroad company has injured stock through its negligence, that it is liable, where the owner has contributed to the injury no further than merely permitting his stock to run at large.

There is a large class of cases, headed by *Davies* v. *Mann*, 10 Mees. & W. 546,—a case much criticised, but which *Judge* Thompson shows has been approved by the great weight of authority (5 South. Law Rev. 835),—in which the principle is upheld as declared by *Lord* Abinger, that, "as the defendant might by proper care have avoided injuring the animal, and did not, he is liable for the consequences of his negligence, though the animal may have been improperly there," and which, as applied to the present case, is conclusive of the result already reached. And it may be observed, further, that that case and others were subsequently reviewed and considered by the court of exchequer in *Tuff* v. *Warman*, 5 C. B. N. S. 573; and it was held that mere negligence or want of ordinary care on the part of the plaintiff would not disentitle him to recover, if the defendant might, by the exercise of ordinary care and caution, have avoided the neglect or carelessness of the plaintiff. And, in a still later and much discussed case (*Radley* v. *London & N. W. R. Co.* L. R. 1 App. Cas. 759), it was held error to instruct the jury, if there was contributory negligence in the plaintiff, they should find for the defendant, without adding the qualification, "unless the defendant could have avoided the mischief by the exercise of reasonable care." *Lord* Penzance said: "The first proposition is a general one, to this effect: that the plaintiff, in an action for negligence, cannot succeed if it is found by the jury that he has himself been guilty of any negligence, or want of ordinary care which contributed to cause the accident. But there is another proposition equally well established, and it is a qualification upon the first; namely, that, though the plaintiff may have been guilty of negligence, and although that negligence may in fact have contributed to the accident, yet, if the defendant could, in the result, by the exercise of ordinary care and diligence, have avoided the mischief which happened, the plaintiff's negligence will not excuse him."

As applied to the facts in hand, the defendant is required to avoid the destruction of life and property, if by ordinary care it may be safely done, or else it will be liable, though the plaintiff may have been negligent. Wharton, Neg. § 879, *note 5*.

So cogently has this principle—that no person or corporation had the right to recklessly inflict wrong, or to destroy the property or animals of another, even when trespassing, if by the exercise of ordinary care it may be avoided, with due regard to the safety of the train—impressed itself upon the justice and humanity of courts, that it has been adopted and applied in some jurisdictions where the common-law rule prevails, which requires the owner to keep his stock within his inclosure. Within the doctrine of these cases, although the present case does not require us to invoke it, the instruction is incontestably sustained by the law. As no other question is presented by the record, or made at the argument, it follows that *the judgment must be affirmed.*

Thayer, *Ch. J.*, dissenting:

I am unable to concur in the result reached by the majority of the members of the court in this case. I cannot assent to the view that an owner of domestic animals can pasture them upon the depot grounds of a railroad company without being chargeable with such a degree of negligence as will preclude his right to a recovery of damages for their injury or destruction by moving trains of cars upon the track of the road, unless done intentionally. There is no stronger evidence to my mind of carelessness and negligence upon the part of such owner than to allow the animals to go at large, and wander about such places, where they are necessarily exposed to being run over and killed. My learned associate who prepared the majority opinion herein has with great care and research collated a large number of both English and American authorities upon the subject, and drawn as a conclusion therefrom that where the common-law rule, which required the owner of stock to keep it within his own inclosure, did not prevail, his permitting it to run at large would not, if it were to stray upon a railroad track, and receive injury, necessarily be such negligence as directly contributed to the injury; and he attempts to show that the common-law rule referred to does not obtain in this State. As an abstract proposition, I make no contention respecting that view; but, in the determination of all this class of cases, we must look squarely at the facts and circumstances, in order to make a just decision. Theories and distinctions, however specious and refined, cannot disprove a self-evident truth.

It appears from the bill of exceptions that the respondent has lost two horses, which have been run over and killed by rail-cars upon the road in question; and it is very evident that if he had a large band, and took no better care of them than he did of the one in question, as shown by the testimony, he would lose them all in the same way, unless the Company ceased to operate its road, and turned its depot grounds into a horse pasture. The bill of exceptions states that "the evidence tended to show that said horse, at the time when he was struck by defendant's locomotive, was running at large on defendant's depot grounds in the Town of Tangent, Linn County, . . . and had at different times previously to said day been seen occasionally pasturing upon said depot grounds; that plaintiff resided at all times in said Town of Tangent, and 700 or 800 feet away from said depot grounds."

This court knows judicially that the railroad in question constitutes a part of a line of road extending from Portland, Or., to San Francisco, Cal., a distance of more than 700 miles, and is the main avenue of transportation of passengers and freight between the two States; that, in operating it, a large number of trains of cars and rolling stock are employed; and that, at all such points as that in question, horses and cattle could not be permitted to pasture upon its depot grounds with any degree of security, however vigilant and careful those having charge of the trains and rolling stock might be in regard to their management. Yet the respondent, living in said Town of Tangent, within a few hundred feet of the place where his horse was killed, permits it to run at large upon the lands of the Company adjoining the depot, which must necessarily be left open, in order to enable the public to transact business with the Company. To conclude that such act, under the circumstances, is not the result of supine indifference and negligence upon the part of the owner of the animal would, it seems to me, be absurd, and to stultify reason. The respondent probably resided upon a town lot, and, having no ground to pasture his horse upon, concluded he might forage upon the Company's land. He knew, of course, that he had no right to allow his horse to run there; knew that he was exposing the animal to imminent peril by doing so. But the opportunity was so favorable for nipping herbage from another's land free of expense that he was willing to take the risk of sacrificing the life of the horse. I can conceive of no carelessness more censurable than to allow horses and cattle to run at large in such a locality; and no prudent man would think of permitting it, out of regard for the beasts themselves. But there are other far more important considerations than the regard for the animals, and their value. These things are incomparable to the damage liable to accrue in consequence of running an engine and train of cars over such animals. Several employés upon railroads have lost their lives during the last year or two from such incidents, and thousands of dollars of damage done. Cars have been thrown from the track, and the lives of passengers jeopardized. A railroad company can ill afford to run its engine and cars over an animal, and will not do so, where it can possibly be avoided, whether liable for its value or not. The respondent had no legal or moral right to suffer his horse to be at large upon a railroad company's depot grounds. He was thereby doing the Company and the public a positive wrong, and I am opposed to his being rewarded for his unjustifiable negligence in that particular. That his act in allowing the animal to go where it did directly contributed to the damage he seeks to recover, and which the jury graciously awarded to him, there can be no doubt, if viewed from a common-sense stand-point. This is not a case involving the right of stock to run at large upon a range or open common. There the land is thrown open, or left open, by the voluntary act of the proprietor, which is construed to be an implied license to the owners of domestic animals to use the same for grazing purposes. But here the Railroad Company is compelled to leave its depot grounds open, for the accommodation of the public, for the purposes of receiving and delivering freight, and for the convenience of persons traveling upon it. The grounds being left uninclosed, under such circumstances, cannot be construed into a license to pasture them, and the conditions are of such a character as to impliedly forbid it.

Nor do I oppose the view expressed in the said opinion regarding the duty of employés of a railroad company to use reasonable effort at all times to prevent the injury or destruction of such animals when found upon the track of the road, although they are there wrongfully. Because cattle or horses go upon a railroad track through the negligence of their owner, it does not follow that the company has the right to kill them. Its employés should always avoid running them down, where they are able to stop the train without injury to it, or without endangering the safety of passengers. But I am decidedly opposed to a trial court referring such a question to a jury, unless there is evidence in the case tending to establish the fact that they could reasonably and safely have stopped the train.

The majority members of the court assume that the evidence in this case tended to prove that the managers of the train, by the exercise of reasonable diligence, could have obviated the casualty in question. I very much doubt, however, whether it warrants that assumption. The statement in the bill of exceptions in regard to that matter is as follows: "That said locomotive was at the time attached to one of defendant's regular passenger trains, which passed through said town and depot grounds, from north to south, about 1 o'clock P. M. of the day, which was the regular time for said train to pass said station at Tangent; that, upon approaching said station, and when about 300 yards distant therefrom, the engineer in charge of the train signaled his approach to said station by sounding the whistle; that said horse was at the time either upon the depot grounds alongside the track, or else was upon the public road, at the north boundary line of the depot grounds, and soon thereafter was seen upon the track of the railroad, on the depot grounds, which track, near the road, was elevated some ten or twelve feet, and at the place where the horse was struck was elevated six or eight feet above the surrounding ground; that soon after the whistle was sounded the horse was so seen upon the track between the last-named two points on the depot grounds, and was walking along towards the approaching train, as if intending to reach said county road, which crosses the railroad track at that point; that when the horse had progressed a few steps in that direction upon the track the engineer sounded the alarm whistle twice or oftener, and turned the steam through the cylinder cocks, to drive the horse from the track; that the horse was at that time from sixteen to sixty feet from said road, and the train was distant from the horse from 180 to 250 feet on the opposite side of the said county road; that when the engineer so sounded the alarm whistle the horse turned immediately around on the track, and started running back along and upon the track, towards the south, and away from the train, but was overtaken and struck by the train within from forty to sixty feet from where he so turned around on the track; . . . that there is a conflict of evidence as to what the speed of the train was when said horse was first seen to go upon the track, and said alarm whistle was sounded, and as to whether or not said speed was slacked before the horse was overtaken and struck by the locomotive, and as to whether or not the engineer endeavored to and could have stopped the train after the horse went upon the track, and before he was struck by the locomotive, the speed of the train when the horse went upon the track being variously estimated by witnesses at from eight to twenty miles per hour, and some of the witnesses testified that the speed of the train was considerably lessened before the horse was struck, while other witnesses testified that they could not perceive that the speed of the train was at all diminished between the sounding of the alarm whistle and the striking of the horse. The engineer testified that immediately upon sounding the alarm whistle he applied the brakes, reversed the engine, and did all that it was in his power to do towards stopping the train, which was running about three miles per hour when the horse was struck. The other witnesses who testified were standing on the depot platform, some 300 feet distant from the point where the horse was struck by the locomotive, and nearly in a direct line with the length of the approaching train; and some of them stated that they did not, and some of them that they did, think the engineer endeavored to check the speed of the train before striking the horse."

I do not think the jury were justified in finding from the facts, under the most favorable construction to the respondent which they could reasonably give him, that the employés of the Company in charge of the train were guilty of violating their duty in the particular referred to. I do not believe that the facts were sufficient to sustain an allegation that said employés, by the exercise of reasonable care and diligence, could have avoided striking the horse with the locomotive. A finding by the jury that a train was running at the maximum or minimum rate supposed by the witnesses, or any intermediate rate, per hour, when the alarm whistle was sounded, and that it was 250 feet from the horse at the time,—the greatest estimated distance,—and that the engineer was not endeavoring to stop it, and could have done so, after the horse went upon the track, and before it was struck by the locomotive, would not have been sufficient to establish such want of care or negligence; as it would have lacked the further essential fact that the train could have been stopped within the distance indicated, and upon that character of grade, without danger of wrecking it, and imperiling the safety of those on board. An engineer of a railroad train is charged with a responsible duty, and he must be the judge, in the event of an emergency, as to the proper course to be pursued. He is often compelled, in cases of threatened danger from causes such as existed in this case, to accelerate instead of retarding the speed of the train, in order to save his own life, and the lives of others depending in a great measure upon his prudence and discretion. It would therefore be highly unjust to impute negligence to his conduct in the performance of his duty, without proof of all the facts necessary to constitute it. It could hardly be supposed that a person intrusted to so important a station as that of engineer upon a passenger train of cars would neglect to check the speed of the train in order to avoid running over a horse discovered upon the track, where it could be effectually and safely done. No one knows better than the engineer himself that his own life is in imminent peril whenever such an occurrence happens; and the law of self-preservation, if no other consideration, would prevent him from voluntarily taking such a risk. I think it may reasonably be claimed, as a rule of evidence in such cases, that the engineer is presumed to have performed his duty, unless the contrary is shown by direct and positive proof. In this case, however, no proof of any neglect on the part of the engineer, or of any of the employés of the Company, was attempted to be established, except by remote inference, not deducible from the facts claimed. It seems to me, therefore, that when the circuit court gave the instruction: "In this case, if you believe from the evidence that the plaintiff was guilty of negligence in allowing his horse to be upon the depot grounds of defendant, and that such negligence contributed to the accident, still, if you believe the accident could have been avoided by the exercise of ordinary care and diligence on the part of the defendant, the defendant is liable,"—it committed error. Cases of this kind are too important to the public to be left wholly to the decision of a jury, who, in ninety-nine cases out of a hundred, will determine them from sympathy, prejudice and caprice. Courts have a responsibility to perform aside from announcing abstract propositions of law. It is the duty of a trial court, and of this court, to see that justice is administered; and it cannot be shirked by a pretext that the case was a proper one to be determined by the jury. In the trial of actions at law, where the testimony in support of the issue is conflicting, it is the province of the jury to determine the facts; but the court should always carefully scan the testimony, and ascertain upon what issues between the parties it is conflicting, and not shuffle the whole responsibility onto the jury. The instruction above set out left the jury, in this case, free to determine it according to their own notions of right, and without regard to the rules of law.

The court had refused to give the instruction requested by the appellant's counsel,—that it was negligence in the owner of a horse to voluntarily permit it to run at large, and seek pasturage upon railroad depot grounds, and, if it were unintentionally injured by the employés of the railroad, through negligence in operating its cars, while the horse was so trespassing upon such grounds, the owner of the horse could not recover damages from the Railroad Company for such injury,—and after such refusal proceeded to tell the jury that, if they believed from the evidence that the plaintiff was guilty of negligence in allowing his horse to be upon the depot grounds of defendant, and that such negligence contributed to the accident, still, etc. By this instruction, the question as to whether or not the plaintiff was guilty of negligence in allowing his horse to be upon the depot grounds of defendant, and that such negligence contributed to the accident,—a very important question of law, indeed,—was left entirely to the belief of the jury from the evidence. Yet this part of the instruction is less objectionable than the latter clause thereof, as it restricts the jury in their finding, whether the plaintiff was guilty of negligence on account of the act referred to, and whether such negligence contributed to the accident, to their belief from the evidence, while the latter clause, to the effect that, if they believed that the accident would have been avoided, etc., would indicate that they might find the defendant liable from general belief, or belief derived from any source. The rule that a railroad company may be liable for killing stock upon its road, although wrongfully there, does not arise out of any new principle. It has always been recognized as a wholesome doctrine that an owner of property had no right to destroy or mistreat another's cattle found trespassing upon the property, but must exercise reasonable care and prudence in removing them.

The issue in this case was to this effect: The plaintiff said to the defendant: "My horse, without any fault of mine, went upon your railroad track; and your agents and servants so carelessly and negligently ran and managed your locomotive and cars upon said track that the same were run against the horse, and thereby killed it, to my damage," etc. The defendant said, in answer thereto: "My agents and servants were not guilty of the alleged carelessness and negligence, but the damage of which you complain resulted from your own carelessness and negligence." Now, the plaintiff having failed to charge an intentional injury to his animal, should, in order to avail himself of the rule which allows a recovery, in such cases, in favor of a party guilty of contributory negligence on his part, have averred in the reply that, notwithstanding the alleged carelessness and negligence charged against him in the answer, he was still entitled to recover the value of his horse, for that the agents and servants of the defendant might and could, by the exercise of reasonable efforts, have avoided running the locomotive against the animal, and that they wholly failed to make such efforts. This would have presented the real issue in the case—an issue tendered by the plaintiff, and which he would have been compelled to maintain by a preponderance of evidence; but he tendered no such issue in his reply. Upon the contrary, he merely denied the allegation of his own carelessness and negligence in the affair. The court, however, cast the burden upon the defendant of proving, not only that the plaintiff was guilty of carelessness and negligence which contributed to the injury, but virtually required the defendant to show that it could not have avoided the accident by the exercise of ordinary care and diligence. The said instruction substantially, went to that effect. It was to the effect that, if the jury found the plaintiff was guilty of negligence in the affair, "and that such negligence contributed to the accident, still the defendant was liable, if the jury believed that it could have been avoided by the exercise of ordinary care and diligence on the part of the defendant." Under that view, a plea on the part of a defendant, in an action against him for negligence, that the plaintiff was also guilty of negligence, which contributed to the injury, would not be good unless it were averred in the plea, also, that the result could not have been avoided by the exercise of ordinary care and diligence on the part of the defendant. Nor would the defendant's proof in support of his plea be of any avail unless it incontestably established that the occurrence could not have been avoided by the exercise of such care and diligence on his part. The logical aspect of the instruction is far beyond my comprehension. If the plaintiff's negligence contributed to the accident, and the defendant was also guilty of negligence in the affair, then it was necessarily the result of their joint wrong; and it certainly could have been avoided by the exercise of ordinary care and diligence on the part of the plaintiff. Why, then, should the defendant be liable to the plaintiff for its wrong, when the plaintiff's wrong was at least equally as instrumental in producing the result?

This will be the first case on record, I imagine, where contribution between wrongdoers has been enforced by a court of justice. If there had been evidence in the case tending to show that the conduct of the agents and servants of the appellant was reckless in the transaction which resulted in the destruction of the respondent's horse, or which indicated a total indifference and disregard of the respondent's rights of property, and such fact had been alleged in the complaint, or set forth in the reply, the trial court might very properly have instructed the jury that, if they found that such had been the conduct of the agents and servants of the appellant, they would be authorized to find him liable, although the plaintiff was guilty of negligence which contributed to the accident; but, in order to admit of a recovery in such a case, the conduct of the defendant must be proven to have been something more than negligent. It must be shown to have been willfully done; for upon no other ground can a plaintiff recover damages against a defendant for an injury resulting from the joint act of both parties. The law will not tolerate so illogical a sequence as the allowance of a recovery of damages by one party against another on account of a transaction in which they are *in pari delicto*. But to submit to a jury questions of fact where there is no evidence in the case which will warrant them in making a finding thereon, or to submit to them questions involving both law and fact in a confused mass, and then send them out to guess at a verdict, is a travesty upon justice.

I do not think the respondent was entitled to recover the judgment appealed from, nor see how it can legally be upheld. It is unjust in principle, and pernicious in its consequences, and was evidently obtained by sham and pretense. The idea that those in charge of the train of cars in question ran it against the horse purposely, or failed to do all in their power which could safely be done to avoid the collision, is too absurd and preposterous to be credited for a moment. The courts of this State cannot afford to tolerate a sentiment which ignores the rights of any parties litigant, whether belonging to natural or artificial persons. Because the appellant is a wealthy railroad corporation, and possibly arbitrary, extortionate and exacting in its dealings with the public, it does not follow that its rights should be ignored. Nor is it good policy on the part of the community to countenance or encourage such practice. We must deal honestly and fairly by railroad companies, whether they do so by us or not. Such a course will be found to be by far the best in the long run. We may succeed in compelling them to pay for a few horses and cattle belonging to thriftless owners, who would probably prefer to have them run over and killed, if they could get anywhere near their estimate of value of the animals, than to exert the slightest effort to prevent the occurrence; but the advantage will be very inconsiderable as compared to the injury which retaliatory measures, if resorted to on the part of the railroads, would occasion, and it would be very unwise to incite any such antagonism. Railroad companies should be required to do their full duty to the public, and, if it need legislation to enforce it, stringent measures should be adopted; but to allow a petty system of illegal and unjust plundering of them will prove to be an indiscreet and short sighted policy.

MISSOURI COURT OF APPEALS (St. Louis).

Julius CONRAD *et al.*, *Appts.*,
v.
John J. FISHER *et al.*, *Respts.*

Julius CONRAD, Admr., etc., of Helena Paulsen, *Appt.*,
v.
John J. FISHER *et al.*, *Respts.*

Henry SCHLOETER, *Appt.*,
v.
John J. FISHER *et al.*, *Respts.*

(37 Mo. App. 352.)

*1. **The right to enforce a vendor's lien in respect of goods sold upon a credit is not a right to rescind** the contract of sale, but is a right to detain the goods until the indebtedness for the purchase price is discharged at or before the expiration of the credit, and, if not so discharged, to sell them and apply the proceeds of their sale to the liquidation of the indebtedness.

2. **It is an additional security** for the payment of the purchase price, and is not waived by the act of the vendor in resorting to any other security which he may have, provided such security is not in itself a security of such a nature as waives or discharges the lien.

3. **A collection of facts stated, in which it appeared that several attachments were sued out** by different creditors of a common debtor, apparently at the same time, all of them acting through the same attorney; that the different writs came into the hands of the sheriff within a few minutes of each other; that

*Head notes by THOMPSON, J.

NOTE.—See *notes* to Farmers Phosphate Co. v. Gill (Md.) 1 L. R. A. 767; Dunn v. Georgia (Ga.) 3 L. R. A. 199; Fenkhausen v. Fellows (Nev.) 4 L. R. A. 732.

See also 37 L. R. A. 166.

they were all levied on the following day, apparently at the same time; and that subsequently, on motions of the several plaintiffs, the suits were consolidated and proceeded to judgment together. *It is held*, that this evidence exhibited such a concert of action as authorized the trier of the facts to find that all the attaching creditors were joint actors, and that either of them was guilty of a conversion in case any of the levies should be adjudged tortious.

4. **The delivery, as collateral security, of a bill of sale,** copies of gaugers' returns and a warehouse receipt of whiskey held in the United States bonded warehouse, creates a pledge, and not a chattel mortgage.

5. **Where, from its situation, personal property is not susceptible of actual delivery,** manual delivery is not essential to the creation of a pledge; it may be created by a symbolical delivery,—as by the delivery of a bill of parcels and a warehouse receipt.

6. **The English doctrine** which, in the case of a pledge by a symbolical delivery, requires an attornment by the warehouseman or other custodian of the goods, in order to create such a delivery as will support the pledge, is not in force in this country.

7. **The owner of goods stored in his own warehouse** cannot make a valid pledge of them, by issuing to another an instrument in the form of a warehouse receipt, in which he professes to hold the goods for that other. Such an attempt to create a pledge is void, as being contrary to the provisions of our Statute relating to chattel mortgages, which requires a delivery of possession or a recording in the office of the recorder of deeds. (Rev. Stat. 1879, § 2503.)

8. **The law of a sister State** of the American Union is a foreign law in the sense that it is not judicially noticed in the tribunals of this State, but must, in order to have effect here, be proved as a fact.

9. **The burden of proving the law of another State** rests upon the party claiming rights under it, and, in the absence of such proof, the trial court is authorized to presume that the same rule of law which obtains in this State obtains in that State, it being founded in the principles of the common law, and not the necessary outgrowth of a local and peculiar statute.

10. **Where a contract is in writing** and is so distinctly drawn as to leave no ambiguities for parol explanation, evidence of a prior course of dealing between the parties to it, and especially of a prior course of dealing between one of the parties to it and the predecessors of the other party, cannot be appealed to to supply an interpretation of it.

11. **But it is competent to show** that the parties in their dealings under the contract varied its terms by a subsequent parol agreement.

12. **Where the facts are numerous and equivocal**—susceptible of different inferences in respect of the question, What was the real intent of the parties?—the question whether there has been such a delivery as devests the vendor's lien, is a question of fact for a jury.

13. **In such a case, in an action at law,** the inferences of fact made by the trial court are not reviewable on appeal, provided they are fairly within the scope of the evidence.

14. **The leading incidents of a vendor's lien are:** that it presupposes title in the vendee; that it is not a right of rescission, but of detention; that it arises by implication of law while the goods remain in the possession of the vendor and the purchase price is unpaid; that it is waived by stipulations in the contract of sale inconsistent with its exercise, as by giving time for payment and taking a negotiable security therefor; that this waiver takes place on the implied condition that the vendee will keep his credit good during the term of the credit; that it revives if, during such term, the vendee becomes insolvent, and that the insolvency which revives it is insolvency in the mercantile sense—an inability to pay one's debts as fast as they mature.

15. **It is not a universal rule that the delivery of the goods** which devests the vendor of his lien must be such a delivery, actual or constructive, as would amount to an "actual receipt" of the goods within the meaning of the seventeenth section of the English Statute of Frauds; nor is it a safe test in determining whether this lien has been devested to consider whether there has been such a delivery.

16. **As between the vendor and vendee,** and in cases where the rights of subsequent purchasers of the vendee are not concerned, this lien is not devested by any species of constructive delivery, so long as the vendor retains the actual custody of the goods, either by himself or by his agent or servant.

17. **This lien is not destroyed** by invoicing the goods to the purchaser.

18. **Nor is it destroyed by marking the packages** with the purchaser's name. *So held*, where the goods consisted of barrels of whiskey distilled in a distillery which, by an arrangement between the contracting parties, sanctioned by the agents of the government, was run in the name of the vendee, and the barrels furnished by the vendor were branded with the name of the vendee as distiller and placed in the distillery warehouse.

19. **Nor is this lien destroyed by an agreement** between the vendor and vendee that the goods shall remain in the warehouse of the vendor subject to the payment of storage by the vendee. The doctrine of *Barrett* v. *Goddard*, 3 Mason, 107, on this subject denied, and the decision criticised.

20. **The fact that by the agreement between the vendor and vendee something remains to be done** to the goods by the vendor, is not conclusive that there has not been such a delivery as cuts off the vendor's lien, but creates a prima facie presumption to that effect, which may be rebutted by circumstances. If the thing remaining to be done was intended to prepare the goods for delivery, the lien continues; but if the facts essential to a delivery have taken place, and the thing remaining to be done is merely in the nature of a subsequent service by the vendor with reference to the goods, the lien is discharged. When, therefore, the goods at the time the contract of sale is made, though in the legal custody and control, are not in the actual possession, of the vendee, but are so situated that he cannot obtain actual possession until a specific act is done by the vendor, if the vendee becomes insolvent before this act has been done, and the actual possession of the goods has not been changed, the vendor may detain the goods as security for the payment of the contract price.

21. **The lien of the unpaid vendor for distilled spirits is not destroyed by placing them in a government warehouse** in charge of a government storekeeper. The custody of the government storekeeper is intended merely to secure the government in its revenue, and not to interrupt or impair the rights of any vendor, vendee or pledgee, beyond what

the terms of the statute under which he holds possession absolutely require.

22. Where the contract stipulated for the doing of three things by the vendor before the delivery should be complete: (1) to give care and attention to the packages while in the government warehouse, the same being the distillery warehouse of the vendor; (2) to place insurance upon the property, if so required by the vendee: (3) and, finally, to complete the delivery of the property itself by placing it free of charge on board the cars,—*It was held*, that, presumptively, there had been no actual delivery until the last of these three things had been performed, unless the other circumstances surrounding the transaction were such as to repel the presumption, and whether they were was a question of fact.

23. In the provisions of the Revenue Laws of the United States, which require the delivery of distilled spirits by the government warehouseman to the owner when the tax is paid, Congress merely intended, by the use of a general word of description, to designate, without circumlocution or needless specification, any person who, upon the payment of the government dues, is in law entitled to the possession of the goods.

24. The lien of an unpaid vendor of goods is not self-executing. It is a right which he may or may not assert, and which if not asserted in time, is lost. If, therefore, the vendor, retaining the goods under a contract with the vendee, in the vendor's distillery warehouse, allows the vendee to call the warehouse his own for the purposes of his trade, and to issue warehouse receipts in respect of the goods, the license thus given to the vendee to issue warehouse receipts does not, *ipso facto*, expire upon the happening of the vendee's insolvency.

25. Where goods which have been sold on credit remain in the possession of the vendor under such circumstances that his lien will revive upon the happening of the insolvency of the vendee, a pledge of the goods by the vendee to his creditor, as collateral security for an antecedent indebtedness, the creditor parting with no new value and making no agreement for delay, does not constitute the pledgee a purchaser for value, in such a sense as gives him a better right in respect of the goods than his pledgor and cuts off the lien of the unpaid vendor.

26. In such a case the pledgee of the vendee cannot be regarded as having a better right than the vendee, on the principle of estoppel, unless he shows that what has been said or done by the vendee has in some way influenced the conduct of the pledgee to his detriment. The law will not presume, in the absence of evidence, that such was the fact.

27. Where the rights of the parties depended upon the law of Kentucky, and this circumstance was not brought to the attention of the trial court by either party, and such law was not proved as a fact, the court declined to affirm the judgment as being for the right party, on the theory that the pledge under which the plaintiffs claimed was not by the law of Missouri a valid pledge, when the court knew, as a matter of general learning, that it was a valid pledge under the law of Kentucky. On the other hand, the court declined to reverse a judgment for the defendants which rested on the ground that the title of the plaintiff was that of a pledgee of warehouse receipts as collateral security for an antecedent debt,—the law of Missouri on the subject being unsettled, and the law of Kentucky, by which the rights of the parties were governed, which had not been put in evidence in the trial court, being, on the analogous subject of commercial paper, that a pledgee for an antecedent debt is not a taker for value, but holds subject to prior equities.

(January 2, 1889.)

APPEALS by plaintiffs from judgments of the Circuit Court for St. Louis City in favor of defendants in actions brought to recover damages for the alleged conversion of certain whiskey. *Affirmed.*

The facts are fully stated in the opinion.

Mr. **David Goldsmith** for appellants.

Mr. **Silas B. Jones** for respondents.

Thompson, *J.*, delivered the opinion of the court:

This case has been argued three times at very great length and with much ability on both sides,—the last time before the two judges who alone participate in this decision. Two other actions, *Julius Conrad, Administrator of Helena Paulsen, Appellant*, v. *John J. Fisher et al., Respondents*, No. 3711, and *Henry Schloeter, Appellant*, v. *John J. Fisher et al., Respondents*, No. 3712,—have also been argued and submitted together with this case. The three actions are of the same nature, arising out of the same transaction and depending upon the same principles of law. They were tried together before the same judge sitting as a jury, and judgments in all of them were entered for the defendants. They are presented in this court for review upon a single bill of exceptions, by a stipulation of the parties. This opinion will dispose of the other two cases, as well as of this case.

Each of these three cases is an action for the conversion of certain whiskey at Silver Creek, in Richmond County, Kentucky. The facts, so far as it seems necessary to state them at the outset, were as follows: During the time when the rights in controversy arose, Charles W. Conrad was doing business in St. Louis, Missouri, under the name and style of C. Conrad & Co. The defendants were partners in two different firms (Gregory, Stagg & Co. and W. S. Hume & Co.) engaged in the business of distillers and rectifiers at Silver Creek, Kentucky. A third firm, Stagg, Hume & Co., and also the two firms above named, of which they were successors, had had a course of dealing with C. Conrad & Co., similar to that which took place under the contract hereafter set out upon which the rights now to be disposed of depend. There is a great amount of testimony in the record as to the nature of this course of dealing, and the facts adduced by this testimony are set out at considerable length by the appellants in their statement, of which we shall speak hereafter.

As introductory to the contract itself, it may be stated that Conrad, doing business at St. Louis under the name of C. Conrad & Co., had acquired an extensive reputation for a certain kind of beer, which had been brewed and bottled for him in St. Louis, and which he had sold under the name of Budweiser beer. He desired to found a similar reputation in respect of certain kinds of whiskey, but as he was not a distiller, it was necessary to find a distiller who would make for him whiskey of the desired grade, and who would assist him in holding himself out to the world as the distiller of it. The defendants were willing to make such whiskey for him and to assist him in representing himself to the public as the distiller of it. In order to carry out this purpose, the following contract was entered into:

"This agreement, made and entered into this 25th day of October, 1882, between Stagg, Hume & Co., of St. Louis, Missouri, of the first part, and C. Conrad & Co., of St. Louis, Missouri, of the second part, witnesseth:

"That the party of the first part agrees to make for the party of the second part, during the months of November and December, 1882, and January, 1883, at the Silver Creek distillery in Madison County, Kentucky, 2,100 barrels of Moss-Rose Sour-Mash Bourbon whiskey and 400 barrels Governor's Choice Rye whiskey, at 46½ cents per proof gallon for the Bourbon and 62½ cents per proof gallon for the Rye—the Bourbon to be invoiced when all made, and the Rye to be invoiced when all made, as per return of United States gauger on duty at distillery.

"That during the manufacture of the whiskey herein contracted for the firm name of the party of the second part (Conrad & Co.) shall be used as distillers, provided that the said party of the second part shall not in any way be held responsible or liable to the United States government for the conduct of the distillery.

"That settlement for the whiskey shall be made as follows: The party of the second part shall give their notes or acceptances, each for $600, payable, the first note on June 16, 1883, and a note payable on the Saturday of each week following until all are paid. That the whiskey shall be of the standard quality of the "Hume" brand, the cooperage first class, eight-iron-hooped barrels, well charred, branded with the firm name of the party of the second part as distillers—all brands required to be furnished by the party of the first part—the packages to contain from forty-six to fifty gallons each, and the proof of the whiskey to run as nearly uniform at 101 per cent as it is possible to make it.

"That storage shall be charged at the rate of five cents per barrel per month from date of entry into United States Warehouse No. 541, Eighth District of Kentucky, and that all care and attention shall be given the packages while in store by the party of the first part.

"That upon the release from bond and payment of United States and state taxes and storage by the party of the second part, packages shall be delivered free of charge by the party of the first part, on board of the cars at Silver Creek, Kentucky.

"That the party of the first part, if desired to do so by the party of the second part, shall place insurance, loss, if any, payable to the party of the second part, who shall pay the premium at not to exceed current rates.

"That if, from fire or other casualty, the party of the first part shall be unable to comply with the terms of this contract in full or in part, the said party of the first part shall not in any way be held liable for such nonfulfillment of contract.

"That when the whiskey is all invoiced and the notes are given for the amount, the party of the first part agrees to pay to the party of the second part $250, in consideration of which the party of the second part agrees to give the party of the first part two cases containing twelve quart bottles of the best French champagne and two casks of Budweiser beer.

"Witness our hands this 25th day of October, 1882, at St. Louis, Mo.

(Signed) "Stagg, Hume & Co.,
"C. Conrad & Co."

The whiskey in controversy was made (or caused to be made, in the manner hereafter stated), by Stagg, Hume & Co., under this contract, and was placed in United States Bonded Warehouse No. 541, as therein provided for. On the 9th of February, 1883, Conrad, being in failing circumstances, and being indebted to these plaintiffs in various amounts which had long been due, delivered to each one of them, without their solicitation, a warehouse receipt for a quantity of this whiskey as collateral security for the indebtedness owing to them, they asking him no questions and he making to them no statements at the time as to why he did this. On the 16th of the same month he suspended payment and his insolvency became known and published; and on the 25th he made an assignment for the benefit of his creditors. Meantime the plaintiffs had taken no steps to withdraw the whiskey from the government warehouse, but merely held the warehouse receipts, parting with no new value for them. The notes given by Conrad to Stagg, Hume & Co. for the whiskey were in their possession, not negotiable, and unpaid at the time of his suspension. Conrad was insolvent to the extent that, although much of his indebtedness was secured, his unsecured creditors received from the administrator of the unpledged assets of his estate no more than ten cents on the dollar.

Soon after his suspension, Stagg, Hume & Co. sued out an attachment in Richmond County, Kentucky, to enforce a vendor's lien upon the whiskey. The other two partnership firms already named (Gregory, Stagg & Co. and W. S. Hume & Co.), of which two firms the defendants were members, being creditors of Conrad on other accounts, sued out other attachments. These attachment suits were, by agreement of the various attaching creditors, consolidated, and, in the consolidation suit, judgment was rendered for the plaintiffs, fixing their respective priorities. The property was sold thereunder; and, although Stagg, Hume & Co. proved up their claim as holders of the notes given by Conrad for the purchase price of the whiskey before the assignee of his estate, and received a dividend in common with the other creditors, yet the total amount which was realized from the sale of the whiskey in Kentucky, in the various attachment suits, added to the dividend thus received by them, was not sufficient to liquidate the indebtedness evidenced by the notes given by Conrad to them for the purchase price of the whiskey.

We understand it to be the settled law that the right to enforce a vendor's lien in respect of goods sold upon a credit is not a right to rescind the contract of sale, but is a right to detain the goods until the indebtedness for the purchase price is discharged, at or before the expiration of the credit, and, if not so discharged, to sell them and apply the proceeds of their sale to the liquidation of the indebtedness. *Babcock* v. *Bonnell*, 80 N. Y. 244; *Chandler* v. *Fulton*, 10 Tex. 2, 60 Am. Dec. 188, 199; *Newhall* v. *Central Pac. R. Co.* 51 Cal. 345, 21 Am. Rep. 713.

It is an additional security, and is not waived by the act of the vendor in resorting to any other security which he may have, provided such security is not in itself a security of such a nature as waives or discharges the lien. Hence, there was nothing incompatible in the act of Stagg, Hume & Co. in proving up their claim before the assignee of Conrad, and receiving a dividend from his estate in its administration, under the Assignment Law of Missouri, in common with other creditors, and in their also proceeding by such means as the law of Kentucky left available to them to enforce their vendor's lien upon the whiskey in the bonded warehouse at Silver Creek in that State; nor is such a contention made on behalf of the plaintiffs. Moreover, as they did not realize enough from both sources—that is, from the dividends received from Conrad's assignee and from the proceeds of the sale of the whiskey under their attachment in Kentucky—to satisfy the notes given for the purchase money, it must follow that, if they had a vendor's lien which they were entitled to enforce against the whiskey, the existence of such a lien is a complete defense to these actions for conversion, provided the title of the plaintiffs is not better than that of Conrad, their transferrer. The strength of this conclusion has been seen by the learned counsel for the plaintiffs, and therefore his chief effort has been to convince the court that Stagg, Hume & Co. had no vendor's lien upon the whiskey in controversy.

Before proceeding to the consideration of the question, it is necessary to get out of the way two other objections raised by the defendant; because, assuming that these objections properly arise upon the record, if they are well taken, they require an affirmance of the judgment, which was given for the defendant, irrespective of the question whether or not Stagg, Hume & Co., had a vendor's lien upon the whiskey.

I. The first of these objections is that there is no evidence in the record tending to show a conversion. In order to understand the grounds upon which this objection is placed, it is necessary to recall the facts that the whiskey was seized under four attachments, simultaneously levied upon it at Silver Creek, Kentucky, by three different firms; that these firms were composed in the aggregate of numerous parties, and that the two defendants who alone are sued in these actions (process having been returned as to the others "not found"), are James A. Gregory and John J. Fisher, neither of whom was a member of the firm of Stagg, Hume & Co., the makers (through the Silver Creek Distilling Company) of the whiskey under the contract with Conrad above set out. These three partnership firms were Stagg, Hume & Co., composed of Stagg, of Hume, and of Taylor, Jr.; W. S. Hume & Co., composed of Fisher, Gregory, Stagg, Hume and Embry; and Gregory, Stagg & Co., composed of Gregory, Stagg, Fisher and Hume. The defendants Fisher and Gregory were members of the firm of W. S. Hume & Co., and also of the firm of Gregory, Stagg & Co. On January 23, 1883, four suits were instituted by these various firms against Charles W. Conrad, in the court of Common Pleas in Madison County, Kentucky, two of them known as No. 1 and No. 2, by Stagg, Hume & Co., the makers of the whiskey and the parties of the first part in the contract above set out; one of them by W. S. Hume & Co., and one by Gregory, Stagg & Co. In all these suits attachments were sued out against the property of Conrad. In the suit of Stagg, Hume & Co., known as No. 1, the effort was to enforce a vendor's lien upon the whiskey in controversy. The writ of attachment issued in this suit came into the hands of the sheriff of Madison County, Kentucky, at three minutes past ten o'clock in the evening of the same day; the writ in the action of W. S. Hume & Co. came into his hands at ten minutes past ten o'clock in the evening of the same day; and the writ in the action of Gregory, Stagg & Co. came into his hands at twelve minutes past ten o'clock in the evening of the same day. The three writs were all levied, on the next day, on the whiskey in controversy, by a notice to the person in charge of the warehouse where it was stored. Possession of the whiskey was never taken nor disturbed under any of the writs. The cases were managed for the several plaintiffs by the same attorneys. They were consolidated for trial, and judgment was given, setting out the rights of each of the plaintiffs, there being other whiskey involved besides that in controversy here, and adjudging a prior right and lien in favor of Stagg, Hume & Co. to the whiskey in controversy, which was sold to satisfy their lien, but which, as already stated, did not bring enough to satisfy it. Neither W. S. Hume & Co., nor Gregory, Stagg & Co., got any part of the proceeds of the sale of the whiskey in controversy. No effort was made in the court below to show that in point of fact the attachment of W. S. Hume & Co. or that of Gregory, Stagg & Co., in any way interfered with the rights of these plaintiffs. But the plaintiffs rested upon the position that what was done under the attachments was *per se* a conversion of the whiskey in controversy, and the defendants now insist that such is not the law. The circuit court adjudged this point against the defendants, and we are unable to say that its conclusion was wrong. It is clear to our minds that there was here evidence tending to show such a concert of action among the four attaching creditors as placed all of them in the position, if the attachments were wrongful, of co-trespassers or joint tortfeasors, within the meaning of the rule laid down by this court at the present term in the case of *Leeser* v. *Boekhoff*, 33 Mo. App. 223, and the cases there cited; and the sufficiency of this evidence was a question of fact for the trial court, sitting as a jury. It is perceived that the attachments were sued out apparently at the same time, by the parties acting through the same attorney; that the different writs came into the hands of the sheriff within a few minutes of each other; that they were all levied on the following day, apparently at the same time, for the hours of the several levies are not specified in the sheriff's return; and that subsequently, on motions of the several plaintiffs, the suits were consolidated and proceeded to judgment together. The fact that the attachment which first came into the hands of the sheriff may, by operation of law, have taken precedence in the first distribution of the fund does not, we think, at all negative the conclusion that there was such concert of action as made all the parties liable as co-trespassers, in case the levies should be adjudged tortious. The levies, it may be assumed, took effect by relation as of the respective dates when the different writs came into the hands of the sheriff. But this doctrine of relation is to be regarded as a fiction resorted to for the purpose of determining the priorities of the attaching creditors as among themselves, and not for the purpose of determining the liability of any one of them as between himself and the defendant in the attachment suit.

II. The next position of the respondent is that the delivery of the bill of sale, copies of gaugers' returns and so-called warehouse receipts created a mere pledge, which was invalid, because there was no delivery. It is not disputed that these papers were delivered to the plaintiffs as collateral security, and not in payment. The transaction, therefore, constituted a pledge or mortgage. That it constituted a pledge, and not a mortgage, can scarcely be the subject of doubt. A bill of sale of chattels, absolute on its face, may, indeed, be shown by parol evidence to have been intended as a mere security for a debt. *Newell* v. *Keeler*, 13 Mo. App. 189. Such was the undisputed evidence here; and whether it was a mortgage or a pledge was a question of law. If it were a mortgage and not recorded, it would not be good against creditors of the mortgagor, unless accompanied by delivery. In that respect it would stand on the same footing as a pledge; for delivery is essential to the validity of a pledge. These warehouse receipts were evidently intended to make a symbolical delivery to the plaintiffs, as security for their respective debts. This would make a pledge, provided a pledge can be created by such an instrument, and by no other delivery, actual or constructive. This is shown by the following case: *Parshall* v. *Eggart*, 52 Barb. 367, affirmed on this point though reversed on another, 54 N. Y. 18. This view is also confirmed by numerous holdings to the effect that taking a bill of sale or bill of parcels of personal property, absolute in its terms, as collateral security merely, amounts only to a pledge. *Walker* v. *Staples*, 5 Allen, 34; *Thompson* v. *Doliver*, 132 Mass. 103; *Kimball* v. *Hildreth*, 8 Allen, 167; *Morgan* v. *Dod*, 3 Colo. 551.

But it does not follow that a valid pledge can be created only by manual delivery of the property pledged. Where, from its situation, the property is not susceptible of actual delivery, a valid pledge may be created by symbolical delivery. *Ex parte Fitz*, 2 Lowell, 519; Jones, Pledges, § 36.

Thus, property in transit may undoubtedly be pledged by the deposit of a bill of lading. *Meyerstein* v. *Barber*, L. R. 2 C. P. 38, affirmed, Id. 661, and in L. R. 4 H. L. 317.

We have held in this court that goods in a warehouse may be pledged by delivery of the warehouse receipt, even without its being indorsed by the pledgor. *St. Louis Nat. Bank* v. *Ross*, 9 Mo. App. 399.

That goods in the hands of a warehouseman may be pledged by a transfer of the warehouse receipt was again held by this court in *Fourth Nat. Bank* v. *St. Louis Cotton Compress Co.*, 11 Mo. App. 341, and has been held by other courts in numerous cases. Jones, Pledges, §§ 280, 298, 302, and cases cited.

That goods detained in the custom house to secure the payment of duties may be pledged by a written contract noted on the books of the chief officer of the custom house without actual delivery, was held by the English Privy Council, reversing the Canadian Court of Queen's Bench, in *Young* v. *Lambert*, L. R. 3 P. C. 142.

This last case, however, involves an idea which seems to be fundamental in the English law, namely, that where goods are in the possession of a third party, in order to constitute such a constructive delivery as will support a valid pledge, there must be an attornment by the actual custodian. *Sir* Joseph Napier, in giving the judgment of the court in the case just cited said: "It appears to their lordships that, by the express agreement of the parties in this case, followed by the acceptance of the chief warehouse keeper, there was a valid constructive delivery of the property comprised in the contract." Id. 156.

But our law does not seem to require an attornment in order to complete a symbolical delivery. *Davis* v. *Russell*, 52 Cal. 611.

The decisions in this State do not give countenance to such an idea, although in Massachusetts they have followed the English rule. *Hallgarten* v. *Oldham*, 135 Mass. 1.

But Mr. Jones in his very satisfactory work on Pledges, speaks of this decision as "contrary to the general rule." Jones, Pledges, § 300.

We should therefore have no difficulty in overruling the contention of the respondents upon this point, if we could regard these instruments as warehouse receipts.

But it has been held by this court, and by several other courts, that a receipt issued by the owner of goods stored in his own store is not a warehouse receipt at all. *Valley Nat. Bank* v. *Frank*, 12 Mo. App. 460; *Thorne* v. *First Nat. Bank*, 37 Ohio St. 254; *Adams* v. *Merchants Nat. Bank*, 2 Fed. Rep. 174, 9 Biss. 396; *Yenni* v. *McNamee*, 45 N. Y. 614; *Farmers Bank* v. *Lang*, 87 N. Y. 209.

In *Valley Nat. Bank* v. *Frank*, *supra*, this court held that the issue by a merchant of a receipt for goods held in his own store, in the form of a warehouse receipt, had not the effect in law of a transfer of title by means of a warehouse receipt, as against a subsequent innocent purchaser.

In *Thorne* v. *First Nat. Bank*, *supra*, it was held that an instrument substantially like a warehouse receipt, issued by a debtor to his creditor, on property owned by the debtor, who was not a warehouseman, for the sole purpose of securing such creditor, was void as against other creditors, where the property remained in the possession of the debtor. In the view which the court took, it was void as an attempt to create a lien upon personal property contrary to the provisions of the Statute making chattel mortgages void unless accompanied by delivery of possession, or unless the mortgage be recorded—which Statute is substantially similar to ours. Rev. Stat. § 2503.

In *Adams* v. *Merchants Nat. Bank, supra*, a similiar ruling was made upon a similar state of facts and based upon similar reasons—the court holding that, in order to create a valid pledge by the transfer of a warehouse receipt, the receipt must be issued and transferred in compliance with the governing statute; otherwise, it will be regarded as in the nature of a mortgage, and void because not recorded or accompanied by the delivery of the property.

A similar ruling was made, and upon similar grounds, in *Yenni* v. *McNamee, supra*. This last case is also authority for the position that such an attempted pledge is not good under our Statute relating to warehouse receipts. That Statute recites: "All receipts issued or given by any warehouseman or other person or firm . . . are hereby made negotiable," etc. Rev. Stat. § 558.

The New York Statute contained the same recitals, using the words "or other persons."

Yet it was held that a receipt issued by the owner of the goods, who held them in his own storehouse, was not a warehouse receipt; that the issuing of it to a creditor did not create a valid pledge, for want of transfer; but that it was an attempt to create a mortgage contrary to the provisions of the Statute (similar to ours), requiring mortgages of chattels to be accompanied by delivery or else recorded.

In another case in the same State, a commission merchant procured a discount of his promissory note upon the following receipt as collateral: "Received in store, for account of Messrs. P. & S , subject to their order, the following named property, as security to pay note given this day" (describing the note and also the property thus attempted to be pledged). There was no manual delivery of the property, and no other symbolical delivery than was effected by the issuing of this receipt, but the property remained in the storehouse of the commission merchant as before. It was held: (1) That the receipt was not a chattel mortgage, and that, if it were, it was void as against the creditors of the mortgagor, because there was neither a delivery nor a recordation as required by the Statute. (2) That the transaction did not, in legal effect, constitute a pledge, because it lacked the essential of delivery. (3) That the fact that the property was delivered to the attempted pledgee, before it was levied upon by the attachment under which the defendant justified, did not validate it as a pledge. *Parshall* v. *Eggart*, 52 Barb. 367. On appeal from this ruling, the court of appeals of the same State held that the transaction was a pledge, and that, considered as a pledge, it was validated by the subsequent delivery before the rights of the attaching creditors supervened—leaving the ruling undisturbed on the other points. See *S. C.* 54 N. Y. 18.

A similar ruling was made under the provisions of the Civil Code of Louisiana (arts. 3125, 3129), where certain attempted pledgees, having allowed the pledgor to remain in possession of the goods which he had attempted to pledge to them, by issuing to them papers by which he professed to have received the goods from them on storage, were held not entitled to the rights of pledgees against subsequent purchasers. *Geddes* v. *Bennett*, 6 La. Ann. 516.

A ruling of *Mr. District Judge* Lowell in a case in bankruptcy is to the general effect that there might be, under circumstances, a valid pledge of cumbrous material, such as locomotive engines, by the delivery of bills of sale, although the property should remain in the possession of the pledgor. *Ex parte Fitz*, 2 Lowell, 519.

But no allusion is made in that case to the existence or effect of any local statute requiring chattel mortgages to be recorded or to be accompanied by delivery, and I do not therefore regard that decision as authority in such a case as that before us. Besides, it does not seem to me to have been well decided upon its circumstances. It invests a bill of sale with the qualities which the Mercantile Law, for purposes of commerce, attaches to bills of lading and to warehouse receipts, and I do not find any well-considered case that has gone to that extent.

But we find that it has been held in Kentucky, construing the Statute of that State (Kentucky Act March 6, 1869), that a person having goods stored in his own warehouse may transfer title in them by issuing warehouse receipts (*Newcombe* v. *Cabe'l*, 10 Bush, 460), and may, by issuing such a receipt, make a valid pledge to them to another,—placing such warehouse receipts on the same footing as similar receipts given by a warehouseman to the owner of the goods and by him transferred in pledge. *Cochran* v. *Ripey*, 13 Bush, 495; *Ferguson* v. *Northern Bank of Kentucky*, 14 Bush, 555. See also *Farmer* v. *Gregory*, 78 Ky. 475; *Greenbaum* v. *Megibben*, 10 Bush, 419.

If the rights of the plaintiffs under these so-called warehouse receipts are governed by the Law of Kentucky, then it is to be observed that the Law of Kentucky is a foreign law which is not judicially noticed in the tribunals of this State, but which must, in order to have effect here, be proved as a fact (*Selking* v. *Hebel*, 1 Mo. App. 340; *Flato* v. *Mulhall*, 72 Mo. 522; *Meyer* v. *McCabe*, 73 Mo. 236; *Bergner* v. *Chicago R. Co.* 13 Mo. App. 499); that the burden of proving what the law of Kentucky was upon this point was upon the plaintiffs; and that, in the absence of such proof, the circuit court was authorized to presume that the same rule of law which obtains in this State obtains in Kentucky, it being founded in the principles of the common law, and not the necessary outgrowth of a local and peculiar statute. *Meyer* v. *McCabe* and *Bergner* v. *Chicago R. Co. supra*.

It is also true that the Supreme Court of Michigan has held (approving the ruling in the Kentucky case of *Cochran* v. *Ripey, supra*) that a warehouseman having property of his own in store may, by issuing a warehouse receipt, make a valid pledge of it to secure his own indebtedness. *Detroit M. & M. Bank* v. *Hibbard*, 48 Mich. 118.

But, as the case stands, we should be bound to hold, following our own decision in *Valley Nat. Bank* v. *Frank, supra*, and believing that attempted pledges in this form, by a person of his own property in his own warehouse, are in contravention of the letter and policy of the

Statute already referred to relating to chattel mortgages—that these warehouse receipts were neither valid as pledges nor as mortgages, and consequently that the plaintiffs have exhibited no title and no standing in court—were it not for the fact that it nowhere appears that this view of the rights of the parties was brought to the attention of the court below during the trial. If it had been, the plaintiffs could have obviated it by putting in evidence the report of the Kentucky case of *Cochran* v. *Ripey, supra*, thereby proving that the law of Kentucky on this subject is different from our own law. In this peculiar state of the record, we do not feel authorized to affirm the judgment on this point, as being for the right party, since we know as a fact that under the law of Kentucky, by which this contract of pledge is to be governed, it was a valid pledge.

III. This brings us to the main question which has been contested, namely, whether there was such a delivery of the property as devested the vendor's lien. In order to a proper understanding of this question, it will be necessary to state at considerable length the manner in which the parties executed the contract above set out. This statement would be less difficult, were it not for the various *aliases* under which the parties did business. The party of the first part was, as already stated, a partnership existing at Silver Creek, Kentucky, called Stagg, Hume & Co., but they executed their contract through a corporation organized under the laws of Kentucky, called the Silver Creek Distilling Company, which corporation was the owner of a distillery at Silver Creek, Kentucky, and also the owner of the government warehouse, number 541, into which, by the terms of the contract, the whiskey was to be and was in fact placed. It is perceived, by reference to this peculiar contract, that Conrad desired to be held out to the world as the distiller of this whiskey, and that Stagg, Hume & Co. were willing to assist him in holding himself out as such distiller. For this purpose, it was absolutely necessary, under the Acts of Congress relating to internal revenue, that the distillery should be run in the name of the assumed distiller, to wit, in the name of C. Conrad & Co., and that the warehouse, which is an integral part of the distillery under such statutes, should be treated as his warehouse. For it must be borne in mind that, by the terms of those laws, each distillery has a warehouse, and that the spirits, as soon as distilled, must be at once conveyed to a receiving cistern (U. S. Rev. Stat. § 3267), whence they must, within three days, be drawn into casks, which casks must be directly removed to the distillery warehouse. As soon as the whiskey is thus removed to the distillery warehouse, each cask must be stamped with what is termed the distillery warehouse stamp, which stamp must contain, among other things, the name of the distiller and the serial number of the cask. With these provisions of the law in force, it would have been obviously impracticable for Conrad to attempt to hold himself out to the public as the distiller of whiskey distilled by someone else, unless he could in some way contrive to have his own name stamped upon the barrels by the officer of the government under the provisions of this law.

It therefore became necessary, in order to maintain before the public the simulation of C. Conrad & Co. being the distillers, that the government should in some sense recognize the fact that the distillery was the distillery of C. Conrad & Co., and the further fact that the warehouse was the warehouse of C. Conrad & Co. Accordingly, the Silver Creek Distilling Company, by whose agency Stagg, Hume & Co. executed the contract, gave the statutory notice to the collector that they proposed to manufacture a certain quantity of whiskey in their distillery at Silver Creek, Kentucky, "doing business as C. Conrad & Co.;" that is to say, for a purpose of their own, the Silver Creek Distilling Company proposed, while manufacturing this whiskey at this distillery, to change their names and take the name of C. Conrad & Co., and the officers of the government, rightly or wrongly, were willing that they should do this.

Touching this matter, the plaintiffs have argued that, under the Federal Statutes, the firm name of C. Conrad & Co. could not be legally used as distillers, nor could the whiskey be lawfully branded with the name of that firm as distillers, nor could any other name be lawfully entered upon the stamps of that of the distiller without actually running the distillery for them and altogether in their name—by which we understand them to mean that, whereas the distillery could not thus be lawfully run in the name of C. Conrad & Co. without their being the distillers, therefore they must have been the distillers. But we confess we cannot understand the force of this reasoning. It seems to us that this is equivalent to saying that whereas a man cannot lawfully do wrong in a given particular, yet if he had done wrong in that particular, therefore he has done right. Whether the distillery could lawfully be run in the peculiar manner in which this distillery was run, is a question between those who so ran it and the government of the United States, with which question we are not concerned. We allude to this merely because it is a branch of a similar line of argument upon which much contention of the plaintiffs rests; and it is just to their learned counsel to say that he seems finally to have abandoned it.

In order to carry out the peculiar provision of this contract by which C. Conrad & Co. should be held out as the distillers of this whiskey, without being in fact the distillers, it was of course necessary to keep up the simulation, in the face of the revenue officers, of C. Conrad & Co. being the distillers. With this end obviously in view, and with no other end in view, as the trial court was at liberty to find,—for any other end in view would contradict the contract and hence be absurd,—the firm name of C. Conrad & Co. was put above the door of the warehouse, and it frequently happened that, when correspondence took place between C. Conrad & Co. at St. Louis and the parties of the first part in this contract at Silver Creek, the letters were addressed by C. Conrad & Co. at St. Louis to C. Conrad & Co. at Silver Creek; and the replies to such letters, generally written by Mr. Embry, the secretary of the Silver Creek Distilling Company, were in like manner signed C. Conrad & Co., though sometimes such letters were addressed to Mr. Embry in his own name and replied to by him in his own name. The parties of the first part to this contract, under the contract the distillers of this whiskey, the vendors acting through the Silver Creek Distilling Company as their agents, or they being the agents of the Silver Creek Distilling Company, it matters little which,—for in either case there was a substantial identity between the parties,—were willing to call themselves C. Conrad & Co. and to be so called themselves. In these letters C. Conrad & Co., writing from St. Louis, would sometimes speak of the warehouse as *our* warehouse, and whoever would reply to the letters from Silver Creek would speak of the warehouse as *your* warehouse.

As has already been stated, the record contains much evidence of a course of dealing in reference to the manufacture of whiskey for Conrad, between him and the two firms which were predecessors in business at Silver Creek, Kentucky, of the firm of Stagg, Hume & Co., the party of the first part to the contract now under consideration, by which the whiskey now in controversy was made. This course of dealing took place under contracts similar in their terms to the present contract, and was a similar course of dealing to that which took place under the present contract. We mention this fact because great stress has been laid upon it in the able argument which has been made at the bar and submitted to us in print by the counsel for the plaintiffs. We do not perceive what precise bearing it has on the questions which we are to consider. It could at most be relevant as bearing upon the inferences of fact which the judge of the trial court, sitting as a jury, might be authorized to draw. But it is to be observed in this connection that the rights of the parties are to be governed by the written contract which they have made, and that a prior course of dealing, especially between one of the parties and other parties, cannot, on any principle with which we are acquainted, be appealed to as affording an interpretation of this contract—and more especially so as this contract is drawn in such distinct terms as to leave no ambiguities for parol explanation. Evidence of a course of dealing under this contract between the parties to it stands on a different footing, since it is competent for the parties to a contract to vary its terms by a subsequent course of dealing.

There is evidence tending to show that its terms were varied, or at least supplemented, in one important particular. It nowhere confers upon C. Conrad & Co. the power to issue warehouse receipts in respect to the whiskey while remaining in the bonded warehouse at Silver Creek. And yet the evidence shows that he did issue such warehouse receipts, that some of them were returned to Silver Creek, and that deliveries of whiskey were made upon them. The evidence in regard to his authority to issue these warehouse receipts is contradictory. The evidence in behalf of the plaintiffs tends to show that Conrad had acquired general authority from Stagg, Hume & Co. to issue warehouse receipts for whiskey in the warehouse at Silver Creek; the evidence of the defendants, on the other hand, tends to show that this authority was limited by the provision that the warehouse receipts should be returned to Silver Creek to be there registered—in other words, that Stagg, Hume & Co., or the Silver Creek Distilling Company, at Silver Creek, should have some sort of control over the matter. Conrad reported the issue of some of these warehouse receipts, by letters addressed to Embry, in "care of C. Conrad & Co.," at Silver Creek, and received replies thereto, signed by Embry, who was at the time the secretary of the Silver Creek Distilling Company.

The whiskey in controversy, when made, was deposited in the bonded warehouse number 541, at Silver Creek, in the name of C. Conrad & Co., in pursuance of the Internal Revenue Statutes, the entry in the warehouse being made by the corporation as "The Silver Creek Distilling Company, doing business as C. Conrad & Co." The warehouse bonds were in like manner given by "The Silver Creek Distilling Company, a corporation organized under the laws of the State of Kentucky, doing business as C. Conrad & Co." These bonds were conditioned for the payment of taxes to the federal government. The whiskey was afterwards invoiced to C. Conrad & Co., of St. Louis, and was settled for by notes in pursuance of the contract. The whiskey was in this condition when, on the 9th of January, 1883, Mr. Conrad, at St. Louis, acting under the name and style of C. Conrad & Co., issued the warehouse receipts already spoken of, under which C. Conrad & Co. purported to have received, into their bonded warehouse at Silver Creek, two hundred and seventy-five barrels of whiskey for Paulina Vogelsang, fifty barrels for Elly Conrad, fifty barrels for Helena Paulsen and forty barrels for Mr. Schloeter. Mrs. Vogelsang was the mother-in-law of Conrad; Elly Conrad was his sister-in-law; Helena Paulsen was his mother-in-law's sister; and Schloeter had formerly been his porter. His evidence tends to show that he was indebted to them in various sums, exclusive of interest, which debts had been of long standing and without security. Without any solicitation whatever upon the part of any of these creditors, he handed to them respectively t... papers purporting to be warehouse receipts, together with bills of parcels and copies of gaugers' certificates, as collateral security for the debts which he owed them respectively. He asked no concessions whatever from them on handing them these papers, and they made no concessions to him whatever.

It should be here stated that the evidence requires us to lay out of view any conception or conjecture that this was a conveyance designed by Conrad to hinder, delay or defraud his creditors; for though the preference of relatives as creditors for alleged past-due indebtedness is one of the common features of business failures, —so much as to require that such preferences should receive careful scrutiny at the hands of triers of the facts,—yet it is to be observed that there is no evidence in this case tending to show that these debts were not bona fide debts, or to take the case out of the ordinary case of a debtor in failing circumstances endeavoring to use his property to prefer some of his creditors. We wish to get the idea out of the way that we proceed upon any conception—the least possible—of these conveyances being simulated, or of their being made to the use of Conrad, and to make it clear that we deal with the rights of the plaintiffs precisely as we would deal with those rights if they were bankers whom Conrad had desired to secure for previous advances, made to him under circumstances which, in his view, rendered it obligatory upon him to secure them at the expense of other creditors. No fraud, either in fact or law, is imputable to the plaintiffs, nor is any imputable to Conrad, unless it be found in an unauthorized use of the authority which had been conferred on him to issue warehouse receipts—of which we shall speak further on.

In this connection it may be best to state, so far as they have not already been stated, the provisions of the Revised Statutes of the United States touching the custody of distilled spirits in bond before the taxes have been paid. The whiskey, removed, as already stated, to the bonded warehouse, must, within the first five days of the next succeeding month, be entered for deposit in the warehouse by the distiller or owner; and the distiller or owner must give bond for the payment, within the next three years, of the taxes due thereon. U. S. Rev. Stat. Sup. p. 530, § 4.

It is also provided that the warehouse shall be provided by the distiller at his own expense, shall be situated on and shall constitute a part of the distillery premises and shall be under the direction and control of the collector for the district, and in charge of an internal revenue store-keeper assigned thereto by the commissioner of internal revenue. U. S. Rev. Stat. §§ 3271, 3273.

There is the further provision that it shall be in the joint custody of the store-keeper and the proprietor, but that it shall not be unlocked or remain open except in the presence of the store-keeper, and that no article shall be received into it, or delivered from it, by the store-keeper, except on the order of the collector. Id. § 3274.

This last provision is supplemented by a regulation of the internal revenue department, as follows: "Whenever any person is allowed access to the distillery warehouse, it must be done under the immediate supervision of the store-keeper. The distiller, or his employés, may be allowed access to the warehouse for the purpose of examining the spirits, repairing the cooperage, or changing the packages to prevent waste." If the commissioner of internal revenue deems the warehouse unsafe, he may require the whiskey stored therein to be removed, under the direction of the collector, to such warehouse as he may designate, and may have it sold if the owner fails to have the removal made. Id. § 3272.

It is further provided that, when the owner shall desire to withdraw the whiskey from the warehouse, he may file with the collector notice thereof, describing the whiskey, and requesting that it be re gauged. U. S. Rev. Stat. Sup. p. 534, § 17.

A "withdrawal entry" must then be made, stating the date of entry into the warehouse and by whom made, together with other matters of description; and thereon, upon the payment of the tax, the collector must issue his order to the store-keeper in charge of the warehouse for the delivery of the whiskey. U. S. Rev. Stat. § 3294.

Thereupon the whiskey is re-gauged, and the cask is branded with the name of the distiller and stamped with the tax-paid stamp. U. S. Rev. Stat. § 3295.

Thereafter it shall not be stored nor shall it be allowed to remain on the distillery premises. Id. § 3288.

There is also a provision for the withdrawal of distilled spirits from the warehouse by the owner for exportation, without the payment of taxes. Id. § 3330.

Upon the foregoing facts the trial court has held that Stagg, Hume & Co., at the time when Conrad delivered the warehouse receipts to the plaintiffs, had such a possession of the whiskey as entitled them to a vendor's lien. The question now to be considered is, whether the facts admit of such an interpretation—not whether they do not admit of a contrary interpretation. For it is to be observed that where the facts are numerous and equivocal—susceptible of different inferences in respect of the question What was the real intent of the parties?—the question whether there has been such a delivery as devests the vendor's lien, or puts an end to the right of stoppage *in transitu*, is a question of fact for a jury. *Chandler* v. *Fulton*, 10 Tex. 2, 60 Am. Dec. 188; *Michigan Cent. R. Co.* v. *Phillips*, 60 Ill. 190, 193.

On the analogous question, whether there has been such a delivery as will pass title and make an executed sale, the rule is the same. "Where the law can pronounce, upon a state of facts, that there is or is not, a delivery and acceptance, it is a question of law to be decided by the court. But where there may be uncertainty and difficulty in determining the true intent of the parties respecting the delivery and acceptance from the facts proved, the question of acceptance is to be decided by the jury." *Houdlette* v. *Tallman*, 14 Me. 400; *Glass* v. *Gelvin*, 80 Mo. 297, 300.

More briefly, it is said: "When there is no dispute as to the facts, it is a question of law; when the evidence is conflicting, the jury must decide." *Glass* v. *Gelvin, supra; Hatch* v. *Bayley*, 10 Cush. 29.

In the case before us the facts were very numerous, and on some points the evidence was conflicting. Interpreted in the light of the contract alone, they become comparatively simple. Interpreted independently of the contract, the inferences to be drawn from them are exceedingly doubtful. So far as they were properly susceptible of interpretation, independently of the contract, the inferences to be drawn from them were inferences of fact which addressed themselves to the judgment of the circuit judge, who tried the case, sitting as a jury. We cannot revise his conclusions of fact on this appeal, unless we see, from his rulings upon the instructions, that he was mistaken in respect of the inferences of law to be deduced from certain facts. Here, as elsewhere, where the law characterizes a fact or a state of facts in a given way, if it appears from the record that the trial judge has characterized such fact or state of facts in a different way, it is within our office to review and correct his decision; but we have no control over his conclusions in respect of mere inferences of fact, provided they are fairly within the scope of the evidence. We shall take up, then, the leading incidents of fact which the evidence tends to show, and inquire whether the learned judge drew from them in any instance a conclusion contrary to that imputed by the law.

It may make our views clearer if, before proceeding to do this, we state some of the established and leading incidents of a vendor's lien. To begin, it should be observed that the existence of a vendor's lien always presupposes that the title to the goods has passed to the vendee; since it would be an incongruous conception that a vendor might have a lien upon his own goods. In this case, the question of title is entirely out of the contest. The defense of a vendor's lien in Stagg, Hume & Co. concedes that the title to the goods had passed to Conrad.

It is next to be observed that a vendor's lien is in no sense a right of rescission. On the contrary, it proceeds in affirmation of the contract, and as a means of its enforcement. It is in the nature of a pledge raised or created by the law, upon the happening of the insolvency of the vendee, to secure the unpaid purchase money to the vendor. It is a mere right of detention and sale, to satisfy the unpaid purchase money. At the outset, in every sale, where the contrary is not stipulated, the implication of law is that the purchase price is to be paid, as a condition precedent, before the vendor shall be obliged to part with his goods. *Bloxam* v. *Sanders*, 4 Barn. & C. 941, 948; *Michigan Cent. R. Co.* v. *Phillips*, 60 Ill. 190, 198; *Arnold* v. *Delano*, 4 Cush. 33, 38.

But this right to retain the goods until the purchase money is paid is waived by any stipulations in the contract of sale which are inconsistent with its exercise. *Pickett* v. *Bullock*, 52 N. H. 354.

It is waived by giving time for payment, and especially by taking a bill or note to secure the payment of the purchase price. *Chambers* v. *Davidson*, L. R. 1 P. C. 305, 4 Moore, P. C. N. S. 158; *Spartali* v. *Benecke*, 10 C. B. 212; *Dixon* v. *Yates*, 5 Barn. & Ad. 313; *Arnold* v. *Delano*, 4 Cush. 33, 39; *Throop* v. *Hart*, 7 Duvall, 512, 521.

But this waiver is said to take place upon the implied condition that the vendee will keep his credit good until the term of the credit shall have expired. *Arnold* v. *Delano*, *supra*; *Thompson* v. *Baltimore & O. R. Co.* 28 Md. 396, 406.

If, therefore, the purchaser becomes insolvent before the goods are delivered, the lien at once revives. *Dixon* v. *Yates*, 5 Barn. & Ad. 313, 341; *Arnold* v. *Delano* and *Throop* v. *Hart*, *supra*.

Although there is some controversy as to the nature of the insolvency which will revive this right, yet it is agreed on all hands that an insolvency in the mercantile sense—an inability to pay one's debts as fast as they mature, evidenced by a stoppage of payment, an assignment for the benefit of creditors, a petition in bankruptcy, or the like—is sufficient. Such an insolvency indisputably supervened in this case before Stagg, Hume & Co. undertook, by levying attachments on the goods, to exercise their supposed right of lien.

There is a controversy in this case in respect of the general theory of the law as to the nature of the delivery which will devest the vendor's lien. The contention of the plaintiffs is that such a delivery, actual or constructive, as would amount to an "actual receipt" of the goods, within the meaning of the seventeenth section of the English Statute of Frauds, will in all cases operate to devest the lien of the vendor. This position is undeniably logical; but the cases in which this statement of doctrine is found are nearly all cases in which the question in judgment was the Statute of Frauds, and not the vendor's lien. It would hence be extremely hazardous to rest our judgment upon what judges, however eminent, have said in cases where they were not considering the question which we are considering. Besides, a little examination will show that this contention is not a sound one. The single case of stoppage *in transitu* proves this. By all the authorities, when a carrier receives goods from a vendor for shipment to the vendee, there has been such an actual receipt as satisfies the Statute of Frauds; and by all the authorities there has not been such a delivery as puts an end to the right of stoppage *in transitu*. If it is answered that the right of stoppage *in transitu* is one thing, and that the vendor's lien is another thing, it is only necessary to appeal to the judicial reports to show that the two are universally regarded as the same right exercised under different circumstances. The right of stoppage *in transitu* is said to be a mere extension of the vendor's lien. *Babcock* v. *Bonnell*, 80 N. Y. 244; *Newhall* v. *Vargas*, 15 Me. 319; *Mohr* v. *Boston & A. R. Co.* 106 Mass. 67, 70; *White* v. *Welsh*, 38 Pa. 396, 420; *Loeb* v. *Peters*, 63 Ala. 243, 35 Am. Rep. 17, 19; *Newhall* v. *Central Pac. R. Co.* 51 Cal. 345, 21 Am. Rep. 713; *Rowley* v. *Bigelow*, 12 Pick. 307, 313; *Benedict* v. *Schaettle*, 12 Ohio St. 515, 521; *Schwabacher* v. *Kane*, 13 Mo. App. 126, 129.

It is simply the right which the law accords to the unpaid vendor, upon the happening of the insolvency of the vendee, to resume his possession and with it his vendor's lien; and when his possession is resumed his rights are worked out by a sale of the goods on notice, and an application of the proceeds to the payment of the purchase price, precisely as in the case of the vendor's lien. *Bloxam* v. *Sanders*, 4 Barn. & C. 941; *Boorman* v. *Nash*, 9 Barn. & C. 145; *Newhall* v. *Vargas*, 15 Me. 341.

It follows from this statement, that, where the right of stoppage *in transitu* exists, the vendor's lien, *a fortiori*, exists. In other words, if there has been such a delivery, before the goods are started on their voyage, as cuts off the vendor's lien, there is no *transitus*, in the sense which supports the right of stoppage *in transitu*.

In view of these and other considerations, eminent judges have denied the proposition that the test, whether there has been a delivery to satisfy the Statute of Frauds, is a safe test of the non-existence of the vendor's lien. Robinson, *Ch. J.*, in *Wegg* v. *Drake*, 16 U. C. Q. B. 252; Miller, *J.*, in *Thompson* v. *Baltimore O. R. Co.* 28 Md. 396, 407; *Townsend* v. *Hargraves*, 118 Mass. 325, 333.

It has been held, on the most obvious grounds, that if a seller of merchandise, in order to maintain his lien for the price, refuses to permit the purchaser to take possession of it, but keeps it in his own personal custody, he thereby prevents an acceptance and receipt of it by the purchaser, such as is necessary to satisfy the Statute of Frauds. *Safford* v. *McDonough*, 120 Mass. 290.

This is in accordance with what was said by Holroyd, *J.*, that, "as long as the seller preserves his control over the goods, so as to retain his lien, he prevents the vendee from accepting and receiving them as his own, within the meaning of the Statute,"—meaning the Statute of Frauds. *Baldey* v. *Parker*, 2 Barn. & C. 37, 44.

This need not be disputed, because the converse of the proposition is not necessarily true. On the other hand, there are decisions which affirm that there may be an acceptance which satisfies the Statute of Frauds in the case of a parol sale, and yet which does not even pass the title to the vendee. *Pinkam* v. *Mattox*, 53 N. H. 600; *Dodsley* v. *Varley*, 12 Ad. & El. 632.

So there may be a delivery such as puts an end to the right of stoppage *in transitu*, and yet no acceptance and receipt such as satisfies the Statute of Frauds. *Smith* v. *Hudson*, 6 Best & S. 431, 445.

From the language of the Statute of Frauds it will be perceived that there must not only be an actual receipt of the goods, but there must also be an acceptance. This draws the question into the domain of intent; and the most cursory reading of the cases will show that the courts regard the question, whether there has been such an acceptance and actual receipt as satisfies the Statute of Frauds, as largely a question of intent. But the existence of the vendor's lien is not in an equal sense a question of intent; because, when a sale is made and executed, so as to pass title to the vendee, the vendor never intends to detain the goods, except in those cases where to do so is in accordance with the course of business which subsists between the parties (of which the books afford some instances), or unless such is the actual agreement; but in nearly all cases the intent is that the title shall pass, and that the vendee shall take the goods at his pleasure, and the corresponding expectation is that he will pay for them according to the terms of the contract. The vendor's lien is thus raised, not in pursuance of the intent of the parties, but by implication of law, in a state of things which the vendor, and presumptively the vendee, never intended nor expected. It is quite clear, therefore, that we cannot regard the test of delivery to satisfy the Statute of Frauds as a safe test by which to determine the existence or non-existence of the vendor's lien.

On the contrary, we affirm that, as between the vendor and vendee, laying out of view the rights of subsequent purchasers from the vendee, the vendor's lien is not devested by any species of constructive delivery, so long as he retains the actual custody of the goods, either by himself or by his own agent or servant.

This doctrine is supported by the best English and American adjudications. In 1877, it was said by *Sir* Barnes Peacock, in giving the judgment of the English privy council, "to be clearly settled, that unless actual possession has been delivered to the purchaser, the vendor is not deprived of his right of lien as against the assignees of the purchaser in the event of his insolvency." *Grice* v. *Richardson*, 3 App. Cas. 319, 323.

"There is," said Shaw, *Ch. J.*, "manifestly a marked distinction between those cases which, as between the vendor and vendee upon a contract of sale, go to make a constructive delivery and to vest the property in the vendee, and that actual delivery by the vendor to the vendee which puts an end to the right of the vendor to hold the goods as security for the price." *Arnold* v. *Delano*, 4 Cush. 33, 38, quoted with approval in *Thompson* v. *Baltimore & O. R. Co.* 28 Md. 396, 406.

To the same effect is *Newhall* v. *Vargas*, 15 Me. 314, 319.

"The lien of the vendor," says Miller, *J.*, "always exists until he voluntarily and utterly resigns the possession of the goods sold, and all right to detain them. So long as the vendor does not surrender actual possession, his lien remains, although he may have performed acts which amount to a constructive delivery, so as to pass the title or avoid the Statute,"—meaning the Statute of Frauds. *Thompson* v. *Baltimore & O. R. Co.* 28 Md. 396, 407.

Speaking upon the same subject, it was said in a later Massachusetts case by *Mr. Justice* Wells: "Regarding the sale and order for delivery as sufficient to make it effectual to pass title as between the parties, still until actual and full delivery, the seller is not deprived of his right to insist upon his lien for the price. Delivery to a carrier for transportation to the purchaser is sufficient to pass the title, and authorize the carrier to complete the delivery and make it absolute. But until so made absolute, the seller may revoke his authority and thus intercept the transmission, restore himself to possession and retain his lien. The same principle applies in all cases of inchoate delivery, or whatever mode of transmission of possession. Until the delivery is actual and absolute, the seller may suspend it and revoke the authority of any intermediary to perfect it." *Keeler* v. *Goodwin*, 111 Mass. 490, 492.

"The rule," said Lowrie, *J.*, "is that, so long as the vendor has actual possession of the goods, or as they are in the custody of his agents, and while they are in transit from him to the vendee, he has the right to refuse or countermand the final delivery, if the vendee be in failing circumstances." It was therefore held that the rejection of evidence tending to show a constructive delivery under a contract of sale was unimportant, where the goods had not been removed after the sale, but continued in the stores and custody of the vendor until the published insolvency of the vendee. *White* v. *Welsh*, 38 Pa. 396, 420.

Even where the goods were ponderous and lay by the road-side, and an agent of the vendor had pointed them out to the agent of the vendee for the purpose of delivery to him, and a minute of the transaction had been entered in the books of the vendor, charging the goods to the vendee,—it was held that this, although a complete delivery to transfer title to the vendee, did not cut off the vendor's lien upon the happening of the insolvency of the vendee, the goods remaining in the same position as when thus pointed out. *Thompson* v. *Baltimore & O. R. Co.* 28 Md. 896, 404.

So, the delivery of a bill of lading, warehouse receipt, bought-and-sold note, delivery order, sale ticket, carrier's receipt or any other writing intended by the parties or made by commercial usage a symbol of the goods themselves, passes constructive possession to the vendee; and yet nothing is more clear than that, as between the vendor and vendee themselves, and in many cases as between the vendor and a sub-vendee, the latter being a bona fide purchaser for a valuable consideration, such symbolical delivery does not devest the vendor's lien, provided the vendor remain in actual custody of the goods. Thus, where the goods are delivered to a carrier by the vendor for shipment to the vendee, the vendor, in the ordinary course of business, transmits the bill of lading to the vendee; but this, on the most familiar grounds, does not cut off the vendor's right of stoppage *in transitu*. In support of this statement of doctrine, we need not go further than refer to the decision of our supreme court, holding that where a sale is not made upon credit, although the goods contracted for have been set apart and identified in the storehouse of the vendor, and although they have been sold by the vendee to a sub-vendee, and a delivery order for them, given by the vendee to the sub-vendee, on the vendor, has been presented by the sub-vendee to the original vendor, and has been by him accepted in writing,—yet, if the original vendee becomes insolvent, leaving the purchase price unpaid, before the original vendor has actually parted with the goods, he may still exercise his right of lien upon them, notwithstanding the rights of the sub-vendee. In such case, the sub-vendee acquires no greater rights than his vendor, the original vendee. *Southwestern F. & C. Exp. Co.* v. *Plant*, 45 Mo. 517, denying *Whitehouse* v. *Frost*, 12 East, 614, reaffirming *Southwestern Freight Co.* v. *Stanard*, 44 Mo. 71, citing and approving *Miles* v. *Gorton*, 2 Cromp. & M. 504, and *Tanner* v. *Scovell*, 14 Mees. & W. 28.

The terms of the sale, it is true, contemplated a cash payment, and this, as already pointed out, was a condition precedent to the right of the vendee to take the goods. But there can be no distinction in principle between the kind of possession which will support the vendor's lien before it is waived, and the kind of possession which will support it after it has revived.

Let us next apply these principles to the salient facts of the present case, and look more closely to see how the judicial decisions have characterized those facts.

The contract already set out required the whiskey to be invoiced, when made, to C. Conrad & Co.; and this, as already stated, was accordingly done. But it has been held that the lien of the vendor is not destroyed by invoicing the goods to the purchaser. *Miles* v. *Gorton*, *supra*; *Dixon* v. *Yates*, 5 Barn. & Ad. 313.

The Superior Court of the City of New York —a court, it may be stated, which has always stood high upon commercial questions,—has gone further than this, and has held, in an able and well-considered opinion by Charles F. Daly, *J.*, that the delivery of a bill of parcels of the goods sold by the vendor to the vendee does not affect the vendor's lien as to so much of the goods as remain in his possession, even as against a sub-vendee. *Hamburger* v. *Rodman*, 9 Daly, 93.

The court was so well assured of the grounds upon which it decided this case that it refused to grant an appeal from its decision. We may therefore dismiss from further view the fact that the goods were invoiced to Conrad, and that bills of parcels, with gaugers' certificates, were delivered to him.

This contract also required the goods to be marked with the name of C. Conrad & Co. as distillers, the brands to be furnished by Stagg, Hume & Co.; and the barrels were so branded. But it has been held, where the subject of the sale was rum in puncheons, which lay in the warehouse of a third person, where they had been deposited by the original vendor, that the act of a sub-vendee, with the consent of the warehouseman, in marking the initials of the sub-vendee upon them, in gauging them, and even in coopering them, did not amount to a taking possession such as devested the original vendor's lien,—though it was conceded that taking samples and coopering were circumstances from which a jury might infer an actual delivery of the whole. *Dixon* v. *Yates*, *supra*.

This contract provided that the goods should be stored in United States Warehouse No. 541, of the Eastern District of Kentucky, and that storage should be charged at the rate of five cents per barrel per month from the date of entry; that is, that storage should be charged by Stagg, Hume & Co. against C. Conrad & Co. But while there is some discredited authority—all of it more than fifty years old—to the effect that the vendor's lien is discharged so that it will not revive on the insolvency of the vendee, by his agreeing to hold the goods as warehouseman for the vendee (*Hurry* v. *Mangles*, 1 Camp. 452; *Barrett* v. *Goddard*, 3 Mason, 107; *Chapman* v. *Searle*, 3 Pick. 38), yet the more recent and better view is that the vendor's lien is not destroyed by an agreement between the vendor and the vendee, that the goods shall remain in the warehouse of the vendor, subject to the payment of warehouse rent by the vendee. *Grice* v. *Richardson*, 3 App. Cas. 319; *Miles* v. *Gorton*, 2 Cromp. & M. 504, 4 Tyrwh. 295.

So it has been held that, where a part of the goods are taken away by the vendee, and warehouse rent paid in respect of such part, this will not prevent the exercise of the right of the vendor's lien upon the remainder. In such a case, it was ruled that the charge of warehouse rent by the vendor did not constitute such a delivery as to devest his lien. *Winks* v. *Hassell*, 9 Barn. & C. 378. See also *Bloxam* v. *Sanders*, 4 Barn. & C. 941.

This is somewhat analogous to a ruling of our supreme court under the Statute of Frauds, where a contract was made for the sale of cattle in the field of the vendor. The purchaser told the vendor to keep the cattle and feed them at the purchaser's expense until he should send for them. This the vendor agreed to do, but upon the condition that if any of them died the purchaser should bear the loss, to which the purchaser assented. It was held that this was no delivery to take the contract out of the Statute of Frauds. *Kirby* v. *Johnson*, 22 Mo. 354.

Nor in such a case will the fact that the vendor gives to the vendee a delivery order, reciting that the vendor holds the goods to the order of the vendee rent free, until a date named, be such a delivery as to devest the vendor's lien. *Townley* v. *Crump*, 4 Ad. & El. 58.

Concerning the decisions which assert the opposing view, it should be said that the earliest of them, *Hurry* v. *Mangles*, 1 Camp. 452, was a *nisi prius* decision of Lord Ellenborough; and it need scarcely be said that a *nisi prius* decision by a judge, however eminent, must have little weight, where the same question has been subsequently ruled otherwise in the same jurisdiction by a court *in banc*. The second of those cases, *Barrett* v. *Goddard*, *supra*, was likewise a *nisi prius* decision of *Mr Justice* Story at circuit. That judge was an eminent commentator, more noted for the exuberance of his learning than for the soundness of his judgment or the accuracy of his statement. His opinion in the case referred to is a singular confusion of the three subjects of delivery to pass title as between vendor and vendee at common law; of delivery to satisfy the Statute of Frauds, and of delivery to devest the vendor's lien or cut off the right of stoppage *in transitu*. It was denied in England, in *Townley* v. *Crump*, *supra*. It was severally criticised in Pennsylvania by Lowrie, *Ch. J.*, in *White* v. *Welsh*, 38 Pa. 396, 421. It was denied in the New York Court of Common Pleas, in *Hamburger* v. *Rodman*, 9 Daly, 93, 98: and it was finally denied in the same circuit where it was pronounced, on the authority of *Arnold* v. *Delano*, 4 Cush. 33,—*Mr. District Judge* Lowell saying: "I take the modern doctrine to be that, if the buyer stops payment before the seller has actually parted with possession, though after he has parted with his title, if no rights of innocent third persons have intervened, his lien revives." *Parker* v. *Byrnes*, 1 Lowell, 539, 540.

The third case, *Chapman* v. *Searle*, 3 Pick. 38, though not overruled in terms, has been overruled in principle, by the subsequent case of *Arnold* v. *Delano*, 4 Cush. 33, and by subsequent cases in the same jurisdiction, which assert that the vendor's lien is not gone so long as he retains actual possession.

In determining whether a contract of sale has been executed so as to pass title to the goods, or whether there has been a delivery such as satisfies the Statute of Frauds, the courts frequently appeal to a principle thus stated by Mr. Chitty: "Although the contract for a sale of goods be complete and binding in other respects, the property in them remains in the vendor and at his risk, if a material fact remains to be done before the delivery, either to distinguish the goods, or ascertain the price thereof." Chitty, Cont. 375, as quoted in *Southwestern F. & C. Press Co.* v. *Stanard*, 44 Mo. 71, 83.

But this is not a conclusive inference. It is rather in the nature of a prima facie presumption, which may be rebutted by circumstances. For instance, the title may pass, although marking, weighing or measuring is thereafter to be performed in order to ascertain the amount to be paid. *Ober* v. *Carson*, 62 Mo. 209, 218; *Thompson* v. *Baltimore & O. R. Co.* 28 Md. 396, 404; *Southwestern F. & C. Press Co.* v. *Stanard*, *supra*.

"Presumptively," says Cooley, *Ch. J.*, "the title does not pass, even though the articles be designated, so long as anything remains to be done to determine the sum to be paid; but this is only a presumption, and is liable to be overcome by such facts and circumstances as indicate an intent in the parties to the contrary." *Byles* v. *Colier*, 54 Mich. 1, 5.

Moreover, the case where such a presumption arises is to be distinguished from the case where there has been such a delivery as would authorize a jury to find that the parties intended that title should pass, and yet where the goods were left in the hands of the vendor to be the subject of some further treatment,—as where a piano sold to the vendee was left in the vendor's shop to be finished in a certain way. *Thorndyke* v. *Bath*, 114 Mass. 116.

By analogy, the courts have appealed to a similar principle for the purpose of determining whether there has been such an actual delivery as cuts off the right of stoppage *in transitu*, or devests the vendor of his lien. Thus, a broker effected a sale of thirty tons of rosin, and notified his principal as follows: "I have this day sold to David Bromer thirty tons of London-made rosin, more or less, at 13s. per cwt., lying in mats at the wharf of Lys & Co., payment by a bill at six months,"—signed by the broker. Still later the plaintiffs (the vendors) sent an order to the wharfingers to weigh and deliver the rosin, upon which the latter gave notice to the vendee that they had received such order from the vendors. Shortly afterwards the vendee became insolvent, and, the rosin still lying at the wharf, the vendors gave the wharfinger notice not to deliver it. It was held that the property had not vested in the vendee, the decision proceeding upon the principle "that the order sent by the vendor to the wharfinger to deliver the goods is sufficient to pass title to the vendee, provided nothing remains to be done but to make the delivery. If it be necessary by the terms of the contract, or by the order to the wharfinger, that anything should be done previous to the delivery, the transfer is not complete till that thing be done. It is impossible to say, in the present case, that something was not to be done. The order was to weigh and deliver; that act, therefore, which was to precede delivery, not having taken place, the property did not pass to Bromer." *Withers* v. *Lys*, 1 Holt. N. P. 18, opinion by Gibbs, *Ch. J.*

It is perceived that, although the judge who decided this case placed his decision upon the ground that the right of property had not passed, the same reasons would have resulted in the conclusion that the vendor had not parted with his possession in a manner so entire as to cut off his lien.

A case was found in one of the legal periodicals where this principle was directly applied in solving the question whether a vendor had lost his right of lien. The decision was made by three referees, all of them eminent in the legal profession. *Hon.* William F. Allen, subsequently a judge of the New York Court of Appeals; *Hon.* Joseph F. Bosworth, subsequently a judge of the Superior Court of the City of New York; and *Hon.* Theodore W. Dwight, president of the law faculty of Columbia College, and some time a judge of the New York Commission of Appeals. These referees delivered an opinion of exceptional ability, in which, on the facts before them, they resolved that the following propositions were established by the authorities: "Where the goods, at the time the contract of sale is made, though in the legal custody and control, are not in the actual possession, of the vendor, but are so situated that the purchaser cannot obtain actual possession until a specific act is done by the vendor, if the vendee becomes insolvent before this act has been done, and the actual possession of the goods has not been changed, the vendor may detain the goods as security for the payment of the contract price, and, as a consequence, will not be compelled by a court of equity to perform the act in question. The right of detention, in case of the intervening insolvency of the vendee, may be exercised by the vendor so long as the vendee has neither obtained actual possession, nor been furnished by the vendor with the exclusive means and power of controlling the possession." *Gill* v. *Pavenstedt*, 7 Am. Law Reg. N. S. 672, 676.

The facts in this case sustain a considerable analogy to the facts of the case now before us. A had purchased a quantity of teas from B. The goods were placed in the bonded warehouse of a third person, and were there entered in the name of B, the vendor. The sale was upon a credit, at a specified price, and the duties were to be paid by the vendee as a part of the price. He had withdrawn, by permission of the vendor, portions of the goods at different times, paying the duties on such portions. Before the credit expired, the vendor gave to him an order on the bonded warehouse, directing the latter to transfer the residue of the goods to the name of the vendee, which was accordingly done. But, as between the parties and the government, the goods still remained in the name of the vendor, and could not be withdrawn from the warehouse under the regulations of the Treasury Department, except by what is termed a "withdrawal entry" signed by the vendor, or by someone authorized by him in writing. While the goods were in this condition, the vendee became insolvent. After his insolvency, he demanded that the vendor should sign the necessary withdrawal entry, which the latter refused to do, except upon full payment of the price. It was held that an act, to wit, the signing of the withdrawal entry by the vendor, remained to be done, as between himself and the vendee, which was of such a nature that there was no delivery, either actual or constructive, and that the vendor's lien for the unpaid purchase money subsisted. *Gill* v. *Pavenstedt, supra.*

We assume that, under the Internal Revenue Statutes above set out, the withdrawal entry, in the case before us, could only be made by the distilling company in whose name the deposit entry was made; and this, as already shown, was—not C. Conrad & Co., simply, but "The Silver Creek Distilling Company, doing business as C. Conrad & Co."

In a case still more like the present, which turned upon this principle, certain distilled whiskey was stored in a government warehouse in Terre Haute, under the provisions of the Internal Revenue Laws, in the name of the vendor, who paid the insurance thereon, and who sold the whiskey, so stored, to the vendee on a credit, and caused it to be inspected and gauged, as is required by the Internal Revenue Laws; whereupon the government store keeper certified that the whiskey was in the store-house, "Mr. Edward Dewey, of Boston (the vendee) being the owner of said whiskey, as *per* Messrs. Mohr & Solomon's (the vendor's) order." It was a part of the contract of sale that the vendor should, from time to time as the vendee should request, ship the goods from the bonded warehouse and pay the warehouse charges, taxes, stamps and insurance, drawing on the vendee at ten days' sight for the amounts so paid. Down to this point, it is perceived that the whiskey was similarly situated to the whiskey in the case before us. It was, as here, in a government warehouse. The title, as here, had been transferred from the vendor to the vendee. The government warehouseman had attorned, so to speak, to the vendee, by issuing the certificates recognizing the vendee as the owner; and yet it was held that, drafts drawn against a shipment of the whiskey having been protested, these facts did not determine the vendor's right of stoppage *in transitu*, but that the vendor might stop them and maintain replevin for them while they were yet in the hands of the carrier in Boston. The court, speaking through *Mr. Justice* Morton, said: "Something remained to be done by the vendors under the contract of sale, before the goods would come into the possession of the vendee at the place of destination. The contract contemplated that they were to forward them to Boston. If the goods had been and remained in their actual possession as vendors until they forwarded them, on the order of Dewey, their right of stoppage *in transitu* would have been unquestionable. The result is the same, though they remained stored in a government warehouse, unless the transfer to Dewey on the records of the warehouse is to be treated as a termination of the transit. But, as we have seen, the terms of the sale provided that the plaintiffs should forward the goods to Boston as their place of destination, and the storage in the warehouse was preliminary to their transit, and not the termination of it. It is no answer to this view to say that there was a constructive delivery of the whiskey to Dewey, which vested the property in him, and that he had the right to take possession of it and withdraw it from the warehouse." *Mohr* v. *Boston & A. R. Co.* 106 Mass. 67, 71.

If this conclusion was a sound one,—and, in favor of the strong equity upon which the vendor's right of lien subsists, we do not see why it was not,—it seems, when applied to the contract in evidence in this case, decisive of the existence of the vendor's lien, unless we are to hold that a vendor has a better right of detainer after the goods leave his warehouse and get into the hands of a carrier, than while they are yet in his warehouse.

Let us next inquire how this principle applies to the contract before us. It stipulated for the doing of three things by the vendor before the delivery should be complete. These were: (1) To give care and attention to the packages while in the government warehouse: "That all care and attention shall be given the packages while in store, by the party of the first part." (2) To place insurance upon the property, if so required by the vendee: "That the party of the first part, if desired to do so by the party of the second part, shall place insurance, loss, if any, payable to the party of the second part, who shall pay the premium at not to exceed current rates." (3) And, finally, to complete the delivery of the property itself: "That, upon release from bond and payment of United States and state taxes and storage, by the party of the second part, the packages shall be delivered, free of charge, by the party of the first part, on board the cars at Silver Creek, Kentucky."

Presumptively, there had been no actual delivery of the property to the vendee until the last of these three things was performed, unless the other circumstances surrounding the transaction were such as to repel the presumption. Whether they were was a question of fact, which has been resolved against the plaintiffs by the trier of the facts, and his resolution is conclusive upon us.

It has been argued with much force that this last-quoted clause of the contract, requiring the delivery of the goods free on board at Silver Creek, is to be regarded, when considered in the light of the facts of the case, as merely a contract to perform an additional service in respect of the property after delivery had in fact taken place. We do not say that the trial court might not have so regarded it. The case of *Cooper* v. *Bill*, 3 Hurlst. & C. 721, required the subject of the sale (certain unsquared logs of timber) "to be delivered to boats when required." They were taken to the side of the canal and deposited on the bank near the landing, but not near enough to the boats, it would seem, to satisfy the requirement of the contract. While so deposited, the vendee, by his agents, took actual possession, marked the logs with his initials and expended five pounds in squaring them. It was held that there had been here such a delivery as devested the vendor of his right of lien. Although the case was very badly considered,—so badly that it would seem that two of the judges had not in their minds any sound conception as to the nature of the vendor's lien,—yet the conclusion was obviously right, on the analogy of the rule in the law of stoppage *in transitu*,—that the vendee may intercept the transit and take possession before the goods have arrived at the place appointed for delivery, which possession will end the right of stoppage of the vendor. If the removal of the whiskey in this case from the distillery to the bonded warehouse and thence to the cars, which the evidence shows would come to a side track by the side of the warehouse, could be regarded as a transit, and if it had appeared that C. Conrad & Co. had, by themselves or agents, intercepted the transit and taken actual possession of the whiskey while it was in the bonded warehouse,—this, of course, would have put an end to the vendor's lien, notwithstanding the provision of the contract requiring the vendors to deliver the goods free on board the cars. But no such facts appear in the record,—unless the collection of facts that the distillery was run in the name of C. Conrad & Co., that the warehouse had above its door the same name, that the whiskey was branded in the same name, and that the correspondence to and fro between Silver Creek, Kentucky and St. Louis, was sometimes conducted as though the warehouse was actually that of C. Conrad & Co.,—were facts from which the trial court was conclusively bound to find an actual delivery of the whiskey to C. Conrad & Co. But to hold, as a conclusion of law, that the facts prove such a delivery, would make them prove too much; because it would make them prove that C. Conrad & Co. were the distillers, in contradiction of the contract under which the whiskey was made, which provided that Stagg, Hume & Co. should make the whiskey, and that, although they should use the name of C. Conrad & Co. as distillers, they should exonerate C. Conrad & Co. from all liability to the government for the conduct of the distillery. It would also involve the absurdity of holding that, while the warehouse was that of C. Conrad & Co., yet they were under obligations by the terms of the contract to pay storage for keeping their whiskey in it to Stagg, Hume & Co. In fact, it would turn the whole transaction upside down, devest the parties of the character of vendor and vendee and turn them into the relation of principal and agent, C. Conrad & Co. being the principals and proprietors, and Stagg, Hume & Co. being merely their agents. Thus, if we do not ignore the language of the contract, throw it away, and get it entirely out of sight, we must, in order to uphold this contention, turn the whole transaction into elemental nonsense.

The question has been presented in another aspect by the very able argument which has been made on behalf of the plaintiffs. The contention is this: That where the goods which have been sold are deposited in the warehouse of a third person, to the use of the vendee, there has been a delivery such as cuts off the vendor's lien, under the English law, where there has been an attornment by the warehouseman to the vendee, and, under the American law, without such attornment; that the goods in this case were warehoused with a third party, which third party was either the government store-keeper, who had the keys and the actual possession of the warehouse, or else the Silver Creek Distilling Company, which was the owner of the warehouse; and that, by thus being placed in the warehouse of a third party, they were placed under the dominion and control of the vendee, so far as could be done while the government tax remained unpaid, which devested the possession of the vendors and with it their lien. We shall consider this question in the alternative aspect of the government store-keeper being the warehouseman, and of the Silver Creek Distilling Company being the warehouseman.

In the first aspect of the question, it is to be observed that the effect of depositing goods in the custom house, or in a bonded warehouse, to secure the payment of government fees, has been several times considered by the courts in respect of a question which is strictly analogous to the question of delivery to devest the vendor's lien, namely the question whether, after goods have arrived at the end of a voyage, there has been such an actual delivery to the consignee as cuts off the right of stoppage *in transitu*; and it has been uniformly held that the fact of a deposit of the goods in a government warehouse does not determine the right. *Northey* v. *Field*, 2 Esp. 618; *Donath* v. *Broomhead*, 7 Pa. 301; *Harris* v. *Pratt*, 17 N. Y. 249; *Mottram* v. *Heyer*, 5 Denio, 629.

And it is well known that in such cases the consignor has generally nothing further to do in order to get the goods out of the warehouse and into the actual possession of the consignee. The consignee really enters the goods at the custom house, as was done by his assignee in the case of *Harris* v. *Pratt, supra.* No strength, therefore, can be derived in favor of the hypothesis of the plaintiffs, from the fact that these goods were in the possession of the government store-keeper. It is to be observed that the government store-keeper is not a warehouseman for any purpose of commerce. He simply holds the goods in the course of transmission, so to speak, between the manufacturer and the consumer, until the government dues are paid. His position ought not to be construed so as to interrupt or impair the rights of vendor, vendee or pledgee, beyond what the terms of the statute under which he holds possession absolutely require. The language of *Judge* Wagner in *Ober* v. *Carson*, 62 Mo. 209, 215, fully justifies us in this conclusion.

But a further argument has been pressed upon us, in favor of the plaintiffs, upon the sections of the federal statute, already quoted, which imply that the store-keeper, on the order of the collector, upon the payment of the government dues, is to deliver the goods to the owner; and, as it is not disputed that Conrad was the owner, the argument derived from this is that the government store-keeper held the goods in a sense as his bailee, to be delivered to him or to his assignee upon the payment of the dues. This argument, like other arguments which have been pressed upon us in this case, proves too much for the case of these plaintiffs. We have already shown that, assuming the warehouse receipts which were delivered to them to be effective to make a symbolical delivery of the goods to them, yet this, under the evidence, did not make them the owners, but it merely made them pledgees. The well-known distinction between a pledge and a chattel mortgage is that, in a chattel mortgage the title passes to the mortgagee, subject to a defeasance; while, in the case of a pledge, the title does not pass to the pledgee, but remains in the pledgor, but the possession passes to the pledgee for the purpose of securing the performance of the obligation intended by the parties. A pledgee, therefore, is not the owner, but the mere holder, of a possessory lien. If this argument were a sound one, then these pledgees would not have had the right, in the event of an attempt upon the part of the pledgor to repudiate the pledge, to pay the taxes and take the goods out of the government storehouse. But such a pledge would be utterly ineffective and nugatory unless the pledgees were accorded this right, and they could not be accorded this right without being regarded as the "owners" within the intendment of the Statute. We hold that Congress, in employing the word "owners," made use of a general word to avoid circumlocution and needless specification, and that this general word was a word of description, intended to designate any person who, upon the payment of the government dues, was in law entitled to the possession of the goods. When, in the cases before us, the sheriff in Kentucky levied upon these goods in the hands of the government store-keeper, and thereafter paid the taxes, they were properly delivered to him as the owner, within the intendment of the Statute. And yet he was not the owner in the sense in which that word is ordinarily employed, though he had the title for a limited and qualified purpose.

But if the Silver Creek Distilling Company is to be regarded as the warehouseman, then the conclusion is the same. The circuit court does not seem to have found, as a fact, what was the relation subsisting between the Silver Creek Distilling Company and Stagg, Hume & Co. Perhaps on the evidence either of the following conclusions was warrantable: (1) that the Silver Creek Distilling Company was the mere agent or servant of Stagg, Hume & Co. for the purpose of carrying out the contract subsisting between them and C. Conrad & Co.; or (2) that, in making this contract with C. Conrad & Co., Stagg, Hume & Co. were agents acting for an undisclosed principal, and that the Silver Creek Distilling Company was that principal. We do not see that it makes any difference in principle which of these views is taken. The fact remains that there was a substantial identity between Stagg, Hume & Co. and the Silver Creek Distilling Company, and that there was no privity between the Silver Creek Distilling Company and C. Conrad & Co. It does not appear that any letter was ever addressed by the Silver Creek Distilling Company to Conrad as such, or by him to them, and it is not clear, from the record, that he even knew of the existence of such a corporation. They were the mere fingers of Stagg, Hume & Co. to carry out their contract with C. Conrad & Co., or else Stagg, Hume & Co. were their mere agents to make the contract without disclosing them; and it does not seem to matter which, for the purposes of the question we are considering. If the Silver Creek Distilling Company were the real principals in the contract, then the case is that of the vendor holding the goods in his own warehouse. If they were the mere agents of Stagg, Hume & Co., then the case is that of Stagg, Hume & Co. holding the goods in the warehouse of their agent, for what a man does by his agent he does by himself. In either case the possession was the possession of the vendor, and carried with it a vendor's lien. That the circuit court has taken this view is shown by the following instructions, given of its own motion:

"If the court finds from the evidence that the contract of October 25, 1882, between Stagg, Hume & Co. and Charles W. Conrad, admitted to evidence, was entered into by Stagg, Hume & Co., and that the whiskey in controversy was made under said contract at the instance and request of Stagg, Hume & Co. by the Silver Creek Distilling Company, and placed by it in its bonded warehouse at Silver

Creek under said contract, and that Charles W. Conrad failed and suspended business in January 1888, and that at the time of such failure Stagg, Hume & Co., or the Silver Creek Distilling Company, jointly with the storekeeper for the United States, were in actual possession of the said whiskey in said bonded warehouse; and that the notes given by Charles W. Conrad in settlement for said whiskey are now, and have always been, held by Stagg, Hume & Co.,—then, the court declares, as a matter of law, that, at the time of said Conrad's failure and suspension of business, the said Stagg, Hume & Co. had a vendor's lien on said whiskey and a right to retain possession thereof, either themselves or by or through said distilling company, until they were paid therefor; provided, the court further finds from the evidence that, at the time the warehouse receipts for the whiskey in controversy were issued to plaintiffs, Charles W. Conrad was, in fact, insolvent, and, further, that neither the distilling company, for itself or on behalf of Stagg, Hume & Co., nor Stagg, Hume & Co., after they, or either of them, became aware of such insolvency, did, with full knowledge of the circumstances under which said receipts were issued, ratify their issuance to Charles W. Conrad."

IV. We come now to the question of the effect of the symbolical delivery of the property to the plaintiffs as determining the vendor's lien. For the purposes of making more clear the view which we take, we shall assume that the evidence establishes that Stagg, Hume & Co. authorized Conrad to issue warehouse receipts in respect of the whiskey on store in the Government Warehouse No. 541, at Silver Creek, Kentucky. Whether the Silver Creek Distilling Company, as such, ever sanctioned the issue of such warehouse receipts, it is not material to inquire, since, as we have already stated, there was no privity of contract between that corporation and Conrad. If Stagg, Hume & Co. gave the authorization, it concluded them, if they were the real vendors; and it equally concluded the distilling company for which they were the agents, if the distilling company were the real vendors.

We ought, perhaps, to state here that we do not take the view upon which the circuit court proceeded, and which is embodied in the above instruction, that the symbolical delivery, which was attempted or effected by means of these warehouse receipts, became inoperative from the circumstance that, at the time of their issue, Charles W. Conrad was in fact insolvent. We can find no such principle in the cases which expound the nature of the vendor's lien and the analogous right of stoppage *in transitu*. Neither of these rights is of such a nature as to be self-executing. It is a right which the vendor may or may not assert; and if he does not assert it in time, it is lost. Stagg, Hume & Co. had not asserted it when these warehouse receipts were issued, and they could not thereafter assert it as against the holders of these warehouse receipts, provided the law placed them, in respect of the rights thereby acquired, on a better footing than that which was occupied by the transferors, C. Conrad & Co.

The general rule of the common law touching transfers of personal property is that the transferee acquires no better title than the transferor had; if the vendor had no title, the vendee gets none; if the pledgor had no title, the pledgee gets none; if the vendor or pledgor had a title, but subject to a lien in behalf of another person, the vendee or pledgee takes it burdened with such lien. This is unquestionably the general rule; but the rule has its exceptions. One exception known to the English common law is the well-known case of sales in market overt; but this exception is a stranger to American law, because in this country there are no markets overt. Another exception, founded in the custom of merchants, arises in the case of strictly negotiable paper, whereby the transferee of a bill of exchange or negotiable promissory note, who receives it in due course of trade, for a valuable consideration, before maturity, and without notice of any infirmities attaching to it, takes it discharged of any equities which may exist in respect of it between the original parties to it. Another exception, founded also in the custom of trade and analogous to the exception relating to commercial paper, relates to the symbolical delivery of goods in the hands of a carrier, effected by a transfer of the bill of lading. Still another exception, having its foundation, in this country, in the general usages of trade, of which the courts take judicial notice (*Gibson* v. *Stevens*, 49 U. S. 8 How. 384, 399 [12 L. ed. 1123, 1129]), but confirmed in nearly all the States of the Union by statutes, relates to symbolical transfers of personal property in warehouses, by the transfer of warehouse receipts. Following the precedent set by the great case of *Lickbarrow* v. *Mason*, 2 T. R. 63, 1 Smith, Lead. Cas. 888, it is now the recognized law of this country that the owner of goods, or one having the legal right to sell or to pledge them, may invest another with the full title and constructive possession of them, by transferring to him a bill of lading or a warehouse receipt which has been issued as their symbolical representative, either by a carrier or a warehouseman in whose custody they are, so as to discharge the vendor's lien or his right of stoppage *in transitu*, if the transferee of the bill of lading or warehouse receipt receives it bona fide and for a valuable consideration.

But what is to be deemed a valuable consideration, within the meaning of this rule, is one in respect of which the decisions are in a very unsatisfactory state. The question whether one who takes an assignment of such a symbol of property merely as collateral security for a past indebtedness, without making any present advance, agreeing expressly or impliedly for an extension of time to the transferor, or, foregoing any benefit or advantage, is to be regarded as a purchaser for value within the meaning of this rule, is the one which we have now to decide; and it is a question upon which there is no direct authority in this State. Unfortunately, the authorities in respect of it in other jurisdictions are conflicting. The question has, within a comparatively short period, been decided both ways in England.

In *Rodger* v. *Comptoir d'Escompte de Paris*, L. R. 2 P. C. 393 (*anno* 1869), it was held by three judges, on an appeal from a colonial court, that one who takes a bill of lading merely as collateral security for a previous obligation is not a purchaser for a valuable consideration in the sense which cuts off the vendor's lien. "Doubtless," said *Sir* Joseph Napier, in giving the opinion of the court, "the vendor's claim cannot prevail against the claim of a transferee for value, given on the faith of a negotiable security fairly and honestly taken; to the extent to which he has so given value he has a prior claim. But the rule is founded on the reason of it, as already stated, *cessante ratione, cessat ipsa lex*. Where there is no advance made or value given upon the faith of the documents, where the object is simply, by a sweeping clause, to gather in whatever may be got to recoup the creditor of a debtor who had become insolvent, for an improvident advance made upon the faith of a totally different security; where, upon the true construction of the assignment, no interest passed that would place the assignee in a better position than the assignor, and the bills of lading which subsequently came to hand were transferred expressly in performance of the agreement in this assignment and without other consideration whatsoever—it appears to their lordships that such a transfer, so made, and under such circumstances, cannot be held sufficient to defeat the vendor's claim."

It is to be observed, however, that the case did not present the naked question we are here considering; since the assignee of the bills of lading knew that the assignment was made in contemplation of insolvency, and this, under a recent decision of our supreme court, would have deprived him of the position of a bona fide purchaser without notice. *Young* v. *Kellar*, 94 Mo. 581.

The question came before the English Court of Appeals, not long afterwards, in the case of *Leask* v. *Scott*, 2 Q. B. Div. 376, in which case the doctrine of the case last cited was denied, in an earnest and somewhat heated opinion by the *Lord Justice* Bramwell, who declared that the decision was "not only a novelty, but a novelty opposed to what may be called the silent authority of all the previous judges and writers who have dealt with the subject." In other words, he inferred that it was the law that one who takes a bill of lading as collateral security merely for an antecedent indebtedness is a purchaser for a valuable consideration, and takes it discharged of the vendor's right of stoppage *in transitu*—simply because the question had never before been decided in England one way or the other. As in the previous case, it is to be observed with reference to this case, that the record did not present the naked question; for there was a present consideration mingling with the antecedent indebtedness, so that the observations of the court upon the question, notwithstanding the positive terms in which they were couched, were really no more than *obiter dicta*,—an opinion upon a case not before them.

In the federal courts we find but two direct decisions upon the question. In *Lesassier* v. *The Southwestern*, 2 Woods, 35, 36, *Mr. Justice* Bradley at circuit ruled the following proposition: "A transfer of a bill of lading as a mere collateral for previous obligations, without anything advanced, given or lost on the part of the transferee, does not constitute such an assignment as will preclude the vendor of the goods from exercising the right of stoppage *in transitu*." The contrary was held by *Mr. District Judge* Nelson, in the Federal Circuit Court in Minnesota, by analogy to the rule laid down by the Supreme Court of the United States in *Brooklyn City & N. R. Co.* v. *N. Y. Nat. Bank of the Republic*, 102 U. S. 14 [26 L. ed. 61], in respect of commercial paper. *St. Paul Roller Mill Co.* v. *Great Western Despatch Co.* 27 Fed. Rep. 434.

We do not find that the question has been distinctly decided in any of the state courts, except in the case of *Loeb* v. *Peters*, 63 Ala. 243, 35 Am. Rep. 17, where it was held that the transfer of a bill of lading by the consignee to his prior creditor, as collateral security merely for the prior indebtedness, does not cut off the vendor's right of stoppage *in transitu* —the creditor of the vendee in such a case not being a bona fide purchaser for value.

In the absence of any direct authority which is controlling upon us, we are thus under the necessity of deciding the question according to the best analogies we can discover in the decisions in this State and in other jurisdictions. There are four analogies which bear directly upon the question: (1) the analogy of goods purchased by means of fraudulent representations, such as will authorize the vendor, on discovering the fraud, to rescind the sale and reclaim the goods; (2) the analogy of conveyances of lands and goods made with the design to hinder, delay or defraud creditors, the purchaser or transferee being innocent of knowledge of the fraudulent design; (3) the analogy of other conveyances of land, subject to unrecorded liens or equities unknown to the transferee; (4) the analogy of the transfer of commercial paper.

First. In respect to the first analogy, it has been unanimously held in the Court of Appeals of New York, in a case twice argued, that one to whom personal property has been delivered by a fraudulent vendor in payment of a precedent debt due him, or (what is tantamount thereto) in performance of an executory contract of sale, made by such fraudulent vendee prior to acquiring possession of the property, or of any symbolical representative of it, is not a bona fide purchaser for value, and cannot hold the property against the original defrauded vendor. *Barnard* v. *Campbell*, 55 N.Y. 456; on re-argument, 58 N.Y. 73.

It is to be observed that this case follows the analogies of the rulings in that State in respect of commercial paper, considered further on, under which a transfer, even in payment of an antecedent indebtedness, does not devest equities subsisting in favor of the payor; which is not the law in this State. *Green* v. *Kennedy*, 6 Mo. App. 577.

Second. The analogy, in respect of conveyances of lands or goods in fraud of the creditors of the transferor, is illustrated by numerous decisions; and, so far as the writer has observed, they are all to the same general effect, which is that, to entitle the transferee to be treated as a purchaser for a valuable consideration, it must appear that he actually paid the purchase money before he had any notice of the fraud; it is not sufficient that he had agreed to pay it, or even that he had given his check in payment, unless the check had been paid. *Arnolt* v. *Hartwig*, 73 Mo. 485; *Dougherty* v. *Cooper*, 77 Mo. 528; *Young* v. *Kellar*, 94 Mo. 581; *McNichols* v. *Rubleman*, 13 Mo. App. 515, 522.

The decisions in other jurisdictions to the same effect are so numerous that we refrain from citing them.

Third. In respect of the third analogy, that of other conveyance of land, subject, in the hands of the grantors, to prior unrecorded conveyances, vendors' liens, resulting trusts or other secret equities, our law, in like manner, speaks only in one way. In order to entitle the innocent grantee to protection against a prior unrecorded conveyance, vendor's lien or other equity, he must have parted with something of value as a consideration, before receiving notice of the prior conveyance of equity. *Aubuchon* v. *Bender*, 44 Mo. 560; *Halsa* v. *Halsa*, 8 Mo. 303; *Chouteau* v. *Burlando*, 20 Mo. 482; *Paul* v. *Fulton*, 25 Mo. 156; *Digby* v. *Jones*, 67 Mo. 107.

Professor Pomeroy, in his great work on Equity Jurisprudence, generalizing on this question, says: "A conveyance of real or personal property, as security for an antecedent debt, does not, upon principle, render the transferee a bona fide purchaser; since the creditor parts with no value, surrenders no right, and places himself in no worse legal position than before. The rule has been settled, therefore, in very many of the States, that such a transfer is not made upon a valuable consideration, within the meaning of the doctrine of bona fide purchase." 2 Pom. Eq. Jur. § 749. To this last statement the learned commentator cites a long list of judicial authorities, pointing out, at the same time, that there are some holdings to the contrary. Since real property has in modern times entered largely into the operations of commerce, it is not perceived why there should be upon such a subject one rule for real property and another rule for personal property; nor is it perceived why there should be one rule for negotiable choses in action and another rule for tangible goods; and while it is desirable that the decisions of the state courts upon questions of commerce, and especially upon questions of commercial paper, should follow those of the federal courts, yet the state judicatories are not bound by the federal judicatories on these questions, and it could easily be pointed out that, on this particular question, so far as it concerns negotiable paper, a majority of the state courts deny the doctrine recently declared in the Supreme Court of the United States in *Brooklyn City & N. R. Co.* v. *N. Y. Nat. Bank of the Republic*, *supra*.

Fourth. Proceeding now to the last and most direct analogy to the question before us, that of the transfer of commercial paper, we regret to find that the question whether the transferee of such paper, who takes it merely as collateral security for an antecedent indebtedness, acquires title to it discharged of prior equities,—is settled differently in different American jurisdictions, and does not seem to be settled at all in this State. The decision of the Supreme Court of the United States in *Swift* v. *Tyson*, 41 U. S. 16 Pet. 1 [10 L. ed. 865], is generally quoted as the leading case in favor of the position that such a taker of negotiable paper takes it discharged of equities. That case did not, however, decide the question; since the question in judgment was whether one who thus takes negotiable paper in payment takes it discharged of equities; although there is a dictum of *Mr. Justice* Story, who gave the judgment of the court, that the rule would be the same in case it were taken as security merely for an antecedent indebtedness. *Mr. Justice* Catron regarded this dictum as so objectionable that he made it the subject of a special dissent. The question remained undecided in that tribunal as late as the case of *Oates* v. *Montgomery First Nat. Bank*, 100 U. S. 239, 249 [25 L. ed. 581, 584], where it was expressly left as an open question; but soon afterwards, in the case of *Brooklyn City & N. R. Co.* v. *N. Y. Nat. Bank of the Republic*, *supra*, it was resolved in favor of the dictum of *Mr. Justice* Story, and contrary to the holdings of the courts of New York and many other States.

The opposing lines of American authority on this question appear to commence with the leading case of *Coddington* v. *Bay*, 20 Johns. 637, where it was held by the highest court of that State, reversing a decision of *Chancellor* Kent (*Bay* v. *Coddington*, 5 Johns. Ch. 54), that one who takes a negotiable instrument merely as collateral security for an antecedent indebtedness due to him from the person indorsing it to him takes it subject to any equities which may exist between the original parties in respect of it. The same court, out of deference to the later decision of the Supreme Court of the United States in *Swift* v. *Tyson*, *supra*, again went over the whole ground, reviewing many authorities, and, while conceding the desirability of the state courts following the ruling of the higher federal tribunals on commercial questions, declined to recede from its previous holdings, but re-affirmed the following proposition: An innocent holder of negotiable paper, who has received it in the usual course of trade, for a valuable consideration, though from a person having no title and no authority to transfer it, will be protected, even as against the claim of the previous owner; but if it appear that the paper was received merely as collateral security for an antecedent debt, due from the person who made the unauthorized transfer, and that the transferee neither parted with value on the credit of receiving it, nor relinquished any previous security, he will not be deemed a purchaser for value, and will not acquire a title to the paper as against the real owner. *Stalker* v. *McDonald*, 6 Hill, 93, 96.

It would not be profitable, in a judicial opinion, to follow through the rulings of the different States the two divergent lines of authority thus started. We shall limit our inquiry to the law of Missouri and the law of Kentucky.

The initial case in this State is *Goodman* v. *Simonds*, 19 Mo. 106. In that case our supreme court had a case before it which, in its judgment, called for a decision of this question. The court, citing the New York decisions above given, and also citing, but not following, *Swift* v. *Tyson*, *supra*, ruled that the transferee of commercial paper as collateral security for an antecedent debt is not a taker

See also 26 L. R. A. 443.

for value. In the opinion of the court by Ryland, *J.*, the following strong language occurs: "A man catching at every chance to save himself never inquires, so he can obtain collateral security, about the fairness of the transaction. He gives nothing for it; he risks nothing for it. Then, common sense and common honesty unite in saying he shall take it with the defenses the other parties have against it in the hands of the original holder and party. We do not say that a bill of exchange, passed to a person in the payment of a pre-existing debt, would be liable in his hands, without notice, to the equities or defenses of the original parties; but that the holder of a bill merely as collateral security for a pre-existing debt, having given no value for it, no consideration for it, holds it liable to such equities. We know that there are authorities whose phraseology may be construed against this view, but we also know that there are authorities in its favor, and we think reason and justice unite in supporting it." Id. 116.

In a case between the same parties and apparently on the same instrument (though how this came about does not appear) which went from the Circuit Court of the United States for the District of Missouri to the Supreme Court of the United States (*Goodman* v. *Simonds*, 61 U. S. 20 How. 343 [15 L. ed. 934]), the court refrained from deciding this question, being of opinion that it was not presented by the record. The question next came before the Supreme Court of Missouri for decision in *Grant* v. *Kidwell*, 30 Mo. 455, and it was ruled, in a short and ill-considered opinion, delivered without referring to the leading authorities on the question, and without making any allusion to *Goodman* v. *Simonds*, that the indorsee of a negotiable promissory note assigned before maturity, as an indemnification against an antecedent liability, takes it discharged of prior equities. The question next came before the supreme court in *Boatman's Sav. Inst.* v. *Holland*, 38 Mo. 49. The plaintiff had taken the note from the payee as collateral security for an antecedent debt, and was now suing the maker upon it. The maker offered certain evidence for the purpose of showing that the note had been given to the original payee upon a consideration which had failed. It was held that the trial court rightly rejected this evidence. Wagner, *J.*, said: "It was wholly irrelevant, and, had it been introduced, it would not have constituted the shadow of a defense. A pre-existing debt, or an antecedent liability, incurred by an indorsee of a negotiable note assigned before maturity, is a sufficient consideration to support the title of such indorsee." The court cited *Swift* v. *Tyson*, *supra*, and also its previous decision in *Grant* v. *Kidwell*, but made no reference to *Goodman* v. *Simonds*, *supra*, although it had been cited in the printed briefs.

If the question rested here, it would be entirely clear that so far as bills of exchange and promissory notes are concerned, the transferee in pledge for an antecedent indebtedness gets as good a title as one who parts with the present value. But these decisions are succeeded by a line of dicta and decision which tend to create the impression that the courts regard the doctrine of *Goodman* v. *Simonds* as still the law of this State. The principle of that decision was recognized by the supreme court in *Logan* v. *Smith*, 62 Mo. 455, 458, and in *Davis* v. *Carson*, 69 Mo. 609, 610; by this court in *Terry* v. *Hickman*, 1 Mo. App. 119, 124, the court saying that it was "controlling authority;" was acted upon by this court as authority in the decision of *Brainard* v. *Reavis*, 2 Mo. App. 490, 493—where the court, with singular inconsistency, cited in the same connection *Grant* v. *Kidwell*, *supra*.

Again in *Hodges* v. *Black*, 8 Mo. App. 394, there is a dictum that "one who takes a note before maturity, merely as collateral for a pre-existing debt, where the facts are such as to raise no new consideration, is not regarded in Missouri as a holder for value free from all equities between the original parties,"—citing *Terry* v. *Hickman*, *supra*. This case was affirmed by the supreme court, adopting the opinion of this court, in 76 Mo. 537.

Again, in *Skilling* v. *Bollman*, 73 Mo. 665, 670, the rule in *Goodman* v. *Simonds* was recognized by the court in the following language from the opinion by Henry, *J.*: "Eminent jurists and judicial tribunals hold that one who, for a prior indebtedness, receives a bill of lading for goods, either as collateral security, or in payment of such indebtedness, has no such title as will avail, even against the vendor's right of stoppage *in transitu*; in other words, that such a one, in such controversy, is not to be regarded as a bona fide purchaser for value (citing cases). And *Goodman* v. *Simonds*, 19 Mo. 106, and *Logan* v. *Smith*, 62 Mo. 455, recognize the principle pronounced in the foregoing cases."

The rule in *Goodman* v. *Simonds* was again recognized and distinguished in *Deere* v. *Marsden*, 88 Mo. 512, the court holding that, where a present consideration, as an agreement express or implied for a delay, however short, supervenes, the rule of that case does not apply. Still later, in *Crawford* v. *Spencer*, 92 Mo. 498, 509, our supreme court made a similar ruling, following *Deere* v. *Marsden*, *supra*, and quoting from the decision in *Goodman* v. *Simonds*, *supra*, the latter portion of the passage which we have quoted from it in this opinion. Finally in *Feder* v. *Abrahams*, 28 Mo. App. 454, 457, where the question was whether a transfer by a failing debtor to one of his creditors, in payment, makes the transferee a purchaser for value, it was said by Rombauer, *J.*: "Plaintiff claims that the decision in *Deere* v. *Marsden*, 88 Mo. 512, questions the rule stated in *Hess* v. *Clark*, 11 Mo. App. 492. This, however, is an obvious mistake. The supreme court in that case simply re-affirmed the proposition, which has been the law of this State since *Goodman* v. *Simonds*, 19 Mo. 107, that one who takes collaterals for a pre existing debt, without any new consideration to support the transfer, is not a purchaser for value of such collaterals." The case which was thus regarded as pronouncing what has ever since been the law of this State was, as I have above shown, twice overruled upon cases in judgment, once thereafter re affirmed and applied, and nine times thereafter expressly or impliedly recognized as the law. The manner in which our courts have thus dealt with a question of such great importance to the commercial community affords a striking illustration of the imperfect way in which judicial work has been done in this State, produced, no doubt, largely by the over-crowded state of the dockets of the courts, and the excessive amount of work thrown upon the individual judges. If the doctrine of *stare decisis* were strictly adhered to, it would unavoidably result in the conclusion that one who takes negotiable paper as collateral security for an antecedent indebtedness takes it as a purchaser for value; for such was ruled in our supreme court in *Boatman's Sav. Inst.* v. *Holland*, 38 Mo. 49, where the question was before the court in judgment, which is the last controlling decision upon the subject. But in view of the manner in which our supreme court has subsequently dealt with the question, I do not think that we are at liberty to hold that it is concluded by that decision. We should rather regard it as still an open question.

If we were to rest our decision upon the analogy of commercial paper and upon the authority of *Boatman's Sav. Inst.* v. *Holland*, *supra*, it would result in a reversal of the judgment of the circuit court in this case; because it would indisputably appear that the plaintiffs became bona fide purchasers for value of the whiskey in controversy, when they received from Conrad the warehouse receipts as collateral security for what he owed them, and especially since the circuit court refused an instruction, tendered by the plaintiffs, asserting this principle. But if we were to take this course, we should place ourselves in the inconsistent position of deciding (perhaps erroneously) the question upon the law of Missouri in one of its controlling aspects, and upon the law of Kentucky in another; for, on the question we are considering, the law of Kentucky is settled that one who takes commercial paper merely as security for an antecedent indebtedness is not a taker for value, but holds it subject to prior equities. *Lee* v. *Smead*, 1 Met. (Ky.) 628; *May* v. *Quinby*, 3 Bush, 96.

When we considered, in a former portion of this opinion, the question of the validity of these warehouse receipts as creating pledges of the property in favor of the plaintiffs, we found that, under a decision of this court, supported by decisions in other jurisdictions, they were invalid; but we also found that they were valid by the law of Kentucky, which law, however, had not been proved as a fact in the trial court. We therefore found that we could not affirm the judgment on that point, since the question had not been raised in the trial court, and, if it had been there raised, the objection could have been obviated by the plaintiffs putting in evidence the law of Kentucky, by which law, it is agreed, the rights of the parties are governed. Upon the same principle, we must now hold that we cannot reverse the judgment as being against the law of Missouri on the point under consideration (the analogy of commercial paper), since, if we were to take this course, the defendants could, on another trial of the cause, put in evidence the law of Kentucky, which on this subject is contrary to the law of Missouri. We cannot, especially, take this course in the unsettled state of the law of Missouri. If the law of Missouri is that the taker of commercial paper, as collateral security merely, is a purchaser for value, within the rule which protects him against prior equities, and if this is a controlling analogy in dealing with the subject of warehouse receipts, nevertheless, knowing as we do that the law of Kentucky, by which the question in this case is governed, is to the contrary, we should be bound to say that the decision of the court upon this point, if erroneous in the precise state of the record, was a harmless error.

We now have to dispose of an argument of counsel for the plaintiffs, based upon the assumption that we are to follow the analogy of commercial paper in deciding the question under consideration. It is this: That the rule, under which the transferee of commercial paper for an antecedent indebtedness takes it subject to equities applies only in the case of accommodation paper where there is a fraudulent deviation, that is to say, where the paper has been given to the payee for a limited or special purpose, and he has, in fraud of the rights of the maker, transferred it for a different purpose. The courts which take this distinction affirm the rule that an indorsee of a negotiable note made for the accommodation of the indorser, but without restriction as to its use, taking the note in good faith as collateral security for an antecedent debt, and without other consideration, is entitled to the position of a holder for value, and is not affected by the defense of want of consideration set up by the maker. *New York City Grocers Bank* v. *Penfield*, 69 N. Y. 502; *Pitts* v. *Vogelsong*, 37 Ohio St. 676; *Dunn* v. *Weston*, 71 Me. 278. See also *Freund* v. *Importers & T. Nat. Bank*, 76 N. Y. 352, 14 Am. Law Rep. 486.

The argument is that, as the evidence of the plaintiffs tends to show that Stagg, Hume & Co. conferred upon Conrad an unlimited authority to issue warehouse receipts in respect of the whiskey in the bonded warehouse at Silver Creek, this unrestricted authority necessarily included the right on his part to pledge it for his antecedent debts. We know of no rule of law which requires us to take this view. The most that can be said in favor of this view is that it would be the conclusion of fact to be drawn from other facts, and whether the conclusion ought to be drawn was a question for the trial court, and not for this court. But it is to be observed that the conclusion would, upon the evidence in this record, be in the nature of a violent presumption. There is no evidence whatever in this record that any member of the firm of Stagg, Hume & Co. ever gave or intended to give to Conrad authority to do what was done—to pledge, in contemplation of insolvency, the whiskey which they had made for him on credit, and which remained in their warehouse, to his relatives and friends for his antecedent debts. Suppose that he had solicited authority from them to do this, could anyone for an instant believe that they would have granted it? It is further to be observed that any course of reasoning, which holds that, because they did authorize him to use warehouse receipts merely as a means of transferring title to these goods while in their warehouse in the ordinary course of trade, they are to be held as having authorized him to use them for the destruction of their own legal rights,—is a course of reasoning which would destroy the vendor's lien in every case; because, as we have observed, the very existence of a vendor's lien always assumes that the title to the goods has passed to the vendee, since a man cannot have a lien on his own goods. The vendor has sold the goods to the vendee on credit, marked them, designated them, set them apart and placed them under his dominion and control in such a sense that the title has passed and that there has been an executed sale. What is this but to say to the vendee: "Take the goods; they are yours; deal with them as you choose; here is a writing saying that I have sold them to you." But notwithstanding all this, if, while they are yet in the actual possession of the vendor, he were to sell them, or to mortgage them, even in the course of trade, by any process which does not amount to a transfer of the possession of them in theory of the law—on the plainest principles, the vendor's lien would revive upon his insolvency, even as against the sub-vendee. The sub-vendee would stand in the shoes of his vendor and get no higher title than his vendor. *Dixon* v. *Yates*, 5 Barn. & Ad. 313; *Hamburger* v. *Rodman*, 9 Daly, 93; *Southwestern F. & C. Press Co.* v. *Stanard*, 44 Mo. 71.

In other words, it is the transfer of possession, and not merely the transfer of title, which cuts off the vendor's lien; and in nearly every case of executed sale the vendor gives the vendee the power of transferring possession, and that was all that was given in this case in the authority to issue warehouse receipts. They were a mere means put into Conrad's hands of delivering constructive possession to others.

Recurring, then, to the analogies in which we have sought for a rule of decision upon the question whether the rights of the plaintiffs as holders of these warehouse receipts are superior to the rights of Stagg, Hume & Co., as unpaid vendors in possession, we find that they are all in favor of the conclusion that the rights of the unpaid vendor are superior, and that the plaintiffs are not to be regarded as purchasers for value, except the one which relates to the assignment of commercial paper; and that, while the law on this subject is unsettled in this State, it is settled in accordance with the other analogies in Kentucky, by the law of which State the rights of the parties are governed. We therefore hold that the plaintiffs are not to be regarded as purchasers for value, and that the vendor's lien of Stagg, Hume & Co., founded on actual possession, took precedence of their constructive possession as pledgees.

In the case already alluded to, which was twice before this court and the supreme court (*Skilling* v. *Bollman*, 6 Mo. App. 76, affirmed 73 Mo. 665, *S. C. sub nom. Skyles* v. *Bollman*, 12 Mo. App. 598, affirmed 85 Mo. 35), the court merely decided that one who takes a bill of lading as collateral security for an antecedent debt gets a better title than one to whom the consignor has subsequently transferred a duplicate exemplification of the same bill of lading in fraud of the rights of the first taker, although the second taker gets actual possession of the property—a principle several times affirmed in the English courts, and a very simple one; for the title of a person to property lawfully acquired is not to be devested, even in favor of an innocent person, by a subsequent fraud of the transferor, for which the first taker is not responsible. The second taker gets nothing, because his vendor has nothing to transfer. *Nemo dat quod non habet.* *Whistler* v. *Foster*, 14 C. B. N. S. 248.

V. One question remains to be considered. It is strongly urged that, even if we take this view, yet, notwithstanding this, the plaintiffs are entitled to be regarded as having a better right on the principle of estoppel. In our opinion the record does not show a state of facts on which an estoppel can be predicated. The doctrine of equitable estoppel cannot be invoked, unless what was said or done by the party to be estopped can be shown to have influenced the conduct of the other. *Eitelgeorge* v. *Mutual House Bldg. Asso.* 69 Mo. 52; *Spurlock* v. *Sproule*, 72 Mo. 503; *Acton* v. *Dooley*, 74 Mo. 63; *Rogers* v. *Marsh*, 73 Mo. 64; *Noble* v. *Blount*, 77 Mo. 235.

It must have had the effect of misleading the party asserting the estoppel. *Hydraulic Press Brick Co.* v. *Neumeister*, 15 Mo. App. 592.

This one element of an estoppel is nowhere presented by the record in this case. It is not shown—and if it was the fact it was for them to show it—that the plaintiffs altered their position in any way to their disadvantage on account of the representation which Stagg, Hume & Co. may have held out to them, by publishing Conrad as the owner of this warehouse and of the whiskey stored therein, and by allowing him to issue warehouse receipts as such owner. If an estoppel, such as is now claimed, can be built upon a presumption or a surmise, it is easy to see that it would totally destroy the rule, applied in so many situations, as already seen, which places a subsequent purchaser in the shoes of his vendor; for a case can scarcely be imagined—and this must be especially true in cases where commercial paper is transferred as collateral security for antecedent debts—where an attenuated estoppel could not be conjured up to destroy the rule of many jurisdictions which deprives such a transferee of the advantages of a bona fide holder for value.

We have thus endeavored to track this most difficult and complicated case over all the ground outlined by the counsel in their arguments. We are greatly indebted to the counsel on both sides for the aid which their learning, ability and industry have afforded us in arriving at the final solution of the questions presented. We have endeavored to decide the case in accordance with settled rules of property, without throwing into the scale any loose conceptions of justice or equity. We cannot, however, refrain from observing in conclusion that the result at which an adherence to legal principles, as we understand them, enables us to arrive, is in consonance with what seems to be the plain justice of the case. The vendor's lien, like the analogous doctrine of stoppage *in transitu*, is favored in the law. *Muller* v. *Pondir*, 55 N. Y. 325, 337; *McEwan* v. *Smith*, 2 H. L. Cas. 309, 328, *per Lord* Campbell; *Callahan* v. *Babcock*, 21 Ohio St. 281, 8 Am. Rep. 63, 65.

It does not rest upon any strictly logical basis. It has been the outgrowth of a struggle for justice. It is founded in the obvious conception of justice that one man's goods ought not to be applied to the payment of another man's debts. *Heins* v. *Railroad Transfer Co.* 82 Mo. 233, 236.

It was, indeed, said by one English judge that "it has always been certain that the owner might retake his goods, on their passage, by any means short of felony, if he had subsequent grounds for believing that the purchaser would not perform his part of the contract by paying for them." Gibbs, *Ch. J.*, in *Litt* v. *Cowley*, 1 Holt. N. P. 338, 7 Taunt. 169.

It was in like manner said by a judge who has been regarded as the father of the system of equity jurisprudence, that if the vendor "had got the goods back again by any means, provided he did not steal them, I would not blame him." *Lord* Hardwicke in *Snee* v. *Prescot*, 1 Atk. 245, 250.

And yet, if the present actions had been allowed to be well founded, the very consequence against which the courts of justice have struggled would have taken place in this instance. One man's goods would have been wrested from his actual possession in order to pay another man's debts.

It results from the foregoing that *the judgment of the Circuit Court must be affirmed.*

Judge **Peers** concurs.

Judge **Rombauer**, having been of counsel, did not sit.

It will perhaps be more satisfactory to the parties to state that *Judge* **Lewis**, who was a member of the court when the cause was first submitted, after examining the record and the printed arguments, was also in favor of affirming the judgment.

[The Reporter is directed by *Judges* Thompson and Biggs to state that, pending a motion for rehearing, *Judge* Biggs succeeded *Judge* Peers as a member of the court; that the motion was taken under advisement for a considerable time, and all the questions involved in the case were gone over by *Judge* Biggs as though the case had been newly presented, and that he concurred in overruling the motion, for the reasons stated in the foregoing opinion.]

GEORGIA SUPREME COURT.

Neal P. MARTIN, *Plff. in Err.*,
v.
George P. JOHNSON.

(......Ga.......)

The law of the State in which a note for money loaned is given governs on the question of usury, where it is secured by a deed of land located in the State, and part of the money, representing the usury, was deducted from the loan, and never paid over to the borrower, although the note is expressly made payable in another State.

(March 1, 1890.)

ERROR to the Superior Court for Muscogee County to review a judgment striking out certain pleas setting up the defense of usury in an action on a promissory note. *Reversed.*

The facts are fully stated in the opinion.

Messrs. **Porter Ingram, J. F. Pou** and **C. R. Russell** for plaintiff in error.

Messrs. **Barrow & Thomas** and **L. F. Garrard** for defendant in error.

Blandford, *J.*, delivered the opinion of the court:

George P. Johnson brought his action against Neal P. Martin on a promissory note, alleging in his declaration that, to secure the payment of said note, Martin had executed to him a deed conveying certain land lying in the County of Muscogee and State of Georgia, wherefore he prayed a special lien on said land according to the Statute in such cases made and provided, as well as a general judgment against Martin.

The note is dated at Columbus, Ga., April 16, 1887, and payable to the order of Johnson

---

NOTE.—*Contract; law of place governs.*

The nature, validity, obligation and interpretation of contracts are to be governed by the *lex loci.* Hochstadter v. Hays, 11 Colo. 118.

In every forum a contract is governed by the law with a view to which it was made. Pritchard v. Norton, 106 U. S. 124 (27 L. ed. 104); Conframp v. Bunel, 4 U. S. 4 Dall. 419 (1 L. ed. 891); Teal v. Walker, 111 U. S. 242 (28 L. ed. 415).

The general rule that the validity of the contract is to be decided by the law of the place where the contract is to be performed, does not apply to cases involving the rate of interest, where it is stipulated in the contract at the place where the loan is made, in conformity with the law of the place, that a higher rate of interest shall be paid than is allowed by the place of performance, but that the *lex loci contractus* governs. Cope v. Alden, 37 How. Pr. 186, 53 Barb. 355; Chapman v. Robertson, 6 Paige, 627, 3 N. Y. Ch. L. ed. 1128.

A contract valid where it is made is to be held valid everywhere. See *notes* to Osgood v. Bauder (Iowa) 1 L. R. A. 655; Bacon v. Horne (Pa.) 2 L. R. A. 355.

Under the Usury Laws.

The illegality of usury is wholly a creature of the Legislature, and parties cannot be relieved from contracts providing for exorbitant rates of interest, except as provided by statute. Coleman v. Commins, 77 Cal. 548.

In a contract for the loan of money, the law of the place where the contract is made is to govern as to the rate of interest, although secured by a mortgage on lands in another State, unless some other circumstance shows that the parties had in view the laws of the latter State. De Wolf v. Johnson, 23 U. S. 10 Wheat. 367 (6 L. ed. 343); Jewell v. Wright, 12 Abb. Pr. 09; Pomoroy v. Ainsworth, 22 Barb. 118; Ballard v. Webster, 9 Abb. Pr. 404.

The law of the State where the agreement was made and the instrument taken to secure its performance decides the fate of a security taken upon a usurious agreement (Andrews v. Pond, 38 U. S. 13 Pet. 65 (10 L. ed. 61); Miller v. Tiffany, 68 U. S. 1 Wall. 298 (17 L. ed. 540); Call v. Palmer, 116 U. S. 98 (29 L. ed. 559); unless some other circumstance shows that the parties had in view the laws of the latter State. De Wolf v. Johnson, *supra.*

These rules are subject to the qualification that the parties act in good faith, and that the form of the transaction is not adopted to disguise its real character. Miller v. Tiffany, *supra.*

If interest at the place of performance of a contract is higher than that at the place of contract,

See also 12 L. R. A. 93.

at the office of the Eastern Banking Company, Boston, Mass. To this action Martin pleaded: (1) The general issue. (2) That the consideration for which said note sued on was given was largely tainted with usury, and that the sum of $80 of usurious interest was added into, and constituted a part of, the $500 for which said note was given; that he actually received from the plaintiff only $420, and that all the balance was for usurious interest at and above the rate of 8 per cent per annum. And defendant further alleges that one William Redd was at the date of the note the duly authorized agent of the plaintiff to negotiate said loan; that he called on Redd, as such agent, and requested said loan of $500 for the term of five years, and that the said Redd then and there agreed to make said loan; that, for the delay of payment of said sum defendant agreed to give his several notes, as alleged by the plaintiff, at the rate of 8 per cent per annum on the said $500 note, and that then and there the said Redd, as such agent, demanded from defendant, for further interest, and in consideration of delay of payment of said note, the further sum of $80, —to all of which exactions and demands defendant agreed and consented, as the same were the only terms upon which the loan could be had; that he received from the plaintiff's authorized agent the sum of $420 and no more, and thereupon gave his note for $500, and the interest notes, plaintiff receiving also the sum of $80, making in all the sum of $263.32 of interest for the delay of payment of the $420 received by defendant for the term of five years; that by said usurious transaction the plaintiff received the sum of $95.22 of usurious interest over and above the lawful rate of 8 per cent interest, for delay of payment of $420 for five years. And defendant pleaded (3) that the plaintiff could not have or enforce any special lien on said land for said purchase money under said deed made by defendant and set forth by plaintiff, because defendant says said deed is void, and conveys no title, the same being tainted with usury; that as part consideration of said deed, defendant paid to the plaintiff the sum of $95.22 of usurious interest over and above the lawful rate of 8 per cent per annum; and that the same entered into, and formed part of, the consideration of said deed. And (4) defendant alleges that on the 16th day of April, 1887, plaintiff made and delivered to defendant his certain obligation in writing, signed with his hand and seal, whereby he bound himself to reconvey to defendant the land described in said obligation, provided that defendant should pay said $500 note sued on, and also the coupon notes described in plaintiff's declaration; which said obligation in writing made by the plaintiff to defendant recites the particulars of said loan of $500; and recites, further, that the loan was made to bear interest at the rate of 8 per cent per annum, defendant averring that said loan of $500 was to and did bear interest at the rate of 16 per cent per annum, defendant receiving only $420, and $80 of said amount being retained by plaintiff as further interest for the delay of payment of $500 for the term of five years. Defendant alleges that said sum of $80 was exacted and retained by the plaintiff as usurious interest over and above the legal rate of 8 per cent per annum, and therefore the deed made by him conveying said land to the plaintiff was made in consideration of said usurious interest, and is null and void; that all the deeds, obligations and contracts between him and the plaintiff concerning said loan are tainted with usury, and each and all of them are null and void. To all of these pleas, except the first, the plaintiff, by his attorneys, demurred, and moved to strike the same. The demurrer was sustained by the court, and said pleas were stricken.

While we think that these pleas were technically incorrect, and that the second and fourth pleas did not constitute a bar to the action, yet, inasmuch as we are of the opinion that the court committed error in striking the third plea, and as the case will have to go back for another trial, and the plaintiff in error may amend his pleas so as to plead a want of consideration in the note as to $80, or a set-off to that amount, we are induced to express some opinion as to the main point which has been argued before us.

---

the parties may lawfully stipulate for the higher interest. *Ibid.*; Andrews v. Pond, *supra*; Peyton v. Heinekin, 131 U. S. Append. Cl. (20 L. ed. 679); Cookle v. Flack, 93 U. S. 344 (23 L. ed. 949); Cromwell v. Sac County, 96 U. S. 51 (24 L. ed. 681).

Where a contract in express terms provides for a rate of interest lawful in one but unlawful in the other State, the parties will be presumed to contract with reference to the laws of the State where the stipulated rate is lawful, and such presumption will prevail until overcome by proof that the stipulation was a shift to impart validity to a contract for a rate of interest in fact usurious. Scott v. Perlee, 39 Ohio St. 67, 48 Am. Rep. 422; Fisher v. Otis, 3 Chand. 102; Butters v. Olds, 11 Iowa, 1; Arnold v. Potter, 22 Iowa, 198; Newman v. Kershaw, 10 Wis. 340; Hosford v. Nichols, 1 Paige, 225, 2 N.Y. Ch. L. ed. 624; Townsend v. Riley, 46 N. H. 300; Fanning v. Consequa, 17 Johns. 511, 8 Am. Dec. 442; Pratt v. Adams, 7 Paige, 615, 4 N. Y. Ch. L. ed. 300; Richards v. Globe Bank, 12 Wis. 692.

Where the contract was made in New York, its construction and validity depend upon the laws of that State. It must be held to have been made with regard to such laws. Meade v. St. Louis Mut. L. Ins. Co. 51 How. Pr. 6.

An agreement for the loan of money, made and consummated in this State by residents thereof, by which the borrower is to give a bond accompanied by a mortgage upon lands in Wisconsin, no place of payment being specified, is governed by the Usury Laws of New York, and not those of Wisconsin. Cope v. Alden, 37 How. Pr. 184; McCraney v. Alden, 46 Barb. 275; Hosford v. Nichols, *supra*; Hull v. Wheeler, 7 Abb. Pr. 411; Goddard v. Sawyer, 9 Allen, 78.

Where persons residing in New York wrote their acceptance upon a draft, and sent it to Illinois to have it negotiated there, it is an Illinois contract, although made payable in New York, and is not usurious, although bearing interest at a greater rate than is allowed in New York, if the rate is lawful in Illinois. Tilden v. Blair, 88 U. S. 21 Wall. 241 (22 L. ed. 632).

Usury in a bond is governed, as a general rule, by the law of the place where payable, although the parties may also stipulate in accordance with the law of the place where the contract is made. Junction R. Co. v. Bank of Ashland, 79 U. S. 12 Wall. 226 (20 L. ed. 385).

It is undoubtedly true, as a general rule, that the interest which a contract should bear is to be governed by the law of the place where the same is to be performed. This rule applies to all legal contracts,—legal where the same are executed and made; but where, according to the law of the place whereat the contract is made, it is unlawful to take or to exact usury, or more than a certain per cent of interest provided by law as the legal rate, such contract will in some instances be construed according to the law of that place.

It appears from the pleas which were stricken that the parties to this case entered into an agreement whereby it was agreed that the plaintiff in error, in consideration that the defendant in error would advance and lend to him the sum of $500, would make and deliver to the defendant in error his promissory note for the sum of $500, and that he would secure the payment of said note by executing a deed to certain land located in this State; the defendant in error to reconvey said land to the plaintiff in error upon payment of the $500 note, and the notes given for usury. To carry out this agreement, the defendant in error advanced to the plaintiff in error the sum of $420, retaining $80 out of the $500 for which the note was given, whereupon the plaintiff in error executed the deed set forth in the record. We are clear in the opinion that a part of this contract or agreement was made in this State, and performed in this State. That is to say, the usurious interest, as alleged in the plea, was paid in this State to the defendant in error. We therefore think that this contract was usurious to some extent, and, under the laws of this State, the defendant in error can recover nothing more than the principal sum loaned, with interest thereon at the rate of 8 per cent, all interest in excess of that being usurious, and not recoverable.

The notes given by the plaintiff in error were only a part of the contract, and it is a well-settled question of law that one contract or agreement may be a good consideration to support another. So, as the part of this agreement which is to be performed in Massachusetts is the payment of the notes sued on, when the courts of this State are called upon to enforce this contract the usury which was exacted and retained by the defendant in error may be pleaded to the action.

In the case of *Andrews* v. *Pond*, 38 U. S. 13 Pet. 77 [10 L. ed. 66], where a draft which contained usury was made in the State of New York, but payable in the State of Alabama, and which, under the laws of the former State, was declared void, whereas, under the laws of the latter State the usury contained in the same alone was void, and could not be collected, the supreme court held that such contract was to be governed by the laws of the State of New York.

In the case of *Holmes* v. *Manning* (Mass.) 19 N. E. Rep. 25, where a note which contained usury was dated at Boston, in the State of Massachusetts, made payable in the State of Massachusetts, but payable to a payee who resided in the State of New York, who was the plaintiff in the case, the court held that the contract was to be governed by the law of New York, and the note was void. See also the case of *Finney* v. *Cadwallader*, 55 Ga. 78.

If this court should hold that a note made in this State, but payable in the State of Massachusetts, for money advanced by the agent of a person who resided in Massachusetts, could be collected notwithstanding it contained 16 per cent usurious and unlawful interest, then the law of this State as to usury would be inoperative and useless. The money lenders of those States which have no usury laws, but which allow to be collected any rate of interest contracted for, could flood this State with their agents, and, by the loan of money, exact the highest rates of interest,—even 100 per cent. The contract of lending and borrowing always includes two agreements,—one, by the lender, to deliver the money; and the other, by the borrower, to repay it. As the pleas do not allege that the agreement to deliver the money was to be performed elsewhere, the place of delivery was Georgia. *Dolman* v. *Cook*, 14 N. J. Eq. 56; *Campion* v. *Kille*, Id. 229; *Andrews* v. *Torrey*, Id. 355.

It was in the performance of this agreement that the usury was reserved. The whole amount of the usury was deducted from the money delivered, and this was done in Georgia. The taint of usury does not result from payment, but from agreement, performed or unperformed. Were payment necessary, the deduction of the usury from the amount of the loan is equivalent to payment, not for the purpose of recovering it back, but for the purpose of affixing the taint, and resisting ultimate payment *pro tanto*. The note bears no usurious interest, but a part of the principal is usury already reserved in Georgia, by holding back a part of the loan. That part of the note represents money now in the creditor's possession, and which he has never delivered to the borrower. Suppose the note were for that money only, with 8 per cent interest on it. Would it be collectible because payable in Boston? Would it not be a contract to pay in Boston usury which had been reserved in Georgia? Is usury reserved in Georgia by deducting it from the loan, less usury because agreed to be actually paid elsewhere?

The parol agreement out of which the note sued on in this case sprung was made in this State. Part of that agreement was performed in this State. The usury set forth in defendant's pleas was paid in this State, and all that was left to be performed of that agreement was the payment of the notes sued on in this State. The maker of these notes resides in this State, and the land which was conveyed as security is located in this State. Whether a contract is made with reference to the place or State or country in which it is to be performed is a question of no easy solution. However this may be, there is enough in this case to show that, in all likelihood, the parties to the contract sued on contemplated the law of the domicil of the maker as the law which should govern this contract in all respects. There is a portion of this contract which under no circumstances could be enforced in the State of Massachusetts,—that as to the land upon which it is sought to set up a lien. Nor can we very readily see how any portion of this contract could be enforced in the State of Massachusetts against a person resident in the State of Georgia. So we think that the second and fourth pleas could be so amended as to be allowed to stand.

As to the third plea, we are satisfied that the court erred in sustaining the demurrer thereto, and striking the same. That plea distinctly alleged that the deed of conveyance was tainted with usury; and this court has frequently held, under our Code, that, wherever a deed is tainted with usury, it is void as a conveyance because the same is illegal. We are satisfied that the striking of this plea was erroneous, and for this reason the judgment of the court below must be reversed.

Judgment reversed.

NEW YORK COURT OF APPEALS.

Jacob B. TALLMAN, *Respt.*,
v.
METROPOLITAN ELEVATED R. CO. *et al.*

(......N. Y.......)

1. **Damages for the permanent diminution in the value of lots** caused by an elevated railway in front of them cannot be recovered in an action for damages after construction of the road, but the damages must be limited to the time preceding the action.

2. **Damages to lots by construction of an elevated railroad** in front of them without compensation to the owner, where he subsequently sues for the damages sustained, are limited to diminished rental or usable value during the time prior to the suit, and must be based on the actual condition of the lots just as they are. What the effect on their value would have been if buildings had been erected thereon, which in fact were not, is immaterial.

(April 15, 1890.)

APPEAL by defendants from a judgment of the General Term of the Court of Common Pleas for the City and County of New York affirming a judgment of the Trial Term in favor of plaintiff in an action brought to recover damages for the alleged diminution in value of plaintiff's lots by reason of the construction of defendant's tracks in front of them. *Reversed.*

The facts are fully stated in the opinion.

Messrs. **Edward S. Rapallo** and **Samuel Blythe Rogers**, for appellants:

The measure of damages should be applied solely with reference to the condition and use of the land during the period sued for.

Taylor v. *Metropolitan Elevated R. Co.* 18 Jones & S. 311; *Greene* v. *New York Cent. & H. R. R. Co.* 12 Abb. N. C. 124, 65 How. Pr. 154; *Seventh Ward Nat. Bank* v. *New York Elevated R. Co.* 21 Jones & S. 412; *Wheelock* v. *Noonan*, 10 Cent. Rep. 512, 108 N. Y. 179; *Hexter* v. *Knox*, 63 N. Y. 561; *Colrick* v. *Swinburne*, 8 Cent. Rep. 701, 105 N. Y. 503; *Hatfield* v. *Central R. Co.* 33 N. J. L. 251; *Dorlan* v. *East Brandywine & W. R. Co.* 46 Pa. 520.

Uncertain and speculative damages cannot be recovered.

Baker v. *Drake*, 53 N. Y. 211; *Wright* v. *Bank of Metropolis*, 1 L. R. A. 289, 13 Cent. Rep. 415, 110 N. Y. 237; *Richardson* v. *Northrup*, 66 Barb. 85; *Woodmansee* v. *Kinnicutt*, 20 N. Y. Week. Dig. 512; *Wehle* v. *Haviland*, 69 N. Y. 448; *Blanchard* v. *Ely*, 21 Wend. 342; *Pollitt* v. *Long*, 58 Barb. 20; *Re La Amistad de Rues*, 18 U. S. 5 Wheat. 385 (5 L. ed. 115); *Wellington* v. *Small*, 3 Cush. 145.

NOTE.—*Elevated street railroads; construction.*

All corporate rights and franchises are lost by an elevated railroad company, by a failure to construct the road within the time fixed in its charter or articles of association. Re Kings Co. Elevated R. Co. 41 Hun, 425.

An application for the appointment of commissioners to appraise property may be defeated by proof of the lease or forfeiture of the corporate rights and franchises of the applicant. *Ibid.*

The failure to locate the columns in the roadway, or their distance from the curb, in streets exceeding forty-two feet in width, does not make the general plan adopted by the commissioners under the Rapid Transit Act defective. Re Kings Co. Elevated R. Co. 112 N. Y. 47.

The omission to prescribe the fixed height of the elevated railroad, by the commissioners under the New York Rapid Transit Act, would not justify condemnation of the plan adopted. *Ibid.*

The omission to fix specific locations of the stations and stairways is not sufficient, standing alone, to make invalid the corporate existence of the elevated railroad company. *Ibid.*

The general plan adopted by the commissioners under the New York Rapid Transit Act is not defective in failing to direct the construction of two tracks in any street, even if the language used is not in fact to be considered as directing them to be constructed. *Ibid.*

Laws authorizing relator to build an experimental section of an elevated railway not less than a quarter of a mile in length are local laws prohibited by the Constitution, and are invalid. People v. Loew, 3 Cent. Rep. 310, 102 N. Y. 471.

Appropriation of right of way; damages.

Depriving the owner of a lot, abutting on a public street, of, or materially interfering with, his enjoyment of the easement in the street to its full width for admission of light and air to his lot, is a taking of his property for public use, within the Minnesota Constitution, for which full compensation must be made. Vanderburgh, J., dissents. Adams v. Chicago, B. & N. R. Co. (Minn.) Oct. 15, 1889.

A banking corporation may recover damages for depreciation in the value of its building, caused by the construction of an elevated railroad in front of its place of business. Fifth Nat. Bank v. New York Elevated R. Co. (N. Y.) 24 Blatchf. 89, 28 Fed. Rep. 231.

The basis of appraisement of damages where the fee of the street is not in the adjoining owners, is the difference in value of the abutting premises before the construction of the railroad and afterwards, including the advantages from the road. Re Brooklyn Elevated R. Co. 55 Hun, 165.

The erection and operation of an elevated railroad on a public street, whereby abutting houses are injured by smoke, their walls cracked, and their

Mr. **James M. Smith,** for respondent:

The evidence of the value of the lots and the cost of building such houses as the plaintiff had made plans for building was properly admitted, for the purpose of showing a basis upon which the jury might form an estimate as to the value of the use of the lots, with and without the road, on the ground that it is fair to presume that a reasonably sensible man will do that which is for his interest.

Matthews, Presumptive Ev. p. 8; Starkie, Ev. 2d Am. ed. p. 1240, *note c.*

Messrs. **John E. Parsons, Joseph H. Choate, G. Willett Van Nest, A. P. & W. Man, Burnett & Whitney, Mitchell & Mitchell,** and **Burrill, Zabriskie & Burrill** submitted a brief in support of the judgment, on behalf of certain persons who had recovered judgments in cases where expert testimony was admitted to prove diminished value.

Earl, *J.*, delivered the opinion of the court:

The plaintiff was the owner of four adjoining lots on the northerly side of West Fifty-third Street in the City of New York. He became the owner of three of them in 1866, and of the other in 1868, and he continued to own them until after the commencement of this action in February, 1884. The elevated railway of the defendants was constructed through Fifty-third Street in front of these lots in 1878, and was thereafter maintained and operated. The plaintiff used a part of his lots for a carpenter shop and the remainder as a lumber yard. This action was commenced to recover damages occasioned to the lots by the construction and operation of the railway, and the only question which it is important for us now to determine relates to the rule of damages.

When the defendant began to construct its railway in front of the plaintiff's lots he could have commenced an action in equity against it and restrained it until it had made compensation to him for the rights and easements which it took from him, or until it acquired them by condemnation proceedings. *Story* v. *New York Elevated R. Co.* 90 N. Y. 122.

In that way he would, at least in theory of the law, have been indemnified for all the damages he would suffer by reason of the construction of the railway. Instead of taking his remedy by an equitable action at that time he could have taken it at any time afterward during his ownership of the lots with the same result.

He was not, however, confined to his remedy by such an action. He could suffer the railway to be constructed and then bring successive actions to recover damages to his lots, caused by the construction, maintenance and operation of the railway. In such an action he would recover his damages to the commencement of the action, and the action would be governed by the principles laid down in *Uline* v. *New York Cent. & H. R. R. Co.* 101 N. Y. 98, 2 Cent. Rep. 116.

In such an action the plaintiff cannot recover for the permanent diminution in the value of his lots. He can only recover the damages he sustains from day to day, or from month to month, or from year to year, in the use of his lots; and the question to be determined in such an action is, How much has the rental or usable value of the lots been diminished by the construction, maintenance and operation of the railway? As a basis for estimating the damages, the lots must be taken as they are used during the time embraced in the action, and the plaintiff's recovery must be confined to the diminished rental or usable value of the lots just as they were. He was in no way pre-

---

occupants disturbed in their sleep, is not an injury for which owners thereof are entitled to compensation, under Pa. Const., art. 16, § 8. Sterrett, *J.*, dissents. Pennsylvania R. Co. v. Marchant, 12 Cent. Rep. 261, 119 Pa. 541, 21 W. N. C. 300.

Aside from the damages to adjacent buildings and lots, the value to the land owner of the right of way taken for an elevated railroad which is at least thirteen feet above the street, on pillars at least thirty feet apart, must be nominal, or nearly so; but any hindrances caused by the railroad in the use of the property that affect its value are proper matters of consideration in determining the damage. Sullivan v. North Hudson Co. R. Co. (N. J.) Nov. 18, 1889.

An abutting owner is entitled to damages, direct and incidental, occasioned by the construction of an elevated railroad. All such damages are recoverable in a single action. The grantee of a municipality by deed containing covenants protecting a street from any other use than that of a public street is entitled to recover such damages. Lahr v. Metropolitan Elevated R. Co. 6 Cent. Rep. 371, 377, 104 N. Y. 268; American P. M. Society v. Brooklyn Elevated R. Co. 46 Hun, 530.

An elevated railroad and its operation imposes upon the street an unauthorized use and is a trespass against abutting owners not duly compensated. Drucker v. Manhattan R. Co. 8 Cent. Rep. 66, 106 N. Y. 157.

The fact that, because a lease of a lot was executed more than six years before the commencement of the action, it is difficult to ascertain the precise amount of damage sustained by the lessee in consequence of the construction of an elevated railroad in front of the lot, is no reason for a refusal to award any damage whatever. Hamilton v. Manhattan R. Co. 30 N. Y. S. R. 17.

A change in the character of the neighborhood, directly or indirectly attributable to the operation of an elevated railroad, cannot be taken into consideration as causing damages for which plaintiff may recover. Moore v. New York Elevated R. Co. 29 N. Y. S. R. 482.

One owning property on a street occupied by an elevated railway has an easement to light from the street, and may maintain an action for damages for any interference with, or interruption of, the light from the street to his property. Pond v. Metropolitan Elevated R. Co. 42 Hun, 567.

Damages for personal injuries.

To maintain an action for injuries to plaintiff's eye by cinders falling from a locomotive of an elevated road, negligence or unskillfulness on the part of the company must be shown. Searles v. Manhattan R. Co. 2 Cent. Rep. 442, 101 N. Y. 661.

Where an elevated railroad company has a right to operate its road over city streets, and to generate steam by the use of coal, any damage necessarily caused by the careful and skillful exercise of its rights can impose no obligation upon it. *Ibid.*

The lease of its road to another company will not relieve from damages by the construction or operation of the road. Pond v. Metropolitan Elevated R. Co. 42 Hun, 567.

Degree of care required to provide safe approaches to train. See *note* to Kelly v. Manhattan R. Co. (N. Y.) 3 L. R. A. 74.

vented from putting his lots to any use he wished. He had the right, acting reasonably, not wantonly or rashly, to put upon them any structures which he deemed most to his advantage; and at any and all times, until the Railway Company acquired as against him the right to maintain and operate its road in Fifty-third Street he had the right to recover the diminished rental value of his lots occasioned to them just as they were by the maintenance and operation of the road. But he could not be permitted to prove or allowed to recover such damages as he might have sustained if he had put his lots to other uses or placed upon them other structures. Such damages would be purely speculative and contingent. The plaintiff had owned these lots for about twelve years before the railway was constructed without making any substantial improvements upon them, and they remained in the same condition down to the commencement of the action. It appears that at some time he made plans for the erection of dwelling-houses upon the lots; but whether he ever intended to build, or would have built, the houses, is mere matter of conjecture. Upon the trial he was permitted to prove what it would have cost to erect the dwelling-houses upon the lots, and what they would have rented for after they were constructed, and also to give evidence of the amount for which they would have rented if the railroad had not been constructed; and the jury evidently took this evidence into consideration in fixing the amount of damages which they awarded the plaintiff. There can be no certainty that the plaintiff would ever have erected dwelling-houses upon the lots, and there could be no certainty as to the rents which could have been obtained from them, either with or without the railroad in the street, and the defendant was permitted by the rule adopted in the court below to have all the advantages which he could derive from keeping his lots substantially vacant and ready to sell as such, and, at the same time, to have all the advantages, without the investment of any money and without any risk, which he could have derived from their improved condition. He was simply entitled to the damages caused to him in the use of his lots from the defendant's interference with his easements of light, air and access, and such damages are necessarily, and from the very nature of the case, such only as flowed from the interference with such easements during the time covered by the action. If he desired a more ample indemnity for the injury he suffered from the railway in front of his lots, he should, by an equitable action, have compelled the defendant either by agreement with him to pay his damages, or to acquire the right by condemnation proceedings to interfere with and take his easements. Any other rule would open upon the trial in every case like this an inquiry into all the possible uses to which the abutting owner might put his premises, and damages, instead of being awarded upon any certain or probable basis, would rest mainly upon conjecture and speculation. Adequate sanction for these views is found in the following authorities: *Green* v. *New York Cent. & H. R. R. Co.* 12 Abb. N. C. 124; *Colrick* v. *Swinburne*, 105 N. Y. 503, 8 Cent. Rep. 701; *Wheelock* v. *Noonan*, 108 N. Y. 179, 10 Cent. Rep. 512; *Hatfield* v. *Central R. Co.* 33 N. J. L. 251; *Dorlan* v. *East Brandywine & W. R. Co.* 46 Pa. 520.

The rule of damages as thus laid down was violated by many rulings upon the trial of this action, and *a new trial must, therefore, be ordered*, costs to abide the event.

All concur.

Theodore THOMAS, *Respt.*,
v.
MUSICAL MUTUAL PROTECTIVE UNION, *Appt.*

(....N. Y.....)

1. **Courts do not sit for the purpose of determining speculative and abstract questions of law,** or laying down rules for the future conduct of individuals in their business and social relations; but are confined in their judicial action to real controversies wherein legal rights of parties are necessarily involved, and can be conclusively determined.

2. **Equity will not entertain jurisdiction** of cases where there is an adequate remedy at law, or grant relief, unless for the purpose of preventing serious and irreparable injury.

3. **Embarrassment in business** resulting to a person by reason of non-membership in a protective union and arising from the refusal of those engaged in or connected with a similar business to deal with or work for him, although influenced by obligations voluntarily assumed by such persons in becoming members of the union, or by representations made to them by individual members thereof, gives no right of action to the person embarrassed against either the union or the individuals so influenced.

4. **An adjudication cannot be obtained in advance** as to the validity of the by-laws of an incorporated association on an application for injunction by a member who has been cited to show cause why he should not be punished for violating such by-laws, unless such punishment would subject him to irreparable injury, and other adequate means of redress are not open to him.

5. **Where the imposition of fines,** payment of which the corporation has no means of enforcing except through the courts, is the only punishment provided for violation of by-laws, a party cited for trial under such by-laws has no right to an injunction restraining such action, since his remedy at law is sufficient.

6. **The possibility that a person may be expelled** from an incorporated association in case of his neglect to pay fines if they should be imposed upon him, where no intention to expel him is shown, is not sufficient to warrant an injunction against proceeding to try him for alleged violation of the by-laws making him liable to fines.

(April 15, 1890.)

APPEAL by defendant from a judgment of the General Term of the Supreme Court, First Department, affirming a judgment of the

---

NOTE.—*Equity will not interfere with exercise of discretionary powers.*

Discretionary power vested by the Legislature in a person or body of men when exercised in good faith cannot be interfered with or be controlled or

See also 18 L. R. A. 190; 48 L. R. A. 272.

New York Special Term adjudging void certain of defendant's by-laws and perpetually enjoining it from proceeding to try plaintiff upon a charge of violating them. *Reversed.*

The case sufficiently appears in the opinion.

Messrs. **Horatio C. King** and **George A. Clement**, for appellant:

The fundamental principle which underlies this case is that the by-laws in question, in their legal operative force, regulate the matter of association as between the members only; they do not purport to interfere with freedom of action outside of the organization. Such an agreement is not inconsistent with or contrary to any existing law.

Master Stevedores Asso. v. *Walsh*, 2 Daly, 1.

Trade combinations or unions for lawful objects are now generally authorized by law, and even for purposes which at one time in this State were held to be unlawful.

People v. *Wilzig*, 4 N. Y. Cr. Rep. 413, cases cited in *note;* Penal Code, § 170.

As no inconsistent law is shown, the exercise of the power in passing the by-laws in question was discretionary, conclusive and lawful.

Williams v. *New York Cent. R. Co.* 18 Barb. 222.

Where the exercise of power is intrusted to the judgment and discretion of a particular body of individuals, no court should interfere with or control that discretion, provided it is exercised in good faith.

Walker v. *Devereaux*, 4 Paige, 230; *People* v. *Troy*, 78 N. Y. 33; *Rex* v. *London*, 3 Barn. & Ad. 255, 271; *Martin* v. *Mott*, 25 U. S. 12 Wheat. 19 (6 L. ed. 537); *United States* v. *Speed*, 75 U. S. 8 Wall. 77 (19 L. ed. 449); *United States* v. *Wright*, 78 U. S. 11 Wall. 648 (20 L. ed. 188); *People* v. *Leonard*, 74 N. Y. 443; *Schanck* v. *New York*, 69 N. Y. 444; *Fudickar* v. *Guardian Mut. L. Ins. Co.* 62 N. Y. 392, 399.

The by-laws in question impose upon the plaintiff no such restraint in trade as would make them void as against public policy.

Curtis v. *Gokey*, 68 N. Y. 300; *Diamond Match Co.* v. *Roeber*, 35 Hun, 421, 427, 428; *Collins* v. *Yorke*, 33 Eng. Rep. (Moak) 463, *note; Oregon Steam Nav. Co.* v. *Winsor*, 87 U. S. 20 Wall. 66 (22 L. ed. 318); Bishop, Cont. last ed. § 576; 2 Parsons, Cont. 7th ed. 747.

If the imposition of a fine or expulsion is illegal, plaintiff has an ample remedy by refusing to pay the fine and defending any proceedings to collect it, or by mandamus in the event of expulsion. Under such circumstances a party is not entitled to relief by injunction.

People v. *Wasson*, 64 N. Y. 167, 170; *Blake* v. *Brooklyn*, 26 Barb. 301, 303; *Davis* v. *American Society for P. of C. to Animals*, 6 Daly, 81, 91; *Wallack* v. *Society for Ref. of Juvenile Delinquents*, 67 N. Y. 23, 29; *Savage* v. *Allen*, 54 N. Y. 458; *Gallatin* v. *Oriental Bank*, 16 How. Pr. 253; *Shrewsbury & B. R. Co.* v. *Stour Valley R. Co.* 2 DeGex, M. & G. 866, 21 Eng. L. & Eq. 628, 636; *McHenry* v. *Jewett*, 90 N. Y. 58; *New York* v. *Mapes*, 6 Johns. Ch. 46; *New York Printing & D. Establishment* v. *Fitch*, 1 Paige, 98; High, Inj. §§ 22, 34, 35, and cases cited.

Vague and uncertain apprehensions do not justify an injunction.

Rochester v. *Erickson*, 46 Barb. 92; *People* v. *Canal Board*, 55 N. Y. 397; *Williams* v. *New York Cent. R. Co.* 18 Barb. 222; *Swett* v. *Troy*, 12 Abb. Pr. N. S. 100; *Bouton* v. *Brooklyn*, 15 Barb. 375; *Phœnix* v. *Emigration Comrs.* 12 How. Pr. 1; High, Inj. § 786.

The court should not interfere by injunction in advance of any action by the defendant under the notice or summons served upon the plaintiff to appear and show cause why he should not be fined.

Hurst v. *New York Produce Exchange*, 1 Cent. Rep. 260, 100 N. Y. 605.

Mr. **Eustace Conway**, for respondent:

Contracts are in restraint of trade which totally prohibit the pursuit of an occupation or the carrying on of a particular business, at any place in this State.

Chappel v. *Brockway*, 21 Wend. 157; *Lawrence* v. *Kidder*, 10 Barb. 641.

Restraints of trade by by-laws are, if made to cramp trade in general, void, and also if to exclude foreigners, unless there is a precedent motion.

Hesketh v. *Braddock*, 3 Burr. 1856.

While a party cannot complain of a breach of his contract which removes competition and restricts trade, he can complain of a wrong arising in direct consequence of such a contract.

Crawford v. *Wick*, 18 Ohio St. 190; *Garret* v. *Taylor*, Cro. Jac. 567; *Proctor* v. *Sargent*, 2

---

aided in law or in equity. Woodruff v. Fisher, 17 Barb. 234; Crocker v. Crane, 21 Wend. 218.

A court of chancery is not the proper tribunal to correct the errors and irregularities of inferior tribunals. Gregg v. Massachusetts Medical Society, 111 Mass. 194, 15 Am. Rep. 27; Mooers v. Smedley, 6 Johns. Ch. 28.

If the ordinances were invalid, and did not render complainants liable to a penalty, they had a complete defense at law. Bouton v. Brooklyn, 15 Barb. 394; Moses v. Mobile, 52 Ala. 208.

When ordinances have been enacted by the proper authority, a court of equity will not interfere by injunction to restrain their enforcement. Nor will that court enjoin such proceedings under the ordinance for the purpose of determining the validity of the ordinance in a court of law, when the defendant has an adequate remedy at law. Desplaines v. Poyer, 11 West. Rep. 770, 123 Ill. 111; Cohen v. Goldsboro, 77 N. C. 2; Devron v. First Municipality, 4 La. Ann. 11; Davis v. American Society for Prevention of Cruelty to Animals, 6 Daly, 81, 75 N. Y. 362; Yates v. Batavia, 79 Ill. 500; Moses v. Mobile, 52 Ala. 198; Burnett v. Craig, 30 Ala. 135; Hamilton v. Stewart, 59 Ill. 330.

Where neither injury to plaintiff's property, inadequacy of his legal remedy, or any pressing or serious emergency, or danger of loss, or other special ground of jurisdiction is shown, complainant is not entitled to final relief by injunction. McHenry v. Jewett, 90 N. Y. 58; Troy & B. R. Co. v. Boston, H. T. & W. R. Co. 86 N. Y. 128; New York P. & D. Establishment v. Fitch, 1 Paige, 98; 3 Pom. Eq. Jur. 368.

The incompleteness and inadequacy of the legal remedy is the criterion which determines the right to the equitable remedy. Jersey City v. Gardner, 33 N. J. Eq. 622; Powell v. Foster, 59 Ga. 790; Johnson v. Connecticut Bank, 21 Conn. 157; Watson v. Sutherland, 72 U. S. 5 Wall. 74 (18 L. ed. 580); New York P. & D. Establishment v. Fitch, *supra;* 3 Pom. Eq. Jur. 368.

A court of equity will sometimes interfere to redress a wrong, but, in general, only where the

Man. & Gr. 87; *Mallan* v. *May*, 11 Mees. & W. 665; *Chesman* v. *Nainby*, 2 Ld. Raym. 1456.

The three by-laws taken together make it impossible for a musician to carry on his business in this country unless he be a member of the defendant Union.

Further, they made it absolutely impossible for the plaintiff to conduct his business according to the requirements of the art of music as there did not happen to be within the membership of the Union a person of the artistic excellence and superiority required by the plaintiff for the conduct of that business.

The result of all this is to take away from plaintiff, and restrain him in, the management and control of his business, and vest it in defendant.

Re Jacobs, 98 N. Y. 98; *Diamond Match Co.* v. *Roeber*, 9 Cent. Rep. 181, 106 N. Y. 482; *Printing & N. Reg. Co.* v. *Sampson*, L. R. 19 Eq. 462; *Leather Cloth Co.* v. *Lorsont*, L. R. 9 Eq. 353; *Leslie* v. *Lorillard*, 1 L. R. A. 456, 110 N. Y. 533; *Central Ohio Salt Co.* v. *Guthrie*, 35 Ohio St. 672; *Stanton* v. *Allen*, 5 Denio, 434; *Hooker* v. *Vandewater*, 4 Denio, 353; *India Bagging Asso.* v. *Kock*, 14 La. Ann. 164; *Clancey* v. *Onondaga F. S. Mfg. Co.* 62 Barb. 395; *Saratoga Co. Bank* v. *King*, 44 N. Y. 87; *Morris Run Coal Co.* v. *Barclay Coal Co.* 68 Pa. 182; *Weller* v. *Hersee*, 10 Hun, 431, affirmed, 74 N. Y. 609; *Arnot* v. *Pittston & E. Coal Co.* 68 N. Y. 558; *Mogul Steamship Co.* v. *McGregor*, L. R. 21 Q. B. Div. 553; *People* v. *Gillson*, 12 Cent. Rep. 616, 109 N. Y. 399; *People* v. *North River Sugar Refining Co.* 16 Civ. Proc. Rep. 1; *Hudson* v. *Thorne*, 7 Paige, 263; *Craft* v. *McConoughy*, 79 Ill. 346; *People* v. *Erie Co. Medical Society*, 24 Barb. 570; *Horner* v. *Graves*, 7 Bing. 743.

Plaintiff brings suit as a member of the defendant corporation, having suffered substantial property damages and injury as the direct result of such adoption, so that unless this suit had been brought the damage would have been irreparable.

See *People* v. *North River Sugar Ref. Co.* 16 Civ. Proc. Rep. 1.

Shareholders may bring suit to declare invalid and restrain improper corporate acts.

Leslie v. *Lorillard*, 1 L. R. A. 456, 110 N. Y. 533, 535. See also *Hawes* v. *Oakland*, 104 U. S. 450 (26 L. ed. 827); Green's Brice, 643 *et seq.* 77; *Manderson* v. *Commercial Bank*, 28 Pa. 379; *Rendall* v. *Crystal Palace Co.* 4 Kay & J. 326; *Hoole* v. *Great Western R. Co.* L. R. 3 Ch. 262; *Pickering* v. *Stephenson*, L. R. 14 Eq. 322; Morawetz, Priv. Corp. § 278. See also Kerr, Inj. p. 505; *Stewart* v. *Erie & W. Transp. Co.* 17 Minn. 372; High, Inj. 3d ed. §§ 1187, 1194, 1200; *Colles* v. *Trow City Directory Co.* 11 Hun, 397; *Emperor of Austria* v. *Day*, 3 DeG. F. & J. 217; *Champlin* v. *New York*, 3 Paige, 573; *Springhead Spinning Co.* v. *Riley*, L. R. 6 Eq. 551; *Thorley's Cattle Food Co.* v. *Massam*, L. R. 6 Ch. Div. 582; *Watson* v. *Sutherland*, 72 U. S. 5 Wall. 74 (18 L. ed. 580); *Riding* v. *Smith*, L. R. 1 Exch. Div. 93; *Dixon* v. *Holden*, L. R. 7 Eq. 488; *Donnell* v. *Bennett*, L. R. 22 Ch. Div. 835.

The proof in our case is sufficient to show that the illegal act is "threatened and imminent," and that is sufficient to maintain the action.

People v. *Canal Board*, 55 N. Y. 390; *Leech* v. *Harris*, 2 Brewst. (Pa.) 571. See also *Springhead Spinning Co.* v. *Riley*, *supra; Garret* v. *Taylor*, Cro. Jac. 567.

Ruger, *Ch. J.*, delivered the opinion of the court:

The remedy afforded for the restraint and punishment of corporations for illegal conduct in the exercise of privileges or franchises not conferred upon them by law is through an action by the attorney-general to suspend their functions or annul their charters. Code Civ. Proc. § 1798.

Individuals who by unlawful combinations seek to interfere with the trade, business or occupation of others, with a view of injuring or embarrassing them in the prosecution of such trade or business, are subject to the penalties of the criminal law and become liable to criminal prosecution on behalf of the people. Penal Code, § 168.

These are the only modes of redress open to parties, generally, for injuries occasioned to them through the voluntary combination of others engaged in similar employments, with a view of influencing and controlling the general conduct and management of such trade and employment. Of course actions may be maintained by individual members of a corporation against it, who have been injured in their property rights by the unlawful action of such corporation, for the purpose of redressing such injuries. Aside from actions of this character, the members of corporations generally cannot

---

wrong is in its nature irreparable. Jones v. Little Rock, 25 Ark. 304; Normand v. Otoe Co. 8 Neb. 21; Thebaut v. Canova, 11 Fla. 169; Mohawk & H. R. Co. v. Artcher, 6 Paige, 83; Reake v. Am. Teleph. & Teleg. Co. 3 Cent. Rep. 73, 41 N. J. Eq. 35; Citizens Coach Co. v. Camden Horse R. Co. 29 N. J. Eq. 299.

By-laws of an association, binding upon its members.

The by-laws of an association are its rules prescribed by a majority of the members for the regulation and management of their joint affairs. Ang. & A. Corp. § 327; Morawetz, Priv. Corp. § 491.

They are binding upon all the members, who are all chargeable with knowledge of the laws and rules of the association and are bound by them. Bauer v. Samson Lodge, K. of P. 102 Ind. 262; People v. St. George's Society, 28 Mich. 261.

They must be reasonable and agreeable to the law of the land. Morawetz, Priv. Corp. § 494; Kent v. Quicksilver Min. Co. 78 N. Y. 159.

Any attempt on the part of an association by its by-laws to deprive a non-consenting member of a right secured to him by the corporate articles is in excess of corporate authority, and *ultra vires.* Ang. & A. Corp. § 345; Diligent Fire Co. v. Com. 75 Pa. 291; Bergman v. St. Paul Mut. Bldg. Asso. 29 Minn. 278; People v. Young Men's F. M. T. A. Benev. Society, 41 Mich. 67; Presbyterian Mut. Assur. Fund v. Allen, 4 West. Rep. 712, 106 Ind. 593; Raub v. Masonic Mut. Relief Asso. 3 Mackey, 68.

Where the association is a voluntary association, the court has no power, in most instances, to pass upon the question as to whether its rules and regulations adopted for the guidance of its affairs are reasonable or unreasonable. Hyde v. Woods, 2 Sawy. 655; Fritz v. Muck, 62 How. Pr. 74; White v. Brownell, 2 Daly, 329.

maintain actions against corporate bodies for the purpose of influencing or controlling their corporate action. However desirable it may be for the members of financial, industrial and social organizations to be acquainted with the legal force and effect of rules and by-laws, adopted by such societies for the purpose of regulating the conduct and action of its members, it furnishes no reason why courts should entertain jurisdiction of actions, either legal or equitable, brought for the mere purpose of obtaining such information, whether they be instituted in behalf of the member bringing the action alone, or in that of all the associates in the corporation. It is only when some injury has been inflicted on the person, or some right of property has been invaded, destroyed or prejudiced by the action of such corporation, that a member is entitled to maintain an action in the courts for redress or protection. Courts do not sit for the purpose of determining speculative and abstract questions of law, or laying down rules for the future conduct of individuals in their business and social relations; but are confined in their judicial action to real controversies wherein the legal rights of parties are necessarily involved and can be conclusively determined. *Bigelow* v. *Hartford Bridge Co.* 14 Conn. 565.

It is said in that case: "It is obviously not fit that the power of the court should be invoked in this form for every theoretical or speculative violation of one's rights."

Legal actions are designed to afford redress for injuries already inflicted and rights of persons or property actually invaded. Equitable actions, however, are not only remedial in their nature, but may also be brought for the purpose of restraining the infliction of contemplated wrongs or injuries and the prevention of threatened illegal action, which may be the occasion of serious injury to others. The creation of equity jurisdiction arose out of the inability of courts of law, through the inflexibility of their rules and want of power to adapt judgments to the special circumstances of cases, to reach and do complete justice in all cases. It is therefore a cardinal rule of equity that it will not entertain jurisdiction of cases where there is an adequate remedy at law, or grant relief, unless for the purpose of preventing serious and irreparable injury. *McHenry* v. *Jewett*, 90 N. Y. 58; *People* v. *Canal Board*, 55 N. Y. 394.

These principles are elementary and lie at the foundation of all equitable jurisdiction. Equity therefore interferes in the transactions of men by preventive measures only when irreparable injury is threatened and the law does not afford an adequate remedy for the contemplated wrong.

As was said by *Judge* Andrews in *McHenry* v. *Jewett*, 90 N. Y. 62, "it is not sufficient to authorize the remedy by injunction, that a violation of a naked legal right of property is threatened. There must be some special ground of jurisdiction, and where an injunction is the final relief sought, facts which entitle the plaintiff to this remedy must be averred in the complaint and established on the hearing."

We think the judgments of the courts below in this case have proceeded in disregard of the elementary rules referred to. We have looked in vain through the findings of the trial court and the evidence given, to discover any grounds, aside from the alleged invalidity of the by-laws, to which the equitable jurisdiction asserted can be referred. A condition of things is indeed indicated by the findings, from which it may be inferred that the plaintiff will be embarrassed in the conduct of his business on account of non-membership in the Union through the action of some of his employés and artists in withdrawing from his employment. Embarrassments in business, however, which arise from the action of those engaged in or connected with a similar business, although influenced by obligations assumed by them voluntarily in becoming members of societies, or by representations made to them by individual members of such organizations generally, give no right of action to persons so embarrassed either against the societies or the individuals so influenced. The action of the employés referred to is not shown to be the consequence of the threatened proceedings against the plaintiff, or to be dictated by any other influence than that of a voluntary determination by them adopted in reference to the management and control of their own business interest.

A brief reference to the undisputed facts in the case shows that the plaintiff's anticipation of injury from the defendant's action is conjectural and based upon insufficient grounds. The defendant was a corporation organized for the general purpose of cultivating "the art of music in all its branches, and the promotion of good feeling and friendly intercourse among the members of the profession and the relief of such of their members as shall be unfortunate." They had power to make and establish by-laws, rules and regulations, not inconsistent with any existing law, as they shall judge proper, and, among other things, to impose, remit and reduce fines, and to suspend or expel "such members as shall refuse or neglect to comply with the said by-laws and regulations." Laws 1864, chap. 168; Laws 1878, chap. 321.

The plaintiff, being a member of such corporation, brought this action to restrain the defendant from enforcing against him certain by-laws of the corporation. The action, confessedly, is based upon the rights given to him as a member of the corporation, and he thereby seeks to retain his membership while endeavoring to exempt himself from the obligations of the rules and by-laws which he voluntarily assumed in joining the society. His complaint is founded upon the theory that certain by-laws are invalid and contrary to law, and he seeks to have them declared void, as he alleges, for his own protection and in the general interests of the corporation. The only by-laws legally involved in the action read as follows:

Art. 3, § 1: "It shall be the duty of every member to refuse to perform in any orchestra or band in which any person or persons are engaged who are not members in good standing, excepting organists and directors of musical societies and members of traveling companies, and, with such, for no longer a period than four weeks; and any member who shall have violated this section shall be deemed to have committed a breach of good faith and fair dealing between the members of this society, and shall be punished according to § 2 of art. 11."

That section provides that an offender "shall, after a fair and impartial investigation by the board of directors, if found guilty, be fined for the first offense $10; for the second offense $20, and for the third offense, be expelled by the board of directors."

The plaintiff was the director of a musical society and a member of a traveling company, and therefore exempt from the operation of the by-law, at least, for a limited time. He was served November 9, 1885, with a notice of which the following is a copy, viz.:

New York November 9, 1885.

Sir,—You are requested to attend a meeting of the board of directors, to be held at Turn Hall, 66 East Fourth Street, New York, on Friday, the 13th inst., at 10 o'clock, A. M., to show cause why you should not be fined for two violations of § 1, article 3, of the by-laws, November 3 and 5.

By order,
M. Papst,
Secretary.

This notice constitutes the only legal evidence of any intended action by the corporation. This suit was commenced on the 10th day of November, 1885, and demands judgment that said by-laws be declared illegal and void, and that said board of directors may be perpetually enjoined and restrained from enforcing the same against the said plaintiff, and against the members of his orchestral company, who are also members of the said defendant Union.

We do not deem it necessary to consider the question of the validity of the by-laws, as they are not necessarily involved in the determination of the action. We are met, *in limine*, by the objection, on the part of the defendant, that no case has been made bringing the action within settled principles controlling courts in the exercise of their equitable jurisdiction over litigants, and there seems to be no answer to the objection. It is not claimed but that the directors were proceeding, in strict accordance with the powers conferred upon them by the by-laws of the corporation, to investigate and determine the questions whether the plaintiff had been guilty of the offense charged, and, if so, the punishment which should be imposed for the offense. So far as the contract rights of the plaintiff are concerned, he admits the jurisdiction of the board of directors, under their charter and by-laws, to try and determine the charge made against him; but claims that he may, in advance of any action on their part, procure an adjudication by the court as to the validity of the by-laws. As we have heretofore seen, he may raise this question, provided its enforcement subjects him to irreparable injury, and other adequate means of redress are not open to him; but in such event only.

It is claimed by the appellant that the action is prematurely brought, inasmuch as the plaintiff has not exhausted his remedies within the society against the infliction of an unjust punishment, and that his remedy at law is amply sufficient to protect him from the injury threatened; and we think this claim is well founded. It becomes necessary, therefore, to see just what it is the corporation proposed to do to the plaintiff. The evidence of the contemplated action is undisputed, and consists solely of the proceedings indicated by the letter summoning the plaintiff for trial before the board of directors, as was found by the trial court. He is thereby notified of an intention to try him for two offenses only; the extreme penalty of which, if found guilty, is the imposition of fines, amounting in the aggregate to $30. This is the extent of the offending proved on the part of the corporation against the plaintiff. There is no question raised, either on the proof or findings, as to the expulsion of the plaintiff from the organization, or any question which looks beyond the exaction of the fines imposed.

If, therefore, the plaintiff is to be injured at all by the action of the corporation it is by the requirement to pay these fines. How is he injured by their imposition? No process is provided by which the corporation can collect them, and their payment, if made at all, must necessarily be by the voluntary action of the plaintiff. If their collection is attempted by legal proceedings, the plaintiff has the same defense to an action therefor that he now seeks to use in restraining this action. It may be claimed that his neglect to pay the fines subjects him to expulsion from the corporation; but it is sufficient to say that the proof does not show any intent by the corporation to expel him, and he is entitled to resort to the remedy by injunction only when the necessity for it clearly appears. The plaintiff voluntarily became a member of the defendant society under a pledge to obey its rules and regulations, and so long as he voluntarily continues such member is bound by them, unless he is subjected to some legal injury for which he has no other redress but an action. It affords him no legal ground of complaint against the corporation that others are members thereof and voluntarily obey its rules and regulations, although such action requires them to refuse, under certain conditions, to transact business with the plaintiff.

We are therefore of the opinion that the only relief which could, under any circumstances, be granted to the plaintiff in this action being a judgment restraining the defendant from prosecuting its charges for violation of by-laws, and as this involves the imposition of a penalty only which the corporation has no means of enforcing, no ground for equitable relief has been established.

It also appears, in addition to the absence of any serious injury to the plaintiff's rights which might follow the infliction of the penalties, that he has not availed himself of the means afforded by the rules of the organization to avoid them. He could have urged the invalidity of the by-laws; his ignorance of them; his exemption therefrom, as the manager of an orchestra, in defense of the charge, or in palliation thereof, and the directors had power to acquit him and remit or reduce the fines. Without waiting to see what the action of the board might be, he assumes that he will be found guilty, his defense disregarded, his excuses ignored, and that the punishment will be inflicted. The case is quite barren of evidence tending to show that any injury is reasonably likely to happen to him. We have not been referred to any authorities holding that an action in equity will be sustained under such circumstances. Even in the case of offenses involving the penalty of expulsion from similar societies, actions have been maintained to enjoin such societies from denying the privileges of membership to a party expelled, only after action by the society expelling such members has been had. No case has been cited where an injunction has been granted in anticipation of such an event, and we think, within settled rules, that suit in equity for such a purpose is not maintainable. *Hurst* v. *New York Produce Exchange,* 100 N. Y. 605, 1 Cent. Rep. 260; *Fisher* v. *Keane,* L. R. 11 Ch. Div. 858; *Labouchere* v. *Earl of Wharncliffe,* L. R. 13 Ch. Div. 346; *Gregg* v. *Massachusetts Medical Society,* 111 Mass. 194; *People* v. *Erie Co. Medical Society,* 24 Barb. 570; *Wolfe* v. *Burke,* 56 N. Y. 118; *West* v. *New York,* 10 Paige, 539.

We practically held in the *Hurst Case,* that the remedy by injunction could not lie, as no violation of plaintiff's rights had happened, or may ever happen, and no injury thereto is threatened in such a sense as justifies a preventive remedy, and the rule there adopted must govern this case.

The judgments of the courts below should be reversed and a new trial ordered, with costs to abide the event.

All concur.

TEXAS SUPREME COURT.

FORT WORTH & RIO GRANDE R. CO., *Appt.,*

v.

Sarah G. JENNINGS.

(....Tex.....)

1. **Building another railroad on a portion of the unused right of way** of a company which has acquired an easement only in the land creates an additional servitude, and the consent of the owner of the land must first be obtained and compensation made to him for the damage.

2. **A defect in a petition** setting up a claim for damages which are too remote to furnish a basis for an action, and an injury which is not special to plaintiff, is not reached by a general demurrer.

(March 4, 1899.)

APPEAL by defendant from a judgment of the District Court for Tarrant County in favor of plaintiff in an action to enjoin defendant from constructing its road along and upon a right of way granted to another company without making compensation to plaintiff. *Affirmed.*

The facts are fully stated in the opinion.

Mr. **N. A. Stedman** for appellant.

NOTE.—*Grant of right of way to railroad; interest acquired.*

A railroad company taking land for its right of way is not the absolute owner of the land taken, but takes and holds the right to occupy it for certain purposes. Trowbridge v. Brookline, 8 New Eng. Rep. 791, 144 Mass. 139.

There is no legal presumption that its occupancy extends to the full legal limit. Philadelphia & R. R. Co. v. Obert, 1 Cent. Rep. 384, 109 Pa. 193.

The grant to a railroad of a right of way conveys to it a mere easement and nothing more. Vermilya v. Chicago, M. & St. P. R. Co. 66 Iowa, 611.

And where it conveys the right of way "for all purposes connected with the construction, use and occupation of said railway," it limits the grant to that railway and its purposes alone. Id. 607.

A railroad company has no power or right to grant an easement even of a foot-way along or by the side of its tracks, and no prescriptive right or presumption of such grant can be asserted. Sapp v. North. Cent. R. Co. 51 Md. 115.

While mere nonuser will not defeat or impair the location of a railroad (Barlow v. Chicago, R. I. & P. R. Co. 29 Iowa, 276; Noll v. Dubuque, B. & M. R. Co. 32 Iowa, 66; Hestonville, M. & F. Pass. R. Co. v. Philadelphia, 89 Pa. 210), yet it may be defeated by permitting another company to take land and actually construct its road thereon. Chesapeake & O. Canal Co. v. Baltimore & O. R. Co. 4 Gill & J. 1; Coe v. New Jersey M. R. Co. 28 N. J. Eq. 100.

A parol license granted by the company to another corporation to pass over the location of its road, or to otherwise use it, is revocable at any time. Illinois Cent. R. Co. v. Godfrey, 71 Ill. 500; Pennsylvania R. Co. v. Jones, 50 Pa. 417; Heyl v. Philadelphia, W. & B. R. Co. 51 Pa. 469.

A railroad company should have such sole and exclusive control of the land within the lines of its road as shall enable it so to keep it as to exclude all probability of any accident resulting from any outside interference with such possession. Hayden v. Skillings, 8 New Eng. Rep. 176, 78 Me. 413.

The mere right of way of a railroad corporation cannot be sold, even on execution, to one who does not own the franchise. East Alabama R. Co. v. Doe, 114 U. S. 340 (29 L. ed. 136).

A railroad company cannot so lease or transfer its interest under its franchises as to rid itself of liability to the owner of land from which it has a right of way, for the improper use of it. Backus v. Detroit, W. T. & J. R. Co. 71 Mich. 645.

A railroad company cannot transfer to an individual or a firm its franchise as a common carrier over a part of its route, with a view and for the purpose of enabling the grantee to operate the road thereon as private property and exclusively for the purpose of his private business. Fanning v. Osborne, 3 Cent. Rep. 453, 102 N. Y. 441.

The Texas & Pacific Railroad Company, under the Act of Congress of March 3, 1871, and the Supplementary Act of May 2, 1872, had no power to transfer its own land grant, road and franchises, or a section thereof, to another corporation. The power to make such a sale was not included in the power given to issue construction and land bonds, and execute mortgages to secure them, on the land grant and other lands the company might acquire. Southern Pac. R. Co. v. Esquibel (N. M.) 5 R. R. & Corp. L. J. 256.

See also 26 L. R. A. 443.

Messrs. **John D. Templeton** and **Hyde Jennings**, for appellee:

A grant of right of way to a railroad or its successors confers no authority on such railroad to convey any part of said right of way except to the purchasers of its franchises, etc.

East Alabama R. Co. v. *Doe*, 114 U. S. 340 (29 L. ed. 136); *Platt* v. *Pennsylvania Co.* 1 West. Rep. 11, 48 Ohio St. 228, 23 Am. & Eng. R. R. Cas. 129; *Sapp* v. *Northern Cent. R. Co.* 51 Md. 51; *Internat. & G. N. R. Co.* v. *Smith Co.* 65 Tex. 21.

The deed of right of way from appellee to the Texas & Pacific Railway Company conveyed nothing but an easement without profit to the Texas & Pacific Railway, and the construction of any other railroad thereon would be an additional burden for which the grantor would be entitled to damages.

Platt v. *Pennsylvania Co. supra; Texas & Pacific R. Co.* v. *Durrett*, 57 Tex. 48; *Southern Pac. R. Co.* v. *Reed*, 41 Cal. 256; *Vermilya* v. *Chicago, M. & St. P. R. Co.* 66 Iowa, 606, 55 Am. Rep. 279; *Tutt* v. *Port Royal & A. R. Co.* 28 S. C. 388; *New Jersey Zinc & Iron Co.* v. *Morris Canal & Bkg. Co.* 1 L. R. A. 133, 44 N. J. Eq. 398; *Imlay* v. *Union Branch R. Co.* 26 Conn. 249; Pierce, R. R. 260, 496, 497.

If said Fort Worth & Rio Grande Railroad had been constructed over said Texas & Pacific right of way it would have been a taking of or damage to plaintiff's land, and she had the right to restrain it by injunction without alleging in her petition that appellant was insolvent or that her damages would be irreparable.

Texas Const. art. 1, § 17; *Gulf, C. & S. F. R. Co.* v. *Eddins*, 60 Tex. 656; *Gulf, C. & S. F. R. Co.* v. *Fuller*, 63 Tex. 467; *Tait* v. *G. H. & S. A. R. Co.* Id. 223; 2 High, Inj. § 622 *et seq.*

Plaintiff is entitled to damage by reason of the construction of defendant's railroad across a street or streets on which plaintiff's lots abut, although such lots may be remote from such crossing.

Gulf, C. & S. F. R. Co. v. *Eddins, Gulf, C. & S. F. R. Co.* v. *Fuller* and *Tait* v. *G. H. & S. A. R. Co. supra; Trinity & S. W. R. Co.* v. *Meadow*, 73 Tex. 34; *Haney* v. *Gulf, C. & S. F. R. Co.* 3 Ct. App. Civ. Cas. § 278 *et seq.*; 3 Sutherland, Damages, 423, 424.

Collard, J., delivered the opinion of the court:

The conveyance of plaintiff to the Texas & Pacific Railway Company of a right of way through her land in the City of Fort Worth vested in the company a perpetual easement for the purposes of right of way for its road. Pierce, Railroads, 130.

The fee was not conveyed, but remained in the vendor. This company, having constructed its road on the right of way designated, and operating the same, transferred a part of its right of way, between its track and adjacent lots, to appellant, the Fort Worth & Rio Grande Railway Company; and the latter Company has taken steps to build its road on this strip without compensation to Mrs. Jennings, whose adjacent lots will be injured or damaged by depreciation in value, if the road is built. Can this be done? The direct question has not been decided in this State; but kindred questions have been decided and discussed by the supreme court, a brief review of which will greatly aid us in deciding the question before us.

In the case of *Houston & T C. R. Co.* v. *Odum*, 53 Tex. 353, *Justice* Gould, delivering the opinion, says: "The use of a street by a railroad, however, is not ordinarily inconsistent with its continued use for the common purpose of a street. The authorities are numerous and conclusive that such an addition to the uses of a street, the fee being in the public, if authorized by the Legislature, gives the lot owner no right to compensation, although his easement in the street be thereby partially impaired and his lots rendered less valuable. The regulation or enlargement of the use of the street—the property of the State—by the Legislature is not a taking of property, within the meaning of the Constitution of 1869, although the lot owner may thereby suffer incidental or consequential inconvenience or injury."

The Constitution of 1869 provided that "no person's property shall be taken or applied to public use without just compensation being made, unless by the consent of such person." Const. 1869, art. 1, § 14; 2 Paschal, Dig. 1101.

The owner's rights in property are better guarded under the Constitution of 1876. It declares that "no person's property shall be taken, damaged or destroyed for, or applied to, public use without adequate compensation being made, unless by consent of such person." Const. 1876, art. 1, § 17.

Construing this language, it has been held that the term "property" as here used, means "not only the tangible thing owned, but also every right which accompanies ownership, and is its incident," and that, where the construction of a railroad inflicts an injury to such property not common to all other property in the same community by reason of the general fact of the existence of the railway, then such property may be said to be damaged, for which there must be compensation to the owner. *Gulf, C. & S. F. R. Co.* v. *Fuller*, 63 Tex. 467.

The court affirmed a judgment for damages in favor of the owner of lots and improvements on a street in which, by legislative authority, a railway company had built its road.

In another later case, decided at the Galveston Term, 1889, *Justice* Gaines, commenting upon the language of the Constitution, says: "Under the provisions of other Constitutions, which merely provided compensation to the owner for property taken for public use, it had been a question whether or not one whose property was immediately and directly damaged by a public improvement, though no part of it was appropriated, could recover for such damages. . . . The insertion of the words 'damaged or destroyed' in the section [of the Constitution] quoted was doubtless intended to obviate this question, and to afford protection to the owner of property by allowing him compensation when, by the construction of a public work, his property was directly damaged or destroyed, although no part of it was actually appropriated." *Trinity & S. W. R. Co.* v. *Meadows*, 73 Tex. 34.

It will now be seen that it is the law of this State that there need be no taking or actual appropriation of property to entitle the owner to damages on account of the construction of a

See also 30 L. R. A. 534.

railroad, or other public works adjacent thereto, but that it is sufficient if the property be thereby directly and specially damaged,—depreciated in value,—as a result not common to all such property in the same community; and it will also be seen that, where land has once been dedicated to the public as a highway, it cannot, even upon authority of the Legislature, be appropriated to other public uses, so as to impose additional burdens upon other adjacent property, without adequate compensation to the owner. Wood, Railway Law, 721 *et seq.*; Pierce, Railroads, 232.

The rights acquired by condemnation of land for public purposes are similar to those ordinarily acquired by contract, unless otherwise stipulated in the deed. Mills, Em. Dom. §§ 110, 111; Pierce, Railroads, 132.

The use of a street for a horse-car railway is not deemed a different use from that intended in its original dedication as a street. *Texas & P. R. Co.* v. *Rosedale St. R. Co.* 64 Tex. 80.

The appellant contends, in this case, that a transfer of a part of its right of way by the Texas & Pacific Railway Company to the appellant did not contemplate a use different from that intended in the deed conveying to it the right of way, and consequently there could be no additional burden upon plaintiff's land by the building and running of defendant's road thereon. We cannot agree to this proposition. The deed of the right of way was to the Texas & Pacific Railway Company, granting it the right to use the same perpetually in operating its road. There is no doubt that a legal sale of the franchise and road would carry everything appurtenant thereto,—the right of way as well as the right to operate the road, and take tolls for freight and passengers; but it may be doubted that it can sever a part of the easement—an incident of the franchise—from the franchise itself, and convey the same to another company.

It has been held by the Supreme Court of the United States that "the right of way could not be sold, on execution or otherwise, to a purchaser who did not own the franchise." *East Alabama R. Co.* v. *Doe*, 114 U. S. 341 [29 L. ed. 137].

The same doctrine is maintained in Ohio. *Platt* v. *Pennsylvania Co.* 43 Ohio St. 228, 1 West. Rep. 11, 22 Am. & Eng. R. R. Cas. 129.

But, where one company sold its entire right of way to another authorized to build and maintain a road between the same points, it was held that the owner of the fee was not injured or affected by the transfer, and that he could not call in question the capacity of the one company to sell, nor the other to purchase. *Crolley* v. *Minneapolis & St. L. R. Co.* 30 Minn. 541.

A railway company pledged its road and appurtenances to the State. The road was sold to satisfy the pledge, and Lane purchased one section of the road. Without deciding whether his purchase included any of the corporate franchises in conjunction with other purchases, it was held that a sale by him to the Junction Company passed title to the right of way, provided it constructed the road as required by the first corporation. *Junction R. Co.* v. *Ruggles*, 7 Ohio St. 1.

Where depot grounds were deeded to a railway company, and, under sanction of the Legislature, the property became vested in another company, it was held that the conditions of the original sale, to the use of the first company, were not violated. *Southard* v. *New Jersey Cent. R. Co.* 26 N. J. L. 13.

A railway company made an assignment of its road and effects, which was adjudged valid by the courts. It was held that purchasers at the trustee's sale, who afterwards incorporated, acquired all rights of the old company under deed to the right of way. *Pollard* v. *Maddox*, 28 Ala. 321.

It has been held that the interest in land acquired by deed to the right of way, within the designated route, may be transferred to another railroad company, into which the original shall merge or consolidate with others by legislative authority. *New Jersey M. R. Co.* v. *VanSyckle*, 37 N. J. L. 496; Pierce, Railroads, 130, 132, 133, 496, 497.

The foregoing four cases are cited in Pierce on Railroads in support of the doctrine as stated in the text, "that a railway company . . . may convey, under authority of law, to another corporation, the interest in land which it has acquired by purchase for a right of way, to be used by the purchaser for the same purpose." And we find that none of the cases support the proposition that a railway company can sell a part of its right of way to another company, so as to enable both companies to build and operate two roads on the same right of way. These authorities only go to the extent of holding that, where there is a legal sale of the road, its corporate rights, or when there is a merger of roads, or where one road is abandoned, and another company is authorized to construct the road on the same line, the right of way may pass by sale.

It may not be necessary, in the case before us, to decide whether a railway company owning the right of way may or may not, with the consent of all interested parties, sell a part of it without at the same time conveying its franchise. It may be only necessary for us to inquire if this can be done without the consent of adjoining land owners, without compensation, by purchase or condemnation, where their lands are damaged specially, and not in common with the general public. Appellant cites the case of *Hatch* v. *Cincinnati & I. R. Co.*, 18 Ohio St. 118, as sustaining its right to take the strip conveyed to it by the Texas & Pacific Railway Company, and construct its road thereon, without compensation to plaintiff for additional damages to her land. The land of plaintiff, in the case cited, was appropriated, under the right of eminent domain, for the purposes of a canal. The canal was made, and used for many years. A railway company, by amicable agreement, had the canal company's interest in the right of way condemned for its use as a railway without the consent of, or compensation to, the owner of adjoining land. The canal was abandoned, and the railroad constructed on the line. It was held that the easement was not abandoned by the canal company to the extent that it reverted to the original owner of the land; but it was also held that the owner was entitled "to recover the value of lands taken, not formerly taken by the original condemnation, and also a fair compensation for additional burdens and inconveniences, not common to the general public, as accrued to him, and his entire tract on which the easement was imposed, by reason of the change of uses." We do not see in what respect this case supports the position of appellant; but, if it is supposed to do so, it was overruled in the later case of *Platt* v. *Pennsylvania Co.*, decided in 1885 by the same court, which is a case almost exactly in point with the one now under consideration. The Lake Shore Railroad Company had appropriated by condemnation a strip of ground 100 feet wide by 1,200 feet in length, and constructed its road on the western half, along which the road was operated. For a consideration of $7,500, the company agreed with another railroad corporation to let it have twenty-five feet wide of the unused half upon which to construct and operate another road, and to so hold the same in perpetuity. The second road was built and operated on the surplus twenty-five feet, but no consideration was paid to the original owner, whose lot was thereby damaged. It was held that the land owner, by the first appropriation (where more land was appropriated than was necessary, an easement, and not a fee, having passed), could not be subjected to the occupancy and burden upon such surplus of another common carrier. It was also held that the original owner could not have recovered the surplus from the first company, but had the right, after its sale, to treat it as abandoned by the first company for its own uses, and that he was entitled to damages as upon an appropriation by the second company. It was also noted by the court that this holding was not in conflict with the recognized right of a railway company to sell or lease its road with its franchises. 43 Ohio St. 228, 1 West. Rep. 11, 22 Am. & Eng. R. R. Cas. 129.

The court also declared that plaintiff's case was supported by the cases of *Junction R. Co.* v. *Ruggles* and *Hatch* v. *Cincinnati & I. R. Co.* There was a dissenting opinion, holding that there was no change in the use of the easement, and therefore no additional servitude upon the owner's land; but we think the reasoning of the majority of the court is conclusive and just. It cannot be doubted that a right of way to one railroad is less onerous than when the same is granted to two, and it must be held that a grant of way to one does not authorize it to operate its road, and to convey a portion of the unused way to another company for the same purpose, without the consent of the owner of adjacent land damaged thereby, and without compensation to him for the damage so caused.

We think injunction to restrain the building of the road by defendant until the plaintiff was compensated, or until the way was properly appropriated under the law, was the proper remedy. Pierce, Railroads, 167, 168, 230.

Appellant contends that the court "erred in overruling its general demurrer to plaintiff's petition, because so much of said petition as alleges damage on account of the contemplated construction and operation of defendant's railway across Hill, Ochiltree, Ballinger and Center Streets, to property not abutting on the right of way of the Texas & Pacific Railway Company, sets up a claim for damages too remote to furnish a basis for an action; and the injury, if any, is not special to plaintiff." If there was error in this part of plaintiff's petition, it being good in other respects, a general demurrer would not reach the defect.

The judgment of the court restrained defendant from building its road on the part of the Texas & Pacific Railway Company's right of way running through any portion of blocks 12, 13, 25 and 29 of Jennings' South Addition to the City of Fort Worth, and also that portion of the right of way occupying Hill and Center Streets, at the intersection of said streets, between the center of said railway track and said block 29. The judgment awards and fixes no damages, but prohibits the building of the road without the consent of the plaintiff, his heirs or assigns, first had and obtained, or without proper appropriation of the same under the laws of the State. Hill and Center Streets intersect at the corner of block 29, where the right of way cuts off a corner of the block. The block abuts on the side of the right of way on which defendant proposes to build its road. We cannot say that there would be no damage to plaintiff by the construction of the road at this point, so causing additional obstruction in these streets. The question of the amount of damage must be settled by the parties, if they consent, or in the proceedings of condemnation, if defendant resort to that method of appropriation, as allowed by the judgment. Our conclusion is, the judgment of the court ought to be affirmed.

Stayton, *Ch. J.*:

Report of commission of appeals examined, their opinion adopted, and *the judgment affirmed.*

MICHIGAN SUPREME COURT.

James T. FLAHERTY
v.
Michael MORAN, *Appt.*

(......Mich.......)

A fence erected maliciously, and with no other purpose than to shut out the light and air from a neighbor's window, is a nuisance.

(May 16, 1890.)

APPEAL by defendant from a decree of the Circuit Court for Kent County in favor of complainant in a suit brought to enjoin the maintenance of a certain fence. *Affirmed.*

The case sufficiently appears in the opinion.

Mr. **L. E. Carroll** for defendant, appellant.

Messrs. **Thompson & Temple** for complainant, appellee.

Long, *J.*, delivered the opinion of the court:

The parties to this cause own adjoining lots in the City of Grand Rapids, complainant's lot being on the northwest corner of Goodrich and

See also 22 L. R. A. 141.

Lagrave Streets, and the defendant's lot adjoining it on the north, both extending westerly to an alley in the rear. The line of the lots was established before either of the parties purchased. The defendant built a house some years ago near the north line of his lot, and standing back some distance from the street. He occupies this property as his home. In August, 1888, the complainant commenced the erection of a house on the front end of his lot. It was to be a double house, facing Lagrave Street, and the north wall being laid about four feet from the line between the two lots, the front wall being much nearer Lagrave Street than defendant's house. After the foundation wall was laid, the defendant built a screen or board fence, about ten feet in height, along the line of the lots, but upon his own premises, extending from the front wall of the complainant's house backward the whole length of complainant's house. It is claimed by the complainant that the screen or fence was built maliciously, and for the purpose of darkening his (complainant's) rooms, and for no useful purpose. The bill is filed to compel the defendant to remove such fence. On the hearing in the court below, the court decreed such removal within sixty days from the decree, and perpetually enjoined the defendant from building or maintaining such a screen or fence. From this decree defendant appeals.

The testimony was taken in open court, and there seems but little dispute of fact, except as to the motive which induced the defendant to build such a fence. It appears that while the complainant was building his house, and during the time the foundation wall was being placed, the wife of the defendant came up and saw Mrs. Flaherty near there, and inquired if the complainant's house was to stand so near the street, and being advised that it was, she remarked that it would spoil the looks of their place and shut off their south view, and, if it was so built, she would build a board fence between them twelve feet high. Soon after this talk the fence was built. Posts were put in the ground, stringers put across, and the boards, extending up and down, were nailed on these stringers, on the defendant's side, the side towards complainant's house being left rough and unplaned. This fence stands within about four feet of complainant's house, and, as the proofs show, darkens his rooms, and obstructs the light and air. The defendant claims not to have known much about the erection of the fence; but it is shown that he brought the posts there, and paid the bill presented for its construction, though his wife looked generally to the height and character of the fence while it was being built. It is not profitable to recite the evidence given on the hearing. The only excuse made by the defense for its erection comes from the wife of the defendant, who testifies that, while the walls of the complainant's house were being erected, she met Mrs. Flaherty on the corner of the lawn, and inquired if the house was to come so near the street as that, and, being told that it did, she responded to Mrs. Flaherty: "Don't you know that you are going to injure the property on the street, and injure ourselves entirely?" when Mrs. Flaherty said: "We are building the house for ourselves, not for other people;" when Mrs. Moran said: "Very well. We will build a fence for ourselves, and we will make it twelve feet high." Soon after this the fence was built, and has ever since been so kept and maintained.

Mrs. Moran says, upon an inquiry being made as to who maintains it: "I do, for my own benefit,—to keep the neighbors from looking through my house, and to protect my lawn. It is not pleasant to live in a house where folks can look right through it, and have another house down in front of you, that you cannot sit down by a window unless your neighbors can see you. There are times when folks want to be alone in their own house; and, furthermore, I want that fence to plant vines on."

The *animus* of the whole matter is plainly discernible from the testimony of Mrs. Moran. The complainant had built his house standing somewhat nearer the street than defendant's house, so that Mrs. Moran's view was obstructed towards the south, and she thought it hurt the looks of her place. It is very evident that the fence serves no useful or needful purpose, and was built, and is now maintained, out of pure malice and spite. The case comes so squarely within the opinion of *Mr. Justice* Morse in *Burke* v. *Smith*,* 69 Mich. 380, 15 West. Rep. 371, that I shall not discuss the questions of law involved. It was there held, by an equal division of the court as then constituted, that "a fence erected maliciously, and with no other purpose than to shut out the light and air from a neighbor's window, is a nuisance."

I fully approve of the reasoning of *Mr. Justice* Morse in that case, and rest this case upon the reason there given by him.

The decree must be affirmed, with costs.

The other Justices concurred.

*The unanimous decision of the court in this case having by the adoption of the opinion of *Mr. Justice* Morse in Burke v. Smith, 15 West. Rep. 371, 69 Mich. 380, now made it for the first time the law of the court, which it was not before, because the court was in that case equally divided, it becomes important to publish that opinion in connection with this case.

By reason of the closeness of the question, and the conflict of decisions upon it in different jurisdictions, the opinions of other members of the court in opposition of that of *Mr. Justice* Morse are also given here. [Rep.]

MORSE, J.:

The parties to this suit own adjoining lots in the City of Kalamazoo. The complainant built two dwelling-houses on his lots for the purposes of rental; one house fronts on Park Street, the other upon Osborn Street. These houses came up within about two feet of the line between him and the defendant. When these houses were built, Smith had a house on his lot fronting on Park Street, with room for a driveway between his house and complainant's premises. About the time complainant erected his houses, Smith built a house on his lot, fronting on Osborn Street. Complainant's houses were about fourteen feet front, with a single tier of rooms running back from the street.

These parties got into a quarrel, and, as a result of petty annoyances on both sides, the defendant finally put up a screen or fence in front of the lower side windows of the complainant, as it is claimed, covering, obscuring and darkening the same, and shutting out the light and air therefrom. The evidence shows these screens to be two in number, and about eleven feet high, coming up to the top of the lower windows of complainant's houses. They were built by setting posts in the ground and nailing boards against them. They were open at the bottom, below the windows.

I think it is established by the evidence that these screens were not put up for a fence, or any other necessary or useful or ornamental purpose, but simply to shut out the view of defendant's premises from complainant's windows.

Smith claims that he did not wish the occupants of complainant's houses to gaze into the windows, or to witness the getting out of and into carriages of his family at the horse block beside the driveway, and for that reason put up the barriers. There is plenty of evidence that when he was erecting these screens he said he was doing it to shut the light out of Burke's windows. I think there was nothing but malice in his motives.

The complainant files his bill of complaint alleging the ownership, value and use of the property belonging to him, the desirability of these houses for rental to families being averred as constituting their chief value. He alleges that these screens were unnecessarily erected from malicious motives, and for the express and avowed purpose of darkening the windows of his two houses, and cutting off the light from entering the windows of said houses, obstructing the view from them, and thereby injuring the value of the houses; avers that they are an intolerable nuisance, that by their existence light and air are prevented from freely entering his houses, the view from the windows is wholly obstructed and cut off, the looks and appearance of the houses greatly injured, their desirability as homes greatly lessened, their rental value depreciated, and their actual market value reduced more than $500; prays that the said screens may be abated as a nuisance, and a perpetual injunction allowed against a continuation or renewal of the same. The court below granted the prayer of complainant's bill.

These screens are erected entirely upon the lot of the defendant; and he appeals to this court, claiming that he has a perfect right to erect and maintain them, and that the question of his motives has nothing to do with the legal aspects of the case, though he disclaims any malice against complainant.

It must be taken for granted, in disposing of this case, that these screens were not erected for the purposes of a fence, or for any other necessary, useful or ornamental purpose. The pretense that they were built to keep prying eyes from observing what was going on in the houses or yard of the defendant is not supported by the proofs. The evidence is clear to my mind that malice alone entered into the reason and motive of their erection. The proofs are conclusive upon this subject.

It is admitted by the counsel for the complainant that he would have no redress had the defendant erected houses or useful buildings or structures as near to complainant's line as these screens are, even though the consequent damage of such erection would have been as great or greater than it has been and now is from the effect of these screens upon the dwellings of complainant, in every respect here complained of.

But his contention is that these screens being a damage to the houses of complainant, and being erected for no good or useful purpose, but with the malicious motive of doing injury, they became and are such a nuisance to the property of complainant that equity will cause their removal and enjoin their future erection or continuance. He invokes the legal maxim that "every man in the use of his own property must avoid injury to his neighbors' property as much as possible," and argues that while it is true that when one pursues a strictly legal right, his motives are immaterial, yet no man has a right to build and maintain an entirely useless structure for the sole purpose of injuring his neighbor. The argument has force, and appears irresistible in the light of the moral law, that ought to govern all human action. And the civil law, coming close to the moral law, declares that "he who in making a new work upon his own estate uses his right without trespassing either against any law, custom, title or possession which may subject him to any service towards his neighbors, is not answerable for the damages which they may chance to sustain thereby, unless it be that he made that change merely with a view to hurt others without advantage to himself."

Thus the civil law recognizes the moral law, and does not permit the owner of land to do an act upon his own premises for the express purpose of injuring his neighbor, when the act brings no profit or advantage to himself.

The law furnishes redress, because the injury is malicious and unjustifiable. The moral law imposes upon every man the duty of doing unto others as he would that they should do unto him. And the common law ought to, and, in my opinion does, require him to so use his own privileges and property as not to injure the rights of others maliciously and without necessity.

It is true that he can use his own property, if for his own benefit or advantage, in many cases to the injury of his neighbor; and such neighbor has no redress, because the owner of the property is exercising a legal right which infringes on no legal right of the other. Therefore, and under this principle, the defendant might have erected a building for useful or ornamental purposes, and shut out the light and air from complainant's windows; but when he erected these "screens" or "obscurers," for no useful or ornamental purpose, but out of pure malice against his neighbor, it seems to me a different principle must prevail. I do not think the common law permits a man to be deprived of water, air or light for the mere gratification of malice. No one has an exclusive property in any of these elements except as the same may exist or be confined entirely on his own premises. If a pond of water lies entirely within his lands, without inlet or outlet, he may do with it as he pleases, while he keeps it upon his own premises. He may also use as he pleases what air or light he can keep and hold within his dominion upon his own lands. But to the air and light between the earth and the heavens the right of each man is more or less dependent upon that of his neighbor. His neighbor must bear the inconvenience and annoyance that the legal and beneficial use of his premises engenders in this respect, if such use falls short of what the law treats as a nuisance; but the right to use one's premises to shut out or curtail the use of either of these elements by his neighbor, out of mere malice and wickedness, when such use is not beneficial to him in any sense, does not exist in law or equity. The complainant in this case had a right to the use of the air and the light about his houses and over defendant's lands, until such right came in conflict with the defendant's enjoyment of his property. This air and light were free and unconfined, and the common property of all.

The leading case relied upon by the defendant, and which has been followed by the courts of several of the States, is Mahan v. Brown, 13 Wend. 261. The action was brought for the obstruction of light. It was averred that the defendant had wantonly and maliciously erected, near to and in front of plaintiff's windows, a fence of the height of fifty feet, without benefit or advantage to himself, and for the sole purpose of annoying plaintiff, by means whereof her house was greatly darkened, and the light and air obstructed from entering the same through the windows, rendering the house uninhabitable, so that her boarders had left her, and her apartments were untenanted, etc. This fence was built, as the screens in this case were, by the defendant under the pretense of preventing his yard from being overlooked by the windows in the plaintiff's house, but in fact from mere malice and with the intent to exclude the light and air from the windows of the plaintiff. The court—Savage, *Ch. J.*, delivering the opinion—held that a person who makes a window in his house overlooking the privacy of his neighbor does an act which strictly he has no right to do, although it is said no action lies for it. "He is therefore encroaching, though not strictly and legally trespassing, upon the rights of another. He enjoys an easement, therefore, in his neighbor's property which in time may ripen into a right. But before sufficient time has elapsed to raise a presumption of a grant, he has no right, and can maintain no action, for being deprived of that easement, let the motive of deprivation be what it may; and the reason is that in the eye of the law he is not injured. He is deprived of no right, but only prevented from acquiring a right, without consideration, in his neighbor's property." The time fixed for acquiring this right or easement in the opinion is twenty years.

I apprehend that at this late day this is not the law in Michigan, and that it never was. A man here has a right to build a window in his house overlooking his neighbor's land, and he gets or gains no easement in his neighbor's property by so doing; and no lapse of time will make his lights "ancient," or prevent his neighbor from the beneficial use of his property, even to the detriment or total obstruction of air and light from his windows, if such windows are so near the premises of his neighbor that his building upon his land will darken or destroy them. Such being the law here, the reason for the decision in Mahan v. Brown, *supra*, does not exist in, and can have no application to, the case under consideration.

This ruling in Mahan v. Brown is followed in Phelps v. Nowlen, 72 N. Y. 39; Chatfield v. Wilson, 28 Vt. 49; Walker v. Cronin, 107 Mass. 555, and many other cases.

In a well-reasoned case in 74 Me. 164 (Chesley v. King), the authorities are reviewed, and the court reaches the conclusion "that it cannot be regarded as a maxim of universal application that malicious motives cannot make that a wrong which in its own essence is lawful." In that case the defendant dug a well upon his own land, which cut off the sources of supply from a spring upon plaintiff's premises. There was a special finding that defendant dug the well for the "mere, sole and malicious purpose of diverting the veins of water which supplied the spring, and not for the purpose of procuring a better supply of water for himself, and improving his estate." The supreme court found that this special finding was not supported by the evidence, but it takes issue with the doctrine of Phelps v. Nowlen, and Chatfield v. Wilson, *supra*, and holds, in substance, that if the special finding had been true, the plaintiff's action would have been sustained.

I am satisfied that the decree of the court below in this case is just and equitable, and can be sustained, if not by the weight of authority, by the better reason and best authority.

In Chasemore v. Richards, 7 H. L. Cas. 387, 388, the court, in laying down the rule that the owner of land has a right to the enjoyment of the land and to the underground waters upon it, and that he may, in order to obtain that water, sink a well to the injury of his neighbor, qualifies the rule by saying that "it seems right to hold that he ought to exercise his right in a reasonable manner, with as little injury to his neighbor's rights as may be;" and alludes to the fact that the civil law "deems an act, otherwise lawful in itself, illegal if done with a malicious intent of injuring a neighbor *animo vicino nocendi*."

In Greenleaf v. Francis, 18 Pick. 117, it is said: "These rights should not be exercised from mere malice." See also Wheatley v. Baugh, 25 Pa. 528; Roath v. Driscoll, 20 Conn. 533; Delhi v. Youmans, 50 Barb. 316-320; Panton v. Holland, 17 Johns. 92-98; Haldeman v. Bruckhart, 45 Pa. 514.

In an Ohio case the inquiry is raised, but not answered, whether, if a hole was dug upon one's premises to the damage of his neighbor, "from motives of unmixed malice, without any object, and, when done, incapable of answering any end, either of ornament, convenience or profit, connected with the enjoyment or use of his property, an action would not lie for the injury." Frazier v. Brown, 12 Ohio St. 294-304.

Mr. Cooley, in his work on Torts, in speaking of nuisances, says: "If a discomfort is wantonly caused from malice or wickedness, a slight degree of inconvenience may be sufficient to render it actionable." Cooley, Torts, 596.

Mr. Washburn, in his work on Easements, quotes with favor the doctrine as to rights in the use of water laid down in Wheatley v. Baugh, *supra*: "Neither the civil nor the common law permit a man to be deprived of a spring or stream of water for the mere gratification of malice. . . . The owner of land on which a spring issues from the earth has a perfect right to it against all the world, except those through whose lands it comes. He has even a right to it against them until it comes in conflict with the enjoyment of their right of property." Washb. Easem. 3d ed. 487, 488.

I cannot see why this principle does not apply with equal force to air and light, which are more free and less capable of confinement than water; and when there is, as in this State, no danger of a prescriptive right being acquired in windows, the reason assigned by Washburn and others for the distinction between the two elements, light and water, is not applicable. See Washb. Easem. 489; Mahan v. Brown, 13 Wend. 264.

If a man has no right to dig a hole upon his premises, not for any benefit to himself or his premises, but for the express purpose of destroying his neighbor's spring, why can he be permitted to shut out light and air from his neighbor's windows maliciously, and without profit or benefit to himself? By analogy it seems to me that the same principle applies in both cases, and that the law will interpose and prevent the wanton injury in each instance.

In Phelps v. Nowlen, 72 N. Y. 39, it is stated that the doctrine is settled in New York "that, if a man has a legal right, courts will not inquire into the motive by which he is actuated in enforcing the same. A different rule would lead to the encouragement of litigation, and prevent in many instances a complete and full enjoyment of the right of property which inheres to the owner of the soil. An idle threat to do what is perfectly lawful, or declarations which assert the intentions of the owner, might often be construed as evincing an improper motive and a malignant spirit, when in point of fact they merely stated the actual rights of the party. Malice might be easily inferred sometimes from idle and loose declarations, and a wide door will be opened, by such evidence, to deprive an owner of what the law regards as well-defined rights."

But it must be remembered that no man has a legal right to make a malicious use of his property, not for any benefit to himself, but for the avowed purpose of damaging his neighbor. To hold otherwise would make the law a convenient engine, in cases like the present, to injure and destroy the peace and comfort, and to damage the property, of one's neighbor, for no other than a wicked purpose, which in itself is—or ought to be—unlawful. The right to do this cannot, in an enlightened country, exist either in the use of property or in any way or manner. There is no doubt in my mind that these uncouth screens, or "obscurers," as they are named in the record, are a nuisance, and were erected without right and for a malicious purpose.

What right has the defendant, in the light of the just and beneficent principles of equity, to shut out God's free air and sunlight from the windows of his neighbor, not for any benefit or advantage to himself, or profit to his land, but simply to gratify his own wicked malice against his neighbor? None whatever.

The wanton infliction of damage can never be a right. It is a wrong and a violation of right, and is not without remedy. The right to breathe the air and to enjoy the sunshine is a natural one, and no man can pollute the atmosphere or shut out the light of heaven for no better reason than that the situation of his property is such that he is given the opportunity of so doing, and wishes to gratify his spite and malice towards his neighbor.

It is said that the adoption of statutes in several of the States, making this kind of injury actionable, shows that the courts have no right to furnish the redress without statutory authority. It has always been the pride of the common law that it permitted no wrong with damage without a remedy. In all the cases where this class of injuries has occurred, proceeding alone from the malice of the defendant, it is held to be a wrong accompanied by damage. That courts have failed to apply the remedy has ever been felt a reproach to the administration of the law; and the fact that the people have regarded this neglect of duty on the part of the courts so gross as to make that duty imperative by statutory law furnishes no evidence of the creation of a new right, or the giving of a new remedy, but is a severe criticism upon the courts for an omission of duty already existing, and now imposed by statute upon them, which is only confirmatory of the common law.

The decree of the court below should be affirmed, with costs of both courts.

SHERWOOD, *J.*, concurred.

CAMPBELL, *Ch. J.*:

This case, assuming all that is claimed for complainant, is one where he opened windows on the side of his house near defendant's line, and defendant built a screen entirely on his own land, high enough to keep his own house—so far as its lower story and side porch and entrances are concerned—from being open to the view from complainant's windows. No authority has been found, and I am satisfied there is no authority,—at least in any region from which we have borrowed our law,—which controverts defendant's right to secure his privacy in that way. If we should grant the complainant relief, we should not only be going beyond the judicial province in making the law, but we should also make a rule in conflict with the universal weight of authority.

It was urged on the argument that there was at least foundation for such relief in the civil law, and that we might follow that if we chose. I have searched diligently, and found no such authority. On the other hand, the civil law reckoned the right of one proprietor to secure a prospect over his neighbor's land as an easement, which could only be obtained by grant, or possibly by such prescription as would be equivalent to a grant. The civil-law countries in Europe have held a rule if anything more stringent. In Scotland it is held that such an easement cannot be gained by prescription, or anything short of express contract. Erskine, 209.

The reason given is that a man cannot be compelled to build on his own land except to suit his own convenience, and that, if a right of prospect could be gained by lapse of time, it would impose a burden on every neighboring proprietor as to the use of his own land, which would be unreasonable.

Domat, in his treatise on the Civil Law, under the head of *Servitudes*, indicates strongly the same doctrine, requiring consent (bk. 1, lib. 12, § 2); and he also refers to the lack of necessity for any extension of privilege. And in his select maxims from the Civil Law it is laid down that no action lies for shutting off light where no servitude exists. Legum Delectus, lib. 8, title 2, § 6.

In the Institutes of Justinian concerning servitude (bk. 2, title 3, § 4), explaining how servitudes may be created, reference is made expressly to this right of prospect; and the methods of obtaining them are in the text confined to contracts and wills. By the French Code it is declared that no servitude can be created except by agreement or prescription, and it is not very clear that such a right as that of a prospect over the grounds of another can be gained by anything but grant. Code Civ. Law, 2, chap. 3, §§ 1, 2; Comte, Traité de la Propriété, 343.

It is expressly declared that no one can, without his neighbor's consent, make windows or other openings in a party wall; and where the wall is on one's own ground, but near the line, no windows can be made except at such a height from the floor as will prevent looking over upon the next lot, and with fixed gratings of not more than four-inch openings, so that a head cannot be reached through them. Code Civ. bk. 2, title 4, § 3.

In this there is substantial resemblance to the customary law of France from which it was borrowed, the custom of Paris declaring that servitudes cannot be treated by prescription; that party walls cannot be pierced; and that windows or lights in walls near the neighbor's land must be nine feet above the ground floor, and seven and a half feet above each other floor, and grated, and not opening. Articles 186, 199-201.

The right to overlook a neighbor's premises seems, by the civil law, to be one depending entirely on whether such a servitude has been created. And if it has not been, there can be no doubt of the right of the neighbor to stop it. This is emphatically declared in Mackenzie's Roman Law, 179. The only occasion for referring to the civil law here arises out of a reference to it on the argument which does not appear to be well founded. Our laws rest on our own American common-law usages. And a somewhat careful search has failed to bring to light any authority for holding that anyone is bound to permit his privacy to be invaded by his neighbors without the right to screen his premises against them.

There seems to be no particular difference in the common-law authorities in holding that a house owner not using a party wall may have as many windows as he chooses opening on his own premises. But there is as little difference in regard to the right of any neighbor to put up such barriers on his own land as will screen it from observation. There can be no question about the character of such a right as complainant claims. It is the right to have his prospect into defendant's property left unobstructed. It is an easement in the strictest sense of the term, and is among those expressly designated as such by all systems of laws. No man can create an easement for himself. If he has no such right, then he cannot complain that it is interfered with, either at law or in equity.

In England it has been held that such an exercise of privilege may, under such circumstances raising a presumption of grant, ripen into the character of an ancient light, which cannot be interfered with. It is there also held that an action will not lie merely for opening such a window, and that the party who desires to prevent it from becoming a right must resort to such measures concerning his own property as will hinder it. There is nothing to prevent the erection of any fence or barrier to reach this result. Mr. Washburn lays it down as the result of the American authorities,—some of which allow prescriptive privileges, while most of which deny them altogether,—that the proper and lawful remedy against such windows is obstructing the view by any efficient means on the premises of the party complaining, and that the motive is of no consequence where there is no contrary right. 2 Washb. Real Prop. 60. See also Washb. Easem.

The English authorities hold this also in respect to cases where the right is not ancient. Wheeldon v. Burrows, L. R. 12 Ch. Div. 31; Davies v. Marshall, 1 Dr. & Sm. 557; Renshaw v. Bean, 10 Eng. L. & Eq. 417; Potts v. Smith, L. R. 6 Eq. 311; Butt v. Imperial Gas Co. L. R. 2 Ch. 158.

It was held in Roberts v. Macord, 1 Moody & R. 230, that there was no easement in a prospect, and that rights in windows did not go so far.

And in Wheeldon v. Burrows, above cited, it was held that the sale of a house by one owning also the adjacent lot involved no implied covenant not to darken the windows.

And in Wynstanley v. Lee, 2 Swanst. 333, it was recognized that in London there never was any presumption of a right to light. This has been always recognized as the custom of London, and was the law there until the passage of an Act of Parliament which changed the disputable presumption which sometimes arose, after long time, into an absolute right after twenty years to have windows left clear, and made the rule applicable in spite of local customs.

In Yates v. Jack, L. R. 1 Ch. 295, it was held that the statute now in force abolished the custom of London and of other cities; and the court—while commenting on the absurd consequences in a city—felt bound to apply the statute, and require the owner of buildings only twenty or thirty feet high on one side of a London street to abstain from raising them higher, and thus lessening the light that would fall on the other side. The result of such a rule is to destroy the value of property, and prevent its owners from using it for natural and proper purposes.

In the nature of things there can be no wrong in preventing another from doing what he has no right to insist upon.

It was held by this court in Allen v. Kinyon, 41 Mich. 281, that the motive is of no consequence when the party does not violate the rights of another. And in support of this doctrine reliance was had on Mahan v. Brown, 13 Wend. 261, where the case was like the present one in its circumstances, but much more serious. There a fence was put up, as the screen was here, for the express purpose of preventing the view from fifteen windows over defendant's ground. The court held that where there was no right to the prospect there was no wrong in fencing it out, and that the defendant's motive was of no consequence, as he was in the exercise of his own right.

In Parker v. Foote, 19 Wend. 309, this doctrine was approved, and it was further held that the doctrine of ancient lights did not apply here.

It was held by this court in Hawkins v. Sanders, 45 Mich. 491, that there was no right of prospect which would prevent the erection of an awning on a neighboring lot.

In Durant v. Riddell, 12 La. Ann. 746, the same rule was applied to a veranda covering the sidewalk.

The doctrine of Mahan v. Brown has been repeatedly enforced in Illinois, in very strong language,—the court holding that a fence or screen of any height was lawful to shut off the view from a neighboring window. Honsel v. Conant, 12 Ill. App. 259. Guest v. Reynolds, 68 Ill. 478.

In Vansyckel v. Tryon, 6 Phila. 401, and Vollmer's App. 61 Pa. 130, it was held that in Philadelphia it was an actionable wrong to open windows over a neighbor's ground in a party wall, and relief was granted in equity.

In Shell v. Kemmerer, 13 Phila. 502, where a bill was filed to prevent tearing down a fence raised to darken a window, and to enjoin the continuance of the window, it appeared the fence was already torn down, and the party was therefore left to his action of trespass, which it was held would be adequate. So far as the window was concerned, the court, inasmuch as it was not governed by the law of Philadelphia, held it must be dealt with by the general law; and while stating it was such a nuisance as ought to be remediable, the judges considered themselves bound by authority not to hold the mere existence of a window actionable, but to consider, in the light of authority, that the proper remedy was by act of the party by putting up obstructions.

It certainly cannot be any man's duty to rebuild, or to build when he has no occasion for so doing, and when an open yard or grounds may be desirable for his comfort. No one disputes his right to shut off windows in that way. And there is no authority for holding that, if he does not wish to build, he may not in any other effective way secure the privacy which is his right on his own premises. That, according to the sense of all civilized nations, is a valuable domestic right, and if we deny it we shall find no standing-point in jurisprudence to justify it.

I think complainant has no right whatever to complain of defendant's screen, and that his bill should be dismissed, with costs of both courts.

CHAMPLIN, J.:

I concur with my brother Campbell that the decree should be reversed. The decisions have been quite uniform to the effect that the motives of a party in doing a legal act cannot form the basis upon which to found a remedy against such party. Under these circumstances it should be left to the Legislature to define and prohibit the act, and declare the remedy, as has been recently done in Massachusetts, Vermont and some of the other States. Mass. Pub. Acts 1887, chap. 348; Vt. Pub. Acts 1886, p. 59.

I think, also, that legislation of the character contained in the Statutes above cited is required, and would meet my hearty approval. We should then have a rule certain in its provisions and operative upon all alike, with due and proper safeguards to the owners of private property.

ARIZONA SUPREME COURT.

Board of Directors of TERRITORIAL INSANE ASYLUM

v.

Lewis WOLFLEY, Governor.

(....Ariz....)

The Governor of a Territory cannot be compelled by mandamus, on the application of the trustees of the Territorial Insane Asylum, who hold his commission as authority for the public duties they perform, to sign a warrant on the treasurer for funds for the asylum.

(*Porter, J., dissents.*)

(July 8, 1889.)

APPLICATION for a peremptory writ of mandamus to compel the Governor to countersign a warrant alleged to have been drawn by the auditor upon the treasurer for funds to meet the expenses of the Territorial Insane Asylum. *Denied.*

The case sufficiently appears in the opinion.

Messrs. **Herndon & Hawkins,** for applicants:

The Board of Directors of the Insane Asylum having made the proper monthly estimate for the current expenses of said asylum as required by law, and presented the same to the auditor, it was his duty to issue the warrant.

See Arizona Rev. Stat. 1887, par. 2483.

Said estimate having been duly made as required, the auditor had no discretion, and certainly the Governor could have none, as the Board of Directors were the parties required by said law to pass upon and make such estimate; and the act required of the Governor, viz., the countersigning of a warrant, was ministerial and in no sense an executive act.

Arizona Rev. Stat. 1887, par. 2966, is as follows: "In all cases of claims audited and allowed against the Territory, and in all cases of grants, salaries, pay and expenses allowed by law, the auditor shall draw a warrant on the treasurer for the amount due, in the form required by law; . . . and every warrant so drawn shall be countersigned by the governor or secretary of the Territory."

Said act is ministerial because the same is authorized to be done by another person, to wit: the secretary of the Territory. And the Legislature could have authorized said warrant to have been issued by the auditor without being countersigned.

See also *People* v. *Brooks*, 16 Cal. 11 *et seq.*; *Middleton* v. *Low*, 30 Cal. 596; *Harpending* v. *Haight*, 39 Cal. 189; *Kendall* v. *United States*, 37 U. S. 12 Pet. 524 (9 L. ed. 1181).

Mr. **Clark Churchill,** *Atty-Gen.*, for respondent:

The chief executive of this Territory is, as to the performance of any and all official duties, entirely removed from the control of the courts.

U. S. Rev. Stat. § 1841; Arizona Rev. Stat. chap. 7, title 60.

He is beyond the reach of mandamus, not only as to the duties of a strictly executive or political nature, but even as to acts purely ministerial, whose performance the Legislature may have required at his hands.

See High, Extr. Legal Rem. § 120. See also dissenting opinion of *Judge* Temple in *Harpending* v. *Haight*, 39 Cal. 216–228.

The Governor has not only the right, power and authority, but it is his duty, to investigate the facts upon which the estimate is made, and exercise his own judgment and discretion and determine whether any warrant should be drawn, and if he decides it should be drawn, then in what amount, before he should or can lawfully countersign it.

See U. S. Rev. Stat. § 1841; Arizona Rev. Stat. chap. 7, title 60, par. 2939.

The word "shall" does not necessarily carry with it a mandatory signification. It is not

NOTE.—Mandamus; when may issue (United States v. Hall (D. C.), 1 L. R. A. 738); as a remedy (Fleming v. Guthrie (W. Va.), 3 L. R. A. 54, *note*); issued only for public purposes. Burnsville Turnp. Co. v. State, 3 L. R. A. 265, 119 Ind. 382.

Nature of the process. State v. Whitesides, 3 L. R. A. 777, and *note*, 30 S. C. 579; Port Royal Min. Co. v. Hagood, 3 L. R. A. 841, and *note*, 30 S. C. 519; State v. Nelson (Minn.) 4 L. R. A. 301

Not allowed to interfere with personal rights. Chaddock v. Day (Mich.) 4 L. R. A. 809.

May issue to enforce public duties. Commercial Union Teleg. Co. v. New England Teleph. & Teleg. Co. (Vt.) 5 L. R. A. 162, *note;* Brown v. Kalamazoo Co. Circuit Judge (Mich.) 5 L. R. A. 226.

Nature of process. Biggs v. McBride (Or.) 5 L. R. A. 115.

construed as "must" except when it is apparent that such was the intent of the Legislature.

Wheeler v. *Chicago*, 24 Ill. 105.

Mandamus will not lie to compel the Governor to perform any act over which he has the right to exercise his judgment or discretion.

Moses, Mand. p. 80; High, Extr. Legal Rem. §§ 119, 120.

Barnes, *J.*, delivered the opinion of the court:

It will be conceded that the governor, the head of the executive department of the government, is not amenable to the judicial department by mandamus to direct him in the exercise of any of the powers intrusted to him as such, whatever the degree or character of the discretion imposed upon him. The executive and judicial departments have separate and distinct functions, clearly marked out, and each is independent of the other. The authority to direct the governor by mandamus is denied by very high authority, and the difficulty of the enforcement of the writ has been suggested with great force. The court ought not to issue the writ unless it is prepared to enforce it. Without the means of enforcement the writ would be idle; yet to enforce it might deprive the territory of the executive, and public safety be jeopardized. *State* v. *Towns*, 8 Ga. 360; *Hawkins* v. *Governor*, 1 Ark. 570.

The right to direct the governor has been limited to the performance of a mere ministerial duty, where such an act has been required of him by law, and where the act is such a one as might have been imposed upon any other person and to enforce a vested private right. This was the limit in the case of *Kendall* v. *United States*, 37 U. S. 12 Pet. 524 [9 L. ed. 1181].

Even in questions affecting private right, if the final decision is with the executive, and the act is a public act, he is independent. *People* v. *Bissell*, 19 Ill. 229; *State* v. *Chase*, 5 Ohio St. 535; *Chamberlain* v. *Sibley*, 4 Minn. 312 (Gil. 228); *Harpending* v. *Haight*, 39 Cal. 189; *People* v. *Hatch*, 33 Ill. 9; *Marbury* v. *Madison*, 5 U. S. 1 Cranch, 170 [2 L. ed. 71].

In the latter case the chief justice declared: "It is not by the office of the person to whom the writ is directed, but the nature of the thing to be done, that the propriety or impropriety of issuing a mandamus is to be determined. Where the head of a department acts in a case in which executive discretion is to be exercised, in which he is the mere organ of executive will, it is again repeated that any application to a court to control in any respect his conduct would be rejected without hesitation. But where he is directed by law to do a certain act affecting the absolute rights of individuals, in the performance of which he is not placed under the particular direction of the president, and the performance of which the president cannot lawfully forbid, the writ may issue."

Here is an application by trustees of one of the territorial charities,—the Insane Asylum,—a branch of the executive department, and whose commission they hold as authority for the public duties they perform, seeking to mandamus the executive to perform a public duty. They have no personal vested rights. They ask as officers, not as individuals. No authority can be found where mandamus has been issued against a governor of a State or Territory in such a case. It is a civil remedy for the protection of purely civil rights. High, Extr. Legal Rem. § 118 *et seq.*, and cases cited, § 430 *et seq.*, and cases cited; *People* v. *University of Michigan*, 4 Mich. 98.

The act which is sought to be enforced upon the Governor in this case is one that is included in the inherent functions of his office. He is the official head of the executive department of the Territory, and, as such, the territorial, penal and charitable institutions are subordinate to him. These trustees hold his commission, and he must see that the laws are faithfully executed by them. One of the means of doing so is to be found in the act sought to be enforced in this case. With it the courts have nothing to do, as the Governor must take the responsibility, and it cannot by him or against him be shifted upon the judicial department.

The writ is denied.

Wright, *Ch. J.*, concurs; **Porter,** *J.*, dissents.

GEORGIA SUPREME COURT.

WESTERN UNION TELEGRAPH CO., *Plff. in Err.*,

v.

F. M. TAYLOR.

(....Ga.....)

*1. **The jurisdiction of justices' courts** being limited by the Constitution to "civil cases arising *ex contractu*, and cases of injuries or damages to personal property," they cannot be invested by the Legislature with jurisdiction over actions to recover a penalty imposed by statute upon telegraph companies for undue delay in the transmission and delivery of messages. The penalty is for the wrongful violation of a public duty, and neither in whole nor in part for a mere breach of contract.

2. **A suit in a court having no jurisdiction** of the subject matter resulting in a judgment for the defendant, is a nullity.

3. **Even payment by the company of the expenses** of the plaintiff, incurred by reason of non-delivery of the message, would not, unless received in full settlement or by way of accord and satisfaction, bar an action for the penalty.

4. **The charge of the court** was substantially correct, and if, in some respects, inaccurate, there was no material error.

5. **The evidence** warranted the verdict.

(February 24, 1890.)

*Head notes by BLECKLEY, *Ch. J.*

See also 9 L. R. A. 744.

ERROR to the Macon City Court to review a judgment in favor of plaintiff in an action to recover the statutory penalty for failure to promptly deliver a telegram. *Affirmed.*

The facts are fully stated in the opinion.

Messrs. **Gustin, Guerry & Hall** for plaintiff in error.

Mr. **Marmaduke G. Bayne** for defendant in error.

Bleckley, *Ch. J.*, delivered the opinion of the court:

The action was by Mrs. Taylor against the Telegraph Company to recover a penalty of $100 for failure to deliver to her a telegram sent from Macon to Brunswick by Bayne, and addressed to her. It was founded on the Act of 1887 (Pamph. Laws, 111), which reads as follows: "Every electric telegraph company with a line of wires wholly or partly in this State, and engaged in telegraphing for the public, shall, during the usual office hours, receive dispatches, whether from other telegraphic lines or from individuals; and on payment or tender of the usual charge, according to the regulations of such company, shall transmit and deliver the same with impartiality and good faith, and with due diligence, under penalty of $100, which penalty may be recovered by a suit in a justice or other court having jurisdiction thereof, by either the sender of the dispatch or the person to whom sent or directed, whichever may first sue; provided, that nothing herein shall be construed as impairing or in any way modifying the right of any person to recover damages for any such breach of contract or duty by any telegraph company; and said penalty and said damages may, if the party so elect, be recovered in the same suit. Such companies shall deliver all dispatches to the persons to whom the same are addressed, or to their agents, on payment of any charges due for the same, provided, such persons or agents reside within one mile of the telegraphic station, or within the city or town in which such station is. In all cases the liability of said companies for messages in cipher, in whole or in part, shall be the same as though the same were not in cipher."

The Company pleaded specially in bar of the action that Bayne, the sender of the message, had sued, prior to the filing of this suit, for the same penalty in a justice's court, and that a recovery was had by the Company. The plea alleged that the justice's court was a court of competent jurisdiction, but upon motion of plaintiff's counsel the plea was stricken, on the ground that the justice's court had no jurisdiction. The jury having found for the plaintiff, the Company moved for a new trial because of this ruling, and on various other grounds. This motion was overruled.

1. The general scheme of the Constitution in conferring jurisdiction upon the inferior courts, which it specifies, is to deal exhaustively with the subjects matter which it mentions and enumerates. This scheme extends also, even as to the superior court, to means and modes of exercising jurisdiction, as, for instance, new trials and writs of certiorari. *Pitts* v. *Carr*, 61 Ga. 454; *Maxwell* v. *Tumlin*, 79 Ga. 570; *Pope* v. *Jones*, Id. 487. Doubtless the Legislature might by statute confer additional jurisdiction on some of the courts and magistrates mentioned in the Constitution, but to do so the material for such superadded jurisdiction would have to be drawn from other subjects matter; that is, from such as the Constitution has not dealt with expressly in making distribution of judicial powers among the inferior courts, etc., which it enumerates. The Act of 1887, above recited, is certainly a legislative attempt to clothe justices' courts with jurisdiction over actions for penalty, and whether the attempt can be held efficacious or not depends upon a right classification of such actions with reference to art. 6, § 7, par. 2 (Code 1882, § 5153), of the Constitution of 1877. The paragraph reads as follows: "Justices of the peace shall have jurisdiction in all civil cases arising *ex contractu*, and in cases of injuries or damages to personal property, when the principal sum does not exceed $100, and shall sit monthly at fixed times and places; but in all cases there may be an appeal to a jury in said court, or an appeal to the superior court, under such regulations as may be prescribed by law." The corresponding provision in the Constitution of 1868 (Code 1873, § 5104) was as follows: "The justices of the peace shall have jurisdiction, except as hereinafter provided, in all civil cases where the principal sum claimed does not exceed $100, and may sit at any time for the trial of such cases; but, in cases where the sum claimed is more than $50, there may be an appeal to the superior court, under such regulations as may be prescribed by law."

It is manifest that the later Constitution intended to narrow the earlier one in respect to the jurisdiction of justices' courts over civil cases. Both Constitutions fix the same limit as to amount, but in one there is no limit whatever as to the nature of the civil cases over which jurisdiction may be exercised, save where exclusive jurisdiction is conferred on some other court, while in the other the cases are such only as arise *ex contractu* or from torts to personal property. Though the Legislature may, perhaps, confer at will jurisdiction upon justices' courts or justices of the peace touching some subjects matter, the subject matter of "civil cases," in so far as these courts or magistrates can take cognizance of the same, is dealt with exhaustively by the Constitution. The Legislature has no more power to invest them with jurisdiction over civil cases not arising *ex contractu*, or from torts to personal property, than over cases involving more than $100 principal, or those arising *ex delicto* from injuries to real property. It follows that, unless an action for a penalty is one arising *ex contractu* within the sense and meaning of the Constitution, the justice's court which entertained and decided the suit brought by Bayne, the sender of the message, against the Company, was without jurisdiction, for it is manifest that the suit was not for injury or damage to personal property.

2. The decisive question, then, is whether an action for the penalty imposed upon telegraph companies by the Act of 1887 is one arising *ex contractu*. Had the expression been "civil cases in form *ex contractu*," there would have been no doubt as to its embracing actions for a penalty, for debt is a form of action *ex con-*

tractu; and that debt upon a statute for a penalty definite in amount was generally, if not always, maintainable, is quite certain. 1 Chitty, Pl. 112, 371-375; *Bullard* v. *Bell,* 1 Mason, 299.

But, though in form *ex contractu,* the action for a penalty was, and still is, founded upon a tort. 1 Chitty, Pl. 45; *Chaffee* v. *United States,* 85 U. S. 18 Wall. 516 [21 L. ed. 908]; *Martin* v. *M'Night,* 1 Overt. (Tenn.) 330.

In *McCoun* v. *New York Cent. & H. R. R. Co.* 50 N. Y. 176, which was a suit brought to recover a penalty or forfeiture under a statute to prevent extortion by railroad companies, Allen, *J.*, said: "Upon the question actually decided by the court below, I am of the opinion that that court erred in holding the summons to have been regularly issued under the first subdivision of section 129 of the Code. The actions within that subdivision must 'arise on contract, and be for the recovery of money only.' This action is for the recovery of money only, and in that respect is within the provisions of the subdivision, but is not upon contract. That term was used in its ordinary and proper sense. A contract is a drawing together of minds until they meet, and an agreement is made to do or not to do some particular thing. It may be express, or it may be implied or inferred from circumstances, and this implication is but the result of the ordinary and universal experience of mankind. If A borrows money of B, the courts may imply a promise to repay the money, for the universal experience is that in such a case a promise is exacted and made. An implied promise or contract is but an express promise, proved by circumstantial evidence. It is quite distinct from that fiction by which a statute liability has been deemed sufficient to sustain an action of assumpsit, upon the ground that a party subjecting himself to the penalty or other liability imposed by statute has promised to pay it. That feature does not suppose a contract, but simply a promise *ex parte.* In this view, every man promises not to trespass on his neighbor's property, or to commit an assault upon his person, and an action of assumpsit might be brought and summons issued, under the first subdivision of section 129, for a breach of this implied contract to observe the laws. The Code was not dealing with a legal fiction in prescribing a form of summons in actions arising on contract. A statute liability wants all the elements of a contract, consideration and mutuality, as well as the assent of the party." And Peckham, *J.*, in the same case, said: "Is this 'an action arising on contract?' It is an action for a penalty for violating a statute. It is claimed to arise on contract, upon the principle stated in 3 Bl. Com. 161, whereby a forfeiture imposed by the by-laws of a corporation, upon any that belong to the body, immediately creates a debt, for which an action of debt will lie by the party injured. This principle is declared by Blackstone to be 'an implied original contract to submit to the rule of the community whereof we are members.' He then adds that the same reason may, with equal justice, be applied to all penal statutes. This principle, if carried out by the same reasoning, would abolish all actions of tort. The implied original contract to obey all statutes, by the same principle and the same reasoning, extends to all laws, whether statutory or common law. It is surely not confined to the obeying of all statute law simply. Thus assumpsit, if not debt, would lie for an assault and battery, or for arson, etc. I incline to think that this provision of the Code had no reference to this fiction of the law of an implied original contract to obey the laws of the land by each member of the community. But it meant what it plainly says. In section 53 of the Code, 'an action for a penalty' is stated as impliedly different from an action on contract for the payment of money and a justice of the peace is expressly given jurisdiction of both. The Code thus recognizes the difference between actions upon contract and an action for a penalty. It is not enough that the recovery is to be for 'money only,' but the action must arise on contract also, to bring the case under the first subdivision. I think it plain that this action does not arise on contract."

The large and loose meaning given to contracts by Blackstone (3 Com. 158-160), as including all obligations, even those arising out of the social compact, is too comprehensive to serve as a guide to the real meaning of the clause of the Constitution which we are considering. Works on contracts generally have confined the term "contract" within much narrower limits. Mr. Bishop is the only writer, so far as we know, who, in a work devoted to contracts solely, has endeavored to broaden his definition of the term so as to make it reach and include what Lowrie, *J.*, in *Hertzog* v. *Hertzog,* 29 Pa. 467, 468, denominates "constructive contracts," which he says are "fictions of law adapted to enforce legal duties by actions of contract, where no proper contract exists, express or implied." For Mr. Bishop's definition, see Bishop, Cont. § 22; and that he intended to include, like Blackstone, the fictitious case of a statutory penalty, see sections 182-206.

But it may be said that there is an actual contract from which the present action arises, namely, that made by Bayne as the sender of the message. That contract, however, with all its consequences except the penalty, is left intact by the Act of 1887. The penalty is not given, in whole or in part, as compensation in damages for a violation of that contract. On the contrary, both the sender, with whom the Company had a contract, and the person to whom the telegram was addressed, and with whom the Company had no contract, are left in full possession of all their rights, outside of penalty in every respect. That the penalty is imposed solely for the wrongful violation of a public duty is manifest, and it seems to us to make no difference that this particular instance of that duty had its origin in contract. The case belongs to that particular class so well described by Mr. Bishop in his work on Non-Contract Law, §§ 73, 74, in which he says: "Though a tort is a breach of a duty which the law, in distinction from a mere contract, has imposed, yet the imposing of it may have been because of a contract, or because of it and something else combining, when otherwise it would not have created the duty. In such a case commonly, . . . the party injured by the nonfulfillment of the duty may proceed against the other for its breach, or for the breach of the contract, at his election. Thus (§ 74), because a common carrier, whether of goods or passengers, is a sort of public servant, the law imposes its duties upon him, a breach whereof is a tort, though there is also a contract which is violated by the same act."

The principle here announced is the one recognized by this court in *Head* v. *Georgia Pac. R. Co.* 79 Ga. 358, and in other cases. A striking instance of its application will be seen in the case of *Tattan* v. *Great Western R. Co.* 2 El. & El. 851, in which the terms "action founded on contract, "and "action of contract," were under construction. See also *Pontifex* v. *Midland R. Co.* L. R. 3 Q. B. Div. 27.

The Supreme Court of Indiana, in adjudicating upon a statute in some respects identical with our own, has held that the penalty is for a breach of duty, and not damages for the breach of contract. *W. U. Teleg. Co.* v. *Pendleton*, 95 Ind. 12.

In *Schaffer* v. *McNamee*, 13 Serg. & R. 44, the words "causes of action arising upon contract, either express or implied," used in conferring jurisdiction upon justices of the peace, were held to be limited to the case of an agreement or understanding immediately between the parties; and Gibson, *J.*, said: "It is evident, therefore, that it is not the form of the action, but the nature of the subject matter of it, which must decide the question of jurisdiction. Actions of debt often arise *ex maleficio*, and where there is not the semblance of a contract, as in all cases of penalties imposed by statute; for there the debt is created by the law, and not by the agreement of the parties." Accordingly it was held in *Zeigler* v. *Gram*, 13 Serg. & R. 102, that a justice of the peace has no jurisdiction of debt for a penalty imposed by a statute for not entering satisfaction of a judgment. While the term "contract," used in its very widest sense, would, as may be seen from Blackstone and Bishop, take in penalties incurred by violating a statute, the ordinary use of the word in the common law is less comprehensive. The use of it in our Code is attended with a precise definition: "A 'contract' is an agreement between two or more parties for the doing or not doing of some specified thing." § 2714.

A "contract of record" is then defined, then "specialty" is defined; and section 2718 adds: "All other contracts than those specified above are termed simple contracts."

It seems obvious that a penalty imposed by statute is not embraced either in the language or the meaning of the Code. What the Code says of actions (§ 3250 *et seq.*) would seem to exclude a certain class of penalties from civil actions altogether, and put them in a class denominated "penal actions." "A civil action is one founded on private rights, arising either from contract or tort." "A penal action is one allowed in pursuance of public justice under particular laws. If no special officer is authorized to be the plaintiff therein, the State or the governor, or the attorney or solicitor general may be the plaintiff." §§ 3253, 3254.

The technical expression, "arising *ex contractu*," used by the Constitution, is found in section 3261 of the Code, which says: "All claims arising *ex contractu* between the same parties may be joined in the same action, and all claims arising *ex delicto* may in like manner be joined." The words "actions *ex contractu*" are found in section 2912, and perhaps in other sections. We think a penalty such as that under consideration arises *ex delicto*, and consequently that a justice's court has no jurisdiction, and can have none conferred upon it by statute, of any suit to recover such a penalty. We are forced to this conclusion, and do not reach it of our own choice; for we agree with the Legislature in thinking it desirable for justices' courts to have jurisdiction of this class of actions. A prompt and cheap remedy in such cases would subserve the public convenience, and be conducive to the attainment of justice in matters of daily concern, embracing almost a countless number of transactions, widely diffused throughout the State.

3. It follows that there was no error in striking the plea; for a previous suit in a court having no jurisdiction could not result in anything but a void judgment, and such a judgment is open to attack any and every where. Code, §§ 3594, 3828. The suit itself was a legal nullity.

4. It seems that the plaintiff, before she brought her action for the penalty, made out and presented to the Company an account for her expenses incurred by a needless trip from Brunswick to Macon, this trip being made in consequence of her failure to receive the message which Mr. Bayne, her attorney, had ordered to be sent by telegraph. It does not appear whether this account for expenses was paid by the Company or not, but no settlement by way of accord and satisfaction is pleaded or proved, nor would the mere payment of such expenses bar an action for the penalty. The Statute leaves the right to damages where it was before the penalty was imposed. It has been correctly held that paying back the amount received for sending a dispatch, unless it is agreed that such payment shall be in full of all the party has a right to recover, will not hinder an action for the penalty. *Western U. Teleg. Co.* v. *Buchanan*, 35 Ind. 430.

5. The action treated the penalty as resulting from a failure to deliver the telegram, and not from a failure to transmit it; nevertheless, delay in transmitting might be considered by the jury as involved in a failure to deliver. But, even if the charge of the court upon this subject was inaccurate, it did no harm, the failure to deliver promptly being fully established by the evidence. The same may be said as to any and all verbal inaccuracies which the charge may have contained.

6. We see no reason to question the sufficiency of the evidence to warrant the verdict. *Western U. Teleg. Co.* v. *McKibben*, 114 Ind. 511, 12 West. Rep. 279

Judgment affirmed.

PENNSYLVANIA SUPREME COURT.

Kate PRICE, *Appt.*,
v.
Josephine M. CONWAY.

(......Pa......)

1. **A publication charging that a teacher** of a certain system of shorthand is incompetent to teach that system, and is using the name of the author of the system without authority, is libelous.

2. **Any written words** which have a tendency to injure a person in his or her office, profession, calling or trade, are libelous.

3. **The office of an innuendo** is to define the defamatory meaning which the plaintiff in a libel suit sets upon the words, and to show how they came to have that meaning and how they relate to the plaintiff.

4. **An averment of special damage** is not necessary in an action for libel, where the words are written of plaintiff in his or her profession or trade.

(April 28, 1890.)

APPEAL by plaintiff from a judgment of the Court of Common Pleas, No. 3, for Philadelphia County, sustaining a demurrer to the declaration in an action to recover damages for the publication of an alleged libel. *Reversed.*

The grounds of complaint sufficiently appear in the opinion.

The grounds of demurrer were:

"*First.* Because the matter contained in said statement is not libelous.

"*Second.* Because said statement does not set forth any cause of action.

"*Third.* Because the alleged libelous matter set forth in the statement does not warrant or justify the innuendoes in said statement.

"*Fourth.* Because the innuendoes contained in said statement enlarge and add to the fair and proper meaning of the matter alleged to be libelous.

NOTE.—*Libel and slander; words tending to injure person in office.*

An action will lie for the publication of words which directly tend to prejudice or injure one in his office, profession, trade or business. Williams v. Davenport (Minn.) Jan. 23, 1890.

Neither the public press nor individuals can discuss the conduct and character of officers and candidates for office, without incurring liability, civil or criminal, for defamatory utterances published, although such publications may be made without malice and upon probable cause. Banner Pub. Co. v. State, 16 Lea, 176.

Any written words are libelous which impute to a man fraud, dishonesty, immorality, etc., or that he is suspected of such conduct, or which suggest that he is suffering from any infectious disease, which have a tendency to injure him in his office, profession or trade, or which hold him up to contempt, hatred, scorn or ridicule. Richardson v. State, 5 Cent. Rep. 766, 66 Md. 205.

Words not otherwise actionable may form the basis of an action for slander when spoken of a party in respect of his office, profession or business; and this principle embraces all temporal offices or trusts, without limitation. White v. Nicholls, 44 U. S. 3 How. 266 (11 L. ed. 591).

The words need not import a charge of crime, yet they must go at least so far as to impute to him some incapacity or lack of due qualification to fill the position, or some positive past misconduct which will injuriously affect him in it, or the holding of principles which are hostile to the maintenance of the government. Sillars v. Collier (Mass.) 6 L. R. A. 680.

The old doctrine of *scandalum magnatum* has never been adopted in Massachusetts as a special remedy. *Ibid.*

A printed publication charging a public officer with culpable neglect of his official duties is libelous *per se*. Larrabee v. Minnesota Tribune Co. 36 Minn. 141.

When a complaint shows that the words were used concerning the plaintiff in an official character, an express averment is unnecessary. Stoll v. Houde, 34 Minn. 193.

A publication containing imputations that a member of the Legislature went there solely for the purpose of passing a bill to enrich himself and his copartners in a certain scheme is libelous. Randall v. Evening News Asso. (Mich.) 7 L. R. A. 309.

But an expression of opinion that a certain person, as a member of the Legislature, is corrupt in his heart and might be induced to change his course from improper motives and inducements, is not actionable without averment and proof of special damages. Sillars v. Collier, *supra*.

A publication charging a county auditor with making a false statement of the financial condition of the county is libelous if the charges are false. Prosser v. Callis, 117 Ind. 105.

It is not necessary that the words used in a published article should be slanderous, to sustain an action for libel. *Ibid.*

The following words spoken of a city attorney: "He is unfit to hold the office of city attorney. His opinion is too easily warped for money consideration,"—do not necessarily indicate dereliction of duty or dishonesty, and are not actionable *per se*. Greenwood v. Cobbey (Neb.) May 16, 1889.

A publication which charges plaintiff, a deputy sheriff, with gross misconduct in office, is libelous, as holding plaintiff up to the scorn and aversion of the public. Bourreseau v. Detroit Evening Journal Co. 6 West. Rep. 151, 63 Mich. 425.

Words tending to injure professional persons.

Words imputing want of integrity or capacity in the conduct of a profession or trade are actionable. Wildee v. McKee, 1 Cent. Rep. 919, 111 Pa. 335.

To charge orally against a minister that he had retained for his own use the whole or part of collections made by him for foreign missions is actionable. McLeod v. McLeod (Super. Ct.) 4 Montreal L. Rep. 343.

Statements concerning a physician, imputing general ignorance of medical science, incompetency to treat diseases and a general want of professional skill, are slanderous and actionable without proof of special damage. Cruikshank v. Gordon, 118 N. Y. 178.

A publication alleging that a physician allowed the decomposing body of a child to remain for several days in the same room with its sick mother, was held actionable without an allegation of special damage. Pratt v. Pioneer Press Co. 35 Minn. 251.

Advice given to one employing a physician to take another doctor, and a declaration that the person giving the advice would not have the physician doctor a dog for him, and that he almost

"*Fifth.* Because there is no averment of special damage."

The demurrer was sustained and judgment was entered for the defendant on the demurrer, and plaintiff thereupon brought the case to this court.

Mr. **Avery D. Harrington,** for appellant:

Though defamatory matter may appear only to apply to a class of individuals, yet if the descriptions in such matters are capable of being, by innuendo, shown to be directly applicable to any one individual of that class, an action may be maintained by such individual in respect to the publication of such matter.

Le Fanu v. *Malcomson*, 1 H. L. Cas. 687.

Where words will bear several meanings, the plaintiff has a right to aver by an innuendo the meaning with which he conceives they were spoken and it is for the jury to decide whether he is right.

Bornman v. *Boyer*, 3 Binn. 517; *Hays* v. *Brierly*, 4 Watts, 392; *Com.* v. *Keenan*, 67 Pa. 208.

There is no employment but that language which concerns the person in such employment will be actionable, if it affects him therein in a manner that may, as a necessary consequence, or does, as a natural or proximate consequence, prevent him deriving therefrom that pecuniary reward which probably he might otherwise have obtained.

Townshend, Slander and Libel, 3d ed. § 182, p. 279; 1 Starkie, Slander and Libel, pp. 127, 129; *Rue* v. *Mitchell*, 2 U. S. 2 Dall. 60 (1 L. ed. 289); *M'Clurg* v. *Ross*, 5 Binn. 221; *Wildes* v. *McKee*, 1 Cent. Rep. 919, 111 Pa. 335.

Even if plaintiff does not aver special damage the action of libel would still be maintainable.

---

killed one of his children,—is slanderous and actionable without proof of special damage. Cruikshank v. Gordon, *supra*.

Words spoken of a lawyer, in reference to what he has done in his profession, charging that he is a "blackmailer," are actionable *per se*. Healy v. Dettra (Pa.) 7 Cent. Rep. 168.

To publish of a lawyer the word "shyster" is libelous. Gribble v. Pioneer Press Co. 34 Minn. 342.

Words tending to injure person in calling or trade.

A mere animadversion in a circular, upon a transaction had with a firm, in which it is stated that the members of the firm, naming them, "are not worthy of our support," even though coupled with the epithets "base treachery," "foul and unfair dealings," —is not actionable *per se*. Donaghue v. Gaffy, 1 New Eng. Rep. 267, 53 Conn. 43.

To publish of and concerning a person, language tending to bring him in ill repute or to destroy confidence in his integrity, is libelous and actionable *per se*. Jones v. Greeley (Fla.) July 15, 1889.

Words accusing a clerk of causing the ruin of another person, by reason of which he lost his situation, are actionable. Wilson v. Cottman, 2 Cent. Rep. 868 65 Md. 190.

Words relating to the quality of articles made, furnished or sold by a person, though false and malicious, are not actionable without special damage, unless they attach to the individual. Dooling v. Budget Pub. Co. 4 New Eng. Rep. 50, 144 Mass. 258.

Where plaintiff advertised for sale as first quality stockings made by defendant, defendant's publication that his stockings should not be judged by those sold by plaintiff, because they had been sold to him at a reduced price because damaged in the dye-house, is not actionable, in the absence of proof of special damage. Boynton v. Shaw Stocking Co. 5 New Eng. Rep. 727, 146 Mass. 219.

A cut or picture of the interior of a saloon, with the word beneath "Kennedy's," together with an article which, taken in its strongest sense, with the aid of proper innuendoes, was a charge that the saloon was the resort of improper characters, and that the influence of the associations there was bad, without any other mention of the plaintiff,—was held a libel on the place, and not on the plaintiff. Kennedy v. Press Pub. Co. 41 Hun, 422.

A publication by a retail seller, concerning wholesale sellers of liquor, charging that the plaintiff, moved to anger because defendant ceased to be a purchaser from him, overbid him in the matter of a lease, and compelled his removal, and recommending retailers "to boycott," is not libelous *per se*; and, in the absence of evidence of special damage, a nonsuit was properly entered. Donaghue v. Gaffy, 3 New Eng. Rep. 545, 54 Conn. 257.

A publication in reply to certain censorious articles that had appeared in the paper respecting a teacher in a normal school, charging a pupil with conduct showing her to be tricky and unreliable, and destitute of womanly characteristics,—was held actionable *per se*, and not a privileged communication. Dixon v. Allen, 69 Cal. 529.

A newspaper article giving the public information as to a man holding himself out as a teacher and seeking to attract pupils by extraordinary advertisements is privileged in such a qualified sense that malice must be proved as a fact in the case before the plaintiff can recover. Press Co. v. Stewart, 12 Cent. Rep. 275, 119 Pa. 584.

The article is not deprived of its privileged character by the fact that it is in the form of an interview which is so altered in details as to render the reporter ridiculous. *Ibid.*

A false publication containing the heading "A School Child Killed by a Teacher," and stating that the teacher had been arrested and lodged in jail, and that threats were made of lynching her,—is libelous *per se*. Doan v. Kelley, 121 Ind. 413.

Any charge of dishonesty against an individual in connection with his business, whereby his character in such business may be injuriously affected, is actionable. Hence the words, "You are a defaulter; all that you have you accumulated by defrauding," spoken of one in his business as a merchant and miller,—are actionable. Noeninger v. Vogt, 5 West. Rep. 390, 88 Mo. 589.

To publish of a merchant or trader that a judgment has been recovered against him is not, in itself, libelous, as an imputation against the soundness of his financial condition, so as to justify an action, without proof of special damages. Woodruff v. Bradstreet Co. 5 L. R. A. 555, 116 N. Y. 217.

A partnership is liable for the act of a partner in slandering the business of another in the course of the partnership business. Haney Mfg. Co. v. Perkins (Mich.) Nov. 15, 1889.

Words spoken or written injurious to a person in his business, and false and malicious, are actionable *per se*, and special damages need not be proved. *Ibid.*

In an action of libel, a verdict of $3,000 will not be set aside as excessive, where the evidence shows that the tendency of the libel was to greatly injure the character, standing and business of the plaintiff, and that the paper in which the publication was made had a wide circulation. Jones v. Greeley (Fla.) July 15, 1889.

Clement v. *Chivis*, 9 Barn. & C. 172; *Bell* v. *Stone*, 1 Bos. & P. 331; *Thorley* v. *Lord Kerry*, 4 Taunt. 355; *LeFanu* v. *Malcomson*, *supra;* Odgers, Libel and Slander, *308; *Rolin* v. *Steward*, 14 C. B. 603.

Mr. **James H. Shakespeare** for appellee.

McCollum, *J.*, delivered the opinion of the court:

The defendant having demurred to the declaration, all relevant matters well pleaded therein must be accepted as true. *Weidee* v. *McKee*, 111 Pa. 335, 1 Cent. Rep. 919.

The facts of the case, as we gather them from the declaration, are, that the plaintiff, at the time of the committing of the grievances therein mentioned, was the proprietor of the Haven College of Shorthand and Typewriting, located at 1322 Chestnut Street, Philadelphia, and was fully competent and authorized to teach the Haven system of shorthand. The defendant was the principal of a rival school, located at 1223 Chestnut Street. These were the only schools in Philadelphia in which the Haven system of shorthand writing was then taught. The defendant, with full knowledge of these facts, published certain certificates over the signature of Curtis Haven, author of Haven's shorthand system, in which it was stated that the only authorized Haven College in Philadelphia was at 1223 Chestnut Street, of which the defendant was the principal; that he could recommend her teaching, but not that of another teacher who was using his name without authority, and for whose teaching he would not be responsible. The defendant also published a circular over her own signature, in which it was stated that there were other teachers of Haven's shorthand in Philadelphia, and that one of them was using the name, Haven College, without authority. The declaration contains *verbatim* copies of these publications, and alleges that they charge and were intended to charge that the plaintiff was incompetent to teach the Haven system of shorthand, and that she was using the name, Haven College, without authority, and that, by means of these accusations, falsely and maliciously made, she has been greatly prejudiced in her reputation and business, and has sustained great loss therein. It specifically describes the injuries inflicted on her business by the publications recited in it, and lays her damages at $5,000.

It is contended in support of the demurrer that the matter set out in the declaration is not libelous, and that the innuendo is not justified by it. Any written words which have a tendency to injure a person in his or her office, profession, calling or trade, are libelous. Odgers, Libel and Slander, p. 19.

An innuendo cannot introduce new matter, or enlarge the natural meaning of words, or put upon them a construction they will not bear. Its office is to define the defamatory meaning which the plaintiff sets upon the words, to show how they come to have that meaning, and how they relate to the plaintiff. If they are capable of the meaning he ascribes to them, it is for the jury to say whether they were used in that sense. Id. p. 100, and authorities cited; *Bornman* v. *Boyer*, 3 Binn. 515; *Thompson* v. *Lusk*, 2 Watts, 17; *Com.* v. *Keenan*, 67 Pa. 203.

As at the time of the grievances mentioned in the declaration there were but two schools in Philadelphia in which the Haven system of shorthand was taught, it is clear that the publications referred to the plaintiff, and we think that they justify the innuendo which defines the meaning she ascribes to them. The declaration contains an averment of special damages, although, in libel, or where words are spoken of another in the way of his or her profession or trade, it is not necessary. Odgers, Libel and Slander, 225.

Judgment reversed, and procedendo *awarded.*

COMMONWEALTH of Pennsylvania, *ex rel.* Arthur BURT,
v.
UNION LEAGUE of Philadelphia.

(....Pa....)

1. **A return will be sufficient to warrant a denial of a writ of mandamus** to reinstate a person in a social club from which he has been expelled, if the club had power to make the expulsion, where it appears therefrom that the proceedings of expulsion were regular and conducted in good faith, that the accused was accorded a full and fair hearing and that a proper judgment was entered on the facts, and the whole proceeding is stated with substantial accuracy, although absolutely technical accuracy of statement is lacking, and it does not appear that the accused was found guilty *in totidem verbis* of the acts for which the by-laws permit expulsion.

2. **The enforcement of the provisions of the charter and by-laws** of a social club which provide for the expulsion of members, in the case of a person who became a member after their adoption, can deprive him of no legal or

NOTE.—*Mandamus to obtain re-instatement in club or other social organization.*

Mandamus is a proper procedure to be invoked by an expelled member seeking to be re-instated. State v. Lipa, 28 Ohio St. 665; Sturges v. Chicago Board of Trade, 86 Ill. 441; Baxter v. Chicago Board of Trade, 83 Ill. 146; People v. New York Benev. Society of O. M. 6 Thomp. & C. 85, 3 Hun, 361; O'Reily v. Mutual L. Ins. Co. 2 Abb. Pr. N. S. 167; State v. Milwaukee Chamber of Commerce, 20 Wis. 63; Otto v. Journeymen Tailors P. & Benev. Union, 75 Cal. 308; Montgomery Co. Med. & S. Society v. Weatherly, 75 Ala. 248; State v. Georgia Medical Society, 38 Ga. 608; Savannah Cotton Exchange v. State, 54 Ga. 668; People v. Mechanics Aid Society, 22 Mich. 86; Erd v. Bavarian Nat. Aid & Loan Asso. 11 West. Rep. 171, 67 Mich. 233; People v. American Institute, 44 How. Pr. 468; People v. St. Franciscus Benev. Society, 24 How. Pr. 216; People v. Erie Co. Medical Society, 24 Barb. 572; Com. v. St. Patrick Benev. Society, 2 Binn. 441; Com. v. German Society, 15 Pa. 251; Green v. African M. E. Society, 1 Serg. & R. 254; State v. Milwaukee Chamber of Commerce, 47 Wis. 670.

The writ of mandamus is applicable to corporations formed for eleemosynary, religious, scientific, benevolent and social societies. State v. Milwaukee Chamber of Commerce, *supra.*

The injured party may, however, pursue his remedy in a common-law suit, and may recover damages for an unlawful expulsion, but cannot afterwards claim to be re-instated. Lamphere v.

constitutional right on the ground that his personal franchise and property rights are subject to the action of a majority of the members.

3. The members of a social club may regulate through their by-laws the causes for expulsion of members and the manner of effecting the same, when such power has been expressly conferred upon them by the Legislature.

4. By-laws of a social club providing for the expulsion of members guilty of acts or conduct which the board of directors shall deem disorderly or injurious to the interests, or hostile to the objects, of the club are not unreasonable, arbitrary or oppressive, nor do they violate any principle of natural justice.

5. Failure of a by-law to designate and define the various and specific acts which will be deemed disorderly within the rule subjecting members of a social club to expulsion therefor, the determination of which question is left to the board of directors, does not render the by-law illegal.

6. A minor offense is sufficient to justify the expulsion of a member from a social club, if the club acts in good faith and exercises only the powers conferred by its charter.

7. A social club in the trial of a charge against one of its members, conviction of which will under its charter and by-laws subject him to expulsion, acts as a judicial tribunal and its judgment therein renders the case *res judicata*, and will preclude its re-examination on its merits by a judicial court.

(May 26, 1890.)

APPEAL by defendant from a judgment of the Court of Common Pleas, No. 3, for Philadelphia County in favor of relator in a proceeding by mandamus to compel defendant to re-instate relator as a member of the defendant club from which he had been expelled. *Reversed.*

The facts are fully stated in the opinion.

Messrs. **A. T. Freedley** and **Joseph B. Townsend,** for appellant:

A sentence of expulsion is conclusive on the merits and cannot be inquired into collaterally either by mandamus or action, or any other mode.

Com. v. *Pike Ben. Society*, 8 Watts & S. 250; *Society for Visitation of Sick* v. *Com.* 52 Pa. 131; *Black and White Smiths Society* v. *Vandyke*, 2 Whart. 309, 313; *Toram* v. *Howard Ben. Asso.* 4 Pa. 519; *Moxey* v. *Stock Exchange*, 9 W. N. C. 441; *Sperry's App.* 8 Cent. Rep. 215, 116 Pa. 391; *Dawkins* v. *Antrobus*, L. R. 17 Ch. Div. 616; *Inderwick* v. *Snell*, 2 Macn. & G. 216; *Hopkinson* v. *Marquis of Exeter*, L. R. 5 Eq. 63; *Hurst* v. *New York Produce Exchange*, 1 Cent. Rep. 264, 100 N. Y. 605; *Lambert* v. *Addison*, 46 L. T. N. S. 23.

In England the by-law is usually framed as follows: "Any conduct in or out of the club which shall, in the opinion of the committee, be injurious to the character and interests of the club."

This is called the "common form of the expulsion clause" (Leach, Club Cas. 16, 61; Wertheimer, Clubs, p. 114), and has been frequently judicially sustained.

Dawkins v. *Antrobus*, *Lambert* v. *Addison* and *Hopkinson* v. *Marquis of Exeter*, *supra*; *Gardner* v. *Fremantle*, 19 Week. Rep. 256; *Lyttelton* v. *Blackburn*, 33 L. T. N. S. 642.

Under similar charter powers, it has been distinctly held that the by-laws may invest the board of directors with determining what is sufficient cause for expulsion.

Pitcher v. *Chicago Board of Trade*, 20 Ill. App. 319; *Dawkins* v. *Antrobus*, *Gardner* v. *Fremantle*, *Lyttelton* v. *Blackburn* and *Hopkinson* v. *Marquis of Exeter*, *supra;* Willcock, Mun. Corp. 634; *Hussey* v. *Gallagher*, 61 Ga. 86;

Grand Lodge, A. O. U. W. 47 Mich. 429; State v. Lipa, *supra*.

He may recover damages, to the extent of his injury. Washington Ben. Society v. Bacher, 20 Pa. 425.

The bringing of an action at law is a waiver of the right to the remedy by mandamus. State v. Lipa, *supra*.

Under the Kentucky Code mandamus will not lie to compel the officers of a benefit society to restore an expelled member. Schmidt v. Abraham Lincoln Lodge, 84 Ky. 490; Cook v. College of Physicians and Surgeons, 9 Bush, 541. And see White v. Brownell, 2 Daly, 329, where it is held that mandamus does not apply to mere voluntary societies.

If the expulsion be without notice the courts will interfere, although the rules may not provide for the giving of notice. Fisher v. Keane, 27 Eng. Rep. (Moak) 586, L. R. 11 Ch. Div. 353.

It is the duty of the courts to construe liberally the rules and regulations of benevolent societies so as to effect their benevolent purposes, and in no case to so construe them as to defeat such purposes, unless their meaning is so clear and certain as to admit of no other construction. Jewell v. Grand Lodge, A. O. U. W. 41 Minn. 405.

An unincorporated mutual benefit association has no right to expel a member for an offense which, by its rules, is punishable only by fine, and thus deprive him of the benefit to which he is properly entitled. Otto v. Journeymen Tailors Protective & Benev. Union, 75 Cal. 308.

Courts will not inquire into the merits of the decision of corporate authorities in expelling a member in regular proceedings, unless the suspension or expulsion has been conducted without authority, when the remedy by mandamus may be invoked (High, Extr. Legal Rem. § 294; Hardin v. Second Baptist Church, 51 Mich. 137; People v. German U. E. St. Stephen's Church, 53 N. Y. 103), and only where civil and property rights are involved. Van Houten v. First Reformed Dutch Church, 17 N. J. Eq. 126; Livingston v. Trinity Church, 45 N. J. L. 230.

Courts entertain jurisdiction only to correct abuses; they do not inquire into the merits of the controversy in a regular course of proceedings, except where property rights are involved. Woolsey v. Lodge No. 23, I. O. O. F. 61 Iowa, 492; Anacosta Tribe, No. 12, I. O. R. M. v. Murbach, 13 Md. 91; Osceola Tribe, No. 11, I. O. R. M. v. Schmidt, 57 Md. 98; Karcher v. Supreme Lodge, K. of H. 137 Mass. 368; Dolan v. Court Good Samaritan, No. 5910, A. O. of F. 128 Mass. 437; Grosvenor v. United Society of Believers, 118 Mass. 78; People v. St. George's Society, 28 Mich. 261; Lafond v. Deems, 81 N. Y. 507; Hutchinson v. Lawrence, 67 How. Pr. 38; Loubat v. Le Roy, 15 Abb. N. C. 1; Olery v. Brown, 51 How. Pr. 92; Com. v. Pike Ben. Society, 8 Watts & S. 247; Sperry's App. 8 Cent. Rep. 215, 116 Pa. 391; Jones v. Nat. Mut. Ben. Asso. (Ky.) Jan. 6, 1887.

But they will interfere for the purpose of protecting property rights in all proper cases, and will follow and enforce as far as applicable the rules applying to incorporated bodies of like character. Otto v. Journeymen Tailors' P. & Benev. Union, 75 Cal. 308.

People v. *New York Commercial Asso.* 18 Abb. Pr. 271; *White* v. *Brownell*, 2 Daly, 329; *People* v. *Chicago Board of Trade*, 45 Ill. 112; *Green* v. *African M. E. Society*, 1 Serg. & R. 254; *Evans* v. *Philadelphia Club*, 50 Pa. 107.

The relator is estopped from denying the validity of the by-laws.

Leach, Club Cas. 45, 46; *Black and White Smiths Society* v. *Vandyke*, 2 Whart. 312; *Lyttelton* v. *Blackburn* and *Pitcher* v. *Chicago Board of Trade*, *supra*; *Toram* v. *Howard Ben. Asso.* 4 Pa. 519; *Moxey* v. *Stock Exchange*, 9 W. N. C. 441; *Hopkinson* v. *Marquis of Exeter*, L. R. 5 Eq. 68; Wertheimer, Clubs, p. 10.

The association possesses an inherent right to expel upon the facts, and for the causes set forth.

Com. v. *St. Patrick Benev. Society*, 2 Binn. 448; *Le Roy* v. *Tidderley*, 1 Siderfin, 14; *Lord Bruce's Case*, 2 Strange, 819; *Rex* v. *Richardson*, 1 Burr. 517.

Messrs. **Bernard Gilpin and John G. Johnson**, for appellee:

A mode of proceedings such as was had in this case was wrong.

Labouchere v. *Earl of Wharncliffe*, L. R. 13 Ch. Div. 354.

The return to the mandamus does not set forth clearly certain facts. A writ of mandamus is not to be answered by a frivolous, evasive or uncertain return.

Com. v. *Pittsburgh*, 34 Pa. 522.

Facts must be set forth clearly, specifically and certainly, and not argumentatively, evasively or inferentially, so that the court may see at once whether, if established, they are sufficient.

Com. v. *Allegheny Co.* 37 Pa. 277. See also *Re Prospect Brewing Co.* 127 Pa. 523.

A personal offense against a fellow member of a club was not sufficient cause for expulsion.

Evans v. *Philadelphia Club*, 50 Pa. 117. See *Com.* v. *St. Patrick Benev. Society*, 2 Binn. 447; *People* v. *Erie Co. Medical Society*, 24 Barb. 570; *Butchers Ben. Asso.* 35 Pa. 151; *Butchers Ben. Asso. No. 1*, 38 Pa. 298.

In the charter of the Union League no express power to expel for such cause is conferred, but simply one to expel for causes not repugnant to law.

A constitution that puts all power over rights into the hands of the majority is really no constitution at all.

Beneficial Asso. of Brotherly Unity, 38 Pa. 299.

Where a charter provides that a corporation shall have the right to admit and expel members, it is a power conferred on the body of corporators, and they cannot delegate the power to the board of directors.

2 Waterman, Corp. p. 554; *State* v. *Milwaukee Chamber of Commerce*, 20 Wis. 63.

Clark, *J.*, delivered the opinion of the court:

This proceeding in the court below was a mandamus, brought by Arthur Burt, to compel the Union League of Philadelphia to re-instate him to membership in the League, from which he had been expelled. The petition was filed, and the alternative writ issued, on the 28th of May, 1888, and on the 23d of June thereafter the defendant's return was filed. The relator thereupon put in a plea traversing the return, but afterwards withdrew the plea, and filed a demurrer; all relevant matters contained in the return must necessarily, therefore, be deemed admitted and accepted as true. By the return it appears that the Union League of Philadelphia was incorporated on the 30th of March 1864, during the War of the Rebellion, "for the purpose of fostering and promoting the love of republican government, aiding in the preservation of the Union of the United States, and extending aid and relief to the soldiers and sailors of the army and navy thereof." By their charter the incorporators were entitled to perpetual succession, and were enabled to take and hold title to real and personal property, and to dispose of the same, "provided that the clear yearly value or income of all the estate and property of said corporation, including interest on all moneys by them lent, shall not exceed the sum of $10,000, exclusive of the real estate in the actual occupancy of the corporation." The officers of the League consist of a president, four vice presidents and fifteen directors, to be elected annually, who are authorized to choose and appoint from their own number a secretary and a treasurer.

The third section of the charter is as follows:

"3. That the duties and rights of the members of the said corporation, the powers and functions of the officers thereof, the mode of supplying vacancies in office, the times of meeting of said corporation or its officers, the number which shall constitute a quorum thereof, respectively, at any such meeting; the mode of electing or admitting members, the terms of their admission and the causes which justify their expulsion, and the manner of effecting the same, and the mode and manner in which the property of said corporation shall be divided and appropriated in case of a dissolution of said corporation, or winding up of its affairs, shall be regulated by the by laws and ordinances of said corporation, which they are empowered to make and alter, in the manner which may be therein mentioned,—provided, that the said by-laws and ordinances shall not be repugnant to, or inconsistent with, the Constitution and laws of the United States or of this Commonwealth."

The first section of the by-laws, afterwards made in pursuance of the charter, provides as follows:

"The members of the Union League of Philadelphia shall support the Constitution of the United States, discountenance, by moral and social influences, all disloyalty to the federal government, encourage and maintain respect for its authority, compliance with its laws and acquiescence in its measures for the enforcement thereof, and for the suppression of insurrection, treason and rebellion, as duties obligatory upon every American citizen."

By the return, moreover, it appears that, "although the purposes for which the corporate defendant was originally created were correctly set forth in the preamble to its said charter, yet the purposes of social intercourse entered as an element into its usefulness, and as the causes which led to its creation ceased to exist, within little more than a year thereafter, the element of social intercourse increased, and although its members are, to a large extent, composed of persons of a certain political faith, as is the case with similar institutions in other cities of the world, yet a chief purpose of the institution is, and long has been, the promotion of social intercourse between the members themselves, and between the latter and the guests of the corporation, and to this end there was and is required the adoption of, and strict compliance with, certain rules of internal discipline, regulating the intercourse within its walls." To advance the purposes of the League, and to promote the social relations of its members, the League became the owner of valuable real estate, upon which is erected a club house, which is maintained and governed according to certain rules and regulations, contained in the by-laws, promulgated under the 3d section of the charter.

The 2d section of the first article, in defining "the duties and rights of the members," provides that the members, "shall have free access to the rooms and library of the League, subject to such rules and regulations as may be prescribed from time to time by the board of directors."

The 1st, 2d, 3d and 4th sections of the second article, defining "the powers and functions of the officers," provides that the board of directors shall consist of the president, vice-presidents and fifteen directors, elected annually, eight of their number to constitute a quorum; that this board of direction shall have power to appoint executive committees to carry into effect the objects expressed in the charter and to prescribe their duties; to "exercise a general superintendence of the affairs of the League, with the control and management of its property and effects;" "to make all rules for the management and regulation of the house, and the maintenance of good order therein, and to provide and enforce penalties for their infraction."

The 5th section of the same article is as follows:

"A majority of the board shall have power to suspend members for a willful infraction of the rules of the house, or of any by-law of the League, or for acts or conduct which they may deem disorderly, or injurious to the interests or hostile to the objects of the League, but the offender may appeal from the sentence of suspension as hereinafter provided; but prior to the suspension of a member, he shall be entitled to notice and a hearing before the board, or before a committee of the same, as he may elect."

The fourth article provides for an appeal, and the trial thereof, as follows:

"1. A member suspended from the League, by sentence of the board of directors, may appeal therefrom, within thirty days after notice thereof posted on the notice board, by filing with the secretary a written notice of his appeal and the reasons therefor. In case of no appeal within the time limited, he shall then cease to be a member of the League.

"2. All appeals shall be tried in a meeting of the League, to be called for the purpose, by the board of directors, within forty days after notice of the appeal shall be filed with the secretary.

"3. The president, or one of the vice-presidents, shall preside at such meetings, and the cause of suspension shall be reported, in writing, by the board of directors, with a statement of facts on which their sentence was founded, a copy of which shall be furnished to the appellant, on his application, to be made to the secretary at least ten days before the meeting. The appellant shall then present his defense in writing, to which one member of the board may reply orally. The appellant, or any one member in his behalf, may then rejoin and a director may a second time speak in support of the charge, and no further discussion shall be allowed. The presiding officer shall then put the question. "Shall the sentence of the board of managers in this case be affirmed?" If a majority of the meeting shall vote in the affirmative, the sentence shall stand as the final judgment of the League, and the appellant shall thereupon forfeit all the rights and privileges of membership. If less than a majority of the meeting vote in the affirmative, then the sentence of the board shall be reversed, and the appellant shall thereupon be restored to membership."

By the fifth section of article 1, it is provided that, "when a person shall cease to be a member from any cause, all the interest he may have in the property of the League by reason of his membership shall be vested in the corporation."

The penalty, in case of conviction of an offense under the 5th section of the by-laws, it will be observed, is, practically, expulsion—the suspension from the privileges of the League is only during the pendency of proceedings, upon conviction by the board, before and after appeal. If no appeal be taken within the time specified, or if one be taken and not sustained, expulsion follows. Suspension indicates merely the status of the member after conviction by the board, pending the time for taking and trial of the appeal. The sentence of the League cannot, therefore, in any proper sense, be said to enlarge the judgment, as intimated by the learned judge of the court below. We have quoted extensively from the charter, to show that the power of expulsion was expressly conferred upon the corporation by the charter, with the right to regulate the causes which would justify the exercise of that power and to define the mode or manner of its exercise, and even more extensively, from the by-laws, to exhibit the rules and regulations, which were made in pursuance of the charter, for the government of the League, and for the trial and expulsion of members offending against them, in order that we may, in the further consideration of the case, see whether or not these by-laws in any way conflict with the charter, or with the Constitution or laws, federal or state.

On the 3d of May, 1870, as we learn from the defendant's return, the relator was elected a member of the League, and, on the 7th of May, signed the book of membership, which contained a copy of the charter and by-laws. On the 30th of December, 1882, a formal charge was preferred against him, by Mr. William E. Littleton, a fellow member, to the effect that the relator was guilty of "conduct unbecoming a gentleman, and a member of the League," specifying, more particularly, that on the Friday preceding, in the restaurant of the League, the relator had used grossly insulting language to the complainant, and that, under the circumstances, the complainant had no recourse but to report the facts to the League. Whereupon, at a meeting of the board of directors, on the 9th of January, 1883, the house committee reported the relator, "for action under article 2, section 5, of the by-laws," and moved that notice be sent to Mr. Burt in accordance therewith; and in the event that Mr. Burt should choose to be tried by a committee, the president was authorized to appoint a committee not exceeding five, to hear the case and report to the board; which was agreed to. The relator having been duly notified, elected to be heard by a committee, and the president thereupon appointed Messrs. E. N. Benson, William C. Houston, Samuel C. Perkins and Edwin H. Fitler, the four vice-presidents, to hear the case. That committee met at the League on the evenings of January 16 and January 24, on both of which occasions Mr. Burt was present and witnesses were examined. A counter-charge of the use of offensive language by Mr. Littleton, as a provocation for Mr. Burt's conduct, having been filed, and an intimation given that Mr. Littleton was under the influence of liquor at the time of the interviews between them, witnesses were called and examined upon that question also.

At a meeting of the board of directors held on the 18th of February, 1883, the committee reported that they were satisfied they had seen and heard everyone who could throw any light on the occurrence, which led to the report of the house committee, and that they found the following facts:

1. That on December 9, 1882, Arthur Burt, in the restaurant of the League, was guilty of rude and ungentlemanly conduct, and told a fellow member, William E. Litttleton, that he was acting like a blackguard.

2. That the offense was without provocation on the part of Mr. Littleton.

3. That Mr. Littleton was not at the time under the influence of liquor.

The committee submitted the following resolution:

"Resolved, That Arthur Burt has been guilty of a violation of art. 2, § 5, of the by-laws of the Union League, and that he be, and is, hereby suspended, from this date, from the privileges of a member."

Whereupon, on motion, the report was accepted by the board and the resolution adopted.

On the 13th of March, 1883, the relator entered and gave notice of an appeal, assigning the following reasons in support of it:

1. That the testimony produced at the hearing in the matter before the committee does not show any sufficient cause for the sentence or suspension imposed by the board.

2. That the offense for which said sentence of suspension was imposed was of such a trifling nature that the punishment by suspension is an unnecessarily harsh and severe one.

A special meeting of the League was thereupon called, upon due and proper notice, for trial of this appeal on the 3d of April, 1883, the trial to be conducted under article 4 of the by-laws. There were present at this meeting 279 persons, which was a quorum; the president, George H. Boker, in the chair, and the trial was proceeded with. The statement of the board, in writing, setting forth the facts as found by the committee, and the action of the board of directors thereon, was first read. In this statement the board set forth that the counter-charge against Mr. Littleton, having been found to be wholly unwarranted, was deemed an aggravation of the relator's offense, and the further fact that the relator had on a previous occasion been suspended for a very gross offense, of a similar character (which is fully set forth in the return), and had only been re-instated upon promise of amendment, and a pledge that there would be no further cause of complaint, was a matter which entered into the consideration of the board in inflicting the sentence of expulsion.

The relator's statement in writing was then read. No witnesses were called; neither of the parties appear to have expressed any desire to that effect; the appeal was submitted upon the facts found by the committee. Mr. Pettitt addressed the meeting on behalf of the board; Mr. McVeigh, in behalf of Mr. Burt, and Mr. Perkins closed the discussion. The president then put the question: "Shall the sentence of the board of managers, in this case, be affirmed?" The result of the vote was 146 ayes, and 75 noes; members present 279. A majority of those present having voted in the affirmative, the president announced that the appeal was not sustained, and that Mr. Arthur Burt ceased to be a member of the Union League.

We give this statement of the relator's arraignment, trial and conviction from the defendant's return, where the facts, we think, are stated, not argumentatively, inferentially or evasively, but with fair and reasonable certainty. The cause of the relator's disfranchisement, and the proceedings by which it was effected, are distinctly and clearly set forth. It is true, the relator does not appear to have been found guilty of "acts or conduct" which by the board were "deemed disorderly," or "injurious to the interests or hostile to the objects of the League," *in totidem verbis;* he was found guilty of rude and ungentlemanly conduct in the League House, in this, that, without cause or provocation, he charged upon a fellow member that he was acting like a blackguard. This was certainly conduct of a disorderly character, especially as it occurred within the club house, a place devoted to the cultivation of friendly political and social relations between gentlemen, and might well be deemed disorderly by the board of directors; that the board did deem the act disorderly, and injurious to the interests, and hostile to the objects, of the League, is shown by their formal resolution to that effect.

It is not expected that the proceedings of a trial of this character, which are conducted in most cases by persons unlearned in the law, will be expressed with absolute technical accuracy, or will be subjected to the severe scrutiny which is applied by persons of critical professional skill in courts of law. If the proceedings are regular, and conducted in good faith; if the accused has been accorded a full and fair hearing, and a proper finding and judgment have been entered upon the facts, and the whole proceeding is stated with substantial accuracy,—it is sufficient. The trial seems to have been conducted in an orderly manner, according to the strict letter of the by-laws of the League. The proceedings are in due form, and the relator, for anything that appears, was allowed the benefit of a full and impartial hearing, before a committee of the board, at his own election. It does not appear that he was denied any right or privilege to which he was entitled. There is no allegation, much less evidence, of fraud or unfairness, and we assume that the action of the League was in good faith.

The only question, as we understand the case, is one of power. Was the League duly and legally authorized by the by-laws to expel the relator from membership for the offense charged, and of which he was convicted?

The case of *Evans* v. *Philadelphia Club*, 50 Pa. 107, bears no analogy, in principle, to the case in hand. In that case there was no express power of expulsion conferred in the charter, and the decision rested wholly upon the ground that the offense was not such as fell within the inherent powers of the corporation at common law. The common-law power of expulsion, as declared in the opinion of *Chief Justice* Woodward, who tried the case at *nisi prius*, may be stated thus:

1. The power of disfranchisment must, in general, be conferred by the charter; it is not sustained as an incidental power, excepting, first, when the member has been legally convicted of an infamous offense, or, second, when he has committed some act tending to the destruction or injury of the society.

2. The power to make by-laws is incidental to corporations, but is generally conferred by charter; by-laws, however, which vest in a majority the power of expulsion for minor offenses are void, and expulsion under them will not be sustained.

3. In joint-stock companies, or corporations owning property, no power of expulsion can be exercised, unless conferred by statute.

On error to this court these rulings at *nisi prius* were affirmed by a divided court. Evans had been convicted of breaking the 65th article of the by-laws of the club, by having an altercation within the walls of the club house with Samuel B. Thomas, and by striking him a blow. "I look upon the occurrence," says the chief justice, "as disorderly and injurious to the club, within the meaning of the 65th by-law, but as one of those minor offenses," etc., "for which a majority have no power even, under the by-laws, to disfranchise a member; and upon the doctrine of the cases I have referred to, I hold the by-law void, so far as it inflicts this extreme penalty for such an offense. I would be very sorry to say that anything short of a statute could confer on a majority of the members of any corporation power to expel a fellow member for merely disorderly conduct." "It is not a joint-stock company at present, for under its by-laws no pecuniary profits are divisible among the members, but it may become so, and whether it does or not, the relator has a vested interest in its estate, and cannot be deprived of it by the proceedings that were had against him. On this point the authorities are clear and without conflict. Nothing but an express power in the charter can authorize a money corporation to throw overboard one of its members. I have shown that the Act of Incorporation contained no such power. On the contrary, it excluded it, for the proviso reads 'that nothing herein contained shall be so construed as to authorize the Philadelphia Association & Reading Room to do any other act or acts, in their corporate capacity, than are herein expressed.'"

These excerpts drawn from the opinion of the chief justice show that, whilst he denied the common-law power of a corporation to disfranchise its members, with the exceptions stated, he conceded that where the power is conferred by the charter it may be exercised even for minor offenses and in money corporations. The Union League, although not a proprietary corporation, cannot in any strict sense be considered a joint-stock or moneyed corporation; its object and purposes, as well as its management, are of a purely patriotic and social, and not a financial or monetary, character. Although authorized to hold property, real and personal, to a certain limited extent, for the promotion of the objects of the League, it is plainly distinguishable from such corporations as are organized for business and for purposes of gain; and this is fully illustrated in the present conduct of its affairs. In the by-laws it is provided that "no member shall receive any profit, salary or emolument from the funds of the League." Members are admitted, not upon payment of the estimated value of a share or interest in the property of the League, but of a merely nominal sum as an admittance fee, and are charged with the payment of an annual tax of $25 for the support of the League, whilst their franchise and property rights are not inheritable but continue for life, or during membership, only. But however this may be, the power of expulsion is expressly conferred by the charter, and the causes which shall justify it, and the manner of effecting the same, are expressly committed to the corporation, to be regulated by the by-laws, which by-laws, "the corporation and its officers are empowered to make, and alter, in the manner therein mentioned." It is plain, also, that according to the by-laws made under this provision of the charter, a majority of the board of directors has the power to suspend a member for acts and conduct which they may deem disorderly, or injurious to the interests, or hostile to the object, of the League, "and this suspension, unless the member is subsequently restored, is equivalent to an expulsion."

It is contended, however, that this provision of the charter, and of the by-laws, is illegal and void, inasmuch as the personal franchise and property rights of each individual member are subject to the action of a majority. We cannot see, nor has it been suggested, how this section of the charter can be said to be in conflict with the Constitution of the State or of the United States; and if it is not, it is more difficult to see how that may be said to be unlawful which the law-making power of the State has expressly declared to be lawful. The relator, at the time of his admission to the League, was bound to know the provisions of the charter and will be held to have assented to its provisions and to the frame of government which was lawfully set up in accordance therewith. By the terms of his admission, the relator voluntarily submitted himself, as to all matters pertaining to the government of the League, to the action of the board, and of the majority; and he could not thereby have been deprived of any constitutional or legal right, for the tribunal was practically one of his own selection.

In the cases of *Butchers Ben. Asso.*, 35 Pa. 151, and 38 Pa. 298, and *Beneficial Asso. of Brotherly Unity*, 38 Pa. 299, applications for charters under the Act of 1833 were refused by this court, for the reason that the provisions of their proposed charters gave entirely indefinite power over its members, and, as this was supposed to be incompatible with the spirit of our institutions, the charters were refused; but if they had been granted no one can doubt that the powers conferred, if exercised in a reasonable manner, and not arbitrarily or capriciously, would have been sustained. Here, however, we have a legislative charter accepted and acted upon; the powers of the corporation have vested and it only remains for us to inquire whether these powers have been exercised in a proper and legal manner.

The case bears a closer analogy to *Society for Visitation of Sick* v. *Com.*, 52 Pa. 125, where the corporation held a charter under the Act of 1791, in which the general power of expulsion was conferred, with the right to enact by-laws, and to alter, amend and repeal the same. The objects of the society were, in case of sickness of a member, to visit and to console him, and to give him advice and assistance; in case of death, to bury him free of charge, and to assist the families of deceased members, according to the circumstances and available means of the society. The relator, Meyer, was convicted of "feigning himself sick without being so," and of "drawing relief after his recovery," which were offenses declared by the by-laws. It was held that the society had a clear right, under the charter, to pass sentence of expulsion for a violation of the by-laws, and, by reason of the nature of the offense, a like power at the common law. Speaking of the force and effect of the charter, *Mr. Justice* Agnew says: "Having the force and effect of law, by the provisions of the Act allowing the incorporation, it is no longer a subject of judicial inquiry as to the fitness of its objects, conditions and articles."

In *Franklin Ben. Asso.* v. *Com.*, 10 Pa. 357, the society was organized under the Act of 1791 for mutual assistance in sickness, etc.; and in order to provide against extraordinary perils, a by-law prohibited members from enlisting as soldiers in the army, and notwithstanding the general and manifest impolicy of such a provision it was said that in a proper case it might be sustained. Such an objection the court said would go to the legal existence of the association. If the articles were against the public policy, it belonged to the court, in the first instance, to withhold the certificate. And as the Legislature, by a direct statute, constituting the charter of the Union League, has expressly given to the members, themselves, the right, through their by-laws, to regulate the causes of expulsion and the manner of effecting the same, we cannot see why the right thus conferred may not be exercised. The wisdom or policy of the provision having been determined by the Legislature, it is not now the subject of judicial inquiry.

Now, in view of the very general and comprehensive powers thus conferred, and of the objects and purposes, conduct and management of the League, can we say that the by-laws, ordained pursuant to the charter, are unreasonable, arbitrary or oppressive, or that they violate any principle of natural justice? We see nothing unreasonable in a by-law of a club, consisting of gentlemen, who are associated for patriotic and social purposes, requiring the observance of a proper decorum and gentlemanly personal intercourse between the members whilst within the walls of the club house. The lack of such regulations would certainly tend to promote such disorder and dissension as would be fatal to the attainment of the objects of the association. Any vilification of a member, or exhibition of personal rancor towards him, or the use of abusive or offensive epithets respecting him, especially in his presence and hearing, within the club house, is, without doubt, disorderly and injurious to the interests of the club. Nor is the by-law in question illegal, or in conflict with the charter, in this, that it does not designate and define the various and specific acts which will be deemed disorderly. To have anticipated in a by-law the various disorderly acts which might or could occur would have required the exercise of a very fertile imagination. Neither the statute nor the common law contains any such ridiculous detail. What is orderly, and what is disorderly, conduct, injurious to the interests and hostile to the objects of the League, must necessarily be determined by some proper tribunal, and the board of directors, to whom the practical management of its affairs is given, constitutes in the first instance the tribunal which the members have themselves set up to have and exercise jurisdiction over such offenses. When Mr. Burt became a member of the League, he voluntarily submitted himself to this jurisdiction; he was admitted upon the terms of the charter, with knowledge that he must submit to all such regulations as the by-laws might reasonably provide, and that for any willful violation or infraction thereof he was liable to be disfranchised.

The offense of which he was convicted, it is true, was a minor offense; not such as would have justified his expulsion at the common law, but such as justified the League, acting in good faith, in the exercise of the powers conferred by the charter, in imposing that sentence, and especially as the relator, on a previous occasion, had been suspended for an offense of a similar character, and was re-instated upon his promise of amendment, and his pledge that there would be no further cause of complaint. Nor is it wholly without significance that the countercharge against Mr. Littleton was wholly groundless, unwarranted and untrue. It does not appear that the board of directors nor the League, in the exercise of their powers, either in the framing of these by-laws or in the trial and conviction of the defendant, acted arbitrarily or oppressively or in any sense unjustly, or that Arthur Burt was disfranchised without cause.

The League in the trial of this cause acted as a judicial tribunal. The offense charged, although a minor offense, was such as brought the relator within the jurisdiction; the trial was conducted in good faith and in due form, and the relator was convicted and sentenced in accordance with the law of the League, which we have said was in conformity with the charter. We may judge of the cause of the expulsion and of the form of the proceedings (*Com.* v. *German Society*, 15 Pa. 251), but we cannot review the case on its merits.

The relator's guilt of the offense charged is *res judicata.* The courts entertain jurisdiction to keep these tribunals in the line of order and to correct abuses, but they do not inquire into the merits of what has passed *in rem judicatum*, in a regular course of proceeding. *Com.* v. *Pike Ben. Society*, 8 Watts & S. 247; *Toran* v. *Howard Ben. Asso.* 4 Pa. 519.

"In *Black and White Smiths Society* v. *Vandyke*, 2 Whart. 312, *Chief Justice* Gibson asserted that the by-laws of a private corporation like the present derived their force from assent, either actual or constructive; and the party assenting to the charter is consequently bound by everything done in accordance with it, and when he has been regularly tried and expelled the sentence of the society, acting in a judicial capacity and within its jurisdiction, is not to be questioned collaterally, whilst unreversed by superior authority. 'If he have been expelled irregularly,' the chief justice adds, 'he has his remedy by mandamus to restore him, but neither by mandamus nor action can the merits of his expulsion be re examined.'"

We quote from the opinion of *Mr. Justice* Agnew, in *Society for Visitation of Sick* v. *Com.*, 52 Pa. 125, where the case in 2 Whart. 312, is followed and the same rule is recognized and approved. No case has been called to our attention in which a different rule is laid down.

We have made no reference to the English cases cited at the argument. The English clubs are not incorporated. They are formed under written articles of agreement, and the rules of law applicable thereto are somewhat different; for there, the members are held upon the footing of a personal contract, whereas in the case of a corporation, as we have already said, the courts will see that the powers conferred, and especially the power of expulsion, are not exercised in an oppressive or arbitrary manner, but in good faith and upon reasonable cause. We have confined our citations to our own cases, which, however, do not differ in any material respect from the cases elsewhere. One case has been brought to our attention, *Pitcher* v. *Chicago Board of Trade*, 20 Ill. App. 319, which appears to bear a very close analogy to the present. The board of trade was a body corporate, created by special Act of the Legislature. It owned a large amount of property. Its object was the promotion of trade, and the admission fee was $10,000. The corporation was authorized to establish such rules, regulations and by-laws for the management of their business, and the mode in which it should be transacted, as they might think proper, and had "the right to admit or expel such persons as they may see fit in manner to be prescribed by the rules, regulations and by-laws thereof." Pitcher was admitted as a member, and paid the price of admission, but was afterwards charged with "fraudulent conduct in a business transaction," an offense declared by the by-laws. He was tried before the board of directors under the by-laws, and, the charge being sustained, he was expelled. On a mandamus it was held that, as the charter conferred a general power of expulsion to be exercised as prescribed by the rules, regulations and by-laws, that power was such as could be delegated to the board of directors. "It seems to us," says *Judge* McAllister, who delivered the opinion, "from a consideration of all the provisions of the Act, that its framers intended to leave the whole subject matter of the expulsion of members to be regulated, both as to method and tribunal, by rules and by-laws of the body, not inconsistent with the principles of natural justice or the laws of the land. In pursuance of that power, the by-laws set out in our statement of the case were adopted, by which appellant on admission agreed to be bound. We are of opinion that such by-laws were authorized by the Act, are not inconsistent with any principle of natural justice or the laws of the land, and are valid; that the trial, conviction and expulsion of the appellant were by a tribunal, not only authorized by the appellee's charter, but by reason of appellant agreeing to be bound by said by-laws."

The case cited presents many points of similarity to the present case. The corporation, in both cases, owns property of large value; members were admitted on payment of a money consideration, the power of expulsion was in both instances conferred by charter and was delegated under the by-laws to the board of directors, not only as to the causes, but as to the manner of its exercise, and in neither case was the particular act or thing charged specifically set forth as an offense in the by-laws, but was, on the trial, so adjudged by the board of directors.

We are of opinion, after a careful examination of the whole case, that the learned court below erred in entering judgment for the plaintiff upon the demurrer.

The judgment is therefore reversed, and judgment is now entered for the defendant.

Rebecca LORD
v.
MEADVILLE WATER CO., *Appt.*

(....Pa.....)

1. **The purchase of land including a spring** will not justify diverting the water flowing therefrom from its natural channel to supply a city with water.

NOTE.—*Right of lower owner to flow of water.*

As to running surface water, the owner can appropriate it to his own use, but he cannot so divert it as to prevent its use by those below him; and even where the water is running underground, if it flows in a natural channel known and ascertained by those deriving its benefits, it cannot be diverted to the injury of the riparian proprietors. Redman v. Forman, 83 Ky. 215.

The upper owner cannot vary the flow of the stream to the injury of the lower owner. See *notes* to Whitney v. Wheeler Cotton Mills, 7 L. R. A. 613; Jordan v. St. Paul, M. & M. R. Co. (Minn.) 6 L. R. A. 573.

2. A defense in an action of trespass that plaintiff is a married woman, and has proved no title, and has no possession except as the wife of her husband, cannot avail where he testifies that the land belongs to her, and is thus estopped from claiming damages in another suit.

(May 19, 1890.)

APPEAL by defendant from a judgment of the Court of Common Pleas for Crawford County in favor of plaintiff in an action of trespass to recover damages for the alleged wrongful diversion of a stream of water that formerly flowed over plaintiff's land. *Affirmed.*

Defendant denied its liability in this action, *inter alia*, upon the grounds that plaintiff was not the owner of the land alleged to have been damaged, and that she had no possession thereof except in the right of her husband.

At the trial plaintiff's husband admitted that she held the title to the land alleged to have been damaged by the diversion of the water.

The court affirmed plaintiff's point to the effect that if the water of the spring had been accustomed to flow across plaintiff's land, and had been diverted by defendant as charged, plaintiff could recover damages to the amount of the difference in the value of the use of the farm with the water in the stream and without it. (First assignment of error.)

Also that if defendant diverted the water without right or authority, punitive damages might be given. (Second assignment of error.)

The court denied defendant's point to the effect that, plaintiff having shown no title to the *locus in quo*, and her husband being admittedly in possession thereof, plaintiff could not recover on any title or possession. (Third assignment of error.)

Also one to the effect that defendant had the right to purchase the water in the spring, and if it did so, the taking and use of the water was not a wrong to the owner of lands on which any waste water from such spring had been wont to flow, and plaintiff was not entitled to recover. (Fourth assignment of error.)

Also one to the effect that under its deed of purchase defendant became the owner of the spring and thenceforth had a right to use the water therefrom for all lawful and necessary purposes, and, if in consequence of such use plaintiff as inferior owner was deprived of the flow of water over her land, it was an evil without remedy, and plaintiff could not recover. (Fifth assignment of error.)

Mr. **Pearson Church**, for appellant:

The person alleged to be aggrieved must show title in fee or a tenancy for life or for years.

Church v. *Northern C. R. Co.* 45 Pa. 339; *Winebiddle* v. *Pennsylvania R. Co.* 2 Grant, Cas. 33.

Where husband and wife are in joint possession or occupancy of personal or real estate, the law presumes the property to belong to the husband, and this presumption continues until the wife shows that she acquired it by means not derived from her husband, and the burden is upon her to prove that she so acquired it.

Pier v. *Siegel*, 107 Pa. 507; *Gamber* v. *Gamber*, 18 Pa. 363; *Rhoads* v. *Gordon*, 38 Pa. 277; *Tripner* v. *Abrahams*, 47 Pa. 220; *Barringer* v. *Stiver*, 49 Pa. 129; *Sixbee* v *Bowen*, 91 Pa. 149.

The Meadville Water Company was chartered for the purpose of supplying the public of the City of Meadville and vicinity with water. It fulfilled that duty by buying land on which there was a spring, the water of which it naturally and lawfully used for the purpose of supplying the same to the public; and if in such use somebody imagined he was damaged, it was *damnum absque injuria.*

Pennsylvania Coal Co. v. *Sanderson*, 4 Cent. Rep. 475, 113 Pa. 126.

A superior owner may improve his lands by throwing increased waters upon his inferior through the natural and customary channels.

Kauffman v. *Griesemer*, 26 Pa. 414.

Why may not the superior owner use his water by decreasing the water upon his inferior?

See *Fletcher* v. *Rylands*, 3 H. L. 330; *Delaware & H. C. Co.* v. *Goldstein*, 125 Pa. 246; *Pennsylvania R. Co.* v. *Marchant*, 12 Cent. Rep. 261, 119 Pa. 542; *Pennsylvania R. Co.* v. *Lippincott*, 8 Cent. Rep. 818, 116 Pa. 472; *Wheatley* v. *Baugh*, 25 Pa. 528.

In this case the Water Company owns the spring which is supplied by percolations spread in every direction through the earth, and if these cannot be gathered together by the owner of the spring and put to a lawful and necessary use, he or it is deprived of the necessary enjoyment of his land.

Wheatley v. *Baugh, supra; Haldeman* v. *Bruckhart*, 45 Pa. 514; *Lybe's App.* 106 Pa. 626; *Collins* v. *Chartiers Valley Gas Co.* 6 L. R. A. 280, 131 Pa. 143.

Mr. **George F. Davenport**, for appellee:

Without compensation made, or secured by bond, the act of the defendant was wrongful, and trespass lies.

Bethlehem S. G. & W. Co. v. *Yoder*, 2 Cent. Rep. 599, 112 Pa. 136.

The Water Company, by purchasing the ground on which is the spring, thereby acquired no right to the use of the water off from the ground purchased nor to the injury of the plaintiff.

2 Bl. Com. p. 18; *Race* v. *Ward*, 4 El. & El. 702.

By the purchase the Water Company only acquired the right to use the water of the spring for ordinary domestic purposes on the ground owned by it.

Arnold v. *Foot*, 12 Wend. 330; *Gillett* v. *Johnson*, 30 Conn. 180; *Wadsworth* v. *Tillotson*, 15 Conn. 366; *Pennsylvania R. Co.* v. *Miller*, 3 Cent. Rep. 126, 112 Pa. 34.

Paxson, *Ch. J.*, delivered the opinion of the court:

We need not discuss the question presented by the second assignment for the reason that an examination of the testimony shows conclusively that the jury did not give punitive damages. The verdict ($41) is within the range of the undisputed testimony.

The remaining assignments refer to the charge of the court and the answers to points. It is not essential to consider them separately. We can better dispose of them by giving our view generally upon the law of the case.

This was an action of trespass brought by

Mrs. Lord, a married woman, against the Meadville Water Company, to recover damages for the diversion of a stream of water which, before the injury complained of, flowed over her land. The Meadville Water Company, appellant, was incorporated under the Act of 1874, and it was alleged had the right of eminent domain for the purpose of supplying the City of Meadville with water. In order to aid in procuring such supply the Company, in the year 1888, purchased an acre of land near said city on which was a flowing spring of water, and carried the water from said spring to the city by means of pipes. The plaintiff owns land near this spring over which the water thereof was accustomed to flow prior to its diversion by the Company. She claims that it no longer flows there, and that by reason of its being diverted out of its natural channel she is deprived of its use for irrigation and other purposes. This suit was brought to recover damages for such injury.

The questions thus presented are not difficult of solution. By the purchase of this acre of land on which the spring is situate the Company acquired the rights of a riparian owner; neither more, neither less. What its rights as riparian owner are were sufficiently defined in the recent case of *Haupt's Appeal*, 125 Pa. 222, where it was said: "If the authority of the plaintiff were measured by its rights as riparian owner it would be slight enough. It might indeed use the water for the domestic purposes incident to the ten acres of land. If there was a tenant thereon he could use it for watering his stock and for household purposes; for any useful, necessary and proper purpose incident to the land itself, and essential to its enjoyment. But that the rights of a riparian owner would justify the plaintiff in carrying the water for miles out of its channel to supply the Borough of Ashland with water is a proposition so palpably erroneous that it would be a waste of time to discuss it."

So we say here. The purchase of the acre of land, including the spring, gave the Company the rights of a riparian owner. But such rights were not a justification for the diversion of the water from its natural channel to supply the City of Meadville. It was conceded upon the argument that the Company had the right to divert it under its power of eminent domain. But it has never exercised such right. To do so involves compensation to those who are or may be injured by such diversion. Compensation was not made nor security tendered.

While a city or borough, or a company having the right of eminent domain, may take a spring or stream of water to supply a municipality, it can only do so by making compensation to those who are deprived of the use of the water, as provided by the Constitution. A taking without compensation is a trespass, as much so as the taking of land by a railroad company to construct its road, without making compensation or filing a bond with security as provided by law. Where the power to take exists, it must be exercised according to law; if it is not, the corporation so taking becomes a trespasser, and may be proceeded against as such.

It is a mistake to assume that the purchase of this acre of land gave the Company an absolute right to the spring of water. The water did not pass by the deed beyond its reasonable use by the vendee as a riparian owner. As was said in *Haupt's Appeal, supra:* "There can be no such thing as ownership in flowing water; the riparian owner may use it as it flows; he may dip it up and become the owner by confining it in barrels or tanks, but so long as it flows it is as free to all as the light and air."

The Company might have taken this spring under its right of eminent domain if it possessed such right; for aught that appears it may do so still; and after having done so, and made compensation to the riparian owners who are injured thereby, it will be free from suits of this nature. Had it done so in this instance it would not have had this judgment against it.

We do not regard the question of the plaintiff's title, under the facts of the case, as of any importance. The plaintiff's husband testified that the farm belonged to her, and he is certainly estopped from recovering damages in another suit.

Judgment affirmed.

William McCLUNG, *Appt.*,
v.
George E. DEARBORNE.

(........Pa........)

Instructions to an employe not to commit an assault and battery on any person, and not to break the law, when sending him to get an organ, which is in the possession of another person, knowing that the errand is likely to excite indignation and resistance, will not relieve him from liability for a wrongful assault made by his employé while engaged in the business of seizing and carrying away the organ.

(April 28, 1890.)

APPEAL by plaintiff from a judgment of the Court of Common Pleas, No. 4, for

---

NOTE.—*Master liable for tortious acts of servant, done in course of the employment.*

Where a servant, in the prosecution of his master's business, deviates from his instructions as to the manner of doing it, and even if he acts directly contrary to his instructions, the master is still liable, if the acts were done in the furtherance of his business. Cosgrove v. Ogden, 49 N. Y. 255; Peck v. New York C. & H. R. R. Co. 8 Hun, 287.

If a trespass is committed in pursuance of the master's orders in defense of the master's property, to maintain its possession or to aid in its protection, the master will be liable for an assault committed by the servant in such employment even though he expressly directed him not to commit it. Barden v. Felch, 109 Mass. 154.

Having set in motion the agency for producing mischief, he is bound at his peril to prevent mischievous results. *Ibid.*; Pittsburg, Ft. W. & C. R. Co. v. Ruby, 38 Ind. 312; Hamilton v. Third Ave. R. Co. 53 N. Y. 25; Shea v. Sixth Ave. R. Co. 62 N. Y. 180; Goddard v. Grand Trunk R. Co. 57 Me. 202; Ramsden v. Boston & A. R. Co. 104 Mass. 117; Bryant v. Rich, 106 Mass. 180; Sherley v. Billings, 8 Bush, 147; Atlantic & G. W. R. Co. v. Dunn, 19 Ohio, 162; Passenger R. Co. v. Young, 21 Ohio, 518; Armstrong v. Cooley, 10 Ill. 509; Crockett v. Calvert, 8 Ind. 127; Douglass v. Stephens, 18 Mo. 362; Arthur v. Balch, 23 N. H. 157; Ayerigg v. New York & E. R. Co. 30 N. J. L. 460; Byram v. McGuire, 3 Head, 530; Wilkins v. Gilmore, 2 Humph. 140.

Philadelphia County in favor of defendant in an action to recover damages for acts committed by defendant's servants in breaking into and entering plaintiff's dwelling-house with force and violence, in violently seizing and taking away a certain cabinet organ and in assaulting plaintiff's wife. *Reversed.*

The case fully appears in the opinion.

Mr **Peter Boyd,** for appellant:

A master is ordinarily liable to answer in a civil suit for the tortious or wrongful acts of his servant, if those acts are done in the course of his employment in his master's service; the maxims applicable to such cases being *respondeat superior* and *qui facit per alium facit per se.*

Smith, Mast. and Serv. 2d ed. p. 188; *Pennsylvania R. Co.* v. *Vandiver,* 42 Pa. 365–370; *Philadelphia Traction Co.* v. *Orbann,* 11 Cent. Rep. 628, 119 Pa. 37; *Drew* v. *Peer,* 93 Pa. 234.

The test of the liability of the master for the tortious acts of his servant is not the instructions given to the servant, but the purpose of the employment.

Bruce v. *Reed,* 104 Pa. 408–414; 1 Shars. Bl. Com. p. 431, *note 1;* 2 Kent, Com. p. 260, *note 1* (*b*); *Philadelphia & R. R. Co.* v. *Derby,* 55 U. S. 14 How. 483 (14 L. ed. 508); *Railroad Co.* v. *Brannen,* 17 W. N. C. 227; Wood, Mast. and Serv. 2d ed. § 283, p. 532; *Heenrich* v. *Pullman Palace Car Co.* 20 Fed. Rep. 100, 23 Am. L. Reg. N. S. 459; Cooley, Torts, 539.

Where a trespass or other tortious act is done by a servant for the benefit of his master, but without his authority, the master may by a subsequent ratification of the act, with knowledge of what the servant has done, become liable for the same, as though the act had been originally authorized by him.

Wood, Mast. and Serv. § 310, p. 590; Wharton, Neg. § 157; *Heenrich* v. *Pullman Palace Car Co. supra.*

Mr. **John S. McKinley,** with *Mr.* **Frederick J. Shoyer,** for appellee:

The moment the servant exceeded the express and directed authority given, that moment defendant was relieved from liability to any person or persons for any consequence of the acts of his servant thus acting in the excess of any and all authority given him by the defendant.

Philadelphia, G. & N. P. R. Co. v. *Wilt,* 4 Whart. 143; *Morley* v. *Gaisford,* 2 H. Bl. 442; *Yerger* v. *Warren,* 31 Pa. 319; *Pennsylvania Co.* v. *Tooney,* 91 Pa. 256; *Kerns* v. *Piper,* 4 Watts, 222; *Snodgrass* v. *Bradley,* 2 Grant, Cas. 43; *Allegheny Valley R. Co.* v. *McLain,* 91 Pa. 442; *McManus* v. *Crickett,* 1 East, 106; *Wright* v. *Wilcox,* 19 Wend. 343; *Foster* v. *Essex Bank,* 17 Mass. 508.

As defendant was in no wise privy to the trespass or responsible for it, his neglect to return to the plaintiff his own property, which had been gotten from him by fraud, cannot make him responsible as a trespasser.

North v. *Williams,* 12 Cent. Rep. 369, 120 Pa. 109.

Williams, *J.,* delivered the opinion of the court:

Dearborne is a dealer in cabinet organs and other musical instruments. It is his habit, and it seems to prevail quite generally among dealers in similar articles, to sell on the installment plan to those who desire it, taking an instrument in the nature of a lease from the purchaser. The several installments of purchase money are to be paid as rent. If they are paid, the article becomes the property of the so-called lessee. If not paid, the vendor reserves the right to seize and retain the article.

Fox was an employé of Dearborne, whose business was to hunt up instruments on which one or more installments were unpaid, whether in the hands of the original purchasers or their vendees, in order that they might be seized or replevied by Dearborne. He had sought and obtained admission to the house of McClung by means of falsehood, and secured the number and description of the cabinet organ in the parlor. His employer alleged that it was an instrument which he had sold or leased to a customer two or three years before, and on which unpaid installments were due. Fox expressed confidence in his ability to invade McClung's home a second time and bring off the organ without a breach of the peace. An expedition was fitted out, consisting of two men and a team, under the direction and control of Fox, for this purpose. Before they set out they were instructed by Dearborne not to commit an assault and battery on any person, and not to break the law. They went to McClung's house, secured admission to the parlor by a false pretense, and began the removal of the organ. Mrs. McClung and her son, who happened to be at home, tried to resist, but were at once overpowered, and the organ and its belongings carried off. The scene is described by one of the witnesses thus: "I came down and saw Mr. Fox. He was holding my mother up against the parlor door. I came forward, and my brother came out and asked what all this meant. He said, 'Just this, if you interfere with my business I will shoot you dead,' and reached in his back pocket . . . he said, 'I come to take this organ out of here. If you interfere with my business I will shoot you.' Then my brother said, 'You do not take this organ out of this house; show your authority. If you don't, you take it over my corpse.' . . . Then he clinched my brother. . . . Then the two colored men came in and began knocking us about. . . . I then went to the corner and saw a policeman, and asked him to come down. He came down, and Fox said arrest this man (meaning my brother), and I will appear against him in the morning. They arrested my brother, and he was taken to the station."

This action was brought by McClung to recover damages for this high-handed and hostile invasion of his home.

On the trial the learned judge of the court below told the jury that the conduct of Fox "was without mitigation, and deserving of the severest condemnation," but that whether Dearborne was responsible for it or not depended on the instructions he gave him when he started out on the expedition. The correctness of this instruction is the point on which this appeal depends. The general doctrine laid down by the learned judge that every man is liable for his own trespass only, must not be taken too literally, for one must be held to do that which he procures or directs another to do for him, as well as that which he does in his own person. *Qui facit per alium facit per se.* Servants and employés are often without the means to respond in damages for the injuries they may inflict on others by the ignorant, negligent or wanton manner in which they conduct the business of their employer. The loss must be borne in such cases by the innocent sufferer, or by him whose employment of an ignorant, careless or wanton servant has been the occasion of the injury; and under such circumstances it is just that the latter should bear the loss. But the master is not liable for the independent trespass of his servant. If a coachman, while driving along the street with his master's carriage, sees one against whom he bears ill will at the side of the street, and leaves the box to seek out and assault him, the master would not be liable. Such an act would be the willful and independent act of the coachman. It was done while in his master's service, but not in the course of that service. But if the coachman sees his enemy sitting on the box of another carriage driving along the same highway, and he so guides his own team as to bring the carriages into collision, whereby injury is done, the master is liable. The coachman was hired to drive his master's horses. He was doing the work he was employed to do, and for the manner of his doing it the master is liable. Wood, Mast. and Serv. 277.

It would be no defense to the master to prove that he had given his coachman orders to be careful, and not drive against others. It was his duty not only to give such orders, but to see that they were obeyed. It will be seen, therefore, that it is the character of the employment, and not the private instructions given by the master to his servant, that must determine the measure of his liability in any given case.

An excellent illustration is afforded by the case of *Garretzen* v. *Duenckel*, 50 Mo. 104. The defendant was a gunsmith. In his absence from his store a clerk was waiting upon a customer who wanted to buy a rifle. The customer desired to see it loaded, and would not buy unless this was done. The orders of the defendant to his clerk were that he should not load a rifle in the store. The customer was so earnest in desiring it that the clerk loaded it, and by accident it was discharged, the ball injuring the plaintiff, who was sitting at a window on the opposite side of the street. The defendant set up his orders to his clerk as a defense, but it did not prevail. The court said: "There is no pretense that the clerk was trying to do anything for himself. He was acting in pursuance of authority and trying to sell a gun, to make a bargain for his master, and in his eagerness to subserve his master's interests, he acted injudiciously and negligently."

In the case now before us, Dearborne sent Fox and his helpers to the house of McClung for the purpose of seizing and bringing away the organ. He says: "I told him to take the men and team when he was ready, and to bring the organ in, but to be careful and not to have any row about it." Black, who drove the team, testifies: "Mr. Dearborne told Fox to go down and get this organ on South Sixteenth Street; to get it as peaceably as possible, and not to have any assault and battery, or any disturbance whatever." These directions show that Dearborne knew that the errand on which he sent his employés was one that was likely to result in trouble, and would require to be managed with great coolness and care in order to avoid collision and a breach of the peace. But however the rule may be held in regard to the criminal liability of the master under such circumstances, it is very clear that he cannot escape liability civilly, by virtue of his instructions to his servant as to the manner of doing an act which the servant is to undertake on his behalf. He knew that the invasion of McClung's house in the manner contemplated was likely to excite indignation and resistance on the part of the inmates, and that what ought to be done might have to be determined under excitement, and without time for consultation or reflection by his employés. Under such circumstances he puts them in his own stead, and he is bound by what they do in the effort to do the thing which was committed to them. *Sanford* v. *Eighth Ave. R. Co.* 23 N. Y. 343; *Lake Shore & M. S. R. Co.* v. *Rosenzweig*, 113 Pa. 519, 4 Cent. Rep. 712; *Pittsburgh, A. & M. P. R. Co.* v. *Donahue*, 70 Pa. 119; *Hays* v. *Millar*, 77 Pa. 238; *Garretzen* v. *Duenckel, supra.*

The defendant was bound not only to give proper instructions to his servants when sending them on such an errand, but he was bound to see that his instructions were obeyed.

In the leading English case of *Seymour* v. *Greenwood*, 6 Hurl. & N. 365, referred to at some length in Wood on Master and Servant, § 297, it is said: "If the act is done within the scope of the servant's employment and is done in the master's service an action lies against the master and he is liable even though he has directed the servant to do nothing wrong."

Here Fox and his helpers were sent to bring away the organ. The acts complained of were committed in the course of, and as a means to, the accomplishment of that for which they were sent. Let it be conceded that they were instructed to do no wrong and that they did what they were warned not to do, the master is nevertheless liable. When he sends them upon an errand that exposes them to resistance and danger and the excitement consequent upon the presence of such a state of things, he must take the chances of their self-control and ability to obey. If he finds the risk inconveniently expensive he may conclude to respect the homes of inoffensive citizens and rely on his legal remedies for the recovery of any property to which he may claim title hereafter.

The jury should have been told that the defendant was liable for what the learned judge aptly characterized as an "unjustifiable outrage" by his employés, and they should have been allowed to assess adequate damages for the breach of the plaintiff's close, if the entry was forcible, and for all the injury done him by any and all the defendant's servants while engaged in the business of seizing and carrying away the organ. All the circumstances may be considered in fixing the compensation to be awarded to the plaintiff.

Judgment reversed, and a venire facias de novo *awarded.*

MICHIGAN SUPREME COURT.

George HANLEY *et al.*
v.
Hiram WALKER, *Appt.*

(....Mich....)

1. **The certificate of architects** which is, by a contract, made a condition precedent to the right to demand payment for labor performed, must be obtained before an action can be maintained on the contract, if the architects have not been guilty of fraud or collusion.

2. **Recovery upon a quantum meruit** cannot be based on a contract which makes a certificate of architects a condition precedent to a right of action, where the certificate has not been obtained.

3. **Remedying the defects pointed out by architects**, but not in the ways suggested by them, and without obtaining from them the certificate made by the contract a condition precedent to a right of action, cannot give a cause of action. Plaintiffs cannot substitute their own assertion, or the opinion of the jury, for the decision of the architects.

4. **Taking possession of real estate**, after work in constructing buildings has been done thereon, and the contractor has left the premises, and appropriating to the owner's use and benefit the labor and materials of the contractor, does not constitute an unequivocal acceptance of the work, although it may be taken into consideration in determining that matter.

(April 11, 1890.)

ERROR to the Circuit Court for Wayne County to review a judgment in favor of plaintiffs in an action to recover the contract price for certain labor and materials furnished by plaintiffs in plastering defendant's houses. *Reversed.*

The facts are fully stated in the opinion.

Messrs. **Atkinson, Carpenter, Brooke & Haigh**, with *Mr.* **William Aikman, Jr.**, for defendant, appellant.

Mr. **J. J. Speed** for plaintiffs, appellees.

Champlin, *Ch. J.*, delivered the opinion of the court:

The plaintiffs composed the firm of George Hanley & Bro., who were house plasterers doing business in the City of Detroit. In 1886 defendant was building brick dwelling-houses situated upon John R. and Watson Streets, in the City of Detroit. They were five in number. On the 26th day of May, 1886, the plaintiffs entered into a contract with defendant to do the plastering in these houses according to certain plans and specifications then prepared for said work by William Scott & Co., architects, which plans and specifications were made a part of the contract. The plaintiffs were to furnish and provide all the good, proper and sufficient materials and labor of all kinds as should be necessary and sufficient for completing and finishing the whole of the lathing and plastering of the five dwelling-houses, for the sum of $2,475. The contract contained this clause: "It is also agreed by and between the parties that the specifications and drawings are intended to co-operate, so that any works exhibited in the drawings and not mentioned in the specifications, or *vice versa*, are to be executed the same as if they were mentioned in the specifications and set forth in the drawings, to the true intent and meaning of the said drawings or specifications, without extra charge; and, should any dispute arise respecting the true construction or meaning of the drawings or specifications, the same shall be decided by William Scott & Co. and decision shall be final and conclusive." It also contained the following: "The contractor, at his own proper costs and charges, to provide all manner of labor, materials, apparatus, scaffolding, utensils and cartage, of every description, necessary for the

NOTE.—*Building contract.*

A contract to build a house implies an obligation to pay for all the work and material that enter into the structure and to defend against all liens of mechanics. State v. Tiedemann, 69 Mo. 515.

Where no time is fixed for the performance of an agreement, a reasonable time will be presumed to have been intended. McCartney v. Glassford (W. T.) Jan. 29, 1889.

Extension of time to complete a contract, and partial alteration in work to be done, not authorize the contractor to abandon it and sue for the value of the work. Hayes v. Second Baptist Church, 8 West. Rep. 829, 88 Mo. 285.

Although a building contract makes the obtaining of the certificate of the architects a condition precedent to the owner's liability, yet where the architects arbitrarily withhold such certificate, the builder may recover by showing that he performed the contract according to its terms. Bentley v. Davidson, 74 Wis. 420.

Where, before a certificate that plumbing and gas fitting had been done according to the plans and specifications could be procured, defendant raised the house and thereby broke and twisted gas and water pipes, he cannot refuse payment because of failure to procure the certificate. Doyn v. Ebbesen, 72 Wis. 284.

Under a contract to construct a brick-kiln in a first-class manner, the contractor is not prevented from recovering if the defects in the kiln are due to the plans and materials furnished by the other party. Birmingham Fire Brick Works v. Allen, 86 Ala. 185.

On a contract to remodel a house according to specifications, with no agreement as to time of payment, where the building is burned when the work is nearly finished, the contractor is entitled to recover the reasonable value of the work so far as completed. Weis v. Devlin, 67 Tex. 507.

In an action for the contract price for erecting a building, an instruction as to *quantum meruit* should limit the recovery to the contract price less the reasonable cost of completing the building according to contract. Phelps v. Beebe, 71 Mich. 554.

One who contracts to do certain work, to be paid for as sections of the work are completed, is, upon the failure of the one for whom the work is done to pay for a section upon its completion, entitled to discontinue the work and recover for that already done. Bennett v. Shaughnessy (Utah) Aug. 20, 1889. See *note* to Boettler v. Tendick (Tex.) 5 L. R. A. 270.

See also 20 L. R. A. 493.

due performance of the several works." The 5th article reads as follows: "Should the owner, at any time during the progress of said works, require any alteration of, deviation from, addition to or omissions in, this contract, consisting of this agreement and the said plans and specifications, made a part hereof, he shall have the right and power to make such change or changes; and the same shall in no way injuriously affect or avoid this agreement, but the difference shall be added to or deducted from the amount of this contract, as the case may be, by a fair and reasonable valuation. No changes shall be made except by written notice from the owner, which may be served on the contractor, sub-contractor or foreman. No omission of work or materials from the plans or specifications shall be deemed extra work if the same is necessary to complete said building in accordance with the general design or purpose for which the same is intended, and the provisions of said plans and specifications, and no work shall in any case be considered extra unless a separate estimate, in writing, for the same shall have been submitted by the contractor to the architect and the owner, and their signatures obtained thereto; and should any dispute arise respecting the true value of any extra work, or of the works omitted by the contractor, the same shall be valued by two competent persons,—one to be chosen by the owner, and the other by the contractor,—and these two shall have the power to name the third, in case they cannot agree, and the decision of the two shall be binding on all parties in case there be no fraud or collusion."

The specifications required the first, second and third stories to be plastered with two coats,—the first of rich brown mortar; the second, excepting coves and splays, to be one hard coat white finish, with plenty of sand; finish composed of cold-run putty and plaster of paris, well mixed and put on,—troweled down hard and smooth. They also require the contractor to put up centers to cost $15 net, in each house, to be selected by the owner or architect. The specifications also contained the following: "Parlors, halls, sitting and dining rooms, to have plaster coves as shown in sketch, rough plastered, and set with pebbles and shells, combed, as may be directed. Second-story halls, and two chambers in each house, to have nine splayed angles rough plastered and coarse combed. Plasterer to run ¾ in beads on angles of all plastered angles, and finish and set ornamental brackets. The plasterer will remove all rubbish, occasioned by his work from the premises, and leave the building broom clean; furnish and put up cotton cloth to the windows, where required; pay for all broken glass while he is performing his work, and furnish heat and labor for drying the plastering."

The contractor was to be paid from time to time, as the work progressed, upon the certificate of the architect, deducting 10 per cent until the whole job was completed and accepted, when the balance and such percentage was to be paid on the architects' certificate after the expiration of thirty days after acceptance and approval by the architect and owner, and the full, satisfactory adjustment of all things pertaining thereto. The contract relative to payment contained this proviso: "That before each and every payment is made a certificate shall be obtained from and signed by William Scott & Co., architects, to the effect that the work has been done, and materials have been furnished, in strict accordance with this agreement, said drawings and specifications, and that he considers the payment properly due. Said certificate, however, is in no way to lessen the total and final responsibility of said contractor."

No time is stated in the contract when the work shall be begun, nor when it shall be completed. Two facts, however, are suggested by the contract: *First* That the buildings were not then so far completed as to be in readiness for plastering. This is apparent from the fact that the contract stipulates that Hanley & Bro. shall build the houses, and furnish all material therefor. But this is not claimed, and explanation is found in the fact that a blank form of building contract was used in making the agreement for plastering. *Second.* The specifications show that the plastering might not be performed until cold weather, as they provide that the contractor shall "furnish heat and labor for drying the plastering." Hence it appears that it was in the contemplation of the parties, on the 26th of May, that the work would be done when the season would require artificial heat to dry the plastering.

The plaintiffs claim that there were two modifications of the written contract: *First.* On account of delay of the builders, the dwellings were not ready for the plasterers until late in the season of 1886. The plaintiff George Hanley testifies that they entered upon the performance of the contract about the middle or last of October; that he had a conversation with defendant about the 1st of October, in which, after mentioning the cause of delay, he said: "'We are into the cold weather and we will have to provide some means of heating;' and he asked me to suggest something to get over the difficulty. I told him that the only way we could do it now would be by using salamanders and coke fires until such times as he would be able to get his proper heating arrangements in shape, and he said he would furnish the coke if I would supply the salamanders. He asked me if I could not make our mortar in the cellar, in order to protect it from the weather. I told him it was not necessary; that we could do it outside as well." He further testified that salamanders were fit only for use in drying out the brown coat; that it is not usual to use them during the progress of the second coat, as it has a tendency to discolor the work; and that he did not use them in this work for that reason. He testified that the second coat was put on after the first coat was dry. From the testimony of Mr. Hanley, it appears that no modification whatever was made in the terms of the contract except that Mr. Walker agreed to furnish coke for the heating, which relieved Mr. Hanley of that expense. The other modification claimed by Mr. Hanley to have been made was in reference to the manner in which the coves were to be finished. The testimony of Mr. Hanley in support of this claim is as follows: "The coves were not put in according to specifications. They were finished in soap-stone, by an arrangement with Mr. Crittenden. I considered that Mr. Crittenden was acting for Mr. Walker in his absence. Previous to Mr. Walker going away, I had an interview with him, and he said to me that anything I needed, to call down and see Mr. Crittenden, and, if there was anything I wanted an explanation about, to come down there and have a talk with Mr. Crittenden. He was in Mr. Walker's office, and apparently in charge of the office business,—bookkeeping, or something of that kind. I called Mr. Crittenden's attention to what would be the appearance of the work if put in according to specifications. So we finished the coves in soap-stone, according to the specimen furnished to Mr. Crittenden. . . . I told Mr. Crittenden that, while soap-stone was more costly work, as Mr. Walker was away, I would not charge anything additional for the change." On cross-examination he testified: "Mr. Walker did not say anything to me with regard to Mr. Crittenden's agency. He merely said, if I needed anything to go down and see him. That was in the latter part of November, as near as I can recollect; just before Mr. Walker went west."

The defendant testified in his own behalf that he never authorized any change in the plans and specifications. He claims that the work was not done according to the contract. That the last coat was not hard finish, but would rub off when touched, leaving a white powder upon the hand, and that the cove and finish were not in accordance with the specifications. On the 23d of February, 1887, Scott & Co., architects, served notice upon plaintiffs that the plastering would not be accepted; that the surface rubbed off; that there was some defect in the last coat, or the frost had touched it; that, in order to make a good job, it would be necessary to calcimine the entire walls. On receipt of this notice, plaintiff sent his men; and they sponged the walls, and claimed that they left them in good order. They received another notice that they had overlooked some closets; and they sent men and sponged these off and heard no more complaint until they called upon defendant to settle, who then claimed that the defect in the walls still existed, and that the cove work was not according to specifications. The plaintiffs admit payment to them of $1,000, but at what time it was made does not appear from the record.

The contract and specifications were introduced by the plaintiffs upon the trial; and the most important question in the case is raised by the eighth request of defendant, that the court instruct the jury as follows: "Under the contract in evidence, it is provided that, before any payment can be demanded by plaintiffs, they shall obtain a certificate from the architect. This they have not obtained, and your verdict should therefore be for the defendant." It is claimed by defendant's counsel that the failure of plaintiffs to complete the work to the satisfaction of the architect, and procure his certificate, is a complete defense to this action. I think the point is well taken. There is no claim upon this record that the architects have been guilty of any fraud, or that there had been any collusion between them and the defendant. There is no pretense that the plaintiffs have applied to or requested the certificate required by the contract.

When parties capable of contracting have deliberately entered into a written agreement in which, by all just rules of construction, the certificate of the architects is made a condition precedent to a right of action, such condition must be performed or its requirements waived. The authorities holding contracts like the one in question here valid are numerous. Leake, Cont. 2d ed. § 640; Benjamin, Sales, 3d Am. ed. § 575; *Morgan* v. *Birnie*, 9 Bing. 672; *Grafton* v. *Eastern Counties R. Co.* 8 Exch. 699; *Clarke* v. *Watson*, 18 C. B. N. S. 278; *Goodyear* v. *Weymouth & Melcombe Regis*, 1 Har. & R. 67; *Ferguson* v. *Galt*, 23 U. C. C. P. 66; *Smith* v. *Briggs*, 3 Denio, 73; *North Lebanon R. Co.* v. *McGrann*, 33 Pa. 530; *Reynolds* v. *Caldwell*, 51 Pa. 298; *O'Reilly* v. *Kerns*, 52 Pa. 214; *Gray* v. *New Jersey Cent. R. Co.* 11 Hun, 70; *Tyler* v. *Ames*, 6 Lans. 280; *Spring* v. *Ansonia Clock Co.* 24 Hun, 175; *Smith* v. *Brady*, 17 N. Y. 173; *Wyckoff* v. *Meyers*, 44 N. Y. 143; *Wangler* v. *Swift*, 90 N. Y. 38; *Tetz* v. *Butterfield*, 54 Wis. 246; *Kirtland* v. *Moore*, 40 N. J. Eq. 106, 1 Cent. Rep. 466; *Hot Springs R. Co.* v. *Maher*, 48 Ark. 522; *Stose* v. *Heissler*, 120 Ill. 433, 8 West. Rep. 441; *Boettler* v. *Tendick*, 5 L. R. A. 270, 73 Tex. 488; *Byrne* v. *Sisters of Charity of St. Elizabeth*, 45 N. J. L. 213; *Elliott* v. *Royal Exch. Assur. Co.* L. R. 2 Exch. 243.

It has also been held that if the certificate is required to be in writing there can be no parol approval. *Lamprell* v. *Billericay Union*, 3 Exch. 283; *Russell* v. *Bandeira*, 13 C. B. N. S. 149; *Goodyear* v. *Weymouth & Melcombe Regis*, *supra*.

Upon this point the authorities are not uniform, and we are not called upon to decide it in this case.

It is the settled law in this State that when a party fails to comply substantially with an agreement, unless it is apportionable, he cannot sue upon the agreement or recover upon it at all. But when anything has been done from which the other party has received substantial benefit, and which he has appropriated, a recovery may be had upon a *quantum meruit* based on that benefit. And the basis of this recovery is not the original contract, but a new, implied agreement deducible from the delivery and acceptance of some valuable service or thing. *Allen* v. *McKibbin*, 5 Mich. 454.

The plaintiffs appeal to this principle, and claim that they are entitled to recover, under the common counts, although they have not obtained the certificate of the architects; and they rely upon *Wildey* v. *Fractional School Dist. No. 1*, 25 Mich. 422, in which this court held that the architect was not made the sole inspector or judge of the work as it progressed, but that a superintendent was expected to be, and was in fact, chosen by the district, and that it was a reasonable inference that the superintendent was expected to supervise the work as it progressed, and to express his dissatisfaction with any portion not in compliance with the specifications. His powers were made, by the contract, as broad as those of the architect, and there was no consent in the contract that his decision should be subject to reversal or review by his nominal superior; and for that reason it was held that whatever passed under his inspection as the work progressed, and was in good faith approved by him, expressly or by implication, was not open to objection on the part of the defendant afterwards, and that as to so much of the work, at least the plaintiff had the same right to recover that he would have had if the proper certificate had been furnished him. And it was also said that, "in a clear case, where the contractor had undertaken, in defiance of the superintendent, to force upon the district one thing, where they had bargained for another,—as, for instance, one kind of roof where another was agreed for,—unless there was a subsequent assent to accept it, express or implied, we do not think the district would be held liable to pay for the thing substituted at all. The district is not to be forced to take what it never wanted or bargained for, on any pretense that it will answer their purpose as well, or that, even if it will not, it is still of some value, and should be paid for accordingly." I do not think the case of *Wildey* v. *Fractional School District No. 1* is an authority in support of plaintiffs' contention. The facts are entirely different. Here there was no superintendent, aside from the architects, agreed upon, and no approval, express or implied, of the architects of the work as it progressed, or after it was completed. It is true that, as to the right of a party, in general, to recover upon the common counts, subject to a recoupment of damages, when he has not strictly complied with his contract, the court expressed its adherence to the views expressed in *Allen* v. *McKibbin;* but the right does not exist in all cases, as was explained in that case, and more particularly in the later cases. *Martus* v. *Houck*, 39 Mich. 431; *Fildeu* v. *Besley*, 42 Mich. 100.

In *Martus* v. *Houck* we stated what was held in *Wildey* v *Fractional School Dist. No. 1*, and upon page 436 the same judge who wrote the opinion in that case, referring to it, said: "We held, explicitly, that one contracting for a building to be put up according to certain specifications had a right to have what he bargained for. Unimportant variances may be overlooked or compensated for under a variety of circumstances which are not in question here, but departures from the contract which are susceptible of correction no one can be compelled to overlook or waive. Protection to equities cannot require it, and the acceptance of such a doctrine as the plaintiff here insists upon would take from an unscrupulous contractor the chief inducement to keep his promises. What is it to him whether or not he lives up to his agreement, if in any event he may collect for such performance as he tenders, and if the party contracting with him has no choice but to take at some price the building the contractor has seen fit to put up? The sanction the law would give to contracts under such a doctrine would, as nearly as possible, be worthless."

These parties are bound by the contract they entered into. The plaintiffs agreed to do the work, strictly in accordance with the plans and specifications, for a round sum. The defendant agreed to pay plaintiffs from time to time, as the work progressed, upon the plaintiffs obtaining a certificate from the architects, deducting 10 per cent, until the job was completed and accepted. The balance and such percentage was to be paid, on the architects' certificate, after the expiration of thirty days after acceptance and approval by the architects and owner; and before each and every payment should be made a certificate was to be obtained from and signed by William Scott & Co., architects, to the effect that the work has been done, and materials have been furnished, in strict accordance with the agreement, drawings and specifications, and that he considers the payment properly due. The fact is undisputed that the plaintiffs have not obtained the certificate required by the contract. They have not applied to the architects for such certificate. They have not obtained the approval or acceptance by the architects of the work. They have not performed it according to its terms. On the contrary, they were notified by the architects that it was not completed according to its terms, and certain defects were pointed out. These defects the plaintiffs claim to have been remedied. This is disputed by defendant. But, if plaintiffs did remedy the defects, they did not do so in the ways suggested by the architects; and they never have obtained the certificate of the architects after they claim the defects were remedied. The plaintiffs' assertion that they had remedied the defects did not give them a right of action. They could not substitute their assertion for the architects' certificate agreed upon between the parties; nor could they change the condition under which the defendant agreed to pay the balance thirty days after the architects' certificate of approval, and of its being completed according to the contract, to an agreement to pay without the certificate, and on their own assertion that it was completed according to contract. As was said in *Clarke* v. *Watson*, 18 C. B. N. S. 285: "This is, in effect, an attempt on the part of the plaintiff to take from the defendants the protection of their architects, and to substitute for it the opinion of a jury."

The principles laid down in *Allen* v. *McKibbin* do not apply to cases where the parties have by their agreement made some act or fact a condition precedent to payment, unless the other party has waived the condition. The waiver may be express, or it may be implied from facts and circumstances, as where the party relying upon the condition has accepted or appropriated the property or fruits of the other party. There is no evidence in the record before us that can be construed into a waiver of the conditions precedent contained in the contract on the part of the defendant. When a person contracts with another to build, or to do some portions of the work in constructing buildings upon real estate belonging to the owner of such real estate, his taking possession after the other has left the premises cannot be construed as an unequivocal acceptance, although he thereby takes possession of, and appropriates to his use and benefit, the labor or materials of the contractor. He must do so, as a matter of necessity, in many cases, or suffer the property to stand idle and unused, to the great detriment of all parties, and especially so of the owner. The most that can be said, in such cases, is that the acts of the party, and all the circumstances, may be taken into consideration in the determination of the question whether there is an implied waiver of the condition precedent. Under the testimony appearing in this record, the fact of the defendant's taking possession was not such an acceptance as relieved the plaintiffs from the terms and conditions of the contract requiring them to obtain the architects' certificate before they were entitled to payment.

As there must be a new trial, it may be well to notice one other matter of controversy between the parties, and that is with reference to substituting the soap-stone finish in the coves for pebbles and shells, as required by the specifications. This substitution cannot be held to have been made with the owner's consent previously obtained. Mr. Crittenden was not defendant's agent for the purpose of making changes in the plans and specifications, and no authority was shown for him to do so. The contract provided that such changes should be made in writing signed by the owner and architect. The change was not made in writing, and Mr. Crittenden was neither owner nor architect. Whether this provision of the contract had been waived, and the substitution ratified, will be, upon a future trial, a question of fact, under all the circumstances, to be submitted to the jury. If any question exists as to what the specifications require, the contract provides that the architects shall determine as to their meaning; and this power cannot be taken away from the architects agreed upon, and left to the construction of other plasterers or architects. The court erred in permitting this to be done upon the trial.

The judgment must be reversed, and a new trial is ordered.

The other Justices concurred.

NEW YORK COURT OF APPEALS.

James J. PHELAN, *Appt.*,

v.

Margaret BRADY, Impleaded, etc., *Respt.*

(......N. Y.......)

1. The title of one in possession of real estate under a valid unrecorded deed must prevail over that of a subsequent mortgagee from the same grantor, although the latter took his mortgage without notice of the prior title and the building upon the premises had been erected for tenement purposes and contained a large number of apartments which were occupied by many lessees, and the grantee in the unrecorded deed had occupied a store and living apartment in the building as a tenant before receiving the

NOTE.—*Title to land; constructive notice by possession.*

Whatever is sufficient to put a party upon inquiry is in equity good notice to bind him. Allegheny First Nat. Bank's App. (Pa.) 5 Cent. Rep. 511; Green v. Slater, 4 Johns. Ch. 38, 1 N. Y. Ch. L. ed. 756. See *note* to Batt v. Mallon (Mass.) 7 L. R. A. 840.

The law imputes notice when parties are put on inquiry. Lovejoy v. Raymond, 1 New Eng. Rep. 405, 58 Vt. 509.

Where a man has sufficient notice to lead him to a fact, he shall be deemed conusant of it. Wright v. Ross, 36 Cal. 437; Jenkins v. Eldredge, 3 Story, 325.

It is good notice, provided the inquiry becomes a duty and would lead to the knowledge of the requisite fact by the exercise of ordinary diligence and understanding. Lodge v. Simonton, 2 Pen. & W. 449, 23 Am. Dec. 42.

It is sufficient notice in equity where the means of knowledge are at hand; and if the party omits to inquire and proceeds to act, he does so at his peril. Angle v. Northwestern L. Ins. Co. 92 U. S. 342 (23 L. ed. 560); Hawley v. Cramer, 4 Cow. 717; Booth v. Barnum, 9 Conn. 286; Pringle v. Phillips, 5 Sandf. 157.

Where a party has notice of such facts as ought to put an ordinarily prudent man on inquiry, a failure to make inquiry is visited with all of the consequences of actual notice. Wood v. Rayburn (Or.) April 21, 1889.

It is also a notice of everything to which it is afterward found such inquiry would have led, although all was unknown for want of the investigation. Frazer v. Western, 1 Barb. Ch. 232, 5 N. Y. Ch. L. ed. 366; Taylor v. Baker, 5 Price, 306; Booth v. Barnum, 9 Conn. 289; Hawley v. Cramer, 4 Cow. 717.

A party having notice sufficient to put him on inquiry cannot become a bona fide purchaser or mortgagee when knowledge of the truth would render him otherwise. Wright v. Ross, 36 Cal. 437; Pendelton v. Fay, 2 Paige, 205, 2 N. Y. Ch. L. ed. 876.

The person in possession may be asked by the purchaser to disclose the right or title by which he holds possession; and the purchaser will be charged with the actual notice he would have received if he had made the inquiry. Matesky v. Feldman (Wis.) Nov. 5, 1889.

Effect of knowledge of possession. See *notes* to Thomas v. Burnett (Ill.) 4 L. R. A. 222; Pittsburgh, C. & St. L. R. Co. v. Bosworth (Ohio) 2 L. R. A. 200; Constant v. Rochester University (N. Y.) 2 L. R. A. 736; Brinser v. Anderson (Pa.) 6 L. R. A. 205.

Actual open possession sufficient to put on inquiry.

Possession under a conveyance from one claiming title is sufficient to put one on inquiry and is equivalent to actual notice in equity. Pitney v. Leonard, 1 Paige, 461, 2 N. Y. Ch. L. ed. 715.

An open and notorious possession under a deed which appears by the records to be from a stranger to the title is sufficient to put a purchaser on inquiry. Mendocino Bank v. Baker, 6 L. R. A. 833, 82 Cal. 114.

Possession of a third party is sufficient to put on inquiry a purchaser contracting with a claimant of the land. Norman v. Bennett, 32 W. Va. 614; Kennedy v. Wible (Pa.) 10 Cent. Rep. 51.

Constructive notice of adverse possession is such notice as will put a prudent man on inquiry, which, if prosecuted with ordinary diligence, will lead to actual notice of the right or title in conflict with which he is about to purchase, and is notice of every right by which the possession is held. Matesky v. Feldman (Wis.) Nov. 5, 1889.

The purchaser of a mortgage upon property in the actual possession of mortgagor's vendor is put upon inquiry. Seymour v. McKinstry, 8 Cent. Rep. 73, 106 N. Y. 230.

See also 19 L. R. A. 105.

grant and made no visible material change in his occupation of the building afterwards, except that he then leased apartments and collected rents.

2. The rule that actual possession of real estate is sufficient notice to a person proposing to take a mortgage on the property, and to all the world, of the existence of any right which the person in possession is able to establish, is not changed by the fact that the property is occupied by numerous tenants.

(March 21, 1890.)

APPEAL by plaintiff from a judgment of the General Term of the Supreme Court, First Department, affirming a judgment of the New York Special Term in favor of defendant in an action brought to foreclose a mortgage. *Affirmed.*

The facts are fully stated in the opinion.

Mr. **N. B. Hoxie**, with *Mr.* **William A. Haggerty**, for appellant:

To defeat the title of the mortgagee it must appear that he was not a purchaser in good faith, but was guilty of a fraudulent intent.

Williamson v. *Brown*, 15 N. Y. 362.

The possession which will amount to notice must be actual, open and visible; it must not be equivocal, occasional or for a special or temporary purpose, neither must it be consistent with the title of the apparent owner by the record.

Pope v. *Allen*, 90 N. Y. 298; *Cook* v. *Travis*, 20 N. Y. 400; *Staples* v. *Fenton*, 5 Hun, 172; 3 Washb. Real Prop. p. 317.

Plaintiff was justified in believing that the persons occupying the premises were tenants of Murphy, the owner.

Claiborne v. *Holmes*, 51 Miss. 146; *Billington* v. *Welsh*, 5 Binn. 129; *Page* v. *Waring*, 76 N. Y. 463; *Brown* v. *Volkening*, 64 N. Y. 76.

Messrs. **Wyatt & Trimble**, for respondent:

Possession is notice and prima facie evidence of the highest estate in the property, viz., a seisin in fee.

Gouverneur v. *Lynch*, 2 Paige, 300, 2 N. Y. Ch. L. ed. 916; *Bank of Orleans* v. *Flagg*, 3 Barb. Ch. 318, 5 N. Y. Ch. L. ed. 916; *Moyer* v. *Hinman*, 13 N. Y. 184; *Tuttle* v. *Jackson*, 6 Wend. 218; *Union College* v. *Wheeler*, 61 N. Y. 88; *Cavalli* v. *Allen*, 57 N. Y. 517; *Chesterman* v. *Gardner*, 5 Johns. Ch. 29, 1 N. Y. Ch. L. ed. 997; *Terrett* v. *Cowenhoven*, 11 Hun, 320; *Troup* v. *Hurlbut*, 10 Barb. 354; *Smith* v. *Jackson*, 76 Ill. 254; *Greer* v. *Higgins*, 20 Kan. 420; *Brown* v. *Volkening*, 64 N. Y. 76.

Knowledge by a purchaser of land of such facts as would put an ordinarily prudent man on inquiry as to the nature of the title of an occupant under a prior unrecorded lease, and lead him to discover the truth respecting the same, is equivalent to actual notice. Drey v. Doyle, 99 Mo. 459.

Whenever inquiry is a duty, a party bound to make it is affected with knowledge of all which he would have discovered had he performed the duty. Means of knowledge, with the duty of using them, are in equity equivalent to knowledge itself. Effinger v. Hall, 81 Va. 94; Davis v. Tebbs, Id. 600; Lyons v. Leahy, 15 Or. 8; Yancy v. Cothran, 32 Fed. Rep. 687; Price v. Reed, 13 West. Rep. 510, 124 Ill. 317; Indiana, B. & W. R. Co. v. McBroom, 13 West. Rep. 833, 114 Ind. 198; Reilly v. Hannibal & St. J. R. Co. 13 West. Rep. 662, 94 Mo. 600; Higgins v. Lodge, 10 Cent. Rep. 554, 68 Md. 229.

Constructive notice by possession.

Actual possession of land is constructive notice of ownership, or of an interest, and is sufficient to put creditors and purchasers on inquiry. Bright v. Buckman, 39 Fed. Rep. 243.

But this never extends beyond the rights of the occupant and those under whom he claims. Roll v. Rea, 11 Cent. Rep. 362, 50 N. J. L. 264.

The possession of land is notice to all the world of the possessor's rights thereunder. Lipp v. South Omaha Land Syndicate, 24 Neb. 692.

Every person dealing with land must take notice of an actual, open and exclusive possession, and when this, concurring with interest in the possessor, makes it homestead, a lender on security of the land stands charged with notice of that fact; and it is immaterial what declarations to the contrary the borrower may make. Texas Land & L. Co. v. Blalock (Tex.) Feb. 11, 1890.

Possession by several purchasers of parcels of land mortgaged, claiming under contracts of purchase, some of whom have fenced and are cultivating their lots, while others have built and are living upon theirs, is sufficiently open and patent to put the mortgagee upon inquiry. Bright v. Buckman, *supra.*

But possession, under an unrecorded bond for title, of a part of the land described in the bond and not in dispute, is not notice of claim to that part in dispute. Wright v. Lassiter, 71 Tex. 640.

Where a person did not occupy the whole of premises, but had actual exclusive possession of a distinct and separate portion thereof, both really and apparently independent and exclusive of any possession of that portion by the mortgagor, and inconsistent with an absolute and unqualified title and right of possession in the mortgagor, such possession is notice to the mortgagee. Bassett v. Wood, 55 Hun, 587.

That a vendor of land is allowed by the vendee to retain possession does not constitute constructive notice to a mortgagee of the vendee of fraud by the latter in purchasing the land of which the vendor was ignorant at the time of such possession and when the mortgage was executed. Matesky v. Feldman (Wis.) Nov. 5, 1889.

Where one who knows of a prior unregistered deed of trust or mortgage procures a mortgage for his own benefit on the same property, which is registered first, he gets the first lien on the property, unless he used fraud to prevent the registration of the mortgage which is first in date. Traders Nat. Bank v. Lawrence Mfg. Co. 96 N. C. 298.

One who takes a mortgage of land from one having a legal title, and subject to a trust in favor of a person in possession, is chargeable, by the fact of such possession, with notice of the rights of the latter. Brooke v. Bordner, 125 Pa. 470.

Occupancy of land under an unrecorded deed, which provides for a reconveyance on payment of a debt to the grantor, is notice to a subsequent purchaser. Seymour v. Hubbard (Vt.) April 12, 1890.

Possession by a tenant of the real owner under an unrecorded deed is sufficient to put a purchaser of the land upon inquiry as to the title. Levy v. Holberg (Miss.) April 21, 1890.

Whether a mortgagee can be held chargeable with notice of a prior unrecorded mortgage in the possession of his attorney in the transaction, who is also the attorney of the prior mortgagee, and whose duties to his clients are therefore conflicting,—*quære.* Constant v. Rochester University, 2 L. R. A. 734, 111 N. Y. 604.

The fact that the property in question is a tenement house has no proper bearing on the question. That fact cannot change the rule.

Crosland v. *Mutual Sav. Fund*, 121 Pa. 82; *Brown* v. *Volkening*, 64 N. Y. 84; *DeRuyter* v. *St. Peter's Church*, 3 Barb. Ch. 556, 5 N. Y. Ch. L. ed. 751.

O'Brien, *J.*, delivered the opinion of the court:

On the 23d day of July, 1886, the plaintiff loaned to the defendant John E. Murphy the sum of $2,000 and took from him his bond, whereby he promised to pay the same, with interest semi-annually, in two years thereafter. On the same day, and as collateral security for the payment of the bond, Murphy and his wife executed, acknowledged and delivered to the plaintiff a mortgage upon certain real estate in the City of New York. The premises thus mortgaged consisted of a tenement building, or block, containing forty-three rooms or apartments, then occupied by twenty different occupants or families, as tenants from month to month, except that three of these apartments were occupied by the defendant Margaret Brady and her husband, who kept a liquor store in part of the building, and they occupied two living rooms in the rear of the store, the wife claiming to be the owner of the premises and collecting rents from the other tenants.

The plaintiff at the time he made the loan had no actual notice or knowledge of any title to the premises in Mrs. Brady, or any claim on her part to be the owner. When the first installment of interest became due upon the mortgage default was made, and the plaintiff brought this action to foreclose under a provision in the mortgage making the whole sum due upon default in the payment of the interest when due.

Margaret Brady, being in possession, was made a party to the action, and she answered, setting up the defense that prior to the execution and delivery of the plaintiff's mortgage, and on or about the 5th of May, 1886, she became the absolute owner in fee simple of the premises described in the complaint and in the mortgage and of the whole thereof, and that upon becoming such owner she took possession of the same, claiming to be the owner and actually owning the same; and that she has ever since continued in actual, open and notorious occupation and possession of the premises as such owner, and has ever since and still owns the same in fee simple.

The trial court found that in March, 1886, Margaret Brady employed one Michael J. Murphy, an attorney, to examine the title to the premises in question and purchase the same for her, and before May 7, 1886, she gave said Murphy, as her attorney, the sum of $6,700 to be used as part of the purchase money; that Murphy procured a contract for the sale of the premises to be made between Mary S. Trimble, who then owned the same, and his son, John E. Murphy, the defendant, in which contract the said John E. Murphy appeared to be the purchaser of the premises; that upon the execution of this contract about March 19, 1886, Michael J. Murphy paid to Mrs. Trimble part of the sum of $6,700 which he had received for that purpose from Mrs. Brady, and the rest of that sum was paid to her on the 7th of May, 1886; that the balance of the purchase price, namely, $16,000, was secured to be paid to Mrs. Trimble by a purchase-money mortgage; that on the same day the purchase price was thus paid, Mrs. Brady's lawyer took from Mrs. Trimble a deed of the premises to his son, John E. Murphy, and the deed was duly recorded on that day; that on the 1st of May, 1886, Mrs. Brady took possession of the premises under the contract, claiming to own the same, and has ever since remained in possession, and occupied the same herself and by her tenants; that she rented certain rooms in the building to tenants immediately thereafter; that she discharged the housekeeper, who had before that date rented the premises and collected the rents for Mrs. Trimble, and moved herself into the rooms formerly occupied by the housekeeper, and that she has received the rents ever since the 1st of May, 1886; that on the 5th of May of that year a deed conveying the premises to Mrs. Brady was executed and duly acknowledged by the defendant, John E. Murphy, and his wife, and by him delivered to his father, Michael J. Murphy, as agent and attorney for Mrs. Brady; that Murphy never had any interest in the premises, never paid any part of the consideration money, and never had possession of the same or any part thereof; that the said Michael J. Murphy retained the deed to Mrs. Brady in his possession until not later than the 25th of August, 1886, when he delivered the same to her, and the same was recorded by her on the 26th of August, 1886, subsequent to the execution, delivery and record of the plaintiff's mortgage.

The trial court held that Mrs. Brady's title and possession were sufficient to defeat any claim under the plaintiff's mortgage, and dismissed the complaint, and this judgment has been affirmed by the general term.

At the time of the execution and delivery of the mortgage to the plaintiff, the defendant, Mrs. Brady, was in the actual possession of the premises under a perfectly valid but unrecorded deed. Her title must therefore prevail as against the plaintiff. It matters not, so far as Mrs. Brady is concerned, that the plaintiff in good faith advanced his money upon an apparently perfect record title of the defendant, John E. Murphy. Nor is it of any consequence, so far as this question is concerned, whether the plaintiff was in fact ignorant of any right or claim of Mrs. Brady to the premises. It is enough that she was in possession under her deed and the contract of purchase, as that fact operated in law as notice to the plaintiff of all her rights.

It may be true, as has been argued by plaintiff's counsel, that when a party takes a conveyance of property situated as this was, occupied by numerous tenants, it would be inconvenient and difficult for him to ascertain the rights or interests that are claimed by all or any of them. But this circumstance cannot change the rule. Actual possession of real estate is sufficient notice to a person proposing to take a mortgage on the property, and to all the world, of the existence of any right which the person in possession is able to establish. *Gouverneur* v. *Lynch*, 2 Paige, 300, 2 N. Y. Ch. L. ed. 916; *Bank of Orleans* v. *Flagg*, 3

Barb. Ch. 318, 5 N. Y. Ch. L. ed. 916; *Moyer* v. *Hinman*, 13 N. Y. 184; *Tuttle* v. *Jackson*, 6 Wend. 213; *Union College* v. *Wheeler*, 61 N. Y. 88, 98; *Cavalli* v. *Allen*, 57 N. Y. 517.

The circumstance that Mrs. Brady and her husband occupied the store and a living apartment in the building prior to the time that she went into possession under her contract of purchase as tenants under Mrs. Trimble, the then owner, cannot aid the plaintiff. It does not appear that he ever heard of that fact till after the commencement of this suit, and we cannot perceive how it would affect the result if he had. The trial court found that prior to making the loan the plaintiff was upon the premises for other purposes, and that then by making inquiry he could have ascertained the rights of Mrs. Brady in the property, and while the absence of such a finding would not change the result, it shows that the plaintiff's loss is to be attributed to his confidence in Murphy, who probably deceived him, and to his failure to take notice of Mrs. Brady's possession.

The judgment should be affirmed, with costs.

All concur.

Amasa R. MOORE, *Appt.*,
v.
John M. FRANCIS *et al.*, *Respts.*

(....N. Y.....)

1. **The question of libel or no libel** in a civil action is one of law which the court must decide, where the publication is admitted, and the words are unambiguous and admit of but one sense.

2. **A publication stating that the teller of a bank had become mentally deranged** from overwork, and while in this condition had made injurious statements in respect to the bank's affairs, which occasioned it trouble, is defamatory in a legal sense, constituting a libel *per se*, although it imputes no crime, and subjects him to no disgrace, reproach or obloquy, for the reason that its tendency is to subject him to a temporal loss by injuring him in his business, character and employment as a teller.

3. **It is not a legal excuse** that defamatory matter was published accidentally or inadvertently, or with good motives, and with an honest belief in its truth.

(April 15, 1890.)

APPEAL by plaintiff from a judgment of the General Term of the Supreme Court, Third Department, affirming a judgment of the Rensselaer Circuit in favor of defendants in an action to recover damages for the publication of an alleged libel. *Reversed.*

The facts sufficiently appear in the opinion.

Mr. **Matthew Hale,** for appellant:

To state in writing that the plaintiff is insane, or that his mind is affected, is libelous.

See Odgers, Libel and Slander, p. 23; *Southwick* v. *Stevens*, 10 Johns. 443; *Perkins* v. *Mitchell*, 31 Barb. 461, 465.

The libelous words were clearly spoken of plaintiff as teller and tended to injure him by the statement that his mental condition was not entirely good, and the further statement that his statements when he was probably not responsible for what he said had caused some bad rumors and are actionable.

Townshend, Slander and Libel, § 181; *Foulger* v. *Newcomb*, L. R. 2 Exch. 327; Newell, Defamation, p. 168, § 1; *Sanderson* v. *Caldwell*, 45 N. Y. 398, 405; *Cruikshank* v. *Gordon*, 118 N. Y. 178.

Mr. **R. A. Parmenter,** for respondents:

The action for a libel injurious to business cannot be maintained in the absence of malice, or a willful purpose to inflict injury, and this must be shown.

Hovey v. *Rubber Tip Pencil Co.* 33 N. Y. Super. Ct. (1 Jones & S.) 522, affirmed, 57 N. Y. 119.

Within the definitions the publication complained of is not libelous unless made with a mischievous and malicious intent towards the person censured.

2 Kent, Com. 16 *et seq.*; *People* v. *Croswell*, 3 Johns. Cas. 337, 354; *Steele* v. *Southwick*, 9 Johns. 214.

It is only where the words of the publication are not susceptible of being understood in any other than a libelous sense that the court is bound to determine its character as matter of law.

Snyder v. *Andrews*, 6 Barb. 43; *Dexter* v. *Taber*, 12 Johns. 240; *Van Rensselaer* v. *Dole*, 1 Johns. Cas. 279; *McKinley* v. *Rob*, 20 Johns. 356; *Dolloway* v. *Turrell*, 26 Wend. 383; *Stanley* v. *Webb*, 21 Barb. 148.

Andrews, J., delivered the opinion of the court:

The alleged libelous publication, which is the subject of this action, was contained in the "Troy Times" of September 15, 1882, in an article written on the occasion of rumors of trouble in the financial condition of the Manufacturers' National Bank of Troy, of which the plaintiff was at the time of the publication, and for eighteen years prior thereto had been, teller. The rumors referred to had caused a "run" upon the bank, and it is claimed by the defendants, and it is the fair conclusion from the evidence, that the primary motive of the article was to allay public excitement on the subject.

NOTE.—*Libel and slander; questions of law and of fact, in action.*

Whether the publication as set out in the complaint is libelous *per se* is properly determined by the court on demurrer, notwithstanding the averment that it was made falsely, maliciously and with the intent to defame plaintiff. Trimble v. Anderson, 79 Ala. 514.

The questions of good faith, or belief in the truth of the statement, and the existence of actual malice, are for the jury. Hinman v. Hare, 6 Cent. Rep. 51, 104 N. Y. 641.

It is for the jury to say whether or not there has been a publication referring to the plaintiff; whether or not it is malicious and false; and whether or not the sense and meaning are as charged. But if the publication is expressed in terms so clear and unambiguous that no circumstances are required to make it clearer, the better rule is that the question of libel or no libel is one of law to be determined by the court. Donaghue v. Gaffy, 3 New Eng. Rep. 548, 54 Conn. 257; Bourreseau v. Detroit Evening Journal Co. 6 West. Rep. 151, 63 Mich. 425; Kedrolivansky v. Niebaum, 70 Cal. 216.

See also 26 L. R. A. 531.

That part of the publication charged to be libelous is as follows:

"Several weeks ago it was rumored that Amasa Moore, the teller of the bank, had tendered his resignation. Rumors at once began to circulate. A reporter inquired of Cashier Wellington if it was true that the teller had resigned, and received in reply the answer that Mr. Moore was on his vacation. More than this the cashier would not say. A rumor was circulated that Mr. Moore was suffering from overwork, and that his mental condition was not entirely good. Next came reports that Cashier Wellington was financially involved, and that the bank was in trouble. A Times reporter at once sought an interview with President Weed of the bank, and found him and Directors Morrison, Cowee, Bardwell and others in consultation. They said that the bank was entirely sound, with a clear surplus of $100,000; that there had been a little trouble in its affairs caused by the mental derangement of Teller Moore, and that the latter's statements, when he was probably not responsible for what he said, had caused some bad rumors."

The complaint is in the usual form and charges that the publication was false and malicious, made with intent to injure the plaintiff in his good name and credit in his occupation as bank teller, and to cause it to be believed that by reason of mental derangement he had become incompetent to discharge his duties and had caused injury to the bank, etc.

The court on the trial was requested by the plaintiff's counsel to rule as a question of law that the publication was libelous. The court refused, but submitted the question to the jury. The jury found a verdict for the defendants, and as the verdict may have proceeded upon the finding that the article was not libelous, the question is presented, whether it was *per se* libelous. If it was, the court erred in leaving the question to the jury. It is the settled law of this State that in a civil action for libel, where the publication is admitted and the words are unambiguous and admit of but one sense, the question of libel or no libel is one of law which the court must decide. *Snyder* v. *Andrews*, 6 Barb. 43; *Matthews* v. *Beach*, 5 Sandf. 256; *Hunt* v. *Bennett*, 19 N. Y. 173; *Lewis* v. *Chapman*, 16 N. Y. 369; *Kingsbury* v. *Bradstreet* Co. 116 N. Y. 211, 26 N. Y. S. R. 520.

Of course, an error in submitting the question to the jury would be harmless, if their finding that the publication was not libelous was in accordance with its legal character. The import of the article, so far as it bears upon the plaintiff, is plain and unequivocal. The words amount to a distinct affirmation: *first*, that the plaintiff was teller of the bank; *second*, that while acting in this capacity he became mentally deranged; *third*, that the derangement was caused by overwork; *fourth*, that while teller and suffering from this mental alienation, he made injurious statements in respect to the bank's affairs which occasioned it trouble.

The cases of actionable slander were defined by *Chief Justice* DeGrey in the leading case of *Onslow* v. *Horne*, 3 Wils. 177, and the classification made in that case has been generally followed in England and this country. According to this classification slanderous words are those which (1) import a charge of some punishable crime, or (2) impute some offensive disease which would tend to deprive a person of society, or (3) which tend to injure a party in his trade, occupation or business, or (4) which have produced some special damage.

Defamatory words, in common parlance, are such as impute some moral delinquency or some disreputable conduct to the person of whom they are spoken. Actions of slander for the most part are founded upon such imputations. But the action lies in some cases where the words impute no criminal offense, where no attack is made upon the moral character, nor any charge of personal dishonor. The first and larger class of actions are those brought for the vindication of reputation, in its strict sense, against damaging and calumnious aspersions. The other class falls, for the most part, at least, within the third specification in the opinion of *Chief Justice* DeGrey, of words which tend to injure one in his trade or occupation. The case of words affecting the credit of a trader, such as imputing bankruptcy or insolvency, is an illustration. The action is maintainable in such a case, although no fraud or dishonesty is charged, and although the words were spoken without actual malice. The law allows this form of action not only to protect a man's character as such, but to protect him in his occupation also against injurious imputations. It recognizes the right of a man to live and the necessity of labor, and will not permit one to assail by words the pecuniary credit of another, except at the peril, in case they are untrue, of answering in damages. The principle is clearly stated by Bayley, *J.*, in *Whittaker* v. *Bradley*, 7 Dowl. & R. 649: "Whatever words have a tendency to hurt, or are calculated to prejudice, a man who seeks his livelihood by any trade or business, are actionable." Where proved to have been spoken in relation thereto, the action is supported, and unless the defendant shows a lawful excuse, the plaintiff is entitled to recover without allegation or proof of special damage, because both the falsity of the words, and resulting damage, are presumed. *Craft* v. *Boite*, 1 Saund. 243, *note*; *Van Vechten* v. *Hopkins*, 1 Am. Lead. Cas. 135.

The authorities tend to support the proposition that spoken words imputing insanity are actionable *per se* when spoken of one in his trade or occupation, but not otherwise without proof of special damage. *Morgan* v. *Lingen*, 8 L. T. N. S. 800; "*Joannes*" v. *Burt*, 6 Allen, 236.

The imputation of insanity in a written or printed publication is *a fortiori* libelous where it would constitute slander if the words were spoken. Written words are libelous in all cases where if spoken they would be actionable, but they may be libelous where they would not support an action for oral slander.

There are many definitions of libel. The one by Hamilton in his argument in *People* v. *Croswell*, 3 Johns. Cas. 336, viz.: "A censorious, or ridiculing writing, picture or sign, made with malicious intent towards government, magistrates or individuals," has been often referred to with approval. But unless the word "censorious" is given a much broader signification than strictly belongs to it, the definition would not seem to comprehend all cases of libelous words. The word "libel," as expounded in the cases, is not limited to written or printed words which defame a man, in the ordinary sense, or which impute blame or moral turpitude, or which criticise or censure him. In the case before referred to, words affecting a man injuriously in his trade or occupation may be libelous, although they convey no imputation upon his character. Words, says Starkie, are libelous if they affect a person in his profession, trade or business, "by imputing to him any kind of fraud, dishonesty, misconduct, incapacity, unfitness or want of any necessary qualification in the exercise thereof." Starkie, Slander and Libel, § 188.

The cases of libel founded upon the imputation of insanity are few. The declaration in *Morgan* v. *Lingen*, *supra*, contained a count for libel and also for verbal slander. The alleged libel was in a letter written by the defendant, in which he states that "he had no doubt the plaintiff's mind was affected, and that seriously," and also that "she had a delusion," etc. It appeared that the defendant had also orally stated, in substance, the same thing. It was claimed that the writing was justified. The plaintiff was a governess. Martin, *B.*, in summing up to the jury, said that "a statement in writing that a lady's mind is affected, and that seriously, is, without explanation, prima facie a libel." In respect to the slander, he said "he thought there was no evidence of special damage. The jury must therefore consider whether the defendant intended to use the expression he did with reference to the plaintiff's profession of governess."

In *Perkins* v. *Mitchell*, 31 Barb. 465, it was held to be libelous to publish of another "that he is insane and a fit person to be sent to the lunatic asylum,"—Emott, *J.*, saying: "Upon this point the case is clear."

Rex v. *Harvey*, 2 Barn. & C. 257, was an information for libel for publishing in a newspaper that the king "labored under mental insanity and that the writer communicated the fact from authority." The judge charged that the publication was a libel and the charge was held to be correct.

The foregoing are the only cases we have noticed upon the point whether a written imputation of insanity constitutes a libel. Several of the text-writers state that to charge in writing that a man is insane is libelous. Addison, Torts, 768; Townshend, Slander and Libel, § 177; Starkie, Slander and Libel, § 164; Odgers, Libel and Slander, § 23.

The publication now in question is not simply an assertion that the plaintiff is or has been affected with "mental derangement," disconnected with any special circumstances. The assertion was made to account for the trouble to which the bank had been subjected by reason of injurious statements made by the plaintiff while in its employment. Words to be actionable on the ground that they affect a man in his trade or occupation, must, as is said, touch him in such trade or occupation; that is, they must be shown, directly or by inference, to have been spoken of him in relation thereto, and to be such as would tend to prejudice him therein. *Sanderson* v. *Caldwell*, 45 N. Y. 405, and cases cited.

The publication did, we think, touch the plaintiff in respect to his occupation as bank teller. It imputed mental derangement while engaged in his business as teller, which affected him in the discharge of his duties. The words conveyed no imputation upon the plaintiff's honesty, fidelity or general capacity. They attributed to him a misfortune, brought upon him by an over-zealous application in his employment.

While the statement was calculated to excite sympathy and even respect for the plaintiff, it nevertheless was calculated also to injure him in his character and employment as a teller. On common understanding, mental derangement has usually a much more serious significance than mere physical disease. There can be no doubt that the imputation of insanity against a man employed in a position of trust and confidence, such as that of a bank teller, whether the insanity is temporary or not, although accompanied by the explanation that it was induced by overwork, is calculated to injure and prejudice him in that employment, and especially where the statement is added that in consequence of his conduct in that condition the bank had been involved in trouble. The directors of a bank would naturally hesitate to employ a person as teller whose mind had once given away under stress of similar duties, and run the risk of a recurrence of the malady. The publication was, we think, defamatory in a legal sense, although it imputed no crime and subjected the plaintiff to no disgrace, reproach or obloquy, for the reason that its tendency was to subject the plaintiff to temporal loss, and deprive him of those advantages and opportunities as a member of the community which are open to those who have both a sound mind and a sound body. The trial judge, therefore, erred in not ruling the question of libel as one of law. The evidence renders it clear that no actual injury to the plaintiff was intended by the defendants, but it is not a legal excuse that defamatory matter was published accidentally or inadvertently, or with good motives, and in an honest belief in its truth.

The judgment should be reversed, and a new trial granted.

All concur.

Francis E. TERRY *et al.*, *Appts.*,

v.

George A. MUNGER, *Respt.*

(.....N. Y.....)

1. The tort in conversion of goods may be waived, and an action brought against the

NOTE.—*Conversion; election of remedy.*

If property be tortiously taken or converted, the injured party may waive the tort and sue in assumpsit; and judgment in such action will bar a further action *ex delicto*. May v. Le Claire, 78 U. S. 11 Wall. 217 (20 L. ed. 50); Saville v. Welch, 2 New Eng. Rep. 788, 58 Vt. 683; Burnap v. Partridge, 3 Vt. 144; 2 Greenl. Ev. § 117; Lindon v. Hooper, Cowp. 419; Moses v. Macferlan, 2 Burr. 1010; Lamine v.

See also 14 L. R. A. 211; 18 L. R. A. 187; 25 L. R. A. 42; 26 L. R. A. 840; 29 L.

wrong-doer upon an implied contract of sale, although he still retains possession of the property.

2. The title to property converted passes to the wrong-doer when the owner elects to treat the transaction as a sale, and brings an action *ex contractu* against him for the price.

3. An election to bring an action ex contractu against one who has converted property, upon the implied contract of sale, precludes a subsequent action for conversion of the same property against other persons who participated in the same acts which have already been treated as constituting a sale of the property.

4. A judgment roll in a former suit by the same plaintiff against other defendants is admissible to show that he had elected to treat as a sale acts which he now claims to constitute conversion of property.

(April 15, 1890.)

APPEAL by plaintiffs from a judgment of the General Term of the Supreme Court, Fifth Department, affirming a judgment of the Genesee Circuit in favor of defendant in an action brought to recover damages for the alleged wrongful taking and conversion of certain machinery belonging to plaintiffs. *Affirmed.*

The case is fully stated in the opinion.

Mr. **W. C. Watson,** with *Mr.* **J. M. Dunning,** for appellants:

The doctrine of a conclusive election of one of several remedies by personal action rests upon an equitable estoppel.

Equitable Co-operative Foundry Co. v. *Hersee,* 33 Hun, 176; *Merrick's Estate,* 5 Watts & S. 9; Herman, Estoppel, § 471; *Smith* v. *Hodson,* 2 Smith, Lead. Cas. *188, 7th Am. ed. 129.

An equitable estoppel is available only between parties and their privies.

See *Jackson* v. *Brinckerhoff,* 3 Johns. Cas 101; *Rathbone* v. *Hooney,* 58 N. Y. 463; *Atlantic Dock Co.* v. *New York,* 53 N. Y. 64; *Lawrence* v. *Campbell,* 32 N. Y. 455; *Dale* v. *Roosevelt,* 1 Paige, 35; *Maybee* v. *Avery,* 18 Johns. 352; *Duchess of Kingston's Case,* 20 How. St. Tr. 355; *Case* v. *Reeve,* 14 Johns. 79; *Gould* v. *James,* 6 Cow. 369; *Lawrence* v. *Hunt,* 10 Wend. 81.

There can be no equitable estoppel although the judgment recovered in the one action is inconsistent with the judgment sought to be recovered in the other without satisfaction.

Lawrence v. *Campbell, supra.*

A record which cannot be used against parties to a suit on trial because some of them were not parties to the record, cannot be used for them.

Chiles v. *Conley,* 2 Dana, 21; *Hurst* v. *McNeil,* 1 Wash. C. C. 70; *Davis* v. *Wood,* 14 U. S. 1 Wheat. 6 (4 L. ed. 22); *Rex* v. *Warden of the Fleet,* Holt, 134.

A judgment not conclusive against a party is not conclusive in his favor.

Southgate v. *Montgomery,* 1 Paige, 41; *Morris* v. *Lucas,* 8 Blackf. 9; Starkie, Ev. 10th ed. p. 97, *note 1,* pp. 317–319; *Fitzhugh* v *Croghan,* 2 J. J. Marsh. 442; *Baring* v. *Fanning,* 1 Paine, 549; *Chapman* v. *Chapman,* 1 Munf. 398.

The rule that parties and privies only are bound applies only to a privity arising after the event out of which the estoppel arises.

Masten v. *Olcott,* 2 Cent. Rep. 93, 101 N. Y. 160.

The plaintiffs are bound by their act as an estoppel only to the extent that Munger acted upon it.

Dorrell, 2 Ld. Raym. 1216; Putnam v. Wise, 1 Hill, 240, and *note;* Hill v. Davis, 3 N. H. 384; Stockett v. Watkins, 2 Gill & J. 326.

Under the Georgia Code, plaintiff in trover who elects to take damages in place of the converted property may recover the value of such property, together with hire thereof for the time during which it has been wrongfully retained by defendant. Ezzard v. Frick, 76 Ga. 512.

A demand for the proceeds of certain Indian trust bonds unlawfully converted is one arising upon an implied contract, or may be so treated by the waiver of the alleged fraud in the conversion of the bonds, and is therefore the proper subject of set-off in a suit. Allen v. United States, 84 U. S. 17 Wall. 207 (21 L. ed. 553).

Election of remedy conclusive.

When a person has two or more remedies for the same wrong, his election and actual prosecution of one is a bar to the others. Hartland v. Hackett, 57 Vt. 92; Goss v. Mather, 46 N. Y. 689; DeGraw v. Elmore, 50 N. Y. 3; Kimball v. Cunningham, 4 Mass. 502; Hooker v. Hubbard, 97 Mass. 177; Sloan v. Holcomb, 29 Mich. 161.

The law does not allow one party to vex and harass another with two different and inconsistent proceedings, carried on at the same time, to produce what in substance must be the same result. Butler v. Wehle, 4 Hun, 56, 6 Thomp. & C. 242; Livingston v. Kane, 3 Johns. Ch. 224.

The remedies are not concurrent, and, the choice between them once made, the right to follow the other is forever gone. See *note* to Fowler v. Bowery Sav. Bank (N.Y.) 4 L. R. A. 145; Riley v. Albany Sav. Bank, 36 Hun, 522; Rodermund v. Clark, 46 N. Y. 354; Borell v. Newell, 3 Daly, 233; Scarf v. Jardine, L. R. 7 App. Cas. 345; Kennedy v. Thorp, 51 N. Y. 174; Bank of Beloit v. Beale, 34 N. Y. 473.

Any decisive act of the party, with knowledge of his rights and of the fact, determines his election, in the case of conflicting and inconsistent remedies. Washburn v. Great Western Ins. Co. 114 Mass. 176; Cheeseman v. Sturges, 9 Bosw. 256; Thwing v. Great Western Ins. Co. 111 Mass. 93, 110.

In peculiar circumstances a party may take either one of these courses, but, having rightfully made his choice, the right to follow the other is extinct and gone. Morris v. Rexford, 18 N. Y. 557; Littlefield v. Brown, 1 Wend. 404; Brown v. Littlefield, 7 Wend. 454, 11 Wend. 467; McElroy v. Mancius, 13 Johns. 121; Junkins v. Simpson, 14 Me. 364; Butler v. Miller, 1 N. Y. 496.

Other applications of the rule.

Parties cannot be permitted to abandon one remedy and adopt another merely on the ground that they had misapprehended their rights. Robb v Voss, 22 Ohio L. J. 338.

If a man once determines his election it is determined forever. Thompson v. Fuller, 28 N. Y. S. R. 4.

Where causes of action differ in substance, the former being on contract and the latter in tort, the law will not permit a recovery on the latter by showing a right to recover upon the former. See *note* to Fowler v. Bowery Sav. Bank (N. Y.) 4 L. R. A. 145.

If a tenant elects his remedy by suit for damages caused by fraud, he so far affirms the contract that

Merrill v. *Tyler*, Seld. Notes, 47; *Catlin* v. *Grote*, 4 E. D. Smith, 296.

An equitable estoppel never takes place where one party does not intend to mislead, and the other party was not actually misled.

Jewett v. *Miller*, 10 N. Y. 402; *Carpenter* v. *Stilwell*, 11 N. Y. 61; *Whedon* v. *Champlin*, 59 Barb. 61; *Frost* v. *Koon*, 30 N. Y. 428.

Proceedings which would not constitute an estoppel are not prima facie evidence of the fact.

Starkie, Ev. 10th ed. p. 340; 2 Phill. Ev. 4th Am. ed. 3, 4, and *notes*.

The cause of action in the former suit is not inconsistent with the cause of action in the present suit, assuming that the plaintiffs waived the tort in the former suit. They are both actions arising in tort.

Chambers v. *Lewis*, 11 Abb. Pr. 210; *Goff* v. *Craven*, 34 Hun, 150; *Hill* v. *Davis*, 3 N. H. 384; *Avila* v. *Lockwood*, 98 N. Y. 33.

The defendant was liable to the plaintiffs for a conversion of the property at the time of the taking, and nothing has been done to extinguish his liability.

Allaire v. *Whitney*, 1 Hill, 488; *Bowman* v. *Teall*, 23 Wend. 309; *Atlantic Dock Co.* v. *New York*, 53 N. Y. 64

Where two are separately sued for the same wrong, if there is no privity between them, a recovery against one, or payment by him, is no bar to a subsequent recovery against the other.

Atlantic Dock Co. v. *New York*, *supra*; *Hyde* v. *Noble*, 13 N. H. 494; *Barron* v. *Davis*, 4 N. H. 338.

Mr. **George Bowen,** for respondent:

The plaintiffs, by bringing their action upon contract against two of the parties who were engaged in removing the property in question, to recover the value of their interest therein as upon a sale of the property with full knowledge of all the circumstances and prosecuting said action to judgment, then and there elected their remedy as upon contract, admitted that they had parted with the title to it at that time, and such election is irrevocable against the world.

Sanger v. *Wood*, 3 Johns. Ch. 416; *Morris* v. *Rexford*, 18 N. Y. 552, 557; *Littlefield* v. *Brown*, 1 Wend. 398; *Rodermund* v. *Clark*, 46 N. Y. 354, 357; *Acer* v. *Hotchkiss*, 97 N. Y. 395; *Bank of Beloit* v. *Beale*, 34 N. Y. 473; *Riley* v. *Albany Sav. Bank*, 36 Hun, 513, 522; *Moller* v. *Tuska*, 87 N. Y. 166; *Boots* v. *Ferguson*, 46 Hun, 129; *Conrow* v. *Little*, 5 L. R. A. 693, 115 N. Y. 387; *Bowker Fertilizing Co.* v. *Cox*, 9 Cent. Rep. 160, 106 N. Y. 555; *Wallace* v. *O'Gorman*, 25 N. Y. S. R. 261; *Floyd* v. *Browne*, 1 Rawle, 125; *Marsh* v. *Pier*, 4 Rawle, 273.

Peckham, *J.*, delivered the opinion of the court:

The plaintiffs commenced an action heretofore against two other persons named, respectively, Kipp and Munger, on account of the same transaction for which this action was brought against the above-named sole defendant. The character of the complaint in that action was before this court, and the case [*Goodwin* v. *Griffis*], is reported in the 88th of New York Reports, at page 629. The defendants in that case were charged with detaching and carrying away from the mill the machinery in question in that case and also in this, and using it for themselves. It was there held, upon a perusal of the complaint, that the action was of a nature *ex contractu* and not *ex delicto*, for the wrong done plaintiffs by the conversion of their property. As the defendants therein had not, after their conversion of it, them-

---

he cannot recover back the consideration. Stevens v. Pierce (Mass.) Feb. 27, 1890.

Assuming that the transaction was fraudulent on the part of the defendant, three remedies were open to the plaintiff: (1) to rescind the contract, treating it as void by reason of the fraud; (2) to enforce the securities as they became due; or, (3) to sue for damages by reason of the fraud. A resort to either of the last two remedies would have been an affirmance of the contract, and consequently a bar to the remedy first suggested, because he could not rescind the contract after having elected to affirm it. Bowen v. Mandeville, 29 Hun, 44; Lloyd v. Brewster, 4 Paige, 537; Field v. Bland, 59 How. Pr. 85.

A suit to redeem from a tax sale is an affirmance of the validity of the tax titles, and an election to defeat them by compliance with the law in relation thereto. Bender v. Bean (Ark.) June 29, 1889.

A party cannot be actively pursuing his remedy in one proceeding and at the same time claim the benefit of another, where the positions are antagonistic. Mills v. Parkhurst, 30 N. Y. S. R. 138.

Where a bank treasurer converts advances obtained on pledge of stock, which is sold by the pledgee, the bank cannot, after repudiating the treasurer's acts, recover the proceeds of the sale from the pledgee. Holden v. Metrop. Nat. Bank (Mass.) Feb. 26, 1890.

Where parties who are entitled to rescind a contract for fraud obtain an attachment against the other party as their debtor they thereby elect their remedy and waive the right to disaffirm their contract; and a subsequent discontinuance of the attachment suit will not restore such right. Conrow v. Little, 5 L. R. A. 693, 115 N. Y. 387.

Garnishing the purchasers of property for the purchase money ratifies the sale and prevents an attack upon it for fraud. Sickman v. Abernathy (Colo.) Dec. 24, 1889.

But an unsuccessful attempt to claim a right, or pursue a remedy, to which a party is not entitled, will not deprive him of the benefit of that to which he is entitled. Re Van Norman (Minn.) Oct. 18, 1889.

So where two actions are not the same either in form or effect, and the measure of liability in each is different, this rule does not apply. Sheble v. Strong, 128 Pa. 315.

In Illinois the fact that plaintiff first sued in assumpsit for goods sold and delivered does not preclude him from changing the form of his action to case for fraud and deceit, pursuant to the Statute. Flower v. Brumbach (Ill.) Jan. 21, 1890.

Following property as far as it can be traced.

Where converted property has assumed altered forms by successive investments, the owner may follow it as far as he can trace it, and sue at law for the substituted property; or he may hold the wrongdoers liable for appropriate damages. May v. Le Claire, 78 U. S. 11 Wall. 217 (20 L. ed. 50). See Thurston v. Blanchard, 22 Pick. 18; Rand v. Nesmith, 61 Me. 111; Shaw v. Coffin, 58 Me. 254; Howe v. Clancey, 53 Me. 130; Boston & W. R. Corp. v. Dana, 1 Gray, 83; Taylor v. Plumer, 3 Maule & S. 562. See *note* to Fowler v. Bowery Sav. Bank (N. Y.) 4 L. R. A. 145.

selves sold or otherwise disposed of the property which they had acquired from the plaintiffs, the fiction of the receipt by defendants of money for the sale of the property, which *ex æquo et bono* they ought to pay back to plaintiffs, and which they therefore impliedly promised to pay back, could not be indulged in, and the position of the parties would have been at one time the subject of some doubt, whether there was any foundation for the doctrine of an implied promise in such case, or any possibility of the waiver of the tort committed by the defendants in the conversion of the property.

In some of the States it has been denied, and such denial placed upon the ground that the property remained in the hands of the wrong-doer, and therefore, no money having been received by him in fact, an implied promise to pay over money had and received by defendant to the plaintiffs' use did not and could not arise. Such was the case of *Jones* v. *Hoar*, 5 Pick. 285. But the great weight of authority in this country is in favor of the right to waive the tort even in such case. If the wrong-doer has not sold the property, but still retains it, the plaintiff has the right to waive the tort and proceed upon an implied contract of sale to the wrong-doer himself, and in such event he is not charged as for money had and received by him to the use of the plaintiff. The contract implied is one to pay the value of the property as if it had been sold to the wrong-doer by the owner. If the transaction is thus held by the plaintiff as a sale, of course the title to the property passes to the wrong-doer when the plaintiff elects to so treat it. See Pom. Rem. 2d ed. §§ 567-569; *Putnam* v. *Wise*, 1 Hill, 234, 240, and *note* by Mr. Hill; *Berly* v. *Taylor*, 5 Hill, 577, 584; *Norden* v. *Jones*, 33 Wis. 600, 605; *Cummings* v. *Vorce*, 3 Hill, 283; *Spoor* v. *Newell*, Id. 307; *Abbott* v. *Blossom*, 66 Barb. 353.

We think this rule should be regarded as settled in this State. The reasons for the contrary holding are as well stated as they can be in the case above cited from Mass. (5 Pick.) and some of the cases looking in that direction in this State are cited in the opinion of Talcott, *J.*, in the case reported in 66 Barb. *supra*. We think the better rule is to permit the plaintiff to elect, and to recover for goods sold, even though the tort-feasor has not himself disposed of the goods.

There is no doubt that the complaint in the former case, reported in 88 N.Y., proceeded upon the theory of a sale of the property to the defendants in that action, and it was so construed by this court, and we have no inclination to review the correctness of that decision. We have then the fact that the defendants in that action were sued by the plaintiffs herein upon an implied contract to pay the value of the property taken by them, as upon a sale thereof by plaintiffs to them.

The plaintiffs having treated the title to the property as having passed to the defendants in that suit by such sale, can the plaintiffs now maintain an action against another person who was not a party to that action, to recover damages from him for his alleged conversion of the same property, which conversion is founded upon his participation in the same acts which plaintiffs in the old suit have already treated as constituting a sale of the property? We think not. The judgment roll in the former action was received in evidence upon the trial of this case, against the objection of the plaintiffs, and notwithstanding the fact that the defendant herein was not a party to such action. It appears that all the facts surrounding the transaction as to the taking of the property were known to the plaintiffs at the time when they commenced their action on the implied contract of sale.

The plaintiffs objected to the introduction of the judgment roll as incompetent and immaterial, and that there was no such defense set up in the answer.

The plaintiffs claim that the admission of such judgment violated the well known general rule that a judgment is not binding upon any but parties and privies. We think the decision does not trench upon the rule in question. If the judgment had been introduced for the purpose of proving any fact adjudicated thereby, any fact in litigation therein, or which properly might have been so litigated, the rule would doubtless apply, and no such fact would or could be proved in favor of the defendant herein as against the plaintiffs by such judgment, because the defendant was not a party or privy to it. It was not by way of estoppel, however, that the judgment was admissible. It was admissible for the sole purpose of showing that the plaintiffs had elected to treat the taking of this property as a sale, and this was shown by a perusal of the complaint therein.

Any decisive act of the plaintiffs, with knowledge of all the facts, would determine their election in such a case as this. *Sanger* v. *Wood*, 3 Johns. Ch. 416, 421.

The proof that an action of that nature had been in fact commenced would have been just as conclusive upon the plaintiffs upon the question of election (proof of knowledge of all the facts at that time being given), as would the judgment have been. It was not necessary that a judgment should follow upon the action thus commenced. In those cases where the commencement of an action has not been regarded as an election of remedies, the fact has appeared that the plaintiff at the time of its commencement was not aware of the facts which would have enabled him to elect, or at least it did not appear that he was acquainted with the facts when he commenced his action. Such is the case in *Equitable Co-operative Foundry Co.* v. *Hersee*, 103 N. Y. 25, 4 Cent. Rep. 189. Here the plaintiffs knew all the facts when they sued the other defendants.

The case of *Conrow* v. *Little*, 115 N. Y. 387, 393, 5 L. R. A. 693, is to the effect that the commencement of the action, where all the facts are known, is conclusive evidence of an election. *Judge* Danforth in that case, in speaking of plaintiffs' election to affirm or avoid the contract therein spoken of, said the plaintiffs could affirm or rescind it. "They could not do both, and there must be a time when their election should be considered final. We think that time was when they commenced an action for the sum due under the contract." It was also held that the discontinuance of that action was immaterial. It was the fact that the plaintiffs once elected their remedy and acted affirmatively upon such election that determined the issue. After that the option no longer existed, and it was of no consequence therefore whether the plaintiffs did or did not make their choice effective. When it becomes necessary to choose between inconsistent rights and remedies, the election will be final, and cannot be reconsidered even where no injury has been done by the choice, or would result from setting it aside. 2 Herman, Estoppel, 1172, § 1045.

The plaintiffs having by the commencement of their former action in effect sold this very property, it must follow that at the time of the commencement of this one they had no cause of action for a conversion in existence against the defendant herein. The transfer of the title did not depend upon the plaintiffs recovering satisfaction in such action for the purchase price. It was their election to treat the transaction as a sale which accomplished that result, and that election was proved by the complaint already referred to.

But it is urged that this election of the plaintiffs is not binding upon them in favor of the defendant herein, because it was only against the defendants in the other action that they made their election. It is said there is no case to be found where an election has been treated as binding in favor of a stranger to the transaction, and that the defendant herein is such stranger so far as the plaintiffs' transaction with the defendants in the other action is concerned.

I do not think this claim can be maintained. In the first place what is the nature of the plaintiffs' act in electing to consider the transaction as a sale? It is a decision or determination upon their part to, in effect, ratify and proclaim the lawfulness of the act of taking the property, and it is an assertion on the plaintiffs' part that in so doing the plaintiffs' interest in the property was purchased, and that thereby their whole title was transferred and they ceased to own any part of the property, and that those who took it impliedly promised the plaintiffs to pay them the value of their interest in such property. This being so, why does not such transfer of title bind the plaintiffs as to the whole world? Surely, the title which plaintiffs once had in the property cannot at the same time rest with them and pass to those who took it. If the title really once passed, that would be a fact actually existing, which anybody ought to have the right to prove if it became material in protecting his own rights, unless there were some equitable considerations in such case which should prevent it. I cannot see that any exist here.

With full knowledge of all the facts the plaintiffs deliberately elected to treat the transaction, in which this defendant's share was well known, as a sale of the property, and now they propose to recover from this defendant damages for the conversion by him of the very same property which they have already said they sold by virtue of the very transaction which they now claim amounted to a conversion of the property by this defendant.

Why should the defendant not be permitted to set up such sale as a complete defense to this action? The plaintiffs have done nothing by reason of defendant's acts which should estop him from setting up this defense. Their situation has not since been altered for the worse by anything the defendant has done. If not, then the fact that the plaintiffs sold the property by virtue of the transaction which they now seek to treat as a conversion of it by this defendant must and ought to operate as a perfect bar to the maintenance of this action. And this is not in the least upon the principle of equitable estoppel. It is upon the principle that the plaintiffs, by their own free choice, decided to sell the property, and having done so, it necessarily follows that they have no cause of action against defendant for an alleged conversion of the same property by the same acts which they had already treated as amounting to a sale.

In *Conrow* v. *Little*, 115 N. Y. 387, 5 L. R. A. 693, already cited, the plaintiffs' election to affirm the contract between them and Branscom, evidenced by their commencement of the attachment suit, was held conclusive upon them, and the defendants were permitted to take advantage of such election, although they were not parties or privies to the plaintiffs' suit against Branscom. The defendants were enabled to take advantage of it, because such election showed that the plaintiffs had affirmed their contract with Branscom, and the plaintiffs' suit against defendants Little could only be maintained upon the assumption that such contract had been rescinded. If the other suit had gone to judgment, would not such judgment have been admissible for the purpose of showing the naked fact of the election of plaintiffs to affirm the contract? I have no doubt of it.

In *Fowler* v. *Bowery Sav. Bank*, 113 N. Y. 450, 4 L. R. A. 145, we held that the action could not be maintained, because the plaintiff by suing the party to whom the bank had already wrongfully paid the money elected to regard such payment as rightfully made, and a cause of action against the bank to recover against it the amount of its former indebtedness to the plaintiff was held to have been forever abandoned because of such election.

In that case, in order to prove the fact of election, the defendant proved the commencement of the former action by the plaintiff, and it was proved, as we assume, by the production of the judgment roll in such former action. It was admissible for the same purpose for which the judgment was admissible in this case, viz., to prove the fact of the plaintiff's election to pursue a totally inconsistent remedy. The defendant was not precluded from availing itself of such defense, although it was neither a party nor privy to the judgment which proved the fact of such election.

In *Bank of Beloit* v. *Beale*, 34 N. Y. 473, the plaintiff put in evidence a judgment roll in which it was neither a party nor privy, to show that Sweet had made an election therein which bound him, and consequently the defendant Beale. This court held the judgment conclusively proved the election.

These views are fatal to the maintenance of this present action for a conversion against the defendant.

If the plaintiffs herein had commenced their action against this defendant, based upon an implied promise by him to pay the value of the property as upon a sale thereof to him in connection with the defendants in the other suit, a totally different question would have arisen, upon which we express no opinion. The plaintiffs in such action might urge that it ought to be sustained upon the ground that the defendant herein was one of the wrong-doers in the transaction resulting in the taking of this property, and that the tort therein committed by him and the defendants in the other suit was a joint and several one for which they were jointly and severally liable, and when the tort was waived by the plaintiffs and an implied contract was based upon such waiver the contract implied was of the same nature as the tort which was waived, and was a joint and several contract. Being a joint and several contract, an action against the other defendants upon their several contract, and a recovery of judgment without satisfaction, would constitute no defense to an action against this defendant, based upon his several and implied contract to pay the value of the property. There may be some authority for this course of reasoning. *City Nat. Bank* v. *National Park Bank*, 32 Hun, 105.

We neither affirm nor deny its soundness, and only refer to it in order to repel any possible implication that in this decision we have held that no such action could be maintained. But even if such an action would lie, we cannot turn the present one for a conversion of the property into one to recover the value thereof as upon a sale to defendant. *People* v. *Dennison*, 84 N. Y. 272; *Romeyn* v. *Sickles*, 108 N. Y. 650, 11 Cent. Rep. 312.

As to the other ground of objection taken by the plaintiffs, we think the evidence was admissible for the reasons stated by the learned judge at general term.

Upon the whole case we are satisfied that no error was committed prejudicial to the plaintiffs, and *the judgment should be affirmed*, with costs.

All concur, **Ruger**, *Ch. J.*, and **Andrews**, *J.*, in result.

NEW YORK COURT OF APPEALS (2d Div.).

Arthur TALAMO, *Respt.*,
v.
August SPITZMILLER, *Appt.*

(....N. Y.....)

1. **The mere fact that a person goes into possession** under a parol lease, which is void because for a longer time than for one year, does not create a yearly tenancy, although payment of an aliquot part of the annual rent would be evidence of such tenancy.

2. **A mere tenancy at will,** subject to the payment of the stipulated rate of rent as for use and occupation, is created by going into possession under an oral lease for more than one year.

(March 18, 1890.)

NOTE.—*Tenancy from year to year; how created.*

A parol lease of real estate for the term of one year to commence *in futuro* is invalid. See Jellett v. Rhode (Minn.) 7 L. R. A. 671, and *note*.

A lease made December 15, 1887, for the year 1888, may be valid, although not in writing, under Miss. Code, § 1292, excepting from the necessity of writing a lease for not longer than one year. McCroy v. Toney, 2 L. R. A. 847, 66 Miss. 233.

A verbal lease of land for a longer term than one year, although invalid, may become a tenancy from year to year if the tenant enters under it, pays rent and remains longer than one year, with the assent of the landlord. Rosenblatt v. Perkins (Or.) 6 L. R. A. 257.

A lessee for a year at a fixed rent, who continues in possession thereafter, with no new arrangement, is a tenant from year to year, not a tenant at will. Second Nat. Bank v. The O. E. Merrill Co. 69 Wis. 501.

An entry into possession and payment of rent inures as a tenancy from year to year. Blumenthal v. Bloomingdale, 1 Cent. Rep. 514, 100 N. Y. 558.

Leases extending three years from the time of making shall have the force and effect of estates at will. Jennings v. McComb, 8 Cent. Rep. 176, 112 Pa. 518.

But renting for a year and holding over for two years is not a tenancy at will. State v. Fort, 24 S. C. 511.

The common-law presumption that, when a tenant for a year holds over with the consent of his landlord and pays rent, a tenancy from year to year is established, is overcome by Iowa Code, § 2014, providing that any person in the possession of real property with the consent of the owner is presumed to be a tenant at will until the contrary is shown. O'Brien v. Troxel, 76 Iowa, 760.

The fact that, after one ceased to be the pastor of a society, he was allowed to remain in possession of the parsonage, did not change his occupancy into a tenancy from year to year or even a tenancy at will, unless his possession was of such duration or under such circumstances as to warrant an inference of consent on the part of the society to a different holding from that which he formerly had. East Norway L. N. E. L. Church v. Froislie, 37 Minn. 447.

Such tenancy is at least a tenancy at will. Goldsmith v. Wilson, 68 Iowa, 685.

When tenancy expires.

A tenancy from year to year of premises in a city, as well as of agricultural premises, expires at the end of the calendar year. Wilson v. Rodeman, 30 S. C. 210.

A lease for one year with the privilege of three years from a certain time is a lease from year to year, not exceeding three years, and the tenant may terminate it at the end of the second year by giving notice. Gillion v. Finley (Pa.) 11 Cent. Rep. 798.

How terminated.

To terminate an estate from year to year by notice requires the giving of such a notice as is prescribed in Or. Code Gen. Laws, § 2987. Rosenblatt v. Perkins (Or.) 6 L. R. A. 257.

The occupancy of premises at an agreed rent per month under a parol lease is a tenancy at will under Vt. Rev. Laws, § 1982; and a notice, before the termination of a year, that the rent would be increased per month, terminated it. Amsden v. Floyd, 6 New Eng. Rep. 854, 60 Vt. 386.

APPEAL by defendant by permission from a judgment of the General Term of the Superior Court of Buffalo affirming a judgment of the Trial Term in favor of plaintiff in an action to recover from defendant the amount realized by him from the sale of certain of plaintiff's personal property out of which defendant claimed the right to reimburse himself for certain rent which he alleged that he had paid for plaintiff's benefit. *Affirmed.*

The case is sufficiently stated in the opinion.

Mr. **Charles B. Wheeler**, for appellant:

It is not necessary in order to bind Talamo that the lease should run directly to him and be taken in his name to make him a tenant.

Van Schaick v. *Third Ave. R. Co.* 38 N. Y. 351.

The statute declaring that "every contract for the leasing for a longer period than one year" shall be void unless the same "be in writing and subscribed by the party by whom the lease or sale is to be made," has no application to this case.

The authority to bind Talamo by the lease may be conferred and shown by parol.

Worrall v. *Munn*, 5 N. Y. 243; *Lawrence* v. *Taylor*, 5 Hill, 107.

If Talamo is not a co-lessee of the house he nevertheless is a sub-tenant under Spitzmiller, and when he entered under a parol lease void by the Statute, and took possession with the consent of Spitzmiller, the occupation inured as a tenancy from year to year.

Laughran v. *Smith*, 75 N. Y. 205; *Reeder* v. *Sayre*, 70 N. Y. 188; *Lounsbery* v. *Snyder*, 31 N. Y. 514; *Greton* v. *Smith*, 33 N. Y. 248; *Craske* v. *Christian U. Pub. Co.* 17 Hun, 320; *Fougera* v. *Cohn*, 43 Hun, 454; *Schuyler* v. *Leggett*, 2 Cow. 660; *Kline* v. *Rickert*, 8 Cow. 226; McAdam, Land. and T. p. 43.

Messrs. **Quinby & Meads**, for respondent:

Where there has been an agreement for a lease, and an occupation without payment of rent, the occupier is a mere tenant at will; although if he subsequently pays rent under that agreement, he thereby becomes tenant from year to year.

Knight v. *Benett*, 3 Bing. 361; *Hegan* v. *Johnson*, 2 Taunt. 48; *Hamerton* v. *Stead*, 3 Barn. & C. 478; *Riseley* v. *Ryle*, 11 Mees. & W. 16; *Richardson* v. *Langridge*, 4 Taunt. 128; *Braythwayte* v. *Hitchcock*, 10 Mees. & W. 494; *Mann* v. *Lovejoy*, Ryan & M. 355; *Lord* v. *Crago*, 6 C. B. 98; *Bishop* v. *Howard*, 2 Barn. & C. 100; *Richardson* v. *Gifford*, 1 Ad. & El. 52; *Thomson* v. *Amey*, 12 Ad. & El. 476; *Arden* v. *Sullivan*, 14 Q. B. 832; *Thomas* v. *Packer*, 1 Hurlst. & N. 672; *Lee* v. *Smith*, 9 Exch. 662.

The law does not infer any particular contract from the mere fact of entry under an agreement for a future lease.

Waring v. *King*, 8 Mees. & W. 575.

If there be no payment of rent, or its equivalent, or other circumstances from which a tenancy can be implied, no such tenancy can be deemed to be created by the mere occupation of the party, nor can he be treated as tenant from year to year.

Archbald, Land. and T. 58, 59, 65, 66; *Dawes* v. *Dowling*, 31 L. T. N. S. 65; *Smith* v. *Eldridge*, 15 C. B. 236; *Coggan* v. *Warwicker*, 3 Car. & K. 40; *Tooker* v. *Smith*, 1 Hurlst. & N. 735; *Lockwood* v. *Lockwood*, 22 Conn. 433; *Berrey* v. *Lindley*, 3 Man. & Gr. 513, *note; De Medina* v. *Polson*, Holt, N. P. 47.

Payment and acceptance of rent, or something equivalent, are deemed an essential ingredient to the creation of a tenancy from year to year.

Rigge v. *Bell*, 5 T. R. 471; *Clayton* v. *Blakey*, 8 T. R. 3; *Thunder* v. *Belcher*, 3 East, 449; *Cox* v. *Bent*, 5 Bing. 185; *Kerr* v. *Clark*, 19 Mo. 132; *Ridgley* v. *Stilwell*, 28 Mo. 400; *Barlow* v. *Wainwright*, 22 Vt. 89; *Thurber* v. *Dwyer*, 10 R. I. 355; *Shepherd* v. *Cummings*, 1 Coldw. 354; *M'Dowell* v. *Simpson*, 3 Watts, 135; *Dumn* v. *Rothermel*, 2 Cent. Rep. 581, 112 Pa. 272; *Koplitz* v. *Gustavus*, 48 Wis. 48; *Singer Mfg. Co.* v. *Sayre*, 75 Ala. 274; *People* v. *Darling*, 47 N. Y. 666; *Blumenthal* v. *Bloomingdale*, 1 Cent. Rep. 518, 100 N. Y. 561; *Thomas* v. *Nelson*, 69 N. Y. 118; *Prial* v. *Entwistle*, 10 Daly, 398.

Bradley, *J.*, delivered the opinion of the court:

The action was brought to recover the proceeds of the sale made by the defendant of the plaintiff's goods. The defendant admits his liability to account to the plaintiff for the proceeds of such sale, and alleges several matters by way of counterclaim, which will be referred to so far as is essential to the determination of the questions presented for consideration on

---

A tenant at will, after notice to quit, has a reasonable time to vacate the premises and procure other accommodations, depending upon the circumstances. *Ibid.*

Where a tenant from year to year holds over after the termination of the term, and the landlord does some act recognizing him as tenant, the tenancy can only be terminated by the agreement of the parties, express or implied, or by notice given, six calendar months ending with the period of the year at which the tenancy commenced. Critchfield v. Remaley, 21 Neb. 178.

Effect of payment of rent.

A lease may be conveyed into a tenancy from year to year, by annual payment, etc. Whether this has been done is for the jury. Dumn v. Rothermel, 2 Cent. Rep. 561, 112 Pa. 272.

Where lands are leased to a tenant for one year for a stipulated rent reserved, and after the expiration of the lease the tenant, without further contract, remains in possession, and is recognized as a tenant by the landlord in the receipt of rent for another year, this will create a tenancy from year to year. Critchfield v. Remaley, 21 Neb. 178.

When a tenant enters under a lease for a term of years, improperly executed, and pays rent according to the terms thereof, the law will infer an intention to create a tenancy from year to year, upon the terms specified in the lease. Fougera v. Cohn, 43 Hun, 454.

A parol continuance of a lease creates a tenancy from year to year or month to month, according to the time of payment of installments of rent. Rev. Stat. § 3078; Vegely v. Robison, 2 West. Rep. 552, 20 Mo. App. 199.

Under Code Civ. Proc., § 373, a tenancy from year to year continues for twenty years from the time of the last payment of rent, before possession becomes adverse. Church v. Schoonmaker, 43 Hun, 225.

this review. The trial court found that on March 13, 1882, by an agreement of lease in writing under seal, made by Catharine Dickman and defendant, she leased to him a dwelling-house for the term of five years from May 1, 1882, at the annual rent of $450 for the first year, and $500 for each subsequent year, payable in equal monthly installments in advance, which the defendant undertook to pay. That the defendant took such lease at the verbal instance and request of the plaintiff, and upon the unwritten understanding and agreement that they should jointly use and occupy the dwelling-house during the term mentioned in the lease; and that the plaintiff should pay to the defendant half the rent; that the defendant and the plaintiff went into the possession of the house in May, 1882, and jointly occupied it until in November following, when the plaintiff quit the house and has not since then occupied any portion of it; that the defendant has paid the monthly installments of rent as they fell due, and that the plaintiff has paid nothing to the defendant on account of the rent. The court allowed to the defendant against the plaintiff a sum equal to one half the rent for the period of the joint occupancy, six and a half months.

And upon the exception to the conclusion of the court that the plaintiff was entitled to recover the amount for which judgment was directed, arises the question whether the defendant was entitled to the allowance of a greater amount against the plaintiff than that given by the court, on account of the rent. The contention of the defendant's counsel is: (1) that the plaintiff became liable to pay the defendant one half the rent which the latter undertook by the lease to pay as the installments should become due; (2) that if not so, the plaintiff became a yearly tenant and was liable to the defendant for one half the amount of the rent for one year. The plaintiff not being a party to the lease assumed no legal obligation to pay rent for the term, as a lease for more than one year not in writing was void. 2 Rev. Stat. 135, §§ 6, 8.

The agreement between the parties and under which the plaintiff entered into joint occupancy with the defendant, being void, gave to the plaintiff no right and imposed upon the defendant no obligation to permit him to go into or remain in possession of any portion of the house, and unless he became a yearly tenant his liability was for use and occupation for the time only which he occupied. *Thomas* v. *Nelson*, 69 N. Y. 118.

The mere fact that a person goes into possession under a lease void because for a longer term than one year does not create a yearly tenancy. If he remains in possession with the consent of the landlord for more than one year under circumstances permitting the inference of his tenancy from year to year, the latter could treat him as such, and the tenant could not relieve himself from liability for rent up to the end of the current year. And the terms of the lease void as to duration of term would control in respect to the rent. *Coudert* v. *Cohn*, 118 N. Y. 309, 28 N. Y. State Rep. 684.

The parol agreement for five years was not effectual to create a tenancy for one year. Nor did the mere fact that the plaintiff went into possession have that effect. He remained in occupation a part of one year only, and the creation of a tenancy for a year was dependent upon something further. While it is not required that a new contract be made in express terms, there must be something from which it may be inferred, something which tends to show that it is within the intention of the parties. The payment and receipt of an installment or aliquot part of the annual rent is evidence of such understanding, and goes in support of a yearly tenancy, and without explanation to the contrary it is controlling evidence for that purpose. *Cox* v. *Bent*, 5 Bing. 185; *Bishop* v. *Howard*, 2 Barn. & C. 100; *Braythwayte* v. *Hitchcock*, 10 Mees. & W. 494; *Mann* v. *Lovejoy*, Ryan & M. 355; *Thomas* v. *Packer*, 1 Hurlst. & N. 672; *Lord* v. *Crago*, 6 C. B. 90.

While there may appear to have been some confusion in the cases in this State upon the subject, this doctrine has been more recently recognized. *Reeder* v. *Sayre*, 70 N. Y. 184; *Laughran* v. *Smith*, 75 N. Y. 209.

In the cases last cited, the tenants had been in possession more than a year when the question arose, but having gone into occupancy under an invalid lease, their yearly tenancy was held dependent upon a new contract, which might be implied from the payment and acceptance of rent, and when once created could be terminated by neither party without the consent of the other, only at the end of a year. The contention, therefore, that by force of the original agreement between the parties, aided by the fact that the plaintiff went into the possession with the consent of the defendant, is not alone sufficient to support an inference of the new contract requisite to create a yearly tenancy. The plaintiff paid no rent, nor while he was in possession was any request of or promise by him made to pay any. He simply went in under the original void agreement, and left within the year. There was no evidence to require the conclusion of the trial court that the plaintiff had assumed any relation to the premises, which charged him with liability other than for use and occupation, during the time he remained in possession. The defendant's counsel, to support his proposition that the entry by the plaintiff with the consent of the defendant made him a yearly tenant, cites *Craske* v. *Christian U. Pub. Co.*, 17 Hun, 319, where it was remarked that a parol lease for a longer term than one year "operated so as to create a tenancy from year to year." If that was intended by the learned justice as a suggestion that such a void lease operated as a demise for one year, it is not in harmony with the view of the court in *Laughran* v. *Smith*, *supra*. That remark in the *Craske Case* was not essential to the determination there made, as rent was in fact paid for a portion of the term, nor can it be assumed that it was intended to have the import sought to be given to it. It must be assumed, upon authority and reason, that a parol lease for more than one year is ineffectual to vest any term whatever in the lessee named, and that when he goes into possession under it with the consent of the lessor without any further agreement, he is a tenant at will merely, subject to liability to pay at the rate of the stipulated rent as for use and occupation. *Barlow* v. *Wainwright*, 22 Vt. 88.

This may be converted into a yearly tenancy by a new contract, which may be implied from circumstances when they permit it. While the mere entry with consent will not alone justify it, a promise to pay and a purpose manifested to accept a portion of the annual rent provided for by the agreement may, as evidence, go in support of such a new contract.

The promise of the plaintiff to pay one half the rent was made preliminary to his entry, and was part of, and not distinguishable from, the parol agreement with the defendant to occupy for five years and pay one half the rent for that term. There does not seem to have been any evidence to require the conclusion that any other than such void agreement was made between the parties, or that the plaintiff became other than a mere tenant at will of the defendant. 1 Woodfall, Land. and T. 1st Am. ed. from 13th Eng. ed. 221.

The other cases cited by the defendant's counsel do not support the proposition asserted by him. There is no opportunity, upon the facts found, or upon any the finding of which the evidence requires, to hold that the defendant took and held the lease as trustee for the plaintiff as to a portion of the demised premises, or that a relation was assumed by the plaintiff to the lease between the lessor and the defendant which legally charged him with liability to the latter for moneys paid by him pursuant to it. The parol agreement between them was void and ineffectual for any such purpose.

The judgment should be affirmed.

All concur.

Charles H. DWINELLE, *Appt.*,

v.

NEW YORK CENTRAL & HUDSON RIVER R. CO., *Respt.*

(....N. Y.....)

1. **If the performance of a railroad company's contract to transport a passenger** is temporarily suspended by a defect in the road-bed, he is entitled, during the time required to overcome the defect, to all the rights of a passenger upon a moving train, including that of protection from the willful misconduct of the company's servants.

2. **The porter of a sleeping or drawing-room car,** which forms a part of the train of a railroad company under a contract with its owner, who sells separate tickets for privileges upon such cars and who furnishes his own servants to collect tickets and assist passengers, is the servant of the railroad company, for whose acts, done in the performance of a contract to carry a passenger, it is responsible, notwithstanding any agreement which may be made upon the subject between the company and the owner of the car.

3. **The question as to whether or not a sleeping-car porter was in the performance of his duties** as servant of a railroad company at the time he committed an assault upon a passenger, so as to make the company liable for his act, must be submitted to the jury, where the evidence shows that an accident rendered it necessary for the passenger to be transferred from the train upon which he took passage to another train; that the porter to whom he had surrendered his ticket and who was the only person who represented the company on the sleeping car assisted in making the transfer; that the passenger demanded a return of his ticket or an introduction to the persons in charge of the new train so that he might receive sleeping-car privileges thereon and that thereupon the porter committed the assault.

4. **A carrier is liable for an unlawful and improper act** and for the natural and legitimate consequences thereof, which is committed by its servant towards its passenger while such servant is engaged in performing a duty which the carrier owes to the passenger, no matter what the motive is which incites the commission of the act.

5. **It is no defense to a suit against a carrier** to recover damages for an assault committed by its servant upon a passenger that at the time the assault was committed the servant had finished the temporary and particular service which he had undertaken to render to the passenger, if the contract of carriage was not yet performed and the duty still rested on the carrier to protect the passenger from the violence of its servants.

(April 15, 1890.)

APPEAL by plaintiff from a judgment of the General Term of the Supreme Court, First Department, affirming a judgment of the New York Circuit dismissing the complaint in an action brought to recover damages for an assault committed on plaintiff by defendant's servant. *Reversed.*

Statement by **Potter,** *J.:*

The facts proven upon the trial were that plaintiff purchased tickets for himself and wife from Geneva to New York for a continuous passage in the ordinary car upon defendant's road, and also tickets for a section in a sleeping car in the same train from the porter, there being no other person acting as conductor thereof, and paid him for the same. In due run, he would have reached the City of New York the next morning, but upon awakening next morning he learned the train was detained at Utica owing to a washout near Amsterdam, and the plaintiff with the other passengers, after waiting until nearly noon, was informed by the porter of the sleeping car that he was required to take another train to the washout and there, after passing the washout, to take still another train to be carried to New York City.

The porter took the hand-baggage of plaintiff and his wife and conducted them to the train they were required to take from Utica to the washout.

NOTE.—Degree of care required of carriers of passengers. See *note* to Goodsell v. Taylor (Minn.) 4 L. R. A. 673.

Right of passenger to proper treatment. See *note* to Conolly v. Crescent City R. Co. (La.) 3 L. R. A. 133.

Carrier undertakes to protect passengers from violence and abuse of its officers. See *note* to South Florida R. Co. v. Rhoads (Fla.) 3 L. R. A. 733.

A master is liable for the tortious acts of his servant. See *note* to McCord v. Western U. Teleg. Co. (Minn.) 1 L. R. A. 143.

The porter carrying their luggage or parcels, conducted them to the sleeping cars which formed a part of the train plaintiff was required to take, but not finding a vacant seat for the plaintiff and his wife in the sleeping car, conducted them into an ordinary coach forming a part of this train, and said to plaintiff very likely another sleeper would be put on to the train and then the plaintiff could have a seat in it. There were no vacant seats in this car, but a gentleman gave his seat to the plaintiff's wife, and the plaintiff remained standing. The porter deposited their luggage at the end of the car near the door.

The porter then turned to go away from plaintiff and walked towards the rear end of the car. Plaintiff then stepped after the porter, pulled his sleeve slightly, whereupon the porter turned towards the plaintiff, and the plaintiff said to the porter, "You have my sleeping-car ticket. I have nothing to show on the other side of the washout that I am entitled to sleeping-car accommodations. I wish you to give me something before you leave me; give me back my ticket so that I can have sleeping-car accommodations on the other side of the washout." The porter replied: "I keep that ticket to show to the Company." The plaintiff said to the porter: "If you cannot give me that, then take me to the ticket office here and tell them how things are and ask them to give me some check or ticket which I can show to the conductor on the other side of the washout."

The porter refused to go to the office with the plaintiff as requested, and then the plaintiff requested the porter to make the plaintiff acquainted with the sleeping-car conductor, who was going upon the train, and the porter replied that he would show the plaintiff the conductor. The plaintiff and the porter thereupon left the car, and walked along by the side of the train, and as they were passing along the porter pointed out a group of men wearing railroad uniforms, and said "There is the conductor." Plaintiff then said to the porter, "He does not know me; take me to him and make me acquainted with him, and tell him I am entitled to a section to New York." The porter turned to go away, saying: "That is none of my business." Plaintiff then said, touching the porter lightly on the arm: "You must not leave me without some satisfaction in this business." The porter thereupon said "Take your hand off me, or I'll hit you," and struck the plaintiff a violent blow in the face, knocking the plaintiff down, and rendering him unconscious.

These acts were done and declarations made in the yard of the defendant at Utica, which at the time contained the depot and station, trains, cars, offices and employés of the defendant, and numerous other passengers who had been detained at this point on account of the washout.

The plaintiff also introduced in evidence an agreement between the defendant and the New York Central Sleeping Car Company, the provisions of which that bear upon the questions in this case will be referred to in the opinion, and rested.

The defendant moved for a dismissal of the complaint upon the grounds that the plaintiff had made out no cause of action against the defendant. That the cause of action stated in the complaint had not been made out. That the act complained of was not done within the scope of the authority of the person who did the act. That the act complained of was not done by any servant of the defendant within the scope of his or any authority he had. That the act complained of was not done by any servant of the defendant while engaged in performing any duty which the defendant owed to the plaintiff. That the act complained of was not an act to be foreseen or provided or guarded against by the defendant.

Mr. **Hugh L. Cole**, for appellant:

Plaintiff's assailant was, for all purposes of this action, the servant of the defendant.

Thorpe v. *New York Cent. & H. R. R. Co.* 76 N. Y. 402; *Ulrich* v. *New York Cent. & H. R. R. Co.* 10 Cent. Rep. 478, 108 N. Y. 80; *Cleveland, C. C. & I. R. Co.* v. *Walrath*, 38 Ohio St. 461; *Kinsley* v. *Lake Shore & M. S. R. Co.* 125 Mass. 54; *Pennsylvania Co.* v. *Roy*, 102 U. S. 457 (26 L. ed. 144).

The assault having been committed during the course of the contract of carriage by one who had been intrusted with some participation in the execution thereof, the defendant is liable. It was not necessary to prove that the servant was acting within the scope of his authority.

Stewart v. *Brooklyn & C. R. Co.* 90 N. Y. 588; *Pennsylvania R. Co.* v. *Vandiver*, 42 Pa. 365; *Nieto* v. *Clark*, 1 Cliff. 145; *Craker* v. *Chicago & N. W. R. Co.* 36 Wis. 657; *Terre Haute & I. R. Co.* v. *Jackson*, 81 Ind. 21; *Peeples* v. *Brunswick & A. R. Co.* 60 Ga. 282; *McKinley* v. *Chicago & N. W. R. Co.* 44 Iowa, 314; *Chicago & E. R. Co.* v. *Flexman*, 103 Ill. 546; *Bryant* v. *Rich*, 106 Mass. 180; *Goddard* v. *Grand Trunk R. Co.* 57 Me. 213; *Sherley* v. *Billings*, 8 Bush, 147.

Even if in fact at the time of the assault the porter was not engaged in performing any duty imposed upon him by the defendant, if third persons had a right to infer from the circumstances that he was so engaged, the defendant is liable.

1 Shearm. & Redf. Neg. § 148; *Tousey* v. *Roberts*, 21 Jones & S. 446; *Bank of Batavia* v. *New York, L. E. & W. R. Co.* 7 Cent. Rep. 822, 106 N.Y. 201; *Walsh* v. *Hartford F. Ins. Co.* 73 N. Y. 5; *Isaacson* v. *New York Cent. & H. R. R. Co.* 94 N. Y. 286.

The question whether the porter was so engaged, or whether the plaintiff had a right to infer that he was so engaged, at the time he committed the assault, should have been submitted to the jury.

Hart v. *Hudson River Bridge Co.* 80 N. Y. 622; *Jackson* v. *Second Ave. R. Co.* 47 N. Y. 274.

The case is precisely the same as if the blow had been struck on the train.

Sherley v. *Billings*, 8 Bush, 147; *Peeples* v. *Brunswick & A. R. Co.* 60 Ga. 282.

Mr. **Frank Loomis**, for respondent:

Defendant undertook to protect the plaintiff against any injury arising from the negligence or willful misconduct of its servants only while they were engaged in performing a duty which the defendant owed to the plaintiff.

Stewart v. *Brooklyn & C. R. Co.* 90 N.Y. 588.

Potter, *J.*, delivered the opinion of the court:

The defendant was under contract obligations to transport the plaintiff with his wife from Geneva to the City of New York, and it had entered upon the performance of the contract, when further performance was temporarily suspended until the defendant could make arrangements to overcome the difficulty and obstruction caused by the washout of its road-bed.

While this was being done the plaintiff was a passenger of the defendant and entitled to all the rights which pertain to a passenger upon a train moving towards the point or destination specified in the contract of carriage. Among the obligations which such a contract imposes upon the carrier are "to protect the passenger against any injury from negligence or willful misconduct of its servants while performing the contract and of his fellow passengers and strangers, so far as practicable, to treat him respectfully and to provide him with the usual accommodations and any information and facilities necessary for the full performance of the contract upon the part of the carrier. And these obligations continue to rest upon the carrier, its servants and employés while such contract continues and is in process of performance." *Thorpe* v. *New York Cent. & H. R. R. Co.* 76 N. Y. 402; *Stewart* v. *Brooklyn & C. R. Co.* 90 N. Y. 588; *Parsons* v. *New York Cent. & H. R. R. Co.* 113 N. Y. 355, 3 L. R. A. 683; Thompson, Car. 50; *Pittsburgh, C. & St. L. R. Co.* v. *Krouse*, 30 Ohio St. 222.

There cannot be any serious question that such are the ordinary duties and obligations between the passenger and the carrier.

The relation of the plaintiff and defendant being that of passenger and carrier, with the duties and obligations to each other resulting from such relation, these questions arise and require consideration in the determination of this case: Was the sleeping-car porter the agent of the defendant? And if so, was he engaged in the performance of his duties as such agent at the time of inflicting the blow upon the plaintiff?

The answer to the first question is that the porter of a sleeping or drawing-room car, even in cases where there is a contract, like the contract put in evidence by the plaintiff in this case, between the railroad company, which sells a passage ticket in its ordinary coaches to a passenger, and the proprietors of a sleeping car, who sell a ticket to the same passenger for a seat and berth in a sleeping car running in the same train, is the servant of the railroad company. This question has been definitely settled by the highest court in this State and of the United States. *Thorpe* v. *New York Cent. & H. R. R. Co.* 76 N. Y. 406; *Pennsylvania Co.* v. *Roy*, 102 U. S. 451 [26 L. ed. 141].

The contracts in those two cases are in all essential respects like the contract in this case. The railroad company, in those cases as in this case, did not own the drawing-room or sleeping car. Nor did it hire or pay the porter. The contract required that the servants employed by the sleeping-car company should be acceptable to the Railroad Company, with other stipulations of a correlative character not necessary to be specified.

In those cases it was held that the law will not permit a railroad company engaged in the business of carrying persons for hire, through any device or arrangement with a sleeping-car company, whose cars are used by the railroad and constitute a part of its train, to evade the duty that is imposed upon it by law, and that the defense that the porter was not the servant of the railroad company, but of the sleeping or drawing-room car company, is not a defense to the railroad company, or rather, in the language of *Judge* Andrews, "that the persons in charge of the drawing-room car are to be regarded and treated in respect to their dealings with passengers as the servants of the defendant (the railroad company) and that the defendant is responsible for their acts to the same extent as if they were directly employed by the company."

And this court in the same case, *Thorpe* v. *New York Cent. & H. R. R. Co.*, *supra*, holds that the Act of 1858, chap. 125, introduced by the plaintiff in the case under consideration, authorizing railroad and sleeping and drawing-room car companies to make contracts of that character, carefully provided that it should not be construed to exonerate the railroad company from the payment of damages for injuries in the same way and to the same extent as if the cars were owned and provided by the railroad company.

These cases hold, as matter of law, that the porter of the sleeping car is, in the performance of the duties and obligations of the railroad company under its contract to carry a passenger, the servant of the railroad.

The second of the above questions is, Was the sleeping-car porter engaged in the performance of his duties as such agent at the time of inflicting the blow upon the plaintiff? That question must in this and similar cases depend upon the evidence, and must be determined by the jury. The office of the court is to determine what facts are proper to be submitted to the jury for its determination of that question.

We think the evidence in this case should have been submitted to the jury. The evidence was to this effect: that the defendant had contracted to carry the plaintiff to New York; that contract had not been performed but was in process of performance; that the porter was actually engaged in the performance of services to that end; that owing to the interruption of the train upon which the defendant was carrying the plaintiff to his destination, it became necessary to transfer the plaintiff to another train; that the porter so informed plaintiff and was transferring the plaintiff to the other train with his luggage; that the porter was the person of whom the plaintiff purchased and paid for his seat and berth and to whom the plaintiff had surrendered it upon demand, and was in short the only person with whom the plaintiff had any business relations upon the train, and was the only person who represented the defendant or whom the defendant had in any manner put forward or presented in the sleeping car to perform the duty and service which the defendant owed the plantiff. Upon these and other facts developed upon the trial, the question should have been submitted to the jury whether or not the porter was not at this time and down to the act of striking the plaintiff the servant of the defendant. *Buffett* v. *Troy & B. R. Co.* 40 N. Y. 168; *Tousey* v. *Roberts*, 21 Jones & S. 446-447; *Althorf* v. *Wolfe*, 22 N. Y. 355; *Isaacson* v. *New York Cent. & H R. R. Co.* 94 N. Y. 278.

But it is urged that if the porter was as matter of law, or if the jury had found upon such submission as matter of fact that the porter was, the servant of the defendant at the time and place of striking the plaintiff, the striking was willful and malicious upon the part of the porter and beyond the scope of his employment; and further, that the porter had finished the service he was performing for defendant towards the plaintiff and that the defendant owed the plaintiff no further duty.

I need not stop to discuss the contention that the master is not liable for the willful and malicious acts of a servant of a carrier towards or upon a passenger. The case of *Stewart* v. *Brooklyn & C. R. Co.*, 90 N. Y. 588, settles that question against the defendant in this case. In that *Judge* Tracy says: "By the defendant's contract with the plaintiff it had undertaken to carry him safely, and to treat him respectfully, and while a common carrier does not undertake to insure against any injury from every possible danger, he does undertake to protect the passengers against any injury from the negligence or willful misconduct of its servants while engaged in performing a duty which the carrier owes to the passenger. A common carrier is bound so far as practicable to protect his passengers, while being conveyed, from violence committed by strangers and co-passengers, and he undertakes absolutely to protect them against the misconduct of its own servants engaged in executing the contract," or, as otherwise therein expressed, "from an assault committed upon a passenger by a servant intrusted with the execution of a contract of a common carrier." *Weed* v. *Panama R. Co.* 17 N. Y. 362.

These and numerous other cases hold that no matter what the motive is which incites the servant of the carrier to commit an unlawful or improper act towards the passenger during the existence of the relation of carrier and passenger, the carrier is liable for the act and its natural and legitimate consequences. *Nieto* v. *Clark*, 1 Cliff. 145; *Com.* v. *Power*, 7 Met. 596; *Goddard* v. *Grand Trunk R. Co.* 57 Me. 202, 2 Am. Rep. 39; *Craker* v. *Chicago & N. W. R. Co.* 36 Wis. 657, 17 Am. Rep. 504; *Chicago & E. R. Co.* v. *Flexman*, 103 Ill. 546.

It is also urged in behalf of defendant in this case, that the porter had performed all the duties which, as the servant of the defendant, he owed to the plaintiff. I think this view of the situation and obligations of the parties in this case is entirely too narrow and is untenable.

The contract of carriage between the plaintiff and defendant was but partially performed, and was in the actual process of performance. The plaintiff had been waiting through the forenoon to enable the defendant to make the necessary arrangements to complete its contract of carriage. The arrangement made by the defendant for that purpose was to start an independent train from Utica. This required the transfer of the plaintiff and his luggage to such train. It was necessary that the plaintiff should be informed of this, and that he with his luggage should be transferred to such other train. The porter was attending to this duty, and to that end had placed the plaintiff in an ordinary car to resume his journey. If the plaintiff had been injured by any negligence or misconduct of the defendant's servant, or from a defect in the defendant's railroad grounds or walks or yard while waiting the making up and taking of the extra train, there could be no question as to the liability of the defendant therefor. *Clussman* v. *Long Island R. Co.* 9 Hun, 618, affirmed in 73 N. Y. 606; *Parsons* v. *New York Cent. & H. R. R. Co.* 113 N. Y. 355, 3 L. R. A. 683.

The passenger is entitled to all necessary information to enable him to pursue his journey with safety and despatch, and he has often been held guilty of contributory negligence, relieving the carrier from liability, for his omission to make such inquiries. *Siner* v. *Great Western R. Co.* L. R. 3 Exch. 150, cited in *note* to the opinion, *Hulbert* v. *New York Cent. R. Co.* 40 N. Y. 154.

If it is the duty of the passenger to make inquiry, it is the corresponding duty of the carrier to give the information sought. The porter had undertaken to furnish such information to the plaintiff, or to introduce him to the conductor of the sleeping car for that purpose, and while so engaged had refused to complete the work, and struck plaintiff the blow complained of.

As we have seen, the defendant owed the plaintiff the duty to transport him to New York, and during its performance to care for his comfort and safety. This duty of protecting the personal safety of the passenger, and promoting by every reasonable means the accomplishment of his journey, is continuous, and embraces other attentions and services than the occasional services required in giving the passenger a seat or some temporary accommodation. Hence whatever is done by the carrier or its servants which interferes with or injures the health or strength or person of the traveler, or prevents the accomplishment of his journey in the most reasonable and speedy manner, is a violation of the carrier's contract, and he must be held responsible for it.

The idea that the servant of a carrier of persons may, in the intervals between rendering personal services to the passenger for his accommodation, assault the person of the passenger, destroy his consciousness and disable him from further pursuit of his journey, is not consistent with the duty that the carrier owes to the passenger, and is little less than monstrous.

While this general duty rested upon the defendant to protect the person of the passenger during the entire performance of the contract, it signifies but little or nothing whether the servant had or had not completed the temporary or particular service he was performing, or had completed the performance of it, when the blow was struck. That blow was given by a servant of the defendant, while the defendant was performing its contract to carry safely and to protect the person of the plaintiff, and was a violation of such contract.

Hence, we think the court should not have dismissed the complaint, but should have submitted these facts and the circumstances attending the blow to the jury, upon the question whether or not the porter was in the performance of his duties as the defendant's agent when the blow was inflicted.

The judgment should be reversed and a new trial granted, with costs to abide the event.

All concur.

INDIANA SUPREME COURT.

STATE of Indiana, *ex rel.* John WORREL, *Appt.*,
v.
William A. PEELLE, Jr.

(....Ind.....)

1. **An incumbent of an office,** whose demurrer to a complaint disputing his title thereto has been sustained by the trial court, is not debarred from setting up by way of answer a different claim of title to the office than the one already considered, in case of the reversal and remanding of the cause by the supreme court, if he in good faith believes he has a different title and has not yet addressed an answer to the complaint.

2. **No valid appointment can be made to an office** in possession of an incumbent whose term has not yet expired; and the surrender of the office by the prior incumbent to the appointee will confer upon him no title thereto.

3. **There can be no valid appointment** to an office so long as the appointing power is not called into exercise.

4. **Records of the official acts of the governor,** which are kept in a public office, are competent evidence upon the question of the title of a person to an office which he claims under the governor's commission.

5. **A commission given by the governor,** who has power to appoint incumbents to a certain office, authorizing a person to serve in such office, which expressly recites that such person derives his claim of title from an election by the Legislature and is commissioned for that reason, does not give the person a valid title to the office as the governor's appointee.

(*Elliott, J., and Mitchell, Ch. J., dissent.*)

(May 15, 1890.)

APPEAL by relator from a judgment of the Circuit Court for Marion County in favor of defendant in a proceeding by information to obtain possession of a certain office in possession of defendant, who was alleged to have no title thereto. *Reversed.*

The facts are fully stated in the opinions.

NOTE.—*Appointment to office.*

The power to appoint to office is not a legislative, but an executive, function. State v. Hyde, 121 Ind. 20.

Appointments to office, by whomsoever made, are intrinsically executive acts. State v. Barbour, 3 New Eng. Rep. 666, 53 Conn. 76.

An appointment is complete when the last act required of the appointing power has been performed. *Ibid.*

The provision of Ind. Const., art. 15, § 1, that all officers whose appointments are not otherwise provided for in the Constitution "shall be chosen in such manner as now is or hereafter may be prescribed by law," while giving the Legislature power to make laws regulating appointments, does not give it power itself to choose the officers. State v. Peelle, 121 Ind. 495; State v. Hyde, *supra.*

The Legislature cannot delegate the power to one state officer to appoint another state officer. State v. Hyde, *supra.*

The term "vacancy" applies to an existing office without an incumbent, although it has never been filled. *Re* Election of District Judges, 11 Colo. 373.

By the appointment of a successor, the appointing power recognizes the fact that a vacancy has occurred. McGee v. State, 1 West. Rep. 468, 103 Ind. 444.

If a vacancy in the office of county treasurer is left by the change of the time of beginning the term, the power to fill it is in the board of county commissioners, under Colo. Const., art. 14, § 9. *Re* House Bill No. 38 (Colo.) Dec. Term, 1886.

The governor of Indiana, in case of vacancy in a state office, can make an appointment until the next general election, when the people may elect an incumbent to the office. State v. Hyde, *supra.*

Under Colo. Const., art. 4, § 6, providing that the governor shall appoint, with the consent of the Senate, all officers whose appointment or election is not otherwise provided for, the consent of the Senate is not required where the appointment of officers is expressly conferred by statute upon the governor alone. *Re* Question Propounded by the Governor (Colo.) March 29, 1889.

The governor's commission is merely prima facie evidence of the facts recited therein. State v. Chapin, 9 West. Rep. 55, 110 Ind. 272.

An [illegible]er appointed by the governor to fill a vacancy will hold, not for the remainder of the term, but only until the qualification of a successor chosen at the next ensuing general election, to be held in accordance with Fla. Const., art. 18, § 9. Vacancies in Elective County Offices (Fla.) Jan. 16, 1889.

An illegal appointment to fill an assumed vacancy confers no protection on the appointee, when coupled with a prior removal in the exercise of quasi judicial discretion. Nichols v. MacLean, 2 Cent. Rep. 500, 101 N. Y. 526.

The legality of an officer's appointment cannot be collaterally attacked. State v. Brooks, 39 La. Ann. 817.

Officer de facto.

If the successor in office is not appointed in conformity with the law, the incumbent will continue in office, not as a mere *de facto* officer, but as officer *de jure.* Smoot v. Somerville, 59 Md. 88.

One cannot be a *de facto* officer unless he is acting as such under color of having been rightfully elected or appointed. East Norway Lake N. E. L. Church v. Halvorson (Minn.) Feb. 10, 1890.

Since there can be no such thing as an officer *de facto* when there is no office to fill, a person, although acting in good faith, cannot be an officer *de facto* where the vacancy caused by the expiration of his term has been filled by the election of another. State v. Lane (R. I.) Oct. 16, 1889.

Trial of title to office.

The proper proceeding to try a title to an office is by *quo warranto,* not certiorari; but it only lies

See also 12 L. R. A. 202, 364.

Messrs. **Louis T. Michener,** *Atty-Gen.*, **Albert J. Beveridge, John H. Gillette, Frank H. Blackledge** and **Leander M. Campbell,** for appellant:

A commission does not constitute the official title, but is merely a certificate of such title. Where it certifies that the person commissioned derived his title from some other source than appointment, it is absolutely conclusive evidence that such person was not appointed.

Marbury v. *Madison*, 5 U. S. 1 Cranch, 156 (2 L. ed. 60); *United States* v. *Le Baron*, 60 U. S. 19 How. 78 (15 L. ed. 527); *State* v. *Askew*, 48 Ark. 86.

The circumstances under which it was issued may be shown in order to explain, establish or overthrow the title to which such commission does certify.

Thompson v. *State*, 21 Ala. 55; *State* v. *Askew*, 48 Ark. 86; *State* v. *Chapin*, 9 West. Rep. 53, 110 Ind. 276.

An appointment is not valid when made while an officer, under good title, is occupying the office.

State v. *Harrison*, 13 West. Rep. 370, 113 Ind. 438.

Mr. **Addison C. Harris,** also for appellant:

One man cannot hold the same office at the same time under two adverse claims or titles or sources of power or authority. The rights or titles are not concurrent, and, the choice between them being once made, the right to follow the other is forever gone.

Rodermund v. *Clark*, 46 N. Y. 357.

The case is analogous to those in which the right to occupy incompatible offices was denied, in which it has been ruled:

That the acceptance of the second office *ipso facto* vacates the first.

Mechem, Pub. Off. § 425, and cases cited; *Rex* v. *Trelawney*, 3 Burr. 1615; *Milward* v. *Thatcher*, 2 T. R. 81; *Rex* v. *Tizzard*, 9 Barn. & C. 418; *People* v. *Hanifan*, 96 Ill. 420; *Foltz* v. *Kerlin*, 2 West. Rep. 670, 105 Ind. 225.

That the acceptance of a second office is conclusive of the officer's election to hold that office.

Mechem, Pub. Off. § 426; *State* v. *Brinkerhoff*, 66 Tex. 45; *Stubbs* v. *Lee*, 64 Me. 195, 18 Am. Rep. 252; *Van Orsdall* v. *Hazard*, 3 Hill, 243.

That the best evidence of this acceptance, which is the election to hold the second office, is the qualification, by taking oath and giving bond if any is required by law.

Mechem, Pub. Off. § 250; *Smith* v. *Moore*, 90 Ind. 294.

Messrs. **McCullough & Harlan** and **Stanton J. Peelle** for appellee.

Berkshire, *J.*, delivered the opinion of the court:

This is the second time this case has been in this court. *State*, ex rel. *Worrell*, v. *Peelle*, 121 Ind. 495.

When the case was first before the circuit court judgment was rendered for the appellee upon a demurrer to the complaint. From the judgment so rendered an appeal was prosecuted to this court. In this court the judgment was reversed, and the cause remanded, with directions to the court below to overrule the demurrer to the complaint. When the cause again came before the circuit court the appellee answered in two paragraphs. The first paragraph

---

against one who has been in actual possession and user. State v. Camden Co. 1 Cent. Rep. 436, 47 N. J. L. 454; People v. Riordan (Mich.) Feb. 1, 1889.

In Michigan *quo warranto* is the only way to try title to office finally and conclusively. Frey v. Michie, 12 West. Rep. 587, 68 Mich. 323.

In Texas, however, it is not the only method to be pursued for the recovery of an office. The right to an office may be determined in an ordinary civil suit brought directly by the claimant against the party in possession. McAllen v. Rhodes, 65 Tex. 348.

Quo warranto will not lie when an office is vacant. Nichols v. MacLean, 2 Cent. Rep. 500, 101 N. Y. 526; State v. McCullough (Neb.) July 3, 1888; Williams v. Clayton (Utah) March 8, 1889.

Conceding that the right to an office may be conferred by mandamus, the writ will not issue unless the person, if any, in possession of the office, is made a party to the proceeding. Kelly v. Edwards, 69 Cal. 460.

Proceedings by *quo warranto* are "remedial cases" of the class denominated in the Constitution "cases at law." State v. Minnesota Thresher Mfg. Co. 3 L. R. A. 510, and *note*, 40 Minn. 213; People v. Reid, 11 Colo. 138.

Proceeding to test right to office.

An action to determine a disputed title to a public office can be brought only in the name of the State by the attorney-general or district attorney on his own information or that of another, who may be joined as plaintiff. Guillotte v. Poincy (La.) 5 L. R. A. 403.

The right of the person elected to the office of senator or representative in the General Assembly may be contested by any elector of the district or county. Rev. Stat. § 3003; Dalton v. State, 1 West. Rep. 784, 43 Ohio St. 652.

A predecessor in office cannot contest the validity of his successor's appointment by refusing to deliver up the records of the office. McGee v. State, 1 West. Rep. 467, 103 Ind. 444.

Giving a full and fair hearing to an officer is insufficient to give validity to proceedings against him for his removal, where the proceedings before the hearing have not been in accordance with the statute. People v. Therrien (Mich.) April 11, 1890.

In a proceeding to contest the right to an office, where the single material issue is whether relator received a majority of the votes, further issues as to whether the returns from certain townships were properly rejected by the board of canvassers are immaterial; and findings of the jury on these, which are inconsistent with their findings on the real issue, may be disregarded. Gatling v. Boone, 101 N. C. 61.

Where the question is whether there was a vacancy to be filled by an election or appointment, or where it is, Did the law authorize the election or appointment in a given case?—courts have jurisdiction to determine the law of the case. Robertson v. State, 7 West. Rep. 494, 109 Ind. 99.

Cal. Penal Code, § 770, providing that from a judgment of removal from office an appeal may be taken in the same manner as from a judgment in a civil action, but until reversal defendant is suspended from office, and that pending the appeal the office must be filled as in case of a vacancy,—is applicable to proceedings under § 772, providing for removal of public officers by summary proceedings. Woods v. Varnum (Cal.) Jan. 30, 1890.

was a special denial and the second paragraph the general denial.

It would have been proper practice had the appellant filed a motion to strike out the first paragraph as an incumbrance to the second, notwithstanding there would have been no available error had such a motion been filed and overruled.

Several paragraphs of reply were filed to the first paragraph of answer, but regarding it as a mere denial of the allegations in the complaint, the reply becomes wholly without importance.

The cause, being at issue, was submitted to the court for trial and a finding made thereafter for the appellee. The appellant moved the court for a new trial, which motion the court overruled and the proper exception was reserved. Judgment was then rendered for the appellee, and from that judgment this appeal is prosecuted. When the case was here the first time the whole contention was as to the power of the Legislature, under the Constitution, to designate the incumbent to the office in question. The appellee rested his claim to the office upon an election by the Legislature, and the appellant's relator relied upon an appointment from the executive of the State. The appellee now claims title to the office by virtue of an appointment from the executive of the State, while the appellant's relator assumes the same position as heretofore.

After the cause had been remanded to the court below, as the appellee had not yet addressed an answer to the complaint, he was not debarred from setting up, by way of answer, a different claim of title than the one already considered by this and the court below, if he in good faith believed he had any different title. And the question now is, Does the appellee hold the office in question by appointment from the executive department of the government? As we understand the position of the appellee, it is that he holds the office (1) by appointment from Gov. Porter, and (2) by appointment from Gov. Gray. For two sufficient reasons the appellee received no appointment to the office in question from Governor Porter, the second of which applies with equal force to the action of Gov. Gray.

First. At the time the appellee claims to have received his appointment from Gov. Porter, John B. Conner, Esq., was rightfully holding the office and his term of office did not expire for one and one half months thereafter. That the governor could make no valid appointment under such circumstances, it is only necessary to cite the well-considered case of *State* v. *Harrison*, 113 Ind. 434, 13 West. Rep. 370.

But the contention is urged that, even if the appointment was void when made, as Conner thereafter surrendered the office to the appellee, his appointment was thereby validated. This position cannot be maintained. The appointment being void at its inception, no act of the governor could thereafter give it validity. It will hardly be expected that we take the time to cite authorities to support so plain a proposition. And it is sufficient to say that if the governor could not validate his own void act, Conner could not do so for him. The surrender of the office by Conner to the appellee we think amounted to an abandonment thereof and created a vacancy therein; but if there were any doubt as to this proposition, both parties have so treated it, and for all the purposes of this case we would be bound to so hold.

After the vacancy had been created, the governor was authorized to fill it by appointment and could have appointed the appellee, and if this had been done the appellee would have held the office by virtue of the appointment then made, and not because of the commission issued to the appellee before Conner abandoned the office.

Upon the question that the surrender of an office by its rightful incumbent to one claiming title thereto without right does not give to the latter title thereto, we refer to *Turnipseed* v. *Hudson*, 50 Miss. 429, 19 Am. Rep. 15.

The second reason why the appellee did not receive an appointment from the executive is that the appointing power lodged with him under the Constitution was never invoked in behalf of the appellee, and so long as it was not called into exercise there could be no appointment, although the governor could at any time call it into action.

It appears that the General Assembly assumed (and it was but an assumption) to take from the executive department the power therein vested under the Constitution to designate the incumbent of the office in question, and not only so, but to legislate the rightful incumbent of said office out of office before the expiration of his term, and to take unto themselves the election of an incumbent to said office, and as the result the General Assembly elected the appellee and gave him a certificate of election. The first election occurred on the 3d day of March, 1883, and upon a certificate thereof being presented to the executive he issued the following commission:

"The State of Indiana, To all who shall see these presents, greeting:

"Whereas, It has been certified by the proper authority that, at a joint convention of the two Houses of the Fifty-third General Assembly, held in the hall of the House of Representatives, March 3d, 1883, that William A. Peelle, Jr., was elected Chief of the Bureau of Statistics.

"Therefore, know ye, that in the name and by the authority of the State aforesaid, I do hereby appoint and commission William A. Peelle, Jr., Chief of the Bureau of Statistics aforesaid, to serve as such for the term of two years from the 8th day of March, 1883, and until his successor shall have been elected and qualified.

In witness whereof, etc.

By the Governor, Albert G. Porter.
W. R. Myers, Secretary of State.

There was no pretense that the appellee held any other title to the office than that which the said election conferred upon him, and when we remember the aggressive attitude of the General Assembly at this time with reference to its power to elect the incumbents to a large class of offices, including the one in question (and of this we take judicial knowledge), the appellee would not have been willing to have recognized the executive department as the source of his title.

The governor was careful to recite in the

commission the nature of the appellee's title, and that he commissioned him as the chosen of the General Assembly.

That it was the purpose and intention of the governor when he issued the commission to deliver to the appellee the evidence of his title as derived from the Legislature, and to make it distinctly appear that he was in no sense the appointee of the executive, is so manifest that there is no ground for a contrary contention to rest upon.

But, in addition to what appears on the face of the commission, the records of the executive office disclose the fact that the commission was issued to the appellee because and on account of his election by the General Assembly. We know of no sufficient reason why these records are not competent evidence. They are the records kept in a public office of the official acts of the chief executive officer of the State. But see *Marbury* v. *Madison*, 5 U. S. 1 Cranch, 137 [2 L. ed. 60].

But it still further appears that after the appellee received his commission from Gov. Porter, he recognized the Legislature, and not the executive, as the source from which he derived title to the office. The following is the oath which was administered to him and indorsed on his commission:

State of Indiana, }
Marion County. } ss.

I, William A. Peelle, Jr., do solemnly swear that I will support the Constitution of the United States and of the State of Indiana, and that I will honestly and faithfully discharge my duties as chief of the Bureau of Statistics, for the term for which I have been elected, to the best of my ability, so help me God.

William A. Peelle, Jr.

Subscribed and sworn to before me this 9th day of March, 1883.

S. P. Sheerin, Clerk Supreme Court.

But it is contended that by some kind of legal fiction the appellee, each time he was commissioned by the governor, became his appointee. This contention is not very clearly defined, but proceeds, as we understand it (in part at least) upon the theory that all persons are presumed to know the law and that this presumption applies as well to public officers as to individuals; and as Governors Porter and Gray are presumed to have known when they commissioned the appellee that the General Assembly had no power to elect him to the office, the presumption must prevail that they intended by their official acts in commissioning him to appoint him to the office, and that this presumption must prevail over their expressed intention to the contrary; or, to express the contention in other language, though they intended by their official acts to do one thing and in fact did what they intended, that in law they did something else. This is carrying the doctrine of presumptions beyond precedent and we think beyond reason. For some purposes the presumption contended for prevails, but it is never applied to a question such as the one here under consideration. It is usually recognized in the construction of contracts and the enforcement of penal statutes, but we know of no case where it has been allowed to give to the official act of a public officer a different legal effect than the act itself expressly declares was intended. See *Citizen's Loan Asso.* v. *Friedley* (Ind.), 7 L. R. A. 669.

On the 9th day of February, 1885, the Legislature again elected the appellee to the office in question, and thereafter, upon a certificate of election, the governor issued to him a commission. In 1887 there was no election and the appellee continued to hold the office until 1889, when the Legislature again elected him to the office, and on presentation of his certificate of election to the governor a commission was refused, and, the governor having appointed the appellant's relator and commissioned him, this controversy arose.

The following is the appellee's commission from Governor Gray:

The State of Indiana, To all who shall see these presents, greeting:

Whereas, it has been certified to me by the proper authority that William A. Peelle, Jr., has been elected to the office of chief of the Bureau of Statistics of the State of Indiana, by the General Assembly on the 9th day of February, A. D. 1885.

Therefore, Know Ye, that in the name and by the authority of the State aforesaid, I do hereby commission the said William A. Peelle, Jr. as said chief of the Bureau of Statistics of the State of Indiana for the term of two years from the 8th day of March, 1885, and until his successor shall have been elected and qualified.

In witness whereof, etc.

By the Governor, Isaac P. Gray.
William R. Myers, Secretary of State.

We have nothing to add with reference to Governor Gray's action, except to say that he seemed to be more careful, if possible, than his predecessor to emphasize the fact that the appellee was not his appointee, but was commissioned as the chosen of the General Assembly. The word "appoint" is found in the commission issued by Gov. Porter, but nowhere appears in that of Gov. Gray.

But the further contention of the appellee is that, as the appointing power was lodged with the executive of the State, his purpose or intention in commissioning the appellee cannot be inquired into; that notwithstanding the purpose is disclosed in the face of the commission all of its recitals must be disregarded, and the commission treated as an appointment made by the executive. Much that we have already said is here applicable. This is but contending for a conclusive presumption that you must take an officer to mean one thing when he does another.

As the appointing power was lodged in the executive when he commissioned the appellee, had the commission recited an appointment or had it been silent as to the source of the appellee's title to the office, then no doubt the commission would have been conclusive for the very good reason that the mental operations of the governor's mind unexpressed in the act could not be inquired into; and if for no other reason, such inquiry would be impracticable. But when the source of title is lodged somewhere else than with the executive his commission is only prima facie evidence of title. *Boone Co.* v. *State*, 61 Ind. 379; *Reynolds* v. *State*, 61 Ind. 392; *Hench* v. *State*, 72 Ind. 297;

State v. *Chapin*, 110 Ind. 272, 9 West. Rep. 53; *Marbury* v. *Madison*, *supra*.

This court has gone so far as to hold that even after the governor has issued a commission, if it appears that he has commissioned a wrongful claimant, to the prejudice of one who is rightfully entitled to the office, he may issue the second commission. *Gulick* v. *New*, 14 Ind. 93.

The same reasons which make the governor's commission conclusive when silent as to the source of title, that the person commissioned is the governor's appointee, where he has the power to appoint an incumbent to such office, render his commission conclusive that such person is not his appointee when it recites that the person commissioned derives his claim of title because of an election by the people or Legislature, and is commissioned because thereof.

We hold that when the appellant's relator was appointed there was a vacancy in the office which the governor was empowered to fill by appointment until there should be an election by the people.

Judgment reversed, with costs.

Elliott, *J.*, dissenting:

I am so strongly convinced that the law is with the appellee that I cannot assent to the prevailing opinion. The importance of the questions involved requires a statement of my reasons for dissenting, and this statement I shall make without elaboration.

Governor Porter issued to Peelle a commission in March, 1883, and under that commission he entered into possession of the office. At the expiration of the term designated in the commission issued by Governor Porter, Governor Gray, then the governor of the State, issued a commission to Peelle, and under these commissions he continued in undisturbed possession of the office, discharging its duties and recognized as an officer *de jure* by all the departments of the government until this action was brought. He entered into office under Governor Porter's commission and continued under that of Governor Gray. He entered office, therefore, by executive sanction, and his continuance in office was by executive authority, for either this must be true, or else it must be true that no executive power or function was exercised in commissioning him; and, surely, in every commission there is some expression of executive judgment.

The law of the case as declared on the former appeal, which controls us now whatever may be our individual opinions, is that the legislative election in 1883 was utterly void, and if it was void Peelle could not have entered into the office nor have held it under that election, for it is absolutely inconceivable that a void act can confer right or title. But Peelle did go into office and has continued there for nearly seven years, and the only power which could put or keep him there was and is that of the chief executive of the State; and the chief executive, by the commissions issued to him, authorized him to enter into the office and to continue in it, so far as it was in the power of the chief executive to do so. The chief executive alone had power to put and keep him in office, and it was the chief executive that did put him into office and continued him there by designating him as the person entitled to the office in the commission issued to him. It seems clear to me that the only power to which Peelle's appointment is referable is the executive power, for there is no other to which it can by any possibility be referred.

The fact that Governors Porter and Gray recited in the commissions issued by them that Peelle was elected by the General Assembly, and that he was commissioned because he was so elected, does not prove that the minds of the chief executives did not assent to and confirm his appointment. They knew the law; they knew that they alone possessed the appointing power, and, knowing this, they designated him as the person to fill the office, and thus gave him the place by their own acts, for it was in their power, and in theirs alone, to withhold the office or to bestow it upon him. No other department of the government could either bestow or withhold the office. The law as declared on the former appeal is not a new law, for, according to the decision, it has existed since the adoption of the Constitution, and it was known to the governors of the State at the time the commissions were issued, for no man can be deemed ignorant of the law, certainly not the highest officers in the State.

Neither Governor Porter nor Governor Gray was the mere agent or clerk of the General Assembly, for in appointing to office the governor exercises a power vested in him by the Constitution. He is beyond legislative control in all cases where he exercises his constitutional prerogative, and that was exercised in this instance.

What may be the power of the governor under a valid statute is a question with which we have here not the remotest concern. Here the commissions were issued because the chief executive had the constitutional power to issue them by virtue of his prerogative. He could not, indeed, issue them by virtue of any other right or power vested in him.

In exercising his constitutional prerogative the governor exercises his own will and judgment. No one can share the power with him nor divide the responsibility. As the issuing of the commissions were executive acts under the Constitution, they express the executive judgment and will, for they can express no other in a case such as this where the governor possesses the whole and the exclusive appointing power.

If either Governor Porter or Governor Gray exercised the constitutional prerogative of the chief executive,—and in this instance no other could have been exercised,—then, what moved them to do it, or what reason, belief, motive or opinion influenced them, is not a question for judicial cognizance, nor can it be under our Constitution. To attempt to ascertain in any mode or under any circumstances, or by any process or procedure, what influence controlled the mind and judgment of the governor, would be an invasion of the executive domain which no authority will warrant nor any principle justify. If the courts can, by one mode, whether by examining the commission or by some other, inquire what belief, motive or opinion influenced the judgment of the governor, they can do so in any mode, and this would subject the exercise of executive power to judicial control. Our Constitution expressly forbids that this ever be done. It cannot be said that there is one mode in which the inquiry may be prosecuted and no other, for once it is granted that the question is a judicial one, then all modes are open to the courts and they may probe the executive mind in every method known to the law. I affirm that the courts cannot prosecute any inquiry for the purpose of ascertaining what influenced the governor to issue a commission in such a case as this, for it is a question over which the courts have no jurisdiction.

In a case where the power to appoint resides exclusively in the governor, and where he writes the name of a person in a commission and delivers it to him, he exercises his constitutional prerogative, for he can exercise no other. When it is ascertained that the governor has issued a commission there the power of the court terminates.

No ingenuity of invention nor any subtility of argument can make it appear otherwise than that in the judgment of Governor Gray and of Governor Porter, Peelle was the man entitled to the office. This was the executive judgment, and the executive judgment is conclusive, for the sole and absolute power of appointing to an office which it is the prerogative of the governor to fill by appointment is in the governor. His judgment, however influenced, no court can supervise. Even if it be true that the executive judgment was misled or was controlled by an erroneous view, still it was the executive judgment, and as such beyond review. The executive judgment was called into exercise and the executive pen wrote the name of the man designated to fill the office. If there was an exercise of executive judgment, no matter how invoked or upon what grounds it proceeds, it is unimpeachable, for there is no tribunal that has jurisdiction to investigate the question of executive conduct in cases where, as in this, the power of deciding resides wholly in the governor.

It is useless to cite as authority or as illustrations cases where the appointing power is not exclusively vested in the governor, for they have not the remotest application in such a case as this. Such cases prove nothing at all to the point, nor prove anything that anybody desires; for all concede that where the governor has not the exclusive appointing power, his commission is not the vehicle for conveying the title to the office. But even in such cases it does convey some expression of the executive judgment.

It must be true that a commission issued by the governor in a case such as this, where he has the whole appointing power, expresses his judgment, or it must be true that it is utterly void. To declare it void is to affirm that the highest officer of the State did a vain and idle thing, and this no court has power to do. Nor can it be assumed that the governor, having the sole power to appoint, has violated his constitutional duty and his oath, and laid down his high constitutional prerogative at the feet of the Legislature. If it be adjudged that he yielded to an unconstitutional statute, surrendered his executive independence and invested a man with the *indicia* of office, it is necessarily asserted that he wrongfully yielded his executive independence and violated his duty; and this assertion no court can rightfully make, for the plain reason that it can do no more than ascertain that the governor has invested the man he names in his commission with the legal *indicia* of title. The act of issuing a commission, of itself and by its own force and vigor, expresses the executive judgment that the man named shall take the office, and no court can inquire what belief or opinion influenced the judgment of the chief executive.

The act of issuing a commission, where the governor has the sole power of appointment, is absolutely, wholly and exclusively executive. It is impossible that it can be partly executive and partly legislative. It embodies the judgment of the governor; this it embodies and this alone, for it cannot embody the judgment of anyone else on earth. If it embodies any part of the executive judgment no court can inquire what influenced that judgment without usurping power that belongs to another department of the government.

It is not within the power of the courts to examine any evidence, whether supplied by the commission, by the books of the governor's office or by the oral statements of the governor, for the purpose of ascertaining whether he was influenced by an insufficient or an illegal cause to clothe the man whose name he wrote on the commission with the *indicia* of office.

President Garfield wrote upon the commission of General Wallace "Ben Hur," and surely no one would assert that it was competent for the courts to inquire whether the presidential judgment was influenced by that great book. If, however, they can inquire into the motives or opinions of the appointing power in any case, they can do so in such a case as that instanced as an illustration as well as in any other. The only defensible conclusion is, that, if the instrument is a commission, what is written in it has no force as evidence, beyond the fact that the person named is designated as the one who in the executive judgment is entitled to the office specified, and the courts have no power to push their investigation beyond that point. I repeat that we are here dealing with a case where the sole right to appoint resides in the governor, for the rule is different where the governor has not the appointing power; back of him in such a case is the source of right and title, but where he has the exclusive power he is the exclusive creator of title and right. He is the sole fountain of right and power. No more need be known, and no more can legally be known, by the courts than that he has designated a person to fill an office by writing his name in a commission and delivering it to him.

But if it be conceded, a concession that is wholly unauthorized, that the courts may search the commission to discover what belief, motive or opinion controlled the mind of the chief executive and induced him to issue and deliver to the person designated the *indicia* of office, the utmost that can be said is that Governor Porter and Governor Gray were influenced by the legislative election to decide in his favor. Grant that this does appear and so appear that the courts can regard it as evidence, and still it does not authorize the inference that the designation or appointment was not that of the governor. All that can be inferred, awarding to the recital the utmost possible force as evidence, is that the legislative election influenced the two governors from whom Peelle holds commissions to designate him for the office, for, upon no principle of law or logic can it be assumed that those high officers yielded their official prerogatives to a void and dead legislative declaration. Those officers were bound by the strongest and highest considerations that can influence men to exercise their judgment and to maintain the executive independence, and it must be assumed that they did their sworn duty and did exercise their judgment. Either this must be true or it must be true that two of the highest officers of the State weakly yielded to legislative usurpation and inexcusably surrendered their executive independence.

But more than this. If it be adjudged that the commissions were issued by the governor, because the Legislature bade them do it, then it is affirmed that two of the governors of the State were ignorant of a principle of constitutional law, and yielded, not to an actual command, but to a legislative declaration having not one spark of vitality. If it be conceded that the courts may search for evidence to prove what opinion, belief or motive operated upon the mind of the governor, it is much more reasonable to assume that the executive judgment simply coincided in the legislative selection or designation and united with the Legislature in designating the person who should fill the office, than it is to assume that the governor yielded to an invalid statute and acted simply as the passive agent of the Legislature. The assumption suggested as the reasonable one leads to no unjust or evil consequences, attributes no ignorance to either of the governors, nor imputes to him any violation of duty; whereas, the assumption that the recitals in the commission show that he issued the commission solely because of the legislative election convicts the chief executive of the State of ignorance of constitutional law or else of a willful violation of duty, and an indefensible surrender of a high prerogative, and, in either event, leads to evil consequences.

To construe the recitals of the commissions as evidence of a breach of duty by the governor, or of ignorance on his part, is a wide stretch of judicial authority, and certainly no such construction should be resorted to where, as here, it is reasonable and natural to infer that the governor yielded to the influence of the legislative election, not because it coerced him, but because it persuaded or convinced him that the choice or selection was a proper one. It is neither unusual nor improper, as everyone knows, for the governor to consult the officers or citizens, and recommendations are often made to the appointing power in behalf of applicants for office. This is illustrated by the cases where postmasters are designated by an election held by the people; for, while such an election may influence the president to make the appointment, it does not coerce his judgment, and if he should recite in his commission that the person so chosen was appointed because of his election, we suppose no one would think of questioning the validity of the appointment. We have no more right in this instance to assume that the election by the Legislature coerced either Governor Porter or Governor Gray than a court would have to assume, in the case supposed, that the election by the people had coerced the president.

If we are to strictly adhere to the words of the commissions and regard only the letter of the instrument, then the commission given Peelle by Governor Porter is conclusive, for it is written therein that "in the name and by the authority of the State aforesaid I do hereby appoint and commission William A. Peelle, Jr., Chief of the Bureau of Statistics."

If the recitals control, then it is impossible to deny that Governor Porter did appoint Peelle to the office.

Under the appointment made by Governor Porter, Peelle was inducted into the office in 1883, and he continued in office undisturbed until this action was brought, nearly seven years afterwards. For almost seven years he has been in office, and it seems to me very doubtful whether, after such a lapse of time, anyone can be heard to aver that when Governor Porter appointed him there was no vacancy. I am, at all events, thoroughly convinced that the relator cannot question the action of Governor Porter. To aver that there was then no vacancy is to aver that Governor Porter was ignorant of the law. And it is more, for it is to aver that for more than six years all of the executive, legislative and administrative officers of the State were ignorant of the fact, if it be fact, as assumed, that Peelle was a usurper. But still more than this, Mr. Conner, who it is assumed was the incumbent when Peelle was appointed by Governor Porter, yielded the office without objection and asserts no title, for the title is here asserted by one who claims through an appointment made more than six years after the appointee of Governor Porter had taken possession of his office. I know of no authority nor of any principle that will authorize any court or any officer to sit in judgment on the action of Governor Porter at the demand of one whose sole and only claim to the office is an appointment made six years and more after Governor Porter's appointee took possession of the office.

Nor do I believe that it can be justly asserted that from the time Mr. Conner yielded the office it has been vacant. When Peelle entered the office six years ago and more under Governor Porter's appointment the vacancy was filled; or else Mr. Conner is still the officer *de jure*. That it was in fact filled no one will deny; that it was so in law is my firm conviction. It may be true that when Governor Porter appointed Peelle there was no vacancy, but when Mr. Conner yielded the office, as it is asserted he did do, there was a vacancy and this vacancy was filled by Mr. Peelle's entrance under Governor Porter's appointment. As the sole power of appointing was at that time in Governor Porter, his commission operated to place Peelle in office as soon as the vacancy occurred, and Governor Gray's commission continued him there. It may be true (it is immaterial whether it be so or not) that if Peelle's right had been challenged by Mr. Conner, or if Governor Porter had commissioned another, Peelle could not have rightfully held the office under Governor Porter's commission; but however this may be, it cannot be true that what occurred under executive sanction twice manifested, more than six years ago, can be reviewed at the suit of one whose claim is founded on a commission only a few months old.

It is assumed that Mr. Conner abandoned the office, and if, therefore, it ever became vacant, it became so when Mr. Conner abandoned it in 1883, if he did abandon it, and at that time the governor of the State had an unquestioned right to fill it, and Governor Porter did attempt, at least, to fill it by appointing Mr. Peelle; and the only person who could legally complain was Mr. Conner, for, if Peele's appointment was invalid, then Mr. Conner, by force of the constitutional provision which rules the question, held over, and he only was wronged.

In this case the relator has the burden of establishing two things: first, the strength of his own title, and, second, the weakness of Peelle's; and if he has weakened Peelle's title it is because he has shown that Mr. Conner was entitled to the office, and has thus shown that he has himself no title. He is "hoist by his own petard." If, as the argument of the relator assumes from beginning to end, the two governors who issued Peelle's commissions were mistaken as to the law, then, so, we must presume, was Mr. Conner; and if he was he did not abandon the office, and he it is who is now, upon the relator's own theory, entitled to the office. If Peelle, by virtue of the unconstitutional statute under which the Legislature assumed to elect him, has kept any person out of office, it is Mr. Conner and not Mr. Worrel. If Mr. Conner were here claiming the office, there would, to my mind, be much more difficulty in vindicating Mr. Peelle's claim; for, if an officer yields to a law believed at the time by the executive and legislative departments of the government to be valid, and is by it coerced out of office, he cannot be adjudged to have abandoned the office. But it is doubtful whether it would be competent, even at the suit of Mr. Conner, to reach back over a period of nearly seven years and review the action of Governor Porter; it is, however, quite clear that it is not competent to do it at the suit of the relator, who was a stranger until May, 1889.

If Peelle wrongfully put anyone out of office by entering into it, that one was Mr. Conner, and if there is anyone who has a claim to the office except Peelle, it is Mr. Conner. If there is, and has been, no vacancy in the office, it must be for the reason that Mr. Conner was never rightfully ousted; and if there was no vacancy when Governor Porter and Governor Gray acted, there was none when Governor Hovey issued the commission to Mr. Worrel six years later.

It is inconsistent to assert that Governor Porter and Governor Gray were coerced into putting Peelle into office and keeping him there by the legislative election, and that all they did was to obey the direction of the Legislature, yielding to it their own judgments and surrendering their own high constitutional prerogatives, and yet hold that Mr. Conner, in yielding to coercive measures that controlled the highest officers of the State, voluntarily abandoned an office to which he was of right entitled. To me it seems illogical to assert that the two governors were so constrained by legislative action that they did not exercise their free judgment and constitutional rights, and yet hold that a subordinate officer, who yielded to the same action of the Legislature, acted of his own free will and uncontrolled judgment, and voluntarily abandoned his office.

If Mr. Conner did not abandon the office he is still the *de jure* officer, and if he is, the appellant's relator has not the shadow of a claim. Conner did not abandon the office if he merely yielded to the same power which, as the relator asserts, controlled and coerced Governor Porter, and left the office because he was forced by law to do so. It is impossible to conceive how it can with consistency be asserted that there was no vacancy in 1883 because Mr. Conner was the officer *de jure*, and yet be asserted that, as Mr. Conner was forced out of the office in that year, it lets the relator in six years later. Nor is it easy to conceive any rational theory upon which the relator can lay hold of Mr. Conner's rights to defeat Peelle; for, as Mr. Conner is not before the court, no question as to him can be determined, and certainly no right of Mr. Conner can be made available to the relator, who had not the remotest connection with the case until six years after Peelle, as the relator now claims, wrongfully asserted title against Mr. Conner.

The case seems to me very clear upon principle, but authorities are not wanting.

That executive powers and duties are beyond review by the courts is firmly settled. *Smith* v. *Myers*, 109 Ind. 1, and authorities cited page 7, 7 West. Rep. 90.

That the commission of an officer who, as is true of this case, has the sole and exclusive appointing power, is a conclusive expression of the judgment of the officer invested with that power, is affirmed in strongly reasoned cases, and, so far as I have been able to ascertain, is denied by none. In a case where the officer having the sole power of appointment erroneously supposed that he must act upon the action of a legislative body, the court said: "The essential thing is the fact of the appointment. That might have been contained in a letter addressed to the persons appointed or to the public. If the paper was signed for the purpose of making or evidencing the appointment, all else is mere matter of form and unimportant." *People* v. *Fitzsimmons*, 68 N. Y. 514.

In another case the court said: "In such a state of case it is only necessary that the person claiming the office shall show that the officer has exercised that power and decided in his favor." *Hoke* v. *Field*, 10 Bush, 144, 19 Am. Rep. 58.

That there is no abandonment of a public office where the person yields it in deference to a statute which is afterwards declared to be unconstitutional is adjudged in the very strongly reasoned case of *Turnipseed* v. *Hudson*, 50 Miss. 429, 19 Am. Rep. 15, where the authorities are collected and ably reviewed.

That the law is that if Mr. Conner did not abandon the office by yielding to an unconstitutional statute the implied or expressed declaration of Governor Porter or of Governor Gray did not and could not create a vacancy is set tled by our own decisions. *Knox Co. Comrs. v. Johnson* (Ind.) 7 L. R. A. 684; *State v. Harrison*, 113 Ind. 434, 13 West. Rep. 370.

Whatever view may be taken of this case, it seems clear to me that the relator has no title to the office, and if he has not, then there can be no question as to the correctness of the judgment of the trial court. Whether Mr. Peelle or Mr. Conner is entitled to the office is a much more doubtful question than the question presented by the relator's assertion of title.

Mitchell, *Ch. J.*, concurs in the opinion of **Elliott,** *J.*

IOWA SUPREME COURT.

William G. PENNYPACKER
v.
CAPITAL INSURANCE CO., *Appt.*

(....Iowa....)

1. **Where a policy of insurance is issued on property in one State** by a company in another State, and it does not appear where it was delivered or payable, or where the contract was made, or the premium paid, it may be inferred that the contract was made in either State as readily as in the other.
2. **A statutory prohibition against insurance** by foreign corporations without compliance with certain requirements, under a certain penalty, does not make a policy issued without such compliance void as to the insured.
3. **Evidence that notice and proofs of loss were sent to a firm** through which the policy was procured, although not agents of the insurer, and that they forwarded the papers by mail to the insurer, is admissible as tending to show that the insurer received them.
4. **Notice and proofs of loss mailed** to an insurer will be presumed to have been duly received in the absence of evidence to the contrary.
5. **Instructions that notice of loss must have been given** within a reasonable time, while the policy requires it to be given "forthwith," are not prejudicial, as the terms are so nearly synonymous.
6. **Proof of the mailing of notice and proofs** of loss addressed to an insurer and properly stamped, opposed by testimony of the insurer's officers and clerks that the documents were never received, presents a question for the

---

NOTE.—*Foreign corporations; law of comity.*

A foreign corporation can exercise none of the functions or privileges conferred by its charter, in any other State of the Union, except by the comity and consent of the latter. Liverpool & L. L. & F. Ins. Co. v. Oliver, 77 U. S. 10 Wall. 566 (19 L. ed. 1029); Runyan v. Coster, 39 U. S. 14 Pet. 122 (10 L. ed. 382).

By general comity, corporations created in one State or Territory are permitted to carry on any lawful business in another, and to acquire, hold and transfer property there equally as individuals. Cowell v. Colorado Springs Co. 100 U. S. 55 (25 L. ed. 547); American & F. C. Union v. Yount, 101 U. S. 352 (25 L. ed. 888).

It may, under the law of comity, make contracts, and sue in the courts of the State in which they transact business. Bank of Augusta v. Earle, 38 U. S. 13 Pet. 519 (10 L. ed. 274); Tombigbee R. Co. v. Kneeland, 45 U. S. 4 How. 16 (11 L. ed. 855).

A state statute which imposes upon a foreign corporation limitations of its right to make contracts in the State for carrying on commerce between the States is an invasion of the exclusive right of Congress to regulate commerce among the States. Cooper Mfg. Co. v. Ferguson, 113 U. S. 727 (28 L. ed. 1137).

Recovery may be had on a policy issued by a company not authorized to engage in business in the State. Ganser v. Fireman's Fund Ins. Co. 34 Minn. 372.

A suit for an account on a tontine policy issued by a stock company can be entertained by the courts of other States than that of the company's domicil. Pierce v. Equitable L. Assur. Society, 4 New Eng. Rep. 876, 145 Mass. 56.

The objection that the defendant company, as well as the plaintiff, has its legal existence in another State than that where sued, and should not be held to answer, is waived by a general answer. *Ibid.* See *note* to State v. West. Union Mut. L. Society, *ante*, 129.

Rule in the various States:

Alabama.

The doing of a single act of business in the State, if it be in the exercise of a corporate function, by a foreign corporation having no known place of business or agent in the State, is prohibited by the State Constitution. Farrior v. New England Mortgage Security Co. 88 Ala. 275.

If, in violation of the Constitution, it lends money and takes a mortgage without having a place of business or agent in the State, it cannot foreclose the mortgage, the promise of the mortgagor being void. *Ibid.*

California.

The Legislature of the State, in attempting to impose a condition upon which foreign corporations shall be permitted to do business within the State, cannot exercise a power denied to it by the State Constitution. San Francisco v. Liverpool & L. & G. Ins. Co. 74 Cal. 113.

By continuing in business they do not waive the right to object to the unconstitutionality of the condition. *Ibid.*

Where the agent of a foreign corporation, which is charged with contempt, willfully conceals himself to avoid service of an order to show cause, service may be made upon its attorney of record. Eureka Lake & Y. Canal Co. v. Yuba Co. Super. Ct. 116 U. S. 410 (29 L. ed. 671).

Colorado.

The State may prescribe the terms upon which a foreign corporation shall be allowed to carry on its business in the State. Cooper Mfg. Co. v. Ferguson, 113 U. S. 727 (28 L. ed. 1137).

The carrying on of business in the State by a foreign corporation without the filing of the certificate and the appointment of an agent as required by the statute is forbidden. *Ibid.*

But the making in Colorado of one contract by

See also 34 L. R. A. 466; 36 L. R. A. 271.

jury as to whether the documents were received or not.

7. A special finding by a jury that notice and proofs of loss sent by mail were received within sixty days, the time limited by the policy, is sufficiently definite without stating the exact day.

(May 13, 1890.)

APPEAL by defendant from a judgment of the District Court for Polk County in favor of plaintiff in an action to recover the amount alleged to be due upon a policy of fire insurance. *Affirmed.*

Statement by **Given,** *J.:*

Action to recover upon a policy of insurance against loss or damage by fire. The petition shows that defendant issued to plaintiff a policy upon property in Pennsylvania, insuring him against loss or damage by fire, for which he paid the premium; that while said policy was in full force the property was totally destroyed by fire, of which he gave notice and proofs of loss as required. The defendant answered in two counts, denying generally in the first, and alleging in the second that it is a corporation organized under the laws of Iowa, with its principal place of business at Des Moines; that it had not, and was not, for want of sufficient capital stock, entitled to qualify under the laws of Pennsylvania to do business in that State, and had no office or agent in that State, and was not soliciting or doing business therein, when said policy was issued, all of which the plaintiff well knew; that said policy was issued in violation of the laws of Pennsylvania, and therefore void.

The requirements of the laws of Pennsylvania, as set out, are "that, before any insurance company not of that State shall be permitted to transact any insurance business within the State of Pennsylvania, or to issue any policies of insurance upon property within said State, either by itself or agents, a certificate must be obtained of the insurance commissioner of said State certifying that it has so complied with the laws of Pennsylvania, and is authorized to transact such business within the State; that any company, not of said State, that shall do an insurance business within said State without having first qualified itself as provided, and without first receiving the certificate required, shall pay a fine and penalty for such offense to said State." The plaintiff demurred to said second count on the following grounds: (1) The defendant is estopped from alleging its want of authority to do business in the State of Pennsylvania; (2) The statute of Pennsylvania does not render the contract of insurance referred to void; (3) The said count shows that the defendant is liable to a penalty for doing an unauthorized business in the State of Pennsylvania, but shows no defense to the claim of the plaintiff herein; (4)

---

an Ohio corporation does not constitute carrying on a business. *Ibid.*

Where the Constitution and statutes provide that foreign corporations shall make and file a certificate designating an authorized agent in the State, residing at its principal place of business, upon whom process may be served, a certificate is in substantial conformity which designates the "general manager" residing at its principal place of business as agent, without giving any particular name. Goodwin v. Colorado Mortgage Invest. Co. 110 U. S. 1 (28 L. ed. 47).

The fact that a foreign corporation has not filed its certificate of incorporation within the State, as required by statute, will not prevent it from bringing a suit within the State, either in the state or federal court. Haley Livestock Co. v. Routt Co. 2 Denver Legal News, 275.

Connecticut.

Stock of a foreign corporation pledged with a citizen of this State is not subject to foreign attachment or garnishment. Winslow v. Fletcher, 2 New Eng. Rep. 322, 53 Conn. 390.

District of Columbia.

A corporation doing business in a foreign territory consents to be sued there. Baltimore & O. R. Co. v. Harris, 79 U. S. 12 Wall. 65 (20 L. ed. 354).

Acts of Congress made the Baltimore & Ohio Railroad Company suable in the District of Columbia. *Ibid.*

The law of Virginia limiting a corporation to the bounds of the State, in performing its functions, could only prevent it from making new contracts subsequent to the separation, but could not release it from contracts in the District of Columbia made before the separation. Korn v. Mutual Assur. Society, 10 U. S. 6 Cranch, 192 (3 L. ed. 195).

A decree of the Virginia Court of Chancery, transferring property of a corporation to trustees, is recognized by the Supreme Court of the District of Columbia under the doctrine of comity. Glenn v. Dodge (D. C.) 3 Cent. Rep. 283.

Florida.

In the absence of prohibitory legislation individual citizens cannot complain because a foreign corporation is doing business in the State. Pensacola Teleg. Co. v. W. U. Teleg. Co. 96 U. S. 1 (24 L. ed. 708).

Georgia.

Under the Georgia Constitution, a purchase, by a railway company in Georgia, of the contract to construct the line of a competitive company, and of the securities of such competitive company, with a view to prevent the construction of such competing line, is illegal and void, and all concerned as to assets resulting therefrom are constituted trustees for those whose rights have been invaded. Langdon v. Central R. & Bkg. Co. 2 L. R. A. 120, 37 Fed. Rep. 449.

Illinois.

A State has power to discriminate between her own corporations and those of other States desirous of transacting business within her jurisdiction, and may determine the degree of discrimination subject to the fundamental law of the Union. Ducat v. Chicago, 77 U. S. 10 Wall. 410 (19 L. ed. 972).

The powers of a corporation need not be exercised at any one place in the State. Saint Clara Female Academy v. Sullivan, 4 West. Rep. 114, 116 Ill. 375.

The object of the Illinois Statute was to produce uniformity in the powers, liabilities, duties and restrictions of foreign and domestic corporations of like character, and to bring them all under the influence of the same law. *Ibid.*; Barnes v. Suddard, 4 West. Rep. 136, 117 Ill. 237.

A foreign corporation cannot be incorporated into another corporation of the same name under the laws of another State, although the stock ownership is the same in both States. Drummond

it does not appear that the alleged contract of insurance was made in the State of Pennsylvania, and therefore the laws of Pennsylvania regarding insurance would have no effect; (5) the defendant, having issued to the plaintiff its policy of insurance, cannot now allege a violation of law on its part to avoid its liability under said policy. This demurrer was sustained, and defendant excepted. The case was tried to a jury, the principal contention being as to whether notice and proofs of loss had been given as required. On the trial, defendant excepted to certain rulings admitting and excluding testimony, and to certain instructions. The jury found for the plaintiff, and returned with their general verdict a special finding submitted at defendant's request, and their answer, as follows: "When were the proofs of loss received by the defendant at its office in Des Moines, Iowa?" "Within sixty days from the date of the fire." The defendant moved to set aside the verdict on the grounds of the rulings already stated, and the further ground that the verdict of the jury is contrary to the law and evidence, is the result of passion and prejudice, misconduct of the jury, and that the jury failed to answer special interrogatories by defendant. This motion being overruled, judgment was entered upon the verdict, to all of which defendant excepted, and from which it appeals.

Messrs. **Read & Read,** for appellant:

It is within the province of each State to determine for itself whether a foreign corporation shall be admitted to do business within the State, and to prescribe the terms and conditions upon which such permission shall be given.

Paul v. *Virginia,* 75 U. S. 8 Wall. 168 (19 L. ed. 357); *Bank of Augusta* v. *Earle,* 38 U. S. 13 Pet. 538 (10 L. ed. 283); *Ducat* v. *Chicago,* 77 U. S. 10 Wall. 410 (19 L. ed. 972).

A contract founded on an act prohibited by the Statute is void and the law will not lend its aid to either party, either for its enforcement or the recovery of damages for its breach.

Bishop, Cont. § 547; *Nellis* v. *Clark,* 4 Hill, 424; *Morck* v. *Abel,* 3 Bos. & P. 35; *Staples* v. *Gould,* 5 Sandf. 411; *Camden* v. *Anderson,* 1 Bos. & P. 272; *Buxton* v. *Hamblen,* 32 Me. 448; *Thorne* v. *Travellers Ins. Co.* 80 Pa. 15; *Brooklyn L. Ins. Co.* v. *Bledsoe,* 52 Ala. 538; *Northwestern Mut. L. Ins. Co.* v. *Elliott,* 5 Fed. Rep. 225; *Lycoming F. Ins. Co.* v. *Wright,* 55 Vt. 526; *Rising Sun Ins. Co.* v. *Slaughter,* 20 Ind. 520; *Cincinnati Mut. Health Assur. Co.* v. *Rosenthal,* 55 Ill. 85; *Re Comstock,* 3 Sawy. 218; *Semple* v. *Bank of British Columbia,* 5 Sawy. 88; *Bank of British Columbia* v. *Page,* 6 Or. 431; *Ætna Ins. Co.* v. *Harvey,* 11 Wis. 394; *Williams* v. *Cheney,* 3 Gray, 215.

This contract, being void under the laws of Pennsylvania, will be held void everywhere.

McDaniel v. *Chicago & N. W. R. Co.* 24 Iowa, 412; Story, Conf. L. § 243 *et seq.*

Where the statute is prohibitory, the con-

Tobacco Co. v. Randle, 2 West. Rep. 91, 114 Ill. 412.

In such case, however, where no injury is shown, injunction will not lie. *Ibid.*

Withdrawing the inhibition of a foreign corporation to take mortgages does not impair the obligation of the contract as to an existing mortgage, even as to one having a subsequent lien on the land. Gross v. United States Mortgage Co. 108 U. S. 477 (27 L. ed. 795).

Whether the power of a foreign corporation is exceeded in purchasing land is a question between the corporation and the State only, and cannot be raised in ejectment by an individual. Shope and Magruder, *JJ.*, dissent. Barnes v. Suddard, 4 West. Rep. 184, 117 Ill. 237.

Indiana.

A railroad corporation of one State does not become a citizen of another by extending its road into the latter with permission, unless the statute giving permission must necessarily be construed as creating a new corporation. Pennsylvania R. Co. v. St. Louis, A. & T. H. R. Co. 118 U. S. 290 (30 L. ed. 83).

A complaint by a foreign corporation in a suit upon a note executed to it in this State need not allege that it has complied with the statute in relation to the duties of its agents doing business in this State before entering upon their agency. Sprague v. Cutler & S. Lumber Co. 3 West. Rep. 649, 106 Ind. 242.

Iowa.

The statute requiring certain foreign corporations desiring to do business in this State to become domesticated and submit to the jurisdiction of the state courts to the exclusion of the federal courts, is not, when applied to foreign railroads, repugnant to the constitutional provision as to impairing the obligations of contracts, nor to the commercial clause of the Federal Constitution, nor to the 14th Amendment thereof; nor is it an interference with the jurisdiction of the federal courts. Goodrel v. Kreichbaum, 70 Iowa, 362.

But a statute whose sole object is to require of a foreign corporation to stipulate not to remove suits into the federal court as a condition of a permit to do business within the State is void. Barron v. Burnside, 121 U. S. 186 (30 L. ed. 915).

The fact that the chief officers of a corporation come into the State with some of its property for advertisement and exhibition does not bring that corporation into the State as an inhabitant. Carpenter v. Westinghouse Air-Brake Co. 32 Fed. Rep. 434.

Louisiana.

A constitutional requirement of a foreign corporation, so far as it interposes a restriction on navigation, is void. New Orleans & M. Packet Co. v. James, 32 Fed. Rep. 21.

Maryland.

A corporation created in one State may exercise within another State the general powers conferred by its own charter and permitted by the laws of its own State not inconsistent with the laws and policy of the other State. Day v. Postal Teleg. Co. 6 Cent. Rep. 441, 66 Md. 354.

So foreign corporations may acquire and hold property in this State necessary to the prosecution and conduct of their business in this State. *Ibid.*

And their creditors in their own State may avail themselves of any of their assets found in this State, which equity will protect and make available. *Ibid.*

Massachusetts.

A State may make a corporation of another State, as there organized and conducted, a corporation of its own *quoad* any property within its territorial jurisdiction. Graham v. Boston, H. & E. R. Co. 118 U. S. 161 (30 L. ed. 196).

A company made up of distinct corporations chartered by different States, which is practically

tract is illegal and not enforcible by either party.

2 Wood, Fire Ins. § 521; *Thorne* v. *Travellers Ins. Co.* and *Rising Sun Ins. Co.* v. *Slaughter*, *supra; Franklin Ins. Co.* v. *Louisville & A. Packet Co.* 9 Bush, 590.

Forwarding proofs of loss through the mails is not sufficient.

Susquehanna Mut. F. Ins. Co. v. *Tunkhannock Toy Co.* 97 Pa. 424; *Hodgkins* v. *Montgomery Co. Mut. Ins. Co.* 34 Barb. 213; *Plath* v. *Minnesota Farmers Mut. F. Ins. Asso.* 23 Minn. 479.

Messrs. **Phillips & Day,** also for appellant:

Where both parties to a contract have sought to circumvent and have aided in violating the law, no reason can be given for refusing to enforce the contract at the instance of one party which does not equally demand that it shall not be enforced at the instance of the other party. The law must enforce the contract at the instance of either party, or must refuse all recognition of, and deny all relief to, both parties. To enforce the contract at the behest of either party is simply to ignore the law, and render its inhibitions a nullity.

See *Thorne* v. *Travellers Ins. Co* 80 Pa. 15; *Rising Sun Ins. Co.* v. *Slaughter*. 20 Ind. 520; *Buxton* v. *Hamblen*, 32 Me. 448; *Camden* v. *Anderson*, 1 Bos. & P. 272; *Re Comstock*, 3 Sawy. 218; *Semple* v. *Bank of British Columbia*, 5 Sawy. 88; *Bank of British Columbia* v. *Page*, 6 Or. 431; *Nellis* v. *Clark*, 20 Wend. 24; *Staples* v. *Gould*, 5 Sandf. 411; *Morck* v. *Abel*, 3 Bos. & P. 35; *Nellis* v. *Clark*, 4 Hill, 424; *Bloxsome* v. *Williams*, 3 Barn. & C. 232; *Roys* v. *Johnson*, 7 Gray, 162.

Messrs. **Cummins & Wright,** for appellee:

Where statutes contain no absolute prohibition, but provide a penalty for the doing of the act, a contract made in violation of the terms of the statute is not necessarily invalid, but the only effect is to compel the payment, by the party, of the penalty prescribed.

Hill v. *Smith*, Morris (Iowa) 70; *Pangborn* v. *Westlake*, 36 Iowa, 546; *Tootle* v. *Taylor*, 64 Iowa, 629; *Fergusson* v. *Norman*, 5 Bing. N. C. 76; *Harris* v. *Runnels*, 53 U. S. 12 How. 79 (13 L. ed. 901); *Fackler* v. *Ford*, 65 U. S. 24 How. 322 (16 L. ed. 690); *Oneida Bank* v. *Ontario Bank*, 21 N. Y. 490; *Strong* v. *Darling*, 9 Ohio, 201; *Geer* v. *Putnam*, 10 Mass. 312; *Dowell* v. *Appelgate*, 7 Fed. Rep. 881; *Union Nat. Bank* v. *Matthews*, 98 U. S. 621 (25 L. ed. 188); *Genesee Nat. Bank* v. *Whitney*, 103 U. S. 99 (26 L. ed. 443); *Fortier* v. *New Orleans Nat. Bank*, 112 U. S. 439 (28 L. ed. 764); *Milford* v. *Worcester*, 7 Mass. 48; Sedgwick, Stat. and Const. L. 73; *Ganser* v. *Fireman's F. Ins. Co.* 34 Minn. 373.

A foreign insurance company doing business in a State is estopped from saying that it was doing business contrary to the law.

Germania F. Ins. Co. v. *Curran*, 8 Kan. 9;

---

one corporation with a capital stock a unit, and with one set of shareholders and one board of directors, although as to either of the States it is governed by the laws of that State, has a domicil in each State and may hold meetings therein and transact corporate business in each State. *Ibid.*

The statute providing that conveyances or mortgages of corporate realty must be authorized by vote of stockholders at a meeting called for that purpose, does not apply to foreign corporations. Saltmarsh v. Spaulding, 6 New Eng. Rep. 598, 147 Mass. 224.

Where directors of a foreign corporation are authorized by the statutes of the State of its creation to mortgage its realty, a mortgage here in the usual form of a mortgage of this State is valid. *Ibid.*

Michigan.

A certificate of service by the proper officer on the agent of a foreign corporation is sufficient prima facie evidence that the agent represented the company in the business; but this may be rebutted. St. Clair v. Cox, 106 U. S. 350 (27 L. ed. 222).

Where the statute authorizes such service it is essential, to support the jurisdiction, to render a personal judgment that somewhere in the record it is said the corporation was engaged in business in that State. *Ibid.*

Minnesota.

A foreign corporation is not made domestic by a state statute authorizing it to operate roads in the State provided it shall be deemed a domestic corporation in all proceedings arising in that State. Chicago, M. & St. P. R. Co. v. Becker, 32 Fed. Rep. 849.

Iowa railway companies accepting the provisions of the statutes of this State permitting them to extend their roads into this State, are required to file articles of association with the secretary of state, and pay the fee prescribed by statute. State v. Sioux City & N. R. Co. (Minn.) Feb. 17, 1890.

Mississippi.

A corporation of one State, when operating a road in another State as lessee, subjects itself, as to that road, to such local legislation as would have been applicable to the lessor had no lease been made. Stone v. Illinois Cent. R. Co. ("Railroad Commission Cases") 116 U. S. 347 (29 L. ed. 650).

Missouri.

A corporation of one State, doing business in another, is suable where its business is done, if the laws make provision to that effect. St. Louis Wire-Mill Co. v. Consolidated Barb-Wire Co. 32 Fed. Rep. 802.

Montana.

Foreign corporations are not prohibited from doing business in Montana. Garfield, M. & M. Co. v. Hammer, 6 Mont. 53.

The prohibition in the Montana Statute against any foreign corporation doing business in the Territory without complying with the terms of the statute does not abridge the right of the foreign corporation to sue. Powder River Cattle Co. v. Custer Co. (Mont.) 22 Pac. Rep. 383.

And an action by it to recover back taxes paid by compulsion is not an action based upon any act or contract of the corporation, within the prohibition of a statute against doing business in the Territory. *Ibid.*

Nebraska.

The Constitution denies to a foreign railroad company the right of eminent domain, until it has become a body corporate under the laws of Nebraska; but this does not prohibit its consolidation with a domestic corporation and thereby becoming itself domestic. State v. Chicago, B. & Q. R. Co. 3 L. R. A. 564, 25 Neb. 156.

A foreign and nonresident railroad corporation under the constitutional prohibition cannot acquire a right of way indirectly through a Nebraska

Clay F. & M. Ins. Co. v. *Huron S. & L. Mfg. Co.* 31 Mich. 346; *Ehrman* v. *Teutonia Ins. Co.* 1 Fed. Rep. 471; *Union Mut. L. Ins. Co.* v. *McMillen*, 24 Ohio St. 67; *Columbus Ins. Co.* v. *Walsh*, 18 Mo. 229; *Hartford L. S. Ins. Co.* v. *Matthews*, 102 Mass. 221; *Washington Co. Ins. Co.* v. *Colton*, 26 Conn. 46; *Gentry* v. *Conn. Mut. L. Ins. Co.* 15 Mo. App. 215; *Columbia F. Ins. Co.* v. *Kinyon*, 37 N. J. L. 33; *Manhattan Ins. Co.* v. *Ellis*, 32 Ohio St. 388; *Behler* v. *German Mut. F. Ins. Co.* 68 Ind. 347; *Cincinnati Mut. H. Assur. Co.* v. *Rosenthal*, 55 Ill. 90; *Swan* v. *Watertown F. Ins. Co.* 96 Pa. 37; *Watertown F. Ins. Co.* v. *Simons*, 96 Pa. 520.

If this contract is valid in Iowa, the laws of Pennsylvania can in no manner determine its validity.

Story, Conf. L. §§ 242, 296; *Davis* v. *Bronson*, 6 Iowa, 410; *Smith* v. *McLean*, 24 Iowa, 329; *Arnold* v. *Potter*, 22 Iowa, 198; *Butters* v. *Olds*, 11 Iowa, 1; *Savary* v. *Savary*, 3 Iowa, 272; *United States Bank* v. *Donnally*, 33 U. S. 8 Pet. 361 (8 L. ed. 974); *Andrews* v. *Herrot*, 4 Cow. 508, and *note; Flanagan* v. *Packard*, 41 Vt. 561; *Lamb* v. *Bowser*, 7 Biss. 315.

Our policy was an Iowa contract, because dated there, and because its existence dated from the time it was mailed.

Lamb v. *Bowser*, 7 Biss. 372; *Columbia F. Ins. Co.* v. *Kinyon*, 37 N. J. L. 33; *Hyde* v. *Goodnow*, 3 N. Y. 267; *People* v. *Imlay*, 20 Barb. 68; *Huntley* v. *Merrill*, 32 Barb. 626; *Williams* v. *Cheney*, 8 Gray, 215; *Hacheny* v. *Leary*, 12 Or. 40; *Hartford L. S. Ins. Co.* v. *Matthews*, 102 Mass. 221.

Given, J., delivered the opinion of the court:

The questions raised and argued on the demurrer may be resolved into the single inquiry, Is the contract of insurance sued upon void? It is alleged that it is void because the defendant had not and was not entitled to qualify under the laws of Pennsylvania, to contract insurance upon property in that State at the time this policy was issued, and because the plaintiff received it knowing that fact. For the purposes of the demurrer these allegations are to be taken as true, and we are to say whether, being true, they render the policy void. Appellant's contention is that the contract was made and policy issued and accepted, in violation of the laws of Pennsylvania, as set out in the answer, and that, the plaintiff having received the policy knowing that fact, the parties are *in pari delicto*, and the law will not enforce the contract at the suit of either. Appellee contends that the policy was issued and is payable in Iowa, and its validity is therefore to be determined by the laws of Iowa, and that the Statute set out did not forbid the issuing the policy in suit, nor make the same void, but simply declares the Company liable to a fine for issuing it.

2. It does not appear from the answer, nor from it and the petition, where the contract was made, premium paid or policy delivered, nor where it is payable. From the facts that the Company is of Iowa, and the insured property in Pennsylvania, we may infer the contract to have been made in either State as readily as the other. Such being the state of the

---

corporation. Koenig v. Chicago, B. & Q. R. Co. (Neb.) Oct. 23, 1889.

The title of a foreign corporation which purchased real estate at a judicial sale in Nebraska while Neb. Laws 1887, chap. 65, § 1, was in force, is valid against everyone but the State, and can be devested only by proceedings brought by the State for that purpose. Carlow v. Aultman (Neb.) Feb. 4, 1890.

A Statute of Limitations begins to run, as against a foreign corporation, from the time it has a person within the State upon whom process to commence a suit may be served. United States Exp. Co. v. Ware, 87 U. S. 20 Wall. 543 (22 L. ed. 422).

New Jersey.

It is just and proper that foreign corporations should be subject to the legitimate police regulations of the State, and should have, if required, an agent in the State to accept service of process when sued for acts done or contracts made therein. Stockton v. Baltimore & N. Y. R. Co. 1 Inters. Com. Rep. 411, 32 Fed. Rep. 9.

But in the pursuit of business authorized by the federal government they cannot be obstructed by any State. *Ibid.*

Where a foreign corporation, without authority, has taken a lease of real estate, it will be estopped from pleading *ultra vires* in an action for the rent. Camden & A. R. Co. v. May's Landing & E. H. C. R. Co. 4 Cent. Rep. 303, 48 N. J. L. 530.

New York.

A foreign corporation within a State under an annual license is subject to the power of the State to change at any time the conditions of admission for the future. It is not within the jurisdiction of the State so as to be within the equal protection of the laws under the Fourteenth Amendment, in respect to an imposition upon it of unequal burdens as compared with foreign corporations of other States. Philadelphia Fire Asso. v. New York, 119 U. S. 110 (30 L. ed. 342).

A corporation with capacity to contract may contract outside the State, unless the law of the other State forbids. Day v. Ogdensburgh & L. C. R. Co. 9 Cent. Rep. 456, 107 N. Y. 129; Saltmarsh v. Spaulding, 6 New Eng. Rep. 593, 147 Mass. 224.

A foreign corporation may enforce the covenant made by a person, to the effect that he will not engage in trade within a certain district. Diamond Match Co. v. Roeber, 9 Cent. Rep. 151, 106 N. Y. 473.

Ohio.

The right of the patent owner to permit or license the use of the invention is not a creature of franchise or statute, but of the common law; and in exercising this common-law right of licensing others to use its patent, the corporation owner is no more nationalized or domesticated than a private owner would be under the same circumstances. United States v. Am. Bell Teleph. Co. 29 Fed. Rep. 17.

Pennsylvania.

The Legislature may prescribe the conditions upon which a foreign corporation shall transact business in the State. List v. Com. 10 Cent. Rep. 586, 118 Pa. 322; Insurance Co. of North America v. Brim, 9 West. Rep. 834, 111 Ind. 281.

It may exclude a foreign corporation entirely, or restrict its business to particular localities. Pembina Consolidated Silver Min. & M. Co. v. Pennsylvania, 125 U. S. 181 (31 L. ed. 650).

The only limitation upon the power of a State to exact conditions allowing a foreign corporation to do business is where it is engaged in interstate commerce. *Ibid.*; State v. Woodruff S. & P. Coach Co. 18 West. Rep. 811, 114 Ind. 155.

pleadings, we are not called upon to determine what effect the law of Pennsylvania would have upon this policy as an Iowa contract.

3. The principle that contracts made in violation of law are void is too well established to require citations. "The well-settled general rule is that, when a statute prohibits or attaches a penalty to the doing of an act, the act is void, and will not be enforced, nor will the law assist one to recover money or property which he has expended in the unlawful execution of it. Or, in other words, a penalty implies a prohibition though there are no prohibitory words in the statute, and the prohibition makes the act illegal and void. . . . But, notwithstanding this general rule, it must be apparent to every legal mind that, when a statute annexes a penalty for the doing of an act, it does not always imply such a prohibition as will render the act void." *Pangborn* v. *Westlake*, 36 Iowa, 548.

The law of Pennsylvania, as set out, provides that no insurance company not of that State shall insure property therein unless it has a certain amount of capital stock, has complied with certain requirements and has obtained a certificate from the insurance commissioner that it is qualified to do business in that State, and that any such company that shall do business in that State without having first qualified itself, and without first having received a certificate, as prescribed, from the insurance commissioner, "shall pay a fine and penalty for such offense." The evident purpose of such a law is the protection of those paying for insurance upon property in that State. The prohibition and penalty are against the company only. No duty is required of the insured, and no act upon his part expressly prohibited. There is nothing in the law declaring what effect it shall have upon policies issued and accepted as this is alleged to have been. A number of cases are cited by appellant where, in actions brought by the insurance company to enforce rights under the contract of insurance, it was held that statutes similar to that set out were prohibitory and the contracts void; but in none of those cases it is held that they are void as to the assured.

The Manistee, 5 Bliss, 383, is a case wherein the Statute of Illinois was under consideration. That Statute required foreign insurance companies to produce certain statements, and to procure authority from the auditor of state to transact business within the State, and declared it unlawful for any agent to do business without having first complied with those laws. It was provided that, upon conviction for violating these requirements, punishment by fine or imprisonment, or both, might be imposed. The court says: "Those Statute Laws do not declare void policies issued by foreign companies, through a local agent, in disregard or violation of them. The object of these Statutes was for the security of citizens doing business with such companies, by bringing them as near as possible to local corporations, and also as a provision for revenue. Where a statute prohibits or annexes a penalty to its commission, the act is made unlawful; but it does not follow that the unlawfulness of the act was meant by the Legislature to avoid a contract

---

The office-license tax upon foreign corporations, imposed by the Act of June 7, 1879, is not in violation of the Federal Constitution or the Constitution of Pennsylvania, and is consequently valid. Norfolk & W. R. Co. v. Com. 5 Cent. Rep. 240, 114 Pa. 256.

Nor does it conflict with the commercial clause of the Federal Constitution, or with the 14th Amendment. Pembina Consolidated Silver Min. & M. Co. v. Pennsylvania, *supra*.

Under the Act prohibiting a foreign corporation from holding real estate, a deed of real estate to a foreign corporation is not void, but grantee takes the land subject to the State's right of escheat. Hickory Farm Oil Co. v. Buffalo, N. Y. & P. R. Co. 32 Fed. Rep. 22.

The State alone can take advantage of the legal disability of a foreign corporation to hold real estate. *Ibid.*

Trustees of a corporation in the State of New York can purchase or hold real estate in the State of Pennsylvania, until some act shall be done by the Commonwealth of Pennsylvania, according to its own laws, to devest that right, and to vest the estate in itself. Runyan v. Coster, 39 U. S. 14 Pet. 122 (10 L. ed. 382).

The statutes providing that where a conveyance has been made by a foreign corporation to a domestic corporation before escheat the title shall be indefeasible as to the State, does not sanction the purchase in trust for the foreign corporation; nor does the Act to aid corporations in the development of coal, etc., authorize such purchase. Com. v. New York, L. E. & W. R. Co. (Pa.) 5 Cent. Rep. 743.

A purchase by a foreign corporation of the capital stock of a Pennsylvania corporation, as a device to enable it to hold real estate in Pennsylvania, is a violation of the law. *Ibid.*

Texas.

The failure of a foreign corporation to procure a permit to do business does not prevent it from asserting rights and recovering property in the state court. Texas Land & Mortgage Co. v. Worsham (Tex.) March 18, 1890.

Tennessee.

A mere license to enter a State, given to a railroad company of another State, does not create a new corporation. Goodlett v. Louisville & N. R. Co. 122 U. S. 391 (30 L. ed. 1230).

The provisions of the Tennessee Code regulating the mode in which corporations may be sued, apply equally to domestic and foreign corporations having an office or agency and a resident local agent in the county in which the suit is brought. Cumberland Teleph. & Teleg. Co. v. Turner (Tenn.) Dec. 5, 1889.

The president of a foreign corporation, who is not made a party defendant to a bill, but only mentioned as the principal officer of the corporation for the service of process, and upon whom the process against the company is served as such, is not a party to the suit, and cannot demur to the bill. Peters v. Neely, 16 Lea, 275.

The fact that a corporation was organized under the laws of another State does not, where its president was a party to the litigation, relieve it from the rule which governs purchasers of property pending litigation about the title. Whiteside v. Haselton, 110 U. S. 296 (28 L. ed. 152).

Vermont.

In the Act prohibiting a company from doing business in the State unless it was "responsible by the laws of the State" in which it was situated for the neglects of its agents, the word "laws" includes not only statutory, but common, law. Lycoming

made in contravention of it. Where a statute is silent and contains nothing from which the contrary can properly be inferred, a contract in contravention of it is void. But the whole statute must be examined in order to decide whether or not it does contain anything from which the contrary can be properly inferred. There is no penalty pronounced against a person for obtaining a policy from, or doing business with, the company that has not complied with the requirements of those Statutes." *Union Mut. L. Ins. Co.* v. *McMillen*, 24 Ohio St. 67, is somewhat in point. That was an action upon a policy of life insurance issued by the plaintiff in error. The company claimed that its failure to comply with a statute similar to that under consideration rendered the policy void. The court says: "Whether the Statute was meant to invalidate policies issued by companies in contravention of its provisions is to be determined from a consideration of the Statute as a whole. The object of the Act is not to make the business of life insurance unlawful. The Statute is designed for the protection of policy holders and others dealing with insurance companies. To this end it is made unlawful for persons to act on behalf of such companies until the provisions of the Statute have been complied with. But we do not think it was intended to devolve on persons dealing with the companies the duty and risk of ascertaining whether they had complied with the Statute. On the contrary, it seems to have been the intention of the Legislature to rely on the penalties imposed as sufficient to insure such compliance."

In *Pangborn* v. *Westlake, supra*, the question was whether a contract for the sale of a lot in a plat that had not been recorded was void because of the Statute providing that any person who shall dispose of, or offer for sale, any lot in any town or addition until the plat was acknowledged and recorded, shall forfeit $50 for each lot sold or disposed of. This Statute is similar in several respects to that in question. It is quite as prohibitory. It is addressed to the seller alone. It is for the protection of the purchasers, and imposes no duty upon or prohibition against them. In passing upon the question, this court said: "We are therefore brought to the true test, which is that while, as a general rule, a penalty implies a prohibition, yet the courts will always look to the language of the statute, the subject matter of it, the wrong or evil which it seeks to remedy or prevent and the purpose sought to be accomplished in its enactment; and if, from all these, it is manifest that it was not intended to imply a prohibition, or to render the prohibited act void, the courts will so hold, and construe the statute accordingly." See also *Hill* v. *Smith*, Morris (Iowa) 70; *Tootle* v. *Taylor*, 64 Iowa, 629.

It is argued that to hold this contract not prohibited is to defeat the purposes of the law; that it will admit foreign companies to do business subject only to such fines as may be assessed. In view of the language of the law as stated, the absence of express prohibition, and the evident purpose to protect the insured, we are clearly of the opinion that it was not intended to render contracts such as that in suit void. To so hold does not necessarily admit foreign companies to do business in that State in disregard of its laws. The power of the courts is ample to compel, by fine and otherwise, compliance with the law of the State. The contract being valid, the matter demurred to is no defense, and the question of estoppel does not arise. We think the demurrer was properly sustained.

4. On the trial the plaintiff was permitted to testify that he received the policy through Rhem & Van Deinse, of Indianapolis, Ind.; that he sent notice by mail, and proofs of loss, to them; and that after sixty days he drew on the defendant, and the draft was returned protested. Anton J. Van Deinse was also permitted to testify, over defendant's objection, to the receipt of the notice and proofs of loss from the plaintiff, and that they were forwarded by mail to the defendant. While it is true that Rhem & Van Deinse were not the agents of the defendant, yet this testimony only tended to show how and when the notice and proofs were transmitted, and was properly admitted, if such notice and proofs may be given in the manner stated. That they were transmitted through Rhem & Van Deinse is immaterial except as it tends to show whether the defendant received them, and when.

5. The court instructed the jury that, if Van Deinse mailed the notice and proofs of loss, properly addressed, to the defendant, the presumption is that they were duly received, but

---

F. Ins. Co. v. Wright, 5 New Eng. Rep. 640, 60 Vt. 515.

The capacity of a British corporation to hold lands in this country was not affected by the Revolution. Society for Propagation of Gospel v. New Haven, 21 U. S. 8 Wheat. 464 (5 L. ed. 662).

Virginia.

States may exclude a foreign corporation entirely, or they may exact security for the performance of its contracts. Paul v. Virginia, 75 U. S. 8 Wall. 168 (19 L. ed. 357).

West Virginia.

A corporation exists only in contemplation of law and by force of law, and can have no legal existence beyond the State or sovereignty by which it is created. Reco v. Newport News & M. V. Co. 8 L. R. A. 572, 32 W. Va. 164.

A corporation created under the laws of the State of New York is sufficiently proved in this State by the production of a copy of the certificate of its incorporation, properly attested and further authenticated by the clerk of the court, in the county where the business is to be carried on, and under the seal of said court in the manner prescribed by § 20, chap. 130, Code. Singer Mfg. Co. v. Bennett, 28 W. Va. 17.

The Code prescribing that foreign corporations shall comply with certain regulations before holding property or doing business does not make contracts made here before such compliance absolutely void and unenforceable. Toledo Tie & L. Co. v. Thomas (W. Va.) 11 S. E. Rep. 37.

If the statute imposes a penalty upon the corporation for failing to comply with such prerequisites, such penalty will be deemed exclusive of any others. *Ibid.*

One State cannot, by mere legislative declaration, deprive the foreign corporation of its right to resort to the federal courts in cases where such right is conferred by the Constitution and laws of the United States. Reco v. Newport News & M. V. Co. 8 L. R. A. 572, and *note*, 32 W. Va. 164.

that this presumption may be overcome by evidence. Appellant concedes that such is the rule as to the notice, but contends that, as the plaintiff had sixty days in which to furnish proofs of loss, he should be held to proof of their actual delivery. We see no reason for the distinction. The plaintiff was under the same obligation to furnish both.

Hodgkins v. *Montgomery Co. Mut. Ins. Co.*, 34 Barb. 213, is relied upon. That case is not in point, as it turned upon certain express provisions in the policy not found in this. The court instructed the jury that they must find that the notice of the loss was given within a reasonable time. Appellant contends that this was erroneous, as the policy requires that it be given forthwith. We think the terms are so nearly synonymous that no prejudice could have resulted therefrom. We see no error in the instructions in either of the respects alleged. Some objection is made to the sufficiency of the proofs of loss claimed to have been forwarded, but, as no such objection appears to have been made in the lower court, it cannot be considered here.

6. In addition to the alleged errors already considered, it is urged that the court erred in not granting a new trial on the grounds that the verdict is not supported by the testimony, and that the special finding was not properly answered. The fact in question was whether the notice and proofs of loss had been furnished as required. For the plaintiff, there was the testimony of Van Deinse as to addressing, stamping and mailing them, and the presumption that arises therefrom. Against this, there was the testimony of the defendant's officers and clerks who received its mail that no such documents were received. It was properly left to the jury to say whether the documents were received, and they have found that they were. There is surely evidence upon which to so find, and therefore the verdict should not be disturbed on that ground. The special finding was answered as definitely as it could be, under the testimony. There was nothing from which to fix the precise day upon which the proofs of loss were received except as it might be inferred from the time and place they were mailed. It was important to decide whether they were received within the sixty days, and this the jury could and did find as a fact from the testimony. They could not have found with the same certainty the precise day, nor was it material that they should. Our conclusion is that *the judgment of the District Court should be affirmed.*

MASSACHUSETTS SUPREME JUDICIAL COURT.

Patrick CURRAN
v.
CITY OF BOSTON.

(......Mass.......)

A city is not liable for injuries resulting from the negligence of officers engaged in the management of a workhouse which it has established purely for the public service and to assist in the performance of its public duty of supporting paupers and criminals, and who also conduct the work incidental to the maintenance of the institution and to the employment of its inmates, although the establishment was voluntarily erected and maintained under legislative permission; and the fact that some revenue is derived by the city from the labor of the inmates is immaterial if the institution is not conducted with a view to pecuniary profit and none is in fact obtained. This is especially true where such officers are appointed and directed by an independent board which is in no way the agent of the city.

(May 23, 1890.)

EXCEPTIONS by plaintiff to a judgment of the Superior Court for Suffolk County (Barker, *J.*), entered upon a verdict directed for defendant in an action brought to recover damages for personal injuries alleged to have resulted from the negligence of defendant's servants. *Overruled.*

The case sufficiently appears in the opinion.

Mr. **E. Greenhood** for plaintiff.

Mr. **R. W. Nason** for defendant.

Devens, *J.*, delivered the opinion of the court:

The plaintiff was an inmate of the workhouse or house of industry belonging to the City of Boston, situate on Deer Island, having been convicted of a misdemeanor and having been legally sentenced to confinement there. He was injured while engaged in unloading coal, and it must be presumed was prepared to prove that he, himself, was in the exercise of due care and that the officers and servants employed in this institution were negligent. The single question presented is, whether these officers and servants engaged in conducting the work incidental to the maintenance of the workhouse of the City and to the employment of the inmates thereof (from whose employment it derives a certain amount of revenue), such officers and servants being also engaged in the management of the City's property employed in the business of the workhouse, are agents of the City for whose negligence in the performance of their duties the City is responsible.

It is a general principle that municipal corporations are not liable to private actions for omissions or neglect in the performance of a

---

NOTE.—While a municipal corporation is liable for its own negligence, it is not liable for the negligence of its agents or licensees; nor is it liable for the malfeasance or negligence of its officers or employés acting under ordinances. See Culver v. Streator, 6 L. R. A. 270, 130 Ill. 238.

Its liability depends on the statute. See *notes* to Chope v. Eureka (Cal.) 4 L. R. A. 325; Lincoln v. Boston (Mass.) 3 L. R. A. 257; Robinson v. Rohr (Wis.) 2 L. R. A. 366; Hines v. Charlotte (Mich.) 1 L. R. A. 844.

corporate duty imposed upon them by law, or that of their servants engaged therein, where such city derives no benefit therefrom in its corporate capacity, unless such action is given by statute. *Oliver* v. *Worcester*, 102 Mass. 489, and cases cited.

The contention of the plaintiff is that the case at bar is distinguishable because, as a mere volunteer, the City has devoted property intended mainly for corporate purposes to other purposes for its own advantage, as in *Oliver* v. *Worcester, supra;* that it has voluntarily undertaken a work partially for the public good with a view to its own advantage and to relieve itself from burdens peculiar to itself, and that it has embarked in an enterprise, partly commercial, from which it receives a partial remuneration for its expenditures out of a special class in the community so that the entire expense of conducting the workhouse is not met by taxation.

While the workhouse was maintained primarily by the City at its own expense, it was not by law compelled to establish this institution. The plaintiff's argument concedes that when established its officers and servants were not selected by the City but by the board of directors of public institutions; but it urges that they are still to be deemed the agents of the City, as the act of establishing such an institution is voluntary, and the imposition of the ministerial duties upon such officers is the act of the municipality, and that it is immaterial, therefore, whether the ministerial duties involved in the administration of such an institution are cast by statute upon a board over whose tenure of office the City has no control.

The authority to erect and maintain a workhouse or almshouse, to relieve therein poor and indigent persons, is given by Pub. Stat., chap. 33, § 1; Gen. Stat., chap. 22, § 1. The same section provides that offenders of the class to which plaintiff belonged are to be there maintained when sentenced thereto by proper authority.

Pub. Stat., chap. 207, § 29, provides that such offenders may be sentenced "for a term not exceeding six months to the house of correction or to the house of industry or workhouse within the city or town where the conviction is had, or to the workhouse if any there is in the city or town in which the offender has a legal settlement, if such town is within the county."

There is no imperative direction that the City shall establish a workhouse, but by law it is responsible for all county charges of the County of Suffolk; and if the convict were sentenced to confinement therein, his expenses would necessarily be paid by it. Pub. Stat. chap. 22, § 1.

By the more general law, any city or town which has in the house of correction an inmate having his settlement in such town is liable for the cost of his support. Pub. Stat. chap. 220, § 61.

By the Statute authorizing the erection and maintenance of workhouses by a city, a mode of performing a strictly public duty is provided for, which cannot be of any pecuniary advantage to the cities or towns instituting them. No such case is presented as exists where a city has undertaken to build particular works, as water-works, sewers, etc., and where a city acts as an agency to carry on an enterprise to some extent commercial in its character for the purpose of furnishing conveniences and benefits to such as choose to pay for them. The element of consideration then comes in and in such cases it is usually held that a liability exists on the part of the city for an injury to an individual through negligence in building or maintaining such works. *Tindley* v. *Salem*, 137 Mass. 171; *Child* v. *Boston*, 4 Allen, 41; *Oliver* v. *Worcester, supra; Emery* v. *Lowell*, 104 Mass. 13; *Merrifield* v. *Worcester*, 110 Mass. 216; *Murphy* v. *Lowell*, 124 Mass. 564.

The action of the City in establishing the workhouse was purely for the public service and for the general good in providing for the care and support of offenders for whose maintenance it was responsible. While in some cases the statute enjoins and directs action similar to this, and in others permits it, in either case as there is no element of corporate advantage or of pecuniary profit to the City, it is not to be held responsible because it exercised the option which was given to it to undertake what it did. *Hafford* v. *New Bedford*, 16 Gray, 297; *Fisher* v. *Boston*, 104 Mass. 87.

In *Tindley* v. *Salem, supra*, the cases in regard to the liability of towns for the acts of servants or agents were carefully collected and considered by *Mr. Justice* C. Allen. Referring to the distinction attempted to be drawn between negligence of the servants of a town or city in the performance of a duty imperatively required, and one voluntarily assumed by authority of the statute, he remarks: "This distinction does not affect the resulting liability. There are many provisions of statute by which all municipal corporations must do certain things, and may do certain other things, in each instance with a view solely to the general good. In looking at these provisions in detail, it is impossible to suppose that the Legislature have intended to make the distinction a material one in determining the question of corporate liability to private actions. For example, towns must maintain pounds, guide posts and burial grounds; and may establish and maintain hospitals, workhouses or almshouses," etc. "In all these cases the duty is imposed or the authority conferred for the general benefit. The motive and the object are the same, though in some instances the Legislature determines finally the necessity or expediency, and in others leaves the necessity or expediency to be determined by the towns themselves. But when determined, and when the service has been entered upon, there is no good reason why a liability to a private action should be imposed where a town voluntarily enters upon such a beneficial work, and withheld when it performs the service under the requirement of an imperative law."

We are of opinion, therefore, that the City cannot be held liable upon the ground that the workhouse was established by it voluntarily.

Upon another ground, also, the City cannot be held liable for the alleged negligence of the officers and servants engaged with the plaintiff in the work in doing which he was injured. When the City established the workhouse, the inspection, ordering and government thereof were placed by law in the hands of "the board of directors of public institutions," for the County of Suffolk. This was a board of public officers whom the city council of Boston were required to elect by concurrent vote. While certain powers are given to this board by statute and certain ordinances may be passed by the city council, not inconsistent with the Statute, as to the performance of their duties, it is an independent body, in whom is vested the administration of the public institutions. It is not an agent of the City, nor does it perform any duties as such. Stat. 1857, chap. 35.

As the board is not in any proper sense the agent or servant of the City, those whom it employs cannot be so considered. Nor do we perceive any reason why the City should be held responsible because some revenue is derived from the labor of the inmates. It is required that these inmates should be kept at work, by the Statute, but the institution is not conducted with a view to any pecuniary profit. It is not suggested that the expenses of maintaining the workhouse are met by what is derived from the labor of the inmates or that any profit above them is made. Even if the entire expense is not met by taxation, by reason of the profit thus derived, such profit is purely incidental. The object and purpose of the workhouse, and the conduct of it, are not thus shown to be of the nature of a business. It only appears that as a public institution it is managed in a judicious and economical manner.

It was therefore correctly ruled that the plaintiff could not maintain his action against the City, and that his remedy, if any, was against the officers and servants alleged to be guilty of negligence, by which he claimed to have been injured.

Exceptions overruled.

NEW YORK COURT OF APPEALS.

Pedro MORA Y LEDON *et al.*, *Appts.*,

v.

Frederick C. HAVEMEYER *et al.*, *Respts.*

(......N. Y.......)

1. **The word "shipment"** in a contract purchasing 1,000 tons of sugar "for shipment within thirty days, by sail or steam, seller's option," and providing for marine insurance by the buyers, means the delivery of the sugar within the time required on some vessel destined to the proper port, which the seller has reason to suppose will sail within a reasonable time after shipment, and does not mean a clearance of the vessel as well as putting the goods on board, where there is nothing to indicate that the seller was expected to exercise any control over the clearance of the vessel or of her subsequent management.

2. **Shipment of goods** which do not constitute a full cargo is sufficiently made by placing them on board a vessel bound for the intended port, and engaged in an honest effort to obtain a cargo for such port.

(April 15, 1890.)

APPEAL by plaintiffs from a judgment of the General Term of the Supreme Court, First Department, affirming a judgment of the New York Circuit in favor of defendants in an action brought to recover the contract price for certain sugar alleged to have been sold and delivered to defendants. *Reversed.*

The facts are fully stated in the opinion.

Mr. **Noah Davis**, with *Messrs.* **Arnold & Greene**, for appellants:

The title of the sugar passed to the buyers on delivery of the same to the steamer for transportation, and the execution by the master of "the shipping documents" completed the sale and delivery on the 7th day of March, 1885, two days before the expiration of the thirty days. The shipment was therefore completed within thirty days.

Caulkins v. *Hellman*, 47 N. Y. 452; *Mee* v. *McNider*, 12 Cent. Rep. 776, 109 N. Y. 500.

The word "shipment," when used in connection with a contract of sale and purchase, means the delivery to the master or carrier for transportation, the putting the same on board and the making by the master and delivery to the shipper of a bill of lading or "shipping documents" therefor.

Bowes v. *Shand*, L. R. 2 App. Cas. 455; *Hill* v. *Blake*, 97 N. Y. 221; *Fisher* v. *Minot*, 10 Gray, 260; *Reuter* v. *Sala*, L. R. 4 C. P. Div. 239; *Gibson* v. *Sturge*, 10 Exch. 622, 29 Eng. L. & Eq. 464; *Bohllingk* v. *Inglis*, 3 East, 381; *Stubbs* v. *Lund*, 7 Mass. 453; *Newhall* v. *Vargas*, 13 Me. 105; *Tobias* v. *Lissberger*, 7 Cent. Rep. 728, 105 N. Y. 404.

Mr. **John E. Parsons**, for respondents:

In this case the contract was for the purchase in New York of sugar to be transported by the plaintiffs from Cuba to New York, and there to be delivered to the defendants. In such a case "shipment within thirty days" means that within that time the sugar shall be started by ship from the place from which it is to be transported.

Tobias v. *Lissberger*, 7 Cent. Rep. 728, 105 N. Y. 404; *Pope* v. *Porter*, 8 Cent. Rep. 451, 102 N. Y. 366; *Norrington* v. *Wright*, 115 U. S. 188 (29 L. ed. 366); *Cunningham* v. *Judson*, 1 Cent. Rep. 274, 100 N. Y. 179; *Hill* v. *Blake*, 97 N. Y. 216; *Hoare* v. *Rennie*, 5 Hurlst. & N. 19; *Phillips* v. *Taylor*, 17 Jones & S. 318.

The cases which hold that "shipment" means loading or putting on board will be found to involve either bills of lading or contracts, the context of which shows that that was what was intended by the parties.

Rommel v. *Wingate*, 103 Mass. 327; *Welsh* v. *Gossler*, 89 N. Y. 540; *Sears* v. *Wingate*, 3 Allen, 103; *Shepherd* v. *Naylor*, 5 Gray, 591; *Portland Bank* v. *Stubbs*, 6 Mass. 422; *Bradstreet* v. *Heran*, 2 Blatchf. 116; *Grant* v. *Norway*, 10 C. B. 665; *Lickbarrow* v. *Mason*, 1 H. Bl. 360; *Berkley* v. *Watling*, 7 Ad. & El. 29.

Ruger, *Ch. J.*, delivered the opinion of the court:

The sole question involved in this case is the interpretation to be given to the language "for shipment within thirty days by sail or steam, seller's option," as used in an executory con tract for the sale by the plaintiffs to defendants of 1,000 tons of Cuba Muscovado sugar, upon which the buyers were to provide marine insurance. The contract was made on February 7. 1885, in New York, where the vendees resided, the vendors being residents of Cuba, and the sugar was intended to be shipped from some port in that island to the defendants at New York. The evidence shows that the shipment of the sugar was begun on the steamer Gladiolus at Sagua, in Cuba, on the 5th and completed on the 7th day of March, 1885, when the master of the vessel delivered to the plaintiffs a bill of lading certifying to the shipment "in good order and condition by Messrs. Mora, Ona & Co. (the plaintiffs), for account and risk of Messrs. Havemeyer & Elder (the defendants), on board the Br. str. called the Gladiolus, whereof Sinclair is master, now lying at the Port of Sagua la Grande, Cuba, and bound for New York, . . . fifteen hundred hogsheads of Muscovado sugar."

The steamer did not, in fact, clear from the port until the 18th of March, and arrived in New York on the 17th of the same month.

It further appears that the full capacity of the Gladiolus was 1,500 tons, and freight room to New York for 1,000 tons only was hired of her charterer by the plaintiffs. It also appeared that the vessel was detained by the charterer, without the knowledge or consent of the plaintiffs, so far as appears, at Sagua for six days after the sugar was shipped, seeking for freight to fill out her complement. The sugar and bills of lading were duly tendered to the defendants in New York by the plaintiffs' agents on the day of the arrival of the Gladiolus in that city, and they refused to receive them upon the grounds stated in a letter, of which the following is a copy:

New York, March 17, 1885.

Messrs. Perkins & Welsh, Agts.:

Gentlemen—We beg to inclose draft and documents for the cargo Gladiolus. We decline to accept the cargo, as the terms of the contract were not complied with. The ship should have cleared the 10th inst. at the latest, and was detained seeking cargo much beyond a reasonable time after shipment.

Yours very truly,
Havemeyer & Elder.

Other evidence was given upon the trial, but none which bears upon the point involved in the case. After the evidence was closed, the defendants asked the court to direct a verdict for them, upon the following grounds:

First. That the plaintiffs failed to comply with the contract of sale.

Second. That the contract required shipment within thirty days, and it appears that the sugar was not shipped until after the expiration of that time.

The court granted the motion and the plaintiffs duly excepted thereto. The judgment entered upon this verdict was affirmed at general term, and from that affirmance this appeal is taken. Upon the trial the plaintiffs objected to the direction of a verdict by the court, and if there was any evidence in the case presenting questions of fact, it was error for the trial court to take it from the jury. The motion for a verdict was put by the defendants upon a single ground, viz.: that the evidence did not show a shipment of the sugar by the plaintiffs within thirty days after the date of the contract, and the determination of this appeal depends upon the question whether such shipment was made within the time mentioned.

If the ground stated be literally construed, it is obvious that it has no support in the evidence, for the sugar was concededly shipped within the thirty days. If we refer to the defendants' letter of refusal, we find that the shipment of the sugar within the stipulated time is distinctly conceded; but they claim that the nonperformance of the contract referred to consisted in the fact that the vessel did not sail immediately after the expiration of the thirty days, and the question to be determined is whether the language of the contract required the clearance of the vessel, as well as the loading of the ship, within the stipulated time. This was the ground upon which the trial court based its judgment, and the general term have placed their affirmance substantially upon the same ground. Some allusions are made in the opinion below to the bona fides of the shipment; but that question, if in the case at all, was a disputed question, and could not be made a reason for sustaining a judgment which might otherwise be erroneous. If there was evidence in the case tending to show bad faith on the part of the plaintiffs in making the shipment, it presented a question of fact for the jury, upon which the parties were entitled to take their verdict. We think the language of the contract is not susceptible of the construction given to it by the courts below. This contract, like all others, must be construed with reference to the intent of the parties making it, and if its language is plain and unambiguous, it must be given that construction which the language fairly imports, and the question of its meaning is a question of law for the court. That meaning, we think, is the putting the goods sold on board a vessel bound for New York, with the intent in good faith to have them cleared for the port of destination in the regular course of trade, or in a reasonable time after the shipment.

The appellants claim that the place of delivery for the goods sold under this contract was the sailing port, and that when they were shipped in conformity to the terms of the contract title passed to the vendees, and the goods were thereafter to be transported at their risk. This is claimed to have been indicated, among other provisions, by that requiring the vendees to make marine insurance. *Mee* v. *McNider*, 109 N. Y. 500, 12 Cent. Rep. 776.

It is unnecessary to decide this question as it has no controlling influence over the signification of the word "shipment," as used in the contract. That question, we think, is made clear by general usage and the uniform course of authority on the point. There is nothing in the language used in the contract, or in the surrounding circumstances, to indicate that the vendors were expected to exercise any control over the clearance of the vessel, or her subsequent management. That event might be governed by the condition of the tide, the direction of the wind, the facilities for clearance and many other circumstances over which the vendors had no control and could not have been supposed to have had when the contract was made. These were matters for the judgment of those navigating the vessel. No qualifying adjectives are prefixed to the word "shipment" in the contract, and it clearly defines the kind of shipment intended to be made, which was one made upon a steam or sailing vessel within thirty days from the date of the contract. It is, of course, implied by this language, and the surrounding circumstances, that the shipment was to be made in Cuba upon a vessel bound for New York, and if there was no regular line making trips to the port of destination from the shipping port, that the plaintiffs would supply, in some way, the means of transportation to perform the service required.

In an ordinary contract for the sale of goods to be shipped from one place to another, between which there are regular lines of transportation, it would not be supposed that the vendor was under obligation to exercise control over the medium of transportation after the goods were delivered to the carrier, or be responsible for delays in forwarding them to their place of destination. In the absence of regular lines of transportation some variations in the obligations of the vendor would be necessary, and those rules should be applied which are reasonable under the circumstances of the case and such as would naturally be indicated by the nature and requirements of the contract. In cases where the vendor is to pay the freight and the goods are not sufficient to complete a cargo, it would seem to be reasonable that, in his own interest, he should be authorized to select a vessel which had or could obtain a full cargo and thus diminish the charges on his consignment.

We think the plaintiffs, under this contract, were not required to hire a special ship for the purpose of transporting the goods, if that object could be otherwise reasonably attained; but they, undoubtedly, would be bound to ship on some vessel destined for the Port of New York, which they had reason to suppose would sail within a reasonable time after shipment had been made. In a case where the goods sold would not constitute a full cargo, it would seem to be a sufficient compliance with the contract to put them, within the specified time for shipment, on board a vessel bound for the intended port and engaged in an honest effort to obtain a cargo for such port. If the vendors in good faith shipped goods upon such a vessel, having reason to suppose she would sail within a reasonable time after shipment, we think it would be all the vendees could require under the contract, and if they desired a more speedy performance it should have been specially provided for by agreement. There is no language in the contract requiring the clearance of the vessel or the arrival of the goods at any particular time, and the option given to the vendors to ship by sail or steam evidently contemplated some latitude in respect to the time for the arrival of the goods in New York. A shipment by steam on the 8th of February, or by sail on the 9th of March, would, either, have brought the vendors within the strict terms of the contract. The possible time for the receipt of the goods by the vendees would, in case of an immediate clearance under these conditions, have fluctuated between the 12th day of February and the last days of the succeeding March, and shows some indifference on their part as to the particular time of their arrival in New York. It seems, therefore, quite clear that the goods arrived in New York and were tendered to the vendees within the time contemplated by the contract for their arrival, and the defendants have not been injured by delay in their shipment, unless the terms of the contract have in some way been violated by the plaintiffs. To bring themselves within this exception the defendants claim that the word "shipment," as used in the contract, means a clearance of the vessel, as well as the putting the goods on board, within the period allowed for shipment. The words "shipment" and "shipped" are now used indifferently to express the idea of goods delivered to carriers for the purpose of being transported from one place to another, over land as well as water, and imply, with respect to carriage by land, a completed act, irrespective of the time or mode of transportation. *Caulkins* v. *Hellman*, 47 N. Y. 452; *Fisher* v. *Minot*, 10 Gray, 260; *Schmertz* v. *Dwyer*, 53 Pa. 335.

The same signification has, so far as we have discovered, uniformly been given to them by lexicographers, when applied to transportation, either by land or water. Thus Webster defines "shipment" to mean "the act of putting anything on board of a ship or other vessel;" Worcester, "the act of shipping or putting on board a ship." Abbott's, Bouvier's and Rapalje & Lawrence's Law Dictionaries each give substantially the same definitions.

We have been referred to no authorities supporting the defendants' contention, and we believe it to be contrary to the invariable meaning of the word, as defined by lexicographers, as understood by the mercantile community generally or as laid down in the decisions of the courts. A leading case on this subject in England is that of *Bowes* v. *Shand*, L. R. 2 App. Cas. 455, H. of L., which seems to us to be in point. The contract in that case provided for the purchase of a quantity of rice "to be shipped at Madras . . . during the months of March and April;" and the question was whether rice mainly put on board during the month of February, with bills of lading taken therefor, was a compliance with this contract, although a small part of the cargo was not put on board, nor did the vessel sail until the month of March; and it was held that it was not. The case was ably and exhaustively discussed by the Lord Chancellor and the law lords generally, and the court were unanimously of the opinion that the word "shipped," according to its natural and ordinary signification, as well as its meaning in the mercantile community, was the putting of the goods on board the vessel and taking a bill of lading therefor; and it was accordingly held that rice put on board in February was not shipped in March or April, although the vessel did not, in fact, sail until March.

Delivering an opinion in that case, *Lord* Hatterly quite emphatically said: "I think the meaning of the word 'shipped' is sufficiently understood by this time in commerce. But if it were needed, I think we have sufficient evidence before us that by the word 'shipped' all the witnesses understand 'put on board.' Evidently if the sailing of the vessel containing the cargo was any part of the act of shipment, that case should have been otherwise decided." To a similar effect was the case of *Reuter* v. *Sala*, L. R. 4 C. P. Div. 239.

Chief Justice Shaw in *Fisher* v. *Minot*, 10 Gray, 260, says: "The word 'shipped,' in common maritime and mercantile usage, means 'placed on board of a vessel for the purchaser or consignee to be transported at his risk'; and such a delivery is a constructive delivery to the purchaser. . . . 'Shipment' means delivery on board." See also *Stubbs* v. *Lund*, 7 Mass. 453; *Newhall* v. *Vargas*, 13 Me. 105.

It has been urged by the respondents that the case of *Tobias* v. *Lissberger*, 105 N. Y. 404, 7 Cent. Rep. 723, is in conflict with this definition; but we do not so regard it. In that case the contract was for the sale of "about 100 tons of old iron vignol rails for prompt shipment by sail from Europe." The term "shipment" was there qualified by the word "prompt" and it was held, the vendor having an option of ports from which to ship, that a delivery of iron on board a vessel in a port blockaded by ice, which could not in the regular course of nature be opened for an indefinite period, was not a "prompt shipment" within the meaning of those terms. The distinction between the cases is too obvious to need comment.

The respondents have referred to certain evidence, which it is suggested tended to show bad faith on the part of the plaintiffs in making this shipment. There is certainly not sufficient evidence of that kind to make a question of law for the court, and it would be going quite as far as is warranted to say there is enough to carry it to a jury.

The judgments of the courts below should be reversed, and a new trial ordered, with costs to abide the event.

All concur.

Malcolm CALHOUN *et al.*, *Appts.*,

v.

DELHI & MIDDLETOWN R. CO. *et al.*, *Respts.*

(......N. Y.......)

1. **A decision in a suit** which is practically carried on by one party, who pays all the expenses of both sides, will not be held conclusive of the question involved when presented in another suit.

2. **The equitable remedy for the cancellation of town bonds** may be refused by reason of long delay and acquiescence on the part of the town and its taxpayers, accompanied by frequent acts recognizing the validity of the bonds, although the delay is not continued for the statutory period of limitation of equitable actions.

3. **The inability of a municipal corporation to make valid,** by acquiescence or recognition, obligations which it had no power to create, will not prevent consideration of such matters in determining whether it shall be denied a remedy because of laches.

4. **A statutory period of limitation of equitable actions** is not, where a purely equitable remedy is invoked, equivalent to a direction that no shorter period shall be a bar to relief in any case, and does not preclude a denial of relief, for unreasonable delay, in accordance with equitable principles.

5. **The failure for nearly ten years** of a town and its taxpayers to give warning or protest against dealing with or taking its void bonds, with affirmative acts of recognition encouraging investment therein as safe and valid securities, is sufficient to defeat an equitable action for their cancellation.

6. **An injunction will not be granted in favor of taxpayers** to restrain payment to the holders of void town bonds of moneys which have been collected without hindrance or protest for the special purpose of paying interest thereon, while the bonds were apparently valid and before any adjudication against them.

(April 15, 1890.)

APPEAL by plaintiffs from a judgment of the General Term of the Supreme Court, Fourth Department, affirming a judgment of the Delaware Special Term dismissing the complaint in an action brought to obtain the cancellation of certain town bonds and to enjoin the payment of interest thereon. *Affirmed.*

The facts are fully stated in the opinion.

Mr. **Isaac H. Maynard,** for appellants:

Taxpayers may maintain actions against bondholders, to restrain the collection of invalid bonds, and to procure their cancellation.

Metzger v. *Attica & A. R. Co.* 79 N. Y. 171; *Ayers* v. *Lawrence*, 59 N. Y. 192; *Latham* v. *Richards*, 12 Hun, 360; *Springport* v. *Teutonia*

NOTE.—*Laches; equitable rule depends on circumstances.*

The court of equity applies the rule of laches according to its own ideas of right and justice. See *note* to Middletown v. Newport Hospital (R. I.) 1 L. R. A. 191.

Where the case was one solely of equitable cognizance and, for any reason, the statute afforded no protection, it is the law of courts of equity, independent of positive legislative limitations, that they will not entertain stale demands. *Re* Accounting of Neilley, 95 N. Y. 390; Platt v. Vattier, 34 U. S. 9 Pet. 416 (9 L. ed. 177); Perry, Tr. § 869; Kane v. Bloodgood, 7 Johns. Ch. 93, 2 N. Y. Ch. L. ed. 233; Hunton v. Davies, 2 Rep. in Ch. 44; St. John v. Turner, 2 Vern. 418; Bean v. Tonnele, 94 N. Y. 381; Kingsland v. Roberts, 3 Paige, 193, 3 N. Y. Ch. L. ed. 370.

Nothing can call forth this court into activity but conscience, good faith and reasonable diligence. Where these are wanting the court is passive and does nothing. Laches and neglect are always discountenanced. United States R. S. Co. v. Atlantic & G. W. R. Co. 34 Ohio St. 463; Brown v. Buena Vista County, 95 U. S. 161 (24 L. ed. 423); Smith v. Clay, 2 Amb. 645; Story, Eq. § 1520 *a*; Sample v Barnes, 55 U. S. 14 How. 70 (14 L. ed. 330); Walker v. Robbins, 55 U. S. 14 How. 584 (14 L. ed. 552); Creath v. Sims, 46 U. S. 5 How. 192 (12 L. ed. 111); Bateman v. Willoe, 1 Sch. & Lef. 201; Callaway v. Alexander, 8 Leigh, 114; Powell v. Stewart, 17 Ala. 719; Riddle v. Baker, 13 Cal. 295; Sanderson v. Ætna I. & N. Co. 34 Ohio St. 444; Twin Lick Oil Co. v. Marbury, 91 U. S. 587 (23 L. ed. 329); Grymes v. Sanders, 93 U. S. 55 (23 L. ed. 798); Clegg v. Edmondson, 8 DeG. M. & G. 787; Jennings v. Broughton, 5 DeG. M. & G. 126; Miller v. Miller, 25 N. J. Eq. 366; Ensign v. Colburn, 11 Paige, 503, 5 N. Y. Ch. L. ed. 212.

Sav. Bank, 75 N. Y. 397; *Hills* v. *Peekskill Sav. Bank*, 2 Cent. Rep. 463, 101 N. Y. 490.

There was no intimation anywhere that an action of this character could not be maintained by the taxpayers against the bondholders where the invalidity of the bonds was established.

See *Alvord* v. *Syracuse Sav. Bank*, 98 N. Y. 599.

The only way by which the waste or injury of the funds of the town can be prevented is through the medium of this action.

People v. *Brown*, 55 N. Y. 180; *Oxford First Nat. Bank* v. *Wheeler*, 72 N. Y. 201.

The bondholders are properly made parties because they can maintain an action against the supervisor to collect the amount of their coupons even though he has been enjoined from paying them, unless they are made parties and bound by the judgment.

Oxford First Nat. Bank v. *Wheeler, supra.* See *Rogers* v. *Stephens*, 86 N. Y. 623; *Osterhoudt* v. *Rigney*, 98 N. Y. 222.

If the bonds are void, as they have been held to be by the decision of this court, and an attempt is being made to divert the funds of the town to their payment, the statutory cause of action is made out and the plaintiffs must have a decree.

Warrin v. *Baldwin*, 7 Cent. Rep. 768, 105 N. Y. 537.

Relief cannot properly be denied upon the ground of any delay in bringing the action.

We fail to find any case holding that where a cause of action is created by express statutory enactment the failure of the plaintiff to bring the action within any specified time less than the limitation prescribed by law can be made use of to prevent a recovery.

See *Alvord* v. *Syracuse Sav. Bank*, 98 N. Y. 599; *Mentz* v. *Cook*, 11 Cent. Rep. 819, 108 N. Y. 504.

Involuntary submission to an unlawful act cannot deprive the citizen of his remedy to prevent a repetition of the injury whenever he may seek to invoke it, unless the Statute of Repose has intervened.

Cruger v. *Dougherty*, 43 N. Y. 107.

There can be no such thing as a bona fide holder of town bonds in the sense in which the term is used in commercial law.

Cagwin v. *Hancock*, 84 N. Y. 532; *Potter* v. *Greenwich*, 26 Hun, 330, 92 N. Y. 662; *Brownell* v. *Greenwich*, 114 N. Y. 518; *Weismer* v. *Douglas*, 64 N. Y. 105.

Mr. **John B. Gleason**, for respondents: The decision in the case of *Craig* v. *Andes*, 93 N. Y. 405, was procured by a fraud upon this court and upon the defendants here, and is of no authority.

Equity will afford no relief to the repudiating taxpayer where his action is commenced for the cancellation of bonds after a long period of acquiescence marked by express recognition of the bonds in a series of successive payments of the interest upon them.

Calhoun v. *Delhi & M. T. R. Co.* 28 Hun, 379, 2 Story, Eq. Jur. §§ 293, 1520, *note 4;* 1 Dillon, Mun. Corp. § 548; *Venice* v. *Woodruff*, 62 N. Y. 465; *Solon* v. *Williamsburgh Bank*, 114 N. Y. 122.

The court ought not to make the adjudication against the defendants because it is equitable for the town to waive any irregularity in the issue of these bonds and pay them.

People v. *Mead*, 36 N. Y. 224.

It was competent for a town to pay the interest on its bonds issued under circumstances creating an equitable claim, although their collection could not have been enforced at law. Such payment, therefore, cannot be said to be waste of the property or funds of the town.

Murdock v. *Aiken*, N. Y. Ct. App. 1863 (not reported), cited in *People* v. *Mead*, 36 N. Y. 224.

Andrews, *J.*, delivered the opinion of the court:

This action was commenced January 6, 1882, by the plaintiffs, certain taxpayers of the Town of Andes, in the County of Delaware, in behalf of themselves and all other taxpayers in said town, against the Delhi & Middletown Railroad Company, the supervisor of said town, and certain other defendants, holders of bonds to the amount of about $50,000, dated September 1, 1871, part of $98,000 of bonds with interest coupons attached, purporting to have been issued by commissioners in behalf of said town, under and in pursuance of chapter 907 of the Laws of 1869, in aid of the construction of the Delhi & Middletown Railroad. The complaint sets forth that the bonds were issued without authority and were void for the reason, among others, that the proper consents required by the Act of 1869 were not obtained, and demanded equitable relief, first, that the defendant Ballantine, supervisor of said town, be restrained and enjoined from paying the interest falling due on such bonds March 1 and September 1, 1882, out of the sum of $6,650, in his hands, levied and collected for the payment of such interest; and second, that the bonds held by the individual defendants be decreed to be delivered up and canceled.

The question of the validity of the bonds of the Town of Andes, issued under the Act of 1869, was presented to and adjudicated by this court in the case of *Craig* v. *Andes*, 93 N. Y. 405. It was there decided, for reasons disclosed in the prevailing opinion, that the bonds were void. That action was brought after the commencement of the present one, to recover interest on certain of the bonds, which fell due March 1, 1882. It now appears from the evidence in this action that the Craig suit was brought at the instance of Ballantine, the supervisor of the town, and the trial judge found "that the coupons on which the action was brought were paid for out of the moneys of said town, and said action was prosecuted by attorneys paid by said town and was defended by attorneys paid by said town; said town paying all the expenses thereof, and the suit was brought and defended for the purpose of procuring the bonds of said town to be declared invalid."

We fully assent to the claim of the counsel for the bondholders, that an adjudication obtained under such circumstances ought not to stand in the way of a re-examination by the court of the grounds upon which it proceeded, and if we were now satisfied either that upon the facts presented in that case the question of law was erroneously decided, or that facts not disclosed on the trial of the *Craig Case*, but now brought out, would, if then disclosed, have led to a different result, the circumstances stated would emphasize the duty of the court to correct its errors, or to conform its judgment in the present case to the new circumstances.

It is claimed that material facts bearing upon the validity of the bonds, not shown on the trial of the *Craig Case*, were proved on the trial of the present one, prominent among which is the fact, which now appears, that the railroad in aid of which the bonds were issued had been in fact legally located on the identical route specified in the conditional consents, prior to May 6, 1871, the date of the presentation of the petition and consents to the county judge. But we deem it unnecessary to determine whether the new facts presented affect the principle of our former decision, for the reason that we think the judgment below dismissing the complaint in this action was properly rendered, assuming the invalidity of the bonds.

It will be convenient to consider separately the two purposes of this action, viz.: the surrender and cancellation of the bonds held by the individual defendants, and the separate and distinct relief by injunction to prevent the defendant Ballantine from applying the money in his hands to the payment of interest. The jurisdiction of a court of equity to compel the surrender and cancellation of written instruments obtained by fraud, or which being void for any reason may, if outstanding, subject the plaintiff to loss or injury, is very ancient and has been frequently exercised. The plaintiff seeking this relief invokes the equitable powers of the court, and the court grants or refuses it in the exercise of a sound discretion, according to the circumstances of the particular case.

The granting of this relief cannot be claimed as a matter of "absolute right *ex debito justitiæ*, such as a party has to recover an amount due on a contract or for damages for a tort." The existence of jurisdiction, and the fact that plaintiff makes out that the instrument of which he seeks the surrender and cancellation is void, are not conclusive of his right to a final decree in his favor. The court may, nevertheless, refuse to exercise the jurisdiction, and leave the party to his defense at law when the instrument is sought to be enforced against him. But in entertaining or declining jurisdiction the court does not act capriciously, but is guided by principles which have gradually been evolved in the course of adjudication. It is apart from our present purpose to arrange or classify the cases upon the subject. The general grounds of jurisdiction, and the circumstances which justify equitable interference, or, on the other hand, the denial of equitable relief, are set forth in the text-books and illustrated by decided cases. We refer to a few of the decisions in this court upon the subject. *Heywood* v. *Buffalo*, 14 N. Y. 540; *Venice* v. *Woodruff*, 62 N. Y. 462; *Springport* v. *Teutonia Sav. Bank*, 75 N. Y. 397.

The facts in the present case present several elements which have entered into the consideration of the court in granting relief for the cancellation of written instruments. The bonds of the Town of Andes are, as we have assumed, void, and since the commencement of this action they have been so adjudicated, but the adjudication is an estoppel only as between the parties to the action in which it was made. The other bondholders are not concluded, and may contest over again the question of the validity of the bonds. There exists also the further element that the bonds are not void on their face, and that in a suit brought thereon the proof of the adjudication of the county judge that the requisite consents had been obtained would presumptively establish performance of the condition as to consents in the Bonding Act, and cast upon the town the *onus* of disproving it, and showing that, in fact, the requisite consents had not been given. *Craig* v. *Andes*, 93 N. Y. 410.

It also appears by the record that the bonds are held by numerous parties, each of whom might bring an action at law to enforce them, unless prevented by the equitable interposition of the court for their cancellation. In the case of *Springport* v. *Teutonia Sav. Bank*, *supra*, 84 N. Y. 403, the court sustained an action for the cancellation of town bonds, upon facts substantially similar to those presented in this case, with the important exception, however, that there the town had acted promptly in repudiating the bonds and in seeking to review the proceedings under which the right to issue them was claimed. In that case the adjudication of the assessor was made March 18, 1871. The town procured a writ of certiorari to review and set aside the bonding proceedings, April 18, 1871, and they were set aside in that proceeding by the judgment of this court in June, 1873. The defendants purchased the bonds in September, 1871, pending the litigation on the certiorari, and in January, 1875, the suit for cancellation was commenced. The town had paid no interest on the bonds and refused in any way to recognize their validity.

This court, also, in the case of *Metzger* v. *Attica & A. R. Co.*, 79 N. Y. 171, affirmed a judgment canceling town bonds issued in aid of the Attica & Arcade Railroad Company, on the ground that they were issued without authority. The bonds in that case were delivered by town commissioners to the railroad company in exchange for its stock March 21, 1874. The suit for cancellation was commenced in January, 1876, less than two years thereafter. The commissioners were joined with the railroad company as defendants in the action, and the complaint alleged collusion between the defendants to impose the bonds upon the town. The bonds had not been transferred by the company and the town had paid no interest.

The case of *Mentz* v. *Cook*, 108 N. Y. 504, 11 Cent. Rep. 819, sustained a decision of the special term of the supreme court decreeing the cancellation of town bonds, on the ground of a defect in the petition by which the proceedings to bond the town were initiated. The road in aid of which the bonds were issued had never been constructed, and after paying interest on the bonds for a single year, the town repudiated its liability and commenced an action for their cancellation.

The present case, for the first time in the history of the litigations growing out of the Town Bonding Acts in the aid of railroads in this State, presents the question whether the equitable remedy for cancellation may be refused by reason of long delay and acquiescence on the part of the town and its taxpayers, accompanied meanwhile by frequent acts recognizing the validity of the obligations of which cancellation is sought, although the delay in bringing the action has not continued for the full statutory period of limitation of equitable actions. It is important to state the material facts bearing upon the question. The adjudication of the county judge that the persons who signed the petition in the bonding proceedings constituted a majority of the taxpayers of the Town of Andes in number and amount of taxable property, was made May 22, 1871. The bonds (except a part not now material) were issued and delivered to the Railroad Company in exchange for its stock between June 13 and December 10, 1872. They were payable in thirty years from date, with semi-annual interest at 7 per cent. In each year for nine years and more a tax was levied on the town to pay the interest on the bonds, and it was regularly paid as it accrued up to September 1, 1881, and in 1878 the town meeting voted a tax of $8,000 to pay that amount of bonds, and they were so paid and retired. The railroad in aid of which the bonds were issued was never put in operation. But the Company during 1872, 1873 and 1874 expended in grading and other construction, within the Town of Andes, a sum greater than the amount of bonds issued by the town. In 1874 a town meeting was held pursuant to chapter 453 of the Laws of 1874, to determine whether the town commissioners should be authorized to sell the stock taken in exchange for the bonds, and it was decided that such authority should not be given. In 1875, on a new vote being taken under chapter 153 of the Laws of 1875, a sale was authorized. The stock was not sold, and in December, 1881, was practically extinguished by a sale of the railroad under foreclosure. This action was commenced December 6, 1881, more than ten years after the adjudication of the county judge, and nine years and more, but less than ten years, after the issue of the bonds. The trial judge found that the individual defendants purchased the bonds held by them in good faith, paying therefor not less than par and accrued interest, without notice of any claim by the officers or taxpayers of the town that there was any defense thereto or any suspicion of their invalidity.

It cannot be doubted that if obligations of an individual having general power to contract had been issued without his authority, but he had afterwards permitted them to be dealt with by the public as valid securities, and had recognized their validity by frequent payment of interest, and by payment of a portion of the principal, these acts would have constituted a ratification of the unauthorized obligations, and have precluded the obligor from denying their validity. Under the decisions in this State similar acts on the part of a town or other municipality, recognizing the validity of bonds issued under the Bonding Acts, would not estop the municipality issuing them from denying their validity on the ground that essential conditions provided in the Bonding Acts had not been complied with. By our decisions, the obtaining of consents to the extent, and in the mode, prescribed in the Acts, is of the very substance of the power conferred upon municipal corporations to issue bonds for the purposes contemplated, and bonds issued without the requisite consents are held to have been issued without authority. Municipal corporations, since they possess no general authority to issue such bonds, cannot by recognition or subsequent ratification validate obligations which they had no power to create. This point was involved in *Craig* v. *Andes*, where the question of estoppel was raised and overruled, and the decision on this point accords with the tenor of the cases in this State. See *Weismer* v. *Douglas*, 64 N. Y. 105; *Cagwin* v. *Hancock*, 84 N. Y. 542; *Starin* v. *Genoa*, 23 N. Y. 439.

The dismissal of the complaint in this action cannot, therefore, rest upon the ground of estoppel or ratification, but the acts of the town, its long acquiescence, without action or protest, in the bonding proceedings, its repeated recognition of the validity of the bonds by payments, are pertinent considerations where the court is called upon, after a long delay, to exert its equitable powers in decreeing their surrender and cancellation.

It is, and always has been, the practice of courts of equity to remain inactive where a party seeking their interference has been guilty of unreasonable laches in making his application. Story, Eq. Jur. § 1520.

The principle is stated with great force and clearness by *Lord* Camden, in *Smith* v. *Clay*, Ambl. 645. "Nothing can call forth this court into activity but conscience, good faith and reasonable diligence. Where these are wanting the court is passive and does nothing. Laches and neglect are discountenanced, and therefore, from the beginning of this court, there was always a limitation to suits in this court."

Courts of equity, it has been said, act not so much in analogy to, as in obedience to, Statutes of Limitation of legal actions, because where the legal remedy is barred, the spirit of the Statute bars the equitable remedy also.

In the present case the cause of action for the cancellation of the bonds was not barred by the ten years' Statute applicable to equitable actions. But a period of nine years had elapsed after the bonds were issued, before the commencement of the action. But we apprehend that the period of limitation of equitable actions fixed by the Statute is not, where a purely equitable remedy is invoked, equivalent to a legislative direction that no period short of that time shall be a bar to relief in any case, or precludes the court from denying relief in accordance with equitable principles for unreasonable delay, although the full period of ten years has not elapsed since the cause of action accrued. The ten years' limitation was primarily designed to shield defendants (*Buffalo & N. Y. C. R. Co.* v. *Dudley*, 14 N. Y. 352), and it must be true that a court, in the exercise of its equitable jurisdiction, could not entertain or enforce a cause of action barred by the Statute, and not within any exception, acting upon any general equitable considerations. But in enforcing purely equitable remedies, depending upon general equitable principles, unreasonable and inexcusable delay is an element in the plaintiff's case which a court of equity always takes into consideration in exercising its discretion to grant or refuse relief, and is not a mere collateral incident. Where there is a remedy at law whereby the plaintiff can prosecute or defend his legal right, the refusal of relief leaves the parties where they were.

If there are special circumstances which may change the situation of the plaintiff to his injury, unless the equitable remedy is interposed, this fact may be considered. But the right of the court to deny relief, upon equitable grounds, for long delay, although short of the statute period of limitation, is in the nature of a defense, and is not we think taken away by the Statute. There may be a well-founded distinction between the case of an application for an equitable remedy in aid of, or to enforce, a legal right not barred by the Statute, and the case where an exclusively equitable remedy is sought, such as to restrain proceedings at law, or, upon the principle *quia timet*, to deprive an adversary of the muniment of his alleged legal right, which he inequitably retains. In cases of the latter class, long delay or acquiescence, although short of the statute period for the limitation of equitable actions, may be a ground for refusing relief. Pom. Eq. Jur. §817.

The cancellation of securities is a purely equitable remedy and cannot be claimed as an absolute right, nor is it applied for or awarded in aid of a legal right or title.

We conclude, therefore, that it was within the power of the court to dismiss the complaint so far as relief was sought for a cancellation of the bonds, on the ground of delay in bringing the action. The circumstances justified the conclusion on this branch of the case. The town and the taxpayers permitted the bonds to be dealt with and taken by the savings banks and others, for nearly ten years. not only without, so far as appears, a word of warning or protest, but by affirmative acts of recognition encouraged investment therein as safe and valid securities. The bonds, resting on the adjudication of the county judge, were apparently valid. The Legislature has still the power to ratify them and make them valid obligations of the town. *Williams* v. *Duanesburgh*, 66 N. Y. 129; *Horton* v. *Thompson*, 71 N. Y. 513; *Rogers* v. *Stephens*, 86 N. Y. 623.

They are now in the hands of bona fide holders, that is, of persons who have paid value for them without notice. The fact that if the plaintiffs are defeated here, the bonds may be sued upon and enforced in another jurisdiction, constitutes no equitable reason for maintaining the action. *Venice* v. *Woodruff*, *supra*.

The judgment denying relief for the cancellation of the bonds is incidentally supported by the opinion in *Craig* v. *Andes*, wherein the learned judge by whom it was pronounced, referring to the judgment in the present case in the supreme court, said: "Nor is the correctness of that decision in question here, for a court of equity might, in its discretion, refuse to interfere and leave the party to his legal rights;" and in *Alvord* v. *Syracuse Sav. Bank*, 98 N. Y. 599, *Judge* Finch recognizes the doctrine that a court of equity would not lend its aid in a case of inexcusable laches of the party seeking relief. The denial of relief in this case may result practically in the enforcement of the bonds in question and also of other town bonds issued and held under similar circumstances. But in contrasting the relative conduct and situation of the town and the taxpayers on the one side and the purchasers of bonds on the other, we cannot say that such a result will be repugnant to any principle of justice or equity.

The right of the plaintiffs to maintain the action, so far as it seeks to enjoin and restrain the defendant Ballantine from paying the interest on the bonds for the year 1882, out of money in his hands, levied and collected for that purpose, depends upon the question whether such payment, if made, would be an illegal act or constitute waste under chapter 531 of the Laws of 1881. This Act, which superseded the original legislation on the subject initiated by chapter 161 of the Laws of 1872, is entitled "An Act for the Protection of Taxpayers," and in its first section authorized an action to be prosecuted by taxpayers against officers, agents, commissioners or other persons acting in behalf of any county, town, village or municipal corporation, "to prevent any illegal act on the part of any such officers, agents, commissioners or other persons, or to prevent waste or injury to any property, funds or estate of such county, town, village or municipal corporation."

By Act, chapter 234, of the Laws of 1879, the office of railroad commissioner in the several towns in Delaware County was abolished, and the duties appertaining thereto were imposed upon the supervisors of the several towns. It was made the duty of the supervisor of each town to report to the board of supervisors, each year, the amount of interest on railroad bonds of the town falling due in that year, and the Act provides "that the said amount shall be raised by tax as now provided by law, and paid by the collectors of the taxes to the said supervisors, and by them applied in payment of the interest and coupons aforesaid." The defendant, Ballantine, as supervisor of the Town of Andes, in the fall of 1881, reported to the board of supervisors of Delaware County the amount required to be raised to pay the interest falling due on the railroad bonds of the town, for the year 1882, viz.: the sum of $6,650, and the board of supervisors, at its annual session in the fall of 1881, included in its warrant for the collection of taxes in the Town of Andes the sum so reported, and this amount was duly collected and paid over to the supervisor pursuant to the direction of such warrant, for the purpose of paying the interest on the bonds, and the sum so collected remains in his hands. The plaintiffs in their character as taxpayers seek to prevent the supervisor of the Town of Andes from performing the duty imposed upon him by the Act of 1879, and from applying the money for the purpose for which it was raised.

We are of opinion that the payment by the supervisor of the interest on the bonds, out of the funds, would neither be an illegal act, nor constitute waste within the Statute of 1881. The bonds were, under the adjudication of the county judge, presumptively valid obligations of the town. When the money in question was raised, their validity had not been impeached by any judicial decision. The town had, for a long time, recognized their validity. The taxpayers acquiesced for many years in the measures taken to raise money by taxation to pay the interest on the bonds. In 1874 and 1875, in their collective capacity in town meetings, they voted upon the question of the sale of the stock held by the town, at elections held under Acts of the Legislature in these years, which Acts, while they did not have the effect of legalizing the bonds which were the consideration for the stock authorized to be sold, nevertheless assumed their validity.

The bonds were not illegal or void in the sense that they were fraudulently issued or issued without consideration. They were exchanged for stock, and the Railroad Company concurrently with the subscription therefor entered into an agreement with the railroad commissioners that the proceeds of the bonds should be used for the construction and equipment of the railroad within the Town of Andes, and this agreement was performed. It is not claimed that there was any fraud or collusion in the bonding proceedings. The bondholders are innocent holders for full value of the securities thus issued. It is very clear, we think, that neither the town nor the taxpayers would be permitted to recover back money actually paid by the town to the bondholders as money illegally paid and received. It was paid upon presumptively valid obligations, under a claim of right on their part to receive it, and if payments actually made by the officers of the town would be valid and binding, it would not, we think, be an illegal act on the part of the supervisor, under the Act of 1881, to apply the money now in his hands according to the direction of the Statute, simply for the reason that the validity of the bonds is now questioned.

The question of the duty of the officer holding money raised to pay interest on bonds issued under the Town Bonding Acts to make such payment, notwithstanding some omission or defect in the bonding proceedings, which rendered the bonds invalid, has been considered by this court in several cases. *People* v. *Brown*, 55 N. Y. 180; *Oxford First Nat. Bank* v. *Wheeler*, 72 N. Y. 201.

We held in each of these cases that an officer who had in his hands money collected to pay interest on town bonds could not be permitted to question their validity when called upon to pay it over to those entitled to it under the Statute. In one case the collector of the town refused to pay the money collected by him to the town commissioners, as required by the Act, and in the other the town commissioners, after they had received it, refused to pay it to the bondholders, and in the case last cited the action of a bondholder to compel such payment was sustained. In both cases the defense was made that the bonds were void, and in both the defense was interposed pursuant to resolutions of the town meeting of the town whose bonds were in question.

The money, the payment of which is sought to be restrained in this action, has been collected in usual course from the taxable property in the Town of Andes. Neither the town nor the taxpayers intervened to prevent its collection. So far as appears the taxpayers paid the money voluntarily and have no recourse to recover it back. The money does not belong to them, nor in a strict sense is it the property of the town. It was raised for a special purpose, and it can be applied legally to no other. The Act of 1881 should have a broad and liberal construction to accomplish the purposes of its enactment. But it is difficult to perceive how that can be treated as an illegal act, or as constituting waste, the performance of which may be compelled by mandamus. We do not doubt that taxpayers may by means of this statutory action arrest the payment of money collected to pay fraudulent or collusive claims against a town having neither a legal nor equitable foundation. We confine our judgment to a case of money raised to pay a claim apparently valid, which has been so treated by the town and its taxpayers, having implied legislative sanction, and where no fraud is imputed. In such case we think the taxpayers cannot arrest the payment under the Act of 1881. If in this case judgment was given for a cancellation of the bonds, then it might follow that the fund would be left where it is, as there would be no debt in fact or in form to which it could be applied. See *Metzger* v. *Attica & A. R. Co. supra.*

We think the judgment should be affirmed.

All concur.

NEW YORK COURT OF APPEALS (2d Div.).

METROPOLITAN ELEVATED R. CO., *Appt.,*
v.
Sylvester H. **KNEELAND** *et al.*, *Respts.*

(......N. Y.......)

1. An allegation of liability to pay, without allegation either of payment or of actual loss, sufficiently shows damage to a corporation for acts of its directors in issuing promissory notes in its name, which have come into the hands of bona fide purchasers for value.

2. Directors of a corporation incur a personal liability to it by voting for a resolution, which they have no power, express or implied, to pass authorizing the issue and negotiation of notes of the corporation, which are in

---

NOTE.—*Personal liability of directors for acts done without authority.*

Ultra vires acts of directors in executing accommodation paper render them personally liable to the creditors of the corporation. Patterson v. Minnesota Mfg. Co. (Minn.) June 18, 1889.

They are personally liable for suffering the corporate funds or property to be wasted or lost by

effect void, where such notes are issued and come into the hands of bona fide purchasers for value.

3. A person who fraudulently places in circulation the negotiable instrument of another, whether made by him or by his apparent authority, and thereby renders him liable to pay the sum to a bona fide purchaser, is guilty of a tort, and, in the absence of special circumstances diminishing its value, is presumptively liable to the injured party for the face value thereof.

(April 15, 1890.)

APPEAL by plaintiff from a judgment of the General Term of the Supreme Court, First Department, affirming a judgment of the New York Special Term sustaining demurrers to the complaint in an action to enforce the alleged liability of defendants for the wrongful issuance of certain negotiable paper in the name of plaintiff. *Affirmed as to some, and reversed as to the other, defendants.*

Statement by **Vann, J.:**

Aside from certain facts alleged by way of inducement, the substantial allegations of the complaint are that from the 8th of November, 1882, until in August, 1884, the defendant, Kneeland, was a stockholder, director and the president of the plaintiff, a railroad corporation, organized under the laws of this State; that as president he was not called upon to perform any duties connected with the active management or operation of the road, and there was no salary attached to his office by any resolution or action either of the stockholders or directors; that his predecessors in office had never received any salary, and that the plaintiff never agreed to pay him a salary as its president, or to pay him for his services; that on the 5th of June, 1884, all of the defendants were directors of the plaintiff, and, with the exception of Mr. Gillett, attended a directors' meeting at which the following resolution was unanimously adopted, viz.:

"*Resolved*, That S. H. Kneeland, the president of this Company, shall be paid a salary of $25,000 per annum from the time of his election as such;" that on the 18th of the same month at another meeting of the directors, all of the defendants being present except Duggin and Slayback, it was unanimously resolved "that the president be and he is authorized to use the credit of the Company by issuing and negotiating its notes, or otherwise, for paying the salary of the said president, said notes to be signed by the president and countersigned by the treasurer in the usual way and form and not to exceed the limit of the amount heretofore authorized;" that prior to the adoption of the latter resolution, as well as subsequently, notes officially signed and countersigned by the president and treasurer, respectively, were issued to the amount, in the aggregate, of $48,950, and are now due and unpaid; that said notes were retained by said Kneeland and applied to his own use, and while some of them are held by certain of the defendants, others were negotiated before maturity and passed into the hands of bona fide purchasers for value without notice; that payment of some of said notes has been demanded of the plaintiff and suits threatened thereon and actions have actually been brought against it upon two thereof; that said Kneeland was never entitled to demand or receive from the plaintiff any salary or compensation for services as such president, and that the Company was under no liability to him either for salary or compensation, as the defendants knew or were bound to know as directors, and that their action in voting to pay him a salary, and in directing the issue of notes for that purpose, was illegal, a breach of trust and a violation of their duty as directors; that said notes are invalid in the hands of all persons except bona fide purchasers, without notice, before maturity and for a valuable and sufficient consideration; that the aforesaid action of the defendants was a fraud upon the plaintiff, and that, in consequence thereof, it has incurred a liability to pay such of said notes as have come into the hands of bona fide purchasers, without notice, for a good consideration and before maturity; that some of said notes were "paid over by the said Kneeland to some of the defendants in payment of or to secure the payment" of precedent indebtedness of said Kneeland to such defendants and that they are still under the control "of the defendants or some of them," and have not passed into the hands of bona fide purchasers.

The relief demanded is that "an account be

---

gross negligence or inattention to their duties. Horn Silver Min. Co. v. Ryan (Minn.) Dec. 20, 1889.

To render a business corporation liable upon a promissory note indorsed by its manager, there must have been prior authority or subsequent ratification, which may be evinced by the general course of business as well as by resolution. Huntington v. Attrill, 118 N. Y. 365.

Notes issued for the purpose of being used and circulated as money, in violation of the statute, are void and cannot be made the basis of recovery (Atty-Gen. v. Life & F. Ins. Co. 9 Paige, 470, 4 N.Y. Ch. L. ed. 780; Lindsey v. Rottaken, 32 Ark. 638; Smith v. Strong, 2 Hill, 241; McCullough v. Moss, 5 Denio, 567; Dively v. Cedar Falls, 21 Iowa, 569); the prohibition only applies to bills and notes which are capable of circulating as money.

A corporation, without any express power in its charter for that purpose, may make a negotiable promissory note or bill of exchange, when not prohibited by law from doing so, provided such note or bill is given for a debt contracted in the course of its proper legitimate business. Halstead v. New York, 5 Barb. 224, 7 N.Y. Leg. Obs. 76; Moss v. Averill, 10 N. Y. 457; McCullough v. Moss, 5 Denio, 577. See Mott v. Hicks, 1 Cow. 513; Barker v. Mechanics F. Ins. Co. 3 Wend. 94; Moss v. Oakley, 2 Hill, 265; Safford v. Wyckoff, 4 Hill, 442; Kelley v. Brooklyn, 4 Hill, 263; Moss v. Rossie Lead Min. Co. 5 Hill, 137; Conro v. Port Henry Iron Co. 12 Barb. 27; Barry v. Merchants Exch. Co. 1 Sandf. Ch. 300, 7 N. Y. Ch. L. ed. 334; Curtis v. Leavitt, 15 N. Y. 67; Jackson v. Brown, 5 Wend. 590; Ketchum v. Buffalo, 14 N. Y. 363.

The policy inducing the imposition of restraints upon corporations not formed to carry on the business of banking was to prevent the recurrence of a series of corporate usurpations which had deluged the State with illegal issues of mere paper obligations, resulting in great derangements to business, and producing numerous cases of financial embarrassment and ruin. New York T. & L. Co. v. Helmer, 12 Hun, 45.

taken of said notes, and that it be ascertained and determined which of said notes came into the hands of bona fide purchasers, . . . and that this plaintiff have judgment against these defendants for . . . $48,950 with interest from June 5, 1884, or for such a sum as plaintiff is liable to pay to the holders of said notes." There is also a prayer for general relief.

The defendants demurred to the complaint, Slayback, Duggin and Kneeland, separately, upon the ground that it does not state facts sufficient to constitute a cause of action; that two causes of action are improperly united, and that there is a defect of parties, both plaintiff and defendant.

Upon the trial an interlocutory judgment was entered sustaining the demurrer as to all of the defendants, with leave to amend in twenty days, but directing that the complaint should be dismissed unless the plaintiff should amend the same during said period. Upon the expiration of twenty days, the plaintiff having omitted to amend, final judgment was entered dismissing the complaint with costs.

Messrs. **Davies & Rapallo**, for appellant:

The defendants, as agents of the corporation, and trustees of the funds of the stockholders, committed a constructively fraudulent act in appropriating trust property to the use of one of their number without consideration. Their action constituted a tort, and rendered them liable to the corporation and stockholders for all resulting damage.

See *Butts* v. *Wood*, 37 N. Y. 319; *Comstock* v. *Comstock*, 57 Barb. 469; *Coleman* v. *Second Ave. R. Co.* 38 N. Y. 201; *Wardell* v. *Union P. R. Co.* 4 Dill. 330; *Aberdeen R. Co.* v. *Blakie*, 1 Macq. H. L. Cas. 462; *Metropolitan E. R. Co.* v. *Manhattan R. Co.* 14 Abb. N. C. 103.

A tortious act, which results in the creation of an outstanding valid pecuniary obligation against the complaining party, even although such obligation is not yet paid, is regarded as constituting the foundation of a complete cause of action against the offender, the element of damage consisting of the existence of the outstanding liability.

Farnham v. *Benedict*, 9 Cent. Rep. 557, 107 N. Y. 159; *Brooklyn Crosstown R. Co.* v. *Strong*, 75 N. Y. 591; *Ontario* v. *Hill*, 33 Hun, 250, *Thayer* v. *Manley*, 73 N. Y. 305; *Decker* v. *Mathews*, 12 N. Y. 313; *Betz* v. *Daily*, 3 N. Y. S. R. 309.

Messrs. **Stickney & Shepard** and **Nelson S. Spencer**, for respondent Kneeland:

An unequivocal allegation that the notes are the notes of the plaintiff is necessary in order to sustain the position that the plaintiff has suffered, or will suffer, any injury, and is therefore essential to maintain any right of the plaintiff to any relief in this action against these defendants, either at law or in equity.

Lord v. *Cheesebrough*, 4 Sandf. 696; *Bank of Geneva* v. *Gulick*, 8 How. Pr. 51.

The omission of such an allegation is fatal. 1 Edwards, Neg. Inst. 3d ed. § 98; 2 Edwards, Neg. Inst. §§ 925, 929, 938; *Nickels* v. *American Railway Signal Co.* N. Y. Daily Reg. Feb. 26, 1884.

Messrs. **Barlow & Wetmore**, for the other respondents:

Where a covenant is to indemnify against "damages" it is not enough that the indemnitee has "incurred damages," but he must have sustained them, by payment.

See *Gilbert* v. *Wiman*, 1 N. Y. 550; *Kohler* v. *Matlage*, 72 N. Y. 267; *Newburgh Nat. Bank* v. *Bigler*, 83 N. Y. 61; *Belloni* v. *Freeborn*, 63 N. Y. 390.

In the case at bar, the directors have made no express covenant, and if one is implied, it certainly can be no broader than that no "damages" shall come from their acts or omissions.

The person injured by a tortious act can only recover for the damages which he has suffered.

Williams v. *Mostyn*, 4 Mees. & W. 145; *Planck* v. *Anderson*, 5 T. R. 40; *Randell* v. *Wheble*, 10 Ad. & El. 728; *Hobson* v. *Thelluson*, L. R. 2 Q. B. 642; *Stimson* v. *Farnham*, L. R. 7 Q. B. 175; *Commercial Bank* v. *Ten Eyck*, 48 N. Y. 305; *Knapp* v. *Roche*, 94 N. Y. 333; *People* v. *Stephens*, 71 N. Y. 557.

It is legally impossible to determine, in this action, that one single one of these notes is owned by a bona fide holder without notice, since none of such holders are parties to the suit.

The holders would not be bound by the judgment in this action (not being parties), and so the plaintiffs would not be bound.

Meltzer v. *Doll*, 91 N. Y. 373.

It cannot be successfully claimed that an allegation that an agent, corporate or otherwise, made (or authorized) a note in the name of his principal without authority or consideration, or fraudulently, shows a conversion of the note.

In trover the plaintiff must show a right of property, either absolute or special, in himself—that is, that he is the owner of the property converted.

Selwyn, Nisi Prius, 7th Am. ed. 1353; *Malcolm* v. *O'Reilly*, 14 Jones & S. 222; *Dodds* v. *Johnson*, 3 Thomp. & C. 217.

Vann, *J.*, delivered the opinion of the court:

This is an action against the directors of a corporation for fraudulently issuing and negotiating promissory notes in its name, which, on reaching the hands of bona fide purchasers for value, became legal obligations against the Company. The substantial question presented by the demurrer is whether such an action can be maintained upon an allegation of liabilty to pay without an allegation either of payment or of actual loss. In an action for the conversion of a promissory note by wrongfully negotiating it to a bona fide holder for value, the maker need neither allege nor prove that he has paid it, but it is sufficient if he avers that he is legally liable to pay it. *Decker* v. *Mathews*, 12 N. Y. 313.

The gravamen of such an action, as was held in the case cited, is the wrongful act of the defendant in causing a note without value, except to a bona fide holder, to become valuable by the sale thereof to such a purchaser as could enforce it against the plaintiff. It was also held in that case that a cause of action accrued to the maker as soon as he became liable upon the note through the transfer thereof, and that neither the right of action nor the measure of damages depended upon the fact of payment.

This case was relied upon by the court when it rendered judgment in *Farnham* v. *Benedict*, 107 N. Y. 159, 9 Cent. Rep. 557, where the defendant, being in possession, without title, of certain town bonds that had been fraudulently issued through his procurement, and which were void in fact, although apparently valid, sold them to bona fide purchasers and thus rendered them valid and binding upon the town so that it was compelled to pay them. It was held that he was liable to the town for the amount of the bonds, and *Judge* Rapallo speaking for the court said that immediately on the negotiation of the bonds a cause of action accrued in favor of the town, either in the nature of an action of trover for the face of the bonds, or as for money had and received, for the money realized by him on the sale, according to the rule laid down in *Comstock* v. *Hier*, 73 N. Y. 269.

In *Thayer* v. *Manley*, 73 N. Y. 305, the defendant by means of false and fraudulent representations induced the plaintiff to execute and deliver to him three negotiable promissory notes, but before any of them became due the plaintiff demanded them from the defendant, who refused to deliver them. He still held the notes at the time of the trial, but one of them had become due after the commencement of the action. It was held that, as the defendant had it in his power, when the suit was commenced, to dispose of the notes to a bona fide holder in whose hands they would have been valid, and as the plaintiff was then entitled to recover the damage which might accrue to him, this right was not impaired by the subsequent maturity of one of the notes before a transfer; that as the judgment and a satisfaction thereof would transfer title to the notes to defendant, plaintiff was entitled to recover the full value, but that to avoid circuity of action a provision should be incorporated in the judgment giving to defendant the right to cancel and return the notes as a satisfaction of the damages. It was also held that the measure of damages in such an action is the face of the note and interest, unless it should appear that it was of less value by reason of payment of the same, insolvency of the maker or some other lawful defense.

In *Betz* v. *Daily*, 3 N. Y. S. R. 309, it was held that in an action by a partner against his copartner and certain third persons for fraudulently making notes in the name of the firm and negotiating them so that bona fide holders could compel the plaintiff to pay them, the cause of action was complete when the wrong was done and that payment of the notes was not essential to a recovery. Some of the notes were paid by the plaintiff after the commencement of the action, and before trial, but a verdict for the amount of all the notes fraudulently negotiated was sustained. The court said: "The plaintiff was not injured to the amount of money which he had paid out in taking up these fraudulent notes at the time of beginning the action. The injury to him was done when the notes were first negotiated."

In *Ontario* v. *Hill*, 33 Hun, 250, the defendants were held liable for wrongfully issuing the negotiable bonds of a town, some of which had fallen into the hands of innocent holders for value. It was determined that the cause of action accrued immediately upon the passing of the bonds into the hands of bona fide purchasers who could enforce them against the town. "In a legal sense," it was said, "the plaintiff had sustained damages by the action of the defendants when the bonds passed into the hands of persons who could enforce their payment against the town. The plaintiffs' alleged right of action springs out of the defendants' breach of duty as public officers, and is in the nature of an action on the case for consequential damages."

This case was subsequently reversed, but not on this point. *Ontario* v. *Hill*, 99 N. Y. 324.

While the case presented by this appeal may not be a strict action of conversion, it bears a close analogy to actions of that character when brought by the makers of negotiable promissory notes for the conversion thereof. What is the nature of the injury for which such an action lies? It is not the loss of the material substance of the note, which is simply a piece of paper with a few words written thereon. Neither is it the loss of a contract, or of the evidence of a contract, that the maker could enforce, because it is his own engagement in form, but not even that in fact. The wrongful destruction of an article is ordinarily a conversion thereof, but the destruction of a note that had had no inception would not be a conversion as to the maker, unless it might be deemed a conversion of the material substance only, which is not now important. The injury consists in the negotiation of the note, so that, according to the law-merchant, it becomes a valid and enforceable contract against the maker, or, as in *Thayer* v. *Manley*, *supra*, in retaining possession after demand made, so that the wrong-doer had the power to put it into lawful circulation. Wrongfully aiding in the negotiation of a note, or wrongfully making a note to be negotiated by others, would appear to be injuries of the same character.

What was the nature of the tortious act of which the defendants by their demurrer admit they were guilty? Those who voted for the resolution which in form authorized one of their number to issue and negotiate notes of the plaintiff, assumed to authorize and, by authorizing, caused some of the notes in question to be issued and negotiated. They had no power, express or implied, to pass that resolution, or its predecessor which provided a salary for the president. They could not thus give away the property of the corporation. They could not bind the stockholders by voting to appropriate the assets of the Company to an illegal purpose. *Butts* v. *Wood*, 37 N. Y. 317; *Coleman* v. *Second Ave. R. Co.* 38 N. Y. 201; *Ogden* v. *Murray*, 39 N. Y. 202; *Kelsey* v. *Sargent*, 40 Hun, 150; *Maux Ferry Gravel Road Co.* v. *Branegan*, 40 Ind. 361; *Holder* v. *Lafayette, B. & M. R. Co.* 71 Ill. 106; *Accomodation Loan & S. F. Asso.* v. *Stonemetz*, 29 Pa. 534; *Kilpatrick* v. *Penrose Ferry Bridge Co.* 49 Pa. 118.

Their action, as admitted on the record, was a violation of their duty as directors, a breach of trust and a fraud upon the plaintiff. The result of their action was to cause notes to be made, purporting to be valid obligations of the plaintiff, although in fact void. While not the notes of the Company they appeared to be such, as they were issued by those having apparent authority. If nothing further had been done, however, the wrong would doubtless have been *injuria absque damno*, but the defendants who adopted the second resolution thereby authorized the negotiation of the notes and some of them were negotiated accordingly and reached the hands of bona fide holders for value. These notes, as is here admitted, the plaintiff has become liable to pay in consequence of the fraudulent conduct of those defendants. Thus the dead pieces of paper were, to this extent, given life and converted into contracts binding upon the Company without its consent. In what respect do these wrongful acts differ from those which, in the cases cited, were held to authorize an action for conversion, or an action in the nature of conversion? Do they differ in the character of the injury inflicted, or loss sustained? Is there not in each the same presumption of damages springing from a liability wrongfully imposed? Were not all of these actions founded upon the fact that the maker, real or apparent, of a negotiable instrument, had, through the wrongful acts of another, become chargeable, so that he could be compelled to pay such instrument, which would not have ripened into a valid obligation against him but for such wrongful act?

We think that the cases relating to this subject rest upon the principle that a person who fraudulently places in circulation the negotiable instrument of another, whether made by him or by his apparent authority, and thereby renders him liable to pay the same to a bona fide purchaser, is guilty of a tort, and, in the absence of special circumstances diminishing its value, is presumptively liable to the injured party for the face value thereof. As the case under consideration fairly comes within this principle, it should be governed by it. The essential injury common to all cases of this character is the fraudulent imposition of liability. Hence there should be a common remedy, whether it is called an action in conversion or in the nature of conversion, or a special action on the case.

These views lead to a reversal of the judgment as to all of the defendants who voted for the resolution authorizing the president of the Company to issue and negotiate its notes for the purpose of paying him a salary to which he was not entitled. The defendants Slayback and Duggin, who demur separately, but through the same attorneys and upon the same grounds as the other defendants, except Kneeland, did not vote for said resolution, although they voted for the resolution to pay the president a salary. This act, although wrongful, was harmless, so far as appears, until supplemented by further action in which they did not participate, and for which, upon the record as presented, they cannot be held responsible. The passage of the resolution for the payment of a salary, without specifying how it should be paid, did not bring the notes into existence nor put them into circulation. No cause of action was set forth, therefore, as to those defendants, who are not alleged to have had any connection with the act that resulted in making and negotiating the notes.

The judgment should be affirmed as to the defendants Slayback and Duggin, but, under the circumstances, without costs.

As to all the other defendants, the judgment should be reversed, and the demurrer overruled, with costs, with leave to such defendants to withdraw their demurrer and serve an answer within thirty days upon payment of costs.

All concur, except **Potter**, *J.*, not sitting.

Jane McKENZIE *et al.*, *Respts.*,

v.

Charles HARRISON *et al.*, *Appts.*

(....N. Y.....)

1. **An executed parol agreement** modifying a contract under seal will be upheld.
2. **A gift may be made of the balance of a debt** after payment of part only, although payment of such part cannot constitute an accord and satisfaction. A receipt in full may be evidence of the gift.

(*Follett*, Ch. J., *and Bradley and Parker*, JJ., *dissent.*)

(April 22, 1890.)

APPEAL by defendants from a judgment of the General Term of the Supreme Court, First Department, overruling exceptions directed to be heard at General Term in the first instance, and ordering judgment to be entered upon the verdict directed by the Trial Term in favor of plaintiffs in an action to recover rent alleged to be due and unpaid. *Reversed.*

The facts sufficiently appear in the opinion.

Mr. **N. B. Hoxie**, with *Messrs.* **Cudlipp & Glover**, for appellants:

The agreements were after breach (*i. e.*, after each quarterly payment became due) and were fully executed.

The situation of the parties was in effect the same as if defendants had on each quarter day paid the full amount specified in the lease, and the plaintiffs had then given to defendants the sum of $250; and the arrangement, having become executed, is not now subject to attack.

See 2 Parsons, Cont. 3d ed. p. 518; *Nicoll* v. *Burke*, 78 N. Y. 580.

A sealed agreement may be modified by an executed parol agreement.

Fleming v. *Gilbert*, 3 Johns. 528; *Pierrepont* v. *Barnard*, 6 N. Y. 279; *Esmond* v. *Van Benschoten*, 12 Barb. 366, 370; *Stone* v. *Sprague*, 20 Barb. 509, 515; *Dearborn* v. *Cross*, 7 Cow. 48; *Delacroix* v. *Bulkley*, 13 Wend. 71; *Horgan* v. *Krumwiede*, 25 Hun, 117; *Keeler* v. *Salisbury*, 33 N. Y. 648, 655; *Strang* v. *Holmes*, 7 Cow. 224; *New York* v. *Butler*, 1 Barb. 325; *Jeffers* v. *Bantley*, 47 Hun, 90; *Lawrence* v. *Barker*, 9 Daly, 140.

The plaintiffs made a gift to the defendants of $250 upon each quarterly payment, and cannot now recover back such gifts.

Heathcote v. *Crookshanks*, 2 T. R. 24; *Fellows* v. *Stevens*, 24 Wend. 299.

The rule that payment of a portion of a debt cannot be pleaded as an accord and satisfaction to the claim for a larger sum, has met with more or less dissatisfaction in the recent cases, and by the simplest device the application of the rule may be evaded or prevented. And it is submitted that at this day in this tribunal administering justice upon equitable as well as legal principles, not sacrificing substance to form, it should not be held that the absence or omission of such a device shall render a transaction illegal or invalid that with such a device would be upheld.

See *Bidder* v. *Bridges*, L. R. 37 Ch. Div. 406; *Goddard* v. *O'Brien*, L. R. 9 Q. B. Div. 37; *Sibree* v. *Tripp*, 15 Mees. & W. 23; *Jaffray* v. *Davis*, 48 Hun, 500; *Milliken* v. *Brown*, 1 Rawle, 391.

Messrs. **Lewis Johnston** and **Edward W. S. Johnston**, for respondents:

The plaintiffs' claim cannot be defeated except by proof of a valid agreement to reduce the rent, and a surrender of the written lease. There was no offer to show any consideration for the alleged parol agreement to reduce, and the parties returned, by defendants' own showing, to the terms of the original written lease.

Coe v. *Hobby*, 72 N. Y. 141, 7 Hun, 157; *Smith* v. *Kerr*, 10 Cent. Rep. 482, 108 N. Y. 31, 33 Hun, 567; *Lynch* v. *McBeth*, 7 How. Pr. 113; *Swain* v. *Seamens*, 76 U. S. 9 Wall. 254, 271 (19 L. ed. 554, 559); *Emerson* v. *Slater*, 63 U. S. 22 How. 42 (16 L. ed. 365); 1 Benjamin, Sales, §§ 240, 245, p. 184 (p. 358, ed. 1888).

The lease was not valid by the Statute of Frauds unless in writing, and it cannot be varied by parol without a violation of the Statute.

Hill v. *Blake*, 97 N. Y. 222.

Haight, *J.*, delivered the opinion of the court:

This action was brought to recover the amount of rent alleged to be due and unpaid upon a lease of real estate in the City of New York. It appears that the parties had made and executed a lease under seal whereby the plaintiffs leased to the defendants the store and premises known as No. 16 Fourth Street for the term of ten years from May 1, 1877, for the annual rental of $4,500, payable quarterly. Upon the trial the defendants offered to prove in substance that after they had occupied the premises for one year under the lease, and paid the rent in full for that year, they reported to the plaintiffs that their business was very dull and that they could not afford to pay so much rent. That thereupon the plaintiffs agreed to reduce the rent $1,000 per year, making it $3,500 a year, or $875 for each quarter. That thereafter the defendants at the end of each quarter paid the plaintiffs $875, and the plaintiffs executed and delivered to them a receipt for that amount in full for balance of rent due at that date as per agreement "until times are better." That this continued for three years, after which the plaintiffs notified the defendants that thereafter they wished them to pay the amount of rent originally provided for by the lease, and that thereafter the full amount of rent was paid until the commencement of this action in December, 1886. This evidence was excluded by the trial court and a verdict ordered for the plaintiffs for the full amount claimed.

The general term was of the opinion that the case of *Coe* v. *Hobby*, 7 Hun, 157, 72 N. Y. 141, disposed of the questions involved in this case. The facts in that case are very similar to those which were offered to be proved in this, but in that case the action was brought for a quarter's rent which had become due, no part of which had been paid, the lessor refusing to any longer accept the reduced amount agreed upon; and he did not seek or claim the right to recover the balance of the quarterly rents which had previously been paid in part under the agreement and for which a receipt had been given in full. The distinction, therefore, between the two cases is apparent. In that case the lessor was seeking to enforce the provisions of his lease, which was under seal, and collect a quarter's rent then due and owing. The lessees were defending under an executory verbal contract to reduce the rent. Whilst in this case the lessees are defending under an executed oral agreement to the effect that the rent has been paid and accepted in full, and is evidenced by a written receipt given therefor.

We shall not question the rule that a contract or covenant under seal cannot be modified by a parol unexecuted contract. *Coe* v. *Hobby*, *supra; Smith* v. *Kerr*, 33 Hun, 567–571, 108 N. Y. 31, 10 Cent. Rep. 842.

Neither shall we question the views of the court below to the effect that the alleged oral agreement in this case to reduce the rent $1,000 per year was void and inoperative in so far as it remained unexecuted. The lessors had the right to repudiate it at any time and demand the full amount of rent provided for by the lease; but in so far as the oral agreement had become executed, as to the payments which had fallen due and had been paid and accepted in full as per the oral agreement, we think the rule invoked has no application.

The reason of the rule was founded upon public policy. It was not regarded as safe or prudent to permit the contract of parties which had been carefully reduced to writing and executed under seal to be modified or changed by the testimony of witnesses as to the parol statements or agreements of parties. Hence the rule that testimony of parol agreements shall not be competent as evidence to impeach, vary or modify written agreements or covenants under seal. But the parties may waive this rule and carry out and perform the agreements under seal as changed or modified by the parol agreement, thus executing both agreements; and where this has been done and the parties have settled with a full knowledge of the facts and in the absence of fraud, there is no power to revoke or remedy reserved to either party. *Munroe* v. *Perkins*, 9 Pick. 298; *Lattimore* v. *Harsen*, 14 Johns. 330; *McCreery* v. *Day*, 6 L. R. A. 503, 119 N. Y. 1.

So in this case, if, as is claimed, the parol agreement was made to reduce the rent $1,000 per year, and that agreement has been carried out and fully executed by the parties, and at the end of each quarter, when the rent by the terms of the lease became due and payable, the reduced sum as agreed upon by the parol agreement was paid, and the parties settled upon that basis, and, as evidence of such settlement, the plaintiff gave a receipt in full for the amount of rent due to that date, it became executed and the plaintiff cannot revoke the same or maintain this action to recover any greater sum than that settled for.

It is also claimed that the oral agreement

was void for the want of a consideration. Assume this to be so, and that the plaintiffs at any time whilst the agreement remained executory had the right to demand the full amount of rent provided for by the lease. They, however, had the right to waive consideration and carry out their parol agreement, and if they did this, executing it, they were brought within the rule to which we have already called attention.

To illustrate: A may give B his promissory note without consideration. As long as it remains in the hands of B, A may interpose the defense that it was given for B's accommodation and was without consideration. But as soon as A executed his promise to B by paying the note his agreement becomes executed and he cannot recover back the money so paid.

It may be claimed that the payment of a less sum than the admitted debt is not a good accord and satisfaction. There are numerous authorities sustaining this doctrine. *Lord* Coke stated the rule to be that where the condition is for the payment of a definite, fixed, liquidated sum, the obligor cannot, at the time appointed, pay a less sum in satisfaction of the whole, because it is apparent that the lesser sum of money cannot be a satisfaction of a greater.

This rule has been criticised as unsound and unjust in cases where the lesser sum is accepted in full satisfaction of the greater. See Coke, Litt. 212 B; *Foakes* v. *Beer*, L. R. 9 App. Cas. 605, 614, 617; *Jaffray* v. *Davis*, 48 Hun, 500.

Whilst in other cases the courts have g. still further and held that the rule applied even in cases where the payment was accepted in full satisfaction and a receipt given therefor. *Harriman* v. *Harriman*, 12 Gray, 341; *Smith* v. *Phillips*, 77 Va. 548; *Bunge* v. *Koop*, 48 N. Y. 225; *Wilkinson* v. *Byers*, 1 Ad. & El. 106; Langdell, Sel. Cas. Cont. 197, 201.

Under the view taken by us of this case, it does not become necessary to approve or disapprove of the doctrine promulgated in these cases, for this rule has no application when the payment is made under an agreement which is recognized as valid by the parties, and has been fully executed.

Again, a debt could be discharged at common law by executing a formal release under seal. The seal imported a consideration, and this has not been questioned by any of the cases.

There undoubtedly is a distinction between releases under seal and an ordinary receipt given on the payment of a sum of money which is not under seal, the latter being subject to explanation and proof showing that it was given without consideration.

But even though there may not be an accord and satisfaction, there may be a gift, and the receipt may be evidence of such gift. A gift is a voluntary transfer of any property or thing by one to another without consideration. To be valid it must be executed. There must be a delivery by the donor, such as will place the property or thing given under the control of the donee, and there must be an intent to vest the title in him. Actual and personal delivery by the donor is not always necessary, for when another person is the custodian an order of the donor to deliver to the donee may constitute a gift. It may be oral or in writing. No formal words or expressions are required. It is a question of intent, and the inquiry is as to what was intended by that which was said and done. A promissory note or other evidence of debt may be the subject of a gift, and the delivery of the note or of the evidence of debt is evidence tending to show an intent to give. A debt may be forgiven, and a receipt in full may be evidence of such forgiveness. 2 Schouler, Pers. Prop. 68-90. See also Bishop, Cont. § 50.

In the case of *Gray* v. *Barton*, 55 N. Y. 68, the defendant was owing the plaintiff the sum of $820. The plaintiff told him that if he would give him $1 to make it lawful he would gi· him the entire debt. Whereupon the defendant delivered $1 to the plaintiff, who thereupon executed and delivered a receipt therefor in full to balance all accounts to date of whatever name and nature. It was held that the executing and delivery of the receipt in full, with the purpose of giving the debt, was such an act that the law would construe the instrument, if necessary, as an assignment to the defendant.

This case is in point and is controlling upon the question under consideration. See *Ferry* v. *Stephens*, 66 N. Y. 321; *Carpenter* v. *Soule*, 88 N. Y. 251-256.

We are therefore of the opinion that the proof offered should have been received, that from it the jury might have found that the plaintiffs gave to the defendant the balance of the rent for which this action was brought.

The judgment should be reversed and a new trial ordered, with costs to abide the event.

All concur except **Follett**, *Ch. J.*, **Bradley** and **Parker**, *JJ.*, who dissent.

NORTH CAROLINA SUPREME COURT.

STATE OF NORTH CAROLINA, *Appt.*,
v.
EAVES.

(......N. C.......)

1. The removal of a certain church will not affect the portion of a statute prohibiting the sale of intoxicating liquor within three miles of such church, where the statute does not show that its object was to protect the church alone.

2. An arrest of judgment can be granted only for a defect appearing upon the face of the record. On motion therefor, knowledge derived from the evidence cannot be considered.

(April 21, 1890.)

APPEAL by plaintiff from an order of the Superior Court for Rutherford County arresting judgment upon a verdict convicting defendant of illegal liquor selling. *Reversed.*

The case sufficiently appears in the opinion

Messrs. **Theodore F. Davidson**, *Atty-Gen.*, and **R. H. Battle** for appellant.

Mr. **J. N. Holding** for appellee.

Clark, *J.*, delivered the opinion of the court:

Chapter 234, Acts 1881, prohibited the sale of spirituous liquor at numerous points named, and, among others, "within three miles of Rutherfordton Baptist Church, in Rutherford County." The defendant was indicted for selling spirituous liquor "within three miles of the old site of the Rutherfordton Baptist Church, in Rutherford County, contrary to the Statute in such case made and provided," and was found guilty. He moved in arrest of judgment, which was allowed, as stated by the court, upon the grounds: "(1) that the indictment was defective in not setting forth the fact that at the time of the ratification of the Statute there was such a church in Rutherford County as the 'Rutherfordton Baptist Church, and that it had since been moved;' (2) that the law had been passed to protect the church, and, as the church had been removed and no longer needed protection at the old site, the law ceased to be operative; the reason ceasing, the law ceased also."

The principle quoted, that, "the reason ceasing, the law ceases also," has reference solely to the application of settled legal principles to a given state of facts, a system which is usually called the "common law." It has no application to the supposed legislative reason for adopting a statute which must speak for itself, and is construed according to its tenor. There are rules for the construction of statutes where their meaning is doubtful, such as considering the mischief to be remedied, or the object to be attained.

Potter's Dwar. Stat. 182, citing Story, Confl. Laws, p. 10, and *Denn* v. *Reid*, 35 U. S. 10 Pet. 524 [9 L. ed. 519], says: "Although the spirit of an instrument is to be regarded no less than its letter, yet the spirit is to be collected from the letter."

The rules for construing the meaning of doubtful language in a statute, by the intention of the Legislature, do not authorize the courts to infer the motive of that body in passing an Act, and when a state of facts which then existed ceases, the courts have no power to hold that such state of facts caused the Act to be passed, and therefore the Act itself is at an end. Here there are no doubtful words to construe. The meaning and intention are clearly to forbid the sale of spirituous liquor within three miles of the point named. There is no intent indicated that the law should cease to operate if the state of facts then existing should change. The rule is, if the language is doubtful and the intention clear, to construe the language by the intention. Here, the language being clear, the supposed policy of the Legislature is too uncertain a ground upon which to found the interpretation of the Statute. *Brown* v. *Brown*, 103 N. C. 213.

If the object was solely to protect the church in the quiet exercise of religious services, and not the people of the adjacent territory as well, it is strange that the Act was to be in force all the time, and is not limited to the days such services are held, as is the case with the Act prohibiting the sale or giving away of intoxicating liquor within five miles of a polling place (Code, § 2740); or the Act prohibiting the same within two miles of a political speaking (Id. § 1079); or the General Act prohibiting it, except by licensed dealers, within one mile of any place where religious exercises are in progress. Id. § 3671.

It may be that the motive with the Legislature was to protect the church. The Statute does not so declare. If such was the motive, and the occasion of it has ceased, another Legislature may see fit to repeal the law. The court cannot do so. If the church had been burned, an accident or an incendiary could not destroy an Act of the Legislature, nor could the removal of the church by vote of a majority of its members nullify the law. The church is merely designated as the locality from which the distance of three miles is to be measured. Its removal can no more repeal the Statute than the destruction of a beginning corner can vitiate a deed. The removal to a new site cannot make it the center of a new district of three miles, but the distance must still be measured from the spot where the church stood when the Act was passed. In Spain, where windmills are common, they have a saying: "Though the mills are down, the winds are blowing there still." Though the church has been removed, people are still living within the three-mile radius of where it stood, and they cannot be deprived of the protection of the Statute upon the assumption that the Legislature meant to protect churches only. Indeed, in this same Act, territory within a given distance of certain mills, mines, factories and railroad stations, and also certain entire townships, are protected. Could the act of a private citizen in closing his mine or removing his mill or factory, or the act of a railroad corporation in changing its depot, or of the county commissioners in the division or absorption of a township, repeal the application of the Statute to the territory described in the Act? With as much force it might be argued that a change of name would have that effect. If the continuing force of a statute depends upon the conduct of individuals, the congregation would take the adjacent territory out of the Statute as certainly by a change of the name of their church as by a removal of the building, possibly, a few yards or more. In both cases the test is, What spot was designated by the Legislature as the point from which the territory exempted is to be measured? and no one except the Legislature can change or repeal the Statute. *State* v. *Moody*, 95 N. C. 656; *State* v. *Patterson*, 98 N. C. 666.

The case of *State* v. *Hampton*, 77 N. C. 526, is not in point; for there the Act prohibited the sale of intoxicating liquor within three miles of Asheville & Spartanburg Railroad during the construction of said road, and the Act was held to be in force only during the time limited. There is no such limitation here. Had the Act prohibited the sale of liquor within three miles of the church during divine services, whenever no services were held there, whether the omission was caused by a removal of the building or otherwise, the Act would not be in operation. *Aliter*, when, as here, the church or the mill or railroad station is only a designation of the central point of the protected territory.

Another objection applies to both of the grounds assigned in arrest of judgment. An arrest of judgment can only be granted for a defect appearing upon the face of the record. Nothing which appears thereon shows that the church had in fact been removed at all, or stands elsewhere than it did the day the Act was ratified. It is true the bill charges "the old site of Rutherfordton Baptist Church." *Non constat*, but that the church named in the Act was built upon such old site. It may or may not be so. It is a matter of surmise, and not a "defect apparent." Probably it would have been better if the additional allegation suggested by the court below had been made in the indictment, but advantage of any supposed defect in that regard could only be taken before verdict. It is cured by verdict, for, apart from the knowledge derived from the evidence, which cannot be considered on a motion in arrest of judgment, there is nothing to show that the words "old site" are anything other than mere surplusage. If, however, those words can be taken as showing a removal of the church since the Statute, there is no defect; for the old site is the proper point from which the three miles are to be measured. The judgment in arrest must be set aside, and the cause remanded, that the superior court may proceed to pass judgment upon the verdict in conformity to this opinion.

Error.

VIRGINIA SUPREME COURT OF APPEALS.

Alice Lee DAVIS *et al.*, *Appts.*,
v.
Thomas V. STRANGE'S EXECUTOR.

(....Va....)

A reconveyance by a natural daughter to her father will be set aside where he had deliberately conveyed her the property as a gift, and after becoming feeble in body and mind was, although unwilling, driven by other members of his family to ask her for a reconveyance, and she gave it without time for reflection, consultation or advice while deeply moved by his distress, and urged by the family lawyer, who had been sent with him and who told her that it would be best for her to do so, although he knew the fact, unknown to her, that her father's latest will had omitted all provisions for her which former wills contained.

(April 10, 1890.)

APPEAL by complainants from a decree of the Circuit Court for the City of Lynchburg dismissing their bill in a suit brought to set aside a deed of certain real estate which was alleged to have been procured through undue influence. *Reversed.*

The facts are fully stated in the opinion.

Messrs. **Kirkpatrick & Blackford** for appellants.

Mr. **R. G. H. Kean** for appellee.

Fauntleroy, *J.*, delivered the opinion of the court:

The petition of Alice Lee Davis and Joseph

NOTE.—*Undue influence.*

To constitute undue influence the testator must be so controlled by persuasion, pressure or fraudulent contrivance that he is not left to act intelligently and voluntarily, but becomes subject to the will or purposes of others. *Re* Mitchell's Estate (Minn.) Feb. 27, 1890.

Undue influence must destroy free agency and amount to moral or physical coercion. Elkinton v. Brick, 18 Cent. Rep. 889, 44 N. J. Eq. 154.

Importunity, which cannot be and is not resisted, is undue influence. The mere suggestion to a testator that an indicated testamentary provision would be productive of justice between the natural objects of his bounty can hardly amount to undue influence. *Ibid.*

It is impossible to distinguish by rule between that which is within the bounds of legitimate influence and that which makes the influence undue. The effect of all acts must depend upon the relations between the parties to them, and the character, strength and condition of each, and be determined by the application of sound sense to each given case. *Ibid.*

When two parties occupy to each other a confidential relation, and a sale is made by the party reposing confidence to the party in whom confidence is reposed, equity raises a presumption against the validity of the transaction. Dunn v. Dunn, 6 Cent. Rep. 91, 42 N. J. Eq. 431.

Undue influence exists wherever, through weakness, ignorance, dependence or implicit reliance of one on the good faith of another, the latter obtains an ascendency which prevents the former from exercising an unbiased judgment. To affect a will it must, in a measure at least, destroy free agency and operate on the mind of the testator at the time of making the will. Herster v. Herster, 122 Pa. 239.

Where there is a suspicion of undue influence, raised by general circumstances, in a suit to set aside a deed of a gift made to one *in loco parentis*, the burden is on the grantee to show grantor's knowledge and the fairness of the transaction. Worrall's App. 1 Cent. Rep. 201, 110 Pa. 349. See Cowee v. Cornell, 75 N. Y. 92.

In determining the question of undue influence, the mental and physical condition of the testator and the provisions of the will itself are proper matters of consideration. Myers v. Hauger, 98 Mo. 433.

Where a son enjoyed the confidence of his aged mother, and exercised great influence over her, and confidential relations existed between them, the burden of proof is on such son to show, aside from the formal way by which a gift passed to his credit, that it was in fact a gift. Parker v. Parker, 4 Cent. Rep. 67, 45 N. J. Eq. 224.

Undue influence as to a gift *inter vivos* may be shown by evidence of influence by the donee in other matters; as, in the relations of physician, advisor, friend and agent. Woodbury v. Woodbury, 2 New Eng. Rep. 90, 141 Mass. 329.

The burden of showing that a will was induced by undue influence is upon the party who alleges the fact. Tyler v. Gardiner, 35 N. Y. 594.

As to wills.

The undue influence to be available to set aside a will must be such as to overpower and subject the will of the testator, thus producing a disposition of property which he would not have made if left freely to act his own pleasure. *Re* Eiler's Will, 29 N. Y. S. R. 58.

It is not necessary to invalidate a will on the ground of undue influence, that the improper influence should have been resorted to at the time of the execution of the will; but it is sufficient if the

S. Davis, her husband, represents that they are aggrieved by a decree of the Circuit Court of the City of Lynchburg, entered on the 3d day of January, 1889, by which it was adjudged and decreed that the bill of the complainants be dismissed; and that the complainant, Alice Lee Davis, formerly Alice Lee Strange, pay to the defendants their costs, etc.

The bill was filed by appellant Alice Lee Strange to vacate and annul and to set aside a deed, executed by her August 26, 1887, by which she conveyed to Thomas V. Strange a house and lot in the City of Lynchburg, Va., of the value of $8,000 or $10,000, without consideration, in a situation of sudden surprise and emergency of action, without the presence or advice of friend or counsel, and when she was rendered wholly unable to exercise a consenting mind, by the undue influence of her father and of his attorney and agent, who pressed her with importunity and strong persuasions, and assurances that she would be otherwise provided for and compensated, that she should not lose anything by it, and that it would be best for her to make the property back to Mr. Strange, as it was threatened to be burned; under the compulsion of which, she hastily and inconsiderately executed the deed, to which she had been already most powerfully moved and induced by the distress and suffering, expressed and exhibited to her, of her aged and devoted father, occasioned to him by the reproaches and importunate remonstrances and interference of his son-in-law and other daughter.

The facts of the case, as disclosed in the record, show the environments of the appellant, and the actual, relative and correlative circumstances in which she was placed, and under which she was improperly induced to the hasty, inconsiderate and unconscionable transaction which she prays to be relieved from by the equitable jurisdiction of this court, reviewing the denial of her prayer and the dismissal of her bill by the circuit court.

Alice Lee Strange, who, since this suit was instituted, has intermarried with Joseph S. Davis, is the natural daughter of the late Thomas V. Strange, of Lynchburg, a white man, by a colored woman named "Belle." She was received into the family of her father as his child, and treated, both by his wife and himself, as the petted daughter of the household, with equal rights and recognition with his legitimate child. Every advantage of education was afforded her; and, when old enough to leave the paternal roof, she was sent to a boarding-school in Washington City, where she remained until she graduated. It is the fact—the status—of this relation of parent and child, and the family recognition and association which obtained between the appellant and her father and his household, which it is important to state and remark, however revolting to the moral sense and offensive against public policy. The relations which existed between her and her father and his wife and the whole family are indicated by a number of letters from her father to her, written during her absence in Washington, which are filed as exhibits with the bill. They show the deepest parental affection and the most anxious and tender solicitude and guardian care over her and for her as his favorite child; and his liberal intentions toward her in regard to his estate, and that he freely conferred with her in regard to his intentions. They not only show her environments and motives, which, through her filial feelings, overmastered her will in the rash and immoderate act into which she was precipitated, and from which she now seeks relief; but they reveal the hidden though powerful influences and agencies which instigated and controlled a transaction in which her father was as unwilling and as much wronged a victim as was the daughter herself.

---

will was afterwards executed under a controlling influence previously put in operation, and which was still controlling the testator to the extent of destroying his free agency. Overall v. Bland, 11 Ky. L. Rep. 871.

Late decisions in reference to deeds.

A deed of land from a woman seventy-seven years of age, of sound mind, but worried and nervous about the matter in question, will be set aside upon a showing that she was unduly influenced, that she was in confidential relation with the grantee, and signed the deed thinking that it was a power of attorney, and that she did not intend to part with the title to the land. June v. Willis, 24 Blatchf. 198, 30 Fed. Rep. 11.

A deed by an aged, feeble and ignorant man cannot be sustained, where the consideration is the future care from a daughter, which arrangement is not embodied in the deed, which the grantor's inability to read made the more necessary; and where there were no terms agreed upon, and the son-in-law accounted to the grantor for the proceeds of a farm conveyed, for a year or more after the deed. McDaniel v. McCoy, 12 West. Rep. 664, 68 Mich. 232.

A conveyance of a farm worth $2,200, by a man seventy-seven years old, and weak in body and mind, to his son-in-law, in consideration of a promise, afterward fulfilled, on the part of the latter, to take care of the grantor as long as he lived and to bury him, will not, in the absence of positive proof of fraud or duress, upon grantor's death within a year after conveyance, be set aside at the instance of his heirs. Travis v. Lowry (Pa.) 7 Cent. Rep. 553.

A deed obtained by children from an aged and infirm parent of failing mind, of property worth $5,000, for a consideration of $10, on a mere vague promise to take care of the grantor, by representing to him that other children are about to place him under guardianship and seize his property, will be set aside as having been obtained by fraud and undue influence, although the other children do subsequently obtain an inquest and have the grantor adjudged of unsound mind, as they had previously proposed to the grantees as the proper course, but not for the purpose of obtaining control of his property. Giles v. Hodge, 74 Wis. 360.

Transactions based on breach of trust, not enforceable.

A person cannot retain the advantage of a transaction which he has promoted through a breach of confidence reposed in him by a party to the transaction, even though the transaction could not have been impeached had no confidential relations existed. Tate v. Williamson, L. R. 2 Ch. 55; Rhodes v. Bate, L. R. 1 Ch. 252; Billage v. Southee, 9 Hare, 534.

This principle extends to every possible case in which a fiduciary relation exists as a fact, where

We cannot extend these letters, in this opinion, as they appear in the record, in their full length and significance; but a few extracts from some of them will illustrate our commentary.

On the 18th of November, 1878, he writes:

"My Dear Alice: Yours to mine of the 11th inst. was read to me last night by Minnie [his wife], so far as she could for sobbing; for she can never read your letters without crying. Please recollect what I have before said to you —that is, to do well for yourself; if you do that, all will be well with you. That means much more, perhaps, than you are aware. It is the great concern of men advanced in life to know what to do with what they have accumulated by industry and economy and prudence; men of my own stamp, for instance, don't leave their effects to fools and spendthrifts."

On the 12th of December, 1878, he writes:

"Dear Alice: Your postal card to Nannie [his daughter, Mrs. Litchford] to hand at the store [of Strange & Litchford]. You know that I have before asked you not to write on p. c. to us. It is a fact, that we have kept secret from you, that you are hated by one in the family with unequalled hatred, and simply because Minnie and myself love and provide for you, and so intend to do. It was because of that that Nannie [Mrs. Litchford] went to the Springs last summer, at a cost of $150, to prevent her from staying in the house with negroes. When you visit Lynchburg, you are not to visit them, tho' Nannie and the children will visit you. I hope and pray that your talents will place you head and shoulders ahead of them; whilst I wish them all good luck, both parties are of my family. I care for all, and wish to place all beyond the powers of this world; but you in particular I wish to see stand prominent in the land because of your worth. We don't hear from Belle and Charlie."

On the 31st of July, 1879, he writes:

"Dear Loved One: Your last of 30th inst. to hand; all three of your letters to hand. Last one causes uneasiness for fear of my letter to you on Monday, 28th, draft for $25, is lost or stolen. . . . Don't think that I will ever forget you. That would be impossible after Minnie and myself having raised you, and the request that I would not forsake you, and still more to stand by and see you complete your studies. Two people were never more devoted to each other than Minnie and myself; and for her sake, if no more, you will not be forgotten or forsaken. Death is one of the uncertain things of the world, and therefore I shall leave in the hands of J. E. Yoder some important papers for you, and with the request, in the event of my death, that you be at once informed of it, that the proper steps may be taken to secure your interest. I have much to say. God bless you."

On the 10th of October, 1879, he writes:

"Dear Child Alice: Some several years since I made a will, which was then my will; but since the death of Minnie [his wife] it is right to make another, which was done yesterday, and is in the hands of J. E. Yoder, who was one of the witnesses of the same, as was also Mr. Work and Mayor Branch, in which you are largely interested. Should I drop off, you will be posted. It is entirely secret, and will so remain until my death. Say nothing of it to anyone, but I have made arrangement for Belle to have $150 per annum, unless she marry; in that event, she has nothing. I mention this to assure you that you will never be forgotten. Not a word from you since the telegram. How is that? God bless you, Belle and Charlie. If you write, and I don't get them, I must get a box to myself."

—Thus showing his apprehension that someone unfriendly to her (meaning his son-in-law and partner) would intercept their correspondence, if his mail continued to come with the general mail of Strange & Litchford.

On the 23d of October, 1879, he writes:

---

there is confidence reposed on one side, and resulting superiority and influence on the other, whether the duties involved be moral, social, domestic or merely personal. It is applied to gifts, whether mere bounties or the effects of liberality based upon antecedent favors and obligations. See Brock v. Barnes, 40 Barb. 521; Todd v. Grove, 33 Md. 188; Falk v. Turner, 101 Mass. 494; Turner v. Turner, 44 Mo. 535; Wistar's App. 54 Pa. 60; Greenfield's Estate, 14 Pa. 489; Taylor v. Taylor, 49 U. S. 8 How. 183 (12 L. ed. 1040); Jenkins v. Pye, 37 U. S. 12 Pet. 241 (9 L. ed. 1070); Prideaux v. Lonsdale, 1 DeG. J. & S. 433; Broun v. Kennedy, 4 DeG. J. & S. 217; Fulham v. McCarthy, 1 H. L. Cas. 703; Savery v. King, 5 H. L. Cas. 627; Morgan v. Minette, L. R. 6 Ch. Div. 638; Turner v. Collins, L. R. 7 Ch. 329.

It is almost impossible in the course of the connection between parties in confidential relations, that a transaction shall stand purporting to be a bounty for the execution of an antecedent duty. Hatch v. Hatch, 9 Ves. Jr. 292.

This rule is applied to all transactions where influence over another has been acquired and abused in which confidence has been reposed and betrayed. Smith v. Kay, 7 H. L. Cas. 750; Huguenin v. Baseley, 14 Ves. Jr. 273, 2 Lead. Cas. in Eq. *556 (4th Am. ed.) 1156.

Any surreptitious dealing between one principal and the agent of the other principal is a fraud on such other principal cognizable in a court of equity. Panama & S. P. Teleg. Co. v. India Rubber, G. P. & T. W. Co. L. R. 10 Ch. 515.

Where all parties to a transaction knew that they were dealing with a trust fund devoted by the donor to a specific purpose, the utmost good faith was demanded on the part of the purchaser. American Emigrant Co. v. Wright, 97 U. S. 339 (24 L. ed. 912).

Purchasers obtaining a contract for the sale of land through a broker, who, with their knowledge and in collusion with them, has concealed material facts from his principal or exerted his skill in the negotiation against his principal, cannot in equity enforce the contract. Young v. Hughes, 32 N. J. Eq. 372; Farnsworth v. Hemmer, 1 Allen, 494; Raisin v. Clark, 41 Md. 158; Walker v. Osgood, 98 Mass. 348; Rice v. Wood, 113 Mass. 133; Dunlop v. Richards, 2 E. D. Smith, 181.

Whenever a purchaser is affected with notice of facts which in law constitute a breach of trust, the sale is void as to him, and the property remains and continues subject to the trust. Wormley v. Wormley, 21 U. S. 8 Wheat. 421 (5 L. ed. 651); Oliver v. Piatt, 44 U. S. 3 How. 333 (11 L. ed. 622); Mechanics Bank v. Seton, 26 U. S. 1 Pet. 300 (7 L. ed. 153); Wilson v. Mason, 5 U. S. 1 Cranch, 45 (2 L. ed. 29); Murray v. Ballou, 1 Johns. Ch. 566, 1 N. Y. Ch. L. ed. 247; Jaudon v. National City Bank, 8 Blatchf. 430; Story, Eq. 395, 1257; Perry, Tr. § 217.

"Yours of the 19th and 20th to hand. Next Monday I will send you amount promised. I want you to keep on with music and drawing, as Minnie requested. Her life was tied up in yours, and if I am to carry out any wish of hers on earth, it is to complete your education, and then to see that you are provided for. Will send the dress as soon as ready. May kind words be with you, and God's blessing rest upon you. If you will start on teaching, you will find that you will rise very fast. If you marry you will be tied down. There is much ahead for you."

On the 20th of November, 1879, he writes:

"Dear Child: Yours of the 16th at hand to-day. Am always glad to hear from you. Am glad your music scholars are on the increase. It afforded me happiness to do or say things to make our angel Minnie happy, and she, as you know, left nothing undone to make me happy or comfortable; and consequently two people never got on better than we did. And from day of our marriage to her sickness our attachment increased for each other, and now soon be five months since her death, and yet I can't realize the fact that she has gone to the spirit land. And if I was the Christian that she was, I would rejoice for the time to come for me to go to meet her. Nannie is all to me that she can be; nothing left undone that can be done for my comfort; yet, after all, if I could be with you and Belle, it seems it would be a paradise to me. I advise you against writing to Nannie, on account of her selfish husband, and his hatred for you, not for any wrong that you have done him, or any other living soul, but because you were loved by Minnie and myself. I expect the day will come when you will soar long above him; and for that end never cease to strive. I enclose X. Will send the other toward the end of the month. May God's blessing rest upon you, dear child, and the other two."

"Lynchburg, April 20th, 1884.

"My Dear Alice: No doubt you think long time my delay in writing. Writing has got to be quite irksome to me, hence one cause of delay; and next to that the pressure upon me. As to my taking up the two notes before they are due, I do not now see how to do it, as we have just got through a $20,000 job, namely the mill. I will take them up, however, as they come due. Our city is making rapid strides of improvement. I expect to be over in June.

"Affectionately, T. V. Strange."

These extracts show that appellant was very dear to her father and his wife; and that his full intent was not only to educate and take care of her while he lived, but to make ample provision for her at his death. With deep parental care for his favorite child, and with solicitude lest she should, by some accident, not be provided for, he made his will in 1879, in which she was provided for, and which he gave to Mr. Yoder for safe keeping. He apprised her of it, and that she was largely interested in it. In the year 1881 he determined to change his scheme of providing for her by will, and placed his bounty to her in grants by deeds; to protect her, no doubt, as far as possible, from the contingencies of his own advancing age, and the machinations of his son-in-law, whose selfish hate he so dreaded, and against whom he, with prophetic wisdom, intended to shield her.

On the 1st of August, 1881, he purchased and conveyed to her a dwelling-house in Washington City, costing $3,500. The deed was drawn by his counsel, Mr. W. D. Branch, and declares that it is made "in consideration of the obligations growing out of the peculiar and near relations existing between him and the said Alice Lee Strange, which relations, under a sense of duty not only to her, but to his God, he feels bound to acknowledge, and takes pleasure in heeding; and also in consideration of personal kindnesses and attention shown and services rendered him by the said Alice Lee Strange; as well as in consideration of the earnest request made of him by his wife before and in her last illness."

On the 22d of December, 1881, he conveyed to his daughter Alice, by a deed, the property in Lynchburg, now in question, reserving a life estate to himself. The consideration for this grant the deed declares to be "valuable services rendered him by said Alice Lee Strange, as well as in consideration of the anxious and earnest request made of him by Minnie N. Strange, deceased, his late wife, in her last illness, to make ample provision for the support, comfort and maintenance of the said Alice Lee Strange, which request, having promised faithfully to comply with, he feels in honor bound to obey, and for other considerations him thereunto moving."

Having executed and delivered this deed, on the next day, December 23, 1881, he made his will, the one which went to probate, and which was written by his friend and legal adviser, W. D. Branch. By this will he gave all his estate to his daughter, Nannie M., the wife of L. E. Litchford, for life, with remainder over to her children. Beside what he gave to Mrs. Litchford by his will, he had already made large advancements and conveyances of valuable realty to her. Thus he had provided for both his daughters; had satisfied his conscience and his own devoted attachment to his child, Alice, by making good his sacred promise to his dying wife, and, as he vainly thought, had protected his best-loved child from the contingencies of fortune, and the dreaded avarice and hate of his selfish son-in-law.

Alice, having entire confidence in her father, did not put the deed for the Lynchburg property to record, and things remained unchanged until the summer of 1887, when some injudicious friend erroneously advised her that both the deeds to her were void, because no money consideration was named in them. She therefore brought them back to her father, who, at her request, re-conveyed both pieces of property—that in Washington and that in Lynchburg—to her, by two other deeds, bearing date August 18, 1887, wherein he repeats the considerations named in each deed for which they were respectively substituted, and adds in each the words: "And in further consideration of $5, in lawful money of the United States, to him in hand paid by the party of the second part."

His willingness to execute, so as to quiet any apprehensions in regard to the validity of the grant, and his solemn re-affirmation of his motives for making the conveyances, attest the fact that his affection and determination to provide for his "dear child" were as warm and fixed in 1887 as in 1881.

Alice placed the deed to the Lynchburg property on record on the day it was executed, and this became the *Iliad* of woes to her, and to her devoted old father. Up to that time the fact of its existence was known only to her father and to W. D. Branch and to herself, and the jealousy of the Litchfords seems to have slept in the comfortable knowledge that, by the will of 1881, Alice was excluded from all participation in her father's large estate; and they rejoiced in the belief that their father had ignored his sense of duty to his God; had broken his sacred promise to his dying wife, and was rapidly closing his days on earth, unmindful of the child of his best affection, whom he had tenderly nurtured, and of whom he was so proud. The recordation of the deed discovered their error, and rudely shocked their fancied security in the exclusive enjoyment of the whole of their feeble old father's large estate, and roused them into jealous and energetic resistance.

Poor old Strange, in lean and slippered pantaloon, and a condition of senile imbecility, lived at Litchford's house. When a copy of the deed was procured from the clerk's office, the family was thrown into a high state of excitement. Litchford at once set off for Mr. W. D. Branch, the family lawyer, and asked him to come to his store, and then sent him over to his house to see Mr. Strange, who he said was wanting him. Litchford had told Mr. Strange, with impassioned violence, that he would rather see the property burned down than that it should go to Alice; and Mr. Branch, with his mind attuned to Litchford's sentiments (of which his burst of indignation to poor old feeble Strange was doubtless a fair sample), went over to Litchford's house to see the culprit, who had shocked the long latent moral complacency of his son-in-law and daughter by the development of a diversion of a small portion of his large property to his darling child, and, so much, from their jealous and selfish expectation. The old man was sitting on the porch alone; but upon Mr. Branch's arrival, Mrs. Litchford came upon the scene, holding up the offensive deed, and exclaiming: "See what father has done; I don't believe he knew what he was doing when he signed it!" This stormy drama wound up with a demand by Mrs. Litchford upon Mr. Branch to know what must be done; and, on his saying that the law had no remedy, the poor old father, impotently shrinking from the selfish ire which was aroused, said: "I believe I can get Alice to re-convey the property to me; I don't think she will refuse me." This suggestion, which was the real object of the interview, was eagerly caught at, and it was arranged that Mr. Strange, and Mr. Branch to accompany him, at the request of Mrs. Litchford, should take the early train the next morning, and seek Alice down at Chatham, in Pittsylvania County (where she momentarily was on a visit), and get her to re-convey the property, by a deed which Mr. Branch was to carry down, ready made, so that there should be no delay, and no time for reflection or consultation or advice. The poor old dying man, who, in a week afterwards, was at rest from his sorrow, was taken down to be made the unwilling instrument—a puppet in the hands of the managers—to sacrifice the rights of his dear child, Alice, that his few remaining days might be passed in peace. Had she been brought to him in Lynchburg, she would have had time to think and to confer with friends—even, perchance, to consult counsel; but in Chatham she was without advisers and a stranger, and would the more easily yield to the piteous plight of her tottering old father, and the persuasive presence of the counsel of those who were the real and potent projectors of the scene, and the expectant beneficiaries of the sacrifice.

To Chatham they went, on the 26th of August, 1887, on the early morning train, and found Alice at the house of Polly Davis, on the side of the road which leads from the depot to the village. Polly Davis, it is important to note, was no relative, nor even an acquaintance of Alice Lee Strange, except as a visitor for a few days to a schoolmate acquaintance in Polly Davis' house. As Mr. Strange and Mr. Branch passed the house, Alice was in the yard, saw her father and called him to her, and he and Mr. Branch took breakfast with her and the family. After breakfast Mr. Strange and Mr. Branch went out on the porch, and Alice, after aiding in household duties which were requisite, joined them on the porch and carried on a conversation, chiefly with her father, about her affairs in Washington. This continued for some time, without a word of reference to the object of the visit, when the old father, shrinking from the unwilling task which had been assigned to him, got up and took Mr. Branch out for a walk. All Mr. Branch has revealed of their conversation during that walk is that he, fearing their trip might be in vain, told Mr. Strange that when he got back to the house he must tell Alice of the object of their visit. Mr. Strange is dead, and Alice's mouth is sealed; while Mr. Branch, who was employed by those who were to receive the benefit, to induce this young and unadvised girl, in a moment of sudden and irresistible importunity, and of sympathetic sorrow at the sight of the halting gait, the trembling frame and quivering voice of the poor old father, whom she tenderly loved and on whom she had implicitly relied and trusted as the devoted and faithful protector and author and guide of her life, without reflection, and without the advice of friends, or the counsel of a lawyer, to give away property which was valued at $8,000 or $10,000, and which she had held for over six years—he, Mr. Branch, with all the bias of his employment, and of the unfortunate position and part which he took in the transaction, is permitted to testify as to all the details of the execution and procurement of the deed.

Polly Davis, who is a wholly disinterested and impartial witness, paid no attention, and heard nothing that was said, until she heard Mr. Branch say to Alice: "It will be best for you to make this property back to Mr. Strange, as it was threatened to be burned;" and Mr. Strange said, "You shall not lose anything by it"—to which Mr. Branch added, "I will insure you shan't lose anything by it." To all this Alice had little to say, but would not consent

Finally after they had teased her, she commenced crying, and so did Mr. Strange. Mr. Strange said he would give her the worth in money, or more than the worth of it; and Mr. Branch added: "If it remained like it was, it would be only the land there, and it would do her no good, because the people near there said no colored person should live there." "He (Mr. Strange) seemed very feeble that morning —so weak that when he went to breakfast and had to step down a little step, Alice had to help him, and he caught the side of the door. As to his mind, I don't know, as I was not well acquainted with him; but he seemed to be very easy to weep that morning, for a gentleman."

This statement of Polly Davis has the verisimiltude of consistency, congruity and truth. These gentlemen had come down from Lynchburg to persuade Alice to execute the deed; and, being there, it may be rationally believed they used every argument and persuasion in possible range.

But laying aside the evidence of Polly Davis, and the allegations of the bill, and confining attention strictly to the glimpses of the transaction which are disclosed by Mr. Branch, and his deposition itself proves a case of unconscionable cunning and cruel wrong which calls loudly and imperatively for the righteous interference of a court of equity. On the return of Mr. Strange from the walk with Mr. Branch, with his purpose nerved and his mind impressed by Mr. Branch's admonition of the danger of a failure in the object of their journey, he again took his seat in the porch, and after waiting a short while, said: "Alice, I want you to re-convey back that property to me." "What property?—the property in Washington?" she replied. "No, the property in Lynchburg," said he. "What do you mean? Why do you want me to re-convey it to you?" asked Alice. "My family in Lynchburg," answered Strange, "are very much disturbed about my having given you this property, and Mr Litchford says he would rather see me burn down all the houses on it than to see me convey it to you. I thought that, as I had done a great deal for you, and had been very kind to you, you would re-convey it to me." "Do you want me to re-convey it to you, without any equivalent?" she replied. "I have no equivalent to offer," said he. After this much, he went out in the yard, and commenced walking backwards and forwards a good deal distressed, says Mr. Branch. But why a good deal distressed, if it was his own hopeful undertaking? Enough to distress him, and to break his faithful heart, and to bring him to the grave into which he sank a few days thereafter, a victim to the mortification, which he keenly felt, of the sacrilegious wrong of violating his solemn promise to his dying wife and robbing a beloved child whom he had pledged his whole life to protect and provide for. The pressure was too great for him; the conflict between his dread of those at home, and his love for the daughter before him, was enough to distress him; knowing, as he did, that he was the helpless instrument in this fraud on her rights; and he abandoned the attempt, fled the scene, and went out into the yard, and walked backwards and forwards in speechless agony; and, while Alice watched him, with pitying eye and wrung heart, from the porch, the cool and cautious Mr. Branch, steady to his undertaking and true to the expectations of those for whom he acted, took up the refrain, and plied the persuasion: "Mr. Strange authorizes me, Miss Alice, to give you $250 if you will re-convey him this property; but I think he relies entirely on your gratitude. Has he not been very kind to you, and given you a great deal? I think, under all the circumstances, you ought to grant his request." "Has Mr. Strange written his will?" she asked. "Yes, I prepared a will for him, which was signed," he replied. He says he did not tell her that in that will there was no provision for her, because she did not ask him. What was the purport and only possible point of her asking him, quickly and sharply, in response to his saying to her that he thought she ought to execute the deed and grant her father's request: "Has Mr. Strange written his will?" But Mr. Branch saw no *suppressio veri* in this cautious reserve, and he says, "she seemed very much disturbed, and looking at her father, as he walked backward and forward, she said: 'I can't think of causing him distress in his old age; he has been too kind to me; I will let him have the property back. I will be up in Lynchburg in a few days, and will fix the deed.'" The victory was won; and the persuasions of Mr. Branch, and the sight of her father's speechless but eloquent distress, as he walked back and forth before her in the yard, had overcome the tender hearted girl, and, yielding to the dominion of her filial love and life-long duty and devotion to her father, she said she would be up in Lynchburg in a few days and fix the deed. But no; there was a *locus penitentiæ* in a few days' reflection; and, if she got to Lynchburg, she might have advice and counsel as to her rights; and to avoid this very danger Mr. Branch presented his ready-made deed—volunteered to go, and did hurriedly go, for a notary, who came and took and certified the acknowledgment of the deed, with which in his pocket Mr. Branch hurried back to Lynchburg and put it on the record that day—he to receive the plaudit of the Litchford instigators and beneficiaries of the unconscionable wrong; poor old Father Strange to lie down and die, and Alice to console herself with Mr. Branch's gratulating chuckle to her, on the consummation of the rape of her father's bounty, that he thought "she had acted very nobly."

Mr. Branch knew that, in the former wills prepared for Mr. Strange, he had lovingly and lavishly provided for his child Alice; and Alice had been freely and frequently informed of his dispositions and unalterable purpose in her favor; and Mr. Branch knew that Alice knew that he was the legal adviser and confidential friend of her father; and yet, when she, in the extreme stringency and overbearing influences operating upon her to induce consent to the sacrifice which he told her he thought she ought to make, quickly, responsively and pertinently asked him if her father had made his will, he, with wily reserve, did not tell her what, really, it then and there concerned her to know, that she was totally unprovided for in that will which, he told her, he had prepared; and, with his confidential knowledge of its provisions, urged upon her as his opinion that, under all the circumstances, she ought to reconvey the property to her father. Equity grants relief wherever influence is acquired and abused, or confidence reposed and betrayed. *Lord* Kingsdowne in *Smith* v. *Kay*, 7 H. L. Cas. 750.

"Equity is especially jealous to guard the welfare of the weaker party in all contracts between parent and child, guardian and ward, attorney and client, trustee and *cestui que trust*, and, indeed, in all persons standing in fiduciary relations to each other. It is especially active and searching in dealing with gifts, voluntary conveyances, and deeds without due consideration, though its range is so wide as to cover all possible dealings between persons holding such relations, or any relations in which dominion, whether physical, intellectual, moral, religious, domestic or of any sort, may be exercised by one party over the other, or in which the parties contracting are not at arm's length." White & T. Lead. Cas. in Eq. ed. 1887, 1184.

In the case of *Dent* v. *Bennett*, 4 Myln. & C. 269, *Lord Chancellor* Cottenham said: "I will not narrow the rule, or run the risk of, in any degree, fettering the exercise of the beneficial jurisdiction of this court, by any enumeration of the description of persons against whom it ought to be most freely used."

In the famous case of *Huguenin* v. *Baseley*, 14 Ves. Jr. 273, *Lord* Eldon said: "The question is, not whether she knew what she was doing, had done or proposed to do, but how that intention was produced; whether all that care and providence was placed around her, as against those who advised her, which, from their situation and relation with respect to her, they were bound to exert in her behalf."

Among the relations, the mere existence of which casts suspicion on all business transactions between parties holding them, the one which most excites the jealous watchfulness of a court of equity is that of parent and child, especially where (as in the case at bar) it is the parent who is the beneficiary of the child's bounty, and when that bounty is large and entirely disproportionate to the means of the donor. See Story, Eq. Jur. § 309.

"In respect of bounties by children in favor of their parents, it is for the parent—father or mother—to show that no advantage was taken of his or her influence or knowledge, and that the transaction was fair and conscionable. And the same is true of those standing in affection and influence *in loco parentis*." Bigelow, Fr. (1888) 354.

"Causes of surprise and sudden action, without due deliberation, may properly be referred to the same head of fraud or imposition. An undue advantage is taken of the party, under circumstances which mislead, confuse or disturb the just result of his judgment, and thus expose him to be the victim of the artful, the importunate and the cunning. The surprise here intended must be accompanied with fraud and circumvention, or, at least, by such circumstances as demonstrate that the party had no opportunity to use suitable deliberation, or that there was some influence or management to mislead him. If proper time is not allowed to the party, and he acts improvidently; if he is importunately pressed; if those in whom he most places confidence make use of strong persuasions; if he is not fully aware of the consequences, but is suddenly drawn into the act; if he is not permitted to consult disinterested friends or counsel, before he is called upon to act in circumstances of sudden emergency or unexpected right or acquisition—in these and many like cases, if there has been great inequality in the bargain, courts of equity will assist the party, upon the ground of fraud, imposition or unconscionable advantage."

If *Judge* Story had been commenting upon the facts of this case, when he wrote this section 251 of his Equity Jurisprudence, he could not have more exactly described every feature, circumstance and character of this revolting transaction.

The leading English cases developing the jurisdiction of courts of equity in cases like the one under review are collected and quoted in the notes to the celebrated case of *Huguenin* v. *Baseley*, *supra*. See also Pom. Eq. §§ 951-957; *Rhodes* v. *Bate*, L. R. 1 Ch. 252, 257; *Billage* v. *Southee*, 9 Hare, 534, 540; *Miller* v. *Simonds*, 72 Mo. 669; *Wood* v. *Rabe*, 96 N. Y. 414; *Archer* v. *Hudson*, 7 Beav. 551; *Woodbury* v. *Woodbury*, 141 Mass. 329, 2 New Eng. Rep. 90; *Hoghton* v. *Hoghton*, 15 Beav. 278.

In the case of *Bridgman* v. *Green*, 2 Ves. Sr. 627, and Wilmot's Notes, 61, the grantee carried his own attorney to the grantor to prepare the conveyance; which fact, coupled with the fact that the grantor had no counsel with him, is one of the grounds on which the conveyance was set aside. In that case *Lord Commissioner* Wilmot, in speaking of Lock's conduct as the attorney of the grantee to procure the conveyance, says: "What was his duty to have done? Why, to have remonstrated, or, at least, with modesty and humility, to have inquired into the principles and motives of such a wild and immoderate act. A man of nice honor would have said in a moment: 'As I am an entire stranger to you and your circumstances, and there is something so extraordinary and uncommon in what you [not I, Mr. Branch] propose to do, I will not be concerned in it on any account whatever.' He should at least have protracted the execution of such an extravagant purpose, and should have given time for deliberation."

In that case Lock finished his exploit in five days; in the case at bar Branch, having by his persuasive urgency induced Alice to the wild and immoderate act of giving away her patrimony, and produced the intention of the extraordinary and uncommon gift, so far from protracting the execution and giving time for deliberation, demurred to Alice's proposition to go up to Lynchburg before she signed the deed; produced one ready-made; went for the notary, and the whole matter was completed and he on his return to Lynchburg, inside of one-half hour from the moment that poor, halting, hesitating and reluctating Mr. Strange opened the extraordinary proposal and request to his surprised, perplexed and helpless daughter.

In the case of *Statham* v. *Ferguson*, 25 Gratt. 38, *Judge* Moncure says: "The first thing that strikes our minds in this investigation is the extraordinary haste [one whole week] which occurred in the execution of so important an act, and the circumstances attending its exe cution." And yet, in that case, Mrs. Ferguson had the presence and advice of counsel and the presence and witness of several of her neighbors, in her own house, who had been called in to explain the matter to her, and to see that all was fair and right. A unanimous decision of this court affirmed the court below in canceling Mrs. Ferguson's deed and declaring it void, upon the grounds of public policy, as a fraud or imposition upon her rights.

In this case the suggestion or proposal to do the wild and immoderate act did not come from Alice, it was proposed to her by her father, under the coaching and urging admonition of Mr. Branch, and when the poor old father sickened and revolted and fled the scene and relinquished the effort, Mr. Branch renewed the contest, and plied the friendless child with persuasions, and, as she alleges in her bill, and as Polly Davis distinctly proves, with assurances that she should lose nothing by executing the deed and relinquishing her recorded and indefeasible right to $10,000 worth of property without consideration.

We are of the opinion that the circuit court erred in denying the relief prayed for and in dismissing the bill, and that the decree appealed from must therefore be reversed and annulled; and the deed of the 26th of August, 1887, from Alice Lee Strange to Thomas V. Strange, be vacated and set aside.

Decree reversed.

UNITED STATES CIRCUIT COURT, NORTHERN DISTRICT OF OHIO.

James B. McMULLEN *et al.*
v.
Samuel J. RITCHIE.

(41 Fed. Rep. 502.)

1. **Defendant's absence,** and his ignorance of the fact that judgment was entered against him, give him no right to impeach it, where he had appeared in the suit by counsel.

2. **A foreign judgment** cannot be reviewed for any reasons other than for fraud or want of jurisdiction, where it was rendered by a court of competent jurisdiction, after due service of process, or entry of appearance, and hearing upon the issues.

(February 17, 1890.)

ACTION to enforce payment of the amount alleged to be due under a foreign judgment. On demurrer to the answer. *Sustained.*

The facts fully appear in the opinion.

Mr. **Samuel E. Williamson,** for plaintiffs, in support of the demurrer:

This judgment cannot be attacked in the manner attempted in the answer.

Wells, Res Adjudicata, §§ 511–522; *Bank of Australasia* v. *Nias*, 16 Ad. & El. N. S. 717; *Godard* v. *Gray*, L. R. 6 Q. B. 139; *Scott* v. *Pilkington*, 2 Best & S. 11; Herman, Estoppel, §§ 491, 498; Bigelow, Estoppel, 203–205; *Lazier* v. *Westcott*, 26 N. Y. 146; *Baker* v. *Palmer*, 83 Ill. 568; *McCoy* v. *Bank of U. S.* 5 Ohio, 548; article in 18 Cent. L. J. 203; *Warrener* v. *Kingsmill*, 8 U. C. Q. B. 407; *Burn* v. *Bletcher*, 23 U. C. Q. B. 28; *New York, L. E. & W. R. Co.* v. *McHenry*, 17 Fed. Rep. 414; *Mellin* v. *Horlick*, 31 Fed. Rep. 865.

Messrs. **Stevenson Burke** and **J. E. Ingersoll** for defendant, *contra.*

Ricks, *J.*, delivered the opinion of the court:

The plaintiffs instituted this suit to recover from the defendant the sum of $238,000, with interest, which they allege the defendant is legally obligated to pay because of a judgment for that sum rendered in plaintiffs' favor in the Queen's Bench Division of the High Court of

---

NOTE.—*Judgment not subject to collateral impeachment.*

It is conclusively settled that a judgment can only be impeached in a court of equity for fraud in its concoction. New York v. Brady, 115 N. Y. 615; Story, Eq. § 1575.

That it is conclusive upon the parties and those in privity with them as to matter within its jurisdiction, is fundamental. New York v. Brady, *supra*; Stilwell v. Carpenter, 59 N. Y. 423.

In collateral proceedings, the validity of judgments of courts of record will not be inquired into. Holliday v. Jackson, 4 West. Rep. 283, 21 Mo. App. 660; Turner v. Malone, 24 S. C. 399; Lowery v. Howard, 1 West. Rep. 487, 103 Ind. 440; Union Trust Co. v. Southern I. N. & I. Co. 130 U. S. 565 (32 L. ed. 1043).

It cannot be questioned except upon the ground of want of jurisdiction. Paul v. Smith, 82 Ky. 451.

If erroneous, they must be corrected by appeal; if irregular, they must be set aside by a motion in the cause, made in a reasonable time. Ward v. Lowndes, 96 N. C. 367.

Irregularities in the course of judicial proceedings do not render them void or the judgment open to collateral impeachment. Kelley v. People, 3 West. Rep. 47, 115 Ill. 583; Lewis v. Morrow, 5 West. Rep. 409, 89 Mo. 174; Mount v. Manhattan Co. 3 Cent. Rep. 353, 41 N. J. Eq. 211; Millard v. Marmon, 4 West. Rep. 192, 116 Ill. 649; Roberts v. Flanagan, 21 Neb. 503; Spoors v. Coen, 6 West. Rep. 812, 44 Ohio St. 497.

Where the court has jurisdiction both of the subject matter and of the parties, the general rule is that the judgment, although erroneous, is valid until reversed on appeal or writ of error. Chicago, M. & St. P. R. Co. v. Hook, 6 West. Rep. 697, 118 Ill. 587; McMillan v. Longoy, 2 West. Rep. 817, 115 Ill. 498; Reid v. Morton, 6 West. Rep. 709, 119 Ill. 196.

When there is any notice, no matter how irregular and defective, it is sufficient. Judgment based thereon will not be treated as void upon collateral attack. McMullen v. State, 2 West. Rep. 785, 105 Ind. 334.

It is sufficient if the record, with its legal intendments and presumptions, shows these facts. Pope v. Harrison, 16 Lea, 82.

A judgment cannot be attacked for fraud, in collateral proceedings, by one privy to it. Brown v. Woody, 4 West. Rep. 326, 22 Mo. App. 253.

But a judgment may be impeached collaterally as void, when rendered against a party that has not been served with process. Blanton v. Carroll (Va.) 13 Va. L. J. 864. See *note* to Wiese v. San Francisco M. F. Society (Cal.) 7 L. R. A. 577.

Justice for Ontario. The amended petition sets forth the provisions of the original contract upon which the judgment was based, and avers that said action was brought upon said agreement; that plaintiffs prayed that said agreement might be specifically performed, or that they might have damages for the breach thereof; that a proper answer was filed by defendant, setting forth fully his defense to said suit; and that, upon a trial, judgment was rendered in favor of plaintiffs for said sum. The defendant in his answer avers that the contract sued upon in Canada was an accommodation contract, with the full understanding that the same was never to be performed, and that, if the defendant was compelled to pay said judgment, he would be compelled to pay the same without any consideration, and seeks to have the issues set forth in his answer in the Canada case presented and tried in this suit. The answer does not deny the authority of the attorney to enter his appearance in the Canada suit, nor does he deny that he filed an answer in said case setting up the same defense now sought to be made in this court. Having by his appearance and answer submitted to the jurisdiction of the Canada court, and having presented matters of defense which that court must have passed upon in rendering the judgment set forth in the amended petition, the question now to be determined is: Can he be permitted in this court to re-try the same matters of defense presented in the Canada suit? It is not material that the judgment in said case was rendered in defendant's absence, and without his knowledge, as he avers in his answer here, because that court had full jurisdiction of the subject matter and of the defendant, through his entry of appearance by his counsel. Every intendment, therefore, is in favor of the regularity of its proceedings and of the validity of its judgment, as it is not now attempted to impeach it for fraud. The case, therefore, fairly presents for consideration the force and effect to be given by this court to a judgment rendered by a foreign court in a suit between the same parties; the jurisdiction of the subject matter and of the person having been properly acquired, and the proceedings being unassailed for fraud.

Counsel for defendant have cited the cases of *Burnham* v. *Webster*, 1 Woodb. & M. 172; *Buttrick* v. *Allen*, 8 Mass. 273; *Bank of Australasia* v. *Harding*, 9 C. B. 686; *Lyman* v. *Brown*, 2 Curt. 559; *Wood* v. *Gamble*, 11 Cush. 8; and *Schuler* v. *Israel*, 120 U. S. 506 [30 L. ed. 707]. In the first case cited the doctrine is recognized that the foreign judgment is only prima facie evidence as between the parties to it; and *Mr. Justice* Woodbury, in that case, granted a new trial because the trial judge had refused to allow testimony to go to the jury impeaching the judgment for mistake and irregularity, although the foreign court in which it was rendered had full jurisdiction of the subject matter and parties. The learned judge in that case said:

"I would allow the opposing party, where a foreign judgment is sued, pleaded or offered in evidence, to rebut its prima facie force and obligation by showing that the merits of the claim now in controversy were not, in truth, at all there considered and adjudged; and I would do that whether it occurred by accident or mistake, or any agreement of the parties, or any other excusable cause, as well as when it arose from the want of personal service."

Other courts, in cases arising about that same period,—nearly half a century ago,—held the same doctrine. But later decisions, in cases more carefully considered and better reasoned, give greater force and dignity to the records of foreign courts, not only as a matter of comity, but for the better reason that when parties have once had their day in a court of competent jurisdiction, after due service of process or after entry of appearance, and have had a full and impartial hearing upon the merits of their case as made in the pleadings, they should be bound by the judgment of that tribunal, unless they can show its proceedings were tainted with fraud. Counsel for plaintiff has cited the following authorities, which fully sustain the doctrine just stated: *Bank of*

Foreign judgments.

The decision of a foreign court of competent jurisdiction is conclusive. Rapelje v. Emery, 2 U. S. 2 Dall. 231 (1 L. ed. 361); Croudson v. Leonard, 8 U. S. 4 Cranch, 434 (2 L. ed. 670).

It is conclusive as to its own jurisdiction so far as it depends on municipal rules. Rose v. Himely, 8 U. S. 4 Cranch, 241 (2 L. ed. 608): Hudson v. Guestier, 8 U. S. 4 Cranch, 293 (2 L. ed. 625).

Where the judgment is conclusive between parties in the State where it was rendered, it is equally so in every other State and court in the United States. Christmas v. Russell, 72 U. S. 5 Wall. 290 (18 L. ed. 475).

A judgment or decree of one State, made by a court having jurisdiction of the parties and the subject, has the same force when pleaded or offered in evidence in the courts of any other State as in the State where it was rendered. Mutual L. Ins. Co. v. Harris, 97 U. S. 331 (24 L. ed. 959).

To make a record of a state judgment valid upon its face, it is only necessary for it to appear that the court had jurisdiction of the subject matter of the action and of the parties, and that a judgment had in fact been rendered. Maxwell v. Stewart, 88 U. S. 21 Wall. 71, 89 U. S. 22 Wall. 77 (22 L. ed. 564).

Judgments and decrees of courts of any State are *res judicata* whenever questioned in any sister State, provided there was personal service or an appearance of the parties to the suit in the State where the judgment was rendered. Sayre v. Harpold (W. Va.) March 15, 1890.

A court of another State in which a judgment was entered is the proper one to redress the wrong if it was entered by fraud or collusion. Wyoming Mfg. Co. v. Mohler (Pa.) March 11, 1889.

In an action on a foreign judgment, where it appears that the court rendering it was a court of record having a judge and clerk and a seal, the presumption is in favor of its jurisdiction and the regularity of its proceedings. Bailey v. Martin, 119 Ind. 103.

The certificate stating that the transcript is a "true and correct copy" of the judgment, is not defective because it does not state that it is a "true and complete copy." *Ibid.*

A personal judgment rendered under a foreign law by a foreign court will not be enforced where, on the face of the record, it appears that jurisdiction of the person was not obtained. Shepard v. Wright, 113 N. Y. 582.

See *note* to Attrill v. Huntington (Md.) 2 L. R. A. 779.

Australasia v. *Nias*, 16 Ad. & El. N. S. 717; *Godard* v. *Gray*, L. R. 6 Q. B. 139; *Scott* v. *Pilkington*, 2 Best & S. 11; *Lazier* v. *Westcott*, 26 N. Y. 146; *Baker* v. *Palmer*, 83 Ill. 568.

In the case of *Godard* v. *Gray*, decided in 1870 in the Court of Queen's Bench, the prior decisions in England are reviewed, and the learned judge concluded that the law was then well settled in the English courts that the judgment of a foreign tribunal having jurisdiction over the party and the cause cannot be impeached on the ground that it was erroneous on the merits, or that to an action on such judgment the judgment debtor could not defend that the tribunal mistook either the law or the facts. The Court of Appeals of the State of New York, in the case above noted, after a thorough review of the decisions of the courts in England and America, approves the reasoning of *Chancellor* Kent and *Justice* Story, and says that the same principles and decisions made as to judgments from the courts of other States of the Union should be applied to foreign judgments. The court, after quoting freely from *Justice* Story in favor of the absolute conclusiveness of the foreign judgments, except in cases in which the court which pronounced the judgment had not due jurisdiction of the case and of the defendant, or the proceeding was in fraud or founded in palpable mistake or irregularity, or bad by the law of *rei judicatæ*, approves his views as eminently correct and most in harmony with sound principles and the best-considered cases. The court in the same opinion quotes from *Justice* Story, and says:

"Holding that the judgment was only to be regarded as prima facie evidence for the plaintiff," he correctly says, "would be a mere delusion if the defendant might still question it by opening all or any of the original merits on his side; for under such circumstances it would be equivalent to granting a new trial."

If the action of the court of original jurisdiction, having the parties and the subject matter properly before it, is to be reviewed and its judgment to be treated as only prima facie evidence for the judgment creditor, in what class of cases is the court of second or third resort to go behind the original judgment and re-try the case on its merits? Is it to do so where, in its opinion, the court of original jurisdiction was not one of equal learning or of equal rank, or where the judgment debtor, through want of diligence, or because of the lack of zeal or ability of his counsel, did not secure as full and intelligent an examination of his defense as he should have had? If the original judgment is to be reviewed for any reasons other than for fraud and for want of jurisdiction, where is the boundary line of the reviewing court to be fixed? *Mr. Justice* Woodbury, in his opinion in the case cited by defendant's counsel, opens the door as wide as possible and authorizes the court to explore the whole field covered by the issues made in the original suit, and to review its proceedings upon all or any one of the issues there made and not fully considered, whether by accident or mistake, or for any excusable cause. I cannot approve such doctrine. It would destroy the force and effect of judicial proceedings and make the judgments of a foreign tribunal, no matter how high its rank or how binding its decisions within its own jurisdiction, of little greater effect than the original contract or promise sued upon. I think the doctrine as maintained by the later English and American cases, to which reference has been made, has advanced the courts one stage in the progress of simplifying the administration of justice. It is important that there should be a limitation to litigation, and that parties, as to matters upon which they had a full hearing in the court of original and competent jurisdiction, should not be permitted to open and re-try issues once fairly determined whenever and wherever they have an opportunity to do so, by defending against judgments rendered in a foreign country to which they were properly made parties. I am therefore of the opinion that the judgment set out in the amended petition in this case has the same force and effect as a judgment of a court of competent jurisdiction in one of the States of this Union, and is conclusive against the defendant of the matters therein adjudged.

The demurrer to the answer will therefore be allowed.

Jackson, *J.*, concurs.

GEORGIA SUPREME COURT.

MAYOR, etc., OF SAVANNAH *et al.*, *Plffs. in Err.*,
v.
Joseph D. WEED *et al.*

(....Ga.....)

A constitutional provision that taxation shall be "ad valorem on all property subject to be taxed" is violated by an ordinance imposing a tax of 2 1-8 per cent on real estate, 3.10 per cent on bank stock and 1.2 per cent upon all other personal property.

(March 14, 1890.)

ERROR to the Superior Court for Chatham County to review a judgment enjoining the collection of certain taxes. *Affirmed.*

NOTE.—*Taxation* ad valorem; *constitutional provision.*

The Constitutions of some States require property to be taxed in proportion to its value; but this does not affect the power of the Legislature to impose indirect taxes on persons, or on business pursuits, or on the franchises of corporations. 1 Desty, Taxn. 204; Mobile v. Dargan, 45 Ala. 310; Mobile v. Royal Street R. Co. Id. 322; O'Kane v. Treat, 25 Ill. 557; People v. Thurber, 13 Ill. 554; St. Louis v. Green, 7 Mo. App. 468; Creamer v. Allen, 3 Mo. App. 545.

Under such a constitutional provision the assessor must ascertain values in the manner provided by law. Hyatt v. Allen, 54 Cal. 353.

The facts sufficiently appear in the opinion.

Messrs. **Chisholm, Erwin & Du Bignon,** for plaintiffs in error:

The Constitution of 1868 provided that "taxation on property shall be *ad valorem* only and uniform on all species of property taxed."

Art. 1, § 27.

Discrimination in rates of taxation was permissible under that Constitution.

Wilson v. *Augusta Factory*, 44 Ga. 388; *Augusta* v. *Augusta Nat. Bank*, 47 Ga. 563; *Waring* v. *Savannah*, 60 Ga. 97.

Paragraph 1 of § 11 of art. 7 of the Georgia Constitution of 1877 was adopted substantially from art. 9, § 1, of the Constitution of Pennsylvania.

The right of all taxing powers in Pennsylvania within their respective territorial limits, to separate property into classes and to impose different rates of taxation thereon, was settled by the highest court of that State before the adoption into the Georgia Constitution of this clause of the Pennsylvania Constitution.

See *Kittanning Coal Co.* v. *Com.* 79 Pa. 100; *Roup's Case*, 81* Pa. 211; *Germania L. Ins. Co.* v. *Com.* 85 Pa. 513; *Northampton County* v. *Lehigh Coal & Nav. Co.* 75 Pa. 464.

When in the Constitution of one State a provision contained in the Constitution of another State, where it has received a settled judicial interpretation, is adopted, that interpretation is deemed to be adopted with it.

Endlich, Interpretation of Statutes, § 530; *People* v. *Coleman*, 4 Cal. 46, 60 Am. Dec. 582; Cooley, Const. Lim. 64. See also *Com.* v. *Delaware Div. Canal Co.* 2 L. R. A. 798, 123 Pa. 594.

It has long been the settled policy and practice in this State to divide property into classes for the purpose of assessing it for taxation.

This construction having been given to the constitutional provision, it has become a settled rule of property; and in such case it is better to let it stand, although subsequent experience may have satisfied members of this court that it is an erroneous one.

Endlich, Interpretation of Statutes, §§ 357-360, 363; Bishop, Written Law, § 104, and cases cited; Cooley, Const. Lim. pp. 65, 66.

Messrs. **O'Connor & O'Byrne,** for defendants in error:

The only classification of property relatively to taxation which is made or authorized is into exempt property and property subject to be taxed; and taxation on all property subject to be taxed is required to be *ad valorem*—that is, according to value. If exempt, it pays nothing; if subject, the amount it shall pay is measured by multiplying the fixed rate into the actual value.

Verdery v. *Summerville*, 82 Ga. 138; *Gilman* v. *Sheboygan*, 67 U. S. 2 Black, 515 (17 L. ed. 308); Burroughs, Taxn. 61, 62; 1 Desty, Taxn. 195-197; 2 Dillon, Mun. Corp. 748-783; *Pine Grove Twp.* v. *Talcott*, 86 U. S. 19 Wall. 675 (22 L. ed. 232); Cooley, Taxn. 180.

Simmons, *J.*, delivered the opinion of the court:

Weed *et al.*, by petition, complained that the marshal of Savannah had levied upon a lot of land belonging to them in that City an execution for the four-quarters tax due by them upon two lots of land, under the tax ordinance of the City. This ordinance was passed by the municipal corporation on December 22, 1888, and

---

It does not require a uniform method of valuation, but only such regulations as shall secure a just valuation of property, both real and personal. Louisville & N. A. R. Co. v. State, 25 Ind. 180; Wisconsin Cent. R. Co. v. Taylor Co. 52 Wis. 79; Johnston v. Macon, 62 Ga. 645.

Such provision does not require that all property in the State shall be taxed, but that any species of property selected for taxation shall be taxed in proportion to its value. State v. North, 27 Mo. 464; Stratton v. Collins, 43 N. J. L. 562; Williamson v. Massey, 33 Gratt. 241.

The words "ought to be taxed," are to be construed as mandatory. State v. Hannibal & St. J. R. Co. 75 Mo. 212; Hamilton v. St. Louis Co. Ct. 15 Mo. 20; St. Louis v. Green, 7 Mo. App. 468; America Life Asso. v. St. Louis Co. 49 Mo. 512.

Local assessments for local improvements are not "taxes" such as are required to be assessed under this provision. Vasser v. George, 47 Miss. 713; White v. People, 94 Ill. 604.

Statutory provisions whereby different classes of property are listed and valued for taxation in and by different modes and agencies are not necessarily in conflict with this provision. German Nat. Bank v. Kimball, 103 U. S. 732 (26 L. ed. 469); Wagoner v. Loomis, 37 Ohio St. 571.

The provision in the Ohio Constitution is that "all property of every description in the State shall be taxed by a uniform rule, and at its true value in money" (Ohio Const. art. 12, § 2; Columbus Exch. Bank v. Hines, 3 Ohio, 15), the rule being more restrictive on the power of the Legislature than the provisions of the Wisconsin Constitution. See Wisconsin Cent. R. Co. v. Taylor Co. 52 Wis. 70; Knowlton v. Rock Co. 9 Wis. 410.

The tax ordinance of the Village of Summerville, Georgia, for the year 1887, imposing a tax of ¼ of 1 per cent *ad valorem* upon real estate only, is void by reason of conflict with the Georgia Constitution in not laying the tax *ad valorem* upon all property, real and personal, subject to be taxed within the territorial limits of the authority levying the tax. Verdery v. Summerville, 82 Ga. 138.

Although the power of a municipal corporation to tax is not conferred by the North Carolina Constitution, when such power is exercised the Constitution compels the taxation of all property therein, and that it shall be taxed according to its true value in money and by a uniform rule. Redmond v. Tarboro (N. C.) 7 L. R. A. 539.

Under the Constitution of North Carolina all property of whatever description, and not merely that selected for taxation by the Legislature, must be taxed. Const. art. 7, § 9; Redmond v. Tarboro (N. C.) 7 L. R. A. 539.

The word "property" includes moneys, credits, investments and other choses in action. Redmond v. Tarboro, *supra*.

The constitutional provisions which declare that "all taxes levied on property shall be assessed in exact proportion to the value of such property," and inhibit the levy of "a greater rate of taxation than three fourths of 1 per cent on the value of taxable property within this State" (art. 11, §§ 1, 4), prescribe a rule and limit of taxation on property, but do not include all the legitimate subjects of taxation, some of which are not susceptible of determinate value. Western U. Teleg. Co. v. State Board of Assessment, 80 Ala. 273.

imposed a tax of 2¼ per cent upon real estate within the corporate limits, and of ½ of 1 per cent upon all personal property, except shares in banks and banking associations, upon which a tax of only $\frac{3}{10}$ of 1 per cent was imposed. This tax ordinance the petitioners alleged to be illegal and void, because it violated the provisions of article 7, § 2, par. 1, of the Constitution (Code, § 5181). They prayed, among other things, that an *ad interim* injunction might issue against the municipal corporation and the marshal, enjoining them from proceeding to enforce the collection of the tax until the final determination of the cause. The defendants answered, and insisted that the ordinance complained of and the execution mentioned in the petition were legal and valid. Upon the hearing, the trial judge granted the injunction. The mayor and aldermen excepted, and assigned the same as error.

The learned and able counsel for the plaintiff in error contended that this judgment was erroneous, because, under the above section of the Constitution, the municipal authorities of Savannah had the power and authority to classify the subjects of taxation, and to require a tax of a different rate upon realty from that required by them on personal property. They also contended that this clause of the Constitution was borrowed from the Constitution of Pennsylvania; that the construction put upon it by the courts of Pennsylvania is binding upon the courts of this State; and that the construction of the Supreme Court of Pennsylvania is that, under this clause of their Constitution, the Legislature has authority to classify property so that one species may be taxed more than another. We are inclined to think that if this clause had been wholly borrowed from the Constitution of Pennsylvania, and the Supreme Court of that State had put this construction upon it before it was adopted into our Constitution, we would be bound by that construction. But we do not agree with counsel that the clause under consideration was taken wholly from the Pennsylvania Constitution. There are qualifying words in the clause as it stands in our Constitution which in our opinion prohibit the Legislature or a municipal council from classifying property as was done in this case, and which render its meaning entirely different from that of the Pennsylvania Constitution.

The Constitution of Pennsylvania on this subject is as follows: "All taxes shall be uniform upon the same class of subjects, within the territorial limits of the authority levying the tax, and shall be levied and collected under general laws." Our Constitution upon this subject reads as follows: "All taxation shall be uniform upon the same class of subjects, and *ad valorem* on all property subject to be taxed, within the territorial limits of the authority levying the tax, and shall be levied and collected under general laws." If our Constitution were an exact copy of the Pennsylvania Constitution upon this subject, we would most certainly agree with the learned counsel for the plaintiff in error, that property might be classified, and different rates of taxation put upon it; but we think that when the framers of our Constitution interjected into the clause the words, "and *ad valorem* on all property subject to be taxed," it was their intention that there should be no classification of property so that it might be taxed at different rates. Property is not the only subject of taxation. "Everything to which the legislative power extends may be the subject of taxation, whether it be person or property, or possession, franchise or privilege, or occupation or right." Cooley, Taxn. 5.

We think that this clause refers to subjects of taxation other than property, and means that if one kind of business, privilege, franchise or right, etc., is taxed, the tax shall be uniform upon all of that class. For instance, if liquor dealers are taxed, the tax as to all liquor dealers shall be uniform; if draymen are taxed for carrying on their business, the tax shall be uniform as to all of that class; or if butchers, lawyers, physicians, dentists and photographers are taxed, the tax need not be the same upon all of these, but shall be uniform as to each one of these classes. Upon this subject, see *Cutliff* v. *Albany*, 60 Ga. 597; *Shepperd* v. *Sumter County*, 59 Ga. 535; *Davis* v. *Macon*, 64 Ga. 128.

The Legislature or municipal authorities are not bound to tax any occupation or business within their territorial limits, but when they undertake to tax one class of business or occupation the same tax must be levied on all members of that class. We think the plain meaning of this clause of the Constitution is that the Legislature or municipal authorities may classify all subjects of taxation, and make the tax uniform on each class. They can tax these classes or not, as they see proper. They can tax one class and exempt the others; but when they do tax a particular class, the rate must be uniform as to all of that class. When, however, they come to deal with property, a different rule prevails. If property is taxed, all of it must be taxed except that exempted in the Constitution. The Legislature or municipal authorities can make no exemption as to property; it must be taxed, and taxed according to its value. Though property is a subject of taxation, the Constitution treats it as but one subject, and prescribes the rule of uniformity as to it by saying that all of it subject to be taxed shall be taxed *ad valorem*. And if it must be taxed, and taxed according to its value, we cannot see how it can be classified anew, and one rate put upon real estate, a lower rate upon personal property generally, and a still lower rate upon shares in banks and banking associations. If one man has a thousand dollars worth of personal property, and another a thousand dollars worth of real estate, and another a thousand dollars worth of shares in a banking company, it must bear the same rate of taxation. Each must bear the same burden in support of the government which protects the owner and his property. This rule is equitable and just to all parties, and the rule prescribed by the ordinance of the City of Savannah is, in our opinion, inequitable and unjust. Under that ordinance a man who owns a thousand dollars worth of real estate has to pay for the support of the government $21.25, the man who owns a thousand dollars worth of personal property other than bank stock has to pay $5, and the man who owns a thousand dollars worth of bank stock has to pay only $3. In our judgment, the words, "*ad valorem* on all property subject to be taxed," were embodied in this clause of the Constitution for the express purpose of prohibiting such unjust and unequal taxation as this. We adopt in this decision that part of the opinion of the chief justice in the case of *Verdery* v. *Summerville*, 82 Ga. 138, which treats of the proper construction of this clause of our Constitution, and for the reasons we have given above, and the reasons assigned in that opinion, we affirm the judgment of the court below. We express no opinion as to injunction being the proper remedy in a case like this, as the point was not made, and we were requested to affirm this judgment if we decided that the constitutional question made was against the plaintiff in error.

Judgment affirmed.

WROUGHT IRON RANGE CO. *et al.*, *Pltfs. in Err.*,
v.
H. J. JOHNSON, Ordinary of Floyd County, *et al.*

(....Ga.....)

*1. **Only the person who itinerates for trading purposes is a peddler.** His employer, though owning the goods, team and vehicle, is not required to obtain a license, nor subject to any penalty or forfeiture for failing to do so.

2. **One whose vocation is to go from place to place** with a sample stove carried upon a wagon, exhibit the sample and procure orders, which his employer afterwards fills by delivering through other agents the stoves so ordered, is a peddler, within the meaning of the Code of Georgia. But though a peddler, if he is a citizen and resident of Virginia, and the orders he solicits and procures are for stoves belonging to a Missouri corporation, which the latter holds in Missouri, and keeps there until they are thus ordered, he is protected by the Constitution of the United States, as lately construed by the supreme court, against the provisions of the Code requiring a license to peddle, and declaring a forfeiture for not procuring such license.

3. **The parts of the record specified in the bill of exceptions** being as follows, "The petition and exhibit thereto attached, marked 'A,' and the answer of the defendants,"—*Held*, that the writ of error covers nothing else, and that an affidavit verifying the petition, an acknowledgment of service on the petition, an order of the judge appointing a time and place for hearing the application for injunction, and a final order denying the injunction, are not included in the specification, and that the clerk had no warrant or authority for incorporating these things in his certified transcript. These superfluous matters are wholly immaterial to the errors assigned, and this court has no use for them.

(April 4, 1890.)

ERROR to the Superior Court for Floyd County to review a judgment in favor of defendants in an action brought to enjoin the enforcement of an execution and to have the same canceled. *Reversed.*

*Head notes by BLECKLEY, *Ch. J.*

NOTE.—*Hawkers and peddlers defined.*

Any method of selling goods, wares or merchandise by outcry on the streets or public places of the city, or by attracting persons to purchase goods by placards or signals, or by going from house to house, selling, or offering goods for sale, at retail, whether the goods be carried along for delivery presently, or whether the sales are made for future delivery, constitutes the person so selling a hawker or peddler, within the meaning of Rev. Stat. 1881, § 3106, subd. 23. Graffty v. Rushville, 5 West. Rep. 858, 107 Ind. 502.

A person selling goods from door to door as an agent of the manufacturers at a salary, with no personal interest in the goods or their proceeds, is a peddler, within the meaning of the Pennsylvania Act prohibiting peddling in Schuylkill County. See *note* to Com. v. Gardner (Pa.) 7 L. R. A. 666.

The right of "acquiring, possessing and protecting property," given by the Pennsylvania Constitution, does not include the right to sell goods as a peddler, when that is prohibited by statute. *Ibid.*

A peddler is an itinerant individual, ordinarily without local habitation or place of business, who travels about the country carrying commodities for sale. Davenport v. Rice, 75 Iowa, 74.

Under the amended Statutes of Alabama the phrase "peddlers of medicines or other articles of like character" does not include a vendor of medicines renting a vacant lot in a city and erecting a tent thereon, and selling medicines without solicitation or delivery outside the tent. Randolph v. Yellowstone Kit, 83 Ala. 471.

One who goes about repairing and erecting lightning-rods for people who employ him, and furnishes the necessary material to do it, but sells nothing that he does not affix to the house, is not a peddler within the meaning of the Georgia Code. Ezell v. Thrasher, 76 Ga. 817.

Taking orders for goods to be manufactured is not peddling; neither is the sale, by the person taking such orders, of a few articles in a law office where there is no evidence of any offer to sell in any other place. Spencer v. Whiting, 68 Iowa, 678.

One who solicits orders for a local firm on samples is not a peddler. Davenport v. Rice, *supra*.

Peddler's licenses.

An ordinance "to license hawkers, peddlers and auctioneers" is not invalid on the ground that it delegates to the licensee the power to determine the time for which the license shall be granted. State v. Redmon (Minn.) May 7, 1890.

Nor is an ordinance invalid, on the ground that it delegates to the village recorder the ministerial or clerical act of issuing it when it has been granted by the council; nor on the ground that the license fee, which is fixed at $3 per day, is excessive. *Ibid.*

Where a tax was levied on a firm for peddling out clocks, cooking stoves or ranges over the county, it can be collected but once, and the number of agents, wagoners or teamsters employed is discretionary. *Ex parte* Butin, 28 Tex. App. 304.

An ordinance requiring hawkers or peddlers not residents of the city to take out a license for the sale of goods not the growth or manufacture of the county is void. Graffty v. Rushville, 5 West. Rep. 858, 107 Ind. 502.

The provision of the Pennsylvania Act, which discriminates in the amount of license for hucksters in certain counties, required from residents and nonresidents, is repealed by the Supplementary Act of March 14, 1867. Com. v. Shaffer, 128 Pa. 575.

License to hawkers and peddlers, see *note* to State v. Richards (W. Va.) 3 L. R. A. 705.

See also 8 L. R. A. 328; 10 L. R. A. 357; 11 L. R. A. 219; 20 L. R. A. 430; 21 L.

The facts were officially reported to this court as follows:

The Wrought Iron Range Company, a corporation of Missouri, and E. N. S. Lee, a citizen of and resident of Virginia, by their petition, made the following allegations:

"The Range Company manufactures and sells ranges made for cooking purposes at the Company's works in St. Louis, and sold by their agents, by samples throughout the United States, in the following manner: The Company furnishes each agent a team and wagon and a sample range, with which the agent travels over the territory allotted to him, and, by exhibiting the sample, takes orders, for the Company, for the purchase of such ranges from persons desiring to buy, and transmits the orders to the superintendent of the Company at his headquarters, which are sometimes in such territory, and sometimes in another State; and the Company thereupon, from its home office and place of business, fills the orders through the superintendent, and delivers the ranges as the orders are taken. But in no case do the agents sell or deliver the sample ranges intrusted to them. The Company has no place of business in Georgia. Ranges are sometimes stored in warehouses, after they are sold by sample, until delivered to the purchasers. On February 5, 1890, the Range Company furnished Lee with two mules and a wagon and sample range, and he went into Floyd County therewith, and by exhibiting the sample, took an order for a range from one of the citizens of the county, and forwarded this order to the superintendent of the Range Company at Rome, and thereupon the Company accepted the order and delivered the range, in the manner above stated, to the purchaser. The Ordinary of Floyd County, having been informed of the facts and circumstances above stated, demanded both of the Range Company and of Lee, under the provisions of sections 529 and 1681 of the Code, $50 for a license to peddle such ranges in Floyd County, and, when petitioners refused to pay the same, issued executions against them for it, which were levied by the deputy sheriff of Floyd County on the mules, wagon and sample range. The Ordinary also issued an execution against them for an alleged forfeiture of $100, under section 536 of the Code, and caused it to be levied on said property; and the sheriff, by direction of the Ordinary, has also levied both the *fi. fas.* on a trunk belonging to Lee, and threatens to arrest Lee under said process if the license fee and forfeiture are not otherwise collected from petitioners, and from each of them. Petitioners denied that they, or either of them, are peddlers of stoves or ranges, or are liable to take out or to pay a license, as peddlers to the Ordinary, under said section of the Code, or otherwise, or that they, or either of them, are liable, on account of their failure to take out and pay for such licenses, to the forfeiture claimed by the Ordinary. Section 1631 of the Code, so far as it applies to them, and each of them, is unconstitutional, in that it contravenes, and is repugnant to, article 1, § 8, par. 3, of the Constitution of the United States."

Petitioners pray for an injunction against the Ordinary and sheriff; that the execution may be canceled; and for general relief. Attached to the petition was a copy of the execution, and the levy thereon.

The defendant admitted the allegations of the petition to be true, but denied the conclusions drawn therefrom, and alleged that the petitioners were both peddlers, and liable to the tax and forfeiture.

The application for temporary injunction was heard on the pleadings, and the injunction prayed for was refused.

To this decision petitioners excepted.

Mr. **J. Branham**, for plaintiffs in error:

The provisions of the Code requiring peddlers to obtain a license are not applicable to petitioners.

Gould v. *Atlanta*, 55 Ga. 685 (e); *State* v. *Agee*, 83 Ala. 110; *Ballou* v. *State*, 87 Ala. 144; *Welton* v. *Missouri* 91 U. S. 275 (23 L. ed. 347); *Robbins* v. *Shelby County Taxing Dist.* 120 U. S. 489 (30 L. ed. 694); *Asher* v. *Texas*, 128 U. S. 129 (32 L. ed. 368); *Leloup* v. *Port of Mobile*, 127 U. S. 648 (32 L. ed. 314).

Mr. **C. Thornwell** for defendants in error.

Bleckley, *Ch. J.*, delivered the opinion of the court:

The facts are sufficiently stated in the official report.

1. The provisions of the Code under which the Ordinary proceeded furnished no warrant or authority for issuing an execution against the owner of goods because they are peddled or sold by sample through an itinerant agent. This question was virtually ruled in *Howard* v. *Reid*, 51 Ga. 328. In that case it was held that the person to whom the license to peddle is to be granted is he who travels and vends the goods, and that a process issued under section 586 of the Code against others on the ground that they, by their agent, peddled, etc., without a license, is upon its face illegal and void. That case governs this, in so far as the nonresident corporation is concerned. A corporation cannot be a peddler, or obtain license to peddle, under the laws of this State. No one can obtain such license who cannot be sworn, for every peddler has to take an oath. Code, § 1634.

Every itinerant trader by sample is treated as a peddler. Id. § 1631.

The itinerant trader is the person who actually travels, or passes from place to place, for the purpose of trading by sample or otherwise. Within the sense and meaning of the Code, when one adopts that vocation, and pursues it, he becomes a peddler, and by that name or description is to be licensed. *Gould* v. *Atlanta*, 55 Ga. 686.

The execution issued in the present case alleges peddling and selling as peddlers, without first obtaining license to peddle, and without paying the charges fixed by section 529 of the Code, which section prescribes a charge of $50 for a license to peddle. The execution is for the collection of $100 as a forfeiture; and the law declaring the forfeiture is found in section 533 of the Code, under which section the person who incurs it is one who peddles without first obtaining a license to do so. From what we have said, it follows conclusively that this execution could not rightfully be enforced against the Wrought Iron Range Company.

Indeed, as to that corporation, it was and is an utter nullity.

2. The next question relates to the validity of the execution as against Lee, the person who actually itinerated, and exhibited a sample stove, for the purpose of obtaining orders in behalf of the corporation for stoves manufactured in the State of Missouri, and to be forwarded from thence to this State in filling orders so obtained. Lee is a citizen and resident of Virginia, and plies his vocation in Georgia to obtain orders for goods manufactured in Missouri, and not brought within this State until after ordered through him by purchasers, or those desiring to purchase. As he carries his sample stove from place to place upon a wagon drawn by mules, and exhibits the same as a means of trading, or inducing offers to trade, he is doubtless a peddler, within the true sense and meaning of the Code.

Section 1631 reads as follows: "Every peddler or itinerant trader, by sample or otherwise, must apply to the ordinary of each county where he may desire to trade for a license, which shall be granted to him on the terms said ordinary has or may impose. They are authorized to impose such tax as they may deem advisable, to be used for county purposes. The license extends only to the limits of the county."

Section 1635 requires a license for every wagon or other vehicle employed or used in vending such goods, wares or merchandise.

Section 538 is as follows: "If any person, except a disabled soldier of this State, peddles, without first obtaining such license, in counties where the ordinaries take no action regulating peddling, he forfeits to the county $100 for the first act of peddling, and for each month thereafter $25 more."

We should consider these provisions decisive of the case as to Lee, could they be held constitutional in their application to him, and the business in which he is engaged. But this cannot be held consistently with the decisions of the Supreme Court of the United States in *Robbins* v. *Shelby County Taxing Dist.*, 120 U. S. 489 [30 L. ed. 694], and *Asher* v. *Texas*, 128 U. S. 129 [32 L. ed. 368]. These cases rule that statutes of Tennessee and Texas, not more obnoxious than our own to the interstate commerce clause of the Constitution of the United States, are void, for their conflict with that Constitution, in so far as they extend to soliciting orders, and making sales, by and for nonresidents of the State within which the business required to be licensed is transacted. After full examination we can have no doubt that these decisions apply to the present case, and control it. This being so, the matter admits of no further discussion at our hands. After the State has yielded to the federal army, it can very well afford to yield to the federal judiciary. Our sister States, Alabama and Louisiana, have so done. *State* v. *Agee*, 83 Ala. 110; *Simmons Hardware Co.* v. *McGuire*, 39 La. Ann. 848.

The doctrine of co-equality and co-ordination between the Supreme Court of Georgia and the Supreme Court of the United States, so vigorously announced by Benning, *J.*, in *Padelford* v. *Savannah*, 14 Ga. 489, regarded now from a practical standpoint, seems visionary. Its application to this or any like case would be a jarring discord in the harmony of the law. Moreover any attempt to apply it effectively would be no less vain than discordant. When we know with certainty that a question arising under the Constitution of the United States has been definitely decided by the supreme court of that government, it is our duty to accept the decision, for the time being, as correct, whether it coincides with our own opinion or not. Any failure of due subordination on our part would be a breach, rather than the administration, of law. The judge of the superior court erred in not granting the injunction prayed for.

Judgment reversed.

IOWA SUPREME COURT.

FIRST NATIONAL BANK of Creston
v.
C. W. CARROLL and Wife, *Appts.*

(......Iowa......)

A guaranty that cattle of another person will sell in market for four cents per pound, made in consideration of the payment of $30, and an agreement by the other party to pay the guarantor any excess in the selling price above four cents per pound, is a gambling contract.

(May 10, 1890.)

NOTE.—Wagering contracts, void. See *notes* to Sprague v. Warren (Neb.) 3 L. R. A. 679; Harvey v. Merrill (Mass.) 5 L. R. A. 200.

A negotiable note growing out of a wager contract is invalid even in the hands of an innocent holder. Snoddy v. American Nat. Bank (Tenn.) 7 L. R. A. 705.

APPEAL by defendants from a judgment of the District Court for Union County in favor of plaintiff in an action to recover the amount alleged to be due upon a promissory note. *Reversed.*

Statement by **Granger**, *J.*:

Action on a promissory note for $150. The execution of the note is admitted, but alleged to be void because given in fulfillment of a gambling contract, of which the following is a copy:

Creston, Iowa, December 5, 1888.

In consideration of $30.00 paid me this day by L. J. Cusick, I hereby guarantee to him that the five cars of cattle shipped by Cusick Bros., on December 3, to Chicago, shall sell in Chicago for four (4) cents per pound, and he having a one-half interest in said cattle, I agree to make good to him any loss by reason of said cattle selling for less than four cents. That is, I am to pay him the difference, if any, between the price the cattle sell for and four cents on his half interest, in case they sell for less than four cents. Said difference to be paid to him on receipt of account sale, and, if said cattle sell for more than four cents, I am to have the difference. C. W. Carroll.

I agree to pay C. W. Carroll whatever said cattle sell for, over four cents, on my half interest. L. J. Cusick.

The answer sets out the contract and contains averments that when the contract was made the cattle were in transit to the Chicago market; that they were sold for less than four cents per pound; and that the note in suit was given to said Cusick to make good to him the four cents per pound for the cattle under the contract, and that there was no other consideration for the note. A demurrer to the answer presents the question as to the validity of the contract. The district court sustained the demurrer, and from a judgment for plaintiff for the amount of the note the defendants appealed.

Messrs. **Maxwell & Leonard,** for appellants:

A wager or bet is a contract by which two or more parties agree that a certain sum of money, or other thing, shall be paid or delivered to one of them on the happening or not happening of an uncertain event.

2 Bouv. L. Dict. 647, 648; 7 Wait, Act. and Def. 83; *Merchants S. L. & T. Co.* v. *Goodrich,* 75 Ill. 554.

The contract under consideration by its express terms is a wager on the prospective price of a commodity and falls clearly within the rule recognized in what might be termed option contract cases.

Bisbee & Simonds, Law of the Produce Exch. § 207; *Crawford* v. *Spencer,* 1 Am. St. Rep. 745; *Lyons First Nat. Bank* v. *Oskaloosa P. Co.* 66 Iowa, 46; *Gregory* v. *Wattowa,* 58 Iowa, 711; *Murray* v. *Ocheltree,* 59 Iowa, 435; *Bigelow* v. *Benedict,* 70 N. Y. 202; *Lyon* v. *Culbertson,* 83 Ill. 33; *Whitesides* v. *Hunt,* 97 Ind. 191.

Messrs. **McDill & Sullivans,** for appellee:

This contract shows that for $30 paid him, Carroll guaranteed Cusick that his cattle then on the way to the market would bring him four cents per pound. This does not differ from an ordinary insurance contract against loss by fire.

Anderson, L. Dict. *Insurance,* p. 555; May, Ins. § 78; Barber, Ins. § 1; Addison, Cont. Phil. Am. ed. 558; Bishop, Cont. ed. 1887, § 530.

Granger, *J.,* delivered the opinion of the court:

Counsel in argument agree that the question for determination is whether or not the contract set out in the answer is a wagering contract. If so, the note in suit, given as it was, in pursuance of the contract, is void under our holdings, even in the hands of the plaintiffs. *Traders Bank* v. *Alsop,* 64 Iowa, 97.

Appellant likens this contract, in its purpose and effect, to "option deals," which are held to be gambling contracts, and void. Appellee, however, urges, as a distinctive feature, that in option deals there is no actual property as a basis for the transaction, and no property is intended to be delivered or received, while in this case the cattle actually on the way to market formed the basis of the transaction, and it urges that by the contract the cattle were sold to Carroll, or, at least, an interest therein. We are unable to find any language in the contract evincing such a purpose. Cusick Bros. shipped the cattle. They are to sell the cattle in Chicago, and the contract in question is an executory one, to be performed after the cattle are sold. The transaction was clearly a speculative one as to prices. The disposition of the cattle is precisely what it would have been had the contract not been made. Cusick Bros. sold the cattle, as they intended to, for what they would bring in the market, and received the pay therefor; and this would have been the situation without the contract in question. The parties to the contract dealt alone with what would be the market price when the cattle should arrive in Chicago. The market price represented the actual value of the cattle. If the market price was above the four cents per pound, and Cusick paid the excess to Carroll, Carroll received something for nothing. If the market price was less, and Carroll paid to Cusick the difference, then Cusick received more than the value of his cattle, or, in other words, something for nothing, and such receipts are the inspiration and soul of gambling enterprises. *Brua's App.,* 55 Pa. 294, gives the following definition: "Anything which induces men to risk their money or property without any other hope of return than to get for nothing any given amount from another, is gambling."

The same court, in the case of *Waugh* v. *Beck,* 114 Pa. 422, 5 Cent. Rep. 536, used this language: "A transaction in stocks by way of margin, settlement of differences and payment of gain or loss, without intending to deliver stocks, is a mere wager."

This transaction was clearly one in which the parties intended to pay the gain or loss as a market price at a future time would require, without intending to deliver property, and, under the rule given in the Pennsylvania case (55 Pa. 294), it was a wager. The mere fact that there was specific property about which the transaction occurred would make no difference. Parties may as effectually gamble with reference to actual property as with reference to the prices of different classes of property. The cases do not turn upon that point, but upon the actual intent of the parties. *Tomblin* v. *Callen,* 69 Iowa, 229.

Appellee gives this illustration to show that Carroll had an interest in the cattle: "Suppose while in transit the cattle had been killed by the negligence of the railroad company, and the market price on the day they should have reached Chicago would have shown that the cattle would have brought five cents per pound, under Carroll's contract he would have been entitled to all the cattle would have brought over four cents per pound;" and follows with a conclusion that Carroll would have had a right of action against the railroad company. The greatest interest that could be claimed under such a state of facts would be an equitable lien for the profits resulting from the contract, and the mere fact that security is specifically given to aid a gambling contract does not make it valid. But we by no means concur in appellee's conclusion as to such an interest. As we have in substance said, the parties did not intend an exchange of the commodity between themselves, but they contracted only with reference to what Cusick Bros. would be able to sell the cattle for in the market on arrival. It was alone a question of gain or loss, depending on the correctness of their judgments as to future prices. Of course, in actual sales, a gain or loss is or may be the result of a correct or erroneous judgment; but the absence of a purpose to deal with actual property marks the distinction between a legal and a gambling contract. It will be observed that the contract specifies that, in consideration of $30 paid by Cusick, Carroll guaranteed that the cattle should sell for four cents per pound, and the validity of the contract is urged because of this payment and of the guaranty, and the case is likened to insurance. If the contract stopped with the guaranty, the case might be different, but the use of the word "guaranty," and the payment of the $30, do not devest the transaction of its gambling characteristics or purpose. The word "guaranty" can have no other effect than an agreement to pay the difference, and the cash payment, while it might constitute a consideration for a valid agreement to make good a loss, will not cure or make valid what appears to be a mere chance speculation upon prices.

We think the *District Court erred in sustaining the demurrer, and its judgment is reversed.*

David VANNEST

v.

Orin FLEMING.

(......Iowa......)

1. A drain made by adjoining proprietors across their lands to conduct the waters that were naturally drained by a swale in which the drain is located, and which carried them in the same direction that the drain does, cannot be stopped up or its course changed by the lower proprietor without the consent of the other after it has been acquiesced in by all parties.

2. The assent of the lower proprietor to the construction of a ditch on his land to connect with another on the land of the upper proprietor for the purpose of carrying off the drainage of a natural swale, having the same general course is in the nature of a license, which, having been accepted, and the rights conferred, assumed and exercised, and money and labor expended in reliance thereon, cannot be set aside or disregarded.

(February 12, 1890.)

CROSS appeals from a decree of the District Court for Mahaska County in an action brought to enjoin defendant from interfering with the flow of water onto his lands from the adjoining lands of plaintiff, defendant appealing from so much of the decree as enjoined his interference with water flowing in one ditch, and plaintiff appealing from so much of the decree as refused to enjoin interference with water flowing in another ditch. *Affirmed on defendant's appeal. Reversed on plaintiff's appeal.*

Statement by **Beck,** *J.:*

Action in chancery to enjoin defendant from interfering with the flow of water from plaintiff's land upon the adjoining lands of defendant. There was a decree granting part of the relief prayed for by plaintiff, and refusing part. Both parties appeal,—the defendant first, and he is therefore designated as "appellant."

Messrs. **Blanchard & Preston,** for plaintiff:

Even in case there was no consideration paid and defendant had no interest in the north drain, if the licensor has stood by and has seen the licensee make expenditures in reliance upon his license, and which will be wholly or in great part lost to him if the license should be recalled, such facts are sufficient to create an estoppel *in pais,* which will preclude him from revoking.

Swartz v. *Swartz,* 4 Pa. 353; *Rerick* v. *Kern,* 14 Serg. & R. 267; *Lacy* v. *Arnett,* 33 Pa. 169; *Cumberland Valley R. Co.* v. *McLanahan,* 59

NOTE.—*Natural easement and servitude.*

Land on a lower level owes a natural servitude to that on a higher level in respect of receiving, without claim for compensation by the owner, the water naturally flowing down to it. Lord v. Carbon Iron Mfg. Co. 4 Cent. Rep. 853, 42 N. J. Eq. 157; Pennsylvania Coal Co. v. Sanderson, 4 Cent. Rep. 480, 113 Pa. 126.

Every owner of land through which a stream of water flows has presumptively a right against owners of land below him to have the stream flow from his land, in its natural channel, unobstructed. Such right is infringed by construction of a dam below which flows the stream back upon the land which naturally it would leave. Scriver v. Smith, 1 Cent. Rep. 763, 100 N. Y. 471.

A person who purchases a lower farm must take notice of the rights of the owner of the upper farm as to drainage. Bellas v. Pardoe (Pa.) Oct. 1, 1888.

Where the normal flow of surface water over the plaintiff's land was but slightly increased by the diversion, which caused no damage, he cannot recover. Jeffers v. Jeffers, 9 Cent. Rep. 845, 107 N. Y. 650.

Prescriptive right to flow of water.

Right to the artificial flow of water through a watercourse can be acquired by prescription. Murchie v. Gates, 2 New Eng. Rep. 435, 78 Me. 300.

It can be acquired by twenty years of adverse user. Chapel v. Smith (Mich.) April 11, 1890.

One who has suffered water to flow through his land in an artificial channel for more than twenty years cannot then divert it, to the injury of riparian proprietors above, who have enjoyed the benefit of its flow in such artificial channel. Murchie v. Gates, *supra.*

The right gained to flow water by adverse user must be limited by the extent of the user. Chapel v. Smith, *supra.*

Abandonment of a drain, or disuse of it, for any time, breaks the continuity of an adverse user, so as to prevent acquiring a right thereby to flow the land of another. *Ibid.*

Riparian rights. See *note* to Whitney v. Wheeler Cotton Mills (Mass.) 7 L. R. A. 613.

Doctrine of *damnum absque injuria* applied. See *note* to Jordan v. St. Paul, M. & M. R. Co. (Minn.) 6 L. R. A. 573.

Pa. 23; *Huff* v. *McCauley*, 53 Pa. 206; *Sheffield* v. *Collier*, 3 Ga. 82; *Cook* v. *Pridgen*, 45 Ga. 331; *Snowden* v. *Wilas*, 19 Ind 10; *Lane* v. *Miller*, 27 Ind. 534; *Wilson* v. *Chalfant*, 15 Ohio, 248; *Ricker* v. *Kelly*, 1 Me. 117; *Russell* v. *Hubbard*, 59 Ill. 335; *Williams* v. *Morris*, 95 U. S. 444 (24 L. ed. 360); *Clark* v. *Glidden*, 60 Vt. 702.

The same principle applies as to a party-wall which parties are to use in common.

Wickersham v. *Orr*, 9 Iowa, 253; *Rawson* v. *Bell*, 46 Ga. 19; *Russell* v. *Hubbard*, 59 Ill. 335; *Wynn* v. *Garland*, 19 Ark. 23.

The same principle applies to a watercourse in which both parties are interested.

LeFevre v. *LeFevre*, 4 Serg. & R. 241; *Rerick* v. *Kern*, *supra; Williams* v. *Earl of Jersey*, 1 Craig & Ph. 92.

The mere "acquiescence and consent of the parties to such arrangements are in the nature of a contract which, when fulfilled by one party at his cost and charge, must be obligatory upon both."

Pratt v. *Lamson*, 2 Allen, 275; Cooley, Torts, 309; *Wickersham* v. *Orr*, 9 Iowa, 253; *Beatty* v. *Gregory*, 17 Iowa, 109; *Anderson* v. *Simpson*, 21 Iowa, 399; *Harkness* v. *Burton*, 39 Iowa, 101; *Cook* v. *Chicago, B. & Q. R. Co.* 40 Iowa, 451; *Decorah Woolen Mill Co.* v. *Greer*, 49 Iowa, 490; *Kipp* v. *Coenen*, 55 Iowa, 63.

The vast agricultural interests of our State, as well as the public good, require that the proprietor of the higher ground shall have the right to tile drain his own land, and the owner of the lower land shall not have the power to prevent it, except to save himself from great damage or material injury.

McCormick v. *Horan*, 81 N. Y. 86; *Peck* v. *Goodberlett*, 12 Cent. Rep. 199, 109 N. Y. 180; *West Cumberland Iron & Steel Co.* v. *Kenyon*, L. R. 11 Ch. Div. 782; *Anderson* v. *Henderson*, 14 West. Rep. 109, 124 Ill. 164.

Messrs. **John F. Lacey**, **William R. Lacey** and **Bolton & McCoy**, for defendant:

The right to concentrate a flow of water has been denied.

Livingston v. *McDonald*, 21 Iowa, 160; Angell, Watercourses, 7th ed. §§ 108 J, 108 K; *Gregory* v. *Bush*, 7 West. Rep. 169, 64 Mich. 37; *Dickinson* v. *Worcester*, 7 Allen, 19.

The south ditch was not a watercourse but a mere wash upon defendant's land. It laid wholly upon defendant's land, and the surface water, after heavy rains, washed it into a crevice or steep slough such as is familiar to all residents of Iowa. To stop such washes, where they are small enough to be controlled, is the common effort of all good farmers, and it seems rather strange that the aid of a court of equity is invoked to prevent the defendant from using his land as good farmers ordinarily do. The right of defendant to thus protect his property is not defeated even although surface water may be impeded in its flow.

Morris v. *Council Bluffs*, 67 Iowa, 346; *Hoard* v. *Des Moines*, 62 Iowa, 326; *Phillips* v. *Waterhouse*, 69 Iowa, 201.

The agreement as to the north ditch is of no validity under the Statute of Frauds. Such contracts must be in writing.

Angell, Watercourses, 7th ed. § 169, and *note*.

Such license is at will, only, revocable at any time.

Angell, Watercourses, 7th ed. § 169, and *note;* Reed, Stat. Fr. § 721.

An easement in the land of another can only be conveyed by deed.

Browne, Fr. 3d ed. § 232.

Beck, *J.*, delivered the opinion of the court:

1. The petition is in two counts. The first alleges that plaintiff owns 160 acres of land, and defendant owns an eight-acre tract adjacent thereto, on the west; that for many years there has been upon plaintiff's land a natural drain, or open ditch, two or three feet deep, being a natural watercourse, which begins near the center of the tract, and runs in southwesterly direction, crossing the division line of defendant's land about twenty rods north of the southwest corner thereof, and thence across it; that this drain or watercourse is the natural outlet of the water falling and accumulating upon a part of plaintiff's land, and is the natural drainage thereof; that the defendant dammed up the drain at or near its entrance upon defendant's land, but the dam was washed out by the floods, and defendant threatens to rebuild it, and that the water arrested in its flow off of plaintiff's land, and caused to remain thereon by the dam, would prove to be a source of great injury thereto, which would prove irreparable if the dam be permitted to remain.

The second count alleges that plaintiff and defendant, at the time being owners of their respective tracts of land, entered into an oral agreement that plaintiff should cause an open ditch to be dug, other than the one referred to in the first count, which should run westerly from the southwest part of plaintiff's land, and cross the line of defendant's land about thirty rods south of the northeast corner thereof and should run thence upon defendant's land according to lines and distances set out in the petition, which need not be repeated here; that the parties should unite in constructing this ditch, each doing a part of the work, as stated in the petition; that each party was to have the right to connect the drains with the ditch; and that defendant threatens to destroy the ditch or drain and render it useless, which would work great injury to plaintiff.

The defendant, in answer to the first count of the petition, after denying, generally, all allegations thereof, admits the existence of the ditch described in the first count of the petition, but alleges that it is not a natural watercourse, but an artificial ditch. He admits that he obstructed the ditch, but denies that the flow of the water was thereby interfered with, and alleges that plaintiff's land, at the place in question, is higher than the defendant's land; that the ditch is not necessary for the proper drainage of plaintiff's land, the natural depression of the land being sufficient therefor; that it is his intention to fill up the ditch on his own land, but not to obstruct the flow of the water upon plaintiff's land; and that the ditch, with steep banks, is an injury to defendant's land.

In answer to the second count of the petition, defendant admits that the other ditch—the more northerly one—was dug at the mutual expense of the parties, pursuant to a verbal agreement made by the parties, which did not provide how long it should remain, but that it should be tiled in the future, if defendant so required, and that the ditch was not dug in compliance with the agreement. It is alleged that defendant now requires the ditch to be tiled, one half of the expense whereof he proposes to pay. Defendant, in a cross-petition, prays that plaintiff may be enjoined from collecting the water into the ditch described in the first count by tile drains, and thereby causing it to flow upon defendant's land. The cross-petition contains allegations in this language: "That defendant's land is lower than plaintiff's, and that the plaintiff's surface is drained naturally upon defendant's land, but that plaintiff has no lawful right, by drainage, to concentrate the under-ground water and to cause it to flow from a single point upon defendant's land, and that by so doing he has attempted to impose upon defendant's land a burden which it is not required by law to bear." The allegations of the cross-petition are denied by plaintiff in a proper pleading.

Upon the final hearing on the merits, the court found the equities with defendant upon the first count of the petition, which was dismissed by the decree; and upon the second count the equities were found with plaintiff, and the relief prayed for thereon was granted. The defendant's cross-petition was dismissed.

2. The evidence and the pleading show that plaintiff's land is the higher, and is naturally drained over defendant's land by two "sloughs," as they are called in the pleadings ("swales" is a better designation), which run from or through plaintiff's land to and over defendant's. There is no other way of carrying the surplus water, caused by snow and rains, off of and away from plaintiff's land, except through these swales. They also drain defendant's land, which has no other drainage. The case is not one of water, which would not naturally run upon defendant's land, being diverted and brought there by the unlawful acts of plaintiff, but is simply the case of the natural drainage of a tract of land through the swales prepared by nature for that very purpose. The two parties happen to own this tract of land; and the defendant, the owner of the servient estate, attempts to resist the undoubted right of plaintiff, the owner of the dominant estate, to have the surplus water falling upon his land conducted by nature's waterway off of his land to the brook, the creek and the river, the great natural drains of the county. The ground of this resistance is that this water from plaintiff's land passes over defendant's farm. But, as the water from defendant's land must pass over his neighbors' lands below him, which are servient to his lands, he is attempting to impose restrictions upon plaintiff which, with the same claim of right, could be imposed upon him, with equally disastrous results. It is insisted that plaintiff is violating the law and rights of defendant by collecting the water—"underground water," it is called in defendant's pleadings—by tiles, and conducting it to defendant's land at one place, which, it is claimed, is not permitted by the law. It will be readily seen, upon a moment's reflection, by one having but a limited acquaintance with the subject, upon the consideration of the facts developed in the evidence, that there is no difference between underground water, collected by tiling, and surface water. The first is water which would run off in a ditch, were one dug, without entering the earth. But it is permitted to enter the earth, and is then, by natural means, attracted and conducted to the tiles, and through them flows away. It must be remembered that the lands of both parties are used for cultivation with the plow.

The fact is known by every intelligent observer who has directed his eyes over the surface of our beautiful and fertile agricultural lands, that the swales are our most productive lands, while the sward of the prairie grass, and of other natural grasses, remains unbroken. There are no ditches or gutters in the swales. They, of course, are of various widths, depending largely upon the abruptness and height of the little hills or elevations of which they constitute the valleys. When the sward is broken by the plow, the water from rains and snows has a tendency to seek a channel down the swale, which will, of course, be no wider than is required to conduct away the surplus water falling on the land drained by the swale. This channel will soon become a ditch after the sward is broken; and, if left to nature, it will be sinuous, directed by the laws of nature, which give all watercourses that character. But the intelligent husbandman will aid water in this regard, and, with his plow or his shovel will keep the ditches straight. He will not act the foolish part of attempting to do that which is impossible, namely, to keep the surplus water flowing over all the surface of the swale; for the reason that it would prove impossible, and, if successful, it would cost him his crops, and finally impoverish his land, by causing the fertile soil to be washed away.

In the case before us, both parties, if they be intelligent farmers, do this very thing. Plaintiff, instead of an open ditch, put in tile, which subserves the same purpose. Now, these farmers are not diverting the water from the waterway provided by nature. They are not seeking to conduct the water contrary to the course of nature, or in a way it did not run before the soil became the property of man. When the use of the soil is changed from nature's husbandry, the production of grasses from meadows and pastures, to the cultivation of grain by means of the plow, nature continues to direct the water in channels. The plaintiff does not conduct the water to and upon defendant's land in a manner differing from that manner in which it was conducted before the land was plowed. The manner in each instance is nature's manner. Of course, the manner, in one instance, under the laws of nature, provides for a ditch; in the other instances, the laws of nature, under which was produced the sward of the prairie grass, dispense with a ditch.

3. It is shown by the evidence—indeed, defendant himself so testifies—that the ditch referred to in the first count was made upon defendant's land, before he owned it, by the farmer who then owned and cultivated the land. It seems that the defendant's grantor, and the plaintiff or his grantor, were in accord in their views as to the ditch, and its course through the two tracts of land, and, either by

express agreement or by mutual and silent acquiescence in the manner pursued by each in the improvement, by drains, of their respective lands, agreed upon the construction of the ditch, and the line it should pursue. Its place of crossing the dividing line of the lands, in this manner, was settled. The law will not permit complaint to be now made of the location and manner of construction of the ditch, after it has been acquiesced in by the parties. The right of the parties demands that the ditch should remain a settled matter. Good husbandry forbids the changing of ditches. Their permanence prevents the washing away of the soil, as well as avoids expenses in the change.

4. Upon the first count of the petition, and defendant's cross-petition, we reach the conclusions: (1) that the ditch is required by the best interest of both proprietors; (2) that the manner of its construction is in accord with the natural flow of the water; (3) that the quantity of the water has not been increased, and its flow has not been diverted, as charged; (4) that the ditch was established by the acquiescence of the proprietors, and that defendant threatens to interfere with, and change, the flow of the water, by building and maintaining a dam in the ditch; (5) that the ditch cannot be dispensed with, nor its course changed, without the consent of the parties interested. This conclusion is in accord with the doctrines of *Livingston* v. *McDonald*, 21 Iowa, 160, and is supported by familiar principles of the law. See *Bratt* v. *Lamson*, 2 Allen, 275.

5. The evidence very plainly leads to the conclusion of fact that the ditch described in the second count was constructed jointly by the parties, under an oral agreement as to its course, etc; each party contributing labor or money to constructing it. The parties have recognized the ditch, have plowed and farmed in accord with it, and have expended money and labor in the performance of the contract. It can be set aside, disregarded and annulled by neither without the consent of the other. The assent of defendant to the construction of the ditch on his land is in the nature of a license which, having been accepted and the rights conferred assumed and exercised, cannot be set aside or disregarded. *Harkness* v. *Burton*, 39 Iowa, 101; *Cook* v. *Chicago, B. & Q. R. Co.* 40 Iowa, 451; *Anderson* v. *Simpson*, 21 Iowa, 399; *Beatty* v. *Gregory*, 17 Iowa, 109.

6. These considerations lead us to the conclusion that the decree of the district court ought to be affirmed as to the second count, and as to the dismissal of defendant's cross-petition, and reversed as to the dismissal of the first count of the petition. A decree ought to have been entered granting the plaintiff all the relief prayed for in his petition, both upon the first and second counts, and dismissing the cross-petition of defendant. The cause will be remanded to the court below for such a decree.

Modified and affirmed, on defendant's appeal. Reversed on plaintiff's appeal.

Petition for rehearing denied June 8, 1890.

TENNESSEE SUPREME COURT.

PALMER *et al.*, *Appts.*,
v.
STATE OF TENNESSEE.

(....Tenn....)

1. **Mere taxation** of an unlawful business does not legalize it.

2. **Selling pools on a horse-race** run outside of the State is not licensed by the Act of 1889, placing a tax on the business of selling pools upon any such race "in this or any other State." That Act does not repeal Code, § 4870, which makes betting a misdemeanor, nor does it enlarge the exemption therefrom made by § 4871 of bets upon a horse-race run upon a licensed track within the State.

(February 22, 1890.)

APPEAL by defendants from a judgment of the Criminal Court for Davidson County convicting them of the offense of gambling. *Affirmed.*

The facts are fully stated in the opinion.

Messrs. **S. Hill** and **J. M. Quarles** for appellants.

Mr. **G. W. Pickle,** *Atty-Gen.*, for the State.

Lurton, *J.*, delivered the opinion of the court:

Appellants have been convicted of gambling. The indictment charged that they had bet, gambled and put to hazard upon a horse-race run upon a track not authorized by this State; and, in a second count, that they had encouraged and promoted gambling upon races upon

---

NOTE.—*Taxation; taxing power, to what limited.*

The power of taxation by any State is limited to persons, property or business within its jurisdiction. Tappan v. Merchants Nat. Bank, 86 U. S. 19 Wall. 490 (22 L. ed. 189); Cleveland, P. & A. R. Co. v. Pennsylvania ("State Tax on Foreign-held Bonds"), 82 U. S. 15 Wall. 300 (21 L. ed. 179); Pittsburg, Ft. W. & C. R. Co. v. Pennsylvania, 82 U. S. 15 Wall. 326, *note* (21 L. ed. 189).

In property there is always present the element of value as the basis on which equality in taxation can be attained by the application of a uniform rate on such values; but in franchises, trades or occupations there is no element of value in common; and hence the rule of equality is not violated by a taxation of these subjects by a rule which is uniform as to each class. Dis. Op. State Board of Assessors v. New Jersey Cent. R. Co. 4 Cent. Rep. 453, 48 N. J. L. 146.

To tax a merchant upon his stock and also upon his gross sales is not unconstitutional. Keystone Bridge Co. v. Pittsburgh (Pa.) 6 Cent. Rep. 168.

Subjecting racing associations to taxation upon their receipts, and prescribing the period during which racing with horses shall be legal, and inferentially declaring at what time pools upon such races shall be sold, legalizes pool selling at the times and places mentioned. Brennan v. Brighton Beach Racing Asso. (Sup. Ct.) 30 N. Y. S. R. 408.

See also 33 L. R. A. 221; 37 L. R. A. 227.

a track not licensed by this State. The case was tried without a jury upon an agreement as to the facts. The agreed state of facts is as follows:

(1) That the defendants did, on the 15th day of May, 1889, and before the presentment in this case was found, and within the City of Nashville, Davidson County, State of Tennessee, and within the jurisdiction of this court, both sell and offer to sell wagers or bets upon horse-races to be run both in and out of the State of Tennessee, upon a race track other than the lawfully chartered or incorporated blood-horse or turf association, or trotting association, or stock or agricultural fair association.

(2) In this case there were four horses to be run in the race. The defendants offered to sell at public outcry the first choice for the winner in said race, when $50 was bid therefor by a by-stander, which, being the highest bid, was accepted, and the money paid over to the defendants; and thereupon the defendants offered the second choice on the horses to be run in said race, whereupon a by-stander bid $40, which bid, being the highest, was accepted, and the money paid over as before; and thereupon the defendants offered for sale in the same manner the third choice of the horses to be run in said race, whereupon a by-stander bid $30, which, being the highest bid, was accepted; and thereupon the defendant offered the remaining and unsold horse in the same manner, whereupon a by-stander bid $20, which, being the highest bid, was also accepted,—these several sums making altogether the gross sum of $140, from which gross sum the defendants deducted 5 per cent, or $7, as their compensation for their services, leaving remaining, net, $133. On the succeeding day the horse-race was run, and the party who had purchased, in the manner hereinbefore stated, the horse that won, or came out ahead, in the race, was entitled to and did receive from the defendants the whole sum of $133, which was accordingly paid over to said party. The defendants kept books or memoranda of each bid made and accepted, as hereinbefore stated. These transactions hereinbefore related all occurred in a room called a "pool-room," or place for selling pools on horse-races. This particular race was run upon a track outside of the State of Tennessee, but in the State of Kentucky, and within the six months next preceding the presentment in this case. This is known as "auction pools."

(3) It is further agreed and admitted that the defendants, at the time of the selling of said pools as stated in paragraph 2, had duly paid to the county court clerk of Davidson County the privilege tax of $500 imposed upon pool-selling by an Act of the General Assembly of the State of Tennessee, entitled "An Act to Provide Revenue for the State of Tennessee, and the Counties thereof," approved April 8, 1889. And that the said clerk of the County Court of Davidson County had, in consideration of the payment of said privilege tax, duly issued and delivered to the defendant a license, as provided in said Act of the General Assembly, for pool-selling, and that said license was in full force and effect prior to the 15th day of May, 1889, and on said day, and continuing until that date.

The question for decision is as to the effect of the alleged license in legalizing the sale on pools upon races run outside of the State.

By section 4870 of the Code of Tennessee, it is made a misdemeanor to "make any bet or wager for money or other valuable thing."

By section 4881, horse-racing "upon a track or path kept for that purpose" is exempt from the provisions of the Statute against gaming. The betting of money upon a horse-race upon a track within the State, not licensed by the State, has been held to be gambling, within section 4870. *Huff* v. *State*, 2 Swan, 279.

The Act legalizing racing upon a licensed track has been held to have been intended to encourage the improvement of domestic stock, and not intended to make gaming lawful upon races run outside of the State, and that betting upon races run in another State was a misdemeanor, under section 4870. *Edwards* v. *State*, 8 Lea, 412; *Daly* v. *State*, 13 Lea, 228; *State* v. *Blackburn*, 2 Coldw. 235.

By the Revenue Act of 1885, a tax of $300 was put upon the occupation of pool-selling. Acts 1885, Extra Sess. p. 43.

By the Assessment Act of 1887, the occupation of pool-selling was declared to be a privilege, and not to be pursued without license. Act 1887, p. 48.

By the Revenue Act of the same year, a tax was placed upon this business. Act 1887, p. 17.

By the Assessment Act of 1889. § 52, the avocation of pool-selling is again declared a privilege, and, as such, not to be pursued without license. Act 1889, p. 168.

By the Revenue Act of same year, a tax is placed upon each person, company or corporation or agent engaged in selling pools upon any running, trotting or pacing race in this or any other State. Acts 1889, p. 260.

If the selling of pools be not a lottery,—a question not here decided, for reasons hereafter noticed,—then the sale of pools upon races to be run upon a track licensed by this State would not be gaming, within our Statute. *Daly* v. *State*, *supra*.

It was, however, within the power of the Legislature to make the business of selling pools a privilege, and to assess upon the privilege such tax as was deemed wise. Both of the Acts erecting pool-selling into a privilege —that of 1887, and that of 1889—designate the business as "pool-selling," without further words describing the limits of the business. To make this business, by its general designation, a privilege, would no more authorize a seller to sell pools upon an unlawful race than does the liquor dealer's license authorize him to sell liquor to minors, or on Sunday, or within four miles of a school-house.

The privilege of "selling pools," which is not to be pursued without a license, is limited to the sale of lawful pools; that is, pools which are in substance bet upon races to be run upon a licensed track or turf within this State. The tax assessed upon the privilege by the Acts of 1885 and 1887 was assessed upon pool selling, no effort being made to designate whether upon races in or out of the State. The change made in the assessment of the tax upon this occupation by the Act of 1889 is made by adding the words, "in this State, or any other State." The contention is that the addition of these words, not in the Act creating the privilege, but in an Act simply fixing the tax upon a privilege created by another and different Act, operates to license the sale of pools upon races run upon unlicensed tracks in this State, and upon all tracks in other States, and that the licensing of an act theretofore criminal operates to make the act legal, and entitles it to the protection of the law. To put this construction upon this clause in a Revenue Act would operate to repeal in part the criminal law of the State, and to make lawful a species of gambling which has been heretofore unlawful. Was it the intent of the Legislature, by words added to the language theretofore used in fixing the amount of tax upon the occupation of pool-selling, to enlarge the privilege of selling pools beyond such pools as were sold upon lawful races? Or was it the intent of the law makers, by the levying of this tax, to create the privilege of selling pools upon races to be run outside of the State? If the Act which enumerated and created privileged occupations had in express words authorized the licensing of the business of selling pools upon races run in other States, we should then have had a very different question to deal with; for in that case there would be no doubt that the intent of the legislation was to make that species of business a privilege. The effect of such legislation in an Assessment Act, in repealing the Statute making such pool-selling criminal, would present a very grave question. But the question we have to deal with here is as to whether the Legislature intended, by the words they have used in describing this business, to authorize or license the sale of pools upon illegal races.

The case of *Dun* v. *Cullen*, 13 Lea, 202, is cited by the learned counsel as settling this question of legislative intent. That cause was this: The business of commercial agencies was not made a privilege in the Act creating and enumerating privileged avocations. In the Revenue Bill, a tax was levied upon the occupation. The court were agreed that the language of the Revenue Act, namely, "that the rate of taxation on the following privileges shall be as follows," naming the avocations, and the rates of tax would ordinarily be sufficient to create a privilege, and forbid its exercise without license. The "difficulty," said *Judge* Cooper, speaking for the court, "grows out of the fact that the Legislature has passed two Acts,—one of them apparently intended, among other things, to designate the taxable privileges, and the other to fix the rate of taxation upon privileges; and the doubt is whether the latter Act was actually intended to create a privilege." "The point," said he, "is one of some nicety." He reaches a conclusion of this question by the suggestion that this business of a commercial agency was "mentioned, unquestionably, with the expectation that [it was] to be taxed; and, if the Legislature have used language sufficient to enable us to carry that intent into effect, it would seem to be our duty to effectuate the intent. We think this the better conclusion, and hold the occupation taxable." 13 Lea, 205.

The sole inquiry in that case was as to whether the intent of the Legislature was to make that occupation taxable; and the duty of the court was to carry out that intent, if made sufficiently plain. There the question of "nicety" is not as to whether the Legislature intended to create pool-selling a privilege. That they have done in express words. But did they intend, by the words used in describing a privilege created by another Act, to enlarge it so as to make legal that which by the general law was criminal, or to create a new and different privilege from the one created by the Act enumerating taxable privileges? This case is distinguishable from that in many obvious particulars.

Neither is the case of *State* v. *Duncan*, reported in 16 Lea, at page 81, a controlling case. By an Act approved March 30, 1883, it was made a misdemeanor to buy or sell futures. By the Assessment Act approved on the same day, the business of selling futures was made a privilege, and a tax assessed by the Revenue Act thereon. The two Acts then passed together were for this reason construed together, for the purpose of arriving at the meaning and intent of each. "The effect of the Acts of 1883, taken together," said *Judge* Cooper, "is to make it a misdemeanor, both in the buyer and seller, to deal in futures without a license, and at the same time legalize the dealing, by taking out a license." 16 Lea, 81.

We have no such case here. By very ancient statute law, betting upon races other than such as were run on licensed tracks was a misdemeanor. This exception in favor of domestic races was, in its evil results, comparatively limited. To extend this exemption to races run everywhere is, as we can very well know from our knowledge of affairs, to open the doors of gambling establishments all the year round. Did the Legislature intend, by the Revenue Act of 1889, to repeal the general and ancient laws of the State, which made such betting criminal? It is not the case of two Acts upon the same subject, passed upon the same day; and the rule of construction applicable in the *Duncan Case* has no application here.

The tax upon the business of selling pools upon races to be run upon licensed tracks within this State is a tax upon a lawful business, if it be not a lottery,—a question which we do not decide, for the reason that a majority of the court are of the opinion that, for the reasons stated, the provisions concerning the sale of pools upon races run outside of the State is ineffectual, whether it did or did not attempt to license a lottery, as it did not in fact license pool-selling on races run outside of the State—but, so far as it seems to be a tax upon the selling of pools upon races not so run, it is at most a tax assessed upon an unlawful occupation. Taxation so imposed will not be construed to operate as a license legalizing such unlawful betting. Taxation, even under the form of a privilege tax, does not necessarily operate to license the business. The Constitution of Michigan prohibited the passing of any law licensing liquor dealers. A specific tax was assessed upon liquor dealers. It was held by the Supreme Court of that State, *Judge* Cooley delivering the opinion, not to be, in its legal effect, a license tax, or in any way to sanction, authorize or countenance the business. "The idea," said *Judge* Cooley, "that the State lends its countenance to any particular traffic by taxing it, seems to us to rest upon a very transparent fallacy. It certainly overlooks or disregards some ideas that must always underlie taxation. Taxes are not favors, they are burdens. They are necessary, it is true, to the existence of government; but they are not the less burdens. . . . It would be a remarkable proposition, under such circumstances, that a thing is sanctioned and countenanced by the government, when this burden, which may prove disastrous, is imposed upon it, while, on the other hand, it is frowned upon and condemned when the burden is withheld. . . . The taxation of a thing may be, and often is, when police purposes are had in view, a means of expressing disapproval, instead of approbation. . . . A business may be licensed, and yet not taxed; or it may be taxed, and yet not licensed. And, so far is the tax from being necessarily a license, that provision is frequently made by law for the taxation of a business that is carried on under a license existing independent of the tax." He concludes a most elaborate discussion by saying: "If one puts the government to special inconvenience and cost by keeping up a prohibited traffic, or maintaining a nuisance, the fact is a reason for discriminating in taxation against him; and, if the tax is imposed on the thing which is prohibited, or which constitutes the nuisance, the Tax Law, instead of being inconsistent with the law declaring the illegality, is in entire harmony with its general purpose, and may sometimes be even more effectual. Certainly, whatever discriminations are made in taxation ought to be in the direction of making the heaviest burdens fall upon those things which are obnoxious to the public interest, wherever that is practicable." *Youngblood* v. *Sexton*, 32 Mich. 406.

An instance of a license which does not carry with it protection is that of the federal tax upon the occupation of liquor dealing, in States or localities where such traffic is illegal. *License Tax Cases*, 72 U. S. 5 Wall. 462 [18 L. ed. 497]. Concerning this class of cases, it is said: "These burdens are imposed in the form of what are called 'license fees;' and it has been claimed that, where the party paid the fee, he was thereby licensed to carry on the business, despite the regulation which the state government might make upon the subject. This view, however, has not been taken by the courts, who have regarded the congressional legislation imposing a license fee as only a species of taxation, without the payment of which the business could not be carried on, but which, nevertheless, did not propose to make any business lawful which was not lawful before, or to relieve it from any burden or restrictions imposed by the regulations of the State." Cooley, Const. Lim. 5th ed. 721.

The tax imposed by the Act of 1889 is, so far as it is imposed upon the illegal business of selling pools upon races run upon unlicensed tracks, not operative as a license, and does not, by necessary implication, repeal the Criminal Law affecting such betting. The defendants could not, therefore, interpose their receipt for this tax as a defense to the criminal charge.

The judgment must be affirmed.

NORTH DAKOTA SUPREME COURT.

STATE of North Dakota, *ex rel.* George F. GOODWIN, *Atty-Gen., et al.,*

v.

NELSON COUNTY.

(....N. Dak.....)

*1. **An Act approved February 14, 1890,** entitled "An Act Authorizing Counties to Issue Bonds to Procure Seed-grain for Needy Farmers Resident therein," examined, and *held* to be valid, and not an abuse of legislative powers, in that it authorizes the issue of bonds and taxation for a public purpose. *Held, further*, that the Act is not an infringement of section 185 of the State Constitution, in this: that it is a measure intended for the "necessary support of the poor."

2. **In the exercise of its original jurisdiction,** under section 87 of the State Constitution, the supreme court, exercising its discretion,

*Head notes by WALLIN, J.

NOTE.—*Taxes must be laid for public purposes, and not for private interests.*

The term "public purpose" is merely a term of classification to distinguish objects for which, according to settled usage, the government is to provide, from those which, by like usage, are left to private inclination, interest or liberality. People v. Salem, 20 Mich. 452.

To constitute a public purpose it is not necessary that there should be a direct benefit to the people of the whole State; the benefit contemplated may be confined to a particular community. Bloomfield & R. Nat. Gas Light Co. v. Richardson, 63 Barb. 437.

The Legislature may interpose a tax on a local district for a public improvement, such as a canal. Thomas v. Leland, 24 Wend. 65.

Where county commissioners are clothed with legislative power their discretion as to the appropriation of the revenue to different purposes will not be controlled. Long v. Richmond County, 76 N. C. 273.

Taxation for the construction of railroads is essentially for a public use, railroads being public improvements, for the advancement of commerce and promotion of the welfare of the people. Stewart v. Polk County, 30 Iowa, 9; Merrill v. Welsher, 50 Iowa, 61; Dyar v. Farmington Village Corp. 70 Me. 515; Sharpless v. Philadelphia, 21 Pa. 147.

Taxes may be imposed for educational purposes in maintaining the common-school system. Felty v. Uhler, 10 Phila. 512, 30 Leg. Int. 330; Com. v. Hartman, 17 Pa. 118; Opinions of the Justices, 68 Me. 582; People v. Trustees of Schools, 78 Ill. 136; Weightman v. Clark, 103 U. S. 256 (26 L. ed. 392); Briggs v. Johnson County, 4 Dill. 148; Richards v. Raymond, 92 Ill. 612; Jones v. State, 17 Fla. 411.

Taxes may be levied for the preservation of the public health and to prevent the spread of disease. Solomon v. Tarver, 52 Ga. 405.

The draining of low lands for preservation of the public health is a public purpose. Anderson v. Kerns D. Co. 14 Ind. 202; *Re* New Orleans Draining

will issue the writs of habeas corpus, mandamus, quo warranto, certiorari and injunction only when applied for as prerogative writs; and where the question presented is *publici juris*, and one affecting the sovereignty of the State, its franchises or prerogatives or the liberties of the people. To invoke the original jurisdiction of this court, the interest of the State must be primary and proximate, and not secondary and remote. This court will judge for itself whether the wrong complained of is one which requires the interposition of this court to protect the prerogatives and franchises of the State in its sovereign character. In all cases where the original jurisdiction of this court is invoked, except in habeas corpus cases, the attorney-general shall proceed only on leave, based upon a prima facie showing that the case is one of which it is proper for this court to take cognizance. In ordinary cases, this court will not exercise its original jurisdiction to restrain local taxation for any reason. The proper jurisdiction for that purpose is lodged in the district courts. *Held*, this being an application made by the attorney-general in behalf of the State to enjoin the issue of bonds upon the alleged ground that the Statute authorizing the bonds is unconstitutional, that the question is one of local concern, and affects only the County of Nelson and its taxpayers, and hence the case does not fall within the limited class of cases in which this court will exercise original jurisdiction. *Held*, that the writ of injunction is denied upon the ground that the Statute in question is a valid law, and also upon the ground that the question presented is one of merely local concern, and hence is not a proper case to call for the issuing of a writ out of this court.

(April 21, 1890.)

APPLICATION for leave to file an information as a foundation for the issuance of an injunction to prohibit the issuance of certain seed-grain bonds. *Refused.*

The facts are fully stated in the opinion.

Messrs. **George F. Goodwin**, *Atty-Gen.*, and **Burke Corbet** for relators.

Messrs. **M. N. Johnson**, *State Atty.*, and **F. R. Fulton** for respondent.

Wallin, *J.*, delivered the opinion of the court:

Upon the return of an order to show cause, application is made to this court for leave to file an information as a foundation for issuing a writ of injunction out of this court prohibiting the County of Nelson and its officials from issuing seed-grain bonds, under an Act of the State Legislature approved February 14,

---

Co. 11 La. Ann. 338; Alcorn v. Hamér, 38 Miss. 652; Daily v. Swope, 47 Miss. 367; Egyptian Levee Co. v. Hardin, 27 Mo. 495; Tide Water Co. v. Coster, 18 N. J. Eq. 521; Woodruff v. Fisher, 17 Barb. 224; Hartwell v. Armstrong, 19 Barb. 166; People v. Nearing, 27 N. Y. 306; Sessions v. Crunkilton, 20 Ohio, 349; Whiting v. Sheboygan & F. du L. R. Co. 25 Wis. 167.

So the removal of dams to facilitate the flow of stagnant and offensive waters is a public purpose. Cypress Pond. D. Co. v. Hooper, 2 Met. (Ky.) 350.

The following have been held to be public purposes, involving the general interests of the State or community:

Payment of bounties to volunteers to aid in the maintenance of government. Booth v. Woodbury, 32 Conn. 128; Taylor v. Thompson, 42 Ill. 9; Moulton v. Raymond, 60 Me. 121; Thompson v. Pittston, 59 Me. 545; Veazie v. China, 50 Me. 518; Stetson v. Kempton, 13 Mass. 272; Freeland v. Hastings, 10 Allen, 570; Kunkle v. Franklin, 13 Minn. 127; Shackford v. Newington, 46 N. H. 415; State v. Delaware Twp. 31 N. J. L. 189; State v. Richland Twp. 20 Ohio St. 362; Cass Twp. v. Dillon, 16 Ohio, 38; Cunningham v. Mitchell, 67 Pa. 78; Kelly v. Marshall, 69 Pa. 319; Brodhead v. Milwaukee, 19 Wis. 625.

So the Legislature has power to raise money by taxation to refund sums contributed by individuals for the general purpose of filling quotas of troops for the war, but not for refunding sums paid by individuals for substitutes (Freeland v. Hastings and State v. Delaware Twp. *supra*), or for voluntary advancements made by individuals, not on the credit or authority of the municipality. Usher v. Colchester, 33 Conn. 567; Pease v. Chicago, 21 Ill. 508; Ferguson v. Landran, 5 Bush, 230; Perkins v. Milford, 59 Me. 315; Thompson v. Pittston, *supra*; Estey v. Westminster, 97 Mass. 324; Miller v. Grandy, 13 Mich. 540; Cover v. Baytown, 12 Minn. 124; Crowell v. Hopkinton, 45 N. H. 9; Tyson v. Halifax Twp. School Directors, 51 Pa. 22. See also State v. Tappan, 29 Wis. 672.

Money for a particular purpose may be raised by taxation if there be a possibility that it will be promotive in any degree of the public welfare. Booth v. Woodbury, 32 Conn. 128.

The interest of the public must be a direct public interest. Curtiss v. Whipple, 24 Wis. 350.

To render a tax void the absence of all possible public interest must be clear and palpable. Stockton & V. R. Co. v. Stockton, 41 Cal. 173; Schenley v. Allegheny, 25 Pa. 128; Brodhead v. Milwaukee, 19 Wis. 625.

Claims founded on equity and justice, and in gratitude, but not for charity, may be referred to the general interest in, or benefits received by, the public. Guilford v. Chenango County, 13 N. Y. 149; Brewster v. Syracuse, 19 N. Y. 116; Curtiss v. Whipple, 24 Wis. 354.

Taxation for the benefit of exempt firemen has been held lawful, as in discharge of a moral obligation resting upon the State. Exempt Firemen's Benev. Fund v. Roome, 93 N. Y. 313.

So where public agents incur liability in performance of their public duties. Nelson v. Milford, 7 Pick. 18; Bancroft v. Lynnfield, 18 Pick. 566; Friend v. Gilbert, 108 Mass. 412; Hadsell v. Hancock, 3 Gray, 526; Fuller v. Groton, 11 Gray, 340; Baker v. Windham, 13 Me. 74; Pike v. Middleton, 12 N. H. 278; Sherman v. Carr, 8 R. I. 431; Briggs v. Whipple, 6 Vt. 95, 7 Vt. 20.

A legislative question.

It is for the Legislature to determine whether a particular purpose concerns the public sufficiently to justify taxation. Booth v. Woodbury, 32 Conn. 118; Harris v. Dubuclet, 30 La. Ann. 662; Bloomfield & R. Nat. Gas Light Co. v. Richardson, 63 Barb. 437; Thomas v. Leland, 24 Wend. 65; Sharpless v. Philadelphia, 21 Pa. 147; Bennington v. Park, 50 Vt. 178; Brodhead v. Milwaukee, 19 Wis. 625.

A tax law must be considered valid unless it be for a purpose in which the community taxed has no interest, and the absence of all possible public interest is so clear and palpable as to be perceptible by every mind at the first blush. Brodhead v. Milwaukee and Sharpless v. Philadelphia, *supra*, Cheaney v. Hooser, 9 B. Mon. 330; English v. Oliver, 28 Ark. 317.

But taxation for exclusively private interests and the building up of private fortunes would be in the nature of a decree under legislative forms, and unconstitutional. Gove v. Epping, 41 N. H. 539; People v. Flagg, 40 N. Y. 401; Tyler v. Beacher, 44 Vt. 651; Hooper v. Emery, 14 Me. 375; *Re* Market Street, 49 Cal. 546; Allen v. Jay, 60 Me. 124.

1890 and entitled "An Act Authorizing Counties to Issue Bonds to Procure Seed-grain for Needy Farmers Resident therein." The information is based upon the complaint of one John Birkholz, which alleges: "*First.* That the above named complainant, John Birkholz, is a taxpayer of the County of Nelson, the respondent above named. *Second.* That said respondent is a political or public corporation, duly organized under existing laws. *Third.* That J. W. Forbes is the duly elected and qualified chairman of the board of county commissioners, and N. F. Webb is the duly elected county auditor of Nelson County, and as such officers are respectively discharging the duties thereof. *Fourth.* That the above-named respondent, on the 26th day of March, 1890, acting through its board of county commissioners and the county auditor of said County, pursuant to a petition signed by 100 freeholders resident in said County, adopted and passed a resolution at a meeting of said board, and thereby resolved to issue the bonds of the said County in the sum of twenty thousand dollars ($20,000), payable in ten (10) years, and bearing interest at the rate of seven (7) per cent per annum, payable semi-annually, claiming their right to so do under an Act of the Legislative Assembly entitled 'An Act Authorizing Counties to Issue Bonds to Procure Seed-grain for Needy Farmers Resident therein,' approved February 14, 1890, and Acts amendatory thereto; that in pursuance to said resolution said respondent, acting through its auditor and the chairman of its board of county commissioners, has taken such steps as are requisite and necessary in the premises to and is about to issue bonds for said amount, in pursuance of said resolution, claiming its right to do so under the Act aforesaid. *Fifth.* That if said bonds are issued they will become the obligation of the County. In order to meet the payment of the interest thereon, and the payment of the principal of the same, it will be necessary to levy taxes from year to year against the tax-paying people of said County, and the proceeds of said bonds, when issued and sold by the said County, will be diverted to and used for the purpose of buying seed grain, to be distributed to private individuals, indigent and poor farmers, resident in said County. *Sixth.* That the Act of the Legislative Assembly aforesaid, under which said respondent claims its right to issue said bonds, is in contravention of section 185 of the Constitution of the State of North Dakota, which said section reads as follows: 'Sec. 185. Neither the State, nor any county, city, township, town, school-district or any other political subdivision, shall loan or give its credit, or make donations to or in aid of any individual, association or corporation, except for necessary support of the poor, nor subscribe to or become the owner of the capital stock of any association or corporation, nor shall the State engage in work of internal improvement, unless authorized by a two-thirds vote of the people.' Wherefore your complainants pray your honorable court that an order in the nature of a rule to show cause be issued to the said respondent, its officers, agents and servants, to be and appear before your honors at Fargo, in the County of Cass and State of North Dakota, at the opening of court thereof on Wednesday the 2d day of April, A. D. 1890, and then and there show cause, if any reason it has, why an injunction should not be issued restraining respondent from issuing the bonds aforesaid."

It clearly appears from the complaint that the County of Nelson has, under the provisions of the Seed-grain Act in question, taken all of the requisite preliminary steps, and is about to issue the bonds of the County, and sell the same; and will apply the proceeds of such sale to the purchase of seed-grain for such farmers of that County as come within the terms of the Seed-grain Law, and who make application for the seed-grain under oath, and in manner and form as prescribed by the law. It is conceded that all action taken by the defendants is warranted by the express terms of the law; nor is it pretended that the bonds, if issued, will create a county indebtedness exceeding in amount the limit presented by the Constitution of the State. Under such circumstances, the writ of injunction will be refused, as a matter of course, unless the Statute under which the bonds are intended to be issued is itself unconstitutional or void for some reason. The question presented must turn upon the validity of the Seed-grain Statute.

The Statute has 20 sections, but it will suffice to give the substance of such of its provisions as bear upon its validity as a law.

Section 1 provides as follows: "In any county of the State where the crops for any preceding year have been a total or partial failure by reason of drought, hail or other cause, it shall be lawful for the board of county commissioners of such county to issue the bonds of the county under and pursuant to the provisions of this Act, and, with the proceeds derived from the sale thereof, to purchase seed-grain for the inhabitants thereof who are in need of seed-grain, and who are unable to procure the same, whenever said board shall be petitioned in writing so to do by not less than 100 freeholders resident in the county; and said board, at a meeting called as hereinafter provided, to consider said petition, shall by a majority vote determine that the prayer of the petitioners shall be granted: provided that all such petitions shall be filed with the county auditor or county clerk on or before the 28th day of February; and thereupon it shall be the duty of said officer to forthwith call a meeting of the board of county commissioners of his county to consider said petition: and provided, further, that the total amount of bonds issued by any county under the provisions of this Act shall not, with the then existing indebtedness of the county, exceed the limit of indebtedness fixed by the Constitution in such case."

Section 4 provides: "The proceeds arising from the sale of said bonds shall be paid by the purchaser thereof to the county treasurer of the county, or to his authorized agent at the time of the delivery thereof, and such proceeds shall be paid out only on the order of the board of county commissioners."

Section 6 provides that, "for the purpose of securing prompt payment of the principal and interest of said bonds, there shall be levied by the board of county commissioners, at the time and in the manner that other taxes are levied, such sums as shall be sufficient to pay such interest: and in addition thereto a sinking-fund tax shall be annually levied sufficient to pay and retire said bonds at their maturity, and it shall be the duty of the county treasurer to pay promptly the interest upon said bonds as the same shall fall due. No tax or fund provided for the payment of such bonds, either principal or interest, shall at any time be used for any other purpose."

Section 7 is as follows: "The fund arising from the sale of said bonds shall be applied exclusively by said board for the purchase of seed-grain for residents of the county who are poor and unable to procure the same; provided, that no more than 150 bushels of wheat, or its equivalent in any grain, shall be furnished to any one person."

Section 8 provides that "all persons entitled to or wishing to avail themselves of the benefit of this Act shall file with the county auditor or county clerk of the county where said applicant resides, on or before the 1st day of March, an application duly sworn to before said county auditor or clerk, or some other officer authorized to administer oaths. Said application shall contain a true statement of the number of acres the applicant has plowed or prepared for seeding; how many acres the applicant intends to have plowed and prepared for seeding; how many bushels and what kind of grain he will require to seed the ground so prepared as aforesaid; how many bushels of grain the applicant harvested in the preceding year; that the applicant has not procured, and is not able to procure, the necessary seed-grain for the current year; that he desires the same for seed, and no other purpose, and that he will not sell or dispose of the same, or any part thereof, but will use the same, and the whole thereof, n seeding the land so prepared, or to be prepared for crop."

Section 9 provides that the commissioners shall examine all applications, and determine "who are entitled to the benefits thereof, and the amount to which each applicant is entitled."

Section 10 provides that the applicants under the Act shall, before receiving the seed-grain, sign a "contract in duplicate, attested by the county auditor or county clerk, to the effect that said applicant, for and in consideration of ——— bushels of seed-grain received from ——— county, promises to pay to said county ——— dollars, the amount of the cost of the seed-grain; that said sum shall be taxable against all the real and personal property of said applicant; that such tax shall be levied by the county auditor or county clerk of his county, and collected as other taxes are collected under the laws of this State; that the amount of such indebtedness shall become due and payable on the 1st day of October, in the year in which said seed-grain is furnished, together with the interest on such amount from the 1st day of April of that year, at the rate of seven per cent per annum; and, if said indebtedness be not paid on or before the 20th day of October of that year, it shall then be the duty of the county auditor or county clerk of the said county to cause the amount of said indebtedness to be entered upon the tax-list of said county for that year as a tax on the land on which said seed-wheat was sown, and upon any other land owned by the applicant, to be collected as other taxes are; and the sum so entered and levied shall be a lien upon the real estate owned by such person until said indebtedness is fully paid, when it shall be the duty of the proper officer to cancel the same."

The objects and purposes contemplated by the Statute may be readily gathered from the above extracts, and they are clear and unmistakable in their character. The Legislature by this enactment, so far as it can do so, has clothed the several counties of the State where there has been a preceding crop failure with authority to lend their aid in procuring seed-grain to such of their citizens as are engaged in farming pursuits, who make it appear, in manner and form as detailed by the law, that they are unable to procure such seed grain by any other means. The law empowers the counties to lend their aid out of money to be obtained by the issue and sale of county bonds, such bonds to be paid, principal and interest, from funds obtained by means of a general tax levy upon all of the taxable property situated within the counties that issue such bonds. Two features of this Statute stand out in conspicuous prominence: *First.* All benefits obtainable under the Act are confined to persons engaged in the pursuit of farming, and among farmers only those who propose to continue the business of farming after the aid in contemplation has been received by them. *Second.* No part of the fund is intended to be used in support or aiding such indigent persons as have already become a county charge, viz., paupers.

The objections which may be made to the validity of this Statute are twofold: *First,* it may be claimed that the tax authorized by the Statute is not for a public purpose, hence not a valid tax; *second,* it may be contended that, under section 185 of the State Constitution, counties are expressly forbidden to make donations, or lend their aid to either corporations or individuals, hence that the proposed aid is unconstitutional, as repugnant to said section. The courts of this country, and of all countries where constitutional liberty exists, agree with the elementary writers upon the science of government that it is essential to the validity of a tax that it be laid for a public purpose. Difficulty has frequently arisen in discriminating between public and private objects; but where the object is primarily to foster private enterprises, and the only benefit to be derived by the public is incidental and secondary, the tax will be annulled by the courts as an abuse of the legislative prerogative. In the first instance the duty devolves upon the legislative branch of the government to determine whether a proposed tax is or is not for a public purpose; and courts are loth to interpose and declare any tax unlawful, and will only do so in case of a palpable disregard of the wise limitations, express and implied, restricting the power of taxation. But where the Legislature assumes, in the guise of taxation, to compel A to advance his private means to aid B in the prosecution of a purely private enterprise, the courts will not hesitate to perform the duty of declaring such tax void, as subversive of fundamental and vested individual rights, and will do so even in cases where there is no express constitutional inhibition. The power of confiscation does not exist in the Legislature. The cases cited below are but a few of the numberless cases which have applied these principles to statutes imposing pretended taxes. *Citizens S. & L. Asso.* v. *Topeka,* 87 U. S. 20 Wall. 655 [22 L. ed. 455]; *Commercial Nat. Bank* v. *Iola,* 2 Dill. 353; *Parkersburg* v. *Brown,* 106 U. S. 487 [27 L. ed. 238]; *Cole* v. *La Grange,* 113 U. S. 1 [28 L. ed. 896]; *Allen* v. *Jay,* 60 Me. 124; *Lowell* v. *Boston,* 111 Mass. 454; *State* v. *Osawkee Twp.* 14 Kan. 422; *Coates* v. *Campbell,* 37 Minn. 498; Cooley, Const. Lim. marg. p. 487; Cooley, Taxn. 2d ed. pp. 55, 126.

Under these authorities, the test to be applied to the Seed-grain Statute is this: Is the tax provided for in the Statute laid for a public purpose? If this question is answered in the negative, the Statute must be declared null and void, without reference to section 185 of the State Constitution, to which the attention of the court has been particularly directed. The Statute makes provision for levying a general tax, in counties issuing the bonds, for the benefit of a numerous body of citizens, who without fault of theirs, and solely by reason of successive crop failures, are now reduced to extremities, and are in fact impoverished to such an extent that they are, for the present time, wholly without the ability to obtain the grain necessary for seeding the lands from which they derive the necessaries of life. It is agreed on all sides that this class of citizens, having already exhausted their private credit, must have friendly aid from some source in procuring seed-grain, if they put in crops this year. The Legislature, by this Statute, has devised a measure which seems well adapted to meet the exigency, and promises to give the needed relief, with little prospect of ultimate loss to the county treasurer. It is reasonable to anticipate that the beneficiaries of the Act will be enabled to tide over their present embarrassments, and, through the aid granted them by this Statute, a wide-spread calamity, both public and private, will be averted. The crisis in the development of the State which renders some measure of wholesale relief imperatively necessary is fully recognized by all well-informed citizens of the State, and this court will be justified in taking judicial notice of the existing status. The stubborn fact exists that a class of citizens, numbered by many thousands, is in such present straits, from poverty, that unless succored by some comprehensive measure of relief they will become a public burden, in other words, paupers, dependent upon counties where they reside for support. It is to avert such a wide-spread disaster that the Seed-grain Statute was enacted, and it should be interpreted in the light of the public danger which was the occasion of its passage.

"The support of paupers, and the giving of assistance to those who, by reason of age, infirmity or disability are likely to become such, is, by the practice and the common consent of civilized countries, a public purpose." Cooley, Taxn. 2d ed. pp. 124, 125.

"The relief of the poor—the care of those who are unable to care for themselves—is among the unquestioned objects of public duty." Opinion of Brewer, *J.,* in *State* v. *Osawkee,* Twp. 14 Kan. 424.

If the destitute farmers of the frontier of North Dakota were now actually in the almshouses of the various counties in which they reside, all the adjudications of the courts, state and federal, upon this subject, could be marshaled as precedents in support of any taxation, however onerous, which might become necessary for their support. But is it not competent for the Legislature, representing the taxpayers, in the exercise of its discretion and within the limits of county indebtedness prescribed by the State Constitution, to clothe county commissioners with authority, to be exercised at their discretion, to make small loans, secured by prospective crops, to those whose condition is so impoverished and desperate as to reasonably justify the fear that, unless they receive help, they and their families will become a charge upon the counties in which they live.

We have carefully examined the authorities above cited, and many others of similar import, and while fully assenting to the principles enunciated by the cases, viz., that all taxation must be for a public purpose, we do not, with the single exception of the Kansas case, regard them as parallel cases, and applicable to the question presented in the case at bar. As we view the matter, the tax in question is for a public purpose, *i. e.,* a tax for the "necessary support of the poor."

The case of *State* v. *Osawkee, Twp., supra,* asserts a doctrine which would defeat the tax in question. This court has great respect for the court which promulgated that decision, and the most sincere admiration for the distinguished jurist, now upon the supreme bench of the nation, who wrote the opinion in that case. Nevertheless we cannot yield our assent to the reasoning of the case, leading to the conclusion that a loan of aid to an impoverished class, not yet in the poor-house, is necessarily a tax for a private purpose. In our view, it is not certain, or even probable, in the light of subsequent experience in the west, that the court of last resort in the State of Kansas would enunciate the doctrine of that case at the present day. The decision was made fifteen years ago. While the fundamental principles which underlie legislation and taxation have not changed in the interval, it is also true that the development of the Western States has been attended with difficulties and adverse conditions which have made it necessary to broaden the application of fundamental principles to meet the new necessities of those States. Under the stress of adversity peculiar to the condition of the frontier farmer, there has come to be an expansion of the legal meaning of the term "poor" sufficient to embrace a class of destitute citizens who have not yet become a public charge. The main features of the Seed-grain Statute are neither new nor novel. It was borrowed from territorial legislation, and long prior to that the State of Minnesota, in aid of agricultural settlers upon its western frontier, enacted a series of statutes which are open to every criticism which can be made upon the Statute under consideration. Dak. Laws 1889, chap. 43. See also Minn. Gen. Stat. 1878, pp. 1024–1030.

The Legislature of Minnesota has frequently, and by a variety of laws, extended aid to the frontier farmers of that State, who, far from being paupers, were yet reduced to extremities by reason of continued crop failures resulting from hailstorms, successive seasons of drought, and from the ravages of grasshoppers. Under one law towns are authorized to vote a tax to defray the expense of destroying grasshoppers; under another statute, the governor, state auditor and state treasurer were authorized to borrow $100,000 on state bonds, to be issued by them, and the proceeds were to be expended in the purchase of seed-grain for the needy farmers. Again, and at the same session, the same state officials were empowered to issue additional bonds to the same amount, to pay a debt contracted for a similar purpose, upon warrants of the state auditor. Section 6 of the Minnesota Act of 1878, chap. 98, provides as follows: "The credit of the State is hereby pledged to the payment of the interest and principal of the bonds mentioned in this Act, as the same may become due." By another section the state auditor is authorized and required to levy an annual tax necessary to meet the interest and principal of the debt created by these bonds. Many of the features of the two Seed grain Statutes passed at the first session of the Legislature of this State are borrowed from Minnesota. In principle, the legislation of the two States is identical. The aid extended is furnished in the form of a loan to individual farmers, secured on their crops, but to be met primarily by taxation. The destitute communities of farmers who were thus assisted in a neighboring State were enabled thereby to tide over their temporary necessities, and are now self-supporting.

This review of legislation in aid of destitute farmers will serve to illustrate the well-known fact that legislation under the pressure of a public sentiment, born of stern necessity, will adapt itself to new exigencies, even if in doing so a sanction is given to a broader application of elementary principles of government than have before been recognized and applied by the courts in adjudicated cases. It is the boast of the common law that it is elastic, and can be adjusted to the development of new social and business conditions. Can a statute enacted for such broadly humane and charitable purposes be annulled by another branch of the government as an abuse of legislative discretion? We think otherwise. Great deference is due from the courts to the legislative branch of the state government, and it is axiomatic that in cases of doubt the courts will never interfere to annul a statute. Cooley, Const. Lim. marg. p. 487.

It will be presumed that the Legislature, in passing the Seed-grain Statute, acted upon the fullest knowledge of the necessities of the situation, and also presumed that they have passed the Statute after due deliberation and with the clearest apprehension of the scope and purpose of the language used in section 185 of the State Constitution. That section is not only restrictive upon counties, but is also permissive. It permits counties to lend aid for "the necessary support of the poor." To our mind, the restrictive words of that section were intended to prevent the loan of aid either to individuals or corporations, for the purpose of fostering business enterprises, either of a public or private nature; but that the people who adopted the Constitution, as well as those who framed the instrument, expressly intended by the language of that section to grant a power affirmatively to the municipal corporations named in section 185, to lend their aid and make donations for the "necessary support of the poor." The attention of the court has been directed to the Constitutions of nineteen of the States, in which the language of section 185 is used *verbatim*, except only that in the States of North and South Dakota the words above quoted are interpolated. Why was this peculiar language introduced into the Constitutions of North and South Dakota, when nothing of the kind was found in that of the other seventeen States? Why did not the conventions which formed the Organic Law for North and South Dakota simply copy the language which, with this exception, is borrowed from the other Constitutions, without inserting the excepting clause under consideration? To our mind, the answer to these questions is found in the peculiar and alarming condition of the people of Dakota Territory in the year 1889, when the two Dakotas assumed the responsibilities of statehood. Such conditions had not before existed, and hence the Constitutions of other States had made no provisions to meet such necessities. When the two States formed and adopted their Constitutions the fact was well known and recognized by the people of Dakota that the condition of many farming communities was such that some comprehensive measure for their relief was an imperative necessity. In such a conjuncture the words were interpolated into section 185 of the Constitution, which permit counties to loan their aid for the "necessary support of the poor." No constitutional grant of power was necessary to give the new governments authority to provide for the support of paupers in the poor-houses. That power is inherent, and exists in all governments as among their implied powers and duties. By universal consent, taxes are valid when laid for the support of paupers, or those likely to become paupers. There was no necessity and no reason for inserting a provision in the State Constitutions of North and South Dakota authorizing counties to loan their aid to maintain the alms-houses. It would be absurd to assume that the framers of the Constitutions and the people who adopted them intended by this provision to enable local municipalities to issue and sell bonds, and loan the proceeds to the inmates of the poor houses; yet the power to loan aid in "support of the poor" is given. In our opinion, this power is conferred in the Organic Law expressly to meet the exigencies of the situation then existing, and that it is our duty to give it that effect. We believe, and so hold, that the class referred to in the exception contained in section 185 of the State Constitution is the poor and destitute farmers of the State, and that the first Legislature which met after the State was admitted has, by the Seed-grain Statute, put a proper construction upon the language in question. We therefore refuse to grant the writ applied for, and hold that the Seed-grain Statute is a valid enactment.

But our refusal to issue the writ can be placed

upon still another ground. This case furnishes the first instance of an application to this court to put forth its original jurisdiction by issuing a writ except in a single habeas corpus case. We deem it expedient, therefore, to now indicate briefly the circumstances under which this court, in the exercise of a discretion vested in it, will deem it its duty to take original cognizance of cases. Section 86 of the Constitution of the State authorizes this court to "issue writs of habeas corpus, mandamus, quo warranto, certiorari and injunction." In the exercise of its appellate and supervisory powers over inferior courts the supreme court may have occasion from time to time to issue certain of the writs above enumerated; but such writs will not issue out of this court, in the exercise of its original jurisdiction, except in a limited class of cases, and such as are not ordinarily of frequent occurrence. All of the original and remedial writs which can be issued out of this court, under the Constitution, may, under section 103 of the State Constitution, be issued, not only by the district courts, but the judges thereof. We think the intention was to devolve upon the district courts, which are readily accessible, and at all times open for public business, the duty of assuming original cognizance of all ordinary cases which are remediable by means of the writs aforesaid; and to confer upon the supreme court, in the exercise of a discretion vested in it, the duty of taking original cognizance only in the limited class of cases where the writs, except the writ of habeas corpus, are sought for on motion of the attorney-general as prerogative writs. Except in cases of habeas corpus, leave to file an information must be obtained by the attorney-general. When the information makes out a prima facie case, the writ will issue only in cases *publici juris* and those affecting the sovereignty of the State, its franchises and prerogatives, or the liberties of its people. In such cases the court will judge for itself whether the wrong complained of is one which demands the interposition of this court. The Constitution of this State, with respect to the original jurisdiction of the supreme court, is substantially the same as that of the State of Wisconsin; and the interpretation given by the supreme court of that State to that part of its State Constitution meets with the full approval of this court. See *Atty-Gen.* v. *Chicago & N. W. R. Co.* 35 Wis. 425; *Atty-Gen.* v. *Eau Claire,* 37 Wis. 400; *Wheeler* v. *Northern Colorado Irrigation Co.* 9 Colo. 248.

The case at bar affects only the local concerns of the County of Nelson and its taxpayers, and hence does not fall within the limited class of cases indicated above, and in which alone this court will assume original jurisdiction. It follows that for this reason, also, *the writ must be denied.*

All concur.

IOWA SUPREME COURT.

Fredrick J. KILLMER

v.

John J. WUCHNER *et al., Appts.*

(....Iowa....)

1. **Purchasers in good faith** of land in a portion of which their grantors have in fact only a life estate, who make valuable improvements while in possession before learning of the defect in their title, should be allowed, on a sale in partition, the value of the improvements before division of the proceeds.

2. **An allowance for improvements,** to which a purchaser in good faith is entitled, may be made in partition proceedings instead of com-

---

NOTE.—*Partition of estates; jurisdiction in equity.*

As early as the reign of Elizabeth, partition became a matter of equitable cognizance, and now the jurisdiction is established, as of right, in England and in the United States. 3 Pom. Eq. Jur. 424, 425, citing Agar v. Fairfax, 17 Ves. Jr. 533, 2 Lead. Cas. in Eq. (4th Am. ed.) 865, 880, 894; Baring v. Nash, 1 Ves. & B. 551; Parker v. Gerard, Amb. 236; Wood v. Little, 35 Me. 107; Bailey v. Sisson, 1 R. I. 233; Donnell v. Mateer, 7 Ired. Eq. 94; Holmes v. Holmes, 2 Jones, Eq. 334; Howey v. Goings, 13 Ill. 95; Sebring v. Mersereau, Hopk. Ch. 501, 2 N.Y. Ch. L. ed. 502, 9 Cow. 344; Harwood v. Kirby, 1 Paige, 469, 2 N.Y. Ch. L. ed. 718; Teal v. Woodworth, 3 Paige, 470, 3 N. Y. Ch. L. ed. 235; Wilkinson v. Parish, 3 Paige, 653, 3 N. Y. Ch. L. ed. 310; Burhans v. Burhans, 2 Barb. Ch. 398, 5 N. Y. Ch. L. ed. 690; Van Arsdale v. Drake, 2 Barb. 599; Green v. Putnam, 1 Barb. 500; Tanner v. Niles, 1 Barb. 560; Scott v. Guernsey, 60 Barb. 163, affirmed in 48 N. Y. 106; Mead v. Mitchell, 17 N. Y. 210; Clemens v. Clemens, 37 N. Y. 59; Gregory v. Gregory, 69 N. C. 522; Tabler v. Wiseman, 2 Ohio St. 207; Williams v. Van Tuyl, Id. 336; Gregory v. High, 29 Ind. 527; Milligan v. Poole, 35 Ind. 64; Larned v. Renshaw, 37 Mo. 458; Waugh v. Blumenthal, 28 Mo. 462; Reinhardt v. Wendeck, 40 Mo. 577; DeUprey v. DeUprey, 27 Cal. 329; Gates v. Salmon, 35 Cal. 576; Wotten v. Copeland, 7 Johns. Ch. 140, 2 N. Y. Ch. L. ed. 247.

In the original jurisdiction of equity, the partition was effected by means of mutual conveyances; and where the land was incapable of exact or fair division, the court had power to compensate for the inequality by awarding what was known as "owelty or partition," by being a pecuniary compensation, or a charge upon the land by way of rent, servitude or easement. 3 Pom. Eq. Jur. 426; Phelps v. Green, 3 Johns. Ch. 302, 1 N. Y. Ch. L. ed. 626; Larkin v. Mann, 2 Paige, 271, 2 N. Y. Ch. L. ed. 798; Clarendon v. Hornby, 1 P. Wms. 446; Turner v. Morgan, 8 Ves. Jr. 143; Story v. Johnson, 2 Younge & C. (Exch.) 586; Horncastle v. Charlesworth, 11 Sim. 315; Mole v. Mansfield, 15 Sim. 41; Smith v. Smith, 10 Paige, 470, 4 N. Y. Ch. L. ed. 1054; Larkin v. Mann, 2 Paige, 27, 2 N. Y. Ch. L. ed. 798; Haywood v. Judson, 4 Barb. 228; Norwood v. Norwood, 4 Harr. & J. 112; Warfield v. Warfield, 5 Harr. & J. 459; Cox v. McMullin, 14 Gratt. 82; Wynne v. Tunstall, 1 Dev. Eq. 23; Graydon v. Graydon, McMull. Eq. 63; Oliver v. Jernigan, 46 Ala. 41.

The American courts were the first to establish the right of courts of equity to do equity by decreeing a sale of the premises when they could not do equity by compelling a partition and division. Knapp, Part. 324.

The application for a sale will be granted when partition cannot be otherwise made without great inconvenience. Baldwin v. Aldrich, 34 Vt. 529.

pelling the claimant to bring an action at law under the Occupying Claimant Act.

3. A court of equity having acquired jurisdiction of the case has power to afford the proper equitable relief which is demanded.

(May 8, 1890.)

APPEAL by defendants, John J. and George G. Wuchner, from a decree of the District Court for Keokuk County allowing the cost of improvements against them in an action brought to secure the partition of certain real estate. *Affirmed.*

The facts sufficiently appear in the opinion.

Messrs. **Mackey & Stockman,** for appellants:

Remaindermen cannot be charged for improvements.

1 Washb. Real Prop. 4th ed. p. 123, and cases cited in *notes;* 4 Kent, Com. 12th ed. p. 77, and cases cited in *note B; Scott* v. *Guernsey,* 48 N. Y. 106, 124; *Ballentine* v. *Spear,* 2 Baxt. 269; *Brooks* v. *Brooks,* 12 S. C. 422; *Merritt* v. *Scott,* 81 N. C. 385; *Pass* v. *McLendon,* 62 Miss. 580; *Patterson* v. *Johnson,* 113 Ill. 559; *Hancox* v. *Meeker,* 95 N. Y. 528; *Elrod* v. *Keller,* 89 Ind. 382; *Morgan* v. *Morgan,* 23 La. Ann. 502; *Francis* v. *Sayles,* 101 Mass. 435; *Curtis* v. *Fowler,* 66 Mich. 696; *Smalley* v. *Isaacson,* 40 Minn. 450.

One deriving title through a life tenant whose interest is plainly shown by the title papers is not entitled to compensation from the remainderman for improvements.

Stewart v. *Matheny,* 66 Miss. 21.

As to the two thirds owned by appellants, neither appellee nor his grantor ever had color of title, and therefore could have no claim of title.

Hamilton v. *Wright,* 30 Iowa, 480.

Under the Occupying Claimant Law, the occupancy must be bona fide, and the improvements must be made in good faith.

Lunquest v. *Ten Eyck,* 40 Iowa, 216.

Mr. **C. G. Johnston,** for appellee:

Whenever a person has an interest in land and a partition of that interest from other interests is brought about by partition, then an opportunity is offered to do equity between the owners of these several interests and the court will see to it that equity is done between the parties.

Carver v. *Coffman,* 8 West. Rep. 396, 109 Ind. 547.

Allowance for improvements will be made on general principles.

Code, § 2298; *Thorn* v. *Thorn,* 14 Iowa, 55; *Ford* v. *Knapp,* 3 Cent. Rep. 411, 102 N. Y. 135; *Cooter* v. *Dearborn,* 2 West. Rep. 399, 115 Ill. 509.

Mr. **E. S. Sampson** for John Beinke, defendant.

Robinson, *J.,* delivered the opinion of the court.

The title of the land in question was considered and determined in *Killmer* v. *Wuchner,* 74 Iowa, 360.

This action was brought for a partition of the land. Plaintiff asks that, in determining the respective interests of the parties to this action, the improvements upon the land be considered, and that an allowance therefor be duly made. Before this action was commenced plaintiff sold, and agreed in writing to convey, the premises in controversy to John Beinke; and he is made a party defendant. The appellants ask for the partition of the real estate, but insist that their interest is not affected by the improvements. The defendant Beinke admits the contract of purchase with plaintiff, and avers that it is an entirety, and that he does not desire to take only a part of the land. He also alleges that he has placed thereon improvements to the value of $675, and asks that in case a sale is ordered the plaintiff's share of the proceeds thereof be paid into court until an adjustment is effected between himself and the plaintiff. To the answer of Beinke, appellants plead that the improvements for which he claims were made without their knowledge or consent, and with knowledge of their rights. The court below found that each appellant was

---

A sale should be ordered when it is for the best interests of all parties concerned. Johnson v. Olmsted, 49 Conn. 609; Tucker v. Parks, 70 Ga. 414; Lenfers v. Henke, 73 Ill. 405; Branscomb v. Gillian, 55 Iowa, 235; Burgess v. Eastham, 3 Bush, 476; Meyer v. Pargoud, 34 La. Ann. 909; Thurston v. Minke, 32 Md. 576; Wilson v. Duncan, 44 Miss. 642; Higginbottom v. Short, 25 Miss. 160; Fleet v. Dorland, 11 How. Pr. 490; Tucker v. Tucker, 19 Wend. 226; Trull v. Rice, 85 N. C. 327; Steedman v. Weeks, 2 Strobh. Eq. 145; Pell v. Ball, Cheves, Eq. 99; Vesper v. Farnsworth, 40 Wis. 361.

When partition cannot be had without injury to the interests of the co-tenants, a sale and division of the proceeds are as much a matter of right as was actual partition under the common-law rule. Richardson v. Monson, 23 Conn. 97; Johnson v. Olmsted, 49 Conn. 517; Hartmann v. Hartmann, 59 Ill. 103; Metcalf v. Hoopingardner, 55 Iowa, 510; Ritchie v. Munder, 49 Md. 12; Parks v. Siler, 76 N. C. 191.

Allowance for improvements.

As a general rule a person in possession of land in good faith, even though wrongfully in possession, is entitled to compensation for improvements placed by him upon the premises. Barlow v. Bell, 1 A. K. Marsh. 248.

Rights acquired by erecting permanent improvements. See *note* to Moore v. Thorp (R. I.) 7 L. R. A. 731.

Where one joint owner has put improvements on the property, he shall receive compensation for his improvements, either by having the part, on which the improvements are, assigned to him at the value of the land without the improvements, or by compensation directed to be made for them. Hall v. Piddock, 21 N. J. Eq. 314; Town v. Needham, 3 Paige, 553, 3 N. Y. Ch. L. ed. 271; St. Felix v. Rankin, 3 Edw. Ch. 323, 6 N. Y. Ch. L. ed. 675; 2 Van Santv. Eq. Pr. 41.

If improvements are made under the mistaken belief that the tenant owns the land, an allowance will be made in proceedings for partition for the amount that the land is enhanced in value. Elrod v. Keller, 89 Ind. 387.

In computation for improvements, the co-tenant against whom they are charged should not be charged with their price, but only his proportion of the amount which they add to the value of the premises, with a deduction, to which he may have a claim, for use and occupation by the co-tenant who made the improvements. Cooter v. Dearborn, 2 West. Rep. 399, 115 Ill. 509.

Co-tenants making improvements are protected in equity. See *note* to Moore v. Thorp, *supra.*

the owner of an undivided $\frac{1}{18}$ of the premises in controversy, including the improvements, subject to a life estate of Dorotha Strohman, now held by Beinke; and that Beinke was the owner of an undivided $\frac{11}{18}$ of the premises, including improvements and the life estate aforesaid. It was ordered that the premises be sold, and $\frac{11}{18}$ of the proceeds be paid to Beinke, and that the remainder be invested under the direction of the court; that the interest thereof be paid to Beinke during the life of Dorotha Strohman, and at her death that such remainder should be paid to appellants.

1. Appellants contend that the court erred in making an allowance against them for improvements made by appellee. Numerous authorities are cited which hold, in effect, that a tenant for life cannot charge the inheritance or remainder estate with the cost or value of improvements; and for the purposes of this case that may be conceded to be the general rule. The question we are required to determine is whether the facts of this case make it an exception to that rule. The land in controversy was purchased from the general government by the father of appellants, who died testate, and a nonresident of Iowa, in the year 1854. He devised to each of the appellants an undivided one third of the land in question, subject to an estate in the mother. *Killmer* v. *Wuchner*, 74 Iowa, 360. By a decree of the Keokuk Circuit Court rendered December 31, 1886, from which the appellants in this case did not appeal, that estate was determined to be a life estate in the shares of appellant, and an undivided one third in fee simple.

In the year 1862 the grantor of plaintiff obtained from the step-father of appellants, who were then minors, a deed which recited the step-father was their guardian, and which purported to convey the land. It was insufficient as a conveyance, but the evidence satisfies us that it was received in good faith, and relied upon and treated as effectual to pass the title of appellants. In the year 1864 plaintiff's grantor acquired the interest devised to the mother, and in the year 1866 he executed to plaintiff a warranty deed for the entire tract of land. Valuable improvements were made upon it, and there is no doubt that plaintiff occupied and treated the premises as his own until the year 1884, when he sold them to Beinke without any knowledge of appellants' claims. When that sale was made an investigation of the title led to a discovery of the claims of appellants. At that time one of them was about thirty-two years of age, and the other was two years younger, and neither had ever resided in Iowa. They did not know of their interest in the land, nor the improvements thereon, until about October, 1884. Beinke first learned of the defect in his title nine months after he had entered into the agreement of purchase, and, as we understand the record, after a large part, if not all, of the improvements had been made. Certainly, all of much value were made before there was any adjudication of his title. It is true, appellee could have ascertained the interests of appellants before making the improvements, but the improvements were made in good faith, and equal in value the worth of the land without them. When made, appellees were rightfully in possession of the land, and only did that which was proper to develop and make it productive. It was taken in a wild, uncultivated state, and by means of the improvements in question was fitted for residence, and made capable of yielding valuable profits. It cannot be partitioned, but must be sold, and the proceeds divided. Appellants have not been injured by the making of the improvements, and they have no just claim to any portion of their value. They will receive the same amount in value under the decree of the district court that they would have received had the improvements not been made, and with that they should be satisfied. Our conclusion is in harmony with the principles of equity, and is not without support of authorities. See *Thorn* v. *Thorn*, 14 Iowa, 55; *Carver* v. *Coffman*, 109 Ind. 547, 8 West. Rep 896; *Cooter* v. *Dearborn*, 115 Ill. 509, 2 West. Rep. 399; *Ford* v. *Knapp*, 102 N. Y. 135, 3 Cent. Rep. 411; 2 Greenl. Ev. § 549, *note 1;* Freem. Co-tenancy, § 509.

2. Other questions are discussed, but evidently not relied upon, by counsel for appellants. It is suggested that the relief demanded by plaintiffs, and given to them by the district court, should have been sought in an action at law, under the Occupying Claimant Act. But a court of equity, having acquired jurisdiction of the case, has power to afford all proper equitable relief which is demanded. *Green Bay Lumber Co.* v. *Ireland*, 77 Iowa, 636.

It is said that the questions involved in this case could have been adjudicated in the case of *Killmer* v. *Wuchner*, 74 Iowa, 359. That was an action to quiet title, and the relief demanded in this case was not made an issue in that.

Appellants ask a partition in this case, and for general equitable relief, and cannot be heard to complain because their prayer is granted. We are of the opinion that the finding of the district court as to the shares of appellants is sustained by the evidence, and is fair to them.

The decree of the District Court is affirmed.

SOUTH CAROLINA SUPREME COURT.

William L. MAULDIN *et al.*, *Appts.*,
v.
City Council of GREENVILLE.

(....S. C.....)

1. Taxpayers may maintain a suit for an injunction, in behalf of themselves and other taxpayers, to prevent illegal acts of municipal authorities which will increase the burden of taxation.

2. An amended city charter providing that the city may borrow money by issuing bonds "not to exceed the sum of $100,000," omitting the words of the former charter "but never in any form to make the city liable for exceeding that amount in the aggregate," gives authority to issue bonds subsequent to the date of the charter to the extent of $100,000, although a bonded indebtedness already existed.

3. A city may own an electric-light

plant and manufacture electricity for lighting the streets, where it is expressly given power to own property, and also has an implied right to light its streets.

4. The purchase of an electric-light plant is beyond the implied authority of a city so far as it is intended to furnish lights for the residences and places of business of private individuals, either with or without compensation.

(April 21, 1890.)

APPEAL by plaintiffs from a judgment of the Common Pleas Circuit Court dismissing the complaint in an action brought to enjoin defendant from purchasing and operating an electric-light plant. *Reversed.*

The case is fully stated in the opinion.

Messrs. **Wells & Orr,** for appellants:

Corporations can exercise only such powers as are expressly conferred upon them, or which arise by necessary implication.

Dillon, Mun. Corp. 3d ed. § 89; *Ottawa* v. *Carey,* 108 U. S. 110, 121 (27 L. ed. 669, 674); *Stetson* v. *Kempton,* 13 Mass. 272; *New York Firemen Ins. Co.* v. *Ely,* 5 Conn. 560; *Zottman* v. *San Francisco,* 20 Cal. 96; *Clark* v. *Des Moines,* 19 Iowa, 199; Cooley, Const. Lim. 233, 235, 236, and *notes; Blake* v. *Walker,* 23 S. C. 522.

No express power being given in the charter to light streets, it cannot be exercised under the police power or general welfare clause.

Dillon, Mun. Corp. §§ 181, 393–407; *East St. Louis* v. *East St. Louis, G. L. & C. Co.* 98 Ill. 415.

Cities and towns are under no obligation to light the streets at night.

Randall v. *Eastern R. Co.* 106 Mass. 276.

Mr. **M. F. Ansel,** also for appellants:

Property holders or taxable inhabitants may resort to equity to restrain municipal corporations and their officers from transcending their lawful powers or violating their legal duties, in any mode which will injuriously affect the taxpayers.

Dillon, Mun. Corp. 3d ed. §§ 914, and *note,* 915, 916, *note,* 917, 918, *note; Crampton* v. *Zabriskie,* 101 U. S. 601 (25 L. ed. 1070); *New London* v. *Brainard,* 22 Conn. 552; *Baltimore* v. *Gill,* 31 Md. 375; *Colton* v. *Hanchett,* 13 Ill. 615; *Place* v. *Providence,* 12 R. I. 1; *Wade* v. *Richmond,* 18 Gratt. 583; *Harney* v. *Indianapolis, C. & D. R. Co.* 32 Ind. 244.

Owners of taxable property can maintain a suit to annul illegal acts of municipal officers when such acts will increase the municipal taxes, and the State is not a necessary party.

Newmeyer v. *Missouri & M. R. Co.* 52 Mo. 81, 14 Am. Rep. 394; *Frewin* v. *Lewis,* 4 Myl. & Cr. 253; Dillon, Mun. Corp. §§ 921, 922.

Suits have been brought that way in South Carolina.

Gage v. *Charleston,* 3 S. C. 491; *Trimmier* v. *Bomar,* 20 S. C. 354.

Messrs. **T. Q. & A. H. Donaldson,** also for appellants:

The City Council of Greenville had no authority, under the terms of their charter, to purchase and operate the electric-light plant for inside lighting of private residences and places of business.

Dillon, Mun. Corp. 3d ed. § 89; Cooley, Const. Lim. 235; Willcock, Mun. Corp. 769; *Clark* v. *Des Moines,* 19 Iowa, 199, 87 Am. Dec. 423; *New York Firemen Ins. Co.* v. *Ely,* 5 Conn. 560, 13 Am. Dec. 100; *Stetson* v. *Kempton,* 13 Mass. 272, 7 Am. Dec. 145; *Com.* v. *Erie & N. E. R. Co.* 27 Pa. 339, 67 Am. Dec. 471.

The doctrine of *ultra vires* is applied with greater strictness to public than to private corporations.

Newbery v. *Fox,* 37 Minn. 141, 5 Am. St. Rep. 830; Dillon, Mun. Corp. § 457.

If an appropriation of money be made for two objects,—one lawful and the other not,—and it cannot be distinguished and separated, then the whole will be held void; otherwise the court will enjoin or relieve against the expenditure which is unlawful.

Roberts v. *New York,* 5 Abb. Pr. 41. See also *Howes* v. *Racine,* 21 Wis. 515; *Stetson* v. *Kempton,* 13 Mass. 272, 7 Am. Dec. 145.

Messrs. **Perry & Heyward,** with *Mr.* **W. A. Williams,** for respondent:

The complaint does not state facts sufficient to constitute a cause of action in behalf of the plaintiffs, and they cannot amend as proposed.

Doolittle v. *Broome County,* 18 N. Y. 155; *Roosevelt* v. *Draper,* 23 N. Y. 328 *et seq.; Georgetown* v. *Alexandria Canal Co.* 37 U. S. 12 Pet. 91 (9 L. ed. 1012); Pom. Eq. Jur. § 1349, and cases cited; *Corning* v. *Lowerre,* 6 Johns. Ch. 439, 2 N. Y. Ch. L. ed. 178; *Bigelow* v. *Hartford Bridge Co.* 14 Conn. 565; *Seley* v. *Bishop,* 19 Conn. 128; *Smith* v. *Boston,* 7 Cush. 254; *Anon.* 3 Atk. 750; *Atty-Gen.* v. *Foundling Hospital,* 4 Bro. Ch. 165; *O'Brien* v. *Norwich & W. R. Co.* 17 Conn. 372; 2 Dillon, Mun. Corp. 3d ed. §§ 912, 914, 920, and cases cited, 921, 922; *Atty-Gen.* v. *Jolly,* 1 Rich. Eq. 99; *State* v. *Mt. Pleasant,* 3 Rich. L. 214; *Atty-Gen.* v. *Clergy Society,* 8 Rich. Eq. 190; *State* v. *Charleston,* 11 Rich. Eq. 432; *State* v. *Columbia,* 12 S. C. 370; *Atty-Gen.* v. *Dublin,* 1 Bligh, N. R. 312; *Atty-Gen.* v. *Eastlake,* 11 Hare, 205; *Atty-Gen.* v. *Boston,* 123 Mass. 460; *Atty-Gen.* v. *Compton,* 1 Younge & C. Ch. 417; *Atty-Gen.* v. *Lea,* 3 Ired. Eq. 302; *Atty-Gen.* v. *Perkins,* 2 Dev. Eq. 38; *Allen* v. *Monmouth County,* 13 N. J. Eq. 68; *Hinchman* v. *Paterson H. R. Co.* 17 N. J. Eq. 75; *Mechling* v. *Kittaning Bridge Co.* 1 Grant, Cas. 416; *Beveridge* v. *Lacey,* 3 Rand. 63; *Walker* v. *Shepardson,* 2 Wis. 384; *Barnes* v. *Racine,* 4 Wis. 454; *Williams* v. *Smith,* 22 Wis. 594; *Ewell* v. *Greenwood,* 26 Iowa, 377; *Morris & E. R. Co.* v. *Prudden,* 20 N. J. Eq. 530; 1 High, Inj. § 762; *Coast Line R. Co.* v. *Cohen,* 50 Ga. 451; *Carey* v. *Brooks,* 1 Hill, L. 365; *McLauchlin* v. *Charlotte & S. C. R. Co.* 5 Rich. L. 583; *South Carolina Steamboat Co.* v. *South Carolina R. Co.* 30 S. C. 539; *State* v. *Chester & L. N. G. R. Co.* 13 S. C. 298; *Kennerty* v. *Etiwan Phosphate Co.* 17 S. C. 411.

The present charter of the City furnishes ample authority for the purchase of the plant and the issuing of the bonds to pay for the same.

Act 1885, §§ 12, 31 (19 Stat. at L. pp. 109, 115); 17 Stat. at L. p. 526, § 2; Dillon, Mun. Corp. 3d ed. §§ 89, 98; 10 Charter of Greenville City, § 32, as amended by Act 1879; Acts 1887, p. 1028; *Amey* v. *Allegheny City,* 65 U. S. 24 How. 364 (16 L. ed. 614); *New Orleans* v. *Clark,* 95 U. S. 644 (24 L. ed. 521); *Read* v.

Plattsmouth, 107 U. S. 568 (27 L. ed. 414); *Hitchcock* v. *Galveston*, 96 U. S. 841 (24 L. ed. 659).

McGowan, *J.*, delivered the opinion of the court:

The plaintiffs, as citizens and taxpayers of the City of Greenville, instituted this proceeding to restrain the City Council from purchasing and operating an electric-light plant to light the streets and public buildings of the City, and from using the same for lighting private residences; and also to enjoin the Council from issuing bonds of the corporation in payment therefor, upon the grounds substantially stated by the circuit judge, as follows: *First.* Because the city charter confers no authority on the Council to purchase this machinery for the purpose of lighting the streets and public buildings. *Second.* Because the power of the City Council to borrow money for the public use of the corporation has already been exhausted, and that to issue bonds to pay for this plant would be *ultra vires.* *Third.* Because 75 cents on the $100 of the assessed value of real and personal property of the corporation is the limit of taxation fixed by the charter, and this enterprise will necessarily force the Council to exceed that limit, and thus increase the burden of the plaintiffs and all the taxpayers. *Fourth.* Because the purchase includes a costly engine and dynamos for producing incandescent lights for the interior of private residences and places of business, and there is no authority conferred on the Council by the charter to purchase and operate an electric plant for this purpose. Such, briefly and substantially, are the grounds on which the plaintiffs ask relief by injunction.

The City Council, the defendant, answered fully to the merits, admitting paragraphs 1 and 2 of the complaint, but denying each and every other allegation contained in it, not specially denied, admitted or explained, making no objection, however, by plea or demurrer, as to the manner in which the action was brought, in the name alone of the plaintiffs as corporators and taxpayers. The plaintiffs offered in evidence the charter of the City; that an effort had been made to obtain additional powers, which failed; the contracts the City Council had made in reference to the electric plant; the value of the taxable property of the City, its bonded indebtedness, etc.; that the incandescent lights were suitable for lighting the interior of private residences and places of business, but not for lighting the public streets, etc. The City Council, the defendant, offered no testimony, but moved orally at the trial to dismiss the complaint, on the ground that it did not state facts sufficient to constitute a cause of action, which motion was considered in connection with the argument on the merits. The circuit judge, remarking, among other things, that he was not willing to depart from what he considered the practice and doctrine of our own courts—if the complaint states good ground for equitable relief, and the injury complained of is peculiar to none, but common to all, the citizens, then the action must be in the name of the State, *ex relatione* the taxpayers, or in the name of the attorney-general. The individual taxpayer, as such merely, can obtain a standing in court only by alleging and proving that the illegal act complained of will inflict damage special and peculiar to himself, etc.—held that the complaint should be dismissed, for the reason that it did not state facts sufficient to constitute a cause of action. But nevertheless the judge proceeded to consider the case on its merits, and dismissed the complaint, also, on the ground that there was no right or equity in it.

From this decree the plaintiffs appeal to this court, upon the following grounds: "(1) Because his honor erred in holding that the complaint did not state facts sufficient to constitute a cause of action. (2) Because, if said complaint was demurrable at all, it was upon the ground that the plaintiffs had not legal capacity to sue, and the objection, not being taken by demurrer on that ground, was waived. (3) Because, in any event, the plaintiffs should have been allowed to amend by making the State a party on the relation of the attorney-general. (4) Because his honor erred in holding that the City Council of Greenville have authority, under the police powers conferred upon them by section 12 of their charter, to purchase an electric-light plant for the purpose of lighting the streets and public buildings of the City. (5) Because his honor erred in holding that said City Council, under the provisions of section 31 of their charter, have authority to issue bonds to the amount of $100,000, exclusive of the $88,000 of bonds heretofore issued in aid of railroads and graded schools. (6) Because the charter of said City having limited the amount of the annual tax to be levied on the real and personal property of the citizens to 75 cents on the $100, and it appearing, by uncontradicted evidence, that the income of the City is just about sufficient to meet the present expenses, his honor should have held that said Council were without authority to levy an additional tax to meet the interest on any additional bonds, and that, therefore, they had no right to issue them. (7) Because it is respectfully submitted that his honor erred in holding that the said City Council have the right to furnish lights to individuals and others for private purposes, thus using the people's money in speculation and trade. (8) Because it is manifest, from the proof, that one of the chief purposes of the defendant in purchasing the incandescent system of the electric-light plant was not simply to light up the public buildings, but to furnish incandescent lights to private residences and places of business for compensation, for which there is no authority in the charter, and to that extent, at least, it is submitted, their contract with the Brush Electric Light Company was clearly *ultra vires*, and not binding on the City, and that his honor erred in not so holding. (9) Because, if the defendant is permitted to carry out its illegal contract, it will inevitably result in a large increase of the debt of the City, and a proportionate increase in the amount of taxes to be paid by the plaintiffs, and this fact, it is submitted, furnishes sufficient grounds for the relief sought by the plaintiffs, and his honor erred in not so holding," etc.

Exceptions 1, 2 and 3 make the point that it was error in the circuit judge to dismiss the complaint, upon verbal motion at the trial, on the ground that it did not state facts sufficient to constitute a cause of action, in that the plaintiffs had not legal capacity to sue in their own name, without inserting as plaintiff the State *ex relatione* the complaining taxpayers. It will not be necessary to consider whether, as a matter of pleading, the defendant waived the objection, by answering to the merits, without making the objection either by answer or demurrer. In the view the court takes, the objection was purely formal, relating merely to the title of the case; for the plaintiffs might have brought their action according to the formula indicated. The State, in such case, never refuses the use of its name, which might have been added *pro forma*, by order of the court, at any stage of the proceeding. It is always desirable, when it can be done without a breach of principle or injury to others, that the controversies between parties should be decided on their merits alone.

In considering whether the plaintiffs, as taxpayers of the City of Greenville, had the right to bring this action in their own name for the benefit of themselves and other corporators, without alleging special damage to themselves, it will be proper to keep clearly in view the nature, scope and object of the action. It must not be overlooked that it is a proceeding in equity, by a number of taxpayers of an incorporated city, to prevent certain acts, by the municipal authorities, alleged to be beyond their authority under the charter, to the injury of plaintiffs and all other taxpayers of the corporation, somewhat in the nature of a bill *quia timet*. Can it be that, in such a case, a number of citizens, taxpayers of a city, cannot be heard against the corporate authorities in a court of equity asking for an injunction against the consummation of the contemplated wrongs, without alleging special damages to themselves individually? There is a certain relation in the nature of agency between the municipal authorities and all taxpayers of the corporation. It does not strike us that the doctrines as to nuisances and public wrongs of that character have any proper application to the case.

We cannot agree that there is any analogy between this case and those of the class of *South Carolina Steamboat Co.* v. *South Carolina R. Co.*, 30 S. C. 539. That was an action at law for damages, on account of the obstruction of a navigable river, which was a public nuisance to all the world. The parties were in all respects strangers to each other. Here the taxpaying citizens of Greenville are not the whole public, but comparatively a small part of it. They are not strangers to the municipality. They, and they alone, are affected by their acts. As to them this is more in the nature of "a private" than "public" matter.

We think the distinction was well stated in the case of *Baltimore* v. *Gill*, 31 Md. 375–394. That was a proceeding to restrain by injunction the mayor and council of Baltimore from carrying out the provisions of an ordinance authorizing the borrowing of money to build certain railroads. The plaintiffs were taxpayers on real and personal property situated in Baltimore, and they sued in behalf of themselves and others similarly situated. It was maintained (as here) that the plaintiffs had no standing in court, and were not entitled to ask the interposition of a court of equity to restrain by injunction the execution of the ordinance. It was further maintained (as here) that the wrong complained of was of "a public nature" affecting the whole public, in which the attorney general, as the representative of the State, was a necessary party. It was held that the interests of the plaintiffs, as taxpayers, were sufficient to entitle them to maintain the action, and that the attorney-general was not a necessary party. Bartol, *Ch. J.*, in delivering the opinion of the court, said: The case is to be distinguished from cases of public wrongs, in which the general public are alike concerned; that the plaintiffs "as taxpayers of the city, and others similarly situated, . . . constitute a class especially damaged by the alleged unlawful act of the corporation, in the alleged increase of the burden of taxation upon their property situated within the city. The complainants have therefore a special interest in the subject matter of the suit, distinct from that of the general public,"—citing the cases of *New London* v. *Brainard*, 22 Conn. 552; *Webster* v. *Harwinton*, 32 Conn. 131; *Merrill* v. *Plainfield*, 45 N. H. 126; *McMillan* v. *Lee County*, 3 Iowa, 311, etc.

In the case of *Newmeyer* v. *Missouri & M. R. Co.*, 52 Mo. 81, *Mr. Justice* Ewing thus vindicates the ruling: "I have examined the cases cited in support of the other side of the question, or such of them as we have had access to, and, upon a careful consideration of the subject, I am of opinion that the decisions, which affirm the right of plaintiffs (or those standing in the same relation to such controversies) to maintain the action rest upon a more solid foundation of principle and reason than those holding the contrary doctrine; and they are commended to our approval as furnishing the only adequate remedy to the injured party for wrongs resulting from unauthorized or illegal acts like those complained of. The injury charged as the result of the acts complained of is a private injury, in which the taxpayers of the County of Macon are the individual sufferers, rather than the public. The people out of the county bear no part of the burden; nor do the people within the county, except the taxpayers, bear any part of it. It is therefore an injury peculiar to one class of persons, namely, the taxpayers of the County of Macon," etc.

It is true, as indicated above, that all the authorities on the subject are not in perfect accord. But, without incumbering this opinion with the numerous authorities, we think it will be sufficient to say that *Judge* Dillon (certainly our greatest authority on municipal corporations), after a careful analysis and examination of the decisions, states, "as resting upon reason and the preponderance of judicial authority," the following propositions: "(2) That, in the absence of special controlling legislative provision, the proper public officer of the Commonwealth, which created the corporation and prescribed and limited its powers, may, in his own name, or in the name of the State, on behalf of residents and voters of the municipality, exercise the authority, in proper cases, of filing an information or bill in equity, to prevent the misuse of corporate powers, or to set aside or correct illegal corporate acts. (3) That the existence of such a power in the State or its proper public law officer is not inconsistent with the right of any taxable inhabitant to bring a bill to prevent the corporate authorities from transcending their lawful powers, where the effect will be to impose upon him an unlawful tax, or to increase his burden of taxation," etc. See 2 Dillon, Mun. Corp. 3d ed. § 922, and the authorities in *note*.

We know of no Act of the Legislature or decided case which declares the law of this State to be as contended for. All that is claimed is that it has been "the practice" of the State until it has ripened into law. It does seem to have been the early practice, but we have not been referred to a case in which an action like this was dismissed, for the reason that it was not brought according to the indicated formula. Certainly, since the Code was adopted, in 1870, the practice has not been uniform and unbroken.

Gage v. *Charleston*, 3 S. C. 491 (1872), was an action for injunction to restrain the city council of Charleston from subscribing to certain railroad companies, brought by "Alva Gage and seven other named persons, 'inhabitants and property holders of the City of Charleston, for themselves and others, inhabitants and property holders of said city.'"

Glenn v. *York County*, 6 S. C. 412 (1873), was an action to restrain the county commissioners from issuing bonds in aid of the construction of a railroad, brought by "E. L. Glenn and others, . . . taxpayers on real and personal property in New York County."

Trimmier v. *Bomar*, 20 S. C. 354 (1883), was an action to restrain the county commissioners of Spartanburg from issuing bonds in aid of a railroad, "brought by Trimmier, Yorborough, Pool, Tillison and Walker," etc. As it seems that the law on the point of the practice "has not been absolutely settled in this State," we have no doubt that the plaintiffs might have given their proceeding the form required by the ruling below; but were they bound to do so on pain of having it dismissed? Was the action brought absolutely inconsistent with the right of the State? We know of no principle or such unbroken "practice" in the State as requires the court to hold that the proceeding was unauthorized. We think the plaintiffs had a standing in court, and were entitled to have their case heard on its merits.

The charter of the City of Greenville, as amended in 1885 (19 Stat. at L. 106), contains the following provisions for the government of the City. Section 12 provides that the Council "may purchase, hold, possess and enjoy to them, and their successors, in perpetuity or for any term of years, any estate, real, personal or mixed, and sell, lease, alien and convey the same: provided, that the same shall not at any time exceed the sum of ($100,000) one hundred thousand dollars; and the said City Council shall have full power and authority to make and establish all such rules, by-laws and ordinances, respecting the roads, streets, market and police department of said City, and the government thereof, as shall appear to them necessary and requisite for the security, welfare and convenience of said City, for preserving health, life and property therein, and securing the peace and good government of the same," etc. Section 19 gives the City Council the right to levy annually a tax on the assessed property of the City "sufficient to discharge and defray all expenses of carrying into effect the ordinances, rules, regulations and laws made and established as above provided: provided, said tax does not exceed 75 cents upon every $100 of real and personal property as assessed and equalized;" and section 31 provides "that the said City Council shall have power to borrow money for the public use of the corporation, by issuing from time to time, as occasion may require, the bonds of said corporation, bearing interest, . . . for an amount not to exceed the sum of one hundred thousand dollars ($100,000), and for the payment of the interest," etc.

In order to prevent confusion, we will first dispose of the preliminary question as to the ordinary expenses of the city government of Greenville, and the prohibition claimed to exist in the charter, against increasing the bonded debt of the City beyond $100,000. It is urged that the debt already amounts to $88,000 (principally for subscriptions to railroads and public schools), and, with the $21,000 now proposed to be added, it will be extended beyond the limit. Upon casually reading the provision, the first impression may be that it was intended to limit the whole bonded debt, for any and all purposes, to $100,000. Indeed, unless such was the purpose, it would hardly seem necessary to fix a limit at all. But upon close examination we cannot say that such is the proper construction. The words are (in 1885), "to borrow money for the public use of the corporation by issuing . . . bonds . . . for an amount not to exceed the sum of $100,000," omitting the words of the old charter (1880), "but never in any form to make the City liable for exceeding that amount in the aggregate."

We agree that the framers of the provision intended to give the authority to issue bonds subsequent to the date of the charter, "for the public use of the corporation," to the extent of $100,000. See *Hitchcock* v. *Galveston*, 96 U. S. 349 [24 L. ed. 661].

Then the question is whether, under the aforesaid provisions of the charter, the City Council had the power to purchase, own and operate, at the expense of the City, an electric-light plant for the double purpose of lighting the streets of the City and providing incandescent lights to individuals for the interior of private residences and business offices and purposes.

Judge Dillon, in his Municipal Corporations, 3d ed. § 89, states as follows: "It is a general and undisputed proposition of law that a municipal corporation possesses and can exercise the following powers, and no others: *first*, those granted in express words; *second*, those necessarily or fairly implied in or incident to the powers expressly granted; *third*, those essential to the declared objects and purposes of the corporation,—not simply convenient, but indispensable. Any fair, reasonable doubt concerning the existence of power is resolved by the courts against the corporation, and the power is denied. Of every municipal corporation, the charter or statute by which it is created is its Organic Act. Neither the corporation nor its officers can do any act, or make any contract, or incur any liability, not authorized thereby. All acts beyond the scope of the powers granted are void," etc.

Now, tested by this principle so clearly stated, how does the matter stand? Clearly, the charter does not give the power to purchase this plant in express words. It does not so give even the power to light the City, but we assume that this latter power may be fairly implied from the grant of the police power. The City Council had previously lighted the City with gas, and we suppose that it might do so with electricity as well. The lighting, however, with gas, was done by contract, and the new feature complained of is that the Council now propose to purchase, own and operate the engines, dynamos and machinery which produce the electricity, and to pay for them by issuing municipal bonds. This seems to be a new question. It strikes us as remarkable that, in the multitude of cases cited by the distinguished counsel who argued the case, there should not be in one of them the least reference to this precise point. We have made diligent search, and have not been able to find one. We must decide it, but without any help from authorities. The City has the express power to own property, and it also has the implied right to light the City. Do these powers necessarily imply the right to make the City the owner of the plant and a manufacturer of electricity? It is quite certain that such power is not "essential" to the declared objects and purposes of the corporation, for heretofore the City has been lighted by contract, without owning the gas fixtures. The purchase of the electric plant was certainly a new departure, and it is to be hoped that it may not prove to be troublesome and expensive to the City. But considering that some discretion, as to the mode and manner, should be allowed the municipality, in carrying out the conceded power to light the streets of the City, we hold that the purchase of the plant was not *ultra vires* and void, so far as it was designed to produce electricity suitable for and used in lighting the streets and public buildings of the City. But we cannot so hold as to the purchase of so much of that plant as furnished the incandescent light for use in the interior of private residences and places of business, which cannot be properly included within the power to light the streets of the City. The uncontradicted testimony was that the incandescent light is not suitable for lighting the public streets. We are therefore unable to agree with the circuit judge when he said that "if the City, from the same plant, can provide incandescent lights to private residences and places of business for compensation, and thus make the system, in part, at least, self-sustaining, economy and good business management should sustain the transaction," etc. As we understand it, all the powers given to the City Council were for the sole and exclusive purpose of government, and not to enter into private business of any kind, outside of the scope of the city government. In that very direction, especially in these latter times, is the dangerous and growing tendency of municipal corporations. It is very important, for the interest of all, to keep them strictly within the legitimate limits of their powers. The power given to the City Council to issue bonds, so as to bind not only all the taxpayers of the City, but their children as well, is a very high confidence and trust, and can be properly exercised for no other purpose than "for the public use of the corporation," no matter how great the temptation may be. Without regard to good "business arrangements," which may present themselves, such a power must be strictly pursued. We cannot suppose that it was intended to give the City Council, as such, the right to go into commerce, to buy for the purpose of selling goods, or to enter into any private business or speculation whatever. As, for instance, if the City Council, owning horses, in the discharge of their police duties should find it necessary to establish a blacksmith shop, we do not think they would be within their corporate duties to open it for the accommodation of the public, with or without compensation.

In the case of *Ottawa* v. *Carey*, 108 U. S. 110 [28 L. ed. 669], the following propositions were announced: (1) "To the extent of their authority, they [municipal corporations] can bind the people and the property subject to their regulation and governmental control, by what they do, but beyond their corporate powers their acts are of no effect." (2) "Power to govern the city does not imply power to expend the public money to make the water in the rivers available for manufacturing purposes." *Chief Justice* Waite, in delivering the judgment of the court, said: "The charter confers all the powers usually granted to a city for the purposes of local government, but that has never been supposed, of itself, to authorize taxes for everything which, in the opinion of the city authorities, would 'promote the general prosperity and welfare of the municipality.' Undoubtedly the development of the water-power in the rivers that traverse the city would add to the commerce and wealth of the citizens, but certainly power to govern the city does not imply power to expend the public money to make the water in the rivers available for manufacturing purposes," etc.

We cannot doubt that the purchase of the system producing incandescent lights, so far as it was to furnish lights to private persons, with or without compensation, was not a corporate act of the City Council, and binding upon the corporators, but was beyond their authority, as the governing body of the corporation.

The judgment of this court is that the judgment of the Circuit Court be reversed, and the cause remanded to the circuit for such further proceedings as may be deemed necessary to carry into effect the conclusion herein announced.

Simpson, *Ch. J.*, and **McIver,** *J.*, concur.

NORTH CAROLINA SUPREME COURT.

STATE OF NORTH CAROLINA
v.
DOWELL, *Appt.*

(....N. C.....)

1. **A husband may be guilty of an assault** with intent to commit rape upon his wife, where by threats of death he compels another man to attempt to ravish her.

2. **There is a sufficient criminal intent** to sustain a conviction of one who compels another through fear of death to make an actual attempt to commit a crime, although the latter acts solely under compulsion.

(*Merrimon, Ch. J., dissents.*)

(May 5, 1890.)

APPEAL by defendant from a judgment of the Superior Court for Rowan County convicting him of an assault with intent to commit rape. *Affirmed.*

The case sufficiently appears in the opinion.

No appearance for appellant.

Mr. **Theodore F. Davidson,** *Atty-Gen.*, for the State.

Shepherd, *J.*, delivered the opinion of the court:

Ordinarily, precedent is grateful to the judicial mind, as something approved and steadfast, on which it may rest with confidence; but sometimes cases arise of such exceptional enormity that, for the fair name of humanity, the judge would hope to find no counterpart in criminal annals. We incline to believe that the case under consideration is one of such bad eminence. Unmatched in iniquity, as it appears to be, it is hoped, however, that the application of a few elementary principles will harmonize the conclusion to which we have arrived, not only with our moral conceptions of what should be the law, but also with its strict, formal administration.

The facts are abhorrently simple. The white husband of a white wife, under menace of death to both parties in case of refusal, and supporting his threat by a loaded gun held over the parties, constrains a colored man to undertake, and his wife to submit to, an attempted sexual connection. The details of this shocking transaction are so disgusting that we will not stain the pages of our reports with their particular recital. Suffice it to say that, under the coercion of the defendant, Lowery, the

---

NOTE.—*Rape defined.*

Rape is the unlawful carnal knowledge of a female by force and without her consent. 4 Bl. Com. 210; 2 Archb. Cr. Pl. 159; 1 Russ. Cr. 9th ed. 904, 912.

It is the ravishing of a woman against her will and without her consent. Reg. v. Fletcher, Bell, Cr. Cas. 71; Hawk. chap. 41, § 2; 1 East, P. C. chap. 4, § 34.

Rape includes an assault to commit rape. Richardson v. State, 54 Ala. 158; Mills v. State, 52 Ind. 187; Com. v. Drum, 19 Pick. 479; Com. v. Bakeman, 105 Mass. 53; Morey v. Com. 108 Mass. 433; State v. Atherton, 50 Iowa, 189; State v. Cross, 12 Iowa, 66; Com. v. Dean, 109 Mass. 349; Reg. v. Neale, 1 Denison, Cr. Cas. 36; People v. Saunders, 4 Park. Cr. Cas. 196.

Rape is an assault on a woman with intent to commit an act of sexual intercourse by force and violence and against her will. People v. Brown, 47 Cal. 447.

Sexual commerce or intercourse and carnal knowledge are synonymous terms. Com. v. Squires, 97 Mass. 59.

Force and resistance.

While force, actual or constructive, is a necessary ingredient in the crime committed on a female over ten years of age (Lewis v. State, 30 Ala. 54; McNair v. State, 53 Ala. 453; People v. Royal, 53 Cal. 62; Bradley v. State, 32 Ark. 704; Cato v. State, 9 Fla. 163; People v. Bartow, 1 Wheeler, Cr. Cas. 378; Walter v. People, 50 Barb. 144; Reg. v. Fletcher, L. R. 1 Cr. Cas. Res. 39; 1 Whart. Cr. L. 8th ed. § 550; McMath v. State, 55 Ga. 303; Stephen v. State, 11 Ga. 226; Carter v. State, 35 Ga. 263); yet no particular amount of force is necessary; nor that the force should create a reasonable apprehension of death, if she had reason to consider resistance dangerous or even absolutely useless. Waller v. State, 40 Ala. 325; Pollard v. State, 2 Iowa, 567; Turner v. People, 33 Mich. 363; Wright v. State, 4 Humph. 194.

Consent extorted by terror or induced by the influence of a person in whose power she feels herself, is not a defense. Pleasant v. State, 13 Ark. 360; Reg. v. Woodhurst, 12 Cox, Cr. Cas. 443; Reg. v. Hallett, 9 Car. & P. 748; Reg. v. Day, 9 Car. & P. 722.

Aiders and abettors guilty as principals.

To be an aider and abettor it is immaterial that the party is disqualified from being the principal actor by reason of age, sex, condition or class. Boggus v. State, 34 Ga. 275; State v. Sprague, 4 R. I. 257; Lord Audley's Case, 3 How. St. Tr. 401; Rex v. Gray, 7 Car. & P. 164; Reg. v. Crisham, 1 Car. & M. 187.

Even a woman may be punishable for aiding and abetting the perpetrator of the crime. Boggus v. State, *supra;* 1 Russ. Cr. 9th ed. 904.

All persons present aiding or abetting the offense, or encouraging its commission, are principals. Strang v. People, 24 Mich. 1. See United States v. Gooding, 25 U. S. 12 Wheat. 460 (6 L. ed. 693); People v. Woodward, 45 Cal. 293; King v. State, 21 Ga. 221; Hawkins v. State, 13 Ga. 322; Boyd v. State, 17 Ga. 194; Smith v. People, 74 Ill. 144; Williams v. State, 47 Ind. 568; Goff v. Prime, 26 Ind. 196; State v. Shelledy, 8 Iowa, 477; Ward v. Com. 14 Bush. 233; Kessler v. Com. 12 Bush, 18; Com. v. Campbell, 7 Allen, 541; Shannon v. People, 5 Mich. 74; State v. Ricker, 29 Me. 84; State v. Davis, 23 Me. 403; State v. Phillips, 24 Mo. 475; United States v. Wilson, Baldw. 101; United States v. Kelly, 2 Sprague, 83; State v. Comstock, 46 Iowa, 265.

Although a husband cannot individually commit rape upon his wife (Lord Audley's Case, 3 How. St. Tr. 401; 1 Hale, P. C. 629), yet he may be liable as principal for aiding and abetting another in the commission of the crime, the offense being a felony. *Ibid.;* Hemanus v. State, 7 Tex. App. 372; Strang v. People and People v. Woodward, *supra;* Com. v. Murphy, 2 Allen, 163; Com. v. Fogerty, 8 Gray, 489; Lord Audley's Case, *supra;* Rex v. Warden of the Fleet, 12 Mod. 340.

colored man, did actually make the attempt. Indeed, he did everything necessary to constitute the crime of rape except actual penetration. Fortunately the fright and excitement rendered him incapable of consummating the outrage, which, as we understand the case, he would otherwise have perpetrated; and, alike fortunately, at, perhaps, the critical moment, the gun discharging itself in the hands of the unnatural husband, the enforced assailant was enabled to effect his escape.

Under the laws of this State, the offense of an assault with intent to commit rape, although subject to very severe punishment, is technically a misdemeanor; and, there being no degrees in this class of crimes, it must follow that, if the defendant is guilty at all, he must be guilty as a principal. The defendant strangely insists that he is not guilty because he is the husband of the prosecutrix; and he relies as a defense upon the marital relation, the duties and obligations of which he has, by all the laws of God and man, so brutally violated. In our opinion, in respect to this offense, he stands upon the same footing as a stranger, and his guilt is to be determined in that light alone. The person of everyone is, as a rule, jealously guarded by the law from any involuntary contact, however slight, on the part of another. The exceptions, as in the case of a parent, or one *in loco parentis*, moderately chastising a child (*State* v. *Harris*, 63 N. C. 1), or a schoolmaster, a pupil (*State* v. *Pendergrass*, 2 Dev. & B. L. 365, and *Boyd* v. *State*, 88 Ala. 169), are strict and rare.

It was at one time held in our State that the relation of husband and wife gave the former immunity to the extent that the courts would not go behind the domestic curtain, and scrutinize too nicely every family disturbance, even though amounting to an assault. *State* v. *Rhodes*, Phil. L. 453. But since *State* v. *Oliver*, 70 N. C. 60, and subsequent cases, we have refused "the blanket of the dark" to these outrages on female weakness and defenselessness. So it is now settled that, technically, a husband cannot commit even a slight assault upon his wife, and that her person is as sacred from his violence as from that of any other person. It is true that he may enforce sexual connection; and, in the exercise of this marital right, it is held that he cannot be guilty of the offense of rape. But it is too plain for argument that this privilege is a personal one, only. Hence if, as in *Lord Audley's Case*, 3 How. St. Tr. 401, the husband aids and abets another to ravish his wife, he may be convicted as if he were a stranger. The principle is thus tersely expressed by *Sir* Matthew Hale: "For, though in marriage she hath given up her body to her husband, she is not to be by him prostituted to another." Hale, P. C. 629; 2 Bishop, Cr. L. 1135; *Lord Audley's Case*, 3 How. St. Tr. 401.

It thus appearing, we think beyond all question, that the defendant in this indictment is to be regarded as a stranger, we will further consider the case in that aspect alone. It is contended that, as Lowery acted under coercion, and was for that reason excusable, there was no intent to commit rape, and therefore the defendant cannot be convicted. It will be observed that the intent of Lowery to commit the offense is not determined alone by the presumption that everyone is presumed to intend the natural consequences of his act; but he testifies that he did actually attempt to have sexual connection. Here, then, we have a specific, actual intent to commit the foul deed; and can it be that he who constrains the will of another to commit such a crime is to be permitted to shield himself upon the ground that there was an entire absence of criminal intent? If this be true, then one who coerces another to shoot down a third person in cold blood is not guilty of murder, because there was no intent for which the person doing the shooting is criminally responsible. The law in such a case couples the act of the instrument with the felonious intent of the instigator, and in this way he is held guilty of murder; and this is true, also, where the instrument is under the age of seven, and conclusively presumed to be incapable of having any criminal intent. So, too, if one is indicted under our Statute for shooting at a railroad train with intent to injure it, and it appears that he coerced another to do the shooting, can it with reason be said that he is not guilty because his instrument did not have an intent to inflict any injury? These and other examples which we could cite from our reports well illustrate the principle upon which our case depends; and especially is this so when, as we have said, the specific intent is expressly shown by the testimony. We are clearly of the opinion that the unlawful act committed in pursuance of the combined intents of the defendant and his enforced instrument are amply sufficient to sustain the conviction.

While placing our decision upon this ground, we are not prepared to say that, under the circumstances, Lowery would have been excusable had he completed the offense. We leave this as an open question, remarking, however, that the *tabula in naufragio* of *Lord* Bacon has been well nigh submerged by judicial and critical casuists. See Whart. Hom. §§ 560, 561, and *notes* to second edition; *United States* v. *Holmes*, 1 Wall. Jr. 1. See also Coleridge, *Ch. J.*, in the *Case of the Migniotte*, decided in 1884.

But mark the diversity: There the displaced struggler for life was, by clinging to the plank, insufficient for two, as much attacking his companion in shipwreck, as if he were firing at him with a pistol. In our case the victim is entirely innocent,—in no way threatening by her act or deed any harm to the attempted ravisher. In this view of the case, let us briefly refer to the authorities.

In Broom, Legal Maxims, 17, 18, it is said: "In accordance with the principle, *necessitas inducit privilegium*, the law excuses the commission of an act prima facie criminal if such act be done involuntarily, and under circumstances which show that the individual doing it was not really a free agent. Thus, if A by force take the hand of B, in which is a weapon, and therewith kill C, A is guilty of murder, but B is excused; though if merely a moral force be used, as threats, duress of imprisonment or even an assault to the peril of his life, in order to compel him to kill C, this is no legal excuse." For this is cited 1 Hale, P. C. 434, which seems to be entirely in point.

East, in his Pleas of the Crown (vol. 1, p.

294), undertakes to argue that, "if the commission of treason may be extenuated by the fear of present death . . . there seems no reason why this offense [homicide, or any of the other capital offenses, of course] may not also be mitigated upon the like consideration of human infirmity." 1 Bishop, Cr. L. 848. To this, however, an answer is found in 4 Bl. Com. 30, where he says: "In time of war or rebellion, a man may be justified in doing many treasonable acts, by compulsion of the enemy or rebels, which would admit of no excuse in the time of peace. This, however, seems only, or at least principally, to hold as to positive crimes, so created by the laws of society, and which, therefore, society may excuse, but not as to natural offenses, so declared by the law of God. . . . And, therefore, though a man may be violently assaulted, and hath no other possible means of escaping death but by killing an innocent person, this fear and force shall not acquit him of murder; for he ought rather to die himself than escape by the murder of an innocent."

If this be so, and the crime of rape is considered so heinous as to be punishable in the same way as murder, it would seem that "human infirmity" ought not to be tolerated by our laws to the extent of excusing one for the violation of female virtue on the plea of danger to himself, however great or imminent. For the reasons first stated, we think that the ruling of his honor was correct, and that *there is no error.*

Merrimon, *Ch. J.*, dissenting:

The horrible and detestable purpose of the defendant in doing the acts which constitute the criminal offense committed by him against his wife cannot warrant what I deem a misapplication of well-established principles of criminal law. In the nature of the marriage relation, the husband himself cannot ravish his wife; nor, for like reasons, can he, in a legal sense, assault her with the intent to commit a rape upon her. He can only commit the offense of rape, or that of assault with intent to commit a rape, against his wife, by procuring, aiding, abetting or encouraging another to commit these offenses. His offense in such case depends, necessarily, upon the perpetration of the principal offense by another party. In this case the negro named did not commit a rape upon the wife of the defendant, nor did he assault her with such intent. There was a total absence of such intent on his part. Then, in the nature of the matter, how can the defendant be chargeable with the particular offense charged against him in the indictment? As the negro committed no assault with intent to commit a rape, so the defendant did not. It is said, Shall the defendant go quit? Has he committed no offense? Most unquestionably he shall not go quit. He has committed an offense,—a very serious one. He is chargeable with an assault upon his wife with a deadly weapon, and with the intent to kill, and a like assault upon the negro. It is said the punishment of the offense last mentioned is not adequate. It may be very severe. But it may be said as well that the punishment for the offense as charged is not adequate. This, however, is no argument; not the slightest reason pertinent here. The courts have nothing to do with the punishment of offenders, further than to impose the same in the cases, and as required and allowed by law. I will not pursue the subject further.

Donald W. BAIN, State Treasurer, *Appt.*,

v.

RICHMOND & DANVILLE R. CO.

(....N. C.....)

Rolling stock of a nonresident railroad company, used in interstate commerce, is not subject to taxation in a State where it is operating a leased railroad.

(March 17, 1890.)

APPEAL by plaintiff from a judgment of the Superior Court for Wake County denying part of the relief claimed in an action to recover taxes alleged to be due and unpaid. *Affirmed.*

The facts are fully stated in the opinion.

Messrs. **Theodore F. Davidson,** *Atty-Gen.*, and **R. H. Battle** for appellant.

Messrs. **D. Schenck** and **C. M. Busbee** for appellee.

Merrimon, *Ch. J.*, delivered the opinion of the court:

The plaintiff is the treasurer of North Carolina. The defendant is a corporation of the State of Virginia, and has a lease of the railroad of the North Carolina Railroad Company, a corporation of this State; and it does the business of transportation in, through and across this State from the State of Virginia and other States to the State of South Carolina and other States. The purpose of this action is to recover the sum of $350 as taxes alleged to be due this State from the defendant, and for costs.

The following are the facts found by the court below, and its judgment thereupon: "(1) The Richmond & Danville Railroad Company was on June 1, 1888, the owner of $17,500 worth of rolling stock, to wit, four switching engines and one coach, which were on June 1, 1888, used exclusively in North Carolina, but owned in Virginia, and which the Company never at any time recall. (2) Upon all the rolling stock of the Richmond & Danville Railroad

---

NOTE.—*Taxation of rolling stock of railroad companies.*

The rolling stock of a railroad is personal property, and constitutes no part of its real estate. Ottumwa W. M. Co. v. Hawley, 44 Iowa, 57; Boston C. & M. R. Co. v. Gilmore, 37 N. H. 410; Randall v. Elwell, 52 N. Y. 521; Hoyle v. Plattsburgh & M. R. Co. 54 N. Y. 314; Meyer v. Johnston, 53 Ala. 237; Coe v. Columbus, P. & I. R. Co. 10 Ohio St. 372; Teaff v. Hewitt, 1 Ohio, 511; Chicago & N. W. R. Co. v. Fort Howard, 21 Wis. 45.

Engines and cars are no more appendages of a railroad than are wagons and carriages of a highway, and they do not constitute a part of it. State v. Somerville & E. R. Co. 28 N. J. L. 21; Williamson v. New Jersey S. R. Co. 29 N. J. Eq. 311.

Pullman palace cars not owned by the railroad company are included in the rolling stock of the railroad and taxed as such to its owners. Kennedy v. St. Louis, V. & T. H. R. Co. 62 Ill. 395.

Under the statutes of some States, however, the

Company the Company is assessed for taxation, and does pay taxes in Virginia. (3) The rolling stock of the North Carolina Railroad Company is used exclusively in North Carolina; and upon all this rolling stock, of the assessed value of $125,000, taxes are assessed and paid in North Carolina by the Richmond & Danville Railroad Company, the lessee. (4) The board of appraisers and assessors of the North Carolina Railroad made the assessment, as set out as an exhibit to complaint, of $175,000 upon the rolling stock of the Richmond & Danville Railroad Company in use in North Carolina on June 1, 1888. (5) On June 1, 1888, there was in use on the North Carolina Railroad, leased by the Richmond & Danville Railroad in North Carolina, rolling stock passing through the State to the value of $175,000. Such rolling stock was owned by the Richmond & Danville Railroad Company; and the trains in which said rolling stock was used were made up outside of North Carolina and went on through to the State of South Carolina. Upon this state of facts, his honor ruled that the defendant Company was liable to pay taxes to the State upon $17 500, on the engines and coach used exclusively in North Carolina, and was not liable to pay upon $157,500 the remainder, used in interstate commerce. Therefore, it is adjudged that the plaintiff recover of the defendant the sum of $35 and interest from July 1, 1888, and costs."

The power and right of the State to tax property of nonresidents, whether these be natural or artificial persons, having its *situs* within the State for the purposes of business, convenience or pleasure of the owners thereof or others, is too well settled to admit of serious question. This important right of the State is surely founded upon the just ground that such property has the protection, advantage and benefit of the laws of the State; and it ought, on that account, to be required to contribute as taxes its fair share towards the support of the government whose benefits extend to it, not merely casually, but regularly and continuously, while it continues to be so located, as to other like property of residents of the State. Upon principles of common justice, every property owner should contribute to the support of the government that protects and renders his property valuable and useful his fair proportion of money as a consideration therefor, unless for some proper cause he is excused from doing so. *Alvany* v. *Powell*, 2 Jones, Eq. 51; *Redmond* v. *Rutherford County Comrs.* 87 N. C. 122, and numerous cases there cited; *Worth* v. *Ashe County Comrs.* 90 N. C. 409; *Gloucester Ferry Co.* v. *Pennsylvania*, 114 U. S. 196 [29 L. ed. 158]; *Thompson* v. *Union P. R. Co.* 76 U. S. 9 Wall. 579 [19 L. ed. 792]; *Union P. R. Co.* v. *Peniston*, 85 U. S. 18 Wall. 5 [21 L. ed. 787]; *Western U. Teleg. Co.* v. *Texas*, 105 U. S. 460 [26 L. ed. 1067]; *Western U. Teleg. Co.* v. *Massachusetts*, 125 U. S. 530 [31 L. ed. 790]; *Leloup* v. *Port of Mobile*, 127 U. S. 640 [32 L. ed. 311].

If the State were absolutely sovereign in all respects, it might tax property coming into it temporarily from another State for the purposes of trade, or property passing across its territory from one State to another or other States in the course of trade, travel and commerce. It might tax such trade and travel, in the discretion of its Legislature. But, as a member and constituent part of the Federal Union, it does not possess unlimited powers of taxation as to all property, matters and things that might otherwise be deemed and made subjects thereof. It and its authorities, including its courts of justice, are bound by that Constitution; and it is its and their duty to observe, administer and enforce its provisions in proper cases and connections,—as much so as its own Constitution and laws. Indeed, the Constitution of the United States is a part of the Organic Law of this State; and, in principle and theory, there is not, and cannot be, any conflict between the Constitution and laws of the United States and the same of this State. If conflict, in fact, exists in any respect, as, unhappily, is sometimes the case, it is so because those who determine what the law is, administer and enforce it, are ignorant of or misapprehend its true meaning and application, or willfully disregard and disobey it.

A leading and very important purpose of the Federal Union was to establish and secure the freedom of trade and commerce, both foreign and domestic, and, particularly for the present purpose, between and among the several States comprising it. To this end, it is provided in

---

rolling stock is considered real estate and assessed with the road as a whole. Sangamon & M. R. Co. v. Morgan Co. 14 Ill. 163; Maus v. Logansport, P. & B. R. Co. 27 Ill. 77; Louisville & N. A. R. Co. v. State, 25 Ind. 177; Dubuque v. Illinois C. R. Co. 39 Iowa, 56; Bangor & P. R. Co. v. Harris, 21 Me. 533; Cumberland M. R. Co. v. Portland, 37 Me. 444; State v. Severance, 55 Mo. 378.

In the absence of legislation to the contrary, the rolling stock of a railroad, being personal property, is to be taxed to the road at the place of its domicil. It cannot be assessed except at the place which contains the home office of the company. Kennedy v. St. Louis, V. & T. H. R. Co. 62 Ill. 395; Louisville & N. A. R. Co. v. State, 25 Ind. 177; Portland, S. & P. R. Co. v. Saco, 60 Me. 196; Appeal Tax Court v. Philadelphia, W. & B. R. Co. 50 Md. 397; Philadelphia, W. & B. R. Co. v. Appeal Tax Court, Id. 416; Appeal Tax Court v. Northern Cent. R. Co. Id. 417; Appeal Tax Court v. Pullman P. C. Co. Id. 452; Pacific R. Co. v. Cass Co. 53 Mo. 17; State v. Person, 32 N. J. L. 134; Pelton v. Northern Transp. Co. 37 Ohio St. 450; Western Transp. Co. v. Scheu, 19 N. Y. 408; People v. McLean, 80 N. Y. 254; Union S. B. Co. v. Buffalo, 82 N. Y. 351; Orange & A. R. Co. v. Alexandria, 17 Gratt. 176; Hays v. Pacific M. S. S. Co. 58 U. S. 17 How. 596 (15 L. ed. 254); St. Louis v. Wiggins Ferry Co. 78 U. S. 11 Wall. 425 (20 L. ed. 192); Kirtland v. Hotchkiss, 100 U. S. 497 (25 L. ed. 582); Gloucester Ferry Co. v. Pennsylvania, 114 U. S. 208 (29 L. ed. 163); Baltimore & O. R. Co. v. Allen, 22 Fed. Rep. 379.

But for purposes of taxation, the *situs* of personal property of a railroad company may be fixed in whatever locality the property may be brought and used by its owner, by the law of the place where it is found. Marye v. Baltimore & O. R. Co. 127 U. S. 117 (32 L. ed. 95).

The rolling stock of the Baltimore & Ohio Railroad Company, a Maryland corporation employed in the operation of other railroads in Virginia, by virtue of leases or contracts, is not taxable under Va. Laws 1881-82, chap. 119, which apply only to Virginia corporations. *Ibid.*

its Constitution (art. 1, § 8, par. 3) that "the Congress shall have power . . . to regulate commerce with foreign nations and among the several States, and with the Indian tribes." The power thus conferred is indefinite as to its scope, and capable of very latitudinous interpretation and exercise, particularly as it is part of the Organic Law, and the subject to which it relates is one of great breadth and compass. It is difficult to determine its just limit in many respects; but it should receive a reasonable interpretation, such as will effectuate the purpose contemplated, trenching as little as practicable upon the powers, rights and convenience of the States. Very certainly the provision implies that Congress should regulate such commerce, and the States shall not; that Congress shall do so effectually, in such way and by such means as will secure, promote and encourage the same, and that the States shall not, if disposed to do so, interfere with, destroy, hinder or delay the same, or divert it in any way, by any legal constraint, for their own advantage, otherwise than, to a very limited extent, as allowed by the Constitution. Hence, it is settled that a State cannot tax commerce, trade, travel, transportation or the privilege to carry on and conduct the same, or the vehicles, means and appliances employed and used in connection therewith, coming into that State from another temporarily, however frequently, and returning to such other State; nor can it tax such commerce, or such incidents thereto, passing across it from another or other States to another or other States, however often this may be done.

And the reason is that to so tax such commerce, and the incidents thereto, including such means of transportation, would tend directly, and have the effect, in a greater or less degree and extent, to interfere with the freedom of commerce among and between the people of the States. It would have the certain effect to embarrass, hinder and delay the free course of such trade. If a State could thus tax such commerce at all, it might, in its discretion, for its own benefit and advantage, tax it so heavily as to practically destroy it within its own borders, and in possible cases prevent it from passing freely into other States. Moreover, if one State might tax it, every State through which it passed might do so likewise; and thus the power of Congress to regulate interstate trade and commerce would be nugatory and a sheer mockery. It is clear that a State has no such power, and the Supreme Court of the United States has authoritatively so decided, directly and in effect, in many cases. *Hays* v. *Pacific M. S. S. Co.* 58 U. S. 17 How. 596 [15 L. ed. 254]; *Morgan* v. *Parham*, 83 U. S. 16 Wall. 471 [21 L. ed. 303]; *Gloucester Ferry Co.* v. *Pennsylvania*, 114 U. S. 196 [29 L. ed. 158], and numerous cases there cited; *Pickard* v. *Pullman S. C. Co.* 117 U. S. 34 [29 L. ed. 785]; *Leloup* v. *Port of Mobile*, 127 U. S. 640 [32 L. ed. 311].

The Statute (Acts N. C. 1887, chap. 137, §§ 44-51), properly interpreted, does not, and was not intended to, embrace and tax the property of the defendant put in question by this appeal. It had reference to, and embraced property of, corporations, whether resident or not, whose property was situated—had a *situs*—in this State, and was thus subject to be taxed. But the property in question was not, in a legal sense, located—situated—in this State. It had no *situs* here. It was the property of a nonresident corporation, employed and used by it, constantly, for the purposes of transportation, in the course of the conduct of interstate trade and commerce coming into and passing across this State, from another and other States to and into another and other States. It was not stationary, but constantly *in transitu* from one State to another. The mere fact that property of the defendant of the value mentioned was continuously within the State did not give it a *situs* here. It was continually changing and *in transitu* in the course of interstate commerce. It was so continuously in this State, day and night, because of the great volume of trade and travel passing over the defendant's road into and across this State, going to other States.

It is true, as suggested on the argument, that such property receives protection from this State, and has benefit of its laws; but, nevertheless, it is not the subject of taxation, because the Constitution of the United States will not, as we have seen, allow it to be made such subject.

Judgment affirmed.

PENNSYLVANIA SUPREME COURT.

COMMONWEALTH of Pennsylvania
v.
Charles CLEARY, *Appt.*

(....Pa.....)

1. **The benefit of the good character of a person** charged with crime is not limited to cases where there is a reasonable doubt of his guilt, but evidence of his good character may itself create the reasonable doubt which will entitle him to acquittal.

2. **It is not competent to prove the intoxication of a person** by showing the condition of one who was with him, and who had taken the same number of drinks.

(May 19, 1890.)

NOTE.—*Criminal law; good character as a defense.*

Evidence of the general good character of one accused of crime, in the community where he is best known, is admissible in his defense (State v. King, 78 Mo. 555; Jones v. State, 10 Tex. App. 552; Brownlee v. State, 13 Tex. App. 255); but the goodness of his character subsequent to the commission of the offense is not provable. Brown v. State, 46 Ala. 175; State v. Kinley, 43 Iowa, 294.

Evidence is admissible to show that his previous good character was such as to render it unlikely that he could be guilty of the particular crime charged against him. People v. Doggett, 62 Cal. 27; Kee v. State, 28 Ark. 155; Hirschman v. People, 101 Ill. 568; State v. Ormiston, 66 Iowa, 143; Young

APPEAL by defendant from a judgment of the Court of Oyer and Terminer for Clinton County convicting him of the crime of murder in the first degree. *Reversed.*

On the evening of March 12, 1889, Cleary, in company with one Belford, encountered on the streets of the Borough of Renovo, Philip Paul, who was the police officer of the borough. Cleary and Belford were both disorderly and under the influence of liquor. Paul for some reason caught Cleary by the coat collar and started with him towards the lock-up. As they reached the lock-up Cleary drew a pistol and shot Paul, killing him instantly.

Defendant introduced evidence as to his good character. He also offered to prove by one Reese that Belford, who was the same person shown to have been drinking with the defendant during the evening of the alleged killing, and to have drunk every time and no oftener than the defendant, and with one exception to have drunk each time the same kind of drink as defendant, when he came to witness' office was very much intoxicated; to be followed by proof that Belford is older than defendant, although under the age of twenty-one years; that defendant is of a nervous temperament, and therefore more susceptible to the influence of intoxicating liquors than Belford.

Objected to by Commonwealth.

Objection sustained. Evidence excluded. Exception. (First assignment of error.)

The court charged, *inter alia*, as follows:

"The intoxication of the prisoner may be material, and is evidence to be considered by the jury for the purpose of enabling them to determine whether at the time of the commission of the crime the prisoner was so much intoxicated, and his intellect clouded, as to deprive him of the power to think and weigh the nature of the act committed." "Was he able to deliberate and premeditate the homicide?" "The mere intoxication of the prisoner will not exclude or palliate his offense, unless he was in such a state of intoxication as to be incapable of conceiving any intent. If he was his grade of offense is reduced to murder in the second degree." (Third assignment of error.)

Messrs. **W. C. Kress** and **C. S. McCormick** for appellant.

Messrs. **A. W. Brungard**, *Dist-Atty.*, and **T. C. Hipple** for appellee.

Paxson, *Ch. J.*, delivered the opinion of the court:

But for a single error this judgment might have been affirmed. The learned judge below instructed the jury, in his general charge, that "good character is always of importance, and is evidence to be duly considered by the jury, and may turn the scale where there is a reasonable doubt as to the degree or grade of the crime." (Second assignment.) This is all the charge contains upon this subject; there was no point put to the court in regard to it.

The fact that the homicide was committed by the appellant was not disputed below nor here, nor was there any attempt to show that the offense was manslaughter. The sole question was as to the degree of murder. The jury convicted appellant of murder in the first degree.

We think the evidence of good character is applicable both to the commission of the offense and the grade of the crime. So far we are in accord with the trial judge. But we think he stated inaccurately the law as applicable to good character.

In *Heine* v. *Com.*, 91 Pa. 145, the court below instructed the jury: "If a man is guilty his previous good character has nothing to do with the case, but if you have reasonable doubts as to his guilt, then character steps in and aids in determining that doubt." This ruling was reversed by this court, *Mr. Justice* Gordon saying: "The effect of this was to give the evidence of good character no weight whatever, for if the other testimony left in the minds of the jury a reasonable doubt of the defendant's guilt, this of itself, without more, entitled him to an acquittal. Evidence of good character is not a mere make-weight thrown in to assist in the production of a result that would happen at all events, but it is positive evidence, and may of itself, by the creation of a reasonable doubt, produce an acquittal"—citing Wharton, Cr. L. § 643.

In *Hanney* v. *Com.*, 116 Pa. 323, 8 Cent. Rep. 184, the court below fell into the same error as in *Heine* v. *Com.*, *supra*, and upon its review in this court the judgment was reversed, *Justice* Gordon repeating and amplifying his remarks in the former case.

It was urged, however, that *Kilpatrick* v. *Com.*, 31 Pa. 198, sustains the ruling of the court below. The portion of the charge assigned as error in that case is as follows: "The evidence proves the defendant to have borne an excellent reputation; originally evidence of good character was not allowed to go to the jury when there was positive proof of the com-

---

v. Com. 6 Bush, 312; State v. Bloom, 68 Ind. 54; Com. v. Worcester, 3 Pick. 462.

Such evidence may, by creating a reasonable doubt, produce an acquittal of the offense. Carson v. State, 50 Ala. 134; State v. Donovan, 61 Iowa, 278; Heine v. Com. 91 Pa. 145.

Such evidence might create a reasonable doubt in favor of the accused. Armor v. State, 63 Ala. 173; Carson v. State, 50 Ala. 134; Fields v. State, 47 Ala. 603; Hall v. State, 40 Ala. 698; Jupitz v. People, 34 Ill. 516; People v. Ashe, 44 Cal. 288; People v. Fenwick, 45 Cal. 287; People v. Raina, 45 Cal. 292; State v. Gustafson, 50 Iowa, 194; State v. Lindley, 51 Iowa, 343; State v. Donovan, 61 Iowa, 278; State v. McMurphy, 52 Mo. 251; People v. Lamb, 2 Keyes, 360; Stover v. People, 56 N. Y. 315; State v. Henry, 5 Jones, L. 65; Heine v. Com. 91 Pa. 145; Lee v. State, 2 Tex. App. 338; State v. Daley, 53 Vt. 442.

So where guilt is doubtful, such evidence may be produced to rebut the presumption arising from facts and circumstances. State v. Ford, 3 Strobh. L. 517; State v. Rodman, 62 Iowa, 456.

The failure of the accused to call witnesses as to his character raises no presumption of bad character. State v. Dockstader, 42 Iowa, 436; Com. v. Webster, 5 Cush. 295; Harrington v. State, 19 Ohio St. 264; Ormsby v. People, 53 N. Y. 472; People v. Bodine, 1 Denio, 282; State v. O'Neal, 7 Ired. L. 251.

Where evidence of good character has been interposed, it may be rebutted by evidence of bad character deduced from his own admissions, but not by proof of particular acts. Smith v. State, 47 Ala. 540; McCarty v. People, 51 Ill. 231; Gordon v. State, 3 Iowa, 410; State v. Williams, 77 Mo. 310.

See also 12 L. R. A. 449.

mission of an offense, for if one was seen to commit a murder with deliberation, although he had borne an irreproachable character, and were even an angel, he would yet be guilty; the rule of the law in this State, however, per mits evidence of good character to be submitted to the jury in every case of homicide, no matter what may be the other evidence in the cause. But when a doubt suggests itself to your minds as to the prisoner's guilt, upon the facts of the case as presented by the evidence, the law casts the whole weight of the prisoner's former good character in mercy's scale, and settles the question in favor of the accused."

In commenting upon this language, this court said, through *Mr. Justice* Strong: "The final exception is that the court erred in the instruction which they gave to the jury respecting the evidence of the prisoner's good character. This, like the former, is based upon a misconception of the charge. We do not understand the purport of the instruction to have been such as it is contended to have been by the counsel for the plaintiff in error. The substance of the charge was that the law permitted evidence of good character to be submitted to the jury (of course for their consideration) in every case of homicide, no matter what might be the other testimony in the cause, and that when a doubt arises as to the guilt of the accused, such doubt was conclusive in his favor. This by no means confined the jury to attaching importance to the evidence only in cases of reasonable doubt; on the contrary, it left them at liberty to make it a basis for the formation of a doubt."

I have been thus careful to quote the exact language of the court below and of this court in *Kilpatrick* v. *Com.*, as I fear it has been misunderstood in some instances.

The distinction between the two cases, briefly stated, is this: In the case in hand the benefit of good character was limited to cases where there is a reasonable doubt of the guilt of the accused; or, in the precise language of the court below, "may turn the scale where there is a reasonable doubt as to the degree or grade of the crime;" while in *Kilpatrick* v. *Com.*, the language of the court below, while not as explicit as in some of the later cases, to repeat again the language of *Justice* Strong, "by no means confined the jury to attaching importance to the evidence only in cases of reasonable doubt; on the contrary, it left them at liberty to make it a basis for the formation of a doubt."

There is nothing in the charge of the court below from which the jury could fairly infer that the evidence of good character might create the reasonable doubt which entitles the prisoner to a safe deliverance.

It is true that the difference in phraseology in the two cases is apparently slight. There is, however, a real and substantial difference, and where a man's life may depend upon a single word, the use of language cannot be attended with too much care.

We might cite numerous other cases upon this point, but the law is too well settled to require it. The rule deducible from the author ities may be briefly stated thus: Evidence of good character is always admissible for the defendant in a criminal case; it is to be weighed and considered in connection with all the other evidence in the cause—it may of itself in some instances create the reasonable doubt which entitles the accused to an acquittal.

The rule itself is not merely merciful; it is both reasonable and just. There may be cases in which, owing to the peculiar circumstances in which a man is placed, evidence of good character may be all he can offer in answer to a charge of crime. Of what avail is a good character, which a man may have been a lifetime in acquiring, if it is to benefit him nothing in his hour of peril?

The vice of this portion of the charge is in the instruction that good character "may turn the scale where there is a reasonable doubt as to the degree or grade of the crime." But if the other evidence is such as to raise a reasonable doubt whether the grade of crime was murder in the first degree, then the jury are bound to acquit of that offense, so that, as was observed in the cases cited, "this was to give the evidence of good character no weight whatever." The evidence of good character is to be considered with the other evidence in the case, and if it all combined creates a reasonable doubt, the defendant is entitled to an acquittal.

The learned judge below evidently was of opinion that the evidence of good character had little bearing upon the case. I gather this from his opinion refusing a new trial, in which he said, in commenting upon this portion of his charge: "Of this instruction the defendant has no cause of complaint; it was as favorable to him as he could ask. In fact, as the commission of the crime by the defendant was not disputed, and the only question for the jury to determine was the grade or degree of the crime, and as the determination of that question depended upon the mental condition of the defendant, whether intoxicated or not, we are of opinion that the evidence of the defendant's good character had little relevancy."

We do not think the premises upon which this conclusion was drawn are entirely accurate. We do not understand that the commission of the crime was undisputed by the defendant. It is true the commission of the homicide was conceded, but not the commission of murder in the first degree. That was the crime for which he was on trial and of which he was convicted. The commission of that offense was disputed below and also in this court. Nor did the question of the degree depend alone "upon the mental condition of the defendant, whether intoxicated or not." The jury found that he was not intoxicated to the extent of preventing his forming the willful, deliberate and premeditated intent to take the life of the deceased. Just here is the place where the evidence of good character was entitled to come in and have its due weight. Here was his supreme peril. The defense of intoxication had failed. If a man's good character is to avail him at all, when does he need it more than when a jury is deliberating upon the question whether he had formed in his mind the deliberate intent to take a human life? It might not have availed anything in this case; we are not considering the weight of the evidence upon this point; that was for the jury, but it should have been submitted to them in such manner as to give them a proper understanding as to how they should apply it.

We cannot treat this as an immaterial matter, which did not prejudice the defendant. It may not have done so, but we cannot say so. The issue of life and death is so vast, both as to this world and the next, that it is our duty to weigh every word carefully, and leave nothing to conjecture.

As the case must go back for another trial it is proper to say that we do not discover any error in the remaining assignments. The testimony of Dr. Reese, referred to in the first assignment, was properly rejected. It was not competent to prove the defendant's intoxication by showing the condition of Belford, who was with him, and had taken the same number of drinks. Some men can drink twice as much as others without showing it. The inquiry would have involved a collateral issue which might have confused if not misled the jury. The remaining assignments refer to the charge. With the single exception above noted we find no error in it.

Judgment reversed, and a **venire facias de** novo *awarded.*

WEST VIRGINIA SUPREME COURT OF APPEALS.

P. L. BRANNON

v.

COUNTY COURT OF KANAWHA COUNTY *et al.*

(....W. Va.....)

***Taxes imposed by the county court for road purposes** in a district under chapter 35, Acts 1881 (Code 1887, p. 338), are taxes assessed by "county authorities," within the meaning of § 7, art. 10, of the Constitution, and are to be included with other taxes levied by the county court, in determining whether the limit of taxation therein fixed will be exceeded.

(March 24, 1890.)

*Head note by BRANNON, *J.*

APPEAL by defendants from a decree of the Circuit Court for Kanawha County in favor of complainant in a suit brought to enjoin the collection of a certain tax. *Affirmed.*

The case sufficiently appears in the opinion.

Messrs. **Brown & Jackson,** for appellants:

The so-called "road tax" is not in fact a "tax," in the sense of the Constitution; but instead, is a local assessment authorized by the Legislature for local improvement; exercised under the police powers, which inherently exist in every government, to assess and collect from the localities benefited, the costs of the improvements made within its territorial limits.

This power and its exercise have been fully sustained by the courts whenever brought before them.

NOTE.—*Taxation for road and highway purposes; in general.*

The Legislature may compel the levy of a tax for the construction of a local road (Wilcox v. Deer Lodge County, 2 Mont. 574. See *Re* Woolsey, 95 N. Y. 135); but it cannot exercise directly the power of assessment for a local improvement in an incorporated city, regardless of the will of the local community. People v. Lynch, 51 Cal. 15; Schumacker v. Toberman, 56 Cal. 508.

The expense of public highways is usually provided for by the general town or county levy, except such important thoroughfares as are constructed by the State at large, and except also where contributions in labor are demanded for the purpose. Cooley, Taxn. 2d ed. 611; Miller v. Gorman, 38 Pa. 309.

The power to define the taxing district for any particular burden is purely legislative, subject to no restraint other than constitutional provisions. Shaw v. Dennis, 10 Ill. 405; Conwell v. Connersville, 8 Ind. 358; Challiss v. Parker, 11 Kan. 394; Malchus v. Highlands, 4 Bush, 547; Hingham & Q. B. & Turnp. Corp. v. Norfolk County, 6 Allen, 353; People v. Brooklyn, 4 N. Y. 419; Howell v. Buffalo, 37 N. Y. 267; Philadelphia v. Field, 58 Pa. 320; Waterville v. Kennebec County, 59 Me. 80; Arnold v. Cambridge, 106 Mass. 352; Cuming v. Grand Rapids, 46 Mich. 150; Alcorn v. Hamer, 38 Miss. 652; Hill v. Higdon, 5 Ohio, 243; Allen v. Drew, 44 Vt. 174.

In laying out a road, the Legislature may apportion the expense of its construction between several towns. Shaw v. Dennis, 10 Ill. 405; Waterville v. Kennebec County, 59 Me. 80; Norwich v. Hampshire County, 13 Pick. 60; Hingham & Q. B. & Turnp. Corp. v. Norfolk County, 6 Allen, 353; Com. v. Newburyport, 103 Mass. 129; Salem Turnp. & C. B. Corp. v. Essex County, 100 Mass. 282; Cambridge v. Lexington, 17 Pick. 222.

A tax on one community for the benefit of a larger community not taxed would be void. *Ex parte* Marshall, 64 Ala. 266.

And even though the work was wholly within the town, as in case of the erection of a costly bridge, the State or county might be determined by the Legislature as the proper taxing district. Will County v. People, 110 Ill. 511.

The State or the county is the proper taxing district for state or county roads, and the town will not be taxed for their cost of repair except as a part of the larger district in which it is located. People v. Dutchess County, 1 Hill, 50.

Where a city duly authorized thereto improves its own streets, a county tax for roads cannot be laid on its inhabitants. Martin v. Aston, 60 Cal. 63.

A tax levy may be made payable in labor, but this is to some extent a police regulation rather than a tax. It is in the nature of a capitation tax and statutory provisions for assessment are not applicable unless expressly so provided. Sawyer v. Alton, 4 Ill. 127; Pleasant v. Kost, 29 Ill. 490; New Orleans Draining Co's Case, 11 La. Ann. 338; Amenia v. Stanford, 6 Johns. 92; State v. Halifax, 4 Dev. L. 345.

A statute imposing a labor tax on persons residing in the district will not embrace transient laborers. On Yuen Hai Co. v. Ross, 8 Sawy. 384.

A tax assessed as labor cannot be carried upon the roll as a money tax without notice given to perform the work. Bliss v. New Haven, 42 Wis. 605.

A city may commute highway labor on the streets for a money payment. Johnston v. Macon, 62 Ga. 645.

See also 11 L. R. A. 835; 29 L. R. A. 416.

Cooley, Taxn. 398; *Goddard, Petitioner*, 16 Pick. 504, 509; *Norfolk* v. *Ellis*, 26 Gratt. 224; *Douglass* v. *Harrisville*, 9 W. Va. 166.

Under a constitutional provision almost identical with § 7, art. 10, of our Constitution, the Supreme Court of Illinois expressly decided that the township road levies were not contemplated by said section, and, though when aggregated with the county levy the aggregate exceeded the limit fixed by the section, the levies were still valid.

Wabash, St. L. & P. R. Co. v. *McCleave*, 108 Ill. 369.

Messrs. **E. B. Knight** and **J. W. Kennedy**, with *Messrs.* **Chapman & Littlepage** and **Mollohan & McClintic**, also for appellants.

Messrs. **Okey Johnson** and **J. H. Ferguson**, for appellee:

County authorities cannot in any year assess any kind of taxes on the property of the citizen, which will in the aggregate exceed ninety-five cents on the $100 valuation.

Arnold v. *Hawkins*, 14 West. Rep. 739, 95 Mo. 569; *Hare* v. *Kennerly*, 83 Ala. 608; *Mix* v. *People*, 72 Ill. 241; *People* v. *Wall*, 88 Ill. 75; *Chiniquy* v. *People*, 78 Ill. 570.

Brannon, *J.*, delivered the opinion of the court:

The District of Cabin Creek, in Kanawha County, adopted the Alternate Road Law provided by chapter 35, Acts 1881 (Code 1887, chap. 43, § 56b). In 1889 the County Court of Kanawha County levied, for general county purposes, ninety-five cents on the $100 taxable property of the County, and, in addition thereto, thirty cents on the $100 of taxable property in Cabin Creek District, for road purposes in that district. P. L. Brannon, a taxpayer in said district, paid to the sheriff all his taxes save this tax levied for road purposes, which he refused to pay, and the sheriff, for its collection, levied upon property of said taxpayer; and he then, suing for himself, and all other taxpayers of the district, obtained an injunction restraining the sheriff from collecting this road tax, making the County Court and Roman Pickens, the sheriff, defendants to his bill, claiming in his bill, as the two levies together exceeded ninety-five cents on the $100 of taxable property, this road levy was illegal. The answers did not deny the facts alleged, but controverted the mere matter of law as to the illegality of the tax. Facts were agreed, and the cause was heard on the bill, answers, facts agreed, and on a motion to dissolve the injunction; and the decree was that the motion to dissolve be overruled, and the injunction perpetuated. The said County Court and Sheriff Pickens appealed to this court.

The ground on which the appellee, Brannon, bases his injunction is that the levy for county purposes of ninety-five cents, and that of thirty cents, under the Alternate Road Law of 1881 (Code 1887, chap. 43, p. 338), in the aggregate, exceed ninety-five cents on the $100 of property, and therefore the tax is in violation of § 7, art. 10, of the Constitution. That section is as follows: "County authorities shall never assess taxes, in any one year, the aggregate of which shall exceed ninety-five cents per $100 valua-

---

Judicial decisions in various States.

State taxes are levied, not under the law, but by the law determining the subjects and the rate of taxation; while county taxes are levied under the law by an order, edict or ordinance legislative in its character. Calhoun County v. Woodstock Iron Co. 82 Ala. 151.

In Connecticut an assessment for laying out a highway is a local special tax limited to a class interested in the improvement. Bridgeport v. New York & N. H. R. Co. 36 Conn. 255.

In Illinois the tax which the commissioners of highways are authorized to levy is payable as other taxes, in money. Mee v. Paddock, 83 Ill. 494; Baird v. People, 83 Ill. 387; People v. Suppiger, 103 Ill. 434.

The phrase "tax levied for road purposes" includes taxes collected for the payment of damages arising from opening and laying out of roads, the purchase of materials and for repairing roads and bridges (People v. Wilson, 3 Ill. App. 368); and it must be applied to the expenditures of the current fiscal year; it cannot be applied to payment of a prior indebtedness. Highway Comrs. v. Newell, 80 Ill. 587.

Where the amount is extended by the county clerk the tax is legally levied. Thatcher v. People, 79 Ill. 597. See also Wabash, St. L. & P. R. Co. v. Binkert, 106 Ill. 298; Leachman v. Dougherty, 81 Ill. 324; Baird v. People, *supra*.

An absolute duty is imposed upon counties by statute to aid in the building of bridges by the town authorities whenever a case is brought within its provisions. Will County v. People, 110 Ill. 511.

The taxes raised cannot be diverted to any other than road purposes. Highway Comrs. v. Newell, *supra*.

In Indiana the commissioners are clothed with jurisdiction to locate, establish and construct free public roads. Million v. Carroll County, 89 Ind. 5; Muncey v. Joest, 74 Ind. 409; Porter v. Stout, 73 Ind. 3; Mullikin v. Bloomington, 72 Ind. 161; Miller v. Porter, 71 Ind. 521; Faris v. Reynolds, 70 Ind. 359.

Taxation by local assessment is applied to the construction of a road through an agricultural district (Goodrich v. Winchester & D. Turnp. Co. 26 Ind. 119), and the same is the rule in Kentucky (Malchus v. Highlands, 4 Bush, 547); but in Pennsylvania the same rule is not applied. *Re* Washington Avenue, 69 Pa. 352.

In Iowa when taxes for road purposes are collected, they are held as a trust fund to be disposed of as the law provides. Butler v. Fayette County, 46 Iowa, 326; Des Moines & M. R. Co. v. Lowry, 51 Iowa, 486.

A mere irregularity in the levy will not defeat its collection. Iowa R. R. L. Co. v. Sac County, 39 Iowa, 124; Iowa R. R. L. Co. v. Carroll County, 39 Iowa, 151; Cedar Rapids & M. R. Co. v. Carroll County, 41 Iowa, 153; Sioux City & St. P. R. Co. v. Osceola County, 45 Iowa, 168.

In Kansas where a township road tax is levied by the township trustees and county commissioners, and the tax is properly entered on the county tax roll, it is valid. Kansas City, Ft. S. & G. R. Co. v. Tontz, 29 Kan. 460.

In Maine to enable the assessor to make the money assessment the selectmen must have the return of the surveyor showing who are delinquent, and then assess the highway tax in the list of next year. Hayford v. Belfast, 69 Me. 65; Patterson v. Creighton, 42 Me. 378; Tufts v. Lexington, 72 Me. 516; Ingalls v. Auburn, 51 Me. 352; Treat v. Orono, 26 Me. 217.

In Massachusetts town assessors are not obliged to levy a separate highway tax, such taxes being abolished by statute. Westhampton v. Searle, 127 Mass. 502.

tion, except for the support of free schools, payment of indebtedness existing at the time of the adoption of this Constitution, and for the payment of any indebtedness, with the interest thereon, created under the succeeding section, unless such assessment, with all questions involving the increase of such aggregate, shall have been submitted to the vote of the people of the county, and have received three fifths of all the votes cast for or against it." What is the meaning of the words used in said section, "County authorities shall never assess taxes in any one year?" What taxes are here meant? Do these words refer only to taxes imposed for general county charges under the levy called "county levy," or do they mean these road taxes also? The language is broad and comprehensive,—"county authorities" and "taxes." It seems to me that the Constitution contemplates four classes of taxes,—state, county, municipal and school-district taxes. Plainly, it contemplates state, county and municipal taxes, and I think, also, district taxes for education, since § 6, art. 12, provides for subdivision of counties into school districts, providing that "the school districts into which any county is now divided shall continue until changed in pursuance of law;" and section 5 of same article provides that the Legislature shall provide for raising in each county or district money for free schools; and § 8, art. 10, provides that no county, city, school district or municipal corporation shall incur debt except as prescribed. The Legislature has so construed the Constitution by creating the board of education of each district a corporation, and vesting it with power to tax for funds in its keeping, and for its distribution. So, I think, the Constitution contemplates district taxes for school purposes, as distinct from taxes assessed by county authorities. If so, we have state taxes, school-district taxes for schools and municipal taxes, but no other district taxes save those levied by the county authorities; and so I know not where we should rank these road taxes, if not as those assessed by county authorities, within the meaning of § 7, art. 10, above quoted,—not levied for general county charges, but by county authorities, though expended for works in the district. Besides those specified, there is no other taxing power.

The section in question says that county authorities shall never assess taxes in any one year, the aggregate of which shall exceed ninety-five cents per $100, except for the support of free schools. If the Constitution contemplated only district taxation for school purposes the mere presence of this exception in the section would be of almost decisive import to show that the section included in its limitation of taxing power district taxes; but the fact that the Constitution contemplates local support for schools either by county or district tax detracts somewhat from the significance of this exception. Still, not without weight may it be said that, as both district and county taxation are allowed for schools, by the Constitution, this exception applies to both. Exceptions prove the rule. The fact that certain exceptions from this limitation are specified tends to show that all other taxes are meant to be included within the limitation. Another feature of this section 7 strikes me as significant of its meaning, and that is the presence of the word "aggregate," the provision being that county authorities shall never assess taxes, "the aggregate of which shall exceed ninety-five cents per $100 valuation," evidently meaning that more than one kind or species of taxes must be added together for the purposes of the limit of taxation here prescribed. What shall be added? Not charges for the many objects of expendi-

---

In Michigan roads and highways are under control of boards of supervisors, the policy of the State being against improvement of highways by taxation of the people. Atty-Gen. v. Bay County, 34 Mich. 46; Benjamin v. Manistee R. I. Co. 42 Mich. 628; People v. Springwells, 25 Mich. 153.

They have no authority to order money to be raised as a part of the county taxes, to be expended upon the highways in a township. Sage v. Stevens (Mich.) Nov. 23, 1888. See Stockle v. Silsbee, 41 Mich. 615.

In Missouri a road tax is a county tax, within the meaning of the special charter of the Hannibal & St. Joseph Railroad Company (Mo. Acts 1847, p. 157, § 4), exempting that company from payment of county taxes. State v. Hannibal & St. J. R. Co. (Mo.) March 10, 1890.

In Nebraska under the Constitution a land road tax levied without regard to valuation at the rate of $4 per quarter-section is void. Dundy v. Richardson County, 8 Neb. 508; McCann v. Merriam, 11 Neb. 241; Covell v. Young, 11 Neb. 510. See Burlington & M. R. R. Co. v. Saunders County, 9 Neb. 507.

But a statute authorizing a road tax not exceeding $4 to the acre, to be paid in labor at option, is not void on the ground of inequality. Burlington & M. R. R. Co. v. Lancaster County, 4 Neb. 293. See Gunnison County v. Owen, 7 Colo. 467.

The requirement of equality in the Constitution is complied with, if observed as to the jurisdiction for whose use the particular taxes are laid. Pleuler v. State, 11 Neb. 547; Miller v. Hurford, 11 Neb. 377, 13 Neb. 13.

In New Hampshire a petition for a highway must be served on parties entitled to notice, but the record of the laying out of a highway, though conveying no statement of notice or award of damages, is evidence of its having been laid out. Sanborn v. Meredith, 58 N. H. 150; Thompson v. Major, 58 N. H. 242.

A vote to raise money to repair highways and bridges and for winter purposes, if needed, is sufficiently definite to authorize assessment of the tax. Taft v. Barrett, 58 N. H. 447. See Tilton v. Pittsfield, 58 N. H. 327; Kimball v. Russell, 56 N. H. 488.

In New Jersey a road becomes a highway either by being laid out under a statute or by being used as a highway for twenty years, or by dedication to public use by the owner and being accepted by the township or city wherein it is laid. Holmes v. Jersey City, 12 N. J. Eq. 299; State v. Union Twp. 44 N. J. L. 603.

The Legislature may provide for the re-assessment of damages and benefits for opening and grading roads included in a scheme for local improvement. State v. Union Twp. 44 N. J. L. 599; State v. Union, 33 N. J. L. 350; State v. Newark, 34 N. J. L. 236; State v. Union Twp. 37 N. J. L. 271.

A city has a right to have an undue apportionment between it and the county reviewed on certiorari, and payment of the tax by individuals will not prevent the setting it aside. State v. Newark, 44 N. J. L. 424.

In New York making and improving highways, and the imposition of taxes therefor, are ordinary subjects of legislation. People v. Flagg, 46 N. Y.

ture which a county may incur, but classes or kinds of taxes. Take all this language, and the prohibition is broad.

But, in addition to the foregoing views, based only on the Constitution, let us examine the Act of the Legislature under which this question arises, that called the "Alternate Road Law," with a view to see what class of taxes we shall denominate the taxes imposed under it, and determine whether we should regard them as raised by "county authorities." It provides that the county court shall appoint three road surveyors in the district, and these surveyors shall report to the county the amount of money necessary to open and keep in repair the roads of the district, payable in the next year; and it is made the duty of the court to examine such report, and the estimates therein, and make such alterations and corrections therein as the court may see proper, and when it levies for the county debts and liabilities, to levy tax on the male inhabitants and property of the district liable for state and county purposes, which "shall be collected and disbursed in the same manner." Claims for work and other road expenses must be certified to the county court; and, if found correct, shall be allowed by the court, and paid, on order or warrant of the court, by the sheriff. The district lays no tax, nor does its board of surveyors. They allow no claims on the fund. All this is done by the county court. The court alters or corrects the estimate sent it by the surveyors. The tax is imposed upon the inhabitants and property of the district, and expended in the district; but it is estimated, laid and disbursed by the county court,—not by district authorities. The county courts, which are certainly county authorities, by § 24. art. 8, of the Constitution, have the superintendence and administration of the internal police and fiscal affairs of their counties, including the establishment and regulation of roads, etc. Thus, both the Constitution and this Statute place roads under this county authority; and it may be said these road taxes are under its authority, both under the power to regulate roads and under its power over the fiscal affairs of the county. I do not see that, because the roads are by the Legislature to be kept up by taxes levied in each district, for the roads therein, that it is any the less a tax levied by the county authorities, within the meaning of § 7, art. 10.

There is another view favoring this conclusion, and, in my opinion, a forcible view. The manifest design of the convention and people in adopting that section was to limit and restrict local taxation; a power very necessary to local administration, but one to be jealously guarded, and one often made the medium or instrument of burdensome exaction. It should be given a construction which will effectuate the end so plainly in view. Is it plausible to say that the Constitution would limit taxation for county purposes, and leave unlimited an equally dangerous taxation for district purposes? The county purpose has as much reason for an unlimited power of taxation as the district purpose, and more. This construction would distrust the county court as to the ordinary county levy, and trust it as to the levy for district purposes. On the opposite theory, keeping the poor, and other duties under present statutes performed by county courts, might be devolved on the districts, and minor duties left the courts; and, as district taxation is unlimited, the people might be ground down by taxation. The Constitution never intended to tolerate such a result. The provision under consideration is found in the Constitution under the chapter "Taxation and Finance." I think section 7 of article 10 was intended to protect the taxpayers against unlimited levy as to all taxes except state and school taxes, and taxes levied by municipal corporations. Municipal corporations, such as cities and towns,

---

401. See Ayers v. Lawrence, 59 N. Y. 192; People v. Ulster County, 93 N. Y. 397; *Re* Church, 92 N. Y. 1; People v. Esopus, 74 N. Y. 310.

In North Carolina road taxes which may be discharged by labor are governed by the principle which governs taxation of the labor itself. Osborne v. Mecklenburg County, 82 N. C. 400.

In Ohio the levying of taxes by the county commissioners for the purchase of toll roads to make them free public roads is a constitutional exercise of the taxing power. Warder v. Comrs. 38 Ohio St. 639.

Where the improvement of a public road is petitioned for, and is found to be a public necessity, the commissioners cannot improve a part only, nor assess for the payment of such part. Robinson v. Logan, 31 Ohio St. 466; Cincinnati v. Cincinnati & S. G. Ave. Co. 26 Ohio St. 345.

A municipal council is not entitled to control any part of the taxes levied for road purposes, except as provided for. Lima v. McBride, 34 Ohio St. 338.

In Oregon the paramount and primary control of highways in a State, and of streets in a city, is vested in the Legislature. East Portland v. Multnomah County, 6 Or. 62.

In Pennsylvania the principle of local assessment cannot be applied to agricultural lands, for the purpose of defraying the expense of constructing roads. *Re* Washington Avenue, 69 Pa. 360.

An assessment according to the frontage rule of valuation in the rural districts for improvement of the public highways is unconstitutional. Craig v. Philadelphia, 89 Pa. 265; Seely v. Pittsburgh, 82 Pa. 360.

Persons must be given an opportunity to work out their highway taxes. Miller v. Gorman, 38 Pa. 309.

In Vermont the county court has jurisdiction to establish a highway extending into two adjoining towns though no application has been made to the selectmen. Platt v. Milton, 55 Vt. 490.

In Wisconsin notice must be given the taxpayer of the time and place to appear and pay his highway tax in labor. Biss v. New Haven, 42 Wis. 607; Matteson v. Rosendale, 37 Wis. 254; State v. Nelson, 57 Wis. 148.

Where owners or occupants are petitioners for the alteration of a highway, notice of meeting of the supervisors need not be served upon them. *Ibid.*

Statutes authorizing the county board to levy a county-road tax for grading, graveling, ditching or otherwise improving highways, do not authorize the rebuilding of a bridge at extraordinary expense. State v. Wood County, 72 Wis. 629.

Abutting property can be assessed for highway improvements only to the extent of actual benefits to be estimated upon actual view by the commissioner of public works. Johnson v. Milwaukee, 40 Wis. 327; Hersey v. Barron County, 37 Wis. 75. See Hebard v. Ashland County, 55 Wis. 145; Judd v. Fox Lake, 28 Wis. 583.

fall under section 9 of article 10, which provides that the Legislature may confer on them powers of taxation. Of course, their authorities are not county authorities, but municipal authorities, wielding to a certain extent powers of local government distinguishing them from counties and districts; and they are distinct therefrom,—have corporate existence unlike counties and districts, which are mere territorial subdivisions. I do not think that the provision that a proposition to levy beyond said limit must be submitted "to the vote of the people of the county" has force to rebut the construction I have expressed. If the levy is to affect the people of the entire county, the question must be submitted to all its people; if to affect those of a district only, it must be submitted to them. They are all people of the county, in a sense,—in the sense contemplated in the section. The major includes the minor. It is impossible to find language entirely exact and rigidly applicable in all contingencies. We must look at the reason and purpose, and apply the language to accomplish them. The construction contended for is too literal and narrow.

A decision of the Supreme Court of Illinois in the case of *Wabash, St. L. & P. R. Co.* v. *McCleave*, 108 Ill. 368, is pressed upon our consideration for the appellant. Section 7, art. 10, of our Constitution is phrased like section 8, art. 9, of the Illinois Constitution, which reads: "County authorities shall never assess taxes, the aggregate of which shall exceed seventy-five cents per $100 valuation;" and our section 7 was borrowed from it. Decisions made by the Illinois court, before the adoption of our Constitution, construing this clause, would be authority to us; but this decision was in 1884, and is not binding authority. It holds that "town taxes levied for township purposes are not county taxes, within the meaning of § 8, art. 9, of the Constitution, prohibiting county authorities from assessing taxes the aggregate of which shall exceed seventy-five cents on the $100 of valuation, except for the payment of indebtedness existing at the adoption of that instrument. Such towns are municipal corporations, and taxes levied by them are for corporate purposes."

This case is not, however, in conflict with this view. The reason it held such taxes not county taxes, as stated in the syllabus, was that such towns are municipal corporations, and taxes levied by them are for corporate purposes. The judge delivering the opinion said: "The towns are municipal corporations, under the Township Organization Law, and these taxes were levied for corporate purposes. But appellant urges that the law does not authorize the levy of taxes for organized townships; that the law authorizing the levy and collection of taxes for towns refers to incorporated villages. To show that there is not the slightest ground for this objection, we have but to turn to almost any section of the Township Organization Law to see that such townships are called 'towns.' . . . The last clause of § 9, art. 9, of the Constitution, recognizes the power of the Legislature to authorize these bodies to levy and collect taxes for municipal purposes. This is the entire section: 'The General Assembly may vest the corporate authorities of cities, towns and villages with power to make local improvements by special assessment, or by special taxation of contiguous property, or otherwise. For all other corporate purposes, all municipal corporations may be vested with authority to assess and collect taxes, but such taxes shall be uniform in respect to persons and property within the jurisdiction of the body imposing the same.'"

This is just like § 9, art. 10, of our Constitution; and, were the tax here in question a tax levied by a municipal corporation, as in the Illinois case, I should reach the same opinion as that court did. There was another reason why that was not a tax assessed by "county authorities." The judge in the opinion gives as another reason for his conclusion the fact that the Illinois Statute required the clerk to estimate the rate per cent on the valuation of property in the several towns, townships, districts and incorporated cities and villages, to produce the amount certified to the county board as needed, and then required the clerk to extend the tax on the collector's book. The judge said: "Thus it is seen that it was not necessary that the board of supervisors should have made any levy of these municipal taxes. These sections impose the duty on the county clerk without any action on the part of the board. The order of the board in reference to these local taxes added nothing to, nor did it detract anything from, their validity. So, if anything more was needed to show these were not county taxes, this is conclusive of that question, as they are not levied by the board. They are levied by the town authorities, by filing their certificate of the amount required with the county clerk."

In West Virginia it is just the reverse as to these road taxes. The court alone levies them. If this decision is to be construed as justifying the Legislature in making what is not essentially a municipal corporation a municipal corporation, by simply calling it such, as, for instance, to make a mere political subdivision, like a district, a municipal corporation, and thus give it taxing power not limited by said § 7, art. 10, we do not approve it. See the later Illinois case of *Wright* v. *Wabash, St. L. & P. R. Co.* 120 Ill. 541, 9 West. Rep. 744.

The question of the constitutionality of this Road Statute has been argued. When that Statute says that road taxes shall be levied, and gives no limit, it must be taken that it means that they shall be levied within the constitutional limit. The county court must have an eye to that limit, and so apportion the assessment as will, in their judgment, best answer the public interest, but must keep within the limit; and, if that be not adequate for public wants, all that can be said is, "So the Constitution is written." I think that § 7, art. 10, has the function of limiting all taxes levied in a county except school taxes, and those of municipal corporations.

It is argued that this road tax is not a tax. It has all the features, qualities and elements of a tax, and is called a tax in the Statute which imposes it. Taxes are defined as being "the enforced proportional contributions of persons and property, levied by the authority of the State, for the support of the government, and for all public needs. They are the property of the citizen, demanded and received by the government, to be disposed of to enable it to carry into effect its mandates, and to discharge its manifold functions." Cooley, Taxn. 1.

"They are burdens or charges imposed by the legislative power of a State upon persons or property to raise money for public purposes." Blackw. Tax Titles, 1.

This road tax is certainly a tax.

The decree of the Circuit Court is affirmed, with $30 damages, and costs to appellee, against said County Court.

Snyder, *P.*, and **English** and **Lucas,** *JJ.*, concurred.

MASSACHUSETTS SUPREME JUDICIAL COURT.

John C. WILSON
v.
MARTIN-WILSON AUTOMATIC FIRE ALARM CO., *Appt.*

(....Mass.....)

Letters-patent may be sold and transferred by a court of equity through its master for the benefit of creditors of their owner under Stat. 1884, chap. 285, even although he is a nonresident of the State, if the court has acquired jurisdiction which will enable it to bind him with a personal judgment.

(*W. Allen and Field, JJ., dissent.*)

(June 17, 1890.)

APPEAL by defendant from a judgment of the Superior Court for Suffolk County in favor of complainant in a suit brought to reach certain letters-patent belonging to defendant and apply them to the payment of its debt. *Affirmed.*

The case sufficiently appears in the opinion.

Messrs. **George Putnam** and **R. D. Weston-Smith** for appellant.

Mr. **Frank T. Benner** for appellee.

Knowlton, *J.*, delivered the opinion of the court:

This case has previously been before us on the defendant's demurrer, and it was decided that the demurrer should be overruled, and that the service was sufficient to enable the court to render a personal judgment against the Company, which would be held good in any other jurisdiction as well as in this. 149 Mass. 24. A hearing has since been had, and the case now comes here on an appeal from the final decree. The defendant concedes that all parts of the decree are well warranted by the law and the facts, except that part which provides that, if the defendant shall refuse or neglect to make and deliver a written assignment of the letters-patent to the purchaser after a sale at public auction by the master under the decree, the master shall "make and deliver such assignment to said purchaser in the name and on behalf of the defendant corporation."

Two objections are made to this part of the decree: first, that an order for a sale of property by a master or other person appointed for that purpose can be made by a court of equity only under the authority of a statute and that there is no statute which authorizes it in this case; secondly, that a patent right is property of such a nature that the title cannot be passed by a sale or assignment made under an order of the court by any other person than the owner, even if it were in other respects within the jurisdiction of the court to make such an order.

It is undoubtedly true that, primarily, jurisdiction in equity is *in personam,* and that as a general rule, when a transfer of property is necessary, the court cannot order a conveyance of it by a person other than the owner, except under the express or implied authority of a statute.

The foundation of the jurisdiction to which the plaintiff appeals is the Statute of 1851, chap. 206 (Pub. Stat. chap. 151, § 2, cl. 11), which authorizes "bills by creditors to reach and apply any property, right, title or interest, legal or equitable, of a debtor within this State, which cannot be come at to be attached or taken on execution in a suit at law against such debtor." This Statute was passed long before the courts of this State were given general jurisdiction in equity, and it was early interpreted as creating rights unknown to the courts of chancery in England. It was held that a suit under it was not like an ordinary creditor's bill, but that any creditor might proceed without making other creditors parties, and without first obtaining judgment, and while he held security, and that it gave him right of equitable attachment for the collection of his debt. *Crompton* v. *Anthony,* 13 Allen, 33, 37; *Barry* v. *Abbot,* 100 Mass. 396; *Tucker* v. *McDonald,* 105 Mass. 423.

In some particulars the court construed it rather strictly, and held that a patent right owned by a resident here was not property within the State within the meaning of the Statute, and that a creditor could not, under this process, reach and apply an equitable remainder of the debtor in a trust fund, upon the future debt of an equitable tenant for life, nor any other property when his claim was for less than $100, and intimated that the Statute would not apply except in cases where there was a third person in possession or control of the property of the debtor, or in some way under obligation to him. *Carver* v. *Peck,* 131 Mass. 291; *Chapman* v. *Banker & T. Pub. Co.* 128 Mass. 478; *Russell* v. *Milton,* 133 Mass. 180; *Bartholomew* v. *Weld,* 127 Mass. 210; *Phœnix Ins. Co.* v. *Abbott,* 127 Mass. 558.

Thereupon the Statute of 1884, chap. 285, was passed with a view to enlarge the jurisdiction of the court. Section 1 of this chapter is as follows: "A bill in equity may be maintained to reach and apply in payment of a debt any property of a debtor, as provided by cl. 11 of § 2 of chap. 151 of the Public Statutes, notwithstanding the fact that the plaintiff's debt

See also 35 L. R. A. 211.

does not equal $100 in amount, or that the property sought to be reached and applied is in the hands, possession or control of the debtor independently of any other person, or that it is not within the State, or that it is of uncertain value, provided the value can be ascertained by a sale or appraisal, or by any means within the ordinary procedure of the court, or that it cannot be reached and applied until a future time." Section 2 relates to suits to reach and apply the interest of a copartner in the partnership property.

The provisions of this Act indicate an intention on the part of the Legislature to give the court power effectually to reach and apply every kind of property which cannot be attached or taken on execution. It changes the Statute from a mere authority to make an equitable attachment of property in the hands of an equitable trustee, and authorizes proceedings in which there is no other defendant but the debtor, and plainly implies that the court may make all such orders and take such measures as may be necessary to apply the property to the payment of the debt. There can be no doubt that under it a court may proceed against an absent defendant so far as to appropriate his equitable interest in property in this State, which cannot be attached or taken on execution, to the payment of his debt. The only way in which that could be done in his absence might be by appointing some person to sell and convey such interest. The Act does not purport to point out the modes of procedure, but it authorizes the courts to do certain things which they could not do under their general jurisdiction, and impliedly authorizes them to take any measures analogous to ordinary proceedings of courts of equity which may be necessary or proper to accomplish the work which they are set to do. We can imagine many cases in which without authority to order a sale by a master or other person, a court would fail utterly to reach and apply the property which the Statute intended it should apply in favor of the creditor. Indeed the present case seems to be such a one. For it appears that when this bill was brought the president and treasurer and all the directors of the defendant corporation resided or had their places of business in Boston in this Commonwealth, and that all these officers have since resigned their offices and others have been elected in their places, who are all residents of the State of Maine.

One clause of the Statute distinctly refers to a sale of property as a means of ascertaining its value under an order of the court in certain cases. It has never been decided that a sale by a master might not be ordered under the Public Statutes, chap. 151, § 2, cl. 11, and some of the reports indicate that it has been done. *Davis* v. *Werden*, 13 Gray, 305.

However that may be, we are of opinion that under the later Statute there is authority to make a sale in that way, whenever it may be necessary for the purpose of applying property, conformably to the Statute. This view is in accordance with our decision in *McCann* v. *Randall*, 147 Mass. 81.

The next question before us is, whether a patent right so differs from other property that it cannot be sold in this way. This question relates merely to the form of transfer; for it is well settled that a court of equity has power to take it and appropriate it to the payment of the owner's debt. *Gillett* v. *Bate*, 86 N. Y. 87; *Ager* v. *Murray*, 105 U. S. 126 [26 L. ed. 942]; *Pacific Bank* v. *Robinson*, 57 Cal. 520; *Wilson* v. *Martin-Wilson Automatic Fire Alarm Co.* 149 Mass. 24.

Under the Revised Statutes of the United States, § 4884, every patent "shall contain a grant to the patentee, his heirs or assigns."

Section 4898, provides that "every patent or any interest therein shall be assignable in law by an instrument in writing."

An assignment in bankruptcy transfers patent rights. U. S. Rev. Stat.

There is no good reason for holding that this Statute should be construed so strictly as to require an assignment to be made by the patentee's own hand. It is better to hold that an assignment made for him and in his name by anyone acting under legal authority is good, notwithstanding the decisions in *Ashcroft* v. *Walworth*, 1 Holmes, C. C. 152, and *Gordon* v. *Anthony*, 16 Blatchf. 234. We understand this to be the effect of the judgment of the Supreme Court of the United States in *Ager* v. *Murray*, *supra*. We are therefore of the opinion the assignment contemplated by this decree will be good in form under the Statutes of the United States.

It is said that the assignment will be void because a patent is property outside of this Commonwealth which cannot be affected by a judicial sale here. It is true that a judgment or a decree of a court cannot *ex proprio vigore* affect property in another jurisdiction. Titles to real estate can be changed only under and in accordance with the laws of the country where the land is situated; and a decree of a foreign court in regard to personal property can be given no effect against the rights or interests of citizens of the State where the property is situated, nor any effect at all except through comity. Is a patent right property of such a kind, and has it such a *situs* in any particular State, that the courts of one State can disregard a decree determining the ownership of it, made by a court of another State having jurisdiction of the owner of it, and a right to apply it to the payment of his debt? *Carver* v. *Peck*, 131 Mass. 291, and *Stevens* v. *Gladding*, 58 U. S. 17 How. 451 [15 L. ed. 156], indicate that it is not.

It seems to us that the rule to which we have referred relates to visible, tangible property, which a State may say is to be governed by its laws, because it has an actual, visible existence there and not elsewhere—perhaps also to property which cannot be made available except by proceedings under its laws. A patent right is not like a material substance. So far as it has location at all, it is within every part of the United States. But it has no such location anywhere that a particular State can say, "This property is within my jurisdiction. I will not allow any other State to deal with it, but I will control it by my own laws for the benefit of my own people." The reason why ordinary choses in action are usually said to be governed by the law of the place of their owner's domicil is not because they have a local *situs* in themselves, but because they follow the person of their owner, and that place is commonly the only one whose courts have jurisdiction over him.

In the case at bar the defendant was subject to the jurisdiction of the court as much as if it had been a Massachusetts corporation. The right of the court to determine the equitable ownership of the patent, as between the defendant and the plaintiff, is unquestioned. The jurisdiction which settles that is strictly *in personam*. The decree requires the defendant to assign the patent, which is an incorporeal right to be exercised in Massachusetts and elsewhere, and which the corporation carried with it when it went into court on the summons of the plaintiff, and which has no local existence except as it accompanies its owner. The subject matter of the suit was the question as to the ownership of the patent, and as to the duty of the defendant to turn it over to the plaintiff. The decree of the court finding such ownership against a defendant within its jurisdiction, and determining that the property should be transferred for the benefit of the plaintiff, showed jurisdiction in the court to convey the legal title to this peculiar property, which it would not have had to convey an ordinary chattel situated in another State. If in a case of this kind a debtor should refuse to convey the property in accordance with its decree, the court could imprison him. A sale by a master under the order of the court is also authorized by our Statute. The law which has power over a debtor's person has power to determine how and on what conditions a right of his shall be devested, unless the right has relation to tangible property within the jurisdiction of another State which may intervene to control it. It is on this ground, but under a different Statute, that sales are made on executions. Such sales are not founded on proceedings *in rem* which determine the title to the *res* against all the world. But when a court has jurisdiction of a debtor and finds that he owes the debt, the Statute authorizes the issuing of an execution under which his rights in property, whatever they are, may be sold for the benefit of his creditors. The sale is incidental to the determination of his liability.

We are of opinion that other States have no such jurisdiction over the defendant's patent as to affect the validity of a decree which confessedly is good so far as it directs a sale to be made by him, and which would be unquestioned if it related to property wholly within this Commonwealth. This question too, or one much like it, is involved, although but little discussed, in the judgment in *Ager* v. *Murray, supra.*

Decree affirmed.

W. Allen, *J.*, dissenting:

Mr. Justice Field and myself are unable to concur in the decision of the court which affirms that clause of the decree which orders an assignment of the patent to be made by a master. The decree assumes that the court has authority to transfer the title to the patent by decree, for it is immaterial whether the decree directly transfers the title or authorizes a master to do so by a written assignment. The suit is not brought by an owner of property to establish his title to it, and obtain possession of it, but it rests upon the ground that the defendant is the owner, and seeks to effect a change of title.

The ordinary jurisdiction of a court of chancery is *in personam* and not *in rem*, and it is not in accordance with the ordinary procedure of the court to act directly upon property and to transfer the title to it. Whatever authority the court may have to order the payment over or the sale and delivery of property which passes by delivery and is under the control of the court in the manual possession of its sequestrators or receivers or master, so that delivery can be made of it, it cannot transfer or assign a chose in action or an incorporeal right, or change the title to any property by decree without special statute authority. This was fully discussed in the dissenting opinion in *McCann* v. *Randall*, 147 Mass. 81, and is assumed in the opinion of the court in this case, and the authority for the decree is vested on the provision of Stat. 1884, chap. 285, in connection with the earlier Statutes of which that was an amendment. The only question I shall consider is whether that Statute authorized the decree. The question was not decided in *McCann* v. *Randall, supra*, and that case did not decide that the draft which was the property sought to be reached could be assigned by the court. The defendant Manning, in whose possession and control the draft was, within the State, sent it, in disobedience of the injunction of the court, to the principal defendant, the debtor, without the State, in order that he might indorse and collect it; which he did, paying to Manning the amount of a lien he had upon it. Defendant Manning was ordered to pay the amount of the draft less the amount of his lien upon it. In considering whether Stat. 1884, chap. 285, authorized the court to assign a chose in action, it is important to look at the history of the Statute. In 1851 the supreme judicial court was, as now, a court of equity, and as such had jurisdiction of the redemption and foreclosure of mortgages, of trusts, of the specific performance of contracts, of the delivery of goods secreted, etc.; of contribution, of cases where more than two parties were liable; of copartnerships, joint tenancies, etc.; of waste and nuisance, of discovery and of account (Rev. Stat. chap. 81, § 7, chap. 118, § 43), and also of twelve other particular matters which are stated in the index to the Revised Statutes under "Bill in Equity." All this jurisdiction it had had for fifteen years, and it also had during all that time an established procedure under "Rules for the Regulation of Practice in Chancery," the last of which adopted as the outline of their practice the practice of the High Court of Chancery in England, so far as not repugnant to the Constitution and laws of the Commonwealth and the rules of the court. 24 Pick. 410.

The jurisdiction was enlarged by Stat. 1855, chap. 194, to include frauds and conveyances of real estate in the nature of mortgages, and by Stat. 1856, chap. 38, to include accident and mistake, and by Stat. 1857, chap. 214, "full equity jurisdiction, according to the usage and practice of courts of chancery," was given to the court. These Statutes enlarging the equity jurisdiction of the court did not change the procedure in equity. In 1851 this court was as distinctively a court of equity having an established procedure as it is to-day.

Jurisdiction in equity was given in order that the subjects should be brought under the distinctive procedure and process of courts of equity, and to secure the relief which such procedure and process afforded. It was for precisely this purpose that the Statute giving jurisdiction in equity to reach and apply property of debtors was first enacted in 1851. The creditor's bill was unknown to our jurisprudence; there was but little occasion for it. The distribution of the estates of deceased and of insolvent persons was otherwise provided for. The law provided for taking and selling on execution all the property of a debtor which could be taken on process and which it was intended should be liable for his debts, and by the trustee process, goods, effects or credits in the hands of third persons might be reached by proceedings against such persons. In regard to property which could not be taken on execution or attached on trustee process, and which belonged to debtors living in this State, the law furnished substantially the same means as were furnished by a creditor's bill to reach such property, namely, the punishment of the debtor by imprisonment if he did not surrender the property. Rev. Stat. chaps. 90, 98.

There were no means of reaching such property in this Commonwealth which belonged to debtors who were not residents and could not be served with process here. It was to meet this particular mischief in the old law which gave to foreign debtors owning equitable property here an advantage over domestic debtors owning such property, that Stat. 1851, chap. 206, was passed. *Davis* v. *Werden*, 13 Gray, 305.

The language of the Statute is: "The supreme judicial court shall have jurisdiction in equity, upon bill of any creditor to reach and apply, in payment of a debt due from any debtor not residing in this Commonwealth, any property, right, title or interest, legal or equitable, of such debtor, within this Commonwealth, which cannot be come at to be attached or taken on execution in a suit of law against such debtor." The property of a nonresident described by the Statute as within this State would naturally, if not necessarily, be in the possession or legal ownership of a resident here, and the intent of the Statute in giving jurisdiction in equity was that the property might be reached through such person by proceedings *in personam* against him. As originally passed, the Statute is plainly what it has been again and again called by this court, an equitable trustee process and intended only equitable proceedings, and it is impossible to find in it any intention to change the ordinary procedure of the court. It is not and cannot be contended that this Statute gave the court authority to assign a patent. Statute 1858, chap. 34, amended Stat. 1851, chap. 206, by striking out the words "not residing in this Commonwealth," thus making the Act apply to resident and nonresident debtors alike; and, as amended, the Statute was re enacted in Gen. Stat., chap. 113, § 2, cl. 11, and in Pub. Stat., chap. 151, § 2, cl. 11, and remained unchanged until Stat. 1884, chap. 285.

The question is whether that Statute changed the procedure of the court of equity as regards its subject matter and authorized the court to assign a chose in action or incorporeal right. The amendment made by Stat. 1858, chap. 34, which was after the enactment of the Statute giving the court full equity jurisdiction, suggests two important changes in the Statute as originally enacted and as construed by the court. The fact that in the original Act the principal defendant, the debtor, could not be a resident of this Commonwealth, and need not be, and presumably would not be, served with process, and that the property which by the Act was to be reached by proceedings in equity must be within the Commonwealth, and by its nature and situation such that it could not be come at to be attached or taken on execution, naturally led to the construction that there must be some third person within the jurisdiction of the court holding such relation to the property that it could be reached by a personal decree against him.

When by the Amendment of 1858, a debtor residing in the State was made amenable to the suit, the chief ground for that construction was taken away. He must be served with process and be actually or constructively in court. If it appeared that he held in his own possession or control property not exempt from execution, but which could not be come at to be taken on process, it could be reached by the ordinary procedure of a court of equity requiring him to transfer it, and this whether the property were within or without this Commonwealth, and it would be carrying out the general intent of the Statute to authorize the court to enter such a decree. Notwithstanding this Statute the court seemed to hold to the equitable trustee-process construction of the Act (*Phœnix Ins. Co.* v. *Abbott*, 127 Mass. 558), and of course the court could not extend the Acts limited in terms to property within the State, to apply to property without the State. When the Statute was made applicable to residents of the State it became in accordance with the principles and procedure of the courts of equity that it should be extended to property in the hands of the debtor, and to property without the State, because he could be compelled to assign it and it was thus within the reach of a court of equity. This is what was done by Statute 1884, chap. 285, § 1.

It provided that a bill might be maintained under Pub. Stat., chap. 152, § 2, cl. 11, notwithstanding the fact that the property sought to be reached was in the hands, possession or control of the debtor independently of any other person, or that it was not within the State. The Legislature, by extending the scope of the Statute after it had been made to apply to debtors within the State to property in the possession of the debtor, and to property without the jurisdiction of the court, gave a jurisdiction to which a decree *in personam* is especially appropriate, and a decree *in rem* especially inappropriate. The other provisions of the section do not seem material to the question under consideration. It will not be contended that the provision that a bill can be maintained although the property is of uncertain value "provided the value can be ascertained by a sale or appraisal or by any means within the ordinary procedure of the court," authorizes an assignment by the court of a chose in action contrary to the ordinary procedure of the court. It seems to me that the Statute evidently contemplated equitable remedies by decrees *in personam*. If the Statute is to be construed as authorizing a judicial assignment of the title of property which does not pass by delivery it would not justify the decree, because the property in question is not within the Commonwealth, and the decree affects to transfer the title to property outside the jurisdiction of the Legislature and of the courts of this State, and the Statute will not be construed to imply such authority. No question is made of the authority of the court to compel the owner of a patent to assign it to a receiver or a master appointed to receive it, or to a purchaser under the order of the court. The objection is that the court cannot itself by decree transfer the title, for the reason that the patent is not within its jurisdiction. If a patent, according to the general rule of personal property, followed the domicil of its owner, the patent in question would be in the State of Maine, for the owner is a corporation under the laws of that State, and though it may by its agent do business and sue and be sued in other States it cannot change its domicil, nor even pass personally out of the State of its creation. *Augusta Bank* v. *Earle*, 38 U. S. 13 Pet. 519 [10 L. ed. 274]; *Lafayette Ins. Co.* v. *French*, 59 U. S. 18 How. 404 [15 L. ed. 451].

If the patent has no locality except the whole country no State has jurisdiction over it as being properly within its limits, and it can only be reached through the personal act of its owner. A State might indeed by statute order it to be sold on execution or under a decree in chancery and declare the title to be in the purchaser, but such sale would have no more effect outside of the limits of the State than the sale of land in another State would have.

In *Stevens* v. *Gladding*, 58 U. S. 17 How. 451 [15 L. ed. 156], *Mr. Justice* Curtis said in reference to patents and copyrights: "Not to repeat what is said in *Stephens* v. *Cady*, 55 U. S. 14 How. 531 [14 L. ed. 529], it may be added that these incorporeal rights do not exist in any particular State or district; they are coextensive with the United States. There is nothing in any Act of Congress or in the nature of the rights themselves, to give them locality anywhere, so as to subject them to process of courts having jurisdiction limited by the lines of States and districts. That an execution out of the Court of Common Pleas for the County of Bristol in the State of Massachusetts can be levied on an incorporeal right in Rhode Island or New York, will hardly be pretended. That by the way of such an execution the entire right could be divided, and so much of it as might be exercised within the County of Bristol sold, would be a position subject to much difficulty."

Mr. Justice Gray says, in *Ager* v. *Murray*, 105 U. S. 130 [26 L. ed. 943], after quoting the above language: "The difficulties of which the learned justice here speaks are of seizing and selling a patent or copyright upon an execution at law, which is ordinarily levied only upon the property, or the rents and profits of property, that has itself a visible and tangible existence within the jurisdiction of the court, and the precinct of the officer, and do not attend decrees of a court of equity which are *in personam*, and may be enforced in all cases when the person is within its jurisdiction."

It is obvious that it can make no difference as respects the jurisdiction of a State, whether it orders an assignment on an execution of law, or on a decree in equity; the dominion over the property and the assumption of jurisdiction over it are the same in both instances. If it cannot sell and assign it upon process at law, it cannot upon process in equity.

In *Carver* v. *Peck*, 131 Mass. 291, it was held that a patent owned by a resident of this Commonwealth was not property within the State and could not be reached, and the Statute of 1884, extending the jurisdiction to property without the State, was passed. Under that Statute jurisdiction is given, in this case, to compel the defendant to assign the patent (see *Wilson* v. *Martin-Wilson Automatic Fire Alarm Co.* 149 Mass. 25); but the court cannot assume jurisdiction to judicially assign it without overruling the opinion in *Carver* v. *Peck*, and holding that a patent is property within the State. If there was not jurisdiction over the property, before the amendment, for the reason that the property was not within the State, there can be no jurisdiction over the property as within the State after the amendment.

If a patent has location in every part of the United States so that no one State has jurisdiction over it by reason of its locality to the exclusion of other States, and every State has equal jurisdiction over it and an equal right to appropriate it to the benefit of its own citizens as every other State, it follows that no State has jurisdiction over the patent itself, and no State can reach it except through the person of the owner of someone duly authorized by him to assign it. Otherwise there must be legally possible as many different lawful assignors besides the owner as there are States and Territories or judicial districts in the United States. The rights of the States by reason of the locality of the patent are equal, and if any one State has jurisdiction to appropriate it because within its limits every other State must have the same jurisdiction, and as that is impossible, it follows that no State can have the jurisdiction. The fact that the property is incorporeal and intangible and has no visible existence makes it possible to conceive of it as existing in the whole country and in every State; but we cannot conceive of the whole patent in its entirety as having its locality in the whole country and in the several States at the same time. The fact that the property is immaterial and has no actual visible location, certainly cannot aid the jurisdiction over it, which is dependent upon its locality. The State cannot have jurisdiction over it except so far as it is within the State, and so far as the patent is within other States it is not within this State.

Again, the Statute will not be construed to give authority to the court to assign patent rights, and the court will not decree an assignment of them, because the title would not pass by such an assignment. A patent right is assignable only because expressly made so by the Statute which created it, and in the manner prescribed by the Statute. The assignment must be by an instrument in writing by the patentee or his assigns or legal representatives, and it will be void as against subsequent purchasers without notice unless recorded in the patent office within three months from its date. U. S. Rev. Stat. § 4898.

The natural construction of this is that a patent cannot be assigned, and that no state law can make it assignable, in any other way than the one prescribed.

In *Stephens* v. *Cady*, 55 U. S. 14 How. 528 [14 L. ed. 528], speaking of copyrights, *Mr. Justice* Nelson said: "No doubt the property may be reached by a creditor's bill and be applied to the payment of the debts of the author, the same as stock of the debtor is reached and applied for the benefit of the creditors. But in the case of such remedy we suppose it would be necessary for the court to compel a transfer to the purchaser in conformity with the requirements of the Copyrights Act, in order to invest him with a complete title to the property."

In *Ashcroft* v. *Walworth*, 1 Holmes, C. C. 152, it was decided that the Statute "clearly contemplated a written assignment signed by the owner of the patent," and that a court of insolvency of Massachusetts, to vest the title to a patent in the assignee, must compel a transfer in conformity with requirements of the Patent Act.

In *Gordan* v. *Anthony*, 16 Blatchf. 234, the same construction of the Statute was adopted, and it was held that a state court could not vest the title to a patent in a receiver except by compelling an assignment by the patentee.

In *Pacific Bank* v. *Robinson*, 57 Cal. 520, the court said of a patent: "As a creation of legislation it is transferable only according to the provisions of the Statute which created it, and the only question is, Has a court of equity power to compel its assignment and sale for the benefit of creditors?".

The decree required the defendant to transfer by a proper instrument. I see no reason for supposing that the patent office, or any United States court or any state court, outside of the State whose court made the decree, would recognize a transfer of a patent by decree of a state court.

Ager v. *Murray*, 105 U. S. 126 [26 L. ed. 942], is the only case where an assignment of a patent was ordered to be made by a trustee, and that case decided nothing as to the form of the decree. That was a bill brought in the courts of the District of Columbia against residents of the District. The prayer of the bill was that the patent be sold and the defendant be required to execute an assignment to the purchaser in conformity with the Patent Laws. The decree was that in default of payment of the amount found due, the patent right be sold and an assignment executed as prayed for, and in default of defendant's executing such assignment, some suitable person be appointed a trustee to execute the same. This was the form of decree authorized by the Statute of Maryland of 1785, chap. 72, which was in force in the District of Columbia. The defendants appealed from the decree. The court says: "The single question argued before us is whether a patent right may be ordered by a court of equity to be sold, and the proceeds applied to the payment of a judgment debt of the patentee." It was decided that it could be sold, but the manner in which it was understood by the court that it could be transferred appears in the extract before given from the opinion and from the reference to the case of *Stephens* v. *Cady*. The court, after reciting the facts, says: "The case is thus brought directly within the opinion delivered by *Mr Justice* Nelson in *Stephens* v. *Cady*, of the soundness of which we entertain no doubt. The clause of the decree below, appointing a trustee to execute an assignment, if the patentee shall not himself execute one, has not been objected to in the argument, and was clearly within the chancery powers of the court as defined in the Statute of Maryland."

The decree of the court below was affirmed. I do not regard the case as deciding that there could be a valid assignment of a patent by a decree of a state court, where the defendant is a resident of the State and its statutes expressly authorize such a decree,—much less when the defendant is a nonresident, and there is no such statute of the State.

There can be no doubt that an assignment by the defendant *lis pendens* would be recognized everywhere, unless in our own court. If the defendant should assign by an instrument duly recorded to a bona fide purchaser for value in Maine, and the question of the title to the patent should come before our courts between him and a subsequent purchaser and assignee under the decree of the court, I do not see why our courts would not have to declare the title they made to be invalid. The court has no control over the property, and no lien or hold upon it. It is not and never has been in the possession of the court, for the appearance in the suit of a foreign corporation by its attorney or agent does not bring its property into court. All that the court can do is to restrain the defendant from assigning, but if it should assign, in contempt of the restraint, to a bona fide purchaser, I understand that the assignment would be good. The court has not obtained possession of the property, nor of the letters-patent, the evidence and symbol of it; and if it attempts to assign the property, it must do so without the possession of it, actual or constructive, and without the means of knowing, except so far as the records in the patent office may show, whether it then belongs to the defendant. It can make no delivery of the property, or of any symbol of it; all that it can do is to give to the purchaser an instrument, in form an assignment, from a person not the owner and send him to the patent office to have his assignment recorded. But if it is entitled to record, so would be the forty like assignments from the States, which might be presented. If record was refused, would any court compel the recording of such assignments? And if they should all be recorded, how would it be determined which was the one valid assignment? And if that were found, would it hold good against a prior or a subsequent assignment from the owner, duly recorded, or even if not recorded? The answer is that no assignment is valid except by an instrument in writing signed by the owner as required by the Statute.

For the reasons that the clause of the decree which orders the master to make an assignment in behalf of the defendant is not warranted by the ordinary procedure of courts of equity, and is not authorized by the Statute, because the Statute does not authorize such an assignment of a chose in action, nor of property without the Commonwealth, nor of a patent right, I think the decree should be modified by striking out that clause.

Whether the decree should be further modified by ordering an assignment to a master before the sale, has not been considered.

J. A. RICE

v.

Sidney SANDERS, *Appt.*

(....Mass....)

1. A grantee who assumes and agrees to pay, as part of the purchase price of land, a mortgage which his grantor has given thereon, thereby undertakes to discharge the mortgagee's lien upon the land and not simply to cancel the mortgage debt so far as it is a claim against individuals, and his failure to do so will render him liable to at least nominal damages.

2. If several mortgages are so assumed and the grantee fails to pay the one first due and permits it to be foreclosed and the property sold for its payment, he will be liable in damages to his grantor for the latter's loss of security against liability upon subsequent mortgages up to the amount of debts secured by them, even though they are not yet due.

(Field, Devens and W. Allen, JJ., dissent.)

3. A set-off cannot be allowed under Pub. Stat., chap. 168, §§ 3-7, in an action brought to recover unliquidated damages for a breach of contract, of a claim which is of the same kind as that to recover which the action is brought.

(Rescript June 27, 1890. Opinions July 16, 1890.)

APPEAL by defendant from a judgment of the Superior Court for Franklin County in favor of plaintiff in an action brought to recover damages for breach of contract to pay a certain mortgage. *Affirmed.*

Plaintiff made a deed of certain land to defendant, excepting therein from the covenant against incumbrances two mortgages for $1,200 and $500 respectively, immediately followed by the clause "which mortgages the said Sanders assumes and agrees to pay."

The $1,200 mortgage was payable on demand. Nothing would become due on the $500 mortgage until January 1, 1890. On June 8, 1889, the first mortgagee sold the premises under his mortgage for $1,800. This action was brought June 4, 1889, to recover damages for loss of security to meet and cover the $500 mortgage.

The case further appears in the opinion.

Mr. **Sidney Sanders,** appellant, *in propria persona:*

If the premises had sold for enough to pay both mortgages and all expenses, the proceeds

---

NOTE.—*Mortgagor may convey premises subject to mortgage debt.*

A mortgagor has always the right to convey his land subject to the mortgage. Northrup v. Hottenstein, 38 Kan. 263.

Where a purchaser of premises assumes the payment of a mortgage as part of the purchase money, the premises purchased are the primary fund for the payment of the debt, and it is his duty to pay it. Drury v. Holden, 9 West. Rep. 799, 121 Ill. 130; Lilly v. Palmer, 51 Ill. 331; Russell v. Pistor, 7 N. Y. 171.

And the rule is the same, although there can be no such assumption if the purchase be made expressly subject to the incumbrance. Drury v. Holden, *supra;* Comstock v. Hitt, 37 Ill. 542; Fowler v. Fay, 62 Ill. 375; Ferris v. Crawford, 2 Denio, 598.

In paying off the mortgage he simply performs the condition, subject to which he succeeded to the mortgage estate. Knowles v. Carpenter, 8 R. I. 552; Ferris v. Crawford, *supra;* Cumberland v. Codrington, 3 Johns. Ch. 229; Waring v. Ward, 7 Ves. Jr. 339.

The obligation of the purchaser when he assumes the debt inures in equity to the benefit of the mortgagee and may be enforced in a bill to foreclose his mortgage. Crawford v. Edwards, 33 Mich. 360.

Or the mortgagee may maintain a personal action against him without foreclosing the mortgage and without joining the mortgagor as defendant. Burr v. Beers, 24 N. Y. 179; Curtis v. Tyler, 9 Paige, 432; King v. Whitely, 10 Paige, 465; Vail v. Foster, 4 N. Y. 312; Belmont v. Coman, 22 N. Y. 438; Meech v. Ensign, 49 Conn. 206; Hoff's App. 24 Pa. 200; Urquhart v. Brayton, 12 R. I. 169; Bissell v. Bugbee, 7 Reporter, 550, 8 Cent. L. J. 272; Crowell v. Currier, 27 N. J. Eq. 152.

A special agreement between the purchaser and the seller of the equity of redemption, by which the amount of the mortgage debt is considered as so much money left in the hands of the purchaser for the use of the mortgagee, would be sufficient ground for a suit at law by the mortgagee. Garnsey v. Rogers, 47 N. Y. 233; Real Estate Trust Co. v. Balch, 13 Jones & S. 534; Higman v. Stewart, 38 Mich. 523.

A purchaser of the equity of redemption by merely accepting without signing the deed, providing he "assumes and agrees to pay" the mortgage debt, is personally liable therefor; and after foreclosure a court of equity will enforce his liability for any deficiency, by subrogating the mortgagee to the contract made by the mortgagor. Davis v. Hulett, 2 New Eng. Rep. 122, 58 Vt. 90; Schley v. Fryer, 1 Cent. Rep. 5, 100 N. Y. 71.

Grantor must be personally liable.

The covenant by the grantee to pay the mortgage debt will support an action by the mortgagee only when the immediate grantor of the covenantor is himself liable for the mortgage debt. Wilbur v. Warren, 6 Cent. Rep. 216, 104 N. Y. 192.

Where a grantor of an equity of redemption in mortgaged premises is not personally liable to pay the mortgage debt, and has no legal or equitable interest in such payment, except so far as the mortgage may be a charge upon the lands mortgaged, his grantee thereof incurs no liability to the holder of the mortgage by reason of a covenant on his part contained in the deed, to assume and pay the mortgage. Vrooman v. Turner, 69 N. Y. 280; Cashman v. Henry, 75 N. Y. 107, 5 Abb. N. C. 232, 12 Jones & S. 97, 55 How. Pr. 238; Norwood v. De Hart, 30 N. J. Eq. 414; Birke v. Abbott, 8 West. Rep. 331, 103 Ind. 1; Wilbur v. Warren, 6 Cent. Rep. 214, 104 N. Y. 196, 40 Hun, 205; Merriman v. Social Mfg. Co. 12 R. I. 186, in dissenting opinion; Huyler v. Atwood, 26 N. J. Eq. 505; National Union Bank v. Segur, 39 N. J. L. 173; Dean v. Walker, 107 Ill. 547; Trotter v. Hughes,

sufficient to pay the second mortgagee would have gone to him and not to plaintiff, though his claim is not due, so completely is the plaintiff out of all right to the property.

Andrews v. *Fiske*, 101 Mass. 422-424.

The defendant's obligation, if anything, was to pay the mortgages when due and not before.

Furnas v. *Durgin*, 119 Mass. 500-507; *Gaffney* v. *Hicks*, 124 Mass. 301-304; *Locke* v. *Homer*, 131 Mass. 93-105; *Reed* v. *Paul*, 131 Mass. 129-132.

This was a personal obligation and nothing more.

Parish v. *Whitney*, 3 Gray, 516; *Martin* v. *Drinan*, 128 Mass. 515.

There was never any breach of the defendant's alleged contract.

Plaintiff's whole claim is barred by his covenant to warrant and defend. This covenant is not simply a covenant real, but a personal contract with all the incidents of personal contract (*Cole* v. *Raymond*, 9 Gray, 217-219), and estops or rebuts the plaintiff from setting up any titles, or, the same thing, claims based on titles, adverse to what he has conveyed and warranted to the defendant.

Somes v. *Skinner*, 3 Pick. 52; *Knight* v. *Thayer*, 125 Mass. 25; *Bates* v. *Norcross*, 17 Pick. 14.

Mr. **S. T. Field** for appellee.

Knowlton, *J.*, delivered the opinion of the court:

By accepting his deed from the plaintiff, the defendant assumed and agreed to pay two mortgages, of which one was then over due, and the other was payable by installments to become due in the future. It was a single but divisible contract, containing a promise, first, to pay one mortgage immediately, and secondly, to pay the other when it should become due. In proceedings to recover damages for a breach of the contract, each part of it should be considered separately. It is agreed that there has been no breach as to the second mortgage, and damages can be recovered in this action only for neglect to assume and pay the first mortgage. The plaintiff claims damages of two kinds: first, those resulting from the defendant's failure to relieve him from personal liability on the mortgage debt, and secondly, those growing out of the defendant's neglect to obtain a discharge of the first mortgage, whereby the plaintiff has been deprived of a benefit which should have resulted to his security for the payment of the second mortgage. If he can recover only for the failure to relieve him from liability on the mortgage debt, the damage should be only nominal; for before the suit was brought, the mortgage was foreclosed, and the debt was paid from the proceeds of the sale of the mortgaged property. If, on the other hand, he can recover on account of the defendant's neglect to do that which would have worked a discharge of the first mortgage, it does not appear that the assessment was erroneous. Our decision, therefore, must depend upon whether a grantee in

---

12 N. Y. 80; Biddel v. Brizzolara, 64 Cal. 361; Cumberland v. Codrington, 3 Johns. Ch. 229.

Though the assumption of the mortgage debt by the subsequent purchaser is absolute and unqualified in the deed of conveyance, it will be controlled by a collateral contract made between him and his grantor, which is not embodied in the deed. Flagg v. Munger, 9 N. Y. 483.

And it will not in any case be available to the mortgagee, unless the grantor was himself personally liable for the payment of the mortgage debt. Crowell v. St. Barnabas Hospital, 27 N. J. Eq. 656.

In such case the promise of the purchaser is held to be a *nudum pactum*, and, of course, without efficacy in favor of either the grantor or mortgagee. Crowell v. Currier, 27 N. J. Eq. 155; Norwood v. De Hart, 30 N. J. Eq. 414; Brewer v. Maurer, 38 Ohio St. 550.

The mortgagee cannot look to the grantee, personally, at all; because the assumption is but an indemnity, and the grantor not being liable, the indemnity is practically a mere nullity. Mount v. Van Ness, 33 N. J. Eq. 265.

To make the promise of a grantee to pay the mortgage available to the mortgagee of land conveyed to him it must be made to a person personally liable for the mortgage debt. Wise v. Fuller, 29 N. J. Eq. 266.

If the real intention of the parties to the agreement was that plaintiff should assume the payment of the bond and mortgage to the then holders thereof, so as to give them the right to claim the benefit of that promise, it was a mere contract of indemnity as between the parties. Halsey v. Reed, 9 Paige, 451.

Estoppel of grantee.

A purchaser of land who assumes to pay a prior mortgage on it as part of the purchase price is estopped to question the validity of the mortgage for any cause although it may be invalid as between the original parties. Millington v. Hill, 47 Ark. 301; Tuttle v. Armstead, 3 New Eng. Rep. 581, 53 Conn. 175; Hancock v. Fleming, 1 West. Rep. 535, 103 Ind. 533.

So the purchaser of the equity of redemption assuming payment of notes secured by the trust deed cannot set up usury. Essley v. Sloan, 4 West. Rep. 162, 116 Ill. 391.

Where after the purchase of a mortgage the mortgaged premises are conveyed subject to the mortgage which the grantee by the deed assumes and covenants to pay, such grantee is not estopped from insisting, as against such purchaser, that he is not liable under the covenant. Real Estate Trust Co. v. Balch, 13 Jones & S. 531.

But where a person accepts a conveyance of real estate subject to a mortgage, which he assumes as a part of the consideration money of the conveyance, he will not be allowed to protect himself against the performance of the obligation so assumed by denying the personal liability of his grantor for the payment of the said mortgage. Thayer v. Marsh, 11 Hun, 504; Van Schaick v. Third Ave. R. Co. 38 N. Y. 346; Campbell v. Smith, 8 Hun, 6; Garnsey v. Rogers, 47 N. Y. 233.

A grantee assuming payment of a mortgage is estopped to set up a title acquired under a prior mortgage. Connor v. Howe, 35 Minn. 518.

But he may purchase a title paramount without its inuring to the benefit of the mortgagee. Hancock v. Fleming, 1 West. Rep. 535, 103 Ind. 533.

Test of personal obligation of grantee.

To constitute a personal obligation upon a party taking a conveyance of land incumbered by a mortgage binding him to the absolute payment thereof, something more is requisite than a mere statement in the deed that the conveyance is made subject to such mortgage. Stebbins v. Hall, 29 Barb. 530.

a deed, who assumes and agrees to pay a mortgage on the property conveyed, undertakes thereby to terminate the vital existence of the mortgage or only to cancel the mortgage debt, so far as it is a claim against individuals, without discharging the mortgagee's lien upon the land.

One who assumes a mortgage in such an agreement takes upon himself the burden of the debt or claim secured by the mortgage, and there is no doubt that, as between him and his grantor, he becomes the principal, and the latter merely a surety, for the payment of the debt. It is said, in many cases, that primarily the mortgage is a charge upon the land, but it would be more accurate to say that it is made primarily a charge upon the purchase money reserved by the grantee to pay it. *Thayer* ads. *Torrey*, 37 N. J. L. 339.

The relation of the parties and the nature of the contract are the same as if the entire consideration had been paid to the grantor, and he had then taken a part of the money sufficient to pay the mortgage and had intrusted it to the grantee upon his promise to carry it to the mortgagee, and pay it over in satisfaction of the mortgage. Performance of the promise would cancel the mortgage and leave the estate discharged from the lien. If, as a part of the contract, another portion of the consideration had been paid by giving a second mortgage on the property, the discharge of the first mortgage by payment of the money as agreed might be a very important part of the arrangement, without which the second mortgage would be valueless. In assuming the mortgage, the grantee not only undertakes to relieve the mortgagor from personal liability for the debt, but from all liability under the mortgage. If the mortgagor were released from the debt while the mortgage was allowed to remain a binding contract, enforceable against the land, he would still be liable on the covenants and agreements contained in the mortgage. The implied contract would not be performed so long as the mortgage was outstanding as a valid instrument, upon which the mortgagor could in any form be liable. None of the cases which have come to our attention imply that the payment to be made by a grantee in such a case is anything less than an ordinary payment, which works a complete discharge of the mortgage. The reasoning upon which it is held that the damage to be recovered for a breach of such a contract is the amount of the mortgage debt, if no part of it has been paid, and the authorities cited in support of that doctrine, rest upon the ground that an absolute payment should be made. And, where there is an express agreement to pay, the word "pay" is used in its usual sense. *Braman* v. *Dowse*, 12 Cush. 227; *Furnas* v. *Durgin*, 119 Mass. 500; *Locke* v. *Homer*, 131 Mass. 93, and cases cited.

It follows that, in an ordinary case of this kind, if a grantee who has assumed a mortgage should procure from the mortgagee a discharge of the mortgagor from personal liability upon the debt, and leave the mortgage still in force, he could be sued by his grantor for a breach of his contract, and nominal damage could be recovered if no actual damage

---

A recital in a deed, that the land is subject to a mortgage, the amount due thereon being part of and deducted from the consideration, without stating that the grantee assumes payment of the mortgage, does not render the grantee personally liable for a deficiency on foreclosure. Equitable L. Assur. Society v. Bostwick, 1 Cent. Rep. 528, 100 N. Y. 628.

The mere covenant with vendor to pay the mortgage debt does not shift the charge from the fund primarily liable. Wilbur v. Warren, 6 Cent. Rep. 216, 104 N. Y. 192.

The essential purpose of a covenant on the grantee's part to pay the mortgage is to indemnify the mortgagor against a contingency that the land may not bring enough to pay the mortgage, and thereby leaves him exposed to a claim for a deficiency. Wilbur v. Warren, 6 Cent. Rep. 216, 104 N. Y. 192.

If by the terms of the deed the plaintiff was to pay the mortgage, and the amount thereof was deducted from the consideration money, it seems, as between him and the mortgagor, in equity, the plaintiff is personally liable for any deficiency. Gilbert v. Averill, 15 Barb. 23; Tice v. Annin, 2 Johns. Ch. 128; Bigelow v. Bush, 6 Paige, 343; Heyer v. Pruyn, 7 Paige, 465; Jumel v. Jumel, 7 Paige, 591; Vanderkemp v. Shelton, 11 Paige, 28; Ferris v. Crawford, 2 Denio, 595; King v. Whitely, 10 Paige, 465.

Where an owner of property, at the time incumbered, assigns it to another, on his agreement to pay the incumbrance and sell the property, he may have judgment against the first and second purchasers upon their promise severally, for the amount agreed upon. But he can have no such judgment against the third purchaser, as he did not personally promise to pay, nor against the fourth purchaser, as his promisee was under no personal liability to pay. Ford v. David, 1 Bosw. 600.

Relation of vendor and vendee as principal and surety.

It is the general principle that where the owner of land mortgages it to secure the payment of a debt, and afterwards sell the equity of redemption subject to the lien of the mortgage, and the purchaser assumes the payment of the mortgage as a portion of the purchase money, the latter becomes personally liable for the payment of the debt of the former to the holder of the mortgage in the first instance; and if the mortgagor is compelled to pay it, he can recover it from the purchaser of the equity of redemption. In such case the mortgagor and purchaser stand in the relation of principal and surety, the latter as security for the former, to the extent of the mortgage debt. Flagg v. Munger, 9 N. Y. 499; Russell v. Pistor, 7 N. Y. 174; Flagg v. Thurber, 14 Barb. 201; Hartley v. Harrison, 24 N. Y. 171; Marsh v. Pike, 10 Paige, 595–597; Cornell v. Prescott, 2 Barb. 16; Ferris v. Crawford, 2 Denio, 595.

The equity of redemption is a legal estate, and a purchaser thereof can maintain a real action for the premises. Cowles v. Dickinson, 1 New Eng. Rep. 613, 140 Mass. 373.

Where a grantee expressly assumes, as part consideration, the payment of a mortgage debt, the fact that the title conveyed was invalid will not, while he remains in undisturbed possession and enjoyment of the premises, avail him as a defense to payment of the deficiency upon the foreclosure of the mortgage. Gifford v. Father Matthew T. A. Ben. Society, 6 Cent. Rep. 33, 104 N. Y. 139.

For a full discussion on this subject, on the sale of mortgaged premises and the remedies of the mortgagee, see *note* to Gifford v. Corrigan (N. Y.) 6 L. R. A. 610, and the exhaustive *note* to Boone v. Clark (Ill.) 5 L. R. A. 276.

was shown. If the grantor had such an interest in the property covered by the mortgage as to be actually damnified by the failure to remove the mortgage, he might recover his actual damages, notwithstanding that he had been relieved from personal liability upon the debt.

In the case at bar, the plaintiff suffered no actual damage by reason of his liability upon the debt, for that was paid by a sale of the mortgaged premises, but under the second mortgage he had security on the property for his liability named in that, and he was interested in having the first mortgage satisfied and discharged for the improvement of his security. As a direct result of the breach of the contract, he was deprived of that security. The damage which he has suffered is not too remote, but must be presumed to have been contemplated by the parties when they made their contract.

The only remaining objection to his recovery of this damage is that it is uncertain whether he will ever be required to pay the debt covered by the second mortgage. But there is much authority for holding that this fact can make no difference in favor of one who has failed to perform his contract. The defendant should have paid a sum of money which would have given the plaintiff perfect security for the payment by the defendant of the debt upon which the plaintiff is liable. The plaintiff's cause of action for this breach has already accrued. There can be but one recovery upon it, and all his damages must be assessed now. He was entitled to a security which would have been perfect for the amount of the debt. Through the defendant's fault he has no security. His damage is the value of the security which he should have had, up to and not exceeding the amount of the debt secured. *Lethbridge* v. *Mytton*, 2 Barn. & Ad. 772; *Brown* v. *Howard*, 2 Brod. & B. 73; *Howell* v. *Young*, 5 Barn. & C. 259; *Loosemore* v. *Radford*, 9 Mees. & W. 657; *Lathrop* v. *Atwood*, 21 Conn. 117; *Port* v. *Jackson*, 17 Johns. 239; *Re Negus*, 7 Wend. 499; *Crofoot* v. *Moore*, 4 Vt. 204; *Wilson* v. *Stilwell*, 9 Ohio St. 467; *Stout* v. *Folger*, 34 Iowa, 71; *Ham* v. *Hill*, 29 Mo. 275; *Locke* v. *Homer*, 131 Mass. 93.

The principle involved is the same as that in *Furnas* v. *Durgin*, 119 Mass. 500, and other similar cases. In that case it was uncertain whether the plaintiff would ever be called upon to pay any part of the money which he recovered, for the note might be paid by a sale of the land under the mortgage. We are of opinion, therefore, that the plaintiff was rightfully allowed to recover damages for the loss of his security, caused by the defendant's neglect to perform his contract.

The defendant cannot maintain his declaration in set-off. The action was brought to recover unliquidated damages for a breach of contract, and the claim sought to be set off is of the same kind and is not within the Statute. Pub. Stat. chap. 168, §§ 3-7.

Judgment affirmed.

Field, *J.*, dissenting:

It is conceded in the opinion of a majority of the court that the debt secured by the first mortgage had been fully paid, before the suit was brought, out of the proceeds of the land which had been sold under the power contained in this mortgage, and that neither the interest nor any part of the principal debt secured by the second mortgage had, when the suit was brought, become payable. The contention is that the promise of the defendant to the plaintiff to assume and pay these mortgages, which is to be implied from the acceptance of the deed, was a promise to pay off, immediately on receiving the deed, the first mortgage and to have it discharged, so that thereafter the second mortgage should be a first mortgage, and the plaintiff should have this additional security; that the defendant would pay the second mortgage when and as it became payable; that the defendant has not kept this promise but has neglected to pay off the first mortgage and to have it discharged; and that therefore the plaintiff is entitled to recover the whole amount of the debt secured by the second mortgage as damages.

This contention seems to me to be founded upon a misconception of the nature of the contract of the defendant. It was, I think, a personal contract by the defendant with the plaintiff that he would pay to the mortgagees respectively the mortgage debts when and as they became payable, so that the plaintiff, who had parted with all his interest in the land, should not be called upon to pay them, but should be discharged from all personal liability. The plaintiff might have taken security from the defendant for the performance of this contract, but he took none. The promise which is implied by the defendant's acceptance of the deed did not convey to the plaintiff any interest in the land. If the plaintiff paid the mortgages he would be subrogated to the rights of the mortgagees against the land in addition to his rights against the defendant on his promise, but this right of subrogation he would have had if the defendant had made no promise to assume and pay the mortgages, but had taken a deed subject to the mortgages. This contract of the defendant with the plaintiff, under our law, gave no additional rights to the mortgagees; they could not sue the defendant upon it in their own names, nor could they, without the plaintiff's consent, bring suit in his name. *Prentice* v. *Brimhall*, 123 Mass. 291; *Coffin* v. *Adams*, 131 Mass. 133.

The contract of the defendant with the plaintiff contained, in effect, two promises, namely, to pay to two different persons two separate debts due to those persons at different times from the plaintiff. If these debts were paid, when they became payable, out of the proceeds of the land, or by the defendant out of any other property, the plaintiff would have no cause of action. As between the successive holders of the equity of redemption, the land was the primary fund for the payment of these debts, although the mortgagees might resort to any and all remedies which the law gave them. Although the first-mortgage debt was payable on demand, and therefore an action accrued immediately to the plaintiff when the defendant refused to pay it, yet as the mortgage debt was fully satisfied before the suit was brought, the plaintiff had, when he brought his suit, no cause of action on account of the first mortgage. *Muhlig* v. *Fiske*, 131 Mass. 110; *Hood* v. *Adams*, 124 Mass. 481.

As nothing was due and payable on the debt

secured by the second mortgage when the suit was brought, the plaintiff had no cause of action on account of the second mortgage. If the plaintiff should pay the second-mortgage debt when and as it becomes payable, he would perform his promise with respect to this mortgage, and it could not be known when the suit was brought that he would not do this. The defendant never made any promise that the second mortgage should become a first mortgage as security to the plaintiff that he would perform his promise to pay the second-mortgage debt when it became due and payable, and never made any promise that the mortgages should not be paid out of the proceeds of the land. It is not contended that he made any such promise in terms, but it is contended that this would be the effect of a performance of the defendant's promise to pay off the first mortgage, and that this must have been contemplated by the parties as one of the results of performance, and that therefore a cause of action arose for not bringing about this result, or that a cause of action arose because the defendant has not paid off the first mortgage out of other property than the land, and that the damages are to be assessed for the whole amount of the second mortgage because this mortgage, since the sale of the land, attaches only to the surplus, if any, of the proceeds of the sale after paying the first-mortgage debt and not as a first mortgage to the land itself. If the land had not been sold and the plaintiff had brought suit for the neglect of the defendant to pay the first mortgage on demand, the damages would have been the amount of the debt secured by this mortgage. The amount of the second mortgage could not be included in the damages because the obligation to pay that mortgage when it became due was a separate obligation. The parties certainly contemplated that the defendant might sell and convey the equity of redemption, subject to the mortgages, and it appears that he had conveyed it to Joseph Lively subject to these mortgages before the mortgage sale. He might have conveyed it to Lively with a promise himself to assume and pay the mortgages, or under a promise from Lively that he would assume and pay them, or simply subject to the mortgages, as the conveyance was in fact made. As Lively took the equity subject to the mortgages, and without any promise on the part of the defendant to pay them, if the defendant paid them he would be entitled to be subrogated to the rights of the mortgagees against the land and thus compel Lively either to pay him what he had paid or to lose the equity of redemption in the land. *Hermanns* v. *Fanning*, 151 Mass. —.

Whether if the defendant had paid the first mortgage out of other property than the land it would have operated as an absolute discharge of the mortgage, would depend upon his relations to the owners of the equity of redemption subject to this mortgage. He was under no obligation to the second mortgagee to make his a first mortgage, and the only promise he had made to the plaintiff was to assume and pay the mortgages when they became payable. If he conveyed the equity of redemption as he might do, he had an interest in having the mortgages ultimately paid out of the land, so far as the proceeds of the land would pay them, and he never agreed with the plaintiff that he would part with the right to have this done.

Before the decisions in *Furnas* v. *Durgin*, 119 Mass. 500, and *Locke* v. *Homer*, 131 Mass. 93, it was a question whether a grantor must not first pay the mortgage debt before he could sue his grantee upon such a promise as is contained in the deed in this case. It was decided in those cases that this need not be done, but that the grantor could recover the amount of the mortgage debt if it was payable, because, as between the parties, it was the duty of the grantee to pay it. But the grantee would have the right to have the money which he was compelled to pay to the grantor applied to the payment of the mortgage debt, and whether this payment would operate as a discharge of the mortgage would depend upon the relation of the grantee to other persons having interests in the land subject to the mortgage. If the grantor retained no interest in the land and his personal liability on the mortgage debt was discharged, he would have no interest in the question whether the grantee should be subrogated to the rights of the mortgagee as against the land. If in the present case the first mortgagee had made an agreement under seal with the defendant to extend the time of payment, and had taken the obligation of the defendant to pay the debt, knowing that the defendant had promised the plaintiff to assume and pay it, this agreement would, perhaps, have discharged the plaintiff from any personal liability on the mortgage debt, but the making of such an agreement would not have constituted a breach of the defendant's promise to the plaintiff. See *Dickason* v. *Williams*, 129 Mass. 182; Sheldon, Subr. § 26; *Murray* v. *Marshall*, 94 N. Y. 611.

On the contract of the defendant, implied from the acceptance of the deed, the plaintiff had the same rights of action which he would have upon a similar contract made upon a valuable consideration by a third person, and he would also, if he were compelled to pay the mortgage debts, be subrogated to the rights of the mortgagees against the land, in the same manner as if he had conveyed the equity of redemption subject to the mortgages, but without any promise on the part of the defendant to pay them. The damages for a breach of the promise to pay the debt secured by the first mortgage could never have been greater than the debt itself, and as this has been paid out of the property which the defendant had a right to have appropriated to its payment before the suit was brought, there were no damages for this breach, and there was when the suit was brought no breach of the promise to assume and pay the second mortgage. See *Gaffney* v. *Hicks*, 124 Mass. 301.

I think that there should be judgment for defendant.

Mr. Justice **Devens** and *Mr. Justice* **William Allen** concur in this dissenting opinion.

AMERICAN ORDER OF SCOTTISH CLANS
v.
George S. MERRILL *et al.*

(......Mass.......)

No suit will lie in favor of one corporation organized under the Act of 1888, chap. 429, to enjoin either the organization of another corporation with a name so similar to the first as to be within the apparent prohibition of § 2 of that Act, or the use of such name, since § 7 makes it the duty of the commissioner of insurance to determine whether the names conflict before the certificate which is made conclusive evidence of the existence of the corporation is issued; nor will the suit lie to protect the first name as a trade-name since it was taken subject to whatever interference might be permitted by the Statute.

(June 18, 1890.)

REPORT from the Supreme Judicial Court for Suffolk County (Devens, *J.*), for the consideration of the full court of a suit brought to enjoin the use by defendants of a certain corporate name. *Bill dismissed.*

The case sufficiently appears in the opinion.

Messrs. **Charles T. Gallagher** and **Hollis R. Bailey**, for plaintiff:

Where a party claims a franchise under a statute, and is in the possession and enjoyment of such franchise, equity will interpose to protect and secure the enjoyment of such franchise, because it affords the only plain and adequate remedy.

Boston Water Power Co. v. *Boston & W. R. Corp.* 16 Pick. 525; *Newburgh & C. Turnp. Road* v. *Miller*, 5 Johns. Ch. 101, 1 N. Y. Ch. L. ed. 1028; *Charles River Bridge* v. *Warren Bridge*, 6 Pick. 405, 406.

Where the persons complained against profess to act by public authority, and exceed their authority, it is held to be a peculiarly proper case for the interposition of a court of equity.

Boston Water Power Co. v. *Boston & W. R. Corp. supra*, and cases cited; *Hart* v. *Jamaica Pond Aqueduct Corp.* 133 Mass. 488; *Winslow* v. *Nayson*, 113 Mass. 421.

Under the general law relating to the use of trade-names, where a corporation is lawfully established under a particular name, other persons cannot commence and do business under a name so similar that it not only is liable to be mistaken therefor, but in repeated instances actually is mistaken therefor, so that the business of the original corporation is prejudiced and is liable to be still further prejudiced thereby.

Celluloid Mfg. Co. v. *Cellonite Mfg. Co.* 32 Fed. Rep. 94, 97.

Messrs. **Edward Avery** and **William H. Hart**, for defendants Ward *et al.*:

Under the provisions of sections 2 and 7 of the Act of 1888, chap. 429, the whole subject matter of this action was committed to the judgment and discretion of the insurance commissioner, and cannot be considered by this court, and made the basis of the relief sought by the plaintiff in this proceeding.

Boston Rubber Shoe Co. v. *Boston Rubber Co.* 149 Mass. 436.

It is not the province of courts in equity on bill filed to compel independent tribunals to exercise their judgment in a given way, nor, even by the writ of mandamus, compel such tribunals to exercise their judgment or discretion.

Boston v. *Shaw*, 1 Met. 130; *Leland* v. *Woodbury*, 4 Cush. 245; *Comrs. of the Poor* v. *Gains*, 3 Brev. 396; *Fitch* v. *Kirkland*, 22 Wend. 132; *Ezekiel* v. *Dixon*, 3 Ga. 146; *Stevens* v. *Evans*, 2 Burr. 1157; *Deehan* v. *Johnson*, 1 New Eng. Rep. 140, 141 Mass. 23; *Peabody* v. *Boston School Com.* 115 Mass. 383; *Lunt* v. *Davison*, 104 Mass. 498; *Gaines* v. *Thompson*, 74 U. S. 7 Wall. 352, 353 (19 L. ed. 64, 65); *Western R. Co.* v. *DeGraff*, 27 Minn. 5.

It was the judgment of the insurance commissioner that the Legislature invoked, and not that of any other person, body or tribunal.

Gregg v. *Massachusetts Medical Society*, 111 Mass. 185.

When an organization is effected under the Acts of 1888, and has adopted a name, the name thus adopted and approved by the insurance commissioner can only be changed by the general court.

Act 1888, chap. 429, § 2; *Boston Rubber Shoe Co.* v. *Boston Rubber Co.* 149 Mass. 436.

The certificate issued by the Secretary of State is conclusive as to private persons of the right to corporate existence by a designated corporate name.

Boston Rubber Shoe Co. v. *Boston Rubber Co. supra*; *Rice* v. *Com. Nat. Bank*, 126 Mass. 300. See also Pub. Stat. chap. 186, § 17.

Holmes, *J.*, delivered the opinion of the court:

This bill was brought by a fraternal beneficiary corporation formed under Stat. 1888, chap. 429, to enjoin certain of the defendants from organizing another corporation under the same Act by the name of "The Order of Scottish Clans," and also to enjoin the insurance commissioner and the secretary of the Commonwealth from issuing to them the certificate and charter provided for in the Act. After the subpœna was served, the organization of the corporation was completed and a charter was issued, whereupon the plaintiff made an amendment to its bill in the nature of a supplemental bill alleging these facts. It is found as a fact that the name "Order of Scottish Clans," is "so similar to the plaintiff's name as to be liable to be mistaken therefor," and it follows that it is within the express prohibition of section 2, if we are at liberty to consider that fact, —that is to say, if we can go behind the effect of the certificate of the insurance commissioner and of the charter consistently with the terms of section 7.

Of course the right of the defendants to use the name might be left subject to revision upon private suit notwithstanding the issue of the charter, after the analogy of patents. The question is one of construction and the language of the Statute is not entirely conclusive. But practically the construction is settled by *Boston Rubber Shoe Co.* v. *Boston Rubber Co.*

NOTE.—Where names of persons are similar. See note to Rumford Chemical Works v. Muth (Md.) 1 L. R. A. 44. See also Gato v. El Modelo Cigar Mfg. Co. (Fla.) 6 L. R. A. 823.

See also 16 L. R. A. 420; 38 L. R. A. 658; 43 L. R. A. 95.

149 Mass. 436. That case arose under Stat. 1870, chap. 224, but the provisions of that Act are followed substantially in the one before us, except that the prohibition against adopting a name previously in use, or so similar as to be liable to be mistaken for it, in section 2 of the latter, is somewhat fuller and more direct than that in section 8 of the earlier, Act. Pub. Stat. chap. 106, § 17.

The condition attached to the granting of a certificate by the insurance commissioner in section 7 of the present Act is, "if it appears (*i. e.*, to the commissioner) that the purposes and proceedings of the corporation conform to law," instead of "that the requirements of the preceding sections of this Act have been complied with," in section 11 of the Acts of 1870 (Pub. Stat. chap. 106, § 21). The certificate of the secretary of the Commonwealth under the present Act "shall be conclusive evidence of the existence of such corporation at the date of such certificate." § 7.

This does not seem to vary materially, so far as the present question is concerned, from "shall have the force and effect of a special charter, and be conclusive evidence of the organization and establishment of such corporation," in Stat. 1870, § 11 (Pub. Stat. chap. 106, § 21).

In the case which we have cited it was said: "The Legislature plainly intended . . . that in a case within the provision of the Statute the certificate should be conclusive as to private persons of the rights to the corporate existence by the designated corporate name." And in the following: "The question whether the franchise was improperly obtained or improvidently granted may arise in proceedings for a forfeiture in behalf of the public, but is not open in proceedings by a private person under Pub. Stat., chap. 186, § 17." 149 Mass. 440. See also p. 439.

By the same principles, this bill could not be maintained if it were brought now. How far one name not absolutely the same as another resembles it is a matter of degree, and whether one is so like the other as to be liable to be mistaken for it is a matter of judgment, not admitting of exact measurement. If the judgment of the commissioner is ever conclusive, we cannot go behind it simply because we think it very plain that he made a mistake.

The plaintiff got no better standing by seeking to anticipate the action of the statutory tribunal. The case is not like those where a court of equity enjoins parties from proceeding with an action at law. That is done to enforce some equitable principle which a court of law would not recognize. But the commissioner is bound to proceed upon the same principles that this court would proceed upon. It is part of his duty to pass on the question whether the name applied for has the prohibited resemblance to that of an existing company. We must assume that he will do his duty and is competent to form a judgment on the question. We cannot prohibit him from doing what the Statute expressly commits to his determination; neither can we prohibit private parties from applying to him to do it in the manner expressly authorized by statute. See *Gregg* v. *Massachusetts Medical Society*, 111 Mass. 185.

The plaintiff attempts to maintain its bill, not merely under the Statute, but also on the ground that it is entitled to have its name protected as a trade-name. We think it plain that if its name can be called a trade-name in any sense the plaintiff gets no additional rights on that account. It received its name in the first instance as a corporate name under the Statute, subject as such to whatever interference by subsequent corporations might be permitted under the Statute. The name remained subject to the same degree of interference whatever importance it might acquire in a business way. The principle is somewhat like that upon which patentees have been denied the exclusive right to the names of their patented articles as trade-marks after their patents have expired. The degree of protection to which the plaintiff is entitled is measured by the rights which the Statute confers upon it. The limit is marked by the adjudication of the insurance commissioner. See *Linoleum Mfg. Co.* v. *Nairn*, L. R. 7 Ch. Div. 834; *Re J. B. Palmer's Trade-Mark*, L. R. 24, Ch. Div. 504, 517, 521; *Re Ralph's Trade-Mark*, L. R. 25 Ch. Div. 194, 199; *Coats* v. *Merrick Thread Co.* 36 Fed. Rep. 324.

When there are no statute provisions as to the choice of names, and parties organize a corporation under general laws, it may be that they choose the name at their peril, and that if they take one so like that of an existing corporation as to be misleading and thereby to injure its business, they may be enjoined if there is no language in the Statute to the contrary. *Holmes* v. *Holmes, B. & A. Mfg. Co.* 37 Conn. 278; *Newby* v. *Oregon Cent. R. Co.* Deady, 609; *Celluloid Mfg. Co.* v. *Cellonite Mfg. Co.* 32 Fed. Rep. 94, 97.

But these decisions do not apply to a case where the plaintiff and defendant both get their names under a statute requiring such an adjudication as was required by the Act of 1888.

Bill dismissed.

TEXAS SUPREME COURT.

MISSOURI PACIFIC R. CO., *Plff. in Err.*,
v.
H. G. WHIPKER.

(......Tex.......)

Failure of a garnishee to state in his answer the facts which show an exemption of the principal defendant under a statute providing that "no current wages for personal services shall be subject to garnishment" will deprive him of the protection of a judgment against him as against the principal defendant, if the latter has not appeared or been formally cited to appear in the garnishment proceedings, although he made default in the principal suit.

NOTE.—See Carson v. Memphis & C. R. Co. post, —.

(April 15, 1890.)

ERROR to the Circuit Court for Bexar County to review a judgment in favor of plaintiff in an action brought to recover wages alleged to be due. *Affirmed.*

The facts sufficiently appear in the opinion.

Messrs. **Carr & Lewis**, for plaintiff in error:

The judgment against defendant in the garnishment proceedings afforded it a complete protection against liability in this suit.

Lalonde v. *Sun Mutual Ins. Co.* 2 Tex. App. 46.

Mr. **T. G. Pray** for defendant in error.

Gaines, *J.*, delivered the opinion of the court:

This suit was brought by the defendant in error against plaintiff in error to recover a balance due him for services as a brakeman. The defendant Company answered, among other things, that, in a certain suit in which this plaintiff was defendant, a writ of garnishment had been served upon it, and that upon the coming in of its answer a judgment had been rendered against it, which it had paid. A transcript of the proceedings in the garnishment suit was introduced in evidence by the defendant upon the trial. They showed that the defendant Company answered that it was indebted to this plaintiff, but did not show that the answer disclosed that the indebtedness was for current wages. The court held that the judgment in the garnishment proceedings, and its payment by the defendant Company, did not diminish the liability of the Company to the plaintiff in this suit, and gave judgment accordingly. The ruling of the court in that particular is here assigned as error.

Our Statutes provide that "no current wages for personal service shall be subject to garnishment, and, where it appears upon the trial that the garnishee is indebted to the defendant for such current wages, the garnishee shall nevertheless be discharged as to such indebtedness." Rev. Stat. art. 218.

The question, then, is, Will the garnishee, who is indebted to the defendant in the suit for current wages, be protected by a judgment against him when he fails to state in his answer the facts which show the exemption? We think this question must be answered in the negative. The garnishment proceeding is ancillary to the main suit, and to it the defendant in the principal action is not a party. He is not required to be served with notice of either the issuing or the service of the writ of garnishment. It is true that our Statutes, literally construed, require the garnishee to answer only whether or not he is indebted to defendant, and whether or not he has any effects of the defendant in his possession, and does not, in terms, direct that he shall say whether such indebtedness or such effects are exempt from a forced appropriation to the payment of debts or not. Id. arts. 188, 189.

The statutes of some of the States require him to answer only as to debts or property not exempt. We think, however, that, since the defendant is not required by the Statute to have notice of the service of the writ, it was not intended that the garnishee should in his answer confine himself to the literal directions of the Statute, when he knows that the debt or property is exempt. Such a rule would place it in the power of the garnishee, in many cases, to deprive the defendant of the exemption which the law affords him. The garnishment may issue after judgment; and, even when it is issued before, the defendant may remain ignorant of the fact, unless he sees proper to defend the principal suit. If, after service of citation, he determines not to defend, he may expect a judgment to be rendered against him, and execution to issue; but we know of no rule which requires him to take notice of any ancillary proceedings. If he fails to appear, and the plaintiff amends the statement of his demand so as to show a cause of action materially different, he must have notice. For this reason, we cannot think that it was the intention of the Legislature that he should be concluded by the judgment in the garnishment proceeding when the garnishee has failed to disclose the facts showing the exemption, and when he has not been formally cited to appear, and has not voluntarily appeared for the purpose of maintaining his right. This ruling we think in accordance with the great weight of authority in the courts of other States. The Statute of Maine provides that "no person shall be adjudged a trustee . . . by reason of any amount due from him to the principal defendant, as wages for his personal labor, for a time not exceeding one month." Rev. Stat. 1841, chap. 119, § 63.

In construing that Statute the Supreme Court of that State says: "The Statute secures to the laborer his claim of payment for one month's labor, and places it beyond the reach of his creditors; and his debtor cannot deprive him of it by his neglect to disclose the whole matter when summoned as his trustee." *Lock* v. *Johnson*, 36 Me. 464. The following authorities are to the same effect: *Chicago & A. R. Co.* v. *Ragland*, 84 Ill. 375; *Winterfield* v. *Milwaukee & St. P. R. Co.* 29 Wis. 589; *Daniels* v. *Marr*, 75 Me. 397; *Jones* v. *Tracy*, 75 Pa. 417.

The case before us illustrates the injustice of a contrary doctrine. The suit in which the writ of garnishment was sued out was brought June 25, 1886, in a justice's court of Williamson County. The writ of garnishment was issued, was served and was answered by the garnishee on the same day the suit was instituted. The citation for the defendant to Williamson County was returned "Not found," when an *alias* issued to Bexar County, and was served upon him. He made default. There is nothing in the record to indicate that he ever had any reason to suspect that a garnishment had issued to subject his wages to the payment of the debt. In saying that the defendant in the principal suit is not a party to the garnishment proceeding, we do not wish to be understood as holding that he has not the right to appear in a case like this, and to make his own defense. On the contrary, our statutes expressly permit this. Rev. Stat. art. 212.

What we do mean to say is that he is not to be held to have constructive notice of the garnishment proceeding.

We will say, in addition, that, in every case of this character, it would be a proper practice for the garnishee, after disclosing the facts which show the exemption, to have the defendant cited, to the end that he should make his own defense. See *Iglehart* v. *Moore*, 21 Tex. 501.

The parties at interest will then have the burden of the litigation; and upon the trial the garnishee will be entitled to recover his costs, and a reasonable attorney's fee, for his answer. This certainly should be the practice when the fact of the exemption is contested by the plaintiff, or when the garnishee is in doubt as to the facts. Such a rule affords ample protection to all parties.

The judgment is affirmed.

GULF, COLORADO & SANTA FÉ R. CO., *Appt.*, *v.* Will LEVI.

(76 Tex. 337.)

Delay in the transportation of goods, which is caused solely by a mob, will not render the carrier liable at common law to make good losses arising from a decline in their market price or from a deterioration in their quality on account of their perishable nature, during time of transit.

(February 14, 1890.)*

APPEAL by defendant from a judgment of the District Court for Tarrant County in favor of plaintiff in an action brought to recover damages for losses alleged to have resulted from defendant's delay in the transportation of certain goods. *Reversed.*

The case sufficiently appears in the opinion.

Mr. **J. W. Terry**, with *Messrs.* **Shepard & Miller**, for appellant:

A common carrier is not and never has been held liable for deterioration in quality or value of the goods, caused by delay, in connection with the inherent infirmity of the property transported, which, so far as the carrier was concerned, was unavoidable, and not contributed to by any negligence of the carrier.

Geismer v. *Lake Shore & M. S. R. Co.* 3 Cent. Rep. 829, 102 N. Y 563; *Pittsburgh, Ft. W. & C. R. Co.* v. *Hazen*, 84 Ill. 36; *Pittsburg, C. & St. L. R. Co.* v. *Hollowell*, 65 Ind. 188; *Lake Shore & M. S. R. Co.* v. *Bennett*, 89 Ind. 457, 6 Am. & Eng. R. R. Cas. 391.

The common-law liability of carriers was placed upon them that they might be safe in their ways of dealing; for else these carriers might have an opportunity of undoing all persons that had any dealings with them, by combining with thieves, etc., and yet doing it in such a clandestine manner as would not be possible to be discovered.

Coggs v. *Bernard*, 2 Ld. Raym. 909. See also *Forward* v. *Pittard*, 1 T. R. 27; *Riley* v. *Horne*, 5 Bing. 217; *Chevallier* v. *Straham*, 2 Tex. 115.

If the carrier has used due and reasonable diligence in the transportation, under all the circumstances, this will sufficiently discharge him, even though delay were occasioned by some accident or misfortune not irresistible or strictly referable to special exception.

Schouler, Bailm. § 488. See also Ang. Carr. § 283, and *notes;* Edwards, Bailm. §§ 608, 609; *Parsons* v. *Hardy*, 14 Wend. 215, 217; *Conger* v. *Hudson River R. Co.* 6 Duer, 375; *Harmony* v. *Bingham*, 12 N. Y. 99; *Wibert* v. *New York & E. R. Co.* Id. 245, 19 Barb. 36; *Taylor* v. *Great Northern R. Co.* L. R. 1 C. P. 385; *Kinnick* v. *Chicago, R. I. & P. R. Co.* 69 Iowa, 665; *Pittsburg, C. & St. L. R. Co.* v. *Hollowell*, 65 Ind. 188; *Pittsburg, Ft. W. & C. R. Co.* v. *Hazen*, 84 Ill. 36; *Lake Shore & M. S. R. Co.* v. *Bennett*, 89 Ind. 457, 6 Am. & Eng. R. R. Cas. 391; *Geismer* v. *Lake Shore & M. S. R. Co.* 3 Cent. Rep. 829, 102 N. Y. 563.

Losses due to natural decay, deterioration and waste of the things carried are excusable.

Schouler, Bailm. § 416; Hutch. Carr. § 216; Edwards, Bailm. §§ 598, 599; *Hudson* v. *Baxendale*, 2 Hurlst. & N. 575; *Powell* v. *Mills*, 37 Miss. 698; *Swetland* v. *Boston & A. R. Co.* 102 Mass. 276; *Lawrence* v. *Denbreens*, 66 U. S. 1 Black, 170 (17 L. ed. 89); *Clark* v. *Barnwell*, 53 U. S. 12 How. 272 (13 L. ed. 985); *Chevallier* v. *Patton*, 10 Tex. 344.

The carrier is not liable for loss to the shipper because of a decline in the market value of goods during the delay in transportation, where such delay is not contributed to by any negligence of the carrier, but is caused by accident or misfortune or circumstances beyond his control.

Helliwell v. *Grand Trunk R. Co.* 10 Biss. 170; *Michigan C. R. Co.* v. *Burrows*, 33 Mich. 6; *Thayer* v. *Burchard*, 99 Mass. 521; *Peet* v. *Chicago & N. W. R. Co.* 20 Wis. 595; *East Tennessee & G. R. Co.* v. *Nelson*, 1 Coldw. 272; *Vicksburg & M. R. Co.* v. *Ragsdale*, 46 Miss. 458.

Mr. **B. P. Ayres**, for appellee:

A common carrier is liable for all losses except such as may arise from the act of God, the public enemy, the fault of the party complaining or the inherent quality of the property.

Rev. Stat. arts. 277, 278; *Chevallier* v. *Straham*, 2 Tex. 122; *Philleo* v. *Sanford*, 17 Tex. 227; *Arnold* v. *Jones*, 26 Tex. 335; *Ryan* v. *Missouri, K. & T. R. Co.* 65 Tex. 19; 3 Wood, Railway Law, § 424, pp. 1571-1576; *Houston & T. C. R. Co.* v. *Burke*, 55 Tex. 323.

The inevitable accident which excuses a carrier is one which springs from physical agency alone, and not from known force or fraud, except the force be exerted by a public enemy.

*An opinion was handed down in this case on December 17, 1889, in conformity with a decision affirming the judgment of the lower court. A rehearing was subsequently granted, the judgment reversed and the opinion given herewith handed down. The former opinion is therefore superseded and is consequently omitted. [Rep.]

NOTE.—*Carrier of freight; liability for failure to transport; mobs no excuse.*

On failure to transport to the destination agreed, the carrier is liable for the excess over the price stipulated and paid to other carriers to complete the transportation, with interest. White v. Missouri P. R. Co. 2 West. Rep. 158, 19 Mo. App. 400.

A contract to a terminal point, with privilege to a point beyond, is binding. *Ibid.*

The fact that a riotous mob existed, preventing the employé from operating the line to the point of election, is no excuse. *Ibid.*

Chevallier v. *Straham* and *Philleo* v. *Sanford*, *supra*; *Haynie* v. *Baylor*, 18 Tex. 498; *Arnold* v. *Jones*, *supra*.

Stayton, *Ch. J.*, delivered the opinion of the court:

A further consideration of this case induces us to believe that the former disposition made of it was erroneous, and the motion for rehearing is sustained. Appellee brought this action to recover damages resulting from delay in transporting a carload of lemons, received by appellant from another railway company at Rosenberg Junction, to be transported to Fort Worth. He alleged, if the lemons had been transported within a reasonable time, they would have reached Fort Worth on September 27, at which time they were then worth in the market $12 per box, but that they were not delivered at Fort Worth until October 2, when they were worth in the market only $4 per box, and that by reason of this delay he was damaged $2,000, there being $250 boxes. He further alleged that the lemons were shipped from New Orleans in a ventilated car, as was necessary for their preservation, but that while *en route* they were transferred from that to a close car, whereby they were caused to heat and rot, and that from this cause fifty boxes were lost, for which he asked $600 as damages. He further alleged that he was compelled to assort the lemons after they were received at Fort Worth, which cost him fifty cents per box, and this he also sought to recover. The petition then proceeds as follows: "Wherefore plaintiff avers and charges that, by reason of said unreasonable delay in the transportation and delivery of said lemons as aforesaid, and the depreciation of the price thereof as aforesaid, and the transferring said lemons from said ventilated car to said close car as aforesaid, he has been damaged in the sum of $2,725," for which he prays judgment. Defendant answered by a general denial, and further specially pleaded as follows: "And for further and special answer the defendant says that, if it ever received the fruit described in plaintiff's petition, the same was received by it at Rosenberg Junction from the G. H. & S. A. Ry. Company, and was immediately forwarded from said station in said car in which the same had been delivered to defendant, without opening the same. That the said carload of fruit was carried with speed and safety to the City of Temple, in Bell County, through which it had to pass to be delivered to plaintiff at Fort Worth. That said car, on its arrival at Temple, was taken from the train, and side-tracked by a mob of persons, who, at the time, were engaged in a riot in the said City of Temple, and in the removal and destruction of defendant's property, including its road-bed, rolling stock, freight, etc., at said place. That said rioters were in great force and number, and that it was impossible for defendant, with its agents and employés, to resist them, or dispossess them of defendant's property. That when the plaintiff's fruit arrived at Temple in the said car the said rioters immediately stopped the train and car bearing the said fruit, and took possession thereof and out of the control of defendant with overpowering force and arms, and against its protest, and notwithstanding its strenuous and exhausting efforts to prevent the same. The said rioters uncoupled the cars, and forced said car of fruit upon a side track, where, by overwhelming force and arms and violence, for the space of, to wit, five days, they held possession of the same, refusing to permit the defendant to remove the same; and using force and violence to prevent defendant, and its agents and employés, from moving said car, as it then offered and wished and was ready to do. Defendant says that it had remaining in its employ at and during said time a sufficient number of competent employés, who would have moved its trains and carried said car of fruit and other freight, had it not been prevented by the force and violence herein charged. Defendant made every possible effort to resume control of its property, and to move its said trains, and ship the car bearing plaintiff's fruit, and through its manager and agents appealed to city, county and state authorities and officers for assistance and force to control said riot, and the prevailing unlawful force, and to assist defendant to repossess itself of its property, and to pursue its lawful business. But defendant says that neither the city, county nor state officers and authorities were able to furnish sufficient force to subdue said riot, and dispossess said rioters, and drive them from the occupation of defendant's property. That this state of affairs existed for the space of, to wit, five days, during which the plaintiff's fruit was in the control and in the possession of said rioters, and could not be handled or transported by defendant. That immediately after the cessation of said riot, and the dispersion of said rioters, which occurred at the end of, to wit, five days, the defendant immediately recovered its property and freight, and took possession of said car, and, as soon as it was possible transported the same to its destination, namely, the City of Fort Worth, in Tarrant County, where it delivered the same at once to plaintiff. Wherefore defendant says that it has not been guilty of any negligence in and about said transportation of said car, and said delay was not due to the neglect of its duties by defendant, but solely and wholly and entirely to the act of the said rioters and unlawful persons, and to the inability of the peace officers of the City of Temple and County of Bell and State of Texas to disperse the said rioters, and restrain them from acts of violence, and permit the defendant to pursue its ordinary and peaceful avocation. And all this the defendant is ready to verify, and prays judgment."

The plaintiff filed a general demurrer to this plea as setting up no lawful defense, which was sustained by the court. There was a judgment for the plaintiff, from which this appeal is prosecuted.

From the statement it will be seen that plaintiff based his claim for damages mainly on the ground that there was an unreasonable delay in the transportation of the lemons. If a defense to a claim for damages resulting from such a cause, other than inevitable accident or the act of God, can prevail, there can be no doubt that the answer sets up such a defense; and, if a good defense to any part of plaintiff's claim was set up in the answer, it was error to sustain a demurrer to it. Under the Statutes of this State the liability of the common carrier is that imposed by the rules of the common law. [Rev. Stat. art. 277.] "He is liable not only for losses occasioned by secret theft or embezzlement, but for those inflicted by highway robbery, by the spoliations and outrages of mobs, rioters and insurgents. The most resistless and destructive conflagration, if occasioned by human agency, without any negligence whatever on the part of the carrier, will furnish no valid ground of exemption." *Chevallier* v. *Straham*, 2 Tex. 122.

For failure to carry and deliver, the carrier cannot excuse himself by reason of the fact that, through human agency, not under his control, this was prevented without fault on his part; but if the property be wholly lost or partially decayed through some inherent quality, without fault on the part of the carrier, this will excuse the failure safely to carry and deliver, for the operation of the laws of nature, working destruction or loss, furnish the same excuse as do tempest, lightning or other cause termed the "act of God." The reasons on which the common-law rule is based are thus stated by the English judges, whose knowledge of the ground-work of that system has never been questioned:

In *Forward* v. *Pittard*, 1 T. R. 27, the reasons are thus stated by *Lord* Mansfield: "But to prevent litigation, collusion and the necessity of going into circumstances impossible to be unraveled, the law presumes against the carrier, unless he shows that it was done by the king's enemies, or by such act as could not happen by the intervention of man, as storms, lightning and tempests. If an armed force came to rob the carrier of the goods, he is liable; and a reason is given in the books, which is a bad one, viz., that he ought to have a sufficient force to repel it; but that would be impossible in some cases, as, for instance, in the riots of the year 1780. The true reason is, for fear it may give room for collusion, that the master may contrive to be robbed on purpose, and share the spoil."

The reasons are thus stated by Best, *Ch. J.*, in *Riley* v. *Horne*, 5 Bing. 220: "When goods are delivered to a carrier, they are usually no longer under the eye of the owner; he seldom follows or sends any servant with them to their place of destination. If they should be lost or injured by the grossest negligence of the carrier or his servants, or stolen by them, or by thieves in collusion with them, the owner would be unable to prove either of these causes of loss. His witnesses must be the carrier's servants, and they, knowing that they could not be contradicted, would excuse their masters and themselves. To give due security to property, the law has added to that responsibility of a carrier, which immediately rises out of his contract to carry for a reward, namely, that of taking all reasonable care of it, the responsibility of an insurer. From his liability as an insurer, the carrier is only to be relieved by two things, both so well known to all the country when they happen that no person would be so rash as to attempt to prove that they had happened when they had not, namely, the act of God and the king's enemies."

The same reasons do not apply when the thing is actually transported and delivered, although when delivered it may be greatly diminished in value by a fall in the market price, or its value partially or entirely destroyed by reason of its inherent perishable nature, which has worked its partial or entire destruction while in transit. The rule is thus stated by a recent text-writer, in accordance with the view expressed by many others: "But the reasons upon which the extraordinary responsibility of the common carrier for the safety of the goods is founded do not require that the same responsibility should be extended to the time occupied in their transportation. The danger of loss by robbery or embezzlement, or theft by collusion and fraud on his part, has no application when the mere time of the carriage is concerned. 'His first duty,' it is said, 'is to carry the goods safely, and the second to deliver them; and it would be very hard to oblige a carrier, in case of any obstruction, to risk the safety of the goods in order to prevent delay. His duty is to deliver the goods within a reasonable time, which is a term implied by the law in the contract to deliver; as Tindal, *Ch. J.*, puts it, when he says: "The duty to deliver within a reasonable time being merely a term ingrafted by legal implication upon the promise or duty to deliver generally."' In this respect, therefore, the common carrier stands upon the same ground with other bailees, and may excuse delay in delivery of the goods by accident or misfortune, although not inevitable or produced by the act of God. All that can be required of him in such an emergency is that he shall exercise due care and diligence to guard against the delay, and that, if it occur without his fault or negligence, he shall omit no reasonable efforts to secure the safety of the goods." Hutch. Carr. § 330. See also sections 292, 331, 335.

Many cases are cited in the notes illustrative of the application of this rule, and we will briefly refer to some more recent.

In *Haas* v. *Kansas City, Ft. S. & G. R. Co.*, 81 Ga. 792, 35 Am. & Eng. R. R. Cas. 572, it was held that the company was not liable for loss resulting from "delay in delivering freight, caused by a strike of its employés, accompanied by intimidation and violence which could not be prevented or suppressed by either the company or the civil authorities."

The loss in that case resulted from a fall in the market price between the time the freight would ordinarily have been delivered, but for the obstruction, and the time when it was delivered.

In the case of *Geismer* v. *Lake Shore & M. S. R. Co.*, 102 N. Y. 563, 3 Cent. Rep. 329, the same ruling was made, and the case distinguished from *Weed* v. *Panama R. Co.*, 17 N. Y. 362, and *Blackstock* v. *New York & E. R. Co.*, 20 N. Y. 48. Case last cited, while affirming the rule quoted from Hutchinson on Carriers, held that the simple fact that employés refused to work did not relieve the carrier from liability for failure to transport freight within the usual time.

Pittsburg, C. & St. L. R. Co. v. *Hollowell*, 65 Ind. 189, was a case in which a carrier was sought to be held liable for failure to receive and transport freight within the usual time, and the company set up a defense similar to that urged in the case before us. After stating the rule as to the liability of carriers for failure to deliver at place of destination, the court said: "But the strict rule contended for by the appellee is applicable to common carriers only after they have received the goods for transportation, and fail to deliver them at their destination, or when they are lost. In cases like the present, for delay in receiving and carrying the goods, the carrier is not an insurer, and is bound only by the general rule of liability for a breach of his contract, or of his public duty as a carrier; and may be excused for delay in receiving the goods, or in transporting them after they have been received, whenever the delay is necessarily caused by unforeseen disaster which human prudence cannot provide against, or by accident not caused by the negligence of the carrier, or by thieves and robbers, or an uncontrollable mob."

In *Pittsburg, Ft. W. & C. R. Co.* v. *Hazen*, 84 Ill. 36, it was held competent for the carrier to show, in a suit for damages resulting from delay in the transit of freight, that the delay was caused solely by irresistible violence of men who are not in the employment of the company; and that when employés suddenly refused to work and were discharged, and others employed who were prevented by lawless violence of those discharged from doing duty, the company was not liable for delay thus caused.

The case of *Lake Shore & M. S. R. Co.* v. *Bennett*, 89 Ind. 457, 6 Am. & Eng. R. R. Cas. 402, decided by the Supreme Court of Indiana, affirms the rule asserted in *Pittsburg, C. & St. L. R. Co.* v. *Hollowell*, though the case was one under contract. Many cases might be cited in which carriers have been held not liable for injury resulting solely from delay, when this was shown to have been caused by misfortune or accident, not such as would relieve the carrier for loss of freight or failure to deliver it. We are of opinion that the answer excluded presented a good defense to so much of the action as sought to recover damages for decline in market price of lemons during time of transit.

It may be true that the answer does not present a defense arising from the fact that the lemons may have become less valuable while in transit by reason of material decay without fault on part of carrier; for there is no averment in the pleadings of either party that there was any diminution in value on that account. Plaintiff does allege that they heated, and on that account rotted to a given extent, but that was attributed to the wrongful act of defendant in putting them in an improper car. To the extent the fruit may have deteriorated, on account of its perishable nature, while in transit, the facts pleaded would furnish a defense, if defendant bestowed upon it proper care; for in such case such a loss would be attributed solely to the delay which the answer excuses. For the error of the court in sustaining the demurrer *the judgment will be reversed, and the cause remanded.*

Re T. W. TIPTON.

(....Tex. App.....)

A bill published as a law after it has been deposited in the office of the Secretary of State, signed by the President of the Senate, Speaker of the House of Representatives and the Governor, cannot be shown by journals of the Legislature, or any other evidence, to be different from the Statute actually enacted, or invalid for failure to comply with any formalities required by the Constitution.

(February 15, 1890.)

APPLICATION for a writ of habeas corpus to inquire into the cause and validity of the detention of applicant in the custody of the sheriff of Smith County. *Applicant remanded.*

The case sufficiently appears in the opinion.

Messrs. **Finlay, Marsh & Butler** and **McLemore & Campbell** for applicant.

Mr. **Davidson,** *Asst. Atty-Gen.*, for the State.

Willson, *J.*, delivered the opinion of the court:

Applicant, T. W. Tipton, being in custody of the sheriff of Smith County by virtue of a *capias* issued from the county court of said county upon an information based upon a complaint charging said applicant with unlawfully selling refined kerosene illuminating fluid without first having the same inspected and branded according to law, applied to the county judge of said Smith County for the writ of habeas corpus, and said judge declined to grant said writ, but, as the question involved in the case was the validity of a statute, referred the application to this court, requesting action thereon. At Tyler this court granted the writ, and upon a hearing thereof took the cause under advisement, and transferred the same to this branch; and, after a thorough investigation of the question presented, we now declare our conclusions.

It is claimed by applicant that the Statute

NOTE.—*Legislature; passage of bills.*

A bill becomes a law when it has gone through all the forms prescribed in the Constitution. Jones v. Hutchinson, 43 Ala. 721.

It becomes a law when it is passed by the Legislature and is approved by the governor. Memphis v. United States, 97 U. S. 293 (24 L. ed. 920).

After its transmission to the governor neither House can recall it. People v. Devlin, 33 N. Y. 269.

Legislative journals are not evidence of the meaning of a statute; this must be ascertained by the Act itself, and from facts connected with the subject on which it is to operate. Southwark Bank v. Com. 26 Pa. 446. See, however, Edger v. Randolph County, 70 Ind. 331.

They are themselves the highest evidence of the enactment of the law and of the time of its enactment. Gardner v. Barney, 73 U. S. 6 Wall. 499 (18 L. ed. 890); People v. Starne, 35 Ill. 121; Blake v. National City Bank, 90 U. S. 23 Wall. 307 (23 L. ed. 119).

The Court may consult the journals of the two Houses of the Legislature to ascertain its will and intention where the statute to be interpreted is ambiguous. Edger v. Randolph County, *supra*. See note to People v. McElroy (Mich.) 2 L. R. A. 609.

for a violation of which he is being prosecuted and is in custody as aforesaid, to wit, the Act approved April 5, 1889, entitled "An Act to Provide for the Inspection of Refined Oils Which Are the Product of Petroleum, and Which May be Used for Illuminating Purposes within this State, and to Regulate the Sale and Use thereof, and to Provide Penalties for Violation of the Same," is not a valid law, because it is not the Statute which was in fact enacted by the Legislature. It is claimed by applicant, and is conceded by the assistant attorney-general, and is shown by the journals of the Senate and House of Representatives, that said Act originated in the House of Representatives, and was designated and known as "House Bill No. 167." It passed the House, and was sent to the Senate. In the Senate, section 3 of the bill was amended, and the bill was returned to the House with the senate amendment thereto. The House concurred in the senate amendment. The bill, as amended, was enrolled. The committee on enrolled bills reported to the House that the bill had been correctly enrolled, and the bill was then signed and presented to the governor, who approved it, and it was deposited in the secretary of state's office. As appears from the senate journals, the amendment to section 3 of said bill, which was adopted by the Senate, was as follows: "Provided, it shall not be necessary to inspect oil which has been inspected under a law of another State, and its quality determined and evidenced by the authentic stamp or mark of the inspector of such State."

In the enrolled bill, which is now the Statute we are considering, the proviso in section 3, corresponding to the amendment above quoted, reads: "Provided, it shall not be necessary to inspect one which has been inspected under a law of another State." It is manifest that the proviso in the Statute and the proviso which is recited in the senate journals are not the same, but are essentially different.

But how far will the courts of this State go in inquiring into the acts of the legislative department of the government? When a bill has been authenticated by the signatures of the president of the Senate, and the speaker of the House of Representatives, and the governor of the State, and has been deposited in the office of the secretary of state, and published as a law of the State, will the courts of this State, from the journals of the Legislature or other evidence, determine that the statute is not a valid law because not enacted in accordance with the formalities required by the Constitution, or because the statute so authenticated is not the one enacted by the Legislature? In several of the American States, it is the established doctrine that the courts will inquire behind the authenticated statute into the manner of its enactment, and will from the journals determine whether or not it is a valid law. Counsel for applicant have referred us to numerous decisions which so hold, and which unquestionably support the propositions contended for in behalf of applicant. But there is much conflict of authority upon the questions above propounded. We shall not take the time to cite and review the vast number of decisions bearing upon the subject, believing, as we do, that the courts of this State have announced the rules by which we should be governed.

In *Blessing* v. *Galveston*, 42 Tex. 641, it is held that the judicial department, on the bare fact that the journals of one or both Houses of the Legislature fail to show the passage of the bill in full and strict conformity to all the directions contained in the Constitution, should not disregard and treat as naught an Act in all other respects unobjectionable. It is further clearly intimated, we think, in that decision that the authenticated statute should be regarded as the best, if not conclusive, evidence that the required formalities were observed in its passage, and that for the courts to exercise the power of going behind such Statute, and inquiring into the manner of its enactment, would lead to most disastrous consequences.

In *Central R. Co.* v. *Hearne*, 32 Tex. 547, it is held that the best evidence of the terms of an Act of the Legislature is a duly certified copy of the enrolled bill.

In *Day, L. & C. Co.* v. *State*, 68 Tex. 526, it is held that it will be conclusively presumed that a bill had been referred to a committee and reported on before its passage, as required by the Constitution.

In *Usener* v. *State*, 8 Tex. App. 177, this court quotes approvingly from *State* v. *Swift*, 10 Nev. 176, as follows: "Where an Act has been passed by the Legislature, signed by the proper officers of each House, approved by the governor, and filed in the office of the secretary of state, it constitutes a record which is conclusive evidence of the passage of the Act as enrolled. Neither the journals kept by the Legislature, nor the bill as originally introduced, nor the amendments attached to it, nor parol evidence can be received in order to show that an Act of the Legislature, properly enrolled, authenticated and deposited with the secretary of state, did not become a law. This court, for the purpose of informing itself of the existence or terms of a law, cannot look beyond the enrolled Act, certified to by those officers who are charged by the Constitution with the duty of certifying, and with the duty of deciding what laws have been enacted."

In *Hunt* v. *State*, 22 Tex. App. 396, this court held that where the Constitution expressly requires that the journals shall show a particular fact or action of the Legislature in the enactment of a statute, as that the bill was signed by the presiding officer of each House, such fact or action must affirmatively appear in the journals, or the Statute will be invalid. But, where there is no express constitutional requirement that the journals shall show affirmatively that a constitutional requirement has been observed, it will be conclusively presumed that such requirement was observed; and neither the journals, nor any other evidence, will in such case be allowed to impeach the validity of the statute.

We conclude, therefore, that we are not at liberty to go behind the authenticated Statute in this instance. Upon its face, it is a valid law, and it is not claimed that the journals fail to show any fact expressly required to be shown in order to make it valid. It must be conclusively presumed that the Statute, as authenticated and deposited in the secretary of state's office, is precisely the same as was enacted by the Legislature. But, were we at liberty to go behind the Statute, and consult the journals, we would be confronted with conflicting evidence as to the amendment. The senate journals show that an amendment to section 8 was adopted in that House, and show what that amendment was, and that the bill and amendment were returned to the House of Representatives. The journals of the House of Representatives show that the amendment adopted by the Senate was concurred in, but does not set forth the amendment. The journals of the House further show that the bill as amended by the Senate was correctly enrolled, and this enrolled bill is the Statute authenticated and published as a law, but it does not contain the amendment as set forth in the senate journals. Which of the journals, those of the Senate or of the House, are correct? They are of equal credit. It may be that the amendment was incorrectly copied into the senate journals, and that the amendment in fact adopted by the Senate and concurred in by the House is that which appears in the enrolled bill. If, then, we were to look to the journals to determine the question, we should hold that the weight of evidence supports the validity of the Statute, because, the journals of the two Houses being of equal credit and weight, the authentication of the bill as enrolled by the presiding officers of the two Houses and by the executive corroborates and confirms the correctness of the house journals as to the amendment in fact adopted. *It is ordered that the applicant be remanded to the custody of the sheriff of Smith County, and that he pay the costs of this proceeding.*

Ordered accordingly.

ILLINOIS SUPREME COURT.

W. H. EMMONS, *Appt.*,
v.
CITY OF LEWISTOWN.

(......Ill. ......)

Canvassers for books are not hawkers or peddlers within the meaning of the Statute which gives municipal corporations power to compel hawkers and peddlers to obtain a license.

(March 31, 1890.)

APPEAL by defendant from a judgment of the Circuit Court for Fulton County convicting him of violating a city ordinance prohibiting the canvassing for books without first procuring a license. *Reversed.*

The case sufficiently appears in the opinion.

Mr. **H. W. Masters** for appellant.

Messrs. **Gray & Waggoner** for appellee.

Shope, *Ch. J.*, delivered the opinion of the court:

The appellant, a resident of Logan County, in this State, was engaged, in the City of Lewistown, in canvassing and taking orders for the sale of religious books and Bibles published by the Historical Publishing Company of St. Louis, Mo., the books so ordered to be paid for when delivered; and while so engaged, as agent of such company, appellant was arrested and brought before a magistrate, and tried upon the charge of violating ordinance No. 45 of said City. That ordinance provides: "Any person or persons or corporation who shall, within the limits of said City, without first procuring a license therefor, exercise or carry on, either directly or indirectly, the trade, business, occupation or employment of auctioneers, peddlers, hawkers, canvassers of books, maps or other publications, canvassers, vendors or solicitors of or for any medicine, invention or other articles of merchandise, to be sold, or taking orders therefor, on the streets or from house to house, or who shall set up, manage, give, hold or conduct a circus exhibition, menagerie, equestrian performance, musical or minstrel party or concert, theatrical or ballet troupes and combinations, exhibitions of wire dancing, puppets, wax figures, paintings, statuary, machinery, tricks of legerdemain, magic lantern exhibitions, skating rink or any other exhibition, show or amusement, for gain or profit, or where pay for admittance is required, shall, on conviction thereof, forfeit and pay for the use of said City not less than $10 nor more than $200 for each offense: provided, the fine shall not in any case be less than would have been required for a license; and provided, also, that no license shall be required for the sale of articles that are exempt from license by the Statutes of the State of Illinois, or for orders and sales at wholesale by drummers."

It was admitted on the trial that appellant, at the time of his arrest, was soliciting and taking orders for books, issued or published by his principal, on the streets, and from house to house, within the limits of said City, and without having procured a license therefor from the city authorities. The trial resulted in the imposition of a fine and costs. On appeal to the Circuit Court of Fulton County, the cause was re-tried, resulting in a judgment against appellant for $10 and costs. From this judgment appellant has prosecuted his appeal to this court.

It is here insisted that, as the defendant below was the agent of a publishing house located in the State of Missouri, and, in the acts complained of as being in violation of said ordinance, was engaged in the business of his nonresident principal, that the ordinance, when applied to him, interfered with the reserved powers given by the 3d clause of the 8th section of the first article of the Constitution of the United States to Congress, to regulate commerce "among the several States." Reliance

NOTE.—Hawkers and peddlers. See *note* to State v. Richards (W. Va.) 3 L. R. A. 705.

Subject to state license. See *note* to Com. v. Gardner, 7 L. R. A. 666; Wrought Iron Range Co. v. Johnson, *ante*, 273.

See also 48 L. R. A. 99.

is placed upon the case of *Robbins* v. *Shelby County Tax. Dist.* 120 U. S. 489 [30 L. ed. 694], as sustaining that contention; and, if the ordinance is otherwise valid, it must be conceded that that question is involved. We do not deem it necessary, however, to discuss or determine this question, for the reason that the ordinance must be held invalid, as applied to the class of offenses with which the appellant was charged, upon other and to us more satisfactory grounds.

It is shown that appellant was canvassing from house to house, within the City, soliciting subscriptions to certain publications, taking orders therefor, to be paid upon the subsequent delivery thereof. It is not shown that he was carrying such publications, and proposing to sell and deliver the same, or any other goods, wares or merchandise, within said City. That he fell within the prohibition of the ordinance is not questioned.

The City of Lewistown is incorporated under the City and Village Act; and the authority to pass this ordinance must be found, if at all, in paragraph 41, § 1, art. 5, chap. 24, of the Revised Statutes, which gives the power to the city council, and the president and board of trustees in villages, "to license, tax, regulate, suppress and prohibit hawkers, peddlers, pawnbrokers, keepers of ordinaries, theatricals and other exhibitions, shows and amusements, and to revoke such license at pleasure." By a subsequent paragraph of the same section the city council is given power to pass all ordinances, and to make all rules and regulations as are proper and necessary to carry into effect the powers granted, and to impose penalties. The power given is to license, tax, regulate, suppress and prohibit "hawkers" and "peddlers," etc.; and, if it shall be found that "canvassers of books or other publications, on the streets or from house to house," are not "hawkers" or "peddlers," within the meaning of these words as used in the Statute, then it is clear that the city council was without authority to pass an ordinance prohibiting such canvassing within the City without first obtaining a license, or imposing a penalty therefor.

It is to be observed that neither the ordinance nor Statute attempts to define who shall be deemed "hawkers" or "peddlers," and we are therefore to determine from authority whether appellant falls within these designations. We said in *Chicago* v. *Bartee*, 100 Ill. 61, that the term "peddler," as used in this Statute, was to be taken in its general and unrestricted sense, and embraced all persons engaged in going through the city from house to house, and selling commodities,—in that case, selling milk.

Abbott's Law Dictionary defines a "hawker" to be "a person who practices carrying merchandise about from place to place for sale, as opposed to one who sells at an established shop. It is equivalent to 'peddler'," the term now more commonly employed.

The same author quotes from the case of *Com.* v. *Ober*, 12 Cush. 493, as follows: "It is not, perhaps, essential to the idea, but it is generally understood from the word, that a hawker is 'one who not only carries goods for sale, but seeks for purchasers, either by outcry, which some lexicographers concede as intimated by the derivation of the word, or by attracting notice and attention to them, as goods for sale, by a actual exhibition or exposure of them, by placards or labels, or by a conventional signal, like the sound of a horn for the sale of fish.'"

Tomlin says: "Hawkers, peddlers and petty chapmen" are "persons traveling from town to town with goods and merchandise."

Bouvier defines "peddlers:" "Peddlers. Persons who travel about the country with merchandise for the purpose of selling."

Webster's definition is: "A traveling trader; one who carries about small commodities on his back, or in a cart or wagon, and sells them."

This list of definitions might be extended almost indefinitely, but enough has been given to show both the legal and popular meaning of the words "hawker" and "peddler." It has never been understood, either by the profession or the people, that one who is ordinarily styled a "drummer," that is, one who sells to retail dealers or others by sample, is either a hawker or a peddler; and the same is true in respect of persons who canvass, taking orders for the future delivery of books and periodicals or other publications. It is a fundamental canon of construction that the Legislature must be presumed to have used these words in their known and accepted signification, and intended thereby to confer upon the city and village authorities power to license, regulate and prohibit only such callings and vocations as might fall within the terms employed in the Act, as thus known and understood. To concede that the power of the City to license, tax or regulate the canvassing for books or publications within the City is doubtful, is to deny the power. "Any fair, reasonable doubt concerning the existence of power is resolved against the corporation, and the power is denied." 1 Dillon, Mun. Corp. §§ 55, 251.

While it must be conceded that the evil resulting from the method of canvassing from house to house may be great,—indeed, as great as that resulting from the vocation authorized by the Statute to be taxed and regulated, and indeed may be even greater,—yet, if the Legislature, as we are constrained to hold, has not conferred upon cities and villages the power to tax or regulate the same, if relief is to be obtained, resort must be had to the legislative department of the State.

We are of opinion that so much of the ordinance as prohibits canvassing for books and publications in said City without obtaining a license therefor is void, for want of power in the city authorities to ordain the same, and appellant, not falling within the designation of a "hawker" or "peddler," was not amenable to prosecution under the valid portions of said ordinance.

The judgment of the Circuit Court is therefore reversed.

Scholfield and **Bailey**, *JJ.*, concurring specially:

We concur in reversing the judgment below upon the ground that the ordinance is in conflict with the Constitution of the United States, as held in *Robbins* v. *Shelby County Tax. Dist.*, 120 U. S. 489 [30 L. ed. 694].

LAKE ERIE & WESTERN R. CO., *Appt.*,
v.
John M. SCOTT.

(......Ill......)

The depreciation in the value of land lying along a highway, due to the construction of a railway on the opposite side of, and next to, it gives the owner a right to compensation, under a constitutional provision that private property shall not be taken "or damaged" without just compensation.

(*Bailey, J., dissents.*)

(March 31, 1890.)

APPEAL by defendant from a judgment of the Appellate Court, Third District, affirming a judgment of the Circuit Court for McLean County in favor of plaintiff in an action to recover damages for trespass upon, and depreciation in the value of his property in and by the construction of a railway. *Affirmed.*

Statement **Per Curiam:**

This case comes to this court on appeal from the appellate court, the judges of that court having certified that it involves questions of law of such importance, on account of principal and collateral interests, that it should be passed upon by this court. The facts and questions of law involved in the case are sufficiently stated in the opinion filed by the appellate court, which is as follows:

"CONGER, *J.*:

"Appellee owns a farm of about 216 acres, bounded on the west by a public highway sixty-six feet wide, running from the City of Bloomington in a northerly direction, known

NOTE.—*Condemnation of land for railroad purposes; measure of damages.*

The measure of damages against a railroad company for land taken under the right of eminent domain is the difference between the market value of the whole property before and after the building of the road. Schuylkill River E. S. R. Co. v. Stocker, 128 Pa. 233; Wabash, St. L. & P. R. Co. v. McDougall, 6 West. Rep. 321, 118 Ill. 229; Dupuis v. Chicago & N. W. R. Co. 1 West. Rep. 656, 115 Ill. 97; Short v. Rochester & P. R. Co. (Pa.) 6 Cent. Rep. 627; Pittsburgh, B. & B. R. Co. v. McCloskey, 1 Cent. Rep. 619, 110 Pa. 436; Setzler v. Pennsylvania S. V. R. Co. 2 Cent. Rep. 357, 112 Pa. 56; Shepherd v. Baltimore & O. R. Co. 130 U. S. 426 (32 L. ed. 970); *Re* Union Elevated R. Co. 30 N. Y. S. R. 164.

Whether the assessment be for damages to the tenant in fee, for life or for years, the rule as to the measure of damages is the difference between the value of the property (that is to say, the tenant's interest therein) unaffected by the injury, and its value as affected by the injury. Philadelphia & R. R. Co. v. Getz, 5 Cent. Rep. 691, 113 Pa. 214.

If the location of a railroad so affects property that it will compel the removal of business conducted by tenants to another place, the difference between the value of the machinery in connection with the business conducted on the property, and its value to be removed and applied to the same or other use, is a proper element of damages. The reasonable expenses of removing the machinery are also proper items of damages. *Ibid.*

It is proper to take into consideration all elements of damage caused by such construction, which tend to diminish the value of the property. Chicago, K. & N. R. Co. v. Hazels (Neb.) April 17, 1889.

Just compensation includes not only the value of the land taken, but also the diminution in the value of that from which it is severed. Laflin v. Chicago, W. & N. R. Co. 33 Fed. Rep. 415; Hyde Park v. Washington Ice Co. 4 West. Rep. 233, 117 Ill. 233.

If the market value of property is depreciated by the promixity of buildings, fences, etc., to the track, or if danger from fire lessens the value of the premises for sale or use, that element may be considered in fixing compensation. Centralia & C. R. Co. v. Brake, 125 Ill. 393.

In estimating the value of land taken in condemnation, the jury are not to determine how it could best be divided into building lots, or conjecture how fast they could be sold, and they are not to inquire what a speculator might be able to realize out of a re-sale in the future, but what a present purchaser would be willing to pay for it in the condition it is in at that time. Pennsylvania S. V. R. Co. v. Cleary, 125 Pa. 442.

Evidence of value of land taken. See *notes* to San Diego L. & T. Co. v. Neale (Cal.) 3 L. R. A. 83; Theobold v. Louisville, N. O. & T. R. Co. (Miss.) 4 L. R. A. 735.

The temporary injury sustained on account of obstructions placed in a street during the building of a railroad constitutes a claim for damages apart from the claim, under the Ohio statute, for permanent depreciation of the property. Shepherd v. Baltimore & O. R. Co. 130 U. S. 426 (32 L. ed. 970).

Where property has been depreciated in value by reason of the street's being occupied by a railroad company, such depreciation is ascertained by the difference in its value before and its value after the final location and construction of the road. *Ibid.*

The owner of property near to the street is entitled to the remedy given by the statute, if the injury to it is the direct and necessary result of the occupancy of the street by the railroad company, or can be fairly attributed to such occupancy. *Ibid.*

Any depreciation in the value of residence property occasioned by the probability that a railroad company, in operating and using its road, will make unusual and loud noises, and emit from its engines smoke and cinders, and cause other like annoyances naturally incident to the operation of cars, is a proper element to be considered in estimating damages to such property by the location and operation of the road. Fort Worth & N. O. R. Co. v. Pearce (Tex.) Dec. 3, 1889.

Any obstruction of communication with the streets, which interferes with his enjoyment to such an extent as to materially depreciate the value of the premises, is liable to the lot owner in the amount of such depreciation. McQuaid v. Portland & V. R. Co. (Or.) Dec. 10, 1889.

Although the railroad is constructed under authority of a municipal ordinance, it is nevertheless liable to an abutting property owner for the actual diminution in the market value of his land, caused by the construction of its track. Denver & R. G. R. Co. v. Bourne, 11 Colo. 59.

But the operation of a railroad on land taken by eminent domain and abutting on a public city street, although diminishing the value of houses on the other side of the street, is *damnum absque injuria* for which owners of houses are not entitled to compensation, under Pa. Const., art. 16, § 8. Pennsylvania R. Co. v. Lippincott, 8 Cent. Rep. 818, 116 Pa. 472; Pennsylvania R. Co. v. Hunter, 8 Cent. Rep. 828, 116 Pa. 472.

See also 14 L. R. A. 533; 35 L. R. A. 583.

as the 'White Oak Grove Road.' The whole of the farm lies east of this highway, except at one point where a corner of one of the tracts composing the farm crosses the highway, making a small triangle containing from three to six one-hundredths of an acre on the west side of such highway. Appellant's railroad was located and constructed in the middle of its right of way, which was one hundred feet wide, lying west of and adjoining the White Oak Grove road. The railroad was separated from the farm by the highway, except where it touched the little triangular piece lying west of the highway. In constructing the railroad at this point, a cut was made and a portion of the earth on this triangle was dug away and removed. Appellant took no steps to have this land condemned. When the sub-contractor was grading at this point, appellee notified him not to go upon this triangle, as it was his property and the right of way had not been secured over it. In explaining their action appellant's counsel say: 'Upon investigation, it appeared so small and trifling, the sub-contractor was advised to go ahead with his work, and that the Railroad Company would settle with appellee.' No settlement, however, was made and appellee instituted the present suit. The amended declaration upon which the case was tried was in the nature of an action on the case, in which damages were claimed for the trespass and excavation upon the triangular piece lying west of the highway, and for damages to all the land lying upon the east side of the highway. In the declaration it is averred that, by reason of defendant entering upon and digging up and carrying away the soil and earth from plaintiff's land, and by reason of defendant constructing its said railroad, as above stated, so near to said highway, and so near plaintiff's land, and continuing to operate the same, defendant thereby became liable to pay to plaintiff all damages that the construction and operation of its said railroad will cause or has caused to the residue of said body of land not in fact entered upon and despoiled. It is then further averred the construction and operation of said railroad in the manner and way it is constructed and operated will and does greatly injure the rest of said body of land not entered upon and despoiled in this: that it makes, and will through all coming time while such lands are used for farming purposes, the approach to and from the dwelling-house and the other buildings on the west side of said lands over said highway unsafe and dangerous to travel on and over in carriages or other vehicles drawn by horses or other animals; that the deep cut and high embankment immediately in front of and near plaintiff's land make the appearance of such farm unsightly, and otherwise injuriously affect it; and that the construction and operation of said railroad as aforesaid render said farm less convenient and comfortable as a place of residence, and also render such land less safe and convenient for farming purposes, particularly in handling stock upon it. It is then averred that by 'reason of the wrongful acts and doings of defendant as aforesaid, and the injuries done to plaintiff's lands as aforesaid, the salable value of said land is thereby greatly decreased.' Pleas were filed by appellant, a trial had before a jury, who returned a verdict for appellee in the sum of $500, upon which judgment was rendered.

"There can be no question but that appellee was entitled to recover damages occasioned by the entering upon and removing or disturbing the soil upon the premises west of the highway; but it is strenuously insisted that for such damages to the remainder of the farm as are claimed in the declaration there can be no recovery. The evidence was conflicting. Appellee's witnesses testified that the construction and operation of the road would damage appellee's farm to the extent of $6 to $10 per acre,—decrease its rental and salable value; while the witnesses for appellant think there would be no substantial damage. Under these circumstances the jury were warranted in their verdict, if the law as applicable to the case was properly applied.

"The instructions given appellee upon this subject were as follows: '(2) The court instructs the jury, on behalf of plaintiff, that the true measure of compensation, where no land is taken for the right of way for a railroad upon which to construct a road bed and track, is the difference between what the whole property would have sold for unaffected by the railroad and what it would sell for as affected by it. (3) The Constitution of this State declares: "Private property shall not be taken or damaged for public use without just compensation;" and the jury are instructed it will be presumed the framers of that instrument used the word "damaged," in that connection, in its ordinary and popular sense, which is, hurt, injury or loss; and "that the damage contemplated by the Constitution," in cases where no land is actually taken, "must be an actual diminution of present value or of price, caused by constructing and operating the road, or a physical injury to property that renders it less valuable in the market if offered for sale." (4) If the jury believe, from the evidence, that plaintiff is the owner in fee simple of the land described in the declaration, and that the defendant Railroad Company, in constructing its road-bed and track, entered upon any portion of plaintiff's said land, and dug up and carried away the soil, and that such acts were a physical injury to such lands, or any part thereof; and if the jury further believe, from the evidence, the construction of defendant's road-bed and track along, near and adjacent to plaintiff's land, and its contemplated maintenance and operation (if the jury believe, from the evidence, they are so constructed, and that defendant intends to maintain and operate the same) are an actual damage to his lands, and do in fact render the same less valuable in the market if offered for sale,—then the law is for plaintiff, and the jury should find for him; and the jury are instructed, as a matter of law, plaintiff is entitled to recover for any depreciation, if the jury believe, from the evidence, there has been any depreciation in the market value of plaintiff's lands not actually entered upon by reason of the construction, maintenance and operation by defendant of its railroad as constructed, and also for any physical injuries done to that portion of plaintiff's land upon which defendant did actually enter, if the jury believe, from the evidence, defendant did enter upon any portion of plaintiff's lands described in the declaration, and did cause any physical injuries to the same. (5) The jury are further instructed, on behalf of the plaintiff, that, in determining whether plaintiff's lands are lessened in value by reason of the construction and the proposed operation of the railroad, then the jury may consider the injury to plaintiff's lands, if any is proved, arising from the inconveniences actually brought about and occasioned by the construction of defendant's railroad, although such damage might not be susceptible of definite ascertainment; and may also consider such incidental injury as the proof may show might or would result from the perpetual use of the track for moving trains, or from the inconveniences in using said lands for farming purposes and in handling stock upon it, if the proof shows such railroad would occasion any such inconveniences; and they may consider generally such damages as the evidence may show, if any are reasonably probable to ensue from the construction and operation of the defendant's said railroad.'

"Witnesses for appellee seem to base their idea of the damages upon the supposition that the construction and operation of the road so near the highway has rendered it dangerous and unsafe to travel upon, made the egress and ingress from the farm onto the highway with teams and stock more dangerous, rendering the farm less safe and convenient, and thereby reduced the value of appellee's farm. Appellant insists that in all this evidence 'appellee has shown no injury or damages not suffered in common with the general public, for which the law affords him no redress.' We cannot assent to this view. The damages spoken of by the witnesses in reference to making the highway more dangerous are, to some extent, shared with appellee by the public; and in so far as they are common to both no right of action exists. But there are elements of damage affecting the value of appellee's farm which do not in any way affect the public. A highway beside a farm may, and generally does, give it an increased value, depending, to some extent, upon the location of the buildings, and the character and degree of use the owner may have for such highway. In so far as its use is interfered with or destroyed, the value of the farm is lessened, and for that the owner should recover, for he sustains some special pecuniary damages in excess of that sustained by the public generally. But it is urged that the damages claimed arise, not from any physical invasion or disturbance of appellee's property, or actual encroachment upon the highway, but alone from the injury to the use and enjoyment thereof caused by the operation of the railroad; that such operation being lawful, and confined to appellant's right of way, the damages arising therefrom to appellee would be *damnum absque injuria*. We admit there is force in this question, and, as far as we are aware, this precise question has not been passed upon by the supreme court. The nearest approach to it is in the case of *Rigney* v. *Chicago*, 102 Ill. 64, where there was no direct interference with the premises of Rigney, but an obstruction placed in the street at a distance therefrom, thereby injuring the use of the street; or, as stated in the opinion, 'it is not claimed or pretended that the plaintiff's possession has been disturbed, or that any direct physical injury has been done to his premises by reason of the obstruction in question.' The gravamen of the plaintiff's complaint in that case was that the defendant, in cutting off his communication with Halstead Street by way of Kenzie Street, has deprived him of a public right which he enjoyed in connection with his premises, and thereby inflicted upon him an injury in excess of that shared by him with the public generally, and it is for this excess he seeks to recover, and nothing more; and the court says: 'If the lot and buildings of appellant are to be regarded as property, and not merely the subject of property, as, strictly speaking, they are, then there has clearly been no physical injury to it; but if by "property" is meant the right of user, enjoyment and disposition of the lot and buildings, then it is evident there has been a direct physical interference with appellant's property; and, when considered from this aspect, it may appropriately be said the injury to the property is direct and physical.'

"We are inclined to think that there is no good reason for distinguishing between an injury arising from an interference with appellee's right to the advantages the highway gave his farm, caused by a physical obstruction placed therein, as in the foregoing case, and where the same kind of an injury is produced by the operation of trains beside it. In either case the advantages given the farm by the highway have to some extent been destroyed, and the land lessened in value. If it be conceded that the result of operating the road has in fact injured appellee's farm in a way not common to the public, and thereby made it less valuable, it would seem to follow as a necessary consequence that it has been damaged for public use. Such operation, being lawful, and confined to the right of way, does not release appellant from liability; for it would clearly be liable for damages caused by an unlawful act, and, as we understand the constitutional provision that private property shall not be taken nor damaged for public use without just compensation, it means to cover cases where damages are caused by acts that are legal, and entirely within the powers of the corporation performing them, but in the doing of which, for the use and benefit of the public, private property is damaged. It follows, therefore, that appellant's proposition that 'a corporation is not liable unless an individual doing the same thing on his private property would be,' as applied to this case, is not sound. An individual cannot legally take or damage private property for public use, but a railroad company can lawfully do either, if in so doing it makes compensation.

"It has been suggested that if this recovery can be sustained, it would authorize repeated suits, upon the theory that a new injury is caused by every passing train, thus giving ground for successive actions. This is a misapprehension of the true grounds upon which the right of recovery rests. The damage to appellee is caused by the construction of the road in such place as that the proper and only way of operating it did of necessity, from that time, injure the farm and lessen its value. It is the right which appellant has at its pleasure, and for all future time, to operate its trains, that at once depreciates the value of the farm, and not the effect produced by the passing of particular trains, or any particular injury or accident that may occur to appellee's property therefrom; hence the damages arose at the time of the construction of the road, and were then capable of being determined once for all. Believing that this view of the law is within the spirit and meaning of the constitutional provision alluded to [art. 2, § 13], and has been fairly applied by the court below, the judgment of the circuit court will be affirmed."

Messrs. **Stevens & Horton** and **James S. Ewing**, for appellant:

There can be no recovery where the elements of damage are speculative and imaginary, such as the danger of having horses frightened, or offensive to a sensitive taste, such as the unsightliness of an object lawful in itself.

McReynolds v. *Burlington & O. R. R. Co.* 106 Ill. 152; *Peoria & P. U. R. Co.* v. *Peoria & F. R. Co.* 105 Ill. 110; *Stone* v. *Fairbury, P. & N. W. R. Co.* 68 Ill. 394; *Cooper* v. *Randall*, 53 Ill. 24; *Re Penny*, 7 El. & Bl. 660: *Favor* v. *Boston & L. R. Co.* 114 Mass. 350; Cooley, Torts, p. 602.

There can be no recovery under our present Constitution where the injury suffered is of the same kind as that suffered by the public.

Chicago v. *Union Bldg. Asso.* 102 Ill. 379; *East St. Louis* v. *O'Flynn*, 8 West. Rep. 85, 119 Ill. 200; *McDonald* v. *English*, 85 Ill. 232; *Guest* v. *Reynolds*, 68 Ill. 478; *Indiana, B. & W. R. Co.* v. *Eberle*, 9 West. Rep. 206, 110 Ind. 542; *Rochette* v. *Chicago, M. & St. P. R. Co.* 17 Am. & Eng. R. R. Cas. 192; *Rude* v. *St. Louis*, 12 West. Rep. 288, 93 Mo. 408.

There can be no recovery unless, under the facts, the damage complained of would give rise to a right of action at common law.

Rigney v. *Chicago*, 102 Ill. 64; *Chicago* v. *Union Bldg. Asso. supra.*

But a railroad operated by authority of law and for a lawful purpose is not a nuisance.

Chicago & E. I. R. Co. v. *Loeb*, 5 West. Rep. 887, 118 Ill. 203; *Illinois C. R. Co.* v. *Grabill*, 50 Ill. 241.

And the acts complained of, viz.: mental disquietude and inconveniences in mere matters of taste, are not actionable.

Cooper v. *Randall*, 53 Ill. 24; *Guest* v. *Reynolds*, 68 Ill. 478; Cooley, Torts, pp. 598-602; *Owen* v. *Henman*, 1 Watts & S. 548; *Sparhawk* v. *Union P. R. Co.* 54 Pa. 401.

Nor is operating the railroad an actionable offense merely because there is a liability to frighten teams.

Favor v. *Boston & L. R. Co.* 114 Mass. 350; *Philadelphia, W. & B. R. Co.* v. *Stinger*, 78 Pa. 219; *Macomber* v. *Nichols*, 34 Mich. 212; *Stone* v. *Fairbury, P. & N. W. R. Co.* 68 Ill. 394; *Hahn* v. *Southern P. R. Co.* 51 Cal. 605; Cooley, Torts, p. 617.

Hence, under the facts in this case, if plaintiff is damaged at all it is *damnum absque injuria.*

Pennsylvania R. Co. v. *Lippincott*, 8 Cent. Rep. 818, 116 Pa. 472; *Pennsylvania R. Co.* v. *Marchant*, 12 Cent. Rep. 261, 119 Pa. 541; *Florida S. R. Co.* v. *Brown*, 23 Fla. 104; *Rude* v. *St. Louis*, 12 West. Rep. 288, 93 Mo. 408; *Re Penny*, 7 El. & Bl. 660.

Messrs. **Robert E. Williams** and **Isaac N. Phillips**, for appellee:

The principles and rules stated in plaintiff's instructions are sustained by the following authorities:

Stetson v. *Chicago & E. R. Co.* 75 Ill. 74; *Chicago & P. R. Co.* v. *Francis*, 70 Ill. 239; *Page* v. *Chicago, M. & St. P. R. Co.* Id. 328; *Eberhart* v. *Chicago & St. P. R. Co.* Id. 349; *Chicago, B. & Q. R. Co.* v. *Bowman*, 11 West. Rep. 598, 122 Ill. 595; *Wabash, St. L. & P. R. Co.* v. *McDougall*, 6 West. Rep. 321, 118 Ill. 235, 126 Ill. 111; *Rigney* v. *Chicago*, 102 Ill. 82.

The true question is whether the property was injured by the improvements. If not, then there is no damage, and there can be no recovery. If there is, then the recovery must be measured by the extent of the loss.

One of the elements of damage distinctly recognized in *Shawneetown* v. *Mason*, 82 Ill. 337, was the physical obstruction of the right and means of access to plaintiff's premises.

See also *Pekin* v. *Brereton*, 67 Ill. 477; *Pekin* v. *Winkel*, 77 Ill. 56; *Elgin* v. *Eaton*, 83 Ill. 535; *Chicago & P. R. Co.* v. *Francis*, 70 Ill. 238.

Per Curiam:

We are satisfied with the reasoning and conclusions of the appellate court, and *the judgment of that court will therefore be affirmed.*

Bailey, J., dissents.

OHIO SUPREME COURT.

Joseph F. STANLEY, *Pltf. in Err.*,
v.
STANLEY, Admr., etc., of Timothy T. Stanley, Deceased, *et al.*

(47 Ohio St.——)

*1. **Where a person who is a nonresident** of this State and absent from it when a cause of action accrues against him in favor of another in this State, afterward, and during the period of the limitation, occasionally comes into this State, such presence in the State will not set the Statute of Limitations to running in his favor, although the plaintiff might, at such times, by the exercise of ordinary diligence, have commenced an action against him.

2. **Under the provisions of section 4989,**

*Head notes by the COURT.

NOTE.—*Statute of Limitations; interruption by absence from State.*

Where from the time of the execution of the contract to the filing of the complaint defendant had been a nonresident of the State, under the provisions of Rev. Stat. 1881, § 297, the Statute has not begun to run against the cause of action. Wood v. Bissell, 6 West. Rep. 267, 108 Ind. 229.

Revised Statutes, presence of the defendant in the State, for the full period of the time limited for bringing an action, either continuously or in the aggregate, is necessary to constitute a bar of the action.

(March 25, 1890.)

ERROR to the Circuit Court for Washington County to review a judgment affirming a judgment of the Court of Common Pleas in favor of defendants in an action to recover a claim against a decedent's estate, which was alleged to be barred by the Statute of Limitations. *Reversed.*

Statement by **Minshall,** *Ch. J.:*

On January 6, 1881, Joseph F. Stanley commenced suit in the Court of Common Pleas of Washington County against the administrator of Timothy Stanley, deceased, and his heirs, the claim having been disallowed by the direction of the latter.

The petition contained a number of causes of action, eight of which accrued in the years 1866 and 1867, and would have been barred but for the following averments contained in the petition:

"That when the cause of actions accrued to this plaintiff, on each and every of said eight counts set forth in this plaintiff's petition against the said Timothy T. Stanley, the said Timothy T. Stanley was absent from the County of Washington, and absent from the State of Ohio; that he then resided in the State of West Virginia, and so remained absent continuously

---

But nonresidence and continued absence from the State do not excuse a want of diligence in ascertaining complainant's rights. Teall v. Slaven, 40 Fed. Rep. 774.

A debtor's voluntary absence from the State suspends the running of the Statute. Brick v. Buel, 73 Tex. 511.

His absence must be such that process cannot be so served upon him that judgment will bind him personally. Quarles v. Bickford, 6 New Eng. Rep. 197, 64 N. H. 425; Bensley v. Haeberle, 4 West. Rep. 913, 20 Mo. App. 648.

The time during which a debtor is absent residing out of the State of his own free will and accord is to be deducted in estimating the time in which an action must be brought against him. Hoffman v. Churchill (Mich.) Feb. 1889.

The term "beyond seas," in the saving clause of a Statute of Limitations, is to be construed as equivalent to "without the limits of the State" where the Statute is enacted. Shelby v. Guy, 24 U. S. 11 Wheat. 361 (6 L. ed. 495); Faw v. Roberdeau, 7 U. S. 3 Cranch, 174 (2 L. ed. 402); Murray v. Baker, 16 U. S. 3 Wheat. 541 (4 L. ed. 454); Alexandria Bank v. Dyer, 39 U. S. 14 Pet. 141 (10 L. ed. 391).

The term "beyond the seas," in a State Statute of Limitation, will be construed according to the decisions of the State. In North Carolina it is construed to mean "without the United States." Davie v. Briggs, 97 U. S. 628 (24 L. ed. 1086).

A Statute of Limitations which excepts creditors "out of the Commonwealth" begins to run as soon as a creditor enters the State, even temporarily, provided the debtor is then in the State. Faw v. Roberdeau, 7 U. S. 3 Cranch, 174 (2 L. ed. 402).

The five years' limitation provided by the Statute of Kansas in favor of the holder of a tax title will not run in his favor while he is out of the State. Watkins v. Reed, 30 Fed. Rep. 908.

The Tennessee Statute suspending the running of limitation during the debtor's absence from the State, after the right of action has accrued, applies to causes of action accruing in another State and between citizens thereof. Kempe v. Bader, 86 Tenn. 189.

Under the Tennessee Code, temporary absence from the State of a resident debtor, after the cause of action has accrued, suspends the running of limitation. *Ibid.*

The absconding of a debtor to prevent the institution of a suit against him does not suspend the Statute unless such obstruction to the suit existed at the time the cause of action accrued. Richardson v. Cogswell, 47 Ark. 170.

The provision of the Statute preserving right of action against one "without the State" is not applicable to one who concealed the place of his residence, and lived for more than six years within the State, under an assumed name. Engel v. Fischer, 8 Cent. Rep. 303, 102 N. Y. 400.

The claim of a resident of Maine, holding a note made by a resident and payable there, is not barred by the Statute of the State, where the maker, within six years after the claim accrued, removed his residence from the State and never returned. McCann v. Randall, 6 New Eng. Rep. 355, 147 Mass. 81.

The return or coming into the State must be open and notorious and under such circumstances that the creditor could, with reasonable diligence, find his debtor and serve him with process. Engel v. Fischer, 8 Cent. Rep. 305, 102 N. Y. 404; Hill v. Bellows, 15 Vt. 727; Hysinger v. Baltzell, 3 Gill & J. 158; Ford v. Babcock, 2 Sandf. 518; Cole v. Jessup, 10 N. Y. 96; Dorr v. Swartwout, 1 Blatchf. 179.

But when the "coming" is to dwell and reside permanently, it is not necessary in order to set the Statute in operation that the creditor should have knowledge thereof. It is enough if he could acquire such knowledge by the exercise of reasonable diligence. Davis v. Field, 56 Vt. 429; Mazozon v. Foot, 1 Aik. (Vt.) 283; Hall v. Nasmith, 28 Vt. 791; Whitton v. Wass, 109 Mass. 40.

Under the Connecticut Statute, a creditor has six years after the debtor has come into the State in which to institute a personal action upon a simple contract against him. Waterman v. Sprague Mfg. Co. 5 New Eng. Rep. 632, 55 Conn. 554.

The creditor's remedy is not affected by the fact that, during the absence of the debtor from the State, he had real estate here open to attachment. *Ibid.*

An unmarried physician, who boarded and had an office, went out of the State for two months, paid rent for the office, but not for board, during his absence, and then returned to the State and soon after left again, leaving furniture in the office, but giving up his room and board, and went to another State, where he died. Such absences are to be added to the statutory period of limitations in a suit against his administrator on a due-bill made by him. Brady v. Potts (N. J.) 10 Cent. Rep. 173.

Where defense to a suit on a note is the Statute of Limitations, the time defendant resided outside of the State will be deducted from the number of years the note has run. Palmer v. Morse (Me.) 5 New Eng. Rep. 309.

Under the proviso in the Statute of Limitations, successive absences might be accumulated and the aggregate deducted. Cutler v. Wright, 22 N. Y. 484; Harden v. Palmer, 2 E. D. Smith, 177; Ford v. Babcock, 2 Sandf. 531, 7 N. Y. Leg. Obs. 285; Graham v. Schmidt, 1 Sandf. 74; Ogden v. Astor, 4 Sandf. 329.

In case of repeated absences of the debtor from the State, the whole were to be combined; and the bar of the Statute was not perfect unless the defendant's residence in the State, for six complete years after his first return, was established. Richardson v. Curtis, 3 Blatchf. 388.

from the State of Ohio before the accruing of the cause of action in this petition in favor of the plaintiff and against the said Timothy T. Stanley, until his death in the State of West Virginia, on or about the 16th of February, 1878."

This the defendants sought to avoid by the following answer:

"2. They admit that at the time the causes of action set up in the 1st, 2d, 3d, 4th, 5th, 6th, 7th and 8th counts in the petition are said to have accrued to plaintiff, said Timothy T. Stanley was absent from Washington County, and absent from the State of Ohio, and that he then resided in the State of West Virginia, but these defendants deny that he so remained absent continuously from the State of Ohio before the accruing of said cause of action until his death. That they admit that on August 1, 1866, said Timothy T. Stanley departed this State, and went to the State of West Virginia; but they deny that he remained continuously in said State of West Virginia until his death, and these defendants aver that after said August 1, 1866, and after the cause of action set up in the 1st, 2d, 3d, 4th, 5th, 6th, 7th and 8th counts of the petition herein, are said to have accrued to plaintiff, and more than six years prior to the presentation of the claim in the petition set up by plaintiff to said administrator, said Timothy T. Stanley came into said State of Ohio, openly and notoriously, and became subject to the process of the courts of said State, all of which plaintiff at the time well knew. And these defendants further say that during said period of time said plaintiff resided in said Washington County, and State of Ohio; that during said period of time said Timothy T. Stanley came frequently into said Washington County, and remained several days therein, with the knowledge of plaintiff; that during said period of time said Timothy T. Stanley was at the house of plaintiff in said Washington County for several days with the knowledge of plaintiff, and was subject to the process of the courts of said county."

The plaintiff demurred to this answer on the ground that it did not state facts sufficient to constitute a defense to the action. The demurrer was overruled and exception taken. The plaintiff then filed a reply controverting the averments. The case was tried to a jury upon the various issues of fact made by the pleadings, and a verdict rendered for the defendants. On the trial the court charged the jury as follows:

"If the jury find from the evidence upon the issue made in the pleadings upon the question of the Statute of Limitation, that after the accruing of the cause of action set up in the petition, or before the accruing of all of said causes of action, the decedent, Timothy T. Stanley, removed to the State of West Virginia about August, 1866, and that he remained there continuously until his death, about the month of November, 1878, then the Statute of Limitation would not run against said causes of action set up in said petition, and be no bar to a recovery by the plaintiff in this action.

"But if the jury find that during said time, from August, 1866, until the date of his death, about November, 1878, the said Timothy T. Stanley returned frequently, openly, occasionally and notoriously to the County of Washington, in the State of Ohio, the place where the contracts in the petition were made, and the place where said plaintiff during said times resided, and the said plaintiff did know, or would have known by ordinary diligence, of the frequent presence in said Washington County and State of Ohio, of said decedent, Timothy T. Stanley, and could have, by ordinary diligence, obtained service of summons in said County of Washington, and State of Ohio, upon said Timothy T. Stanley, in an action founded upon the causes of action set up in the petition, then the Statute of Limitation would run against said demands mentioned in said petition, and the same would be a bar to a recovery by the plaintiff in this action."

This was excepted to at the time, and, with the ruling on the demurrer, was made the ground of a motion for a new trial. The motion was overruled, and judgment entered upon the verdict, to reverse which this proceeding in error is prosecuted.

Mr. **S. S. Knowles** for plaintiff in error.
Mr. **A. D. Follett** for defendants in error.

Minshall, *Ch. J.*, delivered the opinion of the court:

The question in this case arises upon the defense in the answer to which the demurrer was sustained. The defense was intended to avoid the effect of the averments in the petition as to the absence of the decedent from the State at the time the plaintiff's causes of action accrued, and his continued absence thereafter until the time of his death. The question requires a construction of the following section of the Revised Statutes, relating to the Statute of Limitations:

"Sec. 4989. If, when a cause of action accrues against a person, he is out of the State, or has absconded, or concealed himself, the period limited for the commencement of the action shall not begin to run until he comes into the State, or while he is so absconded or concealed; and if, after the cause of action accrues, he depart from the State, or abscond or conceal himself, the time of his absence or concealment shall not be computed as any part of the period within which the action must be brought."

It is necessary to observe that it is not claimed in the defense to which the demurrer was overruled, that the causes of action to which it was pleaded, or any of them, arose in the State of West Virginia, the residence of the deceased, or were to be performed there. Such averments were made as separate grounds of defense, and were met by denials. The gist of the defense to which the demurrer was interposed, is that, although the decedent resided in the State of West Virginia when the causes of action accrued, yet he frequently came into this State, and within the jurisdiction of the courts of the county in which the plaintiff resided, after the causes of action accrued, and more than six years before the action was commenced; and that these occasions were attended with such circumstances of notoriety that the plaintiff could, with the exercise of ordinary diligence, have obtained service upon him. The defense admits that the deceased was a nonresident of the State at the time the causes of action accrued; but it is claimed that if, at any time thereafter, he came into the State so that the plaintiff might have commenced his action, the Statute began to run, and continued to do so, though he may have departed the State the next day, and have remained out of it the residue of his life.

We do not so construe this Statute. Where a defendant is out of the State when a cause of action accrues against him, our construction is that the Statute does not begin to run until he comes into the State. It then begins to run against him, and if he remain in the State it will be barred in the period limited, from that time. But if, after he comes into the State, he again depart from it, the running of the Statute is suspended during his absence. It is not necessary that we should determine, in this case, whether absence upon business—the defendant continuing a resident of the State—is sufficient, or whether it must be limited to absence as a nonresident of the State; for it is admitted that the decedent was a resident of the State of West Virginia, and his absence, therefore, referable to that fact.

The design of the Statute is to give to the plaintiff the full period of the limitation, in available time, for the commencement of his action; so that, in ascertaining this period, the time the defendant is out of the State is not computed as any part of the time given him in which to commence his action. This is in close analogy to the Roman law which, in like cases, counted only the available days, *tempus utile*, on which activity was possible, in ascertaining whether an action was barred by limitation or not; and days on which the action was hindered by the absence of the defendant were excluded from the computation of the term. Poste's Gaius, 255.

This is the only rational construction that can be placed on the Statute, and makes it consistent with itself. Thus in the second clause it is provided, in so many words, that if after the cause of action accrues, the defendant depart from the State, "the time of his absence . . . shall not be computed as any part of the period within which the action must be brought." It could not then have been intended by the Legislature that, where a defendant was absent from the State at the time a cause of action accrued, his return to the State would only set the Statute to running in his favor, but that it would continue to run, whether he remained in the State or not.

The first clause provides for the case where the defendant is absent from the State when the cause of action accrues; the second for the case where he departs from the State after it has accrued. In the first, the Statute begins to run when he comes into the State; in the second, it ceases to run, and is suspended, until he returns to the State. The purpose, then, of the Statute is perfectly plain: Presence of the defendant within the State, so that he may be sued, avails in his favor; absence from the State, whether at the accruing of the action or afterwards, suspends the running of the Statute.

This is the first time the precise question seems to have arisen in this court, so that none of its previous decisions afford any light in determining it. But most of the other States have Statutes of Limitations with provisions similar in this regard to our own, which have been frequently construed by their courts; and the general result of these decisions is, that when a defendant is absent from the State when a cause of action accrues against him, his occasional or frequent visits to the State will be of no avail to him under a plea of the Statute of Limitations, however open and notorious his visits may have been, unless he has been in the State, and the jurisdiction of its courts, for the full period limited by the Statute, either continuously or in the aggregate.

The Statute of the State of Maine is substantially the same as our own: and there, in a suit on a promissory note, which the defendant claimed was barred, he offered to show that though he lived in the Province of New Brunswick, he was frequently in the State to the knowledge of the plaintiff. But the court said: "The defendant was absent from and resided out of the State when the cause of action accrued, and has not since resided within it, though he may have occasionally been within its limits,"—and it was held that he could not avail himself of the bar of the Statute." *Hacker* v. *Everett*, 57 Me. 548.

We cite, in this connection, and to the same effect, *Milton* v. *Babson*, 6 Allen, 322; *Lane* v. *National Bank of the [illegible]ropolis*, 6 Kan. 74; *Smith* v. *Bond*, 8 Ala. 386; *Chenot* v. *Lefevre*, 8 Ill. 637; *Bell* v. *Lamprey*, 57 N. H. 168; *Bassett* v. *Bassett*, 55 Barb. 505, and *Bennett* v. *Cook*, 43 N. Y. 537.

In the last case the defendant resided in Jersey City, but did business in New York City, and was there some eight or ten hours each day. He plead the Statute. But the court said: "If the Statute runs at all during the presence of a nonresident in the State, such presence must, in any view of the case, amount in the aggregate to six years to render the defense available."

And in *Bassett* v. *Bassett* it is said: "The object of the exception in the Statute was to give the creditor the whole of the six years' residence in the State within which to commence his action. He is not obliged to follow the debtor to another State; nor is he called upon to watch him to ascertain whether he comes into the State for a temporary purpose, so long as his residence is elsewhere."

Our conclusion then is, that under the provisions of § 4989, Rev. Stat., the Statute of Limitations does not run in favor of a defendant to a cause of action whilst he is absent from the State; and this principle is not affected by the fact that the defendant may have been absent from the State when the cause of action first accrued against him; for whenever he departs from the State, after having come into it, the running of the Statute is suspended from that time and during his absence, whether the cause of action first accrued whilst he was in or whilst he was absent from the State.

Judgment reversed, and cause remanded, with direction to sustain the demurrer to the second defense in the additional answer, filed June 18, 1884, and for further proceedings.

DELAWARE COURT OF ERRORS AND APPEALS.

John M. FRIESZLEBEN
v.
Sereck F. SHALLCROSS *et al.*

(......Houst.......)

1. There is no natural right to vote. Contributing to the support of the government may be made a condition of the privilege.

2. The exclusion of a person from the assessment list for twelve months on failure to pay his county poll-tax, in consequence of which he may be precluded from being qualified to vote during that year, is not a violation of Const., art. 4, § 1, which provides that a citizen otherwise qualified who has "within two years next before the election paid a county tax which shall have been assessed at least six months before the election, shall enjoy the right of an elector," or of art. 1, § 3, which provides that "all elections shall be free and equal."

(*Houston, J., dissents.*)

(January 29, 1890.)

RESERVATION by the Superior Court for New Castle County for the consideration of the Court of Errors and Appeals of an action brought to recover damages alleged to have resulted from defendant's depriving plaintiff of an opportunity of paying a county tax and thus of qualifying himself to vote at a general election. *Judgment for defendants.*

In February, 1885, the name of the plaintiff was, on a general assessment, duly placed upon the assessment list for the sixth ward of the City of Wilmington, and the Levy Court of New Castle County afterward, in the spring of the same year, duly laid a poll-tax upon him. On the second day of March, 1886, the plaintiff, who had not paid said poll-tax, was returned by the collector of county taxes for the collection district including the sixth ward of said city, to said levy court as a delinquent, and thereafter, on the 29th day of March in the same year, the defendants, composing and sitting as said levy court, allowed said poll-tax

NOTE.—*Citizenship; possession of political rights not essential to.*

The possession of all political rights is not essential to citizenship under the protection of the 14th Amendment of the Federal Constitution. People v. De La Guerra, 40 Cal. 311.

A State may regulate the conditions and tenure of office. Spencer v. Board of Registration, 1 MacArth. 169; Kennard v. Louisiana, 92 U. S. 480 (23 L. ed. 478).

A State may determine the class of inhabitants who may vote. The elective franchise is not a natural right nor an immunity of citizens. Van Valkenburg v. Brown, 43 Cal. 43; United States v. Anthony, 11 Blatchf. 200; United States v. Crosby, 1 Hughes, 448; Minor v. Happersett, 88 U. S. 21 Wall. 162 (22 L. ed. 627); United States v. Cruikshank, 92 U. S. 543 (23 L. ed. 588), 1 Woods, 308.

The 14th Amendment merely declares that all persons born in the United States are citizens thereof, and are capable of becoming voters, but the provision is not self executing. Spencer v. Board of Registration, *supra.*

The first section of the 15th Amendment does not confer on anyone the right of suffrage, but merely invests citizens of the United States with a constitutional guaranty of exemption from discrimination in the exercise of the elective franchise. Le Grand v. United States, 12 Fed. Rep. 577; United States v. Harris, 106 U. S. 629 (27 L. ed. 290); Neal v. Delaware, 103 U. S. 370 (26 L. ed. 567); United States v. Reese, 92 U. S. 214, 218 (23 L. ed. 563, 564); United States v. Cruikshank, 92 U. S. 543 (23 L. ed. 590), 1 Woods, 308; Anthony v. Halderman, 7 Kan. 50; People v. Board of Registration, 26 Mich. 51; United States v. Petersburg Judges of Election, 14 Am. L. Reg. N. S. 105.

As to the nature of the right of suffrage, see *note* to Bloomer v. Todd (Wash. Terr.) 1 L. R. A. 111.

Qualification of voters; Registration Law.

The registrar of an election precinct has power, under Idaho Revised Statutes, to administer the election oath, although he is not named among those having power to administer an oath, in the General Act. Territory v. Anderson (Idaho) March 18, 1889.

The Legislature has the right to authorize and require the registration of voters in a town or city, but the regulation prescribed must be reasonable and impartial and calculated to facilitate and secure the constitutional right of suffrage, and not to subvert or injuriously restrain or impair the right. Stephens v. Albany (Ga.) March 10, 1890.

If the length of time between the closing of registration (which is made a qualification of voters at a municipal election) and the election is unreasonable, such election is void; and two months, in case of a special election of a mayor and aldermen, is unreasonable. *Ibid.*

The Georgia Statute making registration a qualification of voters at charter elections in the City of Albany restricts such qualification to elections for mayor and aldermen, and does not require registration as a qualification to vote at an election to ascertain whether two thirds of the qualified voters desire bonds of the city to be issued for the purpose of erecting a system of waterworks. *Ibid.*

The Legislature has the power to enact a law requiring qualified voters to be registered before the day of election as a condition of the exercise of their right of suffrage; and such a law may be local in its application. Com. v. McClelland, 83 Ky. 686.

It is not essential to the validity of a Registration Law that it should contain a provision for an examination, on the day of election, of the qualification of voters who, from sickness or other cause, have been prevented from registering. *Ibid.*

A residence of one year in a county, next preceding the election, by a male citizen of the age of twenty-one years, gives him a right under the Constitution to vote in any precinct of the county of which he may have been a resident for sixty days next preceding the election; and a Registration Law is not valid if it requires other qualifications to entitle a person to register. *Ibid.*

An explanatory clause in the statute, inconsistent with the part complete in itself of which it is explanatory, may be stricken out without invalidating the statute. *Ibid.*

Male inhabitants residing in the State June 27, 1835, being made citizens of Michigan by the Constitution, although neither native-born nor naturalized, a law which compels registration of voters, and provides only for native-born or naturalized citizens, is not valid. Atty-Gen. v. Detroit (Mich.) 7 L. R. A. 99.

No Registry Law is valid which deprives the elector of his constitutional right to vote, by any

See also 9 L. R. A. 326; 17 L. R. A. 845.

as delinquent and caused the name of the plaintiff to be struck and dropped from the assessment list; whereby no tax was assessed or laid upon the plaintiff for the year 1886, and he was consequently deprived of all opportunity at any time to pay a county tax for that year and thereby qualify himself to vote at the general election in November of that year, although in all respects, save the payment of a county tax, qualified as an elector. The levy court had no evidence that the plaintiff was dead, or had left the State or the sixth ward of said city, or said collection district. The only evidence before said court was the collector's return of the plaintiff as "delinquent."

The action of the defendants in causing the name of the plaintiff to be struck and dropped from the assessment list and continuing to leave it off the same was in strict accordance with the provisions of section 1 of the Act entitled "An Act in Relation to the Collection of Taxes in this State," passed at Dover, April 10, 1873, and the provisions of section 9 of the Act entitled "An Act in Relation to the Duties of Assessors and of the Levy Courts in the Several Counties of the State," passed at Dover, April 9, 1873.

Section 1 of the Act of April 10, 1873, provides that, in the case of persons assessed and liable to pay poll-taxes, upon the return of the collector in form and verified as therein provided, it shall be the duty of the levy court "to allow said collector as delinquencies the taxes uncollected by him, and the names of such delinquents shall be dropped from the assessment list by the levy court and shall not be placed thereon again for a period of twelve months from and after the date of such allowance."

Section 9 of the Act of April 9, 1873, provides that "it shall not be lawful for any assessor or any levy court, upon the personal application of anyone or otherwise, to place upon the assessment in any hundred the name of any person who, having failed to pay the county tax assessed against him or her for the preceding year, was returned and allowed as a delinquent until after the expiration of the twelve months from the time such allowance as delinquent was made by the levy court."

---

regulation with which it is impossible for him to comply. *Ibid.*

The Legislature cannot disfranchise legal voters without their own fault or negligence, in an attempt to prevent fraud. *Ibid.*

The Statute creating a system of registration for the City of St. Louis makes it the duty of the recorder of votes to provide a suitable registration book for each election precinct in the city, and these books are public records. It is declared a felony to allow a person's name to be entered therein without his taking the required oath. United States v. O'Connor, 31 Fed. Rep. 449.

"Qualified voters," as used in the Constitution of North Carolina, must be construed as embracing those whose competency has been passed upon in their admission to registration, as prima facie proof of the number, the list being open to correction for deaths, removals and other causes subsequently occurring, and perhaps for disqualifications existing at the time of registration, and error in admitting their names to the list. McDowell v. Massachusetts & S. Const. Co. 96 N. C. 514; Southerland v. Goldsboro, Id. 49; Duke v. Brown, Id. 127; Markham v. Manning, Id. 132.

The omission from the form of oath prescribed by the Code, and required of the voter, of the words "and laws of the United States," following the word "Constitution," and "laws of North Carolina not inconsistent therewith," following the same word in reference to the State, is immaterial. State v. Nicholson, 102 N. C. 465.

The registration must be accepted as the act of the officer, notwithstanding the irregularity and even if no oath was administered. *Ibid.*

The fact that a registration book was not kept open during the whole prescribed period will not render the election void, where it had been kept open for inspection. *Ibid.*

The board of registration acts in a quasi judicial character, and is exempt from personal liability for errors of judgment without proof of malice or willful disregard of duty in refusing to register a duly entitled elector. Perry v. Reynolds, 1 New Eng. Rep. 647, 53 Conn. 527.

The registration books are prima facie evidence of the number of qualified voters in a town, but they are open for correction on account of deaths, etc., and perhaps for intrinsic disqualifications and errors in admitting persons to register. Markham v. Manning, 96 N. C. 132; Goforth v. Rutherford R. C. Co. Id. 535.

Registry laws must be so construed as to reconcile their provisions to the unimpaired right of suffrages at elections. Daggett v. Hudson, 1 West. Rep. 795, 43 Ohio St. 548.

The Act (82 Ohio Laws, 232) requiring registration in all cases as a condition to the right of suffrage in certain cities is unconstitutional and void, being unreasonable. *Ibid.*

The General Assembly, under the general grant of legislative power secured to it by the Constitution, has power to provide by statute for the registration of voters, and to enact that all electors must register before being permitted to vote. *Ibid.*

Such an Act, however, to be valid, must be reasonable and impartial, and calculated to facilitate and secure the constitutional right of suffrage, and not to subvert, or injuriously, unreasonably or unnecessarily restrain, impair or impede the right. *Ibid.*

A person not yet a citizen of the United States is entitled, under R. I. Pub. Laws 1889, chap. 735, § 2, to register his name on or before the last day of December, provided he may become qualified to vote during the ensuing year by naturalization. Ward v. Joslin, 16 R. I. —.

Territorial Legislatures have the power to prescribe any reasonable qualifications of voters and for holding office, not inconsistent with the limitations of the United States statutes. Davis v. Beason, 133 U. S. 333 (33 L. ed. 637).

A man disqualified to vote by reason of conviction of a felony is guilty of illegal voting if he votes knowing that he has been convicted of such crime, although he does not know that he is not qualified to vote. Thompson v. State, 26 Tex. App. 94.

In Wash. T. Organic Act (U. S. Rev. Stat., § 5506), providing that the qualifications of voters shall be as prescribed by the Legislative Assembly, provided that the right of suffrage shall be exercised only by adult citizens of the United States, the word "citizens" means only male inhabitants, and the Act of January 18, 1888, conferring the right of suffrage upon women, is void. Bloomer v. Todd (Wash. Ter.) 1 L. R. A. 111.

As to the right of voters to be registered, see *note* to Atty-Gen. v. Detroit (Mich.) 7 L. R. A. 99.

The defendants rely upon the foregoing provisions for the justification of their action in causing the name of the plaintiff to be struck and dropped from the assessment list and continuing to leave it off the same.

The plaintiff had not paid any county tax within the space of two years next preceding the general election in 1886.

This suit is an action on the case brought for the recovery of damages resulting to the plaintiff by reason of his having been deprived by the defendants of all opportunity of paying a county tax for 1886, and thereby qualifying himself to vote at said general election.

The questions reserved for the decision of this court are, first, whether or not the above provisions of the Legislation of 1873 are unconstitutional and void; and, secondly, if said provisions be unconstitutional and void, whether or not the defendants are personally liable in damages for their action in the premises.

Messrs. **Edward G. Bradford, Levi C. Bird** and **Anthony Higgins**, for plaintiff:

The provisions of the Legislation of 1873 upon which the defendants rely, considered as a fiscal regulation of the State, are unconstitutional and void.

The whole of a public burden cannot be thrown on a single individual, under pretense of taxing him.

Sharpless v. *Philadelphia*, 21 Pa. 147, 168; *Hammett* v. *Philadelphia*, 65 Pa. 146; *Re Washington Avenue*, 69 Pa. 352.

If a capitation tax be laid, none of the class of persons thus taxed can be constitutionally exempt upon any other ground than that of public service.

Lexington v. *McQuillan*, 9 Dana, 513; Cooley, Taxn. p. 18; *State* v. *Readington Twp.* 36 N. J. L. 66; *People* v. *Brooklyn*, 4 N. Y. 420.

Unequal taxation by States is prohibited by the 14th Amendment to the Constitution of the United States.

Ex parte Virginia, 100 U. S. 339, 347 (25 L. ed. 676, 680); *Minneapolis & St. L. R. Co.* v. *Beckwith*, 129 U. S. 26, 28 (32 L. ed. 585); *Re Ah Fong*, 3 Sawy. 144, 157; *Barbier* v. *Connolly*, 113 U. S. 27, 31 (28 L. ed. 923, 924); *Yick Wo* v. *Hopkins*, 118 U. S. 356, 369 (30 L. ed. 220, 226); *San Mateo County* v. *Southern Pac. R. Co.* 8 Sawy. 238; *Santa Clara County* v. *Southern Pac. R. Co.* 9 Sawy. 165.

The primary purpose of the provisions of the Legislation of 1873, upon which the defendants rely, was not the regulation of taxation, but the regulation of the elective franchise or its exercise, as such purpose is disclosed by the effect of the Statute.

Henderson v. *New York City*, 92 U. S. 258, 268 (23 L. ed. 543, 548); *Soon Hing* v. *Crowley*, 113 U. S. 703, 710 (28 L. ed. 1145, 1147).

The primary function of written constitutions is rather the recognition and regulation of preexisting rights fundamental in their nature, and their protection against assault or encroachment on the part of the State, than the creation of new rights.

2 Webster's Works, 392; Cooley, Const. Lim. 36.

In the United States there are vested in the people certain inherent and inalienable rights essential to the welfare and happiness of mankind.

Butchers Union S. H. & L. S. L. Co. v. *Crescent City L. S. L. & S. H. Co.* 111 U. S. 746, 756 (28 L. ed. 585, 591).

The doctrine of the innate dignity and sovereignty of manhood underlying our distinctive American liberty gives color and breadth and grandeur to our political institutions. It imperatively demands an equality of civil rights among all men.

The Federalist, No. 38; 1 Webster's Works, 77.

The right in the people to participate in the Legislature is the foundation of liberty and of all free government.

1 Delaware Laws, App. 79, XXVIII.

The ballot is the only means by which the people can exercise their inherent sovereignty and enjoy the right of self-government.

Auld v. *Walton*, 12 La. Ann. 129, 139.

The right to vote is the corner stone upon which rest our free institutions and the preservation of our rights and liberties. Where the right exists, it is a supreme and fundamental right vested in the citizen, as sharing in the sovereignty of the people.

Yick Wo v. *Hopkins*, 118 U. S. 356, 370 (30 L. ed. 220, 226); *Brown* v. *Hummel*, 6 Pa. 86, 93.

The constitutional provisions for the exercise of that supreme political right are, from the essential nature of the principles upon which free government is based, to be liberally construed.

United States v. *Slater*, 4 Woods, 356; *Henshaw* v. *Foster*, 9 Pick. 312, 316; Cooley, Const. Lim. 59.

Under the Constitution of Delaware the right of suffrage, although its exercise depends upon compliance with certain constitutional prerequisites or conditions, is vested in the male citizens of the State, of the age of twenty-one years or upwards, except idiots, insane persons, paupers and persons convicted of a crime deemed by law felony; and this right can be devested only through forfeiture as a punishment for crime judicially ascertained.

The specification in the Constitution of the means by which the right may be forfeited is a constitutional prohibition against the forfeiture of the right by any other means.

McCafferty v. *Guyer*, 59 Pa. 109; *Page* v. *Allen*, 58 Pa. 338, 346; *Barker* v. *People*, 20 Johns. 457; Cooley, Const. Lim. 64.

Every male citizen of the State of the age of twenty-one years or upwards, whose right of suffrage has not been forfeited as a punishment for crime, has a constitutional right to comply with the constitutional prerequisites or conditions for his exercise of the right of suffrage.

Patterson v. *Barlow*, 60 Pa. 54, 67.

One entitled to vote shall not be deprived of the privilege by the action of the authorities.

Cooley, Const. Lim. 616; *Capen* v. *Foster*, 12 Pick. 485, 489; *Page* v. *Allen*, 58 Pa. 338, 346, 351; *McCafferty* v. *Guyer*, 59 Pa. 109; *Patterson* v. *Barlow*, 60 Pa. 54, 67, 71; *Daggett* v. *Hudson*, 43 Ohio St. 548; *State* v. *Fitzgerald*, 37 Minn. 26; *Atty-Gen.* v. *Detroit*, 58 Mich. 213; *Dells* v. *Kennedy*, 49 Wis. 555; *Rison* v. *Farr*, 24 Ark. 161, 171; *People* v. *Canaday*, 73 N. C. 198; *Quinn* v. *State*, 35 Ind. 485.

All regulations of the elective franchise,

however, must be reasonable, uniform and impartial; they must not have for their purpose directly or indirectly to deny or abridge the constitutional right of citizens to vote, or unnecessarily to impede its exercise; if they do, they must be declared void.

Cooley, Const. Lim. 602; *State* v. *Constantine*, 42 Ohio St. 437; *State* v. *Corner*, 22 Neb. 265; *State* v. *Tuttle*, 53 Wis. 45; *Kineen* v. *Wells*, 4 New Eng. Rep. 457, 144 Mass. 497; *State* v. *Baker*, 38 Wis. 71; *Monroe* v. *Collins*, 17 Ohio St. 666; *State* v. *Williams*, 5 Wis. 308; *People* v. *Maynard*, 15 Mich. 463; Paine, Elections, § 340; McCrary, Elections, §§ 13, 17.

The Legislature having no constitutional power to deny, abridge or embarrass the exercise of the elective franchise by any direct legislation, such denial, abridgment or embarrassment cannot constitutionally be effected through indirect legislation, although directly relating to other subjects than the right of suffrage.

Cummings v. *Missouri*, 71 U. S. 4 Wall. 277 (18 L. ed. 356); *Woodbridge* v. *Detroit*, 8 Mich. 274, 306; *Re Parrott*, 6 Sawy. 349, 382, 383; *Davies* v. *McKeeby*, 5 Nev. 369.

Messrs. **John H. Rodney** and **George Gray** for defendants.

Comegys, *Ch. J.*, delivered the opinion of the court:

The questions presented in the arguments of this case by the counsel of the plaintiff are many; but they are all within the scope of those made by the case stated, and questions reserved thereon, which, in effect, are whether the legislation of this State in 1878, set forth in counsel's briefs, is a valid exercise of legislative power; and, if not, whether the defendants are liable to the plaintiff in damages in his action.

In order to properly comprehend and decide the first question, it is necessary—at least I think it will be useful—to go back into the political history of the State, or rather of the territory of which it is composed, and ascertain what, down to the time of the Revolutionary War, was the law with regard to the suffrage, or right to vote for public officers at elections. Before doing this, it will be well that a proper understanding should obtain in regard to the participation of men in the government they are under; that is, the power of deciding by ballot, at elections held for that purpose, who shall administer public affairs.

It is not directly denied on behalf of the plaintiff—in fact, it is conceded—that the power to use the ballot is one of those derived from government, or the political society in which the elector resides. At the same time, the contention here is the outgrowth of the idea that the primary object of government is universality of electorate. It is, of course, entirely consistent with the hopes of most men, members of a political body (as one of the States of the Union) that every person recognized by society as acting *sui juris* should participate in the ballot; and all such, it is believed, are accorded that privilege. But in this State, as no doubt in most of the others, it is conferred only upon the condition of contributing to the support of the government. The paramount duty of organized society is not to make the use of the ballot "free" to every such person, but to provide the means for its own sustenance, which is done by taxation, and, after that, but altogether subordinate to it, however, to secure to the payer of taxes, not the mere taxable, the privilege, or "right," as it is generally called, to vote at elections. There is no natural right to vote. It is one conferred by a community at large upon certain of its members, which implies the power and authority to withhold it from others. The whole idea of our original government—that before 1776—was that only those who paid taxes should vote; not that all should vote, but only those who helped to support the government. It was a privilege conferred upon such, and such only. They were the freemen, out of whose body, in the public aggregate mass, the public officers, particularly the Legislative Council and Assembly, were to be chosen. Those who had real estate were rated upon it, and such as had not were assessed upon the poll.

It is a great mistake to suppose that the first law for a poll-tax, as alleged by plaintiff's counsel in argument, was the Act of 1796. The fact is that before William Penn came to America, to take possession of the territory granted him by Charles II. (March, 1681), he promulgated a "frame" of government for his Province of Pennsylvania, and a Code called "Laws Agreed upon in England," which latter defines those who are to be considered as freemen to use the ballot. In the language of the "frame," by the second clause or paragraph, the freemen were to choose the Provincial Council, and, by the fourteenth, the members of the General Assembly. There is, however, no definition therein of a "freeman." The date of this is the 25th of April (then the second month), 1682. On the following 5th of May, the latter rescript was passed, which in the second clause defines the term "freeman," used in the former and in the first clause of the latter, in the following words: "*Second.* That every inhabitant of said Province [Pennsylvania] that is or shall be a purchaser of one hundred acres of land, or upwards, his heirs and assigns, and every person who shall have paid his passage, and taken up one hundred acres of land at one penny an acre, and have cultivated ten acres thereof, and every person that hath been a servant or bondsman, and is free by his service, that shall have taken up fifty acres of land, and cultivated twenty thereof, and every inhabitant, artificer or other resident in the said Province that pays scot and lot to the government, shall be deemed and accounted a freeman of said Province; and every such person shall be, and may be, capable of electing, or being elected, representatives of the people in Provincial Council or General Assembly in the said Province." These documents are to be found in a compilation of the laws established by the Duke of York, and by the Penn government, also, made by authority of the State of Pennsylvania, labelled "Duke of York's Book of Laws, 1676–1682," and the "Charter and Laws of the Province of Pennsylvania, 1682–1700," pp. 93–101.

In the "Act of Union" by which the counties which now form this State were, by the desire of the inhabitants, annexed by Penn (who had become enfeoffed of them by deed of the Duke of York, who succeeded his brother,

Charles II., as James II.) to his Province of Pennsylvania, those inhabitants were guaranteed to be governed by the same laws, and to enjoy the same privileges, in all respects, as the inhabitants of Pennsylvania, etc. Freemen in the counties were then the same as freemen in the Province; that is, those who paid "scot and lot," or "customary contribution laid upon all subjects according to their ability," as it is defined by the lexicographer, Bailey. The date is 7th of December, 1682. Id. 104. On the same date as the "Act of Union," Penn, "with the advice and consent of the deputies of the freemen of this Province and counties aforesaid" (the Delaware counties), enacted what is called "The Great Laws, or Body of Laws," by chapter 58 of which it is provided as follows: "And, that elections may not be corruptly managed, upon which the present and future good of the Province so much depends, be it," etc., "that all elections of members or representatives of the people and freemen of the Province of Pennsylvania, and territories annexed [now Delaware], to serve in the Assembly thereof, shall be free and voluntary; and that the elector that shall receive any reward or gift, in meat, drink, moneys or otherwise, shall forfeit his right to elect; and such person as shall give, promise or bestow any such reward, as aforesaid, to be elected, shall forfeit his election, and be thereby incapable to serve as aforesaid; and the Assembly shall be sole judges of the regularity or irregularity of the election of the members thereof." In chapter 127 following, it is enacted in these words: "And, to the end that due provisions be made to defray the requisite charges incident to the public business and service of this Province, and territories thereof, be it enacted," etc., "that the charges of each county shall be made up in open court by the respective magistrates thereof; and that every such court shall have, and hereby hath, power to assess and lay such taxes upon the county as shall defray the same, so that it be equal, and according to proportion; and that the one half of the said tax to be paid shall be raised upon land, the other half by the poll, on the male from sixteen to sixty years of age, and that all such persons who hold land within the Province and territories thereof, and do not reside therein, and so incapable of giving that attendance, and yielding that service, to the public, as those that live therein, shall pay to all public taxes for such lands so held by them one half more than residents pay for the same portion."

On the 20th of October, 1691, William and Mary took the government of the Province and territories (the Delaware counties) into their own hands. In this State, on dispossession of Penn, they appointed, as captain general and governor, Benjamin Fletcher; one of the first acts of whose administration was to procure the passage of a law for granting a penny in the pound to the sovereigns, towards the support of the government under him. The fourth clause of the Act provides that the tax shall be a charge upon real and personal estate for a year only, and then declares that "all freemen within this Province and territories as have been out of their servitude by the space of six months, and shall not be otherwise rated by this Act, nor worth one hundred pounds, shall pay unto the use aforesaid the sum of six shillings per head, with a proviso that our chief proprietary and his late deputies shall not be assessed or otherwise chargeable by virtue of this Act." Id. 221, 222. By section 17 of this Act (the law about counties levies) it is provided that the grand jury shall present any sum necessary to be raised, either for the paying of any public debt, or other occasion for the public utility of the county, "and the justices [of the quarter sessions] to make the rate or assessment, which shall be raised in the same manner as moneys are by the sessions agreed to be raised for the support of the government, viz., after the rate of one penny per pound [upon property] and six shillings upon the poll." Id. 233.

William Penn was restored to the government of his Province and territories by William and Mary in the sixth year of their reign (21st October, 1698), and appointed his nephew, William Markham, his deputy, who, with the advice and consent of the council and representatives of the Province and territories, passed an Act or body of laws, the first clause of which, after the preamble, defines the term "freemen" (that is, those who were to vote for council and assemblymen), as follows: "That no inhabitant of this Province or territories shall have right of electing or being elected as aforesaid unless they be free denizens of this government, and are of the age of twenty one years of age or upwards, and have fifty acres of land, ten acres whereof are seated and cleared, or be otherwise worth fifty pounds lawful money of this government, clear estate, and have been resident within this government for the space of two years next before such election." Id. 247.

By this law, Penn made the electoral qualification one entirely of property. In the second chapter of the enactment is "An Act for Raising the Rate of One Penny per Pound, and Six Shillings per Head, upon Such as are not otherwise Rated thereby, to be Employed by the Government for the Time being as is hereinafter Limited and Appointed;" the enacting section of which fixes the rate for housekeepers, and then provides that all males within this Province and territories of this Act who have been free of their servitude by the space of six months, and shall be above the age of twenty-one years, being worth £72 and upwards, shall be assessed and pay after the rate of one penny per pound clear estate as aforesaid, and that such of the said males only as be not worth £72 shall pay six shillings per head.

In 1704 the separation between the territories and the Province took place; and thereafter they had separate legislative bodies, though under the lieutenant governors of the Penn proprietorship of the Province as long as the rule of the family lasted, that is, down to the Revolutionary War. The first declaration of those entitled to vote, of electing and being elected, after the separation was made by an Act of the 7th George II. (1736), passed by the then Lieutenant Gov. Patrick Gordon, "by and with the advice and consent of the representatives of the freemen of the said counties [New Castle, Kent and Sussex on Delaware], in General Assembly met," etc, which in its second section confines the suffrage to property holders by this language: "Provided, always, that no inhabitants of this government shall have right of electing or being elected as aforesaid unless he or they be natural-born subjects of Great Britain, or be naturalized in England, or in this government, or in the Province of Pennsylvania, and unless such person or persons be of the age of twenty-two years or upwards, and be a freeholder or freeholders in this government, and have fifty acres of land or more well settled, and twelve acres thereof cleared and improved, or be otherwise worth forty pounds lawful money of this government clear estate, and have been resident therein for the space of two years before such election." 1 Laws Del. 146.

There is no other Act relating to the qualification of elector in the colonial period. In the year 1797 an Act of the General Assembly of the State was passed which established a different rule from that then prevailing for assessing the polls of freemen, that is, the personal rate. This fixed it at not more than £1,000, of the then currency, nor less than £200. This is the Act erroneously supposed to have first created the poll-tax. Hall's Dig. Laws Del. 390.

In the Revision of 1852 the phraseology is changed, the highest rate of poll-tax being $2,700, the equivalent of £1,000, and the lowest $140, the virtual equivalent of £50, Delaware currency. Such is the law of the State at this day.

From this review of the law which has always prevailed here in regard to the qualification of voters, two things seem to be clear—that is, that the right to vote was conditional altogether upon the payment of taxes previously assessed ("scot and lot," as tersely expressed in the homely but perfectly well-understood language of the ancient enactments), and that the poll-tax was adopted 100 years, at least, before 1797, for those who had no property. Under the old system, there could be no privilege of voting by any without payment of tax, without each man paying his part towards the support of government. The theory then was that no man should enjoy the privilege of voting for public officers unless he paid for it, by adding the requirement of tax upon him to the general concession for the maintenance of the State. The privilege was conditional upon his doing that in some form, voluntary or by compulsion. "Pay your tax and you may vote," said the law; which shows that it was only upon compliance with a condition that a citizen could cast a ballot. All arguments, therefore, which are the offspring of any notion of inalienable right, sacred right, indefeasible right, have no place in this discussion. The right to vote was, in the old time as now, conditional upon several things,—citizenship, majority of age, payment of county rates and levies. It was and is but a privilege or right *sub conditione;* and those who fixed the terms of it were strangers to any other idea than *quid pro quo,*—"scot and lot." Such modern ideas as manhood suffrage (if by that be meant a suffrage because of full age), ballot for all and slavery without the ballot, were properly left to be evolved out of the consciousness of visionary theorists, with aspirations for a state of society dreamt of only by those who would substitute our poor humanity for the great Creator.

The law of 7th George II. (1736), continued, as that fixing the qualification of voters, until the Constitution of the State, of 1792, was made; for that of the 20th September, 1776 (1 Laws Del. App. 83), expressly provides that "the right of suffrage in the election of members for both Houses shall remain as exercised by law at present," etc. Article 5.

In the former the right is thus defined. Article 4, §1: "All elections of governor, senators and representatives shall be by ballot; and, in such elections, every white freeman of the age of twenty-one years, having resided in the State two years next before the election, and within that time paid a state or county tax, which shall have been assessed at least six months before the election, shall enjoy the right of an elector, and the sons of persons so qualified shall between the ages of twenty-one and twenty-two years, be entitled to vote, although they shall not have paid taxes." Const. 1792 (1 Laws Del. 88).

The latter clause of the article was a new feature introduced into the canon of electoral qualification. In the year 1831 a state convention was held to revise the Constitution of 1792. By it, elections were made biennial instead of annual, and the electoral qualification was modified by this language: "In such elections every free white male citizen of the age of twenty-two years or upwards, having resided in the State one year next before the election, and the last month thereof in the county where he offers to vote, and having, within two years next before the election, paid a county tax which shall have been assessed at least six months before the election, shall enjoy the right of an elector; and every free white male citizen of the age of twenty-one years and under the age of twenty-two years, having resided as aforesaid, shall be entitled to vote without payment of any tax: provided, that . . . no idiot or insane person or pauper, or person convicted of a crime deemed by law a felony, shall enjoy the right of an elector," etc. Rev. Code 1874, pp. 32, 33.

This change extended the time for payment of tax to two years before the election, to conform it to the biennial system of elections; allowing all men between twenty-one and twenty-two, having the residential qualification, to vote without payment of tax, confined the tax to county rates and excluded the insane, paupers and persons convicted of felony. This constitutional qualification continues in force to this day,—nearly sixty years from the time of its enactment. Under the old system of taxation provided in the 6th section of the "Act Concerning the Levy Court," etc. (Hall's Dig. 576), the general rate of persons and personal property continued for six, and the assessment of real estate for twelve, years. Afterwards the former was reduced to four years (Rev. Code 1874, p. 85), and by a subsequent amendment that of real estate, which before had been first twelve and then eight years, was reduced to four also (18 Laws, chap. 294); so that the assessments of persons and personal property, and of real estate, are now uniform as to duration.

By the law in force prior to the year 1843,

upon the allowance by the levy court to a collector, in its settlement with him at the March session, of a party upon his duplicate as a delinquent, the practice was to drop his name from the assessment list; and it remained off until the next general assessment of persons and personal property, when it was restored. This was in virtue of the rule that a condition once shown to exist is presumed to continue until the contrary be established. If the Statute had not provided that there should be a general assessment of persons and personal property (*quoad ante*), the name would have remained off the list until the delinquent had himself applied to have it restored, which would not, of course, have been done without some proof that the condition no longer existed; and, in accordance with this presumption, a collector was allowed two years to collect the taxes on his duplicate (copy of the assessment list, with calculation of tax), and no more. Then the tax was treated as extinguished entirely. Hall, Dig. 380.

But it was discovered that collectors, in their zeal to promote the interest of the political party to which they owed their appointment, were in the habit, after the expiry of the two years, of allowing the taxes more than two years old of delinquents on their own sides, or on any other side, provided they would vote the ticket of the collector's party, to be paid, with a view of qualifying them to vote. As the collector's receipt was evidence of right to vote, there was no gainsaying it, without resort to the records of the levy court, which was impracticable. To prevent this fraud upon the Election Law, which contemplated, not the payment of taxes allowed as delinquent, and thus extinguished in fact, but payment of existing rates, the Legislature, at the session of 1843, passed an Act entitled "An Act to Amend the Election Laws of the State of Delaware," in the following words (Act 9th vol. 545): "Whereas, it is highly important to preserve the elections in their purity, and to secure the confidence of the people in the integrity of those who conduct them, therefore, . . . Sec. 2. And be it further enacted by the authority aforesaid, that, for the purpose of preventing frauds by the pretended receipt of old taxes, and by the antedating of receipts for tax, that no collector in this State shall collect any tax upon his duplicate after two years from the date of his warrant, but that after the lapse of two years from such date every such tax shall be extinguished, and no collector shall have power to give a receipt therefor. And it is hereby further enacted and declared that every tax which shall have been returned and regularly allowed by the levy court as delinquent shall be, and the same is, utterly extinguished, and no collector, or other person in his name, shall have power to collect the same, or give a receipt therefor, and any receipt given for such tax shall be void; and if any collector shall receive any such tax, or give a receipt therefor, contrary to the provisions of this section, or shall fraudulently antedate or postdate any tax receipt, or shall use any other fraud in giving such receipt, he shall be deemed guilty of a misdemeanor, and, on conviction thereof by indictment, shall forfeit and pay to the State a fine of $100, and shall also forfeit and pay to any person who will sue for and recover the same the further sum of $100, with costs of suit. The levy court shall examine and settle the delinquent lists of each collector at its meeting in March every year, and make allowance of delinquents. Upon the allowance of any delinquency, the name of such delinquent shall be struck from the assessment list, and also from the collector's duplicate, and shall not be again restored until the delinquent is again lawfully assessed. Sec. 8. And be it further enacted by the authority aforesaid, that the assessors for each hundred in this State, in the year 1844, and in every year thereafter, shall make and complete the assessment for their respective hundreds by the 15th day of January, and shall, on or before the 23d day of said month, publish, by posting in at least five of the most public places in such hundred, a list of the names of the persons assessed, arranged in alphabetical order, setting down separately the amounts assessed as real, personal and capitation, or poll, tax and carrying out the aggregate amount so assessed against each name, and shall at the same time, and at the same places, and in the same manner, give notice that they will attend at the place of holding the general election in such hundred on the last Saturday in said month, from the hour of ten o'clock A. M. until the hour of five o'clock P. M., for the purpose of correcting any errors which may then be shown to him by any resident of such hundred in his assessment, and for the purpose of assessing any such resident as he may have omitted. And additions to, and corrections of, the said assessment lists, may also be made by the levy court and court of appeal in session at any stated or regularly adjourned session of the said court before the first day of April in any year. No assessment shall be made after the last day of March, nor shall any alteration of the assessments be made after that time, except in the lawful allowance of delinquencies. If any assessor, collector, clerk of the peace or other person, shall fraudulently add to, or take from, the said assessments, as finally settled by the levy court at its last session in March, such person shall be guilty of a misdemeanor, and, on conviction thereof by indictment, shall forfeit and pay to the State a fine of $500. . . ."

The preambles to the first and second sections show the motive and purpose of the Legislature, the latter being that above ascribed to it. As corroborative of the allegation above made, that the payment of existing rates by a party offering to vote was contemplated, it is only necessary to refer back to the Statute already cited from Hall's Dig. 578, where, near the close of the 4th section, will be found this language in relation to the returns of the assessors of the assessments, correction of them by the court, etc.: "And, in the year in which a general rate of persons and valuation of personal property only shall be returned, the list [assessment list] shall contain the names, in alphabetical order, of all the persons upon the assessment list of the hundred whose personal property shall be valued, or personal rate imposed; and such list shall specify the personal rate, and the number of slaves, and their valuation, and the valuation of the personal property, and the total amount of the rate and valuation, and in all other years [*i. e.*, years other than those of general assessment of persons and personal property, then six years apart] the list shall contain only additions or alterations that shall have been made to or of the assessment list of the hundred," etc. By the 6th section of the same Act it is provided "that the assessor of each hundred shall annually rate the persons of those liable to such rate, who have arrived to the age of twenty-one years since the making of the assessment of the preceding year, or who shall come to reside in the county, or who shall before have been omitted, and personal property acquired by bequest," etc. Here there is no provision for the restoration of delinquents to the assessment list. Having been dropped from the general list by the uniform usage of the levy court, by force of the presumption quoted, they were not to be again rated until a new general assessment was made. The legality of the practice was unquestioned. The objection to one offering to vote, that he was not on the "levy list," as it was called in common speech, was fatal to his application, unless he could show, before the Constitution of 1831, the payment of a state or county tax within a year which had been assessed six months before the election at which he offered to vote, or, since that time, the payment within two years of a county tax assessed six months also before the election. The purpose of the Act of 1843 was to expressly require what had been always theretofore held to be the law with respect to delinquents, with that, in addition, of preventing the pretended receipt of old taxes, etc. The theory had always been, without dispute, to that time, by the men of any party, that delinquency was exclusion from the assessment until another general assessment of persons and personal property was made, when the law required that they should be put on the list again.

The Act of 1843 stood unchallenged upon the statute book until the year 1847, when a supplement to it was passed, the second section of which provides as follows: "That it shall be the duty of each of the assessors of this State, in the annual assessments for their respective hundreds, according to the law of this State, to assess all such persons as may have been returned and allowed as delinquents at any session of the levy court preceding the period fixed by the Act to which this is a supplement, for the completion of his assessment: provided, such persons reside at the time in the hundred for which he is assessor. And any resolution or order of the levy court, in either of the counties of this State, adverse to the provisions of this Act, be, and the same is hereby, declared null and void; and any practice authorizing the said assessors to omit the assessment of such delinquents until the period of the assessment of persons and personal property next following the time when such persons shall have been allowed as delinquents be, and the same is hereby, directed to be discontinued." Vol. 10, p. 171. Though not doing so in terms, this Act virtually repealed that portion of the original Act of 1843 which provided differently with respect to delinquents; but there is no suggestion or hint in it that the repealed feature of the latter Act was in any sense hostile to the constitutional provisions concerning the privilege of suffrage. It therefore should be treated rather in the light of a revenue provision. At the session of 1851 an Act was passed entitled "An Act to Extend the Rights and Privileges of Poor White Taxables within the State." It is in the following words (Act 10, vol. 518): "Whereas, the present law of this State, requiring the names of delinquent taxables to be stricken from the assessment lists, does, in substance, treat poverty as a crime amounting to disfranchisement; and whereas, it may, and frequently does, happen that, from sickness or other misfortune, poor persons become temporarily unable to pay the public taxes assessed against them, who are nevertheless good and worthy citizens, and willing at all times, when able, to pay the public charges against them, and that the inability to pay in any particular year is no proof that such inability will exist the succeeding year; therefore: Section 1. Be it enacted by the Senate and House of Representatives of the State of Delaware, in General Assembly met, that from and after the passage of this Act the allowances of delinquent lists in the several counties of this State shall be deemed, taken and held to have no other design or effect than the crediting of the accounts of the several collectors for the time being with the several amounts by them respectively returned as the assessments against said delinquent taxables, and that, after being so allowed and credited as aforesaid, the same shall all be again placed on the duplicates of the collectors of the several counties for the succeeding year, except such as are returned as being dead or removed from the State. Sec. 2. And be it further enacted that the Act entitled 'A Supplement to the Act Entitled "An Act to Amend the Election Laws of the State of Delaware,"' passed at Dover, February 16, 1847, and so much of the second section of the Act entitled 'An Act to Amend the Election Laws of this State,' passed at Dover, February 27, 1843, as relates to the striking the names of delinquent taxables from the assessment lists and the collectors' duplicates, be, and the same are hereby, repealed, made null and void."

This Act had its inspiration in the desire of the political party which at the preceding general election of representatives, etc., had attained the power through a split in the party dominant since 1838, to increase its voting strength, the delinquent taxables having been always chiefly of their politics. It was not the offspring of any sentiment that prior legislation with respect to delinquents was in derogation of the electoral right, but grew out of the natural wish to magnify the electorate so as to enable the party then in power to remain there. It is true, the preamble has language that would warrant a different view; but it is well known that it was used simply rhetorically, to promote the passage of the Act. If any of the tax laws had been suspected even of infringing the constitutional right of suffrage, the party which passed the Acts now under consideration would have brought them to the bar of judicial decision to be annulled; for their interest, for the reason above given, made them necessarily hostile to them. The law just quoted remained undisturbed until the Legislature of 1873, which gave rise to this controversy. That legislation has provoked much criticism and animadversion; yet it is not much more, so far as delinquent taxables are concerned, than a revival of the Act of 1848, prepared by the then attorney-general of the State, the late *Chief Justice* Gilpin. From the known care and caution with which his legal action generally was characterized, it is fair to suppose that he gave to the preparation all the consideration and reflection the subject required. Although the fact would not of itself justify a positive conclusion as to the validity of the law, yet it is much, in passing upon it, constitutionally considered, to know that the then first law-officer of the State put it forth with the sanction of his professional rank. As the present Assessment Laws are part of the legislation of 1873, it will be well to take a view of the law as it was before that session. There being no other law for the registration of voters than the Assessment Laws, this is the more necessary, the real contention being that the system of law under which we live, with respect to the electoral right, is repugnant to the Constitution of the State, or that of the United States.

I have already pointed out that in this State there are periodic general assessments of persons and personal property, as well as of real estate. Now they are, by modification of former law, to be made every four years; and now, as heretofore, annual assessments of persons and personal property, in addition to the general assessment, are to be made, for the purpose of including newcomers, persons who have arrived at age since the prior assessment, and personal property since acquired, and to correct omissions, etc. The "Act for the Valuation of Property" (Rev. Code, 84) provides for the periodic assessment of property and persons, but it was modified by chapter 394 of volume 13 so as to reduce the time for the duration of the assessment of real property to four years, thus securing a general assessment of all property once every four years. I have stated this before. There was also, by this Act, a provision for annual assessments, as above.

There was no change in these provisions made by the Act of 9th of April, 1873,—part of the legislation under consideration; but some new features were introduced for what would seem to be the purpose of securing to persons who ought to have the right to vote the means of protecting that right, and to prevent others from voting who ought not to be allowed to do so. The first section prevents the assessors from placing upon the assessment list, in addition to the names of those assessed for poll-tax (all male citizens entitled to vote), the name of anyone not the owner in his own right of taxable property within the assessor's limits, unless he be satisfied, from personal knowledge, that he is of age, and a bona fide resident of the hundred or district, except as thereinafter in the Act provided. The second section provides that, in ten days after making his assessment,—which, by section 16 of the chapter concerning assessors (Rev. Code, 78), he is to complete by the 1st day of January,—he is to post it, made alphabetically, in front of the most public places in his territory, and give notice in writing, either attached to it or otherwise, stating that he will attend at the place of holding the general election therein, on some day to be named in said notice, from 10 A. M. till 5 P. M., to correct errors, and assess any who may have been omitted; and shall also state in the notice that persons desiring to be assessed must apply in person at the time and place mentioned therein, and furnish proof of identity, age and residence required by section 8 following. And it is provided in the same section that, if the assessor cannot complete the service on the day named, he may adjourn to the next or some subsequent day, not exceeding three days from that time, to be announced publicly to those present at the time of the adjournment. The third section not only makes it lawful but the duty of the assessor to place upon his assessment list the name of any person who may have been omitted, who shall appear before him at the time and place specified in the notices aforesaid, and prove his right to be assessed by the affidavit of some respectable freeholder of the county, according to the form of the affidavit given. The fourth section enacts a penalty against the assessor, of not less than $100, nor more than $500, to be recovered by indictment for the misdemeanor the offense is declared to be, of refusing or omitting to place the applicant making the aforesaid proof upon the assessment list, and also for placing on the list, knowingly, the name of any fictitious person, or person not at the time a resident of his territory. The fifth section provides that, in case the assessor is unable, from sickness or otherwise, to attend at the time and place stated in his notice, he shall appoint some other man for the purpose, and give notice thereof as in the second section is mentioned. The sixth section makes it unlawful for the levy court, or any member thereof, to take from the assessment list any names appearing thereon, or to add to any assessment returned by the assessor the name of any person, unless upon his personal application and proof so to be made, as aforesaid, before the assessor, of his right to be assessed. A violation of the above by a member of the court is made a misdemeanor, with penalty of a fine of from $100 to $500 on conviction. And, if the clerk of the peace (the clerk of the levy court) shall neglect to place upon the duplicate to be delivered by him to the collector any name on the assessor's list, he shall forfeit and pay to the person whose name is left off the sum of $10. This is to punish him; for the party's right to vote depends upon his assessment, and not on the correcting of the duplicate. The seventh section makes the offense a misdemeanor, punishable by fine of from $100 to $500, by anyone who shall procure or cause to be placed upon the assessment list any person not entitled to be assessed, or any fictitious or fraudulent person. The 8th section makes it perjury to make a false affidavit under the Act. The 9th section makes it unlawful for any assessor or the levy court to place upon the assessment list of the assessor's hundred the name of any person who was returned a delinquent the year preceding, until after the expiration of twelve months from the time of the allowance of the delinquency by the levy court. The 10th section makes it the duty of the clerk of the peace to deliver to the sheriff in the month of August, in the year of holding the general election, an alphabetical list for each of the hundreds of the county of the delinquent list made and returned by the collectors at the March session of the levy court.

By the 10th section of the chapter next succeeding (chap. 12 of *Collectors*), each collector must, on the first Tuesday of March next succeeding the date of his warrant, render to the levy court a true account of all taxes it was his duty to collect, of all payments made, and of all delinquents; and by section 1 of chap. 372 of vol. 14 of the Laws (Rev. Code, 90), it is made the collector's duty, within thirty days after he has received his duplicate, to give public notice by advertisements, posted in ten or more of the most public places of his territory, stating his place of business or residence, and his readiness to receive taxes; and it is also made his duty, in the month of January in each year, again to give public notice, as aforesaid, of at least ten days, said notice to state the times and places at which he will attend to receive unpaid taxes. It is then made the duty of the levy court, upon proof by the collector's affidavit filed in the office of the clerk of the peace, setting forth that he gave the notice required, and that, in accordance with the last required notice, he did attend at the time and place designated, and there remained for the space of five hours each day, for the period of at least three days, for the purpose of collecting the taxes aforesaid, to allow him as delinquencies the uncollected taxes; and then declares that the names of the delinquents shall be dropped from the assessment list by the levy court, and not be placed thereon again for the period of twelve months from the date of the allowance. The section is made applicable to persons liable to pay poll-tax alone; for the reason that those owning real property can always be made to pay by sale of their property, taxes being a prior lien thereon. It is true there is the ultimate remedy by imprisonment of the body in the case of mere poll-tax men; but it is never resorted to, the cost to the county of confinement in jail for a week, even, more than exceeding the tax. The second section provides that the notice shall be a sufficient demand upon taxables for their taxes, and a performance of the duty to make demand. By the law before (§§ 13, 15, chap. 12, Rev. Code, aforesaid), collectors could only proceed to sell property or imprison the body after ten days' demand, to be proved by his oath as competent evidence of that fact. By section 17, chap. 10, Rev. Code, p. 81, every assessor is required to return his assessment—which by the 16th section he is required to complete by the 1st day of January—to the levy court on the first Tuesday of February, and to attend the court on that day, and on the first Tuesday of March, and on such other days as the court may require, under a penalty of $20 to be recovered by indictment. This is to enable the court to perform its duty, mentioned in sections 12 and 13 in the chapter next cited. By section 11, chap. 8, Rev. Code, p. 62, the levy court is required to sit as a court of appeals on the first Tuesday of March of each year, and on such days and times thence next in said month ensuing as it shall be necessary to adjourn to, and examine the assessments returned by the assessors, and the corrections thereof and additions thereto that may have been made, and receive, hear and determine appeals against the same. By the 12th section the court have power, either upon their own examination or upon appeal, to make additions to and corrections of the assessment list; to call before them any person whose name ought to be on it, or who was omitted by the assessor, etc. By the 14th section, an assessment cannot be called in question anywhere than in the levy court; and the same, as it shall stand in that court, is conclusive. The 15th section provides that no assessment shall be made after the last day of March, and the 16th section, that, if any person shall fraudulently add to or take from the assessments as finally settled by the levy court, he shall be guilty of a misdemeanor, and fined $500. The 21st section enacts that, at the meeting in March in every year, the court shall settle the delinquent list of each collector, and make allowance of delinquents, and upon such allowance the collector is to be credited with the amount thereof. Then there is the provision for the re assessment of the delinquent, superseded by the Legislation of 1873.

I think I have now given—in brief in most cases, but in some *verbatim et literatim*—the provisions of law now in force in relation to the assessment and collection of taxes, and the allowance of delinquents, and the requirement when this is to be done. It will now be useful to compare the old with the present legislation, with a view of seeing what is the difference between them,—whether that difference does deprive the citizen of the right or privilege of the suffrage, it being contended by the plaintiff's counsel, not only that the new legislation was designed to disfranchise a certain class of voters, but that such is the necessary effect. Leaving out of view the question of design, which has no place in this discussion, the point to be decided is, Does the Legislation of 1873 necessarily impair the voting right of the citizen? It will be well, in this inquiry, to look at the state of things existing at the time it was passed, as contrasted with that it displaced.

Before emancipation of slaves, and the adoption of the 15th Amendment to the Constitution of the United States, voting in Delaware was confined to white males of over twenty-one years, with the exceptions before given; and so steady and constant was our population everywhere, except in Wilmington, that such persons as were selected to be assessors were usually acquainted personally with nearly all the voting class. It was for this reason, no doubt, that the law made no requirement of notice by the assessors that they were about to proceed, or would proceed, to make the assessment. At the February Session of the levy court, the assessments were returnable, and, by the practice of the court and the law, they were liable to correction by the levy court, in order to perfect them. But the March Term was an appeal term from assessments, at which any person aggrieved at not being assessed at all, or who, or whose property, was unfairly assessed, could appear before the court and obtain redress. When the levy court had made an examination of the assessment list, and corrections in them, at the February Term, it was the duty of the clerk of the peace, by the 20th of that month, to make copies of the hundred lists, and post them for public inspection, with notice of the holding the court of appeal. Section 27, chap. 9, Rev. Code (Hall's Dig. 375).

This publication was the first formal notice to the public of the assessments, and then they had been completed by the assessors. No further notice was given in relation to assessments. On or before the first Tuesday of April following, it was the duty of the court to issue to the collectors duplicates of the assessment lists, with the taxes assessed upon them, together with warrants for their collection; and it was that of the collector, before proceeding to collect his taxes by legal process, to make ten days' previous demand for them. But other notice to the taxpayers there was none. Doubtless it happened, in many cases, that parties were returned delinquent who had never been called upon for their taxes at all, their only notice being that given by the clerk of the peace, as above required, in the publication of the assessment lists. I have already pointed out that, under the old system, prior to the Act of 1843, when a person was returned a delinquent, his name was dropped from the assessment then existing, and have ascribed the practice to the maxim specified. Under it, therefore, if he was returned a delinquent, and allowed as such by the levy court at the March Session next after the year when the assessment was returned, he was off during the residue of the duration of the assessment (then six years), and after it was changed, then the residue of four years. But it was found that many names were restored in some way surreptitiously, which operated to allow the delinquent class, or such of them as the dominant party needed in their service, to vote when their ballots were in requisition, and escaped paying their taxes at other times, thus defeating the requirement of paying "scot and lot," or taxes whenever assessed, as the distinction of a freeman. This Law of 1843 broke up that fraud, or was intended to do so, and required, in terms, that the delinquent's name should not only be dropped, but that it should not go upon the list again until he was again lawfully assessed, which, by the restrictive effect of the provision in the old Statute for annual assessments could not be done until there was a general assessment of persons. In 1847 an Act was passed, the second section requiring the re-assessment of delinquents in the annual assessments. They then were made to stand upon the same footing as persons before omitted. The first section required the delinquent list to be returned by the collectors on the first day of the annual March Term, and prohibited allowance of it by the levy court for five days after return, and secured the public right to inspect it, by indictment of the members of the levy court, or the clerk of the peace, as the case might be, refusing to allow such inspection upon application. Vol. 10, p. 171.

That Act was repealed by that of 1851, before quoted, which provided that the effect of allowance of delinquency should only be to credit the collector with the tax, and required that the name of the delinquent should be again put upon the collector's duplicate. It also repealed expressly so much of the Act of 1843 as required the dropping the name of a delinquent from the assessment list, though that was done by implication. The Act of 1843, by the expression of purpose contained in the second section, shows a motive for passing the provision with respect to delinquent taxes, and to dropping delinquents from the tax-list. It did its work very effectively, so that taxes had to be paid. The condition upon which the elective franchise was to be enjoyed had to be performed, for the legal presumption prevailed.

In the political campaign of 1846, when the dominant party lost its candidate for governor, a fierce assault was made upon it, and chiefly because of the Act of 1843, and the manner in which that law dealt with delinquents. The Legislature, however, was not lost; and accordingly, at the session following the election, the Act of 1847 was passed, which was repealed, as has been stated, by that of 1851, when the power of the party in the Legislature passed into the hands of its opponent. The legislation upon the subject of delinquents was a game of politics, but no one doubted that it was one which might be lawfully played. It did not put it out of the power of any man, really or practically, to obtain and retain the right to vote, but only aimed at compelling him to perform the condition for its exercise as other people had to do who owned property,—pay the county taxes.

The party which passed the Act of 1851 lost its ascendency in the Legislature at the election of 1852, but retained its majority in the Senate. Of course, there was no prospect of repealing that which had been so great a *desideratum* with it,—on whose side the great body of the delinquents was. At the election of 1854 a totally new party came into power, and by what was then a large majority. Both branches of the Legislature were of its members,—the House entirely, and two thirds of the Senate. It was a very strong party, and had no need to concern itself with legislation about delinquents. A great mistake of legislation made at that session so shattered its ranks that the political power of the State passed away from it utterly, and the party itself practically disbanded. Such result restored to power the makers of the Legislation of 1851, which, suiting the dominant party perfectly, remained in force until it was repealed by that of 1873. By the latter, the provision contained in the Law of 1843 for dropping the name of a delinquent from the list, was re-enacted; and by the Assessment Act (14 Laws Del. chap. 371, Rev. Code, p. 82), passed at the same session (on the day preceding the Delinquent Act), or 14 Laws Del. chap. 372, Rev. Code, p. 90, assessors were forbidden to assess a delinquent "until after the expiration of twelve months" from the time allowance as delinquent was made by the levy court. Why was the Act of 1843 practically revived, as to dropping delinquents from the assessment list? That question has been answered before by what was said with respect to the necessity claimed for the Legislation of the 9th of February, 1873. An immense number of voters, and many of them emigrants from the south, had been added, by the 15th Amendment to the Constitution of the United States, to the political ranks of the State. Almost all of these new voters were obscure persons, without any means whatever of a tangible nature to pay their taxes; and it was soon developed that they would content themselves with paying in the year of voting, and not in an "off year," as it was called. They were not, the most of them, persons whom the stigma of delinquency prompted to the avoidance of it by paying every year. It was grossly unjust to those who had property of an assessable nature, and could not, if they desired, escape the payment of "scot and lot," and to others having none, but with manliness above taking advantage of a too liberal statute, and paying biennially, that this state of things should continue. Accordingly, the Legislation of 1878, both for assessment of persons and the collection of taxes, and allowance of delinquents and disposition of them, was passed. I say accordingly, for its obvious import is as I have described it to be. If there was any other motive for adopting it than to secure the better payment of taxes, it does not appear on the face of it, nor are we warranted in inferring it. A court cannot look behind the plain features of an Act of Assembly perfectly simple in itself to hunt for some secret purpose, unless such necessarily exists, as shown by the operation of the Act itself.

The plaintiff's counsel contend that the object of the Legislation of 1878 was the disfranchisement of voters, and that its effect has been to deny the ballot to citizens who should exercise it. In order to make their point good, they have given the court an example to show how a voter is by the law deprived of his right to vote. But the example is impossible, except upon an assumption that the party having the right to vote is defeated, or deprived of it, in spite of his efforts to enjoy it. This is pure assumption; the fact being that the law cannot operate without the co-operation or consent of the complaining party. If he desire to vote at elections, he has nothing to do but see to it that his name is kept upon the assessment list, and it will be retained there; and he will have the right to vote because of that, according to the Constitution, if he will keep up, like other people in like case, the payment of his tax. If he fail to pay within two years of the election he cannot vote, by the Constitution, and ought not to vote. He who will not contribute his part to support the government that protects him ought not to be allowed, by the use of the ballot, to neutralize the vote of another who does. And he who will not give himself the trouble to see that he is assessed sleeps upon his rights; and for him the maxim, *non dormientibus sed vigilantibus, leges subveniunt*, has appropriate application.

Treating the suffrage as a valuable political right, to be exercised conscientiously and intelligently, and for the public, rather than the welfare of a party, it would have been much better for the State if that feature of the Act of 1843 which provided for dropping from the assessment lists those returned delinquent had been re-enacted in the Act of 1878; for it is not true that delinquency is the effect of poverty. There are none so poor that they cannot pay their poll-taxes, which for them is "scot and lot;" less than two days' hire out of the wages of the common laborer being sufficient for that purpose. Labor everywhere, and always among us, is in demand. There is no hardship upon any in requiring him to pay his taxes, which in this State are county taxes alone, there being no general state tax of any kind. Men who live by their labor, or without work, who have no property, are assessed for a poll so low as to be almost insignificant. It is not poverty that creates delinquency, but a want of appreciation of the moral and political nature of the franchise, which privilege is prized by many white men, and the mass of the colored, simply because it enables them to get money by the sale of it. The notorious practice of purchasing votes by all parties here, as well as in other States, attests the truth of this assertion, and justifies the opinion expressed before about the re-enactment of the feature referred to in the Act of 1843. That Act was not repealed, as has been said, because it was deemed unconstitutional; but the real purpose of it was to relieve the party just then accidentally in power from the burden of paying the taxes of their proletariat.

Taxes being necessary to the support of government, a State has the right to adopt any measure short of actual disfranchisement to compel their payment. No one doubts the validity of the provision in our Statute for imprisonment of nonpaying taxables. Would the law be unconstitutional because the collector might choose to take the ultimate course, —upon the eve of an election to shut up in jail nonpaying citizens to whom it applied? Why would it not be? Simply because imprisonment is an extreme remedy for nonpayment of liabilities, as old as the law. Then, if such a provision be valid, why is not that for dropping from the assessment list for twelve months valid? Such an imprisonment as mentioned would effectually cut off, *pro hac vice*, the suffrage right, whereas the dropping from the list would, under the circumstances pointed out by the plaintiff's counsel, do nothing more; and in that case the dropping could not be otherwise taken than as done by the voter's consent, who had almost a whole year in which to pay his poll-tax, and thus save himself from delinquency. If the operation of the Legislation of 1878 was, *proprio vigore*, to disfranchise a voter, by preventing him from paying his taxes as others are obliged to do, there will be force in the argument of the plaintiff's counsel; but, as it does not so act, and never at all except as a consequence of his own neglect, which many others in like condition of circumstances in life do not suffer themselves to be guilty of, it cannot be charged to the law that he loses temporarily the privilege of voting, but only to his own inattention to his opportunity to retain it. He has simply omitted a duty he owed to himself, and to the public, —if such persons can be supposed to be under any obligation to the body politic,—and deserves all the consequences resulting from his indifference to his interest. Without it can be shown, which it was not, and cannot be (and that fact seemed to embarrass the learned counsel in their elaborate argument), that the Legislation of 1878 disfranchises a voter in spite of himself, or takes some advantage of him against which he had no means of protecting himself, it is too much to ask this court to avoid it as unconstitutional, and a violation of the Organic Law of this State.

It seems not necessary to say more than this

in regard to the objection to the legislation on the ground of its alleged hostility to the 14th and 15th Amendments of the Constitution of the United States,—that in this State every man, rich or poor, black or white, has the equal protection of the laws at all times, whether he be a legal voter or not, the ability to vote being no more necessary to secure that protection in his case than in that of women and minors, who, and whose property, are as much under the shield of the law's protection as is that of any man, great or small. A delinquent taxable is as much safeguarded in his personal rights as is he who owns houses and land. The notion that the right to exercise the suffrage is, in Delaware, necessary for the protection of one's person or property, is purely fanciful, and without any reality of reason. The 15th Amendment was meant to secure the right to vote to colored people, and has done it everywhere. Their delinquency generally as taxpayers, or failure to become assessed, is not the fault of the Statute, and cannot properly be charged against it. To hold the Assessment Act void as in conflict with that Amendment would be a strain of interpretation which would seem to be repugnant to plain common sense.

Grubb, *J.*, concurring:

This case is before us upon questions reserved and directed to be heard in this court upon a case stated in an action on the case in the Superior Court in and for New Castle County, for the recovery of damages resulting to the plaintiff by reason of his having been deprived by the defendants, when acting as members of the levy court of said county, of all opportunity of paying a county tax for the year 1886, and thereby qualifying himself to vote at the general election in that year. It is shown by the record, and admitted, that the plaintiff is a white male person, and was, in all respects, except as to the payment of a county tax, qualified to enjoy the right of an elector in this State at said election. It is also admitted that he was duly assessed and rated for a poll-tax for the year 1885 in the north collection district of Wilmington hundred; that the warrant for the collection of said tax was duly issued to Patrick Neary, the collector for said district; and that the said collector of taxes, having given the notices prescribed by law, and having attended, and remained in attendance, pursuant to said notices, and conformably with the statutory requirements for the collection of said tax, duly returned the plaintiff to the levy court of said county, on March 2, 1886, as a delinquent,—the plaintiff not having paid his poll-tax to him as such collector. It is also admitted that the plaintiff was not dead, and had not left the State, and that the said levy court had no evidence on the subject before it except the collector's return of the plaintiff as delinquent, and his affidavit, verified by his oath, and filed as prescribed by law, of his having, prior to said return, given the notices, and attended and remained in attendance, as aforesaid. It is also admitted that subsequently, on March 29, 1886, the said levy court did allow to the said collector the said poll-tax of the plaintiff, and did cause the name of the plaintiff to be struck and dropped from the said assessment list, whereby no tax was assessed or laid upon the person of the plaintiff for the next ensuing year (1886), and the plaintiff was deprived of any and all opportunity, at any time thereafter, to pay a county tax for the said year (1886) then next ensuing, and thereby of the right to qualify himself as an elector to vote at the general election in said county held on Tuesday, November 2, 1886. It is further admitted that the plaintiff had paid no tax, under any preceding assessment, within two years of and prior to said election. The defendants justify their action in dropping and striking the name of the plaintiff from said assessment list, and in failing to levy a tax on him for the year 1886, under the provisions of the Act entitled "An Act in Relation to the Collection of Taxes in This State," passed April 10, 1873, being 14 Laws Del. chap. 372, and also under the provisions of section 9 of an Act entitled "An Act in Relation to the Duties of Assessors and of the Levy Courts in the Several Counties of This State," passed April 9, 1873, being 14 Laws Del., chap. 371, and the defendants also claim that they cannot be held personally liable in damages for their action as members of said levy court, while, on the contrary, the plaintiff claims that the provisions of said Acts under which the defendants justify their action as aforesaid are unconstitutional and void, and that the defendants are personally liable to him for their said action.

In this connection, it is important to note that the plaintiff does not complain that he was deprived at any time of the opportunity to pay his tax for 1885, either before or after he was returned and allowed as a delinquent as to said tax, and thereby of the right to qualify himself as an elector at said election. He rests his case, as the record shows, exclusively upon his exclusion from the assessment list for 1886, and from all opportunity to pay a tax for that particular year. His suit is instituted for damages for his non-assessment for 1886, by reason of the "dropping" of the plaintiff from the assessment list of 1885, and his exclusion from the assessment list of 1886 by the defendants pursuant to the express requirements of the provisions of section 1, chap. 372, and of section 9, chap. 371, vol. 14, aforesaid. It is not instituted because of the "extinguishment" of his tax for 1885 pursuant to the express requirements of the provisions of section 18, chap. 12, Amend. Code (enacted prior to said Acts of 1873), whereby he was prevented from paying said tax at any time prior to the said election of 1886. Therefore, all objections urged at the argument against the validity of said provisions of the Acts of 1873 on the ground that the plaintiff was not permitted to pay his tax for 1885 at any time up to the said election, and was thereby precluded from obtaining a receipt therefor, as the evidence of his being qualified to vote thereat, are not pertinent to the present inquiry. Consequently, the determination of that question upon this occasion would be *obiter dictum* in the case before us. The real question in the case is whether or not the provisions of the Acts of 1873, requiring the exclusion of the plaintiff in March, 1886, from assessment for that year as a poll taxable, because he was, in said month, returned and allowed as delinquent for 1885, are unconstitutional, and not whether the provisions of section 18, chap. 12, Amend. Code, requiring the extinguishment of the tax of such delinquent, are or are not so. Accordingly, the questions actually reserved for the decision of this court are: *first*, whether or not the said provisions of the Acts of 1878, considered with reference to the case of the plaintiff as presented by the record, are unconstitutional and void; and, *second*, if said provisions be so, whether or not the defendants are personally liable to the plaintiff in damages for their action thereunder as members of the said levy court.

The first of these questions raises the following principal inquiries: *First.* Are said controverted provisions of the Acts of 1878, in their primary purpose and design, a regulation of the assessment and collection of county taxes, or a regulation of the qualification of electors? *Second.* If the former, are they a legitimate and appropriate exercise of the taxing power; that is to say, in accord with the inherent nature, essential characteristics and true meaning and purpose of taxation? *Third.* If they be such legitimate exercise of the taxing power by the General Assembly, are said provisions of the Acts of 1878 nevertheless unconstitutional and void because they have caused the plaintiff to be excluded from the assessment list for 1886, and, consequently, precluded him from being qualified to vote at the general election in that year? These inquiries necessitate the consideration of the said Acts of 1878, construed in connection with the pre-existing statutes of the State in force at the time of their enactment, and relating to the appointment, assessment and collection of taxes. They also require the true interpretation of the Constitution of this State in respect to the scope of the legislative authority in the exercise of the taxing power, as well as in regard to the nature of the elective franchise, with the view of ascertaining whether the latter is subordinate or paramount to the legitimate exercise by the Legislature of the taxing power for the purpose of raising, with regularity and certainty, the public revenue necessary for the support of government, and the promotion of the general welfare.

In the exercise of the power of taxation, the General Assembly has designated and empowered certain instrumentalities or agencies for the assessment and collection of county taxes. These are the levy courts and the assessors and collectors in the several counties. Their duties are prescribed, and their powers conferred, by statutory provisions which, in the legislative judgment, are deemed necessary and appropriate. The system of county taxation existing and in operation at the time of the enactment of the said Acts of 1878, under pre-existing statutory provisions then in force, was, substantially, as follows: In each county the assessors were required to assess, in the first instance, and the levy court to correct and complete the assessment of, all real and personal property not exempted by law, and all polls of every freeman above the age of twenty-one. A general assessment was to be made once in every four years, and a supplementary assessment annually. The assessor in each hundred or assessment district was required to complete his assessment by the 1st day of January in every year, and, after posting the same, and giving public notice as prescribed by law, to sit for the purpose of correcting any errors therein, or for the purpose of assessing persons omitted. Thereupon he must return his assessment to the levy court on the first Tuesday of February. It was made the duty of the levy court to sit as a court of appeal on the first Tuesday of March in every year, and such other days as should be necessary, to determine appeals against the assessments returned by the assessors, and to add to and correct the same, and to complete said assessments by the last day of March. Thereupon the levy court was required to ascertain the amount necessary to be raised by taxation for the year, and to apportion and lay the taxes for the same to and upon the assessments in the several hundreds at a certain rate upon every $100 of the said assessments, and also to cause to be issued, on or before the first Tuesday of April, to the collectors of taxes, respectively, a duplicate of the assessment list of his hundred or collection district, with a warrant thereto annexed.

By the provisions of chapter 12, Amend. Code, it was made the duty of every collector of county taxes to enforce payment of any tax unpaid, after due demand by him, by sale of the personal and real property of the taxable, and, in case he should be unable to find property sufficient therefor, he was authorized to enforce payment thereof by imprisonment of his body. The collector was required by section 10 of said chapter 12 to render to the levy court on the first Tuesday of March next after the date of his warrant a true account of all taxes it was his duty to collect, and of all the payments made, and of all delinquents.

By section 21 of chapter 8, Amend. Code, it was provided that "at the meeting in March in every year the levy court shall examine, adjust and settle the accounts of the collectors, making all just allowances, and the adjustment and settlement shall be final: and the court, if deemed expedient, may require other accounts from the collectors. They shall at the said meeting examine and settle the delinquent list of each collector, as well of state as of county taxes, and make allowance of delinquents; and upon such allowance the collector shall be credited with the amount thereof. The name of the delinquent, if he be dead, or have removed from the State, shall be struck from the assessment list, and also from the collector's duplicate; otherwise, it shall remain on the assessment, and be entered on the collector's duplicate for the succeeding year."

It was also provided by section 18 of said chapter 12 that "no collector, nor his executors or administrators, shall collect or receive any tax after two years from the date of the warrant. After that date it shall be extinguished. Nor shall he at any time collect or receive any tax allowed as delinquent, but the same shall be extinguished:"

The foregoing system, and the statutory provisions relating to it, which are material to the present inquiry, are still in operation and full force, except so far as they have been modified by the Acts of 1873, which are, in their purpose and effect, merely amendatory and supplementary thereto.

Under the legislation prior to the enactments of 1873, provision was made expressly requiring the dropping of the names of those who had died or had removed from the State in any year from the assessment lists of the next ensuing year. But no such provision was made for the dropping also of the names of those who had been found by the collector to be incapable of paying any tax, or to be fictitious and non-existent, and therefore incapable of dying or removing from the State. *Humanum est errare.* In the nature of things, therefore, under said legislation, many such names would inevitably creep into and accumulate upon the assessment lists from year to year, for obvious reasons, in the administration, through human agencies, of a system which, though primarily designed for the raising of public revenue, yet also, incidentally, furnished the means for qualifying as voters,—especially for closely-contested elections,—by the payment of a county tax as prescribed by the Constitution of the State. But, unless the assessment of property and polls be accurate and reliable, it must necessarily follow that the tax rate based upon it for raising the amount of revenue needed in any year will be inadequate, and a deficit in the county treasury will consequently ensue.

The clear, explicit, unambiguous provisions of the Acts of 1873, throughout their entire extent and scope, disclose an unmistakable intention, and a pervading purpose, to supply the deficiencies of previous legislation, and secure a more accurate assessment of the property and polls in the several counties, in order to have a more exact basis for fixing an adequate rate of taxation in every year. Accordingly, the Act passed April 9, 1873, and entitled "An Act in Relation to the Duties of Assessors, and of the Levy Courts, in the Several Counties of this State," being 14 Del. Laws, chap. 371, makes express, explicit and very careful provision for the accomplishment of this purpose. It makes it unlawful for any assessor to place on the assessment list the name of any person who is not the owner of taxable real or personal property within his assessment district, unless he shall be satisfied, from personal knowledge, that such person is of lawful age, and is a bona fide resident of his district. It also requires every assessor, within ten days after completing his assessment list, to post the same as prescribed by the Act, and to give notice that he will attend, at the place, day and hours therein specified, to correct any errors in his assessment, and for the purpose of assessing any person who may have been omitted. He shall at the same time give notice that any person desiring to be assessed must apply in person before him, at the time and place mentioned in said notices, and prove his right to be assessed by the oath or affirmation of some respectable freeholder of the county that he (the applicant) is the identical person he represents himself to be, and known to said freeholder personally to be such; that he is twenty-one years of age; and that he is a bona fide resident in the hundred and county of the assessor, and in the State of Delaware. If the assessor cannot complete the correction of his assessment on the day named in said notices, he may adjourn as prescribed in the Act. In case of inability, from any reason, to attend at the time specified in his notices, he shall appoint some other day, and give notice thereof in the same manner as aforesaid. The Act then, by express provisions, imposes severe penalties upon the assessor for the refusal or omission to place upon the assessment the name of any person who appears and makes proof, in the prescribed manner, of his right to be placed thereon. It also imposes penalties upon the assessor for knowingly placing upon the assessment any fictitious name, or the name of any person not at the time resident in the hundred or assessment district, and also upon any person who shall procure or cause to be placed upon the assessment in any hundred or assessment district the name of any person not entitled to be assessed in said hundred or district, or shall knowingly procure or cause to be placed thereon any fictitious or fraudulent name. It further provides "that it shall not be lawful for the levy court in either of the counties of this State, or any member thereof, to take from the assessment returned to the said levy court by any assessor the name of any person appearing thereon; nor shall it be lawful for such levy court, or any member thereof, to add to any assessment returned as aforesaid the name of any person, unless upon the personal application of such person, and upon proof of his right to be assessed" (§ 6), in the manner already stated; and for the violation of this provision a severe penalty is also imposed. The Act further provides, in section 9 thereof, "that it shall not be lawful for any assessor or any levy court, upon the personal application of anyone, or otherwise, to place upon the assessment in any hundred the name of any person who, having failed to pay the county tax assessed against him or her for the preceding year, was returned and allowed as a delinquent, until after the expiration of the twelve months from the time such allowance as delinquent was made by the levy court."

It is clear, beyond question, that the object of this Act was, through very specific provisions, enforced by positive penalties, to secure an accurate assessment, by excluding therefrom, in the first instance, so far as the assessors could detect them, and do so, all fictitious names, as well as the names of those who were disqualified for assessment for want of the prescribed age or residence. But it was manifest that, to make the assessment accurate, for the purpose of preventing a needless deficit, the lists must be purged, not only of these fictitious names which had escaped the vigilance of the assessors, and could subsequently be discovered by the collectors, but also of the names of all those whose tax the collector should find could not be effectually collected, even by means of legal process; in short, of those who should be ascertained to be unproductive as taxables. An Act auxiliary and supplementary to said chapter 371 was therefore needful. Accordingly, on the day next after the enactment of said chapter 371, the General Assembly passed an Act entitled "An Act in Relation to the Collection of Taxes in This State," being chapter 372, vol. 14, aforesaid. The provisions of this Statute are substantially as follows: Section 1 makes it the imperative duty of every collector of county taxes in each hundred or collection district in this State, within thirty days after he shall have received his duplicate list (in April of every year), to give public notice, in the manner prescribed in the Act, stating in such notice his place of residence or of business, and his readiness to receive taxes. They make it also his duty, in the month of January in each year, again to give public notice, as aforesaid, of at least ten days, which last-mentioned notice "shall state the times and places at which such collector will attend for the purpose of receiving taxes then due and unpaid; and it shall be the duty of the levy court in every county, upon proof being made to them by the affidavit of the collector, verified by his oath or affirmation, and filed in the office of the clerk of the peace for the respective county, setting forth that he has given notice as required by this section, and that, in accordance with the notice last above mentioned, he did attend at the times and places designated in such notice for the reception of taxes, and did remain for the space of at least five hours in each day, and for the period of at least three days, in attendance, for the purpose of collection of taxes aforesaid, to allow said collector, as delinquencies, the taxes uncollected by him; and the names of such delinquents shall be dropped from the assessment list by the levy court, and shall not be placed thereon again for a period of twelve months from and after the date of such allowance." Section 1 also declares that these provisions shall apply to persons assessed and liable to pay poll-tax. Section 2 provides "that the notices required to be given in section 1 of this Act by the collector aforesaid shall be deemed and taken to be sufficient demand upon taxables for the payment of taxes standing against them on the collector's duplicate of the several hundreds and collection districts of this State. Such notices, given as aforesaid, shall be considered a performance and full discharge of the duty of the collectors aforesaid to make demand for taxes; and they shall not be required thereafter to make further demand on any taxable for said taxes as a condition precedent to the employment of legal process as now provided by law for the collection of taxes." Section 3 makes it the duty of the collector to give receipt for taxes received, and, in addition to his signature, to make the impression of the seal (for which it makes provision) of the hundred or collection district of which he is collector upon all receipts given by him for county taxes. Sections 4 and 5 impose penalties upon the collector for using, or permitting the unlawful use of, said seal, and upon all others for counterfeiting said seal, or participating in the fraudulent use of the same. The salient feature of this Act is the mandatory provision that the levy court, upon the return of the collector's delinquent list, as provided by section 10, chap. 12, Amend. Code, and upon the evidence of his affidavit made and filed as prescribed in section 1 of the Act, shall allow said collector as delinquencies the taxes uncollected by him; and that the names of such delinquents shall be dropped from the assessment lists by the levy court, and shall not be placed thereon again for a period of twelve months from and after the date of such allowance.

Prior to the enactment of chapter 872, none but the names of delinquents who were dead or had removed from the State were permitted by law to be struck from the assessment list. All others were required to be retained thereon, and to be entered on the collector's duplicate for the next ensuing year. By the requirements of the foregoing provision of said chapter, therefore, in addition to the names of the dead, and of the removed from the State, the names of the fictitious which have been erroneously assessed by the assessors or the levy court, as well as of those whose taxes shall be found uncollectible by legal process, shall, when returned as delinquents by the collector, be dropped from the assessment, and shall not be placed thereon for the next ensuing year. The collector is thus made an efficient auxiliary in purging the lists of unproductive taxables, and securing an accurate assessment, thus preventing a deficit for the next ensuing year. Through the operation of section 1 of chapter 872, and of the penal provisions of section 9, chap. 871, the collector's return is made imperatively binding upon the assessors and the levy court. Each Act is therefore manifestly designed to operate in connection with the other as a component part of the pre-existing county revenue system, and as amendatory of and supplementary thereto. The practical effect of their provisions is to make the collector exclusively the agent of the Legislature in its exercise of the taxing power; to ascertain and determine finally and conclusively, in the mode prescribed by law, whether or not those whom he shall return as delinquents will be productive taxables for the next ensuing year.

In addition to the foregoing, there are other important provisions of the Acts of 1873. They define with greater precision the duties of the county revenue officials, and prescribe specifically what shall be a performance and full discharge of duty in certain respects. In so doing, they relieve public functionaries from embarrassing uncertainty as to their duty, and from harassing anxieties as to their liability, which are unjust to the officer, and detrimental to the public service. At the same time, they afford the individual citizen due notice, and ample opportunity to become assessed and to pay his tax, if he exercise reasonable diligence, and take care to see that the obligations and the penalties which the law imposes are enforced against those officials who presume to violate those provisions which the Legislature has enacted for the vindication of his rights, and the promotion of the public welfare.

Further analysis of these Acts is needless. They speak for themselves. There is no ambiguity in their language, and no room for doubt as to their design. Everywhere throughout them there is apparent, in the natural meaning of their phraseology, and in the plain import of their provisions, a dominating purpose so to amend the revenue system as to provide for the assessment and collection of county taxes with greater exactness and regularity, and to define the duties and liabilities of the revenue officials with greater precision and certainty. This purpose is indicated in their titles, is implied in their reference only to the officers exclusively intrusted with duties pertaining to revenue and is disclosed through their essential and inseparable connection with the entire Code of county revenue legislation, of which, for their own effectual operation, they must necessarily form a constituent part. Hence, it cannot be maintained that they are primarily a regulation of the suffrage, and secondarily only a regulation of taxation. For, if this be true, then it may be maintained with equal reason that the entire county assessment and collection system, since it is necessarily employed for the qualification of voters through the payment of a county tax, is therefore primarily intended and established to regulate the qualification for voting, rather than to provide for the collection of revenue. The mere statement of this proposition is sufficient for its refutation. Accordingly, the conclusion is irresistible that in their primary purpose and design the provisions drawn in question by the plaintiff's case are intended as an exercise of the taxing power by the Legislature with the view of improving the efficiency of the county revenue system. Whether or not it is the wisest and most effective plan for accomplishing this result which could be devised is immaterial to the question of their constitutional validity. They have been adopted as a means for effecting this result, which appeared to the legislative judgment, as we must presume, to be the most suitable and most effectual for its accomplishment. Being so, the said provisions must be presumed to be valid, and of binding force, until their enactment shall be shown to have been, in constitutional contemplation, unwarranted and prohibited. Cooley, Const. Lim. 168, and cases there cited.

We now come to the second general inquiry, whether or not, if the said provisions be considered as primarily a revenue regulation, they are a legitimate exercise of the true function of taxation, that is to say, in accord with its essential characteristics and purpose, and not in conflict with those limitations upon it which have been held by courts of high authority elsewhere to inhere in the very nature of the power of taxation itself, and to be equally imperative whether declared in written constitutions or not. Cooley, Taxn. 41; *Brewer Brick Co.* v. *Brewer*, 62 Me. 62; *State* v. *Readington Twp.* 36 N. J. L. 66; *Sharpless* v. *Philadelphia*, 21 Pa. 168; *Hammett* v. *Philadelphia*, 65 Pa. 151; *Re Washington Avenue*, 69 Pa. 363, 364; *Knowlton* v. *Rock County*, 9 Wis. 410.

Taxes are defined to be, to use the language of *Judge* Cooley, "burdens or charges imposed by the legislative power upon persons or property to raise money for public purposes. The power to tax rests upon necessity, and is inherent in every sovereignty. The Legislature of every free State will possess it under the general grant of legislative power, whether particularly specified in the Constitution among the powers to be exercised by it or not." Cooley, Const. Lim. 479.

Chief Justice Marshall has said of this power: "The power of taxing the people and their property is essential to the very existence of government, and may be legitimately exercised on the objects to which it is applicable to the utmost extent to which the government may choose to carry it. . . . The people of a State, therefore, give to their government a right of taxing themselves and their property; and, as the exigencies of government cannot be limited, they prescribe no limits to the exercise of this right, resting confidently on the interest of the legislator, and on the influence of the constituents over their representative, to guard them against its abuse." *McCulloch* v. *Maryland*, 17 U. S. 4 Wheat. 428 [4 L. ed. 606].

Judge Cooley continues: "Having thus indicated the extent of the taxing power, it is necessary to add that certain elements are essential in all taxation, and that it will not follow, as of course, because the power is so vast, that everything which may be done under pretense of its exercise will leave the citizen without redress, even though there be no conflict with express constitutional inhibitions. Everything that may be done under the name of taxation is not necessarily a tax; and it may happen that an oppressive burden imposed by the government, when it comes to be carefully scrutinized, will prove, instead of a tax, to be an unlawful confiscation of property, unwarranted by any principle of constitutional government. In the first place, taxation having for its only legitimate object the raising of money for public purposes, and the proper needs of government, the exaction of moneys from the citizens for other purposes is not a proper exercise of this power, and must therefore be unauthorized." Cooley, Const. Lim. 487.

"In the second place, it is of the very essence of taxation that it be levied with equality and uniformity, and, to this end, that there should be some system of apportionment. Where the burden is common, there should be common contribution to discharge it." Id. 495.

"But, to render taxation uniform in any case, two things are essential. The first of these is that each taxing district should confine itself to the objects of taxation within its limits." Id. 499.

The second essential is that apportionment of taxes should reach all the objects of taxation within the district. Of the correctness of this as a principle there can be little doubt, though there may sometimes be difficulty in determining whether in practice it has been applied or not. Id. 501.

"Absolute equality and strict justice are unattainable in tax proceedings. The Legislature must be left to decide for itself how nearly it is possible to approximate so desirable a result. . . . The Legislature must also, except when an unbending rule has been prescribed for it by the Constitution, have power to select, in its discretion, the subjects of taxation. The rule of uniformity requires an apportionment among all the subjects of taxation within the districts, but it does not require that everything which the Legislature might make taxable shall be made so in fact. Many exemptions are usually made from taxation, from reasons the cogency of which is at once apparent." Id. 513, 514.

"The constitutional requirement of equality and uniformity only extends to such objects of taxation as the Legislature shall determine to be properly subject to the burden. The power to determine the persons and the objects to be taxed is trusted exclusively to the legislative department; but over all those objects the burden must be spread, or it will be unequal and unlawful as to such as are selected to make the payment." Id. 515.

"It is, moreover, essential to valid taxation that the taxing officers be able to show legislative authority for the burden they assume to impose in every instance. Taxes can only be voted by people's representatives." Id. 517.

The foregoing extracts from *Judge* Cooley's valuable treatise on Constitutional Limitations, present clearly, comprehensively and succinctly the leading principles illustrating the nature and extent of the power of taxation, and the limitations upon its exercise inherent in the nature thereof, which have been approved by courts and text-writers of acknowledged authority. Without being understood either to define or to declare to what extent, in all cases, said principles shall, in all respects, be applicable and authoritative in this State, it is nevertheless proper to consider whether the said provisions which are complained of in this case are not, so far as they affect the plaintiff, in accord, instead of in conflict, with said principles.

By section 1, art. 2, of the Constitution of Delaware, the legislative power of this State is vested in the General Assembly. There being no express grant of the power of taxation, it passed to the General Assembly, under the general grant of legislative power, as an attribute of sovereignty essential to the existence of the government, and indispensable to the promotion of the general welfare. Excepting the provisions of section 14, art. 2, of the Constitution of this State, respecting the mode of framing and passing bills for the raising of revenue, there is no express limitation therein upon the exercise by the Legislature of the taxing power. Unless, therefore, some clearly implied restriction be found, inherent in the nature of taxation itself, or in some express constitutional provision, the statutory provisions in question must be sustained as a valid exercise of the taxing power. It has not been shown that they were enacted for other than a public purpose. Nor does it appear anywhere in the case before us that they impose any fiscal burdens upon the plaintiff, and are for that reason not uniform and equal. As a matter of fact, instead of imposing taxation upon him for the year 1886, they demonstrate that he is incapable of paying a tax. Instead of discriminating arbitrarily and unequally, by making him bear the burdens of others belonging to his own poll class of taxables, the truth is that the non-delinquent taxables were obliged in 1886 to bear the extra taxation necessary to make good his delinquency in 1885. The latter might justly urge the unequal effect of the operation of said provisions, were it not for the fact that, owing to his inability to pay any tax (which must be presumed from the return of the collector), his exclusion from assessment, in reality, neither increased nor diminished their actual burdens thereafter.

But, even if it were otherwise, and the non-delinquents, by operation of the said provisions, could rightfully complain that thereby the non-assessment of the plaintiff because delinquent imposed his share of taxation upon them without due process of law, yet the plaintiff cannot in this case avail himself of their cause of action. He has sued in the case before us for damages, because, by operation of said provisions, no tax was imposed upon him in 1886, and not because he is wronged by an unequal burden of taxation. He cannot successfully urge that which is not an injury to himself as a ground for invalidating these statutory provisions. He does not complain on that ground, nor is he in a situation to so complain as being one who has been obliged to pay an unequal tax. It is well settled that the courts will never pronounce a statute unconstitutional because it may impair the right of others not complaining. A statute is assumed to be valid until someone complains whose right it invades. *Antoni* v. *Wright*, 22 Gratt. 857; Cooley, Const. Lim. 164.

As was said by this court, upon this very point, in *Coyle* v. *Commissioners* (1884, not yet published): "It will be time enough to consider this question, and the rights of the parties that may be affected thereby, when it shall be presented for our consideration by parties capable of making it, and having an interest in its determination. No such parties are before us."

As heretofore stated, the primary purpose of the enactment of said provisions of the Acts of 1873 was to secure a more reliable assessment, by excluding therefrom all unproductive taxables, in order to prevent a constantly recurring annual deficit. It is a well-settled rule of constitutional construction that when a Constitution gives a general power, or enjoins a duty, it also gives, by implication, every particular power necessary for the exercise of the one or the performance of the other. Therefore, the power to raise by taxation sufficient revenue for the needs of government necessarily includes the power to make reasonable provision for preventing a deficit. This, as has been shown, was the object of the Legislature in the enactment of the provisions complained of by the plaintiff. In its judgment, they were deemed necessary and appropriate to the object in view. For this purpose, they have, in effect, made the collector in each hundred and collection district the sole and final judge of the incapacity for the payment of a tax (and consequently of his unproductiveness as a taxable for the next ensuing year) of anyone whom the collector shall return as a delinquent in any year. He has been selected by the Legislature, in the exercise of the taxing power, as its agent, for this duty, because, as must be presumed, he is the most suitable revenue official for the purpose. Being charged by law with the special duty of collecting taxes, and employing legal process in that behalf, and being also under the obligations of his official bond to fully discharge his duty, he is, presumably, in the legislative judgment, the revenue official best qualified and most likely to discover the productiveness or unproductiveness of the taxables on his annual duplicate. Having given bond, and being liable civilly and also criminally for corrupt and malicious conduct in his office, he cannot reasonably be said to be an irresponsible officer. Nor is it true, as was contended for the plaintiff at the argument, that the collector is clothed, under the provisions of the Legislation of 1873, with authority, arbitrarily, and at his mere will and pleasure, to decide what poll taxables shall, and what poll taxables shall not, pay tax for the ensuing year, and with unrestrained power of choice as to whom he will return as delinquent. Under the provisions of sections 11-14, chap. 12, Amend. Code, it is made the imperative duty of the collector to sell the personal and real property of every taxable who shall fail to pay his tax to the collector after ten days' demand, in order to enforce payment thereof; and for the same purpose, in case he shall not find sufficient property, he is authorized by section 15 of said chapter 12 to take and imprison the body of every such taxable.

Again, under the provisions of section 10 of said chapter 12, the collector is also imperatively required, "on the first Tuesday of March next after the date of his warrant, to render to the levy court a true account of all taxes it was his duty to collect, and of all payments made, and of all delinquents." These provisions were not repealed nor altered by the Legislation of 1873, but, on the contrary, were recognized by it as of continuing force and obligation. Accordingly, the provisions of 1873 must be construed in connection with them. This being so, the absolute duty is imposed by law upon the collector to collect from all alike, without favor or discrimination, and to return all as delinquents and unproductive taxables whose tax cannot be collected on demand, or by legal process. If the collector shall act arbitrarily and corruptly, and disregard his duty, he will do so in direct violation of said statutory provisions, and of the meaning and purpose of the Legislation of 1873. He would therefore act not by authority of, but contrary to, the law. While this will be a good reason for the punishment of the offending collector, yet it is not recognized by the courts as a sufficient ground for declaring the provisions of a statute unconstitutional and void. *Patterson* v. *Barlow*, 60 Pa. 54. It is therefore the undeniable duty of the collector to make diligent inquiry, and exhaust legal process. wheresoever effectual, in the effort to collect the tax of the citizen, before he shall return him to the levy court as a delinquent or unproductive taxable. This is the duty which he owes to the public under the mandates of the law, and the obligations of his bond. He also owes to the individual citizen the duty of giving the two several notices prescribed by section 1 of said chapter 372, vol. 14, and the opportunity, in accordance therewith, to pay his tax. Upon the discharge of these several duties, he shall make his said return to the levy court, and the same shall be conclusive that the delinquent, in legislative contemplation, will be unproductive as a taxable for the next ensuing year, and accordingly his name shall be excluded from the assessment list for that year. It is necessary that this return shall be conclusive of this fact, in order to exclude him from the assessment list, and so prevent a deficit, in fulfillment of the purpose of the Statute. Unless such fact be ascertained during March of any year, it would become impossible to complete the assessment, and have the duplicate and warrant in the hands of the collector in April of such year, as prescribed by law. Consequently, unless this fact can constitutionally be ascertained in the mode and at the time prescribed, the provisions of the Act would be nugatory, and their primary purpose frustrated. Hence, this mode of ascertainment of a fact essential to the indispensable collection of public revenue with regularity and certainty is necessary to the proper execution of the taxing power, and is an appropriate and legitimate exercise thereof by the General Assembly. *Hagar* v. *Reclamation Dist.* 111 U. S. 701-715 [28 L. ed. 569-574]; *Wilson* v. *Baltimore & P. R. Co.* 5 Del. Ch. 538, 545; Cooley, Const. Law, 87.

The delinquent cannot complain that he has had no "day in court," and no opportunity to disprove the fact conclusively established by the return. In contemplation of law, he has received notice to appear, through the notices given by the collector at the precise time specified for the giving thereof in said section 1 of chapter 372. Thereby he has his opportunity to show his capacity as a taxable for the next ensuing year by appearing in accordance with said notices, and paying his tax to the collector. Not having done so, he is legally concluded by the determination and the return of the collector. *Hagar* v. *Reclamation Dist. supra.*

In the present instance the plaintiff admits, as the record discloses, that he was duly assessed as a poll taxable, and that he had legal notice and opportunity to appear before the collector, and show his capacity as a taxable for 1886, but that he did not do so. He admits that he had not, within two years next before the general election in that year, paid any tax, and does not allege or show that he was able or willing to pay any tax either for 1885 or 1886. He admits that the collector was in attendance for the reception of his tax, conformably to his notices given as prescribed by the Act; but he does not allege or show that the collector ever refused to receive it, or deprived him of a free and ample opportunity to pay it. Nor does he allege or show that the collector had not fully and in good faith discharged his official duty, and exhausted all lawful and effective means in an earnest effort to collect his tax before he returned him as a delinquent and unproductive taxable. So that the verity of the statutory presumption established by the collector's return is nowhere impeached by the record.

In this connection, some observations may be made which seem both appropriate and material to the present inquiry, as being illustrative of the serious and not trivial importance as well as of the real necessity of these legislative provisions for ascertaining what portion of the citizens belongs to the productive class, and what portion to the unproductive class, of poll taxables, with a view to securing an accurate assessment, and thus prevent, through an exact and business like administration of the county revenue system, an annually recurring deficit. As hereinbefore shown, the Collection Law of 1873 was enacted to be auxiliary to the Assessment Law of that year, for the purpose of excluding from the assessment lists in any year, through the inquiry and return of the collector, all fictitious names, and also the names of all others who would be unproductive taxables in such year, which had been placed upon the assessment list in the preceding year through the error, or otherwise, of the assessor or levy court. It was argued by counsel for plaintiff that thousands of poll taxables are annually returned as delinquents, but that this is done by the collectors arbitrarily, and without just reason or necessity. The fact is true as stated, but the deduction therefrom was unwarranted. The fact that thousands of poll taxables are annually returned as delinquents by the collectors is not shown by the record in the case before us, but it is shown by the official records of the county revenue officers. Careful examination of these shows that, in addition to those who subsequently die, or remove from the State, there have been placed upon the assessment lists in a single year, in Wilmington alone, not only hundreds, but thousands, of names of persons who never existed, and also great numbers of those whose taxes could not be collected even by legal process. That thousands of these were fictitious names of persons who never existed, is demonstrated by the disproportion which the assessment bears to the population as shown by the census reports. That thousands of the remainder were absolutely unproductive taxables, against whom legal process was wholly unavailing, is a fact which, beyond question, can be conclusively established. While this demonstrates the infirmity of human instrumentalities, and the inadequacy of even the present Assessment Laws and their penal provisions, it also significantly demonstrates the necessity for, and emphasizes the value of, the Collection Law of 1873, by operation of which these flagrant faults in the assessment lists are annually corrected through the agency of the collector.

The consideration of the third general inquiry is now reached. It is contended in behalf of the plaintiff that the provisions of the Acts of 1873, of which he complains, by causing his exclusion from the assessment lists for 1886, thereby operated to deprive him of the opportunity to pay a county poll-tax, as his qualification for the enjoyment of the right of an elector of this State at the general election in that year, and therefore that these provisions are unconstitutional and void, as being violative of section 1, art. 4, and of section 3, art. 1, of the Constitution of this State. Section 1, art. 4, provides that a citizen of the age of twenty-two years or upwards (and otherwise qualified), "and having, within two years next before the election, paid a county tax, which shall have been assessed at least six months before the election, shall enjoy the right of an elector." Section 3 of article 1 provides that "all elections shall be free and equal." It has been shown that said provisions of the Acts of 1873 were enacted by the Legislature in the legitimate exercise of the taxing power, and were appropriate and necessary to the due execution thereof, and were, in their primary purpose and design, a regulation of the collection and assessment of county taxes, and but incidentally and secondarily a regulation for the qualification of electors. The plaintiff's contention, therefore, directly raises the question, Has the General Assembly, according to the true meaning and intent of the Constitution of this State, authority to exclude from assessment, in any particular year, a citizen who has been ascertained by a mode appropriate and essential to the effectual exercise of the taxing power, to be, in the legislative judgment, an unproductive taxable for that year? This is the controlling question in the case presented by the record. There is no need, upon the present occasion, of considering or declaring the extent of legislative power and discretion beyond the requirements of this pivotal question. If it shall be decided affirmatively, the controverted provisions of the Acts of 1873 must be sustained as constitutional and valid. The taxing power, and also the privilege of exercising the elective franchise, are both conferred by express but separate provisions of the same Constitution, —the former by section 1 of article 2, and the latter by said section 1 of article 4. No express limitation upon the taxing power in respect to suffrage is found in that instrument. Therefore, if any restriction upon such power exists, it must appear by clear implication from some other express provision of the Constitution. To ascertain this, resort must be had to a proper construction of the entire instrument. Every enactment of the State Legislature is presumed to be constitutional and valid until the contrary is shown. There is no safe rule for construing the extent or limitation of powers in a Constitution "other than is given by the language of the instrument which confers them, taken in connection with the purposes for which they were conferred." *Gibbons* v. *Ogden*, 22 U. S. 9 Wheat. 188 [6 L. ed. 68].

"But it is not on slight implication and vague conjecture that the Legislature is to be pronounced to have transcended its powers, and its Acts to be considered as void. The opposition between the Constitution and the law should be such that the judge feels a clear and strong conviction of their incompatibility with each other." *Fletcher* v. *Peck*, 10 U. S. 6 Cranch, 87, 128 [3 L. ed. 162, 175].

If examined according to these approved rules of construction, can it be said that any restriction upon the taxing power, as exercised by the Legislature in the present instance, appears by clear implication from the said provisions of article 4 relating to the qualifications of electors? The language of said article, "having, within two years next before the election, paid a county tax, which shall have been assessed at least six months before the election," clearly contemplates the necessity of a preceding assessment. The right to qualify for the suffrage, therefore, is by the Constitution itself made dependent upon the action of the Legislature in the exercising of the taxing power. Unless the Legislature has authority to prescribe an appropriate and necessary mode of ascertaining who will be unproductive subjects of taxation in any year, and to exclude such from assessment in that year, it cannot successfully raise, with certainty and regularity, adequate revenue for support of the government, and thus fulfill the purpose for which it was vested with the taxing power; for, if required to assess those who have been ascertained by such mode to be unproductive as taxables, an annual deficit must inevitably result, and the purpose of the taxing power be thus frustrated. To hold, therefore, that the Legislature is imperatively required to assess a citizen so found to be unproductive is to assert that the existence of government is of subordinate importance to the privilege of suffrage. Such a proposition is untenable, as it is absurd. Without organized government, there can be neither qualification for, nor exercise of, the suffrage, nor protection of life, liberty or property, nor promotion of the general welfare. Without adequate revenue, raised with regularity and certainty, efficient and stable government cannot successfully be maintained. It necessarily follows that the authority of the Legislature, in the exercise of the taxing power, to prescribe all appropriate and needful regulations for the selection and assessment of those only who will be productive taxables, is paramount to any alleged right of the unproductive citizen to be assessed. When section 1 of article 2 of the Constitution vested the taxing power in the General Assembly, and gave to the Legislature the general power, and enjoined the duty, to provide for the raising annually, with certainty and regularity, of needful revenue for the support of the several county governments, it also gave by implication every particular power necessary for the exercise of the one, or the performance of the other.

The language of the above-quoted provision of article 4 should be construed, if possible, so as to harmonize with this implication of the general grant of the taxing power, and yet be operative according to its true meaning and purpose. This may be accomplished by construing said provision to mean that those citizens only shall be qualified for assessment in any particular year who have first been ascertained, by an appropriate mode prescribed by the Legislature, to be capable of paying a county tax for said year. In other words, it means that capacity to pay a county tax is the test of fitness to be assessed, and, as the framers of said provision manifestly designed, of the capacity essential to the proper exercise of the elective franchise. That this was the view of those who framed said provision of article 4 admits of no doubt, as will be found by recourse to the Debates in the Constitutional Convention of 1831, which adopted it. In that convention, the proposition was made to abolish the prerequisite of paying a tax as a qualification for voting. In the course of the very able discussion of this question, conducted by the most eminent constitutional lawyers of the State, the principle upon which that prerequisite is based was very forcibly and plainly stated. In reference to this subject, *Judge* Hall said: "I do not regard the tax qualification as making an invidious distinction between the poor and the rich. If I did, I should vote against it. But I look upon the assessment of a tax as the test of the capacity of a person to exercise the right of a voter. If a person has no property, you can, by our laws, tax his capacity. If he has neither property nor capacity to be taxed he ought not to be suffered to dispose of your rights. The tax is the test of capacity. . . . The principle of the Constitution is this: You shall not vote unless you are taxed." Harker's Debates Delaware Convention 1831, p. 18.

Similar views being expressed by Mr. Clayton and others, the principle was adopted by the convention, and imbedded in our present Constitution. In view of this convincing testimony of the authors of our Constitution, and of the additional reasons above stated, it does not seem reasonable to conclude that the said language of section 1, art. 4, can be recognized judicially as an implied inhibition of the enactment by the Legislature of the said provisions of the Acts of 1878, as regulations appropriate and essential to the effectual exercise of the taxing power.

The plaintiff's exclusion from assessment for the year 1886 as an unproductive taxable, pursuant to said enactments as such regulations, was in accord with the true meaning and purpose of the Constitution that he, and all those who have been similarly ascertained to be unproductive taxables for a particular year, shall not be qualified for assessment for such year. Such citizens, in constitutional contemplation, are not permitted, under the said provision of article 4, to qualify as electors by the paying of a tax for such year, and hence cannot belong to the "voting class." For this reason, the said provisions of the Acts of 1873 are not inhibited by the injunction of section 3 of article 1, that "all elections shall be free and equal." This injunction does not apply to those who have neither a right to vote, nor to qualify as electors, under the Constitution of this State, which establishes, exclusively, the qualifications of those entitled to vote therein. In reality, however, said provisions, in their operation, are equal, and do not discriminate between any persons belonging to the same class of citizens who are in like condition, situation or circumstances. The Constitution itself, in its intent, divides all citizens of the State into productive and unproductive classes of taxables, for the purpose of assessment and taxation, and empowers the Legislature to select the productive, and to reject the unproductive, class, as essential to the fulfillment of this purpose. In accordance with this constitutional purpose, said provisions were enacted. Consequently, if they authorize the assessment of the productive, and forbid that of the unproductive, poll taxables, they are not prohibited, but authorized by the Constitution to do so. Also, if they do not operate similarly towards property holders and non-property holders, it is not because of any invidious discrimination between them created by said provisions. It is because of the difference of condition and circumstances existing between them. All citizens, except minors and female citizens, who own property, are subject to poll-tax, as well as non-property holders. Again, said enactments do not exclude from assessment as a punishment or forfeiture for crime, but to prevent a deficit. Nor is their purpose to compel payment of his tax by disfranchising the delinquent taxable. It is to show that he is incapable of paying a tax, and therefore unproductive as a taxable, and that the assessment of him, and those in like condition, will produce a deficiency of revenue.

The conclusion, therefore, seems unavoidable that the said provisions of the Acts of 1878, considered with reference to the case of the plaintiff as presented by the record, are not unconstitutional and void, but the contrary, and that it should be so certified to the court below. The objections to their constitutional validity, with the numerous authorities in support thereof, which were presented by the counsel for the plaintiff so earnestly and so ably, have been carefully examined, and deliberately considered, as was due to the eminent counsel on both sides, and demanded by the gravity of the subject. But they have failed to show that the opposition between said provisions and the Constitution is such that, as *Chief Justice* Marshall observed in *Fletcher* v. *Peck*, 10 U. S. 6 Cranch, 128 [3 L. ed. 175], "the judge feels a strong and clear conviction of their incompatibility with each other." On the contrary, their enactment appears to have been clearly within the constitutional power of the Legislature, as an appropriate and legitimate exercise of the taxing power. Being so, even though they may be unwise in policy, or defective and inefficient for the purpose designed in their enactment, the resort for their annulment or amendment must be, not to the courts, but to the representatives of the people, or, that failing, to the people themselves. The courts cannot annul these enactments, but they can and will enforce the penalties provided for their violation whenever any infraction thereof is properly presented and duly established.

Saulsbury, *Ch. J.*, and **Paynter,** *J.*, concurred. **Houston,** *J.*, dissented.

MICHIGAN SUPREME COURT.

Samuel LYON, *Appt.*,
v.
William C. DENISON *et al.*

(....Mich.....)

Shares of stock in a sporting club, incorporated under How. Stat., chap. 188, which has power to own a certain amount of property, with the general powers of corporations so far as they are applicable, cannot be sold on execution, under How. Stat., § 7697, providing for such sale of shares in any "bank, insurance company or any other joint-stock company," where the club is not compelled to issue any shares of stock, although it has done so, and, having provided for their transfer, has also provided that ownership thereof shall not entitle a person to any of the privileges of the club, unless he be duly elected a member.

(May 2, 1890.)

APPEAL by complainant from a decree of the Circuit Court for Kent County sustaining a demurrer to the bill in a suit brought to compel the transfer to complainant of certain corporate stock upon the books of the corporation and to enjoin a disposition of it by the person in whose name it stood. *Affirmed.*

The facts are fully stated in the opinion.

Mr. **Reuben Hatch,** for complainant, appellant:

The words "joint-stock company," as used in § 7697 of Howell's Statutes, which permits the interest of a stockholder in any joint-stock company to be seized on execution, are synonymous with the word "corporation."

Blair v. *Compton*, 33 Mich. 414.

It can make no difference that the corporation was organized for pleasure or sporting rather than for business purposes, so long as the stock owned by the members of the corporation is an interest possessing value.

Messrs. **Norris & Norris** for defendant L. A. Denison, appellee

Messrs. **Fletcher & Wanty,** for defendant W. C. Denison, appellee:

At common law corporate stocks were not seizable on execution.

Blair v. *Compton*, 33 Mich. 428; *Van Norman* v. *Jackson County Circuit Judge*, 45 Mich. 208.

Complainant's right to levy on this stock depends, then, wholly on the Statute.

2 How. Stat. § 7697.

The club is organized under chapter 188, Howell's Statutes, an examination of the provisions of which shows that no capital stock is provided for, so that if there be any it exists by virtue of the agreement of members and the club's by-laws, and not by virtue of the Statute.

It is not alleged, and does not appear, that the club has any property.

It necessarily follows that this club is not a "joint-stock company," but rather a social organization, and that being such its stock cannot be seized on execution.

Van Norman v. *Jackson County Circuit Judge*, 45 Mich. 211.

Long, *J.*, delivered the opinion of the court:

The bill in this case states, substantially:

(1) That on the 17th day of July, A. D. 1889, he, the complainant, recovered judgment before Thomas Walsh, Esq., one of the justices of the peace of the City of Grand Rapids, against William C. Denison, in an action of assumpsit, for $127.84 damages, and $3 costs of suit; that, upon showing made on oath of complainant to the satisfaction of said justice, execution was ordered issued forthwith on said judgment, and that execution was so issued by said justice on said 17th day of July, 1889, to any constable of said county, which execution was in the usual form; that on July 19, 1889, the said constable levied said execution upon share of the capital stock of the Pottawatomie Club represented by certificate No. 9, issued to said William C. Denison.

(2) That the Pottawatomie Club aforesaid is, and was at the time of said levy, a corporation or joint-stock company, within the meaning of section 7697 of Howell's Statutes, existing under the laws of this State, and organized under and by virtue of chapter 188 of Howell's Statutes.

(3) That said officer made said levy by leaving a copy of said execution, certified by him, with Charles E. Kusterer, then treasurer of the said Pottawatomie Club.

(4) That said constable, having given due notice of the sale of said stock at public vendue, by notices signed by him, and put up on the 24th day of July, 1889, at three public places in the City of Grand Rapids aforesaid, where the said stock was levied upon, advertising the same for sale at public vendue to the highest bidder, at the outer front door of "Court Block," so called, on Lyon Street, in the City of Grand Rapids aforesaid, on the 31st day of July, 1889, at 2 o'clock in the after-

See also 21 L. R. A. 399; 38 L. R. A. 758.

noon, at the place aforesaid, offered said share of stock for sale at public vendue to the highest bidder, and that, said complainant being the highest bidder, the said stock was struck off and sold to him by said constable for the sum of $1, that being the highest sum bid therefor.

(5) That on the 6th day of August, 1889, a copy of said execution, and the return of said constable thereon, certified by said constable, was left with Charles F. Kusterer, treasurer of said Pottawatomie Club, and the officer whose duty it was to keep a record of the transfer of shares, by Reuben Hatch, attorney for said complainant, at the office of said treasurer, in the City of Grand Rapids aforesaid. Reuben Hatch, as attorney for said complainant, then and there demanded of said Charles F. Kusterer, for said complainant, a certificate of the share so bought by him at the said constable's sale, the said Reuben Hatch offering to pay the fees thereof, and for recording the transfer of said certificate to said complainant, which the said Charles F. Kusterer, as treasurer of said Pottawatomie Club, then and there refused.

(6) That on the 8th day of August, 1889, the said Reuben Hatch, as attorney for said complainant, left with Mark Norris, secretary of said Pottawatomie Club, another copy of said execution, and return thereon, certified by said constable, and demanded the certificate of said share of stock so bought by said complainant, at the same time offering to pay the fees therefor, and for recording the transfer, which the said Mark Norris, as secretary of the said club, refused.

(7) The return of said constable indorsed upon said execution, a certified copy of which was indorsed upon the copies of said execution so left with said Charles F. Kusterer, treasurer of the said club, and with Mark Norris, secretary of the said club, was in words and figures following, to wit:

"I do hereby certify and return that on the 31st day of July, A. D. 1889, at 2 o'clock P.M., I sold at the outer front door of 'Court Block,' so called, on Lyon Street, in the City of Grand Rapids, Michigan, at public vendue, one share of the capital stock of the Pottawatomie Club, represented by certificate No. 9, issued to William C. Denison, the defendant within named, being the same stock levied upon by me by virtue of the within writ, to Samuel Lyon, plaintiff within named, for the sum of $1, that being the highest sum bid therefor, and he being the highest bidder; having given due public notice of said sale as required by law, by advertisement signed by me, and put up at three public places in the City of Grand Rapids aforesaid, where said stock was levied upon on the 24th day of July, A. D. 1889.

"J. C. Pitkin, Constable."

That the levy upon said stock was indorsed upon said original execution in words and figures following, to wit:

"July 19, 1889. The within execution levied upon one share of the capital stock of the Pottawatomie Club, represented by certificate No. 9, the property of William C. Denison, the defendant within named. J. C. Pitkin, Constable,"

—a certified copy of which was also indorsed upon said certified copies of said executions so served as aforesaid upon the said Charles F. Kusterer, treasurer, and Mark Norris, secretary, of the said Pottawatomie Club.

(8) That on the day following said levy said Charles F. Kusterer, as treasurer of said Pottawatomie Club, delivered to said constable a certificate in words and figures following, to wit:

"I, Charles F. Kusterer, treasurer of the Pottawatomie Club, a corporation organized under and by virtue of chapter 188 of Howell's Statutes, and the officer of said club appointed to keep a record of the shares of the stockholders therein, do hereby certify that on July 19, 1889, at the hour of noon (at which time there was served on me a certified copy of an execution issued by Thomas Walsh, justice of the peace, in favor of Samuel Lyon, and against the goods and chattels of William C. Denison) and Denison appeared on the books of said club to be the holder and owner of one share of the stock of said club, and that a copy of the certificate of stock issued to said Denison is annexed hereto; and I do further certify that on the same day, and prior to the service on me of said execution, one Lavello A. Denison notified me that said stock had been purchased by him, and said stock certificate assigned and delivered to him, on the 10th day of July, 1889. Charles F. Kusterer, Treasurer of the Pottawatomie Club. July 19, 1889."

"Copy of Certificate. No. 9. 1 share.

"The Pottawatomie Club of Grand Rapids, Michigan.

"This certifies that William C. Denison is entitled to one share, of the par value of $100 each, of the capital stock of the Pottawatomie Club. This certificate may be transferred on the books of the treasurer of the club, who is transfer agent, to any person, on the surrender of this certificate, properly indorsed; but the ownership of said stock shall not entitle the person owning the same to any of the privileges of the club, unless such person be duly elected a member of said club. The club has a lien on this stock for all unpaid dues and assessments. One hundred dollars have been paid on each share of stock represented by this certificate.

"E. S. Holmes, President.

"N. Fred Avery, Treasurer.

"Grand Rapids, August 17, 1887."

That at the time of said levy your orator had no knowledge of the pretended transfer of said stock to said Lavello A. Denison.

(9) That at the time of said levy the capital stock of said Pottawatomie Club was divided into shares, and certificates thereof had been previously issued to the members or stockholders of said club; that the stock so levied upon and sold was at the time of said levy owned by said William C. Denison; that said William C. Denison appeared to be owner thereof on the books of the said club, and that no transfer of the same from said William C. Denison to any other person had been entered on the books of said club so as to show the names of the parties by and to whom the same was transferred, the number and designation of shares, or the date of the transfer, nor in any other manner; that as your orator is informed and believes, at the time of said levy the said Charles F. Kusterer,

who was the transfer officer of said club, and kept the record of the stock and transfer thereof, had received no notice whatever from said William C. Denison, or from any other person, of any transfer of said stock from William C. Denison to the said Lavello A. Denison, neither had the said Mark Norris, as secretary of said club, received notice, at the time of said levy, of any transfer of said stock from said William C. Denison to Lavello A. Denison.

(10) That the said Lavello A. Denison is the son of the said William C. Denison, and was at the time of said levy, and of the pretended transfer of said stock from the said William C. Denison to the said Lavello A. Denison, mentioned in the certificate of Charles F. Kusterer herein before set forth, in the employ of said William C. Denison; that, as your orator is informed and believes, no consideration was ever paid by the said Lavello A. Denison to the said William C. Denison for said stock; and that the pretended transfer of said stock from said William C. Denison to said Lavello A. Denison is fraudulent and void as to your orator, and was made for the purpose, and with the intent on the part of the said William C. Denison and Lavello A. Denison, of defrauding your orator, and defeating collection of said judgment in favor of your orator, and against said William C. Denison.

(11) That said pretended transfer of said stock by said William C. Denison to his said son is, as your orator is informed and believes, merely colorable, and made with a view of protecting the property and effects of the said William C. Denison, and said stock especially, and placing the same beyond the reach of your orator's said judgment, and enabling said William C. Denison to control and enjoy the same.

(12) That your orator is now, by virtue of said constable's sale, and his purchase of said stock thereat, the true and rightful owner of said stock, and entitled to a certificate thereof from the proper officer of the said Pottawatomie Club, and that he was, upon the service of certified copy of said execution, with the return of said constable indorsed thereon, upon Charles F. Kusterer, treasurer of said club, as aforesaid, entitled to a certificate of said stock, and that it was the duty of said treasurer upon such service, and upon the offer of your orator's said attorney to pay the charges therefor, to have issued to your orator a certificate of said stock as such purchaser; that said stock is worth at least $200; that the attorney of Lavello A. Denison attended said sale, and warned all persons not to bid, and that is one reason why said stock brought so little.

(13) But now, so it is, may it please this honorable court, that the said William C. Denison and Lavello A. Denison, combining and confederating together to and with divers other persons as yet unknown to your orator, but whose names when discovered your orators pray may be inserted herein as defendants, and they made parties hereto, with proper and apt words to charge them, how to injure and oppress your orator, the said confederates respectively do refuse to allow to be issued to your orator a certificate of the share of the stock in said club so bought by him at said constable's sale, pretending that before the said levy upon said stock by said constable, under and by virtue of said execution, said William C. Denison assigned and transferred said stock to his said son, Lavello A. Denison, and that the said Lavello A. Denison, by virtue of said transfer and assignment, is a bona fide purchaser thereof; whereas, your orator expressly charges the truth to be that the said Lavello A. Denison is not a bona fide purchaser of said stock, and that the said assignment and transfer are a mere sham and pretense, in order to cheat and defraud your orator out of the collection of said judgment,—all of which actings, doings and pretenses of the said confederates are contrary to equity and good conscience, and tend to the manifest wrong, injury and oppression of your orator. In tender consideration whereof, and for as much as your orator is remediless in the premises at and by the strict rules of the common law, and is only relievable in a court of equity, where matters of this nature are properly cognizable and relievable. The bill calls for answer, the answer on oath being waived, and prays that the pretended assignment and transfer of said stock by said William C. Denison to his said son may be declared void as a fraud upon the rights of the complainant, and that the same may be canceled, and the said club decreed and directed to issue a certificate of the share of stock to the complainant so bought by him at said sale upon his paying the fees therefor, and that William C. Denison and Lavello A. Denison may be enjoined and restrained from selling, assigning, transferring, delivering, negotiating, incumbering or in any way or manner disposing of said stock to any other person, etc. The bill also contains the usual prayer for other and further relief. This bill was duly verified.

The defendant William C. Denison filed a general demurrer to the bill. Defendant Lavello A. Denison appeared and filed his answer, containing a demurrer clause. By consent of parties the cause came on to be heard on the general demurrer of William C. Denison and the answer of Lavello A. Denison, setting up, among other things, that complainant's bill did not make or state such a case as entitled him to the relief prayed, and praying the benefit of a demurrer. The demurrers only were passed upon by the court, who dismissed the bill, with costs, on October 14, 1889. Complainant appeals.

Counsel for defendants Denisons in this court contend (1) that the bill shows no jurisdiction in the justice to render the judgment or to issue the execution; (2) that the stock seized is not subject to levy, even had it not been transferred; (3) that it was equitable assets, and therefore not subject to levy; (4) that complainant ought to have filed his bill to settle the title to his stock before selling it under the execution; (5) that the bill fails to show that complainant's debt was in existence prior to the transfer of the stock, and hence shows no right to maintain this suit.

From the view we take of the case, however, it does not become necessary to discuss but one question, and that is, whether these shares of stock can be sold on execution.

The Pottawatomie Club was organized under chapter 188 of Howell's Statutes. Section 1 provides "that any ten or more persons of full age, at least six of whom shall be citizens of this State, who shall desire to associate themselves for yachting, hunting, fishing, boating, rowing or other lawful sporting purposes, may make, sign and acknowledge . . . and file in the office of the secretary of state . . . a certificate in writing, in which shall be stated the name or title by which such association shall be known in law," etc. Section 2 of the Act provides that such association shall be a body politic and corporate, and in their corporate name "shall, in law and equity, be capable of taking and receiving real and personal estate, either by purchase, gift, grant, lease or bargain and sale, devise and bequest, not exceeding $25,000, in the aggregate, for the purpose of their corporation, but for no other purpose; and the same at pleasure grant, bargain, mortgage, sell or lease for the use of said association; make all needful rules, regulations and by-laws for the management of its affairs," etc., and appoint officers and agents for the management of its business. The Act also provides for succession by the election of officers and a board of directors for the management of its affairs. Section 7 of the Act provides that said association shall possess the general powers conferred by, and be subject to the provisions and restrictions of, chapter 55, title 10, Rev. Stat. 1846 (How. Stat. chap. 191), so far as the same may be made applicable to associations formed under this Act. Section 7, chap. 191, How. Stat., provides that whenever the capital stock of any such corporation is divided into shares, and certificates thereof are issued, such shares may be transferred by indorsement and delivery of the certificates thereof, such indorsement being by the signature of the proprietor or his attorney or legal representative; but such transfer shall not be valid, except between the parties thereto, until the same shall be so entered on the books of the corporation as to show the names of the parties by and to whom transferred, the number and designation of the shares, and the date of the transfer. Section 7697 of Howell's Statutes provides that "any share or interest of a stockholder in any bank, insurance company or any other joint-stock company, that is or may be incorporated under the authority of or authorized to be created by any law of this State, may be taken in execution and sold, in the following manner."

It is insisted that the Pottawatomie Club is not a joint-stock company within the meaning of section 7697, above quoted; that the Act under which it was incorporated does not provide for the issuing of any certificates of shares of stock; and that the bill does not allege that the club has any property. It is evident that the Legislature, by section 7697, did not intend to limit the right of levy under execution to joint-stock companies as they were known at the common law, as it gives the right to levy upon the shares of stock in any bank, insurance company or any other joint-stock company. Banks or insurance companies may be, and usually are, corporations, and yet the shares of stock issued by such corporations may be levied upon and sold under the provisions of this Statute. A joint-stock company, at the common law, lies midway between a corporation and a copartnership. It is an association of persons for the purpose of business, having a capital stock divided into shares, and governed by articles of association, which prescribe its objects, organization and procedure, and the rights and liabilities of its members, except that the article cannot release the members from their liability as partners to the creditors of the company. Cook, Stock and Stockholders, 2d ed. § 504.

There is an essential difference between a joint-stock company as it existed at the common law, and a joint-stock company having extensive statutory powers conferred upon it by the State within which it is organized. It is not within the contemplation of the Statute under which the club was organized that it should carry on a business for profit, but to hold a limited amount of property for the purposes for which it was organized, to wit, "yachting, hunting, fishing, boating, rowing or other lawful sporting purposes;" and it is quite evident the Legislature never intended that its shares of stock, if any were provided for by its articles of association or by-laws, should be regarded merely as property to be bartered and sold like shares of stock in a purely business concern, and to be treated subject to levy and sale under execution, within the provisions of section 7697. They are not, by the terms of the Statute, compelled to issue stock in order to keep up and maintain their corporation. Their privilege and franchises are to be enjoyed by compliance with the Statute under which they were organized. They have, however, issued certificates of shares of stock. Whether this is provided for in their articles or by-laws is not made to appear by the bill. From an inspection of this certificate it appears that the same may be transferred upon the books of the company by a surrender of the certificate properly indorsed, but it is also provided that the ownership of such stock shall not entitle the person owning the same to any of the privileges of the club, unless such person be duly elected a member of the club. That is, one holding and owning a share of stock has none of the rights and privileges of members of the club, of yachting, hunting, etc. Just what rights one holding such a certificate as owner might be entitled to, it is not necessary to determine upon this record. We are satisfied that the case does not come within the provisions of the Statute authorizing the levy and sale of shares of stock of a bank, insurance company or any other joint-stock company.

The decree of the court below sustaining the demurrer must be affirmed, with costs.

The other Justices concurred.

GEORGIA SUPREME COURT.

SMITH, *Plff. in Err.*,
v.
SMITH *et al.*

(....Ga.....)

*The marriage of a boy in his sixteenth year, although declared by the Code to be void in the sense of being absolutely void, may nevertheless be ratified and confirmed by continuing, after arriving at the age of seventeen years, to cohabit with his wife as such. The Code of 1863 required a license, or the publication of banns, as a condition to the validity of any marriage; but this provision of the Code was repealed by the Act of December, 1863, by which repeal the common law as to informal marriages was restored. The power to make marriage by consent and cohabitation being thus reinstated, the power to complete and confirm by like means an inchoate and imperfect marriage was also revived.

(February 24, 1890.)

ERROR to the Superior Court for Muscogee County to review a judgment in favor of defendants in an action brought by an alleged wife to recover possession of her deceased husband's property. *Reversed.*

The case sufficiently appears in the opinion.

Messrs. **C. J. Thornton** and **A. A. Dozier** for plaintiff in error.

Messrs. **McNeil & Levy** for defendants in error.

Bleckley, *Ch. J.*, delivered the opinion of the court:

The actual marriage took place in Alabama in 1880, and was celebrated by a magistrate. Nothing is suggested as to any defect in the magistrate's authority, whether from want of license or otherwise. The groom was between fifteen and sixteen years of age; the bride was older. Both parties resided in Georgia, in which State a license had been applied for, and refused, because of an objection interposed by the groom's mother, his father being dead. After the marriage ceremony, the parties returned immediately to Georgia, where they continued to reside. The evidence indicates that they cohabited as man and wife up to November, 1883, when the husband died, his age being then upwards of eighteen years. The present suit is by the wife against the guardian of the husband and the sureties upon his bond to recover so much of the husband's estate as the guardian may be accountable for, the plaintiff claiming to be the sole heir-at-law of her deceased husband. The action was defended upon the ground, among others, that she was never his lawful wife, and therefore could not inherit. The Statute Law of Alabama as to the ages of consent is the same as our own, namely, seventeen years in males and fourteen in females. Tested by the law of that State, the marriage was not absolutely void, but voidable only, and until disaffirmed was a marriage in fact. *Beggs* v. *State*, 55 Ala. 108.

Our Code (§ 1710), however, declares that "all marriages solemnized in another State, by parties intending at the time to reside in this State, shall have the same legal consequences and effect as if solemnized in this State. Parties residing in this State cannot evade any of the provisions of its laws as to marriage by going into another State for the solemnization of the marriage ceremony." The rights of the plaintiff, therefore, resulting from the marriage, and what followed thereupon, are to be measured by the laws of this State.

Prior to the Code of 1863, the common law prevailed here as to the validity of the marriage relation established by mere act of the parties without any ceremonial observances, civil or ecclesiastical. *Askew* v. *Dupree*, 30 Ga. 173.

Provisions contained in penal statutes treated the marriage of idiots or lunatics as void, and expressly declared polygamous and inter-Levitical marriages void. Cobb, Dig. 814, 818, 819.

By the Act of 1806 (Id. 225) the issue of divorced parents in all cases were declared legitimate. The grounds of divorce remained as at common law (*Head* v. *Head*, 2 Ga. 191) until 1850. By an Act of that year (Cobb. Dig. 226) the antenuptial causes of total divorce recognized were the following: intermarriages within the Levitical degrees of consanguinity or affinity; mental incapacity; impotency; force, menaces or duress; pregnancy of the wife unknown to the husband. These same causes were recognized in the Code of 1863, with two changes, the first substituting "prohibited degrees" for "Levitical degrees," and the second introducing "fraud" as an additional ground. Code 1863, § 1670.

By that Code, which went into effect on the 1st day of January, the following provisions on the subject of marriage (with others not material to this discussion) became part of our written law, viz.: "Sec. 1653. To constitute a valid marriage in this State, there must be (1) parties able to contract; (2) an actual contract; (3) consummation according to law. Sec. 1654. To be able to contract marriage, a person must be of sound mind, if a male at least seventeen years of age, and if a female at least fourteen years of age, and laboring under neither of the following disabilities, viz.: (1) previous marriage undissolved; (2) nearness of relationship by blood or marriage, as hereinafter explained; (3) impotency. Sec. 1655. Persons related by consanguinity within the fourth degree of the civil law are prohibited from intermarrying. Marriages between persons related by affinity in the following manner are prohibited, viz.: A man shall not marry his step-mother, or mother-in-law, or widow of his uncle, or daughter-in-law, or step-daughter, or granddaughter of his wife. A woman shall not marry her corresponding relatives. Marriages within the degrees prohibited by this section are incestuous. Sec. 1656. To constitute an actual contract of marriage, the parties must be consenting thereto voluntarily, and without any fraud practiced on either. Drunkenness at the time of marriage, brought about by art or contrivance to induce consent, shall be held a fraud. Sec. 1657. Marriages of persons unable

*Head note by BLECKLEY, *Ch. J.*

to contract, or unwilling to contract, or fraudulently induced to contract, are void. The issue of such marriages, before they are annulled and declared void by a competent court, are legitimate. In the latter two cases, however, a subsequent consent and ratification of the marriage, freely and voluntarily made, accompanied by cohabitation as husband and wife, shall render valid the marriage. Sec. 1658. To render valid a marriage in this State, there must be either a license previously granted by the proper officer authorizing such marriage, or a publication of the banns of marriage in a neighboring church, in the presence of the congregation, for at least three Sabbath days prior to its solemnization."

The Code, by those provisions, innovated upon the common law in the following particulars: (1) it raised the age of consent for males from fourteen to seventeen, and for females from twelve to fourteen; (2) it brought first cousins, etc., within the prohibited degrees of consanguinity; (3) it virtually obliterated the distinction between canonical and civil disabilities, and consequently between void and void able marriages; and (4) it exacted license, or the publication of banns, as a condition to the validity of any marriage whatsoever, and thereby made marriage impossible without some preliminary from the State or the church. For there to be any marriage at all which the law would treat as valid, it had to take place under a license, or after the publication of banns. In the absence of both these preliminaries, no matrimonial connection could be formed, however competent the parties might be to assume the bonds of wedlock, or however free and voluntary might be their action in attempting to do so. By applying the one word "void" to all the enumerated instances of marriages, the intention, no doubt, was to use it in the same legal sense as to each and every instance enumerated. The safest and most probable construction is that the sense contemplated was the strict and comprehensive one of utter nullity. This construction is borne out in some degree by what is said in section 1682, as to the effect of divorce: "A total divorce annuls the marriage from the time of its rendition, except it be for a cause rendering the marriage void originally, but in no case of divorce shall the issue be rendered bastards, except in case of pregnancy of the wife at the time of the marriage." This use of the words, "except it be for a cause rendering the marriage void originally," carries the implication that any such marriage would be so utterly void as to require no judgment to dissolve or annul it. Still there is some obstacle to this construction, for, though canonical impediments rendered marriages voidable only, yet, "if the cause existed previous to the marriage, and was such a one as rendered the marriage unlawful *ab initio*, as consanguinity, corporal imbecility or the like, in this case the law looks upon the marriage to have been always null and void, being contracted *in fraudem legis*, and decrees not only a separation from bed and board, but *a vinculo matrimonii* itself." 3 Bl. Com. 94.

The Code deals with the subject of ratifying void marriages, expressly allowing it in the two cases of force and fraud. Under the rule that the expression of one thing is the exclusion of another, there is no probability that there was any intention to allow ratification by mere consent and cohabitation at any age whatever, if either of the parties was under the age of consent at the time when the marriage was celebrated. The phrase "consummation according to law," found in the first section above quoted (§ 1658), meant consummation under license, or after the publication of banns; for, as there could be no valid marriage without one of these antecedents, there could, without one or both of them, be no consummation according to law. But these new conditions introduced by the Code were not long acceptable to the Legislature, for, before they had been operative for a single year, the Act of December 14, 1863 (Pamph. Laws, 48), was passed, by which section 1658 of the Code was repealed, the preamble of the Act reciting: "Whereas, by the above-cited paragraph of the Revised Code of Georgia, all marriages not solemnized in conformity with the other provisions of said Code are declared to be invalid; and whereas, said innovation upon the law as it stood before the adoption of said Revised Code will have the effect of giving rise to perplexing questions of legitimacy of children and rights of property, and to domestic unhappiness, therefore," etc. The common law as to informal marriages was thus restored and reinstated. It follows that a lawful marriage may be contracted between parties prematurely married, if at any time after arriving at the age of consent they so agree, and their marriage may become complete without the observance of any prescribed form. If Smith and wife, after he had become seventeen years of age, had actually agreed to live together as husband and wife, and had continued to cohabit accordingly, a true matrimonia relation would have been established between them. If cohabitation based on express agreement would have had this effect, why should not cohabitation based on acquiescence in their premature marriage have a like effect? Cohabitation referable to that marriage would seem to be as free from moral impurity, and as wholesome to private conscience and public order and decorum, as if it followed upon a new affirmative agreement, consciously entered into for the distinct purpose of inaugurating marriage. Indeed, if persons who unite matrimonially while too young to enter wedlock are to remain together at all after coming to the full age of discretion, it would seem that the more delicate and decorous way to do it, if they can be allowed to omit public forms, is to recognize the past as not abruptly severed from the present and the future by the wide chasm which divides illicit intercourse from matrimonial union. The making of a new agreement would necessarily bring into consciousness a suggestion of something gross and repulsive in the past cohabitation. For a young husband, on consummating his seventeenth year, to propose marriage to the wife with whom he had lived for a year or two previously as a wife, might be necessary under a system of law such as that which the Code attempted to introduce; but we cannot think it necessary under the old system, which the Legislature designed to reinstate, and did reinstate, by the Repealing Act of 1863. While the Code put an implied negative upon the power of ratification except in the two instances enumerated, it failed to negative the power in any express terms, and we think the implied negative underwent an implied repeal by the Act of 1868. The only formidable obstacle to this construction is the general leading doctrine that void contracts are not curable by ratification. But marriage is a peculiar contract, and the marriage of infants, when over the age of seven years, but under the full age of consent, is peculiar in the law of marriage itself. Indeed, the distinction between void and voidable, as applied to contracts of infants generally, is involved in much confusion. 2 Kent, Com. 234; Tyler, Infancy, § 8.

In all our books, except the Code, the contracts of infants are treated as generally voidable; yet the Code says (§ 2731): "The contracts of an infant under twenty-one years of age are void, except for necessaries," etc. But coming back to the contract of marriage, the authorities all agree that, under the age of seven, a child (except when reasons of state are involved) is incompetent to marry at all; but between seven and fourteen in males, and seven and twelve in females, they all agree that an inchoate and imperfect marriage may take place, which is subject to be made good by mutual ratification or confirmation after the age of consent is attained. Disability for want of age is classed with civil, not canonical, disabilities.

Shelford says (Mar. and Div. 479) that it makes a marriage contract void *ab initio*, not merely voidable.

Bishop says (1 Mar. and Div. §§ 147, 150, 153) that the marriage is inchoate or imperfect, and may be affirmed; that it is voidable, not void.

Addison (3 Cont. § 1374) says it is inchoate and imperfect, not absolutely void.

Pollock (Cont. *57) says it is not absolutely void, but good, if agreed to at the age of consent.

Story (1 Cont. § 124) says it is voidable at the will of either party.

Schouler (Dom. Rel. § 24) says it is neither strictly void nor strictly voidable, but rather inchoate and imperfect.

Stewart (Mar. and Div. §§ 51, 58, 148) declares it void to all intents and purposes unless and until duly confirmed.

Blackstone, after treating canonical disabilities, and saying that they make marriage voidable, and not *ipso facto* void, until sentence of nullity is obtained, adds (1 Com. 435): "The other sort of disabilities are those which are created, or at least enforced, by the municipal laws. . . . These civil disabilities make the contract void *ab initio*, and not merely voidable; . . . and, if any persons under these legal incapacities come together, it is a meretricious, and not a matrimonial union." He then treats disability consequent upon having a living wife or husband, and proceeds thus: "The next legal disability is want of age. This is sufficient to avoid all other contracts, on account of the imbecility of judgment in the parties contracting; *a fortiori*, therefore, it ought to avoid this, the most important contract of any. Therefore, if a boy under fourteen, or a girl under twelve years of age, marries, this marriage is only inchoate and imperfect; and, when either of them comes to the age of consent aforesaid, they may disagree and declare the marriage void, without any divorce or sentence in the spiritual court. This is founded on the civil law. . . . And in our law it is so far a marriage that, if at the age of consent they agree to continue together, they need not be married again." To the same effect, see 1 Minor, Inst. 263, 264.

Tyler on Infancy, § 224, says: "Of course, if the parties cohabit as husband and wife after attaining the age of consent, the marriage is affirmed, and cannot be avoided."

Lord Coke (1 Inst. 79*a*) uses this language: "The time of agreement or disagreement when they marrie *infra annos nubiles*, is for the woman at twelve or after, and for the man at fourteen or after, and there need be no new marriage if they so agree; but disagree they cannot before the said ages, and then they may disagree and marrie againe to others without any divorce; and, if they once after give consent, they can never disagree after."

From Burn (2 Eccl. Law, 394) it appears that espousals could supervene upon a void marriage, and that, though they who give girls unto boys under the age of seven years do nothing, espousals would begin after the seventh year if it appeared by word or deed that the parties continued in the same mind. The latest, and perhaps the most distinct, instance of void marriage furnishing a basis for the conjugal relation by acquiescence or ratification, is that of slaves after the change of their status from slavery to freedom.

Mr. Bishop (1 Mar. & Div. § 162), in commenting upon this class of cases, says: "If the parties, having been married while slaves in the form usual among this class of persons, live together as husband and wife after they are emancipated, this, their subsequent mutual acknowledgment, should be held to complete the act of matrimony, so as to make them lawfully and fully married from the time at which such subsequent living together commenced. In those localities in which mutual consent constitutes of itself, without any superadded forms, perfect matrimony, the facts thus indicated would seem to be sufficient without any aid from what took place during slavery; and, where a superadded ceremony is necessary, there appears no reason why such ceremony, performed during slavery,—whether it was not the same which the law made necessary to constitute marriage between whites, still it was the ceremony which the law of usage had established for the blacks,—should not be deemed to combine with the consent which passed after emancipation, so as to make the nuptials complete. We have seen that such is the law of marriage celebrated during a temporary insanity of the parties, or celebrated when they were too young to pass the consent which constitutes complete matrimony; and in future pages we shall see that the same rule applies to cases of fraud, of impotence and perhaps of some other impediments."

As in the case of slaves, so in that of children under the age of consent, by our law, there is no penalty imposed upon the matrimonial parties. They do not, by the mere act of marrying or going through the form of marriage, commit any offense. The marriage of such persons is not so much contrary to law as unauthorized by law. Indeed, it stands related to criminal law precisely as did the marriage of boys under fourteen, and of girls under twelve, by the common law. The only change made by the Code, as it now stands, since the repeal wrought by the Act of 1868 above cited, is that the age of consent is moved upward, and the term "void" is applied to the marriage by express statute. But the same Statute applies the term to marriages procured by force or fraud, and yet it expressly allows them to become valid by ratification. This shows there is no absolute incompatibility—no positive incongruity—between a void marriage and a marriage which is susceptible of being ratified, and thereby made valid. Whether its validity is to date from the time of ratification only, or from the original, imperfect and incomplete marriage, we need not undertake now to determine, for the present controversy does not involve that question. All we hold is that such a marriage as we have under consideration is capable of being ratified when the parties arrive at the age of consent, and that continuous cohabitation as husband and wife after the attainment of that age, is, or may be, sufficient evidence of such ratification. Of course, if either of the parties, notwithstanding their competency as to age, should be wanting in mental capacity to agree to the marriage, that would render him or her incapable of confirming it by ratification. The view we take of the main question involved in the case renders a new trial necessary.

Judgment reversed.

INDIANA SUPREME COURT.

John B. WITTY, *Appt.*,

v.

MICHIGAN MUTUAL LIFE INSURANCE CO.

(....Ind....)

Blanks in the body of a note where the amount and place of payment should be named will not render the note non-negotiable, if the amount is expressed in figures at the head of the note, especially under a statute making negotiable any written promise to pay money which is signed by the promisor.

(April 24, 1890.)

APPEAL by defendant from a judgment of the Superior Court for Marion County in favor of plaintiff in an action brought to recover the amount due upon a certain alleged promissory note. *Affirmed.*

The facts sufficiently appear in the opinion.

Mr. **Thomas Hanna,** for appellant:

Bills and notes must express the sum for which they are given in the body of the instrument; and an instrument in the form of a note, given for a blank sum, though superscribed with the correct amount and transferred in that condition, is not a promissory note.

Edwards, Bills and Notes, 153, 168; Chitty, Bills, 150; 1 Daniel, Neg. Inst. 74, 75; *Norwich Bank* v. *Hyde*, 13 Conn. 279; *Mears* v. *Graham*, 8 Blackf. 144; 1 Parsons, Notes and Bills, 27, 28; *Sanderson* v. *Piper*, 5 Bing. N. C. 425.

Mr. **Horace Speed** for appellee.

Berkshire, *J.*, delivered the opinion of the court:

This is an action brought by the appellee against the appellant on the following writing:

$147.70. Indianapolis, Ind., Nov. 28th, 1883.

Four months after date I promise to pay to the order of the Michigan Mutual Life Insurance Company ——— dollars, and five per cent attorney's fees thereon per annum from date until paid, value received, without relief from valuation or appraisement laws of the State of Indiana. The indorsers jointly and severally waive presentment for payment, protest and notice of protest, and nonpayment of this note, and expressly agree, jointly and severally, that the holder may renew or extend the time of payment hereof from time to time, and receive interest, in advance or otherwise, from either of the makers or indorsers for any extension so made, without releasing them hereon. Negotiable and payable at ———.

J. B. Witty.

Nov. 28th—31—84. Indiana.

The appellee in its complaint did not ask for a reformation of the instrument, but relied on it as a promissory note complete in itself. The appellant answered by the general denial only. The cause was submitted to the court at special term, and a finding made for the appellee. The appellant filed a motion for a new trial, which the court overruled, and he excepted. An appeal was taken to general term, and upon the errors assigned the judgment at special term was affirmed, and from the judgment in general term this appeal is prosecuted.

There is but one question presented for our consideration: Is the written instrument, as it appears in the record, an enforceable obligation? We are of the opinion that it is,—if not so otherwise, by virtue of § 5501, Rev. Stat. 1881,*—and is negotiable by indorsement. It is signed by the appellant, and, when taken as an entirety, we think it contains a promise to pay $147.70, together with 5 per cent attorney's fees. By the very terms of the instrument the appellant obligates himself to pay to the appellee "dollars," and it is expressly recited that the promise rests upon a valuable considera-

---

NOTE.—Commercial paper drawn in blank. See *note* to Hopps v. Savage (Md.) 1 L. R. A. 648.

Blank indorsement; effect of. See *note* to Pool v. Anderson (Ind.) 1 L. R. A. 712. See also Bellows Falls Nat. Bank v. Dorset Marble Co. 2 L. R. A. 428, 61 Vt. 106; Temple v. Baker, 3 L. R. A. 709, 125 Pa. 634.

*"All promissory notes, bills of exchange, bonds or other instruments in writing, signed by any person who promises to pay money, . . . shall be negotiable by indorsement."

tion. No one can read the writing without at once coming to the conclusion that the appellant intended to obligate himself to the appellee for the payment of some definite amount of money, and that the appellee understood that it was receiving such an obligation. Though there may be some formal imperfections in the written obligation or contract which parties have entered into, if it contains matter sufficient to enable the court to ascertain the terms and conditions of the obligation or contract to which the parties intended to bind themselves, it is sufficient.

In the language of *Lord* Campbell in *Warrington* v. *Early*, 2 El. & Bl. 763: "The contract must be collected from the four corners of the document, and no part of what appears there is to be excluded." We can imagine no good reason why the marginal figures upon the writing in question should be disregarded. We know, as a part of the commercial history of the country, that the universal practice has been, for a period so long that the memory of man runneth not to the contrary, to represent by superscription in figures upon all obligations for the payment of money the amount or sum which is written in the body of the instrument. The superscription is always intended to represent the amount found in the body of the instrument, and not a different amount. If, therefore, an obligation is found where there is a promise to pay "dollars," but the number of dollars in the body of the instrument is blank, and the margin of the instrument is found to contain a superscription which states a number of dollars, why, in view of the usage or custom which has so long prevailed, should the body of the instrument not be aided by the superscription? We think in such a case the figures found in the margin should be taken as the amount which the obligor intended to obligate himself to pay, and the obligation enforced accordingly.

We do not think in such a case that the courts would be justified in disregarding the evident intention of the parties, as indicated by the superscription upon the paper, and in holding the instrument void for uncertainty, or on the ground that it is not a perfect writing; and especially are we of the opinion stated in view of the liberal Statute which we have on the subject of promissory notes and other written obligations, and their negotiation. Section 5501, *supra*. In the case under consideration, the action is between the original parties to the instrument, and upon it in the form and condition in which it was executed; and therefore we do not think it would be profitable to consider questions which might arise where the obligation is made payable at a bank, the blank number of dollars afterwards filled in by the payee, and indorsed by him to an innocent holder for value before maturity.

As to whether the writing would be a negotiable instrument in its present condition but for our Statute, we find some conflict of authority. We cite the following authorities for and against the proposition. For: *Ives* v. *Farmers Bank*, 2 Allen, 236; *Sweetser* v. *French*, 13 Met. 262; *Petty* v. *Fleisel*, 31 Tex. 169; *Corgan* v. *Frew*, 39 Ill. 31; *Williamson* v. *Smith*, 1 Coldw. 1. Against: *Norwich Bank* v. *Hyde*, 13 Conn. 279; Edwards, Bills and Notes, 168; *Hollen* v. *Davis*, 59 Iowa, 444, 44 Am. Rep. 688, with *note*.

We find no error in the record.

Judgment affirmed, with costs.

UNITED STATES CIRCUIT COURT, NORTHERN DISTRICT OF GEORGIA.

Wyley G. COOPER
v.
RICHMOND & DANVILLE R. CO.

(....Fed. Rep.....)

*__The circuit court will not inquire into the truth of the affidavit__ and grounds for removal where a foreign corporation, defendant in the cause, files a petition for removal accompanied by an affidavit made by a proper person, stating that, of affiant's own knowledge, from prejudice and local influence, the petitioner will not be able to obtain justice in the state courts.

(June 21, 1890.)

MOTION to remand to the state court a case removed therefrom on the alleged ground of prejudice and local influence. *Denied.*

The case sufficiently appears in the opinion.

Messrs. **Hall & Hammond,** for plaintiff, in support of the motion:

The defendant removed this case on the mere affidavit of its superintendent that from prejudice or local influence the defendant would not be able to obtain justice in the state court. This does not sufficiently "make it appear," as required by the Act of 1887. The change of the verbiage from the Local Prejudice Act of 1867 meant something. Under the Act of 1887, the existence of prejudice or local influence should be "made to appear" by competent and sufficient evidence. A mere affidavit that it exists, no matter how strongly it is stated, is nothing more than the opinion or conclusion of the affiant, and is not competent evidence. Facts and circumstances should be shown to exist from which the court could draw its own conclusion. The defendant did nothing more than was required by the Act of 1867 in this case.

Carson & R. L. Co. v. *Holtzclaw*, 39 Fed. Rep. 578, 885; *Robison* v. *Hardy*, 38 Fed. Rep. 49; *Dennison* v. *Brown*, Id. 535; *Amy* v. *Manning*, Id. 536, 868; *Goldworthy* v. *Chicago, M. & St. P. R. Co.* Id. 769; *Hakes* v. *Burnes*, 40 Fed. Rep. 33; *Minnick* v. *Union Ins. Co.* Id. 369; *Malone* v. *Richmond & D. R. Co.* 35 Fed. Rep. 625–628.

Messrs. **Jackson & Jackson** and **Pope & Barrow** for defendant, *contra.*

Newman, *J.*, delivered the opinion of the court:

This is a case removed to this court from the

*Head note by **Newman**, J.

state court under the Act of March 3, 1887, by the defendant corporation, on the ground of "prejudice and local influence." The questions for determination arise over the sufficiency of the affidavit made on behalf of the defendant, and on which the order for removal was made. In connection with the petition, in setting forth the facts as to the amount involved, the citizenship of the parties and the residence of the plaintiff and defendant, the subject matter of the suit and the prayer for removal, which is sworn to by counsel, defendant presented an affidavit made by S. G. Hammond, acting superintendent of the road in Georgia, who states therein that "from very many years' experience in railroad matters, and especially with litigation against the defendant, Richmond & Danville Railroad, in this particular, in the courts of Atlanta, in said Fulton County, State of Georgia, I know that from prejudice and local influence defendant will not be able to obtain justice in the Superior Court of Fulton County of the State of Georgia, nor in any other court to which the petitioner may, under the laws of said State, have the right, on account of such prejudice or local influence, to remove said cause."

The motion of the plaintiff is in these words: "And now comes the plaintiff in the above-stated case and makes application to the court to examine into the truth of the affidavit and grounds for removal of said case to this court, and remand said case to the Superior Court of Fulton County on the ground that it is not true that the said defendant is unable to obtain justice in said state court, from prejudice or local influence."

Two questions have been argued and submitted: first, whether or not the court was justified in signing the order for removal on the affidavit of defendant's acting superintendent, above quoted; second, whether or not the court will now hear evidence as to the existence of prejudice or local influence, or, in other words, ascertain by evidence *aliunde* as to the existence or non-existence of the grounds for removal. There is decided conflict in the decisions and opinions of the various circuit courts upon both of these questions. The following decisions are upon this subject: *Fisk* v. *Henarie*, 32 Fed. Rep. 417; *Short* v. *Chicago, M. & St. P. R. Co.* 33 Fed. Rep. 114; *Hills* v. *Richmond & D. R. Co.* Id. 81; *Whelan* v. *New York, L. E. & W. R. Co.* 35 Fed. Rep. 849; *Fisk* v. *Henarie*, Id. 230; *Taylor County* v. *Baltimore & O. R. Co.* Id. 161; *Malone* v. *Richmond & D. R. Co.* Id. 625; *Southworth* v. *Reid*, 36 Fed. Rep. 451; *Huskins* v. *Cincinnati, N. O. & T. P. R. Co.* 37 Fed. Rep. 504; *Goldworthy* v. *Chicago, M. & St. P. R. Co.* 38 Fed. Rep. 769; *Dennison* v. *Brown*, Id. 535; *Amy* v. *Manning*, Id. 536; *Carson & R. L. Co.* v. *Holtzclaw*, 39 Fed. Rep. 885; *Hakes* v. *Burns*, 40 Fed. Rep. 33; *Minnick* v. *Union Ins. Co.* Id. 369.

After a careful examination of all the cases, we are disposed to adopt the conclusion, and the reasoning by which he arrives at that conclusion, of *Judge* Jackson in the case of *Whelan* v. *New York, L. E. & W. R. Co.*, *supra*, and to hold that where the petition for removal is accompanied by an affidavit on behalf of the defendant, by a person authorized to make it, stating of his own knowledge, as in this case, the existence of prejudice and local influence, it is sufficient to justify the order for removal; in other words, when it is "made to appear" to this court by affidavit made on the affiant's own knowledge, that the prejudice and local influence exist, that it is a compliance with the Statute. There is nothing whatever in the Act of 1887 to show how it shall be "made to appear" to this court that the prejudice and local influence exist, and unless subdivision 3 of section 639 of the Revised Statutes (Act 1867) remains of force, there is no law prescribing a method of procedure.

The language of the court in the *Whelan Case, supra*, is as follows: "It is further contended that no proper proceedings have been had or taken by the defendant, even conceding its right of removal, to effect such removal. By the 3d section of the Act of 1887 the steps required to be taken in removal cases generally are indicated, but that section excepts from its operation cases sought to be removed on the ground of local prejudice, in respect to which clause 4 of amended section 2 prescribes no mode or method of effecting that class of removals. What procedure may, then, be adopted by the party seeking or entitled to remove under this clause? In conferring the right Congress certainly intended that some process for its exercise should be within reach of the party so entitled. We think the method of procedure for effectuating the right so conferred by said clause may be found in the two paragraphs of § 639, Rev. Stat., which succeed the third sub-division of said section. These two paragraphs prescribing the method of accomplishing removals are not in conflict with the Act of 1887, and may therefore be considered as still in force, and furnishing the proper and appropriate remedy to be employed by the party seeking a removal, and in making it appear to said circuit court that from prejudice or local influence he will not be able to obtain justice in the state courts. It is not indicated in the Act of 1887 how, or in what manner, the fact that the removing party cannot obtain justice in the local courts on account of such prejudice or local influence shall be made 'to appear' to the circuit court. *Judge* Deady, in *Fisk* v. *Henarie*, 32 Fed. Rep. 417–421 (Nov. 29 1887), held that the last clause of section 639, Rev. Stat., which immediately follows sub division 3 of said section, might reasonably be looked to as furnishing the machinery for making it 'appear' to the circuit court that the petitioning party could not obtain justice in the state court because of prejudice or local influence. If this suggestion of that learned judge, in which I concur, is not deemed correct, then, in the absence of all provision as to the method or mode of presenting the application for removal, this court would be left free to adopt proper and suitable rules, prescribing and regulating the practice in such cases; and such rule would naturally be made to conform to the practice and procedure heretofore in force in like cases. In either view of the subject, we think the mode adopted by the defendant in this case is not open to any serious objection. A formal petition, properly sworn to, was duly presented to this court, setting forth all the conditions required by the Act to entitle said defendant to remove the suit. This petition was accompanied and supported by the affidavit of the proper officer of the defendant company, stating, not what the affiant had reason to and did believe in respect to the existence of local prejudice, but in direct terms, and in the very language of the Act, 'that from prejudice and local influence said railroad company will not be able to obtain justice in said courts of common pleas, or in any other state court to which it has, under the laws of the State of Ohio, a right, on account of such prejudice or local influence, to remove said cause,' etc. This makes a prima facie showing as to what was required 'to be made to appear to the circuit court.'"

In the case of *Hills* v. *Richmond & D. R. Co.*, 33 Fed. Rep. 81, decided in this court by the district judge presiding therein, and in the case of *Fisk* v. *Henarie, supra*, decided by *Judge* Deady in the Circuit Court of Oregon, it was held that the old Act, so far as the method of procedure for removal was concerned, remained of force, and that when an affidavit was made in accordance with the Act of 1867 it was sufficient to justify removal. It seems the better practice now, however, even if it be that it is not required by the law, that the existence of the prejudice and local influence should be stated of the affiant's own knowledge. That has been done in this case, and we think the affidavit was sufficient to justify the order for removal.

Now, the affidavit named being sufficient to authorize the order for removal, will the court permit the other party to traverse the grounds of the affidavit and hear evidence as to the existence of prejudice and local influence? We adopt the conclusion of the court in the *Whelan Case* upon this subject also. The argument of *Judge* Jackson upon this subject, in the case named (pp. 861-866), leaves nothing to be added by us. It seems to us conclusive upon this question. We have had occasion in this case and in some other similar cases, arising here, to examine a copy of the bill (presented informally and discussed in a former case) which passed the House and after amendments in the Senate was concurred in by the House, and resulted in the Act of March 3, 1887. This shows the bill as it passed the House, and the various particulars in which it was amended, by striking out and inserting language, in the Senate. From this it appears that as the bill went from the House to the Senate, it read, so far as pertinent to the questions here, as follows: "When it shall be made to appear to the satisfaction of the court that from prejudice or local influence," etc. In the Senate, the words "the satisfaction of the" were stricken and the words "said circuit." before court, inserted, so that it read as it went back from the Senate to the House, and was passed as the Act now reads, "When it shall be made to appear to the said circuit court," etc. It will be seen from the history of this part of the Act that by the House Bill it was contemplated that it should be made to appear "to the satisfaction of the court" (probably the state court), that the prejudice or local influence existed, and that the Senate changed it so that it should clearly provide for the application to be made to the circuit court, and refused to agree to the language which was stricken, above quoted.

This undoubtedly indicates an intention not to allow a provision looking to investigation and inquiry as to the existence of prejudice or local influence to become a part of the Act. If this part of the history of the Act of 1887 be a proper matter for consideration, it greatly strengthens the argument in favor of construing the clause in question as indicated above. The Supreme Court of the United States in *Blake* v. *National City Bank*, 90 U. S. 23 Wall. 307 [23 L. ed. 119], adopted this method of interpreting an Act of 1870, taxing incomes from dividends, etc. The rule there announced is that "a badly expressed and apparently contradictory enactment (such as the one above mentioned) interpreted by a reference to the journal of Congress, where it appeared that that the peculiar phraseology was the result of an amendment introduced without due reference to language in the original bill."

If the history of this Act in the respects named be the proper subject for consideration, it seems to us conclusive upon the questions now presented, and clearly negatives the idea that any investigation or inquiry such as we are requested to make here as to the existence of grounds of removal, was contemplated by Congress. Irrespective of this, however, it appears that when Congress came to deal with the cases which had been removed to this court by plaintiff, before the passage of the Act, it provided that "the circuit court shall, on application of either party, examine into the truth of said affidavit, and the grounds thereof, and unless it shall appear to the satisfaction of said court that said party will not be able to obtain justice in such said court, it shall cause the same to be remanded thereto." It appears from this that when an examination into the truth of the affidavit and the ground thereof was contemplated, it was so stated in express terms, and the statement of it there, we think, gives emphasis to its omission in the preceding part of section 2 in making provision for removal by the defendant. So that giving no weight whatever to the history of the Act, and construing it by what appears upon its face, the clear statement of the duty of the court in one case, and its entire omission in the other, is very significant and leads to the conclusion that in the latter case no such duty was intended to be imposed.

Motion denied.

Don A. Pardee, *Circuit Judge:* I concur.

ALABAMA SUPREME COURT.

MAYOR, etc., OF BIRMINGHAM,
Appts.,
v.
John KLEIN *et al.*

(....Ala.....)

A local assessment against property to pay for pavements constructed along its front, to be apportioned with reference to the benefits which are assumed to accrue to the owners of the property, is not a tax within the meaning of constitutional provisions requiring that "all taxes levied on property in this State shall be assessed in exact proportion to the value of the property," and limiting the amount of taxes that can be levied or collected in any one year.

(April 29, 1890.)

APPEAL by plaintiffs from a judgment of the City Court of Birmingham sustaining a demurrer to the complaint in a proceeding to enforce payment of certain local assessments made for street improvements. *Reversed.*

The case sufficiently appears in the opinion.

Messrs. **Cabaniss & Weakley**, for appellants:

The assessment authorized by the Act of the General Assembly is in no just sense a tax, as that term is used in our Constitution.

Illinois & M. Canal Co. v. *Chicago*, 12 Ill. 403; *Greenburg* v. *Young*, 53 Pa. 280; *Hoyt* v. *East Saginaw*, 19 Mich. 89, 2 Am. Rep. 76; *Maloy* v. *Marietta*, 11 Ohio St. 686; *Egyptian Levee Co.* v. *Hardin*, 27 Mo. 497; *Uhrig* v. *St. Louis*, 44 Mo. 458; *Garrett* v. *St. Louis*, 25 Mo. 505; *Lockwood* v. *St. Louis*, 24 Mo. 20; *Crowley* v. *Copley*, 2 La. Ann. 329; *Wilmington* v. *Yopp*, 71 N. C. 76; *Hayden* v. *Atlanta*, 70 Ga. 817; *Edgerton* v. *Green Cove Springs*, 19 Fla. 140; *Wright* v. *Chicago*, 46 Ill. 44; *Hines* v. *Leavenworth*, 3 Kan. 186; *Motz* v. *Detroit*, 18 Mich. 495; *Williams* v. *Cammack*, 27 Miss. 209; *Lexington* v. *McQuillan*, 9 Dana, 513; *King* v. *Portland*, 2 Or. 146; *Tidewater Co.* v. *Coster*, 18 N. J. Eq. 519; *People* v. *Lynch*, 51 Cal. 15, 21 Am. Rep. 677; *Richmond & A. R. Co.* v. *Lynchburg*, 81 Va. 473; *Norfolk* v. *Ellis*, 26 Gratt. 224; *McGehee* v. *Mathis*, 21 Ark. 40; *Merrick* v. *Amherst*, 12 Allen. 500; *Wright* v. *Boston*, 9 Cush. 233; *Wistar* v. *Philadelphia*, 80 Pa. 505; *Yeatman* v. *Crandall*, 11 La. Ann. 220; *Allen* v. *Galveston*, 51 Tex. 302; *Austin* v. *Gulf. C. & S. F. R. Co.* 45 Tex. 234; *Roundtree* v. *Galveston*, 42 Tex. 526; *Palmer* v. *Stumph*, 29 Ind. 329; Burroughs, Taxn. p.435; Cooley, Taxn. p.636 *et seq.*; 2 Dillon, Mun. Corp. p. 752.

Article 13, § 15, Constitution of 1868, was as follows: "It shall be the duty of the General Assembly to provide for the organization of cities and incorporated towns, and to restrict their power of taxation, assessment and contracting of debt."

The use of the word "assessment" showed that the word "taxation" did not include them.

People v. *Brooklyn*, 4 N. Y. 419, 55 Am. Dec.

NOTE.—*Taxation; constitutional restriction of power; valuation, equality and uniformity.*

A constitutional provision that "all property shall be taxed according to its value," the same to be equal and uniform throughout the State in the manner of ascertaining the same, has been held to apply only to state revenue, and not to taxes levied for local purposes. Washington v. State, 13 Ark. 752; Chambers v. Satterlee, 40 Cal. 497; Allen v. Galveston, 51 Tex. 320; Re Casacalvo and Moreau Streets, 20 La. Ann. 497; Hundley v. Lincoln Park Comrs. 67 Ill. 559; Moore v. People, 106 Ill. 376; Francis v. Atchison, T. & S. F. R. Co. 19 Kan. 303.

Such constitutional provisions apply only to taxation for general purposes of government. *Re* Washington Avenue, 69 Pa. 353; 2 Desty, Taxn. 1251-1253; Norfolk v. Ellis, 26 Gratt. 227.

That special assessments for local improvements according to benefits may be laid notwithstanding the restrictions of the Constitution as to valuation of property assessed, and uniformity in the mode of assessment, has been very generally sustained. Chicago v. Larned, 34 Ill. 203; Bedard v. Hall, 44 Ill. 91; Wright v. Chicago, 46 Ill. 44; Bright v. McCullough, 27 Ind. 223; Palmer v. Stumph, 29 Ind. 329; Turpin v. Eagle Creek & L. W. L. G. R. Co. 48 Ind. 45; New Orleans v. Elliott, 10 La. Ann. 59; Yeatman v. Crandall, 11 La. Ann. 220; New Orleans Draining Co's Case, 11 La. Ann. 338; Municipality No. 2 v. Guillotte, 14 La. Ann. 295; Wallace v. Shelton, 14 La. Ann. 503; Bishop v. Marks, 15 La. Ann. 147; *Re* Casacalvo and Moreau Streets, 20 La. Ann. 497; Daily v. Swope, 47 Miss. 367; Macon v. Patty, 57 Miss. 378; Uhrig v. St. Louis, 44 Mo. 458; Hurford v. Omaha, 4 Neb. 336; Marion v. Epler, 5 Ohio St. 250; Ernst v. Kunkle, 5 Ohio St. 520; Reeves v. Wood County, 8 Ohio St. 333; Northern I. R. Co. v. Connelly, 10 Ohio St. 159; *Re* Dorrance Street, 4 R. I. 230; Weeks v. Milwaukee, 10 Wis. 243; Lumsden v. Cross, 10 Wis. 282; Bond v. Kenosha, 17 Wis. 284; 2 Desty, Taxn. 1253.

Taxes distinguished from assessments for local improvements. See *note* to Adams County v. Quincy (Ill.) 6 L. R. A. 155.

Cannot be imposed where the benefit is general. See *note* to Moore v. Barry (S. C.) 4 L. R. A. 294.

That an assessment is called a tax in the statute will not preclude its being sustained as an assessment. People v. Austin, 47 Cal. 353.

Assessment for special benefits.

The city council is solely vested with power to determine what proportion of the total cost of a local improvement shall be paid by the public by general taxation. Watson v. Chicago, 1 West. Rep. 659, 115 Ill. 78.

A provision in an ordinance "that commissioners shall assess to the property benefited," means that the benefited property shall pay the amount of benefits to the property, the public to pay all in excess thereof. *Ibid.*

The determination of the city council that this excess, if any, shall be paid by general taxation, is binding on the commissioners, and they cannot add to or lessen such amount. *Ibid.*

When the ordinance provides how much of the cost shall be paid by general taxation, that amount, neither more nor less, is so to be paid. *Ibid.*

The ordinance providing for an improvement, the cost whereof shall be paid by special assessment of property benefited, the remainder to be paid by general taxation, is authorized by the Act to Incorporate Cities and Villages. The provisions of § 139 do not apply where the city authorities fix the amount paid by general taxation. Watson v. Chicago, 1 West. Rep. 661, 115 Ill. 78.

The fact that a general tax on a city for street

See also 11 L. R. A. 835.

266; *Hines* v. *Leavenworth, supra; Hurford* v. *Omaha*, 4 Neb. 336; *Weeks* v. *Milwaukee*, 10 Wis. 243; *Hill* v. *Higdon*, 5 Ohio St. 243.

Messrs. **Roquemore, White & McKenzie** also filed a brief on behalf of appellant:

An assessment for improvements is not considered as a burden, but an equivalent or compensation for the enhanced value which the property derives from the improvement.

People v. *Brooklyn*, 4 N. Y. 420; *Brooks* v. *Baltimore*, 48 Md. 265; *Sheehan* v. *Good Samaritan Hospital*, 50 Mo. 155; *Stein* v. *Mobile*, 24 Ala. 617.

In the absence of constitutional restrictions, the power of the General Assembly to authorize municipal corporations to improve streets and sidewalks at the expense of adjacent landed proprietors is undoubted.

Irwin v. *Mobile*, 57 Ala. 6; *Stein* v. *Mobile*, 24 Ala. 591; Burroughs, Taxn. § 45, *note 1*, p. 460, and cases cited therein; Cooley, Const. Lim. p. 479; 2 Dillon, Mun. Corp. §§ 616-735 *et seq.*, § 761; *People* v. *Brooklyn*, 4 N. Y. 420.

As opposed to the doctrine laid down in *Mobile* v. *Dargan*, 45 Ala. 310, we have in our own State, and from this court, the following cases: *Stein* v. *Mobile*, 24 Ala. 591; *Irwin* v. *Mobile*, 57 Ala. 6; *Winter* v. *Montgomery*, 83 Ala. 589; *Western U. Teleg. Co.* v. *State*, 80 Ala. 273; *Strenna* v. *Montgomery*, 86 Ala. 340.

Constitutional declarations to the effect that all taxes levied on property must be in proportion to its value do not place an inhibition upon the grant of power to municipal corporations to make "local assessments."

People v. *Brooklyn, supra; Zanesville* v. *Richards*, 5 Ohio St. 589; *Hill* v. *Higdon*, 5 Ohio St. 243; *Reeves* v. *Wood County*, 8 Ohio St 333; *Northern I. R. Co.* v. *Connelly*, 10 Ohio St. 159; *Palmyra* v. *Morton*, 25 Mo. 593; *Egyptian Levee Co.* v. *Hardin*, 27 Mo. 495; *St. Joseph* v. *O'Donoghue*, 31 Mo. 345; *St. Louis* v. *Clemens*, 36 Mo. 467; *People* v. *Lynch*, 51 Cal. 15; *Emery* v. *San Francisco Gas Co.* 28 Cal. 346; *Whiting* v. *Quackenbush*, 54 Cal. 306; *Howell* v. *Buffalo*, 37 N. Y. 267; *Litchfield* v. *Vernon*, 41 N. Y. 123; *Philadelphia* v. *Tryon*, 35 Pa. 401; *Com.* v. *Woods*, 44 Pa. 113; *Hamilton* v. *Ft. Wayne*, 40 Ind. 491; *Alexander* v. *Baltimore*, 5 Gill (Md.) 383; *Moale* v. *Baltimore*, 5 Md. 314; *Williams* v. *Cammack*, 27 Miss. 209; *Alcorn* v. *Hamer*, 38 Miss. 652; *Smith* v. *Aberdeen*, 25 Miss. 458; *State* v. *Dodge County*, 8 Neb. 124; *Chamberlain* v. *Cleveland*, 34 Ohio St. 551; *Tidewater Co.* v. *Coster*, 18 N. J. Eq. 518; *Thomas* v. *Gain*, 35 Mich. 156; *Nichols* v. *Bridgeport*, 23 Conn. 204; *Re William & Anthony Streets*, 19 Wend. 678; *Re Flatbush Ave.* 1 Barb. 286; *Re Fourth Ave.* 4 Wend. 452; *Re Albany St.* 11 Wend. 149; *Stafford* v. *Hamston*, 2 Brod. & B. 691; *Brooks* v. *Baltimore*, 48 Md. 265; *Cruikshanks* v. *Charleston*, 1 McCord, L. 360; *Williams* v. *Detroit*, 2 Mich. 560; *Woodbridge* v. *Detroit*, 8 Mich. 274; *Hoyt* v. *East Saginaw*, 19 Mich. 39; *White* v. *People*, 94 Ill. 604; *Vasser* v. *George*, 47 Miss. 713; *Craw* v. *Tolono*, 96 Ill. 255; *Daily* v. *Swope*, 47 Miss. 367; *Hines* v. *Leavenworth*, 3 Kan. 186; *Macon* v. *Patty*, 57 Miss. 378; *Yeatman* v. *Crandall*, 11 La. Ann. 220; *State* v. *Dean*, 23 N. J. L. 335; *New Orleans Draining Co's Case*, 11 La. Ann. 338; *State* v. *Jersey City*, 24 N. J. L. 662; *Wallace* v. *Shelton*, 14 La. Ann. 503;

---

improvements was levied on certain land will not relieve the land from an assessment for special benefits. State v. Newark, 2 Cent. Rep. 234, 48 N. J. L. 101.

The judgment of commissioners of assessment for an improvement as to an area over which the benefits extend, and as to the amount of the benefits, will prevail, unless evidence against it is convincing. *Ibid.*

An assessment laid upon an erroneous principle will be corrected, under the New Jersey Act of March 23, 1881. State v. Newark, 9 Cent. Rep. 664, 50 N. J. L. 66.

A city assessment without authority of law will be enjoined. Foster v. Kenosha, 12 Wis. 616; Toledo, W. & W. R. Co. v. Lafayette, 22 Ind. 262.

Municipal corporations: authority of under delegated powers.

The Legislature is authorized to vest the corporate authorities of cities, towns and villages with power to make local improvements by means of special assessments without restriction as to the property to be assessed. McLean County v. Bloomington, 106 Ill. 209.

Grants of power to make local assessments are strictly construed, and must be strictly followed. Keese v. Denver, 10 Colo. 113.

Corporate authorities of cities and villages are vested with power to make local improvements by special assessment, or by special taxation, or both, of contiguous property, as they shall by ordinance prescribe; and in such cases the doctrine of equality and uniformity does not apply, as in cases of taxation for all other purposes. Murphy v. People, 8 West. Rep. 452, 120 Ill. 234.

Assessment district.

Where a council is given power to make assessments upon premises abutting on improved streets and upon other premises benefited thereby, it must designate the taxing district, it cannot delegate power to do so. Whitney v. Hudson, 13 West. Rep. 901, 69 Mich. 189.

Under a city charter providing that the common council "shall determine and prescribe the limits within which private property shall be deemed benefited by the proposed improvement and be assessed and charged," the council must define the assessment district; but whether any particular piece of property therein is benefited is a question for the jury. Kansas City v. Baird, 98 Mo. 215.

Assessments for costs of paving streets.

Assessments for benefits may be levied for paving, planking or otherwise improving the streets. Chambers v. Satterlee, 40 Cal. 497; People v. Austin, 47 Cal. 353; Indianapolis v. Mansur, 15 Ind. 112; Lafayette v. Fowler, 34 Ind. 140; Morrison v. Hershire, 32 Iowa, 271; Municipality No. 2 v. Dunn, 10 La. Ann. 57; Williams v. Detroit, 2 Mich. 560; Macon v. Patty, 57 Miss. 378; People v. Brooklyn, 4 N. Y. 419; *Re* Dugro, 50 N. Y. 513; State v. Portage, 12 Wis. 562; Willard v. Presbury, 81 U. S. 14 Wall. 676 (20 L. ed. 719); Huidekoper v. Meadville, 83 Pa. 156; Philadelphia v. Tryon, 35 Pa. 404; Pray v. Northern Liberties, 31 Pa. 69; Sheley v. Detroit, 45 Mich. 431.

Authority to assess the expense of paving includes all that is necessary in paving, including curbing. Schenley v. Com. 36 Pa. 29. See Cooley, Taxn. 618, *note; Re* Burke, 62 N. Y. 224; O'Reilley v. Kingston, 114 N. Y. 439.

Property fronting on a city street is liable to an assessment for the expense of paving the middle portion of the street, which has been left open and unpaved, and used as a boulevard or drive for a long period after the paving of the sides, such paving being an original improvement. Alcorn v. Philadelphia, 8 Cent. Rep. 136, 112 Pa. 494.

Fairfield v. *Ratcliffe*, 20 Iowa, 396; *Richardson* v. *Morgan*, 16 La. Ann. 429; *Goodrich* v. *Winchester & D. Turnp. Co.* 26 Ind. 119; *Cain* v. *Davie County*, 86 N. C. 8; *Norfolk* v. *Ellis*, 26 Gratt. 224; *Roundtree* v. *Galveston*, 42 Tex. 612; Burroughs, Taxn. §§ 3, 145.

Mr. **Jackson E. Long**, for appellees:

An assessment is a tax.

Cooley, Const. Lim. 250, and *note*, 593 *et seq.*, 617-627; *Irwin* v. *Mobile*, 57 Ala. 12; *Hammett* v. *Philadelphia*, 65 Pa. 146, 3 Am. Rep. 615; *People* v. *Brooklyn*, 4 N. Y. 419, 55 Am. Dec. 266; *Mobile* v. *Dargan*, 45 Ala. 310; *Olive Cemetery Co.* v. *Philadelphia*, 93 Pa. 129, 39 Am. Rep. 733; *Taylor* v. *Chandler*, 9 Heisk. 349, 24 Am. Rep. 308.

There is no recognition in our Constitution of a local assessment as not included in the general word "tax."

Ala. Const.; *Stein* v. *Mobile*, 24 Ala. 611; *Mobile* v. *Stonewall Ins. Co.* 53 Ala. 584.

Decisions under constitutions expressly recognizing a local assessment as distinct from and not included in the general word "taxation" can have no weight in the determination of the question here, the condition being different.

Taylor v. *Chandler*, 9 Heisk. 349, 24 Am. Rep. 308; *People* v. *Brooklyn*, 4 N. Y. 420, 55 Am. Dec. 266; *Emery* v. *San Francisco Gas Co.* 28 Cal. 345; Bouvier, L. Dict. *Assessment.*

Where merely the word "taxation" is used, and not "all," the language in its ordinary signification comprehends all taxation.

Mobile v. *Stonewall Ins. Co.* 53 Ala. 583.

The word "tax" or "taxation," when similarly used in a Constitution, applies to all taxes—a tax such as this is included.

Mobile v. *Dargan*, 45 Ala. 310; *Taylor* v. *Chandler, supra*; *Chicago* v. *Larned*, 34 Ill. 203; *Irwin* v. *Mobile*, 57 Ala. 6; *Mobile* v. *Stonewall Ins. Co.* 53 Ala 572; *Peay* v. *Little Rock*, 32 Ark. 31; *Weeks* v. *Milwaukee*, 10 Wis. 242; *Palmer* v. *Way*, 6 Colo. 106; *Stinson* v. *Smith*, 8 Minn. 366; *Olive Cemetery Co.* v. *Philadelphia*, 93 Pa. 129, 39 Am. Rep. 733; *Mobile* v. *Royal St. R. Co.* 45 Ala. 322.

The opinion in *Mobile* v. *Dargan* was rendered in 1871, construing a clause in the Constitution of 1868. Our present Constitution was adopted in 1875 and that identical clause was adopted without change. This was a legislative adoption of that judicial construction.

East Tennessee, V. & G. R. Co. v. *Bayliss*, 74 Ala. 150; *Morrison* v. *Stevenson*, 69 Ala. 448; *Posey* v. *Pressley*, 60 Ala. 243; *Huddleston* v. *Askey*, 56 Ala. 218; *Woolsey* v. *Cade*, 54 Ala. 378; *Ex parte Matthews*, 52 Ala. 51; *O'Byrnes* v. *State*, 51 Ala. 25; Cooley, Const. Lim. 64, 81.

McClellan, *J.*, delivered the opinion of the court:

This appeal involves the constitutionality of an Act "to Authorize and Empower the Mayor and Aldermen of Birmingham to Improve the Sidewalks of the City of Birmingham, Alabama, at the Cost of Parties whose Property Abuts such Sidewalks," approved February 16, 1885. Sess. Acts 1884-85, pp. 620-622.

Those sections of the Act which are necessary to an understanding of the point under consideration are the following: "Section 1. Be it enacted by the General Assembly of Alabama that the Mayor and Aldermen of Birmingham shall have full power and authority

---

For re-paving.

The paving of a street may be renewed at the expense of the owners of abutting lots. Coates v. Dubuque, 68 Iowa, 550.

The question whether the renewal of the paving of a street is demanded for the public good is to be determined by the city council; and their determination is conclusive, except for want of authority, or for fraud or oppression. *Ibid.*

That a street has been once paved, and the cost paid by assessment, does not render invalid an assessment for re-paving with improved pavement. State v. Newark, 2 Cent. Rep. 234, 48 N. J. L. 101.

An assessment, under Act March 27, 1882, is not defeated on the ground that the tax ordinance did not mention particular streets. *Ibid.*

Assessments for benefits may be levied to pay for the re-paving of a street, although the cost of the work is already raised by a general tax. *Ibid.*

Under a general power to construct sidewalks the expense of the removal of a sidewalk and re-pavement of that portion of street, where such action is necessary, may be assigned to the general fund appropriated to the general expenses of the paving department. Atty-Gen. v. Boston, 2 New Eng. Rep. 689, 142 Mass. 200.

In Pennsylvania it has been held that the cost of re-paving a public street cannot be legally charged against the property fronting thereon, notwithstanding the original cost of paving the street was paid out of the public treasury. Williamsport v. Beck, 128 Pa. 147.

The power to assess the expense of re-paving or re-planking a street on the adjacent proprietors, who had borne the expense of the original construction, has been generally affirmed. Gurnee v. Chicago, 40 Ill. 165; Bradley v. McAtee, 7 Bush, 667; Broadway Baptist Church v. McAtee, 8 Bush, 508; Municipality No. 2 v. Dunn, 10 La. Ann. 57; Williams v. Detroit, 2 Mich. 560; Sheley v. Detroit, 45 Mich. 425; Wilkins v. Detroit, 46 Mich. 120; McCormack v. Patchin, 53 Mo. 33; Willard v. Presbury, 81 U. S. 14 Wall. 676 (20 L. ed. 719); *Re* Garvey, 77 N. Y. 523; *Re* Phillips, 60 N. Y. 16; *Re* Astor, 53 N. Y. 617; *Re* Burke, 62 N. Y. 224; *Re* Brady, 85 N. Y. 268; *Re* Smith, 99 N. Y. 424; Hammett v. Philadelphia, 65 Pa. 146; 2 Desty, Taxn. 1237.

Cost of grading.

Special assessments are made for the cost of grading streets, or changing their grade. Buffalo Cemetery Asso. v. Buffalo, 118 N. Y. 61; Wray v. Pittsburgh, 46 Pa. 365; State v. Dean, 23 N. J. L. 335; Holmes v. Jersey City, 12 N. J. Eq. 299; Lafayette v. Fowler, 34 Ind. 140.

The cost of grading a city street, as distinguished from paving it, cannot be assessed to the owners of the abutting lots. Code, § 465.

But where grading is necessary to secure a proper foundation for a pavement, and the grading is done as an incident to the paving, the cost may be regarded as a part of the cost of paving, for which the owners of abutting lots may be taxed. Code, § 466; Schofield v. Council Bluffs, 68 Iowa, 695.

Rule of apportionment.

Every valid assessment must be based on a legally ordained basis of apportionment. Detroit v. Daly, 13 West. Rep. 151, 68 Mich. 503.

Local assessments may be laid either in proportion to the benefits or in proportion to the frontage of the lands benefited. Mots v. Detroit, 18 Mich. 495; Hoyt v. East Saginaw, 19 Mich. 39.

An assessment apportioned according to benefits is a legitimate exercise of the taxing power. State v. Newark, 27 N. J. L. 191; Seattle v. Yesler, 1 Wash. T. 571.

See also 48 L. R. A. 274.

to cause and procure all sidewalks along the streets, avenues and alleys now established, or hereafter to be established, in said city, to be graded, leveled, curbed, graveled, slagged, cindered, paved or macadamized, or to be re-graded, re-leveled, re-curbed, re-graveled, re-slagged, re-cindered, re-paved or re-macadamized, in such manner and by such methods and with such material as they may deem best and proper. Sec. 2. Be it further enacted that the said Mayor and Aldermen of Birmingham shall have the power to have such work done, or cause the same to be done, and the expense thereof shall, after the completion thereof, be by said Mayor and Aldermen of Birmingham assessed upon the abutting owners of lands or lots lying along and adjacent to the streets or alleys along which such work is done, in proportion to the amount of the benefit accruing to such abutting owner; and all such assessments shall be and constitute a lien upon the lands and lots respectively upon which they shall be so assessed."

It thus appears that the purpose of the Act and its effect, if valid, is to authorize local assessments against property to pay for pavements constructed along its front; the cost, as between different owners, to be apportioned with reference to the benefits which are assumed to accrue to them severally from the betterment. However the relative benefits are to be determined in a given case, and the sum to be charged on a particular lot ascertained,—whether by reference to the superficial area of the property or the length of its abutment on the sidewalk, or the uses to which it is devoted as being to a greater or less extent facilitated by the improvement, or the enhancement thereby of its value compared with other property subject to the gross assessment,—one thing is assured: that the assessment is not made with reference to the value of the property, nor with

---

The general rule for determining the amount of the benefit is to ascertain the market value of the property with the improvement and without it; the excess of value with the improvement over that without it being the amount of benefit. Elwood v. Rochester, 43 Hun, 102.

The provisions and policy of the Revised Statutes as to the assessment and valuation of lots for the cost of local improvements were intended to equalize the expense upon all the lots benefited. Parmelee v. Youngstown, 1 West. Rep. 49, 43 Ohio St. 162.

A statute apportioning the cost of street improvements to lots or parcels of ground extending from the street to be improved to the centre of the block, according to the value of the ground exclusive of improvements, is not unconstitutional. Newman v. Emporia, 41 Kan. 583.

When an assessment for a public improvement has been levied under a statute which required the assessors to assess all the lands benefited, the Legislature cannot authorize a further assessment for the improvement to be levied against other lands of the same owners, so long as the original assessment remains valid against those owners. State v. Essex Public Road Board, 51 N. J. L. 166.

If in the judgment of the assessors the special benefits of a public improvement extend at all to a lot of land which is so circumstanced that a reasonable owner would use it or offer it for sale only as an entirety, then they should levy the assessment upon the whole lot, and not merely upon such part of the lot as lies within lines previously fixed by them as the limit of assessable benefits. *Ibid.*

Modes of assessment.

The Legislature is not confined to one mode of assessment but may adopt the front-foot, the square-foot, the square-acre or the *ad valorem* basis, in its discretion. Daily v. Swope, 47 Miss. 367; Sinton v. Ashbury, 41 Cal. 525.

When the charter requires the property to be assessed according to benefits received, it cannot be assessed according to frontage. Ogden v. Hudson, 29 N. J. L. 104; St. John v. East St. Louis, 50 Ill. 92.

In Arkansas paving taxes must be assessed according to the value of the lots assessed, and it is not competent to apportion the assessment according to frontage. Peay v. Little Rock, 32 Ark. 31; Palmer v. Way, 6 Colo. 106. See Weeks v. Milwaukee, 10 Wis. 242; Chicago v. Larned, 34 Ill. 203.

Municipal assessments for the improvement of streets must be *ad valorem*, and not according to frontage, and must be upon both vacant and occupied lots similarly situated. The exception of one violates the constitutional principle of uniformity in the imposition of the burden. Monticello v. Banks, 48 Ark. 251.

The front-foot rule.

It is not unconstitutional to provide for the apportionment of the expenses of local improvements on adjacent property by the "front foot." Rutherford v. Hamilton, 97 Mo. 543.

A delegation of authority to levy assessments for local improvements in proportion to the frontage of the land assessed, and not in proportion to benefits, is not in violation of the California Constitution. Jennings v. Le Breton, 80 Cal. 8.

Assessments for special improvements, under Rev. Stat., §§ 2269, 2270, were intended to equalize the expense upon land benefited. Where there is benefited land not subdivided into lots, and its value is found by the front foot, such value is its value for taxation. Parmelee v. Youngstown, 1 West. Rep. 49, 43 Ohio St. 162.

Prima facie, all land within the city limits is subject to the frontage rule; and the burden of proving land rural rests upon the owner. Stewart v. Philadelphia (Pa.) 4 Cent. Rep. 674.

Where assessment by the front foot has been made, each lot is separately liable. Younglove v. Hackman, 1 West. Rep. 82, 43 Ohio St. 69.

No power exists to charge rural property for paving roads by the foot-front measure applicable to city property. Philadelphia v. Keith (Pa.) 1 Cent. Rep. 896.

The fact that application of the front-foot rule of assessment for municipal improvements will amount to more than the value of a long, narrow lot fronting on the street lengthwise is no objection to the application of such rule in assessing the lot. Harrisburg v. McCormick, 129 Pa. 213.

Where a tax is to be levied upon lots and lands upon the streets to be improved in proportion to frontage, the lots are only those upon the line of the streets upon which they front or abut. Wilbur v. Springfield, 12 West. Rep. 596, 123 Ill. 395.

In California it has been held that the assessment of abutting property in proportion to its frontage is not in violation of the constitutional provision as to valuation, equality and uniformity. Burnett v. Sacramento, 12 Cal. 76; People v. Burr, 13 Cal. 343; Emery v. San Francisco Gas Co. 28 Cal. 345; Emery v. Bradford, 29 Cal. 75; Walsh v. Mathews, 29 Cal. 123; Taylor v. Palmer, 31 Cal. 240; Crosby v. Lyon, 37 Cal. 242; Chambers v. Satterlee, 40 Cal. 497; Reclamation Dist. v. Hagar, 6 Sawy. 569; Oakland Pav. Co. v. Rier, 52 Cal. 270; Whiting v. Quackenbush, 54 Cal. 306.

reference to the limitations on the rate of municipal taxation. It is manifest, therefore, that if the assessment is a "tax," within the meaning of the Constitution of Alabama, the Statute authorizing it is repugnant to section 1 of article 11 of that instrument, which requires that "all taxes levied on property in this State shall be assessed in exact proportion to the value of such property," and also to section 7 of that article, which provides that "no city, town or other municipal corporation . . . shall levy or collect a larger rate of taxation in any one year, on the property thereof, than one half of one per centum of the value of such property as assessed for state taxation during the preceding year."

There is no longer any doubt but that organic limitations on the taxing power, though expressed in general terms, apply as well to the exercise of that power through the medium of municipal corporations and for municipal purposes as to its exercise directly by the Legislature for state purposes; and hence the requirement that all taxes levied on property in this State shall be assessed *ad valorem* would obtain, with respect to municipal taxation, even in the absence of the other provision quoted, requiring such taxation to be based on the value of property as assessed for state taxation. *Mobile* v. *Stonewall Ins. Co.* 53 Ala. 570.

Both the sections noted therefore bear upon assessments for municipal purposes; and, if either covers the local assessment under consideration, the law authorizing it must fail. It is a fair, if not necessary, inference that the terms "taxes" and "taxation" have respectively the same meaning wherever found in article 11 of the Constitution. The "taxes" which must be laid on a basis of value in section 1 constitute the "taxation" referred to for state purposes in section 4, for county purposes in section 5 and for municipal purposes in section 7; and therefore the only municipal taxation which the Constitution requires to be assessed in exact proportion to the value of property is that embraced in the terms of section 7. The most liberal construction of which the language of that section is susceptible will not admit of its application to local assessment to provide for local improvements of sidewalks. By the very terms employed throughout the article, the taxes and taxation, whether state, county or municipal, are those which make up the general revenues of the one or the other political division, as the case may be,—revenues which come from all the property in the territory and go to defray general governmental expenditures, as distinguished from special outlays to provide for purely local exigencies. With respect to section 7, this is made to appear with great clearness by its reference to the property to which the limitation it imposes is made to apply, and by its requirement as to the assessment upon which the municipal levy must be predicated. Not only is the levy by any city to be made "on the property thereof," *i. e.*, the whole taxable property thereof, but it must be made on "such property as assessed for state taxation during the preceding year." No such thing is known, or was known when the Constitution of 1875 was adopted, or had ever been known, as local assessments of property for state taxation. The state assessment upon which the only municipal levy treated of in the Organic Law is required to be based is a general assessment of all property within the corporate limits, and is intended, as the provisos to section 7 show, to provide a fund for the general expenses of the city government. The city's levy there limited must be put upon the whole property taxed by the State, at the valuation fixed by the State's agents. This necessarily and wholly excludes any idea of a local assessment of particular property for any purpose, or to be laid in any manner, under the Constitution. Nothing in that instrument refers, or can be made applicable, to such a local charge. If this species of taxation—for it is taxation and referable to the taxing power, though differing, as we shall see, from the "taxes" and "taxation" regulated in State Constitutions—is to be upheld, it must be referred to the sovereign power of the General Assembly, which has been curtailed only to the extent of express constitutional limitations. If article 11 contains no inhibition upon the power of the Legislature in respect to local assessments by cities and towns, the Act under consideration is valid and the assessment involved here was well laid; for no proposition is now better established in the law than that Constitutions are not in the nature of Enabling Acts, but are limitations upon the otherwise boundless powers of Legislatures, or, in other words, that the General Assembly is not to look to the Organic Law to ascertain what is permitted it to do, but only to find what inhibitions are thereby put on its action. Cooley, Const. Lim. 479; Burroughs, Taxn. § 145; 2 Dillon, Mun. Corp. § 737; *Irwin* v. *Mobile*, 57 Ala. 6; *Dorman* v. *State*, 34 Ala. 231; *Hare* v. *Kennerly*, 83 Ala. 608.

Having attempted to demonstrate that the assessment here could not have been made under the provisions of the Constitution either as it was made, on a basis of benefits, or even on a basis of the value of the particular property, it next becomes necessary to determine whether the Organic Law is exclusive of all other assessments against property than those of which it treats, in such sort as to amount to a prohibition upon the Legislature in respect to an assessment of the class under consideration. It is not questioned but that the power which this Statute undertakes to delegate to the municipality of Birmingham is a part of the taxing power inherent in all government, and without limitations other than those expressed in the Organic Law. It is equally free from doubt that the power of taxation is never to be taken to be surrendered by intendment or implication, and that, without an expressed surrender, clear and explicit in its terms, it must be held to reside undiminished in the Legislature. *Glasgow* v. *Rowse*, 43 Mo. 479–489; *Baltimore* v. *Baltimore & O. R. Co.* 6 Gill, 288, 48 Am. Dec. 531; *Battle* v. *Mobile*, 9 Ala. 234, 44 Am. Dec. 438, *note* 441; 2 Dillon, Mun. Corp. § 752.

Are the provisions of article 11, referring, as we have seen, to general taxes and taxation, and to such only, expressed limitations on the power of the Legislature with respect to local assessments on property to pay for local improvements which benefit that particular property? We think not. The overwhelming weight of authority is against such a construction and in favor of the validity of such assessments. In considering the question, jurists and judges have proceeded on the theory that such charges were not taxes in the ordinary sense, or within the meaning and intent of constitutional provisions similar to those of Alabama, but that they are in the nature of compensation for a benefit peculiar to the owner of the abutting property, and traceable to him; that such assessments are not exacted for the general public welfare, and do not go to the support of governmental agencies, from the existence and maintenance of which each citizen derives a like benefit, but that they are demandable because the government has expended an equivalent sum in improving the property against which they are laid, and thereby, not the public, but the individual owner of the property improved, has been to that extent the gainer.

A tax, it is said, is a contribution to the general fund. The amount of it is taken from the individual, and nothing which benefits him individually as distinguished from the mass of citizens is given in the place of it. He pays, and by the amount he pays is poorer than he was before. Not so with an assessment of the class we are considering. The property owner pays it, but, in legal contemplation, he loses nothing. He receives the value of his money in the betterment of his property; and, in addition to this, he is benefited to the same extent that all other citizens are, in that a thoroughfare of the city in which his property is situated, and he probably lives, is improved. The authorities almost universally take such an imposition, though confessedly laid under the taxing power, out of the category of "taxes" and "taxation," as those terms are employed in organic limitations on legislative power to levy or authorize the levying of taxes, and in general statutes. Cooley, Taxn. 626–637; Burroughs, Taxn. 460–463; 2 Dillon, Mun. Corp. §§ 752, 753, 761 *et seq.*; *People* v. *Brooklyn*, 4 N. Y. 420; *Sheehan* v. *Good Samaritan Hospital*, 50 Mo. 155; *Dorgan* v. *Boston*, 12 Allen, 223; *Nichols* v. *Bridgeport*, 23 Conn. 189; *Garrett* v. *St. Louis*, 25 Mo. 505; *Cain* v. *Davie County*, 86 N. C. 8; *Shuford* v. *Lincoln County*, Id. 552; *Hill* v. *Higdon*, 5 Ohio St. 243; *King* v. *Portland*, 2 Or. 146; *Norfolk* v. *Ellis*, 26 Gratt. 227; *Roundtree* v. *Galveston*, 42 Tex. 612; *Baltimore* v. *Green Mountain Cemetery Co.* 7 Md. 517; *Chambers* v. *Satterlee*, 40 Cal. 497; *Edgerton* v. *Green Cove Springs*, 19 Fla. 140; *Goodrich* v. *Winchester & D. Turnp. Co.* 26 Ind. 119; *Hines* v. *Leavenworth*, 3 Kan. 186; *Municipality No. 2* v *Dunn*, 10 La. Ann. 57; *Motz* v. *Detroit*, 18 Mich. 495; *Williams* v. *Cammack*, 27 Miss. 209; *Macon* v. *Patty*, 57 Miss. 378; *People* v. *Austin*, 47 Cal. 353; *Bridgeport* v. *New York & N. H. R. Co.* 36 Conn. 255; *Hayden* v. *Atlanta*, 70 Ga. 817; *Barber Asphalt Pav. Co.* v. *Cogreve* (La.) 5 So. Rep. 848; *Excelsior P. & Mfg. Co.* v. *Green*, 39 La. Ann. 457.

On the other hand, the decisions in three or four States are to the effect that local assessments of this character cannot be made under constitutional provisions requiring equality and uniformity of taxation and assessments in proportion to the value of property. The leading case maintaining this view is that of *Chicago* v. *Larned*, 34 Ill. 203. The conclusion in that case may perhaps find some justification in the peculiar phraseology of the constitutional provisions supposed to bear on the question, though an opposite conclusion was reached by the Virginia court on substantially the same provisions. *Norfolk* v. *Ellis*, *supra*.

The effect of this Illinois decision was subsequently remedied by an amendment of the Constitution. The Supreme Court of Arkansas, in *Peay* v. *Little Rock*, 32 Ark. 31, followed this Illinois decision, and another by the Wisconsin court (*Weeks* v. *Milwaukee*, 10 Wis. 243), which is, perhaps, also referable to peculiar terms of the Constitution, and which, at most, only imports doubt as to whether the requirement for uniformity of taxation applied to and defeated local assessments,—and held such local assessments could not be authorized under a constitution which required property to be taxed uniformly and according to value. This Arkansas decision is not reconcilable with the earlier case of *McGehee* v. *Mathis*, 21 Ark. 40, on substantially the same point. A like conclusion has been reached in Tennessee and Colorado; but, as in the Illinois case, the terms of the Organic Law which were supposed to enforce the result were something more than general requirements for uniformity and equality of taxation, and assessments on the basis of value. *Palmer* v. *Way*, 6 Colo. 110; *Taylor* v. *Chandler*, 9 Heisk. 349.

When to these cases are added those of *Mobile* v. *Dargan* and *Mobile* v. *Royal St. R. Co.*, decided by this court, which will be presently considered more particularly, it is believed that the full array of adjudications against the constitutionality of laws like that involved here is presented. After marshalling the authorities pro and con. on this question, *Judge* Cooley concludes: "The fact very clearly appears that, while there is not such a concurrence of judicial opinion as would be desirable, the overwhelming weight of authority is in favor of the position that all such provisions for equality and uniformity in taxation, and for taxation by value, have no application to these special assessments" against abutting property to pay for the construction of sidewalks. Cooley, Taxn. 634.

We now recur to the two cases decided by the Supreme Court of this State, and noted above. They each involve the validity of the same Statute, and were decided at the same term, the one being cited as the authority to support the other, and the one thus cited itself being, on this point, unsupported by reference to any authority. Not only is this true, but the opinion essays no argument in support of the conclusion reached, nor enters upon any consideration, which it might be supposed a question so important—decided, for aught that appears, as upon first impression—would have elicited.

In the opinion in *Mobile* v. *Royal St. R. Co.*, moreover, there is an intimation that, had the assessment been by benefits instead of by frontage, the Act authorizing it would not have been open to the objection of unconstitutionality. Very clearly, if the Constitution applied at all, it would have been equally fatal whether the assessment were by frontage or by benefits, since neither mode would meet the organic requirement of assessment in exact proportion to the value of property. *Mobile* v. *Dargan*, 45 Ala. 310; *Mobile* v. *Royal St. R. Co.* Id. 322.

Not only are these cases opposed to the great weight of judicial opinion in other States and to all authoritative texts, but they are in conflict with the later adjudication of this court.

In the case of *Irwin* v. *Mobile*, 57 Ala. 6, the Act declared in *Mobile* v. *Dargan* to have been repealed by the Constitution of 1868 again came under review with reference to an assessment which had been made before that Constitution became the supreme law of the State. This court intimated such doubt of the correctness of the decision in *Dargan's Case* as is implied by citing a preponderating run of authorities holding the opposite view, and by declining to again decide the point, because it was not necessary to the case in hand. The court then proceeds to pass on the validity of the law authorizing the levy of local assessments against lands to pay for improvements upon which they abut, as brought to the touch of constitutional provisions of force before the Constitution of 1868. The conclusion was that such a law was not repugnant to the provisions of the Organic Law theretofore in force. Inasmuch as the Constitutions of 1819, 1861 and 1865 each contained a clause requiring that "all lands liable to taxation in this State shall be taxed in proportion to their value," we are unable to escape the conclusion that the court took the view held by nearly all other courts, that general organic provisions for taxation by valuation have no application to local assessments for local street improvement; otherwise, it could not have reached the conclusion announced. That conclusion, therefore, is in irreconcilable conflict with the opinion in *Dargan's Case*, and is no more or less, in effect, than a later adjudication by this court that the former decision is unsound.

But, aside from this, the cases of *Mobile* v. *Dargan* and *Mobile* v. *Royal St. R. Co.* are unsound in principle, and opposed to the great weight of authority. It is true the clause of the Constitution involved in those cases was re-ordained after that decision was made; and ordinarily the re enactment of a law after it has been judicially interpreted will be held to impress the judicial construction upon it. But this is not a universal canon of construction, even where identically the same language has been employed; and in this case, while section 1 of article 11 of the Constitution of 1875 is identical with section 1 of article 9 of the Constitution of 1868, yet the presumption that the convention of 1875 intended that section should bear the construction put on it in *Dargan's Case* is rebutted by the succeeding sections of that article, which are new to the Constitution of 1875, and which demonstrate that the framers of the present Organic Law had in mind, and intended to provide for, regulate and limit, in and by the ordinance of article 11, only general taxation for general governmental purposes,—state, county and municipal. The rule of construction referred to, it thus appears, rests upon a presumption of intention which is rebutted by the language employed by the makers of the present Constitution. We cannot give it any operation in this case; and we cannot follow the cases relied on, and would not, even had their soundness not been already drawn in question in the case of *Irwin* v. *Mobile, supra.*

The sounder view is that taken in the very numerous cases cited above,—and, though very numerous, they are by no means all that so hold,—to the effect that provisions, whether in statutes or constitutions, relating to general taxation for state, county and municipal purposes, or either, have no application to special assessments laid against abutting property to pay for street improvements which have benefited and enhanced the value of the property so assessed. The Statute authorizing such assessments in the City of Birmingham is a valid enactment.

The judgment of the City Court, involving a contrary ruling, is reversed, and the cause remanded.

SOUTH CAROLINA SUPREME COURT.

Margaret B. WHEAT *et al.*, *Appts.*,
v.
G. W. DINGLE, Admr., etc., of G. J. Luhn, Deceased, *Respt.*

(....S. C.....)

A dividend from a decedent's assets, which are not sufficient to pay creditors in full, can be computed in favor of a mortgage creditor only on the balance of the mortgage debt, where he has accepted the proceeds of the mortgaged premises on a sale thereof to pay debts as part payment of his claim.

(April 10, 1890.)

APPEAL by complainants from a decree of the Common Pleas Circuit Court for Charleston County in favor of defendant in a controversy submitted to the court without action for the purpose of determining the amount of the dividends to which complainants were entitled, to be paid out of the assets of the estate of defendant's intestate. *Affirmed.*

The agreed statement of facts upon which the controversy was submitted is as follows:

"Margaret B. Wheat claims to recover of G. W. Dingle, as administrator of G. J. Luhn, a dividend upon $16,082.93; and the said administrator resists said claim, but is willing to pay her a dividend upon $6,082.93.

"The Paragon Building & Loan Association claims to recover of G. W. Dingle, as administrator as aforesaid, a dividend upon $11,237.62, which claim said administrator resists, but is willing to pay a dividend upon $5,317.76.

"B. F. Simmons claims to recover of G. W. Dingle, as administrator as aforesaid, a dividend upon $8,284.40, which claim said administrator resists, but is willing to pay him a dividend upon $6,014.

"H. M. Harmon, executrix of Eleazer Harmon, claims to recover of G. W. Dingle, as administrator as aforesaid, a dividend upon $13,-

803.47, which claim said administrator resists, but is willing to pay her a dividend upon $5,-985.20.

"The following are the facts upon which the said controversy depends:

"(1) Margaret B. Wheat is a creditor of the said G. J. Luhn upon a claim, which at the time of his death, with interest to the 1st of June, 1889, amounted to the said sum of $16,-082.93, upon which a dividend is claimed.

"(2) For this claim she held as collateral security a policy of insurance effected by the said G. J. Luhn in his own name upon his own life, and which he assigned in his lifetime to his said creditor to secure said debt. Mrs. Wheat since his death has realized $10,000 from this security and applied the same towards her claim.

"(3) The administrator of G. J. Luhn has in his hands a large amount, the proceeds of assets for distribution, and is willing to pay the proper dividend upon $6,082.93, being the deficiency upon Mrs. Wheat's claim after the application thereto of the proceeds of the security as aforesaid; but the said Mrs. Wheat claims she is entitled to a proper dividend upon the entire amount of the indebtedness as it stood at the time of the death of the said G. J. Luhn, together with the interest thereon up to the time of distribution, regardless of what was realized upon the security.

"(4) If the said claim by Mrs. Wheat is well founded, and distribution be made accordingly, she will not receive from all sources more than the amount of the debt to her by G. J. Luhn.

"(5) The other parties named as plaintiffs in this controversy are each and all bond creditors of said G. J. Luhn, who held mortgages given by him upon his real estate to secure his respective bonds to them.

"(6) The said administrator filed his complaint against the heirs of G. J. Luhn for a sale of his real estate in aid of personal assets in an action to which all the mortgagees were parties. In this action they set up their mortgages, the real estate was sold by order of the court, and the proceeds applied to said liens according to their priorities. No one of the said bonds was paid in full from the proceeds of the sale of the mortgaged premises applicable thereto.

"In the case of the Paragon Building & Loan Association the deficiency was $5,317.76.

"In the case of B. F. Simmons the deficiency was $6,014.

"In the case of H. M. Harmon, executrix, deficiency was $5,985.20.

"(7) The said administrator has in his hands a large amount of the proceeds of personal assets for distribution, and is willing to pay the proper dividend upon said deficiencies; but the said creditors claim that they are each entitled to a proper dividend upon the entire amount of the indebtedness as it stood at the time of the death of the said G. J. Luhn, together with interest thereon up to the time of distribution, regardless of what was realized from the mortgage of each respectively.

"(8) If the said position of the creditors be correct, and distribution be made accordingly, no one of them will receive from all sources more than the total of the said indebtedness to each by G. J. Luhn.

"The questions submitted to the court upon this are as follows:

"Are the aforesaid creditors, or any of them, entitled to a dividend from the said administrator upon the aforesaid respective deficiencies only?

"Or are they, or any of them, entitled to a dividend upon their entire indebtedness to each as it stood at the time of the death of the said G. J. Luhn, with interest up to the time of distribution?

"And the administrator is to be directed by the court according to its determination of the same.

"It is further agreed as a part of this case that, in the case of *G. W. Dinkle, Administrator*, v. *H. M. Harmon, Executrix, et al.*, to which all the mortgagees were parties, which said case was for the sale of the real estate, and did not concern the personalty, an order was made that, if the proceeds of the sale of the mortgaged property were insufficient to pay the several amounts reported due to the respective mortgagees, with interest and costs, as aforesaid, that the master specify the amount of said deficiencies, respectively, in his report of sales, and that the parties respectively entitled to such amounts so deficient have leave to enter up judgment therefor against the administrator, the same to be paid, according to the priorities of the respective debts upon which they are granted, out of the assets of the estate of said intestate which may be applicable thereto, either in the hands of the master or of the said administrator."

Mr. **J. E. Burke,** for the Paragon B. & L. Association, appellant:

Appellants are entitled to a proportion of the assets based upon the amount of their respective debts as they existed at the death of the intestate, and before the securities had been applied thereto, always providing that in no event can more than the debt be paid.

Wilson v. *McConnell*, 9 Rich. Eq. 500; *Morton* v. *Caldwell*, 3 Strobh. Eq. 161; *Wilson* v. *Kelly*, 19 S. C. 167.

The amount to be paid at any time by an estate is one thing, and the debt or amount upon which a creditor's share for the payment thereof is to be based is another thing; and these two things are separate and independent. The debt is as fixed in amount at the moment of death as it is in character, and no payment out of the assets of an estate to the debt of a decedent can alter the amount of the debt to which each and every part of the estate is applicable according to priorities of that debt.

Morton v. *Caldwell, supra.*

A creditor cannot use the two-fund doctrine to injure another creditor.

State Sav. Bank v. *Harbin*, 18 S. C. 431; *Witte* v. *Clarke*, 17 S. C. 323.

A mortgagee has a double security; he has a right to proceed against both, and to make the best he can of both; why he should be deprived of this right because the debtor dies insolvent, it is not easy to see.

See *note* to *Aldridge* v. *Cooper*, 2 Lead. Cas. in Eq. *78, and cases there noted; *Mason* v. *Bogg*, 2 Myl. & Cr. 443.

Messrs. **Mitchell & Smith** for Margaret B. Wheat, appellant.

Mr. **John F. Ficken** for B. F. Simmons, appellant

Mr. **J. N. Nathans** for H. M. Harmon, appellant.

Messrs. **Lord & Hyde** for respondent.

McGowan, *J.*, delivered the opinion of the court:

This was a controversy without action. The agreed statement of facts should appear in the report of the case. It seems that one G. J. Luhn, being largely indebted by mortgage and otherwise, died intestate, and G. W. Dingle administered upon his estate, and took proceedings to sell the real estate in aid of assets. Upon nearly every parcel of the intestate's real estate there was a mortgage securing a debt. The different mortgage creditors were made parties to these proceedings, and the respective pieces of realty were sold, the proceeds applied to the liens in each case, and a balance left unpaid, for which balances the parties were by decree entitled to enter up judgment against the administrator, to be paid out of the assets of the estate which may be applicable thereto. All the appellants, creditors of the intestate, save Mrs. Wheat, were mortgage creditors in the condition above stated; and Mrs. Wheat had as security a policy of insurance upon the life of the intestate, assigned to her in his lifetime; and that, being realized upon after his death, left a balance still due her upon simple contract. She had no part in the proceedings to sell the lands. All the appellants claim that they are entitled, there being a deficiency of personal assets, to a proportion thereof based upon the amounts of their respective debts as they existed at the death of the intestate, and before the securities (mortgages) had been applied thereto, always providing that in no event more than the debt be paid. The administrator contests this view, and claims that they are only entitled to prove for the deficiency which may remain after exhausting their respective securities. The facts were submitted to *Judge* Pressley, who held and "adjudged that the plaintiffs, creditors, are entitled to prove only the balance of their respective debts in prorating with the general creditors out of the remaining assets." The plaintiffs appeal upon the ground that his honor erred in holding that the plaintiffs were entitled to prove only the balance of their respective debts in prorating with the general creditors out of the remaining assets, but, on the contrary, should have adjudged that, in accordance with the rule of law in this State, they, and each of them, were entitled to prove for the full amount of their respective debts as they existed at the death of the intestate, provided only that in no event should the entire amount obtained by any creditor out of the estate exceed the debt as it stood at the time of such death," etc.

In the ground of appeal, as in the argument, reference was made to "a rule of law as established in this State," which, if adhered to, must be considered as conclusive of this case; and in that connection were cited the cases of *Morton* v. *Caldwell*, 3 Strobh. Eq. 166, and of *Wilson* v. *McConnell*, 9 Rich. Eq. 500. We have examined these cases carefully, and we fail to find their supposed analogy to this case. In both those cases the debts were divided into two distinct parts as against the partnership and an individual member of the partnership, and it was held that, "in ascertaining the *pro rata* due a copartnership creditor from the separate estate of a deceased copartner, who died insolvent, the debt should be regarded as standing in the precise condition in which it stood at the death of the copartner, without regard to any subsequent payments derived from the copartnership assets, though, to avoid double satisfaction, such creditor is not entitled to receive more than the balance due after deducting such payments," etc. *Wilson* v. *McConnell, supra.*

This was manifestly on the ground that the payments by the partnership assets were by a person other than the individual debtor.

As was stated by *Chancellor* Johnston in *Morton* v. *Caldwell, supra:* "It would appear from all these views that the proper mode for determining the proportions of assets liable to the respective creditors of a deceased debtor is to assign them according to the amount of the debts as they exist at his death. If, upon any of the demands thus taken into consideration, any payments had been subsequently made by a third party, that does not release the proportion of the deceased's assets originally liable to the creditors if there still remain due on the demand a balance requiring that proportion to satisfy it."

This seems to us, considering the facts, strictly correct; but suppose that the payments referred to, instead of having been made by a third party, had been made out of the estate proper of the debtor himself. Would it be for a moment contended that such payments did not release that much of the deceased's assets originally liable to the creditor? It seems to us that such result would not only be in violation of all principle, but entirely unjust. As we understand it, the cases above cited did not involve the precise point now under consideration, which, as far as we are able to see, is now for the first time raised in this State. Here there is no pretense or allegation that anyone is liable for those debts, or any part of them, except the estate of the intestate himself. All are creditors of his estate alone. Some have mortgages upon particular parcels of land, while others have none, but there is no doubt that the whole of the debtor's estate, real and personal, mortgaged and not mortgaged, is liable for his debts; and it does seem to us that, when any part of his debts is paid by the sale of lands belonging to the estate, that cannot, in any proper sense, be called a payment by a third party, as the payment by the partnership in *Morton* v. *Caldwell, supra.*

Besides, it is settled in this State that a mortgage has priority over specialty and simple-contract debts only to the extent of the property mortgaged. *Piester* v. *Piester*, 22 S. C. 146.

After the property mortgaged has been sold and applied to the debt, leaving a balance of the debt unpaid, as to that balance the creditor is no longer a mortgage creditor, but stands only where his evidence of indebtedness places him; and he gets judgment for the balance alone on his claims, whatever it may be, from which has already been eliminated what was a mortgage debt. In this controversy without action, the case states that "the administrator filed his complaint against the heirs of G. J. Luhn for a sale of his real estate, in aid of personal assets, in an action to which all the mortgagees were parties. In this action they set up their mortgages. The real estate was sold by order of the court, and the proceeds applied to said liens according to their priorities," etc. So that the respective mortgagees, in effect, assented to that application; and it is therefore now too late to present their whole bonds, withholding their mortgages, as suggested by *Lord* Cottenham in the English case cited of *Mason* v. *Bogg*, 2 Myl. & Cr. 447.

The judgment of this court is that *the judgment of the Circuit Court be affirmed.*

Simpson and McIver, *JJ.*, concur.

NEW MEXICO SUPREME COURT.

David ABRAHAMS
v.
CALIFORNIA POWDER WORKS, Impleaded, etc., *Appt.*

(....N. M.....)

Ownership of gunpowder consigned for sale on commission does not render the owners liable for an explosion which occurs while it is in the hands of the consignee.

(February 12, 1890.)

APPEAL by defendant, the California Powder Works, from a judgment of the District Court for Grant County in favor of plaintiff in an action brought to recover damages for injuries resulting from the explosion of certain powder alleged to have belonged to defendant. *Reversed.*

The case sufficiently appears in the opinion.

Messrs. **Catron, Knaebel & Clancy,** for appellant:

Commission merchants, with no right of charging storage, clerk-hire, or other expenses, are not agents of the consignor within the rule which imposes liability on the principal for the consequences of imperfect or negligent conduct of the agent.

Slack v. *Tucker & Co.* 90 U. S. 23 Wall. 329, 330 (23 L. ed. 146); *St. Paul Water Co.* v. *Ware*, 85 U. S. 16 Wall. 576 (21 L. ed. 488); *Blake* v. *Ferris*, 5 N. Y. 48-60 *et seq.; Seymour* v. *Wychoff*, 10 N. Y. 216.

Mr. **Gideon D. Bantz** for appellee.

Lee, *J.*, delivered the opinion of the court:

This is an action of trespass on the case, by the plaintiff, David Abrahams, against the defendant, the California Powder Company, and also the Safety Nitro-Powder Company, corporations organized under the laws of California, to recover damages for an alleged injury to a brick hotel building situated in the Town of Silver City, in the County of Grant, from an explosion of a certain lot of powder stored in a powder-house in said Town of Silver City, which powder-house, it is alleged, was erected, kept and maintained, and which powder was stored in said house, by the defendants. The defendants pleaded not guilty. There was a trial by jury, and a verdict for $300 against the California Powder Company, and, by direction of the court, not guilty as to the Safety Nitro Powder Company. The California Powder Company brings this case to this court by appeal.

The evidence on the part of the plaintiff tended to show that there were eighty kegs of powder in the house, at the time of the explosion, belonging to defendant, the California Powder Company, which was consigned to Neff & Stevens for sale on commission. Evidence was introduced on the part of the defendant tending to show that the powder in question, the eighty kegs, was not a consignment, but an absolute sale, to Neff & Stevens. We will consider the case as if the position of the plaintiff was the correct one, in this respect.

As to the ownership and control of the powder-house, the evidence on the part of the plaintiff is indefinite and uncertain. The witness Neff testifies that Higbee and Cohn told him it belonged to the defendant, the California Powder Company, but says he does not know of any connection Cohn had with the defendant Company; that his understanding is that Higbee had been an agent of the Company, and that he built the house. The nature and character of the agency of Higbee, if one existed, is not shown; nor does it appear what authority either Higbee or Cohn had for giving him the information, or what source of knowledge they possessed on the subject. Neither does it appear that Gould had any authority to make any statement as to ownership. The building of the magazine took place many years before the explosion occurred. There appear to have been several transfers of the business with which it was connected before reaching Neff & Stevens. It does not appear in the evidence that these defendant companies agreed to, or were consulted in regard to, the transfers. No attempt was made to prove that the defendants authorized, or assented to, or had any knowledge of, the storage of any powder in the building in question; but, on the part of defendant, the California Powder Company, it was shown that it not only never authorized nor assented to such storage, but that it had no knowledge whatever of the manner in which Neff & Stevens kept the powder; that they never owned the building, or had any interest in it. Taking the facts as shown on the part of the plaintiff to be true, if the defendants are liable for the damages resulting from the explosion of the powder in question, such liability must attach to them from the fact that they were owners of the powder which was consigned to Neff & Stevens, to be sold by them on commission.

The vital question—that upon which the case hinges—is whether, upon such a state of facts, the defendant Companies stood in relation to Neff & Stevens, the parties who stored the powder in the house, and appear to have had full control of it, so that the maxim, *respondeat superior*, will apply.

The rule is adopted by Wharton, in his Law of Negligence, § 176, in which he quotes as follows: "The principle to be extracted from the cases is said to be that a person, natural or artificial, is not liable for the acts or negligence of another, unless the relation of master and servant, or principal and agent, exist between them, and that when an injury is done by a person exercising an independent employment the person employing him is not responsible to the person injured."

Again, in section 183, the same author says: 'We strike, when pursuing the distinctions which have been taken by the courts in this relation, on the fundamental principle, elsewhere fully discussed, that, wherever there is liberty to act, there, to the party thus free, liability for a tort committed by him is imputable. If the master is at liberty to act in a particular matter, then the tort is imputable to the master. If the servant is at liberty to act, then, if this liberty be one of entire emancipation in the particular relation of the master's control, the tort is imputable, not to the master, but to the servant."

In a very able review of this question in the case of *De Forrest* v. *Wright*, 2 Mich. 368, the court says: "This greatly vexed question, as an eminent judge has pronounced it, has been very much discussed, not only in the English courts, but in our own. The difficulty in deciding cases involving the question presented has been in determining what facts and circumstances legally constitute the relation of master and servant, or under what circumstances one person will be held liable for injuries occasioned by the negligence or unskillfullness of another employed in his behalf. To hold that every person, under all circumstances, would be responsible for injuries committed by another person while employed in his behalf, involves an absurdity no one would countenance. It would create a penalty from which few could escape; for every man is, or ought to be, directly or indirectly, nearly or remotely, engaged in the service, or on behalf, of his fellow men. But, from an examination and comparison of the adjudged cases, the rule now seems very clearly to be this: that where the person employed is in the exercise of an independent and distinct employment, and not under the immediate control, direction or supervision of the employer, the latter is not responsible for the negligence or misdoings of the former."

So, in the case of *Gulzoni* v. *Tyler*, in 64 Cal. 334, which was a suit for damages against the owners of a steamboat, it was proven on the trial that the owners did not have control and management of the boat at the time the damages occurred. The court says: "The rule as stated by Shearman & Redfield on Negligence, § 501, is that if the owner of property lets or lends it, and transfers the entire possession and control of it to another, the owner is not responsible for the wrongful use or mismanagement of it by the transferee. Whoever had the exclusive possession, management and control of the boat, its officers and men, was alone responsible for its mismanagement; and, whether rightfully or wrongfully in such possession, the liability would rest on them alone. Under the rule, *respondeat superior*, this must be so."

The act of the servant is not the act of the master, even in legal intendment or effect, unless the master previously directs or subsequently adopts it. *Parsons* v. *Winchell*, 5 Cush. 592.

In order to clearly understand the application of the foregoing principle to this case, it may be well to refer more particularly to the evidence as to the relationship as proven. Gould, an agent of the California Powder Company, in 1884 called upon Neff & Stevens, requesting them to take the agency of the Company, which they declined, for the reason that they had a large amount of powder of the other company on hand. They desired a certain amount of black powder, which they were short of, which he agreed to have sent them; and it was sent, and billed as follows:

"Tucson, Arizona, November 11th, 1884.
"Messrs. Neff & Stevens, Silver City:
"Bot. of the California Works, 30 California Street. Consigned, eighty kegs blasting, $4.00, $320.00."

It is contended on the part of the plaintiff that this powder was sent as a consignment, to be sold on commission, as other powder belonging to the defendant that had been turned over to them by Cohn, assignee of Crawford. The defendant claims that these eighty kegs were an absolute sale. There was also a letter from William A. Scott, agent at Tucson, Ariz., dated March 13, 1885, which is as follows:

Messrs. Neff & Stevens, Silver City, N. M.
Gentlemen: Your favor of the 10th inst. is at hand. Please to send account sales at $4.00 per keg, and send draft on me for 10 per cent of the amount of the same, as if the draft was cash, for so I will count it. The account sales must be at $4.00 per keg, and I need your receipt for the commission of 10 per cent. You are duly credited with account for $16.85.
Respectfully, Wm. A. Scott, Agent.

The above bill and letter, together with the oral evidence introduced on the trial, clearly show that Neff & Stevens were handling this powder as factors, commission merchants or consignees. There is no evidence in any way limiting their power as such, or directing the manner of handling it. As factors, under the law, they would have full possession of the goods, with a special property therein. Story Ag. § 97.

The court instructed the jury: "If they should find that said black powder was kept and maintained by the defendant or their agents at the time," etc. The word "agents" in the instruction, must be understood in the sense in which it appears from the evidence; and, if instruction No. 6, which was asked by the defendant, and refused by the court, had been given, the issues would have been fairly presented to the jury; which instruction was: "If you believe from the evidence that the defendant corporations each owned a portion of the powder stored in the powder-house at the time of the explosion, but that such powder and powder-house was under exclusive control of Neff & Stevens, as consignees of said corporations, respectively, at the time of the explosion, then, in that case, unless you further believe from the evidence that such explosion was caused by some willful and malicious act of defendant, the California Powder Company, you will find the defendant not guilty."

The first part of this instruction would have brought the case under the rule laid down by the authorities we have referred to, and which is unquestionably the correct law, as applicable to this case. The evidence does not show anything upon which the doctrine of *respondeat superior* could be based. So far as the evidence shows, the relationship of Neff & Stevens to the defendant was that of an independent employment, free of action. There is a total lack of all the elements of master and servant, which must exist to constitute responsibility on the part of the defendant. We think the court should have given the first part of this instruction, or instructed the jury in accordance with the views herein expressed.

The case will be reversed, and remanded for a new trial.

Whiteman and **McFie,** *JJ.*, concur.

NORTH CAROLINA SUPREME COURT.

Lewis COLEMAN, *Appt.*,

v.

D. W. FULLER *et al.*

(....N. C....)

The words "I guarantee payment of the foregoing bond," with signature and seal, written at the foot of the bond of another person under seal, constitute a separate sealed instrument, the signer of which can be sued as a principal obligor and not merely as surety to the preceding bond; and such action therefore is not barred in three years by the Statute of Limitations applicable to sureties, but may be brought at any time within ten years, under Code, § 152, par. 2, relating to actions against principal obligors on sealed instruments.

[(*Davis, J., dissents.*)

(February 24, 1890.)

APPEAL by plaintiff from a judgment of the Superior Court for Johnston County in favor of defendant in an action brought to enforce the alleged liability of the guarantor of a sealed bond. *Reversed.*

The bond and the guaranty were as follows:

$100.

Smithfield, N. C., September 27, 1881.

Twelve months after the completion of the Midland North Carolina Railway from Goldsboro to Smithfield, and the arrival of the first train at the depot, within three fourths of a mile of the court-house at Smithfield, I promise to pay W. J. Best, president of said railway company, one hundred dollars, with interest from the date of said completion, in consideration of the running of said road to or near Smithfield.

[Signed] J. E. Earp. [Seal.]

I guarantee payment of the foregoing bond, Sept. 27, 1881.

[Signed] D. W. Fuller. [Seal.]

Mr. **R. O. Burton, Jr.**, for appellant.

Mr. **C. M. Busbee** for appellees.

NOTE.—*Contract of guaranty.*

A guaranty is a solemn assurance, covenant or stipulation that something shall be or shall be done, a promise "to answer for the debt, default or miscarriage" of another. Anderson, Law Dict.

A contract by which one person is bound to another, for the fulfillment of the promise or engagement of a third party, is a contract of guaranty. 2 Parsons, Cont. 3; Story, Prom. Notes, § 457; 3 Kent, Com. 121.

So a collateral undertaking to pay the debt of another in case he does not pay is a guaranty. Dole v. Young, 24 Pick. 252; Hill v. Smith, 62 U. S. 21 How. 286 (16 L. ed. 114).

A guaranty is an undertaking by one person that another shall perform his contract or fulfill his obligation, or that if he does not the guarantor will do it for him. Gridley v. Capen, 72 Ill. 13.

Construction of contract of guaranty.

The contract of guaranty, although that of a surety, is to be construed as a mercantile instrument, in furtherance of its spirit, and liberally, to promote the use and convenience of commercial intercourse. Davis v. Wells, 104 U. S. 159 (26 L. ed. 686).

Generally, all instruments of suretyship are construed strictly as mere matters of legal right; but the rule is otherwise where they are founded upon a valuable consideration. Mauran v. Bullus, 41 U. S. 16 Pet. 528 (10 L. ed. 1056).

The general rule is that the words of a guaranty are to be taken as strongly against the guarantor as the sense will admit. Drummond v. Prestman, 25 U. S. 12 Wheat. 515 (6 L. ed. 712).

Where a mercantile guaranty is preceded by a recital definite in terms, to which the general words obviously refer, the liability is limited within the terms of the recital in restraint of the general words. Bell v. Bruen, 42 U. S. 1 How. 169 (11 L. ed. 89).

In construing a contract the court will look at the surrounding circumstances to ascertain the intention of the party, and will not be controlled by the technical meaning of the word "guarantee." Weller v. Henarie, 15 Or. 28.

Guaranties are to be interpreted and enforced according to the meaning and intent, and in the manner, designed by the parties at their execution, giving due effect to every part of the same. People v. Lee, 7 Cent. Rep. 88, 104 N. Y. 441.

Where the plain intention of the parties to an agreement appears to have been to jointly bind themselves to pay for brick delivered for the erection of a certain building, it will be construed accordingly. Goldner v. Finn, 11 West. Rep. 177, 67 Mich. 340.

A letter of guaranty written in the United States to a house in England is construed according to the laws of that country (which are the same as in this). Bell v. Bruen, *supra.*

Letters of recommendation requesting, in favor of the persons recommended, "that you will endeavor to render them every assistance in your power," do not constitute a contract of guaranty. Russell v. Clark, 11 U. S. 7 Cranch, 69 (3 L. ed. 271).

It seems that a clause in a letter of introduction, "You may be assured of their complying fully with any contracts or engagements they may enter into with you," does not import an undertak-

See also 17 L. R. A. 652.

Shepherd, J., delivered the opinion of the court:

The single question presented in this appeal is whether the action is barred, as to the defendant Fuller, by the Statute of Limitations. Code, § 152, par. 2, provides that "an action upon a sealed instrument, against the principal thereto," must be commenced within ten years after the cause of action accrues The guaranty executed by the defendant Fuller is under seal, and is written at the foot of the bond, which was executed by the defendant Earp. It is contended by Fuller, the appellant, that he is not a principal to "a sealed instrument," within the above provision of the Code, but that he is simply a surety to the bond, and as such is within the principle of *Welfare* v. *Thompson*, 83 N. C. 276, and other similar decisions, which apply the three-years Statute of Limitations. This leads us therefore to the consideration of the nature and liability of the contract of guaranty. A guaranty is a contract in and of itself, but it also has relation to some other contract or obligation, with reference to which it is collateral. Anderson, Law Dict.; *Carpenter* v. *Wall*, 4 Dev. & B. 144.

"A surety is bound with his principal as an original promisor. . . . On the other hand, the contract of a guarantor is his own separate contract. . . . It is in the nature of a warranty by him that the thing guaranteed to be done by the principal shall be done, and not merely an engagement jointly with the principal to do the thing." Baylies, Sur. 4.

A "guarantor is not an indorser or surety." 2 Randolph, Com. Paper, § 849.

"The surety's promise is to pay a debt, which becomes his own debt when the principal fails to pay it. . . . But the guarantor's promise is always to pay the debt of another." "But he 'is not an indorser nor a surety.'" 2 Parsons, Notes and Bills, 117, 118.

"A guaranty is a special contract, and the guarantor is not in any sense a party to the note." *Lamourieux* v. *Hewit*, 5 Wend. 307; *Ellis* v. *Brown*, 6 Barb. 282; *Miller* v. *Gaston*, 2 Hill, 188, 190; Story, Prom. Notes, § 3.

It is a special contract, and must be specially declared on. Baylies, Sur. 4.

These authorities very abundantly show that the contract of a guarantor is a separate and distinct obligation. Fuller is no party to the bond of Earp, and as to his contract of guaranty he cannot be regarded otherwise than as principal. If this were not so, we would have the anomaly of a contract with only one contracting party. It is said, however, that there is a distinction growing out of the fact that the guaranty is written upon the same paper as the bond. This does not in the least alter the character of the obligation. *Lamourieux* v. *Hewit*, *supra*.

"This engagement or contract of guaranty may be, and often is, written on the back of the note or bill; but it may as well, so far as the guaranty is concerned, be written on a separate piece of paper." 2 Parsons, Notes and Bills, 119.

This feature becomes material only upon questions arising upon the negotiability or assignment of such contracts. No such questions are involved in this appeal. We conclude that Fuller is not a surety to the bond, but a principal to the guaranty, "a sealed instrument;" and, this being a separate contract, the suit is not barred until ten years after the cause of action accrued.

---

ing or guaranty. Clark v. Russel, 3 U. S. 3 Dall. 415 (1 L. ed. 660).

Contract of guaranty construed. See *notes* to Kernochan v. Murray (N. Y.) 2 L. R. A. 183; King v. Bates (Mass.) 4 L. R. A. 268; Hyland v. Habich (Mass.) 6 L. R. A. 383; National Exch. Bank v. Gay (Conn.) 4 L. R. A. 343.

Continuing guaranty.

An undertaking to be responsible for moneys to be advanced, or goods to be sold to another from time to time, is a continuing guaranty. Addison, Cont. 668; Buck v. Burk, 18 N. Y. 343.

Where a person agrees to guarantee a stated sum for goods sold his principal, and, after the latter has purchased a larger amount, agrees to become his surety in twice the original sum, instead of the sum "as heretofore," the agreement is a continuing guaranty. Gardner v. Watson (Tex.) Feb. 4, 1890.

A reply by one person to a letter of another asking if the former is financially responsible for a third person, to the effect that if the latter is unable at any time to pay his bills promptly the former will see that the inquirer is taken care of, constitutes a continuing guaranty that such third person will pay his bills at maturity. Dover Stamping Co. v. Noyes (Mass.) April 2, 1890.

A guaranty of 7 per cent per annum in dividends so long as the purchaser should retain the stock sold him, given by a firm as an inducement for the purchase from them of shares of stock, is not limited to the duration of the partnership or the lives of the copartners. Kernochan v. Murray, 2 L. R. A. 183, 111 N. Y. 306.

A guaranty of the amount of dividends that shall be received from stock, made by the seller as an inducement to the purchase of the stock, is an original, and not a collateral, undertaking, and the guarantors are principals, and not sureties, in such obligation. *Ibid.*

The following writing: "You will send P a full line of samples, suitable for spring and summer, at the lowest figures, and I will guarantee payment of the goods you may sell him,"—is not a continuing guaranty, but only for the sale of goods ordered from samples suitable for the ensuing spring and summer. Schwartz v. Hyman, 10 Cent. Rep. 268, 107 N. Y. 560.

Parol evidence; when not admissible to show a guaranty a continuing one. See *note* to Kernochan v. Murray (N. Y.) 2 L. R. A. 183.

A sealed continuing guaranty is revoked by the death of the guarantor. Slagle v. Forney (Pa.) 23 W. N. C. 457.

So the death of the mortgagor revokes the authority to sell goods to a third person on the security of a mortgage given in part to secure indebtedness arising from future sales to him by the mortgagee. Hyland v. Habich, 6 L. R. A. 383, 150 Mass. 112.

Effect of death of guarantor. See *note* to Kernochan v. Murray, *supra*.

A guaranty to secure a running account at a bank, where consideration is separable, is terminated by the guarantor's death. National Eagle Bank v. Hunt, 5 New Eng. Rep. 777, R. I. Index BB, 117.

Upon a collateral undertaking, as a continuing guaranty, no action is maintainable under a count for money lent and money had and received. Douglass v. Reynolds, 32 U. S. 7 Pet. 113 (8 L. ed. 626).

In an action upon a letter of guaranty, evidence is admissible to establish that credit had been given

Davis, *J.*, dissenting:

At the bottom of Earp's note or bond is the following:

I guarantee payment of the foregoing bond, Sept. 27, 1881.

[Signed] D. W. Fuller. [Seal.]

There is only one promise to pay, and that is by Earp to Best. Earp is, unquestionably, the only principal to that obligation. Fuller guarantees the payment, and that, it is said, is a distinct undertaking,—a special contract,—to which he is principal. But the guaranty itself is only for the payment of the debt, which Earp, the principal, was promised to pay, and is not a primary obligation. Earp is principal to the thing guaranteed, and, if you eliminate his promise, Fuller was promised to do nothing. He is not primarily liable for the debt. He is not the principal to any promise to pay money. He is not the principal in the one, and only one, "sealed instrument" promising to pay money; and, if he is to be held liable on a separate and independent contract or undertaking, then there was a collateral security, and as insisted in the answer, as it was by Mr. Busbee in his argument, it was not assignable. We are construing the instrument in view of a statute which, it seems to me, was plainly intended to limit only the liability of the "principal" to a contract under seal to ten years, and to limit the liability of all persons secondarily liable, whether under seal or not, to three years. It seems to me that there was only one principal to the obligation to pay Best the $100, and that principal was Earp. I am not sure that a guarantor is ever called a principal as to the thing guaranteed to be done, and, whether you call him guarantor or surety to the original and principal obligation, I think neither the spirit nor the letter of section 152, par. 2, Code, makes him "principal thereto." *Judge* Daniel says: "A guaranty is a promise to answer for the payment of some debt, or the performance of some duty, in case of the failure of another person who is himself, in the first instance, liable to such payment or performance." *Carpenter* v. *Wall*, 4 Dev. & B. 144.

I think this other person is everywhere and in all cases spoken of as the principal. I do not think a case can be found in which the guarantor for the payment of another is spoken of as principal. It is said that the contract of guaranty is co-extensive with that of the principal. The answer is, So is that of any other surety under seal, but for our Statute; and it is that which makes the distinction between the limit of the liability of the principal and the person bound to answer for him, whether as surety or (I think) guarantor for the judgment.

Baylies, on Sureties and Guarantors, throughout speaks of the relation between the parties as surety and principal, guarantor and principal, and of contracts of guaranty and contracts of surety; and he also says that, "if the guaranty is made with one person, it cannot be extended to another." Pages 113, 133, 146, 147.

Would not Fuller, in an action against him and Best, or against him and Best's assignee, be entitled to the benefits of sections 2100 and 2101 of the Code? Would he not have the right to show in what relation he stood to the parties, and that he was only surety for the payment of the $100, and that it was so understood by the parties,—that he was not principal? *Welfare* v. *Thompson*, 83 N. C. 276; *Lowder* v. *Noding*, 8 Ired. Eq. 208.

I think that in this case it sufficiently appears that the guarantor, as is often the case in single guaranties for the payment of money by another, is really a surety, and only a surety, for the principal; and, if that were not the fair and necessary construction of the instrument, he would have a right to show that it was so intended and so understood by the parties, and that he would have the right to show this by parol. *Welfare* v. *Thompson*, *supra*.

I think there was no error in the ruling of the judge below.

---

on the faith of the guaranty, and that it was treated as a continuing guaranty. *Ibid.*

Continuing guaranty. See *note* to National Exch. Bank v. Gay (Conn.) 4 L. R. A. 343.

Liability of guarantor; severable.

In a contract of guaranty, the liability of the principal and that of the guarantor are several, and they cannot be joined as parties in the same action. Tyler v. Tualatin Academy & Pacific Univ. 14 Or. 485.

A guaranty of a certain sum per month payable in advance for a specified period, aggregating a stated sum, for rent of premises, is a severable contract of guaranty, and the guarantor is liable upon default of the lessee in making any payment. Weller v. Henarie, 15 Or. 28.

A guaranty, for a valuable consideration, of the punctual payment of principal and interest of bonds which have coupons attached, is an original undertaking which gives the holders of the coupons a right to proceed at once against the guarantor. Philadelphia & R. R. Co. v. Knight, 124 Pa. 58.

Where a person purchases of an association several bonds secured by mortgage, upon the procurement of another, who gave a written guaranty of the payment of three of the bonds, and after the purchaser's death his widow assented to an adjustment and a surrender of the bonds upon the execution of a guaranty that in case the bonds or former guaranty be canceled, destroyed or otherwise disposed of, the guaranty shall remain in full force and effect, and be a continuing running guaranty for the payment of the par value of the bonds and interest, the latter agreement is an instrument of guaranty, and nothing more. Miller v. Rinehart, 119 N. Y. 368.

In an action upon a bond to answer for the debt or default of an agent of the obligee, the defendant may aver and prove the original transaction and agreement between the obligee and the agent. The bond and the contract of agency, having been executed contemporaneously, are to be read together. Weed Sewing Mach. Co. v. Winchell, 5 West. Rep. 824, 107 Ind. 260; Singer Mfg. Co. v. Forsyth, 5 West. Rep. 550, 108 Ind. 334.

Where a contract of guaranty is entered into concurrently with the principal obligation, a consideration which supports the principal contract supports the subsidiary one also; and the consideration may be shown by parol. Authorities cited in Erie County Sav. Bank v. Coit, 7 Cent. Rep. 41, 104 N. Y. 532.

A guaranty must have a consideration to support it. If it is made at the time of the contract to which it relates, so as to constitute a part of the consideration of that contract, it is sufficient. Singer Mfg. Co. v. Forsyth, *supra*; Briggs v. Latham, 36 Kan. 205.

NEW HAMPSHIRE SUPREME COURT.

GARDINER
v.
Edward L. B. GARDINER *et al.*, *Appts.*

(........N. H.........)

1. **An interlineation and erasure** by a testatrix, changing a provision in her will, where the word erased is not so obliterated as to be illegible, is not a revocation, but an alteration; and if the instrument, as altered, is not executed as required by the Statute to make a valid will, codicil or instrument of revocation, the will remains intact as before.

2. **The presumption in favor of the revocation of a portion of a will** by canceling is repelled, where the cancellation is made with a view to a new disposition of the property, which fails to be carried into effect, and partial intestacy will result by such cancellation. In such case the will will stand as originally framed.

(March 14, 1890.)

APPEAL by defendants from a decree of the Probate Court for Rockingham County admitting to probate the will of Elizabeth D. Cutler, deceased, and adjudging that defendants were cut off from participation in its provisions by reason of the erasure of their names therefrom. *Reversed.*

The third article of the will originally provided as follows: "All the estate of which I shall die seised and possessed . . . I give, devise and bequeath in manner following: One undivided fourteenth part thereof to each of the following persons, to wit, Edward L. B. Gardiner, Susan I. Gardiner, both of Passaic, New Jersey, children of my nephew, George A. Gardiner," and seven other persons named and described,—thus disposing of nine fourteenths of the estate.

The remaining five fourteenths are subsequently specifically disposed of and there is no residuary clause.

After the will was executed testatrix drew a light line with a pencil through the word "fourteenth" in the above quotation and wrote the word "twelfth" above it.

She also drew a light pencil mark through the following words:

" Edward L. B. Gardiner, Susan I. Gardiner, both of Passaic, New Jersey, children of my nephew George A. Gardiner."

The will came up for probate in solemn form, and the judge of probate entered a decree approving and allowing it, to which decree was added the following: "And whereas the said Elizabeth D. Cutler, after making said will, made certain erasures and interlineations in the same, it is adjudged and decreed that the word 'twelfth' interlined is not in law a part of said will, not having been inserted in the presence of three witnesses, as required by law, and that the word 'fourteenth' erased, for which said word 'twelfth' was substituted, is a part of said will, and the following words erased, namely, 'Edward L. B. Gardiner, Susan I. Gardiner, both of Passaic, N. J., children of my nephew George A. Gardiner,' are not, in law, a part of said will, said words having been erased with the intention on the part of the said Elizabeth D. Cutler to revoke the legacies to said persons whose names are erased, and that said instrument be proved and allowed as the last will and testament of Elizabeth D. Cutler, and so be recorded in accordance with this decree."

Edward L. B. Gardiner and Susan I. Gardiner thereupon took this appeal.

Messrs. **Frink & Batchelder** for appellants.

Messrs. **Marston & Eastman** and **Wiggin & Fernald** for the executor.

Blodgett, *J.*, delivered the opinion of the court:

The Statute of Wills provides that "no will shall be effectual to pass any real or personal estate, or to change or in way affect the same, unless made by a person of the age of twenty-one years, of sound mind, in writing, signed and sealed by the testator, or by some person in his presence, and by his express direction, and attested and subscribed in his presence by three or more credible witnesses;" and that "no will or clause thereof shall be revoked unless by some other valid will or codicil, or by some writing executed in the same manner, or by canceling, tearing, obliterating or otherwise destroying the same, by the testator, or by some person by his consent and in his presence." Gen. Laws, chap. 193, §§ 6, 14.

The mode of revoking a will is therefore as definitely prescribed by the Statute as the mode of making it; and no essential part of the one can be dispensed with any more than the other.

The first question for adjudication presented by this case arises from the attempt of the testatrix to increase a smaller devise to a larger one by substituting "twelfth" for "fourteenth," by interlineation and erasure. While, in one sense, this was a revocation by the testatrix of what she had previously done, in the true sense it was an alteration. To revoke a testamentary disposition is to annul it, so that, in legal contemplation, it ceases to exist, and becomes as inoperative as if it had never been written. But when, by the substitution of certain words for others, a different meaning is imported, there is not a mere revocation. There is something more than the destruction of that which has been antecedently done.

NOTE.—*Interlineations in will.*

Where there is nothing to explain obliterations and interlineations appearing on the face of a will, it will be presumed they were made after its execution. Burgoyne v. Showler, 1 Robt. Eccl. 5, 8 Jur. 814; Cooper v. Bockett, 4 Moore, P. C. 419; Greville v. Tylee, 7 Moore, P. C. 320.

As bearing upon the question of revocation or no revocation by an act done to the instrument, the declarations of the testator may be shown at the probate as evincing the intent. Evans' App. 58 Pa. 238.

Under the Alabama Code a will cannot be revoked *pro tanto* by expunging the name of a single legatee by drawing a pen through it (Law v. Law, 83 Ala. 432); but if made with intention to revoke the whole will as manifested by declarations of the testator, it is effectual for that purpose. *Ibid.*

See also 36 L. R. A. 176.

There is a transmutation, by which a new clause is created. There is another and a different testamentary disposition, which, to have validity, must be authenticated by the observance of the statutory requirements. *Eschbach* v. *Collins*, 61 Md. 478.

It follows that the failure of the testatrix to execute her purpose in the manner prescribed by the Statute (§ 6) prevented it from going into effect as a testamentary disposition; and, as it is apparent that she had no intent to revoke except by way of alteration, and the word erased not having been so obliterated as to be illegible, there was no revocation, and the will remained intact as before (*Jackson* v. *Holloway*, 7 Johns. 394; *McPherson* v. *Clark*, 3 Bradf. 92; *Quinn* v. *Quinn*, 1 Thomp. & C. 437; *Wolf* v. *Bollinger*, 62 Ill. 368; *Wright* v. *Wright*, 5 Ind. 389; *Re Penniman's Will*, 20 Minn. 245 (Gil. 220); *Stover* v. *Kendall*, 1 Coldw. 557; *Bethell* v. *Moore*, 2 Dev. & B. L. 316; *Wheeler* v. *Bent*, 7 Pick. 61; *Short* v. *Smith*, 4 East, 419; *Kirke* v. *Kirke*, 4 Russ. 435; *Martins* v. *Gardiner*, 8 Sim. 73; *Locke* v. *James*, 13 L. J. N. S. Exch. 186; *Lawson* v. *Morrison*, 2 Am. Lead. Cas. 5th ed. 501; 1 Redf. Wills, 325, 326; *Eschbach* v. *Collins*, *supra; Pringle* v. *McPherson*, 2 Brev. 279); in other words the effect of the alteration is the same as it would have been had it been made by a codicil imperfectly executed.

The remaining question is as to the effect upon the appellants of the cancellation of their names from the list of legatees named in the first clause of the third article of the will. The appellants contend that it had no effect, while the executor contends that it effected a revocation. We think the contention of the appellants must be sustained. Canceling and obliterating have always been considered peculiarly equivocal acts of revocation (*Dan* v. *Brown*, 4 Cow. 490; *Smith* v. *Cunningham*, 1 Addams, Eccl. 455); and eminent authorities hold that where a pencil instead of a pen is used, the cancellation is prima facie deliberative, and not final. 1 Jarm. Wills, 5th Am. ed. 291; 2 Greenl. Ev. § 681, and cases cited.

If this be so, it is decisive of the contention, because no collateral evidence is presented which rebuts the presumption. On the contrary the lightness of the pencil lines, and the failure to change "fourteenths" to "twelfths" in the succeeding clause, tend strongly to show that the act of the testatrix was conditional merely.

But it is not necessary to invoke the doctrine of Jarman and of Greenleaf. There are other and more satisfactory reasons which lead to the same result. The competency of a testator to make revocation of a devise by the simple erasure or cancellation of the name of the devisee is undoubted; but when the act of cancellation is not a substantive, independent act, but is connected with and dependent upon another, and both form but one transaction, the entire design and purpose must be considered, in order to ascertain whether a revocation has been accomplished. When this is done in the case before us, it is at once apparent that the cancellation in question must be considered in connection with the preceding erasure and interlineation, and may properly be treated as relative or dependent thereon, because all the evidence indicates that the only purpose of the testatrix was to make a new disposition as to a portion of her property. There is no reason whatever to suppose that she would have revoked the legacies to the appellants if she had been aware that the proposed disposition could not be carried into effect; but, on the other hand, the fair presumption is that her wishes with regard to her property, as originally expressed, would have remained unchanged, in the absence of any known reason for changing them. And this presumption is further strengthened by the fact that otherwise there would be an intestacy as to the two fourteenths of the estate bequeathed to the appellants; for there is no residuary clause into which it can properly fall, or into which the testatrix intended it should fall. It is clear that the testatrix did not contemplate an intestacy as to any part of her estate. She evidently intended to make a testamentary disposition of the whole of it; and, upon well-settled principles, her intention may be effectuated.

"When a portion of a will is canceled with a view to a new disposition of the property, and the proposed disposition fails to be carried into effect, the presumption in favor of a revocation by the canceling will be repelled, and the will will stand as originally framed." *Re Penniman's Will*, *supra; Lawson* v. *Morrison*, 2 Am. Lead. Cas. 501; *Short* v. *Smith*, *Bethell* v. *Moore*, *McPherson* v. *Clark*, *Wolf* v. *Bollinger* and *Eschbach* v. *Collins*, *supra*.

We are therefore of opinion, and without regard to the presumption arising from the manner of its performance, that, as the cancellation was not done with intent to revoke the bequests to the appellants simply, but with intent to make a new disposition of a porti n of the testatrix's estate, which failed of accomplishment, the canceling which was done only in the view of, and in order to effect, that object, should be esteemed for nothing, and be considered as not having been done absolutely, but only conditionally, and upon the proposed disposition being made effectual. To give it effect, under the circumstances, would not only be against the authorities, but would thwart the actual intention of the testatrix, and make her intestate as to one seventh of her estate, when a contrary intent is plainly manifested in her will. *Wolf* v. *Bollinger*, *supra*.

The decree of the Probate Court upon this branch of the case is reversed, and the appeal sustained.

Bingham, *J.*, did not sit; the others concurred.

KANSAS SUPREME COURT.

MISSOURI PACIFIC R. CO., *Plff. in Err.,*
v.
J. W. SHARITT.

(....Kan.....)

**Where an employe and resident of this State performs labor* in this State for a railway company, a corporation of another State, but also doing business in this State, and the wages of such employé are exempt in this as well as in the other State,—*Held,* in an action by the employé to recover such wages in this State, the fact that the corporation has been garnished in such other State by a creditor of such employé before the bringing of this action in this State, and service of summons obtained upon the employé only by publication, is no defense to such action.

(*Horton, Ch. J., dissents.*)

(November 9, 1889.)

ERROR to the District Court for Franklin County to review a judgment rendered upon appeal from a justice's court in favor of plaintiff in an action to recover wages alleged to be due and which had been garnished in a foreign jurisdiction. *Affirmed.*

Statement by **Clogston,** *C.:*

Sharitt, plaintiff below, commenced this action on the 27th day of July, 1887, against the plaintiff in error, the Missouri Pacific Railway Company, to recover wages due him. The action was brought before a justice of the peace in Franklin County, and judgment was rendered against the defendant. An appeal was taken to the District Court of Franklin County, and trial was had by the court, and the court made findings of fact and conclusions of law which are as follows: "(1) Plaintiff was in the employ of the defendant at Council Grove, Kan., during the month of June, 1887, performing manual labor in and about coupling cars and making up trains, and the like, and was styled a 'yard-master.' (2) As such laborer, he earned, and became and was entitled to receive from the defendant for such month's services, the sum of $79, $75 of which sum has not been paid. (3) That plaintiff is a citizen, resident and householder of the State, and has been for more than two years last past. During said month of June, 1887, and ever since, the plaintiff had a family, to wit, a wife and three children, supported by his labor, and his said earnings were necessary for the support of said family. (4) While the action was pending before the justice, it appeared that certain garnishee proceedings were pending in Morris County, Kan., whereby it was sought to subject said wages to the claim of a certain party there; and it was then agreed between the attorneys for the respective parties in this case that the suit here should be continued ten days, and that if, in the meantime, said garnishee proceedings were dismissed, the defendant would pay plaintiff's claim, or submit to judgment thereon, if plaintiff would pay costs. Accordingly, at the expiration of said ten days, said proceedings having been dismissed, the justice entered judgment accordingly. On the 13th day of July, 1887, at St. Louis, Mo., the defendant Company was garnished by and before a justice of the peace of that State at the suit of W. P. Stewart, a resident of Missouri, against said J. W. Sharitt, and ordered to answer therein, in which it did on July 28, 1887; and the Company was, on September 29, 1887, ordered to pay into that court the amount so due the plaintiff. The plaintiff, Sharitt, defendant in that suit, was not served in said action otherwise than by publication. From the order so requiring said Company to pay said moneys the said Company appealed to the Circuit Court of St. Louis County, Mo., which said action is now pending and undetermined. Neither party or their attorneys had notice or knowledge of these proceedings in St. Louis when the agreement referred to in the fourth finding was made. I conclude, as matter of law, that said personal earnings were and are exempt from the payment of plaintiff's debts, and that he is entitled to recover the same in this action; and judgment will be rendered accordingly."

Judgment thereon was rendered for the plaintiff. Defendant now brings the case here.

Messrs. **John W. Deford** and **Waggener, Martin & Orr,** for plaintiff in error:

That court which first acquires jurisdiction over the fund, whether in this State or another, is justly entitled to deal with it until its jurisdiction is exhausted by the exercise of it, or lost by dismissal or other proper method.

Wallace v. *M'Connell,* 38 U. S. 13 Pet. 136 (10 L. ed. 95); 2 Kent, Com. 122; *Embree* v. *Hanna,* 5 Johns. 101; *Renner* v. *Marshall,* 14 U. S. 1 Wheat. 215 (4 L. ed. 74); *Beaston* v. *Farmers Bank,* 37 U. S. 12 Pet. 102 (9 L. ed 1017); *Connor* v. *Hanover Ins. Co.* 28 Fed. Rep. 549, and cases cited; *East Tennessee, V. & G. R. Co.* v. *Kennedy,* 83 Ala. 462, 3 Am. St. Rep. 755; *Ferguson* v. *Bank of Kansas City,* 25 Kan. 333.

A prior judicial proceeding in another jurisdiction should be respected, and no violence to the rights of a party by a subsequent proceeding here tolerated.

U. S. Const. art. 11, § 1; *Ferguson* v. *Bank of Kansas City,* 25 Kan. 333.

The fact that the service on Mr. Sharitt in the case in Missouri was by publication only is irrelevant. Under our statutes and those of Missouri such service is just as good and effectual as personal service to bind the fund in the hands of the garnishee.

Kansas Justice's Code, §§ 35, 37, 43, 51, 54*a*, 54*d;* Kansas Code Civil Proc. §§ 72, 198, 200, 206, 215–219; Attachment in Justice Courts, 1 Mo. Rev. Stat. §§ 473–479; Attachments in Courts of Record, 1 Mo. Rev. Stat. §§ 420, 434, 435, 3494.

It has never heretofore been hinted that if the defendant was a nonresident absentee, a credit due him by a resident of this State could not be subjected here because of an imaginary *situs* of the credit in the State of the residence of the defendant.

*Head note by CLOGSTON, C.

See also 23 L. R. A. 650; 36 L. R. A. 640; 40 L. R. A. 237; 41 L. R. A. 331; 42 L. R. A. 283; 44 L. R. A. 101; 45 L. R. A. 257; 48 L. R. A. 452.

See *Burlington & M. R. R. Co.* v. *Thompson*, 31 Kan. 180; *Missouri Pac. R. Co.* v. *Maltby*, 34 Kan. 125; *Johnson* v. *Brant*, 38 Kan. 754.

The garnishment lien attaches when the garnishee is served with notice and continues until the attachment is dissolved, or the plaintiff's claim is satisfied.

Atchison Board of Education v. *Scoville*, 13 Kan. 29.

Mr. **Enoch Harpole** for defendant in error.

Clogston, *C.*, filed the following opinion:

It is not contended that the claim sued on is not exempt under the Exemption Laws of this State, but it is contended that, because the garnishment proceedings were commenced in Missouri, and the court of that State obtained jurisdiction of the subject matter before this suit was brought in Kansas, for that reason the defendant Company became liable under its answer in Missouri under said proceedings, and should not again be held liable in this State in this action. The plaintiff in error recognizes the rule laid down by this court that, if the garnishment proceedings had been commenced in this State, no question could have been raised, and also recognizes the rule, adopted in this State, that the garnishee has the same right in his answer to raise all the questions that the debtor himself might raise, and plead the Exemption Law as completely as the debtor might plead it. But plaintiff in error says no such rule exists in Missouri; that, under the decisions of that State, it is precluded from asserting this right, and therefore, if it is compelled to pay this judgment, it will again have to pay the claim under its answer in Missouri. This seems to present a hardship; but, as the claim is exempt under the laws of this State, and presumably exempt under the laws of Missouri,—for it is presumed, in the absence of any showing to the contrary, that the laws of Missouri are the same as the Statute of this State—therefore, if this claim is exempt under both the laws of Missouri and of Kansas, it would be unjust to the defendant in error if, by reason of some construction of the Statute of Missouri, he should be prevented from securing the benefit of the exemption.

It has been held in this State that the garnishee may plead the Exemption Laws, and be protected thereby as completely as the debtor would be. See *Mull* v. *Jones*, 33 Kan. 112.

This seems to be the well-recognized doctrine elsewhere; and, while there is some conflict in the authorities on this subject, the great weight of authority is with our court. We see no reason why an exception should be made in this case to a rule so well established. Under the rule laid down in *Missouri Pac. R. Co.* v. *Maltby*, 34 Kan. 131, and *Kansas City, St. J. & C. B. R. Co.* v. *Gough*, 35 Kan. 1, this judgment must be affirmed. See also *Drake* v. *Lake Shore & M. S. R. Co.* 69 Mich. 168, 18 West. Rep. 720.

Under those decisions, this claim would be exempt to the plaintiff below had he resided either in the State of Missouri, or, as he does, in Kansas; and such exemption ought to be a good defense for the defendant Company in Missouri. *It is therefore recommended that the judgment of the Court below be affirmed.*

Per Curiam: *It is so ordered.*

Horton, *Ch. J.*, and **Johnston,** *J.*, concur.

Valentine, *J.:*

I concur in the decision of this case for the reason that I believe it is sustained by reason and the weight of authority. It seems to be generally held that the laws of any country where a debt is created enter into the contract upon which the debt is founded, so far as they are applicable and material, and form a part thereof. *Greer* v. *McCarter*, 5 Kan. 18, 22; *Deering* v. *Boyle*, 8 Kan. 532 *et seq.*, and cases there cited.

Also, in the absence of anything to the contrary, it will be presumed by the courts that the laws of all the other States are similar to their own. *Furrow* v. *Chapin*, 13 Kan. 107; *Dodge* v. *Coffin*, 15 Kan. 285 *et seq.*, and cases there cited; *Kansas Pac. R. Co.* v. *Cutter*, 16 Kan. 568; *Baughman* v. *Baughman*, 29 Kan. 284.

And, when the *situs* of a debt is changed from the State or jurisdiction in which the debt was created to some other State or jurisdiction, all its incidents and conditions materially affecting it will be transferred with it, and its interpretation, scope and validity will be governed by the *lex loci contractus.* For instance, if the debt is exempt from judicial process in the State where it is created, the exemption will follow the debt, as an incident thereto, into any other State or jurisdiction into which the debt may be supposed to be carried. *Drake* v. *Lake Shore & M. S. R. Co.* 69 Mich. 168, 18 West. Rep. 720; *Wright* v. *Chicago, B. & Q. R. Co.* 19 Neb. 175; *Baylies* v. *Houghton*, 15 Vt. 626; *Pierce* v. *Chicago & N. W. R. Co.* 36 Wis. 283. And see, especially, the opinion in the case of *Missouri Pac. R. Co.* v. *Maltby*, 34 Kan. 125, 128.

In the language of the Michigan case above cited, the exemption of the debt from judicial process "becomes a vested right *in rem*, which follows the debt into any jurisdiction where the debt may be considered as going." Also, the *situs* of a debt is either with the owner thereof or at his domicil, or where the debt is to be paid; and it cannot be subjected to a proceeding in garnishment anywhere else. See the numerous authorities hereafter cited, commencing with the case of *Louisville & N. R. Co.* v. *Dooley*, 78 Ala. 524.

I shall now proceed to consider this case with reference to its facts.

The Missouri Pacific Railway Company, a Missouri corporation doing business in Missouri and Kansas and other States, and operating over 2,000 miles of railway in Kansas, owes a debt, not evidenced by any instrument in writing, to J. W. Sharitt, a resident of Kansas, for wages earned by him as yard-master for the Railway Company at Council Grove, Kan., and presumably payable at that place, which wages are, under the laws of Kansas, and presumably under the laws of Missouri, as nothing appears to the contrary, exempt from execution, attachment, garnishment and other process. W. P. Stewart, a resident of Missouri, who puts forth the claim that Sharitt owes him, instituted a garnishment proceeding before a justice of the peace of that State against the Railway Company to procure the payment to him of the debt which the Railway Company owes to Sharitt. Such proceeding is now pending in the Circuit Court of St. Louis, Mo. No service of summons was ever made upon Sharitt in that case except by publication. The question now arises, and it is the principal question involved in this case, whether Sharitt is bound by such garnishment proceedings or not. Now, unless the Missouri court has jurisdiction of Sharitt, or of something belonging to him, of course the proceeding is void as to him; and, as no personal service or summons was ever made upon him, it will be admitted that the proceeding is without jurisdiction and void as to him personally. But the further question remains, is the proceeding without jurisdiction and void as to any property belonging to Sharitt? Or, in other words, has the Missouri court any jurisdiction, as against Sharitt, over the debt which the Railway Company owes to Sharitt? Sharitt is not a resident of Missouri, nor is he in that State; but, on the contrary, he is a resident of Kansas, and in Kansas, and he has never been served, personally, with any summons in the garnishment proceeding. The debt is not evidenced by any written instrument; but, if it were, the instrument would presumably be in Kansas and in the hands of Sharitt. It is not payable in Missouri, but on the contrary, it is presumably payable in Kansas, where it was created, and where Sharitt resides; and in Kansas, and presumably in Missouri, it is exempt from all judicial process. It is not claimed that the Railway Company has ever set apart any fund, either in Missouri, or in Kansas or elsewhere, for the purpose of paying this particular debt. Hence there is no specific fund connected with this debt, nor any tangible thing to which any jurisdiction could attach. But, if it should be supposed that any particular fund had been set apart to pay this debt, then it should be supposed that it was so set apart in Kansas, as the debt was created in Kansas, is already due in Kansas and is payable in Kansas; and probably the Railway Company could not set apart a fund in Missouri so as to defeat Sharitt's claim in Kansas. The debt is really and in fact a mere chose in action, resting wholly in parol, and is of such an intangible character that it could not be actually seized by any kind of process. And it can hardly be said to have any actual *situs* anywhere; but, if it should be considered as having any actual *situs* anywhere, then its more natural *situs* is where it is to be paid,—in Kansas, and to Sharitt.

It is seldom, and perhaps never, held that the property in a debt, a mere chose in action, can be carried around with the debtor wherever he may go, and exist wherever he may be. Drake, Attachm. §§ 474, 481; Wade, Attachm. § 344; *Wheat* v. *Platte City & Ft. D. R. Co.* 4 Kan. 370.

But, on the contrary, the *situs* of a debt is generally held to be with the creditor, or at his domicil, or at the place where it is made payable. It is the creditor that owns the debt, and not the debtor, and the *situs* of the debt must be considered as being either with the owner or at his domicil, or where it is to be paid. Indeed, the more natural *situs* of any contract, whether a debt or not, would seem to be where it is to be performed. Even tangible property is not subject to garnishment proceedings in a State or jurisdiction in which the property is not situated. See the above authorities, and also *Bates* v. *Chicago, M. & St. P. R. Co.* 60 Wis. 296, 304, 305. See also *Sutherland* v. *Second Nat. Bank*, 78 Ky. 250.

Now, under the facts of this case, we do not think that the Missouri court has any jurisdiction, either of Sharitt, or of anything belonging or appertaining to him: and hence the garnishment proceeding is void as to him. We think the weight of authority sustains this view of the case. See the authorities already cited, and also the following: *Louisville & N. R. Co.* v. *Dooley*, 78 Ala. 524; *Lovejoy* v. *Albee*, 33 Me. 414; *Lawrence* v. *Smith*, 45 N. H. 533; *Miller* v. *Hooe*, 2 Cranch, C. C. 622; *Hamilton* v. *Rogers*, 67 Mich. 135, 10 West. Rep. 903; *Drake* v. *Lake Shore & M. S. R. Co.* 69 Mich. 168, 13 West. Rep. 720; *Baylies* v. *Houghton*, 15 Vt. 626; *Towle* v. *Wilder*, 57 Vt. 622; *Wright* v. *Chicago, B. & Q. R. Co.* 19 Neb. 175; *Pierce* v. *Chicago & N. W. R. Co.* 36 Wis. 283; *Tingley* v. *Bateman*, 10 Mass. 343; *Nye* v. *Liscombe*, 21 Pick. 263; *Sawyer* v. *Thompson*, 24 N. H. 510; *Western R. Co.* v. *Thornton*, 60 Ga. 300; *Green* v. *Farmers & C. Bank*, 25 Conn. 452; *Cronin* v. *Foster*, 13 R. I. 196; *Bates* v. *New Orleans, J. & G. N. R. Co.* 4 Abb. Pr. 72; *Willet* v. *Equitable Ins. Co.* 10 Abb. Pr. 193; *Noble* v. *Thompson Oil Co.* 79 Pa. 354; *Myer* v. *Liverpool, L. & G. Ins. Co.* 40 Md. 595; *Wheat* v. *Platte City & Ft. D. R. Co.* 4 Kan. 370.

As before stated, it is not the debtor who can carry or transfer or transport the property in a debt from one State or jurisdiction into another. The *situs* of the property in a debt can be changed only by the change of location of the creditor who is the owner thereof, or with his consent.

It will be seen from what has been said that my concurrence in the decision in this case is founded almost wholly upon the theory that the Missouri court has no jurisdiction of Sharitt or of anything belonging or appertaining to him, and therefore that there can be no such thing as a *lis pendens* by virtue of the Missouri proceeding, with regard to the subject matter of this action, which is the debt, and nothing in the Missouri proceeding that can be considered as valid or binding as against Sharitt. And all my argument is also based upon the theory that the court first obtaining jurisdiction of the subject matter of an action has the superior right to exercise jurisdiction over such subject matter. But, not wishing to be misunderstood in this case, I will be a little more explicit as to some matters. I think that the Missouri court has jurisdiction of Stewart, the plaintiff in the Missouri action, and of the Railway Company, the garnishee; and that any judgment or order which might be rendered or made by the Missouri court as against Stewart or the Railway Company would be valid and binding as against them. And if Stewart, the plaintiff in that action, had obtained personal service of summons in Missouri upon Sharitt, then any judgment or order which might be rendered or made by the Missouri court as against Sharitt, or against the garnishee, would also be valid and binding as to Sharitt. And, even without personal service of summons upon Sharitt, if he had any tangible property in Missouri, which the Missouri court could seize, even money in the hands of some other person, any judgment or order of such court which might be made or rendered after the seizure of such property would be valid as against Sharitt. And, further, if it could be considered that the debt owing by the Railway Company to Sharitt had a *situs* in Missouri, then any judgment or order made or rendered by such court respecting such debt would be valid; and, if Sharitt were a resident of Missouri, or was even temporarily there, at the time of the attempted seizure of the debt, or if the debt was made payable in Missouri, it might perhaps be considered that the debt had such a *situs* in Missouri that it might be subject to the order or judgment of the Missouri court. But none of these things exist in this case; and hence, in my opinion, the Missouri court has no jurisdiction of Sharitt, or of anything appertaining or belonging to Sharitt.

Of course, the laws of a State can have no extraterritorial force; and therefore, if exempt tangible property, such as could be seized by process, were carried into another State or jurisdiction, such property might cease to be exempt, and might be seized and held in attachment or garnishment proceedings for the payment of debts, but debts existing in Kansas are not at the same time that kind of property in Missouri. Whether what we have just said with respect to tangible property would apply to debts created under contracts made under laws exempting such debts from all judicial process, it is not necessary, in this case, to express any opinion. But, generally, contracts with respect to everything of substance inhering in them—and the laws of the country where the contracts are made, so far as such laws affect the contracts, are generally considered as inhering in the contracts—are governed and determined by the *lex loci contractus*, in whatever jurisdiction the construction or character of such contracts comes into consideration. Several cases are referred to as enunciating doctrines adverse to the views herein expressed, to wit: *Ferguson* v. *Bank of Kansas City*, 25 Kan. 333; *Burlington & M. R. R. Co.* v. *Thompson*, 31 Kan. 180; *Zimmerman* v. *Franke*, 34 Kan. 650; *Stark* v. *Bare*, 39 Kan. 100; *Daniels* v. *Clark*, 38 Iowa, 556; *Moore* v. *Chicago, R. I. & P. R. Co.* 43 Iowa, 385; *Leiber* v. *Union Pac. R. Co.* 49 Iowa, 688; *Mooney* v. *Union Pac. R. Co.* 60 Iowa, 346; *Green* v. *Van Buskirk*, 74 U. S. 7 Wall. 139 [19 L. ed. 109]; *Connor* v. *Hanover Ins. Co.* 28 Fed. Rep. 549; *Morgan* v. *Nevil e*, 74 Pa. 53; *Osborne* v. *Schutt*, 67 Mo. 712; *Blake* v. *Williams*, 6 Pick. 286; *Sturtevant* v. *Robinson*, 18 Pick. 175; *Baltimore & O. R. Co.* v. *May*, 25 Ohio St. 347; *Snook* v. *Snetzer*, Id. 516; *East Tennessee, V. & G. R. Co.* v. *Kennedy*, 83 Ala. 462.

Scarcely any of the above cases have any application to the question whether a court of one State, by virtue of a garnishment proceeding against a resident garnishee, but against a nonresident and absent defendant, residing in another State, and owning a debt created and payable to him in his own State, and by virtue of a service of summons upon the defendant only by publication, could obtain sufficient jurisdiction over the nonresident and absent defendant, or over the debt created and payable to him in the State of his residence, that such court could render a judgment or make an order against the garnishee that would be valid and binding as against the defendant.

The case of *Burlington & M. R. R. Co.* v. *Thompson*, 31 Kan. 180, is relied upon principally among the Kansas cases; but no such question was presented or decided in that case. In the opinion in that case, it is said, among other things: "Again, no question arises here as to the effect of a judgment against the garnishee in the courts of this State, as against proceedings to collect the debt in the State of Nebraska, where the debt was created. As to that question, the cases of *Pierce* v. *Chicago & N. W. R. Co.*, 36 Wis. 283, and *Moore* v. *Chicago, R. I. & P. R. Co.*, 43 Iowa, 385, *supra*, seem to be divergent. As to which states the law correctly, we need not now inquire. The question in this case is not what is the effect of a judgment against a garnishee, but what ought to be such judgment." 31 Kan. 194.

In the leading Iowa case of *Moore* v. *Chicago, R. I. & P. R. Co.*, 43 Iowa, 385, jurisdiction was conceded. See opinion, p. 387.

This was also the case in the case of *Baltimore & O. R. Co.* v. *May*, 25 Ohio St. 347. In that case, jurisdiction was admitted by the pleadings.

In the case of *Blake* v. *Williams*, 6 Pick. 286, the question was not one of jurisdiction, but one of assignment. Besides, the actual *situs* of the debt in that case was, in all probability, just where the proceedings were commenced. The debt was probably payable there.

The case of *Green* v. *Van Buskirk*, 74 U. S. 7 Wall. 139 [19 L. ed. 109], has no application to this case. No debt was attempted to be taken in attachment or garnishment in that case.

The case of *Connor* v. *Hanover Ins. Co.*, 28 Fed. Rep. 549, has perhaps some application to this case, though it certainly does not furnish much authority against the views herein expressed. It also criticises unfavorably the decision made by this court in the case of *Burlington & M. R. R. Co.* v. *Thompson*, 31 Kan. 180.

The case of *Morgan* v. *Neville*, 74 Pa. 52, is probably applicable. And yet the owner of the debt in that case was served personally with notice the next morning after the garnishment proceeding was instituted. This service of notice, however, was probably, for reasons not necessary to mention, not sufficient to give the foreign court jurisdiction.

In the case of *East Tennessee, V. & G. R. Co.* v. *Kennedy*, 83 Ala. 462, the owner of the debt was served personally with summons in the foreign jurisdiction. It is unnecessary to mention more particularly the other cases cited for the Railway Company.

The principal argument urged against holding that the Railroad Company is liable in the present case is that by such holding, and by the possible judgment of the Missouri court, the Company might be required to pay the debt twice. This would certainly be wrong, but wherein would the wrong consist? If this court is right, should it refrain from doing its duty because of some possible wrong somewhere else? Should this court violate its own laws because some foreign court may ignore them? Besides, is the Railroad Company the only party entitled to sympathy? Is not the owner of the debt, with his family, also entitled to some consideration? The debt is his personal earnings, for his own personal services for less than three months—indeed, for less than one month—next preceding the issuing of the garnishment process, and is necessary for the support of his family, and, by the laws of his own State, is exempt from the payment of his debts, and from all judicial process. Now, notwithstanding the fact that this fund is set apart by the laws of the State for the support of himself and family, and is necessary for their support, may it be taken away from them by a foreign jurisdiction four or five hundred miles away,—and it might be thousands of miles away,—and, possibly, upon some false or trumped-up charge, without any personal service of summons upon him? Is he not entitled to have his day in court, and in a court that has first rightfully obtained jurisdiction of him personally, or of his debt? If it be said that the garnishee should serve notice upon him, then what is such notice for? Is such notice necessary in order to give the foreign court jurisdiction of the owner of the debt, or of the debt? Will it be admitted that, without such a notice from the garnishee, the judgment or order rendered or made by the foreign court would be without jurisdiction and void as to the owner of the debt, and still claimed that, with such notice, such judgment or order would be valid and binding as to him? Besides, the garnishee might be unable to give the notice; and, if he could not, then what? I would hardly think that such a notice could give jurisdiction to the foreign court, if it did not have jurisdiction prior to that notice. Besides, why compel the owner of the debt, upon such a notice, to go four or five hundred miles or more to defend an action, and thereby spend more money than the amount of his debt? It might be better for him and his family to lose the debt entirely, and let the laws of the State setting it apart for the benefit and support of himself and family become nugatory and inoperative. Of course, the debt in this case is small,—only $75; but it is a great deal to the laborer who earned it, and his family, and the State has set it apart for the support of his family; and the principle as to jurisdiction is the same as though the debt amounted to many thousands of dollars. If the rule contended for by the Railroad Company should be adopted, then it would be prudent for every creditor to continually watch his debtor, and to follow him around into every jurisdiction into which he might go, for fear that some unscrupulous person, who really had no just claim, might institute a garnishment proceeding and obtain the debt before the creditor could have an opportunity to prevent it. I concur in affirming the judgment of the court below.

A motion for rehearing was subsequently filed and in response thereto the following opinions were filed:

Per Curiam:

Now comes on for decision the motion for a rehearing of this cause, and thereupon it is ordered that the said motion be overruled.

Horton, *Ch. J.*, dissenting:

When the judgment of affirmance was rendered in this court, I had grave doubts whether the law had been properly declared. Since then, I have re-examined the facts disclosed by the record, the decisions referred to by the attorneys and the authorities in the opinions heretofore filed. My opinion now is that a rehearing should be granted, and that the judgment of the trial court should be reversed. My reasons are as follows:

It appears that Sharitt, the employé, during the month of June, 1887, performed manual labor for the Missouri Pacific Railway Company, which system extends through Missouri and Kansas. For these services the Railway Company owed its employé wages,—a debt. These wages are exempt from attachment or garnishment under the laws of this State. W. P. Stewart, a creditor of Sharitt, who resided in St. Louis, Mo., brought an action against him by attachment in St. Louis on the 18th day of July, 1887, and garnished the Railway Company, which answered on July 28, 1887, to the facts of its indebtedness to the employé; and, upon its answer, judgment was rendered against the Company. The employé was served by publication. From the order of judgment requiring the Company to pay the wages or debt to the creditor, the Company appealed to the Circuit Court of St. Louis, Mo., where the action is now pending. Subsequent to the commencement of the action by attachment in St. Louis, Mo., and on the 27th day of July, 1887, Sharitt commenced his action before a justice of the peace in Franklin County, of this State, to recover the same wages or debt which had been garnished in St. Louis, Mo. The justice of the peace rendered judgment against the Railway Company. The Company took an appeal to the District Court of Franklin County, and that court also rendered judgment in favor of the employé, and against the Railway Company. This is complained of.

The question in the case therefore is, Can the employé of the Railway Company bring his action in this State, and recover his wages, notwithstanding the defendant Company has been garnished for the same wages by the employé's creditor in Missouri? Although the amount in dispute is small, the principles involved are important. Several great lines of railroad, like the Atchison, the Missouri Pacific, the Rock Island and others, extend through this into other States. These railroads have thousands of employés in their service whose wages are liable to be garnished, and the law ought not to compel them to pay for the services of an employé twice,—once to the creditor, and afterwards to the employé. Again, many of the employés of these railroads go from State to State in search of work, and often change their employer as well as their residence. These wage workers ought to be protected in the payment of their personal earnings to themselves, which generally are exempt under the statutes of most of the States, so far as the law will permit. "The laborer is worthy of his hire." If the Railway Company is compelled to satisfy the judgment rendered against it in Missouri, then the employé ought not to recover, and the action commenced in this

State should be delayed until the final disposition of the attachment or garnishee proceedings in Missouri. *Ferguson* v. *Bank of Kansas City*, 25 Kan. 333.

"Of course, no debtor should be required to pay his debt twice; but, at the same time, if he goes into a State outside the State of his residence, and transacts business therein, he must expect, as to all matters of procedure and remedy, to abide by the laws of that State. . . . It cannot be doubted that the courts of the State where he resides will respect a judgment rendered against him in this State, provided he has made a perfect and full disclosure, and a reasonable defense, against the claim presented." *Burlington & M. R. R. Co.* v. *Thompson*, 31 Kan. 180.

Kent says: "A *lis pendens*, before the tribunals of another jurisdiction, has, in cases of proceedings *in rem*, been held to be a good plea in abatement of a suit. Thus, where a creditor of A, a bankrupt, had, bona fide and by regular process, attached in another State a debt due to A, and in the hands of B, it has been held that the assignees of the bankrupt could not, by subsequent suit, recover the debt of B. The pendency of the foreign attachment is a good plea in abatement of the suit. In such a case, the equity of the maxim, *qui prior est tempore, potior est jure*, forcibly applies. Unless the plea in abatement was allowed in such a case, the defendant would be left without protection, and would be obliged to pay the debt twice." 2 Kent, Com. 122, 123, 125. See *Morgan* v. *Neville*, 74 Pa. 52; Thompson, Homesteads and Exemptions, §§ 21–23; *Connor* v. *Hanover Ins. Co.* 28 Fed. Rep. 549; Freeman, Executions, 2d ed. § 209.

Pierce v. *Chicago & N. W. R. Co.*, 36 Wis. 283, is in conflict with some of the foregoing decisions, but that case has been severely criticised. 2 Cent. L. J. 378.

But, upon examination, that cases does not, I think, militate against the conclusion I have reached. It is said in that case: "The garnishee must bring the fact of the exemption to the notice of the court where the attachment is pending, or notify the employé of the pendency of the proceedings. In the State of Missouri the supreme court holds that the exemption of property from judicial process is a personal privilege of its owner, and that the debtor of such owner cannot assert it for him by way of defense to a garnishment proceeding. *Osborne* v. *Schutt*, 67 Mo. 712. Therefore the Railway Company could not, under the decisions of Missouri, have protected itself or its employé by alleging the exemption of the wages attached. As the attachment proceedings are still pending in Missouri, and the employé has notice now of these proceedings even within the Wisconsin rule, the garnishee has done all that it could do. If the law is decided otherwise, it is manifest that the Railroad Company will be subjected to a double liability, which does not comport with justice.

It is argued in the concurring opinion that, as Sharitt is not a resident of Missouri, and has not been personally served with any summons in the garnishment proceeding, the action in Missouri by Stewart, a resident of Missouri, and the creditor of Sharitt, against the Missouri Pacific Railway Company, a Missouri corporation, is void as being without jurisdiction, and therefore that the garnishment proceeding is no defense to the action of Sharitt in this State. This view of the law is not, I think, sustained by the weight of the authorities.

Drake, in his work on Attachment, § 597, says: "Where the garnishee is indebted, it will not vary his liability that his contract with the defendant is to pay the money in another State or country than that in which the attachment is pending. Thus, where it was urged as a ground for discharging a garnishee, that his debt to the defendant was contracted in England, and was payable there only, so that the defendant could not, and therefore the plaintiff could not, make it payable elsewhere, the court said: 'We do not perceive any legal principle upon which the objection rests. This was a debt from the garnishee everywhere, in whatever country his person or property might be found. A suit might have been maintained by the defendant here, and therefore the debt may be attached here.'"

In *Blake* v. *Williams*, 6 Pick. 286, it was held that "where W., a banker in England, having advanced money to pay a bill of exchange drawn upon him by M., a citizen of this State, became a bankrupt, and, after an assignment of his effects by commissioners of bankruptcy, but before notice of it had reached this country, the debt due from M. (he not having remitted funds to replace the money advanced) was attached in his hands, by virtue of our trustee process, by B., a citizen of the State, and a creditor of the bankrupt, the attachment was held valid as against the assignment." In the opinion in that case it is said: "By our law the service of a trustee process upon one who is indebted to the defendant in the suit creates a lien upon the debt in favor of the plaintiff in the action, so that, if he recovers judgment against the principal, he shall have execution against the trustee to the amount of the effects in his hands or the debt which he owes; and no distinction is made, in the application of this law, between citizens who may be trustees of other citizens, and those citizens who may be indebted to a person residing in a foreign country, who is indebted to citizens of the United States."

In *Baltimore & O. R. Co.* v. *May*, 25 Ohio St. 347, it was decided that, "in an action to recover money due on contract, it is a sufficient defense to show that the money sought to be recovered has been attached by process of garnishment duly issued by a court of a sister State, in an action there prosecuted against the plaintiff by his creditors, although it appear that the plaintiff and such creditors are all residents of this State."

So, where the debt was contracted where the garnishment took place, but the garnishee agreed to pay the money in another State, he was nevertheless charged. *Sturtevant* v. *Robinson*, 18 Pick. 175. See also *Leiber* v. *Union Pac. R. Co.* 49 Iowa, 688; *Mooney* v. *Union Pac. R. Co.* 60 Iowa, 346.

The concurring opinion, it seems to me, attempts to establish a rule which ignores the fact that the proceedings in garnishment in Missouri are entitled to full faith and credit as a judgment of a sister State, and that, being proceedings *in rem*, and the debt being condemned by a court having jurisdiction, the judgment cannot be contested in this State. Stewart, the creditor in the garnishment proceedings, is a resident of Missouri. The Missouri Pacific Railway Company is a corporation of Missouri. At the time of the garnishment proceedings that corporation owed money to J. W. Sharitt. Sharitt was duly served by publication. The court of Missouri had jurisdiction both of Stewart and the Railway Company, and had full authority to condemn any money owing by that Company to any of its employés, whether residents or nonresidents, if payable in Missouri. "Every country [State] may regulate as it pleases the disposition of personal property found within it, and may prefer its attaching creditor to any foreign assignee; and no authority has a right to question the determination." *Blake* v. *Williams, supra.*

This point was expressly decided in *Connor* v. *Hanover Ins. Co., supra.* The syllabus in that case is as follows: "The defendant, an insurance company under the laws of New York, but doing business also in Illinois and Michigan, became indebted to the nominal plaintiff, a resident of Michigan, for a loss under one of its policies, which loss was, after adjustment, assigned by her to the actual plaintiff, also a resident of that State. Creditors of the nominal plaintiff, citizens of Illinois, commenced suit in that State by attachment against her, and garnished the defendant there. Subsequently to the service of garnishment in Illinois, the assignee of the plaintiff began suit against the defendant in Michigan, and obtained judgment before the case in Illinois was tried. Judgment was soon afterwards had in Illinois. Held, (1) that, as a general rule, the *situs* of a debt is either at the domicil of the creditor, or at the place where it is payable; (2) that, under the laws of Illinois, suit having been first commenced there, and the courts of that State having obtained by garnishment control of the subject matter, there was no jurisdiction in the courts of Michigan."

Of course, between courts of concurrent jurisdiction, the court first acquiring jurisdiction will retain, and the other will not interfere with, it. The courts of Missouri first acquired jurisdiction of the debt or money due to Sharitt, and the courts of this State ought not to interfere in that case until the cause is finally disposed of.

If the rule is established as stated in the opinion, then the Railway Company is twice liable for the same debt,—once to Stewart, the creditor in Missouri, and then again to Sharitt, in this State. The Company has done and is doing all it can to defeat and escape any liability in the garnishment proceeding. It has appealed from the judgment of the justice of the peace of St. Louis to the Circuit Court of St. Louis County, and has notified Sharitt of the pendency of the garnishment proceedings. The Company is helpless. In Missouri, exemption is a personal privilege. The Company cannot assert the exemption for Sharitt. *Osborne* v. *Schutt, supra.*

Sharitt can alone exercise this personal privilege. If he will assert his rights in the Missouri court, the debt or money will be declared exempt. It all lies with Sharitt. Under the circumstances, ought the Company to pay twice, when the action of Sharitt will prevent any judgment against him or the Railway Company in Missouri? Ought the Railway Company to suffer a double liability because Sharitt refuses to answer in a case in which he has been served by publication, and in which he has been personally notified by the Railway Company? I think not. It is stated in one of the foregoing opinions that "the debt is really and in fact a mere chose in action, resting wholly in parol, and is of such an intangible character that it could not be actually seized by any kind of process; and it can hardly be said to have any actual *situs* anywhere." *Ante*, p. 387.

It is further stated in one of the opinions: "I think that the Missouri court has jurisdiction of Stewart, the plaintiff in the Missouri action, and of the Railway Company, the garnishee, and that any judgment or order which might be rendered or made by the Missouri court as against Stewart or the Railway Company would be valid and binding as against them." *Ante*, p. 387.

It was said by *Mr. Justice* Brewer in *Burlington & M. R. R. Co.* v. *Thompson*, 31 Kan 180, that "a mere debt is transitory, and may be enforced wherever the debtor or his property can be found; and if the creditor can enforce the collection of his debt in the courts of this State, a creditor of such creditor should have equal facilities."

I think that Sharitt, as a creditor of the Railway Company, could have enforced the collection of his debt in the courts of Missouri; and if he could have an action in that State, his creditor is entitled to equal facilities. It is not shown anywhere in the record that the debt was payable in the place or county where Sharitt performed his labor; and, if the decision is carried to its logical results, Sharitt should have brought his suit at Council Grove, or in the county where he worked, and not in Franklin County. If his debt was created in Morris County according to the decision, it was payable in Morris County; and therefore, according to the decision, he had no right to bring his action at Ottawa. This, however, is not the law. "A mere debt is transitory, and may be enforced wherever the debtor or his property can be found."

If it be decided by this court, under the facts of this case, that the Missouri court has no jurisdiction either of Sharitt, or of anything belonging to him, or of any money due to him, and that therefore the garnishment proceeding in Missouri is void as to him, then there can be no garnishment of a person in this State owing a debt to a person residing in another State. The practice among the profession is contrary to this decision. Very often persons in this State owing debts to nonresidents are garnished by the creditors of the nonresidents in this State, and the only service had on the nonresidents is by publication; being the same service had in the Missouri court upon Sharitt. §§ 28–54, pp. 702–706, Comp. Laws 1885.

Section 72 of the Civil Code of this State expressly provides, the same as the Missouri Code, that "service may be made by publication in . . . actions brought against a nonresident of this State, or a foreign corporation, having in this

State property or debts owing to them, sought to be taken by any of the provisional remedies, or to be appropriated in any way." I think, however, that this court is foreclosed by its previous decisions, and that the rule stated in the concurring opinion cannot be adopted unless the prior cases are overruled.

In *Burlington & M. R. R. Co.* v. *Thompson*, 31 Kan. 180, the railroad corporation was organized, and had its principal place of business in Nebraska, but its line extended into this State. It was garnished in the courts of this State for a debt due to one of its employés for wages, at the suit of the creditor of the employé. The employé resided in Nebraska, had earned his wages there, and those wages were exempt to him and his family by the laws of that State. No service of process was had on the principal defendant. It did not appear where the plaintiff resided. The able district judge at Atchison County (*Judge* Martin) held in that case "that under our Statute, when a railroad company incorporated under the laws of a sister State leases a line of railroad in this State, and keeps local agents, and operates its lines, within this county, it is liable to the process of a garnishment here for all indebtedness which may be owing to a defendant, although, by the usual course of its business, such indebtedness is payable at the principal office of the corporation in the sister State, the corporation, in such case, being an inhabitant of this State for the purpose of business, and the service of process upon it, and the indebtedness not being of a local character, but enforceable in any jurisdiction in which service may be had." The railroad company prosecuted its writ of error to this court, and expressly made the point "that a foreign corporation cannot be garnished in this State, as the debtor of a nonresident, for a debt contracted and payable in a foreign State, by service on a servant or on the officers of the corporation." The judgment of the trial court was affirmed. *Mr. Justice* Brewer, speaking for the court, said: "He [the plaintiff] is a citizen of Kansas, appealing only to the laws and the courts of this State for the collection of his debt, and simply denying that the laws of another State shall prevent the collection of his debt according to the laws and procedure of his own State." The syllabus states the following proposition of law: "A foreign corporation coming into this State, and leasing property and doing business here, may be garnished for a debt due to one of its employés, although such employé is not a resident of this State, and although the debt was contracted outside of the State." At the time of the rendition of this decision, the members of this court were *Mr. Justice* Valentine, *Mr. Justice* Brewer and the writer. *Mr. Justice* Brewer delivered the opinion in this case. All of the justices concurred in affirming the judgment of the trial judge.

In *Zimmerman* v. *Franke*, 34 Kan. 650, Franke was perpetually enjoined from prosecuting garnishment proceedings in Nebraska against the Missouri Pacific Railway Company by Zimmerman, who was indebted to Franke, and who had personal earnings coming to him from the railway company. Both Franke and Zimmerman resided at Atchison, in this State; but Zimmerman was an employé of the railway company, running between Kansas City and Omaha. He was the head of a family. Zimmerman was not personally served with any process in or from Nebraska, and Franke was proceeding, before the injunction, to collect his claim against Zimmerman, by garnishment in Nebraska, from the Missouri Pacific Railway Company. If the garnishment proceeding in Nebraska was without jurisdiction and void as to any debt or money coming or belonging to Zimmerman, why was this court asked to interfere with its strong arm to forbid Franke from carrying on a void and useless proceeding in Nebraska? That decision, as I understand it, was rendered upon the theory that, if Franke was permitted to prosecute his proceedings by garnishment in Nebraska, he would thereby deprive Zimmerman of his personal earnings, which were exempt under the laws of this State.

In *Stark* v. *Bare*, 39 Kan. 100, the latter was a married man, living in this State, and engaged in the service of the Atchison, Topeka & Santa Fé Railroad Company. He was indebted to Stark; and Stark, to evade the Exemption Laws of this State, sold his claim to John W. Leatherbury, of Kansas City, Mo., for the purpose of permitting Leatherbury to bring an action in Missouri, by garnishment against the railroad company, to appropriate the personal earnings due from the railroad company to Bare. This court sustained a judgment in favor of Bare against Stark upon the ground that the garnishment proceedings instituted by Leatherbury against the railroad company in Missouri deprived Stark of his personal earnings from the railroad company. This decision was also rendered upon the theory that the garnishment proceedings of Missouri deprived Bare, the employé, of the debt due from the railroad company to him in Kansas. Both of these decisions follow *Snook* v. *Snetzer*, 25 Ohio St. 516.

In *Baltimore & O. R. Co.* v. *May*, Id. 347, it was decided, as already stated, that, "in an action to recover money due on contract, it is a sufficient defense to show that the money sought to be recovered has been attached by process of garnishment, duly issued by a court of a sister State, in an action there prosecuted against the plaintiff by his creditors, although it appear that the plaintiff and such creditors are all residents of this State."

I do not think the decisions cited in the opinion and in the concurring opinion, adversely to the views herein expressed, have very much application to this case.

In the cases of *Missouri Pac. R. Co.* v. *Maltby*, 34 Kan. 131, and *Kansas City, St. J. & C. B. R. Co.* v. *Gough*, 35 Kan. 1, about all that was decided was that, where the debt of the garnishee to the defendant is by the laws of Kansas and Missouri exempt, the debt is exempt in this State from garnishment, and no distinction is to be made between residents and nonresidents.

In *Bates* v. *Chicago, M. & St. P. R. Co.*, 60 Wis. 296, a carload of hogs was attempted to be attached by garnishment. It was held in that case that "property outside of the State is not the subject of garnishment under our Statute, and that a common carrier cannot be held liable as a garnishee for goods in actual transit when the process is served."

In *Sutherland* v. *Second Nat. Bank*, 78 Ky. 250, a carload of oats was attached, and the attachment was held wrongful, because the oats were beyond the jurisdiction of the court.

In *Wheat* v. *Platte City & Ft. D. R. Co.*, 4 Kan. 370, an attempt was made to attach or garnish $300,000 of Leavenworth bonds, which were in the State of Missouri, and in the possession of the treasurer of the railroad company. Many of the other decisions cited in the concurring opinion are like these. Of course no one contests but that these are the law as to the points decided, but the *situs* of personal property, like "hogs, oats and bonds," is somewhat different to the *situs* of debts owing to employés and other persons.

In *Wright* v. *Chicago, B. & Q. R. Co.*, 19 Neb. 176, the case was very similar to *Missouri Pac. R. Co.* v. *Maltby, supra*, and disposed of the same way, that decision being fully cited and approved. Something, however, was said in that decision and in several of the other cases cited, about debts not being liable to garnishment where the corporation or person garnished is not owing the debtor money payable in the State where the proceedings are commenced. Again, some of these decisions go to the effect that debts are local, and remain at the residence of the debtor. I need not review these cases, because they do not meet the question presented as to the jurisdiction of the Missouri court, under the laws of that State, over the debt of the Railway Company due to Sharitt. They are nearly all cases where the garnishment proceedings have been commenced and disposed of in the States where the decisions have been rendered. The decisions are constructions of Garnishment Laws of the States where the decisions have been rendered. The question whether proceedings in garnishment of a sister State are entitled to full faith and credit as a judgment, where the corporation or person owing the debt has been garnished in such sister State, and service has been made by publication upon the debtor, is not discussed in but one or two, and those cases are very different from this. I think, if Sharitt had brought his action in Missouri, instead of Kansas, and the Railroad Company had not been garnished, he could have recovered his wages in that State; and, if he could have recovered his wages by an action brought there, his claim or wages could be attached or garnished there.

SOUTH DAKOTA SUPREME COURT.

E. C. HEGELER, *Appt.*,
v.
Edwin W. COMSTOCK, *Respt.*

(....S. D.....)

*1. **The term "negotiable instrument"** has a definite signification in the law-merchant, and the meaning of the term has not been changed by the Code. A negotiable instrument is one that is simple, certain and unconditional.

2. **Certainty as to the payer and payee,** the amount to be paid and the terms of payment, is an essential quality of a negotiable promissory note, and that certainty must continue until the obligation is discharged.

3. **The following is a copy of a note held to be non-negotiable:** "On or before the 1st

*Head notes by BENNETT, J.

NOTE.—*Negotiable instruments.*

A negotiable instrument must be a complete and perfect instrument when it is issued, or there must be authority reposed in someone afterwards to supply anything needed to make it perfect. Davis S. M. Co. v. Best, 7 Cent. Rep. 63, 105 N. Y. 59.

One drawing the form of a promissory note which is unsigned, and which falls into the hands of another, does not thereby authorize the holder to attach the maker's signature. *Ibid.*

The instrument must be certain as to payment in order to be negotiable. Chapman v. Wight, 5 New Eng. Rep. 787, 79 Me. 595. See *note* to Wright v. Traver (Mich.) 3 L. R. A. 50.

A note which contains other provisions than the unconditional payment of money is non-negotiable. South Bend Iron Works v. Paddock, 37 Kan. 510.

Conditions in a promissory note, other than for the payment of money only, are nugatory. Dwelling House Ins. Co. v. Hardie, 37 Kan. 674.

A bill not payable absolutely in money but which may be paid in demand bills on London, and which conditions the liability to pay on the arrival of a vessel at her destination, is not negotiable. The Lykus, 36 Fed. Rep. 919.

That an instrument may be a promissory note it must contain on its face an express promise to pay money. Hence an instrument in the following form: "I. O. U. the sum of $17.05 for value received," signed by the maker, is not a promissory note. Gay v. Rooke (Mass.) 7 L. R. A. 392.

A written instrument, wherein the maker states that there will be due to the other party a stated sum on "final settlement" of a designated transaction between them, is an expression of the obligation of the maker in the amount stated, but qualified as respects the payment, the amount not being payable at once, but chargeable against the maker upon settlement as specified. Rhodes v. Pray, 36 Minn. 392.

An instrument as follows: "Due to [a certain person] and payable when the suit now in court between him and [another] is settled," a stated sum,—is not a promissory note. Burgess v. Fairbanks, 83 Cal. 215.

Orders for delivery of oil drawn upon one holding it as bailee are not negotiable instruments. Barse v. Morton, 43 Hun, 479.

A school order is not a negotiable instrument such as to have any greater validity in the hands of a transferee than in the hands of the first holder. Shakespear v. Smith, 77 Cal. 638.

A note payable at a future day certain, or earlier, at the option of the holder, is not negotiable. Richards v. Barlow, 1 New Eng. Rep. 578, 140 Mass. 218.

To render a note unnegotiable it must show on its face that the promise to pay is conditional, and renders the amount to be paid uncertain. *Ibid.*

The lack of indorsement by the payee of a negotiable note renders it, in the hands of a third person, non-negotiable. Weber v. Ortan, 10 West. Rep. 861, 91 Mo. 677.

See also 11 L. R. A. 860; 12 L. R. A. 483.

day of December, 1884, for value received, I or we, the undersigned, living 5 miles of Howard P. O., County of Miner, Territory of Dakota, promise to pay Marsh Binder Manufacturing Company or order one hundred dollars, at the Miner County Bank, in Howard, with interest from date until paid at the rate of ten per cent per annum, eight per cent if paid when due. The indorsers, signers and guarantors severally waive presentment for payment, protest and notice of protest, and notice of nonpayment of this note, and diligence in bringing suit against any party to this note, and sureties agree that time of payment may be extended without notice or other consent. Edwin W. Comstock."

(May 12, 1890.)

APPEAL by plaintiff from a judgment of the District Court for Miner County in favor of defendant in an action to recover the amount alleged to be due on certain promissory notes. *Affirmed.*

The facts sufficiently appear in the opinion.

Mr. **D. D. Holdridge,** for appellant:

If the amount can be ascertained from the face of the paper, the form of expression is immaterial.

1 Daniel, Neg. Inst. p. 57; *Parsons* v. *Jackson*, 99 U. S. 440 (25 L. ed. 460).

The spirit of the rule requiring precision in the amount of negotiable instruments applies rather to the principal amount than to the auxiliary and incidental additions of interest or exchange.

1 Daniel, Neg. Inst. § 44.

It may be said the clause "if paid when due" brings an element of uncertainty into the note. But a note made payable "on or before" a certain date is just as uncertain, yet it is nevertheless negotiable.

Ackley School Dist. v. *Hall*, 113 U. S. 135 (28 L. ed. 954); 1 Daniel, Neg. Inst. § 48.

All the authorities sustain the negotiability of these notes unless it be the case of *Lamb* v. *Story*, 45 Mich. 488.

That case cites no authorities and is very brief, yet it is essentially different from this case, and is not against any position here taken.

Mr. **Gottleib Engel** for respondent.

Bennett, *J.*, delivered the opinion of the court:

This is an action brought by the plaintiff and appellant against the defendant and respondent upon two promissory notes. The following is a copy of said notes:

"On or before the 1st day of December, 1884, for value received, I or we, the undersigned, living five miles of Howard P. O., County of Miner, Territory of Dakota, promise to pay to Marsh Binder Manufacturing Company or order one hundred dollars, at the Miner County Bank, in Howard, with interest from date until paid at the rate of 10 per cent per annum, 8 per cent if paid when due. The indorsers, signers and guarantors severally waive presentment for payment, protest and notice of protest, and notice of nonpayment of this note, and diligence in bringing suit against any party to this note, and sureties agree that time of payment may be extended without notice or other consent.

"Edwin W. Comstock."

Upon the trial the cause was submitted to the court, sitting as a jury, upon the following agreed statement of facts: "(1) That on the 18th day of August, 1883, the defendant, Ed-

A promise in writing to pay money, upon condition that "this note is to be given up" if the sum is paid to a third person within a time specified, is not a promissory note, and is barred by the Statute of Limitations in six years. Chapman v. Wight, 5 New Eng. Rep. 787, 79 Me. 595.

A promissory note may be negotiable without expressing the time at which it will become payable. Hall v. Toby, 1 Cent. Rep. 54, 110 Pa. 318.

A note payable to bearer is negotiable as commercial paper, if it possesses the other essential requisites of such negotiable instruments. New v. Walker, 6 West. Rep. 873, 108 Ind. 365.

An instrument may be negotiable in one State which yet may be incapable of negotiability by the laws of another State; and the remedy must be in the courts of the latter, on such instrument, according to its own laws. United States Bank v. Donnally, 33 U. S. 8 Pet. 361 (8 L. ed. 974).

Requisites to negotiability. See *note* to Siegel v. Chicago Trust & Sav. Bank (Ill.) 7 L. R. A. 537.

Stipulations and agreements which destroy negotiability.

An ordinary promissory note with an added stipulation that "this note is given for part payment of rent of certain pasture fields, and is not to be paid unless I have the use of said premises, in accordance with a certain lease and agreement,"—is not negotiable. Jennings v. Colorado Springs First Nat. Bank, 13 Colo. 417.

A promissory note, on the face of which, across one end, is written an agreement that the note will be renewed at maturity, is not negotiable. Citizens Nat. Bank v. Piollet, 4 L. R. A. 190, 126 Pa. 194.

An additional agreement in a promissory note, that the holder may sell certain collateral securities and apply the proceeds in payment, and that the maker will pay any deficiency that may exist forthwith, makes the instrument non-negotiable because of the uncertainty as to the sum payable and the time of payment. Continental Nat. Bank v. Wells, 73 Wis. 332.

A clause in a note binding the maker to pay exchange between two places renders the amount payable uncertain and defeats its negotiability, where there is no fixed rate of exchange established by law or by the terms of the note. Windsor Sav. Bank v. McMahon, 3 L. R. A. 192, 38 Fed. Rep. 283.

To render a note negotiable under the law-merchant, the amount to be paid at maturity must be ascertainable by the face of the note without resort to evidence *dehors* the instrument. *Ibid.*

A condition in a promissory note, that if it is not paid when due the property described therein for which it is given shall belong to the payee, destroys the character of the instrument as a promissory note, and reduces it to a mere contract. See *note* to Wright v. Traver (Mich.) 3 L. R. A. 50.

A provision in a note for a percentage of the amount due as attorney's fees destroys its negotiability. Adams v. Seaman (Cal.) 7 L. R. A. 224.

A provision in a note for a percentage of the amount due, as attorney's fees "on suit by himself or an attorney employed," destroys its negotiability, under Cal. Civ. Code, § 3088, providing that "negotiable instruments must be without any condition not certain of fulfillment." *Ibid.*

A statement or recital in a note that it is given for the privilege of hanging advertising signs in street cars for three months from a certain subsequent date will not destroy its negotiability. Siegel v. Chicago Trust & Sav. Bank (Ill.) 7 L. R. A. 537.

win W. Comstock, made, executed and delivered to the Marsh Binder Manufacturing Company or order his two certain promissory notes of $100 each. A copy of said notes is set out in the complaint hereto attached. (2) That said notes were given in part payment for a machine. That said machine was warranted by said company, and that said Comstock purchased said machine on the faith of said warranty, and the consideration for said notes wholly failed. That the said defendant had a good and sufficient defense to said notes in the original parties' hands. (3) That on the 9th day of November, 1888, the Marsh Binder Manufacturing Company borrowed of the plaintiff, E. C. Hegeler, the sum of $22,500. That to secure the payment of said sum of money so borrowed the said company, on the 9th day of November, 1888, the same day the said sum was so borrowed, transferred to the plaintiff, E. C. Hegeler, a large number of notes, amounting to about $30,000, and among the notes so transferred were the above-described notes. (4) That said notes were so transferred as above stated before they were due, and that the plaintiff had no notice of any defense to the same, but received them in perfect good faith. (5) That at the time of the transfer above mentioned, the Marsh Binder Manufacturing Company properly indorsed said notes to the plaintiff. (6) That at the commencement of this action several thousand dollars of the $22,500 borrowed by the Marsh Binder Manufacturing Company of the plaintiff, E. C. Hegeler, as before stated, and for which the above-described notes were taken as security, was still unpaid. (7) That at the commencement of this action the said notes were the property of the plaintiff, due and unpaid. (8) That at the commencement of this action, to wit, February 11, 1888, there was due on both of the above-described notes the sum of $290.80."

The following were the stipulations entered into by the parties as to the legal questions involved in said action, to wit: "(1) Whether the plaintiff, under the above statement, was a bona fide holder. (2) Whether said notes are negotiable instruments so as to cut off in the hands of said plaintiff, procured by him as above stated, all defenses that might have been set up and proven between the original parties to the notes."

Upon the hearing the court found the following conclusions of law: "(1) That said notes are not negotiable instruments, and that said defendant is entitled to prove any defense to said notes that he could have proven in an action between the original parties to said instruments. (2) That the defendant has a good and valid defense against said notes, and to the whole thereof, and is entitled to a judgment of dismissal of plaintiff's action, and for costs,"—and rendered a judgment dismissing the plaintiff's complaint, and that the defendant recover of said plaintiff the costs and disbursements of this action.

Whereupon the plaintiff perfects his appeal, and makes the following assignment of errors: "(1) The court erred in finding that said notes were not negotiable. (2) The court erred in finding that the defendant is entitled to prove any defense to said notes that he could have proven in an action between the original parties to said instruments. (3) The court erred in finding that the plaintiff, under the statement and stipulation of the parties, was not a bona fide holder. (4) The court erred in finding that the defendant has a good and valid defense against said notes, and that defendant is entitled to a dismissal of plaintiff's action. (5) The judgment is erroneous, and against law."

By stipulation of the parties, and the assignment of errors, the only legal questions involved in this action are these: *First.* Are the written instruments sued upon negotiable notes? *Second.* Is the plaintiff a bona fide holder of the same? It is claimed that the following clause renders these notes non-negotiable: "With interest from date until paid, at the rate of 10 per cent, 8 per cent if paid when due."

1. Are said instruments negotiable? The statutes of Dakota, independent of the common law and decisions of state courts, define negotiable instruments and settle their ingredients. We quote from Compiled Laws: "Sec. 4456. A negotiable instrument is a written promise or request for the payment of a certain sum of money to order, or bearer, in conformity to the provisions of this article. Sec. 4457. A negotiable instrument must be made payable in money only, and without any condition not certain of fulfillment." "Sec. 4462. A negotiable instrument must not contain any other contract than such as is specified in this article."

The term "negotiable instrument" has a definite signification in the law-merchant, and the meaning of the term has not been changed by the Code. The principal importance which is to be attached to the question of negotiability arises from the rule of law which subjects all non-negotiable bills and notes to any equities which may exist between prior parties, even when they are transferred before due to a bona fide purchaser for value. A negotiable instrument is one that is simple, certain and unconditional.

Lord Ellenborough, in *Smith* v. *Nightingale*, 2 Starkie, 375, held that an instrument wherein the promise "to pay J. S. the sum of sixty-five pounds, with lawful interest for the same, and all other sums which should be due him," was not a promissory note. Byles, Bills, 147.

Lord Kenyon, in *Carlos* v. *Fancourt*, 5 T. R. 485, observed: "It would perplex the commercial transactions of mankind, if paper securities of this kind were issued out into the world incumbered with conditions and contingencies, and if the persons to whom they were offered in negotiation were obliged to inquire when these uncertain events would probably be reduced to a certainty."

In *Ayrey* v. *Fearnsides*, 4 Mees. & W. 168, Parke, *B.*, held that the words "and all fines according to rule" destroy the negotiability.

In *Thompson* v. *Sloan*, 23 Wend. 71, the court held that a promise to pay a certain sum in Canada money is not negotiable.

In the case of *Jones* v. *Radatz*, 27 Minn. 240, the Supreme Court of Minnesota held the following not a negotiable promissory note:

$135. P. O. St. Paul, County of Ramsey, State of Minnesota, September 7, 1878.

Three months after date we, or either of us, promise to pay to H. K. White & Co. or bearers $135, payable at the Second National Bank of St. Paul, Minnesota, for value received, with 12 per cent interest per annum from date, and reasonable attorney's fees, if suit be instituted for the collection of this note. ————.

Chief Justice Gilfillan, in this case, said: "The instrument before us has this certainty as to the $135 and the interest. But the whole instrument must be taken together. The promise to pay the $135, and interest, is not the whole of the promise, not the entire obligation created. The entire promise and obligation is to pay absolutely that sum, and interest, and in a particular contingency, to wit, the bringing suit by the payee after default, to pay a further amount not fixed, and not capable of being ascertained from the instrument itself."

The Supreme Court of Pennsylvania, in the case of *Woods* v. *North*, 84 Pa. 407, held the following instrument to be a non-negotiable promissory note:

$377. Huntington, Pa., May 5th, 1875.

Sixty days after date I promise to pay to the order of W. H. Woods, at the Union Bank of Huntington, three hundred and seventy-seven dollars, and five per cent collection fee, if not paid when due, without defalcation, value received. Samuel Steffey.

Indorsed: W. H. Woods.

In this case *Justice* Sharswood said: "In the paper now in question there enters as to the amount, an undoubted element of uncertainty. . . . If this collateral agreement may be introduced with impunity, what may not be? It is the first step in the wrong direction which costs. These instruments may come to be lumbered up with all sorts of stipulations, and all sorts of difficulties, contentions and litigation result."

In *Cayuga County Nat. Bank* v. *Purdy*, 56 Mich. 6, the supreme court decided that the following was not a negotiable promissory note:

$366.66. Coldwater, Mich., Feb. 27, 1883.

On the 1st day of November, 1883, we the undersigned, whose postoffice address is Algansee, County of Branch, and State of Michigan, jointly and severally, for value received, promise to pay E. M. Birdsall & Company or order three hundred and sixty six 66-100 dollars, with interest at 7 per cent per annum if paid when due; if not so paid, then the interest shall be 10 per cent per annum from date. We also agree to pay exchange and all expenses, including attorney's fee incurred in collecting, payable at the First National Bank in Coldwater, Mich. We do hereby relinquish and waive the benefit of all laws exempting real and personal property from levy and sale, and all benefit or relief from valuation and appraisement laws.

George R. Purdy,
Elnathan George.

Mr. Justice Champlin in this case says: "The modern tendency to interpolate into such instruments, engagements and stipulations not recognized by the law-merchant, affecting the certainty as to the amount due and payable thereon, or the time of maturity, . . . should be discountenanced and held to destroy their negotiability and deprive them of the character of promissory notes, and they should be relegated to the domain of ordinary contracts."

In the case of *Altman* v. *Rittershofer*, 68 Mich. 287, 12 West. Rep. 581, the note before the court was as follows:

$130. Bay City, Michigan, October 17, 1885.

Six months after date I promise to pay to the order of M. Cohn one hundred and thirty dollars, at the Bay National Bank of Bay City, Michigan, for value received, without any relief whatever from valuation or appraisement laws, with eight per cent interest from date until paid, and attorney fees.

Frederick Rittershofer.

Indorsed: M. Cohn.

Mr. Justice Long, in delivering the opinion, says: "A promissory note is an unconditional written promise, signed by the maker, to pay absolutely and at all events a sum certain in money, either to the bearer, or to a person therein designated, or his order. The only question upon the negotiability of this instrument is whether the words 'and attorney's fees,' added thereto, renders the sum to be paid uncertain. . . . The better reasoning in my judgment, holds such instruments non-negotiable."

In *Bank of Carroll* v. *Taylor*, 67 Iowa, 572, the instrument sued on was as follows:

$40.00. Coon Rapids, Iowa, 5-4-1881.

On the twenty-fifth day of December, 1881, for value received, I promise to pay J. W. Stoddard or bearer forty dollars with interest, at ten per cent payable annually from date until paid, and ten per cent is to be added to the amount if this note remains unpaid after maturity, and is collected by suit. For the consideration mentioned above, the undersigned hereby sells and conveys to J. W. Stoddard the following property: one Triumph Drill No. ——, upon condition, however, that if this note and mortgage shall be paid on or before the maturity thereof, then this mortgage to be void, otherwise in full force; and it is further agreed that in case of failure to pay the amount due thereon at maturity, or whenever the holder hereof may deem himself insecure, then he may take said property by virtue of this mortgage, and sell the same at public auction as by law provided; the proceeds of said sale, after deducting all expenses, to be applied on this note and mortgage, the residue, if any, to be returned to the undersigned.

Justice Reed, of the Supreme Court of Iowa, in deciding the case, says: "The question presented is whether these [this] instruments are [is] negotiable. Certainty as to the payer and payee, the amount to be paid and the time of payment, is an essential quality of a negotiable promissory note. The first provision of the instruments in suit is an undertaking by the maker to pay to the person named as payee, or to bearer, a specified sum of money, with interest thereon, at a certain date. This provision, standing alone, contains all the elements of negotiability. If the instruments are not negotiable, then it is because the undertaking of the maker is qualified, and some element of uncertainty in these respects is created by the subsequent provision. By this subsequent provision of the contract a mortgage of certain personal property for the security of the debt, evidenced by the preceding provision, is created. It does not by any express terms modify the undertaking of the maker in the preceding provision, either as to the amount which is to be paid, the time of payment or the person to whom it is to be made. But it is contended that as it confers upon the payee or the holder of the instrument the right to take possession of the mortgaged property and, as is claimed, sell it, even before the maturity of the debt, and apply the proceeds in satisfaction thereof, it has the effect to render the instrument uncertain as to the amount which may be recovered upon it at maturity. . . . In determining the effect of the instruments both conditions must be considered, and when they are considered together we think that while they empower the holder to take possession of the mortgaged property before the maturity of the debt, if he deemed himself insecure, they did not empower him to sell it until after its maturity. . . . The debt evidenced by the instruments was not subject to be diminished before its maturity, and there is no uncertainty as to the amount to be recovered thereon at maturity. The fact that by these terms a mortgage is created by which the debt is secured, and under which payment in whole or in part may be enforced after maturity, does not; in our opinion, affect the question whether or not the instruments are negotiable. They possess all the elements of negotiability."

In the case of *Second Nat. Bank* v. *Wheeler*, 75 Mich. 546, the instrument sued on was as follows:

$150. Richmond, Ind., July 22, 1886.

On or before the 1st day of November, 1887, the subscribers, of Alamo Postoffice, Kalamazoo County, State of Michigan, jointly and severally promise to pay to the Incorporated Company of Gaar, Scott & Co. or order, one hundred and fifty dollars, payable at Kalamazoo National Bank, with 7% interest from date, and 10% after date, and 5% attorney's fees, without relief from homestead, valuation or appraisement laws, for value received. The makers and indorsers of this note hereby severally waive presentment for payment, protest and notice of payment and nonpayment; and the payee or holder of this note may renew or extend the time of payment of the same from time to time, as often as required, without notice and without prejudice to the rights of such payee or holder to enforce payment against the makers, sureties and indorsers, and each of them, parties hereto, at any time when the same may be due and payable.

The instrument called a "note," and the chattel mortgage given to secure the payment of the same, were assigned to the plaintiffs before the time of payment named therein. They were shown to be innocent purchasers for value, in the regular course of business. The court held the instrument to be not a negotiable promissory note, and cited the following cases as authority: *Lamb* v. *Story*, 45 Mich. 488; *Cayuga County Nat. Bank* v. *Purdy*, 56 Mich. 6; *First Nat. Bank* v. *Carson*, 60 Mich. 432; *Altman* v. *Rittershofer*, 68 Mich. 287, 12 West. Rep. 581; *Altman* v. *Fowler*, 70 Mich. 57, 14 West. Rep. 77,—and that the same defenses were therefore open to defendant as if suit had been brought by Gaar, Scott & Co.

In *Lamb* v. *Story*, 45 Mich. 488, the action was founded on an instrument payable on or before two years, with interest at 10 per cent, and contained a clause that if paid within one year it would not draw interest. The court says: "We are of opinion that the instrument sued upon cannot be considered a negotiable promissory note. While it is made payable on or before two years, with 10 per cent interest, and is thus far definite and certain, yet the subsequent clause, that, if paid within one year, it shall not draw interest, destroys the element of certainty which otherwise would exist."

In *First Nat. Bank* v. *Bynum*, 84 N. C. 24, the counsel fees and expenses of collection were promised, but were left uncertain, and the time of payment, which is also important, was left to the option of the payee. There the note was held non-negotiable.

In *First Nat. Bank* v. *Larsen*, 60 Wis. 206, it is decided squarely for the defendant that a provision for the payment of 10 per cent attorney's fees for collection destroys the negotiability of the note; and this decision is placed upon the authority of the opinion of *Mr. Justice* Sharswood, in *Woods* v. *North*, 84 Pa. 407, and of *Maryland F. & Mfg. Co.* v. *Newman*, 60 Md. 584.

A promissory note, or note of hand, as it is often called, is an open promise in writing by one person to pay another person, or to his order, or bearer, a specified sum of money, absolutely and at all events. 1 Daniel, Neg. Inst. § 28.

"In order to fulfill the definition given, the paper must carry its full history on its face, and embrace the following requisites: *first*, it must be open, that is unsealed; *second*, the engagement to pay must be certain; *third*, the fact of payment must be certain; *fourth*, the amount to be paid must be certain; *fifth*, the medium of payment must be money; *sixth*, the contract must be only for the payment of money; and, *seventh*, it is essential to the operation of the instrument that it should be delivered." Id. § 30.

To constitute an instrument negotiable as a promissory note, the maker's liability must be absolute and unconditioned for the payment of a definite sum of money. *Bank of Carroll* v. *Taylor*, 67 Iowa, 572; *Merchants Nat. Bank* v. *Chicago R. Equip. Co.* 25 Fed. Rep. 809; *Hall* v. *Toby*, 110 Pa. 318, 1 Cent. Rep. 54; *McComas* v. *Haas*, 107 Ind. 512, 5 West. Rep. 689; *First Nat. Bank* v. *Carson*, 60 Mich. 432; *Grimison* v. *Russell*, 14 Neb. 521; *Edwards* v. *Ramsey*, 30 Minn. 91; *Smith* v. *Marland*, 59 Iowa, 645; *Miller* v. *Poage*, 56 Iowa, 96; *Third Nat. Bank* v. *Armstrong*, 25 Minn. 530.

Judge Brewer, of the United States Circuit Court for the Eastern District of Missouri, in the case of *Hughitt* v. *Johnson*, 28 Fed. Rep. 865, held that a note otherwise negotiable is rendered non-negotiable by this stipulation in it, viz., a promise to pay "with interest and exchange," and says: "This stipulation renders uncertain the amount to be paid at the maturity of the paper. It is interest and exchange, and what that exchange will be no one can tell."

By a careful review of these cases it seems that the basis of the decision is that of uncertainty in the amount to be recovered. In most of them, if not all, it is not sufficient that the amount necessary to liquidate the note on the day when due is certain, and can be determined, but that certainty must continue till the obligation is discharged.

In the case of *Jones* v. *Radatz*, above cited, the court uses the following language, viz.: "We think the certainty requisite to the negotiablity of the instrument must continue until the obligation is discharged, and that any provision which before that time removes such certainty prevents the instrument being negotiable at all." The same principle is enunciated by the Supreme Court of Michigan, in the case of *Lamb* v. *Story*, 45 Mich. 488.

The Supreme Court of the Territory of Dakota, in *Garretson* v. *Purdy*, 3 Dak. 178, arrived at the same conclusion, not only on account of the uncertainty of such an instrument, but also on account of the lack of the simplicity required by our statute law in relation to negotiable instruments. Applying the principles above cited, are the instruments in question sufficiently simple, certain and unconditional to constitute them negotiable under the Statutes? Are they certain as to intent? The rate of interest is not only uncertain, but depends upon the contingency of prompt or not prompt payment. The instruments must be construed either as meaning: *first*, that they shall bear 10 per cent interest, but if paid promptly when due, only 8 per cent; *second*, that they shall bear 8 per cent interest, but if not paid promptly when due, 10 per cent. There is no certainty until after due as to the amount that will discharge the instruments, the amount depending upon the fact whether paid then or not. This element of uncertainty, not conforming to one of the essential requisites of a negotiable instrument, renders them non-negotiable. Our Code has defined a negotiable instrument to be a written promise or request for the payment of a certain sum of money to order or bearer, made payable in money only, and without any condition not certain of fulfillment, and it must contain no other contract. The design of the Statute is to keep negotiable promissory notes clearly confined within the limits of such paper as required by the law-merchant, and allowing no outside agreement or collateral understandings to enter into the main promise. Otherwise these instruments may be lumbered up with all sorts of stipulations which do not properly belong to promissory notes, but to written contracts. Taking both facts into consideration, we must hold the instrument upon which this action was founded as non-negotiable, and *the judgment of the court below is affirmed.*

Kellam, *J.*:

I concur in the decision of this case because the predecessor of this court, in *Garretson* v. *Purdy*, 3 Dak. 178, adopted a principle and rule which is probably controlling as to the negotiability of the instrument before us. If the question were a new one in this court, I should dissent from the doctrine that the certainty as to the amount represented by a promissory note must be a certainty, continuing until the obligation is discharged, either by payment or by the Statute of Limitations. So far as negotiability means the quality of being transferable by delivery, freed from adverse equities,—and as a rule that is now the practical difference between negotiable and non-negotiable paper,—that quality is lost in passing the line of maturity. The immunity which comes with and attends negotiability is withdrawn the moment the instrument crosses the threshold of dishonor. If certainty is required as a condition of negotiability, I can see no good reason for holding that the certainty must be one which will still exist after the instrument has lost all the incidents and advantages of negotiability. I believe that if the amount of money which the instrument represents at its maturity, and which will then be required to discharge it, is plainly apparent on its face, it is all the certainty, in that respect, contemplated by the rule of the law-merchant or by our Code, defining negotiable instruments, and that the courts ought so to hold. I concur in the decision of this case only under the rule of *stare decisis.*

NEBRASKA SUPREME COURT.

Re Bertie ROBINSON.

(.....Neb.....)

***When a person is arrested in a sister State,** and without being extradited is forcibly brought into the jurisdiction of this State to answer to a criminal offense, and is committed to jail to await trial on such charge,—*Held*, that such person is unlawfully deprived of his liberty, and is entitled to be discharged on habeas corpus.

(March 11, 1890.)

PETITION for a writ of habeas corpus to inquire into the cause for the detention of petitioner in custody and to procure his discharge therefrom. *Petitioner discharged.*

The case sufficiently appears in the opinion.

Messrs. **McClure & Anderson, W. K. Brown** and **Joseph R. Webster** for petitioner.

Mr. **A. Y. Wright** for respondent.

Norval, *J.*, delivered the opinion of the court:

A petition was filed in this court on the 6th day of February, 1890, on behalf of Bertie Robinson for a writ of habeas corpus. It appears from the petition and evidence that a complaint in writing was made before the county judge of Furnas County, on September

*Head note by NORVAL, J.

10, 1889, charging the petitioner with stealing a horse, the property of one Ira B. Huff, and that on the 24th day of the same month one E. M. Matson filed a complaint before a justice of the peace of Sherman County, Kan., charging the petitioner with stealing, in said Furnas County, the aforesaid horse. The said justice issued a warrant for the arrest of said petitioner, who was afterwards arrested and taken before said justice of the peace. On motion of the county attorney the prosecution was dismissed. Robinson was, by order of said justice, delivered to the custody of said Matson, a constable of Red Willow County, Neb., who forcibly, and against the will and consent of Robinson, and without any warrant, requisition or other legal process, conveyed said Robinson out of the State of Kansas into the State of Nebraska, where he delivered said Robinson up to the sheriff of Furnas County for prosecution for said crime. The petitioner was taken before the county judge of said Furnas County, who held the petitioner to the district court of said county to answer said charge, and, in default of bail, said petitioner was committed to the jail of said county, where he has ever since been deprived of his liberty by the respondent, as sheriff of said county. On the 9th day of December, 1889, an information was filed in said district court, charging said Robinson with the crime of horse stealing. On the following day, on being arraigned in said court, he pleaded not guilty to said charge, and on the same day he prayed said district court to discharge him from custody, because he was arrested in the State of Kansas, and was brought forcibly, and without any requisition, into this State, and delivered to the sheriff of said county to answer said accusation. The motion was overruled, and an exception was entered. On the 11th day of December Robinson was tried for said crime in said district court, and, the jury failing to agree upon a verdict, it was discharged, and Robinson was remanded to the custody of the respondent, to await further trial.

But a single question is presented for our consideration, and that is whether or not, under the foregoing facts, the District Court of Furnas County had jurisdiction of the person of the petitioner in the criminal case pending therein against him. We think the answer should be in the negative. There can be no doubt that jurisdiction cannot be acquired in a civil case when the summons is served upon a defendant who was brought into the jurisdiction of the court by force, fraud or deceit, for the purpose of obtaining service of summons upon him. *Wanzer* v. *Bright*, 52 Ill. 35; *Williams* v. *Reed*, 29 N. J. L. 385; *Dunlap* v. *Cody*, 31 Iowa, 260; *Van Horn* v. *Great Western Mfg. Co.* 37 Kan. 523; *Townsend* v. *Smith*, 47 Wis. 623; *Allen* v. *Miller*, 11 Ohio St. 374; *Compton* v. *Wilder*, 40 Ohio St. 130.

The same rule obtains in criminal prosecutions. Nearly the entire current of authority in this country is to the effect that, when a fugitive from justice has been extradited from one State to another, he cannot be prosecuted in the State to which he has been surrendered on an offense other than the one for which he was extradited, before he has had an opportunity to return to the State from whence he was brought. *Re Cannon*, 47 Mich. 481; *State* v. *Vanderpool*, 39 Ohio St. 273; *Ex parte Hibbs*, 26 Fed. Rep. 421; *United States* v. *Rauscher*, 119 U. S. 407 [30 L. ed. 425]; *State* v. *Hall*, 40 Kan. 338; *W[illegible]terman* v. *State*, 116 Ind. 51, 15 West. Rep. 545.

In principle there is no difference between the case at bar and where a person is held for an offense other than the one he was extradited for. In either case it is an abuse of judicial process, which the law does not allow. Ample provisions are made for the arrest and return of a person accused of crime, who has fled to a sister State, by extradition warrants issued by the executives of the States. There is no excuse for a citizen or officer arresting, without authority of law, a fugitive, and taking him forcibly, and against his will, into the jurisdiction of the State for the purpose of prosecution.

We cannot sanction the method adopted to bring the petitioner into the jurisdiction of this State. He did not come into the State voluntarily, but because he could not avoid it. The district court, therefore, did not acquire jurisdiction of the person of the petitioner, and his detention is unlawful. *State* v. *Simmons*, 39 Kan. 262; *State* v. *Hall*, 40 Kan. 338; *Re Cannon*, 47 Mich. 481.

While many authorities hold to the contrary doctrine, we prefer to adopt the rule that seems to be based upon reason, and which recognizes honesty and fair dealing.

The prisoner will be discharged. Judgment accordingly.

The other Judges concur.

MASSACHUSETTS SUPREME JUDICIAL COURT.

MURDOCK PARLOR GRATE CO.
v.
COMMONWEALTH OF MASSACHUSETTS.

(......Mass.......)

An action to recover damages for injuries resulting from the negligence of a servant of the Commonwealth in the performance of his duties is not a claim within the meaning of Acts 1887, chap. 246, which authorizes the maintenance of a suit against the Commonwealth to recover "all claims" against it whether at law or in equity.

(June 20, 1890.)

REPORT from the Superior Court for Suffolk County of a suit to recover damages

---

NOTE.—*State not liable for negligence of its servants or agents.*

No action or claim on behalf of a citizen can be maintained against the State for injuries occasioned by the negligence or misfeasance of its agents except where it has by voluntary legislative enactment assumed such liability. Lewis v. State, 96 N. Y. 71; State v. Hill, 54 Ala. 67; Ray v. Bentley, 49

See also 43 L. R. A. 703.

for injuries alleged to have resulted from the negligence of defendant's servant. *Petition dismissed.*

The case sufficiently appears in the opinion.

Mr. **Frederick D. Ely**, for plaintiff:

The Commonwealth can by its own consent, clearly manifested by Act of the Legislature, be impleaded in its own courts.

Troy & G. R. Co. v. *Com.* 127 Mass. 43; *Wesson* v. *Com.* 3 New Eng. Rep. 778, 144 Mass. 60; *Milford* v. *Com.* 3 New Eng. Rep. 781, 144 Mass. 64; *Green* v. *State*, 73 Cal. 29; *Bowen* v. *State*, 10 Cent. Rep. 517, 108 N. Y. 166; *Splittorf* v. *State*, 10 Cent. Rep. 699, 108 N. Y. 205.

Such an Act is Stat. 1887, chap. 246, and it extends to the cause of action alleged in plaintiff's petition.

In legislative Acts, the natural import of words according to their common use, when applied to the subject matter of the Act, is to be considered as expressing the intention of the Legislature.

Hittinger v. *Westford*, 135 Mass. 258.

The natural import of the words, "all claims against the Commonwealth whether at law or in equity," is to embrace actions of tort as well as contract.

Prigg v. *Pennsylvania*, 41 U. S. 16 Pet. 615 (10 L. ed. 1089); *Fordyce* v. *Godman*, 20 Ohio, 1, 15.

The title of Stat. 1887, chap. 246, cannot be held to qualify the words "all claims whether at law or in equity."

The title of an Act does not constitute a part of the Act.

Charles River Bridge v *Warren Bridge*, 7 Pick. 345; *Parker* v. *Barnard*, 135 Mass. 116.

If the Commonwealth uses property owned or leased by it in such a manner as to materially injure the property of a citizen, it is bound in justice to make compensation.

Thurston v. *Hancock*, 12 Mass. 220; *Mears* v. *Dole*, 135 Mass. 508.

Stat. 1887, chap. 246, is wise and prudent legislation. It is not the first Statute by which a State has allowed itself to be impleaded in an action of tort.

N. Y. Stat. 1870, chap. 321; *Sipple* v. *State*, 99 N. Y. 284; *Bowen* v. *State*, 10 Cent. Rep. 517, 108 N. Y. 166; *Splittorf* v. *State*, 10 Cent. Rep. 699, 108 N. Y. 205.

Messrs. **A. J. Waterman**, *Atty-Gen.*, and **H. C. Bliss**, *Asst. Atty-Gen.*, for defendant:

The derogation of the sovereign powers of a State by an Act of Legislature is not to be assumed.

Gilman v. *Sheboygan*, 67 U. S. 2 Black, 510 (17 L. ed. 304).

Statutes granting special privileges are to be construed strictly, and whatever is not given in unequivocal terms is withheld.

Moran v. *Miami County*, 67 U. S. 2 Black, 722 (17 L. ed. 342).

Statutes which strip a government of any portion of its prerogative, or give of its prerogative, should receive a strict interpretation.

Academy of Fine Arts v. *Philadelphia County*, 22 Pa. 496.

Statutes made in derogation of the common law are to be strictly construed.

Melody v. *Read*, 4 Mass. 471; *Gibson* v. *Jenney*, 15 Mass. 205; *Com.* v. *Knapp*, 9 Pick. 496, *Wilbur* v. *Crane*, 13 Pick. 284; *Lock* v. *Miller*, 3 Stew. & P. (Ala.) 13; *Dwelly* v. *Dwelly*, 46 Me. 377; *Burnside* v. *Whitney*, 21 N. Y. 148; *Sullivan* v. *La Crosse & M. S. Packet Co.* 10 Minn. 386; *Smith* v. *Moffat*, 1 Barb. 65; *Young* v. *McKenzie*, 3 Ga. 31; *Schuyler County* v. *Mercer County*, 9 Ill. 20; *Millered* v. *Lake Ontario, A. & N. Y. R. Co.* 9 How. Pr. 238; *Bailey* v. *Bryan*, 3 Jones, L. (N. C.) 357; *Esterley's App.* 54 Pa. 192; *Rose* v. *Governor*, 24 Tex. 496; *Hearn* v. *Ewin*, 3 Coldw. 399; *Souter* v. *The Sea Witch*, 1 Cal. 162.

Where a limited jurisdiction is given by statute the Act should be construed strictly as

---

Ala. 236; People v. Russell, 4 Wend. 570; Seymour v. Van Slyck, 8 Wend. 403; Clark v. State, 7 Coldw. 306; Clodfelter v. State, 86 N. C. 51; United States v. Kirkpatrick, 22 U. S. 9 Wheat. 720 (6 L. ed. 199); United States v. VanZandt, 24 U. S. 11 Wheat. 186 (6 L. ed. 449); United States v. Nicholl, 25 U. S. 12 Wheat. 505 (6 L. ed. 709); Dox v. Postmaster-General, 26 U. S. 1 Pet. 317 (7 L. ed. 160); Gibbons v. United States, 75 U. S. 8 Wall. 269 (19 L. ed. 453); Story, Ag. 3d ed. § 319.

A State cannot be sued without its consent. Board of Liquidation v. McComb, 92 U. S. 531 (23 L. ed. 623); Nathan v. Virginia, 1 U. S. 1 Dall. 77 (1 L. ed. 44); Briscoe v. Bank of Kentucky, 36 U. S. 11 Pet. 257 (9 L. ed. 709); Curran v. Arkansas, 56 U. S. 15 How. 304 (14 L. ed. 705); Beers v. Arkansas, 61 U. S. 20 How. 527 (15 L. ed. 991); Memphis & C. R. Co. v. Tennessee, 101 U. S. 337 (25 L. ed. 960).

Neither a State nor the United States can be sued as defendant in any court in this country without their consent, except in the limited class of cases in which a State may be made a party in the Supreme Court of the United States by virtue of the original jurisdiction conferred on this court by the Constitution. Cunningham v. Macon & B. R. Co. 109 U. S. 446 (27 L. ed. 992).

Parties cannot sue the State except for the causes of action prescribed by the Constitution or statute. Baltzer v. State, 104 N. C. 265.

The State can only be sued with its own consent, and for liabilities which it chooses to assume. Rexford v. State, 7 Cent. Rep. 762, 105 N. Y. 229.

A State cannot be sued by a citizen of another State or of a foreign state. Hans v. Louisiana, 134 U. S. 1 (33 L. ed. 842).

A State cannot be sued in a circuit court of the United States by one of its own citizens, upon the ground that the case is one that arises under the Constitution or laws of the United States. *Ibid.*; North Carolina v. Temple, 134 U. S. 22 (33 L. ed. 849).

A State may be sued by its own consent. It may, if it thinks proper, waive its privilege and permit itself to be made a defendant in a suit by individuals or by another State. Hans v. Louisiana and Beers v. Arkansas, *supra*; Clark v. Barnard, 108 U. S. 436 (27 L. ed. 780).

The sovereignty may prescribe the terms and conditions on which it consents to be sued, and the manner in which the suit shall be conducted, and may withdraw its consent whenever justice to the public requires it. Beers v. Arkansas, *supra*.

In exercising this latter power, the State violates no contract with the parties; it merely regulates the proceedings in its own courts. *Ibid.*

The supreme court of a State having decided that, in a certain case, that State was liable to suit, this court in the same case follows that decision. Curran v. Arkansas, *supra*.

The appearance of a State in a court of the United States is a voluntary submission to its jurisdiction. Clark v. Barnard, *supra*.

Under the Articles of Confederation, a State could be sued only in cases of boundary. Briscoe v. Bank of Kentucky, 36 U. S. 11 Pet. 257 (9 L. ed. 709).

to the extent of the jurisdiction, but liberally as to the mode of proceeding.

Russell v. *Wheeler*, 1 Hemp. 8. See *Stevens* v. *Ross*, 1 Cal. 94; *Walker* v. *Wynne*, 3 Yerg. 62; *Wakefield* v. *State*, 5 Ind. 195; *O'Brian* v. *State*, 12 Ind. 369.

In the cases where it has been sought to hold towns and cities liable for the injuries resulting generally from the negligence of its agents and officers the law has been strictly construed in favor of the immunity of towns and cities from such liabilities.

Dunbar v. *Boston*, 112 Mass. 75; *Hill* v. *Boston*, 122 Mass. 344; *Waldron* v. *Haverhill*, 3 New Eng. Rep. 683, 143 Mass. 582; *Morrison* v. *Lawrence*, 98 Mass. 219; *Hawk* v. *Charlemont*, 107 Mass. 414; *Sullivan* v. *Boston*, 126 Mass. 540; *Hafford* v. *New Bedford*, 16 Gray, 297; *Buttrick* v. *Lowell*, 1 Allen, 172; *Rossire* v. *Boston*, 4 Allen, 57; *Wesson* v. *Com.* 3 New Eng. Rep. 778, 144 Mass. 60; *Wild* v. *Patterson*, 1 Cent. Rep. 190, 47 N. J. L. 406; *Walsh* v. *New York*, 41 Hun, 299; *Sussex County* v. *Strader*, 18 N. J. L. 108; *Niles Highway Comrs.* v. *Martin*, 4 Mich. 557; *Hamilton County* v. *Mighels*, 7 Ohio, 109; *Eastman* v. *Meredith*, 36 N. H. 384; *Hill* v. *Boston*, 122 Mass. 344; *Bigelow* v. *Randolph*, 14 Gray, 541; *White* v. *Phillipston*, 10 Met. 108; *Sawyer* v. *Northfield*, 7 Cush. 490.

Devens, *J.*, delivered the opinion of the court:

The question presented by the report in the case at bar is whether, on a petition brought by the plaintiff in the superior court, the Commonwealth is responsible, under Pub. Stat., chap. 195, as enlarged by Acts of 1887, chap. 246, for a tort committed by its servants by negligent management and overloading the floor of an apartment which had been hired by the Commonwealth, by which injury was done to another tenant who was in occupation at another apartment in the same building. The Commonwealth can be sued in its own courts undoubtedly where clear statutory authority for that purpose has been given by the Legislature, but in view of its sovereignty the intent to confer such authority should be clearly manifested. *Troy & G. R. Co.* v. *Com.* 127 Mass. 43.

It may be assumed that the facts reported would constitute ground for an action of tort against a natural person, had a similar injury been done by his servants. The contention of the defendant is that the Statutes cited have not in such a case made the Commonwealth liable in this proceeding.

It was held in *Wesson* v. *Com.*, 144 Mass. 60, 3 New Eng. Rep. 778, that the jurisdiction given to the supreme court by Pub. Stat., chap. 195, § 1, of "all claims against the Commonwealth which are founded on contracts for the payment of money did not extend to a claim for damages for a breach of a contract."

It was further held in *Milford* v. *Com.*, 144 Mass. 64, 3 New Eng. Rep. 781, that such jurisdiction did not extend to the obligation imposed by Pub. Stat., chap. 86, § 26, upon the Commonwealth to reimburse the expense incurred by a town in support of a state paper. By these decisions the interpretation of the statute remedy was confined to actual contracts for the payment of money. Subsequently to these decisions the Statute of 1887, chap. 246, was passed which gave to the superior court "jurisdiction of all claims against the Commonwealth, whether at law or equity," with an exception not necessary to be considered. In effect, although not in terms, Pub. Stat., chap. 195, § 1, was amended by striking out the words "which are founded on contracts for the payment of money," and in lieu thereof, inserting the words, "whether at law or in equity." The title of the amendatory Act is "An Act for the Collection of Claims against the Commonwealth," and it provides that "all claims shall be subject to the same set-off and recoupment as they would be if the Commonwealth was a private person." While the words "all claims" may, in their colloquial use, include a demand for damages occasioned by a tort to person or property, in its more proper judicial sense it is a demand of some matter as of right, made by one person upon another for some particular thing or compensation therefor or to do or to forbear to do something as a matter of duty. *Prigg* v. *Pennsylvania*, 41 U. S. 16 Pet. 615 [10 L. ed. 1039].

In view of the fact that the Statute was passed shortly after the decisions in *Wesson* v. *Com.* and *Milford* v. *Com.*, *supra*, it is reasonable to infer that its object was to extend the jurisdiction of the courts to claims which had not been included in the previous Statute, such as those which had been considered in the cases referred to, but not necessarily to claims of a different and distinct character. There are many obligations of the State not coming within the definitions of a contract, all of which definitions require a consent or agreement of the parties. Where a statute imposes an obligation which is enforced as if it arose *ex contractu*, there is not a contract but the obligation arises *ex lege*.

In *Milford* v. *Com.*, above cited, the claim was of this class. The amended Statute was intended to cover claims of this class not arising under contract, those of a breach of contract such as the subject of the suit in *Wesson* v. *Com.*, contracts other than those for the payment of money and perhaps other claims not convenient now to enumerate. This gives to the Statute a full and sufficient meaning without holding, as the plaintiff urges, that a remedy in the nature of an action of tort against the Commonwealth is afforded thereby for neglect or misfeasance of its officers or servants while engaged in the performance of their duties. The object of the Statute cannot have been to create a new class of claims for which a sovereignty has never been held responsible, and to impose a liability therefor, but to provide a convenient tribunal for the determination of claims of the character which civilized governments have always recognized, although the satisfaction of them has been usually sought by direct appeal to the sovereign, or in our system of government, through the Legislature. It is therefore to be considered whether a demand or claim for an injury done or tort committed by a public servant in the performance of his duty is one for which a liability has been held to have been incurred by governments, even if there existed no tribunal competent judicially to pass upon it.

States have always found it necessary to take and use the property of their citizens for the purposes of their government; they have assumed various responsibilities on behalf of their citizens or others; they have also always been parties to contracts for the borrowing of money, the purchase of property, the employment of labor; and the duties arising from such acts have always been fully recognized even if judicial tribunals have not always been provided to make proper compensation for, or adjustment or payment of, the demands arising from such acts. But we do not find that demands founded on the neglect or torts of ministerial officers engaged as servants in the performance of duties which the State as a sovereign has undertaken to perform, have ever been held to render it liable. Nor does this rest upon the narrow ground that there are no means by which such obligations can be enforced, but on the larger ground that no obligations arise therefrom. Municipalities, such as cities and towns, are created by the Commonwealth in order that it may exercise, through them, a part of its power of sovereignty. Where they are engaged in the performance of public duties imposed upon them by statute, they are not liable to private actions of tort for the negligence of their agents employed for this purpose, unless such action is provided by the Statute. *Hill* v. *Boston*, 122 Mass. 344: *Curran* v. *Boston* (Mass.) May 23, 1890.

Had the Legislature intended to create such an obligation and voluntarily to assume in the administration of the State all the responsibility which an individual must incur in his private business, it certainly would have done so in express terms. An intent so to do, as it is in violation of the ordinary principles by which the administration of less important bodies is ordinarily regulated, would not have been left to inference but would have been explicitly stated.

"No government," says *Mr. Justice* Miller, "has ever held itself liable to individuals for the misfeasance, laches or unauthorized exercise of power by its officers or agents." *Gibbons* v. *United States*, 75 U. S. 8 Wall. 269 [19 L. ed. 453].

"The government," says *Mr. Justice* Story, "does not undertake to guarantee to any person the fidelity of any of the officers and agents whom it employs, since that would involve it in all its operations in endless embarrassment and difficulties and losses, which would be subversive of the public interests." Story, Ag. § 319.

The cases of *United States* v. *Kirkpatrick*, 22 U. S. 9 Wheat. 720 [6 L. ed. 199], and *Dox* v. *Postmaster-General*, 26 U. S. 1 Pet. 318 [7 L. ed. 160], cited in *Gibbons* v. *United States*, *supra*, establish the principle that even in regard to matters connected with the cause of action, the government is not responsible for the laches, however gross, of its officers. In the cases thus cited it would seem that no question of jurisdiction could have intervened to disturb the inquiry, as the government was the plaintiff and the defendant was entitled to set off certain claims.

The plaintiff urges that this legislation as construed by him is not novel and that this is not the first Statute by which a State has allowed itself to be impleaded in actions of tort. But the Statute of New York of 1870, chap. 321, and cases cited by him, fortify the position that the assumption of a liability so unusual could not have been left to inference.

It was held (*Lewis* v. *State*, 96 N. Y. 71), that no principle of law nor any adjudged case would make the State liable "for the negligence or misfeasance of its agents in like manner as a natural person is responsible for the acts of his servants," unless the State by its Legislature had voluntarily assumed it.

The cases of *Bowen* v. *State*, 108 N. Y. 166, 10 Cent. Rep. 517, and *Splittorf* v. *State*, 108 N. Y. 205, 10 Cent. Rep. 699, are to the same point.

In *Sipple* v. *State*, 99 N. Y. 284, where the board of canal claims had by the terms of the Statute of New York jurisdiction of claims for damages for injuries in the management of the canals, such as the plaintiff had sustained, *Chief Judge* Ruger remarks: "It must be conceded that the State can be made liable for injuries arising from the negligence of its agents or servants, only by force of some positive statute imposing such liability." In the case there considered, the Legislature, which, in certain events, made the State liable for injuries to an individual, was connected with its administration of the canals of the State, which was an enterprise managed by it as a State, controlled by its own servants, from which a revenue was intended to be derived, as well as a public benefit received, and it was deemed proper, therefore, to incur the same responsibilities as those of private individuals. We have been referred to no legislation by which a State, in the performance of its purely public duties, in administering its government has undertaken to incur responsibility for the negligence or misfeasance of its servants engaged in such administration. Such legislation would be in contravention of what has usually been deemed the rule of public policy.

The Act we are discussing discloses no intention to create against the State a new, and heretofore unrecognized, class of liabilities, but only an intention to provide a judicial tribunal whose well-recognized existing liabilities can be adjudicated.

Where wrongs are done to individuals by those who are the servants of the government, those injured are not remediless, as such persons may be sued as may be other citizens for the torts which they commit. There may be cases also where it would be entirely just that a remedy should be extended by the public to an individual for the injury he had sustained by the negligence of a public servant, but cases of this character the Legislature yet reserves for its own determination.

Petition dismissed.

MONTANA SUPREME COURT.

STATE of Montana, *ex rel.* Louis ROTWITT,

v.

Richard O. HICKMAN, State Treasurer.

(....Mont.....)

An appropriation is "made by law" for the salary of an officer by a state constitution which plainly declares what amount of compensation he shall receive, and no legislative appropriation is necessary in that case to authorize payment.

(February 15, 1890.)

APPLICATION for a writ of mandamus to compel the payment of money alleged to be due and payable to relator as compensation for the performance of his duties as secretary of state. *Granted.*

The case fully appears in the opinion.

Messrs. **McCutcheon & McIntire,** for relator:

Section 4 of article 7 of the Constitution is itself an appropriation, and of course is "one made by law." The appropriation having therefore been made in the Constitution, it is not essential that the Legislature should act to give it validity.

Thomas v. *Owens*, 4 Md. 199; *State* v. *Weston*, 4 Neb. 216; *State* v. *Bordelon*, 6 La. Ann. 68.

The constitutional provision relating to salaries is self-executing.

Endlich, Interpretation of Statutes, 340; Cooley, Const. Lim. p. 100.

Where the salary of a public officer is fixed and the times of payment prescribed by law, no special annual appropriation is necessary to authorize its payment out of the treasury.

Reynolds v. *Taylor*, 43 Ala. 420.

Upon the presentation of the warrant to the Treasurer, it became his duty to pay it out of the funds in his possession "not otherwise appropriated."

Comp. Stat. p. 960, § 1123.

When a plain official duty, requiring no exercise of discretion, is to be performed, and performance is refused, any person who will sustain personal injury by such refusal may have a mandamus therefor.

Fisk v. *Cuthbert*, 2 Mont. 604.

Mr. **Henri J. Haskell,** *Atty-Gen.*, for respondent.

Blake, *Ch. J.*, delivered the opinion of the court:

This is an application to the court for a writ of mandate to be issued to Richard O. Hickman, as the State Treasurer of the State of Montana, commanding him to pay forthwith, out of such moneys as may be in the treasury of the State, and not otherwise appropriated, a certain warrant hereinafter described. It appears from the affidavit on the application of Louis Rotwitt, the party beneficially interested, and is admitted by the respondent, that Rotwitt is the duly elected, qualified and acting secretary of state of Montana. That he entered upon the discharge of his duties upon the 11th day of November, 1889, and has ever since that date continued to perform the same. That upon the 10th day of February, 1890, he presented his account in the sum of $416.67 against the State for his compensation or salary as such secretary of state for the quarter ending on the 31st of December, 1889, to Edwin A. Kenney, who was then and is now the duly elected, qualified and acting auditor of the State of Montana, for settlement, audit and allowance. That thereupon the said Kenney, as such state auditor, settled, audited and allowed said account for the said sum, and then drew his warrant therefor on the said State Treasurer as follows:

No. 9,204. State of Montana, County of Lewis and Clarke, Helena, M. T., Feb. 10th, 1890.

Territorial warrant. Original.

The treasurer will pay to L. Rotwitt or order four hundred and sixteen and 67-100 dollars, for salary as secretary of state for quarter ending Dec. 31st, 1889, out of any moneys in the treasury not otherwise appropriated.

$416.67-100. E. A. Kenney, State Auditor.

Indorsement: Feby. 10th, 1890. Presented, but not paid for want of an appropriation.
R. O. Hickman, State Treasurer.

That he presented the said warrant to the said Hickman, as such State Treasurer, and demanded payment thereof, and that payment thereof was refused, and the same is wholly unpaid; and that there is now in the treasury of the State, and in the possession of the said Hickman, as such State Treasurer, the sum of $40,000. The alternative writ was issued, and on the return thereof said Hickman made the following answer, to wit: "That no provision has been made by law for the payment of this or any other warrant issued to the state officers of Montana for their services, rendered as such officers." The relator then demurred to this answer upon the ground that it does not state facts sufficient to constitute a defense.

There is no statute which makes an appropriation or otherwise provides for the payment of this warrant, and the sole question for decision depends upon the interpretation of the following clauses of the Constitution: "Until otherwise provided by law, the governor, secretary of state, state auditor, treasurer, attorney-general and superintendent of public instruction, shall quarterly, as due, during their continuance in office, receive for their services compensation, which is fixed as follows: . . secretary of state, $3,000 per annum. . . . The compensation enumerated shall be in full for all services by said officers respectively rendered in any official capacity or employment whatever during their respective terms of office, and the salary of no official shall be increased during his term of office. No officer named in this section shall receive for the performance of any official duty any fee for his own use. . . . Article 7, § 4.

"Except as otherwise provided in this Constitution, no law shall extend the term of any public officer, or increase or diminish his salary

See also 24 L. R. A. 266.

or emolument after his election," etc. Article 5, § 31.

"No money shall be paid out of the treasury except upon appropriations made by law, and on warrant drawn by the proper officer in pursuance thereof, except interest on the public debt." Id. § 34.

"The state auditor and state treasurer shall perform such duties as are prescribed in this Constitution and by the laws of the State." Article 7, § 1.

This court, in the cases of *State* v. *Ah Jim* (Mont.), Jan. 4, 1890, and *Thompson* v. *Kenney* (Mont.), Jan. 28, 1890, inquired into the effect of the provisions of the Constitution upon the statutes of the Territory and State and a repetition of the citations and conclusions therein will be avoided. We content ourselves with the observation that the foregoing language of the Constitution and the laws concerning the territorial treasurer are applicable to this proceeding. What, then, are "appropriations made by law?" A majority of the States of the American Union have not adopted Constitutions which specify the salaries that should be paid to their officers. Numerous cases can be found in their courts which determine the necessity of an appropriation by the law-making department before the payment of money can be authorized by the custodian of the public funds. But the fundamental law of this State constitutes an exception in this important feature, and the decisions of such courts do not enlighten us. All the adjudications which construe constitutional phrases similar to those of Montana concur in their declaration of principles.

The leading case is that of *Thomas* v. *Owens*, 4 Md. 189, which was decided in 1853 by the court of appeals, and the opinion was delivered by the profound jurist, *Chief Justice* Le Grand, after a thorough examination. Thomas was the comptroller of the State, and applied for a writ of mandamus to be directed to Owens, the state treasurer, commanding him to pay the amount of a draft drawn in payment of his salary. Owens refused payment on several grounds, including the following: "That no sufficient appropriation has been made by law specifying a sum applicable to the payment of the amount claimed by the petitioner." The gravity of the investigation, and the lucid reasoning of the court, induce us to be liberal in the use of excerpts. "The inquiry, then, is, Is there an appropriation for the period intervening between the 10th of December, 1851,—the time from which we think he is entitled to pay,—and the 1st day of January, 1852? We are of opinion the Constitution, *proprio vigore*, makes such appropriation. Under our system of government, its powers are wisely distributed to different departments. Each and all are subordinate to the Constitution, which creates and defines their limits. Whatever it commands is the supreme and uncontrollable law of the land. This is not denied directly, although it is inferentially, substantially and practically. It is said that, inasmuch as the 20th section of the 3d article of the Constitution declares, 'No money shall be drawn from the treasury of the State except in accordance with an appropriation made by law,' that an Act of Assembly must precede the withdrawal; and inasmuch as none such has been passed covering the period antecedent to the 1st of January, 1852, there is therefore no appropriation by law for that time. To this reasoning we cannot yield our consent. In the construction of any instrument, the whole paper ought to be considered, that the will of its framers may be truly and accurately ascertained. The objects contemplated, and the purposes to be subserved, should be constantly kept in view, and the language used interpreted in reference to the manifest intent. Now, what could have been the purpose of the clause in the Constitution to which we have referred? It was obviously inserted to prevent the expenditure of the people's treasure without their consent, either as expressed by themselves in the Organic Law, or by their representatives in constitutional Acts of legislation."

After citing Story, Const., 3d ed. § 1348, and 1 Tuck. Bl. Com., 362, the opinion continues: "These being the purposes and objects of the clause, the question is, Have the people given their consent to the payment of the salary of the comptroller? That they have done so is palpably manifest. They have said he 'shall receive an annual salary of $2,500.' They have not merely said he may claim such a sum, but, emphatically, that he 'shall receive' it. It is impossible for human language to be less ambiguous or more positive. The people, in their Organic Law, which is paramount to all other law, have not only given their consent, but they have imperatively issued their commands, that the particular officer 'shall receive' it. How is their will obeyed if it be within the power of the treasurer, or anyone else, to withhold it from caprice, unfaithfulness to duty or from mistaken judgment? To allow of such a power in that officer would be to put him above the Constitution, whose creature he is. It would be to invest him with authority to annul the sovereign will, in fact, to stop the wheels of government, and reduce things into the wildest confusion. The Constitution has said the officer 'shall receive' his salary; and this fiat of the supreme will is not to be nullified by the mere *ipse dixit* of a mere ministerial officer; for such, and none other, is the treasurer. In assigning the powers of government to three different departments, the Constitution intended to secure to each its independency of action; and, the more certainly and effectually to insure this, it has ascertained and appropriated the salary they are severally to receive, and it has inhibited the Legislature from diminishing it. Were it not for such a provision, the whole government would exist only by permission of the Legislature. It can only be carried on through the instrumentality of individuals, and their services can only be obtained by being paid for. The framers of the Constitution, and the people who adopted it, aware of this, determined not to submit the durability of their work to the caprice, passion or prejudice which possibly might, at times of great excitement, triumphantly rule the action of the Legislature, and therefore wisely did the work themselves, by ingrafting in the Organic Law a provision for the protection of those who should be charged with its execution. In other words, they made the appropriation. An opposite interpretation would countenance this paradox: that a co-ordinate branch of the government could stop its whole machinery, by refusing to pay the salaries of those upon whom is devolved the discharge of the duties of the other branches; and this, too, when the Constitution expressly declares that these officers 'shall receive' their salaries, and that they 'shall not be diminished!' 'It would be giving to the Legislature a practical and real omnipotence with the same breath which professes to restrict their powers within narrow limits. It is prescribing limits, and declaring that those limits may be passed at pleasure.' *Marbury* v. *Madison*, 5 U. S. 1 Cranch, 178 [2 L. ed. 73]. Now, it is presumed it would not be contended by anyone, however hazardous, that if the Legislature were to pass an Act diminishing the salary of the governor, or of any other officer whose salary is fixed by the Constitution, that such an exercise of power would be rightful and constitutional. If it be not competent to the Legislature to take away a part, by what process of reasoning can it be maintained that they can take away the whole? And yet this is the extent to which the argument addressed to us goes. It seems to us to be but necessary to state the proposition to cause its instantaneous rejection. We hold, for the reasons we have assigned, the people have given their consent to the payment of the salaries fixed in the Constitution, by declaring the amount 'shall' be 'received' by the particular officer; and that this is an appropriation by law,—by the supreme law of the State."

The case of *Thomas* v. *Owens*, *supra*, is commented on in *Green* v. *Purnell*, 12 Md. 333, and the court said: "There, the petition asked for a mandamus requiring the treasurer of the State to pay the comptroller, upon his warrant, the amount of his salary, which is regulated by the Constitution, and, of course, duly appropriated by law."

In *State* v. *Weston*, 4 Neb. 216, the "case raises the question of the authority of the state auditor to draw warrants upon the state treasurer for the payment of the salaries of the state officers when no appropriation therefor has been made by the Legislature." The Constitution of that State provides that "no money shall be drawn from the treasury except in pursuance of a specific appropriation made by law." If this clause, says *Chief Justice* Lake, "had limited the appropriation which it requires to an Act of the Legislature, there might be some force in the objection urged. But it only requires a specific appropriation 'made by law;' and we are clearly of the opinion that this may be accomplished just as effectually by the Constitution as by legislative enactment." The court further says: "In the case of *Reynolds* v. *Taylor*, 43 Ala. 420, it was held that if the salary of a public officer is fixed, and the times of payment prescribed, by law, no special annual appropriation is necessary to authorize the auditor to draw his warrant for its payment. But the case of *Thomas* v. *Owens*, 4 Md. 189, seems to be more directly in point. It was there held that when the Constitution declared the amount to be paid an officer, that it was an appropriation made by law, and no legislative Act was necessary."

In *State* v. *Weston*, 6 Neb. 16, the court explains the decision in *State* v. *Weston*, *supra*, and asserts that "it reaches only those officers who hold by virtue of the Constitution itself, and not to those who hold their offices at the will of the Legislature;" and the "appropriation made by law . . . may be done either by direction of the Constitution itself—that being the supreme law in the State—or by the Legislature."

We do not know of any rule to the contrary where the same constitutional provisions exist which are embodied in the supreme law of this State. An illustration of the principles which are applied where salaries of the officers are not prescribed by the Constitution, and the case of *Thomas* v. *Owens*, *supra*, is not followed, may be found in *Myers* v. *English*, 9 Cal. 348. This was an application for a writ of mandamus to compel the state treasurer to pay certain warrants drawn by the comptroller on account of the salary of a district judge. The Constitution provided that the judges of the district court shall severally, at stated times during their continuation in office, receive for their services a compensation, to be paid out of the treasury, which shall not be increased or diminished during the term for which they shall have been elected. Article 6, § 15.

Another clause is the following: "No money shall be drawn from the treasury but in consequence of appropriations made by law." Article 4, § 23.

It was correctly held by the court that it was necessary for the Legislature to define the amount of the salary, and make an appropriation for the payment thereof, before this remedy could be enforced. This view of the Constitution of a State has been adopted by the Supreme Court of the United States, in construing the clause of the Federal Constitution which declares that no State shall pass any "law impairing the obligation of contracts."

Mr. Justice Swayne, in *Mississippi & M. R. Co.* v. *McClure*, 77 U. S. 10 Wall. 515 [19 L. ed. 998], asserts that "the Constitution of a State is undoubtedly a law, within the meaning of this prohibition."

In *White* v. *Hart*, 80 U. S. 13 Wall. 652 [20 L. ed. 687], the court holds "that a State can no more impair the obligation of a contract by adopting a Constitution than by passing a law. In the eye of the constitutional inhibition, they are substantially the same thing." *Gunn* v. *Barry*, 82 U. S. 15 Wall. 623 [21 L. ed. 215]; *Concord* v. *Portsmouth Sav. Bank*, 92 U. S. 630 [23 L. ed. 630]; *New Orleans Gas Co.* v. *Louisiana Light Co.* 115 U. S. 672 [29 L. ed. 524].

We cannot add anything to the discussion of this vital proposition. The doctrines which were announced in *Thomas* v. *Owens*, *supra*, have been accepted for years without a question, and have remained inflexible under every test. The framers of the Constitution of this State numbered upon their roll most eminent jurists and lawyers. They studied with wisdom and ability the charters which the people had granted to the States of the Union, in their efforts to obtain the best articles from all. They knew the precedents which have been enumerated, and the canons of interpretation which had been formulated by the courts, and deliberately created the sections of the Constitution which fix the salaries of many state officers. In their action upon this subject they did not incorporate the provisions which are frequently in force in the instruments of this solemn character, and did not permit the Legislature to have this great power. In order that there should be no erroneous construction of the clauses under examination, the following section was adopted: "The provisions of this Constitution are mandatory and prohibitory, unless by express words they are declared to be otherwise." Article 8, § 29.

When, therefore, it is plainly declared that the secretary of state, or any other officer, shall receive a certain sum as compensation for his services, an appropriation is "made by law," and the proper officer is empowered to draw his warrant on the State Treasurer in pursuance thereof; and the respondent is required to pay the above-described warrant to the relator.

The demurrer (the respondent abiding by his answer and return) is sustained, and *it is therefore ordered that a peremptory writ of mandate be issued forthwith according to the prayer of the application herein.*

Harwood and **De Witt**, *JJ.*, concur.

INDIANA SUPREME COURT.

William A. MILLER, Exr., etc., *Appt.*,
v.
Isabelle SHIELDS.

(....Ind.....)

The defense arising under § 5119, Rev. Stat. 1881, which makes contracts of suretyship exceptions to the general power conferred by § 5115 upon married women to enter into contracts, must be affirmatively proved when interposed to a suit upon a promissory note which bears on its face no evidence of coverture or suretyship and no attempt is made to negative the existence of those facts in the complaint.

(May 29, 1890.)

APPEAL by plaintiff from a judgment of the Circuit Court for Jackson County in favor of defendant in an action brought to recover the amount alleged to be due upon a promissory note. *Reversed.*

The facts are fully stated in the opinion.

Messrs. **Applewhite & Applewhite** for appellant.

Mr. **B. H. Burrell** for appellee.

NOTE.—*Married woman incapable to contract as surety.*

Where no question of fraud or estoppel has intervened, any contract of suretyship, whatever its form, entered into by a married woman since the Act of 1881, is, under the provisions of this section, wholly void. Allen v. Davis, 101 Ind. 187; Warey v. Forst, 102 Ind. 205; Brown v. Will, 1 West. Rep. 130, 108 Ind. 71; Engler v. Acker, 8 West. Rep. 673, 106 Ind. 223; McLead v. Ætna L. Ins. Co. 5 West. Rep. 633, 107 Ind. 394; Bennett v. Mattingly, 7 West. Rep. 912, 110 Ind. 197; Crooks v. Kennett, 10 West. Rep. 256, 111 Ind. 347; Bartholomew v. Pierson, 11 West. Rep. 848, 112 Ind. 430; State v. Kennett, 13 West. Rep. 818, 114 Ind. 160; Ellis v. Baker, 116 Ind. 411.

So where a married woman guarantees the payment of a promissory note by written indorsement, it is a contract of suretyship, and is void under this section. Nixon v. Whitely, 120 Ind. 361.

A married woman is incapable to bind herself by recognizance of replevin bail, and may be discharged from such contract on motion in the court where judgment was rendered. Eberwine v. State, 79 Ind. 268.

Mortgage by wife of her separate estate to secure her husband's debt is void.

A mortgage executed by a married woman upon her separate real estate to secure her husband's debt is void. Brown v. Will, 1 West. Rep. 130, 108 Ind. 71; Allen v. Davis, 99 Ind. 216, 101 Ind. 187; Cupp v. Campbell, 1 West. Rep. 255, 103 Ind. 213; Engler v. Acker, 8 West. Rep. 673, 106 Ind. 223.

Since the Statute of 1881 went into effect a married woman cannot execute a mortgage binding her real estate to secure her husband's debt. Allen v. Davis, 101 Ind. 189, 99 Ind. 217; Dodge v. Kinzy, 101 Ind. 109; Levering v. Shockey, 100 Ind. 560.

Such a mortgage given to secure a debt on which the husband was liable as surety only is invalid although executed at a time when married women could have incumbered their property for the debt of a third person. Bridges v. Blake, 4 West. Rep. 176, 106 Ind. 333.

Where the married woman's husband joined her in such a mortgage before the Statute of 1881 and while the prior Statute was in force, it was valid and binding. Frazer v. Clifford, 94 Ind. 487; Mathes v. Shank, 94 Ind. 505; Post v. Losey, 9 West. Rep. 616, 111 Ind. 74; Gardner v. Case, 10 West. Rep. 800, 111 Ind. 494.

But under the Statute of 1881 a married woman is incapable of entering into a contract of suretyship for her husband or for any other person. Crooks v. Kennett, 10 West. Rep. 256, 111 Ind. 347.

Suit to foreclose wife's mortgage.

In a suit to enforce such a mortgage it should be alleged that the debt was contracted by her and that it inured to her benefit or that of her estate. Jouchert v. Johnson, 6 West. Rep. 890, 108 Ind. 436.

The loan must be made by her for her benefit or that of her property; a mere temporary receiving the money, or a recital in the mortgage that she is principal and her husband surety, is not sufficient. Orr v. White, 4 West. Rep. 482, 106 Ind. 341.

A contract executed by a married woman is one of suretyship to the extent that the consideration was received by any other person than herself. Vogel v. Leichner, 102 Ind. 55.

The test of whether she was a principal or a surety is determined by the inquiry whether or not she was to receive the consideration for her own benefit or for that of her estate. It does not depend on the form of the contract. *Ibid.*

One who takes such a mortgage with knowledge that her title is fraudulent as to her husband's creditors is estopped in a suit by her to cancel the mortgage, to prove the fraud for any purpose. Warey v. Forst, 102 Ind. 205.

One who knows that a debt is that of the husband, and that the property belongs to the wife, is chargeable with knowledge of the capacity in which she contracts. Keller v. Orr, 4 West. Rep. 707, 106 Ind. 411.

Coverture a personal defense.

Coverture, like infancy, is a personal defense which third parties cannot make for their own benefit. Ætna Ins. Co. v. Baker, 71 Ind. 102; 1 Wait, Act. & Def. 158.

Berkshire, *Ch. J.*, delivered the opinion of the court:

This action is bottomed on a promissory note executed by the appellee to the appellant's testator. The appellee answered in three paragraphs: first, the general denial; second, want of consideration; third, coverture and suretyship.

The appellant replied in general denial.

The cause was submitted to the court for trial, and after the evidence had been concluded a finding was returned in favor of the appellee. The appellant filed a motion for new trial, which was overruled by the court and an exception saved and judgment rendered for the appellee. The record presents but one question for our consideration: Is the finding of the court sustained by sufficient evidence? Notwithstanding the well-established rule of this court that it will not disturb the judgment of a trial court because the evidence which supports it is weak and unsatisfactory, we are compelled to reverse the judgment here involved for the reason that there was a failure of proof as to one vital fact.

In Indiana, since the year 1881, the disabilities which the common law imposed upon married women as to the making of contracts with certain limitations have been removed. Rev. Stat. 1881, §§ 5, 115 *et seq.*

As this court has frequently announced, ability, and not disability, is the rule as to the capacity of married women to enter into contracts. *Vogel* v. *Leichner*, 102 Ind. 55.

In this case it is said: "By the more comprehensive enactment of 1881, above referred to, the Legislature abrogated all legal disabilities of married women, except such as are expressly saved in the Act."

In *Rosa* v. *Prather*, 103 Ind. 191, 1 West. Rep. 267, it is said: "The three most notable respects in which the disability of coverture was felt at common law were in the inability of the wife to sue, in her inability to enter into a contract and in her inability to control her own property. These separate disabilities have all been in general terms removed. . . . The disabilities upon these and other subjects which still remain are special and exceptional, and no longer constitute a part of a category of general disabilities."

In *Arnold* v. *Engleman*, 103 Ind. 512, 1 West. Rep. 482, it is said: "The question here is as to the sufficiency of the facts pleaded to avoid the disability of coverture. We have decided that in cases of married women ability is now the rule and disability the exception.

This is the only reasonable interpretation of our Statute, for its language is broad and comprehensive. Section 5115 provides that all the

---

Although a wife may plead her coverture as a defense under the Statute of 1881, yet her coverture is not a legal disability, except in certain special cases (Bennett v. Mattingly, 7 West. Rep. 912, 110 Ind. 197); it is a personal defense and cannot be pleaded by a third party for his own benefit. *Ibid.*; Rosa v. Prather, 1 West. Rep. 267, 103 Ind. 191.

If a married woman dies intestate leaving children, they may defeat a mortgage executed by her upon her separate estate to secure her husband's debt, by pleading coverture of their mother, being privies both in blood and in estate; but her husband cannot avail himself of the plea although he joined with her in the mortgage. Ellis v. Baker, 116 Ind. 408.

Code, § 5119, construed.

Section 5119 of the Code was enacted for a married woman's protection alone, and cannot be invoked by a purchaser to defeat a mortgage executed to him by a husband and wife as tenants by entireties to secure the husband's debts. Dodge v. Kinzy, 101 Ind. 102, distinguished in Bennett v. Mattingly, 7 West. Rep. 912, 110 Ind. 197.

To bring a mortgage executed by husband and wife, upon land held by entireties, to secure a loan made upon their joint application, within the prohibition of this section, it must affirmatively appear that the money received did not inure to the benefit of the wife, or to the benefit of the joint estate. Security Co. v. Arbuckle, 119 Ind. 69. See Vogel v. Leichner, 102 Ind. 55; Cupp v. Campbell, 1 West. Rep. 255, 103 Ind. 213; Ward v. Berkshire L. Ins. Co. 6 West. Rep. 596, 108 Ind. 301.

Where a husband's note was accepted for the purchase money of land conveyed to husband and wife by entireties, the debt is his, not hers, and a mortgage by both, made to secure the debt, is void as against the wife. Jackson v. Smith, 120 Ind. 520.

Where a wife joins with her husband in a mortgage of his real estate, it is not, as to her inchoate interest, a contract of suretyship within the meaning of this section of the Code. Cupp v. Campbell, 1 West. Rep. 255, 103 Ind. 216; Dodge v. Kinzy, 101 Ind. 102; Grave v. Bunch, 83 Ind. 4; Leary v. Shafter, 79 Ind. 567.

As to tenancy by entireties, rule in the several States, see *note* to Baker v. Stewart (Kan.) 2 L. R. A. 434.

Estoppel of wife.

A married woman may be estopped by her affirmative representations, yet she cannot by her own act or representations remove her legal incapacity to make a contract which coverture alone disqualifies her from making except in a prescribed way. Carpenter v. Carpenter, 45 Ind. 142; Levering v. Shockey, 100 Ind. 558; Bank of America v. Banks, 101 U. S. 240 (25 L. ed. 850); Sims v. Everhardt, 102 U. S. 300 (26 L. ed. 87); Keen v. Coleman, 39 Pa. 299; Klein v. Caldwell, 91 Pa. 140; Morrison v. Wilson, 13 Cal. 494; Todd v. Pittsburgh, Ft. W. etc. R. Co. 19 Ohio St. 514; Behler v. Weyburn, 59 Ind. 143; Cupp v. Campbell, 1 West. Rep. 255, 103 Ind. 213.

But where a wife transfers her separate real estate to her husband by conveyance importing a money consideration, to enable him to mortgage it as his property to secure a loan for his benefit, she is estopped as against the mortgagee, who is not shown to have had knowledge that the conveyance was a mere contrivance to evade the statute, from asserting that the transfer was not bona fide. Long v. Crosson, 119 Ind. 3.

So she is estopped, where she makes a representation by affidavit that the loan is for her own use and benefit, to deny the truth of such representation. Ward v. Berkshire L. Ins. Co. 6 West. Rep. 596, 108 Ind. 301.

Where such a mortgage is foreclosed in a proceeding to which she is a party, and the land is ordered sold, she cannot afterwards in a collateral proceeding question the consideration upon which the mortgage rested. Watson v. Camper, 119 Ind. 60. See Carrico v. Tarwater, 1 West. Rep. 144, 103 Ind. 86; Elwood v. Beymer, 100 Ind. 504; Sanders v. Douglas, 46 Ind. 522; McCaffrey v. Carrigan, 49 Ind. 175; Bates v. Spooner, 45 Ind. 489; State v. Manly, 15 Ind. 8; Perkins v. Bragg, 29 Ind. 507; McMahan v. Newcomer, 82 Ind. 565; Spencer v. McGonagle, 5 West. Rep. 663, 107 Ind. 410.

As to estoppel of married woman, see *note* to Speier v. Opfer (Mich.) 2 L. R. A. 347; Yerkes v. Hadley (Dak.) 2 L. R. A. 363.

legal disabilities of married women to make contracts are hereby abolished, except as herein otherwise provided. This confers a general power to make executory contracts except such as are prohibited by the Statute. There is no provision prohibiting married women from purchasing wearing apparel and executing notes for its value. It is true that in section 5117 it is provided that she may make contracts concerning her separate personal property, but this is merely permissive and cumulative, and is not a limitation upon the general power conferred by the section quoted. It would be a great stretch to affirm that in buying personal property she was not contracting concerning it, and if the provision found in section 5117 stood alone it would be quite doubtful whether a married woman's contract for the purchase of wearing apparel for herself were not valid; but the provisions of section 5115 make it very clear that such contracts are valid and enforcible. Our conclusion is that a married woman may purchase wearing apparel for herself, and that notes executed by her for the price which she agreed to pay for it are valid and may be enforced." See *Barnett* v. *Harshbarger*, 105 Ind. 410, 8 West. Rep. 750.

In *McLead* v. *Ætna L. Ins. Co.* 107 Ind. 394, 5 West. Rep. 633, the court said: "The notes and mortgages were jointly executed by the appellant on the 18th day of November, 1882, at which time the Act of April 16, 1881, concerning husband and wife, which took effect on September 19, 1881, was a part of the law of this State."

Section 5115 of said Statute is then set out, and the court goes on to say: "In *Arnold* v. *Engleman*, 103 Ind. 512, 1 West. Rep. 482, after quoting section 5115 as above, the court said: 'This confers a general power to make executory contracts, except such as are prohibited by the Statute.' . . . In § 5117, Rev. Stat. 1881, it is provided that a married woman 'shall not enter into any executory contract to sell or convey or mortgage her real estate, nor shall she convey or mortgage the same unless her husband join in such contract, conveyance or mortgage.' Section 5119, Rev. Stat. 1881, reads as follows: 'A married woman shall not enter into any contract of suretyship, whether as indorser, guarantor or in any other manner, and such contract as to her shall be void.'" See *Lane* v. *Schlemmer*, 114 Ind. 296 (bottom of page 301), 12 West. Rep. 922.

In *Phelps* v. *Smith*, 116 Ind. 387 (at bottom of page 402), 15 West. Rep. 824, it is said: "The decision in *Phipps* v. *Sedgwick*, 95 U. S. 3 [24 L. ed. 591], if conceded to be otherwise relevant, is not in point because the court placed its judgment upon the disability created by coverture, saying that 'such a proposition would be a very unjust one to the wife still under the dominion, control and personal influence of her husband.' Manifestly this rule cannot apply in jurisdictions where a married woman possesses nearly all the rights of a *feme sole*, and where ability is the rule and disability the exception."

In the quotation which we have made from *Arnold* v. *Engleman*, *supra*, said section 5115 is set out, and we need not copy it again. The exception involved in the case now under consideration is found in section 5119, which section appears in the quotation from *McLead* v. *Ætna L. Ins. Co.*, *supra*, and need not be again quoted.

It is a general rule of pleading applicable alike to civil actions and criminal prosecutions that when an exception or proviso is embodied in the enacting clause of a statute or contract, it must be negatived in the complaint or indictment, but if it is found in a subsequent distinct clause or section of the statute or covenant, as is the case with the Statute before us, then there need be no negation. Gould, Pl. pp. 514, 515; Stephen, Pl. (Heard) pp. 443, 444.

In *Com.* v. *Jennings*, 121 Mass. 47, Gray, *Ch. J.*, speaking for the court, said: "On the other hand, it appears to us to be established by a great preponderance of authority that when an exception is not stated in the enacting clause otherwise than by merely referring to other provisions of the Statute, it need not be negatived unless necessary to a complete definition of the offense."

In *Hart* v. *Cleis*, 8 Johns. 43, the court said: "The action below was brought for a penalty incurred under the 6th section of the Act concerning slaves and servants. The special causes of demurrer stated upon the record are not material; but the defendant relies upon what he alleges to be defects in substance in the declaration, viz.: that the plaintiff does not negative the excepted cases in the section, and that he does not aver that the defendant was master of the slave or acted with his privity. It is a sufficient answer to the first objection that the exception forms no part of the plaintiff's title or right of action, but is merely matter of excuse for the defendant. The excepted cases are not incorporated into the body and substance of the enacting clause, but are given as exceptions, and the instances are not specified in that, but in the subsequent sections." See *Com.* v. *Tuttle*, 12 Cush. 502; *Com.* v. *Hill*, 5 Gratt. 682; *State* v. *Miller*, 24 Conn. 522; *United States* v. *Cook*, 84 U. S. 17 Wall. 168 [21 L. ed. 538]; *State* v. *Abbey*, 29 Vt. 60; *Fleming* v. *People*, 27 N. Y. 329; *Harris* v. *White*, 81 N. Y. 532.

Our own cases are to the same effect. *Russell* v. *State*, 50 Ind. 174; *State* v. *Maddox*, 74 Ind. 105; *Mergentheim* v. *State*, 107 Ind. 567, 5 West. Rep. 851.

The action in this case was upon a promissory note executed by the appellee alone. The complaint did not allege that the appellee was under coverture, but had this fact appeared therein we think it would have been good in the absence of an allegation in negation of section 5119, *supra*. We think so in view of the rule as supported by the authorities cited above. The precise question has never been before this court.

It was held in the case of *Vogel* v. *Leichner*, *supra*, that where the husband and wife jointly executed a promissory note and a mortgage upon the separate real estate of the wife the burden of proof was on the plaintiff seeking to foreclose the mortgage to show that she was liable.

The foregoing case was followed in the case of *Cupp* v. *Campbell*, 103 Ind. 213, 1 West. Rep. 255.

In that class of cases the presumption which naturally arises because of the peculiar relation that exists between husband and wife is that he is the principal debtor and she but his surety, and hence it was well ruled in those cases that the obligation could not be enforced against her nor against her property specifically pledged for its payment, it not appearing affirmatively that she was a principal debtor.

But when a married woman, as she has full power to do under the Married Woman's Act, executes her individual note whereby she promises to pay a given sum of money, the question is very different. No presumption such as that announced in the cases above can prevail. To hold that when a married woman has executed her individual promissory note she is presumed to stand as surety for her husband or some other person until the contrary is made to appear would be to carry the doctrine of presumptions beyond the border line.

It is quite difficult to imagine the relation of principal and surety without a principal, and equally so to find a substantial reason on which to rest the presumption that whenever a married woman executes her individual promissory note she occupies the position of a surety for her husband or some other person. It is true that it may be shown that the individual note of a married woman was given solely for the benefit of the husband or someone else, but when this is claimed by her it must be made to appear affirmatively. The following cases we think support our conclusion:

Arnold v. *Engleman, supra,* was an action on a promissory note executed by a married woman alone and included an account for merchandise sold and delivered to her. And at this point we feel that it is not improper to quote for the second time a small portion of what was said by the court in that case: "It would be a great stretch to affirm that in buying personal property she was not contracting concerning it." But it would not be more so than to presume when a married woman executes her separate promissory note, reciting that for value received she promises to pay so many dollars, that the consideration has moved to someone else, and that she has received no benefit therefrom.

In *McLead* v. *Ætna L. Ins. Co.*, 107 Ind. 896, 5 West. Rep. 638, the court said: "Except as prohibited in these two sections 5117 and 5119, . . . a married woman had and has the same power to make executory contracts, and was and is as much bound thereby, as if she had been or was unmarried at the time of their execution. If the appellee's complaint in the case in hand had shown that the appellant Molinda was the surety of her co-appellant in the notes in suit, or that the mortgaged real estate was her separate estate, it would have been necessary, perhaps, to have alleged the further fact, in order to state a cause of action against her, that she had received either in person or in benefit to her estate the consideration of such notes and mortgage, or some part thereof. . . . But as no such showing was made in the complaint, it was sufficient to withstand appellant's assignments of errors, and would have been good, we think, even upon demurrers for the alleged want of facts."

In *Bennett* v. *Mattingly*, 110 Ind. 199, 7 West. Rep. 912, Niblack, *J.*, for the court, said: "An argument is submitted against the sufficiency of the complaint upon demurrer upon the ground that it showed Mrs. Dingman to have been a married woman at the time she executed the notes and mortgage, and did not aver a state of facts creating a liability on her part notwithstanding the disabilities imposed by her coverture. This would at one time have been a valid objection to the complaint, but the law in that respect has been materially changed by the Revised Statutes of 1881. Coverture is no longer a disability in this State, except in some special cases, and hence upon the facts averred no disability on the part Mrs. Dingman could have been fairly presumed. The complaint was consequently sufficient upon demurrer."

In view of these authorities no such presumption can arise as that contended for by the appellee. But *Elliott* v. *Gregory*, 115 Ind. 98, 14 West. Rep. 830, is still a much stronger case against the said contention. There a married woman was sued for medical services rendered to her at her special instance and request and upon her express promise to pay for the same. She answered coverture, averring in addition that the debt was her husband's for the reason that she could not enter into a binding contract for such services. The answer was demurred to, the cause of demurrer being want of facts, which was overruled. This court reversed the ruling of the trial court and said: "It was an answer in confession and in avoidance. It impliedly admitted the rendition of the services sued for and Mrs. Gregory's promise to pay for the same and then set up her coverture as a protection against her liability to pay for such services. These made the pleading a formal as well as a substantial answer of coverture to the action. This, under existing statutes and our decisions upon them, was not a good defense to the complaint." Section 5115, *supra*, is then quoted, and the court goes on to say: "In the construction of this section we have held that a married woman's ability to contract is now the rule and that her disability to do so constitutes the exception. . . . The answer under consideration did not base Mrs. Gregory's defense upon any of the exceptional disabilities still imposed on married women; on the contrary, the allegations of the complaint, which were impliedly admitted by the answer, made a case affirmatively in which coverture was no disability."

That case seems to cover the case at bar. Here the gravamen of the action, as we have already said, is a promissory note, and at this point we desire to set the note out.

$500.

Brownstown, January 25, 1883.

One year after date I promise to pay to the order of Henry G. Smith five hundred dollars for value received, without any relief whatever from valuation or appraisement laws, with eight per cent interest from date until paid and attorney's fees. Isabelle Shields.

In the case at bar, as in the case last cited, the promise is the express and individual promise of a married woman and differs only in the fact that in the former case the promise rested in parol while in the present case it is in writing.

In the former case the character of the consideration upon which the promise rested is stated, as was necessary because of the fact that the promise rested in parol, but in the case at bar the action is bottomed upon a written obligation which implies a consideration.

Who is presumed to have received the consideration? Necessarily the party or parties who executed the instrument. The question of consideration can only be of consequence to the parties to the obligation. Whether others were or were not benefited because of the giving of the obligation is wholly unimportant because in no event can it be enforced against them. But the obligation here sued upon upon its face expressly states that the note was given for value received. Value received by whom? The note itself states: "I promise to pay," etc., "for value received,"—value received by the promisor. But suppose in the last cited case the answer had been good and at the point where it failed the proof had failed, the result must necessarily have been the same. Why the same? Because in an action upon the separate and express promise of a married woman where a valuable consideration appears, the burden is upon her to show that she is not liable. And we think it can make no difference whether the consideration is affirmatively shown or arises by implication. But the principle here involved has been further settled by this court against the contention of the appellee.

In *Security Co.* v. *Arbuckle*, 119 Ind. 69, Matthew and May E. Arbuckle, husband and wife, owned by entireties certain real estate; they executed their joint notes and a mortgage upon the said real estate to secure the same. The application for the loan for which the notes and mortgage were executed was executed by them jointly. The mortgagee drew his check for the money loaned to them jointly, but delivered it to Matthew Arbuckle, the husband, and he drew the money. The special finding of the court failed to show for what purpose the money was borrowed, or how used. The court said: "The mortgaged estate being the joint property of both, and the loan having been made on the joint application of both mortgagors, the burden is upon them to make it appear that the consideration of the notes was not obtained and used for the benefit of the joint estate. This is not the case of a married woman mortgaging her separate estate to secure a debt which appears to be the obligation of herself and another. This is the case of the owners of a joint estate who joined in a mortgage thereon to secure the apparent obligation of both and it must affirmatively appear that the debt was not for their joint benefit."

The reasoning in that case meets the question before us. This is not the case of a married woman mortgaging her separate estate to secure the apparent debt of herself and another, but it is her separate obligation that she is sued upon and apparently her own debt, and hence the burden is on her to show that her husband and not herself received the consideration for the note. See *Jenne* v. *Burt*, 121 Ind. 275.

And we may add further that we have found no case where a married woman has been sued on her individual promise in which she has been discharged on the ground of coverture and suretyship, except where it has appeared upon the face of the obligation that she occupied the relation of a surety or guarantor, or where the fact has been established by affirmative evidence.

The appellee's husband testified as a witness in her behalf to a conversation which he had with the executor and to the payment of interest due on the note; but there is nothing in his evidence to show to whom the consideration for the note moved. In fact the transaction with the executor after the testator's death, or what may have been said by him, could not have been considered by the court as tending to throw light upon the original transaction. The executor was called as a witness by the appellee, but he made no statement material to the question in issue. The appellee was called as a witness in her own behalf, but testified to nothing material to the issue. The note sued on was secured by a mortgage on the separate real estate of the wife. It is true it was executed jointly by the appellee and her husband, but this could not be otherwise, for she could not mortgage her estate to secure any debt which she might contract except her husband joined in the mortgage.

For the error in overruling the motion for a new trial the judgment must be reversed.

Judgment reversed, with costs.

Mitchell, *J.*, concurs in the conclusion reached, but not with all of the reasoning found in the opinion.

GEORGIA SUPREME COURT.

STANDARD OIL CO., *Plff. in Err.*,
v.
GILBERT & CO.

(......Ga.......)

***A written contract creating a commercial agency** for one year, and fixing the agent's compensation for services, wharfage, storage and paying for the goods sold at a gross sum per month, having been renewed expressly for the next year, and the agency having in fact continued for several successive years afterwards, both parties in all their dealings conforming to the terms of the original contract, there was a tacit renewal of the same from year to year, and the principal could not, by notice given pending the last year's services, terminate the contract before the expiration of that year, so as to deprive the agent of his stipulated monthly compensation for the unexpired portion of the year. Though the mere power of revocation existed, the right to revoke did not exist, neither party having retired from or ceased to do business, and the alleged reason for the revocation being only that the price of goods dealt in had become and might possibly remain low.

(March 31, 1890.)

*Head note by BLECKLEY, *Ch. J.*

ERROR to the City Court of Savannah to review a judgment in favor of plaintiffs in an action brought to recover compensation alleged to be due plaintiffs for personal services performed by them under a contract. *Affirmed.*

The case sufficiently appears in the opinion.

Messrs. **Denmark, Adams & Adams** for plaintiff in error.

Messrs. **Garrard & Meldrin** for defendants in error.

Bleckley, *Ch. J.*, delivered the opinion of the court:

There was no dispute or controversy as to the facts. Their legal significance—nothing else—was for determination; the parties having agreed that the only question should be whether the contract could be terminated before October 1 by the notice of December 15, 1886. The presiding judge decided this question in the negative, and directed a verdict accordingly. The notice referred to, dated December 15, 1886, was in these terms: "Owing to the present low prices of oil, and the possibility of a continuance of the same, we cannot, after December 31, 1886, continue to allow you $75 per month rebate, as heretofore. We solicit a continuance of your orders, and will be glad to allow you jobbers' rebate, the same we are now paying the other merchants."

The contract between the parties, as originally made, was in writing. It bore the date October 1, 1880. The obligations which it imposed on the agents (Gilbert & Co.) were these: (1) To sell coal oil for their principals at such prices as the latter might fix from time to time; (2) to handle no other oil for the period of one year from the date of the contract; (3) to receive the oil at their wharf, and store it in their warehouse, without charge for wharfage or storage; (4) to pay on the 10th of each month for all oil sold during the previous month. The obligations imposed upon the principals were, (1) to pay to the agents $75 per month for one year from the date of the contract; (2) to keep them supplied with merchantable oil at all seasons of the year; (3) to deliver the oil at their wharf or warehouse; (4) to pay them one dollar per barrel on the excess, if any, over 900 barrels sold by them during the year for which the agreement was made. Within a month or two after the year expired the contract was renewed, as the result of written correspondence, for a second year, terminating October 1, 1882. No subsequent negotiations took place, but the parties continued to deal in harmony with the terms of the written contract through all subsequent years, up to December 15, 1886, when the notice above recited was given. Afterwards, and until October of the following year, their dealings went on, but the oil sent during that period was furnished and received without prejudice to the claim of either party. The credit of $75 per month in the oil account, as kept by the principals, ceased with December, 1886, and from that time forward the credits entered as rebates amounted in the aggregate to only $18.84. In other words, compensation for nine months, which, according to the written contract, would be $675, was reduced to $18.84. To which of these sums were the agents entitled?

According to its letter, the notice did not seek to terminate the contract in any respect except as to the amount of compensation. It merely warned the agents that the principals would not pay as they had done theretofore, but would substitute the ordinary rebates allowed the trade. It did not propose to discharge the agents from any of their obligations, which, as we have seen, were not to handle any other oil, to receive and store without charge, and to pay unconditionally on the 10th of each month for all oil sold during the previous month. It admits of no doubt that the notice thus construed would not be effective for any purpose. But construing it, as both parties probably did, to be an effort to terminate the agency altogether, and release both parties from any and all obligation as to future dealings after January 1, 1887, the question is, Was there a legal right so to do? We think not. It is clear that during the first or second year both parties were bound, not from month to month only, but throughout the year, as there was an express undertaking on the part of the Oil Company to keep the agents supplied with oil at all seasons of the year, and to pay them $75 per month for one year. The case does not fall within the principle of such cases as *Burton* v. *Great Northern R. Co.*, 9 Exch. 507; *Rhodes* v. *Forwood*, L. R. 1 App. Cas. 256, and *Orr* v. *Ward*, 73 Ill. 318,—in which it was ruled that it was not obligatory on the employer to furnish business to the agent or employé throughout the whole period embraced in the contract, the reason of such ruling being that the employer had not stipulated so to do. Here, on the contrary, the stipulation was no less express on behalf of one party than of the other. If such a notice as we are considering would not have dissolved the engagement pending the first or second year of the service, it could not have that effect pending the seventh year, unless, by reason of not having been expressly renewed or continued after the second year, it ceased to be a contract for a whole year, and became indefinite as to time, or a contract at will only. Tested by the law of ordinary hiring, or of master and servant, there can be no doubt that services rendered without a new agreement, after the contract term has expired, are to be compensated at the same rate, and to that extent the prior contract is renewed or continued in force. *N. H. Iron Factory Co.* v. *Richardson*, 5 N. H. 294; *Wallace* v. *Floyd*, 29 Pa. 184; *Ranck* v. *Albright*, 36 Pa. 367; *Nicholson* v. *Patchin*, 5 Cal. 474; *Vail* v. *Jersey Little Falls Mfg. Co.* 32 Barb. 564; *Weise* v. *Milwaukee County Suprs.* 51 Wis. 564.

And, where the term of employment does not exceed one year, the authorities seem to us decisive that the prior contract is renewed or continued for an equivalent time, as well as at an equal rate. "Where the hiring is under a special agreement, the terms of that agreement must, of course, be observed. If there be no special agreement, but the hiring is a general one, without mention of time, it is considered to be for a year certain. If the servant continue in employment beyond that year, a contract for a second year is implied, and so on." Smith, Merc. Law, 266; Pomeroy's Smith, Merc. Law, § 508.

"Where a person has been employed by another for a certain definite term at fixed wages, if the services are continued after the expiration of the term in the same business, it is presumed that the continued services are rendered upon the same terms; but this is a mere presumption, which may be overcome by proof of a new contract, or of facts and circumstances that show that the parties in fact understood that the terms of the old contract were not to apply to the continued services." Wood, Mast. and Serv. § 96.

"A person who has been previously employed by the month, year or other fixed interval, and who is permitted to continue in the employment after the period limited by the original employment has expired, will, in the absence of anything to show a contrary intention, be presumed to be employed until the close of the current interval, and upon the same terms." Mechem, Ag. § 212.

"Tacit relocation is a doctrine borrowed from the Roman law. It is a presumed renovation of the contract from the period at which the former expired, and is held to arise from implied consent of parties, in consequence of their not having signified their intention that the agreement should terminate at the period stipulated. . . . Though the original contract may have been for a longer period than one year, the renewed agreement can never be for more than one year, because no verbal contract of location can extend longer." Fraser, Mast. and Serv. 58.

This last is a Scotch authority, but on this question the law of Scotland seems to coincide with our own, and with the law of Louisiana. See *Alba* v. *Moriarty*, 36 La. Ann. 680; *Lalande* v. *Aldrich* (La.) 6 South. Rep. 28; *Tallon* v. *Grand Portage Copper Min. Co.* 55 Mich. 147; *Sines* v. *Wayne County Poor Superintendents*, 58 Mich. 503; *McCullough Iron Co.* v. *Carpenter*, 67 Md. 554, 10 Cent. Rep. 118; *Tatterson* v. *Suffolk Mfg. Co.* 106 Mass. 56; *Capron* v. *Strout*, 11 Nev. 304; *Beeston* v. *Collyer*, 4 Bing. 309.

In the argument notice was taken of the difference between the English and the American rule as to presuming that an indefinite hiring is for a whole year. It was said that in the former country this presumption holds, but in the latter it does not. Wood, Mast. and Serv. § 136.

We think, however, this presumption has nothing to do with the matter; for whether the first hiring has its duration fixed by express or implied contract, if it be fixed in either way, the term (if not longer than one year) admits of duplication by tacit as well as express agreement. When we have a definite term of service, no matter how we get it, subsequent service of the same kind, where no new contract is made and nothing appears to indicate a change of intention, may be referred to the previous understanding, and to a tacit renewal of the engagement.

Thus far we have dealt with the question without any special reference to the law of agency, as distinguished from that of master and servant generally. This was a commercial agency, comprehending not only personal services, but the use of a wharf for landing the oil, and of a warehouse for storing it, and attended with a guaranty of the proceeds of all sales, the agents being obliged to pay within ten days for the oil sold in each month. The agents, if not *del credere* agents technically, were upon the same footing as such; they had to pay for all the goods they sold. No doubt the power of revoking the agency pending a current year's business existed, but the right to revoke it without sufficient cause did not exist, and a wrongful revocation leaves the principal liable to make reparation to the agent. Mechem, Ag. §§ 209, 614, 620, 621; Code, § 2183.

Here no cause was assigned but the low price of oil, and the prospect of its continuance. Neither of the parties had retired, or so far as appears wished to withdraw from business; and, according to the evidence, fifteen days' notice would be too short a time within which to make arrangements with other dealers for oil. To do that would require several months. We can see nothing whatever in the record to justify a revocation of the agency by such a notice as was given, and we agree with the presiding judge in the opinion that the Oil Company had no legal right to terminate the contract before October 1, 1887, without mutual consent. The engagement was one from year to year, and not merely at the will of either party. There was no contention that the amount claimed by the defendants in excess of the plaintiff's demand was more than they ought to recover upon their plea of set-off, if they were entitled to recover at all; and, the verdict being for that amount, it was correct, and the court did not err in refusing a new trial.

Judgment affirmed.

TENNESSEE SUPREME COURT.

Sam CARSON, *Appt.*,
v.
MEMPHIS & CHARLESTON R. CO.

(....Tenn.....)

1. **A garnishee is not bound to set up an exemption** law in favor of the principal defendant, who, with actual knowledge of the proceedings, fails to make a defense.

2. **An exemption law of one State has no** effect in an action brought in another State.

(April 17, 1890.)

APPEAL by plaintiff from a judgment of the Circuit Court for Shelby County in favor

NOTE.—*Garnishment; statutes no extraterritorial effect.*

A court will not give effect to the Exemption Laws of another State. Boykin v. Edwards, 21 Ala. 261; Newell v. Hayden, 8 Iowa, 140; Helfenstein v. Cave, 3 Iowa, 287; Baltimore & O. R. Co. v. May, 25 Ohio St. 347; Morgan v. Neville, 74 Pa. 52; Thompson, Homesteads and Exemptions, § 20.

See also 8 L. R. A. 321.

of defendant in an action brought to recover wages alleged to be due. *Affirmed.*

The case sufficiently appears in the opinion.

Messrs. **Watson & Hirsch** for appellant.

Messrs. **Poston & Poston**, for appellee:

The Company was subject to garnishment, and the judgment is valid and binding upon it and its employé, the garnished debtor.

National Bank v. *Huntington*, 129 Mass. 444; *Mooney* v. *Union Pac. R. Co.* 60 Iowa, 346, 9 Am. & Eng. R. R. Cas. 131; *Eichelburger* v. *Pittsburg, C. & St. L. R. Co.* (Ohio) 9 Am. & Eng. R. R. Cas. 158; *Burlington & M. R. R. Co.* v. *Thompson*, 31 Kan. 180, 16 Am. & Eng. R. R. Cas. 480; *Fithian* v. *New York & E. R. Co.* 31 Pa. 114; *Pennsylvania R. Co.* v. *Peoples*, 31 Ohio St. 537; *Barr* v. *King*, 96 Pa. 486; Thompson, Homesteads and Exemptions, § 21; Freeman, Executions, § 209; Morawetz, Priv. Corp. § 961; *Libbey* v. *Hodgdon*, 9 N. H. 396; *Newby* v. *Von Oppen*, L. R. 7 Q. B. 293; *City F. Ins. Co.* v. *Carrugi*, 41 Ga. 670; *St. Louis P. Ins. Co.* v. *Cohen*, 9 Mo. 441; *Hannibal & St. J. R. Co.* v. *Crane*, 102 Ill. 250.

A garnishee is not a party to an action in the sense that he is required to make defense as between the plaintiff and defendant.

Moore v. *Chicago, R. I. & P. R. Co.* 48 Iowa, 385; *Walters* v. *Washington Ins. Co.* 1 Iowa, 411.

The Company was not bound to plead in the Alabama court that such wages were exempt. The law is otherwise.

Walters v. *Washington Ins. Co. supra;* Thompson, Homesteads and Exemptions, § 23.

Exemption Laws have no extraterritorial effect.

Burlington & M. R. R. Co. v. *Thompson*, 31 Kan. 180, 16 Am. & Eng. R. R. Cas. 480; *Helfenstein* v. *Cave*, 3 Iowa, 287; *Moore* v. *Chicago, R. I. & P. R. Co.* 48 Iowa, 385; *Baltimore & O. R. Co.* v. *May*, 25 Ohio St. 325, 347; *Morgan* v. *Neville*, 74 Pa. 52; *Lock* v. *Johnson*, 36 Me. 464; *Chicago & A. R. Co.* v. *Ragland*, 84 Ill. 375.

The garnishee is not compelled to claim the exemption, as it is a personal privilege to be claimed by the employé or not, as he chooses, and the garnishee cannot, in most cases, know whether he desires to claim it or not.

Thompson, Homesteads and Exemptions, § 23.

A garnishee cannot insist on matter by plea which would be good only in abatement of the attachment. That must come from the defendant.

Cheatham v. *Trotter*, Peck (Tenn.) 198.

Caldwell, *J.*, delivered the opinion of the court:

This is an action of debt, tried below and here on an agreed state of facts. The plaintiff, Sam Carson, was in the service of the defendant, the Memphis & Charleston Railroad Company, as brakeman on one of its trains running from Memphis to Chattanooga, and back again through Mississippi and Alabama. He was a citizen of Tennessee, made his contract of employment here, and usually received his wages at Memphis, though no place of payment was named in the contract. While so employed the plaintiff, in the month of May, 1888, earned $20.45, which, by the custom of the Company, became due and payable on the 10th of June following. On the 28th of May, Prout, a citizen of Alabama, sued out an original attachment in that State against Carson, on the ground of nonresidence, to collect a debt of $21 contracted there; and on the same day a writ of garnishment issued on the attachment against the Memphis & Charleston Railroad Company to reach a sufficiency of Carson's wages to pay his debt to Prout. Proper publication was made for Carson, and by that means, or some other, he had actual notice of the pendency of the attachment and garnishment proceedings; but he failed to make defense. The garnishment process was served on the Company's agent at Tuscumbia, and on the 11th of June, one day after Carson's wages became due and payable, the Company answered that it owed him $20.45 for wages due him as brakeman. Trial was duly had, and judgment rendered against the garnishee for the $20.45. This judgment the Company paid. Thereafter, on the 28th of June, 1888, Carson brought the present suit before a justice of the peace, at Memphis, to recover the same wages from the Railroad Company. The fact of the proceedings in Alabama, and the payment of the judgment there, were interposed as a defense to the action. The justice of the peace, and after him the judge of the circuit court, adjudged the defense a good one, and rendered judgment for the defendant. Carson has appealed in error.

It is agreed that the attachment and garnishment proceedings were in strict conformity to the laws of Alabama. From this concession, it follows that the garnishee was completely discharged from all liability by payment of the garnishment judgment, unless there be something in the question of exemption to take the case out of the usual rule, and prevent that result. It is earnestly urged by Carson's counsel that this is an exceptional case, made so by the fact that, under the law of this State (Mill. & V. Code, § 2931), his wages to the extent of $30 were exempt from seizure by garnishment or otherwise. The position, briefly stated, is that it was the duty of the garnishee to claim the exemption for Carson, and thereby prevent judgment against it on the garnishment process, and that, having failed to do this, the Company's indebtedness to him remains unchanged and unsatisfied. To our mind, this position seems altogether untenable, for more reasons than one.

1. There was no peculiarity about this indebtedness to Carson,—no inherent quality or

---

In Wisconsin it has been held that it is the duty of the garnishee to notify the debtor of the proceedings, and to set up the defense that the wages were exempt from execution by the law of the State of the debtor's residence (Pierce v. Chicago & N. W. R. Co. 36 Wis. 283); but this doctrine has been denied by the Supreme Courts of Iowa and Ohio. Moore v. Chicago, R. I. & P. R. Co. 43 Iowa, 385; Conley v. Chilcote, 25 Ohio St. 320. See Chicago & A. R. Co. v. Ragland, 84 Ill. 375, 5 Cent. L. J. 169; Winterfield v. Milwaukee & St. P. R. Co. 29 Wis. 589; Snook v. Snetzer, 25 Ohio St. 516; Missouri & P. R. Co. v. Whipler, post,——

superadded responsibility to distinguish it from any other debt, so far as the Company was concerned. It owed this debt as it owed any other debt. It had assumed no other obligation than that of payment of a particular sum at a specified time. The contention of Carson would make the obligation greatly more burdensome, by throwing upon the Company the additional responsibility and expense of knowing, at its peril, that there was an exemption law in his favor, and of claiming the benefit of it for him. Such a requirement would be unjust and unreasonable.

In *Davenport* v. *Swan*, 9 Humph. 186, the garnishee stated in his answer that a horse of a debtor in his possession was exempt from execution, whereupon he was discharged, because his answer, which was conclusive, did not contain a sufficient admission to charge him. That case does not stand in the way of the views just expressed. There the garnishee volunteered to set up the fact of exemption. He was not required to do it; nor was it decided or intimated that it was his duty to do so, or that, in case of failure to do so, he would have been liable to the garnishment debtor for the value of the horse. No such question was before the court.

The question of the right or duty of a garnishee in this State to plead the Exemption Law of another State in favor of its creditor, the garnishment debtor, who resided in the other State, was expressly reserved by this court in the case of *Holland* v. *Mobile & O. R. Co.*, 16 Lea, 418, 419.

2. Had the Railroad Company made the claim of exemption ever so formally for Carson, it would have availed him nothing. Exemption Laws have no extraterritorial effect. Their operation is restricted to the States in which they are enacted. Freeman, Executions, § 209; Thompson, Homesteads and Exemptions, § 20.

Carson was a citizen of Tennessee, and in the courts of this State would have been entitled to the exemption, had he claimed it; but the suit was in Alabama, where even he could not have made the claim successfully. Then, of course, the garnishee could not have done so for him, and ought not to suffer for failing to make the effort. Nonresidents of this State cannot avail themselves of the benefit of our Exemption Laws, either as to personalty (*Hawkins* v. *Pearce*, 11 Humph. 45; *Lisenbee* v. *Holt*, 1 Sneed, 50), or as to homestead. *Prater* v. *Prater*, 87 Tenn. (3 Pickle) 83; *Emmett* v. *Emmett*, 14 Lea, 370.

Learned counsel for Carson relies on certain authorities which are yet to be noticed.

Mr. Smyth, in his work on Homesteads and Exemptions (§ 562), says: "A garnishee who pays over money which constitutes a part of the personalty exemption of the debtor does so at his own risk. He will be liable to the debtor (his creditor) for the full amount of the money he has paid. A person who has been brought into court as garnishee may answer that the property of the debtor in his hands, or his indebtedness to such debtor, is exempt by law from seizure on attachment or execution, and he is bound to bring the fact to the notice of the court; otherwise the judgment against such garnishee, and the satisfaction thereof, will not bar an action against him by the attaching debtor." For these propositions the author cites *Watkins* v. *Cason*, 46 Ga. 444, and *Pierce* v. *Chicago & N. W. R. Co.* 36 Wis. 283. We have not had access to the former of these cases, but the latter we find to be an authority for the text, and very similar to the one at bar, the difference being that the creditor of the garnishee in that case had no notice of the suit pleaded in bar. That case has attracted wide attention, and received very unfavorable comments from courts of last resort and text-writers. It cites no precedent to support it, and, so far as we know, has not itself been followed by any subsequent case. In *note 2* to section 209 of his work on Executions, Mr. Freeman says it is "utterly indefensible."

Mr. Thompson likewise assails it as unsound, and assigns his reasons at some length in section 866 of his work on Homesteads and Exemptions.

The cases of *Burlington & M. R. R. Co.* v. *Thompson*, 31 Kan. 180; *Mooney* v. *Union Pac. R. Co.*, 60 Iowa, 346, and *Eichelburger* v. *Pittsburg, C. & St. L. R. Co.* (Ohio), 9 Am. & Eng. R. R. Cas. 158, decided, respectively, by the court of last resort in Kansas, Iowa and Ohio, are in conflict with the Wisconsin case (the last one expressly denying its soundness), and in harmony with our holding herein.

Let the judgment be affirmed.

ILLINOIS SUPREME COURT.

Hattie POND, *Appt.*,
v.
David SHEEAN, Exr., etc., of Bradner Smith, Deceased, *et al.*

(.......Ill.......)

1. A parol promise by a person to leave all his property, real, personal and mixed, to a child in consideration of her becoming a member of his family and taking his name, is void under the Statute of Frauds.

2. Becoming a member of a man's family, and taking his name, and living with him as his child until his death in consideration of a parol promise by him to leave all his property, real, personal and mixed, to such child, is not such a part performance of the contract as to

---

NOTE.—*Parol promise to leave property by will is within the Statute of Frauds.*

Where an agreement concerns land, and is in parol, it is void by the Statute of Frauds. If it so appears on the face of the bill, such defense may be taken advantage of on demurrer. Randall v. Howard, 67 U. S. 2 Black, 585 (17 L. ed. 269).

An executory contract to devise real estate must be in writing. Roehl v. Haumesser, 12 West. Rep. 901, 114 Ind. 311.

8 L. R. A.

See also 9 L. R. A. 129.

make it amount to a fraud to refuse performance of the promise, on the ground that it is within the Statute of Frauds.

3. **An entire contract** relating to personal as well as real estate, if void as to the real estate under the Statute of Frauds is void as to the personal property also.

(March 29, 1890.)

APPEAL by plaintiff from a judgment of the Circuit Court for Jo Daviess County in favor of defendants in an action to compel specific performance of an alleged parol contract by which plaintiff was to receive certain property at the death of Bradner Smith. *Affirmed.*

The facts are fully stated in the opinion.

Messrs. **Hopkins, Aldrich & Thatcher** and **E. L. Bedford** for appellant.

Mr. **John J. Jones,** for appellees:

The contract alleged is obnoxious to the Statute of Frauds. In order to take a parol contract respecting lands out of the Statute of Frauds there must be exclusive possession, taken under the contract, by the party seeking its enforcement.

Updike v. *Armstrong*, 4 Ill. 566; *Shirley* v. *Spencer*, 9 Ill. 600; *Ramsey* v. *Liston*, 25 Ill. 114; *Stevens* v. *Wheeler*, 25 Ill. 309; *Mason* v. *Bair*, 33 Ill. 207; *Keyes* v. *Test*, Id. 319; *Fitzsimmons* v. *Allen*, 39 Ill. 440; *Laird* v. *Allen*, 82 Ill. 43; *McNamara* v. *Garrity*, 106 Ill. 387; *Bright* v. *Bright*, 41 Ill. 97; *Kurtz* v. *Hibner*, 55 Ill. 514; *Bohanan* v. *Bohanan*, 96 Ill. 591; *McDowell* v. *Lucas*, 97 Ill. 498; *Gudgel* v. *Kitterman*, 108 Ill. 50; *Hart* v. *Carroll*, 85 Pa. 508; *Ballard* v. *Ward*, 89 Pa. 358; *Detrick* v. *Sharrar*, 95 Pa. 521; *Miller* v. *Zufall*, 4 Cent. Rep. 490, 113 Pa. 317; *Recknagle* v. *Schmaltz*, 72 Iowa, 63; *Wood* v. *Thornly*, 58 Ill. 464; *Padfield* v. *Padfield*, 92 Ill. 198; *Pickerell* v. *Morse*, 97 Ill. 224; *Cronk* v. *Trumble*, 66 Ill. 428.

Full payment of the purchase money for real estate verbally agreed to be conveyed is not of itself sufficient to take the agreement out of the Statute of Frauds.

Fitzsimmons v. *Allen, supra; Temple* v. *Johnson*, 71 Ill. 13; *Gorham* v. *Dodge*, 11 West. Rep. 602, 122 Ill. 528.

The contract should also be established, by competent proofs, to be clear, definite and unequivocal in all its terms. If the terms are ambiguous, or not made out by satisfactory proofs, a specific performance will not be decreed.

Worth v. *Worth*, 84 Ill. 442; *Gosse* v. *Jones*, 73 Ill. 510; *Langston* v. *Bates*, 84 Ill. 525; *Bohanan* v. *Bohanan*, 96 Ill. 595; *Ferbrache* v. *Ferbrache*, 110 Ill. 210.

A court of equity interferes to enforce a contract within the Statute of Frauds only where there have been such acts of performance by the party asking relief that he would suffer an injury amounting to a fraud by a refusal to execute the agreement.

Wallace v. *Rappleye*, 103 Ill. 231; *Preston* v. *Casner*, 104 Ill. 264; *Kaufman* v. *Cook*, 114 Ill.

An executory contract to bequeath personal property exceeding $50 in value must be in writing. *Ibid.*

An oral promise to make a will of all the testator's property, real and personal, in favor of a person, who in consideration thereof agrees to make a similar will in favor of the first testator and makes one accordingly, is a contract for the sale of lands, within the Statute of Frauds. Gould v. Mansfield, 103 Mass. 408.

Where a promise rests in parol its performance could not be enforced in equity if lands were to be devised, unless under such circumstances as would justify the enforcement of a parol contract for the conveyance of land. DeMoss v. Robinson, 46 Mich. 65; Gould v. Mansfield, *supra;* McClure v. McClure, 1 Pa. 374.

An oral agreement, that if a niece would live with her uncle as his child, taking his name and performing housework, she should receive all his property after his death, is within the Statute of Frauds. Specific performance will not lie; but an action will lie to recover the value of services rendered. Wallace v. Long, 3 West. Rep. 870, 105 Ind. 522.

Where a mother verbally promised that at her death certain property should belong to her daughter if she would live with her, the mother furnishing the house and paying the expenses, no such possession is acquired by the daughter, in executing the agreement, as takes the contract out of the Statute. Gorham v. Dodge, 11 West. Rep. 716, 122 Ill. 528.

Negotiations between a father and daughter, by which the father was to deed to his daughter certain property in consideration of his maintenance and support during his life, and which were never consummated, the deeds prepared not being executed, will not give the daughter the right to retain possession of the land against the father. Zenor v. Johnson, 9 West. Rep. 378, 111 Ind. 42.

Performance and possession take it out of the Statute.

A valid oral agreement may be made to leave a sum of money by will to a particular person in consideration of services thereafter to be rendered by the promisee to the promisor, provided such services are in fact thereafter rendered and accepted in pursuance of such contract. Wellington v. Apthorp, 4 New Eng. Rep. 383, 145 Mass. 69.

An agreement resting in parol, to devise real estate in consideration of services in caring for the testator, is binding and enforceable when the promisee has performed the consideration. Pflugar v. Pultz, 9 Cent. Rep. 488, 43 N. J. Eq. 440.

Where a proposal by an uncle, in a letter to his niece, that if her daughter would take care of him and his wife he would devise to the niece one half of his estate, was accepted and fulfilled, it will be enforced against his estate. Roehl v. Haumesser, 12 West. Rep. 899, 114 Ind. 311.

In an action to enforce the agreement made on the adoption of a child, where it appears plaintiff has fully performed the contract on her part, and the same has also been performed in part by the other parties thereto, and to the extent of providing for and maintaining plaintiff during many years, the Statute of Frauds has no application. Sharkey v. McDermott, 8 West. Rep. 737, 91 Mo. 647.

An oral agreement by a father to convey land to a daughter, if she would maintain her grandmother during life, is taken out of the Statute by possession, and complete performance of the agreement, and the making of valuable improvements on the land, by the daughter. Burns v. Fox, 12 West. Rep. 117, 113 Ind. 205.

A parol agreement by a father, that if his two sons would pay the interest and balance of the purchase money of land, and take care of their parents during life, they should have the land after his death, executed by the sons for fifteen or twenty years, is binding, and is not within the Statute of Frauds. Carney v. Carney, 14 West. Rep. 783, 95 Mo. 353.

11; *Clark* v. *Clark*, 11 West. Rep. 896, 122 Ill. 388; *Warren* v. *Warren*, 105 Ill. 569; *Wallace* v. *Long*, 3 West. Rep. 570, 105 Ind. 522.

The alleged contract, being entire as to realty and personalty, cannot be enforced as to the personalty alone where the Statute of Frauds applies to that portion of the contract which relates to realty.

Thayer v. *Rock*, 13 Wend. 53; *Cooke* v. *Tombs*, 2 Anstr. 420; *Lea* v. *Barber*, 2 Anstr. 425, *note; Meyers* v. *Schemp*, 67 Ill. 471; *Prante* v. *Schutte*, 18 Ill. App. 62; *Hall* v. *Loomis*, 6 West. Rep. 617, 63 Mich. 709.

As a general rule specific performance will not be enforced of a contract relating to personalty.

Parker v. *Garrison*, 61 Ill. 250; *Pierce* v. *Plumb*, 74 Ill. 331; *Cohn* v. *Mitchell*, 2 West. Rep. 63, 115 Ill. 131.

Craig, *J.*, delivered the opinion of the court:

This was a bill in equity, brought by Hattie Pond, to set aside the last will of Bradner Smith, deceased, and to enforce the specific performance of a parol agreement alleged to have been made on or about the 1st day of December, 1857, between Marshall B. Pierce, father of complainant, and Bradner Smith, under which the complainant claims all the property, both real and personal, which the said Bradner Smith owned at the time of his death. The bill sets out the contract, substantially, as follows:

"Bradner Smith, after consultation with his wife, Mary Smith, and with her full consent and approval, in order to induce oratrix's father to consent to the separation, and permit her to become a member of the family of said Bradner Smith, made a proposition to your oratrix's father that if he would permit them, the said Bradner and wife, to take your oratrix to their home, and would permit her to assume the name of 'Smith,' instead of 'Pierce,' and allow her to live with them as their child, the said Bradner Smith, in consideration thereof, would give your oratrix at his death [amended to read 'at their,' viz., Bradner and Mary Smith's 'death'] all his property—real, personal and mixed—that he might have in his name, or under his control, at the time of decease; that, in consideration of these promises, her father consented and agreed to said proposition, and then and there entered into a contract with said B. Smith, with the knowledge and consent of his wife, Mary Smith, that oratrix should go and live with them, as their child, assume the name of 'Smith' instead of 'Pierce,' take the place of their child, live with them as such, and, in consideration thereof, at the death of said B. Smith [amended to read 'at their death,' namely, Mary and Bradner Smith, instead of 'at his death'] all of his estate—real, personal and mixed—was to become and be the property of your oratrix; that, in compliance with said contract, oratrix then and there, to wit, December 1, 1856, did leave her father's home, and go to the home of B. Smith and wife, and became a member of their family, and assumed the name of 'Smith' instead of 'Pierce,' and was known as 'Smith,' from thence until oratrix's marriage, and oratrix faithfully carried out her part of said contract, and was a true and faithful child of said Mary and B. Smith during their lives, and performed her part of above contract."

It is also alleged that complainant lived with the Smiths, under said agreement, until she was twenty-nine years of age, when she was married to Dr. Frederick L. Pond. It is also alleged that Mary Smith died May 21, 1885, and that Bradner Smith died March 31, 1887. It is also alleged that "in violation of said contract," etc., "and in fraud of your oratrix's rights in the premises, B. Smith was induced, December 19, 1885, to execute a purported will, and on January 7, 1887, shortly before his death, executed a purported codicil thereto, as appears by copies attached to Exhibits A and B, by which will and codicil he deprived oratrix of any part of his property whatever; that Bradner Smith, at the time of executing said purported will and codicil, was weak in mind, and in his dotage, and by reason of said condition was induced, in fraud of oratrix's rights, to execute the same."

The complainant sets out in the bill a list of property—real, personal and mixed—owned by the deceased at the time of his death, valued at $20,000. The bill then prays that the will and codicil may be declared null and void; that complainant be declared to be the owner and entitled to the possession of the personal property and notes; and that deeds may be executed conveying the lands to her. The executor and devisees under the will put in answers to the bill in which they deny the making of the alleged contract, and plead the Statute of Frauds thereto. They also denied all the substantial allegations of the bill. A cross-bill was also filed by one of the legatees, Clara A. Smith; but, as that has no bearing on the decision of the case, it is not necessary to set out its contents here. Replication having been filed, the cause proceeded to a hearing on the pleadings and evidence, and the court entered a decree dismissing the bill for want of equity; and the complainant appealed.

The complainant's mother was a sister of Mary A. Smith, the wife of Bradner Smith. She died May 10, 1854, when complainant was about two years old. Bradner and Mary Smith had no children of their own, and soon after the death of complainant's mother they took complainant to their home; and she there remained until the second marriage of her father, July 28, 1856, when she returned home to her father. It seems that during the two years' residence of complainant with the Smiths they became very much attached to her, and made an effort to arrange with complainant's father for her return to their home. Pierce, the father of complainant, resided at Savanna, and the Smiths at Galena. The contract under which complainant was taken into the Smith's family was claimed to be proven by one witness,—who was present when the contract was made, —Mrs. Pierce, now the widow of complainant's father. She stated that she was married, July 28, 1856, to Marshall B. Pierce, who at the time of their marriage had six children, Hattie, the youngest, being four years old at the time. "She continued to reside in our family six or eight months after our marriage. At the end of that period of eight months, arrangements were made by my husband, Marshall B. Pierce, with Bradner Smith and Mary A. Smith, his wife, through Mary A. Smith, with respect to the future care, custody, nurture and services of the complainant, Hattie Pond, then Pierce, by which they were to keep her, and raise her as their own child, giving her the advantage of a good education, and were to leave her their property, whatever it was, when they were done with it, in consideration of the future care, nurture and services of the complainant. This agreement was entered into at our house in Savanna. I was present when the arrangement was made. I think it was in 1857. I don't know that anyone was present except Mr. Pierce, myself and family. Mrs. Smith made the contract on the part of Bradner Smith and herself. They resided at Galena at that time. Mrs. Smith at that time said, concerning when Hattie, the complainant, was to have the property of the Smiths, that she was to receive the property when they were done with it,—she was to have all they had. She had always expected to take Hattie, but never had claimed her until Mr. Pierce was married, when she thought she ought to have her. Mary A. Smith meant by that expression, 'when they were done with it,' referring to their property, at their death. Marshall Pierce, my husband, and I supposed them to refer to the death of Mr. and Mrs. Smith. After the arrangement was entered into as above, Mrs. Smith took the complainant home with her to Galena."

The declarations of the Smiths, on different occasions during the time that Hattie resided with them, were proven by several witnesses, to the effect that what they had would be hers when they were through with it; that she would be an heir, etc.,—but no person now living heard the contract except Mrs. Pierce, whose evidence is given above. At the time the arrangement relied upon was made, Smith owned real and personal property; and, as heretofore shown, he owned real and personal property at the time of his death. Mary Smith, the wife of Bradner, died May 21, 1885; and the latter died March 31, 1887. There is no controversy in regard to the fact that complainant, from the time she was four years of age until she married, at the age of twenty-nine, on October 10, 1880, resided with the Smiths as a member of their family. She was boarded, clothed and educated by them: and at the same time she performed such services as are usual in a family occupying the position in society that the Smiths occupied. So far as appears, she was treated as a child, and no doubt performed the same services, and received the same advantages, in education, clothing and other respects, that she would have received if she had been a child of the Smiths. Whether Bradner Smith, in raising complainant from infancy to womanhood, in clothing and educating her, in aiding her to consummate an advantageous marriage, in giving her property, did all that, in morals, he should have done, is not a question which we are called upon to determine. The complainant seeks by her bill the specific performance of a parol contract. Under the contract she claims personal property, choses in action and real estate; but, as she never was in possession of any of the property under the contract, the Statute of Frauds being pleaded, is she entitled to a decree? While other questions are involved, this is the most important one.

The law may be regarded as well settled that a parol contract for the sale of lands will be enforced where the purchase money has been paid, possession taken under the contract and lasting and valuable improvements made on the lands. *Stevens* v. *Wheeler*, 25 Ill. 309; *McNamara* v. *Garrity*, 106 Ill. 387; *Fitzsimmons* v. *Allen*, 39 Ill. 440; *Laird* v. *Allen*, 82 Ill. 43.

So, also, where the owner of real estate makes a parol promise to his child to convey lands to him, and, relying on such promise, the child goes into possession of the lands, and makes valuable and lasting improvements, such a promise rests upon a valuable consideration, and may be enforced in equity. *Kurtz* v. *Hibner*, 55 Ill. 514.

In the case last cited, it was held that no important distinction exists between such a promise and a sale. But we are aware of no well-considered case holding that a court of equity will decree the specific performance of a parol agreement to convey lands where the purchaser has not entered into possession under the contract; but, on the other hand, this court has held in a number of cases that possession under the contract must be established in order to take the case out of the Statute of Frauds. *Wood* v. *Thornly*, 58 Ill. 465.

In the case cited it is said: "To constitute such performance as will avoid the Statute, it must clearly and distinctly appear that the party entered into possession under the agreement itself. . . . The mere possession of land under a parol agreement of sale, even with the superadded fact of valuable improvements, will not be deemed part performance, if the possession was obtained otherwise than under the contract."

In *Temple* v. *Johnson*, 71 Ill. 14, the question arose whether full payment of the purchase money, without taking possession of the premises, was sufficient to take a case out of the Statute of Frauds; and in disposing of the question it is said: "In the case of *Fitzsimmons* v. *Allen*, 39 Ill. 440, it was held that the payment in full of the purchase money, and the possession of the property purchased, took the case out of the Statute of Frauds. This is the greatest relaxation of the requirements of the Statute that has been made by this court, nor do we incline to go any further in that direction."

While the decisions of the various courts are not entirely uniform, the general rule seems to be, as stated by Story in his work on Equity Jurisprudence, § 761, that the general ground upon which courts proceed to execute parol contracts for part performance, as the governing rule, is "that nothing is to be considered as a part performance which does not put the party into a situation which is a fraud upon him, unless the agreement is fully performed;" and he says that, although formerly a payment of the purchase money was considered a sufficient part performance to take the case out of the Statute, the rule is now otherwise settled: and in this he is fully sustained by the adjudged cases both in the British and American courts.

In *Ferbrache* v. *Ferbrache*, 110 Ill. 210, this court again held that by the Statute of Frauds all contracts for the transfer of title to land must be in writing; and, to take a case out of the Statute, it is indispensable that the contract shall be established by competent proof, to be clear, definite and unequivocal in all its terms, and that possession shall have been taken of the land under the contract, and payment of the purchase money made. See also *Kaufman* v. *Cook*, 114 Ill. 13; *Clark* v. *Clark*, 122 Ill. 388, 11 West. Rep. 396; *Gorham* v. *Dodge*, 122 Ill. 528, 11 West. Rep. 602.

A case of much point is *Wallace* v. *Long*, 105 Ind. 522, 8 West. Rep. 870. In that case a child seven years old was taken under an agreement that, if she would live with decedent and her husband until their death, they would make her their heir, and at their death they would will her their entire estate. Property, real and personal, was left, of the value of $6,000; but no will was made as per the contract. In deciding the case, it is said: "If the Statute of Frauds presents no obstacle to the enforcement of the contract, then, so far as the record discloses, none exists. It cannot, of course, be denied that if the contract had been in writing, or if, in pursuance of an oral contract, the plaintiff had been put in complete possession, and she had otherwise fully performed on her part, specific performance could have been enforced. It would then have presented a case analogous in principle to *Mauck* v. *Melton*, 64 Ind. 414.... This much has been said to show that the only impediment in the way of a specific enforcement of the contract involved in this case is the Statute of Frauds. When the title to property . . . is to be acquired by purchase, the Statute of Frauds will operate upon and affect the contract, in precisely the same manner, whether the consideration for the purchase is to be paid in services, money or anything else. In either case, such a contract, being in parol, and entirely executory, cannot be enforced by either party. That the evidence in this case tends to support the view that it was the purpose of the intestate to make provision for the plaintiff's ward by a will, may be conceded; but, as the agreement to do so was never manifested in writing, signed by her, and as it involved an agreement for a sale of real estate, and for the transfer of personal property, . . . such agreement was subject to the operation of the Statute of Frauds equally with all other agreements for like sales. Because the agreement was not withdrawn from the operation of the Statute by part performance, it cannot be specifically enforced; neither can it be the foundation of an action for damages."

It will be observed that in the case cited, while the agreement was one of the same character as the agreement involved here, the same rule was held to apply as if it was a mere verbal sale of real estate, where no possession had been taken under the contract.

In view of the authorities, we are able to arrive at but one conclusion; and that is that the contract relied upon, resting in parol, is within the Statute of Frauds, and void. Conceding that complainant was taken into the family of the Smiths under an arrangement as testified to by Mrs. Pierce, and that they were to leave her their property when they were done with it, "in consideration of the future care, nurture and services" of complainant, and treating the surrender of complainant by her father, and such services as she may have rendered, as a payment for the property agreed to be given her, still, as she never obtained possession of any of the property under the contract, under the authorities the agreement, resting in parol, was void by the Statute of Frauds, and cannot be enforced in a court of equity. It is imposing no hardship upon parties, where the title to real property is involved, to require their contracts to be reduced to writing; and it is the safer rule. Where the terms and conditions of a contract depend upon the recollection of witnesses after the lapse of many years, as is the case here, there is always much uncertainty in regard to what the contract really was; and, where the title to real property is involved, no rule ought to be adopted which will encourage the making of such contracts. There are cases cited in appellant's brief which seem to lay down a different rule, and which seem to support appellant's position; but we have not the time to review them here, nor do we think it would serve any useful purpose to do so. It is sufficient to say that the cases referred to are not in harmony with the principle announced by the decisions of this court, and we are not inclined to follow them.

But it is contended in the argument that the services rendered by complainant, and the facts, as they appear from the record, that the whole course of her subsequent life was changed in consequence of the agreement, prevent the Smiths from relying on the Statute of Frauds. In other words, by the acts of performance, complainant would suffer an injury amounting to a fraud unless relief is granted under the contract. The rule on this subject is laid down in *Wallace* v. *Rappleye*, 103 Ill. 231, and the cases there cited. But we do not regard the acts of performance proven in this case such as would authorize a court in holding that complainant has suffered an injury amounting to a fraud unless she is granted relief. When the father of complainant consented that she might enter the Smith family, he was a man in very moderate circumstances. He had a wife and six or seven children to support, and for several years relied upon a salary, as clerk of a steamboat on the Mississippi River, for the support of himself and family, while, on the other hand, Bradner Smith was in good circumstances—alleged to be worth $40,000. He had no family but himself and wife. He was therefore in a condition to afford complainant many advantages in her raising and education that she would not receive if she resided with her parents. So far, therefore, as being placed in a worse condition on account of the agreement, it is without foundation. Indeed, the manner in which complainant was raised and educated, and the marriage she subsequently contracted through the influence of the Smiths, seem to show that her condition in life was improved, rather than injured, by the arrangement.

It will, however, be observed that complainant seeks by her bill to recover personal property as well as real estate; and it may be claimed that as to the personal property the agreement is not within the Statute. The contract, however, must be regarded as an entirety; and, if void as to real estate, it must also be held void as to personal property. This is a rule of law well established. *Meyers* v. *Schemp*, 67 Ill. 469.

The decree of the Circuit Court will be affirmed.

MINNESOTA SUPREME COURT.

Andrew JOHNSON, *Appt.*,
v.
ST. PAUL & DULUTH R. CO., *Respt.*

(....Minn.....)

*1. **Railroad Employer's Liability Act.** *Held*, following *Lavallee* v. *St. Paul, M. & M. R. Co.*, 40 Minn. 249, that chapter 13, Laws 1887, applies only to employés of railway corporations exposed to the peculiar hazards connected with the use and operation of the road.

2. **A crew of men**, of which plaintiff was one, was engaged in repairing a bridge on defendant's road, and in performing the work it was necessary to leave the draw partly open. Through the negligence of one of the crew, the draw was left unfastened, and was blown shut by the wind, and injured the plaintiff while at work between the stationary part of the bridge and draw. *Held*, that defendant was not liable.

(April 30, 1890.)

APPEAL by plaintiff from an order of the District Court for St. Louis County denying his motion for a new trial in an action brought to recover damages for personal injuries alleged to have resulted from the negligence of defendant's servants, in which the complaint had been dismissed. *Affirmed.*

Plaintiff was a carpenter in the employ of defendant, engaged in the occupation of repairing bridges that were out of order. While working upon a drawbridge over the St. Louis River near Duluth, he was injured by reason of the draw, which had been negligently left unfastened, swinging shut, owing to the force of the wind, and catching him between the stationary part of the bridge and the draw.

This action was brought to recover damages for such injuries under chapter 13 of the Session Laws of 1887, which reads as follows:

"Every railroad corporation owning or operating a railroad in this State shall be liable for all damages sustained by any agent or servant thereof, by reason of the negligence of any other agent or servant thereof, without contributory negligence on his part, when sustained within this State; and no contract, rule or regulation between such corporation and any agent or servant shall impair or diminish such liability: *Provided*, that nothing in this Act shall be so construed as to render any railroad company liable for damages sustained by any employé, agent or servant while engaged in the construction of a new road or any part thereof, not open to public travel or use."

Messrs. **Draper & Davis** for appellant.

Messrs. **White & Reynolds, James Smith, Jr.**, and **W. H. Bliss** for respondent.

*Head notes by MITCHELL, J.

NOTE.—Construction of Massachusetts Employer's Liability Act, Stat. 1887, chap. 270. See *notes* to Ryalls v. Mechanics Mills (Mass.) 5 L. R. A. 667; Mellor v. Merchants Mfg. Co. (Mass.) 5 L. R. A. 792. And see Ashley v. Hart, 1 L. R. A. 355, 147 Mass. 573.

Mitchell, *J.*, delivered the opinion of the court:

The injury to plaintiff having been caused by the negligence of his fellow servant, he cannot recover unless under chapter 13, Laws 1887.

In *Lavallee* v. *St. Paul, M. & M. R. Co.*, 40 Minn. 249, in which this Statute was very fully considered, we held that it applied only to the peculiar hazards incident to the use and operation of railroads; that it must be construed as designed exclusively for the benefit of those who are in the course of their employment exposed to such hazards, and whose injuries are caused by them. And the more we consider the question the more are we confirmed in the opinion that it is only when construed as subject to some such limitation that the Statute can be sustained as a valid law. As was said in the case referred to, to avoid the imputation of "class" legislation, the classification, in cases of special legislation, must be made upon some apparent, natural reason,—some reason suggested by necessity, by such a difference in the situation and circumstances of the subjects placed in different classes as suggests the necessity or propriety of different legislation with respect to them. If a distinction is to be made as to the liability of employers to their employés, it must be based upon a difference in the nature of the employment, and not of the employers. One rule of liability cannot be established for railway companies, merely as such, and another rule for other employers, under like circumstances and conditions, unless upon the theory suggested in *Missouri P. R. Co.* v. *Mackey*, 127 U. S. 205 [32 L. ed. 107], that the State may "prescribe the liabilities under which corporations created by its laws shall conduct their business in the future, where no limitation is placed upon its power in this respect by their charters,"—a proposition which, as thus broadly stated, that court, in view of its later utterances, could hardly have intended to announce. Indeed, the particular question now under consideration was not before the court, and, presumably, was not in mind. Neither would it relieve the Act from the imputation of class legislation that it applies alike to all railroads. It has been sometimes loosely stated that special legislation is not class, "if all persons brought under its influence are treated alike under the same conditions." But this is only half the truth. Not only must it treat alike, under the same conditions, all who are brought "within its influence," but in its classification it must bring within its influence all who are under the same conditions. Therefore, if a distinction is to be made between railway corporations and other employers as respects their liability to their employés, it must be based upon some difference in the nature of the employment, and can only extend to cases where such difference exists. Hence most courts, as notably in Iowa and Kansas, have held that similar statutes, although general in their terms, embrace only "the peculiar hazards of railroading." But, when we come to examine the adjudicated cases, we confess we are unable to discover any definite, consistent or logical rule which the courts have applied in determining whether, upon the facts of a particular case, it fell within or without the Statute. In some cases it has been held that the Statute applied because the duty of the employés required them to ride upon the cars to the place of work, although the injury was not sustained while thus riding, and was not caused by, or in any manner connected with, the operation of the road. Such a position seems to us wholly illogical. Other cases have been held within the Statute because the work being performed was necessary to the use and operation of the road, although the injury sustained was not caused by, or connected with, such use and operation. This, we think, is equally illogical. In fact, the proposition is so broad and indefinite as to bring within the Act all employés, regardless of the nature of their employment; for the work of all, even clerks in offices, is, in a sense, necessary to the use and operation of the road. Therefore, after mature consideration, our conclusion is that, if any limitation is to be placed by the courts upon the application of this Statute (and on constitutional grounds there must be), the only one which will furnish any definite or logical rule is to hold that it only applies to those employés who are exposed to the peculiar hazards incident to the use and operation of railroads, and whose injuries are the result of such dangers. We do not mean to say that there may not be reasons suggested by some differences in the nature of the employment which would warrant the Legislature in placing some other hazards within the provisions of such a law; but, if the courts should attempt to impose upon the general language of this Statute any other limitation than the one suggested, they would be all at sea, without either rudder or compass. Applying the test suggested, it is clear that plaintiff's case is not within the provisions of the Act.

A crew of men, of which plaintiff was one, was engaged in repairing a drawbridge on defendant's railroad. In doing this work it was necessary to leave the draw partly open. Plaintiff was at work between the stationary part of the bridge and the draw, when the wind blew the draw shut, and injured him. The draw might and should have been fastened open, which was omitted to be done through the negligence of the foreman of the crew. Plaintiff was not engaged in operating the road, nor was his injury caused by any of the hazards incident to its operation, any more than in the case of the helper in the repair-shops in the *Lavallee Case*. As suggested by counsel for defendant, suppose there had been a wagon bridge over the St. Louis River, alongside of this railroad bridge, and one of a crew engaged in repairing it had been injured under like circumstances. He could not have recovered from his employer. Yet the actual situation, both as to the nature of the employment and the cause of the injury, would have been the same in either case.

Order denying a new trial affirmed.

WISCONSIN SUPREME COURT.

Mary R. DUFFIES, *Respt.*
v.
Mary DUFFIES, *Appt.*

(.....Wis.....)

Enticing a husband away from his wife and depriving her of his society and support give her no right of action.

(*Cassoday, J., dissents.*)

(April 8, 1890.)

APPEAL by defendant from a judgment of the Superior Court for Milwaukee County in favor of plaintiff and from an order denying a motion for a new trial in an action brought to recover damages for the alleged enticing away of plaintiff's husband and depriving plaintiff of his society and support. *Reversed.*

The facts are sufficiently stated in the opinion.

Messrs. **Van Dyke & Van Dyke,** for appellant:

At common law a wife could not maintain an action against one who wrongfully and maliciously enticed her husband from her.

2 Bl. Com. p. 142; *Lynch* v. *Knight*, 9 H. L. Cas. 577; Reeve, Dom. Rel. 110; Schouler, Dom. Rel. § 41; *Van Arnam* v. *Ayers*, 67 Barb. 544; Action of a Wife for the Alienation of her Husband's Affections, 9 Wash. L. Rep. 513, 530.

No statute of this State has changed this common-law rule.

Laws of 1881, chap. 99, which enables a married woman to maintain an action, as if unmarried, "for an injury to her person or character," does not confer a right to maintain this action.

Logan v. *Logan*, 77 Ind. 559; *Van Arnam* v. *Ayers*, *supra.*

There is a wide distinction between an "injury to the person" and "an injury to personal rights."

Wagner v. *Lathers*, 26 Wis. 436; *Calloway* v. *Laydon*, 47 Iowa, 456; *Freese* v. *Tripp*, 70 Ill. 496, 500; *Meidel* v. *Anthis*, 71 Ill. 241; *Fentz* v. *Meadows*, 72 Ill. 540; *Keedy* v. *Howe*, Id. 134; *Confrey* v. *Stark*, 73 Ill. 187; *Gibbs* v. *Larrabee*, 23 Wis. 495; *Peterson* v. *Knoble*, 35 Wis. 80; *Mulford* v. *Clewell*, 21 Ohio St. 191.

Messrs. **Williams, Friend & Bright,** for respondent:

The right of a husband to maintain an action

NOTE.—*Action for alienation of husband's affections.*

A married woman can maintain an action for damages for enticing away her husband, and consequent deprivation of his comfort and aid, protection and society. Bennett v. Bennett, 6 L. R. A. 553, 116 N. Y. 584.

She may maintain an action against another woman for alienating her husband's affections. Foot v. Card, 6 L. R. A. 829, 58 Conn. 1; Seaver v. Adams (N. H.) March 14, 1890.

See also 8 L. R. A. 833; 10 L. R. A. 468; 14 L. R. A. 545; 26 L. R. A. 412; 27 L.

for the loss of the *consortium* of the wife through the malicious interference of a third person is not questioned. And the gist of the action is the loss of the comfort and society of the wife, and not the loss of her services. At any rate, loss of services is not an indispensable element.

Winsmore v. *Greenbank*, Willes, 581; *Philp* v. *Squire*, Peake, N. P. Cas. 82, Buller, N. P. 78, 79; *Bartelot* v. *Hawker*, Peake, N. P. Cas. 7; *Weedon* v. *Timbrell*, 5 T. R. 357; *Jaynes* v. *Jaynes*, 39 Hun, 40; *Baker* v. *Baker*, 16 Abb. N. C. 293, and authorities cited; *Lynch* v. *Knight*, 9 H. L. Cas. 577, 588; Cooley, Torts, 224; *Heermance* v. *James*, 47 Barb. 120; *Rhinehart* v. *Bills*, 82 Mo. 534.

This action, like every other tort action, rests upon the broad principle that where a legal right is impaired or lost by the wrongful act of another, the wrong-doer must answer for the injury in damages.

Cooley, Torts, 20; *Ashby* v. *White*, 2 Ld. Raym. 938; 1 Smith, Lead. Cas. *342, 7th Am. ed. 455; *Chapman* v. *Pickersgill*, 2 Wilson, 145; *Pasley* v. *Freeman*, 3 T. R. 51; *Lumley* v. *Gye*, 2 El. & Bl. 216; *Bowen* v. *Hall*, L. R. 6 Q. B. Div. 333; *Walker* v. *Cronin*, 107 Mass. 555; *Benton* v. *Pratt*, 2 Wend. 385; *Rice* v. *Manley*, 66 N. Y. 82.

Whatever disability the married woman was under at common law with respect to actions was due to the fiction that the husband and wife were one person—*i. e.* the husband.

Ball v. *Bullard*, 52 Barb. 143.

Prior to the marriage the parties were equal in the law. The promise of the woman to marry the man was as good as his promise to marry her.

Harrison v. *Cage*, 5 Mod. 411.

Our Constitution precludes any discrimination which will afford help to the strong and leave the weak without redress.

Art. 1, § 9.

The married woman had a legal right to the *consortium* of her husband—at the common law—as much as to her separate estate which she held under the protection of a court of chancery. She might not have her remedy in the common-law courts because of the fiction of the law, therefore she sought redress in the ecclesiastical court where she might have a remedy.

Westlake v. *Westlake*, 34 Ohio St. 621.

If there is any doubt that the right of *consortium* was a legal right of the wife by the common law, there is no such doubt as to our law. It springs from the marriage contract. When the Statute made desertion a cause for divorce, it likewise made the *consortium* a legal right in the wife.

She also has a remedy for a malicious injury to that right.

Ashby v. *White*, 2 Ld. Raym. 938; *Winsmore* v. *Greenbank*, Willes, 581; Const. art. 1, § 9; *Flanders* v. *Merrimack*, 48 Wis. 567-575.

The right of each party in the marriage contract is *res* and subject to ownership; the term "property" in its broad sense includes this right.

Jaynes v. *Jaynes*, 39 Hun, 40.

By looking at the general scope of the legislation it is clear that the intention was to give the married woman the same remedy for every injury or wrong which any other person would have for a similar injury or wrong. No other conclusion is possible without resorting to a strict and technical construction of these provisions of the statutes which this court has held are to be liberally construed.

Krouskop v. *Shontz*, 51 Wis 204; *Shanahan* v. *Madison*, 57 Wis. 278; *Carney* v. *Gleissner*, 62 Wis. 493; *McLimans* v. *Lancaster*, 63 Wis. 596.

This right of action has been upheld by the following decisions of New York, whose statutes are substantially like our own:

Jaynes v. *Jaynes*, 39 Hun, 40; *Breiman* v. *Paasch*, 7 Abb. N. C. 249; *Baker* v. *Baker*, 16 Abb. N. C. 293; *Warner* v. *Miller*, 17 Abb. N. C. 221; *Churchill* v. *Lewis*, Id. 226; *Bennett* v. *Bennett*, 6 L. R. A. 553, 116 N. Y. 584. See also *Clark* v. *Harlan*, 1 Cin. Super. Ct. Rep. 418; *Westlake* v. *Westlake*, *supra; Lynch* v. *Knight*, 9 H. L. Cas. 577.

Orton, *J.*, delivered the opinion of the court:

This action is brought by the plaintiff, as the wife of one Frank W. Duffies, against the defendant, the mother of said Frank, to recover damages by reason of the defendant having wrongfully induced, persuaded and caused the said Frank W. Duffies to refuse further to live and cohabit with the plaintiff, and to support and maintain her, and to support and maintain their child, and maliciously enticed him away from her, intending thereby to deprive her of his society, and support, maintenance, aid and assistance. The action was tried, and the plaintiff recovered, by the verdict of the jury, $2,000, of which the plaintiff remitted $1,000, and judgment was rendered for the residue thereof. Errors are assigned for admitting irrelevant testimony, refusing to submit certain questions to the jury, to give certain instructions and for denying motions for nonsuit and for a new trial, but they will not be considered any further than some of them may involve the question whether the action itself will lie. The learned counsel for the appellant, before the trial was commenced, objected to the introduction of any evidence under the complaint, on the ground that it stated no cause of action, which objection was overruled. On this demurrer, *ore tenus*, the learned counsel contended that this action would not lie at common law, and that there is no statute allowing it. From the examination of the authorities we have been able to make, and considering the reason thereof, we have concluded that such contention is correct, and that the action cannot be maintained.

The learned counsel of the respondent contends that the action lies (1) at the common law; and (2) by the terms and liberal interpretation of our statutes; and (3) by analogy to similar cases. The learned counsel does not contend that any such action was maintained at the common law, but that by the principles of the common law, and in analogy to similar actions at the common law, the right of action existed, and was not maintainable only on account of the wife's disability to bring the action. But the wife was not only unable to bring the action to recover damages for the loss of her husband's society, but the damages themselves were the property of the husband, the same as in case of personal injury, or for defamation, even before marriage. *Gibson* v. *Gibson*, 43 Wis. 23; *Barnes* v. *Martin*, 15 Wis. 241.

How can she be said to have had a right of action to recover damages which she could neither own nor enjoy? More properly the right of action was in the husband, in the interest or on account of his wife. The common law could not recognize a right of action in the wife to sue for the loss of her husband's society, without involving the absurdity that the husband might also sue for such a cause. The wife having no right of property, at common law, in any damages recovered on her account for any cause, neither could she have any right of action to recover them. This may have been grossly wrong, but such was the theory of the common law, and, to make it consistent, the wife had no such right of action. The wife was not only inferior to the husband, but she had no personal identity separate from her husband. It is not proper to say that the common law was inconsistent in denying to the wife the right to bring such an action, and at the same time allowing the husband to sue for the loss of the society of his wife. Her disability in this respect was consistent with all of her disabilities.

When the learned counsel cites the case of *Winsmore* v. *Greenbank*, Willes, 581, decided in the nineteenth year of George the Third, in which the husband sued for enticing away his wife, *per quod amisit* the comfort and society of his wife, as furnishing the same reason for the wife bringing such an action, he ignores all these common-law disabilities of the wife, which are consistent with each other. *Chief Justice* Willes admitted that there was no precedent for such an action, but, as the action on the case had been invented for similar cases, he claimed that this was only another case with new facts, and as there were "injury and damage," and the violation of a right, and the action ought to lie, it would lie within the reason of other cases. And so the learned counsel argues from *Philp* v. *Squire*, Peake, N. P. Cas. 82, in the 31st year of George the Third, in which *Lord* Kenyon held that the action by the husband was not for the loss of the services of the wife, but of her society.

In *Pasley* v. *Freeman*, 3 T. R. 51, the action was for making a false affirmation with intent to defraud. *Lord* Kenyon held that the action would lie, although a new case, because there was *damnum cum injuria*.

In *Ashby* v. *White*, 2 Ld. Raym. 938, decided in 1701, the action was against an officer for refusing to receive the plaintiff's vote. It was a case of *prima impressionis*, but *Chief Justice* Holt, against the other judges, held that the action would lie at common law, on the ground that where there is a wrong there should be a remedy.

In *Chapman* v. *Pickersgill*, 2 Wilson, 145, the action was for falsely and maliciously suing out a bankrupt commission and it was held that the action would lie at common law on the same ground.

In *Lumley* v. *Gye*, 2 El. & Bl. 216, the action was for enticing away a singer employed to sing in a theater, and in *Bowen* v. *Hall*, L. R. 6 Q. B. Div. 333, for enticing away a common laborer employed by the plaintiff. These are all new cases predicated upon the same general principles of the common law. The argument is, if these actions can be sustained, and the action of the husband for the loss of his wife's *consortium*, why may not an action by or on behalf of the wife, for the loss of her husband's society, support and protection, be maintained on the same principles? The reason is obvious, and suggested above. The wife had no property in the *consortium* of her husband that is lost, nor any right to it that has been violated at common law. If the same able judges who were free to invent actions, and to sustain new cases in an old action, and were quick to see the justice and humanity of all cases, could have found a right of action of the wife in such a case, we may believe that old forms and fictions would not have stood in the way. Her relative position and conditions as a wife at common law precluded the recognition of any such right of action. Under the civil law the husband and wife were distinct persons. The wife had a separate estate, the right to contract debts and to bring actions for injuries. Her position was so nearly equal to that of her husband that her right to his society was recognized, and she had a remedy for its loss. But that remedy was confined to the ecclesiastical courts, and consisted only in having her husband returned to her. 1 Bl. Com. 442.

The wife had a right of action for defamation, by the civil law, but it was denied her in the common-law courts, because she would then have two actions or a double remedy. *Palmer* v. *Thorpe*, 4 Coke, 20; *Byron* v. *Emes*, 12 Mod. 106, 2 Salk. 694.

Another reason was that an action for defamation would not lie without special damages, and the wife could have no special damages. In looking into the books of the common law, we can find no such action or right of action of the wife, and they are both denied on principle as well as want of precedent. In the genial light of modern times, the true situation and position of the wife in the marriage relation are seen more clearly than formerly, and the place assigned her by the law and by common consent is much higher and more suitable to her intrinsic character, ability and worth. She is placed on a nearer equality with her husband in her rights of person, property and character. Under the just and genial laws of married women, she has resumed her position of a *feme sole*, as nearly as is compatible with natural law. It is not therefore surprising that so great and gallant, learned and humane, a judge and chancellor as *Lord* Campbell should hold in *Lynch* v. *Knight*, 9 H. L. Cas. 577, that the wife had the same right to the *consortium* of her husband that he had to hers, and might allege special damage for its loss, caused by defamation of her character. The Lord Chancellor said that it was a case of first impressions, and rested his opinion upon the great changes that had taken place in the position and relations of the wife under modern legislation. The opinion is by no means positive, and placed the right on the condition that it might be shown that the wife's "loss and injury" concurred. But the opinion is *obiter* in that case, and off-hand, and can hardly be accepted as authority. But the remedy of the wife was of no use or benefit to her, for she had to join her husband in the suit, and the damages recovered belonged exclusively to him. The plaintiff obtained judgment in Queen's Bench in Ireland. It was affirmed in Exchequer by a divided court, and reversed in the House of Lords, but on another question. It is, however, a decision that no such case had ever been sustained at common law.

In *Westlake* v. *Westlake*, 34 Ohio St. 621, it was held that the action would not lie at common law, and it was only allowed in Ohio by the Statute that gave the wife a right of action for all violations of or injury to the wife's "personal rights" *Judge* Cooley said he could see "no reason why such an action might not exist, when the Statute allowed her to sue for personal wrongs." Cooley, Torts, 228.

"Personal rights" are not rights of person. The latter are physical, and the former are relative and general, and embrace all the rights any person may have and all the wrongs he may suffer. The court held correctly that the right to the society of her husband was a personal right, under the Statute. It was so held also in *Clark* v. *Harlan*, 1 Cin. Super. Ct. Rep. 418. It is said in the opinion that the wife had no such right at common law as a personal right, and therefore she could not sue, but she may by force of the Statute.

But it was held in *Mulford* v. *Clewell*, 21 Ohio St. 191, that, under the Statute that allowed the wife to sue for "injury to her property or person," she could not bring this action for the *consortium* of her husband, nor at common law.

In many cases, as in *Ashby* v. *White*, *supra*, it has been held that the action might be brought, because there should be "no wrong without a remedy," as *Chief Justice* Holt said in that case. But we must not forget that to entice away her husband was no wrong to the wife, and she had no right to his society, and the damages, if any, belonged to him at common law.

In *Van Arnam* v. *Ayers*, 67 Barb. 544, it was held that the action would not lie at common law, nor under the Statute, "for injury to her person and character," or her separate property.

In *Jaynes* v. *Jaynes*, 39 Hun, 40, it was held that the action would lie under the Statute of "Civil Procedure," but not at common law.

In *Breiman* v. *Paasch*, 7 Abb. N. C. 249, it was held that the action would lie, if not under the Statute, under the authority of *Lynch* v. *Knight*, *supra*, since the wife's disability to sue alone had been removed.

In *Baker* v. *Baker*, 16 Abb. N. C. 293, the right is predicated upon the wife's separate property, and the right to sue for injury to her person and character.

In *Logan* v. *Logan*, 77 Ind. 559, the action by the wife was for defamation, and she counted *per quod* for loss of the society of her husband. It was held that she might bring the action under the Statute, of "injury to her person or character," but it could not be extended for loss of the society of her husband.

In *Calloway* v. *Laydon*, 47 Iowa, 456, an action under the Liquor Law like ours in chapter 127, Laws 1872, in which the wife might recover "for injury to her person, property or means of support, and for all damages sustained, and for exemplary damages," it was held that she could not recover for the loss of her husband's society. And so in *Freese* v. *Tripp*, 70 Ill. 503, and in *Confrey* v. *Stark*, 73 Ill. 187, and in *Mulford* v. *Clewell*, *supra*.

The recent case of *Foot* v. *Card*, 58 Conn. 1, 6 L. R. A. 829, is sustained by the authority of *Lynch* v. *Knight*, *supra*, and on the ground that the wife is in a condition of perfect equality with her husband, and "her right is the same as his in kind, degree and value." It is said that even if the damages go to the husband, he would hold them as trustee for the wife. This case would be of greater authority if the expressions of the wife's absolute equality with her husband were less general, sweeping and unlimited.

The still more recent case of *Bennett* v. *Bennett*, 116 N. Y. 584, 6 L. R. A. 553, holds that the action will lie at common law, and cites *Lynch* v. *Knight*, *supra*, and under the statutes which allow her to recover for "injury to her person or character," and give her separate property. It is held, in the leading opinion, that the wife can sue alone for all injuries to her person, and the damages recovered will belong to her.

It will be seen that there is very little conclusive authority on this question by the decisions of the courts in this country or in England. The doctrine may be said to be unsettled. Those courts which hold that the action will lie at common law do so because the Statute has placed the wife on an equality with the husband or removed her disabilities. This would seem to imply that the action would not lie at common law, but by Statute. Other courts hold that the right of action existed at common law, and would therefore lie as soon as the Statute removed the wife's disability to sue alone. The question may be said to be a new one in this court, although the effect of some of our decisions may have a direct bearing upon it.

The case of *Peterson* v. *Knoble*, 35 Wis. 80, was an action under the Liquor Law, commonly called the "Graham Law," to recover for injury to the "person, property or means of support" of the wife. The husband was made drunk, and turned his wife out of doors. The question was raised whether injury to her feelings and for the indignity could be recovered in the action. The court cites *Mulford* v. *Clewell*, *supra*, as holding that nothing could be recovered, except for actual violence, or physical injury to the person or health, not even for her disgrace or loss of society of her husband, and, while approving that case, holds that for injury to the feelings, and for the indignity, she may recover, because it is a part of the actual damages in the action, and connected with the injury to her person, and because "exemplary damages" may also be recovered under the Statute. This limitation to the actual damages for the physical injury would seem to imply that the loss of her husband's society could not be recovered for under the Statute. The cases in Ohio and Illinois, under the same law, hold that damages for the loss of her husband's society cannot be recovered, as we have seen.

The case of *Dillon* v. *Linder*, 36 Wis. 344, was brought under the same Statute (chap. 127, Laws 1872). While it was pending, and before trial, chap. 179, Laws 1874, repealing the above chapter, was passed, and the question was whether, by such repeal, the action was defeated or abated, or saved by § 33, chap. 119, Rev. Stat. 1858, now § 4974, Rev. Stat. It was held, *Chief Justice* Ryan writing the opinion, that the section referred to related only to "new forms of remedy for old rights," and that the Statute created the cause of action itself, and that the repeal took away the right of action, and that was not saved by the Statute, and was therefore gone. The important and pertinent effect of this decision is that the Statute created the cause of action or right of action to recover damages by reason of any person causing, through drunkenness of the husband, any injury to the wife's "person, property or means of support, and any damages sustained, and exemplary damages."

Then it follows that such a cause of action or right of action did not exist at common law, but is purely statutory. If, then, such damages could not be recovered at common law, much less could a more remote and speculative class of damages, for the loss of the husband's society by such means, be recovered at common law, or without a statute creating such a cause of action or right of action. It follows also, as before said, that the right of action of the wife, in such a case, did not exist at common law. It was not a mere common-law disability to bring the action. The only two statutes now in force in this State allowing the wife to bring an action alone, and to have the damages recovered her own separate property, are said chapter 179, Laws 1874 (Rev. Stat. § 1560), which gives her an action against any person who causes, through the drunkenness of the husband, "injury to her person, property or means of support;" and chapter 99, Laws 1881, which gives her an action for any "injury to her person or character." According to common reason and the decided weight of authority, neither of these Statutes gives the wife any right of action for the *consortium* of her husband. The loss of her husband's society is not an injury to her person, property, means of support or character, and such an action cannot be forced, within the terms or spirit of the statutes, by the most strained and liberal construction. Such a right of action does not exist by law, nor can it be inferred from the ameliorated and changed conditions of the wife, and her equality with her husband, produced by modern legislation in her behalf. Whatever equality of rights with her husband she may have, it is not proper to say that "her right to the society of her husband is the same in kind, degree and value as his right to her society." There are natural and unchangeable conditions of husband and wife that make that right radically unequal and different. The wife is more domestic, and is supposed to have the personal care of the household, and her duties in the domestic economy require her to be more constantly at home, where the husband may nearly always expect to find her, and enjoy her society. She is purer and better by nature than her husband, and more governed by principle and a sense of duty and right, and she seldom violates her marriage obligations or abandons her home, or denies to her husband the comforts and advantages of her society by any inducement or influence of others, without just cause. Actions against others for enticing her away from her home and her husband's society are not frequent. She is protected from such wrong, not only by her integrity of character, but by greater love for her family and the comforts and genial influences of home life. With the husband the case is different. He may not be his wife's superior in the sense of the common law, or in anything, and may be her inferior in many things, but he is charged with the duty of providing for, maintaining and protecting his wife and family. He is engaged, for this purpose, in the business and various employments of the outside world, that must necessarily more or less deprive his wife of his society. The exigencies of even his legitimate business may keep him away from her and his home for months or years. He is exposed to the temptations, enticements and allurements of the world, which easily withdraw him from her society, or cause him to desert or abandon her. Others may entice or induce him to do many things, for business or pleasure, which may deprive his wife of his society. The wife had reason to expect all these things when she entered the marriage relation, and her right to his society has all these conditions, and is not the same in "degree and value" as his right to hers. For these reasons and many others, if actions by the husband for the loss of the society of his wife are not frequent, actions by the wife for the loss of his society would be numberless. This right of action in the wife would be the most fruitful source of litigation of any that can be thought of. The loss of his society need not be permanent for a cause of action. For a longer or shorter time, if caused by improper inducements or enticements, the right would accrue. There would seem to be very good reason why this right of action should be denied. The justice and advantages of such an action are at least doubtful. For these reasons, this action cannot be sustained on the ground of the wife's equality in right, or of "a remedy for every wrong," or of the coincidence of "injury and damage," or of the constitutional right of a remedy for "injury to person, property or character." The right is at least so doubtful that the courts may well await a direct Act of the Legislature conferring it. There are questions of public policy and expediency involved that may well be considered by the Legislature. The court should have sustained the objection of the defendant to any evidence under the complaint on the ground that it did not state a cause of action.

The judgment of the Superior Court is reversed, and the cause remanded, with directions to dismiss the complaint.

Cassoday, *J.*, dissenting:

I am not prepared to give my assent to the opinion of the court filed in this case. There seems to be high authority for saying that at common law an action for damages could be maintained for the alienation and loss of the affection and society of the husband from his wife. *Lynch* v. *Knight*, 9 H. L. Cas. 577; *Bassett* v. *Bassett*, 20 Ill. App. 543; *Foot* v. *Card*, 58 Conn. 1, 6 L. R. A. 829; *Bennett* v. *Bennett*, 116 N. Y. 584, 6 L. R. A. 553, affirming 41 Hun, 640, and *Mehrhoff* v. *Mehrhoff*, 26 Fed. Rep. 13.

In such action, however, it was necessary for the husband to join, as it was said, for conformity's sake. *Ibid.*

So, in an action for damages for a tortious injury to the wife, it was held necessary in this State, prior to the recent Statute on the subject, for both husband and wife to join in the action. *Gibson* v. *Gibson*, 43 Wis. 23; *Meese* v. *Fond du Lac*, 48 Wis. 323; *Shanahan* v. *Madison*, 57 Wis. 276.

But, in addition to the rights of property and business previously possessed, "chapter 99, Laws 1881, gave to a married woman, as though she were sole, the right to maintain an action for any injury to her person or character, and took from the husband all right to or control over such action, and all right to or interest in any judgment recovered therein." *Shanahan* v. *Madison, supra.*

Prior to that enactment, such action, for personal injury to the wife, if brought in her own name alone, could only be defeated on such ground, by showing the fact of such marriage in abatement, and then proving the same. *McLimans* v. *Lancaster*, 63 Wis. 596.

That action was commenced in the name of the wife alone, some time prior to that Statute, but no objection on that ground was taken by plea in abatement or otherwise, until after two trials at the circuit court and the case had been brought to this court on a second appeal; and it was held in effect that the irregularity in commencing the suit in the name of the wife alone was cured by that Statute. In so holding, this court followed *Weldon* v. *Winslow*, L. R. 13 Q. B. Div. 786, where Brett, *M. R.*, speaking for the court, said: "For such a cause of action no action could ever have been brought by the husband alone without joining his wife as a plaintiff. . . . The injury to the wife was the meritorious cause of action, and, if she had died before the commencement of the action, the husband would not have been entitled to sue. If damages should be given, they would belong, in the first place, to the wife alone; and if they should not be reduced to possession by the husband, and he should die, the damages would be hers, and would not go to his executors." *McLimans* v. *Lancaster*, 63 Wis. 600.

In that case the right of action had been created and given by Statute.

In this State it has frequently been held that compensatory damages include mental suffering, and that no distinction is to be made between other forms of mental suffering and that which consists in a sense of wrong or insult arising from an act really or apparently dictated by a spirit of willful injustice, or by a deliberate intention to vex, degrade or insult. *Craker* v. *Chicago & N. W. R. Co.* 36 Wis. 658; *Grace* v. *Dempsey*, 75 Wis. 323, and cases there cited.

Within the rulings of this court in the cases cited, no good reason is perceived why this action is not maintainable; especially is this so if such right of action existed in favor of the husband and wife jointly at common law, as indicated in the authorities cited. I have not had the time to verify, by careful examination, whether that is so or not.

CALIFORNIA SUPREME COURT.

H. P. STONE, *Respt.*,

v.

James HAMMELL, *Appt.*

(83 Cal. 547.)

1. **A surety who merely gives his note** for his share of the original debt to a co-surety, who has paid the debt, does not thereby acquire any right of action against his principal; at least where any cause of action against the latter in favor of the co-surety was barred by time.

2. **After a cause of action against the principal debtor is barred** a surety, as to whom the Statute has not run because he has been absent from the State, cannot acquire any right of action against the principal by payment of the demand.

(April 2, 1890.)

APPEAL by defendant from a judgment of the Superior Court for Santa Barbara County in favor of plaintiff and from an order denying a motion for a new trial in an action brought by a surety upon a promissory note to recover from his principal the amount of certain promissory notes which he had given a co-surety in satisfaction of a claim for contribution towards the payment of the original note. *Reversed.*

*An opinion was handed down in this case on September 2, 1889, affirming the judgment of the lower court. After re-argument the judgment was reversed and the opinion filed which is given herewith, and the former opinion thereby rendered useless, in consequence of which it is omitted. [Rep.]

The case sufficiently appears in the opinion.

Messrs. **W. S. Bouton** and **Wells, Guthrie & Lee,** for appellant:

The Statute having commenced to run against the remedy of Newell for contribution from Stone, before his departure from the State, Newell's remedy for contribution against Stone was barred July 1, 1880.

An action upon a contract obligation or liability, not founded upon an instrument in writing, is barred in two years.

Code Civ. Proc. § 339; *Chipman* v. *Morrill*, 20 Cal. 131.

When the Statute begins to run, a subsequent disability does not stop it.

Quivey v. *Hall*, 19 Cal. 98; *Crosby* v. *Dowd*, 61 Cal. 597.

A cause of action against the principal debtor does not accrue to the surety till the surety has paid the debt.

Walker v. *McKay*, 2 Met. (Ky.) 294; *Romine* v. *Romine*, 59 Ind. 846; *Bonham* v. *Galloway*, 13 Ill. 78; *Shepard* v. *Ogden*, 3 Ill. 257; *Swift* v. *Crocker*, 21 Pick. 241; *Power* v. *Butcher*, 10 Barn. & C. 329; *Reynolds* v. *Doyle*, 1 Man. & Gr. 753; *Estate of Hill*, 67 Cal. 243.

Acceptance of a note payable at a future day for a pre-existing debt does not extinguish the debt.

Brewster v. *Bours*, 8 Cal. 506; *Crary* v. *Bowers*, 20 Cal. 86; *Mitchell* v. *Hockett*, 25 Cal. 542; *Crawford* v. *Roberts*, 50 Cal. 236.

Mr. **B. F. Thomas** for respondent.

McFarland, *J.*, delivered the opinion of the court:

After further consideration, upon argument on rehearing, we are satisfied that the judgment in this case should be reversed.

The plaintiff, with three other persons,—Newell, Hamilton and Hayman,—were sureties on a promissory note made by defendant, Hammell, to one Byron Stevens for $3,000, dated July 1, 1877, and payable one year after date. Plaintiff claims that one of said sureties, Newell, paid on said note something over $2,000, and that plaintiff paid to Newell, as his *pro rata* contributive share, $1,000; and this action was brought to recover said $1,000 of defendant, the principal on the note. There are a number of interesting questions in the case, which, under the views which we take of it, need not be determined. For instance, defendant contends that he gave a mortgage to the sureties to secure them, and that the mortgage should have been foreclosed, and that the mortgaged property was sufficient in value to satisfy the note; that defendant was discharged from the liability sued on by a decree in insolvency; and that the $1,000 was more than plaintiff's contributive share. We will assume, however, that the property was not held by way of mortgage, and was faithfully applied by Newell, as far as it would go, to the payment of the note; that the decree in insolvency did not include the liability sued on; and that $1,000 was the correct amount of plaintiff's contributive share.

It is not averred in the complaint, or found by the court, that the plaintiff, Stone, ever paid to his co surety Newell any money, or gave him any property, in satisfaction of Newell's claim for contribution. The only averment on the subject is as follows: "That on the 1st of March, 1884, this plaintiff, in full satisfaction of the amount of money which he should contribute to said P. N. Newell for his aforesaid payments on the aforesaid note, made, executed and delivered to said P. N. Newell his promissory notes in the sum of $1,000, whereupon the said P. N. Newell gave to plaintiff his receipt in full for plaintiff's liability to contribute to him for the aforesaid payments on said promissory note."

This is not a very clear averment that Newell took the notes in absolute payment of his former claim, but we will assume it to be sufficient for that purpose. There is no averment that plaintiff ever paid the notes, or any part of either of them. It appears from the findings that they were payable two years after date, and would not mature until more than a year after this action was commenced. The court below held that the giving of these notes, and their acceptance as payment by Newell, constituted a cause of action in favor of plaintiff against defendant. In this holding, under the facts in the case at bar, at least, the court, in our opinion, erred. The general rule is, undoubtedly, that a surety can recover of the principal only the amount or value which the surety has actually paid. If he has paid in depreciated bank notes taken at par, he can recover only the actual value of the bank notes so paid and received. If he has paid in property, he can recover only the value of the property. If he has compromised, he can recover only what the compromise cost him. The rule is that he shall not be allowed to "speculate out of his principal." Brandt, Sur. § 182, and cases there cited; *Estate of Hill*, 67 Cal. 243.

There is authority, however, and perhaps a preponderance of authority, to the point that if a surety, by giving his negotiable promissory note, satisfies the claim of the creditor, and extinguishes the debt of the principal to the creditor, he may recover from the principal the amount of the debt without showing that he has paid his promissory note. Brandt, Sur. § 181, and cases cited.

But the authorities are not uniform upon the subject. In Indiana and North Carolina, and some other States, it is held that the surety cannot recover of the principal until he has paid the money, and that the giving of a note is not sufficient. *Brisendine* v. *Martin*, 1 Ired. L. 286; *Nowland* v. *Martin*, Id. 307; *Romine* v. *Romine*, 59 Ind. 851, and cases there cited.

Many of the cases hold that, if the surety discharges the debt by a negotiable note, he can maintain an action against the principal, while, if he does so by means of a bond, or any non-negotiable instrument, he cannot, upon the theory that a negotiable note is analogous to money,—a distinction which is founded upon no apparent good reason. *Boulware* v. *Robinson*, 8 Tex. 327, 58 Am. Dec. 117; *Peters* v. *Barnhill*, 1 Hill, L 237.

The rule is founded on the reason that if the surety, by giving his own obligation, discharges the original debt of the principal, the latter is as much benefited as if he had discharged it by actually paying the money. Its weakness lies in the possibility of the surety recovering the whole amount of the principal, and never paying his own note, thus violating the cardinal rule that the surety shall not speculate out of the principal. But, if we assume the rule to be as first above stated, it is not so clearly commendable as to deserve pushing further than adjudicated cases have already carried it; and in all cases to which our attention has been called the rule has been enforced against the principal in favor only of the surety who has extinguished the debt to the original creditor. We have seen no case in which the rule has been applied to a surety who had not satisfied the original debt, but had only given his note to another surety, who had satisfied it. Moreover, the reason of the rule, if it be held to be the rule, is that the principal is benefited to the extent of the original debt or liability which has been extinguished by the new obligation of the surety; and the reason ceases when there is no such benefit. Now, in the case at bar, defendant was in no manner benefited by the notes given by plaintiff to Newell, nor was any debt or liability of defendant thereby extinguished, because, at the time the notes were given, there was no legal liability from the defendant to Newell, for the reason that any cause of action which the latter might have had against the defendant for moneys which he had paid to Byron Stevens had long been barred by the Statute of Limitations. The last payment made by Newell on the note to Stevens, as averred and found, was on January 10, 1881; and, as his cause of action for the payments which he had made was not "founded on a written instrument," it was barred in two years,—that is, on January 10, 1883. *Chipman* v. *Morrill*, 20 Cal. 136.

But plaintiff did not give his notes to Newell until March 1, 1884. At that time defendant was under no legal obligation to anyone which plaintiff could discharge by giving said notes. The original note given to Stevens had itself been long since outlawed. Therefore, by giving said notes, plaintiff acquired no cause of action against the defendant herein.

We think, also, that the cause of action averred in the complaint would have been barred by the Statute of Limitations, which was pleaded by defendant, even though plaintiff, on March 1, 1884, had actually paid Newell the $1,000 in money. Plaintiff seeks to avoid the running of the Statute through the fact that, within a month after the original note to Stevens matured, he left the State, and resided out of the State for several years. His contention is that, as Newell's cause of action against him for contribution would not be barred while he remained out of the State, therefore his cause of action which he had against defendant, or which he proposed at some future time to have, by paying his contributive share to Newell, would not be barred during his absence from the State, though such absence should be for 50 years. He contends that by returning at any time, and subjecting himself to Newell's claim, and paying it, he could recover his part of it against defendant, although in the hands of Newell it had been outlawed for a quarter of a century. We do not think that the law of limitation of actions contemplates any such an anomaly. When a man leaves the State, the Statute of Limitations does not run during his absence as to any cause of action against him, but his absence does not prevent the Statute from running as to any cause of action in his favor. At any time within two years after Newell had paid the original note, plaintiff could have paid his contributive share to Newell, and maintained an action for it against defendant. But he could not wait until the whole of Newell's cause of action against defendant was barred, and then revive one half of the claim by coming back years afterwards, and making a real or pretended payment of it to Newell. The whole claim was, as to defendant, dead, and the breath of life could not be blown into one half of it by any such legal hocus-pocus.

For the reasons above stated, *the judgment and order appealed from are reversed*, and the cause remanded for such further proceedings as respondent may be advised to take.

We concur: **Fox, J.; Sharpstein, J.; Paterson, J.**

Beatty, Ch. J.:

I concur. A surety who pays the debt of his principal has an undoubted right to recover the amount paid. But such is not the case here. The liability of the principal had been extinguished by the Statute of Limitations before any payment by the surety. The absence of the plaintiff from the State had kept the claim alive as to him, though it was extinguished as to the defendant. The plaintiff therefore did not pay the defendant's debt. He merely paid his own debt. By so doing, he could not possibly acquire a right of action against the defendant.

MAINE SUPREME JUDICIAL COURT.

Maria E. SULLIVAN
v.
MAINE CENTRAL R. CO.

(......Me.......)

Riding in a carriage on Sunday for exercise and for no other purpose is not a violation of the Statute in relation to the observance of the Lord's Day, which contains a prohibition against unnecessary walking or riding.

(December 28, 1889.)

EXCEPTIONS by defendant to a judgment of the Supreme Judicial Court for Kennebec County in favor of plaintiff in an action brought to recover damages for personal injuries alleged to have resulted from defendant's negligence. *Overruled.*

Plaintiff was riding with her brother in a carriage on one Sunday afternoon when the horse caught his foot between the planking and the rail while attempting to cross defendant's tracks and was thrown down, thus overturning the carriage and throwing both the plaintiff and her brother to the ground. She brought this action to recover damages for the injuries resulting from that fall. Defendant contended that she could not maintain the action for the reason that she was traveling on Sunday in violation of law.

Messrs. **Wilson & Woodard** for defendant.

Messrs. **Heath & Tuell** for plaintiff.

Foster, J., delivered the opinion of the court:

The defendant's contention in support of the

NOTE.—Sunday. See *notes* to Henderson v. Reynolds (Ga.) 7 L. R. A. 327; Anderson v. Bellinger (Ala.) 4 L. R. A. 680; W. U. Teleg. Co. v. Yopst, (Ind.) 3 L. R. A. 224; Porter v. Pierce (N. Y.) 7 L. R. A. 847.

A non-juridical day. See *note* to Parsons v. Lindsay (Kan.) 3 L. R. A. 658.

See also 11 L. R. A. 63, 563; 26 L. R. A. 605.

single question raised by the exceptions is founded upon the erroneous assumption that riding upon Sunday for exercise, and for no other purpose, is a violation of the Statute in relation to the observance of the Lord's Day. The Statute is not to be so construed. Such an interpretation would be contrary to the spirit as well as the letter of a statute which expressly excepts from its prohibition works of necessity or charity. Rev. Stat. chap. 124, § 20.

And this exception may properly be said to cover everything which is morally fit and proper, under the particular circumstances of the case, to be done upon the Sabbath.

Tested by this rule, our own court, in *O'Connell* v. *Lewiston*, 65 Me. 34, and *Davidson* v. *Portland*, 69 Me. 116, has held that walking out in the open air upon the Sabbath for exercise is not a violation of the Statute.

In other jurisdictions, also, it has been held not to be unlawful to ride to a funeral (*Horne* v. *Meakin*, 115 Mass. 326); walking to prepare medicine for a sick child (*Gorman* v. *Lowell*, 117 Mass. 65); riding to visit a sick sister (*Cronan* v. *Boston*, 136 Mass. 384); traveling to visit a sick friend (*Doyle* v. *Lynn & B. R. Co.* 118 Mass. 195); a servant riding to prepare needful food for her employer (*King* v. *Savage*, 121 Mass. 303); a father riding to visit his two boys (*McClary* v. *Lowell*, 44 Vt. 116); walking for exercise (*Hamilton* v. *Boston*, 14 Allen, 475), and walking partly for exercise and partly to make a social call. *Barker* v. *Worcester*, 139 Mass. 74.

The Statute was never intended as an arbitrary interference with the comfort and conduct of individuals, when necessary to the promotion of health, in walking or riding in the open air for exercise. The prohibition is against unnecessary walking or riding. As a general rule, the jury, under proper instructions from the court, must determine this question from the circumstances presented to them.

In this case we can perceive no error in the instructions, and the exceptions must be overruled.

Nor do we think the verdict should be disturbed under the motion for a new trial. A very careful examination of the evidence satisfies us that upon the questions of fact submitted to the jury no interference by this court is necessary. The plaintiff was clearly entitled to some damages. The amount awarded does not appear to be excessive.

Motions and exceptions overruled.

Peters, *Ch. J.*, and **Walton, Virgin, Emery** and **Haskell**, *JJ.*, concurred.

MICHIGAN SUPREME COURT.

George T. MILLER
v.
James OTTAWAY *et al.*, *Appts.*

(......Mich.......)

Knowledge of a warranty on a sale in which a promissory note was given for the purchase price will not affect the rights of a bona fide purchaser of such note for value before maturity, if he had no knowledge of the breach of the warranty.

(June 6, 1890.)

ERROR to the Circuit Court for Genesee County to review a judgment in favor of plaintiff in an action brought to recover the amount alleged to be due on a promissory note. *Affirmed.*

The facts are fully stated in the opinion.

Messrs. **Howard & Gold,** for defendants, appellants:

The burden of proof was upon plaintiff to show not only that he bought the note before maturity, but also that he was a bona fide holder without notice of defendants' equities.

Conley v. *Winsor*, 41 Mich. 256; *Carrier* v. *Cameron*, 31 Mich. 378; *New York Iron Mine* v. *Citizens Bank*, 44 Mich. 344.

Messrs. **Durand & Carton** and **Ira T. Sayre** for plaintiff, appellee.

Champlin, *Ch. J.*, delivered the opinion of the court:

This suit was brought to recover the amount of a promissory note dated November 15, 1887, due in one year, payable to Archibald Carmichael or bearer, for $407. The consideration for which the note was given was one span of mares and two colts, purchased by James Ottaway at an auction sale. Ottaway bid off the span of mares for $285, and the colts for $122, and gave his note for the amount. Defendants claim that at the time of sale the mares were warranted to be with foal, and, if they proved to be so, then he was to pay the further sum of $16 for the service of the horse. Plaintiff purchased the note of the payee on December 8, 1887, and paid full value for it. It turned out that the mares were not with foal. The plaintiff was present at the auction sale, and acted as clerk for Mr. Carmichael, who was confined to his house by sickness, and had general control of the auction. If the warranty was made as claimed by the defendants, plaintiff was fully aware of it at the time. No question is made that the mares were not served with the horse in the proper season. Defendants claim to have become satisfied that the mares were not with foal in the spring or summer following. The plaintiff denied that the sale was with the warranty claimed by defendants.

The first question to be decided is whether, conceding there was a warranty, it can be set up in recoupment of damages against the notes in plaintiff's hand. Restating the facts for the purposes of this question, it presents a case where no fact exists which impugns the title of the holder, nor the honesty, good faith or validity of the original transaction of which the note was a part. There was simply a warranty on the sale that the mares were with foal, and, if they proved to be so, the purchaser was to pay $16 more for the service of the horse. The purchase of the note was for full value, with a knowledge of the warranty, but without knowledge of its breach before the note matured, and before it was known that there would be a breach. The promise of the defendants was not conditioned; neither was there fraud nor imposition connected with the inception of the note. The plaintiff, having paid value before maturity, held the note by an independent title.

It was said by this court in *Nichols* v. *Sober*, 38 Mich. 681, that "the law has always been solicitous to exclude any rules calculated to hinder the free circulation of mercantile paper having legitimate inception, as in this case; and it is settled in this State that a transferee cannot be deprived of his right as a bona fide holder in this class of cases, except upon evidence sufficient to show his participation in the fraud, or equivalent misconduct of the party who transfers to him."

It is laid down by Parsons on Bills and Notes (vol. 1, p. 261) that "knowledge on the part of the holder, at the time he took the note, that it was not to be paid on a specified contingency, is not sufficient to defeat his right to recover, although the contingency had then happened, if he was ignorant of this fact,"—citing *Adams* v. *Smith*, 35 Me. 324; *Ferdon* v. *Jones*, 2 E. D. Smith, 106; *Davis* v. *McCready*, 4 E. D. Smith, 565. See also *Kelso* v. *Frye*, 4 Bibb, 493; *Dow* v. *Tuttle*, 4 Mass. 414; *State Nat. Bank* v. *Cason*, 39 La. Ann. 865; *Patten* v. *Gleason*, 106 Mass. 439; *Davis* v. *McCready*, 17 N. Y. 230; *Craig* v. *Sibbett*, 15 Pa. 238; *Bond* v. *Wiltse*, 12 Wis. 612.

From the foregoing authorities, and upon reason, the correct doctrine appears to be that it is not a good ground of defense against a bona fide holder for value that he was informed that the note was made in consideration of an executory contract, unless he was also informed of its breach. If he had knowledge of the breach, the defense may be interposed. *Wagner* v. *Diedrich*, 50 Mo. 484; *Coffman* v. *Wilson*, 2 Met. (Ky.) 542; *Bowman* v. *Van Kuren*, 29 Wis. 218; *Sutton* v. *Beckwith*, 68 Mich. 303, 12 West. Rep. 647.

The note in question being valid in its inception, and not subject to any condition, a collateral agreement to warrant the mares to be with foal cannot be set up as a defense to the action in this case, where the plaintiff purchased in good faith for value, and without notice or knowledge of any breach of the warranty. A mere collateral agreement or warranty made at the time the note was given does not affect the validity or negotiability of the note, although the purchaser before maturity may know of such agreement. It is common knowledge that in many executory contracts, involving large sums of money, such as drafts drawn against bills of lading, and also such as the purchase of real estate, lumbering contracts, construction of buildings and roads, and other business dealings, notes are given, and often negotiated to those familar with the terms of the contracts; and it would unnecessarily hamper the transfer of such paper, and affect its value injuriously, to hold that the purchaser, before breach of such contract, although he had notice of the contract under which it was given, takes such paper subject to any damages that may arise to the maker from failure of the payee to perform such contract. There is neither reason nor necessity for so holding. Indeed, the defendants in this case set up in their notice of defense the warranty and its breach, and that plaintiff purchased the note with knowledge of such warranty and its breach before he so purchased. The jury found, in answer to a special question, that the plaintiff, George Miller, bought the note in question of Archibald Carmichael before his death; and it was in proof that he died January 6, 1888. This is an end of the case. The defense is not made out, and it is immaterial if testimony tending to show a warranty by Carmichael was erroneously ruled out. Under the special finding, which has the force of a special verdict, no other general verdict could have been rendered by the jury than the one they did.

The judgment must be affirmed.

The other Justices concurred.

VIRGINIA SUPREME COURT OF APPEALS.

WESTERN UNION TELEGRAPH CO.,
Plff. in Err.,
v.
James K. WILLIAMS.

(......Va.......)

1. The creation of a public road through land of a private owner does not devest him of the fee, but gives the public merely a right of way.

2. The Act of February 10, 1880, authorizing a telegraph company to construct a line along county roads, provided the ordinary use of the road was not obstructed, does not give any right to build such line without compensation to the owner of the fee. If the Act is intended to give such right it is in violation of the

NOTE.—*Condemnation of land for highway does not devest owner of the fee.*

On condemnation of private property for roads and streets the general rule is that, subject to the easement of the public, the fee of the land taken is in the owner of the adjoining soil. Suffield v. Hathaway, 44 Conn. 521; Old Town v. Dooley, 81 Ill. 255; Cox v. Louisville, N. A. & C. R. Co. 48 Ind. 178; Terre Haute & I. R. Co. v. Scott, 74 Ind. 29; Vaughn v. Stuzaker, 16 Ind. 338; Overman v. May, 35 Iowa, 89; Small v. Pennell, 31 Me. 267; Thomas v. Ford, 63 Md. 346; Nicholson v. Stockett, Walker (Miss.) 67; Williams v. Natural Bridge Pl. R. Co. 21 Mo. 580; Copp v. Neal, 7 N. H. 275; Higbee v. Camden & A. R. Co. 19 N. J. Eq. 276; Gidney v. Earl, 12 Wend. 98; Rogers v. Bradshaw, 20 Johns. 735; State v. Howell, 90 N. C. 705.

In taking land for a highway only the easement is taken, and, subject thereto, the title and all consistent uses remain in and belong to the owner. Hagaman v. Moore, 84 Ind. 496.

On discontinuance of its use as a highway the

constitutional provision against taking private property without just compensation.

3. **The erection of a telegraph line upon a highway** is an additional servitude for which compensation must be made to the owner of the soil.

(*Lewis, P., and Richardson, J., dissent.*)

(March 27, 1890.)

ERROR to the Circuit Court for New Kent County to review a judgment in favor of plaintiff in an action to recover damages for the erection by defendant of telegraph poles, etc., upon a highway in which plaintiff claimed to own the fee. *Affirmed.*

The facts are fully stated in the opinions.

Messrs. **Waller R. Staples** and **Robert Stiles** for plaintiff in error.

Messrs. **Pollard & Sands, R. T. Lacy** and **W. W. Gordon**, for defendant in error:

The erection of telegraph poles imposes an additional burden which must be compensated for by a new condemnation.

Board of Trade Tel. Co. v. *Barnett*, 107 Ill. 508; *Atlantic & P. Teleg. Co.* v. *Chicago, R. I. & P. R. Co.* 6 Biss. 158; *Southwestern R. Co.* v. *Southern & A. Teleg. Co.* 46 Ga. 43; *Western U. Teleg. Co.* v. *Rich*, 19 Kan. 517; *Willis* v. *Erie Teleg. & Teleph. Co.* 37 Minn. 347. See also *Reg.* v. *United Kingdom Electric Teleg. Co.* 9 Cox, Cr. Cas. 174; *Dickey* v. *Maine Teleg. Co.* 46 Me. 483.

Lacy, *J.*, delivered the opinion of the court:

This is a writ of error to a judgment of the Circuit Court of New Kent County rendered on the 30th day of October, 1888. The plaintiff in error constructed its telegraph line upon the county road in New Kent County, where the said road ran over the lands of the defendant in error, without his consent, and without condemnation proceedings, and without tendering compensation, and refusing to pay compensation, therefor. As is alleged in the declaration, the defendant, "against the will of the plaintiff, and violently, against the protest of the plaintiff, entered upon the said land, and cut down and destroyed the trees and underwood,—fifty pine trees, twenty oak trees, and other trees, of the value of $1,950, —and broke down and prostrated a great part of the fences of the said plaintiff, and dug holes in the land of the plaintiff, and put posts there and kept the same there, etc., and incumbered the land, and hindered the plaintiff in the free use and enjoyment thereof." The defendant pleaded "Not guilty," and moved the court to remove the case to the federal court, which motion to remove the case the court overruled, and the case proceeded to a trial; and upon the trial the jury rendered a verdict in favor of the plaintiff for the sum of $550, upon which judgment was rendered accordingly, whereupon the defendant, the plaintiff in error here, applied for and obtained a writ of error to this court.

There were sundry exceptions taken at the trial which were assigned as error here. The first assignment which we will consider is as to the refusal of the court to give to the jury certain instructions asked by the defendant, and the giving by the court of certain other instructions.

The plaintiff moved the court to instruct the jury to the following effect: That, "if the jury believe from the evidence that the defendant was, at the time of the committing of the alleged trespass in the declaration mentioned, and still is, a telegraph company chartered by this or any other State, and that the road along which it has constructed and maintained, and still is maintaining, its telegraph line in the County of New Kent, was at said time, and still is, a county road, then the said defendant had at said time, and still has, the right to construct and maintain its said line along said county road, upon any part thereof, to the width or extent of thirty feet, whether the road-bed actually used by the public was and is of such width or not, provided the ordinary use of said road be not thereby obstructed; and said defendant had at said time, and still has, the right to cut down and trim out such trees or limbs, within such width or extent of thirty feet, as might interfere with the proper and effective construction, maintenance and operation of its said line. (2) For the exercise of such right as aforesaid, the defendant is not required to obtain permission from, or to make compensation to, the owner or owners of the land upon which said road is located, whether the fee-simple title to the soil upon which the road is located, or the mere easement thereon, be vested in the public. (3) The jury are further instructed that, although the road bed of said road actually used by the public may not be or have been of the width of thirty feet, and although the overseer of said road may not have complied with the law in keeping said road clear and smooth, and free from obstructions, to the legally required width of thirty feet, yet, under the laws and statutes of the Commonwealth, the defendant Company was authorized to use any part of said legal road of thirty feet to the same extent as if said overseer had strictly complied with the provisions of law requiring him to keep said road

---

soil and freehold revert to the owner, who cannot be compelled to return the price paid for the easement. Westbrook v. North, 2 Me. 179; Nicholson v. Stockett, Walker (Miss.) 67; Hampton v. Coffin, 4 N. H. 517; Taylor v. Armstrong, 24 Ark. 102; San Francisco v. Spring Valley Water Works, 48 Cal. 493; Brown v. Freeman, 1 Root (Conn.) 118; Buel v. Clark, Id. 49; Morris v. Schollsville Branch R. R. Turnp. Road, 6 Bush, 671; Westbrook v. North, Nicholson v. Stockett and Hampton v. Coffin, *supra*; Jackson v. Hathaway, 15 Johns. 447; Whitbeck v. Cook, 15 Johns. 483; Phillips v. Dunkirk, W. & P. R. Co. 78 Pa. 177; Mitchell v. Bass, 33 Tex. 259.

Construction of telegraph lines, an additional servitude.

The construction of a telegraph and telephone line on a railroad company's right of way imposes an additional servitude or burden on the land, for which the owners are entitled to compensation. See *note* to Baltimore City Am. Teleph. & Teleg. Co. v. Smith (Md.) 7 L. R. A. 200, and *note*.

The petition for the assessment of damages caused by telegraph poles must indicate the size of the poles to be erected and the positions in which they will be placed. State v. New York & N. J. Teleph. Co. 8 Cent. Rep. 589, 49 N. J. L. 624.

clear of timber and other obstructions to the required width, and the whole thirty feet been actually used by the public as a road."

But the court refused to give these instructions of the defendant, and gave the following: "(1) The court instructs the jury that the law presumes that the ownership of lands along the side of a public road in Virginia extends to the middle of said road, and the burden of proof is on the party who claims otherwise to show that such is not the case along the road where the right is controverted; and the owner has the exclusive right to the soil, subject to its use for the purposes of the public, and to the right of passage of the public over the same; and, being owners of the soil, they have a right to all of the ordinary remedies for disturbing of, or injury to, their freehold or possession; and any Act of the Legislature which devests such owners of their rights is unconstitutional and void. (2) The fact that a road is a public road or highway does not authorize the digging of holes for the purpose of erecting telegraph posts, and the erecting of posts, and the establishing a telegraph line, over the lands of a person, without his consent, although the same may be erected or done on that part of his premises which is used as a public road."

It thus appears that the claim of the defendant is that, by reason of the Act of Assembly of February 10, 1880 (Acts 1879-80, pp. 53, 54), it was authorized to construct its telegraph poles and line along the land over which the county road runs, without making compensation therefor, and that it maintains its right to exercise, as to these lands, the right of eminent domain thereon,—to take and enjoy what belongs to another, in the exercise of the sovereign power, not only without making any compensation therefor, but without any formal proceedings looking to condemnation of this property under any of the forms of law whatever.

If it is once conceded, or in any wise established, that the land in question belonged to the plaintiff, it was his private property, his freehold; as entirely his own, throughout all its parts, as the shelter which he had erected around and over his hearthstone, for his habitation and home, and as entirely under the protection of the laws against intrusion as the very hearthstone itself. That these lands are the lands of the plaintiff, unless he has lost them by the creation of a public road across them, is undeniable,—is, indeed, not denied. Does the creation of a public road through the land devest him of the fee in the same?

As to the extent of the right acquired by the public upon opening a highway in Virginia, Mr. Minor, in his Institutes (vol. 1, p. 120), says: "The public acquires merely a right of passage. The freehold and all the profits of the soil (that is, trees, mines, etc.) belong still to the proprietor from whom the right of passage was acquired. He may therefore recover the freehold in ejectment, subject to the right of way, and may maintain an action of trespass for digging the ground. If it be unknown from which of two adjacent proprietors a highway was at first taken, or if the highway be the boundary between them, they are understood to own each *ad medium filum viæ*,"—citing Bacon, Abr. *Highways*, *b*; *Bolling* v. *Petersburg*, 3 Rand. (Va.) 563; *Home* v. *Richards*, 4 Call (Va.) 441; *Harris* v. *Elliott*, 35 U. S. 10 Pet. 25 [9 L. ed. 333].

And this subject is again referred to by Mr. Minor in his second volume, p. 20, as to the ownership of land adjacent to highways, when he says: "The ownership usually extends to the middle of the road, as in the case of a private stream; or, if the same party owns on both sides, the whole road belongs to him, subject to the public easement of the right of passage in either case,—citing 3 Kent, Com. 432."

In the case of *Home* v. *Richards*, *supra*, all the judges delivered opinions, and all held that the grant of the right of way does not convey the soil, but only the right to a way over.

In the case of *Bolling* v. *Petersburg*, *supra*,—a case fully and ably argued in this court by the foremost lawyers of that day,—*Judge* Carr delivered the unanimous opinion of the court. Speaking as to the public highway, he said: "Does this disable the demandant from recovering the land? It certainly would not in England, as many cases show,"—citing *Lade* v. *Shepherd*, 2 Strange, 1004.

In that case the defendant rested one end of a bridge upon the highway. Upon trespass brought, the court said: "It is certainly a dedication to the public so far as the public has occasion for it, which is only for a right of passage; but it never was understood to be a transfer of the absolute property in the soil."

In *Goodtitle* v. *Alker*, 1 Burr. 143, in ejectment, a special verdict finding that the land was a public street and public highway, *Lord* Mansfield says: "1 Rolle, Abr. 392, is express 'that the king has nothing but the passage for himself and his people, but the freehold, and all profits, belong to the owner of the soil.' So do all the trees upon it, and mines under it. . . . The owner may get his soil discharged of this servitude or easement of a way over it by a writ of *ad quod damnum*. It is like the property in a market or fair. There is no reason why he should not have a right to all remedies for the freehold, subject still, indeed, to the servitude or easement. . . . An action of trespass would lie for an injury done to it. . . . I see no ground why the owner of the soil may not bring ejectment as well as trespass." *Northampton* v. *Ward*, 1 Wilson, 107; *Harrison* v. *Parker*, 6 East, 154.

But it is said that in this country we act on a more liberal scale; that the court will look to the great principles of public policy and give them effect; that, the conveniences of the community requiring highways, they must be had; and, as a mere right of way is not sufficient for the full enjoyment of them, we must consider the Commonwealth as vested with a base fee in all public highways.

Our business is with the law as it is; and, where the power to be exercised is one of so important a character as the taking away the property of a citizen, devesting him of his eminent domain in the soil, I could not consent to take the step unless I saw myself justified by some clear principle of the common law, or some plain enactment of the statute. The English cases are pretty strong evidence that the common law confers no such power. I have looked into our statutes, and I can find nothing there to countenance the idea that where a road is established the fee in the soil, either simple or base, is vested in the Commonwealth. On the contrary, I think it is obvious that a right of way is all that the public requires, leaving the whole fee in the owner of the soil. It is for the use of the land by the Commonwealth that the owner is compensated. There can be no question as to what the law is in this State. It is well settled.

In *Warwick* v. *Mayo*, 15 Gratt. 528, *Judge* Allen delivered the unanimous opinion of this court to the same effect. Speaking of a highway, he says: "The easement comprehends no interest in the soil," and cites *Judge* Swift as saying, in *Peck* v. *Smith*, 1 Conn. 103: "The right of freehold is not touched by establishing a highway, but continues in the original owner of the land in the same manner it was before the highway was established, subject to the easement." He says, further: "Nothwithstanding the easement, the owner retains many and valuable interests. . . . He may make any use of it not inconsistent with the enjoyment of the easement." Hare & Wallace's *notes* to *Doraston* v. *Payne*, 2 Smith, Lead. Cas. *199, where the authorities are collected.

After speaking of the English rule, and the decisions of some of the States, he says: "In Virginia the rule has been established by an authoritative decision of the very point in accordance with the settled doctrine of the English courts,"—and refers to *Bolling* v. *Petersburg*, *supra*.

If these principles are thus settled in Virginia, as they certainly are, they are equally as firmly inbedded in the jurisprudence of numerous other States of this country. These are collected and cited by Mr. Angell in his work on Highways, p. 396, § 301 *et seq.*, and *notes*. At page 398, § 303, this author says: "The principles of the common law in this respect have been recognized and adopted by the American courts,"—citing *Perley* v. *Chandler*, 6 Mass. 454.

Under these principles the plaintiff was entitled to maintain trespass against the defendant when the said defendant stopped upon his land, instead of passing along, and dug up his soil, and cut down his trees, and tore down and scattered his fence, unless such taking of his property was by due process of law, for public uses, upon just compensation. If the use for which the land was taken was a private use, it could not be lawfully taken without his consent. But the use may be conceded to be a public use, and yet to take without just compensation was unlawful. Such taking without authority of law was a trespass, and such taking could find no justification in any Act of the General Assembly. Art. 5, § 14, Const. Va.

It is claimed that the Act of Assembly passed February 10, 1880 (Acts 1879-80), authorized this Company to so construct its works upon the land of the plaintiff. That Act should receive a reasonable construction, and be so construed, if possible, as to avoid repugnance to the Constitution; and while, by that Act, these companies are authorized to construct their lines and fixtures along the county roads, provided the ordinary use of the road was not obstructed, it is not expressly provided that this may be done without compensation. But the provision is so as not to obstruct the ordinary use. The Commonwealth had and has in these roads nothing but the use to pass over and along, and the Act provides that this use shall not be obstructed by virtue of that Act. But at the conclusion of this paragraph, constituting the last words in it, are these words, "upon making just compensation therefor;" and then follow the provisions of the law which provide for the proceedings necessary to ascertain what is just compensation by condemnation proceedings. This was certainly the provision of the Act as to lands of persons generally; and, if the land upon which the highway runs is the private property of the citizen, which it clearly is, should not this language be held to apply to such land as well as to others? Why not? The Commonwealth has no more power to grant the one than the other. To grant either is to take private property, and this can only be done upon just compensation. If this is the true construction of this Act, the same is in accordance with the Constitution of the State; and the plaintiff was entitled to maintain his suit against a corporation which neither took lawfully, nor paid just compensation. But if the Act does provide for the taking of this private property without compensation, then it is void for repugnancy to the Constitution of the State, and the plaintiff was entitled to recover and the instruction of the court was right.

However, it is claimed by the plaintiff in error that, granting that the rights of the plaintiff are what we have stated, and the Commonwealth has only the right to use by going over, still his case is good, because his works are only a use of the easement, and constitute no new taking,—no additional servitude. We will now briefly consider this argument.

The right in the Commonwealth is to use by going along over. This is the extent of the right. If the right was granted to the defendant to go over simply to carry its messages, then the right granted was in existence before the grant, and the right to go over is not only not disputed, but distinctly admitted. This is the servitude over the land fixed upon it by law, and the whole extent of it. If anything more is taken, it is an additional servitude, and is a taking of the property, within the meaning of the Constitution. To take the whole subject,—the land in fee, is a taking. This, however, is the meaning of the term only in a limited sense, and in the narrowest sense of the word. The constitutional provision which declares that property shall not be taken for public use without just compensation was intended to establish this principle beyond legislative control, and it is not necessary that property should be absolutely taken, in the sense of completely taking, to bring a case within the protection of the Constitution. As was said by a learned justice of the Supreme Court of the United States: "It would be a very curious and unsatisfactory result, if, in construing a provision of constitutional law always understood to have been adopted for protection and security to the rights of the individual as against the government, and which has received the commendation of jurists, statesmen and commentators, as placing the just principles of the common law on that subject beyond the power of ordinary legislation to change or control them, it shall be held that, if the government refrains from the absolute conversion of real property to the uses of the public, it can destroy its value entirely; can inflict irreparable and permanent injury to any extent; can, in effect, subject it to total destruction,—without making any compensation, because, in the narrowest sense of that word, it is not taken for the public use. Such a construction would pervert the constitutional provision into a restriction upon the rights of the citizen, as those rights stood at the common law, instead of the government, and make it an authority for invasion of private right under the pretext of the public good, which had no warrant in the laws and practices of our ancestors." *Justice* Miller in *Pumpelly* v. *Green Bay & M. Canal Co.* 80 U. S. 13 Wall. 166 [20 L. ed. 557].

It is obvious, and it is so held in many cases, that the construction of a railroad upon a highway is an additional servitude upon the land, for which the owner is entitled to additional compensation. Cooley, Const. Lim. 548; *Ford* v. *Chicago & N. W. R. Co.* 14 Wis. 616; *Pomeroy* v. *Milwaukee & C. R. Co.* 16 Wis. 641.

And the power of a Legislature to authorize a railroad to be constructed on a common highway is denied upon the ground that the original appropriation permitted the taking for the purposes of a common highway, and no other. The principle is the same when the land is taken for any other purpose distinct from the original purpose, and the reasoning in the two cases is applicable to each.

In the case of *Imlay* v. *Union Branch R. Co.*, 26 Conn. 255, it is said: "When land is condemned for a special purpose, on the score of public utility, the sequestration is limited to that particular use. Land taken for a highway is not thereby convertible into a common. As the property is not taken, but the use only, the right of the public is limited to the use—the specific use—for which the proprietor has been devested of a complete dominion over his own estate. These are propositions which are no longer open to discussion." *Nicholson* v. *New York & N. H. R. Co.* 22 Conn. 85; *South Carolina R. Co.* v. *Steiner*, 44 Ga. 546.

In the case of a telephone company, the chancellor, in the case of *Broome* v. *New York & N. J. Teleph. Co.* 42 N. J. Eq. 141, 5 Cent. Rep. 814, held that, in order to justify a telephone company in setting up poles in the highway, it must show that it has acquired the right to do so, either by contract or condemnation, from the owner of the soil, saying: "The complainant seeks relief against an invasion of his proprietary right to his land. The defendants, a telephone company, without any leave or license from, or consent by, him, but, on the other hand, against his protest and remonstrance, and in disregard of his warning and express prohibition, and without condemnation, or any steps to that end, set up their poles upon his land. . . . What has been said is sufficient of itself to establish the right of the complainant to relief; for, in order to justify the defendants in setting up the poles, it is necessary for them to show that they have acquired the right to do so, either by consent or condemnation, from the owner of the soil." As to these rights of the owner of the soil, see 9 Am. & Eng. Cyclop. Law, title *Highways*, 7, § 2; *Board of Trade Tel. Co.* v. *Barnett*, 107 Ill. 508; *Southwestern R. Co.* v. *Southern & A. Teleg. Co.* 46 Ga. 48; *W. U. Teleg Co.* v. *Rich*, 19 Kan. 517; *Willis* v. *Erie Teleg. & Teleph. Co.* 37 Minn. 347.

That the erection of a telegraph line upon a highway is an additional servitude is clear from the authorities. That it is such is equally clear upon principle, in the light of the Virginia cases cited above. If the right acquired by the Commonwealth in the condemnation of a highway is only the right to pass along over the highway for the public, then, if the untaken parts of the land are his private property, to dig up the soil is to dig up his soil; to cut down the trees is to cut down his trees; to destroy the fences is to destroy his fences; to erect any structure, to affix any pole, or put it in and upon the land, is to take possession of his land; and all these interfere with his free and unrestricted use of his property. If the Commonwealth took this without just compensation, it would be a violation of the Constitution. The Commonwealth cannot constitutionally grant it to another.

It is true that the use of the Telegraph Company is a public use. That Company is a public corporation, as to which the public has rights which the law will enforce. But these public rights can only be obtained by paying for them. The use, while in one sense public, is not for the public generally. It is for the private profit of the corporation. It is its business enterprise, engaged in for gain. Its services can only be obtained upon their being paid for. There is no reason, either in law or in common justice, why it should not pay for what it needs in the prosecution of its business. Upon this burden being placed upon it, it can complain of no hardship. It is the common lot of all. If the said Company has use for the private property of a citizen of this Commonwealth, and it is of advantage to it to have the same, it is illogical to argue that the property is of small value to the plaintiff, and, in the aggregate, a great matter to the plaintiff in error. This argument is not worth considering. It cuts at the very root of the rights of property. It would apply with equal force to all the transactions of life. It is sufficient to say the ægis of the Constitution is over this as over all other private property rights, and there is no power which can devest it without just compensation.

We think the instructions of the circuit court were clearly right, and there is no error therein.

There is no error in the process in the case. It was made as provided by law against a nonresident corporation having no officer or agent resident in the county.

There was no error in the refusal of the court to remove the case from New Kent County. Not the slightest ground is shown for it. And it may be remarked that the plaintiff in error selected its forum when it thus unlawfully invaded the property rights of one of the citizens of that county.

As to the contention concerning the summoning of the jury by the sheriff, because he was interested in the suit, there is no error in that action of the court below: (1) because the sheriff does not appear to be in any wise interested in the suit; and (2) because the sheriff did not in fact select the jury. Upon objection made, the judge made out the list, and gave it to the deputy sheriff, to summon the required *venire.*

Upon the whole case, we are of opinion that there is no error in *the judgment appealed from,* and the same *must be affirmed.*

Fauntleroy and **Hinton,** *JJ.*, concur.

Lewis, *P.*, dissenting:

I take a very different view of the case from that taken in the opinion of the court just read; and, as the case is an important one, I will state the reasons for my dissent. I agree that the Act of February 10, 1880, does not provide for additional compensation to the owners of lands abutting on highways along which telegraph lines may be constructed, and, therefore, that the question in the case is whether, on that account, the Act is constitutional. But, before proceeding to discuss that question, I will remark that the case, as presented by the record, is quite an extraordinary one. The plaintiff sued to recover damages to the amount of $1,500. Although the assessed fee-simple value of his land abutting on the highway is only $175, yet the jury returned a verdict for $550 damages; and the alleged injury consists, as far as I can ascertain from the record, in planting a single pole, strung with wire, on so much of the highway as passes over the plaintiff's land, and "cutting trees and underwood" that grew upon the highway,—from all which the inference seems to have been drawn by the jury and the court below that, if the plaintiff's land is worth little or nothing for taxation, its value for telegraph purposes is enormous. Inasmuch, however, as no formal bill of exceptions was filed to the action of the court in overruling the defendant's motion to set aside the verdict, although the record recites that an exception was taken, and there is no certificate of the facts proven, or of the evidence, I will confine myself to the question of the constitutionality of the Act, and that depends upon whether the use of the highway for a telegraph line is a new servitude upon the soil, or whether it is included in the original appropriation. If the latter view be the correct one, then there has been no taking of the plaintiff's property, within the meaning of the Constitution, under the Act in question, but simply the grant of a privilege to use a public easement, which has already been paid for, and which is subject to the regulation and control of the Legislature.

What, then, are the nature and extent of the public easement in land condemned for a highway? The plaintiff contends that it is merely a right of passage, and nothing more; and *Bolling* v. *Petersburg,* 3 Rand. (Va.) 563, is referred to in support of this position. That case, which adopts the language of the ancient authorities on the subject, does indeed so hold; and when it was decided the language used was sufficiently comprehensive to cover every then known mode of enjoying the public right. But since that time civilization has advanced. New modes of using the public highways have been discovered, and, as the common law adapts itself to the constantly changing wants and conditions of society, the courts have held—and rightly, I think—that the view contended for by the plaintiff is altogether too narrow and restricted. So that the principle, as now established, is that the highways of a State are not only open and free for travel and traffic, but that, with the assent of the Legislature, they may be devoted, under the original appropriation, to such other public uses as are consistent with their use as public thoroughfares. "The more ancient decisions," says Angell, "limited the rights of the public [in highways] to that of passage and re passage, and treated any interference of the soil other than was necessary to the enjoyment of this right as a trespass. But the modern decisions have very much extended the public right, and particularly in the streets of populous cities." And then he goes on to say that, "whether the corporation be the user of the fee, . . . or whether it be merely the trustee of the streets and highways as such, irrespective of any title to the soil, it has the power [with the sanction of the Legislature] to authorize their appropriation to all such uses as are conducive to the public good, and do not interfere with their complete and unrestricted use as highways; and, in doing so, it is not obliged to confine itself to such uses as have already been permitted. As civilization advances, new uses may be found expedient." Ang. & D. Highw. § 812.

Another author, in treating of the same subject, uses this language: "The use of property taken by the right of eminent domain is not confined to the precise mode or kind of use which was in view at the time of the taking, but may extend to other modes, which were then unpracticed and unknown. When property has been taken for a public use, and full compensation made for the fee or a perpetual easement, its subsequent appropriation to another public use—certainly, if one of a like kind—does not require further compensation to the owner." Pierce, Railroads, 238.

One of the numerous cases in which this principle has been decided is *Chase* v. *Sutton Mfg. Co.* 4 Cush. 152, in which case *Chief Justice* Shaw said that where, under the authority of the Legislature, in virtue of the sovereign power of eminent domain, private property has been taken for a public use, and a full compensation for a perpetual easement in land has been paid to the owner therefor, and afterwards the land is appropriated to a public use of a like kind, no new claim for compensation can be sustained by the owner of the land over which it passes. And to the same effect is *Peddicord* v. *Baltimore, C. & E. M. Pass. R. Co.*, 34 Md. 463, in which case it was held that the use of the bed of a turnpike for the purpose of a passenger railway was not a new and distinct servitude, which entitled the abutting owners to new compensation, because, in the opinion of the court, such use did not exclude, or seriously interfere with, the original modes in which the highway was used, but simply added another in furtherance of the same general object. "It is true," said the court, "that when the right of way was originally acquired, and when it was granted to the turnpike company, it was not actually contemplated by any of the parties to the acquisition and grant that it would be used for a passenger railway, yet it may be said to have been within the legal contemplation of all that it was to be used for all the purposes by which the object of its creation as a public highway could be promoted. The parties looked to the future . . . as well as to the then present; and it cannot be supposed that the authors of its existence intended otherwise than that it should respond to whatever demands new improvements and increased facilities might make upon it, so only that such demands must be always consistent with its character and purpose as a public highway."

The same principle is laid down with great force and clearness by *Chief Justice* Shaw in *Com.* v. *Temple*, 14 Gray, 69. In that case it was held that all public easements intended for common and general benefit, whatever may be their nature and character, are under the control and regulation of the Legislature, exercising the sovereign power of the State, and therefore it was competent for that body to authorize a street railway to be constructed and maintained by a private corporation in the public highway. "It is the great merit of the common law," said the eminent jurist who spoke for the court, "that it is founded upon a comparatively few broad, general principles of justice, fitness and expediency, the correctness of which is generally acknowledged, and which at first are few and simple, but which, carried out in their practical details, and adapted to extremely complicated cases of fact, give rise to many, and often perplexing, questions. Yet these original principles remain fixed, and are generally comprehensive enough to adapt themselves to new institutions and conditions of society, new modes of commerce, new usages and practices, as the progress of society, in the advancement of civilization, may require."

So, in the subsequent case of *Atty-Gen.* v. *Metropolitan R. Co.*, 125 Mass. 515, it was again decided that it is within the power of the Legislature to authorize the construction of a street railway without the consent of the adjoining proprietors, and without additional compensation to them; that the future alteration and use of public streets for public travel must always be subject to reasonable modification by future legislation; that the compensation of the adjoining land owners must be presumed to have been adjusted to such future changes; and that their convenience may be affected thereby without impairing any constitutional right to additional compensation; in other words, that any inconvenience or annoyance resulting from such changes is a merely incidental injury, or *damnum absque injuria*, just as this court has repeatedly decided with respect to incidental injuries to land owners caused by the alteration in a lawful manner of the grade of a public street. *Smith* v. *Alexandria*, 33 Gratt. 208; *Kehrer* v. *Richmond City*, 81 Va. 745.

In Cooley, Const. Lim., 552, 555, the author after remarking that when property is appropriated for a public way, and the proprietor is paid for the public easement, the compensation is generally estimated, in practice, at the value of the land itself, says, further, that "a strong inclination is apparent to hold that, when the fee in the public way is taken, . . . it is taken for any public use whatever to which the public authorities, with the legislative assent, may see fit afterwards to devote it in furtherance of the general purpose of the original appropriation; and, if this is so, the owner must be held to be compensated at the time of the original taking for any such possible use." There is no material difference in principle, however, as the author points out in a note, with regard to the extent of the rights of the public in a highway, whether the fee is in the public or in the adjacent land owner, or in some third person. In either case the Legislature may, without providing for additional compensation, authorize such uses to be made of the highway as are conducive to the public convenience, and not repugnant to the purposes of the original appropriation. *Barney* v. *Keokuk*, 94 U. S. 324 [24 L. ed. 224].

In many of the States of the Union it has been held that the use of the highway even for a steam railway is not an additional burden upon the land of the adjoining proprietor which entitles him to increased compensation; and so it was held in the case last mentioned, the supreme court, in that particular, following the local law of Iowa, in which State the case arose and was decided. The weight of authority, however, is the other way, the idea being that such a use of the highway is inconsistent with its use by the general public, to which it had been legally appropriated. And *Judge* Dillon says that, while there is solid ground to distinguish between steam and horse railways, yet there is much to recommend as sound the view that, where property is acquired for a street, it may be used as a street under the original appropriation, in such way as the Legislature, representing the public, and best acquainted with the public needs, may authorize. 2 Dillon, Mun. Corp. 3d ed. § 722.

This was substantially the view taken by *Chief Justice* Gibson, with whom the whole court concurred, in the *Case of the Philadelphia & T. R. Co.*, 6 Whart. 25, where it is said that, as in England a highway is the property of the king, as *parens patria*, so here it is subject to the paramount authority of the Legislature in the regulation of its use by carriages or means of locomotion "yet to be invented," and that the remedy for an abuse of this power is with the people, who by changing their rules may change the law. And it is not easy to see why, upon principle, this should not be regarded as the true solution of this whole matter.

In some of the cases a distinction is suggested between highways in the county and streets within the limits of cities or towns, according to which the latter may be used for more various uses than the former, as for laying gas and water pipes, the construction of horse railways, sewers, levees, wharves and other accommodations for the public. But, as both the highway and the street are opened for the same general purpose,—and a street is a highway,—there would seem to be no sound basis for such a distinction.

Much of the confusion in the decisions on the subject of the constitutional power of the Legislature over highways is owing, it seems to me, to a failure to discriminate between the use for which a highway is appropriated and the modes of using it. Hence, in passing upon such questions, a clear idea of what a highway is ought always to be kept in view. And what is a highway? Perhaps no better definition of it, in the light of reason and the modern decisions, can be given than to say that it is a road or thoroughfare for the use of the general public, for the purpose of intercommunication, which embraces the right to use the highway not only for passage, but for the transmission of intelligence. Formerly, as before remarked, the only mode by which intelligence could be transmitted over a highway was by passing over it. But it is not so now. The discovery of the telegraph and the telephone has revolutionized the methods of intercommunication; and I am unable to perceive why, when a message is sent over a telegraph or telephone wire erected on the public highway, the same, or substantially the same, use is not made of the highway as when a message is sent over it by a messenger on foot or on horseback. In the one case, as was well said in the argument at the bar, the message goes with the messenger; in the other, it goes without the messenger,—the only difference being in the mode of sending it. And it hardly seems in keeping with the progressive spirit of the common law, in eulogy of which so much has been justly written, to say that the new method is not admissible, though with the assent of the Legislature, because it was not known to Bracton or Blackstone.

Said the court in *Dickerson* v. *Colgrove*, 100 U. S. 578 [25 L. ed. 619]: "The common law is reason dealing by the light of experience with human affairs." And what experience had our fathers with electricity as an element of intercommunication in 1825, when *Bolling* v. *Petersburg* was decided? None whatever. That the new method is not inconsistent with the ordinary use of the highway is to my mind obvious. Indeed, it is in aid of it; for it not only furnishes vastly increased facilities of intercommunication, but it tends to the relief of the highway, by lessening travel over it, which in populous cities, and even in the country, is no small consideration. And here it may be remarked that the Statute expressly provides that in no case shall a telegraph or telephone erected along a highway obstruct the ordinary use of the highway. Acts 1879–80, p. 53; Code, §§ 1287–1290.

As to the complaint that, in constructing its line, the defendant cut down trees of the plaintiff, it is enough to say that it appears from the record that no poles were planted, or trees cut, except on the highway; and this it was as competent for the defendant to do, under the authority conferred by the Legislature to construct its line, as it was for the public authorities, in the first instance, to cut down such trees as stood in the way when the road was being opened and constructed. The record recites that "all of the acts complained of as done by the defendant upon the lands of the plaintiff were confined to the said legal road of thirty feet, and were necessary to the proper and effective construction, maintenance and operation of the said telegraph line of the defendant."

In the argument a number of authorities were cited to show that it is not competent for the Legislature to authorize a telegraph company to construct its line over the right of way of a railroad company, without making just compensation therefor; and this, I take it, no one will deny. The road-bed and right of way of a railroad company, at least in this State, are as much its property as its rolling stock, or the money in its treasury; and the one can no more be lawfully taken without just compensation than the other. But that is a very different case from this, for here I have endeavored to show that the plaintiff's property has not been taken; that nothing has been granted but the right to use a public easement, which right, under no circumstances, can last longer than the easement itself.

Fortunately, direct authority is not wanting in support of these views. The precise question has been adjudicated in two well-considered opinions,—one by the Supreme Judicial Court of Massachusetts in the case of *Pierce* v. *Drew*, 136 Mass. 75; the other by the Supreme Court of Missouri in the case of *Julia Bldg. Asso.* v. *Bell Teleph. Co.*, 88 Mo. 258, 5 West. Rep. 357, in both of which cases it was distinctly held that an additional servitude is not imposed by the erection on a public highway of a telegraph or telephone line under a statute of the State, and that such statute is not unconstitutional because it makes no provision for additional compensation to the owners of the fee in the highway. In the first-mentioned case the court, in an able and learned opinion by *Mr. Justice* Devens, said: "The discovery of the telegraph developed a new and valuable mode of communicating intelligence. Its use is certainly similar to, if not identical with, that public use of transmitting information for which the highway was originally taken, even if the means adopted are quite different from the post-boy or the mail-coach. It is a newly discovered method of exercising the old public easement, and all appropriate methods must have been deemed to have been paid for when the road was laid out." And he added that, "under the clause to regulate commerce among the States, conferred on Congress by the Constitution of the United States, although telegraphic communication was unknown when it was adopted, it has been held that it is the right of Congress to prevent the obstruction of telegraphic communication by hostile state legislation, as it has become an indispensable means of intercommunication," — citing *Pensacola Teleg. Co.* v. *W. U. Teleg. Co.* 96 U. S. 1 [24 L. ed. 708]. See also *W. U. Teleg. Co.* v. *Texas*, 105 U. S. 460 [26 L. ed. 1067]; *W. U. Teleg. Co.* v. *Seay*, 132 U. S. 472 [33 L. ed. 409], and cases cited.

In *Julia Bldg. Asso.* v. *Bell Teleph. Co.*, *supra*, it was said: "If a thousand messages were daily transmitted by means of telephone poles, wires and other appliances used in telephoning, the street, through these means, would serve the same purpose which would otherwise require its use either by a thousand footmen, horsemen or carriages, to effectuate the same purpose. In this view of it, the erection of telephone poles and wires for transmission of oral messages, so far from imposing a new and additional servitude, would, to the extent of each message transmitted, relieve the street of a servitude or use by a footman, horseman or carriage."

In opposition to these views the case of *Board of Trade Tel. Co.* v. *Barnett*, 107 Ill. 507, has been cited. That case was disapproved of by both the Massachusetts and Missouri courts, and, I think, with good reason. The case decides that there is no difference in principle between a telegraph and a steam railway in a country highway, so far as the abstract question of servitude is concerned, and that, as the railway is an additional servitude, so also is the telegraph. This reasoning, to my mind, is fallacious. In the nature of things, the use of a highway for operating a steam railway more or less excludes the ordinary methods of travel, and is attended with other inconveniences besides. But can this be said of the telegraph? In what way does a telegraph, erected on the side of a highway, in the country, interfere with the rights of the abutting owner, or with its use as a public thoroughfare? Does it exclude or obstruct travel? On the contrary, it is obviously much less an obstruction than travelers on horseback or in vehicles over the road usually are to one another; and, as to any increased dangers or annoyance resulting from the use of streets in a city for the stringing of numerous wires, of which much has been said, that is not a direct but an incidental injury, which is a matter for the Legislature, and not for the courts, to consider; for nobody doubts that in such cases the Legislature may, if it sees fit, require additional compensation to the owners of the fee to be made.

It has never been questioned, so far as I am informed, that the Legislature may authorize telegraph wires to be laid beneath the surface of a street without additional compensation therefor; and, if this can be lawfully done, the power to authorize the wires to be put above the surface would seem to be equally clear, the difference being a mere matter of regulation, as to which, as we have seen, the power of the Legislature is unqualified.

As to the case of *Warwick* v. *Mayo*, 15 Gratt. 528, decided in 1860, and to which our attention has been called, I have only a word to say. In that case, Allen, *P.*, announced the elementary principle that the right of freehold is not touched by establishing a highway, but continues in the original owner of the land, subject to the public easement; and he referred, as authority, to the case in 3 Rand. (Va.) 563. But no question that arises in the present case arose in that case, or was, probably, dreamed of; and, even if it had been decided that no mode of using the public easement is lawful, without additional compensation to the owner of the fee, than such as was known and practiced a half century ago, that would be no reason, if the decision were wrong, for perpetuating the error. Until a comparatively recent period, no one ever heard of an instrument under seal being negotiable; and yet, at the present day, there are sealed instruments the negotiability of which is recognized everywhere, not by virtue of statutes, but because an advanced civilization, and the consequent necessities of commerce, require it; in other words, because the common law is expansive, or rather comprehensive, enough to adapt itself to the wants and conditions of modern society.

Another illustration may be drawn from the course of decision in admiralty. For more than fifty years after the adoption of the Constitution, the subordinate federal courts, following the English decisions defining the jurisdiction in admiralty, held that the admiralty jurisdiction of the United States was confined to tide-water; and so the supreme court itself decided in *The Thomas Jefferson*, 23 U. S. 10 Wheat. 428 [6 L. ed. 358]. But in the case of *The Genesee Chief* v. *Fitzhugh*, 53 U. S. 12 How. 443 [13 L. ed. 1058], which was a case of collision on Lake Ontario, *Chief Justice* Taney, speaking for the court, in one of his most celebrated opinions, pointed out that while the definition of the jurisdiction, so far as it related to England, was a sound and reasonable one, because in that country there were no navigable streams beyond the ebb and flow of the tide, and that at the time the Constitution was adopted the definition was, for all practical purposes, a proper one for this country also, yet that it had ceased to be so; and accordingly the court declared that the jurisdiction extends to all waters that are in fact navigable, whether tide-waters or not, thus overruling its own previous decision on the subject as being erroneous because not going far enough. In the course of his opinion, the chief justice used language which with propriety may be quoted here. He said: "It is the decision in the case of *The Thomas Jefferson* which mainly embarrasses the court in the present inquiry. We are sensible of the great weight to which it is entitled. But, at the same time, we are convinced that, if we follow it, we follow an erroneous decision into which the court fell, when the great importance of the question, as it now presents itself, could not be foreseen, and the subject did not therefore receive that deliberate consideration which at this time would have been given to it by the eminent men who presided here when that case was decided. For the decision was made in 1825, when the commerce on the rivers of the west, and on the lakes, was in its infancy, and of little importance, and but little regarded, compared with that of the present day."

I refer to this merely to show into what errors courts sometimes fall by blindly following decisions that are not applicable to our own times and circumstances, forgetting that the world is moving onward, and that common law is common sense dealing by the light of experience with human affairs. And it is into just such an error, it seems to me, that the court has fallen in the present case.

My opinion, therefore, is that the Act in question is constitutional and valid, and that the judgment of the circuit court should be reversed.

Richardson, *J.*, concurring.

Petition for rehearing denied.

INDIANA SUPREME COURT.

STATE OF INDIANA, *Appt.*
v.
Sidney ROBBINS.

(....Ind.....)

1. **Gaming devices** seized by the sheriff while executing a warrant for the arrest of their owner upon the charge of unlawfully keeping such devices for the purpose of gain are as properly subject to the order of the court trying the offender as if they had been seized by authority of a search warrant.

2. **Unless articles seized because used for violating law** are of such a character that the law will not recognize them as property entitled as such to its protection under any circumstances, they cannot be summarily destroyed without affording the owner an opportunity to be heard upon the subject of their lawful use and to show whether or not they are intrinsically useful or valuable for some lawful purpose.

3. **An order by the court,** which must be passed before or at the time of the final sentence of a person convicted of unlawfully keeping gaming devices for gain, is necessary to justify a destruction of such person's gaming apparatus, which has been seized by the sheriff, under the Statute which provides that "upon conviction of the person offending the sheriff shall forthwith destroy or cause to be destroyed the apparatus used for unlawful purposes.

(June 7, 1890.)

APPEAL by the State from orders of the Circuit Court for Cass County overruling a motion to direct the destruction of certain gaming apparatus, and directing its return to the owner. *Affirmed.*

The facts are fully stated in the opinion.

Messrs. **L. T. Michener,** *Atty-Gen.*, **John T. McGreevy,** *Pros. Atty.*, and **D. H. Chase** for appellant.

No appearance for appellee.

Mitchell, *J.*, delivered the opinion of the court:

Upon information of the prosecuting attorney within and for the County of Cass, Sydney Robbins was arrested upon the charge of unlawfully keeping and exhibiting for gain, and for the purpose of winning money thereon, a roulette table and wheel and a faro table and box for dealing cards contrary to the provisions of § 2086, Rev. Stat. 1881. The sheriff took the defendant into custody upon a warrant, upon which the officer made return, among other things, that he had seized one faro table complete, and one roulette table complete, adding that he had seized the devices above named on sight, while the game was in progress. The defendant appeared in court on the 10th day of May, 1889, and pleaded guilty and a fine of $25 was assessed against him. Afterwards, on the 27th day of May, 1889, the prosecuting attorney moved the court for an order directing the sheriff to destroy the gaming apparatus or devices theretofore seized and remaining in the possession of the officer. Thereupon Robbins appeared and moved the court for an order directing the sheriff to return the property to him. The court overruled the motion of the prosecutor and ordered that the property be returned to the owner. From these several rulings this appeal is prosecuted by the State.

It is provided in section 2086, in substance, that whoever keeps or exhibits for gain, or to win or gain money, any gaming table or any apparatus, device or machine of any kind or description, for the purpose of betting or gaming, shall be fined, etc. Provision is made in the Code regulating criminal procedure whereby, upon proper affidavit, justices of the peace are authorized to issue warrants to search any house or place for, among many other things, "any gaming table, establishment, device or apparatus, kept or exhibited for the purpose of unlawful gaming," etc. It is provided, when the warrant is executed by the seizure of the property or things described therein, that the property or things shall be delivered by the justice to the sheriff to be securely held by him, "subject to the order of the court trying the offender," and upon conviction of the person offending the sheriff shall forthwith destroy or cause to be destroyed the apparatus, devices, etc., used for unlawful purposes; and as to all other property, "he shall, after such conviction, deliver the same, under the order of the court, to the proper owner thereof."

On behalf of the State, it is insisted that it was the duty of the court to order the destruction of the gaming devices for the unlawful keeping and exhibition of which the owner had been convicted and which had been taken by the sheriff, in whose custody they remained. We have no doubt of the authority of a sheriff, or other officer authorized to make arrests, to seize articles which he knows or has good reason to believe are being employed in violating the criminal law, or as instruments for the commission of crime. Things which may supply evidence of an offense of which one has been accused may be taken into the possession of the officer making the arrest, to be disposed of under the direction of the court. 1 Bishop, Crim. Proc. §§ 210, 211.

An officer has no authority to take money from the person of a prisoner, or to take from him any other property or thing, unless it is in some way connected with the crime with the commission of which he is charged, or unless it renders his arrest or detention hazardous, or might facilitate his escape. It is not only the right, but it is the duty, of every peace officer to seize any property or thing that is being used in the commission of crime or in the violation of law enacted for the protection of the health, morals and welfare of the community. *Spaulding* v. *Preston*, 21 Vt. 9.

The gaming devices in question having been lawfully seized and taken into the possession of the sheriff, they were as properly subject to the order of the court trying the offender as they would have been in case they had been seized by a constable armed with a search war-

NOTE.—The destruction by a public officer of nets for catching fish, set in violation of law, is proper and reasonable exercise of official power, and may be done summarily under the authority of the statute. See Lawton v. Steele (N. Y.) 7 L. R. A. 134, and note.

See also 24 L. R. A. 355.

rant, and afterwards turned over to the sheriff. The Statute authorizing the issuance of a search warrant was designed as a means of discovering and securing possession, by the officers of the law of articles or things the use of which was immoral and unlawful. If, without resorting to the Statute, the proper officer of the court obtained possession of the articles or things used in the commission of a crime, in some other manner equally lawful and legitimate, the jurisdiction of the court over the subject would be the same as if it had been first taken by a search warrant and turned over to the sheriff. In other words, so far as the court has jurisdiction over the property or thing, its jurisdiction depends upon the fact that the apparatus shall be property in the custody of the sheriff when the offender is before the court for trial, and not that he shall have obtained the custody by means of a search warrant. The material part of the Statute in that regard is that the thing seized "shall be securely held by the sheriff, subject to the order of the court trying the offender."

No definite or precise mode of procedure is pointed out by the Statute, in order to enforce the forfeiture of the things seized. The provision is that the sheriff shall securely hold the articles seized, "subject to the order of the court trying the offender," and upon conviction of the person offending destroy or cause to be destroyed the articles used for unlawful purposes. The inquiry then is, Was it necessary, in order to warrant the destruction of the property, that an order to that effect should have been made by the court?—and, If it was, had the court jurisdiction to make it after the case was ended?

It is fundamental that no person can be deprived of any article which is recognized by the law as property, without a judicial hearing, after due notice. No degree of misconduct or wrong can justify the forfeiture of the property of a citizen, except in pursuance of some judicial procedure, of which the owner shall have notice, and in which he shall have the opportunity to contest the ground upon which the forfeiture is claimed. *Lowry* v. *Rainwater*, 70 Mo. 162, 35 Am. Rep. 420; *People* v. *Copely* (Ill. C. C.) 4 Crim. Law Mag. 187; 8 Am. & Eng. Cyclop. Law, 1081.

There are, however, some articles which cannot be kept, exhibited or used for any lawful or innocent purpose, such as spurious coin or bills, obscene pictures, books or prints, and other articles or devices, the exhibition, use or possession of which in any form and under all circumstances is unlawful or corrupting and prejudicial to public morals or health. Such articles are regarded as nuisances *per se*. Property cannot exist in them and an officer into whose hands they come may be authorized by statute or ordinance to destroy them summarily without process. It has been held, however, that such articles cannot be destroyed by an officer in the absence of a law or ordinance authorizing their destruction. *Ridgeway* v. *West*, 60 Ind. 371.

There are other articles which are not in and of themselves nuisances, which may be used for an illegal or immoral purpose, and which may yet be regarded as property. It may be a question whether implements or articles seized in a particular case are honest, lawful tools or things for innocent amusement, or whether they are devices for counterfeiting, burglar's tools or apparatus for gambling. Differences of opinion may arise as to the character of books or prints. As has been said: "Pictures and illustrations, that might be considered unobjectionable in scientific and philosophical treatises upon medicine and surgery, might be highly indecent and immoral if intended for public circulation. Some of the finest works of art in painting and sculpture, though greatly admired by artists and critics, might be considered by a portion of the community as wholly improper for public exhibition." *Atty-Gen.* v. *Boston Municipal Court*, 103 Mass. 456.

In many instances property may or may not exist in a thing according to the use to which it is or may be applied, or the purpose for which it is kept or exhibited, or the intrinsic value of the materials out of which it is constructed. Gaming apparatus may be made of valuable material, capable in some other form of being applied to useful and lawful purposes, or it may be used for innocent and harmless amusement in the form in which it exists. It cannot always be determined by inspection, or disclosed as matter of law, that articles used for the illegal and immoral purpose of gaming may not also be used for innocent and lawful purposes, or that in honest hands they may not constitute lawful merchandise. Unless, therefore, articles seized are of such a character that the law will not recognize them as property, entitled as such to its protection, under any circumstances, they cannot be summarily destroyed without affording the owner an opportunity to be heard upon the subject of their lawful use, and to show whether or not the articles are intrinsically useful or valuable for any other purpose than gambling, or whether their only recognized value and customary use is as implements for gaming.

If, upon inquiry by the court trying the offender, it should appear that the property seized is such as is of no substantial or practical use or value, except in connection with a gambling room, or if the use to which it is customarily devoted by the owner is unlawful gaming, its destruction should be ordered upon application to the court as part of the judgment in the case, provided the defendant be found guilty; and as to all other property seized, that is, such as is adapted to a lawful use, it should be ordered returned to the owner, in accordance with the provisions of § 1623, Rev. Stat. 1881. *Com.* v. *Gaming Implements*, 119 Mass. 332; *Atty-Gen.* v. *Boston Municipal Court*, *supra*.

This last section, so far as applicable to gaming apparatus or devices, is to be construed in connection with section 2086. When so construed it is apparent that the inquiry in respect to the character of the property seized and "the order of the court trying the offender," referred to in section 1623, must be made by the court before or at the time final judgment is pronounced against the defendant. The destruction of the implements employed in the commission of the crime must be regarded as, in some sense, a part of the penalty to be adjudged by the court against the offender, and the order of forfeiture must be part of the judgment pronounced in the case. After the penalty has been assessed and final judgment has been pronounced and the case ended, the court cannot again take jurisdiction upon a mere motion, and proceed with another hearing and make another order enforcing punishment in the nature of an additional penalty against the defendant or his property. The conclusion follows, that after having pronounced final judgment the court had no jurisdiction to enter upon an inquiry and make an order for the destruction of the articles seized. The application should have been made before or at the time judgment was pronounced. The order for the destruction of the property was therefore correctly refused, for the reason that it was made too late.

The judgment is affirmed.

MONTANA SUPREME COURT.

George R. NEWELL *et al.*, *Respts.*,
v.
Michael A. MEYENDORFF, *Appt.*

(....Mont.....)

1. A contract giving a person an exclusive agency for the sale of a brand of cigars in a certain Territory is not void as in restraint of trade.

2. Where a defendant was totally deprived of his defense by the action of the court in first sustaining a demurrer to his answer, which set up a contract for the sole agency of the goods purchased by him, and a breach thereof by plaintiffs, and then on his amended answer setting up the invalidity of the contract as an absolute defense, making a ruling, after the case was submitted on the pleadings, to the effect that the contract was valid, although the latter ruling was correct, the judgment will be reversed.

(February 4, 1890.)

APPEAL by defendant from a judgment of the District Court for Lewis and Clarke County in favor of plaintiffs and from an order denying his motion for a new trial, in an action to recover the contract price for certain cigars sold and delivered to defendant. *Reversed.*

The facts are fully stated in the opinion.

Mr. **John B. Clayberg**, for appellant:

A party is not permitted to take inconsistent positions in court in the same suit.

Smith v. *Babcock*, 3 Sumn. 584. See *Ohio & M. R. Co.* v. *McCarthy*, 96 U. S. 258 (24 L. ed. 693); *Philadelphia, W. & B. R. Co.* v. *Howard*, 54 U. S. 13 How. 307 (14 L. ed. 157); *Avendano* v. *Gay*, 75 U. S. 8 Wall. 376 (19 L. ed. 422); *Bushnell* v. *Kennedy*, 76 U. S. 9 Wall. 387 (19 L. ed. 736); *Irwin* v. *Miller*, 23 Ill. 401; *Braidwood* v. *Weiller*, 89 Ill. 606; *Belanger* v. *Hersey*, 90 Ill. 70; *Glover* v. *Benjamin*, 73 Ill. 42; *Hemphill* v. *Holley*, 4 Minn. 233; *Sweezey* v. *Stetson*, 67 Iowa, 481; *McQueen* v. *Gamble*, 33 Mich. 344; *Beam* v. *Macomber*, 35 Mich. 455; Bigelow, Estoppel, 601; 1 Herman, Estoppel, § 822.

The court had no power at a subsequent term to change its rulings, as to the validity of the contract, thereby depriving defendant of his defense of recoupment.

Kemper v. *Waverly*, 81 Ill. 278; Freeman, Judgm. §§ 15-23; *Williams* v. *Hayes*, 68 Wis. 248; *Territory* v. *Christensen* (Dak.) Jan. 31, 1887; *Schobacher* v. *Germantown F. Mut. Ins. Co.* 59 Wis. 86; *Sels* v. *First Nat. Bank*, 60 Wis. 246; *Exchange Bank* v. *Ford*, 7 Colo. 314; *Newman* v. *Newton*, 14 Fed. Rep. 634; *Breed* v. *Ketchum*, 51 Wis. 164; *United States Bank* v. *Moss*, 47 U. S. 6 How. 31 (12 L. ed. 331); *Jackson* v *Ashton*, 35 U. S. 10 Pet. 480 (9 L. ed. 502); *Washington Bridge Co.* v. *Stewart*, 44 U. S. 3 How. 413 (11 L. ed. 658); *Cameron* v. *M'Roberts*, 16 U. S. 3 Wheat. 591 (4 L. ed. 467); *Latimer* v. *Morrain*, 43 Wis. 107; *Wise* v. *Frey*, 9 Neb. 217; *Hansen* v. *Bergquist*, 9 Neb. 269.

If this contract was void as being contrary to public policy, and the goods were purchased under it, no recovery can be had upon it.

Collins v. *Blantern*, 2 Wilson, 341; *Roll* v. *Raquet*, 4 Ohio, 400; *Miller* v. *Larson*, 19 Wis. 486; *Jerome* v. *Bigelow*, 66 Ill. 452; *Foster* v. *Thurston*, 11 Cush. 322; *Martin* v. *Wade*, 37 Cal. 168; *Knowlton* v. *Congress & E. S. Co.* 57 N. Y. 518; *St. Louis, J. & C. R. Co.* v. *Mathers*, 71 Ill. 592; *King* v. *Brown*, 2 Hill, 485; *Peck* v. *Burr*, 10 N. Y. 204; *Saratoga County Bank* v. *King*, 44 N. Y. 87; *Arnot* v. *Pittson & E. Coal Co.* 68 N.Y. 558; *Gregg* v. *Wyman*, 4 Cush. 322; *Way* v. *Foster*, 1 Allen, 408; *King* v. *Green*, 6 Allen, 139; *Wight* v. *Rindskopf*, 43 Wis. 344; *Clarke* v. *Lincoln Lumber Co.* 59 Wis. 655.

Messrs. **Sanders, Cullen & Sanders** for respondents.

De Witt, *J.*, delivered the opinion of the court:

The record in this case presents the following history: The complaint is for the price of cigars sold and delivered by plaintiffs to defendant. Defendant answered, and admitted the sale and delivery, and set up in recoupment a contract, the terms of which were, generally, that in 1886 he was dealing in cigars; that plaintiffs approached him to sell their "Flor de B. Garcia Cigars," agreeing that defendant should have the sole and exclusive right of selling, handling and dealing in said cigars in Montana; that plaintiffs would not sell said cigars to anyone else in the Territory; that defendant would cease advertising and selling various other valuable brands of cigars in which he was dealing, and from the sale of which he was deriving much profit; that he would accept said sole agency, would purchase said brand of

NOTE.—Contracts reasonable as to space, and as to time, and not in derogation of public rights, are not contracts in restraint of trade. See *note* to Leslie v. Lorillard (N. Y.) 1 L. R. A. 456.

But an agreement between steamers to prevent or impede fair competition in trade is void as against public policy. See Anderson v. Jett (Ky.) 6 L. R. A. 390; and see exhaustive *note* to People v Chicago G. T. Co. (Ill.) *post*, —.

cigars from plaintiffs, and would introduce and promote the sale thereof to the best of his ability. The answer further alleges, in detail, the performance by defendant of his part of the contract, and the expenditure of large sums of money in placing said cigars upon the market. Then follows the allegation of breach by plaintiffs, in that they sold the said brand of cigars to other dealers in the Territory, by which breach the defendant suffered great damage in his business, which damage he recoups against the plaintiff's account for the cigars sold. The court below sustained a demurrer to this answer, on the ground that the contract pleaded was void, as against public policy, being in restraint of trade, and could not be pleaded in recoupment. Defendant accepted the ruling of the court, and took leave to amend, which he did by pleading the same contract, not in recoupment, but as an absolute defense, on the ground that, if the contract were void, the plaintiffs could not recover thereunder. The case went to trial in this condition, before the court without a jury. The theory of the case seems to have been preserved until the court made findings and conclusions of law, at which time he held that the contract was not void. Defendant presumably had not introduced evidence of damages by reason of breach, as he was not entitled to under the pleadings; and judgment was made and entered for plaintiffs for the amount claimed. Defendant seems not to have had a day in court. His motion for a new trial was denied. From that order, and the judgment as well, he appeals, having saved his errors complained of by exception.

We will first construe the contract as to whether it must be considered void as in restraint of trade. The rule that contracts that are in restraint of trade shall be void, as against public policy, is among our most ancient common-law inheritances. In *Alger* v. *Thacher*, 19 Pick. 51, Morton, *J.*, says: "As early as the second year of Henry V. (A. D. 1415), we find, by the Year Books, that this was considered to be old and settled law. Through a succession of decisions, it has been handed down to us, unquestioned, till the present time." The learned judge traces the history of the rule to its modern modification, that "contracts in restraint of trade, generally, have been held to be void; while those limited as to time or place or persons have been regarded as valid, and duly enforced." He gives the reasons for the rule in the following language: "(1) Such contracts injure the parties making them, because they diminish their means of procuring livelihoods, and a competency for their families. They tempt improvident persons, for the sake of present gain, to deprive themselves of the power to make future acquisitions, and they expose such persons to imposition and oppression. (2) They tend to deprive the public of the services of men in the employment and capacities in which they may be most useful to the community as well as themselves. (3) They discourage industry and enterprise, and diminish the products of ingenuity and skill. (4) They prevent competition, and enhance prices. (5) They expose the public to all the evils of monopoly; and this especially is applicable to wealthy companies and large corporations, who have the means, unless restrained by law, to exclude rivalry, monopolize business, and engross the market. Against evils like these, wise laws protect individuals and the public, by declaring all such contracts void." See also cases in that opinion cited.

The doctrine is again well stated in *Lawrence* v. *Kidder*, 10 Barb. 641, in which case the court, Selden, *J.*, cites with approval Bronson, *J.*, in *Chappel* v. *Brockway*, 21 Wend. 157, as follows: "There may be cases where the contract is neither injurious to the public nor the obligor, and then the law makes an exception, and declares the agreement valid."

In *Oregon Nav. Co.* v. *Winsor*, 87 U. S. 20 Wall. 68 [22 L. ed. 315], *Mr. Justice* Bradley says: "There are two principal grounds on which the doctrine is founded that a contract in restraint of trade is void as against public policy. One is the injury to the public by being deprived of the restricted party's industry; the other is the injury to the party himself by being precluded from pursuing his occupation, and thus being prevented from supporting himself and his family. It is evident that both these evils occur when the contract is general, not to pursue one's trade at all, or not to pursue it in the entire realm or country. The country suffers the loss in both cases; and the party is deprived of his occupation, or is obliged to expatriate himself in order to follow it. A contract that is open to such grave objections is clearly against public policy. But if neither of these evils ensues, and if the contract is founded on a valid consideration, and a reasonable ground of benefit to the other party, it is free from objection, and may be enforced."

We have cited these reasons for the rule in full, in order to apply them to the contract under consideration. They embody the modern doctrine, as held by the authorities. A recitation alone, of the rule and its reasons, seems to us sufficient to take the contract under consideration out of the operation of its prohibitions. The contract is not general; it is limited as to place and person. The public is not deprived of the alleged restricted party's industry. On the contrary, the contract provides for the placing upon the Montana market the product of the plaintiffs' industry, by the selection and services of a local Montana agent, interested in the success of sales, and to be rewarded by such success. Nor is there any injury to the party himself, the plaintiffs, by their being precluded from pursuing their occupation. Rather, by the contract, they seem to have sought a means of extending the field of their operations, and not of restricting them. In the light of the authorities, the rule and the reasons therefor and the facts, we are clearly of the opinion that the contract was not in restraint of trade, and not void. It was simply a contract, for a consideration, for the enlistment of the services of an agent for the plaintiffs in their business. The court below was therefore correct in his last view of the contract. It follows that he was wrong in his first position in sustaining the demurrer to the original answer.

Respondent urges that all the proceedings and pleadings, prior to the amended pleadings, on which the case was tried, are *dehors* the case on appeal,—citing Sawyer, *J.*, in *Barber* v. *Reynolds*, 33 Cal. 501: "The old complaint, in the form first filed, ceases to be the complaint in the case, or to perform any further function as a pleading, but the amended complaint falls into its place, and performs the same, and not different, functions." Upon an examination of this case, we find the judge further saying, "The identity of the action is in no respect affected;" and it was preliminary to arriving at the conclusion last quoted that the previous utterance was made. The law, as counsel cites it, is true, as far as he goes. The old answer in the case at bar does not "perform any further function as a pleading;" but we are not precluded from examining that answer, and the sustaining of the demurrer thereto, for the purpose suggested *infra*. We are mindful of the consequences of defendant answering over, after demurrer sustained (*Francisco* v. *Benepe*, 6 Mont. 243), and we, at this time, recur to that ruling, and review the same, not as if an appeal had been taken therefrom to this court, but for the purpose of ascertaining whether the court in such decision, together with his latter reversal of his position, in the same case, did not deprive defendant of a substantial right, and exclude him from his day in court. If that be true, defendant has a remedy. *Ubi jus, ibi remedium.* If the contract be valid, defendant certainly has the right to recoup his damages. If the contract be void, defendant has the right to plead it in bar. But the court below changed front as often as defendant aligned himself with the court's last evolution. It was impossible for the defendant to keep pace with the movements of the court, who finally left him a judgment debtor, after having twice declared that he had a good defense, but each time when the court had placed defendant in a position where he could not avail himself of such defense. For the defendant's disasters, thus resulting, there must be a remedy. We find it as follows: A party in an action is bound by his pleadings. He is also bound by the ruling of the court which he obtains upon his own motion, and is estopped from claiming such ruling as error. 2 Herman, Estoppel, § 823, and *note*.

A party is bound by his theory and presentation of his case. "A party cannot get relief on one basis, and then seek a new chance to litigate, on the suggestion that he has a defense, which he did not see fit to rely on before." *Beam* v. *Macomber*, 35 Mich. 457. See also *Belanger* v. *Hersey*, 90 Ill. 73; *Sweezey* v. *Stetson*, 67 Iowa, 481.

"Where a party gives a reason for his conduct and decision touching anything involved in a controversy, he cannot, after litigation has begun, change his ground, and put his conduct upon another and a different consideration. He is not permitted thus to mend his hold. He is estopped from doing it by a settled principle of law." *Ohio & M. R. Co.* v. *McCarthy*, 96 U. S. 267 [24 L. ed. 696]. See also *Dreyfous* v. *Adams*, 48 Cal. 131; *Long* v. *Fox*, 100 Ill. 43; *McQueen* v. *Gamble*, 33 Mich. 344; *Callaway* v. *Johnson*, 51 Mo. 33; *Edward's App.* 105 Pa. 103.

When the plaintiffs in the case at bar had procured the ruling of the court that the contract was void, they placed their theory of the case upon record. Might they then, "upon after-thoughts, new suggestions and new aspects of the case, change their position of the case from that on which they deliberately chose originally to present it to the court?"—and especially after defendant had accepted the construction of the contract demanded by plaintiffs, and held by the court. Plaintiffs were estopped by the position they had assumed, and into which they had forced defendant, when, to change that position, in the time and in the manner that it was changed, deprived defendant of all defense whatsoever. The decision of the court holding the contract valid was made after the testimony was closed and the case argued and submitted, and submitted on pleadings which forbade evidence in recoupment. If the court had made his reformed ruling before the close of the case, defendant could have obtained leave to amend himself back to his original position, and obtain a continuance on the ground of surprise, if necessary, to enable him to obtain and produce his evidence of damages. It would seem that the action of the court was accident and surprise, against which no ordinary prudence could have guarded. We are of opinion that plaintiffs were estopped from asserting that the contract was valid, or of receiving the benefit of the ruling of the court to that effect, when such ruling came at the time, in the manner and under the circumstances that it did, and to the total deprivation to the defendant of his defense to the action. Therefore the latter ruling of the court, although correct by construing the contract, under the circumstances described, and entailing the results that it did, and taken with the former position assumed by the court, and depriving defendant of a substantial right, was error.

We make no reflection upon the distinguished judge who tried the cause. His reformation of his first opinion is a credit as well to his eminent and conceded ability as to his known sense of justice and probity. His action complained of was more in the nature of a misfortune, which happened to be fatal to the defendant.

Respondent urges that the statement on motion for a new trial cannot be considered, as it was not settled by the judge who tried the case, but by his successor in office. It is not necessary to consider this objection, as the data for our conclusion are all found in the judgment roll, and the appeal is from the judgment, as well as the order denying the motion. We cannot leave this case without animadverting upon the record as it is presented. This court has heretofore had occasion to remind counsel that the preparation of a record is their duty, and it is not for them to leave the supreme court to grope through a disorderly mass of immaterial matter to ascertain that which counsel relies upon. *Upton* v. *Larkin*, 7 Mont. 462; *Raymond* v. *Thexton*, Id. 305; *Fant* v. *Tandy*, Id. 443; *Sherman* v. *Higgins*, Id. 479.

In the record in this case, the complaint, second amended complaint, replication, judgment, notice of motion and specification of errors all appear twice in full, instead of being once inserted, and afterwards noticed by appropriate reference. Where reference is made, pages are omitted. It is difficult to refer to page ——. The matter is not presented in that orderly, systematic, chronological method that presents to the court an intelligent view of the case at a reading. When we do arrive at the gist of the matter, it is after such labor as caused the learned compilers of the Institutes of Justinian to say, in the dedication of that work, "*et opus desperatum, quasi per medium profundum euntes cœlesti favore ad implevimus.*"

The judgment is reversed, and the cause remanded for a new trial.

Blake, *Ch. J.*, and **Harwood,** *J.*, concur.

NORTH CAROLINA SUPREME COURT.

D. L. GORE, *Appt.*,
v.
D. L. TOWNSEND and Wife.

(....N. C....)

*1. **Where a wife joined her husband in a mortgage** conveying his land, together with personal property belonging to him, to secure his debt, and afterwards the husband alone executed a second mortgage, conveying the same and other personal property, to secure a second note executed by him, and before the personal property was sold directed that the proceeds of sale of the personal property, except so much as should arise from the sale of a mule and wagon, about which there was no direction, should be applied to the payment of the debt secured by the second mortgage,—*Held*, that the fund arising from the sale of the mule and wagon should be paid upon the debt secured by the first mortgage, in exoneration of the wife's inchoate dower interest.

2. **The inchoate right of the wife to dower** in her husband's land, under Code, chap. 53, has a present value as property, depending on the ages, health and habits of both, and other circumstances competent to show the probabilities as to the length of life of each; and when she incumbers it by joining in a mortgage of his land to secure his debt she becomes his surety.

3. **The mortgagee cannot, because the husband failed to direct the application** of the fund arising from the sale of the mule and wagon, apply it in discharge of the debt secured by the second mortgage, but must pay it on that secured by the first mortgage, for which the property is primarily liable, and in exoneration of the wife's dower.

*Head notes by AVERY, J.

(April 7, 1890.)

APPEAL by plaintiff from a judgment of the Superior Court for Robeson County applying a certain fund in reduction of the mortgage which the action was brought to foreclose, in exoneration of the female defendant's liability as surety thereon. *Affirmed.*

Statement by **Avery,** *J.*:

This was a civil action tried before Shipp, *J.*, at the Fall Term, 1889, of Robeson Superior Court, and was brought to foreclose a mortgage set out in the pleadings. The mortgage was executed to secure a note for $750, dated 19th of March, 1884, and was made the same day, and in addition to the land conveyed therein, which was the individual property of D. L. Townsend, two mules and one wagon were also mortgaged therein to secure said debt, which was the individual debt of said Townsend. One of the mules died subsequently. The land was acquired by D. L. Townsend in 1884, and he intermarried with the *feme* defendant in 1875, and they were then, and have been ever since, citizens and residents of this State, and it is on the land on which they were living at the time that they executed the mortgage, and on which they are now living, and neither of said defendants owns any other land in the State of North Carolina.

On the 12th of March, 1887, D. L. Townsend, to secure further advances from plaintiff, executed his note for $1,119.10, due on the 1st day of January, 1888, and secured same by a mortgage on personal property therein set out, of even date with the note, in which was in-

---

NOTE.—*Dower right of wife protected.*

The dower right of the wife cannot be conveyed away by the husband, nor can it be taken by his creditors on execution. Rundlett v. Ladd, 59 N. H. 15; Doty v. Baker, 11 Hun, 222; Bartlett v. Van Zandt, 4 Sandf. Ch. 396, 7 N. Y. Ch. L. ed. 1147.

A wife's inchoate right of dower in lands is substantial and valuable interest, which will be protected and preserved to her, and she has a right of action to that end, and the only exception to that rule is where the State or its agents, exercising the right of eminent domain, take for public use the lands affected by said inchoate right of dower. Douglas v. Douglas, 11 Hun, 406; Simar v. Canaday, 53 N. Y. 304; Mills v. Van Voorhies, 20 N. Y. 412; Matthews v. Duryee, 4 Keyes, 525; Denton v. Nanny, 8 Barb. 618; Vartie v. Underwood, 18 Barb. 561; Duncan v. Terre Haute, 85 Ind. 104.

The rule for computing the present value of a wife's inchoate right of dower during the life of the husband is to ascertain the present value of an annuity for her life equal to the interest in the third of the proceeds of the estate to which her contingent right of dower attaches, and then to deduct from the present value of the annuity for her life the value of a similar annuity depending upon the joint lives of herself and her husband, and the difference between those two sums will be the value of her contingent right of dower. Doty v. Baker, 11 Hun, 225; Gordon v. Tweedy, 74 Ala. 232, 49 Am. Rep. 814.

The claim of the wife of the mortgagor, who joined in the execution of the mortgage, upon the surplus moneys arising on foreclosure, for the value of her inchoate right of dower, is superior to the claims of judgment creditors of the mortgagor, notwithstanding a provision in the mortgage for the return of the surplus, if any, to the mortgagor, his heirs or assigns. New York L. Ins. Co. v. Mayer, 19 Abb. N. C. 103.

The inchoate right of the wife to dower attaches to the surplus which, *pro hac vice*, is still to be deemed real estate, and entitles her to claim that such inchoate and contingent right be recognized and protected by a reservation of one third of such surplus until it shall be known whether she will survive her husband, and that in case she so survive she may, as widow, receive the thereafter accruing income of such one third during her life. Matthews v. Duryee, 4 Keyes, 540, 3 Abb. App. Dec. 225.

Dower right of wife subordinate to vendor's lien. See *note* to Seibert v. Todd (S. C.) 4 L. R. A. 606.

cluded the mule and wagon also conveyed in first mortgage. About January 1, 1888, it was mutually agreed between plaintiff and defendant D. L. Townsend that all the property conveyed in the second mortgage, dated 12th of March, 1887, should be surrendered to plaintiff, and, on a sale thereof on the best terms possible, the proceeds, except mule and wagon, were to be credited on note and mortgage, dated 12th of March, 1887, the defendant, D. L. Townsend, however, not giving any directions as to how the proceeds of the sale of the mule and wagon above referred to, conveyed in both mortgages, were to be applied. This property, including the mule and wagon, was sold, and the proceeds of sale of mule and wagon, amounting to $144.10, were applied by D. L. Gore to the note and mortgage dated March 12, 1887. The mule and wagon were the property of D. L. Townsend at the time of the execution of both mortgages. The *feme* defendant joined with her husband in the execution of the mortgage of 1884, and her privy examination was regularly taken. There was a verdict in response to the issues submitted to the jury as to the value of the land as appears in the record. Upon these facts, a trial by jury being waived, except as to the value of the land, his honor was of opinion that the *feme* defendant, having joined in the execution of the mortgage conveying her husband's land, became a surety to the debt, and the proceeds of the sale of the mule and wagon, amounting to $144.10, should be applied as of January 1, 1888, the time of sale, to the note and mortgage of March 19, 1884, and so adjudged, and the plaintiff excepted.

Messrs. **T. A. McNeill** and **S. C. Weill** for plaintiff.

Mr. **W. F. French** for defendants.

Avery, *J.*, delivered the opinion of the court:

In all cases where the wife executes a mortgage on her property for her husband's debts, or for money loaned to him, it is well settled that she occupies the position of, and is entitled to all the rights and privileges of, surety for her husband. Kelly, Cont. Married Women, 105.

She "assumes, in the eye of a court of equity, the character of a surety for the husband. Properly speaking, she is not a surety, but she is so called by analogy. She has a title to call upon the husband to exonerate her estate from the debt." 1 Bishop, Married Women, § 604; *Purvis* v. *Carstaphan*, 73 N. C. 575.

It is true that the inchoate right of dower was never considered an estate or interest in a court of law, which did not even concede the power of the widow to convey her unassigned dower after the right had become consummate by the husband's death, but she might make a contract for the sale that would be enforced in a court of equity. *Potter* v. *Everitt*, 7 Ired. Eq. 152; *Bayler* v. *Com.* 40 Pa. 37.

It must be remembered, however, that the discussion of the nature of the wife's interest in her husband's land has assumed a new phase since the enactment of the law restoring the common-law right of dower in North Carolina.

In *Gwathmey* v. *Pearce*, 74 N. C. 398, *Justice* Reade, after citing *Purvis* v. *Carstaphan* as establishing the doctrine that the wife, when she joins her husband in a mortgage of her separate property to secure his debt, sustains the relation of his surety in that transaction, says, in reference to the former case: "Here the wife joined her husband in the conveyance of his land in trust to pay his debt, in which land she had, under our Dower Statute, a vested right to dower, to be allotted after her husband's death; and she joined in the deed for the purpose of binding her dower. After her husband's death, the whole land, her dower included, was sold under the trust deed to pay the debt. This made the wife a creditor of her husband's estate to the amount of the value of her dower in the land." The Dower Statute referred to by the court was the Act of 1868-69 (chap. 93, §§ 32-37), and was substantially the same as sections 2102, 2104, 2106 and 2107 of the Code; and therefore, if the inchoate right to dower was a "vested right," then it is of equal dignity and importance now, and the mortgage in which the defendant's wife joined in the present case passed an interest that imputed additional present value to the mortgagee's security in proportion to the worth of her life estate in one third of the land, estimated according to the life tables, or certainly to a sum that an expert could ascertain, having as data for his calculation the value of the land and the chances of survivorship on her part after the husband's death.

Although in *Gwathmey* v. *Pearce*, *supra*, the wife was declared a creditor of the husband's estate after his death to the value of her dower, the ruling could have been sustained only on the principle, upon which it is explicitly made to rest, that the wife was a surety, and she did not sustain that relation to the original contract because her husband died, but because she signed a deed that subjected her interest in the land conveyed. It would seem, therefore, that this court has settled the principle that the wife, by joining in a mortgage of the husband's land to secure his debt, becomes then a surety, and in case she survive him, and the land is sold to satisfy the debt, she becomes also a creditor to the value of the life estate. The language of sections 2106 and 2107 of the Code seems to recognize the right during the husband's life as a valuable interest, that may pass by a conveyance, rather than a naked right, that the claimant may be barred by the estoppel of her deed from enforcing; and this interpretation follows the line of more modern legislation to make every valuable interest transferable and convertible into money, while it is in accord with the older idea that the claim of the wife to dower is favored by the law. While there is conflict of opinion as to the nature and qualities of the wife's inchoate interest, there is much authority that, either directly or indirectly, sustains the view advanced by this court, apart from any peculiarity in the language of our Statute; and it is strongly supported, too, by analogy.

The right of exoneration in equity grows out of the suretyship, and must exist so soon as the interest conveyed is about to be subjected to sale, and it appears that there is a fund or property belonging to the principal debtor equally liable with such interest for the debt. The contract of suretyship, or the conveyance of one's property to secure the debt of another, is a transaction primarily between, not the principal and the surety, but the surety and the third person. 2 Bishop, Married Women, § 370.

In *Bullard* v. *Briggs*, 7 Pick. 533, it was held that the relinquishment of the right of dower was a valid consideration for the conveyance of the equity of redemption, even as against the claim of creditors; and Parker, *Ch. J.*, in discussing the nature of the wife's interest during the husband's life, says: "The consideration for this intended settlement on the wife was her right of dower in the estate, which the husband was about to mortgage. Without her relinquishment, he could not raise the money wanted for his support and his debts. His days were numbered by intemperance and disease. Though she had no actual estate in the dower during the life of her husband, yet she had an interest and a right of which she could not be devested but by her consent or crime, or her dying before her husband. It was a valuable interest, which is frequently the subject of contract and bargain. It is an interest which the law recognizes as the subject of conveyance by fine in England, and by deed with us."

In *Vartie* v. *Underwood*, 18 Barb. 561, the court held that "the wife's inchoate right of dower in the husband's land follows the surplus moneys raised by a sale in virtue of the power of sale in a mortgage executed by her with her husband, and will be protected against the claims of the husband's creditors, by directing one third of such surplus moneys to be invested, and the interest only to be paid to the creditors during the joint lives of husband and and wife." See also *Denton* v. *Nanny*, 8 Barb. 618.

In the later case of *Wedge* v. *Moore*, 6 Cush. 8, *Chief Justice* Shaw delivering the opinion of the court, it was held that where the husband executed three mortgages upon his land, his wife joining only in the second one, she was entitled, after his death, to dower against the third mortgagee, who had paid the debts secured by the two first mortgages.

In the case of *Kelly* v. *Harrison*, 2 Johns. Cas. 29, the court held that a wife who remained a subject of Great Britain, while her husband took part with the Colonies in the Revolution, was entitled to dower after the death of the husband in all land acquired by the husband up to the beginning of the war. Kent, *J.*, says: "But the right could not attach till the land was purchased, and I distinguish between the capacity to acquire and the vested right. The Revolution took away the one, and did not impair the other."

Scribner, in his work on Dower (vol. 2, p. 8), says: "Although, therefore, an inchoate right of dower cannot be properly denominated an estate in lands, nor indeed a vested interest therein, and notwithstanding the difficulty of defining with accuracy the precise legal qualities of the interest, it may nevertheless be fairly deduced from the authorities that it is a substantial right, possessing, in contemplation of law, the attributes of property, and to be estimated and valued as such."

It has many of the incidents of property. It has a present value that can be computed. *Jackson* v. *Edwards*, 7 Paige, 386, 408, 4 N. Y. Ch. L. ed. 200; *Buzick* v. *Buzick*, 44 Iowa. 259; 1 Scribner, Dower, 519; *Stoppelbein* v. *Shulte*, 1 Hill, L. (S. C.) 200.

It is a valuable consideration for a conveyance to the wife. *Bullard* v. *Briggs*, *supra; Reiff* v. *Horst*, 55 Md. 42.

The wife may maintain an action for its protection. *Petty* v. *Petty*, 4 B. Mon. 215; *Burns* v. *Lynde*, 6 Allen, 305; *Simar* v. *Canaday*, 53 N. Y. 298; *Bissell* v. *Taylor*, 41 Mich. 702; *Benoist* v. *Murrin*, 47 Mo. 537.

She may file a bill or bring an action for the redemption of a mortgage covering it. *Davis* v. *Wetherell*, 13 Allen, 60.

It has been repeatedly declared by the courts an incumbrance, within the meaning of a usual covenant in a deed. *Hill* v. *Ressegieu*, 17 Barb. 162; *Shearer* v. *Ranger*, 22 Pick. 447.

The right of dower is favored by the law; and, apart from the idea of suretyship, a widow may maintain an action for dower in equity, and may demand that a lien upon the land be discharged out of the personal estate, or that a portion of a tract of land shall be sold to relieve the dower of the lien of a mortgage, or an equitable estate of the lien for the purchase money. 1 Scribner, Dower, 521.

It is true that it was held in *Jenness* v. *Cutler*, 12 Kan. 500, that where the wife joined the husband in a mortgage deed conveying his land, and waiving the homestead right, she was not a surety, but the ruling rested upon the undefined nature of the homestead right. It was not only not an estate, but not a right peculiar to the wife. Brandt, Sur. § 22.

It must be recollected that the restoration of the common-law right of dower by our Statute worked a change in the nature of the wife's present interest in her husband's lands. It is no longer subject to the double contingency of survivorship and failure by the husband to alienate before death, but only to the former; and, if he venture to sell without the joinder of the wife, a prudent purchaser, in fixing the price, will deduct from the actual value such sum as, looking to the ages of husband and wife, their habits, etc., he estimates the chances of the wife's dower to be worth. Hence this court, in holding in the case of *Gwathmey* v. *Pearce*, *supra*, that the widow was a creditor after the death of the husband to the extent of the value of the land mortgaged, because she had become his surety when she incumbered her inchoate right of dower, assigned as a reason that the then recent changes in the law had made her interest a "vested right," and imparted to it a value, even during the life of the husband.

We concur with the court below in the opinion that the wife was a surety, and the proceeds of the sale of the mule and wagon should have been applied to the payment of the debt secured by the first mortgage in exoneration of the land, in which she had a valuable interest. Her right to exoneration could not be defeated by the failure of the husband to direct the application of the proceeds of the sale of the mule and wagon which was primarily liable under the first mortgage, in exoneration of the land. The inchoate right of the wife to dower in her husband's land has a present value as property, depending on the ages of both, their health, habits and other circumstances tending to show the probabilities as to the length of the life of each; and, where she incumbers it by joining in a mortgage of his land to secure his debt, she becomes his surety. Her right to exoneration could not be defeated by the failure of the husband to direct the application of the proceeds of the sale of the mule and wagon, that fund being primarily liable under the first mortgage.

There is no error.

MAINE SUPREME JUDICIAL COURT.

CARLETON MILLS CO.
v.
Joshua E. SILVER *et al.*

(....Me.....)

1. If it is doubtful from the terms of a grant whether the kind of mill or particular machiney mentioned therein, for which water is to be furnished, indicates the quantity of water and measures the extent of the power intended to be conveyed, or is referred to as a limit of the use to the particular kind of mill or specified machinery, the former construction will be favored.

2. A grant of a certain water privilege for the purpose of propelling a factory and its machinery and appurtenances, the building to be of a certain size with necessary appurtenances and machinery, will be construed to measure the quantity of water, and will not limit the use of water to carry only such machinery as may be in the main building, if some of the machinery is in an annex and no more power is required to propel it than if it were in the main building, where it could all be placed.

3. Parties have the right to run their factory as many hours a day as they consider proper where they have a grant of water for the purposes of their factory with no limitation therein upon the number of hours per day in which they can run the factory.

(December 30, 1889.)

EXCEPTIONS by defendants to a judgment of the Supreme Judicial Court for Piscataquis County in favor of plaintiff in an action brought to recover damages for an alleged interference by defendants with plaintiff's water rights. *Overruled.*

The case sufficiently appears in the opinion.

Mr. **A. G. Labroke,** with *Messrs.* **Crosby & Crosby,** for defendants:

The measure of power on our construction is simple, clear, easily understood. But on plaintiff's theory it is complicated, mixed, uncertain, indefinite. What certainty can there possibly be that the plaintiff does not exceed its rights of power when it deserts the simple 98 x 48 and extends, divides and diffuses it in numerous ways?

It is not right to subject the defendants to perplexing difficulties.

Drummond v. *Hinckley,* 80 Me. 483.

Ten hours a day is a legal day's work unless there be a special agreement for a larger day's work. Williams in the deed never made any agreement for a longer time. The statute must govern.

Bachelder v. *Bickford,* 62 Me. 526; *Barrett* v. *Parsons,* 10 Cush. 372.

Mr. **Henry Hudson** for plaintiff.

Foster, J., delivered the opinion of the court:

On June 8, 1881, Owen B. Williams was the owner of the premises, land and water privilege about which this contention has arisen, situated upon Carleton Stream, in the Village of Sangerville. Upon that day he conveyed by metes and bounds a specific part of the premises to the plaintiff, and in the conveyance, immediately following the description of the boundaries, is this language: "Together with the Williams dam, and all the water privileges of the 'Carleton Mill Stream,' so called, for all the purposes of propelling a factory, and its machinery and appurtenances, to be built on said privilege, said factory building to be ninety-eight feet in length, and forty-eight feet in width, with all necessary appurtenances and machinery for working the same up to its full capacity."

Subsequently the plaintiff built a woolen factory on the privilege conveyed by this deed, two stories high besides a basement, the main building being the same dimensions as that named in the deed. On the easterly side of

---

NOTE.—*Conveyance of water privilege.*

A mere convenience is not sufficient to create or convey a right or easement, or impose burdens on lands other than those granted, as incident to the grant. In all cases the question of necessity controls. Ogden v. Jennings, 62 N. Y. 532; Holmes v. Seely, 19 Wend. 507; Nicholas v. Chamberlain, Cro. Jac. 121; French v. Carhart, 1 N. Y. 96; Voorhees v. Burchard, 55 N. Y. 98; Oakley v. Stanley, 5 Wend. 523; Tabor v. Bradley, 18 N. Y. 109; LeRoy v. Platt, 4 Paige, 77, 3 N.Y. Ch. L. ed. 350; New York L. Ins. & T. Co. v. Milnor, 1 Barb. Ch. 353, 5 N. Y. Ch. L. ed. 414; Warren v. Blake, 54 Me. 276; Pierce v. Selleck, 18 Conn. 321.

By the conveyance of a mill lot, with a mill turned by water upon it, the right to use the dam and the necessary pondage would pass as appurtenant, if the dam and pond were upon the remaining lands of the grantor. Central R. Co. v. Valentine, 29 N. J. L. 567. See Leonard v. White, 7 Mass. 6; Wetmore v. White, 2 Cal. Cas. 87.

The conveyance of land would pass a mill and millpond and canal upon the same; and the latter would pass the flowage of water and water-privileges enjoyed and used with it and often giving to it its chief value. Babcock v. Utter, 1 Keyes, 428, 1 Abb. App. Dec. 56; Oakley v. Stanley, *supra;* Burr v. Mills, 21 Wend. 290.

The conveyance in terms of a "mill" or "mill-race" or "privileges" would undoubtedly pass the right to flow sufficient to raise the necessary head of water to carry the mill. Tabor v. Bradley, 18 N. Y. 113.

Where grantor had imposed the burden upon the land adjoining for his own benefit, it would continue to be attached unless the right to subvert it was expressly reserved. Green v. Collins, 86 N. Y. 251; Lampman v. Milks, 21 N. Y. 505; Simmons v. Cloonan, 47 N. Y. 3. See *note* to Bowling v. Burton (N. C.) 2 L. R. A. 285.

the main building, but connected with it, a tower eighteen feet by twelve feet was erected, in which were the stairways to the main building, and an elevator operated by power from the factory wheel.

On the northerly end of the main building, and connected with the same, outside the ninety eight feet in length, was erected an annex, in which were placed the factory wheel, two pickers, a duster and a force pump, which were run by the factory wheel; also dye kettles, rinsing tubs, boiler to heat the factory and chimney. The only wheel which run the factory was built under this annex.

The case shows that, while the main building contained sufficient room for the wheel, pickers and duster, yet no more power was required to propel them in this annex than if located in the main building.

The points in controversy, so far as they are raised by the bill of exceptions, pertain to the legal construction of this deed, and may be determined by the answer to this single question, whether the language in the deed shall be construed to measure the quantity of water to which the plaintiff is entitled, or to limit the use of water to carry only such machinery as may be in the main building.

The plaintiff's contention is for the former, that the grant is of water sufficient or necessary to propel a particular factory, reference to the mill being made only to indicate and measure the quantity of power intended to be conveyed.

The defendants, upon the contrary, contend that the deed is to be so construed as to limit the power for the special purpose of propelling only such machinery as may be contained in the main building.

It is undoubtedly competent for the owner of the whole of the mill privilege to convey any part of the power he pleases, and limit its use to any particular purpose which he may see fit to express in the grant, and the other party is willing to accept. Where such purposes are plain from the terms of the conveyance, courts will so construe the contract as to carry into effect the expressed intention of the parties. Oftentimes, however, where such rights are derived solely from grant, particularly where they are a part only of a larger waterpower, it is a question of some difficulty, in construing the grant, to determine whether the power granted was intended to be applied to a specific use only, or whether a reference to the purposes named in the grant was made for the sole purpose of defining and measuring the quantity of power granted. If the parties, from the terms of the grant, have left it doubtful whether the kind of mill or particular machinery mentioned indicates the quantity of water, and measures the extent of the power intended to be conveyed, or is referred to as a limit of the use to the particular kind of mill or specified machinery, the former construction will be favored, as being more favorable to the grantee, more for the general interest of the public, and as being more probably the intention of the parties. This is the general doctrine adopted by the courts and adhered to in grants of this nature, whenever the description of the rights conveyed is in such terms as to leave it in doubt which of these two kinds or species of grants was intended. *Deshon* v. *Porter*, 38 Me. 289, 293; *Pratt* v. *Lamson*, 2 Allen, 275; *Tourtellot* v. *Phelps*, 4 Gray, 370, 374; *Ashley* v. *Pease*, 18 Pick. 268, 275; *Covel* v. *Hart*, 56 Me. 518.

In this case the court instructed the jury that the "plaintiff's rights are not confined to such machinery alone as it might put into the main building, for the true construction of that deed does not restrict the water to such machinery as is in there, but the language of the deed is simply used to express the measure of the water to which it is entitled."

This instruction, we think, presented the law correctly to the jury. In construing the plaintiff's deed from Williams, the intention of the parties must first be sought from the language of the deed, taken in connection with the situation of their business, the subject matter to which it relates and the object to be obtained. *Sumner* v. *Williams*, 8 Mass. 162; *Deshon* v. *Porter*, *supra*.

When we consider, therefore, the objects and purposes for which the power was granted, we think it clear that the language of the deed does not restrict the grantee to the use of the water for the specific purpose of propelling such machinery only as might be in the main building, but that by the terms of the deed, so far as they relate to the machinery to be used in a factory of the dimensions named, the intention was to describe the quantity of water, the use of which is thereby conveyed. Hence, if some of the machinery required in a factory like this is located in an annex, instead of being in the main building, and no more power is required to propel it than if it were situated in the main building, it would certainly be within the terms of the plaintiff's deed.

The power intended to be conveyed, as expressed in the deed, is "for all the purposes of propelling a factory and its machinery and appurtenances" essential to the successful operation of a building of the size mentioned in the terms mentioned in the grant, "with all the necessary appurtenances and machinery for working the same up to its full capacity."

The annex and tower situated upon the plaintiff's land, and thus connected with the factory building proper, considering the nature of the grant, and the purposes to which the power was to be applied, may properly be considered as embraced within the terms of the deed. The case discloses the fact that there was sufficient room in the main building for such machinery as was placed within this annex. If, therefore, the plaintiff considered it for its interest or convenience to place some portion of the machinery necessary to the operation of its factory in this separate apartment, provided no more power was required to operate it than if it had all been under the same roof, it had a right so to do. The instructions of the court to which exceptions are taken were in accordance with the views we have here expressed, and were therefore correct.

Nor were the defendants' rights affected by the refusal of the court to instruct the jury that the plaintiff could not operate the factory more than a reasonable time, and that ten hours a day through the year is a reasonable time. The plaintiff's rights are not thus circumscribed. It is expressly stated that the plaintiff "has the first right to, and control of, all the water in said stream at the said dam and privilege, at all times and seasons of the year, for propelling its said factory and machinery for the factory building as before described." Having the right to the use of the water for the purposes of its factory, at all times and seasons of the year, it had a right to run its factory as many hours a day as it considered proper. Its deed contains no limitation upon the number of hours out of the twenty-four each day in which it can run its factory. It is not for the court to restrict the time when the factory shall be operated, when the parties have not seen fit to do so.

Exceptions overruled.

Peters, *Ch. J.*, and **Danforth, Virgin, Libbey** and **Emery**, *JJ.*, concurred.

Isaac H. JAMES
v.
Thomas P. WOOD.

(......Me.......)

1. **Possession of animals reclaimed** from a wild state is prima facie evidence of title.

2. **Liberating an animal captured during close time** in violation of statute interferes with no legal right or title of the person illegally holding it captive, and gives him no right of action.

3. **Following a moose** in a forest until it becomes snow-bound and then capturing it during close time is a violation of Rev. Stat., chap. 30, § 9, prohibiting hunting, killing or destroying a moose during that time.

(December 11, 1889.)

EXCEPTIONS by defendant to a judgment of the Supreme Judicial Court for Franklin County in favor of plaintiff in an action brought to recover damages for an alleged trespass by defendant in entering upon plaintiff's premises and liberating a moose and deer there confined. *Sustained.*

The case sufficiently appears in the opinion.

Mr. **Prince A. Sawyer** for defendant.

Messrs. **Stubbs & Fog** and **J. J. Parlin**, for plaintiff:

The plaintiff had lawful possession of moose and deer, not having killed or destroyed them in violation of law.

Maine Rev. Stat. chap. 30, § 12.

Whether plaintiff's possession was lawful or not, it was sufficient to enable him to maintain an action of trespass against a mere wrong-doer.

Craig v. *Gilbreth*, 47 Me. 416; *Brown* v. *Ware*, 25 Me. 411.

NOTE.—*Property in animals* feræ naturæ.

Occupancy of animals *feræ naturæ* is actual corporal possession of them. 4 Puffen. chap. 6, §§ 2, 10.

Wild animals when captured and under the control of the capturer are his property. State v. House, 65 N. C. 315.

Pursuit alone vests no property or right in the huntsman, even when accompanied with wounding. 2 Justin. Inst. title 1, § 13; 3 Fleta, chap. 2, p. 175; 2 Bracton, chap. 1, p. 8.

Pursuit alone gives no right of property in animals *feræ naturæ.* Occupancy in wild animals can be acquired only by possession; but such possession does not signify manucaption, though it must be of such a kind, as by nets, snares or other means, as to so circumvent the creature that he cannot escape. Pierson v. Post, 3 Cai. 177.

Though property in such animals may be acquired by occupancy, or by wounding so as to bring it within the power or control of the pursuer, yet if thereafter the hunter abandons the pursuit he acquires no property therein although his dogs continue the chase. Buster v. Newkirk, 20 Johns. 75.

When wild animals have been killed and labor has been bestowed upon their carcasses, the product of that labor is property subject to larceny. Norton v. Ladd, 5 N. H. 203.

Bees are animals *feræ naturæ*, but when hived and reclaimed a qualified property may be acquired in them. Gillet v. Mason, 7 Johns. 16.

Wild bees in a bee tree belong to the owner of the soil where the tree stands. Ferguson v. Miller, 1 Cow. 243.

Though a person obtains a license from the owner to take them this does not confer ownership upon him until he has taken actual possession of the bees, and another person under such a license, first obtaining possession, acquires the title. Gillet v. Mason and Ferguson v. Miller, *supra*; Idol v. Jones, 2 Dev. L. 162.

A qualified property may be obtained in them by reclaiming them and making them tame by art, or otherwise, or by confining them so that they cannot escape. 2 Bl. Com. 390.

If a person finds a tree containing a hive of bees on the land of another, and marks the tree, he does not thereby reclaim the bees, and vest a right of property in himself, and he cannot maintain an action for carrying away the bees and honey. Gillet v. Mason, *supra.*

Bees when hived are the property of the one who has reclaimed them, although they temporarily escape. Goff v. Kilts, 15 Wend. 550; Wallis v. Mease, 3 Binn. 546.

Geese when tamed are the property of the one who tames them. Amory v. Flyn, 10 Johns. 100.

So a buffalo calf when domesticated is property (Ulery v. Jones, 81 Ill. 403); and so of pea fowls and turkeys (Com. v. Beaman, 8 Gray, 497); and so of a canary. Manning v. Mitcherson, 69 Ga. 447.

But fish, unless reclaimed, are not property. State v. Krider, 78 N. C. 481.

Oysters planted in a bed and separately marked are property. State v. Taylor, 27 N. J. L. 117; Decker v. Fisher, 4 Barb. 592; Lowndes v. Dickerson, 34 Barb. 586; Fleet v. Hegeman, 14 Wend. 42. See Brinckerhoff v. Starkins, 11 Barb. 248.

If a whale is killed, anchored and left with marks of appropriation it is by law and custom the property of the captors, even if it should drift to another place. Swift v. Gifford, 2 Low. 110; Taber v. Jenny, 1 Sprague, 315.

A sable caught in a trap is not property subject to larceny. Norton v. Ladd, 5 N. H. 203. See 2 Bishop, Cr. L. § 773.

Any bird after it is tamed is property and the subject of larceny. Haywood v. State, 41 Ark. 479; Manning v. Mitcherson, *supra.*

Whoever undertakes to keep an animal *feræ naturæ* in places of public resort is liable for the injuries inflicted by it on a party who is not guilty of negligence. But if the animal is of a tame nature, there must be proof of notice to the owner of its vicious habits, in order to make him liable. Congress & E. Spring Co. v. Edgar, 99 U. S. 645 (25 L. ed. 487).

Plaintiff having been attacked and injured in a park by a male deer belonging to the proprietors of the park, the owners were held liable, upon a

See also 35 L. R. A. 279.

Haskell, *J.*, delivered the opinion of the court:

Trespass *q. c.* and *d. b.* for entering upon the plaintiff's land, and liberating a moose and deer there confined. The plaintiff had captured the moose and purchased the deer during close time. The defendant justifies as game warden.

1. The defendant cannot be considered as having seized the game under any provision of statute, inasmuch as he held no precept either to arrest the plaintiff, or to seize the game, nor does he pretend that he ever had any intention of procuring one. His testimony that he acted by the consent of the plaintiff was not believed by the jury; and, as the evidence is conflicting upon that point, the court cannot say that the finding of the jury was wrong.

2. No property exists in wild animals so long as they remain in a state of nature, but when killed or reclaimed they become property,—absolutely when killed, and qualifiedly when reclaimed; for, when restored to their natural, wild and ferocious state, the dominion of man over them is at an end, and all property in them is extinguished. *Case of Swans*, 7 Coke, 16; Finch, Com. Law, 176; Kent, Com. pt. 5, lect. 35, § 2; *Blades* v. *Higgs*, 11 H. L. Cas. 621.

Since they are the subjects of property, their possession must be prima facie title, as with all other chattels, and sufficient to support an action concerning them against any wrong-doer. *Union State Co.* v. *Tilton*, 69 Me. 244; *Adams* v. *McGlinchy*, 66 Me. 474; *Craig* v. *Gilbreth*, 47 Me. 416; *Brown* v. *Ware*, 25 Me. 411; *Burke* v. *Savage*, 13 Allen, 408; *Magee* v. *Scott*, 9 Cush. 148; *Armory* v. *Delamirie*, 1 Strange, 505.

The burden is therefore upon the defendant to justify his act if he would defeat the action. *Hodsdon* v. *Kilgore*, 77 Me. 155.

He has not justified the taking of the deer, for the plaintiff's possession of it is sufficient evidence of title until impeached. Moreover, the evidence shows that the plaintiff purchased the deer, and fails to show that it had been captured in violation of law. He therefore is entitled to recover the value of the deer. The instructions of the presiding justice relating to the deer were correct, and the evidence sustains the verdict for its value.

3. One cannot justify the taking of a chattel to which he has no title by showing that the person from whom he took it is not the owner. *Fiske* v. *Small*, 25 Me. 453.

But, if the subject of the asportation had not become property at all, then the loss of it occasioned no damage. A poacher who has killed game, and thereby made it absolutely property, takes no title to it as against the owner of the

---

verdict of the jury establishing their knowledge of the animal's vicious propensities. *Ibid.*

Fisheries; power of State Legislature to regulate. See *note* to Lawton v. Steele (N. Y.) 7 L. R. A. 134.

Decisions on the Game Laws of the various States.

Illinois.

The Illinois Game Laws make the possession or sale of quail unlawful during a certain period of time, although such quail were taken or killed beyond the state limits: and such Act is constitutional. Magner v. People, 97 Ill. 320.

Maine.

Complaint for penalty, for use of State, for killing game out of season need not allege to whom penalty goes. State v. Thrasher, 8 New Eng. Rep. 613, 79 Me. 17.

Massachusetts.

Under the Massachusetts Statute a person is not punishable for having in his possession offering for sale a game bird lawfully taken or killed in another State. Com. v. Hall, 128 Mass. 410.

Michigan.

The only punishment for violation of How. Stat., § 2208, for the protection of game, is $50; and no punishment can be inflicted under § 9261. Robison v. Judge of Recorder's Court of Detroit, 14 West. Rep. 190, 69 Mich. 608.

Missouri.

A statute prohibiting the killing or having in possession certain game within certain periods of time is constitutional; it neither deprives one of his property, nor is it in restraint of trade. State v. Judy, 7 Mo. App. 524.

New Jersey.

A fishwarden may, as a common informer, prosecute for violation of the Game Laws, although the chosen freeholders of his county may not have determined to employ him to do so. State v. Peters, 51 N. J. L. 244.

New York.

The New York laws prohibit having in possession game birds after the first of March, although killed at a time when, by the Act, the killing is not prohibited, or brought from another State. Phelps v. Racey, 60 N. Y. 10.

Such laws are constitutional. *Ibid.*

The New York Laws of 1883 authorize the fish and game protectors to sue for penalties in the same circumstances as actions therefor "might now or may hereafter be brought by any individual" under existing statutes. It was held that a judgment in an action brought by an individual was a bar to an action brought by the fish and game protectors. People v. Robbins, 39 Hun, 137.

Mandamus lies to compel the district attorney to sign the certificate required by the Game Laws to enable the game protector to obtain from the county treasurer the sum due him for the penalties recovered, but not where criminal proceedings only were instituted. *Ex parte* Roberts, 40 Hun, 53.

Under the provisions contained in Laws 1883, chap. 317, § 1, an action to recover the penalties imposed for a violation of the Game Laws may, upon the request of a game protector, be brought by any district attorney, where the offense was committed in his county or in an adjoining county. People v. McDonald, 44 Hun, 592.

Under N. Y. Laws 1883, chap. 317, a district attorney cannot sue for the violation of Game Laws occurring outside of his own county. People v. McDonald, 11 Cent. Rep. 281, 108 N. Y. 655.

Ohio.

Under the Ohio Crimes Act it is unlawful to kill wild ducks on the land of another person, although within the channel of a navigable river, when the owner has set up a notice "No shooting or hunting allowed on these premises." State v. Shannon, 36 Ohio St. 423.

The right reserved to the owner of premises to use and employ ferrets to catch rabbits thereon, is personal to himself and those acting for him; he cannot permit their use to another, nor would his permission relieve the latter from the penalty prescribed by statute. Hart v. State, 29 Ohio St. 666.

soil, whose property it would have been, had he killed it. *Blades* v. *Higgs, supra.*

This court has said, in substance, that the law protects the title or claim of no one that arises from a violation of law. It has held that no action can be maintained upon a contract executed on Sunday; that the price of chattels sold in violation of law cannot be recovered, and that no action can be maintained on a note given for goods bought to be peddled contrary to law; that no action for a tort arising from transactions done by the plaintiff in violation of the Sunday laws can be maintained. The court says: "The law distinguishes between rights acquired in conformity with and arising under its provisions, and claims originating in their clear and palpable violation; that it will not enforce claims made in contravention of its mandates, nor protect property held against, and being used for, the deliberate purpose of disobeying its enactments. A different course would be suicidal. The law cannot lend its aid to the destruction of its own authority, and to the disobedience of its own commands." *Lord* v. *Chadbourne,* 42 Me. 429, 439.

Damages were claimed for preventing the plaintiffs from doing an illegal act which, if done, would have been criminally punishable, and the court says: "It is difficult to perceive how the prevention of an offense constitutes a valid cause of action on the part of the would-be offender, who is interfered with in the commission of his intended offense. It is still more difficult to understand how any damages can have been sustained by reason of such interference." *Bangor, O. & M. R. Co.* v. *Smith,* 49 Me. 9.

Suppose a hunter has his rifle leveled at game in close time, and some one shoves it aside so that the game is missed. Shall the hunter have damages? He has only been prevented from continuing a criminal act.

Suppose lobsters illegally taken are thrown overboard alive. Is he who does it a trespasser? Shall the taker of them have damages for his illegal catch? Or suppose one lands a salmon in violation of law, and a bystander, while it is yet alive, throws it back into the water. Shall the fisherman have the value of the salmon that the law forbids his having at all?

When game is killed, it absolutely becomes property, but, when taken alive, only conditionally so; for, when released, property in it is gone. So long, then, as the possession of live game is illegal, qualified property in it is illegal also, and the releasing of such game interferes with no legal right or title of the person illegally holding it captive.

The plaintiff's possession of the moose was prima facie title, but, when it appears that his possession was gained in violation of law, it cannot be that the same law will say that his illegal act gave him a legal title; and if he had no legal title to the moose he has suffered no damages from its being set loose.

The plaintiff's illegal act prevented the moose from becoming property at all. Not so with the illegal act of a thief who may have stolen a coat; for the coat was already property, and had an owner, who alone could lawfully take it from the thief. The public, whose servant the defendant was, stands in the place of the owner of the coat. Care should be taken, therefore, not to confound the doctrines of this case with the well-settled rule of law that possession of property is a good title against everybody but the true owner.

4 Rev. Stat., chap. 30, § 9, provides: "No person shall [during close time] in any manner hunt, kill or destroy any moose, under the same penalty," of $100. The plaintiff followed the moose in the forest until it became snow-bound, and then, by the use of a rope, tied it to a tree, and finally bound it upon a sled, and hauled it some fifteen miles to his home, when he confined it until it was released by defendant. Without doubt, this conduct, resulting in capture, was in violation of the Statute. The plaintiff did not destroy or kill the animal, but he did hunt and thereby capture it.

The purpose and scope of the Statute is to give moose absolute immunity from the vexations of men during a portion of each year deemed by the Legislature necessary for their preservation and protection, and to prevent their decimation and extinction. The defendant's act, therefore, was meritorious, and in the aid of the purpose of the Statute; and, while his authority gave him no especial protection, still duty as an officer called him to interfere and prevent a continued violation of the Statute.

The contention that the game had been bonded by the plaintiff is not sustained. No bond signed and conditioned as provided by statute was ever given. It was so irregular that it was absolutely void.

Motions and exceptions sustained, unless plaintiff remits $100.

Peters, *Ch. J.*, and **Walton, Virgin, Emery** and **Foster,** *JJ.*, concurred.

John B. HARE
v.
Stephen McINTYRE.

(....Me.....)

1. **The words "all persons,"** in Rev. Stat., chap. 17, §§ 23, 24, requiring notice by those engaged in blasting before an explosion so that "all persons" or teams shall have time to retire to a safe distance, do not apply to the workmen in the quarries.

2. **Fellow servants owe to each other the duty** to exercise ordinary care and prudence in the prosecution of their work, and for failure to do so are liable at common law to each other for resulting personal injury.

(January 4, 1890.)

REPORT from the Supreme Judicial Court for Knox County for the opinion of the full court of an action brought to recover damages for personal injuries resulting from defendant's alleged negligence in firing a blast in a granite quarry without giving notice of it *Nonsuit.*

The facts fully appear in the opinion.

Mr. **Joseph E. Moore** for plaintiff.

Mr. **Charles E. Littlefield** for defendant.

Virgin, *J.*, delivered the opinion of the court:

An action by one workman in a granite

quarry against his fellow workman, to recover damages for a personal injury alleged to have been caused by a rock thrown from a blast discharged by the defendant. The case comes up on a report of the evidence; and, if the action is maintainable, it is to stand for trial for the assessment of damages.

The action is founded on Rev. Stat., chap. 17, §§ 23, 24, the material provisions of which, including the words in brackets found in the original Act of 1852, chap. 257, are as follows: (23). "Persons engaged in blasting lime rock, or other rocks, shall, before each explosion, give seasonable notice thereof, so that all persons or teams [that may be] approaching shall have [a reasonable] time to retire to a safe distance from the place of said explosion. (24). Whoever violates the preceding section . . . is liable for all damages caused by any explosion [when seasonable notice thereof was not given]; and if the persons engaged in blasting rocks are unable to pay, or after judgment and execution avoid payment . . . by the poor debtor's oath, the owners of the quarry, in whose employment they were, are liable for the same."

Is this statutory remedy intended to apply to workmen in quarries?

A literal construction of the words "all persons" would doubtless include them. Still, when read in connection with the other clauses of the Statute, we do not think the Legislature so intended. "Persons that may be approaching" seem rather intended to apply to those only who are not engaged in and about the quarry, and who, therefore, being ignorant of their proximity to danger, are seen coming within the danger line, instead of including with them such persons, also, as are constantly engaged there, and have personal knowledge of what is taking place there. That clause apparently limits the remedy to such outsiders as might unsuspectingly be approaching within the possible range of the blast, and the object of the "seasonable notice" to them is "so that they and their teams may have a reasonable time to retire to a safe distance."

Moreover, if the real intention of these provisions, derived from their language alone, left any doubt on this question, it is entirely removed by the further consideration that the other construction would make it in derogation of the common law; and, to warrant such a result, the intention should be clearly expressed. *Dwelly* v. *Dwelly*, 46 Me. 377; *Carle* v. *Bangor & P. C. & R. Co.* 43 Me. 269.

By the universally acknowledged rule of common law, when an employé, of age and intelligence, enters another's service, he is presumed to understand, and therefore, as between himself and his employer, and in the absence of any agreement to the contrary, to assume, all the ordinary risks incident thereto, and to measurably predicate his wages upon the extent of the perils he is to encounter and assume, among which are those which he knows are more or less likely to occur through the occasional negligence of his co-employé. And, as it is utterly impracticable for the employer to absolutely prevent such negligence, and the best thing he can do in that direction is to employ such prudent workmen as are least likely to act negligently, therefore, if he has used proper care in respect of their selection, the employer is not responsible to any one of them for an injury resulting from the negligence of any other. But, if the Statute in question is intended to include workmen in quarries, then this long-established, salutary rule of the common law is thereby reversed; for the Statute expressly makes the employers liable for an injury occasioned by the negligence of a fellow servant, if the one who causes it is unable to pay, or avoids. If such a radical change of the law governing the duties and liabilities of employers to their employés had been in the mind of the Legislature, we think the law-makers would have clearly and directly expressed such intention, and, even, not limited it to workmen in quarries, but extended it to other kinds of business involving more or less danger, and in which large numbers of employés are engaged.

This view finds apposite illustration in a decision of this court construing a statute defining the liability of railroad companies. Chapter 81, Rev. Stat. 1841, after providing for the erection of sign-boards and gates, and stationing agents at crossings, and fixing penalties for non-compliance therewith, continued as follows: "Every railroad corporation shall be liable for all damages sustained by any person in consequence of any neglect of the provisions of the foregoing section, or of any other neglect of any of their agents, or by any mismanagement of their engines, in an action on the case by the person sustaining such damages." Rev. Stat. 1841, chap. 81, § 21.

In an action by an employé against a railroad company to recover damages for an injury caused by another employé, the court, in deciding that the Statute did not apply, says: "Notwithstanding its literal construction [of the Statute] might entitle . . . any servant to recover for injuries occasioned by the fault of a fellow servant, still such a construction is wholly inadmissible. Statutes, unless plainly to be otherwise construed, should receive a construction not in derogation of the common law." And, after expressing the opinion that the Statute was not intended to change the nature of contracts between such corporations and their servants, the court continues: "If such had been the intention, we think it would have been more plainly or directly expressed. The words 'any person' . . . must be limited in their application to such persons as were not the servants of the corporation, . . . leaving such servants, who are presumed to have arranged their compensation with their eyes open, and to have assumed the relation with all its ordinary dangers and risks, without any remedy against the corporations for such injuries as may be incident to the service they have engaged to perform." *Carle* v. *Bangor & P. C. & R. Co. supra.*

Can the action be maintained at common law?

Some of the elementary writers seem inclined to the opinion that one servant is not liable to a fellow servant for negligence. Wharton, Neg. § 245; Wood, Mast. and Serv. § 325.

To maintain his action, the plaintiff must prove some contract or obligation from which, in legal contemplation, arises a duty, the breach whereof is alleged against the defendant, or facts establishing such a relation between himself and the defendant that such a duty will thence result, together with a breach thereof. Broom, Com. Law, 670.

There is no subsisting contract between fellow servants, and neither receives any compensation from the other. Neither is a party to, or has any interest or privity in, the other's contract with their common master. Their separate, independent contracts with him are only material as showing that they are, individually, rightfully on the premises, and engaged in the performance of their service there The action cannot, therefore, be founded on any contract, but, if at all, on the defendant's misfeasance, which, even if it could be deemed a breach of his contract with his master, would not for that reason exempt him from liability to others injured thereby, provided such misfeasance was a violation of a duty springing from the relation between them. And we are of opinion that where two or more persons are engaged in the same general business of a common employer, in which their mutual safety depends somewhat upon the care exercised by them, respectively, each owes to the other a duty, resulting from their relation of fellow servants, to exercise such care in the prosecution of their work as men of ordinary prudence usually use in like circumstances, and he who fails in that respect is responsible for a resulting personal injury to his fellow servant. Such a liability would necessarily have a salutary influence in inducing care on their part.

The great weight of authority lies in this direction. Thus, where the plaintiff sued a railroad company to recover damages for the death of her husband, one of its employés, killed by the negligence of one of the defendant's engine drivers, *Barons* Pollock and Huddleston, while they exempted the company because the death was caused by a fellow servant, said: "It is clear that an action would well lie against the driver of the engine, by whose negligent act the death was occasioned." *Swainson* v. *North-Eastern R. Co.* L. R. 3 Exch. Div. 341, 343.

A like dictum was made by *Baron* Alderson in *Wiggett* v. *Fox*, 11 Exch. 832, 839, and by *Baron* Bramwell in *Degg* v. *Midland R. Co.* 1 Hurlst. & N. 773, 780. And it has been directly adjudicated in *Wright* v. *Roxburgh*, 2 Ct. Sess. Cas. 3d Series (Macpherson, L. & B.) 748; *Hinds* v. *Harbou*, 58 Ind. 121; *Hinds* v. *Overacker*, 66 Ind. 547; *Griffiths* v. *Wolfram*, 22 Minn. 185, and in *Osborne* v. *Morgan*, 130 Mass. 102, which last case expressly overrules *Albro* v. *Jaquith*, 4 Gray, 99.

The contrary doctrine "is not only destitute of sense," says the eminent author of "Thompson on Negligence," "but it involves the monstrous conclusion that one servant owes no duty of exercising care to avoid injuring his fellow servants." 2 Thomp. Neg. 1062. See also Addison, Torts, § 245; Shearm. & Redf. Neg. § 144.

Facts. In September, 1882, the defendant, a quarryman of twelve years' experience, was engaged in opening a new place in the quarry, by blasting off the outside layer of soft stone so as to uncover those fit for use which lay beneath, in sheets about two feet thick. He sunk his first hole fifteen inches deep in the front edge of the top layer, and charged it with "a little more than half a pound of powder." Next north was a table rock six or seven feet high. South, southeast and southwest of this place of blasting were two tiers of long, narrow sheds, extending easterly and westerly, seven or eight feet high, divided into bands, where quarried rocks were shaped and dressed. These sheds had narrow doors in each end for ingress and egress, with two sets of doors on their north and south sides,—the lower ones two and one half feet wide, and so constructed as to be taken out, and the upper ones three and one half feet wide, hung at their upper edges by hinges, and were opened by being swung upward.

The plaintiff was a quarryman and stonecutter. He had cut stone there in May and June, and, after working July and August in the crew of one who then had charge of blasting, he returned to cutting again in September, when he was engaged in the extreme west end of shed No. 3, 265 feet south of the place of blasting. The north side doors, towards the blast, were closed to keep out the north wind, while the upper south door was open, and the lower one closed. When the blast exploded, a piece of rock weighing about ten pounds came through the north wall of the shed, above the closed upper door, and hit the plaintiff's back, while in a stooping attitude, and thence out of the south open door to an iron rail, where it broke.

The injury caused by this rock is the foundation of the action, and the particular complaint is that no notice was given to the plaintiff previous to the firing of the blast.

A careful examination of the mass of evidence reported satisfies us that the general notice usually given when a small blast is to take place was seasonably given, to wit, a cry of "Fire!" three times made, with short intervals of time between them, before applying the fire, and that the explosion did not take place for several minutes thereafter. It also appears that when heavy blasts, which seldom occur, with twenty-five to fifty pounds of powder, are made, the custom is to send word to the several sheds. Frequently, when light blasts are fired, many workmen, on hearing the alarm, go into the sheds for protection, and those already in remain; and hence has grown up a sort of careless feeling of security on their part.

The plaintiff and some others in the same shed testify that they heard no alarm,—accounted for, perhaps, by reason of the din of their hammers, and the fact that the doors on the side next to the blast were closed. Still others in the same direction, and much further away, distinctly heard it.

But we think the plaintiff mistook his form of remedy, and that the real fault of the defendant was not in failing to give sufficient notice, but in not sufficiently covering the blast. It is absurd to say that rocks from a blast properly covered will fly as did those which rained down upon shed 3, one of which went through its board wall. The gross carelessness of such omission appears upon its face, —*res ipsa loquitur*. But there is no such claim in the declaration, and evidence thereof was therefore excluded. Neither is there any allegation, in terms, of negligence on the part of the defendant, or due care on the part of the plaintiff. We are of opinion, therefore, that this action is not maintainable.

Plaintiff's nonsuit.

Peters, *Ch. J.*, and **Walton, Emery, Foster** and **Haskell,** *JJ.*, concur.

NEW YORK COURT OF APPEALS.

Philander W. FOBES, *Respt.*,
v.
ROME, WATERTOWN & OGDENSBURG R. CO., *Appt.*

(....N. Y.....)

The construction and operation of a surface railroad along and upon a city street, substantially upon the same grade therewith, under authority from the Legislature and by permission of the city, is not a taking of any property of an abutting land owner, who has no title to any portion of the street which will entitle him to compensation either for interference with any of his easements in the street or for consequential damages to his adjoining property necessarily resulting from a reasonable operation of the road, where the use of the street is not exclusive in its nature and the passage through and across it is left free and unobstructed for the public.

(June, 1890.)

APPEAL by defendant from a judgment of the General Term of the Supreme Court, Fourth Department, affirming a judgment of the Onondaga Special Term in favor of plaintiff in an action brought to enjoin defendant from operating its road in front of plaintiff's property until it should make compensation to him for the damages thereby occasioned. *Reversed.*

The case sufficiently appears in the opinion.

Mr. **William B. Hornblower,** with *Mr.* **Edmund B. Wynn,** for appellant:

A steam surface railroad may be built and operated in the street of a city without any compensation to the owner of abutting property for injury to his property or its easements, provided the abutting owner has no title to the fee under the bed of the street, and provided the railroad is built without causing any unnecessary obstruction to the use of the street as a public street, and provided the railroad is operated in a reasonably prudent and careful manner.

Drake v. *Hudson River R. Co.* 7 Barb. 508; *Greene* v. *New York Cent. & H. R. R. Co.* 65 How. Pr. 154; *Corey* v. *Buffalo, C. & N. Y. R. Co.* 23 Barb. 482; *Hamilton* v. *New York & H. R. Co.* 9 Paige, 171, 4 N. Y. Ch. L. ed. 653; *Plant* v. *Long Island R. Co.* 10 Barb. 26; *Chapman* v. *Albany & S. R. Co.* Id. 360; *Adams* v. *Saratoga & W. R. Co.* 11 Barb. 414, reversed in 10 N. Y. 328, but not on these points; *Hentz* v. *Long Island R. Co.* 13 Barb. 646; *People* v. *Kerr*, 27 N. Y. 188; *Kellinger* v. *Forty-Second St. & G. St. F. R. Co.* 50 N. Y. 206; *Washington Cemetery* v. *Prospect Park & C. I. R. Co.* 68 N. Y. 591.

The overwhelming weight of authority in other States is against the right of an abutting owner on a city street to compensation for the

NOTE.—*Street railroad; right to construct and operate its line.*

It is within the power of a city to grant a railroad company the right to construct and operate its road over its streets. Atchison & N. R. Co. v. Manley, 42 Kan. 577.

The right of a street railroad company to construct and operate its line is a franchise emanating from the sovereign power. See *notes* to Arbenz v. Wheeling & H. R. Co. (W. Va.) 5 L. R. A. 371; People v. O'Brien (N. Y.) 2 L. R. A. 255; People v. Newton (N. Y.) 3 L. R. A. 174.

The city may authorize a railroad company to lay a track at grade and use it for the passage of its cars in common with other conveyances, although the contiguous property may be depreciated and egress be difficult, if the owners are not excluded entirely. For such incidental injury there is no redress, either public or private, unless in case of unreasonable delay in passing so as to incumber the street. Dwenger v. Chicago & G. T. R. Co. 98 Ind. 157; Tate v. Ohio & M. R. Co. 7 Ind. 479.

This court cannot restrain the construction of a railway for the benefit of the residents along streets and squares; if such residents are damaged by the construction they will be heard by the courts upon a proper case made. Savannah & T. R. Co. v. Savannah, 45 Ga. 608.

So held in a case brought by the city authorities to recover pecuniary compensation for the additional servitude placed upon streets and squares by the Legislature, where the corporation had the right to run a street railway. See 1 Am. L. Reg. N. S. 198.

To allow a street in a city or village to be used for a railroad track, either upon its natural surface, or by tunneling, is not a misappropriation of it, provided that such use does not interfere with its free and unobstructed use by the public, as a highway. Adams v. Saratoga & W. R. Co. 11 Barb. 450; Williams v. New York C. R. Co. 18 Barb. 246; Hudson & D. Canal Co. v. New York & E. R. Co. 9 Paige, 323, 4 N. Y. Ch. L. ed. 718.

A street railroad which does not materially interfere with the use of the street is not a nuisance *per se.* Hamilton v. New York & H. R. R. Co. 9 Paige, 171, 4 N. Y. Ch. L. ed. 653; Harris v. Thompson, 9 Barb. 364; Drake v. Hudson River R. Co. 7 Barb. 556; Anderson v. Rochester, L. & N. F. R. Co. 9 How. Pr. 553; Lexington & O. R. Co. v. Applegate, 8 Dana (Ky.) 289; Hentz v. Long Island R. Co. 13 Barb. 656.

The right to establish a railroad at the places where it was proposed to be constructed was challenged on the ground that compensation had not been provided for the taking of, or the injury to, private property, but the exception in that respect was not allowed. Davis v. New York, 14 N. Y. 518; Lexington & O. R. Co. v. Applegate, *supra;* Drake v. Hudson River R. Co. 7 Barb. 508; Plant v. Long Island R. Co. 10 Barb. 26; Adams v. Saratoga & W. R. Co. 11 Barb. 414; Milhau v. Sharp, 15 Barb. 244, 17 Barb. 437; Chapman v. Albany & S. R. Co. 10 Barb. 360; Williams v. New York Cent. R. Co. 18 Barb. 222; Stuyvesant v. Pearsall, 15 Barb. 244. See *note* to Trinity & S. R. Co. v. Meadows (Tex.) 3 L. R. A. 565.

use of the street by a steam surface railroad, where the abutting owner does not also own the fee.

Dillon, Mun. Corp. § 723; *Lexington & O. R. Co. v. Applegate*, 8 Dana (Ky.) 289; *Severy v. Central Pac. R. Co.* 51 Cal. 194; *Barney v. Keokuk*, 94 U. S. 324 (24 L. ed. 224); *Perry v. New Orleans, M. & C. R. Co.* 55 Ala. 413; *Carson v. Central R. Co.* 35 Cal. 325; *Hogan v. Central Pac. R. Co.* 71 Cal. 83; *Colorado Cent. R. Co. v. Mollandin*, 4 Colo. 154; *Florida Southern R. Co. v. Brown*, 23 Fla. 104; *South Carolina R. Co. v. Steiner*, 44 Ga. 547; *Moses v. Pittsburgh, Ft. W. & C. R. Co.* 21 Ill. 517; *Indianapolis, B. & W. R. Co. v. Hartley*, 67 Ill. 439; *Chicago, B. & Q. R. Co. v. McGinnis*, 79 Ill. 269; *Dwenger v. Chicago & G. T. R. Co.* 98 Ind. 153; *Clinton v. Cedar Rapids & M. R. R. Co.* 24 Iowa, 455; *Davis v. Chicago & N. W. R. Co.* 46 Iowa, 389; *Atchison & N. R. Co. v. Garside*, 10 Kan. 552; *Central Branch Union Pac. R. Co. v. Twine*, 23 Kan. 585; *Central Branch Union Pac. R. Co. v. Andrews*, 30 Kan. 593; *Cosby v. Owensboro & R. R. Co.* 10 Bush, 288; *Hill v. Chicago, St. L. & N. O. R. Co.* 38 La. Ann. 599; *Grand Rapids & I. R. Co. v. Heisel*, 38 Mich. 62; *Donnaher v. State*, 8 Smedes & M. 661; *Tate v. Missouri, K. & T. R. Co.* 64 Mo. 149; *Cross v. St. Louis, K. C. & N. R. Co.* 77 Mo. 322; *Morris & E. R. Co. v. Newark*, 10 N. J. Eq. 352, 357; *Cleveland & P. R. Co. v. Speer*, 56 Pa. 325; *Struthers v. Dunkirk, W. & P. R. Co.* 87 Pa. 282; *McLauchlin v. Charlotte & S. C. R. Co.* 5 Rich. L. 583; *Tennessee & A. R. Co. v. Adams*, 3 Head, 596; *Houston & T. C. R. Co. v. Odum*, 53 Tex. 343; *Richardson v. Vermont Cent. R. Co.* 25 Vt. 465; *Hatch v. Vermont Cent. R. Co.* 28 Vt. 142; *Heiss v. Milwaukee & L. W. R. Co.* 69 Wis. 555.

Mr. **C. P. Ruger**, for respondent:

Every abutting owner is, by the mere fact of such ownership, the owner of an easement in the highway without regard to the nature of its origin.

Fritz v. Hobson, L. R. 14 Ch. Div. 542; *Adams v. Chicago, C. B. & N. R. Co.* 39 Minn. 286; *Grand Rapids & I. R. Co. v. Heisel*, 38 Mich. 62.

The simple fact that the lot owner is liable to taxation, for the purpose of maintaining the adjacent highway, gives him an interest therein in the nature of an easement.

Lahr v. Metropolitan E. R. Co. 6 Cent. Rep. 371, 104 N. Y. 268; *Abendroth v. New York Elevated R. Co.* 22 Jones & S. 417.

Any interference with the highway which substantially impairs the abutter's easement is a taking of his property, unless such interference is by the proper authorities, directly or indirectly, for some ordinary street purpose, such as the establishment or change of a grade.

Drucker v. Manhattan R. Co. 8 Cent. Rep. 66, 106 N. Y. 157.

The owner of an easement can complain of the permanent appropriation of the street to uses which destroy or substantially impair his easement. The steam railway is such a use and the street permanently appropriated therefor.

Hussner v. Brooklyn City R. Co. 114 N. Y. 433.

The elevated railway decisions have established a general rule of law under which the construction and operation of a steam surface railway is a taking of the abutter's easement.

Fanning v. Osborne, 34 Hun, 121, reversed in the Court of Appeals, 3 Cent. Rep. 453, 102 N. Y. 441, but upon another point.

The abutting owner's easement of light, air and access in and to the highway is private property, and, like other property, entitled to the benefit of the constitutional protection.

Story v. New York Elevated R. Co. 90 N. Y. 122; *Lahr v. Metropolitan Elevated R. Co.* 6 Cent. Rep. 371, 104 N. Y. 268; *Drucker v. Manhattan R. Co.* 8 Cent. Rep. 66, 106 N. Y. 157; *Arnold v. Hudson River R. Co.* 55 N. Y. 661; *White's Bank v. Nichols*, 64 N. Y. 65.

This rule is not confined merely to elevated railways.

Oswego v. Oswego Canal Co. 6 N. Y. 257; *Uline v. New York Cent. & H. R. R. Co.* 2 Cent. Rep. 116, 101 N.Y. 98.

Some cases hold that any material obstruction, whether by the ordinary operation of the road or not, is considered a taking of property, for which compensation must be made.

South Carolina R. Co. v. Steiner, 44 Ga. 547; *Central Branch Union Pac. R. Co. v. Twine*, 23 Kan. 585; *Central Branch Union Pac. R. Co. v. Andrews*, 30 Kan. 590; *Scioto Valley R. Co. v. Lawrence*, 38 Ohio St. 41; *Elizabethtown, L. & B. S. R. Co. v. Combs*, 10 Bush, 382; *Theobold v. Louisville, N. O. & T. R. Co.* 66 Miss. 279; *Phipps v. Western Maryland R. Co.* 66 Md. 320; *Burlington & M. R. R. Co. v. Reinhackle*, 15 Neb. 279; *Denver & R. G. R. Co. v. Bourne*, 11 Colo. 59; *Adams v. Chicago, B. & N. R. Co.* 39 Minn. 286; *St. Paul & P. R. Co. v. Schurmeier*, 74 U. S. 7 Wall. 272 (19 L. ed. 74).

The modern tendency throughout the country manifestly is toward the protection of private property rights in these cases as being equally important to those of corporations. In several States late decisions have come out squarely in line with the principles of *Story v. New York E. R. Co.*, 90 N.Y. 122, in their application to steam surface railways.

Theobold v. Louisville, N. O. & T. R. Co., Scioto Valley R. Co. v. Lawrence and *Denver & R. G. R. Co. v. Bourne, supra.*

Peckham, *J.*, delivered the opinion of the court:

We think that the defendant has, by its exceptions, duly raised the question argued before us. We are also of the opinion that the plaintiff's lot is bounded by the exterior line of the street in question, and that he has no title to the land to the centre of the street, subject to the public easement. The courts below held that the occupation and appropriation by defendant of a part of plaintiff's easement in Franklin Street is and always has been unlawful. To that conclusion the defendant excepted.

It admits that plaintiff had an easement in that street, but it denies that it has occupied or appropriated it.

Whether it has taken any portion of the plaintiff's easement in the street in question is what the defendant asks shall be decided by us, and it denies *in toto* any taking whatever of the plaintiff's property or any portion thereof.

For many years prior to the decision of the case of *Story* v. *New York Elevated R. Co.*, 90 N. Y. 122, I think the law was that a duly incorporated railroad company, having authority from the State to build its road, and laying its tracks and operating its road through and upon the surface of the streets of a city under the protection of a license from such city, took thereby no portion of the property of an individual who owned land adjoining the street, but bounded by its exterior line. The company was therefore not liable to such an owner for any consequential damages to his adjoining property arising from a reasonable use of the street for railroad purposes, not exclusive in its nature and substantially upon the same grade as the street itself, and leaving the passage across and through the street free and unobstructed for the public use.

The first case in this State upon that subject, and decided more than forty years ago, is that of *Drake* v. *Hudson River R. Co.*, 7 Barb. 508. This was a case decided by the General Term of the Supreme Court, sitting in the City of New York, and composed of three most able and learned judges, and I do not find that the principle involved in that decision has been reversed or overruled by any judgment of this court. That case holds the doctrine which I have above stated. It was elaborately argued on both sides by counsel as eminent at the bar as the State afforded, and the opinions of the learned judges are conclusive proof of the ability with which the case was considered by them.

In *Williams* v. *New York Cent. R. Co.*, 16 N. Y. 97, it was held that the dedication of land to the use of the public for a highway is not a dedication of it to the use of a railroad, and such a road cannot be built upon it without compensation to the owner of the fee. It was in that case held to be another and an additional burden upon the land if used for railroad purposes, not covered by the dedication for ordinary street purposes, and hence the owner of the fee was entitled to a compensation for an additional burden to which he had never dedicated his property. It was not a mere additional use of an easement, but it was an actual taking of the land for railroad purposes (though not absolutely exclusive), and hence the owner was protected by the Constitution from such a taking without a compensation. The *Drake Case* was alluded to, but only for the purpose of pointing out the clear distinction between the two cases, and the court said the *Drake Case* involved simply the right of an adjoining owner on the street, who did not own the fee, to recover for incidental damages unavoidably resulting from the construction of the railroad in the street under authority of the law and with the permission of the city authorities, where no land or easement of the adjoining owner was taken. It was also stated that the *Drake Case* might be considered as settling the question that a railroad in a populous town is not a nuisance *per se* (of course when legally authorized), and that when the company has acquired the title to the land upon which its road is located, such company is not liable, unless guilty of some misconduct, for consequential damages resulting from the operation and use of its road. It has been regarded as having such title so far as the adjoining owner is concerned, who has no fee in the street, when, by authority of law and the consent of the city owning the street, its rails are therein laid upon the surface, and the use of the street for ordinary street purposes is not thereby prevented.

In *Wager* v. *Troy Union R. Co.*, 25 N. Y. 526, it is assumed that there is no difference in kind or species between a railroad in a city street, operated by horse power, and one operated by steam. Smith, *J.*, in writing the opinion in that case, says that such difference would present simply a question of degree in respect to the enlargement of the easement, and would not affect the principle. He also said that if the title to the Troy Street were in that city as the fee in the streets in New York is in the city itself, the mayor and common council of Troy might perhaps have authorized such appropriation of the street without compensation to the adjoining owners.

The case of *Wager* was followed in this court by that of *People* v. *Kerr*, 27 N. Y. 188. It was there held that the legislative permission to lay down street railroad tracks without change of grade in those streets in the City of New York where the city owned the fee, was a sufficient justification for such action by the company, and that no compensation was necessary to be paid to the owner of the adjoining property. It was an appropriation to public use to provide for the construction of a street railroad through a street without change of grade. As this was a horse railroad the decision of the court must be regarded in the light of that fact. But still it is apparent that although a horse railroad was regarded as a different public use for a street from that which had heretofore obtained, yet it was such a public use as was not inconsistent with its continuous use as an open and a public street. There was no change of grade, and no continuous and exclusive possession of the street, except in a limited sense, by the mere laying of the rails therein.

I think there is no authority in this court which holds that there is any real difference between a railroad operated by horse power and one operated by the power of steam in the streets of the city. If the Legislature can authorize the one it can, under the same circumstances, authorize the other. I refer to railroads on the same grade as the street itself and where the chief difference lies in the different motive powers which are used.

In *Craig* v. *Rochester City & B. R. Co.*, 39 N. Y. 404, it was held that the owner of a lot on a street, who owned a fee thereof subject only to the public easement for a street, was entitled to compensation for the new and additional burden upon the land so used as a street, by the erection of even a horse railroad thereon. In this case *Judge* Miller said he saw no distinction in the application of the rule between cases of steam and cases of horse power.

In *Kellinger* v. *Forty-Second St. & G. St. F. R. Co.*, 50 N. Y. 206, it is held that one who did not own the fee of the street could not recover damages for inconvenience of access to his adjoining lands caused by the lawful erection of a street railroad through the street.

By these last two decisions it is seen that to

construct even a horse railroad in a city street is to place a new and additional burden upon the land, the right to do which does not exist by reason of the general right of passage through the street; but if the adjoining owner of land is not the owner of the fee in the street, and the railroad company has obtained the proper authority, he has no right to compensation for such added burden, nor to complain of such use so long as it is not exclusive or excessive. The same reasoning applies, as we have seen, in the case of a steam surface railroad. Such a use of the streets would be an additional burden upon the land, and, of course, if the adjoining owner had title in fee to the centre of the street, subject only to the public easement, he would have a right of action, as held by the *Williams* and other cases, while if he did not, no such right would exist in his favor merely because it was a steam instead of a horse railroad which was to be constructed. The authority of the law and the consent of the city would be enough to authorize the building of either, and the difference between the steam and the horse railroad would not be one of such a nature as to require or permit any difference in the decision of the two cases. If the use of either became unreasonable, excessive or exclusive, or such as not to leave the passage of the street substantially free and unobstructed, then such excessive, improper or unreasonable use would be enjoined, and the adjoining owner would be entitled to recover damages sustained by him therefrom, in his means of access, etc., to his land. *Mahady* v. *Bushwick R. Co.* 91 N. Y. 149.

In *Washington Cemetery* v. *Prospect Park & C. I. R. Co.*, 68 N. Y. 591, 593, Andrews, *J.*, assumes the right of the Legislature to authorize the construction of a railroad on a street without exacting compensation from the corporation authorized to construct it, to the owner of adjoining land, provided such owners did not own the fee in the street. The Statute in the case cited permitted the use of steam on some portion of this road, so that *Judge* Andrews' remarks were not confined to horse railroads.

Assuming that the plaintiff had no title whatever to the land in the street through which the defendant laid its rails, and ran its trains under legislative and municipal authority, I think it is clear that prior to the decision of this court in the *Story Case*, 90 N. Y. 122, he had no cause of action against the defendant, based upon any alleged taking of the plaintiff's property or easement by defendant. If its user of the street became excessive, or exclusive, and hence degenerated into a nuisance, the plaintiff had another remedy.

The claim is now made that the *Story Case*, *supra*, and those cases which followed and are founded upon it, so far altered the law as to permit a recovery in all cases where the easement of the adjoining lot owner, through the building and operation of the road, is injuriously affected by any deprivation, or diminution of light, air or access to his lot, even though he do not own the fee to the centre of the street; and where such injury occurs, it is claimed that the property of the owner in his easement of light, air or access has been taken to a greater or less extent, and compensation is guaranteed to him therefor by the Constitution.

The *Story Case* did not intend to overrule or change the law in regard to steam surface railroads. The case embodied the application of what was regarded as well-established principles of law to a new combination of facts, such facts amounting, as was determined, to an absolute and permanent obstruction in a portion of the public street, and in a total and exclusive use of such portion by the defendant; and such permanent obstruction, and total and exclusive use, it was further held, amounted to a taking of some portion of the plaintiff's easement in the street for the purpose of furnishing light, air and access to his adjoining lot. This absolute and permanent obstruction of the street, this total and exclusive use of a portion thereof by the defendant, was accomplished by the erection of a structure for the elevated railroad of defendant, which structure is fully described in the case as reported. The structure, by the mere fact of its existence in the street, permanently and at every moment of the day, took away from the plaintiff some portion of the light and air which otherwise would have reached him, and, in a degree very appreciable, interfered with and took away from him his facility of access to his lot; such interference not being intermittent and caused by the temporary use of the street by the vehicles of the defendant while it was operating its road through the street, but caused by the iron posts and by the superstructure imposed thereon, and existing for every moment of the day and night. Such a permanent, total, exclusive and absolute appropriation of a portion of the street as this structure amounted to was held to be illegal and wholly beyond any legitimate or lawful use of a public street. The taking of the property of the plaintiff in that case was held to follow upon the permanent and exclusive nature of the appropriation by the defendant of the public street or of some portion thereof. If that appropriation had been held legal, any merely consequential damage to the owner of the adjoining lot, not having any title to the street, would have furnished no ground for an action against the defendant. It was just at this point that the disagreement existed between the members of this court in the *Story Case*. The judge who wrote one of the dissenting opinions did not think that the facts presented any different principle from that of any ordinary steam surface railroad operating its road through the streets of a city under the authority of the Legislature and of the municipality, in a case where the adjoining lot owner did not own the fee in the street. The character of the structure and all the facts incident thereto were regarded by him as simply resulting in an additional burden upon the street, somewhat greater in degree, it is true, than a steam surface railroad; but still it was such a use of the street as the Legislature might permit, and the Legislature having in fact granted it such power, the defendant was not responsible for the incidental damage resulting to one whose property was not in fact taken within the meaning of the constitutional provision, and the defendant did him therefore no actionable injury. The other dissenting judges were of the same opinion.

A majority of the court, however, saw in the facts existing in that case what was regarded as a plain, palpable and permanent misappropriation of the street or some portion of it to the exclusive use of the defendant corporation, and as resulting from it the court held that there was a taking of property belonging to the plaintiff without compensation, which no Legislature could authorize or legalize. But this taking, it cannot be too frequently or strongly asserted, resulted from the absolute, exclusive and permanent character of the appropriation of the street by the structure of the defendant. There is no hint in either of the prevailing opinions in the *Story Case* of any intention to interfere with or to overrule the prior adjudications in this State upon the subject now under discussion, as to steam surface railroads. In the *Story Case* it was argued that no real distinction in principle existed between a steam surface and an elevated railroad resting on such a structure as was proved in that case. This court, however, made the distinction, and the two prevailing opinions are largely taken up with arguments going to show that the distinction was obvious, material and important, and was so real and tangible in fact as to call for a different judgment than would have been proper and appropriate in the case of the ordinary steam surface railroad such as the *Drake Case* was.

Judge Tracy, in the *Story Case*, said that the conclusion reached in that case was based upon the character of the structure there involved, and that the language of *Judge* Wright in the *Kerr Case, supra*, where he asserted that the abutting owners had no property or estate in the land forming the bed of the street in front of their premises, must be construed with reference to the point then considered. In another portion of his opinion *Judge* Tracy said that no structure upon the street can be authorized which is inconsistent with the continued use of the street as an open public street. He also added that whatever force the argument may have as applied to railroads built upon the surface of the street, without change of grade, and where the road is so constructed that the public is not excluded from any part of the street, it has no force when applied to a structure like that authorized in the present case. This, he says, is an attempt to appropriate the street to a use essentially inconsistent with that of a public street, and hence illegal. He does not pretend that the ordinary steam railroad, laid on the same grade as the street, and not excluding others from its use, appropriates the street to a use essentially or at all inconsistent with that of a public street. The use may be an additional burden laid upon the street, but nevertheless it is such a use as is entirely consistent with its continued use as a public street.

Judge Danforth, in his opinion, views the structure in much the same light. He cites the case of *Corning* v. *Lowerre*, 6 Johns. Ch. 439, 2 N. Y. Ch. L. ed. 178, where *Chancellor* Kent restrained the defendant by injunction from obstructing Vesey Street, in New York City, by building a house thereon, and he says that the railroad structure designed by the defendant for the street opposite the plaintiff's premises is liable to the same objection, that is, it is as permanent in its character and as exclusive in its possession of that portion of the street, as was the defendant's building in the case cited. He further says that the street railway cases are in no respect in conflict with the doctrine announced in his opinion.

Other citations might be made from both opinions of those most learned and able judges, but enough has been shown to enable us to say with entire correctness that there was no intention in deciding the *Story Case* to reverse or overrule the cases in regard to steam surface railroads which have been already cited. Those cases include just such a case as is the one at bar.

Following the *Story* comes the *Lahr Case*, 104 N. Y. 268, 6 Cent. Rep. 371, and the principles decided in the former were reiterated in the latter case. It is difficult to see that any enlarged rule as to awarding damages in that class of cases has been definitely announced in the *Lahr Case*. The general rule to be adopted was agreed upon by the parties and involved an award once for all. The particular damage which the defendant was liable for, growing out of the existence of the defendant's structure, was held by three of the five members of the court then voting, to embrace any injury or inconvenience resulting from the unlawful structure, or any such injury or inconvenience as was incidental to the use thereof. Two of the five members were in favor of a more restricted rule, and they agreed simply in the result which affirmed the judgment of the court below.

Then came the *Drucker Case*, 106 N. Y. 157, 8 Cent. Rep. 66, and in it the principle was announced, as stated in the head note, that in awarding damages it was proper to prove and take into consideration as elements of damages the impairment of plaintiff's easement of light caused by the road itself and the passage of trains, and the interference with the convenience of access caused by the drippings of oil and water. This was held as a fair result from a holding that the structure was an illegal one, and to the extent above described the court held the plaintiff entitled to an award of damages. But the foundation for the recovery in all the cases above cited of any damages whatever, lies in the fact of the illegality of the structure.

Looking carefully over the cases involving the elevated railroads and their rights and liabilities, we cannot see that any new rule was adopted in any of those cases which would hold the defendant herein liable under the facts proved, for the taking of any property or any portion of an easement belonging to the plaintiff. On the contrary, we think the plaintiff's case is still governed by the case of *Drake* and the other cases in this court which have already been cited, and in which the principle decided in the *Drake Case* has been assented to and affirmed. Upon such facts it has been held that there was no taking of any property or easement of an adjoining owner who had no title to any portion of the land upon which the street was laid out, where the Company was authorized by law and licensed by the city to so use the street.

Plaintiff's counsel cites the case of *Hussner* v. *Brooklyn City R. Co.*, 114 N.Y. 433, as bearing upon this question. We cannot see that it does. The use of steam on the portion of the road spoken of in that case was not permitted, and it was therefore unlawful, and for the damages caused to an abutting owner by reason of the nuisance the defendant was held liable.

We are of the opinion that the plaintiff made out no legal ground for an action against defendant based upon any alleged taking of his property by the defendant. If there are any facts which go to show that the use of the street by the defendant is excessive and in that way a nuisance, the recovery herein was not based upon any such liability and it cannot be sustained on that ground now.

The judgments of the Special and General Terms of the Supreme Court must be reversed and a new trial granted, with costs to abide the event.

All concur, except **Ruger,** *Ch. J.*, and **Andrews,** *J.*, not voting.

PEOPLE OF the State of NEW YORK
v.
E. REMINGTON & SONS, *Appts.*

Re Proof of Claim of ILION NATIONAL BANK, *Respt.*

(....N. Y.....)

A creditor of an insolvent has the right to prove and have dividends upon his entire claim, irrespective of collateral securities held by him.

(June 3, 1890.)

APPEAL by defendant's receivers from an order of the General Term of the Supreme Court, Fourth Department, affirming an order of the Onondaga Special Term overruling exceptions to the report of a referee allowing a claim against defendant in insolvency proceedings. *Affirmed.*

Statement by **Gray,** *J.:*

This is an appeal by the receivers of E. Remington & Sons, an insolvent corporation, from an order of the general term affirming an order of the special term, which overruled their exceptions to the report of a referee upon the claim of the Ilion National Bank, a creditor. The defendant corporation was proceeded against by the people in an action for its dissolution on the ground of insolvency. Receivers were appointed and a reference ordered to take proof of claims.

The Ilion National Bank, this respondent, was a creditor to a large amount, and as collateral security for the payment of the indebtedness to it had received pledges of properties and securities. It made proof of its full claim against the insolvent corporation on the indebtedness theretofore created. The receivers objected that there should be deducted from the proof of claim the sums already realized by the respondent from the collateral securities and the value of the securities still held, and that the claim should be allowed for the balance only. But the referee allowed and reported the claim at the full amount, without regard to the securities or the sums realized therefrom.

Mr. **William Kernan,** for appellants:

Where one creditor has two funds of his debtor to which he can resort for payment, and another creditor has a lien on one of the funds only, equity will compel the first creditor to resort to that fund to which the lien of the other does not extend.

Bishop, Insolv. Debtors, 2d ed. § 356; Story, Eq. § 633; *Halsey* v. *Reed*, 9 Paige, 446, 4 N. Y. Ch. L. ed. 768; *Besley* v. *Lawrence*, 11 Paige, 581, 5 N. Y. Ch. L. ed. 241; *Aldrich* v. *Cooper*, 8 Ves. Jr. 382.

NOTE.—*Rule of distribution of insolvent's estate among creditors, secured and unsecured.*

The rules of the Bankrupt Law, that where a creditor holds the securities of third persons he may prove his whole debt, but in case he realizes on the security before proving he can prove only the balance remaining unpaid (Blumenstiel, Bankruptcy, 287), have not been uniformly applied in distributions under State Insolvent Laws; for in Massachusetts it is held that the creditor can share only on the deficiency of his debt after exhausting the security (Amory v. Francis, 16 Mass. 308), without recognizing the distinction as made in the Bankrupt Act between securities on the debtor's estate and those of third persons. See Cabot Bank v. Bodman, 11 Gray, 134; Richardson v. Wyman, 4 Gray, 553; Lanckton v. Wolcott, 6 Met. 305.

In Iowa, and by the earlier decisions of New York and Rhode Island, a creditor who has a claim secured by a lien is entitled to a dividend from the voluntary assignee of his debtor only on such residue of his claim as may remain unpaid after he has exhausted the property subject to his lien. *Re* Knowles, 13 R. I. 90; Strong v. Skinner, 4 Barb. 560; Besley v. Lawrence, 11 Paige, 581, 5 N. Y. Ch. L. ed. 240; Midgeley v. Slocomb, 32 How. Pr. 426; Dickson v. Chorn, 6 Iowa, 19; Wurts v. Hart, 13 Iowa, 519.

This rule is in accordance with the established rule in equity that where one creditor has a lien on two funds, and another has a lien only on one of them, the former must exhaust the fund upon which the latter has no lien. *Re* Knowles, *supra.*

But the equitable rule that where one creditor has a lien upon two funds, and another creditor a lien upon only one of them, the former will be compelled to resort, in the first instance, to the fund upon which he has an exclusive lien, will not be enforced where it would operate to the prejudice of the party entitled to the double security. Bates v. Paddock, 7 West. Rep. 222, 118 Ill. 527; Sweet v. Redhead, 76 Ill. 374; Brown v. Cozard, 68 Ill. 178; United States v. Duncan, 12 Ill. 523; 3 Pom. Eq. Jur. § 1414.

In proceedings under the Insolvent Law, a secured creditor, not having sold or surrendered his security to the assignee, has no right to prove the secured debt, unless the assignee can treat the act of the creditor as a conclusive election to prove the debt, and a waiver and equitable release of the security to him. Nichols v. Smith, 3 New Eng. Rep. 507, 143 Mass. 455.

When the creditor who holds the security which comes within the terms of the statute inadvertently, by mistake either of law or fact, proves his whole debt without disclosing his security, and, before he has derived any advantage, or the creditors have suffered any detriment from his act, takes proper measures to waive or abandon his proof, and to pursue his rights as a secured creditor, according to law, he does not thereby waive

See also 11 L. R. A. 841; 21 L. R. A. 822.

A mortgagee petitioned for the sale of his security and to be permitted to prove the full amount of his debt in the suit for the administration of the assets of the deceased mortgagors. It was held he could prove only for so much of his debt as might remain unpaid by the proceeds of the mortgaged estate.

Greenwood v. *Taylor*, 1 Russ. & M. 185; *Brocklehurst* v. *Jessop*, 7 Sim. 438.

The same rule is enforced as against creditors of insolvent estates.

Amory v. *Francis*, 16 Mass. 308; *Farnum* v. *Boutelle*, 13 Met. 159; *Wurtz* v. *Hart*, 13 Iowa, 515; *Third Nat. Bank* v. *Lanahan*, 6 Cent. Rep. 425, 66 Md. 461; *Re Knowles*, 13 R. I. 90.

Upon principles of equity and justice between the creditors, the rule is as we maintain. It was provided for by the statute in cases of bankruptcy, for the reason that it was just and equitable. It was enforced in England before any statutory provision.

Jervis v. *Smith*, 7 Abb. Pr. N. S. 220.

Mr. **A. M. Mills**, for respondent:

The creditor is entitled to prove and have dividends upon his entire debt, irrespective of his collateral security.

Putnam v. *Clark*, 17 Vt. 84; *West* v. *Rutland Bank*, 19 Vt. 403; *Moses* v. *Ranlet*, 2 N. H. 488; *Findlay* v. *Hosmer*, 2 Conn. 350; *Logan* v. *Anderson*, 18 B. Mon. 114; *Kramer & Rahm's App.* 37 Pa. 71; *Patten's App.* 45 Pa. 151; *Bates* v. *Paddock*, 7 West. Rep. 222, 118 Ill. 524; *Yates* v. *Dodge*, 11 West. Rep. 628, 123 Ill. 50; *Allen* v. *Danielson*, 4 New Eng. Rep. 106, 15 R. I. 480; Story, Eq. Jur. § 564*b*; Bishop, Insolv. Debtors, 373; *Mason* v. *Bogg*, 2 Myl. & Cr. 443; *Aldrich* v. *Cooper*, 8 Ves. Jr. 382; 2 Lead. Cas. in Eq. *78; *Kellock's Case*, L. R. 3 Ch. 769, 39 L. J. N. S. Ch. 112; *Re Barned's Bkg. Co.* (*Ex parte Bank of England*) 39 L. J. N. S. Ch. 759, 18 Week. Rep. 944, 22 L. T. N. S. 895; *Re Joint Stock Discount Co.* (*Warrant Finance Co's Case*) L. R. 5 Ch. 86, 39 L. J. N. S. Ch. 122, 21 L. T. N. S. 626.

The doctrine that where one creditor has a lien upon two funds for the payment of his debt, while other creditors of the same debtor have a lien upon one of the two funds, the first creditor will be obliged to resort to that fund upon which the second creditor has no lien, is never applied when it will in any manner trench upon the rights or in the least operate to the prejudice of the double-fund creditor.

Cheesebrough v. *Millard*, 1 Johns. Ch. 409, 1 N. Y. Ch. L. ed. 190; *Brinkerhoff* v. *Marvin*, 5 Johns. Ch. 320, 1 N. Y. Ch. L. ed. 1096.

Where the sufficiency of the fund, to which the junior creditor cannot resort, to pay the prior creditor's debt in full, is doubtful, or the prior creditor refuses to run the hazard of getting his pay out of that fund, the rule does not apply.

Evertson v. *Booth*, 19 Johns. 486; *Bernhardt* v. *Lymburner*, 85 N. Y. 172.

The rule in bankruptcy, which requires that the collateral security be exhausted before the creditor draws a dividend, was purely statutory and does not govern us.

Mason v. *Bogg*, 2 Myl. & Cr. 443; *Jervis* v. *Smith*, 7 Abb. Pr. N. S. 217.

Gray, *J.*, delivered the opinion of the court:

The only question presented for our consideration and determination by this appeal is whether the creditor of this insolvent corporation was entitled to prove and receive a dividend upon the full amount of the debt due from the insolvent estate, or whether the receivers, as the personal representatives of the insolvent, could reduce the claim of the creditor, for the purposes of a dividend, by com-

---

or forfeit his security; nor do the unsecured creditors acquire an equitable right to it which can be enforced by the assignee. *Ibid.*

That he is entitled to a dividend only on that portion of his claim which remains unpaid after deducting the moneys received from the securities, is held in Third Nat. Bank v. Lanahan, 6 Cent. Rep. 425, 66 Md. 461.

The obligation of the trustee of an insolvent assignor to pay the latter's debt depends upon the state of the account between the creditor and the assignor at the time when payment is made. *Ibid.*

The creditor of an insolvent, holding a mortgage to secure notes given by the debtor, cannot claim to enforce the lien of the mortgage, and at the same time claim allowance from the estate for the face value of the notes. He will be deemed to have elected to claim his right under the mortgage. Gummersell v. Hanbloom, 1 West. Rep. 717, 19 Mo. App. 274.

The authorities are in conflict, and a plausible reason can be given for either view; but the weight of authority is in favor of the proposition that the dividend should be allowed on the whole claim. Paddock v. Bates, 19 Ill. App. 470; Findlay v. Hosmer, 2 Conn. 350; Moses v. Ranlet, 2 N. H. 488; Logan v. Anderson, 18 B. Mon. 114; Patten's App. 45 Pa. 151; Keim's App. 27 Pa. 42; Putnam v. Russell, 17 Vt. 54; West v. Bank of Rutland, 19 Vt. 403; Jervis v. Smith, 1 Sheld. 189, 7 Abb. Pr. N. S. 217.

The Pennsylvania decisions hold that a creditor is entitled to a dividend under an assignment not merely as a creditor but as an equitable owner of the assigned estate, and that the extent of his ownership is fixed by the amount of his claim when the assignment is made. Re Bates, 118 Ill. 529; Shunk's App. 2 Pa. 309; Keim's App. 27 Pa. 42; Brough's Estate, 71 Pa. 460.

So a creditor by bond and mortgage was held entitled to a *pro rata* dividend on his whole claim, even though he had collected the greater part of it out of the mortgaged property. Morris v. Olwine, 22 Pa. 441; Miller's App. 35 Pa. 481; Graeff's App. 79 Pa. 146; Bates v. Paddock, 7 West. Rep. 222, 118 Ill. 524.

A creditor may prove his whole debt without regard to any collateral security he may hold. If the dividend so reduces the debt that the collateral security will more than pay for it, the personal representative is bound to redeem for the benefit of the general creditors. Bates v. Paddock, *supra.*

Where a creditor held a trust deed to secure her claim, which had never been foreclosed, and her whole debt was provided for in the assignment, and was listed as one of the liabilities of the debtor, the whole is to be paid *pro rata* from the assets; and the amount of her dividend must be credited on the whole debt, and the mortgage foreclosed on the balance; and, should there be a surplus, it would go to the assignee. *Ibid.*

One having a lien on property for securing the payment of a debt against an insolvent debtor may retain the property and enforce his lien, if the assignee does not require it to be sold. Rogers v. Heath (Vt.) Jan. 6, 1890.

pelling a deduction from the amount of the proved debt of the value of collateral securities or of any proceeds thereof.

There are conflicting decisions upon this question in the courts of the United States; and in England, if we look back, up the current of opinions, we may find some differences in views. But the preponderance of authority is in favor of the view that the creditor has the right to prove and have dividends upon his entire debt, irrespective of the collateral security. In this State the precise question is without any controlling precedent. Two cases decided by the special term of the supreme court are to be found in the reports which perhaps bear upon the question. They arose under general assignments for the benefit of creditors and are conflicting. It may be said, therefore, that the field is open to us for review and determination. I think we must conclude that the view which I have mentioned as having the weight of authority in its favor is the one best according with the principles and established rules of equity jurisprudence, to which department of legal science the question pertains. Some confusion of thought seems to be worked by the reference of the decision of the question to the rules of law governing the administration of estates in bankruptcy; but there is no warrant for any such reference. The rules in bankruptcy cases proceed from the express provisions of the Statute, and they are not at all controlling upon a court administrating in equity upon the estates of insolvent debtors. The Bankrupt Act requires the creditor to give up his security in order to be entitled to his whole debt; or, if he retains it, he can only prove for the balance of the debt, after deducting the value of the security held. The jurisdiction in bankruptcy is peculiar and special, and a particular mode of administration is prescribed by the Act. To administer, in cases of insolvency coming within the jurisdiction of courts of equity, by analogy with the modes of bankruptcy courts, is not required, and their precedents are not to be deemed as causing any change in the rules established by courts of equity for the marshaling and distribution of assets.

Suggestion is also made of a principle of equity, as controlling upon the question. It is, that where the creditor has two funds of his debtor to which he can resort for payment, and another creditor has a lien on one fund only, equity will compel a resort by the first creditor to that fund to which the lien of the other does not extend. But that is not exactly this case; nor is the principle, if it were, decisive. The author, whose statement of the principle is quoted from, has limited its application to such cases, where, to compel the first creditor to resort to the one fund, will not operate to his prejudice, or trench upon his rights. Story, Eq. Jur. § 633.

Judge Story assigns as a reason for the application of the principle, that by so compelling the creditor to satisfy his claim out of one of the funds no injustice is done to him in point of security or payment. The learned author's reason negatives the proposition that a secured creditor shall lose or forego any advantage which he may have by reason of security, and through which the fullest satisfaction of his debt can be obtained.

In *Evertson* v. *Booth*, 19 Johns. 486, Spencer, *Ch. J.*, held, with reference to the equitable rule invoked by the appellants here, that it is not to be enforced if it will "in the least impair the prior creditor's right to raise his debt out of both funds." And he emphatically remarked: "I know of no principle of equity which can take from him any part of his security until he is completely satisfied."

Where could any such principle have its origin? The agreement between the debtor and the creditor was that a debt should be paid. That debt is a definite quantity, and nothing less than its full amount can be said to be the debt. It is not altered or affected in its amount because the creditor may hold some collateral security. That is not a factor of the debt; but merely an incident to the debt. The very force and meaning of a collateral security are in the idea of a guaranty of the performance of the principal agreement which was to pay the debt. The property which a creditor holds as collateral to the indebtedness of his debtor secures him to that extent, in case his debt is not paid in full by the debtor, or by his estate.

As between the creditor and his debtor, the latter could not compel the former to resort first to his collaterals before asserting his claim by a personal suit. The debtor has no control over the application of the collaterals. It is the general rule of equity that the creditor is not bound to apply his collateral securities before enforcing his direct remedies against the debtor. Story, Eq. Jur. § 640; *Lewis* v. *United States*, 92 U. S. 618 [23 L. ed. 518].

Then on what principle can we hold that because the debtor becomes insolvent the contract with his creditor is changed, and that the creditor cannot, under those circumstances, enforce his direct claim against the debtor until he has realized on his securities? Is the rule capable of such inversion? I cannot see any reason in the proposition. I do not see why, in the absence of intervention by positive or statutory law, the engagements of parties should be varied.

If in bankruptcy another method was prescribed by the Statute for the proof and payment of debts, it was a matter purely within the discretion of the Federal Legislature. Its constitutional right to establish uniform laws on the subject of bankruptcies throughout the United States obviously included the power to prescribe the mode of marshalling the insolvents' assets for distribution among creditors, and, being the law of the country, it becomes a part of every contract. But this furnishes no reason why the established rules of courts of equity should be changed in the administration of the estates of insolvents.

In *Kellock's Case*, L. R. 3 Ch. App. 769, decided in 1868, it was held that in the winding up of a company, under the Companies Act of 1862, a creditor holding security might prove for the whole amount due to him, and not merely, as in bankruptcy, for the balance remaingd ue after realizing upon or valuing his security.

In *Greenwood* v. *Taylor*, 1 Russ. & M. 185, decided in 1830, it had been held that the practice in bankruptcy furnished a precedent, which should be followed in the administration of assets; but, in *Mason* v. *Bogg*, 2 Myl. & Cr. 447, decided in 1837, *Lord Chancellor* Cottenham said: "That the principle which the decision in *Greenwood* v. *Taylor* professes to follow cannot be the principle of a court of equity, is further proved by the circumstance that in bankruptcy a particular mode is prescribed. A creditor may there prove; but then he must give up his security; or he may obtain an order that his security should be sold and that he should prove for the difference. In equity, however, a party may come in and prove without giving up or affecting his securities, except so far as the amount of his debt may be diminished by what he may receive."

Mason v. *Bogg* was a case of the administration of the insolvent estate of a deceased person, and *Lord* Cottenham further remarked, as to the rights a mortgage creditor, "a mortgagee has a double security; he has the right to proceed against both and to make the best he can of both. Why he should be deprived of this right because the debtor dies and dies insolvent is not very easy to see."

Then *Sir* Wm. Page Wood, speaking in *Kellock's Case, supra*, of the decision in *Greenwood* v. *Taylor*, said: "This court is not to depart from its own established practice, and vary the nature of the contract between the mortgagor and mortgagee by analogy to a rule which has been adopted by a court having a peculiar jurisdiction, established for administering the property of traders unable to meet their engagements; which property the court found it proper and right to distribute in a particular manner, different from the mode in which it would have been dealt with in the court of chancery. . . . We are asked to alter the contract between the parties by depriving the secured creditor of one of his remedies, namely, the right of standing upon his securities until they are redeemed."

So in this country we find that rule more generally prevailing which allows the creditor holding securities to prove and to receive his dividend on the whole debt. It is asserted in *Judge* Story's work on Equity Jurisprudence, § 524, and in the following cases: *Re Bates*, 118 Ill. 524; *West* v. *Rutland Bank*, 19 Vt. 403; *Moses* v. *Ranlet*, 2 N. H. 488; *Findlay* v. *Hosmer*, 2 Conn. 350; *Logan* v. *Anderson*, 18 B. Mon. 114.

In *Patten's App.*, 45 Pa. 151, it was held, in relation to an assignment made for creditors, that the unsecured creditor has no right to the benefit of the securities held by another creditor, until that other's whole debt was paid.

In *Allen* v. *Danielson*, 15 R. I. 480, 4 New Eng. Rep. 106, which was a case arising under an insolvent assignment, Durfee, *Ch. J.*, delivering the opinion of that court, said: "According to the decided weight of authority the rule is to allow creditors to bring in their claims in full and have dividends accordingly."

That opinion is both well considered and able; and it deliberately overruled a prior decision of the court in the case of *Knowles' Petition*, 13 R. I. 90. The learned chief justice admitted the error into which they had previously fallen, and remarked that they would have decided the case differently, if they had then, as now, the same array of authorities presented, and that, in adopting the other view, not only the correct rule would be established, but the rule which was generally prevalent elsewhere. The counsel for the appellants finds decisions by the courts of Massachusetts, Iowa and Maryland, which undoubtedly conflict with the views we incline to. But I think that, whether we look at this question in the light of reason, or of the adjudged cases, the rule which best commends itself to our judgment is that which leaves the contractual relations of the debtor and his creditors unchanged when insolvency has brought the general estate of the debtor within the jurisdiction of a court of equity for administration and settlement. The creditor is entitled to prove against the estate for what is due to him, and to receive a dividend upon that amount. If the collateral securities are more than sufficient to satisfy any deficiency in the payment of the debt from the dividends, the personal representatives may redeem them for the benefit of the estate.

The order appealed from should be affirmed, with costs.

All concur, **Ruger**, *Ch. J.*, in result, except **Earl** and **O'Brien**, *JJ.*, taking no part.

INDIANA SUPREME COURT.

Board of Commissioners of MONTGOMERY COUNTY, *Appts.*,

v.

Theodore H. RISTINE, Admr., etc.

(.....Ind.....)

1. **Insanity which leads the person afflicted** with it to make indecent exposure of his person in public renders him dangerous to community within the meaning of Rev. Stat. 1881, §§ 5142-5150, which provide for the restraint of such persons at public expense and the re-imbursement of the public treasury out of their estates.

2. **County commissioners are not authorized to enter into contracts** for the care and support of persons in the county asylums for the poor, which are organized solely for the purpose of public charity and benevolence; hence no recovery can be had by them upon a contract to pay for care and support furnished to an insane person.

3. **The law raises no implied obligation** on the part of one received into a charitable institution for support or treatment to pay therefor in the absence of a contract; such relief is referred to motives of charity unless the charter or by-laws of the institution provide that compensation may and shall be demanded.

(*Berkshire, Ch. J., and Olds, J., dissent.*)

(June 5, 1890.)

APPEAL by plaintiffs from a judgment of the Circuit Court for Montgomery County in favor of defendant in an action brought to recover compensation for care and support furnished to an insane person. *Affirmed.*

The facts are fully stated in the opinion.

Mr. **John H. Burford** for appellants.

Messrs. **Kennedy & Kennedy** for appellee.

Mitchell, *J.*, delivered the opinion of the court:

In the year 1878 John W. Hulett was adjudged a person of unsound mind, incapable of managing his estate, and was accordingly placed under guardianship by order of the Circuit Court of Montgomery County. At the September Term, 1874, the guardian appeared before the Board of Commissioners of the County and represented that his ward was possessed of an estate amply sufficient to pay for his board and care, and that, as guardian, he was willing to enter into an agreement with the County Board to pay $3 a week for the board and care of his ward. It was thereupon agreed between the Board and the guardian that the insane ward should be received into the county asylum for the poor, to be boarded and cared for under the supervision of the superintendent of the asylum at the price of $3 per week, and an order was made upon the Commissioners' record accordingly. The ward died in 1887, leaving an estate valued at $3,000. The Board of Commissioners thereupon filed a claim against his estate, in which they set out the foregoing order and agreement, and alleged that the Board had fully complied with its agreement, and that there remained due the County something over $400 on account of board and care furnished the decedent.

By way of inducement it is alleged that the insane ward was wholly incapable of taking care of himself; that he was dangerous and indecent in his habits; that the guardian had no suitable or safe place in which to confine him; that he had been unable, after repeated efforts, to procure anyone to take charge of and care for him, and that he therefore made application to the Board of Commissioners, as above, to have him admitted into the county asylum, where a suitable place had been prepared to keep and take care of such persons as he was.

The question is whether or not the Board of Commissioners was entitled to recover for what remained unpaid at the death of the ward, either upon the contract specially pleaded or for the value of the board and necessaries furnished as upon an implied promise to pay.

The facts as presented make it apparent that the person against whose estate this claim is being prosecuted was insane and dangerous to community, within the meaning of the Statute. One whose insanity is of such a character as to lead him to make indecent exposure of his person in public, and who, on that account, becomes a constant menace to public morality and decency, is as certainly dangerous to community, if suffered to remain at large, as is one who threatens physical injury to others. The Statute, §§ 5142–5150, makes provision whereby such persons may be restrained, under the order of the circuit court, at the public expense. Provision is also made whereby the public treasury may be reimbursed out of the estate of a person dangerously insane, in case he is possessed of an estate. This Statute looks to the protection of the public from those whose insanity makes them dangerous to the community. It has in it no feature of charity to the individual, nor was it enacted with a view to benevolence. If proceedings had been taken under this Statute and the person adjudged insane and dangerous to community had become a charge upon the public treasury, it would have been within the power of the County Commissioners, by the very terms of the Statute, to collect the charges out of the estate of the insane person. Rev. Stat. 1881, § 5147.

No regard was paid to the above Statute. The Constitution provides for the establishment and support of certain benevolent institutions, and confers power upon county boards "to provide farms as an asylum for those persons who, by reason of age, infirmity or other misfortune, have claims upon the sympathy and aid of society." Const. art. 9, § 3.

The Legislature, in devising a charitable scheme for the care and support of the poor, enacted that "every county should relieve and support all poor and indigent persons lawfully settled therein," and that it should be lawful for county commissioners to purchase a tract of land, and to build, establish and organize an asylum for the poor, and employ some humane and responsible person to take charge of them. Rev. Stat. 1881, §§ 6069–6090.

The Statute provides that all poor persons who have become permanent charges on the county may be received into and supported in the county asylum, and the county commissioners are authorized to assess a tax for the support of the poor and for the establishment and maintenance of an asylum; but we find no authority for a county board to admit anyone into the county asylum by contract or to receive pay for the care and support of anyone admitted into the institution. The organization and maintenance of county asylums for the poor, and the care and support of those who are admitted into them, is a part of a scheme of unmixed public charity and benevolence which was inaugurated under the express sanction of the Constitution.

An institution organized for the avowed purpose of bestowing or administering charity, unless specially authorized by its charter to do so, cannot contract to bestow what purports to be a benefaction for a price or to dispense charity for pay. The Statute nowhere authorizes county commissioners to enter into contracts for the care and support of persons in the asylums organized for the care and support of the poor, nor is there any implication that persons who are admitted into those asylums can be so admitted by contract with the county commissioners. In *Switzerland County v. Hildebrand*, 1 Ind. 555, it was held that the provision made by law for the support of the poor was purely charitable, and that a husband could not be held liable for board, lodging and support furnished in the county asylum to his wife. Again in *Noble County v. Schmoke*, 51 Ind. 416, it was held that a contract made by the husband of an insane wife with a board of commissioners for her support in the county asylum was invalid, and that no recovery could be had by the county, even though it had performed the contract. The case first cited was decided in 1849, before the adoption of the present Constitution. The doctrine distinctly enunciated in that case is that the county commissioners have no power to convert an institution that was intended as a public charity into a boarding house for such as wished accommodation for themselves, or for their relations, for pay.

A convention to revise our Constitution, and more than twenty successive Legislatures, have met and adjourned since that decision was promulgated, and all have accepted it as a correct exposition of the spirit and purpose of the Constitution and laws under which provision has been made for the relief of the poor. All the existing laws in relation to those asylums have either been enacted or re-enacted since the decisions above mentioned were promulgated, and yet there is nowhere, even by implication, any power conferred upon county boards to admit persons of any degree or station into a county asylum for pay or by contract. More than forty years ago this court declared, in effect, that these institutions were organized for purely charitable and benevolent purposes; that the work done in them was to be the part of the public in the great labor of love for the unfortunate, that was to be done without money and without price; and the Legislature, the immediate representative of the people, during all this time, has accepted the decisions of this court as correct interpretations of the spirit and purpose of the Constitution and laws. After this great lapse of time we are now asked to overturn the decisions thus acquiesced in, so as to authorize an institution that has all this time been regarded as a noble public charity, to be converted, in part at least, into a house of private entertainment by contract with the county commissioners. If county commissioners may make a contract with the guardian of an insane ward, or the husband of an insane wife, to care for and board the ward or wife, they may enter into contracts with guardians of minor children to have them boarded at the asylum for the poor at an agreed price, or they may enter into contracts with husbands whose wives are not insane for a like purpose. When it is thought advisable to change the policy of the State so as to authorize county asylums to be converted into places for confining and keeping insane persons by contract, or for boarding those who are not agreeable to other members of the family, the change ought to be made by the Legislature, and not by the courts. Our conclusion is that the contract relied on was unauthorized and beyond the power of the County Commissioners, and that no recovery can be had thereon. Nor can there be any recovery upon the *quantum meruit* as upon an implied contract or promise. It is a thoroughly settled proposition that where one is received into a charitable institution for support or treatment the law raises no implied obligation to pay in the absence of a contract. When an individual is received into an institution established solely for benevolent purposes, the law refers his reception and the relief administered to him to motives of charity, unless the charter or by-laws of the society or institution provide that compensation may and shall be charged. An institution or society, no more than an individual, can assume to be dispensing charity and at the same time create a pecuniary obligation against one to whose necessities it ministers. The way-faring man who fell among thieves may have been as rich as Dives, but became under no implied obligation to reimburse the good Samaritan, who set an example of charity by pouring oil and wine into his wounds, and by lodging him at an inn at his own expense. Services which were intended to be gratuitous at the time they were rendered cannot afterwards be used as the basis of an implied promise to pay. *Ramsey* v. *Ramsey*, 121 Ind. 215–222.

In *St. Joseph's Orphan Society* v. *Wolpert*, 80 Ky. 86, it appears that a charitable institution organized for the purpose of educating and maintaining orphan children sought to recover from a guardian the value of raising and maintaining his wards, the children of a deceased soldier. The wards had been raised by the society, with the avowed purpose of bestowing upon them an education as a matter of charity. Learning afterwards that the guardian had in his hands a considerable sum of money which had been paid him by the United States government as pension money, the society brought suit. It was held that, the society having been created for charitable and benevolent purposes, it could not recover for board, care and education of orphans, whose control it had taken with the avowed purpose of bestowing charity. County asylums having, as we have seen, been organized for purposes of charity and benevolence only, the commissioners having no power to admit persons by contract for pay, the law will not raise an implied obligation or promise on the part of one admitted to pay for the value of his board and support. The law will imply that he was admitted through motives of charity. We are aware that there are decisions in some of the States that seem to hold a contrary view. Courts in other States, however, hold to the views enunciated by this court in the cases cited. Our opinion is that the subject is not now open to the courts of this State for further examination, until the Legislature shall have intervened. Whether an overseer of the poor who has furnished temporary relief to a wife or child wrongfully deserted by a husband or parent, can recover from the person in default upon an implied or constructive promise we do not inquire. What we hold is that a person who is admitted into a county asylum organized for the support of the poor cannot be charged therefor either upon an express or implied contract.

The judgment is affirmed with costs.

Berkshire, *Ch. J.*, **and Olds,** *J.*, dissenting:

We are compelled to dissent from the opinion of the court, and briefly state some of the reasons which lead us to a different conclusion.

Conceding that under the law the contract alleged in the appellant's complaint was one which it had no legal right to make, it does not follow that the appellant might not enforce it or recover upon a *quantum meruit*. The guardian of the decedent might, under the circumstances, enter into such a contract, and after his ward was taken into the county asylum and cared for pursuant to the contract, it did not lie in his mouth during the lifetime of the decedent, nor of his administrator thereafter, to deny the authority of the appellant to enter into the contract. It appears that the parties all acted in good faith, and in the light of the circumstances, that which was done was for the best, not only for the decedent, but for the public.

The decedent was an insane person and his condition was such that the public good as well as his own benefit required that he be confined. He had an ample estate to compensate those who might care for him, but no private person could be found prepared and willing to assume the burden and responsibility. The appellant was so situated that it could take the decedent to its poor asylum and give him proper care and attention without in any way abridging the rights and privileges of others supported at said institution. Under such circumstances we can imagine no satisfactory reason why the appellant should not be reimbursed. Every element of an estoppel is present.

The opinion of the court in the main rests upon two former cases decided by this court: *Switzerland County* v. *Hildebrand*, 1 Ind. 555; *Noble County* v. *Schmoke*, 51 Ind. 416.

The last of these cases was decided by a divided court, two out of three of the judges dissenting.

Not only are we of the opinion that these cases are not sound in principle, but we find them to be out of line with the great weight of authority. See *Howard* v. *Whetstone Twp.* 10 Ohio, 365; *Springfield Twp.* v. *Demott*, 13 Ohio, 104; *Hanover* v. *Turner*, 14 Mass. 227; *Jasper County* v. *Osborn*, 59 Iowa, 208; *Templeton* v. *Stratton*, 128 Mass. 137; *Bangor* v. *Wiscasset*, 71 Me. 535; *Dakota* v. *Winneconne*, 55 Wis. 522; *Chester County* v. *Malany*, 64 Pa. 144; *Turner* v. *Hadden*, 62 Barb. 480; *Wertz* v. *Blair County*, 66 Pa. 18; 2 Kent, Com 148; *Ashland County* v. *Richland County Infirmary*, 7 Ohio St. 71; *Goodale* v. *Lawrence*, 88 N. Y. 513; *Arlington* v. *Lyons*, 131 Mass. 328.

In our opinion the judgment ought to be reversed.

OHIO SUPREME COURT.

PITTSBURGH, CINCINNATI & ST. LOUIS R. CO., *Pltf. in Err.*,

v.

William L. D. SHIELDS, by Next Friend.

(47 Ohio St. ....)

*1. **The law requires of those who use dangerous agencies** in the prosecution of their business to observe the greatest care in the custody and use of them.

2. **This duty cannot be shifted** by a master from himself to his servant, so as to exonerate him from the negligence of the servant in the use and custody of them. Where they are so intrusted, the proper custody, as well as the use of them, becomes a part of the servant's employment by the master, and his negligence in either

NOTE.—*Master liable for injuries caused through negligence of servant.*

A party under an antecedent obligation to do a thing, or to do it in a particular way, cannot get rid of his responsibility by deputing it to somebody else. Fowler v. Saks (D. C.) 7 L. R. A. 649, 18 Wash. L. Rep. 206.

To render a person liable for the acts of another the relation of master and servant must exist between them. Ames v. Jordan, 71 Me. 540; Joslin v. Grand Rapids Ice Co. 50 Mich. 516; Hexamer v. Webb, 2 Cent. Rep. 489, 101 N. Y. 377.

A master is not liable for every act of negligence of his servants, but only for such acts of negligence as are permitted while in his service, and in some way connected with such service. Wabash R. Co. v. Savage, 6 West. Rep. 800, 110 Ind. 156.

A principal or master is liable for the acts and negligence of his agent or servant in the course of his employment, although he did not authorize or know of the acts complained of (New Orleans, M. & C. R. Co. v. Hanning, 82 U. S. 15 Wall. 649, 21 L. ed. 220); and even though the servant disobeyed instructions (French v. Creswell, 13 Or. 418; Mound City Paint & C. Co. v. Conlon, 10 West. Rep. 100, 92 Mo. 221); and although the acts were done in disobedience of express orders. Cook v. Houston Direct Nav. Co. (Tex.) Feb. 28, 1890; Driscoll v. Carlin, 10 Cent. Rep. 176, 50 N. J. L. 28.

But this rule does not apply to exemplary damages. Texas Trunk R. Co. v. Johnson, 75 Tex. 158; International & G. N. R. Co. v. McDonald, 75 Tex. 41.

Corporations are liable for the acts of their servants while engaged in their employment, in the same manner and to the same extent that individuals are liable under like circumstances. Merchants Nat. Bank v. State Nat. Bank, 77 U. S. 10 Wall. 604 (19 L. ed. 1008); Weightman v. Washington, 66 U. S. 1 Black, 39 (17 L. ed. 52); Orleans v. Platt, 99 U. S. 676 (25 L. ed. 404).

The master is shielded from responsibility only when the servant steps outside his general duty, and does an act to subserve his own interest or gratify his passions. French v. Cresswell, 13 Or. 418. See *note* to Doyle v. Chicago, St. P. & K. C. R. Co. (Iowa) 4 L. R. A. 420.

Doctrine of *respondeat superior*. See *note* to Ford v. Kendall School Dist. (Pa.) 1 L. R. A. 607.

Instances.

A livery-stable keeper is liable for damage to a horse boarding in a stable, caused by an employé's negligence in the performance of his duties. Eaton v. Lancaster, 4 New Eng. Rep. 772, 79 Me. 477.

A livery-stable keeper is liable for the negligence of his driver temporarily engaged in the service of an undertaker. Hershberger v. Lynch (Pa.) 10 Cent Rep. 389.

The Missouri Statute awarding a penalty whenever any person shall die from an injury occasioned by the negligence of any officer, agent, servant or employé, while running or managing any locomotive, car or train of cars, includes the negligence of any and all servants, and is not limited to that of a superior in command. Rine v. Chicago & A. R. Co. (Mo.) Dec. 21, 1889.

To run a train towards a hand car after warning, without keeping any lookout ahead, is a neglect of duty on the part of the trainmen, for which the railroad company is liable in case of injuries from a collision. Howard v. Delaware & H. Canal Co. (Vt.) 6 L. R. A. 75, 40 Fed. Rep. 195.

See also 11 L. R. A. 773.

regard is imputable to the master, in an action by one injured thereby. And where the injury results from the negligence of the servant in the custody of the instrument, it is immaterial, so far as the liability of the master is concerned, as to what use may have been made of it by the servant.

(May 20, 1890.)

ERROR to the Circuit Court for Preble County to review a judgment, affirming a judgment of the Court of Common Pleas, in favor of plaintiff in an action brought to recover damages for personal injuries alleged to have resulted from the negligence of defendant's servants. *Affirmed.*

The facts sufficiently appear in the opinion.

Mr. **Charles Darlington** for plaintiff in error.

Messrs. **Foos & Fisher,** for defendant in error:

The failure of the servant to do the business or perform a duty imposed on the master is the failure of the master, and if injury results the master is liable.

Weed v. *Panama R. Co.* 17 N. Y. 362; *Philadelphia & R. R. Co.* v. *Derby*, 55 U. S. 14 How. 469 (14 L. ed. 502); *Pittsburgh, Ft. W. & C. R. Co.* v. *Hinds*, 53 Pa. 512; *Stephen* v. *Smith*, 29 Vt. 160; *Goddard* v. *Grand Trunk R. Co.* 57 Me 202; *Craker* v. *Chicago & N. W. R. Co.* 36 Wis. 657, 17 Am. Rep. 504; *Bryant* v. *Rich*, 106 Mass. 180; *Flint* v. *Norwich & N. Y. Transp. Co.* 34 Conn. 554; *Venables* v. *Smith*, L. R. 2 Q. B. Div 279; *Garretzen* v. *Duenckel*, 50 Mo. 104.

When it is said that the master is not responsible for the willful wrong of the servant the language is to be understood as referring to an act of positive and designed injury not done with a view to the master's service or the purpose of executing his orders.

Rounds v. *Delaware, L. & W. R. Co.* 64 N. Y. 129.

This element is not in the case at bar; no injury resulted from the act of using the torpedoes.

Philadelphia & R. R. Co. v. *Derby* and *Craker* v. *Chicago & N. W. R. Co. supra.*

The court held in *Toledo, W. & W. R. Co.* v. *Harmon*, 47 Ill. 298, and in *Chicago, B. & Q. R. Co.* v. *Dickson*, 63 Ill. 151, that when the engineer used the whistle to frighten horses the company was liable for the injury resulting.

Cooley, Torts, pp. 537, 538.

The injury did not result from the direct and positive act of the servant in using the torpedoes, but from a failure on the part of the servant to do the master's business, with which he was intrusted.

Heenrich v. *Pullman Palace Car Co.* 10 Sawy. 80, 20 Fed. Rep. 100, 23 Am. L. Reg. N. S. 459.

Minshall, *Ch. J.*, delivered the opinion of the court:

The suit below was an action by Shields, a small boy, prosecuted by his next friend, against the Pittsburgh, Cincinnati & St. Louis Railway Company for an injury caused by the explosion of a torpedo, wantonly and negligently left on its track by one of its servants, at a point where the children and inhabitants living along the line of the track were daily in the habit of passing with the knowledge and acquiescence of the Company. The torpedo, a dangerous instrument, used by the Company as a signal in the operation of its road, was picked up by a companion of the plaintiff, carried some distance away and caused to explode by one of them hitting it. They were ignorant of its character, and at the time trying to satisfy their curiosity about it. The same accident caused the injury for which the original action in *Harriman* v. *Pittsburgh, C. & St. L. R. Co.*, 45 Ohio St. 11, 9 West. Rep. 438, was brought, the judgment in which was reversed by this court, for error in sustaining a demurrer to the petition; and the petition in the *Harriman Case* is substantially the same as in this case.

After the decision in the *Harriman Case*, the defendant below filed an answer in this case, the second defense of which, and to which a demurrer was sustained, is as follows:

"The defendant, for its second defense, says that it carries upon its trains signal torpedoes to be used in addition to its regular signals, when, from fog or other cause, the other signals cannot be seen or relied upon, and that if said torpedo was placed upon the track as alleged in said amended petition, by the employés of this defendant (a fact which defendant wholly denies), that then said employés placed the same upon the track, at a time and place in broad daylight, when and where there was no necessity for the use thereof, or of any signals of any kind whatsoever, and that said use was without the knowledge or consent or authority, express or implied, of the defendant; was against and contrary to its rules and regulations, as said employés well knew, and that said torpedo was so used by them outside and beyond the scope of their employment, and in no wise connected with the control, management or operation of said train of cars or railroad, and was so placed for the accomplishment of an independent and wrongful purpose of their own, in this, to wit: that said employés, or one of them, while said train was taking water at said water tank, for the purpose of having sport with some lady passengers who were upon said train, took torpedoes from the place where kept on said train, and without the knowledge of said lady passengers, with whom said employés were well acquainted, placed the same upon the iron rails of the track, in front of the wheels of the caboose in which said lady passengers were riding, with the intention to frighten them by the sudden and unexpected explosion of said torpedoes, which would result with a loud noise by the passage of the caboose over them; when said train started forward, one of said torpedoes failed to explode, and was found as stated in said amended petition."

The sustaining of the demurrer to this defense is assigned for error. There is also an exception to the ruling of the court in refusing to charge as requested. But this ruling need not be noticed, as it presents simply the same question as is presented by the demurrer to the answer.

It would seem that the question raised by this defense was presented by the demurrer to the petition in the *Harriman Case*, and determined by the decision of this court therein,—the fourth proposition of the syllabus being, in substance, that the Railroad Company was liable for the negligence of its servant, in placing and leaving the torpedoes on its track at a point where the public, including children, were permitted to pass, "notwithstanding such negligent acts of the servant were wanton, reckless and needless."

But the counsel for the plaintiff in error think that it was not, and claim that there is clear error in the case for the reason that the act of the conductor in placing the torpedoes on the track was a mere caprice of his own, outside of his employment as a servant, and contrary to the rules of the Company; and that therefore the Company is not liable.

We do not adopt this view, and shall show that the negligence of the conductor in this regard, though wanton and contrary to the rules of the Company, occurred within his employment, and is therefore imputable to the Company.

The law requires of persons having in their custody instruments of danger that they should keep them with the utmost care. 1 Hilliard, Torts, 3d ed. 127.

"Sometimes," says Pollock, "the term 'consummate care' is used to describe the amount of caution required, but" he says, "it is doubtful whether even this is strong enough. At least, we do not know any English case of this kind (not falling under some recognized head of exception) where unsuccessful diligence on the defendant's part was held to exonerate him." Pollock, Torts, 407. See also Wharton, Neg. § 851.

And it stands to reason that one charged with a duty of this kind cannot devolve it upon another, so as to exonerate himself from the consequences of injury being caused to others by the negligent manner in which the duty in regard to the custody of such an instrument may be performed. Speaking of the absolute duty imposed by statute in certain cases, or, also, the duties required by common law "of common carriers, of owners of dangerous animals or other things involving by their nature or position special risk or harm to neighbors," Pollock observes, "The question is not by whose hand an unsuccessful attempt was made, whether that of the party himself, or of his servant, or of an 'independent contractor,' but whether the duty has been adequately performed or not." Pollock, Torts, 64.

We in no way limit nor question the soundness of the general rule, which exonerates the master from liability for the acts of his servant done outside of his employment. What has been stated is strictly within the reason and principle of the rule, which is that whatever the servant is intrusted by the master to do for him must be done with the same care and prudence that would be required of the master, acting in that regard for himself; if it be the custody of dangerous instruments, he must observe the utmost care.

The inability of the master to shift the responsibility connected with the custody of dangerous instruments, employed in his business, from himself to his servants intrusted with their use, is analogous to, and may be said to rest upon the same principle as that which disenables him from shifting to an independent contractor liability for negligence in the performance of work that necessarily tends to expose others to danger, unless the work is carefully guarded. It seems by the great weight of authority and reason that this cannot be done. See *Ohio Southern R. Co.* v *Morey*, 47 Ohio St. —, 7 L. R. A. 701, and cases there cited. Also see *Lawrence* v. *Shipman*, 39 Conn. 586, 589; Cooley, Torts, 2d ed 644, 646.

And the relation of master and servant and that of employer and independent contractor are, in this regard, treated in one view by Pollock in his work on Torts, as will appear from consulting his work at page 64.

Now, in this case, it must be observed that the duty intrusted by the Railway Company to the conductor in regard to these torpedoes was, not only to use them as signals with the requisite care and caution, but to observe like care and caution in the custody of them, when not in use. The servant's custody of them when not in use was as much a part of his employment as was the use of them as signals when required. In taking them from the place where they were carried when not in use, and, in mere caprice, placing them on the track for the purpose of frightening the ladies, he was not, it is true, within his employment as to the use of them; but, in so doing, he violated the duties connected with his employment as the custodian of them, and thereby made his master liable for the consequences of his neglect, in the same manner, and to the same extent, as if it had been done by the Company itself.

It is necessary in this and in all similar cases to distinguish between the departure of a servant from the employment of the master, and his departure from, or neglect of, a duty connected with that employment. A servant may depart from his employment without making his master liable for his negligence when outside the employment of the master; and he so departs whenever he goes beyond the scope of his employment and engages in affairs of his own. But he cannot depart from the duty intrusted to him, when that duty regards the rights of others in respect to the employment of dangerous instruments by the master in the prosecution of his business, without making the master liable for the consequences; for the first step in that direction is a breach of the duty intrusted to him by the master, and his negligence in this regard becomes at once the negligence of the master; otherwise the duty required of the master in respect to the custody of such instruments employed in his business may be shifted from the master to the servant, which cannot be done so as to exonerate the master from the consequences of a neglect of the duty.

To better illustrate the ground of this distinction, we may, for example, suppose a servant, with others under his control, employed with a construction train repairing the track of his master. He may, for a time, quit his employment, and, with his men, go off on affairs of his own. Whilst thus out of the master's employment, he may build a fire, which, through his negligence, may consume the property of another; and, in the meantime, loss of life and property may result from a collision with the train negligently left standing on the track. Now whilst, as has been held, the master would not be liable for the loss resulting from the fire, because the act was done outside the servant's employment (*Morier* v.

St. Paul, M. & M. R. Co. 31 Minn. 351), yet it is equally certain that, for the loss occasioned by the servant's negligence in leaving the train on the track, the master would be liable in damages, for the plain reason that, in abandoning the custody of the train, he was guilty of negligence in the employment of the master, whilst, in building the fire, he was not.

That what was done by the conductor contravened the purpose and instructions of the Company, in regard to the use of these torpedoes, does not vary its liability for the negligence of the conductor in the custody of them.

In discussing the master's liability for his servant, it is said by Professor Wharton: "It is not necessary, in order to make the master liable, that there should be specific directions as to the particular act. It is enough if the general relation of master and servant, within the range of such act, exists. The question is simply whether the wrong inflicted was incidental to the discharge of the servant's functions. It may have been capricious. It may have contravened the master's purposes or directions. But a master who puts in action a train of servants, subject to all the ordinary defects of human nature, can no more escape liability for injury caused by such defects than can a master, who puts machinery in motion, escape liability, on the ground of good intentions, for injury accruing from defects of machinery. Out of the servant's orbit, when he ceases to be a servant, his negligences are not imputable to the master. But within that orbit, they are so imputable, whatever the master may have meant." Wharton, Neg. § 160. See also Wood, Mast. and Serv. § 283; Cooley, Torts, 632 (539*).

The custody of these torpedoes was within the servant's orbit. Negligently leaving them on the track was a negligence within that orbit, and therefore imputable to the master. If a master has a duty to perform and intrusts it to a servant, who disregards it to the injury of another, it is immaterial, so far as the liability of the master is concerned, with what motive or for what purpose the servant neglects the duty. This is illustrated by the case of *Weed v. Panama R. Co.*, 17 N.Y. 362, which was an action against the company for a failure to carry the plaintiff to her destination with reasonable dispatch. The delay was caused by the willful act of the conductor in wrongfully detaining the train at a station, and which the defendant claimed exonerated it from liability. But the court held otherwise, it being observed, among other things, in the opinion, that "the obligation to be performed was that of the master, and delay in performance, from intentional violation of duty by an agent, is the negligence of the master."

We do not see that this in any way conflicts with the decision in *Little Miami R. Co.* v. *Wetmore*, 19 Ohio St. 110. There the plaintiff got into a quarrel with the baggage-master of the company about checking his baggage; and under the influence of anger, the latter struck the plaintiff with a hatchet, and it was held that the company was not liable for the injury. A hatchet is not an instrument of danger, within the rule above stated—it includes only such instruments as are such within themselves. The danger of a hatchet is in the hand and spirit of the man who may use it. If, in this case, the instrument left on the track had been a hatchet, the Company would not have been liable to a child who might afterwards have picked it up and been injured by it. For the Company would have been under no such duty, as to its custody, as it was under in regard to this dangerous explosive.

Judgment affirmed.

WISCONSIN SUPREME COURT.

Julius BELOW, *Respt.*,

v.

T. H. ROBBINS, *Appt.*

(.....Wis.....)

1. **A judgment for conversion** of exempt property, including costs, is itself exempt.

2. **The right to pay a debt to the sheriff,** if he has an execution against the creditor for the amount due, under Rev. Stat., § 3028, does not extend to a judgment which is exempt because rendered for the value of exempt property.

3. **Trover and replevin** being concurrent remedies, the fact that a party could have replevied exempt property will not prevent him from claiming as exempt a judgment for the conversion thereof.

4. **Costs on motion** are regarded on appeal as in the discretion of the court below.

5. **Orders entered after decision** of motions will not be set aside to try issues then raised for the first time.

(April 29, 1890.)

APPEAL by defendant from certain orders of the Circuit Court for Langlade County denying defendant's motion to quash an execution, granting plaintiff's motion to cancel the satisfaction of the judgment, and denying defendant's motion to re-open the first two orders, in an action to recover damages for a wrongful levy upon, and sale of, certain property exempt from execution sale. *Affirmed.*

The case sufficiently appears in the opinion.

Messrs. **Bloodgood, Bloodgood & Kemper,** for appellant:

Section 3028, Rev. Stat., provides that "after the issuing of execution against property, any person indebted to the judgment debtor may pay to the sheriff the amount of his debt, or so much thereof as shall be necessary to satisfy the execution, and the sheriff's receipt shall be a sufficient discharge for the amount so paid."

A judgment is the highest form of indebtedness, and if this Statute provides a valid release from a simple-contract obligation (*Kibbee* v. *Howard*, 7 Wis. 150; *Judd* v. *Littlejohn*, 11 Wis. 176), how much more must it apply to a debt the amount of which is judicially found and determined by a court of competent jurisdiction.

A judgment for the conversion of exempt property is not itself also exempt.

Temple v. *Scott*, 3 Minn. 419; *Mallory* v. *Norton*, 21 Barb. 424; Thompson, Homesteads and Exemptions, § 893.

Granting that the value of the exempt property might still be held exempt, a part of the judgment is for damages and costs and does not in any way represent the exempt property.

Tilloteon v. *Wolcott*, 48 N. Y. 190.

Messrs. **Lynch & Latta**, for respondent:

The judgment debtor in this case had no right to pay the amount of the judgment to the sheriff in satisfaction of the execution issued upon the Mock judgment.

Thompson, Homesteads and Exemptions, § 894; *Tilloteon* v. *Wolcott*, 48 N.Y. 188; *Naumburg* v. *Hyatt*, 24 Fed. Rep. 898; *Montgomery County* v. *Riley*, 75 N. C. 144; *Gaster* v. *Hardie*, 75 N. C. 460; *Comstock* v. *Bechtel*, 63 Wis. 656; *Maxwell* v. *Reed*, 7 Wis. 582.

Articles exempted from sale on execution by § 2982, Rev. Stat., of chapter 78, are exempt absolutely to all persons.

Knapp v. *Bartlett*, 23 Wis. 68; *Humphrey* v. *Taylor*, 45 Wis. 251; *Spikes* v. *Burgess*, 65 Wis. 428; *Puett* v. *Beard*, 86 Ind. 172, 44 Am. Rep. 280; *Curlee* v. *Thomas*, 74 N. C. 51; *Wilson* v. *McElroy*, 32 Pa. 82; *Duff* v. *Wells*, 7 Heisk. 17.

There are clear distinctions between the proceeds of exempt property, exempt from attachment, where said property has been voluntarily sold by a debtor, and where taken from him by proceedings against his will, and changed into money.

Thompson, Homesteads and Exemptions, § 748; *Stebbins* v. *Peeler*, 29 Vt. 289; *Keyes* v. *Rines*, 37 Vt. 263; *Mitchell* v. *Milhoan*, 11 Kan. 617; *Houghton* v. *Lee*, 50 Cal. 101; *Cooney* v. *Cooney*, 65 Barb. 524; *Tilloteon* v. *Wolcott*, 48 N. Y. 190; *Watkins* v. *Blatschinski*, 40 Wis. 347.

Plaintiff was entitled to have the pretended satisfaction of the judgment set aside.

Flanders v. *Sherman*, 18 Wis. 575; *Andrews* v. *Rowan*, 28 How. Pr. 126.

Cole, *Ch. J.*, delivered the opinion of the court:

It is not denied that the judgment against the defendant in this case was for the wrongful conversion of property exempt from sale upon execution. In other words, it was for the conversion of a stock of goods, selected and kept by the plaintiff for the purpose of carrying on his trade or business, not exceeding $200 in value. The Statute expressly exempts that amount of stock. Subd. 8, § 2982.

The defendant, as sheriff, had wrongfully seized and sold the stock upon an execution issued on a prior judgment against the plaintiff in favor of S. T. and F. E. Mock, judgment creditors.

After the judgment for the conversion of the exempt property was rendered and docketed, the defendant therein attempted to discharge it by paying the amount thereof to the sheriff of Langlade County, taking a receipt for the same, who had in his hands an *alias* execution issued on the Mock judgment. This was done in pursuance of § 3028, Rev. Stat., which, it is claimed, authorizes such payment. Therefore the question presented is, Does that section of the Statute authorize such a payment and discharge of this judgment for the conversion of exempt property? The section reads: "After the issuing of execution against property, any person indebted to the judgment debtor may pay to the sheriff the amount of his debt, or so much thereof as shall be necessary to satisfy the execution; and the sheriff's receipt shall be a sufficient discharge for the amount so paid." We are clearly of the opinion that this provision was not intended to include, and should not be applied to, a judgment for the value of exempt property. If such a judgment could be discharged by applying the amount on another judgment against the person claiming the exemption, the spirit and policy of the Statute would be defeated, in many cases. This court has uniformly held that the Exemption Laws must have a liberal construction, so as to secure their full benefit to the debtor. It would be useless to grant the privilege contained in these laws if it could be defeated or rendered of no possible value by allowing the judgment for the conversion of exempt property thus to be satisfied. Unless the judgment itself is held exempt, or enjoys the privileged position which the property had which it represents, the debtor is not protected. This is very obvious. Public policy requires such a construction of the above provision that it will not impair in any degree the beneficent intent of the Exemption Law.

In the language of *Commissioner* Leonard, when considering a kindred question in *Tilloteon* v. *Wolcott*, 48 N. Y. 188: "Public policy requires such a construction of the Statute as will insure its full benefit to the debtor. It would be useless to grant the privilege contained in the Statute if it could be rendered of no effect by refusing an adequate remedy for the invasion of the exemption, or by permitting a recovery, when obtained for such invasion, to be wrested from the debtor by proceedings on behalf of creditors. The judgment, when recovered by the debtor for the wrongful invasion of his privilege of the exemption of his property from levy and sale, represents the property for the value of which it was recovered." Page 190.

In the case where this language was used, it was sought to reach by proceedings supplementary to execution a judgment recovered for the value of exempt property, and it was held that it could not be done. *Montgomery County* v. *Riley*, 75 N. C. 144.

It is said the party entitled to the exemption could in this case have fully protected himself by bringing his action of replevin, and have recovered the exempt property. But the counsel on the other side gives a complete answer to this position by saying that the action of trover and replevin are concurrent remedies, and that the plaintiff could pursue either remedy; and further, that, under the Statute of Replevin, the defendant could bond the property, in which case the plaintiff's judgment would be for the recovery of the property or its value. We do not think the plaintiff lost his exemption by bringing the action in the form he did. The judgment for the exempt property is exempt, we think, contrary to the intimation in *Mallory* v. *Norton*, 21 Barb. 424.

In *Temple* v. *Scott*, 3 Minn. 419 (Gil. 306), the Supreme Court of Minnesota reached a different conclusion, and held that the exemption did not attach to the judgment which represented the value of the exempt property. But we must hold otherwise, because we think that the exemption of the Statute must attach to it, in order to give full effect to the intention of the legislation upon the subject.

In *Watkins* v. *Blatschinski*, 40 Wis. 347, it was decided that the money due a judgment debtor from the purchaser of his homestead as a part consideration therefor, and which the debtor intended in good faith to apply to the purchase of another homestead, was not liable to garnishment. It was said that the right given by the law to a debtor to sell and convey the homestead free from all liens would be a barren right, so far as the owner was concerned, if the proceeds of the sale could not be protected until they reached the hands of the vendor, or while in transition from one homestead sold to another purchased. So here it may be said the privilege of the exemption of the stock of goods would be a barren right if the judgment rendered for its value could be discharged by applying the amount on another judgment against the debtor.

The entire judgment, in this case, was exempt, including the costs taxed in the action brought to vindicate the right which the law secured the debtor.

It follows from these views that the orders entered on the 21st day of October, 1889,—one denying the defendant's motion to set aside and quash the execution in the action, and the other granting the plaintiff's motion to set aside and cancel the satisfaction of judgment, and declaring the judgment in full force,—must both be affirmed. The costs on the motion were in the discretion of the court, and we shall not disturb the action of the court on that point. Counsel says, on the motion to set aside the execution, there was not the slightest allusion in the motion papers to the matter of exemption. This position is not sustained by the record. Robbins says, in substance, in his affidavit, that he tendered the balance due on the judgment to the attorneys of the plaintiff, and that they refused the tender "upon the ground that the judgment herein was for exempt property belonging to the plaintiff."

We do not think there was any error in the ruling of the court denying the defendant's motion to re-open the first two orders. The court had already decided and entered these orders, and it would have been irregular to set them aside and try a new issue raised at that stage of the proceedings, as to whether or not the plaintiff had other exempt property.

The three orders appealed from are affirmed.

Lyon, *J.*, took no part.

RHODE ISLAND SUPREME COURT.

Julien L. HERRESHOFF
v.
A. BOUTINEAU.

(.....R. I.....)

1. A contract restraining the exercise of one's calling for a certain time is not necessarily void upon grounds of public policy simply because the restraint extends throughout an entire State.

2. A contract not to teach the French or German language, or aid or advertise to teach them, or be connected in any way with any person, persons or institutions that teach them, in the State of Rhode Island during the year

---

NOTE.—*Contracts in partial restraint of trade.*

Contracts for a limited restraint of trade are valid if entered into for good reasons, such as to afford fair protection to the purchaser of a business. Chappel v. Brockway, 21 Wend. 157; Nobles v. Bates, 7 Cow. 307; Heichew v. Hamilton, 3 G. Greene (Iowa), 596, 4 G. Greene, 317; Hedge v. Lowe, 47 Iowa, 137; Smalley v. Greene, 52 Iowa, 241; Jenkins v. Temples, 39 Ga. 655; Pierce v. Fuller, 8 Mass. 223; Pierce v. Woodward, 6 Pick. 206; Perkins v. Lyman, 9 Mass. 522; Pike v. Thomas, 4 Bibb, 486; Story, Eq. Jur. § 292; 1 Addison, Cont. §§ 272, 508; Powell, Cont. 102.

Where the restraint contracted for appears to have been for a just and honest purpose, for the protection of the legitimate interests of the party in whose favor it is imposed, reasonable as between the parties, and not specially injurious to the public, the restraint will be held valid. Hubbard v. Miller, 27 Mich. 15, 19; Guerand v. Dandelet, 32 Md. 562. Beal v. Chase, 31 Mich. 490; Ewing v. Johnson, 34 How. Pr. 202; Pierce v. Woodward, 6 Pick. 206; Hedge v. Lowe, 47 Iowa, 137, 140.

An agreement between partners, that one of them alone shall conduct the business, is not void as in restraint of trade. Kinsman v. Parkhurst, 59 U. S. 18 How. 289 (15 L. ed. 385).

Secrets of art, not patented, are not within the scope of the law against restraint of trade. Thus, it has been decided that a trader may sell a secret in his trade, and restrain himself, personally, from the use of it. Bryson v. Whitehead, 1 Sim. & Stu. 74; Vickery v. Welch, 19 Pick. 523. See also Jones v. Lees, 1 Hurlst. & N. 189; Metcalf, Cont. 275.

Restrictions as to time.

It is no objection to a covenant in partial restraint of trade that it is unlimited as to time. Diamond Match Co. v. Rœber, 9 Cent. Rep. 181, 106 N. Y. 473.

A contract in restraint of the exercise of a profession, unlimited as to time, but in other respects reasonable, is valid. French v. Parker (R. I.) 6 New Eng. Rep. 494.

Whether a contract in restraint of trade, which is to endure during the life of the promisor or covenantor, is reasonable or not is an undecided question in this State, and such contract is not therefore enforceable by injunction. Mandeville v. Harman, 5 Cent. Rep. 625, 42 N. J. Eq. 185.

The presumption is that a contract in restraint of trade is void. *Ibid.*

A contract not to engage in a particular trade or business in a certain place within a specified time is valid. Arnold v. Kreutzer, 67 Iowa, 214; Hedge v. Lowe, 47 Iowa, 137; Smalley v. Greene, 52 Iowa, 241; Baumgarten v. Broadaway, 77 N. C. 8; Tallis v. Tallis, 1 El. & Bl. 391.

An agreement by a vendor of a mercantile business and its good will, as part consideration, that he will not for five years engage in the same business in the same village, is valid. Washburn v. Dosch, 68 Wis. 436.

See also 12 L. R. A. 428; 14 L. R. A. 80; 15 L. R. A. 598; 18 L. R. A. 657; 20

after the end of a term of employment as teacher, is unreasonable because the restraint extends beyond any apparently necessary protection to the other party, unless it is shown that the latter would be seriously injured by such teaching in any part of the State.

(April 14, 1890.)

SUIT to enjoin the breach of a contract not to teach the French or German language for a certain time within the State of Rhode Island. On demurrer to bill. *Demurrer sustained.*

The facts are fully stated in the opinion.

Mr. **Albert A. Baker** for respondent, in support of the demurrer.

Mr. **Amasa M. Eaton** for complainant, *contra.*

Stiness, *J.,* delivered the opinion of the court:

The complainant, director of a school of languages in Providence, employed the respondent to teach French from January 7, 1889, to July 1, 1889

The contract, in writing, provided that the respondent would not, during the year after the end of his service, "teach the French or German language, or any part thereof, nor aid to teach them, nor advertise to teach them, nor be in any way connected with any person or persons or institutions that teach them, in the said State of Rhode Island."

The respondent's service ended July 1, 1889, after which time he gave lessons in French, in Providence. This suit is brought to restrain him from so doing within the time covered by this contract. The respondent demurs to the bill, contending, *first,* that the contract is void on the ground of public policy, because it imposed a general restraint throughout the State; and, *secondly,* because it is unreasonable. Is the contract void? For a long time, beginning with the Year Books, contracts limiting the exercise of one's ordinary trade or calling met with much disfavor in the courts. Any limitation whatever was considered, in the first reported case (Year Book, 2 Hen. V.,5, pl. 26), so far contrary to law that a plaintiff suing thereon was sworn

---

In Whittaker v. Howe, 3 Beav. 383, an agreement by a solicitor, for valuable consideration, not to practice as a solicitor in any part of Great Britain for twenty years, was held valid. See also Davis v. Mason, 5 T. R. 119.

An agreement by a physician, in consideration of purchase of office and business, not to practice medicine or surgery in a given vicinity thereafter, was held to be valid and binding in Doty v. Martin, 32 Mich. 462.

In Holbrook v. Waters, 9 How. Pr. 335, it was held that an agreement, upon sufficient consideration, not to practice medicine, nor in any manner to do business as a physician in the County of Oswego, at any time from the first day of May, 1851, was valid.

In Mott v. Mott, 11 Barb. 127, a physician sold his interest in an office, furniture, etc., and an established practice, to his partner for a given consideration, and agreed not to practice medicine in the town where the office was located for five years; and the court held the restriction, as to extent of territory and length of time, reasonable for the protection of the party, and the contract binding, citing, in support of this position, Chappel v. Brockway, 21 Wend. 157; Ross v. Sadgbeer, 21 Wend. 166; Hitchcock v. Coker, 6 Ad. & El. 438; Leighton v. Wales, 3 Mees. & W. 545; Horner v. Graves, 7 Bing. 743; Mallan v. May, 11 Mees. & W. 653; 1 Story, Eq. Jur. § 292; Chitty, Cont. 576, Perkins' ed. and cases there cited.

The test to be applied in determining whether a restraint is reasonable or not is to consider whether it is only such as is necessary to afford a fair protection to the interest of the party in whose favor it is given, and not so large as to interfere with the interest of the public. Mandeville v. Harman, 5 Cent. Rep. 629, 42 N. J. Eq. 185.

Restriction as to locality.

A contract in restraint of trade as to a particular place is valid. Chappel v. Brockway, 21 Wend. 157; Jenkins v. Temples, 39 Ga. 655; Smalley v. Greene, 52 Iowa, 241; Hedge v. Lowe, 47 Iowa, 137; Guerand v. Dandelet, 32 Md. 562; Beal v. Chase, 31 Mich. 490; Ewing v. Johnson, 34 How. Pr. 202; Pierce v. Woodward, 6 Pick. 206.

Where a contract is divisible, and is valid as to the place in which made, although void as to the stipulation not to do business "elsewhere," the consideration being sufficient, inquiry will not be made into its adequacy. Smith's App. 5 Cent. Rep. 208, 113 Pa. 579.

A contract restraining one of the parties thereto from the exercise of a trade within a limited locality, when there is reasonable ground for the restriction, is valid. *Ibid.*

In consideration that A would take B as an assistant in his business as a surgeon, for as long a time as should please A, B agreed not to practice on his own account for fourteen years within ten miles of the place where A resided; and the court held the contract valid. See Bunn v. Guy, 4 East, 190; Gale v. Reed, 8 East, 80.

In Smalley v. Greene, 52 Iowa, 241, 243, the defendant had, for a valuable consideration, agreed not to practice law in a specified town, and the contract was held to be valid.

In Bunn v. Guy, 4 East, 190, a contract entered into by a practicing attorney to relinquish his business and recommend his clients to two other attorneys, for a valuable consideration, and that he would not himself practice in such business within 150 miles of London, was held to be valid. See also Heichew v. Hamilton, 3 G. Greene, 596, 4 G. Greene, 317.

If a physician, under a valid contract not to practice in a certain place, is visited at a neighboring place, without his solicitation, by patients from the former place, he has the right to treat them, but their solicitation is no excuse for doing so in the place prohibited. Raub v. Van Horn (Pa.) March 20, 1890.

On the sale of a business, a covenant not to engage in the same business anywhere in the United States, excepting Nevada and Montana, is a partial restraint of trade, and valid. Peckham, *J.,* dissents. Diamond Match Co. v. Roeber, 9 Cent. Rep. 181, 106 N. Y. 473.

The successor and assignee of the purchaser may enforce the covenant. *Ibid.*

A restraint of trade, embracing an entire State, is not necessarily general. *Ibid.*

Where a barber, without shop, patronage or good will to sell, forms a partnership of indefinite duration, and stipulates never to do any barbering in the town outside the shop of his partner, the stipulation is unreasonable and will not be enforced. See *note* to Carroll v. Giles (S. C.) 4 L. R. A. 154.

Contracts in partial restraint of trade may be valid, and if divisible they are not vitiated by one illegal provision. See *note* to Carroll v. Giles, *supra.*

Consideration essential. See *note* to Leslie v. Lorillard (N. Y.) 1 L. R. A. 456.

at by the judge and threatened with a fine. But it was soon found that, to some extent at least, such contracts help, rather than harm, both public interests and private welfare; that they are necessary to trade itself, in order to secure the sale, at fair value, of an established business, by protecting it against the immediate competition of the seller; also to enable one to learn a trade or to get employment from another, free from the risk of having the knowledge and influence thus gained used to the employer's damage; to encourage investment in business enterprises under reasonable safeguards and for other equally evident reasons. Accordingly, exceptions to the early doctrine were recognized from time to time, until the leading case of *Mitchell* v. *Reynolds*, 1 P. Wms. 181, when the court established the rule that a contract in restraint of trade, upon consideration which shows it was reasonable for the parties to enter into it, is good; "that wherever a sufficient consideration appears to make it a proper and a useful contract, and such as cannot be set aside without injury to a fair contractor, it ought to be maintained; but with this constant diversity, viz., where the restraint is general not to exercise a trade throughout the kingdom, and where it is limited to a particular place,—for the former of these must be void, being of no benefit to either party, and only oppressive."

It is to be observed that the contract in this case was limited in time to five years, the term of the lease of a bakehouse, which the plaintiff had bought of the defendant, and also limited in space to the Parish of St. Andrew's, Holborn. The case, therefore, did not call for decision upon a contract running throughout the kingdom. Nevertheless it has since been commonly assumed, as the settled rule of law, that such a restraint is contrary to public policy, and void. The principle upon which this rule is put is, that the public have the right to demand that every person should carry on his trade freely, both for the prevention of monopoly and of unprofitable idleness. The argument is, if the restraint is general throughout the realm, the public interest is interfered with, since the party restrained can only resort to his trade for a livelihood by expatriation. But, if the restraint be local and partial, the party and the public may still have the benefit of his services in his own land, in some other place. While this distinction has frequently been recognized, the cases in which it has had the sanction of a decision have been few.

In *Rousillon* v. *Rousillon*, L. R. 14 Ch. Div. 351, Fry, *J.*, mentions only two, and these, he says, seem to have been decided upon the ground of unreasonableness, rather than upon the ground of universality. In other words, the universality was held to be unreasonable. This case, following *Whittaker* v. *Howe*, 3 Beav. 383; *Jones* v. *Lees*, 1 Hurlst. & N. 189, and *Leather Cloth Co.* v. *Lorsont*, L. R. 9 Eq. 345,—expressly holds that there is no absolute rule that a covenant in restraint of trade is void, if it is unlimited in regard to space.

The respondent urges that *Rousillon* v. *Rousillon* has been overruled by the recent case of *Davies* v. *Davies*, L. R. 36 Ch. Div. 359; but we do not think this is so. While Cotton, *L. J.*, showing great willingness, if not anxiety, to overrule it, based his opinion upon the ground that the restriction was void, because unlimited in space, Bowen, *L. J.*, did not put his decision on that ground, and Fry, *L. J.*, adhered to his opinion in *Rousillon* v. *Rousillon*. That *Davies* v. *Davies* was not received in England as overruling the last-named case, see *note* to this case in Law Quarterly Review, vol. 4, 240. In view of these cases, we do not think it is now the rule in England that restraint throughout the kingdom is absolutely void.

In this country the cases have been quite similar to those in England. In the recent case of *Diamond Match Co.* v. *Roeber*, 106 N. Y. 473, 9 Cent. Rep. 181, Andrews *J.*, says: "It is worthy of notice that most, if not all, the English cases which assert the doctrine that all contracts in general restraint of trade are void, were cases where the contract before the court was limited or partial. The same is generally true of the American cases." In that case the defendant covenanted, for the period of ninety-nine years, not to engage in the manufacture or sale of friction matches, within any of the States or Territories of the United States, except Nevada and Montana. The complainant sought to restrain a breach of that covenant in New York, the respondent claiming that the covenant, being general as to New York, was void. But the court declared it to be valid, in a strong and thorough opinion, showing the history of litigation, and the tendency of recent judicial decisions upon this subject. Taking this case in connection with *Oregon Steam Nav. Co.* v. *Winsor*, 87 U. S. 20 Wall. 64 [22 L. ed. 315], we think it cannot be said here, any more than in England, that a restraint is absolutely void, upon grounds of public policy, because it extends throughout a State.

Public policy is a variable test. In the days of the early English cases, one who could not work at his trade could hardly work at all. The avenues to occupation were not as open nor as numerous as now, and one rarely got out of the path he started in. Contracting not to follow one's trade was about the same as contracting to be idle, or to go abroad for employment. But this is not so now. It is an every-day occurrence to see men busy and prosperous in other pursuits than those to which they were trained in youth, as well as to see them change places and occupations without depriving themselves of the means of livelihood, or the State of the benefit of their industry. It would therefore be absurd, in the light of this common experience now, to say that a man shuts himself up to idleness or to expatriation, and thus injures the public, when he agrees, for a sufficient consideration, not to follow some one calling within the limits of a particular State. There is no expatriation in moving from one State to another, and from such removals a State would be likely to gain as many as it would lose. We do not think public policy demands an agreement of the kind in question to be declared void, and we do not think such a rule is established upon authority. We therefore hold that the agreement set out in the bill is not void simply because it runs throughout the State.

Is the contract unreasonable? Courts should be slow to set aside as unreasonable a restriction which has formed a part of the consideration of a contract; yet, when it is a restriction upon individual and common rights, which only oppresses one party without benefiting the other, all courts agree that it should not be enforced. In determining the reasonableness of a contract, regard must be had to the nature and circumstances of the transaction. For example, if one has sold the good will of a mercantile enterprise, receiving pay for it, upon an agreement not to engage in the same business in the same State, for a certain time, such a stipulation would stand upon quite a different footing from a similar stipulation of a mere servant in an ordinary local business. In many undertakings, with modern methods of advertising and facilities for ordering by telegraph or mail, and sending goods by railroad or express, it would matter little whether one was located at Providence or Boston or some other place. In such cases a restriction embracing the State, or even a larger territory, could not be said on that account to be unreasonable; for without it the seller might immediately destroy the value of what he sold and was paid for. But it is unreasonable to ask courts to enforce a greater restriction than is needed. So it has been uniformly held that restrictions which go too far are void. As was said in the *note* of the Law Quarterly Review, above cited: "Covenantees desiring the maximum of protection have, no doubt, a difficult task. When they fail, it is commonly because, like the dog in the fable, they grasp at too much, and so lose all."

Besides the matter of protection, the hardship of the restriction upon the party and the public should also be considered. In the present case, we think the restriction is unreasonable,—not as a rule of law because it extends throughout the State, but because it extends beyond any apparently necessary protection which the complainant might reasonably require, and thus, without benefiting him, it oppresses the respondent, and deprives people in other places of the chance which might be offered them to learn the French and German languages of the respondent. The complainant urges that he has established a school in Providence, at great expense, to teach languages by a new method, where scholars come from all parts of the State, and that by reason of the small extent of the State, and the ease of passing to and fro within it, such a restriction is reasonable and necessary to keep teachers from setting up similar schools, and enticing away his scholars. All this may be true with reference to Providence and its vicinity. But while, as is averred, many pupils from all parts of the State may come to Providence, as a center, for the same reason few would go to other places. For example, a school in Westerly or Newport would not be likely to draw scholars from Providence, or places from which Providence is more easily reached. Indeed, the complainant says he offered after the contract was made, and now offers, to allow the respondent to teach in Newport, thereby admitting that the restriction is greater than the necessity. The people of Newport, Westerly and other places have the right to provide for education in languages without coming to Providence. It is hard to believe, and the bill does not aver, that losing the few, if any, from some such place who might leave the complainant, if the respondent were to teach there, would seriously affect the complainant's school. Teaching in Providence, or in any place from which the complainant receives a considerable number of pupils, might affect it, and a restriction limited accordingly might be reasonable; but we think it is unreasonable to go further. The complainant bought nothing of the respondent whose value he now seeks to destroy. He hired the latter as a teacher at no more than fair wages. He needs and has the right only to be secured against injury to his school, from teachers who may entice away his scholars, after leaving his employ. The contract clearly goes beyond this.

The demurrer must be sustained.

MICHIGAN SUPREME COURT.

PEOPLE OF the State of MICHIGAN
v.
Herman FOSS, *Appt.*

(....Mich.....)

1. **A strip of grass** left to grow in a rural or country road on the side of the beaten track belongs to the owner of the fee, and he has the right to harvest it.

2. **A person has no right from mere caprice or express malice to drive** upon and destroy a strip of grass growing between the two ditches on the sides of a highway, in the space usually known as the wrought or traveled part of the road, but on the portion of which another person owns the fee.

3. **Merely pushing off the horses of another** from grass which one is entitled to cut in a highway, where the other is wantonly endeav-

NOTE.—*Easement; owner of soil right to use of highway.*

By the common law, the fee in the soil remains in the original owner where a public road is made upon it; but the use of the road is in the public. Barclay v. Howell, 31 U. S. 6 Pet. 498 (8 L. ed. 477).

If the road should be vacated by the public, the owner resumes the exclusive possession of the ground. *Ibid.*

Title remains in the owner of the soil, on its appropriation for a public highway. See *note* to Illinois Cent. R. Co. v. Houghton (Ill.) 1 L. R. A. 213; New Jersey Z. & I. Co. v. Morris Canal & Bkg. Co. (N. J.) 1 L. R. A. 133.

In Massachusetts, where a mere easement is taken for a public highway, the soil and freehold remain in the owner of the land; and upon the discontinuance of the highway, the soil and freehold revert to the owner of the land. Harris v. Elliott, 35 U. S. 10 Pet. 25 (9 L. ed. 333).

On the appropriation of land for an easement the owner retains every right in the soil not inconsist-

See also 17 L. R. A. 626.

ering to spoil the grass, and then defending against the latter's attack, does not make one guilty of assault and battery.

(May 9, 1890.)

APPEAL by defendant from a judgment of the Circuit Court for St. Clair County convicting him of an assault and battery. *Reversed.*

The facts are fully stated in the opinion.

Messrs. **Avery, Jenks & Avery,** for defendant, appellant:

Defendant, being the owner of the fee, was the owner of this grass, and being the owner of it and having property rights in it, he had all the rights incident to the ownership of property and among these the right to protect and preserve it; and for the purpose of harvesting it he had a right to go into the highway, and the complaining witness had no right to interfere with defendant in the exercise of this right.

Woodruff v. *Neal,* 28 Conn. 167; *Suffield* v. *Hathaway,* 44 Conn. 521; *Stackpole* v. *Healy,* 16 Mass. 33; Cooley, Torts, 318; *Holladay* v. *Marsh,* 3 Wend. 142; *Campau* v. *Konan,* 39 Mich. 362.

It was a question of fact for the jury to determine whether it was necessary for the complaining witness to drive on this grass in order to have the usual rights of one of the public in the free and ordinary use of the public highway; he did not as a matter of law have the absolute right to go on this grass and destroy it and render it worthless merely because his fancy or caprice might lead him there.

Adams v. *Rivers,* 11 Barb. 390; *Phifer* v. *Cox,* 21 Ohio St. 255; *Adams* v. *Emerson,* 6 Pick. 57; *People's Ice Co.* v. *The Excelsior,* 44 Mich. 229.

The defendant and his father had a perfect right to protect their own property and prevent complainant from destroying it, which he was doing at the time the assault occurred.

Drew v. *Comstock,* 57 Mich. 181.

Mr. **Seward L. Merriam,** for the State, appellee:

The fact that grass was growing in the highway where intended and prepared for public travel, is simply the result of public caprice in selecting generally one track instead of many while exercising the continuous right, at all times, that each person enjoys of traveling such portion of the wrought highway as he sees fit so long as he does not interfere with the lawful public (not private) rights of others.

Daniels v. *Clegg,* 28 Mich. 36; *Pigott* v. *Engle,* 60 Mich. 228.

A highway is a public way for the use of the public, and the restrictions on its use are only such as are calculated to secure to the general public the largest practical benefit from the enjoyment of the easement.

Macomber v. *Nichols,* 34 Mich. 216.

Any part of a highway may be used by the traveler, and in such direction as may suit his convenience or taste.

Stinson v. *Gardiner,* 42 Me. 248, 66 Am. Dec. 283.

In *Tonawanda R. Co.* v. *Munger,* 5 Denio, 255, 49 Am. Dec. 244, it was held that grass in the highway was private property as against the right of another to graze or pasture it. This is as far as the court could be expected to go. Grazing and pasturing are not the public rights to which highways are dedicated, but on

---

ent with the easement. Platt v. Pennsylvania Co. 1 West. Rep. 17, 43 Ohio St. 228.

As against the public the owner may make any use of the land which does not interfere with the paramount right of the public to the easement. Palatine v. Kreuger, 9 West. Rep. 759, 121 Ill. 72; Jackson v. Hathaway, 15 Johns. 447; Baker v. Shephard, 24 N. H. 208; Adams v. Emerson, 6 Pick. 57; Barclay v. Howell, 31 U. S. 6 Pet. 498 (8 L. ed. 477); Angell, Highw. chap. 7.

The owner of the soil has a right to all above ground except only the right of passage for the king and his people. Goodtitle v. Alker, 1 Burr. 133.

The owner of the soil over which another has an easement is entitled to the herbage. Smith v. Langewald, 1 New Eng. Rep. 449, 140 Mass. 205; Perley v. Chandler, 6 Mass. 454; Adams v. Emerson, 6 Pick. 57; Atkins v. Boardman, 2 Met. 457.

The owner has a right to the herbage growing on the right of way. Blake v. Rich, 34 N. H. 282. But see Troy & B. R. Co. v. Potter, 42 Vt. 265.

The herbage on the highway belongs to the owner of the soil, and where another grazes his cattle thereon he is liable to an action for the trespass. Woodruff v. Neal, 28 Conn. 165; Cool v. Crommet, 13 Me. 250; Stackpole v. Healy, 16 Mass. 33; Avery v. Maxwell, 4 N. H. 36.

While it is used as a highway the owner is entitled to the timber and grass which may grow upon the surface, and to all minerals which may be found below; and he may bring an action of trespass against anyone who obstructs the road. Barclay v. Howell, 31 U. S. 6 Pet. 498 (8 L. ed. 477).

The owner of the fee is the owner of the minerals under the surface, and of the soil, gravel, trees and herbage, except as needed in constructing or repairing the road. Platt v. Pennsylvania Co. 1 West. Rep. 17, 43 Ohio St. 228; Kansas Cent. R. Co. v. Allen, 22 Kan. 285; Taylor v. New York & L. B. R. Co. 38 N. J. L. 28; Preston v. Dubuque & P. R. Co. 11 Iowa, 15; Aldrich v. Drury, 8 R. I. 554; Hasson v. Oil Creek & A. R. R. Co. 8 Phila. 556.

May maintain and defend his rights to use of soil.

As against a stranger not using the land as a highway, the rights of the owner of the soil are the same as though the highway had never been established, and he may maintain his rights against such stranger by the usual remedies. Taylor v. Armstrong, 24 Ark. 102; Peck v. Smith, 1 Conn. 103; Read v. Leeds, 19 Conn. 182; Thomas v. Ford, 63 Md. 346; Gidney v. Earl, 12 Wend. 98; Piollet v. Simmers, 106 Pa. 95; Bolling v. Petersburg, 3 Rand. (Va.) 563. See Lewis, Em. Dom. § 589.

A person may resist an aggression upon his property if he uses no more force than is necessary to expel the invader. Harrison v. Harrison, 43 Vt. 417; Drew v. Comstock, 57 Mich. 176.

The question whether the force employed was excessive is generally one of fact. Hanson v. European & N. A. R. Co. 62 Me. 84; Currier v. Swan, 63 Me. 323; Com. v. Bush, 112 Mass. 280; Com. v. Mann, 116 Mass. 58; State v. Taylor, 82 N. C. 554; Edwards v. Leavitt, 46 Vt. 126.

Where a party exceeds the limits of necessary protection he becomes himself a trespasser. Dole v. Erskine, 35 N. H. 503; Trogden v. Henn, 85 Ill. 237; Steinmetz v. Kelly, 72 Ind. 442; Bartlett v. Churchill, 24 Vt. 218.

the contrary are a hindrance and annoyance thereto.

Morse, *J.*, delivered the opinion of the court:

Defendant was convicted of assault and battery upon one August Steiman in justice's court. Upon appeal to the Circuit Court for the County of St. Clair, he was again convicted by the verdict of a jury. He brings his case to this court upon exceptions before judgment.

The place of the alleged assault was in a public highway, and, as the defendant claims, upon that portion of the same within the half adjoining his father's lands. The farm of the complainant lies opposite his father's, and on the other side of this highway. There is a ditch running close to the fence on defendant's father's side of the road. Between this ditch and the usually traveled track of the highway there was a strip of grass land, from a rod to a rod and a half in width, extending the whole length of the father's premises. Grass had grown there many years, and, when in condition, had been cut, sometimes by defendant and his father, and occasionally by Steiman. There had been more or less controversy about this grass, which finally culminated in the affray causing this suit. The defendant lived with his father. On the 15th of June, 1889, Steiman was drawing rails from his fence, on the Smith side of the road, to his orchard, using the highway for that purpose. He was drawing the rails upon a crotch between three and four feet wide. Steiman, after loading, drove on the north side of the center of the road, outside of the beaten or traveled track, and upon the grass. Defendant was mowing. Steiman claims that he told defendant to get out of the way. The elder Foss was there with a bushel basket and rake, gathering the cut grass into the basket. They acted as if they did not hear Steiman, and he "told his horses to git up, and the boy then went on the north side of the road, and the old man stood on the south side of the road; . . . and as I went by the boy cut my horse on the back side with the scythe with which he had been mowing." They had some hard words, and Steiman testifies that as he was driving on defendant came up behind him, and struck him twice on the neck. Steiman was corroborated in his testimony by his son. Defendant testified that Steiman came across the road and drove his team upon him; that he threw his scythe into the fence corner, and shoved the horses back with his hands. Steiman dropped his lines "and hauled off," and said: "I will kill you." "When I see he was going to hit me, I pushed him back. I gave him two pushes,—one after the other; and, when he see I was pushing him, he went straight across the road and got a scythe, and came up to me, and hauled off three times, and says: 'I cut you in two.'" Defendant stepped back out of his way, and finally Steiman went away, with threats of future hurt to defendant. Defendant was supported in his testimony by the evidence of his father.

The record also states that other witnesses were produced by the prosecution who gave testimony in corroboration of the facts testified to by Steiman and his son; and the defendant produced other witnesses who gave evidence in corroboration of the facts sworn to by himself and his father. The excuse of Steiman for driving on the grass was that the road was muddy. He admitted that there was grass on his own side, but claimed that it was n t wide enough to drive on. The testimony on the part of the defendant showed that the road was sandy, and, although it had rained two days before, the road was not muddy. The beaten track was somewhat nearer Steiman's fence than it was that of Foss; but it is clear that Steiman drove over the grass for the express purpose of damaging it, as there was room between the beaten track and the uncut grass to drive upon the sward where the grass had been cut. It is also evident upon the record that there was bad blood between the parties, growing out of their rights in the highway as claimed by each. It was claimed by Steiman that Foss had pastured his cattle in the road, and that he had forbid it, because they trespassed upon his side of the highway, but that he did not quarrel with Foss about the grass on Foss' side of the road. He admitted, however, that he cut it one year, and pastured it an ther. Foss and his son testified that Steiman told them that, if they would let him have one swath on their side of the road, he would make them no trouble, and that, when he drove upon the grass, he also purposely stamped it down with his feet.

The defendant's counsel requested that the following instruction be given to the jury, which was refused: "That the defendant had a legal right to cut the grass on his side of the highway; that the grass there growing belonged to him,—as much so as the grass growing on any other part of his farm,—and, for the purpose of harvesting the grass so growing on his side of the highway, he had a right to be there, in person, for that purpose, either of his own right or as the servant of his father, who appears to be the owner of the land, so long as he did not interfere with the free and ordinary use of the highway for public travel. And also that defendant had a right to protect the grass, and in so protecting it from being run over and destroyed by Steiman, he would be justified in using as much force as would be necessary to keep Steiman from destroying it; and, if the jury found that no more force was used than was necessary to protect it, their verdict should be for the defendant."

The court was also asked to charge, in substance, that Steiman was a trespasser on that side of the highway, and liable to be put off by the defendant, if no more force was used than was necessary to protect the grass, unless the jury found that it was necessary for Steiman to drive there in order to have the free and customary use of the highway for public travel. The circuit judge refused to so charge, and instructed the jury that, as to the question of the right of Steiman to travel where he did in the highway, as a matter of law, a person had a right to travel where he pleased upon any part of the wrought portion of the highway; that it was usual to dig ditches on each side, and throw the earth taken from that, and construct a road-bed; and that the travel is usually between these ditches; and that any person, in traveling along the highway about his business, has the right, absolutely, to go where he pleases, so long as he does not interfere with other persons traveling on the highway." I think the public, or any one of the public, has a right to go wherever their judgment might dictate, or their caprice may lead them to go; that, because it happens that the beaten track is in a certain locality, it need not always remain just there, and we know, as a matter of fact, it changes according to the caprice of the public or circumstances, of which I might enumerate many, and one person has a right to commence to change that track as well as another. There may be reasons why a person may desire to go upon grass ground instead of the beaten track; and, whatever the reason may be, I instruct you, as a matter of law, that a person has a right to go where he chooses along that wrought portion of the road. And, if it is a fact that the defendant in this case made an assault upon Mr. Steiman because he persisted in exercising that right, and in driving upon the grass, and struck him, then he is guilty of assault and battery as charged in the complaint."

The point in controversy is thus sharply defined by defendant's requests and the charge of the court above stated. It seems to me a novel and interesting question. It is undisputed that Steiman was driving upon growing grass within the wrought portion of the highway, but outside of the beaten or customary track of wagons, and within that portion of the highway the fee of which was in defendant's father. The defendant was under age, and working for his father. The father had the right to this grass not only as against Steiman, but all the world, unless it was necessary to destroy it for the needs of public track. If Steiman had cut the grass and carried it away, Foss could have sued him in trespass for so doing, and recovered from him in trover the value of the grass thus converted. This is certain, within all the authorities. The fee of the land was in Foss, subject only to the easement of the public to use it for the purpose of highway. He had the right to use it, and to enjoy the profits of it, in any way not incompatible with the public enjoyment of the right of way. *Woodruff* v. *Neal*, 28 Conn. 169; *Suffield* v. *Hathaway*, 44 Conn. 521, 527; *Starkpole* v. *Healy*, 16 Mass. 33; Cooley, Torts, 318; *Holladay* v. *Marsh*, 3 Wend. 142; *Campau* v. *Konan*, 39 Mich. 362, 365; *Adams* v. *Emerson*, 6 Pick. 57; *Clark* v. *Dasso*, 34 Mich. 86; *People* v. *O'Brien*, 60 Mich. 8-13; *Ellsworth* v. *Lord*, 40 Minn. 337; *Wolf* v. *Holton*, 61 Mich. 550-553; Washb. Easem. 4th ed. 10; *Coburn* v. *Ames*, 52 Cal. 385.

It is plain enough from this record that the complaining witness Steiman drove where he did without necessity, and for the express purpose of destroying the grass.

The question arises whether he had the right, from mere caprice or express malice, to destroy this grass by driving upon it, and stamping it under his own and his horses' feet, because it happened to be between the two ditches, and in a space usually known as the wrought or traveled part of the road, when he would have no right to go and cut and carry it away for his own use. I think not. If the jury had found that Steiman drove on this grass, when it was not necessary, for the purpose of damaging or destroying it, and that all defendant did was to push the horses off from it, and, when attacked by Steiman for this, did no more than was necessary in order to push him away from him, it would have been their duty to have acquitted him. It may not be desirable that grass should grow and be harvested in the wrought portion of the highway, but when, upon a rural or country road, the travel has been in a uniform beaten track, leaving grass to grow and ripen undisturbed upon the sides of such track, no one but the abutting landowner, who owns the fee, has the right to harvest it; and he can not only maintain trespass or trover against any person cutting and taking it away against his will, but he has the right to protect it against wanton or malicious damage or destruction, whether it is attempted to be done under the guise of travel upon the highway or in some other way. In this case the complaining witness could not have destroyed this grass by turning his cattle upon it to pasture it. Neither, in my opinion, could he drive his horses and wagon upon it to trample it under foot, when it was not at all necessary to do so, and while he knew Foss and his son were at work gathering it. The law does not permit or encourage any "dog in the manger" business of this kind.

In *Phifer* v. *Cox*, 21 Ohio St. 248, the plaintiff brought an action to recover damages for the destruction of a hedge within the limits of a highway. The court held that, so long as the enjoyment of a right of way was unobstructed, there was no reason why the easement of a highway should afford a justification to an individual for the needless destruction of property belonging to the owner of the land merely because it happened to be within the bounds of the road as laid and established. And in *People's Ice Co.* v. *The Excelsior*, 44 Mich. 229-233, *Judge* Marston says: "Ordinarily, it may be said that the entire width of the highway may be used, yet the owner of the land over which it passes may, within the limits thereof, plant trees, set posts and do such other acts as will add to his convenience or assist in beautifying his premises. He is encouraged in doing this by public sentiment. . . . Public convenience may in time, in particular locations, require the removal of some of these things; and, whenever the necessity arises, and the public authorities request their removal, then the private must give way to the public or paramount right. But, while permitted to remain, no one traveling the highway could willfully injure or destroy them; and, should anyone do so, he would justly be held responsible notwithstanding his plea of a claim of right to travel over any part of the highway." And at page 234, 44 Mich., speaking of the relative rights of the steamer and the riparian proprietor, he says: "The right of navigation, while paramount, is not exclusive, and cannot be exercised to the unnecessary or wanton destruction of private rights or property, where both can be freely and fairly enjoyed."

So, in this case, while the right of travel upon the highway was paramount, Steiman could not exercise that right, in caprice or wantonly, to destroy the property—the grass—without any necessity of Foss, where both the right of travel and the harvesting and preservation of this grass could be freely and fairly enjoyed.

The Circuit Court was in error; and the verdict of the jury must be set aside, and a new trial granted the defendant.

The other Justices concurred.

Cornelius KNIGHT
v.
Henry U. LINZEY *et al.*

(......Mich.......)

1. **If an innocent party has been defrauded into giving notes** he is not obliged to contest them in the hands of a stranger on any information short of a certainty that the latter is not a bona fide holder before bringing an action against the party defrauding him.

2. **If a person having no knowledge of the scheme** of the Bohemian oat business, or of the corporate existence of the pretended company, or of the want of integrity of its purpose, and the honesty of its business, relies entirely upon and believes the statements of another that there is such a corporation, and that its business is honest, he is not precluded on the ground of guilty participation from maintaining an action for fraud against the person who induced him to give his notes in pursuance of such scheme, although it is fraudulent.

3. **If a man, knowing that a scheme is fraudulent,** and that the natural outcome of it will be to defraud some innocent person, goes into it solely for the purpose of making money out of it, though he may not be equally in fault with another, who is the moving party in the fraud and influences him by his persuasions and representations, a court will, on the ground of public policy, deny him any relief against the other party.

(May 2, 1890.)

ERROR to the Circuit Court for Shiawassee County to review a judgment in favor of plaintiff in an action brought to recover from defendants the amount of certain notes alleged to have been procured by them through fraud and sold to third persons. *Reversed.*

The facts are fully stated in the opinion.

Messrs. **Watson & Chapman,** for defendant Linzey, appellant:

Whenever a note, of the kind mentioned in this case, is obtained by fraud, the note is void between the parties, and the presumption of fraud follows the note all along its way, and cannot be recovered upon until evidence is introduced sufficient to overthrow such presumption of fraud, and satisfy a jury that the holder of the same is a bona fide owner, and an innocent purchaser.

Davis v. *Seeley*, 15 West. Rep. 412, 71 Mich. 209.

When a party, with full knowledge of all the facts, pays a demand unjustly made upon him, it is a voluntary payment, and cannot be recovered, and it makes no difference if the transaction out of which it grew was illegal and fraudulent; his payment is voluntary, and he cannot recover the amount paid.

Chitty, Cont. pp. 933, 934, and cases there cited.

A man who goes into a transaction of this kind, as the plaintiff testifies he did, knowing that it was a fraudulent scheme, should not be allowed by the courts to recover for the money paid out on account of it.

Story, Eq. Jur. 3d ed. p. 199; *Ætna Ins. Co.* v. *Reed*, 33 Ohio St. 283; *Slaughter* v. *Gerson*, 80 U. S. 13 Wall 379 (20 L. ed. 627); *Brown* v. *Leach*, 107 Mass. 364; *Long* v. *Warren*, 68 N.Y. 426; *Parker* v. *Moulton*, 114 Mass. 99; *Chrysler* v. *Canaday*, 90 N.Y. 272; *Mamlock* v. *Fairbanks*, 46 Wis. 415; *Schwabacker* v. *Riddle*, 99 Ill. 343.

When a man has full knowledge of a transaction and knows all about it, he cannot be allowed to shut his eyes to the facts and rely upon representations made to him by another

NOTE.—*Relief from contract obtained by fraud.*

The maker of a note given for Bohemian oats, induced to give it by persistent acts and misrepresentations, will not be denied relief on the ground that he is *in pari delicto.* See *notes* to Hess v. Culver (Mich.) 6 L. R. A. 498; Evans v. Stuhrberg (Mich.) 6 L. R. A. 501.

The maker of negotiable paper may defend an action brought by a bona fide purchaser for value before maturity, upon the ground that he was induced to sign the paper by false representations as to its character. The burden of proving this, and his freedom from laches, rest upon him. National Exch. Bank v. Veneman, 43 Hun, 241.

It is against the policy of the law to enable either party to enforce an agreement in fraud of the law or which was made to injure another. Randall v. Howard, 67 U. S. 2 Black, 585 (17 L. ed. 269).

A defendant who seeks to share in the fruits of a contract cannot complain that it was fraudulently procured. Bissell v. Foss, 114 U. S. 252 (29 L. ed. 126).

A party to a fraudulent contract may forfeit his right to treat it as void by his conduct in relation to it. Burton v. Stewart, 3 Wend. 236.

The general rule is, in cases of executed contracts, where both parties are guilty of actual fraud, a court of equity will not lend its aid to either. Anderson v. Merideth, 82 Ky. 564.

The exception to the general rule applies where the mind of one of the actors of the fraud exercises an undue influence on the other. In this state of the case, although the grantor has been guilty of fraud, equity will adjudge rescission and adjust the equities between them, and will allow the grantee his expenses in managing the estate while it was in his hands. *Ibid.*

Where parties are concerned in illegal agreements or other transactions, whether they are *mala prohibita* or *mala in se,* courts of equity, following the rule of law as to participators in crime, will not grant relief in accordance with the maxim, *in pari delicto potior est conditio defendentis.* Bromley v. Smith, 2 Hill, 517; Vandyck v. Hewitt, 1 East, 96; Howson v. Hancock, 8 T. R. 575; Browning v. Morris, Cowp. 790; Osborne v. Williams, 18 Ves. Jr. 379; Buller, N. P. 131; Harrington v. Bigelow, 11 Paige, 349, 5 N. Y. Ch. L. ed. 158; Warburton v. Aken, 1 McLean, 460; Foley v. Greene, 1 New Eng. Rep. 17, 14 R. I. 618; Green v. Corrigan, 3 West. Rep. 627, 87 Mo. 359; Keel v. Larkin, 83 Ala. 142; Le Warne v. Meyer, 38 Fed. Rep. 191.

Where the scheme or contract is *malum in se* and the parties to it are *in pari delicto,* the law refuses to aid either of them against the other, but leaves them where they have placed themselves by their own acts. Smith, Cont. 3d Am. ed. *187-191; Burt v. Place, 6 Cow. 431; Nellis v. Clark, 20 Wend. 24, 4 Hill, 424; Thomas v. Richmond, 79 U. S. 12 Wall. 349 (20 L. ed. 453); Smith v. Hubbs, 10 Me. 71; Schermerhorn v. Talman, 14 N. Y. 94; Knowlton v. Congress & E. Spring Co. 57 N. Y. 518; Howson v. Hancock, 8 T. R. 575.

See also 14 L. R. A. 405; 38 L. R. A. 176.

party and be allowed to recover upon those representations, no matter how fraudulent they are.

Whiting v. *Hill*, 23 Mich. 399; *Bridge* v. *Penniman*, 7 Cent. Rep. 742, 105 N. Y. 642; *Pratt* v. *Philbrook*, 41 Me. 132.

The benefits and burdens growing out of the illegal business cannot be distributed or equalized. The law will have nothing to do with the transaction in any way except to declare it void.

Ward v. *Doane* (Mich.) Nov. 1, 1889.

Such a scheme as the one developed in this case is against public policy, and plaintiff being a party to the fraud, the law will leave him where it found him.

Davis v. *Seeley*, *supra; McNamara* v. *Gargett*, 12 West. Rep. 650, 68 Mich. 454.

Mr. **A. L. Chandler**, for plaintiff, appellee:

This case is like other Bohemian oat cases, except in the degree of moral turpitude shown by this defendant.

Hess v. *Culver* (Mich.) 6 L. R. A. 498.

The defense do not pretend the representations made by them were true. There was no corporation such as they claimed there was, and consequently no president, secretary, seal, agents or assets. This was fraudulent.

Holcomb v. *Noble*, 14 West. Rep. 56, 69 Mich. 396.

If this was a gambling contract the party who lost is entitled to recover back what he paid to defendant, which in this case was two notes of the value of $300 and interest.

Hess v. *Culver*, *supra*.

As Linzey enjoyed the fruits of this transaction as of a sale of valid notes, he ought to be estopped from invoking any infirmity in it for his own benefit.

Daniels v. *Tearney*, 102 U. S. 415 (26 L. ed. 187); *Cook* v. *Finkler*, 9 Mich. 133.

He must be held to intend the consequences of his own act.

Allison v. *Chandler*, 11 Mich. 542; *McNamara* v. *Gargett* and *Davis* v. *Seeley*, *supra; Merchants Bank* v. *McClelland*, 9 Colo. 608; *National Bank* v. *Young*, 5 Cent. Rep. 118, 41 N. J. Eq. 531.

Whiting v. *Hill*, 23 Mich. 404, does not decide that Knight could not rely on Linzey's representations, and must rely on independent knowledge. Knight sought the best information he could get.

Picard v. *McCormick*, 11 Mich. 74; *Converse* v. *Blumrich*, 14 Mich. 121; *Eaton* v. *Winnie*, 20 Mich. 166.

When a charge covers the entire case it must all be read and considered together.

Dibble v. *Nash*, 47 Mich. 592.

Mr. **S. S. Miner**, also for plaintiff, appellee:

This being a Bohemian oat scheme, the transaction was void on the grounds of public policy, and Knight had his action against Linzey and Davison for the fraud.

Hess v. *Culver* (Mich.) 6 L. R. A. 498.

Linzey and Davison having transferred the notes before they were due, and a few days after they were given, and having received pay for them and appropriated the money to themselves, will not be heard to say that "Knight did not use sufficient diligence in trying to avoid payment of the note."

Evans v. *Stuhrberg* (Mich.) 6 L. R. A. 501.

Morse, *J.*, delivered the opinion of the court:

This is another Bohemian oat case, and comes here from the Shiawassee Circuit Court, where the plaintiff recovered judgment. The declaration is framed upon the same theory as those in the cases of *Hess* v. *Culver* (Mich.) 6 L. R. A. 498, and *Pearl* v. *Walter*, 45 N. W. Rep 181 (present term). The plea was the general issue. The same objection was made to the introduction of proof under the declaration as we have recently noticed in the last case above mentioned, and will need no further attention.

The principal points raised in the case relate to the charge of the court. It was alleged in the declaration that the plaintiff was induced to make two notes, one for $100 and one for $200, and that these notes were sold before due, by the defendant Linzey, to an innocent purchaser for value. It appeared upon the trial that the $200 note was sold before due to one Edward Rose, and the $100 note to one Silas Frye, and that the plaintiff had paid them to these parties before bringing suit. Linzey sold the note to Rose, and Davison the note to Frye. Linzey testified that he told both Rose and Frye, before they purchased the notes, that they were given for Bohemian oats, and that he informed plaintiff of this fact before he paid the notes. Plaintiff, however, denies that Linzey told him anything of the kind; and Rose swears that he did not know the note was given for Bohemian oats until after he purchased it. Frye was not sworn. Reuben Johnson testified that he heard Linzey tell Rose that the note was given for Bohemian oats before Rose bought it; and two other witnesses swore that they heard Linzey tell plaintiff that, if he was in Knight's place, he would not be in a hurry about paying the notes, as Rose knew what they were given for before he purchased.

The counsel for the defendants insisted upon submitting to the jury the question whether or not Rose and Frye, or either of them, were innocent purchasers of the notes, and requested the court to instruct the jury that, if they found both of them not to be innocent purchasers, and plaintiff knew it, his payment of the notes to them was voluntary, and he could not recover, or, if either of them was not an innocent purchaser, and plaintiff knew it, he could not recover for the note held by such one, and also submitted the following request, in addition: "*Ninth*. The notes in question in this suit were void, and the purchasers thereof are supposed to know for what they are given, and could not recover upon the notes of plaintiff until they first proved, by a preponderance of evidence, that they were innocent purchasers of the same; and it became the plaintiff's duty to make a fair and diligent inquiry into the facts, and ascertain whether they were innocent purchasers before he paid the notes, and, if he paid them without making such inquiry, then he made the payment voluntarily, and cannot recover in this case; and, before he can recover, he must prove, by a preponderance of evidence, that said Rose and Frye were innocent purchasers of the notes."

The court gave these requests, but qualified the last or ninth by adding: "Unless the jury should find that there was fraud practiced on the plaintiff in obtaining the notes from him by Linzey and Davison, and of which fraud plaintiff had no knowledge or information at the time he gave said notes."

Counsel also requested a charge, as to each note, that, if they found the purchaser (Rose or Frye) not an innocent purchaser, and that he knew for what the note was given, then the plaintiff, if before payment he had been reliably informed of facts which showed that such purchaser was not a bona fide one for value, was not obliged to pay the same, and it became a voluntary payment, and he could not recover of Linzey the amount of such payment. This was given, with the qualification annexed to the ninth request.

These directions were, if anything, more favorable to the defendants than the law is. If the plaintiff, an innocent party, was defrauded into giving these notes, he was not obliged, upon information obtained from the party who had defrauded him, or any other information short of a certainty, to contest these notes in the hands of a stranger to the transaction of their inception, and who would be presumably an innocent holder of them. He was not compelled to take the chances of two lawsuits to obtain relief from, or redress for, the fraud committed upon him. The court charged the jury, substantially, as requested by the defendants, that, if the plaintiff entered into the transaction, knowing that in the end some person or persons must be defrauded, and knew how the oats were bought and sold, then plaintiff and defendants were engaged in a transaction against public policy, and therefore void; and the law would leave each of them, where they had left themselves, without redress, and the plaintiff could not recover if he knew of the common fraud. This charge was correct, but it is claimed that the circuit judge entirely neutralized the effect of it by stating subsequently in his charge as follows, it being the plaintiff's third request: "Knight had a perfect right to rely upon the statements of Linzey, and was not bound to seek information elsewhere, and Linzey was bound to make true statements to Knight; and, if he made false statements to Knight which were material, and Knight relied upon such statements, and believed them, and parted with his two promissory notes, and afterwards paid said notes, and Knight was not equally in fault with Linzey, then Knight would be entitled to recover."

The court further said in his general charge, in reference to this subject: "I charge you that if two men, of equal knowledge, enter into a contract, deliberately, for the purpose of doing an act which is fraudulent, and the tendency of which is to contravene the principles of the common law, or in violation of the Statute, then each would be equally in fault: and, so long as the contract remains unperformed, neither party would be aided at law or in equity to its enforcement. The law would leave them where they have placed themselves. But if they were not equally in fault,—and this doctrine applies where the action is brought upon the contract,—if one of them was influenced by the judgment of the other, did not act upon his own knowledge of the facts, and was ignorant of the facts until he was informed by the other party of their existence, and relied upon the judgment of the other party, and upon his statements of the facts communicated to him by the other party, and believed them to be true, and then relied upon the judgment of that other person, he at the time believing and relying upon that other person as to the existence of the facts communicated to him, as to the honesty of the subject matter of the contract entered into,—of its being lawful,—he would not in such case be a knowing and guilty participant in the violation of law, or in contravention of public policy. If the plaintiff in this case had no knowledge of the scheme of the Bohemian oat business,—had no knowledge or information of the corporate existence of the pretended company, or the want of integrity of its purpose, and the honesty of its business,—and relied entirely upon the defendant's statement, from his long acquaintance with him, and believed that the corporation was organized as stated, and believed that its business was an honest one, and his own judgment was subordinated to that of the defendant and the man Davison, or either of them, he could not be as equally to blame as those from whom he got his information, and on whose judgment he relied." This part of the general charge was certainly good law, well and clearly expressed.

But following this the court referred to the Legislative Act of 1887 as being aimed, not at the man who made the note, but at the one who procured it and put it in circulation. He said the Act did not apply to or govern the case in hand, as the notes were made long before it passed, but that he referred to it as illustrating the views of the prominent men who composed the Legislature. "It makes a man a criminal who procures a note by falsehood, and puts it in circulation, but does not say anything about the man who gives the note." He then closed his directions as follows: "I therefore charge you that if you find that Linzey, in the presence of Davison, made the representations stated in the declaration,—whether he knew them to be false or not would make no difference,—and the plaintiff was influenced thereby, and relied upon them, and believed them to be true, and acted upon them, then he would not be equally at fault; and if the plaintiff has been injured thereby, he will be entitled to recover the amount he actually paid, with interest at six per cent from the time of payment to date. But if he had knowledge, and he acted upon his own knowledge and judgment, knew that the scheme was fraudulent, and made a contract for gain, and was equally guilty of contravening public policy, then your verdict should be for the defendant. The action is brought for the fraud which he alleges was practiced upon him, and not upon the contract that was made, and the contract is referred to for the sole purpose of proving the extent of the injury sustained, in case of fraud practiced. The plaintiff must prove fraud by a preponderance of evidence that satisfies you of that fact, and you must find that the plaintiff did not knowingly participate in it. A man cannot very well be said to participate in an unlawful act when his mind is a blank so far as the facts are concerned; and where the facts are stated by another, and impressed upon his mind, his act is built upon the declarations and information conveyed by that other, and of which he has no independent knowledge. The conduct and representations of the defendants Linzey and Davison may be considered by you in determining the relations of this party to the fraud, if one was committed; and you may consider, also, what took place soon after between these two men, in the absence of the plaintiff, in disposing of the notes."

It is very plain to me that the jury must have been misled by the instructions of the circuit judge, taken as a whole. The third request of the plaintiff, as given, is not sound law. It must be conceded that Knight was not equally in fault with the defendant Linzey, as Linzey was the moving party in the fraud, and by his persuasion and representations influenced Knight more or less in the transaction. But if Knight knew it was a fraud, and went into it solely for the purpose of making money out of it, knowing that, if he made any money some innocent third party must be defrauded thereby, and that this was the natural outcome of the scheme, the law will not permit him to recover back from Linzey what he paid to him, as it would be money knowingly paid in furtherance of fraud; and a recovery, under such circumstances, would be against public policy. "The benefits and burdens growing out of the illegal business cannot be disturbed or equalized. The law will have nothing to do with the transaction in any way, except to declare it void." *Ward* v. *Doane*, 48 N. W. Rep. 982.

Under this third request the jury may well have inferred that Knight had a right to rely upon the statements of Linzey, independent of his own knowledge and belief, and, being not equally in fault, might recover back the money paid upon the notes, although he knew at the time he gave them that the whole scheme was a fraud, and that, if he won, it must be that someone else would lose by a like transaction, out of which he must obtain his profit. This is not the law. The latter part of the general charge was also misleading. When the court said: "But, if he had knowledge, and he acted upon his own knowledge and judgment,—knew that the scheme was fraudulent, —and made a contract for gain [and was equally guilty of contravening public policy], then your verdict should be for the defendant,"—the insertion of the clause which I have inclosed in brackets made that bad law which would have been good law without it; for, if he knew the scheme was a fraud, and acted upon his own knowledge and judgment, he could not well have been deceived by the defendants, and whether or not he was equally guilty with them of contravening public policy became of no moment. In such a case the plaintiff would take his chances, as does one upon the throw of a dice-box.

Unless the jury was misled by the charge of the court, it would naturally seem, from the plaintiff's own testimony, that they must have found against him. He testified on cross-examination as follows:

Q. You are a school-teacher, or was?

A. I taught school a few terms.

Q. Until you found you could make more money as a farmer than a teacher? Why did you go into the Bohemian oat business,—for what purpose? What was the object of it?

A. I supposed I would make a little money out of it according to their representation.

Q. You went into the Bohemian oat business, knowing it was a fraud and a swindle, for the purpose of making money,—thought you could, the way it was represented to you?

A. Yes, sir.

Q. You didn't go into it for any other purpose than to make money?

A. Not a bit; no, sir.

Q. You understood it to be a fraudulent, but a money-making, scheme, by which you were going to have sold forty bushels of oats at $15 per bushel—did you not?

A. Yes, sir.

Q. And that was the inducement that led you to get into it, believing that you could make that much money out of it, though you knew it was a fraud?

A. I thought I could make some money out of it.

Q. I asked you if you knew it was a fraud, and that to make money was the inducement that led you to go into it?

A. Yes, sir.

Q. You didn't expect the Bohemian oat business could run always, did you? You thought it would go down at some time?

A. I didn't know it would.

Q. I ask you, didn't you think that it would have to go down some time?

A. I didn't know but it might.

Q. Didn't you expect it was going down at some time?

A. I didn't know whether it would or not.

Q. Didn't you expect it was going down at some time?

A. Yes, sir.

Q. But you didn't expect it was going down before your bond was raised?

A. I didn't know anything about that.

Q. You didn't think it was going down before your bond was raised, did you?

A. I didn't know that it would.

Q. You didn't think it would?

A. No, I did not.

Q. But finally you thought someone would get caught just as you have been caught now?

A. I didn't know they would.

Q. I am not asking you what you knew, but if you thought that.

A. Yes, sir.

Q. At the time that you went into it?

A. No, sir; I did not know that anybody was going to get caught.

Q. I am not asking you what you knew about the scheme. Did you know how the business was done?

A. Yes, sir.

Q. I ask you now, and you have told me you expected it was going down,—that thing could not run always. You expected it would go down,—that somebody would lose on it,—didn't you?

A. Yes, sir.

Q. You knew they must lose, didn't you?

A. Yes, sir.

Q. So you knew, if your contract was carried out, someone would, in the end, lose his money?

A. Yes, sir.

Q. And you thought you would make some out of it?

A. Yes, sir; I thought I would make a little.

Q. You went into a speculation to make something for nothing, and got left, didn't you?

A. Yes, sir; a $300 note.

It is suggested that many of these questions were double, and therefore misleading; that the answers might have referred to the first part of these double questions, and not to the whole; and that plaintiff did not understand the full import and meaning either of the questions, or the questions and answers taken as a whole. But the testimony above quoted was the last evidence he gave as to the reasons that actuated him in going into this transaction, and remains unexplained in the record. It may be that he was led into these statements by the skill and ingenuity of the attorney who cross-examined him; but, if so, his attorney did not, for some reason, attempt to get him out of the trap into which he had fallen, if trap it was. But, unexplained, the logic of this testimony was that Knight well knew what the scheme was,—that it was a fraud and a swindle for the purpose of making, and the inducement for going into it was to make, money fraudulently; and he also knew that, if his contract was carried out, somebody, in the end, must lose money by his gain. He went into this fraud "expecting to get something for nothing, and got left." What matter is it to the courts, under this testimony, whether or not Linzey made false representations to the plaintiff? Upon this evidence, unexplained, the plaintiff plainly barred himself from recovery. While the Legislature has wisely shaped the law so as to punish criminally the men who are traveling about the country procuring notes like these, and as Linzey procured this one, there still is no redress for the plaintiff, under his own showing, against these defendants, until the Legislature shall see fit to provide him a remedy by statute. The unwritten law will give him no relief, and, in my opinion, very properly leaves him where he has put himself, because he went into it with full knowledge of what he was doing, and that the transaction was unlawful. His testimony does not show a case "where he was influenced by the judgment of other" or that he "did not act upon his own knowledge of the facts, and was ignorant of the facts until he was informed by the other party of their existence, and relied upon the judgment of the other party, and upon his statements of the facts, and believed them to be true, and then relied upon the judgment of that other person as to the existence of the facts communicated to him as to the honesty of the subject matter of the contract entered into," and believed it to be lawful. In view of his testimony above quoted, it cannot be said that the representations to plaintiff that the company was incorporated could have influenced him to believe the transaction lawful; for it is not to be presumed that, knowing what he says he did about the scheme, he would believe that such a fraud could be legalized by incorporation, or that such a swindle as the plaintiff admits that he knew this to be would be permitted, much less made lawful, by the State.

This is a different case from that shadowed forth in the declaration in *Pearl* v. *Walter* (present term), where the plaintiff was afraid there was "something wrong" in it at first, but had his fears overcome and his suspicions removed by the representations of those who seemed to know more than he did about the matter. Here the plaintiff says he knew it was a fraud, and that he could not gain unless some other person than defendants lost, and that, really, the only inducement that led him into it was his cupidity and greed. He was not actually deceived, and he was "consciously wrong." See *Hess* v. *Culver* (Mich.) 6 L. R. A. 498.

He knew what the fraud was, but thought he might get his money out of it, and the profit with it, before the scheme collapsed. He took the chances that the fraud might not be operated upon him, but upon someone else for his benefit.

The verdict should have been, as the record stands, for the defendants. It may be that on another trial the plaintiff may make a better showing as to his want of knowledge of the fraud, and his reasons for entering into it; but, as the case appears here a new trial must be granted to the defendants, with costs of this court, and *the judgment of the lower court reversed.*

The other Justices concurred.

TENNESSEE SUPREME COURT.

Barnett R. HUGHES, *Appt.*,
v.
Benjamin F. BROWN *et al.*

(......Tenn.......)

1. **A disclaimer by a person sued as trustee** long after his appointment, and who has never executed a bond as such, relates back to the time of his appointment.

2. **An action against cestuis que trustent** may be maintained without having any trustee as a party, where there is a vacancy in the trusteeship.

3. **The bar of the Statute of Limitations** against a suit brought against a woman and her

---

NOTE.—*Statute of Limitations; application to trusts.*

The Statute of Limitations has no application to an express trust where there is no disclaimer. Seymour v. Freer, 75 U. S. 8 Wall. 218 (19 L. ed. 310).

It has no application until disavowal by the trustee. Horne v. Ingraham, 14 West. Rep. 567, 125 Ill. 198.

The Statute does not run against a trust until disavowed by the trustee. Reynolds v. Sumner, 13 West. Rep. 327, 126 Ill. 58; Thomas v. Merry, 12 West. Rep. 672, 113 Ind. 83; Ward v. Harvey, 10 West. Rep. 223, 111 Ind. 471; Bent v. Priest, 1 West. Rep. 752, 86 Mo. 475; Rucker v. Dailey, 66 Tex. 284; Dyer v. Waters (N. J.) Feb. 3, 1890.

Where the relation of parties is that of trustee and

children, all being *cestuis que trustent*, there being no trustee, is not saved, under Code, § 2755, by the pendency of a suit until within one year preceding against the woman and her husband and a person as trustee who was no longer such, which suit was dismissed because of the failure to make the children, who were remaindermen, as well as *cestuis que trustent*, parties to the proceeding.

4. **A suit to charge the payment of an equitable claim** upon a trust estate, although purely equitable, is subject to the Statute of Limitations.

5. **A remedy at law on the bond of a trustee having proved inadequate** by reason of the insolvency of the sureties, a remedy in equity to reach property not subject to execution is barred when delayed until the bond and also the decree thereon are barred.

(February 27, 1890.)

APPEAL by complainant from a decree of the Chancery Court for Williamson County in favor of defendants in a suit to enforce payment out of a trust estate, of a debt alleged to have been created by the trustee for the benefit of the trust. *Affirmed.*

The facts sufficiently appear in the opinion.

Mr. **Jesse G. Wallace** for appellant.

Mr. **N. N. Cox**, for appellees:

Although the claim may be purely equitable, yet it is sought to raise an implied lien or equity as security for the debt. Such implied lien, although the creature of equity and enforcible only in equity, is barred in seven years.

Thompson v. *Thompson*, 3 Lea, 126; *Fisher* v. *Fisher*, 9 Baxt. 72; *Armstrong* v. *Campbell*, 3 Yerg. 231.

Lurton, *J.*, delivered the opinion of the court:

Complainant's bill is filed for the purpose of enforcing out of the trust estate payment of a debt created by the trustee for the benefit of the trust. The property which he seeks to charge is a tract of land, with the improvements, held in trust for the support and maintenance of the defendant, Mrs. Virginia Brown, and her children, remainder at death of Mrs. Brown to her children then living and the representatives of such as are dead. In default of such issue, then the remainder is devised to the surviving sisters of Mrs. Brown, and on the death of such survivors to the issue of such. This land was purchased by the trustee at a chancery sale had for the purpose of enforcing a vendor's lien in favor of complainant as the executor of the will of Mrs. Brown's father. The bid of Davis, as trustee, was, upon application of Mrs. Brown, credited with what was then supposed to be the interest of Davis' *cestui que trust* under the will of complainant's testator. To protect complainant in event it should turn out that this credit was in excess of the share of his *cestui que trust*, Davis was required to execute a refunding bond, with two sureties, conditioned, upon final settlement of complainant's account as executor, to refund to him any sum in excess of the true share of the *cestui que trust* by reason of this credit. Upon execution of this bond, title was vested in T. H. Davis as trustee, no lien being retained by reason of the circumstances under which the purchase money was paid. Upon the final settlement of the executor's accounts in the chancery court, it was ascertained that the interest of Mrs. Brown had been largely overpaid, and on October 24, 1870, summary judgment was rendered on the refunding bond theretofore executed against Davis as trustee and his sureties on the bond, and execution was awarded. The children of Mrs. Brown were not parties to any of the consolidated causes in which the proceedings just recited were had, though their mother and the trustee

cestui que trust, the Statute of Limitations does not commence to run until there has been an open denial and repudiation of the trust by the trustee, brought home by the *cestui que trust* in such manner as will require the latter to act as upon an asserted adverse title. Key v. Hughes, 32 W. Va. 184.

Time begins to run against a trust only from the time when it is openly disavowed by the trustee, who insists upon an adverse right or interest which is fully and unequivocally made known to the *cestui que trust*. Chicago & E. I. R. Co. v. Hay, 7 West. Rep. 720, 119 Ill. 507; Speidel v. Henrici, 120 U. S. 377 (30 L. ed. 718).

In the absence of open disavowal of the trust by the trustee, a bar to an action against him can only be created by the lapse of twenty years. De Bardelaben v. Stoudenmire, 82 Ala. 574.

The trusts to which the Statute does not apply are: (1) direct and continuing; (2) exclusively cognizable in equity; (3) arising between trustee and *cestui que trust*. Yorks' App. 1 Cent. Rep. 660, 110 Pa. 77.

As between trustee and *cestui que trust*, direct trusts are not reached by the Statute. Somerset County Bank v. Veghte, 4 Cent. Rep. 407, 42 N. J. Eq. 39. See Rucker v. Dailey, 66 Tex. 284.

It is only to pure or direct trusts that the equitable rule denying the validity of the defense of the Statute applies. It does not apply to implied trusts, where there is concurrent equity and law jurisdiction. Newsom v. Bartholomew County, 1 West. Rep. 475, 103 Ind. 526; Rush County v. State, 1 West. Rep. 536, 103 Ind. 497.

The Statute of Limitations runs in favor of a defendant chargeable as a trustee of an implied trust, and it is not necessary, in order to set the Statute in motion, that he should have denied or repudiated the trust. In such case the Statute begins to run when the wrong complained of is done, and the limitation is four years. Hecht v. Slaney, 72 Cal. 363.

In case of an implied or constructive trust, unless there has been a fraudulent concealment of the cause of action, lapse of time is as complete a bar in equity as at law. Speidel v. Henrici, 120 U. S. 377 (30 L. ed. 618).

One who becomes a trustee merely by construction of law may plead the bar of the Statute. Mathews v. Simmons, 49 Ark. 463.

Application of Statute to equitable actions.

Application of the Statute in equity is by way of analogy. Yorks' App. 1 Cent. Rep. 354, 110 Pa. 69.

Where there is both a legal and equitable remedy for the same cause of action, if the legal remedy is barred by lapse of time, the equitable remedy will also be held to be barred. Smith v. Wood, 6 Cent. Rep. 316, 42 N. J. Eq. 563.

If a party has a legal title and a legal right of action, and, instead of proceeding at law, resorts to equity, the same period of time that would bar him at law will bar him in equity. Butler v. Johnson, 111 N. Y. 204.

See *note* to Dieffenbach v. Roch (N. Y.) 2 L. R. A. 829.

Davis were. A part of this decree of October, 1870, has been paid off. Davis, as trustee, received no fund whatever, and the entire trust fund is represented by the lands so purchased by him. He and his sureties are insolvent, so that nothing has been or can be made off of them. This bill is filed against all of the *cestuis que trustent* for the purpose of collecting the balance due on the decree as a charge upon the trust estate.

The first defense to be considered is that the necessary parties are not before the court. Davis, the trustee, in 1874 passed his accounts in the original case in which he had been appointed, and tendered his resignation. This was accepted, and by the same decree B. F. Brown, the husband of Virginia Brown, was appointed in his room and place, and required to execute a bond as such. This it appears that he has never done. He is now sued as trustee. By answer, he now disclaims having accepted the appointment. After so long a lapse of time, even in the absence of proof indicating an acceptance, he might, but for this disclaimer, be presumed to have accepted. The disclaimer, however, must be taken to relate back to the time of the appointment. *Goss* v. *Singleton*, 2 Head, 79; Hill, Trustees, 206-219.

The objection that the legal title was not vested in him formally by decree would be unimportant if he had accepted the appointment, for by implication vestiture of title would have resulted from his appointment without formal words. *Wooldridge* v. *Planters Bank*, 1 Sneed, 297.

The decree denuding Davis of his trust probably operated to devest him of the legal title, and the refusal of Brown to accept the trust leaves the title in abeyance. It is clearly a case of a vacancy in the trusteeship. The property is within the jurisdiction of the court, and all of the *cestuis que trustent* are parties defendant. There being no trustee, the court has the power to make a decree binding the property. 2 Perry, Tr. § 878.

A much more serious defense is that of the Statute of Limitations. The decree on the refunding bond was rendered October 24, 1870. This bill was filed May 21, 1887, nearly seventeen years after the cause of action accrued. Manifestly, upon the facts stated, the complainant would have been entitled to the relief he seeks if the bill had been filed in time. To meet this defense the complainant first relies on the fact that in 1879, and within the time limited for action on judgments and decrees, he filed a bill in equity seeking the same relief, and this case was a pending suit until December, 1886, when it was dismissed by this court without prejudice. Within one year thereafter this bill was filed, and he now insists that the case falls under section 2755 of the Code, which provides that when a suit is commenced in time, and a decree is rendered against the complainant on any ground not concluding his right of action, a new suit may be brought within one year. This is a good answer to the plea of the Statute, provided that suit and this are substantially for the same cause, and the parties in each suit are identical. The defendants to the former suit were Brown and wife and F. H. Davis. The remaindermen were not parties, and for this very reason that cause was dismissed. Davis was sued as trustee in the former case. He did not answer, and no *pro confesso* seems to have been taken against him. It now appears that when that suit was begun Davis was not the trustee. Though B. F. Brown was a defendant in that case, yet, as we have seen, he was not the trustee, and was not sued as such. Thus we have a case where it was sought to reach and fasten a charge upon that property, when only one of a number of *cestuis que trustent* were before the court, and where there was no trustee. There are cases where the trustee may stand for and be treated as a representative of his *cestui que trust*, but the general rule is that all the *cestuis que trustent*, and the trustee, if there be one, should be made parties to a suit affecting the trust estate. 2 Perry, Tr. §§ 873, 874.

The fact that there was no trustee before the court, and only one of the *cestuis que trustent* was a party, ought not to and cannot have the effect of suspending the Statute of Limitations. Neither can that suit have any effect, as against Mrs. Brown, for the reason that neither in that nor in this was it sought to reach and subject any particular interest that she had to the satisfaction of this debt. In that case and in this the effort is to subject the trust property as an entirety to the satisfaction of a demand against it, and not to subject the interest of Mrs. Brown to a debt for which she was personally bound. Neither has Mrs. Brown any such separate interest as can be distinguished from that of her children without injury to them and their interest. The trust is for the support of Mrs. Brown and her children, and so long as they constitute a part of her family their interest in the trust cannot be affected by assuming that the mother has a life estate, which can be taken from her without injury to them. *Hix* v. *Gosling*, 1 Lea, 568.

This suit is therefore not against the same parties who were defendants to the former suit, and the two suits cannot be so connected as to save the bar of the Statute.

The learned counsel for the complainant very earnestly insists that the Statutes of Limitation do not operate upon claims and demands purely equitable, and for which there is no adequate remedy at law, and the demand which he represents is one exclusively cognizable in a court of equity. This presents a question of great interest to the profession, for it is important to know whether there are cases other than express trusts which are unaffected by the legislation limiting the time within which suits may be brought. This question has been a matter of controversy from the earliest history of equity, and, while we have much dicta, there are no reported cases in this State which are controlling in the determination of the point. The earlier English and American Statutes of Limitations alike operated in terms on the form of action. Thus our Act of 1715, which continued in force in this State until the codification of our Statute Law in 1858, prescribed that all actions of trespass, detinue, trover and replevin, all actions of account and upon the case, all actions of debt for arrearages of rent, actions of assault, menace and battery, should be brought within the time therein specified. These were actions at law, and hence it was said the Statute was not in terms applicable to bills in equity, that form of suit not being mentioned.

The conclusions to be drawn from the precedents of controlling influence as to the applicability of the Statutes of Limitations to courts of equity before the change made by the Code of 1858, whereby they were made to apply to the cause rather than to the form of action, are these:

1. That courts of equity, having at all times discouraged laches, did after the Legislature had prescribed a bar to legal actions, and upon the maxim, *equitas sequitur legem*, adopt the time prescribed in such statutes as barring a suit in equity upon any cause of action on which an action at law might have been maintained. *Elmendorf* v. *Taylor*, 23 U. S. 10 Wheat. 168 [6 L. ed. 294]; *Smith* v. *Clay*, 3 Bro. Ch. 640, *note; Hovenden* v. *Annesley*, 2 Sch. & Lef. 632; *Porter* v. *Cocke*, Peck (Tenn.) 48; *Shelby* v. *Shelby*, Cooke, 184; *Armstrong* v. *Campbell*, 3 Yerg. 232; *Hickman* v. *Gaither*, 2 Yerg. 200.

2. The application of the Statutes in equity was determined by the cause of action, rather than the nature of the equitable relief sought. The fact that the legal action was inadequate to obtain the relief which a court of equity could administer did not take the case out of the bar prescribed for the legal action on the same cause. "In all cases," said *Lord* Camden in *Smith* v. *Clay*, "when the legal right has been barred by Parliament, the equitable right to the same thing has been concluded by the same bar." Or, as stated by *Chancellor* Kent: "When the same subject matter of the demand in equity can also be made the subject of an action at law, the rule of analogy applies in all its force; as *Lord* Redesdale observed in *Bond* v. *Hopkins*, 1 Sch. & Lef. 413, . . . the Statute of Limitations does not apply in terms to proceedings in courts of equity, but equitable titles are affected by analogy to it. If the equitable title be not sued upon within the time within which a legal title of the same nature ought to be sued upon to prevent the bar of the Statute, the court, acting by analogy to the Statute, will not relieve." *Kane* v. *Bloodgood*, 7 Johns. Ch. 120, 2 N. Y. Ch. L. ed. 241.

So this court, speaking through Overton, *J.*, said that it had been argued that the Statute did not apply "unless the relief sought in this court is of the same nature of that which would be obtained at law. This position is not supported by any of the books. Compensation in damages would have been the relief administered at law, but in this court a decree *in specie* may be obtained. This difference in the mode of redress has no effect upon the Statute of Limitations; it is pleadable in this court as well as at law. . . . In every case where an action could have been sustained at law, and to which the Statute might have been made to apply, so it would apply in equity if relief were sought there. Nor is it material whether that relief be of one kind or another. It is the nature of the cause of action that must determine the application of the Statute, and not the nature of the relief which can be afforded." *Shelby* v. *Shelby*, Cooke, 184.

3. The Statute does not operate as between the trustee and *cestui que trust* in that class of direct and peculiar trusts cognizable alone in courts of equity. This is so for the reason that the possession of one is the possession of the other, and, until the trust relation has ceased by repudiation with notice, there can be no such thing as an adverse holding. The principle upon which the doctrine rests is precisely the same as that which prevents the Statute from running at common law as between tenants in common and landlord and tenant. The legal rule in regard to legal relations, so like the relations between trustee and *cestui que trust* in equity, is the very foundation of what is so often mistaken for an exception peculiar to courts of equity concerning the application of the Statute. To quote the observation of *Lord* Redesdale, which very clearly states this principle: "In the case of a strict trustee, it was his duty to take care of the interest of his *cestui que trust*, and he was not permitted to do anything adverse to it. A tenant also had a duty to preserve the interests of his landlord, and many acts, therefore, of a trustee and a tenant, which, if done by a stranger, would be acts of adverse possession, would not be so in them from its being their duty to abstain from them." *Cholmondeley* v. *Clinton*, 2 Jac. & W. 1,190; *Armstrong* v. *Campbell*, 3 Yerg. 201.

4. But when the trust was not a direct technical trust, springing out of contract, but was imposed on the conscience of the party by operation of equitable principles, and, as some of the judges put it, dependent upon evidence, then, in all such cases, the Statute did operate as a bar, notwithstanding such constructive and implied trusts were creations of a court of equity, and the remedy for their enforcement exclusively equitable. *Cocke* v. *M'Ginnis*, Mart. & Y. 361, and other authorities.

The reason for the distinction between the effect of the Statute upon express and implied trusts lies in the fact that in the latter kind of trust the element of trust and confidence is absent.

The relation of trustee and *cestui que trust* does not in fact exist, and the holding of an implied or constructive trustee is for himself, and therefore at all times adverse. *Beckford* v. *Wade*, 17 Ves. Jr. 98; *Hickman* v. *Gaither*, 2 Yerg. 200.

From the foregoing principles it manifestly follows that, in all that large class of express trusts where the remedy at law is concurrent, the Statute which operates to bar the concurrent legal remedy will likewise bar equitable suit. It would be intolerable that equity should maintain a suit when the legal right was barred.

In the early and well-considered case of *Cocke* v. *M'Ginnis*, *Judge* Catron for this court said: "The history of English jurisprudence, it is believed, furnishes not an instance where it was holden that the relation of *cestui que trust* and trustee prevents the Statute from creating a bar in a case where an action at law can be sustained. In every case where an action of assumpsit will lie, there even courts of chancery, having concurrent jurisdiction with courts of law, will apply the Statute. This has been the settled rule of decision in the English courts for a century."

We very lately had occasion to review our

own decisions on this question, and to repeat and apply the rule so clearly announced in the case last cited to the suit of the distributees against an administrator for an account, and to recover their distributive shares. The action at law being barred, the equitable suit was held likewise barred. *Alvis* v. *Oglesby*, 87 Tenn. 172, and other cases.

Now, in view of the well-settled principles concerning the operation of the Statute upon bills in equity, is there any foundation for the proposition that because the remedy of complainant, as against this trust estate, is purely equitable, therefore his suit is not subject to the bar of the Statute? The rule which we deduce from a consideration of the English and Tennessee cases is that, with the exception of suits between trustees and *cestuis que trustent*, concerning those direct technical trusts cognizable alone in equity, the Statute which would bar the demand, if it were the subject of a legal action, will likewise bar the equitable remedy. There is no more reason for holding that a bill to charge the payment of an equitable claim upon a trust estate should be taken out of the Statute which bars all suits upon contracts within six years, than there was for holding that a suit upon an equitable title, or to declare and enforce a constructive or implied trust, was without the Statute. In both the cases last put the remedies were purely equitable, and yet it was held that the Statute applied. Cases cited.

The cases cited by complainant's counsel to support his proposition are not in point. They are all cases of suits between trustee and *cestui que trust*, and upon demands at that time cognizable only in equity. Cases cited.

The only authority to which we have been referred that seems to support the proposition that a purely equitable demand is not within the bar of the Statute is the statement of Mr. Perry that suits against the separate estate of a married woman, "the remedy being wholly equitable," are not barred by the Statute. Perry, Tr. § 663.

To support this brief statement he cites two Irish chancery cases, and the case of *Norton* v. *Turvill*, 2 P. Wms. 144. The first two cases are not accessible, and would not, at best, be of any controlling effect. The case of *Norton* v. *Turvill* was a decision by the Master of the Rolls, who, in reply to the defense of the Statute, said: "But in this case all the separate estate of the *feme covert* was a trust estate for payment of debts, and a trust is not within the Statute of Limitations."

Now, if it be conceded that the separate estate was a separate estate for the payment of debts, and complainant was one of the creditors thereby provided for, then the decision that the Statute did not apply was right. A separate estate may be, however, as between the *feme covert* and her trustee, a trust estate, and the Statute have no application, as between the *cestui que trust* and the trustee; but precisely how the creditor of the married woman becomes a *cestui que trust* is not explained by the decision. As to strangers to the trust, the Statute manifestly must apply. The exception is in favor of the *cestuis que trustent* and upon the ground that the possession of the trustee is their possession. A married woman's contract does not bind her personally, and only operates to charge her separate estate. This charge may have been regarded as constituting the separate estate a trust estate for the payment of such engagements. However that may be as to a separate estate, the doctrine is not applicable to a trust of the character of that before us. It was not a trust for the payment of debts. Whatever doubt might have existed as to the application of the Statute to a purely equitable demand would seem to be removed by the change made in our statutes by the Code. These statutes no longer apply to legal actions in terms, or address themselves to the form of suit. They apply directly to all civil actions, and to the cause of action, and not the form of the remedy. The cause of action here is a contract between the trustee and complainant. All actions upon contract are barred in six years. This contract was put in judgment. Actions upon judgments and decrees are barred in ten years. Assuming that the implied lien of complainant as a vendor was not lost by his taking bond with personal security, then his implied lien was barred in seven years. *Sheratz* v. *Nicodemus*, 7 Yerg. 12.

But upon another ground the suit of complainant is barred. To secure himself against overpaying the legacy to Mrs. Brown and her children, he took a refunding bond, with two personal sureties. His remedy upon this bond against the trustee and the sureties at law was clear. Indeed, he obtained a summary judgment thereon and was awarded the legal writ of *fieri facias*. The insolvency of the sureties alone defeated its satisfaction. The remedy at law proving inadequate, he now resorts to a court of equity to reach property not subject to execution. If he had filed his bill in time, his relief was easy. He has delayed until his bond is barred, and the decree thereon is barred likewise. That the remedy in equity is in kind different from that afforded at law is no reason why the Statute which barred his legal remedy shall not likewise bar the equitable relief.

Affirm the decree, with costs.

KENTUCKY COURT OF APPEALS.

CITY OF NEWPORT, *Appt.*,
v.
NEWPORT & CINCINNATI BRIDGE CO.

(......Ky.......)

1. **A penal ordinance to enforce a contract** with a city is void, where it does not relate to the morals, health or safety of the people.
2. **An ordinance to compel a bridge company to sell one hundred tickets for** $1 according to its contract with a city is not an exercise of police power, but relates merely to a contract in respect to a financial matter.
3. **Issuing five cards** each good for twenty crossings is a substantial compliance by a bridge company with a contract to sell one hundred tickets for $1.

(May 10, 1890.)

APPEAL by defendant from a judgment of the Chancery Court for Campbell County enjoining it from enforcing a certain ordinance. *Affirmed.*

The facts sufficiently appear in the opinion.

Mr. **E. W. Hawkins** for appellant.

Messrs. **Ramsey, Maxwell & Ramsey** for appellee.

Holt, *J.*, delivered the opinion of the court:

The appellee, the Newport & Cincinnati Bridge Company, was incorporated in 1868. Its charter authorized it to charge reasonable tolls, the maximum rate, however, not to exceed that charged by the Covington & Cincinnati Bridge Company. Desiring the use of a portion of one of the streets of the appellant the City of Newport, for the purpose of constructing its bridge, or the approach to it, the city council, on May 12, 1868, passed "an ordinance granting the Newport & Cincinnati Bridge Company the use of a portion of a street for the purpose of a bridge," the fourth section of which provides: "In consideration of the foregoing grant, the rates of toll over said bridge shall be as follows, viz.: Packages of one hundred tickets to foot passengers for $1 to all persons applying for the same; one horse and dray, ten cents for a single crossing; one horse and express wagon, ten cents; one horse and buggy, fifteen cents." The Bridge Company accepted the terms of this ordinance in the construction of its bridge. There is nothing in it relating to tolls for foot passengers, save the provision relating to the sale of packages of one hundred tickets for $1. The other rates for a foot passenger charged by the Company are three cents for a single crossing; two and a half cents each way to go and return; or he can purchase what are termed seven and twenty coupon crossings, entitling him to cross, the one seven, and the other twenty, times, for ten and twenty-five cents respectively.

In and perhaps prior to 1882 the Bridge Company, instead of furnishing packages of one hundred tickets for $1, began issuing packages of five cards for that price, each card being good for twenty crossings, and one perforation being made in it upon each crossing. The city council in the year last named passed an ordinance subjecting any officer or agent of the Bridge Company to a fine for failing or refusing to sell packages of one hundred tickets for $1; and one of the Company's agents having been arrested, charged with its violation, and the City threatening to have arrested and to prosecute all of the Company's agents until it should furnish and sell packages of one hundred tickets for a dollar, it brought this action, enjoining the City from enforcing the ordinance. The lower court perpetuated the injunction.

If the ordinance was invalid, then the Company had the right, in order to prevent irreparable injury and a multiplicity of prosecutions, to go into a court of equity for relief. The chancellor often interferes to prevent an illegal use of power by municipal authorities; and where such consequences follow the enforcement of an ordinance as will result in this instance, a proper case is presented for equitable relief, if the ordinance be invalid. *Brown* v. *Catlettsburg*, 11 Bush, 435.

The passage of the ordinance of May 12, 1868, was the tender of a grant by the City to the Bridge Company, upon the condition that the tolls should be as therein fixed. Upon its acceptance by the Company, a contract arose between it and the City, and such a contract must be enforced by the judicial department of the government. It stands upon the same footing as one between individuals. It would be exceedingly dangerous to individual right and liberty, which the common law so highly regards, to permit municipalities to enforce their own construction of their contracts by pains and penalties. Whether the Legislature could confer such a power we need not inquire, inasmuch as it is not pretended that it has been attempted in this instance. Where an ordinance is penal in character, the right of the municipality to enact it must clearly appear.

The enforcement of this ordinance would not be an exercise of the police power. While it is difficult, if not impossible, to concisely define the extent of this power, yet it certainly should not be extended so far as to permit a city to enforce its view of its contracts by penal ordinances, in cases involving neither the morals, health nor safety of its people. It may by ordinance limit the speed of railroad trains or street-cars through its streets, and in the same manner regulate any matter which is conducive to the health or safety or morality of its citizens. The public welfare demands the existence of such a power, and, when properly directed, the municipality should not be restricted to a narrow limit in its exercise. But where it is a matter of contract, affecting merely the pockets of its citizens, or it financially, it must resort to the courts for relief in the same manner as individuals.

A construction of the contract between the parties was not necessary in order to afford the appellee proper relief. This was given by enjoining the enforcement of the ordinance. Its petition, however, asks that the issual of the five-card packages be adjudged a compliance with the clause in the ordinance relative to the one hundred ticket packages, while the answer of the appellant not only asks a dissolution of the injunction, but in counterclaim form requests the court to order the appellee to furnish and sell packages of one hundred tickets for a dollar. The lower court determined this question, holding that the issual of the five cards was a compliance with the spirit of the contract; and, as this judgment would be binding upon the City in any case where it would have the right to sue the Company, it is proper to consider it.

The law looks to the spirit of a contract, and not the letter of it. The question therefore is not whether a party has literally complied with it, but whether he has substantially done so. The ordinance in question was not designed to enable persons to purchase tickets for resale at an advanced price. The Statute prohibited any such traffic. Its object was a commutation of fare to those who desired to cross the bridge frequently. The mere form of the ticket is immaterial. The purpose was to regulate the price for one hundred crossings, and the issual of the five cards, each good for twenty crossings, for $1, was a substantial compliance with the contract.

Judgment affirmed.

MASSACHUSETTS SUPREME JUDICIAL COURT.

GOODYEAR DENTAL VULCANITE CO.
v.
Thomas H. BACON.

(....Mass.....)

1. **A surety is not liable** on a bond signed by him alone, but purporting to be signed by the principal also, where he did not consent to a delivery of the bond without the principal's signature.

2. **The burden of proof** to show that a surety consented to the delivery of a bond, purporting to be signed by the principal, without the latter's signature, is on the obligee.

(May 10, 1890.)

EXCEPTIONS by plaintiff to a judgment of the Superior Court for Suffolk County in favor of defendant in an action brought to enforce defendant's alleged liability as surety upon the official bond of plaintiff's treasurer. *Overruled.*

The case sufficiently appears in the opinion.

Messrs. **Blackmar & Sheldon** for plaintiff.

Mr. **J. R. Bullard** for defendant.

Devens, *J.*, delivered the opinion of the court:

The instrument in suit purports to be the bond of Caduc as principal, and of the defendant and others as sureties, in different sums, respectively, for the faithful performance by Caduc of his duties as treasurer of the plaintiff Company. It was held at a former hearing that a demurrer to the declaration thereon, based upon the reason that it did not appear thereby that the principal had ever signed the bond upon which it was sought to hold the defendant as surety, could not be sustained. *Goodyear Dental Vulcanite Co.* v. *Bacon,* 148 Mass. 542.

"If the defendant," it was said, "knowing that Caduc had not signed it as principal, but intending, nevertheless, to be himself bound as surety, executed the bond, and delivered it as it is, . . . he may be held liable upon it. Caduc was liable without a bond." At the subsequent trial the defendant testified, without contradiction, that "he had not consented to the principal not signing, nor to the delivery without such signature; that he signed at the request of the proposed principal and relied on his signing; that nothing was said on the subject." He also added, the plaintiff objecting, "that he did not understand he was to be bound unless the principal signed." Upon this evidence the plaintiff asked the court to rule that it was entitled to judgment; but the court held that upon this evidence it was not bound to find for the plaintiff, and found for the defendant.

When the so-called bond was delivered to the plaintiff, it was in an imperfect condition. While purporting to be signed by the principal, it was not so signed, and while purporting to be under seal, no seals had been affixed. The plaintiff had possession of and produced the instrument, which is evidence of a delivery to it, but not necessarily of any delivery by the defendant, who, without contradiction, denied any delivery by himself, or any authority from him to deliver the same in its then condition. Even if the testimony, as the plaintiff contends, shows simply that the defendant signed the bond, and left it with the principal, "without imposing any restriction upon its delivery, or making any condition that it should not be delivered until signed by the principal or somebody else," it was still competent for the judge to find from the facts stated by the defendant, in connection with the usual habits of business, and the obviously unfinished condition of the instrument itself, that no intention was shown that it should be delivered to the obligee except after it was completed, and thus that the signature of the defendant was provisional only. An instrument like that in suit ordinarily is and should be executed by all the intended parties. It was for the plaintiff to show that, although not thus executed, the defendant had consented to its delivery under such circumstances that it would bind him even if it were inoperative and invalid as against the principal. *Russell* v. *Annable,* 109 Mass. 72; *Wood* v. *Washburn,* 2 Pick. 24; *Bean* v. *Parker,* 17 Mass. 591; *Adams* v. *Bean,* 12 Mass. 137.

The case at bar is readily distinguishable from those cases where the bond has been delivered in a perfect condition to the obligee, and where he has had no notice that it contemplated that it should have signatures and seals which it did not bear. *White* v. *Duggan,* 140 Mass. 18; *Wild Cat Branch* v. *Ball,* 45 Ind. 213.

The view we have taken of the question discussed renders it unnecessary to consider whether the instrument could properly be declared on as a bond, no seals having been affixed thereto.

Exceptions overruled.

NOTE.—*Bond; what essential to bind surety.*

It is essence of a bond to have an obligee as well as an obligor. Garrett v. Shove, 4 New Eng. Rep. 747, 15 R. I. 538.

The signing, sealing and delivery of a bond are prima facie evidence of its acceptance and approval by the obligee. Coggeshall v. Pollitt, 1 New Eng. Rep. 806, 15 R. I. 168.

Delivery is an indispensable requisite to the validity of a voluntary bond. Harris v. Regester, 70 Md. 109.

An actual or implied acceptance of a bond is essential to constitute a delivery. Authorities cited in Bell v. Pierce, 5 New Eng. Rep. 547, 146 Mass. 58.

Delivery, by the maker, of a bond payable to the holder, is presumed from the fact of possession. State v. Suwannee County Comrs. 21 Fla. 1.

A surety may make any conditions he chooses in signing a bond, before its delivery; and where it is not signed by a party whose signature was required as a condition to his signing, the surety will not be bound. Hessell v. Johnson, 6 West. Rep. 392, 63 Mich. 623.

A bond signed only by the sureties is insufficient to bind them. State v. Austin, 35 Minn. 51.

Rule as to liability of surety. See *note* to Tyler v. Sanborn (Ill.) 4 L. R. A. 218.

Liability of surety on penal bond. See *note* to Frink v. Southern Exp. Co. (Ga.) 8 L. R. A. 482.

OPINION OF THE JUSTICES.

Re MANUFACTURE OF GAS AND ELECTRIC LIGHT BY MUNICIPAL CORPORATIONS.

(150 Mass. 592.)

1. **Power to manufacture and distribute gas and electricity for public use** in lighting streets and public buildings may lawfully be conferred by the Legislature on cities and towns together with the power to raise money by taxation for the construction and maintenance of the necessary works, as such service is a public one.

2. **Such power may also be lawfully conferred** to enable the cities and towns to produce gas and electricity to be sold to their own citizens for the lighting of their private property if the Legislature is of opinion that the common convenience and welfare of such citizens will be promoted thereby, at least where all inhabitants of a city or town are given the same, or similar, rights to be supplied so far as is reasonably practicable, and are compelled to pay therefor a sum sufficient to reimburse to the cities and towns the reasonable cost of what is furnished.

(May 27, 1890.)

SUBMISSION by the House of Representatives of the question whether or not the Legislature has the constitutional right to enact laws conferring on cities and towns the power to manufacture gas and electric light for public use and also for sale to their own citizens. *Answered in the affirmative.*

Per Curiam:

To the Honorable House of Representatives of the Commonwealth of Massachusetts:

We received on the 24th inst. your order of the 22d inst., a copy of which is annexed, and we respectfully submit the following opinion:

In considering the questions asked we assumed that the power to be conferred is not merely a power to receive and use property given in trust for the purposes named, but is a

NOTE.—*Municipal authority to light streets.*

A municipal corporation having the power by legislative grant to erect and maintain gas works for the purpose of lighting its public streets, and to furnish its inhabitants with the means of obtaining gas at their own expense, has the implied power to contract with others to furnish it in like manner, and may, by contract, grant to a corporation the exclusive right to the use of its streets for that purpose for a term of years. Newport v. Newport Light Co. 84 Ky. 166.

A city has the right to make and enforce ordinances, and to make and apply any conditions precedent which it may choose relative to the carrying on of the business of furnishing residents with gas, in the same manner that any private corporation may do. Com. v. Philadelphia (Pa.) Feb. 17, 1890.

A city ordinance providing that the use of gas may be refused until all arrears for gas consumed on the premises have been paid is reasonable. *Ibid.*

Power conferred by charter upon the city council, by ordinances, "to erect lamps and to provide for lighting the city, and to create, alter and extend lamp districts," requires the exercise of judgment and discretion, and cannot be delegated to a committee of the council. Minneapolis Gas-Light Co. v. Minneapolis, 36 Minn. 159.

A city given power by its charter to make, amend or repeal ordinances for lighting streets, but not given exclusive power over them, cannot grant the exclusive use of the streets for fifteen years for wires and poles for electric lights. Grand Rapids E. L. & P. Co. v. Grand Rapids E. E. L. & F. G. Co. 33 Fed. Rep. 659.

The power of a city or village, under Ohio Rev. Stat., § 2486, to erect or purchase gas works whenever deemed expedient and for the public good, is not limited by §§ 2480 and 2482, authorizing such action where a gas company has refused or neglected to furnish gas. State v. Hamilton, 47 Ohio St. —, 23 Ohio L. J. 190.

A gas company having no exclusive franchise has no vested rights which are interfered with by the construction of gas works by a city in which the company has for many years had the entire business of furnishing gas. *Ibid.*

Manufacture and distribution of gas a public franchise.

The manufacture of gas and its distribution by means of pipes laid, under legislative authority, in the streets and ways of a city, is not an ordinary business in which everyone may engage as of common right, upon terms of equality, but is a franchise relating to matters of which the public may assume control, and when not forbidden by the Organic Law of the State, may be granted by the Legislature, as a means of accomplishing public objects, to whomsoever, and upon what terms, it pleases. New Orleans Gas Light Co. v. Louisiana Light & Heat P. & Mfg. Co. 115 U. S. 650 (29 L. ed. 516); Louisville Gas Co. v. Citizens Gas Light Co. 115 U. S. 683 (29 L. ed. 510).

The grant of an exclusive privilege is none the less a contract because the manufacture and distribution of gas, when not subjected to proper supervision, may work injury to the public; for such a grant does not restrict the power of the State to establish and enforce regulations not inconsistent with the essential right given to the company by its charter. New Orleans Gas Light Co. v. Louisiana Light & Heat P. & Mfg. Co. *supra.*

The right to use the streets and other public thoroughfares of a city for the purpose of placing therein or thereon pipes, mains, wires and poles for the distribution of gas, water or electric lights for public and private use is not the ordinary business in which anyone may engage, but is a franchise belonging to the government, the privilege of exercising which can only be granted by the State or the municipal government of the city acting under legislative authority. Grand Rapids E. L. & P. Co. v. Grand Rapids E. E. L. & F. G. Co. 33 Fed. Rep. 659; Newport v. Newport Light Co. 84 Ky. 166.

A company incorporated under the General Laws of Ohio in 1855, authorized to lay its mains and pipes in the streets and alleys of a city, to provide the city with gas at a price not to exceed a maximum figure, to be fixed by the council, does not have an exclusive right to the use of the streets for laying pipe for the conveyance of gas. Hamilton Gas-Light & Coke Co. v. Hamilton, 21 Ohio L. J. 94.

A gas company incorporated under the Pennsylvania General Incorporation Act of 1874, having, prior to the Act of May 29, 1885, laid a pipe and supplied with gas one mill in a city, and having since become incorporated under the latter Act, may lay other pipes in the city without first obtaining its consent. Allegheny v. Chartiers Valley Gas Co. (Pa.) 10 Cent. Rep. 281.

While a grant of an exclusive privilege to lay and maintain gas pipes in a city for fifty years, with a provision for a sale of the plant to the city at the end of twenty-five years if the city wishes to buy, will not bind the city to maintain such exclusive privilege where a sale of the plant on application is refused; yet the city must elect whether or not it

See also 8 L. R. A. 602; 15 L. R. A. 240; 27 L. R. A. 514.

power to raise money by taxation and by means of it to construct and maintain works for the manufacture and distribution of gas or electricity to be used by the municipalities for lighting the public streets and buildings, and by the inhabitants for lighting the land and buildings which are their private property.

We also assume that the gas or electricity to be furnished to the inhabitants for their private use is to be paid for by them at rates to be established, which shall be deemed sufficient to reimburse to the cities and towns the reasonable cost of what is furnished and that all the inhabitants of a city or town are to have the same, or similar, rights to be supplied with gas or electricity so far as is reasonably practicable, and the capacity and extent of the works which it is deemed expedient to maintain will permit.

Whether cities and towns can be authorized to give gas and electricity to their inhabitants, or to sell either to them at varying and disproportionate prices, selecting their customers, selling to some and arbitrarily refusing to sell to others, are questions which it is not necessary to consider.

By the Constitution full power and authority are given to the General Court to make "all manner of wholesome and reasonable orders, laws, statutes and ordinances" not repugnant to the Constitution, which "they shall judge to be for the good and welfare of this Commonwealth," etc., and "to impose and levy proportional and reasonable assessments, rates and taxes upon all the inhabitants of and persons resident, and the estates lying within the said Commonwealth. . . . for the public service, in the necessary defense and support of the government of the said Commonwealth, and the protection and preservation of the subjects thereof," etc. Part 2, chap. 1, § 4.

The extent of the right of taxation is not necessarily to be measured by that of the right of eminent domain, but the rights are analogous.

---

will purchase at the price fixed by referees before they are chosen; and it is not a breach of contract for the gas company to refuse to appoint its referees until the city has so agreed. Montgomery Gas-Light Co. v. Montgomery, 87 Ala. 245.

A council exceeds its powers in agreeing to grant to a gas company an exclusive privilege. Cincinnati Gas-Light & Coke Co. v. Avondale, 1 West. Rep. 94, 43 Ohio St. 257.

Courts of common pleas may hear disputes between municipal authorities and natural-gas companies as to the manner of laying such pipes. Pittsburgh's App. 6 Cent. Rep. 225, 115 Pa. 4.

Right to lay pipes in streets.

A right granted by charter to a gas company to lay gas pipes in the streets of a city is an easement, and not a mere license. Providence Gas Co. v. Thurber, 2 R. I. 15.

A natural-gas company duly incorporated, with power to lay pipes, has the power of eminent domain, and the grant of a right to exercise this power is constitutional. McDevitt v. People's Natural Gas Co. (Pa.) 6 Cent. Rep. 885; Johnston v. People's Natural Gas Co. (Pa.) 5 Cent. Rep. 564.

It is invested with the right to enter on any public street to lay down pipes, but cannot lay them down in the street of a city without the assent of its council. Pittsburgh's App. 6 Cent. Rep. 225, 115 Pa. 4.

It has, however, no right to lay pipes without first making or securing payment of damages to the land owner. Sterling's App. 2 Cent. Rep. 51, 111 Pa. 35.

Such councils are only authorized to give or withhold their assent, and cannot couple their assent with any condition or restriction not imposed by the Act, unless the company agrees thereto; and they may adopt reasonable regulations as to the manner, etc., of laying such pipes, with respect to safety and public convenience. Pittsburgh's App. *supra.*

An ordinance granting a right to lay pipes in a street is valid; but such a grant is a franchise to be strictly construed, and in a certain sense is a contract with the public, and becomes void by force of the legislative declaration contained in the grant, if the conditions are not complied with. State v. Boyce, 1 West. Rep. 96, 43 Ohio St. 46.

Under a city ordinance giving a light company for twenty-five years the exclusive privilege of using any or all of the streets of the city for the purpose of laying pipes to convey and supply gas to the city, a grant of the streets for any other use should not be implied, and in case of introduction of a light other than gas, requiring a different use of the streets, consent of the city is necessary. Newport v. Newport Light Co. 11 Ky. L. Rep. 840.

If, after permission is granted to lay pipes in a street upon condition that a bond be given and work commenced within one year, a suit is brought to enjoin action under the ordinance, the pendency of such action and proceedings may excuse the delay of the grantee, and prevent a forfeiture, and may be regarded as postponing the beginning of the time prescribed for forfeiture until the date of such final judgment, from which date the time given by ordinance begins to run. State v. Boyce, *supra.*

A bond duly presented within one year from the date of such judgment should be acted on, and, upon refusal to act, the board may be compelled by mandamus. *Ibid.*

Injunction will not lie to restrain laying of pipes.

Under the Public Statutes the mayor, aldermen or selectmen have authority to regulate, restrict and control the laying of gas pipes in streets, and an owner of private property cannot ask an injunction to restrain the acts of a company in laying gas pipes until after he has made application to the public officers to restrain such acts and they have refused to act. Kenney v. Consumers Gas Co. 2 New Eng. Rep. 816, 142 Mass. 417.

Nor can one gas company restrain by injunction a second company authorized by the city to lay its pipes in the streets. Meadville Fuel Gas Co. v. Meadville Natural Gas Co. (Pa.) 8 Cent. Rep. 921; Jersey City Gaslight Co. v. Consumers Gas Co. 4 Cent. Rep. 330, 40 N. J. Eq. 427.

A municipal corporation cannot sustain a bill for perpetual injunction against a natural-gas fuel company on the ground that the corporation has laid its pipes in the borough without permission, and that such pipes are defective, where the averments of the bill are denied, and the court upon examination finds the matter complained of is not a public nuisance. Borough of Butler v. Butler Gas Co. (Pa.) 5 Cent. Rep. 669.

When gas furnished by gas companies becomes a nuisance, by reason of defective pipes, the municipality can prohibit its continuance; and an injunction restraining abatement of the nuisance by the municipality will be dissolved. *Ibid.*

Private property can be taken without the consent of the owner only for public uses, and the owner must be paid full compensation therefor; otherwise he would contribute more than his proportionate share toward the public expenses.

By taxation the inhabitants are compelled to part with their property, but the taxation must be proportional and reasonable and for public purposes.

Taxes may be imposed upon all the inhabitants of the State for general public purposes, or upon the inhabitants of defined localities for local purposes, and when distinct private benefits are received from public works special assessments may be laid upon individuals.

We have no doubt that, if the furnishing of gas and electricity for illuminating purposes is a public service, the performance of this service can be delegated by the Legislature to cities and towns for the benefit of themselves and their inhabitants, and that such cities and towns can be authorized to impose taxes for this purpose upon their inhabitants, and to establish reasonable rates which the inhabitants who use the gas and electricity can be compelled to pay. The fundamental question is whether the manufacture and distribution of gas or electricity to be used by cities and towns for illuminating purposes is a public service.

The maintenance of public streets and buildings is a public service, and it may be reasonably necessary to light them in order that the greatest public benefit may be obtained from using them.

To say nothing of the usefulness of lighting streets as a means of promoting order and of affording protection to persons and property, the common convenience of the inhabitants may require that they be lighted.

Cities and thickly settled towns have for a long time been accustomed to light their public buildings and some of their streets at the public expense. If the streets and public buildings are to be lighted, the means are a matter of expediency. If the Legislature can authorize cities and towns to light their streets and public buildings, it can authorize them to do this by any appropriate means which it may deem expedient.

As a question of constitutional power, we cannot distinguish the right to authorize cities and towns to buy gas or electricity for their use, from the right to authorize them to manufacture it for their use.

We therefore answer the first question in the affirmative.

The second question is one of more difficulty.

It is impossible to define with entire accuracy all the characteristics which distinguish a public service and a public use from services and uses which are private. The subject has been considered many times in the opinions of the court of which we are now the justices, and *Lowell* v. *Boston*, in 111 Mass. 454, is a leading case. It is there said that "an appropriation of money raised by taxation or of property taken by the right of eminent domain by way of gift to an individual for his own private uses exclusively would clearly be an excess of legislative power;" that "the promotion of the interests of individuals, either in respect of property or business, although it may result incidentally in the advancement of the public welfare, is in its essential character a private, and not a public, object;" and that the appropriation of property for turnpikes and railroads "can only be justified by the public service thereby secured in the increased facilities for transportation of freight and passengers of which the whole community may rightfully avail itself." It is said that the essential point is that a public service or use affects the inhabitants "as a community, and not merely as individuals."

It was early decided that "the prevention of damage by fire is one of the objects affecting the interests of the inhabitants generally, and clearly within the scope of municipal authority." *Allen* v. *Taunton*, 19 Pick. 485.

Although the property to be protected is private property, the need of protection is felt by every owner in the city or town: the property of one may be endangered by the burning of that of another; efficient means of protecting his property cannot well be furnished by every inhabitant, and there is a necessity of common action which makes the expenditure of money for the purpose properly a municipal expense.

The maintenance of sewers and drains is a public service. One object is the preservation of the public health; but apart from this they are of great convenience to the inhabitants whose estates can be drained by them. It is impracticable for every owner of land in cities and towns to construct and maintain sewers and drains, exclusively on his own account. They cannot ordinarily be constructed over any considerable territory without using the public ways or exercising the right of eminent domain; they are therefore regarded as of common convenience and are constructed at the public expense.

The furnishing of water for cities and towns for domestic use affords, perhaps, the nearest analogy to the subject we are considering. It was long ago declared that "the supply of a large number of inhabitants with pure water is a public purpose." *Lumbard* v. *Stearns*, 4 Cush. 60.

The statutes are well known which authorize cities and towns to maintain water-works for supplying their inhabitants with water, and the constitutionality of these statutes has not been doubted.

Water cannot ordinarily be supplied to a large city or town from ponds or streams without the exercise of the right of eminent domain and the use of the public ways.

Every inhabitant needs water, and often the only practicable method of obtaining it is by the agency of corporations or of the municipality. The land for the public ways having been taken for a public use, it may be subjected to other public uses, but it cannot be subjected to strictly private uses without the consent of the owners of the fee when the fee remains in the abutters.

There is therefore often a necessity of having water common to the inhabitants of a community, which cannot well be met except by the exercise of public rights, and therefore the furnishing of water has been considered a public service.

In the case of water, as in that of sewers and drains, a portion of the service is exclusively public, and the benefit to individuals cannot be separately estimated from that of the community; but a part of the service is rendered to individuals, and the benefit of this can be separately estimated. The inhabitants are therefore required to pay for the water furnished for their private use, and special assessments for the use of sewers and drains are laid upon estates specially benefited; and, for the same reasons, while in laying out highways the expense is public betterment, assessments may be laid upon the owners of lands specially benefited.

Artificial light is not perhaps so absolutely necessary as water, but it is necessary for the comfortable living of every person. Although artificial light can be supplied in other ways than by the use of gas or electricity, yet the use of one or both for lighting cities and thickly settled towns is common, and has been found to be of great convenience, and it is practically impossible for every individual to manufacture gas or electricity for himself.

If gas or electricity is to be generally used in a city or town, it must be furnished by private companies or by the municipality, and it cannot be distributed without the use of the public streets or the exercise of the right of eminent domain.

It is not necessarily an objection to a public work maintained by a city or town that it incidentally benefits some individuals more than others, or that from the place of residence, or for other reasons, every inhabitant of the city or town cannot use it, if every inhabitant who is so situated that he can use it has the same right to use it as the other inhabitants.

It must often be a question of kind and degree whether the promotion of the interests of many individuals in the same community constitutes a public service or not. But in general it may be said that matters which concern the welfare and convenience of all the inhabitants of a city or town and cannot be successfully dealt with without the aid of powers derived from the Legislature, may be subjected to municipal control when the benefits received are such that each inhabitant needs them and may participate in them, and it is for the interest of each inhabitant that others as well as himself should possess and enjoy them.

If the Legislature is of opinion that the common convenience and welfare of the inhabitants of cities or towns will be promoted by conferring upon the municipalities the power of manufacturing and distributing gas or electricity for the purpose of furnishing light to their inhabitants, we think that the Legislature can confer the power.

We therefore answer the second question in the affirmative.

We notice that the bill, a copy of which was inclosed with your order, relates to the manufacture and distribution of gas or electricity, not only for furnishing light, but also for furnishing heat and power.

We have not considered whether the furnishing of gas or electricity for supplying either heat or power can be regarded as a public service. We have confined our opinion to the questions asked, which, as we understand them, relate to the manufacture and distribution of gas or electricity solely for the purpose of furnishing light.

Marcus Morton,
Walbridge A. Field,
Charles Devens,
William Allen,
Charles Allen,
Oliver Wendell Holmes, Jr.,
Marcus P. Knowlton,
Justices of the Supreme Judicial Court.

ILLINOIS SUPREME COURT.

HINCKLEY, *Appt.*,
v.
HORAZDOWSKI.

(....Ill......)

1. A boy twelve years old employed to take lumber away from a flooring machine and load it on a wagon who is injured in attempting, under orders of the foreman of the mill, to oil dangerous machinery while in motion, which service was disconnected from that for which he was employed, may recover damages from his employer.

2. A statement by the court to the jury, made in open court without objection by either

NOTE.—*Master and servant; duty of master to instruct and caution minor employés.*

A person who employs children to work with or about dangerous machinery, or in dangerous places, should so instruct them concerning the dangers that they may, by the exercise of such care as ought reasonably to be expected of them, guard against and avoid injuries arising therefrom. Cleveland Rolling Mill Co. v. Corrigan, 3 L. R. A. 385, 46 Ohio St. 283.

He must give proper instructions to make him understand and appreciate the danger attending his employment. Glover v. Dwight Mfg. Co. 148 Mass. 22.

Mere formal instructions are not sufficient, but the person employed must be brought to an actual understanding of the dangers, and be made to appreciate them and the consequence of want of care. Ogley v. Miles, 28 N. Y. S. R. 896.

But it is not necessary to instruct a boy twelve years old, on his going to work at a machine, that the cogs, which are open to view, are dangerous, because the danger is obvious. Buckley v. Gutta Percha & R. Mfg. Co. 113 N. Y. 530.

Where a young boy is inexperienced in the use of or in working about machinery, it is incumbent on the experienced master to caution him when he puts him in a place of danger. Neilon v. Marinette & M. Paper Co. 75 Wis. 579.

The rule that a servant cannot recover for the

party, that certain facts stated are admitted, is not in any sense an instruction to the jury, and therefore the fact that it was not made in writing, as instructions are required to be, is not error, especially where it was immaterial in the case.

3. It is not conclusive against the right of a child to recover against his employer for negligence in giving him dangerous work, that he had done it for some time before he was injured.

4. The rule that the common master is not liable for an injury caused by the negligence of a fellow servant does not apply where the injured servant is a child incapable of comprehending the risk of the employment arising from the possibility of such negligence.

5. An instruction that a master is not liable for injuries to one servant resulting from the negligence of his fellow servant is properly refused if it is not limited to cases in which the master used due care in selecting him.

(January 21, 1890.)

APPEAL by defendant from a judgment of the Appellate Court, First District, affirming a judgment of the Superior Court of Cook County in favor of plaintiff in an action brought to recover damages for personal injuries alleged to have resulted from the negligence of defendant's servant. *Affirmed.*

The case sufficiently appears in the opinion.

Messrs. **McKenzie & Wood** for appellant.

Messrs. **Jones & Lusk** for appellee.

Magruder, *J.*, delivered the opinion of the court:

This is an action of case, brought in the Superior Court of Cook County by the appellee, a minor, by his next friend, against the appellant and two others, to recover damages for a personal injury. The present appellant was the only one of the three defendants named in the declaration who was served with process. In the trial court the verdict and judgment were in favor of the plaintiff below, which judgment has been affirmed by the appellate court, and is brought here for review by appeal.

At the time of the accident, the defendants

---

negligence of fellow servants applies to infant servants. Pittsburg, C. & St. L. R. Co. v. Adams, 3 West. Rep. 387, 105 Ind. 151.

The contributory negligence of a fellow servant will not prevent recovery for injury to a servant, where the master was negligent. Hunn v. Michigan Cent. R. Co. (Mich.) 7 L. R. A. 500.

A master is liable for the negligence of a foreman in requiring a minor employé to clean machinery while in motion, although such work was within the scope of his employment. Robertson v. Cornelson, 34 Fed. Rep. 716.

But he is not liable where a minor is injured while acting in disobedience to an order of his foreman. *Ibid.*

Minor employé takes risks of employment.

The fact that an employé is a minor does not vary the law as to his assumption of risk, if he has sufficient intelligence to comprehend the dangers incident to his service. Goff v. Norfolk & W. R. Co. 36 Fed. Rep. 299; Buckley v. Gutta Percha & R. Mfg. Co. 113 N. Y. 530.

A boy fourteen or fifteen years old cannot recover of his employer for injuries received in consequence of allowing his hand to be caught under a stamping machine at which he was employed, as the danger was as obvious to him as to an adult. O'Keefe v. Thorn (Pa.) 24 W. N. C. 379.

Contributory negligence defeats recovery.

A master is not liable for injuries to a boy thirteen years old who voluntarily undertook to do something not within the scope of the work to which he was assigned, and which was neither difficult nor dangerous if he had used ordinary care. Gillen v. Rowley (Pa.) April 14, 1890; Rock v. Indian Orchard Mills, 3 New Eng. Rep. 69, 142 Mass. 522.

A boy fourteen years old who had received necessary instructions from the master to qualify him to work on a machine in a spinning-mill, which was not dangerous in itself if he had used ordinary care, cannot recover from the master where his arm and hand were caught by a band and injured. Zurn v. Tetlow (Pa.) April 14, 1890.

In an action for damages for the death of a minor employé, evidence that, when shoving a car from a side to a main track, he was looking towards the engine, when he should have been looking ahead at the car before him, demands a verdict for defendant. Littlejohn v. Central Railroad Co. 74 Ga. 396.

A boy seventeen years old working at a stamping-press, with which he was familiar, cannot recover for the crushing of his hand because the upper die accidentally fell, on the ground that the machine was defective, where, in placing his hand between the dies, he violated a well-known printed rule posted on the press, and also the instructions of the superintendent and of the foreman of the establishment, especially when he had been recently warned, by a prior fall of the die, of the danger of putting his fingers between the dies. Cullen v. National Sheet Metal Roofing Co. 114 N. Y. 45.

For an injury sustained thereby after proper precautions and instructions, the master will not be liable. Hayes v. Bush & Denslow Mfg. Co. 2 Cent. Rep. 876, 102 N. Y. 648.

Where a boy employed to keep culm in motion down a chute in a coal-breaker enters the chute elsewhere than at the regular place, contrary to instructions, the master is not liable for injuries; but it is otherwise if he is not forbidden to use such place. Pennsylvania Coal Co. v. Nee (Pa.) 12 Cent. Rep. 524.

Where a boy employed in a boiler shop to work in a tool-room, being out of work, was directed by the boss of the tool-room to go into the adjoining boiler-room for work, where he sustained the injuries sued for, the boss of the tool-room, being merely authorized to direct the work in that room, had no authority to direct plaintiff to seek employment in the boiler-room, and the master was not liable. Fisk v. Central Pac. R. Co. 72 Cal. 38.

A boy's capacity is the measure of his responsibility; and if he has not the ability to foresee and avoid the danger to which he may be exposed, negligence will not be imputed to him if he unwittingly exposes himself to the danger. Strawbridge v. Bradford, 128 Pa. 200.

A child who has not been properly instructed as to dangers of the employment, and who, while in the discharge of his duty as he understands it, suffers an injury in consequence of his employer's negligence, may maintain an action against the employer therefor, notwithstanding that, by reason of his youth and inexperience and the failure of the employer to properly instruct him, he did some act in the performance of his duty, according to the judgment and knowledge he possessed, which contributed to the injury, but which he did not know, and was not advised, would be likely to injure him. Cleveland Rolling Mill Co. v. Corrigan, 3 L. R. A. 385, 46 Ohio St. 283.

below owned and controlled a planing-mill in the lumber district near the corner of Robey Street and Blue Island Avenue, in the City of Chicago. Certain machines were used in the mill for planing wood. The plaintiff, then a boy twelve years old, was employed at the mill to take the lumber away from a flooring-machine, and load it on a wagon back of the machine. When the accident occurred, he had been instructed by the foreman in charge of the mill to oil one of the machines, and, in doing so, while the machine was in motion, he received the injuries for which the suit is brought. His arm was caught in the machinery, and, after being treated a considerable length of time, failed to heal, and was finally amputated. All the facts are settled by the judgment of the appellate court.

Appellant objects to an instruction given by the trial court because it predicated the finding of the jury upon their believing from the evidence, among other things, "that the defendant was guilty of negligence as charged," and because it said to the jury: "In determining whether or not the defendant was guilty of negligence as charged, you will likewise consider the age, apparent intelligence and experience of the plaintiff at the time of the accident; also, the nature of the work he was required to do,—that is, whether dangerous or otherwise,—and whether or not he fully understood its character; and, if he did not, then whether or not the defendant should, under all the circumstances proven in this case, have known the fact."

The portion of the declaration referred to as charging negligence is as follows: "Plaintiff, then a minor of the age of, to wit, twelve years, was then and there employed and engaged by said defendant in and about his said business; and, while so employed and engaged, the plaintiff was then and there, by said defendant, negligently and improperly ordered and directed to attend to and oil one of the machines then and there used and operated, and being used and operated, by said defendant, which said direction and order of said defendant was then and there dangerous and hazardous to this plaintiff, because of his tender age, as aforesaid, and well known so to be by said defendant."

The evidence tends to show that, under the original contract of employment, the plaintiff was not required to oil machinery, but to take lumber away, and put it on a wagon; that, in so taking away lumber, he "was four to six feet away, and didn't have to go about the machinery;" that he was directed by the foreman of the defendant to go outside of the regular work embraced in his contract, and oil revolving machinery; that the work of oiling such machinery was hazardous and dangerous, especially to a boy only twelve years old, and without experience in such work; that there was another employé, called a "feeder," with an experience of several years, whose business it was to oil the machinery. With evidence of this character before them, the instruction given to the jury as above stated was not erroneous.

If it should be conceded that the foreman of the mill and the plaintiff, who was under his control and direction, were fellow servants of the defendant, yet the rule that an employer is not liable for injuries resulting from the negligence of co-employés in the same line of duty has no application to this case. The reason of the rule is that the employé, in entering upon the service of the employer, takes upon himself the natural and ordinary risks and perils incident to the service, among which is the carelessness of his fellow servants. But the reason fails where the risk is not within the contract of service, and the servant, in making the contract, has no reason to believe that he will encounter such a risk. The injury did not occur while the boy was taking away lumber, and loading it upon a wagon, but while he was engaged in a service outside of his contract, and disconnected from it. He was too immature to form a correct idea of the danger of the task assigned to him, and relied entirely upon the judgment of the foreman. It was certainly an act of negligence on the part of the foreman to order a little boy to oil such dangerous machinery while it was in motion. Having intrusted the foreman with the management of his mill, the defendant is responsible for his conduct. This case is on all fours with the case of *Union Pac. R. Co.* v. *Fort*, 84 U. S. 17 Wall. 553 [21 L. ed. 739], and is governed by the principles there announced.

In *Gartland* v. *Toledo W. & W. R. Co.*, 67 Ill. 498, it does not appear that the minor, whose age is not given, was engaged in work not embraced within his contract of service. It would appear from the statement of facts in that case that the operating of the cars, which caused the injury, was directly within the scope of the minor's regular contract of employment.

It is claimed that the trial court gave the jury an oral instruction in violation of the Statute requiring instructions to be in writing. This claim is not sustained by the record. The defendant at the close of the trial admitted that the premises where the accident occurred were owned and controlled by him. The court merely repeated, in the hearing of the jury and of the counsel on both sides, the admission so made, so that the jury could understand what it was. We perceive no error in the record.

The judgment of the Appellate Court is affirmed.

The case was subsequently reargued and on May 14, 1890, **Wilkin**, *J.*, delivered the opinion of the court:

This is an action on the case by appellee against appellant, and other defendants not served, to recover for a personal injury alleged to have been received by him through their negligence. The declaration is of one count only, and avers that defendant was on the 4th of July, 1886, the owner of and operating a planing-mill in the City of Chicago, wherein he used and employed certain machines for planing wood; and said plaintiff, then a minor, of the age, to wit, twelve years, was then and there employed and engaged by said defendant in and about his said business, and while so employed and engaged the plaintiff was then and there, by said defendant, negligently and improperly ordered and directed to attend to and oil one of the machines then and there used and operated, and being used and operated by said defendant, which said direction and order of said defendant was then and there dangerous and hazardous to this plaintiff, because of his tender age, as aforesaid, and well known so to be by said defendant; and while said plaintiff was engaged in attending to and oiling said machine, in obedience to said order and direction of said defendant, and using all due care and diligence, the arm of said plaintiff was caught, crushed and mangled in and by said machine, so that plaintiff is and will be a cripple for life because thereof, and deprived of the use of said arm. The plea was the general issue. Plaintiff below recovered a judgment for $3,000, and costs, which the appellate court has affirmed.

It must be admitted, we think, that the declaration is rather an unusual one, and somewhat loosely drawn. It does not proceed upon the theory that the injury was received while plaintiff was performing labor outside of his contract of employment, although his counsel so treat it in their argument. The negligence complained of in the declaration is that the defendant wrongfully ordered the plaintiff, he being a child without experience in such matters, to oil a piece of machinery, the doing of which exposed him to great peril of life and limb. It is not the case merely of a minor being set at dangerous work, for in such cases the master is not liable for the risk, if the servant has sufficient capacity to take care of himself, and knows and can properly appreciate the risk. 1 Shearm. & Redf. Neg. 4th ed. § 218.

It belongs to the other class of cases mentioned by the authors, in the same section, of which it is said: "But, while the mere fact of minority is deemed immaterial, it is well settled, in America at least, that any actual incapacity of a minor to understand and appreciate the perils to which he is exposed is to be fully considered, and that he can recover from his master for injuries suffered from any peril the nature of which he did not know, or could not properly appreciate, if he did nominally know, and to which a prudent and right-minded master would not have allowed him to be exposed."

And says Wharton, in his work on Negligence, § 216: "Hence we may hold that where a child is employed the employer must look out for the child, and must see that it is not exposed to danger arising from the structure of building or machinery which an operative of ordinary intelligence and experience would perceive. Notice of danger is not enough. The child must have sufficient instructions to enable him to avoid danger."

Many cases are cited by both these authors in support of the text.

The rule is so just and humane, when applied to a case clearly falling within its principles, that no court would hesitate to enforce it, as of first impression. Children of tender years are often employed about factories in which are used pieces of complicated and dangerous machinery. If one of these is sent by the master or his superintendent, with or without instructions, where he will be exposed to revolving wheels, belts and pulleys, anyone may know that, by reason of his inexperience and immature judgment, he is liable to be killed or maimed, and, if he is injured while using due care for one of his capacity, it would seem too clear for argument that the master should be held liable. To say that such a child takes the risk of his employment,—that if he is not willing to take the hazard of obeying the command he must refuse,—is idle, if not cruel. By his inexperience he is unable to comprehend the risk. By his childish instincts he implicitly obeys. Of the existence of the rule, and its pre-eminent justice, there can be no doubt. Does this case fall within it? This question with us is not, Does the evidence bring plaintiff clearly and satisfactorily within the rule? for, unless we can say there is no evidence tending to support a material element of the case, we must accept the judgment of affirmance in the appellate court as having settled the facts necessary to make out plaintiff's case in his favor. It is contended, however, that the evidence wholly fails to show that the foreman of defendant ordered the plaintiff to oil the machine by which he was hurt, but that the boy's own testimony proves the contrary. We do not so construe it. It certainly tends to prove that he was attempting to oil the machine, because he had been told to do so by Joseph Knourek, the foreman. True, the foreman did not, at that moment, command him to do so, but he testified that he had general instructions from the foreman to attend to that duty when the machine needed oil, and his evidence, at least, tends to show that he was, at the time he received his injury, attempting to obey those instructions.

It does not very clearly appear from the evidence how the injury was incurred. The knee, as we understand the evidence, was first caught by a revolving plate, and then the hand was drawn between the rollers, but just how the knee came in contact with the plate, or how the hand was brought between or within the rollers, does not appear. It is, however, shown by the boy's testimony that, in oiling the machine while in motion, he was exposed to a running belt, and compelled to extend his arm over it. In other words, the effect of his evidence is that to oil that machine while running was attended with danger. It is doubtless true that the foreman, or other experienced person, with mature judgment, could do so with comparative safety; but it is clear from the evidence, especially from the painful results, that it was hazardous for a child to attempt it. The fact that appellee had done that work for some time prior to the accident, and the number of times he had done so, were very proper facts to be considered by the jury in determining whether or not it was negligence in the foreman to require him to continue to do so, and also for the purpose of determining whether or not the injury resulted from inexperience and want of judgment, or from his own negligence; but such proof cannot be held to be conclusive against his right to recover. A child exposed to danger may escape for a time, but sooner or later an injury will in all probability occur.

The case of *Gartland* v. *Toledo, W. & W. R. Co.*, 67 Ill. 498, strenuously insisted upon as governing this case, is not in point. There the question was whether a minor employé should be held bound by the rule which prevents a recovery from the common master for an injury resulting through the negligence of a fellow servant. It was held that the mere fact that the plaintiff in that case was under twenty-one years of age did not relieve him from the risk of negligence on the part of co-employés. Here it was a question of fact for the jury whether or not appellee was a child within the rule stated.

It appears from an amended bill of exceptions that on the trial the court stated to the jury: "It is admitted, by and between counsel, that this defendant was owning and controlling the planing-mill when the injury occurred, and that this foreman was his foreman." It is said this statement amounted to an oral instruction as to the law of the case, and was therefore erroneous. It is not denied that the statement as to the ownership of the planing-mill was authorized by a stipulation of counsel, but it is insisted that the further statement, that the foreman was defendant's foreman, was a conclusion which, if properly drawn from the stipulation, could only have been properly given to the jury in writing. In the first place, the statement was not in any sense an instruction to the jury; again, it was made in open court, and no objection was made to it, either as a statement of the agreement or as an oral instruction; and, finally, it was immaterial. It was not denied on the trial that the foreman who gave the order complained of to appellee was the foreman of appellant. His own testimony shows it.

It is also insisted that the court below improperly refused the following instruction: "If the jury believe from the evidence that the plaintiff was injured by following the direction, or obeying the orders, or through the carelessness or by the fault of his fellow servant, Willie Knourek, then the plaintiff cannot recover." The reason why the common master is not held liable for an injury caused by the negligence of a fellow servant is because that is one of the ordinary risks of the employment. But if the injured employé is a child, incapable of comprehending that risk, the rule ought not to apply. However, this instruction does not announce the rule correctly, as applied to fellow servants generally. It not only assumes that Willie Knourek was a fellow servant of appellee, but that the master had used due care in the selection and employment of him. The instruction attempts to set up an affirmative defense, and, to make it available, it was not only necessary to show that the injury was caused by the negligence of a fellow servant, but also that the master had used ordinary care and prudence in employing such fellow servant. In the foregoing view of the law applicable to the facts of this case, the instructions given to the jury are not subject to the criticism made upon them, and, in our opinion, they are free from substantial error. We repeat, this is not the case merely of a minor under twenty-one years of age, suing for an injury, but of a child to whom the employer owed a special duty. After a careful re-examination of this case we have reached the conclusion that our former judgment of affirmance was right.

CHICAGO CITY R. CO., *Appt.*,
v.
Frank WILCOX.

(......Ill.......)

1. **The negligent omission of duty by its parent,** in permitting a child to go at large unattended, is not to be imputed to the child in a suit by it to recover damages for personal injuries occasioned by the negligence of a third person.
2. **Instructions** that a child about seven years of age cannot be guilty of negligence are erroneous. That is a question for the jury.
3. **Erroneous instructions** are not cured by others contradicting them.

(May 14, 1890.)

APPEAL by defendant from a judgment of the Appellate Court, First District, affirming a judgment of the Circuit Court for Cook County in favor of plaintiff in an action brought to recover damages for personal injuries alleged to have resulted from defendant's negligence. *Reversed.*

The case sufficiently appears in the opinion.

Mr. **C. M. Hardy** for appellant.

Messrs. **Charles E. Pope** and **E. F. Masterson** for appellee.

Wilkins, *J.*, delivered the opinion of the court:

Action on the case begun in the Circuit Court of Cook County, to the September Term, 1887. The declaration charges that appellant was on the 24th day of June, 1887, running a line of street "grip-cars" on Wabash Avenue, in the City of Chicago, and that plaintiff, in crossing its track on Harmon Court, using due care, was, by the negligence of defendant's employés in charge of one of its cars, run over, and one of his legs so bruised and wounded that it became necessary to amputate it. He

NOTE.—*Doctrine of imputed negligence.*

The contributory negligence of a carrier is no bar to the right of a passenger to recover from another party for injuries received in consequence of the latter's negligence. New York, P. & N. R. Co. v. Cooper, 13 Va. L. J. 290; Flaherty v. Northern Pac. R. Co. 39 Minn. 328; Whelan v. New York, L. E. & W. R. Co. (Ohio) 38 Fed. Rep. 15. See *note* to Nisbet v. Garner (Iowa) 1 L. R. A. 152.

Where a husband, at his wife's request, called at a drug store for a harmless medicine, and the agent of the druggist carelessly put up and delivered a poisonous drug, which the wife drank, causing her instant death, the druggist is liable. Davis v. Guarnieri (Ohio) 13 West. Rep. 438, 45 Ohio St. 470.

The contributory negligence of the husband in the purchase of the drug to be used by the wife is not imputable to her, the doctrine of imputable negligence not prevailing in Ohio. *Ibid.*

The rule that the negligence of the driver of a wagon is not imputable to one riding with him when an accident occurs at a railroad crossing, is applicable only to cases where the relation of master and servant, or principal and agent, does not exist, or where the passenger is seated away from the driver, or is separated from him by an inclosure, and is without opportunity to discover danger and to inform the driver of it. Brickell v. New York, C. & H. R. R. Co. 30 N. Y. S. R. 982.

The rule as to imputed negligence as asserted in Thorogood v. Bryan, 8 C. B. 114, the leading case, has

recovered a judgment for $15,000, which was affirmed by the appellate court. At the time of the injury, plaintiff was but six years of age, living with his parents near the place of his injury.

On the trial the court gave to the jury the following instruction: "The court instructs the jury for the plaintiff that if they, from the evidence, believe that the parents are working people, and that the father was not present at the time of the accident, and that the mother was attending to her usual occupation, in attending their little store on Harmon Court, in such event the law does not require that persons in their station in life shall keep constant watch over their children, nor can the want of such care be imputed to them as negligent conduct; nor can negligence be imputed to the child on account of its age,—he being seven years of age, or about that, at that time." This, appellant insists, was error. No other question of law is presented for our decision. We need only direct our attention to the propositions of law announced in it.

The first part of this instruction assumes that, in an action by a child so young, negligence cannot be imputed to it, to recover for a personal injury received through the negligence of another, want of proper care by its parent, guardian or other custodian, in suffering it to go at large unattended, cannot be charged to the child as contributory negligence, so as to defeat the action. If this hypothesis is incorrect, that part of the instruction could only have operated to the plaintiff's prejudice, and the defendant cannot complain of its inaccuracy. The instruction also lays it down as a rule of law that a child of seven years of age cannot in such case be chargeable with personal negligence. Thus two legal questions are presented for decision, upon either of which there is to be found a conflict of authorities. On the first, two well-defined lines of decisions appear, each in direct conflict with the other. In Shearman & Redfield on Negligence the rule established by one line of these decisions is denominated the "New York rule," the other the "Vermont rule." Sections 74, 78. The first is based upon *Hartfield* v. *Roper*, 21 Wend. 615, in which it is said: "An infant is not *sui juris*. He belongs to another, to whom discretion in the care of his person is exclusively confided. That person is keeper and agent for this purpose, and, in respect to third persons, his act must be deemed that of the infant. His neglect is the infant's neglect." The other or Vermont rule "holds that the contributory negligence of a parent, guardian or other person having control of the child is not to be imputed to the child itself," so as to defeat an action by it for an injury caused by the negligence of another. *Robinson* v. *Cone*, 22 Vt. 213.

It is insisted by counsel for the appellant that we are committed to the first-named rule. Messrs. Shearman and Redfield seem to have so understood some of our former decisions, and so cite them in their valuable work on the Law of Negligence. 4th ed. vol. 1, § 74, *note 6*.

It will be found upon examination that the cases cited do not bear that construction. *Hund* v. *Geier*, 72 Ill. 393, was a suit by a father for an injury to his infant son. *Toledo, W. & W. R. Co.* v. *Grable*, 88 Ill. 441; *Chicago* v. *Hesing*, 83 Ill. 204; *Chicago* v. *Starr*, 42 Ill. 174; *Chicago & A. R. Co.* v. *Becker*, 76 Ill. 25; and the same case in 84 Ill. 483,—in each of which cases the action was by an administrator for the benefit of the parents as next of kin. These cases are so clearly distinguishable from those in which the child himself sues that they must have been cited by mistake. See Id. § 71.

The two remaining cases cited in *note 6* were

---

been criticised in England (The Milan, Lush. 388), and has been pronounced unsound by many of the American courts. See Little v. Hackett, 116 U. S. 366 (29 L. ed. 652); Wabash, St. L. & P. R. Co. v. Shacklet 105 Ill. 364; Bennett v. New Jersey R. & Transp. Co. 36 N. J. L. 225; New York, L. E. & W. R. Co. v. Steinbrenner, 47 N. J. L. 161; Chapman v. New Haven R. Co. 19 N. Y. 341; Dyer v. Erie R. Co. 71 N. Y. 228; Transfer Co. v. Kelly, 36 Ohio St. 86; See *notes* to Nisbet v. Garner (Iowa) 1 L. R. A. 153, Wymore v. Mahaska County (Iowa) 6 L. R. A. 545, Chicago City R. Co. v. Robinson (Ill.) 4 L. R. A. 126.

Negligence of parent not imputable to child.

In an action by a child itself for personal injuries the negligence of its mother in allowing it to go upon the public streets unattended by a person of mature years constitutes no defense. Winter v. Kansas City Cable R. Co. 6 L. R. A. 536, 99 Mo. 509.

A child of tender years is not precluded from recovering damages for an injury which might have been avoided by the exercise of ordinary care by defendant, from the fact that his parent or guardian allowed him to place himself in a position of danger without a custodian. Bisaillon v. Blood, 6 New Eng. Rep. 908, 64 N. H. 565.

In Iowa, the contributory negligence or wrongful act of the parent, without volition on the part of the child, is not imputable to the latter. Wymore v. Mahaska County, 6 L. R. A. 545, 78 Iowa, 396.

If the parents were negligent, but the child was not, such negligence on the part of the parents would not absolve the defendant from liability. Ihl v. Forty-Second Street & G. St. Ferry R. Co. 47 N. Y. 317; McGarry v. Loomis, 63 N. Y. 107.

It cannot be said that it was, as matter of law, under the circumstances proved, negligence for the parents to permit her to go on to the sidewalk to play; and whether it was or was not was a question for the determination of the jury. Oldfield v. New York & H. R. R. Co. 14 N. Y. 310; Ihl v. Forty-Second Street & G. St. Ferry R. Co. and McGarry v. Loomis, *supra*.

The right of recovery in favor of the estate of a child killed by another's negligence is not affected by the fact that his parents, who are entitled to his estate by inheritance, contributed to the accident. Wymore v. Mahaska County, *supra*.

An action by a child three years old for personal injuries on the public streets is not defeated by the negligence of another child ten years old, who was the only protector for the injured child present at the time. Winter v. Kansas City Cable R. Co. *supra*.

But in an action by a parent for injury to his child, the contributory negligence of a third person, to whom he intrusts the custody or care of such child, is imputable to him and he is charged with the consequences; so where he placed his child in the care and custody of its grandmother her negligence in permitting the child to trespass on the railroad track is imputable to him and bars his recovery. Pratt Coal & Iron Co. v. Bradley, 88 Ala. 371.

suits by the child in its own name, but neither of them holds that negligence on the part of the parents would have defeated the action.

In *Gavin* v. *Chicago*, 97 Ill. 66, Gavin recovered a judgment in the Circuit Court of Cook County against the City of Chicago for an injury to his person alleged to have been occasioned by the city in negligently maintaining a swing bridge. That judgment was reversed by the appellate court of the first district, and Gavin prosecuted a writ of error to this court. The judgment of the appellate court was affirmed on the broad ground that the evidence showed no negligence on the part of the city. It appeared, however, that on the trial the care bestowed upon the plaintiff by his parents, he being a child but four years of age, was submitted to the jury; and *Justice* Scott, rendering the opinion of the court, said: "Under the circumstances proven, the jury found there was no negligence on the part of the mother touching the care she bestowed upon her child."

In *Chicago & A. R. Co.* v. *Gregory*, 58 Ill. 226, the defendants offered proof of the negligence of the plaintiff's mother in permitting him to go unattended in a place of danger. The competency of such evidence was not raised either on the trial below or in this court. In affirming the judgment of the circuit court, it was said the evidence failed to establish such negligence; but that fact in no way controlled in the decision of the case. All that can be fairly said in regard to these cases is that the question now under discussion might have been raised in them, but counsel did not see fit to do so; and, as its decision did not become necessary to a proper determination of the cases, the court was not called upon to express any opinion upon it, and did not.

In Wharton on Negligence, *Ross* v. *Innis*, 26 Ill. 260; *Chicago* v. *Starr*, *supra*, and *Pittsburg, Ft. W. & C. R. Co.* v. *Bumstead*, 48 Ill. 221,—are cited, in a *note* to section 311, as holding "that, when a child is negligently permitted by its parents or guardians to stray on a thoroughfare or railroad track, this negligence may be regarded, even when the child brings suit through a guardian or *prochein ami*, as the contributory negligence of the child."

The citation of *Ross* v. *Innis* is evidently a mistake, as the case has no relation whatever to this question.

Chicago v. *Starr*, as already stated, was an action by an administrator for the benefit of the next of kin.

Pittsburg, Ft. W. & C. R. Co. v. *Bumstead*, *supra*, like *Hund* v. *Geier*, *supra*, was an action by the father to recover for an injury to his minor son. It is also to be borne in mind that there is a distinction between cases in which a parent having the immediate custody and control of a child negligently contributes to its injury, as in *Ohio & M. R. Co.* v. *Stratton*, 78 Ill. 88, and those in which the negligence consists in merely permitting it to stray beyond such immediate custody and control into a place of danger. If these distinctions are observed, it will be found that the question now raised has never been decided by this court. So treating it, we are clearly of opinion that the weight of authority and better reasoning is in support of the doctrine that in a case like this the child is not chargeable with a negligent omission of duty by its parent. There was therefore no reversible error in giving the first part of the third instruction. Bishop, Non-Cont. Law, §§ 581–583; Wharton, Neg. §§ 310, 314; 1 Shearm. & Redf. Neg. § 78.

The question as to whether, as a matter of law, personal negligence can be attributable to a child seven years of age, as before stated, is also one upon which the authorities are not harmonious. In 1 Shearman & Redfield on Negligence, § 73, it is said: "In analogy to the rule which holds a child under seven years of age incapable of crime, some courts have considered them also incapable of negligence; but we think that this is not to be conclusively presumed. Juries may be depended upon not to overrule this presumption except in perfectly clear cases."

In *Toledo, W. & W. R. Co.* v. *Becker*, *supra*, the first branch of one of the instructions given on behalf of the plaintiff told the jury "that the law does not require that a boy six or seven years of age should exercise that degree of diligence that would be required of a grown person." This was held to be error, and *Justice* McAllister, delivering the opinion of the court, said: "The age, capacity and discretion of the deceased to observe and avoid danger were questions of fact to be determined by the jury; and his responsibility was to be measured by the degree of capacity he was found to possess. The first branch of the instruction was erroneous in assuming facts and drawing conclusions of law from them. When taken in connection with what followed in the second branch, the jury would be likely to infer that only slight negligence could be imputed on account of his being a boy six or seven years of age."

That decision is in conformity with the well-recognized rule that a child can only be chargeable with want of care for his personal safety in proportion to his age and intelligence. 1 Shearm. & Redf. Neg. § 73; Bishop, Non-Cont. Law, § 586; Wharton, Neg. § 309; *Kerr* v. *Forgue*, 54 Ill. 482; *Chicago, R. I. & P. R. Co.* v. *Eininger*, 114 Ill. 79.

When the case of *Chicago & A. R. Co.* v. *Becker* came up on a second appeal (84 Ill. 483), a reversal was insisted upon on the sole ground that the evidence did not sustain the verdict; and it was then said, in commenting upon the evidence: "While the deceased was no doubt possessed of ordinary intelligence, and was as capable of using as much caution for his safety as other boys of his age, yet it is not to be expected of a boy between six and seven years of age that the same caution and care will be used for personal safety as will be exercised by a person of mature age; and the law will not impute negligence to an infant of such tender years."

The appellate court seems to have understood this case to hold that negligence cannot, as a matter of law, be imputed to a child of the age of six or seven years. Such is not the purport of the decision. In the very same case, it has been expressly held that the question of the child's negligence was one of fact to be determined by the jury.

In *Chicago & A. R. Co.* v. *Murray*, 62 Ill. 326, it was held that a little girl about seven and a half years of age was guilty of contributory negligence, and a judgment in her favor reversed because instructions given on her behalf did not tell the jury to consider whether she had not been guilty of a high degree of negligence even for a person of her age. We think the true rule is that a child is to be held to the exercise of care for its personal safety according to its age, experience and intelligence, and the circumstances by which it was surrounded at the time of the alleged injury; that it cannot be arbitrarily said that negligence may be imputed to a child seven and a half years of age, but not to one of six or seven. Many children of six years of age, by their intelligence and experience, are far more capable of taking care of themselves and avoiding danger than others much older. Certainly no great degree of care for its personal safety is to be expected of a child six or even eight years of age; but we think it safe in each case to submit the question as to whether negligence shall be imputed to a child to the jury, as one of fact, to be determined from the particular circumstances in evidence.

The third instruction took from the jury all question of the plaintiff's negligence,—in fact, told them that, as a matter of law, he could not be guilty of any negligence,—and for that reason was erroneous. Other instructions given on behalf of defendant are directly contradictory to this one, but they do not cure the error contained in it. It is impossible for us to say which direction the jury followed. For the error indicated the *judgment of the Circuit and Appellate Courts must be reversed.*

PEOPLE of the State of Illinois, *ex rel.* Francis B. PEABODY, *Appt.*,

v.

CHICAGO GAS TRUST CO.

(130 Ill. 268.)

1. **Permission to purchase the "capital stock"** of other corporations, found in a corporate charter, will, if properly conferred, enable its recipient to purchase shares of such stock, although there exists under certain circumstances a distinction between "capital stock" and "shares of stock."

2. **Pleas to an information** charging a corporation with purchasing and holding a majority of the shares of stock of other corporations, which admit the holding of capital stock without setting out whether such stock is a majority or less than a majority of the shares, are demurrable.

3. **Since incidental powers of a corporation** must be directly and immediately appropriate to the execution of the specific power granted to it, and power to purchase stock in other gas companies is not necessary to accomplish the power to make and sell gas and operate gas works, the former power cannot exist as incidental to the latter, but express legislative authority is necessary to warrant its exercise.

4. **The provisions of the law** enter into and form a part of the charter of a corporation formed under a General Incorporation Act.

5. **Merely naming a power in the statement** filed with the secretary of state is not sufficient to warrant its exercise by a corporation organized under a General Incorporation Act, if it is not essential to the accomplishment of the object for which the corporation is formed, and is not expressly permitted by the terms of the Act; the law, and not the statement or the license or the certificate, must determine what incidental powers can be exercised.

6. **Power to purchase, hold and sell stock** in other gas companies cannot be exercised by a corporation organized under the General Incorporation Act for the purpose of erecting or operating gas works and manufacturing and selling gas, although such power is specified in its articles of incorporation.

7. **The purpose of purchasing and holding all the shares of the capital stock** of companies engaged in a certain kind of business of a public character in a city or State is not a "lawful purpose" for which a corporation can be organized under the General Incorporation Act (Rev. Stat. chap. 32), as it tends to the creation of a monopoly.

8. **Although the determination of questions of public policy** is ordinarily a legislative function, yet it is the duty of the judiciary to

---

NOTE.—*Contracts against public policy are void.*

The common law will not permit individuals to oblige themselves by contract either to do or not to do a particular thing when the thing to be done or omitted is in any degree injurious to the public. West Virginia Transp. Co. v. Ohio River Pipe Line Co. 22 W. Va. 617; W. U. Tel. Co. v. Am. U. Tel. Co. 65 Ga. 160; Hazlehurst v. Savannah, G. & N. A. R. Co. 43 Ga. 13; Raymond v. Leavitt, 46 Mich. 447; Colles v. Trow City D. Co. 11 Hun, 397; Watson v. Harlem & N. Y. Nav. Co. 52 How. Pr. 348; Faulds v. Yates, 57 Ill. 416; Falls' App. 91 Pa. 434.

All contracts prejudicial to the interests of the public, such as a contract tending to prevent free competition, are void. See *note* to Chippewa, V. & S. R. Co. v. Chicago, St. P. M. & O. R. Co. (Wis.) 6 L. R. A. 601.

The manufacture and distribution of gas by means of pipes placed in the streets of a city is business of a public character. Chicago Gaslight & Coke Co. v. People's Gaslight & Coke Co. 11 West. Rep. 65, 121 Ill. 530.

A contract tending to create and perpetuate a monopoly in furnishing gas to a city is void as against public policy. *Ibid.*

The supplying of illuminating gas is a business of a public nature, to meet a public necessity; and where such business cannot be restrained without prejudice to the public interest, contracts imposing such restraints, however partial, will not be enforced or sustained, because in contravention of public policy. Gibbs v. Baltimore City Consol. Gas Co. 130 U. S. 396 (32 L. ed. 979).

The rule that contracts in partial restraint of trade are not invalid does not apply to a corporation engaged in furnishing that which is a matter of public concern to the inhabitants of a city. Chicago Gas Light & Coke Co. v. People's Gas Light & Coke Co. *supra.*

It is against the general policy of the law to destroy or interfere with free competition, or to permit such destruction or interference. Stewart v. Erie & W. Transp. Co. 17 Minn. 395; Wright v. Ryder, 36 Cal. 342.

If the object of a contract is to prevent or impede free and fair competition in trade, and it may in fact have that tendency, it is void as against public policy. Anderson v. Jett (Ky.) 6 L. R. A. 390.

Where a contract belongs to a class which is reprobated by public policy, it will be declared void, although in that particular instance no injury to

See also 12 L. R. A. 563; 29 L. R. A. 839.

refuse to sustain that which is against the public policy of the State when such policy is manifested by its legislation or fundamental law.

9. The business of manufacturing and distributing illuminating gas by means of pipes laid in the streets of a city is a business of a public character and any unreasonable restraint upon the performance of their duty to the public by companies engaged therein is prejudicial to the public interest and in contravention of public policy.

(November 26, 1889.)

APPEAL by relator from a judgment of the Circuit Court for Cook County in favor of defendant in a proceeding in the nature of a *quo warranto* to determine by what warrant it exercises certain powers, privileges and franchises. *Reversed.*

The case fully appears in the opinion.

Messrs. **George Hunt**, *Atty-Gen.*, and **James K. Edsall**, for appellant:

The capital stock of a corporation is the fund or property of the corporation; while the shares of stock in the corporation are the property of its individual stockholders. The two are not identical. Power to purchase one is not, therefore, power to purchase the other.

Porter v. *Rockford, R. I. & St. L. R. Co.* 76 Ill. 563, 566, 567; *Pacific Hotel Co.* v. *Lieb,* 83 Ill. 602; *Oswego Starch Factory* v. *Dolloway,* 21 N. Y. 449; *Williams* v. *W. U. Teleg. Co.* 93 N. Y. 162, 188; *Minot* v. *Philadelphia, W. & B. R. Co.* 85 U. S. 18 Wall. 206, 229 (21 L. ed. 888, 895); *Burrall* v. *Bushwick R. Co.* 75 N. Y. 211; *VanAllen* v. *Nolan,* 70 U. S. 8 Wall. 583 (18 L. ed. 235): Cook, Stock and Stockholders, § 3, *note 2.*

One corporation cannot become a stockholder in another, unless that power has been specially granted by statute.

Boone, Corp. § 107; Field, Ultra Vires, p. 80; Green's Brice, Ultra Vires, 2d ed. p. 91, *note b; Franklin Co.* v. *Lewiston Sav. Inst.* 68 Me. 43; *New Haven M. & W. M. Mut. Sav. Bank & Bldg. Asso.* v. *Meriden Agency Co.* 24 Conn. 159; *Milbank* v. *New York, L. E. & W. R. Co.* 64 How. Pr. 20, 22, 25, 29; *New Jersey Cent. R. Co.* v. *Pennsylvania R. Co.* 31 N. J. Eq. 475, 484, 494; *Berry* v. *Yates,* 24 Barb. 199; *Sumner* v. *Marcy,* 3 Woodb. & M. 105; *Central R. Co.* v. *Collins,* 40 Ga. 582; *Hazlehurst* v. *Savannah, G. & N. A. R. Co.* 43 Ga. 13; *Franklin Bank* v. *Commercial Bank,* 36 Ohio St. 350, 354; 1 Morawetz, Priv. Corp. §§ 431, 433, 434; *Woods* v. *Memphis & C. R. Co.* (Ala. Ch. Ct.) 5 R. R. & Corp. L. J. 372, 378.

A corporation formed under the general law cannot acquire corporate powers not granted by statute, by the insertion of such powers in its "statement" filed with its secretary of state.

Rev. Stat. chap. 32, §§ 1, 2; *Oregon R. & Nav. Co.* v. *Oregonian R. Co.* 130 U. S. 1, 25 (32 L. ed. 837, 841).

The power to purchase and hold a majority and controlling interest in the shares of stock of four competing corporations, engaged in a public employment, is not a "lawful purpose" for which a corporation may be organized under the laws of this State. What constitutes a "lawful purpose" for which to form a corporation, within the meaning of these terms as used

---

the public may have resulted. Firemen's Charitable Asso. v. Berghaus, 13 La. Ann. 209.

Corporate franchises are public grants.

The sovereign authority is vested in Congress and the Legislatures of the various States, each having its proper and limited sphere of action. Hence corporate franchises must be secured by either an Act of Congress or of the Legislature of the State where the corporation is to be created. Franklin Bridge Co. v. Wood, 14 Ga. 80; Falconer v. Campbell, 2 McLean, 195.

In this country corporate rights can only be conferred by legislative Acts. 1 Dillon, Mun. Corp. § 17; 2 Kent, Com. 277; United States Trust Co. of N. Y. v. Brady, 20 Barb. 119; Pennsylvania R. Co. v. Canal Comrs. 21 Pa. 9; Field, Corp. 20.

Corporate franchises, whether resulting from general or special laws, are grants from the sovereignty of the people. Benefit to the country at large, from the objects for which the corporations are created, constitute the consideration, and in most cases the sole consideration, of the grant. Marshall, *Ch. J.*, in Dartmouth College Case, 17 U. S. 4 Wheat. 518, 637 (4 L. ed. 629, 659).

It is the general rule that corporate franchises are granted upon a trust or condition that the corporate privileges shall not be abused; that the corporation undertakes and agrees, upon condition of forfeiture, that it will so manage and conduct its affairs that it shall not become dangerous or hazardous to the safety of the State or community in and with which it transacts business (Ward v. Farwell, 97 Ill. 593); and that the franchise may be forfeited and the corporation dissolved for acts *ultra vires*, or for breach of the trust condition and perversion of the objects of the grant. Chicago L. Ins. Co. v. Needles, 113 U. S. 574 (28 L. ed. 1084); People v. Dispensary & H. Society of the Women's Inst. 7 Lans. 306; People v. Bristol & R. Turnp. Road, 23 Wend. 225; People v. Fishkill & B. Pl. Road Co. 27 Barb. 445; State v. Milwaukee, L. S. & W. R. Co. 45 Wis. 590; Chesapeake & O. Canal Co. v. Baltimore & O. R. Co. 4 Gill & J. 1, 106; People v. North River Sugar Ref. Co. 2 L. R. A. 33, and *note*, 54 Hun, 355.

Grants by the public are to be strictly construed, and an intention to grant an exclusive privilege or monopoly is not to be implied. State v. Hamilton, 47 Ohio St. —, 23 Ohio L. J. 190.

The principle that, as between the State and its grantee of a franchise, the grant must be construed most strongly against the grantee, is not to be invoked in support of the forfeiture of the franchise. People v. Broadway R. Co. (Sup. Ct.) 29 N. Y. S. R. 343.

Corporations, being mere creatures of the law, possess those powers only which are given to them by their charters. See *note* to Chewacla Lime Works v. Dismukes (Ala.) 5 L. R. A. 100.

The grantee of a public grant can take nothing but what his grant plainly gives. See *note* to Memphis & C. R. Co. v. Woods (Ala.) 7 L. R. A. 605.

Forfeiture and dissolution for misuser of franchise.

In the creation of every corporation there is a tacit condition that the franchise may be forfeited for willful misuser or nonuser in regard to matters which go the essence of the contract between it and the State. Darnell v. State, 48 Ark 321.

Corporate franchises cannot be forfeited except in clear cases of violation of the Statute. People v. O'Brien, 2 L. R. A. 225, 111 N. Y. 1; Crawfordsville & S. W. Turnp. Co. v. Fletcher, 1 West. Rep. 247, 104 Ind. 97.

A corporation which has entered into an illegal combination, creating a monopoly, is by reason thereof liable to forfeiture and dissolution, at the suit of the people, under N. Y. Code Civ. Proc.,

in the Statute, is a judicial question, to be determined by the courts in each case as it shall arise.

Ill. Rev. Stat. chap. 32, §§ 1, 2; *Oregon R. & Nav. Co.* v. *Oregonian R. Co. supra.*

To permit a corporation or trust company to be formed for the purpose of concentrating in its hands a controlling interest in the shares of stock of other competing corporations exercising a public employment like these gas companies, would necessarily so combine and blend their interest as to prevent competition between them, and thus injuriously affect the public interest.

Chicago Gas-Light & Coke Co. v. *People's Gas Light & Coke Co.* 11 West. Rep. 63, 121 Ill. 530; *Craft* v. *McConoughy*, 79 Ill. 346; *Weidenger* v. *Spruance*, 101 Ill. 278, 285; *Milbank* v. *New York, L. E. & W. R. Co. supra; Gibbs* v. *Baltimore City Consol. Gas. Co.* 130 U. S. 396, 408 (32 L. ed. 979, 984).

Whatever tends to prevent competition among those engaged in a public employment, or business impressed with a public character, is opposed to public policy, and is therefore unlawful, *ipso facto*, without proof of evil intention, or actual injury to the public.

Chicago Gas Light & Coke Co. v. *People's Gas Light & Coke Co.* and *Gibbs* v. *Baltimore City Consol. Gas Co. supra;* Cook, Tr. pp. 21, 28-31; *Hooker* v. *Vandewater*, 4 Denio, 349, 353; Greenhood, Pub. Pol. 655, 656; *Central Ohio Salt Co.* v. *Guthrie*, 35 Ohio St. 666; *Gibbs* v. *Smith*, 115 Mass. 592; *Swan* v. *Chorpenning*, 20 Cal. 182.

This combination of the four competing gas companies of Chicago, through the intervention of this Gas Trust Company, is against the policy of the Consolidation Laws of this State.

New Orleans Gas Co. v. *Louisiana Light & Heat P. & Mfg. Co.* 115 U. S. 650 (29 L. ed. 516); 1 Starr & C. Stat. p. 626, par. 53, § 4.

Messrs. **Goudy, Green & Goudy,** for appellee:

There is nothing in the common law to prevent one corporation from taking or accepting shares in another corporation.

Royal Bank of India's Case, L. R. 4 Ch. 252; *Booth* v. *Robinson*, 55 Md. 419; *Central R. Co.* v. *Collins*, 40 Ga. 583; *Hazlehurst* v. *Savannah, G. & N. A. R. Co.* 43 Ga. 13; *Chicago, P. & S. W. R. Co.* v. *Marseilles*, 84 Ill. 643; *Clapp* v. *Peterson*, 104 Ill. 26; *Fraser* v. *Ritchie*, 8 Ill. App. 554.

The charter of the Chicago Gas Trust Company is a complete warrant for the purchase of the stock mentioned in the pleas.

Morawetz, Priv. Corp. § 318; *Ashbury R. C. & Iron Co.* v. *Riche*, L. R. 7 H. L. 653.

The proposition is not sound, that anything that tends to relax competition is unlawful.

Central Shade Roller Co. v. *Cushman*, 3 New Eng. Rep. 505, 143 Mass. 353; *Com.* v. *Hunt*, 4 Met. 111; *Snow* v. *Wheeler*, 113 Mass. 179; *Dolph* v. *Troy Laundry Mach. Co.* 28 Fed. Rep. 553; *Skrainka* v. *Scharringhausen*, 8 Mo. App. 522; *Ontario Salt Co.* v. *Merchants Salt Co.* 18 Grant, Ch. 540; *Wickens* v. *Evans*, 3 Younge & J. 318; *Chappel* v. *Brockway*, 21 Wend. 157; *Diamond Match Co.* v. *Roeber*, 9 Cent. Rep. 181, 106 N. Y. 473; *Leslie* v. *Lorillard*, 1 L. R. A. 456, 110 N. Y. 519; *Marsh* v. *Russell*, 66 N.

---

§ 1798, for the abuse of its powers and for the exercise of privileges and franchises not conferred upon it by law." *Note* to People v. North River Sugar Ref. Co. (N. Y.) 2 L. R. A. 33.

The charter of a corporation will not be declared to be forfeited except in a proceeding instituted directly for that purpose by the government granting the charter. Jersey City Gaslight Co. v. Consumers Gas Co. 4 Cent. Rep. 331, 40 N. J. Eq. 427; Broadwell v. Merritt, 2 West. Rep. 185, 87 Mo. 95; Thompson v. People, 23 Wend. 576.

The remedy against a corporation for misuser or nonuser of its corporate franchises is an action at law by *scire facias*, prosecuted at the instance and on behalf of the government. Atty-Gen. v. Stevens, 1 N. J. Eq. 369; Merrick v. Brainard, 38 Barb. 595; Patrick v. Ruffners, 2 Rob. (Va.) 209; State v. Fourth N. H. Turnp. 15 N. H. 162; Com. v. Cullen, 13 Pa. 133; Silver Lake Bank v. North, 4 Johns. Ch. 373, 1 N. Y. Ch. L. ed. 872; John v. Farmers & M. Bank, 2 Blackf. 367.

The forfeiture can only take effect upon a judgment of a competent tribunal on a proceeding in behalf of the State. Allen v. New Jersey S. R. Co. 49 How. Pr. 17; New York Marbled Iron Works v. Smith, 4 Duer, 362; Kincaid v. Dwinelle, 5 Jones & S. 326; Cary v. Schoharie Valley Mach. Co. 2 Hun, 110; Bradt v. Benedict, 17 N. Y. 99; N. Y. Code, § 430.

Dissolution of a corporation can take place only: (1) by an Act of the Legislature, where power is reserved for that purpose; (2) by a surrender, which is accepted, of the charter; (3) by a loss of all its members, or of an integral part, so that the exercise of corporate functions cannot be restored; (4) by forfeiture, which must be declared by judgment of court. Penobscot Boom Corp. v. Lamson, 16 Me. 231; Vernon Society v. Hills, 6 Cow. 23; Bank of Niagara v. Johnson, 8 Wend. 645; Wilde v. Jenkins, 4 Paige, 481, 3 N. Y. Ch. L. ed. 524; Chesapeake & O. Canal Co. v. Baltimore & O. R. Co. 4 Gill & J. 121; Russell v. M'Lellan, 14 Pick. 63; Revere v. Boston Copper Co. 15 Pick. 351; Peter v. Kendal, 6 Barn. & C. 703; 2 Kent, Com. 312.

The power which may have been abused or abandoned cannot be taken away but by regular process. Vernon Society v. Hills, 6 Cow. 26; Morley v. Thayer, 3 Fed. Rep. 748; State v. Real Estate Bank, 5 Ark. 595; Boston Glass Manufactory v. Langdon, 24 Pick. 49; Chesapeake & O. Canal Co. v. Baltimore & O. R. Co. 4 Gill & J. 1; Wilde v. Jenkins, *supra.*

It can only be effected by judicial trial and judgment; and so it has been held even where the Act provided that in default of fulfilling the condition the corporation should be dissolved. People v. Manhattan Co. 9 Wend. 354; Bank of Niagara v. Johnson, 8 Wend. 645; Briggs v. Penniman, 8 Cow. 387; Rex v. Amery, 2 T. R. 515; People v. Runkle, 9 Johns. 147; Terrett v. Taylor, 13 U. S. 9 Cranch, 43 (3 L. ed. 650); Verplanck v. Mercantile Ins. Co. 1 Edw. Ch. 84, 6 N. Y. Ch. L. ed. 68; Doyle v. Peerless Petroleum Co. 44 Barb. 239; Gilman v. Green Point Sugar Co. 61 Barb. 9.

Whenever there is a nonuser or misuser of its franchises, the corporation may be adjudged dissolved for a breach of trust. Rex v. London, 1 Show. 274; Exeter v. Glide, 4 Mod. 33.

Consolidation of corporations, creating a trust, is ultra vires.

Corporations can only consolidate with the consent of the Legislature, and when a consolidation is thus effected, it amounts to a surrender of the old charters and the formation of a new corporation out of such portions of the old as enter into the new. State v. Bailey, 16 Ind. 46.

The authority for two or more corporations to consolidate is derived from the statute. See *note*

Y. 288; *Kellogg* v. *Larkin*, 3 Pinney, 123; Morawetz, Priv. Corp. §1181; *Illinois Cent. R. Co.* v. *People*, 10 Cent. Rep. 582, 121 Ill. 319; *Collins* v. *Locke*, L. R. 4 App. Cas. 674; *Leather Cloth Co.* v. *Lorsont*, L. R. 9 Eq. 345; *Mogul Steamship Co.* v. *McGregor*, L. R. 15 Q. B. Div. 476; *Mogul Steamship Co.* v. *McGregor*, L. R. 21 Q. B. Div. 544; *Perkins* v. *Lyman*, 9 Mass. 521; *Havemeyer* v. *Havemeyer*, 11 Jones & S. 506, 86 N. Y. 618.

Defendant's charter is a determination by the executive department of the government that the organization was for lawful purposes: it is only in cases of clear infringement that courts will interpose to hold such acts nugatory.

People v. *Hatch*, 33 Ill. 9; Cooley, Const. Lim. 69.

In the ordinary acceptation of terms, to purchase and hold stocks of gas companies is a lawful purpose.

Healy, Joint-Stock Companies, p. 182.

The Legislature, not the courts, has the right to declare the public policy of a State.

State v. *Clarke*, 54 Mo. 17; *Carroll* v. *East St Louis*, 67 Ill. 568; *Santa Clara Female Academy* v. *Sullivan*, 4 West. Rep. 114, 116 Ill. 375; *Stevens* v. *Pratt*, 101 Ill. 206; *Cowell* v. *Colorado Springs Co.* 100 U. S. 55 (25 L. ed. 547).

Magruder, *J.*, delivered the opinion of the court:

The Chicago Gas Trust Company, appellee herein, was organized under the General Incorporation Law of this State. The statement filed by the original incorporation with the secretary of state sets forth that the Trust Company was formed for two objects, or for one object of a two-fold character. The object named in the first clause of the second specification of the "statement" is, in brief, the erection and operation of works in Chicago, and other places in Illinois, for the manufacture, sale and distribution of gas and electricity. The object named in the second clause of the second specification of the statement is, in brief, "to purchase and hold or sell the capital stock" of any gas or electric company or companies in Chicago, or elsewhere in Illinois.

In this proceeding no attack is made upon the validity of the organization of the Gas Trust Company as a corporation. That it was formed in strict conformity with the requirements of the General Incorporation Law is not denied by the People. Nor does the State here question the right of the appellee Company to acquire and operate works for the manufacture and sale of gas and electricity, in pursuance of the object designated in the first clause above mentioned. Hence the controversy arising upon the demurrer to the pleas in this case is not as to the right of appellee to exist as a corporation, nor as to its right to exercise the first one of the powers sought to be conferred upon it by its charter. The controversy presented by the record relates solely to the authority of the appellee to carry out the object designated in the second

---

to State v. Chicago, B. & Q. R. Co. (Neb.) 2 L. R. A. 564.

It can only be effected through the express sanction of law. See *note* to Botts v. Simpsonville B. C. Turnp. Co. (Ky.) 2 L. R. A. 594.

A trust which is in effect the uniting of several corporations into a practical consolidation or partnership not authorized by their charters or effected under the statutes in reference to consolidation of corporations, is *ultra vires*, and warrants the forfeiture of corporate existence. *Note* to People v. North River Sugar Ref. Co. (N. Y.) 2 L. R. A. 33.

The centralization of corporate franchises in a single irresponsible power furnished with every delegated facility for regulating and controlling at will, throughout the country, the production and price of a particular and necessary article of commerce, creates a monopoly which is unlawful. *Ibid.*

Combinations to control trade are illegal.

The uniting of corporations into a particular consolidation or partnership, not authorized by their charters or effected under statutes in reference to consolidation of corporations, is *ultra vires*, and warrants the forfeiture of their corporate existence. *Note* to People v. North River Sugar Ref. Co. (N. Y.) 2 L. R. A. 33.

Such combinations have frequently been condemned by courts as unlawful and against public policy. Craft v. McConoughy, 79 Ill. 346; Alger v. Thacher, 19 Pick. 51; Hannah v. Fife, 27 Mich. 172; Hooker v. Vandewater, 4 Denio, 349; Stanton v. Allen, 5 Denio, 434, Hoffman v. Brooks, 11 Cin. W. L. Bull. 258; Central Ohio Salt Co. v. Guthrie, 35 Ohio St. 672; Morris Run Coal Co. v. Barclay Coal Co. 68 Pa. 186.

The possibility that other business enterprises in the same pursuit may be set on foot to counteract the effect of a combination to control the market in a commodity, will not relieve such combination from illegality. People v. North River Sugar Ref. Co. 5 L. R. A. 386, 54 Hun, 354.

The organization of a corporation for the purpose of controlling the manufacture and trade in matches, by getting all manufacturers of matches to enter into a combination, giving it the whole control of the business, and by buying out all others who might be competitors, is an unlawful enterprise, being an attempt to create a monopoly. Richardson v. Buhl (Mich.) 6 L. R. A. 457.

Monopolies in trade or business, against public policy, are illegal.

Public policy encourages fair dealing, honest thrift and enterprise, and is opposed to monopolies and combinations, because unfriendly to such thrift and enterprise; and it declares all combinations whose object is to destroy or impede free competition in business as utterly void. Bennett, J., in Anderson v. Jett (Ky.) 6 L. R. A. 390.

Monopoly in trade or in any kind of business in this country is odious to our form of government. It is sometimes permitted to aid the government in carrying on a great public enterprise, or public work, under governmental control, in the interest of the public. Its tendency is, however, destructive of free institutions, and repugnant to the instincts of a free people, and contrary to the whole scope and spirit of the Federal Constitution, and is not allowed to exist under express provision in several of our state constitutions. It is alike destructive of both individual enterprise and individual prosperity, whether conferred upon corporations or individuals, and therefore public policy is, and ought to be, as well as public sentiment, against it. All combinations among persons or corporations for the purpose of raising or controlling the prices of merchandise, or any of the necessaries of life, are monopolies, and are intolerable, and ought to receive the condemnation of all courts. Sher-

clause above mentioned. It is claimed on the part of the People that the charter or articles of association of the Gas Trust Company did not and could not confer upon it the power "to purchase and hold . . . the capital stock" of other gas companies. It is averred in the information, and admitted in eight of the eleven pleas, that appellee has purchased, and now holds, a majority of the shares of the capital stock of four gas companies, to wit, the Chicago Gas-Light & Coke Company, the People's Gas-Light & Coke Company, the Equitable Gas-Light & Fuel Company and the Consumer's Gas Company; and it is admitted in three of the pleas that the appellee has purchased, and now holds, some portion of the capital stock of said four companies. The information charges that, by so purchasing and holding a majority of the shares of the capital stock of each of the four companies, the appellee usurps and exercises "powers, liberties, privileges and franchises not conferred by law." The appellee pleads, in justification, that the power so to purchase and hold the stock is granted by the terms of its charter.

Can the Chicago Gas Trust Company lawfully purchase and hold the stock of other gas companies? A distinction is sought to be drawn between "capital stock" and "shares of stock." It is said that capital stock means the entire property owned by the corporation, while a share in the stock is the right to partake, according to the amount put into the fund, of the surplus profit obtained from the use and disposal of the capital stock of the Company to those purposes for which the Company is constituted. It is therefore insisted by the appellant that, even if the charter of the appellee can be held to confer the power to purchase and hold the general property or funds of other gas companies, it does not for that reason confer the power to purchase and hold shares of stock in such other companies.

The distinction contended for undoubtedly exists under certain circumstances, and for certain purposes; but we think that, in the present case, the words, "the capital stock of any gas company or companies," are broad enough to include shares of stock. In the General Incorporation Act, under which the appellee and Consumers' Gas Company and the Equitable Gas-Light & Fuel Company are all organized, the statement is required to set forth "the name of the proposed corporation, the object for which it is to be formed, its capital stock, the number of shares of which such stock shall consist," etc. The original charter of the Chicago Gas-Light & Coke Company provides that "the capital stock of said company shall not exceed $300,000, to be divided into shares of $25," etc. The charter of the People's Gas-Light & Coke Company, as amended in 1865, also provides that its capital stock may be divided into shares. The terms thus used designate the capital stock of a corporation as that which consists of, or may be divided into, shares. Hence, for the purposes of the present discussion, "the capital stock of any gas company" may be regarded as the aggregate of all the shares of such stock.

---

wood, *Ch. J.*, in Richardson v. Buhl (Mich.) 6 L. R. A. 466.

No remedy on such contracts at law or in equity.

Contracts growing out of illegal or immoral acts are not enforceable; the governing principle being *ex dolo malo non oritur actio.* See *notes* to Cobbs v. Hixson (Mich.) 4 L. R. A. 682; Bowman v. Phillips (Kan.) 3 L. R. A. 631.

Neither law nor equity will afford relief between the parties to such contracts, who are *in pari delicto.* See *note* to Leonard v. Poole, 4 L. R. A. 728.

Wherever two or more persons are engaged in a fraudulent transaction to injure another, neither law nor equity will interfere to relieve either of those persons, against the other, from the consequences of their own misconduct. Dent v. Ferguson, 132 U. S. 50 (33 L. ed. 242).

No one shall, by the aid of a court of justice, obtain the fruits of an unlawful contract. Gibbs v. Baltimore City Consol. Gas Co. 130 U. S. 396 (32 L. ed. 979).

It is well settled that if a contract be void as against public policy the court will neither enforce it while executory, nor relieve a party from loss by having performed it in part. Foote v. Emerson, 10 Vt. 344; Hanson v. Power, 8 Dana, 91; Pratt v. Adams, 7 Paige, 616, 4 N. Y. Ch. L. ed. 303; Piatt v. Oliver, 1 McLean, 300, 2 McLean, 277; Stanton v. Allen, 5 Denio, 434.

Contracts tending to the injury of public interests will not be enforced. See *note* to Bowman v. Phillips, *supra.*

Where a business is of such a character that it presumably cannot be restrained to any extent whatever, without prejudice to the public interest, courts decline to enforce or sustain contracts imposing such restraints, however partial, because in contravention of public policy. Gibbs v. Baltimore City Consol. Gas Co. 130 U. S. 408 (32 L. ed. 984); Woodstock Iron Co. v. Richmond & D. Extension Co. 129 U. S. 644 (32 L. ed. 819); Arnot v. Pittston & E. Coal Co. 68 N. Y. 558; Morrill v. Boston & M. R. Co. 55 N. H. 537.

An agreement between parties unequivocally a combination in restraint of trade, and to enhance the price in the market of bagging, an article of prime necessity to cotton planters, cannot be enforced in a court of justice. India Bagging Asso. v. Kock, 14 La. Ann. 164; Glasscock v. Wells, 23 La. Ann. 517; Cummings v. Saux, 30 La. Ann. 207.

An agreement to advance the price of lard by in part withholding from the market that which was owned or controlled by the association is not enforceable in a court of justice. Keene v. Kent, 4 N. Y. St. Rep. 431; Leonard v. Poole, 4 L. R. A. 728, 114 N. Y. 371.

Courts will take notice, of their own motion, of illegal contracts which come before them for adjudication. Richardson v. Buhl (Mich.) 6 L. R. A. 457.

A criminal offense.

Persons who participate in an unlawful scheme to raise the price of a commodity of trade are all principals, although some may act as mere agents, and are to profit less than others, or even not at all. Leonard v. Poole, 4 L. R. A. 728, 114 N. Y. 371.

This was held under a penal statute of the State which provides that if two or more persons conspire to commit any act injurious to trade or commerce each of them is guilty of a misdemeanor. 2 Rev. Stat. 692, § 8, subd. 6; People v. Fisher, 14 Wend. 9; Hooker v. Vandewater, 4 Denio, 349; Stanton v. Allen, 5 Denio, 434; Arnot v. Pittston & E. Coal Co. 68 N. Y. 558.

Agreements to stifle competition in trade are void, and conspiracies to injure trade are indictable at common law. People v. North River Sugar Ref. Co. 3 L. R. A. 33, and *note*, 54 Hun, 355. See *note* to Richardson v. Buhl (Mich.) 6 L. R. A. 457.

The first, third and seventh pleas aver that the defendant uses and exercises "the power, liberty, privilege and franchise of purchasing and holding the capital stock of gas companies in the State of Illinois," and that in such use and exercise thereof "it has purchased, and still holds, capital stock of four companies," etc., without stating how much capital stock it holds. The demurrer to these pleas might well have been sustained, on the ground that they do not answer the information. The information charges that the defendant has purchased and holds a majority of the shares of stock in each of the four companies, while the pleas answer by saying that defendant holds "capital stock," and do not set forth whether the stock so held is a majority, or less than a majority, of the shares. If it be conceded, however, that the three pleas are not defective for the reason thus specified, they present the question whether appellee can lawfully purchase and hold shares of stock in other gas companies, the number of such shares being less than a majority, and therefore too small to give a controlling interest in such other companies.

There are two views which may be taken of the power to purchase and hold the capital stock of other gas companies, as designated in said second clause: Must it be regarded as an original, independent power, intended to exist exclusively and in addition to the power named in the first clause, or may it be considered as merely ancillary to the other power of maintaining and operating works for the manufacture and sale of gas? If the latter view be correct, the main object for which the Gas Trust Company was formed would be that it might itself maintain and operate works for the manufacture and sale of gas, while the purchase of shares of stock in other companies would be merely a subordinate object, incidental only to the main purpose of the corporate formation. An illustration of this idea may be found in the general law of this State in regard to life insurance companies, which makes it lawful for a life insurance company, organized in the State, to "invest its funds or accumulations in the stocks of the United States, . . . or in such other stocks or securities as may be approved by the auditor." The main object of forming such a company is to engage in the business of life insurance, but the power to invest surplus funds in certain stocks is given as an incident to such business.

Can the power to purchase and hold the stock of other gas companies be lawfully exercised by the appellee, as incidental to the main purpose of maintaining and operating works for the manufacture and sale of gas? Corporations can only exercise such powers as may be conferred by the legislative body creating them, either in express terms or by necessary implication; and the implied powers are presumed to exist to enable such bodies to carry out the express powers granted, and to accomplish the purposes of their creation. *Chicago, P. & S. W. R. Co.* v. *Marseilles*, 84 Ill. 643; *Chicago Gas-Light & Coke Co.* v. *People's Gas-Light & Coke Co.* 121 Ill. 530, 11 West. Rep. 63.

An incidental power is one that is directly and immediately appropriate to the execution of the specific power granted, and not one that has a slight or remote relation to it. *Hood* v. *New York & N. H. R. Co.* 22 Conn. 1; *Franklin Co.* v. *Lewiston Sav. Inst.* 68 Me. 43.

Where a charter, in express terms, confers upon a corporation the power to maintain and operate works for the manufacture and sale of gas, it is not a necessary implication therefrom that the power to purchase stock in other gas companies should also exist. There is no necessary connection between manufacturing gas and buying stocks. If the purpose for which a gas company has been created is to make and sell gas and operate gas-works, the purchase of stock in other gas companies is not necessary to accomplish such purpose. "The right of a corporation to invest in shares of another company cannot be implied, because both companies are engaged in a similar kind of business." 1 Morawetz, Priv. Corp. § 431.

It is true that a gas company might take the stock of another corporation in payment of a debt, or perhaps as security for a debt; but the actual purchase of such stock is not directly and immediately appropriate to the execution of a specifically granted power to operate gas-works and manufacture gas. Some corporations, like insurance companies, may find it necessary to keep funds on hand for the payment of losses by death or fire, or to meet other necessary demands; but it is questionable whether even these can invest their surplus funds in the stocks of other corporations without special legislative authority. But there is nothing in the nature of a gas company which renders it proper for such a company to accumulate funds for outside investment. Its surplus profits belong to the stockholders, and, when distributed among them, can be used by them as they see fit.

If, then, the power to purchase outside stocks cannot be implied from the power to operate gas-works, and make and sell gas, a company to whom the latter power has been expressly granted cannot exercise the former without legislative authority to do so. This is the law, as settled by the great weight of authority. Boone, on the Law of Corporations, says: "Without a power specifically granted or necessarily implied a corporation cannot become a stockholder in another corporation, and especially where the object is to obtain the control or affect the management of the latter." § 107.

In Green's Brice's Ultra Vires (p. 91, *note b*) it is said: "In the United States a corporation cannot become a stockholder in another corporation unless by power specifically granted by its charter, or necessarily implied in it."

So, also, 1 Morawetz on Private Corporations (§§ 431, 433) says: "A corporation has no implied right to purchase shares in another company for the purpose of controlling its management. . . . A corporation cannot, in the absence of express statutory authority, become an incorporator by subscribing for shares in a new corporation, nor can it do this indirectly, through persons acting as its agents or tools."

The authorities referred to by these text-writers sustain the conclusions announced by them. It has been held in many cases that "in the United States corporations cannot purchase or hold or deal in the stocks of other corporations, unless expressly authorized to do so by law;" and that "one corporation cannot become the owner of any portion of the capital stock of another corporation, unless authority to become such is clearly conferred by statute." *Franklin Co.* v. *Lewiston Sav. Inst. supra; Franklin Bank* v. *Commercial Bank*, 36 Ohio St. 350; *Milbank* v. *New York, L. E. & W. R. Co.* 64 How. Pr. 20; *Sumner* v. *Marcy*, 3 Woodb. & M. 105; *New Haven M. & W. M. Mut. Sav. Bank & Bldg. Asso.* v. *Meriden Agency Co.* 24 Conn. 159; *Central R. Co.* v. *Collins*, 40 Ga. 582; *Hazlehurst* v. *Savannah, G. & N. A. R. Co.* 43 Ga. 13; *Berry* v. *Yates*, 24 Barb. 199.

The special charters of the Chicago Gas-Light & Coke Company and of the People's Gas-Light & Coke Company, which are set out in full in the information, and not called in question in any of the pleas, confer, by express grant, the power to erect gas-works, and manufacture and sell gas, etc., but do not confer the power to buy shares of stock in other companies. Upon the latter subject they are silent. It will not be denied that, under the authorities already cited, these two companies cannot buy and hold stock in other gas companies. The same would undoubtedly be admitted to be true of the Chicago Gas Trust Company, if it held under a special charter of like tenor and effect, granted before the adoption of the Constitution of 1870. Does it make any difference that the appellee was organized under the General Incorporation Act? The General Incorporation Act of this State does not, in express terms, confer upon the corporations organized under it the power to purchase and hold shares of stock in other corporations. It is silent upon that subject. The only powers granted by it are the ordinary corporate powers, such as the rights to be bodies corporate and politic, to sue and to be sued, to have a common seal, etc. The charter of a corporation formed under such a general law does not consist of the articles of association alone, but of such articles taken in connection with the law under which the organization takes place. 1 Morawetz, Priv. Corp. § 318. The provisions of the law enter into and form a part of the charter. It certainly cannot be true that a corporation formed under the General Incorporation Act, for a purpose other than that of dealing in stocks, can exercise the power of purchasing and holding stock in other corporations, where such power cannot be necessarily implied from the nature of the power specifically granted, and is not necessary to carry the latter into effect. The power to purchase and hold stock in other companies must be the subject of legislative grant, if not in all cases, at least in cases where it cannot be implied from the powers expressly granted. The General Incorporation Law contains no grant of such power by the Legislature. Can a corporation organized under that Law be clothed with such a power by merely naming it in the statement filed with the secretary of state? We think not. The action of the secretary of state in issuing the license and the certificate of organization is necessarily, to a large extent, merely ministerial. *Oregon R. & Nav. Co.* v. *Oregonian R. Co.* 130 U. S. 1 [32 L. ed. 837]; 4 Am. & Eng. Cyclop. Law, title *Corporations*, p. 192, *note 1*.

Whether the articles of association, consisting of the statement, the license, the report of the commissioners, the certificate of organization, etc., do or do not confer such rights and powers as are authorized by the law is a matter for judicial determination. Counsel for appellee says: "We do not claim, of course, that the action of the secretary of state is conclusive, and not subject to review by this court," etc.

The question whether or not the power to purchase stock is a lawful purpose, under section 1 of the Incorporation Act, which provides that "corporations may be formed in the manner provided by this Act, for any lawful purpose" [Ill Rev. Stat. chap. 32, § 1], does not arise under this branch of the discussion. It will be pertinent, when we come to consider the right to buy and hold stock, as an original and independent power or object of formation. It is not denied by the appellant that the organization of appellee for the purpose of erecting gas-works and making and selling gas is an organization for a lawful purpose. Viewing that as the main purpose for which appellee was formed, the incorporators could not tack on and connect with such main purpose the power to buy and hold stock in other gas companies, by merely describing such power in the statement. To hold that they could confer such power by writing it down in the statement would be to hold that the General Assembly could clothe them with a part of its legislative functions. When a corporation is formed under the General Incorporation Act, for the purpose of carrying on a lawful business, the Law, and not the statement or the license or the certificate, must determine what powers can be exercised as incidents of such business. Even if shares of stock be regarded as personal property, as claimed by counsel for appellee, section 5 of the General Law provides that corporations formed under it "may own . . . so much . . . personal estate as shall be necessary for the transaction of their business, and may sell and dispose of the same when not required for the uses of the corporation, . . . and may have and exercise all the powers necessary and requisite to carry into effect the objects for which they may be formed." [Ill. Rev. Stat. chap. 32, § 5.]

This language negatives the idea that a corporation formed under the General Law can exercise the power of buying and holding the stock of other companies. A company engaged on its own account in manufacturing and selling gas does not need the stock of other gas companies in order to transact its business. Hence it is forbidden to own such stock, the same being "personal estate."

The language of the Act, as thus quoted, expressly restricts the powers of a corporation organized under it to such powers as are necessary and requisite to carry into effect the object for which it was formed. We have already seen that, where the object of forming a gas company is to engage in the business of making and selling gas, the purchase of stock in other companies is not necessary to carry such object into effect. Therefore the General Incorporation Act not only does not expressly authorize the purchase of such stock, but impliedly forbids it in cases where the main purpose of the corporate creation is other than the purchase and sale of stocks. It has been held that the powers obtained by the corporations organized under general laws are necessarily restricted to those mentioned in the Act (*Philadelphia Medical College Case*, 3 Whart. 445); that in such cases the charter is void as to all powers and privileges granted beyond the provisions of the Statute (*Heck* v. *McEwen*, 12 Lea, 97); that, if unauthorized provisions are added to the articles of incorporation, all acts done pursuant to such provisions will be void (*Eastern Pl. R. Co.* v. *Vaughan*, 14 N. Y. 546); that anything in such articles not warranted by the Statutes authorizing the formation of corporate bodies is void for want of authority (*Oregon R. & Nav. Co.* v. *Oregonian R. Co. supra*), and that such articles must be construed strictly and against the grantee, and in favor of the government or the general public. *Ibid.*

Our conclusion upon this branch of the case is that, if the Chicago Gas Trust Company be regarded as a corporation formed for the purpose of erecting or operating gas-works and manufacturing and selling gas, it has no power to purchase and hold or sell shares of stock in other gas companies as an incident to such purpose of its formation, even though such power is specified in its articles of incorporation.

We come, now, to the second view of the right to purchase and hold the stock of other companies, which is involved in the issue presented by demurrers to all of the eleven pleas, including the first, third and seventh. The language of the statement imports an intention to create the Chicago Gas Trust Company for two independent objects. The clauses describing these objects are connected by the conjunction "and." Both were designed to be of equal importance, and to be carried out independently of each other. According to the plain meaning of terms in which they are set forth, neither was to be regarded as secondary or incidental. The first of these objects is stated as follows: "To build, erect, purchase, lease, establish, maintain, enlarge, extend and operate or demise works in . . . Chicago, . . . and in such other place or places in . . . Illinois as said corporation may, by the vote of the majority of its stockholders, elect, for the manufacture, supply, sale and distribution of gas and electricity, or either, for the furnishing of light, heat, fuel and power," etc. There is nothing in this record to show that appellee has ever done anything towards the accomplishment of this first object. The second of the two objects is stated as follows: "And to purchase and hold or sell the capital stock, or purchase or lease or operate the property, plant, good will, rights and franchises, of any gas-works, or gas company or companies, or any electric company or electric companies, in . . . Chicago, . . . or elsewhere, in . . . Illinois, as said corporation may, by vote of the majority of the stockholders, elect," etc.

Manufacturing and selling gas is one kind of business; dealing in stocks is another and different kind of business. If it appeared that the appellee was engaged in both, under its present charter, a serious question might arise as to the power to organize one corporation for two distinct purposes, under the General Incorporation Act of this State. This record, however, only shows that the appellee is exercising the power designated by the declaration of the second object of its formation. What is the power which it is so exercising? If appellee can "purchase and hold the capital stock" of other gas companies, it can hold all the capital stock of such companies. "The capital stock" does not mean a part, but the whole. We have already seen that the "capital stock," as those words are here used, includes all the shares of stock. This view is strengthened by the use of the words, "or purchase or lease or operate the property, plant, good will, rights and franchises" of any gas company. If "capital stock" meant nothing but property, the right to purchase property would not be mentioned in separate words.

Counsel for appellee say in their brief: "It is a pretty nice distinction to say that the power to buy capital stock of a corporation does not include the power to purchase certain of the shares of that stock." If power to purchase "capital stock" includes the power to purchase "certain of the shares of the stock," then power to purchase "the capital stock" includes the power to purchase all the shares of such stock. The power sought to be conferred by these articles of association is something more than the mere right of purchasing certain shares of stock of other gas companies as an investment. An attempt has been made to vest the Chicago Gas Trust Company with the tremendous power of purchasing and holding all the shares of stock, and purchasing and operating all the property, rights and franchises, of every gas company, not only in Chicago, but in the State of Illinois. What has been done under the power thus claimed to have been lawfully granted?

There were four gas companies in the City of Chicago, whose names have already been mentioned. One of them, under an old charter of 1849, had the right to lay its mains and pipes in the streets without permission of the city. The other three had permission to do so under ordinances passed by the city council. All of them laid their pipes and mains, and were engaged in making gas and furnishing it to the inhabitants. They were the only gas companies who were so engaged, and who had undertaken to make such use of the public streets. The Chicago Gas Trust Company has purchased and now holds a majority of all the shares of stock of these four companies. It was itself organized with a capital stock of $25,000,000. The capital stock of the four companies was $16,984,200. How great a majority of such stock is held by the appellee does not appear from the record. What results must necessarily follow from such ownership of a majority of the shares of stock of these four companies? One result is that the Chicago Gas Trust Company can control the four other companies. The question is not whether it has attempted to exercise such control; the law looks to the general tendency of the power conferred. Greenhood, Pub. Pol. 5; *Richardson* v. *Crandall*, 48 N. Y. 348; *Central Ohio Salt Co.* v. *Guthrie*, 35 Ohio St. 666.

The 6th section of the General Incorporation Act provides that the corporate powers shall be exercised by a board of directors or managers, and that the number of such directors or managers, and their terms of office, shall depend upon "the consent of the owners of a majority of the shares of stock." It cannot be denied that the appellee, as owner of the majority of the shares of stock of these four companies, can control them, in the exercise of all their corporate powers, through a board of managers of its own selection.

In *Weidenger* v. *Spruance*, 101 Ill. 278, this court, speaking through *Mr. Justice* Scholfield, said: "The stockholders elect the directors, and, through them, carry into effect the corporate functions. Presumably, the directors act in obedience to the aggregate wishes of the stockholders," etc. *Milbank* v. *New York, L. E. & W. R. Co.* 64 How. Pr. 29.

The control of the four companies by the appellee—an outside and independent corporation —suppresses competition between them, and destroys their diversity of interest, and all motive for competition. There is thus built up a virtual monopoly in the manufacture and sale of gas. The fact that the appellee, almost immediately after its organization, bought up a majority of the shares of stock of each of these companies shows that it was not making a mere investment of surplus funds, but that it designed and intended to bring the four companies under its control, and, by crushing out competition, to monopolize the gas business in Chicago. The General Incorporation Act provides "that corporations may be formed, in the manner provided in this Act, for any lawful purpose, except banking, insurance, real estate, brokerage, the operation of railroads and the business of loaning money." Ill. Rev. Stat. chap. 32, § 1.

The purpose for which a corporation is formed, under the Act, must be a lawful purpose. So far as appellee was organized with the object of purchasing and holding all the shares of the capital stock of any gas company in Chicago or Illinois, it was not organized for a lawful purpose, and all acts done by it towards the accomplishment of such object are illegal and void. The word "unlawful," as applied to corporations, is not used exclusively in the sense of *malum in se* or *malum prohibitum*. It is also used to designate powers which corporations are not authorized to exercise, or contracts which they are not authorized to make, or acts which they are not authorized to do; or, in other words, such acts, powers and contracts as are *ultra vires*. *Franklin Co.* v. *Lewiston Sav. Inst.* and *Oregon R. & Nav. Co.* v. *Oregonian R. Co. supra.*

The business of manufacturing and distributing illuminating gas, by means of pipes laid in the streets of a city, is a business of a public character. It is the exercise of a franchise belonging to the State. The services rendered and to be rendered for such a grant are of a public nature. Companies engaged in such business owe a duty to the public. Any unreasonable restraint upon the performance of such duty is prejudicial to the public interest, and in contravention of public policy. *Chicago Gas Light & Coke Co.* v. *People's Gas Light & Coke Co.* 121 Ill. 530, 11 West. Rep. 68; *Gibbs* v. *Baltimore City Consol. Gas Co.* 130 U. S. 396 [32 L. ed. 979].

Whatever tends to prevent competition between those engaged in a public employment or business impressed with a public character is opposed to public policy, and therefore unlawful. Whatever tends to create a monopoly is unlawful, as being contrary to public policy. 2 Addison, Cont. 748; Greenhood, Pub. Pol. 180, 643, 654, 655, 670; *Morris Run Coal Co.* v. *Barclay Coal Co.* 68 Pa. 173; *Craft* v. *McConoughy*, 79 Ill. 346; *Central R. Co.* v. *Collins*, 40 Ga. 582; *Hazlehurst* v. *Savannah, G. & N. A. R. Co.* 43 Ga. 13; *West Virginia Transp. Co.* v. *Ohio River Pipe Line Co.* 22 W. Va. 600.

In *Craft* v. *McConoughy*, *supra*, where the opinion was delivered by *Mr. Justice* Craig, we said: "We understand it to be a well-settled rule of law that an agreement in general restraint of trade is contrary to public policy, illegal and void. . . . Whatever is injurious to the interest of the public is void on the ground of public policy."

In *Central Ohio Salt Co.* v. *Guthrie*, *supra*, the Supreme Court of Ohio said: "Public policy unquestionably favors competition in trade, to the end that its commodities may be afforded to the consumer as cheaply as possible, and is opposed to monopolies, which tend to advance market prices to the injury of the general public."

We are reminded by counsel that the application by the courts of public policy to the law is a usurpation of legislative functions. And undoubtedly some courts have gone so far as to deserve the charge of such usurpation. But it is the duty of the judiciary to refuse to sustain that which is against the public policy of the State, when such public policy is manifested by the legislation or fundamental law of the State. *Santa Clara Female Academy* v. *Sullivan*, 116 Ill. 375, 4 West. Rep. 114.

By chapter 28 of our Revised Statutes, it is provided that "the common law of England, so far as the same is applicable and of a general nature, . . . shall be the rule of decision, and shall be considered of full force until repealed by legislative authority." Public policy is that principle of law which holds that no subject or citizen can lawfully do that which has a tendency to be injurious to the public, or against the public good. This principle owes its existence to the very sources from which the common law is supplied. Greenhood, Pub. Pol. 2, 3.

The common law will not permit individuals to oblige themselves by a contract either to do or not to do anything, when the thing to be done or omitted is in any degree clearly injurious to the public. *Chappel* v. *Brockway*, 21 Wend. 159; *West Virginia Transp. Co.* v. *Ohio River Pipe Line Co.* 22 W. Va. 600.

In *Stanton* v. *Allen*, 5 Denio, 434, an agreement, whose tendency was to prevent competition, was held to be void by the principles of the common law, because it was against public policy, and injurious to the interests of the State. "Contracts creating monopolies are null and void as being contrary to public policy." 2 Addison, Cont. 748.

All grants creating monopolies are made void by the common law. 7 Bacon, Abr. 22.

In the *Case of the Monopolies*, 11 Coke, 84, it was decided, as long ago as the forty-fourth year of the reign of Queen Elizabeth, that a "grant to the plaintiff of the sole making of cards within the realm was utterly void, and that for two reasons: (1) that it is a monopoly, and against the common law; (2) that it is against divers Acts of Parliament," etc. *Bell* v. *Leggett*, 7 N. Y. 176; *Burke* v. *Child*, 88 U. S. 21 Wall. 441 [22 L. ed. 623].

If contracts and grants whose tendency is to create monopolies are void at common law, then, where a corporation is organized under a general statute, a provision in the declaration of its corporate purposes, the necessary effect of which is the creation of a monopoly, will also be void. Speaking of the articles of association of corporations formed under general laws, the Supreme Court of the United States says: "We have to consider, when such articles become the subject of construction, that they are, in a sense, *ex parte*. Their formation and execution—what shall be put into them, as well as what shall be left out—do not take place under the supervision of any official authority whatever. They are the production of private citizens, gotten up in the interest of the parties who propose to become corporators, and stimulated by their zeal for the personal advantage of the parties concerned rather than the general good. . . . These articles, which necessarily assume by the sole action of the corporators enormous powers, many of which have been heretofore considered of a public character, sometimes affecting the interests of the public very largely and very seriously, do not commend themselves to the judicial mind as a class of instruments requiring or justifying any very liberal construction. Where the question is whether they conform to the authority given by statute in regard to corporate organizations, it is always to be determined upon just construction of the powers granted therein, with a due regard for all the other laws of the State upon that subject. . . . The manner in which these powers shall be exercised, and their subjection to the restraint of the general laws of the State, and its general principles of public policy, are not in any sense enlarged by inserting in the articles of association the authority to depart therefrom." *Oregon R. & Nav. Co.* v. *Oregonian R. Co. supra.*

In the *Oregon Railway Case, supra*, a railroad corporation had been organized under a general law of the State of Oregon which contained the following provision: "Whenever three or more persons shall desire to incorporate themselves for the purpose of engaging in any lawful enterprise, business, pursuit or occupation, they may do so in the manner provided in this Act;" and it was declared in the articles of association that the company might exercise the power to lease the railroad. The court there held that the power to lease its road, and turn over the use of its franchises to another company, was not authorized by the General Incorporation Act of the State, nor by the course of legislation therein, and that therefore such power could not be conferred by the declaration contained in the articles of association. The leasing of the road, in the absence of statutory authority therefor, was not sanctioned as being a "lawful enterprise," within the meaning of the language above quoted.

The public policy of a State may be indicated by the provisions of its Constitution as related to past and present legislation.

In *New Orleans Gas Light Co.* v. *Louisiana Light & Heat P. & Mfg. Co.*, 115 U. S. 650 [29 L. ed. 516], a gas company had been given, in 1835, the exclusive privilege of making and selling gas in New Orleans for some fifty years, and the question was whether such exclusive privilege was abrogated by the new Constitution of 1879, which contained a provision abolishing the monopoly features in all existing charters. The United States Supreme Court said in that case: "The monopoly clause only evinces a purpose to reverse the policy, previously pursued, of granting to private corporations franchises, accompanied by exclusive privileges, as a means of accomplishing public objects." We have been referred to more than fifty special charters granted by the Legislature of this State, in the years 1853, 1854, 1855, 1857, 1859, 1861, 1865, 1867 and 1869, to gas companies in various cities and towns in the State, each one of which confers the exclusive privilege of laying gas-pipes in the streets for a number of years. But when the Constitution of 1870 was adopted, it provided in section 22, art. 4, that the General Assembly should pass no local or special law for "granting to any corporation, association or individual any special or exclusive privilege, immunity or franchise whatever;" and in section 1 of article 11, that "no corporation shall be created by special laws, . . . but the General Assembly shall provide, by general laws, for the organization of all corporations hereafter to be created." Manifestly the Constitution of 1870 reversed the old policy of granting exclusive privileges to gas companies. After 1870 the public policy of the State was against the granting of exclusive privileges to corporations of any kind. The General Incorporation Act of 1872 was passed in pursuance of section 1, art. 11. The prohibition of special charters granting exclusive privileges, and the authorization of incorporations under a general law, followed by the passage of such a law, put the people of this State on record as being opposed to the creation of monopolies of all kinds.

But of what avail is it that any number of gas companies may be formed under the General Incorporation Law, if a giant trust company can be clothed with the power of buying up and holding the stock and property of such companies, and, through the control thereby attained, can direct all their operations, and weld them into one huge combination? The several privileges or franchises intended to be exercised by a number of companies are thus vested exclusively in a single corporation. To create one corporation for the express purpose of enabling it to control all the corporations engaged in a certain kind of business, and particularly a business of a public character, is not only opposed to the public policy of the State, but is in contravention of the spirit, if not the letter, of the Constitution. That the exercise of the power attempted to be conferred upon the appellee Company must result in the creation of a monopoly results from the very nature of the power itself. If the privilege of purchasing and holding all the shares of stock in all the gas companies of Chicago can be lawfully conferred upon appellee under the General Incorporation Act, it can be lawfully conferred upon any other corporation formed for the purpose of buying and holding all the shares of stock of said gas companies. The design of that Act was that any number of corporations might be organized to engage in the same business, if it should be deemed desirable. But the business now under consideration could hardly be exercised by two or three corporations. Suppose that, after appellee had purchased and become the holder of the majority of shares of stock of the four companies in Chicago, another corporation had been organized with the same object in view; that is to say, for the purpose of purchasing and holding a majority of the shares of stock of the gas companies in Chicago, there being only four of such companies. What would there be for the corporation last formed to do? It could not carry out the object of its creation, because the stock it was formed to buy was already owned by an existing corporation. Hence to grant to the appellee the privilege of purchasing and holding the capital stock of any gas company in Chicago is to grant to it a privilege which is exclusive in its character. It is making use of the General Incorporation Law to secure a special "privilege, immunity or franchise;" it is obtaining a special charter under the cover and through the machinery of that Law, for a purpose forbidden by the Constitution. To create one corporation that it may destroy the energies of all other corporations of a given kind, and suck their life-blood out of them, is not a "lawful purpose."

It may be here stated, as showing the policy of the State to be against the purchase by one gas company of stock in other corporations, that the power to purchase such stock is not granted in any of the more than fifty special charters above named. On the contrary, in each of these charters the power of the gas company to acquire and hold personal property is limited to such personal estate "as may be necessary and proper for the construction, extension and usefulness of the works of said company, and for the management and good government of the same." The power of purchasing and holding the capital stock of the four gas companies in question tends to relieve appellee of a proper share of its legal obligations, and to enable it to carry on a gas business without subjecting itself to the restrictions imposed by the Statute. To this extent the exercise of such power is not lawful.

The successful operation of a gas company in any city requires the use of the public streets for the purpose of laying pipes and mains. Section 1, art. 5, of the General Act for the Incorporation of Cities and Villages confers upon the city council the power to regulate the use of the streets, to provide for the lighting of the same, and to regulate the openings therein for the laying of gas pipes and mains, and erecting gas-lights. By the same section it is also provided that any company "organized for the purpose of manufacturing illuminating gas to supply cities or villages, or the inhabitants thereof, with the same, shall have the right, by consent of the common council (subject to existing rights), to erect gas factories, and lay down pipes in the streets or alleys of any city or village in this State, subject to such regulations as any such city or village may by ordinance impose." The General Act for the Formation of Corporations, considered with reference to the powers conferred by it upon gas companies organized under it, must be construed in connection with the City Incorporation Act. The provisions of the latter Act, as above quoted, are to be considered as a part of every charter granted to a gas company under the former Act. The charter, or, speaking more accurately, the articles of association, of every such gas company can only be issued or accepted subject to the foregoing provisions. Hence the appellee Company could not exercise the power of operating works for the manufacture and sale of gas in Chicago without submitting to such regulations as the common council of the city might by ordinance impose, nor could it erect a gas factory and lay its pipes in the streets without the consent of the common council. It accepted its certificate of organization subject to the condition that it would obtain such consent and submit to such regulations, if it engaged in the business of making and selling gas in that city. As between it and the State, it was bound to fulfill this condition in its capacity as a separate and independent organization, and not as the governing influence in the directories of other organizations. But it either does or may engage in the business of making and selling gas in Chicago without obtaining the consent of the council, and without submitting to the regulations of the city, by operating through the four companies, a majority of whose stock it owns, and whose business it can therefore control. It thus indirectly makes use of privileges granted to the four companies, but never granted directly to itself. The regulations which the common council might have deemed it necessary to make, with reference to the use of the streets by appellee, may not have been the same as those which the four companies were required to submit to. But this is not all. By the terms of the provision above quoted, appellee could only obtain the consent of the council to erect gas factories and lay pipes in the streets of the city "subject to existing rights." What were "existing rights?" The rights already secured by the four companies to use the streets and alleys, and make and sell gas. But the appellee, through the controlling interest which it owns in the stock of the four companies, can use the streets, and make and sell gas, independently of the existing rights of the four companies; and not only so, but it either does or may absorb, combine and use the rights of said companies, and subordinate them to its own purposes. In the mode thus indicated, the appellee, in the exercise of the extraordinary power sought to be conferred upon it, may avoid the wholesome restrictions of the law applicable to the circumstances under which gas companies are permitted to use the public streets. By the use of the words "subject to existing rights" in the City Incorporation Act the Legislature plainly indicated its intention that there should be no combination between gas companies, but that each should separately pursue its business of furnishing gas to the inhabitants. If every new company seeking the consent of the council to its use of the streets for laying gas-pipes is required to accept such consent, "subject to existing rights," the companies already existing, and already exercising the rights of using the streets and furnishing light, must be allowed to continue to do so, and to do so independently of the new company, and as separate organizations under their respective charters. Gas companies, being engaged in a business of a public character, are charged with the performance of public duties. Their use of the streets whose fee is held by the municipal corporation, in trust for the benefit of the public, has been likened to the exercise of the power of eminent domain. *Chicago Gas Light & Coke Co.* v. *People's Gas Light & Coke Co. supra.*

In *Gibbs* v. *Baltimore City Consol. Gas Co., supra*, the Supreme Court of the United States, in an able opinion delivered by *Mr. Chief Justice* Fuller, uses these words: "These gas companies entered the streets of Baltimore under their charters, in the exercise of the equivalent of the power of eminent domain, and are to be held as having assumed an obligation to fulfill the public purposes to subserve which they were incorporated."

The privileges awarded to the four gas companies under their respective charters were given them in return for and in consideration of services to be rendered by them to the public. When they entered the streets of Chicago, they assumed the performance of the public duty of furnishing light to the inhabitants. That they should be permitted or required or forced to abandon the performance of such public duty is against the policy of the law. The public duty is imposed upon each company separately, and not upon the four when combined together. Each for itself, when it accepted the articles of association, assumed an obligation to perform the objects of its incorporation. But the appellee, through the control which it does or may exercise over the four companies by reason of its ownership of a majority of their stock, renders it impossible for them to discharge their public duties, except at the dictation of an outside force, and in the manner prescribed by a corporation operating independently of them. They are thus virtually forced to abandon the performance of their duty to the public. The freedom and effectiveness of their action in carrying out the purposes of their creation are seriously interfered with, if not actually destroyed. A power whose exercise leads to such a result cannot be lawfully intrusted to any corporate body.

We held in *Chicago Gas Light & Coke Co.* v. *People's Gas Light & Coke Co., supra*, that for the reasons there stated a contract between two of these four companies, the effect of which was to stifle competition between them, and necessitate an abandonment of their public duties, was against public policy, and could not be enforced. The attempt to consolidate the two companies by placing the majority of their stock in the hands of the appellee would accomplish the same unlawful result which was sought to be obtained by the forbidden contract. In ordinances passed by the common council of the City of Chicago, granting permission to the other two of the four companies, to wit, the Equitable Gas-Light & Fuel Company and the Consumers' Gas Company (or its predecessor), to lay pipes in the streets for the purpose of supplying gas to the inhabitants of the city, it was provided that such permission should not take effect until the two last-named companies had given bond not to "sell, lease or transfer their franchises and privileges to any other gas company," and not to "enter into any combination with any other company concerning the rate (or price) to be charged for gas." But the Chicago Gas Trust Company, by reason of its ownership of the majority of the shares of stock of the Consumer's Company and the Equitable Company, can effect a virtual transfer of their franchises and privileges to itself, in spite of the condition imposed by the ordinance, and in utter disregard of the public interests.

We concur in the following views expressed by the Supreme Court of Georgia in the case of *Central R. Co.* v. *Collins, supra:* "All experience has shown that large accumulations of property in hands likely to keep it intact for a long period are dangerous to the public weal. Having perpetual succession, any kind of a corporation has peculiar facilities for such accumulation, and most governments have found it necessary to exercise great caution in their grants of corporate powers. Even religious corporations, professing, and in the main, truly, nothing but the general good, have proven obnoxious to this objection, so that in England it was long ago found necessary to restrict them in their powers of acquiring real estate. Freed, as such bodies are, from the sure bound to the schemes of individuals,—the grave,—they are able to add field to field, and power to power, until they become entirely too strong for that society which is made up of those whose plans are limited by a single life."

We are of the opinion that the court below erred in overruling the demurrers to the pleas.

The judgment of the Circuit Court is reversed, and the cause is remanded to that court, with directions to sustain the demurrer to the pleas, and for further proceedings in accordance with the views here expressed.

Petition for rehearing denied.

CHICAGO & NORTHWESTERN R. CO., *Appt.*,

v.

Samuel W. CHAPMAN.

(....Ill....)

1. **A common carrier cannot,** even by express contract, exempt itself from liability for losses resulting from its gross negligence or willful misconduct.

2. **An amount named in a bill of lading as the limit of liability** will not restrict recovery for a loss due to gross negligence, where the amount was inserted by the carrier's agent without asking any questions as to the value of the property, and without notice to the shipper of any difference in rates in case of such limitation.

(May 14, 1890.)

APPEAL by defendant from a judgment of the Appellate Court, Second District, af-

NOTE.—Carrier may limit or restrict his liability by contract. See *notes* to Richmond & D. R. Co. v. Payne (Va.) 6 L. R. A. 849; Hull v. Chicago, St. P. M. & O. R. Co. (Minn.) 5 L. R. A. 587, Hartwell v. Northern Pac. Exp. Co. (Dak.) 3 L. R. A. 342; North America Ins. Co. v. Easton (Tex.) 3 L. R. A. 424; Missouri Pac. R. Co. v. Ivey (Tex.) 1 L. R. A. 500.

firming a judgment of the Circuit Court for Kane County in favor of plaintiff for $3,290 in an action to recover damages for the loss of plaintiff's horse while in defendant's possession for purposes of transportation under a contract limiting defendant's liability in case of loss to $100. *Affirmed.*

The case sufficiently appears in the opinion.

Mr. **W. C. Goudy**, with *Messrs.* **W. B. Keep** and **R. N. Botsford**, for appellant.

Mr. **A. H. Barry**, with *Messrs.* **Sherwood & Jones**, for appellee.

Shope, *Ch. J.*, delivered the opinion of the court:

This is an action on the case by appellee against appellant, as a common carrier, to recover damages for the loss of the plaintiff's horse while being shipped over appellant's railroad. There is little dispute as to the facts of the case. There was ample evidence to show gross negligence on the part of the servants of the defendant from which the injury to the horse resulted. By the ruling of the trial court in giving an instruction for the plaintiff, and in the modification of one asked by the defendant, the question of law is presented whether it is competent for a railway carrier to limit or restrict by contract its liability for an injury to property, during its transportation, against the gross negligence of the carrier or its servants. The Act in respect of common carriers, approved March 27, 1874, provides "that, whenever any property is received by a common carrier to be transported from one place to another within or without this State, it shall not be lawful for such carrier to limit his common-law liability safely to deliver such property at the place to which the same is to be transported, by any stipulation or limitation expressed in the receipt given for such property." This is substantially re-enacted in § 32, chap. 114, relating to railroads. Rev. Stat. 1889, chap. 114, § 32.

These Statutes do not in terms prohibit common carriers from limiting their common-law liabilities by contract with the owner of property delivered for transportation. Formerly the restriction of a carrier's liability, when expressed in a mere receipt, often gave rise to the question as to whether the shipper had knowingly assented thereto, and this enactment was doubtlessly intended to obviate the difficulty growing out of that condition. In many respects a railway carrier may, by express contract, limit its strict common-law liability. It may by special contract limit the liability to such damage or loss as may occur on its own line of carriage. *Illinois Cent. R. Co.* v. *Frankenberg*, 54 Ill. 88; *Chicago & N. W. R. Co.* v. *Montfort*, 60 Ill. 175; *Field* v. *Chicago & R. I. R. Co.* 71 Ill. 458; *Erie R. Co.* v. *Wilcox*, 84 Ill. 239; *Wabash, St. L. & P. R. Co.* v. *Jaggerman*, 115 Ill. 407, 2 West. Rep. 863.

The carrier may limit its liabilities against loss by fire without his fault (*Van Schaack* v. *Northern Transp. Co.* 3 Biss. 394); and the liability may thus be limited as an insurer, and against other loss, not attributable to its negligence or that of its servants, and may require the value of goods offered for transportation to be fixed by the shipper, to protect itself against fraud in case of loss.

The courts of this State have never held that the carrier may limit or restrict its liability for loss or damage resulting from its own gross negligence, or the gross negligence of its servants. On the contrary, it has been repeatedly and uniformly held that it cannot do so, even by express contract with the shipper. The question first arose in *Illinois Cent. R. Co.* v. *Morrison*, 19 Ill. 136, and it was there said: "We think the rule a good one, as established in England and in this country, that railroad companies have the right to restrict their liability as common carriers by such contracts as may be agreed upon specially, they still remaining liable for gross negligence or willful misfeasance, against which good morals and public policy forbid that they should be permitted to stipulate." And substantially the same language is used in *Illinois Cent. R. Co.* v. *Read*, 37 Ill. 484, and in *Illinois Cent. R. Co.* v. *Adams*, 42 Ill. 474.

In *Illinois Cent. R. Co.* v. *Smyser*, 38 Ill. 354, it was held that a railroad company may restrict its liabilities for loss or injury occurring during the transportation of property, the carrier being still held liable for gross negligence or willful misfeasance.

So in *Illinois Cent. R. Co.* v. *Adams*, *supra*, it is said "that, although a railroad company might protect itself by contract against certain risks assumed by common carriers and belonging to their vocation, it was contrary to good morals and public policy that they should be allowed to stipulate against their own gross negligence, or that of their employés, or their willful default."

In *Oppenheimer* v. *United States Exp. Co.*, 69 Ill. 62, the court holds that the contract exempting carriers from liabilities is not to be construed as providing against loss or injury occasioned by actual negligence on their part.

In the subsequent case of *Arnold* v. *Illinois Cent. R. Co.*, 83 Ill. 273, it was said: "The doctrine is settled in this court that railroad companies may by contract exempt themselves from liability on account of the negligence of their servants, other than that which is gross or willful."

In the *Read Case*, *supra*, the question arose where the plaintiff was riding on a free ticket, on the back of which was an indorsement to the effect that the person accepting the same assumes all risks of accident and expressly agrees that the company shall not be liable under any circumstances for injury to the person or property of the passenger while using the ticket. It was held that the acceptance and use of the ticket made the indorsement thereon a special contract, but that the contract did not exempt the company from liability for injury caused by gross negligence.

In *Erie R. Co.* v. *Wilcox*, *supra*, we said: "The law has wisely, and for reasons that concern the public welfare, inhibited a common carrier of passengers or freight from contracting against its own negligence, or that of its servants and employés." See also *Toledo, W. & W. R. Co.* v. *Beggs*, 85 Ill. 80.

In *Adams Exp. Co.* v. *Stettaners*, 61 Ill. 184, goods were shipped from Chicago to New York, worth in fact $400, for which the company gave the shipper a receipt, limiting its liability to $50 in case of loss, of which the shipper had notice. It was there said that "even if it should be conceded that the shipper in this case must be considered as having assented to the terms of the bill of lading, we cannot hold the carrier excused from the exercise of reasonable and ordinary care. Courts have often had occasion to express their regret that common carriers have been permitted, even by contract, to discharge themselves from the obligations imposed by the salutary rules of the common law. . . . It is very unreasonable in the carrier to say that it will in no event be liable beyond the sum of $50, in the absence of a special contract, though it may have received much more than that sum merely in the way of freight. . . . It would be very easy for them to require the shipper to specify the value of the merchandise, . . . making their charges in proportion to their liability. If the shipper should falsely state the value, he could not complain of being held to his own valuation. In order to prevent the carrier from releasing himself by contract from all liability, courts have laid down the rule above stated, that he cannot, even by contract, exempt himself from the exercise of reasonable care."

And the same rule was laid down in *Boscowitz* v. *Adams Exp. Co.*, 93 Ill. 523, and it was there held that the defendant was liable for the full value of the goods, if the loss was owing to negligence on the part of the railway company, who was the servant of the express company in the transportation of the goods.

We have thus given an epitome of cases decided by this court, to which others might be added, for the purpose of showing that we are committed to the doctrine that a common carrier cannot, even by express contract, exempt itself from liability resulting from gross negligence or willful misconduct, committed by itself, or by its servants or employés. Whatever may be the rule elsewhere, in this State the common carrier cannot contract for exemption from responsibility for a failure on its part, or that of its servants, to exercise ordinary care in the transaction of its business. If the carrier may by contract limit its liability for gross negligence or willful misfeasance to any extent, it may contract for total exemption. A contract for exemption from liability for its torts being void as against public policy, it cannot shield itself, as to any portion of the damages to persons or property, occasioned by its gross negligence or willful misconduct. As we have seen, it may protect itself against fraud by requiring the consignee to state the value of the thing shipped; but when it receives property for transportation it must exercise reasonable care until it reaches its place of destination, and will not be permitted to absolve itself from that responsibility.

By the strict rule of the common law, the carrier was liable for injuries resulting from causes beyond his control, and which were not the result of his act or the omission of his duty, the exception being that he was not liable for injury or loss resulting from the act of God or the public enemy. Thus he must account for goods received for transportation, even though they be destroyed by fire without his fault. The rule has generally been so far relaxed that the carrier may, by special contract, exempt himself from this strict liability imposed by the common law; but the weight of authority, in our judgment, holds, as this court has uniformly held, that he may not exempt himself from liability for damages resulting from the gross negligence or willful misconduct of himself or of his servants. The law does not authorize common carriers to fix arbitrarily the value of goods delivered to them for transportation, and thereby limit their liability in case of loss. If a value should be fixed by the carrier, as before stated, and the contract of shipment was based thereon, the amount thus fixed would ordinarily determine the liability of the carrier. It would not, however, if untruthfully given, in respect of property that the carrier had less opportunity to inspect and know the value of than the shipper, estop the carrier to show that the value was less than that fixed.

It cannot be said that the clause in this contract, attempting to limit a recovery to $100, amounts to an admission on the part of the shipper that the horse was worth no more than that sum. It was not made by the shipper, or intended as a statement of the value of the property, but was intended to fix a limit to the defendant's liability in case of loss; and if the contract had not been void, and had been knowingly entered into by the shipper or his authorized agent, it might have furnished the measure of recovery. If the injury to the property and damage resulting had been caused by any casualty against which the carrier might contract, the tender made by the defendant of the amount named in the contract might have been a bar to recovery, if it had been kept good. It is manifest from the foregoing that the tender was not effectual to defeat a recovery by the plaintiff. As before said, we are not unmindful that a contrary rule has been announced by courts of the highest respectability, and among them the Supreme Court of the United States. Notwithstanding the great respect we entertain for the very learned and eminent tribunals which have thus held, we are so strongly committed to the doctrine before announced that we feel compelled to adhere to the rule so long and firmly established in this State. And notwithstanding the persuasive weight of the rulings of these eminent tribunals, and of the reasons given for their decisions, we are still satisfied that the rule laid down in this State is based upon sound reason and a wise public policy, and is also supported by the decided weight of authority. In this case the agent of appellant came to the agent of the appellee and others, and offered special inducements to ship their animals over appellant's road. No representation was made by appellee or his agent to induce the fixing of the value either of the property shipped or of the services of the appellant for its carriage. It is insisted that the Company had two classifications at the time under which live stock was shipped; that one limited the amount of recovery for a horse to $100 in case of loss, and that in the other class there was no limitation, but a higher freight rate was charged. At the same time of this shipment no notice was given of any such classification. The appellant's agent received the property, charged what he saw proper, and made out the bill of lading without asking any questions as to the value of the property. The fact that such classification existed could in no way affect the plaintiff's right of recovery, unless notice thereof had been brought home in some way to the plaintiff or his agent. But it cannot avail in any event as against the right of recovery here. Plaintiff was guilty of no misconduct, which would estop him from asserting his right to recover the value of his property, and it was unlawful for the railway carrier to contract for exemption from liability resulting from the gross negligence of its servants. Some other minor points are made, which, however, have been disposed of by what has already been said, and no further discussion need be indulged.

We find no substantial error in the record, and *the judgment of the Appellate Court will be affirmed.*

Susie KIRKPATRICK, *Appt.*,
v.
Frank H. CLARK.

(....Ill....)

1. A witness cannot be asked in an action of ejectment whether the plaintiff was ever the owner of the premises.

2. Conveyance to a third person of land purchased by a married woman according to her directions does not violate any right of the husband.

3. Parties concerned in illegal agreements are to be left without remedy against each other if they are *in pari delicto.*

4. A deed given to defraud the grantor's creditors will not support an action of ejectment against him.

(March 31, 1890.)

APPEAL by defendant from a judgment of the Circuit Court for Morgan County in favor of plaintiff, in an action of ejectment. *Reversed.*

The facts are sufficiently stated in the opinion.

Messrs. **Morrison & Whitlock,** for appellant:

Appellant could not go into a court of equity and procure the cancellation of this deed, and appellee is estopped from obtaining affirmative relief at law. The court will leave the parties where it finds them, giving relief to neither.

Story, Eq. Jur. § 298; *M'Cullum* v. *Gourlay,* 8 Johns. 147: *Phelps* v. *Decker,* 10 Mass. 274; *Gregory* v. *King,* 58 Ill. 169; *Miller* v. *Marckle,* 21 Ill. 152; *Winston* v. *McFarland,* 22 Ill. 88. See also *Jamison* v. *Beaubien,* 4 Ill. 113.

A court of law in an action of ejectment will take cognizance of fraud.

Jamison v. *Beaubien,* 4 Ill. 113; *Rogers* v. *Brent,* 10 Ill. 573.

The plaintiff must recover on the strength of his own title.

Boyer v. *Thornburg,* 115 Ill. 540, 8 West. Rep. 38.

If the evidence offered had been admitted, then it would have appeared that Clark had no title cognizable in law. That evidence *aliunde* the deed is admissible in ejectment.

See *Sloan* v. *Petrie,* 16 Ill. 262; *Stow* v. *Russell,* 36 Ill. 35.

Mr. **Edward L. McDonald,** for appellee:

It is not competent, in an action of ejectment, to show who paid the consideration money on the conveyance of the premises to the plaintiff, with the view to establish a trust.

Chiniquy v. *Catholic Bishop of Chicago,* 41 Ill. 148.

No question of consideration can ever be admissible.

Escherick v. *Traver,* 65 Ill. 381.

In ejectment the legal title must prevail, and no equitable title can be shown in defense.

2 Greenl. Ev. § 331; Adams, Ejectment, 32; *Roundtree* v. *Little,* 54 Ill. 323; *Johnson* v. *Watson,* 87 Ill. 535; *Fleming* v. *Carter,* 70 Ill. 286.

While in a suit on a simple contract fraud is a good defense, it is not generally pleadable in bar when the action is founded on a specialty.

Escherick v. *Traver,* 65 Ill. 381; *Dyer* v. *Day,* 61 Ill. 337; *Williams* v. *Claytor,* 2 Ill. 502; *Roundtree* v. *Little,* 54 Ill. 324.

The sudden springing of such defense upon the trial as that attempted in this case would operate as a surprise, and tend to mar the system of common-law pleading, which intends that a party must have some notice of the questions which must be met.

Escherick v. *Traver,* 65 Ill. 381.

Bailey, *J.,* delivered the opinion of the court:

This was an action of ejectment, brought by Frank H. Clark against Susie Kirkpatrick, to recover lot 27, in Tilton & Cassell's Addition to Jacksonville. A trial was had on a plea of not guilty, resulting in a verdict and judgment in favor of the plaintiff; and the defendant now appeals to this court.

NOTE.—*Parties* in pari delicto *are without remedy.* Where parties are concerned in illegal agreements or transactions, whether they are *mala prohibita* or *mala in se,* courts of equity, following the rule of law as to participators in crime, will not grant relief to either party in accordance with the maxim, *in pari delicto,* etc. Harrington v. Bigelow, 11 Paige, 349, 5 N. Y. Ch. L. ed. 158; Warburton v. Aken, 1 McLean, 460; Atwood v. Fisk, 101 Mass. 363; Swartzer v. Gillett, 1 Chand. 207; Davies v. London & P. M. Ins. Co. L. R. 8 Ch. Div. 469; Bromley v. Smith, 2 Hill, 517; Vandyck v. Hewitt, 1 East, 96; Howson v. Hancock, 8 T. R. 575; Browning v. Morris, Cowp. 790; Osborne v. Williams, 18 Ves. Jr. 379; Buller, N. P. 131.

Where the scheme is *malum in se,* and the parties to it are *in pari delicto,* the law refuses to aid either of them against the other, but leaves them where they have placed themselves by their own act. Thomas v. Richmond, 79 U. S. 12 Wall. 349 (20 L. ed. 453); Smith v. Hubbs, 10 Me. 71; Schermerhorn v. Talman, 14 N. Y. 94; Knowlton v. Congress & E. Spring Co. 57 N.Y. 518; Nellis v. Clark, 20 Wend. 24; Smith, Cont. 3d Am. ed. 187; Burt v. Place, 6 Cow. 431; LeWarne v. Meyer, 38 Fed. Rep. 191; Keel v. Larkin, 83 Ala. 146.

The only exception to this rule is where one party acts under oppression, injustice, hardship, undue influence or great inequality of age or condition; although he may be *in delicto,* he is not *in pari delicto,* and may have relief in equity. Phalen v. Clark, 19 Conn. 421; Pinckston v. Brown, 3 Jones, Eq. 494; Freelove v. Cole, 41 Barb 318; Goodenough v. Spencer, 15 Abb. Pr. N. S. 248, 46 How. Pr. 347; 1 Story, Eq. Jur. § 300; Foley v. Greene, 1 New Eng. Rep. 17, 14 R. I. 618; Bagley v. Williams, 4 Giff. 638.

See also 14 L. R. A. 508; 33 L. R. A. 750.

The plaintiff, at the trial, made proof, under the twenty fifth section of the Statute in relation to ejectment, that he claimed title through one Matthew Ashelby, a common source of title with the defendant, and then read in evidence a warranty deed from said Ashelby and wife, duly acknowledged and recorded, conveying said lot to him. The defendant's counsel then called the defendant as a witness in her own behalf, and, after she had testified that she had been acquainted with the plaintiff for about eleven years, and that, when she first became acquainted with the lot in question, it was the property of Mr. Ashelby, she was asked the following questions: "State whether or not, at the time this deed was made to Mr. Clark, you were in a controversy with your husband, and whether or not the deed was made to Mr. Clark by arrangement between you and Mr. Clark, so as to prevent any claim your husband might have on the property if the deed was in you." "You may state whether or not Mr. Clark at any time, in fact, was the owner of and in possession of that property."

These questions, being both objected to by the plaintiff's counsel on the ground of incompetency and immateriality, were excluded; and thereupon the defendant's counsel made to the court the following statement and offer: "We expect and offer to prove by this witness and two other witnesses, Mr. and Mrs. Rogers, who have been sworn and are now in court, that they heard a conversation between Mr. Clark and Mrs. Kirkpatrick in which it was stated that Mr. Clark had no interest in the property, and never had any; that the deed was made to him for the purpose of hindering and defrauding creditors and the husband of Mrs. Kirkpatrick, and that Mr. Clark then admitted that every cent that Mrs. Kirkpatrick ever owed him had been paid, and that he had no claim to the property,—no right to it,—and that the property in controversy in this case was held by him only for the purpose of hindering and delaying creditors; that she asked him to give her a deed to the property, and he refused to do it, but admitted that he had no title in it, and that he only held it to cover it up so that the creditors could not get it, and also to prevent her husband from having any right to it."

The evidence thus offered, being objected to as incompetent, was excluded; and counsel then further offered to prove by Mrs. Kirkpatrick "that she went, in company with Mr. Clark, to Mr. Ashelby, and requested Mr. Ashelby to make the deed to Mr. Clark for the property, but did not tell Mr. Ashelby the reason for its being made to Mr. Clark; that Mrs. Kirkpatrick paid in full the consideration of said deed."

This evidence also, being objected to for the same reason, was excluded. Exceptions were duly preserved by the defendant to the rulings of the court excluding said evidence, and said rulings are the only errors now assigned upon the record.

A considerable portion of the evidence offered was clearly incompetent or immaterial, or both. Thus, the question put to the witness as to whether the plaintiff had ever been, in fact, the owner of the property in question, if understood as calling for the legal ownership of the lot, was incompetent, as the legal title to lands cannot be proved in that mode. If understood as calling for the equitable title, it was immaterial, as in this form of action only legal titles can be investigated. So of the question whether the deed was not made to the plaintiff, by arrangement between him and the defendant, with a view to keeping said lot free from any claim the defendant's husband might have thereon in case the title was taken in her name. The evidence called for by that question would simply have tended to show that the plaintiff took and was holding the title to said lot as trustee for the defendant. Her equitable title thus attempted to be shown was quite immaterial, since it constituted no defense to the action. The rule is well settled that a trustee may recover in ejectment the lands affected by the trust, even as against the *cestui que trust*.

In *Reece* v. *Allen*, 10 Ill. 236, this court said: "A court of law may, indeed, investigate some questions of fraud, and, when proved, treat a deed as a nullity and conveying no title, as where a party was induced to execute a deed supposing it was another paper; but in general it will not go behind the naked legal title, and inquire where the equities are. Even in case of a naked trustee, the law is so strenuous for the legal title that it enables the trustee to recover in ejectment against the *cestui que trust*." See also *Kirkland* v. *Cox*, 94 Ill. 400; Sedgw. & W. Trial of Title to Land, § 222, and cases cited in *notes*.

If it be said that the purpose of said question was to elicit evidence tending to show that said conveyance to the plaintiff was a fraud upon the rights of the defendant's husband, it may be answered that, even admitting that proof of such fraud would have been material, said evidence would have had no tendency to prove it. If the lot in question had been conveyed directly to the defendant, it would have vested in her husband no right of interest except an inchoate right of dower; and it was no fraud upon him if his wife, in purchasing the lot, had the title conveyed to a trustee for the express purpose of preventing such right from attaching. Even at common law, where the husband was entitled to the possession and enjoyment of his wife's lands during their joint lives, it was never supposed to be a fraud upon his rights for his wife to have lands purchased with her separate means, or derived from sources other than her husband, conveyed to a trustee for the sole purpose of placing them beyond his control, and having them held for her separate use; and such trusts were habitually resorted to for that purpose. But under our Statute a married woman is entitled to the sole possession and enjoyment of her lands free from the interference and control of her husband, the husband's right of dower, even after it has become vested, being imperfect and incapable of assertion or beneficial enjoyment until after her death. How, then, can he be said to have rights in lands which his wife does not yet own, but which she contemplates purchasing, which it would be a fraud upon him to deprive him of? Dower in lands which the wife does not yet own is an interest to which the husband has neither a legal, equitable nor moral right; and the wife is entirely at liberty to so manage her purchases made with her own means, if she can, as to prevent his acquiring such right.

A more difficult question is raised by that portion of the offer of the defendant's counsel in which they propose to prove by said witnesses that the lot in question was paid for by the defendant, but that, by arrangement between her and the plaintiff, the conveyance was made by Ashelby to the plaintiff with intent to hinder and defraud the defendant's creditors; such intention being participated in by both the plaintiff and the defendant.

It is a general rule, subject, it is true, to certain exceptions, that, where parties are concerned in illegal agreements, they are left without remedy against each other, provided they are *in pari delicto*. The law, in such cases, refuses to lend its aid to either party, but leaves them where it finds them, to suffer the consequences of their illegal or immoral acts. This rule is ordinarily expressed by the maxim, *ex dolo malo*, or *ex turpi causa, non oritur actio*, or by the maxim, *in pari delicto potior est conditio defendentis et possidentis*. These maxims are applied to executed transactions as well as to those which are executory, and are enforced by courts of law as well as courts of equity.

As said by the chancellor in *Bolt* v. *Rogers*, 3 Paige, 154, 3 N.Y. Ch. L. ed. 95, "Wherever two or more persons are engaged in a fraudulent transaction to injure another, neither law nor equity will interfere to relieve either of those persons, as against the other, from the consequences of their own misconduct."

In *Smith* v. *Hubbs*, 10 Me. 71, the court says: "There is a marked and settled distinction between executory and executed contracts of a fraudulent or illegal character. Whatever the parties to an action have executed for fraudulent or illegal purposes, the law refuses to lend its aid to enable either party to disturb. Whatever the parties have fraudulently or illegally contracted to execute, the law refuses to compel the contractor to execute, or pay damages for not executing, but in both cases leaves the parties where it finds them. The object of the law in the latter case is, as far as possible, to prevent the contemplated wrong, and in the former to punish the wrong-doer, by leaving him to the consequences of his own folly or misconduct." See also *Miller* v. *Marckle*, 21 Ill. 152; *Nellis* v. *Clark*, 20 Wend. 24; *Howell* v. *Fountain*, 3 Ga. 176; *Carey* v. *Smith*, 11 Ga. 539; *White* v. *Crew*, 16 Ga. 416; 1 Story, Eq. Jur. § 298.

If it be true, as the evidence offered would tend to show, that the defendant purchased the lot in question of Ashelby with her own money, but, for the purpose of hindering and defrauding her creditors, entered into a fraudulent arrangement or conspiracy with the plaintiff to have said lot conveyed to him, said transaction was illegal, and within the condemnation of the fourth section of our present Statute of Frauds. The transaction being consummated by the execution of the conveyance to the plaintiff, leaving the defendant in the possession which she had previously obtained under a demise from Ashelby, the law should leave them both where it finds them. The defendant, clearly, could not be permitted to go into a court of equity to compel an execution by the plaintiff of his trust; and it would seem that, upon the same principle, the plaintiff should be debarred from coming into a court of law to use his ill-gotten title for the purpose of recovering of the defendant the possession.

We know of no case where this precise question has been decided by this court, but cases are to be found where the reasoning adopted has a tendency to support the view above expressed. The case of *Rogers* v. *Brent*, 10 Ill. 573, was ejectment, brought by the holder of a patent from the United States, issued to him as assignee of the certificate of entry, against the holder of a title derived through a sheriff's deed executed upon a sale of the land on execution against the original holder of said certificate prior to its assignment to the plaintiff. The court, in holding that the assignment of the certificate and the patent subsequently issued thereon were fraudulent and void as to the defendant, said: "The law is that the common-law courts may entertain jurisdiction of questions of fraud, and that a conveyance, whether it be by deed from an individual or by a patent from the government, although executed with all the forms of law, when obtained in fraud of the rights of others may, in an action of ejectment, be disregarded by the court as void at the instance of the injured party, or those holding under him." In the course of the opinion it is said, by way of argument, that "it would hardly have been denied that a court of law would treat as a nullity a deed to the assignee of Samuel, when it was established that the assignment was made and the deed obtained to defraud creditors, or to defeat a title previously obtained by a sale under an execution against Samuel [the assignor]."

In *Jamison* v. *Beaubien*, 4 Ill. 113, which was also an action of ejectment, the plaintiff's proof of title consisted of a certificate of pre-emption; and, certain evidence tending to impeach the pre emption on the ground of fraud being excluded by the trial court, this court, in holding that such exclusion was erroneous, said: "Fraud, it is said, vitiates all acts as between the parties to it; nor can there be a doubt that fraud is cognizable in a court of law as well as equity. It is an admitted principle that a court of law has concurrent jurisdiction with a court of equity in cases of fraud. The evidence offered went directly to the validity of the certificate of pre-emption purchase. If it had its inception in fraud, it was certainly competent for the defendant to show the fact; and, if the officers granting it were parties to the fraudulent act, it was no doubt void, and might be impeached in an inquiry in which the preemptor was a party."

The case of *Miller* v. *Marckle*, 21 Ill. 152, was a bill in equity for the foreclosure of a mortgage alleged by the mortgagor to have been executed without consideration, for the purpose of securing his property against his creditors until he could get means to settle with them; and this court, in holding that the defense should have been sustained, said: "If money has been actually paid or property transferred, and the grantee put in possession, courts will not compel the money or property to be restored or the party ousted. They will not, on the one hand, undo what has been done, nor, on the other, perfect what has been left unfinished. Suppose the position of these parties reversed, and the appellant was seeking by bill in chancery to rescind the mortgage, and for a surrender of the notes. . . . The court would not interfere. It would leave the parties where it found them, aiding neither. We would say: 'You executed the notes and the mortgage for a fraudulent purpose. The act is binding on you, and you cannot have our aid to compel their surrender.' So we say to the appellee here: 'You have the notes and mortgage. You were a willing party to a proposed fraud. We will give you no assistance to enforce the one or the other. Equity aids not iniquity.' Had an absolute deed of the premises been made, and the party put in possession, the court would not interfere to oust him." See also *Tyler* v. *Tyler*, 126 Ill. 525.

In the first two of the three cases last above cited the fraud was set up by parties not *in pari delicto* with the parties against whom the fraud was charged. Those cases sustain the rule, however, that a court of law will, in an action of ejectment, on proper proof, hold a conveyance upon which a party relies to establish his title to be fraudulent and void, at least where the fraud is charged by one who is not a party to it. In the case last cited the court held that it was proper to grant relief at the instance of a participant in the fraud. In the present case, if the facts are as the evidence offered would tend to show, the fraudulent transaction has been consummated, to the extent of vesting the title in the plaintiff and leaving the possession in the defendant. Here, according to the rules of law above discussed, they should be left. The defendant, clearly, can have no remedy to recover the title; and, if the defendant is permitted in this action to recover the possession, said rules will be applied in all their rigor to the defendant, while the plaintiff will be exempted from their application. His present title, without the possession or the means of obtaining it, is a barren right. But, if a court of law can lend him its aid to recover the possession, his title becomes perfect, at least as against the defendant; and the law, notwithstanding his participation in the fraud, will be to him both a sword and a shield. We are not inclined to so apply the law as to involve an absurdity of this character.

In *Harrison* v. *Hatcher*, 44 Ga. 638, the precise question before us was presented, and we are disposed to concur with the conclusion reached by the court in that case. The action was ejectment, and the plaintiff claimed title under a deed executed to him by the defendant; and the evidence tended to show that said deed was executed by defendant without consideration, and for the purpose of defrauding the grantor's creditors. The defendant asked the court to charge the jury, among other things, in substance, that if said deed was executed by him to defraud his creditors, and that he remained in possession, the transaction was fraudulent, and the defendant could not be ousted of possession, as the court would not aid a party to a fraud to assert rights against the other party, and would not disturb the possession. This charge the court refused to give; and, there being a verdict and judgment for the plaintiff, it was held on appeal that the refusal of the court to charge as requested was error. The point thus raised is discussed in its opinion as follows: "On looking into the cases upon this subject, we are satisfied that the rule *in pari delicto* applies to the condition of a defendant in a suit, even though he sets up his own fraud. He is in possession, and the courts will not aid the other party to get possession under a fraudulent deed. They will even permit the defendant to say: 'The deed under which the plaintiff claims is a fraud,—the result of evil practices between him and me;' and if this be made out by the proof the plaintiff cannot recover."

It follows that in the present case the evidence offered, so far as it tended to show that the deed under which the plaintiff claims title was executed in fraud of the defendant's creditors, was proper, and should have been admitted, and that its exclusion was error. For said error *the judgment will be reversed, and the cause remanded.*

GEORGIA SUPREME COURT.

M. P. HARWELL, *Piff. in Err.*,
v.
James SHARP *et al.*

(......Ga.......)

*That a creditor transferred to his attorney a just debt, and caused attachment and garnishment to issue and be prosecuted in an adjoining State, thus coercing payment, though both parties were citizens of Georgia, and though the motive for proceeding elsewhere was to evade the laws of this State exempting the debtor's wages from process of garnishment, constitutes no cause of action in favor of the debtor against the creditor.

(April 14, 1890.)

*Head note by BLECKLEY, *Ch. J.*

ERROR to the Atlanta City Court to review a judgment sustaining a demurrer to the petition in an action brought to recover damages for an alleged contempt and abuse of law in the collection of a certain claim by attachment. *Affirmed.*

Petitioner alleged that he was in the employ of the Western & Atlantic R. Co.; that several members of his family being sick, he purchased drugs of defendants to the amount of $9.70, upon which he afterwards paid a small amount. When asked to pay the remainder he informed defendants that he was earning but $1.25 per day, with which amount he was hardly able to support his family, but that he would pay the amount as soon as possible; that defendants thereupon made a pretended transfer of their claim to a Tennessee attorney, who instituted a garnishment proceeding and attached petitioner's wages; that petitioner was forced to go to Tennessee, and, in order to feed his family, pay said attorney $13 out of the wages so sequestered; that the amount so squeezed from his daily wages did not leave him enough to pay his house rent and provide sufficient food and clothing for his family, and that the $13 taken from his wages under the circumstances is blood money; that both parties were residents of Georgia and that the drugs were sold and the wages earned there; that the proceeding was a trick to evade the laws of Georgia and treat them with contempt; that the proceeding was an abuse of legal process; and that, petitioner's wages being free from garnishment in Georgia, defendants were guilty of a breach of legal duty because of which petitioner ought to recover.

Messrs. **Haygood & Douglas,** for plaintiff in error:

If plaintiff and defendant to a suit in another State both live in Georgia, the plaintiff may be restrained from using process in that other State to collect a debt exempt under the laws of Georgia.

Story, Eq. Jur. § 899; *Foster* v. *Vassall*, 3 Atk. 589; *Mackintosh* v. *Ogilvie*, 3 Swanst. 365; *Hunter* v. *Potts*, 4 T. R. 182; *Cranstown* v. *Johnston*, 3 Ves. Jr. 183; *Massie* v. *Watts*, 10 U. S. 6 Cranch, 148 (3 L. ed. 181); *Teager* v. *Landsley*, 69 Iowa, 725; *Hager* v. *Adams*, 70 Iowa, 746; *Mumper* v. *Wilson*, 72 Iowa, 163, 2 Am. St. Rep. 238; *Dehon* v. *Foster*, 4 Allen, F'', 7 Allen, 57; *Snook* v. *Snetzer*, 25 Ohio St. 516; *Keyser* v. *Rice*, 47 Md. 203, 28 Am. Rep. 448; *Wright* v. *Chicago, B. & Q. R. Co.* 19 Neb. 175, 56 Am. Rep. 747; *Engel* v. *Scheuerman*, 40 Ga. 206, 2 Am. Rep. 573; *Wilson* v. *Joseph*, 5 West. Rep. 681, 107 Ind. 490.

If plaintiff could use injunction to restrain defendant from levying on exempt wages outside of the State, much more should he have a common-law remedy against defendant.

Story, Eq. Jur. §§ 862, 864; *Lawrence* v. *Batchelder*, 131 Mass. 504; Freeman, Executions, § 489; Ga. Code, § 3219; *Morgan* v. *Neville*, 74 Pa. 52.

Breach of legal duty gives an action.

Ga. Code, §§ 2953, 3588.

Damages may be recovered for malicious abuse of process when there is want of probable cause and malice.

Wilcox v. *McKenzie*, 75 Ga. 73; *Cook* v. *Walker*, 30 Ga. 519; *Juchter* v. *Boehm*, 67 Ga. 534.

Damages may be recovered for illegal levy without showing malice and want of probable cause.

Holton v. *Taylor*, 80 Ga. 508; *Patterson* v. *Phinizy*, 51 Ga. 33; *Bodega* v. *Perkerson*, 60 Ga 516; *Boyd* v. *Merriam*, 58 Ga. 561; *McDougald* v. *Dougherty*, 12 Ga. 613.

Messrs. **Arnold & Arnold,** for defendants in error:

The action in the Tennessee court was legal and proper, and defendants would not be liable to an action in the Tennessee courts.

Burlington & M. R. R. Co. v. *Thompson*, 31 Kan. 180, 47 Am. Rep. 497.

The fact that they reside in this State can make no difference. The law of the place of the injury invariably governs.

Bleckley, *Ch. J.*, delivered the opinion of the court:

By the statute law of this State, "all journeymen, mechanics and day laborers shall be exempt from the process and liabilities of garnishment on their daily, weekly or monthly wages, whether in the hands of their employers or others." Code, § 3554.

We are not informed by anything directly alleged in the plaintiff's declaration whether or not any similar law prevails in the State of Tennessee. The fair inference from what is alleged would be that there is no like exemption in that State, or at least none of which nonresident debtors could avail themselves. It appears that the defendants, who were creditors of the plaintiff, for the purpose of resorting to a Tennessee forum, and to evade this provision in the laws of Georgia, transferred their account to their attorney, and caused attachment to issue in Tennessee, and a garnishment to be served on the Western & Atlantic Railroad Company, who was indebted to the plaintiff for wages earned as a daily laborer. The effect of this garnishment was to constrain the plaintiff to pay the debt, in whole or in part, which he owed to the defendants, the sum paid being $13. This is the grievance of which he complains, alleging that he was injured and damaged thereby in the sum of $2,500. Both parties being citizens of Georgia, it is not unlikely that, if application had been made in time, an injunction might have been obtained, restraining the defendants from prosecuting their attachment and garnishment in Tennessee. Ample and apparently sound authority for so doing may be found. *Snook* v. *Snetzer*, 25 Ohio St. 516; *Keyser* v. *Rice*, 47 Md. 203; *Teager* v. *Landsley*, 69 Iowa, 725; *Hager* v. *Adams*, 70 Iowa, 746; *Mumper* v. *Wilson*, 72 Iowa, 163; *Wilson* v. *Joseph*, 107 Ind. 490, 5 West. Rep. 681.

It does not follow, however, that because the plaintiff might have asserted his exemption in this way, and claimed the benefit of the law of his own State, it was in any sense unlawful, or legally wrongful, for the defendants to bring their attachment in Tennessee, and use there the remedy of garnishment furnished by the laws of that State. Unless restrained by some tribunal of their own State, they were but exercising a privilege common to all citizens of the United States. While left free to act according to their own will in the use of remedies they had as much right to sue in Tennessee as they would have had if they were citizens of that State. *Morgan* v. *Neville*, 74 Pa. 52.

In dealing with a somewhat similar question, the Supreme Court of Massachusetts, in *Lawrence* v. *Batchelder*, 131 Mass. 504, speaking by Field, *J.*, said: "The argument of the plaintiffs in the case at bar is that, as it was contrary to equity for the defendant to proceed with his suits to judgment, and to a satisfaction of the judgments from the funds attached, so it is contrary to equity for him to retain the money so obtained, and that they can maintain an action at law against the defendant for money had and received to their use, because the money, *ex æquo et bono*, belongs to them. This argument rests on the assumption that courts of law will afford a remedy in damages for all wrongs done, which courts of equity, if seasonably applied to, will prevent; but this is not true. Courts of equity recognize and enforce rights which courts of law do not recognize at all; and it is often on this ground that defendants in equity are enjoined from prosecuting actions at law." The plaintiff may have had his election to bring the defendants' rights, as against his wages, to the test of Georgia law, or allow them to be tested by Tennessee law. This election could be exercised, however, only in due time and proper manner. He could not allow the law of Tennessee to be applied to the case, and afterwards, by such an action as this, have the law of Georgia applied to it. His remedy, if he had any, was to prevent, by injunction upon his adversary, the application of Tennessee law as a rule of adjudication. This he did not do otherwise than by paying the debt. Although it is not distinctly stated, we think it is to be inferred from the language of the declaration that he paid before the proceeding in Tennessee reached a conclusion by judgment. Had it resulted in a judgment, there can be no doubt, assuming that the attachment and garnishment were regular according to the laws of Tennessee, that such judgment would have to be treated in Georgia as having the same effect as would be ascribed to it in Tennessee. *Green* v. *Van Buskirk,* 72 U. S. 5 Wall. 310 [18 L. ed. 600], 74 U. S. 7 Wall. 139 [19 L. ed. 109].

A case very similar to the present has been decided in Indiana; and it was held that, even though there was a statute making the act complained of penal, no recovery could be had for the transfer of a just debt, and proceeding upon it by attachment in another State, though the effect was to deprive the debtor of his exemption allowed by the laws of his own State, of which State the creditor also was a citizen. *Uppinghouse* v. *Mundel,* 103 Ind. 238, 1 West. Rep. 204.

The soundness of that adjudication may be questioned, inasmuch as there was an express statute violated. But with us there is no such statute, and we are therefore not required to go the full length of this Indiana precedent.

Upon no recognized theory of a malicious abuse of process, or the malicious prosecution of a civil action, can the declaration before us be upheld. There was a just debt, and a lawful resort to a competent forum (nothing to the contrary being alleged) for its collection, and payment was made either pending the suit or after judgment. The debt was thus, in whole or in part, extinguished. The money paid is no longer that of the debtor, but has become the property of the creditor. While there may have been damage, there has been no legal injury—no wrong done to the plaintiff—for which any court adjudicating upon legal principles can afford redress. There was no error in sustaining the demurrer to the declaration.

Judgment affirmed.

NORTH CAROLINA SUPREME COURT.

STATE OF NORTH CAROLINA
v.
J. B. STEELE, *Appt.*

(......N. C.......)

*1. **Where an innkeeper made a regulation that "no livery-man** or agent of any transportation or baggage company, no washer-woman or sewing-woman, not connected with the house, or loafer or lounger or objectionable person will be allowed in the hotel," and gave notice to the agent of a livery stable who had previously been in the habit of "drumming" for custom at his hotel not to come upon the hotel premises again,—*Held,* that the innkeeper had a right to expel said agent from the hotel without using unnecessary force, if he entered it after such notice, and engaged in drumming for custom, although at the time the hotel-keeper had made an arrangement with another keeper of a livery stable, by which the former should receive 10 per centum of the proceeds of the business derived from the guests of the hotel, and notwithstanding the further fact that a third livery-man representing his own stable, and who had received a similar notice, was actually in the hotel at the time of the expulsion, and had been soliciting patronage for his business among the guests, but was not shown to have had actual license from the innkeeper to approach the guests.

2. **Guests of an hotel, and travelers or other persons entering it with the bona fide intent** of becoming guests, cannot be lawfully prevented from going in or put out by force after entrance, provided they are able to pay the charges and tender the money necessary for that purpose, if requested by the landlord, unless they be persons of bad or suspicious character, or of vulgar habits, or so objectionable to the patrons of the house, on account of the race to which they belong, that it would injure the business of the house to admit them, or unless they attempt to take advantage of the freedom of the hotel to injure the landlord's chances of profit, derived either from his inn or any other business incidental to and connected with its management, and constituting a part of the provision for the wants or pleasure of his patrons.

3. **When persons, unobjectionable** on account of character or race, enter an hotel, not as guests, but intent on pleasure or profit, to be derived from intercourse with its inmates, they are there not of right, but under an implied license that the landlord may revoke at any time.

4. **Regulations,** such as that made by the Battery Park Hotel, of which the defendant was the manager, are reasonable, and any person violating them may be expelled, after notice to desist from violating them, if it be done without using excessive force.

5. **An innkeeper has the right to establish a livery stable** in connection with his hotel, as he can a barber shop, a news stand or a laundry, or he may contract with the proprietor of a livery stable in the vicinity to secure for the latter, as far as he legitimately can, the patronage of his guests for a per centum of the proceeds or profits derived by the owner of such vehicles and horses from dealing with the patrons of the public house; and where he enters into such contract

*Head notes by AVERY, J.

NOTE.—Innkeeper and guest; relations between. See *note* to Coskery v. Nagle (Ga.) 6 L. R. A. 483.

he may, after notice, enforce such a regulation as that made by the Battery Park Hotel, by expelling the agents or representatives of livery stables, who enter to solicit the patronage of guests, or, where such agent persists in visiting the hotel for that purpose after notice to desist, the landlord may expel him without excessive force, if he refuses to leave, and may eject him, even though he enter for a lawful purpose, if he does not disclose his true intent when requested to leave, or whatever may have been his purpose, if he has in fact engaged in soliciting the patronage of the guests.

6. **The rule is that the proprietor of a public house has the right to request a person,** who visits it not as a guest or on business with guests, to depart, and if he refuse the innkeeper may expel him, and if he do not use excessive force, may justify, on a prosecution for assault and battery, in removing him.

7. **If the prosecutor went into the hotel at the request of a guest,** and for the purpose of conferring with the latter on business still if, while in the hotel, he engaged in "drumming" for his employer, after notice to desist from it, the defendant might expel him in the same way; and if the prosecutor, having entered to see a guest, did not then solicit business from the patrons of the hotel, but had done so previously, the defendant, seeing him there, had the right to use sufficient force to eject him, unless he explained, when requested to leave, what his real intent was. The guest, by sending for a hackman or carriage driver, could not delegate to him the right to do an act for which even the guest himself might be lawfully put out of the hotel.

8. **If it be admitted that the rule laid down in Markham v. Brown,** 8 N. H. 523, is correct, our case comes under the exception in that case; because it appears that the conduct of the prosecutor was calculated to injure the business of the hotel by diminishing its profits derived from the contract made with the keeper of the other livery stable.

9. **The defendant as manager of the hotel could make a valid contract,** for a valuable consideration, with Sevier to give him the exclusive privilege of remaining in the house and soliciting patronage from the guests in any business that grew out of providing for the comfort or pleasure of the patrons of the house. The proprietor might contract for a per centum of the amount realized from doing a livery business with the guests, and expel without excessive force the agents of rival establishments, who, after notice to desist, persisted in soliciting business from the guests, on the ground that they were entering his inn to injure him in his business connected with the hotel.

10. **The proprietor could permit** S., who contracted to pay the hotel 10 per centum of the proceeds of his business with the guests, to remain, or omit to order C. the livery-man who had received a notice similar to that sent to the prosecutor, or to put C. out and expel the prosecutor without violating the constitutional inhibition against monopolies.

(May 5, 1890.)

APPEAL by defendant from a judgment of the Criminal Court for Buncombe County adjudging him guilty of an assault and battery, and overruling his motion for a new trial. *Reversed.*

Statement by **Avery,** *J.:*

This was a criminal action for an assault and battery tried before Charles A. Moore, *Judge,* and a jury, at the October Term of the Criminal Court of Buncombe County, on an appeal from a court of a justice of the peace of said county. The defendant pleaded not guilty.

Joseph Weaver, the prosecutor, swore that a Mr. Dawson, who was a guest at the Battery Park Hotel, in the City of Asheville, Buncombe County, called to him, the witness, to supply him some horses from a livery stable, in the City of Asheville, with which stable the witness was connected as the agent of the manager and owners thereof. That because of this he went up on the porch of the hotel, when the defendant, who was the manager of the hotel, came up to him, and asked him to get off the porch. The witness said he replied, "All right, sir," and then started off, but before he could get off the defendant pushed him, and he would have fallen and been hurt had he not caught on the railing of the porch. Witness stated, on his cross-examination, that he did not know whether the defendant knew he was drumming for a livery stable or not. That the defendant had notified him in writing previous to that time not to go on the grounds of the hotel (see "Exhibit C," *infra*). That the defendant had told him before that day to go on the back side of the hotel, when he had livery business to transact with the guests of the hotel, to a place designated for livery-men to conduct such business. That he had been notified by the defendant to keep off the porch before that day. That on that day he was standing on the steps of the hotel porch. That the defendant did not give him time to get off. That the defendant was within two feet of him, when he said, "Get off of here," and that before he could get off the defendant pushed him off, as he above described. That the defendant pushed him after he was down off the steps, where he was permitted to stay. The defendant introduced in evidence the rules and regulations of the hotel, which were printed on a heavy piece of card-board. See "Exhibit A," *infra.*

The defendant, being introduced to testify in his own behalf, said he was the manager of the Battery Park Hotel and its business. That the prosecutor, on the day of the alleged assault, was on the porch of the hotel, interfering with parties working on the hotel. That he told the prosecutor to go away, and to go off the porch, and that he might stay at the place designated for livery-men. The prosecutor was a livery-man. That he kept two persons to receive orders for all livery-men from said place so designated from guests at the hotel, and that it was the duty of these two persons to transact all business between the guests of the hotel and the livery men, and that he made no charge against livery-men or anyone else on account of the services of such persons. That the prosecutor knew of this rule and regulation of the hotel, and was on the porch in violation of the rule. That he told him to go away, and he did not go. That he then put his hands gently on the prosecutor, and pushed him gently down the steps off the porch. That he only used such force as was necessary to put the prosecutor off the porch. That he used no violence whatever.

Witness further testified that the prosecutor

constantly came into the hotel, and would "hang around." That he would go on the porch and "hang around" there, spitting tobacco juice around on the floor and on the railing of the porch. That on the morning of the difficulty the prosecutor had a stick under his arm. That it was the duty of the witness, under the rules of the hotel, to keep all livery-men out of the hotel. On cross examination, the witness testified that the prosecutor was interfering with the men at work on the hotel by talking to them and taking up their time. That the prosecutor told him that the painters had asked him for a chew of tobacco. That he thinks the painters were working by the day. That they were working for a Mr. Lee, but that he paid the hands on that job by the day. That his impression is that the prosecutor was in the office of the hotel that day also. That the prosecutor told him that he had come there to see his customers, and that he told the prosecutor, "You must get off of here;" and that the prosecutor said that he would not, and resisted him. That he had told Weaver and other livery-men not to come there. That he saw the prosecutor spitting on the floor. That he had some time before that made a contract with one Sevier, a livery-man, to do the livery business for the hotel, and that Sevier was to pay him 10 per cent of the proceeds of the business. That he had never complained to the prosecutor of his spitting on the floor. That the prosecutor was there on that morning drumming for the livery stable he was connected with. That he had come there to annoy him, and that it did annoy him to see him there. That he had torn up the contract with Sevier by order of Col. Coxe, the owner of the hotel. That he heard the prosecutor drumming that morning. That he was talking about horses and carriages, and talking loud. That Mr. Sevier and all other persons in the livery business could get orders to and from the guests of the hotel. That he had never seen the prosecutor drunk. That he does not know for certain that Sevier is now, and was then, paying 10 per cent of the proceeds of the livery business of the hotel to Col. Coxe.

The defendant then proposed to offer in evidence two ordinances of the City of Asheville, as follows: "Sec 681. Any porter who shall enter the general passenger depot, or any passenger depot in this city, for any hotel or boarding house, or eating-house, without the consent of the railroad authorities in charge of such depot, shall, upon conviction, be fined five dollars. Sec. 682. If any person or persons shall enter any passenger depot, hotel, boarding-house or other place of business, and violate the rules thereof, or hinder or obstruct the business therein, he may be ordered out by the person in charge, and upon refusal to go shall be punished as provided in the preceding section, provided said rules shall be reasonable, and shall have been approved by the mayor and board of aldermen."

The defendant then offered in evidence other ordinances of the City of Asheville ("Exhibit B," *infra*) for the purpose of showing that the rules of the hotel had, by an ordinance of the said city, been duly approved. The solicitor for the State objected to the introduction of these ordinances. The objection was sustained by the court, and the defendant excepted.

Henry Nettles was then introduced by the defendant, and swore that he was employed at the Battery Park Hotel. That it was his duty to announce carriages when ready, to take orders from guests of the hotel, and to send orders to any livery stable in town desired by the guests, and to take orders to and from livery-men at places designated for them by the hotel authorities. That a Mr. Reynolds was also employed for the same purpose. That he had seen the prosecutor there; had seen him often spitting tobacco juice on the floor, and drumming among the guests. That he had seen him when pretty full of liquor at the hotel, but not down drunk. That he saw the difficulty between the defendant and the prosecutor. Defendant told the prosecutor to get off a half dozen times. The prosecutor said he would not go. The defendant put his hand on the prosecutor's shoulder, and pushed him down the steps. That the way he pushed him would not have pushed a baby down the steps. On cross-examination, he stated that the prosecutor was drinking. That his face was red, and his breath smelled bad. That the prosecutor said that he had a warrant for the defendant. Prosecutor also said that he had not touched a drop of liquor. As the defendant pushed him he caught hold of the "bannisters," but the defendant did not push him violently. He also said that he had collected bills for the prosecutor from guests of the hotel. That when he was asked by a guest to order a carriage, that he would ask what stable he wanted it from, and, if no particular stable was mentioned, he would give it to the one he (the witness) wanted to have it.

In reply, the State introduced one H. S. Loomis, who swore that he was the room and bill clerk at the Battery Park Hotel. That the written contract between Sevier and the defendant as to the livery business of the hotel had been destroyed, but the agreement was still in force, the only difference in the terms being that, under the contract originally, he collected the money, while now Sevier collected it. That he knows the hotel gets 10 per cent of the proceeds of the business done by Sevier, and not of the business done by other livery-men.

The prosecutor was recalled, and testified as follows: That he never spit on the floor at the hotel. That his conduct was gentlemanly in every respect, and that he had not drank a drop. That Mr. Woodbury, his employer, had at one time before this had the same contract with the hotel that Sevier had. That when Mr. Woodbury had the contract, he complained about other livery-men doing livery business at the hotel.

E. C. Chambers swore that he was a livery-man doing business in the City of Asheville. That he had received the same notice received by the prosecutor. That he drummed at the hotel among the guests for custom since he had received the notice, and that he had not been put out of the hotel, or ordered to leave. That he had also had a man employed to drum for him since the notice had been given him.

Because of a disagreement of counsel, and because requested by them so to do, all the evidence, except as to character, is sent up as part of the case. No special instructions were asked of the court by the defendant.

The court charged the jury as follows:

"It is admitted by the defendant that he did, against the will of the prosecutor, Weaver, put his hands upon him, and push him off the porch of the Battery Park Hotel, and down the steps thereof, to the ground. Nothing else appearing, this, in law, would constitute an assault and battery. But the defendant insists that he was justified in so putting his hands on the prosecutor, and so pushing him off the porch and steps of the hotel: (1) Because he, the defendant, was on his own premises, where he had a right to be; that the prosecutor, Weaver, was a trespasser there; that he ordered him to go away which he refused to do; and that he then gently put his hands upon him, and gently pushed him down off the porch and steps of the hotel, using no unnecessary force whatever. (2) Because he was the manager of the Battery Park Hotel, in the City of Asheville, in Buncombe County, and in control of the same at the time he so put his hands on the prosecutor and pushed him off the porch and steps of the hotel, and that, as such manager, it was his duty to keep all disorderly persons from the hotel, and to keep therefrom all such persons as are, because of their conduct, habits, manners, business, etc., nuisances, and an annoyance and discomfort to the guests of the hotel; that the prosecutor went to the hotel, after having been forbidden to do so, and so conducted himself as to become such nuisance, annoyance and discomfort, by spitting tobacco juice upon the floor, by becoming intoxicated, and other conduct; that the law devolved it upon him, and that it was his duty, as manager of the hotel, to the guests thereof, to make such rules and regulations as were necessary to procure the exclusion therefrom of disorderly persons, and such as, by their conduct, manner, habits and business, are nuisances and an annoyance and a discomfort to the guests of the hotel; and that he had made a rule, which was known to the prosecutor, and which was necessary and proper to procure the comfort of his guests, and to secure quiet and good order; that the prosecutor violated this rule, and when requested to leave the hotel and premises refused to do so, and that then the defendant gently put his hands upon him, and put him off the porch and steps of the hotel, using no excessive or unnecessary force or violence whatever.

"To these positions of defense relied upon by the defendant the State replies that the prosecutor, Weaver, was where he had the right to be; that he was at the Battery Park Hotel, which was a public inn, for a lawful purpose, to wit, to attend and serve the customers of his employer's livery stable; that others engaged in the same business he was in were permitted by the defendant to go and be there for the same purpose, and that therefore the defendant had no right lawfully to remove him from the hotel unless he was so conducting himself as to become a nuisance, an annoyance and discomfort to the guests and officers of the hotel; and that, in fact, he was not so conducting himself, nor was he such nuisance, annoyance or discomfort. The court charges you that, ordinarily, when one is on his own premises, he has the right to order another person who may come upon the same to go away, and upon a refusal to go he may put his hands gently upon him, and gently remove him therefrom, and, in the event of resistance, to use such force as may be necessary to eject him. But this is not always so when the premises are those of a public inn or hotel, such as it is admitted the premises were in this case. It being admitted by both the State and the defendant that the premises from which the defendant put the prosecutor in this case were those of a public inn or hotel, and that the defendant was at the time the manager thereof, and in control of the same, the court charges you that it was the duty of defendant, and the law devolved it upon him, to prescribe such reasonable rules and regulations as were necessary to the comfort of his guests, to secure quiet and good order, and to procure the exclusion from the hotel of disorderly persons, and such as by their conduct, manner and habits or business are nuisances, and an annoyance and discomfort to the guests of the hotel. It was also the duty of the defendant to his guests, and he had the right, to prevent all such persons coming into the hotel, and after they should come into the hotel, or upon the porch thereof, to order them to go away, and upon a refusal to go to put his hands gently upon them, and gently remove them, and, in the event of resistance, to use such force as would be necessary to remove them. It is admitted by the State that the defendant had, prior to the time he pushed the prosecutor off the porch and steps of the hotel, made the rules and regulations which have been read in your hearing, and that the prosecutor, Weaver, knew of them. It is also admitted by the State that the prosecutor had received a written notice from the defendant not to come upon the premises of the hotel prior to such time. This written notice has also been read to you. It is also admitted by the State, as insisted by the defendant, that the prosecutor went to the hotel for the purpose of transacting business connected with his employer's livery stable.

"The questions, then, for consideration and determination, are: (1) Did the prosecutor have the right to go to the Battery Park Hotel to transact the business of his employer, that of a livery-man, with the guests of the hotel? (2) If he did have such right, did he so conduct and demean himself while there as to forfeit his right to be there? (3) If he had no right to go to the hotel to transact his business as a livery-man, or if, while there, having such right to go and to be there, he so conducted himself as to forfeit such right, did the defendant use only such force as the law permitted him to use in removing the prosecutor, or was the force excessive and unlawful? The court charges you that, if you shall find from the evidence that others engaged in the same business as the prosecutor were permitted by the defendant to go to the Battery Park Hotel for the same purpose for which the prosecutor went there,—that is, to secure and transact business for his employer's livery stable,—then the prosecutor had also the right to go there for that purpose at reasonable times, and to remain there a reasonable length of time for the transaction of such business; and it would not matter that the rules of the hotel forbade his entering the premises of the hotel for that purpose, or that he had been previously forbidden, in writing, to come upon the premises of the hotel, nor would it matter that the defendant had designated a place at the back of the hotel where livery-men could transact their livery business with the guests of the hotel, through the servants and employés of the hotel, even though the prosecutor knew of such place being so designated. He would not, however, have the right to go there at all times, nor would he have the right to remain there all the time, or an unreasonable length of time, for the transaction of such business, against the will of the owner or manager. Unless you find from the evidence that other persons in the same business as the prosecutor were permitted by the defendant to go to the hotel for the same purpose for which the prosecutor went there, then the prosecutor had no right to go or be there for the purpose of transacting the business of his employer in connection with his livery stable, after notice from defendant to keep off the premises, and after the rule forbidding livery-men to come there to transact their business had been made known to him. Whether or not others, engaged in the same business as the prosecutor, were permitted by defendant to go to the Battery Park Hotel for the same purpose for which the prosecutor went there; whether the prosecutor went there at a reasonable time; whether he remained there only a reasonable length of time for the transaction of his business with a guest or guests of the hotel,—are matters for the consideration of the jury alone, and they must find how such facts are from the evidence adduced in the case. If the jury shall find from the evidence, under the charge of the court, that the defendant permitted others engaged in the same business as the prosecutor, to wit, the livery business, to go to the hotel to transact such business, and that other persons did go there, and there transact such business, although the prosecutor would then have the same rights at the hotel as such other person, yet if while at the hotel the prosecutor so demeaned himself, by becoming intoxicated, by spitting tobacco juice on the floor, loud and boisterous talking, cursing, swearing and other conduct, as to become a nuisance, an annoyance and discomfort to the guests and officers of the hotel; or if he went there at an unreasonable time for the transaction of such business, or remained there an unreasonable length of time for the transaction of such business, against the will of the defendant,—he lost all right to be at the hotel for any purpose, and it became the duty and right of the defendant to order him away, and upon his refusal to go to first put his hands gently upon him, and gently put him away, and, in the event of resistance, to use such force as would be necessary to eject him. The defendant would, in no event, have the right to use excessive force in putting the prosecutor off the porch and steps of the hotel. As to whether the prosecutor so conducted and demeaned himself, whether he went to the hotel at an unreasonable time for the transaction of his business, and whether the defendant used excessive force in removing the prosecutor, are matters of fact for the determination of the jury from the evidence."

The defendant excepted in writing to the charge of the court, as follows: "The defendant excepted to the charge of the court, as hereinbefore set forth, for that—(1) The court erred in submitting the question to the jury as to whether or not the rules and regulations adopted by the Battery Park Hotel were reasonable and proper. (2) That the court erred in submitting the question to the jury as to whether or not other persons engaged in the same business as the prosecutor were permitted by the defendant to go to the hotel for the purpose of carrying on this business, for that there was no evidence that the defendant permitted or allowed such to be done. (3) That the court erred in the following instructions given to the jury: 'If you shall find from the evidence that others engaged in the same business as the prosecutor were permitted by the defendant to go to the Battery Park Hotel for the same purpose for which the prosecutor went there,—that is, to secure and transact business for his employer's livery stable,—then the prosecutor had also the right to go there for that purpose at reasonable times, and to remain there a reasonable length of time for the transaction of such business; and it would not matter that the rules of the hotel forbade his entering the premises of the hotel for that purpose, or that he had been previously forbidden in writing to come upon the premises of the hotel.' (4) That the court erred in the following instructions given to the jury: 'Nor would it matter that the defendant had designated a place at the back of the hotel where livery-men could transact their livery business with the guests of the hotel through the servants and employés of the hotel, even though the prosecutor knew of such place being so designated.'"

Verdict of guilty, and judgment thereon. Motion for new trial. Motion overruled. Appeal by the defendant to the supreme court. Case settled on a disagreement of counsel.

Exhibit A: "No livery-man or agent of any transportation or baggage company, no washerwoman or sewing-woman not connected with the house, or loafer or lounger or objectionable person, will be allowed in the hotel."

Exhibit B: "At the meeting of the board of aldermen of the City of Asheville, on the 16th day of August, 1889, the following proceedings were heard: 'It was moved and seconded that the following rules for the regulation and government of the Battery Park Hotel be approved by the board. The motion was carried,—ayes, 5; noes, 1.' Among these rules is the following: 'No livery-man or agent of any transportation or baggage company, no washer woman or sewing-woman not connected with the house, or loafer or lounger or objectionable person, will be allowed in the hotel.'"

Exhibit C: "Battery Park Hotel, Asheville, N. C. J. B. Steele, Manager. July 18th, 1889. Mr. Joseph B. Weaver: On and after July 18th, 1888, parties engaged in the livery business will be indicted for trespass if found inside the Battery Park Hotel or grounds, unless by permission of J. V. Sevier, lessee of livery privilege of said hotel. [Signed] J. B. Steele, Manager."

Messrs. **D. Schenck, H. A. Gudger** and **Batchelor & Devereux** for appellant.

Messrs. **Theodore F. Davidson,** *Atty-Gen.*, and **G. A. Shuford** for the State.

Avery, *J.*, delivered the opinion of the court:

It was formerly held by the courts of England that where an innkeeper allured travelers to his tavern by holding himself out to the public as ready to entertain them, and then refused to receive them into his house when he had room to accommodate them, and after they had tendered the money to pay their bills, he was liable to indictment. But this doctrine, says Bishop (vol. 1, § 532, Crim. Law), "has little practical effect at this time, being rather a relic of the past, than a living thing of the present." *Rex* v. *Luellin*, 12 Mod. 445.

In a dictum in *State* v. *Mathews*, 2 Dev. & B. L. 424, this old principle was stated with some qualification, viz., that "all and every one of the citizens have a right to demand entertainment of a public innkeeper, if they behave themselves, and are willing and able to pay for their fare; and, as all have a right to go there and be entertained, they are not to be annoyed there by disorder, and if the innkeeper permits it he is subject to be indicted as for a nuisance." *Rommel* v. *Schambacher*, 120 Pa. 579, 9 Cent. Rep. 742.

The duty and legal obligation resting upon the landlord are to admit only such guests as demand accommodation, and he has the right to refuse to allow even travelers who are manifestly so filthy, drunken or profane as to prove disagreeable to others who are inmates, and thereby to injure the reputation of his house, to enter his inn for food or shelter, though they may be abundantly able to pay his charges. 2 Whart. Crim. Law, § 1587; *Reg.* v. *Rymer*, 13 Cox, Cr. Cas. 378.

The right to demand admission to the hotel is confined to persons who sustain the relation of guests, and does not extend to every individual who invades the premises, not in response to the invitation given by the keeper to the public, but in order to gratify his curiosity by seeing, or his cupidity by trading with, patrons who are under the protection of the proprietor. 1 Whart. Crim. Law, § 625.

The landlord is not only under no obligation to admit, but he has the power to prohibit the entrance of, any person or class of persons into his house for the purpose of plying his guests with solicitations for patronage in their business; and especially is this true when the very nature of the business is such that human experience would lead us to expect the competing "drummers," in the heat of excitement, not only to trouble the guests by earnest and continued approaches, but by their noise, or even strife. The guest has a positive right to demand of the host such protection as will exempt him from annoyance by such persons as intrude upon him without invitation and without welcome, and subject him to torture by a display of their wares or books, or a recommendation of their nostrums or business.

That learned and accomplished jurist, *Chief Justice* Shaw, delivering the opinion in *Com.* v. *Power*, 7 Met. 600, said: "An owner of a steamboat or railroad, in this respect, is in a condition somewhat similar to that of an innkeeper, whose premises are open to all guests, yet he is not only empowered, but he is bound, so to regulate his house as well with regard to the peace and comfort of his guests, who there seek repose, as to the peace and quiet of the vicinity, and to repress and prohibit all disorderly conduct therein; and of course he has a right and is bound to exclude from his premises all disorderly persons, and all persons not conforming to regulations necessary and proper to secure such quiet and good order."

This principle was stated as an established one, and used by the court as an argument to sustain by analogy its ruling announced in a subsequent portion of the opinion, that a railroad company had a right by its regulations to exclude from its depot and cars, at any station, persons who visited them for the purpose of soliciting passengers to stop at particular hotels; and one of the reasons given for holding the regulation reasonable was that, where the agents urged the claims of their respective hotels "with earnestness and importunity, it was an annoyance to passengers." The doctrine is there laid down, too, that persons other than passengers prima facie have the right to enter the depot of a railroad company, as others besides guests may go into hotels, without making themselves trespassers, because in both instances there is an implied license given to the public to enter. But such licenses in their nature are revocable, except in the one case as to passengers, and in the other as to guests, who have the right to enter the train, ticket-office or hotel, as the case may be, if they are sober, orderly and able to pay for transportation or fare. The court went further in that case, and held that, in enforcing the reasonable regulation against "drummers" for hotels at the depot, the servants of the railway company were not guilty of an assault for expelling by force, not excessive, a person who had repeatedly violated the regulation by going upon the platform and soliciting for a hotel, though on the particular occasion when he was ejected from it he had a ticket, and intended to take the train destined for another town, but failed to disclose to such servants the fact that he entered for "another purpose, when it was in his power to do so."

Were we to follow the analogy to which the principle laid down in that case would lead, an innkeeper could not only make and enforce a regulation forbidding persons to come on his premises for the purpose of soliciting his guests to patronize the livery stables that they might represent, but he might, in enforcing the rule against one who had previously violated it after notice that he should not do so, put such person off his premises, without excessive force, though at the particular time the person had entered with the bona fide intent to become a guest at the hotel, but failed to announce his purpose; or, under the same principle, he might expel by force one who becomes a guest, and takes advantage of his situation to subject other inmates of the house to the annoyance of "drumming" for such establishments. The same distinction is drawn between guests and others who enter a hotel intent on business or pleasure by the courts of Pennsylvania.

In *Com.* v. *Mitchell*, 1 Phila. 63, and *Com.* v. *Mitchell*, 2 Pars. Eq. Cas. 431, it was held that an innkeeper is bound to receive and furnish food and lodging for all who enter his hotel as guests, and tender him a reasonable price for such accommodation; but "if an individual [other than a guest] has entered a public inn, and his presence is disagreeable to the proprietor or his guests, he has a right to request the person to depart, and, if he refuses, the innkeeper has the right to lay his hands gently upon him, and lead him out, and, if resistance is made, to employ sufficient force to put him out," without incurring liability to indictment "for assault and battery."

Justice Story, in *Jencks* v. *Coleman*, 2 Sumn. 224, discussed the doctrine to which we have referred, that the right even of one who pays for his passage on a steamboat or railway is subject not only to the limitation that he shall be sober, and shall not be guilty of such nuisance or make such disturbance as shall annoy other passengers, but to the further restriction that he may be refused admittance or expelled, after he enters the boat or car, if it appears that "his object is to interfere with the interest or patronage of the proprietors (or company) so as to make the business less lucrative to them."

In the case last cited the proprietors of the boat Franklin had entered into a contract to run a line of stages between Boston and Providence in connection with the boat, which was running from New York to Providence. The plaintiff, Jenks, had been in the habit of coming on board the boat at Newport to solicit passengers for an opposition line of stages between Providence and Boston, thus interfering with the business of the owners of the boat, and the arrangement made by them for their own profit and advantage with a different line from that represented by said plaintiff, just as in the case at bar the proprietors of the hotel had entered into a contract with one Sevier by which they were to receive 10 per centum of the amount realized by him for the hire of carriages to the guests of the Battery Park Hotel.

Justice Story, too, runs the parallel between the hotel and boat line just as *Chief Justice* Shaw did between the inn and the railway company, but with the marked difference that the former goes much further in tracing the analogy that makes the public house subject to some of the same liabilities created, and entitled to the full measure of protection afforded by law to companies engaged in transporting passengers. In discussing the principle he says: "A case still more strongly in point, and which, in my judgment, completely meets the present, is that of an innkeeper. Suppose passengers are accustomed to breakfast or dine or sup at his house, and an agent is employed by a rival house, at the distance of a few miles, to decoy the passengers away, the moment they arrive at the inn; is the innkeeper bound to entertain and lodge such agent, and thereby enable him to accomplish the very objects of his mission, to the injury or ruin of his own interests? I think not."

In the case of *Barney* v. *Oyster Bay & H. S. B. Co.*, 67 N. Y. 302, the court of appeals held that a company running a line of steamboats for transporting passengers had a right to establish, in connection with their boats, an agency for the delivering of baggage at the terminus, and that one who had had the contract to transfer such baggage upon similar terms, two years before, could be expelled and refused as a passenger, if after notice he would not discontinue his efforts to induce passengers to employ him in the same capacity, rather than an expressman with whom the company had entered into a later agreement for their own pecuniary interest to deliver the baggage of its passengers.

All of the authorities that we have cited above are collated and approved in Angell on Carriers, in sections 530, 530*a* and 530*b*.

In the case of *Harris* v. *Stevens*, 31 Vt. 79, it was held that when a railway company erected station-houses it impliedly opened the doors of them to every person to enter, but that the license was revocable as to all persons except those who had legitimate business there, growing out of the operation of the road, and with the officers or employés of the company, and that the corporation had the right to direct all other persons to leave the depot or ticket office, and, on their refusal to depart, to remove them. It was further held in the same case that it was a reasonable regulation to require everyone who expected to take the train, and desired to remain in the station house for that purpose, to purchase a ticket, and that the servants of the company would be justified in expelling, without excessive force, one who did not declare his purpose to buy a ticket, and actually buy it within a reasonable time, or one who had bought a ticket even, if he failed to disclose that fact when requested to leave.

In the recent case of *Old Colony R. Co.* v. *Tripp*, 147 Mass. 35, 6 New Eng. Rep. 366, the court laid down the rule in reference to the rights of persons at depots as follows: "Passengers taking and leaving the cars at the station, and persons setting down passengers or delivering merchandise or baggage for transportation from stations or taking up passengers or receiving merchandise that had been transported to the station, had a right to use the station building and grounds superior to the right of the plaintiff (corporation) to exclusive occupancy." And it is further held to be the correct construction to be placed on a statute passed by the Legislature, giving to all persons equal terms, facilities and accommodations for the use of its depot and other buildings and grounds, that it was intended only to govern the relation between the common carrier and its patrons, and hence that a railroad company, even in the face of such a statute, had a right to contract with an individual to furnish the means to carry incoming passengers or their baggage and merchandise from its stations, and may grant to him the exclusive right to solicit the patronage of such passengers.

Upon a review of all the authorities accessible to us, and upon the application of well-established principles of law to the admitted facts of this particular case, we are constrained to conclude that there was error in the charge given by the court to the jury, because:

1. Guests of a hotel, and travelers or other persons entering it with the bona fide intent of becoming guests, cannot be lawfully prevented from going in or put out by force, after entrance, provided they are able to pay the charges and tender the money necessary for that purpose, if requested by the landlord, un-

less they be persons of bad or suspicious character, or of vulgar habits, or so objectionable to the patrons of the house, on account of the race to which they belong, that it would injure the business to admit them to all portions of the house, or unless they attempt to take advantage of the freedom of the hotel to injure the landlord's chances of profit derived either from his inn or any other business incidental to or connected with its management, and constituting a part of the provision for the wants or pleasure of his patrons. *Jencks* v. *Coleman*, *Com.* v. *Mitchell* and *Com.* v. *Power*, *supra; Pinkerton* v. *Woodward*, 33 Cal. 557, 91 Am. Dec. 660; *Barney* v. *Oyster Bay & H. S. B. Co.* *supra;* 1 Whart. Cr. Law, § 621; Ang. Carr. §§ 525, 529, 530; *Briton* v. *Atlanta & C. A. L. R. Co.* 88 N. C. 536.

When persons unobjectionable on account of character or race enter an hotel, not as guests, but intent on pleasure or profit, to be derived from intercourse with its inmates, they are there, not of right, but under an implied license that the landlord may revoke at any time; because, barring the limitation imposed by holding out inducements to the public to seek accommodation at his inn, the proprietor occupies it as his dwelling-house, from which he may expel all who have not acquired rights, growing out of the relation of guests, and must drive out all who, by their bad conduct, create a nuisance and prove an annoyance to his patrons. *Harris* v. *Stevens*, 31 Vt. 79; 1 Whart. Cr. Law, § 625.

3. The regulation, if made by any innkeeper, that the proprietors of livery stables, and their agents or servants, shall not be allowed to enter his hotel for the purpose of soliciting patronage for their business from his guests, is a reasonable one, and, after notice to desist, a person violating it may be lawfully expelled from his house, if excessive force be not used in ejecting him. *Com.* v. *Power* and *Harris* v. *Stevens*, *supra*. See also *Griswold* v. *Webb*, 16 R. I.—, 7 L. R. A. 302; *Old Colony R. Co.* v. *Tripp*, *supra*.

4. An innkeeper has unquestionably the right to establish a news stand or a barber shop in his hotel, and to exclude persons who come for the purpose of vending newspapers or books, or of soliciting employment as barbers; and, in order to render his business more lucrative, he may establish a laundry or a livery stable in connection with his hotel, or contract with the proprietor of a livery stable in the vicinity to secure for the latter, as far as he legitimately can, the patronage of his guests in that line for a per centum of the proceeds or profits derived by such owner of vehicles and horses from dealing with the patrons of the public house. After concluding such a contract, the innkeeper may make, and, after personal notice to violators, enforce, a rule excluding from his hotel the agents and representatives of other livery stables who enter to solicit the patronage of his guests; and where one has persisted in visiting the hotel for that purpose, after notice to desist, the proprietor may use sufficient force to expel him if he refuse to leave when requested, and may eject him, even though on a particular occasion he may have entered for a lawful purpose, if he does not disclose his true intent when requested to leave, or whatever may have been his purpose in entering, if he in fact has engaged in soliciting the patronage of the guests. *Barney* v. *Oyster Bay & H. S. B. Co.*, *Jencks* v. *Coleman* and *Harris* v. *Stevens*, *supra;* Ang. & A. Corp. § 530.

5. The broad rule laid down by Wharton (1 Cr. Law, § 625) is that "the proprietor of a public inn has a right to request a person who visits it, not as a guest or on business with a guest, to depart, and if he refuse the innkeeper has a right to lay his hands gently upon him, and lead him out, and, if resistance be made, to employ sufficient force to put him out; and for so doing he can justify his conduct on a prosecution for assault and battery." It will be observed that the author adopts in part the language already quoted from the courts of Pennsylvania.

6. If it be conceded that the prosecutor went into the hotel at the request of a guest, and for the purpose of conferring with the latter on business, still, in any view of the case, if, after entering, he engaged in "drumming" for his employer when he had been previously notified to desist in obedience to a regulation of the house, the defendant had a right to expel him if he did not use more force than was necessary; and if the prosecutor, having entered to see a guest, did not then solicit business from the patrons of the hotel, but had done so previously, the defendant, seeing him there, had a right to use sufficient force to eject him, unless he explained, when requested to leave, what his real intent was. *Harris* v. *Stevens* and *Com.* v. *Power*, *supra*.

The guest, by sending for a hackman, could not delegate to him the right to do an act for which even the guest himself might lawfully be put out of the hotel.

7. If we go further, and admit, for the sake of argument, that the principle declared in *Markham* v. *Brown*, 8 N. H. 530, and relied on to sustain the view of the court below, is not inconsistent with the law on the same subject, as we find it laid down by Wharton and other recognized authorities, still our case will be found to fall under the exception to the general rule stated in express terms in that case. The court said: "If one comes to injure his [the innkeeper's] house, or if his business operates directly as an injury, that may alter the case; but that has not been alleged here; and perhaps there may be cases in which he may have a right to exclude all but travelers and those who have been sent for by them. It is not necessary to settle that at this time." There was no evidence in *Markham* v. *Brown* that the proprietor of the hotel had any contract with another stage line, or would suffer pecuniary loss or injury, if the agent who was expelled was successful in his solicitations; and it seems that Angell and others, who cite as authority that case, as well as *Jencks* v. *Coleman* and *Barney* v. *Oyster Bay & H. S. B. Co.*, reconcile them by drawing the distinction that in the latter cases, and in the hypothetical case of an innkeeper, put by *Justice* Story, the person whose expulsion was justified was doing an injury to the proprietor, who had him removed, by diminishing his profits derived legitimately from a business used as an adjunct

to that of a common carrier or innkeeper. In using the language quoted above, *Justice* Parker seems to have had in his mind, without referring to it, the opinion of *Justice* Story, delivered in the circuit court but two years before (*Jencks* v. *Coleman, supra*).

8. The defendant, as manager of the hotel, could make a valid contract, for a valuable consideration, with Sevier, to give him the exclusive privilege of remaining in the house and soliciting patronage from the guests in any business that grew out of providing for the comfort or pleasure of the patrons of the house. The proprietors of the public house might legitimately share in the profits of any such incidental business as furnishing carriages, buggies or horses to the patrons, and for that purpose had as full right to close their house against one who attempted to injure the business in which they had such interest as the owner of a private house would have had; and this view of the case is consistent with the doctrine enunciated in *Markham* v. *Brown*.

There was no evidence tending to show that Chambers had actual permission from the proprietors to approach the inmates of the hotel on the subject of patronizing him, nor that they had actual knowledge of the fact that he had continued his solicitations after receiving a similar notice to that sent to the prosecutor. The fact that he was overlooked or passively allowed to remain in the hotel (it may be under the impression on the part of the defendant that he had desisted from his objectionable practices) cannot, in any view of the law, work a forfeiture of the right to enforce a reasonable regulation, made to protect their legitimate business from injury. If, therefore, a permit on the part of the defendant to Chambers to "drum" gratuitously in the house would at once have opened his doors to all of the competitors of the latter (a proposition that we are not prepared to admit), the defendant did not, so far as the testimony discloses the facts, speak to him on the subject; and the soundness of the doctrine that, without interfering with the legal rights of the guests, the proprietor of a hotel is prohibited by the Organic Law from granting such exclusive privileges to any individual, as to the use or occupancy of his premises, as any other owner of land may extend, is not drawn in question. We therefore sustain the second and third assignments of error. His honor erred, for the reasons given, in instructing the jury that the guilt of the defendant depended upon the question whether he permitted Chambers or Sevier to solicit custom in the house. He had a lawful right to discriminate, for a consideration, in favor of Sevier, while it does not appear from the evidence that he granted any exclusive privileges to Chambers. We hold that the regulation was such a one as an innkeeper had the power to make, and must not be understood as approving the idea that the sanction of the municipal authorities could impart validity to it, if it were not reasonable in itself, and within the powers which the law gives to proprietors of public houses in order that they may guard their own rights and protect their patrons from annoyance. For the reasons given *the defendant is entitled to a new trial.*

MASSACHUSETTS SUPREME JUDICIAL COURT.

Louis O. MORASSE

v.

G. Elz BROCHU.

(......Mass.......)

1. A declaration in a suit for slander, which claims special damages because of loss of trade, will not be held insufficient for failing to set out the names of persons who ceased or refused to employ plaintiff, after defendant has proceeded to trial without noticing such failure. An objection raised for the first time by a request for instructions comes too late.

2. An action will lie to recover damages for the utterance of a false imputation, although not actually defamatory, if it was made with the express purpose of injuring plaintiff in his profession, and such injury actually follows as the probable and natural result of the speaking of the words, just as was intended by defendant.

3. A statement by a clergyman to his congregation in effect that a certain physician was excommunicated by reason of his marriage, that he should be debarred from being employed as a physician in the parish and the patients who employed him could not in their sickness have the ministrations of the clergyman, may properly be given to the jury to determine whether or not it was made of the physician in respect to his profession so as to render them actionable *per se.*

4. Evidence of special damage may be given in an action for slander although the words spoken were actionable *per se*; it is also admissible although a necessary allegation of special damage has been insufficiently made if defendant has waived the defect.

5. Defendant's declarations made after the commencement of a suit against him for slander may be admitted in evidence upon the question of malice.

6. Where the evidence substantially supports the declaration an instruction that plaintiff cannot recover by reason of a variance is properly refused.

7. It is competent for a jury to find that words spoken by a clergyman to his congregation, to the effect that a certain physician had been excommunicated and should be no longer employed by them, were spoken maliciously and for the purpose of injuring the physician in his business.

(June 20, 1890.)

EXCEPTIONS by defendant to a judgment of the Superior Court for Worcester County in favor of plaintiff in an action to recover damages for the alleged publication of a slander. *Overruled.*

NOTE.—Slander. See Nissen v. Cramer (N. C.) 6 L. R. A. 780, and cases referred to in *note.*

Plaintiff was a practicing physician in Southbridge. His wife left him, went to Michigan and procured a divorce, to which plaintiff consented for the purpose of saving her honor. He was afterwards married to another woman by a justice of the peace.

Defendant was pastor of the Roman Catholic Church to which plaintiff belonged. At the time of the marriage he was absent in Europe. After his return he was invited to attend a dinner party at which plaintiff was to be present, but refused to do so. On Sunday, February 27, 1887, in the course of his sermon he said, according to his own testimony:

"Upon my return from the Holy Land, I learned with sorrow that a scandal had taken place among my congregation. I have kept silent until this day, but I see with sorrow that certain members of my congregation strive to have me publicly approve the object of the scandal. I was invited, recently, to seat myself at a table of friends, at which were the authors of the scandal. I blame those members of the congregation who endeavor to have me approve of that which the Church condemns, and punishes by excommunication. I should state to you, upon the subject of excommunication, that if you have need of the priest for your sick, and if you should have in your service an excommunicant, please call the priest before or after, seeing that the priest, in his sacred function, cannot remain at the same time as an excommunicant beneath the same roof."

Evidence was admitted against defendant's objection that after the commencement of the suit he stated to the congregation as follows:

"An action has been brought against me. I am not the party sued; everything falls upon the congregation. Be not disturbed—the congregation is worth $60,000. We will see if the church shall destroy the vermin, or if the vermin the church."

The jury returned a verdict in favor of plaintiff and defendant alleged exceptions.

The points of the case sufficiently appear in the opinion.

Messrs. **John Hopkins** and **Charles Haggarty,** for defendant:

The language relied upon, read and interpreted as it would ordinarily be understood by mankind, does not mean what the plaintiff says it means in his *innuendo.* An *innuendo* cannot add to, enlarge or change the sense of the previous words, and the matter to which it alludes must always appear from the antecedent parts of the declaration.

Goodrich v. *Hooper,* 97 Mass. 1; *York* v. *Johnson,* 116 Mass. 482; *Adams* v. *Stone,* 131 Mass. 133; *Thomas* v. *Croswell,* 7 Johns. 264; *Sanderson* v. *Caldwell,* 45 N. Y. 398.

Words not actionable in themselves do not become so when spoken of one in his profession unless they touch him in his profession.

Van Tassel v. *Capron,* 1 Denio, 250.

In case of a physician they do not touch him professionally, unless they impute misconduct or incapacity in the discharge of his professional duties.

Ayre v. *Craven,* 2 Ad. & El. 2.

Where the words can bear but one meaning, and that is obviously not defamatory, no *innuendo* or other allegation in the pleadings can make the words defamatory.

Hunt v. *Goodlake,* 29 L. T. N. S. 472; *Mulligan* v. *Cole,* 33 L. T. N. S. 12.

The fact that special damage is alleged and that actual damage has in fact followed from the publication is immaterial in considering what is the true construction of the language.

Hart v. *Wall,* L. R. 2 C. P. Div. 150.

Where special damage is the foundation of the cause of action it is a material allegation and must be fully and accurately stated.

Havemeyer v. *Fuller,* 60 How. Pr. 316; *Hallock* v. *Miller,* 2 Barb. 630.

Loss of the society of friends and neighbors, expulsion from religious society or suffering "annoyance, trouble, disgrace, loss of friends, credit and reputation," are not special damage.

Roberts v. *Roberts,* 10 L. T. N. S. 602; *Weldon* v. *De Bathe,* L. R. 14 Q. B. Div. 339, 53 L. T. N. S. 520; *Dwyer* v. *Meehan,* 18 L. R. (Ir.) 138.

Loss of custom is special damage, and must be specifically alleged and the customers' names stated on the record.

Odgers, Libel and Slander, 299; *Swan* v. *Tappan,* 5 Cush. 104; *Cook* v. *Cook,* 100 Mass. 194; *Fitzgerald* v. *Robinson,* 112 Mass. 371; *Tilk* v. *Parsons,* 2 Car. & P. 201.

Where words imputing misconduct to another are spoken by one having a duty to perform, and the words are spoken in good faith in the belief that it comes within the discharge of that duty, or when they are spoken in good faith to them who have an interest in the communication, no presumption of malice arises and no action can be maintained without proof of express malice.

Bradley v. *Heath,* 12 Pick. 164.

No inference of malice is to be drawn from the fact that the words used were intemperate or excessive from over-excitement.

Brow v. *Hathaway,* 13 Allen, 239.

In actions of slander evidence cannot be given of words spoken on another occasion, and of a different import from those charged in the declaration, although offered only for the purpose of showing malice.

Bodwell v. *Swan,* 3 Pick. 376; *Taylor* v. *Kneeland,* 1 Doug. (Mich.) 67; *Howard* v. *Sexton,* 4 N. Y. 157; *Howell* v. *Cheatham,* Cooke (Tenn.) 248.

Messrs. **W. S. B. Hopkins** and **A. J. Bartholomew,** for plaintiff:

Such words as must injure the plaintiff's reputation to disparage him in his means of living—such as reflect upon the moral character or conduct of the plaintiff—always fall within the range of defamatory and actionable words, if false or maliciously uttered (Odgers, Libel and Slander, 1st Am. ed. pp. 64-85, 308-318; *Burtch* v. *Nickerson,* 1 Am. Lead. Cas. 5th ed. 103, and cases cited), and need not impute crime.

Gove v. *Blethen,* 21 Minn. 80; *Swan* v. *Tappan,* 5 Cush. 104; *Fitzgerald* v. *Robinson,* 112 Mass. 381.

It is a fact for the jury to determine whether the words were spoken of the plaintiff in the way of his business.

Odgers, Libel and Slander, p. 69; *Ramsdale* v. *Greenacre,* 1 Fost. & F. 61; *Bloss* v. *Tobey,* 2 Pick. 328; *Van Tassel* v. *Capron,* 1 Denio, 250; *Terry* v. *Hooper,* 1 Lev. 115; Starkie, Slander and Libel, 3d Eng. ed.; Bigelow, Torts, p. 106.

A general averment of damage by loss of clients is sufficient.

Odgers, Libel and Slander, pp. 318, 319, and cases cited; *Chaddock* v. *Briggs*, 13 Mass. 251; *Phillips* v. *Hoyle*, 4 Gray, 571; *Burt* v. *McBain*, 29 Mich. 260; *Ashley* v. *Harrison*, 1 Esp. 48; *Cook* v. *Field*, 3 Esp. 133.

Here there was a count alleging special damage, and at the trial the defendant asked for no specifications of names which perhaps might have been ordered, nor was that objection taken on demurrer.

Clark v. *Munsell*, 6 Met. 382, 387; *Clay* v. *Brigham*, 8 Gray, 162; *Chace* v. *Sherman*, 119 Mass. 391.

The jury alone could decide the following questions:

Did he speak them concerning the plaintiff in the way of his profession?

Allen v. *Hillman*, 12 Pick. 104.

Were the words spoken false, and did the defendant utter them with a deliberate intent to injure the plaintiff's business?

Gassett v. *Gilbert*, 6 Gray, 98; *Brow* v. *Hathaway*, 13 Allen, 239; *Remington* v. *Congdon*, 2 Pick. 310; *Sheckell* v. *Jackson*, 10 Cush. 26.

Were the words, taking them in the connection in which they were used and the circumstances under which they were used, defamatory words?

Odiorne v. *Bacon*, 6 Cush. 188.

The words spoken after suit were competent to prove malice, or the intent with which the words were uttered.

Baldwin v. *Soule*, 6 Gray, 322; *Markham* v. *Russell*, 12 Allen, 573.

C. Allen, *J.*, delivered the opinion of the court:

1. The defendant contends that there is no sufficient averment of special damages. The averment in respect to the plaintiff's loss of practice as a physician is, that members of the church and other persons have refused to have transactions with him or to employ him in his profession, whereby he has been deprived of the profits, income and emoluments thereof. The only omission of any needful averment which is suggested is, that the names of the persons who have ceased or refused to employ the plaintiff should have been set out.

Where there is merely an accusation of immorality, in words which might be spoken of anyone, whether having any particular occupation or not, it has often been held that a charge of special damages from loss of custom or society must include the names of those who have cut off from the plaintiff in consequence of the imputation. This rule has not been so strictly held in cases where the accusation has been made for the express purpose of injuring the plaintiff in his trade or profession, and has had that effect; and in various cases, and for differing reasons, the rule in such cases has been relaxed, and a general averment of loss of customers has been held sufficient. *Evans* v. *Harries*, 1 Hurlst. & N. 251; *Riding* v. *Smith*, L. R. 1 Exch. Div. 91; *Clarke* v. *Morgan*, 38 L. T. N. S. 354; *Hopwood* v. *Thorn*, 8 C. B. 303, 309, per V. Williams, *J.*, *interloc.*; *Weiss* v. *Whittemore*, 28 Mich. 366; *Trenton Mut. L. & F. Ins. Co.* v. *Perrine*, 23 N. J. L. 402, 415. See also *Hargrave* v. *LeBreton*, 4 Burr. 2422; *Hartley* v. *Herring*, 8 T. R. 130.

In this Commonwealth, this question has not been decided.

In *Cook* v. *Cook*, 100 Mass. 194, the charge was general, and had no relation to any particular occupation of the plaintiff, and there was no question of loss of custom or of society.

In *Fitzgerald* v. *Robinson*, 112 Mass. 371, the averments were full, and no question arose.

In the present case there was a demurrer to the declaration. The Practice Act requires that in case of a demurrer the particulars in which the alleged defect consists shall be specially pointed out. Pub. Stat. chap. 167. In view of this requirement, the defendant specially and at length assigned five different grounds of demurrer, but there was no intimation of an objection on the ground that the names of the persons who would not employ the plaintiff were omitted. If the demurrer had contained this ground of objection, the plaintiff might have applied for leave to amend. Moreover, the Practice Act provides that no averment need be made which the law does not require to be proved, and that the substantial facts may be stated without unnecessary verbiage (Pub. Stat. chap. 167, § 2); and the court may in all cases order either party to file a statement of such particulars as may be necessary to give the other party and the court reasonable knowledge of the nature and grounds of the action or defense. § 61.

The demurrer having been overruled, no motion was made by the defendant for an order that the plaintiff be required to specify the names of persons referred to in the declaration. So far as the matter of pleading, therefore, is concerned, it must be considered that the defendant was content to go on trial without an averment of the names of these persons, and his request, at the close of the evidence, for an instruction to the jury that there was no sufficient allegation of special damage to make the words actionable, came too late, even if otherwise it could be considered as the proper way to raise the objection.

It must now be taken, therefore, that there was a sufficient averment of special damages.

2. If there was a sufficient averment of special damages, then the question is, whether an imputation of the kind made by the defendant upon the plaintiff, when false and when made for the express purpose of injuring the plaintiff in his profession, and when such injury is the probable and natural result of the speaking of the words, and when such injury actually follows, just as was intended by the defendant, will support an action by the plaintiff against the defendant.

It is sometimes said that it will not, unless the words are defamatory. But the better rule is, that such an imputation, whether defamatory of the plaintiff or not, will support an action under the circumstances above mentioned. There were all the elements of a wrongful act deliberately done for the purpose of working an injury and actually working one, even though the words have no meaning which, strictly speaking, could be called defamatory. *Riding* v. *Smith*, L. R. 1 Exch. Div. 91; *Lynch* v. *Knight*, 9 H. L. Cas. 600, per *Lord* Wensleydale; *Barley* v. *Walford*, 9 Q. B. 197; *Green* v. *Button*, 2 Cromp. M. & R. 707; *Trenton Mut. L. & F. Ins. Co.* v. *Perrine*, 23 N. J. L. 402. See also Odgers, Libel and Slander, 89, 92 (at bottom), where the question is fully discussed.

It may not be technically an action for slander, if the words are not defamatory, but the name of the action is of no consequence.

In *Kelly* v. *Partington*, 5 Barn. & Ad. 648, Littledale, *J.*, suggested the following illustration: "Suppose a man had a relation of a penurious disposition, and a third person, knowing that it would injure him in the opinion of that relation, tells the latter a generous act which the first had done, by which he induces the relation not to leave him money, would that be actionable?" And *Sir* John Campbell answers: "If the words were spoken falsely, with intent to injure, they would be actionable."

In Odgers on Libel and Slander, the following illustration is given: "If in a small country town where political or religious feeling runs very high, I maliciously disseminate a report, false to my knowledge, that a certain tradesman is a radical or a dissenter, knowing that the result will be to drive away his customers, and intending and desiring that result, then if such result follows, surely I am liable for damages in an action on the case, if not in an action of slander." P. 91.

In such a case there is an intentional causing of temporal loss or damage to another without justifiable cause and with the malicious purpose to inflict it, which will sustain an action of tort. *Walker* v. *Cronin*, 107 Mass 555.

And under this doctrine, in the opinion of a majority of the court, the present action may well stand.

3. But even if the averment of special damages is to be regarded as insufficient, for want of naming the persons who would not employ the plaintiff as a physician, the question remains, whether the words are actionable *per se*, as containing a defamatory imputation upon the plaintiff, or rather, whether there was enough in them to warrant the judge in submitting them to the jury.

Words are held to be actionable *per se* which convey an imputation upon one in the way of his profession or occupation, and in such case there need be no averment of special damages. The old phraseology of Comyn's Digest, which has often been followed or repeated, is that "words not actionable in themselves are not actionable when spoken of one in an office, profession or trade, unless they touch him in his office;" and many cases turn upon the question whether words spoken of one who has a particular profession or trade touch him in it—that is, whether they have such a close reference to such profession or trade that it can be said they are defamatory by means of an imputation upon him in that character, as, *e. g.*, an imputation upon him as a clergyman, a physician or a tradesman, distinctly and independently of being an imputation upon him as an individual. Some of the cases have gone very far to negative such a construction. Thus, for example, it was said by Bayley, *B.*, in *Lumby* v. *Allday*, 1 Cromp. & J. 301 (1831), that it was his opinion (for the time being) that the words must go to the length "of showing the want of some necessary qualification, or some misconduct, in the office." And in *Ayre* v. *Craven*, 2 Ad. & El. 2, words imputing adultery to a physician were held not actionable *per se*, and without special damage, there being nothing to show that the adultery was committed by him while acting as a physician, or in connection with his medical practice. These two cases are perhaps the most striking of any in that direction. But see also *Pemberton* v. *Colls*, 10 Q. B. 461, and *Gallwey* v. *Marshall*, 9 Exch. 294, for instances where imputations upon clergymen were held not to reflect upon him in his profession.

The case of *Ayre* v. *Craven* has not escaped criticism and comment, both from the bar and bench, though perhaps it has never been overruled.

In *Hopwood* v. *Thorn*, 8 C. B. 293, Cockburn and E. James said in argument: "*Ayre* v. *Craven* has confessedly gone to the very verge of absurdity."

In *Gallwey* v. *Marshall*, 9 Exch. 294, Willes said in argument: "The case of *Ayre* v. *Craven* is an extreme case;" to which Alderson, *B.*, replied from the bench: "There are certain professions, the proper exercise of which depends on morality; and except for the case of *Ayre* v. *Craven*, I should have thought that that of a physician was one of them." P. 297.

It may well be suggested that the doctrine of that and kindred cases has a distinct tendency to lower the estimation in which clergymen and physicians are naturally and properly held. At any rate, they do not correctly represent the law of Massachusetts.

In *Chaddock* v. *Briggs*, 13 Mass. 248, which was decided when drunkenness was not a crime in Massachusetts, and when the habits in respect to drinking intoxicating liquors were freer than at present, it was held that to charge a clergyman with a single act of drunkenness was actionable *per se*. The decision of course rested on the ground that it injured him in his profession, the court saying, "a pure and even unsuspected moral character being necessary to their usefulness in the community." That case has never since been questioned in this State, and it is inconsistent with the general doctrine that the words must impute either ignorance or want of skill, or some misconduct while actually performing the duties or functions of the profession or office.

In the present case it must now be assumed that the jury found, under the instructions which were given to them, that the defendant falsely and with a deliberate purpose and intent of injuring the plaintiff in his profession, and for the purpose of gratifying his ill will towards the plaintiff, spoke the words in question. These words did not merely instruct the congregation that the effect of a second marriage, under the circumstances which existed, was to excommunicate the plaintiff from the Catholic Church, but they proceeded to impute against the plaintiff that such marriage or such excommunication should debar him from being employed as a physician in the parish, and that patients who employed the plaintiff as a physician could not in their sickness have the ministrations of the defendant as their priest. The question is, Does this imputation affect him or, in the words of Comyn, touch him, in his capacity as a physician? It seems to be a palpable straining of language to say that it does not. It imports not only that the plaintiff was not in himself a suitable person for a Catholic community to employ as a physician, but that if employed the patient must lose the attendance of a priest. But the jury might well find that the plaintiff was a suitable person to be employed there as a physician, notwithstanding his marriage and its ecclesiastical consequence. The defendant assumed to stand in a position of authority. By virtue of this position he was able to exert a special influence upon his people. He assumed to assert and to exercise this influence; and his words amounted, in the opinion of the jury, to a plain departure from the proper exercise of such influence, and virtually to an instruction that the plaintiff was an unsuitable and improper person to be employed as a physician, and a direction not to employ him, on pain of losing caste in the church, and of losing the benefit of his ministrations as priest if they should be sick. The words were also susceptible of the meaning that the plaintiff was an unfit man even to be met socially, and that the defendant would not sit at the same table with him. Under these circumstances the court cannot lay down a rule that the words did not touch the plaintiff in his profession. According to the verdict of the jury, they were designed to touch him, and did touch him, effectually in his profession.

The language of Parke, *B.*, in *Southee* v. *Denny*, 1 Exch. 196, 202, 203, supports this view.

In the opinion of a majority of the court the words might therefore properly be found by the jury to have been spoken of the plaintiff in respect to his profession as a physician, and they might properly be found to be defamatory and actionable without an averment of special damages. See, as supporting this result, *Sanderson* v. *Caldwell*, 45 N. Y. 398, 405, where the court formulates a rule which would include this case.

The minor questions in the case may be briefly disposed of.

If an averment of special damages was necessary, or if the words set forth were actionable *per se*, in either case the evidence of special damage was properly received.

The evidence of what the defendant said after the commencement of the action was competent upon the question of malice. *Beals* v. *Thompson*, 149 Mass. 405.

The judge properly refused to instruct the jury that the plaintiff could not recover by reason of a variance. Taking the testimony of the various witnesses, there was from some one or other of them evidence substantially in support of all the words set forth in the declaration.

It was competent for the jury to find that the defendant spoke the words maliciously, for the purpose of injuring the plaintiff as a physician.

Exceptions overruled.

NORTH CAROLINA SUPREME COURT.

STATE OF NORTH CAROLINA
v.
HUNTER, *Appt.*

(....N. C.....)

1. Merely standing still on a sidewalk and refusing to move at the command of a policeman does not make one guilty of a nuisance.

2. If all except one of those who are obstructing a sidewalk disperse upon request of an officer, the one remaining is not subject to arrest for obstructing the free passage of the street "and failing to disperse upon notice."

3. An ordinance providing that a person may be arrested and taken, without warrant or hearing, to the station-house because he refuses to "move on," and, in the opinion of an officer, "unreasonably persists in remaining so as to incommode others passing," violates a constitutional provision that "no person should be taken, imprisoned . . . or in any manner deprived of his life, liberty or property, but by the law of the land."

4. An officer must determine at his peril whether an offense has been committed, before making an arrest without a warrant, where his power to arrest without warrant is expressly confined to cases where he has seen an offense committed, or where he knows it has been committed, and has reasonable ground to apprehend an escape.

5. The mere fact that a person is drunk on the streets will not authorize his arrest, under an ordinance permitting arrest for being "found drunk in the streets, hallooing or making an unusual noise."

(*Davis, J., dissents.*)

(April 28, 1890.)

NOTE.—*Constitutional protection of personal rights.*

Under the constitutional clause which declares that no person shall be deprived of life, liberty or property "without due process of law," no arrest can be made without warrant, except in cases of felony, or breaches of the peace, committed in the presence of the arresting officer. People v. Haug, 13 West. Rep. 471, 68 Mich. 549.

In cases of ordinary misdemeanors, a constable cannot arrest the offender without warrant, unless he is present at the time of the offense. Webb v. State, 51 N. J. L. 189.

The fact that a warrant has issued, directed to any constable of the county, will not avail such officer, unless such precept be in his possession at the time the arrest be made. *Ibid.*

An individual, unless taken in the criminal act, cannot be arrested without complaint on oath made before a committing officer and charging him with crime. State v. Dill (Del.) Nov. 6, 1889.

Nor can an officer arrest without process for a misdemeanor or violation of a city ordinance, not involving a breach of public order, although the offense is committed in his view. Danovan v. Jones, 36 N. H. 246; Wood v. Brooklyn, 14 Barb. 425; Philadelphia v. Campbell, 11 Phila. 163.

An officer has no right to arrest without a warrant, after the offense has been committed, in any case where the punishment is only a fine or imprisonment, or both. Bright v. Patton, 8 Cent. Rep. 711, 5 Mackey, 534.

One charged with a misdemeanor cannot be arrested after the commission of the act, without the proper warrant. People v. McLean, 13 West. Rep. 144, 68 Mich. 480.

A sheriff cannot send a deputy to one place to make arrest without a warrant, while he goes to another place for the same purpose with a warrant. *Ibid.*

He must be present, in sight or hearing, to justify an arrest by the deputy without a warrant. *Ibid.*

An officer cannot arrest without a warrant for a previous breach of the peace, even if it had been committed in his presence, however short the interval of time he was absent. The arrest must be immediate. *Ibid.*; Krulevitz v. Eastern R. Co. 3 New Eng. Rep. 310, 143 Mass. 228; Wahl v. Walton, 30 Minn. 506; Meyer v. Clark, 9 Jones & S. 107; Taylor v. Strong, 3 Wend. 384; State v. Sims, 16 S. C. 486.

In Massachusetts an officer who releases an intoxicated person on his promise to go directly home may retake him on his going into a bar room in sight of the officer. Com. v. Hastings, 9 Met. 259.

Arrest under warrant.

A warrant is a legal process issued by competent authority, directing the arrest of a person or persons upon grounds stated therein. Drennan v. People, 10 Mich. 169.

The warrant is directed to regular officers of the law, but in unusual emergencies the magistrate may direct his warrant to private persons named therein, as well as to officers of the law. Noles v. State, 24 Ala. 672; Kelsey v. Parmelee, 15 Conn. 260; Com. v. Foster, 1 Mass. 488; Com. v. Keeper of Prison, 1 Ashm. 183; Meek v. Pierce, 19 Wis. 300.

Where a warrant is issued against a person whose name is unknown the best description possible of the person to be arrested, sufficient to indicate clearly on whom it is to be served, must be given, by stating his occupation, personal appearance and peculiarities, the place of his residence or other circumstances by which he can be identified. Com. v. Crotty, 10 Allen, 403; Mead v. Haws, 7 Cow. 332.

The officer receiving the warrant for service must see that upon its face it appears to have been issued by a magistrate having jurisdiction, and upon legal cause shown. Grumon v. Raymond, 1 Conn. 40; Gurney v. Tufts, 37 Me. 130; Sandford v. Nichols, 13 Mass. 286; Drennan v. People, 10 Mich. 169.

A warrant in due form, issued by competent authority, is a complete justification and protection of an officer effecting the arrest. Clarke v. May, 2 Gray, 410; Mangold v. Thorpe, 23 N. J. L. 134.

But a warrant issued in blank, where the name of the person arrested was afterwards written in without authority, is no protection to an officer. Rafferty v. People, 69 Ill. 111; Alford v. State, 8 Tex. App. 545.

An officer cannot justify an arrest made under a warrant which does not give the first name of the person. Prell v. McDonald, 7 Kan. 426.

Nor under a warrant giving a name different from that of the person arrested. Alford v. State, 8 Tex. App. 545; Griswold v. Sedgwick, 6 Cow. 456.

Nor under a warrant issued against "persons who are suspected" of the crimes alleged in the warrant. Grumon v. Raymond, 1 Conn. 40. Consult Hawley, Law of Arrest on Criminal Charges.

Arrest without warrant, for crime committed within view.

An officer has a right to arrest without a warrant for any crime committed within his view. It was his duty to do so at common law, and this is still the law. Phillips v. Trull, 11 Johns. 486; State v. Brown, 5 Harr. (Del.) 505; Derecourt v. Corbishley, 5 El. & Bl. 188; Rex v. Hunt, 1 Moody, C. C. 93; 2 Hale,

See also 8 L. R. A. 846; 10 L. R. A. 607; 15 L. R. A. 63, 558; 19 L. R. A. 449;

APPEAL by defendant from a judgment of the Criminal Court for Buncombe County convicting him upon an an indictment for false imprisonment. *Affirmed.*

Statement by **Avery, J.:**

This was an indictment for false imprisonment, tried at the January Term, 1890, of the Criminal Court of Buncombe County, before Moore, *Judge.*

The defendant was a policeman of the City of Asheville, and arrested one Samuel Bennett, without warrant, for alleged violation of city ordinances in the following words: "Any persons assembling and loitering on the streets in sufficient numbers, or in such manner, as to cause an obstruction to free passage of the streets or sidewalks or crossings, and failing to disperse upon notice by any officer or any member of the police, shall, on conviction, be fined $10." "Whenever three or more persons obstruct the sidewalk, it shall be the duty of the officer to courteously request them to move on, and, if such persons unreasonably persist in remaining, so as to incommode others passing, he shall take them to the station-house."

After several witnesses had been examined for the State, the defendant testified in his own behalf as follows: "Four or five months ago Bennett and four or five others were standing on the sidewalk in front of Powell & Snider's store when people were passing, and they had to step out on the curbing to get around them. He asked them politely to get off the sidewalk and not obstruct it; and they all went off except Bennett, who said to him: 'There is room.' He told the prosecutor for the third time to move, and he refused to do it. He had no warrant or other process for the prosecutor at the time, but the next morning he swore out a warrant, which was produced in evidence. He was at that time a policeman. The prosecutor was drunk, and acted like a drunken man. Witness told him that he was drinking. The

---

P. C. 90-94; 2 Hawk. P. C. chap. 13, § 7; 1 East, P. C. 307. But see Butolph v. Blust, 5 Lans. 84, where it was held that an officer could exercise his authority to arrest outside his jurisdiction only in cases of felony. See Boyleston v. Kerr, 2 Daly, 220; Lancaster v. Lane, 19 Ill. 242; O'Brian v. State, 12 Ind. 369; Reg. v. Mubel, 9 Car. & P. 474.

In such case he must act promptly, for if he leaves and returns, however short the interval of time, he cannot make a legal arrest. Wahl v. Walton, 30 Minn. 506, 28 Alb. L. J. 168.

His authority to arrest without a warrant is limited to felonies and breach of the peace. State v. Oliver, 2 Houst. 585; Tiner v. State, 44 Tex. 128; Reg. v. Walker, Dearsly, C. C. 358; Galliard v. Laxton, 2 Best & S. 363; Reg. v. Chapman, 12 Cox, C. C. 4.

At common law a constable had power to arrest without warrant for breach of peace, or for felony, committed or in act of commission. Ballard v. State, 1 West. Rep. 79, 43 Ohio St. 340.

To justify an arrest without a warrant it must be made to appear that the accused will escape if the procurement of a warrant is attempted. O'Connor v. State, 64 Ga. 125; Ross v. State, 10 Tex. App. 455; Staples v. State, 14 Tex. App. 136.

In cases of felony a peace officer may arrest without warrant upon information where he has reasonable cause. Cahill v. People, 106 Ill. 621; Doering v. State, 49 Ind. 56; Rohan v. Sawin, 5 Cush. 281; Eanes v. State, 6 Humph. 53; Rex v. Birnie, 1 Moody & R. 160.

An official proclamation by the governor is sufficient evidence that a felony has been committed to warrant an officer in arresting one whom he reasonably believes is the person described in the proclamation. Eanes v. State, *supra.*

Instructions and information by telegraph from a public officer are sufficient ground for procuring an arrest. Castro v. De Uriarte, 16 Fed. Rep. 93.

Arrests are authorized, either by warrant or by the verbal order of a magistrate, for an offense committed in his presence. Lancaster v. Lane, 19 Ill. 242; Com. v. McGahey, 11 Gray, 194; Forrist v. Leavitt, 52 N. H. 481.

Knowledge that a warrant has been issued and is in the hands of another officer is sufficient ground for arrest for felony by an officer who does not have the warrant. Drennan v. People, 10 Mich. 169.

Petit larceny being a felony at common law, an officer may arrest a person on reasonable ground that he has committed the offense. Hernann v. Seneschal, 11 Week. Rep. 184; Orchard v. Roberts, 12 Week. Rep. 253; People v. Wilson, 55 Mich. 506; Drennan v. People, *supra;* State v. Grant, 76 Mo. 236; Hawley, Law of Arrest on Criminal Charges.

A mere belief that a crime has been or is being committed, without some basis of facts and circumstances on which to rest, is not sufficient. People v. Burt, 51 Mich. 199; State v. Grant, 79 Mo. 113.

If the officer acts in good faith he has a right to arrest a person without a warrant, whom he has good reason to believe is guilty of felony, even though it should afterwards appear that no felony had been committed. State v. Grant, 76 Mo. 236; McCarthy v. De Armit, 99 Pa. 63; Boyd v. State, 17 Ga. 194; Rex v. Woolmer, 1 Moody, C. C. 334.

To constitute a reasonable belief there must be a strong conviction from the circumstances that the party arrested is the felon. Marsh v. Smith, 49 Ill. 396.

There should be a reasonable ground of suspicion, supported by circumstances sufficient to warrant a cautious man to believe that the party is guilty. McCarthy v. De Armit, *supra.*

The right to arrest without warrant upon reasonable suspicion of felony is absolute and not dependent upon the probability of the suspected person's escape before a warrant can be procured. Rohan v. Sawin, 5 Cush. 281; Holley v. Mix, 3 Wend. 350.

The right exists as much in case of a statutory felony as in case of a felony at common law. Firestone v. Rice, 71 Mich. 377.

Belief, however well founded, will not justify arrest without a warrant for a mere misdemeanor. Com. v. Carey, 12 Cush. 246; Com. v. McLaughlin, 12 Cush. 615. *Contra,* State v. Brown, 5 Harr. (Del.) 505.

Arrest for breach of the peace.

An officer can arrest one committing a breach of the peace in his presence, without a warrant. People v. Rounds, 11 West. Rep. 507, 67 Mich. 482; Shanley v. Wells, 71 Ill. 78; Pow v. Beckner, 3 Ind. 475; Vandeveer v. Mattocks, 3 Ind. 479; Quinn v. Heisel, 40 Mich. 576; People v. Pratt, 22 Hun, 300; McCullough v. Com. 67 Pa. 30; Com. v. Deacon, 8 Serg. & R. 47; State v. Bowen, 17 S. C. 58; Ross v. State, 10 Tex. App. 455; Staples v. State, 14 Tex. App. 136; United States v. Hart, Pet. C. C. 392.

The breach, however, must actually occur in his presence. People v. Haley, 48 Mich. 495; Sternack v. Brooks, 7 Daly, 142.

Where a breach of the peace is merely threatened, or where it has been fully committed, he is not authorized to arrest without a warrant. Quinn

prosecutor only remained in the calaboose twenty or thirty minutes; and he told him that if he, or any of his friends, would deposit $5 in lieu of bond, he would let him go until next morning, and then appear before the mayor. One Smith deposited with the defendant the $5. The prosecutor did not demand to be permitted to give bond; nor did he offer bond, nor deposit any money in lieu thereof. No one offered to go his bail, and Smith deposited the $5 after the prosecutor was confined in the calaboose. On cross examination the defendant stated that Bennett was standing nearly in front of the store door, and about three and a half feet from the edge of the sidewalk; and when he asked him to move he said: 'There's eight feet;' but there was not so much as eight feet between the place where the prosecutor was standing and the edge of the sidewalk, which is not more than eight feet wide at that place. The arrest was made about sunset for a violation of the city ordinance, for blocking the sidewalk; and people were passing at the time. He did not decline to tell the prosecutor for what he arrested him, but did tell him. Prosecutor said something about going to Thrash's or somewhere else, to get bond. Defendant declined to go with him, but told him he could give bond, but would not take him to hunt it up. Prosecutor did not offer to go to procure bail before he got into the calaboose. Pulliam, one of the aldermen of the city, was at that time mayor *pro tem*. His place of business is in the Bank of Asheville, two hundred yards away, and it was about the same distance to the calaboose from where the arrest was made. Pulliam was not in the bank at that time, but was at his residence, about a half mile distant. Upon re-direct examination the defendant stated that Thrash's place of business was between said bank and the place of arrest. No surety was present to go on the bond, and prosecutor only suggested that he could give bond."

---

v. Heisel, 40 Mich. 576. But see Spaulding v. Preston, 21 Vt. 9.

A constable is bound to use his best efforts to suppress an affray, but he has no power to arrest for an affray not done in his presence, without a warrant, unless a felony is done or is likely to be done. Cook v. Nethercote, 6 Car. & P. 741; Rex v. Curvan, 1 Moody, C. C. 132; 1 Russ. Cr. 9th ed. 410; 1 Hawk. P. C. chap. 63, § 13.

An officer may arrest one making an assault upon him, while he is interposing to prevent an impending breach of the peace. McIntyre v. Raduns, 14 Jones & S. 123; Levy v. Edwards, 1 Car. & P. 40; Mosley v. State, 23 Tex. App. 409.

The attempt by force to prevent the servants of a municipality from laying pipe in the street authorizes an arrest without a warrant. Crosland v. Shaw (Pa.) 11 Cent. Rep. 665.

The wanton discharge of a firearm in a street of a city is a breach of the peace. People v. Bartz, 53 Mich. 493.

So, forcibly breaking open the door of a lodger in the exercise of a claim of right to pass through the room is a breach of the peace. Taaffe v. Kyne, 9 Mo. App. 15.

An officer may arrest, without a warrant, parties engaged in disturbing a religious meeting. Vandeveer v. Mattocks, 3 Ind. 479; Hutchinson v. Sangster, 4 Greene (Iowa) 340.

A special officer or policeman, in making an arrest without warrant for breach of the peace or violation of an ordinance, cannot act outside of his jurisdiction. Com. v. Hastings, 9 Met. 259; Butolph v. Blust, 41 How. Pr. 481.

Under the North Carolina Code authorizing the constable of a town to execute any lawful warrant issued by the mayor of a city or incorporated village, and giving the mayor the jurisdiction of a justice of the peace in all criminal matters, a warrant regular on its face, issued by the mayor, will protect the town constable in its proper execution anywhere within the county. State v. Sigman (N.C.) April 15, 1890.

Arrest for misdemeanors, without warrant.

A peace officer has the right to arrest without warrant for a misdemeanor, where the arrest is made *flagrante delicto*. State v. McNally, 2 West. Rep. 421, 87 Mo. 644.

In determining the power of the marshal of a municipal corporation to arrest without warrant, sections 1849 and 7129 of the Revised Statutes should be construed together to determine the extent of such power. Ballard v. State, 1 West. Rep. 79, 43 Ohio St. 340.

Public and disorderly drunkenness, when committed in view of the officer, has been held to be ground of arrest without warrant. Bryan v. Bates, 15 Ill. 87; State v. Bowen, 17 S. C. 58; Charleston v. Payne, 2 Nott & McC. 475; Mosley v. State, 23 Tex. App. 409; Shanley v. Wells, 71 Ill. 78; State v. Lafferty, 5 Har. (Del.) 491; State v. Russell, 1 Houst. 122; Bryan v. Bates, 15 Ill. 87; Main v. McCarty, 15 Ill. 442; Com. v. Coughlin, 123 Mass. 436; Phillips v. Fadden, 125 Mass. 198; Roberts v. State, 14 Mo. 138; People v. Pratt, 22 Hun, 300; State v. Freeman, 86 N. C. 683; White v. Kent, 11 Ohio St. 550; Thomas v. Ashland, 12 Ohio St. 127.

A peace officer in making an arrest for drunkenness must exercise his judgment, and determine whether it is his duty, under all the circumstances, to do so. But when he has exercised his discretion, and acts without rashness or negligence, his acts cannot be regarded as criminal because he is found to be mistaken. Com. v. Cheney, 2 New Eng. Rep. 227, 141 Mass. 102.

To justify the arrest of idle persons and vagrants walking the streets, there must be reasonable grounds for suspicion. See Roberts v. State, 14 Mo. 138; Reg. v. Tooley, 2 Ld. Raym. 1296; Lawrence v. Hedger, 3 Taunt. 14; 1 Whart. C. L. 8th ed. § 441.

In New York it is held that a common prostitute is not a vagrant unless she has no lawful means of support. People v. Forbes, 4 Park. C. C. 611. See *Ex parte* Birchfield, 52 Ala. 378.

An officer has no right to arrest, without a warrant, one accused merely of being a common prostitute. *Re* Way, 41 Mich. 299; People v. Pratt, 22 Hun, 300. *Contra*, Shaker v. Mumma, 17 Md. 336. See Hawley, Law of Arrest on Criminal Charges.

A public officer may arrest a person without a warrant for the public exhibition of an obscene picture, or for a public indecent exposure of his person. State v. Freeman, 86 N. C. 683.

The Texas Code authorizes an arrest without warrant for unlawfully carrying weapons, not only when the offense is committed within the officer's knowledge and presence, but also when he is informed of it by a credible person, even if there are time and opportunity to obtain a warrant. Jacobs v. State, 28 Tex. App. 79.

A marshal of a municipal corporation is authorized, without warrant, to arrest a person found on the public streets of the corporation carrying concealed weapons. Ballard v. State, 1 West. Rep. 79, 43 Ohio St. 340.

A police officer has no right, at the request of the

Other witnesses were examined, and a number of exceptions taken to the charge that became immaterial in the view of the case taken by the court. The defendant appealed from the judgment pronounced on the verdict of guilty. N. C. Const., art. 1, § 17, provides that "no person ought to be taken, imprisoned or disseised of his freehold, liberties or privileges, or outlawed or exiled or in any manner deprived of his life, liberty or property, but by the law of the land.

Mr. **George A. Shuford** for appellant.
Mr. **Theodore F. Davidson,** *Atty-Gen.*, for the State.

Avery, *J.*, delivered the opinion of the court:

In the case of *State* v. *Freeman*, 86 N. C. 683, the court distinctly recognized the right of a police officer to arrest without warrant, not only for felonies, riots and breaches of the peace, but for violation of a city or town by-law prohibiting nuisances, and which the municipality has the power to make, when the offense is committed in his presence. The Code, § 3820, makes it a misdemeanor to violate any valid city or town ordinance. The city law relied upon by the defendant to justify the arrest is not very happily and clearly expressed. The first section offered, numbered 348, makes the gravamen of the offense created by it consist in the failure on the part of the persons who, by assembling in sufficient numbers in the streets, have caused an obstruction, "to disperse upon notice by any officer or any member of the police." According to the defendant's own account of the transaction, the prosecutor, Bennett, and four or five others, were standing in front of Powell & Snider's store, when they were asked politely not to obstruct the sidewalk; and all of the others immediately went away, leaving Bennett alone. Bennett then said, "There's room," whereup-

---

keeper of a restaurant, to arrest without a warrant one who, taking a meal, fraudulently substitutes for the check given him one of a smaller amount, which he pays. Boyleston v. Kerr, 2 Daly, 220.

Right of private person to arrest.

At common law it is the duty of any person, in whose view a felony is committed, to arrest the offender. Long v. State, 12 Ga. 293; Brockway v. Crawford, 3 Jones, L. 433; Ruloff v. People, 45 N. Y. 213; Keenan v. State, 8 Wis. 132.

So, the owner of property, finding a person in the act of taking it unlawfully, may arrest the taker without a warrant. Smith v. Donnelly, 66 Ill. 465.

A private person may, in a temperate manner, in good faith and without a warrant, arrest one who has just committed a felony. State v. Mowry, 37 Kan. 369.

A private person may arrest without a warrant if he is sure that a felony has been or is about to be committed. See Burns v. Erben, 40 N. Y. 463; Hawley v. Butler, 54 Barb. 490; Samuel v. Payne, Doug. (Eng.) 359; Doughty v. State, 33 Tex. 1; *Ex parte* Krans, 1 Barn. & C. 261; Rex v. Hunt, 1 Moody, C. C. 93; Hadley v. Perks, L. R. 1 Q. B. 456; Allen v. London & S. W. R. Co. L. R. 6 Q. B. 65; Rex v. Jackson, referred to in 1 East, P. C. 298.

He may arrest another who is guilty of an affray or breach of the peace, without a warrant (Knot v. Gay, 1 Root, 66), but he cannot arrest for a breach of the peace after it is over. Phillips v. Trull, 11 Johns. 486.

Any person may suppress an affray, but he cannot of his own authority arrest either fighter after the affray is over, unless there is reason to apprehend the affray will be renewed. Price v. Seeley, 10 Clark & F. 28, 1 Lead. Cr. Cas. (Bennett & H.) 143; Phillips v. Trull, 11 Johns. 486; 1 Russ. Cr. 9th ed. 408, 411; 1 Hawk. P. C. §§ 11, 13, 19.

Distinction between private person and peace officer.

There is a distinction, as to the right to arrest, between a peace officer and a private person; the officer is justified in arresting one whom he has good reason to believe to be guilty of a felony, while a private person is not justified, however reasonable his belief, unless it appears that a felony was actually committed. Wrexford v. Smith, 2 Root, 171; Long v. State, 12 Ga. 293; Holley v. Mix, 3 Wend. 350; Burns v. Erben, 40 N. Y. 463; State v. Bryant, 65 N. C. 327; Brooks v. Com. 61 Pa. 352.

A private person cannot arrest another on mere suspicion, however strong the suspicious circumstances may be. Long v. State, 12 Ga. 293; Teagarden v. Graham, 31 Ind. 422; Doering v. State, 49 Ind. 56; Somerville v. Richards, 37 Mich. 299; Reuck v. McGregor, 32 N. J. L. 70; Brockway v. Crawford, 3 Jones, L. 433; Hanes v. State, 6 Humph. 53 Ashley v. Dundas, 5 U. C. Q. B. (O. S.) 754; McKenzie v. Gibson, 8 U. C. Q. B. 100.

When there is only probable cause of suspicion a private person, without a warrant, makes an arrest at his peril, as nothing short of proof of a felony will justify the arrest. Wakely v. Hart, 6 Binn. 316.

Where a warrant has been issued, a private person has no right to arrest for the crime included in the warrant. Kirbie v. State, 5 Tex. App. 60.

A private person has no right to arrest another without a warrant upon information of the commission of a felony upon which he had reason to rely. Such arrest is illegal and he makes it at his own risk, although an officer would be justified if he had acted upon such information. Cary v. State, 76 Ala. 78; Carr v. State, 43 Ark. 99; Long v. State, 12 Ga. 293; Ryan v. Donnelly, 71 Ill. 100; Allen v. Leonard, 28 Iowa, 529; People v. Burt, 51 Mich. 199; Simmerman v. State, 16 Neb. 615; Reuck v. McGregor, 32 N. J. L. 70; Burns v. Erben, 40 N. Y. 463; Holley v. Mix, 3 Wend. 350; Wakely v. Hart, 6 Binn. 316; Brooks v. Com. 61 Pa. 352; Brockway v. Crawford, 3 Jones, L. 433.

Arrest; how made.

Although manual seizure of the person is not always necessary, there must be that or its equivalent; but it is no arrest where there is no personal coercion, or deprival of liberty. Hill v. Taylor, 50 Mich. 549.

Anything which subjects a person to the actual control and will of another constitutes an arrest and imprisonment, whether a physical control, locking the door of a room where a person is found or a voluntary submission to words of arrest. United States v. Benner, 1 Bald. 240; Field v. Ireland, 21 Ala. 240; Strout v. Gooch, 8 Me. 127; Brushaber v. Stegemann, 22 Mich. 267; Gold v. Bissell, 1 Wend. 210.

An arrest is effected by an officer laying his hand on the person whom he has authority to arrest, though he may fail to stop or hold him. Whithead v. Keyes, 3 Allen, 495.

In a case of felony, where a person may lawfully be arrested without a warrant, the officer need not exhibit a warrant, but in cases of misdemeanor, where an arrest cannot lawfully be made without a warrant, the law requires the officer to have the warrant in his possession at the time of the arrest, that the person arrested may know whether the ar-on the defendant, after the prosecutor had been requested three times "to move," and had not done so, arrested him. A man cannot be guilty of a nuisance by merely standing still on a sidewalk, and refusing to move at the command of a policeman. Even under the phraseology of the ordinance, he was not guilty if the failure to "disperse" which was essential to constitute guilt. An obstruction may be removed, and a crowd dispersed, if all save one go off in different directions and he stands his ground. The act of one person halting on the streets for a reasonable time without misbehaving himself in any way is not such a nuisance as the city had a right to forbid by its laws under the general power delegated to it. Cooley, Const. Lim. *200.

The section referred to imposes a fine of $10 for a violation; and if its provisions are within the purview of the powers granted to the corporation the violation was also a misdemeanor. The other ordinance, Rule 15, is not materially different as to what it professes to prohibit and prevent; but it is amenable to objection, as legislation *ultra vires*, in that, instead of a fine, it imposes the punishment of imprisonment in the station-house, to be inflicted at the discretion of an officer, without a previous preliminary examination. Not only is the right of municipalities to make by-laws restricted to the express legislative grant of authority given in the charters or contained in the general laws defining the rights, duties and powers of all such corporations, but they are subject to the limitations contained in the Constitution of the United States, and that of the State in which they may be situate. Cooley, Const. Lim. *198, 199.

The second ordinance relied upon for the protection of the officer, Rule 15, is clearly in violation of the Constitution, art. 1, §§ 12, 13, 17, in providing that a person may be arrested because he refuses to "move on," and, in the opinion of the officer, who is left to judge of

---

rest is legal or not. State v. Phinney, 42 Me. 384; Com. v. Cooley, 6 Gray, 350; Drennan v. People, 10 Mich. 169; State v. Spaulding, 34 Minn. 361.

Notice to be imparted to person arrested.

The person arrested should have notice that he is arrested by lawful authority. State v. Phinney, 42 Me. 384; Drennan v. People, 10 Mich. 169.

Any actual notice of arrest by lawful authority is sufficient, and in such case the officer need not exhibit or read his warrant. State v. Townsend, 5 Harr. (Del.) 487; Com. v. Cooley, 6 Gray, 350; People v. Wilson, 55 Mich. 506; Arnold v. Steeves, 10 Wend. 514; Wolf v. State, 19 Ohio St. 248; Reg. v. Davis, Leigh & C. Cr. Cas. 64; State v. Garrett, 1 Winst. L. 144; 2 Hawk. P. C. chap. 13, § 18.

Notice of arrest is imparted where the person making the arrest is a known officer, or by seeing his uniform or badge of office. Yates v. People, 32 N. Y. 509.

Being arrested while in the act of committing a breach of the peace or other offense is notice of arrest. Wolf v. State, 19 Ohio St. 248.

Notice of the purpose to arrest and the reason for it, or immediate pursuit from the scene of the crime, is notice of arrest. People v. Pool, 27 Cal. 572.

Notice, to one who has committed a felony, of the purpose of pursuit, is necessary only to give the pursued an opportunity to desist from flight and unlawful action and to peaceably surrender, and is not necessary if he necessarily knows the purpose of the pursuit and the attempted arrest. State v. Mowry, 37 Kan. 369.

Where a party has been apprehended in the commission of a felony or on fresh pursuit, notice is not necessary. *Ibid.*

A private person who fails to give notice of his purpose to arrest is guilty of a trespass. State v. Bryant, 65 N. C. 327.

Right to use necessary means to effect arrest.

An officer in making a lawful arrest has the right, and it is his duty, to use every necessary means to make the arrest, and if resisted he may use sufficient force to overcome the resistance, and if the person resisting is killed by the officer it is justifiable homicide. United States v. Fayette County Jailer, 2 Abb. U. S. 265; State v. Fuller, 96 Mo. 165.

An officer has the right to use force to overcome resistance or prevent the escape of a fleeing criminal. People v. Carlton, 115 N. Y. 618.

He has no right, however, rudely and with violence to seize and collar his prisoner, unless resistance be offered, or an attempt be made to escape. State v. Mahon, 3 Harr. (Del.) 568; Burns v. State, 80 Ga. 544.

Unnecessary harshness or violence should be avoided. Fulton v. Staats, 41 N. Y. 498; Skidmore v. State, 2 Tex. App. 20; Beaverts v. State, 4 Tex. App. 175.

An officer has no right to use handcuffs, unless, without them, there is danger of the prisoner's escape. Cochran v. Toher, 14 Minn. 385.

He has a right to use his discretion as to the necessity for using handcuffs, and is liable only in case of a clear abuse of such discretion. Firestone v Rice, 15 West. Rep. 356, 71 Mich. 377.

After a prisoner has twice escaped, the officer is justified in using handcuffs upon him, and is not indictable for assault on account of having done so. State v. Sigman (N. C.) April 15, 1890.

Authority to break in doors.

The verbal order of a magistrate justifies the officer in breaking doors to make the arrest when the authority to arrest is lawful. Com. v. McGahey, 11 Gray, 194.

The officer has the right to break open the outer and inner doors of a house to effect an arrest under a criminal warrant or on an arrest for felony on reasonable suspicion, or to quell an affray, and will be justified although it should transpire that the person sought is not in the house at the time. Kelsey v. Wright, 1 Root, 83; Hawkins v. Com. 14 B. Mon. 395; State v. Smith, 1 N. H. 346.

Where an officer has reasonable cause to believe that the person named in the warrant, or a person whom he seeks to arrest on a charge of felony, is in the dwelling-house of another, he has a right to search the house, and, after demand for admittance and notice of his purpose, to break open doors if necessary to prosecute the search. Com. v. Reynolds, 120 Mass. 190; Com. v. Irwin, 1 Allen, 587.

The officer should first demand admittance, and explain the purpose of his entry. Barnard v. Bartlett, 10 Cush. 501.

If a person escapes while under arrest the officer may re-arrest him, and, if necessary, may break open the doors of his house to effect the arrest. Cahill v. People, 106 Ill. 621.

An officer may break open doors to prevent an affray, or to follow with fresh pursuit when affrayers flee into a house. 1 Russ. Cr. 9th ed. 410; 1 Hawk. P. C. chap. 63, § 13.

Upon fresh pursuit a private person has a right to break open the doors of any house in which the

his conduct, "unreasonably persists in remaining, so as to incommode others passing," and can be taken, without warrant or hearing, to the station-house. Under this law, he may be deprived of his liberty, and sent to a dungeon, not only without trial, but without even a preliminary examination, or an opportunity to give bail for his appearance at an investigation to be had in future, because, in the opinion of a policeman, he consumes an unreasonable time in exchanging greetings with two friends whom he meets upon the sidewalk of the city.

In the case of *Judson* v. *Reardon*, 16 Minn. 431 (Gil. 387), the defendant justified, in an action brought against him to recover damages for arresting the plaintiff, under an ordinance of the City of St. Paul, which provided that anyone who refused, without sufficient excuse, to obey any order or direction given at a fire by a person duly authorized to order or direct, should pay a fine not exceeding $50, and that "any member of the common council or any fire warden may arrest and detain such person, . . . until such fire is extinguished."

The court held that the clause permitting the arrest and detention during the fire was unconstitutional and void, and that, if the plaintiff had violated any valid city ordinance, he might have been arrested without warrant. This case has been cited with approval by both Cooley and Dillon. Cooley, Const. Lim. *201, 245, *note 3;* Dillon, Mun. Corp. § 414, *note.*

It was held, also, that an ordinance providing for the destruction of property as a nuisance, without a judicial hearing, was void under a section in the Constitution of Illinois substantially the same as that already cited from our own Organic Law. Article 1, § 17; *Darst* v. *People*, 51 Ill. 286.

The by-law distinguished as "Rule 15" is unconstitutional and void. If the other section is sufficiently intelligible to be enforced under a strict construction of its language in in any conceivable case, it is certain that the

---

felon has taken refuge. Brooks v. Com. 61 Pa. 352; Hawley, Law of Arrest on Criminal Charges.

But upon mere suspicion a private person has no right to break open doors or kill the suspected person to prevent his escape. Brooks v. Com. 61 Pa. 352; State v. Bryant, 65 N. C. 327.

Right of officers to call on citizens to assist.

An officer has a right to call upon any citizen to assist him in the execution of his warrant, and any-one refusing to assist is subject to prosecution. Coleman v. State, 63 Ala. 93; State v. Denniston, 6 Blackf. 277; Coyles v. Hurtin, 10 Johns. 85; State v. Shaw, 3 Ired. L. 20.

A person assisting an officer at his request or command, although the latter be a trespasser, is protected by law against suits for trespass and false imprisonment, if in his acts he confines himself to the order and directions of the officer. Watson v. State, 83 Ala. 60; Firestone v. Rice, 71 Mich. 377; McMahan v. Green, 34 Vt. 69. *Contra*, Mitchell v. State, 12 Ark. 50.

One aiding in making an arrest must himself have reasonable grounds for belief that the accused is guilty of a felony. Salisbury v. Com. 79 Ky. 425.

Persons coming to the aid of officers are entitled to the same protection as the officers themselves. State v. Oliver, 2 Houst. 585; People v. Moore, 2 Doug. (Mich.) 1; Coyles v. Hurtin, 10 Johns. 85; State v. Alford, 80 N. C. 445; Brooks v. Com. 61 Pa. 352; Galvin v. State, 6 Coldw. 283; 1 Hale, P. C. 462; Fost. Cr. L. 309.

A private person coming to the aid of an officer is not justified in killing where no felony has in fact been committed. See East, P. C. 297; Fost. Cr. L. 309.

Killing by officer in making arrest.

In no case must a felon be killed in attempting to effect his arrest if the officer can capture him by obtaining assistance or otherwise. Williams v. State, 44 Ala. 41.

It has been held that so long as the person sought to be arrested on a charge of murder was content peaceably to avoid arrest, the pursuing party had no right to kill him. State v. Anderson, 1 Hill, L. 327.

If an officer acts without a warrant he must be prepared to show the fact of a felony committed in order to justify taking the life of a person whom he is endeavoring to arrest or secure; his own belief of the commission of a felony, on however reasonable a ground, will not justify the killing. Conraddy v. People, 5 Park. C. C. 234.

The killing of an actual felon by a private person in his endeavor to arrest may be justified where the felon has notice of the intention to arrest him. State v. Roane, 2 Dev. L. 58.

A peace officer, in overcoming resistance to arrest for a misdemeanor *flagrante delicto*, is not restricted to the use of force necessary to self-defense, but may resort to the taking of life if necessary. State v. McNally, 2 West. Rep. 481, 87 Mo. 644.

An officer upon a warrant is justified in killing one accused of felony if he resists or flees; and so without warrant on the probable suspicion founded on his own knowledge or the information of others. Compare United States v. Rice, 1 Hughes, 560; Clements v. State, 50 Ala. 117; State v. Garrett, 1 Winst. L. 144; Wolf v. State, 19 Ohio St. 248; State v. Anderson, 1 Hill, L. 327; Reg. v. Dadson, 2 Denison, C. C. 35; 1 East, P. C. 298; 2 Hale, P. C. 85.

An officer seeking to arrest a felon, who refuses to stop when ordered to, may kill him, to prevent his escape, if he cannot otherwise capture him. Brooks v. Com. 61 Pa. 352.

A well-grounded belief that a felony is about to be committed will extenuate homicide committed in prevention, but not in pursuit, by a volunteer. State v. Rutherford, 1 Hawks, 457; State v. Roane, 2 Dev. L. 58. See Ruloff v. People, 45 N. Y. 213.

Killing by officers in routs, riots and unlawful assemblies, if necessary in arrest of offenders, is justifiable. Pond v. People, 8 Mich. 150; 4 Bl. Com. 180; 1 Hale, P. C. 495.

Not authorized in cases of misdemeanor.

In misdemeanors, the voluntary killing of the accused in the effort to arrest him is murder. Williams v. State, 44 Ala. 41.

In making an arrest for misdemeanor the officer can kill or inflict great bodily harm upon the person only when, by reason of resistance, he is placed in danger of like harm. Dilger v. Com. 11 Ky. L. Rep. 67.

So an officer has no right to kill a prisoner in custody for a misdemeanor to prevent his escape, and if he does so he is guilty of murder or manslaughter, according to circumstances. Reneau v. State, 2 Lea, 720; Forster's Case, 1 Lewin, Cr. Cas. 187.

In a case in Texas it was held that a penitentiary guard had no right to shoot an escaped convict who continued to flee when called upon to stop. Wright v. State, 44 Tex. 645.

So in making arrests in misdemeanors and in civil actions, life can be taken only where the party sought to be arrested resists by force, not when he merely escapes. A mere attempt to resist, not

conduct of the prosecutor in failing "to disperse" after his comrades had deserted him did not, according to defendant's own account of the transaction, subject him to liability either for the penalty prescribed, or to indictment under the general law making it a misdemeanor to violate a town ordinance.

The charter of the city (chap. 111, §§ 25, 27, 59, Priv. Laws 1883) gave the city marshal the powers, as a peace officer, of the sheriff or constables of the County of Buncombe, and to both the marshal and a policeman the authority to make arrests "(1) whenever he shall have in his hands a warrant duly issued by the mayor of the City of Asheville or a justice of the peace of the County of Buncombe; . . . (3) whenever a misdemeanor or violation of any ordinance has been committed, and he has reasonable cause to believe that the suspected party may make his escape before a warrant can be obtained."

The power to arrest without warrant is, in express terms, confined to two classes of cases: where he sees an offense committed; or where he knows it has been committed, and has reasonable ground to apprehend an escape. The latter provision enlarges his authority beyond that of a sheriff or constable, but upon condition that the ordinance has certainly been violated. *Judge* Dillon, in his work on Municipal Corporations (vol. 1, § 211), says: "Charters authorizing municipal officers to make arrests upon view, and without process, are to be viewed in connection with the general statutes of the State, and, being in derogation of liberty, are strictly construed." *Pesterfield* v. *Vickers*, 3 Coldw. 205; *White* v. *Kent*, 11 Ohio St. 550.

In the exercise of the extraordinary power given him by the charter, it was the duty of the defendant, before he touched the person of the prosecutor and demanded a surrender of his liberty, to know that the misdemeanor had been committed, either from seeing, or from

---

amounting to an assault, will not justify killing. Clements v. State, 50 Ala. 117. See Fost. C. L. 271; 1 Hale, P. C. 481; 1 East, P. C. 302; State v. Bryant, 65 N. C. 327; Tinor v. State, 44 Tex. 128; Hawley, Law of Arrest on Criminal Charges.

But killing to prevent an escape after a felony actually committed is justifiable. State v. Rutherford, 1 Hawks, 456; State v. Roane, 2 Dev. L. 58.

But an officer who, in attempting to recapture a person charged with a misdemeanor after the latter's escape, fires a pistol the ball from which passes near such person, is guilty of an assault, no matter what may have been his intention as to shooting him. State v. Sigman (N. C.) April 15, 1890.

After the escape of a prisoner charged with a misdemeanor, the officer cannot lawfully use any means to recapture him that he would not have been justified in employing in making the first arrest. *Ibid.*

Right to resist illegal arrest.

Illegal official action may be forcibly resisted. 1 Wharton, Cr. L. 8th ed. 3646.

A person may resist an illegal arrest. People v. Rounds, 11 West. Rep. 507, 67 Mich. 482; State v. Wimbush, 9 S. C. 309; Alford v. State, 8 Tex. App. 545.

But a person may not lawfully offer forcible resistance to an attempted wrongful arrest, until all other means of peaceably avoiding it have been exhausted. People v. Carlton, 115 N. Y. 618; Rafferty v. People, 72 Ill. 37; State v. Belk, 76 N. C. 10.

An arrest for improper purposes without just cause, or for a just cause without lawful authority, and for unlawful purposes, excuses acts committed under it. Strong v. Grannis, 26 Barb. 122; State v. Learnard, 41 Vt. 585.

Where an officer and a posse attempt to arrest a person for theft without a warrant, he not being caught in the act, he is justified in using his whip to compel them to release his horse, and so avoid arrest. Massie v. State, 27 Tex. App. 617.

If the person making the arrest is not known to be an officer, resistance is justified, even to the taking of life. Alford v. State, *supra.*

There is a clear distinction in the right to resist an arrest, between cases where the arrest is made by officers known to be such, and those made by private persons. Yates v. People, 32 N. Y. 509.

Under the Kentucky Criminal Code an officer who does not inform the person of the offense charged against him, or that he is acting under a warrant, may be lawfully resisted. Hamlin v. Com. 11 Ky. L. Rep. 348.

And persons assisting in the arrest, who were not duly summoned, may be lawfully resisted. *Ibid.*

If a person undertakes to resist an officer after he has made known his authority, he does so at his peril. State v. Oliver, 2 Houst. (Del.) 585.

If a party assists in resisting a criminal's arrest for felony, he may become an accessory after the fact, by endeavoring to shelter the accused. United States v. Tinklepaugh, 3 Blatchf. 425; McQuoid v. People, 8 Ill. 76; Slicker v. State, 13 Ark. 397; Reg. v. Marsden, L. R. 1 C. C. 131, 11 Cox, Cr. Cas. 90; 4 Bl. Com. 129; 1 Hale, P. C. 619; 2 Hawk. P. C. chap. 29, § 26; Dalt. Just. 530.

Even where arrest is lawful, if the officer illegally shoots at the person whom he is seeking to arrest, the latter is justified in shooting in self-defense. State v. Oliver, 2 Houst. (Del.) 608; Tiner v. State, 44 Tex. 128.

So, in case of an illegal arrest a person may resist, and if he kills the officer in so doing, it is only manslaughter. Noles v. State, 26 Ala. 31; State v. Oliver, *supra;* Galvin v. State, 6 Coldw. 291; Com. v. Drew, 4 Mass. 391; Com. v. Carey, 12 Cush. 246; Roberts v. State, 14 Mo. 146; Rafferty v. People, 69 Ill. 111, 72 Ill. 37; State v. Belk, 76 N. C. 10. See Tackett v. State, 3 Yerg. 392.

Killing officer in resisting arrest; when murder.

The law does not sanction the taking of life to repel every threatened trespass or invasion of personal rights. Williams v. State, 44 Ala. 41; Noles v. State, 24 Ala. 672; Roberts v. State, 14 Mo. 138; Com. v. Drew, 4 Mass. 391; Tackett v. State, 3 Yerg. 392.

When a person in resisting an officer or those engaged in assisting an officer to make a lawful arrest in a lawful way, slays one of the arresting party, it is murder. Dill v. State, 25 Ala. 15; Johnson v. State, 30 Ga. 426; Milner v. State, 30 Ga. 137; State v. Oliver, 2 Houst. (Del.) 585; Reg. v. Porter, 12 Cox, Cr. Cas. 444; 1 East, P. C. 299; Fost. Cr. L. 270, 308; 1 Wharton, Cr. L. 8th ed. § 413; 1 Russ. Cr. 9th ed. 732.

If the officer had the right to make the arrest the killing would be murder although done in the heat of blood. Galvin v. State, 6 Coldw. 283.

If the party having authority to arrest or imprison, using the proper means, happens to be killed, it will be murder for all who take part in such resistance. State v. McNally, 2 West. Rep. 481, 87 Mo. 644.

The intentional killing of an officer, acting under proper warrant of arrest, is murder in the first degree. State v. Spaulding, 34 Minn. 361; Rafferty v. People, 72 Ill. 37.

such information as made him willing to incur the risk of indictment, or of being mulcted in damages, if no ordinance had been violated. The question of good faith on the part of the policeman comes to his aid when he is resisted in making an arrest that he has an undoubted right to make, if there be resistance, and the question arise whether excessive force was used to overcome it; but policemen of Asheville must determine at their peril, preliminary to proceeding without warrant, whether a valid ordinance has been violated within or out of their view. The principle recognized in the cases of *State* v. *McNinch*, 90 N. C. 695, and *State* v. *Pugh*, 101 N. C. 737, was never intended to apply in any case except where an officer is making a lawful arrest.

In the case of *Judson* v. *Reardon*, *supra*, another principle was laid down which seems to have met with approval also. It was held that the arrest having been made under a void by-law, and being without authority, the officer making it could not rely upon his good faith as a defense to an action brought by the party imprisoned for malicious prosecution, and that, if the arrest was made upon the first part of the ordinance, which was not unconstitutional, the honest purpose of the defendant would not protect him because the plaintiff had violated that part of the ordinance by crossing the hose. There two distinct provisions, one valid and the other void, were embodied in one paragraph, while in our case they are the subjects of distinct sections. The difference in that respect can give rise to no distinction between that case and the one before us; for a legislative or a municipal law may be valid in part and void in part, and the portion not repugnant to the Organic Law will be enforced just if it had been a distinct statute.

There was no suggestion in the evidence that the prosecutor was "found drunk in the streets, hallooing or making an unusual noise," so as to bring him within the letter or even the spirit of the only other ordinance offered in evidence, designated as "number 645." The fact that the prosecutor told the defendant that he had been drinking, or acted like a drunken man, or that he even was drunk, without making any noisy demonstration, neither subjected him to liability for the penalty nor to indictment, because, under a strict construction of the law, he must have been both drunk and noisy.

This case may be distinguished from that of *State* v. *McNinch*, 87 N. C. 567, in the fact that in the latter the arrest was made under an ordinance declaring "public drunkenness and loud and profane swearing to be a nuisance." The court held that, where one was found drunk and swearing in an open space in rear of a bar-room, it was public drunkenness, though in a private place, and that the defendant was therefore liable under the letter of the law. That case went to the extreme limit in sustaining the right to declare any act a nuisance that was not a nuisance at common law, and especially when no specific power to enact the by-law was shown to be in the city charter.

We conclude that according to the defendant's own evidence he was guilty; and therefore, though the judge may have failed to state the law correctly in submitting to the jury the whole case, still the defendant is not entitled to a new trial if he was guilty in the aspect of the testimony most favorable to himself, and founded upon the conception that his own statement was true.

The judgment must be affirmed.

Davis, *J.*, dissents.

One who kills a peace officer to prevent arrest, knowing, or having reasonable grounds to believe, that he is a peace officer, is guilty of murder. Creighton v. Com. 83 Ky. 142; Brooks v. Com. 61 Pa. 352; Angell v. State, 36 Tex. 542.

It is for the court, and not the jury, to determine whether one attempting to make an arrest had the right to do so. Creighton v. Com. *supra*.

One who kills a private individual assuming to act as an officer in resisting arrest by him is to be tried as if the deceased had not been acting as an officer. *Ibid.*

It is murder for a felon to kill a person pursuing him for a felony which he committed. Brooks v. Com. 61 Pa. 352. See Galvin v. State, *supra*.

Where after commission of a felony the wrongdoers flee and are overtaken, and the officer points a gun at them and orders them to surrender, if they fire upon and kill him, it is murder. People v. Pool, 27 Cal. 572.

A policeman may arrest, without warrant, for disorderly conduct or other violation of city ordinances, or for crime, in order to prevent escape. In such a case, to attempt to kill the policeman is an assault with intent to murder, although no malice toward the policeman be proved other than the use of a weapon likely to produce death. Harrell v. State, 75 Ga. 842.

When killing is manslaughter.

Killing of an officer, attempting to make an unlawful arrest, is not justifiable, in the absence of a reasonable apprehension of bodily harm. State v. Cantieny, 34 Minn. 1.

The killing of the officer will be manslaughter, if the arrest be attempted without authority (Noles v. State, 26 Ala. 31; Rafferty v. People, 72 Ill. 37, 69 Ill. 111; State v. Oliver, 2 Houst. (Del.) 585; Com. v. Drew, 4 Mass. 391; Com. v. Carey, 12 Cush. 246); or if the officer exceeds his authority, or the process is defective (Rafferty v. People, *supra*); or if the warrant is without seal (Rex v. Stockley, referred to in 1 East, P. C. 310; Rex v. Harris, referred to in 1 Russ. Crimes, 8th Am. ed. *621); or if the person arrested be ignorant of the official character of the officer (Rex v. Higgins, 4 U. C. Q. B. (O. S.) 83); or if the officer be involved in a quarrel disconnected with his official duties. United States v. Gleason, 1 Woolw. 75, 128.

It is manslaughter where he attempts to kill the officer, but by accident kills a third person. Angell v. State, 36 Tex. 542; Com. v. Carey, *supra*; Com. v. McLaughlin, 12 Cush. 615; Roberts v. State, 14 Mo. 138; Jones v. State, 14 Mo. 409; Com. v. Drew, 4 Mass. 391. See Yates v. People, 32 N. Y. 509; Reg. v. Porter, 12 Cox, Cr. Cas. 444.

J. S. MOSSELLER, *Appt.*,
v.
W. I. S. DEAVER *et al.*

(........N. C.........)

1. **Even the owner of real estate** has no right to make a forcible entry upon the actual possession of another who is not a recent trespasser or intruder.

2. **In addition to nominal damages** for a forcible entry upon the peaceable possession of plaintiff, even by the owner, he can recover for any injury inflicted upon his person or personal property.

3. **Exemplary damages** for forcible entry may be recovered if the unlawful act is done in a wanton and reckless manner.

(May 19, 1890.)

APPEAL by plaintiff from a judgment of the Superior Court for Buncombe County in favor of defendants in an action brought to recover damages for an alleged forcible entry and detainer. *Reversed.*

The case sufficiently appears in the opinion.

Mr. **Theodore F. Davidson** for appellant.

Mr. **M. E. Carter** for appellees.

Shepherd, *J.*, delivered the opinion of the court:

The plaintiff had been in possession of the strip of land in controversy from 1884 to March, 1888. Whether he entered under the defendant Wilson, the owner, and the terms under which he entered, are disputed questions. It is admitted, however, that in March, 1887, Wilson, after giving the plaintiff notice to quit, agreed that he should remain upon the land until the succeeding October. The plaintiff continued in possession until March, 1888, when, without any further notice, he was forcibly ejected by the defendant Deaver and a negro, who were acting under the direction and authority of the said Wilson. The entry was made while the plaintiff was in the actual possession of his house, and in his presence, and was done under such circumstances as to constitute a forcible entry under the Statute, if not, indeed, an indictable forcible trespass. His honor charged the jury that, if the plaintiff was not the tenant of Wilson, the latter, and those acting under him, "had the right to go there and put him out by force, if no more force was used than was necessary for that purpose." Under the circumstances of this case (the plaintiff not being a recent trespasser or intruder), we cannot approve of the instruction given, as it is not only opposed to the public policy which requires the owner to use peaceful means or resort to the courts in order to regain his possession, but is directly contrary to a statute which condemns the violent act as a criminal offense.

In *Dustin* v. *Cowdry*, 23 Vt. 631, Redfield, *J.*, said: "We entertain no doubt that such a principle of law . . . did exist in England from the time of the Norman conqueror until the Statute of 5 Richard II., chap. 8, of 'Forci-

NOTE.—*Forcible entry and detainer, as a remedy.*

The remedy of forcible entry and detainer was designed to protect the actual possession, whether right or wrong; and it is no defense that defendant was entitled to the possession. Logan v. Lee (Ark.) March 29, 1890.

It is a civil action (Taylor v. De Camp, 68 Wis. 162); but it does not lie for a mere trespass on land. Castro v. Tewksbury, 69 Cal. 562.

Actual possession is sufficient to sustain the action against a wrong-doer. Mears v. Dexter, 14 Va. L. J. 240.

In order to maintain an action of forcible entry, the plaintiff must show that he was in the actual and peaceable possession of the property entered upon, that the defendant, by some kind of violence or circumstance of terror, entered into or upon the property, and so turned the plaintiff out, and took and held possession of it himself: or that, after making a peaceable entry, the defendant, by force, threats or menacing conduct, turned the plaintiff out and took the possession. Castro v. Tewksbury, 69 Cal. 562.

The plaintiff must be, at the time of the alleged entry, in the actual possession of the premises; neither the right of nor constructive possession is sufficient. Dills v. Justice, 10 Ky. L. Rep. 547.

But it is not necessary for plaintiff to prove actual personal presence on the land for five days continuously preceding the unlawful entry. Giddings v. 76 Land & Water Co. 83 Cal. 96.

The action cannot be brought unless the plaintiff has had peaceable possession; and a scrambling possession obtained by tying horses in an unfinished stable which is in the hands of the contractor is not sufficient. Blake v. McCray, 65 Miss. 443.

Possession means that position or relation which gives an occupant the use and control of land, excluding all others from a like use or control. Seisin means possession with intention of asserting a claim to a freehold estate. Ft. Dearborn Lodge v. Klein, 2 West. Rep. 33, 115 Ill. 177.

Proceedings under the Forcible Entry and Detainer Act decide the right of possession only; one having a right to enter may do so peaceably. "Force," as used in the statutes, means actual force. *Ibid.*

Under the Arkansas Statute relating to forcible entry and detainer, a contractor may recover possession of a part of a railroad, where he has been turned out of possession by force and violence after its completion and before payment. Iron Mountain & H. R. Co. v. Johnson, 119 U. S. 608 (30 L. ed. 504).

Title to property not in issue.

The title to the property cannot be inquired into for any purpose. Riverside Co. v. Townshend, 10 West. Rep. 580, 120 Ill. 9; Kepley v. Luke, 106 Ill. 395; McGuirk v. Burry, 93 Ill. 118; Smith v. Hoag, 45 Ill. 250; McCartney v. McMullen, 38 Ill. 237; Shoudy v. School Directors, 32 Ill. 290.

Title cannot be shown in defendant to prevent a restitution of the premises. Respublica v. Shryber, 1 U. S. 1 Dall. 68 (1 L. ed. 40); Peyton v. Stith, 30 U. S. 5 Pet. 485 (8 L. ed. 200).

The immediate right of possession is all that is involved, and hence a judgment in such action is not a bar to ejectment. Riverside Co. v. Townshend, 10 West. Rep. 580, 120 Ill. 9. See Cromwell v. Sac County, 94 U. S. 351 (24 L. ed. 195).

Neither the title nor the right to possession is at issue, nor can they be put in issue in such action. Sheehy v. Flaherty, 8 Mont. 365.

A forcible entry upon the actual possession of plaintiff in forcible detainer being proved, he will be entitled to restitution though the fee simple and present right of possession are shown to be in defendant. Giddings v. 76 Land & Water Co. 83 Cal. 96.

Evidence of title in action of forcible detainer is

See also 14 L. R. A. 206.

ble Entry and Detainer,' a period of nearly three hundred years; . . . and it is certain, we think, that such a mode of reducing rights of action to possession is more suited to the turbulence and violence of those early times, when no man whose head was of much importance to the state felt secure of retaining it upon his shoulders for anhour, than to the quiet and order and general harmony of the nineteenth century. . . . But as men advanced towards equality, and claimed to have their rights respected and guaranteed to them, and more carefully defined, this state of the law became intolerable and was among the first to be abrogated by Parliament." This was done by the statute of 5 Richard II., which is substantially enacted in North Carolina (see Code, § 1028) and in many other States of this Union.

"A contrary rule," says Lawrence, *J.*, in *Reeder* v. *Purdy*, 41 Ill. 279, "befits only that condition of society in which the principle is recognized that—

> He may take who has the power,
> And he may keep who can.

If the right to use force be once admitted, it must necessarily follow as a logical sequence that so much may be used as shall be necessary to overcome resistance, even to the taking of human life."

Nearly all of the authorities agree that such forcible entries on the part of the owner are unlawful; but there is a great diversity as to whether an action of trespass *quare clausum fregit* may be maintained, and also whether the defendant can justify under the plea of *liberum tenementum.*

Erskine, *J.*, in *Newton* v. *Harland*, 1 Man. & Gr. 644, said that "it is remarkable that a question so likely to arise should never have been directly brought before any of the courts sitting in banc," until that case, which was tried in 1840; and it is also worthy of remark that Ruffin, *Ch. J.*, in *State* v. *Whitfield*, 8 Ired. L. 317, regarded it as still an open question in North Carolina. In the conflict of authorities we must adopt that rule which in our judgment rests upon the sounder reason. This is so well expressed by the court in *Reeder* v. *Purdy*, *supra*, that we will reproduce the language of the learned justice who delivered the opinion. He says: "The reasoning upon which we rest our conclusion lies in the briefest compass, and is hardly more than a simple syllogism. The Statute of Forcible Entry and Detainer, not in terms, but by necessary construction, forbids a forcible entry, even by the owner, upon the actual possession of another. Such entry is therefore unlawful. If unlawful, it is a trespass, and an action for the trespass must necessarily lie. . . . Although the occupant may maintain trespass against the owner for a forcible entry, yet he can only recover such damages as have directly accrued to him from injuries done to his person or property, through the wrongful invasion of his possession, and such exemplary damages as the jury may (under proper instructions) think proper to give. But a person having no title

---

inadmissible, the inquiry being confined to the actual, peaceable possession of plaintiff, and the unlawful or forcible ouster or detention by defendants. *Ibid.*

Pleadings and proceedings in action.

A return of service of summons in forcible entry and detainer, which fails to show that a copy of the complaint was certified to by the justice of the peace, or by the plaintiff or his agent or attorney, is insufficient to maintain a judgment by default. Belfils v. Flint, 15 Or. 158.

A defendant in a proceeding under the Oregon Forcible Entry and Detainer Act may be required to answer not less than two, or more than four, days after service. *Ibid.*

A complaint alleging in substance that the defendant broke and entered the premises rented by plaintiff from defendant, and by force and menace refused to permit plaintiff to enter the same, and has ever since held, and now forcibly holds, possession, wrongfully and illegally, and claiming damages for such wrongful acts, and the consequent injury to plaintiff's business, was held to state a cause of action in tort, and not upon contract. Medcraft v. Dartt, 67 Wis. 115.

An allegation that prosecutor was seized, etc., is good, although not stating when he was seised. An additional allegation of peaceable possession is merely surplusage. Respublica v. Shryber, 1 U. S. 1 Dall. 68 (1 L. ed. 40).

It is not necessary for plaintiffs in forcible detainer to show that defendants held possession by force or threats of force. Giddings v. 76 Land & Water Co. 83 Cal. 96.

To constitute a forcible entry, it is sufficient if the entry, in the presence or absence of the possessor, is attended with such a display of force as manifests an intention to intimidate the party in possession, or to deter him from defending his rights, or to excite him to repel the invasion. Ely v. Yore, 71 Cal. 130.

Unless there is evident force against the person in actual possession, indictments should be discouraged. Thompson v. Com. 7 Cent. Rep. 861, 116 Pa. 155.

Entering a house under claim of right and in occupant's absence, and substituting a new lock for the occupant's, does not amount to forcible entry and detainer. *Ibid.*

The mere filing, by the defendant, of an answer claiming title to the premises, will not deprive the court in which the action is pending of jurisdiction; but if it should appear from the evidence that the question involved was one of title, and not for possession of the premises alone, the case should be dismissed. Lipp v. Hunt, 25 Neb. 91.

In an action of trespass for forcible dispossession of one claiming as tenant, evidence of the temper and character of the one making personal assaults was admissible in evidence, to show the knowledge plaintiff had of such temper and disposition, and the effect which threats might have upon him. Champlin and Sherwood, *JJ.*, dissenting. Baumier v. Antiau, 8 West. Rep. 115, 65 Mich. 31.

Evidence of personal assaults made by defendant's wife in his presence are admissible, while those made in his absence should be excluded. *Ibid.*

Evidence of the character of the premises, to show the value of the lease, was held admissible; and evidence of the cost of machinery which plaintiff had purchased for the purpose of working the premises was not admissible. *Ibid.*

There being evidence that the parties had made a settlement by which the plaintiff had surrendered possession, the charge of the court should have submitted to the jury to determine whether a settlement had in fact been made; but not whether it had been made on a good and sufficient consideration. *Ibid.*

to the premises clearly cannot recover damages for any injury done to them by him who has title." "He may, however," says the court, "recover nominal damages in all cases of forcible entry and detainer;" and this, in our opinion, is the correct view of the law. It is strongly sustained in *Newton* v. *Harland*, *supra*, though the point is not distinctly decided. In that case, Bosanquet, *J.*, agrees with Tindall, *Ch. J.*, in holding that, "if the act be expressly prohibited by statute, it must . . . be illegal and void." See also Cooley, Torts, 323, 324.

Our conclusion, therefore, is that, there having been a forcible entry upon the peaceable possession of the plaintiff, he is entitled to recover nominal damages for the trespass. He is also entitled to recover damages for any injury inflicted upon his person, his furniture, his tools, and even his house, if it is a fixture only. There may also be awarded exemplary damage if the unlawful act be done in a wanton and reckless manner. The complaint alleges such injuries, and it was error on the part of the court in making the case turn upon the question whether the force used was necessary to the expulsion of the plaintiff, as we have seen that the forcible entry was unlawful, without reference to the amount of force necessary to effectuate the purpose of the plaintiff. We are also of the opinion that the incompetent collateral matter admitted by the court must have had a prejudicial effect against the plaintiff.

For the reasons given, *there must be a new trial.*

INDIANA SUPREME COURT.

INDIANAPOLIS CABLE STREET R. CO.,
Appt.,
v.
CITIZEN'S STREET R. CO.

(....Ind.....)

1. **The rule which prohibits the granting of monopolies** applies only to such things as are of common right, and is never applied to things which are monopolies in their nature; hence it will not prevent the granting for a reasonable and fixed period of the exclusive right to operate a railway line in certain streets.

2. **A mere agreement by a municipal corporation** not to grant any rights or privileges which will impair or destroy those conferred by its ordinance giving a certain corporation permission to operate a street railway system in its streets will not prevent it from granting like permission to others.

3. **Where two rival companies have each received permission** to construct a railway system in the streets of a city, the one which first begins work on a line involving a certain street, in good faith and acting within the terms of its grant, has the better right to the use of that portion of the street which its tracks will cover; and this right will continue so long as money is expended and the work diligently prosecuted with a view to its completion.

4. **A municipality** having control over its streets may prescribe the motive power to be used in propelling street cars thereon; and when it prescribes one kind of power no other can be used.

5. **A street railway company having authority to use a cable** for motive power acquires no right to the exclusive use of a street by entering thereon and laying tracks upon which it intends to use a different motive power.

6. **A street railway company may,** for the purpose of defeating the rights which its rival claims to have acquired by reason of prior occupation of a street in which both companies have equal rights, allege and prove that such occupation was not in conformity to such rival's charter powers, in that the tracks were laid with the intention of using motive power different from that permitted by the charter.

7. **A grant of permission to use a certain motive power** upon street railway tracks wrongfully constructed with the intention of using such power when another was prescribed by the company's charter, will not relate back to the time of the construction of the tracks so as to cut off intervening rights.

8. **A company having power to own and operate** a street railway in a particular city may use the tracks, cars and other property which it purchases from another company previously chartered with like power, although the latter had no power to sell and transfer its franchise.

(June 19, 1890.)

APPEAL by defendant from a judgment of the General Term of the Superior Court

---

NOTE.—*Electric railways in city streets.*

A charter permitting a street railway to use horses or other power will permit the use of electricity as a motive power. Taggart v. Newport St. R. Co. (R. I.) 7 L. R. A. 205.

Where authority is given to use electricity as a motive power, by any system of application approved as suitable, the placing of poles in the streets will not be held prohibited by a clause in the charter prohibiting the incumbering of any part of the streets not occupied by its tracks. *Ibid.*

The New York Statutes authorizing a turnpike company to operate a street railroad, and to use "the power of horses, animals or any mechanical or other power, or the combination of them, which such company might choose to employ, except the force of steam,"—embraces electricity as a motive power. Hudson River Teleph. Co. v. Watervliet Turnp. & R. Co. 29 N. Y. S. R. 694.

The Rapid Transit Act (Laws 1875, chap. 606) authorized the organization of companies to construct street railways on the surface, to be operated by any power other than animal. Earl, *J.*, dissents. New York Cable R. Co. v. New York, 6 Cent. Rep. 56, 104 N. Y. 1.

Street railways; grant of franchise to. See *note* to People v. Newton (N. Y.) 3 L. R. A. 174.

Cable lines. See *note* to Weber v. Kansas City Cable R. Co. (Mo.) 7 L. R. A. 819.

City ordinance authorizing construction of railway. See *notes* to People v. O'Brien (N. Y.) 2 L. R. A. 255; Taggart v. Newport St. R. Co. (R. I.) 7 L. R. A. 205.

for Marion County affirming a judgment of the Special Term in favor of plaintiff in a suit brought to enjoin defendant from constructing a street railway upon certain streets, and from interfering with plaintiff in its construction of a railway upon the same streets. *Affirmed.*

The facts are fully stated in the opinion.

Messrs. **James B. Black, Shepard & Martindale** and **Hammond & Rogers,** for appellant:

In this State, power to confer a monopoly does not exist.

Const. art. 1, § 23.

A grant which gives to one or to an association of persons an exclusive right to use a given thing, or pursue a given employment, is a monopoly, though it do not continue indefinitely or in perpetuity.

Brenham v. *Brenham Water Co.* 67 Tex. 542.

The granting of the right to build and operate a street railway for the transportation of passengers for hire is a "special privilege" not enjoyed by the people in common.

Denver & S. R. Co. v. *Denver City R. Co.* 2 Colo. 681; *People's Pass. R. Co.* v. *Memphis City R. Co.* 77 U. S. 10 Wall. 38, 51 (19 L. ed. 844, 849); *Augusta Bank* v. *Earle*, 38 U. S. 13 Pet. 595 (10 L. ed. 311); *New York & H. R. Co.* v. *New York*, 1 Hilt. 562.

The Constitution prohibits the granting of an exclusive right to a street railroad company.

Birmingham & P. M. St. R. Co. v. *Birmingham St. R. Co.* 79 Ala. 465; *Louisville Gas Co.* v. *Citizens Gas Light Co.* 115 U. S. 683 (29 L. ed. 510); *Citizens G. & M. Co.* v. *Elwood*, 14 West. Rep. 92, 114 Ind. 332.

No franchise is ever construed to be exclusive, whether it be in the nature of a contract or not, unless it be so declared in clear terms, or be necessarily implied, or unless the terms of the grant render such construction imperative.

Stein v. *Beinville Water Supply Co.* 34 Fed. Rep. 145; *Com.* v. *Erie & N. E. R. Co.* 27 Pa. 351; *Fort Worth St. R. Co.* v. *Rosedale St. R. Co.* 68 Tex. 169; *Crawfordsville & E. Turnp. Co.* v. *Smith*, 89 Ind. 290; *Auburn & C. Pl. R. Co.* v. *Douglass*, 9 N. Y. 453, 454; *Chenango Bridge Co.* v. *Binghampton Bridge Co.* 27 N. Y. 93, 104; *Jackson County H. R. Co.* v. *Interstate R. T. R. Co.* 24 Fed. Rep. 306; *Sixth Ave. R. Co.* v. *Kerr*, 45 Barb. 138; *Wright* v. *Nagle*, 101 U. S. 791 (25 L. ed. 921).

The courts will, if possible, construe a grant to a corporation as not being exclusive.

Chenango Bridge Co. v. *Binghampton Bridge Co. supra; Charles River Bridge* v. *Warren Bridge*, 36 U. S. 11 Pet. 420 (9 L. ed. 773). See *note* to 3 Parsons, Cont. 536.

A municipal corporation cannot, by virtue of its general power over the streets, grant the right to construct a street railroad thereon. It must be authorized by the State Legislature.

Davis v. *New York*, 14 N. Y. 506; *Milhau* v. *Sharp*, 27 N. Y. 611; *Jersey City* v. *Jersey City & B. R. Co.* 20 N. J. Eq. 360; *Eichels* v. *Evansville St. R. Co.* 78 Ind. 261; *Coleman* v. *Second Ave. R. Co.* 38 N. Y. 201; *Saginaw Gas-Light Co.* v. *Saginaw*, 28 Fed. Rep. 529; *State* v. *Hilbert*, 72 Wis. 184.

A by-law which creates a monopoly is void.

Saginaw Gas-Light Co. v. *Saginaw, supra; Logan* v. *Pyne*, 43 Iowa, 524, 22 Am. Rep. 261; *Stein* v. *Bienville Water Supply Co.* 34 Fed. Rep. 145, 153; *Citizens G. & M. Co.* v. *Elwood*, 14 West. Rep. 92, 114 Ind. 332, 336; *Davenport* v. *Kleinschmidt*, 6 Mont. 502; *Logan* v. *Pyne*, 43 Iowa, 524, 22 Am. Rep. 261; *Memphis City R. Co.* v. *Memphis*, 4 Coldw. 406.

Even if appellee had a valid grant of an exclusive use of all the streets of the city for its horse railways, it has no right to complain of the use by the appellant of any street for the purpose of a cable or electric railway.

Saginaw Gas-Light Co. v. *Saginaw* and *Stein* v. *Bienville Water Supply Co. supra; Bridge Proprietors* v. *Hoboken L. & I. Co.* 68 U. S. 1 Wall. 116 (17 L. ed. 571); *Bush* v. *Peru Bridge Co.* 3 Ind. 21; *Omaha Horse R. Co.* v. *Cable Tramway Co.* 30 Fed. Rep. 324; *Savannah S. & S. R. Co.* v. *Coast Line R. Co.* 49 Ga. 202; *Louisville & P. R. Co.* v. *Louisville City R. Co.* 2 Duvall, 175; *Des Moines St. R. Co.* v. *Des Moines B. G. St. R. Co.* 73 Iowa, 513, 524; *Teachout* v. *Des Moines B. G. St. R. Co.* 75 Iowa, 722.

It is competent for the Legislature, after granting a franchise to one person or corporation, which affects the rights of the public, to grant a similar franchise to another person or corporation.

Fort Plain Bridge Co. v. *Smith*, 30 N. Y. 44, 61, 62; *Charles River Bridge* v. *Warren Bridge*, 36 U. S. 11 Pet. 420 (9 L. ed. 773); *Chenango Bridge Co.* v. *Binghampton Bridge Co.* 27 N. Y. 93; *New York & H. R. Co.* v. *Forty-Second Street & G. St. F. R. Co.* 50 Barb. 285; *Washington & B. Turnp. Road* v. *Baltimore & O. R. Co.* 10 Gill & J. 392; *White River Turnp. Co.* v. *Vermont Cent. R. Co.* 21 Vt. 590; *Thorpe* v. *Rutland & B. R. Co.* 27 Vt. 140, 152; *Washington & B. Turnp. Co.* v. *Maryland*, 70 U. S. 3 Wall. 210 (18 L. ed. 180); *Illinois & M. Canal Co.* v. *Chicago & R. I. R. Co.* 14 Ill. 314; *East St. Louis C. R. Co.* v. *East St. Louis U. R. Co.* 108 Ill. 265; *Lafayette Pl. R. Co.* v. *New Albany & S. R. Co.* 13 Ind. 90; *Bush* v. *Peru Bridge Co.* 3 Ind. 21; *State* v. *Noyes*, 47 Me. 189; *Baltimore & O. R. Co.* v. *State*, 45 Md. 596.

No condition has been imposed on appellant as to the portion of the street which it shall use.

See *Burrow* v. *Terre Haute & L. R. Co.* 5 West. Rep. 626, 107 Ind. 432, 436.

Until the appellee has built or commenced to build a railroad on a particular street, it cannot object to the use of any particular portion of a street by another company, or claim that it has an exclusive right to a particular portion of a particular street.

Fort Worth St. R. Co. v. *Rosedale St. R. Co.* 68 Tex. 169.

The attempt of a municipal corporation to create a monopoly is an attempt to devest itself of its legislative power, which it cannot do.

Gale v. *Kalamazoo*, 23 Mich. 344, 9 Am. Rep. 80; *Nash* v. *Lowry*, 37 Minn. 261; *Citizens St. R. Co.* v. *Jones*, 34 Fed. Rep. 579; *Birmingham & P. M. St. R Co.* v. *Birmingham St. R. Co.* 79 Ala. 465; *Brenham* v. *Brenham Water Co.* 67 Tex. 542; *Davis* v. *New York*, 14 N. Y. 506; *Milhau* v. *Sharp*, 27 N. Y. 622; *Eichels* v. *Evansville St. R. Co.* 78 Ind. 261.

If, having obtained such consent, a company locates and surveys a line definitely designated by the city in granting its consent, such locating and surveying give it vested right to the use of the street.

Denver & R. G. R. Co. v. *Alling,* 99 U. S. 463 (25 L. ed. 438); *Titusville & P. C. R. Co.* v. *Warren & V. R. Co.* 12 Phila. 642; *Troy & B. R. Co.* v. *Potter,* 42 Vt. 265, 272; *Old Colony R. Co.* v. *Miller,* 125 Mass. 1; *Drury* v. *Midland R. Co.* 127 Mass. 571; *Davis* v. *East Tennessee & G. R. Co.* 1 Sneed, 94.

A court has no right to interfere with a railroad company's location of its road, on the score of preference within the limit of its charter.

Parke's App. 64 Pa. 137; *Morris & E. R. Co.* v. *Blair,* 9 N. J. Eq. 635; *Waterbury* v. *Dry Dock E. B. & B. R. Co.* 54 Barb. 388.

The making of a binding contract for the construction of a line of railroad is a commencement of its construction, as is also the purchasing of materials for the particular work.

See *Citizens St. R. Co.* v. *Jones,* 34 Fed. Rep. 579.

The appellee may not in this action question the right of the appellant to construct a cable or an electric road, or raise any inquiry as to what motive power will be used upon a line in course of construction by the appellant when it shall have been completed.

West Jersey R. Co. v. *Cape May & S. L. R. Co.* 34 N. J. Eq. 164; *New York & H. R. Co.* v. *Forty-Second St. & G. St. F. R. Co.* 50 Barb. 285; *Market St. R. Co.* v. *Central R. Co.* 51 Cal. 583; *Christopher & T. St. R. Co* v. *Central C. T. R. Co.* 67 Barb. 315; *New York Cable Co.* v. *New York,* 6 Cent. Rep. 56, 104 N. Y. 1; *Jackson County H. R. Co.* v. *Interstate R. T. R. Co.* 24 Fed. Rep. 306; *New York & H. R. Co.* v. *Forty-Second St. & G. St. F. R. Co.* 50 Barb. 309; *Brooklyn, C. & J. R. Co.* v. *Brooklyn City R. Co.* 33 Barb. 420; *Fort Plain Bridge Co.* v. *Smith,* 30 N. Y. 63; *Citizens Street R. Co.* v. *Jones,* 34 Fed. Rep. 579; *Methodist Episcopal Union Church* v. *Pickett,* 19 N. Y. 482, cited in *Williamson* v. *Kokomo Bldg. & L. F. Asso.* 89 Ind. 390; *Re Petition of New York E. R. Co.* 70 N. Y. 327; *Barren Creek Ditching Co.* v. *Beck,* 99 Ind. 247; *Logan* v. *Vernon, G. & R. R. Co.* 90 Ind. 552; *State* v. *Woodward,* 89 Ind. 118; *Planters Bank* v. *Alexandria Bank,* 10 Gill & J. 346, 356.

Advantage cannot be taken of nonuser or misuser of an Act of Incorporation in any collateral action.

Union Branch R. Co. v. *East Tennessee & G. R. Co.* 14 Ga. 327; *Hammett* v. *Little Rock & N. R. Co.* 20 Ark. 204; *Vernon Society* v. *Hills,* 6 Cow. 23; *Vermont* v. *Society for Propagation of Gospel,* 1 Paine, 652.

The present intention of a corporation, even fraudulently, to omit a future duty, is not ground for an injunction.

Aurora & C. R. Co. v. *Lawrenceburg,* 56 Ind. 80; *State* v. *Kingan,* 51 Ind. 142; *State* v. *Beck,* 81 Ind. 500.

When two railroad companies have authority to build and run a railroad between the same terminal points, neither can take exception to any irregularity or unlawfulness in the exercise of such franchise by the other, unless it can show a particular injury to itself from such course.

Erie R. Co. v. *Delaware, L. & W. R. Co.* 21 N.J. Eq. 283; *Kinealy* v. *St. Louis, K. C. & N. R. Co.* 69 Mo. 658; *Omnibus R. Co.* v. *Baldwin,* 57 Cal. 160, 165; *Hudson & D. Canal Co.* v. *New York & E. R. Co.* 9 Paige, 323, 4 N. Y. Ch. L. ed. 718; *Taggart* v. *Western Md. R. Co.* 24 Md. 563; *City Hotel* v. *Dickinson,* 6 Gray, 586; *Humbert* v. *Trinity Church,* 24 Wend. 587, 630.

Messrs. **Winter & Elam** and **Henry C. Allen,** for appellee:

The ordinance granting the Citizens' Company a license to occupy the streets of Indianapolis, when accepted and acted upon, is a contract which cannot be impaired by subsequent legislation.

New Orleans Gas Light Co. v. *Louisiana L. & H. P. & Mfg. Co.* 115 U. S. 650 (29 L. ed. 516); *New Orleans Water Works Co.* v. *Rivers,* 115 U. S. 674 (29 L. ed. 525); *Louisville Gas Co.* v. *Citizens Gas Light Co.* 115 U. S. 683 (29 L. ed. 510); *Des Moines St. R. Co.* v. *Des Moines B. G. St. R. Co.* 73 Iowa, 513; *Indianapolis* v. *Indianapolis G. L. & C. Co.* 66 Ind. 396; *People* v. *Mutual Gas Light Co.* 38 Mich. 154; *Buchanan* v. *Logansport, C. & S. W. R. Co.* 71 Ind. 265; Cooley, Const. Lim. 337, 338, and *notes; People* v. *Chicago W. D. R. Co.* 18 Ill. App. 125; *Grand Rapids E. L. & P. Co.* v. *Grand Rapids E. E. L. & F. G. Co.* 33 Fed. Rep. 659; *St. Tammany Water Works Co.* v. *New Orleans Water Works Co.* 120 U. S. 64 (30 L. ed. 563); *Citizens Street R. Co.* v. *Jones,* 34 Fed. Rep. 579.

Where a particular method of forfeiture has been provided, it must be strictly pursued, and there can be no forfeiture in any other way.

Dillon, Mun. Corp. § 345; *Detroit* v. *Detroit & H. Pl. R. Co.* 43 Mich. 140; *Everett* v. *Marquette,* 53 Mich. 450.

By the ordinance in question the Citizen's Company was given the right, as against all others, to occupy the centre of the streets of Indianapolis for a limited time, and it is a contract that cannot be violated by granting to any other company the right to occupy precisely the same ground, the rights of the Citizen's Company not having been forfeited.

Dartmouth College v. *Woodward,* 17 U. S. 4 Wheat. 518 (4 L. ed. 629); *Vincennes University* v. *Indiana,* 55 U. S. 14 How. 268 (14 L. ed. 416); Wait, Insolv. Corp. § 17, and cases hereinbefore cited.

Where a corporation or an individual suffers a special and peculiar injury, the right exists to challenge the authority of the person or corporation inflicting it.

Tate v. *Ohio & M. R. Co.* 7 Ind. 479.

Coffey, *J.,* delivered the opinion of the court:

This was an action by the appellee against the appellant, brought for the purpose of enjoining the appellant from constructing a street railroad on certain streets in the City of Indianapolis, and to enjoin it from interfering with the appellee in its construction of a street railroad on said streets.

It is alleged in the complaint that the Citizen's Street Railway is a corporation organized under the laws of this State for the purpose of building, maintaining and operating street railways propelled by animal power in the streets in the City of Indianapolis; that after the organization of said corporation the common council of said city, on the 18th day of January, 1864, passed an ordinance by section 2 of which, and by the terms of section 3 of a subsequent ordinance passed on the 18th day of September, 1865, said corporation was granted power and authority to construct and lay a single or double track for such railway lines upon and along the course of all the streets of the City of Indianapolis, including Meridian, Circle, Market, Georgia and Alabama Streets, and Home, Central and Lincoln Avenues; that by the terms of said ordinance said tracks were to be laid in the center of said streets where practicable, except where a double track was contemplated, in which case the tracks were to be laid so as to make the center of said tracks the center of the street; that the grant of said right was to extend for the full term of thirty-seven years; that said city was not to grant to any person or corporation any privilege which would impair or destroy the rights and privileges of said corporation; that said corporation promptly accepted said ordinance and the other ordinances amendatory thereof, and at once laid and commenced operating a system of street railways in the City of Indianapolis, and complied with the terms of said ordinance, and has never at any time given to the authorities of said city any cause of forfeiture, and has been continuously extending said system, at an expense of many hundreds of thousands of dollars, and has never abandoned any of its rights; that the appellee is a corporation organized for the purpose of constructing, maintaining and operating street railways in the City of Indianapolis propelled by animal power, and that in April, 1888, it purchased from said Citizen's Street Railway Company all its property of every nature and description, including its cars, tracks, rights, franchises, real estate, horses, mules, harness, etc., with a view to succeeding to the rights of said Company in the continuation, maintenance and operation of its system of street railways in said city; that in April, 1888, said city, by a duly adopted ordinance, granted to the appellee all the rights, franchises and privileges of every nature and description belonging to said Citizen's Street Railway Company in the streets of said city, and thereupon appellant took possession of all such property, rights, franchises, etc., and has ever since been operating the said road under and in accordance with the authority conferred on it by its charter from the State of Indiana, and by its contract with said Citizen's Street Railway Company, and by the said ordinance granting and confirming to it, as the successor of said Citizen's Street Railway Company, all the rights of said last-named Company in the premises; that the appellant is a corporation organized under the laws of this State for the purpose of constructing, operating and maintaining lines of street cars in the City of Indianapolis, and is claiming the right to construct, operate and maintain such lines of cars in said city upon the streets hereinbefore named; that appellee has begun the construction of a line of street railway commencing and communicating with a track, or an existing and completed line, known as the Illinois Street line, at the junction of Illinois and Georgia Streets, extending thence east on Georgia Street to Meridian, thence north on Meridian to Washington Street, and connecting on Washington Street with the Washington Street line, and also, thence north on Meridian to Circle; thence east on Circle to Market, and thence east on the Market Street line; and, also, diverging at Maryland Street from said Meridian Street line, and extending thence east on Maryland Street to Pennsylvania Street, and thence north on Pennsylvania Street to Washington Street, and connecting with said Washington Street line; that it has also commenced another line commencing at the intersection of Pennsylvania and Market Streets, extending thence east on Market S reet to Alabama, thence north on Alabama Street to Home Avenue, thence east on Home Avenue to Central Avenue and thence north on Central Avenue to the State Fair Grounds; that on said last-named line it has done a large part of the work for the construction of the same, and is still at work prosecuting the same with the greatest diligence; that on Tuesday, the 24th day of July, 1888, it commenced work on said Georgia and Meridian Street line, and is diligently prosecuting the same; that by the contract as set forth in said ordinances it is required to lay its said tracks in the center of said streets, and in case of double tracks the same must be laid at such distance from the center of said streets as will make the central point between the two tracks the center of the street; and that under its said contract and ordinances it has no right to lay said tracks at any other points in said streets; that the appellant, claiming to have authority or license from said city, has entered upon some of the same streets, to wit, Meridian and Market Streets, and is threatening to enter upon others of said streets, and is building and is threatening to build a double-track street railroad in the center of said streets, occupying precisely the same ground that the appellee is required by its ordinance to occupy, and is thereby seeking to, and will, if it is permitted so to lay its tracks and to maintain the same, exclude the appellee from the use of said streets; that in 1877 said city, by an ordinance duly passed, granted or attempted to grant to appellant the right to build and operate a line of street cars on Meridian, Circle, Market and Alabama Streets, and on Home and Central Avenues, the same to be operated as cable cars, that is, being cars propelled by a cable revolving under ground and moved by a stationary steam engine at the termini of said lines; that long before it attempted to lay any track on said streets, or any of them, it disclaimed any purpose to accept said ordinance or license, and refused to accept the same; that on the —— day of June, 1888, it did enter upon Meridian Street between Circle and Maryland Streets, and proceeded to construct along the center of said street, upon the very ground the appellee is entitled to occupy, a double-track line to be used and propelled by animal power, or possibly by electrical motors, and at the time it thus tore up said street and constructed its track thereon it had no license or authority whatever in the premises to build any line whatever except said cable line, which it disclaimed any purpose of building; that on the —— day of ——, 1888, said city passed an ordinance authorizing the appellant to build a line of street railroad on said streets to be operated by electric motors, the wires for said motors to be under ground; that said ordinance was general in its terms, simply permitting said lines on said streets and not specifying the parts of said streets to be occupied by said lines; that after the appellee had commenced, as it had the right to do, to build its said tracks on Georgia and Meridian Streets, and on the other streets named, the appellant commenced to tear up said streets, and has commenced laying track on Market and Meridian Streets, and is threatening to lay its said track on the other streets hereinabove named, along the center of the same, thereby excluding the appellee from said streets.

The appellant filed an answer in two paragraphs, and also a counterclaim, and on a subsequent day filed a third paragraph of answer; but as no question is made on these pleadings they need not be set out. The appellee also filed a second paragraph of complaint; but we deem it unnecessary to refer now to the allegations contained therein, as all the questions arising on this paragraph arise upon the special finding of facts hereinafter referred to in this opinion.

Upon issues formed the cause was tried at special term of the superior court, resulting in the granting of a perpetual injunction against the appellant, from which it appealed to the general term and assigned error. The judgment of the special term was affirmed, from which the appellant appeals to this court. The court at special term made a special finding of the facts in the cause and stated its conclusions of law thereon. In this special finding are set out the several ordinances of the City of Indianapolis under which the respective parties to this suit claim the right to construct and operate street railroads on the streets of said city.

It appears by the special finding of facts in this cause, among other things, that on the 18th day of January, 1864, the common council of the City of Indianapolis passed an ordinance by which it granted to the Citizen's Street Railway Company of Indianapolis, and its successors, the right to lay a single or double track for passenger railway lines, with all necessary and convenient tracks for turn-outs, side tracks and switches, in, upon and along the course of the streets and alleys of the City of Indianapolis. The ordinance required the company to use animals only as a motive power. The track is required to be laid in the center of the street in all cases where it is practicable to so lay it, except where a double track is contemplated, in which case the track may be laid at such distances from the center of the street as will make the center point between the two tracks the center of the street. No track is to be laid within twelve feet of the sidewalk upon any street, in any case where it is practicable to avoid it. The rights and privileges granted by the ordinance are to extend over a period of thirty years from its passage, and the city thereby binds itself, during said period, not to grant to or confer upon any other person or corporation any privileges which will impair or destroy the rights and privileges granted to the Citizen's Street Railway Company. It is provided that if at any time during said period of thirty years the common council of the City of Indianapolis should be of the opinion that a line of street railroad should be constructed upon any street in said city over which no line exists, it may so declare by resolution; and if said company shall fail for a period of thirty days after service of notice, by the delivery of a copy of such resolution to it, to certify to the common council of said city a copy of a resolution of its directors ordering the construction of said line, with the affidavit of the president attached, that it is the design, in good faith, of said company to proceed immediately with the construction of said line of railway, the common council may, by resolution, declare all privileges and right of way over and in said line of street railway forfeited, and may grant the same to some other person or company.

By an ordinance passed by said council on the 18th day of September, 1865, it is declared to be the true intent and meaning of the ordinance of January 18, 1864, to grant to the Citizen's Street Railway Company the right to construct and operate street railways on any and all streets in the City of Indianapolis, whether named in said ordinance or not, and by the latter ordinance such permission is granted as to all the streets then in said city as well as to all streets that might thereafter be added by the extension of the corporate limits of the city. Immediately after the passage of these ordinances the Citizen's Street Railway Company commenced the construction and operation of a system of street railways in the City of Indianapolis under said ordinances, and continued to construct and operate such system until the 24th day of April, 1888, at which time it had thirty-eight miles of street-railroad track. On the 24th day of April, 1888, it sold and transferred all its property, including said track, cars, mules, harness, etc., to the appellee, which transfer was duly approved by the common council of the City of Indianapolis. At the time of the approval of said transfer the council passed an ordinance granting to the appellee all the right and privileges possessed by the Citizen's Street Railway Company. Immediately after obtaining possession of the property the appellee began to extend the system of street railroads already existing, and between the time of its purchase and the 1st day of September, 1889, built near fifteen miles of additional track.

On the 22d day of June, 1887, the common council of the City of Indianapolis, by an ordinance duly passed, granted to the appellant permission and authority to lay, construct, operate and maintain a single or double track street railway, with all the necessary and convenient tracks for turn-outs, side-tracks, switches and terminals in, upon and along all streets and alleys of said city then existing or which might thereafter be laid out. The ordinance required the appellant to construct, by the 1st of November, 1888, what was known as a cable line, operated by underground cable in connection with stationary engines on the following portions of said streets: one line commencing at the Union Passenger Station at Jackson Place, thence north on the new fifty-foot street leading from Jackson Place to Georgia Street, thence east upon Georgia Street to Meridian Street, thence north on Meridian Street to Circle Street, thence west on Circle Street to Market Street, thence west on Market Street to Tennessee Street, thence north on Tennessee Street to New York Street, thence west on New York Street to Mississippi Street, thence north on Mississippi Street to Seventh Street, thence east on Seventh Street to Tennessee Street, thence north on Tennessee Street to Twelfth Street, and thence east on Twelfth Street to the State Fair Grounds; one line commencing at the intersection of Meridian Street and the south boundary of Circle Street, thence east on Circle Street to Market Street, thence east on Market Street to Alabama Street, thence north on Alabama Street to Home Avenue, thence east on Home Avenue to Central Avenue, thence north on Central Avenue to Clyde Street, thence east on Clyde Street to College Avenue; and one line commencing at the intersection of Georgia Street and Meridian Street, thence east on Georgia Street to Pennsylvania Street, thence south on Pennsylvania Street to Madison Avenue, and southwardly on Madison Avenue to Minnesota Street.

On the 23d day of June, 1887, the appellant filed notice of its acceptance of the terms of this ordinance, but nothing was done looking to the construction of railway tracks until about the 1st of January, 1888. At that time John W. Dudley, a civil engineer, made some surveys for the New York Cable Railway Construction Company, which work he prosecuted at intervals between the 1st of January and the 18th day of March, 1888. During this time he surveyed a line called the Michigan Street line extending from Fall Creek Bridge southwesterly to West Street, and thence southerly to Michigan Street, and eastward on Michigan Street to the United States Arsenal grounds, and thence northerly on Keystone Avenue to Clifford Avenue, thence easterly on Clifford Avenue to Rural Street. He made a profile of this line. He was employed to do this work by W. W. Dudley, the general manager of the New York Cable Railway Construction Company, who was at the time president of the Indianapolis Cable Street Railroad Company. Between the 1st and 6th of May, 1888, said John W. Dudley resumed his surveys for the New York Cable Railway Construction Company, and within a few days thereafter the angle formed by the central line of Georgia Street and the central line of Meridian Street was measured and a wooden stake driven at the intersection of these two lines to form a basis upon which to order curve construction at said intersection. A similar stake was driven at the intersection of the central line of Meridian Street and the street-car tracks of the Citizen's Street Railroad Company on Washington Street, and the angle was measured there in like manner. The same measurements were made at the intersection of the central line of Circle Street and Meridian Street, and a line was measured around the southeast quarter of Circle Street. There was also a similar stake driven at the intersection of the center line of Market Street and the center line of the Citizen's Street Railroad Company's tracks on Pennsylvania Street, and the angle there measured. At the intersection of the center line of Market and Alabama Streets a similar stake was driven and the angle of intersection measured. At the intersection of the center line of Alabama Street and center line of the Citizen's Street Railroad Company's tracks on Massachusetts Avenue a similar stake was driven and a like measurement of angle made. At the intersection of the center line of Morrison Street and Alabama Street a similar stake was driven, and also, both at the intersection of the center line of Alabama Street south of Morrison Street and north of Morrison Street, there being an off-set or jog on Alabama Street at Morrison of about fifteen feet. The angles were also measured on Morrison Street. Like measurements and stakes were driven at the intersection of Sixth and Alabama Streets, Sixth Street and Central Avenue, Central Avenue and Ninth Street, Ninth Street and the central line of the Citizen's Street Railroad Company's tracks upon College Avenue on Ninth Street, and at a point about two hundred feet east of College Avenue on Ninth Street, a similar peg was driven in the center of Ninth Street. Plats were made showing these measurements. All said surveying, measuring, platting were begun between the 1st and 6th of May, 1888, and continued for and done within three or four days, by John W. Dudley and his assistants. During the last eight days of May, 1888, John W. Dudley resumed work for the New York Cable Railway Construction Company, and made a survey beginning on Market Street, on the east side of Circle Street, extending to the intersection of the center line of Alabama Street and Market Street, and thence north on Alabama Street nearly to New York Street. This survey consisted of a measurement of the distance along the center line of the street, and pegs were driven at intervals of one hundred feet. These pegs were driven to furnish reference marks for a double line of track of street railroad extending along the line of the route measured. In the latter part of May, 1888, the New York Cable Railway Construction Company became insolvent, and, after the 1st of June that year, no more work was done for it in Indianapolis. The work done by or for said company was done for and on behalf of the appellant. The first of June, 1888, a contract was made between W. W. Dudley and associates, subscribers for the majority of the stock of the Indianapolis Cable Street Railroad Company, and Mr. Tom. L. Johnson and his associates, by which the latter obtained an assignment of said stock subscriptions, none of the stock of said company having then been issued. On the 1st of June, 1888, W. W. Dudley arranged with Tom. L. Johnson to order for the appellant a mile of single-track material, and on short notice to procure materials of three miles of double track, in all seven miles of single track. In pursuance of this order, a mile of track material was sent immediately, and at the same time he made arrangements for tools and employed agents and workmen for laying track on Meridian Street and other streets. On the 2d or 3d day of June, 1888, said John W. Dudley began work for the Indianapolis Cable Street Railroad Company upon the streets of Indianapolis. He drove stakes at intervals of fifty feet upon the center line of Meridian Street, between the south line of Circle Street and the north line of Pearl Street, by direction of W. W. Dudley, the president of the appellant.

These stakes were driven for the purpose of furnishing reference points by which to align tracks of a street railroad. On the 4th day of June, 1888, the appellant began laying street railroad track, beginning at the south line of Circle Street, and extending southward on Meridian. The track laid at this time on Meridian Street, south of Circle Street, was a double-track street railway, the two tracks being laid at equal distances from the center of the street, with their inner rails about four feet and four inches apart, each track occupying, with the ties supporting it, a space of eight feet. It was not a cable street railroad, and was not built for the purpose of being operated as such, the idea of building a cable road having been abandoned about the 1st of June of that year. The work of laying this double-track road on Meridian Street, extending south from the Circle, was continued until the north line of Washington Street was reached, when Washington Street itself was omitted, and work resumed on the south side of Washington Street, extending said tracks southward on Meridian until they reached Pearl Street, making a distance of about two hundred and twenty feet between Circle Street and Washington Street, and about one hundred and sixty-two feet between Washington Street and Pearl Street. This work was completed between Washington Street and the Circle, and was in progress south of Washington Street, when work was suspended by the request of the city attorney of Indianapolis, which request was based upon the ground that the track being laid on Meridian Street, south of Circle Street, was not a cable street railroad, and not authorized by the ordinance giving the appellant Company authority to lay street railroad tracks where those were laid. These tracks laid on Meridian Street, between Circle and Pearl Streets, could be used to run cars drawn by animals or propelled by the overhead-wire-and-pole system of electricity, or by cars operated by an electrical storage battery, and could not be operated by cables or underground wires, as there was no excavation in the street below said tracks to constitute a chamber in which any underground wires could be operated. The appellant, at the time it constructed these tracks, did not construct them to be operated by underground cables or wires.

Soon after the transfer to the appellee of the right of its predecessor hereinbefore mentioned, the general manager of that Company gave orders to construct a number of additional street-car lines in the City of Indianapolis, and among other lines was a line extending from the Union Station to the State Fair Grounds.

On the 6th day of June, 1888, the appellee began work on Market at the east line of Pennsylvania Street, and continued to excavate and lay track toward the east on Market Street, until the square between Market and Delaware Streets was completed; and the square between Delaware and Alabama Streets was well advanced towards completion, when work was stopped by the street commissioner of the City of Indianapolis. And on the 10th of June, 1888, an injunction suit was brought by the appellee to prevent further interference with the work by the city authorities, and upon this injunction being granted, work was resumed on Market Street between Delaware and Alabama, and continued upon Alabama Street between Market and New York Streets, said work on Alabama Street being well advanced towards completion on the 24th day of July, 1888. The appellant caused its said engineer and his assistants, on the 24th day of July, 1888, between the hours of eight and twelve in the morning, to survey Georgia Street between Illinois and Meridian Streets, and to drive stakes similar to those hereinbefore mentioned on the center line of Georgia Street from a point therein east of Illinois Street and west of Meridian Street, and at about one third of the distance eastward between Illinois and Meridian Streets, said point being at the west side of a street running north from the Union Depot and Jackson Place to Georgia Street and named McCrea Street, thence eastward, to the intersection of the center lines of Georgia and Meridian Streets, said stakes being driven into the surface of the street at intervals of fifty feet along said course, for the purpose of furnishing a reference mark for the construction by the appellant of a double track street railroad upon Georgia and Meridian Streets, to connect with the line of street railroad which the appellant had built, as before stated, between Circle and Pearl Streets, upon Meridian Street.

At the time the appellant caused said survey and staking, commencing about the 1st and 6th days of May, 1888, and continuing for three or four days, there was no street railway track of any company upon and along Meridian Street between Louisiana Street and Circle Street, or on and along Circle, or on and along Market Street between Circle Street and Alabama Street, or on and along Alabama Street between Market Street and Sixth Street, or on and along Sixth Street between Alabama Street and Central Avenue, or on and along Central Avenue between Sixth Street and Ninth Street, or on and along Ninth Street.

At the time the surveying and staking, within the last eight days of May, 1888, was done, there was no street railroad track of any company on and along Market Street between Circle Street and Alabama Street, or on and along Alabama Street between Market Street and Seventh Street.

On the 6th day of June, 1888, at 1 o'clock P. M., the appellee first began work upon a line of street railway on Market Street, between Pennsylvania and Alabama Streets, by placing a force of men there and commencing the digging up of the street to put in a double-track street railroad, and laid there some ties and track between that time and the third day thereafter, when said work stopped for the time being, no work having been done at that time on any other part of the line of which the track so put in was to constitute a part.

On the 24th day of July, 1888, the appellant, beside causing the survey and staking on Georgia Street, made arrangements for assembling its workmen to resume construction the next morning on Georgia Street between Illinois and Meridian Streets, and on Meridian Street between Louisiana Street and Circle Street, and for such purpose caused its tool boxes to be deposited at the northeast corner of Meridian and Georgia Streets between 3 and 4 o'clock in the afternoon. About the same hour a force of the appellee's workmen commenced work on Georgia Street, at or near its intersection with Illinois Street, and began digging up said Georgia Street eastward from Illinois Street, and constructing upon said Georgia Street at that place toward Meridian Street a double track street railway. About seven o'clock on the evening of the same day the appellant placed its force of workmen upon Meridian Street at the crossing thereof with Georgia Street, and commenced digging up said Meridian Street and constructing on and along the same a double-track street railway, beginning said digging and construction at the north side of said crossing and extending the same southward across said crossing and on Meridian Street toward Louisiana Street, there being then no street-railroad track constructed or in course of construction upon Meridian Street, except said portion constructed by the appellant heretofore mentioned. That on the same evening, and immediately after the appellant had commenced said digging and construction, the appellee, dividing its force of workmen so working upon Georgia Street, and transferring a portion of its said force of workmen from Georgia Street to Meridian Street north of Georgia Street, caused its said workmen to dig up Meridian Street between Georgia and Maryland Streets, and to construct thereon a double-track street railway, and the same night the appellee caused its said force of workmen to place its double-track iron curve for said railway at said crossing of Georgia and Meridian Streets, partly upon cross-ties placed by the appellant in excavations made by it, but did not fasten them, and, for the purpose of so placing said curve, drove and pushed from said place the workmen of the appellant, and afterward appellee removed the ties of appellant and replaced them with its own.

Thereupon, on said night of the 24th of July, 1888, and on succeeding days, the appellant constructed and finished its double-track railway upon Meridian Street between Georgia and Louisiana Streets. On the 25th day of July, 1888, the appellee caused its workmen to continue the work of constructing a double-track street railway on and along Meridian Street between Georgia and Maryland Streets. On the 25th day of July, 1888, the appellant, besides continuing its work of construction on Meridian Street between Louisiana and Georgia Streets, also proceeded to and did dig up and prepare Meridian Street from Pearl Street to and beyond Maryland Street, and place and construct there a double track street railway. Also, on the same day, the appellant dug up and prepared Market Street from Circle Street eastward to Pennsylvania Street, and placed cross-ties and rails, and partly constructed a double-track street railway on and along said portion of Market Street, there being then no other railroad track upon said portion of Market Street.

On the evening of the 27th day of July, 1888, the appellant's workmen, being at work on Circle Street between its southern intersection with Meridian Street and its eastern intersection with Market Street, and having been notified of the issuance of a restraining order, which on that date was granted in the cause against it, restraining it from work on said line, and, because thereof, ceased work upon its said line, the same being the first line designated in section 2 of said General Ordinance No. 19 of 1887, as amended by section 1 of said General Ordinance No. 34 of 1888.

After the issuing of the said restraining order herein, and after the granting of a temporary injunction, which was issued herein against the appellant on the 28th day of July, 1888, enjoining it from working upon said line, and while said restraining order and said temporary injunction were pending and in force, the appellee continued its work of construction, and constructed and finished, and has been and is using and operating with animal power, a continuous double-track street railway on and along the following streets: Georgia Street from Illinois Street to Meridian Street, Meridian Street from Georgia Street to Circle Street, Circle Street from Meridian Street south of Circle Street to Market Street east of Circle Street, Market Street from Circle Street eastward to Alabama Street, Alabama Street from Market Street to Home Avenue, Home Avenue from Alabama Street to Central Avenue, Central Avenue from Home Avenue to Tenth Street.

In the construction of its said line mentioned in the nineteenth paragraph of the special finding, while said restraining order and said temporary injunction were in force against the defendant, the appellee took up and wholly removed from their places in the streets all the tracks so constructed by the appellant on Meridian Street and Market Street, placing the material thereof in the street gutters, and placing and constructing its tracks of said line in the same places from which it had so removed the appellant's said tracks.

In constructing said line of street railway track from Illinois Street to Tenth Street, upon the route before described, and in extending its line on Meridian Street south of Georgia Street, appellee removed from its position 2,600 feet estimated as single-track street railroad, which was worth $1.75 a foot when in place in the street, and 75 cents a foot when removed and lying upon the side of the street as hereinbefore stated, except 400 feet on Market Street, between Circle and Pennsylvania Streets, which had only been partially completed, and was worth $1.50 as it lay in the street before removed to the sides thereof.

The city council of the City of Indianapolis, by an ordinance passed on the 2d day of July, 1888, granted to the appellant further time, extending to the 1st day of January, 1889, within which to complete certain designated lines of cable street railway, with the right to construct either a cable or electric railway, which ordinance was accepted by the appellant on the 23d day of July, 1888.

As a part of said system of street railways of which the appellee took possession and proceeded to operate on the 3d day of April, 1888, there was and is a line of street railway extending on Washington Street along its entire course through said city; also a double-track street railway extending from Louisiana Street northward on Illinois Street to Seventh Street, connecting at Washington Street with said line thereon; also a double-track street railway connecting with said Washington Street line at the intersection of Washington and Pennsylvania Streets, and running thence northward on Pennsylvania Street to Seventh Street, and thence east on Seventh Street to Alabama Street, thence north on Alabama Street to Ninth Street; also a street railway connecting the said Pennsylvania Street line at the intersection of Pennsylvania and Ohio Streets, and running thence northeasterly on Massachusetts Avenue to New Jersey Street, thence north on New Jersey Street to Fort Wayne Avenue, thence northeasterly on Fort Wayne Avenue to Central Avenue, thence north on Central Avenue to Christian Avenue, thence east on Christian Avenue to College Avenue, thence north on College Avenue to Ninth Street; also a line of street railway connecting the said Washington Street line at the intersection of Washington and East Streets, and running thence north on East Street to Ohio Street, thence east on Ohio Street to Noble Street, thence north on Noble Street to Massachusetts Avenue, thence northeast on Massachusetts Avenue to Peru Street, thence north on Peru Street to Home Avenue.

The appellant has never disclaimed, abandoned or consented or agreed to the surrender or repeal of its rights or privileges under and through its said ordinances numbered 19 and 84, hereinbefore mentioned.

The double-track street railways commenced and constructed by the appellant on Meridian and Market Streets, as hereinbefore stated, were of such construction as to be capable of and suitable for operation as electrical street railways using the storage battery system for propelling the cars thereon, and were suitable for or capable of being operated by means of poles or overhead wires. Said storage battery system is one method of propelling cars run on street railways, but as yet is mostly experimental, not in general use, and expensive when used to propel cars over street railways. The purpose of the appellant to use such storage system as a motive power in propelling its cars over the line of its railways in the city was not declared in writing, or in any way made known to the city or its officers. It was, however, orally so declared about the 1st of June, 1888, by some of the officers of the defendant.

Upon these and other facts set out in the special finding, not necessary to be here repeated, the court stated as a conclusion of law that the appellee was entitled to an injunction against the appellant enjoining it from constructing a street railroad in the center of the streets named in the complaint, and entered a decree accordingly.

It is not denied that the common council of a city in this State has the exclusive control and management of the streets and alleys within the corporate limits of the city. Indeed, it is conceded on all sides that the common council of the City of Indianapolis possessed the power to grant to the appellee, as well as to the appellant, the privilege of building and operating street railroads upon the streets of said city.

It is contended by the appellant, however, that the appellee is claiming that the City of Indianapolis by its common council granted to it the exclusive right to occupy, for street railroad purposes, the center of all the streets in the city, and it is argued that such grant, if made, amounts to a monopoly, and that it is for that reason void.

As a general rule neither the State nor a municipal government can grant or create a monopoly. *Citizens Gas & Min. Co. v. Elwood*, 114 Ind. 332, 14 West. Rep. 92.

In that case it was said by this court that "the spirit and policy of the law forbid municipal corporations from creating monopolies, by favoring one corporation to the exclusion of another."

Our Constitution provides that "the General Assembly shall not grant to any citizen or class of citizens privileges or immunities which upon the same terms shall not equally belong to all citizens."

But it must not be understood that all monopolies are unlawful. Many things which are lawful are, from their nature and of necessity, monopolies, such are patent rights, copyrights, the right to keep a ferry, and many other things which might be mentioned. As a street railroad company has no legal right to lay its track upon the streets of a city without the permission of the common council, if the city should grant such right to one company and refuse to grant it to another, the company to which the right was granted would have a monopoly, until such time as the common council should grant a similar right to some other person or company. So if the common council should grant to a street railroad company the right to lay its track on certain streets which were too narrow to admit of being occupied by other street railroad tracks, such company would have a monopoly of such streets. It is plain, therefore, that while monopolies, as a general rule, are unlawful, there are many exceptions to the rule. The rule applies only to such things as are of common right, and is never to be applied to such things as are in their nature a monopoly.

Judge Elliott, in his valuable work on Roads and Streets, in discussing this question at page 566, says: "To deny the power of the Legislature to make a grant that is of necessity of a monopolistic character, would lead to the unwarranted conclusion that in no case can the Legislature grant the right to lay or operate a street railway in a road, or street; for, if the power to make such grant be conceded, it necessarily and unavoidably results that the occupancy of the part of the road or street is exclusive, as two railways cannot occupy the same space."

It is held in many respectable authorities that an exclusive right in such cases may be granted for a reasonable and fixed period. *New Orleans Gas Light Co. v Louisiana, L. & H. P. & Mfg. Co.* 115 U. S. 650 [29 L. ed. 516]; *New Orleans Water Works Co. v. Rivers*, 115 U. S. 674 [29 L. ed. 525]; *Des Moines, St. R. Co. v. Des Moines, B. G. St. R. Co.* 73 Iowa, 513; *St. Tammany Water Works Co. v. New Orleans Water Works Co.* 120 U. S. 64 [30 L. ed. 563].

This brings us to a consideration of the ordinance passed by the common council of the City of Indianapolis, granting to the Citizen's Street Railway Company the right to construct and operate street railroads upon the streets of the City of Indianapolis, and to whose rights the appellee claims to have succeeded. This ordinance, together with the ordinance subsequently passed declaratory of the intention of the parties at the time of its passage, grants to the Citizen's

Street Railway Company the right to lay its track, either single or double, on all the streets of the City of Indianapolis, confining it to the center of the street where practicable. This right is not declared in the ordinance to be exclusive.

Grants of franchises by public corporations to individuals or private corporations are to be strictly construed, and no exclusive privilege passes unless it be plainly conferred by express words or necessary implication. *Citizens St. R. Co.* v. *Jones*, 34 Fed. Rep. 579.

A grant made by the Commonwealth, or by a municipal corporation under authority from the Commonwealth, is to be taken most strongly against the grantee, and nothing is to be taken by implication against the public, except what necessarily flows from the nature of the terms of the grant. *Allegheny* v. *Ohio & P. R. Co.* 26 Pa. 355; *Birmingham & P. M. St. R. Co.* v. *Birmingham St. R. Co.* 79 Ala. 465.

The ordinance granting to the Citizen's Street Railway Company the right to construct street railways on the streets of the City of Indianapolis does not grant to it the exclusive right to construct street railways thereon.

Indeed, it is not claimed by the appellee, as we understand the briefs on file, that it possesses the exclusive right to construct street railroads on the streets of said city, but it is conceded that the common council may grant to other persons or corporations the same right. Where the sovereign has granted a special charter to a corporation to conduct a particular business, without granting any exclusive privileges over that business, the same sovereign may in like manner grant special charters to other corporations to carry on the same business; and where there is a conflict of profits between them the first has no remedy. *Crawfordsville & E. Turnp. Co.* v. *Smith*, 89 Ind. 290; *Charles River Bridge* v. *Warren Bridge*, 36 U. S. 11 Pet. 420 [9 L. ed. 773].

Acting upon this well-known principle, the common council of the City of Indianapolis granted to the appellant the right, also, to construct, maintain and operate street railroads upon the streets of the City of Indianapolis.

At this point the question arises as to what were the rights of the appellant and the appellee, in so far as they had the right to occupy the streets of the city, as between themselves. As to unoccupied streets, our opinion is that they stood upon an equality, and that the controversy resolves itself into a question of first occupancy.

Judge Elliott, in discussing this question in his work on Roads and Streets, page 570, says: "If the company which secures the first grant actually occupies the street it is authorized to use, then there is much reason for affirming that its right to the part of the street actually occupied and used is paramount and exclusive. By actually taking possession of the street and using it for the accommodation of the public, the company first in point of time does such acts as vest its right. But, to have this effect, the company, as it seems to us, must take possession in good faith and for the purpose of constructing and operating such a railway as the grant contemplates. . . . While it is, as we believe, true that some act must be done vesting the inchoate right conferred by a general grant, still we do not regard it as essential that manual possession should be taken of all the streets or roads embraced in the general grant or license. If the company having the prior right enters upon the work of constructing a system, and with reasonable diligence and in good faith does actually construct a considerable part of the system, it ought not to lose its rights, unless it has failed to comply with a proper demand to complete the system, or has unreasonably delayed its completion. . . . Conflicting claims asserted by rival companies claiming under general grants must often be settled by applying the rule that the first to rightfully occupy the street has the better right."

We have thus copied copiously from the work above referred to because we think it states the law accurately and concisely. See also *Waterbury* v. *Dry Dock, E. B. & B. R. Co.* 54 Barb. 388; *Titusville & P. C. R. Co.* v. *Warren & V. R. Co.* 12 Phila. 642; *Morris & E. R. Co.* v. *Blair*, 9 N. J. Eq. 635; *Denver & R. G. R. Co.* v. *Cañon City & S. J. R. Co.* 99 U. S. 463 [25 L. ed. 438].

Where a company has entered upon the construction of a particular system of street railroads, and has expended its money in the prosecution of the work, it would be manifestly unjust to permit some other person or company, after the commencement of the work, to jump in and appropriate any portion of the streets involved in such system, while the former was diligently prosecuting the work, and thus destroy the system, to the ruin of the company engaged in its construction. If this could be done no person or company would undertake the construction of a system of street railroads; but to hold the right to such system, money should be expended in its construction, and the work, with a view of its completion, should be diligently prosecuted without intermission, unless stopped by circumstances over which the projector has no control.

In this case, as we understand the special finding, the appellee, in the early part of June, 1888, entered upon the construction of a system of street railroads in the City of Indianapolis, which appropriated a portion of the streets described in the complaint. Such system was determined upon and ordered by the general manager of the appellee soon after the transfer made to it by the Citizen's Street Railway Company.

It does not appear that the appellant did anything under its charter prior to the 24th day of July, 1888.

Disregarding its charter, which authorized the construction of a cable road, it proceeded to construct one of an entirely different character. Indeed, it wholly abandoned the idea of constructing a cable road, and when engaged in constructing one of a different character, in violation of its charter, it was stopped by the city attorney, for the reason that it was acting wholly without authority. In our opinion the appellant, by taking possession of the streets of Indianapolis, with a view of constructing a street railroad other than a cable road, acquired no rights in such streets, either as against the appellee or the city. It was a mere trespasser. A municipal power having control over the streets may prescribe the motive power to be used in moving street cars, and when it prescribes one kind of power the company cannot use another.

As the grant of a special charter or franchise to a corporation is construed strictly against the corporation, where the right to use one motive power is prescribed the company cannot successfully maintain its right to use another or different power. Elliott, Roads and Streets, p. 360; *People* v. *Newton*, 48 Hun, 477, 112 N. Y. 396, 3 L. R. A. 174; *Denver & S. R. Co.* v. *Denver City R. Co.* 2 Colo. 681; *Citizens Street R. Co.* v. *Jones*, 34 Fed. Rep. 579; *Birmingham & P. M. St. R. Co.* v. *Birmingham St. R. Co.* 79 Ala. 465; *Allegheny* v. *Ohio & P. R. Co.* 26 Pa. 355; *North Chicago City R. Co.* v. *Lake View*, 105 Ill. 207.

It is urged, however, that the appellee cannot inquire as to the motive power by which appellant intended to move its cars, as that was a question entirely between the appellant and the City of Indianapolis. We are not inclined to adopt this view. If the appellee had no interest in the question other than any other citizen of the City of Indianapolis, doubtless it could not raise the question now under consideration; but the appellant and the appellee had equal rights in the streets in controversy. Neither had the exclusive right to the streets or any portion thereof until occupied under its charter. The first to take possession in good faith under the charter granted to it acquired the superior right. When the appellant claims, therefore, that it entered the streets of Indianapolis and took possession under the terms of its charter, in good faith, with a view of constructing the line of street railroad which it had the right to construct under the terms of its charter, we think it competent for the appellee to allege and prove that it did not enter under the terms of its charter, and that, instead of constructing a line of cable street railroad, it was acting in violation of its grant and was a mere trespasser. There can be no pretense that the appellant did any work conforming to the rights granted it by the City of Indianapolis prior to the 24th day of July, 1888, as it did not accept the right granted it to construct an electric railroad until the 23d day of that month. In the meantime the appellee had taken possession of the streets in controversy, and was diligently prosecuting the work of constructing a system of street railroad which included these streets. The rights acquired by the appellant on the 23d day of July could have no retroactive operation so as to affect the rights of the appellee, vested by its possession.

It follows from what we have said that, as the appellee commenced the construction of a system of street railroads under the terms of its charter, which included the streets in controversy, and was in good faith diligently prosecuting the work to completion prior to the time the appellant commenced work to construct a system of street railroads pursuant to the terms of its charter, the appellee has the superior right.

It is claimed, however, that the Citizen's Street Railway Company could not sell and transfer to the appellee its franchises, and that appellee by its franchise acquired no rights. We regard this as an immaterial question. The appellee is a duly organized corporation for the purpose of owning and operating a street railroad in the City of Indianapolis. It is not denied that by its purchase it acquired all the property of the Citizen's Street Railway Company, except its franchises. The City of Indianapolis, about the date of the transfer of the property, granted to the appellee all the rights, privileges and franchises possessed by the Citizen's Street Railway Company. Assuming, without deciding, that the Citizen's Street Railway Company could not sell and transfer its franchises, and still the right of the appellee to own, construct and operate its railroad upon the streets of the City of Indianapolis is complete.

We have carefully examined all the questions presented by the record and argued in the able briefs of counsel in this case, and find no error for which the judgment should be reversed.

Judgment affirmed.

MISSOURI SUPREME COURT.

Jacob N. STANLEY, *Respt.*,

v.

WABASH, ST. LOUIS & PACIFIC R. CO., *Appt.*

(....Mo.....)

1. **A statute will not be presumed** to have been intended by the Legislature to have any extraterritorial force, where such intention would make it void.

2. **A statute compelling railroad companies to furnish double-decked cars** for sheep, under a penalty for failure to do so, and limiting the price per carload, is void as an attempted regulation of commerce when applied to interstate shipments.

(May 19, 1890.)

APPEAL by defendant from a judgment of the Circuit Court for Macon County in favor of plaintiff in an action brought to recover back an alleged overpayment of freight charges for the transportation of certain sheep. *Reversed.*

Statement by **Sherwood**, *J.:*

The second count of the petition is as follows:

"(2) Plaintiff, for another and further cause of action, states that the defendant, in shipping said sheep as aforesaid, placed and carried them in twelve single-decked cars, and failed and refused and neglected to furnish plaintiff with double-decked cars, as it was its lawful duty to do; and the defendant, in violation of the Statute in such cases made and provided, charged and collected of plaintiff, for the carrying of said sheep from said La Plata, Mo., to East St. Louis, Ill., at the rate of $25 per car for twelve cars, making the sum of $300 received by the defendant for the transportation of said sheep, which was the full legal rate of freight allowed for the shipment of stock, and was $150 in excess of the amount that the defendant could lawfully charge for such transportation of said sheep in a single-decked car. Wherefore the plaintiff says an action hath accrued to him to have and recover of defendant the sum of $150, the excess so charged as aforesaid, for which plaintiff demands judgment."

This count is based upon the Statute entitled "An Act to Require Railroad Companies to Furnish Double-decked Cars for the Shipment of Sheep, and Providing a Penalty for Failing so to Do," approved March 18, 1881.

A trial by the court, without the intervention of a jury, resulted in a judgment for plaintiff in the sum of $105, which caused an appeal by the defendant to the Kansas City Court of Appeals, from which court the cause was transferred to this court on a jurisdictional ground. Other points are unnecessary to be set forth now, as they will be sufficiently stated in the opinion.

Mr. **George S. Grover**, with *Mr.* **Wells H. Blodgett**, for appellant:

The Statute relied on for recovery has no extraterritorial force and does not apply to shipments from a point within to a point without the State of Missouri.

Mo. Sess. Acts 1881, p. 83; *Gilbreath* v. *Bunce*, 65 Mo. 349; *Vawter* v. *Missouri Pac. R. Co.* 84 Mo. 679, and cases cited; *Merrill* v. *Boston & L. R. Co.* 63 N. H. 259, 21 Am. & Eng. R. R. Cas. 48, and cases cited in *note* p. 50; *Hyde* v. *Wabash, St. L. & P. R. Co.* 61 Iowa, 441; 3 Rorer, Railroads, p. 1149, and cases cited; 3 Wood, Railway Law, § 411, p. 1532; Rorer, Interstate Law, pp. 149–154; *Branley* v. *Southeastern R. Co.* 12 C. B. N. S. 63.

If, as held by the court below, this Statute applies to an interstate shipment, then it is a regulation of commerce, and, as such, is a violation of section 8 of article 1 of the Constitution of the United States.

Gibbons v. *Ogden*, 22 U. S. 9 Wheat. 1 (6 L. ed. 23); *Brown* v. *Maryland*, 25 U. S. 12 Wheat. 419 (6 L. ed. 678); *Passenger Cases*, 48 U. S. 7 How. 283 (12 L. ed. 702); *The Daniel Ball*, 77 U. S. 10 Wall. 557 (19 L. ed. 999); *Ward* v. *Maryland*, 79 U. S. 12 Wall. 418 (20 L. ed. 449); *State Freight Tax Cases*, 82 U. S. 15 Wall. 232 (21 L. ed. 146); *Welton* v. *Missouri*, 91 U. S. 275 (23 L. ed. 347); *Henderson* v. *New York*, 92 U. S. 259 (23 L. ed. 543); *Inman Steamship Co.* v. *Tinker*, 94 U. S. 238 (24 L. ed. 118); *Foster* v. *New Orleans*, 94 U. S. 246 (24 L. ed. 122); *Hannibal & St. J. R. Co.* v. *Husen*, 95 U. S. 465 (24 L. ed. 527); *Hall* v. *De Cuir*, 95 U. S. 485 (24 L. ed. 547); *Pensacola Teleg. Co.* v. *Western U. Teleg. Co.* 96 U. S. 1 (24 L. ed. 708); *Lord* v. *Goodall, N. & P. S. S. Co.* 102 U. S. 544 (26 L. ed. 220); *Webber* v. *Virginia*, 103 U. S. 351 (26 L. ed. 567); *Western U. Teleg. Co.* v. *Texas*, 105 U. S. 460 (26 L. ed. 1067); *New York* v. *Compagnie Générale Transatlantique*, 107 U. S. 59 (27 L. ed. 383); *Moran* v. *New Orleans*, 112 U. S. 69 (28 L. ed. 653); *Head Money Cases*, 112 U. S. 580 (28 L. ed. 798); *Cooper Mfg. Co.* v. *Ferguson*, 113 U. S. 727 (28 L. ed. 1137); *Gilmore* v. *Hannibal & St. J. R. Co.* 67 Mo. 323.

No appearance for respondent.

Sherwood, *J.*, delivered the opinion of the court:

1. The second count of the original petition charged that the contract was made to ship the sheep from La Plata, Mo., to St. Louis, Mo., but the amended petition charged the contract was to ship the sheep from La Plata, this State, to East St. Louis, Ill.; and upon this it is claimed that there was a change in plaintiff's cause of action. This point need not be discussed, because it appears that the answer of the defendant to the original petition was considered as refiled to the amended petition, and this, being done without objection, cannot be objected to here for the first time. Nor need the action of the trial court as to plaintiff's first count be considered, seeing that it was in favor of the defendant, and the plaintiff does not appeal. The statutory provisions upon which this action is brought are as follows:

"Section 1. All railroad companies, private companies or individuals owning or operating a railroad or railroads in the State of Missouri are required to furnish a sufficient number of double-decked cars for the shipment of sheep to supply the demand for such cars on their respective lines, and to allow shippers to load both decks in said cars with sheep to the aggregate extent of (20,000) twenty thousand pounds; which cars, so loaded, shall be received and transported by such railroad companies, or private companies or individuals, as one carload of stock; and it shall not be lawful for said railroad companies, private companies or individuals to charge or receive for the transportation of a double-decked car of sheep more than the legal rate of freight allowed for the shipment of stock.

"Sec. 2. Should any railroad company, or private company or individuals, owning or operating a railroad or railroads in the State of Missouri, refuse or neglect to furnish cars as provided in the preceding section, it shall not be lawful for them to charge or receive for the transportation of a car of sheep more than one half the legal rate of freight allowed for the shipment of stock."

It will not be intended that this Statute was to have any extraterritorial force, since this would be beyond the power of the Legislature of this State. General presumptions of this sort always attend legislative Acts. *Merrill* v. *Boston & L. R. Co.* 63 N. H. 259, 21 Am. & Eng. R. R. Cas. 48, and cases cited; 2 Rorer, Railroads, 1151; Rorer, Interstate Law, 149–154.

2. But if, as held by the trial court, the Statute under discussion can be held to apply to interstate shipments, then it is an attempted regulation of commerce, and violates article 1, § 8, of the Constitution of the United States. *Gibbons* v. *Ogden*, 22 U. S. 9 Wheat. 1 [6 L. ed. 23]; *Welton* v. *Missouri*, 91 U. S. 275 [23 L. ed. 347]; *Hannibal & St. J. R. Co.* v. *Husen*, 95 U. S. 465 [24 L. ed. 527]; *Hall* v. *De Cuir*, 95 U. S. 485 [24 L. ed. 547]; *Cooper Mfg. Co.* v. *Ferguson*, 113 U. S. 727 [28 L. ed. 1137]; *Hardy* v. *Atchison, T. & S. F. R. Co.* 32 Kan. 698, 18 Am. & Eng. R. R. Cas. 432, and cases cited; *Carton* v. *Illinois Cent. R. Co.* 59 Iowa, 148; *Louisville & N. R. Co.* v. *Tennessee Railroad Commission*, 19 Fed. Rep. 679, 16 Am. & Eng. R. R. Cas. 1

"The legislative authority of every State must spend its force within the territorial limits of the State." Cooley, Const. Lim. 151.

Controlled by these considerations, *we reverse the judgment.*

All concur.

MARYLAND COURT OF APPEALS.

Frank O. SINGER, *Plff. in Err.*,

v.

STATE OF MARYLAND.

(........Md........)

1. **A government has an inherent right** to impose such restraints and to provide such regulations in regard to the pursuits of life as the public welfare may require.

2. **Prohibiting any but registered plumbers,** who have received a certificate of competency from a state board, to engage in the business of plumbing is but the ordinary exercise of the police power of the State, and does not violate any constitutional rights of individuals.

(June 19, 1890.)

ERROR to the Criminal Court for Baltimore City to review a judgment convicting defendant upon an indictment for refusing to comply with the provisions of a statute requiring plumbers to receive a certificate of competency before engaging in the plumbing business. *Affirmed.*

The case sufficiently appears in the opinion.

Argued before Alvey, *Ch. J.*, and Miller, Bryan, Fowler, Briscoe, McSherry and Robinson, *JJ.*

Messrs. **John Stewart** and **David Stewart** for plaintiff in error.

Messrs. **W. Pinkney White,** *Atty-Gen.*, and **Charles G. Kerr** for the State.

Robinson, *J.*, delivered the opinion of the court:

The traverser is a plumber by trade and was indicted for refusing to comply with the requirements of the Act of 1886, chap. 439, which provides that no person shall engage in the business of plumbing in the City of Baltimore unless such person shall have received from the State Board of Commissioners of Practical Plumbing a certificate as to his competency and qualification.

This Act the traverser contends is in violation of his constitutional rights under the 14th Amendment of the Constitution of the United States and of the Constitution of this State, both of which declare that no person shall be deprived of his life, liberty or property without due process of law. These constitutional safeguards have been so fully considered and discussed by the supreme court, especially since the adoption of the 14th Amendment, by which the restraint upon the power of the States to pass laws affecting personal and private rights was made a part of the Federal Constitution that it can only be necessary to refer to the conclusions reached by that court as affecting the question before us. *Dent* v. *West Virginia,* 129 U. S. 114 [32 L. ed. 623]; *Barbier* v. *Connolly,* 113 U. S. 27 [28 L. ed. 923]; *Mugler* v. *Kansas,* 123 U. S. 623 [31 L. ed. 205]; *Soon Hing* v. *Crowley,* 113 U. S. 703 [28 L. ed. 1145]; *Powell* v. *Pennsylvania,* 127 U. S. 678 [32 L. ed. 253].

No one questions the right of every person in this country to follow any legitimate business or occupation he may see fit. This is a privilege open alike to everyone. His own labor and the right to use it as a means of livelihood is a right as sacred and as fully protected by the law as any other personal or private right.

But broad and comprehensive as this right may be, it is subject to the paramount right inherent in every government to impose such restraint and to provide such regulations in regard to the pursuits of life as the public welfare may require. This paramount right rests upon the well recognized maxim, *salus populi est suprema lex,* and whatever difficulty there may be in defining the precise limits and boundaries by which the exercise of this power is to be governed, all agree that laws and regulations necessary for the protection of the health, morals and safety of society are strictly within the legitimate exercise of the police power. *Powell* v. *Pennsylvania* and *Mugler* v. *Kansas, supra; Minneapolis & St. L. R. Co.* v. *Beckwith,* 129 U. S. 26 [32 L. ed. 585].

As to the common and ordinary occupations of life, little or no regulation may be necessary; but if the occupation or calling be of such a character as to require a special course of study, or training, or experience, to qualify one to pursue such occupation or calling with safety to the public interests, no one questions the power of the Legislature to impose such restraints and prescribe such requirements as it may deem proper for the protection of the public against the evils resulting from incapacity and ignorance. And neither the 14th Amendment of the Federal Constitution, nor article 23 of the Bill of Rights of the Constitution of this State, was designed to limit or restrain the exercise of this power. It is in the exercise of this power that no one is allowed to practice law or medicine or engage in the business of a druggist unless he shall have been found competent and qualified in the mode and in the manner prescribed by the statute. And although the business and trade of a plumber may not require the same training and experience as some other pursuits in life, yet a certain degree of training is absolutely necessary to qualify one as a competent and skillful workman. We all know that in a large city like Baltimore, with its extensive system of drainage and sewerage, the public health largely depends upon the proper and efficient manner in which the plumbing work is executed. And this being so, the Legislature not only has the power, but it is eminently wise and proper that it should pro-

---

NOTE.—*Police power of State.*

The police power of the State embraces its whole internal affairs and its civil and criminal polity. See *note* to State v. Marshall (N. H.) 1 L. R. A. 51.

vide some mode by which the qualifications of persons engaged in that business shall be determined.

In considering the power of the Legislature to impose restraints upon all persons engaged in certain pursuits, the supreme court says:

"The nature and extent of the qualifications required must depend primarily upon the judgment of the State as to their necessity. If they are appropriate to the calling or profession and attainable by reasonable application no objection to their validity can be raised." *Dent* v. *West Virginia*, 129 U. S. 114 [32 L. ed. 623].

The Act of 1886, now before us, provides in the first place that no one shall engage in the business of plumbing except those qualified to work as registered plumbers; and further that no one shall be qualified to work as a registered plumber unless he shall have made application to and received from the State Board of Practical Plumbers appointed by the government a certificate as to his competency.

These requirements are appropriate, and relate to the business of plumbing, and are such as the Legislature deemed necessary and proper for the protection of the health of the people of Baltimore against the consequences resulting from the work of incompetent and inexperienced plumbers. They are in themselves fair and reasonable, and impose no restraint or qualification which may not be complied with by reasonable training and experience. Such an Act is but the ordinary exercise of the police power of the State, and does not violate in any sense the constitutional rights of the traverser.

Judgment affirmed.

KENTUCKY COURT OF APPEALS.

JOHNSON *et al.*, *Appts.*,
v.
David ELKINS and Wife.

(......Ky.......)

1. The fact that land was purchased with pension money and a conveyance thereof made to the pensioner's wife does not exempt it from liability for his debts, under U. S. Rev. Stat., § 4747.

2. The words "process in an action" include an execution.

3. A coroner cannot execute process directed to the sheriff, under Code of Practice, § 667. Where the coroner is authorized to act the process must be directed to him.

(April 17, 1890.)

APPEAL by plaintiffs from a judgment of the Circuit Court for Larue County dismissing the complaint in an action brought to subject property, alleged to have been fraudulently assigned, to the payment of a debt. *Affirmed.*

The facts sufficiently appear in the opinion.

Messrs. **H. S. Johnson** and **John W. Gore** for appellants.

Mr. **D. H. Smith** for appellees.

Holt, *J.*, delivered the opinion of the court:

The appellants, having a judgment in the Green Circuit Court against the appellee David Elkins, sued out an execution to the County of Larue, where the debtor then resided. It was directed to the sheriff, but, there being none at the time in the county, it was received and returned by the coroner "No property found." This action was then brought in the Larue Circuit Court to subject to the payment of the judgment a tract of land of sixty three acres, situate in said county, which had been conveyed to the wife of the debtor Elkins by one Noe. The petition avers that the land was in fact paid for by the debtor, and that it was conveyed to the wife to defraud his creditors. The copy of the execution which issued to Larue County shows, at least prima facie, that the appellant's debt was created before the land was purchased. It bears interest according to it from October 14, 1887, and the purchase was not made until November 1, 1887. It appears that the land was paid for with pension money of the debtor, drawn from the United States government. The money itself never came to his hands. The check for it did, and was indorsed by him to one Hoover, who, for the debtor, drew the money upon it, and out of it paid Noe for the land. It is now claimed that the money, when paid to Noe, was in the course of transmission to the pensioner, and, being therefore exempt from seizure for the debts of the pensioner by the United States Statute, it was no fraud upon his creditor to invest it in the land, and have the deed taken to the wife.

Section 4747 of the Revised Statutes of the United States provides: "No sum of money due or to become due to any pensioner shall be liable to attachment, levy or seizure by or under any legal or equitable process whatever, whether the same remains with the pension office, or any officer or agent thereof, or is in course of transmission to the pensioner entitled thereto, but shall inure wholly to the benefit of such pensioner."

It has been repeatedly decided by this court that after the money reaches the hands of the pensioner it is no longer exempt. *Robion* v. *Walker*, 82 Ky. 60; *Hudspeth* v. *Harrison*, 6 Ky. L. Rep. 304.

In the last-named case it was held that the fact that land was purchased with pension money did not exempt it from liability for the pensioner's debts.

In the case of *Sims* v. *Walsham*, 7 S. W. Rep. 557, the money itself did not come to the hands of the pensioner, but a check did; and he transferred it to another person, with directions to draw the money, and pay it to his sons, to be, and which was, used by them in paying for

---

NOTE.—*Pension money.*

Protection from attachment. See *note* to Holmes v. Tallada (Pa.) 8 L. R. A. 219.

Proceeds mingled with other funds not exempt. See Yates County Nat. Bank v. Carpenter, 7 L. R. A. 557, 119 N. Y. 550.

See also 11 L. R. A. 110.

land, which was conveyed to them. It was held that the land, so held by them by voluntary conveyance, was liable for the pensioner's debt.

These cases are decisive of this one, so far as this question is concerned. Another one presents itself, however, which doubtless controlled the lower court in dismissing the action of the appellants. A creditor may sue in equity to set aside a conveyance of land by his debtor as fraudulent, upon a return of *nulla bona* upon an execution issued from a court having jurisdiction to sell land; or he may do so without it, provided he sues out an attachment upon any of the grounds mentioned in our Code of Practice, and in conformity to its provisions. He may adopt either course, but one or the other must be pursued. *Martz* v. *Pfeifer*, 80 Ky. 600; *Kyle* v. *O'Neil*, 10 Ky. L. Rep. 70.

In this instance the averments of the petition are not sufficient to sustain the action upon the last-named ground.

It is evident the action is attempted to be based upon the return of "No property" upon the execution which issued to Larue County. By section 667 of the Code of Practice every process in an action must be directed to the sheriff of the county. If he be a party to the suit, or interested in it, then it must be directed to the coroner; or, if he be interested, then to the jailor; or, if all these officers be interested, then to any constable; and a summons or an order for a provisional remedy may, at the request of the party in whose behalf it is issued, be directed to any one of the officers above named, if he be not a party to nor interested in the action.

It was held in the case of *Menderson* v. *Specker*, 79 Ky. 509, that an attachment must be executed by the officer to whom it is directed, and that it cannot be executed by any officer to whom it might have been directed, as is specially provided by section 47 of the Code as to a summons. The word "process," as used in the Code, includes an execution. It was so decided in the case of *Gowdy* v. *Sanders*, 10 Ky. L. Rep. 912, where it is also held that an execution from a circuit court or a court of like jurisdiction must be directed to the sheriff, unless he be a party to the action, or interested in it, and that it must be directed to the officer by whom it is to be executed. The return by the coroner, therefore, upon the appellants' execution is a nullity. He had no right to handle it. It was not directed to him, and could be executed only by the officer to whom it was directed. It results, therefore, that there was in fact no return of *nulla bona* to support this action. This objection has not been waived by the appellees. It was raised in the lower court, and insisted upon in the answer. It is therefore available here, and *the judgment must be and is affirmed.*

RHODE ISLAND SUPREME COURT.

Julia J. HOLLAND *et al.*

v.

CITIZENS' SAVINGS BANK *et al.*

(16 R. I. ....)

1. Notice of the pendency of a bill affecting land is not notice to a purchaser thereof *pendente lite* of matters set up by a subsequent amendment to the bill.

2. Where two or more persons are interested in mortgaged property subject to the mortgage, and one of them pays the mortgage debt for his own protection, he is entitled, not to have the mortgage assigned to him, but simply to succeed to the lien of the mortgage against the others in equity, to the extent of his claim against them for indemnity, by way of subrogation.

3. One who pays a mortgage is not entitled

NOTE.—*Notice of pendency of suit; effect of.*

Lis pendens, which in a chancery suit begins with the filing of the bill and service of subpœna, and continues until the final orders are taken in the case, is notice of every fact contained in the pleadings which is pertinent to the issue, and of the contents of exhibits to the bill which are produced and proved. Murray v. Lylburn, 2 Johns. Ch. 441, 1 N. Y. Ch. L. ed. 440; Murray v. Finster, 2 Johns. Ch. 155, 1 N. Y. Ch. L. ed. 329; Cook v. Mancius, 5 Johns. Ch. 89, 1 N. Y. Ch. L. ed. 1019; Sedgwick v. Cleveland, 7 Paige, 287, 4 N. Y. Ch. L. ed. 159; Van Hook v. Throckmorton, 8 Paige, 33, 4 N. Y. Ch. L. ed. 333; Jackson v. Losee, 4 Sandf. Ch. 381, 7 N. Y. Ch. L. ed. 1142; Griffith v. Griffith, Hoffm. Ch. 153, 6 N.Y. Ch. L. ed. 1097; White v. Carpenter, 2 Paige, 217, 2 N. Y. Ch. L. ed. 882; 2 Pom. Eq. Jur. 74, 75; Walker v. Goldsmith, 14 Or. 149; Center v. Planters & M. Bank, 22 Ala. 743; King v. Bill, 28 Conn. 593; Low v. Pratt, 53 Ill. 438; Miller v. Sherry, 69 U. S. 2 Wall. 237 (17 L. ed. 827); Jones v. Lusk, 2 Met. (Ky.) 356; Lewis v. Mew, 1 Strob. Eq. 180; Stone v. Connelly, 1 Met. (Ky.) 652.

The rule is that notice arising from a bill filed is notice of what that bill contains and nothing more, and should not be extended beyond the property which is the subject of the suit. If land is affected by collateral proceedings in a cause where the bill itself does not affect it, actual notice of such proceedings must be proven to charge a purchaser. Griffith v. Griffith, Hoffm. 159, 6 N.Y. Ch. L. ed. 1100; Carr v. Callaghan, 3 Litt. 365; Frakes v. Brown, 2 Blackf. 295; Edmonds v. Crenshaw, 1 McCord, Eq. 264.

A purchaser of real estate while a suit is pending concerning it is bound by the result of the suit, when, at the time of the purchase, the nature of the claim upon the property was disclosed by the pleadings. Wilson v. Heffin, 81 Ind. 41; Kern v. Hazlerigg, 11 Ind. 443; Britz v. Johnson, 65 Ind. 561; Leitch v. Wells, 48 N. Y. 585.

Lis pendens affects a purchaser with constructive notice of all the facts that are apparent on the face of the pleadings at the time he takes his deed, and of such other facts, as those facts necessarily put him upon inquiry for, and as such inquiry, pursued with ordinary diligence and prudence, would bring to his knowledge. Jones v. McNarrin, 68 Me. 341.

Doctrine of *lis pendens* generally. See *note* to Houston v. Timmerman (Or.) 4 L. R. A. 716.

What indispensable to give effect to doctrine. See *note* to Benton v. Shafer (Ohio) 7 L. R. A. 812.

See also 44 L. R. A. 479.

to an assignment thereof on the ground that it covers other property than his own, and because complications have arisen in the settlement of the mortgagor's estate making it important for him to have an assignment, where the divided ownership and the complications have arisen after the mortgage was given.

4. **The title of a bona fide purchaser** for value without notice at a mortgage sale is not affected by the fact that the holder of the mortgage had prevented a tender by refusing to accept payment except on conditions which he had no right to make.

5. **A sale under a power** in a mortgage will not be enjoined or set aside on the ground of a perversion of the power to improper purposes, where the mortgagee is acting within the letter of his power, unless the perversion is very clearly shown.

6. **Perversion of the power** to sell land under a mortgage is not shown by the fact that some advantage may accrue to the mortgagee besides the payment of the debt, or an advantage may incidentally accrue thereby to others.

(March 1, 1890.)

BILL in equity to procure cancellation of certain mortgage sales and to compel a transfer of the mortgages to the owner of the mortgaged premises, or to redeem the premises from the sales. On demurrer to bill. *Sustained.*

The facts are fully stated in the opinion.

Messrs. **John E. Lester, Amasa M. Eaton** and **Herbert Almy** for complainants.

Mr. **James M. Ripley** for respondent, the Citizens' Savings Bank.

Messrs. **Simon S. Lapham, Charles E. Salisbury** and **Daniel W. Fink** for the other respondents.

Durfee, *Ch. J.*, delivered the opinion of the court:

The bill shows that John K. Lester, late of Providence, died January 20, 1880, leaving a will by which he devised the larger part of his homestead estate, subject to certain conditions, to his son John Erastus Lester; that said homestead estate, when said John K. died, was subject to two mortgages, for $8,000 each, given to the Mechanics' Savings Bank, one dated September 10, 1875, and the other March 2, 1876; that said bank transferred them, August 18, 1884, to the Citizens' Savings Bank; that September 29, 1888, said Citizens' Savings Bank advertised said homestead estate for sale on October 20, 1888, under the powers in said mortgage; and that, previous thereto, said John Erastus Lester had conveyed his interest in said estate to the complainant Julia J. Holland. This bill was filed October 19, 1888. It set forth that said Julia had offered to pay said Citizens' Savings Bank the amount due on the mortgages and expenses, provided the Bank would assign the mortgages to her, or to some person named by her, but that the Bank had refused to do so. The bill repeated the offer, and prayed that the Bank might be compelled to accede to it, and also that the sale might be enjoined. The complainant prayed for a preliminary injunction, which the court denied. The bill also showed that John K. Lester died leaving other real estate, likewise mortgaged, and two other sons, to one of whom, James C. Lester by name, he devised, subject to certain conditions, besides other real estate, that portion of the homestead estate which he did not devise to said John Erastus, so that the two $8,000 mortgages covered the estate devised to said John Erastus, and overlapped upon that which was devised to said James C. Lester. The bill as originally filed set forth certain complications, which it alleged had arisen in the settlement of the estate, affecting the rights of said John Erastus and the said Julia, his grantee, making it difficult for her to pay off the mortgages, and, at the same time, important for her to have them assigned to her. The bill has been amended, and as amended sets forth that the homestead estate was sold at mortgagee's sale October 20, 1888, to one Orrin E. Jones, and afterwards was conveyed by him to one Roswell O. Whitney. Jones and Whitney have been made parties to the bill as amended. The bill now asks that the sales may be canceled, and that said Julia may have said mortgages transferred to her on paying the amount due thereon, or that she may be allowed to redeem. The Bank has demurred to the bill generally for want of equity, and the case is before us on said demurrer.

The amended bill sets forth reasons for relief not set forth in the original bill; but it alleges nothing to show that the sale, as such, was improperly conducted. The purchaser, therefore, acquired a good legal title to the estate, and communicated it to his grantee; and the grantee, as legal owner, is entitled to hold the estate, unless the complainant Julia can show some equity which gives her a right, as against him, to the relief prayed for. But she can have no equity against him unless he and his grantor had notice thereof when they purchased. The amended bill simply avers, in regard to Jones, the purchaser at the mortgagee's sale, that he had notice of the pendency of this bill, which means, of course, the bill before it was amended, the amendment having been made since the sale. The averment in regard to Whitney, the present owner, is that he purchased with notice of the complainants' rights. The averment is very general. Story, Eq. Pl. § 263.

But, whatever notice Whitney may have had, he would take the estate subject only to the equities which it was subject to in the hands of his grantor, who, as we have seen, is simply alleged to have had notice of the pendency of the bill as originally filed. The question, then, supposing such notice sufficient, is whether the bill as originally filed disclosed equities entitling said Julia to the relief now prayed for.

We will first consider whether the bill as originally filed showed that the said Julia had any right to have the mortgages assigned to her upon paying to the holder the amount due thereon, together with the expenses incurred by the holder in advertising, etc. The rule which is the more generally recognized is that a mortgagee cannot be required to assign the mortgage upon receiving the amount due thereon unless the person making payment is entitled to such assignment for some equitable reason, but can only be required to release or discharge the debt and mortgage, or, if the person making payment prefers, to surrender them to him, uncanceled. This is because the mortgagee, like any other creditor, is not under any obligation to sell and transfer his claim to another, but is only under obligation to accept payment thereof when duly tendered, and because he is entitled, under his mortgage, if the debt is not paid as stipulated, to sell the estate for its payment, or to foreclose in some other mode, as provided by law. *Chedel* v. *Millard*, 13 R. I. 461; *Butler* v. *Taylor*, 5 Gray, 455; *Lamson* v. *Drake*, 105 Mass. 564; *Lamb* v. *Montague*, 112 Mass. 352; *Hamilton* v. *Dobbs*, 19 N. J. Eq. 227; *Bigelow* v. *Cassedy*, 26 N. J. Eq. 557; *Gatewood* v. *Gatewood*, 75 Va. 407; *Chase* v. *Williams*, 74 Mo. 429; *Ellsworth* v. *Lockwood*, 42 N. Y. 89.

The question, then, is, What is such a reason as will give a right to the assignment, and does any such apply in favor of said Julia? The cases hold that a surety paying the debt is entitled to have the mortgage assigned to him, and it has been said that the equity would likewise reach to anyone else personally bound to pay the debt by reason of a similar relation to it. *Gatewood* v. *Gatewood*, *supra.*

And so, doubtless, the mortgagee might become subject to the equity by reason of his own contract or conduct. Further than this we do not find that the cases, except in New York, admit the equity, their doctrine being that where two or more persons are interested in mortgaged property subject to the mortgage, and one of them pays the mortgage debt for his own protection, he is entitled, not to have the mortgage assigned to him, but simply to succeed to the lien of the mortgage against the others in equity, to the extent of his claim against them for indemnity, by way of subrogation. This seems to us to be the correct doctrine. The right of the mortgagee originates in the mortgage; and we do not see how, on principle, after the mortgage has been given, any other person, by acquiring an interest in the mortgaged property, can acquire an equity against him at variance with his right, so long as he himself does nothing to create it. 2 Jones, Mort. §§ 1086, 1087.

The bill as originally filed shows only two grounds on which the complainant Julia could claim to have the mortgages assigned to her, namely: *first*, because the mortgages cover other property than her own; and, *second*, because certain complications set forth in the bill had arisen in the settlement of the mortgagor's estate. But said divided ownership and said complications are both matters arising after the mortgages were given, and matters with which, so far as appeared by said bill, neither the original mortgagee nor its assignee, the Citizens' Savings Bank, had had anything to do. The bill as originally filed, therefore, did not show any equitable ground on which said Julia was entitled to have the mortgages assigned to her.

The said Julia contends that she is entitled, if not to have the mortgages assigned to her, to redeem them, notwithstanding the sale. She admits that when she filed her bill, and when the sale occurred, she had not paid, or tendered payment of, the mortgage notes then overdue; but her claim is that no tender was necessary, because the Bank, then holding the mortgages, prevented her making tender by informing her that payment of the two $8,000 mortgages would not be received unless she also paid a mortgage for $8,000 given to the Bank by James C. Lester aforenamed, after his father's death, upon the portion of the estate devised to him by his father's will, and therefore covering a part of the homestead estate covered by said two mortgages. If this was so, the effect was, in our opinion, not to defeat the power of sale, but only to make the sale under it offensive and inequitable on the part of the Bank; and a bona fide purchaser for value, without notice, would still get a good title. For the purchaser to be affected, he must have had notice. *Jenkins* v. *Jones*, 2 Giff. 99; *Montague* v. *Dawes*, 12 Allen, 397; *Cranston* v. *Crane*, 97 Mass. 459.

The question is, therefore, whether the bill as originally filed gave such notice, notice in no other form being alleged. We do not find that it did. It made no mention of the mortgage for $8,000, the same being first set forth in one of the amendments. It did not allege any previous tender or even offer of payment, simply as such, but only an offer to pay the amount due on the mortgages for an assignment of them. It is not clear that the bill itself offered payment unconditionally, though it contained a formal prayer to redeem. Of course, the mere pendency of a bill to redeem would not suspend the power; for that would defeat the purpose of the power, which is to avoid the delay of a suit. *Adams* v. *Scott*, 7 Week. Rep. 213; 2 Jones, Mortg. § 1797.

We do not think the said Julia is entitled to redeem as against the present owner for the second ground assigned.

The said Julia claims a right to redeem on another ground, namely, a perversion of the mortgage power to purposes for which it was not given. The power is given to the mortgagee for the purpose of enabling him to collect his debt more readily than he could by suit, and if, instead of using it for that purpose, he attempts to use it from an ill motive, to oppress the debtor, or to acquire the property himself, or to serve the purposes of others, the court considers it a fraud upon the power, and may enjoin the sale, or, if the sale has been made, may set it aside, in a proper case. 2 Jones, Mortg. § 1801; *Robertson* v. *Norris*, 1 Giff. 421; *Foster* v. *Hughes*, 51 How. Pr. 20.

But it is a delicate matter for the court to interfere on this ground, where the mortgagee is acting within the letter of his power, and, to warrant it, the perversion should be very clearly and specifically alleged. 2 Jones, Mortg. § 1804; *Vaughan* v. *Marable*, 64 Ala. 60.

Of course, it does not follow, because some advantage may accrue to the mortgagee from the sale besides the payment of the debt, or because an advantage may incidentally accrue to others, that the power is perverted; and the mortgagee cannot be required to forego the exercise of it simply for that reason. 2 Jones, Mortg. § 1802.

The bill as originally filed set forth that John K. Lester, when he died, was indebted to his son John Erastus in about $21,000; that James C. became executor of the will; and that, as such, and as devisee under it, he procured from John Erastus a release of said John's claims against the estate in consideration of an agreement on his part to pay to said John certain sums of money, and to deliver to said John the portion of the estate devised to him, at the time appointed by the will for delivery, freed from the mortgages; that said James paid said money in part, but died before carrying out the rest of said agreement; that Warren R. Perce, one of the defendants, who survived him in the administration, has refused to complete carrying it out; and that said Julia has brought suit in equity against him to compel him to carry it out. The bill also set forth that said Perce had collected the rents of the estate to a large amount, and that, though having money enough to pay the interest on the mortgages, he had refused to do so, and suffered the estate to be advertised for sale under them, and that said Julia "is informed and believes, and therefore charges it to be true, that said Perce and others and said Bank have combined together for the purpose of allowing said property to be sold under said mortgages, and thereby defeat the purposes of said former bill brought against said Perce and others."

The charge, it will be observed, is not that the Bank either sold or intended to sell under the mortgage for the purpose of defeating said suit, but that said Perce and others and the Bank combined together for the purpose of allowing the sale to be made, and thereby defeating the suit. It is not clear how far the charge was intended to affect the Bank; for certainly the Bank had no need to combine with any person for the purpose of allowing itself to sell under the mortgages after default. It is not such a charge as would entitle the complainants to relief against the Bank or the present owner; nor can it, in our opinion, amount to notice. For either purpose, it should be more direct and determinate. It is, at best, a mere averment on information and belief, with nothing definite alleged to substantiate it. Indeed, the counsel for the complainants rely in support of this point rather on matter set forth in the amendments than on said charge; but, insomuch as there is no allegation that the purchaser at the mortgage sale had notice thereof, we have not considered the sufficiency of the matter so set forth.

The demurrer is sustained.

ILLINOIS SUPREME COURT.

William HAMSHER, *Appt.*,
v.
Anna HAMSHER *et al.*

(....Ill.....)

1. A Young Men's Christian Association not exercising any ecclesiastical control over its members, or prescribing any form of worship for them, or subjecting them to any discipline for failure to conform to its rules, is not a corporation "formed for religious purposes," *i. e.*, for purposes of religious worship, so as to be forbidden by the Corporation Act of 1872 to acquire more than ten acres of land. The association contemplates benevolent and missionary work rather than religious worship.

2. The power of a corporation to acquire and hold title to certain real estate cannot be questioned by any party except the State, where it has power to hold real estate for some purposes.

(March 31, 1890.)

APPEAL by defendant William Hamsher from a judgment of the Circuit Court for Macon County dismissing his cross-bill setting up a right in himself to certain lands of which partition was sought by the original bill. *Affirmed.*

David F. Hamsher, the husband of Anna Hamsher and son of William Hamsher, died testate, February 15, 1889, seised, *inter alia*, of 160 acres of farm land.

His will, after making a number of special bequests, devised to the board of directors of the Young Men's Christian Association of Decatur all the estate then remaining.

The widow and father were the only surviving heirs and next of kin of decedent. The widow renounced under the will and elected to take the one half of all of decedent's property which would remain after payment of debts.

Anna Hamsher in her own right and as executrix, together with Milton Johnson, her co-executor, filed a bill asking that homestead be set off to the widow and that the remainder of the real estate be divided between the widow and executors so that she might have the moiety going to her and the executors might retain the other moiety for the purposes and trusts of the will.

William Hamsher, who had been given an annuity out of the income of the estate, and the other beneficiaries under the will, were made parties defendant. William Hamsher answered and filed a cross-bill claiming that the devise to the Christian Association was void and that the land so devised descended to him as heir; that he was tenant in common with the widow of all the real estate; and praying that partition might be made between himself and the widow.

The court dismissed the cross-bill and entered a decree as prayed in the original bill, and William Hamsher thereupon took this appeal.

Messrs. **Bunn & Park** for appellant.

Messrs. **Isaac R. Mills, Andrew H. Mills** and **W. C. Outten,** for appellees:

The Young Men's Christian Association of Decatur, Ill., does not come within the limitation of § 42, chap. 32, Ill. Stat. (1 Starr & C. Stat. p. 623), for the reason that it is evident from its organization that it is a corporation of the class "not for pecuniary profit," and because its purposes are, as shown by its charter, educational, humanitarian and charitable rather than those of religious worship.

Gilmer v. *Stone*, 120 U. S. 586 (30 L. ed. 734); *Alexander* v. *Tolleston Club*, 110 Ill. 65; 4 Am. & Eng. Encyclop. Law, p. 207, title *Powers and Liabilities of Corporations*, and cases cited.

The rights of a corporation to receive and hold property can only be called in question by the State in a direct proceeding, and this is particularly true where the grant, if invalidated, can only be invalidated as to part.

Alexander v. *Tolleston Club*, 110 Ill. 65; *Barnes* v. *Suddard*, 4 West. Rep. 184, 117 Ill. 237; *Vidal* v. *Girard*, 43 U. S. 2 How. 189 (11 L. ed. 230); *Cowell* v. *Colorado Springs Co.* 100 U. S. 55 (25 L. ed. 547); *American & Foreign C. U.* v. *Yount*, 101 U. S. 352 (25 L. ed. 888); *Jones* v. *Habersham*, 107 U. S. 174 (27 L. ed. 401); Perry, Tr. § 45; *Baker* v. *Neff*, 73 Ind. 68; *Hayward* v. *Davidson*, 41 Ind. 214; *Bogardus* v. *Trinity Church*, 4 Sandf. Ch. 663, 7 N. Y. Ch. L. ed. 1247.

The appellant cannot inquire whether certain property is necessary for the purposes of a corporation, where by law it is capable of taking, purchasing, holding and disposing of real estate for purposes of its organization.

Hayward v. *Davidson*, 41 Ind. 214; *Cowell* v. *Colorado Springs Co. supra; Natoma Water & Min. Co.* v. *Clarkin*, 14 Cal. 552; Dillon, Mun. Corp. § 444.

Under the law and under its charter, the Young Men's Christian Association of Decatur, Ill., is a charitable corporation, and this residuary legacy is a charitable bequest, and as such is valid.

Heuser v. *Harris*, 42 Ill. 425; *Germain* v. *Baltes*, 113 Ill. 29; *Andrews* v. *Andrews*, 110 Ill. 223; *Hunt* v. *Fowler*, 121 Ill. 269; *Santa Clara Female Academy* v. *Sullivan*, 4 West. Rep. 114, 116 Ill. 375.

Magruder, *J.*, delivered the opinion of the court:

The appellees in this case make many points, some of which may be stated as follows: *first*, that the appellant has not, and never can have, a vested interest in the lands in controversy, but that the title, possession and control of the interest claimed by him is vested in the executors, and remains there until after his death; *second*, that appellant is not a tenant in common with appellee Anna Hamsher, the widow of the deceased, and therefore not entitled to the partition prayed for in his cross-bill, but that the widow, as owner in fee of one half of the lands by virtue of her renunciation and election, and the executors, as being vested with the title in fee of the other half by operation of the will, are tenants in common, and the only parties entitled to partition; *third*, that the right of the board of directors of the Young Men's Christian Association of Decatur to receive and hold so much of the real estate devised by item 11 of the will as exceeds in quantity ten acres can only be called in question by the State in a direct proceeding; *fourth*, that the appellant, by accepting the bequest of $600 per year to himself during his life, is estopped from setting up any right of his own that will defeat the full effect and operation of every part of the will; *fifth*, that the Young Men's Christian Association of Decatur, Ill., does not come within that class of religious corporations which are forbidden by our Statute to receive by devise more than ten acres of land, including land already held. As the view which we take of the fifth and last point disposes of the material issues involved in the cause, we do not deem it necessary to decide either of the other positions taken by counsel for appellees.

David F. Hamsher died testate, leaving no child, or descendants of a child. His surviving wife, Anna Hamsher, by reason of her renunciation and election under sections 11-18 of the Dower Act, is entitled to take one half of all the real and personal estate, subject to the payment of debts. The theory of the cross-bill filed by the appellant in the court below is that item 11 of the will attempts to devise to the Young Men's Christian Association of Decatur, Ill., 160 acres of land, reduced by such renunciation and election of the widow to an undivided one half of 160 acres of land; that such devise is void under section 42 of our Act Concerning Corporations, which is hereinafter set forth; that, by reason of the void character of the devise, the land embraced in it must be regarded as intestate estate, and belongs to the appellant, as the father and sole surviving heir of the deceased testator. Assuming the contention of the appellant to be correct,—that the will devises to the association in question land exceeding ten acres in quantity, including that already held by the association,—we are brought to the consideration of the question whether or not the association can hold the land so devised. Section 42 of the "Act Concerning Corporations," approved April 18, 1872, in force July 1, 1872 (Starr & C. Stat. 623; Rev. Stat. 1874, chap. 32, § 42), is as follows: "Any corporation that may be formed for religious purposes under this Act, or under any law of this State, for the incorporation of religious societies, may receive, by gift, devise or purchase, land not exceeding in quantity, including that already held by such corporation, ten acres, and may erect or build thereon such houses, buildings or other improvements as it may deem necessary for the convenience and comfort of such congregation, church or society, and may lay out and maintain thereon a burying-ground; but no such property shall be used except in the manner expressed in the gift, grant or devise, or, if no use or trust is so expressed, except for the benefit of the congregation, church or society for which it was intended."

From an examination of the sections which precede, and of those which follow, section 42, it becomes manifest that the corporations intended to be designated by the latter section are those churches, congregations or societies which are organized for the purposes of "religious worship." Sections from 29 to 34, inclusive, of the Act, have reference to "corporations not for pecuniary profit," providing for the mode of their organization, defining the nature and extent of their powers, specifying the methods of electing their trustees, of effecting their dissolution, of distributing their property, of changing their articles of association, etc. Sections from 35 to 46, inclusive, have reference to "religious corporations." Section 35 begins as follows: "The foregoing provisions shall not apply to any religious corporations; but any church, congregation or society formed for the purpose of religious worship may become incorporated in the manner following, to wit."

The mode of organizing such a religious corporation is essentially different from that prescribed for organizing a corporation "not for pecuniary profit." In the latter case, three or more persons desiring "to associate themselves for any lawful purpose other than for pecuniary profit" make a certificate stating the name of the association, its business, the objects of its formation, the number and names of its trustees, managers or directors, etc., and file such certificate with the secretary of the State, who thereupon issues a certificate of organization, etc. But, in the organization of the religious corporations referred to in the Statute, the church, congregation or society holds a meeting, and elects or appoints two or more of its members "as trustees, wardens and vestrymen," etc., and adopts a corporate name; and when the chairman or secretary of the meeting has made, and filed in the recorder's office of the county, an affidavit as to the holding of such meeting, and its action as aforesaid, the body politic and corporate is created. The words "such congregation, church or society," as used in sections 36, 41, 42 and 46, refer back to section 35, where the "church, congregation or society," intended to be designated, is described as being "formed for the purpose of religious worship."

The view here expressed has been adopted by the Supreme Court of the United States.

In *Gilmer* v. *Stone*, 120 U. S. 586 [30 L. ed. 734], that court had occasion to construe the section (42) now under consideration; and *Mr. Justice* Harlan, in delivering the opinion in that case, uses the following language: "The counsel for the plaintiff in error seem to lay stress upon the more general words, 'formed for religious purposes,' in the 42d section of the Act; but, manifestly, the other parts of the same section, and previous sections, show that the only corporations intended to be restricted in the ownership of land to ten acres were those formed for the purpose of 'religious worship,' and not organizations commonly called 'benevolent' or 'missionary' societies."

It now becomes necessary to inquire whether or not the Young Men's Christian Association of Decatur, Ill., is a corporation organized for the purposes of "religious worship." If it is not such a corporation, then the Legislature, whether wisely or unwisely, has failed to place any restriction upon its receiving, by "gift, devise or purchase," a quantity of land greater than ten acres. The best evidence of the purposes of its formation is the declaration of such purposes as found in its charter or articles of association. These articles are made a part of the cross-bill, and attached thereto as an exhibit. They consist of a certificate, in writing, made, signed and acknowledged as required by section 29 of the Corporation Act, and of a certificate of organization issued by the secretary of state in accordance with section 30 of that Act. From the very nature of these articles, it is apparent that the Young Men's Christian Association of Decatur, Ill., was organized as a corporation "not for pecuniary profit." If it had been organized under the Act as a "religious corporation," the evidence of its incorporation would not be such articles of association as are above described, but would be the affidavit, or a certified copy thereof, mentioned in sections 35 and 36. We agree with counsel for appellant that a corporation whose purpose is to engage in "religious worship" cannot circumvent the statutory restriction of its ownership of land to ten acres by effecting its organization under the sections in relation to corporations "not for pecuniary profit." Hence its character is to be determined not so much by the mode of its formation, as by the object and purposes of its formation. The written certificate filed with the secretary of state states, among other things, that "the name of such corporation is 'The Young Men's Christian Association of Decatur, Illinois.' The object for which it is formed is to promote growth in grace and Christian fellowship among its members, and aggressive Christian work, especially by and for young men, and to seek out and aid the worthy poor. The management of the aforesaid association shall be vested in a board of directors consisting of the officers of said association and one active member from each religious denomination represented in said association, who are to be elected annually."

It is manifest, from the provision thus made for the composition of the board of directors, that the association is not under the control of one religious denomination, but is made up of representatives from a number of such denominations, while the corporation, which is forbidden by section 42 to receive more than ten acres of ground, is one which embodies the ideas and principles of a single religious or ecclesiastical organization. The written certificate of the association does not state, in express terms, that it is formed "for the purpose of religious worship," nor can we say that the objects of its formation as declared in such certificate are necessarily the equivalents of certain forms of religious worship.

Webster defines "worship" to be "the act of paying honors to the Supreme Being; religious reverence and homage; adoration paid to God, or a Being viewed as God." The association in question seems, however, to contemplate a practical missionary and benevolent work, not only among its own members, but among the young and the poor who may need help outside of its membership. The object for which it was formed, according to the description of such object in its articles of association, does not approach so nearly the definition of "religious worship" as do the announced objects of the two societies mentioned in *Gilmer* v. *Stone, supra*. There it appeared that a board of foreign missions was formed "for the purpose of establishing and conducting Christian missions among the unevangelized or pagan nations, and the general diffusion of Christianity," and that a board of home missions had for its object "to assist in sustaining the preaching of the gospel in feeble churches," etc., and "to superintend the whole of home missions in the behalf" of certain churches, and "to receive . . . and disburse . . . funds . . . for home missionary purposes;" and it was there held that neither of said boards was "a church, congregation or society formed for the purpose of religious worship."

It does not appear that the Young Men's Christian Association of Decatur, Ill., exercises any ecclesiastical control over its members, or prescribes any form of worship for them, or subjects those who fail to conform to its rules to ecclesiastical discipline. Therefore a limitation upon the extent of its ownership of real estate is not so imperatively demanded by those considerations of public policy which apply to corporations formed for the purpose of public worship. We are of the opinion that said association is not subject to the restriction contained in section 42 of the Corporation Act, and that the devise to it of a greater quantity of land than ten acres is not invalid. It follows that the appellant takes nothing as heir, and that his cross-bill was properly dismissed.

Counsel for appellant claim that, even if the association was properly organized as a corporation "not for pecuniary profit," it can only take and hold so much real estate as is necessary for the purposes of its organization, and that the will gives it more land than it needs for such purposes. By section 31 of the Corporation Act, corporations "not for pecuniary profit" are made capable, in law, "of taking, purchasing, holding and disposing of real estate and personal estate for purposes of their organization." Such corporations are thus clothed with the capacity of holding real estate. If the Young Men's Christian Association of Decatur "has exceeded in extent its power of holding real estate, appellant, we conceive, cannot take advantage of the fact." *Alexander* v. *Tollecton Club*, 110 Ill. 65.

When a corporation may, for some purposes, acquire and hold the title to real estate, it cannot be made a question by any party, except the State, whether the real estate has been acquired for the authorized uses or not. *Hayward* v. *Davidson*, 41 Ind. 214.

There being capacity to purchase or to receive by devise, whether the corporation, in so purchasing or receiving, exceeds its power, is a question between it and the State, and does not concern appellant. Dillon, Mun. Corp. § 444.

We perceive no error in the record.

The judgment of the Circuit Court is affirmed.

ARKANSAS SUPREME COURT.

ST. LOUIS, IRON MOUNTAIN & SOUTHERN R. CO., *Appt.*,
v.
William RAMSEY *et al.*

(....Ark....)

1. **The title to lands covered by rivers** which are navigable in fact is in the State, whether the tide ebbs and flows in them or not; hence the holder, under a United States patent of land bordering on such river, cannot maintain an action to recover damages for the removal of gravel from the river bed in front of his land below high-water mark.

2. **High-water mark** or the dividing line between the proprietors of lands bordering on a navigable stream and the State is the point beyond which the presence and action of water are so common and usual and so long continued in all ordinary years as to mark upon the soil a character distinct from that of the banks in respect to vegetation as well as in respect to the soil itself.

3. **A gravel bar** in a river bed which is covered by the ordinary stage of high water, at which time steamers pass over it in safety, but which is bare at low water, upon which no vegetation grows and which is not covered by soil, is the property of the State and not of the riparian proprietor.

(May 24, 1890.)

APPEAL by defendant from a judgment of the Circuit Court for Independence County in favor of plaintiffs in an action to recover the value of certain gravel removed by defendant from a river bed and alleged to belong to plaintiffs. *Reversed.*

The facts sufficiently appear in the opinion.

Messrs. **Dodge & Johnson,** for appellant:

The territory which included Arkansas at the time of its acquisition from France was subject to the civil law, and by that law the riparian owner's title on streams actually navigable extended only to the bank or high-water mark.

Pollard v. *Hagan*, 44 U. S. 3 How. 220 (11 L. ed. 569).

The riparian proprietor on navigable waters owns to high-water mark only.

Woolrych, Waters, 40–44; Angell, Tide Waters, 22–24; *Chapman* v. *Kimball*, 9 Conn. 40, and cases cited; *McManus* v. *Carmichael*, 3 Iowa, 54; *Gould* v. *Hudson River R. Co.* 6 N. Y. 522; *People* v. *Canal Appraisers*, 33 N. Y. 461; *Barney* v. *Keokuk*, 94 U. S. 325 (24 L. ed. 224); *Pollard* v. *Hagan*, 44 U. S. 3 How. 217 (11 L. ed. 568).

The true definition of a navigable stream is a stream which is actually navigable.

Houck, Rivers, § 45, p. 26 *et seq.*; *The Genesee Chief* v. *Fitzhugh*, 53 U. S. 12 How. 454, 455 (13 L. ed. 1058); Gould, Waters, § 76; *St. Paul & P. R. Co.* v. *Schurmeier*, 74 U. S. 7 Wall. 272 (19 L. ed. 74); *Martin* v. *Waddell*, 41 U. S. 16 Pet. 367 (10 L. ed. 997); *Pollard* v. *Hagan*, 44 U. S. 3 How. 212 (11 L. ed. 565); *Goodtitle* v. *Kibbe*, 50 U. S. 9 How. 471 (13 L. ed. 220).

By common law the riparian proprietor on navigable waters owns to high-water mark only; and this rule applies to the Mississippi River.

McManus v. *Carmichael*, 3 Iowa, 1; *Haight* v. *Keokuk*, 4 Iowa, 212; *Wood* v. *Fowler*, 26 Kan. 682; *Hoboken* v. *Pennsylvania R. Co.* 124 U. S. 656 (31 L. ed. 543); *Gould* v. *Hudson River R. Co.* 6 N. Y. 522; *Langdon* v. *New York*, 93 N. Y. 144; *Re Staten Island R. T. Co.* 4 Cent. Rep. 515, 103 N. Y. 260; *People* v. *Canal Appraisers*, 33 N. Y. 499, 500; *Carson* v. *Blazer*, 2 Binn. 475; *La Plaisance Bay Harbor Co.* v. *Monroe*, Walk. Ch. (Mich.) 168; *Bowman* v. *Wathen*, 2 McLean, 376; *Black River Imp. Co.* v. *La Crosse, B. & Transp. Co.* 54 Wis. 684; *Chicago, B. & Q. R. Co.* v. *Porter*, 72 Iowa, 426; *Steele* v. *Sanchez*, Id. 65; *Trus-*

NOTE.—Title to soil below ordinary high-water mark where the tide ebbs and flows is in the State. See *notes* to Miller v. Mendenhall (Minn.) 8 L. R. A. 89; Swanson v. Mississippi & R. R. B. Co. (Minn.) 7 L. R. A. 673; Parker v. West Coast Packing Co. (Or.) 5 L. R. A. 61; Case v. Loftus, 39 Fed. Rep. 730; Fulmer v. Williams (Pa.) 1 L. R. A. 603.

See also 21 L. R. A. 62.

tees of Schools v. *Schroll*, 9 West. Rep. 741, 120 Ill. 509; *Stockton* v. *Baltimore & N. Y. R. Co.* 32 Fed. Rep. 19.

Messrs. **H. S. Coleman** and **J. C. Yancey**, for appellees:

When a deed calls for a corner standing on the bank of a creek, "thence down said creek with the meanders thereof," the boundary is low-water mark.

McCullouck v. *Aten*, 2 Ohio, 309; *Handly* v. *Anthony*, 18 U. S. 5 Wheat. 385 (5 L. ed. 115).

A person whose land is bounded by a stream of water which changes its course gradually by illuvial formation, shall still hold the same boundry, including the accumulated soil.

New Orleans v. *United States*, 35 U. S. 10 Pet. 662 (9 L. ed. 578); *St. Clair* v. *Lovingston*, 90 U. S. 23 Wall. 46 (23 L. ed. 59).

The riparian proprietors of land bounded on the Ohio River, in West Virginia, own the fee in the land to low-water mark, subject to the easement to the public in that portion lying between high and low-water mark, with the right of the State to control the same for the purposes of navigation and commerce, without compensation to the owner.

Barre v. *Fleming*, 29 W. Va. 314.

When the subject of controversy is created by accretion, there is no distinction in the riparian rights between navigable and unnavigable streams.

Warren v. *Chambers*, 25 Ark. 120.

A grant from the United States to land upon the Mississippi River extends to the thread of the current.

Houck v. *Yates*, 82 Ill. 179.

The riparian owner has also, by law of this State, an exclusive right as against the public to the river banks to low-water mark, subject to the right of easement for commerce.

Ensminger v. *People*, 47 Ill. 384; *Chicago* v. *Laflin*, 49 Ill. 172.

That the corner of the lands bounded on one side of the Mississippi River is entitled to accretions made thereto by the gradual filling up or receding of the river is not an open question in this State. Land thus formed belongs to the riparian owner.

Campbell v. *Laclede Gas Light Co.* 84 Mo. 372; *Smith* v. *St. Louis Pub. Schools*, 30 Mo. 290; *Garnier* v. *St. Louis*, 37 Mo. 556; *Benson* v. *Morrow*, 61 Mo. 345; *St. Louis Pub. Schools* v. *Risley*, 40 Mo. 357; *Buse* v. *Russell*, 86 Mo. 209; Gould, Waters, §§ 85, 155, 156, 159; 2 Bl. Com. 268; 3 Kent, Com. 428; 2 Washb. Real Prop. 58, 452.

Battle, *J.*, delivered the opinion of the court:

Appellees, being the owners, as tenants in common, by inheritance from an ancestor, who derived title under a patent from the United States Government, of N.W. frl. part of sec. 21, T. 13, N. R. 6 W., on the bank of and bordering on White River, in Independence County, containing according to the patent $22\frac{56}{100}$ acres, the patent for which bears date 12th of December, 1823, brought suit against the Railway Company to recover the value of 3688 carloads of gravel, which the appellant took from a gravel bar, which the appellees alleged in their complaint was lying immediately adjacent to and between the high bank and the water in the main channel of White River. They alleged that this bar had formed against said bank by long years of accretion; and that it is not now part of the main or ordinary channel of the river, but it has become a part of their said tract of land by accretion, and lies immediately in front of the same between the banks of said stream.

The appellant answered, admitting the location, as described, of the tract of land, and the taking of the gravel from the bar, but denied that the gravel bar was a part of the tract of land owned by the plaintiffs.

The proof showed that the gravel bar was not a part of the N. W. frl. 1-4 of sec. 21, T. 13 N. R. 6 W., but that it laid "in the river bed, in front of the tract of land;" that twenty-five years ago the bed of White River ran where the gravel bar now is; that before that time the river ran along the edge of the bank; that the gravel bar had formed slowly for years; that it is not now above the ordinary stage of high water, and is bare at low water, and that a rise in the river of from six to eight feet would cover it; that from ten to fifteen feet is an ordinary high-water rise, and would leave the gravel bar from five to eight feet under the water; that no trees or soil grow on the bar; that the position is this: first, there is a high bank, then a second bottom, then a gravel bar, and then the water; that the second bottom is five or six feet higher than the bar; that any year, at some time, the water in the river rises from fifteen to twenty-two feet; that in ordinary high water steamboats can pass right over the gravel bar in controversy; that there is a swag between the gravel bar and the bank, in which minnows have often been caught; that the water often rises over this gravel bar in one night.

The cause was submitted to the jury upon the evidence and instructions of the court, and there was a verdict for appellee, which upon motion by appellant for a new trial the court refused to disturb; whereupon appellant, having saved exceptions to the giving and refusing of instructions by the court, appealed.

The main question to be determined is, how far the ownership of the appellees in the land between the banks of the river, in front of their tract, extends, by virtue of their ownership of the land upon the bank of the river, under the patent from the government of the United States.

At common law, "as a general principle, the soil of ancient navigable rivers, where there is a flux and reflux of the sea, belongs to the crown, and that of other streams to the subject, that is to the owners of adjacent grounds, to each respectively as far as the middle of the stream." Woolrych, Waters, 44.

The ebb and flow of the tide in a river was at common law the most usual test of its navigability, but was not a conclusive test. Woolrych, Waters, 40.

The soil under navigable streams, at common law, belonged to the king as *parens patriæ*, for the same reason that the waters did, that is as a trust for the public use and benefit. Woolrych, Waters, chaps. 1, 2; Angell, Tide Water, 19-67; Hale, De Jure Maris, cited in *note* 6 Cow. 539; *Chapman* v. *Kimball*, 9 Conn. 88.

Many of the States of the United States have held to the common-law test of the navigability of rivers, and to the doctrine that only those rivers are navigable in a legal sense in which the tide ebbs and flows; and there has been much discussion and conflict of authority upon this question, a majority in number, perhaps, of the courts of last resort maintaining the common law doctrine. But the more reasonable test, as we conceive, of the navigability of a river is its use as a navigable stream, or its capability of being used as such.

The ebb and flow of the tide is merely an arbitrary test, since many waters where the tide flows are not in fact navigable, and many, especially on this continent, where it does not flow, are navigable.

"It is navigability in fact that forms the foundation for navigability in common law." *McManus* v. *Carmichael*, 3 Iowa, 1; *The Genesee Chief* v. *Fitzhugh*, 53 U. S. 12 How. 443 [13 L. ed. 1058].

While in England the ebb and flow of the tide is the most convenient, certain and usual test of the navigability of rivers, as the tide in fact does ebb and flow in all its navigable rivers,—it is wholly inapplicable in this country, where there are large fresh-water rivers thousands of miles long, flowing almost across the entire continent, bearing upon their bosom the commerce of the outside world in part, as well as of the continent.

The largest river in England, the Thames, is only about 250 miles, and the Severn is only about 210 miles, in length.

If we apply the principle of the common law, that the soil under the navigable waters belongs to the sovereign for the benefit and use of the public, and are not governed by the common-law test of the navigability of streams, but by their navigability in fact, we are constrained to maintain that the true doctrine is, that the beds of navigable rivers belong to the government, notwithstanding the tide does not ebb and flow in them.

In *Pollard* v. *Hagan*, 44 U. S. 3 How. 213 [11 L. ed. 566], it is held that "the shores of navigable waters and the soils under them were not granted by the Constitution of the United States, but were reserved to the States respectively; and that the new States have the same rights, sovereignty and jurisdiction over this subject as the original States; and *Mr. Justice* McKinley, delivering the opinion of the court, at page 229 [573], says: "Then to Alabama belong the navigable waters and the soils under them, in controversy in this case, subject to the rights surrendered by the Constitution to the United States;" and on page 230 [574] he says: "To give to the United States the right to transfer to a citizen the title to the shores and the soils under the navigable waters would be placing in their hands a weapon which might be wielded greatly to the injury of the state sovereignty, and deprive the State of the power to exercise a numerous and important class of police powers."

Goodtitle v. *Kibbe*, 50 U. S. 9 How. 471 [13 L. ed. 220], affirms the doctrine of this case, and holds that the title to the soil in navigable waters below high-water mark is in the State.

In the case of *McManus* v *Carmichael*, *supra*, the court said: "By the Acts of the United States relating to the survey and sale of the public lands (see Act of May 18, 1796, etc.), also the laws establishing the general land office, it is well known that the whole bed of navigable rivers is excepted from the surveys, and that the lands of the United States are sold with reference to the plats and field notes of the survey."

It is also held in the same case that the rule that grants are to be construed most strongly against the grantor does not apply to public grants; but that the government being but a trustee for the public, its grants are to be construed strictly. This is familiar law.

In *Middleton* v. *Pritchard*, 4 Ill. 510, *Mr. Justice* Wilson in a dissenting opinion says, in regard to the sale of lands by the government: "The land authorized to be sold, and the mode of selling it, are prescribed by law, and all sales in violation of that are void. These surveys and plats are the guides of the land officers in making their sales; they have no authority to sell a single acre that has not been surveyed."

In *Barney* v. *Keokuk*, 94 U. S. 324 [24 L. ed. 224], *Mr. Justice* Bradley in discussing this question says, on page 336 [227]: "In this country, as a general thing, all waters are deemed navigable which are really so;" and on page 338 [228] he says: "In our view of the subject the correct principles are laid down in *Martin* v. *Waddell*, 41 U. S. 16 Pet. 367 [10 L. ed. 997]; *Pollard* v. *Hagan*, 44 U. S. 3 How. 212 [11 L. ed. 565], and *Goodtitle* v. *Kibbe*, 50 U. S. 9 How. 471 [13 L. ed. 220]. These cases relate to tide water, it is true, but they enunciate principles which are equally applicable to all navigable waters. And since this court in the case of *The Genesee Chief* v. *Fitzhugh*, 53 U. S. 12 How. 443 [13 L. ed. 1058], has declared that the great lakes and other navigable waters of the country, above as well as below the flow of the tide, are in the strictest sense entitled to the denomination of navigable waters, and amenable to the admiralty jurisdiction, there seems to be no sound reason for adhering to the old rule as to the proprietorship of the beds and shores of such waters. It properly belongs to the States, by their inherent sovereignty; and the United States has wisely abstained from extending (if it could extend) its survey and grants beyond the limit of high water. The cases in which this court has seemed to hold a contrary view depended on the local laws of the State in which the lands were situated."

But it is necessary to a full understanding of the rights of a riparian owner and of the public in the lands between the banks of a river to determine the legal meaning of the phrase "high water."

It does not mean, as has been sometimes supposed, the line reached by the great annual rises, regardless of the character of the lands subject at such times to be overflowed. But, as decided in the case of *Houghton* v. *Chicago, D. & M. R. Co.* 47 Iowa, 370: "High-water mark is the line between the riparian proprietor and the public,—is to be regarded as co-ordinate with the limit of the river bed."

Whatever difficulty there may be in determining it in places, this doubtless may be said: "What the river does not occupy long enough to revert from vegetation, so far as to destroy its value for agriculture, is not river bed."

In *Howard* v. *Ingersoll*, 54 U. S. 13 How. 381

[14 L. ed. 189], *Mr. Justice* Curtis gave a satisfactory definition of the banks and bed of a river. He says: "The banks of a river are those elevations of land which confine the waters when they rise out of the bed; and the bed is that soil so usually covered by water as to be distinguishable from the banks or both, produced by the common presence and action of flowing water. But neither the line of ordinary high-water mark or ordinary low-water mark, nor of a middle stage of water can be assumed as the line dividing the bed from the banks. This line is to be found by examining the bed and banks, and ascertaining where the presence and action of water are so common and usual, and so long continued in all ordinary years, as to mark upon the soil of the bed a character distinct from that of the banks, in respect to vegetation, as well as in respect to the nature of the soil itself. Whether this line between the bed and the banks will be found above or below or at a middle stage of water, must depend upon the character of the stream."

"But, in all cases, the bed of a river is a natural object, and is to be sought for, not merely by the application of any abstract rules, but as other natural objects are sought for and found, by the distinctive appearances they present, the banks being fast land on which vegetation appropriate to such land in the particular locality grows wherever the bank is not too steep to permit such growth, and the bed being soil of a different character and having no vegetation, or only such as exists where commonly submerged in water."

The owner of land on the margin of a navigable stream in this State holding under a grant from the United States government, does not take *ad medium filum aquæ*, but to high-water mark, as limited and defined above, and the beds of all navigable rivers in the State belong to the State, in trust for the use of the public. Was this gravel bar an accretion to appellee's land?

Accretion to land on a stream navigable or unnavigable belongs to the owner of land; therefore, if appellee's contention that this bar has become a part of his land by accretion has been maintained, the judgment of the circuit court is correct. *Warren* v. *Chambers*, 25 Ark. 120; *New Orleans* v. *United States*, 35 U. S. 10 Pet. 662 [9 L. ed. 573]; *Jones* v. *Soulard*, 65 U. S. 24 How. 41 [16 L. ed. 604]; *Saulet* v. *Shepherd*, 71 U. S. 4 Wall. 502 [18 L. ed. 442]; Am. & Eng. Encylop. Law, § 3, p. 37, and cases cited. Accretion is the increase of real estate, by the addition of portions of soil by gradual deposition through the operation of natural causes, to that already in possession of the owner. The term "alluvion" is applied to the deposit itself, while accretion rather denotes the act. 3 Washb. Real Prop. 60, 61; Bouvier, Law Dict. title, *Accretion;* Woolrych, Water, lateral p. 29.

Fleta says: "We acquire a right to things, according to the Law of Nations, by accession. That which a stream has added to our land by alluvion, for instance, belongs to us by virtue of the same law." Fleta, liber 3, chap. 2, § 6.

Does the testimony in this case show that the gravel bar is alluvion added to the land of the appellees by accretion? We think not; on the contrary the evidence shows that the gravel bar is a part of the bed of White River within the above definition.

Reversed and remanded.

SOUTH DAKOTA SUPREME COURT.

Margaret BUETER, *Respt.*,
v.
BUETER, *Appt.*

(....S. D.....)

***1. In this case the evidence examined,** and *held*, to sustain the allegation of respondent that she executed the articles of separation between herself and her husband, appellant herein, under menace, entitling her to rescind, and to support the judgment of the court below in annulling and setting the same aside.

2. In this State a wife, justified by her husband's misconduct towards her in living separate from him, may maintain an independent action against him for her support, without regard to the question of divorce.

3. In such an action, if the wife is destitute, the court has power to include in its judgment an allowance of attorney's fees, as necessaries for the wife.

(April 1, 1890.)

APPEAL by defendant from a judgment of the District Court for Lawrence County in favor of plaintiff in a suit brought to set aside certain articles of separation and to obtain an allowance for support and maintenance and for counsel fees. *Affirmed.*

The facts sufficiently appear in the opinion.

Mr. **Granville G. Bennett** for appellant.

Messrs. **McLaughlin & Steele** for respondent.

Kellam, J., delivered the opinion of the court:

This was an action brought by respondent against appellant in the District Court of Lawrence County, to set aside and annul certain articles of separation between said parties, who are husband and wife, and for other specific relief, hereinafter noticed, alleging in her complaint that she signed the articles reluctantly and unwillingly, under menace and duress exercised towards her by appellant; that she revoked and renounced said articles of separation, and claims all her rights as the lawful wife of appellant, and offers to return and be reconciled to him wherever it will be safe for her to do so. The complaint further charges extreme and repeated acts of violence towards respondent for a long time before and at the time of signing such articles; alleges that she is old, infirm and destitute; and that appellant is in possession of all the property accumulated by their joint industry and economy. The

*Head notes by KELLAM, J.

other specific relief asked for was a decree requiring the appellant to pay her monthly a reasonable allowance for her support, and a reasonable sum as attorney's fees and expenses of the action. The appellant answered, denying all the allegations of ill treatment and violence, and of menace and duress as to the execution of the articles of separation, and set up such articles as a defense to the action. Upon the trial the court decreed the articles of separation null and void, because obtained from respondent by menace and duress; and, further, that appellant should pay to respondent, or to the clerk of the court for her use, for her support and maintenance, the sum of $40 per month, until the further order of the court, and the sum of $150 for attorney's fees in the action. From this judgment and decree the appellant appeals.

All the alleged errors which are brought to the attention of this court by the assignment and the record may be considered under two distinct heads: (1) Is the evidence sufficient to support and justify the court in its decree setting aside and annulling the articles of separation between appellant and respondent? and, if so, (2) Had the court jurisdiction to entertain so much of this action as sought to compel appellant to make an allowance for the support of respondent?

Does the evidence show that these articles of separation were executed by respondent under the coercion of menace and duress? "Duress" is declared by our Statute (§ 3504, Comp. Laws) to consist in (1) unlawful confinement of the person of the party, or of husband or wife of such party, or of an ancestor, descendant or adopted child of such party, husband or wife; (2) unlawful detention of the property of any such person; or (3) confinement of such person, lawful in form, but fraudulently obtained, or fraudulently made unjustly harassing or oppressive.

By section 3505, menace consists in a threat (1) of such duress as is specified in the first and third subdivisions of the last section; (2) of unlawful and violent injury to the person or property of any such person as is specified in the last section; or (3) of injury to the character of any such person.

Much of the evidence tending to show violent and active cruelty towards respondent by appellant did not immediately connect such acts with the execution of this agreement. Indeed, many of them occurred months before, and had no relation to the agreement, or its execution, and can only be considered in connection with their probable, or, rather, inevitable, effect upon respondent, in inspiring a fear of their repetition. A woman who had never known or felt her husband's hand in violence against her would doubtless be less moved by an angry threat than one who, remembering the experience of the past, would at once connect the threat with its execution, and instinctively measure its meaning by the recollection of the bruises she had before received. The testimony of the respondent, Margaret Bueter, Mrs. Rewman, her daughter, and at least five or six other witnesses, establishes beyond doubt the violent and wicked conduct of appellant towards respondent. He had himself educated her to know and appreciate the force and meaning of his threats. The proof of his general ill treatment of respondent is so abundant and convincing that we shall not refer to it in detail. In the examination of respondent, the following questions and answers occur:

Q. What was his conduct just before that [signing articles of separation], for some days, towards you?

A. Cruelness, meanness and violence. He kicked me with his boots that I was black and blue all over, days and days before,—you might say for months.

Q. What was the last time before signing; how long before?

A. That same morning.

Q. (By the Court.) Did he make any threats against you?

A. Yes, sir; he did.

Q. (By the same.) In order to make you sign it?

A. Yes, sir.

Q. (By the same.) What threats did he make against you? Did he threaten to do any violence to you if you did not sign it?

A. Yes, sir.

Q. (By the same.) What did he say?

A. He knocked me down, and kicked me.

Q. (By the same.) Did he kick you because you would not sign this writing?

A. Yes, sir; that is what he did.

We make the following extract from the testimony of Mrs. Rewman:

Q. What took place between them as to the signing of that [articles of separation] in your presence?

A. I know he abused her when she said she would not sign it.

Q. What do you mean by abuse?

A. Well, he slapped her, and pulled her around.

Q. Do you know who brought these articles of separation to the house?

A. No, sir; I do not. I first saw them—papa handed them to me, and asked me to read them to mamma. I read them to her. I started to read them. I don't know whether I finished them or not; and she said she would not sign them at the time I read it. My mother cannot read English writing. I don't think I finished reading them. I read them over half through, though. She listened to it, and she said she wouldn't sign them, and did not care to hear any more after she had heard half of it.

Q. Tell the judge why she signed the articles after her expressing her unwillingness.

A. Because there was not any peace at home unless she would sign them,—to make peace she signed them. There would be no peace at the house unless she signed them.

Q. (By the Court.) How long after they were brought to the house was it before she signed them?

A. It was two or three days. I think he brought them here on Tuesday, and they were signed on Thursday, I think.

Q. During the interval from the time they came to the house until they were signed by your mother, state what you know about any pressure being brought to bear upon her, either by violence or otherwise, to induce her to sign them.

A. I know he kicked her once when they quarreled about her not signing the paper, and she said she would not sign it, and in the evening of that night, before she signed them, they were quarreling, and he slapped her, and abused her.

Q. What was the condition of your mother at the time she signed the paper? Was she in good health or unwell?

A. She was feeling very poorly.

There is considerable other testimony in the same line, though possibly not quite so directly connected with the execution of these papers; and while we are not disposed to limit the force, as evidence, of the certificate of the officer who took respondent's acknowledgment, and while her evidence cannot be taken to impeach his certificate, it strongly corroborates the testimony of respondent and her witnesses as to her reluctance to signing the agreement. He says there was much contention and angry talk between them, and that he must have been there an hour, at least, before she agreed. Without more particular discussion, we content ourselves with saying generally that the evidence bearing upon this immediate question, carefully read and thoughtfully considered, impresses us as it did the trial court; and we are fully convinced that the execution of the articles of separation of April 15, 1884, by the respondent, was caused by threats of bodily injury, and accomplished by menace, as alleged in the complaint.

Having reached the conclusion that the court below was right in annulling the articles of separation, we approach the next question with more reluctance, because it involves a question of jurisdiction never before, to our knowledge, presented to the courts of this State or Territory. The proposition is clean cut, and, plainly stated, is this: Can a wife, justified by the conduct of her husband towards her in leaving her home, maintain an independent action against her husband for her maintenance? And can a court of equity entertain such an action, and by its decree compel the husband to make provision for her support during such separation? It must be conceded that little support is found for such an action in the books of the text-writers, and the adjudications of the courts, in number, at least, preponderate against it. The question is important. It is squarely presented in this case, and it must be answered.

Both at common law and under our Statute the wife is entitled, by virtue of the marriage contract, to support and maintenance from her husband, and he, in turn, is under obligation to supply such support and maintenance, commensurate with his ability, until relieved from such duty, either by the law, or by the voluntary act of the parties to the contract. Comp. Laws, § 2588.

But while this mutual and correlative duty and right, as between husband and wife, have been recognized by the courts from an early day, it was never in the English courts, I think, not even the ecclesiastical, allowed as an independent right or cause of action. It was only asserted and allowed as an incident or appendage to some other proceeding, generally for a divorce.

In *Ball* v. *Montgomery*, 2 Ves. Jr. 191, *Lord* Loughborough said: "I take it to be now the established law that no court, not even the ecclesiastical court, has any original jurisdiction to give a wife a separate maintenance. It is always as incidental to some other matter that she becomes entitled to a separate provision;" and this was probably the nearly uniform holding of the English courts, except that upon *supplicavit* for security of the peace, against her husband, it was said, in the case just cited, the wife might be allowed a separate maintenance, if necessary that she should live apart from her husband; but even this authority was questioned in subsequent cases, and it is very doubtful, if not altogether improbable, that a case like the one at bar could have been maintained in any of the courts of England.

In Bishop on Marriage and Divorce the author declares that the doctrine and practice of the English courts were strongly against it, and to the same purpose is the declaration of *Judge* Story in the second volume of his Equity Jurisprudence, § 1422.

An examination of the earlier American cases shows a strong disposition to follow the same rule, but it did not command universal obedience. In an early Virginia case (*Purcell* v. *Purcell*, 4 Hen. & M. 507), a broader jurisdiction was asserted; and it was there held that if a husband abandon his wife, and separate himself from her, without any reasonable support, a court of equity may, in all cases, decree her a suitable maintenance and support out of his estate, upon the very ground that there is no adequate or sufficient remedy at law in such a case. Mr. Bishop speaks disapprovingly of the chancellor's conclusion as to the jurisdiction of a court of equity in such a case, but *Judge* Story says of it: "There is so much good sense and reason in this doctrine that it might be wished it were generally adopted." Story, Eq. Jur. § 1423*a*.

The same doctrine was again recognized and maintained in Virginia in *Almond* v. *Almond*, 4 Rand. (Va.) 662.

In South Carolina the same rule as to the jurisdiction of a court of equity is asserted in *Prather* v. *Prather*, 4 Desaus. Eq. 33; and later, in the same State, in *Rhame* v. *Rhame*, 1 McCord, Eq. 197.

In Alabama the rule is broadly stated, in *Glover* v. *Glover*, 16 Ala. 440, to be: "Where a husband abandons his wife without just cause, and casts her upon society destitute of the means of subsistence, a court of chancery, as an original ground of equity, will entertain a bill filed against him for alimony;" and this case was followed in *Kinsey* v. *Kinsey*, 37 Ala. 393.

In *Butler* v. *Butler*, 4 Litt. (Ky.) 202, this question was elaborately reviewed, and in his opinion *Judge* Mills says: "Suppose the case of abandonment by the husband, and that the separation is complete, without any sentence, and that the wife is left to the humanity of the world, without support, has the chancellor, without the Statute, or in cases not embraced by it, no authority to direct a portion of the husband's estate to be set apart for the support of the wife, leaving the marriage contract as obligatory as ever? This is a question different from the power of separation, and deserves further consideration. . . . It is clear that strong moral obligations must lie on every husband, who has abandoned his wife, to support her. The marriage contract and every principle binds him to this. To fail to do it is a wrong acknowledged at common law, though that law knows no remedy, because there the wife cannot sue the husband. But in equity the wife can sue the husband, and it is the province of a court of equity to afford remedy where conscience and law acknowledge a right, but know no remedy."

In 1869 this precise question was before the Supreme Court of California, in *Galland* v. *Galland*, 38 Cal. 265; and, though the case was decided by a divided court, *Judge* Crockett, in the prevailing opinion, says: "Whatever reason may have prevailed at common law to induce the courts to withhold their aid from the wife under these circumstances [separation and destitution], none exists in this State why a court of equity should refuse to compel an offending husband to provide out of their common property for the support of an ill-used wife, who has been forced to seek protection elsewhere than under the husband's roof."

Again, in *Garland* v. *Garland*, 50 Miss. 694, after a very thorough examination of this question, and the cases bearing upon it, the court in its opinion uses this language: "Courts of equity in America will always interpose to redress wrongs when the complainant is without full, adequate and complete remedy at law. Here there is no such process as *supplicavit*, nor a distinct proceeding for the restitution of the conjugal relation. If a wife is abandoned by her husband without means of support, a bill in equity will lie to compel the husband to support the wife without asking for a decree of divorce."

In the case of *Graves* v. *Graves*, reported in 36 Iowa, 310, *Judge* Cole, delivering the opinion of the court, states the question thus: "The main question involved in the controversy is whether a court of equity has the authority or jurisdiction to entertain an action brought for alimony alone, and to grant such alimony where no divorce or other relief is sought;" and after an examination of the question, and the history of its treatment by the courts, both in England and America, he concludes: "It seems to us that, upon well-settled equity principles, as well as upon considerations of public policy, the action may be maintained without asking a divorce or other relief."

And very recently this distinct question was presented to the Supreme Court of Nebraska in *Earle* v. *Earle*, 43 N. W. Rep. 118. In that case, as in *Galland* v. *Galland*, *supra*, it was contended—and the appellant so insists in this case—that the Statute affirmatively authorizing alimony and support to the wife, as an incident or appendage to divorce proceedings, impliedly negatives the power or jurisdiction of the court to make such allowance in other cases, but in neither case was such argument convincing. The syllabus of this case, prepared by the court, says: "The law of the land having made it the legal duty of a husband to support his wife and children, courts of equity within this State have the power, in a suit by the wife for alimony and support, to enforce the discharge of such duty, without reference to whether the action is for a divorce or not."

These cases, while possibly not strictly in line with the prevailing current of judicial decisions, either in England or this country, commend themselves to our judgment. Their reasoning seems to us logical and safe, and their conclusions in harmony with the present legal status of married women. A denial of such jurisdiction would seem to expose the law and the courts to the just criticism of having squarely asserted the wife's right to support from her husband, yet denying her a remedy when such support is refused. Our Statute allows the husband and wife to agree upon terms of immediate separation, and, if such terms provide for the support of the wife by the husband, the courts will enforce such support, at the suit of the wife. But how can this second agreement add to the original obligation, deliberately undertaken and assumed by him, as a part and parcel of his marriage contract? Can a repetition of such agreement, or a further recognition of such obligation, in articles of separation, add anything to its force? A substantial and inseparable part of the marriage contract was his undertaking to support and maintain his wife, and this obligation continued upon him while living in separation, provided such separation was justified by his own misconduct. The law always and without reserve declares this obligation absolute. Is it made more so by his again assenting to it in articles of separation? True, the agreement may fix the amount of support, and how it shall be supplied, but that does not affect the principle upon which her cause of action rests. It only attempts to fix the measure of relief, which would otherwise be left entirely to the court. It is difficult to see how the agreement, which adds no duty *in specie* to that already imposed by the law, can supply a cause of action in favor of the wife, if none existed before. If the parties to this action had voluntarily agreed upon terms of separation, by which the husband was bound to support the wife, any court of equity would, without hesitation, have entertained her action to compel performance, and the court would not confine itself to the terms of the agreement, but would make such allowance as was equitable. This is nearly the language of *Judge* Mills in *Butler* v. *Butler*, *supra*.

Marriage being the result of a civil contract between the parties, and the law positively declaring that such contract covers and imposes the obligation of support, we are unable to perceive, on any principle of reason or justice, why a wife who agrees to separate from her husband should be more favored by the law than one who clings to him in spite of his ill usage, until aged in years, infirm in body and broken in spirit, she is finally driven from her home by his unbearable misconduct. It is no adequate response to say that the law makes the husband liable for necessaries which may be furnished the discarded wife under such circumstances. What if no tradesman would furnish such supplies, and take the risk of collecting against her husband? It would be extremely improbable that any wife could long maintain herself in that way. Such a support would be too uncertain, precarious and humiliating. It neither meets the rights of the wife, nor the duties of the husband. It is equally unfair, unjust and inequitable to tell the destitute, and possibly unoffending, wife that the law will compel her husband to provide for her if she will couple her application for maintenance with a complaint for divorce. There may be abundant reasons, controlling with her, and which the law ought to respect, why she does not want a divorce. There may be objections in conscience,—a vital and unyielding principle and rule of her religion. She may unselfishly desire to avoid a public notoriety and scandal that would involve her children, or she may still have such affection for, and faith in, her husband as will feed the hope of his reformation and their reconciliation,—reasons, all of them, which the law ought not to ignore or disrespect. The husband owing this duty of maintenance to the wife, we perceive no good reason why she may not, independent of any other ground, maintain an action against him for its enforcement. In this case, the evidence shows such misconduct towards his wife, and illusage of her, by the appellant, as would, and does, in our opinion, justify the separation and the bringing of this action. No complaint is made as to the amount of the allowance decreed by the court, except as to the item of $150 attorney's fees, and as to this the learned counsel for appellant vigorously says: "There is no shadow of legal authority for the judgment awarding plaintiff an attorney fee of $150, or any sum whatever. No attorney fees are ever allowed except when clearly provided by statute, or where they are subject of contract." This allowance cannot be defended as a substitute for statutory costs, and was not so intended by the trial court, and in that sense is not costs at all. The Statute regulates the amount of costs in any action, when allowed. In this case the court had found from the evidence that the wife was justified in living separate and apart from her husband, and was entitled to maintenance during such separation; that the husband was able to furnish such support, but refused; and that the wife was destitute. Upon these facts, it is the husband's undisputed duty to furnish necessaries. If it was necessary that this woman have support, and necessary to bring this action to obtain it, then the action, with its proper expense, was a necessary chargeable against the husband. The law furnishes no inflexible definition of the term "necessaries."

In *Shepherd* v. *Mackoul*, 3 Campb. 326, a husband was held liable upon an attorney's bill for services rendered in exhibiting articles of the peace against him. In that case *Lord* Ellenborough said that the wife "had a right to appeal to the law for protection, and she must have the means of appealing effectually. She might therefore charge her husband for the necessary expense of this proceeding as much as for necessary food and raiment;" and this rule was followed in numerous English cases.

Morris v. *Palmer*, 39 N. H. 123, holds the same doctrine in a similar case.

In *Porter* v. *Briggs*, 38 Iowa, 166, the question was whether the husband was liable for services rendered by an attorney in establishing the innocence of the wife upon a charge of adultery, made by the husband himself, in an action for divorce, and the court says: "In our opinion, he is liable for such services upon an implied promise, which the law raises, to pay therefor as necessaries for the wife;" and, upon a reargument of the case, the court adhered to this opinion.

In *Warner* v. *Heiden*, 28 Wis. 517, the court held that a husband who prosecuted his wife to compel her to find sureties to keep the peace, and failed to sustain the charges brought against her, was liable for the reasonable fees of attorneys employed by her to defend her against such prosecution, on the ground that such legal services were necessaries.

In the case of *Graves* v. *Graves*, 36 Iowa, 310, an action very similar to the one at bar, referred to above on another branch of this case, the supreme court of Iowa affirmed a decree of the court below requiring the husband to pay an attorney's fee of $150 for services in bringing the action. These cases are sufficient to illustrate the principle, and to justify our application of it to this case. We think the attorney's fees in this case were properly considered by the court as necessaries, and, as they do not appear to be unreasonable in amount, we are not disposed to disturb the decree in this respect.

The last objection appellant makes to this decree is that it provides that a failure for thirty days, on the part of appellant, to make the payments at the times required, shall be deemed contempt. This objection is not substantial. This provision adds nothing to the force of the judgment. The court makes its decree, and the law provides the means for its enforcement. If non-observance, by appellant, of the requirements of this decree would be contempt, it would be so, not because it was so recited in the judgment, but because it was an act of disobedience which the law made contempt. Punishment as for contempt is not an unusual means of enforcing orders in equity. If at any time appellant is unable to comply with the requirements of the decree, and such disability has not been voluntarily created by his own act, he will not be liable to be punished as for contempt.

The judgment of the District Court is affirmed.

All the Judges concurred.

Petition for rehearing denied.

ILLINOIS SUPREME COURT.

Walter L. PEASE, *Appt.*,
v.
William C. RITCHIE *et al.*

(....Ill....)

1. Where one of several judgment debtors, for whom the judgment debt has been secretly purchased in another's name, holds the judgment out to the world as valid, and procures a sale of his own land on execution under it, becoming the purchaser himself in another's name, he is estopped from claiming that the judgment was paid before the sale, in order to prevent the exercise of a right of redemption by another judgment creditor.

2. An execution cannot be said to be issued, within the meaning of a statute requiring it to be issued within one year in order to preserve the lien of a judgment, until it is delivered to an officer to execute.

3. A discharge of a judgment debtor in bankruptcy, although the judgment has ceased to be a lien, does not render it unavailing for the purpose of redeeming the debtor's lands from sale under a prior judgment.

(May 14, 1890.)

APPEAL by plaintiff from a judgment of the Circuit Court for Cook County in favor of defendants in a suit brought to quiet title to certain real estate. *Affirmed.*

Plaintiff was the original owner of the land. One Chisholm recovered a judgment against him and certain other persons under which an execution was issued and levied on the land in controversy and the land was sold at execution sale. Subsequently Wells, Norton & Walker, judgment creditors of Pease, redeemed the lands from that sale and obtained a sheriff's title thereto. Defendants claimed under the title so obtained.

Further facts appear in the opinion.

Messrs. **Cook & Upton** and **Gregory, Booth & Harlan** for appellant.

Messrs. **Frederick Ullmann** and **Charles A. Dupee** for appellee.

Craig, *J.*, delivered the opinion of the court:

Under the facts as they appear from the record, appellant contends that the Chisholm judgment was paid, and as to him a sale thereunder was a nullity, and a redemption thereupon conferred no title whatever on the party seeking to redeem; second, that the Wells, Norton & Walker judgment against him was not a lien on the premises in controversy, because no execution had issued thereon within a year under the Statute, and that, though a judgment may be used to redeem when not a lien, this judgment could not be so employed, because, at the time redemption was attempted, the appellant had obtained his discharge in bankruptcy, and therefore the judgment could not be made the basis of redemption any more than it could be sued over or execution issued thereon, and appellant's property sold, if he insisted on the protection of his discharge, and that Wells, Norton & Walker were not therefore judgment creditors within the meaning of the Statute.

Various other questions have been raised and discussed in the argument of counsel, but, in the view we take of the record, it will not be necessary to consider them, as, in our opinion, the sheriff's title obtained by Wells, Norton & Walker under the redemption from the sale on the Chisholm judgment, disregarding all other questions, is conclusive of the rights of the parties.

As respects the first proposition, that the Chisholm judgment was paid, upon an examination of the evidence, it will be found that the judgment was rendered against Pease, Dobbins and others, who were partners. By an arrangement between the partners, the equitable obligation to pay the judgment devolved upon Dobbins and the other defendants, and not upon Pease. On the 30th day of January, 1876, Fuller, on behalf of Pease, purchased the judgment, the latter furnishing the money. On the 1st day of June, 1877, by the direction of Pease, Fuller assigned the judgment to Edward F. Lawrence, and he assigned to Chisholm, the original judgment plaintiff. These assignments were not of record. The transaction was a secret one, known only to Pease and those connected with him acting in his interest. In the schedule attached to Pease's bankrupt proceedings, his oath shows that the judgment was still subsisting against him. The attorneys of Pease sued out an execution, and caused it to be levied on the premises, and caused the premises to be sold on the execution. At the sale Pease had the property bid off in the name of Inslee. A short time before the execution issued, Pease, in answer to a letter of inquiry by appellee Ritchie, in regard to the judgment, wrote as follows: "Yours of 25th received. R. B. Chisholm is the owner of the judgment you mentioned, and I understand Mr. Perry represents him in the matter."

Under the facts, we think Pease is now estopped from claiming that the Chisholm judgment was paid. He held the judgment out to the world as a valid subsisting judgment. He sold the land on an execution issued upon it, and became the purchaser in another name. After having done these acts, and invited the redemption and subsequent sale by a judgment creditor, it is too late now for him to assert that the judgment was paid, and the sale an idle ceremony. If authority is needed to sustain this position, *Niantic Bank* v. *Dennis*, 37 Ill. 385, is a case in point. The Statute conferred the right of redemption upon Wells, Norton & Walker, judgment creditors, and in the exercise of that right they had every reason to believe that the sale under the Chisholm judgment was in all respects valid, and obligatory upon Pease and all other persons claiming any interest in the premises under or through him; and, having acted in good faith, they and their grantees ought to be protected.

But it is insisted that, if the sale under the Chisholm judgment is to be treated as valid, it is then claimed that there was no right of redemption in the judgment creditors, Wells, Norton & Walker, because their judgment was not a lien, and the discharge in bankruptcy of Pease was a satisfaction of the judgment. The Statute provides that a judgment of a court of record shall be a lien on the real estate of the person against whom it is obtained, in the county for which the court is held, for seven years from the time it is rendered, provided that, when execution is not issued on a judgment within one year from the time it becomes a lien, it shall thereafter cease to be a lien. Rev. Stat. chap. 77, § 1.

The first question to be considered is whether, within the meaning of the Statute, an execution issued on the judgment in favor of Wells, Norton & Walker within one year from the time it was rendered. As before observed, the clerk made out an execution within the year, but it was never delivered to the sheriff to execute, and when found an indorsement was found on the back of the execution, "Not called for." We do not think what was done here can be regarded as a compliance with the Statute.

The Statute requires something more than the mere writing of an execution by the clerk, and placing it among the files in his office. The word "issued," as used in the Statute, has a more comprehensive meaning, and we think that the fair construction of the word as used in the Statute requires an execution to be made out, properly attested by the clerk, and delivered to the sheriff to be executed by him. The object of issuing an execution is to collect the judgment; but that object cannot be carried out unless the execution is placed in the hands of an officer for collection. The only conclusion we are able to reach, when the purpose of the Statute is kept in view, is that an execution cannot be said to be issued within the meaning of the Statute until it is delivered to the sheriff to execute. From what has been said, it seems plain that the judgment of Wells, Norton & Walker was not a lien from the time it was rendered, and did not become a lien until October 30, 1880, when the execution was issued upon which the redemption was made, but that fact did not prevent them from redeeming.

This court has held that a judgment creditor may redeem from a prior sale, although his judgment may not be a lien. *Sweezy* v. *Chandler*, 11 Ill. 449.

But while appellant concedes that, in an ordinary case, a judgment creditor may redeem, although his judgment may not be a lien, yet it is claimed that appellant's discharge in bankruptcy rendered the judgment unavailing for the purpose of redemption. It is conceded that, if the judgment had been a lien, the appellant's discharge in bankruptcy would have had no effect upon it. It is no doubt true that appellant's discharge in bankruptcy operated as a bar to any action which might be brought to recover any debt or obligation existing at the time he was declared a bankrupt, and after-acquired property was exempted from being taken in satisfaction of any such debts. But, if any creditor had a lien or an equitable claim, by mortgage or otherwise, upon any property of the bankrupt, such right or rights would remain unaffected by the proceedings in bankruptcy.

In *Tallcott* v. *Dudley*, 5 Ill. 435, the effect of a decree in bankruptcy is somewhat discussed. It is there said: "I take it to be a well settled principle of law that by a decree of bankruptcy the assignee succeeds immediately to all the rights and interests of the bankrupt, to just the same extent that the bankrupt himself had them, subject to and affected by all the equities, liens and incumbrances existing against them in the hands of the bankrupt. The assignee is not a bona fide purchaser for a valuable consideration, but he rather acquires a title by operation of law, and the title comes into his hands in no more perfect a condition than it left the hands of the bankrupt. Indeed, the assignee may be considered rather as a volunteer than a purchaser, and takes the title devested of no lien or equity previously created, either by operation of law or the act of the bankrupt. These are familiar and well-established rules under the English Bankrupt Law, . . . and have been repeatedly recognized and adopted under the Bankrupt Law of the United States."

When appellant was adjudged a bankrupt, the Chisholm judgment was in full force, and a lien on all real estate owned in Cook County by appellant. The assignee succeeded to the title to that lot in question, subject, however, to the right of Chisholm to sell the property in satisfaction of the judgment, and, in the event that the assignee failed to redeem within one year, also subject to the right of Wells, Norton & Walker, judgment creditors, to redeem. These rights of redemption conferred upon judgment creditors by the public laws of the State may be regarded as valuable property rights which have not been taken away or destroyed by the proceedings in bankruptcy. In many cases they may be as valuable as a mortgage.

In *Hardin* v. *Osborne*, 94 Ill. 571, it was held that "an assignee in bankruptcy does not take the title to the property of the bankrupt as an innocent purchaser without notice, free from latent equities, etc.; but he takes as a mere volunteer, standing in the shoes of the bankrupt as respects the title, having no greater rights in that regard than the bankrupt himself could assert." The same rule is declared in *Jenkins* v. *Pierce*, 98 Ill. 646, and *Yeatman* v. *New Orleans Sav. Inst.*, 95 U. S. 766 [24 L. ed. 590]. Here the right of redemption in favor of judgment creditors was not affected by the proceedings in bankruptcy. The judgment in favor of Wells, Norton & Walker was not paid, discharged or released. It remained in full force and effect. The discharge in bankruptcy released the bankrupt personally from its payment, and operated to protect his after-acquired property from being taken in satisfaction of the judgment; but in other respects it remained in full force, and Wells, Norton & Walker had the right to resort to all means conferred by law to enforce its collection, and among these was the right of redemption as judgment creditors.

The decree of the Circuit Court will be affirmed.

MAINE SUPREME JUDICIAL COURT.

ANDERSON
v.
ROBBINS.

(....Me.....)

A mortgagor who, while in possession, verbally leased the premises at a rent payable quarterly, cannot recover from the lessee for the two-and-one-half months' use and occupation preceding the mortgagee's entry and the lessee's attornment to him, where the mortgagee fifteen days before the expiration of the current quarter duly entered and took possession for condition broken, and the tenant on his demand

NOTE.—*Rights of mortgagee in possession.*

Where the prior mortgagee enters upon the land for condition broken, and the lessee thereof attorns to him, the lessee becomes the tenant of the mortgagee; but until such entry and attornment, or until the mortgagee requires the lessee to pay

thereupon agreed to, and at the expiration of the quarter did, pay to him the rent for the whole quarter.

(February 27, 1890.)

RESERVATION upon agreed statement of facts by the Supreme Judicial Court for Waldo County for the opinion of the full court, of an action brought to recover rent alleged to be due and unpaid.

Judgment for defendant.

The case sufficiently appears in the opinion.

Messrs. **Thompson & Dunton** for plaintiff.

Mr **W. H. Fogler** for defendant.

Virgin, *J.*, delivered the opinion of the court:

Assumpsit by a mortgagor of real estate against his tenant under a verbal lease, made after the mortgage, at a rent payable quarterly, for the recovery of two-and-one half months' rent.

The principal question presented is. When a mortgagor in possession verbally leases the premises at a rent payable quarterly, and the mortgagee, fifteen days before the expiration of a current quarter, duly enters and takes possession for condition broken, whereupon, on demand by the mortgagee, the tenant agrees to pay, and, at the end of the current quarter, does pay, to him the rent for the whole quarter, can the mortgagor recover from the lessee for the two-and-one-half months' use and occupation next preceding the mortgagee's entry and lessee's attornment to him.

We are of the opinion that he cannot.

To be sure, a verbal lease of land creates only a tenancy at will, which can be terminated by the parties thereto only in the mode prescribed by Rev. Stat., chap. 94, § 2. Still, until determined, it is sufficient to establish between them the relation of landlord and tenant, the amount of rent to be paid, and the times when payable. *Cameron* v. *Little*, 62 Me. 550.

But, while such a tenancy can be determined by the parties only in the mode mentioned, it may be by one holding the paramount title of mortgagee at any time. *Crosby* v. *Harlow*, 21 Me. 499; *Hill* v. *Jordan*, 30 Me. 367.

For the legal title vests in the mortgagee upon the delivery of the mortgage, and thereupon he is regarded as having all the rights of a grantee in fee, subject to the defeasance. Hence, in the absence of any express or implied agreement in the mortgage or other writing between the parties, the mortgagee has the right of immediate possession before as well as after condition broken. *Gilman* v. *Wills*, 66 Me. 273; Rev. Stat. chap. 90, § 2.

On account of the peculiar relation subsisting between the parties to a mortgage, the mortgagor, though the title be in the mortgagee, cannot be required to pay rent to the latter so long as he is allowed to remain in possession, since his contract is to pay interest and not rent (*Chase* v. *Palmer*, 25 Me. 341, 346; *Noyes* v. *Rich*, 52 Me. 115; *Long* v. *Wade*, 70 Me. 358); "nor has he any power, express or implied," said *Lord* Mansfield, "to let leases not subject to every circumstance of the mortgage." *Keech* v. *Hall*, 1 Doug. 21, 1 Smith, Lead. Cas. *653, 7th Am. ed. 879; *Pope* v. *Biggs*, 9 Barn. & C. 254; Jones, Mortg. §§ 708, 776.

And, if a lease is made by the mortgagor, the lessee becomes liable to the mortgagee for rent accruing due after the latter's entry and the lessee's promise to pay, but not for rent due before such entry and promise, as prior thereto there would be no privity between them. *Evans* v. *Elliot*, 9 Ad. & El. 342; *Crosby* v. *Harlow* and *Hill* v. *Jordan*, *supra; McKircher* v. *Hawley*, 16 Johns. 289; *Stone* v. *Patterson*, 19 Pick. 476; *Smith* v. *Shepard*, 15 Pick. 147; 2 Washb. Real Prop. 3d ed. 131, and cases in *notes*.

After entry by the mortgagee, the lessee cannot be liable to the mortgagor for rent which should thereafter accrue, for rent payable quarterly is in no part due until the stipulated quarter day. *Countess of Plymouth* v. *Throgmorton*, 1 Salk. 65; *Fitchburg Cotton Manufactory Corp.* v. *Melven*, 15 Mass. 268; *Wood* v. *Partridge*, 11 Mass. 488; *Perry* v. *Aldrich*, 13 N. H. 343; *Russell* v. *Fabyan*, 28 N. H. 543.

And while there may be an apportionment of rent as to estate (*Salmon* v. *Matthews*, 8 Mees & W. 827; *Boston & W. R. Corp.* v. *Ripley*, 13 Allen, 421), there can be none as to time (*Ex parte Smyth*, 1 Swanst. 337, note *a;* 2 Greenl. Cruise, title 28, chap. 3; 3 Kent, Com. 470), for the contract is entire,—the rent for the period of time agreed upon is regarded as an indivisible item. *Cameron* v. *Little*, 62 Me. 550.

Hence at common law, if a tenant at will determines the tenancy before rent day, he is bound to pay the whole sum which would have been payable had he continued tenant till that day (*Bowe's Case*, Aleyn, 4); whereas, if the lessor himself determines before the rent day, no rent will be due. Bacon, Abr. 573; *Robinson* v. *Deering*, 56 Me. 357; *Cameron* v. *Little*, *supra*.

But it is urged that the lessor did not terminate this tenancy, and that hence the rule last mentioned does not apply; and furthermore, that the dicta in *Fitchburg Cotton Manufactory Corp.* v. *Melven*, *supra*, and in *Zule* v. *Zule*, 24 Wend. 76, 78, suggesting that a count on *quantum meruit* might be maintained for use and occupation enjoyed by the lessee prior to the mortgagee's entry, should apply. But the tenancy between the mortgagor and his lessee was completely determined by the mortgagee's entry and the lessee's attornment to him, which was equivalent to an eviction by a paramount title. 3 Kent, Com. 464; *Smith* v. *Shepard*, *supra; Welch* v. *Adams*, 1 Met. 494; *Knowles* v. *Maynard*, 13 Met. 352; *Nicholson* v. *Munigle*, 6 Allen, 215; *Fuller* v. *Swett*, Id. 219, *note*.

The tenant's attornment to the mortgagee was no violation of the principle which estops a lessee from denying his lessor's title. *Ryder* v. *Mansell*, 66 Me. 167.

By promising to pay to the mortgagee upon

rent to him, the mortgagee and the lessee are strangers. Holmes v. Turner's Falls Lumber Co. 3 New Eng. Rep. 177, 142 Mass. 590; Smith v. Shepard, 15 Pick. 147; Russell v. Allen, 2 Allen, 42; Welch v. Adams, 1 Met. 494; Haven v. Adams, 4 Allen, 80; Ellis v. Boston, H. & E. R. Co. 107 Mass. 1; Massachusetts H. L. Ins. Co. v. Wilson, 10 Met. 126; Cook v. Johnson, 121 Mass. 326. See note to Cook v. Cooper (Or.) 7 L. R. A. 273.

the latter's rightful entry, the tenant saved the trouble and expense of ejection, which he could not lawfully prevent, and thereby became tenant of the mortgagee, and paid to him the subsequently accruing rent; and neither law nor equity requires him to pay any part of it over again. *Kimball* v. *Lockwood*, 6 R. I. 138, 140.

Moreover, the lease having been made after the mortgage, it was subject to it, and to the entry at will by the mortgagee. Still it was an express agreement, and excluded an implied one. It was not mutually rescinded, but so long as it continued the parties were bound by its terms. No rent became due under its provision which was not paid by the lessee to the lessor. For a part of the last quarter's rent there was no express or implied promise on the part of the lessee to pay to the lessor. *Knowles* v. *Maynard*, 13 Met. 352, 355, is expressly in point.

Judgment for the defendant.

Peters, *Ch. J.*, and **Libbey, Emery** and **Foster,** *JJ.*, concurred.

Joseph W. SYMONDS *et al.*, Walter G. Davis *et al.*, Intervenors,

v.

John Winslow JONES.

(....Me.....)

1. **Labels and trade-marks may be sold and transferred** by the proprietor of a business together with the plant and good will thereof, so as to prevent him from afterwards using them, as formerly, to the detriment of his vendee; and the fact that such proprietor's name or initials form part of them is immaterial.

2. **The breach of a stipulation in an agreement for the sale of the plant,** good will, labels and trade-marks of a business, that the seller shall be employed by the buyer for a certain length of time to manage the business, will not cause a forfeiture of the buyer's exclusive right to use the labels and trade-marks.

3. **An injunction and accounting** will not be granted against one who has wrongfully used labels and trade-marks, in favor of one who has purchased the right to their exclusive use, if the latter has exercised his right in such manner as to mislead the public by causing them to believe that the goods upon which they were placed were the product of his vendor, and had in no way indicated that he had succeeded the original producer and originator of the marks.

4. **Prior improper and misleading use of labels,** afterwards corrected and made right, will not prevent the maintenance of a bill in equity for the protection of the corrected label, at least in favor of mortgagees in possession, the improper use having been by the mortgagors before they were deprived of possession.

5. **New parties complainant** may be admitted from time to time in an equity proceeding as their interests arise, if such admission is for the protection of present rights and does not increase the burden of the defense.

6. **Purchasers of labels and trade-marks** will be restrained from using them so as to lead the public to suppose the goods upon which they appear were packed by their vendors.

(February 1, 1890.)

APPEAL by defendant from a decree of the Supreme Judicial Court for Cumberland County in favor of complainants in a suit brought to enjoin the alleged wrongful use of certain labels and trade-marks, and the engaging in certain business. *Affirmed.*

The facts are fully stated in the opinion.

Messrs. **Benjamin F. Hamilton** and **George F. Haley,** for appellant:

Complainants by their own fraud and misrepresentation have deceived and misled the public, and thereby have forfeited their right to the trade-mark, and all claim for protection in a court of equity.

Upton, Trade-Marks, 98; *Manhattan Medicine Co.* v. *Wood*, 108 U. S. 218 (27 L. ed. 706); *Leather Cloth Co.* v. *American Leather Cloth Co.* 4 DeG. J. & S. 137, 11 H L. Cas. 523; *Connell* v. *Reed*, 128 Mass. 477; *Parlett* v. *Guggenheimer*, 8 Cent. Rep. 796, 67 Md. 542; *Siegert* v. *Abbott*, 61 Md. 276; *Buckland* v. *Rice*, 40 Ohio St. 526; *Stachelberg* v. *Ponce*, 23 Fed. Rep. 430, 128 U. S. 686 (32 L. ed. 569); *Sherwood* v. *Andrews*, 5 Am. L. Reg. N. S. 588; *Delaware & H. Canal Co.* v. *Clark*, 80 U. S. 13 Wall. 311 (20 L. ed. 581).

The inquiry is not only whether the defendant, from his own showing or by proof, has acted unjustly and inequitably, but also whether the complainants, by their allegations and proof, have shown that they are entitled to relief.

Knox v. *Smith*, 45 U. S. 4 How. 298 (11 L. ed. 983).

Mr. **Arthur Steuart,** also for appellant:

Generic names cannot be appropriated as trade-marks.

Lea v. *Deakin*, 11 Biss. 23; *Leclanche Battery Co.* v. *Western Electric Co.* 23 Fed. Rep. 276, and cases cited; *Goodyear's India Rubber Glove Mfg. Co.* v. *Goodyear Rubber Co.* 128 U. S. 598 (32 L. ed. 535).

The words "Winslow's Green Corn," being clearly generic, are public property.

A name alone is not a trade-mark when it is applied to designate, not the article of a particular maker or seller, but the kind or description of thing which is being sold.

Delaware & H. Canal Co. v. *Clark*, 80 U. S. 13 Wall. 311 (20 L. ed. 581); *Thomson* v. *Winchester*, 19 Pick. 214; *Wolfe* v. *Goulard*, 18 How. Pr. 64; *Sherwood* v. *Andrews*, 5 Am. L. Reg. N. S. 588; *Candee* v. *Deere*, 54 Ill. 439; *Singer Mfg. Co.* v. *Wilson*, L. R. 2 Ch. Div. 434; *Cocks* v. *Chandler*, L. R. 11 Eq. 446; *Ford* v. *Foster*, L. R. 7 Ch. 611; *Burke* v. *Cassin*, 45 Cal. 467; *Burnett* v. *Phalon*, 9 Bosw. 192; *Binninger* v. *Wattles*, 28 How. Pr. 206; *Singleton* v. *Bolton*, 3 Doug. 293; *Canham* v. *Jones*, 2 Ves. & B. 218; *Goodyear's India Rubber Glove Mfg. Co.* v. *Goodyear Rubber Co.* 128 U. S. 598 (32 L. ed. 535).

Mr. **W. L. Putnam,** for appellees:

The evidence in this case shows that the com-

NOTE.—Trade-marks and trade-names. See *note* to Gato v. El Modelo Cigar Mfg. Co. (Fla.) 6 L. R. A. 723; Laughman v. Piper (Pa.) 5 L. R. A. 599; Cigar Makers Protective Union v. Conhaim (Minn.) 3 L. R. A. 125; Rumford Chemical Works v. Muth (Md.) 1 L. R. A. 44; Coats v. Merrick Thread Co. (N. Y.) 1 L. R. A. 616.

mon words "Globe" and "World Renowned," in the connection in which they are here used, answer all the conditions necessary to constitute them proper trade-marks.

Royal Baking Powder Co. v. *Royal Chemical Co.* Am. Trade-Mark Cas. (Price & S.) 1; *Royal Baking Powder Co.* v. *Mason*, Id. 86; *Royal Baking Powder Co.* v. *Sherrill*, 59 How. Pr. 17; *Royal Baking Powder Co.* v. *Jenkins*, 2 N. Y. Monthly L. Bull. 53; *Royal Baking Powder Co.* v. *McQuade*, Am. Trade-Mark Cas. (Price & S.) 401; *Royal Baking Powder Co.* v. *Vouwie*, Id. 1065; *Royal Baking Powder Co.* v. *Davis*, 33 Pat. Off. Gaz. 1391, 26 Fed. Rep. 293; *McLean* v. *Fleming*, 96 U. S. 245 (24 L. ed. 828).

An infringer cannot avail himself of another person's trade-mark by simply adding to it that the article was manufactured by himself.

Menendez v. *Holt*, 128 U. S. 514 (32 L. ed. 526).

When a person owns a business, the establishment at which the business is carried on and trade-marks which carry his own name, disposition of the establishment, the business and the trade marks in one lump, as was done in this case, will entitle the purchaser to use the name of the seller on the trade-mark, and the seller cannot use the trade-mark with his own name on it.

Hoxie v. *Chaney*, 3 New Eng. Rep. 709, 143 Mass. 592; *Kidd* v. *Johnson*, 100 U. S. 617 (25 L. ed. 769); *Manhattan Medicine Co.* v. *Wood*, 108 U. S. 218 (27 L. ed. 706).

Jurisdiction to restrain the publishing of notices and the issuing of circulars is merely incidental to the larger jurisdiction to protect trade-marks and good will.

High, Inj. § 1181; *Boston Diatite Co.* v. *Florence Mfg. Co.* 114 Mass. 69; *Bradbury* v. *Dickens*, 27 Beav. 53; 3 Chitty, Eq. Index 4th ed. p. 2770; *Mogford* v. *Courtenay*, 45 L. T. N. S. 303; *Harper* v. *Pearson*, 3 L. T. N. S. 547; *Stevens* v. *Paine*, 18 L. T. N. S. 600; *Massam* v. *Thorley's Cattle Food Co.* L. R. 14 Ch. Div. 748.

Emery, J., delivered the opinion of the court:

This is an equity appeal. The material facts found by the court are these:

John Winslow Jones, the respondent, for several years prior to 1880 had been carrying on extensively the business of preserving or "canning" meat, fish and vegetables at various factories in Maine, New Brunswick and Prince Edward Island, and had built up a large trade in the canned products in the United States and Canada. The particular process of canning was known as the "Winslow Process," having been originated by one Isaac Winslow. The business above stated was started by Nathan Winslow & Co., and was succeeded to by the defendant, who greatly extended it. Among the labels used by him to designate the products were two in particular. One was known as the "red" label, being of a red color, and bearing the figure of an ear of corn, the words "Winslow's Green Corn," and "John Winslow Jones, Portland, Maine," and also the figure of a globe, with the words "World Renowned" and "Trade-Mark" thereon. The other was known as the "yellow" label, being of a yellow color, and bearing the figure of a globe, with the letters "J. W. J." thereon, and the words "Globe Trade-Mark Brand," "Winslow's Green Corn," "World Renowned," etc. While these particular labels were used on canned corn, the figure of the globe and the various words and phrases on these labels were used on labels for other products, and on the letter-heads and circulars used in the business.

In the latter part of 1879, Jones procured the organization in England of the J. Winslow Jones Company, Limited, for the purchasing, carrying on and further extending the same business; and in pursuance of an agreement he conveyed to the new company, March 1, 1880, all his said factories, machinery and plant generally, and also, as admitted by Jones in his answer, all the labels, trade marks and good will of the business. Jones further admits that such conveyance included the "red" label and the "yellow" label above described.

It was stipulated in the agreement referred to that Jones should be employed by the limited company as its managing director in America, for ten years, at a fixed salary, and should not for the same time carry on a similar business within fifty miles of any factory of the company, nor send any similar canned goods to any part of Europe.

To secure certain debentures, the limited company made to trustees, Bacon and Herring, a conveyance of all the property received from Jones, including the business, good will, labels and trade-marks. The limited company, subject, of course, to this trust deed, took possession of all the property and plant conveyed, and carried on the same business, with Jones as managing director in America, until 1882, and during that time made use of the same labels and trade marks to designate their products. In 1882 the limited company, becoming financially embarrassed, transferred all the property, plant and business, including labels and good will, to Charles P. Mattocks, subject, of course, to the trust deed to secure debentures. It was agreed by the company, the trustees and Mattocks that the last-named should take charge of the property and carry on the business, which he did, using the same labels and trade-marks to designate the products of the factories so managed by him. This arrangement for Mattocks to take charge of the business was assented to by the debenture holders, including Jones, who was a large holder. In 1883 Mattocks leased the property, plant and good will to the Winslow Packing Company, and gave it written licenses to use, during the lease, the labels and trade marks which had been used in the business. Mattocks was president and manager of this new company. The company used to some extent these "red" and "yellow" labels, among others, as they had been before used, until 1885, when they had printed across the face of the labels the words, "Winslow Packing Company, Successor to."

December 8, 1886, the original trustees, under the deeds to secure the debentures, transferred the trust, and conveyed all the properties, including good will and labels, etc., to J. W. Symonds and Edward Moore, the complainants, who thereafterwards held the properties, etc., under the same trusts.

After the assignment of the J. Winslow

Jones Company, Limited, in 1882, Jones was no longer employed as managing director, and subsequently, as early as 1884, he at various places in the United States, and within the limits of the trade or custom of the former business, but not within fifty miles of any of its factories, engaged in the same kind of business. In this new business, to designate his new products, he made use of some labels, similar in color and style to the old "red" and "yellow" labels of the former business. The figure of an ear of corn, the figure of a globe, the words, "John Winslow Jones, Portland, Maine," "Successor to Nathan Winslow & Co." "Winslow's Green Corn," "World Renowned," "Trade-Mark," "Globe Brand," and the initials "J. W. J.," were used on these new labels. There were some minor differences between the old and new labels, but they were practically similar. Jones also used in his new business practically the same style of letter-heads that he had used in the old business, and which had been used by his assignees, the limited company, and its successors. The letter-heads had on them the words "Winslow's World Renowned Green Corn," and the figure of a globe, with the words "Trade-Mark." Jones also issued circulars, claiming the right to the sole use of the globe trade-mark and the old labels, and denying any right in the assignees of the limited company.

This conduct of Mr. Jones, as to labels, letter-heads, etc., disturbed the trade, and lessened the sale of the product of the old factories, and injured the business of those claiming under his assignees, the limited company. Whereupon Messrs. Symonds and Moore, as trustees for the debenture holders, and joining Mattocks and the Winslow Packing Company as parties, filed this bill in equity against Jones, praying for an injunction to restrain Jones from engaging in a similar business within fifty miles of any of their factories, from selling canned goods in Europe, and from using letter-heads or labels similar to or in colorable imitation of those used by him in the old business, and by him sold to the limited company. The bill also prayed for an account. The court, held by a single justice with the equity powers of a chancellor, sustained the bill, and granted a perpetual injunction as prayed for, but made no order for accounting. The respondent thereupon appealed to the law court, sitting as an appellate equity court.

All controversies over the facts are settled by our finding of facts, as above stated, and it only remains to consider the legal and equitable principles by which, upon the facts found, the case is to be determined.

Every business man feels a natural and honorable pride in the articles produced by him, and in the business he builds up. He naturally gives some particular name to the product of his invention, of his factories, farms, mines or vineyards, to distinguish them from similar products of others, and uses peculiar labels and marks upon his products to identify them as his own. The public come to associate these names labels and marks with the products of some particular origin or ownership, or of some particular factory, farm, etc. It is clear that such names, etc., thus become convenient for the consumer, and valuable to the producer, and that both the consumer and the producer should be protected against their use by other parties upon other similar products. They become valuable according to the familiarity of the public with them, and the excellence of the product designated by them. The law justly recognizes such names, labels and marks as important attributes or appurtenances of a business, and as proper to be transferred with any sale or transfer of the business and its plant.

Words, descriptive of the article, or indicative of the general locality of its production, cannot, of course, be appropriated by one producer to his exclusive use. Every producer of the same kind of articles can use upon his products any words descriptive of the quality of the articles, or indicative of the county or town where produced, however long time the same words may have been used by others. A man may always describe his products, and tell where they were produced. The same may be said of any color upon a label, for every label must have some color, and the number of colors is limited. Such words and marks, however, as by their own meaning, or by association in the public mind, indicate, not the quality of an article, but its origin or ownership,—the person by whom, or the factory in which, it was produced,—become appropriated in their use exclusively to the originator or owner of such articles. No other person can lawfully use them to designate other similar articles of different origin or ownership. *McLean* v. *Fleming*, 96 U. S. 245 [24 L. ed. 828]; *Delaware & H. Canal Co.* v. *Clark*, 80 U. S. 13 Wall. 311 [20 L. ed. 581]; *Goodyear's India Rubber Glove Mfg. Co.* v. *Goodyear Rubber Co.* 128 U. S. 598 [32 L. ed. 535]; *Amoskeag Mfg. Co.* v. *Trainer*, 101 U. S. 51 [25 L. ed. 993]; *Godillot* v. *Harris*, 81 N. Y. 263.

The respondent urges that most, if not all, the words and symbols on the "red" and "yellow" labels in question are such as cannot, under the principles above stated, be exclusively appropriated by the complainants as against him. He claims that such of the words and symbols as are generic, or descriptive, or do not indicate the origin, or that the ownership is in the complainants, are free to all, and that he cannot be restrained from using them. In this class he places "World Renowned," "Trade-Mark," "Only Reliable Brand," etc. The complainants practically concede that such words could not be exclusively appropriated by one producer.

The respondent further claims that the words, "Winslow's Green Corn," do not, under the facts, indicate the origin or ownership of the products, but simply that they are prepared by a process originated by Isaac Winslow, and known to the trade as the "Winslow Process;" that this process was never effectually patented, and was not patentable; and hence anyone could use it, and could use any apt words to indicate that his product was by that process. He argues that "Winslow's Green Corn" are apt words for that purpose, and that they indicate the process only. The complainants concede that the process originated with Isaac Winslow, and was never effectually patented, but they insist that the words "Winslow's Green Corn," under the facts, do in themselves and by association indicate that the articles upon which they are placed are produced from the plant of Winslow or his successors in the business. Many authorities are cited by counsel on each side of this controversy.

The respondent further urges that the words "John Winslow Jones" constitute his name, and that the letters "J. W. J." are the initials of his name, and were intended to represent his name and initials; and that no one else can acquire the right to use them, or to prevent his using them. The complainants insist that the respondent should not use the words "John Winslow Jones, Portland, Maine," since he no longer carries on this business in Portland, Me., and they do carry it on there; that the use by the respondent of these words combined injures their business, in that it tends to mislead the public into believing that the respondent's goods are the product of the old, well-known factories. The complainants further reply that, whatever other use the respondent may make of the letters "J. W. J.," for him to use them on the figure of a globe has the same injurious effect.

The complainants, however, do not rest their case on the ground that they have appropriated and used these words and symbols on the "red" and "yellow" labels, and that such words and symbols are capable of exclusive appropriation. They place their case on the ground that, whatever the character of these words and symbols, they were devised and used by the respondent as the labels and trade marks of his business, and as such were sold by him for a valuable consideration to the purchasers of his plant and business. The complainants, representing these purchasers, urge, and the facts show, that the respondent—by selling the good will of the business, and the labels and marks used by him to designate the products of the business—promised, for a consideration, not to use such labels or marks for himself, and, for the same consideration, promised that the purchasers should have the exclusive use, so far as he was concerned. It is argued that whatever may be the rights of the complainants against third parties, unaffected by any contract, they have acquired, by valid contract from this respondent, the right to the exclusive use, as against him, of these labels, and the words and symbols upon them; and that his use of them, or of any colorable imitation of them, is a violation of his contract, which an equity court can and should prevent.

What is known as the "good will" of the business is recognized by the law as a proper subject of sale or contract, in connection with a transfer of a business plant. An established business, with plants and products well known to the trade, has a money value often far above that of its mere plant, and this is often the controlling motive for the purchase. Labels, trade-marks, particular words and phrases devised or used to distinguish or identify the products of the plant, and associated with such products in the public mind, are in like manner usually transferred with the plant, and are regarded as valuable acquisitions for the purchasers. They are, equally with the good will, proper subjects of such sale and contract. The name or initials of the originator or owner of the business, when used on labels and as trade-marks in the business, may thereby have a value, and so may be included in a sale of the business, so far at least as to prevent the vendor afterwards using them in like manner on other similar products, to the detriment of his vendee.

These propositions are supported and illustrated by authorities.

In *Kidd* v. *Johnson*, 100 U. S. 617 [25 L. ed. 769], S. N. Pike adopted as a trade mark for his whiskey the words, "S. N. Pike's Magnolia Whiskey, Cincinnati, Ohio," inclosed in a circle. He took several partners into the business, but retained his individual ownership of the plant and the trade-mark. The firm, Pike being a member, removed the business to New York, and Pike sold the Cincinnati plant and trade-marks to Mills, Johnson & Co., who entered upon the business with that plant, and used the same label and trade-mark before used by S. N. Pike, and the various firms with which he was associated. Pike dying, his surviving partners undertook to use the trade-mark above described. The court held that the purchasers from S. N. Pike had the exclusive right to use the trade-mark, and enjoined the defendants' use.

In *Burton* v. *Stratton*, 12 Fed. Rep. 696, two brothers, Stratton, originated a yeast, and adopted as a trade-mark the figures of two heads (portraits of one of them with a twin brother) in an oval setting, with the words, "Twin Brothers' Improved Dry Hop Yeast." The brothers, the proprietors, sold the business and the trade-mark to Burton, who carried on the same business, and used the same trade-mark. Subsequently one of the Strattons began making yeast, and used the words or name, "Twin Brothers' Dry Hop Yeast." The use of this trade-mark by Stratton was enjoined. Brown, *J.*, said that the cases were numerous in which it had been held that a party may lawfully sell, not only a trade-mark indicative of origin in himself, but even the right to use his own name, in connection with a particular business.

In *Pepper* v. *Labrot*, 8 Fed. Rep. 29, the right to use the words "Old Oscar Pepper" was held to pass by an assignment of the plant and business, even as against Pepper himself, the former proprietor, who had set up a separate establishment in another county.

In *Skinner* v. *Oakes*, 10 Mo. App. 45, Oakes had originated a business of making and selling a candy called "Oakes' Candy." He took a partner, Probasco, and the firm carried on the same business. He afterwards sold to Probasco all his interest in the property, business and trade-marks. Probasco's title passed to Skinner. It was held that Oakes should be restrained from using the name "Oakes' Candy," in a new candy business set up by him.

In *Hoxie* v. *Chaney*, 143 Mass. 592, 3 New Eng. Rep. 709, A. N. Hoxie had originated and carried on a business of making and selling soaps, and used for label and trade-mark the phrases "A. N. Hoxie's Mineral Soap," and "A. N. Hoxie's Pumice Soap." He took Pegram into partnership, and afterwards sold to him all the plant, business and good will. Pegram then formed a partnership with Chaney. It was held that Hoxie, having sold and been paid for the names and marks applied to the soap, could not use them in a new soap business.

In *Churton* v. *Douglas*, Johns. Eng. Ch. 174, the complainant and respondent had carried on a manufacturing business under the firm name of "John Douglas & Co." Douglas sold to Churton all his interests in the plant, business and good will, and afterwards formed a new partnership with another person in the same kind of business, under the same firm name, "John Douglas & Co." The new firm was restrained from using that name.

But the respondent contends that this case is not within the above principles, even if they are correctly stated. He contends that any transfer of good will, labels and trade-marks by him to the limited company was conditional upon his being employed for ten years as managing director of that company in America; and that his discharge at the end of two years worked a forfeiture of the right to the exclusive use of the labels and trade-marks. No such condition of forfeiture was expressed in words in the instrument of conveyance, nor in the preliminary agreement of sale, and forfeitures are not favored in the judicial interpretation of writings. We think the agreement for hiring was an independent agreement, so far as the conveyance and transfer of the property, good will and trade-mark were concerned. As well, we think, might Jones claim a forfeiture of all the property conveyed as of this part of it. We do not think it was intended that the property or the business or its good will should revert to Jones, if for any reason he should be discharged from the employ of the limited company before the expiration of the ten years.

The respondent again contends, and stoutly, that the complainants should not have the protection of the law and of this court for these labels, for the reason that they, or the persons managing the property and the business, since he left the employ of the limited company, have so used the labels and marks as to mislead the public into believing that the goods were manufactured or prepared by him. The facts do show that the limited company, and, after it, Mattocks and the Winslow Packing Company, used the "red" or "yellow" labels more or less without change up to 1885, when the latter company printed across the face of such of these labels as it did use the words, "Winslow Packing Co., Successor to." Such use of the labels, without words indicating that Jones had personally left the business, and indicating a change of ownership, would evidently mislead the public as to the manufacturer of the goods, and hence should not receive protection from the court. It would wrong Jones, as well as the public. *Stachelberg* v. *Ponce*, 23 Fed. Rep. 430, 128 U. S. 686 [32 L. ed. 569]; *Manhattan Medicine Co.* v. *Wood*, 108 U. S. 218 [27 L. ed. 706].

It is plain that, while thus using the labels, the parties complainant in interest could not maintain a bill for an injunction against their use by the respondent.

The facts further show, however, that, before the filing of the bill, the proprietors of the labels refrained from using them, or made such additions to those they did use as clearly to indicate that the ownership of the business had changed, and that the successors to Jones, instead of Jones himself, were producing the goods. At the time of filing this bill, none of the complainants were offending in this respect, but all seem to have been dealing fairly with the public. Of course they cannot have any damages or accounting for things done by the respondent while they were themselves offending, but, if they are now themselves doing equity, they may ask the court to require the respondent to do equity also.

In *Manhattan Medicine Co.* v. *Wood*, *supra*, the decision adverse to the complainant was put on the ground that the misrepresentation had been and was being continued. We find no authority deciding that a prior improper and misleading use of labels, afterwards corrected and made right, should bar a bill in equity brought for the protection of the corrected label. In this case we think the improper use was inadvertent; and, now that such use has been corrected for several years, it seems to us inequitable that Jones should continue to make use of the labels and trade-marks (or colorable imitations of them) which he sold for a satisfactory consideration to the complainants' predecessors.

In coming to this conclusion upon this question, however, we bear in mind that the improper use complained of was not by the complainant trustees, nor their predecessors in the trust, nor by the debenture holders, but by Mattocks and the Winslow Packing Company, who were practically mortgagors in possession, while the trustees and debenture holders were mortgagees out of possession. The innocent debenture holders have taken possession since the filing of this bill, as will hereafter be stated, and are now asking for protection. Perhaps, had the original complainants or those now prosecuting been guilty of the misconduct, the result might have been different. We do not say.

The respondent also raises a question of equity pleading which we have maturely considered. Pending this suit, the debenture holders have caused all the property held by the original complainants as trustees, including the labels, trade-marks, etc., to be sold by the trustees to enforce the trusts and realize on the assets. At such sale, duly held, Messrs. Davis, Baxter & Davis were the purchasers, and the trustees conveyed to them all the property and rights held by them under the various trust deeds. These purchasers thereupon applied to the court for leave to come in as parties complainant, and further prosecute the suit. Leave was granted, and they were admitted as intervening complainants. To which order the respondent excepted. We do not see any objection to the admission of these new parties. Equity procedure is sufficiently elastic to admit new parties as their interests accrue. The purpose of their admission in this case is not to obtain a declaration of future rights, as argued by the respondent, but to obtain a declaration of present rights, and the prevention of future wrongs. The respondent is not prejudiced. The burden of the defense is not increased. The issues are not changed. The subject matter remains the same, and the judgment must be the same, it being apparent that no accounting can be had in either case.

Our conclusion is that the intervening complainants are properly made parties, and that equity requires in their behalf that the respondent should be perpetually restrained by injunction as set forth in the decree appealed from.

We think, however, it is the duty of the complainants to the respondent, as well as to the public, to refrain from using the labels in such manner and form as might lead the public to suppose that the goods packed by them were packed by the respondent. They should strike from their letter-heads, circulars and labels any words indicating that the goods were prepared by John Winslow Jones, and, if they use his name, should add such words as clearly indicate that the goods are not prepared by him, but by them as his successors. This duty should be declared and made imperative in the decree, or in the supplemental decree, modifying the former decree. As the respondent was compelled to appeal to obtain this modification of the decree, so as to prevent improper, misleading use of his name,—a modification we think he is entitled to,—we think he should recover the costs since the appeal, to be set off against the complainants' costs to the time of the appeal.

Decree affirmed, and case remanded for additional decree in accordance with this opinion.

Peters, *Ch. J.*, and **Walton, Virgin, Foster** and **Haskell,** *JJ.*, concurred.

CALIFORNIA SUPREME COURT.

E. McDANIEL, *Appt.*,
v.
M. CUMMINGS, *Respt.*

(83 Cal. 515.)

1. **An easement for the discharge of surface water** upon lower land adjoining is not given by Code Civ. Proc., § 801. That section is a mere definition of easements appurtenant, and does not prescribe or regulate the manner of acquiring them.

2. **Overflow water from the river** may be kept off from land at a distance from the river by a barrier or embankment, although this may set it back on land nearer the river, if the owner of the latter will not co-operate with those behind him in erecting a levee on the bank to protect all the lands from such overflow.

(March 13, 1890.*)

APPEAL by plaintiff from an order of the Superior Court for Colusa County dissolving a temporary injunction restraining defendant from maintaining an embankment or dam in such a manner as to cause certain water to set back onto plaintiff's land. *Affirmed.*

*An opinion was handed down in this case September 12, 1889, in conformity to a decision reversing the order of the lower court. A rehearing was subsequently had and the opinion given here handed down. The former opinion is therefore omitted. [Rep.]

The case sufficiently appears in the opinion.

Mr. **H. M. Albery,** for appellant:

The superior or dominant owner has an easement in the land of the inferior or servient owner for the free and uninterrupted flowage upon and across the lands of the latter of all surface waters naturally collecting or accumulating upon the lands of the former and the interference by either owner with the natural flowage of such waters in such manner as to cause detriment to the other is actionable.

Osburn v. *Connor*, 46 Cal. 347; Gould, Waters, § 266 and *note 7;* Angell, Watercourses, 7th ed. §§ 108 *a*–108 *k;* Washb. Easem. pp. 427–433, *Livingston* v. *McDonald*, 21 Iowa, 160; *Ross* v. *Clinton*, 46 Iowa, 606; *Tootle* v. *Clifton*, 22 Ohio St. 247; *Butler* v. *Peck*, 16 Ohio St. 334; *Martin* v. *Riddle*, 26 Pa. 415; *Kauffman* v. *Griesemer*, 26 Pa. 407; *Hays* v. *Hinkleman*, 68 Pa. 324; *Earl* v. *De Hart*, 12 N. J. Eq. 280; *Martin* v *Jett*, 12 La. 501, 32 Am. Dec. 121; *Gillham* v. *Madison County R. Co.* 49 Ill. 484; *Alton & U. A. H. R. & C. Co.* v. *Deitz*, 50 Ill. 210, *Gormley* v. *Sanford*, 52 Ill. 158; *Hicks* v. *Silliman*, 93 Ill. 255; *Beard* v. *Murphy*, 37 Vt. 99; *Overton* v. *Sawyer*, 1 Jones, L. 308, 62 Am.

NOTE.—*Easement and servitude; flowage of water.*

An easement is a right which one person has to the use of the land of another for a specific purpose. See *note* to Nowlin v. Whipple (Ind.) 6 L. R. A. 159.

Land on a lower level owes a natural servitude to that on a higher level. See *note* to Vannest v. Fleming (Iowa) 8 L. R. A. 277.

Easements generally. See *note* to Illinois Cent. R. Co. v. Houghton (Ill.) 1 L. R. A. 213.

The term "natural easement" is applicable, especially to the case of flowing water; but an easement, when technically considered, is an interest which one man has in an estate of another, by grant or by prescription. Scriver v. Smith, 1 Cent. Rep. 767, 100 N. Y. 471.

An easement may be acquired by prescription, by which water collecting upon the land of one person must be allowed to overflow the lands of an adjacent proprietor; but a land owner has no right, by digging ditches or tiling drains, to empty out sag holes into this ravine upon the land of an adjacent proprietor; and the latter is entitled to an injunction to restrain the flowage in excess of the natural overflow. Gregory v. Bush, 7 West. Rep. 169, 64 Mich. 37.

The owner of land upon a natural stream has no right to construct an embankment which will at times of ordinary floods cause the swollen current to overflow, invade and destroy the lands of another proprietor. Crawford v. Rambo, 4 West. Rep. 445, 44 Ohio St. 279.

A person having the right of flowage through another's land, while not exercising his right, has no right to interfere with ordinary farm fences maintained by the owner of the servient estate for the protection of his land. Smith v. Langewald, 1 New Eng. Rep. 449, 140 Mass. 205.

The superior owner may improve his lands by throwing increased waters upon his inferior, through the natural and accustomed channels; which is a most important principle, in respect not only to agriculture, but to mining operations also. Pennsylvania Coal Co. v. Sanderson, 4 Cent. Rep. 481, 113 Pa. 126.

A land owner upon whose lands surface water accumulates by the natural elevation of the land cannot, by means of drains and ditches, concentrate the water and discharge it upon the land of a lower owner to the latter's damage. Weddell v. Hapner (Ind.) May 15, 1890.

Dec. 170; *Gillison* v. *Charleston*, 16 W. Va. 298; *Gannon* v. *Hargadon*, 10 Allen, 106, 87 Am. Dec. 625, and *note*; *Gibbs* v. *Williams*, 25 Kan. 210, 37 Am. Rep. 241; *Burnett* v. *Nicholson*, 72 N. C. 334; *Porter* v. *Durham*, 74 N. C. 767; *Little Rock & Ft. S. R. Co.* v. *Chapman*, 39 Ark. 463, 43 Am. Rep. 281; *Inman* v. *Tripp*, 11 R. I. 520; *Goldsmith* v. *Elsas*, 53 Ga. 186; *McCormick* v. *Kansas City, St. J. & C. B. R. Co.* 70 Mo. 359, 35 Am. Rep. 431; *Shane* v. *Kansas City, St. J. & C. B. R. Co.* 71 Mo. 237, 36 Am. Rep. 481; *Boynton* v. *Longley*, 19 Nev. 69, 3 Am. St. Rep. 781; *Brown* v. *McAllister*, 39 Cal. 573; *West* v. *Girard*, not reported but given in table of unreported cases in 65 Cal.

One must so use his own rights as not to infringe upon the rights of another.

Civ. Code, § 3514; *Little Rock & Ft. S. R. Co.* v. *Chapman*, 39 Ark. 463; Pothier, Customs of New Orleans, title 13; Angell, Watercourses, § 108*e*; *Gillham* v. *Madison County R. Co.* 49 Ill. 488, 95 Am. Dec. 628.

The right of the servient tenant to manage the surface waters must be exercised in such way as not to interfere with the free flowage of surface waters from the lands of the dominant owner.

Civ. Code, § 3514; *Livingston* v. *McDonald*, 21 Iowa, 160.

The waters flowing across plaintiff's land were surface waters, within the proper meaning of that expression.

McCormick v. *Kansas City, St. J. & C. B. R. Co.* 70 Mo. 359, 35 Am. Rep. 435; *Gormley* v. *Sanford*, 52 Ill. 160; *Shane* v. *Kansas City, St. J. & C. B. R. Co.* 71 Mo. 237, 36 Am. Rep. 485; *Taylor* v. *Fickas*, 64 Ind. 167, 31 Am. Rep. 117.

While a riparian owner has a legal right to protect himself and his property against the encroachments of a navigable river, yet in so doing he must exercise due care and caution that he cause the adjacent land owner no direct or immediate damage: neither must he obstruct the flow of the water in the stream.

Montgomery v. *Locke*, 72 Cal. 75; *Barnes* v. *Marshall*, 68 Cal. 569; *West* v. *Taylor*, 16 Or. 165. See also *Livingston* v. *McDonald*, 21 Iowa, 160.

Messrs. **John H. Harrington** and **Edwin Swinford**, for respondent:

The doctrine of the common law is that there exists no natural easement, or servitude, in favor of the owner of the superior or higher ground or fields, as to mere surface water.

Chatfield v. *Wilson*, 28 Vt. 49; *Dickinson* v. *Worcester*, 7 Allen, 19; *Greeley* v. *Maine Cent R. Co.* 53 Me. 200; *Bowlsby* v. *Speer*, 31 N. J. L. 351; *Swett* v. *Cutts*, 50 N. H. 439, 9 Am. Rep. 276.

The tendency is to limit the servitudes which a lower field owes to an upper one in respect to water, to such as flows in a defined watercourse, and not to extend it to such as falls upon the surface in the form of rain or melting snow, although from the nature of the surface such water, when it does fall, flows in a uniform course or direction.

Washb. Easem. 3d ed. p. 454; *Franklin* v. *Fisk*, 13 Allen, 211; *Taylor* v. *Fickas*, 64 Ind. 167; *New Albany & S. R. Co.* v. *Peterson*, 14 Ind. 112; *Greencastle* v. *Hazelett*, 23 Ind. 186; *Emery* v. *Lowell*, 104 Mass. 16; *Turner* v. *Dartmouth*, 13 Allen, 291, 293; *Flagg* v. *Worcester*, 13 Gray, 601; *Parks* v. *Newburyport*, 10 Gray, 28; *Hoyt* v. *Hudson*, 27 Wis. 656, 9 Am. Rep. 473; *Pettigrew* v. *Evansville*, 25 Wis. 223; *Delhi* v. *Youmans*, 50 Barb. 316; *Waffle* v. *New York Cent. R. Co.* 58 Barb. 413; *Chatfield* v. *Wilson* and *Bowlsby* v. *Speer*, *supra*; *Swett* v. *Cutts*, 50 N. H. 439; *Stewart* v. *Clinton*, 79 Mo. 603; *Benson* v. *Chicago & A. R. Co.* 78 Mo. 504; *Abbott* v. *Kansas City, St. J. & C. B. R. Co.* 83 Mo. 271, 53 Am. Rep. 581; *Greeley* v. *Maine Cent. R. Co.* 53 Me. 200; *Lamb* v. *Reclamation Dist.* 73 Cal. 125.

Ogburn v. *Connor*, 46 Cal. 347, has already been overruled in part, and should be *in toto*.

See *Osgood* v. *Eldorado W. & D. G. Min. Co.* 56 Cal. 571; *Broder* v. *Natoma Water & Min. Co.* 100 U. S. 274 (25 L. ed. 790).

In the case at bar the waters came from the Sacramento River, where the adjacent owner has an undisputed right to confine them by means of levees. The adjacent owner has control of the source.

See *Lamb* v. *Reclamation Dist. supra*.

Having control over the source, he cannot refuse to prevent the flow himself and then enjoin others from protecting themselves against it.

Ibid.; *Rex* v. *Sewer Comrs.* 8 Barn. & C. 355.

Beatty, *Ch. J.*, delivered the opinion of the court:

Defendant owns the west half of a certain section, No. 26, in Colusa County. Plaintiff owns land adjoining on the west. Still further to the west, at a distance of about two miles from plaintiff's land, the Sacramento River flows from north to south. The land next the river is the highest, there being a gradual descent from the river bank to and beyond the land of defendant. When the river rises above the level of its banks, as it generally does several times during every rainy season, the water flows off to the east or southeast, across the land of plaintiff and other lands similarly situated, to and across the land of defendant and other lands in the same relative situation. It does not flow in any narrow or defined channel or channels, but in a broad sheet, covering a wide surface. When the river falls below the level of the banks the overflow cannot, of course, find its way directly back into the stream, and consequently the lands near the river are drained by the spread and flow of water towards the east and southeast, across the lower lands, such as those of defendant. Left unobstructed in their natural and accustomed flow, these waters soon pass beyond the plaintiff's lands, leaving them fit for cultivation. But recently the defendant, without intending to injure the plaintiff, and acting upon the bona fide belief that he had the right so to do, commenced, and was proceeding to complete, a levee or embankment along his west line, the necessary effect of which will be to prevent the flood water from passing over his land, and to set it back upon the plaintiff's land, causing it to cover a larger area thereof, and to remain thereon for a longer period, than it otherwise would. The plaintiff thereupon commenced this action to enjoin the defendant from erecting or maintaining said levee. A temporary injunction was issued upon the filing of the complaint. Afterwards, on motion of the defendant, and upon affidavits showing the state of facts above set forth, the superior court dissolved the injunction on the ground that the defendant, in erecting and maintaining his levee, was acting within and according to his rights. From this order dissolving the injunction plaintiff appealed, and on September 12, 1889, an opinion was filed by this court reversing the order, upon the authority of *Ogburn* v. *Connor*, 46 Cal. 346.

A rehearing was subsequently granted upon petition filed on the part of the defendant in which the correctness of the decision in *Ogburn* v. *Connor* is assailed, as is also the construction which we gave to section 801 of the Civil Code.

I think there can be no doubt that we were in error in holding that section 801 of the Civil Code gives to the owner of higher land an easement for the discharge of surface water upon lower land adjoining. That section merely enumerates the different kinds of burdens or servitudes upon lands that may be attached as incident or appurtenant to the other lands; or, in other words, it is a mere definition of easements appurtenant, and makes no pretense of prescribing or regulating the manner of acquiring them. Among the other easements defined are: "(9) The right of receiving water from or discharging the same upon the land. . . . (11) The right of having water flow without diminution or disturbance of any kind."

Undoubtedly these are easements which may exist as appurtenant or incident to the lands of one, and as servitudes or burdens upon the land of another; but the question here is not as to what an easement or a servitude is, but as to how it is created, and when it attaches. In the solution of this question we derive no assistance from section 801 of the Civil Code. That section is no more authority for saying that the plaintiff has an easement for the discharge of surface water according to its natural flow from his land to that of defendant than it is for saying that he has any other of the seventeen kinds of easements enumerated; as, for instance: "(1) the right of pasture; (2) the right of fishing; (3) the right of taking game; . . . (17) the right of burial." How, then, is the existence of an easement in any particular case to be determined? Ordinarily, an easement is created by contract between the owners of different parcels of land,—that is to say, by grant, either express or implied; but with respect to rights such as that in controversy here, the question of easement or no easement depends upon the law defining the mutual rights and obligations of the owners of land in the relative situations of the tracts belonging to the plaintiff and defendant. What, then, was the law applicable to these lands at the date of their acquisition? It does not appear when either of the parties acquired his land, but it is to be presumed it was subsequent to the 18th of April, 1850, at which date it was enacted that "the common law of England, so far as it is not repugnant to or inconsistent with the Constitution of the United States, or the Constitution or laws of the State of California, shall be the rule of decision in all the courts of this State." Stat. 1850, p. 219.

This rule continues in force. Pol. Code, § 4463.

As there is nothing in the Constitution of the United States, or in the Constitution or statute law of this State, to which the common-law rule on this subject—whatever it may be—can be repugnant, it is manifest that the whole question is solved whenever it is determined what the common-law rule is.

In the case of *Ogburn* v. *Connor* this precise question was presented, and it was then determined that "when two parcels of land, belonging to different owners, are adjacent to each other, and one is lower than the other, and the surface water from the higher tract has been accustomed by a natural flow to pass off over the lower tract, the owner of the lower tract cannot obstruct this flow. The owner of the upper tract has an easement to have the water flow over the land below, and the land below is charged with a corresponding servitude." This, of course, was intended as a statement of the common-law rule, for otherwise it could not have been the law of this State. But counsel for respondent contends, and counsel for appellant seems to admit, that it is really a statement of the rule of the Roman civil law, and that it is the exact opposition of the common-law rule. It must be confessed that this proposition seems to be sustained by many of the cases cited in the briefs, and if the question were now to be decided for the first time I should certainly find great difficulty in arriving at the conclusion reached by the court in the case referred to. But that decision was rendered seventeen years ago, following a previous case, not reported, entitled *Castro* v. *Bailey*, and has stood unchallenged ever since. Necessarily, it has become the rule of property and of right respecting interests which have vested during that long interval, and it cannot now be disturbed without manifest injustice to all who have acted upon the faith of it. If it be erroneous, it must nevertheless be upheld upon the principle of *stare decisis*, and so far as our action is concerned, the rule must continue to obtain as it is there laid down.

But counsel for respondent, although originally conceding that the order appealed from must be reversed unless the decision in *Ogburn* v. *Connor* was repudiated, now contend that the cases may be distinguished, and that this order should be affirmed on the principle applied in *Lamb* v. *Reclamation Dist.*, 73 Cal. 125.

In that case this court adopted and applied to the flood waters of our large rivers the principle laid down in the English case of *Rex* v. *Sewer Comrs.*, 8 Barn. & C. 355, with respect to the waters of the sea, viz., that they are a common enemy, against which every man has a right to defend himself, regardless of the fact that the barriers he erects for the protection of his land may cause the flood to rise higher, or flow with greater force upon his neighbor. We think this is the true principle to apply to the case of parties in the relative situation of the plaintiff and defendant here, especially in view of the policy of all our state legislation respecting our overflowed lands. If the owner of the land next to the river will not, either by himself, or in combination with those behind him, erect a levee on the bank, he ought not to be allowed to prevent them from protecting themselves merely because by so doing they prevent his higher land from being drained of the flood waters as rapidly as it otherwise would be. Because his land may be cultivated without artificial protection, he ought not to be allowed to prevent others from using proper means to make their lands productive; and what is true of the owner of the river bank is true in the same sense of each successive owner back of him. It is the interest of all to combine and share the expense of placing a levee on the bank, by which all will be protected; but if those in front will not co-operate with those behind, and will do nothing for themselves, they must not be allowed to stand in the way of those whose necessities compel them to act. There is no necessary conflict between these views, or the principles they sustain, and the decision in *Ogburn* v. *Connor*. That decision refers to surface water having its sources in springs, or descending from the clouds in the form of rain or snow waters; waters, that is to say, which the owner of the higher land cannot keep out by any practicable means. It does not apply to flood waters which the owner of the higher land can restrain by the same means employed by his neighbor. In this case it does not appear that defendant's dam will cause the plaintiff any injury by holding back the rain water falling on his land, or any water except the overflow of the Sacramento River. As against that, we think the defendant is entitled to protect himself, and that the plaintiff, if he finds it necessary, may do the like.

Order affirmed.

We concur: **Paterson, *J.*; Sharpstein, *J.*; Fox, *J.*; McFarland, *J.***

OHIO SUPREME COURT.

LEMBECK, *Plff. in Err.*,
v.
John NYE.

SAME, *Plff. in Err.*,
v.
E. E. ANDREWS.

(47 Ohio St.......)

*1. (a) **A non-navigable inland lake** is the subject of private ownership; and where it is so owned, neither the public, nor an owner of adjacent lands, whose title extends only to the margin thereof, have a right to boat upon, or take fish from, its waters.

(b) **Such riparian proprietor, however, is of right entitled** to the use of the water therein for domestic and agricultural purposes connected with the adjacent land upon which he may reside or be engaged in cultivating.

2. (a) **Where one who owns a tract of land that surrounds and underlies a non-navigable lake,** the length of which is distinguishably greater than its breadth, conveys a parcel thereof that borders on the lake, by a description which makes the lake one of its boundaries, the presumption is that the parties do not intend that the grantor should retain the title to the land between the edge of the water and the center of the lake, and the title of the purchaser, therefore, will extend to the center thereof.

(*Spear and Williams, JJ., dissent.*)

(b) **If, however, the call in the description be to and thence along the margin** of the lake, no such presumption arises, and the title of the purchaser will extend to low-water mark only.

(c) **Or, if the description be by metes and bounds,** no reference being made therein to the lake, then only the land included within the lines as fixed by the terms used by the parties to the deed will pass to the grantee.

3. **Where numerous acts are being committed,** and their continuance threatened, under a claim of right, by one person on the land of another, which acts constitute trespass, and the injury resulting from each act is or would be trifling in amount as compared with the expense of prosecuting actions at law to recover damages therefor, the owner may resort, in the first instance, to a court of equity for appropriate relief.

*Head notes by the COURT.

(May 20, 1890.)

NOTE.—*Property in unnavigable lakes.*

An unnavigable lake, although of considerable size, may be private property, and be subject to the common-law rule as to fresh-water streams. Ledyard v. Ten Eyck, 36 Barb. 102; Gould, Waters, §§ 83, 84.

Although the presumption exists of title in the crown, with respect to the shore and soil under tide waters, yet no such presumption exists in respect to vacant land, like the bed of a lake. Bristow v. Cormican, L. R. 3 App. Cas. 641.

In New Jersey the test by which to determine whether waters are public or private is, at common law, the ebb and flow of the tide. Cobb v. Davenport, 32 N. J. L. 369.

So a fresh-water pond or lake of sufficient depth to float large vessels, but with no navigable outlet and never navigated by large vessels, is private property with respect to its soils and fishings. *Ibid.*

In Pennsylvania a pond is an entirety, and the whole or none of it is private property: if it covers the soil of several owners it is not a private pond. Reynolds v. Com. 93 Pa. 458.

In Massachusetts a licensee from the State to use the waters of a great pond will be protected in such right. Proprietors of Mills v. Braintree Water Supply Co. 4 L. R. A. 272, 149 Mass. 478. See note to Ulbricht v. Eufaula Water Co. (Ala.) 4 L. R. A. 572.

The common-law doctrine of riparian rights is unsuited to the condition of the State of Nevada; there the right of a riparian owner should be determined by the application of the principle of prior appropriations. Reno S. M. & R. Works v. Stevenson (Nev.) 4 L. R. A. 60; Colorado Farmers H. L. C. & Reservoir Co. v. Southworth, 4 L. R. A. 767, 13 Colo. 111.

In some of the Western States owners of lands bordering upon unnavigable lakes own the bed of the lake to its center. Forsyth v. Forsyth, 7 Biss. 201; Ridgway v. Ludlow, 58 Ind. 248; Edwards v. Ogle, 76 Ind. 302; Gould, Waters, § 85.

WRITS of error to the Circuit Court for Medina County to review judgments in favor of defendants in actions brought to enjoin defendants from trespassing upon property alleged to belong to plaintiff. *Reversed.*

Statement by **Bradbury,** *J.:*

The plaintiff in error, who was also the plaintiff in the courts below, brought in the Court of Common Pleas of Medina County two actions, one against the defendant E. E. Andrews, and the other against the defendant John Nye, the pleadings in the two actions being substantially alike, if not exact copies, one of the other.

The plaintiff in his petition set forth that he owned in fee simple, and was entitled to the exclusive possession of, the land that underlies and forms the natural bed of Chippewa Lake in Medina County, Ohio, together with a narrow strip of land that surrounds the same; that the lake was valuable for the purpose of keeping boats and fishing tackle for hire to persons who resort to it for recreation and pleasure; that the defendants, who respectively occupy certain lands that border on the lake, in violation of the rights of the plaintiff, have each fitted out and keep for hire boats and fishing tackle, have let the same to excursionists and pleasure seekers for hire and intend to continue to do so, whereby repeated and constant acts of trespass are being committed and will continue to be committed upon his said property by transient, and in many instances irresponsible, persons; that the defendants are each irresponsible pecuniarily, and that the ordinary actions at law would furnish him no adequate remedy. Whereupon he prays for an injunction and general equitable relief.

Each defendant by an answer filed in the action against him denied that the plaintiff owned in fee simple, or was entitled to the exclusive possession of, the premises in dispute; admits that he keeps and lets for hire boats and fishing tackle from the front of his premises to persons who resort to the lake for pleasure, and claims a right to continue to do so, averring that the same has been done by himself and predecessors for more than twenty-one years, and that for more than forty years the public has resorted to said lake for boating and fishing.

The record does not disclose any of the proceedings in the court of common pleas, but shows that the two actions were tried in the Circuit Court of Medina County upon an agreed statement of facts and a judgment rendered against the plaintiff in each action, who thereupon instituted proceedings in this court to reverse those judgments.

Excluding certain immaterial matters, the agreed statement of facts shows that the Chippewa Lake has an area of about four hundred acres, is oval in form, its length from north to south being about twice as great as its width from east to west, its principal tributary emptying into it at its northerly end and its surplus water escaping by a stream flowing from its southern extremity; its bottom sloping gradually from the shore to its center, where the depth is "considerable;" that its waters are valuable not only for the purpose of letting boats and fishing tackle to pleasure seekers thereupon for hire, but to gather ice from its frozen surface; that it has never been used for navigation but that from very early times hunters and fishermen have resorted to it without license to fish and hunt, and for more than forty years the public have had free access to it for boating, hunting and fishing; that the defendants and their grantors have for more than forty years occupied continuously their respective lands to the water in all its variations, and have enjoyed the free use of the water, in connection with their lands, for the purpose of watering cattle, washing sheep, boating and fishing, and without license or consent from anyone. That the defendants, Andrews and Nye, have constructed on the premises occupied by each buildings and appliances such as are found at pleasure resorts, to which their places are adapted, and the value of which, for such purposes, is dependent upon their right of access to and use of the lake for the purpose of boating and fishing. They keep for hire a large number of small boats, which they let to pleasure seekers and sportsmen resorting to the place, and they derive some profit from such hiring of their boats. In the use of the lake, in connection with the hiring of their boats, they have constructed a temporary dock, extending from the shore occupied by them, into the lake far enough to get beyond shallow water, and at such docks they keep their boats tied when not in use, and from them the public take such

In Wisconsin the owner of land which borders upon a lake is entitled only to the accretions, and to the soil which may be left by recessions of water, and he has no title to the submerged soil. Delaplaine v. Chicago & N. W. R. Co. 42 Wis. 214; Boorman v. Sunnuchs. 42 Wis. 233; Diedrich v. Northwestern U. R. Co. 42 Wis. 248, 47 Wis. 662; Olson v. Merrill, 42 Wis. 203; Wright v. Day, 33 Wis. 260; Shufeldt v. Spaulding. 37 Wis. 662; Mariner v. Schulte, 13 Wis. 692; Jones v. Pettibone, 2 Wis. 308.

Ownership of a strip of the shore of a pond gives no right to fish in the pond as against the owner of the land under the water. Decker v. Baylor (Pa.) March 10, 1890.

Private streams, what are. See *note* to Haines v. Hall (Or.) 3 L. R. A. 610.

Conveyance of land bordering on unnavigable waters.

Deeds in a chain of title plainly indicating that the boundary of the land is the bank of a pond pass no title to the land under the pond, either to the grantees in such deeds or to their grantees or assigns. Holden v Chandler, 61 Vt. 291.

The boundary of land "on the edge of the pond" is not a boundary by a stream which may change by gradual washings and deposits, but the territory is limited by a defined boundary, without regard to the contingent subsidence of the water constituting the pond and thereby leaving the land dry. *Ibid.*

A grant of land bounded on rivers above tide water carries the exclusive right and title of the grantee to the centre of the stream, subject to the easement of navigation. School Trustees v. Schroll, 9 West. Rep. 743. 120 Ill. 509.

An entirely different rule applies when land is conveyed bounded along or upon a natural lake or pond. In such case the grant extends only to the water's edge. *Ibid.*, and authorities cited.

A deed conveying land adjoining a private freshwater stream may make the bank or margin of the water a monument. Gould, Waters, § 200, citing, in *notes*, many cases as instances.

boats for hire. That a public road is opened to the lake along the line between the lands of the two defendants, and they having fitted up their lands for places of resort, and being situated on such public road, resort to the lake was, at the time of the commencement of this action, substantially confined to persons who reached it over the defendants' grounds, they being the only ones having boats for hire and grounds open to the public.

The lands, the title of which is immediately in dispute in these actions, lying between the water's edge of the lake and its center, and in front of the shore land occupied by the defendants, as well as the entire lake and its surrounding lands, as a part of the Western Reserve lands, were, at the time of the division of the Connecticut Land Company, allotted to Samuel Fowler and three others and as early as 1815, by virtue of sundry conveyances of interests and proceedings in partition, the ownership of all such lands was in James Fowler and Samuel Fowler.

That sales of parcels of the entire tract were made from time to time by the Fowlers until all the lands immediately surrounding, or bordering on, the lake were conveyed away by them, the last conveyance thereof bearing date of Jan. 24, 1868. That on Aug. 11, 1876, the Fowlers conveyed to D. H. Ainsworth and A. W. McClure whatever title they then had to the bed of the lake and the lands surrounding it, which title, by subsequent conveyance, is now vested in the plaintiff in error. That the descriptions in the several deeds by which the Fowlers conveyed to purchasers thereof the several parcels of land that surround and border on the lake are not uniform. Some of these descriptions were by metes and bounds only, containing no words referring to, or indicating the existence of, the lake, while others made the margin of the lake a boundary. The descriptions in two of the deeds, however, that to Fred B. Chamberlain and the one to Delanson DeForrest, under whom the defendant Nye claims title by mesne conveyances, expressly make Chippewa Lake one boundary of the land conveyed, though the deed to the lessor of Nye makes the margin of the lake the boundary of the lands which it conveys to him.

Messrs. **Harrison, Olds & Henderson** and **Henderson & Clide** for plaintiff in error.

Messrs. **Boynton, Hale & Horr** for defendants in error.

Bradley, *J.*, delivered the opinion of the court:

The contention between the parties to this action is over their respective rights to and in Chippewa Lake, a non-navigable body of water in Medina County, in this State, having an area of about four hundred acres, oval in form, though its extension from north to south is about twice as great as that from east to west. It is true that the plaintiff in error claims that the waters of the lake have subsided by reason of the deepening of the channel of its natural outlet, whereby a narrow strip of land entirely around the lake has been recovered; but as this claim is not sufficiently supported by the agreed statement of facts to require any consideration of the principles or authorities upon which he founds his claim to title thereto, it will not be further noticed in the decision of the cause.

The lake is situated in the Western Reserve lands, and upon the division of the lands of the Connecticut Land Company was, together with a body of land entirely surrounding it, allotted to Samuel Fowler and three others, and which by sundry conveyances and certain proceedings in partition became the property, in fee simple, of Samuel Fowler and James Fowler as early as the year 1815, to whom all the parties to this proceeding trace title. By the conveyances and proceedings above noticed, the title to the lake, as well as the title to the lands inclosing it, vested in the Fowlers, if it is susceptible of private ownership, which we think it clearly is. *Bristow* v. *Cormican*, L. R. 3 App. Cas. 641, 652.

"A lake which is not really useful for navigation, although of considerable size compared with ordinary fresh-water streams, may be private property." Gould, Waters, § 83; *Ledyard* v. *Ten Eyck*, 36 Barb. 102; *Hogg* v. *Beerman*, 41 Ohio St. 81.

Many other authorities could be cited in support of this proposition, but it is too well settled to require it to be done, even if controverted, which it is not in this action, although material to its determination.

It is agreed that, from an early period in the history of the State, hunters and fishermen, without license, resorted at will to the lake to hunt and fish, and that for more than forty years the public has had free access to it for boating, hunting and fishing. It is not readily perceived how this early and continued custom can be said to cast any material light upon the intention of the parties in respect of the deeds by which the lands around the lake were from time to time conveyed; it can only be material, therefore, as tending to show a dedication of the lake by its owners to the public, and a consequent extinguishment of their private property therein. These facts may constitute a link in the chain of evidence necessary to prove a dedication of the lake to the public, but fall far short of establishing that fact. In truth, when consideration is given to the early customs of the people of this State in this respect —their well-known habit of hunting and fishing upon all lands and waters where fish or game might be found, irrespective of their ownership, or whether inclosed with fences or not—it is apparent that this class of evidence ought to be received and weighed with extreme caution as proof of a dedication to such uses. Private owners are not to be deemed to have devoted their property to uses of this kind simply because they interposed no objections to their neighbors, or even to strangers, hunting and fishing upon it; other circumstances must appear manifesting that it was his intention to do so. Dedication depends upon the intention of the owner to devote his lands to a public use and should be made to appear clearly and satisfactorily. 5 Am. & Eng. Encyclop. Law, 400, 401; *Smith* v. *State*, 23 N. J. L. 712; Washb. Easem. 209.

Here the owner did no act indicating an intention to devote the lake to the use of the public; it does not even appear that the owner had any knowledge that the public was using it in the manner that the agreed statement shows it to have been, in fact, used; and as dedication by parol, or *in pais*, acts by way of estoppel on the proprietor, uses by the public unknown to him can have no appreciable probative force to establish a dedication against him.

The lake, as we have seen, being susceptible of private ownership, and having been allotted to the Fowlers, or to them and others whose title they obtained, upon the division of the Western Reserve lands, and not having been dedicated to the use of the public, passed by the deed made by the Fowlers August 11, 1876, to Ainsworth and McClure, under whom the plaintiff derives title, unless it had already passed to some, or all, of the purchasers of the lands surrounding the lake by virtue of the prior deeds of the Fowlers made to such purchasers. This depends upon the descriptions in those deeds and the rules of law that apply to conveyances of lands bounded upon non-navigable inland lakes. By a series of deeds, the first of which bears date of October 16, 1823, and the last of January 24, 1868, the Fowlers conveyed all the lands that surrounded the lake to various parties, under which the same are now held, and such parts of the lake as may have passed by virtue of these conveyances could not, of course, have been conveyed by a subsequent deed of the Fowlers under which the plaintiff in error derives title; and it is therefore of the first importance to ascertain what those conveyances in fact include, which necessitates a construction of their respective descriptions.

These descriptions may be divided into three classes. In the first class are two deeds, one from James Fowler *et al.* to Delanson De Forrest, the other from James Fowler and wife to Fred B. Chamberlain, wherein the lake itself is made one boundary of the land thereby conveyed; in the second class are four deeds, one from James Fowler to Catharine and Sally Trump, one from James Fowler to Charles Wheeler, one from James Fowler to William Walter and the other from James Fowler to Charles Wright, wherein the margin of Chippewa Lake is made either a corner or one of the boundary lines of the lands conveyed by them respectively; while in the third class are two deeds, one from James Fowler *et al.* to Abraham Fritz; the other from James Fowler *et al.* to Conrad Snyder, in which the lands conveyed are described by metes and bounds only, no reference whatever being made to the lake.

The rule that lands, one boundary of which is a navigable river running through this State, extend to the middle of the stream subject to easement of navigation, was laid down by this court as early as the year 1828. *Gavit* v. *Chambers*, 3 Ohio, 496.

The same rule was applied to calls in a survey bounding lands upon a non-navigable stream, shortly thereafter (*Benner* v. *Platter*, 6 Ohio, 505); since which time the doctrine therein announced has been firmly maintained by this court. *Curtis* v. *State*, 5 Ohio, 324; *Lamb* v. *Rickets*, 11 Ohio, 311; *Walker* v. *Board of Public Works*, 16 Ohio, 540; *June* v. *Purcell*, 36 Ohio St. 396; *Day* v. *Pittsburgh, Y. & C. R. Co.* 44 Ohio St. 406, 5 West. Rep. 206.

The rule, however, is otherwise in respect to calls in a deed bounding the lands conveyed by it on the waters of Lake Erie. *Sloan* v. *Biemiller*, 34 Ohio St. 492.

And in the case of lands bounded on the Ohio River the clear tendency of judicial opinion in this State is to limit the title of the riparian proprietor to low-water mark (*Benner* v. *Platter*, 6 Ohio, 508; *Blanchard* v. *Porter*, 11 Ohio, 138, 142; *Booth* v. *Hubbard*, 8 Ohio St. 247); but the effect to be given to a call in a deed that makes a non-navigable lake one boundary of the lands conveyed by it has not heretofore received the attention of this court. The authorities upon the question are in conflict, and seem to be incapable of reconciliation. In some of the States, and in England, the rule is to limit the operation of the conveyance to the water edge. Gould, Waters, § 80, p. 155; *Bloomfield* v. *Johnston*, Ir. R. 8 C. L. 68; *Bradley* v. *Rice*, 13 Me. 198; *Wood* v. *Kelley*, 30 Me. 47; *Wheeler* v. *Spinola*, 54 N. Y. 377.

In other States, notably Indiana and Michigan, the contrary rule may be considered as established. *Ridgway* v. *Ludlow*, 58 Ind. 248; *Stoner* v. *Rice*, 121 Ind. 51, 6 L. R. A. 387; *Clute* v. *Fisher*, 65 Mich. 48, 8 West. Rep. 121.

In this conflict of authority we are at liberty to adopt such rule on the subject as best comports with the presumed intention of the parties, a sound public policy and the analogies of the rules in force in this State respecting boundaries upon running streams. It may be conceded that the numerical weight of authority supports the rule that a call in a deed making a non-navigable lake a boundary only passes title to the land to low-water mark; but, be that as it may, no solid ground is readily perceived for limiting, in that case, the deed to the waters' edge, and in the case of a running stream, extending its operation to the center or thread thereof; and in this State, where the rule is so firmly established that a boundary on a running stream carries the land to the middle or thread thereof, principles of analogy afford strong grounds for applying it to non-navigable lakes. The main reasons for the rule in one case apply equally to the other. The existence of "strips or gores" of land along the margin of non-navigable lakes, to which the title may be held in abeyance for indefinite periods of time, is as great an evil as are strips and gores of land along highways or running streams; the litigation that may arise therefrom after long years, or the happening of some unexpected event, is equally probable, and alike vexatious in each of the cases, and that public policy which would seek to prevent this by a construction that would carry the title to the center of a highway, running stream or non-navigable lake that may be made a boundary of the lands conveyed, applies indifferently, and with equal force, to all of them. It would seem, also, that whatever inference might arise, from the presumed intention of the parties, against the reservation of the land underlying the water, would be as strong in one case as in either of the others.

That practical difficulties in the application of the rule may arise where the lake is so nearly round that it cannot be said to have any length as distinguishable from its breadth, or when the side lines of the respective parcels of land bounding on the lake approach it in such direction that if they should be extended to the center thereof they would cross each other, is apparent.

The latter difficulty is not at all unusual in the case of lands bounding on running streams, but does not prevent the application of the rule. 8 Washb. Easem. 459, star *note;* Angell, Watercourses, § 55,—where the subject is learnedly discussed by those able authors, and this difficulty overcome.

Whether there are in Ohio non-navigable lakes of such shape that no length can be affirmed of them does not appear; if there are any such, and the rule applicable to running streams and to non-navigable lakes distinctly longer than they are wide cannot be applied to them, other appropriate rules must be adopted, which, in the light of all the circumstances, may be regarded as effectuating the intention of the parties, and are consistent with public policy, one main object in all cases of this kind being to adopt and apply such rules as will accomplish those important ends.

Whatever difficulties may be conjectured as liable to arise in possible cases to the application of the rule we have adopted, in fact none do arise in the case before us, for Chippewa Lake is distinctly longer than it is wide, and a prolongation to its center of the side lines of the respective parcels lying along its sides will not cause them to cross each other. The rule, of course, excludes those lands which merely touch the end of the lake and do not at all extend along its sides.

This rule, however, is applicable to but two of the conveyances,—that to Delanson DeForrest and that to Fred B. Chamberlain. While, if the parties to a deed make a running stream, a non-navigable lake or a highway one boundary of the lands conveyed by it, public policy and the presumed intention of the parties will extend the line to the middle of such monument, yet it is competent for them to limit the conveyance to the side of the highway, the top of the bank of the running stream or to the edge of the water of the lake (*Blanchard* v. *Porter*, 11 Ohio, 138; *Lough* v. *Machlin*, 40 Ohio St. 332), and the question is whether the parties to the other deeds conveying the land surrounding Chippewa Lake have not done so. As has been shown, in four of the conveyances of the Fowlers of the lands bordering on the lake, the "margin" of the lake is made a boundary or corner instead of the lake itself. "Margin of the lake" is a term of unequivocal import, meaning the line where the earth and water meet around the lake; by the use of these words the parties have declared their intention to make, not the middle, but another part, of the lake,—the edge of the water,—the boundary line. No other construction can be given to the words the parties themselves have chosen, without doing violence to their meaning; and an intention contrary to the one expressed by the very words selected by the parties themselves cannot be presumed. *McCullock* v. *Aten*, 2 Ohio, 308; *Lamb* v. *Rickets*, 11 Ohio, 311; *Hopkins* v. *Kent*, 9 Ohio, 13; Gould, Waters, § 199.

In the remaining deeds from the Fowlers to the lands around the lake the lands were described by metes and bounds, no mention of the lake being made. In descriptions of this class only the lands within the bounds pass. "Where lands are granted by metes and bounds all the area within those bounds and no more passes." *Lockwood* v. *Wildman*, 13 Ohio, 430.

Indeed, where the parties have by their deed inclosed the land by agreed lines, without any reference whatever to adjacent natural objects, it is difficult to conceive of a principle that would extend those lines to include those natural objects, however convenient they might be to the enjoyment of the land actually conveyed.

From the construction we have given to the descriptions contained in deeds made by the Fowlers conveying away the several parcels of land that surround the lake, it follows,—that the deeds made to Delanson DeForrest and Fred B. Chamberlain make the center of the lake one boundary of the tracts conveyed to them respectively, and that the other deeds carry title no farther than the edge of the water, and that therefore the title to all the bed of the lake except what was covered by the De Forrest and Fred B. Chamberlain deeds remained in the Fowlers, and by their deed of Aug. 11, 1876, was conveyed to D. H. Ainsworth and A. W. McClure, and is now owned by the plaintiff in error by virtue of mesne conveyances from Ainsworth and McClure, as set forth in the agreed statement of facts.

It also follows that as the defendant Andrews claims title under conveyances which constitute the margin of the lake a boundary, he has no title to any portion of the bed of the lake, nor has the defendant John Nye a title to any portion thereof, for the reason that although the deed from the Fowlers to Delanson De Forrest, and the mesne conveyances from the latter to J. H. Barrett, conveyed title to the center of the lake, yet the deed from J. H. Barrett to Levi Nye, the lessor of defendant John Nye, limits its operation to the edge of the lake by expressly making the margin thereof its boundary on the side, or end, of the tract abutting thereon. We therefore hold that the plaintiff in error is the owner in fee simple of all that part of the bed of Chippewa Lake not covered by the deeds made by the Fowlers to Delanson DeForrest and Fred B. Chamberlain, and that those two deeds cover such parts thereof as are inclosed by a prolongation, to its center, of those lines of the description that approach the sides of the lake.

The bed of the lake being private property the public has no right to fish in, and boat upon, its waters; nor have the defendants the right to engage in the business of letting for hire boats and fishing tackle to such portions of the public as may resort to the lake to boat and fish for their pleasure and recreation. That the latter right is one that can be acquired by prescription may be admitted, but the facts agreed upon fall short of establishing it by that method, even if that contention was maintained on behalf of the defendants in error, which we do not understand is the fact, in view of the arguments presented in the able brief of their counsel.

The agreed statement of facts in respect to this question is as follows:

"The defendants and their grantors have for more than forty years occupied continuously their respective lands to the water in all its variations, and have enjoyed the free use of the water in connection with their lands for the purpose of watering cattle, washing sheep, boating and fishing, and without license or consent from anyone."

This does not show that the enjoyment was adverse or under any claim of right. Both of these elements must exist, according to the current of authority, in connection with the prescribed period of enjoyment, to create a right by prescription. Washb. Easements, 150; *Toole* v. *Clifton*, 22 Ohio St. 247.

However, conceding that these are not necessary elements of prescription, and that the defendants had acquired a prescriptive right to water cattle, wash sheep, boat and fish in the lake, yet it by no means follows that, because they may do these things, they may also erect docks extending into the water and embark in the business of keeping boats and fishing tackle to let for hire to pleasure seekers who may resort to the lake to boat and fish for recreation upon its waters. The two rights are clearly distinguishable from each other; and the contention is over the latter right only, in respect to which the agreed statement of facts, while it states that the defendants are exercising it, is silent as to the duration of their enjoyment thereof, and therefore does not establish the right by prescription.

That a riparian proprietor by virtue of his ownership to the edge of the water of a private stream or lake has access to and the right to use the water for domestic and agricultural purposes, is not controverted by the plaintiff in error. Such use may fairly be considered as within the presumed intention of the parties.

That the lake is valuable for the purpose of gathering ice from its frozen surface appears from the agreed statement of facts, and the right of the defendant to gather it was asserted on one side and denied by the other in the course of the argument, but the question is not made by the parties in their pleadings and therefore cannot be noticed in the decree.

The agreed statement of facts shows that the defendant Nye is insolvent, and the financial condition of Andrews doubtful; but aside from this, and were they both solvent and fully able to respond to any damages that might be recovered against them in actions of trespass, yet it is apparent from the whole record that such actions would not afford an adequate remedy for the violations of the rights of the plaintiff in error in the past; and those threatened in the future were, and are, during certain seasons of the year, of daily, if not of hourly, occurrence under the claim of a right to do so; besides the injury resulting from each separate act would be trifling, and the damages recoverable therefore scarcely equal to a tithe of the expenses necessary to prosecute separate actions therefor.

It follows from the holding of the court respecting the effect to be given the several descriptions in the conveyances made by the Fowlers and others to the various parcels of land that surround the lake, that neither of the defendants has shown a right to erect docks and let to hire for use thereon boats and fishing tackle. It also follows that in so far as these acts affect those portions of the lake to which the title of plaintiff does not extend, he is not entitled to relief against them, but is entitled to have so much thereof as his title covers protected from those unwarranted violations. There should be a decree, therefore, finding that, as against the defendants herein, the plaintiff in error is the owner in fee simple and entitled to the exclusive possession of all the lands underlying the waters of Chippewa Lake except those parts thereof that, according to the rules hereinbefore laid down, were conveyed by the Fowlers to Delanson DeForrest and Fred B. Chamberlain, and restraining the defendants from letting to hire either boats or fishing tackle, to be used on the water overlying the lands so found to belong to him.

Judgment accordingly.

Spear, *J.*, dissenting:

I concur in the foregoing except as to one point. I am of opinion that the title of neither defendant in error should be held to extend to the middle of the lake.

The decision in *Gavit* v. *Chambers*, 3 Ohio, 496, is the foundation of the doctrine in Ohio that the ownership of lands bounded by an inland stream carries the title of the owner to the middle. It was held in that case to be "vitally essential to the public peace and to individual security, that there should be distinct and acknowledged legal owners for both the land and the water of the country. . . It cannot be reasonably doubted that, if all the beds of our rivers supposed to be navigable, and treated as such by the United States, in selling the lands, are to be regarded as unappropriated territory, a door is open for incalculable mischiefs. Intruders upon the common waste would fall into endless broils among themselves, and involve the owners of the adjacent lands in controversies innumerable. Stones, soil, gravel, the right to fish, would all be subjects for individual scramble, necessarily leading to violence and outrage."

The rule that the lands covered by such waters should not be public water rests upon the ground of public policy, and it is in recognition of this rule that the lands underlying Chippewa Lake are considered to be the subject of private ownership. This being determined, the only question remaining is, What part of the lake shall be held to be the bound intended when the lake generally is given as the boundary? As to streams, the center, or thread, is the established bound, where the language of the deed does not contradict such construction, because the center is the most conspicuous part. The water is a moving body, and, as to the depth and breadth, is subject to constant change, which produces variations on the opposite sides. The thread, or current, however, shifts but little, and is, in the main, stationary, so that a line running to the thread would be a reasonably certain line, and would be easily ascertained. This is not true as to natural lakes and ponds. Such bodies do not have any thread or current. The water is the most conspicuous portion, but no rule of convenience or certainty requires that the line, where the lake itself is mentioned as the boundary, should be extended to the center. Indeed, the application of such rule would be attended, in most cases, with practical difficulties in the running of lines beyond the water's edge. If lakes were always found in the shape of a square, or a parallelogram, these difficulties would be slight, perhaps, but more frequently they are nearer a circular shape. The difficulties in such case are apparent. They may be theoretically overcome by an engineer on a diagram, but practically, in the water, they would always exist, and would prove a fruitful source of contention and quarrel.

The rule which, it is submitted, is the true rule, is stated by Gresham, *J.*, in *Indiana* v. *Milk*, 11 Fed. Rep. 389, as follows:

"Non-navigable streams are usually narrow, and the lines of riparian owners can be extended into them at right angles without interference or confusion, and without serious injustice to anyone. It was therefore natural, when such streams were called for as boundaries, to hold that the real line between opposite shore owners was the thread of the current. The rights of the riparian proprietors in the bed of the stream, and in the stream itself, were thus clearly defined. But when this rule is attempted to be applied to lakes and ponds, practical difficulties are encountered. They have no current, and, being more or less circular, it would hardly be possible to run the boundary lines beyond the water's edge so as to define the rights of shore-owners in the beds. Beaver Lake is seven and a half miles east and west, and less than five miles north and south. Extending the side and end lines into the lake, there being no current, when would they meet? This rule is applicable, if at all, whether there be one or more riparian proprietors. I do not think the mere proprietorship of the surrounding lands will, in all cases, give ownership to the beds of natural non-navigable lakes and ponds, regardless of their size. It would be unfair and unjust to allow a party to claim and hold against his grantor the bed of a lake containing thousands of acres solely on the ground that he had bought and paid for all the small surrounding fractional tracts—the mere rim."

In my view there is no difference, in law, in the two cases now under consideration, and a like judgment should be rendered in each. But the judgment in the case of Nye is assented to as the best practical solution under the circumstances.

Williams, *J.*, concurs in the above.

OREGON SUPREME COURT.

STATE OF OREGON, *Respt.*,
v.
E. J. KAISER, *Appt.*

(......Or.......)

***1. Acts and omissions deemed to be contempts** of the authority of courts, under the laws of Oregon, are only those which are specified as such under the subdivisions of section 650 of the Civil Code, and in other sections thereof, and can be punished only in the mode therein prescribed.

2. The publication of an article in a newspaper is not a contempt unless it reflects upon the conduct of the court in reference to a pending suit or proceeding, and tends in some manner to influence its decisions therein, or to

*Head notes by THAYER, *Ch. J.*

NOTE.—*Contempt of court, in presence of court.*

Any willful act tending to obstruct justice is a contempt of court. Cheadle v. State, 9 West. Rep. 88, 110 Ind. 301.

A breach of the peace in open court is a direct disturbance and a palpable contempt of the authority of the court. *Re* Terry, 128 U. S. 289 (32 L. ed. 405).

The court, when in session, is present in every part of the place set apart for its own use and for the use of its officers, jurors and witnesses; and misbehavior anywhere in such place is misbehavior in the presence of the court. *Re* Savin, 131 U. S. 267 (33 L. ed. 150).

Disorderly conduct, insulting demeanor, etc., *in facie curiæ*, constitute a direct contempt. Ill temper of the judge is no excuse for contempt. Holman v. State, 2 West. Rep. 761, 105 Ind. 516.

It is competent for the circuit court, immediately upon the commission in its presence of such a contempt, to proceed upon its own knowledge of the facts and to punish the offender, without further proof and without issue or trial in any form. *Re* Terry, *supra*.

Where a man in the court room struck the marshal a violent blow in his face, and thrust his hand under his vest where his bowie knife was concealed, apparently to draw it, it is a contempt of court. *Re* Terry, 36 Fed. Rep. 419.

A court is not dissolved by a mere recess or necessary adjournment from one day to the next; and misbehavior affecting public justice, in the court-room and in the immediate presence of the judge, while he is attending there to resume business when the hour of recess expires, is misbehavior in the presence of the court. Baker v. State, 4 L. R. A. 128, 82 Ga. 776.

When a party is guilty of a contempt by using insulting language to the judge while holding court, he may be punished therefor without any rule being issued against him; and in such case the judge may act upon his own knowledge of what has been said, and absolutely refuse to hear any other evidence as to the language used by said party. State v. Gibson (W. Va.) Sept. 14, 1889.

Where the insulting language was not used in the court room, a rule should be issued, and defendant be allowed to prove by witnesses the actual language used. *Ibid.*

Where persons disclaimed any intent to use disrespectful language, and asked permission to withdraw the paper, the court allowed them to do so on payment of the costs of the proceedings for contempt. United States v. Late Corporation of Church of Jesus Christ, etc. (Utah) Feb. 1889.

Under the Act of Congress of 1789, the question whether particular acts constitute a contempt is to be determined according to the rules and principles of the common law. *Re* Savin, 131 U. S. 267 (33 L. ed. 150).

Attempting, while a witness is in the witness-room, or in the hallway of the court room, to deter him from testifying, by offering him money, is a misbehavior in the presence of the court, and punishable, without indictment, by fine and imprisonment, as a contempt. *Ibid.*

See also 28 L. R. A. 242; 44 L. R. A. 159.

impede, interrupt or embarrass the proceedings of the court in reference thereto.

3. A court has no authority to proceed against a party for contempt on account of acts not committed in the immediate view and presence of the court, unless the facts constituting the contempt are shown by an affidavit presented to the court.

(May 1, 1890.)

APPEAL by defendant from a judgment of the Circuit Court for Jackson County finding him guilty of contempt of court and sentencing him to fine and imprisonment. *Reversed.*

Statement by **Thayer,** *Ch. J.:*

Said Circuit Court, at a term thereof held on the 13th day of December, 1889, proceeded of its own motion to make and enter the following order:

"In the Circuit Court for Jackson County, Oregon. Whereas, you, E. J. Kaiser and N. A. Jacobs, as editors and publishers of the Valley Record, a newspaper published at the City of Ashland, Jackson County, Oregon, on Thursday, the 12th of December, 1889, in an issue of said Valley Record published on said day, did publish of and concerning the above court, and the judge and officers thereof, the following, to wit: 'The circuit judge has ordered an investigation into the whys and wherefores of a material witness disappearing in a criminal case, in which his important testimony was needed to convict. While the honorable court is at the investigation business, it might not be more than common justice to go into the wholesale business of investigating itself, and everybody else connected with the management and manipulation of the jurisprudence of southern Oregon. If some of the methods employed could be sifted to the bottom a system of debauchery would be unearthed that may be very warm and interesting to some of the executors. In fact, then, the evidence would be laid bare to the people of southern Oregon, and they would know just why one man can be convicted of murder in the first degree, and "hung by the neck until he is dead," on strong circumstantial evidence; and why another crime, of the same foul magnitude, is committed, and the courts fail to find the author, when the circumstantial evidence that made the first man stretch hemp was far less convicting in its circumstantialness than was the case that the blind Goddess of Justice could not find guilty; why attorneys can offer bribes to even such august personages as grand jurors to bring in suitable verdicts; and why—yes, why—a lot of other things, just as queer, irregular and delicate, and too numerous to mention, are occurring as periodically as there are exigencies that make them. In fact the court would have an all year's job on its hands. The practicing condition of jurisprudence in this section of the world is as corrupt and criminal in its methods, in proportion to population, amount and magnitude of crime, and purse of criminals, as it is in the cities where these cases are regularly "handled" by the political boss who "makes" the officials, "fixes" the juries and attends to the case, for a large sum. These irregular methods are becoming so numerous that it seems as though they have encysted themselves upon, and are a part of, the—unwritten—works of Blackstone. This is one of the conditions and dangerous consequences of the political methods in vogue in Jackson County, an immediate result of

---

Approaching a person summoned as a juror, with a view of improperly influencing his actions in the event of his being sworn as a juror in the case, if done in the presence of the court, is a contempt punishable by fine or imprisonment, at the discretion of the court, without indictment. *Re* Cuddy, 131 U. S. 280 (33 L. ed. 154).

An attempt to bribe a juror to bring about a disagreement of the jury is punishable as for a contempt, although no prejudice is shown to have resulted to either party. Langdon v. Wayne Circuit Ct. Judges, 76 Mich. 358.

A contempt committed in the presence of the petit jury while they are engaged in performing the functions devolved upon them by law, and which must be performed out of the sight and hearing of the judge or anybody else, is committed in the immediate view and presence of the court. People v. Barrett, 56 Hun, 351, 30 N. Y. S. R. 728.

Where an attempt was made, according to the affidavit on which the motion was founded, to confer upon the district court, by a false and fraudulent averment, a jurisdiction to which it was not entitled under the Constitution, this was a gross contempt of court. Eberly v. Moore, 65 U. S. 24 How. 147 (16 L. ed. 612).

Any attempt, by a mere colorable dispute, to obtain the opinion of the court upon a question of law which a party desires to know for his own interest or his own purposes, when there is no real and substantial controversy between those who appear as adverse parties to the suit, is an abuse which courts of justice have always reprehended, and treated as a punishable contempt of court. Lord v. Veazie, 49 U. S. 8 How. 251 (12 L. ed. 1067).

Contempt; power to punish for.

Power to punish for contempt is inherent in courts of superior jurisdiction. It is not regulated by statute alone. The Legislature can neither create nor destroy the power. Holman v. State, 2 West. Rep. 761, 105 Ind. 516; *Re* Terry, 128 U. S. 289 (32 L. ed. 405); *Re* Robinson, 86 U. S. 19 Wall. 513 (22 L. ed. 205).

So United States courts have power to punish for contempts. *Re* Savin, 131 U. S. 267 (33 L. ed. 150).

So have the district courts of Colorado. Cooper v. People, 6 L. R. A. 430, 13 Colo. 352.

The superior courts of New Jersey, modeled after the English courts of common law, have authority to punish summarily by proceedings for contempt. *Re* Cheesman, 4 Cent. Rep. 576, 49 N. J. L. 115.

Under the Revised Statutes, courts of the United States have power to proceed summarily for contempt. *Re* Savin, *supra.*

Under the Act of Congress of 1789, the question whether particular acts constitute a contempt is to be determined according to the rules and principles of the common law. *Ibid.*

The courts of the United States have power to punish for contempts of court committed in the presence of the said courts, or so near thereto as to obstruct the administration of justice. *Ibid.*

But territorial courts are not United States courts, within the meaning of U. S. Rev. Stat., § 725, defining the power of United States courts to punish for contempt. Territory v. Murray, 7 Mont. 251.

U. S. Rev. Stat. invest the district courts of Mon-

which is shown in the shameless way in which its representative officials are allowed to sell out their constituency for a beggarly fee. Another direct result of this condition of affairs has placed an indebtedness of from $100,000 to $150,000—such a magnitude that no one does know the actual amount—over the county, that is bearing practically ten per cent interest (mighty large returns and safe investment for big capital); and no effort is being made to stop it from climbing right along up. When will the cupidity, indifference and lack of courage of the people in public affairs cease, and an effort made to at least put a check to these grasping vultures?' It is therefore now hereby ordered that you, and each of you, be and appear before said court, at the courthouse in Jacksonville, said county and State, on Monday, 16th December, 1889, at 9 o'clock in the forenoon, then and there to show cause, if any you have, why you should not be punished for contempt of said court for having so published and circulated the matter above set out as aforesaid. Done in open court on Friday, 13th December, 1889. Lionel R. Webster."

A certified copy of the order and citation having been personally served upon the said E. J. Kaiser on the 17th day of December, 1889, he appeared in accordance with the requirements thereof, and filed an answer duly verified by him, of which the following is a copy.

"E. J. Kaiser comes, and, in answer to a citation issued out of the above-entitled court, and heretofore served on him, says that he is engaged in publishing a newspaper of general circulation at Ashland, Or.; that, in publishing said article that appears in said citation, he did not make any reference to any action or proceeding then pending in said court, or before any grand jury, nor was there any grand jury in session at said time, as defendant is informed; that said article was, so far as the same relates to the courts of this county, a criticism of past acts therein, and the same was not intended to have, and would not have, any tendency to interfere with the proper and unbiased administration of the law in any case or cases then or now pending in said court; and that said article was published only, as the defendant believed, in the interest of society, and defendant earnestly disclaims any intentional disrespect towards said court, or the officers thereof, in the publishing of said article. And, further answering, defendant avers that said court has no jurisdiction of the person of this defendant under this proceeding, and denies that this court has any jurisdiction to punish this defendant, or to adjudge him in contempt, for the publishing of said article set forth in said citation."

The said circuit court, upon the said order, citation and answer, adjudged the said Kaiser guilty of contempt of the court in the publication of said article, and sentenced him to pay a fine of $50, and also that he be imprisoned in the county jail for the period of fifteen days, from which adjudication the said Kaiser brought this appeal.

Mr. **H. K. Hanna,** for appellant:

In the proceeding had in this cause before the lower court no jurisdiction whatever had

---

tana with all the chancery power which formerly belonged to chancery in England; and they are not limited to the punishment provided by the statutes of the Territory. Zimmerman v. Zimmerman, 7 Mont. 114.

The Legislature may aid the jurisdiction or enlarge the powers of courts by declaring certain improper conduct to be contempt, and may regulate the practice in proceedings for contempt. Cheadle v. State, 9 West. Rep. 48, 110 Ind. 301.

While the power to punish contempts ought to be exercised promptly, yet it is an arbitrary power which ought to be kept within prudent limits, especially in regard to indirect contempts in any way involving the freedom of the press. *Ibid.*

Summary punishment for contempt.

There is a distinction between a commitment by precept for the nonpayment of money and a commitment upon a conviction and fine as punishment for a contempt in misconduct punishable by fine and imprisonment. In the latter case the prisoner is not entitled to the jail liberties, and in the former "he is in execution in a civil action," and is entitled thereto. People v. Cowles, 3 Abb. App. Dec. 514; People v. Cowles, 4 Keyes, 50; Van Wezel v. Van Wezel, 3 Paige, 38, 3 N. Y. Ch. L. ed. 48; Ford v. Ford, 41 How. Pr. 173; People v. Bennett, 4 Paige, 282, 3 N. Y. Ch. L. ed. 437; Patrick v. Warner, 4 Paige, 397, 3 N. Y. Ch. L. ed. 486. See Rose v. Tyrell, 25 Wis. 565.

Summary punishment for contempt is held not to be an infringement of the Constitution, which guarantees to every citizen a trial by jury. This power, however, is to be exercised only where no other adequate remedy can protect public justice from obstruction. Gandy v. State, 13 Neb. 451; State v. Doty, 32 N. J. L. 403; State v. Matthews, 37 N. H. 450; *Ex parte* Grace, 12 Iowa, 208; State v. Anderson, 40 Iowa, 207; *Re* Hirst, 9 Phila. 216. See *note* to Baker v. State (Ga.) 4 L. R. A. 128.

The right of trial by jury in cases of contempt has been always denied. Arnold v. Com. 80 Ky. 304, 44 Am. Rep. 483; Neal v. State, 9 Ark. 259; State v. Matthews, 37 N. H. 450; People v. Bennett, 4 Paige, 282, 3 N. Y. Ch. L. ed. 437.

The Act to abolish imprisonment for debt only precludes an attachment to enforce payment of money decreed to be paid by final decree. Dusenberry v. Woodward, 1 Abb. Pr. 452; Patrick v. Warner, 4 Paige, 397, 3 N. Y. Ch. L. ed. 486. See People v. Kelly, 35 Barb. 462; Watson v. Nelson, 69 N. Y. 544.

The court has control over its own proceedings and may refuse to the defendant the benefit of them, when asked as a favor, until he purges himself of his contempt. Brinkley v. Brinkley, 47 N. Y. 49; Johnson v. Pinney, 1 Paige, 646, 2 N. Y. Ch. L. ed. 785; Rogers v. Paterson, 4 Paige, 450, 3 N. Y. Ch. L. ed. 511; Evans v. Van Hall, Clarke, Ch. 22, 7 N. Y. Ch. L. ed. 41; Ellingwood v. Stevenson, 4 Sandf. Ch. 366, 7 N. Y. Ch. L. ed. 1136; Robinson v. Owen, 46 N. H. 40; 1 Dan. Ch. 655.

This principle does not apply to an application which is a matter of strict right, as a motion to set aside proceedings for irregularity. Kaehler v. Dobberpuhl, 56 Wis. 491; King v. Bryant, 3 Myl. & C. 191; Mead v. Norris, 21 Wis. 315.

Publishing court proceedings in newspapers.

A newspaper reporter who conceals himself in a jury-room, and takes notes of the proceedings, and subsequently publishes his recollections thereof, although he surrenders his notes to the judge when discovered, is guilty of contempt of court. *Re* Choate, 24 Abb. N. C. 430, 41 Alb. L. J. 287.

been acquired of the person of the appellant for the reason that the essential requirements of the Statute relative to the punishment of contempts had not in any manner been complied with. Consequently the whole proceeding in this matter is void.

Hill Code, §§ 652, 653; *Whittem* v. *State*, 36 Ind. 196; *Wilson* v. *State*, 57 Ind. 71.

Our Legislature has designated and limited the acts, the omission or commission of which shall be deemed contempts of the authority of the court, and our courts cannot assume that acts other than those enumerated, however libelous they may be toward a presiding judge, shall be deemed contempt, or be punished as such.

Storey v. *People*, 79 Ill 45; *People* v. *Wilson*, 64 Ill. 195; Rapalje, Contempt, pp. 70, 71, § 56; *Dunham* v. *State*, 6 Iowa, 245; *Ex parte Hickey*, 4 Smedes & M. 751.

Messrs. **William M. Colvig**, *Dist. Atty.*, and **A. S. Hammond**, for respondent:

The power to punish for contempt being inherent, each court is its own exclusive judge as to whether contempt has been committed.

Rapalje, Contempt, 1; 1 Thompson, Trials, § 124; *Cooper* v. *People*, 6 L. R. A. 430, 13 Colo. 352; 3 Am. & Eng. Encyclop. Law, 800.

The powers of courts of record in this respect, being necessary to their very existence, are given by the Constitution that created them, and the Legislature, being a co-ordinate branch of government, cannot deny or restrict them.

Holman v. *State*, 2 West. Rep. 761, 105 Ind. 513; 1 Thompson, Trials, p. 133, § 125; Rapalje, Contempt, § 11.

Contempts *in facie curiæ* are punishable in a summary manner without a hearing.

1 Thompson, Trials, § 133; 3 Am. & Eng. Encyclop. Law, 790; Rapalje, Contempt, 111, 393; *United States* v. *Green*, 3 Mason, 482; *Com.* v. *Dandridge*, 2 Va. Cas. 408; *State* v. *Matthews*, 37 N. H. 450; *Re Percy*, 2 Daly, 530; *People* v. *Nevins*, 1 Hill, 154; *People* v. *Kelly*, 24 N. Y. 75; 4 Bl. Com. 286; *Easton* v. *State*, 39 Ala. 552; *Middlebrook* v. *State*, 43 Conn. 257; *Ex parte Wright*, 65 Ind. 504.

Where the contempt is not committed in the presence of the court, the usual method of bringing the party into court is, upon the filing of affidavits showing the commission of the offense, to issue an attachment. But the only object of the affidavits and attachments is to bring the party into court.

Rapalje, Contempt, § 93; 3 Am. & Eng. Encyclop. Law, 792; *Com.* v. *Dandridge*, 2 Va. Cas. 408; *People* v. *Kelly*, 24 N. Y. 75; *State* v. *Gibson*, W. Va. Sept. 14, 1889.

And it is immaterial what method is pursued, so that the defendant has his day in court. So, where he comes in and answers, he waives all irregularities.

Rapalje, Contempt, p. 148, § 109; *Ex parte Savin*, 131 U. S. 267 (33 L. ed. 150). See also article by S. D. Thompson in 5 Crim. Law Mag. 506; *Golden Gate C. H. M. Co.* v. *Yuba County Super. Ct.* 65 Cal. 191; *Ex parte Cottrell*, 59 Cal. 418; *Re Cheesman*, 4 Cent. Rep. 576, 49 N. J. L. 115; *Ex parte Kilgore*, 3 Tex. App. 247; *McConnell* v. *State*, 46 Ind. 298; *Whittem* v. *State*, 36 Ind. 196; *Ex parte Wiley*, 36 Ind. 528.

The summary power to commit and punish

Where he refuses to promise that he will not publish any of the deliberations, upon which he is discharged from custody, and afterwards publishes the deliberations, his discharge is not a bar to a subsequent proceeding to punish him for criminal contempt. People v. Barrett, 56 Hun, 351, 30 N. Y. S. R. 728.

A contempt by thus concealing himself is committed in the immediate view and presence of the court, and is summarily punishable. Re Choate, *supra*.

A fair and reasonable review and comment upon court proceedings, as they take place from time to time, is not a contempt of court. Cooper v. People, 6 L. R. A. 430, 13 Colo. 352.

A press reporter who obtains information about a verdict by eaves-dropping, and reports it to the newspaper he represents, without knowing whether it is true or false, is guilty of a flagrant contempt of the court, and should be promptly and severely punished. Orman v. State, 24 Tex. App. 495.

Under the statute, the false or grossly incorrect publication of a pending case, trial or proceeding tending to prejudice the public as to the merits, and to corrupt or embarrass the administration of justice, is an indirect contempt. Re Graves, 29 Fed. Rep. 60; Respublica v. Oswold, 1 U. S. 1 Dall. 319, (1 L. ed. 155).

An attempt by wanton publication to prejudice the rights of litigants in a pending cause, degrade the tribunal, and impede, embarrass, or corrupt the due administration of justice, is a contempt of court. Cooper v. People, *supra*; Re Cheesman, 4 Cent. Rep. 576, 49 N. J. L. 115.

If a contempt consists in publishing grossly inaccurate accounts of proceedings of the court, the findings must show that the publication was made with intent to bring the court into contempt, and the language used must be found and set out. Re Deaton, 105 N. C. 59.

Comments, however stringent, in relation to proceedings passed and ended, are not contempts. They may constitute a libel upon the judge or some other officer of the court, but cannot be treated as in contempt of its authority. Cheadle v. State, 9 West. Rep. 43, 110 Ind. 301.

A circuit court has no power, under W. Va. Code, regulating punishment for the classes of contempts therein mentioned, to summarily fine an attorney for writing and causing to be published in a newspaper a libelous charge against the judge of such court. State v. McClaugherty (W. Va.) Nov. 21, 1889.

Disobedience of order of court.

When a party sought to be bound by an order had actual knowledge or notice of its existence, although there might have occurred some slip in the formal method of bringing it home to him, the effect of such order cannot be wholly lost and he is guilty of contempt in disobeying it. People v. Sturtevant, 9 N. Y. 278; Watson v. Citizens Sav. Bank, 5 S. C. 166; McNeil v. Garratt, 1 Craig & P. 98; Ewing v. Johnson, 34 How. Pr. 206.

Even parties simply hearing that an order for injunction has been granted and disregarding it can be adjudged guilty of contempt. New York v. New York & S. I. Ferry Co. 8 Jones & S. 315; Osborne v. Tennant, 14 Ves. Jr. 136.

If an order is served on the solicitor and knowledge thereof is brought home to the party he may be punished for a willful disobedience of the order in the same manner as if it had been personally served on himself. Watson v. Citizens Sav. Bank, *supra*.

One who refuses to obey a lawful order of a court,

for contempts tending to obstruct or degrade the administration of justice is inherent in courts of chancery and other superior courts, as essential to the execution of their powers, and to the maintenance of their authority, and is part of the law of the land.

Cartwright's Case, 114 Mass. 238, quoted in article in 22 Crim. Law Jour. 466; Howes, Jur. § 221, *note 1; People* v. *Turner*, 1 Cal. 152; *Williamson's Case*, 26 Pa. 9, 67 Am. Dec. 376, 380; *Arnold* v. *Com.* 80 Ky. 300, 44 Am. Rep. 480; *United States* v. *Late Corporation Church of Jesus Christ, etc.* (Utah) Feb. 1889; *Cooper* v. *People*, 6 L. R. A. 430, 13 Colo. 352; *Little* v. *State*, 90 Ind. 338; Rapalje, Contempt, § 1; Criminal Contempts, 5 Crim. Law Mag. (May) 151

That the publication, in a newspaper of general circulation in the immediate vicinity of the court, of scandalous and libelous matter concerning the court or its officers, constitutes a contempt, cannot be doubted.

Rapalje, Contempt, § 56; Desty, Am. Crim. Law, § 73 *b*, citing *State* v. *Morrill*, 16 Ark. 384; 4 Bl. Com. 285; 2 Bishop, Crim. Law, 6th ed. § 259; *Stuart* v. *People*, 4 Ill. 405; *Respublica* v. *Oswald*, 1 U. S. 1 Dall. 319 (1 L. ed. 155), 1 Am. Dec. 246; *People* v. *Wilson*, 64 Ill. 219; *State* v. *Morrill*, 16 Ark. 384; *Myers* v. *State*, 46 Ohio St. 473; *Re Buckley*, 69 Cal. 1.

Thayer, *Ch. J.*, delivered the opinion of the court:

Two questions are presented for our consideration upon this appeal: *first*, whether the matter published by the appellant was punishable as a contempt of the circuit court; *second*, whether said court had authority of its own motion to cite the appellant to appear before it, and inflict punishment upon him for the alleged offense.

The Civil Code of this State, section 650, prescribes what acts and omissions in respect to a court of justice, or proceedings therein, shall be deemed to be contempts of the authority of the court. They are as follows: Disorderly, contemptuous or insolent behavior towards the judge, while holding the court, tending to impair its authority, or to interrupt the due course of a trial or other judicial proceedings; a breach of the peace, boisterous conduct or violent disturbance tending to interrupt the due course of a trial or judicial proceeding; misbehavior in office, or other willful neglect or violation of duty, by an attorney, clerk, sheriff or other person appointed or selected to perform a judicial or ministerial service; deceit or abuse of the process or proceedings of the court by a party to an action, suit or special proceeding; disobedience of any lawful judgment, decree, order or process of the court; assuming to be an attorney or other officer of the court, and acting as such, without authority, in a particular instance; rescuing any person or property in the custody of an officer by virtue of an order or process of such court; unlawfully detaining a witness or party to an action, suit or proceeding while going to, remaining at or returning from the court where the same is for trial; any other unlawful interference with the process or proceedings of a court; disobedience of a subpœna duly served, or refusing to be sworn or answer as a witness; when summoned as a juror in a court, improperly conversing with a party to an action, suit or other proceeding to be tried at such court, or with any other person, in relation to the merits of such action, suit or proceeding, or receiving a communication from a party or other person in respect to it without immediately disclosing the same to the court; disobedience by an inferior tribunal, magistrate or officer of the lawful judgment, decree, order or process of a superior court, or proceeding in an action, suit or proceeding, contrary to law, after such action, suit or proceeding shall have been removed from the jurisdiction of such inferior tribunal, magistrate or officer. There are various other acts in the Code which are specially declared punishable as contempt; and it au-

---

saying in its presence that he will go to jail before he will obey its order, is guilty of contempt. *Ex parte* Robinson, 71 Cal. 608.

But it is not a contempt to disobey an order of court which is not authorized by law. Lester v. People (Ill.) Jan. 21, 1890. See *note* to Com. v. Perkins (Pa.) 2 L. R. A. 223.

It is not contempt for defendant in a divorce suit to refuse or fail to obey an order to pay temporary alimony. Allen v. Allen, 72 Iowa, 502.

But it has also been held that a person refusing to pay alimony as ordered is guilty of contempt where he had been advised not to pay, and it is evident that he did not intend to pay. Potts v. Potts, 13 West. Rep. 147, 68 Mich. 492.

So nonpayment of alimony, as ordered, by a defendant who absents himself from the State and renders personal service impossible, is punishable as contempt, where service is made upon his solicitor. Fairchild v. Fairchild (N. J.) 11 Cent. Rep. 750; Ford v. Ford, 10 Abb. Pr. N. S. 79.

A husband who refuses to comply with an order of the court to give security for alimony may be adjudged guilty of contempt. Wright v. Wright, 74 Wis. 439.

In a divorce suit, a district court in Montana has power to order a defendant's answer stricken from the file, in punishment of his disobedience of an order to pay alimony, where the defendant is a nonresident and absent from the Territory, and no other punishment can be resorted to. Zimmerman v. Zimmerman, 7 Mont. 114.

Under the California Code of Civil Procedure, proof of inability of a person imprisoned for contempt in refusing to pay alimony as directed by the court, to comply with such order, entitles him to his discharge. *Re* Wilson, 75 Cal. 580.

A failure to pay alimony as directed by the court is a civil contempt: and a person imprisoned therefor is in custody as under an execution. *Ibid.*

An assignee in insolvency who refuses to comply with an order to pay into court the money in his hands may be punished for contempt. Buhlert v. Superior Court, 72 Cal. 97.

The failure to produce the body of the person named in a writ of habeas corpus, who was in the custody of the person served with the writ, is a contempt committed in the face of the court. *Ex parte* Sternes, 77 Cal. 156.

A sheriff who refuses to release a prisoner ordered to be discharged on habeas corpus is guilty of contempt of court. *Re* Vanvaver (Tenn.) Jan. 10, 1890.

A party to a suit, who is bound by the decree, may be guilty of contempt by a pertinacious opposition to it, or by a refusal to obey it, and asserting a different right or title from the one alleged and enforced by him in the suit. Texas v. White ("*Re* Chiles") 89 U. S. 22 Wall. 157 (22 L. ed. 819).

thorizes every court of justice, and every judicial officer, to punish contempt by fine or imprisonment, or both, but provides that such fine shall not exceed $300, nor the imprisonment six months, and that, when the contempt is not one of those mentioned in subdivisions 1 and 2 of section 650, or subdivision 1 of section 916, which empowers every judicial officer to preserve and enforce order in his immediate presence, etc., it must appear that the right or remedy of a party to an action, suit or proceeding was defeated or prejudiced thereby before the contempt can be punished otherwise than by a fine not exceeding $100. § 651.

Section 652 of the Code provides that "when a contempt is committed in the immediate view and presence of the court or officer, it may be punished summarily, for which an order must be made, reciting the facts as occurring in such immediate view and presence, determining that the person proceeded against is thereby guilty of a contempt, and that he be punished as therein prescribed;" and section 653 provides that "in cases other than those mentioned in section 652 [642], before any proceedings can be taken therein, the facts constituting the contempt must be shown by an affidavit presented to the court or judicial officer, and thereupon such court or officer may either make an order upon the person charged to show cause why he should not be arrested to answer, or issue a warrant of arrest to bring such person to answer in the first instance."

Section 655 provides that, "in the proceeding for a contempt, the State is the plaintiff. In all cases of public interest the proceeding may be prosecuted by the district attorney on behalf of the State; and in all cases where the proceeding is commenced upon the relation of a private party, such party shall be deemed a co-plaintiff with the State."

These various sections of the Code not only provide what acts shall be deemed contempts, and point out the mode of procedure for their punishment, but strongly indicate that, when the act constituting the contempt is not committed in the immediate view and presence of the court or officer, it must be such an one as is calculated to affect the right or remedy of a party in a litigation.

Section 651, which limits the punishment to a fine not exceeding $100, unless it appear that the right or remedy of a party to an action, suit or proceeding was defeated or prejudiced by the contempt, clearly shows this. If this view be correct, it follows, then, that, unless the matter published by the appellant constituted a contempt under subdivision 1 or 2 of said section 650, or under subdivision 1 of section 916, or affected, or tended to affect, the right of a party to a litigation pending in said court, or before the judge thereof, it does not come within the purview of the Code. But counsel for the respondent urge that a court of justice has power to punish for contempt, and that its power in that respect cannot be limited by statute. This is undoubtedly true, so far as it is necessary to maintain order in the conduct of its business, and in the enforcement of its jurisdiction. The Legislature could as well abolish the courts outright as to deprive them of the power to punish for contempt those who impeded, obstructed and embarrassed the administration of the law. It would paralyze their functions, and render their process, orders, decrees and judgments mere *brutum fulmen*. But whether they possess inherit authority to punish as contempt acts which do not affect causes actually pending before them, although the acts tend to degrade the court, and bring the administration of justice into disrepute, has never been conceded in this country. Counsel for respondent have cited in support of that doctrine from the American decisions, *State v.*

Violation of injunction.

The power to punish for the violation of an injunction is incident to the power to grant an injunction. Mourer v. State, 5 West. Rep. 807, 107 Ind. 539. See *Re* Nichols, 54 N. Y. 72; People v. Campbell, 40 N. Y. 138; Albany City Bank v. Schermerhorn, 9 Paige, 372, 4 N. Y. Ch. L. ed. 736; *Re* Smethurst, 4 How. Pr. 369.

The purpose of the Statute for the punishment of contempt is to enforce obedience to the orders of the court, not to punish, but only after the contempt is proved to imprison the delinquent until the order of the court is complied with or he discharged according to law. *Ex parte* Wright, 65 Ind. 512; M'Credie v. Senior, 4 Paige, 378, 3 N. Y. Ch. L. ed. 477.

In a proceeding for contempt for violation of an injunction, it is the satisfaction of the offended dignity of the law and the vindication of the respect due to tribunals of justice which call for the interposition and punishment. Conover v. Wood, 5 Abb. Pr. 90.

Courts exercising both common-law and chancery jurisdiction may issue final orders of injunction which cannot be disputed and their validity brought into question in proceedings on an attachment for contempt. Central U. Teleph. Co. v. State, 9 West. Rep. 242, 110 Ind. 205.

Although an injunction be irregularly obtained, it is still an order of the court, and must be discharged before it can be disobeyed. Howe v. Willard, 40 Vt. 662.

However hastily or improvidently an injunction may be granted, it is valid until annulled by the court granting it, or reversed on appeal, and until such time it is entitled to obedience. If it is disobeyed the party can be punished for contempt. Erie R. Co. v. Ramsey, 45 N. Y. 654.

That he was advised by counsel and believed that the order of injunction was null and void, and that he acted upon such advice and belief, is not an answer to the proceeding for contempt. Roosevelt v. Edson, 1 How. Pr. (N. S.) 250; People v. Edson, 19 Jones & S. 257; People v. Compton, 1 Duer, 522; Lansing v. Easton, 7 Paige, 364, 4 N. Y. Ch. L. ed. 190, Rogers v. Paterson, 4 Paige, 456, 3 N. Y. Ch. L. ed. 514; Hawley v. Bennett, 4 Paige, 163, 3 N. Y. Ch. L. ed. 387; *Re* Fenny, 4 Nat. Bankr. Reg. *70.

In equity a party may be punished as for a contempt when he has knowingly and designedly done acts which he knew, at the time, the court had, by an order, prohibited him from doing, although at the time no order had been served, or in fact entered, but had only been directed to be entered. People v. Brower, 4 Paige, 405, 3 N. Y. Ch. L. ed. 491; Hull v. Thomas, 3 Edw. Ch. 236, 6 N. Y. Ch. L. ed. 640; State v. Dwyer, 41 N. J. L. 95; Livingston v. Swift, 23 How. Pr. 2; Stafford v. Brown, 4 Paige, 360, 3 N. Y. Ch. L. ed. 470; Vansandau v. Rose, 2 Jac. & W. 264; Endicott v. Mathis, 9 N. J. Eq. 110; Cape May & S. L. R. Co. v. Johnson, 35 N. J. Eq. 424; People v. Compton, 1 Duer, 553.

Morrill, 16 Ark. 384, and *Stuart* v. *People*, 4 Ill. 405; but it is well understood that the courts of the latter State have since held quite to the contrary. *Storey* v. *People*, 79 Ill. 45.

In *State* v. *Anderson*, 40 Iowa, 207, the Supreme Court of that State held that the publication by an attorney of an article in a newspaper criticising the rulings of a court in a cause tried and determined prior to the publication did not constitute contempt punishable by the court, and referred approvingly to *Dunham* v. *State*, 6 Iowa, 245, in which it was held that the publication of articles in a newspaper reflecting upon the conduct of a judge in relation to a cause pending in court, which had been disposed of before the publication, however unjust and libelous the publication might be, did not amount to contemptuous or violent behavior towards the court, under chapter 94, Code 1851, of that State, nor that such articles were so calculated to impede, embarrass or obstruct the court in the administration of the law as to justify the summary punishment of the offender under that chapter. The inherent power of a court of justice to punish for contempt one who commits acts which have a direct tendency to obstruct or embarrass its proceedings in matters pending before it, or to influence decisions regarding such matters, is undoubted; but it can hardly be maintained, from the adjudications had upon the subject in the various States, that such power is broad enough to vest in the court the authority to so punish anyone for criticising the court on account of its procedure in matters which have fully terminated, however much its dignity and standing may be affected thereby, however unjust, rude or boorish may be the criticism, or whatever may be its effect in bringing the administration of the law in disrepute. In any event, it seems to me that the Legislature has authority to limit the power of courts in regard to matters of contempt to the punishment only of such acts as are specified in the sections of the Code above set out. Nor can I discover any reason why the Legislature does not possess authority to prescribe the mode of procedure to be observed by the courts in the exercise of their power to punish in such cases. The proceeding is not a personal matter of the court. The State is a plaintiff in all cases of that character. But, when the acts constituting the contempt are committed in the presence of the court, it may take judicial cognizance of them, and inflict summary punishment. It is, however, required to make an order reciting the acts as occurring in its immediate view and presence, and determine that the person proceeded against is thereby guilty of a contempt and that he be punished, etc. As I view the said sections of the Code, they are little more than declaratory of the law upon the subject of contempt as understood by a large portion of the courts of the several States at the time of their adoption. They provide every means necessary to the preservation of order and decorum in the presence of the courts of the State, while engaged in the transaction of their business, for the enforcement of obedience to their lawful judgments, decrees, orders and processes, and for the performance of official duty upon the part of their officers. Whether, therefore, the said matter published by the appellant constituted a contempt depends upon whether it falls within any of the cases specified in said sections; and whether the circuit court had authority, of its own motion, to cite the appellant to appear before it, and inflict upon him the punishment imposed, depends upon whether the offending was done in the immediate view and presence of the court.

For what purpose or with what intent the appellant published the said matter, unless it were to create an idle, silly sensation, is an enigma. His doing so probably resulted from a freak or spleen. He certainly could not have expected to gain any advantage from such a profusion of extravagancy, nor have supposed that a half-witted person, even, would give any credence to his grotesque account of the affairs of Jackson County referred to in his production. Why any man other than an addle-brained lunatic should print such absurd, ridiculous stuff in a newspaper is difficult to imagine. The indulgence in such shilly-shally by managers of newspapers indicates a mania on their part to abuse, vilify and insult officials selected to administer the affairs of government, however devoted and faithful to the public interests those officials may be. Such a course only tends to incite anarchy, the most dangerous and dreaded enemy with which a republican government has to contend. It is well known to this court, and to the community generally, that no such condition in the judicial matters of "southern Oregon" as the appellant endeavored to represent exists, and that no such abuses as he depicted prevail there, but, upon the contrary, that justice is as well and faithfully administered in that locality as in any other part of the State. Yet the appellant, the editor of the newspaper, whose desire should only be to have upright and competent officials in the administration of the local affairs of his section, where he consistently can take pride in having them so regarded by the community and the world at large, makes use of his position to traduce and degrade them. Instead of attending to his business of imparting useful information,—instead of assisting in building up the community and its institutions,—he acts the part of an iconoclast. The course pursued by such persons is a positive damage and injury to society. It is a poor requital for the faithful services of the learned judge who presides in the first judicial district, and whom the people thereof selected to determine the law in their matters of difference, to subject him to a wholesale charge of dereliction of duty, coming from whatever source it may.

The publication, according to the general definition given by Blackstone, and by some of the more modern law-writers, upon the subject, would probably constitute contempt, but, under the Code of this State, it does not; nor do I think it would according to the weight of decisions made under the Constitutions of the various States. If it had reflected upon the conduct of the court with reference to a pending suit, and tended in any manner to influence its decision therein, it would unquestionably have been a contempt; but it was not shown that any suit was then pending by which the rights of any litigant were, or could have been, affected by it. The article itself states that the court had ordered an investigation into the "whys and wherefores" of a material witness disappearing in a criminal case, in which his testimony was needed to convict; but it does not appear in the proceeding for contempt that such was the fact, nor, as I can see, that it was calculated to influence the decision in that matter. It appears to have been a vague, wanton fault-finding in regard to the general manner in which official duty in that part of the State had been performed, not arising to the dignity of a criticism, nor entitled to any notice whatever. If the publishers of such contemptible articles are left alone to breathe and scent their own fetid exhalations, it will be the most suitable punishment which can be inflicted upon them. If the act were such an one as could have been in the immediate view and presence of the court, it would doubtless have been what is termed a "direct contempt;" but, it not having been so committed, and not involving a direct disobedience to any order of the court, it comes within the class denominated "constructive contempts." 20 Am. Law Reg. 147.

In proceedings to punish that class of contempts, it is necessary that a proper information should be filed before the court is authorized to act in the matter. Said section 658 of the Code, above set out, makes it imperative that the facts constituting the contempt in such cases must be shown by an affidavit presented to the court, etc., before the proceeding can be taken. "The power of a court," said Wallace, *J.*, in *Batchelder* v. *Moore*, 42 Cal. 414, "to punish for an alleged contempt of its authority, though undoubted, is in its nature arbitrary, and its exercise is not to be upheld except under the circumstances and in the manner prescribed by law."

I am of the opinion, therefore, that the court was not authorized to proceed in the matter of its own motion; nor was the court empowered to punish the appellant by imprisonment. Section 651 of the Code, above referred to, is decisive upon that point.

The decision appealed from must therefore be reversed.

NEW YORK COURT OF APPEALS (2d Div.).

James T. VOUGHT *et al.*, *Appts.*,
v.
Joseph S. WILLIAMS, *Respt.*

(......N. Y.......)

1. A provision in a contract for the sale of real property that the title is to be passed upon by the purchaser's lawyer or conveyancer does not make his decision that the title is good a condition precedent to the vendor's right to enforce the performance of the contract.

2. A stipulation that the title to real estate shall be "first class" means nothing more than it shall be marketable.

3. The presumption of death of one who left home for causes unknown and has not been seen or heard of by his family or friends for upwards of twenty-four years, and who, when last seen, was about twenty-three years old, unmarried, dissipated, in feeble health and in destitute condition, being in want of clothing, is not sufficiently strong to make marketable a title to real estate which depends on his death.

(April 15, 1890.)

APPEAL by plaintiffs from a judgment of the General Term of the Supreme Court, Fifth Department, affirming a judgment of the Monroe Equity Term in favor of defendant in an action to enforce specific performance of a contract for the purchase of certain real estate. *Affirmed.*

Statement by **Brown**, *J.:*

Appeal from a judgment of the General Term of the Fifth Department affirming a judgment entered upon a decree of the Special Term. The action was for the specific performance of a contract to purchase real estate. In March, 1858, Giles B. Richardson died intestate, seised of the property in question, leaving, surviving him, his widow, Mary P. Richardson and two sons, William H. and Giles B., Jr. Giles B., Jr., was born on May 16, 1840, and lived with his mother at Pittsford, Monroe County, until 1863. At that time he was unmarried, was in poor health, was very dissipated and had no business. In May, 1863, he left home and about a week thereafter was seen by an acquaintance in the City of Albany. He was then in a destitute condition, and in want of clothing, and stated that he was going to Troy to procure work. From that time until the trial of the action he had not been seen, and none of his friends or members of his family ever heard anything of him. In April, 1875, his mother and brother, by deed, conveyed the property in question to the plaintiff's grantors. The deed recited that the grantors were the sole heirs at law of Giles B. Richardson, deceased, and that it was intended to vest the absolute title to said lands in the party of the second part; that the deed was executed upon the assumption that Giles B. Richardson, Jr., was actually dead. The contract between the parties to this action for the sale of the land provided that the title was to be "first class," and was to be passed upon by a lawyer or conveyancer to be designated by the defendant. The defendant refused to take the property on the ground that the title was not a marketable one.

Further facts appear in the opinion.

Mr. James Breck Perkins, for appellant:

The Statute says (Code, § 841) that a person who absents himself for seven years is presumed to be dead, unless it is affirmatively proved that he was alive within that time.

The legal presumption is apart from any statutory rule, that as Richardson has not been heard from for seven years and more, by persons, who, if he had been alive, would naturally have heard of him, he is presumed to have died.

Lawson, Presump. Ev. Rule 43, pp. 200-205.

And, having been unmarried when last known to be alive, he will be presumed to have died without lawful issue.

Lawson, Presump. Ev. Rule 41, p. 197; Phillips, Ev. pp. 238, 239.

The presumption alone is enough to make a title merchantable.

Hillary v. *Waller*, 12 Ves. Jr. 239; *Emery* v. *Grocock*, 6 Madd. 54; *Prosser* v. *Watts*, 6 Madd. 59; *Dixon* v. *Dixon*, 3 Bro. Ch. 510; *Lyddea* v. *Weston*, 2 Atk. 20; *Ten Broeck* v. *Livingston*, 1 Johns. Ch. 357, 1 N.Y. Ch. L. ed. 170; *M'Comb* v. *Wright*, 5 Johns. Ch. 263, 1 N. Y. Ch. L. ed. 1077; *Brooklyn Park Comrs.* v. *Armstrong*, 45 N. Y. 234; *Gerry* v. *Post*, 13 How. Pr. 118; *Shriver* v. *Shriver*, 86 N. Y. 575; *Stapylton* v. *Scott*, 16 Ves. Jr. 274; *Schultz* v. *Rose*, 65 How. Pr. 75; *Fleming* v. *Burnham*, 1 Cent. Rep. 267, 100 N. Y. 1; *Ottinger* v. *Strasburger*, 33 Hun, 466; *Kip* v. *Hirsh*, 5 Cent. Rep. 375, 103 N. Y. 565.

Mr. **George F. Yeoman**, for respondent:

The decision of the defendant's attorneys that the title was not good is a bar to this action whether the attorneys were right or wrong as to the fact.

Hudson v. *Buck*, L. R. 7 Ch. Div. 683; *Williams* v. *Edwards*, 2 Sim. 78; *Gray* v. *Central R. Co.* 11 Hun, 70.

Where there is an executory contract to purchase, and in it the vendee has reserved the right to examine and decide as to some fact before executing the contract, his decision is conclusive, if made in good faith.

Note on stipulations to satisfy, 18 Abb. N. C. 48; *McCormick H. Mach. Co.* v. *Chisrown*, 33 Minn. 32, 31 Alb. L. J. 357; *Singerly* v. *Thayer*, 1 Cent. Rep. 52, 108 Pa. 291, 33 Alb. L. J. 82; *McClure* v. *Briggs*, 1 New Eng. Rep. 621, 58 Vt. 82, 33 Alb. L. J. 223; *Exhaust Ventilator Co.* v. *Chicago, M. & St. P. R. Co.* 66 Wis. 218, 34 Alb. L. J. 77.

A presumption from the lapse of time will not arise in support of a title as against a purchaser.

Shriver v. *Shriver*, 86 N. Y. 584; Atkinson, Marketable Titles, pp. 419, 420; *Wood* v. *Squires*, 1 Hun, 481; *Morey* v. *Farmers L. & T. Co.* 14 N. Y. 308; Pomeroy, Spec. Perf. § 205.

Where a party leaves home temporarily, with the intention of returning, the presumption of death will arise after the lapse of seven years, if he is not heard from; but where he left with the intention of remaining away, the presumption does not arise until inquiry has been made at the place to which he went, and it then appears that he has been absent from that place for more than seven years without being heard of. Where it does not appear what the intent was at the time of leaving, the court will not presume the intent of returning in order to be able to presume the death. A presumption will not be made to base a presumption upon.

Wharton, Ev. 3d. ed. § 1285.

The statutory presumption does not apply, except as against the owner of a life estate.

Code, § 941; *Gerry* v. *Post*, 13 How. Pr. 120; *Merritt* v. *Thompson*, 1 Abb. Pr. 223; *McCartee* v. *Camel*, 1 Barb. Ch. 462, 5 N. Y. Ch. L. ed. 456.

Brown, *J.*, delivered the opinion of the court:

The provision that the title was to be passed upon by the defendant's lawyer or conveyancer did not make the decision of the conveyancer that the title was good a condition precedent to the right of the plaintiff to enforce the performance of the contract. If a decision to that effect was refused unreasonably, the failure to obtain it would not defeat a recovery; and it would have been unreasonably refused if in fact, and beyond all dispute, the title was good. *Folliard* v. *Wallace*, 2 Johns. 395; *Thomas* v. *Fleury*, 26 N.Y. 26; *Brooklyn* v. *Brooklyn City R. Co.* 47 N. Y. 475; *Bowery Nat. Bank* v. *New York*, 63 N. Y. 336; *Duplex Safety Boiler Co.* v. *Garden*, 101 N.Y. 388, 2 Cent. Rep. 379; *Doll* v. *Noble*, 116 N. Y. 230.

The stipulation that the title should be "first class" could mean nothing more than that it should be marketable. The trial court refused to find that Giles B. Richardson, Jr., was dead, and it did find that there was no evidence "as to whether or not he was dead, except the presumption, if any, which is raised from the facts hereinbefore stated with regard to him." It found as conclusion of law "that the title of the plaintiff to said premises, depending, as it does, upon the disputed question of fact, is not a marketable title, and that the defendant was entitled because of said defect to refuse to carry out the said contract."

It is an established principle of law that every purchaser of real estate is entitled to a marketable title, free from incumbrances and defects, unless he expressly stipulates to accept a defective title. *Burwell* v. *Jackson*, 9 N. Y. 535; *Delavan* v. *Duncan*, 49 N. Y. 485.

A marketable title is one that is free from reasonable doubt. There is reasonable doubt when there is uncertainty as to some fact appearing in the course of its deduction, and the doubt must be such as affects the value of the land, or will interfere with its sale. A purchaser is not to be compelled to take property, the possession of which he may be compelled to defend by litigation. He should have a title that will enable him to hold his land in peace, and, if he wishes to sell it, be reasonably sure that no flaw or doubt will arise to disturb its market value. *Brooklyn Park Comrs.* v. *Armstrong*, 45 N. Y. 234; *Shriver* v. *Shriver*, 86 N. Y. 575, and cases cited; *Hellreigel* v. *Manning*, 97 N. Y. 56; *Fleming* v. *Burnham*, 100 N. Y. 1, 1 Cent. Rep. 267; *Ferry* v. *Sampson*, 112 N. Y. 415; *Moore* v. *Williams*, 115 N. Y. 586; *Swayne* v. *Lyon*, 67 Pa. 436; *Dobbs* v. *Norcross*, 24 N. J. Eq. 327.

"If a title depends upon a fact which is not capable of satisfactory proof, a purchaser cannot be compelled to take it." *Shriver* v. *Shriver*, *supra*.

It was said, however, in *Ferry* v. *Sampson*, *supra*, that "the rule is not absolute that a disputable fact not determined by the judgment is in every case a bar to the enforcement of the sale. It depends in some degree upon discretion. If the existence of the alleged fact which is supposed to cloud the title is a possibility merely, or the alleged outstanding right is a very improbable and remote contingency, which, according to ordinary experience, has no probable basis, the court may compel the purchaser, in such a case, to complete his purchase."

In that case the decisions of the general and

special term were reversed, and the purchaser was compelled to take the title, although one to whom the property had been devised by his father's will was not shown to be dead, or, if dead, that he had not left a widow or children surviving him. It was shown, however, that he had not been heard from for forty years before the trial of the action, and if living would have been about sixty-one years of age. If the reasoning of the opinion in the case just cited is to be applied in this case, it would lead to a reversal of the judgment appealed from. In respect only to the length of time that had elapsed since the absent owner was heard from do the cases differ. Here we have a young unmarried man, of feeble health, and of dissipated habits, leaving home from causes unknown. When last seen, he was in a destitute condition and in want of clothing; and for upwards of twenty-four years no one of his family or friends have seen or heard of him. Is it reasonable to suppose that, if living, he would have made no effort to obtain the property that he left behind? The presumption of death does not depend on length of time alone.

Here, as in *Ferry* v. *Sampson*, there was a valuable interest in property which, according to common experience, the owner would, if living, have probably asserted and claimed. These circumstances all point to Richardson's death, as in the case cited they indicated the death of Armstrong, the devisee. *Ferry* v. *Sampson* is not an authority, however, for anything further than that forty years' absence, under the circumstances there proven, raised a presumption of death. In that respect it is like the case of *M'Comb* v. *Wright*, 5 Johns. Ch. 263, 1 N. Y. Ch. L. ed. 1077, where *Chancellor* Kent made a similar ruling.

But I am not prepared to decide that a purchaser of real estate should be compelled to take title when there is an outstanding right in a man who, if living, would be only forty-seven years of age, and of whose death there is no evidence except the presumption arising from an absence from his friends of twenty-four years, and his failure to communicate with them and to claim property which he left behind him upon his departure from home. It is very probable that the man is dead. The chances are very largely in favor of that conclusion. But his death is not proven, and the plaintiff's title to the real estate, which necessarily depends upon his death, cannot be said to be free from a reasonable doubt. Why should we compel the purchaser to take all the risk involved in that doubt? There is no title by adverse possession. The only act of his cotenant hostile to his title that appears in the record before us is the deed of his mother and brother, which purported to convey the whole land in April, 1875; and if there has been adverse possession it dates from the delivery of that deed. *Culver* v. *Rhodes*, 87 N. Y. 348.

No decision made in this action can bind Richardson or his descendants, if he left any. The cloud on the title would remain, whatever decision the court might make upon the question whether Richardson was or was not living; and the title cannot be made marketable by determining that fact in this action.

In *Fleming* v. *Burnham*, *supra*, it was said: "It would be unjust to compel a purchaser to take a title, the validity of which depended upon a question of fact, when the facts presented upon the application might be changed on a new inquiry, or are open to opposing inferences." That statement is very applicable to this case. Richardson, or some descendant of his, might appear at any time and destroy all the reasoning built upon his absence and abandonment of his property. The parties contracted with reference to a "first-class title." They did not rely upon the agreement which the law would imply to that effect. They expressly stipulated for it. The consideration to be paid for the land was based upon it; and the court should not compel the defendant to execute the contract unless it is clear, beyond a reasonable doubt, that he will receive what he contracted to buy. There must be some point of time, of course, when the presumption of death would arise; but we have been referred to no case in this State in which that presumption has prevailed where the absence was less than forty years. We do not think that it should prevail in this case. The circumstances do not point unequivocally to Richardson's death, and the special term decided correctly in refusing to enforce the contract.

The judgment should be affirmed.

All concur, except **Bradley and Haight**, *JJ.*, not sitting.

INDIANA SUPREME COURT.

CINCINNATI, INDIANAPOLIS, ST. LOUIS & CHICAGO R. CO., *Appt.*,
v.
Mary C. HOWARD.

(....Ind.....)

1. **An objection to the admission of evidence** in answer to a question propounded to a witness on the ground that it is "improper and incompetent" or that it is "irrelevant and immaterial and does not rebut anything" is too general to raise any question for the consideration of the appellate court.

2. **Where a railroad company for the purpose of showing** that a train sounded a whistle when it approached a road crossing at which an accident occurred, gives evidence that there were other crossings in the vicinity at which the whistle was also sounded, witnesses living near such other crossings may be permitted to testify that no whistle was sounded near them.

3. **A person who was present** when others started out upon a drive, during which they came into a collision with a railroad train upon a railroad crossing and were injured, may be permitted to testify as to where they were going, such testimony being part of the *res gestæ*.

4. **A party who has answered interrogatories** propounded before trial, under § 359,

See also 9 L. R. A. 521; 22 L. R. A. 33; 30 L. R. A. 684; 32 L. R. A. 149.

Rev. Stat. 1881, cannot object to the introduction of the answers in evidence at the trial upon the ground that they are irrelevant.

5. **In order to entitle a person injured by a collision** with a railway train at a highway crossing to recover damages for such injuries from the company he must show by a preponderance of evidence that both he and his driver vigilantly used their eyes and ears to ascertain if a train was approaching; he has no right to assume that no train is approaching, if his view is obstructed, from the fact that no whistle is sounded, and such fact cannot be considered in determining the question of his negligence.

6. **When a person crossing a railroad track** is injured by collision with a train the fault is prima facie his own and he must show affirmatively that his fault or negligence did not contribute to the injury before he can recover therefor; this is done, however, if all the facts and circumstances illustrating his conduct at the time of the accident are shown and the inference that he exercised proper caution arises therefrom.

7. **The fact that a train is behind time** and is running faster than its usual speed does not excuse one attempting to cross the track from exercising all the care and caution required of him when the train is on time and running at its usual speed.

8. **Obstructions to sight or hearing** in the direction of an approaching train as a traveler upon a highway nears a railroad crossing require increased care on his part, the care required being in proportion to the increase of danger that may come from the use of the highway at such place.

9. **An instruction which has no application** to the evidence in the case should not be given, although it contains a correct statement of the law in the abstract.

(June 6, 1890.)

APPEAL by defendant from a judgment of the General Term of the Superior Court for Marion County affirming a judgment of the Special Term in favor of plaintiff in an action brought to recover damages for personal injuries alleged to have resulted from the negligence of defendant's servants. *Reversed.*

The injury resulted from a collision between plaintiff, who was traveling upon a highway, and defendant's train, and was alleged to have been the result of the negligent running of the train.

It was shown at the trial that another road crossed the railroad track about a mile north of the one where the accident occurred, near which was a whistling post. Oliver Klingensmith, who lived about a quarter of a mile from that crossing, was asked by plaintiff, against defendant's objection, with reference to the train which caused the accident:

Q. 27. I will ask you to state whether that train did or did not whistle at the first crossing north of the crossing where the accident occurred?

A. I never heard none.

Mrs. Sarah F. Howard was asked by plaintiff, against defendant's objection, with respect to the parties who were injured:

Q. 17. Where were they going?

A. Well, they started to church.

Q. 18. To what place?

A. To Crooked Creek, to the Baptist Church.

The other material facts sufficiently appear in the opinion.

Messrs. **Baker, Hord & Hendricks,** for appellant:

If there are obstructions to sight the duty exists to use increased care in the use of the sense of hearing.

Bellefontaine R. Co. v. Hunter, 33 Ind. 335; *St. Louis & S. E. R. Co. v. Mathias,* 50 Ind. 65; *Terre Haute & I. R. Co. v. Graham,* 95 Ind. 286.

When a person has been killed at a railroad crossing, and there are no witnesses of the accident, the circumstances must be such as to show that the deceased exercised proper care for his own safety. When the circumstances point just as much to the negligence of the deceased as to its absence, or point in neither direction, the plaintiff should be nonsuited.

Cordell v. New York Cent. & H. R. R. Co. 75 N. Y. 330; *Hart v. Hudson River Bridge Co.* 84 N. Y. 56.

The burden was upon the plaintiff to establish that there was no contributory negligence.

Hale v. Smith, 78 N. Y. 483; *Warner v. New York Cent. R. Co.* 44 N. Y. 471; *Reynolds v. New York Cent. & H. R. R. Co.* 58 N. Y. 248; *Toledo, W. & W. R. Co. v. Brannagan,* 75 Ind. 490.

The fact that a train was behind time, and was running faster than its usual speed, at the crossing, to make up time, did not excuse the plaintiff or her father from exercising the care and caution required of them, when the train was on time and running at its usual rate of speed at that crossing.

Salter v. Utica & B. R. R. Co. 75 N.Y. 273, 281; *Wilcox v. Rome, W. & O. R. Co.* 39 N. Y. 358, 376; *Schofield v. Chicago, M. & St. P. R. Co.* 2 McCrary, 268.

If there were any obstructions to sight or hearing in the direction of the approaching train, as the plaintiff and her father neared the crossing, the obstructions required increased care on the part of the plaintiff and her father on approaching the crossing.

Terre Haute & I. R. Co. v. Clark, 73 Ind. 168; *Pittsburgh, C. & St. L. R. Co. v. Martin,* 82 Ind. 484; *Lake Shore & M. S. R. Co. v. Miller,* 25 Mich. 274; *Toledo & W. R. Co. v. Goddard,* 25 Ind. 185; *Toledo, W. & W. R. Co. v. Brannagan, supra; Pittsburg, C. & St. L. R. Co. v. Yundt,* 78 Ind. 373; *Huntington v. Breen,* 77 Ind. 29; *Nave v. Flack,* 90 Ind. 205, 212; *Porter County Comrs. v. Dombke,* 94 Ind. 72.

Mr. **John T. Dye,** also for appellant:

Contributory negligence is not a matter of defense, and the plaintiff must show affirmatively, by pleading and proof, that his negligence did not contribute to the injury before he is entitled to recover therefor.

Cincinnati, H. & I. R. Co. v. Butler, 1 West. Rep. 110, 103 Ind. 32; *Lyons v. Terre Haute & I. R. Co.* 101 Ind. 419; *Cincinnati, W. & M. R. Co. v. Hiltzhauer,* 99 Ind. 486.

When a person crossing a railroad track is injured by a collision with a train, the fault is, prima facie, his own, and he must show affirmatively that his fault or negligence did not contribute to his injury before he is entitled to recover for such injury.

Hathaway v. Toledo, W. & W. R. Co. 46 Ind.

25, cited and approved in *Cincinnati, H. & I. R. Co.* v. *Butler, supra.*

Where obstacles interpose which obstruct sight and sound it is the plain dictate of ordinary prudence that the traveler on the highway should approach the crossing with a degree of caution much above that which would be required at a point where no obstacles intervened.

Cincinnati, H. & I. R. Co. v. *Butler, supra,* and cases cited; *Indiana, B. & W. R. Co.* v. *Greene,* 8 West. Rep. 883, 106 Ind. 279.

Where the circumstances point just as much to the negligence of the deceased as to its absence, or point in neither direction, the plaintiff should be nonsuited.

Toledo, W. & W. R. Co. v. *Brannagan,* 75 Ind. 490; *Warner* v. *New York Cent. R. Co.* 44 N. Y. 465; *Cordell* v. *New York Cent. & H. R. R. Co.* 75 N. Y. 330; *State* v. *Maine Cent. R. Co.* 76 Me. 357; *Lesan* v. *Maine Cent. R. Co.* 77 Me. 85; *State* v. *Maine Cent. R. Co.* 77 Me. 538; *Hinckley* v. *Cape Cod R. Co.* 120 Mass. 257; *Allyn* v. *Boston & A. R. Co.* 105 Mass. 77; *Hathaway* v. *Toledo, W. & W. R. Co. supra; Sherlock* v. *Alling,* 44 Ind. 204; *Bellefontaine R. Co.* v. *Hunter,* 33 Ind. 335; *Haas* v. *Grand Rapids & I. R. Co.* 47 Mich. 401; *Lake Shore & M. S. R. Co.* v. *Miller,* 25 Mich. 274; *Pennsylvania R. Co.* v. *Beale,* 73 Pa. 504; *Chicago, R. I. & P. R. Co.* v. *Houston,* 95 U. S. 697 (24 L. ed. 542); *Schofield* v. *Chicago, M. & St. P. R. Co.* 114 U. S. 615 (29 L. ed. 224); *Chicago & E. I. R. Co.* v. *Hedges,* 118 Ind. 5; *Tully* v. *Fitchburg R. Co.* 134 Mass. 499; *Butterfield* v. *Western R. Corp.* 10 Allen, 532.

Messrs. **Levi Ritter, E. F. Ritter** and **B. W. Ritter,** for appellee:

The rule that requires the plaintiff to prove, as a part of his own case, that he was himself guilty of no contributory fault, does not necessarily require this proof to be made by direct affirmative evidence.

Pittsburgh, C. & St. L. R. Co. v. *Wright,* 80 Ind. 182; *Salem* v. *Goller,* 76 Ind. 291, 292; *Pittsburgh, C. & St. L. R. Co.* v. *Noel,* 77 Ind. 110, 118; 2 Thomp. Neg. p. 1178; 2 Redfield, Railways, p. 253; Pierce, Railroads, p. 346; *Prentiss* v. *Boston,* 112 Mass. 43, 47; *Foster* v. *Dixfield,* 18 Me. 380, 381; *Johnson* v. *Hudson River R. Co.* 20 N.Y. 70; *Solen* v. *Virginia & T. R. Co.* 13 Nev. 106; *Gay* v. *Winter,* 34 Cal. 153, 163; *Lane* v. *Crombie,* 12 Pick. 177; *Mayo* v. *Boston & M. R. Co.* 104 Mass. 137, 140; *Greenleaf* v. *Illinois Cent. R. Co.* 29 Iowa, 14, 4 Am. Rep. 181; *Nelson* v. *Chicago, R. I. & P. R. Co.* 38 Iowa, 564; *Murphy* v. *Chicago, R. I. & P. R. Co.* 45 Iowa, 661; *Rusch* v. *Davenport,* 6 Iowa, 443; *French* v. *Brunswick,* 21 Me. 29; *French* v. *Taunton Branch R. Co.* 116 Mass. 537; *Richey* v. *Missouri Pac. R. Co.* 7 Mo. App. 150.

The failure to give the statutory signals was a circumstance to be considered in determining the question of contributory negligence on the part of the plaintiff.

Pittsburgh, C. & St. L. R. Co. v. *Martin,* 82 Ind. 476, 483; *Pittsburgh, C. & St. L. R. Co.* v. *Yundt,* 78 Ind. 373, 376; *Gaynor* v. *Old Colony & N. R. Co.* 100 Mass. 208; *Indianapolis & V. R. Co.* v. *McLin,* 82 Ind. 452; Abbott, Tr. Ev. 597; *Pennsylvania R. Co.* v. *Ogier,* 35 Pa. 71; *Milwaukee & C. R. Co.* v. *Hunter,* 11 Wis. 161; *Continental Imp. Co.* v. *Stead,* 95 U. S. 161 (24 L. ed. 403); 2 Thomp. Neg. p. 1173; *Massoth* v. *Delaware & H. Canal Co.* 64 N.Y. 524.

The second instruction given on the motion of appellee is well sustained by the authorities of this State as well as of other States.

Indianapolis & V. R. Co. v. *McLin, Pittsburgh, C. & St. L. R. Co.* v. *Martin* and *Pittsburgh, C. & St. L. R. Co.* v. *Yundt, supra;* Pierce, Railroads, 342, 350; *Gaynor* v. *Old Colony & N. R. Co.* 100 Mass. 208, 212; *Pennsylvania R. Co.* v. *Ogier,* 35 Pa. 71. See also *Kennayde* v. *Pacific R. Co.* 45 Mo. 255; *Tabor* v. *Missouri Valley R. Co.* 46 Mo. 353; *Ernst* v. *Hudson River R. Co.* 35 N.Y. 9, 39 N.Y. 61.

Berkshire, *Ch. J.,* delivered the opinion of the court:

The appellee was the plaintiff below and the appellant the defendant. The gravamen of the action is negligence, and in the complaint there is the proper negation of contributory negligence. The appellant answered in general denial. The cause was submitted to a jury for trial, a verdict returned in favor of the appellee and over a motion for a new trial judgment was rendered upon the verdict. From the judgment at special term an appeal was taken to general term, and from its judgment affirming the judgment in special term this appeal is prosecuted.

Several errors have been assigned, but we are only concerned with certain questions arising out of the court's action in overruling the motion for a new trial. It is not our province to determine whether the 26th question put by the appellee to the witness, John Kissel, and his answer thereto, were or were not improper, for the reason that no specific objection was made to the same. It has been held time and again that a general objection to the admission of evidence in answer to a question propounded to a witness raises no question for our consideration. The objection which we find in the record is that the evidence "is improper and incompetent." This is a stereotyped objection to the admission of offered evidence that is without value for any purpose.

There is no available error in the record as to the ruling of the court in allowing the witness Oliver Klingensmith to answer question 27, propounded to him by the appellee. The objection made was: "We object to it as not rebutting anything, and as incompetent and irrelevant and immaterial, and having nothing to do with the matter."

The objection is too general, but in view of the testimony as to the distance the road crossings were from each other, introduced by the appellant, and the further testimony introduced by the appellant as to the different points at which the whistle was sounded, we are of the opinion that the question and answer were proper.

The illustrations given by counsel for the appellant in their original briefs are not parallel cases. What we have said as to the question put and the answer given thereto by the witness Oliver Klingensmith, applies equally to the question propounded to Francis Mathis, and his answer to the same. The objection to the 21st question asked of Mrs. Sarah F. Howard and her answer thereto is that the evidence "is incompetent, irrelevant and immaterial. The objection is unavailing. The objections to questions 17 and 18, propounded to this witness, and her answer thereto, are unavailing. The testimony was not improper. The witness was the mother of the appellee and the wife of Dr. Howard, who lost his life in the accident involved in this controversy. When the husband and daughter left their home, which was also the home of the witness, on the fatal evening, she was present. What was said when they were about to depart as to their destination was not mere hearsay, but was a part of the *res gestæ*. It was pertaining to what afterwards happened. Such testimony is always competent.

The appellee was permitted by the court to introduce in evidence certain answers given to certain interrogatories propounded by the appellee to the appellant.

Section 359 entitled the appellee to propound interrogatories to the appellant relative to the matter in controversy, and required the appellant to answer the same. After the interrogatories had been answered, by virtue of the same section of the Statute, it was the appellee's right to introduce the answers in evidence if she so desired. If the interrogatories were not relevant the appellant should have moved their rejection; if the appellant gave irrelevant answers to the interrogatories that was its own fault, and it cannot complain that they were introduced in evidence.

This brings us to the questions arising in the record because of the instructions given to the jury by the court and those refused.

This is an action to recover damages because of injuries to the appellee occasioned by an accident occurring at a point where appellant's railway crosses a certain highway located in Marion County, Indiana. The appellee and her father, Dr. Howard, were in a buggy drawn by one horse, and were in the act of passing over the railroad track when struck by one of the appellant's locomotive engines pulling a train of cars along its said railroad and across said highway. The correctness of the instructions depends upon the duties and liabilities of the parties under the recognized rules of law in such cases.

And at this point, as well as at any other, we may say that there was a conflict in the evidence as to whether the whistle was sounded and the bell rung, as the statute law of the State then required, and, the jury having found that they were not, we are concluded by the finding, and in the further consideration of the case shall take it for granted that the appellant was guilty of negligence contributing to the disaster. This will leave but the one main fact and the questions which are involved relating to it,—the want of contributory negligence on the appellee's part.

In *Hathaway* v. *Toledo, W. & W. R. Co.*, 46 Ind. 25, the following instruction was held to be correct as a statement of the law: "When a person crossing a railroad track is injured by a collision with a train the fault is prima facie his own, and he must show affirmatively that his fault or negligence did not contribute to the injury, before he is entitled to recover for such injury."

In the case of *Cincinnati, H. & I. R. Co.* v. *Butler*, 103 Ind. 31, 1 West. Rep. 110, it is said: "In cases where contributory negligence may be claimed it is settled in this court that the absence of contributory negligence is part of the plaintiff's case both as to averment and proof."

In *Lyons* v. *Terre Haute & I. R. Co.*, 101 Ind. 419, it is said: "It is too well settled to admit of debate that a party who sues for an injury to person or property resulting from negligence must prove that he was himself without negligence. *Cincinnati, W. & M. R. Co.* v. *Hiltzhauer*, 99 Ind. 486, and cases cited."

In *Indiana, B. & W. R. Co.* v. *Greene*, 106 Ind. 279, 3 West. Rep. 888, it is said by this court: "It may suffice to say, since it is the established rule of this court, as it is of the courts in a large majority of the States, that it must be affirmatively shown that the injured party was in the exercise of due care at the time the accident occurred. At least it must be made to appear that want of care on his part in no way contributed to bring about the injury or helped to produce the accident for which compensation is sought."

In view of these authorities the following instructions asked by the appellee and given by the court were erroneous:

"No. 2. A traveler upon a public highway in this State has a right to assume that a railroad company, whose track crosses such highway, will obey the law and give the signals required by law upon the approach of trains to such crossing, and (although the failure to give such signals does not release the traveler from exercising due care), if no such signals are given, and the view is obstructed and there are no indications to the contrary, the traveler is not guilty of contributory negligence in assuming that no train is advancing upon such crossing within eighty rods thereof."

"No. 4. The burden is upon the plaintiff to show that there was no negligence upon her part contributing to the injury complained of; but this need not necessarily be shown by directly affirmative evidence, but may be shown by proving the facts and circumstances from which it may be inferred. If all of the circumstances under which the said injury occurred are put in evidence, and upon the examination of them nothing is found in acts or omissions showing contributory negligence, or grounds for suspecting or inferring such negligence on the part of the plaintiff, the inference of care upon her part may be drawn from the absence of all appearance of fault, either positive or negative, on the part of plaintiff, in the circumstances under which the injury was received; and in considering the question of due care on her part, you have a right to take into consideration, together with the other facts and circumstances in the case, the instinct of self-preservation and the known and ordinary disposition of all persons to guard themselves against danger."

"No. 5. It was the duty of the defendant, by its employés in the charge of such train, in approaching said crossing, when not less than eighty (80) nor more than one hundred (100) rods distant therefrom, to sound the whistle on such engine distinctly three (3) times, and to ring the bell upon such engine continuously from the time of sounding such whistle until such engine had fully passed said crossing; and although the failure to give such warning of the approach of such train did not relieve the plaintiff from exercising due care to avoid the injury, yet if no such warning was given, the absence of such warning is a circumstance to be considered in determining whether such care was exercised by the plaintiff."

The second instruction could have led the jury to no other conclusion; if the view was in some way obstructed between that part of the highway over which the appellee was approaching the crossing and the railroad, and there had been a failure to sound the whistle attached to the locomotive engine or ring its bell within eighty rods of the crossing, and if she could have crossed in safety had the approaching train been eighty roads away, she was not guilty of contributory negligence, even though she drove upon the crossing without stopping to look or listen for an approaching train. In other words, from a slight obstruction of the view and a failure to ring the bell or sound the whistle the jury might infer want of contributory negligence in attempting to cross the railroad track under any circumstances which would have made it reasonably safe on the supposition that the engine and train were eighty rods away.

By the fourth instruction the jury are told substantially that if there is nothing in the evidence tending to show contributory negligence they may without proof infer that there was no such negligence.

By the fifth instruction the jury are told that if the whistle was not sounded nor the bell rung, this was a circumstance tending to show want of contributory negligence; and as a logical sequence, if it was a circumstance in that direction, then the jury might have found therefrom that it was sufficient to establish the fact, as it was for them to determine as to the weight of the evidence. This very instruction may have misled the jury and caused them to find want of contributory negligence.

The court should have given instructions numbered three, eight and eleven, or their equivalent, asked by the appellant, as they stated the law correctly and were applicable to the evidence.

"No. 3. The burden is on the plaintiff to show, by a preponderance of the evidence, that she and her father vigilantly used their eyes and ears to ascertain if a train of cars was approaching, and if this has not been shown to you by a preponderance of the evidence the the plaintiff cannot recover."

"No. 8. When a person crossing a railroad track is injured by collision with a train, the fault is prima facie her own, and she must show affirmatively that her fault or negligence did not contribute to the injury, before she is entitled to recover tor such injury."

"No. 11. The fact that the train was behind time, and was running faster than its usual speed, at the crossing to make up time, did not excuse the plaintiff or her father from exercising the care and caution required of them, when the train was on time and running its usual rate of speed at that crossing."

In *Allyn* v. *Boston & A. R. Co.*, 105 Mass. 77, it is said: "Mere proof that the negligence of the defendant was a cause adequate to have produced the injury will not enable a plaintiff to recover, as it does not necessarily give rise to the inference of due care upon his part, proof of which is essential in the case." See *Sherlock* v. *Alling*, 44 Ind. 184, 204.

In *Indiana, B. & W. R. Co.* v. *Greene, supra*, it is further said: "The facts and circumstances illustrating the conduct of the injured person at the time of the accident must be made to appear. If from these the inference can be drawn that proper caution was exercised it may then be said the presumption of contributory negligence has been affirmatively removed."

The trial court in that case gave the following instructions: "The allegation that the injury occurred without fault or negligence of the plaintiff's intestate must be proved by the plaintiff; but at the same time it is a negative averment, and if the plaintiff has shown by evidence that the injury occurred as charged, resulting in the death of the plaintiff's intestate, and that it was caused by the negligence of the defendant as charged, without showing any contributory negligence or ground for inferring or reasonably suspecting such negligence, she will be entitled to recover without making direct or affirmative proof on that subject. In the absence of circumstances to show or suggest it there is no presumption of contributory negligence."

This instruction was held to be erroneous, and the court said, speaking of the appellant: "He must show the facts, as well those which relate to his share in the transaction as those which relate to the defendants, and if upon the whole case the inference of negligence arises against the defendant, and of due care on his part, he may recover. The fact that a person traveling on a highway comes in collision with a train on a railway crossing is of itself sufficient to suggest a presumption of contributory negligence against him in a suit for compensation. *Cincinnati, H. & I. R. Co.* v. *Butler*, and *Hathaway* v. *Toledo, W. & W. R. Co. supra.*" See *Toledo, W. & W. R. Co.* v. *Brannagan*, 75 Ind. 490, upon the last proposition above.

It is the rule that a person before crossing a railroad track must stop, look and listen, and applies to pedestrians as well as to others. *Aiken* v. *Pennsylvania R. Co.* 130 Pa. 380; *Butler* v. *Gettysburg & H. R. Co.* 126 Pa. 160.

In *Allen* v. *Maine Cent. R. Co.* (Me.), 19 Atl. Rep. 105, it is said: "The evidence shows that at twenty-five or thirty feet from the crossing the approaching train from Bath might have been seen by the plaintiff several hundred feet distant from the crossing. The plaintiff did not look in that direction until his horse's fore feet were between the rails. Was the neglect on his part to look in that direction a want of ordinary care and prudence? Is a traveler justified in traveling upon a railroad crossing in the absence of safety signals giving him the right to cross without looking for an approaching train? It has been many times decided by this court that the traveler before crossing a railroad must look and listen? If the crossing at which the plaintiff was injured is so constructed that an approaching train cannot be seen until a traveler comes very near to the railroad track, common prudence requires him to approach at such speed that when an approaching train may be seen he may be able to stop and allow such train to pass." To the same effect are our own cases. *Cincinnati, H. & I. R. Co.* v. *Butler, supra*, and cases cited; *Indiana, B. & W. R. Co.* v. *Greene, supra*. See, upon these different propositions, *Chicago & E. I. R. Co.* v. *Hedges*, 118 Ind. 5; *Cones* v. *Cincinnati, I. St. L. & C. R. Co.* 114 Ind. 328, 14 West. Rep. 101; *Ohio & M. R. Co.* v. *Hill*, 117 Ind. 56; *Lake Shore & M. S. R. Co.* v. *Pinchin*, 112 Ind. 592, 11 West. Rep. 247; *Indiana, B. & W. R. Co.* v. *Hammock*, 113 Ind. 1, 12 West. Rep. 297.

In the light of these authorities the following instruction requested by the appellee and given by the court was erroneous:

"No. 8. There is no rule of law which requires a traveler upon a public highway in approaching a railroad crossing to stop his team still. But, in determining the question of plaintiff's contributory negligence it is for you to say whether the course pursued by the plaintiff was such as would have been adopted by an ordinarily cautious and prudent person, in the exercise of reasonable care to avoid injury, under the facts and circumstances in this case as disclosed by the evidence. And I leave it for you to say whether there were such obstructions to the view of the train that did the injury, and such lack of warning on the part of defendant of its approach, as would lead an ordinarily cautious and prudent man, in the exercise of reasonable care to avoid injury, to believe that no train was approaching within such distance of the crossing as to make his endeavor to pass the same dangerous."

From this instruction the jury could well infer, if it appeared that there was some lack of warning, that the train was approaching the crossing and that the view between the appellee and the approaching train was obstructed, that it then became a question for their determination as to whether such lack of warning, together with the obstructed view, were sufficient to lead a person of ordinary prudence and judgment to the conclusion that there was no train approaching within such a distance as to render it unsafe for the appellee and her father to attempt to pass over the track, and if so, then they were not guilty of negligence in attempting to pass over without first stopping and exercising their senses of hearing and sight. In our opinion instruction number fifteen, asked by the appellant, contained a correct statement of the law, and should have been given. This instruction reads thus:

"No. 15. If there were any obstructions to sight or hearing in the direction of the approaching train, as the plaintiff and her father neared the crossing, the obstructions required increased care on the part of the plaintiff and her father on approaching the crossing. In such case the care must be in proportion to the increase of the danger that may come from the use of the highway at such a place."

When applied to the evidence in the case all of the foregoing instructions asked by the appellant were exceedingly pertinent as well as proper.

While we do not condemn instruction numbered one, asked by the appellee, and given by the court in the abstract, we think that there was no evidence which made it pertinent, and that it was calculated to mislead the jury. The said instruction is as follows:

"No 1. If you find from the evidence that the plaintiff was injured by the defendant's train while traveling upon a public highway, as alleged in her complaint, that the whistle was not sounded and the bell rung as required by law, as said train approached said crossing, and that plaintiff was misled by defendant's failure to give such warning, and without fault or negligence on her part, and, without notice of the approach of said train, was placed in a position of great peril, and, in the excitement of that peril, and in the effort to escape, made a mistake as to the proper course to be pursued, and injury resulted, such error of judgment is not contributory negligence, and will not bar a recovery by her for the injury sustained."

We may add further that we find no evidence tending to rebut contributory negligence on the appellee's part,—in view of the authorities, not a circumstance.

As to the circumstances which found the appellant and her father on the crossing when the misfortune overtook them, the evidence is an entire blank. Whether or not they saw the train approaching, or heard the sound which a moving train gives out, and were deceived as to the distance it was from them and attempted to cross the track notwithstanding, we do not know. The rate of speed at which they approached the crossing, and whether or not they stopped and exercised their senses of hearing and sight, are facts which do not appear in the evidence.

In view of the authorities which we have cited, and especially the cases of *Indiana, B. & W. R. Co.* v. *Greene* and *Cincinnati, H. & I. R. Co.* v. *Butler, supra*, the case at bar seems to have been tried upon a theory entirely erroneous.

The case of *Pittsburgh, C. & St. L. R. Co.* v. *Martin*, 82 Ind. 476, and relied upon by the appellee, is not in harmony with our earlier cases and is out of line with those more recent, the later cases following the earlier ones, and upon the questions involved in the present case cannot be regarded as authority since the case of *Cincinnati, H. & I. R. Co.* v. *Butler, supra*.

The judgment must be reversed.

Judgment reversed, with costs.

ILLINOIS SUPREME COURT.

LOCEY COAL MINES, *Pff. in Err.*,

v.

CHICAGO, WILMINGTON & VERMILLION COAL CO.

(131 Ill. 9.)

1. No exception can be made from the right allowed by Rev. Stat., chap. 77, § 16, of redemption from sale under execution, decree, etc., in the case of a sale, on a creditor's bill, of both the real and personal property of an insolvent mining corporation, at least where the severance of the personal property from the real estate will not materially impair its value or usefulness, although the property is more available and valuable when in combination, and although a large

expense will be necessary to keep the mines from deterioration during the period of redemption, when no one can be permitted to operate them.

3. A court, by requiring conveyance to its receiver in a creditor's suit of real property which might have been seized and sold on an execution at law, cannot thereby take it out of the operation of the Statute in relation to redemption.

Wilkin, J., dissents.

(October 31, 1889.)

ERROR to the Appellate Court, Second District, to review a judgment affirming a decree of the Circuit Court for Will County directing the sale of defendant's property without privilege of redemption. *Reversed.*

The facts are fully stated in the opinion.

Messrs. **H. S. Monroe** and **George H. Locey,** for plaintiff in error:

The sale of the entire property of the corporation without redemption would be improper.

Rev. Stat. chap. 77, §§ 16-18; *Stone* v. *Gardner,* 20 Ill. 309; *Suitterlin* v. *Com. Mut. L. Ins. Co.* 90 Ill. 483; *Wetherbee* v. *Fitch,* 4 West. Rep. 220, 117 Ill. 67; *Peoria & S. R. Co.* v. *Thompson,* 103 Ill. 187; *Hammock* v. *Farmers Loan & Trust Co.* 105 U. S. 77 (26 L. ed. 1111).

Mr. **George S. House,** for defendant in error:

Where property will sell for more as a unit than if sold separately, it may be sold together.

McLean County Bank v. *Flagg,* 31 Ill. 290; Rev. Stat. 1845, chap. 57; *Hammock* v. *Farmers Loan & Trust Co.* 105 U. S. 77 (26 L. ed. 1111).

Bailey, *J.*, delivered the opinion of the court:

This was a creditor's bill, brought by the Chicago, Wilmington & Vermillion Coal Company against the Locey Coal Mines, to enforce the collection of a certain judgment at law against the defendant.

It appears from the bill, which, for want of an answer, was taken *pro confesso* and from the proofs adduced at the hearing, that on the 8th day of February, 1887, the complainant obtained a judgment against the defendant by confession for $6,903.65 and costs, and that execution issued on said judgment has been returned wholly unsatisfied.

It further appears that the defendant is a corporation organized under the laws of this State for the purpose of carrying on the business of mining and selling coal, and that, in the prosecution of its business, it had acquired, and at the time of filing said bill held and owned, certain mining lands situate in Bureau County, consisting of 280.81 acres, and, in addition thereto, the coal under 211.71 acres of other land adjoining, and had sunk upon said land a coal-mining shaft and an escapement or air-shaft, and erected some thirty dwelling-houses, a boarding-house, a store house, and various other buildings, and set a steam-engine, steam-boiler, coal-hoisting apparatus and machinery, pumps, coal-car tracks, railroad and switch tracks, screens, pit scales and car scales, and constructed on the Illinois River a loading dock, and procured for the transportation of coal one coal boat and a steam barge or towing boat,—all of which were desirable and necessary for carrying on its business of mining and selling coal. This property was owned by the defendant subject to a trust deed executed by the defendant to Charles S. Hinchman, to secure the payment of $30,000 and interest, and also a mortgage to Edward Lewis to secure the payment of $1,838.35.

The bill further alleges that the defendant has carried on its business at a large expense, and has acquired a valuable trade for its mining products and a standing in the market which should not be lost; that the defendant's property is of that character that its chief value consists in maintaining it as it now exists, for the transaction of the business for which it was brought together, and that the interests of all concerned will be better promoted by preserving all of said property as a unit; that the defendant is greatly embarrassed financially, and is unable to meet its debts due and to become due, and that the interests on said incumbrances remain due and unpaid; that the defendant is about $7,000 in arrears in the payment of the wages of its miners, and has no means with which to pay the same; and that, by reason of such nonpayment, said miners have quit their work and refuse to resume the same until proper arrangements are made for the payment of their wages.

Upon the filing of said bill an order was entered, the defendant by its counsel consenting thereto, appointing a receiver and requiring the defendant to turn over to such receiver all its assets and property, and by the same order the receiver was directed to continue the defendant's business of mining and selling coal. In pursuance of said order, the defendant conveyed and transferred to the receiver all of its said property, and the latter thereupon entered into possession and undertook to carry on the business of operating the mine. To enable him to commence operations, an order was entered, on his petition, authorizing him to borrow $10,000 and issue receiver's certificates therefor; and the money thus borrowed was expended in paying the operatives their arrearages and in defraying the expenses of continuing the business.

On petition of the defendant, the receiver was authorized to buy 300 acres more of mining rights, which purchase was accordingly made at a cost of $3,200. Subsequently the complainant, having become the owner of the indebtedness secured by the $30,000 deed of trust, and also all of the certificates then issued by the receiver, filed its petition asking for an order authorizing the receiver to borrow a further sum, to be expended in improvements of said property, and offering to advance the same on receiver's certificates; and, the defendant consenting thereto, an order was entered in accordance with the prayer of said petition, and in pursuance of said order the receiver borrowed of the complainant the sum of $15,900.

Said cause coming on for hearing on the bill taken as confessed, a large amount of evidence was introduced as to the value of the property and assets of the defendant in the hands of the receiver, said evidence being to a very large degree conflicting. The decree found "that the property is of that kind and character, all so related to the other, and thus gathered together and obtained for the transaction of the business of the mining and sale of coal, that the said property cannot well be sold separately without manifest injury to the interests of all interested therein, and that all said property, including the personal property on hand at the time of sale, of every kind and character, should be sold as an entirety and as one property,—as a unit,—to better conserve the interests of all parties interested therein; that the value of all of said property rights does not exceed the sum of $60,000, and that the said corporation defendant is entirely insolvent and wholly unable to pay its debts; that the claims now existing against the said corporation defendant, now proven in this cause, together with the expenses, costs and charges still likely to accrue and arise under the receiver, will reach the sum of at least $85,000, and the property is of that kind and character that, for its proper preservation, its operation as a coal mine is absolutely necessary and essential; that its continued operation under a receiver is not only unwise and injudicious, but may be greatly prejudicial to the rights and interests of the creditors of said corporation; and that all said property, both real and personal, should be sold without unreasonable delay; and on account of the property and its value, as compared with the claims due, and the scant security thus afforded for such claims, it should be sold without redemption and free and clear of any and all claims of any and all parties to this cause, whether intervenors or otherwise."

Said decree has been affirmed by the appellate court, and the record is now brought here by writ of error. The errors assigned in this court relate: *first*, to that portion of the decree which orders the sale of the real estate in question without redemption; and, *second*, to that portion of the decree which finds the value of all the property in question to be only $60,000. The second assignment of error does not seem to be insisted upon; and the only question, therefore, presented for our consideration is whether the circuit court properly ordered the sale of the real estate without redemption.

There can be no question that the property transferred to the receiver, and which the decree ordered to be sold, is, in the main, real property. Such is, of course, the character of the 280.81 acres of land to which the defendant had obtained the title in fee; and that character appertains, not only to the soil and the buildings erected thereon, but to the coal lying beneath the surface, and the various shafts and mines by means of which the coal is reached and the mining operations carried on. The right which the defendant had acquired prior to the filing of the bill to the coal under the 211.71 acres is an interest in land, and is in its nature real property. The same is true of the mining rights acquired by the receiver under the order of the court. The thirty dwelling-houses, the boarding-house, the store-house and the other buildings are all, presumptively at least, parts of the realty. The same thing may perhaps be said of the engine and boiler, railroad and switch tracks, coal tracks, docks and most of the other apparatus and machinery erected upon and attached to the land for the purpose of carrying on the defendant's mining operations. There is, it is true, a considerable amount of property owned by the defendant, and procured by it for use in and about its mines, which is in its nature personal property. Of this character is its machinery, not so attached to the soil as to become fixtures, its tools, boats, mules and the stock of goods in the defendant's store. All of these, however, constitute relatively but a small portion of the entire mining establishment, as the inventory of the movable property shows that the goods in the store amounted only to $1,-915.31 in value, the mining property to only $1,924, and the boats only $632.40. The bill alleges, and the decree finds, that the various portions of the entire property are so related to each other, and the business purpose for which it is chiefly valuable is such, that the best interests of all concerned will be best promoted by having the entire property kept together and treated as a unit. This is because its principal value consists in its being operated as a coal mine. Upon this feature of the case there was no controversy at the hearing, and there need be none now. We are of the opinion, however, that the conclusions sought to be drawn from it do not necessarily follow.

It need not be questioned that a division of the mining lands embraced in the decree into a number of parcels, and selling them in such parcels, would not be the best course to pursue in order to realize the highest price. Such division would doubtless greatly impair, if not altogether destroy, the value of said lands as mining lands. The expense of sinking the necessary shafts, and erecting and supplying proper machinery and appliances, is doubtless too great to make mining profitable if limited to a small tract of land. In case the lands in question should be divided, and go into the hands of several proprietors, this large expense would need to be incurred upon each tract, in order to make it available as mining property. It may therefore be admitted that, in order to obtain the highest price, the mining lands of the defendant, including the shafts, mines, buildings, machinery and other improvements appertaining to the realty, should be sold together, and not in parcels. But, so far as we are able to perceive, the same considerations do not necessarily apply to the comparatively small amount of personal property of the defendant which it has purchased and brought together for use in and about the mines. If that should be sold separately, and thus go into the hands of a purchaser different from the one who buys the mines, there would be no material injury thereby occasioned to the mines, or to the parties interested therein, since other personal property equally serviceable could doubtless be obtained in the market at its fair cash value. Such would unquestionably be the case with the stock of goods, the tools, portable machinery, mules, and indeed all the goods and chattels which may be said to form a part of the property appurtenant to the mines. It does not necessarily follow, therefore, that the case presents any such combination of real and personal property into an indissoluble unit as will make it impracticable to sell each species of property separately, and in accordance with the general rules of law applicable thereto, without destroying or greatly impairing the value of the entire property.

Our present Statute provides that, when any

real estate is sold by virtue of an execution, judgment or decree of foreclosure of a mortgage, or enforcement of a mechanic's lien or vendor's lien, or for the payment of money, it shall be the duty of the sheriff, master in chancery or other officer making the sale to deliver to the purchaser a certificate entitling him to a deed in case the property is not redeemed within the statutory period of redemption. Rev. Stat. chap. 77, § 16.

The language of the Statute is imperative, and seems to contemplate no exceptions. Why, then, should the real estate, which constitutes the great bulk of the property in question, be sold without redemption? In support of the decree authorizing such sale, we are referred to *Hammock* v. *Farmers Loan & Trust Co.*, 105 U. S. 77 [26 L. ed. 1111], and *Peoria & S. R. Co.* v. *Thompson*, 103 Ill. 187. These were suits in chancery, each brought for the foreclosure of a mortgage executed by a railway company, conveying its railroad, with the appurtenances, franchises, equipments, tools, incomes, assets and property belonging thereto, then possessed or thereafter acquired by the company, and in each case a decree for the sale of the entire mortgaged property as a unit, and without redemption, was sustained. This conclusion was reached upon the theory that, while a railway track, considered by itself, was real estate, yet, when viewed in connection with its public character and the franchises usually connected with it, it could not be regarded as lands and tenements within the meaning of the Statute. On this point, in *Peoria & S. R. Co.* v. *Thompson*, it is said: "A number of reasons suggest themselves to us why they should not be so considered. In the first place, when a railway, its appurtenances, privileges and franchises, are mortgaged as a whole, there is, in our opinion, no power or authority to sell them separately. From the very nature of the property, one would be useless without the other. The franchise could not be used at all without the road, and the road could not lawfully be used, as against the State, without the franchise. Under such circumstances, to avoid the possibility of conflicting ownerships, the law has wisely determined that both must be sold as an entirety."

Again: "While a railroad franchise, when considered by itself, will be treated as personal property, and the road itself, when so viewed, will be treated as realty, yet, when considered as an entirety, as they must be when so mortgaged and sold, they are, strictly speaking, neither the one nor the other, within the meaning of the law pertaining to redemptions. From a sale of land a redemption is allowed; from a sale of personal property no such redemption is permitted. And since the two are indissolubly combined, by virtue of the mortgage, decree and sale, there is just as much reason, so far as the question depends upon the two kinds of property, when separately considered, for contending the right of redemption is denied, as there is that it is given."

A further consideration bearing upon the question is drawn from the public character of railway companies. On that point it is said: "In view of the public character of the road, it will not be questioned that the public generally have a direct interest in keeping it continuously open, without any material diminution of its capacity to meet all the legitimate wants of the public. It is therefore but just and proper that the foreclosure proceedings should be conducted in such a manner, having due regard to the private interests of all parties concerned, as to cause the least possible injury or inconvenience to the public, and we are of opinion that this will be more effectually accomplished by the method adopted than it can be in any other way. To have ordered a sale of the personal property separately, from which it is conceded there would be no redemption, and a sale of the realty with the right of redemption, as is claimed should have been done, it would most likely have resulted either in a sacrifice of the property, or some portion of it, or in embarrassing complications seriously affecting, at least for a while, the public interests."

It is clear that very little, if any, of the foregoing reasoning can have an application to the present case. Here there is no question of a franchise, the existence and exercise of which are essential to the legal use and enjoyment of the tangible property. No personal property is involved, the severance of which from the real estate will materially impair the value or usefulness of the latter. No question arises of any public use, nor has the public any interest in the continued operation of the mines, beyond what it has in the continued prosecution of any other private business enterprise. Every circumstance which may be held to take the case out of the operation of the statutory mandate, which requires judicial sales of real property to be made subject to the statutory right of redemption, seems to be wanting. While we are disposed to adhere to the doctrine of the cases above cited, we are not inclined to extend the rule there laid down to cases which do not come clearly within the reasons upon which the rule is based. The mere fact that real and personal property are so brought together in a particular business enterprise, and are so related to each other, as to be more available and more valuable in combination than when taken separately, will not of itself authorize the sale of both as a unit without redemption. If this were otherwise, the right of redemption which the Statute gives in all ordinary cases of judicial sales of real property might be denied or set aside almost with impunity. Thus, in case of a farm well stocked with domestic animals, agricultural implements and other chattel property specially adapted to its profitable tillage, we might have a combination of real and personal property more valuable when treated as a unit than when separated. A well-furnished house, with carpets, furniture and other belongings specially purchased, adapted and fitted for use in such house, would constitute a combination of real and personal property more valuable to the proprietor, and more available, perhaps, for sale, if it could be sold as a single item of property. But it has never been held that in either of these cases the real estate becomes anything but real estate, and subject to judicial sale as such. Nor has it ever been held that a separation of the personal from the real property would be unauthorized, even though its effect would be to essentially diminish the market value of both. So long as the law recognizes the distinction between these two classes of property, and subjects them to different rules, those rules must apply, and cannot be dispensed with by the courts, even though their application may work some inconvenience.

It is suggested as a further argument *ab inconvenienti*, in support of the decree, that, if the statutory redemption is allowed, neither the receiver, the defendant nor the purchaser can be permitted to mine coal after the sale, and while the period of redemption is running; and that, in order to keep the mines from deterioration and injury during that period, the water must be kept out, fresh air supplied, etc., at a cost of about $400 per month. This expense should not be borne by the receiver, as he can no longer work the mines, since his doing so would simply be a subtraction or taking away of a portion of the property sold. The defendant, being insolvent and presumably unable in any event to redeem, would have no inducement to incur such expense, since, for the same reason above stated, it could not be permitted to operate the mines during the period of redemption. The purchaser, on the other hand, would be entitled to possession only after the period of redemption has expired, and so could not legally enter upon the mines for the purpose of protecting them from deterioration. These inconveniences doubtless may arise, but they do not, in our opinion, justify the court in disregarding or overriding a plain and positive mandate of the Statute. Inconveniences the same in character, though perhaps less in degree, not unfrequently grow out of the possession and use of real estate during the period of redemption; but the Statute is general in its terms, and makes no exceptions because of them.

Counsel also seek to sustain the decree on the ground that the court, through the receiver, had the entire control of both the equitable and legal title to the real estate in question, and could dispose of it in such manner as it saw fit. Said property was conveyed to the receiver by the defendant in obedience to an order of the court requiring such conveyance. It is true, said order was entered with the consent of the defendant; but the validity and effect of the order, and the power of the court to enter it, in no way depended upon such consent. The control which the court obtained over the property was no different or greater than it would have been if the order had been entered as the result of adversary proceedings, and against the opposition and protest of the defendant. The question then arises, whether, on a creditor's bill, a court, by requiring real property, which might have been seized and sold on an execution at law, to be conveyed to a receiver, can thereby take it out of the operation of the Statute in relation to redemption. A creditor's bill may be viewed as a species of process for the execution and enforcement of a judgment at law, and it is difficult to see why real property seized and sold in that proceeding should not be subject to redemption the same as when sold on execution. Our present Statute is somewhat broader than the one previously in force. The former Statute seemed to limit the right of redemption to sales upon execution upon foreclosure decrees, and proceedings to enforce mechanic's liens; but by the Revision of 1874 it is made to apply to all cases of real estate sold "by virtue of an execution, judgment or decree of foreclosure of a mortgage, or the enforcement of a mechanic's lien or vender's lien, or for the payment of money;" and it is made the duty of the sheriff, master in chancery or other officer making the sale to execute to the purchaser a certificate of purchase made expressly subject to the right of redemption. It seems very clear that the Statute, since the Revision, is broad enough to embrace cases like the present. The sale ordered by the decree is to be made by an officer of the court, viz., the receiver, and is to be made for the payment of money, viz., the amount due on the complainant's judgment. In no view we are able to take of the case can the decree be sustained. It should have provided for the sale of the real estate separately, and subject to the statutory right of redemption.

The judgment of the Appellate Court and the decree of the Circuit Court will be reversed, and the cause will be remanded to the latter court for further proceedings not inconsistent with this opinion.

Wilkin, *J.*, dissenting:

I do not concur. I think the evidence in the record fully justified the finding of the circuit court, and that in such a case a court of equity may properly order property belonging to a corporation, used by it in carrying on its corporate business, to be sold as a unit, and without redemption, notwithstanding a part of such property may be real estate. It is unlike a case in which individual property is ordered sold.

Petition for rehearing denied.

INDIANA SUPREME COURT.

James K. KINCAID, *Appt.*,

v.

INDIANAPOLIS NATURAL GAS CO. *et al.*

(....Ind.....)

1. **Pipes for the transportation of natural gas** cannot be laid in a country road without making compensation to the owner of the fee, although the right to do so has been granted by the board of county commissioners.

2. **An injunction will not be granted** to restrain the use of pipes laid in a highway for the transportation of natural gas, at the instance of the owner of the fee, who has received no compensation, where he knowingly permitted the work to proceed under a license from the board of county commissioners until large sums of money had been expended and it would be ruinous to the company to stop it, and where many citizens have acquired rights on the faith of the successful completion of the work, especially where compensation can be recovered by the land owner in an appropriate action for that purpose.

(June 25, 1890.)

APPEAL by plaintiff from a judgment of the Circuit Court for Hamilton County in favor

NOTE.—See Opinion of the Justices (Mass.) *ante*, 487.

of defendants in a suit brought to enjoin the use of pipes laid in a country road for the transportation of gas without making compensation to the owner of the fee. *Affirmed.*

The case sufficiently appears in the opinion.

Messrs. **J. A. New, S. E. Urmston** and **Stephenson & Fertig** for appellant.

Messrs. **Kane & Davis** for appellee.

Elliott, *J.*, delivered the opinion of the court:

The board of commissioners of Hamilton County granted to the Indianapolis Natural Gas Company the right to lay pipes in a free gravel road constructed under the Statute of this State at the expense of the land owners. The appellant is an abutting owner in fee of land along the line of the highway. Prior to the time this suit was brought the Company had constructed a system of gas works and had laid in the highway a line of pipes for the purpose of supplying the citizens of the City of Indianapolis and others with natural gas. In the prosecution of this work the Company had expended many thousands of dollars. To make the system effective and to successfully supply gas, as it had undertaken to do, it became necessary for the Company to extend its line of pipes so as to connect its main line and system with additional gas wells, which it had drilled and of which it was the owner. This it was undertaking to do at the time the appellant sued out the injunction issued in this case. The trial court dissolved the temporary injunction and refused to grant a perpetual injunction. From this judgment the appellant prosecutes his appeal.

The license granted by the board of commissioners was effectual to convey the right of the county, such as it had, in the highway, but it did not affect private property rights. *Burkham* v. *Lawrenceburg* (this term).

The owner of the fee in a suburban highway has a special proprietary right distinct from that of the public, and this right cannot be taken without compensation. In a case decided in 1855 it was held that abutters have a private right distinct from that of the public, which even the Legislature cannot take away except to appropriate to a public use upon payment of compensation. *Indianapolis* v. *Croas*, 7 Ind. 9.

This doctrine has been steadily adhered to by this court. *Haynes* v. *Thomas*, 7 Ind. 38; *Cox* v. *Louisville, N. A. & C. R. Co.* 48 Ind. 178; *Pettis* v. *Johnson*, 56 Ind. 139; *State* v. *Berdetta*, 73 Ind. 185; *Ross* v. *Thompson*, 78 Ind. 90; *Cummins* v. *Seymour*, 79 Ind. 491; *Logansport* v. *Shirk*, 88 Ind. 563; *Indianapolis* v. *Kingsbury*, 101 Ind. 211; *Terre Haute & L. R. Co.* v. *Bissell*, 108 Ind. 113, 6 West. Rep. 253; *Rensselaer* v. *Leopold*, 106 Ind. 29, 8 West. Rep. 874; *Lafayette* v. *Nagle*, 113 Ind. 425, 12 West. Rep. 637.

The rule declared by our own cases is in harmony with the very ancient and well-settled rule that the public acquires, except in cases where the seizure of the fee is authorized, nothing more than a right to pass and repass, and the great weight of authority sustains the doctrine laid down by our decisions.

There is an essential distinction between urban and suburban highways, and the rights of abutters are much more limited in the case of urban streets than they are in the case of suburban ways. We note the distinction between the classes of public ways and declare that the servitude in the one class is much broader than it is in the other, but it is not necessary to here mark with particularity the difference between the two classes of public ways, for we are here concerned only with suburban ways.

Subject to the right of the public the owner of the fee of a rural road retains all right and interest in it. He remains the owner, and, as such, his rights are very comprehensive. *Brookville & M. Hydraulic Co.* v. *Butler*, 91 Ind. 136; *Shelbyville & R. Turnp. Co.* v. *Green*, 99 Ind. 214; *Dovaston* v. *Payne*, 2 H. Bl. 527; *Peck* v. *Smith*, 1 Conn. 103; *Presbyterian Society* v. *Auburn & R. R. Co.* 3 Hill, 567.

That the appellant has a special private interest in the lands upon which the highway is located, which cannot be taken from him without compensation, is quite clear upon principle and authority.

The appropriation of the land for a rural highway did not entitle the local officers to use it for any other than highway purposes, although they did acquire a right to use it for all purposes legitimately connected with the local system of highways. A use for any other than a legitimate highway purpose is a taking within the meaning of the Constitution, inasmuch as it imposes an additional burden upon the land; and whenever land is subjected to an additional burden the owner is entitled to compensation. The authorities, although not very numerous, are harmonious, upon the question that laying gas pipes in a suburban road is the imposition of an additional burden, and that compensation must be made to the owner. *Bloomfield & R. N. Gas Light Co.* v. *Calkins*, 62 N. Y. 386, 1 Thomp. & C. 549; *Bloomfield & R. N. Gas-Light Co.* v. *Richardson*, 63 Barb. 437; *Stumpf's App.* 116 Pa. 35, 8 Cent. Rep. 112; *Webb* v. *Ohio Gas Fuel Co.* 16 West. L. Bull. 121.

The same principle is declared in the cases which hold that drainage pipes cannot be laid in rural highways except for public drainage purposes connected with the system of highways. *Murray* v. *Gibson*, 21 Ill. App. 488; *Indianapolis, B. & W. R. Co.* v. *Hartley*, 67 Ill. 439; *Board of Trade Teleg. Co.* v. *Barnett*, 107 Ill. 507.

The cases to which we have referred are well reasoned and are founded on solid principle. We have no hesitation in concluding that the laying of the pipes in the highway was a taking of the appellant's property within the meaning of the Constitution, and that he is entitled to compensation.

It does not follow, however, that a land owner entitled to compensation for property appropriated to a public use can always maintain injunction. It remains, therefore, to inquire and decide whether the appellant can maintain this suit, for if he is not entitled to an injunction he cannot succeed.

The use to which the line of the highway was appropriated was a public one. There can be no doubt that the work of supplying cities with natural gas is a public one for which property may be appropriated under the right of eminent domain. *State* v. *Indiana & O. O. G. & M. Co.* 120 Ind. 575; *Carothers* v. *Philadelphia Co.*

118 Pa. 468, 11 Cent. Rep. 48; *Pennsylvania Natural Gas Co.* v. *Cook*, 123 Pa. 170; *Johnston's App.* (Pa.) 5 Cent. Rep. 561.

There was an assertion of a right to use the highway, and the Gas Company had expended large sums of money on the faith of the license granted to it by the board of commissioners. It had assumed to use the highway for a public purpose, and many citizens had acquired rights upon the faith of the successful and effective prosecution and conduct of the work and business undertaken by the Company. The appellant, with knowledge of the facts, made no objection until the completion of the main line and system, but delayed until they had been completed and then asked for an injunction. To grant the relief he seeks will, it is clearly inferable, seriously impair the rights of the public as well as those of the Gas Company. We are satisfied that, upon the case made by the evidence, the appellant is not entitled to an injunction. In adjudging that he has no right to an injunction we do not hold that he may not in a proper case recover damages for the invasion of his legal rights. What we here decide is that the case made is not one justifying resort to the extraordinary remedy of injunction. The effect of our decision is that he has mistaken his remedy.

The work in which the Gas Company is engaged is one in which the general community have an interest, and to arrest the work by injunction would do great injury to many citizens. Persons other than the Gas Company have an interest, and they are so numerous that it is the duty of the courts to protect that interest where it can be done without materially impairing the rights of any private citizen; and that can be done in this instance, for the appellant, in the appropriate action, and upon making a proper case, can be fully compensated in damages for all injury that he may have suffered. There is present here an element of public policy which exerts a controlling influence. The good of the community forbids that one who occupies such a position as the appellant does should be permitted to arrest work essential to the successful discharge of the Company's duty to supply the community with fuel in the form of natural gas. Public policy, as has been demonstrated in analogous cases, requires that the rights of the community should be protected and the land owner left to his remedy at law. *Louisville, N. A. & C. R. Co.* v. *Beck*, 119 Ind. 124; *Louisville, N. A. & C. R. Co.* v. *Soltweddle*, 116 Ind. 259; *Bravard* v. *Cincinnati, H. & I. R. Co.* 115 Ind. 1, 14 West. Rep. 817; *Sherlock* v. *Louisville, N. A. & C. R. Co.* 115 Ind. 22, 14 West. Rep. 843; *Midland R. Co.* v. *Smith*, 113 Ind. 233, 12 West. Rep. 699; *Indiana, B. & W. R. Co.* v. *Allen*, 113 Ind. 581, 12 West. Rep. 887.

Nor does this rule operate unjustly, for the land owner is not deprived of compensation; on the contrary, the right to compensation is left open to him, and it is his own fault if he does not recover full compensation for all the loss he has actually sustained. Blended with the element of public policy is another influential one, and that is this: The appellant, without objection, knowingly permitted the work to proceed until it reached a stage at which it would be ruinous to the Company, which had invested such large sums of money, to stop it by injunction. These two elements in their combined strength certainly make a case in which an injunction should, upon plain principles of equity, be denied. *Logansport* v. *Uhl*, 99 Ind. 534-544; *Dodge* v. *Pennsylvania R. Co.* 43 N. J. Eq. 351, 10 Cent. Rep. 655, 36 Am. & Eng. R. R. Cas. 180.

Judgment affirmed.

MIDLAND R. CO., *Appt.*,
v.
James FISHER.

(....Ind....)

1. A purchaser, at a foreclosure sale, of a railroad company's interest under a deed granting it a right of way over certain lands in which is incorporated, as part of the consideration therefor, an agreement by the company to build a fence, is bound to carry out the agreement; and its liability to do so may be enforced by a subsequent grantee of the fee in an action of covenant, although the company merely accepted the deed without acknowledging it.

NOTE.—*Deed-poll defined.*

A deed made by one party only, as a sheriff, the edges of the instrument being "polled," or shaven even, is a deed-poll. Anderson, Dict. See 2 Bl. Com. 296; Giles v. Pratt, 2 Hill, L. 439.

A deed-poll is designed simply to transfer the grantor's interest, and is executed by him alone. 3 Washb. Real Prop. 311; Dyer v. Sanford, 9 Met. 395.

A deed-poll is in the first person, while deeds of indenture are in the third person; but although the deed is in the form of an indenture, it will be good as a deed-poll if the grantor executes it alone. Hallett v. Collins, 51 U. S. 10 How. 174 (13 L. ed. 376); Hipp v. Huchett, 4 Tex. 20.

A deed-poll raises all the estoppels necessary for the protection of the grantor's interest. Tiedeman, Real Prop. § 894.

It seems that the grantee in a deed-poll is bound by covenants therein to be performed by him; and an action of covenant may be maintained against him. The acceptance of the deed and enjoyment of the estate estop him and those claiming under him from denying his covenants, and from denying that the seal attached is his as well as that of the grantor. Atlantic Dock Co. v. Leavitt, 54 N. Y. 35.

In some of the States where the common-law pleading still prevails, the action of the grantor for nonperformance of the duties reserved in a deed-poll must be assumpsit, and the promise, being raised by the law, is not within the Statute of Frauds. Goodwin v. Gilbert, 9 Mass. 510; Jackson v. Matsdorf, 11 Johns. 91; Jackson v. Mills, 13 Johns. 463; Jackson v. Morse, 16 Johns. 197; Allen v. Pryor, 3 A. K. Marsh. 306; Hills v. Eliot, 12 Mass. 26; Fletcher v. M'Farlane, 12 Mass. 46; Nugent v. Riley, 1 Met. 117; Newell v. Hill, 2 Met. 180; Hinsdale v. Humphrey, 15 Conn. 431; Johnson v. Muzzy, 45 Vt. 419; Maule v. Weaver, 7 Pa. 329. But see Black v. Black, 4 Pick. 234; Boyd v. Stone, 11 Mass. 342.

But in the code States this distinction has passed away with the abolition of specific forms of action. Atlantic Dock Co. v. Leavitt, 54 N. Y. 34.

Whether covenant can be brought in any case against a person who has not become a party to the deed by signing and sealing, see Harper v. Burgh, 2 Lev. 206; Burnett v. Lynch, 5 Barn. & C. 596.

2. A deed-poll, when accepted by the grantee, becomes the mutual act of the parties, and the grantee is as much bound by its covenants as the grantor is.

3. The acceptance, by the grantee, of a deed-poll gives it the effect of a written contract in respect to the obligations assumed by him, and it will be so regarded in determining the bar of the Statute of Limitations.

(June 19, 1890.)

APPEAL by defendant from a judgment of the Circuit Court for Madison County, in favor of plaintiff in an action brought to enforce an alleged agreement to build a fence. *Affirmed.*

The facts sufficiently appear in the opinion.

Messrs. **Henry Crawford** and **M. A. Chipman** for appellant.

Messrs. **Stephenson & Fertig** for appellee.

Elliott, *J.*, delivered the opinion of the court:

In May, 1873, the then owners of the land described in the appellee's complaint conveyed to the Anderson, Lebanon & St. Louis Railway Company a right of way. In consideration of the grant of the right of way the company, by an agreement incorporated in the deed, promised to construct a board fence five boards in height on each side of the railroad as soon as it should be completed. The deed conveying the right of way was signed by the grantors, but not by the grantees. The railroad was completed in 1876, and the action was brought in 1886. In 1875 the company mortgaged all of its property and rights, and in 1883 the mortgage was foreclosed by a decree of the circuit court of the United States. A sale of all of the property and franchises of the company was made upon the decree of foreclosure, and the Midland Railway Company purchased all of the rights of the mortgagor. Under the title thus acquired the Midland Company entered into possession and began to operate the road purchased by it as soon as it acquired title. No fence had been erected as provided in the deed granting the right of way. Fisher became the owner of the land in August, 1884.

The contention of the appellant's counsel is that its client did not become liable for the general debts of its predecessor, and that the debt which the appellee seeks to enforce is a general debt. We agree with counsel that the rule is that a corporation which succeeds to the property and rights of another corporation through the medium of a sale upon a decree of foreclosure is not responsible for the general debts of the corporation whose property and franchises it acquires. *Lake Erie & W. R. Co.* v. *Griffin*, 92 Ind. 492; *Hoard* v. *Chesapeake & O. R. Co.* 123 U. S. 222 [31 L. ed. 130]; *Gilman* v. *Sheboyan & F. du L. R. Co.* 37 Wis. 317.

But we cannot agree that the assumption that the claim of the appellee is a mere general debt is valid, for we regard the performance of the agreement to build a fence as a condition of the right to enjoy the easement granted by the owners of the land. The right which the appellee seeks to enforce is more than a general claim for money, for it is a right blended with that of the appellant to use and occupy the land with its track. The appellant's liability does not rest upon the claim against the old company, but upon the duty which arises out of the occupancy of the land. It cannot, in equity, be permitted to enjoy the easement and yet refuse to perform the agreement which created and conferred the easement.

We think the principle declared in *Lake Erie & W. R. Co.* v. *Griffin, supra; Bloomfield R. Co.* v. *Van Slike*, 107 Ind. 480, 5 West. Rep. 655; *Lake Erie & W. R. Co.* v. *Griffin*, 107 Ind. 464, 5 West. Rep. 807; *Bloomfield R. Co.* v. *Grace*, 112 Ind. 128, 11 West. Rep. 368; *Indiana, B. & W. R. Co.* v. *Allen*, 113 Ind. 308, 12 West. Rep. 910, and *Donald* v. *St. Louis, K. C. & N. R. Co.* 52 Iowa, 411,—governs this phase of the case. The appellant is in the possession of the right of way as the grantee of the original contractor, and it must take the benefit it enjoys subject to the burden annexed to it by the contract which gave existence to that benefit. It cannot enjoy the benefit and escape the burden, for the burden and the benefit are so interlaced as to be inseparable. The right to the benefit is so blended with the burden that equity and justice forbid a severance.

One who takes a privilege in land to which a burden is annexed has no right to assert a claim to the privilege and deny responsibility for the burden. A party who acquires such a privilege acquires it subject to the conditions and burdens bound up with it, and must, if he asserts a right to the privilege, bear the burden which the contract creating the privilege brought into existence. The one he cannot have at the expense of the other.

In *Louisville, N. A. & C. R. Co.* v. *Power*, 119 Ind. 269, we said of a railroad company: "Holding the land under the deed as it did it was bound to perform its contract. To permit it to retain the land and repudiate the deed would be against equity and good conscience."

In this instance the covenant written in the deed was an essential part of it, and the agreement to construct the fence was part of the consideration for the land. The case is near akin to that of a suit to enforce a vendor's lien, for here the deed upon its face exhibited the contract, and the facts open to observation showed that the covenant had not been kept. The facts open to observation did more than put the appellant upon inquiry, but had they done no more than put it upon inquiry it could not justly claim the rights of a purchaser without notice. It must be held that the covenant in the deed through which the appellant claims and the facts open to observation imparted notice of the covenant, and notice also of its nonperformance.

The covenant is, as we have indicated, an integral part of the deed upon which rests the rights of the appellant. The deed which creates the asserted right discloses the covenant which burdens the right. In excepting the right under such a deed and asserting a claim to the privileges conferred by its subsequent grantees the original covenantor became bound to perform the agreement. The covenant passed with the land. The easement which burdened the fee was an incumbrance, and the party that took the land took it subject to the incumbrance, but in taking subject to the incumbrance of the easement that party acquired the benefit interwoven with the incumbrance. Both the burden and the benefit—the easement and the covenant—essentially inhere in the land. One burdens the estate, the other benefits it. The party who acquires the estate necessarily acquires it with both the burden and the benefit. He must submit to the one, but he has a right to the other.

In *Hazlett* v. *Sinclair*, 76 Ind. 488, the question was examined with care, the authorities collected and the judgment of the court was that a covenant very similar to the one under consideration was a real covenant running with the land. In the case referred to the court quoted with approval from the case of *Carr* v. *Lowry*, 27 Pa. 257, the following statement of the law: "The liability to perform and the right to take advantage of this covenant both pass to the heir or assignee of the land, to which the covenant is attached. The covenant can by no means be considered as merely personal or collateral and detached from the land."

In *Hazlett* v. *Sinclair* the case of *Bloch* v. *Isham*, 28 Ind. 37, was shown not to rule such a case as this. The question in *Junction R. Co.* v. *Sayers*, 28 Ind. 318, must for many reasons be regarded as radically different from that here presented, but it is enough to say that in that case the burden was not annexed to the easement conveyed, but was created by an independent agreement. The question received careful attention in the case of *Conduitt* v. *Ross*, 102 Ind. 166, and the rule there declared is substantially the same as that laid down in the case of *Hazlett* v. *Sinclair*, *supra*.

In *Bronson* v. *Coffin*, 108 Mass. 175, the authorities are reviewed at great length and a covenant such as that here under consideration was held to run with the land, so that the earlier cases in that court, conceding them to be in point, are not of controlling force.

The very fully considered and strongly reasoned case of *Burbank* v. *Pillsbury*, 48 N. H. 475, adjudges that a covenant to build a fence around granted estate will create an incumbrance on the land, and this doctrine harmonizes with that of the cases to which we have referred. If it be true, and it is true, that the agreement constitutes a real covenant against incumbrances, then it must be true that it runs with the land. It is a covenant inhering in the granted easement of a right of way, and as such runs with that estate. Applying this doctrine to the case before us, and it clearly results that the estate in the land which the appellant's grantor took—the easement of a right of way—was burdened with the incumbrance created by the covenant to fence the granted property. The ultimate conclusion, therefore, is that the covenant to fence binds the appellant and inures to the grantee of the servient estate in which the easement with its incumbrance inheres. In addition to the cases we have here cited and those collected in *Hazlett* v. *Sinclair*, may be cited the following: *Huston* v. *Cincinnati & Z. R. Co.* 21 Ohio St. 235; *Atlantic Dock Co.* v. *Leavitt*, 50 Barb. 135; *Duffy* v. *New York & H. R. Co.* 2 Hilt. 500; *Woolliscroft* v. *Norton*, 15 Wis. 198.

The authorities are well agreed upon the proposition that a deed-poll when accepted by the grantee becomes the mutual act of the parties. *Newell* v. *Hill*, 2 Met. 180; *Goodwin* v. *Gilbert*, 9 Mass. 510; *Huff* v. *Nickerson*, 27 Me. 106; *Tripe* v. *Marcy*, 39 N. H. 439; *Stevens* v. *Morse*, 47 N. H. 532; *Burbank* v. *Pillsbury* and *Atlantic Dock Co.* v. *Leavitt*, *supra*.

The appellant's grantor by accepting the deed made its covenants binding upon it, and acquired the estate incumbered and burdened by the agreement, and the appellant, as the deed is in his chain of title, took the grantee's easement with its burden and its incumbrance. *Tripe* v. *Marcy*, *Stevens* v. *Morse* and *Burbank* v. *Pillsbury*, *supra*.

The promise of the appellant's grantor is not a verbal one, and the case is not governed by the provision of the Statute of Limitations respecting verbal contracts. The acceptance of the deed by the grantee named in it made it a written contract, and the obligations created by the deed are therefore express and are evidenced by a writing. The adjudged cases very fully and satisfactorily sustain this doctrine. In one case it was said: "Nor is it material that this contract is not signed by the grantee. The acceptance of the deed makes it a contract in writing binding upon the grantee just as the acceptance by a lessee of a lease makes it a written contract binding upon such lessee, and suit can be maintained upon it as though it were also signed by the grantee." *Schmucker* v. *Sibert*, 18 Kan. 104.

The rule thus stated is sanctioned by many other cases. *Ricard* v. *Sanderson*, 41 N. Y. 179; *Atlantic Dock Co.* v. *Leavitt*, 54 N. Y. 35, 13 Am. Rep. 556; *Rogers* v. *Eagle Fire Co.* 9 Wend. 618; *Spaulding* v. *Hallenbeck*, 35 N. Y. 206; *Newell* v. *Hill*, 2 Met. 180; *Goodwin* v. *Gilbert*, 9 Mass. 510; *Huff* v. *Nickerson*, 27 Me. 106; *Burbank* v. *Pillsbury*, *supra*.

The doctrine is a very ancient one. In Sheppard's Touchstone it is said: "If feoffment or lease be made to two, and there are divers covenants in the deed to be performed on the part of the feoffees or lessees, and one of them doth not seal, and he that doth not seal doth notwithstanding accept of the estate and enjoy the lands conveyed or demised, in these cases as touching all inherent covenants, they are bound by these covenants as much as if they do seal the deed."

Some of the authorities deny that the technical action of covenant will lie against the grantee of a deed-poll, but an English author who favors the technical rule concedes that the weight of the English decisions is the other way, saying: "Perhaps, however, the doctrine has been too long sanctioned to be now reversed. At all events, it is an introduction of an equitable principle into a court of law, the acceptance of a deed being considered equivalent to an actual execution by the grantee." Platt, Covenants, 18.

The equitable rule has much to commend it, while the technical rule is the product of the slavish adherence to forms which did so much to deform the common law, and is without any merit entitling it to favor. But we need not discuss this question at length, for it has been discussed again and again and the better reasoned cases support the equitable doctrine. *Finley* v. *Simpson*, 22 N. J. L. 331; *Harrison* v. *Vreeland*, 38 N. J. L. 366; *Sparkman* v. *Gove*, 44 N. J. L. 252; *Maynard* v. *Moore*, 76 N. C. 158; *Bowen* v. *Beck*, 94 N. Y. 86; *Atlantic Dock Co.* v. *Leavitt*, *supra*; *Maine* v. *Cumston*, 98 Mass. 317; *Martin* v. *Drinan*, 128 Mass. 515.

Judgment affirmed.

STATE of Indiana, *ex rel.* Simon W. TAYLOR, *Appt.*,
v.
Board of Commissioners of WARRICK COUNTY.

(....Ind.....)

The fact that a county superintendent of schools was elected by means of corruption cannot be relied upon to prevent the issuance of a mandate to compel the board of county commissioners to approve his school-book bond, if, upon his receiving the required number of votes, a certificate of election has been issued to him, and he has duly qualified and entered upon the discharge of the duties of his office; his right to hold the office cannot be inquired into except by a direct proceeding instituted for that purpose.

(June 24, 1890.)

APPEAL by relator from a judgment of the Circuit Court for Warrick County in favor of respondents and from an order denying a motion for a new trial in an action brought to compel the approval of relator's school-book bond. *Reversed.*

The case sufficiently appears in the opinion.

Messrs. **D. B. Kumler, J. A. Heminway** and **John L. Taylor** for appellant.

Messrs. **G. H. Hazen** and **Gilchrist & DeBruler** for appellees.

Coffey, *J.*, delivered the opinion of the court:

The relator was duly elected county superintendent of schools in Warrick County by the trustees of said County on the 3d day of June, 1889.

He immediately filed his bond, to the approval of the county auditor, took the oath of office and entered upon the discharge of the duties of his office as such superintendent. The appellant did not file the bond required by the Statute, known as the school-book bond, acting under the belief that it was not necessary to file such bond until after the governor of the State should issue his proclamation, as provided for in section 10 of said Law. The governor issued his proclamation on the 29th day of July, 1889, and on the 9th day of August following the relator tendered to the Board of Commissioners of Warrick County a good and sufficient bond under the terms of said Law, and demanded its approval, which was refused. This suit was brought to compel, by mandate, the approval of said bond.

The Board of Commissioners answered in substance that prior to his election as county superintendent the relator was trustee of one of the townships in Warrick County; that at said time the County had ten trustees, five of whom were of one political faith and five of another political faith; that the relator belonged to one political party and the auditor of said County to another; that the relator and said auditor entered into a corrupt agreement, by the terms of which the relator was to resign his said office of trustee and the said auditor was to appoint a trustee as his successor of the same political faith as said auditor; and that in consideration of his resigning his said office of trustee it was agreed that the relator should be elected by the trustees of said County superintendent of the schools of said County; that pursuant to the terms of said corrupt agreement the relator did resign his said office of trustee, said auditor did appoint his successor and the relator was elected by the trustees of the several townships of said County superintendent of the schools thereof; that the relator was elected by means of said corrupt agreement, and without it he could not have been elected.

Upon issues formed the cause was tried by the court, resulting in a finding and judgment for the appellees over a motion for a new trial.

We are not favored with a brief by the appellees, and are not advised of the ground upon which the court based its judgment, but in our opinion the court erred in overruling the appellant's motion for a new trial.

In all of its essential features this case is like the case of *Knox County* v. *Johnson* (Ind.) 7 L. R. A. 684 (decided at last term), except in the matter of defense set up by the appellees. The appellant, at the time he tendered his special bond to the Board of Commissioners of Warrick County, had been duly elected, qualified and was acting as county superintendent of schools; was in the possession of the office and was discharging the duties pertaining thereto. Such being the case, the appellees could not attack his title in the collateral manner attempted by their answer. The public have an interest in the discharge of the duties of the office, and until such time as the appellee shall be ousted by a proper proceeding for that purpose, every-one must recognize him as the legally elected and qualified county superintendent. *Leach* v. *Cassidy*, 23 Ind. 449; *State* v. *Jones*, 19 Ind. 356; *Redden* v. *Covington*, 29 Ind. 118; *Gumberts* v. *Adams Exp. Co.* 28 Ind. 181; *Creighton* v. *Piper*, 14 Ind. 182; *Kisler* v. *Cameron*, 39 Ind. 488; *McGee* v. *State*, 103 Ind. 444, 1 West. Rep. 467; *Parmater* v. *State*, 102 Ind. 90; *Mannix* v. *State*, 115 Ind. 245, 18 West. Rep. 109.

The certificate of election issued to the appellant and his qualification as county superintendent bar all inquiry into his right to hold the office, except in a direct proceeding for that purpose. *Parmater* v. *State, supra.*

It is not denied that the appellant was elected county superintendent by the votes of a majority of the trustees of Warrick County, and that he duly qualified and entered upon the discharge of the duties of his office. No one is contesting his election and no proceeding is pending to oust him.

It is settled by the case of *Knox County Comrs.* v. *Johnson, supra*, that he was entitled to have the bond in question approved at the time it was tendered. The appellees could not go behind his election and inquire into his title to the office. It was their duty to approve his bond. Having refused to do so, mandate is the proper remedy to compel them to perform that duty. *Gulick* v. *New*, 14 Ind. 93; *McGee* v. *State, supra.*

The circuit court erred in overruling the motion for a new trial.

Judgment reversed, with directions to the Circuit Court to grant a new trial.

MISSOURI SUPREME COURT.

STATE OF MISSOURI, *Respt.*,
v.
Gustus P. HOPE, *Appt.*

(....Mo.....)

1. **Objections to the admission of testimony** in criminal as well as in civil cases must state opportunely the reasons therefor in order to preserve the rulings for a review.

2. **A party cannot in general demand** the exclusion of evidence called out in fair response to questions asked without objection.

3. **The fact that a witness testified** on behalf of the State in a criminal case without having first been sworn is not ground for error, where no objection was made at the hearing before he was fully cross-examined.

4. **A statute permitting a verdict** when defendant is voluntarily or willfully absent does not violate his constitutional right to be present at the trial.

(March 22, 1890.)

APPEAL by defendant from a judgment of the Circuit Court for Scotland County sentencing him for the crime of unlawfully assaulting, stabbing and wounding another. *Affirmed.*

Statement by **Barclay**, *J.*:

This cause is here upon an indictment, in the usual form, charging defendant with an assault upon Walker Hale with intent to kill. He was convicted of unlawfully assaulting, stabbing and wounding Hale, and was sentenced in accordance with that verdict. He then appealed to this court, after the customary motions. The evidence on the part of the State tended to prove that defendant and Hale had an altercation on the public road, during the course of which defendant inflicted certain wounds on Hale with a knife. That there was abundant testimony to support the verdict is not denied. The defendant relied upon self-defense, and, furthermore, offered evidence of good general reputation as a peaceable and quiet boy, as well as for veracity. In this branch of the case, during the examination of a witness for defendant, the following questions on his behalf were asked, and answers given:

"B. Riley, sworn on the part of the defendant. Direct examination. (1) Do you live in the neighborhood of Mr. Hope? *A.* Yes, sir. (2) Are you a relation of his? *A.* No, sir. (3) How long have you lived there? *A.* I have lived there, within half of a mile, for ten or twelve years. (4) Have you been acquainted with the family? *A.* Yes, sir. (5) Are you acquainted with his reputation for truth and veracity in the neighborhood? *A.* Yes, sir. (6) Is it good or bad? *A.* I think it is good. (7) Are you acquainted with his reputation as being a quiet and peaceable boy? *A.* It is considered good."

NOTE.—*Exceptions to ruling; when must be taken.*

Exceptions in criminal prosecutions stand on the same footing as those in civil causes. State v. Day (Mo.) Nov. 18, 1889; State v. Meyers, 99 Mo. 107.

Exceptions must distinctly present the ruling of the court, or they cannot be considered. Young v. Martin, 75 U. S. 8 Wall. 354 (19 L. ed. 418); Springfield F. & M. Ins. Co. v. Sea, 88 U. S. 21 Wall. 158 (22 L. ed. 511).

Objections to the admission or rejection of evidence must be taken at the trial, or by bill of exceptions. Thomson v. Madison B. & A. Asso. 1 West. Rep. 269, 103 Ind. 279; Roberts v. Hershiser, 20 Neb. 594; Pittsburgh, C. & St. L. R. Co. v. Heck, 102 U. S. 120 (26 L. ed. 58); Zeller v. Eckert, 45 U. S. 4 How. 289 (11 L. ed. 979); Phelps v. Mayer, 56 U. S. 15 How. 160 (14 L. ed. 643); Bryan v. Forsyth, 60 U. S. 19 How. 334 (15 L. ed. 674); Barton v. Forsyth, 61 U. S. 20 How. 532 (15 L. ed. 1012); Campbell v. Boyreau, 62 U. S. 21 How. 223 (16 L. ed. 96); Dredge v. Forsyth, 67 U. S. 2 Black, 563 (17 L. ed. 253); Houghton v. Jones, 68 U. S. 1 Wall. 702 (17 L. ed. 503); Hutchins v. King, 68 U. S. 1 Wall. 53 (17 L. ed. 544); Belk v. Meagher, 104 U. S. 279 (26 L. ed. 735).

Assignments of error to the admission of testimony, which do not state that the objection was made at the time of the trial, cannot be considered on appeal. Griffin v. Johnson (Ga.) Jan. 17, 1890.

A ruling made during the progress of a trial, either admitting or excluding evidence, is not an order, and it must therefore be excepted to when made. McGuire v. Drew, 83 Cal. 225; Abbey v. Ferris, 31 N. Y. S. R. 59; Benepe v. Wash, 38 Kan. 407.

A point not brought to the attention of the court at the trial cannot be raised in the supreme court for the first time. Talbot v. Taunton, 1 New Eng. Rep. 615, 140 Mass. 552; Keith v. Wells (Colo.) March 28, 1890; Chapman v. Moore, 5 West. Rep. 270, 107 Ind. 223; Thomson v. Madison B. & A. Asso. *supra*; Miller v. Bradish, 69 Iowa, 279; Shafer v. Ferguson, 1 West. Rep. 129, 103 Ind. 90; Miles v. Albany, 8 New Eng. Rep. 473, 59 Vt. 79.

Where a question was not objected to until the answer had been given, and there is nothing to show that it could not have been, the objection will not be considered. State v. Ward, 61 Vt. 153.

An exception to the admission of evidence is not available, where the objection was not made until after it had gone to the jury, and where there was no motion to strike out. Hangen v. Hachemeister 5 L. R. A. 137, 114 N. Y. 566; Wright v. State, 81 Ga. 745; United States v. Breitling, 61 U. S. 20 How. 253 (15 L. ed. 900); Scott v. Lloyd, 34 U. S. 9 Pet. 418 (9 L. ed. 178).

In such case the right to make the objection is waived. Roberts v. Graham, 73 U. S. 6 Wall. 578 (18 L. ed. 791).

Where improper testimony was admitted without objection, it is too late to make the objection for the first time on a motion for a new trial. Feidler v. Motz, 42 Kan. 519; Steffy v. People, 130 Ill. 98.

Where the grounds for excluding testimony appear by cross-examination, which is followed by a motion to exclude such testimony, the objection is taken in time. Comes v. Chicago, M. & St. P. R. Co. 78 Iowa, 391.

General exceptions not considered on appeal.

Vague and general exceptions make no issue of law that can be passed upon by this court. Central R. Co. v. Freeman, 75 Ga. 331; Cureton v. Westfield, 24 S. C. 457; Coln v. Coln, Id. 597.

Objections presented by bill of exceptions, when too general, present no question for review on error or appeal. Peck v. Chouteau, 8 West. Rep. 318, 91 Mo. 138; Clark v. Conway, 23 Mo. 438.

To a general objection to evidence, the only question is whether it is admissible for any purpose. Dow v. Merrill, 65 N. H. ——.

A general objection to evidence is sufficient only

In rebuttal, the State offered some evidence regarding defendant's reputation, in the course of which the question (referred to in the opinion) arose on a motion to exclude a part of the testimony of witness Zugg. The passage from the record presenting this point is as follows:

"Ernest Zugg, recalled, on the part of the plaintiff. (1) Are you acquainted in the neighborhood in which the defendant, Gustus P. Hope, resides? *A.* Yes, sir. (2) Are you acquainted, in the neighborhood in which he resides, with his general reputation as to being a quiet, law-abiding boy? *A.* Yes; I guess I am. By the Court. Is his general reputation good or bad? *A.* I don't know what general reputation is. I don't know what you mean. By the Court. It is the estimation in which he is held by the people generally. Is that general reputation good or bad? *A.* I don't know what you call good or bad. (3) What is the estimation of him? *A.* It is quarrelsome. (Objected to.) By the Court. That will not do. By the Court. General reputation consists in the estimation in which a man is held by the people generally. (4) They were relatives of Mr. Hale's? *A.* Not all of them wasn't. (5) Wasn't it a fact that this talk was from the relatives of Mr. Hale? *A.* I don't know that it was; it wasn't all from them. (6) Wasn't the principal talk that you heard from them? *A.* I don't know but one family that were relatives. Here Mr. Smoot (counsel for defendant) asked that the court exclude all this testimony from the jury, as not being founded on any time with reference to this difficulty. By the Court. Objection overruled. To the said action of the court, in not excluding the said testimony from the jury, the defendant, by his counsel, did then at the time except."

Another witness (Mr. Goslin) for the State was examined on the same subject, and the following questions asked, and answers made, without any objection or exception: "(5) Are you acquainted with his general reputation for peace and quiet in the neighborhood in which he lives? *A.* Yes, sir; I am. (6) Is it good or bad? *A.* It is bad."

The opinion states the other facts bearing upon the questions discussed in it.

Messrs. **Smoot & Pettingill** and **R. F. Walker** for appellant.

Mr. **John M. Wood**, *Atty-Gen.*, for respondent.

Barclay, *J.*, delivered the opinion of the court:

The points made by the defendant upon the rulings of the trial court on the evidence are not well taken.

1. Most of these rulings were made over objections to testimony which assigned no ground or reason for excluding it. Section 1907 of our Statutes concerning criminal procedure (Rev. Stat. 1879) declares that "the provisions of law in civil cases, relative to compelling the attendance and testimony of witnesses, their examination, the administration of oaths and affirmations, and proceedings as for contempt, to enforce the remedies and protect the rights of parties, shall extend to criminal cases, so far as they are in their nature applicable thereto, subject to the provisions contained in any statute."

where the evidence is inadmissible in its nature. Tozer v. New York Cent. & H. R. R. Co. 7 Cent. Rep. 389, 105 N. Y. 659; State v. Meyers, 99 Mo. 107; Everdson v. Mayhew (Cal.) April 25, 1889; Chicago & R. I. R. Co. v. People, 9 West. Rep. 740, 120 Ill. 667.

Where the objection could not be obviated by any means within the power of the party offering the evidence, in order to raise the question of its admissibility it is sufficient to make a general objection thereto. Holcombe v. Munson, 5 Cent. Rep. 402, 108 N. Y. 682.

A general objection to evidence only saves the right to specific rulings on the defects that are called to the court's attention before the case is submitted to the jury. Willard v. Pike, 4 New Eng. Rep. 608, 59 Vt. 202.

A party cannot, on appeal, under a general objection to the admission of evidence, object to its admission on grounds not specified, and which, if they had been specified, might have been obviated. Earl v. Lefler, 46 Hun, 10; Farman v. Ellington, 46 Hun, 47.

A general exception to the admission of testimony, unless the whole of it is incompetent, will not be considered. The objectionable portion must be specifically pointed out. Smiley v. Pearce, 98 N. C. 185. See Cincinnati, I. St. L. & C. R. Co. v. Howard (Ind.) *ante*, 593.

Objections to evidence too indefinite to save question for review.

An objection to evidence that it is incompetent, immaterial and irrelevant, is not sufficient to present any question on appeal. Stringer v. Frost, 2 L. R. A. 614, 116 Ind. 477; Clark Civil Twp. v. Brookshire, 18 West. Rep. 379, 114 Ind. 437; Chicago & E. I. R. Co. v. Holland, 11 West. Rep. 51, 122 Ill. 461; Vickery v. McCormack, 117 Ind. 594; Louisville, N. A. & C. R. Co. v. Falvey, 1 West. Rep. 876, 104 Ind. 409; McCullough v. Davis, 6 West. Rep. 579, 108 Ind. 292; Byard v. Harkrider, 6 West. Rep. 867, 108 Ind. 376; Metzger v. Franklin Bank, 119 Ind. 359; Bundy v. Cunningham, 5 West. Rep. 540, 107 Ind. 360.

That a question is "irrelevant and inadmissible" will not raise the question of its competency, where it is relevant to a certain point in issue. Burke v. Koch, 75 Cal. 356.

Blending an objection to the admissibility of evidence in the same application which questions its sufficiency is not proper. Columbian Ins. Co. v. Lawrence, 27 U. S. 2 Pet. 25 (7 L. ed. 335).

An objection to evidence as incompetent must state the reasons which make it incompetent. Helena v. Albertose, 8 Mont. 499.

An objection to evidence as "incompetent and immaterial" is sufficient to apprise the court of the real nature of the objection, when it immediately succeeds eight previous objections to similar evidence, made upon the ground that the witness was not competent to testify to transactions and conversations with a deceased person. *Re* Eysman's Will, 3 L. R. A. 599, 113 N. Y. 62.

Exceptions must be specific.

Exceptions to the admission of evidence must be specific. Fuller v. Smith, 74 Ga. 335; Brunswick v. Moore and Hall v. Huff, 74 Ga. 409; House v. Alexander, 3 West. Rep. 316, 105 Ind. 109; Landwerlen v. Wheeler, 3 West. Rep. 639, 106 Ind. 523; Northwestern Mut. L. Ins. Co. v. Hazelett, 2 West. Rep. 693, 105 Ind. 212; Smythe v. Scott, 3 West. Rep. 750, 106 Ind. 245; Louisville, N. A. & C. R. Co. v. Grantham, 2 West. Rep. 281, 104 Ind. 353.

A particular objection is necessary to raise the question of the admissibility of evidence as part of the *res gestæ*. Hughes v. State, 27 Tex. App. 127.

The appellate court cannot consider an error in the admission of evidence to which no specific ob-

This has been a part of the law of Missouri from a date as early, at least, as 1835. It has been re-enacted repeatedly in the various revisions of the statutes that have taken place since then. Its language to-day is substantially, if not identically, the same that it has been for some fifty years. Rev. Stat. 1835, 3d ed. p. 490, § 15; Rev. Stat. 1845, p. 880, chap. 138, § 16; Rev. Stat. 1855, p. 1191, chap. 127, § 18; Gen. Stat. 1865, p. 850, chap. 213, § 17; Rev. Stat. 1879, § 1907; Rev. Stat. 1889, § 4207.

In civil cases it has been uniformly ruled by this court, from a very early period of its history, that it is not sufficient, for the purposes of review, to object generally to improper testimony when offered, but that the grounds must be stated to the court with the objection. *Fields* v. *Hunter*, 8 Mo. 128; *Roussin* v. *St. Louis Perpetual Ins. Co.* 15 Mo. 244; *Clark* v. *Conway*, 23 Mo. 438; *Western & P. R. Co.* v. *Cox*, 32 Mo. 456; *Lohart* v. *Buchanan*, 50 Mo. 201.

That rule has thus become a fixed part of our jurisprudence governing the trial of civil causes, and must be regarded as having been in contemplation of the law-makers when the revision of the Statutes alluded to occurred. Section 1907, Rev. Stat. 1879, should therefore be considered as having been re-enacted from time to time with the then prevailing rule relative to the examination of witnesses in civil cases as part of it, in accordance with an established principle of interpretation of laws. *Sanders* v. *St. Louis & N. O. Anchor Line*, 97 Mo. 27, 3 L. R. A. 390.

We hence consider it necessary in criminal, as well as in civil, causes for a party objecting to the admission of testimony to state opportunely the reasons for the objection in order to preserve the ruling for review, should it be adverse to the objector. If the ruling be favorable to the latter, however, and thus the evidence be excluded, generality in the objection would furnish no cause for reversing the ruling of the trial court. It would be sustained, if defensible on any grounds.

In *State* v. *O'Connor*, 65 Mo. 374, views are expressed somewhat at variance with those above indicated. In so far as they conflict, that decision should no longer be regarded as authoritative.

2. Referring to the other rulings of the trial court on the evidence, as to some no exceptions were saved, which precludes reviewing them, as this court has often held; and as to others the objections were interposed too late,—that is to say, after the testimony had been admitted, unchallenged, in response to pertinent questions. A party cannot, in general, demand the exclusion of evidence called out in fair response to

---

jection was made, and which is not within the purview of a general objection. Wilson v. Kings County Elevated R. Co. 114 N. Y. 487.

Objections to evidence must be reasonably specific, to be available on appeal. Ohio & M. R. Co. v. Walker, 12 West. Rep. 731, 113 Ind. 196; Smith v. James, 72 Iowa, 515.

An exception to evidence which does not point out the particular part objected to is not sufficient, where some of the evidence is competent. Prindle v. Campbell (D. C.) 18 Wash. L. Rep. 254.

A party objecting to a certain class of evidence need not object specifically to each question and answer, to raise the question on appeal. Oppenheimer v. Barr, 71 Iowa, 525.

The overruling of objections to evidence which are not specific will not be reviewed on appeal. Boston v. Murray, 13 West. Rep. 261, 94 Mo. 175; Binford v. Young, 13 West. Rep. 815, 115 Ind. 174.

A general objection will not be considered on appeal, when evidence was received, without specific objection, to prove the allegations wanting in the complaint. Bowman v. Eppinger (N. D.) April 1, 1890.

A general objection to testimony is not sufficient where it is admissible as to one defendant, but not as to another. Taylor v. Deverell (Kan.) April 4, 1890.

Insufficiency of evidence will not be considered on an assignment that the decision is against law, without specifying the particulars in which the evidence is insufficient. Malone v. Del Norte County, 77 Cal. 217.

Grounds of objection must be stated.

The only mode to get evidence or objections to evidence in the record is by a bill of exceptions. Thomson v. Madison B. & A. Asso. 1 West. Rep. 269, 108 Ind. 279.

An exception can be reserved only by having it embodied in a "bill of exceptions," or by having it noted in the record of the decision to which it relates. State v. Leach, 71 Iowa, 54.

Objections to evidence must specify in a direct and positive manner the ground which was presented to the court below on the trial. Cole v. Byrd (Ga.) April 29, 1889; Woodbury v. District of Columbia (D. C.) 3 Cent. Rep. 788, 5 Mackey, 127; Adler v. Land, 4 West. Rep. 269, 21 Mo. App. 516; Safety Fund Nat. Bank v. Westlake, 4 West. Rep. 881, 21 Mo. App. 565; Talbott v. Padgett, 30 S. C. 167; Bray v. Parker, 82 Ga. 234; Wilhelm v. Burleyson (N. C.) May 13, 1890; Dale v. See, 5 L. R. A. 583, 51 N. J. L. 378; Tucker v. Jones, 8 Mont. 225.

They must be stated, by pointing out some definite or specific defect in its character, or it will be without weight before an appellate court. Camden v. Doremus, 44 U. S. 3 How. 515 (11 L. ed. 705); United States v. McMasters, 71 U. S. 4 Wall. 680 (18 L. ed. 311); Moore v. Bank of Metropolis, 38 U. S. 13 Pet. 302 (10 L. ed. 172).

Without specifying the ground, an exception will not be sustained. Mooney v. Peck, 8 Cent. Rep. 637, 49 N. J. L. 232; Merkle v. Bennington, 12 West. Rep. 516, 68 Mich. 133.

Nor will it be ground for reversal, unless the testimony is wholly inadmissible. Turner v. Newburgh, 12 Cent. Rep. 215, 109 N. Y. 301.

Nor will the objection be considered on appeal. Hughes v. Griswold, 82 Ga. 299; L'Hommedieu v. Cincinnati, W. & M. R. Co. 120 Ind. 435.

It is the right of the court to know upon what ground the objector relies. Blackmore v. Fairbanks (Iowa) Feb. 3, 1890.

Rulings of the court, admitting or rejecting evidence, can be brought to this court for revision only by a bill of exceptions. They cannot properly be included in a special verdict or in an agreed statement of facts. Suydam v. Williamson, 61 U. S. 20 How. 427 (15 L. ed. 978); Pomeroy v. Bank of Indiana, 68 U. S. 1 Wall. 592 (17 L. ed. 638); Phœnix Ins. Co. v. Lanier, 95 U. S. 171 (24 L. ed. 383); Buscher v. Scully, 4 West. Rep. 725, 107 Ind. 246.

Rulings not the subject of a bill of exceptions will not be reviewed. Passenger Conductors L. Ins. Co. v. Birnbaum (Pa.) 7 Cent. Rep. 635.

Rulings of the trial court cannot be brought into the record by mere reference to them in a bill of exceptions (State v. Griffin, 98 Mo. 672); nor can they be preserved in the record by a recital by the clerk that exception was taken thereto. Steffy v. People, 130 Ill. 98.

questions asked without objection. Nothing exceptional is shown here affecting the application of that rule. When the legal objection to testimony is not apparent from the question that educes it, but is developed later in any way (for instance on cross-examination), the omission to object, at the time it came in, is no waiver of the right to have it excluded. It is only when the exceptional nature of the testimony has become apparent that the failure to object may constitute a waiver of objection. The reason of this rule is thus stated in a recent case: "To allow a party to permit, without objection, the admission of evidence, and for the first time make his objection in instructions, would be intolerable practice. If he had an opportunity to interpose an objection, he cannot take the chances that the testimony will be favorable to him, and when it turns out otherwise raise his objection, but must be held to have waived it." *Maxwell* v. *Hannibal & St. J. R. Co.* 85 Mo. 95.

The rule itself merely involves an application of the principle, frequently declared of late, that, on appeal, parties are bound by the theories of law they asserted or acquiesced in at the trial. Whether such theories take the form of instructions asked (*M. Foster Vinegar Mfg. Co.* v. *Guggemos*, 98 Mo. 391), or of instructions unexcepted to (*State* v. *Griffin*, 98 Mo. 672), or of rulings on evidence, the nature of which is clear at the time, we think the principle equally applies. In the case before us it appears that defendant's objection to the testimony of witness Zugg in rebuttal (to the effect that defendant was generally reputed to be quarrelsome) was that the question eliciting it did not fix any time with reference to the difficulty. The objection itself was not valid. The question, by the use of the present tense, did fix the time as that of the trial; but construing it broadly as an objection to receiving the testimony because it did not fix the time as that of the difficulty, then it was too tardy for recognition, under the rule we have discussed. Moreover, defendant made the same inquiry, as that against which his objection under discussion was directed, during the examination of his witness, Mr. Riley, and interposed no objection to the same question when asked Mr. Goslin, a prior witness for the State. (The statement preceding this opinion presents the exact language used in each of these instances). There is respectable authority for holding that either of these

---

Where a party merely objects to evidence, but fails to state all the grounds of his objection, he is deemed to waive his objection (see cases cited in Thompson, Trials, 560, *note*), and all grounds not specified are waived. Id. 561.

Bill of exceptions; what should show.

A bill of exceptions failing to show the objections made to the evidence cannot be considered on appeal. Goforth v. State, 22 Tex. App. 405.

Specific grounds of objection must be embodied in the bill of exceptions. Ringensberger v. Hartman, 3 West. Rep. 363, 102 Ind. 537.

It should point out the evidence complained of. Wiley v. Logan, 95 N. C. 358; Clements v. Rogers, 95 N. C. 248.

It should show enough of the evidence rejected to make its relevancy apparent. Indiana, B. & W. R. Co. v. Adams, 11 West. Rep. 668, 112 Ind. 302.

A bill should show what the evidence excluded would have been. Moss v. Cameron, 66 Tex. 412; Vance v. Upson, 66 Tex. 476.

A bill of exceptions to the exclusion of testimony should show that the testimony would have benefited the party excepting (McKay v. Overton, 65 Tex. 82), and that the party was actually injured by the exclusion of the testimony of a witness. Warren v. Spencer Water Co. 3 New Eng. Rep. 502, 143 Mass. 155.

On exception to admission of evidence it must appear from facts shown that the evidence was admitted to the injury of the excepting party. Noyes v. Smith (Me.) 4 New Eng. Rep. 788.

The mere statement, in a bill of exceptions, of an objection made to evidence, does not establish that the ground of objection existed, but it must be made to appear that it in fact existed. Huffman v. State, 28 Tex. App. 174.

Evidence or statements of fact not contained in the bill of exceptions nor made a part thereof, though appended thereto, will not be regarded by the court. National Bank of Metropolis v. Kennedy, 84 U. S. 17 Wall. 19 (21 L. ed. 554); Reed v. Gardner, 84 U. S. 17 Wall. 409 (21 L. ed. 665).

A bill of exceptions to the admission in evidence of certain small slips of paper "written in bad Spanish and without names or any signature," without showing what was written on them, is insufficient. Livar v. State, 26 Tex. App. 115.

Where documentary evidence is excluded, or a portion admitted, it must be made part of a bill of exceptions, so the court can judge of its admissibility. People v. Coughlin, 11 West. Rep. 556, 67 Mich. 466.

Record on appeal; what must show.

The record must set forth the objections specifically. Grubbs v. Morris, 1 West. Rep. 187, 103 Ind. 166; Shafer v. Ferguson, 1 West. Rep. 130, 103 Ind. 90; Osburn v. Sutton, 6 West. Rep. 903, 108 Ind. 443; Ketcham v. Barbour, 3 West. Rep. 856, 102 Ind. 576; Louisville, N. A. & C. R. Co. v. Jones, 7 West. Rep. 83, 108 Ind. 551; Chapman v. Moore, 5 West. Rep. 269, 107 Ind. 223; Louisville, N. A. & C. R. Co. v. Thompson, 5 West. Rep. 833, 107 Ind. 442.

Where the record fails to show what ruling was made, or any exception to it, no question as to such ruling can be presented on appeal. Burns v. People, 126 Ill. 282.

The record on appeal must specify the particulars in which the evidence is claimed to be insufficient, or that ground for setting aside the verdict will not be considered. Alpers v. Schammel, 75 Cal. 590.

An objection as to the competency of evidence will not be considered on appeal, where the record shows that the lower court did not certify that ground of objection to be true. De Vaughn v. McLeroy, 82 Ga. 687.

Errors in admitting or rejecting testimony will not be noticed, unless the evidence is sent up with the record. Wilson v. Gerhardt, 9 Colo. 585; First Nat. Bank v. Leppel, Id. 594.

Where no exceptions appear in the transcript, except such as appear from the minutes of the clerk, this court cannot take any notice of them. Young v. Martin, 75 U. S. 8 Wall. 354 (19 L. ed. 418).

A stenographer's report of the evidence, not signed or attested by the judge, is not a part of the record. Louisville, N. A. & C. R. Co. v. Kane, 120 Ind. 140.

Excluded evidence which derives its materiality alone from parts of a plea stricken out need not be considered on appeal, when not set forth in the record except by an exhibit of a long extract from the stenographic report of the trial. McGee v. Long (Ga.) July 8, 1889.

acts on defendant's part was a waiver of the objection in question. *Hinds* v. *Longworth*, 24 U. S. 11 Wheat. 206 [6 L. ed. 455]; *Hayden* v. *Palmer*, 2 Hill, 205; *Gale* v. *Shillock* (Dak.) 29 N. W. Rep. 631; *McCormick* v. *Laughran*, 16 Neb. 87.

But, without expressly deciding that point, we think the trial court committed no reversible error in the ruling, considered in all its bearings.

3. The next assigned error rests on the claim that a witness testified on behalf of the State at the trial without having first been sworn. No objection on this ground was made at the hearing. It appears for the first time in the motion for a new trial, and nothing in the record shows when the fact was discovered by defendant or his counsel. Had the point been suggested when the witness began his statement or during his examination, the irregularity or oversight of permitting him to testify, unsworn (if it existed), could have been easily and promptly rectified. But it was not suggested. After the witness had been examined in chief he was fully cross-examined on the part of defendant. Thus was he treated by both parties as in all respects fully qualified to testify. It has been held by other courts, as well as our own, that where an oath is requisite to qualify a person as a trier of the facts or of law, it may be waived by the competent parties in interest, either expressly (*Howard* v. *Sexton*, 4 N.Y. 157; *Tucker* v. *Allen*, 47 Mo. 488; *Grant* v. *Holmes*, 75 Mo. 109), or by going forward in the matter without inquiry or objection. *Arnold* v. *Arnold*, 20 Iowa, 275; *Merrill* v. *St. Louis*, 83 Mo. 244; *Cochran* v. *Bartle*, 91 Mo. 636, 8 West. Rep. 707.

We think the principle on which these rulings are based is applicable also to the case of a witness in the circumstances here shown. *Lawrence* v. *Houghton*, 5 Johns. 129.

This assignment of error has been considered on the assumption that the facts alleged were as claimed by defendant, but it is not thereby conceded that an affidavit accompanying a motion for new trial, though uncontradicted, is necessarily to be accepted as establishing the facts it recites, where they are such as have occurred in the immediate presence of the court.

4. The record shows that defendant was "willfully and voluntarily absent" when the verdict of the jury was returned in open court, though his counsel was present at the time, and defendant had been personally in attendance, until then, during the entire trial. He was afterwards brought in, and the sentence of the court was pronounced in his presence, after his motions for new trial and in arrest had been overruled.

By section 1891, Rev. Stat. 1879, in force when the alleged offense was committed, and when the trial of defendant occurred, it is provided as follows: "No person indicted for a felony can be tried unless he be personally present during the trial; nor can any person be tried or be allowed to enter a plea of guilty in any other case unless he be personally present, or the court and prosecuting attorney shall consent to such trial or plea in the absence of the defendant; and every person shall be admitted to make any lawful proof by competent witnesses or other testimony in his defense, provided, that in all cases the verdict of the jury may be received by the court, and entered upon the records thereof, in the absence of the defendant, when such absence on his part is willful or voluntary, and, when so received and entered, shall have the same force and effect as if received and entered in the presence of such defendant: and provided, further, that, when the record in the appellate court shows that the defendant was present at the commencement or any other stage of the trial, it shall be presumed, in the absence of all evidence in the record to the contrary, that he was present during the whole trial."

The provisos in this section first became a part of our law at the Revision of 1879. Prior to that time, and ever since 1835, the Statute declared that "no person indicted for a felony can be tried unless he be personally present during the trial," etc., omitting any such qualifications of that rule as are contained in the provisos of the present law. Rev. Stat. 1835; Gen. Stat. 1865, p. 850, § 15.

While the Statute was in that form, prior to the Revision of 1879, this court had held it error to receive a verdict in the absence of defendant, even though he had escaped from custody after the cause had been submitted to the jury. *State* v. *Buckner*, 25 Mo. 167; *State* v. *Braunschweig*, 36 Mo. 397.

It had further been held that the record must affirmatively show the presence of defendant at the rendition of the verdict (*State* v. *Cross*, 27 Mo. 332; *State* v. *Dooly*, 64 Mo. 146), though in some instances that fact had been taken as established by inferences from other entries in the record. *State* v. *Schoenwald*, 31 Mo. 147; *State* v. *Lewis*, 69 Mo. 92.

The important change made in the Statute by the Revision of 1879 (§ 1891) was probably induced by a consideration of the decisions mentioned. In view of the history of the law on the subject, there can be no doubt of the legislative purpose in the amendment. It was, among other things, to prevent a defendant from securing a mistrial and continuance by escaping if in custody, or absconding if on bail, after the cause had been submitted to the jury, and before verdict rendered. Whether that purpose was accomplished will appear presently.

The language of the law so plainly sanctions the reception of a verdict by the court in defendant's absence, when willful or voluntary, that no difference of opinion is likely to arise as to its meaning. The difficulty, if any there be, appears upon the suggestion that the enactment in question may be in conflict with the Organic Law, particularly with that section of the Bill of Rights which declares that, "in criminal prosecutions, the accused shall have the right to appear and defend in person and by counsel; to demand the nature and cause of the accusation; to meet the witnesses against him face to face," etc. Const. 1875, art. 2, § 22.

The Statute, in permitting a verdict when defendant is voluntarily or willfully absent, evidently proceeds on the assumption that by such willful or voluntary absence the defendant waives the right to be present, which otherwise he might constitutionally insist on. Is such waiver valid? In considering this question, we start from the postulate that the courts will not declare a statute unconstitutional unless it is manifestly so, and that all fair and reasonable doubts on that point will be resolved in favor of its constitutionalty. The presumption is that the Legislature acted within the proper sphere of its powers, and, until the contrary is clearly and satisfactorily made to appear to the court, the law will be upheld. That the accused may waive some rights secured by the Constitution is a proposition supported by the authority of so many adjudicated cases that a citation of them now seems unnecessary. But there is great diversity of opinion respecting the particular constitutional rights that may be waived. Numbers of cases hold that certain rights cannot be waived by the accused for reasons of public policy. It would probably tend to confuse, rather than to elucidate, the present case to attempt any summary of the principles applicable to the waiver of constitutional rights generally. The issue actually before us requires only a decision upon the validity of a waiver, by defendant's own act, of his right to be personally present at the rendition of verdict. Defendant undoubtedly has a right to be heard, and for that purpose to be present when the verdict against him on a charge of felony is given; but if, being on bail, he sees fit to run away at that stage of the trial, on whom shall the consequences of such misconduct fall? It is a "fundamental legal principle," of far-reaching scope in its practical application (*Mutual L. Ins. Co.* v. *Armstrong*, 117 U. S. 591 [29 L. ed. 997]; *Reynolds* v. *United States*, 98 U. S. 161 [25 L. ed. 248]; *Riggs* v. *Palmer*, 115 N. Y. 506, 5 L. R. A. 340), that "no one should have an advantage from his own wrong." 1 Co. Litt. 148*b*; Broom, Legal Max. 8th ed. Yet to hold that, in such a state of facts as we have supposed, defendant during his willful absence retains the right, while he endeavors to increase the impossibility, of his being heard in the cause, would seem to us a clear instance of giving him a great advantage from his own wrong. The maxim is founded on principles of common fairness and good faith, as is also the idea expressed in section 1891 of the Revised Statutes, that defendant, by voluntarily withdrawing from the court when the verdict is rendered, should be held to relinquish the right to be present and heard, which, but for his own wrongful act, he might freely enjoy. In such case he is deprived of no right. He merely refuses to avail himself of one, just as he may in various ways waive his constitutional right to confront the witnesses against him under repeated rulings of the court. *State* v. *Wagner*, 78 Mo. 644; *Merrill* v. *St. Louis*, 83 Mo. 252; *State* v. *Houser*, 26 Mo. 431.

In *State* v. *Smith*, 90 Mo. 37, 6 West. Rep. 651, the present Statute was considered, and no intimation of its unconstitutionality was made. In other cases it has been further held, even under the old Statute (Gen. Stat. 1865, p. 850, § 15), that defendant's absence at the trial during part of the argument of counsel to the jury was not a prejudicial error requiring a reversal. *State* v. *Bell*, 70 Mo. 633; *State* v. *Grate*, 68 Mo. 22.

In other States, without such a statute as our present one, and under constitutional provisions in most instances substantially like those in force here, it has been repeatedly held that where defendant was absent by his own voluntary act, *e. g.*, by escape or by absconding while on bail, at the rendition of verdict in cases other than capital, the court might properly receive it, notwithstanding his absence. *Sahlinger* v. *People*, 102 Ill. 241; *State* v. *Kelly*, 97 N. C. 404; *Price* v. *State*, 36 Miss. 531; *Gales* v. *State*, 64 Miss. 105; *Barton* v. *State*, 67 Ga. 653; *Hill* v. *State*, 17 Wis. 676; *Fight* v. *State*, 7 Ohio, pt. 1, 180; *Jackson* v. *State*, 49 N. J. L. 252, 8 Cent. Rep. 581; *State* v. *Peacock*, 50 N. J. L. 34, 10 Cent. Rep. 175; *Lynch* v. *Com.* 88 Pa. 189.

The principle on which those decisions rest has been declared in others in its application to different phases of court proceedings in criminal cases. *People* v. *Bragle*, 88 N. Y. 585, as explained in *People* v. *Lyon*, 99 N. Y. 224; *United States* v. *Davis*, 6 Blatchf. 464; *State* v. *Paylor*, 89 N. C. 539.

We do not think the court loses jurisdiction of the cause by reason of defendant's getting beyond the confines of the court-room when the verdict comes in. *State* v. *Kelly*, 97 N. C. 404.

If that were the effect of such action on his part, the court would not have power to enter an order for his arrest thereafter, so long as he remained away. That result certainly could not have been intended by the constitutional provision in question as now worded. In interpreting the fundamental law of the State it is proper to consider the effect and consequences of any proposed construction of it in ascertaining what was probably the intention designed to be expressed by the instrument. Constitutions, like other laws, are governed by established rules of interpretation, and among others by that just mentioned. To hold that the flight of defendant while on bail, just before verdict, must necessarily produce a continuance of the cause, would make it possible for anyone able to give bond, by repeating that performance at each successive trial, to finally defeat the ends of justice. Such conduct would not deprive defendant of his constitutional right to bail or of his freedom of action during every recess of the court while the trial lasted; but (if now sanctioned here) it would introduce a new and novel mode for securing continuances, having some advantage over the ordinary methods heretofore in use. It would have, at least, the merit of simplicity, But we do not think those who framed or the people who adopted the Constitution contemplated such a construction of it in this regard as would make it ever possible for any defendant in a criminal case to avoid and escape altogether a verdict, otherwise just and correct, by any such acts of his own. We believe that no language used in that instrument will bear a construction which would make such results possible. We are of opinion that section 4191, Rev. Stat. 1889 (§ 1891, Rev. Stat. 1879), in so far as it relates to the subject under discussion, is entirely constitutional, and that the trial court committed no error in proceeding in accordance with its terms.

We find no error in any of the rulings of the court, to which exceptions were saved, in the giving or refusal of instructions, and, after a car ful examination of the record, observe no.hing c lling for further remark.

The judgment is affirmed, for the reasons stated, with the concurrence of all the members of the court except **Sherwood, J.**, who dissents.

OHIO SUPREME COURT.

NEW VIENNA BANK, *Plff. in Err.*,
v.
Edward F. JOHNSON *et al.*

(47 Ohio St. ....)

*1. **The Statutes of the State regulating the mode of signing, sealing, acknowledging and recording mortgages** are limited in their application to these particulars; the legal or equitable effect of the instrument and its contents are unaffected thereby; and the rights of the parties and of third persons subsequently dealing with the land are to be determined by the general rules of law and equity, applicable to the subject in analogous cases.

2. **In order to mortgage land as security for a debt,** it is not necessary, in all cases, to clothe the creditor with the legal title; it is sufficient if the intent to pledge the land as a security clearly appears from the instrument, and the instrument is duly executed and recorded, as required by statute.

3. **A mortgage upon real estate,** made by the owner to a partnership in its firm name, to secure an indebtedness to it, duly executed and recorded, as required by statute, constitutes a valid lien upon the property in favor of the firm as a security for the indebtedness to it.

(April 29, 1890.)

ERROR to the Circuit Court for Clinton County to review a judgment sustaining demurrers to the answer and cross-petition setting up a mortgage lien on the property in a suit to enjoin the sale of certain property by an assignee for benefit of creditors and to compel a transfer thereof to complainant. *Reversed.*

The facts sufficiently appear in the opinion.

Mr. **H. B. Lindley, Jr.,** for plaintiff in error.

Messrs. **Mills & Van Pelt** for defendant in error.

Minshall, *Ch. J.*, delivered the opinion of the court:

Joshua W. Johnson, being indebted to the New Vienna Bank in the sum of $1,628, executed, December 30, 1885, a mortgage to the Bank to secure the same, which was duly filed for record the following day. The Bank was a partnership doing business in that name. The mortgage covered two tracts of land, one containing seventy-one and a fraction, and the other thirty-eight and a fraction, acres, and purported to convey "all the estate, title and interest" of said Johnson in and to said lands "to the said New Vienna Bank, its successors and assigns forever," without other words of limitation. Afterwards, in the month of January, 1886, Johnson and his son Edward entered into an agreement for an exchange by which the father agreed to convey to the son the thirty-eight-acre tract covered by the mortgage, and the son agreed to convey to the father twenty-six acres owned by himself. In accordance with this agreement the son at once conveyed the twenty-six acres owned by him to his father, who, on the 4th of February following, mortgaged it to one Morris to secure an indebtedness. But the father by reason of sickness, as is alleged, failed to convey the thirty-eight-acre tract to the son, as by the terms of the agreement he was bound in equity to do. On the day following the mortgage to Morris, he executed a mortgage to one Woolard to secure an indebtedness of $1,995, on the other tract of seventy-one acres covered by the mortgage to the Bank. And afterwards, on June 24, 1886, being in failing circumstances, he made an assignment of all his property, for the benefit of his creditors, to Edwin Arthur, which was duly filed on the same day in the probate court. The assignee, under the order of the probate court, being about to sell the thirty-eight-acre tract with the other lands assigned to him, Edward, the son, commenced an action in the common pleas to enjoin the sale, and compel the conveyance of the tract to him under the agreement for an exchange which had been executed on his part by the conveyance of the twenty-six acres to his father, he also averring that he had taken possession of the thirty-eight acres at the time of the exchange, and had continued in the possession and occupation of it as his own ever since, whereby all parties had notice of his rights.

All parties in interest were finally made parties to the suit and answered setting up their rights. To the answer and cross-petition of the Bank, setting up its mortgage and claiming a lien prior to all others upon the thirty-eight and seventy-one acre tracts covered by it, the plaintiff and the administrator of Woolard (he having died) demurred, claiming that the mortgage, having been executed to the Bank by name, instead of to the members composing

*Head notes by the COURT.

NOTE.—*Mortgage; formalities as to execution; statutory requirement.*

The formalities as to the execution of a mortgage prescribed by statute cannot be dispensed with without making it invalid as to third persons. Dodd v. Bartholomew, 8 West. Rep. 125, 44 Ohio St. 171.

A mortgage signed and recorded, but omitting seals, may be reformed by the addition of seals, against a subsequent attaching creditor having notice. Bullock v. Whipp, 1 New Eng. Rep. 809, 15 R. I. 190.

The Pennsylvania Act of 1881 affects the immediate parties to the transaction. Sankey v. Hawley, 11 Cent. Rep. 785, 118 Pa. 30.

Under Cal. Civ. Code, § 1962, subd. 2, the parties to a mortgage are estopped by recitals therein. Waldrip v. Black, 74 Cal. 409.

the firm, was of no avail as a security, and that therefore the cross-petition of the Bank failed to state facts entitling it to any relief.

The case, having been heard and determined by the rendition of judgment in the common pleas, was appealed to the circuit court, where, upon a renewal of the demurrers, they were sustained, and the answer and cross-petition of the Bank dismissed. The action of the circuit court in this regard is assigned for error here. Hence the only question to be decided upon the record is, whether the mortgage executed to the New Vienna Bank can be made available to it as a lien on the land as a security in its favor against the claim of the plaintiff and those of the other mortgagees, all of whom are subsequent in time. It is claimed that it cannot for the reason that the Bank is not a legal entity; that it is simply a partnership of certain natural persons doing business in that name, and incapable of holding the legal title to lands in their firm name. Conceding this to be true, does it follow that the instrument is not available to the Bank as a lien on the land to the extent of the debt intended by the maker to be secured thereby? If so, it must be for the reason that, in order to create a lien on land as security for a debt, the legal title must, in all cases, be transferred to the person intended to be secured, or that such a lien cannot exist independent of the legal title. But this is not the case.

There are what are termed equitable as well as legal mortgages. The distinction is that a legal or common-law mortgage is a conveyance of the land accompanied by a condition contained either in the deed itself, or in a separate instrument executed at the same time. And, to quote the language of Mr. Jones, which has been frequently quoted with approval by the courts, "in addition to these formal instruments which are properly entitled to the designation of mortgages, deeds and contracts which are wanting in one or more of these characteristics of a common-law mortgage are often used by parties for the purpose of pledging real property, or some interest in it, as security for a debt or obligation, and with the intention that they shall have effect as mortgages." These kinds of mortgages are, as he says, "as many as there are varieties of ways in which parties may contract for security by pledging some interest in lands." And he adds, "Whatever the form of the contract may be, if it is intended thereby to create a security, it is an equitable mortgage." Jones, Mortg. § 162.

We are not unmindful of the fact that, under the decisions that have been made in this State, giving a construction to our Statutes regulating the execution and recording of mortgages, many instruments that would be treated elsewhere as equitable mortgages could have no effect given them here as against third persons, whether they had notice of their existence or not. But these Statutes and the construction placed upon them do not go beyond what they require as to the signing, acknowledgment and recording of the instrument. They prescribe no requisites as to the contents of the instrument—as to how lands shall be charged as a security, or the intent manifested. The character of the instrument in this regard, and its effect, are left to be determined by the application of the general principles of law and equity on the subject. So that any instrument that would, by the application of these principles, be regarded as constituting a lien on land as against third persons with notice, will have the same effect under our Recording Statutes, where it has been duly executed and recorded. *Strang* v. *Beach*, 11 Ohio St. 283; *Hura* v. *Robinson*, Id. 232, and *Dodd* v. *Bartholomew*, 44 Ohio St. 171, 3 West. Rep. 123.

By the record of the instrument it becomes notice to others of the equitable as well as legal rights of the parties. It may, as against third persons, be corrected to give effect to the intent apparent upon the face of the instrument, or the courts may, in a proceeding to enforce it, regard that as done which ought to have been done, and treat the instrument as if corrected Pom. Eq. § 1235.

A few instances may be selected to illustrate the doctrine and show its application to this case. An instrument which does not transfer the legal estate has been held to operate as an equitable transfer of it in the nature of a mortgage. Thus, a mortgage to certain executors from which the word "heirs," creating a fee, was omitted, and the word "successors" used instead, was held to be an equitable mortgage in fee, and was reformed in a proceeding to foreclose it, against a subsequent mortgagee of the same land with notice. *Gale* v. *Morris*, 29 N. J. Eq. 222.

And so, in *Brown* v. *First Nat. Bank*, 44 Ohio St. 269, 3 West. Rep. 601, effect was given to an instrument as a mortgage in fee, although words of inheritance were not used in it. The instrument had been executed in the State of Indiana upon lands in this State, and had therefore to be construed by the laws of this State. By it the debtor simply mortgaged and warranted his land to his creditor as a security for the debt, with a provision for foreclosure in case of nonpayment. The purpose to secure the debt by a mortgage upon the land was apparent from the instrument, and of this intention all persons dealing with the land were held to have notice by the record of the instrument. See the opinion by Owen, *Ch. J.*, p. 276. And so in California it is held that the words "we mortgage the property," accompanied by a provision for the sale of it, upon nonpayment of money thus secured, are sufficient to create a mortgage. *De Leon* v. *Higuera*, 15 Cal. 483, and *Barroilhet* v. *Battelle*, 7 Cal. 450.

So, too, when, by the terms of his deed, a grantor reserves a lien on the land as a security for the unpaid purchase money, it operates as a mortgage, and the record of the deed is constructive notice to all others of his rights. Pom. Eq. § 1255.

But the lien so secured is independent of the legal title, as that passes by the deed to the purchaser, who is said to hold in trust for the grantor until the purchase money has been paid. For many other similar instances, see Jones, Mortg. §§ 163–171.

It is true that some of these could not, for reasons before stated, be made available as liens in this State against third persons.

Holding the legal title may, in some cases, be of much advantage to the mortgagee, as thereby, on condition broken, he may recover the land and hold it until his debt is satisfied. And this may be said to be the distinguishing feature of a common-law mortgage. It is, however, seldom resorted to—the remedy by foreclosure and sale (and which may be had in all cases) being more generally adopted. In a proceeding by foreclosure, it is not material where the legal title resides. A sale is required in all cases (Rev. Stat. § 5316) and the purchaser takes thereby all the interest of both the mortgagor and mortgagee in the land. As the passing of the legal title is not necessary to affect land as a security for a debt, no reason can be assigned why the debtor may not create, and the creditor accept, such a security, provided compliance is had with the Statutes regulating the execution and recording of similar instruments. Such form of security certainly contravenes no rule of law or public policy, and is in harmony with the purpose and intention of the parties in all cases where the whole object is, on the one hand to give, and on the other to obtain, a security.

The execution of a mortgage in the usual form is now generally regarded as only a security, and not as a conveyance. Like the debt it secures, it is treated throughout as a chose in action. That a partnership may make contracts in its firm name is a matter of elementary law. It may make a note in its firm name, or may accept one payable to itself. It may be formed to deal in land, and may make valid contracts therefor. And if the firm cannot hold the legal title, the vendor holds it in trust for the firm. *Sherry* v. *Gilmore*, 58 Wis. 324, 332.

In this case the court says: "There does not seem to be any reason for holding that a partnership, in making a purchase of real estate for the benefit of the firm, may not do so in the same manner that they make other purchases, viz., in the firm name."

A number of cases are cited, where it has been held that a general description of the grantee is sufficient to support the deed—as the "heirs", or "children" of a given person—on the principle that that is certain which can be made certain, and therefore applicable to the members of a firm. See also Bates, Partn. § 296, and cases cited.

And it has been held in some cases that a conveyance to a firm is a conveyance to the members as tenants in common, who hold the title in trust for the firm. *Jones* v. *Neale*, 2 Pat. & H. (Va.) 339; *Beaman* v. *Whitney*, 20 Me. 413.

That a partnership may acquire an equitable estate in real property is decided in *Rammelsberg* v. *Mitchell*, 29 Ohio St. 22, 52.

Therefore, to say that a partnership cannot contract for an interest in land in its firm name as a security only, would be to establish an exception, with neither reason nor necessity for its existence. There are quite enough conflicting principles in the law, or what the Romans would have termed "inelegancies," without adding to their number, in the absence of any controlling necessity for so doing.

The instrument, the validity of which is questioned in this case, was designed by both parties to be a mortgage. This is apparent on the face of it. The only objection made to it is the incapacity of the partnership in its firm name to take and hold the legal title to real estate. But this is not material, for if it were so, then, as already shown, Johnson, the mortgagor would hold the legal title in trust as a security for the firm. In such case there would be no need of a formal reformation, as it would be the duty of the court, in the exercise of its equity powers, to treat that as done which ought to have been done, and give effect to the instrument in a proceeding to enforce it, according to the priority of its record, by awarding to the Bank a lien upon the land for the satisfaction of the amount due it.

The case of *Hughes* v. *Edwards*, 22 U. S. 9 Wheat. 489 [6 L. ed. 142], has a close analogy to this case. There by the laws of Kentucky an alien could not hold the title to lands in that State, and, the mortgagees being subjects of Great Britain, objection was taken to the mortgage on this ground. But the court said: "The objection is deprived of all its weight in a case where the mortgagee, instead of seeking to obtain possession of the land, prays to have his debt paid, and the property pledged for its security sold, for the purpose of raising the money. Under this aspect, the demand is, in reality, a personal one, the debt being considered as the principal, and the land merely as an incident; and, consequently, the alienage of the mortgagee, if he is a friend, can, upon no principle of law or equity, be urged against him."

In *Chicago Lumber Co.* v. *Ashworth*, 26 Kan. 212, a mortgage, taken in the firm name of partners, was held to be a valid security. The court said: "Ashworth was cognizant of the name and style under which the partners transacted their business, and executed the mortgage to the Chicago Lumber Company for the benefit of the partners composing the partnership transacting business in that name. The mortgage was therefore taken in the name of the partnership; hence there was an actual grantee in the mortgage, although such grantee was merely the name and style of the partnership;" and the legal title was regarded as held in trust for the real grantees, the partners, which, as we have seen, is all that is necessary where a sale, and not the possession of the land, is sought, in proceedings to enforce the mortgage as a security.

The case of *Stambaugh* v. *Smith*, 23 Ohio St. 596, is not in point. The real question there was, not whether a firm could hold the title to a lease in its firm name, but whether it could be released by the firm in its own name, the legal title being not in it, but in a member in trust for it. It was held that it could not, for the very plain reason that the *cestui que trust* can in no case transfer the legal title. That can only be done by the trustee. The case does not decide, nor was it intended to decide, that a partnership may not hold a lease in its firm name, so as to be protected in the enjoyment of it according to the intention of the parties. That it may hold the equitable title in fee simple was held in *Rammelsberg* v. *Mitchell*, *supra*.

We think the court erred in sustaining the demurrer to the answer and cross-petition of the Bank.

Judgment reversed, and cause remanded for further proceedings.

WISCONSIN SUPREME COURT.

Julius REISE, Impleaded, etc., *Respt.*,
v.
Frances H. ENOS, Impleaded, etc., *Appt.*

(....Wis....)

1. **A right of way across a lot** given by a conveyance of an adjoining lot to be used in common with the grantors and the owners and occupants of the former lot, is a right appurtenant to the lot conveyed, and the grantee after he has conveyed the lot cannot claim to be still entitled to use the right of way in connection with any other lot subsequently acquired.

2. **An easement of a right of way** is not presumed to be personal, where it can fairly be construed to be appurtenant to some other estate.

3. **A reservation in a conveyance of a lot** which has a right of way appurtenant of such right of way to the grantor is ineffectual. He cannot enlarge the right, or retain any interest in the right of way as separate and distinct from the lot to which it belongs.

(*Orton, J., dissents.*)

(April 29, 1890.)

APPEAL by defendant, Frances H. Enos, from a judgment of the Circuit Court for Waukesha County in favor of plaintiff, Reise, in an action brought to enjoin defendant from obstructing or closing up a certain alleged alley, and to recover damages on account of temporary obstruction of the same. *Reversed.*

The alley was alleged to exist across the rear ends of lots 3 and 4 of Kimball's plat of subdivision of a part of the Mill Reserve in the Village of Waukesha. Said plat consists of a triangular parcel of ground bounded by Mill Street and Clinton Street, which streets intersect at its northwest corner, and by "block J," of N. W. Addition. It is divided into lots 1, 2, 3 and 4, all fronting on Mill Street. Lot 4 lies next to Clinton Street and the alleged alley or right of way extends across the rear ends of lots 4 and 3 to lot 2

The following is a diagram of the premises in controversy:

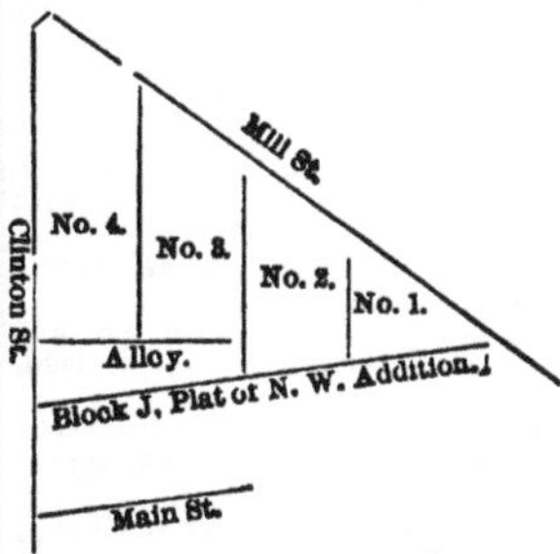

The further facts sufficiently appear in the opinion.

Messrs. **Parks & Robinson** and **Griswold, Chafin & Martin,** for appellant:

The way so granted was clearly appurtenant to lot 3, and the respondent, under the grant, obtained no personal right to the use of said way, apart from his ownership of said lot.

Spensley v. *Valentine*, 34 Wis. 160; *Cahill* v. *Layton*, 57 Wis. 600, 610; Washb. Easem. 40, 232; *Dennis* v. *Wilson*, 107 Mass. 591; *Louisville*

NOTE.—*Easement defined.*

An easement is an interest in land created by grant or agreement, express or implied, which confers a right upon the owner thereof to some profit, benefit, dominion or lawful use out of or over the estate of another. Huyck v. Andrews, 3 L. R. A. 789, 113 N. Y. 81.

It is an estate or interest in lands within the Statute of Frauds requiring contracts affecting real property to be in writing. North Beach & M. R. Co's App. 32 Cal. 506; Foster v. Browning, 4 R. I. 51; Rice v. Roberts, 24 Wis. 465; Cayuga R. Co. v. Niles, 13 Hun, 173; Day v. New York Cent. R. Co. 31 Barb. 548. See Sands v. Thompson, 43 Ind. 24; Wolfe v. Frost, 4 Sandf. Ch. 72, 7 N. Y. Ch. L. ed. 1027.

Easement defined. See *note* to Nowlin v. Whipple (Ind.) 6 L. R. A. 159.

How created.

An easement is generally and naturally and properly created by words of grant, but words of covenant may be equivalent to a grant if such be the clear intention. Norfleet v. Cromwell, 64 N. C. 12; Watertown v. Cowen, 4 Paige, 510, 3 N. Y. Ch. L. ed. 536.

There is a distinction between a servitude or easement imposed upon land, and a covenant real running with the land; but this difference has not always been kept in view. West Virginia Transp. Co. v. Ohio River P. L. Co. 22 W. Va. 600, 46 Am. Rep. 543; Tulk v. Moxhay, 2 Phil. Ch. 774; Whatman v. Gibson, 9 Sim. 196; Schreiber v. Creed, 10 Sim. 35; Woodruff v. Trenton Water Power Co. 10 N. J. Eq. 489; Barrow v. Richard, 8 Paige, 351, 4 N. Y. Ch. L. ed. 457; Brewer v. Marshall, 18 N. J. Eq. 337; Hills v. Miller, 3 Paige, 254, 3 N. Y. Ch. L. ed. 141.

A grant of an easement will pass by assignment or conveyance. Columbus, H. & G. R. Co. v. Braden, 9 West. Rep. 194, 110 Ind. 558.

An easement can only be created by a conveyance under seal, or by long user, from which a conveyance is presumed. Cagle v. Parker, 97 N. C. 271.

Whoever grants a thing is understood also to grant that without which the grant itself would be of no effect. Boody v. Watson, 4 New Eng. Rep. 563, 64 N. H. 162.

When the use of anything is granted, everything is granted by which the grantee may have and enjoy such use. Salem Capital Flour Mills Co. v. Stayton W. D. & Canal Co. 33 Fed. Rep. 146.

Only such incorporeal easements as are strictly essential and necessary to the enjoyment of the estate granted pass with the word "appurtenances." Root v. Wadhams, 9 Cent. Rep. 874, 107 N. Y. 384; Griffiths v. Morrison, 7 Cent. Rep. 773, 106 N. Y. 165.

A mere convenience is not sufficient to create such right of easement. Root v. Wadhams, *supra.*

Where a deed reserves a right in the nature of a servitude for the benefit of other land owners, such right, if not against public policy, is appurtenant to the land of the grantor and binding on that conveyed to the grantee, and will pass with the lands to all subsequent grantees. Coudert v. Sayre (N. J.) Jan. 4, 1890.

Where a right of way is granted, it becomes an

See also 11 L. R. A. 134.

& N. R. Co. v. *Koelle*, 104 Ill. 455; *Kramer* v. *Knauff*, 12 Ill. App. 115; *Potter* v. *Iselin*, 31 Hun, 134.

Lot No. 2 was acquired by Reise subsequent to the grant to him of lot 3, with its appurtenant right of way; and the servitude could not be extended thereto.

Smith v. *Porter*, 10 Gray, 66.

If a man have a right of way over another's land to a particular close, he cannot enlarge it to other closes.

Kirkham v. *Sharp*, 1 Whart. 323, 29 Am. Dec. 57; Washb. Easem. 3d ed. 60, 185-187; *Lewis* v. *Carstairs*, 6 Whart. 193; *Shroder* v. *Brenneman*, 23 Pa. 348; *Rexford* v. *Marquis*, 7 Lans. 249; *French* v. *Marstin*, 24 N. H. 440, 57 Am. Dec. 294; *Com.* v. *Wood*, 10 Pa. 97; *Watson* v. *Bioren*, 1 Serg. & R. 227, 7 Am. Dec. 617; *Davenport* v. *Lamson*, 21 Pick. 72; *Leach* v. *Hastings*, 7 New Eng. Rep. 146, 147 Mass. 515; *Case of Private Road*, 1 Ashm. (Pa.) 417; *Carter* v. *Page*, 8 Ired. L. 190.

The right being appurtenant to the land conveyed by Reise, and only to that land, passed with its conveyance.

Garrison v. *Rudd*, 19 Ill. 558; *Gunson* v. *Healy*, 100 Pa. 42; *Dennis* v. *Wilson*, *supra;* Washb. Easem. 9; *Louisville & N. R. Co.* v. *Koelle*, *Potter* v. *Iselin* and *Kramer* v. *Knauff*, *supra*.

Messrs. **Ryan & Merton**, for respondent:

From the language in the deed there can be no question as to the intention of the grantor to grant an assignable interest to grantee, in the said right of way.

Pentland v. *Keep*, 41 Wis. 490; *Poull* v. *Mockley*, 33 Wis. 482.

In order to pass as appurtenant there must, as a general proposition, be an existing easement in the technical sense of the word, meaning thereby the right to use another's land for special and temporary purposes, in connection with the land for the use and enjoyment of which the right is exercised.

2 Washb. Real Prop. 623.

Counsel cannot claim the right of way across lot 4, as an appurtenance within the legal and ordinary meaning of the word, that would make it necessary to the enjoyment of said lot 3, without which the grant itself would be of no effect.

Broom, Legal Maxims, 362; *Mabie* v. *Matteson*, 17 Wis. 1; 2 Washb. Real Prop. 26; *Gayetty* v. *Bethune*, 14 Mass. 49; *Cary* v. *Daniels*, 8 Met. 466.

Cole, *Ch. J.*, delivered the opinion of the court:

There does not appear to be any sufficient ground for holding, upon the undisputed facts, that the plaintiff, Reise, as owner of lot 2, acquired a right of way over lot 4 by prescription, because he had not owned that lot twenty years when this action was commenced, and it does not appear that his grantors ever had or claimed the right to pass across lots 3 and 4 to Clinton Street. Indeed, one of his grantors, Mr. Hill, distinctly testified that, while his wife owned lot 2, there was no right of way across these, and that they never went through in that direction, but that the ordinary way was out from the back of lot 2, and, he adds, there was a high fence built up to Mr. Reise's store, and at the rear of the store came down to this double privy. This evidence effectually disposes of any claim or pretense to a right of way from lot 2 over lot 4 founded upon adverse user of twenty years, if such claim were seriously insisted upon, as it is not. The right of way, if it exists, must rest upon grant; and

appurtenance to the land, following it into the hands of each successive grantee. Parish v. Caspare, 7 West. Rep. 370, 109 Ind. 586.

Right to use an alley which is the only approach from the highway to land sold passes as an appurtenance. Zell v. First Universalist Society, 12 Cent. Rep. 148, 119 Pa. 390.

Where the deed conveyed the right of way, of undefined width, with a stipulation to have and hold said rights and privileges to the use of the company as long as required, nothing more passes than an easement in or right of way over the land. Douglass v. Thomas, 1 West. Rep. 171, 103 Ind. 187.

Grant of right of way, when personal, is not assignable or inheritable, and cannot pass to a trustee in insolvency, or to a corporation succeeding the individual grantees. Hall v. Armstrong, 1 New Eng. Rep. 831, 53 Conn. 554.

An easement or servitude created by deed is never presumed to be personal or in gross, when it can be fairly construed to be appurtenant to some other estate; and when the reservation naturally operates to enhance the value of the other adjacent lands of the grantor, it is a strong circumstance to indicate that it was intended to be appurtenant to the estate, and not merely personal to the grantor. McMahon v. Williams, 79 Ala. 288.

As to way of necessity, see *note* to Logan v. Stogdale (Ind.) 8 L. R. A. 58.

Rights of parties.

To constitute an easement there must be two distinct tenements, the dominant to which the right belongs, and the servient upon which the obligation rests. Pierce v. Keator, 70 N. Y. 421; Wolfe v. Frost, 4 Sandf. Ch. 72, 7 N. Y. Ch. L. ed. 1027; Wagner v. Hanna, 38 Cal. 116.

Where the owner of a tract of land makes one part of it servient to another by an alteration which is obvious and permanent, and then conveys one of the parts, three things are essential: (1) a separation of the title; (2) that before the separation takes place the use which gives rise to the easement shall have been so long continued and so obvious as to show that it was meant to be permanent; and (3) that the easement shall be necessary to the beneficial enjoyment of the land granted or retained. Kelly v. Dunning, 8 Cent. Rep. 600, 43 N. J. Eq. 62; Wetmore v. Fiske, 4 New Eng. Rep. 796, 15 R. I. 360.

The grantee of such part takes it benefited or burdened by the easement which the alteration created. *Ibid.*

If the owner of land annexes to part of it a right of way, as appurtenant to the land, and then conveys such land, his grantees acquire an easement. Parish v. Caspare, 7 West. Rep. 369, 109 Ind. 586.

The vendor of a lot carved out of a larger plot owned by him can impose no servitude upon the lot in favor of the portion retained by him, in derogation of his grant, without an express reservation to that effect in the grant. Sloat v. McDougall, 30 N. Y. S. R. 912.

The rights of a party having an easement in the land of another are measured and defined by the purpose and character of that easement. See *note* to Illinois Cent. R. Co. v. Houghton (Ill.) 1 L. R. A. 213.

there in fact is where the plaintiff's counsel does rest it. It appears that Reise was at the commencement of the action the owner of lot 2; it having been conveyed to him by Hill and wife in August, 1870. He was formerly the owner of lot 3; it having been conveyed to him in 1864 by Cook and wife, who then owned both lots 3 and 4. In this deed from Cook to Reise of lot 3, there is granted, among other things, "a right of way from Clinton Street across the rear of said lot 4 to the rear end of lot 3, to be used in common with the owners and occupants of said lot 4 and with the said parties of the first part, and their heirs and assigns," reserving a room in the privy, which was on the back end of lot 3, for the use of the grantors and assigns.

In May, 1887, Reise conveyed lot 3 to the grantor of the defendant, Elihu Enos, by a deed which contained this clause: "Saving and reserving to the said parties of the first part, from the operation of this conveyance, the right of way being in use in and across the rear of lot 3 for their use in common, and the use of their heirs and assigns forever, with the owners and occupants of said lot 3, for use as a passageway to the right of way in the rear of lot 4, in said plat of said subdivision of said mill reserve running across said lot 4 to Clinton Street, in said village; also, giving and granting to said parties of the second part the use of the right of way from Clinton Street across the rear of said lot 4 to the rear end of said lot 3, in common with the parties of the first part, their heirs and assigns forever, and the owners and occupants of said lot 4. It is intended to specially reserve hereby from the operation of this conveyance the right of way to the parties of the first part, their heirs and assigns, forever, the free and uninterrupted right of way across the rear of said lots 3 and 4."

In April, 1874, Cook and wife executed a deed to the appellant, Frances H. Enos, conveying lot 4, in effect, with this reservation, subject to the right of way and passage from Clinton Street across the rear of said lot 4 to the rear end of lot 3.

Now, it is on the language of these deeds that the plaintiff predicates his right, as owner of lot 2, to the right of way from that lot across lot 3, and also across the rear of lot 4 to Clinton Street; and the simple question presented is, Can that right be maintained upon the language of the deeds? So far as lot 3 is concerned, there can be no doubt, as he expressly reserved that right in his conveyance to the grantor of Elihu Enos. He owned lot 3, and could reserve such right of way in his grant. There is no controversy upon that point. But, after he had conveyed away lot 3, can he still claim the right to a passageway across lot 4? The contention of appellant's counsel is that the right of the grantee in the deed from Cook to Reise in 1864, when lot 3 was conveyed, of a right of way from Clinton Street across the rear of lot 4 to the rear end of lot 3, was a right of way appurtenant to lot 3, and that this right cannot be enlarged so that it can be used or maintained in connection with any other lot to which he subsequently acquired a title; for, he says, the easement granted was not one in gross, but was to be enjoyed by the owner of lot 3, and could not be applied to another estate. We think this position is correct, and is sustained by the cases to which counsel refers. It is very clear that the easement is not what is called in the books an "easement in gross," that is, a personal right only, which might be assigned by the grantee to another person, but that it is an easement or right of way which is appurtenant to the land conveyed, and which will pass with that lot to another, where proper words of conveyance are used. Such an easement is not presumed to be personal where it can fairly be construed to be appurtenant to some other estate. Washb. Easem. *29, 161; *Dennis* v. *Wilson*, 107 Mass. 591; *Louisville & N. R. Co.* v. *Koelle*, 104 Ill. 455.

In the language of the authorities, lot 3, to which the easement is appurtenant, is the dominant estate, and lot 4, over which the easement is enjoyed, is a servient estate. It scarcely need be remarked that it is essential that the two estates should belong to different persons; for if the two estates belong to the same individual, he would have the right, as owner, to use each in any manner that might suit his convenience or pleasure. But, as to the point that Reise had, by the original deed of 1864, an easement or right of way over lot 4 as appurtenant to the lot conveyed to him, that is to say, lot 3, it seems to us there can be no doubt upon the authorities; and it appears to be equally well settled in the law that where, by one and the same deed, for one consideration, a man conveys a parcel out of a larger tract of land, and grants a right of way to him and his heirs in his own land obviously useful and necessary to the beneficial enjoyment of the land granted, the grantee takes the right of way therein as appurtenant to the land granted only, and has no right to use it as appurtenant to other land afterwards acquired. This is substantially the language of *Chief Justice* Shaw in *Stearns* v. *Mullen*, 4 Gray, 151. To the same effect are the decisions in *Davenport* v. *Lamson*, 21 Pick. 72; *Cotton* v. *Pocasset Mfg. Co.* 13 Met. 433; *Smith* v. *Porter*, 10 Gray, 66; *French* v. *Marstin*, 24 N. H. 440; *Shroder* v. *Brenneman*, 23 Pa. 348; *Gunson* v. *Healy*, 100 Pa. 42.

It is said that the right of way from Clinton Street across the rear of lot 4 to the rear end of lot 3, contained in the deed from Cook to Reise, is granted in general terms, and does not restrict the right to lot 3, or expressly declare it appurtenant to that lot. But still the legal implication is that the right was to be used and enjoyed by the owner of lot 3, and in connection with that lot. It is therefore appurtenant to lot 3, to which it is annexed, and cannot be enjoyed separate and distinct from the lot to which it belongs. Nor could Reise, to whom the right was originally granted, enlarge the right, and subject the servient estate to a new species of burden. But it is a general principle that, where an easement has become appurtenant to an estate, it follows every part of such estate, into whosesoever hands the same may come, by purchase or descent, providing the burden on the servient estate is not thereby increased. This doctrine is fully discussed and illustrated in Washb. Easem. 3d ed. 34-36; Goddard, Easem. 324. And it is well settled that, if a person has a right of way over the land of another to a particular close, he cannot enlarge it or extend it to other closes. That doctrine is decisive of this case.

It follows that the plaintiff, Reise, had no right to the use of the way over the rear of lot 4 except as the owner of 3, and could not, by virtue of the grant, use the way in connection with lot 2, which he subsequently acquired; for he had parted with his estate in lot 3. This point is so clearly and distinctly decided by the cases to which we have referred, and others which might be added to the same effect, that it is unnecessary to discuss the question further here.

We do not see that Reise's right is affected, so far as lot 4 is concerned, by the reservation in his deed to the grantor of Elihu Enos. Of course, he had the right of way through lot 3, which he had conveyed; but that was of no practical value to him unless he could use it in connection with the right of way across lot 4 to Clinton Street. But, as that right of way was only appurtenant to lot 3, he could not use it as a right of way to and from lot 2, because to do so would enlarge and extend the right over the servient estate to another lot. The right of way from lot 2 across lots 3 and 4, as we have said, rests upon grant, or on the language of the deeds referred to. There is no claim that, by the recorded plat which is mentioned in the conveyances, such right of passage existed by dedication. Indeed, the latter claim, if made, would be fully set at rest by the testimony of Hill, who says that, while his wife owned lot 2, there was no passageway across in that direction which was used. This satisfactorily shows that no such way in fact existed, or was supposed to exist, in consequence of an alley being marked on a plat extending from Clinton Street to the southwest corner of lot 2. In many cases where lots are platted and conveyed according to the recorded plat, which shows an alley or street abutting or bounding the lot, an inference arises that it was intended to dedicate the alley or street for the benefit of the adjoining lot owners. But from the undisputed facts in this case no such inference can be made.

In any view which we have been able to take of the case, we think *the judgment of the Circuit Court must be reversed, and the cause be remanded with directions to dismiss the complaint.*

Orton, *J.*, dissents.

Lyon, *J.*, took no part.

NEW YORK COURT OF APPEALS.

Mary IRVING, Trustee, etc., *Respt.*,

v.

James J. CAMPBELL, *Appt.*

(....N. Y.....)

1. The record of a deed cannot be read in evidence if such deed was acknowledged and proved by a subscribing witness whose place of residence does not appear from any part of the deed, acknowledgment or notarial certificate.

2. A title to land is not marketable if one link in the chain consists of a deed, the execution and delivery of which can be established only by parol evidence.

(June, 1890.)

APPEAL by defendant from a judgment of the General Term of the Superior Court of the City of New York affirming a judgment of the Special Term in favor of plaintiff in an action brought to compel specific performance of a contract to purchase certain real estate. *Reversed.*

The case is sufficiently stated in the opinion.

Mr. **Alexander Thain,** with *Mr.* **James P. Campbell,** for appellant.

Mr. **James B. Dill,** for respondent:

The record supplies the fact of the residence of the subscribing witness. Tucker conveyed the property to Lawrence, and Lawrence's deed describes Tucker as of the City of New York. Clerical errors, changes in phraseology or omissions of words clearly not of the substance of the Statute may be disregarded.

West Point Iron Co. v. *Reymert,* 45 N. Y. 703; *Canandaigua Academy* v. *McKechnie,* 90 N. Y. 618, 628.

Substantial compliance with the Statute is sufficient.

Canandaigua Academy v. *McKechnie,* 90 N. Y. 618; *Jackson* v. *Gumaer,* 2 Cow. 552; *Troup* v. *Haight,* Hopk. Ch. 239, 2 N. Y. Ch. L. ed. 407; *Duval* v. *Covenhoven,* 4 Wend. 561; *Meriam* v. *Harsen,* 4 Edw. Ch. 70, 6 N. Y. Ch. L. ed. 801; *M'Intire* v. *Ward,* 5 Binn. 296.

The omission of the words "described in" has been held to be unimportant.

West Point Iron Co. v. *Reymert,* 45 N. Y. 706.

The omission of the words "the foregoing instrument" has been held to be immaterial.

Smith v. *Boyd,* 101 N. Y. 475.

Whatever doubt exists relates to the record, not to the title. The title is the substance and the record is merely one of the sources of evidence of that title.

Fryer v. *Rockefeller,* 63 N. Y. 268.

A party in actual possession under color of title is presumed to have title even against an adverse claim of title supported by a deed and a record.

Rev. Stat. pt. 2, chap. 1, title 2, art 4, § 147 (7th ed. p. 2196); *Union College* v. *Wheeler,* 61 N. Y. 98; *Brown* v. *Volkening,* 64 N. Y. 76; *Phelan* v. *Brady,* 21 Abb. N. C. 286.

Even if the record is insufficient, the evidence proves the execution of the deed from Lawrence and shows that the plaintiff has a good and valid title to the premises in question.

Defects in the record or paper title may be cured or removed by parol evidence.

Hellreigel v. *Manning,* 97 N. Y. 60.

When the judicial doubt as to the validity of a title depends upon a question of fact, the test is whether, upon all the evidence, in a trial at law, the court would order a verdict in favor of the title.

Heck v. *Volz*, 14 N. Y. S. R. 409.

In order to throw doubt upon a title, it is necessary to show facts which tend to question the proof of the plaintiff's title.

Moser v. *Cochrane*, 9 Cent. Rep. 427, 107 N. Y. 35.

Ruger, *Ch. J.*, delivered the opinion of the court:

The object of this action was to compel the specific performance by the defendant of a contract made April 18, 1887, to purchase from the plaintiff certain real estate in the City of New York. Upon May 18, 1887, the day appointed for the performance of the contract, the plaintiff duly tendered to the defendant a deed sufficient in form to convey the premises described, executed by her as grantor. The defendant objected to the proposed title, among others, upon the ground that there was no legal evidence of the transfer of title by Thomas Lawrence, through whom the plaintiff claims.

It was conceded on the trial that Thomas Lawrence had title to the premises previous to and in the year 1871, and it was claimed that on November 23 of that year he conveyed the same to Eliza Irving, the plaintiff's grantor, by warranty deed.

This deed was attempted to be proved by a copy of the record in the register's office of the City of New York, duly certified by him to be a correct copy thereof. From such certificate it appeared that a deed from Thomas Lawrence to Eliza Irving of the premises in question, purporting to have been acknowledged and proved by Gideon J. Tucker, the subscribing witness thereto, had been recorded in such register's office.

This acknowledgment did not state the place of residence of the subscribing witness, neither did that fact appear from any part of the deed or the notarial certificate.

Thomas Lawrence, the grantor, died unmarried and childless, in 1875 or 1876, and the original deed was shown to have been lost at about that time; so that the only written evidence of its execution consisted of the record referred to.

At the time fixed for the performance of the contract, the plaintiff and her grantor had occupied the premises for about sixteen years only, and failed by about four years from completing the possession necessary to perfect title by adverse possession.

That the deed from Lawrence to Eliza Irving was actually made and delivered to the grantee by Lawrence was satisfactorily proved upon the trial of this case, but such proof rested altogether in parol, and might or might not be available to the holders of title under the plaintiff in any subsequent litigation between them and adverse claimants under Lawrence.

It is not disputed by the respondent but that the purchaser under this contract was entitled to a marketable title, free from any reasonable doubt, and she undertakes to sustain the contention that this is such title, mainly by the claim that the Lawrence deed was properly recorded. The question as to what constitutes a marketable title has been the frequent subject of discussion in this court in recent cases, and may be regarded as settled by authority. The rule as to the quality of such title is quite fully stated by *Judge* Earl in *Moore* v. *Williams*, 115 N. Y. 586. He there says: "There is no record or document which precludes Barnes from enforcing his judgment against the lot. The recitals in the deed of Guion to these defendants do not bind him and are not evidence against him, a prior incumbrancer. All the evidence to defeat his lien rests in parol and depends upon the memory of living witnesses. Whenever Barnes attempts to enforce his lien against the lot he can be defeated only by a resort to the evidence of such witnesses, who may then be dead or inaccessible. . . . Is a purchaser bound to take a title which he can defend only by a resort to parol evidence, which time, death or some other casualty may place beyond his reach? . . . Aside from the language used in the contract, it is familiar law that an agreement to make a good title is always implied in executory contracts for the sale of land, and that a purchaser is never bound to accept a defective title, unless he expressly stipulates to take such title, knowing its defects. . . . A good title means not merely a title valid in fact, but a marketable title which can again be sold to a reasonable purchaser or mortgaged to a person of reasonable prudence as a security for a loan of money. A purchaser will not generally be compelled to take a title when there is a defect in the record title which can be cured only by a resort to parol evidence."

It was also said by *Judge* Andrews, in *Fleming* v. *Burnham*, 100 N. Y. 10, 1 Cent. Rep. 267: "A title open to a reasonable doubt is not a marketable title. The court cannot make it such by passing upon an objection depending on a disputed question of fact or a doubtful question of law, in the absence of the party in whom the outstanding right was vested. He would not be bound by the adjudication and could raise the same question in a new proceeding. . . . It would especially be unjust to compel a purchaser to take a title, the validity of which depended upon a question of fact, where the facts presented upon the application might be changed on a new inquiry or are open to opposing inferences." See *Vought* v. *Williams*, 120 N. Y. 253, *ante*, 591.

Whatever conclusion might be reached by us in this case as to the validity of the plaintiff's title must therefore be unavailing to her grantee in any future contest with claimants under Lawrence, either by inheritance or purchase. In the absence of a good record title, he must necessarily be driven to rely for a defense upon parol evidence, which might then be accessible or not, according to circumstances beyond his control. It would seem, therefore, from the authorities, that the title tendered to the defendant was not so free from reasonable doubt as to require him to accept it, unless we conclude that the Lawrence deed was properly acknowledged so as to entitle it to be recorded. It therefore becomes material to consider the sufficiency of the acknowledgment of this deed. These Acts (3 Rev. Stat. 7th ed. p. 2215, §§ 1–17) provided, among other things, that an unrecorded deed shall be void as against any subsequent purchaser, in good faith and for a valuable consideration, of the same real estate. § 1, chap. 8, pt. 2.

Such deed may be so acknowledged as to be entitled to be recorded by the person executing it, or by a subscribing witness. § 12.

When the proof is made by a subscribing witness, he shall state his place of residence and that he knew the person described in and who executed such conveyance. *Ibid.*

"Every officer who shall take the acknowledgment or proof of any conveyance shall indorse a certificate thereof, signed by himself, on the conveyance, and in such certificate shall set forth the matters hereinbefore required to be done, known or proved on such acknowledgment or proof, together with the names of the witnesses examined before such officer, and the places of their residence, and the substance of the evidence given by them." § 15.

"Every conveyance acknowledged or proved and certified in the manner above prescribed, by any of the officers before named, may be read in evidence without further proof thereof, and shall be entitled to be recorded." § 16.

"The record of a conveyance duly recorded, or a transcript thereof duly certified, may also be read in evidence with the like force and effect as the original conveyance." § 17.

It would thus appear by the express language of the Statute that a conveyance of lands can be proved only by the acknowledgment to a public officer of its execution by the person making it, or by the affidavit of a subscribing witness having a place of residence, which must be stated to the officer taking the proof, and be inserted by him in the certificate required to be made and indorsed on the conveyance.

The provisions of the Revised Statutes were mostly new, and effected radical changes in respect to the laws relating to the proof and acknowledgment of conveyances, and especially in regard to such proof when made by a subscribing witness. The revisors, in their notes upon section 15, say that so much thereof as refers to the residence of witnesses is new, and was "deemed desirable in order to detect fraud, or to sustain an honest deed." 5 Stat. at L. 345.

The established canons for the construction of statutes require the courts to examine the condition of the law prior to the adoption of the statute, in order to discover its reason and purpose, and to so interpret it as to give effect to such purpose and object. *Waller* v. *Harris*, 20 Wend. 555.

The imperative language of the Statute respecting the residence of subscribing witnesses, as well as its plain object, would seem to preclude the court from considering its requirements as either directory or immaterial. It was plainly intended to remedy defects in the pre-existing law, which experience had shown to be dangerous.

Proof of a conveyance by a subscribing witness being liable to be rebutted by evidence that he was interested or incompetent (§ 17), it became important that parties interested should have some means of identifying such witness, aside from his mere name, which, in many cases, would be misleading and unreliable. The witness is therefore expressly required to state his residence, and that fact must also be incorporated in the certificate. This requirement has, in the safeguard it affords the public against possible frauds, a plain and obvious purpose to serve, which cannot be disregarded without opening the door to the most manifest abuse and imposition. To consider this provision as directory or immaterial violates the language of the Statute, deprives it of its efficacy, and puts in the power of unknown and unascertainable persons the opportunity to foist upon the record evidence of important transactions in real estate without any adequate security against imposition and fraud. It is not necessary that this certificate should be expressed in the language of the Statute, or according to any precise form; but in respect to its substantial provisions, it is indispensible that they should in some way be contained in it, and convey to all persons knowledge of the required information.

In the certificate in question no attempt is made to comply with the requirement of the Statute in respect to the residence of the witness, and there is nothing in the circumstances surrounding the transaction which can properly supply the omission to do so. We have not been referred by the respondent to any authority on the point holding such an acknowledgment to be valid or sufficient.

In *Dibble* v. *Rogers*, 13 Wend. 536, it was held, where a deed was acknowledged by the grantor, that the identity of the person making the acknowledgment was not required to be proved to the officer taking it, by the subscribing witness; but that other persons acquainted with him might make the necessary proof, and the certificate would be sufficient although the residence of such witness was not stated therein. It was assumed, however, in the opinion, that the Statute required the residence of the witness to be imperatively stated only in the case of a subscribing witness making proof himself of the execution of the deed.

It was held in *Fryer* v. *Rockefeller*, 63 N. Y. 268, that an acknowledgment which failed to state that the persons making it were known to the officer as the persons described in and who executed the deed, although it did state they were "grantors of the within indenture," was fatally defective, and did not entitle the deed to be recorded.

We find no authorities holding that a material provision of the Statute, expressly required to be stated, can be wholly disregarded, and a deed thus acknowledged lawfully admitted to record. That a deed improperly recorded cannot be read in evidence has been determined in numerous cases. *Morris* v. *Keyes*, 1 Hill, 540; *Clark* v. *Nixon*, 5 Hill, 36.

The cases of *Jackson* v. *Gumaer*, 2 Cow. 552; *West Point Iron Co.* v. *Reymert*, 45 N. Y. 703, and *Canandaigua Academy* v. *McKechnie*, 90 N. Y. 618, referred to by the respondent, are not authorities on the point. These cases all arose under deeds executed previous to the adoption of the Revised Statutes, and under a statute which did not require the residence of the subscribing witness to be stated in the certificate of acknowledgment.

We should have been gratified in this particular case if we could have reached a conclusion in favor of the sufficiency of the plaintiff's title, because we feel convinced that the lapse of time will soon cure any defects in her title; but a careful regard for the salutary provisions of the Statute has seemed to us to forbid such a result. The mere fact that in this case the subscribing witness was a well-known and respected citizen, whose residence was widely known, cannot work a change in a general rule provided by Statute, and we are therefore constrained to hold that the acknowledgment in this case does not entitle the Lawrence deed to be read in evidence.

The judgment of the General and Special Terms should therefore be reversed, and a new trial ordered, with costs to abide the event.

All concur.

MASSACHUSETTS SUPREME JUDICIAL COURT.

George W. VENABLE *et al.*, *Appts.*,
v.
Charles RICKENBERG and Traders' National Bank.

(....Mass.....)

1. **If an equitable attachment** of a debtor's property is prohibited by statute, the property cannot be reached in equity and the statute avoided merely by a change in the form of proceedings.

2. **A suit in equity to reach and apply property** to the payment of a debt cannot be maintained either under the general equity jurisdiction or under a statute which permits such suit in case the property "cannot be come at to be attached or taken on execution in a suit at law," where the property is in its nature attachable by trustee process, but cannot be attached in the particular case because of a statute prohibiting the collecting of that particular kind of debt by attachment, "either by trustee process or otherwise."

(June 21, 1890.)

APPEAL by plaintiff from a decree of the Superior Court for Suffolk County dismissing a bill filed to reach and apply certain property to the payment of a debt. *Bill dismissed.*

The case sufficiently appears in the opinion.

Messrs. **Warren & Brandeis** and **William H. Dunbar**, for appellants:

The effect of the discharge in bankruptcy, so far as the plaintiffs were concerned, was merely to exempt Rickenberg thereafter from arrest, and to exempt his subsequently acquired property "from attachment by trustee process or otherwise" upon any proceeding to enforce the payment of the debt due by him to the plaintiffs.

Mass. Pub. Stat. chap. 157, § 83; *Maxwell* v. *Cochran*, 136 Mass. 73.

A judgment creditor's bill will lie, to reach and apply in satisfaction of the judgment a debt due the judgment debtor, at least when the remedy by trustee process is not available.

Edgell v. *Haywood*, 3 Atk. 352; *Edmeston* v. *Lyde*, 1 Paige, 637, 641, 2 N. Y. Ch. L. ed. 781, 783. See *Hadden* v. *Spader*, 20 Johns. 554; *Powell* v. *Howell*, 63 N. C. 283.

Where by statute garnishment proceedings have been introduced, judgment creditor's bills are frequently resorted to to reach debts due the debtor, whenever an obstacle exists to the maintenance of proceedings at law.

Hinsdale D. G. Co. v. *Tilley*, 10 Biss. 572; *Pendleton* v. *Perkins*, 49 Mo. 565; *Furlong* v. *Thomssen*, 1 West. Rep. 729, 19 Mo. App. 364.

As our courts now possess full equity powers, the existence of the statutory remedy by trustee process, even if available, would not abridge the powers of this court as a court of general equity jurisdiction.

Carver v. *Peck*, 131 Mass. 291–293; *Maxwell* v. *Cochran*, 136 Mass. 73, 74; *Powers* v. *Raymond*, 137 Mass. 483, 484; *Weil* v. *Raymond*, 2 New Eng. Rep. 506, 142 Mass. 206, 213.

If Mass. Pub. Stat., chap. 157, § 83, be construed as denying to a nonresident judgment creditor the right to reach, in equity, after return of nulla bona, property of the debtor not otherwise exempt from being taken on execution, and of such a nature that it cannot be taken at law, the Statute is, in that respect, in derogation of the Federal Constitution, and therefore void.

Ogden v. *Saunders*, 25 U. S. 12 Wheat. 213 (6 L. ed. 606); *Cook* v. *Moffat*, 46 U. S. 5 How. 295 (12 L. ed. 159); *Baldwin* v. *Hale*, 68 U. S. 1 Wall. 223 (17 L. ed. 531); *Springer* v. *Foster*, 2 Story, 383.

A State cannot by statute discharge a debtor from pre-existing debts due to citizens of the State itself, such a law being deemed to impair the obligation of the contract.

Sturges v. *Crowninshield*, 17 U. S. 4 Wheat 122 (4 L. ed. 529); *Farmers & M. Bank* v. *Smith*, 19 U. S. 6 Wheat. 131 (5 L. ed. 224).

Whatever will be an impairment of the obligation of a pre-existing contract between citizens of the State passing a particular law, as operating to discharge the debt, will equally be an impairment of the obligation of a contract subsequently made between a citizen of that State and a citizen of a different State.

See *M'Millan* v. *M'Neill*, 17 U. S. 4 Wheat. 209 (4 L. ed. 552); *Kenyon* v. *Stewart*, 44 Pa. 179.

NOTE.—It is within the general jurisdiction of a court of chancery to assist a judgment creditor to reach and apply to the payment of his debt any property of the judgment debtor which, by reason of its nature only, and not by reason of any positive rule exempting it, cannot be taken on execution at law; as in case of trust property, on which the judgment debtor has the entire beneficial interest of shares in a corporation, or of choses in action. Ager v. Murray, 105 U. S. 126 (26 L. ed. 942); M'Dermutt v. Strong, 4 Johns. Ch. 687, 1 N. Y. Ch. L. ed. 981; Spader v. Davis, 5 Johns. Ch. 280, 1 N. Y. Ch. L. ed. 1083; Hadden v. Spader, 20 Johns. 554; Edmeston v. Lyde, 1 Paige, 637, 2 N. Y. Ch. L. ed. 781; Wiggin v. Heywood, 118 Mass. 514; Sparhawk v. Cloon, 125 Mass. 263; Daniels v. Eldredge, 125 Mass. 356; Drake v. Rice, 130 Mass. 410; Storm v. Waddell, 2 Sandf. Ch. 494, 7 N. Y. Ch. L. ed. 675.

See also 35 L. R. A. 211.

The obligation of the contract may not be impaired, under the guise of merely altering the remedy.

Bronson v. *Kinzie*, 42 U. S. 1 How. 311 (11 L. ed. 143); *Curran* v. *Arkansas*, 56 U. S. 15 How. 304 (14 L. ed. 705); *West* v. *Sansom*, 44 Ga. 295; *Planters Bank* v. *Sharp*, 47 U. S. 6 How. 301 (12 L. ed. 447); *Taylor* v. *Stearns*, 18 Gratt. 244; *Oatman* v. *Bond*, 15 Wis. 20.

No statute is valid which so changes the remedy as to impair the substantive rights of the creditor.

Antoni v. *Greenhow*, 107 U. S. 769 (27 L. ed. 468); *Tennessee* v. *Sneed*, 96 U. S. 69 (24 L. ed. 610); *Penniman's Case*, 103 U. S. 714 (26 L. ed. 602); *Von Hoffman* v. *Quincy*, 71 U. S. 4 Wall. 535 (18 L. ed. 403); *Walker* v. *Whitehead*, 83 U. S. 16 Wall. 314 (21 L. ed. 357); *Roberts* v. *Cocke*, 28 Gratt. 207.

Therefore an unreasonable exemption of property, or the imposition of conditions and limitations that unreasonably clog the plaintiff's efforts to enforce his rights, or any change rendering his remedy nugatory, will be held invalid as impairing the obligation of the contract.

Green v. *Biddle*, 21 U. S. 8 Wheat. 1 (5 L. ed. 547); *Grimes* v. *Bryne*, 2 Minn. 89; *Lockett* v. *Usry*, 28 Ga. 345; *Hardeman* v. *Downer*, 39 Ga. 425; *Lessley* v. *Phipps*, 49 Miss. 790; *Johnson* v. *Fletcher*, 54 Miss. 628; *Huntzinger* v. *Brock*, 3 Grant, Cas. 243; *Riggs* v. *Martin*, 5 Ark. 506; *Oliver* v. *McClure*, 28 Ark. 555; *Lapsley* v. *Brashears*, 4 Litt. 47.

If the Legislature changes the remedy, it must provide another effective remedy.

Farnsworth v. *Vance*, 2 Coldw. 108, 111; *Bruce* v. *Schuyler*, 9 Ill. 221; *Stephenson* v. *Osborne*, 41 Miss. 119; *Smith* v. *Morse*, 2 Cal. 524; *Robinson* v. *Magee*, 9 Cal. 81.

Mr. **George Fred Williams**, for appellee:

Pub. Stat., chap. 151, § 2, cl. 11, has never been treated as a provision in aid of an execution, but is simply an extension of the trustee process to reach property so situated as to be unavailable to the creditor by reason of the nature, kind, condition, situation or title of the property.

Ager v. *Murray*, 105 U. S. 126 (26 L. ed. 942); *Schlesinger* v. *Sherman*, 127 Mass. 206; *Crompton* v. *Anthony*, 13 Allen, 33, 37.

There is no general equity jurisdiction available to a creditor except in the aid of the law. That which is claimed in this case is in contravention of the law in that it is sought to provide a remedy from which the creditor is by law definitely excluded.

Petts v. *Bagley*, 12 Pick. 572; *Choteau* v. *Richardson*, 12 Allen, 365; *Carpenter* v. *King*, 9 Met. 511; *Murphy* v. *Manning*, 134 Mass. 488.

Where the statutes of the Commonwealth provide a remedy by trustee process and in equity against every description of property, applicable to the payment of debts, the general equity powers of the courts should not be called to the aid of a nonresident creditor, who, by refusing to put himself within the scope of the Insolvency Laws, is cut off from a plain statutory remedy.

Emery v. *Bidwell*, 140 Mass. 271, 275, 1 New Eng. Rep. 281.

Field, *J.*, delivered the opinion of the court:

The plaintiffs recovered judgment against Rickenberg on December 23, 1887. The claim on which the judgment was recovered became due and payable before the first publication of the notice of the issuing of the warrant in the proceedings in insolvency which were instituted by Rickenberg on April 7, 1886, and although this claim was provable against the estate of Rickenberg in insolvency it was not proved. The debt due from the Traders' National Bank to Rickenberg, which the plaintiffs seek to reach and apply to the payment of their judgment, is "property and estate" acquired by Rickenberg subsequently to the time of the first publication of the notice of the issuing of the warrant. The plaintiffs, at the time of the first publication of the notice, were, and ever since have been, residents of the State of New York, and Rickenberg was and is a resident and citizen of the Commonwealth of Massachusetts. It is conceded, as we understand, by the counsel for the plaintiffs, that but for the provisions of Pub. Stat., chap. 157, § 83, the debt due from the Bank to Rickenberg could be attached by the plaintiffs by trustee process, and it must be inferred from the allegations of the bill that this debt is of such a nature that it could be attached by trustee process, by any person who has a similar cause of action on which he has a right to attach the property of Rickenberg. If Pub. Stat., chap. 157, § 83, is a constitutional and valid Statute, the plaintiffs cannot attach this debt in a suit on their judgment "by trustee process or otherwise;" if this section is void in its application to nonresident creditors, the plaintiffs can attach this debt by trustee process. Under either view there is no jurisdiction in equity. The Statute prohibits certain remedies to these plaintiffs for the collection of a debt due from an insolvent debtor in Massachusetts who has obtained his discharge. An attachment in equity is within the prohibition, and the Statute cannot be avoided by a change in the form of proceedings. *Maxwell* v. *Cochran*, 136 Mass. 73.

This suit cannot be regarded as a method of levying an execution on a judgment obtained at law. Jurisdiction in equity to entertain bills like this is expressly limited to bills to reach and apply property "which cannot be come at to be attached or taken on execution in a suit at law." Pub. Stat. chap. 151, § 2, cl. 11.

This means property which is of such a nature that it cannot be attached or taken on execution in a suit at law. We must hold that the same limitation attaches in this Commonwealth to suits brought under the general equity jurisdiction of the court to collect a judgment obtained at law. If the property in its nature is attachable by trustee process, a suit in equity cannot be maintained to reach and apply it in payment of a debt of a special kind which by the statutes cannot be collected by an attachment of this property either "by trustee process or otherwise." Debts can be attached in action at law only by trustee process, and only certain actions at law can be begun by trustee process. Pub. Stat. chap. 183, § 1.

Legal causes of action, which cannot be prosecuted by trustee process, cannot be prosecuted in equity to reach property in its nature attachable by trustee process, because trustee process will not lie. To hold otherwise would be to contravene the will of the Legislature. For the same reason, if it be true that Pub. Stat., chap. 157, § 85, does not leave the plaintiffs in this case any adequate remedy at law, equity cannot supply the deficiency. *Emery* v. *Bidwell*, 140 Mass. 271, 1 New Eng. Rep. 231; *Schlesinger* v. *Sherman*, 127 Mass. 206; *Wilson* v. *Martin-Wilson Automatic Fire Alarm Co.* 149 Mass. 24.

We must decline to consider whether Pub. Stat., chap. 157, § 83, is inconsistent either with the Constitution of the United States or with the Constitution of the Commonwealth, because a determination of these questions is not necessary to the decision of the case.

Bill dismissed.

SOUTH CAROLINA SUPREME COURT.

Elias A. B. McCARTER *et al.*, *Respts.*,
v.
Lawson K. ARMSTRONG, *Appt.*

(......S. C.......)

Specific performance will not be granted of a contract to clear out the channel of a creek so as to allow running water to flow freely, and make a ditch of sufficient size to drain the lands of another party, and to keep such ditch open and unobstructed forever. The case is one in which the injury can be redressed by damages in an action at law.

(March 3, 1890.)

APPEAL by defendant from a judgment of the Circuit Court for York County decreeing specific performance of a contract. *Reversed.*

The contract, the specific performance of which was sought, is as follows:

"This indenture between Lawson K. Armstrong, of the first part, and Elias A. B. McCarter, D. W. McCarter, J. R. McCarter, Joseph Herndon, Curtis M. Parrott and James B. Woods, of the second part, witnesseth: Whereas the party of the first part is the owner of a certain mill and mill-site on Allison Creek, in said county and State, extending up to high-water mark, as indicated by the pond, and formerly known as the 'Patton Mill;' and whereas the parties of the second part are the owners of lands lying above the said creek from said mill, the McCarters together, and the others severally, owning separate tracts, and each tract being injured by said pond in this: that it is wholly impracticable to drain the bottoms thereon without letting and keeping down the dam, and ditching the stream that lies within the boundaries of the said pond; and whereas the boundary of the said high-water mark has just been ascertained by a survey, as evidenced by a plat made by Sur-

---

NOTE.—*Specific performance, not a matter of right.*

Specific execution of a contract is not a matter of right, but rests in the discretion of the court. Willard v. Tayloe, 75 U. S. 8 Wall. 557 (19 L. ed. 501); Rutland Marble Co. v. Ripley, 77 U. S. 10 Wall. 339 (19 L. ed. 955).

It rests in judicial discretion exercised according to the principles of equity and with reference to the facts of the case. Hennessey v. Woolworth, 128 U. S. 438 (32 L. ed. 500); Nickerson v. Nickerson, 127 U. S. 668 (32 L. ed. 314); Hamilton v. Harvey, 10 West. Rep. 924, 121 Ill. 469; Eckstein v. Downing, 4 New Eng. Rep. 387, 64 N. H. 248; Stevens v. Comstock, 12 Cent. Rep. 327, 109 N. Y. 655.

Such discretion is not an arbitrary or capricious one, but controlled by the settled principles of equity. Willard v. Tayloe, *supra.*

A court of chancery will often refuse to enforce a contract when it would also refuse to annul it. In such a case the parties are left to their remedy at law. Jackson v. Ashton, 36 U. S. 11 Pet. 229 (9 L. ed. 698); Hepburn v. Dunlop, 14 U. S. 1 Wheat. 179 (4 L. ed. 65).

If the contract is vague and uncertain, the court will not decree a specific performance, but will leave the party to his remedy at law. Smith v. Taylor, 82 Cal. 533.

The delay of a party in taking proceedings to enforce a contract, for a period which would bar an action at law for the property, is such laches as disentitles him to the aid of a court of equity. Preston v. Preston, 95 U. S. 200 (24 L. ed. 494).

Not decreed when there is adequate remedy at law.

Where land or any estate therein is the subject of contract, the remedy for its specific performance is purely equitable and is a substitute for the legal remedy where such legal remedy is inadequate or impracticable. Johnson v. Johnson, 40 Md. 189; McNamee v. Withers, 37 Md. 171; Au Gres Boom Co. v. Whitney, 26 Mich. 42; Reese v. Lee County Police Board, 49 Miss. 639; Williams v. McGuire, 60 Mo. 254; Hayes v. Harmony Grove Cemetery, 108 Mass. 400; Riddle v. Cameron, 50 Ala. 263; Warren v. Daniels, 72 Ill. 272; Yoakum v. Yoakum, 77 Ill. 85; Page County v. American Emigrant Co. 41 Iowa, 115; Warren v. Ewing, 34 Iowa, 168; Law v. Henry, 39 Ind. 414; Kuhn v. Freeman, 15 Kan. 423; Green v. Richards, 23 N. J. Eq. 32; Colgate v. Colgate, Id. 372; Reynolds v. O'Neil, 26 N. J. Eq. 223; Wynn v. Smith, 40 Ga. 457; Porter v. Allen, 54 Ga. 623; Chartier v. Marshall, 51 N. H. 400; McClaskey v. Albany, 64 Barb. 310; Olney v. Eaton, 66 Mo. 563; Gartrell v. Stafford, 12 Neb. 545; Bonner v. Little, 38 Ark. 397; Wormley v. Wormley, 98 Ill. 544; Coffman v. Robbins, 8 Or. 278; Grier v. Rhyne, 69 N. C. 346; Wright v. Pucket, 22 Gratt. 370; Ambrouse v. Keller, 22 Gratt. 769; Bleakley's App. 66 Pa. 187; Seichrist's App. Id. 237; 3 Pom. Eq. Jur. 442; Love v. Welch, 97 N. C. 200.

Equity will not retain jurisdiction where an adequate remedy can be had by legal proceedings, nor for the purpose merely of affording compensation in damages. Genet v. Howland, 30 How. Pr. 360, 45 Barb. 560; Bradley v. Bosley, 1 Barb. Ch. 125, 5 N. Y. Ch. L. ed. 324.

Where any rights which the vendee may have arising out of the transaction can be protected by an action at law, specific performance ought not to be decreed. Emrich v. White, 66 How. Pr. 158; Winne v. Reynolds, 6 Paige, 407, 3 N. Y. Ch. L. ed. 1041.

See also 11 L. R. A. 143; 35 L. R. A. 167.

veyor W. B. Allison, May 4, 1886, which is attached to and made a part of this indenture, to the end that the dam may be removed without having said boundary in doubt: I. That, in consideration of the covenants, agreements, grants and quit-claims of the parties of the second part, hereinafter specifically recited, the first party, for himself, his heirs and assigns, does by these presents covenant and grant with and to the parties of the second part, their several heirs and assigns, as follows, to wit: 1. That the said first party is to take down so much of the mill-dam as may be necessary for the purpose hereinafter stated, and never again to erect the same, or to do or to suffer any other act that will interfere with the full flow of water along the channel of said creek, over the land that the said mill is situated upon, and, further, to dig out, ditch and open the channel of said creek up to the 'Scruggs' line, so as to allow all running water to flow freely. The ditch to be sufficient in size to drain the lands of the parties of the second part above, by carrying off all the ordinary water from the lands of the second parties, and to be completed by the first day of July, 1886, unless prevented by rocks that require blasting, and then in a reasonable time thereafter, and to be kept open and unobstructed forever, unless obstructions below the line of the first party cause a common fill of the ditch above said line. 2. That for the faithful performance of these covenants, and every of them, the first party hereby binds himself to the second parties in the penal sum of six hundred dollars. 3. That, the better to secure the rights hereby intended to be given to the parties of the second part, the first party does hereby grant to the parties of the second part the right to the full, free and uninterrupted enjoyment of the natural flow of water along the said watercourse, as the same will naturally run over the lands of the first party after the removal of the dam, and the ditching as aforesaid, and to the extent of the boundary of said land below the said dam, together with such free ingress and egress as may be necessary to insure the proper enjoyment of the easement hereby granted: To have and to hold, all and singular, the privileges aforesaid to the parties of the second part, their respective heirs and assigns, forever. II. That, in consideration of the above covenants and grants, the parties of the second part hereby agree to pay, at the execution of this indenture do pay (the first party acknowledging its receipt), the sum of six hundred dollars to the first party; and, in addition thereto, they, for themselves and their respective heirs and assigns, do by these presents covenant and grant with and to the party of the first part, his heirs and assigns, as follows, to wit: 1. That it shall be lawful for the said party of the first part, and the right is hereby granted to him, (1) to use and enjoy, as a way to and from the bottoms of the first party, the 'old track' leading from the main road to the said bottoms; and (2) to remove all growing timber around the edges of the 'pond bottoms' shading and injuring the growing crops: To have and to hold said privileges, to the said party of the first part, his heirs and assigns, forever. 2. That the parties of the second part do by these

---

If the objection to the title of the defendant is sound, this is not a case in which a court of equity can decree a specific performance, providing that compensation be made to the purchaser. Emrich v. White, 66 How. Pr. 158.

If it turns out that defendant cannot make a title to that which he has agreed to convey, the purchaser is left to seek his remedy at law in damages for the breach. Refeld v. Woodfolk, 63 U. S. 22 How. 318 (16 L. ed. 370).

Jurisdiction will not be exercised where adequate compensation can be recovered by an action at law. Roundtree v. McLain, Hemp. 246.

If there is an adequate legal remedy the court will refuse specific performance, unless, under all the circumstances, it would be inequitable and unjust to do so. Simon v. Wildt, 84 Ky. 157.

Specific performance will not be decreed on a contract relating to personal property, unless relief at law is inadequate, and unless the thing contracted for has some intrinsic or special value. Cohn v. Mitchell, 2 West. Rep. 62, 115 Ill. 124.

Specific performance of a contract for personal services will not be enforced, especially where there is any remedy at law. Ikerd v. Beaver, 4 West. Rep. 547, 106 Ind. 483; Wollensak v. Briggs, 7 West. Rep. 673, 119 Ill. 453; Willingham v. Hooven, 74 Ga. 233; Hamblin v. Dinneford, 2 Edw. Ch. 529, 6 N. Y. Ch. L. ed. 493; Rhodes v. Rhodes, 3 Sandf. Ch. 284, 7 N. Y. Ch. L. ed. 854. See *notes* to Cort v. Lassard (Or.) 6 L. R. A. 653; William Rogers Mfg. Co. v. Rogers (Conn.) 7 L. R. A. 779.

Especially is this true where the services stipulated for require the exercise of mechanical skill, intellectual ability and judgment. Wollensak v. Briggs, 7 West. Rep. 673, 119 Ill. 453.

But where there has been a part performance, so that defendant is enjoying the benefit *in specie*, contracts for personal acts will be enforced. Stuyvesant v. New York, 11 Paige, 414, 5 N.Y. Ch. L. ed. 182; Birchett v. Bolling, 5 Munf. 442; Whitney v. New Haven, 23 Conn. 624; Gregory v. Ingwelsen, 32 N. J. Eq. 199.

A bill in the federal court failing to make out a case for specific performance of a contract, but making out a case for damages for breach thereof, will be dismissed without prejudice to an action at law on the same cause of action. Zeringue v. Texas & P. R. Co. 34 Fed. Rep. 239.

So specific performance will not be granted of covenants by the licensee of a patent to render monthly reports, to pay royalties and perform personal duties. Washburn & M. Mfg. Co. v. Freeman Wire Co. 41 Fed. Rep. 410.

In cases of specific performance, parties are sometimes remitted to a court of law; but this is never done where the remedy is not as effectual and complete there as a chancellor can make it. May v. Le Claire, 78 U. S. 11 Wall. 217 (20 L. ed. 50).

Specific performance will not be decreed where the party who asks for it has an adequate remedy provided by the reservation in his deed and by the contract itself. Rutland Marble Co. v. Ripley, 77 U. S. 10 Wall. 339 (19 L. ed. 555).

Specific performance is never decreed where the party can be otherwise fully compensated. Memphis v. Brown, 87 U. S. 20 Wall. 289 (22 L. ed. 264).

The court ought not to adjudge a specific performance, by the defendant, of the duty imposed upon it by the statute: the plaintiff should be left to his remedy for damages. Clarke v. Rochester, L. & N. F. R. Co. 18 Barb. 350; Morss v. Elmendorf, 11 Paige, 277, 5 N. Y. Ch. L. ed. 135.

As to specific performance generally, see Hodges v. Kowing (Conn.) 7 L. R. A. 87, and cases referred to in *note*.

presents remise, release and forever quit-claim unto the first party all their joint and several rights, title or estate in and to the land heretofore covered by the said pond up to high-water mark, as indicated by the survey aforesaid, to have and to hold the same, to the said first party, his heirs and assigns, forever. Witness our hands and seals of the parties hereto this 11th May, A. D. one thousand eight hundred and eighty-six. Done in duplicate. Signed, sealed and delivered in the presence of C. E. Spencer, G. W. S. Hart.

"L. K. Armstrong, [Seal.]
"E. A. B. McCarter, [Seal.]
"David M. McCarter. [Seal.]
"J. R. McCarter. [Seal.]
"J. Herndon. [Seal.]
his
"C. M. × Parrott. [Seal.]
mark
"James B. Woods. [Seal.]"

The case sufficiently appears in the opinion.

Messrs. **Hart & Hart**, for appellant:

Equity should not entertain this bill as one for specific performance.

Equity will never assume the enforcement of a contract where there is doubt or uncertainty as to time, mode or manner of performance. It will not assume to command the doing of an act by another where it cannot through its own ministerial officers perform it. It will not decree a performance that cannot be commanded *in specie*, instantly, directly and in definite terms.

Reed v. *Vidal*, 5 Rich. Eq. 289; *Church of the Advent* v. *Farrow*, 7 Rich. Eq. 378; Story, Eq. Jur. §§ 725–727; *Rayner* v. *Stone*, 2 Eden, 128; *Gervais* v. *Edwards*, 2 Dru. & W. 80; *Blackett* v. *Bates*, L. R. 1 Ch. 117; *Paris Chocolate Co.* v. *Crystal Palace Co.* 3 Sm. & G. 119; *Blanchard* v. *Detroit, L. & L. M. R. Co.* 31 Mich. 43; *Rankin* v. *Maxwell*, 2 A. K. Marsh. (Ky.) 488; *Colson* v. *Thompson*, 15 U. S. 2 Wheat. 336 (4 L. ed. 253); Fry, Spec. Perf. § 229; *Phillips* v. *Thompson*, 1 Johns. Ch. 149, 150, 1 N. Y. Ch. L. ed. 95; *Parkhurst* v. *Van Cortlandt*, 1 Johns. Ch. 283, 1 N. Y. Ch. L. ed. 142; *Beard* v. *Linthicum*, 1 Md. Ch. 348, and other cases; *Preston* v. *Preston*, 95 U. S. 202 (24 L. ed. 495); *Rutland Marble Co.* v. *Ripley*, 77 U. S. 10 Wall. 358 (19 L. ed. 961); *Flint* v. *Brandon*, 8 Ves. Jr. 162.

Mr. **C. E. Spencer**, for respondents:

The remedy of specific performance is applicable when the thing contracted to be done, and not pecuniary compensation, is the thing practically required.

Adams, Eq. *78, 84; *Sarter* v. *Gordon*, 2 Hill, Ch. 121; *Farley* v. *Farley*, 1 McCord, Ch. 506; *Mosely* v. *Virgin*, 3 Ves. Jr. 185.

Simpson, *Ch. J.*, delivered the opinion of the court:

Some time in 1886 the plaintiffs, respondents, and the defendant, appellant, entered into a certain written agreement, a copy of which is hereto appended, in which it was stipulated that a certain mill-dam across Allison's Creek, in the County of York, at a point where the defendant had a mill, should be taken down by the defendant and the channel of the creek above said dam dug out, ditched and opened up to the Scruggs line, so as to allow all running water to flow freely, the ditch to be of sufficient size to drain the lands of the respondents, which, it was stated, were greatly injured by the pond, this said work to be completed by the 1st day of July then ensuing, in 1886, unless prevented by rocks requiring blasting, and then in a reasonable time, and when completed to be kept open and unobstructed forever, etc., which the defendant bound himself faithfully to perform in the penal sum of $600, the plaintiffs agreeing to pay the defendant $600 at the execution of the agreement, which payment was acknowledged by the defendant; and also stipulating for some other privileges to the defendant, all of which appears in the agreement appended. The work not having been done, as it is alleged, although frequently requested by the plaintiffs, the action below was commenced in September, 1887, in which the plaintiffs prayed judgment: "(1) That the defendant be forthwith required to cut the said ditch in manner and form as he had undertaken to do, that is to say, so that it would allow all ordinary water to flow freely through it from off the plaintiffs' lands above, and to be of sufficient size for that purpose, and, further, that he be required to keep the same open and unobstructed forever; and, failing in this, that the plaintiffs be allowed to do the said work at the defendant's expense. (2) For the sum of $900, special damages suffered by the plaintiffs from the defendant's failure of performance up to the present time, as well as for damages to follow hereafter up to the time of performance, and for the costs of this action."

The defendant answered, denying certain allegations of the complaint, but averring that he had performed the work which the agreement required of him, according to the stipulation therein, and further averring that the failure of the ditch to drain plaintiffs' lands was due to other causes than the imperfect construction of the ditch. Before the case came up for trial the defendant gave notice, under Rule 29 of the circuit court, that an order would be applied for submitting certain issues to a jury, and at the November Term, 1888, his honor, *Judge* Kershaw, upon hearing the motion, made an order appointing a referee to frame jury issues, and continued the case. These issues were framed and afterwards reported to the court. They will be found in the case. When the case afterwards came up for trial, his honor, *Judge* T. B. Fraser, presiding, "announced (against the objection of the plaintiffs, who contended that the case was one in equity, for specific performance) that he would remit the whole case to a jury and let them find a general verdict; that he was inclined to the opinion that it was not a case of equity jurisdiction for specific performance, but, if he should conclude later that it was such, he would hear the case on calendar 2, when reached on that calendar. The jury found for the defendant, and when the case was reached on calendar 2 the plaintiffs moved for a new trial in the event that his honor still thought the case was a case at law. His honor then announced that he would hear counsel on the prayer for specific performance, after which he filed a decree giving judgment for specific performance and granting such orders as were necessary to enforce said judgment.

The defendant has appealed upon several exceptions, all of which will be found in the case; but, from the view which we have taken of the appeal, we think that exception 5 is the only one that raises any question proper for our consideration. That exception alleges error to his honor "in reversing his first conclusion at the opening of the trial, that the case presented by the pleadings was not one for specific performance, but an action sounding in damages for breach of contract, especially as the trial had been conducted under that ruling." The remedy of specific performance is an equitable remedy; and when the court of equity had a separate existence in this State it attached to that court, or whenever it has a separate existence now this remedy belongs to that court exclusively. "Their distinctive object is to specifically enforce the complainant's equitable right, and to compel the defendant to specifically perform the actual equitable obligation which rests upon him." 3 Pom. Eq. Jur. § 1400.

This equity may exist in reference to certain contracts, and also to enforce the performance of trusts; but, whatever may be the character of the case, some equitable feature is necessary in order to entitle the complainant to invoke the aid of the court of equity. Since the adoption of the Code in our State, blending the two courts of law and equity, the same necessity exists. In fact, there has been no change as to equity jurisdiction. The change has been merely as to the mode of procedure. The court of common pleas has an equity side as well as a law side, but neither one of these branches has been extended, or authorized to encroach upon the other. What was a law cause of action before is still a law case, and what was an equity cause is still an equity case. So that to determine the question here, whether or not the plaintiff is entitled to his demand for specific performance, we have only to consider whether he would have been thus entitled under the old court of equity. The matter in contest here is a contract or an agreement for the performance of certain work by the defendant, in order to drain or carry off water from the lands of the plaintiffs. Now, as stated above, the old court of equity had jurisdiction to enforce the performance of certain classes of contracts. Does this belong to one of the classes? is the question here. The marked cases in which there was no doubt as to the jurisdiction of the old court were in reference to contracts for the sale of lands, and also for the sale of certain specific chattels, where the said chattels had some special value to the claimant over and above any pecuniary estimate. Id. § 1402.

But still the jurisdiction did not depend entirely upon the nature of the contract, nor upon its subject matter, but upon some equitable feature or element belonging thereto, and this feature was generally the inadequacy of a legal remedy, and, where this existed clearly, there was an equitable jurisdiction for the interpretation of the court of equity, for specific performance. If the breach of the contract, however, could be reasonably satisfied with damages, then the court of equity could not interfere. So that in all these cases in reference to contracts, the underlying principle is the practicability or impracticability of a sufficient and adequate legal remedy. Now, the ordinary legal remedy for the breach of contracts is an action for damages; and, where proper damages can be assessed by a jury, it is a law case, and the court of equity has not and cannot take jurisdiction. Here the injury complained of is alleged to be the result of a failure on the part of the defendant to perform his part of the agreement mentioned in the complaint. Admit the failure. Where is the difficulty in proving and recovering the subsequent damages? And why is it that the remedy at law is insufficient or inadequate? We do not see this. The value of the work stipulated in the agreement to the plaintiffs was some $600, the amount paid by them to the defendant, and the allowance of some specific privileges to him; and for the performance of the work the defendant bound himself in the penal sum of $600. Thus it seems the parties themselves, in the agreement, determined to some extent the value of said work, if properly performed, and also what amount would cover damages in the event that defendant failed on his part; and we see no reason growing out of the facts, either alleged in the complaint or proved on the trial, which could prevent a jury from giving an adequate redress for such damages, if any, as may have been sustained by the plaintiffs. The injury complained of was upon lands. The value of land can certainly be estimated, and we suppose it could be determined whether it had been injured in whole or in part only; and there seems to be no special reason in this case why the extent of the injury could not have been ascertained, and why a sufficient pecuniary compensation for whatever injuries the plaintiffs have sustained, if any, would not be satisfactory. But, besides, contracts for building and construction, and for personal acts, etc., will not usually be enforced in a court of equity; but the parties will generally be left to an action of law for their breach, unless under some peculiar circumstances, and unless, too, the work to be done is well defined and specific, and is such as to be within the power of the court to enforce by its decree. Where, however, the work consists of personal acts, requiring protracted supervision and discretion, *e. g.*, such as building contracts for construction of railroads, mining, quarries and the like, the court will not generally interfere. See 3 Pom. Eq. Jur. § 1405, and numerous cases in the *notes*.

Here the work was to be kept up forever.

We have reached our conclusion with some hesitation and doubt, but we think this case was one sounding in damages, and could be redressed, if there has been a breach and injury sustained, by a verdict of a jury; the facts necessary thereto being peculiarly for a jury. We are therefore of the opinion that his honor, the trial judge, erred in reversing his first conclusion, and after a verdict had been rendered for the defendant, in opening the case, and trying it anew upon the equity side of the court.

It is the judgment of this court that the judgment of the Circuit Court be reversed, and that the case be remanded, with the right of the defendant to enter judgment upon his verdict, without prejudice, however, to plaintiffs to take such action in reference thereto as they may be advised.

McIver and **McGowan**, *JJ.*, concur.

A petition for rehearing was subsequently filed and on June 2, 1890, the following opinion was delivered:

Per Curiam:

After a careful examination of the allegations set forth in the petition, the supreme court decides that it does not appear therefrom that any question, either of fact or of law, involved, has been overlooked by the supreme court.

Petition dismissed.

MONTANA SUPREME COURT.

Dennis O'DONNELL, *Appt.*,
v.
John H. GLENN *et al.*, *Respts.*

(......Mont.......)

1. **The existence and effect of an alleged common error** are for the court and not for the jury.

2. **A common error having the force of law** is not shown by the fact that 88 per cent of the mining prospectors of one county in a vast Territory during about two years used a form of verification for location notices which was fatally defective under a law of Congress by reason of omitting to state of the date of the location, where it does not show that any considerable number of persons have relied upon, or sought to fix their rights upon, the alleged common error, or that large property interests depend upon upholding such notice.

(May 2, 1890.)

APPEAL by plaintiff from a judgment of the District Court for Silver Bow County in favor of defendants in an action brought to determine adverse claims to a certain mining lode. *Reversed.*

Statement by **DeWitt**, *J.*:

This action is the ordinary one, between claimants of quartz mining ground, brought to determine the right of possession, and the right to proceed in the United States land office to obtain a patent to the premises. The plaintiff founds his rights upon a location of a claim called the "Flapjack;" defendants, upon their Argonaut claim. The respective locations are in geographical conflict. The validity of the Argonaut location notice was contested upon the trial. The notice and verification thereto are as follows:

"Notice is hereby given that the undersigned, having complied with the requirements of chapter 6, title 32, of the Revised Statutes of the United States, and the local laws, rules and regulations and customs of miners, have located 1,500 linear feet on the Argonaut lode (——acres plain mining ground) situated in Summit Valley Mining District, Deer Lodge County, Territory of Montana, and being more particularly described as follows, to wit: Begining at a stake, southeast corner, and running west 1,500 feet; thence north 600 feet; thence east 1,500 feet; thence south 600 feet, to place of beginning. Said lode is bounded on the south by the Silversmith, and southwest by the Goldsmith, and on the east by what is known as the 'Rooney Lode.' Above lode runs 900 feet easterly, and 600 feet westerly, from discovery shaft, and 300 feet on each side. Located Dec'r 22, 1880.

John H. Glenn,
"Attest: John Hall,
John B. Cameron.

"Territory of Montana, }
"County of Deer Lodge. } ss:

"J. B. Cameron, first being duly sworn according to law, deposes and says that we are citizens of the United States, and are the locators of the following described mining premises; that the description therein contained, as beginning at a stake at the southeast corner, running west 1,500 feet; thence north 600 feet; thence east 1,500 feet; thence south 600 feet, to the place of beginning,—is true, and that the locators, whose names are subscribed thereto, are bona fide residents of Montana Territory. John B. Cameron.

"Subscribed and sworn to before me this 24th day of December, 1880. A. H. Barret, Notary Public.

"Filed for record Dec'r 27th, 1880, at 11½ o'clock A. M. Jas. S. McAndrews, County Recorder."

This case was before this court at the July

NOTE.—*Common error may pass for right.*

A common error in some cases passes for right. Broom, Leg. Max. 128; Noy, Max. 37; 4 Inst. 240; Waltham v. Sparkes, 1 Ld. Raym. 42; Phipps v. Ackers, 9 Clark & F. 598; Earl of Waterford's Claim, 6 Clark & F. 172; Devaynes v. Nobles, 2 Russ. & M. 506.

Where a common opinion has been made the groundwork and substratum of practice it is evidence of what the law is. Isherwood v. Oldknow, 3 Maule & S. 396; Garland v. Carlisle, 2 Cromp. & M. 95; Co. Litt. 186a.

This maxim, however, was met by a protest from *Lord* Kenyon, *Ch. J.*, in Rex v. Eriswell, 3 T. R. 725; and see Smith v. Edge, 6 T. R. 563; Broom, Leg. Max. 104.

The mere statement and re-statement of a doctrine—the mere repetition of the *cantilena* of lawyers—cannot make it law, unless it can be traced to some competent authority, especially if it be irreconcilable to some clear legal principles. O'Connell v. Reg. 11 Clark & F. 373.

It has been held that in the acknowledgment of a deed by a married woman the frequent omission of showing and explaining to her the deed she has executed will not make the practice right, under a statute requiring her to examine the instrument privately and apart from her husband. Paine v. Baker, 1 New Eng. Rep. 154, 15 R. I. 100.

The maxim was held to apply where deeds were for seventeen years made by an official town plat, although incomplete in not being accompanied by its field notes. Ming v. Foote (Mont.) Jan. 28, 1890.

Term, 1888, and the location notice above recited was then held to be fatally defective by reason of the verification omitting to state the date of the location. *O'Donnell* v. *Glenn*, 8 Mont. 248.

On the new trial granted by this court, from which trial this appeal is now prosecuted, the district court admitted this notice in evidence upon testimony and a theory that were not before this court at the hearing, July, 1888. Defendants introduced testimony for the purpose of showing that large numbers of mining-location notices with verifications of the sort annexed to the above were used and recorded in the county about the time this notice was filed, and urged that the fault of the verification was common among the people at that period, and that large property interests were involved in the construction of the verification, and invoked the maxim, *communis error facit jus.* The evidence introduced for this purpose from the records of Deer Lodge County, in which the location was made, was as follows: At about the time of the filing of the location notice in question, it seems that three forms of verification were in use in Deer Lodge County. For the sake of definition, counsel call them the "Old Form," the "Correct Form" and the "Glenn Form," the latter being the form used in the notice above recited. In the year 1878, 75 per cent of the notices recorded in the county were in the correct form, with 25 per cent divided between the old form and the Glenn, the latter being, therefore, some fraction of 25 per cent not stated. In February, 1879, 46 out of a total of 50 were in the old and Glenn forms. In March there were 25 Glenns against 35 of the two others. In April, one half were Glenn and old forms. In the two years 1879 and 1880 there were 914 locations, of which 283 were Glenn, 97 old and 534 correct, form. The Glenn and old together form 42 per cent of the whole. The Glenn alone is 31 per cent of the whole. Leaving out of consideration the old form, and computing the Glenn and correct form, the Glenn is 33 per cent of the total. From and after March, 1880, the use of the Glenn form steadily and rapidly decreased. In March the Glenn form was 27 out of a total of 60; in April, 22 out of 100; May, 11 out of 65; June, 7 out of 40; July, 2 out of 80; August, 1 out of 45; September, 2 out of 35; October, 2 out of 25; November, none. December 22d we meet the notice in controversy, and with that the use of the form disappears from the records.

For six months preceding the date of the record of the Argonaut location the objectionable form was used fourteen times in 190 location notices. This analysis is taken from the brief of appellant, and was admitted by respondent to be correct. The district court admitted the evidence, and upon the subject gave the following instruction: "The burden of proof is on the defendants to show that the Argonaut was a valid location, and that in making the same they complied with all that the law requires to make a valid location, as defined to you above [referring to preceding instructions], and that such location included within its boundaries the ground in controversy. If the jury believe from the evidence that the defendants, or their predecessors in interest, prior to the location made by plaintiff, located the premises in controversy as the Argonaut claim, and in the affidavit of the location failed to state the date of said location, and to verify the same, but said Argonaut claim was in all other respects located and recorded as required by law, the court instructs you that the failure or omission to give the date of the location in the verification did not render the location invalid, the error or omission having been one of frequent or common occurrence at the time; and if the jury believe that the location of the Argonaut was in all other respects regular, and such as the law requires, their verdict should be for the defendants for the possession of the premises in controversy." The verdict and judgment were for the defendants. Plaintiff appeals from the judgment. Among his exceptions saved is his objection to the admission of the above testimony as to the alleged common error, and the construction of the court, in the foregoing instruction, that the alleged error was a common one at the time, and, as such common error, made the location notice of the Argonaut good, for the purposes of the action, notwithstanding that the location notice was, intrinsically, fatally defective, as held in *O'Donnell* v. *Glenn*, 8 Mont. 248. Respondent still insists, upon this hearing, that the location notice and verification were good, notwithstanding the decision of this court that they may preserve their point in case an appeal should lie from the present decision of this court.

Mr. **William Scallon** for appellant.

Mr. **John F. Forbis** for respondents.

DeWitt, *J.*, delivered the opinion of the court:

The sufficiency of the location notice of the Argonaut claim is no longer an open question in this case. It was decided to be invalid on the former appeal. *O'Donnell* v. *Glenn*, 8 Mont. 248.

That decision is now the law of this case. The other consideration is whether the common error sought to be proved, and relied upon by defendants, was in fact a common error, and whether, as such, it was of a nature to make good, for the purposes of the action, the defective location notice.

The district court held that both the existence and effect of a common error of this sort is a question for the court, and not the jury. The matter is one of mixed law and fact. In the application of the maxim, *communis error facit jus*, the inquiry is whether the law is made. If the fact of the existence of a common error is to be submitted to the jury, and the jury finds its existence, then the court has no province but to complete the maxim, and say, "*facit jus.*" But that is the very question for a court; that is, to say what is the law. The court must say what the law has been made, whether by a common error or by a Legislature. We are therefore of opinion that the lower court was correct in holding that both the existence and effect of the alleged common error were for the court, and not for the jury. To hold otherwise would be to make the jury the judges of the law. See *M'Keen* v. *Delancy*, 9 U. S. 5 Cranch, 22 [3 L. ed. 25], and cases cited below.

We will now endeavor to determine whether the court erred in its decision that such a common error existed as should be held to make the law that the controverted location notice was good for the purposes of the case on trial. The application of the maxim under consideration, like that of all abstract generalizations, is attended with difficulty and danger. A review of the authorities leads us to the conclusion that each case of the invocation of the rule must stand largely upon its own facts.

In Coke upon Littleton we find that the learned author often prefaces the announcement of a legal principle with the words: "It is commonly said." By these words, we understand, is meant: "It is commonly the legal opinion." To the expression cited, Littleton adds: "That is, it is the common opinion, and *communis opinio* is of good authority in law. *A communi observantia non est recedendum*,"—which we may read: "There must not be a departure from a common or general observation or practice." The annotator to Coke upon Littleton adds at this point: "Other rules immediately connected with this are, that *communis error facit jus*, and *res judicata pro veritate habetur*, and also that *minime mutanda sunt quæ certam interpretationem habuerunt*." 186*a*. The two latter may, perhaps, be well rendered, "An adjudicated matter shall be deemed to be correct," and "Those matters shall be least changed which have attained a certain interpretation." The language of these maxims carries the idea of an observance, an interpretation, a construction, and to some extent a judicial one at that, as evidenced by the words "*observantia*," "*res judicata*" and "*interpretationem*." Thus we find our maxim under purview, at an early day, in company with language tending to the view that the common error that makes the law is an error in the observing, the construing, the interpreting law, and not an error in totally disregarding, and in practice repealing, a positive statute; and, furthermore, that the error is general, and not confined to a portion of one class of the inhabitants of one geographical or political division of the jurisdiction, as was the case with the error being considered, which was confined to 33 per cent of the prospectors of the County of Deer Lodge, in the Territory of Montana.

In the year 1764 the Supreme Court of Pennsylvania says: "These deeds, and this mode of examination of *femes covert* on conveying their estates, have generally prevailed in this Province from its settlement, and undergone from time to time the notice of the courts of justice. It would be very mischievous now to overturn them. The maxim, *communis error facit jus*, cannot operate more properly than in this case." *Davey* v. *Turner*, 1 U. S. 1 Dall. 14 [1 L. ed. 16].

Here a general practice had received tacit judicial approval for years. The same court in 1768 applies the maxim to a "constant usage," the individual instance of which having occurred forty-one years prior to the controversy before the court. *Lloyd* v. *Taylor*, 1 U. S. 1 Dall. 17 [1 L. ed. 18].

The Supreme Court of the United States in 1809 applies and discusses the doctrine. Says *Mr. Chief Justice* Marshall: "The first question which presents itself in this case is, Was this deed properly proved? Were this Act of 1715 now for the first time to be construed, the opinion of this court would certainly be that the deed was not regularly proved. A justice of the supreme court would not be deemed a justice of the county, and the decision would be that the deed was not properly proved, and therefore not legally recorded. But, in construing the statutes of a State on which land titles depend, infinite mischief would ensue should this court observe a different rule from that which has been long established in the State; and, in this case, the court cannot doubt that the courts of Pennsylvania consider a justice of the supreme court as within the description of the Act. It is of some weight that this deed was acknowledged by the chief justice, who certainly must have been acquainted with the construction given to the Act, and that the acknowledgment was taken before another judge of the supreme court. It is also recollected that the gentlemen of the bar . . . spoke positively as to the universal understanding of the State on this point, and that those who controverted the usage on other points did not controvert it on this. But what is decisive with the court is that the judge who presides in the Circuit Court for the District of Pennsylvania reports to us that this construction was universally received." *M'Keen* v. *Delancy*, 9 U. S. 5 Cranch, 22 [3 L. ed. 25].

In this case there was a "universal understanding in the State," and the learned chief justice refers to "the judicial and professional construction in the State."

In *M'Ferran* v. *Powers*, 1 Serg. & R. 101, the same question was before the Supreme Court of the State of Pennsylvania, and was decided upon the authority of the case last above cited; and here, again, we find the idea of a universal and judicial or professional construction.

In the Supreme Court of the United States, in 1803, in the case of *Stuart* v. *Laird*, 5 U. S. 1 Cranch, 299 [2 L. ed. 115], the court, Patterson, *J.*, says: "To this objection, which is of recent date, it is sufficient to observe that practice and acquiescence under it for a period of several years, commencing with the organization of the judicial system, affords an irresistible answer, and has indeed fixed the construction. It is a contemporary interpretation of the most forcible nature. This practical exposition is too strong and obstinate to be shaken or controlled. Of course the question is at rest, and ought not now to be disturbed." This case is another instance of the universal and judicial character of the error. See also *Green* v. *Neal*, 31 U. S. 6 Pet. 291 [8 L. ed. 402], which reviews many of the cases.

The Supreme Court of Massachusetts says in *Rogers* v. *Goodwin*, 2 Mass. 475: "Of these Statutes a practical construction early and generally obtained,—that in the power to dispose of lands was included a power to sell and convey the common lands. Large and valuable estates are held in various parts of the Commonwealth, the titles to which depend on this construction. Were the court now to decide that this construction is not to be supported, very great mischief would follow. . . . We cannot shake a principle which in practice has so long and so extensively prevailed. If the practice originated in error, yet the error is now so common that it must have the force of law. The legal ground on which this provision is now supported is that long and continued usage furnishes a contemporaneous construction which must prevail over the mere technical import of the words."

We cite *Mr. Justice* Blackburn as follows in *Reg.* v. *Justices of Sussex*, 2 Best & S. 664: "I think, also, that there are cases in which a mistaken notion of the law has, no matter why, become so generally accepted, and been so acted upon, as to render it probable that business has been regulated, and the position of parties altered, in consequence; and in such cases we may hold that the general acceptation of the mistake has made that law which was originally error. *Communis error facit jus.* But, then, I think that, before we act upon this principle, we ought to see it clearly made out that the error has been commonly accepted, and that the nature of the case is such that parties are likely to have acted upon the mistake, and so altered their rights and position."

Lord Brougham, *Ch.*, says, in *Devaynes* v. *Noble*, 2 Russ. & M. 495: "If it be true that even a prevailing error—what has been called a common or universal error—may be said to make the law, this at least may be allowed to be a sound foundation of the doctrine I am referring to, namely, that, unless a great and manifest deviation from principle shall have been committed, it may create much further mischief to reverse an individual case by way of correcting a slight error, if that error has been acted upon for a long series of years, than to leave it as it stands; more especially if the opinions of lawyers and the decisions of judges have been ruled by it, and if, upon the analogies of that case, the same principle has been recognized and adopted in other cases connected with and relating to it." The learned chancellor above calls a common error a universal error, and speaks of the opinions of lawyers and the decisions of judges being ruled by it.

In *Re Will of Warfield*, 22 Cal. 71, the court says: "Courts feel themselves constrained to uphold, where it is possible, contemporaneous interpretation of statutes, under which interpretation rights of property have for many years been acquired."

In the case of *Panaud* v. *Jones*, 1 Cal. 488, the court cites with approval a Spanish authority, Esriche's Derecho Espanol, as follows: "Legitimate custom acquires the force of law, not only when there is no law to the contrary, but also when its effect is to abrogate any former law which may be opposed to it, as well as to explain that which is doubtful. Hence it is said that there may be a custom without law, in opposition to law and according to law."

Counsel for respondent has urged this opinion in his argument. We hesitate to adopt the views therein contained, however, to the extent that a common error can have the effect to abrogate a positive statute, except under most extraordinary circumstances, of which we now have no knowledge. The California decision was made in the earliest history of the jurisprudence of that State, when it had just fallen heir to much that was Spanish, and, along with the rest, perhaps some customs that were not so valuable as other portions of the inheritance. We have reviewed some of the leading cases in which the maxim under consideration has been discussed and applied, with the view of discovering what the current opinion would be as to the facts in the case at bar. See also the cases cited in the foregoing authorities, and also Broom, Leg. Max. *141; *Corn Exch. Bank* v. *Nassau Bank*, 91 N. Y. 74; *Hazard* v. *Martin*, 2 Vt. 77.

It is not possible to deduce from the authorities inflexible rules governing the practical scope of the maxim, *communis error facit jus.* The decisions tend, however, towards a few general principles, each of which principles has at some time been invoked in some case, but not all of them, perhaps, in the same case. In every case we find some of them applied, while in some cases some of them may be disregarded. We cannot lay down rules, any one of which would be decisive of every case. But we state the following principles, with the suggestion that, if an individual case fell within the purview of all of them, there would be no difficulty with the maxim, and that, in proportion as the facts of a case depart from the principles announced, the difficulty of application is increased. Every case depends upon its own facts. The rules, as we conceive them to be,—rules flexible in their nature, and subject to the qualifications above suggested,—are: (1) The common error must be one having some judicial or professional recognition, approved or tolerated by decisions of judges or opinions of lawyers; or, to put the rule less positively, such judicial or professional recognition adds to the law-making force of the common error. We further qualify the rule in this, that common error may possibly have the law-making power, when supported by lay opinion only, provided that other rules may be forcibly applied. (2) Courts will not lightly or inconsiderately allow a common error to subvert a rule of law, or abrogate a positive statute. (3) The error must be a universal or very general one. The nearer universal, the more forcibly will it address itself, as a law-maker, to the approval of courts. (4) The acquiescence in the common error has involved, or there depends upon it, large property interests. (5) The error must be one that people have relied and acted upon, and have fixed their rights and positions thereby. (6) The longer the error has existed, the greater force it has. (7) The error must be clearly proved. (8) The error must be one in the observing, construing or interpreting law, and not an error in directly disobeying and abrogating that which is law.

We have called the above suggestions "rules," but the word "rules" must be received with the limitations above laid down. If the facts in the case at bar met the requirements of all these rules, or if they fell fairly within them, we should affirm the judgment below. But let us examine the facts in the order in which we have stated the rules: (1) The alleged common error in the location notice in question never received approval or toleration by judicial decision or legal opinion. The form of verification was adopted simply by a few prospectors in a part of the Territory, without any assurance from any source that it was correct. (2) The United States and territorial laws as to the requirements of a location notice, as construed in 8 Mont. 248, are peremptory. We hesitate to admit that 33 per cent of the mining locators of one county of a vast territory can by their own unauthorized practice abrogate, repeal and nullify a positive law. (3) So far from the error being general or universal among the people, it was limited to a very small number. (4) It is not shown that large property interests depend upon the upholding of this location notice. Only 288 of these notices are found, and these all in two years. This was ten years ago. In the history of mining prospecting, ten years will see the valuable mines patented, and the others abandoned or re-located. They are, in either instance, beyond the necessity of relying upon the defective location notice. (5) It does not appear that any considerable number of persons have relied upon, or sought to fix their rights upon, the alleged common error. (6) The error existed but a short time. It attained its height months before the location of defendants. From March, 1880, it rapidly waned into desuetude, and disappeared with the defendants' location, December 22. (7) The error was clearly enough proved so far as it went. (8) The error did not consist in any effort to observe, construe or interpret the law of Congress or the Territory. It was rather a direct disobedience of those laws. To construe or interpret a statute is to read it for the purpose of ascertaining its meaning and effect. He cannot be said to construe or interpret who clearly disregards the law. That is not construing. It is refusing to do so. It is defying the law. We arrive at the opinion that the facts in the case at bar are almost wholly in conflict with all the principles governing the application of *communis error facit jus.* The district court erred in instruction No. 3, recited above, upon the subject of common error. The action of the court in this matter of the alleged common error was objected to, and exception saved in other manner as well as in the instruction referred to.

The judgment is reversed, and the case remanded for a new trial.

Blake, *Ch. J.*, and **Harwood,** *J.*, concur.

IOWA SUPREME COURT.

J. A. SMITH

v.

CITY OF OSAGE, *Appt.*

(....Iowa....)

1. A common source of title will not prevent a subsequent grantee in possession of property from claiming adversely to a prior one, where, although he claims under a deed from the same person, each insists that the deed of the other is invalid and passes no title.

2. A city is estopped to set up any claim to land dedicated to public use, but never used by the public, where it has permitted a person to occupy it, and has levied and collected city taxes thereon as his private property.

(May 15, 1890.)

APPEAL by defendant from a judgment of the District Court for Mitchell County in favor of plaintiff in an action brought to quiet the alleged title of plaintiff to certain lands. *Affirmed.*

The case sufficiently appears in the opinion.

Mr. **L. M. Ryce,** for appellant:

A party cannot recall a statutory dedication once made in any way except that provided by statute; this, too, where there had not even been any act of acceptance by the City or public.

Lake View v. *Le Bahn*, 120 Ill. 92, 6 West. Rep. 786; *Weeping Water* v. *Reed*, 21 Neb. 261; *Baker* v. *St. Paul*, 8 Minn. 491.

Until the time arrives when any street or part of a street is required for actual use, and when the public authorities may be properly called upon to open it, no mere nonuser for any length of time will operate as an abandonment.

Reilly v. *Racine*, 51 Wis. 526; *Lee* v. *Mound Station*, 6 West. Rep. 329, 118 Ill. 304; *Derby* v. *Alling*, 40 Conn. 410; *Henshaw* v. *Hunting*, 1 Gray, 210; *Meier* v. *Portland Cable R. Co.* 1 L. R. A. 856, 16 Or. 500; *Lake View* v. *Le Bahn*, *supra; Shea* v. *Ottumwa*, 67 Iowa, 39; *Waterloo* v. *Union Mill Co.* 72 Iowa, 437.

Were this an action between individuals, it is exceeding doubtful at least if appellee could recover here upon his plea of adverse possession and Statute of Limitations. The presumption of law is that such possessions are taken and held in subordination to the true owner's title.

Sydnor v. *Palmer*, 29 Wis. 251; *Grube* v. *Wells*, 34 Iowa, 148; *Pownal* v. *Taylor*, 10 Leigh, 172, 34 Am. Dec. 725; *Irvine* v. *McRee*, 5 Humph. 554, 42 Am. Dec. 468; *Rung* v. *Shoneberger*, 2 Watts, 23, 26 Am. Dec. 95; *St. Luke's Church* v. *Mathews*, 4 Desaus. 578, 6 Am. Dec. 627; *Schwallback* v. *Chicago, M. & St. P. R. Co.* 69 Wis. 292.

This entire so-called adverse possession has not been one essentially hostile. Mere fencing, ordinary occupancy for farming purposes, are not alone sufficient.

Plimpton v. *Converse*, 42 Vt. 712, 44 Vt. 158; *Kerns* v. *McKean*, 65 Cal. 411.

The law construes such acts alone as being permitted by, and subordinate to, the true owner.

Cheek v. *Aurora*, 92 Ind. 107; *Carter* v. *La Grange*, 60 Tex. 636.

So the law construes or presumes the continued possession of the original grantor as against the original grantee.

McDunn v. *Des Moines*, 34 Iowa, 467; *Livermore* v. *Maquoketa*, 35 Iowa, 358; *Rowe* v. *Beckett*, 30 Ind. 154, 95 Am. Dec. 676, and *note; Schaferman* v. *O'Brien*, 28 Md. 565, 92 Am. Dec. 708; *Henry* v. *Stevens*, 6 West. Rep. 577, 108 Ind. 281.

This presumption continues to obtain until said original grantor, or some one of his grantees after the first grantee, makes an express claim of a hostile title,—"expressly denies that of said first grantee."

Hayes v. *Frey*, 54 Wis. 520; *Lake View* v. *Le Bahn*, *supra*; *Allen* v. *Allen*, 58 Wis. 210; *Roebke* v. *Andrews*, 26 Wis. 344; *Kerns* v. *McKean*, 65 Cal. 411; *Kerns* v. *Dean*, 77 Cal. 555; *Mayes* v. *Blanton*, 67 Tex. 245; *Barnard* v. *Roane Iron Co.* 85 Tenn. 139; *Hinkle* v. *Davenport*, 38 Iowa, 358.

And due knowledge or notice thereof must be brought or proven home to the holder of the legal title.

Dayton v. *Fargo*, 45 Mich. 155; *Smith* v. *Stevens*, 82 Ill. 554; *Davis* v. *Bowmar*, 55 Miss. 671; *Morrill* v. *Titcomb*, 8 Allen, 100; *Alexander* v. *Wheeler*, 69 Ala. 332; *Bartlett* v. *Secor*, 56 Wis. 520; *Sherman* v. *Kane*, 86 N. Y. 57; *Wheeling* v. *Campbell*, 12 W. Va. 36, 17 Am. L. Reg. N. S. 390.

And the adverse holding must be under color of title or claim of right not derived from the original grantor or grantors but from some other foreign, independent source.

Schwallback v. *Chicago*, *M. & St. P. R. Co.* *supra*; *House* v. *McCormick*, 57 N. Y. 310; *Pope* v. *Haumer*, 74 N. Y. 240; *Wilklow* v. *Lane*, 37 Barb. 244; *Gilliam* v. *Bird*, 8 Ired. L. 280, 49 Am. Dec. 379, and *note*; *Carbrey* v. *Willis*, 7 Allen, 364, 83 Am. Dec. 688; *Hunt* v. *Amidon*, 4 Hill, 345, 40 Am. Dec. 283, and *note*.

Payment of taxes for city and county purposes does not conclude the public from claiming the use of the land for a public street.

Chicago v. *Wright*, 69 Ill. 319; *Lemon* v. *Hayden*, 13 Wis. 159; *Wyman* v. *State*, Id. 663; *Lake View* v. *Le Bahn*, *supra*; *Winona* v. *Huff*, 11 Minn. 119; *San Leandro* v. *Le Breton*, 72 Cal. 170; *Lee* v. *Mound Station*, *supra*; *Hamilton* v. *Chicago*, *B. & Q. R. Co.* 124 Ill 235; *Kennedy* v. *Cumberland*, 65 Md. 514; *Baker* v. *Johnston*, 21 Mich. 319; *Wilder* v. *St. Paul*, 12 Minn. 209, 210.

The plea of adverse possession and the Statute of Limitations is of no avail against the City and the public.

Alton v. *Illinois Transp. Co.* 12 Ill. 38; *Quincy* v. *Jones*, 76 Ill. 231; *Logan County* v. *Lincoln*, 81 Ill. 158; *Lee* v. *Mound Station*, *supra*; *Piatt County* v. *Goodell*, 97 Ill. 84; *Vicksburg* v. *Marshall*, 59 Miss. 563; *Sims* v. *Frankfort*, 79 Ind. 446; *Com.* v. *Moorehead*, 10 Cent. Rep. 611, 118 Pa. 344, 4 Am. St. Rep. 599; *Hoadley* v. *San Francisco*, 50 Cal. 265; *People* v. *Pope*, 53 Cal. 437; *Grogan* v. *Hayward*, 4 Fed. Rep. 161; *San Leandro* v. *Le Breton*, *supra*; *St. Vincent Female Orphan Asylum* v. *Troy*, 76 N. Y. 108; *Reilly* v. *Racine*, 51 Wis. 526; *Henshaw* v. *Hunting*, 1 Gray, 203; *Arundel* v. *McCulloch*, 10 Mass. 70; *Jay* v. *Whelchel*, 78 Ga. 786; *Cowart* v. *Young*, 74 Ga. 694; 2 Dillon, Mun Corp. par. 533; *Waterloo* v. *Union Mill Co.* 72 Iowa, 437; *Wheeling* v. *Campbell*, 12 W. Va. 36, 17 Am. L. Reg. N. S. 898, *note*.

Mr. **G. E. Marsh**, for appellee:

By reason of the levy and collection of taxes upon said property, including the streets, alleys and public square, the defendant City and public cannot now deny plaintiff's title thereto.

Adams County v. *Burlington & M. R. R. Co.* 39 Iowa, 507; *Audubon County* v. *American Emigrant Co.* 40 Iowa, 460; *Austin* v. *Bremer County*, 44 Iowa, 155; *Simplot* v. *Dubuque*, 49 Iowa, 630; Dillon, Mun. Corp. § 533; *Bullis* v. *Noble*, 36 Iowa, 618; *Getchell* v. *Benedict*, 57 Iowa, 121.

The actual, open, hostile and continuous possession of the property in dispute by plaintiff and his grantors for thirty years or upwards makes plaintiff's title thereto full, complete and absolute. Knowledge or notice of such possession need not be brought home to the holder of the legal title.

Close v. *Samm*, 27 Iowa, 503, 510; *Teabout* v. *Daniels*, 38 Iowa, 158, 161.

Plaintiff could claim adversely although he derived his title through subsequent grantees of defendant's grantor.

Schwallback v. *Chicago*, *M. & St. P. R. Co.* 69 Wis. 292. See also *Kennebeck Purchase* v. *Springer*, 4 Mass. 416, 3 Am. Dec. 227.

The Statute of Limitations may be invoked against a municipality or the public under certain circumstances.

Wheeling v. *Campbell*, 12 W. Va. 36, 17 Am. L. Reg. N. S. 386; *Manchester Cotton Mills* v. *Manchester*, 25 Gratt. 825; *Richmond* v. *Poe*, 24 Gratt. 149; *Cincinnati* v. *First Presbyterian Church*, 8 Ohio, 298; *Cincinnati* v. *Evans*, 5 Ohio St. 594; *Lane* v. *Kennedy*, 13 Ohio St. 42; *St. Charles County* v. *Powell*, 22 Mo. 525; *St. Charles Twp. School Directors* v. *Goerges*, 50 Mo. 194; *Peoria* v. *Johnston*, 56 Ill. 45; *Chicago*, *R. I. & P. R. Co.* v. *Joliet*, 79 Ill. 40; *Illinois Cent. R. Co.* v. *Houghton*, 1 L. R. A. 213, 126 Ill. 233; *North Hempstead* v. *Hempstead*, 2 Wend. 109; *Denton* v. *Jackson*, 2 Johns. Ch. 320, 1 N. Y. Ch. L. ed. 394; *Hayward* v. *Manzer*, 70 Cal. 476; *Gregory* v. *Knight*, 50 Mich. 61; *Scheuber* v. *Held*, 47 Wis. 340; *Pella* v. *Scholte*, 24 Iowa, 283, sustained and followed by implication in *Livermore* v. *Maquoketa*, 35 Iowa, 358; *McDunn* v. *Des Moines*, 34 Iowa, 467; *Brown* v. *Painter*, 44 Iowa, 368, and expressly followed in *Davies* v. *Huebner*, 45 Iowa, 574; *Simplot* v. *Dubuque*, 49 Iowa, 630; *Bell* v. *Burlington*, 68 Iowa, 296, 299; *Orr* v. *O'Brien*, 77 Iowa, 253.

Nonuser coupled with an adverse holding by a claimant for the statutory period of ten years is conclusive of forfeiture and abandonment.

Waterloo v. *Union Mill Co.* 72 Iowa, 437.

The rule applicable between individuals should be enforced here.

Lucas v. *Hart*, 5 Iowa, 415; *Bullis* v. *Noble*, 36 Iowa, 618; *Foster* v. *Bigelow*, 24 Iowa, 379; *Campbell* v. *Mayes*, 38 Iowa, 9.

Beck, *J.*, delivered the opinion of the court:

1. The plaintiff claims to hold the title to the land in controversy, and alleges that defendant sets up an adverse title thereto. The defendant in its answer alleges that the land in question was platted and laid off in lots, streets, alleys and a public square, and that the streets, alleys and public square were in that way dedicated to the public use. It is not claimed that defendant holds the title of any of the lots, and the only claim or interest it has is as a representative of the public, or as a municipal corporation having charge and control, for the benefit of the public, of land dedicated to public use, as streets, alleys and public

grounds. It does not appear that any of the lots laid off on the land in question have been sold, or that defendant is the representative of the owners of such lots, or the guardian of their interests. The plaintiff pleads various defenses to defendant's claim that a part of the land has been dedicated to the public use, and is held subject thereto. We find it necessary to consider but two defenses, as, in our opinion, the decision of the case turns thereon. Other defenses will not be stated nor considered in this opinion.

2. Plaintiff, in his answer to defendant's claim, pleads the Statute of Limitations as a defense to the action, alleging that he has been for thirty years in the actual, open and notorious possession of the land, which has been adverse to defendant, and the claim it sets up to the land. The facts, briefly stated, are these: Sarah E. Moore entered the land in 1854. In 1855 she united with her husband in conveying the land to Eaton and Jenkins for the purpose, expressed in the deed, of causing the land to be laid off into village lots by the grantees in the deed. It seems to be a deed with conditions creating a power and trust. This deed is not acknowledged. It was duly recorded. The owners of other tracts of land united with Eaton and Jenkins in laying off a large tract of land into village lots, and for that purpose caused a plat of the land to be filed, showing lots, streets, alleys and a public square. This was in 1855. Objections are made to the regularity and sufficiency of the plat, and the act of dedication by the owners of the land, indorsed on the plat. Mrs. Moore continued in the possession of the land until 1871, when she conveyed it to one under whom plaintiff claims. Plaintiff now claims that he and his grantor, and those under whom they claim, have been in the actual, open and notorious possession of the land, claiming the title thereto against all men. It appears that the land has been used and cultivated as a part of a farm. The streets and alleys have never been opened, and the public square has not been occupied by the public, but has been in cultivation as a part of a farm. Plaintiff insists that he and those under whom he claims have been in adverse possession of the land, and that defendant's claim to the land is barred by the Statute of Limitations. Defendant maintains that, as plaintiff claims under Mrs. Moore by a subsequent conveyance, his title cannot be adverse to the City, whose claim is based upon a prior conveyance executed by her; that, as plaintiff's and defendant's title have a common source, from the same grantor, Mrs. Moore, plaintiff's title cannot be adverse to defendant's claim. We know no rule recognized in this State extending so far. If there were, no case of adverse holding could arise in this State, where all titles are derived from the government. No title not capable of being traced back to the government is valid here, for all titles have their origin in the government, which is often reached through fewer mean conveyances than were executed in this case. The rule which counsel presents, we think, cannot extend further than to exclude the doctrine of adverse holding from cases wherein the parties hold under the same title, these titles meeting in a common source, in such a manner as that one is held to be in subordination to, or dependent upon, the other, and not independent of, or in conflict thereto.

In the case before us, plaintiff's and defendant's title nowhere meet in a common source. It is true they are both traced to Mrs. Moore. Each party claims under a deed executed by her, but each insists that her deed under which the other claims is invalid, and does not pass title, and the party acquires no title under it. With the deeds executed by Mrs. Moore the conflict of title begins. The respective parties holding the titles originally under her deeds hold adversely, and in conflict with each other. It cannot be said that plaintiff does not hold adversely to defendant, because Mrs. Moore herself, while in possession of the land, would not be regarded as holding adversely to defendant. But the same cannot be said of her grantee, under whom plaintiff claims. He entered upon the land under a title in conflict with defendant's claim, and held it adversely thereto. He held color of title, for his claim was based upon a deed valid in form, under which he entered and held the land. His possession thereto was adverse as to defendant. The public, whose right to the use and occupancy of the land is attempted to be established by defendant, as the representative of the public, bases it in this action upon the facts and doctrines of the law above recited. *Pella* v. *Scholte*, 24 Iowa, 283; *Davies* v. *Huebner*, 45 Iowa, 574.

Waterloo v. *Union Mill Co.*, 72 Iowa, 437, is not in conflict with these views.

3. The defendant was not organized as a City until 1871, and has taken no steps to open the streets and alleys, or to secure the occupancy by the people of the public square, but during all the time has assessed the land, and levied taxes thereon, and collected them. Prior to the incorporation of defendant as a City the plaintiff, or those under whom he claims, paid the taxes. Prior to 1867 the land was sometimes taxed as lots, sometimes described on the tax-list according to the government subdivisions, and the conveyances of the land described it as lots, according to the plat. The deed executed by Mrs. Moore and her husband describes the land by the congressional subdivisions, and also as lots, according to the plat. Subsequent to 1867 the land was described upon the tax-list by the government subdivisions. The public square and the streets and alleys were in this manner subjected to taxation. It does not clearly appear for what years the corporation taxes were levied and collected, but we think each year after the incorporation of the City in 1871, and certainly after 1876, it levied and collected taxes upon the land, describing it according to the government subdivisions. Defendant is charged by law with the control of the streets, alleys and public grounds within its borders, and may vacate them and restore them to private use. Code, § 464.

It may exercise the authority and power of taxation over private property and land held by individuals. It does not exercise such power over streets, alleys and public grounds within its limits. In the case before us, it has permitted plaintiff, and those under whom he claims, to occupy the land, which has never been subject to public use, and it levies and collects city taxes thereon. The law regards this as a declaration by its acts that it holds no claim to the land, and as an abandonment of all claim to the public use of the lands. The City may vacate streets and other public lands, and restore them to private owners by proper action. The same end may be attained by abandonment and nonuse, and by taxation, and in other ways treating the land as private property. The City will be estopped to set up any claim to land to which the right of public use has been abandoned by subjecting it to taxation as private property. *Simplot* v. *Dubuque*, 49 Iowa, 630.

Upon this point see *Getchell* v. *Benedict*, 57 Iowa, 121; *Adams County* v. *Burlington & M. R. R. Co.* 39 Iowa, 507; *Audubon County* v. *American Emigrant Co.* 40 Iowa, 460; *Austin* v. *Bremer County*, 44 Iowa, 155.

We reach the conclusion that the action is barred by the Statute of Limitations, and that defendant is estopped to set up the claim of the public to the land in controversy. Other questions discussed by counsel need not be considered.

The judgment of the District Court is affirmed.

INDIANA SUPREME COURT

LOUISVILLE, NEW ALBANY AND CHICAGO R. CO., *Appt.*, v. George CORPS.

(....Ind....)

1. An attack upon one of several paragraphs of a complaint made for the first time in the assignment of errors will be unavailing, even although the paragraph assailed is radically defective.

2. An averment that plaintiff had no knowledge of the danger of continuing in the service of his employer, which existed because of the latter's failure to provide suitable machinery and competent workmen, is necessary to warrant a recovery for injuries alleged to have resulted from such failure; otherwise it will be assumed that the danger was known to and assumed by the employé. An allegation of freedom from fault is not sufficient for this purpose.

3. In pleading, plaintiff must state all the facts essential to a cause of action; if any material fact is lacking the complaint will go down before a demurrer.

(June 20, 1890.)

APPEAL by defendant from a judgment of the Circuit Court for Clark County overruling a demurrer to the complaint in an action brought to recover damages for personal injuries alleged to have resulted from defendant's negligence. *Reversed.*

NOTE.—*Master and servant; knowledge by servant of defective and dangerous machinery.*

A servant does not assume any risk incident to the use of defective machinery or appliances of which he is ignorant. See *notes* to Myhan v. Louisiana E. L. & P. Co. (La.) 7 L. R. A. 172; Davis v. St. Louis, I. M. & S. R. Co. (Ark.) 7 L. R. A. 283; Foley v. Pettee Machine Works (Mass.) 4 L. R. A. 51.

It is the duty of the master to inform his servant of risks to which he is subjected in the course of his employment. See *note* to Brazil Block Coal Co. v. Gaffney (Ind.) 4 L. R. A. 850.

Burden of proof on servant.

Negligence on the part of an employer is not to be presumed. Authorities cited in Louisville, N. A. & C. R. Co. v. Sanford, 117 Ind. 265.

An employé, to recover for injuries caused by defective appliances, must prove that he did not know, and had not equal means with the master of knowing, that the appliances were defective. *Ibid.*

A servant seeking to recover for an injury has the burden of establishing negligence on the part of the master, and due care on his own part. Texas & N. O. R. Co. v. Crowder (Tex.) March 18, 1890.

The burden is on a servant alleging that injuries were sustained by him in consequence of defective machinery or appliances, to prove that the same was defective. Humphreys v. Newport News & M. V. Co. 33 W. Va. 135.

A railroad employé suing the company for damages sustained in his employment has the burden to overcome the presumption of law that defendant has discharged its duty toward him, by showing negligence on its part. Murray v. Denver & R. G. R. Co. 11 Colo. 124.

To establish contributory negligence of a servant, the burden of proof as to his knowledge of latent danger is on the master. Myhan v. Louisiana E. L. & P. Co. (La.) 7 L. R. A. 172.

It is incumbent upon a railroad employé who attributes his injury to the fact of brake-shoes being worn thin, to prove the fact permitting the inference that the brake could not be applied, or that when applied it was not as effective as it should or would have been with thicker brake-shoes. Smith v. New York Cent. & H. R. R. Co. 118 N. Y. 645.

The question of negligence is one of fact for the jury, taking into view all the circumstances of the case. Nolan v. Brooklyn City & N. R. Co. 87 N. Y. 67; Morrison v. Erie R. Co. 56 N. Y. 307; Maguire v. Middlesex R. Co. 115 Mass. 239; West Chester & P. R. Co. v. McElwee, 17 P. F. Smith, 311; Messel v. Lynn & B. R. Co. 8 Allen, 234; Wharton, Neg. p. 366.

Injury from defective or dangerous appliances.

There can be no relief, without proof, on a controverted question. Hughes v. Hughes, 87 Ala. 652.

The general rule of pleading is that when an issue is properly joined, he who asserts the affirmative must prove it. Simonton v. Winter, 30 U. S. 5 Pet. 141 (8 L. ed. 75).

When an affirmative fact is averred, on which the title to relief is founded, and is denied, the burden of proof rests on the complainant; and it is incumbent on him to produce sufficient evidence to satisfy the mind. Long v. Gill, 80 Ala. 408.

The party on whom the burden of proof in any cause rests may be determined by considering which would succeed if no evidence were offered by either side, and by examining what would be the effect of striking out of the record the allegation to be proved. The *onus* must be on the party who, under such tests, would fail in the suit. Porter v. Still, 63 Miss. 357.

The facts sufficiently appear in the opinion.

Messrs. **James K. Marsh** and **Ward H. Watson** for appellant.

Messrs. **M. Z. Stannard** and **Frank B. Burke** for appellee.

Elliott, *J.*, delivered the opinion of the court:

It has been often ruled by this court that an attack upon one of several paragraphs of a complaint made for the first time in the assignment of errors will be unavailing, even though the paragraph assailed may be radically defective. This settled doctrine renders it unnecessary for us to consider the objections urged against the first paragraph of the appellee's complaint.

The second paragraph of the complaint was assailed by demurrer in the court below, and we are required to give judgment upon it. The paragraph named alleges that the plaintiff was in the service of the defendant as a laborer in its repair shops at New Albany; that the defendant negligently employed an inexperienced, unskillful and incompetent person to superintend and direct the work in its shop and the work upon which the plaintiff was engaged at the time of his injury; that the work which the plaintiff was then performing was that of moving the large driving wheels of one of the defendant's locomotives; that the defendant negligently failed to provide a sufficient number of competent men to do the work of moving such wheels; that the defendant negligently failed to furnish sufficient machinery for such work, in that it failed to furnish blocks to hold such wheels; that by reason of the careless and negligent acts of the defendant a pair of driving wheels of one of its locomotives ran upon the plaintiff's hand and arm, and so injured them as to deprive the plaintiff of their use; that the driving wheels ran upon the plaintiff without fault on his part, and the injury to him could not have been avoided by the exercise of care or prudence on his part.

It is settled law that an employer must use reasonable care to provide his employés with safe working places and appliances. It is also settled that the employer must use reasonable care to select competent and skillful persons for service. *Indiana Car Co.* v. *Parker*, 100 Ind. 181; *Cincinnati, I. St. L. & C. R. Co.* v. *Lang*, 118 Ind. 579; *Taylor* v. *Evansville & T. H. R. Co.* 121 Ind. 124; *Lake Shore & M. S. R. Co.* v. *Stupak* (Ind.) 23 N. E. Rep. 246; *Pennsylvania Co.* v. *O'Shaughnessy*, 122 Ind. 588.

But it is quite as well settled that an employé cannot recover from the employer for an injury produced by some cause incident to the nature of his services, and that the master is not responsible for the known risks incident to the service in which the servant engages. For anything that appears in the complaint the peril was a known incident of the service and was one assumed by the plaintiff; and if it was, there can be no recovery. *Indianapolis & St. L. R. Co.* v. *Watson*, 114 Ind. 275, 12 West. Rep. 285; *Pennsylvania Co.* v. *O'Shaughnessy*, *supra*, and cases cited.

In order to make a good complaint in such a case as this it is essential that it should be averred that the plaintiff has no knowledge of the danger, since if he did have knowledge and voluntarily continued in the master's service he is deemed to have assumed the risk as an incident of his service. *Louisville, N. A. & C. R. Co.* v. *Sandford*, 117 Ind. 265; *Brazil Block & Coal Co.* v. *Young*, 117 Ind. 520; *Lake Shore & M. S. R. Co.* v. *Stupak*, 108 Ind. 1, 6 West. Rep. 244; *Indiana, B. & W. R. Co.* v. *Dailey*, 110 Ind. 75, 8 West. Rep. 516; *Philadelphia & R. R. Co.* v. *Hughes*, 119 Pa. 301, 11 Cent. Rep. 822; *Wilson* v. *Winona & St. P. R. Co.* 37 Minn. 326; *Gaffney* v. *New York & N. E. R. Co.* 15 R. I. 456.

Remaining in the master's service with knowledge of the dangers of the service is not simply contributory negligence; for, as Mr. Beach says: "The servant is deemed to assume the risks of such danger, and to waive any claim upon his master for damages in case of injury." Beach, Contrib. Neg. § 140.

There is, in such a case, no right of recovery, for the employer is absolved from liability. It is therefore a necessary conclusion, as shown by the authorities to which we have referred, that the allegation that the plaintiff was free from fault does not supply the place of averments showing that the risk was not one knowingly assumed as an incident of his service. It may be true that an employé exercised the utmost care, and yet be true that the risk assumed was an incident of the service in which he engaged.

We are here dealing with a question of pleading and not of evidence. There is, as is well known, an essential difference between matters of pleading and matters of evidence; in pleading, facts must be directly and positively averred, while, as matter of evidence, conclusions may be inferred, without positive statements, from facts and circumstances. In pleading, it is incumbent upon the plaintiff to state all the facts essential to a cause of action, and if any material fact is lacking the complaint will go down before a demurrer. A material fact is here absent, and that is the fact that the danger was not an incident of the service in which the plaintiff voluntarily engaged. This fact must be averred as the rules of pleading require, although if the question were one of evidence it might be inferred.

Judgment reversed.

CONNECTICUT SUPREME COURT OF ERRORS.

NAUGATUCK WATER CO.

v.

A. J. NICHOLS.

(58 Conn. 403.)

A premature and void contract made by a corporation before there had been paid in the amount of capital stock required by statute to be paid in before corporate powers could be exercised, the contract being to promote the purposes of the corporation, and being carried out after the corporation became enabled to make it valid, does not release a subscription for corporate stock.

(Pardee and Loomis, JJ., dissent.)

(March 3, 1890.)

APPEAL by defendant from a judgment of the Waterbury District Court in favor of plaintiff in an action brought to recover an assessment upon a stock subscription. *Affirmed.*

The facts are sufficiently stated in the opinion.

Messrs. **Morris W. Seymour** and **Howard H. Knapp**, for appellant:

Every subscription, no matter how formal or informal, by implication incorporates the terms of the charter of the proposed company; and every subscriber agrees to become associated with the others only upon condition that the formalities of the charter shall be observed.

1 Morawetz, Priv. Corp. pp. 66, 136–138; *Indianapolis Furnace & Min. Co.* v. *Herkimer*, 46 Ind. 142.

Where the corporation has the authority to begin business or exercise its privileges on a certain amount of stock subscribed or paid in, the subscription becomes binding when the prescribed amount has been reached.

Boston, B. & G. R. Co. v. *Wellington*, 113 Mass. 79; *Lexington & W. C. R. Co.* v. *Chandler*, 13 Met. 311; *White Mountain R. Co.* v. *Eastman*, 34 N. H. 145.

The corporation began business before receiving the required payments upon the stock subscriptions, and thereby released the subscribers.

Morawetz, Priv. Corp. p. 158.

Nor does it avail this plaintiff that subsequently the payment of twenty-five per cent was made.

Ticonic Water Power & Mfg. Co. v. *Lang*, 63 Me. 480.

Failure to perform the condition precedent, prescribed in the charter, was fatal to a recovery.

Lexington & W. C. R. Co. v. *Chandler*, 13 Met. 311; *White Mountain R. Co.* v. *Eastman*, 34 N. H. 145; *Penobscot & K. R. Co.* v. *Dunn*, 39 Me. 587; *Troy & G. R. Co.* v. *Newton*, 8 Gray, 596; *Penobscot & K. R. Co.* v. *Whittier*, 12 Gray, 244; *New Hampshire Cent. R. Co.* v. *Johnson*, 30 N. H. 390; *Katama Land Co.* v. *Holley*, 129 Mass. 541.

Mr. **H. C. Baldwin**, for appellee:

Defendant is estopped by his own acts from denying the legal existence of the plaintiff. His subscription was part of the basis relied upon to put the corporation in working condition. It was partly on the strength of that subscription that contracts were entered into and the preliminary arrangements made for the immediate construction of the works.

See *West Winsted Sav. Bank & Bldg. Asso.* v. *Ford*, 27 Conn. 282; 2 Morawetz, Priv. Corp. §§ 741, 743, and authorities cited.

Litchfield Bank v. *Church*, 29 Conn. 137, is conclusive of this case.

Andrews, *Ch. J.*, delivered the opinion of the court:

The plaintiff is a corporation created by a Special Act of the General Assembly passed at its January Session, 1887, "for the purpose of supplying the Town of Naugatuck with a supply of pure water for domestic and other uses." The charter is found in the Special Acts of that Session at page 571. It grants to the corporation the privilege to take springs of water, to make dams for reservoirs, to construct aqueducts in any of the streets, to enter upon land and to collect rents, and empowers it to borrow money, to give mortgages, to make contracts and to do very many other things thought to be necessary or convenient to enable it to carry out the purpose of its creation. In addition to these things the charter provides that "twenty-five per cent of the capital stock shall be paid in before said company can exercise the privileges and powers herein granted."

Within the time limited by law the corporators named in the charter, and certain other persons associated with them, one of whom was the defendant, met, voted to accept the charter, chose directors and other officers, enacted by-laws, and organized themselves into a corporation under and pursuant to it. The defendant subscribed for twenty shares of the capital stock, of which the par value was twenty-five dollars a share. On the 25th day of July, 1888, the directors voted to call for, and issued a call for, an installment of twenty-five per cent of the stock, to be payable on or before the 20th day of August then next. Of this call the defendant received due notice, but has at all times neglected and refused to pay it. On the 15th day of July, 1888, the plaintiff entered into a verbal contract with one Snow to construct for it its water-works. This contract was put into writing on the first day of August, and it was on that day executed by the parties. By the terms of that contract the plaintiff agreed to pay, and has since paid, to Snow, over $17,000 for work done by him. The whole of the twenty-five per cent was not paid in until after the said first day of August.

The trial court rendered judgment for the plaintiff to recover the installment. The defendant has appealed. The substance of his reasons of appeal is, that he is absolved from his promise to pay for the stock for which he subscribed because the plaintiff undertook to contract with Snow for the construction of its water-works before the whole of the twenty-five per cent had been paid in.

In the formation of a private civil corporation there are two classes of contracts to be considered. One is the contracts which the corporators or promoters make each with all the others in order to bring the corporation into existence, of which a subscription to the capital stock is an example, and which necessarily antedate its completed existence. These are the organizing contracts. The other class is the contracts which the corporation itself, after it comes into a complete existence, makes with third persons. Both these classes of contracts depend upon the provisions of the charter; and it is usual that the charter of every corporation contains provisions relating to each. The organizing contracts are made primarily by each of the subscribers with each of the others. They are also in a sense made with the corporation. But the making them is not an exercise of any of the powers or privileges granted to the corporation, because they are the steps necessary to be taken before the corporation is qualified to exercise any of the powers or privileges granted to it. It needs hardly to be said that there must be a full compliance with all the charter provisions relating to the organizing contracts before the corporation comes into such a legal existence as to be able to make contracts with third persons at all. Until these preliminary steps have been taken there is no legal person in being capable of exercising any power or privilege whatever.

It is obvious enough that any omission or failure to complete the organization would affect any contract with a third person. How any premature contract with a third person could interrupt or hinder the organization is not so plain. If any organizing contract was by its terms conditioned that no such contract should be entered into, or if it was so made conditional by the provisions of the charter, then it would appear.

The contract of subscription signed by the defendant is not by its terms conditioned upon anything relating to contracts which the plaintiff might make with third persons, unless the reference in it to the charter puts it in such a condition. If, then, the charter of the plaintiff contains no provision making a subscription to its capital stock dependent for its validity upon the time when the Company might enter into contracts with third persons, then there is no such condition in this case. There certainly is no express condition in the charter to that effect. The defendant claims that the provision of the charter above quoted is such a condition by implication, because it forbids the plaintiff to exercise any of the granted privileges and powers until the required part of the capital stock should be paid in. It does not seem to us that this claim can be sustained. Some of the powers and privileges granted to the plaintiff in its charter are hereinbefore enumerated. Prohibiting the exercise of any of these is quite a different thing from discharging a subscriber from the payment for his stock. The contract with Snow is foreign to the defendant's subscription contract. It purports, indeed, to have been made by the corporation; but in law it was not and could not have been, as at that time the corporation had no power to make it. It is not, however, a case of *ultra vires*. A case of *ultra vires* is where a fully existing corporation attempts to act upon some subject matter not within its charter powers. In this case the subject matter was within the powers conferred by the charter, but the corporation was not qualified to exercise those powers. Hence the executory contract, so far as the corporation was concerned, was inoperative. It was as though it had not been. In a case of *ultra vires* a corporation may become bound by the principles of estoppel. In this case it could only be bound by subsequent transactions from which a contract might be implied. Snow, the contractor, might, perhaps, have looked through the corporation and held those who assumed to act for it and in its name without authority liable as individuals. Beyond this we cannot see that any effect can be given to it as an executory contract.

The argument made on behalf of the defendant admits that his subscription was valid and lawful except for the contract with Snow. The provision of the charter clearly forbade such a contract. Being forbidden it was void. Can it be so that a void contract with Snow will release the defendant from his lawful one? If the defendant is not bound on his subscription then none of the subscribers are. All or none are bound. It cannot be that those who paid promptly are holden and the defendant who refused to pay is released. If all are released the consequence is that those who paid one installment can be compelled to pay no more; on the contrary, it would seem that they ought to have the amount refunded to them, otherwise they would be in a worse condition than those who refused to pay. The inevitable result of the defendant's claim, if granted, would be disaster complete and overwhelming to the enterprise.

The provision of the charter under consideration forbids the exercise of any granted power until the installment was paid in. A careful regard for the public interest might naturally prompt the Legislature to enact such a prohibition, while nothing but an injury done or threatened to the subscriber would be likely to suggest relieving him from making payment. Between these two things there is no legal connection. The relation of cause and effect does not exist. Neither implies the other. Either may well stand without the other, as either might be omitted without affecting the other.

It must not be inferred that we regard the provision of the charter as in the interest of the public alone; nor for the benefit merely of third persons. We entertain no doubt that it was designed to protect the stockholder as well. If the premature exercise of any granted power operated to the injury of any subscriber he ought not to be held to pay. But, on the other hand, if it was an advantage to him, and if it also tended to promote the purposes for which the corporation was chartered, it would be very unreasonable that he should not pay according to his promise. When any subscriber really suffers from such cause a remedy will not be wanting.

We think a compliance with this provision is not a condition precedent to the right of the plaintiff to recover in this action; and that a disobedience to it does not operate to release the defendant from his promise.

In this opinion **Carpenter** and **Fenn**, *JJ.*, concurred.

Pardee, *J.*, dissenting:

It is provided in the plaintiff's charter that "twenty-five per cent of the capital stock shall be paid in before said Company can exercise the privileges and powers herein conferred." This provision, therefore, of legal necessity is written as a condition precedent in every subscription made to the capital stock. Indeed, each subscription was expressly made "upon the terms and under the conditions and limitations" imposed by the charter. Each subscriber secured whatever measure of protection there may be in it to himself. All other subscribers combining cannot deprive him of it. The law of the plaintiff's being requires the subscription of the capital stock, the organization, the call for, and the actual payment into the treasury of one quarter of the capital, prior to the making of contracts for the construction of its water works. But this law was disregarded. The organized corporation, not having either called for or received a dollar from the subscriptions to its capital, entered into a contract for the construction of its works. It was the privilege of the defendant to annex to his subscription the condition that he would not become a member of the corporation if it should do that thing.

It is not an answer to his defense to say that all other subscribers have waived the violation of the charter, have paid and have ratified the contract. Each of them could waive or ratify for himself; no one, nor all of them, could waive or ratify for him. Nor to say that in this case the contract was an advantageous one and therefore neither the corporation nor the defendant suffered any pecuniary injury. The latter is not to be made to bear the burden of proving that he was not injured. The question is one of construction of a contract. What condition did the defendant annex to his subscription? Has the plaintiff so far met the condition as to be entitled to enforce the contract of subscription? Indeed the question is far reaching; it is, in reality, whether it is possible in making a contract of subscription to the capital of a corporation to impose thereon any condition which will protect the subscribers from an absolute liability.

In this opinion **Loomis, J.**, concurred.

MASSACHUSETTS SUPREME JUDICIAL COURT.

Leon WEENER *et al.*, *Appts.*,
v.
Lester BRAYTON.

(......Mass.......)

1. A label cannot be treated as a trade-mark which does not indicate by what person the articles upon which it is used were made, but only that he was a member of a certain association, which membership confers the right to use the mark, and of which there is no exclusive use, its rightful use not being connected with any business, but belonging to many persons not connected in business and unknown to each other.

2. To entitle one to an injunction to restrain an alleged invasion of his right of property in a trade-mark, he must show that he is in some way the owner thereof by reason of some business which he is transacting and to which its use is incident, and that its use is not merely a personal privilege which he possesses as a member of a particular association of wide extent and embracing many members of varied interests.

3. The fraudulent use of marks and labels for the purpose of deceiving the public will not be enjoined at the instance of one who does not show that he is himself a manufacturer or owner of, or dealer in, the articles which are fraudulently represented by the counterfeited labels to be his; hence the fact that persons are

NOTE.—*Title and right to exclusive use of a trade-mark.*

Three things are requisite to the acquisition of a title to a trade-mark: *first*, the person desiring to acquire title must adopt some mark not in use to distinguish goods of the same class or kind already on the market belonging to another trader; *second*, he must apply his mark to some article of traffic; and *third*, he must put his article, marked with his mark, on the market. Schneider v. Williams, 13 Cent. Rep. 255, 44 N. J. Eq. 391.

Where children on the death of their father continued the use of his trade-mark, their mark cannot be interfered with by one who has never acquired a right to use it. Pratt's App. 10 Cent. Rep. 596, 117 Pa. 401.

The right to a trade-mark is a property right, for the violation of which damages may be recovered in an action at law; and the continued violation of it will be enjoined by a court of equity. United States v. Steffens, ("Trade-Mark Cases") 100 U. S. 82 (25 L. ed. 550).

At common law the exclusive right to the ordinary trade-mark grows out of its use, and not from its mere adoption. *Ibid.*

The adoption by plaintiff of the words "La Normandi" as a trade-mark, in his business of manufacturing and selling cigars of a certain kind, cannot take the right previously acquired by the public in the use of the words "La Normanda" as indicating a particular kind of cigars. Injunction denied. Stachelberg v. Ponce, 128 U. S. 686 (32 L. ed. 569).

Manufacturers and merchants have severally the right to distinguish their productions and goods by a peculiar mark or device that they may secure the profits which superior repute may be the means of giving to them. Gillott v. Esterbrook, 48 N. Y. 376; 2 Story, Eq. 951.

Right to protection in use of trade-mark.

The right to protection is not exclusively in the manufacturer. The person for whom the goods are manufactured (Amoskeag Mfg. Co. v. Spear, 2 Sandf. 599; Walton v. Crowley, 3 Blatchf. 440; Godillot v. Hazard, 12 Jones & S. 430, 49 How. Pr. 7), and the vendor who sells and who may have no direct relation to the manufacturer, have such right. Godillot v. Hazard, 12 Jones & S. 430, 49 How. Pr. 7; Amoskeag Mfg. Co. v. Spear, 2 Sandf. 599; Walton v. Crowley, 3 Blatchf. 440.

A party having a valuable interest in trade or business is entitled to protection against any other person who attempts to pirate upon the good will of his customers, or of the patrons of his trade or business, by sailing under his flag without his authority or consent. Amoskeag Mfg. Co. v. Trainer, 101 U. S. 62 (25 L. ed. 997).

The court proceeds upon the ground that complainant has such valuable interest (Fetridge v. Merchant, 4 Abb. Pr. 160), and protects the title of the author and inventor of any names, marks, letters or other symbols which any manufacturer, trader or other person has devised and appropriated or been accustomed to use in his trade or business, and restrains by injunction any unauthorized use thereof to his prejudice. Bloss v. Bloomer, 23 Barb. 609.

To entitle a complainant, in cases relating to trade-marks, to protection, the right must be clearly established by the evidence (Ball v. Siegel, 3 West. Rep. 41, 116 Ill. 147); and the question is not whether the complainant was the original inventor or proprietor; anyone is entitled to protection against one who attempts to deprive him of his trade or customers by using his labels, signs or trade-mark without his knowledge or consent. McLean v. Fleming, 96 U. S. 252 (24 L. ed. 831); Coats

See also 9 L. R. A. 576; 13 L. R. A. 377; 23 L. R. A. 821.

officers or members of an association which has adopted a label to show that the articles bearing it were manufactured by its members does not, without more, entitle them to maintain a bill to enjoin the fraudulent use of such label.

(June 24, 1890.)

APPEAL by plaintiffs to the full court from a decree of the Supreme Judicial Court for Suffolk County sustaining a demurrer to the bill in a suit brought to enjoin an alleged unlawful use by defendant of plaintiffs' trade-mark. *Affirmed.*

The case sufficiently appears in the opinion.

Messrs. **Benj. F. Butler** and **Frank L. Washburn,** for appellants:

Plaintiffs adopt the whole label for their trade device or trade-mark, and are entitled to protection.

Holmes v. *Holmes B. & A. Mfg. Co.* 37 Conn. 278; *Pierce* v. *Guittard,* 68 Cal. 68.

This la[bel] and the right to use it as used are the subject of property.

Colman v. *Crump,* 70 N. Y. 573; *Newman* v. *Alvord,* 51 N. Y. 189.

Protection extends to one who may not have even the exclusive right to the use of the label.

Newman v. *Alvord,* 51 N. Y. 189; *Collins* v. *Reynolds Card Mfg. Co.* 7 Abb. N. C. 17.

The members of the union, including the plaintiffs herein, have a common valuable pecuniary interest in the labels in question, which is entitled to protection in a court of equity.

Strasser v. *Moonelis,* 11 Cent. Rep. 461, 108 N. Y. 611.

Where trade-marks have not been infringed, courts of equity have granted injunctions against the use upon goods of certain marks, labels and wrappers, when there appeared to be a design to deceive the public by concealing the true origin of the goods and make it appear they were the goods of another.

Croft v. *Day,* 7 Beav. 84; *McLean* v. *Fleming,* 96 U. S. 245 (24 L. ed. 828); *Brown Chemical Co.* v. *Myer,* 31 Fed. Rep. 453.

Mr. **Stephen H. Tyng,** for appellees:

The plaintiffs fail to state a case, and the bill should be dismissed.

See *Cigar-Makers Protective Union* v. *Conhaim,* 3 L. R. A. 125, 40 Minn. 243; *Schneider* v. *Williams,* 13 Cent. Rep. 255, 44 N. J. Eq. 391; *Rogers* v. *Taintor,* 97 Mass. 291, 297.

Devens, J., delivered the opinion of the court:

This case comes before us upon a demurrer which concedes, for the purposes of this hearing, the truth of the allegations of the bill. From these it appears that the plaintiffs are officers and members of the Cigar-Makers' Union, No 97; that said Union, No. 97, is a member of the International Cigar-Makers' Union of America, which is a voluntary association composed wholly of local unions; that said International Union has authorized and directed its president to furnish to all local unions a trade mark label to be pasted upon the outside of each box containing cigars made by members of the union; that cigars made by such members have acquired a valuable reputation, and that in consequence the right to the exclusive use of such labels is of great value; that

---

v. Holbrook, 2 Sandf. Ch. 586, 7 N. Y. Ch. L. ed. 718.

In an action for an injunction to restrain defendants from using a certain trade-mark for flour, which consisted of the words "La Favorita," the fact that plaintiffs were not the actual manufacturers of the flour upon which they placed such words does not deprive them of the right to be protected in the use of that brand as a trade-mark. Menendez v. Holt, 128 U. S. 514 (32 L. ed. 526).

Where consent by the owner to the use of his trade-mark by another is to be inferred from his knowledge and silence merely, it lasts no longer than the silence from which it springs; it is, in reality, no more than a revocable license. *Ibid.*

Labels protected.

A party may, under certain circumstances, be restrained from using another's label which does not rise to the rank of a trade-mark. No one has a right to represent his goods as the goods manufactured by another. To do this by using another's label is actionable. Adams v. Heisel, 31 Fed. Rep. 279.

Where a party engaged in canning and packing salmon, having a contract with another as sole agent for the sale of the canned fish, had a label to be placed on the cans, in one division of which was the name of the other party as sole agent, a purchaser of all the property of such party, including the labels, has no right, as against the party named as agent, to use that part of the label referring to such agency. Coleman v. Flavel, 40 Fed. Rep. 854.

The word "Elk," printed upon the face of a label for a box of cigars, with the head of an elk, is not invalid as a trade-mark because not designating origin or ownership, when it has words printed on it showing that it is made at the Elk Cigar Factory. Lichtenstein v. Goldsmith, 37 Fed. Rep. 359.

The use of the same or similar colors of wrappers and of boxes in putting up packages of goods cannot be claimed as an infringement of trade-mark, where there are marked differences in the labels and in all other particulars except in the colors. Philadelphia Novelty Mfg. Co. v. Blakesley Novelty Co. 40 Fed. Rep. 588; Philadelphia Novelty Mfg. Co. v. Rouss, Id. 585.

The use of a rose-colored capsule upon bottles of wine cannot be claimed as a trade-mark; nor can another be prevented from using them, where there is no attempt to deceive by labels or otherwise. Mumm v. Kirk, 40 Fed. Rep. 589.

Where the labels of complainants and defendants are so entirely dissimilar that one cannot readily be mistaken for the other, the fact that the word "Tycoon" is found in both of them does not make a case of infringement of a trade-mark. Corbin v. Gould, 133 U. S. 308 (33 L. ed. 611).

An order overruling a demurrer to the complaint in an action by the "Officers and Members of the Cigar Makers' Union, a branch and member of the Cigar Makers' International Union of America," was affirmed by a divided court. Allen v. McCarthy, 37 Minn. 349.

Injunction to restrain violation of right.

Where a manufacturer of nails has made use of labels of combinations of numbers,—as, "60," "70," "80" and "111," he should be protected by injunction in the exclusive use of such numbers. American Solid Leather Button Co. v. Anthony, 3 New Eng. Rep. 630, 15 R. I. 338.

Where one Le Page formed a corporation to which he sold his business, with the right to use his trade-mark "Le Page's Liquid Glue," and subsequently left the corporation, the use of the name "Le Page's Improved Liquid Glue" by him will be enjoined. Russia Cement Co. v. Le Page, 6 New Eng. Rep. 577, 147 Mass. 206.

See also 31 L. R. A. 374.

the defendant has caused to be put on boxes containing inferior cigars, and not made by members of the union, a counterfeit label so closely resembling said union label as to deceive purchasers: that for the purpose of deceiving the purchasers and obtaining higher prices, he has sold cigars in boxes on which he has pasted such counterfeit labels, well knowing the cigars contained therein were not made by members of the union and were inferior in workmanship and quality to those made by them and which are rightfully sold under the so-called union label.

A trade-mark is a peculiar name or device by which a person dealing in an article designates it as of a peculiar kind, character or quality, or as manufactured by or for him, or dealt in by him, and of which he is entitled to the exclusive use. *Rogers* v. *Taintor*, 97 Mass. 291; *Chadwick* v. *Covell*, 6 L. R. A. 839, 151 Mass. —.

There is no exclusive ownership of the names, devices, symbols or marks which constitute a trade-mark apart from the use or application of them, but the word "trade-mark" is the designation of them when applied to a vendible commodity. The exclusive right to make such use or application is rightly treated as property. While property in these names, devices, etc., for all purposes cannot exist, yet property as applied to particular, vendible articles may exist when such articles have gone into the market identified by them and have thus obtained reputation or currency by them, as indicating a special or superior quality, or as the work of a particular manufacturer, or some other circumstance which commends them to the public. Kerr, Injunc. 895.

The jurisdiction of a court of equity to restrain the wrongful use, by persons not entitled thereto, of such trade-marks, is founded, not upon the imposition upon the public thus practiced, but on the wrongful invasion of the right of property therein which has been acquired by others. A remedy is afforded only to the owner of the right of property in such trade-marks, on account of the injury which is thus done to him. The wrong done to him consists in misrepresenting the vendible articles sold as being those of the true owner of the mark, and thus, to a greater or less extent, depriving him of the benefit of the reputation he has given to the articles made or dealt in by him. To the validity of a trademark so as to entitle anyone to a remedy for an invasion thereof, three things have been held necessary: that he must show that he has adopted some marks or signs not in use by others, to distinguish the goods manufactured or sold by him, from those of other manufacturers or traders; that these must be applied to some articles of traffic, and that such articles must have been placed on the market. *Schneider* v. *Williams*, 44 N. J. Eq. 391, 13 Cent. Rep. 255; *Chadwick* v. *Covell*, *supra*.

The right to a trade-mark cannot exist as a mere abstract right independent of and disconnected from a business. It is not property as distinct from, but only as incident to, the business. It cannot be transferred except with the business, may be sold with it, and ordinarily passes with it. *Cigar-Makers Protective Union* v. *Conhaim*, 40 Minn. 243, 3 L. R. A. 125.

In the case above cited the allegations of the bill were, apparently, the same as those in the case at bar, and the bill was brought by certain persons, members of the Cigar-Makers' International Union, through their membership of one of the local unions, which compose the larger body. It appeared from the complaint that a device claimed to be a trade-mark, but in its form rather an advertisement, had been adopted by the International Union, which was furnished to all local unions for use on the boxes of cigars made by their members;—that the right to use it would continue as long as they were members; that such right would cease when they ceased to be such, and that a manufacturer could only use it by employing

---

Where a publisher of a newspaper, having suspended, sold the plant to a purchaser, who leases it, the lease reciting that it has been used in the publication of a certain paper, and containing a covenant to use it for the continuance of such publication, an injunction will lie to restrain the lessee from continuing the publication of a paper by that name. Lane v. Smythe (N. J.) Feb. 3, 1890.

A label resembling in six distinct points a label used by another person in the same business is such an imitation as should be enjoined, if at least two persons were deceived thereby, and defendant's sales have increased thereby. McCann v. Anthony, 3 West. Rep. 436, 21 Mo. App. 83.

To entitle plaintiff to relief against an alleged infringement of a trade-mark, the evidence must be clear. Ball v. Seigel, 8 West. Rep. 43, 116 Ill. 137.

Positive proof of fraudulent intent is not required to give a right to an injunction, where the proof of infringement is clear. McLean v. Fleming, 96 U. S. 245 (24 L. ed. 828).

Use of the defendant's name on a spurious trademark is no defense to a bill for an injunction, but only a circumstance to be considered in determining whether the public are likely to be deceived. Pratt's App. 10 Cent. Rep. 596, 117 Pa. 401.

Where there is a similitude to the substantial parts of a trade-mark, there is an infringement; and an evasive attempt to hide the similarity, or a colorable explanation which appears to be made for the purpose of escaping the effects of a wrongful use of the trade-mark, will not defeat the owner's right to an injunction. Keller v. B. F. Goodrich Co. 117 Ind. 556.

A trade-mark used in connection with certain articles of dentistry, consisting of the words "The Akron Dental Rubber," is infringed by the use, upon similar articles, of the words "Non-Secret Dental Vulcanite, made according to our analysis of the Akron Dental Rubber." *Ibid.*

Injunction; when not granted.

In suits in trade-mark cases an injunction is never granted in the first instance, if the exclusive title of plaintiff is denied, unless the grounds upon which it is denied are manifestly frivolous. When the title is disputed the course is to let the motion for an injunction stand over until plaintiff has established his legal right in an action at law. Samuel v. Berger, 4 Abb. Pr. 89, 13 How. Pr. 344, 24 Barb. 165; Fetridge v. Merchant, 4 Abb. Pr. 157; Amoskeag Mfg. Co. v. Spear, 2 Sandf. 619, 7 N. Y. Leg. Obs. 313; Wolfe v. Goulard, 18 How. Pr. 69; Motley v. Downman, 3 Mylne & C. 14; Partridge v. Menck, 2 Barb. Ch. 101, 5 N. Y. Ch. L. ed. 572, 2 Sandf. Ch. 622, 7 N. Y. Ch. L. ed. 729.

That the words used to designate a particular

members of the union, and would have no right so to do if he ceased to employ its members. It did not there appear, nor is it alleged in the case at bar, that either the plaintiff or any one of the unions was a business corporation, association or partnership for the purpose of manufacturing and selling or engaging in the manufacture or sale of cigars. It was held that the device in question (which in all substantial respects was the same with that here considered) was not a trade-mark, and the right to use it was not property but a personal privilege. Its object was simply to indicate membership in the union, and, to obtain whatever advantage the fact of membership might give its members, they had agreed on a certain device which might be placed on their productions. The right to use such a device was obtained merely by joining the association, and did not at all depend upon whether the person had earned a reputation for the manufacture of the particular article. It was therefore held that it could not be protected as a trade-mark. For similar reasons we are of opinion that the label alleged by the bill in the case at bar to have been counterfeited cannot be treated as a trade-mark. However disreputable and dishonest it may be falsely to represent goods made by other persons to have been made by members of the union, upon which subject there can be but one opinion, those who do not carry on any business to which the use of the label is incident, who have not applied it to any vendible commodity which has been placed upon the market, in which they deal or of which they are the owners or manufacturers, cannot maintain a bill to restrain the use by the defendant of the label as a trade-mark. It wants many essential elements of such a mark; it does not indicate by what person articles were made, but only membership in a certain association; there is no exclusive use of it, but many persons not connected in business, and unknown to each other, may use it. Its rightful use is not connected with any business. It cannot be transferred with any business, but such use is dependent only on membership in the association. Upon the question whether labels of this character are valid trade-marks, there has been some contrariety of opinion.

In *People* v. *Fisher*, 50 Hun, 552, under the New York Penal Code, which does not define a trade-mark in essential particulars differently from that usually adopted independent of the Statute, it was held that the label was a valid trade-mark; but we are of opinion that it cannot be so treated and considered, unless a quite different definition is given to this word from that which it has heretofore received, and quite different conditions from those heretofore recognized are held sufficient to justify proceedings for an injunction against one who dishonestly seeks to make a market for his wares by advertisements thereof which are false and unjustifiable. Without discussing the rights which a purchaser may have who has been deceived by such an advertisement or label, it is necessary for those who claim that their right of property in a trade-mark has been invaded, to show that they are in some way by themselves, or with others, the owners thereof by reason of some business which they are transacting together, and to which its use is incident, and not merely a personal privilege which they possess as members of a particular association of wide extent and embracing many persons of varied interest, to advertise, or have advertised by those by whom they are employed, the articles made by them as being made by members of such association.

It is urged by the plaintiffs, even if the label in question cannot be considered technically a trade-mark, that even where trade-marks have not been infringed, courts of equity have granted injunctions against the use, on various grounds, of certain marks, wrappers and labels, where there appeared to be a design to deceive the public by concealing the true origin of the

---

kind of goods in both labels are inclosed in a floral wreath of the same description is not of itself enough to constitute a fraudulent imitation. Merrimack Mfg. Co. v. Garner, 2 Abb. Pr. 325.

A man cannot be enjoined from giving his own name to a medicine or other article of which he is in good faith the manufacturer, although the result may be to confound the article to some extent in the public mind with a similar article previously manufactured by some other person of the same name, unless the use of his own name is merely colorable, accompanied with some artifice to mislead the public. Brown Chemical Co. v. Myer, 31 Fed. Rep. 453; William Rogers Mfg. Co. v. Simpson, 4 New Eng. Rep. 75, 54 Conn. 527.

The use of the words "patent roofing," merely designating the kind of business one is engaged in, cannot be protected as a trade-mark. Fay v. Fay (N. J.) 4 Cent. Rep. 241.

Plaintiffs, having stamped upon silver spoons "*Rogers & Bro. A," were not entitled to enjoin defendants from stamping "C. Rogers & Bros. A," it being a fair and honest use of the owner's name. Loomis, *J.*, and Park, *Ch. J.*, dissenting. Rogers v. Rogers, 1 New Eng. Rep. 411, 53 Conn. 121.

A purchaser, at assignee's sale, of wrappers, sacks, etc., used in a seed business, marked with the name of the assignor's firm, is not entitled to enjoin the assignor from using the firm name. Iowa Seed Co. v. Dorr, 70 Iowa, 481.

Forfeiture of right to injunction.

Where tea is put up in a package encased in tinfoil like imported teas, and marked "Standard He-No," on the front of the package, with statements which lead the public to suppose that it is pure tea, if, instead of this being true, the tea is compounded in Baltimore of several varieties, although purified by a secret process, the misrepresentation will defeat an injunction for infringement of the trade-mark. Kenny v. Gillet, 70 Md. 574.

An injunction will not be granted to restrain the infringement of a trade-mark which is accompanied with statements in the label plainly calculated to deceive and mislead purchasers. *Ibid.*

One seeking to palm off on the public a spurious for a genuine article, under guise of his trade-mark, forfeits his right to have such trade-mark protected. Parlett v. Guggenheimer, 8 Cent. Rep. 796, 67 Md. 542.

An exclusive privilege to deceive the public by means of a trade-mark containing misrepresentations is not one that a court of equity will aid or sanction. Manhattan Medicine Co. v. Wood, 108 U. S. 218 (27 L. ed. 706).

Allowing cigar boxes to be labeled with the names of dealers to whom the cigars are sold or for whom they are made is not deception or false representation when stamped with the name and the trade-mark of the factory which makes them. Lichtenstein v. Goldsmith, 37 Fed. Rep. 359.

goods, and to make it appear that they were the goods of another. *Croft* v. *Day*, 7 Beav. 84; *McLean* v. *Fleming*, 96 U. S. 245 [24 L. ed. 828]; *Brown Chemical Co.* v. *Myer*, 31 Fed. Rep. 453; *Thomson* v. *Winchester*, 19 Pick. 214.

We have no occasion to question this principle or the authorities by which it has been sustained. It will be found that where, under such circumstances, an injunction has been granted or an action maintained, it has been at the instance of one who was himself a manufacturer, dealer in or owner of the articles which were fraudulently represented by the counterfeited labels, wrappers or advertisements, to be his. In such case the fraud complained of would have a natural and inevitable tendency to lessen the sales, affect the reputation of the articles manufactured or dealt in, injure the business of the complainant, and would thus afford him a ground for relief by reason of the special and peculiar damage which he would sustain or to which he might be exposed. The plaintiffs show by their bill that they have a right to use the label in question and that it is a valuable privilege; but although they aver that they have suffered loss by the use of it by the defendant, they do not show that any business which they pursue has been affected, or that they have sustained any definite loss or any injury except that which must be extremely remote and purely speculative.

In *Carson* v. *Ury* (U. S. C. C. Mo.), 5 L. R. A. 614, it was held that a union label (answering in all respects to the one annexed to the plaintiff's bill, and there averred to have been counterfeited by the defendants) did not answer to the definition ordinarily given to a technical trade-mark, because it did not indicate with any degree of certainty by what particular person or firm the cigars were manufactured to which it might be affixed, or serve to distinguish the goods of one cigar manufacturer from another, and also because the complainant did not appear to have any vendible interest in the label, but merely a right to use it so long and only so long as he might remain a member of the union. In all these respects it lacked the characteristics of a valid trade-mark. In that case, however, the complainant had averred himself to be a manufacturer of cigars entitled to use the union label, who had used and was actually using it on the cigars manufactured by him, thus guaranteeing the character and quality of his cigars; that he had made profits thereby and that he had been greatly injured and was liable to be greatly injured by the defendants, who had prepared for sale counterfeit labels in the similitude of those he had used and which he was entitled to use. It was there deemed that the cases of *Cigar-Makers Protective Union* v. *Conhaim* and *Schneider* v. *Williams*, cited *supra*, were distinguishable in this, that in those cases the bills were framed upon the theory that the label was a technical trade-mark and as such the property of all the members of the union, and that any one or more members of the union might maintain a suit to restrain any unauthorized person from using the label whether they were themselves engaged in the manufacture and sale of cigars on their own account or not. It was deemed, therefore, properly to have been held in those cases that the plaintiffs could not be considered to have such a property in the label that they could maintain a bill upon the ground that they were injuriously affected by the fraudulent acts complained of, while in the case then before the court the complainant had averred himself to be a manufacturer of cigars who had built up a profitable trade and business, which business was liable to be and was damaged by the fraudulent acts complained of. In the case at bar there is no allegation that the plaintiffs are themselves, on their own account or with others, manufacturers or dealers in cigars as a business, or even persons actually employed by others in their sale or manufacture, or that the union of which they are members and officers is engaged in any business of that description. They do not by their bill show that they apply or have applied this label to any vendible commodity of which they are the owners or which they manufacture for the market or place thereon for sale, or in which they deal. Where an association such as the Cigar-Makers' Union, embracing many members and many divisions as subordinate unions, has adopted a symbol or device to be used on boxes of cigars made by its members, such device or symbol not indicating by whom the cigars are made, but only that they are made by some of the members of the union; and where the right to use the device or symbol belongs equally to all the members, and continues only while they are members,—a bill cannot be maintained by individual members or officers of such association to restrain others wrongfully and fraudulently using such device or symbol from so doing. Any injury to such members or officers is not direct or immediate, nor does it affect them in any business which in some form they conduct. It is upon this ground that such invasions of that which has been held to be property have heretofore been restrained.

Whether if the bill had contained allegations similar to those which were found in the case of *Carson* v. *Ury*, *supra*, it might have been maintained, we have no occasion now to consider.

Bill dismissed.

PHŒNIX NATIONAL BANK of Providence

v.

Alfred H. BATCHELLER *et al.*

(......Mass.......)

1. When a state court has yielded its opinion and adopted that of the United States Supreme Court upon a given subject, and such decision has been acquiesced in for many years, it will not be departed from unless the court is very sure it is wrong, and also that the United

NOTE.—*Insolvent Laws have no extraterritorial efficacy.*

It is the general rule that Insolvent Laws have no extraterritorial efficacy, and are wholly ineffectual against nonresidents of the State, even though the contract, by its terms, was to be performed in the State granting the discharge, unless the nonresident creditor voluntarily becomes a party to the insolvent proceedings, or claims or accepts a dividend thereunder. Ogden v. Saunders,

See also 16 L. R. A. 159; 28 L. R. A. 451.

States Court either will not regard the state decision as subject to review by it or will change its own decision.

2. **A discharge under State Insolvency Laws** will not release existing debts due to nonresident creditors who do not come in and prove their claims in the insolvency proceedings.

3. **There is nothing in the Massachusetts Insolvency Law indicating an intent** to refuse foreign creditors access to the local courts to enforce their claims after a discharge as a merely local rule of procedure, or otherwise than as a consequence of the substantive right having been barred by the discharge; hence since the right cannot be barred the action may be maintained.

(June, 1890.)

REPORT from the Superior Court for Suffolk County of a suit brought by a foreign creditor to enforce payment of its claim by a debtor who had been discharged in insolvency. *Judgment for plaintiff.*

The case sufficiently appears in the opinion.

Mr. **Lauriston L. Scaife** for plaintiff.

Messrs. **John Lowell, M. F. Dickinson, Jr.,** and **Hollis R. Bailey,** for defendants:

In the courts of Massachusetts, if not elsewhere, said discharge in insolvency constitutes a good defense to any action upon the note in question.

Pub. Stat. chap. 157, § 81; Stat. 1884, chap. 236, § 9.

Previous to *Kelley* v. *Drury*, 9 Allen, 27, it was settled in Massachusetts that a discharge in insolvency, obtained in Massachusetts by a resident of Massachusetts, was a good defense to an action on a contract made and to be performed here, even though the plaintiff was a nonresident.

Scribner v. *Fisher*, 2 Gray, 43; *Burrall* v. *Rice*, 5 Gray, 539.

Baldwin v. *Hale*, 68 U. S. 1 Wall. 223 (17 L. ed. 531), which *Kelley* v. *Drury* follows, was decided on no constitutional ground.

See *Baldwin* v. *Bank of Newbury*, 68 U. S. 1 Wall. 239 (17 L. ed. 535); *Ogden* v. *Saunders*, 24 U. S. 12 Wheat. 279 (6 L. ed. 628); *Gilman* v. *Lockwood*, 71 U. S. 4 Wall. 409 (18 L. ed. 432).

The question involved in the case was one of comity, and not of right.

The views of the United States courts on this matter of comity or international law have long been different from those of the courts of Massachusetts.

Marsh v. *Putnam*, 3 Gray, 551.

The laws which subsist at the time and place of making a contract enter into and form a part of it, as if they were expressly referred to or incorporated in its terms.

Edwards v. *Kearzey*, 96 U. S. 601 (24 L. ed. 797); *United States* v. *Quincy*, 71 U. S. 4 Wall. 550 (18 L. ed. 409).

By international law a debt is discharged by a certificate in bankruptcy duly granted at the place where the contract was made; *a fortiori* if it was expressly made payable in the same place.

Story, Confl. L. § 340; Westlake, Private Internat. Law, § 225; *Gardner* v. *Houghton*, 2 Best & S. 743; *Mansfield* v. *Andrews*, 41 Me. 591; *Peck* v. *Hibbard*, 26 Vt. 698; *May* v. *Breed*, 7 Cush. 15; *Mather* v. *Bush*, 16 Johns. 233.

The courts of a State or country are bound to obey the command of its Legislature, whether it agrees with international law or not, unless the Legislature has exceeded its constitutional power.

Story, Confl. L. § 348; *Murray* v. *De Rottenham*, 6 Johns. Ch. 52, 2 N. Y. Ch. L. ed. 52; *Sidaway* v. *Hay*, 3 Barn. & C. 12; *Ellis* v. *M'Henry*, L. R. 6 C. P. 228.

Accordingly it has been held that our late Bankrupt Law discharged a debt held by a foreigner who took no part in the proceedings.

Ruiz v. *Eickerman*, 5 Fed. Rep. 790; *Pattison* v. *Wilbur*, 10 R. I. 449.

The plaintiff is not deprived of any rights under this contract, since it still has all that it ever had. That has happened which the parties contemplated might happen: the debtors have failed, and obtained a discharge under Massachusetts laws, and this discharge is a good defense against any action in the state courts of Massachusetts.

See *Blanchard* v. *Russell*, 13 Mass. 1, 5, 6; *United States* v. *Quincy* and *Edwards* v. *Kearzey, supra.*

Holmes, *J.*, delivered the opinion of the court:

This is an action by a Rhode Island National Bank upon a promissory note payable in Massachusetts, and made here by the defendants, citizens of this State. The defense is a discharge in insolvency in this State. It is admitted that the plaintiff did not prove its claim upon the note, and the only question is whether, under these circumstances, the discharge is a bar. It was argued for the defendant that the decisions of the Supreme Court of the United States, that discharges in such cases are not generally valid against citizens of other States, do not go upon any constitutional ground, but upon mistaken views of what is called private international law, and therefore are not binding upon us; and we were asked to reconsider *Kelley* v. *Drury*, 9 Allen, 27, in which this court yielded its earlier expressed opinion and followed the precedent of *Baldwin* v. *Hale*, 68 U. S. 1 Wall. 223 [17 L. ed. 531]. See also *Guernsey* v. *Wood*, 130 Mass. 503; *Maxwell* v. *Cochran*, 136 Mass. 73.

There is no dispute that the letter of the discharge and of our Statute covers the plaintiff's claim. Pub. Stat. chap. 157, §§ 80, 81.

And the argument in favor of giving them

25 U. S. 12 Wheat. 215 (6 L. ed. 606); Cook v. Moffat, 5 How. 309 (12 L. ed. 166); Boyle v. Zacharie, 31 U. S. 6 Pet. 348 (8 L. ed. 423); Baldwin v. Hale, 68 U. S. 1 Wall. 223 (17 L. ed. 531); Gilman v. Lockwood, 71 U. S. 4 Wall. 409 (18 L. ed. 432); Kelley v. Drury, 9 Allen, 27; Soule v. Chase, 39 N. Y. 342; Donnelly v. Corbett, 7 N. Y. 500; Smith v. Gardner, 4 Bosw. 54; Ballard v. Webster, 9 Abb. Pr. 404; Canada Southern R. Co. v. Gebhard, 109 U. S. 545 (27 L. ed. 1027); Newton v. Hagerman, 10 Sawy. 462; Satterthwaite v. Abercrombie, 23 Blatchf. 309, 24 Fed. Rep. 544; Stevenson v. King, 2 Cliff. 3; Springer v. Foster, 2 Story, 387; Cleveland, P. & A. R. Co. v. Pennsylvania, 82 U. S. 15 Wall. 326 (21 L. ed. 189); Van Glahn v. Varrenne, 1 Dill. 519; Letchford v. Convillon, 20 Fed. Rep. 609; Torrens v. Hammond, 4 Hughes, 600; Mather v. Nesbit, 4 McCrary, 506; Mississippi Mills Co. v. Ranlett, 19 Fed. Rep. 196.

effect according to their letter is that, unless the Statute is void, we are bound to follow it; that the law of the place where the contract is made, and is to be performed, which is in force at the time of making and for performing it, enters into the contract so far as to settle everywhere what acts done at that place shall discharge it (*May* v. *Breed*, 7 Cush. 15); and that a discharge in accordance with that law cannot be said to impair the obligation of a contract which contemplated it, or to deprive the contractee of property without due process of law, when that property was created subject to destruction in that way. We express no opinion upon the weight of this argument. Although it formerly prevailed with this court (*Scribner* v. *Fisher*, 2 Gray, 43; *Burrall* v. *Rice*, 5 Gray, 539), it may be that there is a distinction as to a discharge by legal proceedings. It may be that statutes providing for a discharge by an insolvency court do not enter into the contract in such a sense as to bind the contractee to adopt and submit himself to the jurisdiction as an implied condition of the promisor's undertaking. It does not follow, because the discharge, if effective, does not impair the obligation of the contract, that absolute liability to it is a part of the substantive obligation. The substantive promise and the obligation of the contract are different things. And apart from this consideration it may be that by sound principle the plaintiff is to be taken to have subjected itself to Massachusetts proceedings only to the extent that if the Massachusetts courts could acquire jurisdiction over it in the ordinary modes by which jurisdiction of the person is acquired, it would be bound everywhere by a discharge granted here.

However this may be, we see no sufficient reason for departing from what has been accepted as the law for a quarter of a century. We agree that, consistently with our duty, we cannot yield our opinion upon new questions not subject to the final jurisdiction of the Supreme Court of the United States solely out of a desire for uniformity. But when we are asked to overrule a decision of our own court which has been acquiesced in for so long, we should have to be very sure before doing so, not only that the decision was wrong, but also that the Supreme Court of the United States, whatever we may think about it, either would not regard our decision as subject to review by them, or would abandon opinions which they have expressed repeatedly and down to the latest volume of their Reports.

We should hesitate to overrule *Kelley* v. *Drury*, even if we were ready to say that we disagreed with the principle of *Baldwin* v. *Hale*, and that we thought our decision not subject to review. For when in a particular case the precedents are settled in favor of uniformity, the fact that they do conform to the decisions of the Supreme Court of the United States is a most powerful secondary reason for not disturbing them and would be likely to outweigh our private opinions upon the original matter. There is, too, a particular reason for uniformity in the present case, because it is manifest that, practically at least, the general validity of the discharge,—that is, its effect outside this Commonwealth,—depends upon the decision of other courts than this, and that the decision of the United States court upon that question is of more importance than that of any other. The often-repeated view of the Supreme Court of the United States is that discharges like the present are void for want of jurisdiction, and that statutes purporting to authorize them are beyond the power of the States to pass. *Baldwin* v. *Hale*, 68 U. S. 1 Wall. 223, 233 [17 L. ed. 531, 534]; *Baldwin* v. *Bank of Newbury*, 68 U. S. 1 Wall. 234 [17 L. ed. 534]; *Gilman* v. *Lockwood*, 71 U. S. 4 Wall. 409 [18 L. ed. 432]; *Denny* v. *Bennett*, 128 U. S. 489, 497 [32 L. ed. 491, 494]; *Cole* v. *Cunningham*, 133 U. S. 107, 115 [33 L. ed. 539, 542].

Whether that court would regard a decision to the contrary by a state court as subject to review by them upon constitutional grounds does not appear very clearly from any language of theirs which has been called to our attention, unless it be the following, repeated in *Baldwin* v. *Hale*, 68 U. S. 1 Wall. 231 [17 L. ed. 533], from *Ogden* v. *Saunders*, 24 U. S. 12 Wheat. 213, 369 [6 L. ed. 606, 659]: "But when in the exercise of that power, the States pass beyond their own limits and the rights of their own citizens, and act upon the rights of citizens of other States, there arises a conflict of sovereign power and a collision with the judicial powers granted to the United States, which renders the exercise of such a power incompatible with the rights of other States, and with the Constitution of the United States." This is somewhat emphasized as the deliberate view of the court, not only by its original mode of statement, but by their adhesion to it after the dissent of *Chief Justice* Taney in *Cook* v. *Moffat*, 46 U. S. 5 How. 295, 310 [12 L. ed. 159, 166]. See *Scribner* v. *Fisher*, 2 Gray, 43, 47.

This language certainly gives the impression that our decision would be regarded as subject to review, possibly on the ground of an implied restriction on the power to pass Insolvent Laws reserved to the States (*Denny* v. *Bennett*, 128 U. S. 489, 498 [32 L. ed. 491, 495]); possibly on the ground that the discharge would impair the obligation of contracts with persons not within the jurisdiction (*Cook* v. *Moffat*, 46 U. S. 5 How. 295, 308 [12 L. ed. 159, 165]); possibly by reason of the Fourteenth Amendment (*Pennoyer* v. *Neff*, 95 U. S. 714 [24 L. ed. 565]); possibly on some vaguer ground. We feel the force of the reasoning quoted from *Stoddard* v. *Harrington*, 100 Mass. 87, 89, but that case did not profess to weaken the authority of *Kelley* v. *Drury*, and moreover the question which we are now considering is not what would be our own opinion, but what seems to be the opinion of the Supreme Court of the United States.

The decision in *Kelley* v. *Drury* did not go upon any nice inquiry whether it was subject to review, but upon the ground that this court deferred to the decision of the Supreme Court of the United States, that discharges like the present were not binding outside the jurisdiction, and that, this being so, a discrimination should not be made in favor of our citizens in proceedings in the state court in distinction from proceedings in the courts of the United States.

This last proposition was conceded by the senior counsel for the defendant. But as some doubt was thrown upon it in the printed brief we repeat what was again intimated in *Murphy*

v. *Manning*, 134 Mass. 488, that there is nothing in the law affecting the question before us which indicates an intent to refuse foreign creditors access to the courts of Massachusetts as a merely local rule of procedure, or otherwise than as a consequence of the substantive right having been barred by the discharge. The form of the discharge in Pub. Stat., chap. 157, § 80, and the language of § 81, address themselves directly to the substantive right and declare the debtor discharged from the specified debts. It being settled that the plaintiff's debt is not barred, an action can be maintained to recover it in the state court.

Judgment for plaintiff.

CONNECTICUT SUPREME COURT OF ERRORS.

William R. CONE *et al.*, Exrs., etc., of James R. Averill, Deceased,

v.

Austin C. DUNHAM *et al.*, Exrs. of Austin Dunham, Deceased, *et al.*, *Appts.*

(....Conn.....)

1. **Express continuing trusts** are excluded from the operation of Statutes of Limitation, while implied trusts are subject thereto.
2. **Leaving corporate stock in the possession and name of the seller,** the sale being evidenced only by a declaration thereof in a receipt given for the money paid, and there being no agreement as to the future disposition of the stock or the dividends thereon, creates an implied trust in the seller which is enforceable at law and subject to the operation of the Statute of Limitations.
3. **There is no legal presumption of the** death of a person who has left home and has not since been heard from until after the expiration of seven years.
4. **The pendency of an appeal** from an order admitting a will to probate will not excuse a delay of over two years on the part of executors who have qualified thereunder to present for payment claims of testator against the estates of other deceased persons.
5. **A claim against a deceased person's estate** is forever barred if it is not exhibited within the time limited by the court of probate for the presentation of such claims. Disability of claimant is no excuse for failure to present a claim.
6. **An award** made upon a submission to arbitrators by executors of a question as to the ownership of certain corporate stock which was in the possession of testator and had been distributed under his will before the agreement to arbitrate was made is not admissible in evidence against the distributees in an action to recover possession of the stock.

(June, 1890.)

NOTE.—*Statute of Limitations; trust not within bar of.*

Trusts which are mere creatures of a court of equity are not within the Statute. Kane v. Bloodgood, 7 Johns. Ch. 90, 2 N. Y. Ch. L. ed. 231; McClane v. Shepherd, 21 N. J. Eq. 80.

The trusts not within the Statute are those which are the creatures of courts of equity, and not within the cognizance of a law court; and as to those other trusts which are the ground of an action at law the Statute is as much a bar in one court as the other. Buckingham v. Ludlum, 37 N. J. Eq. 144; Young v. Wiseman, 7 T. B. Mon. 270, 18 Am. Dec. 177. See Wanmaker v. Van Buskirk, 1 N. J. Eq. 685; Morse v. Oliver, 14 N. J. Eq. 259; McClane v. Shepherd, 21 N. J. Eq. 76; Roosevelt v. Mark, 6 Johns. Ch. 266, 2 N. Y. Ch. L. ed. 121.

To exempt a trust from the bar of the Statute, it must be a direct trust and of the kind belonging exclusively to the jurisdiction of equity. People v. Oran, 11 West. Rep. 422, 121 Ill. 650.

Trusts not affected by Statutes of Limitation are those technical and continuing trusts not at all cognizable at law, but which fall within the peculiar and exclusive jurisdiction of courts of equity. Tinnen v. Mebane, 10 Tex. 252; Cocke v. McGinnis, Mart. & Y. 363.

Trusts intended by courts of equity not to be reached by the Statute are those technical and continuing trusts which are not cognizable at law, but fall within the proper, peculiar and exclusive jurisdiction of this court. Love v. Watkins, 40 Cal. 547, 570; Bourne v. Hall, 10 R. I. 144; Finney v. Cochran, 1 Watts & S. 112, 37 Am. Dec. 452. See Prevost v. Gratz, 19 U. S. 6 Wheat. 481 (5 L. ed. 311); Raymond v. Simonson, 4 Blackf. 77; Payne v. Hathaway, 3 Vt. 212; Cook v. Williams, 2 N. J. Eq. 209; Baylor v. Dejarnette, 13 Gratt. 152; Hemenway v. Gates, 5 Pick. 321; Greenwood v. Greenwood, 5 Md. 334; Clifton v. Haig, 4 Desaus. 330; Farnam v. Brooks, 9 Pick. 212; Staniford v. Tuttle, 4 Vt. 82; Collard v. Tuttle, 4 Vt. 491; Codman v. Rogers, 10 Pick. 112; Oliver v. Piatt, 44 U. S. 3 How. 411 (11 L. ed. 658); Hostetter v. Hollinger, 10 Cent. Rep. 771, 117 Pa. 606, 21 W. N. C. 73.

It does not apply to actions founded on a direct or strict trust such as are not cognizable at law, but fall within the proper, peculiar and exclusive jurisdiction of a court of equity. Partridge v. Wells, 30 N. J. Eq. 179.

The custodian of a fund which has been created for the benefit of a particular person, the contributors having wholly relinquished their control over it, is within the operation of the Statute of Limitations. Hostetter v. Hollinger, *supra.*

No lapse of time bars a direct or an express trust.

The rule is well settled that no lapse of time is a bar to a direct trust, as between executor and trustee and *cestui que trust.* Robison v. Robison, 5 Lans. 169; Bigelow v. Catlin, 50 Vt. 410; Goodrich v. Pendleton, 3 Johns. Ch. 384, 1 N. Y. Ch. L. ed. 657; Chicago & E. I. R. Co. v. Hay, 7 West. Rep. 720, 119 Ill. 493; Decouche v. Savetier, 3 Johns. Ch. 190, 1 N. Y. Ch. L. ed. 587; Coster v. Murray, 5 Johns. Ch. 522, 1 N. Y. Ch. L. ed. 1162; Beckford v. Wade, 17 Ves. Jr. 87; Parmele v. McGinty, 52 Miss. 481; Cholmondeley v. Clinton, 2 Jac. & W. 1.

The Statute of Limitations is not a bar to a trust where the *cestui que trust* is the trustee's wife. Rusling v. Rusling, 7 Cent. Rep. 129, 42 N. J. Eq. 594.

Money received by the husband from his wife's separate estate was received by him as statutory trustee, against which the Statute of Limitations would not run. Comstock's App. 4 New Eng. Rep. 592, 55 Conn. 214.

Limitation does not run in favor of a trustee as against his *cestui que trust* while the latter is in pos-

APPEAL by defendants from a judgment of the Superior Court for Hartford County in favor of plaintiff in an action brought to recover possession of certain corporate stock alleged to have been the property of plaintiff's testator. *Reversed.*

The facts are fully stated in the opinion.

Messrs. **A. P. Hyde** and **C. J. Cole,** for appellants:

The limitations against an estate are an absolute bar and there is no provision for suspension during the disability of the plaintiff.

Atwood v. *Rhode Island Agricultural Bank,* 2 R. I. 196; *Pratt* v. *Northam,* 5 Mason, 95; Lewin, Tr. p. 866; *Morgan* v. *Hamlet,* 113 U. S. 449 (28 L. ed. 1043); *Rowell* v. *Patterson,* 76 Me. 196; *Hall* v. *Bumstead,* 20 Pick. 8; Schouler, Exrs. § 419.

The Statute of Limitations as to claims against estates is highly favored.

Ang. Lim. 5th ed. p. 161; 3 Wms. Exrs. 2184; *Sugar River Bank* v. *Fairbanks,* 49 N. H. 139.

Equity follows the analogies of the law in the matter of the Statute of Limitations.

2 Lewin, Tr. 864; *Kane* v. *Bloodgood,* 7 Johns. Ch. 113, 2 N. Y. Ch. L. ed. 239; *Belknap* v. *Gleason,* 11 Conn. 162; Lewin, Tr. 1159, *note,* and cases cited.

The plaintiff cannot, by a mere change of forum, avoid the limitation of the Statutes. If he has two remedies, one at law and the other in equity, the bar which operates in one also operates in the other.

Kane v. *Bloodgood, supra; Johnson* v. *Smith,* 27 Mo. 591; *Governor* v. *Woodworth,* 63 Ill. 254; *Barton* v. *Dickens,* 48 Pa. 518; *Prewett* v. *Buckingham,* 28 Miss. 95; *Zacharias* v. *Zacharias,* 23 Pa. 452; *Trecothick* v. *Austin,* 4 Mason, 30; *Hayward* v. *Gunn,* 82 Ill. 385; *Johnson* v. *Ames,* 11 Pick. 182; *Morgan* v. *Hamlet, supra.*

If the trust is implied or constructive, that is, created by construction, implication or by operation of law, the Statute runs and operates as a bar, because in such cases the holding is adverse.

Perry, Tr. § 865, p. 786; *Hart's App.* 32 Conn. 537; *Wilmerding* v. *Russ,* 33 Conn. 76; *Phalen* v. *Clark,* 19 Conn. 434; *Belknap* v. *Gleason, supra; Burditt* v. *Grew,* 8 Pick. 108; *Jones* v. *Lightfoot,* 10 Ala. 17; *Trecothick* v. *Austin,* 4 Mason, 16; Ang. Lim. §178, p. 169; *Strimpfler* v. *Roberts,* 18 Pa. 300; *Prewett* v. *Buckingham, supra; Manion* v. *Titsworth,* 18 B. Mon. 582; *Barton* v. *Dickens* and *Hayward* v. *Gunn, supra; Wells* v. *Perry,* 62 Mo. 573; *McClane* v. *Shepherd,* 21 N. J. Eq. 76; *Ashhurst's App.* 60 Pa. 290; *Johnson* v. *Smith* and *Zacharias* v. *Zacharias, supra; Murdock* v. *Hughes,* 7 Smedes & M. 219; *Kane* v. *Bloodgood,* 7 Johns. Ch. 90, 2 N. Y. Ch. L. ed. 231; 2 Lewin, Tr. pp. 863, 864.

In cases of express, technical and continuing trusts, if the trust be repudiated, then, the holding being adverse, the Statute runs from the time of repudiation.

Perry, Tr. § 868, p. 785, and cases cited; *Wickliffe* v. *Lexington,* 11 B. Mon. 161; Ang. Lim. §174, p. 164.

The eight shares as held by Dunham, if held in trust, were held as a deposit or bailment, and the claim was recognizable in a court of law.

3 Bl. Com. p. 431; *Sturt* v. *Mellish,* 2 Atk. 610; *Kane* v. *Bloodgood,* 7 Johns. Ch. 110, 2 N.

---

session of the trust estate. Gilbert v. Sleeper, 71 Cal. 290; Jackson v. Jackson (Pa.) 7 Cent. Rep. 850.

A pledgee who retains the pledged property may at any time be compelled to restore it, upon tender of the debt; and the Statute does not run against it. Humphrey v. Clearfield Co. Nat. Bank, 5 Cent. Rep. 135, 113 Pa. 417.

The Statute does not apply in favor of a trustee as to funds held in trust. Lawrence v. Warwick (N. J.) 3 Cent. Rep. 470.

Since the possession of the trustee is the possession of the *cestui que trust,* and no action at law will lie by the latter against the former for any money payments due, the Statute of Limitations does not apply to express trusts. Dyer v. Waters (N. J.) Feb. 3, 1890.

The Statute of Limitations is not a bar to an action, founded on an express trust, to compel an accounting. Anderson v. Meredith, 10 Ky. L. Rep. 460; Reeves v. Beekman, 7 Cent. Rep. 453, 42 N. J. Eq. 613.

An action against a trustee to compel an accounting and for judgment for the amount of trust funds converted is not subject to the six years' Statute of Limitations. Colglazier v. Colglazier, 117 Ind. 460.

The Statute of Limitations does not apply in cases of direct and express trusts or cases of fraud. App v. Dreisbach, 2 Rawle, 287, 21 Am. Dec. 450.

Deposit; a direct trust.

Every deposit is a direct trust; and every person who receives money to be paid to another, or to be applied to a particular purpose, is a trustee. App v. Dreisbach, 2 Rawle, 287, receding from Coster v. Murray, 5 Johns. Ch. 522, 1 N. Y. Ch. L. ed. 1162.

He is a trustee in a limited sense, and no other; so the corporation is a trustee of the dividend unpaid to the stockholder. King v. Paterson & H. R. R. Co. 29 N. J. L. 507.

Where defendant bank took certain stocks from the trustee thereof and held them, and afterwards the proceeds of their sale, as a trust fund, under a trust to return them to the trustee, the latter and the *cestui que trust* both had an equitable remedy against defendant which could not be affected by the Statute of Limitations. Blake v. Traders Nat. Bank, 4 New Eng. Rep. 624, 145 Mass. 13.

Executor and administrator as trustees.

An administrator, being a trustee, cannot set up the Statute of Limitations in bar to the next of kin, or persons entitled to the distribution of assets. Rubey v. Barnett, 12 Mo. 3, 49 Am. Dec. 115.

A cause of action against an administrator does not depend upon the debts, but upon their collection; and the application of the Statute to the original debts has no bearing. Swift v. Martin, 2 West. Rep. 146, 19 Mo. App. 488.

The Statute will not bar action for a legacy against an executor or an administrator holding assets. Collins v. Collins, 2 New Eng. Rep. 35, 140 Mass. 502.

The rule that the Statute will not bar a suit for a legacy applies only when the suit is against an executor or another who is charged by the will with an express trust in relation to the legacy. Millington v. Hill, 47 Ark. 301.

The acceptance of a devise binds the devisee personally for the payment of a legacy charged upon the devise. But the obligation is an implied one, not in writing, and an action on it is barred by the Statute of Limitations of three years. *Ibid.*

It seems that where an executor has settled his account, exhibiting a balance in his hands, he ceases to be a trustee, and becomes a debtor for

Y. Ch. L. ed. 238; *Murray* v. *Coster*, 20 Johns. 576; *Trecothick* v. *Austin*, 4 Mason, 30; 5 Wait, Act. and Def. 170, § 2; *Wilson* v. *Little*, 2 N. Y. 443; *Ayres* v. *French*, 41 Conn. 142; *Seymour* v. *Ives*, 46 Conn. 113; *Derome* v. *Vose*, 140 Mass. 575.

Ignorance of his rights on the part of a person against whom the Statute has begun to run will not suspend its operation.

2 Lewin, Tr. p. 866; *Bank of Hartford County* v. *Waterman*, 26 Conn. 324.

Messrs. **George G. Sill, Lewis Sperry** and **George Eliot Sill**, for appellees:

The Statute of Limitations does not affect an express and subsisting trust.

Wilmerding v. *Russ*, 33 Conn. 67; *Philippi* v. *Philippe*, 115 U. S. 151 (29 L. ed. 337); Perry, Tr. § 863; 2 Lewin, Tr. p. 863; *Snyder* v. *McComb*, 39 Fed. Rep. 292.

This is an express trust.

Pom. Eq. § 152.

Property once impressed with an express trust always remains an express trust into whosesoever hands it may pass, except a bona fide purchaser without notice and for value.

2 Pom. Eq. § 1048.

Averill may have been dead when Dunham died. If he was and it was unknown, the Statute of Limitations did not begin to run against his claim until his death was legally presumed and executors were qualified to act.

Wood, Lim. p. 254, § 117; *Hobart* v. *Connecticut Turnp. Co.* 15 Conn. 145; *Amy* v. *Watertown*, 130 U. S. 320 (32 L. ed. 954).

That executors have the power to make a submission is established beyond controversy.

Alling v. *Munson*, 2 Conn. 694; Schouler, Exrs. §§ 387, 389, and *note 2;* 1 Encyclop. Law, p. 658, and *note 1;* Wms. Exrs. pp. 1800, 1801, *note; Chadbourn* v. *Chadbourn*, 9 Allen, 173; *Bean* v. *Farnam*, 6 Pick. 269; Rev. Stat. § 595.

Defendants are bound by the award.

1 Encyclop. Law, p. 711, and *note 2; Strodes* v. *Patton*, 1 Brock. 228; *Wheatley* v. *Martin*, 6 Leigh, 62.

An award of an arbitrator is conclusive upon the parties as to all the facts submitted and decided by the award.

Curley v. *Dean*, 4 Conn. 259.

Seymour, *J.*, delivered the opinion of the court:

It appears from the findings in this case that on and before August 14, 1850, Austin Dunham owned twenty-one shares of the Ætna Life Insurance Company's stock, on which $10 a share had been paid. On or about said date he "sold to, or subscribed or bought for, James R. Averill, eight shares of said stock, and said Averill paid him therefor $10 a share and took a receipt as follows, viz.:

Hartford, Aug. 14, 1850. Received from James R. Averill eighty dollars, being the first installment on eight shares of the Ætna Life Insurance Company's stock standing in my name, but owned by him and he remaining responsible for the balance of the installments when called in. Austin Dunham.

The object of said Averill was to conceal his interest in said stock, and it continued standing in the name of said Austin Dunham on the books of the Ætna Life Insurance Com-

---

such balance, to the legatees; and is therefore protected by the Act of Limitations. App v. Dreisbach, 2 Rawle, 302, 21 Am. Dec. 450.

Limitation of rule; repudiation of trust.

The rule is subject to limitations, and whenever a trustee sets up an open, public, adverse claim against a *cestui que trust*, and denies that the trust any longer subsists, or where a trustee recognizes another person as *cestui que trust*, long possession and continued enjoyment of the property, under such recognition, will be a bar in equity. Needles v. Martin, 33 Md. 619. See Robinson v. Hook, 4 Mason, 152; Farnam v. Brooks, 9 Pick. 212.

The general rule is that when a trustee unequivocally repudiates the trust, and claims the estate as his own, and such repudiation and claim are brought to the notice or knowledge of the *cestui que trust*, the Statute of Limitations begins to run from the time such knowledge is brought home to him. United States v. Taylor, 104 U. S. 222 (26 L. ed. 723); Perkins v. Cartmell, 4 Harr. (Del.) 270, 42 Am. Dec. 753; Ricords v. Watkins, 56 Mo. 554. See Willison v. Watkins, 28 U. S. 3 Pet. 52 (7 L. ed. 600); Boone v. Chiles, 35 U. S. 10 Pet. 223 (9 L. ed. 404).

The possession of the trustee not being adverse to the *cestui que trust*, as between them there is no limitation of time, unless there is a clear repudiation of the trust, brought home to the party so as to require him to act as upon a clearly asserted adverse title. Merriam v. Hassam, 96 Mass. 522; Wright v. Ross, 36 Cal. 433. See Baker v. Whiting, 3 Sumn. 486; Boone v. Chiles, *supra;* Keaton v. Greenwood, 8 Ga. 103; Kemp v. Westbrook, 1 Ves. Sr. 278.

Although length of time is no bar to a trust clearly established, and express trusts are not within the Statute of Limitations, time begins to run as soon as the trust is openly disavowed by the trustee insisting upon an adverse right and interest which is clearly and unequivocally made known to the *cestui que trust*. Speidel v. Henrici, 120 U. S. 377 (30 L. ed. 718); Reynolds v. Sumner (Ill.) 1 L. R. A. 327, 12 West. Rep. 327; Thomas v. Marry, 12 West. Rep. 672, 113 Ind. 83; Ward v. Harvey, 10 West. Rep. 223, 111 Ind. 471; Horne v. Ingraham, 14 West. Rep. 567, 125 Ill. 198.

A *cestui que trust* cannot be held to have slept upon his right to relief in equity against the trustee until the latter has assumed some position of antagonism to, or denied, all the former's rights, of which he has notice. Dyer v. Waters (N. J.) Feb. 3, 1890.

A mere retention by the trustee of a portion of the income of the trust, with the consent of the *cestui que trust*, and without any pretense that it is so retained upon a claim of right, does not produce such a hostile attitude as will set the Statute of Limitations in motion. *Ibid.*

Parties to administrator's proceeding to sell land cannot recover proceeds of the sale on the ground that, thirty years before, intestate had invested their money with his own in the purchase of the land, taking title in his own name, where it appears that there was an open disavowal of the trust twenty years prior to the action. Ward v. Harvey, *supra.*

The Statute of Limitations does not run in favor of a trustee under a valid parol agreement to hold property in trust, until he repudiates it. Broder v. Conklin, 77 Cal. 330.

Where jurisdiction concurrent in law and equity.

Where jurisdiction is concurrent the Statute runs. Newsom v. Bartholomew Co. Comrs. 1 West.

pany down to the time of his death. There was nothing on the books of said company, or on the certificates of stock, or on the books of said Dunham, or on any of his papers, to indicate that said Averill had any claim or demand against any of said stock, and no notice was given to said insurance company that he had any interest in or claim to the same, and said stock was never separated from other stock owned by said Dunham, but remained in said Dunham's name with the knowledge and consent of said Averill, who never made any demand for the delivery thereof. Between August 14, 1850, and February 25, 1874, additional installments, amounting to fifty-eight per cent, were paid upon said stock, to wit, thirty per cent in dividends and twenty-eight per cent in cash, which cash was paid by said Dunham and repaid to him by said Averill.

On February 25, 1874, the remaining thirty-two per cent was called in and paid by said Dunham, who then held fifty-eight shares. He has since received from said insurance company, in cash dividends on said stock, enough to repay said thirty-two per cent installment as paid by him, and the same has been repaid in no other way.

About September 15, 1875, Mr. Averill made his will, and named Wm. R. Cone, Roland Mather and Robert E. Day, the plaintiffs in this suit, as his executors. About September 20, 1875, he left Hartford, and has never returned or been heard from. Just before leaving he delivered to said Robert E. Day a sealed envelope which contained said will and certain instructions to said Cone, Mather and Day, written upon a separate paper.

September 30, 1882, when the presumption of his death, arising from his seven years' absence without having been seen or heard from, was established, said Averill's will was probated and his executors duly qualified. An appeal was taken from the probate of the will, which was continued in the superior court until February 17, 1885, when judgment was given for the appellees. On March 3, 1885, the executors of said Averill made demand of the executors of said Dunham for said eight shares of stock, with the increment and dividends thereon, and they refused to deliver the same.

The instructions which were in the sealed envelope delivered to Robert E. Day, and which had not been read by the parties to whom they were directed until about September 30, 1882, contained what purported to be a list of said Averill's securities, and among them the following item: "Also eight shares Ætna Life Insurance stock in name of Austin Dunham, on which $68 per share has been paid by *me*, worth $450 to $500 per share."

Austin Dunham died March 12, 1877, leaving a will, which was proved March 19, 1877, and the executors thereof qualified on said day. At his death fifty-eight shares of said insurance stock were standing in his name, including the eight shares claimed by the plaintiffs, and the defendants had no knowledge that any right or claim existed, or was claimed to exist, against said shares or any part thereof.

May 12, 1877, the executors of Mr. Dunham filed an inventory of his estate in the court of probate, and included in it the whole of said fifty-eight shares of stock, and then claimed, and ever since have claimed, that the whole of said stock belonged to said estate absolutely.

The court of probate limited six months

Rep. 476, 108 Ind. 526; Carpenter v. Canal Co. 35 Ohio St. 317; Jones v. Jones, 91 Ind. 379; *Re* Accounting of Neilley, 95 N. Y. 389; Wilmerding v. Russ, 33 Conn. 77. See Robinson v. Hook, 4 Mason, 152; Tinnen v. Mebane, 10 Tex. 252; Wingate v. Wingate, 11 Tex. 433; Hovenden v. Lord Annesley, 2 Sch. & Lef. 607; Lockey v. Lockey, Prec. in Ch. 518; Murray v. Coster, 20 Johns. 576; Smith v. Calloway, 7 Blackf. 86.

A distinction has been taken where the trust is a continuing trust between the parties, or where the trust has been created by will; in such cases the Statute will not apply. Albrecht v. Wolf, 58 Ill. 190; Finney v. Cochran, 1 Watts & S. 112.

It is a case where there is concurrent jurisdiction, the Statute may be pleaded with the same effect in equity as at law. Dugan v. Gittings, 3 Gill, 138, 43 Am. Dec. 317.

In such case the Statute comes *in proprio vigore* and must receive the same construction, and can be answered by no other disabilities than if the remedy had been sought at law. M'Crea v. Purmort, 16 Wend. 460; Roosevelt v. Mark, 6 Johns. Ch. 266, 2 N. Y. Ch. L. ed. 121.

Where remedies are concurrent.

Even where the jurisdiction in equity is exclusive, the limitation applies, if the remedy sought is analogous to a remedy at law. Hancock v. Harper, 86 Ill. 450. See Carpenter v. Carpenter, 70 Ill. 457; 2 Story, Eq. § 1520.

Rule applied in a case of trust which is limited in its duration, or in a case where a party has a legal remedy, and a court of law concurrent jurisdiction. The Statute operates whether the suit is at law or in chancery. Lexington & O. R. Co. v. Bridges, 7 B. Mon. 556, 46 Am. Dec. 524.

Where a party has a legal and an equitable remedy in regard to the same subject matter, courts of equity obey the law and give to the Statute the same effect and operation in the one court as in the other. Estate of Leiman, 32 Md. 225; Quayle v. Guild, 91 Ill. 384; Gelston v. Thompson, 29 Md. 600; Dugan v. Gittings, 3 Gill, 138; Hertle v. Schwartze, 3 Md. 383.

Courts of equity, equally with courts of law, are bound by the Statutes of Limitation, in all the varieties of bailment, pawns, deposits, etc., although express trusts, where there are convenient remedies in cases at law, or by bill in equity. Armstrong v. Campbell, 3 Yerg. 201; Lockey v. Lockey, Prec. in Ch. 518; Sturt v. Mellish, 2 Atk. 610; Hovenden v. Lord Annesley, 2 Sch. & Lef. 607; Cocke v. McGinnis, Mart. & Y. 361; Rowe v. Bentley, 29 Gratt. 760; Somerset Co. Bank v. Veghte, 4 Cent. Rep. 407, 42 N. J. Eq. 39.

One who is not actually a trustee, but upon whom that character is forced by a court of equity, only for the purpose of a remedy, may avail himself of the Statute. Baxter v. Moses, 77 Me. 481. See Baker v. Atlas Bank, 9 Met. 182; Peabody v. Flint, 6 Allen, 52; Farnam v. Brooks, 9 Pick. 212; Stringer's Case, L. R. 4 Ch. App. 475; *Re* Alexandra Palace Co. L. R. 21 Ch. Div. 149; Carrol v. Green, 92 U. S. 509 (23 L. ed. 738).

Exception, as to implied, constructive and resulting trusts.

The rule exempting trusts from the operation of Statutes of Limitation does not apply to a resulting trust. Dale v. Wilson, 39 Minn. 330; Ward v. Harvey, 10 West. Rep. 223, 111 Ind. 471.

Long lapse of time will defeat the enforcement of a resulting trust. Smith v. Turley, 32 W. Va. 14.

In case of an implied or constructive trust, unless

from March 19, 1877, for the presentation of claims against said estate. No claim was presented within the time so limited, either by said Averill or by any person acting for him, for said eight shares of stock or for any interest or claim therein; and no claim or demand was made, or notice of claim given, that said Averill or his estate had any interest, right or claim in or to any of said stock or the dividends thereon—either to or upon said Dunham's executors or to or upon any other person, until March 3, 1885, when the plaintiffs notified the executors of said Dunham, in writing, and demanded a transfer to them of said stock, with payment of interest and dividends thereon, together with a proper account of the same; which demand they refused to comply with.

November 18, 1878, the Ætna Life Insurance Company made a stock dividend of four shares of increased stock for each share of original stock, so that the fifty-eight shares of stock in the hands of Mr. Dunham's executors were increased to two hundred and ninety shares. July 5, 1879, and June 15, 1882, Mr. Dunham's executors distributed said two hundred and ninety shares, under the provisions of the will, to and among the defendants. Said distribution was made voluntarily and pursuant to the will, without any order of distribution by the court of probate. Mr. Dunham's estate has not been settled. A large amount of property is still in the hands of his executors and no final account has been rendered by them. Since said distribution further stock dividends have been made by said insurance company, which would increase the eight shares mentioned in the writing of August 14, 1850, to sixty-six and two thirds shares.

After the refusal of the executors of said Dunham to comply with the demand made upon them March 3, 1885, by the executors of said Averill, this suit was commenced, namely, on November 24, 1886, against said Dunham's executors and those to whom said stock had been distributed as hereinbefore stated. The superior court rendered a joint judgment against all the defendants, that they deliver and transfer at once to the plaintiffs sixty-six shares of the capital stock of the Ætna Life Insurance Company, and also pay to the plaintiffs the sum of $5,485.20, together with the further sum of $182, the same being the value of two thirds of one share of said stock, and all dividends which may hereafter be declared and paid on the above shares until the delivery thereof to the plaintiffs as adjudged, and their costs, taxed at ——— dollars; from which judgment an appeal is taken to this court.

Among the defendants' reasons for appeal are the following, viz.: "Because the court held that the plaintiffs were not barred by their failure, and the failure of their testator, to present their claim against the estate of Austin Dunham within the time limited by the court of probate, and were not barred by their neglect and failure to bring their suit within the limitations of the Statute; and because the court held that the plaintiffs' claim and suit were not barred by the Statutes of Limitation, either general or special."

The pleadings raised these issues; they were ably argued by counsel, and, inasmuch as, in our judgment, a correct decision of them is

---

there has been a fraudulent concealment of the cause of action, lapse of time is as complete a bar in equity as at law. Speidel v. Henrici, 120 U. S. 377 (30 L. ed. 718).

The liability growing out of an implied trust which the law would raise for the purposes of justice is within the ordinary rules of limitation. Mills v. Mills, 115 N. Y. 80; Kane v. Bloodgood, 7 Johns. Ch. 90, 2 N. Y. Ch. L. ed. 231; Lammer v. Stoddard, 103 N. Y. 672.

In cases of implied trusts, relief is refused to parties who come into a court of equity after long acquiescence. Hendrickson v. Hendrickson, 8 Cent. Rep. 209, 42 N. J. Eq. 657.

The Statute begins to run from the time the wrong was committed, by which the party became chargeable as trustee by implication. Lammer v. Stoddard, *supra*. See Wilmerding v. Russ, 33 Conn. 67; Ashhurst's App. 60 Pa. 290; McClane v. Shepherd, 21 N. J. Eq. 76; Decouche v. Savetier, 3 Johns. Ch. 190, 216, 1 N.Y. Ch. L. ed. 587, 597; Ward v. Smith, 3 Sandf. Ch. 592, 7 N. Y. Ch. L. ed. 968; Higgins v. Higgins, 14 Abb. N. C. 13; Clarke v. Johnston, 85 U. S. 18 Wall. 493 (21 L. ed. 904); Hecht v. Slaney, 72 Cal. 363.

The Statute of Limitations runs against an action brought by a judgment creditor of an insolvent to establish and enforce a constructive trust in land set aside to him in insolvency proceedings as a homestead; and the order setting aside the homestead being a matter of public record, plaintiff's ignorance of the fraud will not bar the running of the Statute. *Ibid.*

The six years' limitation under New York Code Civ. Proc. is a defense to an action for money had and received under circumstances raising an implied trust; otherwise with a direct or express trust. Price v. Mulford, 9 Cent. Rep. 866, 107 N. Y. 303.

In the case of a trustee *ex maleficio*, or by implication or construction of law, the Statute begins to run against the beneficiary seeking to enforce the trust from the time the wrong was committed by which the party became chargeable as trustee by implication. Lammer v. Stoddard, *supra*.

Claims against estate of decedent.

An action may be maintained against an administrator, on a claim against the estate, if commenced within two years and six months after notice of the appointment of the administrator. Gould v. Whitmore, 4 New Eng. Rep. 670, 79 Me. 383.

An action against an administrator *de bonis non* may be brought within two years from the time of his giving bond. Eddy v. Adams, 5 New Eng. Rep. 426, 145 Mass. 489.

Under the Mississippi Code all actions against executors must be brought within four years and six months after they have qualified, and by virtue of § 2172, the fact may be pleaded in any case where a bar has accrued under the Code. Gibbs v. Bunch, 63 Miss. 47.

The Statute limiting actions in assumpsit to six years begins to run in favor of executors and administrators as soon as they are qualified. They may reduce this time to three years by giving the notices provided in the last section. Knowles v. Whaley (R. I.) 1 New Eng. Rep. 150.

An executor sued more than six years after a cause of action accrued against his testator may plead the Statute. Miskey v. Miskey (Pa.) 10 Cent. Rep. 829, 20 W. N. C. 470.

He is not prevented from pleading the Statute by omission to give notice of having taken out letters. York's App. 1 Cent. Rep. 659, 110 Pa. 69.

A trust by which assets of an estate are received

decisive of the case, we shall confine ourselves mainly to their consideration.

Do the Statutes of Limitation, relied upon by the defendants, defeat the plaintiffs' right of action?

This question requires, for its correct answer, a thorough examination of the character of the trust raised between the parties by the transaction of August 14, 1850,—a transaction which, the plaintiffs claim, raised an express, technical and continuing trust, not cognizable at law, but within the proper, peculiar and exclusive jurisdiction of a court of equity, and therefore not subject to the Statutes of Limitation; and which the defendants claim, on the contrary, raised only an implied trust, cognizable at law, and therefore subject to the Statutes of Limitation.

Bouvier defines express trusts as those which are created in express terms in the deed, writing or will; and implied trusts as those which, without being expressed, are deducible from the nature of the transaction as matter of intent, or which are superinduced upon the transaction by operation of law as matters of equity, independently of the particular intention of the parties; and adds that the term is used in this general sense, including constructive and resulting trusts, and also, in a more restrictive sense, excluding those classes.

Perry, in the 4th edition of his work on Trusts, says: "Trusts are divided into simple and special trusts. A simple trust is a simple conveyance of property to one upon trust for another, without further specifications or directions. In such case the law regulates the trust and the *cestui que trust* has the right of possession and of disposing of the property, and he may call upon the trustee to execute such conveyances of the legal estate as are necessary. A special trust is where special and particular duties are pointed out to be performed by the trustee. In such cases he is not a mere passive agent, but he has active duties to perform; as where an estate is given to a person to sell and from the proceeds to pay the debts of the settlor." See vol. 1, § 18.

"Implied trusts are such as arise by operation of the law for the purpose of carrying out the presumed intention of the parties, or, without regard to the intention of the parties, for the purpose of asserting rights of parties or of frustrating fraud; they include the two classes of trusts known as resulting and constructive trusts." 10 Am. & Eng. Encyclop. Law, p. 2.

"In implied trusts, instead of the idea of permanence, the substantial right of the beneficiary is that the trust should be ended by a conveyance of the legal title to himself. All trusts by operation of law consist, therefore, in a separation of the legal and equitable estate, one person holding the legal title for the benefit of the equitable owner, who is regarded in equity as the real owner and who is entitled to be clothed with the legal title by a conveyance." 2 Pom. Eq. Jur. § 603.

"As between trustee and *cestui que trust*, in the case of an express trust, the Statute of Limitations has no application and no length of time is a bar . . . It does not run until re-

---

by executors and administrators is not of the class of trusts exclusively cognizable in equity, but includes the relation of debtor and creditor, and either party may plead the Statute. *Ibid.*

Creditors of a decedent do not become the owners of the personal estate of their debtor, so as to prevent the plea of the Statute of Limitations as against their debt. Heft's App. (Pa.) 7 Cent. Rep. 593, 19 W. N. C. 302.

Where he gives such notice as he thinks sufficient without any order in relation thereto by the court or clerk, he cannot be heard to say that such notice was insufficient and in law no notice, for the purpose of saving a claim filed by him against the estate from the Statute. Clark v. Tallman, 68 Iowa, 372.

Where he neglected, without excuse, to file his claim until within a few days of the expiration of the year next following the giving of the notice of his appointment, and there was not time within such year to give due notice of the claim, and for the parties adversely interested to prepare for trial, and so the claim was not proved within the year, the claim was barred by the Statute at the time the trial was reached. *Ibid.*

Where the administration of an estate has been closed and the administrator discharged, the right of a creditor to apply for a sale of the decedent's lands for payment of a probate claim accrues upon the discharge of the administrator; and unless the application is filed within ten years from that time it is barred by the Statute. Brown v. Hanauer, 48 Ark. 277.

A promise by an administrator to pay a claim against the estate does not bind either the estate or the sureties on his bond, so as to take the case out of the three years' limitation contained in the Statute. Probate Judge v. Ellis, 1 New Eng. Rep. 238, 63 N. H. 366.

If no right of action accrued prior to the death, none accrues until the grant of administration, and the Statute runs from such grant. Kulp's App. (Pa.) 6 Cent. Rep. 886.

Suits to recover legacies.

Inasmuch as an action at law lies by statute to recover a legacy, a suit in equity for a legacy not charged on land may be barred by the Statute of Limitations. Hedges v. Norris, 32 N. J. Eq. 194. See Pratt v. Northam, 5 Mason, 95; Phares v. Walters, 6 Iowa, 106; Dugan v. Gittings, 3 Gill, 138; Young v. Mackall, 3 Md. Ch. 398.

The Statute begins to run against a legacy charged on real estate one year after the issuing of letters testamentary. Butler v. Johnson, 41 Hun, 206.

Where by the terms of a will the executor does not take the fee, and there is no equitable conversion of the real estate into personalty, but merely a power in trust to sell for the payment of debts and legacies, the Statute will run against the execution thereof, and may be interposed in favor of an heir or devisee or their assigns. *Ibid.*

Where more than ten years had elapsed between the probate of a will and the advertisement of a sale of a portion of decedent's estate to pay certain debts and legacies, as against residuary devisees such claims were barred by the Statute, notwithstanding judgments had been recovered on them against the executor. *Ibid.*

If an executor pays a legacy, a suit by him to recover the amount, on the ground of overpayment, etc., may be barred by the Statute. Ely v. Norton, 6 N. J. L. 187; Frost v. Frost, 4 Edw. Ch. 733, 6 N. Y. Ch. L. ed. 1036; Myers v. Skrine, Harp. Eq. 179; Shelburne v. Robinson, 8 Ill. 597.

pudiation or adverse possession by the trustee and knowledge thereof on the part of the *cestui que trust.*" See 1 Perry, Tr. § 863, etc.

"All trusts arising by operation of law, whether implied, resulting or constructive, are subject to the Statute of Limitations."

"To exempt a trust from the bar of the Statute of Limitations it must first be a direct trust; second, it must be of the kind belonging exclusively to the jurisdiction of a court of equity; and third, the question must arise between trustee and *cestui que trust.*" *Hayward* v. *Gunn*, 82 Ill. 385.

"The Statute of Limitations is a good defense in equity as well as at law. When it does not by its terms apply to courts of equity they have adopted it by analogy to the defense at law, in all cases in which it would be a defense in courts of law. But it is no defense in matters of a purely equitable nature, and of which courts of equity have an exclusive jurisdiction. Trusts are held to be within this exception, being matters of pure equity jurisdiction. But this exception is confined to express and technical trusts, and not to such as arise by implication." *McClane* v. *Shepherd*, 21 N. J. Eq. 79.

In *Cook* v. *Woolley*, 2 N. J. Eq. 209, A. executed a power of attorney to W. and thereby placed her whole property at the disposal of the attorney, with full power to collect her choses in action and to make sale of her goods and chattels, and, out of the principal as well as interest of the proceeds, to maintain and support her, with a special provision that W. should account whenever required. A bill for an account was filed by A's administrator, to which, among other defenses, the Statute of Limitations was pleaded. Respecting this plea the chancellor says, in giving the opinion: "As to the general principle on this subject there is no difficulty. It is well settled that no time can bar the claim in the case of a direct trust as between the trustee and *cestui que trust.* But whether this is a trust of such a character has created the doubt." He concludes, however, that the facts before him raise an express direct trust, and gives as the reasons for such conclusion that "the power of attorney placed the whole property of this woman at the disposal of her trustee, not only her choses in action, but her goods and chattels, with full power to collect the one and sell the other, and out of the proceeds, as well principal as interest, to maintain and support her, and with a special provision that the trustee should account whenever required."

"This (he says) is unlike a delegated power conferred on a person for a single or limited object; it reached her entire property, related to her whole living and, by its very terms, was a continuing fiduciary engagement. There would be no security if the Statute might be pleaded in a case like this. It would defeat its very object. But (he adds) there is enough here, even if the Statute did apply, to take this case out of its operation."

We need not discuss this point further. The difficulty is not with the rule which excludes express continuing trusts from the operation of the Statute of Limitations and subjects implied trusts to its operation, but with its application; and we have cited somewhat freely from the authorities, not because we were in doubt about the existence or propriety of the rule, but to aid in its application.

This is in some respects a peculiar case. In most of the cases from which the principles applicable to it are extracted there are three parties to the transaction, namely, a settlor, a trustee and a *cestui que trust.* Here the trust is created by the transactions between the trustee and the *cestui que trust.* Mr. Dunham owned twenty one shares of stock. Of this Mr. Averill purchased eight shares, which, for reasons of his own, he did not want transferred to himself, but did want them to remain standing in the name of Mr. Dunham and ostensibly his. Hence arose the necessity of the writing of Aug. 14, 1850. If the stock had been regularly transferred, upon receipt of the $80, of course, the transferee would have been thereafter responsible for the balance of the installments when called in, and, the transaction being complete, no writing would have been needed. The writing was in the nature of a receipt, to furnish evidence, not only of the payment of the $80, but also that of the twenty-one shares of said stock standing in Mr. Dunham's name, Mr. Averill was the owner of eight, having paid $80 therefor and become responsible for the balance of the installments when called in. It contained no agreement as to the future disposition of the stock or the dividends therefrom; that was left where the law left it. Mr. Dunham assumed no trust respecting such disposition other than that implied by the law upon the facts.

It seems certain, then, that the trust raised by the transactions of July 14, 1850, was an implied one. It would have been terminated, and the trustee discharged, upon a delivery of the stock, with its increments and such dividends as had not been necessary to pay installments, to Mr. Averill or his representative. The trustee had no other duty respecting it. Instead of the idea of permanency, the substantial right of the beneficiary was that the trust should be ended by a conveyance of the legal title to himself. It was a claim enforceable at law and subject to the Statutes of Limitation.

As already stated, Mr. Dunham died March 12, 1877. His executors qualified March 19, 1877. The court of probate limited six months from said March 19 for the presentation of claims against his estate. No claim was presented by or in behalf of Mr. Averill or his estate until March 3, 1885. In other words, the claim upon which this suit is based was first presented against Mr. Dunham's estate about seven and a half years after the expiration of the time limited by the court of probate for the presentation of claims and nearly two and a half years after the executors of Mr. Averill's will had qualified. This suit was brought more than nine years after Mr. Dunham's decease. If, as suggested by the plaintiffs, the law would excuse the failure to present the claim within the time limited by the court of probate when there was no one to present it, yet that excuse could not prevail here. There is no legal presumption that Mr. Averill died before September 20, 1882; no presumption that he was not living when the time limited for the presentation of this claim expired.

Then, again, if the law would excuse a failure to present the claim until after the executors of Mr. Averill's will had qualified, yet there is nothing in the fact that an appeal was taken to the superior court from the probate of his will to excuse the delay of two years and over before presenting it.

The failure to exhibit a claim within the time limited by the court of probate for the presentation of claims against a deceased person's estate forever debars the demand. There is no provision for suspension during the disability of the claimant. It is a statutory bar which, to quote the language of Lewin in his work on Trusts, p. 866, "affords a substantial, insuperable obstacle to the plaintiff's claim, and no plea of poverty, ignorance or mistake can be of any avail." However clear and indisputable the title, could the merits be inquired into, the limited time has elapsed and the door of justice has closed. The language of *Judge* Story, quoted in the defendants' brief, suggests a reason for the strict application of the Statute. He says: "This Statute of Limitations as to executors and administrators is not created for their own security or benefit, but for the security and benefit of the estates which they represent; it is a wholesome provision designed to produce a speedy settlement of estates and the repose of titles derived under persons who are dead." If it appears to work harshly in this case the law is nevertheless so that whenever this Statute comes in, it applies, regardless of any hardships which it may work, and we must regard this claim as barred by the failure to present it against Mr. Dunham's estate within the time limited by the court of probate.

Again, and independent of the failure to present the claim within the time limited by the court of probate, the failure to commence suit upon it until November 24, 1886, must be held to be a good defense. It would seem that Mr. Averill could have compelled Mr. Dunham to deliver to him eight shares of said stock immediately after his purchase, and could have had the same transferred to his name on the books of the insurance company, thus assuming with the company the responsibility for the payment of further assessments. The defendants claim that at any rate he could have so compelled Mr. Dunham, and that the general Statutes of Limitation began to run from the time when Mr. Dunham had been repaid by cash and dividends, for the installments paid by him, which made the stock full-paid stock. This time, they say, appears from the finding to have been previous to Mr. Dunham's death, which was March 12, 1877, more than nine years before this suit was brought.

Upon the facts already recited we see no valid answer to this claim. Indeed the decision that the trust assumed by or imposed upon Mr. Dunham was an implied, instead of an express continuing, trust disposes of the claim that the Statutes of Limitations cannot be effectually pleaded, and, in connection with the disposition we make of the questions arising upon the submission and award, is decisive of the case.

Soon after the demand of March 3, 1885, the plaintiffs and the executors of Mr. Dunham entered into a written agreement to submit the matter in dispute, being the same matter involved in this suit, to arbitration, and agreed upon an arbitrator to whom the matter was referred. The arbitrator made and published his award. On the trial the plaintiffs offered this submission and award as evidence of title. The defendants objected on the ground, among others, that it purports to be a submission on the part of the executors, and by the executors only, and can have no bearing except so far as it affects the executors, in any event; that it purports to be a submission and award in June, 1886, long after the distribution of the stock to all of the parties, without any notice to them, and without any authority on the part of the executors to bind them. The court overruled the objections, and received said submission and award as tending to show in whom was the equitable title.

We think the court erred in overruling said objection. The award was offered as evidence against all the defendants. Several of them were not parties to it, and, so far as appears, in no wise authorized it or ratified it. It could not, therefore, affect them so far as any question of title was in issue in this suit. If it could affect the executors and through them the estate, it could only affect the other defendants indirectly by diminishing the assets of the estate. It was no foundation for the judgment against the defendants jointly, that they deliver and transfer at once to the plaintiffs sixty-six shares of the capital stock of said company, and make further payments as therein provided—a judgment which proceeded upon the ground, of course, that the equitable title to said sixty-six shares was in Mr. Averill's executors, and which was influenced by the award which was admitted in evidence. In the way and for the purpose for which it was offered, said submission and award were not admissible evidence. It nowhere appears from the finding that objection was made in the superior court to the admissibility of the award in evidence, upon the ground that the executors of Mr. Dunham had no power, either directly or indirectly, by submitting a stale claim to arbitration, to waive the bar of the Statute of Limitations. The court below was not called upon to consider that question, and it is therefore not before us, though alluded to in the defendants' brief.

There is error in the judgment appealed from, and *it is reversed.*

In this opinion the other Judges concurred.

ILLINOIS SUPREME COURT.

John MITTEL *et al.*, *Appts.*,
v.
Johann KARL *et al.*

(....Ill....)

A deed to a woman and her husband, and "the survivor of them, in his or her own right," gives each a life estate, with a fee to the survivor.

(May 14, 1890.)

APPEAL by defendants from a judgment of the Circuit Court for Cook County in favor of plaintiffs in a suit brought for the partition of certain lands. *Reversed.*

The facts are fully stated in the opinion.

Messrs. **William Vocke** and **Arnold Heap**, for appellants:

In *Ewing* v. *Savary*, 3 Bibb, 235, the grantor made a deed to two persons and "the survivor of them, his heirs or assigns." The court held that the grant conveyed an estate for life and a contingent remainder in fee to the survivor.

See also *Hannon* v. *Christopher*, 34 N. J. Eq. 459; 1 Brightly, Purdon's Dig. p. 939, title *Joint Tenancy; Arnold* v. *Jack*, 24 Pa. 57; *Lentz* v. *Lentz*, 2 Phila. 117; *Stimpson* v. *Batterman*, 5 Cush. 153.

Messrs. **Francis Lackner** and **Otto C. Butz**, for appellees:

The statutes of the State of Delaware upon this question are similar to our own, and in that State it was held in the case of *Davis* v. *Smith*, in which the question arose upon a devise, that the devisees took as tenants in common, and not as joint tenants.

Davis v. *Smith*, 4 Harr. 68.

In *Cheney* v. *Teese*, 108 Ill. 473, it was held that the devisees took as tenants in common and not as joint tenants, or as life tenants with remainder to the survivor.

If there be a doubt whether an estate was, at its creation, a joint tenancy or a tenancy in common, or if, conceding the estate to have been a joint tenancy at its creation, there be a doubt whether there has not been a subsequent severance of the jointure, in all such cases equity will resolve the doubt in favor of tenancy in common.

Freeman, Co-ten. § 13.

Craig, *J.*, delivered the opinion of the court:

This was a bill by appellees for partition of certain lands in Cook County. Originally the title to the lands was vested in Michael Jobst and Maria Jobst, his wife, who on July 7, 1875, conveyed by warranty deed of that date to John Mittel. On July 8, 1875, John Mittel, by warranty deed, conveyed the premises to Maria Jobst and Michael Jobst, her husband, and "the survivor of them, in his or her own right." On February 28, 1885, Maria Jobst died intestate, leaving her surviving no issue, but her husband and the complainants in the bill, her next of kin. Afterwards, on April 19, 1886, Michael Jobst died, leaving no children, but leaving a will in which he devised his property to his brothers and sisters, who claim the whole of the property conveyed to Jobst and his wife by the deed of July 8, 1875; while, on the other hand, appellees, complainants in the bill, claim that, upon the death of Maria Jobst, an undivided one-quarter of the property descended to Michael Jobst as surviving husband, and the other undivided quarter descended to appellees, her next of kin.

From the foregoing statement it is apparent that the decision of the case rests entirely upon the construction to be placed upon the deed of July 8, 1875, wherein the premises are conveyed to Maria Jobst and Michael Jobst, her husband, and the survivor of them, in her or his own right. If, under the deed in question, Maria Jobst and Michael Jobst took the fee as tenants in common, then it is plain that, upon the death of Maria, the undivided one half of the lands which was held by her would descend, one half thereof to her husband, and the other half to appellees. Prior to the adoption of the Act of 1861, commonly known as the "Married Women's Law," under a deed made to a man and his wife, upon the death of one the whole estate passed to the survivor. *Mariner* v. *Saunders*, 10 Ill. 124; *Lux* v. *Hoff*, 47 Ill. 425.

This rule is predicated upon the principle that in law husband and wife are but one person, and hence cannot take an estate by moities, but both are seised of the entirety, so that neither can dispose of the estate without the consent of the other, but the whole must remain to the survivor. 2 Bl. Com. 182.

Both of the cases cited followed the law as declared by Blackstone: It was held that, where an estate was granted to a man and his wife, they are neither properly joint tenants nor tenants in common. But after the adoption of the Act of 1861, conferring upon married women the right to acquire property, and hold and enjoy the same free from the husband's control, this court held that the reason for the rule, holding that a conveyance to husband and wife made them tenants by the entirety with right of survivorship, had ceased to exist, and they will now take and hold as tenants in common. *Cooper* v. *Cooper*, 76 Ill. 57.

Under the rule as declared in the case last cited, had the land been conveyed to Maria Jobst and Michael Jobst without the words, "and the survivor of them, in his or her own right," it is clear they would have held the fee as tenants in common, and upon the death of either the land held would have descended to his or her respective heirs. The question, then, to be determined is, What construction is to be placed on the words found in the deed, "and the survivor of them, in his or her own right?" It is suggested that they may be rejected as surplusage. That cannot be done. These words were placed in the deed by the contracting parties for a purpose, and they cannot arbitrarily be rejected.

In the construction of written contracts it is the duty of the court to ascertain the intention of the parties, and the intention when ascer-

NOTE.—Conveyance to husband and wife; common-law and state rules. See *note* to Baker v. Stewart (Kan.) 2 L. R. A. 434.

See also 18 L. R. A. 329; 22 L. R. A. 42.

tained must control; but, in arriving at the intention, effect must be given to each clause, word or term employed by the parties, rejecting none as meaningless or surplusage. *Lehndorf* v. *Cope*, 122 Ill. 317, 11 West. Rep. 618.

But it is said, if the words cannot be rejected as surplusage, the deed created a joint tenancy, which has, in effect, been extinguished by our Statute, leaving the parties occupying the relation of tenants in common.

Section 5, chap. 30, Rev. Stat., provides that "no estate in joint tenancy, in any lands, tenements or hereditaments, shall be held or claimed under any grant, devise or conveyance whatsoever, heretofore or hereafter made, other than to executors and trustees, unless the premises therein mentioned shall expressly be thereby declared to pass, not in tenancy in common, but in joint tenancy; and every such estate, other than to executors and trustees (unless otherwise expressly declared as aforesaid), shall be deemed to be in tenancy in common." Section 1 of chapter 76 of the Statute provides: "If partition be not made between joint tenants, the parts of those who die first shall not accrue to the survivors, but descend or pass by devise, and shall be subject to debts, dower, charges, etc., or transmissible to executors or administrators, and be considered to every intent and purpose in the same view as if such deceased joint tenants had been tenants in common."

A joint tenancy may be created in the manner provided in section 5, *supra;* but by the terms of section 1 the right of survivorship is taken away, and the estate, except where it is conferred upon executors and trustees, is practically destroyed. If, therefore, the grantees in the deed in question took strictly as "joint tenants," as that term is known and recognized at common law, they might be regarded as tenants in common, and the interest in the lands held by Maria Jobst might pass by descent, as declared in section 1, *supra.* A joint tenancy is said to be distinguished by unity of possession, unity of interest and unity of time of the commencement of such title. Williams, Real Prop. 132.

The same author says tenants in common are such as have a unity of possession, but a distinct and several title to their shares. Between a joint tenancy and tenancy in common the only unity that exists is therefore the unity of possession. A tenant in common is, as to his own undivided share, precisely in the position of the owner of an entire and separate estate. One principal element of an estate of joint tenancy is unity of interest. 2 Bl. Com. chap. 12.

Was there unity of interest created by the deed in question? The fee was not conveyed to the two parties with right of survivorship by the deed. The one first dying took only a life estate, while the survivor took the fee. Under such a conveyance, we do not think unity of interest existed; if not, an estate of joint tenancy was not created. But, aside from this, it will be observed that our Statute in plain language declares that no estate in joint tenancy shall be held or claimed unless the premises shall expressly be thereby declared to pass, not in tenancy in common, but in joint tenancy. The deed in question contains no such declaration. It provides for a survivorship, it is true, which is regarded as one characteristic of a joint tenancy; but the declaration which the Statute requires to establish the estate is nowhere found in the deed, and, in the absence of such a declaration, we are inclined to hold that the estate was not created. We think the language of the deed, when properly understood, will admit of but one construction, and that is that the premises were conveyed to Maria and Michael Jobst for life, with a contingent remainder in fee to the survivor. The language of the grant is to Michael Jobst and Maria Jobst and the survivor of them, in his or her own right. It was doubtless intended that the one who should die first should take only a life estate in the premises, with remainder in fee to the survivor and his heirs.

Ewing v. *Savary*, 3 Bibb, 235, is a case in point. There the grantor made a deed to two persons, and "the survivor of them, his heirs and his assigns." The court held that the grant conveyed an estate for life and a contingent remainder in fee to the survivor. It is there said: "Although there is no express limitation to them for life, the express limitation of the fee to the survivor necessarily implies it. Nor can there be any doubt that the contingent remainder is good, for there was a particular estate of freehold to support it, and *eo instante* that the particular estate determined the estate in remainder commenced."

In the State of Pennsylvania, where they have a statute similar to our own, in *Arnold* v. *Jacks*, 24 Pa. 57, it was held that, although survivorship as an incident to joint tenancy was abolished by the Statute, it may be given by will or deed. As to the purpose and object of the deed in question, there can be no reasonable doubt. In the first instance Jobst and his wife held the fee to the premises as tenants in common. They conveyed to a third party, who reconveyed to them, with the clause in the deed providing that the survivor should take the fee. If it had been intended that the fee should remain in Jobst and wife as tenants in common, why the necessity of a conveyance to Mittel, and a reconveyance, with the added words providing the fee should go to the survivor? There is no way in which it can be held that Jobst and his wife took the fee as tenants in common without rejecting the clause in the deed providing that the survivor should take the fee, and we are aware of no rule of construction under which that can be done.

As is said in *Riggin* v. *Love*, 72 Ill. 556, a construction which requires us to reject an entire clause of a deed is not to be admitted, except from unavoidable necessity; but the intention of the parties, as manifested by the language employed in the deed, should, so far as practicable, be carried into effect. Here the grant of an estate for life, and a contingent remainder in fee to the survivor, violates no rule of the common law, or any Statute of the State, and we perceive no reason why it should not be sustained, and the evident intent of the parties carried out.

The decree will be reversed, and the cause remanded for further proceedings in conformity to this opinion.

CONNECTICUT SUPREME COURT OF ERRORS.

Margaret B. TYLER
v.
Wilson WADDINGHAM.

(58 Conn. 375.)

1. **The ruling of a court sustaining a demurrer** to a complaint for misjoinder of parties and causes of action cannot be reviewed upon appeal if plaintiff, after such ruling, withdraws the case against all but one of the defendants and files a new complaint against him, upon which the case is tried and the judgment entered from which the appeal is taken.

2. **A partnership is created** by an agreement under which one person advances money to another for investment in land on their joint account, the profits to be shared between them in a certain proportion.

3. **A person is liable as partner on a note** given in the name of another as part of the purchase price of land purchased in pursuance of a scheme for profits to be shared between them, although he authorized the other only to procure options and not to complete any purchase of land, where after he knew of the facts he accepted the benefits of the purchase, continued to furnish money to effectuate the common object and was active in schemes for the development of the property.

4. **Prima facie liability of partners** for a debt contracted by one of them may be rebutted by evidence that credit was given to the individual partner alone.

5. **A finding at the conclusion of a special finding** of facts which says: "And upon said finding I further find," etc., is not a finding of fact on independent evidence, but is only an application of the special facts previously stated, and is not conclusive.

6. **An election to give exclusive credit** to one partner is not established in the absence of full knowledge of the relation of the parties between whom the choice is to be made, and the knowledge must be actual in contradistinction to that which is constructive.

NOTE.—*Partnership; what constitutes.*

A partnership is a civil person, and in contemplation of law a moral being distinct from the persons who compose it. Pilcher's Succession, 39 La. Ann. 362.

It is a combination, by two or more persons, of capital, labor or skill, for the purpose of business for their common benefit. Kelley v. Bourne, 15 Or. 476.

A partnership may exist and the parties be bound, although there is no partnership name. Meriden Nat. Bank v. Gallaudet, 30 N. Y. S. R. 999.

It is a voluntary association of two or more persons for the purpose of lawful trade, and may be inferred from facts and circumstances. Whiting v. Leakin, 6 Cent. Rep. 456, 66 Md. 255.

As between partners, the ultimate facts whence a partnership is deduced are the agreement and its execution, summed up as the executed agreement. Shriver v. McCloud, 20 Neb. 474.

The existence of a partnership depends, as between the parties themselves, upon the intention of the parties. Bush v. Bush, 4 West. Rep. 670, 89 Mo. 360; Kellogg Newspaper Co. v. Farrell, 4 West. Rep. 51, 88 Mo. 594; Kelley v. Bourne, 15 Or. 476.

A community of interest does not make a partnership. Morgan v. Farrel, 58 Conn. 413.

The test of partnership is a community of profit; a specific interest in the profits, as profits, in contradistinction to a stipulated portion of the profits as a compensation for services. Hackett v. Stanley, 115 N. Y. 630; 3 Kent, Com. 25; Leggett v. Hyde, 58 N. Y. 272.

It is not necessary that there should be an express stipulation to share profit and loss, in order to constitute a partnership. If it were understood between the parties that there was to be a communion of profit, that would be a partnership. Bloomfield v. Buchanan, 13 Or. 108.

A participant in profits directly as such is, as to third persons, a partner, whatever may be the arrangement between the partners. Caldwell v. Miller, 127 Pa. 442.

A mere participation in profit and loss of a venture, by one who has no other interest in the property, does not constitute a partnership. Clifton v. Howard, 5 West. Rep. 327, 89 Mo. 192; Kellogg Newspaper Co. v. Farrell, 4 West. Rep. 51, 88 Mo. 594.

Participation in the profits as such is prima facie evidence of partnership; and when such prima facie evidence is not rebutted by any proof tending to show that the participants in such profits only received them as compensation for services rendered, then it becomes conclusive; and in such a case it is proper for the court to so instruct the jury. Fourth Nat. Bank v. Altheimer, 8 West. Rep. 562, 91 Mo. 190.

An agreement which shows no community of interest between the parties as to profits and losses in the business, but merely a loan of credit to one party, a clause at the end stating that "failure to comply will forfeit all interest in this firm," and that "the name of the firm will be," etc.,—does not create a partnership. Klosterman v. Hayes, 17 Or. 325.

Partners in real estate speculation.

Where two persons are equally interested in the profits to be derived from a sale of lands by one of them, they are in a sense partners in the lands. Boone v. Clark, 5 L. R. A. 276, 129 Ill. 466.

One member of a partnership formed for the purpose of buying and selling land has authority to sell the land. Young v. Wheeler, 34 Fed. Rep. 98.

A written contract by a real-estate agent and the owner of land to put land upon the market, advertise and sell it, for a share in the surplus of profits, is one of agency, and not of partnership. Durkee v. Gunn, 41 Kan. 496.

Where one of several parties to an oral partnership contract to buy and sell real estate realizes, by means of a secret agreement with a purchaser, an amount in excess of that received by his partners, they are entitled to an accounting and share of the excess. Newell v. Cochran, 41 Minn. 374.

A purchaser from parties buying and selling land under an oral contract of partnership, who, by a secret agreement, pays to one of the partners more than the others receive, cannot be compelled by the others to pay to each of them sums equal to the excess. Their remedy is against their copartner. *Ibid.*

One who advances money to a firm under an agreement that he is to have a share in the profits of the land purchased therewith, and who, during the temporary illness of a member, takes title to the lands and afterwards reconveys them, does not thereby become a partner so as to render him liable for material furnished during the time he held title. Keogh v. Minrath, 30 N. Y. S. R. 129.

See also 9 L. R. A. 421; 11 L. R. A. 149; 20 L. R. A. 776; 27 L. R. A. 1

7. Facts admitted by a demurrer to one count are not admitted for the purposes of evidence at all, and can have no bearing upon questions arising on the trial under other counts.

8. A guaranty in consideration of forbearing collection of a note for two years of "the punctual payment of each and every installment of interest on said note as they shall become due, and also of each and every installment of interest that shall become due" on a certain other note, cannot be limited to interest before maturity of the notes, especially where the first note was already overdue when the guaranty was made.

9. Parol negotiations on Sunday have no effect on the validity of a contract within the Statute of Frauds which is actually executed in writing and delivered on a secular day.

10. A demand upon the principal is not a condition precedent to the maintenance of an action against the guarantor upon a guaranty which is absolute in its terms.

11. A court does not abuse its discretion in interfering to prevent questions to be asked of counsel as a witness for his client in such form as to call out certain facts and exclude others connected with the same transaction.

12. A conversation relative to the construction of a written contract is properly excluded if the contract is unambiguous in its terms.

13. The exclusion of a question designed only to show the bias of a witness already effectually impeached by record evidence is not prejudicial error.

14. The withdrawal of a claim against the estate of a principal debtor does not discharge a guarantor from liability under an unconditional guaranty.

(February 7, 1890.)

CROSS-APPEALS from a judgment of the Superior Court for New Haven County in an action to recover the amount payable upon an overdue promissory note, and the interest upon another note not yet due, payment of all of which sums defendant was alleged to have guaranteed,—plaintiff appealing from so much of the judgment as held defendant not liable for the principal of the note, and defendant appealing from so much as held him liable for interest. *Affirmed on defendant's appeal. Reversed on plaintiff's appeal.*

The facts are fully stated in the opinion.

Messrs. **Simeon E. Baldwin** and **Talcott H. Russell**, for plaintiff:

A partnership existed between Kimberly and Waddingham. The money was not loaned to Kimberly. It did not become his property, but was deposited in trust for the parties. The profits were to be divided in a certain proportion between the parties, and Waddingham exercised control in the management of the affairs of the concern and took an active interest in promoting the objects of the scheme. This arrangement possessed all the features of a partnership.

See *Parker* v. *Canfield*, 37 Conn. 250; *Citizens Nat. Bank* v. *Hine*, 49 Conn. 236.

An undisclosed partner may be held for a note given in the name of another partner.

Morse v. *Richmond*, 97 Ill. 303; *Hulett* v. *Fairbanks*, 40 Ohio St. 233; *Dale* v. *Hamilton*, 5 Hare, 369; *City Bank's App.* 3 New Eng. Rep. 549, 54 Conn. 269.

A ratification of the action of Kimberly is as good as an original agreement.

Stillman v. *Harvey*, 47 Conn. 26.

Waddingham is liable for the notes as an undisclosed principal.

National Shoe & Leather Bank's App. 5 New Eng. Rep. 604, 55 Conn. 494.

No demand on the maker of the notes before suit against guarantor was necessary. The instrument guarantees "the punctual payment of each and every installment of interest . . . as they shall come due." Such a guaranty requires no action on the part of the plaintiff against the maker to hold the guarantor.

See *City Sav. Bank* v. *Hopson*, 2 New Eng. Rep. 556, 53 Conn. 454; *Breed* v. *Hillhouse*, 7 Conn. 528; Brandt, Sur. § 8, p. 119; *Hungerford* v. *O'Brien*, 37 Minn. 306.

The withdrawal of the claim against Kimberly's estate was equivalent to the discontinuance of an attempt to collect against the principal. This does not discharge the surety.

See *Cilley* v. *Colby*, 61 N. H. 63; *McKenzie* v. *Wiley*, 27 W. Va. 658; *Banks* v. *State*, 62 Md. 88; *Brown* v. *Chambers*, 63 Tex. 131; *Knight* v. *Charter*, 22 W. Va. 422; *Concord Bank* v. *Rogers*, 16 N. H. 9; *Barney* v. *Clark*, 46 N. H. 514.

The plaintiff was not bound to present the claim.

Wasson v. *Hodshire*, 5 West. Rep. 843, 108 Ind. 26; *Villars* v. *Palmer*, 67 Ill. 204; *Clopton* v. *Spratt*, 52 Miss. 251; *Mitchell* v. *Williamson*, 6 Md. 210; *Sibley* v. *McAllaster*, 8 N. H. 389.

The acceptance of the note of Kimberly did not release the claim against Waddingham, because it is found that Mrs. Tyler did not know the relation between them at the time.

Maneely v. *M'Gee*, 6 Mass. 143; *Merrill* v. *Kenyon*, 48 Conn. 315.

Messrs. **Henry Stoddard, Charles K. Bush** and **Charles Kleiner**, for defendant:

Even if defendant was the principal and Kimberly the agent, and if defendant and Kimberly were partners in the purchase of plaintiff's farm, yet, she having accepted the notes of Kimberly in payment, she has no further claim on defendant.

Bonnell v. *Chamberlin*, 26 Conn. 487; *Bulwinkle* v. *Cramer*, 27 S. C. 376; *Briggs* v. *Partridge*, 64 N. Y. 357, 363; *Parker* v. *Canfield*, 37 Conn. 271.

She testifies that Kimberly told her that he was defendant's agent, and that she contracted with Kimberly for that reason, and she voluntarily takes Kimberly's notes in payment; under these circumstances there is no element of misinformation or suppression, so that the question whether Kimberly was the agent of defendant, as a partner or otherwise, is wholly unimportant and immaterial.

Merrill v. *Kenyon*, 48 Conn. 319; *Paterson* v. *Gandasequi*, 15 East, 62, 2 Smith, Lead. Cas. *348; *Addison* v. *Gandasequi*, 4 Taunt. 573, 2 Smith, Lead. Cas. *358; *Thomson* v. *Davenport*, 9 Barn. & C. 78, 2 Smith, Lead. Cas. *358; *Raymond* v. *Crown Eagle Mills*, 2 Met. 319; *Jones* v. *Ætna Ins. Co.* 14 Conn. 508.

After the note became due, no interest, considered as interest, could accrue on it, but only damages for the detention of the money after it was payable.

Beckwith v. *Hartford, P. & F. R. Co.* 29 Conn. 270.

A guarantor is never answerable beyond the clear scope of his engagement; courts will not presume a continuing guaranty where the terms of the contract are doubtful.

Morgan v. *Bryce*, 16 Rep. 760; *Hall* v. *Rand*, 8 Conn. 572.

A party who takes an agreement prepared by another, and upon the faith of it incurs obligations or parts with property, should have a construction given to the instrument favorable to himself.

Noonan v. *Bradley*, 76 U. S. 9 Wall. 394 (19 L. ed. 757).

Ambiguities in a written contract should in general be construed against the writer.

Huidekoper v. *Douglass*, 7 U. S. 3 Cranch, 1-71 (2 L. ed. 347-369).

Loomis, *J.*, delivered the opinion of the court:

The record in this case as it comes to this court is unnecessarily voluminous and complicated.

The complaint as first brought to the September Session, 1887, of the Superior Court for New Haven County, was against three defendants, namely: the West Shore Land Improvement Company, a New York corporation, having an office and doing business in Orange in this State; Edward A. Anketell of New Haven, as administrator of the estate of Edward L. Kimberly, late of said Orange, deceased; and Wilson Waddingham of said Orange,—all of whom remained defendants until the 23d day of February, 1888.

Meanwhile sundry voluminous motions to strike out and expunge portions of the complaint were heard by the court and in part sustained. Also sundry demurrers by the defendants to the complaint for multifariousness and misjoinder of defendants were heard and sustained by the court. After which, on the date last mentioned, the plaintiff by written withdrawal signed by her attorney, and made part of the record, wholly discontinued the action against all the defendants mentioned except Waddingham, and filed a new complaint, called in the record the "second amended supplemental complaint," upon which the trial proceeded against Waddingham alone.

This complaint consisted of two counts. The first count sought to make Waddingham liable, either as unnamed principal or as a partner with Kimberly, to pay a note of $5,000 described in the complaint and given by Kimberly on the purchase by him of certain real estate belonging to the plaintiff.

The second count was based upon an express contract by Waddingham as guarantor for the payment of the interest on the note for $5,000, and also on another note for $30,000 given by Kimberly to the plaintiff on account of the purchase mentioned.

The court found for the defendant on the first count and for the plaintiff on the second, and both parties have appealed to this court.

The facts found by the court are in substance as follows: In 1881 Kimberly entered into an agreement with the defendant Waddingham, by which the latter was to furnish money to procure options to purchase land (including the plaintiff's) on or near the shore of Long Island Sound in the Towns of Orange and Milford, and then during the life of the options to organize a corporation to take the lands at an advanced price. Waddingham was to have two thirds and Kimberly one third of the profits, and the former agreed to advance to Kimberly, and did so, $15,000 toward the accomplishment of said objects. The sums so advanced were to be and were deposited in a bank mutually agreed on, in the name of E. L. Kimberly, trustee. The defendant between the 6th day of September, 1881, and the 28th day of February, 1883, inclusive, at different times advanced to Kimberly in the aggregate the sum of $45,359, of which $5,000 was paid back.

The plaintiff owned a large farm, as described in the complaint, which was a part of the land the agreement between Kimberly and the defendant had reference to. Kimberly at first went to the plaintiff accompanied by a real estate broker to negotiate for the purchase of her farm, but as they were not financially responsible she refused to negotiate with them until they announced themselves as agents, and gave her to understand they were agents of a company of which the defendant was the head. Afterwards, on the 6th of October, 1881, she entered into an agreement in writing, signed by her and Kimberly, by which she agreed to convey the land to Kimberly, or his appointees, on or before March 1, 1882, and Kimberly on his part agreed to make payment and give security as specified in the agreement. The price first agreed to be paid for the farm was $50,000, but afterwards, before the day for the giving of the deed, in February, 1882, by reason of Kimberly's representation made to the plaintiff that he would not be able to carry out the contract at the price first agreed, she reluctantly consented to reduce the purchase price to $40,000, and the agreement was so modified. In February, 1882, the conveyance was made to Kimberly, who made part payment in money out of the funds furnished by the defendant, and for the remainder of the purchase price executed and delivered to the plaintiff notes described in the complaint, and mortgaged the land so purchased as security for their payment to the plaintiff.

In fact the defendant did not authorize Kimberly to make any purchases of land or give notes and mortgages for such purchases, either in his name or in Kimberly's, or on account of either or both, except to the extent of the purchase of options. He was not aware that Kimberly had done more until the summer of 1882, when he was informed of the facts by Kimberly, who urged him to assist in the formation of a company, which the defendant consented to do, hoping thereby to get some of his money back.

On the 28th of October, 1882, Kimberly, at the request and solicitation of the defendant, deeded all the lands purchased by him, or the equities therein, to the West Haven Shore Land Improvement Company, and the company issued to him paid-up capital stock to the amount of nearly $800,000, being all except five shares of the capital of the company, in return for the lands; and the defendant gave Kimberly a writing stating that he was entitled to one-third interest in the profits of the lands so conveyed by him.

The court also finds that, after the defendant knew that Kimberly had obtained deeds of land in his own name, he continued to loan him money to assist him, and endeavored to induce others to become interested in the scheme for the development of the lands, and tried to secure the construction of a railroad to benefit the property, but without success. Kimberly paid the interest on the plaintiff's notes to February 28, 1883, inclusive, and the defendant paid it from that time to August 28, 1886, inclusive; and since October 1, 1886, the defendant has been in exclusive possession and control of all the property in question, taking all the rents and profits.

In reference to the seventh paragraph in the first count of the plaintiff's complaint, which alleged that "the plaintiff when she accepted said notes did not know of the nature of the agreement between Kimberly and Waddingham, and did not intend to release any claim against Waddingham," the finding is as follows:

"The plaintiff testified in her deposition that when she took these notes the only knowledge she had of the nature and terms of any agreement then existing between Kimberly and Waddingham was that she 'understood they were only agents for a land improvement society, of which Waddingham was the head and formed the responsible party;' and that she did not intend, by so doing, to release Waddingham or any other person from any claim she might have against him or them; and that in taking the notes and mortgages (she also took and holds a mortgage from Kimberly of a one-third interest in other property valued at $11,400 as additional security for the $5,000 notes), she did not give exclusive credit to Kimberly, and did not consider that she in any way released any rights against Waddingham or any company that might be liable to her. On the whole evidence, however, I am of opinion, and find, that the sole influence which the understanding and belief on the part of the plaintiff that Kimberly was acting, not on his own sole and unassisted responsibility, but upon that of Mr. Waddingham or of some company formed or to be formed in which he was interested, exerted over her, was that she was thereby convinced that the scheme would be carried through and the notes and mortgages discharged; but I do not find that when she accepted the notes and mortgages from Kimberly she had any understanding or belief that, apart from the security upon the real estate, there was any other individual or company personally bound or liable to her for the contract price or any part thereof."

The court also adds: "And upon said finding I further find the second defense to the first count true;" which defense was as follows:

"1. The plaintiff elected to give, and did give, sole and exclusive credit to Kimberly in the transactions set up in the fifth and sixth paragraphs of said count.

"2. The plaintiff accepted, in payment of the property described in plaintiff's Exhibit A, the notes of Kimberly set up in paragraph six, secured by a first mortgage from Kimberly to the plaintiff upon the property.

"3. The plaintiff still holds and owns said mortgages."

The plaintiff, in support of her appeal, claims that the trial court erred in its rulings in four respects: (1) in sustaining the demurrer for misjoinder of parties and causes of action; (2) in holding that the relationship of partners or principal and agent did not exist between Kimberly and the defendant; (3) in allowing Bush, the attorney, the privilege of counsel in refusing to answer certain inquiries; (4) in striking out certain paragraphs from the amended supplemental complaint.

In regard to the questions as to misjoinder, they are not properly before this court for review, for the reason that the plaintiff withdrew her case against the West Haven Shore Land Improvement Company and against the administrator of Kimberly, and filed a new complaint against the present defendant alone. The action was discontinued against the other two parties; so that it was no longer in the superior court, and therefore it could not be appealed from that court to this court. The motives for withdrawal are of no consequence. It is equally immaterial whether it was because the plaintiff thought she had no case, or because she knew the court thought so. In contemplation of law the case was taken out of court by the voluntary action of the plaintiff, and placed beyond the reach of all courts, unless upon some appropriate proceedings for its reinstatement.

We come next to the question whether, upon the facts contained in the finding, the relation of partners, or of principal and agent, existed between Kimberly and the defendant, so that the debts contracted by Kimberly in dealing with the plaintiff were the debts also of the defendant. The form of the question implies not only that the true answer to be given is in doubt, but that the relation of the parties must be either that of principal and agent or copartners.

We discover very few indications of ordinary agency. In the light of the few facts given it is extremely difficult to point out the principal who is to command or the servant who is to obey. Although Kimberly invented the scheme and first proposed it to Waddingham, and the form of proposal at first indicated that all that was expected of Waddingham was to furnish him money for a consideration, yet as finally launched, it entirely loses the appearance of being Kimberly's sole enterprise, and he no longer seems a mere borrower of money from Waddingham, who is to receive two thirds of the profits in lieu of interest; for Kimberly's receipt, which the court finds was executed at the same time as a part of the transaction, shows that the money so furnished was "to be deposited in a bank agreed upon, to his credit as trustee, for the purpose of making contracts for land," etc., and the writing concludes: "Following is the interest each party shares in the profits." Then after the signature and date there was added: "The profits from the above investments are to be divided as follows: one third to E. L. Kimberly; two thirds to Wilson Waddingham & Co. (Signed) E. L. Kimberly," —thus showing, if not directly, by necessary inference, that there were two equal parties, regarded as principals, each of whom was a sharer in the profits, and that there was a common investment, a common adventure on the joint account of the two concerned, with a definite agreement as to the division of the profits.

It is true that Kimberly was not at first expressly authorized to take deeds in his own name and give his own notes, and that the scheme as first proposed contemplated the purchase of options to obtain the land and afterwards selling the same at an advance to a corporation to be formed for the purpose of purchasing it. But after the defendant knew all the facts as to Kimberly's transactions, he immediately accepted all the benefits, continued to furnish money to effectuate the common object, was active in promoting schemes for the development of the property and the enhancement of its value, procured, or assisted in procuring, the formation of a corporation as contemplated and induced Kimberly to convey the land in question and other lands purchased in the same way to the corporation, at the enormous valuation of $800,000, for which stock was issued to Kimberly nominally representing that sum. And immediately upon the consummation of all these transactions the defendant wrote to Kimberly as follows:—

West Haven, Conn. Oct. 30, 1882.

E. L. Kimberly, Esq.,

In reply to your inquiries, I beg to state that you are entitled to one-third interest of the profits of all the lands purchased by you and this day deeded by you to the West Shore Land Improvement Company. Yours sincerely,

Wilson Waddingham.

In the light of all these facts will not the law recognize the features of a partnership, especially in behalf of a third person?

Let us ascertain and apply the sharpest and most approved legal tests of this relation.

In *Loomis* v. *Marshall*, 12 Conn. 69, this court said: "The test of partnership is a community of profit, a specific interest in the profits as profits, in contradistinction to a stipulated portion of the profits as a compensation for services."

Smith, in his Mercantile Law, p. 26, says: "To constitute such a community of profit as is requisite to a partnership, the partner must not only share in the profits of his companions, but share in them as a principal; that is, he must not be a mere agent, factor or servant, receiving in lieu of wages a sum proportional to the profit gained by his employers. Still, if a servant or agent stipulate for a share in the profits and so entitles himself to an account of them, he becomes as to third persons a partner."

Parsons, in his treatise on Partnership (2d ed. p. 149), says: "We should hold the test of partnership to be . . . Has the party lending or contributing the money acquired by his bargain a proprietary interest in the profits while they remain undivided? If he has, he is liable as a partner; otherwise he is not so liable."

In 3 Kent's Commentaries, p. 22, *note a*, it is said: "It is not essential to a partnership that there should be a communion of interest in the capital stock and also in the profit and loss. If there be a community of profit, or of profit and loss in the adventure or business between the parties, they will be partners in the profit and loss, though not partners in the capital stock. If, however, there be no agreement between the parties on the point, the presumption will be a community of interest in the property as well as in the profit and loss. . . . There is also a distinction between a stipulation for a compensation for labor proportioned to the profits, without any specific lien upon such profits, and which does not make a person a partner, and a stipulation for an interest in such profits, which entitles the party to an account as a partner."

This *Chancellor* Walworth, in *Champion* v. *Bostwick*, 18 Wend. 185, and *Mr. Justice* Wilde, in *Denny* v. *Cabot*, 6 Met. 82, held to be a sound distinction as regards the rights of third persons.

In all these citations we may recognize one and the same test—a proprietary interest in the profits while they remain a part of the undivided stock; and we ask, After Kimberly had sold the lands in question, could not Waddingham have maintained an action of account against him to have their relative rights in the avails of the sale adjusted, or must he content himself with an action at law for the use of money? Could he not even have followed the profits into the common reservoir created by the parties to receive them,—namely, this corporation, to which the lands were sold, and have the stock of the corporation distributed according to their respective proprietary interest in the profits? Or, on the other hand, if the corporation had issued to Waddingham all the stock which represented the value of the lands sold, could not Kimberly have maintained account to determine his interest, or must he have simply sued Waddingham for his services?

It is now well established that there may be a partnership to trade in land. *Brady* v. *Colhoun*, 1 Penr. & W. 140; *Morse* v. *Richmond*, 97 Ill. 303; *Hulett* v. *Fairbanks*, 40 Ohio St. 233; *Dale* v. *Hamilton*, 5 Hare, 369.

In *Richards* v. *Grinnell*, 63 Iowa, 44, by an oral agreement A was to furnish money with which B was to buy land, taking the title in A's name. A was to receive for his capital ten per cent interest and half the profits from the sale of the land. A brought an action of account against B, which was sustained on the ground that A and B were partners.

In *Hill* v. *Sheibley*, 68 Ga. 556, B received the money of A, to be invested on joint account in buying land. If no investment should be made the money was to be returned. A died and his administrator sued B and obtained a verdict, which the higher court set aside on the ground that B was not a trustee or agent, but a partner, of A.

If, then, we have established the position that Waddingham and Kimberly were partners, there being no question that the contracts for the purchase of the plaintiff's land and the notes given in payment therefor were strictly in pursuance of the purpose and business of the partnership, the liability of Waddingham, prima facie, is established in favor of the plaintiff. But this prima facie liability, based on the presumption that all the partners are equally liable for the obligations of the copartnership, may be rebutted by direct evidence that the credit was not given to the partnership, but to an individual member of it. *Smith* v.

Watson, 2 Barn. & C. 401; *Ensign* v. *Wands*, 1 Johns. Cas. 171.

If, then, the finding shows that the plaintiff elected to give exclusive credit to Kimberly at the time of the making of the contract in question, she cannot proceed against the defendant now. The counsel for the defendant claims that this point is settled as a question of fact by the finding of the court that the second defense to the first count is true, which presents this precise issue. This claim would be unanswerable if intended to be so found as a question of fact based on appropriate evidence before the court. But it is to be noticed that this is at the conclusion of what the court calls its special finding of facts, and the court in terms says: "And upon said" (special) "finding I further find the second defense to the first count true." It was not therefore intended as a finding of a fact based on independent evidence, but only as an application of the special facts previously stated to the determination of the legal issue raised by the second defense. The question is therefore controlled by the special facts referred to and the legal conclusions to be drawn therefrom.

Such a finding was held reviewable in *Mead* v. *Noyes*, 44 Conn. 487, and in *Hayden* v. *Allyn*, 55 Conn. 280, 5 New Eng. Rep. 87, this point was even more fully considered. The finding there concluded: "Upon the facts set forth it is found that said transfer was not made in good faith in the regular course of business, and was made in view of insolvency and with intent to prefer a creditor, the defendant company,"—in regard to which we then said: "If this had been a conclusion of fact from the evidence before the court it could not be reviewed; but it is very clearly an inference of law from the facts specifically found. The evidence had exhausted itself in producing the facts thus found. Nothing remained but for the court in the exercise of its legal judgment to draw its inference from the facts. This the judge himself distinctly states in saying that this conclusion is upon the facts set forth. In such a case the conclusion of the court can always be reviewed by the appellate court. An erroneous conclusion is an error of law and not an error in an inference of fact."

The question then for review in the case at bar is, whether the conclusion of the court that the plaintiff had elected to give exclusive credit to Kimberly was warranted by the special facts found.

It seems to us that these facts, when examined in the light of well-established legal principles, will be found to lack at least one essential element of a binding election, which is, full knowledge as to the relation of the parties between whom the choice is to be made. If we reason merely from the nature of the act the necessity of such knowledge would be implied, for without it it would be impossible to make a selection from two or more persons. But, however this may be, no rule of law is better established than this.

Parsons, in his treatise on Partnership, 2d ed. p. 110, says, speaking of the effect of giving credit to one partner alone: "It must, however, be remembered that this credit, to exonerate the other partners, must be given knowingly and voluntarily. For if one sold goods actually to a firm, but through the agency of a partner whom he did not know to be a partner, and accordingly charged the same to that partner alone, the firm would still be bound. We think this rule applies equally to all simple contracts, whether oral or written."

The rule applicable to an after-disclosed partner is identical with that as to an after-disclosed principal. In *Merrill* v. *Kenyon*, 48 Conn. 314, this court insisted upon the necessity of full and actual knowledge in order to debar a seller of goods to an agent from his right to make the principal his debtor on discovering him, and held that where the seller took the promissory note of the buyer for the goods, with knowledge that he was an agent, but without knowing who the principal was, he was not thereby debarred from afterwards electing to make the principal his debtor.

The knowledge which the plaintiff possessed, as found by the court, falls far short of the full measure required by law. It is found that the plaintiff testified that she understood Kimberly to be only agent of a land improvement society, of which Waddingham was the head and formed the responsible party, but she did not intend to give exclusive credit to Kimberly, nor release rights she might have against Waddingham or any company that might be responsible to her. The court however in effect found on the whole evidence that her belief was that Waddingham was not legally holden, but that his connection with an interested company was such that the scheme would be carried out, but at the same time she had no idea that any other individual or company was personally bound to pay her for the land.

If it be suggested that the mention of Waddingham as having some influential connection with the matter was sufficient to put the plaintiff on inquiry and give her the means of knowledge, we reply that the rule requires actual knowledge in contradistinction to that which is constructive, and full knowledge in contradistinction to that which is partial. *Thomson* v. *Davenport*, 9 Barn. & C. 78; *Raymond* v. *Crown Eagle Mills*, 2 Met. 319. Both these cases are cited with approval in *Merrill* v. *Kenyon*, *supra*.

It will not suffice to disclose the name of one who was in fact partner or principal unless his true position as such be also disclosed. There seems to have been an utter misconception on the part of the plaintiff of the true position of Waddingham relative to the case; and furthermore there was one material fact that it was impossible for her to know at the time she took the notes of Kimberly, namely, that Waddingham would ratify, as he did in the summer of 1882, the unauthorized act of Kimberly in making an absolute purchase of land instead of buying mere options to purchase, as the agreement first made contemplated.

We do not know, and there is nothing to suggest, how this fact was met or disposed of in the court below, or whether it was considered at all in this connection. The form of the special finding, that when the plaintiff accepted the notes and mortgages she had no belief that there was any other person or company liable to her, indicates that it may have been assumed on the trial that the true and conclusive test of the question whether exclusive credit was given to Kimberly was the actual intent and belief of the plaintiff at the time, irrespective of her knowledge of the material facts. We have already seen that what the law deems giving exclusive credit, may be very different from the actual belief of the party at the time. All the numerous cases where a vendor has been permitted to resort to an after-discovered partner or principal are founded on this distinction, and the phrase "after-discovered" implies it.

There is no fact found showing when the plaintiff first knew of the defendant's actual connection with this matter, or what she did after that date in the way of giving credit to Kimberly. There is a suggestion of the possible existence of facts bearing upon this point in the allegations of the second defense to the second count, which was demurred to by the plaintiff and the demurrer sustained. A demurrer admits facts that are well pleaded, but only for the purpose of determining their legal sufficiency. Facts so admitted are not admitted for the purposes of evidence at all, and therefore can have no bearing upon the questions referred to. *Pease* v. *Phelps*, 10 Conn. 68; *Gray* v. *Finch*, 23 Conn. 495; *Havens* v. *Hartford & N. H. R. Co.* 28 Conn. 90; Gould, Pl. 461, 462.

As this part of the case which we have been considering may not have been fully investigated in the trial court and as the record suggests the possibility of other evidence in the case, we prefer to grant a new trial of this issue rather than to reverse the judgment.

The alleged errors, predicated upon the striking out by the court of certain paragraphs in the amended supplemental complaint, inserted originally as the plaintiff claims to lay the foundation for showing the relation between Waddingham and the West Haven Shore Land Improvement Company, and between Waddingham and Kimberly, have all been rendered immaterial, partly in consequence of the voluntary withdrawal of the action against two of the parties, and partly in consequence of the construction we have placed on the finding of the court that Kimberly and the defendant were partners in the transaction.

This last-mentioned fact also renders it immaterial to discuss the question whether Mr. Bush, the counsel for the defendant and for the West Haven Shore Land Improvement Company, was properly excused from answering the questions put to him by the plaintiff, upon the ground of his professional privilege. The utmost result which the plaintiff claimed from the evidence desired was to establish the partnership between Kimberly and the defendant and that the corporation was duly organized under the laws of the State of New York,—facts already established upon our construction of the finding.

This brings us to the consideration of the questions arising upon the defendant's appeal under the second count of the complaint, which predicates his liability solely upon a written guaranty signed by him, as follows:

"In consideration that Mrs. Margaret B. Tyler, of Springfield, Massachusetts has at my request agreed to forbear for a period of two years from the present time to take any steps to collect by legal process the principal of the note of $5,000, dated February 28, 1882, signed by Edward L. Kimberly, payable to said Margaret B. Tyler one year from date, with interest at the rate of six per cent per annum, payable semi-annually, together with all taxes assessed upon said sum against said Tyler, or the holder of the note, unless requested by me to take such steps, I hereby guarantee the punctual payment of each and every installment of interest on said note as they shall become due, and also of each and every installment of interest that shall come due on the note of said Kimberly for $30,000, payable ten years from date, but otherwise of the same date and tenor as said first-mentioned note. Dated at New Haven, October 2, 1883.

(Signed) Wilson Waddingham."

The construction of this contract and the extent of obligation it imposed on the defendant, is the important question raised by this appeal.

There was a counterclaim filed by the defendant for the reformation of this contract, and the court has found in detail the verbal negotiations of the parties that preceded the execution of the writing, as follows:

"On Sunday, September 23, 1883, Mr. Russell, acting for Mrs. Tyler, called on Mr. Waddingham at his residence in West Haven, introduced himself, and stated that he called in reference to the Tyler matter. He mentioned the $5,000 note, which was then overdue, and also installments of interest overdue on both notes, saying further that Mrs. Tyler, while she had considerable property, was land-poor, so to speak; she had her children to support, and she needed her interest; she must have it; she depended upon it. Mr. Waddingham said: 'That matter will be all right. You need have no trouble about it,'—adding: 'I will give you a check for the interest now.' Mr. Russell stated that he did not care to receive that then: he would prefer to wait until some arrangement could be made about the whole matter. As Mr. Waddingham had friends to dinner he excused himself, asking Mr. Russell to come again the following Sunday. Mr. Russell did so. At this interview Mr. Russell told Mr. Waddingham that he had looked into the matter to some extent, and as far as he could see there was a good chance of holding him liable as a partner on these notes. Mr. Waddingham said there was no such chance at all, that there was no such thing, but that he had advanced or loaned Kimberly a very large sum of money, and now proposed to go through with the scheme in some form. After more conversation Mr. Russell finally said that if the interest was guaranteed he would be satisfied, and that he would prepare a form of guaranty and send it to Mr. Waddingham for signature. To this Mr. Waddingham agreed. Nothing was said about the time of extension, or directly as to length of time of guaranty, during their interview. The entire substance of the interview is hereinbefore recited. On October 1st, 1883, Mr. Russell sent the guaranty recited in paragraph 2 of said count to Mr. Waddingham, accompanied by the following note:—

"'New Haven, Conn., Oct. 1, 1883.

"'Wilson Waddingham, Esq., Dear Sir:— The amount of the interest on the Tyler notes, due September 1, 1883, is $1,050, being six months' interest at six per cent on $35,000. I inclose form of guaranty for your signature, drawn to correspond with the oral understanding already arrived at. Yours very respectfully. Talcott H. Russell.'

"To which Mr. Waddingham, having signed and inclosed the guaranty, replied as follows:

"'New York, Oct. 2, 1883.

"'Talcott H. Russell, Esq., Dear Sir:—Your esteemed favor of first instant duly received, and inclosed herewith I hand you my No. A 180 check on the Wall Street National Bank, this city, for $1,050, in accordance with our understanding, and also inclose herewith the guaranty, with my signature attached, which you desire me to send. Very truly yours, Wilson Waddingham, per C. F. Madison.'

"This constitutes the entire negotiations in reference to said guaranty."

This evidence was pertinent to the issue upon the defendant's counterclaim for a reformation of the contract, but it failed to establish the facts necessary to grant the relief prayed for, and it was properly denied by the court, and no error is alleged in this respect. But the facts as to the verbal negotiations of the parties resulting in the written contract have been referred to by counsel on both sides as having some bearing upon the question as to the construction of the written contract. Some of the facts may have a remote bearing upon this question; still in our judgment there appears no such ambiguity in the language of the contract as to give any controlling importance to any of the extrinsic facts of the case.

The plaintiff claims that the agreement is a guaranty of the interest upon both of the notes mentioned until the principal shall be paid. The defendant, on the other hand, claims that he is not liable to pay interest on either note for a longer period than the expiration of the extension on the five-thousand-dollar note, to wit, October 2, 1885, or for such time prior to that date as the defendant should cause such note to mature, by calling upon the plaintiff to collect it.

The main argument in support of the defendant's contention is founded upon the fact that the contract states the consideration as confined simply to the five-thousand-dollar note and the forbearance to collect that note for two years unless requested by the defendant. It is claimed to be incredible that a man of wealth, for the mere purpose of securing a two years' extension on a five-thousand-dollar note, would have knowingly bound himself to pay, in addition to the interest on that note, the interest also as it might come due on the thirty-thousand-dollar note that had nine years longer to run.

If the consideration named was the only thing that moved the defendant to his undertaking, the argument would have great force. But in drawing up the written agreement the statement of the consideration was immaterial, except that a good consideration must appear. It is to be noticed that in the verbal negotiations nothing was said as to consideration. We know from the extrinsic facts found by the court that there was another motive at this time operating on the mind of the defendant. It was his intention then to pay these notes in full, or, as he expressed it to Mr. Russell, he had advanced so much money already that he then proposed to go through the scheme in some form.

But if we knew nothing of the defendant's motives except as indicated in the statement of the consideration, it is absolutely certain that his guaranty was not confined to the five-thousand-dollar note, but embraced also the thirty-thousand-dollar note. But the defendant contends that as the smaller note was only extended two years the guaranty for the payment of the interest on that note was by implication limited to that time, and if so, that all the expressions relative to paying interest on the large note are to be controlled and limited by the expressions in regard to the first-mentioned note, in the absence of other distinguishing words.

This reasoning might well apply were the language of the contract vague and ambiguous. But the undertaking of the defendant is here expressed with unusual clearness. It is to pay the future interest on two notes described and precisely identified, and all the future interest that may thereafter accrue is included. It would seem impossible to mistake the meaning and application of the words—"punctual payment of each and every installment of interest on said note as the same shall become due," "and also of each and every installment of interest that shall come due on the note of said Kimberly for $30,000, payable ten years from date." In order to test what is within the scope of this contract it would seem absurd to ask whether the installment had become due within two years, when each and every installment coming due in the future is in terms included.

But the further claim is made that the contract only requires the defendant to pay the interest; and that after the five-thousand-dollar note became due there was no legal liability on anyone to pay interest as such, but only damages for the detention of the principal. This obviously is not the case for any such distinction, for it is demonstrable that the parties did not use the term in this extremely technical sense. The five-thousand-dollar note became due February 28, 1883, while the contract of guaranty was not executed till October 2, 1883. The former therefore had been seven months overdue when the defendant agreed to pay each and every installment of interest as it should become due. The fact that the plaintiff had agreed not to collect the note for two years did not change damages for the detention of money back into interest for that time, leaving it to change again into damages when the time expired.

We would not, however, rest the argument upon this narrow view. If neither note had been due when the contract in question was made we should still think that such a distinction was never contemplated by the parties, but that interest, as such, would be recoverable on the notes according to their terms as long as they remained outstanding and unpaid, although the principal might be overdue. *Hubbard* v. *Callahan*, 42 Conn. 528.

The defendant claimed upon the trial that the contract of guaranty was illegal and void because it was made upon Sunday, upon which the court makes the following finding: "Although the preliminary oral discussions took place on two several Sundays, as duly appears, I do not find that the agreement was made or executed on Sunday." The defendant contends that this is not equivalent to a finding that it was not made on Sunday, and that as all the facts appear this court may determine the question as matter of law. Assuming for the purposes of this case that this position is correct, it is certain from the finding that the written guaranty was not executed or delivered on Sunday. It is an undertaking to answer for the debt of another, and to be binding it must be in writing, under the Statute of Frauds. The parol negotiations therefore which took place on Sunday could not under the Statute amount to a completed and binding agreement. The only binding contract in this case was made on a secular day. The plaintiff was under no necessity of proving, as part of her cause of action, her own or her agent's illegal desecration of the Sabbath. Her case began with the execution and delivery of the written contract, and that was perfectly valid. *Frost* v. *Plumb*, 40 Conn. 111.

The mere fact that a contract grows out of a transaction which took place on Sunday will not render it void. *Stackpole* v. *Symonds*, 23 N. H. 229; *Adams* v. *Gay*, 19 Vt. 358; *Goss* v. *Whitney*, 24 Vt. 187; *Butler* v. *Lee*, 11 Ala. 885.

Where a horse was bought (by parol) on Sunday, but was not delivered until Monday, it was held a valid sale, because the sale was not made binding on Sunday under the Statute of Frauds. *Bloxsome* v. *Williams*, 3 Barn. & C. 232; *Williams* v. *Paul*, 6 Bing. 653; *Lovejoy* v. *Whipple*, 18 Vt. 379.

A deed signed and acknowledged on Sunday, but not delivered till Monday, has been held good, upon the ground that it could only take effect from delivery. *Love* v. *Wells*, 25 Ind. 503; *Beitenman's App.* 55 Pa. 183; *Flanagan* v. *Meyer*, 41 Ala. 132.

So a note signed upon Sunday but delivered on a secular day has been held valid. *Hilton* v. *Houghton*, 35 Me. 143; *Clough* v. *Davis*, 9 N. H. 500; *Hill* v. *Dunham*, 7 Gray, 543.

The defendant's claim that a demand of the maker of these notes was necessary as a condition precedent to the maintenance of this action against the guarantor was properly overruled by the court. The guaranty was absolute and not conditional within the decisions of this court. *City Sav. Bank* v. *Hopson*, 53 Conn. 454, 2 New Eng. Rep. 556; *Breed* v. *Hillhouse*, 7 Conn. 523.

The judgment is also claimed to be erroneous in amount, in that the court made a mistake in computing the interest at $1,050, when it should have been only $1,038.50. The only color for such a claim is found in the last date given in the statement that the court gives "damages to the amount of the interest on both notes from said 28th day of August, 1886, accruing prior to the date of the commencement of this suit, namely, interest to February 26, 1887, amounting to $1,050." The only mistake was in giving the date under the videlicit as February 26, instead of February 28. There was in fact no mistake in the amount of interest found due. The record shows that there was six months' interest due February 28, 1887, upon $35,000, which amounts to the precise sum for which the court rendered judgment. It will be noticed that the suit was not commenced till July 26, 1887, so that the six months' interest had been overdue about five months.

The rulings of the court relative to the form of the questions to be put to Mr. Bush, one of the defendant's counsel, respecting his taking possession of the land in controversy, were fairly within the discretion of the presiding judge. The defendant was allowed to question the witness fully as to the circumstances under which possession was taken, and was only interfered with when it was obvious that the skillfully framed questions were designed to call out certain facts and exclude others connected with the same transaction. The counsel confessed finally that if he could not confine the witness exclusively to the arrangement had with Mr. Russell, he did not care to inquire at all.

The excluded questions relative to the talk between Russell and Bush as to the meaning of the guaranty, and the self-serving declarations of Waddingham relative to his contract, if admitted, could not properly have affected the legal construction of the written contract, which was unambiguous in its terms as we have seen.

The testimony of Scott offered by the plaintiff "to matters," (as the finding states) "material to the claimed liability of Waddingham under the second count," must have been as to some extrinsic circumstances favorable to the plaintiff's construction of the contract. Counsel for the defendant in their brief say in effect that such was the object of this testimony. But our construction of the contract is based entirely upon the language of the contract itself, which is so clear in its meaning that no extrinsic evidence can vary it. The exclusion therefore of a question designed only to show the bias of the witness, who had already been, as it would seem, effectually impeached by record evidence, could not have materially affected the defendant.

It is also assigned as error that the court sustained the demurrer to the second defense to the second count. The allegations of that defense were: 1. That on the — day of ——, 1887, Edward A. Anketell was duly appointed administrator on the estate of said Edward L. Kimberly, deceased, by the Court of Probate for the District of New Haven. 2. That on or about the — day of ——, 1887, the plaintiff duly presented said notes for payment to Edward A. Anketell, as such administrator, and claimed the payment of the same from said estate. 3. That on or about the 20th day of January, 1888, and after the time limited for the presentation of claims had expired, the plaintiff withdrew all claims against said estate for the payment of said notes or either of them or the interest thereon. 4. That the estate of said Kimberly was finally settled by said administrator on the 26th day of January, 1888, as a solvent estate.

It is too manifest to require discussion that the demurrer to this defense was properly sustained. These acts of the plaintiff could not have injuriously affected the defendant. As the plaintiff was not obliged to present her claim she had the right also either to withhold it or withdraw it. In order to discharge a surety there must be a release of "some mortgage, pledge or lien,—some right or interest in property which the creditor can hold in trust for the surety and to which the surety if he pay the debt can be subrogated,—and the right to apply or hold must exist and be absolute." *Glazier* v. *Douglass*, 32 Conn. 393.

We find no error upon the defendant's appeal, and the judgment in favor of the plaintiff upon the second count is affirmed.

There was error upon the plaintiff's appeal, and a new trial is granted under the first count, upon the issue whether the plaintiff knowingly elected to take Kimberly as her sole debtor for the payment of the price of the land.

In this opinion the other Judges concurred.

Richard B. LEAKE, Trustee, etc.,
v.
Thomas L. WATSON *et al.*

(58 Conn. 332.)

1. **One who sells trust securities,** knowing that the sale is for unauthorized purposes in violation of the trust, although he makes the sale simply as an agent, is liable to the beneficiaries for the breach of the trust.

2. **Knowledge that property is held in trust** is sufficient to put one dealing with it as agent upon inquiry as to the origin and nature of the trust, and to charge him with all the knowledge that inquiry properly directed would bring.

3. **Brokers who, at the request of the trustee** and one of the *cestuis que trustent*, sell stocks which they know belong to the trust fund, knowing also that the proceeds are to be used in stock speculation, are liable to account to the other *cestuis que trustent* for their share of the proceeds of the sale so far as they have been diverted from the legitimate purposes of the trust.

4. **Distribution by the probate court** of property to trustees in trust for a certain person, under a will giving her a life interest only, does not authorize persons dealing with the property to regard her as sole beneficiary.

5. **Property purchased from a fund,** which includes moneys held under different trusts, the title being taken as under one of the trusts only, is chargeable with the same trusts that attached originally to the fund as against those who deal with it knowing it to be trust property.

6. **The right of a trustee to sue for property,** which it is his duty to hold in trust for a certain person during her life, and which will then go to her heirs, does not depend on her interest in the property. He is under obligation to keep it safely until her death.

7. **No notice of the resignation of a trustee** and the appointment of his successor is required to be given to the heirs of one for whom, during her life, the trust is held, and whose heirs on her death are entitled to the property absolutely, since she has no heirs until after her death.

See also 30 L. R. A. 290.

(February 7, 1890.)

RESERVATION by the Superior Court for Fairfield County for the opinion of the Supreme Court of Errors of an action brought to recover the value of certain stocks and bonds which had been sold by defendants as brokers with alleged knowledge that the sale was in violation of a trust. *Judgment for plaintiff.*

Plaintiff was the substituted trustee under the will of Charles Bulkley, deceased.

Defendants defended upon the ground that at the time they made the sale they were ignorant of the existence of the will by which the trust was constituted; that the stocks and bonds were received by defendant Watson as a broker in the regular course of business from Mrs. Georgiana Nichols, *cestui que trust*, and Elizabeth Bulkley, then trustee, with orders to sell the same, and that he sold them in good faith without notice of plaintiff's claim.

The court below made the following finding of facts:

Charles Bulkley of Fairfield in this State died in 1875, leaving a will, which was duly probated, and which, after providing for his widow, proceeded as follows:

"*Fourth.* All the rest, residue and remainder of my estate, real and personal, I give, devise and bequeath unto trustees, as hereinafter named, for the uses and purposes hereinafter set forth, as follows:

"One fifth to be held in trust; and the income, use, interest and improvement thereof to be paid over annually, or in more frequent installments if deemed expedient and convenient by the trustees, unto and for the use and benefit of my daughter, Mary Elizabeth, wife of Isaac Jennings, the remainder to go to her heirs forever; provided that said Mary Elizabeth may, if she shall deem it expedient and necessary, from time to time take and receive portions of the principal, not exceeding in all one half of such principal, and not to exceed the sum of one thousand dollars in any one year; such portion of the principal to be paid over by the trustees upon notice in writing so to do, and the receipt of said Mary Elizabeth to be a sufficient voucher to the trustees in the premises. Three other parts, of one fifth each, to be held in trust in the same manner as aforesaid, with the same privilege of receiving portions of the principal, for the use and benefit respectively of my other daughters, Elizabeth Whitney, wife of Rev. Frederick S. Hyde, Georgiana, wife of William B. Nichols, and my aforementioned daughter, Catharine, with remainder to their heirs forever."

The remaining fifth was given to trustees for the benefit of the children of a deceased son. The will appointed Elizabeth Bulkney, the wife of the testator, and Oliver Bulkley, his nephew, executors and trustees, with a direction that no bond should be required of them.

The property was afterwards on the 1st day of February, 1876, distributed by order of the probate court, the distribution commencing as follows: "Estate of Charles Bulkley. The subscribers, distributors on said estate, having been legally sworn, have set out and distributed the same according to law and to the will of the said deceased, as follows:"

The distribution to Mrs. Nichols was headed as follows: "We set to Elizabeth Bulkley and Oliver Bulkley, trustees for Georgiana Nichols"—and then followed a list of stocks and bonds, amounting to $44,981.81. All the property thus set out to trustees for Mrs. Nichols was received and taken into possession by Oliver Bulkley, one of the trustees, being received by him as trustee from himself as executor. On the 21st day of August, 1885, Mr. Bulkley rendered his account as trustee to the court of probate, which was accepted, and he was on the same day, upon his application previously made, discharged from the trust. By his account thus rendered it appeared that $17,480.58 in value of the trust property then in his hands was made up of new investments since the commencement of the trust, the rest being the same property that was described in the distribution. New certificates of the stock had been taken in 1876 in the names of the two trustees. Upon his resignation as trustee Mr. Bulkley surrendered the certificates (with one exception) and procured new ones issued in the name of "Elizabeth Bulkley, Trustee for Georgiana Nichols," which were delivered by him to Mrs. Bulkley.

Mr. Bulkley, while acting as trustee, made ten annual payments of $1,000 each, commencing March 9, 1876, ending January 30, 1885, to Mrs. Nichols, from the principal of the fund, designed by him and accepted by her as payments of principal under the provisions of the will in reference to the $1,000 per year.

Georgiana Nichols was born in 1838, married in 1857, became single again in 1877, and has since so remained. She has three daughters, the youngest born in 1864, now the wife of Richard P. Leake, the plaintiff trustee, and one son aged fifteen. The defendant Watson resides in Bridgeport, and carries on business there under the name of T. L. Watson & Co. There is in fact no company, the business being his own exclusively. The defendant Smith is not a partner, but only an employé at a fixed salary. Watson is also a partner in the firm of Watson & Gibson, doing business in the City of New York. His business in Bridgeport has been established over twenty years, that in New York about ten years. The business is that of private bankers, brokers and dealers in stocks. The defendant Smith became an employé in May, 1884. He resides in New Haven. He has been the cashier, manager and confidential agent of Watson in the conduct of the Bridgeport business, to the details of which the latter, being occupied with his New York business, has given little attention, except an oversight of its general conduct. Watson has never been a member of the New York Stock Exchange, but his stock transactions were conducted through a firm called Prince & Whitely, members of the Exchange, having an office in New York with which Watson's Bridgeport office was connected by private wire. Prince & Whitely were the representatives of Watson on the floor of the New York Stock Exchange. In buying and selling stocks for customers Watson charged three sixteenths of one per cent, or eighteen and three-quarter dollars for each one hundred shares, of which one sixteenth was his own share, and the remaining two sixteenths was paid to Prince & Whitely, being the established rate paid to members of the Exchange on transactions,—all of which early became known to Mrs. Nichols; and she also knew that the securities held on margins were from time to time, as the exigencies of the margin account required, sent and transferred, in accordance with the custom of such business, by the defendants to Prince & Whitely. The defendant Smith first became personally acquainted with Mrs. Nichols in the early part of September, 1885, when she called at the banking office, and with her mother, Mrs. Bulkley, some two or three weeks later. Watson became acquainted with them in the spring of 1886. [Here followed a detailed statement of the particular transactions with the defendants.]

During the entire time covered by the transactions above detailed, from September, 1885, down to the summer of 1887, both Mrs. Bulkley and Mrs. Nichols had stock accounts with Watson, as a broker, doing business under the name of T. L. Watson & Co., and their stock transactions with him in his Bridgeport office, conducted mainly through Smith acting for him, in buying or selling on margin or speculation, were frequent and numerous. The accounts were kept in their individual names respectively, each having stock or margin accounts in addition to the bank, check or deposit account of Mrs. Nichols. There was also still another account in the name of Elizabeth Bulkley, trustee for Georgiana Nichols, which was a mixed account, commenced by paying in some cash with which stocks were bought as investment. Then more stocks were bought and the former used as margin to float the latter. There was no other account of this nature with any customer on the defendant's books. All stocks on margin were held on condition that the defendants should have a right to dispose of them without notice whenever the margin was reduced below a stipulated per cent. These stock speculations through the defendants were mainly directed by Mrs. Nichols, both on her own account and that of her mother, who was an aged lady, apparently fully dominated by her. Mrs. Nichols had had a previous experience in stock speculations and relied unduly upon her own judgment and sagacity. Her orders to the defendants were peremptory, and were complied with quite as fully as margins would allow. I do not find that the defendants ever induced or encouraged her to speculate; she needed no such inducement. On the contrary, they in some moderate measure endeavored to dissuade and restrain her. She made some fortunate speculations, but the general result was total disaster, both to the trust fund, which constituted her only individual resource, and to her mother's private means. All these transactions with the trust property were with her full knowledge and approval. All certificates transferred were signed by the trustee in form to correspond with the description in the certificate, and such signature to the power of transfer was generally witnessed by both Mrs. Nichols and by Smith. These powers were signed and witnessed in blank, when the certificates were left in pledge, on margin, or for disposition, and filled out whenever there was occasion to sell out the margin or otherwise dispose of them.

In addition to the transactions which appear herein, the defendants received other money and stocks as margin, being the private property of Mrs. Bulkley, and received money as dividends on trust stocks while held, and credited it to Mrs. Nichols, and also paid out money to and for her, for insurance, living expenses and otherwise, in checks and other ways, so that the above is not a complete statement of all the transactions between the parties; but I find generally that if it is lawful for the defendants to charge Mrs. Nichols for money advanced to or for her personally, or credited on her margin, or on her private account, as a counter-charge or offset for money received by them derived from the sale of trust certificates and property, with the approval or concurrence of Mrs. Bulkley, then, but not otherwise, they have fully accounted for the items hereinbefore specified and set forth.

I find that both the defendants at all times knew that the securities belonged to, and stood in the name of, "Elizabeth Bulkley, Trustee for Georgiana Nichols;", but they did not know, nor did they inquire with regard to, or use any means whatever to ascertain, the origin, nature, terms or limitations of the trust, and neither of them had actual, as distinguished from constructive, notice and knowledge of the existence of the will of Charles Bulkley, or the proceedings of the probate court in reference thereto. They knew where Mrs. Bulkley and Mrs. Nichols resided, which was in the Town of Fairfield, and both on one occasion visited them in their house, and on another occasion in their rooms, while temporarily residing at the Atlantic Hotel in Bridgeport. Both ladies, especially Mrs. Nichols, were well known in Bridgeport and Fairfield, and were members of a family of large reputed means. Although the business of T. L. Watson & Co. was very large and their customers numbered by the hundreds, yet the circumstance of having women customers as stock speculators was quite exceptional, though not without a precedent, in their business. There was no other such customer at the time these transactions took place. If the law is so that, upon these facts, and as a conclusion therefrom, the defendants can be charged with notice of the facts relating to the trust, its nature and terms, I am of the opinion, and therefore find, that they should be so charged.

I find by evidence offered by the defendants and objected to by the plaintiff, but received, if such evidence is admissible, that it is the custom of brokers and bankers, in the financial community where these transactions took place, in dealing with and transferring certificates of stock and other securities, standing in the name of a trustee named in the instrument, with transfer and blank power of attorney accompanying the same, regularly executed by such trustee, and acquiesced in by the person named as beneficiary, to transfer the same without any further information, knowledge or inquiry whatever.

I find that the expectation of life of Mrs. Nichols on November 19, 1887, was twenty-two years. The value of her life interest in an estate, according to recognized tables of such expectancy, is sixty-three per cent, and she is apparently in good health and vigor.

On November 10, 1887, Elizabeth Bulkley was removed by the probate court from the trust, and the plaintiff was appointed trustee in her place.

Messrs. **C. R. Ingersoll** and **W. L. Bennett**, for plaintiff:

A person coming into possession of property bound by a trust, with notice of the trust, holds subject to the trust.

Goddard v. *Prentice*, 17 Conn. 546.

When a person deals with another in regard to property known to be held by the party in a representative capacity, he is put upon inquiry as to the power of the fiduciary and is held to know all that inquiry would have taught him.

Shaw v. *Spencer*, 100 Mass. 382; *Loring* v. *Brodie*, 134 Mass. 453; *Smith* v. *Burgess*, 133 Mass. 511; *Graff* v. *Castleman*, 5 Rand. 195; *Strong* v. *Strauss*, 40 Ohio St. 87; *Sigourney* v. *Munn*, 7 Conn. 324; *Boswell* v. *Goodwin*, 31 Conn. 74; *Blatchley* v. *Osborn*, 33 Conn. 226; *Duncan* v. *Jaudon*, 82 U. S. 15 Wall. 165 (21 L. ed. 142); *Central Nat. Bank of Baltimore* v. *Connecticut Mut. L. Ins. Co.* 104 U. S. 54 (26 L. ed. 693); *Earl of Sheffield* v. *London Joint-Stock Bank*, L. R. 13 App. Cas. 333.

The fact alone of the offer by Mrs. Bulkley to pledge these stocks was sufficient to put these defendants on inquiry.

Anderson v. *Kissam*, 35 Fed. Rep. 699; *Merchants Bank of Canada* v. *Livingston*, 74 N. Y. 223; *Deobold* v. *Opperman*, 2 L. R. A. 644, 111 N. Y. 531; *Smith* v. *Ayer*, 101 U. S. 320 (25 L. ed. 955); *Prall* v. *Hamil*, 28 N. J. Eq. 66; *Carter* v. *Manufacturer's Nat. Bank of Lewiston*, 71 Me. 453; *Bayard* v. *Farmers & M. Bank of Phila.* 52 Pa. 232.

A trustee may not hazard the trust fund in a trade or business.

1 Perry, Tr. § 454; *King* v. *Talbot*, 40 N. Y. 76; *Loring* v. *Brodie*, *supra*.

Defendants could not safely assume that even together the trustee and *cestui que trust* had the power which they claimed to have.

Deobold v. *Oppermann*, *supra*.

Messrs. **H. Stoddard** and **G. Stoddard**, for defendants:

Defendants were mere agents, selling the securities in the open market as brokers. They sold in good faith, without notice of any *cestui que trust* except Mrs. Nichols.

2 Pom. Eq. § 1048; 1 Perry, Tr. § 246.

An agent is accountable to his principal only.

2 Perry, Tr. § 813; 1 Lewin, Tr. 191. See also 1 Lewin, Tr. 482; 2 Lewin, Tr. 641.

In order to establish the liability of bankers and brokers there must be: "(1), a misapplication or breach of trust actually intended," and "(2), the bankers must be privy to such intended misapplication or breach of trust."

Maw v. *Pearson*, 28 Beav. 196; *Keane* v. *Robarts*, 4 Madd. 332; *Bardy* v. *Caley*, 33 Beav. 366; *Gray* v. *Johnston*, L. R. 3 H. L. 1; *Barnes* v. *Addy*, L. R. 9 Ch. App. 244.

Where the trustee, having the legal right, pledges or disposes of property for a purpose apparently proper, the title of the pledgee will be perfect even if the trustee intended a fraud, if the loan was made for a purpose apparently proper, without knowledge, actual or implied, of such intention.

Goodwin v. *Am. Nat. Bank*, 48 Conn. 550;.

Duncan v. *Jaudon*, 82 U. S. 15 Wall. 176 (21 L. ed. 145); *Shaw* v. *Spencer*, 100 Mass. 382.

It is no answer for the plaintiff to say that these ladies were speculating and that the defendants knew it. They had a perfect right to speculate.

Hatch v. *Douglas*, 48 Conn. 116.

The judgment of the court of probate that Mrs. Nichols is the beneficiary of the trust in question is conclusive upon all persons, including the plaintiff, until it is reversed.

Rev. 1875, p. 371, § 16; Gen. Stat. 1888, § 628; *Pinney* v. *Bissell*, 7 Conn. 21; *Davenport* v. *Richards*, 16 Conn. 310; *Bissell* v. *Bissell*, 24 Conn. 241; *Brush* v. *Button*, 36 Conn. 292; *Beach* v. *Norton*, 9 Conn. 182; *Am. Bible Society* v. *Wetmore*, 17 Conn. 181; *Ashmead's App. from Probate*, 27 Conn. 241; *Mix's App. from Probate*, 35 Conn. 121; *Vail's App. from Probate*, 37 Conn. 185.

Notice of an unsuspected trust, an undisclosed beneficiary and a doubtful equity, is not to be imputed to the defendants.

2 Perry, Tr. §§ 833, 834; *Goodwin* v. *Am. Nat. Bank*, 48 Conn. 550; *Wilson* v. *Wall*, 73 U. S. 6 Wall. 83 (18 L. ed. 727); *Williams* v. *Jackson*, 107 U. S. 478 (27 L. ed. 529).

The certificate in this case stood in the name of a trustee for a particular person. There was nothing to suggest inquiry. The certificate exhausted the subject.

See *Duncan* v. *Jaudon*, 82 U. S. 15 Wall. 165 (21 L. ed. 142).

The plaintiff is not a trustee for the heirs of Mrs. Nichols.

Noble v. *Andrews*, 37 Conn. 346.

The active concurrence of the *cestui que trust* in a breach of trust bars his right of complaint.

1 Perry, Tr. § 467; 2 Perry, Tr. § 849; *Evans* v. *Benyon*, L. R. 37 Ch. Div. 329; *Fyler* v. *Fyler*, 3 Beav. 555; *note* to *Brice* v. *Stokes*, 2 White & T. Lead. Cas. in Eq. 4th Am. ed. 1748.

Carpenter, *J.*, delivered the opinion of the court:

Counsel for the respective parties have argued this case upon distinct and widely different theories,—for the defendants, on the theory that they were merely agents; for the plaintiff on the theory that the defendants were purchasers or pledgees. Each party, in his chosen position, is strongly intrenched. Grant his premises, and his position is well nigh impregnable; grant the premises of both, were it possible, and a decision of the case would be very difficult. But both cannot be right. The defendants cannot be entitled to the immunities of agents and at the same time liable as purchasers.

Our first inquiry then is, Were they purchasers or agents? So far as they sold the securities as mere agents, in good faith, without knowledge, actual or constructive, that other persons interested in the trust were being prejudiced; in other words, so long as they did not knowingly participate in a breach of the trust, and have fully accounted,—they are not liable. In that case they conveyed no title of their own, but only such title as the principal could convey. The principal and the purchasers were the contracting parties. For the purposes of re-investment, and of paying Mrs. Nichols such portions of the principal as she might be entitled to, Mrs. Bulkley as trustee had a right to sell, and the defendants might safely act as her agents for that purpose. If she sold for other purposes, in violation of the trust, with the defendants' knowledge, even though they may have sold as agents, still we think they are liable.

If Mrs. Bulkley sold the trust estate for the purpose of using the proceeds in stock speculations, or of permitting Mrs. Nichols so to use them, it was a clear breach of trust. If the defendants were the purchasers, knowing the purpose, they participated in the breach of trust. If they were holding stocks or other securities on margins for Mrs. Bulkley or Mrs. Nichols, or both, and received the trust estate as security, and subsequently sold it, using the avails to make good the losses, their liability cannot be questioned.

So long as trust property improperly sold can be traced and identified, the holder taking it with knowledge, it remains trust property. When it is sold pursuant to the terms of the trust, or apparently so, and the purchaser takes it in good faith, he takes it freed from the trust. In this case the finding shows that most of the property passed from the trustee to the defendants as trust property, in gross violation of the trust, with the defendants' full knowledge. We say with the defendants' full knowledge, because the defendants, knowing that it was trust property, were put upon inquiry, and the law imputes to them such knowledge as they would have obtained had they made inquiry. The trust, its terms, conditions and limitations, were matters of record. Inquiry, properly directed, would have brought to them full knowledge as to the origin and nature of the trust, and that other parties besides Mrs. Bulkley and Mrs. Nichols were interested in it. They had no moral or equitable right to assume, as they manifestly did, that Mrs. Nichols was the owner of the entire beneficial interest. They knew, or were bound to know, that her interest was only for life; consequently that at her death the trust would cease and that the whole estate would pass into other hands.

That the defendants participated in the breach of trust can admit of no doubt. They knew that Mrs. Bulkley and Mrs. Nichols were using the property in hazardous business—stock speculations; that they themselves were taking the only certain profits, their commissions, while doubtful profits, almost certain losses, and probably complete disaster in the end, were the perquisites of the other party.

It seems very clear to us that the defendants are liable for the trust property, if any, now in their hands, and for the avails of that which they have disposed of, less the amount which appears to have been used for the legitimate purposes of the trust.

We will consider more in detail some of the objections raised by the defendants.

1. They contend that under the circumstances no constructive notice of an unknown and unsuspected trust can be made the basis of an action. Here doubtless they refer to the interest of the remaindermen. The defendants, knowing that the property with which they were dealing was trust property, were bound to inquire and ascertain the nature and

extent of the trust. Inquiry would have informed them that the same instrument which created the trust in favor of Mrs. Nichols gave the remainder to her heirs at law. It matters not, so far as the question of notice is concerned, whether the gift over is valid or void. It is enough that there are possible parties who have an interest in the property besides Mrs. Bulkley and Mrs. Nichols. As that fact clearly appears on the face of the will, the trust is neither unknown nor unsuspected.

2. It is insisted that the action of the court of probate in distributing to trustees in trust for Mrs. Nichols is conclusive that she is the sole beneficiary. It is conclusive as to the property constituting the trust estate, but it is not conclusive as to the parties interested in the estate. The distribution is in terms made under the will, which gave Mrs. Nichols only a life estate. A life estate is necessarily followed by a remainder, and the will disposes of the remainder. The court of probate makes no distribution of the remainder.

3. That the equity, if any, of the plaintiff, or any other possible beneficiary, was not only secret, unknown and unsuspected, but was at least so doubtful that no implied or constructive notice can be imputed to the defendants. There is no doubt or uncertainty as to the equities of the reversioners. There may be a question as to who they are, but that is not such a doubt as will justify the application of the rule invoked.

4. It appears that Oliver Bulkley, while he was trustee, sold portions of the various trusts which he held and mingled the avails in one common fund. With a part of this fund he purchased other property, taking the title in himself and Elizabeth Bulkley as trustees for Mrs. Nichols. The defendants claim that they are not liable for any of that property which came into their hands. That cannot be so. Any property purchased by the trustees to take the place of that sold by them is trust estate, so far as the defendants are concerned.

5. It is further contended that the plaintiff is not trustee for the heirs of Mrs. Nichols; that the remainder never was in trust; that the trust was created for the daughters alone, and that the heirs receive a title in fee. But the trust attaches to the property and continues until the property is delivered to the remaindermen. The trustees are chargeable with the duty of safely keeping the property until then. The law undertakes that that duty shall be performed. If a trustee proves unfaithful he is removed, and another appointed, who is clothed with the necessary powers to maintain the integrity of the trust. Therefore the plaintiff's right to recover does not depend upon Mrs. Nichols' interest in the property.

6. The last objection we care to consider is that, as no notice was given to the children of Mrs. Nichols of the resignation of Oliver Bulkley, that resignation, and the action of the probate court in accepting the same and in appointing another trustee, are inoperative so far as the trust relates to the heirs; that to that extent Oliver Bulkley is still trustee, and legally responsible; and that the defendants cannot be held responsible until it is demonstrated that he cannot make the fund good.

We do not think that the heirs were beneficiaries in such a sense that notice to them was necessary. The express or principal trust will terminate on the death of Mrs. Nichols. The resulting trust will enable the trustees to hold the property until it can be delivered to the heirs. Strictly speaking, the latter could not and did not exist during the trusteeship of Oliver Bulkley, and cannot come into existence during the lifetime of Mrs. Nichols. It is difficult therefore to see how he could have been regarded as trustee for the heirs. It is doubtless true that if he had been guilty of wasting the trust estate he would be liable, either to his successor or to the heirs; but there can be no justice in holding him liable for the squandering of the estate by his successor.

It is the contention of the defendants that there should be no judgment against them in the present proceeding, even if they applied the proceeds of sales of trust shares upon their account against Mrs. Nichols in her own name, for the reason that these shares were her absolute property; that the gifts in remainder by the testator to the heirs of his daughters respectively are void by force of the Statute against Perpetuities, and that therefore the daughters took the fee in such shares as were put under the several trusts for their benefit.

It is the further contention of the defendants that Mrs. Nichols requested them to sell the trust shares and apply the proceeds for her sole use and benefit, upon their account against her for the purchase of shares upon margins for her profit, and that, so far forth as that may have been done, the *corpus* of the fund has been paid to and consumed by her; and that, to the extent to which she was such absolute owner because of the invalidity of the remainder over, the defendants are to be protected by a court of equity against a judgment compelling them to make a payment to the fund which by any possibility should inure solely to her benefit.

These claims upon the part of the defendants virtually call for the judicial interpretation of the will of Charles Bulkley; for a determination of the question as to the validity of the several remainders over; of the question to what extent, if to any, Mrs. Nichols was the absolute owner of the shares which were for her use and upon her request taken from under the trust.

That these questions may be properly considered and finally determined, it is deemed best to remand this case, reserved for our consideration, for the purpose of giving opportunity to these defendants, if they may choose to avail themselves of it, by bill in the nature of interpleader or cross-bill, to summon into court Mrs. Nichols and the other children of Charles Bulkley, deceased, and the heirs of each of them, and make them parties, so far as they may choose to be heard, and thus obtain a judicial construction of the will in question, to the end that the measure of right in Mrs. Nichols in the shares set apart in trust for her may be determined, and all questions presented by the respective parties may have final determination in one proceeding.

In this opinion the other Judges concurred.

MARYLAND COURT OF APPEALS.

Max BALLOCK, *Appt.*,
v.
STATE OF MARYLAND.

(....Md....)

1. **Any device whereby money or any other thing is to be paid** or delivered on the happening of any event or contingency in the nature of a lottery is illegal under the laws relating to lotteries and lottery tickets.

2. **The fact that there are no blanks** to be drawn but that the holder of every number or ticket obtains something of value, does not prevent a distribution of prizes by lot or chance from being a lottery.

3. **Nor will the fact that the scheme provides for a return of the entire investment** with interest prevent its being condemned as a lottery, if the time for such return is dependent on the revolution of a wheel, and the inducement for investing is the possibility of getting a bonus which is to be determined in the same manner.

4. **Bonds of foreign governments** coupled with conditions and stipulations which change their character from simple government bonds for the payment of a certain sum of money to a species of lottery ticket are within the condemnation of statutes against lotteries and subject to state laws on the subject.

(July 1, 1890.)

APPEAL by defendant from a ruling of the Criminal Court for Baltimore City admitting certain evidence upon the trial of an indictment for a violation of the Lottery Laws. *Affirmed.*

The facts sufficiently appear in the opinion.

Argued before Alvey, *Ch. J.*, and Bryan, McSherry, Fowler, Briscoe and Irving, *JJ.*

Messrs. **William S. Bryan, Jr.**, and **Peter J. Campbell** for appellant.

Messrs. **William Pinkney Whyte** and **C. G. Kerr** for appellee.

Irving, *J.*, delivered the opinion of the court:

Section 172 of article 27 of the Code of Public General Laws of this State is in these words: "No person shall draw any lottery or sell any lottery ticket in this State; nor shall any person sell what are called policies, certificates or anything by which the vendor or other person promises or guarantees that any particular number, character, ticket or certificate shall, in any event or on the happening of any contingency, entitle the purchaser or holder to receive money, property or evidences of debt."

Section 173 of the same article provides that "all devices and contrivances designed to evade the provisions of the preceding section shall be deemed offenses against it."

Section 176 makes provision for punishing anyone who may keep a house, office or other place for the purpose of selling or bartering any lottery ticket, policy certificate or any other thing by which the vendor or other person promises or guarantees that any particular number, character, ticket or certificate shall in any event or in the happening of any contingency in the nature of a lottery entitle the purchaser or holder to receive money, property or evidence of debt.

The next section punishes the owner of any house for permitting it to be used "as a place for selling lottery tickets or any of the things in the nature thereof mentioned in the preceding section."

The appellant was indicted in the Criminal Court of Baltimore for violating these Lottery Laws of the State. The first count charges the appellant with selling to Bernard C. Winckler "a lottery ticket." The second count charges the sale of a "lottery policy." The third charges the sale of a "lottery certificate." The fourth count charges him with selling "a certain thing by which the vendor thereof promised that a particular number should, on the happening of a contingency in the nature of a lottery, entitle the holder of said thing to receive money contrary to the form of the Act of Assembly in such case made and provided," etc. Other counts charged him with keeping "a room," "a place," "a house," for the sale of such things, and for permitting such room, place or house to be kept for such purpose.

No question arises upon the form or sufficiency of the indictment. The appeal presents but a single question, whether certain evidence was properly admitted by the trial court in support of any of these charges against the appellant.

The case was tried before the court without the aid of a jury, and the only exception in the case is to the admission of the testimony set out in the exception which was objected to *en masse*. The witness testified that the appellant sold to him for the sum of $95 an instrument called an "Austrian Government Bond," which provides that the Austrian government will pay to its bearer the principal sum of 100

NOTE.—*Lottery schemes defined.*

See *note* to Yellowstone Kit v. State (Ala.) 7 L. R. A. 599; People v. Elliott (Mich.) 3 L. R. A. 403.

A lottery, within the meaning of statutes against carrying on lotteries, embraces only schemes in which a valuable consideration of some kind is paid directly or indirectly for the chance to draw a prize. Yellowstone Kit v. State (Ala.) 7 L. R. A. 599, 41 Alb. L. J. 392.

Distributing prizes by lot or chance to holders of tickets given away is not carrying on a lottery, although it may be done with the view of drawing a large crowd together in the hope of profit from such of them as may choose to buy medicines from the distributor, or tickets to performances given by him, or to pay for seats in the tent where the prizes are selected, where no payment for any purpose is necessary as a condition of receiving a prize. *Ibid.*

The game, practiced in aid of fairs and charities, of voting, with tickets purchased at fixed prices, for candidates, of whom one in whose name the most tickets are voted is to receive some article which the whole number of tickets pays for, is not illegal, either under the statute or at common law, in Maine. Dion v. St. John Baptiste Society (Me.) Feb. 11, 1890.

See also 31 L. R. A. 792, 835.

gulden (Austrian value) in accordance with its condition set forth on the back of the instrument, together with one fifth-part of any such sum of money as may be allotted to the prize number of the bond, and which sum must amount to at least 120 gulden (Austrian value) with interest semi annually on the bond until the same is drawn at the rate of five per cent per annum; and by the rules and regulations concerning the drawing and redemption of these bonds, indorsed on the instrument in question, it is, in substance, provided that the bonds issued on the loan of March 15, 1860, are divided into 20,000 equal series, and each series to the amount of 10,000 gulden is subdivided into twenty numbers, marked from 1 to 20. Each of the bonds contains on its left heading the number of the series, and on its right its prize number; the drawing of the series numbers it is provided shall take place on the first day of February and August in each year; that of the prize number on the first day of May and the second day of November in each year. For the purpose of the drawing of the series 20,000 numbers are deposited in a wheel from which the fixed number of series to be redeemed for the half year is drawn.

The series numbers so drawn are then deposited in a second wheel to await the next drawing of prize numbers. On the day when the drawing of prize numbers takes place twenty numbers, from 1 to 20, are deposited in a separate wheel, whereupon the wheel wherein the series numbers are deposited is unlocked, and one number drawn therefrom. This number designates the series of the bond which is entitled to the highest prize. Thereupon the number from the wheel containing the twenty prize numbers is to be drawn, and this number designates the bond which is entitled to the highest prize. In this manner the drawings are to be continued until all the prizes above 600 gulden are exhausted. All other bonds receive the principal and interest, twenty per cent, in addition.

At every drawing the following prizes are drawn: first one of 300,000 gulden, one of 50,-000 gulden, one of 25,000 gulden, two of 10,-000 gulden, fifteen of 5,000 gulden, and thirty of 1,000 gulden. Drawn bonds are to be paid three months after the drawing. The holder of a bond receives in any event the face value thereof with interest at five per cent up to the drawing and a premium prize of twenty per cent. He has also the chance to draw one of the highest prizes. The chance varied from 60,000 to 200 gulden. This statement of the offer is in the bill of exceptions, and the translated bond furnished the court does not materially vary the statement.

Our Statute allows the sale of nothing which, on the happening of a contingency in the nature of a lottery, brings pecuniary benefit, which would not be enjoyed but for the chance falling to the holder. Courts are required by section 184 to construe the provisions liberally in order to reach and suppress the evil, and they are required to hold "anything" to be a lottery ticket, which, on the happening of such event or contingency in the nature of a lottery, entitles the holder to money or property.

In *Smith* v. *State*, 68 Md. 170, this court decided that it was the duty of the courts to hold any device whereby money or any other thing is to be paid or delivered on the happening of any event or contingency in the nature of a lottery to be a lottery ticket. The same view is reiterated in *Boyland* v. *State*, 69 Md. 512. Every possible phase of such transaction seems to have been provided against in our Statute. Section 183 of article 27 of the Code provides that these sections relating to lotteries shall apply to all lotteries, "whether authorized by any State, District or Territory, or by any foreign country." This provision effectually disposes of the contention that the word "person" in the Statute does not include a sovereign State or country. The Statute provides that it shall.

Webster defines a lottery to be "a distribution of prizes by lot or chance," and Worcester says: "It is a distribution of prizes and blanks by chance; a game in which small sums are ventured for the chance of obtaining a larger value."

It has been strenuously and ably contended that because there are no blanks in the wheel, but something of value must always come to the holder of any particular number, it is no lottery ticket. Such does not seem to be the legal acceptation; and under our law it certainly cannot be.

In *Hull* v. *Ruggles*, 56 N. Y. 424, it is said: "Where pecuniary consideration is paid and it is determined by lot or chance, according to some scheme held out to the public, what and how much he who pays the money is to receive for it, that is a lottery." Something very inconsiderable could be substituted for the blank, if the defendant's argument was sound, and this would entirely destroy its character as a lottery. Its vicious character would be entirely purged by such substitution. Our Statute certainly prohibits such evasion and prevents a ruling which would sanction such evasion or make it possible. The law of this State for the purpose of preventing the mischiefs lotteries are thought to produce makes anything partaking of the nature of a lottery a lottery. It has been vigorously argued that because the money ventured must all come back, with interest, so that there can be no final loss, it cannot be a lottery, even within the meaning of our law. At some uncertain period, determined by the revolution of a wheel of fortune, the purchaser of a bond does get his money repaid; but we do not think this deprives the thing of its evil tendency or robs it of its lottery semblance and features. The inducement for investing in such bond is offered of getting some "bonus," large or small, in the future soon or late according to the chances of the wheel's disclosures. The investment may run one year, or it may run thirty years, according to the decision of the wheel. It cannot be said this is not a species of gambling, and that it does not tend in any degree to promote a gambling spirit, and a mode of making gain through the chance of dice, cards, wheel or other method of settling a contingency. It certainly cannot be said that it is not in the "nature of a lottery," and that it has no tendency to create desire for other and more pernicious modes of gaming. Our Statute does not justify a court, expressly directed to so construe the law as to prevent every possible evasion, whether designedly or accidentally adopted, in deciding a thing is not a lottery, simply because there can be no loss, when there may be very large contingent gains; or because it lacks some element of a lottery according to some particular dictionary's definition of one, when it has all the other elements with all the pernicious tendencies which the State is seeking to prevent. Striking at the root of the evil and to prevent all its possible mischiefs, the Statute lays down a different rule from that applied to the construction of other criminal statutes, which is a rule of strict construction. Instead of that rule the law says this Statute is to be construed liberally in order to prevent the introduction and use of anything in the nature of a lottery, for the making of money or securing property.

The case of *Kohn* v. *Koehler*, 96 N. Y. 362, was a civil suit under the New York Statute to recover double the amount paid by plaintiff for a bond exactly like the one here involved, and does decide that it did not fall under the condemnation of the New York Statute; and the *Shobert Case*, 70 Cal. 632, follows it in construing the California Statute.

We have examined the Statutes of those States, and do not think those cases can or ought to control us in the construction of our Statute, which is so essentially different from both the New York and the California Law. Even upon the New York Statute we think the reasoning of *Judge* Davis in the supreme court, in *Kohn* v. *Koehler*, 21 Hun, 466–470, more convincing and sounder than that of the appellate court which reversed the supreme court's decision in the case; and we approve the reasoning of the supreme court. Our State has such a well-defined policy respecting lotteries and regards them or anything in the nature of them so detrimental to public and private morals, and so much in the way of the certain and substantial thrift of its citizens, that it has forbidden the dealing in anything partaking of their nature. It has expressly included, as we have already noted, anything of that nature authorized by other States and foreign governments. Its dignity and laws, therefore, ought to be upheld unless the law be plainly violation of constitutional obligation or treaty and stipulation. We cannot see that our law is so. It is true the Austrian government bonds are vendible, and ought to be treated as other articles of commerce, as a rule; but when those bonds are coupled with conditions and stipulations which change their character from simple government bonds for the payment of a certain sum of money to a species of lottery ticket which falls under the condemnation of our Statutes, it must be classed as its conditions characterize it, and then it is not vendible under our law, and it does not violate constitutional provision or a treaty stipulation to so hold. All the decisions of the supreme court make a saving in favor of police regulations, as within constitutional authority. Such bonds as this should be no more protected in their sale than diseased meat or diseased cattle, which no one would contend could not and should not be restricted and punished. They are property, of course, and their possession would be protected, and, if disturbed, the law would redress. So it would be with Louisiana lottery tickets, which are confessedly not salable; and such bonds should be no more protected in sale than the lottery tickets, pure and simple.

The case has been argued as if this defendant was charged to be and is an Austrian subject, and entitled by treaty stipulation to sell and dispose of his property. He is not so charged to be, and if he was, he would have to be treated exactly as if he were a citizen of the United States and the State of Maryland. The criminal laws operate alike and equally upon residents and nonresidents. As an Austrian he could not sell lottery tickets in the Louisiana lottery, although he might own them, with any more immunity and right than one of our own citizens. Constitutional provisions and treaty stipulations never could have been intended to prevent a State from forbidding that which was deemed injurious to its people. We think the evidence excepted to was properly admitted. The ruling will be affirmed.

Ruling affirmed and cause remanded.

PHILADELPHIA, WILMINGTON & BALTIMORE R. CO., *Appt.*,

v.

Charles H. ANDERSON.

(....Md....)

1. **Passenger carriers are bound to exercise** the utmost degree of care, skill and dili-

---

NOTE.—*Carriers; duty to use care for safety of passengers.*

In respect to carrying passengers a railroad company is bound to exercise all the care and skill which human prudence and oversight can suggest to secure the safety of its passengers. Diabola v. Manhattan R. Co. 29 N. Y. S. R. 149.

They are bound to use the best precautions in known practical use, to secure the safety of their passengers; and this is the measure of their duty whether they carry them on freight or mixed trains, or on exclusively passenger trains. Oviatt v. Dakota Cent. R. Co. (Minn.) May 19, 1890.

They are bound to keep the platforms at their passenger stations in a safe condition for persons to enter and leave the cars; and failure to do so will render the company liable to persons injured, without fault on their part, on account of the defect. See *note* to Pennsylvania Co. v. Marion (Ind.) 7 L. R. A. 687.

All that is required of a carrier to overthrow the presumption of negligence on its part, arising through injury to a passenger, and to exonerate itself from liability, is to show that, in the conduct of its business, it had employed the utmost skill, prudence and circumspection practically and usually applied to railroad carrying. Louisville, N. A. & C. R. Co. v. Jones, 7 West. Rep. 83, 108 Ind. 551.

A railroad company is liable for actual damages for failing to announce or give notice in some way of the station, and to stop its train long enough for a passenger to get off with safety. Dorrah v. Illinois Cent. R. Co. 65 Miss. 14.

It is liable if a reasonable time to leave is not afforded the passenger and he is injured in an attempt to alight after it has started and while in motion, if he does not, in getting off, incur a danger obvious to the mind of a reasonable man. Central R. & Bkg. Co. v. Miles, 88 Ala. 256.

The fact that the conductor did not know that a

gence, consistent with the nature of their business, in providing safe and convenient modes of access to their trains and of departure from them.

2. **Where a passenger is injured while attempting to alight from a train** at a regular station, by another train belonging to the same carrier and in charge of its servants, which runs past the station platform while the passengers of the former train are being received and discharged, the carrier, to relieve itself from liability for damages, must show that it used the degree of care which the law imposed upon it.

3. **The existence of negligence** cannot be determined as a matter of law unless the inference of it from the facts is certain and incontrovertible.

4. **Whether or not a passenger was guilty of negligence** who, in the night, after the name of his station had been called and the train stopped, attempted to alight from the car, is a question for the jury, although the car stopped before reaching the platform, which fact he might have discovered by looking for the station lights, and had, after a momentary pause, begun to move again slowly before he made the attempt, at least if there is nothing to show that he knew the purpose of the renewed movement of the train.

5. **A passenger is justified in assuming** that no train will be permitted to pass a station at which a passenger train has stopped for the discharge and receipt of passengers in such manner as to interfere with them; hence he cannot be held guilty of contributory negligence as matter of law because he failed, before leaving the car on which he was traveling, to look out for an approaching train by which he was injured.

(*McSherry, J., dissents.*)

(June 19, 1890.)

APPEAL by defendant from a judgment of the Circuit Court for Cecil County in favor of plaintiff in an action brought to recover

---

passenger intended to leave the car, and did not see him leaving it, does not excuse the company for not giving such passenger reasonable time to get off the train, unless he was so situated as to conceal himself from the conductor's observation. McDonald v. Long Island R. Co. 116 N. Y. 546.

If after a train stops at a station a passenger remains in his seat after a reasonable opportunity to get up, it is not necessarily negligence for the conductor to assume that he did not intend to leave at that station. *Ibid.*

Calling the name of a station and stopping the train soon after to take a side track while another train passes, will not make the carrier liable for injuries to a passenger who attempts to get off at that place, where all the surroundings indicate that it is not the proper place for alighting. Smith v. Georgia Pac. R. Co. 7 L. R. A. 323, 88 Ala. 538.

A railroad company cannot be held liable for failure of its train to come to a full stop at a station where a passenger alights, where, before the train has stopped, another passenger pulls the bell rope, causing it to acquire speed again, the alighting passenger being aware of such action and of its effect. Mississippi & T. R. Co. v. Harrison, 66 Miss. 419.

A passenger on a railroad train has the right to assume that he will be given reasonable opportunity to get off the train before it starts, and his omission to retain hold upon the railing at the moment he is about to step from the car onto the platform of the station is not a ground for imputing negligence to him. McDonald v. Long Island R. Co. 116 N. Y. 546.

A passenger, in attempting to alight or jump from a moving train, may be justified in a particular case in relying upon the superior knowledge of the conductor as to the speed or movements of the train and other circumstances, in following his directions, particularly when notified to act promptly to prevent being carried beyond the station. Jones v. Chicago, M. & St. P. R. Co. (Minn.) Dec. 20, 1889.

For a conductor to notify or advise a passenger to leave a train while in motion, under circumstances likely to expose him to accident or injury, is negligence and unwarrantable conduct. *Ibid.*

A passenger who sustained no injury by jumping from a train which failed to stop at a flag station, where he had instructed the conductor to stop, can recover nominal damages only. Kansas City, M. & B. R. Co. v. Fite (Miss.) Jan. 27, 1890.

Exemplary damages cannot be recovered of a railroad company for failure to announce or give notice of a station and to stop its trains long enough for a passenger to alight with safety, unless such action is accompanied by willfulness or other aggravating conduct. Dorrah v. Illinois Cent. R. Co. 65 Miss. 14.

Contributory negligence of passenger.

It cannot be said, as a matter of law independently of any statute, that it would under all circumstances be an act of negligence for a passenger to attempt to alight from a moving train. Raben v. Central Iowa R. Co. 74 Iowa, 732.

But the attempt on the part of a passenger to get off from a moving train, in the absence of any evidence of necessity, apparent or real, is contributory negligence as a matter of law. New York, L. E. & W. R. Co. v. Enches, 4 L. R. A. 482, 127 Pa. 316.

While it is the duty of a railroad company to stop at the station and land a passenger safely and conveniently, yet, if the company neglects this duty and passes the station without stopping, it does not justify a passenger in jumping from a moving train, unless expressly invited by the employés of the company to do so. Walker v. Vicksburg, S. & P. R. Co (La.) 7 L. R. A. 111.

Where he was impelled to jump simply from his unwillingness to be carried beyond his destination he was guilty of contributory fault. *Ibid.*

Unless a train is moving very slowly and the circumstances are especially favorable, it is prima facie negligence for a passenger to attempt to alight or jump from a moving train. Jones v. Chicago, M. & St. P. R. Co. (Minn.) Dec. 20, 1889.

If a passenger gets off of a moving train by his own volition without being instructed to do so, being left free to remain and get off when he pleases, and is injured in so getting off, he cannot recover against the company. Whelan v. Georgia, M. & G. R. Co. (Ga.) March 1, 1890.

Negligence of passenger in getting on and off cars while in motion. See *notes* to Hunter v. Cooperstown & S. V. R. Co. (N. Y.) 2 L. R. A. 832; New York, P. & N. R. Co. v. Coulbourn (Md.) 1 L. R. A. 541.

Duty to land passenger safely. See *note* to De Kay v. Chicago, M. & St. P. R. Co. (Minn.) 4 L. R. A. 632; Missouri Pac. R. Co. v. Wortham, 3 L. R. A. 368, *note*, 73 Tex. 25.

Degree of care required of carriers of passengers. See Dodge v. Boston & B. S. S. Co. 2 L. R. A. 83, *note*, 148 Mass. 207; Goodsell v. Taylor, 4 L. R. A. 673, 41 Minn. 207. See *note* to Cincinnati, I. St. L. & C. R. Co. v. Cooper (Ind.) 6 L. R. A. 241.

damages for personal injuries alleged to have resulted from defendant's negligence. *Affirmed.*

The facts sufficiently appear in the opinion.

Argued before Alvey, *Ch. J.*, and Robinson, Bryan, McSherry, Fowler and Briscoe, *JJ.*

Mr. **William J. Jones**, with *Messrs.* **John J. Donaldson, L. Marshall Haines** and **William Ward**, for appellant:

There is no liability upon the defendant because, under the ruling in *Lewis* v. *London, C. & D. R. Co.*, L. R. 9 Q. B. 70, 71, there was no negligence in stopping for an instant, where the plaintiff testifies he might have seen where he was if he had looked.

The plaintiff does not bring himself within any of the cases, for they all relate to passengers leaving the train while at rest, upon the invitation of the railroad company. But this man left the train after it had resumed its journey.

His right to recover rests entirely upon the cases which have been decided of passengers leaving moving trains; and no court has gone further than to say that where the plaintiff looks, and believes from what he sees that he may alight in safety, he may go to the jury, if the court can see that the risk was one that a reasonable man would take. Here he did not look when he leaped.

Mr. **Albert Constable** for appellee.

Bryan, *J.*, delivered the opinion of the court:

Anderson recovered a judgment against the appellant, who was defendant below, for injuries received whilst he was a passenger on its railroad. The circuit court left it to the jury to find on the evidence whether the injuries were caused by the negligence of the defendant; and whether the plaintiff's own negligence contributed to produce them. The defendant contended that the case ought not to have been submitted to the jury; that there was no evidence of negligence on its part, and that the court ought to have ruled that the negligence of the plaintiff directly contributed to the injury.

The plaintiff testified at the trial that he was a passenger in the defendant's cars, and that he left Philadelphia on the night of the 11th of January, 1889, having a ticket which entitled him to passage to the City of Chester. That when they reached this place, "Chester" was called out, and the train was stopped; that he supposed that the train was at the Chester depot; that he got up and started to go out, and when he reached the platform the train started again; that he thought that the train was then leaving Chester, and, as he did not wish to be carried to the next station, he stepped off, and just then the Philadelphia and Washington express came along, and knocked him down, broke his leg and crushed his foot. The train in which the plaintiff was traveling was going west or south, and the express train which injured him was going east or north. It appears that Welsh Street is at the east end of the station platform, and Market Street is at the west end of it. The plaintiff testified that the train stopped at Welsh Street; but that he thought at the time it was at Market Street, which was at the other end of the platform, and that he stepped off on the left-hand side of the train; that at Market Street, on the right side of the train, there are safety gates; that on the east side of the street they are four feet nine inches from the cars, and on the west side about twenty-four inches from them; that the place where he stepped off is between the east and west bound track, and is called the six-foot way, but he had never measured the space, and did not know its exact width; that there are two platforms at Chester Station, running the whole distance from Welsh to Market Streets, one of them on each side of the railroad tracks. He further testified that when the train slowed up and the name of "Chester" was called out, and the train stopped, he understood that he was at the station, and that the passengers for that station were to get off; that he was in a hurry to get off, as the train had started, and he thought that unless he got off at once he would be carried on to the next station; that no one called out or gave notice that the train had not reached the station, or told the passengers to keep their seats, and that he heard no warning of any kind; that the train was moving very slowly, and he alighted safely and secure on his feet; that just as he got his foot on the ground, he saw the headlight of a locomotive coming east; that he had barely time to turn around when he was struck,—he was knocked down, but he was not on the track. On cross-examination, he testified that he did not look to see where he was, because he was so positive that he was at Chester depot, or Market Street crossing; that if he had looked from the right side of the car forward, he supposed that he would have seen the lights there (that is the station lights); that he was getting off very near the middle of Market Street; that he supposed that he was safe in getting off there; that he had no chance to look; that he knew all about the location of the station. He also testified that passengers get on or off the trains at Chester indifferently on either side of it; if they live south of the station, they generally get off on the left-hand side; if they live north of the station they generally get off on the right-hand side, except ladies, who take the right-hand side because the platform comes up higher on that side, and the step is shorter; that fully one third of the passengers arriving at Chester from the east get off on the left hand side; that he never knew or understood that there was any rule of the Company against it, and never heard of any notice forbidding it, or of any protest from any agent of the Company against it; that he knew that there was a rule of the defendant which forbade trains to pass a station when a train was receiving or discharging passengers.

There was other evidence corroborating the plaintiff's statements about the habit of passengers in getting on or off the train on either side. One of the witnesses says he never knew of any rule of the defendant which forbade it, and never saw or heard of any notice to that effect; another witness, a policeman, testified that he had acted as officer for the defendant at the Chester depot when their officer was absent; that his practice was to help passengers on and off the trains on either side, and such was the practice of the regular railroad officer, and that there was no rule of defendant which he ever knew or heard of that was against leaving the cars on the side away from the platform.

Rule 112 of the defendant was offered as evidence as follows: "A train approaching a station where a passenger train is receiving or discharging passengers must be stopped before reaching the passenger train."

We have not stated all the evidence, nor have we stated it in the order in which it was given at the trial. But the portions which we have quoted will suffice to illustrate the judgment which we have formed on the questions presented by this record. Carriers of passengers have in their charge the lives and safety of the persons whom they undertake to transport, and are subjected to a responsibility proportioned to the gravity of the trust reposed in them. They are bound to use the utmost degree of care, skill and diligence in everything that concerns the safety of passengers; nor are their duties limited to the mere transportation of them. They are bound to provide safe and convenient modes of access to their trains, and of departure from them.

In *Gaynor* v. *Old Colony & N. R. Co.*, 100 Mass. 208, it was said: "The plaintiff was a passenger, and while that relation existed, the defendants were bound to exercise towards him the utmost care and diligence in providing against those injuries which can be avoided by human foresight. He was entitled to this protection so long as he conformed to the reasonable regulations of the Company, not only while in the cars, but while upon the premises of the defendants; and this requires of the defendants due regard for the safety of passengers, as well in the location, construction and arrangement of their station buildings, platforms and means of egress, as in their previous transportation." *Vide* also *Hauer's Case*, 60 Md. 462, 468.

But the degree of care which is exacted of these carriers is subject to a reasonable limitation; it is not the utmost and highest absolutely, but the highest which is consistent with the nature of their business; and there must be a due regard to its necessary requirements. The plaintiff was injured whilst he was a passenger, that is, during the time when he was under the defendant's protection; and the injury was inflicted by a train of cars running on the defendant's track and under the control and management of its servants. It seems to us that under these circumstances the defendant ought to be required to show that it used on the occasion the degree of care which the law imposed upon it; and that we may apply to this case the language of the late chief justice in *Worthington's Case*, 21 Md. 283:

"The cases of *Stokes* v. *Saltonstall*, 38 U. S. 13 Pet. 181 [10 L. ed. 115], and *Stockton* v. *Frey*, 4 Gill, 414, conclusively establish the law, that in such case the occurrence of the accident is prima facie evidence of negligence on the part of the defendants, throwing upon them the *onus* of rebutting the presumption by proving there was no negligence. Of course, that can be done only by proving that fact and circumstances explaining the cause of the accident showing it to be such as could not have been guarded against by the utmost care and diligence; or in other words by proving, in the language of *Chief Justice* Shaw, 'the most exact care and diligence, not only in the management of the trains and cars, but also in the structure and the care of the track, and in all the subsidiary arrangements necessary to the safety of the passengers.'"

But the question still remains whether the plaintiff by his own negligence contributed to the production of the injury. Before we express an opinion on this point, it is fit to take into view the incidents of the entire transaction. As the train approached the City of Chester, it slowed up; the name "Chester" was then called out, and the train stopped at the eastern end of the station platform; the plaintiff started to leave the car in which he was traveling, but when he reached the car platform the train had commenced to move on slowly; nevertheless he stepped from the car, and was immediately struck by a train coming from the opposite direction. If he had looked ahead before he left the step of the platform, he would have seen the light of the advancing train, and could have avoided the danger. It is difficult to see why, after the speed was slackened, the name of the station was called out and the train was stopped, unless it was intended that the passengers for that place should alight. The passenger who should draw this conclusion cannot be considered as forming an opinion which no reasonable man could entertain. The evidence does not inform us why the name was called out, and why the train was stopped, unless this was the purpose; nor does it show why, after a momentary pause, it afterwards slowly proceeded. If the discovery of the approaching train caused any change of purpose on the part of the conductor, it would have been reasonable to communicate this change to passengers, whose safety might be affected by it. If any reason had been made known to the plaintiff for the stoppage of the train, and the announcement of the name of the station, we would have had more light on the nature and character of his act. But without some aid of this kind, we are unable to say that the inference of negligence on his part is certain and incontrovertible, and consequently we cannot declare it as a question of law. *Cumberland Valley R. Co.* v. *Maugans*, 61 Md. 53.

He made his exit from the car in safety, but was immediately confronted by a great danger. If he had looked forward he might have seen and avoided it. But here we must bear in mind the circumstances attending his exit from the cars. He was getting off at a place which, with the knowledge and permission of the defendant, was habitually used for this purpose; and he knew, moreover, that it was the defendant's duty to use all possible care to make this place safe for him. And he knew that by a special rule it had declared that when his train was discharging passengers, any approaching train must be stopped, and not be allowed to reach it. Now, assuming that he supposed that he was to be discharged as a passenger at that place, he would necessarily and unavoidably infer that he would be safe, if the Railroad Company observed this rule. Undoubtedly he had a right to assume that this rule would be enforced, and, relying upon the assurance guaranteed by the rule, he was dispensed from the necessity of using the degree of care ordinarily required of persons who go on or near railroad tracks. This was decided in *Baltimore & O. R. Co.* v. *State*, 60 Md. 449. In that case a passenger was killed at a railroad station while attempting to cross a track on his way from one train to another. The question was on the degree of care which he was bound to use. The circuit court refused any instruction prayed by the railroad company to the effect that, if the deceased left a place of absolute safety and voluntarily went on the track in order to board a passenger train; and that if by the exercise of ordinary care, caution and prudence on his part, he could have known of the danger of attempting to cross the track, or of being on it for any purpose at that time; and that if he did not exercise such care, caution and prudence,—then he was guilty of contributory negligence. This court decided that the prayer was properly refused.

In a very clear and well-reasoned opinion, the present chief justice pointed out the distinction between the obligations of passengers in this regard and other persons, not sustaining this relation to the carriers. He says: "In leaving the train from Hagerstown, at the station, and in crossing over the intervening track from one platform to the other, in order to take the east-bound train, the deceased might well assume that the defendant would not expose him to any danger which, by the exercise of due care, could be avoided. And though the deceased himself was required to exercise reasonable care, yet we may suppose that his watchfulness was naturally lessened by his reliance upon the faithful observance by the employers of the defendant of such precautionary rules and regulations as would secure to passengers a safe transfer from one train to the other. And, except in the presence of immediate apparent danger, he was authorized to act upon such reliance. For the general rule that applies in ordinary cases of parties crossing railroad tracks, that they should stop, look and listen before making the venture, does not apply in a case like the present. In such case as this, the rule is, as established by a number of well-considered cases, that the passenger of the railroad is justified in assuming that the company has, in the exercise of due care, so regulated its trains that the road will be free from interruption or obstruction when passenger trains stop at a depot or station to receive and deliver passengers." *Baltimore & O. R. Co.* v. *State*, 60 Md. 463.

And in dealing with the prayer which we have quoted, he says: "It entirely ignored the fact that the deceased was a passenger, and was entitled to the protection of a passenger in passing over the intervening track to board the train that was to take him on his way to Frederick. It required of the deceased the exercise of care and caution to ascertain whether there was danger of a passing train before attempting to cross the track to board the train that he was required to take; whereas he was, unless he saw or knew of the approaching train, justified in acting upon the implied assurance that no train would be allowed to pass the station to obstruct the transfer of passengers from one train to another." 60 Md. 465.

We do not see how we can hold, as matter of law, that the plaintiff was guilty of contributory negligence, because he did not look out for the approaching train before he left the car in which he was traveling. In our opinion the whole question was properly left to the jury by the instructions given at the trial.

Judgment affirmed.

McSherry, *J.*, dissents.

John HARRIS, *Appt.*,

v.

MAYOR, etc., OF BALTIMORE.

(......Md.......)

There is no implied authority in members of a partnership formed for taking and executing paving and curbing contracts, to borrow money and execute promissory notes therefor to bind the firm, unless there be proof to show the actual necessity, or usage, for the exercise of such power by the individual members of the firm in conducting the work.

(*Bryan, J., dissents.*)

(July 1, 1890.)*

APPEAL by plaintiff from a judgment of the Superior Court for Baltimore City in favor of defendants in an action brought to recover the amount alleged to be due under a paving contract, but which defendants claimed to have paid to a third party. *Reversed.*

The case sufficiently appears in the opinion.

Argued before Alvey, *Ch. J.*, and Miller, Robinson, Irving, Briscoe, Fowler and Bryan, *JJ.*

Mr. **Albert Ritchie**, for appellant:

The distinction in law in respect to the powers of trading and non-trading partnerships is as thoroughly recognized and established as it is possible to be, and this case cannot be decided on the law applicable to "ordinary" or commercial partnerships without undermining the settled law, both of the United States and England.

1 Lindley, Partn. p. 302, § 130.

Between the injured partner and the appellant on the one side, and the bank on the other, the former ought to recover, because of the laches of the bank.

Cocke v. *Mobile Branch Bank*, 3 Ala. 175.

It is the duty of parties dealing with a non-trading partnership to make inquiry, and they take the note of the firm at their peril.

Benedict v. *Thompson*, 33 La. Ann. 196.

There is a presumption against the taker of the note of a non-trading firm from his knowledge of the nature of the business.

Pooley v. *Whitmore*, 10 Heisk. 629.

In non-trading partnerships, the doctrine of general agency does not apply, and there is no presumption of authority to support the act of one partner.

Pease v. *Cole*, 53 Conn. 58-60.

*A decision was reached in the case affirming the judgment below and an opinion handed down June 12, 1889. Subsequently a re-argument was granted and the opinion given herewith handed down. The former opinion has therefore become of no importance upon the particular point herein decided, and it is consequently omitted. [Rep.]

The need of money does not create the power in one partner to borrow, give notes or pledge.

Dickinson v. *Valpy*, 10 Barn. & C. 128; *Brown* v. *Byers*, 16 Mees. & W. 252; *Judge* v. *Braswell*, 13 Bush, 67; *Pease* v. *Cole, supra; Breckinridge* v. *Shrieve*, 4 Dana, 375, 379.

The question of the power to borrow money in the case of a non-trading firm is not one of law for the court but one of fact for the jury.

Winship v. *Bank of United States*, 30 U. S. 5 Pet. 529 (8 L. ed. 216); *Kimbro* v. *Bullitt*, 63 U. S. 22 How. 256 (16 L. ed. 313); *Pease* v. *Cole, supra; Wagner* v. *Simmons*, 61 Ala. 143; *Ulery* v. *Ginrich*, 57 Ill. 531; *Davis* v. *Richardson*, 45 Miss. 499; *Dickinson* v. *Valpy*, 10 Barn. & C. 138; *Judge* v. *Braswell*, 13 Bush, 67; *Irwin* v. *Williar*, 110 U. S. 506 (28 L. ed. 228); *Kimbro* v. *Bullitt*, 63 U. S. 22 How. 269 (16 L. ed. 317).

Collateral security is "a separate obligation attached to another contract to guarantee its performance; the transfer of property or other contracts to insure the performance of the principal engagement."

Bouvier, Dict.; *Munn* v. *McDonald*, 10 Watts, 270; *Shoemaker* v. *National Mechanics Bank*, 2 Abb. U. S. 416; *Swift* v. *Beers*, 3 Denio, 70.

If there was no power to make the original contract, the guaranty is invalid.

Colebrook, Col. Security, § 260; *Heidenheimer* v. *Mayer*, 10 Jones & S. 506, affirmed in 74 N. Y. 607; *Joslyn* v. *Dow*, 19 Hun, 497; *Workingmen's Bkg. Co.* v. *Rautenberg*, 103 Ill. 460.

In an action at law, a part assignment is invalid, and vests no title or lien, unless it has been accepted by the debtor. And this acceptance must be before other parties have acquired rights.

Wilson v. *Carson*, 12 Md. 54; *Rosenstock* v. *Ortwine*, 46 Md. 388; *Gibson* v. *Finley*, 4 Md. Ch. 75.

There must be proof of "a promise by the defendant (drawee) to the plaintiff (assignee) to pay him."

Papineau v. *Naumkeag S. C. Co.* 126 Mass. 372; *James* v. *Newton*, 2 New Eng. Rep. 820, 142 Mass. 371, 374; *Small* v. *Sproat*, 3 Met. 305.

Messrs. **Bernard Carter, F. S. Hoblitzell** and **William A. Hammond** for appellee.

Alvey, *Ch. J.*, delivered the opinion of the court:

This case has been re-argued and upon reconsideration the majority of the court are decidedly of opinion that the judgment of the court below ought to be reversed, instead of being affirmed, as was done upon the first argument.

The action was brought by the plaintiff, the present appellant, as assignee of William R. Weaver and Charles H. Harris, contractors for and doing the work of paving and curbing of streets, in the partnership name of William R. Weaver & Company, against the Mayor and City Council of Baltimore, to recover a balance of $9,000, alleged to be due the assignors on contracts executed by them for the City, and which was by said contractors assigned to the plaintiff. The City occupies the position of a mere stakeholder, and depends for indemnity on the National Farmers and Planters' Bank of Baltimore, that bank claiming, and having received, the funds under a prior assignment to that made to the plaintiff, the bank having indemnified the City against the result of this suit.

The plaintiff was defeated in his right to recover upon the application of the general principle in the law of partnership that applies in cases of trading or commercial partnership, but not in cases of non-trading partnership. Hence Weaver as partner was held by the court to be general agent of the firm, with power by implication to act for and bind the firm in all matters as fully as a trading partner could do, including the power to borrow money, to make and pass promissory notes and to pledge the assets of the partnership as collateral security for money borrowed, even though it was without the knowledge of his copartner, and the money was in fact applied to his own use. This is the principle of the instruction given by the court to the jury, at the instance of the defendant, and it is also the principle of the ruling of the court on the proffer of evidence by the plaintiff,* as set out in the second bill of exceptions. In both of these rulings we think there was error.

The partnership here is not claimed or asserted to be a trading or commercial partnership in any proper sense of the term; nor is there the least pretense to assert that there was any express authority from the copartner Harris to Weaver to borrow money of the bank, and to make and to pass the promissory notes of the firm payable to the bank or order, and at the same time to pledge by assignment the assets of the firm as collateral security for the money thus borrowed; nor is there any pretense to say that those acts of Weaver were ever ratified by Harris.

But the defendant relies alone upon an implied authority, supposed to result from the relation of the partner and what is asserted to be the necessity of the business.

There was no proof, however, of the manner of conducting the business, nor as to any necessity for the exercise of power to borrow money to carry it on, nor as to any custom or usage in the manner of raising funds for the due prosecution of the work under contracts such as those made and performed by this firm. No such question was put to the jury; but the court simply assumed as matter of law that there was, in such cases, an actual necessity for the exercise of the power to borrow money to enable the firm to perform the contracts, and therefore there was authority, by implication, in each of the partners to borrow money, make notes and pledge the property of the partnership as collateral security, in the name and on account of the firm. This we do not understand to be the law in regard to partnerships of the character of the one in question. The text-writers of the highest authority, as do also many decided cases, maintain a doctrine directly the reverse.

In Story on Partnership, § 102*a*, the learned author, after stating the general principle ap-

*This evidence was intended to show that Weaver did not apply the money to partnership purposes. [Rep.]

plicable to trading or commercial partnerships, goes on to say that "we are to understand that this doctrine is not applicable to all kinds of partnerships but is generally limited to partnerships in trade and commerce, for in such cases it is the usual course of mercantile transactions, and grows out of the general customs and laws of merchants, which is a part of the common law, and is recognized as such. But the same reason does not apply, or at least may not apply, to other partnerships, unless indeed it is the common custom or usage of such business to bind the firm by negotiable instruments, or it is necessary for the due transaction thereof."

And so in 1 Lindley on Partnership, *130 (Ewell's ed.), it is laid down as the settled law that "one partner in a non-trading partnership cannot bind his copartner by a bill or note drawn, accepted or indorsed by him in the firm name, even though it be for a debt of the firm, unless either he has express authority therefor from his copartner, or giving of such instruments is necessary to the carrying on of the partnership business, or is usual in similar partnerships; and the burden is upon the party suing on such note or bill to prove such authority, necessity or usage." See *note 1*, and cases there cited on same page.

There are other text-writers of high authority, to whom reference could be made, who have been equally explicit in noting the distinction between the powers of a partner in a trading or commercial partnership, and the powers of a partner in a non-trading partnership; but it is unnecessary to cite them.

The qualification of the general principle thus stated by the text-writers is fully supported by the decisions,—as will appear by an examination of the cases of *Dickinson* v. *Valpy*, 10 Barn. & C 128; *Brown* v. *Byers*, 16 Mees. & W. 252; *Brettle* v. *Williams*, 4 Exch. 623; *Smith* v. *Sloan*, 37 Wis. 285; *Davis* v. *Richardson*, 45 Miss 499; *Pease* v. *Cole*, 53 Conn. 53, and many other cases, some of which are referred to in the brief of the counsel for the plaintiff.

In the leading case of *Dickinson* v. *Valpy*, *supra*, a copartnership formed to purchase and operate mines, and where the question was whether the copartners were liable on a instrument drawn by a member in the name of the company, and in the form of a bill of exchange, but which the court held to be in effect a promissory note, it is held to be incumbent on the plaintiff to prove that a member of the company had authority to bind other members by the making of such an instrument; and the plaintiff having failed to give evidence to show that it was necessary for the purpose of carrying on the business of that mining company, or usual for other mining companies, to draw or accept bills of exchange, or make promissory notes, he was not allowed to recover. And Mr. *Justice* Littledale, concurring with the rest of the court, in the course of his opinion said: "Evidence of the nature of the company ought to have been given to show that, in order to carry into effect the purposes for which it was instituted, it was necessary that individual members should have the power of binding the others by drawing and accepting bills of exchange. In the absence of any such evidence, I am of opinion that it is not competent to individual members of a mining company (which is not a regular trading company) to bind the rest by drawing or accepting bills."

And in the case of *Brettel* v. *Williams*, *supra*, where persons were partners as railway contractors and had contracted to do certain works, and there was a sub contract for the doing of part of the work, for the doing of which coals were required to make brick, it was held that one of the partners had no authority to guarantee, in the name of the firm, payment for coals to be furnished to those with whom the firm had contracted for making the bricks, there being no evidence that the guaranty was necessary for carrying into effect the contract of the firm. In that case *Mr. Baron* Parke, in the course of a carefully considered opinion for the whole court, after referring to some previous cases, said: "In the present case no evidence was given to show the usage of the defendants in this particular business, or of others in a similar business; nor was there any evidence of the sanction by the other defendants of the act of their copartner; for a witness, who was called to prove the latter fact, would not, on cross-examination, swear that he was authorized by them to write a letter, which if proved to have been so written, would have been sufficient. Simply as railway contractors they could not have any such power." And it would therefore seem to be very clear that if partnerships formed for operating mines, to construct railways, and, as shown by the cases, for farming, for hotel keeping, for conducting theatres and the like, are not to be regarded as in the class of trading or commercial partnerships, for the same reason partnership formed for taking and executing paving and curbing contracts are not, *per se*, in such class; and therefore there is no implied authority in the members to borrow money and make promissory notes therefor to bind the firm, unless there be proof to show the actual necessity or usage for the exercise of such power by the individual members of the firm, in conducting the work. See case of *Kimbro* v. *Bullitt*, 63 U. S. 22 How. 256 [16 L. ed. 313].

The bank had knowledge of the nature of the partnership; that was disclosed on the face of the transaction by which the money was obtained by Weaver. And with that knowledge it was its duty to inquire as to the authority of Weaver to make the notes and assignments, and failing to make such inquiry it took the notes and collateral security at its peril. *Cocke* v. *Mobile Branch Bank*, 3 Ala. 175; *Judge* v. *Braswell*, 13 Bush, 67; *Pooley* v. *Whitmore*, 10 Heisk. 629; *Benedict* v. *Thompson*, 33 La. Ann. 196.

The note constitutes the primary claim of the bank, and the assignments are only collateral and subsidiary to the principal debt. If the notes were made without authority, and not therefore binding on the firm, the assignments, which, by express terms, are only intended as collateral security for the notes, would, upon the authorities, equally fail to bind the firm. But the assignments would be good and effective to bind and transfer any interest of Weaver in the claims against the City, after payment of partnership debts and liabilities, but to that extent only. It would appear, however, that there is no such interest upon which the assignments can operate.

In our opinion the court below should have

ruled in the testimony offered by the plaintiff in the second exception, and should have rejected the prayer of the defendant, and granted the first and fourth prayers of the plaintiff; and therefore the judgment ought to be reversed.

Judgment reversed and new trial awarded.

Bryan, *J.*, dissents.

John B. WOLF, *Appt.*,

v.

Dora BAUEREIS.

(....Md.....)

1. **The provision that a married woman may sue** "upon any cause of action in her own name," in the proviso to Code, art. 45, § 7, which makes a wife liable for debts contracted in her separate business, and authorizes suits against her for such debts as if she was a *feme sole*, must be restricted by the preceding part of the section, and does not extend to an action for injury to her person.

2. **A proviso in a statute** should always be construed with reference to the immediately preceding part of the clause or section to which it is attached.

3. **Failure to allege the continuance of the absence and desertion** of plaintiff's husband at the time of the trial will not make a replication to a plea of coverture insufficient, where it alleges "that at the time the wrongs and injuries complained of were committed" he had deserted and abandoned her and abjured the State, and ceased to reside therein.

4. **A married woman may sue for injuries** to her person without joining her husband, where, without her fault, he has deserted her, and left the State without intention of returning.

5. **The amendment of a declaration** does not extend the running of the Statute of Limitations to the time it is made so as to permit a cause of action to be barred which was good at the time suit was brought, if it is not founded upon a new cause of action.

(June 19, 1890.)

APPEAL by defendant from a judgment of the Court of Common Pleas for Baltimore City in favor of plaintiff in an action brought to recover damages for an alleged assault and battery with an attempt to commit rape. *Affirmed.*

The case is fully stated in the opinion.

Argued before Alvey, *Ch. J.*, and Robinson, McSherry, Fowler and Bryan, *JJ.*

Mr. **Frederic C. Cook** for appellant.

Messrs. **William S. Bryan, Jr.**, and **John T. Ensor** for appellee.

Alvey, *Ch. J.*, delivered the opinion of the court:

The plaintiff in this case is a married woman, and the action is for an assault and battery of her person, with the charge of an outrageous forcible attempt on the part of the defendant to have carnal connection with her. The action was originally instituted in the joint name of husband and wife, but by an amendment of the declaration the name of the husband was omitted, and the suit was thence conducted in the name of the wife alone. The defendant pleaded in abatement of the amended declaration the coverture of the plaintiff, to which plea the plaintiff demurred and the demurrer was overruled. The plaintiff then replied to the plea of coverture, and alleged "that at the time the wrongs and injuries complained of were committed, her husband had permanently and voluntarily, and without her knowledge or consent, deserted and abandoned her, and ceased to render her any maintenance or support, and had abjured the State of Maryland, and had ceased to reside therein, without any fault on the part of the plaintiff." To this replication the defendant demurred but the demurrer was overruled.

The defendant then pleaded two pleas: (1) that he did not commit the wrong alleged; and (2) that the cause of action sued on did not occur within one year next prior to the filing of the amended declaration. To the second plea the plaintiff demurred, and the demurrer was sustained. The case was then tried on the issue made by the first plea, and the verdict and judgment being against the defendant he has appealed. And the questions presented by the record are those only which are raised by the demurrers to the pleadings.

There are three questions presented: (1) whether a married woman, for a cause of action such as that declared on in this case, can maintain a suit in her own name, under the provision of the Code, as if she were *feme sole*; (2) if she cannot maintain the action in her own name, by virtue of the provision of the Statute, whether the replication to the plea

---

NOTE.—*Action by wife for damages for personal injuries.*

Abandonment by her husband gives the wife the right to sue for her earnings and those of her children. Harris v. Bohle, 2 West. Rep. 169, 19 Mo. App. 529.

Correspondence between husband and wife, in which the wife speaks of receiving his welcome letters, and expresses an earnest hope that they will soon be united, conclusively disproves her claim that he has abandoned her. Brunner v. Brunner, 70 Md. 105.

In an action by husband and wife for personal injury to the wife, evidence that the husband and wife were not living together at the time of the injury, and had not been for some time, is inadmissible on the defense. Northwestern Union Packet Co. v. Clough, 87 U. S. 20 Wall. 528 (22 L. ed. 406).

Damages for negligently diminishing the earning capacity of a married woman are presumed to belong to her husband; and when she seeks to recover such damages the complaint must allege that for some reason she is entitled to the fruits of her own labor; and if she seeks to recover for an injury to her business, the complaint must allege that she was engaged in business on her own account, and by reason of the injury was injured therein as specifically set forth. Uransky v. Dry Dock, E. B. & B. R. Co. 118 N. Y. 304.

The loss of a woman's capacity to earn money should be considered in estimating damages for alleged injuries, in an action by herself and husband, where her marriage had taken place after receiving the injuries. Such damage accrued to her individually, as it was caused before the marriage. Reading v. Pennsylvania R. Co. (N. J.) Feb. 22, 1890.

of coverture furnished a sufficient answer to that plea; and (3) whether the plea of the Statute of Limitations, in the form pleaded, constituted a bar to the action.

1. With respect to the first question, that depends upon the proper construction of section 7 of article 45 of the Code. Of course, it is a familiar principle of the common law that for any injury to the person of the wife during coverture, by battery, slander, etc., the wife cannot sue alone, but the husband and wife must join; and in such case, the declaration must conclude to their damage, and not to that of the husband alone; for the damages will survive to the wife if the husband die before they are recovered, and so if the wife die after judgment, the judgment survives to the husband. 1 Chitty, Pl. 82; *Stroop* v. *Swartz*, 12 Serg. & R. 76.

But it is insisted by the plaintiff that this principle of the common law has been changed by the section of the Code to which we have referred. The court below, in overruling the demurrer to the plea of coverture, held otherwise, and in so holding we think the court was clearly right. The question, however, was again raised by the subsequent demurrers ruled by the court.

Section 7 of article 45 of the Code had its origin in the Act of 1842, chap. 293, entitled "An Act to Regulate Conjugal Rights as They Regard Property." The Act was an enabling statute, conferring upon a married woman the right to acquire property in certain ways, and to hold the same exempt from the debts of her husband; and by the eighth section of the Act, a married woman was authorized by her own skill, industry or personal labor to earn money or other property to the value of $1,000 or less, and to hold the same to her own use, with a proviso that such money or property should be liable for debts contracted by any such married woman, to be collected by attachment.

This eighth section of the Act of 1842 was embodied in the Code of 1860, article 45, as section 7, and which section was, by the Act of 1882, chap. 265, repealed and re-enacted so as to be made to read as we now find it in section 7 of article 45 of the present Code. The modifications introduced by the Act of 1882 were, first, to dispense with the limit to the amount of the earnings of the wife; second, to confine the liability of such earnings to debts contracted "in and about the business, occupation or enterprise in which said money or other property shall be earned or invested;" third, that for any such debts a married woman may be sued as if she were *feme sole;* and fourth, that any such property so acquired may be taken in execution to satisfy any judgment rendered on such cause of action, etc. And at the end of the section, without other break or stop in the context than a mere semi-colon, it is added, "and provided further that any married woman may sue in any court of law or equity in this State upon any cause of action in her own name, and without the necessity of a *prochein ami*, as if she were *feme sole.*"

This general language, "upon any cause of action," if read dissociated from the context and general purview of the section, would certainly furnish strong color for the contention of the plaintiff, that a married woman is now placed upon the same footing as a *feme sole*, in respect to all causes of action whatever in which she may have an interest. But that construction is certainly too broad. If such construction were adopted the wife might maintain actions against her husband on contracts, or for wrongs to her person or property. It is not to be supposed that such a radical change was intended by the Legislature. Moreover, if such general, unqualified right of maintaining actions, as if she were a *feme sole*, had been intended to be conferred upon the wife, we can hardly suppose that the codifier or the Legislature would have deemed it necessary to retain, as part of article 45, the section 4 of that article, which provides that if a married woman has no trustee, she may, by her next friend, sue in any court of law or equity in all cases for the recovery, or security, or protection of her property, as fully as if she were a *feme sole.* The general language in the proviso of the section under consideration must be taken and read in connection with the preceding part of the section. It was intended, manifestly, to supply what had been omitted from the Act of 1842, and the Code of 1860,—that is to say, the giving to a married woman a right to maintain an action in her own name, to a corresponding extent that she was made liable to suit, upon any cause of action arising from or growing out of "the business, occupation or enterprise," in which she is allowed to engage, or in respect to the money or other property that she may earn or invest, under the Statute. The ability to maintain such action was essential to the complete protection and security of the rights that she might acquire by her skill and industry; and to confer upon her that power was the object, doubtless, of the proviso incorporated in the section by the re-enactment of 1882. It is said that the function of a proviso is that of limiting and qualifying the language of the statute, and not that of enlarging or extending the Act or section of which it is a part; and that a proviso should always be construed with reference to the immediately preceding part of the clause or section to which it is attached. *Re Webb*, 24 How. Pr. 247; *Kensington* v. *Keith*, 2 Pa. 218; *Ex parte Partington*, 6 Q. B. 649, 658; Endlich, Interpretation of Statutes, § 186.

And so construing the proviso in the section of the Code before us, we cannot resist the conclusion that the plaintiff is not in this case entitled to maintain the action in her own name alone, by virtue of the provision of the Statute relied on.

2. The next question is whether the replication to the plea of coverture, alleging desertion and abandonment of the wife by her husband, afforded a sufficient answer to the plea, and alleged facts sufficient to entitle the plaintiff to maintain the action without the joinder of her husband.

It is objected that the replication is defective in the manner of alleging the facts; that it fails to allege the continued absence and desertion of the husband at the time of trial. And it must be conceded that the replication does not, in this respect, conform to good precedent. *Boggett* v. *Frier*, 11 East, 302.

But still, by fair construction and reasonable intendment, we think the facts are sufficiently alleged to raise the issue of the continued and

he ever knew or heard of that was against leaving the cars on the side away from the platform.

Rule 112 of the defendant was offered as evidence as follows: "A train approaching a station where a passenger train is receiving or discharging passengers must be stopped before reaching the passenger train."

We have not stated all the evidence, nor have we stated it in the order in which it was given at the trial. But the portions which we have quoted will suffice to illustrate the judgment which we have formed on the questions presented by this record. Carriers of passengers have in their charge the lives and safety of the persons whom they undertake to transport, and are subjected to a responsibility proportioned to the gravity of the trust reposed in them. They are bound to use the utmost degree of care, skill and diligence in everything that concerns the safety of passengers; nor are their duties limited to the mere transportation of them. They are bound to provide safe and convenient modes of access to their trains, and of departure from them.

In *Gaynor* v. *Old Colony & N. R. Co.*, 100 Mass. 208, it was said: "The plaintiff was a passenger, and while that relation existed, the defendants were bound to exercise towards him the utmost care and diligence in providing against those injuries which can be avoided by human foresight. He was entitled to this protection so long as he conformed to the reasonable regulations of the Company, not only while in the cars, but while upon the premises of the defendants; and this requires of the defendants due regard for the safety of passengers, as well in the location, construction and arrangement of their station buildings, platforms and means of egress, as in their previous transportation." *Vide* also *Hauer's Case*, 60 Md. 462, 468.

But the degree of care which is exacted of these carriers is subject to a reasonable limitation; it is not the utmost and highest absolutely, but the highest which is consistent with the nature of their business; and there must be a due regard to its necessary requirements. The plaintiff was injured whilst he was a passenger, that is, during the time when he was under the defendant's protection; and the injury was inflicted by a train of cars running on the defendant's track and under the control and management of its servants. It seems to us that under these circumstances the defendant ought to be required to show that it used on the occasion the degree of care which the law imposed upon it; and that we may apply to this case the language of the late chief justice in *Worthington's Case*, 21 Md. 283:

"The cases of *Stokes* v. *Saltonstall*, 38 U. S. 13 Pet. 181 [10 L. ed. 115], and *Stockton* v. *Frey*, 4 Gill, 414, conclusively establish the law, that in such case the occurrence of the accident is prima facie evidence of negligence on the part of the defendants, throwing upon them the *onus* of rebutting the presumption by proving there was no negligence. Of course, that can be done only by proving that fact and circumstances explaining the cause of the accident showing it to be such as could not have been guarded against by the utmost care and diligence; or in other words by proving, in the language of *Chief Justice* Shaw, 'the most exact care and diligence, not only in the management of the trains and cars, but also in the structure and the care of the track, and in all the subsidiary arrangements necessary to the safety of the passengers.'"

But the question still remains whether the plaintiff by his own negligence contributed to the production of the injury. Before we express an opinion on this point, it is fit to take into view the incidents of the entire transaction. As the train approached the City of Chester, it slowed up; the name "Chester" was then called out, and the train stopped at the eastern end of the station platform; the plaintiff started to leave the car in which he was traveling, but when he reached the car platform the train had commenced to move on slowly; nevertheless he stepped from the car, and was immediately struck by a train coming from the opposite direction. If he had looked ahead before he left the step of the platform, he would have seen the light of the advancing train, and could have avoided the danger. It is difficult to see why, after the speed was slackened, the name of the station was called out and the train was stopped, unless it was intended that the passengers for that place should alight. The passenger who should draw this conclusion cannot be considered as forming an opinion which no reasonable man could entertain. The evidence does not inform us why the name was called out, and why the train was stopped, unless this was the purpose; nor does it show why, after a momentary pause, it afterwards slowly proceeded. If the discovery of the approaching train caused any change of purpose on the part of the conductor, it would have been reasonable to communicate this change to passengers, whose safety might be affected by it. If any reason had been made known to the plaintiff for the stoppage of the train, and the announcement of the name of the station, we would have had more light on the nature and character of his act. But without some aid of this kind, we are unable to say that the inference of negligence on his part is certain and incontrovertible, and consequently we cannot declare it as a question of law. *Cumberland Valley R. Co.* v. *Maugans*, 61 Md. 53.

He made his exit from the car in safety, but was immediately confronted by a great danger. If he had looked forward he might have seen and avoided it. But here we must bear in mind the circumstances attending his exit from the cars. He was getting off at a place which, with the knowledge and permission of the defendant, was habitually used for this purpose; and he knew, moreover, that it was the defendant's duty to use all possible care to make this place safe for him. And he knew that by a special rule it had declared that when his train was discharging passengers, any approaching train must be stopped, and not be allowed to reach it. Now, assuming that he supposed that he was to be discharged as a passenger at that place, he would necessarily and unavoidably infer that he would be safe, if the Railroad Company observed this rule. Undoubtedly he had a right to assume that this rule would be enforced, and, relying upon the assurance guaranteed by the rule, he was dispensed from the necessity of using the degree of care ordinarily required of persons who go on or near railroad tracks. This was decided in *Baltimore & O. R. Co.* v. *State*, 60 Md. 449. In that case a passenger was killed at a railroad station while attempting to cross a track on his way from one train to another. The question was on the degree of care which he was bound to use. The circuit court refused any instruction prayed by the railroad company to the effect that, if the deceased left a place of absolute safety and voluntarily went on the track in order to board a passenger train; and that if by the exercise of ordinary care, caution and prudence on his part, he could have known of the danger of attempting to cross the track, or of being on it for any purpose at that time; and that if he did not exercise such care, caution and prudence,—then he was guilty of contributory negligence. This court decided that the prayer was properly refused.

In a very clear and well-reasoned opinion, the present chief justice pointed out the distinction between the obligations of passengers in this regard and other persons, not sustaining this relation to the carriers. He says: "In leaving the train from Hagerstown, at the station, and in crossing over the intervening track from one platform to the other, in order to take the east-bound train, the deceased might well assume that the defendant would not expose him to any danger which, by the exercise of due care, could be avoided. And though the deceased himself was required to exercise reasonable care, yet we may suppose that his watchfulness was naturally lessened by his reliance upon the faithful observance by the employers of the defendant of such precautionary rules and regulations as would secure to passengers a safe transfer from one train to the other. And, except in the presence of immediate apparent danger, he was authorized to act upon such reliance. For the general rule that applies in ordinary cases of parties crossing railroad tracks, that they should stop, look and listen before making the venture, does not apply in a case like the present. In such case as this, the rule is, as established by a number of well-considered cases, that the passenger of the railroad is justified in assuming that the company has, in the exercise of due care, so regulated its trains that the road will be free from interruption or obstruction when passenger trains stop at a depot or station to receive and deliver passengers." *Baltimore & O. R. Co.* v. *State*, 60 Md. 463.

And in dealing with the prayer which we have quoted, he says: "It entirely ignored the fact that the deceased was a passenger, and was entitled to the protection of a passenger in passing over the intervening track to board the train that was to take him on his way to Frederick. It required of the deceased the exercise of care and caution to ascertain whether there was danger of a passing train before attempting to cross the track to board the train that he was required to take; whereas he was, unless he saw or knew of the approaching train, justified in acting upon the implied assurance that no train would be allowed to pass the station to obstruct the transfer of passengers from one train to another." 60 Md. 465.

We do not see how we can hold, as matter of law, that the plaintiff was guilty of contributory negligence, because he did not look out for the approaching train before he left the car in which he was traveling. In our opinion the whole question was properly left to the jury by the instructions given at the trial.

Judgment affirmed.

McSherry, J., dissents.

John HARRIS, *Appt.*,
v.
MAYOR, etc., OF BALTIMORE.

(......Md.......)

There is no implied authority in members of a partnership formed for taking and executing paving and curbing contracts, to borrow money and execute promissory notes therefor to bind the firm, unless there be proof to show the actual necessity, or usage, for the exercise of such power by the individual members of the firm in conducting the work.

(*Bryan, J., dissents.*)

(July 1, 1890.)*

APPEAL by plaintiff from a judgment of the Superior Court for Baltimore City in favor of defendants in an action brought to recover the amount alleged to be due under a paving contract, but which defendants claimed to have paid to a third party. *Reversed.*

The case sufficiently appears in the opinion.

Argued before Alvey, *Ch. J.*, and Miller, Robinson, Irving, Briscoe, Fowler and Bryan, *JJ.*

Mr. **Albert Ritchie**, for appellant:

The distinction in law in respect to the powers of trading and non-trading partnerships is as thoroughly recognized and established as it is possible to be, and this case cannot be decided on the law applicable to "ordinary" or commercial partnerships without undermining the settled law, both of the United States and England.

1 Lindley, Partn. p. 302, § 180.

Between the injured partner and the appellant on the one side, and the bank on the other, the former ought to recover, because of the laches of the bank.

Cocke v. *Mobile Branch Bank*, 3 Ala. 175.

It is the duty of parties dealing with a non-trading partnership to make inquiry, and they take the note of the firm at their peril.

Benedict v. *Thompson*, 33 La. Ann. 196.

There is a presumption against the taker of the note of a non-trading firm from his knowledge of the nature of the business.

Pooley v. *Whitmore*, 10 Heisk. 629.

In non-trading partnerships, the doctrine of general agency does not apply, and there is no presumption of authority to support the act of one partner.

Pease v. *Cole*, 53 Conn. 53–60.

---

*A decision was reached in the case affirming the judgment below and an opinion handed down June 12, 1889. Subsequently a re-argument was granted and the opinion given herewith handed down. The former opinion has therefore become of no importance upon the particular point herein decided, and it is consequently omitted. [Rep.]

tiff lost his child, Barbara K. Kern, who died from disease caused and produced by the noxious and deadly fumes and odors arising from said cess-pool or well. And also, by means of the premises, the said plaintiff hath been and is hindered and prevented from exercising and carrying on his trade and business of a grocer and saloon-keeper in so beneficial a manner as he, before the committing of the said grievances by the said defendant, had been used and accustomed to do, and would have continued to do, and hath thereby been deprived of divers great gains and profits which he otherwise might and would have derived and acquired, to wit, in the County of Wayne, at 219, 221, 223 Croghan Street, in the City of Detroit, aforesaid, by reason of the loss of time of said plaintiff and his wife, caused by the illness directly produced by the divers noisome, noxious, offensive and poisonous stenches arising from said cess-pool or open well, as aforesaid, and by the driving away of the patrons and customers of the plaintiff by reason of the said smells, vapors and stenches. And also, by means of the premises, the said plaintiff hath been compelled to pay out in expense large sums of money, in paying doctors' bills for the attendance upon the plaintiff and his family during their illness caused by said cess-pool or open well, a large sum of money, to wit, the sum of $500. And also, by means of the premises, the said plaintiff hath been subjected to a great expense in hiring nurses to attend to and watch the plaintiff and his said family in their illness caused by said cess-pool or open well to a large amount, to wit, the sum of $500. Therefore, the said plaintiff says that he is injured, and has sustained damage, to the amount of $10,000.

"*Second count.* And whereas, also, the said plaintiff, being so possessed of his dwelling-house, grocery store and saloon, with the appurtenances aforesaid, the said defendant, before and at the time of the committing of the grievances hereinafter mentioned, was the owner and proprietor of the said premises Nos. 219, 221, 223 Croghan Street, upon which was the said cess-pool or open well under the said dwelling, grocery store and saloon of the said plaintiff, and by reason thereof the said defendant, before and at the time of the committing the grievance by the said defendant as hereinafter mentioned, ought not to have filled said well with rubbish, and erected said dwelling upon the same, but ought to have torn down said well, and filled the same with solid earth, and prevented the drowning of rats in said well or cess-pool, and prevented the excrement, filth, water and dead vermin, from time to time, being in the said cess-pool or open well, and to have prevented thereby divers noxious, noisome, offensive, unwholesome and poisonous smells, vapors and stenches from proceeding therefrom unto and into, and permeating through, the entire dwelling-house, grocery store and saloon, with the appurtenances, of the said plaintiff, to wit, in the County of Wayne, at Nos. 219, 221, 223 Croghan Street, in the City of Detroit. Nevertheless the said defendant, well knowing the said last-mentioned premises, but contriving, and wrongfully and unjustly intending, to injure, prejudice and aggrieve the said plaintiff, and to incommode, make sick and kill him, the said plaintiff, and his family, in the possession, use, occupation and enjoyment of his dwelling-house, grocery and saloon, with the appurtenances, heretofore, to wit, on the 1st day of May, A. D. 1885, and on divers other days and times between that day and the day of the commencement of this suit, to wit, in the County of Wayne, at Nos. 219, 221, 223 Croghan Street, in the City of Detroit, aforesaid, wrongfully and unjustly suffered, permitted, concealed and refused to disclose the source of danger well known by said defendant, and caused by him, by neglecting to fill up said well, and the same not being discoverable by the said plaintiff, and the said plaintiff having no knowledge of the existence of the said source of danger to the health and life of the plaintiff and his family, permitted and caused divers large quantities of dead rats and other vermin, decayed wood and rubbish, and large quantities of filth and water, to remain in said last-mentioned cess-pool or open well, from which whereby divers noisome, noxious, offensive, unwholesome and poisonous smells, vapors and stenches, during all the time aforesaid, ascended and came onto and into and permeated into every part of the entire premises of the said plaintiff, as aforesaid, and on those several days and times, thereby sowing seeds of disease and death in the body of the plaintiff and his said family, and also thereby causing the death of his child as aforesaid, and the expenditures for nurses and doctors, and lost time of the plaintiff and his wife aforesaid. Therefore the said plaintiff says that he is injured, and has sustained damages, to the amount of $10,000."

When this cause was heard, we intimated that we only desired argument upon the point whether it was necessary for the plaintiff to allege that defendant had notice or knowledge of the noxious odors, and had neglected or refused to remove them, or disclose their cause. Upon further consideration of the declaration, we are of opinion that it discloses a cause of action. The cause alleged does not rest upon any covenant, express or implied, of the landlord to repair the premises, nor that they were habitable at the time the lease was made; nor does it rest, necessarily, upon the relation of landlord and tenant, although the lease is set up by way of inducement, to show the right of plaintiff to possession of the premises. But the cause of action is based upon the maxim that every person must so use his own premises as not to injure others, either in person or property, rightfully in the vicinity. The declaration sets up the construction and continuance of a nuisance by the defendant upon his own land to the injury of the plaintiff, the existence and cause of which were unknown to the plaintiff, and were known to, but were concealed from him by, defendant. It discloses a cause of action in tort, resting upon the duty of the defendant to disclose to the plaintiff defects in the premises amounting to nuisances, known to defendant and concealed from plaintiff, which were calculated to impair, and did impair, the health of the plaintiff. Wood, Land. and T. 284; *Minor* v. *Sharon*, 112 Mass. 477; *Scott* v. *Simons*, 54 N. H. 426.

How well the plaintiff may be able upon the trial to connect the cause with the consequences alleged is not involved in the inquiry before us.

The judgment is reversed, and a trial ordered. The other Justices concurred.

PEOPLE OF the State of MICHIGAN

v.

MORRIS *et al.*, *Appts.*

(.....Mich.....)

1. **A plea of guilty to an information** charging larceny, under a general statute, in one count and horse stealing in another applies to both counts and authorizes sentence for horse stealing.

2. **A minimum punishment of three years for horse stealing,** except in cases of the first offense, when it may be two years or less, with a maximum of fifteen years, is not cruel or unusual punishment, although it must be greater than it may be for manslaughter.

(May 9, 1890.)

ERROR to the Circuit Court for Kalamazoo County, to review a judgment imposing a sentence upon defendants after a plea of guilty to an information charging them with the crime of horse stealing. *Affirmed.*

The facts sufficiently appear in the opinion.

Mr. **D. G. F. Warner** for appellant.

Mr. **George P. Hopkins**, *Pros. Atty.*, for the People.

Grant, *J.*, delivered the opinion of the court:

The respondents were charged with the larceny of a horse of the value of $150. The information contained two counts,—one framed under the general Statute for larceny, and the other charging the larceny under section 9180 of Howell's Statutes, which is an Act to Provide for the Prevention and Punishment of Horse Stealing. The respondents, upon being arraigned, pleaded guilty. The court made the customary investigation, for the purpose of determining whether their plea was made freely, with the full knowledge of the accusation against them and without undue influence. The court therefore sentenced Morton to the state's prison for six years and nine months, and Morris for seven years.

Under the first count, respondents' sentence could not have been more than five years. Under the second count, their sentence could have been not less than three nor more than fifteen years, unless it was their first offense, in which case the court might have sentenced them to the state house of correction for a term not exceeding two years. It is contended that the sentence is erroneous for two reasons, viz.: (1) because the plea of guilty applied only to the first count, under which the maximum penalty is five years; (2) because § 9180, How. Stat., is unconstitutional in that the punishment provided by it is "cruel or unusual."

1. The first contention cannot be maintained. Where there are two counts charging different grades of the same offense, under a conviction or plea of guilty, it has been the general practice in England and in this country to pass judgment according to the count charging the highest grade of offense. In this case the offense was the same set up in both counts. It must be presumed that the respondents understood the information read to them, and that the judge, as required by law, correctly explained the charge against them before passing sentence. It must therefore be presumed that they pleaded guilty to all that the information contained. We find no authorities to the contrary. *Dean* v. *State*, 43 Ga. 218; *Adams* v. *State*, 52 Ga. 565; *Estes* v. *State*, 55 Ga. 131; *People* v. *Shotwell*, 27 Cal. 394; *State* v. *Tuller*, 34 Conn. 280; *Scott* v. *State*, 31 Miss. 473; *State* v. *Core*, 70 Mo. 491; *Com.* v. *Hope*, 22 Pick. 1; *Lyons* v. *People*, 68 Ill 271; *Manly* v. *State*, 7 Md. 135; *Conkey* v. *People*, 1 Abb. App. Dec. 418.

Re Franklin (Mich.), 43 N. W. Rep. 997, is not in point. In that case there were four counts, containing two distinct offenses, viz.: larceny and the receiving of stolen goods. If convicted as a receiver, he could under our Statute have avoided state's prison by satisfaction. A proper regard for the rights of a citizen under such circumstances requires that the record should show of which crime the party is convicted. But the reason of that decision does not apply to cases where the law makes different grades of the same offense, nor where by statute the same offense may receive different punishments; nor does the Act providing for a distinct punishment for horse stealing supersede the general Statute for larceny. A respondent cannot be prejudiced by a proceeding under the first Statute named, nor by counts embodying both Statutes. We have statutes providing a different punishment for larceny from the person, from a dwelling house, at a fire, etc. But it has never been contended that these superseded the general Statute for larceny, nor that a person could not be convicted under this general Statute, although the facts might warrant a prosecution under the others.

2. Article 6, § 31, of the Constitution of this State provides that cruel or unusual punishment shall not be inflicted. It is to the credit of our country that its courts have seldom been called upon to determine whether legislative enactments infringe this clause of the Constitution. The question under this Statute is for the first time directly before this court. Indirectly, this Statute has been brought before the court on former occasions, but the point has never been decided, though the opinions in those cases contain some expressions hostile to the policy of such legislation. With the policy of the law it is not our province to deal. That belongs to the Legislature, which is composed of representatives direct from the people, and who alone have the right to voice the sentiments of the people in the public enactments. When those sentiments are enacted into law, the only province of the court is to determine their validity under the Constitution. The rule by which courts must be governed in such cases is as follows: "When a statute is challenged as in conflict with the fundamental law, a clear and substantial conflict must be found to exist to justify its condemnation." By this sound rule, and with but little light to be gathered from the authorities, so few are they, we must approach the discussion and the determi-

See also 30 L. R. A. 734.

nation of this question. The difficulty in determining what is meant by "cruel and unusual punishments," as used in our Constitution, is apparent. Counsel for defendant claims that, as properly understood, it means, when used in this connection, punishment out of proportion to the offense. If by this is meant the degree of punishment, we do think the contention correct. When, in England, concessions against cruel and unusual punishments were first wrested from the crown, slight offenses were visited with the most extreme punishment, and no protest was made against it. But our concern is to ascertain how this language is to be understood in the constitutional sense.

In *Re Bayard*, 25 Hun, 546, it is said: "We first find the injunction against cruel and unusual punishment in the Declaration of Rights presented by the convention to William and Mary before settling the crown upon them in 1688. That Declaration recites the crimes and errors which had made the revolution necessary. These recitals consist of the acts only of the former king and the judges appointed by him, and one of them was that 'illegal and cruel punishment had been inflicted.' The punishments complained of were the pillories, slittings and mutilations which the corrupt judges of King James had inflicted without warrant of law, and the Declaration was aimed at the acts of the executive, for the judges appointed by him, and removable at pleasure, were practically part of the executive. It clearly did not then refer to the degree of punishment, for the criminal law of England was at that time disgraced by the infliction of the very gravest punishment for slight offenses, even petit larceny then being punishable with death. But the Declaration was intended to forbid the imposition of punishment of a kind not known to the law or not warranted by the law." *Justice* Cooley says: "Probably any punishment declared by statute for an offense which was punishable in the same way at the common law could not be regarded as cruel or unusual, in the constitutional sense; and probably any new statutory offense may be punished to the extent and in the mode permitted by the common law for offenses of similar nature. But those degrading punishments, which in any State had become obsolete before its existing Constitution was adopted, we think may well be held forbidden by it as cruel and unusual. We may well doubt the right to establish the whipping post and pillory in States where they were never recognized as instruments of punishment, or in States whose Constitutions, revised since public opinion had banished them, have forbidden cruel and unusual punishments. In such States the public sentiment must be regarded as having condemned them as cruel, and any punishment which, if ever employed at all, has become altogether obsolete, must certainly be looked upon as unusual." Const. Lim. 408.

But for the disposition of this case we may adopt the rule contended for and then we must find (in order to declare the law unconstitutional) that the minimum punishment provided by the law is so disproportionate to the offense as to shock the moral sense of the people. Imprisonment for larceny is, and always has been, in this country and in all civilized countries, one of the methods of punishment. There may be circumstances surrounding the commission of larceny where fifteen years would not be considered too severe a punishment. When punishment is commensurate with the depravity of the criminal, as shown in the commission of the act, justice is done. Under most of our criminal laws, cases may arise when the punishment inflicted might be considered cruel, but that does not condemn the law. The judge in such cases has acted within the jurisdiction of constitutional law, and other means must be resorted to to right the wrong. Appellate courts cannot interfere if the proceedings have been regular. The law itself must therefore be cruel or unusual to warrant the interposition of the courts. It is argued that under this law a prisoner must be sentenced from three to fifteen years, while under other statutes for the larceny of property of the same value, he could only be imprisoned for one year. This is not a fair or legitimate test. Our statutes, and so probably the statutes of all the States, recognize this distinction. Under our statutes larceny from the person, larceny from a dwelling-house, or at a fire, may be punished by imprisonment for five years. The cashier or any officer or servant of a bank, who takes any of the property intrusted to his care, and thereby commits larceny, may be imprisoned for ten years. Any officer, clerk or person employed in the state treasury may, for larceny therefrom, be imprisoned for fourteen years. So, too, any person who shall, at the same term of court be convicted of three distinct larcenies, may be imprisoned for fifteen years. In all these cases the property stolen may not exceed the value of a dollar. It has never been contended that any of the punishments imposed by these statutes were cruel or unusual. It is also argued that under this Statute a man must be imprisoned for a longer period than may one who is convicted of manslaughter. The larceny of a horse usually, if not necessarily, implies a bad and wicked disposition. A person may be guilty of manslaughter without possessing any such disposition. He may be convicted of manslaughter when engaged in doing an act which is only *malum prohibitum*, and not *malum in se*. He may be found guilty of manslaughter under circumstances which do not have any tendency to show a wicked intent or purpose. I cannot therefore see that this law can be held unconstitutional, because the punishment inflicted must be greater than may be the punishment for manslaughter. This was expressly held in *Ex parte Mitchell*, 70 Cal. 1.

In *Re Bayard*, above cited, the law provided a greater punishment for the same crime in the city than in the country, and it was held constitutional. It will be conceded that the Legislature has the constitutional power to fix the minimum as well as the maximum of the punishment. It has also the exclusive jurisdiction to define "crime," and prescribe the punishment. It is supposed to represent the sentiment and wishes of the people. In these days of intelligence and improvement, extraordinary, indeed, must be the terms of a criminal law which would shock the average judgment of the people. The horse is an animal of peculiar value. His owner becomes attached to him because of his intelligence, and the use made of him. The thief makes him a means of escape by one of many roads. In a few hours he may perhaps drive him into another State. Organized bands of these thieves have existed in various parts of the country, and so extensive have been their depredations that vigilance committees have been organized to accomplish what the authorities seemed powerless to do. Under these circumstances, it seems to me clear that it would be almost a usurpation of authority for the courts to hold that a minimum punishment of three years, even, is so disproportionate to the offense as to be cruel or unusual. But for the first offense the person convicted may be sent to the house of correction for any period not exceeding two years. Certainly here is discretion enough left to the trial court to protect the rights of anyone. The policy of inflicting greater punishments for the second or more offenses has long been adopted, and is not questioned. A few authorities may be referred to bearing upon the subject. In 1816 the Legislature of New York passed an Act to suppress dueling, the punishment being that the convicted person should be incapable of holding or being elected to any post of profit, trust or emolument, civil or military. The court held that the punishment did not come within the constitutional prohibition as cruel or unusual. *Barker* v. *People*, 3 Cow. 686.

A similar statute of the Territory of New Mexico, for horse stealing, imposed the punishment of not less than thirty nor more than sixty lashes on the bare back. Under the provisions organizing the Territory, it was provided that the laws passed by the Legislative Assembly should be submitted to the Congress of the United States, and, if disapproved, should be null and of no effect. The act was submitted to Congress, and had never been disapproved. The law was held constitutional. *Garcia* v. *Territory*, 1 N. M. 415. See also *Ligan* v. *State*, 3 Heisk. 159.

This law was enacted in 1877, and no demand appears to have been made for its repeal or modification. We may therefore infer that it meets the approval of the people of this State, who, we are confident, would not permit a criminal law shocking to their moral sense, and imposing a cruel punishment, to remain long upon the statute book. The crime of horse stealing has generally been regarded from the earliest times as involving a greater degree of criminality than the larceny of other property. In England, by Statute (1 Edw. VI. chap. 12, § 10), in 1547 the horse thief was deprived of the benefit of clergy, and this distinction was preserved in later statutes. 1 Steph. Crim. Law 465-468.

Statutes similar to our own have been enacted, and are still in force in many of the States. In Texas this crime is punished by imprisonment for not less than five nor more than fifteen, years; in Georgia, not less than four, nor more than twenty, years; in Arkansas, not less than five, nor more than fifteen, years; in Tennessee, not less than three, nor more than ten, years; in Kentucky, not less than two, nor more than ten, years; in Maryland, not less than two, nor more than fifteen, years; in Wisconsin, not less than two, nor more than fifteen, years; in Virginia, not less than three, nor more than eighteen, years; in Illinois, not less than three, nor more than twenty, years; and in many other States the punishment is from one to ten years. We are not pointed to a single decision which condemns such Statutes as unconstitutional. Our conclusion therefore is that this Statute cannot be condemned by the courts as imposing a cruel or unusual punishment, either in the popular or the constitutional sense.

Conviction and sentence affirmed.

The other Justices concurred.

SOUTH CAROLINA SUPREME COURT.

J. H. AMAKER, *Appt.*,
v.
Frances NEW *et al.*, *Respts.*

(....S. C.....)

1. The period of six years from the discovery of the fraud, within which an action to set aside a fraudulent conveyance must be brought, under Code, § 112, does not apply where a judgment creditor, who has purchased the land on execution sale made in disregard of the fraudulent deed, brings an action to recover possession after the death of a widow having a superior claim of dower, to whom he had been obliged temporarily to surrender possession.

2. One who has made out a prima facie case for the recovery of land is not prevented

NOTE.—*Statute of Limitations in case of concealed fraud.*

In cases of fraud the Statute of Limitations begins to run, in equity, not at the time the fraud is perpetrated, but from the time of its discovery. Peck v. Bank of America, 7 L. R. A. 826, 16 R. I.—; Binney's Appeal, 8 Cent. Rep. 124, 116 Pa. 169: Caswell v. Caswell, 9 West. Rep. 158, 120 Ill. 377; Yancy v. Cothran, 32 Fed. Rep. 687; Moses v. Taylor, 11 Cent. Rep. 724, 6 Mackey, 255.

Laches cannot be imputed to plaintiffs in the absence of all knowledge of the facts of which it is predicated. Tunstall v. Withers, 14 Va. L. J. 298.

In a case of fraud upon the part of an administrator, in which each of the defendants participated, a court of equity should be slow in denying relief upon the mere ground of laches in bringing suit. Bryan v. Kales, 134 U. S. 126 (33 L. ed. 829).

Where the party against whom a cause of action existed in favor of another, by fraud or actual fraudulent concealment, prevents another from obtaining knowledge thereof, the Statute would commence to run only from the time the right of action was discovered, or might, by the use of due diligence, have been discovered. Bradford v. McCormick, 71 Iowa, 129.

Where fraudulent concealment by a justice of the peace prevented the Statute of Limitations

See also 26 L. R. A. 864.

from attacking as fraudulent a deed set up in defense, because the time for bringing an action to set aside the conveyance as fraudulent has expired.

(*Simpson, Ch. J., dissents.*)

3. A case cannot be affirmed on other grounds, where erroneous instructions on one branch of it have been given to the jury.

(April 21, 1890.)

APPEAL by plaintiff from a judgment of the Common Pleas Circuit Court for Orangeburg County in favor of defendants in an action brought to recover possession of certain real estate. *Reversed.*

The facts are fully stated in the opinions.

Messrs. **Izlar & Glaze,** for appellant:

At the time of the execution of the voluntary deed by the donor Sistrunk was his creditor, and he was therefore warranted by law in treating the conveyance as void in law, and in subjecting the property embraced in it to the execution of judgment rendered for the recovery of his debt.

Richardson v. *Rhodus*, 14 Rich. L. 101; Freeman, Executions, § 186; Wait, Fraud. Conv. § 59.

The deed of the sheriff transferred to Sistrunk the legal title to said land, and not merely the right to the legal title, and to have the said voluntary conveyance set aside by proper proceedings in a court of competent jurisdiction.

A purchaser at sheriff's sale, or one claiming under such purchaser, can, in an action to recover the possession of the land bought, assail for fraud a conveyance of the judgment debtor, executed before the sale.

Burch v. *Brantley*, 20 S. C. 509; *Lowry* v. *Pinson*, 2 Bail. L. 324; *Thomas* v. *Jeter*, 1 Hill, L. 380; *Smith* v. *Culbertson*, 9 Rich. L. 106; *Richardson* v. *Rhodus*, 14 Rich. L. 95.

Messrs. **Glover & Bowman,** for respondents:

When a charge of fraud is made against a deed, the Statute will commence to run when the right of action accrues, and the moment a cause of action arises the right of action will accrue. The action in the present case was commenced March 18, 1887, nineteen years after Sistrunk had personal knowledge of the deed, or fifteen years at least after the return of *nulla bona* on his execution, and was barred.

Plaintiff claims under Sistrunk's title, and therefore he is barred.

Suber v. *Chandler*, 18 S. C. 526; *Newberry Nat. Bank* v. *Kinard*, 28 S. C. 110.

If the plaintiff was not barred by the Statute of Limitations, fraud cannot be relieved against after twenty-three years.

Myers v. *O'Hanlon*, 12 Rich. Eq. 208; *Hovenden* v. *Annesley*, 2 Sch. & Lef. 630; *Riddlehoover* v. *Kinard*, 1 Hill, Ch. 378; *White* v. *Moore*, 23 S. C. 463; Wait, Fr. Conv. §§ 288, 289.

The court will not entertain a charge of fraud after the lapse of twenty years on account of the laches of the plaintiff.

Eigleberger v. *Kibler*, 1 Hill, Ch. 120; Wait, Fr. Conv. § 287.

McIver, J., delivered the opinion of the court:

I understand it to be well settled that an existing creditor who wishes to subject property to the payment of his debt, which has been conveyed by his debtor, by a voluntary deed to another, before judgment obtained, has two remedies, to either of which he may resort, to wit: he may disregard the conveyance as fraudulent and void, and proceed to sell the property under his execution, leaving the validity of the deed to be determined in an action of the purchaser at such sale to recover possession of the land; or he may, by an action on the equity side of the court, have the deed set aside on the ground of fraud, and the land conveyed by it subjected to the payment of his debt. If he resorted to the latter mode of relief, then it was settled in the court of equity that he must commence his action within four years after the discovery of the fraud, or such action would be barred: and this equity rule is now made statutory by section 112 of the Code, the time being enlarged from four to six years. But I do not see how this doctrine can be made applicable in a case where the creditor resorts

---

from running in his favor, it also prevented it from running in favor of his sureties. *Ibid.*

The Statute of Limitations does not run against a party to bar his right of action for the correction of a mistake until he discovers the mistake, or until he might discover it by pursuing inquiries suggested by facts within his knowledge; but he is not obliged to pursue such inquiries when the defendant has so conducted himself as to justify him in believing that no mistake has been made. Manatt v. Starr, 72 Iowa, 677.

The Minnesota Statutes limiting the time of actions for relief from fraud embrace both legal and equitable actions. Humphrey v. Carpenter, 39 Minn. 115.

The Statute does not run against a suit by an administrator for discovery of assets conveyed in fraud, until discovery of the fraud, due diligence for its discovery having been used by plaintiff. Preston v. Cutter, 6 New Eng. Rep. 398, 64 N. H. 461.

A creditors' bill in New York, founded on fraud, is barred only by the lapse of six years from the discovery of the fraud. Decker v. Decker, 10 Cent. Rep. 509, 108 N. Y. 128.

A suit in equity by an assignee in bankruptcy to recover bonds fraudulently transferred by the bankrupt must be brought within two years from the discovery of the transfer, under U. S. Rev. Stat., § 5057. Phelps v. Elliott, 35 Fed. Rep. 455.

If not brought within six years after the time plaintiff first had knowledge of the sale, the bill will be dismissed, although six years have not yet elapsed since the reversal on appeal of the order in the original cause. *Ibid.*

Where an attorney receives from his client a claim against an estate for collection, and files it against the estate in his own name, concealing such fact from his client, limitation does not begin to run against the client until he discovers the cause of action, or might discover it by the use of reasonable diligence; but he is not required to make an examination of the records, as the attorney's obligation is to inform him. Wilder v. Secor, 72 Iowa, 161.

In cases of fraud, the Statute of Limitations does not begin to run until discovery of the concealed fraud. See *notes* to Carrier v. Chicago, R. I. & P. R. Co. (Iowa) 6 L. R. A. 799; Peck v. Bank of America (R. I.) 7 L. R. A. 826.

to the former mode of relief from the fraud. In such a case, the creditor brings no action to set aside the deed, and there is nothing to which the plea of the Statute of Limitations can be made applicable. That Statute confers no rights except simply that of immunity from suit, and therefore, until some action is brought against one who seeks to avail himself of the benefits of the Statute, there is no room for its application. For example, where an action is brought on a note after the time limited for the commencement of such action, while the Statute affords perfect immunity from such action, it does not operate as payment of the debt evidenced by such note, and if the holder thereof can obtain payment in any other way than by resort to an action he has the right to do so. See *Wilson* v. *Kelly*, 16 S. C. 216.

The Statute of Limitations is nothing but a "statute of repose," as it has been called, founded on motives of public policy; it is best for the general welfare that, after the lapse of a prescribed time, fixed arbitrarily, a person shall not be allowed to enforce a claim by the use of the legal machinery of the courts,—that is, the doors of the courts are no longer open to him for the enforcement of a claim which he has neglected to assert within the prescribed time.

Now, in this case, treating it as though the action was brought by Sistrunk, in whose shoes the real plaintiff stands, where has there been any delay on the part of the creditor in asserting his rights? The voluntary deed was made in November, '866. Sistrunk recovered his judgment, on cause of action arising prior to the deed, in August, 1867. The land was levied on and sold by the sheriff in January, 1868, and possession was surrendered to the purchaser at such sale, Sistrunk, of the entire tract of 300 acres. By proceeding instituted in March, 1869, that portion of the tract (158 acres) now in dispute was laid off to the widow of the grantor as her dower, and she held possession until her death, in March, 1886, and within about a year thereafter this action was commenced. From this statement it appears that the creditor proceeded promptly, after obtaining his judgment, to subject the land to the payment of his debt, in one of the modes permitted by law, to wit, a sale under his judgment, notwithstanding the prior voluntary deed, and, having thus acquired possession, retained the same until required to surrender the portion now in dispute, temporarily, to the superior claim of dower, and, very soon after that estate terminated by the death of the widow, this action was commenced to regain possession of that part of the land which had thus been temporarily surrendered under the superior claim of dower. There never was, therefore, any occasion for the creditor to bring his action to set aside the deed for fraud (and such is not the nature of the present action); for he had availed himself of the other remedy afforded by law, by selling the land under his execution as the property of the grantor, notwithstanding the prior execution of the voluntary deed. This being an action to recover possession of real estate, and not an action to set aside a deed for fraud, I am unable to see how the plea of the Statute of Limitations can be applied; for certainly the right of action did not arise until the estate of dower fell in by the death of the widow, and the action was commenced within a year after that event occurred. The plea of the Statute, as it is called (improperly, as I think, for such a plea must be directed to the cause of action set forth in the complaint), is not directed to the plaintiff's cause of action, but is interposed as a protection against an attack made by the plaintiff upon the defense set up by defendants.

The plaintiff having made out a prima facie title, as is shown by the refusal of the motion for a nonsuit, to which no exception was taken, the defendants undertook to show a superior title in themselves under the deed in question, and, surely, the plaintiff was entitled to show any defect in that deed which would render it insufficient to vest title in the defendants, either by showing that it was not under seal, or not executed in the presence of two subscribing witnesses, or that the grantor was *non compos*, or that it was not recorded. If so, why may it not also be shown that it was void for fraud? I do not understand that it ever was the rule that a deed or other instrument could not be attacked for fraud after the lapse of the prescribed time, in any way, but only that it could not be attacked by an action instituted for that purpose. I can very well understand how the law, from consideration of public policy, may forbid one from invoking its aid by bringing an action to set aside a deed for fraud, after the time limited for the purpose, but I am unable to understand upon what principle, either of law, equity or good morals, one who has made out a prima facie case for the relief he demands can be forbidden from showing that the defense set up against his claim is founded in fraud, simply because such fraud had been committed so long ago as to bar an action brought to obtain relief from such fraud; but I do not think any case can be found which would sanction such a doctrine. It seems to me that any other view would render the conceded right of the creditor to disregard the fraudulent deed and sell the land under his execution absolutely nugatory; for, in such a case, all that the grantee under the fraudulent deed would have to do would be to wait until the expiration of six years, and then assert his claim under such deed, when, under the view contended for, it would be shielded from attack on the ground of fraud by the Statute of Limitations. If it should be said that the creditor, after purchasing the land under his execution, could protect himself by bringing an action to remove a cloud from his title, by having the deed declared void for fraud, this is only saying that one of the conceded modes of relief which a creditor has cannot be made effectual without resorting also to the aid of the other mode of relief; which practically amounts to saying that the only effectual mode of relief is by an action to set aside the deed for fraud, and that the other mode is but a delusion.

I agree with the chief justice that the deed cannot be regarded as a marriage settlement, because it does not appear to have been made in pursuance of any arrangement entered into prior to the marriage, or that it was in any way founded upon or connected with the contract of marriage.

As to the position taken by counsel for respondents, that the judgment below may be sustained upon other grounds, even if there was error in charging the jury with respect to the Statute of Limitations, it is only necessary to to say that this cannot be done in a case tried by a jury, for the reasons stated in *Bonham* v. *Bishop*, 23 S. C. 105. The judgment of this court is that *the judgment of the Circuit Court be reversed, and that the case be remanded to that court for a new trial.*

McGowan, *J.*:

I concur. It is clear that the plaintiff could not sue for the land during the life of Mrs. Inabnet, for she held it by a legal title,—her dower right. Within a year after her death, the plaintiff did sue for the land; but it appears that, in the mean time, other parties took possession, claiming under another and different right, which the widow, as to herself, disclaimed when she took dower. It seems to me that no action for the land accrued to the plaintiff, in respect to this new claim, until after it was set up by the defendants after the death of the widow. Until the new claim was asserted by taking possession under it, no right of action for the land existed in the plaintiff which required him to sue the defendants.

Simpson, *Ch. J.*, dissenting:

This is a contest over a tract of land of 158¼ acres situate in Orangeburg County. Both parties claim from a common source, and the question below was, Which had the better title? The facts, so far as necessary to be stated here, were as follows: One Absalom Inabnet, in 1866, was indebted to several parties; among them, to one N. E. W. Sistrunk. While thus indebted he conveyed to his son-in-law, William H. Bennett, a tract of land containing 800 acres, of which the 158¼ acres were a part, in trust for the sole and separate use of the grantor's wife, Mary A. Inabnet, for her life, and at her death to be equally divided among all of his children, etc., the consideration of this deed, as expressed therein, being natural love and affection and $10. The deed was duly recorded. Judgments were obtained by the aforesaid creditors, including N. E. W. Sistrunk, against the said Absalom Inabnet, after the execution of this deed, to wit, in 1866, and in 1868 the land was levied upon and sold by the sheriff after the return of *nulla bona* upon the execution of Sistrunk. At this sale Sistrunk became the purchaser, who, it seems, went into possession. In 1869, Mary Inabnet, the widow of Absalom, and the certain *cestui que trust* for life under the deed to W. H. Bennett, by proceeding in the probate court, obtained dower in the land, to wit, the 158¼ acres mentioned above, and now in dispute. In 1884, Sistrunk having died, the 158¼ acres was included in partition proceedings between his heirs at law, and at a sale ordered in said proceeding the plaintiff here became the purchaser, receiving a deed from the master, 2d of March, 1885. Sistrunk in his lifetime had sold off the remainder of the 800 acres. In 1886, Mary Inabnet, the widow of Absalom, and the dowress of the 158¼ acres in dispute, died, and the defendant Frances New, a daughter of Absalom, took possession, and with her husband, Picken New, has continued in possession up to this time, claiming under the trust deed to Bennett. Under this state of facts, the plaintiff brought the action below for the recovery of the said 158¼ acres. Under the charge of his honor, *Judge* Hudson presiding, the verdict was for the defendants.

The gist of plaintiff's action was that the deed under which defendants claimed was a voluntary deed, executed while the grantor was in debt to plaintiff and others, and, it having been developed by a return of *nulla bona* that this debtor had no other sufficient property to pay said debts, that said deed was null and void and fraudulent, and consequently that the sale by the sheriff to Sistrunk was a valid sale and conveyed the land free from said voluntary deed. The defendants relied upon the Statute of Limitations, contending that, Sistrunk not having instituted proceedings within the statutory period to vacate and set aside the Bennett trust deed, neither he, if he was alive, nor those claiming under him, could now, at this late date, do so. His honor sustained this defense, instructing the jury "that, after six years after Sistrunk got title, he was barred and deprived of assailing the deed on the ground of fraud upon creditors, and that the plaintiff, with constructive notice of this deed, is affected by the neglect of Sistrunk, under whom he claims, and that, if more than six years had elapsed from the time this deed was put on record to the time he instituted suit he is debarred from assailing the deed on the ground of fraud against existing creditors, and, this deed being assailed in this way, the defendant has a superior title, and must prevail." The plaintiff also claimed that the Bennett deed was a marriage settlement, and, not having been recorded in the office of the secretary of state, was void as to him. This position was overruled by his honor. The counsel of appellant in his argument states the questions involved in his exceptions as follows: "(1) Is not property, voluntarily transferred in fraud of existing creditors, subject to execution in favor of such creditors, precisely as if such transfer had not been made? (2) Does not the title of the sheriff to lands sold as the property of one who has voluntarily conveyed the same to another, in fraud of existing creditors, transfer to the purchaser the legal title to the lands sold, and not merely the right to the legal title, and to have the fraudulent transfer vacated and set aside, by appropriate proceedings in a court of competent jurisdiction, within six years after said fraudulent transfer? (3) Under the circumstances of this case, is the plaintiff barred by the Statute of Limitations from assailing the voluntary deed of conveyance made by Absalom Inabnet to William H. Bennett, on the ground that the same was executed in fraud of the then existing creditors of the said Absalom Inabnet? (4) Is the voluntary deed of conveyance from Absalom Inabnet to William H. Bennett void for want of recording in the office of secretary of state?"

The first and second propositions above may be affirmed without argument, upon the general principle that fraud will vitiate anything. In both of said propositions it is assumed and conceded that the deed is to be voluntary and in fraud of existing creditors. Such a deed is of course void, and a purchaser at sheriff's sale of land conveyed in such deed gets a superior title to such land. This is unquestionably sound legal doctrine, as well as good morals. But while this is true, yet there is another doctrine which holds that a party may lose a perfect title by delay in asserting it. Statutes of Limitation, for the sake of peace and repose, have been adopted and enforced in almost every country, certainly everywhere where regular judicial systems have been built up and justice is administered under settled principles of law. Admitting here that the voluntary deed in question was fraudulent as to the existing creditors of Absalom Inabnet, and that at the sale Sistrunk obtained a perfect title, if the court could now get at these facts; but the question is, Can the court now get at these facts? It is established doctrine of equity that, in order to set aside a fraudulent deed on the ground of fraud, it must be assailed within six years from the discovery of the fraud. It cannot be attacked afterwards, if, during this time, there is a party who can sue and a party who can be sued. Whatever may be the real merits of the case and the truth of the alleged facts, this principle closes the door and forbids the court from going back behind the statutory period, so that in such case it is not competent for the assailant to prove the fraud upon which he relies; and hence, in the absence of such testimony, the deed stands before the court unaffected and must take rank from its date, having priority to all subsequent conveyances. Suppose that in this case Sistrunk was alive, and had instituted an action on the equity side of the court to vacate this deed for fraud at the date of the action below, fifteen years or more after his purchase at sheriff's sale, could the court have entertained the action for a moment? We think not. What is the difference between such a case and the one below? True, the plaintiff is not Sistrunk, but he stands in Sistrunk's shoes. True, too, the action below was not in terms to vacate defendants' deed, but still plaintiff's claim depends upon vacating that deed. It is set up by the defendants in opposition to plaintiff's deed, and the plaintiff attacks it on the ground of fraud, and he must sustain his attack or his claim fails. In other words, he must have it adjudicated fraudulent in order to succeed in his action for the recovery of the land. This is nothing more than an effort to set aside said deed for fraud, which, as we have seen, cannot be done after the lapse of the statutory period; certainly not in a direct proceeding to that end, much less so in a collateral attack. The fact that Bennett yielded possession to Sistrunk at the sheriff's sale, and that the widow of A. Inabnet, the life tenant *cestui que trust* under that deed, came in and claimed dower, was well calculated to lull Sistrunk into security and mislead him, but we do not see how this could bind the present defendant, a remainderman under that deed. Her active rights had not attached, and did not attach until upon the death of her mother, in 18—, when she immediately took possession. Under these views, we see no error in the charge of his honor on the subject of fraud. See the following cases: *Eigleberger* v. *Kibler*, 1 Hill, Ch. 118; *Prescott* v. *Hubbell*, Id. 212; *Farr* v. *Farr*, Id. 387; *Shannon* v. *White*, 6 Rich. Eq. 96; *Godbold* v. *Lambert*, 8 Rich. Eq. 162-164; *Beck* v. *Searson*, 8 Rich. Eq. 132; *Cox* v. *Cox*, 6 Rich. Eq. 275.

Nor do we think there was error in his ruling as to the necessity of this deed being recorded in the office of secretary of state; nor was his charge, when taken as a whole, vulnerable, as complained in the last exception, "in that it charged on the facts," in violation of article 4, § 26, of the Constitution.

NEW MEXICO SUPREME COURT.

Alvah E. WOLCOTT *et al.*, *Piffs. in Err.*,
v.
Singleton M. ASHENFELTER and Wife.

(....N. M....)

1. **Each of several rooms in a building occupied by separate tenants** is a "house" within the meaning of a statute which gives a lien on the property of a tenant while it remains in the house rented; and a removal of such property with the landlord's consent from one room to another in the same building taken under a new contract defeats the lien.

2. **A mere general creditor without any specific lien,** although made a party defendant in a suit to foreclose a mortgage on the debtor's chattels, for the purpose of determining the question of the existence of a lien claimed by him, cannot question the validity of the mortgage.

(January 29, 1890.)

ERROR to the District Court for Grant County to review a judgment in favor of plaintiffs in an action brought to foreclose a chattel mortgage. *Affirmed.*

The facts are fully stated in the opinion.

Messrs. **Elliott & Pickett,** for plaintiffs in error:

The chattel mortgage is void as against Wolcott, because it was not renewed by an affidavit stating the amount due, etc., as required by the statutes of New Mexico.

See Prince's Rev. Ed. Laws of New Mexico, p. 64. See also 2 Wait, Act. and Def. p. 199, § 18; *Newell* v. *Warren*, 44 N. Y. 244; *Paine* v. *Mason*, 7 Ohio St. 198; *Edson* v. *Newell*, 14 Minn. 228; *National Bank of the Metropolis* v. *Sprague*, 20 N. J. Eq. 13.

In *Seaman* v. *Eager*, 16 Ohio St. 209, the court held that the fractions of a day are to be counted.

Griffin v. *Forrest*, 49 Mich. 309; *Briggs* v. *Mette*, 42 Mich. 12.

NOTE.—*Dwelling-house; part of house may be.*

A part of a dwelling-house may be so severed from the rest of it, by being let to a tenant, as to constitute of itself a dwelling-house. See Quinn v. People, 71 N. Y. 561; Com. v. Bulman, 118 Mass. 456; Reg. v. Pierson, 1 Salk. 382, 2 Ld. Raym. 1197.

Wolcott's claim of landlord's lien for $1,300 is prior to the chattel mortgage. Said lien commenced to run or attach to the property the first of October, 1883, and continued down until the hearing of this cause in the court below, the property never having been removed from his building.

Fowler v. *Rapley*, 83 U. S. 15 Wall. 337 (21 L. ed. 37); *Webb* v. *Sharp*, 80 U. S. 13 Wall. 14 (20 L. ed. 478); *Holdane* v. *Sumner*, 82 U. S. 15 Wall. 600 (21 L. ed. 254); *Longstreth* v. *Pennock*, 87 U. S. 20 Wall. 575 (22 L. ed. 451).

Mr. **Gideon D. Bantz**, for defendants in error:

Landlords shall have a lien on the property of their tenants which remains in the house rented, for the rent due.

Comp. Laws 1884, § 1537.

The words "house rented" are used in the sense of premises rented. And where, therefore, the premises rented consist, as in this instance, of a part of the house—two rooms—the lien is lost by the landlord if he consents to the tenant's removal of his chattels from the leased premises.

Bouvier, L. Dict. title *House*, citing 6 Mod. 214; Wood. Land and T. 178; *Rex* v. *Great and Little Usworth*, 5 Ad. & El. 261; *Henrette* v. *Booth*, 15 C. B. N. S. 500; *Fenn* v. *Grafton*, 2 Bing. N. C. 617; Taylor, Land. and T. 7th ed. § 66.

The lien conferred by the statute arises out of the common-law doctrine of distraint. At common law distress must be made upon some part of demised premises out of which the rent issued.

Taylor, Land. and T. § 573.

Mrs. Ashenfelter had a valid mortgage as against Wright, even though it had never been recorded, and after she filed her bill for foreclosure of it, her lien was perfected as against a mere general creditor of Wright.

Boone, Mortg. § 251; Jones, Chat. Mortg. § 245; Bump, Fr. Conv. ed. 1872, § 458.

Long, *Ch. J.*, delivered the opinion of the court:

This cause is in this court on writ of error to the District Court of Grant County. There Singleton M. Ashenfelter and Nettie A. Ashenfelter, his wife, brought their action to foreclose a chattel mortgage, and made parties thereto Frank J. Wright and Alvah E. Wolcott, who are the plaintiffs in error in this court. As against Wright, it is alleged in the bill of complaint that on the 24th day of February, 1886, Frank J. Wright made and delivered to Nettie A. Ashenfelter, wife of S. M. Ashenfelter, his promissory note in the sum of $250, and at the same time that he also made, executed and delivered to her to secure said note a chattel mortgage on a library situated in Silver City, in said county; that the mortgage was duly acknowledged, and also properly recorded in time in the said County of Grant. It is also averred that the debt was, at the commencement of the action, unpaid and past due. It is further alleged that the other defendant in the action, Wolcott, also claimed to hold a lien on the same library for $1,300, but that his lien, if any existed, was for a much smaller sum, and was subsequent to that claimed by the complainants. Wolcott was made a party, that he might be required to set up and establish his lien, so that the court could ascertain and discover the amount thereof, and decree as to priorities. The complainants made the usual prayer for judgment, decree fixing their priority and for sale of the mortgaged property. Wolcott filed demurrer to the complaint, which was overruled by the court. Both Wolcott and Wright then answered the bill, and upon the answers issue was joined, and the cause referred to a master.

It is assigned here for error that the demurrer should have been sustained, but as no reason for such contention is shown in the oral argument or brief, and we are unable to perceive any defect in the bill of complaint, we hold that assignment to be not well taken. The master made a very careful and elaborate report. He found, and so reported to the court, that in 1883 Alvah E. Wolcott owned a building in the Town of Silver City, and on the 1st day of October made a written lease to his codefendant, Frank J. Wright, of two certain rooms in said building, said rooms to be used by Wright for a law office, and the lease to run for two years, at $45 per month, payable monthly; that Wright occupied the two rooms until the 1st of February, 1886, under said lease; and at that date, on account of the nonpayment of rent for the two rooms during his occupancy under the written lease, owed Wolcott the sum of $945, as rent due and unpaid for said rooms to that date. The master further found that Wolcott, at that date, desired to make other arrangements respecting said two rooms, and so he rented them then to another tenant, who took possession of them. Wright, at that date, with Wolcott's consent, moved out of the two rooms the library, which, before that date, had been in them, and altogether ceased to occupy them as a tenant. Through the building in which the two rooms are situated is a central hall. The two rooms occupied by Wright as aforesaid are in the building on the north side of the hall, and entered from it. Wright, when he moved his library out of the two rooms, moved into and occupied a single room on the south side of the central hall, by and with the consent of Wolcott. Possession was taken by Wright, February 1, 1886, of the single room. At that time it was verbally agreed between Wright and Wolcott that the former should pay, as rent for the single room, $20 per month, nothing being said as to the time of payment. Wright, after he moved into the single room, paid as one month's rent therefor, in February, $20. He paid no further rent, but continued to occupy the room south of the hall to the rendition of the decree in the court below, and at that date, for rent of the single room, was indebted to Wolcott in the sum of $420, being the rental for said room to December 1, 1887. The note and mortgage given by Wright to Mrs. Ashenfelter were executed on the 24th day of February, 1886, and the mortgage was duly recorded the next day. At that time the library described in the mortgage was situated in the single room south of the central hall, and had been there at least twenty-three days. There was then due and unpaid, as rent for the two rooms on the north side of the hall, by Wright the sum of $945. All these facts are found by the master, and reported to the court.

The master found and the court decreed the priorities, as between the two lienholders, Wolcott and Mrs. Ashenfelter, to be as follows: that Wolcott held, to the extent of $420, the prior and first lien over Mrs. Ashenfelter; that Mrs. Ashenfelter, to the amount of her mortgage, held the next and second lien. It seems to have been apparent to the court that, after payment of costs and expenses and the liens thus created, there would be nothing left; so nothing is decreed as to any residue. Wright does not assign any separate error on his own behalf separately, but joins in the assignment by Wolcott. These do not relate to any matter affecting Wright separately, but only refer to priorities.

The first question to consider is whether the court erred in refusing to decree the $945 as a lien on the library prior in time to the mortgage lien. The court held, and in effect so decreed, that this lien was lost on the library when Wright removed, by the landlord's consent, out of the two rooms, and into the single room. If this ruling is correct, then, as to that sum, Wolcott would be only a general creditor, or, as it is sometimes expressed, "a creditor at large," without any specific lien for the rent thus accrued on the library. The two rooms first occupied by the tenant and the single room last occupied are entirely separate and distinct apartments, but plaintiffs in error contend, inasmuch as they are all under one roof, in the same building, that the rent which had accrued for the occupancy of the two rooms, and which had attached as a lien on the library there situated, followed the library to the other room, and continued there, also, as a lien. The defendants in error contend that the term "house" in the Statute applies to the separate apartments in the same building, where these are rented separately; that where there are several rooms in one building, and each room is occupied by a separate tenant, as between the landlord and the several tenants, each apartment so occupied is a "house," within the meaning of the Statute; and that when the landlord consents to a removal of a tenant's property from the separate room so occupied it is, in legal contemplation, a removal from the house, and the lien is lost. This question arises on the following section of the Compiled Laws:

"Sec. 1587. Landlords shall have a lien on the property of their tenants, which remains in the house rented, for the rent due; and said property may not be removed from said house, without the consent of the landlord, until the rent is paid or secured."

The lien is upon the property of the tenant which remains in the house, not upon the property which, with the landlord's consent, is removed from the house. The tenant may not remove the property from the house until the rent is paid. This is a right which the landlord may insist upon, but, if he voluntarily consents to the removal, he waives his lien. This Statute is a substitute for the old remedy of distress for rent, a right exercised by the landlord during an early period. Says Mr. Taylor: "The common law of England, and most of her statutory provisions regulating a distress for rent, have been generally adopted in the United States." "In order to sustain a distress, the relation of landlord and tenant must be actually completed and exist between the parties. . . . It will, however, only continue so long as that relation subsists." Taylor, Land. and T. §§ 558, 563.

The rule of the common law is well stated in *Williams* v. *Terboss*, 2 Wend. 151, as follows: "At the common law, the landlord could only distrain property which was actually on the demised premises when he came for that purpose. His right to distrain must also have been exercised during the . . . term. . . . If the tenant fraudulently removed his property and effects from the demised premises, either before or after the rent became due, the landlord could not follow and seize them for rent, unless they were removed by the tenant after the landlord had actually come to distrain, and had view of the goods on the premises."

Our Statute is an outgrowth of this principle of common law of distress for rent, and, if the landlord voluntarily consents to a removal of the goods from the demised house, his lien is lost, because the Statute expressly provides the lien attaches against the goods which remain in the house. The right is itself an incident of a particular tenancy, and arises out of it. This Statute contemplates there must be, to create the lien, a landlord, a tenant, a house rented and goods in that particular house. In case of a building, erected with many rooms, for the purpose of letting separate apartments to different tenants, no occupant is a tenant of the whole building, but only of a particular apartment, which apartment is the tenant's house. Over that he has full control. One entering there without his consent is a trespasser. It is his house. The lien grows out of the tenancy as to a house rented. Wright did not occupy the whole building, and he had no house rented, if the word "house" can apply only to the whole building. This question, however, is settled on authority.

Taylor, in his work on Landlord and Tenants, vol. 2, p. 187, quotes from the case of *Winslow* v. *Henry*, 5 Hill, 481, with approval: "As rent cannot issue out of a mere easement, or incorporeal hereditament, upon the demise of a room, with a right of common passage along an entry leading from such room into the public street, it was held that the landlord could not seize goods of the tenant kept in such common passage."

Bukup v. *Valentine*, 19 Wend. 554, is exactly in point. The facts of that case are as follows. The defendant, Valentine, demised to the plaintiff, for a term which ended May 1, 1845, the lower part of a house in Mulberry Street, New York, consisting of all the lower story, the two front joint bedrooms, the front basement kitchen, with half the cellar and privilege in the yard. Valentine, at the same time, rented to one Merit the upper part of the same house, consisting of certain rooms, and also the back basement kitchen and half the cellar. May 1, 1835. Merit left that part of the house he had previously occupied; and the plaintiff, under a lease from Valentine for one year, removed into those apartments vacated by Merit. At the same time one Marshall became tenant of the apartments which Valentine had at first occupied. The plaintiff had failed to pay his rent for the lower part of the house which he first occupied, and for rent due for those apartments Valentine distrained the plaintiff's goods located in the upper part of the building, in the apartments he last occupied. The plaintiff brought replevin for the goods, and failed in the court below. He appealed to the supreme court, and it was contended there by Valentine that plaintiff had not removed from the demised premises. The court held otherwise, and reversed the case. The court says: "It is now said that the removal to another part of the same building was not a removal from the demised premises. I cannot yield to this argument. Both before and after the rent fell due there were two tenants in the house, each having the exclusive enjoyment of a different part of the building. On the 1st of May, the plaintiff gave up the rooms he had previously occupied, and removed into other apartments. He ceased to be a tenant of the rooms he had occupied in 1884, as fully as though he had removed into an adjoining building owned by the same or another landlord."

So this court says with respect to Wright. The case is exactly in point, correct, as we think, in principle, and we are content to follow it, and therefore hold the rent accrued for the two rooms did not follow as a lien on the library to the single room across the hall. As to the $945 rent due Wolcott for the two rooms occupied by Wright, the former having waived his landlord's lien by consenting to the removal of the property, at least as between himself and a subsequent mortgagee, it is a question whether in the court below Wolcott, being only a general creditor, was in a position to attack the mortgage of Mrs. Ashenfelter, on the ground that she had not complied with the Statute requiring an affidavit to be filed within thirty days next preceding the expiration of one year from the filing of the chattel mortgage. Mrs. Ashenfelter had filed her affidavit, but not within the thirty days. She filed it several days too early, as at the time of such filing the thirty days specified in the Statute had not yet commenced to run. If the affidavit is filed or exhibited too soon, or before the thirty days begin to run, such filing is nugatory, and of no effect. Jones, Chat. Mortg. § 287; Boone, Mortg. § 250; *National Bank* v. *Sprague*, 20 N. J. Eq. 13; *Newell* v. *Warner*, 44 Barb. 258.

The chattel mortgage must be regarded as if the affidavit had not been filed. Our Statute provides as follows:

"Sec. 1589. Every mortgage, so filed, shall be void as against the creditors of the person making the same, or against subsequent purchasers or mortgagees in good faith, after the expiration of one year after the filing thereof, unless, within thirty days next preceding the expiration of the term of one year from such filing, and each year thereafter, the mortgagee, his agent or attorney, shall make an affidavit exhibiting the interest of the mortgagee in the property at the time last aforesaid, claimed by virtue of such mortgage, and, if said mortgage is to secure the payment of money, the amount yet due and unpaid; such affidavit shall be attached to and filed with the instrument or copy on file to which it relates."

The record in the case before us discloses that Mrs. Ashenfelter had not taken possession of the mortgaged property, so at the commencement of the action, in the absence of the statutory affidavit, and without possession having been taken by the mortgagee, her mortgage under the Statute would be of no effect as to such creditors of Wright as were in a situation to assert its invalidity. The authorities before cited give construction to a statute like our own, and under them it is clear, as against creditors who are in a position to raise the question, the chattel mortgage is void. Was Wolcott in that position in the court below? He had not reduced his claim to judgment. He had no specific lien on the library in any form. At best, he had only the right to sue his debtor. In the meantime, Mrs. Ashenfelter had the right, if she could peaceably obtain possession to do so, or to proceed and foreclose her mortgage. Is there any rule which would require that she should be restrained of her right to foreclose, and wait the movements of the general creditors, so long as the mortgage remained valid as between her and the debtor? The mortgage contained a provision that, upon default in payment, she might take actual possession of the property wherever she could find it. Default was made, and her right as against Wright to possession was perfect. If she had taken actual possession, her right under the mortgage would have been as complete as if she had filed the affidavit required by statute. Controversy arose as to possession between Mrs. Ashenfelter and Wolcott, so she procured a receiver to be appointed to hold the property, and the court decreed a sale thereof. As to the $945, Wolcott had not then procured either a judgment or lien by attachment. In this state of things, if Wright had turned over possession to the mortgagee, notwithstanding her failure to comply with the Statute, she would have been preferred to the general debt of Wolcott, not so as to the specific landlord's lien for the single room. That, however, is decreed to be prior to Mrs. Ashenfelter's, and is out of the case. If, then, she could have received possession, and thus have perfected her right, which had become suspended by failure to file the statutory affidavit, we can see no reason why she might not have properly invoked the aid of the court to reduce the property to cash, and apply it to the discharge of her specific lien as against Wright, unless some lienholder, with a right to question the legality of her mortgage, interposed. If Wolcott could attack the chattel mortgage, then any general creditor could do so. It would, to say the least, be illegal to hold that a creditor, without any lien upon a chattel, or right thereto, in the absence of a judgment which might by execution be enforced against such chattels, could call upon a court of equity to remove even a void lien from the property, constituting an apparent cloud upon it. Without a specific lien on the chattel, what benefit could such a creditor derive? He could not sell the chattel without judgment and execution. A consideration of some of the cases will indicate the construction which should be placed upon the words of the Statute, "shall be void against creditors."

In *Van Heusen* v. *Radcliff*, 17 N. Y. 580, the court says: "When a conveyance is said to be void against creditors, the reference is to such parties when clothed with their judgments and executions, or such other titles as the law has provided for the collection of debts."

Mr. Bump, in his work on Fraudulent Conveyances, 3d ed. p. 460, gives a clear elucidation of this subject: "It is commonly said that a fraudulent conveyance is void against creditors, but this must be taken in a limited sense. The law provides a mode for determining the rights of all parties, and does not permit even a creditor to act as judge in his own case. . . . A fraudulent conveyance, moreover, does not confer any additional rights upon creditors. They cannot seize the property of their debtor without any legal process, and appropriate it of their own accord to the satisfaction of their demands. . . . They may cause it to be appropriated to the payment of their debts, but they can do this only in the mode which the law prescribes. . . . Consequently the expression that a fraudulent transfer is void against creditors simply means that the rights of creditors as such are not, with respect to the property, affected by such transfer; but that they may, notwithstanding the transfer, avail themselves of all the remedies for collecting their debts out of the property, or its avails, which the law has provided in favor of creditors, and that in pursuing those remedies they may treat the property as though the transfer had not been made, that is, as the property of the debtor. The transfer is ineffectual to shield the property in the hands of the grantee from the just claims of the creditors of the grantor, when those claims are prosecuted against it in the manner pointed out by the law. His title, however, is good against even creditors, unless they protect themselves against him by pursuing that prescribed course by which alone the property can be made available for the satisfaction of debts. A 'creditor at large,' as it is termed, cannot impeach the conveyance, but only a creditor having some process on which the property may be lawfully seized, and by which it is made liable, either immediately or ultimately, to be appropriated in satisfaction of his debt. . . . Before he can impeach the transfer, he must have an execution, attachment or some other legal process which authorizes the seizure of the property. This process may be a warrant of distress or an attachment, as well as an execution."

Although unable to examine all the cases cited by Mr. Bump in support of this position, one which we believe to be well established, we append them for reference: *Andrews* v. *Durant*, 18 N. Y. 496; *Rinchey* v. *Stryker*, 26 How. Pr. 75; *Schlussel* v. *Willett*, 34 Barb. 615, 12 Abb. Pr. 397, 22 How. Pr. 15; *Tiffany* v. *Warren*, 37 Barb. 571, 24 How. Pr. 293.

In *Owen* v. *Dixon*, 17 Conn. 496, a well-considered opinion is given, from which the following quotation is made: "It is a familiar principle that a fraudulent conveyance of property is void as to the creditors of the vendor. By this is meant that the rights of a creditor as such are not, with respect to the property, affected by such conveyance. . . . A 'creditor at large,' as it is termed, cannot impeach the conveyance, but only a creditor having some process on which the property may be lawfully seized, and by which it is made liable" for the debt.

We think the same rule of construction established with respect to conveyances fraudulent as to creditors should be applied to the term "void as against creditors," used in our Statute. There is authority, however, more directly in point, giving that construction to statutes to the same effect as the one quoted. In New York the Statute on the subject under consideration is much like our own.

In *Thompson* v. *Van Vechten*, 27 N. Y. 582, in considering who might attack a chattel mortgage for want of the statutory affidavit, the court says: "It is true the mortgage cannot be legally questioned until the creditor clothes himself with a judgment and execution, or with some legal process against his [the debtor's] property; for creditors cannot interfere with the property of their debtors without process."

It seems to us clear that, until Wolcott had by some legal means procured a lien on the property, being only a general creditor, or, as some books express it, a "creditor at large," he could not appeal to a court of equity to remove by its decree a mortgage good against the debtor. The conclusion reached on this point is much strengthened by the terms of section 1590 of the Compiled Laws. This section and section 1589 must be construed together, as they clearly relate to the same subject.

"Sec. 1590. If such affidavit be made and filed before any purchase of such mortgaged property shall be made, or other mortgage deposited, or lien obtained thereon in good faith, it shall be as valid to continue in effect such mortgage as if the same had been made and filed within the period above provided."

This must remove all substantial doubt. If the affidavit provided for in section 1589 is not filed within the thirty days required, then the mortgage is void as to creditors; but if such a creditor omits to take such action as to obtain a lien thereon before the affidavit is thereafter filed, and the mortgagee files his affidavit as required by section 1589, it operates to revive the mortgage against all creditors who have not in the meantime obtained liens. Failure to file the affidavit required within the thirty days suspends the operation of the mortgage as against general creditors, and if they reduce their debts to judgment against the mortgagor, and levy on the property of the mortgagor, while the mortgage is suspended for want of the statutory affidavit, they secure priority, or, if they levy attachments, the same result is reached; but, if they omit to take some action, the mortgage lien may be revived. This latter section gives construction to the term "creditors," as used in the preceding one, and limits that term to such as may, by some legal means, secure a lien on the mortgaged property. As to the $945, Wolcott, being only a general creditor, without specific lien on the library, and being without judgment upon which execution might issue, could not attack the mortgage of Mrs. Ashenfelter, the same being good and valid against the mortgagor.

We find no error in the record of the court below, and accordingly *the judgment and decree there entered are affirmed.*

Whiteman, Lee and **McFie**, *JJ.*, concur.

IOWA SUPREME COURT.

Irene BILLS
v.
Daniel B. BILLS *et al.*, *Appts.*

(....Iowa....)

A clause in a will declaring that testator "desires" that a certain disposition should be made of all that remains at his wife's death of the real and personal property given her by previous clauses of the will is merely precatory, and will not prevent her from taking the fee-simple title of the land, and the absolute property in the subject of the bequest.

(May 26, 1890.)

APPEAL by defendants from a judgment of the District Court for Jones County overruling a demurrer to the petition in an action brought by the widow of a testator, she being executrix of his will and a devisee and legatee thereunder, to obtain a judicial construction of the will. *Affirmed.*

The case sufficiently appears in the opinion.

Mr. **John S. Stacy,** for appellants:

Conflicting provisions in a will should be reconciled so as to conform to the manifest general intent, and it is only in cases where such provisions are wholly and absolutely repugnant that either of them should be rejected.

Baxter v. *Bowyer*, 19 Ohio St. 490; *Worman* v. *Teagarden*, 2 Ohio St. 380.

According to its context and manifest use an expression of desire or wish will often be equivalent to a positive direction when that is the evident purpose and meaning of the testator.

Burt v. *Herron*, 66 Pa. 400; *Colton* v. *Colton*, 127 U. S. 300 (32 L. ed. 138).

When there are two conflicting and irreconcilable clauses, the last governs as being the latest declaration of the testator.

Johnson v. *Mayne*, 4 Iowa, 180–194; *Felton* v. *Hill*, 41 Ga. 554; *Armstrong* v. *Crapo*, 72 Iowa, 604; *Heidlebaugh* v. *Wagner*, 72 Iowa, 601; 1 Redf. Wills, 451; 1 Jarm. Wills, 472; *Van Vechten* v. *Keator*, 63 N. Y. 52; *Van Nostrand* v. *Moore*, 52 N. Y. 12, and cases before cited.

In all adjudicated cases in Iowa or elsewhere, where the first clause in a will was held to give an estate in fee, the language was invariably much stronger than in this.

See *Williams* v. *Allison*, 33 Iowa, 278; *Benkert* v. *Jacoby*, 36 Iowa, 273; *Rona* v. *Meier*, 47 Iowa, 607.

The words, "remaining at her decease," are to be construed "to mean such as use has not destroyed."

Goudie v. *Johnston*, 109 Ind. 427; *Harbison* v. *James*, 90 Mo. 411; *Howard* v. *Carusi*, 109 U. S. 725 (27 L. ed. 1089); *Giles* v. *Little*, 104 U. S. 291 (26 L. ed. 745); *Green* v. *Hewitt*, 97 Ill. 113.

Even if the words "except as hereinafter specified" had not been used in the first clause, there would not be an absolute devise in fee.

Lowrie v. *Ryland*, 65 Iowa, 584. See *Colton* v. *Colton*, 127 U. S. 300 (32 L. ed. 138).

Messrs. **Sheean & McCarn** and **W. G. Thompson,** for appellee:

When an interest is given or an estate conveyed in one clause of an instrument, in clear and decisive terms, such interest or estate cannot be taken away or cut down by raising a doubt upon the extent and meaning and application of a subsequent clause, nor by inference therefrom, nor by any subsequent words that are not as clear and decisive as the words of the clause giving that interest or estate.

Thornhill v. *Hall*, 2 Clark & F. 22; *Macnab* v. *Whitbread*, 17 Beav. 299; *Reid* v. *Atkinson*, 5 Ir. Eq. 373; *Greene* v. *Greene*, 3 Ir. Eq. 90, 17 Week. Rep. 487; *Mackett* v. *Mackett*, L. R. 14 Eq. 49; *Perry* v. *Merritt*, L. R. 18 Eq. 152, 9 Eng. Rep. (Moak) 702; *Parnall* v. *Parnall*, L. R. 9 Ch. Div. 96, 25 Eng. Rep. (Moak) 801; *Doe* v. *Lewis*, 4 Nev. & M. 696; *McKenzie's App.* 41 Conn. 607, 19 Am. Rep. 525; *Jackson* v. *Bull*, 10 Johns. 20; *Ramsdell* v. *Ramsdell*, 21 Me. 288; *Harris* v. *Knapp*, 21 Pick. 416; *Homer* v. *Shelton*, 2 Met. 202; 1 Jarman, Wills, Perkins' ed. p. 677, *note 2; Lynde* v. *Estabrook*, 7 Allen, 68; *Fiske* v. *Cobb*, 6 Gray, 144; *Jones* v. *Bacon*, 68 Me. 34, 28 Am. Rep. 1.

An absolute power of disposal in the first taker will render a subsequent limitation repugnant and void.

Gifford v. *Choate*, 100 Mass. 343; *Ide* v. *Ide*, 5 Mass. 500; 4 Kent, Com. 270; *Mitchell* v. *Morse*, 77 Me. 423, 52 Am. Rep. 781; *Williams* v. *Worthington*, 49 Md. 572, 33 Am. Rep. 286; *Fowe* v. *Whitmore*, 82 N. Y. 405; *Stowell* v. *Hastings*, 59 Vt. 494, 59 Am. Rep. 743; 1 Eq. Cas. Abr. 176; 4 Kent, Com. 2d ed. 535; *Smith* v. *Van Ostrand*, 64 N. Y. 278; *Campbell* v. *Beaumont*, 91 N. Y. 464; *Seibert* v. *Wise*, 70 Pa. 147; *Ramsdell* v. *Ramsdell*, 21 Me. 288; *Moore* v. *Sanders*, 15 S. C. 440, 40 Am. Rep. 703; *Canedy* v. *Jones*, 19 S. C. 297, 45 Am. Rep. 777; *Anderson* v. *Cary*, 36 Ohio St. 506, 38 Am. Rep. 602; *Spooner* v. *Lovejoy*, 108 Mass. 532; Bispham, Eq. pp. 115, 116.

The Iowa cases fully sustain the claim of appellee.

Williams v. *Allison*, 33 Iowa, 278; *Benkert* v. *Jacoby*, 36 Iowa, 273; *Rona* v. *Meier*, 47 Iowa, 607; *Allen* v. *Johnson*, 63 Iowa, 124; *Re Burbank's Will*, 69 Iowa, 378.

Beck, *J.*, delivered the opinion of the court:

1. The will presented for interpretation is in the following language: "In the name of God, amen: I, Sidney Elijah Bills, of the Town of Strawberry Hill, in the County of Jones, and State of Iowa, of the age of sixty-one years, and being of sound mind and memory, do make public and declare this my last will and testament, in manner following; that is to say: *first*, I give and bequeath to my wife, Irene Bills, all of my real and personal property situated in Jones County, Iowa, except as hereinafter specified; *second*, I give and bequeath to my nephew Sanford H. Brownell all that real estate conveyed to me by him, containing (134) one hundred and thirty-four acres, more or less, situated in Decatur County, Iowa, and also all that real estate owned by me situated in the Town of Sabula, Jackson County, Iowa; and, *third*, I give and bequeath to said Sanford H. Brownell the bay mare known by name

See also 45 L. R. A. 53.

'Nellie,' now in Jones County, Iowa, also one hundred dollars in money, same to be taken in payment for what I owe him at this time; *fourth*, I give and bequeath to my brother, Daniel B. Bills, the sum of one hundred dollars in money; *fifth*, all the real and personal property herein bequeathed to my wife, Irene Bills, remaining at her decease, I desire to be divided into five equal shares,—to Daniel B. Bills and Abigail E. Diviney, and remaining shares to my brother's two sons, Frank E. Bills and Frederick A. Bills, and Sanford H. Brownell. All of which said several legacies or sums of money I direct and order to be paid to said respective legatees within one year after my decease; and I hereby appoint as my executors of this my last will and testament, my wife, Irene Bills, and John Bender, of Jones County, Iowa, hereby releasing them from giving bonds, and hereby revoking all former wills by me made."

2. Plaintiff claims in his petition, and insists that under the will she takes an absolute estate, in fee simple, in the lands, and the absolute property in the personalty, of the estate, and that the fifth item of the will simply uses precatory language, and does not limit the estate and interest vested in plaintiff by the first item. Defendants maintain the contrary, insisting that plaintiff takes but a life estate in the property, with the right to possess, enjoy and use it, but, after such estate and right shall be terminated by her death, the property shall be distributed under item 5 of the will.

3. In our opinion, the books teach these rules for the interpretation of wills: (1) When an estate or interest in land is devised, or personalty is bequeathed, in clear and absolute language, without words of limitation, the devise or bequest cannot be defeated or limited by a subsequent doubtful provision inferentially raising a limitation upon the prior devise or bequest. (2) When there is an absolute or unlimited devise or bequest of property, a subsequent clause expressing a wish, desire or direction for its disposition after the death of the devisee or legatee will not defeat the devise or bequest, nor limit the estate or interest in the property, to the right to possess and use during the life of the devisee or legatee. The absolute devise or bequest stands, and the other clause is to be regarded as presenting precatory language. The will must be interpreted to invest in the devisee or legatee the fee-simple title of the land, and the absolute property in the subject of the bequest. *Williams* v. *Allison*, 33 Iowa, 278; *Benkert* v. *Jacoby*, 36 Iowa, 273; *Rona* v. *Meier*, 47 Iowa, 607; *Alden* v. *Johnson*, 63 Iowa, 127; *Re Burbank's Will*, 69 Iowa, 378; *McKenzie's App.* 41 Conn. 607; *Jackson* v. *Bull*, 10 Johns. 20; *Mitchell* v. *Morse*, 77 Me. 423; *Ramsdell* v. *Ramsdell*, 21 Me. 288; *Jones* v. *Bacon*, 68 Me. 34; *Harris* v. *Knapp*, 21 Pick. 412; *Lynde* v. *Estabrook*, 7 Allen, 68; *Fiske* v. *Cobb*, 6 Gray, 144; *Gifford* v. *Choate*, 100 Mass. 343; *Williams* v. *Worthington*, 49 Md. 572; *Foose* v. *Whitmore*, 82 N. Y. 405; *Campbell* v. *Beaumont*, 91 N. Y. 465; *Stowell* v. *Hastings*, 59 Vt. 494; *Seibert* v. *Wise*, 70 Pa. 147; *Moore* v. *Sanders*, 15 S. C. 440; *Canedy* v. *Jones*, 19 S. C. 297; *Anderson* v. *Cary*, 36 Ohio St. 506.

Cases cited by defendants' counsel are not in conflict with the doctrines we have stated, in that the instruments interpreted therein, by their express language, did not vest the devisee with the fee of the land, nor the legatee with the absolute property in the subject of the bequest, a contrary purpose clearly appearing in the wills.

These views lead us to the conclusion that the district court rightly overruled the demurrer to plaintiff's petition.

Its judgment is affirmed.

NEW JERSEY SUPREME COURT.

STATE OF NEW JERSEY, Jesse R. LEEDS, *Prosecutor*,

v.

MAYOR, etc., of ATLANTIC CITY *et al.*

(....N. J. L....)

*1. **When an office is full de facto** of a person claiming it under color of right, the proper remedy to test the claimant's title is quo warranto, and not mandamus.

2. **An office is deemed to be full** *de facto* whenever a person elected has been admitted to it, notwithstanding the election may, upon legal grounds, turn out to be invalid; provided such election is consistent with an honest misapprehension of the law, and not evidence of a palpable disregard of its provisions.

3. **When a relator in office** *de jure et de facto* is interfered with by one whose lack of title *de jure* is *res judicata*, mandamus, and not quo warranto, is the proper remedy.

4. **Where a mandamus is applied for** to compel a corporation to restore relator to an office to which he is prima facie entitled, the incumbent is not a necessary party to the allowance of a peremptory mandamus.

*Head notes by GARRISON, J.

(March 12, 1890.)

APPLICATION for a writ of mandamus to compel the restoration of applicant to the duties and privileges of an office from which an illegal attempt had been made to exclude him. *Granted.*

The facts fully appear in the opinion.

Argued before Van Syckel, Magie and Garrison, *JJ.*

Mr. **J. W. Westcott** for prosecutor.
Mr. **A. B. Endicott** for defendants.

Garrison, *J.*, delivered the opinion of the court:

This cause is before us upon a rule for a mandamus. The facts are briefly these: The relator was elected sergeant of police in Atlantic City at a meeting of city council held November 24, 1885. He took the prescribed oath of office, and entered upon his official duties. At the meeting of city council held November 23, 1886, the office thus held by the relator was,

See also 14 L. R. A. 643.

upon motion, declared vacant, and an election held to fill the same, which resulted in the selection of one Samuel Loder, who was thereupon declared elected "sergeant of police, instead of Jesse R. Leeds, removed;" since which time the said Loder has performed the duties of the office with the concurrence of the city authorities, who declined to recognize the relator, notwithstanding his refusal to surrender his equipments, and his occasional performance of official duty. These proceedings of city council, in so far as they resulted in the removal of the relator, were carried by him into the court by certiorari, and were here set aside, as being in contravention of the provisions of "An Act Respecting Police Departments of Cities, and Regulating the Tenure of Office of Officers and Men Employed in Said Departments," and the supplement thereto (Pub. Laws 1886, p. 48). The action of city council by which relator was removed from his office having thus been declared illegal, he now asks for a writ of mandamus to compel the City to restore him to the duties and privileges of his said office. The rule, which is directed against the municipality alone, is by it opposed upon four grounds:

(1) That mandamus is not the proper remedy.

(2) That the present incumbent is a necessary party.

(3) That relator served the full term for which he was elected.

(4) Because he accepted his discharge.

In considering these objections in their inverse order, it is sufficient to say of the last one that it is not sustained by the proofs, and of the third that it is *res judicata*. The first and second reasons have more substance, and may be dealt with together.

The contention raised is that quo warranto, and not mandamus, is the proper remedy in the present case.

The appropriate use of these remedies, in cases of amotion from public office, has been a fruitful source of discussion, and the result, so far as the American cases are concerned, is a contrariety of judicial opinion and practice.

At an early period it was established by the court of king's bench that quo warranto, and not mandamus, was the proper remedy where the office was full *de facto*. *Rex* v. *Colchester*, 2 T. R. 259; *Rex* v. *York*, 4 T. R. 699; *Rex* v. *Oxford*, 6 Ad. & El. 349.

It is likewise to be gathered from the English cases that an office is deemed full *de facto* whenever a person elected has been admitted to it, whether the election was or was not of such a character that it could be supported at law. Thus in the case of *Rex* v. *Lisle*, which is reported at length by Andrews, and briefly by Strange, it is said: "In order to constitute a man an officer *de facto*, there must be, at least, the form of an election, though that, upon legal objections, may afterwards fall to the ground." Andrews, 163; 2 Strange, 1090.

The language of Wightman, *J.*, in *Frost* v. *Chester*, 5 El. & Bl. 531, which was an application for mandamus, presents the view of the same court at a later period. "We may assume," he says, "that the office is not full *de jure* but only *de facto*, and, for the purpose of the present argument, we may assume that the election has been holden in a way not warranted by law, and is therefore bad, and such as could not be supported on quo warranto. But the office is not the less full *de facto*, and the party elected has been admitted." To the same effect were the opinions of Coleridge, *J.*, and *Chief Justice* Campbell in the same case; the court being unanimous that, where an office was thus full, quo warranto, and not mandamus, was the remedy.

But, while it is true that the illegality of the election by virtue of which an incumbent has gained entrance to an office does not prevent the office from being full of him *de facto*, it is also to be noted that from the earliest periods it has been held requisite that the illegality in question must be consistent with honesty of purpose. Elections based upon mistakes of fact or misconceptions of law may impart a color of right which will bar the allowance of a mandamus, but palpable disregard of law renders the action by which an office is seized merely colorable, and in a clear case will be brushed aside, as affording no obstruction to the exercise of a plain legal duty. Thus, in *Rex* v. *Bankes*, 3 Burr. 1452, *Lord* Mansfield proposed, upon the argument, that affidavits be laid before him, that he might determine whether it was a doubtful election, and fit to be tried upon an information in the nature of a quo warranto, or whether it was merely colorable, and clearly void,—saying that in the former case the court might not grant a mandamus, while in the latter case they ought. And from a *note* by Burrows (p. 1454) it appears that *Lord* Hardwicke, in *Rex* v. *Holmes*, Hil. T. 9 Geo. II., K. B., cites the *Case of Tintagel*, Hil.T. 8 Geo. II., K. B., 2 Strange, 1003, as the first case in which a mandamus had been granted under such circumstances, adding, as if in apology, that it had been done because it was "a quite clear case." See also *Rex* v. *Cambridge*, 4 Burr. 2008.

The distinction thus early indicated has become incorporated in the modern English rule upon this subject, which is stated by Mr. Shortt (on Quo Warranto Informations, 122) as follows:

"Wherever the office is full *de facto*, the proper method of proceeding is by quo warranto to oust the occupant, if he is not in possession *de jure*. And the office is full *de facto*, though the election to it was illegal, provided it was a real and not merely a colorable election. If, on the other hand, the election was merely colorable so as to be really no election at all, it does not confer even a *de facto* possession, and the remedy of the person ousted by it is not quo warranto, but mandamus."

In this country the courts of New York have adopted the English rule without substantial change. In the leading case, however, an additional reason is given, viz., that the corporation, being a third party, may admit or not at pleasure, and the rights of the party in office may be injured. *People* v. *New York*, 3 Johns. Cas. 79.

This is obviously rather a matter of practice than an error in principle.

So in the later cases we find the writ refused upon grounds adopted from the English cases. *People* v. *Lane*, 55 N. Y. 217; *Re Gardner*, 68 N. R. 467; *People* v. *Ferris*, 76 N. Y. 326.

A similar course obtains in Connecticut. *Duane* v. *McDonald*, 41 Conn. 517.

On the contrary, other state courts, notably those of Massachusetts, have relaxed the rigidity of the rule, and to a certain extent permit the right to an office actually filled to be raised upon an alternative mandamus. *Re Strong*, 20 Pick. 484; *Ellis* v. *Bristol County*, 2 Gray, 370; *Conlin* v. *Aldrich*, 98 Mass. 557; *Putnam* v. *Langley*, 133 Mass. 204; *Dew* v. *Judges*, 3 Hen. & M. 1.

The rule, as it obtains at present in the various States, will be found with citations of numerous cases in Angell & A. Corp. § 702 *et seq.*

In this State, so far as any expression of judicial sentiment is to be found, it is favorable to retaining the distinction upon which the English rule is founded, *i. e.*, that quo warranto, and not mandamus, is the remedy in all cases in which an office is full *de facto*, excepting only those cases in which the office has been filled by proceedings palpably without legal warrant. *Hoboken* v. *Gear*, 27 N. J. L. 265; *State* v. *Miller*, 45 N. J. L. 251; *State* v. *Camden*, 39 N. J. L. 416; *State* v. *Camden*, 42 N. J. L. 335.

There are in particular two cases in which this court has evidently proceeded upon this view of the rule of law.

In *State* v. *Paterson*, 35 N. J. L. 190, the office of city treasurer could, under the city charter, be filled only by a majority meeting of the board of aldermen. The defendant, who had been admitted to the office by an election in which less than a legal number of aldermen were present, claimed, against the relator's application for a mandamus, that as he was in office *de facto*, and under color of an election, quo warranto, and not mandamus, was the proper remedy. The court held, however, that the election by the aldermen in violation of their own organic law was merely colorable, and all the facts being before the court, a peremptory mandamus went in the first instance.

In *State* v. *Jersey City*, 51 N. J. L. 240, the discharge of a person, under a debatable construction of a recent legislative enactment, and the filling of his position, did not prevent the allowance of a peremptory mandamus for his restoration to office. All of the facts necessary for the determination of the legality of his discharge appear to have been before the court on the rule to show cause, and the propriety of the proposed remedy does not seem to have been questioned, nor does the reported case show that the incumbent was a party to the proceedings. The present case possesses elements of strength for the relator not to be found in the reported cases, in that it is *res judicata* that his removal from office was illegal.

The authority of these two cases would appear to be conclusive upon the relator's right to a peremptory mandamus restoring him to his office.

There is, however, an aspect of this case which, while it leads to the same result, appears to me more surely consonant with the rule of law which we seem to have adopted.

That rule, in its rigidity, is applicable to cases only in which a relator, clearly out of office *de facto*, is seeking to oust an incumbent who is clearly in. In such cases, the reason for the rule makes the fullness of the office *de facto* the test as to whether quo warranto is or is not the only remedy.

There is, however, a class of cases in which this reason for the rule is wanting. I refer to those cases in which the facts before the court, or within its judicial knowledge, show that the relator was in office *de jure et de facto*, and that the defendant while claiming to be in *de facto*, can make no claim to be in *de jure*. Here the relator is not called upon to test the title to the office, for that is not in dispute. The office is not *de facto* full against him, unless by his conduct he elect to consider himself out. In contemplation of law, his title to the office *de jure* draws to it the possession *de facto*, as in cases where simultaneous acts of occupancy are exercised by contestants over a legal title. In such cases there is nothing to be tried by quo warranto. The law being settled, and the facts undisputed, the duty of the court is clear. *People* v. *Scrugham*, 20 Barb. 302, presents such a state of facts, and is directly in point. This case was subsequently reversed, but not upon the ground for which it is here cited.

In the case in hand this court has, upon certiorari, annulled the only thing which challenged the relator's right to this office. The testimony taken under this rule shows that the relator was in office at the time of this unlawful attempt at his amotion, and that he has not elected to consider himself out. Under these circumstances, the municipality can interpose no objection to the proposed mandamus.

The only remaining question is the right of the defendant municipality to object to this application because the incumbent is not a party to it.

The incumbent of an office is undoubtedly a necessary party to proceedings brought for the purpose of testing his title thereto.

By the certiorari suit it was decided that, at the time of the appointment of the incumbent, there existed no legal vacancy in the office he still purports to fill.

Without discussing the questions which might have arisen if the incumbent himself had made application to be made a party to the certiorari, it is sufficient for present purpose to say that the defendant cannot now avail itself of the non-joinder of the incumbent in the proceeding now before us.

As to the City of Atlantic City, the prima facie right of this relator to be admitted to this office is *res judicata*.

A peremptory mandamus will be allowed.

UNITED STATES CIRCUIT COURT, DISTRICT OF OREGON.

GIANT POWDER CO.
v.
OREGON PACIFIC R. CO. *et al.*

(......Sawy.......Fed. Rep. ......)

*1. **The general phrase in the Act of 1885—"any other structure"**—following, as it does, a specific enumeration of works declared to be subject to a lien for labor and materials furnished for their construction, such as a "building," "ditch," "flume" and "tunnel,"—*Held*, to include a railway.

2. **A person entitled to a lien on a railway** for materials furnished for its construction may in his notice of lien confine his claim to that portion or section of the road in the construction of which his material was used.

3. **Giant powder** furnished by the manufacturer to a contractor for the construction of a railway, and used by the latter in the progress of such work, is "material" within the purview of the Lien Law of 1885, for the value of which such manufacturer is entitled to a lien on the railway, or such portion thereof as the powder was used in the construction of.

(June 16, 1890.)

SUIT to enforce an alleged lien for material furnished for use in the construction of a certain line of railway. On demurrer to bill. *Demurrer overruled.*

The case is fully stated in the opinion.

Mr. **L. Flinn** for defendants in support of the demurrer.

Mr. **George H. Williams** for plaintiff, *contra.*

Deady, *J.*, delivered the following opinion:

This suit is brought by the Giant Powder Company, a corporation of California, against the Oregon Pacific Railway Company and the Wallamet Valley & Coast Railway Company,

* Head notes by DEADY, *J.*

NOTE.—*Mechanic's Lien Law applicable to railroads; late decisions in the various States.*

Arkansas.

The Statute must be fully complied with, and the accounts must be filed within ninety days. Arkansas Cent. R. Co. v. McKay, 30 Ark. 682.

California.

But one mechanic's lien can be acquired on a section of a railroad to be graded under an entire contract; successive liens cannot be filed as payments fall due. Cox v. Western Pac. R. Co. 47 Cal. 87, 44 Cal. 18.

Where material was furnished at divers times, at the request of or under sub-contracts of different persons, it is not sufficient for a materialman to file a claim for the gross sum, without any designation of the amounts furnished for the several persons. Gordon Hardware Co. v. San Francisco & S. R. Co. (Cal.) Oct. 4, 1889.

A description of materials furnished for the construction of a railroad, as "nails, spikes, iron, steel, picks, shovels and other like material," is too indefinite and uncertain to sustain a lien, especially as some of the articles mentioned are merely tools, and not properly materials for the road. *Ibid.*

Filing a lien for too much, if done without fraud, will not defeat a right to recover the amount due. Harmon v. San Francisco & S. R. Co. (Cal.) Oct. 4, 1889.

Colorado.

A mechanic's lien cannot be obtained under the Colorado Act of 1881, where no statement or notice is made as required by § 4 of the Act. Greeley, S. L. & P. R. Co. v. Harris, 12 Colo. 226.

The proceeding to enforce a mechanic's lien is purely statutory, and no lien attaches unless the Statute is complied with, at least substantially. *Ibid.*

Connecticut.

The Statute giving mechanics a lien upon buildings applies to buildings of a railroad company. Botsford v. New Haven, M. & W. R. Co. 41 Conn. 454.

The lien of a contractor attaches to the land of a railroad held under an equitable title, and takes precedence over a mortgage covering the entire franchise and property of the company. Botsford v. New Haven, M. & W. R. Co. 41 Conn. 454.

Where the lien claimed was invalid the bill should be dismissed. Benedict v. Danbury & N. R. Co. 24 Conn. 320.

Georgia.

The lien given by the Code upon property manufactured or repaired by mechanics does not attach in favor of a workman hired by another to do the work. Quillian v. Central R. & Bkg. Co. 52 Ga. 374.

Though contractors may be mechanics, yet this fact does not entitle them to the benefit of the Statute, if the work is done through others employed by them for that purpose. Savannah & C. R. Co. v. Callahan, 49 Ga. 506; Savannah, G. & N. A. R. Co. v. Grant, 56 Ga. 68.

Suit must be brought within twelve months from the date of record of the lien; the mere filing of the declaration is not commencement of the suit. Cherry v. North & S. R. Co. 65 Ga. 633.

Illinois.

Under the Act of 1861, no one is entitled to a lien unless his contract was directly with the company, and unless he proceeds to enforce it within three months after his cause of action accrues. Arbuckle v. Illinois M. R. Co. 81 Ill. 429.

The Act of 1872, which gives sub-contractors a lien for labor and materials, gives no right to a lien for labor and materials furnished before its passage. Arbuckle v. Illinois M. R. Co. 81 Ill. 429.

A contract between a construction company and a railroad company, that certain rails and other materials shall be used in the construction of a railroad in Illinois, and that, until fully paid for, the seller shall have a lien thereon and constructive possession of them, is not a waiver of a statutory lien in favor of the seller. Chicago & A. R. Co. v. Union Rolling Mill Co. 109 U. S. 702 (27 L. ed. 1081).

One furnishing materials to a sub-contractor has no lien against the railroad company or its property. Cairo & St. L. R. Co. v. Watson, 85 Ill. 531; Smith Bridge Co. v. Louisville, N. A. & St. L. A. L. R. Co. 72 Ill. 506.

A party who, at the request of the railway company, takes up its certificates of indebtedness to its laborers for the boarding of its hands, is not entitled to any lien under the Statute. Cairo & V. R. Co. v. Fackney, 78 Ill. 116.

See also 11 L. R. A. 580.

corporations of Oregon, and James Searle and E. B. Deane, doing business under the firm name of Searle & Deane, citizens of Oregon, to enforce a lien for material on a certain section of the Wallamet Valley & Coast Railway.

It is alleged in the bill that the defendant, the Wallamet Valley & Coast Railway Company, is the owner of said railway, which extends from Yaquina Bay, Oregon, eastward through Corvallis, into the Cascade Mountains; that in 1888 and 1889 said Company contracted with the defendant, the Oregon Pacific Railway Company, to construct said road eastward from Albany, Oregon; that on August 25, 1888, the Oregon Pacific Railway Company contracted with the defendants, Searle and Deane, to construct the portion of said road, commencing at station numbered 2659, plus 78, in Marion County, and extending from there eastward for fifteen miles along the established route of the same, in which contract it was provided that Searle and Deane should furnish all the material and labor for such construction; that Searle and Deane commenced work on the road on September 1, 1888, and completed said section thereof, according to the contract, on January 15, 1889, and there remained due them and unpaid thereon, the sum of $111,893.62.

That the plaintiff, between September 26 and December 31, 1888, furnished Searle and Deane "electrical material, powder, fuse and caps necessary and proper materials to use in the prosecution of said work," and the said defendants (S. and D.) agreed to pay the plaintiff the sum of $7,148.82 therefor; that said material was used by Searle and Deane in the construction of said road, and the value thereof, namely, $7,148.32, is now due from them to the plaintiff.

That on January 22, 1889, the plaintiff filed with the clerk of Marion County its claim for such material, under the Lien Law of Oregon, for the purpose of establishing a lien upon said section of said road, and the land for thirty feet on either side of the centre line thereof; which claim was duly recorded; and, that the plaintiff has obtained a judgment against Searle and Deane for said money, but nothing has been or can be made on the same.

In a proceeding by a sub-contractor to obtain a lien, it must appear that all the steps required by the Statute have been taken. Cairo & St. L. R. Co. v. Cauble, 4 Ill. App. 133.

As to sufficiency of notice to owner, see Cairo & St. L. R. Co. v. Cauble, 85 Ill. 555.

An intervening defendant who fails to show title or interest in the property has no such standing in court as will enable him to question a decree establishing the lien. Lake Shore & M. S. R. Co. v. McMillan, 84 Ill. 208.

A laborer's statutory lien is not assignable at law. Cairo & V. R. Co. v. Fackney, 78 Ill. 116.

Indiana.

In the Railroad Mechanic's Lien Law of 1883 the Legislature intended to give a lien on the railroad and not on mere parcels of it. Midland R. Co. v. Wilcox, 122 Ind. 84.

In the Lien Law of 1885, amending and explaining the Law of 1883, providing that the lien shall be on the railroad within the county in which the labor and material is performed and furnished, it was not the intention of the Legislature to limit the lien to a single county; and a lien may be enforced as to the entire line or unfinished road, in any county into which the work extends. Midland R. Co. v. Wilcox, *supra.*

Under this later Act a contractor having due notice of the pendency of actions against the railroad by his sub-contractors, materialmen and laborers is bound by the judgments recovered in such actions, and his lien is abated to the amount of such judgments. Midland R. Co. v. Wilcox, *supra.*

A contractor expending money and labor in building a railroad, under an agreement with the company that he shall have possession of the road until he is fully paid, does not thereby acquire a priority over an elder valid mortgage. Dunham v. Cincinnati, P. & C. R. Co. 68 U. S. 1 Wall. 254 (17 L. ed. 584).

Iowa.

Under the laws of Iowa a mechanic's lien for work done under a contract takes precedence of all incumbrances on the property after the work was commenced. "Removal Cases," 100 U. S. 457 (25 L. ed. 593); Taylor v. Burlington, C. R. & M. R. Co. 4 Dill. 570; Brooks v. Burlington & S. W. R. Co. 101 U. S. 443 (25 L. ed. 1057).

Where the holder of a mechanic's lien acquires the legal title to the property with the intention that the lien should not be merged, the intention of the lienholder will prevail as against junior incumbrancers. Delaware R. Const. Co. v. Davenport & St. P. R. Co. 46 Iowa, 406.

A mechanic's lien for ties attaches from the commencement of the building and takes precedence over a mortgage executed after that time, although the work was not commenced until after the execution of the mortgage. Neilson v. Iowa Eastern R. Co. 44 Iowa, 71.

That a contractor who files a mechanic's lien for work on a railroad in Iowa is a stockholder of a construction company which guaranteed bonds and a mortgage to secure them, on the road, does not estop him from setting up that his lien is superior to that of the mortgage. Meyer v. Egbert, 101 U. S. 728 (25 L. ed. 1078).

The entire road is subject to a lien for work done on one part of it, although the road was built in sections. Brooks v. Burlington & S.W. R. Co. 101 U. S. 443 (25 L. ed. 1057); Meyer v. Egbert, 101 U. S. 728 (25 L. ed. 1078).

The filing of a statement of account by a subcontractor within thirty days, and the claim for a lien within sixty days, do not entitle him to his lien unless he gives written notice of the filing to the owner, his agent or trustee. Lounsbury v. Iowa, M. & N. P. R. Co. 49 Iowa, 255.

If the contractors entered into an agreement by which they became personally liable to pay the claim of the sub-contractor, the contractors were not entitled to a change of venue to the county of their residence. Vaughn v. Smith, 58 Iowa, 553.

Where, under the contract, payment is to be made before completion of the railway, and such payment is made without notice, it will cut off the lien of the sub-contractor. Roland v. Centerville, M. & A. R. Co. 61 Iowa, 380, 11 Am. & Eng. R. R. Cas. 47.

A mechanic's lien not filed till after the lapse of ninety days cannot be enforced as against the purchasers at foreclosure at suit of the bondholders, and by them transferred to another company. Bear v. Burlington, C. R. & M. R. Co. 48 Iowa, 619.

Where on a foreclosure suit parties intervene and seek to enforce a claim for materials without claiming a mechanic's lien, the purchaser at the foreclosure sale is not bound to look beyond what appears on the face of the record. Hale v. Bur-

The prayer of the bill is, that it be adjudged that the plaintiff has a lien on said section of the road for the amount due it for said material and costs of suit, including the cost of preparing such lien and a reasonable attorney fee, and that the property may be sold to satisfy the same.

The defendants, the Railway Companies, demur to the bill.

On the argument the following points were made in support of the demurrer:

1. At and prior to the filing of the alleged lien, the law of the State did not give a lien on railways to materialmen.

2. A lien cannot be had on a part or section of a railway.

3. The material in question did not enter into the construction of the road, but was merely used by the contractors as a part of their plant or means in performing their contract.

Section 1 of the Act of February 11, 1885 (Comp. 1887, § 3669), provides that every person "furnishing material of any kind to be used in the construction . . . of any building, wharf, bridge, ditch, flume, tunnel, fence, machinery or aqueduct or any other structure or superstructure, shall have a lien upon the same for the . . . material furnished, at the instance of the owner of the building or other improvement or his agent; and every contractor . . . shall be held to be the agent of the owner for the purpose of this Act."

Section 5 of the Act (Comp. 1887, § 3673) provides that any materialman desiring to claim the benefit of the Act must, within a certain time, "file with the county clerk of the county in which such building or other improvement or some part thereof shall be situated, a claim containing a true statement of his demand" with the name of the owner of the property and the person "to whom he furnished the materials; and also a description of the property to be charged with said lien, sufficient for identification."

Section 12 of the Act (Comp. 1887, § 3681) declares:

"The words 'building or other improvement,' wherever the same are used in this Act, shall be held to include and apply to any wharf, bridge, ditch, flume, tunnel, fence, ma-

---

lington, C. R. & N. R. Co. 13 Fed. Rep. 203, 2 McCrary, 558.

The requirement of a written settlement with the sub-contractor is sufficiently complied with by filing it with the clerk within the thirty days allowed for filing the lien. Bundy v. Keokuk & D. M. R. Co. 49 Iowa, 207.

The lien for repairs upon a completed railway is not paramount to the lien of a mortgage executed before completion of the road; nor will such lien take precedence of the mortgage, when the improvements made constitute an integral part of the road. Bear v. Burlington, C. R. & M. R. Co. 48 Iowa, 619.

A lien attaches at the commencement of the work, and the time for notice expires ninety days from the date of the conclusion of the work. Delaware R. Const. Co. v. Davenport & St. P. R. Co. 46 Iowa, 406.

A lien for materials furnished embraces only the completed portion of the road, but the fact that the road as projected at the time was not fully completed will not defeat the lien. Neilson v. Iowa Eastern R. Co. 51 Iowa, 184.

A clause in a contract reciting that "all the money for the work hereinbefore specified should be paid by the citizens of Delaware County" does not constitute the contractor the holder of collateral security so as to prevent him from acquiring a mechanic's lien on the road. Delaware R. Const. Co. v. Davenport & St. P. R. Co. 46 Iowa, 406. See Removal Cases, 100 U. S. 457 (25 L. ed. 593).

If the contractor has fully paid the sub-contractor the employé of the latter cannot enforce a lien against the company. Utter v. Crane, 37 Iowa, 631.

A day laborer is entitled to a mechanic's lien upon a railway for his wages. Mornan v. Carroll, 35 Iowa, 22.

Kansas.

Laborers and mechanics employed by a sub-contractor are within the protection of the Compiled Laws of 1879, and if the company fails to take the bond required may maintain their action against it. Mann v. Corrigan, 28 Kan. 194.

One in the employ of a contractor simply as timekeeper is not a laborer in the sense of the Statute, and cannot recover the amount due him by the contractor although the company failed to take the bond required by statute. Missouri, K. & T. R. Co. v. Baker, 14 Kan. 563.

The statute applies, not merely when the company is engaged in the construction of its first and main track, but where it is enlarging its road by side tracks. Missouri, K. & T. R. Co. v. Brown, 14 Kan. 557.

A company failing to take the bond required by statute is liable personally, not merely to laborers, but to any person to whom they transfer their claims. Missouri, K. & T. R. Co. v. Brown, 14 Kan. 557.

The bond is not vitiated by an additional stipulation to save the company harmless from all trouble, damage, costs, suits, judgments, etc. The liability of the company is purely statutory, and one seeking to enforce it must show all the facts required. Atchison, T. & S. F. R. Co. v. Cuthbert, 14 Kan. 212.

Kentucky.

Under the Statutes of Kentucky, a lien does not attach to railway bridges and like structures. Graham v. Mt. Sterling Coal Road Co. 14 Bush, 425.

The Kentucky & Great Eastern Railroad Construction Company acquired no ownership of, or lien on, the constructed road between Newport and Catlettsburgh, under its contract of May 22, 1873, with the Kentucky & Great Eastern Railway Company for the construction of said road. The vague provision for giving the construction company all the earnings of the road "during construction" and "until accepted" cannot be construed as giving a lien, since that would be inconsistent with the whole tenor of the instrument. Wright v. Kentucky & G. E. R. Co. 117 U. S. 72 (29 L. ed. 821).

Louisiana.

To maintain a privilege where the amount exceeds $500 a party must show that no claim was duly recorded. State v. Mexican Gulf R. Co. 5 La. Ann. 333.

Maryland.

Machinery used for the manufacture and hoisting of artificial stone is not within the Statute giving materialmen a lien for material used for the construction of bridges. Basshor v. Baltimore & O. R. Co. 2 Cent. Rep. 850, 65 Md. 99.

Coal cars are not subject to the lien, the word "machine" in the Statute applying only to fixed and stationary machinery. New England C. S. Co. v. Baltimore & O. R. Co. 11 Md. 81.

chinery, aqueduct to create hydraulic power or for mining or other purposes; and all other structures and superstructures, whenever the same can be made applicable thereto."

By section 1 of the Act of February 25, 1889 (Sess. Laws, 75), any sub-contractor, materialman or laborer, who "shall furnish to any contractor to any railroad corporation, any fuel, ties, materials or supplies or other article or thing, or who shall do or perform any work or labor for such contractor in conformity with any terms of any contract, express or implied, which such contractor may have made with any such railroad corporation, shall have a lien upon all property, real, personal and mixed, of said railroad corporation."

This is a most extraordinary Act. The lien of the materialman or laborer is declared to exist against all the property of the corporation, including "personal," without limit as to situation or place of existence, on the furnishing of materials or the performing of labor, without any record being made of the same, or notice to anyone of the claim, except in the case of a laborer, when notice is required to be given to the corporation that he will hold its property for his "pay."

It is contended by counsel for the demurrer that the passage of the Act of 1889 amounts to a legislative declaration that the Act of 1885 did not include or apply to railways.

The subsequent Act might have been passed out of abundance of caution, and not upon any well-grounded or serious impression that the former was wanting or insufficient in this respect. Be this as it may, the opinion of the Legislative Assembly of 1889 as to the scope and purpose of the Act of 1885 is of very little moment, and can have no weight in the construction of the latter one, concerning rights and transactions which were vested or transpired before its existence.

The intention of the Legislature of 1889 in passing the Act of that year is a proper subject of judicial inquiry and determination, but its opinion of the scope and effect of the Act of 1885, if it had any, is not material in this case. Considering the peculiar provisions of the Act of 1889, the most obvious reason for its passage is that the Legislature thereby intended to take

---

Massachusetts.

The Massachusetts Statute applies to anyone performing labor under a contract with a sub-contractor. Hars v. Boston, R. B. & L. R. Co. 121 Mass. 510.

Under the Statute of 1878, the employé of a contractor whose contract was made before the passage of the Act has no right of action against the owner although the labor was performed after the Statute took effect. Parker v. Massachusetts R. Co. 115 Mass. 580.

Michigan.

Contractors and sub-contractors are not "laborers," within the Statute giving a right of action for labor debts. Chicago & N. E. R. Co. v. Sturgis, 44 Mich. 538.

Time checks issued by a sub-contractor are inadmissible in an action for a labor debt, being mere hearsay. Chicago & N. E. R. Co. v. Sturgis, 44 Mich. 538.

A corporation is not liable for labor to persons hired by a contractor or sub-contractor except so far as it is indebted to the latter. Bottomley v. Port Huron & N. W. R. Co. 44 Mich. 542.

Where the plaintiff's claims against the railroad company were based upon orders drawn by a sub-contractor upon plaintiff in favor of a laborer, these orders did not constitute an assignment of the claim of the laborer for the amount due him from the sub-contractor. Dudley v. Toledo, A. A. & N. M. R. Co. 9 West. Rep. 334, 65 Mich. 655.

A laborer may sue for work done by his team, where no right arises by its service to any other person. Chicago & N. E. R. Co. v. Sturgis, 44 Mich. 538.

A statutory right of action for labor and materials follows the assignment of the claim. Chicago & N. E. R. Co. v. Sturgis, 44 Mich. 538.

A suit against a company for labor will not admit of the theory that defendant is merely an agent of the owner. Chicago & N. E. R. Co. v. Sturgis, 44 Mich. 538.

Missouri.

The Act of 1878, giving a lien to contractors and others, applies to horse railroads laid in the streets of a city, as well as steam railroads. St. Louis Bolt & Iron Co. v. Donahoe, 3 Mo. App. 559.

Under the Statute of 1878 a lien for labor or material cannot be fixed upon a part only of the roadbed of a public railway. It must be upon the whole. Knapp v. St. Louis, K. C. & N. R. Co. 6 Mo. App. 205.

Prior to the Act of 1878 a strip of land granted to a railroad company for a right of way could not be subjected to a mechanic's lien. It was not the design of the Mechanic's Lien Law to allow a railroad to be sold out in detached parcels. Schulenburg v. Memphis, C. & N. W. R. Co. 67 Mo. 442.

A party furnishing material under a contract with the president of the company is an original contractor, and as such is entitled to a mechanic's lien. Hearne v. Chillicothe & B. R. Co. 53 Mo. 324.

A person furnishing materials under one contract on an open account is entitled to a lien for items furnished more than ninety days before filing the lien, if other items were furnished within the ninety days. Hetzell v. Chicago & A. R. Co. 2 West. Rep. 556, 20 Mo. App. 435.

One who sells materials to a contractor for building a railroad is entitled to a lien upon the road only for the amount of the material used. *Ibid.*

The provision of the Statute requiring notice to be given does not relate to the enforcement of a lien, but the establishment of a personal liability. Morgan v. Chicago & A. R. Co. 76 Mo. 161.

Service of notice upon the station agents of a foreign railway company is service of notice upon the company. Morgan v. Chicago & A. R. Co. 76 Mo. 161.

Claims for work done or materials furnished on a part of a great system managed by a single corporation constitute a lien upon the whole of the system superior to mortgages of all kinds. Central Trust Co. v. Wabash, St. L. & P. R. Co. 30 Fed. Rep. 332.

Where the workman's contract is not with the owner the building cannot be bound for more than the reasonable value of the work and materials. Kling v. Railway Const. Co. 7 Mo. App. 410.

Materials furnished for temporary structures, and never incorporated into the permanent work, are not subjects for a lien under the statutes. Knapp v. St. Louis, K. C. & N. R. Co. 6 Mo. App. 205.

A laborer employed by a sub-contractor is entitled to the benefit of the Statute. Peters v. St. Louis & I. M. R. Co. 24 Mo. 586.

It is not necessary that the thirty days' work required by statute should be done on thirty consecutive days. *Ibid.*

The assignee of such claim may sue in his own name. *Ibid.*

the subject of claims against railway corporations for materials and labor furnished out of the operation of the General Lien Law of 1885, and put it under this special Act, which does not require any notice of the claim to be filed with any clerk or other officer, and provides a special proceeding in which all such claims must be enforced, as in one suit.

It must be admitted that if the Legislature intended to include railways in the Act of 1885, it is not apparent why so important a subject was not mentioned in the long list of those expressly named.

Still the language of the Act is certainly broad and comprehensive enough to include a railway. It is certainly a "structure," if not a "superstructure." A lien can as conveniently be imposed upon it as upon a "ditch," "flume" or "tunnel." These instances of lienable property are expressly mentioned in the Statute, and the scope and operation of this general term, "structure," immediately following this specific enumeration, must be ascertained by reference to the latter. The doctrine of *noscitur a sociis* applies; and the significance of the word "structure" in this Statute is indicated by the company it is found in—"ditch," "flume" and "tunnel." If the language of the Act was "building or other structure" only, then it might not be construed as including a railway. But the words, a "ditch or any other structure," cannot consistently with this established rule of construction be held to exclude a railway. A railway is literally and technically a "structure." It consists of the bed or foundation, which may be of earth, stone or trestle work, on which are laid the ties and rails. These taken together constitute a "structure" in the full sense of the word—a something joined together, built, constructed. Freund, Lat. Lex., *Structura Struo*; Worcester's Dict. *Structure.*

In 2 Jones on Liens (§ 1618) it is said that statutes giving a lien for labor and materials furnished for the construction of "buildings" are not usually regarded as being applicable to railways. But, he says (§ 1624), where the term "structure," "erection," "improvement" are used in the Statute, it is possible to establish a lien for anything that can be attached

---

Failure of the clerk of the circuit court to forward to the secretary of state a copy of an account filed for a lien will not defeat the lien. St. Louis Bridge & Const. Co. v. Memphis, C. & N. W. R. Co. 72 Mo. 664.

A petition for enforcement may be amended at any time, in furtherance of justice. Nauman v. Jefferson City, L. & S. W. R. Co. 1 West. Rep. 390, 391, 19 Mo. App. 100.

Where an amended petition is similar in all respects to one already filed, with the exception that the time of filing the lien, which was omitted in the first petition, was averred, it is error in the court to strike it out. *Ibid.*

A justice of the peace has no jurisdiction to enforce a mechanic's lien against a railway. Cranston v. Union Trust Co. 75 Mo. 29.

New Jersey.

The lien given to laborers by statute cannot be extended so as to impair the obligation of contracts or lien of duly recorded incumbrances antecedent to the Act. Coe v. New Jersey M. R. Co. 31 N. J. Eq. 105.

A depot building, as against a mechanic's lien, is part of the mortgaged premises under a prior mortgage. Coe v. New Jersey M. R. Co. 31 N. J. Eq. 105.

Laborers in the employ of the corporation at the time of its insolvency have a lien upon its assets for their wages, but persons holding such claims but not in its employ at that time have no lien upon the property. Delaware, L. & W. R. Co. v. Oxford Iron Co. 33 N. J. Eq. 192.

New York.

It is only to the extent of what is due or to become due to the sub-contractor upon his contract that the lien can attach. Lumbard v. Syracuse, B. & N. Y. R. Co. 55 N. Y. 491.

To render the company liable, it must be shown that it was, at the time of filing notice, indebted to the contractor. Sampson v. Buffalo, N. Y. & P. R. Co. 18 Hun, 233.

The certificate of the county clerk stating when the notice of the lien was filed in the county clerk's office is not proper evidence of that fact, in an action to foreclose a lien. Sampson v. Buffalo, N. Y. & P. R. Co. 4 Thomp. & C. 600.

North Carolina.

Ordinary mechanic's lien laws should not be interpreted as giving a lien upon the roadway, bridges or other property of a railroad company, that may be essential in the operation and maintenance of its road for the public purpose for which it was established. Buncombe County v. Tommey, 115 U. S. 122 (29 L. ed. 305).

Claims of contractors or laborers for labor performed subsequent to the execution of a mortgage are postponed to the bondholders, although the lien was filed before the registration of the mortgage in the State where the labor was performed. Tommey v. Spartanburg & A. R. Co. 7 Fed. Rep. 429.

Ohio.

The Mechanic's Lien Law of Ohio does not authorize a lien upon a railroad for "erecting, altering, repairing or removing any building, appurtenances," etc. Rutherfoord v. Cincinnati & P. R. Co. 35 Ohio St. 559.

The law does not provide a remedy in favor of the creditor of a sub-contractor against funds in the hands of the owner due or to become due to the original contractor. Stephens v. United R. Stock Yard Co. 29 Ohio St. 227.

A substantial compliance with the condition of the statute providing for the service of written notice upon the company is essential to create its obligation to the employé of the contractor or sub-contractor. Scioto Valley R. Co. v. Cronin, 38 Ohio St. 122.

Pennsylvania.

In Pennsylvania an unpaid contractor, laborer or workman employed in the construction of a railroad has a lien of indefinite duration, which has precedence over every right acquired by mortgage made after the debt to the contractor was incurred. Fox v. Seal, 89 U. S. 22 Wall. 424 (22 L. ed. 774).

A stable built by a street railway company is subject to a mechanic's lien. McIlvain v. Hestonville & M. R. Co. 5 Phila. 13.

In order to create a mechanics' lien for materials furnished to a contractor for a particular building, the credit must be given to the building, and not to the contractor. Poole v. Union Pass. R. Co. (Pa.) 24 W. N. C. 376.

Material furnished to a contractor for the erection of a particular building is prima facie upon the credit of the building. *Ibid.*

A railway constructed in the slope of a mine, by a lessee, is not an improvement or fixture to which a mechanics' lien will attach under the Act of 1858. Esterley's App. 54 Pa. 192.

to the realty; and cites *Neilson* v. *Iowa Eastern R. Co.*, 44 Iowa, 71, where it appears to have been held, under such a statute, that a lien existed against a railway for ties used in its construction.

In *Forbes* v. *Wallamette Falls Electric Co.* (Or.), 23 Pac. Rep. 670, it was held by the Supreme Court of this State that poles set in the ground and connected together by wire in the usual way for the transmission of electricity between Portland and Oregon City constitute a "structure" within the meaning of that term, as used in section 3669 (Comp. 1887), and therefore a lien attached thereto for work done thereon, at the instance of a contractor. In delivering the opinion of the court, *Mr. Justice* Strahan said: "Do these poles planted in the ground, connected together with wires and insulators, constitute a structure, within the true intent and meaning of the Statute? In answering this question, but little aid can be had from the decisions of other States, for the reason that no general principle of law is involved, and such decisions have generally turned on the special or peculiar phraseology of the particular Statute."

A railway is certainly a "structure" within the authority of this decision. The railway and the wireway, notwithstanding the different uses to which they are subject, are both structures, upon which a lien may be had as security for the labor and materials that entered into their composition.

The case of *Buncombe County* v. *Tommey*, 115 U. S. 122 [29 L. ed. 305], cited on behalf of the demurrer, is not in point. It turned on the construction of a Statute of North Carolina, that gave a lien on a "building . . . lot, farm or vessel, or any kind of property not therein enumerated," for "the payment of all

---

A judicial sale under foreclosure of a mortgage given subsequently to work done by a contractor without his knowledge or assent is void so far as regards the paramount lien of the contractor. Shamokin Valley & P. R. Co. v. Malone, 85 Pa. 25.

A mortgage of a railroad, given subsequently to work done by a contractor, is invalid as against such contractor. Tyrone & C. R. Co. v. Jones, 79 Pa. 60; Woods v. Pittsburg, C. & St. L. R. Co. 99 Pa. 101, 3 Am. & Eng. R. R. Cas. 525.

A bill in equity for the enforcement of a lien, so framed that it disclosed the presumption of payment, and containing no allegation of facts in rebuttal of the presumption, will be dismissed on demurrer. Hayes v. Bald Eagle Valley R. Co. 4 Cent. Rep. 457, 113 Pa. 380.

Texas.

Mechanic's Lien Laws have not been extended to railroads in Texas. Galveston, H. & H. R. Co. v. Cowdrey, 78 U. S. 11 Wall. 459 (20 L. ed. 199); Tyler Tap. R. Co. v. Driscol, 52 Tex. 13; Central & M. R. Co. v. Henning, 52 Tex. 466.

The word "labor," in Sayles' (Tex.) Civ. Stat., art. 3179a, giving a lien to those performing labor in the construction, operation or repair of a railroad, means one who performs manual services in the construction, repair or operation of the road, and does not embrace one who may work in preparing something of his own to sell a railway company. St. Louis, A. & T. R. Co. v. Mathews, 75 Tex. 92.

The assignment of the debt passes with it the liens that secure it. That the debt is a simple promissory note, or that the assignee was ignorant of the existence of the lien, does not affect the rule. Houston & T. C. R. Co. v. Bremond, 66 Tex. 159.

Vermont.

The mechanic's lien on a railway is not lost by taking a promissory note for the same. Poland v. Lamoille Valley R. Co. 52 Vt. 144.

An action cannot be maintained under Vt. Rev. Laws, § 3372, which makes railroads liable to day laborers employed by contractors for labor in constructing their roads, where the work was done and the contract made and to be performed in New York. Cartwright v. New York, R. & M. R. Co. 4 New Eng. Rep. 361, 59 Vt. 675.

If New York has a statute imposing a similar liability on railroads, the action should have been based upon that Statute. *Ibid.*

Virginia.

Furnishing materials creates an incipient lien, which is perfected by filing one's claim according to the provisions of the statute. Boston v. Chesapeake & O. R. Co. 76 Va. 180, 12 Am. & Eng. R. R. Cas. 263.

Notice and affidavit having been furnished, as required by law, by the sub-contractor to the owner, it makes the latter liable for the amount named in the affidavit, without regard to the state of accounts between him and the general contractor. Norfolk & W. R. Co. v. Howison, 81 Va. 125.

A sub-contractor may give notice as soon as the materials are furnished, and may furnish the required affidavit at the same time or at any time thereafter, if within twenty days after the work is completed. *Ibid.*

West Virginia.

A sub-contractor in the second degree, who shows no privity of contract with the owner of the land or with his duly authorized agents, who furnishes material or labor in the erection of a building on the land, can acquire no lien, either on the lot or building, by giving the notice provided for in W. Va. Code, chap. 75, § 5, within thirty days after the labor was performed or material furnished. McGugin v. Ohio River R. Co. (W. Va.) Sept. 14, 1889.

Wisconsin.

The law of mechanic's lien does not apply to railway bridges or tracks, a bridge not being a "building" within the meaning of the Statute. La Crosse & M. R. Co. v. Vanderpool, 11 Wis. 120.

The doctrine that a railroad is an entirety cannot be applied so as to cut off a mechanic's lien upon a depot building. Hill v. La Crosse & M. R. Co. 11 Wis. 215.

Where claim for a lien is filed by a sub-contractor of a materialman the contractor as well as the owner of the building should be made defendants so that all equities may be adjusted. Carney v. La Crosse & M. R. Co. 15 Wis. 503.

Priority of lien gives priority of legal right. Howard v. Milwaukee & St. P. R. Co. 101 U. S. 837 (25 L. ed. 1081).

Where a fund was by law required to be paid to the "laborers" upon a railway, members of a corps of engineers were not included. State v. Rusk, 55 Wis. 465. See Pennsylvania & D. R. Co. v. Leuffer, 84 Pa. 168. But compare Leuffer v. Pennsylvania & D. R. Co. 11 Phila. 548.

The relation of the company to the employé of its contractor in construction of its road is that of guarantor, upon certain statutory conditions, and the employé's action may be brought in the justice's court to the extent of its jurisdiction. Redmond v. Galena & S. W. R. Co. 39 Wis. 426.

debts contracted for work done on the same or material furnished."

Of the specific terms used in this Statute, only two—"building" and "vessel"—include structures; and they do not in the nature of things suggest or show that the following general phrase—"any kind of property"—was intended to include such a structure as a railway. On the contrary, it is manifest that the general term "property" has reference to, and is to be interpreted as, a mere expansion of the specific kinds of "property" or land just mentioned —"lot" and "farm."

The objection that a lien cannot be had on a part or section of a railway for labor or material furnished for its construction does not strike me favorably.

In 2 Jones on Liens (§ 1619) decisions to that effect are referred to, but they appear to have been made on the language of a statute giving a lien on "the road" as a whole; and also on the ground of public policy, which it is said will not permit a sale of a portion of a road on execution. It is easy to say a thing is against public policy. But that does not make it so. Public policy is manifested by public Acts, legislative and judicial, and not private opinion. however eminent. I have no knowledge of any such public policy prevailing in this State. A railway is nothing but private property devoted to public use, the same as a warehouse, and is so far and no farther the subject of public policy. The owner, be he a natural person or a private corporation, can disuse or dispose of it, in whole or in part, at his or its pleasure.

True, it was held in *Brooks* v. *Burlington & S. W. R. Co.*, 101 U. S. 443 [25 L. ed. 1057], that a person who furnished labor and materials used in the construction of a certain portion of a railway had a lien on the whole of it. This ruling was made in favor of the lienor, and it does not follow, from anything decided in that case, that he might not have limited his lien to the portion on which he bestowed his labor and materials, and enforced it accordingly.

But there is a public policy of this State, as shown by its legislation, that should be considered in this connection; which is, that persons who furnish labor or materials, to be used in the construction of railways, shall have a lien thereon, as a security for the value of such labor and materials. To promote this policy and to produce the practical results intended by the Legislature, the Statute giving this lien should be construed, so far as in reason and right it may, and all mere doubts as to the extent and manner of its application should be so resolved.

The Statute (Comp. 1887, § 3678) only requires the notice of the lien to be filed with the clerk of one county—that in which the "building or other improvement (structure) or some part thereof shall be situated." That was done in this case. If the effect of the transaction is to give the plaintiff a lien on the whole road, it may sell the whole road. But my own judgment is, that even if the plaintiff might claim a lien on the whole road, it may, nevertheless, limit its lien by its notice to the part or section of the road for the construction of which it furnished material.

The notice also contains the name of the owner of the road and the persons to whom the plaintiff furnished the material, as provided in said section, and also a description of the property "to be charged with said lien, sufficient for identification," in these words: "The railroad known as the Wallamette Valley & Coast Railroad, being built by the Oregon Pacific Railroad Company, and being that portion of said railroad commencing at station No. 2659, plus 78, on the line of said road in Marion County, State of Oregon, and extending from there in an easterly direction a distance of fifteen miles along the surveyed and located route of said road in said" county and State, "as shown by the maps . . . of the permanently located line of said railroad in the office of said Company."

If there is no Wallamette Valley & Coast Railway in the State of Oregon which passes through Marion County, then this alleged lien does not exist. But if there is, and I suppose of this fact there is no doubt, at least on this demurrer, then the description given of it and the section on which the plaintiff claims a lien sufficiently identified it. A conveyance of a farm, said to be situate in Marion County, Oregon, belonging to the Oregon Pacific Railway Company, and known as "Blackacre," would be good, so far as description goes.

Was this material "used" in the construction of this section of this road within the meaning of this Statute?

In *Rasshor* v. *Baltimore & O. R. Co.*, 65 Md. 99, 2 Cent. Rep. 850, cited by counsel for the demurrer, it was held, under a Statute giving a lien on a bridge for all materials "used in or about" its construction, that a person furnishing a contractor with machinery wherewith to build a bridge could not have such lien.

Admitting the correctness of this decision, as I do, the cases are not in my judgment parallel. The machinery and appliances furnished the contractor in that case, although "used" in the construction of the bridge, did not enter into the structure and become a part of it. They were the contractor's "plant" and retained their identity and fitness for further use, saving the limited and gradual wear and tear incident to such use.

This powder was not only "used" in the construction of this road, but it was thereby necessarily consumed; and it was so intended. It was furnished to be so used, in the construction of this road. Nice questions may arise as to whether material is "used" in the construction of a road, as a tool or plant simply, or so used and consumed as to entitle the furnisher to a lien on the result for its value.

The food furnished a contractor for his workmen may be said to be "used" and "consumed" in the construction of the road on which they work. But this is only so in a remote and consequential way or sense. The food does not enter directly into the structure, and is not so used. Mason work may be done on a road in a dry country or season, when large quantities of water must be hauled many miles for the preparation of the necessary mortar. Upon the completion of the structure and the hardening of the mortar, the water has as thoroughly disappeared as the powder after the blast. Again, lumber may be used in the construction of a building for the purpose of scaffolding. However, it does not thereby literally enter into the composition of the building, nor, so to speak, become a part of it. But, in my judgment, both it and the water have been "used" in the construction of the building and mason work within the meaning of the Lien Law and the purpose for which it was enacted.

And so I think this powder was "used" in the construction of this section of the road, whereby it was consumed, not gradually and incidentally, as a tool or part of a contractor's plant, but wholly and at once, in aiding to clear and fit the roadway for the reception of the ties and rails.

The demurrer is overruled.

VERMONT SUPREME COURT.

ESTATE OF Madison S. MANLEY

v.

Miriam A. STAPLES.

(......Vt.......)

An adjudication that a person is not in such mental condition as to be incapable of taking care of himself by denial of an application to appoint a guardian for him is not necessarily an adjudication that he is not insane at all, and does not estop the applicant from claiming that such person is incompetent to make a will.

(April 27, 1890.)

EXCEPTIONS by contestant to a judgment of the Rutland County Court affirming a decree of the Probate Court admitting to probate the will of Madison S. Manley, deceased. *Reversed.*

Before testator's death contestant, who was his daughter, applied to the probate court for the appointment of a guardian over him on the ground that he was an insane person. This application was after a full hearing denied. Shortly after this, with no change in testator's mental condition, the will in controversy was made. When it was offered for probate contestant objected on the ground of the mental incapacity of testator. The court held that the question of his mental capacity was determined by the decree in the guardianship proceedings, and that contestant was precluded from showing that he then lacked sufficient testamentary capacity.

The case further appears in the opinion.

Messrs. **Butler & Moloney,** for contestant:

The testator may have been utterly incompetent to make a valid will, and the probate court might so consider him and yet not have considered it necessary to appoint a guardian under Rev. Laws, § 2436.

The property or rights of this defendant were not involved in the petition before the probate court.

Nimblet v. *Chaffee*, 24 Vt. 629.

That decision cannot conclude parties as to pecuniary interests that were not therein involved.

Abbott v. *Dutton*, 44 Vt. 546.

The appointment of a guardian would not have been conclusive against the validity of a will made during such guardianship; neither is the refusal to appoint one conclusive against her so as to debar her from contesting the will.

The causes of action are not the same.

Gates v. *Gorham*, 5 Vt. 317. See also *Clark* v. *Harrington*, 4 Vt. 69; *Stewart* v. *Martin*, 16 Vt. 397; *Newbury* v. *Connecticut & P R. Co.* 25 Vt. 377; *Williams* v. *Robinson*, 39 Vt. 267.

The measure of proof is entirely different.

Riker v. *Hooper*, 35 Vt. 457; *Davenport* v. *Hubbard*, 46 Vt. 200.

The burden rests with a party setting up a judgment as an estoppel to show that the matters in question were adjudged in the adjudication set up.

Parker v. *Roberts*, 1 New Eng. Rep. 158, 63 N. H. 431; *Lorillard* v. *Clyde*, 2 Cent. Rep. 882, 102 N. Y. 59; *Zoeller* v. *Riley*, 1 Cent. Rep. 8, 100 N. Y. 102.

The matter of the sanity of the testator is not *res judicata;* the requisites to constitute it such are lacking.

Freeman, Judgm. 252, 259; *Burton* v. *Barlow's Estate*, 55 Vt. 434; *Reading* v. *Ludlow*, 43 Vt. 628.

Messrs. **Joel C. Baker** and **D. E. Nicholson,** for proponent:

The issue of fact that the probate court had to decide upon the petition of the daughter, in her application for a guardian for her father, was the truth of the representation that he was an insane person.

Cleveland v. *Hopkins*, 2 Aik. 394; *Holden* v. *Scanlin*, 30 Vt. 177.

Although the probate court on the subject of inquisitions for the appointment of guardians is a court of special and limited jurisdiction, yet a decree of that court acting within the sphere of its jurisdiction is conclusive upon all matters which appear from the record to have been adjudicated upon.

Rix v. *Smith*, 8 Vt. 365; *Sparhawk* v. *Buell*, 9 Vt. 41; *Probate Court* v. *Van Duzer*, 13 Vt. 135; *Bennett* v. *Camp*, 54 Vt. 36; *White* v. *Palmer*, 4 Mass. 147; *Stone* v. *Damon*, 12 Mass. 488.

When a right or a fact has been judicially tried and determined by a court of competent jurisdiction, the judgment thereon, so long as it remains unreversed, shall be conclusive upon the parties and those in privity with them in law or estate.

Merriam v. *Whittemore*, 5 Gray, 316; *Sawyer* v. *Woodbury*, 7 Gray, 499; *Jennison* v. *West Springfield*, 13 Gray, 544; *Morse* v. *Elms*, 131 Mass. 151; *Mussey* v. *White*, 58 Vt. 45; *Stout* v. *Lye*, 103 U. S. 66 (26 L. ed. 428).

All matters which might have been urged by the party before the adjudication are concluded by the judgment, as to the principal parties, and all privies in interest or estate.

Danaher v. *Prentiss*, 22 Wis. 311; *Parkhurst* v. *Sumner*, 23 Vt. 538; *Spencer* v. *Dearth*, 43 Vt. 98.

The rule of *res judicata* applies not only to

judgments by courts, but to all judicial determinations, whether made by courts in ordinary actions or in summary or special proceedings, or by judicial officers in matters properly submitted for their determination.

Brown v. *New York*, 66 N. Y. 385.

If this testator was not so far insane that he required a guardian to manage his business and care for his property, clearly an adjudication of that condition ought to be conclusive upon his capacity to make a will.

Converse v. *Converse*, 21 Vt. 168; *Thornton* v. *Thornton*, 39 Vt. 122.

Rowell, J., delivered the opinion of the court:

This is an appeal from the probate of a testamentary writing as the last will and testament of Madison S. Manley. The exceptions show that the contestant, who is a daughter of the testator, filed several pleas, which were replied to; but the pleadings are lost, and we do not know what they were, except that it is conceded that one of the pleas set up want of testamentary capacity. The proponent claims, but it is not conceded, that to this plea he replied, by way of estoppel, the decree of the probate court hereinafter mentioned, and that the replication was traversed. But, as it is uncertain just what issue was formed by the pleadings, and as it seems to have been the purpose below to send the case here for decision on the merits of the question that has been argued, we decide it accordingly.

The Statute provides that the probate court may appoint guardians of insane persons on application of a relative or friend of such person representing to the court that such person is insane, and incapable of taking care of himself, and praying that a guardian be appointed. Rev. Laws, § 2436.

The contestant made such an application for the appointment of a guardian of her father, which, after full hearing, was dismissed a short time before the making of this will; and the question is whether that decree concludes the contestant from showing that before and at the time of its rendition the testator was of unsound mind, and incapable of making the will,—it being conceded that there was no change in his mental condition after the making of the decree, and before the making of the will. In order to make the decree conclusive, if otherwise it would be, it must appear that the matter here involved, namely, the testamentary capacity of the testator, was necessarily there involved and decided. The fact that one is under guardianship as an insane person is not conclusive against his capacity to make a will while the guardianship continues. *Williams* v. *Robinson*, 39 Vt. 267.

But it does not follow from this that the dismissal on the merits of an application for the appointment of a guardian of one as an insane person is conclusive in favor of his capacity to make a will. This is manifest when we consider the reasons for the decision in the case referred to. The ground of appointing a guardian of a person as insane is that, by reason of mental weakness or distraction, or both, he is incapable of taking care of himself; and the object of it is to secure proper care of his person and property. *Williams* v. *Robinson*, *supra*.

It follows, therefore, that to refuse the appointment of a guardian of a person as insane is an adjudication that he is not in such mental condition aforesaid as to be incapable of taking care of himself. It is not necessarily an adjudication that he is not insane at all, but only that he is not insane in a respect nor to an extent that renders him incapable of taking care of himself. Insanity differs in kind and character as well as in extent and degree. A man may be insane on some subjects, and not on others. He may be insane on one subject, and sane on all others. His insanity may be of such a character, and run along such a line, as in no wise to affect his capacity to take care of himself and his property. The insanity last mentioned would not warrant the appointment of a guardian over him, as it would not constitute the statutory cause for the appointment, and yet it might consist of such a delusion in respect of a disinherited child as to defeat a will that was the direct offspring of the partial insanity. It seems clear, therefore, that the question here involved was not necessarily involved in the proceedings before the probate court, and that its decree is not conclusive in the respect claimed.

Judgment reversed, and cause remanded.

Darius H. ROWELL

v.

TOWN OF VERSHIRE.

(......Vt.......)

1. **A girl of weak mind, incapable of exercising any choice as to the place of her residence,** and suffering from such mental infirmity as makes it necessary that she should remain under the care and control of her parents, and who has never been emancipated, takes the settlement of her father, though acquired after she reached the age of majority, and he is, if able to do so, bound to furnish her with support.

2. **The promise of aid** by the overseer of the poor to a man who is charged with the duty of supporting his daughter, if he will give her such support, is without consideration, and legally unenforcible.

(May 28, 1890.)

EXCEPTIONS by defendant to a judgment of the Orange County Court in favor of plaintiff in an action brought to recover compensation for support furnished to a pauper under an alleged contract with the overseer of the poor by which plaintiff was to be paid for furnishing such support. *Reversed.*

The facts sufficiently appear in the opinion.

Messrs. **J. K. Darling** and **John H. Watson**, for defendant:

There is no implied contract on the part of the Town to pay for services or relief afforded to a pauper which was not afforded at their special request.

Aldrich v. *Londonderry*, 5 Vt. 441; *Ives* v. *Wallingford*, 8 Vt. 228; *Houghton* v. *Danville*,

See also 31 L. R. A. 461.

10 Vt. 587; *Putney* v. *Dummerston*, 13 Vt. 370; *Churchill* v. *West Fairlee*, 17 Vt. 447.

The daughter, Lomyra, having always been a part of the plaintiff's family and never emancipated, it was by law the duty of the plaintiff, as her father, to support her.

Reeve, Dom. Rel. 283; *Swain* v. *Tyler*, 26 Vt. 9; *Rockingham* v. *Springfield*, 59 Vt. 521.

This being so, the plaintiff, when aided by the Town in the support of the said Lomyra, himself, in legal sense, became and was the pauper.

Rockingham v. *Springfield, supra; Gilmanton* v. *Sanbornton*, 56 N. H. 336; *Croydon* v. *Sullivan County*, 47 N. H. 179.

A promise by a party to do what he is bound in law to do is the same as no consideration at all, and is merely void.

Cobb v. *Cowdery*, 40 Vt. 28; Chitty, Cont. 51, 52, and *notes; Crowhurst* v. *Laverack*, 8 Exch. 208; *Laboyteaux* v. *Swigart*, 1 West. Rep. 562, 108 Ind. 596.

It may be said that the plaintiff relied upon this promise and therefore it ought to be held binding, but the very meaning of the requirements of a consideration for a promise or other agreement is that if that element is wanting the party relies on the agreement at his peril.

Bragg v. *Danielson*, 1 New Eng. Rep. 727, 141 Mass. 195. See also *Kent* v. *Rand*, 2 New Eng. Rep. 858, 64 N. H. 45; *Wennall* v. *Adney*, 3 Bos. & P. 249; *Smith* v. *Ware*, 13 Johns. 257; *Mills* v. *Wyman*, 3 Pick. 207; *Goodright* v. *Straphan*, 1 Cowp. 201; *Littlefield* v. *Shee*, 2 Barn. & Ad. 811; *Meyer* v. *Haworth*, 8 Ad. & El. 467; *Eastwood* v. *Kenyon*, 11 Ad. & El. 438; *Jennings* v. *Brown*, 9 Mees. & W. 496; 1 Parsons, Cont. 432–446; *Hubbard* v. *Bugbee*, 58 Vt. 172; *Hayward* v. *Barker*, 52 Vt. 429.

It is the duty of the court to charge fully upon all the points of law in the case; and exceptions can be taken to the charge as given, or the neglect to charge, upon any question.

State v. *Hopkins*, 56 Vt. 261; *Buck* v. *Squiers*, 23 Vt. 498.

What took place between the overseer of the poor and the plaintiff did not constitute a contract upon which the plaintiff could recover, and the jury should have been so instructed.

Putney v. *Dummerston*, 13 Vt. 370; *Churchill* v. *West Fairlee*, 17 Vt. 447; *Houghton* v. *Danville*, 10 Vt. 537; *State* v. *Gaffney*, 56 Vt. 451; *Company of Carpenters* v. *Hayward*, Doug. 374; 1 Greenl. Ev. § 49; 1 Best, Ev § 82; *Noyes* v. *Rockwood*, 56 Vt. 647; *Reed* v. *Reed*, 56 Vt. 492; *Mixer* v. *Williams*, 17 Vt. 457; *Rothchild* v. *Rowe*, 44 Vt. 394.

Mr. **Roswell Farnham** for plaintiff.

Ross, *J.*, delivered the opinion of the court:

This is an action of assumpsit, in which the plaintiff seeks to recover for supporting his daughter Lomyra A. on an alleged contract with the overseer of the poor of the defendant. The daughter was twenty-three years old when the suit was brought, and presumably over eighteen years old when the claimed contract was made. It is stated in the exceptions that it appeared that this daughter had, from a child, been of weak mind, and incapable of exercising any choice or intention in regard to the place of her residence, had always lived with the plaintiff as a part of his family, and during all said time was suffering from such mental disability and infirmity as rendered it necessary that she should remain with, and under the care, protection and control of, her parents, and had never been emancipated. On this state of facts, she was incapable of gaining any settlement in her own right. *Ryegate* v. *Wardsboro*, 30 Vt. 746.

She would take the settlement of her father, though acquired after she reached the age of majority. *Hardwick* v. *Pawlet*, 36 Vt. 320; *Topsham* v. *Chelsea*, 60 Vt. 219. "Upon the ground of humanity," as said in the case first cited, she remained a part of the plaintiff's family after she reached the age of majority as much as she did before, and the same policy which prohibits the separation of the father from his unemancipated children for the purposes of support prohibited the separation of this daughter from the plaintiff for such purpose. An order of removal upon the plaintiff, with his family and effects, would be operative to remove the daughter with him. *Landgrove* v. *Plymouth*, 52 Vt. 503.

While, *ex necessitate*, she remained a member of the family of the plaintiff, he was bound, if of sufficient ability, to support her. When any member of the legally constituted family is in need of support, and the legal head of the family, on whom the duty to support the family legally rests, is unable, pecuniarily, to furnish it, the legal head of the family becomes a pauper, and the whole family take their status from him, and the aid furnished to the needy member is legally furnished to him, because on him rests the legal duty of furnishing the support, not only of himself, but of any member of the family. *Newbury* v. *Brunswick*, 2 Vt. 151; *Gilmanton* v *Sanbornton*, 56 N. H. 336; *Croydon* v. *Sullivan County*, 47 N. H. 179.

In this last case may be found cited a large number of cases from other New England States supporting this doctrine, and applying it to the case of support furnished to an unemancipated child who had passed the years of majority. Hence the charge of the court was correct when it instructed the jury that the aid furnished by the defendant for the support of this unfortunate daughter was furnished to the plaintiff, and that in legal significance the plaintiff was the pauper aided, because it was his duty, if of sufficient pecuniary ability, to support the daughter. The support of her furnished by the Town was in relief of his legal duty, and so in relief of him.

Until the court thus charged, in substance, the case on both sides had been tried upon the question whether the overseer of the poor of the defendant had contracted with the plaintiff to pay him for supporting this daughter for more time than it had paid him. It had proceeded upon the basis that the plaintiff was under no legal duty, even if of sufficient ability as between him and the Town, to support the daughter, and that he, in this respect, stood related to the Town like any other person under no legal duty to furnish the support. As soon as the learned judge had closed his charge, the counsel of the defendant requested the court to further charge the jury, in substance, that the plaintiff, being the real pauper, although made so by the needs of this daughter, having furnished the support himself, could not recover of the defendant, although the jury should find that the overseer of the poor of the defendant agreed that he would pay him for supporting the daughter. The court did not comply with this request, and did not charge upon this subject at all. To this neglect to charge the defendant excepted. The plaintiff contends that this request was out of season, having been made at the close of the charge. If the request as such, was out of time, it is well settled that, without request, the court is bound to charge upon every branch of the case. Hence if this is an essential part of the case, an exception to its failure to charge unrequested is well taken. But, if the request were necessary, the court might well waive the rule requiring requests to be made earlier in the trial. It has done so, because it allows the exception without condition, and without regard to the rule relative to requests to charge. Hence the question remains, whether it was the duty of the court to charge the jury on this subject. This raises, in legal effect, the question: A person claiming to be a pauper applies to the overseer of the poor of the town where he is residing for aid, and the overseer tells him, "You continue to support yourself, and, as the agent of the town, I will pay you a given sum per week," or, to be strictly analogous to this case, "I will aid you," without naming any sum. The person claiming to be a pauper does support himself, and the overseer neglects to furnish any aid. After the lapse of the period when the aid should have been furnished, can the real or pretended pauper recover of the town upon the promise of the overseer? In other words, is there any consideration for such promise? We think not.

It was the legal duty of the plaintiff, if of sufficient ability, to support this daughter. He had no right to cast any of it upon the public. If, by the promise of aid, he was induced to make an extra effort to support her, and did so, he did no more than his legal duty. The Town received no benefit, and he no detriment, by the discharge of this duty, because he relieved the Town from the performance of no legal duty. It owed him no duty to support the daughter, if he could support her. In supporting her, he suffered no legal detriment, because he only discharged his legal duty. If the promise of aid was an inducement to the discharge of this legal duty, it was without consideration, and legally non-enforceable.

In *Cobb* v. *Cowdery*, 40 Vt. 25, Kellogg, *J.*, speaking for this court, says: "A promise by a party to do what he is bound in law to do is not an illegal consideration, but is the same as no consideration at all, and is merely void. In other words, it is insufficient, but not illegal. Thus, if the master of a ship promise his crew an addition to their fixed wages in consideration of, and as incitement to, their extraordinary exertions during a storm, or in any other emergency of the voyage, this promise is a *nudum pactum*, the voluntary performance of an act which it was before legally incumbent on the party to perform being, in law, an insufficient consideration. And so it would be in any other case where the only consideration for the promise of the one party was the promise of the other party to do, or his actual doing, something which he was previously bound in law to do. Chitty, Cont. 10th Am. ed. 51; Smith, Cont. 87, 88; 3 Kent, Com. 185."

The principle here announced clearly shows that the promise of the defendant through its overseer of the poor was without consideration, and not enforceable. For this promise the plaintiff promised to support this daughter,—just what and no more than he was legally bound to do without the defendant's promise. That the plaintiff performed his promise adds nothing by way of consideration, because he was legally bound to support the daughter, as much before as after he promised the overseer to do so. Applications of this principle may be found in the following cases: *Smith* v. *Bartholomew*, 1 Met. 276; *Rix* v. *Adams*, 9 Vt. 233; *Ferrill* v. *Scott*, 2 Speers, L. (S. C.) 344, 42 Am. Dec. 371; *Keith* v. *Miles*, 39 Miss. 442; *Jones* v. *Ashburnham*, 4 East, 455; *Hawley* v. *Farrer*, 1 Vt. 420; *Barlow* v. *Smith*, 4 Vt. 139; *Stotesbury* v. *Smith*, 2 Burr. 924.

It was therefore error for the court to neglect to instruct the jury upon this branch of the case, as it was one of the vital points in the case as made up.

Without taking up the other exceptions in the case, *the judgment is reversed, and cause remanded.*

NEW YORK COURT OF APPEALS (2d Div.).

George R. BRISTOR, *Respt.*,
v.
Stephen H. BURR *et al.*, *Appts.*

(.........N. Y.........)

The occupation of a parsonage by a minister of the gospel after his suspension by the church authorities is not that of a servant of the church or trustees in such sense as to render him a trespasser on his refusal to leave it, or permit his forcible eviction by church officers; at least this is true in regard to ministers in the Methodist Episcopal Church in which the minister is not hired by the church or the trustees, but is appointed by the annual conference.

(*Follett, Ch. J., dissents.*)

(June 3, 1890.)

APPEAL by defendants from a judgment of the General Term of the Supreme Court, Second Department, affirming a judgment of the Circuit Court for Rockland County in favor of plaintiff in an action brought to recover damages for an alleged assault upon, and forcible eviction of, plaintiff from a house in which he resided. *Affirmed.*

The facts sufficiently appear in the opinion.

Mr. **Garrett Z. Snider**, for appellants:

The plaintiff was not a tenant of the parsonage. His occupation was that of a servant or licensee. Either as a servant or licensee he was entitled to no notice to quit. The possession of the parsonage was always in the trustees of the

Methodist Episcopal Church, and they might remove him at any time.

People v. *Annis*, 45 Barb. 304; *Haywood* v. *Miller*, 3 Hill, 90; *Kerrains* v. *People*, 60 N.Y. 222; *Hanford* v. *People*, 7 N. Y. Week. Dig. 528; *Comstock* v. *Dodge*, 43 How. Pr. 97; *People* v. *Fields*, 1 Lans. 222; *Jackson* v. *Babcock*, 4 Johns. 418; *Ives* v. *Ives*, 13 Johns. 235.

The fact that plaintiff continued in possession of the parsonage for some weeks after his suspension did not change the character of his holding from that of a servant or licensee to that of a tenant.

Kerrains v. *People*, *supra;* *Doyle* v. *Gibbs*, 6 Lans. 180.

Mr. **William J. Groo,** with *Mr.* **Irving Brown,** for respondent.

Bradley, *J.*, delivered the opinion of the court:

The action was brought to recover for an alleged assault upon, and forcible eviction of, the plaintiff from a house in which he was residing, and for the alleged conversion of certain of his personal property then in the house at Spring Valley, in the County of Rockland. The plaintiff was a member of the Newark Conference of the Methodist Episcopal Church, by which he was stationed as a preacher in March, 1885, at Spring Valley, and continued to preach in the church at that place until the 15th of January, 1886, when he was suspended from all ministerial services and church privileges. This was done in accordance with the rules and Discipline of the Methodist Church, and was effectual as a suspension until the then next annual conference in March following. From the time he went to that place to preach, the plaintiff with his family resided in a house which had for several years been occupied by the Methodist ministers as a parsonage.

On March 17, 1886, the defendants forcibly ejected the plaintiff from the house. It is of that act and the alleged conversion of his goods then in the parsonage that the plaintiff complains. The trial court held as matter of law, and instructed the jury, that the eviction of the plaintiff was illegal; and that upon that branch of the case the question was one of damages only, for them to determine. And upon the exception to that instruction and exception to the refusal of the court to charge and submit to the jury, as requested by the defendants' counsel, certain propositions bearing upon that subject, arise the main questions presented for consideration. They pertained not only to the relation of the plaintiff to the premises, but to the persons assuming to act as trustees of the church, and to the right of the trustees to assume any control of the parsonage.

Although it was not directly proved that the Spring Valley Church was a corporation, it may from what did appear be inferred and assumed that it was such, as no question was raised to the contrary. The temporalities belonging to the church were under the control of the trustees. Laws 1813, chap. 60, § 4.

The parsonage was owned by the Mutual Life Insurance Company, and was held for a parsonage under a demise from that company, and whether it was rented to the trustees or to a society known as the Ladies' Guild, was one of the questions upon which evidence was given. While the defendants contended that the church or the trustees of it as such were the tenants of the insurance company, it was claimed on the part of the plaintiff that such society rented the premises; and that it was not within the control of the trustees. If this society could be treated as an independent one outside of the authority of the church, and the fact as to where the tenancy from the insurance company was located became material, there would upon the evidence have been a question for the jury. It is at least very questionable whether that society could be treated otherwise than as an instrumentality within the church organization to aid in the accomplishment of its legitimate objects, and for that purpose a mere agency of the religious corporation. In the view taken of the case the determination of that question does not, nor does the official character of those defendants who assumed to act as trustees in what they did, seem to be essential here for consideration.

Sufficient appears by the record before us to indicate that an unfortunate controversy arose in the church and congregation, and that there was a want of that generous Christian spirit which should characterize the action of religious societies. But it is not the province of the court to deal with those considerations. It is the legal aspect only of the situation which can have treatment here.

When the plaintiff went to Spring Valley pursuant to the direction of the conference to perform the services as minister of the church there, the house was furnished to him as a place of residence. He lawfully went into occupancy of the parsonage. If that occupancy was the actual possession of it by him at the time of his eviction, the defendants were chargeable with liability for assaulting and forcibly expelling him from the house. And this was so irrespective of the mere right to the possession, as in that case there was no justification for the application of such force to eject the plaintiff, although the defendants, as trustees, may have had the right to reduce the premises to possession by means of legal process and proceedings. *Parsons* v. *Brown*, 15 Barb. 590; *Bliss* v. *Johnson*, 73 N. Y. 529; *McMillan* v. *Cronin*, 75 N Y. 474.

It is, however, contended on the part of the defendants that the plaintiff was a mere servant of the church, and that in that relation only he resided in the house. If that were so, and if the trustees as lessees of the insurance company had the control of the house, the plaintiff had no possession of it and the trustees had the right to remove him from it, and on his refusal to go to use all the force essential to do so. In such case the possession would be theirs and not his. *Haywood* v. *Miller*, 3 Hill, 90; *Comstock* v. *Dodge*, 43 How. Pr. 97; *Kerrains* v. *People*, 60 N. Y. 221.

But it is difficult to see that the relation of master and servant existed between the trustees or the church they represented and the plaintiff. It does not appear that he was hired by that religious corporation, or that it assumed any legal obligation to pay him for his services as minister. He was placed there by the conference pursuant to the regulation and discipline of that church denomination, and no contractual relation existed between the Spring

Valley church and the plaintiff. *Landers* v. *Frank Street M. E. Church*, 97 N. Y. 120.

This church, being subject to such disciplinary regulations, had not within itself legitimately the power to deny to the plaintiff, when so stationed there, the right to exercise his ministerial duties or to exclude him from its church edifice devoted to that service. *People* v. *Conley*, 42 Hun, 98.

This, it seems, is deemed essential to the maintenance of the system of church government and its integrity. And to assure the application of its property and revenues to the uses of the church and purposes connected with it, the Statute has prohibited their diversion to other objects. Laws 1875, chap. 79, § 4.

The articles of the Discipline of the Methodist Episcopal Church were put in evidence but are not set forth in the record. It may be assumed that they furnished no aid to the defendants in their bearing upon the relation between the local church and its minister. While the church could not itself, through its own officers, exercise power over its minister, it was not without the means of relief from his ministrations when for sufficient cause they should become otherwise than religiously fit for or satisfactory to the congregation. This relief for some reason, of no concern here, was accomplished through the constituted authority. Whether his suspension would effectually result in the severance of the plaintiff's relation as the minister of this church was dependent upon the action of the annual conference, which was then to go into session in the latter part of March. This was the situation at the time of his eviction from the parsonage. It evidently was contemplated that when he ceased to be the minister of the church he would leave the parsonage. But in the occupation of the house his relation was not that of a servant of the church or trustees in the sense sought to be applied to render him a trespasser on his refusal to leave it. No other relation than that of possession was consistent with the use and enjoyment of it as a parsonage in view of his duties as pastor, which are not supposed to be wholly discharged in the public service at the church. Otherwise, his occupancy and its privileges would be at the will of the trustees, and he be liable, or might be subjected to intrusion at their pleasure.

There appears to have been nothing, so far as appears in the circumstances under which he went into the house, or in his relation to the church or its trustees, which so qualified his occupancy as to render it otherwise than possession by him. This is presumptively the relation assumed to premises by a party who lawfully enters upon them as a place of abode, and occupies them as such; and any less right than that which possession furnishes is dependent upon some understanding, express or implied, denying such relation. None appears in this case so qualifying the character of the occupancy of the plaintiff, and he had the right to protection against eviction by violence without the aid of legal process. It is unnecessary to consider the question whether he was a tenant at will and entitled to a month's notice, or whether legal proceedings may have been effectually taken with a shorter or without any notice for his removal.

In view of the fact that the plaintiff was in actual possession of the house at the time in question, the use of the force used by the defendants to expel him from the house was without justification.

Whether the plaintiff had established his alleged claim for the conversion of the property was treated as a question of fact, which was submitted to the jury. We do not understand that any question of law was raised by any exception bearing specially upon this branch of the case. Nor is it seen that there was any error in leaving that question to the jury.

No other exceptions seem to require consideration.

The judgment should be affirmed.

All concur, except **Follett**, *Ch. J.*, who dissents.

FIFTH AVENUE BANK, *Respt.*,
v.
James B. COLGATE, Impleaded, etc., *Appt.*

IMPORTERS & TRADERS' BANK of New York, *Respt.*,
v.
James B. COLGATE, Impleaded, etc., *Appt.*

(.....N. Y.....)

1. **The renewal or continuance of a limited partnership** operates merely as an extention, for the designated period, of the partnership already formed, and in practical effect is the same as if such time had been embraced within the term of the original formation.

2. **The impairment of the capital fur-**

NOTE.—*Limited partnerships.*

Limited partnerships exist only under warrant of statute. See *notes* to Vauhorne v. Corcoran (Pa.) 4 L. R. A. 386; Jenning's App. (Pa.) 2 L. R. A. 43.

In order to obtain the privilege of a limited partnership, the formalities of the special laws relating thereto must be strictly complied with. Davidson v. Frechette, Montreal L. Rep. 5 Super. Ct. 282.

Upon noncompliance with the terms of the statute, the members of a limited partnership become personally liable to creditors as general partners, but between themselves are special partners bound by their contract. Clement v. British America Assur. Co. 2 New Eng. Rep. 57, 141 Mass. 298.

Under the Missouri statutes a limited partnership is formed after the recorded statement shall have been published once a week for four consecutive weeks in a newspaper in each of the places in which the business is carried on, if there be any such paper published there. Selden v. Hall, 4 West. Rep 782, 21 Mo. App. 452.

The statement required must be strictly true, but it is not necessary for the statement to set forth the amounts contributed by the general partners; and a false statement thereof will not affect the liability of special partners. *Ibid.*

It is unnecessary that the cash contributed by the special partner should be actually paid prior to the formation of the partnership; and where the statement filed recited that the contribution by the special partner had not been actually paid, the Act will be satisfied by a subsequent payment before the formation of the partnership shall have been completed. Ellison, *J.*, dissenting. *Ibid.*

In New York it is held that Limited Partnership Acts should receive a reasonable construction.

See also 27 L. R. A. 684; 38 L. R. A. 791.

nished to a limited partnership by a special partner, without his fault, does not prevent the renewal or continuance of the partnership, and a statement in the certificate or affidavit of renewal that the capital is unimpaired is mere surplusage, which, although false, does not render him liable as a general partner to one who has not been induced thereby to give credit to the firm.

(June 3, 1890.)

APPEALS by defendant Colgate from judgments of the General Term of the Superior Court for the City of New York overruling his motion for a new trial upon exceptions taken during the trial at the Trial Term of actions brought to recover upon certain partnership notes, in which he was held liable as a general partner. *Reversed.*

Statement by **Bradley**, *J.:*

The first action was brought upon two promissory notes made by Humphrey & Co., in October and December, 1882, amounting to $11,958.57. The second action was brought upon six promissory notes made by Humphrey & Co., in September, 1882, amounting to $35,-882.16.

The alleged defense of the defendant, Colgate, was that he was a special partner of the firm of which the other defendants, Theodore E. Humphrey, James Humphrey and Correl Humphrey, were general partners. This firm was formed for a term commencing on March 11, 1874, and terminating February 28, 1877, and Colgate as special partner contributed to it $100,000. At its termination it was renewed or continued for a further term ending on February 28, 1882, and on February 18, 1882, a certificate was made by all the parties to it and an affidavit by one of the general partners for the further renewal or continuance of the partnership until February 28, 1885. In February, 1883, the firm failed and made an assignment for the benefit of its creditors. The last-mentioned certificate contained the following provision:

"*Fourth.* The amount of capital which the said James B. Colgate, the said special partner, heretofore contributed to the common stock of the said copartnership is the sum of one hundred thousand dollars ($100,000) in cash, and the said capital stock of the said special partner remains in the said limited partnership wholly unimpaired, and the said amount, namely one hundred thousand dollars ($100,000), has been contributed by the said special partner to the common stock of the renewed and continued partnership."

And the accompanying affidavit of the general partner stated "that the sum of $100,000 specified in the said certificate to have been contributed by James B. Colgate, the special partner therein named, as capital to the common stock of the said partnership, has been heretofore actually and in good faith paid in cash as capital to the common stock of the said copartnership, and remains in the said limited partnership wholly unimpaired, and the said amount, namely $100,000, has been contributed by the said special partner to the common stock of the renewed and continued partnership."

The defendant Colgate alone defended. The plaintiffs recovered.

Messrs. **Butler, Stillman & Hubbard**, for appellant:

The Statute should be construed as allowing a renewal, regardless of the condition of the association; the statutory certificate, record, affidavit and publication need contain no new

---

Manhattan Co. v. Laimbeer, 11 Cent. Rep. 329, 108 N. Y. 578.

The failure of the county clerk to record the certificate of a limited partnership will not render a special partner liable as a general partner. Ruger, *Ch. J.*, and Gray, *J.*, dissent. *Ibid.*

Where a certificate states that its business is that of "general commission business, buying and selling grain, etc., on commissions," and the terms of the partnership as published state that it is for the purpose of conducting a "general commission business," the variance is immaterial. Manhattan Co. v. Phillips, 12 Cent. Rep. 624, 109 N. Y. 383.

Payment by a special partner of his contribution to capital, simultaneously returned to him to make good his contribution to a previous partnership, cannot be upheld as made in good faith. *Ibid.*

In forming or renewing a limited partnership, strict compliance with statutory provisions is necessary. The general test of sufficiency of certificate and affidavit that special capital has been paid in is, Do they furnish adequate information to creditors? Haddock v. Grinnell Mfg. Corp. 1 Cent. Rep. 360, 109 Pa. 372.

The statement should show where and in what amount subscriptions are to be paid, and the subscription-list book should thereafter show payment or nonpayment of installments falling due after recording the statement. Hill v. Stetler (Pa.) 12 Cent. Rep. 138.

And where the certificate contained false statements as to payments by subscribers, they are liable as general partners. Hite Nat. Gas Co's App. 10 Cent. Rep. 505, 118 Pa. 436.

The articles of association or statement of a limited partnership organized under the Pennsylvania Act of 1874 and the Supplement of 1876 are fatally defective if they do not contain such a detailed description and valuation of the property as is required by the Supplement. Sheble v. Strong, 128 Pa. 315.

Articles to create a limited partnership, under Act June 2, 1874, not showing full names of all members, how subscriptions were to be paid, location of business, etc., are wholly insufficient: and the subscribers are personally liable as ordinary partners. Pears v. Barnes (Pa.) 1 Cent. Rep. 569.

An affidavit of renewal must show in what shape the capital stock remains in the firm, whether in cash, merchandise, bad debts, etc. Creditors are entitled to know whether the capital is held in a shape to respond to their claims. Haddock v. Grinnell Mfg. Corp. *supra.*

Affidavit filed upon renewal of a limited partnership, that the capital specified in the original articles as contributed by special partner "has been so contributed, and remains in the common stock of the firm," is insufficient. *Ibid.*

Persons who have failed to make their concern a limited partnership by reason of a non-compliance with the law providing for such partnerships are liable to be sued as general partners for the debts of the firm; and creditors are not confined to the mode pointed out by the Pennsylvania Act of 1874 for rendering them so liable. Vanhorne v. Corcoran, 4 L. R. A. 386, 127 Pa. 255.

As to liability of special partner in limited partnership, see *note* to Imperial Refining Co. v. Wyman (Ohio) 8 L. R. A. 503.

matter not in the original certificate, except the statement that the partnership is renewed for a certain further time, and any other matter analogous to recording of a mortgage of personalty is practically a re-statement of the original facts.

Bates, Partn. 160; Crary, Lim. Partn. p. 39; *Arnold* v. *Danziger*, 30 Fed. Rep. 898; *Ropes* v. *Colgate*, 17 Abb. N. C. 136.

A renewal certificate under section 11, stating only the facts required by section 4 of the Limited Partnership Statute, on the formation of the partnership, is a compliance with the requirements of section 11.

Metropolitan Nat. Bank v. *Sirret*, 97 N. Y. 320.

The requirements of the Statute respecting the conduct of a limited partnership once duly formed and in operation are not, like those relating to the formation of the partnership, conditions precedent to its continuance, but regulations as to the exercise of its privileges under the Statute.

Madison County Bank v. *Gould*, 5 Hill, 309; *Van Ingen* v. *Whitman*, 62 N. Y. 513; *Sharp* v. *Hutchinson*, 1 Cent. Rep. 717, 100 N. Y. 533; *Singer* v. *Kelly*, 44 Pa. 145; *Lachaise* v. *Marks*, 4 E. D. Smith, 610; *Haviland* v. *Chace*, 39 Barb. 283; *Manhattan Co.* v. *Laimbeer*, 11 Cent. Rep. 329, 108 N. Y. 578; *Benton* v. *Wickwire*, 54 N. Y. 226; *Johnson* v. *Hudson R. R. Co.* 49 N. Y. 462; *Bonnell* v. *Griswold*, 80 N. Y. 128.

A false statement in the renewal certificate or affidavit required by section 11 does not entail the liability of a general partnership.

Chase v. *Lord*, 77 N. Y. 1.

The special partner cannot be held for violations of the Statute by acts done after the legal formation of the partnership, unless proved to have been intentional, or with knowledge on his part.

Madison County Bank v. *Gould*, *Van Ingen* v. *Whitman* and *Singer* v. *Kelly*, *supra*.

He cannot be made the victim of a fraud practiced on him.

Troubat, Lim. Partn. p. 128.

Mr. **John E. Parsons,** with *Messrs.* **Stern & Myers,** for respondents:

If a special partnership is not created as provided by statute it does not exist; and if business is done it is done by the members as general partners.

Sharp v. *Hutchinson*, 1 Cent. Rep. 717, 100 N. Y. 533; *Bowen* v. *Argall*, 24 Wend. 496; *Abendroth* v. *Van Dolsen*, 131 U. S. 66 (33 L. ed. 57); *Haviland* v. *Chace*, 39 Barb. 283; *Loomis* v. *Hoyt*, 20 Jones & S. 287; *First Nat. Bank* v. *Lenk*, 32 N. Y. S. R. 191.

Where the partnership is renewed there must be a declaration that at the beginning of the renewed period there is at the risk of the business the designated amount of special capital, and that the fact shall correspond with the statement; otherwise the contract of the business would operate as a fraud on third parties which the law will not allow.

Hackett v. *Stanley*, 115 N. Y 625.

Both the purpose of the Statute and its language show that the necessity for an affidavit upon a renewal is that information may be given about the special capital. There is to be a present affidavit; it must swear to the present condition of the capital.

Durant v. *Abendroth*, 69 N. Y. 148; *Andrews* v. *Schott*, 10 Pa. 47; *Haddock* v. *Grinnell Mfg. Corp.* 1 Cent. Rep. 360, 109 Pa. 372; *Lineweaver* v. *Slagle*, 64 Md. 480.

Mr. Colgate is responsible for the statement of the certificate and affidavit. If they were true he is protected, if they were not true he is not.

Continental Bank v. *National Bank*, 50 N. Y. 575; *Manufacturers & T. Bank* v. *Hazard*, 30 N. Y. 226; *Van Ingen* v. *Whitman*, 62 N. Y. 513.

In the cases where the courts have striven to protect a special partner the objection relied upon to make him a general partner was technical.

Madison County Bank v. *Gould*, 5 Hill, 309; *Johnson* v. *McDonald*, 2 Abb. Pr. 290; *Bowen* v. *Argall*, 24 Wend. 496; *Levy* v. *Lock*, 5 Daly, 46; *Lawrence* v. *Merrifield*, 10 Jones & S. 36, affirmed, 75 N. Y. 590; *Metropolitan Nat. Bank* v. *Sirret*, 97 N. Y. 320; *Manhattan Co.* v. *Laimbeer*, 11 Cent. Rep. 329, 108 N. Y. 578; *Manhattan Co.* v. *Phillips*, 12 Cent. Rep. 624, 109 N. Y. 383.

Here the claim is substantial, and in such cases the courts have rigidly enforced the liability of a special partner

Haviland v. *Chace*, 39 Barb. 283; *Argall* v. *Smith*, 3 Denio, 435; *Bulkley* v. *Marks*, 15 Abb. Pr. 454; *Beers* v. *Reynolds*, 11 N. Y. 97; *Van-Riper* v. *Poppenhausen*, 43 N. Y. 68; *Van Ingen* v. *Whitman*, 62 N. Y. 513; *Maginn* v. *Lawrence*, 13 Jones & S. 235; *Durant* v. *Abendroth*, 69 N. Y. 148, 97 N. Y. 132; *Loomis* v. *Hoyt*, 20 Jones & S. 287; *Benedict & B. Mfg. Co.* v. *Hutchinson*, 21 Jones & S. 486; *Manhattan Co.* v. *Phillips*, 12 Cent. Rep. 624, 109 N. Y. 383; *Hennessey* v. *Farrelly*, 13 Daly, 468; *Sharp* v. *Hutchinson*, 1 Cent. Rep. 717, 100 N. Y. 533.

Mr. **George A. Strong,** with *Messrs.* **Martin & Smith,** filed a brief by leave of court on behalf of a party similarly situated with respondents.

Bradley, *J.*, delivered the opinion of the court:

The question presented is whether the defendant, Colgate, as a special partner in a limited partnership, had protection against liability. Without the aid of the Statute upon the subject, there was no relief for him against the responsibilities of a general partner. And to render it available as an exemption from liability, compliance with the provisions of the Statute was essential in the formation of the limited partnership and its renewal or continuance. The view of the trial court upon the evidence was that it was legally and regularly formed and the contribution of $100,000 by Colgate duly made, which afforded to him the rights of a special partner, and that the first renewal was effectual; but that the statement in the certificate for the further continuance made in February, 1882, to the effect that the special capital remained wholly unimpaired, was false, inasmuch as the firm was then insolvent, and for that reason the defendant was liable as a general partner. If the solvency of the firm was essential to a renewal or continuance of the limited partnership and to the exemption of the special partner from liability as a general partner, or if it was necessary for that purpose to embrace in the certificate a statement truly made of the then actual condition of such capital, the recovery must be sustained. The conclusion was fairly required that the firm was then insolvent in fact, although it did not so appear by the books of the firm or by any information which the special partner had obtained from the balance sheets furnished him or otherwise.

The question becomes one of construction of the Statute, which provides that the certificate of formation shall contain: (1) the name of the firm under which such partnership is to be conducted; (2) the general nature of the business intended to be transacted; (3) the names of all the general and special partners interested therein, distinguishing which are general and which are special partners, and their respective places of residence; (4) the amount of capital which each special partner shall have contributed to the common stock; (5) the period at which the partnership is to commence and the period at which it will terminate. 2 Rev. Stat. 764, § 4.

The certificate shall be acknowledged, certified, filed and recorded. Id. § 6.

And with it shall be filed an affidavit of one of the general partners, stating that the sums specified in the certificate to have been contributed by each of the special partners to the common stock have been actually and in good faith paid in cash. Id. 765, § 7.

And it is further provided that "no such partnership shall be deemed to have been formed until a certificate shall have been made, acknowledged, filed and recorded, nor until an affidavit shall have been filed as above directed; and if any false statement be made in such certificate or affidavit, all the persons interested in such partnership shall be liable for all the engagements thereof as general partners." Id. § 8.

Then follows provision for publication of notice. Id. § 9.

Thus far the provisions of the Statute apparently have relation to the formation of a limited partnership. It is further provided that "every renewal or continuance of such partnership beyond the time originally fixed for its duration shall be certified, acknowledged and recorded, and an affidavit of a general partner be made and filed and notice given in the manner herein required for its original formation; and every such partnership which shall be otherwise renewed or continued shall be deemed a general partnership." Id. § 11.

This is the only provision for the renewal or continuance, and in it must be found whatever is essential to the extension of the existence of the partnership beyond the period originally given to it. The evidence of the renewal or continuance must be furnished in the same manner as that of its formation. The same formality must be observed. And because the last-mentioned section does not contain within itself the requisites of the certificate and affidavit, reference must be had to §§ 4 and 7, in which appears the manner of the formation so far as relates to the certificate and affidavit. The provisions there must be followed in the renewal or continuance. The only thing essential to be considered here has relation to the special capital. It is provided in § 4 that the certificate shall contain a statement of the amount of capital which the special partner shall have contributed, and in § 7, that it shall appear by the affidavit that the amount so specified in the certificate has been actually and in good faith paid in cash.

The inquiry arises whether the statement in the certificate and affidavit, or in either of them, that the special capital remained unimpaired, was essential to the renewal or continuance of the limited partnership, or whether in fact such condition of the capital was necessary to effectually accomplish it. It is not so expressed in the terms of the Statute, nor is it necessarily within its import. The manner in which the renewal is to be represented is that required to form the partnership originally.

The evidence of the latter is in the certificate, affidavit and proof of publication of notice, all of record. The original certificate states the amount of capital which has been contributed by the special partner to the common stock, and the affidavit declares that the amount so certified has been in good faith paid in cash. The repetition of those statements in the certificate and affidavit of renewal or continuance would, in that respect, seem to be a literal compliance with the Statute, at least in form. In that sense the manner of doing it was the same as, or like, that provided for the creation of the partnership; and in that view no statement of the condition of the capital at the time of renewal or continuance would be deemed essential. But it is contended on the part of the plaintiffs that something must appear in the papers required for the continuance, to show that the capital is then unimpaired, else the requirement of the certificate and affidavit is in that respect useless, and can serve no beneficial purpose by way of information to the then and future creditors of the firm, or those dealing with it. The purpose of this provision of the Statute is not that a new partnership be created, but that one already existing may be continued; that its life may at the option of the partners be prolonged. No new capital is to be contributed by the special partner. His right and relation as such, so far as they are dependent upon capital, are supported by the contribution made by him in the outset. There may be reasons for the denial of the right to renew or continue the partnership, unless the capital remains intact and unless the evidence of it be furnished by the record required to be made of the renewal, and the contrary may not be wholly without the claim of rational contention. But which view has the support of the better reason or would be productive of the better rule applicable to it under all circumstances, is not now the subject of consideration further than it may have a bearing upon the question of construction of the Statute. If it is not required by the Statute that the fact be made so to appear by them, the statement in the certificate and affidavit that the capital remained unimpaired would seem to have been surplusage, and the fact that it was not so was unimportant for the purposes of the question here, unless the effectual renewal or continuance of the limited partnership was dependent upon the capital then so remaining.

It may be observed that the provision of § 8 declaring the effect of any false statement relates only to the certificate and affidavit made on the original formation of the partnership, and that there seems to be no provision of that character applicable to the proceedings taken for the renewal or continuance. But whatever the Statute directs to be done is essential to accomplish it without reference to the existence or want of any penal provision, as all the rights and privileges qualifying the obligations and liabilities incident to a general partnership according to the common law or law-merchant are wholly derived from the Statute, which, for their support, must be substantially, in all respects, observed. *Haviland* v. *Chace*, 39 Barb. 283; *Sharp* v. *Hutchinson*, 100 N. Y. 533, 1 Cent. Rep. 717.

And this in the formation of the partnership is not satisfied by the sufficiency of the certificate and affidavit with the requisite notice, but the essential facts upon which they purport to be founded must exist and be truly stated in them to give efficiency to the statutory partnership. *Van Ingen* v. *Whitman*, 62 N. Y. 513; *Durand* v. *Abendroth*, 69 N. Y. 148.

The only provision for the contribution of capital by the special partner is found in § 2, which provides that it be made "in actual cash." This has relation to the formation of the partnership, and contribution of capital at any other time or during its continuance is not only not provided for, but by § 12 it is declared that every alteration "in the capital or shares thereof contributed, held or owned, or to be contributed, held or owned by any of the special partners," shall be deemed a dissolution of the partnership. The contribution of capital, therefore, by which the interest of the special partner is represented during the time of the continuance of the partnership is unchangeably fixed by that made on its formation. *Lineweaver* v. *Slagle*, 64 Md. 465.

And this capital is guarded against the act of the special partner by statutory inhibition of its withdrawal (§ 15), and by the penalty if it be so withdrawn by him, wholly or partially, during the continuance of the partnership, that his relation and protection as such cease, and he becomes a general partner. *Bulkley* v. *Marks*, 15 Abb. Pr. 454; *Beers* v. *Reynolds*, 11 N. Y. 97.

The renewal or continuance provided for operates as an extension for the designated period, a mere continuance of the life for that time of the originally formed partnership, and in practical effect is the same as if such time had been embraced within the term of the original formation. Troubat, Lim. Partn. § 122.

This was evidently the purpose of the Statute, and the renewal or continuance, so far as respects the reference to the special capital, has relation only to that which was originally contributed; and the proceedings had to extend the time of existence are assurance that nothing has been done to defeat the right of renewal and of the protection of the special partner as such. If, however, it be requisite to a renewal or continuance that it be made to appear in the certificate and affidavit that the capital remains unimpaired, it follows that unless the capital so remain the existence of the partnership cannot be extended. The consequence of such requirement to protect the special partner against the liability of a general partner would render it imprudent for him to consent to renew or to permit the business to proceed, but his safety would be only in an immediate liquidation. The books of the firm would not necessarily afford him accurate or full information of its actual financial condition. Nor would the appearances of the ability of the debtors of the firm to pay be any protecting information, if it turned out that they were at the time insolvent. While he may examine into the state and progress of the partnership concerns, and may "negotiate sales, purchases and other business," subject to the approval of a general partner, he shall not, except as so provided, transact any business on account of the partnership, nor be employed for that purpose as agent or otherwise without being subjected to the liabilities of a general partner. 2 Rev. Stat. 766, § 17, as amended by Laws 1857, chap. 414.

He therefore must rely mainly upon the information he may obtain from the books and the general partners about the condition of the firm at any time during its existence. The situation in that respect of a special partner may be well illustrated by what appears in this case. He had nothing to do with the business. He was furnished annually with balance sheets taken from the books, showing what purported and as then appeared to be the financial condition of the firm. The statement furnished him near the time of the renewal or about the 1st of March, 1882, represented the firm as solvent with a balance of over $250,000 to the credit of the general and special partners. This was the situation appearing on the books. The special partner had done nothing to impair the capital. The deficiency in value of the bills receivable and accounts among the assets of the firm placed it in a state of insolvency. These facts, of themselves, are of no moment. They are referred to by way of illustration of the embarrassment to a special partner, which may attend the continuance of a partnership beyond the term originally designated, if the capital must remain unimpaired to permit it, and as bearing, if any it may have, upon the construction of the Statute. It is urged that the certificate and affidavit required to renew or continue must have been intended to speak of the situation as of the time they are made, and that the statutory adoption of the manner of certifying and verifying the original formation as the method of doing it must be taken as applicable *mutatis mutandis* to the renewal or continuance. This may be properly so in the formality of distinguishing it from the creation of the partnership. But a substantial difference would be a departure from the manner prescribed. It is no more essential to add anything not within the provisions of the Statute than it is permissible to omit anything within its provisions. The manner as directed of certifying and verifying imports substantial uniformity with that required by §§ 4 and 7, and not necessarily anything more. Troubat, Lim. Partn. § 110.

If the purpose of the requirement to accomplish the continuance was to inform the future creditors of the firm, or those dealing with it, of its then financial condition, the Legislature signally failed, in the language employed, to express such intent. The only reference made to capital in the Statute is that relating to its contribution and amount as of the time of the formation. And the consequences upon it of the hazards of the trade to which the capital may have been exposed in the business of the partnership does not seem by the Statute to be made the subject of information to be furnished by the certificate and affidavit essential to the continuance, and they in not containing any reference to the then condition of the capital cannot operate as a fraud upon the creditors any more than that to which the creditors might be subjected in the midst of an unexpired term.

If it had been within the legislative purpose that such further information be furnished, it may, and seems that it would, in some manner have been so indicated in the Statute. And to say that it was within its contemplation that the papers made to continue the partnership must import that the special capital remains unimpaired, and if not so no continuance of it can be effectually had, requires an implication not warranted by any language of the Statute.

In *Metropolitan Nat. Bank* v. *Sirret*, 97 N. Y. 320, no statement to that effect was contained in the certificate or affidavit of renewal or continuance, and the court held that the certificate stated all the facts required to be stated by the 4th section of the Statute. The court there did not consider the question whether it was essential to a renewal or continuance that the capital should then remain unimpaired. It may be assumed that the continuance as well as its former existence must have for its support a valid formation of the partnership. It takes from its creation the life which sustains its properly continued existence. It is argued that the Statute has within its purpose an unexpressed meaning which should govern its construction. Upon that subject it may be said that when there is obscurity in the words used, or if the language employed does not completely express the evident purpose of a statute, the legislative intent may be sought for in its title or in the cause or necessity for making it, and effect given as within its meaning, although not within the letter of the statute. *People* v. *Utica Ins. Co.* 15 Johns. 358, 380.

But the intention of the framers must first be sought for in the language used, and if that is free from ambiguity and has a plain meaning it will be presumed to express their intent, and there is no occasion to go further for interpretation. The language of a statute should be given its natural and obvious import. The court cannot correct errors or cure supposed defects in legislation. *McCluskey* v. *Cromwell*, 11 N. Y. 593; *Johnson* v. *Hudson R. R. Co.* 49 N. Y. 455, 462; *Benton* v. *Wickwire*, 54 N. Y. 226; *Bell* v. *New York*, 7 Cent. Rep. 263, 105 N. Y. 144.

There does not seem to be anything in the Statute in question, or in its apparent purpose, to warrant the conclusion that the intent of its makers was to deny to a partnership constituted in pursuance of it the right to continue its existence unless the capital remained undiminished, or that its condition, other than by reference to the capital originally contributed, must essentially be certified or represented in the papers upon which the continuance is founded. While such restriction might wisely be applied to stay speculation on exhausted capital, it may be seen that such a rule might have the effect to force a partnership into liquidation at much sacrifice as a precautionary means for the protection of a special partner. In some of the States the statutes require a statement to be made on renewal of the partnership of the condition of the capital, and in many of them the statutes are similar in that respect to ours. The right to form limited partnerships was first introduced into this State by chapter 244 of Laws of 1822, which required no certificate, but provided for a registry of substantially the requisites of the certificate now required, and following in that connection was the provision that "all renewals or continuances of partnerships shall be registered in like manner." § 7.

And by the next section it was provided that it should be the duty of a general partner at the time of registering to file an affidavit made by him of the actual bona fide advance of the sum by the special partner according to the registry of the amount of the same. § 8.

The main features there were substantially the same as they are in the Revised Statutes. But the provisions of the Act of 1822 may be so construed as not to have required an affidavit on renewal or continuance. In the present Statute the words "certified, acknowledged and recorded, and an affidavit of a general partner be made and filed, and notice given in the manner herein required for its original formation," are substituted for the method provided in that respect by the prior Act. Then, as now, there was no qualification of the right to renew or continue, founded upon the remaining condition of the special capital provided by the Statute. But it was then given the same protection as now against interference of the special partner with it.

It has been suggested that, in the view taken here, an affidavit could serve no important purpose on renewal, as it would furnish no information not before given by that filed on the formation, and therefore the appearance in it of something further was contemplated. While it is not seen how the implication contended for can arise from that cause, it may be assumed that the certification and verification as directed might be treated as assurance that the capital originally contributed or any part of it had not been withdrawn by the special partner, since those are by the Statute made the essential facts to support the continuance of the partnership, and the only ones in respect to the capital provided for by the Statute. There is nothing in the revisers' notes to indicate any design to produce any substantial modification in that respect of the provisions of the prior Statute (3 Rev. Stat. 2d ed. 608), which may properly be referred to in construing the revision. *McDonald* v. *Hovey*, 110 U. S. 619 [28 L. ed. 269], 100 U. S. 508 [25 L. ed. 631]; *Waterford & W. Turnp.* v. *People*, 9 Barb. 161.

This system of partnership was at an early day adopted in continental Europe, and became part of the modern civil law. And *Chancellor* Kent informs us that the provisions of our Statute upon this subject "have been taken in most of the essential points from the French regulations in the Commercial Code; and it is the first instance in the history of the legislation of New York, that the statute law of any other country than that of Great Britain has been closely imitated and adopted." 3 Kent, Com. 36.

By reference to the French Code it is seen that the continuance of a partnership beyond its prior designated term required authentication according to the same forms as for its creation, and they were essentially to be observed for its accomplishment. The policy of this law was to bring into trade and commerce funds of those not inclined to engage in that business, who were disposed to furnish capital upon such limited liability, with a view to the share of profits which might be expected to result to them from its use. And the fact that the law has been in operation in this State for nearly seventy years, and has been adopted in most if not all the States of the Union, indicates that it is deemed to have its advantages, and that it serves a purpose consistent with the public welfare. It is entitled to a reasonable construction for the protection of the special partners as well as others that the Statute in its design may be rendered effectual. *Van Riper* v. *Poppenhausen*, 43 N. Y. 78; *Manhattan Co.* v. *Laimbeer*, 108 N. Y. 578, 582, 11 Cent. Rep. 829.

There seems to be but very little adjudication bearing upon the question under consideration. In Louisiana the Statute provides that "the prorogation which may be agreed upon between the parties shall be made and proved in the same manner as the contract of partnership itself."

In *Arnold* v. *Danziger*, 30 Fed. Rep. 898, the question arose whether the prorogation which the partners sought to make was effectual to continue the existing partnership inasmuch as the special capital had been impaired and the general partner was insolvent. The action was there by creditors of the firm, who alleged that they were induced by the renewal of the partnership to give it credit; and the relief sought was that the special partner should advance sufficient to make up the amount originally contributed by him. The court held that the renewal or continuance was not the creation of a new partnership, but an extension of the one before then existing; and that the special partner had hazarded only the amount contributed and was not liable to do more. The determination of that case was to the effect that the diminution or impairment of the capital was not in the way of the renewal or continuance of the partnership.

In *Haddock* v. *Grinnell Mfg. Corp.*, 109 Pa. 375, 1 Cent. Rep. 360, there was no new certificate making any reference to the special capital, but the affidavit stated the amount originally contributed and that it remained in the common stock. While it appeared by the certificate and affidavit made on the formation that the amount had been paid in cash, there was nothing in either the agreement for renewal or the affidavit then made that the contribution was made in cash. The court held that the affidavit was insufficient to support the continuance of the limited partnership and that the liability of the special partner was that of a general partner, for the reason that it was not stated in what shape the capital remained, whether "in cash, in merchandise," or was represented by "bad debts, a margin in stock or speculation in real estate," and added the remark that "the creditors are entitled to know when the partnership is renewed whether the special capital is a reality or a myth."

It may be observed that while the provision of the Pennsylvania Statute relating to renewal or continuance is the same in that respect as in this State, it is different in relation to the nature of capital furnished. There the contribution may be made in cash, goods or merchandise, and when made in goods, their nature and value shall be fully set forth in the certificate. The view expressed in the opinion in that case was to the effect that the affidavit should give as full information upon the renewal as upon the original formation, and that when renewed or continued the partnership must be in the same condition, so far as the special capital is concerned, as when originally formed. While that view is not entirely in harmony with *Metropolitan Nat. Bank* v. *Sirret*, and is not adopted here, it is unnecessary to say of that case more than that it is distinguishable from the present one in the fact that the requisite certificate and affidavit within the meaning of the Statute were not made for renewal, and upon that ground the decision there made was placed.

We think that the impairment of the capital without the fault of the special partner did not deny the right to renew or continue the partnership, nor is the statement of the condition of the special capital in the certificate or affidavit essential to effect a renewal. It follows that those instruments contained all that was required by the Statute to accomplish such continuation, and whatever was in excess of it was, for that purpose, surplusage. What might be the consequences of such additional statement in the certificate, as bearing upon the liability of the special partner to creditors who have been induced by it to give credit to the firm, is a question not here for consideration. Nor is the question considered whether or not the trial court was right in holding, as matter of law, that the contribution of capital was duly and in good faith made by the special partner in the formation of the partnership.

These views lead to the conclusion that *the judgments should be reversed and new trials granted, costs to abide the event.*

All concur.

NEW YORK COURT OF APPEALS.

Martin LIPMAN, Surviving Partner, etc., *Respt.*,
v.
NIAGARA FIRE INSURANCE CO., *Appt.*

(....N. Y.....)

1. **A binding slip** containing a memorandum to identify the parties to a contract of insurance, the subject matter and the principal terms to be "binding until policy is delivered" is a contract for temporary insurance subject to the conditions contained in the ordinary policy in use by the company.

2. **A notice to brokers** is a good notice of a cancellation of insurance obtained by them, where it is subject to a condition that it may be terminated by notice to the "person who procured the insurance."

3. **The cancellation of an insurance policy,** which provides that it may be terminated on notice, is effected *eo instanti* on notice given in good faith by the insurer, if no premium has been paid.

(June 3, 1890.)

APPEAL by defendant from a judgment of the General Term of the Supreme Court, First Department, affirming a judgment of the New York Circuit in favor of plaintiff in an action brought to recover the amount due under an alleged policy of fire insurance. *Reversed.*

Statement by **Andrews** *J.*:

On the 2d of September, 1885, plaintiffs instructed certain insurance brokers to procure insurance on their property. The brokers took what is known as a binding slip to the defendant, which was accepted by it and which was as follows:

Pell, Wallack & Co., Insurances, 55 Liberty Street.

New York, September 2, 1885.

The undersigned do issue for account of Shaped Seamless Stocking Co., amounts specified below at one and one quarter for twelve months from September 2, 1885, on machinery and stock, building No. 3 (as per form, building situate Randall's Island, N. Y.). This receipt binding until policy is delivered at the office of Pell, Wallack & Co.

Company.	Amount.
Niagara	$2,500
Sun, England	2,500
New Hampshire	1,250
Buffalo, German	1,250
Citizen, German, } Pitts.	1,250

T. J. Temple & Co., C.

Accepted by Pollock. Vallette for M.

The brokers upon receiving the binding slip immediately sent it to their principals in this action, and it remained in their possession until the day of the fire.

NOTE.—*Termination of contract of insurance; notice.*

To terminate a contract of insurance requires notice to the assured or to someone who is his agent to receive such notice. Grace v. Am. Cent. Ins. Co. 109 U. S. 278 (27 L. ed. 932).

Where an agent directed by the company to cancel a policy informs the assured that it is canceled, who thereafter takes the policy to the agent's place of business to be surrendered, but does not deliver it because of the agent's absence, and negotiates for other insurance in place of the canceled policy, such policy is to be regarded as canceled by both parties. Hopkins v. Phœnix Ins. Co. 78 Iowa, 344.

Where a parol contract of insurance made by an agent of the insurance company was reported by him to the company, whose officer wrote him to cancel the risk or obtain a higher rate; and the agent was afterwards discharged; and the policy which had been written was canceled without notice to the assured,—the company is liable upon the contract of insurance for a fire occurring in the following year. Commercial Union Assur. Co. v. State, 13 West. Rep. 47, 113 Ind. 331.

A return of a corrected policy to, and a retention of it by, the insurance company, in pursuance of an offer, which was known to the company, to rescind the contract, is evidence that the company acceded to the proposition to rescind. German Ins. Co. v. Davis (Ark.) Oct. 5, 1889.

An insurance company which has given credit for premium has no right to cancel the policy for nonpayment thereof, except after putting the insured in default by giving him personal notice of the intended cancellation. Farnum v. Phœnix Ins. Co. 83 Cal. 264.

An insurance company which has received and retains the premium from its general agent who issued the policy is estopped to set up that its rules forbid the issuing of policies to the class of persons to which the insured belongs. Esch v. Home Ins. Co. 78 Iowa, 334.

Where a written agreement provided that an insurance policy should continue in force from the date of expiration until notice of discontinuance, the assured to pay *pro rata* for the time used, sending a check for an additional month's insurance was not a notice of discontinuance at the end of that month. Greenwich Ins. Co. v. Providence & S. S. Co. 119 U. S. 481 (30 L. ed. 473).

Under a condition in a policy that it may be canceled upon payment of unearned premium, the assured is estopped to set up the nonpayment of such premium, after having induced the company's agent to believe that cancellation was recognized by him without such payment. Hopkins v. Phœnix Ins. Co. *supra.*

If a notice of intention to cancel an insurance policy on account of the nonpayment of the premium was sent by mail and not received by the insured, the cancellation is ineffective. Farnum v. Phœnix Ins. Co. *supra.*

A policy given upon condition that if any of its terms are violated by the insured the insurer may refund to insured a ratable proportion of the premium for the unexpired term of the policy gives the insurers the option of terminating the policy at will. Sun Fire Office v. Hart, L. R. 14 App. Cas. 98.

Conditions in fire policy; effect of breach of. See *notes* to Russell v. Cedar Rapids Ins. Co. (Iowa) 4 L. R. A. 538; Phœnix Ins. Co. v. Copeland (Ala.) 4 L. R. A. 848.

Notice, and payment back, or tender of premium requisite.

Notice of cancellation of policy, and actual payment or tender of a ratable proportion of the premiums for the unexpired time of the policy, can alone suffice to terminate the contract. Griffey v. New York Cent. Ins. Co. 1 Cent. Rep. 528, 529, 100 N. Y. 417.

The fire took place on the 3d of September at three o'clock in the afternoon. On that day, and at half past twelve o'clock, the Company sent to the brokers a notification that they did not want to write the risk, and the brokers thereupon sent a boy in their employment to ascertain why the defendant did not want to take the risk. He was also instructed to tell the clerk in charge that the brokers had not the binding slip, but would try to replace the risk that afternoon; and when the boy came back he said all right, and the brokers thereupon tried to get the insurance elsewhere.

Messrs. **DeForest & Weeks,** for appellant:

The law will imply the contract of insurance to have been in the terms of the "usual policy" of the Company from the binding slip alone.

De Grove v. *Metropolitan Ins. Co.* 61 N. Y. 594; *Van Loan* v. *Farmers Mut. F. Ins. Asso.* 90 N. Y. 285; *Hubbell* v. *Pacific Mut. Ins. Co.* 1 Cent. Rep. 73, 100 N. Y. 46; *Hubbard* v. *Hartford F. Ins. Co.* 33 Iowa, 325; *Eureka Ins. Co.* v. *Robinson,* 56 Pa. 256.

The notice of termination of the contract of insurance given to the persons who procured the insurance to be taken by the Company terminated the contract of insurance prior to the time of the fire.

Grace v. *Am. Cent. Ins. Co.* 109 U. S. 283 (27 L. ed. 934); *Hermann* v. *Niagara F. Ins. Co.* 1 Cent. Rep. 707, 100 N. Y. 415.

The insurance was to be terminated without qualification "on giving notice," not on giving notice of an hour, or a day, or a week. For the court to insert the word "reasonable" before the word "notice," and then to decide as matter of law that notice at half-past twelve was not "reasonable," is in effect to make a new contract between the parties.

See *McLean* v. *Republic F. Ins. Co.* 3 Lans. 421; *Home Ins. Co.* v. *Heck,* 65 Ill. 111.

Mr. **Adolph L. Sanger,** for respondent:

The contract of insurance made by the defendant with the plaintiffs was absolute. It was evidenced by the binding slip, pursuant to which the same was binding until the delivery of the policy.

Post v. *Ætna Ins. Co.* 43 Barb. 352, 362, 363; Ang. Ins. § 33; *Ellis* v. *Albany City F. Ins. Co.* 50 N. Y. 402; *Train* v. *Holland Purchase Ins. Co.* 62 N. Y. 602; *Angell* v. *Hartford Ins. Co.* 59 N. Y. 171.

Until the policy is delivered, the binding slip is in force, and so remains and is not discharged.

1 Phill. Ins. § 16; *Audubon* v. *Excelsior Ins. Co.* 27 N. Y. 223; *Kelly* v. *Commonwealth Ins. Co.* 10 Bosw. 95, 100.

A mere request to return the policy, and a promise to return the premiums, are not effective. A tender should accompany the notice. *Ibid.*

The right to cancel is not effectively exercised by the company's giving a mere notice to a broker or agent of the insured that it desires to cancel the policy. Herman v. Niagara F. Ins. Co. 1 Cent. Rep. 707, 100 N. Y. 411.

Where there is a power to cancel on giving notice and a return of premium there must be an actual return or tender of the money. Ætna Ins. Co. v. Maguire, 51 Ill. 342; Franklin F. Ins. Co. v. Massey, 33 Pa. 221; Hathorn v. Germania Ins. Co. 55 Barb. 28; Goit v. National Protection Ins. Co. 25 Barb. 189; Peoria M. & F. Ins. Co. v. Botto, 47 Ill. 516; Hollingsworth v. Germania N. H. & H. F. Ins. Co. 45 Ga. 294.

Where the policy provided that the company had the right to cancel it for neglect to pay the premium, and it did so and notified the plaintiff of the fact, it is not liable on the policy. Boatmen's F. & M. Ins. Co. v. James, 10 Ky. L. Rep. 816.

Where a policy contained the provision that it might be terminated at the option of the company by giving notice to that effect, the notice meant is notice to the insured. London & L. F. Ins. Co. v. Turnbull, 86 Ky. 230.

Where the defense to an action is that the company gave notice of a desire to cancel the policy, it must be shown that notice of cancellation was given to the assured or a duly accredited agent; notice to one who had merely secured the policy for assured is not sufficient. Com. v. Pelican Ins. Co. (La.) 17 Ins. L. J. 444.

Such a notice must be accompanied by an actual tender of the unearned premium to the assured or his proper agent. *Ibid.*

Agency; notice.

A provision in a policy, that it may be terminated by notice to the person who may have procured it, does not cover a case in which the agent of the company gives notice to himself as the person who procured the insurance. Niagara F. Ins. Co. v. Raden, 87 Ala. 311.

An agency to procure insurance is ended when the insurance is procured and the policy delivered to the principal; and the agent has no power thereafter to consent to a cancellation of the policy. North America Ins. Co. v. Forcheimer, 86 Ala. 541; Niagara F. Ins. Co. v. Raden, *supra.*

Where the policy stated that it was procured by a broker, the broker was not the agent of the assured to receive notice of cancellation. Mutual Assur. Society v. Scottish U. & N. Ins. Co. 84 Va. 116.

Where the company's agent allows an insurance broker to take the insurance and pay therefor when it suits his convenience, a notice of cancellation, under a proviso in the policy reserving to the company the right to return the unexpired premium *pro rata,* at any time, with the effect of canceling the policy, is effectual without returning part of the premium, where the premium had not in fact been paid to the company. Stone v. Franklin Ins. Co. 7 Cent. Rep. 749, 105 N. Y. 543.

An insurance broker was held so far the agent of the assured that notice to him of the cancellation of the policy was notice to the assured. *Ibid.*

Evidence of a general custom in fire insurance business to consider the broker obtaining insurance as the agent of the insured for the purpose of giving notice of termination is inadmissible, when it contradicts the manifest intent of the parties. Grace v. American Cent. Ins. Co. 109 U. S. 278 (27 L. ed. 932).

A clause in an insurance policy that "any person other than the assured, who may have procured the insurance to be taken by this company, shall be deemed to be the agent of the assured named in this policy," makes him such agent only as to matters immediately connected with the procurement of the policy; it does not authorize service upon him of a notice of cancellation of the policy. *Ibid.*

An agent will be liable to the company for a loss incurred through his delay in obeying imperative orders to cancel. Washington F. & M. Ins. Co. v. Chesebro, 35 Fed. Rep. 477.

The design is to give immediate effect to the insurance, or to supply the place of a formal policy until one can be procured.

Perkins v. *Washington Ins. Co.* 4 Cow. 645; *Lightbody* v. *North American Ins. Co.* 23 Wend. 18, 25.

The insurance could only have been terminated, if at all, in the manner claimed, after the issuing and delivery of the policy. The clause as to the termination of the policy imports nothing more than that the person obtaining the insurance was to be deemed the agent of the assured in matters immediately connected with the procurement of the insurance.

Stilwell v. *Mutual L. Ins. Co.* 72 N. Y. 385; *Hodge* v. *Security Ins. Co.* 33 Hun, 583; Wood, Fire Ins. 2d ed. § 118.

The binding contract to give a policy could not be terminated by notice to the brokers, and, as there was no such provision in the binding slip, notice to the brokers was not notice to the assured.

Hermann v. *Niagara F. Ins. Co.* 1 Cent. Rep. 707, 100 N. Y. 411; *Grace* v. *American Cent. Ins. Co.* 109 U. S. 278 (27 L. ed. 932); *White* v. *Connecticut F. Ins. Co.* 120 Mass. 330; *Von Wein* v. *Scottish U. & N. Ins. Co.* 20 Jones & S. 490.

The plaintiffs could not be bound by provisions contained in a policy of insurance in no way referred to in the binding slip, and of which plaintiffs could not be supposed to have any knowledge.

Pattison v. *Mills*, 1 Dow & C. 342, 361; Wood, Fire Ins. 2d ed. §§ 157, 158, 160; *King* v. *United States Life Ins. Co.* 20 N. Y. Week. Dig. 203; *Von Wein* v. *Scottish U. & N. Ins. Co. supra.*

As no policy was ever issued or delivered by the one party, or accepted by the other, it is in vain to say that their contract was embodied in such an instrument, and that the terms can only be known by its tenor.

Pattison v. *Mills, supra; Post* v. *Ætna Ins. Co.* 43 Barb. 351; *Guggenheimer* v. *Greenwich F. Ins. Co.* 44 Hun, 629; *Justice* v. *Lang*, 42 N. Y. 493, 497.

The brokers who procured the insurance were the agents of the plaintiffs only for that specific transaction; they were not the agents of the plaintiffs for the purpose of receiving notice of cancellation.

Hermann v. *Niagara F. Ins. Co., Grace* v. *American Cent. Ins. Co., White* v. *Connecticut F. Ins. Co.* and *Von Wein* v. *Scottish U. & N. Ins. Co. supra.* See also *Ellis* v. *Albany City F. Ins. Co.* 50 N. Y. 402.

The plaintiffs could not, in any event, be bound by the alleged notice of cancellation, because such notice was not a reasonable notice.

McLean v. *Republic F. Ins. Co.* 3 Lans. 421; Wood, Fire Ins. § 113.

The facts being undisputed, the question of reasonable time was a question of law which the court had the right to determine in plaintiffs' favor.

Bennett v. *Lycoming Co. Mut. Ins. Co.* 67 N. Y. 274; *Aymar* v. *Beers*, 7 Cow. 705, 710, 711.

Andrews, *J.*, delivered the opinion of the court:

The binding slip signed by the defendant was not a mere agreement to insure, but was a present insurance to the amount specified therein. The instrument is informal. It states on whose account the insurance is made, the property covered, the amount insured, the term of insurance and the date. But it does not specify the risk insured against, nor does it contain any conditions such as are usually found in insurance policies. The evident design of the writing, as disclosed by the testimony, was to provide temporary insurance pending an inquiry by the Company as to the character of the risk, or, if that was known, during any delay in issuing the policy.

The secretary of the defendant signed the binding slip upon the solicitation of Pell, Wallack & Co., insurance brokers of the plaintiffs, in the afternoon of September 2, 1885. The officers of the defendant having made inquiry as to the risk, notified the plaintiffs' brokers before one o'clock on the afternoon of September 3 that the defendant declined it. The property described in the binding slip was destroyed by fire in the afternoon of September 3, the fire having commenced about three o'clock.

The claim on the one side is that the binding slip was a complete and perfect contract, binding the defendant, according to its language, "until policy is delivered at the office of Pell, Wallack & Co.," and not terminable therefore by notice prior to that time, or if so terminable, then only upon reasonable notice, which, as is claimed, was not given, nor in any event upon notice to the plaintiffs' brokers, they not being agents of the plaintiffs for the purpose of receiving such notice.

It is insisted on the other side that the contract evidenced by the binding slip was a contract subject to the conditions contained in the ordinary policy in use by the Company, one of which contained the following clauses:

"This insurance may be determined at any time by request of the assured, or by the Company, on giving notice to that effect to the assured, or to the person who may have procured this insurance to be taken by this Company."

The notice given on the 3d of September prior to the fire terminated, as is insisted, the contract of insurance pursuant to this condition. We think there can be no doubt that the true construction of the binding slip only obligated the defendant according to the terms of the policy in ordinary use by the Company. There is no other reasonable interpretation of the transaction. The binding slip was a short method of issuing a temporary policy for the convenience of all parties, to continue until the execution of the formal one. It would be unreasonable to suppose either that the brokers expected an insurance except upon the usual terms imposed by the Company, or that the secretary of the Company intended to insure upon any other terms. The right of an insurance company to terminate a risk is an important one. It is not reserved in terms in the binding slip and could not be exercised at all so long as no policy should be issued, unless the condition in the policy is deemed to be incorporated therein.

Upon the plaintiffs' contention the Company could not cancel the risk so long as the binding slip was in force, and the only remedy of the Company to get rid of the risk would be to issue the policy and then immediately cancel it. The binding slip was a mere memorandum to identify the parties to the contract, the subject matter and the principal terms. It refers to the policy to be issued. The construction is, we think, the same as though it had expressed that the present insurance was under the terms of the usual policy of the Company to be thereafter delivered.

The trial judge was of opinion that the binding slip was not a complete and independent contract of insurance subject to no conditions, but he ruled that the obligation of the defendant was to be determined by the question, whether the condition in the defendant's policy, that the Company might terminate the policy by notice to the "person who procured the insurance," was a usual one, and submitted the case to the jury on that issue.

The case of *De Grove* v. *Metropolitan Ins. Co.*, 61 N. Y. 594, is, we think, a decisive authority against the view of the learned trial judge. The general term dissented from the ruling of the trial judge on this point and held that notice to Pell, Wallack & Co., the brokers who procured the insurance, was authorized by the condition in the policy. It, however, sustained the judgment on the ground that notice did not terminate the contract until a reasonable time had elapsed after it was given; and that the two and a half hours which intervened between the notice and the happening of the fire was not such reasonable time; and that consequently the insurance was then in force.

We think there can be no reasonable doubt upon the language of the condition that notice to the brokers was a good notice, and that if otherwise sufficient, it terminated the defendant's liability. The brokers procured the insurance. In fact their duties in respect to it had not terminated. The binding slip provided that the policy when issued should be delivered at their office. The notice was given to persons to whom notice might be given by the express language of the policy. The special language of the condition in the defendant's policy upon this point was, it is said, inserted to meet the objection pointed out by this court in *Hermann* v. *Niagara F. Ins. Co.*, 100 N. Y. 415, 1 Cent. Rep. 707.

It remains to consider whether, under the condition, the policy terminated *eo instanti* on notice by the Company. There is no language which postpones the effect of notice until the lapse of a reasonable time thereafter. The rule is well settled that where a person undertakes to do an act upon notice from another, it is implied that he shall have a reasonable time after he is called upon to do the thing or render the service, and, no time for performance being specified, the law gives him a reasonable time. But where a contract fixes the time of performance, the rule of reasonable time has no application. We have been referred to no case, nor have we found any, which sanctions the doctrine that where one has assumed an obligation which is to continue until notice given to the other party, the obligation continues after notice.

If in this case the premium had been paid beyond the period when notice was given, then the bare notice would not have terminated the risk. But this, for the reason that the Company is bound in such case in order to terminate the policy, not only to give notice, but to refund or offer to refund the insurance premium. This is the construction placed on clauses like the one in question. The cancellation in such case only takes place on notice and return of the premium for the unexpired term. *Van Valkenburgh* v. *Lenox F. Ins. Co.* 51 N. Y. 465; Wood, Fire Ins. § 106, and cases cited.

The privilege reserved by the Company to terminate the policy on notice cannot be exercised under circumstances which would make it operate as a fraud on the insured, as in case of notice given pending an approaching conflagration, threatening to destroy the property insured. *Home Ins. Co.* v. *Heck*. 65 Ill. 111.

In the present case no premium had been paid. The notice was given in good faith. There was no special emergency at the time. It was given during business hours, in ordinary course.

The contract provides that it should be terminated on notice. We perceive no reason why the contract should not be construed according to its terms. The parties might have provided that the risk should be carried by the Company after notice for a reasonable time to enable the insured to place it elsewhere. But they did not do so, and even if a custom of that kind had been proved, which was not, it would have been inadmissible to change or extend the explicit language of the contract. We think the cancellation was effected at the time of the service of the notice. See *Mueller* v. *South Side F. Ins. Co.* 87 Pa. 399; *Grace* v. *Am. Cent. Ins. Co.* 16 Blatchf. 433, but reversed on another point, 109 U. S. 278 [27 L. ed. 932].

The judgment should therefore be reversed, and a new trial granted.

All concur.

TEXAS SUPREME COURT.

MOTON & Son, *Appts.*,
v.
Otis HULL.

(....Tex.....)

1. **A citizen may be restrained** from proceeding in another State by garnishment to seize the wages of a fellow citizen in evasion of the laws of their own State, by which such wages are exempt.

2. **An allegation that both parties to a suit reside** in a certain city and county "where they now are, and for several years have been, residents," and that for many months plaintiff has been engaged in railroad shops at that place, and that a garnishment suit was instituted against him, sufficiently alleges his residence at that place at the time such suit was commenced.

(April 29, 1890.)

APPEAL by defendants from a judgment of the District Court for Grayson County in favor of plaintiff in an action brought to enjoin defendants from maintaining a garnishment suit in a foreign jurisdiction to collect a claim out of plaintiff's exempt wages. *Affirmed.*

Messrs. **S. S. Fears** and **J. W. Finley,** for appellants:

The petition fails to show that the appellee, Hull, was a resident of Texas, or nonresident of Missouri, at the time suit was brought in Sedalia, and is therefore bad.

Malone v. *Craig,* 22 Tex. 609; *Carter* v. *Griffin,* 32 Tex. 212; *Martin* v. *Sykes,* 25 Tex. Supp. 197; *Jennings* v. *Moss,* 4 Tex. 452; *Hall* v. *Jackson,* 8 Tex. 309; *Denison* v. *League,* 16 Tex. 408.

If neither appellants nor appellee were residents of Missouri at the time suit was brought there, or subsequent thereto, and neither were temporarily there, and the appellee did not submit to the jurisdiction, and no property was brought under the court's control, the courts of Missouri had and have no jurisdiction, and no judgment can be rendered against appellee or the Missouri Pacific Railway Company, and no injunction is necessary.

Pana v. *Bowler,* 107 U. S. 545 (27 L. ed. 430); *St. Clair* v. *Cox,* 106 U. S. 353 (27 L. ed. 223); *Pennoyer* v. *Neff,* 95 U. S. 714 (24 L. ed. 565); 2 Civ. Cas. Ct. App. §§ 91-94; Drake, Attachm. §§ 451*b*, 460, 461, 677; Rev. Stat. arts. 194, 205; Wade, Attachm. §§ 399, 405; *Laidlaw* v. *Morrow,* 44 Mich. 547.

The courts of Missouri having no jurisdiction, the appellee had a legal remedy by: (1) pleading to the jurisdiction there; (2) bringing suit in Texas against either the appellants Moton & Son or the Missouri Pacific Railway Company, and no injunction should have been issued or perpetuated.

1 Civ. Cas. Ct. App. § 991; Hilliard, Inj. 178; *Purinton* v. *Davis,* 66 Tex. 456; 1 High, Inj. §§ 28, 89, 90-93, 125; *Richards* v. *Kirkpatrick,* 53 Cal. 433; *People* v. *Wasson,* 64 N. Y. 167; *St. Louis, I. M. & S. R. Co.* v. *Reynolds,* 4 West. Rep. 628, 89 Mo. 146; *Metcalf* v. *Gilmore,* 59 N. H. 417, 47 Am. Rep. 217; *Mead* v. *Merritt,* 2 Paige, 404, 2 N. Y. Ch. L. ed. 964; *Bicknell* v. *Field,* 8 Paige, 443, 4 N. Y. Ch. L. ed. 496; *Venice* v. *Woodruff,* 62 N. Y. 462; *Laidlaw* v. *Morrow,* 44 Mich. 547.

Appellee did not offer to do equity by paying appellants what he justly owed them, and was not entitled to the writ of injunction.

Goldfrank v. *Young,* 64 Tex. 438; High, Inj. §§ 443, 1116-1121, 1130; Story, Eq. §§ 64*e*, 301.

Messrs. **Standifer & Moseley,** for appellee:

Equity will not permit a citizen of this State to resort to courts of other States to do any act forbidden by the laws of this State, or for the purpose of evading the Exemption Laws of this State.

Wilson v. *Joseph,* 5 West. Rep. 681, 107 Ind. 490; *Snook* v. *Snetzer,* 25 Ohio St. 516; High, Inj. 2d ed. § 106; *Keyser* v. *Rice,* 47 Md. 203, 28 Am. Rep. 448; *Dehon* v. *Foster,* 4 Allen, 545; *Engel* v. *Scheuerman,* 40 Ga. 206, 2 Am. Rep. 573; *Cunningham* v. *Butler,* 2 New Eng. Rep. 838, 142 Mass. 47; *Zimmerman* v. *Franke,* 34 Kan. 650; *Missouri Pac. R. Co.* v. *Maltby,* 34 Kan. 125.

Hobby, J., filed the following opinion:

The appellee brought suit in the District Court, April 18, 1887, to restrain appellants from prosecuting a garnishment suit in Justice Court, Sedalia, Mo., in which the Missouri Pacific Railway Company was garnishee and appellee defendant. The petition alleged that all parties reside in Grayson County, Texas; that appellee's claim against said railway company was current wages for personal service, and that the resort to the Missouri court was in fraud of our laws and to subject exempt property to the payment of appellants' claim.

Appellants moved to dissolve the injunction: (1) for want of jurisdiction to issue it; (2) because no ground is shown for equitable interference, the plaintiff having a complete remedy at law; (3) for the reasons set forth in the sworn answer, said answer alleging, amongst other things, that plaintiff was justly indebted to defendant, which he refused and failed to pay, and that the sole object of bringing the suit in Missouri was to collect said debt, and not in fraud of our courts or laws.

This motion was overruled by the court. A trial was had and judgment was rendered June 2, 1887, in favor of plaintiff for costs and perpetuating the injunction. From this judgment defendants appeal.

The leading question in the case presented under assignments in proper form is whether the courts of this State have the power, upon the petition of a resident of this State, to whom current wages for personal services are due, to restrain, through the process of injunction, a citizen of the county in which the suit by injunction is commenced, from proceeding in another State by a writ of garnishment to seize such current wages for personal service, with the purpose of evading, by such garnishment proceeding, the Constitution and laws of this State, which expressly exempt from such seizure or attachment said current wages.

The correct rule upon this subject we understand to be: That if the averments of the petition for injunction are of such a character as to make it the duty of the court to restrain or enjoin the party from instituting or conducting like proceedings in a court of this State, it would be a proper case for restraining him by a similar process from prosecuting such suit in the courts of another State. *Dehon* v. *Foster,* 4 Allen, 550.

In the cases of *Snook* v. *Snetzer,* 25 Ohio St. 519, and *Dehon* v. *Foster, supra,* it was declared to be clear and indisputable that a court of chancery, upon the statement of a proper case, possessed the power to restrain persons within its jurisdiction from prosecuting suits either in its own courts or of other States or foreign countries. This power or authority is exercised upon the ground of the right of the State to compel its citizens to respect its laws beyond its territorial jurisdiction.

"Although the courts of one country have no authority to stay proceedings in the courts of another, they have an undoubted authority to control all persons and things within their territorial limits. When, therefore, both parties to a suit in a foreign country are resident within the territorial limits of another country, the courts of equity in the latter may act *in personam* upon those parties and direct them by injunction to proceed no further in such suit." Such is the principle laid down by *Mr. Justice* Story. Story, Eq. § 899.

The exercise of this power does not proceed upon any claim of right to interfere with or in any manner control or stay the proceedings in the courts of another State, but upon the ground that the person to whom the restraining process is directed is residing within the court's jurisdiction, and that he is in the power of the court issuing such process. *Keyser* v. *Rice*, 47 Md. 213.

The decree acts directly upon the person, and its validity as to him is not affected by the fact that it does not extend to the court in which the proceedings are directed to be restrained.

In *Snook* v. *Snetzer*, 25 Ohio St. 516, it was decided that a citizen of Ohio could be enjoined from prosecuting an attachment in another State against a citizen of Ohio to subject to the payment of his claim the earnings of the debtor, which by the laws of Ohio were exempt from the payment of such claim. See also *Engel* v. *Scheuerman*, 40 Ga. 209.

In *Keyser* v. *Rice*, *supra*, it was held in effect that it was against equity for a creditor to evade the laws of his own country in order to thereby obtain a preference over other creditors. As such was the necessary effect of the garnishment proceeding in Missouri, such will be presumed to have been the purpose of the creditor in this case.

We are of opinion that the court rightly perpetuated the injunction. See Wharton, Confl. L. § 711*a*.

The petition, we think, sufficiently alleged that the residence of plaintiff was at the time of the proceedings in garnishment in this State. The petition was filed April 18, 1887, and alleged that appellants and appellee reside in the City of Denison in said County of Grayson, "where they now are, and for several years have been, residents; that on March 18, 1887, and for many months hitherto, appellee had been engaged in the employ of the Missouri Pacific Railway Company, in the shops of said company in the City of Denison, said County and State; that on March 12, 1887, the garnishment suit was instituted in Sedalia," etc. The evidence fully sustained these averments.

There is no error in the judgment, and we think it should be affirmed.

Stayton, *Ch. J.*:

Report of the commission of appeals examined, their opinion adopted and *the judgment affirmed.*

ILLINOIS SUPREME COURT.

E. SANFORD *et al.*, *Piffs. in Err.*,
v.
Cassa KANE.

(....Ill.....)

1. **The assignee of a mortgage** cannot execute a power of sale thereby given unless the debt secured has been transferred to him so as to pass the legal title thereto.
2. **A transaction cannot be devested of the taint of usury** caused by the lender's acceptance of a sum, which he calls a commission, by the fact that he subsequently sells the securities taken in his own name, if he was in fact the actual lender.
3. **A married woman is not estopped by covenants** of warranty in a deed, in which she joined with her husband merely for the purpose of releasing her dower right, so as to make a title subsequently acquired by her inure to the grantee's benefit, although she is given by statute power to contract as if unmarried; at least such estoppel will not prevent her from relying upon a title so acquired to enable her to redeem the lands from a foreclosure sale.

(May 14, 1890.)

ERROR to the Circuit Court for Iroquois County to review a judgment in favor of plaintiff in an action brought to set aside a sale of lands under a mortgage and to redeem from the mortgage. *Affirmed.*

The facts are fully stated in the opinion.

Mr. **B. C. Cook** for plaintiffs in error.

Mr. **Robert Doyle** for defendant in error.

Shope, *Ch. J.*, delivered the opinion of the court:

This bill was filed to set aside the sale of land made under a power in the mortgage given by Morris Kane, joined by his wife, Cassa Kane, October 15, 1875, to E. Sanford, appellant, and to redeem from said mortgage. The mortgage secures the payment of $500 three years after date, with interest at 10 per cent, payable semiannually. There was executed contemporaneously with the mortgage by Kane and wife a note for $500, signed by Kane and wife, payable to Sanford, and bearing interest as mentioned in the mortgage. While the mortgage does not mention a note, the proof shows that they were parts of the same transaction, and given to secure the same loan, the note being required as further security, should there be any deficiency on a sale under the mortgage. The mortgage provided that, in case of default in the payment of the debt, or any part thereof, "the said grantee, his heirs or assigns," may sell the mortgaged premises," etc., "and in his name, or in my name, or as my attorney in fact," make a deed to the purchaser or pur-

NOTE.—*Assignee of mortgage.*

In States where a mortgage is regarded as a mere security, and not an estate in land, and the mortgage gives mortgagee or his assigns power to sell upon default of payment, an assignment of the note secured will vest the power of sale in the assignee. Pardee v. Lindley, 31 Ill. 174; Olds v. Cummings, 31 Ill. 188. Compare Hamilton v. Lubukee, 51 Ill. 417.

Such power thereby passes from the mortgagee and cannot be executed by him. Kilgour v. Gockley, 83 Ill. 109.

chasers. September 15, 1876, Sanford indorsed the note to one Edgar F. Whittlesy, and on the same day made to Whittlesy a separate written instrument, purporting to assign and transfer the mortgage, and also placed his name in blank upon the mortgage. September 2, 1879, Whittlesy made a similar written assignment of the mortgage to George Wilkinson, but no assignment of the note, and delivered the note and mortgage to him. The interest was paid to July 20, 1878, the maturity of the note. Default was made in the payment of principal, and on October 16, 1879, Wilkinson, claiming to be the assignee of the mortgage debt, sold the land under the power contained in the mortgage, having previously given notice, according to the terms of the mortgage, of the sale to take place on that day, at 2 o'clock P. M. Just before the hour of sale, Morris, Kane and Wilkinson met, and the proof tends to show that it was agreed that the sale should be postponed until 4 o'clock, to enable Kane to procure the money to pay off the debt; but during his absence, and before the hour of postponement had arrived, Wilkinson sold the property to Sanford for $800, and refused to do anything further, referring Kane to Sanford.

The first and one of the principal questions is whether the power of sale was executed by a person authorized by the mortgage to execute the same. If it was, the sale must stand, in the absence of other grounds of objection; but, if made by one not authorized by the mortgage, then it was void, and no title passed by the sale and deed. The power of sale was given by the mortgage to the mortgagee, or to his heirs or assigns. If there was no transfer of the debt, so as to pass the legal title thereto, the power could be executed only by the mortgagee, but, if the debt was legally assigned, the assignee was the one authorized to make the sale.

In *Hamilton* v. *Lubukee*, 51 Ill. 415, the mortgage contained a power of sale given to "the mortgagee, his heirs or assigns," in case of default. The notes in that case were never assigned, but were sold and delivered to Eisendrath & Co. The mortgage was assigned by an indorsement made thereon. The court said: "The mortgage not being an assignable instrument either at common law or under the Statute the power to sell remained with the mortgagee." And the court referred to *Olds* v. *Cummings*, 31 Ill. 188; *Pardee* v. *Lindley*, Id. 174. See also *Strother* v. *Law*, 54 Ill. 413; *Mason* v. *Ainsworth*, 58 Ill. 163; *Dempster* v. *West*, 69 Ill. 618; *Bush* v. *Sherman*, 80 Ill. 160; *Union Mut. L. Ins. Co.* v. *Slee*, 123 Ill. 93, 10 West. Rep. 154; *Delano* v. *Bennett*, 90 Ill. 533.

If the note was secured by the mortgage, its legal holder would be authorized to execute the power of sale. Whittlesy, being its assignee, alone could make it, if the note was secured by the mortgage; and the sale by Wilkinson, the note not having been indorsed to him, was unauthorized and void. A mortgage of real estate is not negotiable or commercial paper, either at common law or under our statutes, and an assignment of it does not convey or transfer the legal ownership. The right acquired is an equitable right only, so that, in any event, Wilkinson was not the legal assignee of Sanford. As we have seen, the legal title to the note was in Whittlesy by its indorsement to him by the payee Sanford, and not in Wilkinson. The mortgage being a mere chose in action, and not assignable, the right to make the sale, if the mortgage is to be treated independently of the note, would remain in the mortgagee. The sale, having been made by Wilkinson, was therefore void, and there has been no valid foreclosure of the equity of redemption. It follows that the mortgagors have a right to redeem from the mortgage by the payment of the sum legally due thereon. It will be unnecessary to consider, in this view, whether Wilkinson was guilty of such conduct at the sale as would equitably entitle the complainant below to the relief sought by her bill.

The right to redeem from the mortgage being established, the question of usury presented by the pleadings becomes material. It is conceded that Kane received only $475 of the $500 for which the note and mortgage were given. Sanford contends that the $25 retained by him out of the loan was not usury, but was commission paid him by Kane for procuring the loan. Undoubtedly a broker, negotiating loans in good faith from others, may charge the borrower commission without rendering the loan at full rate of legal interest usurious. *Hoyt* v. *Pawtucket Sav. Inst.* 110 Ill. 392; *Phillips* v. *Roberts*, 90 Ill. 492; *Boylston* v. *Bain*, Id. 283; *Ballinger* v. *Bourland*, 87 Ill. 513.

The question here made is one of fact. Was the loan made by Sanford or by Whittlesy? Looking at the papers executed by the Kanes, and the acts of the parties, the conclusion that it was in fact made by Sanford seems irresistible. He took the note and mortgage to himself, and furnished the money by his draft, long before the assignment to Whittlesy. If Sanford was loaning money for Whittlesy, or if the latter had agreed to make the loan, the usual course would have been to have taken the securities directed to him. Sanford, it appears, controlled the securities, and finally became the purchaser of the property. Without entering into detail, we are not satisfied that the money in fact loaned belonged to Whittlesy, or to anyone other than Sanford. The transaction was evidently one, not infrequent, where a loan is taken at a high rate of interest, and subsequently sold to investors of money. If Sanford in fact made the loan, he could not devest the transaction of the taint of usury by afterwards selling the note and mortgage to Whittlesy. To sanction such a transaction would be to uphold a palpable evasion of the Statute. We think the court below properly held that the evidence shows the transaction to be usurious. The defendant in error, having sought relief in a court of equity, was bound to submit to equitable terms, and the court, therefore, very properly decreed that she should pay 6 per cent interest per annum on the loan, as a condition of her right to redeem.

The point is made that Cassa Kane, when she filed this bill, October 15, 1881, had no interest in the land, and therefore had no standing in a court of equity to set aside the sale and redeem from the mortgage. The facts upon which the contention is based are substantially as follows: Morris Kane was the owner of the land, said Cassa having only an inchoate right of dower. After their mortgage to Sanford, February 21, 1876, Morris Kane, his wife not joining in the deed, conveyed the land to his father, John Kane. No conditions were inserted in this deed, and the grantee assumed no obligations in respect to the Sanford mortgage. On March 27, 1879, the title to the land then being in John Kane, Morris and Cassa Kane, his wife, by warranty deed, purported to convey the land to one John C Parr, subject to the Sanford mortgage. It is clear that at that time Cassa had no interest in the land, other than, perhaps, her inchoate right of dower, and not that interest as against the Sanford mortgage. The title not being in either Morris or Cassa Kane, Parr took nothing by his deed. It is unnecessary for us to determine here what obligation he assumed in respect of this mortgage, or what would have been the effect of his deed in a suit by Sanford or the holder of this mortgage to fix liability upon him under said deed. On the 3d of October, 1881, John Kane, the holder of the equity of redemption, and having the right to redeem from the Sanford mortgage, conveyed all his estate, right, title and interest in this property to Cassa Kane, and it is by virtue of the title thus acquired that she claims the right to file this bill. Her right to do so would not be disputed if she had not united with her husband in the warranty deed to Parr. It is contended, however, by plaintiff in error, that whatever title she acquired by the deed from John Kane inured to the benefit of her former grantee, Parr; and that she is estopped by her covenants of warranty from disputing that the title is vested in him under her deed. At common law, a married woman was not estopped by the covenant in her deed, or in those of her husband in which she joined. 2 Devlin, Deeds, § 1287; Bigelow, Estoppel, 3d ed. 277; *Strawn* v. *Strawn*, 50 Ill. 33; *Patterson* v. *Lawrence*, 90 Ill. 174.

It is claimed that section 6, chap. 68, Rev. Stat., relating to husband and wife, has changed this rule of the common law. That section reads: "Contracts may be made and liabilities incurred by a wife, and the same enforced against her, to the same extent, and in the same manner, as if she were unmarried; but, except with the consent of her husband, she may not enter into or carry on any partnership business," etc. The question is directly presented whether this change in the rule of the common law subjects the defendant in error to estoppel by the covenants in her deed to Parr. If it does, then the title subsequently acquired will inure to the benefit of her grantee holding her deed containing covenants of warranty. The Statutes enlarging the rights and obligations of married women are of comparatively recent date, and we have been unable to find any considerable authority bearing upon the question. By the Statute of Massachusetts (Gen. Stat., chap. 108, § 3), every married woman is made capable of selling and conveying her separate real and personal property, entering into contracts in respect to the same, and of suing and being sued in respect of all matters relating thereto, in the same manner as if she were sole.

In *Knight* v. *Thayer*, 125 Mass. 25, an analogous question was presented, and the court says: "By the common law of Massachusetts the warranty deed of a married woman, though executed in such form as to convey her title, did not operate against her by way of covenant or of estoppel, because she was incapable of binding herself by covenant of warranty, or by agreement to convey her real estate." After giving the substance of the Statute, the court further says: "Any conveyance or contract executed by a married woman in accordance with the power thus conferred is binding upon and may be enforced against her, to the same extent as if she were unmarried." The court then held that a warranty deed of a married woman of her land would pass to her grantees a subsequently acquired title.

Under our Statute, married women may make contracts that will be enforced against them, but their conveyances, in order to bind them in respect of their real estate, must have for their object the disposition, in some form, of their lands, or of some right or interest relating to their lands. Where a married woman joins with her husband in his deed, for the sole purpose of enabling him to pass the title, free from her inchoate right of dower, such deed cannot be said to be her contract for any other purpose than to release her dower. A court of equity, when its power is invoked, will look beyond the mere form, and into the substance, of the transaction, and give effect to the contracts of parties, according to the true intent and meaning which the parties themselves understood attached to them at the time they were made. It cannot be said, at least in equity, that, by signing and acknowledging the deed of her husband for the sole purpose of releasing her dower, she makes the deed her own, and subjects herself to liability on the covenants of title. The deed may operate as a conveyance, release or acquittance only, or it may create a contract obligation, as where the party covenants in respect of the estate granted.

In *Strawn* v. *Strawn*, *supra*, Strawn and his wife by their deed conveyed land of the husband to their daughter, and the heirs of her body, forever, and the grantors covenanted for themselves, their assign and assigns, to forever warrant and defend the same. The usual acknowledgment of its execution was taken, in which the wife formally relinquished her dower. The daughter died without issue. After the husband's death, the wife claimed the land by right of survivorship. The fact that Mrs. Strawn joined in the deed was claimed to be evidence establishing the joint ownership in herself and husband. It was also claimed that the heirs of Jacob Strawn, the grantor, were estopped by the covenants in the deed. This court, however, held that the wife joined in the execution of the deed in compliance with the Statute in order to release her dower, and for that purpose only, and that the covenants therein could not have the effect insisted upon. It is there said: "But is it true that, by force of the Act of 1861, the appellant [the wife] could be bound by the covenants in this deed? Had it been her own land, and her husband had united in a conveyance of it [by deed] containing covenants, she could not be held responsible upon them any further than that they should be held to convey from her and her heirs her right and interest in the land. And this immunity is not destroyed by the Act of 1861. If that Act makes her responsible on covenants contained in a deed she may execute for her own land, how it can be said to make her liable on covenants on deed for land to which she set up no title, and joined in its execution for the sole and only purpose of releasing any future right she might have as a wife surviving her husband, the owner of the fee, we fail to perceive."

We have not failed to note the difference between the rights of married women under the Statutes in force when these deeds were made and those given by the Act of 1861. The foregoing case aptly illustrates the view that will be taken in the construction of the deeds of married women.

Before proceeding further, it should be said that the deed to Parr did not purport to be that of the wife, Cassa Kane. She had and claimed to have no title or interest in the land other than her inchoate dower. She had nothing that could be conveyed by deed. The Conveyance Act provides the mode by which she may relinquish her dower "in any of the real estate of her husband or in any real estate," by joining him in a deed. If she join with her husband in a conveyance of his land merely for the purpose of releasing her dower, she will not in equity be held liable upon the covenants of the deed. It should also be observed that Parr is making no claim to this land. He does not claim that the title was vested in him by the deed from John Kane to Cassa Kane. Plaintiff in error does not claim by, through or under Parr, and we are unable to perceive upon what principle he can be permitted to insist upon the estoppel. There is no proof that Parr paid anything for the deed to himself, or has at any time attempted, or is now attempting, to assert any title thereunder.

We are of the opinion that Mrs. Kane, defendant in error, is not estopped, by the deed to Parr, from asserting title under the deed from John Kane to herself. We are of the opinion that, under the facts here shown, she having joined in making the deed to Parr for the single purpose of relinquishing her dower right, if she had any, in the land, the title subsequently acquired by her would not inure to the grantee in such deed.

We find in this record no substantial error, and *the decree is therefore affirmed.*

MISSISSIPPI SUPREME COURT.

I. S. WEST, Jr.,
v.
PEOPLE'S BANK of New Orleans.

(......Miss......)

1. **A return on a writ of attachment** that it was levied upon lands described, and executed personally upon defendant by giving him a copy, without stating that the officer went upon the lands, or to the house of the person in whose possession they were, and then and there declared the levy of the writ, as required by Code, § 2424, in case of a levy on occupied premises such as the levy is made upon, is insufficient to sustain the validity of the attachment, even after judgment, as against the intervening rights of other persons.

2. **The judgment of a court** in an attachment case cannot create a lien operating retroac-

---

NOTE.—*Removal of cloud on title; jurisdiction of court of equity.*

The jurisdiction of courts of equity to remove clouds from title is well settled (Apthorp v. Comstock, 2 Paige, 482, 2 N. Y. Ch. L. ed. 997; Pettit v. Shepherd, 5 Paige, 493, 3 N. Y. Ch. L. ed. 801; Petrsoll v. Elliott, 31 U. S. 6 Pet. 95 (8 L. ed. 332); Colchester v. Lowten, 1 Ves. & B. 226; Hayward v. Dimsdale, 17 Ves. Jr. 111), and is fully maintained by the modern decisions of the courts. Ward v. Chamberlain, 67 U. S. 2 Black, 445 (17 L. ed. 326).

All the authorities agree in conferring jurisdiction where the claim, whose shade is cast upon the plaintiff's title, is not utterly void upon the face of the instrument itself, but is shown to be so by extrinsic evidence, or where it is shown to be against the plaintiff's title. "Such jurisdiction," says Story, "is founded on the true principles of equity jurisprudence, which is not merely remedial, but is also preventive of injustice." Chautauque Co. Bank v. White, 6 Barb. 606; Lawrence v. Zimpleman, 37 Ark. 643; Detroit v. Martin, 34 Mich. 170; Briggs v. Johnson, 71 Me. 237; Brooks v. Howland, 58 N. H. 98; Guest v. Brooklyn, 69 N. Y. 513; Bockes v. Lansing, 74 N. Y. 437; Smith v. New York, 6 Daly, 402; Beach v. Hayes, 58 How. Pr. 17; Lewis v. Buffalo, 1 Sheld. 80; Dows v. Chicago, 78 U. S. 11 Wall. 108 (20 L. ed. 65); Hannewinkle v. Georgetown, 82 U. S. 15 Wall. 547 (21 L. ed. 231); Coulson v. Portland, Deady, 481; Huntington v. Central Pac. R. Co. 2 Sawy. 503; Shell v. Martin, 19 Ark. 139; Chaplin v. Holmes, 27 Ark. 414; Palmer v. Boling, 8 Cal. 384; Cohen v. Sharp, 44 Cal. 29; Gage v. Rohrbach, 56 Ill. 262; Barnett v. Cline, 60 Ill. 205; Reed v. Reder, 62 Ill. 240; Lee v. Ruggles, Id. 427; Harrison v. Haas, 25 Ind. 281; Sapp v. Morrill, 8 Kan. 678; Leigh v. Everheart, 4 T. B. Mon. 379; Kinyon v. Duchene, 21 Mich. 498; Weller v. St. Paul, 5 Minn. 95; Fowler v. St. Joseph, 37 Mo. 228; South Platte Land Co. v. Buffalo County, 7 Neb. 253; Oakley v. Williamsburgh, 6 Paige, 262, 3 N. Y. Ch. L. ed. 978; Van Doren v. New York, 9 Paige, 388, 4 N. Y. Ch. L. ed. 743; Hanlon v. Westchester County, 57 Barb. 383; Newell v. Wheeler, 48 N. Y. 486; Judd v. Fox Lake, 28 Wis. 583; Wals v. Grosvenor, 31 Wis. 681; Brooklyn v. Meserole, 26 Wend. 138.

The courts of Pennsylvania have adopted and recognized the equity jurisdiction to remove clouds upon title, as fully and as broadly as it is described in the equity text-books and decisions. Dull's App. 5 Cent. Rep. 187, 113 Pa. 510.

Jurisdiction founded on inadequacy of legal remedy.

The jurisdiction of a court of equity to remove a cloud upon title is founded on the inadequacy of the remedy at law, and it does not arise when the plaintiff has a remedy by an action at law. Byerly v. Humphrey, 95 N. C. 151; Walker v. Walker, 1 New Eng. Rep. 250, 63 N. H. 321; United States v. Wilson, 118 U. S. 86 (30 L. ed. 110); Gage v. Mayer, 5 West. Rep. 496, 117 Ill. 632; Benner v. Kendall, 21 Fla. 584; Maisch v. Hoffman, 5 Cent. Rep. 632, 42 N. J. Eq. 116.

When the estate or interest to be protected is equitable, jurisdiction in equity should be exercised whether the plaintiff is in or out of possession. 3 Pom. Eq. Jur. 438; Hager v. Shindler, 29 Cal. 47;

tively so as to cut out intervening rights of others.

3. A cross-bill in a suit to remove a cloud from title will not be dismissed because defendant denies the title to have been in the person under whom both parties claim, at the time of the levy of a writ of attachment under which plaintiff claims, where this denial is qualified and explained by allegations showing that a conveyance canceled at suit of defendant was the foundation of the denial.

4. Relief will not be denied on a cross-bill in a suit to remove a cloud on title because defendant shows a perfect title on which he might maintain ejectment.

(June 2, 1890.)

CROSS APPEALS from a decree of the Chancery Court for Harrison County dismissing the bill and cross-bill in an action brought to quiet title to a certain piece of real estate. *Reversed on defendant's appeal.*

The facts sufficiently appear in the opinion.

Messrs. **Nugent & McWillie, Percy Roberts, R. Seal** and **Calvit Roberts,** for complainant:

The Attachment Law provides: "This Act shall be construed in all courts of judicature, in the most liberal manner, for the detection of fraud, the advancement of justice and the benefit of creditors."

Rev. Code 1880, art. 2476.

Attachments have been habitually upheld whenever there has been a substantial compliance with the prescriptions of the Statute.

Dandridge v. *Stevens*, 12 Smedes & M. 723; *Saunders* v. *Columbus L. & G. Ins. Co.* 43 Miss. 596.

Defendant is absolutely without right to stand in judgment on any one of the defects and irregularities alleged by him. Defects and irregularities in the bond, affidavit and levies of the writ in attachment proceedings are matters which the defendant in attachment, and the defendant alone, can put at issue.

Drake, Attachm. 8272; *Emerson* v. *Fox*, 3 La. 182; *Mayer* v. *Stahr*, 35 La. Ann. 57; *Camberford* v. *Hall*, 3 McCord, L. 345; *Seibert* v. *Switzer*, 35 Ohio St. 661; *Van Arsdale* v. *Krum*, 9 Mo 397; *Fridenburg* v *Pierson*, 18 Cal. 152.

If there is a bond, no matter how insufficient, an affidavit, no matter how imperfect, a levy, no matter how defective, the attachment exists, although irregular, infirm and defeasible by the defendant; and a judgment of court based on such an attachment, although voidable on a motion to quash, or writ of error, is impregnable to any collateral attack leveled against it by a third person.

Freeman, Judgm. par. 126; *Voorhees* v. *Jackson*, 35 U. S. 10 Pet. 449 (9 L. ed. 490); *Thompson* v. *Tolmie*, 27 U. S. 2 Pet. 162 (7 L. ed. 383); *New Lamp Chimney Co.* v. *Ansonia B. & C. Co.* 91 U. S. 659 (23 L. ed. 336); *Crizer*

Castro v. Barry, 79 Cal. 443; Hyde v. Redding, 74 Cal. 493; Thompson v. Lynch, 29 Cal. 189; More v. Steinbach, 127 U. S. 70 (32 L. ed. 51); Jones v. Smith, 22 Mich. 360; Almony v. Hicks, 3 Head, 39; Bunce v. Gallagher, 5 Blatchf. 481; Ely v. New Mexico & A. R. Co. 129 U. S 291 (32 L. ed. 688); Holland v. Challen, 110 U. S. 15 (28 L. ed. 52).

When a party is in possession and is unable to obtain adequate legal relief he may obtain his remedy in equity. Branch v. Mitchell, 24 Ark. 431; Gage v. Rohrbach, 56 Ill. 262; Gage v. Billings, Id. 268; Hinchley v. Greany, 118 Mass. 595; Clouston v. Shearer, 99 Mass. 209; Sullivan v. Finnegan, 101 Mass. 447; Pierce v. Lamson, 5 Allen, 60; Martin v. Graves, Id. 601.

Where a party out of possession has an equitable title, or where he holds the legal title under such circumstances that the law cannot furnish him full and complete relief he may resort to a court of equity for relief. Plant v. Barclay, 56 Ala. 561; Lawrence v. Zimpleman, 37 Ark. 643; Thompson v. Lynch, 29 Cal. 189; Hager v. Shindler, 29 Cal. 47; Booth v. Wiley, 102 Ill. 84; Redmond v. Packenham, 66 Ill. 434; Kennedy v. Northup, 15 Ill. 148; King v. Carpenter, 37 Mich. 363; Ormsby v. Barr, 22 Mich. 80; Low v. Staples, 2 Nev. 209; Pier v. Fond du Lac, 38 Wis. 470.

Possession essential to right of action.

The cases are not uniform on the above propositions, some of them broadly stating that a person seeking this relief must, under all circumstances, be in possession. Daniel v. Stewart, 55 Ala. 278; Smith v. Cockrell, 66 Ala. 64; Baines v. Barnes, 64 Ala. 375; Tyson v. Brown, 64 Ala. 244; Arnett v. Bailey, 60 Ala. 435; Miller v. Neiman, 27 Ark. 233; Keane v. Kyne, 66 Mo. 216; Clark v. Covenant Mut. L. Ins. Co. 52 Mo. 272; Haythorn v. Margerem, 7 N. J. Eq. 324; Busbee v. Lewis, 85 N.C. 332; Herrington v. Williams, 31 Tex. 448; Orton v. Smith, 59 U. S. 18 How. 263 (15 L. ed. 393); Johnson v. Huling, 127 Ill. 14; Peacock v. Stott, 104 N. C. 154; Sheppard v. Nixon, 12 Cent. Rep. 74, 43 N. J. Eq. 627.

Peaceable possession in the complainant is a jurisdictional fact in an action to quiet title to lands. Beale v. Blake, 45 N. J. Eq. 668; Nixon v. Walter, 4 Cent. Rep. 875, 41 N. J. Eq. 103.

Either actual possession or legal title is necessary to entitle one to maintain an action to quiet title. Wood v. Nicolson (Kan.) April 4, 1890.

Under the statute of Oregon, that "any person in possession of lands by himself or his tenant may maintain suit to quiet the possession," the possession must be accompanied with a claim of right, that is, must be founded upon title, legal or equitable. Stark v. Starr, 73 U. S. 6 Wall. 402 (18 L. ed. 925).

Equity will not entertain a bill to remove a cloud from a title, unless complainant is in possession under a conveyance or incumbrance valid on its face. Curry v. Peebles, 83 Ala. 225.

Before chancery will quiet title, plaintiff must have been in possession and possession must have been assailed. Marks v. Main, 2 Cent. Rep. 701, 4 Mackey, 559.

A bill to quiet title cannot be maintained in equity independent of the statute, without clear proof of both possession and legal title in the complainant. Frost v. Spitley, 121 U. S. 552 (30 L. ed. 1010); Harland v. Bankers & M. Teleg. Co. (N. Y.) 32 Fed. Rep. 305.

To entitle a complainant to relief, he must show possession, a legal or equitable title in himself, a claim set up by some other person, and his title must be substantiated. Hatch v. St. Joseph, 12 West. Rep. 560, 68 Mich. 220.

Party out of possession must pursue remedy at law.

But a person out of possession holding the legal title will be left to his remedy—ejectment. Crane v. Randolph, 30 Ark. 579; Munson v. Munson, 28 Conn. 582; Burton v. Gleason, 56 Ill. 25; Polk v. Pendleton, 31 Md. 118; King v. Carpenter, 37 Mich. 363; Moran v. Palmer, 13 Mich. 367; Odle v. Odle, 73 Mo. 289; Graves v. Swart, 99 Mo. 13; Davis v. Sloan, 11 West.

v. *Gorren*, 41 Miss. 564; *Harrington* v. *Wofford*, 46 Miss. 31; *Campbell* v. *Hays*, 41 Miss. 562; *Christian* v. *O'Neal*, 46 Miss. 669; *Loughridge* v. *Bowland*, 52 Miss. 546.

The trial court expressly finds the two great jurisdictional facts of the case, viz.: That there had been a citation and also an "attachment," and this finding is conclusive.

Saffarans v. *Terry*, 12 Smedes & M. 690; Rorer, Jud. Sales, § 797.

Messrs. **E. Howard McCaleb** and **E. J. Bowers**, for respondent:

The levy was insufficient to create a lien and was utterly void, because it was not made as directed by law, but was a levy such as is prescribed for the seizure and sale of unoccupied land.

Sherman v. *Union Nat. Bank*, 66 Miss. 648.

The judgment obtained by West on the confession of the defendant Carriere released the lien created by the attachment in so far as other creditors' rights were affected. The taking of the deed to the property attached, on which he had only a lien, and that an inchoate lien, was necessarily a discharge of the attachment.

Waples, Attachm. pp. 490, 491; *Cole* v. *Wooster*, 2 Conn. 203, *Murray* v. *Eldridge*, 2 Vt. 388; *Brandon Iron Co.* v. *Gleason*, 24 Vt. 228; *Hall* v. *Walbridge*, 2 Aik. 215; Drake, Attachm. § 283; *Clark* v. *Foxcroft*, 7 Me. 348; *Fairbanks* v. *Stanley*, 18 Me. 296; *Hill* v. *Hunnewell*, 1 Pick. 192.

When each of two parties claims from one person, as a common source, neither is at liberty to deny that such person had title.

Gaines v. *New Orleans*, 73 U. S. 6 Wall. 643 (18 L. ed. 950).

The issues raised by the pleadings in this controversy show that an equity court has jurisdiction to unravel the frauds complained of in appellant's cross-bill and grant the relief demanded.

Smith v. *Gettinger*, 3 Ga. 140; *Whipple* v. *Cass*, 8 Iowa, 126; *Reed* v. *Ennis*, 4 Abb. Pr. 393; *Hale* v. *Chandler*, 3 Mich. 531.

Cooper, *J.*, delivered the opinion of the court:

The controversy in this cause is between I. S. West, Jr., and the People's Bank of New Orleans, each claiming to be the owner of the land described in the pleadings by title derived under judicial proceedings against the former owner, Charles J. Carriere. On the 25th of June, 1884, West sued out a writ of attachment returnable to the Circuit Court of Harrison County against Carriere, as a nonresident. To this writ the sheriff of Harrison County made return, as follows: "Executed within process this 26th day of June, 1884, by levying upon the following described real estate situated in Harrison County, Mississippi, as that of C. J. Carriere, deft., to wit [describing lands by metes and bounds]. Further executed by hand-

---

Rep. 455, 95 Mo. 552; Dyer v. Baumeister, 3 West. Rep. 262, 87 Mo. 134; Weaver v. Arnold, 1 New Eng. Rep. 129, 15 R. I. 53; United States v. Wilson, 118 U. S. 86 (30 L. ed. 110); Orton v. Smith, 59 U. S. 18 How. 263 (15 L. ed. 393); Hipp v. Babin, 60 U. S. 19 How. 271 (15 L. ed. 633); Ellis v. Davis, 109 U. S. 485 (27 L. ed. 1006); Killian v. Ebbinghaus, 110 U. S. 568 (28 L. ed. 246); Fussell v. Gregg, 113 U. S. 550 (28 L. ed. 993); McDonald v. White, 130 Ill. 493; Moses v. Gatliff, 11 Ky. L. Rep. 856; Russell v. Barstow, 8 New Eng. Rep. 782, 144 Mass. 130.

A bill to obtain possession of property in the adverse possession of another will not be entertained in equity, although relief in the nature of removing a cloud on the title is sought. Harland v. Bankers & M. Teleg. Co. 32 Fed. Rep. 305.

A suit in equity cannot be sustained on behalf of heirs to remove a cloud on their title by declaring an administrator's sale void, where the heirs were out of possession and defendants in possession when suit was commenced. Thompson v. Newberry, 10 West. Rep. 385, 93 Mo. 18.

A person out of possession cannot maintain a bill to remove a cloud upon title, whether his title is legal or equitable; for if his title is legal, his remedy at law by action of ejectment is plain, adequate and complete; and if his title is equitable, he must acquire the legal title, and then bring ejectment. Harland v. Bankers & M. Teleg. Co. *supra*.

Owner out of possession cannot maintain action *quia timet* to remove cloud upon title nor to establish legal title or possession, unless other circumstances give equitable jurisdiction. Moores v. Townshend, 3 Cent. Rep. 441, 102 N. Y. 387.

Preventive remedy by injunction.

It is equally well settled that equity may prevent by injunction the casting of a cloud on title. Pettit v. Shepherd, 5 Paige, 493, 3 N. Y. Ch. L. ed. 801; Thomas v. Simmons, 1 West. Rep. 118, 103 Ind. 583.

The court may in a proper case interpose to prevent the illegal act from which such cloud must necessarily arise. Brooklyn v. Meserole, 26 Wend. 132; Oakley v. Williamsburgh, 6 Paige, 265, 3 N. Y Ch. L. ed. 280; Hare v. Carnall, 39 Ark. 196; Ottawa v. Walker, 21 Ill. 605; Barnard v. Hoyt, 63 Ill. 341; Litchfield v. Polk County, 18 Iowa, 70; Holland v. Baltimore, 11 Md. 186; Folkerts v. Power, 42 Mich. 283; Thomas v. Gain, 35 Mich. 155; Fowler v. St. Joseph, 37 Mo. 228; Mechanics Bank v. Kansas City, 73 Mo. 555; Leslie v. St. Louis, 47 Mo. 474; Burnet v. Cincinnati, 3 Ohio, 73; Culbertson v. Cincinnati, 16 Ohio, 574; Red v. Johnson, 53 Tex. 288; Harrison v. Vines, 46 Tex. 22; Dean v. Madison, 9 Wis. 403.

The court will enjoin the casting of a cloud upon a title in a case wherein the cloud itself, when cast, would be removed. Huntington v. Central Pac. R. Co. 2 Sawy. 514. See Palmer v. Boling, 8 Cal. 388; Fremont v. Boling, 11 Cal. 380; Pixley v. Huggins, 15 Cal. 127; Hibernia S. & L. Society v. Ordway, 38 Cal. 681, 682; Shattuck v. Carson, 2 Cal. 588; Guy v. Hermance, 5 Cal. 73; Englund v. Lewis, 25 Cal. 337; Alverson v. Jones, 10 Cal. 9–11.

But it will never interfere to enjoin a sale of land upon an idle or groundless suspicion, an unreal fear or the mere possibility of its casting a cloud over the title of one in actual possession of the land under an unchallenged title. Archbishop of San Francisco v. Shipman, 69 Cal. 590. See Hartman v. Reed, 50 Cal. 485; Schroeder v. Gurney, 73 N. Y. 430; Sanders v. Yonkers, 63 N. Y. 489.

A sale of lands under execution which would confer no title, and whose only effect would be to cloud the title of others, will be enjoined. Knightstown First Nat. Bank v. Deitch, 83 Ind. 133; Groves v. Webber, 72 Ill. 607. See Oakley v. Williamsburgh, 6 Paige, 262, 3 N. Y. Ch. L. ed. 978; Tibbetts v. Fore, 70 Cal. 242; Culver v. Phelps, 130 Ill. 217.

The court may interpose its aid to prevent such a shade from being cast upon the title, when the defendant evinces a fixed determination to proceed with the sale. Hotchkiss v. Elting, 36 Barb. 49; Johnson v. Hahn, 4 Neb. 148. See Marsh v. Clark County, 42 Wis. 502; Cotzhausen v. Kaehler, Id. 332; Schettler v. Fort Howard, 43 Wis. 48; Irwin v Lewis, 50 Miss. 370.

ing to C. J. Carriere, deft., in person a true copy of within process."

This writ was returnable to the November Term of the Circuit Court, and at that time the defendant appeared and pleaded in abatement to the attachment. At a subsequent term of the court the defendant withdrew all defense, and judgment by consent was rendered in favor of the plaintiff, and the land attached directed to be sold. Under this judgment a writ of *vend. ex.* was issued, and the property described in the writ was sold, and the plaintiff in attachment, West, became the purchaser. On the 1st of July, 1884 (after the levy of the attachment, and before the return day of the writ), the People's Bank exhibited its bill in the Chancery Court of Harrison County against Charles J. Carriere and Mamie Adele Carriere, his wife, and against the infant children of the said Charles J. Carriere, in which it was averred that on the 30th day of May the said Charles J. Carriere was indebted to said Bank in a large sum; that he was then insolvent, and, for the purpose of defrauding his creditors, on that day made a voluntary conveyance of the property here in controversy to his said wife and infant children. The property was described in said bill, and, under sections 1848, 1845, Code, a lien was fixed by the filing of the bill against the property proceeded against. This proceeding resulted in a final decree in favor of the Bank, canceling the conveyance from Carriere to his wife and children, and subjecting the land to sale for the payment of the complainant's debt. Under this decree the land was sold by a commissioner of the chancery court, and at this sale the People's Bank became the purchaser.

It will be seen that both parties to the present litigation claim to have secured the title of Charles J. Carriere, West claiming title under the attachment suit, and the Bank under the chancery proceeding. The regularity and validity of the chancery suit of the Bank against Carriere and others is not controverted, and it is conceded by West that the title of Carriere passed under the sale thereunder, unless he (West) secured a title under his attachment, and the sale under the judgment rendered therein. The present suit was commenced by West, who avers that he is the owner and in possession of the land, and that the claim of title asserted by the Bank casts a cloud and suspicion on his title; wherefore he prays its cancellation. The Bank answered the bill, and also exhibited a cross bill, by which it seeks to cancel the title of West as a cloud upon its title. On final hearing the court dismissed the original and cross-bills, and both parties appeal.

Two questions are presented by the record: (1) In whom is the title of Carriere vested? (2) Is the holder of that title entitled to a decree canceling that of his adversary? The cross-bill exhibited by the People's Bank avers that, at the date of the levy of the attachment sued out by West against Carriere, the lands in controversy were not wild, uncultivated or unoccupied, but that they were then occupied as a residence by Carriere and his family. This allegation of the cross-bill is not denied, and its truth must be accepted as established, if it be competent to aver the fact in this proceeding.

Section 2424 of our Code prescribes how writs of attachment shall be levied upon real estate. It provides that "every writ of attachment shall be executed in the following manner: that is to say, in case of a levy on real estate, the officer shall go to the house or land of the defendant, or to the person or house of the person in whose possession the same may be, and then and there shall declare that he attaches the same at the suit of the plaintiff in the writ named. But, in the event the land is wild, uncultivated or unoccupied, a return upon the writ by the proper officer, that he has attached the land, giving a description thereof by numbers, metes and bounds, or otherwise, shall be a sufficient levy, without going upon the land." Section 2425 declares that "the officer serving an attachment shall make a full return thereon of all his proceedings, on or before the return day of the writ."

The contention of the Bank is that the levy of the writ of attachment, as shown by the return of the officer, was invalid, and fixed no lien upon the land; that the only act done by the officer was to note the levy on the writ; and, while this would have been sufficient to fix the lien if the land had been "wild, uncultivated or unoccupied," it had no effect upon the property in controversy, since it was at the time of the levy occupied by the defendant in attachment and his family. West responds to this assault by replying that the defect in the levy, if any exist, is a mere irregularity which might have been and was waived by the defendant; and again, that, in this collateral controversy, it is not competent for the Bank to attack the validity or effect of the judgment in the attachment suit, which, as he contends, adjudicated the validity of the levy, and condemned the land to sale for the debt found due to him.

We have examined many cases touching the position assumed by counsel for West, and though the rule is very generally declared to be that mere irregularities in the proceedings cannot be availed of by third persons, or by the defendant himself in a collateral controversy, it is not clear what defects are to be considered as irregularities only, within the rule announced. The earlier South Carolina Reports contain many cases in which the distinction is drawn between those omissions or defects which are considered irregularities only, and those which are held to vitiate the proceedings, and entitle third persons to contest the validity of the judgment.

It has been held in that State that the following defects are irregularities only, and do not annul the judgment: an omission by the plaintiff to make affidavit of his debt (*Foster* v. *Jones*, 1 McCord, L. 116); omitting to give the requisite bond (*Chambers* v. *McKee*, 1 Hill, L. (S. C.) 229); in giving the attachment bond in double the debt, instead of double the damages or sum sued for (*Camberford* v. *Hall*, 3 McCord, L. 345); the omission of the magistrate to return into court the attachment bond. *Kincaid* v. *Neall*, Id. 201.

On the other hand, it has been decided in the same State that the following defects are fatal to the validity of the judgment, and that junior attachers may set aside the prior attachment, and subject the property to their demands: an illegal service of the writ (*Byne* v. *Byne*, 1 Rich. L. 438; *Gardner* v. *Hust*, 2 Rich. L. 601); suing out a writ against one not liable to that process (*Weyman* v. *Murdock*, Harp. L. 125); that the cause of action is not suable by attachment (*Sargeant* v. *Helmbold*, Id. 219); a writ issued by one partner against another on a partnership demand (*Rice* v. *Beers*, 1 Rice, Dig. (S. C.) 75); that the fund has not been attached. *Burrell* v. *Letson*, 1 Strob. L. 239.

In Louisiana it has been decided that a junior attacher cannot intervene to allege informality in the senior proceedings consisting in a failure of the first attacher to make the affidavit required by law, the affidavit being a substantial compliance with the Statute. *Clamageran* v. *Bucks*, 4 Mart. (N. S.) 487.

It seems, however, to be generally held that a junior attacher or other third person may show that the officer failed to make a valid levy upon the property attached.

In *Southern Bank of Mo.* v. *McDonald*, 46 Mo. 31, after the return day of an execution the creditor sued out a writ of garnishment (not being permitted by the Statute so to do), and the garnishee appeared and answered, and submitted to judgment. Another creditor subsequently sued out his writ of garnishment, and served it upon the same garnishee. It was held that he could show the invalidity of the first garnishment, and the fund was directed to be paid to him.

In the following cases junior attachers have been given priority over prior attachers because of the defects named in the first proceedings:

In *Stone* v. *Miller*, 62 Barb. 430, because the officer levying the first writ failed to leave a copy of the writ with the party in whose possession the goods were found, as directed by statute; in *Lindau* v. *Arnold*, 4 Strob. 290, because a domestic attachment had been issued for $56, when the Statute authorized such attachments to run for not more than $20; where the debt of the first attacher was not due at the time of the commencement of this action (*Henderson* v. *Thornton*, 37 Miss. 448; *Walker* v. *Roberts*, 4 Rich. Law, 561); where the officer fails to levy the writ upon real estate in the manner required by law, as by failing to give the defendant a copy of the writ, or to go upon the land, or to levy in the presence of witnesses (*Schwartz* v. *Cowell*, 71 Cal. 306; *Watt* v. *Wright*, 66 Cal. 202; *Tiffany* v. *Glover*, 2 G. Greene, 387; *Sherman* v. *Bank*, 66 Miss. 648); or because the officer failed to take possession of personal property levied on. *Gates* v. *Flint*, 39 Miss. 365.

Our own case of *Sherman* v. *Bank*, in 66 Miss. 648, might have been sufficient for the decision of this question, but in that case there was no service upon or appearance by the defendant, and it is contended here by counsel for West that the appearance and confession of judgment by Carriere was a waiver of any defect appearing in the levy. We have therefore cited other cases to show that such appearance and waiver cannot cure defects of this character. The point here made was insisted upon in the case of *Gardner* v. *Hust*, 2 Rich. L. 601, and the court said: "Such illegal service creates no lien in cases of attachment. If there was no lien, then the confession of judgment by Hust to Miller is not the revival of a lien by waiving an irregularity, but the creation of a lien by relation back to the illegal service. If the levy had been set aside at the instance of Hust, and it had been a mere irregularity, then it may be that, as between him and Miller, he might, by confessing judgment, waive the irregularity and remove the objection to the levy. He, at least, would not, after the confession, be allowed to question the regularity of the previous proceedings. But the doctrine contended for in this case, that such waiver, by relation back, can defeat rights which had accrued in the mean time, has no support from any case or any legal analogy. In this view of the case, Miller's confession of judgment can only (as to Gardner) be regarded as a common confession, and has no lien except that created by the *fi. fa.*, which was not lodged until October. In the mean time Gardner had acquired a lien by his attachment."

It will be noted that our Statute requires the officer to return into court the writ, with a full return thereon "of all his proceedings." The officer here returned that he levied the writ upon the lands described, and executed it personally upon the defendant, and gave him a copy. It is not stated that the officer went upon the lands, or to the house or person in whose possession they were, and then and there declared the levy of the writ. It does not appear that the defendant was notified that a levy had been made. All that was done was to indorse a levy of the land upon the writ, and to serve the defendant with a copy of the writ. We must assume that the officer's return contains a full statement of "all that he did in the execution of the writ," and, if this be true, no levy was made upon the land. It is by the levy that the lien arises, and that is not a legal levy which does not conform, in substance at least, to the statutory requirements. The judgment of the court cannot create a lien operating retroactively so as to cut out intervening rights of others. It can only give effect to a lien already secured by conformity to the law by which it is provided. The People's Bank, by the institution of its suit in chancery, secured a lien upon the property at a time when no sufficient levy had been made of the attachment writ, and the title derived by it under the decree in that cause related back to the inception of the lien. The consequence is that the Bank, and not West, secured the title of Carriere.

The remaining question is whether the Bank is entitled to have cancellation of the title of West in this proceeding. West by his bill avers that the title to the property was in Carriere at the time his writ of attachment was issued and served. The chancellor dismissed the bill of West, because he thought the children of Carriere (grantees in the conveyance made by Carriere on the 24th of May, 1884) were necessary parties to the bill. He then dismissed the cross-bill of the People's Bank, because the complainant therein had a full and complete remedy at law to recover the property described, and because it denied the title to have been in Carriere at the time of the levy of the writ of attachment. In this we think the court erred. It is true that the answer denies the title to have been in Carriere, but the effect of this denial is qualified and explained by the statements of the answer and cross-bill, in which it clearly appears that the conveyance of May 24th, which had been canceled at the suit of the Bank, was the foundation of the denial. Manifestly the whole controversy between the Bank and West is as to which party acquired the title of Carriere. Both parties admit that he once had title, and both claim to have derived that title It is well settled in this State that one who seeks concellation of a cloud upon his title must show that he is the owner of the land in controversy. But, where both parties claim under a common source, there is an admission by each that the title was in that source, and this is sufficient to uphold the right of that party who proves that he has secured that title to the relief of cancellation. If the Bank were suing West in ejectment for the recovery of the land, it might show that he claimed under Carriere, and then that it was the true owner of his title. This being proved, a recovery would be had by the Bank, without any other proof of title in Carriere. *Gordon* v. *Sizer*, 39 Miss. 805; *Smith* v. *Utley*, 26 Miss. 291; *Griffin* v. *Sheffield*, 38 Miss. 359.

Nor do we think that the cross-bill should have been dismissed on the ground that the complainant therein might by ejectment try the validity of the title of West, who is in possession of the land. The right is conferred by Statute (Code, § 1833) upon the real owners, whether such real owners be in possession, or be threatened to be disturbed in his possession, or not," to cancel, to have cancellation decreed, of any conveyance or evidence of title, or any claim or pretense of claim of title, "which may cast doubt or suspicion on the title of the real owner." It has sometimes been declared by the court that the jurisdiction conferred upon courts of chancery should not be exercised to try conflicting legal titles.

In *Huntington* v. *Allen*, 44 Miss. 663, many expressions of this sort were used, but the court finally disposed of the case by doing precisely what it declared should not be done,—putting its conclusion upon the invalidity of the complainant's title. But we are not aware of any case in which, a clear legal or equitable title being shown in the complainant, the court has declined to cancel the adversary title or claim on the ground that it is in form a legal title, or because of its apparent strength or weakness.

In *Glazier* v. *Bailey*, 47 Miss. 396, the court refused to intervene because there was already pending an action of ejectment in which the titles of the parties could be tested. We know of no line by which the jurisdiction of the court is limited other than that prescribed by the law which confers it. When the complainant shows a perfect title, legal or equitable, and the title of the defendant is shown to be invalid, it is, in the nature of things, a cloud upon the title of complainant, and should be canceled.

The decree dismissing the cross-bill of the People's Bank must be reversed. A decree will be entered here, granting the relief prayed by it, and canceling the title derived by West under his attachment proceedings as a cloud upon the title by the Bank.

Decreed accordingly.

ARKANSAS SUPREME COURT.

Laura A. JOHNSON, *Appt.*,

v.

Supreme Lodge of KNIGHTS OF HONOR *et al.*

(....Ark.....)

1. The word "heirs" in a certificate of life insurance, where there is no context to explain it, means those who would, under the Statutes of Distribution, be entitled to the personal estate of the insured.

2. A widow is not one of the heirs of her deceased husband within the meaning of an insurance policy so as to be entitled to share in the proceeds, under Arkansas statutes, which give her half of the husband's personal estate as dower, absolutely and independently of creditors, and provide for distribution subject to debts and the widow's dower.

3. No one except the insurer by a benefit certificate can object to the right of brothers and sisters of a person insured to take the proceeds of his certificate, on the ground that the constitution of the insurer limits the right to take the benefits to members of the family of the insured, or those dependent on him.

(May 10, 1890.)

NOTE.—"*Heirs*" *construed.*

The word "heirs" means such persons as the law points out to succeed to personal property. Wright v. Methodist Epis. Church, Hoffm. Ch. 202, 6 N. Y. Ch. L. ed. 1115.

It may be construed to mean children or next of kin. Cushman v. Horton, 1 Hun, 602, 4 Thomp. & C. 104.

But without other words to fix the meaning the word "heirs" cannot be read "next of kin." Mason v. Bailey (Del.) 12 Cent. Rep. 331.

In construing the meaning of the word "heirs" as used in any legal document the intent will be construed and regarded if possible. Addison v. v. New England C. T. Asso. 4 New Eng. Rep. 639, 144 Mass. 591; Bradlee v. Andrews, 137 Mass. 50; Sweet v. Dutton, 109 Mass. 591; Tillman v. Davis, 95 N. Y. 17; Greenwood v. Murray, 28 Minn. 120; Criswell v. Grumbling, 107 Pa. 408.

The word "heirs" when uncontrolled by the expressed intent of the testator vests a legacy which otherwise would be contingent. Muhlenberg's App. 103 Pa. 593; McGill's App. 61 Pa. 46; Patterson v. Hawthorn, 12 Serg. & R. 112.

The heirs-at-law are those who answer the description at the time of the testator's death. Whall v. Converse, 5 New Eng. Rep. 823, 146 Mass. 345.

The right heir of a person deceased is he of the blood of the deceased upon whom the law casts the inheritance. Mason v. Bailey (Del.) 12 Cent. Rep. 331.

A husband or administrator is not the right heir of a wife or person dying intestate. *Ibid.*

In a statute concerning the succession of person-

See also 24 L. R. A. 664; 39 L. R. A. 351.

APPEAL by plaintiff from a judgment of the Circuit Court for Prairie County in favor of interpleaders in an action brought to recover the amount alleged to be due upon a benefit insurance certificate. *Affirmed.*

The facts sufficiently appear in the opinion.

Messrs. **U. M. Rose, G. B. Rose** and **George Sibley,** for appellant:

Under the designation of "heirs," the widow was entitled to at least one half the amount of the policy. When personalty is spoken of the word "heirs" means those entitled under the Statute of Distributions.

Houghton v. *Kendall*, 7 Allen, 77; *Wright* v. *Methodist Epis. Church*, Hoffm. Ch. 202, 6 N. Y. Ch. L. ed. 1115; *Holloway* v. *Holloway*, 5 Ves. Jr. 403; *Lowndes* v. *Stone*, 4 Ves. Jr. 649; *White* v. *Stanfield*, 6 New Eng. Rep. 56, 146 Mass. 425; *Re Stevens' Trusts*, L. R. 15 Eq. 110, 5 Eng. Rep. (Moak) 746; *Wingfield* v. *Wingfield*, L. R. 9 Ch. Div. 658, 26 Eng. Rep. (Moak) 417; *Re Thompson's Trusts*, L. R. 9 Ch. Div. 607, 26 Eng. Rep. (Moak) 384; *McKinney* v. *Stewart*, 5 Kan. 392; *McCabe* v. *Spruil*, 1 Dev. Eq. 189; *Corbitt* v. *Corbitt*, 1 Jones, Eq. 117; *Kiser* v. *Kiser*, 2 Jones, Eq. 28; *Henderson* v. *Henderson*, 1 Jones, L. 221; *Evans* v. *Salt*, 6 Beav. 266; *Jacobs* v. *Jacobs*, 16 Beav. 560; *Doody* v. *Higgins*, 2 Kay & J. 729; *Low* v. *Smith*, 2 Jur. N. S. 344; *Eby's App.* 84 Pa. 241; *Welsh* v. *Crater*, 32 N. J. Eq. 180; *Alexander* v. *Wallace*, 8 Lea, 569.

The subsequent amendment of the Constitution confining the benefits to the family of the member, or to persons dependent on him, deprived the intervenors of any vested rights. They had no vested rights prior to his death.

4 Kent, Com. 336; *Fugure* v. *Mutual Society of St. Joseph*, 46 Vt. 362; *Gundlach* v. *Germania Mechanics Asso.* 4 Hun, 339; *Poultney* v. *Bachman*, 62 How. Pr. 466; *Supreme Commandery K. of G. R.* v. *Ainsworth*, 71 Ala. 436; *Byrne* v. *Casey*, 70 Tex. 247; *Splawn* v. *Chew*, 60 Tex. 532; *St. Patrick's Male Benef. Soc.* v. *McVey*, 92 Pa. 510.

The grown-up brothers and sisters of the deceased, living in their own houses miles away, were not members of his family.

Elsey v. *Odd Fellows Mut. Relief Asso.* 2 New Eng. Rep. 667, 142 Mass. 224.

The Association is now existing under laws which prohibit payment to any but members of the family of the deceased, or those dependent on him, and a contract to pay to his heirs generally is *ultra vires* and void, and the benefit would have to go to such persons as might be prescribed in the charter, the supreme law of the order.

Addison v. *New England C. T. Asso.* 4 New Eng. Rep. 639, 144 Mass. 591.

There is no valid designation, and the widow is the only one entitled to take under the constitution and charter of the Association.

Ballou v. *Gile*, 50 Wis. 614; Hirschl, Fraternities, 23.

Mr. **J. E. Gatewood,** for appellees:

The word "heirs" has no different signification when used in reference to personal property from what it has when used in reference to real estate in this State. Here the estate, both real and personal, descends to the kindred, male and female, subject to widow's dower, clearly not recognizing the widow as kindred.

Mansf. Dig. § 2522, subds. 1-3, §§ 2523-2525.

The wife can only be made heir by declaration in writing.

Id. §§ 2344, 2345.

The only case in which she can inherit is under section 2528, where there is a total failure of kindred.

Kelly v. *McGuire*, 15 Ark. 555. See also *Robinson* v. *Bishop*, 23 Ark. 378; *Cox* v. *Britt* 22 Ark. 567; *Hill* v. *Mitchell*, 5 Ark. 608.

Appellant could take one half of the benefit certificate only in case it was the property of her deceased husband's estate, and then only as dower.

See Mansf. Dig. § 2593.

If there is no person designated in the certificate who can take the benefit, then the policy either lapses and must be covered into the widow's and orphan's fund of the order, or be collected by the administrator of Johnson and paid to his creditors.

Weil v. *Tafford*, 3 Tenn. Ch. 108.

The Knights of Honor alone could complain of Johnson's want of obedience to the laws of the order.

Prentice v. *Knickerbocker L. Ins. Co.* 77 N.Y. 483.

After having received dues, the Knights of Honor, if a party to the suit, could not defend it on plea of *ultra vires.*

Niblack, § 7; Brice, Ultra Vires, 729; *Ohio & M. R. Co.* v. *McCarthy*, 96 U. S. 258 (24 L. ed. 693); *Hitchcock* v. *Galveston*, 96 U. S. 351 (24 L. ed. 662); *Bloomington Mut. L. Ben. Asso.* v. *Blue*, 8 West. Rep. 642, 120 Ill. 121; *Holland* v. *Taylor*, 9 West. Rep. 606, 111 Ind. 121.

---

al estate the word "heirs" does not include the widow of the decedent (Drake v. Pell, 3 Edw. Ch. 251, 6 N. Y. Ch. L. ed. 646), nor the husband. Wright v. Methodist Epis. Church, Hoffm. Ch. 202, 6 N. Y. Ch. L. ed. 1115.

There is no reason for holding that the word "heirs," when applied to personal estates, has a broader or more comprehensive signification than the words "next of kin." Tillman v. Davis, 95 N. Y. 17.

In a few cases in this country, however, it has been held that the word "heirs" when applied to personal property means those that by the Statute of Distribution take the personal property in case of intestacy, and hence embraces widows. Sweet v. Dutton, 109 Mass. 579; Welsh v. Crater, 32 N. J. Eq. 177; Freeman v. Knight, 2 Ired. Eq. 72; Croom v. Herring, 4 Hawks, 393; Corbitt v. Corbitt, 1 Jones, Eq. 114; Henderson v. Henderson, 1 Jones, L. 221; Collier v. Collier, 3 Ohio St. 369; McGill's App. 61 Pa. 46; Eby's App. 84 Pa. 241; Alexander v. Wallace, 8 Lea, 569.

In Murdock v. Ward, 67 N. Y. 387, it was held that the next of kin meant relatives in blood and consequently excluded the widow. So in Luce v. Dunham, 69 N. Y. 36; Keteltas v. Keteltas, 72 N. Y. 312.

The legal rights of the heirs or distributees to property of deceased persons cannot be defeated, except by valid devise of such property to other persons. Chamberlain v. Taylor, 7 Cent. Rep. 221, 105 N. Y. 185.

The beneficiary cannot be changed except in the manner provided in the contract.

Supreme Council L. of H. v. *Smith*, 45 N. J. Eq. 466; *Luhrs* v. *Luhrs*, 24 N. Y. S. R. 252.

Though the constitution of an association provides that certificates shall be payable only to the family or some one dependent on members, yet this question can only be raised by the association; and payment by them into court of the amount of the certificate waives the objection.

Knights of Honor v. *Watson*, 64 N. H. 517.

Battle, J., delivered the opinion of the court:

On the 4th day of September, 1883, the Supreme Lodge of the Knights of Honor issued to James W. Johnson, a member of DeVall's Bluff Lodge, No. 2,172, a local lodge of the Knights of Honor located at DeVall's Bluff, in this State, a benefit certificate for the sum of $2,000, payable to his heirs at his death. At that time Johnson was unmarried, and the constitution of the Supreme Lodge authorized the issuing of a benefit certificate payable on the death of a member to his family, or as he might direct. In 1884 the constitution was changed so as to authorize the issuing of a certificate to a member "payable to some member or members of his family, or person or persons dependent on him, as he may direct or designate by name, to be paid as provided by general law." After this, on the 7th of December, 1884, James W. Johnson and Laura A. Johnson, the plaintiff in this action, married; and on the 27th of February, 1886, a child was born to them, who died on the 10th of August of the same year. On the 24th of November following, James W. Johnson died without descendants, leaving Laura A., his widow, and S. M. Pate and O. T. Carr, sisters of the whole blood, and George W. Price and Salvona T. Hurt, half sister and brother, his nearest kindred, him surviving. The beneficiaries named in the certificate of the 4th of September, 1883, were never changed. The Supreme Lodge has paid the $2,000 into court; and the sisters and half sister and brother, defendants in this action, claiming to be the heirs of Johnson, and Laura A., litigate its disposition.

The first question presented for our consideration is, Who are meant by the word "heirs" in the certificate in controversy? It is a technical word. When used in any legal instrument, and there is no context to explain it, as in this case, it should be understood in its legal and technical sense. *Moody* v. *Walker*, 3 Ark. 147; *Myar* v. *Snow*, 49 Ark. 129; *Hascall* v. *Cox*, 49 Mich. 440; *Mounsey* v. *Blamire*, 4 Russ. 384; *De Beauvoir* v. *De Beauvoir*, 3 H. L. Cas. 553, 557; *Doody* v. *Higgins*, 2 Kay & J. 729; *Holloway* v. *Holloway*, 5 Ves. Jr. 401.

At law it was used to designate the persons on whom an inheritance in real estate was cast by the law on the death of the ancestor. Originally, it could not be used to designate those on whom the goods or chattel property were cast, because the law cast them upon no one. No one "was appointed by law to succeed to the deceased ancestor. On his death they became *bona vacantia*, and were seized by the king on that account, and by him, as grand almoner, applied to pious purposes, now considered superstitious, for the good of the souls of their former owner." But, since the enactment of Statutes of Distribution, it has often been used in gifts and bequests of personal property to designate the donee or legatee. As to its meaning when used in this connection, courts are not in harmony, and there is much confusion and conflict in the decisions. No useful purpose can be served by a review of the cases upon the question in this opinion. Suffice it to say that the weight of authority holds that the word "heirs," when used in any instrument to designate the persons to whom personal property is thereby transferred, given or bequeathed, and the context does not explain it, means those who would, under the Statute of Distributions, be entitled to the personal estate of the persons of whom they are mentioned as heirs in the event of death and intestacy. *Doody* v. *Higgins*, 2 Kay & J. 729; *Gittings* v. *McDermott*, 2 Myl. & K. 69; *Wingfield* v. *Wingfield*, L. R. 9 Ch. Div. 658, 26 Eng. Rep. (Moak) 422; *Sweet* v. *Dutton*, 109 Mass. 590; *Wright* v. *Methodist Epis. Church*, Hoffm. Ch. 211, 213, 6 N. Y. Ch. L. ed. 1119, 1120; *McCabe* v. *Spruil*, 1 Dev. Eq. 190; *Evans* v. *Salt*, 6 Beav. 266; *Jacobs* v. *Jacobs*, 16 Beav. 557, 560; *White* v. *Stanfield*, 6 New Eng. Rep. 56, 146 Mass. 425; *Low* v. *Smith*, 2 Jur. N. S. 344; *Houghton* v. *Kendall*, 7 Allen, 77; 2 Jur. N. S. (pt. 2) 211; *Croom* v. *Herring*, 4 Hawks, 393; *Eddings* v. *Long*, 10 Ala. 203; *Rawson* v. *Rawson*, 52 Ill. 62; *Richards* v. *Miller*, 62 Ill. 423; *Hascall* v. *Cox*, 49 Mich. 440, 441. See *Tillman* v. *Davis*, 95 N. Y. 17.

In many States where the widow is entitled to take under the Statute of Distribution, she is held to be an heir of her deceased husband as to his personal estate. But it is different in this State. Section 2522, Mansfield's Digest, provides: "When any person shall die, having title to any real estate of inheritance or personal estate not disposed of, nor otherwise limited by marriage settlement, and shall be intestate as to such estate, it shall descend and be distributed in parcenary to his kindred, male and female, subject to the payment of his debts and the widow's dower, in the following manner: *first*, to children or their descendants, in equal parts; *second*, if there be no children, then to the father, then to the mother, if no mother, then to the brothers and sisters, or their descendants, in equal parts," etc. The Statutes provide that relations of the half blood shall inherit equally with those of the whole blood in the same degree, unless the inheritance come to the intestate through an ancestor. In only one event does the widow take as an heir or distributee of her deceased husband, and that is when he died intestate, and leaves no children or their descendants, father, mother, nor their descendants, or any paternal or maternal kindred capable of inheriting. Our statutes virtually declare that she shall not take the real or personal property of her deceased husband as heir in any other event, if then. Mansf. Dig. § 2528.

It is true that section 2592, Mansfield's Digest, provides: "If a husband die, leaving a widow and no children, such widow shall be endowed of one half of the real estate of which such husband died seised, and one half of the personal estate, absolutely and in her own right." But she takes the one half of the personal estate as dower, absolutely and independently of creditors, and not as a distributive share.

In *Hill* v. *Mitchell*, 5 Ark. 618, this court said: "Distribution and dower are two separate and distinct things. One is a lien created by law on the property of the husband at the time of the marriage, which necessarily takes precedence over all other subsequent accruing rights, and attaches to the specific property, and is carved out of it. Distribution occurs after administration and the payment of debts, and the estate is then divided between the heirs and legatees. The widow is not entitled to any portion or distributive share after her dower has been allotted to her; for all that goes to the heirs or legatees after payment of debts, and the administrator is bound to distribute the residue in his hands. We have no statute giving her any portion of the personal estate as a distributive share, and that part of the common law which is in force here allows her no such interest in the personal effects of her husband."

In Illinois a statute was enacted which provides: "When there is a widow or surviving husband, and also a child or children, or descendants of such child or children, of the intestate, the widow or surviving husband shall receive as his or her absolute personal estate one third of all the personal estate of the intestate." Rev. Stat. chap. 39, par. 4.

In *Gauch* v. *St. Louis Mut. L. Ins. Co.*, 88 Ill. 251, the court held that this Statute was not intended to, and did not, make the widow an heir of her intestate husband, but defined what shall be taken as dower, and held that a policy of life insurance payable to the "legal heirs" of the person whose life was insured was payable to his children, if he left any, and that his widow was not included in the words "legal heirs."

We do not think that Laura A. was an heir of her husband, or included in the word "heirs" in the certificate in controversy. But it is contended that the brothers and sisters of Johnson are entitled to no part of the $2,000, because the constitution of the Supreme Lodge of 1884 limits the right of a member of any lodge of the Knights of Honor to name beneficiaries in a certificate issued to him to the members of his family, or those dependent on him, and they belong to neither of these classes. But this question can be raised by no one except the Supreme Lodge, and it does not. By paying the money into court, it has expressed its willingness to have it paid to Johnson's heirs. The money forms no part of his estate. The widow has no interest in it. The constitution of the Supreme Lodge of 1884 provides: "In the event of the death of all the beneficiaries designated by the member before the decease of such member, if he shall make no other disposition thereof, the benefit shall be paid to the heirs of the deceased member." The child having died before its father, Johnson left his brother and sisters his only heirs. As the Supreme Lodge by its certificate promised to pay them the $2,000, and do not object to paying, and no other person can, lawfully, they are entitled to a judgment that it be paid to them.

Judgment affirmed.

MISSOURI SUPREME COURT.

STATE OF MISSOURI, *Appt.*,
v.
William P. MCGONIGLE, Admr., etc., of Peter H. Early, Deceased, *et al.*, *Respts.*

(........Mo.........)

1. **Parol evidence may be given** to show what was said and done in the presence of the court acting in a ministerial capacity, as in the matter of approving an official bond, in order to show notice.

2. **Erasing the name of a surety** at his request and substituting another before the approval of an official bond, and without the consent or knowledge of the other sureties, discharges them, where the approval of the bond by the court was made with knowledge of the substitution, and of the fact that the other sureties had no knowledge thereof.

3. **Signing a bond as surety** and leaving it with the principal to procure other signatures and present it for acceptance and approval does not authorize the principal to discharge a person who had, or who might thereafter, become a party to the instrument.

4. **A surety who signs a bond in ignorance** of the fact that the other sureties thereon have been released by the erasure of the name of a surety cannot be held liable on the bond, as he did not intend to become the sole surety.

NOTE.—*Suretyship.*

Parol evidence may be given to show that a bond was made on condition that it should be void in a certain emergency. Field v. Biddle, 2 U. S. 2 Dall. 171 (1 L. ed. 335).

The acknowledgment of a bond by two or three sureties and its delivery will rebut any inference against its validity which might arise from the simple fact of its not having been signed by the other surety. Duncan v. United States, 32 U. S. 7 Pet. 435 (8 L. ed. 739).

A surety who signs a bond knowing that it has not been signed by the principal, but intending, nevertheless, to be himself bound as surety, may be liable on the bond. Goodyear Dental Vulcanite Co. v. Bacon, 148 Mass. 542.

The fact that a surety on a bond signed it in the expectation that his partner also would sign the bond as surety, but that for some reason he failed to do so, will not relieve him from liability. Whittaker v. Richards (Pa.) 7 L. R. A. 749.

Where an erasure of one of the sureties' names in an official bond was made after another surety signed the instrument, and without knowledge or consent of the latter, he is discharged. United States v. Conklin ("Rogers v. The Marshal") 68 U. S. 1 Wall. 644 (17 L. ed. 714).

After a surety has received and approved a bond given in a claim suit, the subsequent signature of another surety thereto will not vitiate the bond or release the former surety. But the signature of the additional surety is without consideration and without effect, as the right of the obligor to the possession of the property in suit was perfected when the bond was first approved. Anderson v. Bellenger, 87 Ala. 334.

See also 41 L. R. A. 823.

5. The doctrine of spoliation has nothing to do with the question of the effect of erasing the name of a surety, before the approval of a bond, upon the liability of other sureties.

6. An estoppel cannot arise to prevent sureties on an official bond from insisting upon their release from liability on account of the alteration of the bond before approval, from the fact that they permitted the principal to perform his official duties without objection for two years after the bond was approved, if it is not shown that they had knowledge of the alteration.

(*Sherwood and Barclay, JJ., dissent.*)

(May 19, 1890.)

APPEAL by plaintiff from a judgment of the Circuit Court for Knox County in favor of defendants in an action brought to recover the amount due by a defaulting tax collector from the sureties on his official bond. *Affirmed.*

The facts are fully stated in the opinion.

Messrs. **John M. Wood,** *Atty Gen.*, **L. F. Cottey** and **O. D. Jones,** for appellant:

The Statute requires county courts to "keep just and faithful records of their proceedings." The record does not show that Dailing's name was ever on the bond, or erased therefrom. The acts and proceedings of the county court are known alone by its record.

Medlin v. *Platte County*, 8 Mo. 235; *Milan* v. *Pemberton*, 12 Mo. 599; *Dennison* v. *St. Louis County*, 33 Mo. 168; *Reppy* v. *Jefferson County*, 47 Mo. 66; *Maupin* v. *Franklin County*, 67 Mo. 327; *Mobley* v. *Nave*, 67 Mo. 546; *Johnson County* v. *Wood*, 84 Mo. 515; *Bank of Commerce* v. *Hoeber*, 8 Mo. App. 171; *Riley* v. *Pettis County*, 96 Mo. 318.

Reid did not make the erasure. He had nothing to do with it. The bond was in the possession of the court for its approval and the erasure was spoliation and not alteration.

Medlin v. *Platte County*, *supra*.

After a bond has been delivered to the proper court or officer, it is entirely out of the power of anyone to release the bondsmen by merely erasing their names therefrom.

Jones v. *State*, 7 Mo. 82; *James* v. *Dixon*, 21 Mo. 538; *State* v. *Farmer*, 54 Mo. 439; *Graves* v. *McHugh*, 58 Mo. 500; *Brown* v. *Weatherby*, 71 Mo. 152; *State* v. *Richardson*, 29 Mo. App. 595.

The county court had no authority to release a solvent surety; and if it exceeds its authority, the county or State will not be bound by its unauthorized act.

Wolcott v. *Lawrence County*, 26 Mo. 275; *State* v. *Clark County*, 41 Mo. 49; *State* v. *State Bank*, 45 Mo. 538; *Steines* v. *Franklin County*, 48 Mo. 177; *State* v. *Hays*, 52 Mo. 579; *Wood* v. *Williams*, 61 Mo. 63; *Saline County* v. *Wilson*, Id. 239; *Maupin* v. *Franklin County*, 67 Mo. 330; *Dixon* v. *Livingston County*, 70 Mo. 240; *Book* v. *Earl*, 3 West. Rep. 340, 87 Mo. 256; *Sturgeon* v. *Hampton*, 3 West. Rep. 844, 88 Mo. 218; *State* v. *Harris*, 96 Mo. 37.

Defendants must be held on the ground of estoppel. They had notice of the record of approval of said bond by the county court, since all men are bound to take notice of the public records of all courts. They knew that Reid was holding office by virtue of their suretyship for him, and they kept silent while the public revenues were being squandered by their principal.

State v. *Potter*, 63 Mo. 212; *State* v. *Williams*, 77 Mo. 463; *Lionberger* v. *Krieger*, 4 West. Rep. 431, 88 Mo. 160; *Wright* v. *Lang*, 66 Ala. 389; *Burns* v. *Campbell*, 71 Ala. 271; *Herring* v. *Skaggs*, 73 Ala. 446; *Evans* v. *Daughtry*, 84 Ala. 68; *Crawn* v. *Com.* 84 Va. 282; *Middleton* v. *State*, 120 Ind. 166; *Dair* v. *United States*, 83 U S. 16 Wall. 1 (21 L. ed. 491); Bigelow, Estoppel, 3d ed. 454, and cases cited.

Dailing's name was not signed to the bond, nor written in the body thereof, when the others signed, and they cannot be released by its erasure.

Taylor County v. *King*, 73 Iowa, 153; *State* v. *Potter*, 63 Mo. 212.

The surety invested the principal with an apparent authority to deliver the bond, and there was nothing on its face or in any of the attending circumstances to apprise the officials who accepted it that there was anything to preclude its acceptance. The surety is therefore alone in fault in the matter.

State v. *Potter*, 63 Mo. 212-226; *Hern* v. *Nichols*, 1 Salk. 289; *State* v. *Baker*, 64 Mo. 167; *State* v. *Modrel*, 69 Mo. 152; *State* v. *Hewitt*, 72 Mo. 604; *Wolff* v. *Shaeffer*, 74 Mo. 155, 156.

Whenever an alteration has been made by common consent of the parties or before delivery, the instrument will not be avoided.

1 Am. & Eng. Encyclop. Law, p. 503; *Ravisies* v. *Alston*, 5 Ala. 297; *Stewart* v. *Preston*, 1 Fla. 10; *Wickes* v. *Caulk*, 5 Harr. & J. 36; *Boston* v. *Benson*, 12 Cush. 61; *Den* v. *Wright*, 7 N. J. L. 175; *Campbell* v. *Roe*, 2 Hawks, 33; *Britton* v. *Stanley*, 4 Whart. 114.

An alteration, although material, cannot invalidate a written instrument when made by a stranger to the contract.

1 Am. & Eng. Encyclop. Law, p. 505; *Bigelow* v. *Stilphen*, 35 Vt. 521; *Boyd* v. *McConnell*, 10 Humph. (Tenn.) 68; *Robertson* v. *Hay*, 91 Pa. 242; *Williams* v. *Moseley*, 2 Fla. 304; *Van Brunt* v. *Eoff*, 35 Barb. 501; *Hunt* v. *Gray*, 35 N. J. L. 227; *Drum* v. *Drum*, 133 Mass. 566; *Adams* v. *Frye*, 3 Met. 103; *Lubbering* v. *Kohlbrecher*, 22 Mo. 596.

If a surety permits his principal, with his knowledge and consent, by means of the bond unauthorizedly delivered, to possess the fund and fill the office, he will be estopped to make the defense made here.

Wright v. *Lang*, 66 Ala. 389; *Burns* v. *Campbell*, 71 Ala. 271; *Herring* v. *Skaggs*, 73 Ala. 446; *Dair* v. *United States*, 83 U. S. 16 Wall. 1 (21 L. ed. 491); *Canon* v. *Grigsby*, 3 West. Rep. 87, 116 Ill. 151; *Prouty* v. *Wilson*, 123 Mass. 297.

Mr. **G. R. Balthrope,** for respondents:

The evidence clearly and emphatically shows a material alteration and change made in the obligations and responsibilities resting upon these respondents by virtue of said bond, and said bond by reason of said alteration and changes so made is void as to these respondents.

Martin v. *Thomas*, 65 U. S. 24 How. 315 (16 L. ed. 689); *Smith* v. *United States*, 69 U. S. 2 Wall. 219 (17 L. ed. 788); *State* v. *Craig*, 58 Iowa, 238; *State* v. *Churchill*, 48 Ark. 426; *Osborne* v. *Van Houten*, 45 Mich. 444; *Bracken County Comrs. Sinking Fund* v. *Daum*, 80 Ky. 388.

Kearns, having signed the bond after Dailing, will in law be presumed to have signed it upon the faith of Dailing's signature being upon it and upon the belief that he would be held as a co-surety.

Martin v. *Thomas* and *Smith* v. *United States*, *supra*.

And those who signed before Dailing were released because of failure to secure the proper number of sureties.

State v. *Craig*, *supra;* Murfree, Official Bonds, §§ 53, 760; Brandt, Sur. § 385; *Osborne* v. *Van Houten*, *Bracken County Comrs. Sinking Fund* v. *Daum* and *State* v. *Churchill*, *supra*.

The county court being the agent for the State in receiving and approving the bond, its acts and knowledge in the premises should be imputed to the State.

Hord v. *Taubman*, 79 Mo. 101, 108.

The doctrine of estoppel will not apply, for the sureties knew nothing of the alteration having been made.

Frederick v. *Missouri River, Ft. S. & G. R. Co.* 82 Mo. 402; *Burke* v. *Adams*, 80 Mo. 504; *St. Louis & S. F. R. Co.* v. *Evans & H. F. B. Co.* 85 Mo. 307.

Messrs. **Blair & Marchand** also for respondents.

Black, *J.*, delivered the opinion of the court:

The State, as plaintiff, brought this suit against the sureties on the official bond of Peter J. Reid, who was elected collector of Knox County in November, 1884. Reid seems to have paid over the county revenues collected by him, but he made default to the State in the amount of $14,092, and hence this suit. The case was tried by the court without a jury, the trial resulting in a judgment for the defendants, to reverse which the State prosecutes this appeal. Many matters of defense were set up in the answer filed by the defendants, and evidence was received in support of them; but the court at the close of the trial excluded the evidence bearing upon these defenses, except that offered in support of that part of the answer which, in effect, states that the bond sued upon is not the obligation of the defendants. This is therefore the only defense before us on this appeal.

In August, 1885, Reid presented to the County Court of Knox County a bond, in the penal sum of $30,000, for approval, signed by himself and the following sureties, in the following order: P. H. Early, Patrick Flemming, I. D. McPike, Thomas Bresnen, George Dailing and Thomas Kearnes. At the same time, Dailing, one of the sureties, appeared before the court, which was then in session, and asked that his name be taken off the bond, assigning as a reason therefor that he signed upon the understanding that James Kelly would also sign, and that Kelly's name had not been procured. The matter was talked over in the presence of the court, and the name of Dailing was erased by the clerk in the presence of all of the judges, and of Dailing and of Reid, but in the absence of, and without the knowledge or consent of, any of the other sureties. Some of the evidence is to the effect that the erasure was made by the clerk at the instance of the court, the other parties present consenting. The presiding justice then told Reid he must procure other sureties. Thereupon Reid took the bond, and in one or two days again presented it to the court, with the name of John Cain signed on the line, and at the place, from which Dailing's name had been erased. The court then approved the bond by an order dated the 4th of August, 1885. Cain, who signed by making his mark, did not know that Dailing had ever been a party to the instrument. The other sureties signed at different dates, and at the office of Reid. Nothing is said about any erasure in the body of the bond, and the inference is that the names of the sureties had not been inserted at that place when the bond was first presented for approval. Dailing was a substantial property owner, while Cain appears to have been in debt to the amount of the full value of all of his property. The defendants asked no instructions. The State asked one only on this branch of the case, to the effect that the evidence concerning the erasure of the name of Dailing constituted no defense, which the court refused. The plaintiff is therefore here standing on a demurrer to the evidence of the defendants.

1. The State places much reliance upon the proposition that the circuit court should have excluded all of the parol evidence of what was said and done in the presence of the judges of the county court. This contention is based upon the ground that the acts of the county court can be shown alone by the record. These courts are required to keep a just and faithful record of their proceedings, and must speak by and through the record. The county courts, however, in approving these official bonds, act in a ministerial, and not a judicial, capacity. *State* v. *Lafayette County Ct.* 41 Mo. 221; *State* v. *Howard County Ct.* Id. 248; *Re Thompson*, 45 Mo. 55.

They are made the agents of the State and counties for the purpose of accepting such bonds. The parol evidence was not offered in this case for the purpose of showing any order or judgment of the court, but for the purpose of showing that the court had full notice and knowledge of the fact that the name of one of the sureties had been erased, and that, too, without the knowledge or consent of the other sureties. For this purpose the evidence was properly received. Notice to the court, when thus acting in a ministerial capacity, may be shown by evidence which would be sufficient in case of other agents. It is not to be expected that all the information which the court may have while transacting such business will be spread upon the record. The law does not require it.

2. The plaintiff cites, and with confidence relies upon, a line of authorities, of which *State* v. *Potter*, 63 Mo. 212, is the leading one in this court. That was a suit on the bond of Turley, as guardian of certain minors, with Potter and another as sureties. Potter's defense was that he signed the bond on the condition that it would be signed by one Bothrick as surety and that it was filed by Turley without having procured the signature of Bothrick. Says the court: "Here the surety who defends this action had invested the principal with an apparent authority to deliver the bond; and there was nothing on the face of the bond, or in any of the attending circumstances, to ap-

prise the official who accepted it that there was any secret agreement which should preclude the acceptance of the bond." The defense was accordingly overruled, and the doctrine of that case overruling former cases has been followed in subsequent cases. *State* v. *Baker*, 64 Mo. 167; *State* v. *Modrel*, 69 Mo. 152; *State* v. *Hewitt*, 72 Mo. 604; *Wolff* v. *Schaeffer*, 74 Mo. 154.

It is now well-established law in this and other jurisdictions that, where a surety signs a bond, and leaves it in the hands of the principal to be delivered only upon the condition that it is signed by another person, and the principal delivers the bond to the obligee without complying with the condition, and the obligee takes it without notice of the conditional agreement, the surety will be bound. *Dair* v. *United States*, 88 U. S. 16 Wall. 1 [21 L. ed. 491]; *State* v. *Peck*, 53 Me. 284; *Taylor County* v. *King*, 73 Iowa, 153; *State* v. *Pepper*, 31 Ind. 76; *Millett* v. *Parker*, 2 Met. (Ky.) 608.

The same rule applies where the surety signs a bond leaving a blank space for the penalty, and the principal fills it with a larger amount than that agreed upon by the principal and surety. *Butler* v. *United States*, 88 U. S. 21 Wall. 274 [22 L. ed. 615].

In these cases of conditional agreements, it is the surety who puts trust and confidence in the principal, and not the obligee, and, if anyone is to be the loser, it should be the surety; for he puts it in the power of the principal to create the mischief complained of. The bond having been accepted and acted upon, the surety is estopped from setting up an unperformed and undisclosed condition. The cases before cited all proceed upon the ground that there is nothing upon the face of the bond, as disclosed by the attending circumstances, to apprise the obligee or accepting officer of a state of facts which should prevent its acceptance. When the county court accepted the bond in question, it had full knowledge of the fact that the name of Dailing as one of the sureties had been erased, and the name of Cain substituted therefor. The circumstances all tend to show that the court knew this had been done without the knowledge or consent of the other sureties. The court was in no manner misled or deceived, and there is no room or ground for the application of any principle of estoppel as against the sureties. The cases before cited, and the principles of law upon which they are ruled, do not meet the question which we are bound to decide in this case.

3. The surety has the right to stand upon the very terms of his contract; and it is well-settled law that any material variation or alteration in the obligation or contract upon which he is bound will discharge him, unless he consents to the alteration before made, or by some subsequent act ratifies it. Burge, Suretyship, 214; Baylies, Sureties, 260.

The principle of law just stated is not controverted by the plaintiff, but its application to the case in hand is denied. It is therefore deemed best to make a concise statement of the facts of some of the cases relied upon by the defendants.

Martin v. *Thomas*, 65 U. S. 24 How. 315 [16 L. ed. 689], was a suit upon a delivery bond executed to a marshal in a replevin suit. After the bond had been executed by the principal and three sureties, the principal, with the consent of the marshal, and without the consent of the sureties, erased his name. This erasure, it was held, constituted a variation of the contract of the sureties, and discharged them from all liability on the bond.

Smith v. *United States*, 69 U. S. 2 Wall. 219 [17 L. ed. 788], was a suit upon a bond given by Pine as marshal, the bond having been approved by the district judge. Smith, one of the sureties, defended on the ground that the bond was not his deed. The evidence showed that Smith, Hoyne and others had signed the bond as co-sureties for Pine. Hoyne became dissatisfied, and requested Pine to erase his name, which was done, but by whom did not appear. The name of Hoyne was erased when the bond was presented to the judge for approval and the judge had been told by Hoyne that he wanted his name erased. The remaining sureties, except Smith, appeared before the judge, and acknowledged the execution of the bond. Smith did not acknowledge it, and did not know that Hoyne's name had been erased. It was held that the sureties who acknowledged the bond after the erasure were estopped from interposing the alteration as a defense; but, as to Smith, it was held that the erasure was a material alteration of the obligation to which he became a party, and that he was therefore discharged.

The suit in *State* v. *Craig*, 58 Iowa, 238, was upon the bond of the warden of the penitentiary. There were some eleven sureties as the bond stood when produced in evidence, and the defense was material alteration. The evidence showed that one Smith signed it as a surety after the first seven signatures had been obtained, and the other sureties signed after Smith. Before the names of the sureties had been inserted in the body of the bond, and before approval, Smith's name was erased without the consent of any of the other sureties. The persons signing before Smith did not know that he had signed until after the suit had been commenced. It was held that though Craig, the principal, had been intrusted with the bond to procure signatures, and present it for approval, yet, as to the sureties signing subsequent to Smith, Craig was not authorized to deliver the bond after it had been altered to their prejudice, and that those sureties were discharged because the instrument sued upon was not their contract. The sureties who signed before Smith were also discharged on the ground that it would be presumed that they signed with the understanding that other sureties would be procured in such a way that all would be held and bound as co-sureties.

In the case of *Bracken County Comrs. Sinking Fund* v. *Daum*, 80 Ky. 388, the suit was based upon a sheriff's bond, and the defense was *non est factum*. Ten persons signed a power of attorney authorizing the county clerk to sign their names to the bond. At least two of the names were erased before the power of attorney was delivered to the clerk. It was held that, if the names were erased without the knowledge or consent of the other sureties, and with the knowledge or by the direction of the county judge, whose duty it was to take and approve the bond, then the plaintiff could not recover. The court said, in substance, that it was the duty of officers intrusted with authority to take and approve official bonds to use ordinary care and prudence to protect the sureties, as well as to protect the public. Here the bond, when first presented to the county court for its approval, was a completed bond. As then presented, it expressed the contract of the sureties. They agreed to be jointly and severally bound, but they did not agree that the name of Cain should be substituted for Dailing. The alteration in the obligation was a material one, and was made in the presence of the county court, and without the knowledge or consent of the sureties; and the bond as approved is not the obligation of the defendants. The authorities cited are in point, and all lead to the conclusion just stated. Some of them, and others which we have not cited, go further in favor of the discharge of sureties than we are disposed to go. If the name of Dailing had been erased, and that of Cain substituted, without the knowledge of the county court, then we have no hesitancy in saying that the sureties should not be discharged, because, by intrusting the bond to Reid, they put it in his power to mislead and deceive the court, and they should suffer the consequences. Here the court was not misled, but accepted the bond knowing that it had been altered without the knowledge or consent of the other sureties. Under these circumstances the court had no right to disregard the rights of the other sureties.

The argument is made that when these sureties signed the bond, and left it with Reid, the principal, to procure other signatures, and present it to the county court, they thereby made him their agent, and are bound by his acts. It is to be remembered that the county court had full knowledge of all of the facts. So that the argument, to have any bearing on this case, must go to the extent of saying that Reid had invested in him the right to discharge at pleasure any one or more of the persons who became parties to the bond; that for this purpose he could of right represent the sureties as well as himself. This is carrying the doctrine of implied powers entirely too far. Each of the sureties, when signing the bond and leaving it with Reid, did doubtless make him their agent, for the purpose of procuring other sureties, and for the purpose of presenting the bond for acceptance and approval. But it cannot be said they thereby gave him authority to discharge anyone who had, or might thereafter, become a party to the obligation.

As said in *State* v. *Craig, supra*, the principal was not authorized to deliver the instrument after it had been altered to the prejudice of the sureties. Nor does the fact that the sureties knew the bond had to be approved furnish any ground for the inference that they authorized the alteration. *Smith* v. *United States, supra*.

It is true the defendant Cain signed the bond after the alteration had been made, but the evidence is to the effect that he was wholly ignorant of the fact that Dailing had ever been a party to the bond. As to him the bond is void, because he signed it upon the supposition that the other parties were in fact co-sureties, and he never undertook to become the sole surety. *Howe* v. *Peabody*, 2 Gray, 556.

But it is further argued that the erasure of Dailing's name was spoliation only, and did not affect the liability of anyone on the bond. If the bond had been delivered, and the erasure thereafter made by county officials, then *Medlin* v. *Platte County*, 8 Mo. 235, would be an authority for the position thus taken by plaintiff. It is, in effect, said in that case that the term "alteration" is usually applied to the act of a party entitled under the instrument, and imports an improper design; but spoliation is the act of a stranger, without the participation of a party interested. It is also held that county officials who have the custody of instruments in writing are strangers, within the meaning of the rule, so that, if these officials deface such instruments, their acts are but spoliation. To the same effect is *State* v. *Berg*, 50 Ind. 496. Here there never was a time when the State or county held Dailing as a surety, for the evidence is all to the effect that his name was erased before the bond was delivered or accepted. The question in this case is whether the bond sued upon is the deed of the sureties, and we do not see that the doctrine of spoliation has anything to do with this controversy.

4. The plaintiff insists that the court erred in refusing an instruction to the effect that, if the bond was approved by the court on 4th August, 1885, and the defendants knew that Reid occupied the office of collector, and collected the revenues, for the years 1885 and 1886, and made no objection thereto, then they are estopped from making the defense that the bond was altered by the erasure of Dailing's name. There is an abundance of evidence tending to establish all the facts stated in this refused instruction, but there is not a word of evidence tending to show that the defendants during this time knew that Dailing's name had been erased. The only evidence to which our attention is called is that they knew nothing about the erasure. An estoppel cannot arise until it is shown that they knew of the alteration, and thereafter made no objection to the performance by Reid of official duties by virtue of having given the bond in question. No such state of facts is shown, or hypothetically stated, in the instruction; and it was therefore properly refused.

It is useless to notice the other minor suggestions made by the plaintiff. They do not meet the real and only question in this case. The case has been twice argued, and we can come to no other conclusion than that before indicated. We have endeavored to lay it down as the better law that sureties on these official bonds ought not to be discharged until they show knowledge on the part of the accepting officers of a state of facts which should have precluded the acceptance of the bond, be it a conditional contract between principal and surety, or an alteration of the bond as executed by the surety. That has been done in this case. Common information, without any special knowledge of the law, ought to have told these county judges that it was an improper thing to strike off the name of one of the sureties without the consent of the other sureties.

The judgment is affirmed.

Sherwood and **Barclay**, *JJ.*, dissent; the other Judges concur.

Petition for rehearing overruled.

MASSACHUSETTS SUPREME JUDICIAL COURT.

BOSTON SAFE DEPOSIT & TRUST CO.
v.
Benjamin F. COFFIN *et al.*

(....Mass.....)

1. The true meaning of words used in a will is to be arrived at by considering them not only in their relation to the clause immediately in question but to the whole will.

2. The mere grammatical or ordinary sense of words used in a will is not to be adhered to if it would be repugnant or inconsistent with the remainder of the instrument.

3. Where an intention to dispose of the whole of an estate appears in a will a partial intestacy should not be recognized unless the deficiencies of expression are such as will compel it.

4. When a conviction that a testator must necessarily have intended an interest to be given which is not bequeathed by express and formal words is produced by a reading of the whole will, the court will supply the defect by implication and so mould the language of the testator as to carry into effect as far as possible the

NOTE.—*Construction of will; intention of testator governs.*

The first and great rule in the exposition of wills, to which all other rules must bend, is that the intention of the testator expressed in his will shall prevail, provided it be consistent with the rules of law. Smith v. Bell, 31 U. S. 6 Pet. 68 (8 L. ed. 322); Lambert v. Paine, 7 U. S. 3 Cranch, 97 (2 L. ed. 377).

It is the cardinal rule, and if that intent can be clearly perceived, and is not contrary to some positive rule of law, it must prevail, although in giving effect to it some words should be rejected, or so restrained in their application as to change the literal meaning of the particular sentence. Finlay v. King, 28 U. S. 3 Pet. 346 (7 L. ed. 701).

The intention of the testator must prevail unless it is in conflict with some fundamental principle of law. Randall v. Josselyn, 4 New Eng. Rep. 909, 59 Vt. 557; *Re* Cayuga County Surrogate, 46 Hun, 657; *Re* Boardman, 5 New Eng. Rep. 781, R. I. Index BB, 101; Decker v. Decker, 10 West. Rep. 344, 121 Ill. 341; Emery v. Union Society, 4 New Eng. Rep. 542, 79 Me. 334; Randall v. Josselyn and *Re* Cayuga County Surrogate, *supra;* Myrick v. Heard, 31 Fed. Rep. 241; Davenport v. Sargent, 2 New Eng. Rep. 549, 63 N. H. 538; Kennard v. Kennard, 1 New Eng. Rep. 168, 63 N. H. 303; McKelvey v. McKelvey, 1 West. Rep. 69, 43 Ohio St. 213; Summit v. Yount, 6 West. Rep. 921, 109 Ind. 506; Allen v. Craft, 7 West. Rep. 518, 109 Ind. 476; Wetter v. United Hydraulic C. P. Co. 75 Ga. 540; Middleswarth v. Blackmore, 74 Pa. 414; Schott's Estate, 78 Pa. 40; Reck's App. Id. 432; Webb v. Hitchins, 105 Pa. 91; Banta v. Boyd, 6 West. Rep. 87, 118 Ill. 186; *Re* Stewart, 74 Cal. 98; Jasper v. Jasper, 17 Or. 590; Covenhoven v. Shuler, 2 Paige, 122, 2 N. Y. Ch. L. ed. 839; Tuttle v. Heidermann, 5 Redf. 202; Crosby v. Wendell, 6 Paige, 548, 3 N. Y. Ch. L. ed. 1096; Pond v. Bergh, 10 Paige, 140, 4 N. Y. Ch. L. ed. 919; Parks v. Parks, 9 Paige, 107, 4 N. Y. Ch. L. ed. 627; Van Nostrand v. Moore, 52 N. Y. 12; Betts v. Betts, 4 Abb. N. C. 317; Amory v. Lord, 9 N. Y. 419; Irving v. DeKay, 9 Paige, 521, 4 N. Y. Ch. L. ed. 800; Wetmore v. St. Luke's Hospital, 56 Hun, 313.

A rule of law may overrule the intention of a testator in four instances: (1) where the devise would make a perpetuity; (2) where it would put the freehold in abeyance; (3) where chattels are limited as inheritances; (4) where a fee is limited on a fee. Ruston v. Ruston, 2 U. S. 2 Dall. 243 (1 L. ed. 365).

Effect is to be given to the intent of a testator, irrespective of the particular phraseology of the will, when not repugnant to the terms of the instrument. McLean v. Freeman, 70 N. Y. 88; Pearsall v. Simpson, 15 Ves. Jr. 29; Hutton v. Simpson, 2 Vern, 722; Meadows v. Parry, 1 Ves. & B. 124; Murray v. Jones, 2 Ves. & B. 313; Mackinnon v. Sewell, 5 Sim. 78; Avelyn v. Ward, 1 Ves. Sr. 420; Bainbridge v. Cream, 16 Beav. 25.

When the language of a will is plain, no intention of testator, except that expressed, is sought after. Greenough v. Cass, 5 New Eng. Rep. 53, 64 N. H. 326.

The intention of the testator when clear must prevail over the grammatical meaning of words. Williams v. Western Star Lodge, 38 La. Ann. 620.

The intent is not to be overcome by an ambiguous direction in a subsequent part of the will. McGuire's App. (Pa.) 9 Cent. Rep 650.

All mere technical rules of construction must give way to the plainly expressed intention of the testator, if that intention be lawful. Reck's App. 78 Pa. 432; Colton v. Colton, 127 U. S. 300 (32 L. ed. 138).

Construction of will. See Dougherty v. Rogers (Ind.) 3 L. R. A. 849.

Rules of construction; intention to govern.

It is the duty of the court to determine the meaning from the will itself. *Re* Huntington, 6 Cent. Rep. 217, 103 N. Y. 677; Kirkland v. Conway, 3 West. Rep. 478, 116 Ill. 438; Banta v. Boyd, 6 West. Rep. 87, 118 Ill. 186; Thomas v. Thomas, 7 West. Rep. 67, 108 Ind. 576; Pugh v. Pugh, 3 West. Rep. 661, 105 Ind. 552; Campbell v. Crater, 95 N. C. 156.

It is the duty of the court to reconcile all the language defined, if possible; and the intention derived from the language is to be the polar star, to guide in the construction to be given. Lynch v. Pendergast, 67 Barb. 506; Auburn Theolog. Sem. v. Kellogg, 16 N. Y. 83; Hawley v. James, 7 Paige, 213, 4 N. Y. Ch. L. ed. 129.

It is bound to give that construction which shall carry out the intention of the testator, if such intention can be gathered from the terms of the will. Ford v. Ford (Mich.) April 11, 1890.

It is authorized to put itself in the position occupied by a testator, in order, in view of the circumstances then existing, to discover from that standpoint what the testator intended by his will. Lee v. Simpson, 134 U. S. 572 (33 L. ed. 1038).

It should not seek the intention in particular words and phrases, or confine it by technical objections, but should find it by construing the provisions of the will with the aid of the context, and by considering what seems to be the entire scheme of the will. Riker v. Cromwell, 113 N. Y. 115.

The court will look at the circumstances under which the devisor made the will, as, the state of his property, of his family and the like. Kaufman v. Breckinridge, 5 West. Rep. 154, 117 Ill. 305; Sager v. Galloway, 4 Cent. Rep. 681, 113 Pa. 500; Worth v. Worth, 95 N. C. 239; Byrnes v. Stillwell, 5 Cent. Rep. 402, 103 N. Y. 453.

The interpretation, being the ascertainment of the fact of the testator's intention, is ordinarily determined by the natural weight of competent evidence of that fact, and not by artificial technical

See also 14 L. R. A. 125.

intention which it is of opinion that be has on the whole sufficiently declared.

5. If a testator divides his estate into a number of parcels equal to the number of his children living and deceased, and manifests a purpose to have each branch of his family have one portion, only providing for a devise over in case a particular branch becomes extinct, and in disposing of the portion of a deceased child provides that the income of it shall be divided among her three children during their lives and in case one dies leaving issue one third of the principal shall be given to them absolutely, but in case there is no issue his share of the income shall be divided between the survivors, but does not dispose of the principal in such event, in case two die without issue and the other afterwards dies leaving issue the principal will all be divided between such issue, and no part of it will be given to the heirs and next of kin of the testator.

(June, 1890.)

RESERVATION from the Supreme Judicial Court for Suffolk County (Holmes, *J.*) for the opinion of the full court of a suit for the construction of a certain clause in the will of Jared Coffin, deceased.

The case sufficiently appears in the opinion.

Mr. **John E. Farnham** for the children of William F. Hastings.

Messrs. **J. Willard** and **Henry G. Nichols** for certain of testator's heirs and next of kin.

rules. Bodwell v. Dickerman, 2 New Eng. Rep. 282, 63 N. H. 446.

The law does not decide upon conjectures, but upon plain, reasonable and certain expressions of intention, found on the face of the will. Wright v. Page, 23 U. S. 10 Wheat. 204 (6 L. ed. 803).

Neither does it speculate on the motives which might have governed the testator. Towle v. Delano, 4 New Eng. Rep. 178, 144 Mass. 95.

When the intention is in doubt, courts will favor such intent as will hold to the vesting of the estate, and a literal interpretation of the words may be departed from. The court frequently rejects strictly grammatical sense to carry into effect such intent. McKinstry v. Sanders, 2 Thomp. & C. 191.

It was said by *Sir* William Jones, more than two hundred years since, that a case upon a will had no brother and therefore that authorities in point in such cases could not be expected. Clark v. Hornthal, 47 Miss. 499.

Each case which involves judicial construction, presenting its peculiar facts, must be controlled by the general statement that the testator's intention, clearly expressed, or necessarily implied, must be carried out. Manson v. Manson, 8 Abb. N. C. 123; Lupton v. Lupton, 2 Johns. Ch. 614, 1 N. Y. Ch. L. ed. 512.

If effect cannot, consistently with the rules of law, be given to the entire will, or an entire provision in a will, any part of it may be sustained which is conformable to the rules of law, and which can be separated from the residue without doing violence to the testator's general intention. Oxley v. Lane, 35 N. Y. 349; Cane v. Gott, 24 Wend. 641, 666; DeKay v. Irving, 5 Denio, 646; Lang v. Ropke, 5 Sandf. 363, 371; Williams v. Williams, 8 N. Y. 525; Savage v. Burnham, 17 N. Y. 561, 572.

General and particular intent.

Where there is a general and particular intent apparent upon the face of the will, the general intent, although first expressed, shall control and overrule the particular. Sheriff v. Brown, 3 Cent. Rep. 770, 5 Mackey, 172.

If the court can see a general intention consistent with the rules of law, but the testator has attempted to carry it into effect in a way that is not permitted, the court is to give effect to the general intention though the particular mode shall fail. Inglis v. Sailor's Snug Harbor, 28 U. S. 3 Pet. 99 (7 L. ed. 617).

The general intention of the testator in the disposal of his estate can be carried into effect, although his directions to delay the final division should be illegal, and consequently invalid in whole or in part. Converse v. Kellogg, 7 Barb. 595; Irving v. DeKay, 9 Paige, 521, 4 N. Y. Ch. L. ed. 800.

The failure of a particular trust or direction should not invalidate the residue of the will. Manice v. Manice, 43 N. Y. 384; Kane v. Gott, 24 Wend. 666; Savage v. Burnham, 17 N. Y. 576; Oxley v. Lane, 35 N. Y. 349; Harrison v. Harrison, 36 N. Y. 543; Schettler v. Smith, 41 N. Y. 328.

Full effect should be given to the particular intent, as well as to the general intent, of the testator, so far as his particular intent can be ascertained by the will and is consistent with the rules of law, and with his general intent, which general intent must control in a will. Bonard's Will, 16 Abb. Pr. N. S. 204; Clark v. Hornthal, 47 Miss. 239.

A general intent is of weight in determining what was intended by particular devises or bequests. Given v. Hilton, 95 U. S. 591 (24 L. ed. 458).

Where, from the language of a will, there is no doubt as to the testato:'s intention, the mandatory provisions of the will may be broadened and supplied by the chancellor, in order to carry out the intention of the testator. Peynado v. Peynado, 82 Ky. 5.

Although a clear gift cannot be cut down by a doubtful expression in the will, yet when a predominant purpose is apparent, but a doubt arises as to the method devised to effect that purpose, such doubt should be so resolved as to accomplish the object of testator, by presuming that he intended a legal and not an illegal method. Crozier v. Bray, 120 N. Y. 366.

Intent must be clear.

The intention to supply the lack of technical terms in a will must be clear and manifest. Busby v. Busby, 1 U. S. 1 Dall. 226 (1 L. ed. 111).

The rule of construction which seems to have prevailed is, that the inference from the will need not be irresistible or such as to exclude all doubts possible to be raised, but must nevertheless be such as to leave no hesitation in the mind of the court, and must not rest upon mere conjecture. The intention must be clear so that no other reasonable inference can be made. *Re* Vowers, 113 N. Y. 572; Grout v. Hapgood, 13 Pick. 164.

Devises by implication are sustainable only upon the principle of carrying into effect the intention of the testator; and unless it appears, upon an examination of the whole will, that such must have been the intention, there is no devise by implication. Post v. Hover, 33 N. Y. 599.

An expression in a will of an intention on the part of the testator to convey property, at a future time, to his daughter-in-law, cannot be construed to be a devise. Hurlbut v. Hutton, 4 Cent. Rep. 409, 42 N. J. Eq. 15.

To create a devise by inference the implication must be a necessary one; there must be such a strong probability of an intention to devise that an intent to the contrary cannot be supposed. *Ibid.*

No legacy will be implied unless it is necessary to carry out the manifest and plain intent of the testator, which would fail unless such implication be allowed. Bartlett v. Patton, 5 L. R. A. 523, 33 W. Va. 71.

Devens, *J.*, delivered the opinion of the court:

The whole of the testator's estate was devised and bequeathed to three trustees, and the sixth clause of the will of Jared Coffin, the construction of which is sought by the bill in the case at bar, is as follows: "Sixth: That they, the said Whitney, Nickols and Kelly, and the survivor of them, shall, during the lifetime of George N. Hastings, William F. Hastings and Henry H. Hastings, children of my deceased daughter Emeline Hastings, wife of Thomas Nelson Hastings of Cambridge in the said County of Middlesex, pay over to them respectively in equal shares the interest, rents, income, dividends and profits of one other seventh of my said estate, real, personal and mixed, and, on the death of either of them, shall distribute and divide one-third part of such portion of my estate to and among the children of such of them as shall so die, share and share alike, the descendants of any such child or children to take the same share or portion which his, her or their parents would be entitled to if living. In case either of them, said George, William and Henry, shall die, leaving no lawful descendants, then the share or portion of such interest, rents, income, dividends and profits payable to such of them as shall so die is to be paid to the survivor and survivors, and if they all die leaving no children or descendants of children living at their decease, then the said

---

So long as there is no satisfactory evidence to the contrary, the law looking to the relationship and rights of others will ascribe to the donor that intention most favorable to an equal distribution of his property among all his children. Parks v. Parks, 19 Md. 323; Clark v. Wilson, 27 Md. 693; Dutch's App. 57 Pa. 461; Ruch v. Biery, 9 West. Rep. 215, 110 Ind. 449.

Intention to be carried into effect.

The intention of the testator, when it shall have been ascertained from an examination of the will in connection with the situation of his property, etc., at the time of making such will, must be carried into effect by the courts so far as that intention is consistent with the rules of law. Amory v. Lord, 9 N. Y. 419; Irving v. DeKay, 9 Paige, 528, 4 N. Y. Ch. L. ed. 804; Harrison v. Jewell, 2 Dem. 33; Chrystie v. Phyfe, 19 N. Y. 344; Hawley v. James, 5 Paige, 318, 3 N. Y. Ch. L. ed. 734.

Where the general intent is clear, it will be carried out at the expense of any particular intent which cannot be carried out consistently with it, the paramount purpose being entitled to prevail. Pell v. Mercer, 14 R. I. 430; Finlay v. Riddle, 3 Binn. 139, 162; Purnell v. Dudley, 4 Jones, Eq. 203; Jesson v. Wright, 2 Bligh, 1, 56; Thellusson v. Woodford, 4 Ves. Jr. 227, 329.

That testatrix's plan of division of her property fails to effectuate her purpose will not justify the court in disregarding the plain provisions of the will. Terry v. Smith, 7 Cent. Rep. 127, 42 N. J. Eq. 504.

Where there is no ambiguity in the terms of the will, a doubt suggested by extraneous circumstances cannot be permitted to affect its construction. Sponsler's App. 107 Pa. 85.

In construing wills, the most unbounded indulgence has been shown to the ignorance, unskillfulness and negligence of testators. Weeks v. Cornwell, 6 Cent. Rep. 779, 104 N. Y. 325.

Rule of construction.

In construing a will the words are to be construed according to their natural import, unless the context evidently points out that in the particular instance there should be some other construction. Sheriff v. Brown, 3 Cent. Rep. 770, 5 Mackey, 172; *Re* Hallet, 8 Paige, 378, 4 N. Y. Ch. L. ed. 469; Puryear v. Edmondson, 4 Heisk. 51.

A testator must be presumed to have used words in their ordinary primary sense or meaning. *Re* Woodward, 7 L. R. A. 367, 117 N. Y. 522.

All doubts are to be resolved in favor of the testator's having said exactly what he meant. Cody v. Bunn, 46 N. J. Eq. 131.

Where the provisions of the will are clear and simple no reason exists for taking the testator's words in any other than their natural sense. Wylie v. Lockwood, 86 N. Y. 301; Lovett v. Buloid, 3 Barb. Ch. 137, 5 N. Y. Ch. L. ed. 847.

The question in expounding a will is, not what testator meant, but what is the meaning of his words. Barry's App. (Pa.) 8 Cent. Rep. 132; Bates v. Woodruff, 11 West. Rep. 567, 123 Ill. 205.

The technical rules or import of words used will not be allowed to defeat testator's manifest intention. Albert v. Albert, 10 Cent. Rep. 570, 68 Md. 352; Myrick v. Heard, 31 Fed. Rep. 241; Rhein's App. (Pa.) 7 Cent. Rep. 491; Suydam v. Thayer (Mo.) 12 West. Rep. 611.

Technical words reconcilable with the context of the will will not be expunged on mere conjecture. Simes's App. (Pa.) 11 Cent. Rep. 173.

The testator's intention, when ascertained, will control technical terms. Jouroimon v. Massengill, 86 Tenn. 81.

Courts, in construing wills, should give effect to the intention of the testator to the extent, if necessary, of modifying the meaning of terms employed and of rejecting words. Dulany v. Middleton (Md.) Oct. Term, 1889.

Where construction of a clause is difficult on account of meagre or contradictory phraseology, the true meaning of testator may be sometimes ascertained by examining other provisions. Towle v. Delano, 4 New Eng. Rep. 178, 144 Mass. 95.

Where the meaning of words is doubtful as to beneficiaries or proportions, the interpretation will be aided by the general rules of inheritance. Dunlap's App. 8 Cent. Rep. 845, 116 Pa. 500.

While rules of construction may aid somewhat the way to a conclusion, they are not to be used to frustrate the intention of the testator, but when that is ascertained the language and mode of expression, if of doubtful import, may be subordinated to such intention. Rich v. Hawxhurst, 114 N. Y. 515; Lytle v. Beveridge, 58 N. Y. 592; Hoppock v. Tucker, 59 N. Y. 202; Phillips v. Davies, 92 N. Y. 199.

The whole will to be taken together.

No rule is better settled than that the whole will is to be taken together and is to be so construed as to give effect, if it be possible, to the whole. Smith v. Bell, 31 U. S. 6 Pet. 68 (8 L. ed. 322); Robinson v. Adams (Ct. Er. and App. Del.) 4 U. S. 4 Dall. Appx. xii. (1 L. ed. 920).

It may be taken as a well-settled general rule that the will and a codicil are to be construed together as parts of one and the same instrument speaking from the date of the codicil, and that a codicil is no revocation of a will further than it is so expressed. Newcomb v. Webster, 113 N. Y. 196; Westcott v. Cady, 5 Johns. Ch. 343, 1 N. Y. Ch. L. ed. 1104; Haven v. Haven, 1 Redf. 375; Willet v. Sandford, 1 Ves. Sr. 186; Gelbke v. Gelbke, 88 Ala. 427; Sturgis v. Work, 122 Ind. 134.

The intention of the testator is to be gathered from the whole will. Suydam v. Thayer, 12 West. Rep. 612, 94 Mo. 49; Randall v. Josselyn, 4 New Eng. Rep. 909, 59 Vt. 557; Emery v. Union Society, 4 New

one seventh of my estate shall be held by the said trustees for the use and benefit of my surviving children or their issue, in the same way and manner as is herein provided for as in respect of the other portions of my estate which I have herein disposed of, and which said trustees are to hold in trust in the way and manner herein set forth." In terms only two events are provided for by which the principal of the one seventh of the testator's estate which is the subject of that clause is disposed of. One is the death of either of his three grandsons, children of his daughter Emeline, leaving issue, in which case the one third of such portion or seventh is to be divided and distributed "to and among the children of such of them as shall so die, share and share alike, the descendants of any such child or children to take the same share or portion which his, her or their parents would be entitled to if living." The other event is the death of all these grandsons without issue. If this had occurred the one seventh of the testator's estate held for their benefit was to be held for the benefit of the testator's surviving children or their issue. In the event which actually took place, the death of two of the grandsons leaving no issue, provision was made that the income of their shares should be paid to the survivors or survivor. These payments have actually been made to the surviving grandson, William F. Hastings, as his brothers have respectively deceased.

Eng. Rep. 542, 79 Me. 334; Walker v. Pritchard, 10 West. Rep. 146, 121 Ill. 221; Rhein's App. (Pa.) 7 Cent. Rep. 491; McGuire's App. (Pa.) 9 Cent. Rep. 650; *Re* Cayuga County Surrogate, 46 Hun, 657; Sheriff v. Brown, 3 Cent. Rep. 770, 5 Mackey, 172; Kirkland v. Conway, 8 West. Rep. 478, 116 Ill. 438; Sager v. Galloway, 4 Cent. Rep. 681, 113 Pa. 500; Wiggin v. Perkins, 2 New Eng. Rep. 896, 64 N. H. 36; Crosby v. Wendell, 6 Paige, 548, 3 N. Y. Ch. L. ed. 1096; Bayeaux v. Bayeaux, 8 Paige, 333, 4 N. Y. Ch. L. ed. 450; Hartnett v. Wandell, 60 N. Y. 346, 19 Am. Rep. 197; Carpenter v. Cameron, 7 Watts, 51; Tuttle v. Heidermann, 5 Redf. 292; Simpson v. English, 1 Hun, 560, 4 Thomp. & C. 81; Crosby v. Wendell, 6 Paige, 548, 3 N. Y. Ch. L. ed. 1096; Pond v. Bergh, 10 Paige, 140, 4 N. Y. Ch. L. ed. 919; Van Nostrand v. Moore, 52 N. Y. 12; Betts v. Betts, 4 Abb. N. C. 317; Covenhoven v. Shuler, 2 Paige, 122, 2 N. Y. Ch. L. ed. 839; Pond v. Bergh, 10 Paige, 140, 4 N. Y. Ch. L. ed. 919; Parks v. Parks, 9 Paige, 107, 4 N. Y. Ch. L. ed. 627.

The construction of a will must depend upon the intention of the testator, to be ascertained from everything contained within the four corners of the instrument. Clark v. Hornthal, 47 Miss. 499; Hoxie v. Hoxie, 7 Paige, 192, 4 N. Y. Ch. L. ed. 120; Wms. Exrs. 1541. See further, as to intention, Broom, Leg. Max. 409 *et seq.*; Watson v. Woods, 3 R. I. 226; Perry v. Hunter, 2 R. I. 80; Hall v. Chaffee, 14 N. H. 215; Hall v. Hall, 27 N. H. 275; Fogg v. Clark, 1 N. H. 163; Decker v. Decker, 3 Ohio, 157; King v. Bock, 15 Ohio, 559; Brasher v. Marsh, 15 Ohio St. 103; Gandolfo v. Walker, Id. 251; Jones v. Robinson, 17 Ohio St. 171; Moore v. Beckwith, 14 Ohio St. 129; Ripple v. Ripple, 1 Rawle, 386; Rathbone v. Dyckman, 3 Paige, 9, 3 N. Y. Ch. L. ed. 87; Banks v. Walker, 3 Barb. Ch. 448, 5 N. Y. Ch. L. ed. 967; Doe v. Smith, 7 T. R. 531; Bradhurst v. Bradhurst, 1 Paige, 331, 2 N. Y. Ch. L. ed. 668; Hoxie v. Hoxie, 7 Paige, 187, 4 N. Y. Ch. L. ed. 118; Ackerman v. Ernott, 4 Barb. 638, 3 N.Y. Legal Obs. 340.

In arriving at testator's intent, effect is to be given to every part of the will. McDevitt's App. 4 Cent. Rep. 83, 113 Pa. 103; Miller v. Pugh, 5 Cent. Rep. 239, 113 Pa. 459; Finney's App. 3 Cent. Rep. 597, 113 Pa. 11; Banta v. Boyd, 6 West. Rep. 87, 118 Ill. 186; St. John's Mite Asso. v. Buchly, 6 Cent. Rep. 298, 5 Mackey, 406.

The intention of the testator is not to be determined from one clause or provision of the will, but each and every clause of it must be considered, and the intention be determined from the whole will. Suydam v. Thayer, 12 West. Rep. 611, 94 Mo. 49.

Effect should be given to every clause, and proper force to every word, of a will. Shepard v. Shepard, 6 New Eng. Rep. 541, 6 Vt. 109.

The interpretation must give effect to every provision of the will and codicil, in accordance with a cardinal rule to be observed in the construction of wills. Crozier v. Bray, 39 Hun, 125.

When an intention is revealed in the entire structure of a will, individual clauses are to be construed with reference to that intention. Goddard v. Whitney, 1 New Eng. Rep. 196, 140 Mass. 92.

Where a gift is to persons *nominatim*, the intention to give a right of survivorship may be deduced from other parts of the will. Collins v. Bergen, 4 Cent. Rep. 406, 42 N. J. Eq. 57.

In ascertaining what the intention of the testator was, the words used are to be taken according to their meaning as gathered from the consideration of the whole instrument and a comparison of its various parts. Jasper v. Jasper, 17 Or. 590.

In arriving at testator's intention words and limitations in the will may be rejected, accepted or transposed. *Re* Huntington, 6 Cent. Rep. 217, 108 N. Y. 677; Quin v. Skinner, 49 Barb. 134, 33 How. Pr. 235; Pattorson v. Read, 5 Cent. Rep. 812, 42 N. J. Eq. 146.

Or they may be supplied or left out in a clear case. McGuire's App. (Pa.) 9 Cent. Rep. 650.

Or they may be transposed, supplied or entirely rejected. Killam v. Allen, 52 Barb. 613; Treadwell v. Montanye, 2 Dem. 571; Rathbone v. Dyckman, 3 Paige, 9, 3 N. Y. Ch. L. ed. 87; Mason v. Jones, 2 Barb. 229; Bradley v. Amidon, 10 Paige, 235, 4 N. Y. Ch. L. ed. 938; Jackson v. Hoover, 26 Ind. 521; Marshall v. Hopkins, 15 East, 309; Pond v. Bergh, 10 Paige, 140, 4 N. Y. Ch. L. ed. 919.

Full meaning can be given to both contingencies of death and marriage by transposing them, as is often done where such provisions are connected by the conjunction "and," when that is necessary to make them sensible. Chrystie v. Phyfe, 19 N.Y. 350.

If the reading of the whole will produces a conviction that testator must necessarily have intended an interest to be given which is not bequeathed by express and formal words, the court must supply the defect by implication. Phelps v. Phelps, 4 New Eng. Rep. 187, 143 Mass. 570.

If transposition gives effect to all the provisions of the will and renders them all harmonious and consistent with each other and with the general purpose and intent of the will, it affords satisfactory ground of presumption that it reaches the source of the difficulty and explains the mode in which it arose. Jackson v. Hoover, 26 Ind. 521; Rathbone v. Dyckman, 3 Paige, 9, 3 N. Y. Ch. L. ed. 87.

The law upon the subject of implied devises is thoroughly settled. The policy of the law and the leaning of the courts is against the doctrine of devises by implication. Holton v. Den, 23 N. J. L. 330.

To create a devise by inference the implication must be a necessary one: there must be such a strong probability of an intention to devise that an intent to the contrary cannot be supposed. 2 Pow. Dev. 199.

Words in a will will be supplied, in order to effectuate the intention, as collected from the context, and this may be done by the court in order to give the will effect. Kelly v. Kelly, 5 Lans. 447.

What was to be done with the principal of the two thirds to the income of which the other grandsons had been entitled upon the decease of the surviving grandson leaving issue was not explicitly provided for. The surviving grandson, William F., had now deceased leaving issue. It is not disputed that his children are entitled to the one third of the portion of which he originally enjoyed the income, but it is contended on behalf of the next of kin and the heirs-at-law of the testator that the two thirds of which he has enjoyed the income since the decease of his brothers are to be treated as intestate property undisposed of by the will except so far as the income during the life of the surviving grandson was concerned, and that it is impossible to introduce into the clause a bequest over to the children of the surviving grandson of the principal of the shares of the brothers of their father.

The general principles which apply to the construction of a clau e similar to the one in question are well settled. While care must be taken that courts do not undertake to make wills for testators, and while their meaning is not to be ascertained by mere conjecture as to what they may have intended, the true meaning of words used is to be arrived at by considering them not only in their relation to the clause immediately in question but to the whole will. Their more grammatical or ordinary sense is not to be adhered to if it would be re-

---

Punctuation must give way whenever it interferes with the proper and reasonable construction of a will. Rhein's App. (Pa.) 7 Cent. Rep. 491.

Must be so construed as to avoid partial intestacy.

Words may be read in their natural sense to effect intent and avoid partial intestacy, although some remote consequences may not have been in testator's mind. Dove v. Johnson, 1 New Eng. Rep. 729, 141 Mass. 287.

When one undertakes to make a will it will be presumed that his purpose is to dispose of his entire estate. Snyder v. Baker, 7 Cent. Rep. 347, 5 Mackey, 443; Scofield v. Olcott, 9 West. Rep. 133, 120 Ill. 362; Phelps v. Phelps, 4 New Eng. Rep. 467, 143 Mass. 570; Leigh v. Savidge, 14 N. J. Eq. 124; Gilpin v. Williams, 17 Ohio St. 396; Gourley v. Thompson, 2 Sneed, 387; Jarnagin v. Conway, 2 Humph. 50; Boyd v. Latham, Busb. L. (N. C.) 365, cited in *notes* to 2 Wms. Exrs. 1088; Appeal of Boards of Missions, 91 Pa. 507.

No presumption of an intent to die intestate as to any part of his property is allowable, when the words of a testator's will may fairly carry the whole. Given v. Hilton, 95 U. S. 591 (24 L. ed. 458).

Where it is apparent that it was testator's purpose at the time of making his will to dispose of his entire estate, the will should be construed, if possible, so as to prevent intestacy as to any part of his property. Shuck v. Shook, 24 Abb. N. C. 463.

The introductory clause of a will, "As to such worldly estate wherewith it has pleased God to intrust me, I dispose of;" and the final clause, "If anything is omitted, I leave it to be conducted by my executors,"—reinforce the legal presumption of the testator's intention to dispose of his entire estate. Reynolds v. Crispin (Pa.) 9 Cent. Rep. 544.

It is essential, in order that the intention of the testator may be made effectual, that the established rules of law in respect to the transmission and descent of property be not disregarded. Bailey v. Sanger, 6 West. Rep. 556, 108 Ind. 264.

Construction in case of repugnancy.

Every testator is presumed to have framed his bequests and devises in view of the general rules for the construction of wills adopted by courts; but this presumption must give way if it will defeat what otherwise appears to have been the testator's intention. Griggs v. Veghte (N. J. Eq.) May 22, 1890.

A will is to be so construed as to avoid, if possible, all repugnancy and give effect to all its language; rule applied to case where in one part of the will an estate is given in clear and decisive terms, and there are subsequent words not so clear and decisive. Roseboom v. Roseboom, 81 N. Y. 359; Auburn Theological Seminary v. Kellogg, 16 N. Y. 83; Van Nostrand v. Moore, 52 N. Y. 20.

A will ought to be construed so as to make it, so far as practicable, a harmonious whole. Harris v. Carpenter, 7 West. Rep. 907, 109 Ind. 540.

Where clauses conflict, the rule requiring a construction permitting every part to stand, if possible, must be departed from; later clauses must prevail. Hendershot v. Shields, 2 Cent. Rep. 225, 42 N. J. Eq. 317.

Courts almost always succeed in reconciling the clauses or gifts alleged to be inconsistent; but they recognize the existence of the rule and the necessity of its application in a proper case. Van Nostrand v. Moore, 52 N. Y. 21.

The latter of two conflicting clauses in a will prevails. Lindenkohl v. Just (D. C.) 12 Cent. Rep. 397; Kulp v. Bird (Pa.) 7 Cent. Rep. 576.

A later clause of a will, repugnant to a former provision, is to be considered as intending to modify or abrogate the former. Authorities cited in Walker v. Pritchard, 10 West. Rep. 146, 121 Ill. 221.

The exceptions to this rule are, where the latter clause is void for uncertainty for illegality, or where the cause assigned for the change, in the will, is a mistake or is false. Moore v. Moore, 47 Barb. 262; Auburn Theological Seminary v. Kellogg, *supra*.

If after all reasonable endeavors to preserve both provisions, it be found impossible to do so, the one which occurs latest in the instrument is allowed to govern, rather than that both should fail (Norris v. Beyea, 13 N. Y. 284; Bonard's Will, 16 Abb. Pr. N. S. 206; Rona v. Meier, 47 Iowa, 607; Sherratt v. Bentley, 2 Myl. & K. 149; Constantine v. Constantine, 6 Ves. Jr. 100; Smith v. Bell, 31 U. S. 6 Pet. 68 (8 L. ed. 322); Bradstreet v. Clarke, 12 Wend. 665; Johnson v. Mayne, 4 Iowa, 180), unless the intention of the testator, as apparent from other parts of the will, requires a different construction. Parks v. Parks, 9 Paige, 124, 4 N. Y. Ch. L. ed. 634.

Where the intention of the testator to limit an estate apparently given in the earlier part of a will to a lesser estate is clear from subsequent clauses of the will, the later clause will determine the extent of the estate. Temple v. Sammis, 16 Jones & S. 327; Williamson v. Daniel, 25 U. S. 12 Wheat. 568 (6 L. ed. 731); Smith v. Bell, 31 U. S. 6 Pet. 68 (8 L. ed. 322); Parks v. Parks, 9 Paige, 107, 4 N. Y. Ch. L. ed. 627; Bradstreet v. Clarke, 12 Wend. 602; Mason v. Jones, 2 Barb. 229; Chrystie v. Phyfe, 19 N. Y. 344; Terry v. Wiggins, 47 N. Y. 512; Taggart v. Murray, 53 N. Y. 233; Colt v. Heard, 10 Hun, 189; Van Nostrand v. Moore, 52 N. Y. 12; Bundy v. Bundy, 38 N. Y. 410; Striker v. Mott, 28 N. Y. 82.

Where there is an invincible repugnance between two paragraphs in a will, the latter must prevail, as being the latest expression of the intent of the testator. Heidlebaugh v. Wagner, 72 Iowa, 601; Armstrong v. Crapo, 72 Iowa, 604.

A subsequent clause, apparently irreconcilable with precedent provisions, will be construed in connection with them, and may be rejected if repugnant to the intention of the testator as derived

pugnant or inconsistent with the remainder of the instrument. Where there has been a failure also in such a clause to use the technical or positive language appropriate to express a meaning which is evident from the whole will taken together, and where the language for that purpose is defective, the necessary words may be supplied or words may be transposed to effectuate the obvious intention. *Barrus* v. *Kirkland*, 8 Gray, 512; *Baxter* v. *Baxter*, 122 Mass. 87.

The whole of the testator's estate was devised to trustees for the various purposes which appear in the successive clauses of his will. It was to be divided in seven equal parts, each of which was to be held as a separate and distinct fund. Of seven shares the interest, income, etc., of five of them was bequeathed respectively to his five children then living for their natural lives, and at their deaths to be divided among their children or the issue of such children. If either of them died and left no issue, the seventh of which such child had enjoyed the income was to be held and finally disposed of for the benefit of his surviving children or their issue if they should have deceased. Two of the testator's children, both daughters, had deceased at the time of making the will, leaving children, and to these children he gives respectively, and as representing what would have been their mother's share of his property, the interest, income, etc., of one of these seven

---

from the whole will. Bonard's Will, 16 Abb. Pr. N. S. 207.

To render a subsequent provision repugnant to a previous one the last must be entirely incompatible with the first, so that if effect be given to the last the other must entirely fail. Conover v. Hoffman, 1 Bosw. 223; Sweet v. Chase, 2 N. Y. 73; Covenhoven v. Shuler, 3 Paige, 122, 3 N. Y. Ch. L. ed. 839.

Interpretation of language of will.

The interpretation, being the ascertainment of the fact of the testator's intention, is determined by the natural weight of competent evidence proving that fact, and not by artificial and technical rules. Kimball v. Lancaster, 60 N. H. 264; Bodwell v. Dickerman, 2 New Eng. Rep. 282, 63 N. H. 446.

The rule equally applicable to all written instruments is that the terms of it are to be understood in their plain, ordinary and popular sense, unless they have in respect of the subject matter, or by the known usage of trade, or the like, acquired a peculiar sense distinct from the popular use of the same words, or unless the context evidently points out, in the particular instance and in order to effectuate the immediate intention of the parties, that it should be understood in some other or peculiar sense. 1 Greenl. Ev. § 278.

In the interpretation of wills, the first and natural impression conveyed to the mind on reading the clause involved is entitled to great weight. The testator is not supposed to be propounding riddles, but rather to be trying to convey his idea in the simplest manner, so as to be correctly understood at first view. When this impression is confirmed by the application of grammatical rules to the clause as constructed, it derives great additional support. Bobb's Succession (La.) Jan. 7, 1889.

The plain and unambiguous words of the will must prevail, and are not to be controlled or qualified by any conjectural or doubtful constructions growing out of the situation, circumstances or conditions, either of the testator, his property or his family. Bonard's Will, 16 Abb. Pr. N. S. 204; Mann v. Mann, 14 Johns. 1; Parsons v. Winslow, 6 Mass. 175; Dawes v. Swan, 4 Mass. 208; Gibson v. Seymour, 1 West. Rep. 253, 102 Ind. 488.

Language susceptible of two constructions.

Where language is susceptible of two constructions, that interpretation is to be preferred which would render valid the provision of the will. Matteson v. Matteson, 51 How. Pr. 278; Thorn v. Coles, 3 Edw. Ch. 330, 6 N. Y. Ch. L. ed. 678; Moon v. Stone, 19 Gratt. 278; Mason v. Jones, 2 Barb. 229; Dubois v. Ray, 35 N. Y. 165; Edwards v. Bibb, 43 Ala. 673; Pruden v. Pruden, 14 Ohio St. 254; Farnam v. Farnam, 1 New Eng. Rep. 315, 53 Conn. 261.

Where the words of a will are capable of a twofold construction, that should be adopted most consistent with the intention as ascertained by the other provisions of the will. Conover v. Hoffman, 1 Bosw. 221.

That construction is to be preferred which inclines to the inheritance of the children of a deceased child. Bowker v. Bowker, 148 Mass. 198.

A will should not be so read as to contradict itself, if any other reasonable interpretation is possible; but if it is capable of two constructions, one consistent and the other inconsistent with the law, the former should be preferred, as it is to be presumed that the testator intended to comply with the law. Crozier v. Bray, 120 N. Y. 366.

Interpretation of specific terms.

Where words are used which have a settled legal meaning, full effect must be given to them. Allen v. Craft, 7 West. Rep. 517, 109 Ind. 476.

When it is apparent that technical words are not used in their legal signification, such interpretation must be given to them as will give effect to the testator's intention. Gambrill v. Forest Grove Lodge, 8 Cent. Rep. 883, 66 Md. 17.

The words "all my property," used in a will, mean the testator's realty and personalty, subject to the payment of his debts. Smith v. Terry, 10 Cent. Rep. 694, 43 N. J. Eq. 659.

The word "effects" (French "*effets*"), when used indefinitely in wills, but in connection with something particular and certain, is limited by its association to other things of a like kind. Ennis v. Smith, 55 U. S. 14 How. 400 (14 L. ed. 472).

"Estate" is *genus generalissimum*, and comprehends both the land and the inheritance. It is sufficiently descriptive both of the subject and the interest existing in it. Lambert v. Paine, 7 U. S. 3 Cranch, 97 (2 L. ed. 377).

It includes all real and personal estate. Weatherhead v. Baskerville, 52 U. S. 11 How. 329 (13 L. ed. 717); Archer v. Deneale, 26 U. S. 1 Pet. 585 (7 L. ed. 272).

"Every movable," in a will, following a list of household articles, does not include debts due the testatrix. Jackson v. Vanderspreigle, 2 U. S. 2 Dall. 142 (1 L. ed. 323).

The term "furniture" embraces everything about the house that has usually been enjoyed therewith, including plate, linen, china and pictures. Endicott v. Endicott, 4 Cent. Rep. 872, 41 N. J. Eq. 93; 2 Jarman, Wills, R. & T. ed. 352.

The word "issue" is regarded primarily as a word of limitation, and is synonymous with the technical words "heirs of the body." Allen v. Craft, 7 West. Rep. 517, 109 Ind. 476.

Where a testator devised his estate "to the issue or children" of his said two daughters who may then be living, "to be equally divided among all such issue or children, share and share alike," the words "issue or children" cannot be read as meaning "child or children," but that all issue of the said daughters take *per stirpes*. Hall v. Hall, 1 New Eng. Rep. 293, 140 Mass. 267.

shares to be divided between them equally for their lives, providing that if either grandchild died without issue the income which it enjoyed should be enjoyed by the survivor or survivors of the same family, while if such child left issue the portion of the seventh of which it had enjoyed the interest and income should be received by them. These sevenths of the estate are disposed of by the first and sixth clauses of his will in similar language with the exception of those changes rendered necessary by the fact that there were four grandchildren, daughters of his deceased daughter Rebecca S. French, and three grandchildren, sons of his deceased daughter Emeline Hastings. There were therefore three beneficiaries under the sixth clause, which is the one under consideration, and the income which was to be divided between them was the same which their mother would have received if living at the time of the will and if the same provision had been made for her which was made for the living children. It is only in case all these grandchildren die leaving no children or issue that the one seventh of the income of which they or the survivors of them enjoy will pass by the will to the trust for the benefit of the testator's surviving children or issue. In case either of these grandchildren die leaving issue it is provided that the trustees "shall distribute and divide one-third part of such portion of my estate to and among the children of such of

---

Where testator intended in his will, providing for equal distribution among issue, that issue should take in a representative way, the word "issue" will be construed to mean children alone, and not children and their descendants *per capita*. Dexter v. Inches, 6 New Eng. Rep. 607, 147 Mass. 324.

Where a legatee was to receive the income of property during life and upon his death the property was to be distributed to his "personal representatives who would be entitled to his personal estate according to law," those words were intended to describe his next of kin. Davies v. Davies, 5 New Eng. Rep. 407, 55 Conn. 319.

The word "money," in a bequest, must be understood in its legal and popular sense to mean gold or silver, or the lawful currency of the country, or bank notes. Smith v. Burch, 92 N. Y. 234; Judah v. Harris, 19 Johns. 145; Dusenberry v. Woodward, 1 Abb. Pr. 454; Danville v. Sutherlin, 20 Gratt. 583; Green v. Sizer, 40 Miss. 543; Beck v. McGillis, 9 Barb. 59; Klauber v. Biggerstaff, 47 Wis. 550, 32 Am. Rep. 778; Thompson v. Riggs, 72 U. S. 5 Wall. 663 (18 L. ed. 704); Veazie Bank v. Fenno, 75 U. S. 8 Wall. 533 (19 L. ed. 482); Hepburn v. Griswold, 75 U. S. 8 Wall. 603 (19 L. ed. 513); Legal Tender Cases, 79 U. S. 12 Wall. 457 (20 L. ed. 287), Wood v. Bullens, 6 Allen, 516; Bush v. Baldrey, 11 Allen, 367; Frothingham v. Morse, 45 N. H. 545; Frank v. Wessels, 64 N. Y. 155; Legal Tender Cases, 52 Pa. 9; Buchegger v. Shultz, 13 Mich. 420; Williams v. Rorer, 7 Mo. 556; Seawell v. Henry, 6 Ala. 226; Cooley v. Weeks, 10 Yerg. 141.

Confederate treasury notes never did come up to the standard of money. Hill v. Erwin, 44 Ala. 666.

The words "my land" in a will are sufficient to convey the lands then owned by the testator. Funk v. Davis, 1 West. Rep. 304, 103 Ind. 281.

Family.

For definition of the term "family," see *note* to Miller v. Finegan, 6 L. R. A. 814.

"Children" defined.

The word "children," as well as all other similar descriptive terms of classes or relations, must be understood in wills in its primary and simple signification. Sherman v. Sherman, 3 Barb. 387; Hughes v. Sayer, 1 P. Wms. 534; Fosdick v. Cornell, 1 Johns. 440; Jackson v. Staats, 11 Johns. 337; Anderson v. Jackson, 16 Johns. 382; Wilkes v. Lion, 2 Cow. 384.

The word "children" in a bequest or legacy must be understood in its primary or simple signification, where there are many persons in existence at the date of the will, or when the bequest or legacy takes effect, answering such meaning of the term; and in such case, the word will never include grandchildren. Pugh v. Pugh, 3 West. Rep. 681, 105 Ind. 552.

It must be taken in its accustomed sense and limited to offspring in the first degree, in the absence of indications that the testator intended to give it some other meaning. Kirk v. Cashman, 3 Dem. 244; Sherman v. Sherman, 3 Barb. 387; Lawrence v. Hebbard, 1 Bradf. 255; Hone v. Van Schaick, 3 N. Y. 540; Guernsey v. Guernsey, 36 N. Y. 272; Magaw v. Field, 48 N. Y. 668; Palmer v. Horn, 84 N. Y. 516; Wylie v. Lockwood, 86 N. Y. 291; Pugh v. Pugh, *supra*.

The settled rule in the construction of wills is, that the word "children" will not be construed to include grandchildren, unless there is something in the context to show that the testator intended that it should include grandchildren, or unless the provision will be inoperative without such construction. Feit v. Vanatta, 21 N. J. Eq. 85; Mowatt v. Carow, 7 Paige, 328, 4 N. Y. Ch. L. ed. 175; Moor v. Raisbeck, 12 Sim. 123; Cutter v. Doughty, 23 Wend. 522; Hone v. Van Schaick, 3 Edw. Ch. 474, 6 N. Y. Ch. L. ed. 730, in error, 3 N. Y. 538; Tier v. Pennell, 1 Edw. Ch. 354, 6 N. Y. Ch. L. ed. 170; *Re* Hunt's Estate (Pa.) 25 W. N. C. 450.

The term "children" is primarily and technically used as a word of purchase and not of limitation, and means the immediate descendants of the person named as the ancestor. In such sense the words must be taken as used in the will, unless a different signification is imposed upon them by the testator by other parts and clauses of the will. Lytle v. Beveridge, 58 N. Y. 605.

A mere marginal note or memorandum on a will devising all testator's property to his children, to the effect that the personal estate is to be divided equally among the "heirs," will not have the effect of extending the sense of the word "children" so as to comprehend grandchildren. *Re* Hunt's Estate, *supra*.

The word "children" includes only the immediate legitimate descendants and not a step-child. Lawrence v. Hebbard, 1 Bradf. 255; *Re* Hallet, 8 Paige, 375, 4 N. Y. Ch. L. ed. 468.

The words "such child or children" are not necessarily limited to the immediate offspring, but embrace grandchildren, where the other portions of the will show such to be the intention of the testator, or where such a view is necessary to carry into effect his provisions. *Re* Brown, 29 Hun, 417; Prowitt v. Rodman, 37 N. Y. 42; Scott v. Guernsey, 48 N. Y. 106; Lawrence v. Hebbard, 1 Bradf. 252; Bowne v. Underhill, 4 Hun, 130.

The word "children" it is said means prima facie legitimate children, as much so as if the word "legitimate" were written before it. Bolton v. Bolton, 73 Me. 309; Collins v. Hoxie, 9 Paige, 81, 4 N. Y. Ch. L. ed. 616; *Re* Hallet, *supra*; Cromer v. Pinckney, 3 Barb. Ch. 466, 475, 5 N. Y. Ch. L. ed. 974, 978; Dorin v. Dorin, L. R. 7 H. L. 568; Hill v. Crook, L. R. 6 H. L. 265. See Gelston v. Shields, 16 Hun, 154.

In short wherever the term "children" has received a construction synonymous with issue, it has generally been based upon something in the will, unless it resulted from the fact that there were no children in existence. Cummings v. Plummer, 94 Ind. 407; Cromer v. Pinckney, 3 Barb. Ch. 466, 5 N.

them as shall so die, share and share alike, the descendants of any such child or children to take the same share or portion which his, her or their parents would be entitled to if living." While the latter portion of this clause applies grammatically to the one third originally bequeathed, it is loosely used, as their parents were not entitled to any share of the principal if living. It indicates, however, that all of which the parent had enjoyed the income, and which might properly be termed his share, would pass to his children or issue. It is more important that the whole scheme of the testator's will shows that he intended that if by the death of some of these grandchildren the income of the survivors or survivor was augmented, the portion as thus augmented and from which the survivor derived his income was to be treated as and to pass in the same way as the original third, of which alone he had the benefit while his brothers survived.

The intention of the testator to dispose of his whole estate is manifest. He so devises and bequeathes it in express terms to the trustees whom he names. He divides it into sevenths, appropriating one in the administration of the trust to each branch of his family. He makes no provision for any residuum, as he believes there can be none under the cross-remainders he has made in case one branch of his family should have become extinct when the time for the division of the principal has arrived. When

---

Y. Ch. L. ed. 974; Churchill v. Churchill, 2 Met. (Ky.) 466; Gardner v. Heyer, 2 Paige, 11, 2 N.Y. Ch. L. ed. 792; Gable's App. 40 Pa. 231; Ward v. Sutton, 5 Ired. Eq. 421; Hallowell v. Phipps, 2 Whart. 376; Dickinson v. Lee, 4 Watts, 82; Cutter v. Doughty, 23 Wend. 513; Izard v. Izard, 2 Desaus. or Dean's Eq. 308; Phillip v. Beall, 9 Dana, 1; Ewing v. Handley, 4 Litt. 346; Osgood v. Lovering, 33 Me. 464; Thomson v. Ludington, 104 Mass. 194; Low v. Harmony, 72 N. Y. 408; Feit v. Vanatta, 21 N. J. Eq. 84; Castner's App. 88 Pa. 478.

So where it appears there were no persons in existence who would answer to the description of children, in the primary sense of the word, at the time of making the will; or where there could not be any such at the time or in the event contemplated by the testator; or where the testator has clearly shown, by the use of other words, that he used the word "children" as synonymous with descendants or issue, or to designate or include illegitimate offspring, "grandchildren or stepchildren" —these may be included in the term (Palmer v. Horn, 84 N. Y. 521. See Reeves v. Brymer, 4 Ves. Jr. 698; Magraw v. Field, 48 N. Y. 668); or unless the provision will be inoperative without such construction. Feit v. Vanatta, 21 N. J. Eq. 85; Crooke v. Brookeing, 2 Vern. 106; Moor v. Raisbeck, 12 Sim. 123; Cutter v. Doughty, 23 Wend. 522; Tier v. Pennell, 1 Edw. Ch. 354, 6 N. Y. Ch. L. ed. 170; Hone v. Van Schaick, 3 Edw. Ch. 474, 6 N. Y. Ch. L. ed. 730, in error, 3 N. Y. 538.

Sometimes, it is true, grandchildren and issue, or descendants generally, are permitted to take under an enlarged construction of the term "children;" but the general rule is that where there are children who properly answer the description, grandchildren cannot be permitted to share along with them. Guernsey v. Guernsey, 36 N. Y. 272, 2 Trans. App. 156.

"Children" has a legal significance, extending, as the case may be, to grandchildren and even illegitimate children, but never permitting the term "sons" to be substituted to the exclusion of daughters, unless such be the clear intent. Weatherhead v. Baskerville, 52 U. S. 11 How. 329 (13 L. ed. 717).

A devise to A and B or their legal representatives was construed to mean children taking by substitution. Albert v. Albert, 10 Cent. Rep. 572, 68 Md. 352.

Adopted children.

Under the Kentucky statutes a judgment adopting children makes them heirs-at-law, to the exclusion of collateral kindred. Hence, when such adopted children are sole devisees, a collateral relative has no such interest as to enable him to contest the probate of the will. Tinker v. Ringo, 11 Ky. L. Rep. 120.

In Texas an adopted child of a man who dies without descendants of his own is entitled to all of his separate property and one half of his community property. Eckford v. Knox, 67 Tex. 200.

In Massachusetts, by Pub. Stat., chap. 148, § 7, an adopted child will take the same share of property which the parent owns, but he cannot take property which would come to a natural child by right of representation. Wyeth v. Stone, 4 New Eng. Rep. 462, 144 Mass. 441.

He can inherit directly from parents, but he cannot inherit in lieu of them. *Ibid.*

Under said Statute, § 8, the term "child," in a grant, trust, settlement or devise, will include a child adopted by the settlor, grantor or testator, unless the contrary plainly appears. *Ibid.*

Where the settlor, etc., is not the adopting parent, the adopted child will not have the right of a child born in lawful wedlock to the adopting parent, unless the intention plainly appears. *Ibid.*

The statutory adoption of an illegitimate child does not render it "issue" of the father, so as to defeat a testamentary remainder made contingent upon his leaving no issue. Jenkins v. Jenkins, 6 New Eng. Rep. 390, 64 N. H. 407.

The devise of the residue to "my lawful heirs" does not include a child who has been adopted by testator and his wife, and whose adoption has been undone by proceedings in the probate court, by testator and its natural mother, after the death of the testator's wife. Morrison v. Sessions, 14 West. Rep. 665, 70 Mich. 297.

Where one half of the testator's property was given to an adopted daughter after the death of the widow, and the other half to the "nearest and lawful heirs" of the testator and those of his wife, the adopted daughter is not included in the words "nearest and lawful heirs," nor is an adopted heir of the wife. Reinders v. Koppelman, 13 West. Rep. 614, 94 Mo. 338.

Where a will devised the remainder of an estate to testator's adopted daughter in her own right; but if she died without issue before the death of the testator's wife, then to the heirs at law of the said wife; and the adopted daughter died without issue before the death of the wife, who had no natural children, but, after testator's death adopted another child that survived her, the burden is on the latter, as testator was not the adopting parent, to show that it was his intention to include an adopted child. Wyeth v. Stone, 4 New Eng. Rep. 462, 144 Mass. 441.

"Heir" defined.

The word "heir" of itself imports succession to property *ab intestato.* Blackstone's definition is this: "An heir, therefore, is he upon whom the law casts the estate immediately on the death of the ancestor." 2 Com. 201; Fabens v. Fabens, 2 New Eng. Rep. 380, 141 Mass. 395, 399, 400; Lincoln v. Perry, 149 Mass. 373.

The word "heirs," used in a will in the devise of a contingent remainder, must be construed in its technical sense, unless the will shows clearly that it

an intention to dispose of the whole of an estate appears a partial intestacy should not be recognized unless the deficiences in the expressions of the will are such as to compel it. That there could have been no intention to deprive the issue of Emeline of any part of the seventh which he had appropriated to her children in pursuance of his scheme of dividing his estate into seven parts, one for each living child and one for the children of each of his own children who had deceased leaving issue, is further shown by the equality which he sought to establish in these shares by requiring the debts due from any child to be treated as a part of i's share. It cannot be supposed that the testator intended that in the contingency that has occurred only one third of a seventh should go to the issue of his daughter Emeline, while the issue of the other children received a full seventh.

We are satisfied that a construction of this will by which it shall be held that the whole of the seventh the income of which passed to William (the son of Emeline who survived his brothers and is now himself deceased) should now become the property of his children is necessary to effectuate the intention of the testator and should be adopted. It renders the will harmonious in its provisions; it makes the equal division between his children or the representatives of each child contemplated by the testator and does not, by depriving the grandchildren of Emeline of a portion of the share of their grandmother, leave any intestate estate.

When the reading of a whole will produces a conviction that the testator must necessarily have intended an interest to be given which is not bequeathed by express and formal words, the court will supply the defect by implication and so mould the language of the testator as to carry into effect, as far as possible, the intention which it is of opinion that he has on the whole sufficiently declared. *Metcalf* v. *First Parish in Framingham*, 128 Mass. 375.

An examination of the decisions in similar cases will show that such implication has been made where the intention of the testator has appeared less strongly than in the case at bar. Many of them were considered in the case of *Metcalf* v. *First Parish in Framingham*, *supra*. In that case a testator had bequeathed

---

was used by the testator in a different sense. Irvine v. Newlin, 63 Miss. 192.

The word "heirs" cannot be held a word of purchase, unless testator's intent to so use it appears manifest. Allen v. Craft, 7 West. Rep. 517, 109 Ind. 476.

When the word "heirs" is used in a will, not to denote succession, but to describe a legatee, and there is no context to explain it otherwise, the natural and ordinary sense of the word "heirs" should not be departed from. Wallace v. Minor (Va.) Dec. 12, 1889.

Naming devisees shows that testator intended the word "heirs" in the limited sense of "heirs of the body," which at common law would create a fee tail, but under the Pennsylvania statute a fee simple. Knoderer v. Merriman (Pa.) 5 Cent. Rep. 852.

The word "heirs" in a will, when uncontrolled by the expressed intent of the testator, has the effect to vest a legacy which otherwise would be contingent. It is to be taken as a word of limitation limiting the bequest in case of the death of the legatee or of time fixed for payment to his or her representatives. Muhlenberg's App. 103 Pa. 593; McGill's App. 61 Pa. 46, followed and approved in Patterson v. Hawthorn, 12 Serg. & R. 112; King v. King, 1 Watts & S. 205; Reed v. Buckley, 5 Id. 517; Buckley v. Reed, 15 Pa. 83; Manderson v. Lukens, 23 Pa. 31.

The word "heirs" may be read to mean "children" if the context distinctly shows that it was employed in that sense by the testator. But there must be no doubt as to the intention of the testator to affix to the word "heirs" a meaning different from that assigned it by law. Allen v. Craft, 7 West. Rep. 516, 109 Ind. 476; Eldridge v. Eldridge, 3 Cent. Rep. 844, 41 N. J. Eq. 89; Anthony v. Anthony, 5 New Eng. Rep. 41, 55 Conn. 256; McCartney v. Osburn, 6 West. Rep. 793, 118 Ill. 403.

A devise "to the heirs of his body bequeathed (*sic*) in lawful wedlock" construed to mean heirs begotten in lawful wedlock. Millett v. Ford, 6 West. Rep. 424, 109 Ind. 159.

"Heirs of A," A being then alive, may mean the children of A. Campbell v. Rawdon, 19 Barb. 500.

In a provision directing executors, in case of the death of either of testator's sons, "to pay over to the widow, if living, $3,000, providing he (the son) leaves no heirs," etc., the word "heirs" means "children." Anthony v. Anthony, 5 New Eng. Rep. 41, 55 Conn. 256.

In the clause, "that if either son should die without heirs of his own," the latter word means lineal descendants or issue living at his decease. Abbott v. Essex County, 59 U. S. 18 How. 202 (15 L. ed. 352).

Under the Act of Assembly of Virginia which provides that the heirs or legal representatives of an officer shall receive a certain quantity of land, the devisees of the officer cannot take the land unless the Act itself describes them as the legal representatives of the officer. The term "legal representatives" was intended to provide for the case of a person who may have purchased the right of the officer. Stevenson v. Sullivant, 18 U. S. 5 Wheat. 207 (5 L. ed. 70).

Next of kin, who alone can take real estate, under Act of April 27, 1883, must be entirely within the blood of the ancestor from whom the realty descended, without regard to other relationship they may bear to intestate. Ranck's App. 4 Cent. Rep. 46, 113 Pa. 98.

Where a legatee under a will providing that, in case he should die before testatrix, the sum given to him should go to those persons living at the time of testatrix's death who shall be next of kin, died in testatrix's lifetime, leaving as next relations a brother and three nephews, sons of another brother, all of whom survived testatrix, the legacy was payable, under the words "next of kin," to the brother. Swasey v. Jaques, 4 New Eng. Rep. 43, 144 Mass. 135.

Ambiguities in will; proof of intention.

In the construction of a will a latent ambiguity may be removed by extrinsic evidence. Patch v. White, 117 U. S. 210 (29 L. ed. 860).

Where it consists of a misdescription if it can be struck out and enough remain in the will to identify the person or thing, the court will so deal with it; or, if it is an obvious mistake, will read it as if corrected. *Ibid.*

A court may look beyond the face of the will, where there is an ambiguity as to the person or property to which it is applicable, but not to enlarge or diminish the estate devised. King v. Ackerman, 67 U. S. 2 Black, 408 (17 L. ed. 292).

So a legacy to Samuel may be explained to mean a legacy to William. Powell v. Biddle, 2 U. S. 2 Dall. 70 (1 L. ed. 293).

certain stock to a trustee for the benefit of Nancy Green, a sister of a deceased wife, and William Green, her husband, for and during their natural lives, as follows: During her life to pay the net income to her semi-annually; in case she should die before him to transfer one half of the principal to a certain charitable institution and to pay the income of the remainder to him for life; in case he should die before her then at her death to transfer the whole of the principal to the same institution. She died before her husband and one half of the principal was paid to the institution and the other half kept in trust for him. While in this will there were residuary devisees, provision for whom is not made in the will we are considering, it was held that on the death of the husband the institution was entitled to this part of the principal also. It was held that the chief purposes of the testator were to provide for the wife during life (a provision for the husband being made in case he survived her), with an ultimate gift of the whole bequest to the institution, although in express words the gift of the whole bequest to the institution was in case of the death of the wife after the husband.

In the case at bar we find that the testator intended to divide his estate equally between his children and the children of his deceased daughters representing respectively their mothers, to provide for his children during life and at the decease of each child to divide the share of which it received the income among the issue of such children, and, in the case of the deceased daughters, to provide for their children during their respective lives and at their decease to divide among the children of each the principal of that share or portion of a share of which its parent had enjoyed the income, whether such income had or had not been augmented by the death of brothers or sisters.

We are of opinion that the trust, so far as the property affected by the sixth clause of the will is concerned, is now terminated and the trustees should now be directed to divide and distribute the seventh part of the testator's estate, of which William F. Hastings has received the income, among his children or their guardians representing them, if they are still in their minority.

Instructions accordingly.

The time when the will was made, the circumstances surrounding the testator, the subject matter of the devise and the beneficiaries, may be considered in determining the object of testator's bounty. Reinders v. Koppelman, 13 West. Rep. 614, 94 Mo. 338; Staigg v. Atkinson, 4 New Eng. Rep. 851, 144 Mass. 564; Noe v. Kern, 12 West. Rep. 235, 93 Mo. 367.

Extrinsic evidence is admissible only to explain ambiguities arising out of extrinsic circumstances, —as to persons, objects and the like. But evidence is not admissible to show a different intention from what the words of a will disclose. Wilkins v. Allen, 59 U. S. 18 How. 385 (15 L. ed. 396).

An expressed intention in a will may serve to explain language afterwards used therein; but the intention must be found in the acts or dispositions of the testator, and not alone in any previously expressed purpose. Blake v. Hawkins, 98 U. S. 315 (25 L. ed. 139).

Evidence of the situation of the parties may be received when it is necessary to a correct understanding of a bequest, together with the facts and circumstances. Little v. Giles, 25 Neb. 313; Smith v. Bell, 31 U. S. 6 Pet. 68 (8 L. ed. 322). See *note* to Dougherty v. Rogers (Ind.) 3 L. R. A. 847.

Parol evidence not admissible where no ambiguity exists.

Parol evidence is not admissible to supply, contradict, enlarge or vary the words of a will, or to explain testator's intention, except in cases of latent ambiguity or to rebut resulting trusts. *Re* Huntington, 6 Cent. Rep. 217, 108 N. Y. 679; Brome v. Pembroke, 5 Cent. Rep. 604, 66 Md. 193; Bunner v. Storm, 1 Sandf. Ch. 357, 7 N. Y. Ch. L. ed. 358; Myres v. Myres, 23 How. Pr. 411. See *note* to Dougherty v. Rogers (Ind.) 3 L. R. A. 847.

A mere doubt suggested by extraneous circumstances cannot be permitted to affect its construction. Baker's App. 7 Cent. Rep. 158, 115 Pa. 590.

But the court may, in a proper case, be aided by extrinsic circumstances surrounding its execution, revealing more clearly the motive or intention of the testator. Jasper v. Jasper, 17 Or. 590.

Extrinsic circumstances which aid in the interpretation of the language of a will and help to disclose the actual intention may be considered. McCorn v. McCorn, 1 Cent. Rep. 727, 100 N. Y. 511.

When the construction of a devise is doubtful, the reasons given therefor may be looked to in order to solve the doubt; but when the meaning of the language employed is clear, it cannot be controlled by the reason assigned for making it. Evans v. Opperman, 76 Tex. 293.

Parol evidence is not admissible to enlarge or alter the estate devised by a will. Robinson v. Randolph, 21 Fla. 629.

So parol evidence of the good will and affection of a testator toward a person is inadmissible for the purpose of demonstrating his intention in a bequest. The paper must speak for itself, and its meaning and effect be ascertained by the court. Mackie v. Story, 93 U. S. 589 (23 L. ed. 986).

Patrol testimony to show that clauses were put into a will contrary to the instructions of the testator must be of facts unconnected with any general declaration or wishes expressed by a testator for the disposition of his property by will. Weatherhead v. Baskerville, 52 U. S. 11 How. 329 (13 L. ed. 717).

Parol proof cannot be produced in a court of construction to contradict a will, nor to correct a mistake, nor to show the intention of the testator, unless to apply the description in the will to one of several subjects or persons. Mistakes and variances between the will as prepared and the instructions given for preparing it can only be reformed by the probate court. Burger v. Hill, 1 Bradf. 372; Gardner v. Heyer, 2 Paige, 13, 2 N. Y. Ch. L. ed. 793; Marriot v. Marriot, 1 Strange, 666; Segrave v. Kirwan, 1 Beatty, 166; Murray v. Jones, 2 Ves. & B. 318; Newburgh v. Newburgh, 5 Madd. 364; Powell v. Mouchett, 16 Madd. 216; Story, Eq. §§ 164, 179; Collins v. Hoxie, 9 Paige, 81, 4 N. Y. Ch. L. ed. 616.

Where there is nothing in a will upon which to predicate a construction that the land was different from that described in the will, no evidence is admissible to show the intent of the testator. Funk v. Davis, 1 West. Rep. 302, 103 Ind. 281.

Harold W. WINDRAM, *Appt.*,
v.
Peter W. FRENCH *et al.*

(......Mass......)

1. Officers of a corporation who sign and issue certificates of its stock in the usual form, stating upon their faces that the corporation is incorporated according to the laws of a particular State, and that the stock is non-assessable, thereby represent that the stock is not spurious nor invalid because of their known acts or omissions, and also that everything has been done which is necessary to make the stock rightfully exempt from further assessment; and if such representations are false the officers will be liable in damages to one who has taken the certificates in good faith and for value relying upon the representations.

2. A declaration which, taken as a whole, was apparently intended to present a certain case, will not be pronounced bad for want of technical accuracy of allegation, unless the specific defect is unmistakably pointed out; hence an allegation that plaintiff took certain stock relying on its validity may be taken to mean that he relied upon representations made in the certificate, which it appears he had seen.

(June, 1890.)

APPEAL by plaintiff from a judgment of the Superior Court for Suffolk County sustaining a demurrer to the declaration in an action to recover damages for losses which were alleged to have resulted to plaintiff by reason of his paying value for certain stock in reliance upon defendant's representations as to its validity. *Demurrer overruled.*

The case sufficiently appears in the opinion.

Messrs. **Thomas F. Nutter** and **George R. Nutter**, for appellant:

If directors of a corporation knowingly issue unauthorized and void certificates of shares, or invalid transferable obligations of the company, they are liable to any purchaser or subsequent transferee of the certificates or obligations who takes them relying on their apparent validity.

Morawetz, Priv. Corp. 2d ed. § 574; *Bruff* v. *Mali*, 36 N. Y. 200; *Clark* v. *Edgar*, 12 Mo. *App.* 345, 84 Mo. 106; *Eaglesfield* v. *Londonderry*, L. R. 4 Ch. Div. 693; *Cross* v. *Sackett*, 6 Abb. Pr. 247; *Bartholomew* v. *Bentley*, 15 Ohio 659.

The action is properly brought against these defendants and need not be brought against the corporation.

Bruff v. *Mali, supra.*

Even if this is a statutory liability, it should be enforced. A statutory liability should be enforced where the foreign statute is like the domestic.

Leonard v. *Columbia Steam Nav. Co.* 84 N. Y. 48; *Stoeckman* v. *Terre Haute & I. R. Co.* 15 Mo. App. 503; *Knight* v. *West Jersey R. Co.* 108 Pa. 250; *Dennick* v. *New Jersey Cent. R. Co.* 103 U. S. 11 (26 L. ed. 439).

The statutes of Massachusetts and New Hampshire are in substance similar.

See Pub. Stat. chap. 105, §§ 17-19.

Defendants are liable upon an implied warranty.

Lobdell v. *Baker*, 1 Met. 193, 3 Met. 469; *Hecht* v. *Batcheller*, 6 New Eng. Rep. 610, 147 Mass. 335, 339; *Potts* v. *Chapin*, 133 Mass. 276, 281; *Matthews* v. *Massachusetts Nat. Bank*, 1 Holmes, 396.

A person is liable who has in his possession substances which may work harm and negligently suffers them, improperly labeled, to get abroad.

Thomas v. *Winchester*, 6 N. Y. 397, quoted in 36 N. Y. 206; *Norton* v. *Sewall*, 106 Mass. 143; *Boston & A. R. Co.* v. *Shanly*, 107 Mass. 568.

A representation borne upon the instrument itself is a representation to each successive holder.

Lobdell v. *Baker*, 3 Met. 469, 473; *Morgan* v. *Skiddy*, 62 N. Y. 319; *Clark* v. *Edgar, supra*; *Bedford* v. *Bagshaw*, 29 L. J. Exch. 59; *Swift* v. *Winterbotham*, L. R. 8 Q. B. 244, 253; *Com.* v. *Harley*, 7 Met. 462.

Messrs. **Hutchins & Wheeler**, for appellees:

The gist of an action for fraudulent representations is fraud and deceit in the defendant, and damage to the plaintiff, and the *scienter* must be alleged in the declaration and proved at the trial.

Pearson v. *Howe*, 1 Allen, 207; *Tryon* v. *Whitmarsh*, 1 Met. 1; *Dyer* v. *Lewis*, 7 Mass. 284; *Hartford L. S. Ins. Co.* v. *Matthews*, 102 Mass. 221.

It must also appear that the plaintiff was deceived, and that he acted in whole or in part in reliance on the representations.

Emerson v. *Brigham*, 10 Mass. 197; *Matthews* v. *Bliss*, 22 Pick. 48; *Safford* v. *Grout*, 120 Mass. 20; *Eastwood* v. *Baine*, 28 L. J. Exch. 74.

The declaration cannot be supported as a declaration in tort for breach of a warranty, for there is no allegation of a warranty, or promise, or any breach thereof.

Cooper v. *Landon*, 102 Mass. 58; *Stone* v. *Denny*, 4 Met. 151; *Salem India Rubber Co.* v. *Adams*, 23 Pick. 256; *Mahurin* v. *Harding*, 28 N. H. 128.

Holmes, J., delivered the opinion of the court:

It appears from the declaration that the defendants knowingly and fraudulently signed, as president and treasurer respectively, and issued, invalid certificates of stock in a New Hampshire corporation, which were afterwards acquired by the plaintiff in good faith and for value in Massachusetts. The certificates were in the usual form of stock certificates, and bore upon their face the words "Incorporated under the Laws of the State of New Hampshire. Non-assessable." There is no doubt that by thus authenticating and issuing the certificates the defendants made certain representations which accompanied them, and which, like the offer in a letter of credit, addressed themselves to whoever should purchase those certificates thereafter, whoever he might be. *Bruff* v. *Mali*, 36 N. Y. 200, 205. See *Bartholomew* v. *Bentley*, 15 Ohio, 659; *Clark* v. *Edgar*, 84 Mo. 106; *First Nat. Bank of South Bend* v. *Lanier*, 78 U. S. 11 Wall. 369, 378 [20 L. ed. 172, 175]; *Matthews* v. *Massachusetts Nat. Bank*, 1 Holmes, 396; *Lobdell* v. *Baker*, 3 Met. 469, 471.

The scope of these representations is matter of construction. They certainly went to the point that the stock was not spurious, and that it was not invalid by reason of the fraudulent or known acts or omissions of the officers in question. In view of the word "Non-assessable," they went further. That word affirmed that such things had been done as were required by the New Hampshire law to be done in order to make the stock rightfully exempt from further assessment. This is not the case of an original subscriber to whom the facts were made known, upon which the conclusion non-assessable was based, and who seeks to avoid liability to an assessment, as in *Upton* v. *Tribilcock*, 91 U. S. 45 [23 L. ed. 203]. See *Eaglesfield* v. *Londonderry*, L. R. 4 Ch. Div. 693.

Here the facts were unknown, and a statement of the conclusion imported a statement that facts existed which justified it, just as when a man states that he owns a thing, or that two persons are husband and wife, or that goods are attached, or that a pauper has a settlement in a certain place. *West Bridgewater* v. *Wareham*, 138 Mass. 305; *Varns* v. *Lane*, 138 Mass. 350, 354; *Rosenberg* v. *Doe*, 148 Mass. 560, 562. See *Eaglesfield* v. *Londonderry*, L. R. 4 Ch. Div. 693, 703.

The representations thus made by the defendants were false.

It is suggested that unless the plaintiff knew the New Hampshire law, which is not alleged, there was no representation that the stock was full paid. But there was an express representation that somehow or other the stock was non-assessable, and that is enough. For if that does not imply that it was full paid, and if some other mode by which it might become non-assessable can be conceived, the declaration discloses by reasonable implication that the only mode in fact under the New Hampshire law was by the par value having been fully paid in. It also alleges that in truth nothing had been paid in, and thus that the representation was false, if the certificate represented stock at all. There is a further allegation that the stock was invalid by reason, as we understand it, of the defendants' acts and omissions set forth. This, so far as it involves a conclusion of law, is an allegation of New Hampshire law, and therefore of matter of fact which we must take to be true. In this respect, also, the representations imported by the face of the certificates set forth were false.

If, as we must assume, the stock was void, the damage to the plaintiff is apparent. The same would be true if, though not void, it was subject to assessment, although it is not distinctly alleged that the plaintiff believed it to be non-assessable. We need not consider, at this stage of the case, what his position would be if it should turn out to have been the law of New Hampshire that a bona fide purchaser of the stock was entitled to hold it as full paid, so that the stock was not void and was not subject to assessment in the plaintiff's hands, even in favor of the creditors of the company. It would not follow necessarily that the plaintiff had suffered no damage. In the market, if an attempt were made to sell, the difference might be material between a title based on payment to the company and one based on bona fides and the absence of notice, a question of fact liable to be disputed.

We have, then, fraudulent representations and damage. The weak point in the declaration is in the connection between these two elements. The allegation is that the plaintiff indorsed, etc., "relying on the validity of said stock as security," but not that he relied on the defendants' representations that it was valid or non-assessable. If the demurrer had pointed out this specific defect and the plaintiff had not seen fit to amend, it might have been questionable whether the declaration ought to be sustained. But the only ground of demurrer that could be taken to support this objection is that it does not appear that the plaintiff was deceived by any false representations made by this defendant. This would seem to have been addressed, and to have been understood to be addressed, to a somewhat different point, viz.: that the representations on the face of the stock, for one reason or another, did not amount to false representations by the defendants to the plaintiff. We therefore give the plaintiff the benefit of a somewhat liberal construction. When we can gather from the whole declaration that it is intended to present a certain case, we do not pronounce it bad for a want of technical accuracy of allegation unless the specific defect is unmistakably pointed out. While it is true that the declaration does not aver in terms that the plaintiff relied upon the representations made in the certificate, it does allege that the defendants delivered the stock to Meacom for the purpose of enabling him to raise money upon it: that Meacom applied to the plaintiff to lend him $300 on the security of the stock; that the plaintiff, relying on the validity of the stock, etc., indorsed the note of Meacom for $300 and obtained that sum "by placing said stock as collateral security for the payment of said amount." These last words import that at the time of the transaction the plaintiff had the certificates, and we think that the declaration may be taken to mean that he knew their purport. We have, then, the representations which we have recited, made by the defendants to the plaintiff, and the plaintiff's belief that the facts represented were true. Still, if we were to be very precise, we have not the fact that these representations were the cause of the belief; but as it is not necessary that they should be the sole cause, the declaration may be assumed to mean that they contributed to the result. *Safford* v. *Grout*, 120 Mass. 20, 25; *Matthews* v. *Bliss*, 22 Pick. 48, 53.

In this view, it is unnecessary to consider whether the declaration does or does not state a cause of action valid in this Commonwealth for an omission to give the warning required by the New Hampshire statute to be placed upon the face of the certificates.

Demurrer overruled.

CONNECTICUT SUPREME COURT OF ERRORS.

George E. GAYLORD and Wife
v.
CITY OF NEW BRITAIN, *Appt.*

(58 Conn. 398.)

The failure of city authorities to clean out a gutter which has become improperly obstructed so that it fails to carry off water resulting from the melting of snow piled between the sidewalk and the curb of the street, within a reasonable time after due notice that the melting of the snow permits the formation of ice from day to day on the sidewalk, renders the city liable for injuries occasioned by slipping on ice which had thus formed upon the walk.

(*Pardee and Loomis, JJ., dissent.*)

(January 6, 1890.)

APPEAL by defendant from a judgment of the Court of Common Pleas for Hartford County in favor of plaintiffs in an action brought to recover damages for injuries alleged to have resulted from defendant's negligence in permitting ice to accumulate upon a certain sidewalk. *Affirmed.*

The facts sufficiently appear in the opinions.

Mr. **Philip J. Markley**, for appellant:

In this rigorous climate the duties of cities and towns in respect to snow and ice are and must be very limited.

Congdon v. *Norwich*, 37 Conn. 414; *Landolt* v. *Norwich*, Id. 615; *Dooley* v. *Meriden*, 44 Conn. 117.

The law does not require a municipal corporation to respond in damages for every injury that may be received on a public street, nor is the corporation required to have its sidewalks so constructed as to secure absolute immunity from danger in using them, nor is it bound to use the utmost care and exertion to that end.

2 Dillon, Mun. Corp. § 1006.

Although ice has accumulated upon a sidewalk to a dangerous extent, it is not the duty of a municipality to remove or cover it in any less than a reasonable time after its formation.

Hartford v. *Talcott*, 48 Conn. 532.

Mr. **Lyman S. Burr**, for appellees:

A duty was imposed upon the defendant to keep the streets, highways and walks within its limits free from ice, snow or obstruction of any kind, and that duty was a sole and exclusive one, and the defendant is liable for any damage arising from its neglect of this duty. A sidewalk is a part of the highway and the space between the sidewalk and curb or gutter is also a part of the highway.

Manchester v. *Hartford*, 30 Conn. 118; *Cusick* v. *Norwich*, 40 Conn. 375; *Ely* v. *Parsons*, 2 Conn. 384; *Hartford* v. *Talcott*, 48 Conn. 525.

Ice formed by the freezing of melted snow by the side of the highway is a defect.

Morse v. *Boston*, 109 Mass. 446.

It is no defense that the defendant used ordinary care and diligence if by such care the difficulty was not removed and the defect still remains.

Horton v. *Ipswich*, 12 Cush. 488.

Cloughessey v. *Waterbury*, 51 Conn. 405, is decisive of this case.

See also *Tripp* v. *Lyman*, 37 Me. 250.

Fenn, *J.*, delivered the opinion of the court:

On the evening of February 19, 1888, Mrs. Gaylord received injuries occasioned by slipping on ice which had accumulated on a flagged walk in the defendant City. This ice had formed the same day from the melting of snow piled between the sidewalk and curb, in a space seven feet in width. For several weeks the sidewalk had been covered with water for a considerable distance at and east and west of the place of the injury, whenever the weather was warm enough to melt the adjacent snow. The residents would clear off or cover the ice in the morning, but ice would form anew toward evening from the snow melted by day. Of this condition of things the defendant was fully informed, and the street commissioner had been twice notified, once at least ten days before February 19, 1888, that the sidewalk was inconvenient and unsafe by reason of the constant accumulation and re-accumulation of ice, and that an accident was probable in consequence.

The difficulty could have been removed and the sidewalk made safe if the gutter on the same side of the street had been kept properly cleaned, or if the snow between the sidewalk and curb had been removed, either of which things could have been done without unreasonable trouble and expense; and the defendant had ample time after notice to make the sidewalk safe, but neglected to do so. The gutter on that side of the street and in front of the place of the accident had been cleared by the defendant on the 8th, and again on the 15th, of February, 1888, but at the time of the accident was so clogged as to prevent the flow of water.

On these facts the court found negligence in the defendant, and that such negligence consisted in not removing the cause of the trouble, which was the snow between the curb and sidewalk, or in allowing the gutter to become improperly obstructed, though fully aware that the sidewalk from the ice formations had been a long time, and was likely to continue to be, dangerous to travelers. Is there manifest error in such finding?

The liability of cities and boroughs for injuries occasioned by icy walks has been fully enunciated and explained by this court in repeated decisions, and the nature and limitations of such liability have been clearly defined and are undoubtedly well understood. It requires no further discussion here. It is sufficient to say that we are aware of no case, in this or any other jurisdiction, wherein the liability of a corporation is extended in such regard beyond responsibility for existing defective conditions within the limits of a walk of which it had, or ought to have had, knowledge, or in which it has been held that a duty devolved upon any such corporation to remove snow or ice, so long as it existed in the state and situation in which it originally fell, or was formed outside the actual limits of the walk by reason of mere proximity and consequent liability to spread over and thereby render dangerous the walk itself. If such a duty can ever exist we confess that we should be slow to find it; and if it were necessary in order to vindicate the judgment of the court below to so hold, we should scarcely hesitate to declare such judgment erroneous.

Such necessity, however, does not exist. For whether in strict consistency with the statement we have just made, the decision, under the peculiar and exceptional facts disclosed in the finding, should be sustained, as based upon the negligence of the defendant in failing to remove the adjacent snow which had been piled and left between the sidewalk and the curb, such snow not existing in the situation where it fell, but having been there accumulated, it is unnecessary to determine, for there is another ground upon which we think the decision of the court below can be clearly vindicated, perhaps in more strict conformity to the allegations of the complaint, which alleges that on February 19, 1888, and long prior thereto, the defendant had permitted ice and snow to accumulate upon the walk described, and that they were so allowed to accumulate by reason of the negligence of the defendant in caring for the sidewalk and the gutter contiguous thereto, and by reason of the refusal of the defendant to properly care for the same, though often requested.

The court below, as we have seen, found that at the time of the accident the gutter was so clogged as to prevent the flow of water, and that the difficulty could have been removed and the sidewalk made safe if the gutter had been kept properly cleared, which could have been done without unreasonable trouble and expense, and that the defendant had ample time after notice and before the accident to do so, and that the defendant was guilty of negligence in allowing the gutter to become improperly obstructed.

So that, leaving the decision of all questions of fact, where by law they pertain, to the trial court, the sole question of law which remains for us to review is, whether the court erred in holding that a duty rested upon the defendant to clear the gutter from improper obstructions, when it could be done without unreasonable trouble or expense, and when it possessed full actual knowledge of its condition, had ample time to do it, and knew that the direct and immediate result of such condition of the gutter was to render the sidewalk inconvenient and unsafe by reason of the constant accumulation and re-accumulation of ice, and that an accident was probable in consequence; a question which it seems to us needs only to be stated to carry upon its face its own manifest answer in the negative.

It will not be denied that a city is under some obligation in reference to the construction of necessary gutters to drain its walks, and a like obligation may exist to care for such gutters when constructed. In either case the duty is preventive in character.

There is no error in the judgment appealed from.

In this opinion **Andrews,** *Ch. J.*, and **Carpenter,** *J.*, concurred.

Pardee, *J.*, dissenting:

There was no structural defect in the highway; neither in the part adapted to the passage of vehicles, nor in that to foot passengers, nor in the gutter.

The defendant moved snow from the inner to the outer edge of the sidewalk, but placed none in the gutter; it did not increase the quantity of the water in the gutter. It only omitted to foresee that water from snow melting where it fell might run upon the walk and might thus become ice dangerous to passengers.

Of course some of the water resulting from the melting of snow which has fallen upon a city of undulating surface will run over the sidewalks. Possibly a portion of this will there become ice dangerous to the traveler. But, because of all this, the obligation is not upon the city, by way of prevention, to remove the snow from its entire surface. This would involve an intolerable expense, but no precaution less thorough than this would suffice, for equal protection must be provided for all places.

The City assumes no legal responsibility by permitting snow to melt where it falls; none when it melts, by leaving the water to find its way into a properly constructed gutter, even if a part flowed upon the sidewalk. There is no legal obligation upon the City to foresee and prevent the freezing of water from melted snow. The responsibility upon it in reference to the ice in question is precisely that which is upon it in reference to ice from water from snow which fell upon adjacent land; that is, to remove or cover it upon reasonable notice. Of the ice in question the City had not such notice. It formed at nightfall and the plaintiff fell in the evening. It is of no legal significance that the City had knowledge that in repeated instances ice had formed at the same place. The ice which caused the fall of the plaintiff was a new and independent formation. In reference to it the City was entitled to the same notice as if it had not previously formed there.

Loomis, *J.*, concurred in this opinion.

MONTANA SUPREME COURT.

MONTANA UNION R. CO., *Appt.*,
v.
Charles LANGLOIS *et al.*, *Respts.*

(....Mont.....)

The exclusive right to use the platform of a railway company for receiving and discharging passengers cannot be granted by the company to one hack owner.

(May 1, 1890.)

APPEAL by plaintiff from an order of the District Court for Silver Bow County set-

NOTE.—*Dominion of railroad over its stations and grounds.*

The dominion of a railroad corporation over its trains, tracks and right of way is no less complete or exclusive than that which every owner has over his own property. Hence the corporation may exclude whom it pleases, when they come to transact their own private business with passengers or other

ting aside a temporary injunction and dismissing the bill in an action brought to enjoin defendants from trespassing upon plaintiff's station grounds and platform. *Affirmed.*

The case is fully stated in the opinion.

Mr. **J. S. Shropshire,** with *Messrs.* **William H. DeWitt** and **M. L. Wines,** for appellant:

The station grounds are the private property of the Company.

Comp. Laws, § 692, p. 816; *Barker* v. *Midland R. Co.* 18 C. B. 46; *Hall* v. *Power,* 12 Met. 482; *Harris* v. *Stevens,* 31 Vt. 79; *Gillis* v. *Pennsylvania R. Co.* 59 Pa. 129; *Illinois Cent. R. Co.* v. *Godfrey,* 71 Ill. 500.

The Railroad Company may make all reasonable regulations for the management of its grounds.

Com. v. *Power,* 7 Met. 596, 1 Am. R. Cas. 389; *Hall* v. *Power, supra; Barker* v. *Midland R. Co.* 18 C. B. 46, 86 Eng. L. & Eq. 253; *Caterham R. Co.* v. *London, B. & S. C. R. Co.* 1 C. B. N. S. 410, 40 Eng. L. & Eq. 259.

It is not unlawful, nor against public policy, for a railroad company to carry passengers by stage to and from one of its stations and an adjacent village, in connection with and as a part of its business of transporting passengers upon its road.

Buffit v. *Troy & B. R. Co.* 36 Barb. 420, 40 N. Y. 168.

For a consideration, it may give this right to enter to one, and exclude all others.

Beadell v. *Eastern Counties R. Co.* 2 C. B. N. S. 509.

The Railroad Company may exclude hackmen and others not there for the purpose of taking passage on the train.

Summitt v. *State,* 8 Lea, 413; *Johnson* v. *Chicago, R. I. & P. R. Co.* 51 Iowa, 25; *Barker* v. *Midland R. Co.* 18 C. B. 46, 86 Eng. L. & Eq. 253.

Hackmen have no right in the station grounds, and may be excluded.

Summitt v. *State, supra; Landrigan* v. *State,* 31 Ark. 50; *Barker* v. *Midland R. Co.* 18 C. B.

---

third persons. This applies to selling lunches to passengers or soliciting orders from them for the sale of lunches. Fluker v. Georgia R. & Bkg. Co. 2 L. R. A. 843, 81 Ga. 461.

While such ownership carries with it a right of control in most respects, the same as in private property, a railroad station or steamboat wharf is to some extent a public place. The public have the right to come and go there for the purpose of travel, for taking and leaving passengers and for other matters growing out of the business of the company as a common carrier. Griswold v. Webb (R. I.) 7 L. R. A. 303.

A hackman conveying passengers to a railroad depot for transportation, and aiding them to alight upon the platform of the corporation, is as rightfully upon the same as the passengers alighting. Tobin v. Portland, S. & P. R. Co. 59 Me. 183.

But the company has the right to say that no business of any other character shall be carried on within the limits of its property; and to say that no one shall come there to solicit trade, simply because it may be convenient for travelers, and to say that none except those whom it permits shall solicit in the business of hacking or expressing. Griswold v. Webb, *supra.*

And when notice of such prohibition has been given the license which otherwise might be implied is at an end, and it is the duty of persons engaged in any such business to heed the notice and to retire from the premises. Barney v. Oyster Bay & H. Steamboat Co. 67 N. Y. 301; Com. v. Power, 7 Met. 596.

In Barney v. Oyster Bay & H. Steamboat Co. it was said that a common carrier of passengers may establish on its car or vessel an agency for the delivery of passengers' baggage, and may exclude all other persons from entering upon it for the purpose of soliciting or receiving orders from passengers in competition with such agency.

So an innkeeper would not be bound to entertain an agent of a rival inn who sought to decoy away his customers. Jencks v. Coleman, 2 Sumn. 221.

But an innholder has no right to exclude from his inn a stage driver who entered it to solicit guests to patronize his stage, in opposition to a driver of a rival line, who had been admitted for a like purpose. Markham v. Brown, 8 N. H. 523.

Regulations for use of depot and grounds.

In Old Colony R. Co. v. Tripp, 6 New Eng. Rep. 366, 147 Mass. 35, it was held that a railroad corporation may contract with one to furnish the means to carry incoming passengers or their baggage and merchandise from its stations, and may grant to him the exclusive right there to solicit the patronage of such passengers; and that such an agreement was not within the Statute which provides that such a corporation "shall give to all persons or companies reasonable and equal terms, facilities and accommodations . . . for the use of its depot and other buildings and grounds." The court held that the Statute applied only to the relations between common carriers and their patrons, or those who had the right to use the station, and did not give others the right to go there and solicit business because another had the right. Morton, *Ch. J.,* Field and Devens, *JJ.,* dissenting. See also Harris v. Stevens, 31 Vt. 79.

If the contract is reasonable, and the exclusion of the party is a reasonable and proper regulation to carry it into effect on the part of the corporation, the regulation may be sustained. Jencks v. Coleman, 2 Sumn. 222.

But a regulation which does not give to all persons or companies reasonable and equal terms, facilities and accommodations for the use of its depot and other buildings and grounds in the transportation of persons and property would be in effect the establishment of a monopoly not granted by its charter, and which might be solely for its own benefit, and not for the benefit of the public. New England Express Co. v. Maine Cent. R. Co. 57 Me. 188; Parkinson v. Great Western R. Co. L. R. 6 C. P. 554; Palmer v. London, B. & S. C. R. Co. L. R. 6 C. P. 194.

In the case of Summitt v. State, 8 Lea, 413, notwithstanding the rule of the company forbidding hackmen to enter the building, the right of a hackman to go into a part of the depot to obtain the baggage of a passenger whose check he had was not controverted.

An unlicensed hackdriver specially ordered for a steamboat passenger is not a trespasser in going with his carriage for the purpose of meeting such passenger upon a wharf used by the steamboat company to receive and discharge all passengers, although the rules of the wharf forbid any but private carriages or hackney carriages which are licensed to stand upon the wharf. Griswold v. Webb (R. I.) 7 L. R. A. 302.

If a passenger orders a carriage to take him from the terminus such carriage is *pro hac vice* a private carriage, in the sense that it is not standing for hire. Masterson v. Short, 43 How. Pr. 451.

46; *McKone* v. *Michigan Cent. R. Co.* 51 Mich. 601; Patterson, Railway Accident Law, 219.

No inconvenience to the public being shown, a railroad company will not be enjoined at the suit of a hackman to admit him; and, of course, an injunction should be granted to the company to exclude such hackmen.

Beadell v. *Eastern Counties R. Co. supra; Painter* v. *London, B. & S. C. R. Co.* 2 C. B. N. S. 702; *Barker* v. *Midland R. Co. supra; Marriott* v. *London & S. W. R. Co.* 1 C. B. N. S. 499; *Dubuque & S. C. R. Co.* v. *Richmond*, 86 U. S. 19 Wall. 584 (22 L. ed. 173); *Old Colony R. Co.* v. *Tripp*, 6 New Eng. Rep. 366, 147 Mass. 35, and cases cited.

Mr. **Charles O'Donnell**, with *Mr.* **John J. McHatton**, for respondent:

Although the depot grounds and platforms may be private as to ownership, they are not so as to the purposes to which they are appropriate. And while they are used mainly with a view to the convenience of those who travel or transport their goods by the road, still others, against whom no special objections exist, should not be unreasonably or unequally excluded.

Hutchinson, Carr. § 523, p. 424; Rorer, Railroads, par. 4, p. 480.

Defendants, in common with all citizens of the Commonweath, have the right, at all reasonable and proper times, to go upon the plaintiff's premises, when necessary to the transaction of their business, unless by so doing they in some way obstruct or interfere with said Company in the discharge of its legitimate business.

Worcester v. *Western R. Corp.* 4 Met. 564; *Com.* v. *Power*, 7 Met. 596; *Cambios* v. *Philadelphia & R. R. Co.* 9 Phila. 411.

A railroad company cannot monopolize the business of transporting passengers and freight from its stations.

Summitt v. *State*, 8 Lea (Tenn.) 413, 9 Am. & Eng. R. R. Cas. 302; *Cambios* v. *Philadelphia & R. R. Co. supra; Markham* v. *Brown*, 8 N. H. 523.

Whatever may be plaintiff's right to exclude all common carriers of passengers or merchandise from its depot and grounds, it cannot arbitrarily admit to its grounds and platform one common carrier and exclude all others.

Parkinson v. *Great Western R. Co.* L. R. 6 C. P. 554; *Palmer* v. *London, B. & S. C. R. Co.* L. R. 6 C. P. 194; *New England Exp. Co.* v. *Maine Cent. R. Co* 57 Me. 188; *Marriott* v. *London & S. W. R. Co.* 1 C. B. N. S. 499.

Harwood, *J.*, delivered the opinion of the court:

This is an action for an injunction. The complaint sets forth: That the appellant is a railway corporation, organized under the laws of the Territory of Montana. That it is the owner of, and operating as a common carrier, a line of railroad running from Garrison, in Deer Lodge County, and divers other stations, to its station known as "South Butte," in Silver Bow County, Mont., the latter station being about one and one half miles from the United States postoffice in the City of Butte, in said Silver Bow County. That at the said station of South Butte the appellant is the owner of and in possession of a large number of railway tracks, yard, station grounds and buildings; that the appellant has at said depot or station building at South Butte a long platform for the accommodation of passengers, whom the appellant transfers to and from said station; and that said depot grounds are surrounded by a board fence, inside of which hacks and wagons are accustomed to drive for the purpose of conveying passengers to appellant's passenger trains, and receiving passengers from said trains. That at the time stated, and for a long time prior thereto, the appellant had a contract with the government of the United States whereby the appellant was obliged to carry upon its trains the United States mail matter to said station at South Butte, and thence to the postoffice at the City of Butte. That appellants contracted with Geoffrey and Thomas Lovell, in the name of Lovell Bros., to carry said United States mail from said station at South Butte to the United States postoffice at Butte City; and appellant further contracted with said Lovell Bros. to have an ample supply of backs and omnibuses at said station of South Butte, at the arrival of all trains, for the safe and comfortable transportation of all passengers who desire such transportation from said station of South Butte to the City of Butte and points adjacent thereto. And in consideration thereof the appellant granted and agreed with said Lovell Bros. to give them the exclusive right to drive and stand their hacks, carriages and omnibuses along the edge of the said platform. That respondents are the owners or drivers of hacks and carriages, and at the times complained of, and against the will and protest of plaintiff, have forcibly driven their hacks and carriages into said depot yard of plaintiff, and driven and stood said hacks adjacent to and against the platform aforesaid, and have forcibly kept from such platform the hacks of Lovell Bros. That plaintiff, by its agents and servants, has often protested to defendants against their conduct in that respect, and repeatedly told defendants that they could not occupy said platform privileges; but that plaintiff did offer defendants the privileges of driving into plaintiff's said depot at said station, and standing their hacks in said yard, to deliver and receive passengers, provided the defendants would keep away from the said platform a distance of fifty feet, which place was clearly indicated to the defendants; and further that defendants might have the privilege of driving and standing their hacks and carriages at a point on said platform east of the passenger depot not occupied by the hacks of said Lovell Bros. That, notwithstanding these protests and concessions of plaintiff, the defendants continue to drive and stand their hacks next to said platform, and within said fifty-feet limit; and defendants expressly decline to desist from driving and standing their hacks at said forbidden place, and expressly declare that they will persist in placing their hacks at the platform reserved, as aforesaid, to Lovell Bros. That if the defendants continue to do those acts complained of, or any of them, the plaintiff will be prevented from carrying out its part of the said contract with Lovell Bros., and the latter will decline to transport the said United States mail from the station aforesaid, and to the postoffice at Butte

City, and to care for plaintiff's railway passengers, as aforesaid. That plaintiff has not a plain, speedy and adequate remedy at law. Upon the facts set forth, the plaintiff prays that the defendants be restrained by injunction from driving or standing backs, cabs, carriages or busses at the said platform of plaintiff at the west side of its depot buildings, or within fifty feet thereof.

The defendants answer, and admit that defendant Charles Langlois is the owner of a line of hacks, vehicles and carriages, with which he is engaged in carrying passengers in and about the City of Butte, and to and from the station and trains of plaintiff, and that the other defendants named are in his employ as drivers of said hacks, carriages, etc.; but the defendants deny that they, or either of them, ever in any manner interfered with the said plaintiff in the conduct of its said railroad or passenger business at South Butte or elsewhere, or that they, or either of them, interfered with the comfort or convenience of passengers of plaintiff at said station. The defendants further allege that plaintiff never had any contract with any of its passengers to carry or transport them further than its said station at South Butte; and that plaintiff's contract for transportation of its passengers to said station ends and is fully executed when such passengers are landed on said platform; and that all such passengers are obliged to procure and pay for their transportation from said platform to the City of Butte or elsewhere. That the defendants, in their conduct in running their line of hacks and carriages for the transportation of passengers and baggage to and from the said station, have always conducted the same in a quiet and orderly manner, and have not gone upon the platform of plaintiff, nor solicited nor annoyed plaintiff's passengers, but have driven their hacks and carriages up to said platform on the west side of said station, and stood them there to receive and carry any and all such passengers as might wish to employ them to do so. That they never have at any time interfered, nor attempted to interfere, with the hacks of said Lovell Bros. at said station. That defendants have only driven their hacks up to said platform when there was a vacancy thereat, and had only refused to remove their hacks therefrom to make way for the hacks of said Lovell Bros. The defendants further allege that the portion of plaintiff's platform which is west of the said passenger station, as described in plaintiff's complaint, is the portion of the platform where passengers alight from plaintiff's trains at said station. That the portion of the said platform east of said station building which plaintiff alleges to have offered to allow defendants to drive their hacks to for the purpose of landing and receiving passengers is used almost entirely for handling freight and baggage, and the ground along-side thereof is always used by baggage and freight wagons. That if said Lovell Bros. are allowed the exclusive use of said platform west of said station-house it will give the said Lovell Bros. the entire control of the business of carrying passengers from the said station, to the discomfort, inconvenience and detriment of said passengers, and to the injury and destruction of defendants' passenger carrying business from said station. That defendants have not in any manner interfered with or hindered the plaintiff or Lovell Bros. in the handling or transportation of the United States mails over said railroad, or from said station to the postoffice in the City of Butte or elsewhere; but have always allowed and conceded to the said plaintiff and to the said Lovell Bros. sufficient ground and space at and against said platform for the use of said Lovell Bros.' baggage wagon, omnibus, two carriages or hacks and their wagon used in carrying United States mails, without any interference or hindrance for defendants, or either of them. The defendants deny that if said acts of defendants complained of be allowed to continue, the plaintiff will thereby suffer irreparable injury, or any injury whatever; or that, if defendants continue said acts complained of, it will hinder, prevent or delay the plaintiff in its business. And the defendants allege that it is not for the convenience of plaintiff's business that they have entered into said contract with said Lovell Bros. as alleged in said complaint, but for the purpose of giving said Lovell Bros. an undue advantage over these defendants and other hackmen in the said passenger carrying business from said station, and to exclude defendants and other hackmen from any competition in said business.

The foregoing facts are substantially the allegations of the complaint and answer, respectively. No other pleadings were filed. Final hearing of the cause was had upon the facts set forth in the complaint and answer, and determined in the court below by an order setting aside the temporary injunction, and denying the relief prayed for by plaintiff, from which order plaintiff appealed. The whole question involved in this controversy is compassed by the proposition, on the part of the plaintiff, "that it is the owner of said grounds, depot buildings and platform, and that it may regulate the use of said platform as it desires, providing the traveling public is not inconvenienced; that it may, if it desires, engage in carrying passengers in hacks to and from its trains; that, if it was so engaged, it would have the right to its own property for such purpose; that, if it has such rights, it can as well employ Lovell Bros. with hacks to do such service as to own the hacks; that, if the plaintiff has the right to its platform, it has the right to sell that right to the Lovells for a valuable consideration," and should be protected in the exercise and benefits of these rights. These propositions are controverted by defendants in so far as they affirm the right of the plaintiff to grant exclusive use of a portion of said platform to one party to approach and occupy the same, to convey passengers thereto and receive passengers therefrom, and exclude all others from so doing. No complaint is made that any reasonable rule or regulation made by plaintiff for the government of its depot platform or grounds has been violated, or that defendants have committed any act which interferes with the transaction of plaintiff's business, except in so far as defendants interfere with the exclusive use of said portion of plaintiff's platform granted to Lovell Bros. In respect to the delivery of the United States mail matter at said platform, and transportation thereof to the

United States postoffice in the City of Butte, it is admitted that ample space for that purpose is left to the use of the Company and its employés, according to its requirements. The question of handling the United States mail matter, it seems, is incidentally brought into this controversy; the transfer of this mail matter for the plaintiff being principally the consideration performed by Lovell Bros. for the grant of exclusive use of the designated portions of the railway platform to them, at which place Lovell Bros. may ply for passengers to patronize their hacks and carriages.

If the plaintiff has the right to grant the exclusive use of its platform in the respect mentioned, it may be granted for any other valid consideration as well. It is not denied that a railway company may make and enforce all reasonable rules and regulations necessary to govern persons coming to its station buildings, platform and grounds. It is highly proper and beneficial to all concerned that this be done. The law recognizes this right on the part of the common carrier, and the courts enforce it. Upon this point the learned counsel for appellant cites many authorities, with which this court agrees; but we conceive that the matter under consideration is a far different proposition. The grant of a special privilege to Lovell Bros. to use the specified portion of plaintiff's platform at said station, and the exclusion of all from approaching thereto, to land or receive passengers, is not a rule or regulation, in the common acceptation of these terms as used in the legal authorities, and applied to this subject. We therefore find in the numerous and valuable authorities cited on that theory only general aid in solving this controversy. A general rule or regulation, as applied to the government of the conduct of persons, or of a class of persons, contemplates uniformity, and not discrimination, in its requirements. This controversy must be solved by a consideration of the mutual rights of the appellant as a common carrier and its passengers. All passengers in common are entitled to equal opportunities and conveniences of place to approach and depart from plaintiff's trains. At the station mentioned the railway company either commences or terminates its engagement to transport its passengers to and from said station, as the case may be. The contract of the railway company does not require that it either furnish conveyance to bring the passenger to said platform, or transport him therefrom. The passenger may employ whom he desires to bring him there for the departure on plaintiff's trains, or to meet and receive him on his arrival at said station. But the plaintiff contends that it may grant the exclusive use of a large portion of its platform to one party, at which to land passengers for departure on said trains, or to receive passengers from said trains, and, if the passenger is willing to contract with this one party for transportation thereto or therefrom, such passenger may have the convenience of landing or departing from that portion of said platform; otherwise, he must land fifty feet away from said platform, or go to another portion of the platform, incumbered with express and baggage wagons and the handling of freight and baggage matter.

Suppose a passenger travels every day from this station, and returns, he is entitled to the same convenience and facilities for approaching and leaving this depot as other passengers. If he contracts with another than Lovell Bros., or the party to whom the Railway Company has granted the exclusive use of said portion of the platform, to bring him there, and be there to receive him on his return, he must alight from his carriage, or be received by it, fifty feet away from said platform, or be landed where the express and baggage matter is handled; while the passenger who employs Lovell Bros. for the same purpose may land at and depart from this convenient portion of said platform. Or if a party desired to use his own carriage to bring him to said station, or receive him on his return, it seems the same conditions would prevail.

Certainly, if the plaintiff has the right to grant the exclusive use of said platform to one, and exclude the public hackmen therefrom, it would apparently have the right to exclude the private hackmen therefrom. To the strong it would perhaps make no difference, as a matter of convenience, just where they were landed at or received from said station; but to the feeble and the helpless, and those incumbered with their care, it would be a matter of great discomfiture and inconvenience. Still other conditions which directly result from the position demanded by plaintiff, and which militate against the equal rights of passengers, may be suggested. Suppose all other hackmen who desire to compete with Lovell Bros. for the carrying passengers to and from this depot will perform the service for half the sum charged by Lovell Bros., are the passengers entitled to the benefit of this competition? Has not the passenger the right to call these other hackmen to his service, and, if he does call them, has he not a right to have such other hackmen approach the platform at the same place, or at least have an equal and common chance to approach at this same convenient place, as his co-passenger who employs Lovell Bros.? If any of the passengers do accept these better terms, they must suffer the discrimination of being denied a landing at that portion of the platform granted exclusively to Lovell Bros., or, when they alight from plaintiff's trains, they either go fifty feet away from that portion of said platform, or to the east side of the depot building, for transportation with a hackman at the less rate. It is a rule of universal application that the public is entitled to whatever competition may grow out of the public demands, on the one hand, and the contest of others to supply such demands, and receive the compensation therefor. Are not the conditions here sought to be so controlled by the plaintiff as to stifle the natural development of such competition?

It is alleged by the plaintiff that by its arrangement with Lovell Bros. the latter engage to have a sufficient number of hacks and carriages, at the arrival of all passenger trains, to transport such passengers to the City of Butte from said station. But the plaintiff does not contract to carry its passengers destined to said station beyond that point, nor to see that such passengers are provided with transportation beyond that point. The plaintiff simply undertakes to reap a benefit from the necessity of its passengers to procure on their own account, and from such party, and on such terms as they may, transportation to the city. This benefit is sought to be derived by the plaintiff from a grant of the most favorable portion of the platform, where plaintiff sees fit to land its passengers, exclusively to one party to solicit their patronage, and, for this grant, such party aids plaintiff in carrying out its contract to deliver the United States mails at the postoffice in the City of Butte On principle, we cannot reconcile these conditions which are demanded by appellant with the rule that all who come to take passage or who arrive at the station of a common carrier are entitled to equal convenience and opportunity to approach said station or depart therefrom. It seems to us that the direct effect of appellant's position is to say to its passengers, "You must employ Lovell Bros., or suffer certain inconveniences in taking passage with another."

These observations are not to be confounded with the question as to whether the railway company may not exclude all hackmen from its station buildings, or even from the platform, or set bounds on its grounds beyond which they should not come, as the exigencies of the situation and business might reasonably require, or to make and enforce any other reasonable rule as to the government of its depot buildings and grounds. It is not a general question of that character which here engages the consideration of the court. The Constitution of this State (art. 15, § 7) provides that "no discrimination in charges or facilities for transportation of freight or passengers of the same class shall be made by any railroad or transportation or express company between persons or places within the State."

The reported cases, involving like or similar facts as the one at bar, which have come to our attention, are few in number. The recent case of *Old Colony R. Co.* v. *Tripp*, 147 Mass. 35, 6 New Eng. Rep. 366, is the nearest in point. The facts involved in that case are quite similar to the case at bar, although it appears from the statement of facts and the opinion that while exclusive grant was made by the railroad company to Porter & Sons to come upon the depot premises to solicit passengers and baggage for transportation, and all other hackmen were forbidden to come there for that purpose, still all hackmen were allowed equal privileges to come to the station to deliver passengers and baggage, and to receive such as they had a previous order for. While we concur in the general principles of law applicable to common carriers, announced by the majority of the nearly evenly divided court in that case, we cannot subscribe to the conclusions drawn by the majority. On the contrary, after a careful consideration of that case, we are inclined to adopt the reasoning and conclusion of the dissenting opinion delivered by the three minority judges. The majority opinion in that case very clearly and forcibly states the general principles of law governing common carriers applicable to the present consideration. The court says: "The plaintiff is obliged to be a common carrier of passengers. It is its duty to furnish reasonable facilities and accommodations for the use of all persons who seek for transportation over its road. It provides its depot for the use of persons who were transported on its cars, to or from the station, and holds it for that use; and it has no right to exclude from it persons seeking access to it for the use for which it was intended and is maintained. It can subject the use to rules and regulations; but by statute, if not by common law, the regulations must be such as secure reasonable and equal use of the premises to all having such right to use them." We do not find it consonant with reason, based upon those general propositions, to draw the conclusion that the Railroad Company may bring its passengers to a common landing, where the necessity, comfort or convenience of their situation compels them to obtain on their own account transportation to some place beyond, and there introduce them to one favored party, saying: "If you engage transportation from this party, you may do so here on the spot, without delay or inconvenience, and take passage from this platform without delay or inconvenience, provided you will engage this particular party, and pay his demands; otherwise, you must suffer the importunity of this party to take passage with him, and if you will not, you must suffer the inconvenience and delay of going to some other point to engage conveyance and take passage."

All this the Railroad does, not for a benefit to the passengers, but for a benefit to itself, over and above what the passenger has paid for transportation over the railroad. If the Railroad Company set bounds beyond which all hackmen were forbidden to come, and undertook to forbid all solicitation within the depot or on the platform on the part of hackmen or others for employment, this would be an entirely different proposition. The Company does not undertake to protect the passenger from that annoyance in these cases, but invites it and farms out the exclusive privilege and opportunity to do this. In the case cited *supra* the majority of the court bases its conclusion on the ground that the hackman has no right or license to be in plaintiff's depot without the express or tacit permission of plaintiff; and this license, if granted, may be revoked at pleasure. We may grant this premise. The right which the Railroad has to exclude all hackmen from its depot buildings and platform may rest upon the same principle. But has the Railroad Company, in dealing with its passengers, and exercising a control over their movements and the conditions which surround them for the time being, a right to place one hackman in their midst, with exclusive control over the common conveniences and facilities of the place at which the passenger may land, or from which he may depart, so that, if the passenger obtain the use of these conveniences and facilities, he must purchase the privilege from such hackmen or suffer discrimination? The use of these common conveniences and facilities belongs to the passengers alike, in the order in which they may come to occupy them; whereas the Railroad Company has granted away what belonged to the passengers in common, and the one holding the grant may use it as an advantage over the passenger, to compel his employment. It is said in the opinion cited *supra:* "If a railroad company allows a person to sell refreshments or newspapers in its depots, or to cultivate flowers on its station grounds, the Statute does not extend the same right to all persons." Upon this proposition it might be suggested that the passenger has no common interest or rights which meet and intermingle with the rights of the common carrier on this subject, or which are affected by such a grant. The same reply may be made, we think, with good reason, to the proposition as to a place to serve refreshments on the premises of the plaintiff. The passenger has no common rights which are taken away or interfered with by the Company in this respect. It is true, the passenger's necessities may require that he have food at proper times on his journey; but all passengers have an equal right to provide supplies, under regulations which apply to all alike as to the amount of baggage allowed to each. Moreover, this question has no relation to the mutual engagements existing between the common carrier and its passengers. The passenger has purchased, or proposes to purchase, from the common carrier, transportation, and he must come to the station to receive such transportation, and on arriving at his destination he must depart from the station. The right to come to the station, and depart therefrom, under reasonable regulations which apply alike to all passengers, without special conditions, is incidental to the main contract; while the supply of refreshments or newspapers, or the cultivation of flowers, at the station grounds, has, as we conceive, no appropriate connection with the engagements of the passenger and the common carrier.

The case cited *supra* is the only American case brought to our attention which passes upon points directly involved herein. The subject is apparently a new one in this country. The English cases involving the main subject of controversy are also few in number.

In the case of *Marriott* v. *London & S. W. R. Co.*, 1 C. B. N. S. 499, the complainant, Marriott, alleged that he brought passengers to defendant's railway station, and the latter refused him access to the station grounds to deliver his passengers there, while at the same time this privilege was granted to other omnibuses; and, upon this showing, an injunction was granted. Other English cases bearing upon the main subject here under consideration have been examined. *Beadell* v. *Eastern Counties R. Co.* 2 C. B. N. S. 509; *Painter* v. *London, B. & S. C. R. Co.* Id. 702; *Barker* v. *Midland R. Co.* 18 C. B. 46.

The demands in the case at bar on the part of plaintiff go beyond those urged in any of the cases so far examined by us.

Upon grounds of sound reason, public policy and the general principles of law governing common carriers, as well as the provisions of the Constitution, we believe *the order of the court below ought to be affirmed, and it is so ordered.*

Blake, *Ch. J.*, concurs.

Associate Justice **DeWitt,** having been counsel for plaintiff in this action in the court below, did not sit in the consideration thereof in this court.

WEST VIRGINIA SUPREME COURT OF APPEALS.

J. M. GUFFEY *et al.*

v.

R. M. HUKILL, *Piff. in Err.*

(....W. Va.....)

*1. **Where a lease for years contains a clause of forfeiture** for breach of its covenant to pay rent, or other covenant, but no clause of re-entry for such forfeiture, demand and re-entry is not the only mode by which the landlord may enforce the forfeiture.

2. **A lease for years for drilling for petroleum oil and gas** contains provision: "The parties of the second part covenant to commence operations for said purposes within nine months from and after the execution of this lease, or to thereafter pay to the party of the first part $1.33⅓ per month, until work is commenced—the money to be deposited in the hands of John Kennedy for each and every month. And a failure on the part of said second parties to comply with either one or the other of the foregoing conditions shall work an absolute forfeiture of this lease;" and there is no covenant for re-entry, and there is failure to commence operations and to pay money in lieu thereof, and the lessor leases to another person. *Held*, the first lease is thus avoided, and the second lease is good against it, as the execution of the second lease is a sufficient

*Head notes by BRANNON, J.

NOTE.—*Lease; re-entry of landlord, on forfeiture of tenant's estate.*

In case of forfeiture by nonperformance of the covenants of a lease the lessor may avail himself of the right of re-entry or not, and if he does not the term will continue, for the lessee cannot elect that it shall cease or be void. Rede v. Farr, 6 Maule & S. 121; Arnsby v. Woodward, 6 Barn. & C. 519.

A tenant cannot insist that his own act amounted to a forfeiture. Belloc v. Davis, 38 Cal. 251; Canfield v. Westcott, 5 Cow. 270; Williams v. Talbot, 16 Tex. 1.

A clause in a lease which provides for its termination at the election of the lessors, upon default in payment of rent, although in the form of a mere stipulation or contract, is still a condition, since it provides for ending the term, and forfeiture of the estate in case of default. Horton v. New York Cent. & H. R. R. Co. 12 Abb. N. C. 30; Beach v. Nixon, 9 N. Y. 35; Clark v. Jones, 1 Denio, 516.

In a lease for years it depends upon the question whether the estate was made absolutely to terminate on the determination of a condition subsequent contained in it, or whether only a right of re-entry was given, as in the former case it would cease at once. Towle v. Palmer, 1 Abb. Pr. N. S. 95, 1 Robt. 453.

If the condition in the lease was merely that the landlord might re-enter, the lease was voidable only and might be affirmed by acceptance of rent. Chalker v. Chalker, 1 Conn. 79; Jackson v. Andrews, 18 Johns. 431; Clark v. Jones, *supra;* Pennant's Case, 3 Coke, 64 *a;* Duppa v. Mayo. 1 Saund. 287b; Co. Litt. 215 *a;* Reid v. Parsons, 2 Chitty, 247; Roberts v. Davey, 1 Nev. & M. 448.

The mere receipt of rent due before forfeiture,

declaration of forfeiture, without demand and re-entry.

3. **The second lessee** may maintain unlawful detainer against the first lessee in possession.

(June 24, 1890.)

ERROR to the Circuit Court for Monongalia County to review a judgment in favor of plaintiffs in an action brought to recover possession of a certain tract of land. *Affirmed.*

The facts sufficiently appear in the opinion.

Mr. **Okey Johnson**, for plaintiff in error:

The plaintiffs never having been in possession, unlawful detainer would not lie. Nor will it lie to enforce a forfeiture of a lease, but the remedy is by ejectment under chapter 93 of the Code.

Hawkins v. *Wilson*, 1 W. Va. 117; *Raleigh County* v. *Ellison*, 8 W. Va. 308; *Bowyer* v. *Seymour*, 13 W. Va. 18; *Duff* v. *Good*, 24 W. Va. 685.

In any view of the case the plaintiffs below are estopped to set up any claim to the premises, because they stood by and saw Hukill spend large sums of money without setting up any claim to possession under their pretended lease.

Philadelphia, W. & B. R. Co. v. *Dubois*, 79 U. S. 12 Wall. 47 (20 L. ed. 265); *Erwin* v. *Lowry*, 48 U. S. 7 How. 172 (12 L. ed. 655); *Kirk* v. *Hamilton*, 102 U. S. 68 (26 L. ed. 79); *Close* v. *Glenwood Cemetery*, 107 U. S. 466 (27 L. ed. 408); *Green* v. *Biddle*, 21 U. S. 8 Wheat. 1 (5 L. ed. 547); *Bank of United States* v. *Lee*, 38 U. S. 13 Pet. 107 (10 L. ed. 81).

Besides they were bound to take notice of the rights of Hukill, because he was openly on the land boring for oil from early in May, 1889, until July 5, 1889, before he had any notice that plaintiffs below set up any claim to the possession.

Indiana & I. C. R. Co. v. *Sprague*, 103 U. S. 756 (26 L. ed. 554); *Bowman* v. *Wathen*, 42 U. S. 1 How 189 (11 L. ed. 97); *Lea* v. *Polk County Copper Co.* 62 U. S. 21 How. 493 (16 L. ed. 203); *Landes* v. *Brant*, 51 U. S. 10 How. 348 (13 L. ed. 449); *Hughes* v. *United States*, 71 U. S. 4 Wall. 232 (18 L. ed. 303); *Townsend* v. *Little*, 109 U. S. 504 (27 L. ed. 1012).

A clause in a lease declaring that if the rent is not paid when due the tenant's rights and privileges under the lease shall become absolutely forfeited does not have the effect on the happening of the default of avoiding the lease, but renders it voidable at the option of the lessor.

Creveling v. *West End Iron Co.* 51 N. J. L. 34; *Galey* v. *Kellerman*, 123 Pa. 491; *Wills* v. *Manufacturers Natural Gas Co.* 5 L. R. A. 603, 130 Pa. 222.

If the lessor does not avail himself of the right to forfeit, the term will continue, for the lessee cannot elect that it shall cease or be void.

Arnsby v. *Woodward*, 6 Barn. & C. 519; *Rede* v. *Farr*, 6 Maule & S. 121; *Reid* v. *Parsons*, 2 Chitty, 247.

The lease does not fall without action on the part of the lessor.

Taylor, Land. and T. § 492; *Doe* v. *Bancks*, 4 Barn. & Ald. 401; *Arnsby* v. *Woodward*, *supra; Doe* v. *Birch*, 1 Mees. & W. 402; *Porter* v. *Merrill*, 124 Mass. 534; *Ludlow* v. *New York & H. R. Co.* 12 Barb. 440; *Phelps* v. *Chesson*, 12 Ired. L. 194; *Bowman* v. *Foot*, 29 Conn. 331; *Read* v. *Tuttle*, 35 Conn. 25.

The common law clearly and specifically declares that upon breach of the covenant to pay rent, before advantage can be taken by the lessor of a clause that on nonpayment of the rent when due the lease shall be void, the lessor must first make a demand for the actual sum due, on the day it is due, shortly before sunset of the day, at the most notorious place on the land; demand must be made in fact though no one is there, and in the absence of sufficient distress on the premises, re-entry is made by going on the land with witnesses and declaring that for want of sufficient distress, and nonpayment of rent demanded, mentioning the amount, he re-enters and re-possesses himself of the premises.

Jackson v. *Harrison*, 17 Johns. 66; *Connor* v. *Bradley*, 42 U. S 1 How. 211 (11 L. ed. 105); *Rede* v. *Farr*, 6 Maule & S. 121; *Doe* v. *Bateman*, 2 Barn. & Ald. 168; *M'Cormick* v. *Connell*, 6 Serg & R. 151; *Lesley* v. *Randolph*, 4 Rawle, 123; 8 Am. & Eng. Encyclop. Law, 443; *Roe* v. *Davis*, 7 East, 363; *Doe* v. *Paul*, 3 Car. & P. 613; *Jackson* v. *Kipp*, 3 Wend. 230; *Prout* v. *Roby*, 82 U. S. 15 Wall. 471 (21 L. ed. 58); *Gage* v. *Bates*, 40 Cal. 384; *Collins* v. *Hasbrouck*, 56 N. Y. 157; *Van Rensselaer* v. *Jewett*, 2 N. Y. 141; *Boyd* v. *Talbert*, 12 Ohio, 214; Co. Litt. 201; *Duppa* v. *Mayo*, 1 Wms. Saund. 287, *note 16; Smith* v. *Whitbeck*, 13 Ohio St. 471; *Sheets* v. *Selden*, 74 U. S. 7 Wall. 420 (19 L. ed. 168); Taylor, Land. and T. § 493, *note 6; Bowman* v. *Foot*, *Read* v. *Tuttle* and *Doe* v. *Birch*, *supra; Garnhart* v. *Finney*, 40 Md. 449; *Rogers* v. *Snow*, 118 Mass. 118; *Miller* v. *Sparks*, 4 Colo. 303; *People* v. *Dudley*, 58 N. Y. 323; *Gaskill* v. *Trainer*, 3 Cal. 334; *Jenkins* v.

after the lease had been forfeited, will not be a waiver of the forfeiture. Pendill v. Union Min. Co. 7 West. Rep. 452, 64 Mich. 172; Jackson v. Allen, 3 Cow. 220; Bleecker v. Smith, 13 Wend. 553.

And certainly the mere payment of rent or royalty, unless fully paid, would not waive the forfeiture, as it would be a continuing cause of forfeiture. Alexander v. Hodges, 41 Mich. 691; Doe v. Woodbridge, 9 Barn. & C. 376; Doe v. Allen, 3 Taunt. 78; Doe v. Jones, 5 Exch. 498.

The estate of the tenant would still continue subject to the right of re-entry. Garner v. Hannah, 6 Duer, 270.

Election of remedies.

Where the controversy related to the sinking and boring of oil wells in land, in violation of rights therein claimed by the plaintiff, a court of equity would grant relief by an injunction (Allegany Oil Co. v. Bradford Oil Co. 21 Hun, 32); yet a party, by insisting upon his claim of forfeiture, and to recover the land, must waive the claim for damages for breach of the covenant, and cannot be allowed to pursue both remedies at the same time and in the same action. Underhill v. Saratoga & W. R. Co. 20 Barb. 467.

Where a landlord elects to proceed at law against a tenant to enforce a forfeiture of the lease for nonperformance of its conditions, or for a violation of a covenant, he cannot, during the pendency of the suit at law against the tenant, have relief in equity against him, as upon a subsisting tenancy. Conger v. Duryee, 90 N. Y. 599; Linden v. Hepburn, 3 Sandf. 668; Hall v. Gould, 13 N. Y. 135.

Jenkins, 63 Ind. 415; *Philips* v. *Doe*, 8 Ind. 132; *Ment* v. *Rathbone*, 21 Ind. 454; *Bacon* v. *Western Furniture Co.* 53 Ind. 229; *O'Connor* v. *Kelley*, 41 Cal. 432; *Chapman* v. *Harney*, 100 Mass. 353; *Chapman* v. *Kirby*, 49 Ill. 211; *Becker* v. *Werner*, 98 Pa. 555; *Bowyer* v. *Seymour*, 13 W. Va. 12; *Gage* v. *Bates*, 40 Cal. 384; *O'Connor* v. *Kelley*, 41 Cal. 434.

The mere giving of a new lease would not affect the old one.

Wartenby v. *Moran*, 3 Call, 491; *Bowyer* v. *Seymour*, 13 W. Va. 12; *Leonard* v. *Henderson*, 23 Gratt. 331.

Mr. **John W. Donnan,** also for plaintiff in error:

By failure to commence operations the contingent obligation to pay rental had become an absolute continuing liability for its payment during the balance of the twenty years, from which the lessee could only be relieved by the bona fide commencement of operations.

Taylor, Land. and T. § 492; *Wills* v. *Manufacturers Natural Gas Co.* 5 L. R. A. 603, 130 Pa. 222.

The primary obligation of the lessee was thereafter the payment of the rent and no forfeiture of the lease could ever take place except for a failure to pay this rent. The right of the plaintiffs then depends upon their establishing that the Hays lease had become forfeited for the nonpayment of the monthly rent, and the burden is upon them to show such facts as are required under the law to establish such forfeiture.

1 Washb. Real Prop. p. 321*; *M'Cormick* v. *Connell*, 6 Serg. & R. 152; *Bowman* v. *Foot*, 29 Conn. 331; *Tate* v *Crowson*, 6 Ired. L. 67.

To warrant a forfeiture demand for the rent must be made in fact although there should be no person on the land to pay it.

Taylor, Land. and T. § 492; *Bowyer* v. *Seymour*, 13 W. Va. 12; *Chapman* v. *Kirby*, 49 Ill. 211; *Chapman* v. *Harney*, 100 Mass. 353; *McMurphy* v. *Minot*, 4 N. H. 251; *Chapman* v. *Wright*, 20 Ill. 120; *Jones* v. *Reed*, 15 N. H. 72; *Jackson* v. *Harrison*, 17 Johns. 70; *Gage* v. *Bates*, 40 Cal. 384; *Smith* v. *Whitbeck*, 13 Ohio St. 471, and cases cited in *note* to *Spencer's Case*, 1 Smith, Lead. Cas. *132–134; *Prout* v. *Roby*, 82 U. S. 15 Wall. 476 (21 L. ed. 60); *Connor* v. *Bradley*, 42 U. S. 1 How. 215 (11 L. ed. 107).

Where a tenant has forfeited his lease by failure to pay rent, courts of law and equity alike interfere in the tenant's behalf, although all the formalities of a common-law demand may have been complied with upon his paying the rent, and the costs and damages which the landlord may have incurred.

Taylor, Land. and T. § 495; *Mactier* v. *Osborn*, 6 New Eng. Rep. 35, 146 Mass. 399, 4 Am. St. Rep. 323; *Smith* v. *Mariner*, 5 Wis. 551, 68 Am. Dec. 85, *note*.

Messrs. **Keck & Son** also for plaintiff in error.

Mr. **Alfred Caldwell,** for defendants in error:

The instruments under which both parties claim are intended to give an interest and estate in the land and vest in the lessees corporeal hereditaments and constitute leases and not mere licenses.

2 Am. Lead. Cas. 549, *et seq.*; 1 Washb. Real Prop. 542; *Kitchen* v. *Smith*, 101 Pa. 452; *Chicago & A. O. & M. Co.* v. *United States Petroleum Co.* 57 Pa. 83; *Duke* v. *Hague*, 107 Pa. 57; *Stoughton's App.* 88 Pa. 198.

Breach of a covenant will work an absolute forfeiture with the necessity of a demand and entry.

Munroe v. *Armstrong*, 96 Pa. 307; *Brown* v. *Vandergrift*, 80 Pa. 142.

The Hays lease, under which the plaintiff in error claims, has been forfeited.

Allegany Oil Co. v. *Bradford Oil Co.* 21 Hun, 26, affirmed in 86 N. Y. 638.

If the grantor has an estate in possession, he may convey the same at once, as the forfeiture will be completed without entry or claim.

Dumpor's Case, 1 Smith, Lead. Cas. *109; *Porter* v. *Noyes*, 47 Mich. 55; *Conrad* v. *Morehead*, 89 N. C. 31.

There was a stipulation for the money to be deposited with Kennedy, and, if this was not done and the work was not commenced as agreed, the forfeiture was complete.

Cowan v. *Radford Iron Co.* 83 Va. 547.

Messrs. **Berkshire & Sturgiss,** also for defendants in error:

That an entry, even for condition broken, is unnecessary where he who has the right to enter is already in possession, is both common law and common sense.

Littleton, Inst. 218 *a*; Cruise, Dig. title 13, chap. 2, § 45; *Hamilton* v. *Elliott*, 5 Serg. & R. 375; *Van Rensselaer* v. *Ball*, 19 N. Y. 100; *Allegany Oil Co.* v. *Bradford Oil Co.* 21 Hun, 26, 86 N. Y. 638.

Mr. **A. F. Haymond** also for defendants in error.

Brannon, *J.*, delivered the opinion of the court:

This was an action of unlawful detainer in the Circuit Court of Monongalia by Guffey and Murphy against Hukill for possession of thirty acres of land for drilling for petroleum oil and gas, in which there was judgment for plaintiffs, to which judgment Hukill obtained this writ of error.

The case was decided upon a demurrer to evidence from which it appears to be a contest between those claiming under two conflicting leases made by Wise for drilling for oil and gas. Wise made to Hays a lease of this thirty acres dated the 30th of June, 1886, for twenty years, which on the 10th of January, 1889, was assigned to Hukill. Under this lease Hukill defends. By lease dated the 11th of July, 1888, Wise leased the thirty acres to Rezin Calvert for twenty years, and Calvert assigned this lease to Ida C. and Vinnie Calvert on the 16th of March, 1889, and they assigned it to Guffey and Murphy on the 8th of May, 1889. Under this lease the plaintiffs claim. It is claimed by the plaintiffs that the hostile lease to Hays became forfeited under provisions contained in it, and therefore the later lease to Calvert confers a valid right. This Hays lease contains this clause: "The parties of the second part covenant to commence operations for said purposes within nine months from and after the execution of this lease, or to thereafter pay to the party of the first part $1.33⅓ per month until work is commenced, the money to be deposited in the hands of John Kennedy for each and every month; and a failure on the part of the said second parties to comply with either one or the other of the foregoing conditions shall work an absolute forfeiture of this lease."

Hays' lease was recorded the 26th of October, 1886, before the execution of the Calvert lease. About the 1st of May, 1889, Hukill began boring for oil under the Hays lease, and continued the work until November, 1889, when he obtained large quantities of oil in two wells.

No rent was paid under the provision for the monthly payment of $1.33⅓ on the Hays lease until about the 4th of January, 1889, when or later Hays paid it to Wise. Kennedy, in October, 1888, offered to pay Wise this rent, but he declined to receive it then, but received it afterwards from Hays. All the rent due Wise under the Hays lease was paid him. Hukill took possession under the Hays lease and began boring for oil with the knowledge and consent of Wise.

No demand was ever made by Wise on Hays for the rent, except that he called once on Kennedy for it.

An important question in this case is, whether or not the lease to Hays became forfeited and of no further force by reason of the failure to bore for oil or pay the monthly sum of $1.33⅓ in lieu thereof and the subsequent lease by Wise to Calvert; for if the Hays lease be still in life, Hukill can defend his possession, but if dead, it affords him no defense. Such boring or the monthly payment of $1.33⅓ as its commutation is made by the Hays lease an express condition for noncompliance with which its life is to cease. But it is earnestly contended for the appellant that such failure does not *ipso facto* end the lease, but that demand must have been made for the payment of said money as rent, and on failure of payment, re-entry on the premises by the lessor, Wise, under the principles of common law thus stated in Lomax's Digest, 710, 711: "The third remedy for rent is by re-entry. The condition of re-entry for rent was the remedy by the ancient law, afterwards changed into a distress. But it is yet allowable at law, where the party provides it by deed; as if a man make a feoffment, gift or lease, reserving rent, with a condition that if the rent be behind, it shall be lawful for the feoffor, etc., and his heirs into the lands to re-enter." "When the lessor is about to re-enter for nonpayment of rent, the common law requires a previous demand of rent, with circumstances of great particularity. On the very day upon which the rent becomes due, at a convenient time before sunset, the lessor must make an actual demand of the exact amount of the rent due at the particular place at which the rent may be made payable by the terms of the lease; or, if there be no place stipulated in the lease, the demand must be made at the most notorious place upon the land demised, which, if there be a dwelling-house, is the front door."

Does this law apply to this lease? It declares that failure of the lessee to commence operations or pay $1.33⅓ per month in lieu of so doing "shall work an absolute forfeiture of this lease," but contains no provision for reentry for such omission. Where there is not only a declaration that a certain act or omission shall work a forfeiture, but also that for it the landlord may re-enter, it may plausibly be said that the landlord may or may not choose to enforce the forfeiture by re-entry, and if he elects to so enforce it, he must make such reentry, as that is the act pointed out by the express terms of the lease as the mode of enforcement of the forfeiture; whereas, when there is no provision for re-entry, it is not required. Is, then, this common-law method of enforcing a forfeiture by demand and re-entry applicable to a lease which simply provides for forfeiture for breach of its covenants, but contains no clause of re-entry? Or, rather, in such case, are demand and re entry the only mode of declaring the will of the lessor to enforce the forfeiture?

Kent, in his Commentaries, vol. 4, side p. 128, lays down the rule thus: "There is this further distinction to be noticed between a condition annexed to an estate for years and one annexed to an estate of freehold, that in the former case the estate *ipso facto* ceases as soon as the condition is broken, whereas, in the latter case, the breach of the condition does not cause the *cesser* of the estate without an entry or claim for that purpose. It was a rule of the common law that where an estate commenced by livery, it could not be determined before entry. When the estate has *ipso facto* ceased by the operation of the condition, it cannot be revived without a new grant; but a voidable estate may be confirmed and the condition dispensed with."

This rule of the common law is well settled. 1 Lomax, Dig. 238; 1 Minor, Inst. 229.

"If the estate be an estate only for years, it is otherwise. No entry (unless it be so stipulated) is necessary to determine it, for as a term of years may begin without ceremony, it may end without ceremony." 2 Minor, Inst. 229, citing 2 Bl. Com. 155; 2 Tho. Co. Litt. 3, 4, 87, 88, 95-97. See Adams, Eject. 197; *Stuyvesant* v. *Davis*, 9 Paige, 431, 4 N. Y. Ch. L. ed. 762; *Parmelee* v. *Oswego & S. R. Co.* 6 N. Y. 74.

The only exception to this rule was where the lease provided for re-entry, in which case there must be re-entry. *Stuyvesant* v. *Davis*, *supra;* Taylor, Land. and T. § 493.

Taylor's Landlord and Tenant, § 492, states the rule as above, but says that the distinction between the estates for years and freehold "has been almost, if not quite, abated by modern decisions, which establish that the effect of a condition making a lease void upon a certain event is to make it void at the option of a lessor only, in cases where the condition is intended for his benefit, and he actually avails himself of this privilege. The English law in this respect has been generally followed in this country, and such lease is therefore held good until avoided, though the lessee is estopped to set it up against the lessor."

In a *note* to § 492, Taylor says that the original rule that breach of the condition in a lease for years *per se* forfeits it, prevails in Pennsylvania, and there have been contrarient decisions in New York, and cites decisions in a few other States that there must be some declaration by the lessor of his election to forfeit. I am not aware of any decision in Virginia to tell us whether the original rule as above stated prevails. But let us take the law to be as Taylor states it. It is only a partial modification, or, as he states, an abatement, of the original rule.

He says that the effect of these later decisions is to make the lease void at the option of the lessor only, in cases where the condition is intended for his benefit, that is, that the lessor may waive the forfeiture, and if he choose not to declare the lease forfeited, it does not lie in the mouth of the tenant who has broken his covenant to set up the breach of the condition as destroying the lease, but he remains liable for rent. He further says that until the lease be avoided by the landlord it continues good, though the lessee is estopped to set it up against the lessor. The lessee is in the wrong, and he cannot set up the lease as continuing against the landlord who elects to insist on the forfeiture. Under the law as it had stood, so dead was the lease upon the mere breach of the condition that the landlord could not recognize it as existing or revive it but by new lease, but it was dead as to both him and his tenant; but under the modification of the rule wrought by the later decisions, the lease continued good until the landlord avoided it, but so far as the tenant's rights were concerned it was void, and he could not set it up against the landlord. The cause of forfeiture only renders the lease void as to the lessee, and it may be affirmed by the lessor, and the rights and obligations of both parties will continue in that case. *Clark* v. *Jones*, 1 Denio, 516.

Thus, no re-entry is necessary in case of a lease for years which contains a clause of forfeiture for breach of covenant but no clause of re entry.

There is in this case another reason why no re-entry was necessary. The lease let to Hays only the right to bore for oil, and reserved the use of the land to Wise for tillage, and he was in actual possession. No man can enter upon himself. A man need not make a re-entry when he is in possession himself. *Notes* to *Dumpor's Case*, 1 Smith, Lead. Cas. *109; *Hamilton* v. *Elliott*, 5 Serg. & R. 375; Co. Litt. 216 *b*, 218; *Shaffer* v. *Shaffer*, 37 Pa. 525; *Allegany Oil Co.* v. *Bradford Oil Co.* 21 Hun, 26, 86 N. Y. 638.

If it be said that though re-entry is not necessary, yet demand for payment is, I respond that demand is only necessary as a pre-requisite to re-entry, where there must be re-entry. Wise did go to Kennedy, to whom Hays had contracted to pay, and asked him if any money had been left with him for him, but none had been left. Were any demand necessary, it might be said, not without force, that this was a demand.

Thus, this rule as it exists to-day, as stated by Taylor, recognizes the power of the lessor to treat the lease as void. In what way shall he do so? Taylor's Landlord and Tenant, § 488, says: "The relation of landlord and tenant will be dissolved when the tenant incurs a forfeiture of his lease in consequence of the breach of some condition therein contained and the landlord re-enters or signifies his intention to treat the lease as void, if it is so expressed in the lease."

So, where no re-entry is required, he may signify his intention.

What did Wise do to manifest his intention to avoid the lease? He refused back rent and executed a subsequent lease of the land for oil purposes to Calvert, thus in a signal and unmistakable manner declaring his purpose to end the Hays lease. The common-law rule above stated required no re-entry, and its modification as stated by Taylor, and also the last quotation given above from Taylor, only required a declaration of the landlord to treat it as forfeited. And in the case of *Allegany Oil Co.* v. *Bradford Oil Co.*, *supra*, it was held by both the supreme court and the Court of Appeals of New York, that where a lease for boring for oil provided that unless the lessee commence a well within nine months the lease was "to become void and cease to be of any binding effect," and there was failure to commence, that no re-entry was necessary, as the lessor was in possession, and that no notice of the landlord's intention to enforce the forfeiture was necessary, and that if even any overt act or notice was necessary, the execution of a second lease to another party was a sufficient declaration of the landlord's intention to enforce the forfeiture. The deed of an infant is voidable, not void, but requires an act to disaffirm it. A deed for the land to a second purchaser is a destruction of the first deed, and vests title in the second purchaser. *Mustard* v. *Wohlford*, 15 Gratt. 329.

For these reasons I hold that by reason of the failure to either bore for oil or to pay money in lieu thereof, under the Hays lease and the execution of the lease to Calvert, the former lease to Hays was at an end.

The case of *Bowyer* v. *Seymour*, 13 W. Va. 12, is urged upon us as decisive in favor of Hukill. The lease in that case was made for coal mining, and provided that a failure to pay money which it stipulated was to be paid for coal should be considered an abandonment of the lease, and it was held that notwithstanding nonpayment of such money, the lessor must make a demand for the rent and a re-entry to make the forfeiture complete. But there is a marked line of distinction between that case and this, in the fact that, as *Judge* Haymond says, that was a lease in fee, or at least for life, and under the original common-law rule above given, a freehold estate could not be forfeited for breach of a condition without demand and re-entry; whereas the lease in this case is a lease for years, which under said rule does not require re-entry. Anything said in that case as to a lease for years would be *obiter*.

I think that case was decided correctly.

The reasons given above are sufficient, I think, to show that the Hays lease is forfeited, and render it unnecessary for us to pass on the question discussed in argument as to the effect of a lease for years for the purpose of producing petroleum oil or gas containing provision for its forfeiture on breach of condition and a clause of re-entry, or to say whether we would approve the decision of the Supreme Court of Pennsylvania in *Brown* v. *Vandergrift*, 80 Pa. 142, so confidently relied on by appellee.

That lease provided that the lessee should begin to bore for oil in sixty days, and that if he should not commence within the time specified, he should pay $30 per month until drilling should commence; and that a failure of the lessee to comply with any of its conditions and agreements should work a forfeiture of his rights, and the lessor might enter upon the land and dispose of it as if the lease had not been made.

The lessee failed to commence work or pay money, and the land owner made a subsequent lease to other parties. The court held that the covenant of forfeiture was modified, not abrogated, by the clause for payment of rent; that the landlord might refuse payment of back rent and insist on the forfeiture; that time was of the essence of the contract, and equity would enforce the forfeiture. The lessor, as here, remained in possession, and it does not appear that any such thing as re entry was insisted on, and the court below said that no demand of the commutation money was necessary, and this was held no error.

The opinion of *Chief Justice* Agnew says: "The discovery of petroleum led to new forms of leasing land. Its fugitive and wandering existence within the limits of a particular tract was uncertain, and assumed certainty only by actual development upon experiment. The surface required was often small compared with results, when attended with success; while these results led to great speculation, by means of leases covering the lands of a neighborhood like a flight of locusts. Hence it was found necessary to guard the rights of the land owner, as well as public interest, by numerous covenants, some of the most stringent kind, to prevent their lands from being burdened by unexecuted and profitless leases, incompatible with the right of alienation and the use of the land. Without these guards lands would be thatched over with oil leases by sub-letting, and a farm riddled with holes and bristled with derricks, or operations would be delayed so long as the speculator would find it hopeful or convenient to himself alone. Hence covenants became necessary to regulate the boring of wells, their number and time of succession, the period of commencement and completion and many other matters requiring special regulation. Prominent among these was the clause of forfeiture to compel performance and put an end to the lease, in case of injurious delay or want of success. The lease was not valuable, except by development, unlike the ordinary terms for the cultivation of the soil."

If that case was correctly decided, it follows *a fortiori* that our decision upon this lease, having no clause of re entry, is correct. In *Munroe* v. *Armstrong*, 96 Pa. 307, the opinion says: "What is there in the circumstances calling for a fiction to defeat the covenant against delay in searching for or producing oil? The subject of the lease was a fluid likely to flow for a considerable distance through the crevices and loose sand where it is found. A small tract of land could be nearly or entirely drained by wells on adjoining lands, and it is common that leases contain covenants for diligent operation and forfeiture in case of suspension. An oil lease yields nothing to the land owner when not worked, and is an incumbrance on his land, tying his hands against selling or leasing to others; but when idle it costs the lessee nothing and is valuable, or may prove so, if he can hold it awaiting developments in the vicinity."

These cases draw a distinction between oil leases and leases of other kinds.

The payment of the rent or commutation money to Wise and his consent to Hukill's taking possession under the Hays lease could have no effect to waive the forfeiture, because such payment and taking possession occurred after the execution by Wise to Calvert of the second lease, which operated as a declaration of forfeiture and to devest all estates under the Hays lease and invest it in Calvert, and the after act of payment did not destroy Calvert's rights.

It is said that the lease of the plaintiff is itself forfeited because of nonpayment and failure to bore for oil within the time specified in it; but that lease is dated the 11th of July, 1888, and provides for boring a well within six months and, on failure, then payment of fifty cents per acre, payable within six months "from the time of completing such well." A tender of $7.50 was made the 10th of July, again on the 11th of July, 1889, and refused by Wise, and a tender of $15 was made the 10th of January, 1890, and refused. The only acts of disaffirmance by Wise of said lease were such refusals and assent to the entry under the Hays lease. Forfeiture of this lease could not revest title under the Hays lease, though it might show that the plaintiffs had no title on which to maintain their action; but there was no forfeiture, as the tenders saved it.

The contention that chapter 93 of Code 1887 provides the only means of enforcing a forfeiture for nonpayment of rent or breach of condition, is not tenable in my opinion. I think the action of ejectment therein provided for is remedial and accumulative remedy to dispense with demand and re entry, and that it does not destroy the common-law mode of demand and re-entry. But, however that may be, it applies only where there is necessity to make demand and re-entry; and in this case, for reasons above given, there was no duty on the lessor to re-enter.

I think the action of unlawful entry lies. It is true it is designed to protect the actual possession. It applies when a tenant holds over after his right has expired. After a declaration of forfeiture by Wise, he could have maintained such an action against Hukill, because he would have held after his right expired; and he having let to Calvert the right to possession for oil purposes, I do not see why the action does not lie for the plaintiff. It seems hardly necessary to say that the contention that plaintiffs are estopped by standing by and seeing Hukill spend money in developing oil without setting up claim is not good. Hukill began operations early in May, 1889, and it is admitted that on the 5th of July Guffey and Murphy sent him a formal notice in writing that they had the sole right to drill for oil under their lease, telling him the very page and book where he would find it on record, and warning him not to drill. He did not produce oil until November.

The evidence offered by defendant of the amount of money expended by him in developing oil was properly rejected, as the question was one of right between the parties under their respective claims, and the proposed evidence was immaterial.

As to the complaint that plaintiffs were allowed to give evidence that when they acquired their right they had no notice of defendant's claim, I think it immaterial. If the Hays lease had become forfeited there was no right under it of which they could have notice. *Central Land Co.* v. *Laidley*, 32 W.Va. 134.

As to the exclusion as evidence of the deed of the 14th of May, 1889, from Wise to Hukill, conveying absolutely all the oil and gas under said tract, it could not affect the right of plaintiffs, under the Rezin Calvert lease, made and recorded long before its date, and was irrelevant to the case.

I am of opinion that the evidence sustained the plaintiffs' case, and that the court below properly refused to exclude their evidence and rendered judgment for them.

Judgment affirmed.

ILLINOIS SUPREME COURT.

CITY OF CHICAGO, *Appt.*,
v.
Sarah A. T. McLEAN.

(......Ill.......)

1. **Suffering in mind** as well as in body is ground for damages for a personal injury.

2. **An averment that plaintiff suffered** "great pain and agony" is sufficient to cover any effect upon the mind that resulted from an injury to the body.

3. **No allegation of special damage,** in a suit for a personal injury, is necessary in order to permit a recovery for mental suffering which was inseparable from the bodily injury.

4. **Instructions that if plaintiff stepped, without looking,** into a dangerous place, or failed to observe the condition of the sidewalk on which she was walking, she cannot recover for injuries received, are properly refused as virtually telling the jury that certain facts constitute negligence.

(May 14, 1890.)

APPEAL by defendant from a judgment of the Appellate Court, First District, affirming a judgment of the Circuit Court for Cook County in favor of plaintiff in an action brought to recover damages for personal injuries alleged to have resulted from a defect in defendant's sidewalk. *Affirmed.*

The case sufficiently appears in the opinion.

Mr. **W. E. Hughes,** with *Messrs.* **George F. Sugg** and **Charles S. Cameron,** for appellant:

There was no averment of special damages in the declaration, alleged to have been sustained by the plaintiff because of suffering in her mind; such allegation was necessary to warrant a recovery.

Joch v. *Dankwardt*, 85 Ill. 331.

The court erred in refusing the fourth instruction asked by the appellant,—that if plaintiff failed to use her eyes to direct her footsteps, she has no cause of action.

Kewanee v. *Depew*, 80 Ill. 119.

It also erred in refusing the sixth instruction, that if plaintiff was injured because of the fail-

---

NOTE.—*Damages for personal injuries; mental anguish.*

That physical and mental sufferings, both present and future, are proper elements of damages, see South & North Alabama R. Co. v. McLendon, 63 Ala. 266; Porter v. Hannibal & St. J. R. Co. 71 Mo. 66; Ransom v. New York & E. R. Co. 15 N. Y. 415; Curtis v. Rochester & S. R. Co. 18 N. Y. 534, 20 Barb. 282; Hamilton v. Third Ave. R. Co. 8 Jones & S. 376; Walker v. Erie R. Co. 63 Barb. 260; Drinkwater v. Dinsmore, 16 Hun, 250; De Forest v. Utica, 69 N. Y. 614; Texas M. R. Co. v. Douglas, 73 Tex. 325; Giblin v. McIntyre, 2 Utah, 384; Spicer v. Chicago & N. W. R. Co. 29 Wis. 580; Whelan v. New York, L. E. & W. R. Co. 38 Fed. Rep. 15.

In estimating the damages for personal injuries, when the injury produces mental as well as bodily suffering, the mental suffering may be taken into consideration by the jury in estimating the damages. Kennon v. Gilmer, 131 U. S. 22 (33 L. ed. 110); Toledo, W. & W. R. Co. v. Baddeley, 54 Ill. 19, 5 Am. Rep. 71; Matteson v. New York Cent. R. Co. 62 Barb. 364; Hamilton v. Third Ave. R. Co. 53 N.Y. 28. *Contra*, Covington St. R. Co. v. Packer, 9 Bush, 455, 15 Am. Rep. 725; Robertson v. Cornelson, 34 Fed. Rep. 716; Ridenhour v. Kansas City C. R. Co. (Mo.) June 2, 1890.

The damages should include a reasonable sum for pain and suffering. Vicksburg & M. R. Co. v. Putnam, 118 U. S. 545 (30 L. ed. 257).

Pain and suffering that may reasonably be expected in the future may be considered in giving damages for personal injuries, if the evidence shows that they will be experienced as a result of the injury. Feeney v. Long Island R. Co. 5 L. R. A. 544, 116 N. Y. 375.

Where bodily injuries are alleged and proved, physical pain and mental anguish are proper elements of damage, though not stated in the petition. Brown v. Hannibal & St. J. R. Co. 99 Mo. 310.

In an action for negligently shooting and wounding plaintiff, it is not error to charge the jury that, in computing the damages, they may take into consideration "a fair compensation for the physical and mental suffering caused by the injury." McIntyre v. Giblin, 100 U. S. (25 L. ed. 572).

The jury may consider the character of the injuries received, how far they will disable the plaintiff from pursuing his occupation, his physical and mental condition, and they may allow such damages as, in their judgment, would be a fair and just compensation for the same. Baltimore & O. R. Co. v. Kean, 3 Cent. Rep. 716, 65 Md. 394.

Only mental anguish or suffering which can be proved is such as is endured as the direct consequence of the injury; and anxiety of mind about the safety of others who may be in danger of injury from the same cause cannot be considered. Keyes v. Minneapolis & St. L. R. Co. 36 Minn. 290.

A woman is not entitled to recover for mental anguish, in an action for injury to her means of support by selling intoxicating liquors to her husband, where it is shown that before defendant sold him any liquors she had sworn to a bill drawn for divorce charging him with being an habitual drunkard. Johnson v. Schultz, 74 Mich. 75.

Municipal corporation; liability for injuries caused by its negligence. See *notes* to Chope v. Eureka (Cal.) 4 L. R. A. 325; Lincoln v. Boston (Mass.) 3 L. R. A. 257.

ure on her part to look where she was going, or observe the condition of the sidewalk on which she was walking, the jury should find the defendant not guilty.

Chicago v. *McGiven*, 78 Ill. 347; *Aurora* v. *Brown*, 12 Ill. App. 122.

Mr. **James Frake,** with *Mr.* **Frederick Peake,** for appellee:

Mental, as well as bodily, suffering is proper to be considered.

Hannibal & St. J. R. Co. v. *Martin*, 111 Ill. 219; *Indianapolis & St. L. R. Co.* v. *Stables*, 62 Ill. 313.

Appellant's instructions numbered 4 and 6 should not have been given.

Owen v. *Chicago*, 10 Ill. App. 465.

Magruder, *J.*, delivered the opinion of the court:

This is an action of case commenced by the appellee against the appellant in the Circuit Court of Cook County on March 13, 1888, to recover damages for a personal injury. The trial resulted in a verdict and judgment for the plaintiff, which judgment has been affirmed by the appellate court. The cause is brought here by appeal from the appellate court.

The declaration avers, in substance, that the City wrongfully and negligently suffered the sidewalk of Hermitage Avenue to be and remain in an unsafe and dangerous condition; that a part of the sidewalk, about four feet in length, had been "torn down," or the sidewalk had never been built, so as to extend over said space of four feet in length, as it should have been, and would have been had the sidewalk been complete; that such space was open and uncovered, except by one plank laid lengthwise with the sidewalk, across said open space, which plank was loose and insecure; that in the evening of March 15, 1886, plaintiff was passing along said sidewalk, it being then dark, and there being a driving snow-storm; that, while plaintiff was using all due care to prevent injury to herself, she stepped into said open space, and fell to the ground, and was injured, etc. The facts are settled by the judgment of the appellate court.

Appellant complains of an instruction given by the trial court, which told the jury that if they found the defendant guilty, and that plaintiff had sustained damages by reason of the injury, they had a right, in estimating such damages, to "take into consideration all the facts and circumstances in evidence before them; the nature and effect of the plaintiff's physical injuries, if any, shown by the evidence to have been sustained from the cause alleged in the declaration; her suffering in body and mind, if any, resulting from such injuries," etc. The part of the instruction which is particularly objected to is that which allows damages for "suffering in mind."

The instruction here complained of is substantially the same as the fifth instruction in *Hannibal & St. J. R. Co.* v. *Martin*, 111 Ill. 219, which was held to be good. In that case we said: "Where suffering in body and mind is the result of injuries caused by negligence, it is proper to take it into consideration in estimating the amount of damages." The decision in the *Martin Case* is conclusive upon the point here made, and we must hold that the instruction given by the trial court was not erroneous.

Upon her direct examination plaintiff was asked this question: "How has your mind been since that time,—your faculties?"—to which she answered as follows: "Very poor; very different from what it was before." An objection to this question and answer by defendant's counsel was overruled, and exception was taken. Counsel for appellant urge, as a reason why their objection should have been sustained, that the effect of the injury upon the plaintiff's mind was matter of special damage, and should have been specially pleaded in the declaration. In the first place, the language of the declaration is broad enough to cover such effect upon the mind as may have resulted from the injury to the body. It is averred that plaintiff "suffered great pain and agony." "Agony" has been defined to be violent pain of body or mind. In the second place, the plaintiff is always entitled to recover all damages which are the natural and proximate consequence of the act complained of; and those damages which necessarily result from the injury are termed "general," and may be shown under the general allegations of the declaration. Only those damages which are not the necessary result of the injury are termed "special," and required to be stated specially in the declaration. *Quincy Coal Co.* v. *Hood*, 77 Ill. 68.

But the body and mind are so intimately connected that the mind is very often directly and necessarily affected by physical injury. There cannot be severe physical pain without a certain amount of mental suffering. The mind, unless it is so overpowered that consciousness is destroyed, takes cognizance of physical pain, and must be more or less affected thereby. *Indianapolis & St. L. R. Co.* v. *Stables*, 62 Ill. 313.

We do not understand that the instruction, or the admitted proof in this case, contemplated any other mental suffering than that which was inseparable from the bodily injury. Therefore no allegation of special damage was necessary. Any mental anguish which may not have been connected with the bodily injury, but caused by some conception arising from a different source, could not properly have been taken into consideration by the jury. We are of the opinion that it was not error to overrule the objection.

Appellant also assigns as error the refusal of the court to give the fourth and sixth instructions asked by it. In the fourth it was stated that "a person in the full possession of her faculties, passing over a sidewalk when there was light, with no crowd to jostle or disturb her, and no intervening obstacle to hide a dangerous place which she is approaching, and no sudden cause to distract her attention, is bound to use her eyes to direct her footsteps; and if she failed to do so, and is negligent therein, she has no cause of action against the City for injuries received by her because she stepped, without looking, into such dangerous place." In the sixth it was said that "ordinary care requires that the foot passenger shall use her eyes as well as her feet, and therefore, if you believe from the evidence that the plaintiff was injured because of the failure on her part to look where she was going, or observe the condition of the sidewalk on which she was walking, you should find the defendant not guilty." These instructions were properly refused. They virtually tell the jury that certain facts constitute negligence. Negligence is a question of fact, and not one of law, and "it is for the jury to determine from the evidence whether one or both of the parties may have been negligent in their conduct, and not for the court to take the question from them, and declare, if certain facts exist, negligence is established." *Myers* v. *Indianapolis & St. L. R. Co.* 113 Ill. 386, and cases there cited.

The plaintiff in this case was bound to make a reasonable use of her faculties when walking along the sidewalk, in order to avoid danger; but what was such reasonable use was a question of fact to be determined by the jury, under all the circumstances disclosed by the evidence. A number of instructions which were given told the jury that the plaintiff could not recover unless she "was at the time of such injury exercising reasonable care and caution." Several instructions given at the request of defendant embodied all that was material or important in the refused instructions. Among these was the eleventh, which is as follows: "(11) If, after considering all the evidence, you should believe the defendant's servants in charge of the street in controversy failed to exercise ordinary care in keeping its sidewalks on that street in safe condition, yet if you also believe from the evidence that plaintiff, at the time of the injury, failed to exercise ordinary care for her own safety to prevent or to avoid the injury complained of, then there can be no recovery by the plaintiff in this case, and the jury should find the defendant not guilty." What particular facts amounted to an exercise of ordinary care, or what particular facts amounted to a want of ordinary care, it was for the jury, and not for the court, to determine. *Wabash R. Co.* v. *Elliott*, 98 Ill. 481.

Some of the phraseology used in the fourth instruction was made use of by this court in *Kewanee* v. *Depew*, 80 Ill. 119. That case was decided before it had become the law of this State that questions of fact in actions of this kind are settled by the judgment of the appellate court. Moreover, it appeared there that the plaintiff had seen the defect in the sidewalk four or five days before he was injured, and several times subsequently, and that at the time of the injury, instead of looking at the hole in the sidewalk of the existence of which he had knowledge, he was observing a passing buggy, to satisfy his curiosity as to the style of harness on the horse. In the present case there was evidence tending to show that the plaintiff had no previous knowledge of the open space in the sidewalk before she fell into it. By omitting all reference to this circumstance, the language of the refused instructions required of her the same degree of care in case she was ignorant of the defect as though she had known of it. Hence the phraseology which may have been appropriate in the *Depew Case* was not adapted to the circumstances of the case at bar. We perceive no such error in the record as would justify a reversal.

The judgment of the Appellate Court is affirmed.

IOWA SUPREME COURT.

STATE OF IOWA, *Pltf. in Certiorari*,
v.
Claus VOSS.

SAME *v.* George TANNA.

SAME *v.* Henry KAHLER.

SAME *v.* T. BOE.

SAME *v.* Edward CONERY.

(....Iowa....)

A condition in a judgment sentencing defendant for contempt in violating an injunction against the unlawful sale of intoxicating liquors, that "the execution of this judgment is to be suspended during the pleasure of the court," is unlawful and void.

(June 3, 1890.)

CERTIORARI to the District Court for Clinton County to determine the validity of certain conditions in judgments sentencing defendants to fine or imprisonment for contempt of court, by which the execution of the judgments was suspended during the pleasure of the court. *Judgment for plaintiff.*

The facts fully appear in the opinion.

Messrs. **W. A. Maginnis** and **W. L. Smith,** for plaintiff in certiorari:

Section 12 of chap. 143 of the Acts of the 20th General Assembly gives the court no power such as it assumed to exercise in this case. That section provides that "Any person violating the terms of any injunction granted in such proceedings shall be punished as for contempt by a fine of not less than $500 nor more than $1,000, or by imprisonment in the county jail not more than six months, or by both such fine and imprisonment, in the discretion of the court."

Mr. **P. B. Wolfe,** for defendants in certiorari:

The power of the court to suspend sentence is fully established.

People v. *Mueller*, 15 Chicago Leg. News, 364.

The following authorities sustain the action of the court in these causes:

Com. v. *Dowdican*, 115 Mass. 136; *State* v. *Addy*, 43 N. J. L. 113; *Weaver* v. *People*, 33 Mich. 297.

Beck, *J.*, delivered the opinion of the court:

These cases, arising upon like facts, and involving the same principles of law, are submitted for decision in this court together, upon one abstract. The records of all the cases are alike. There is no dispute upon the facts in-

See also 23 L. R. A. 856; 29 L. R. A. 260; 40 L. R. A. 109; 41 L. R. A. 472; 42 L. R. A. 190.

volved in the cases, which, briefly stated, are these: The defendants were, by proper proceedings under the Statute, enjoined from selling unlawfully intoxicating liquors, of which they were found guilty, in the proceedings, whereby they maintained a nuisance, which by decrees they were enjoined from maintaining. After these decrees were rendered, defendants continued to sell intoxicating liquors contrary to law, and proceedings were thereupon instituted to punish them for contempt. They continued in contempt of the injunction until after these proceedings were instituted; but, before the citation for them to answer in the proceedings was served, they ceased to disobey the injunction, and quit selling intoxicating liquors, thus abating the nuisance. Upon the hearing in these proceedings the court found that defendants had violated the injunction by selling intoxicating liquors, and were in contempt, and subject to punishment therefor, and in each case entered a judgment for a fine of $500 against the defendant therein, and an order that he stand committed to the county jail for thirty days unless the fine and costs be sooner paid. The judgment contains a condition in this language: "The execution of this judgment is to be suspended during the pleasure of the court; but whenever the court, or one of the judges thereof, so directs, execution and warrant of commitment are to issue. The clerk is to pay W. A. Maginniss and W. L. Smith, attorneys in said cases, ten per cent of the fine paid, whenever the said fine, or any part thereof, is paid." The validity of this condition is involved in the only question arising in the case.

2. Certiorari is provided by statute for the review of proceedings to punish for contempt, and appeal does not lie in such cases. Code, § 3499.

3. The question of the case is a simple one, and demands but brief discussion. The condition of the judgment puts its execution wholly within the discretion of the court below, whether that discretion be exercised with or without justice or reason. If it be the pleasure of that court, process may never be issued upon the judgment. The case is this: We find a judgment for a fine against defendant, which can only be enforced at the pleasure of the court. The judgment is thus suspended, and the State is defeated of the remedy provided by law upon the exercise of the pleasure of the district court. If the power to do this exists in a case of contempt, it must exist in all cases punishable by fine and imprisonment. The law is no respecter of persons. One violator of law possesses no rights or immunities not held by another. It follows, then, that all fines and penalties prescribed by law may be collected only when it accords with the pleasure of the court in which judgment is rendered therefor. The claim of the validity of the condition of the judgment leads to the most absurd results. It is hardly necessary to say that it is based upon no statute.

4. It is shown by a stipulation filed in the case that the defendants had, before the entry of the judgments, but after the proceedings were begun wherein they were entered, ceased to violate the law by maintaining a nuisance for the unlawful sale of intoxicating liquors. The same stipulation shows that they were guilty of contempt, and continued to violate the law and disobey the injunction of the court until after the contempt proceedings had been executed. The fact that the defendants had ceased to violate the law is urged as the ground upon which the order suspending the judgment was rightly made. It has never been understood that the reformation of a violator of the law—the turning away from crime to an honest life—will defeat punishment for past offenses. It may mitigate punishment, but will not wholly defeat it. It may be the ground of a pardon. But in this case the punishment is not mitigated, but suspended. If it be the pleasure of the court never to direct execution, the effect of a pardon is had without the authority of law. It is simply the case of the court arresting execution during the pleasure of the judge, without authority of the law.

5. The court, in a proper case, may arrest judgment to attain the ends of justice, but not to defeat the remedy sought by plaintiff, which is the effect of the order suspending the execution. If judgment be suspended, the action stands for disposition in the future as provided by law. In this case the action is disposed of, —is ended by judgment; and the plaintiff's remedy is indefinitely suspended or wholly cut off, by the order suspending execution during the pleasure of the judge of the court. The distinction between suspending judgment and suspending execution is obvious, and need not be further pointed out. Counsel for the defendants cite in support of the action of the court below the following cases: *People* v. *Mueller*, 15 Chicago Legal News, 864; *Com.* v. *Dowdican*, 115 Mass. 136; *State* v. *Addy*, 43 N. J. L. 113; *Weaver* v. *People*, 33 Mich. 297.

These are cases wherein sentence after the verdict was suspended,—a very different thing from the suspension of execution after judgment on sentence.

In our opinion, the order of the district court suspending execution is without the authority of law, and should be declared null and void.

Judgment for plaintiff.

NORTH DAKOTA SUPREME COURT.

TRAVELERS INSURANCE CO., *Respt.*,
v.
CALIFORNIA INSURANCE CO. of San Francisco *et al.*

(....N. D.....)

*1. **Where a policy of fire insurance provides that action** thereon must be brought within a specified time after the loss occurs, the limitation runs from the date of the fire, although, under other provisions of the policy, the cause of action does not accrue until some time after the fire.

2. **A mortgagee,** to whom the policy to mortgagor is made payable, may sue alone, where his claim exceeds the amount of the insurance.

3. **A mere contract of re-insurance** creates no privity between the original insured and the re-insurer; but, where the loss or risk is expressly assumed by another company, the original insured may sue upon such contract as having been made for his benefit.

(May 6, 1890.)

*Head notes by CORLISS, *Ch. J.*

APPEAL by defendants from a judgment of the District Court for Cass County in favor of plaintiff in an action brought to recover the amount alleged to be due on a policy of fire insurance. *Reversed.*

The facts sufficiently appear in the opinion.

Messrs. **Miller, Cleland & Cleland** and **W. L. Wilder**, for appellants:

The parties acting in Minnesota might contract for a limitation of action, and the contract in this respect will be upheld and enforced by the courts of this State. Such a stipulation is valid.

Peoria M. & F. Ins. Co. v. *Whitehill,* 25 Ill. 466; *Williams* v. *Vermont Mut. Ins. Co.* 20 Vt. 230; *Wilson* v. *Ætna Ins. Co.* 27 Vt. 101; *Portage County Mut. F. Ins. Co.* v. *West,* 6 Ohio St. 602; *Nute* v. *Hamilton Mut. Ins. Co.* 6

NOTE.—*Fire insurance; limitation of action on policy.*

Where a policy limits the time for suing upon it to a "term of twelve months next after the loss or damage shall occur," the twelve months' term does not begin to run until after the loss becomes payable by the terms of the policy, and the right of action accrues. Steen v. Niagara F. Ins. Co. 89 N. Y. 315; Ames v. New York Union Ins. Co. 14 N. Y. 253; New York v. Hamilton F. Ins. Co. 39 N. Y. 45; Hay v. Star F. Ins. Co. 77 N. Y. 235; Spare v. Home Mut. Ins. Co. (Or.) 17 Fed. Rep. 568; Barber v. Fire & M. Ins. Co. of Wheeling, 16 W. Va. 658; Chandler v. St. Paul F. & M. Ins. Co. 21 Minn. 85; May, Ins. § 479; Killips v. Putnam F. Ins. Co. 28 Wis. 472; Friezen v. Allemania F. Ins. Co. (Wis.) 30 Fed. Rep. 352; Vette v. Clinton F. Ins. Co. (Mo.) 30 Fed. Rep. 668.

The cause of action does not accrue until after the furnishing of the proof of loss. Chandler v. St. Paul F. & M. Ins. Co. *supra.*

Where it is provided in a policy of insurance that action must be brought within one year after loss, and that the company will pay the loss in sixty days after proof of loss, the limitation begins to run after the expiration of sixty days from the furnishing of the proof of loss. Ellis v. Council Bluffs Ins. Co. 64 Iowa, 507, followed in Miller v. Hartford F. Ins. Co. 70 Iowa, 704. See Stout v. City F. Ins. Co. 12 Iowa, 384; Longhurst v. Star Ins. Co. 19 Iowa, 364.

Suit on a policy of insurance, which is payable sixty days after due notice and proof of loss, cannot be maintained if begun before the expiration of the sixty days. German Am. Ins. Co. v. Hocking, 6 Cent. Rep. 911, 115 Pa. 319. See *notes* to Murdock v. Franklin Ins. Co. (W. Va.) 7 L. R. A. 572; Case v. Sun Ins. Co. (Cal.) 8 L. R. A. 48.

A contrary view.

The decisions, however, are not harmonious, for while all the authorities concede that such stipulations in a policy of fire insurance are valid (see Wilkinson v. First Nat. F. Ins. Co. of Worcester, 72 N. Y. 499; May, Ins. § 478; *note* to Case v. Sun Ins. Co. (Cal.) 8 L. R. A. 48), the weight of authority, as developed in the preceding citations, treats these provisions for limitation of the action or suit as being for the benefit of the insurer, to be subject to the rules of construction, and to be construed together; while in other States the provision limiting the right of action to a shorter period than that prescribed by the general Statute of Limitations is held binding on the insured. Fullam v. New York Union Ins. Co. 7 Gray, 63; Cray v. Hartford F. Ins. Co. 1 Blatchf. 280; Ketchum v. Protection Ins. Co. 1 Allen, N. B. 136; Wilson v. Ætna Ins. Co. 27 Vt. 99; Amesbury v. Bowditch Mut. F. Ins. Co. 6 Gray, 596; Virginia F. & M. Ins. Co. v. Wells, 83 Va. 736; Chambers v. Atlas Ins. Co. 51 Conn. 17.

In Illinois and Massachusetts it is held to take effect from the time of the destruction of the property from the cause insured against. Johnson v. Humboldt Ins. Co. 91 Ill. 92; Fullam v. New York Union Ins. Co. 7 Gray, 61. See *note* to Murdock v. Franklin Ins. Co. (W. Va.) 7 L. R. A. 572.

In the absence of any evidence of bad faith or unreasonable delay on the part of the insurance company there is nothing to authorize the court to relieve the insured from the consequences of his own express contract. Fullam v. New York Union Ins. Co. *supra;* Grant v. Lexington F. L. & M. Ins. Co. 5 Ind. 26; Ames v. New York Union Ins. Co. 4 N. Y. 264.

Under a policy which provided that no action should be sustained unless commenced within six months after the loss should occur, and also that no suit should be maintained until arbitrators had fixed the amount of the loss, it was held that the action could be commenced within six months after the arbitrators had fixed the amount of the loss. Barber v. Fire & M. Ins. Co. of Wheeling, 16 W. Va. 658. *Contra* in Johnson v. Humboldt Ins. Co. 91 Ill. 92, where it is held that the time does not continue twelve months after the award, and that in no event should a suit or action be commenced after the expiration of twelve months from the date of the fire producing the loss.

Unless the assured was prevented by the action or non-action of the insurer in the matter of arbitration, the insured must commence his action within the time specified in the stipulation. Thompson v. Phœnix Ins. Co. (Or.) 25 Fed. Rep. 296.

This rule, however, would not obtain in case of bad faith on the part of the insurer or unreasonable delay on his part, in which case the action would not be barred. Little v. Phœnix Ins. Co. 123 Mass. 380; Gooden v. Amoskeag F. Ins. Co. 20 N. H. 73.

See also 16 L. R. A. 138; 21 L. R. A. 743; 27 L. R. A. 48.

Gray, 178; *Humboldt Ins. Co.* v. *Johnson*, 1 Ill. App. 309.

In the following cases such a stipulation has been construed and held to be a bar to the action:

Riddlesbarger v. *Hartford Ins. Co.* 74 U. S. 7 Wall. 386 (19 L. ed. 257); *Arthur* v. *Homestead F. Ins. Co.* 78 N. Y. 462; *Virginia F. & M. Ins. Co.* v. *Wells*, 83 Va. 736; *Boon* v. *State Ins. Co.* 37 Minn. 426; *Thompson* v. *Phœnix Ins. Co.* 25 Fed. Rep. 296; *Chandler* v. *St. Paul F. & M. Ins. Co.* 21 Minn. 85; *O'Laughlin* v. *Union Cent. L. Ins. Co.* (Mo.) 11 Fed. Rep. 280; *Garretson* v. *Hawkeye Ins. Co.* 65 Iowa, 468; *Peoria M. & F. Ins. Co.* v. *Whitehill, supra; Ripley* v. *Ætna F. Ins. Co.* 30 N. Y. 164.

Mr. **Alf. E. Boyesen,** for respondent:

The time in which the action must be brought under the limitation clauses reading like the one in this policy does not commence to run until sixty days after the proofs of loss are furnished to the company.

Ellis v. *Council Bluffs Ins. Co.* 64 Iowa, 507; *Friezen* v. *Allemania Ins. Co.* 30 Fed. Rep. 352; *Mix* v. *Andes Ins. Co. of Cincinnati*, 9 Hun, 397; *Chandler* v. *St. Paul F. & M. Ins. Co.* 21 Minn. 88; *Mayor* v. *Hamilton F. Ins. Co.* 39 N. Y. 45; *Barber* v. *Fire & M. Ins. Co. of Wheeling*, 16 W. Va. 658; *Steen* v. *Niagara F. Ins. Co.* 89 N. Y. 315; *Spare* v. *Home Mut. Ins. Co.* 17 Fed. Rep. 569; *Hay* v. *Star F. Ins. Co.* 77 N. Y. 235; *Longhurst* v. *Star Ins. Co.* 19 Iowa, 364; *Hennessey* v. *Manhattan F. Ins. Co.* 28 Hun, 98.

The Company defended the first action on the ground that it was prematurely brought, because instituted within less than sixty days after proofs of loss were received by the defendants. Plaintiff then dismissed the first action, and on the 24th day of March, 1887, commenced the action now pending. If Mr. Sprague did not commence his action within a year he was barred, and if the Company elected to retain the proofs of loss and to accept them, the first action was prematurely brought. Mr. Sprague under this state of facts could do nothing else than commence his first action as he did and then if the Company by its pleadings indicated that it elected to stand on the proofs, the only thing he could do was to dismiss and commence over again. When the defendants interposed the answer pleading the receipt of the proofs of loss, and claimed an abatement of the first action by reason of such facts, they certainly should be held to their election.

Dyckman v. *Sevatson*, 39 Minn. 132.

Corliss, *J.*, delivered the opinion of the court:

The alleged liability of the defendant, the California Insurance Company of San Francisco, rests upon a fire insurance policy issued by it covering buildings owned by one E. C. Sprague; and the other defendant, the Phœnix Insurance Company, is sought to be held by virtue of a contract between it and its co-defendant whereby it re-insured the risk, and assumed the same. If this contract were strictly one of re-insurance, there would be no such privity between the original insured and the re-insurer as would create a liability on the part of the latter to the former. *Strong* v. *Phœnix Ins. Co.* 62 Mo. 289; *Consolidated R. E. & F. Ins. Co.* v. *Cashow*, 41 Md. 59; *Herckenrath* v. *Am. Mut. Ins. Co.* 3 Barb. Ch. 63, 5 N. Y. Ch. L. ed. 818; *Commercial Mut. Ins. Co.* v. *Detroit F. & M. Ins. Co.* 38 Ohio St. 11–16; *Gantt* v. *Am. Cent. Ins. Co.* 68 Mo. 533.

This doctrine has been embodied in our Code. Comp. Laws, § 4186. But this contract appears to have been more than one of re-insurance. The Phœnix Company assumed the risk, and there is respectable authority holding that under such an agreement the original insured may sue directly the company that assumes the loss. *Johannes* v. *Phenix Ins. Co. of Brooklyn*, 66 Wis. 50; *Glen* v. *Hope Mut. L. Ins. Co.* 56 N. Y. 379; *Fischer* v. *Hope Mut. L. Ins. Co.* 69 N. Y. 161.

No question having been made in the court as to the liability of the Phœnix Company directly to the insured, we will not discuss the point any further.

The plaintiff sues as the mortgagee of the insured, whose debt exceeds the amount due under the policy. The policy makes the loss payable to the mortgagee as its interest may appear. It is not claimed that the mortgagee cannot maintain this action without joining with it the insured as a party plaintiff. That the mortgagee may sue alone, where his claim exceeds the amount of the insurance, has the support of several cases. *Hammel* v. *Queen Ins. Co. of London*, 50 Wis. 240; *Cone* v. *Niagara F. Ins. Co.* 60 N. Y. 619; *Martin* v. *Franklin F. Ins. Co.* 38 N. J. L. 140; *Coates* v. *Pennsylvania F. Ins. Co.* 58 Md. 172.

If the owner lays claim to any part of the insurance money, the company may protect itself by interpleader. But the better practice is for the mortgagor and mortgagee both to sue. See *Winne* v. *Niagara F. Ins. Co.* 91 N. Y. 185; *Appleton Iron Co.* v. *British America Assur. Co.* 46 Wis. 23.

The defendants claim that the cause of action was destroyed by the lapse of time before the commencement of the action. The policy contains the usual limitation clause providing that no action shall be maintained upon the policy "unless commenced within twelve months next after the loss shall have occurred," and that the lapse of that time shall be taken as conclusive evidence against the validity of any claim under the policy. The loss occurred May 24, 1885, and this action was not brought until March 24, 1887. It is claimed by plaintiff, however, that proofs of loss were not furnished until April 1, 1886, and that the twelve months' limitation did not commence to run before that date, and therefore the action was brought in time. This presents the question of the construction of such limitation clauses, which has often vexed the courts. It is undoubtedly true that a majority of the adjudications so interpret these limitations as to allow the full time to sue after the right of action has accrued, although more than the limited time has elapsed since the loss occurred. We cannot assent to the doctrine of these cases. They rest upon the alleged necessity of harmonizing conflicting provisions. In these cases, as in this, the policies provided that the loss should not be payable until a specific number of days after proofs of loss. There is no conflict between such a provision and another part of the same policy requiring the action to be brought in twelve months, or any other time, after loss shall have occurred, provided, of course, a reasonable time is left after the cause of action has become perfect in which to sue. The error which appears to this court to lie at the foundation of these decisions is the assumption that the insurance company intended to give the insured the full time specified, during every moment of which he might institute his action. What right has any tribunal to find hidden somewhere in the contract a privilege to have the full time to sue after the cause of action has accrued, when the policy gives it only from the time the loss occurs? There are two distinct provisions,—one that the insured shall not sue before a certain time, and another that he shall not sue after a certain time. These do not clash. They merely necessitate the construction that the intention was to give the insured such period in which to maintain his action after he could sue as would be left after deducting from the time limited, the time which must elapse before the right to sue could accrue. But we find in these cases this extraordinary reasoning: They assert that this doctrine will often kill the action before it could have life. The answer is short and simple. Every limitation in a contract is void which does not leave the plaintiff a reasonable time in which to sue after his right to sue has become perfect. When an insurance company has declared that a suit must be brought within forty days after a loss has occurred, and that no action shall be maintained until thirty days after proof of loss, the duty of the court is not to interpolate into the contract a provision that the limitation runs from the date the cause of action accrues in place of one expunged by the same process, to wit, the provision that the time runs from the time the loss occurs, which is the date of the fire; but the court should invoke against the Company the rule that a right of action shall not, in effect, be destroyed by a limitation which leaves the plaintiff an unreasonably short time to sue after his cause of action has accrued, and declare the limitation clause void. If other provisions of the policy make it appear that in every case a reasonable time will not be left after the right to sue has become perfect, the limitation is void. If, acting in good faith, and with all proper diligence, it transpires in any particular case that other provisions of the policy to be complied with as conditions precedent to a right of action could not be performed in time to leave a reasonable time thereafter in which to sue, the limitation is inoperative in such a case; and, if the Company has induced the insured to believe that the loss will be paid, or that the limitation will not be insisted on, until it is too late to sue, the limitation is waived. Thus the insured is fully protected by the application of known and established principles. The contract is construed as it is written, and the time when the limitations begin to run, if at all, is fixed, and not uncertain.

In *Johnson* v. *Humboldt Ins. Co.*, 91 Ill. 92, the limitation provision required the action to be brought within twelve months after the "loss occurred," and it was declared that no action should be commenced until sixty days after proof of loss. Said the court. "The two clauses, considered together, obviously provide that the company shall have sixty days within which to make payment after notice and proof of loss, but in no event should a suit or action be commenced after the expiration of twelve months from the date of the fire producing the loss. Any other meaning attached to the language, it seems to us, would be strained, unreasonable and in direct violation of the plain intention of the parties, clearly expressed." To same effect are *Virginia F. & M. Ins. Co.* v. *Wells*, 83 Va. 736; *Chambers* v. *Atlas Ins. Co.* 51 Conn. 17.

Chandler v. *St. Paul F. & M. Ins. Co.*, 21 Minn. 85, apparently supports this view. There were two distinct clauses in the limitation provision of the policy in that case, one of which clearly contemplated that the insured should have twelve months after the cause of action accrued, and the other of which declared that the action must be brought within twelve months after the loss had occurred. The court held that the limitation began to run from the date when the right to sue became perfect, on the ground that the clauses were inconsistent, and therefore that must prevail which was most favorable to the insured. But, by holding that the two clauses were inconsistent, it necessarily adjudged that the clause which required the action to be brought within the time specified after the loss had occurred referred to the date of the fire, and did not refer to the accruing of the cause of action as the date from which such language would make the limitation run, as that was what the other clause was construed to, and clearly did, mean.

The court in *Semmes* v. *City F. Ins. Co. of Hartford*, 80 U. S. 13 Wall. 160 [20 L. ed. 490], appears to have adopted the same construction, although this precise question was not in the case; the court saying: "It is not said, as in a statute, that a plaintiff shall have twelve months from the time his cause of action accrued to commence suit, but twelve months from the time of loss; yet by another condition the loss is not payable until sixty days after it shall have been ascertained and proved. The condition is that no suit or action shall be sustainable unless commenced within the time of twelve months next after the loss shall occur," etc. The whole trend of this opinion, and the decision of the court, show that such a provision was regarded, not as giving the insured a specific time during all of which he might sue, but simply as fixing a period beyond which he could not sue.

It appears that a former suit, brought within a year after the loss occurred, was dismissed, and this action instituted after the year had elapsed. But it is well settled that the bringing of an action within the time limited, and which is afterwards dismissed, will not save the second action, commenced subsequently to the expiration of the time, from the operation of the limitation. *O'Laughlin* v. *Union Cent. L. Ins. Co.* 11 Fed. Rep. 280; *Riddlesbarger* v. *Hartford F. Ins. Co.* 74 U. S. 7 Wall. 386 [19 L. ed. 257]; *Wilson* v. *Ætna Ins. Co.* 27 Vt 99; *Arthur* v. *Homestead F. Ins. Co.* 78 N. Y 462.

To the former action the defendant pleaded as a defense that it was prematurely brought, in that sixty days had not elapsed since the receipt by it of proofs of loss. This defense the

Company had a perfect right to make without waiving the limitation clause. See *Arthur* v. *Homestead F. Ins. Co. supra.*

The two provisions are independent of each other. If the insured places himself in a position where he cannot sue within the time limited without suing prematurely, and cannot, on the other hand, wait until he has a right to sue after making proofs of loss without having his claim destroyed by the limitation provision, it is his own fault; and the Company had an undoubted right to urge the defense that the action was prematurely brought without being held to waive the other defense to the second action, commenced too late. Moreover, the time had not run when the first action was brought, and the limitation defense could, therefore, not have been interposed to that action. It cannot be said that the defendant the California Company has estopped itself from setting up the defense by holding out to the insured the hope of a settlement without suit. Assuming that all that was said and done by its own agent, and also by the agent of the Phœnix Company, was sufficient to justify the insured in refraining from suing, there came a time when he became satisfied that the Companies did not intend to pay; and this was in December, 1885, five months before his right to sue was extinguished. Certainly after that time nothing was said or done by either Company to lead the insured to believe that payment without suit was intended.

In this connection the case of *Garido* v. *Am. Cent. Ins. Co.* (Cal.) 8 Pac. Rep. 512, is important. In this case the year's limitation expired February 15, 1881. Negotiations for settlement continued until January 21, 1881, when insured was informed that the company would not pay. In answer to the claim of waiver, the court said that he had ample time in which to bring his action after the company had ceased to lead him to believe that suit would not be necessary. It will be noticed that in that case the insured had only twenty-five days left, whereas in the case at bar he had five months. To same effect is *Garretson* v. *Hawkeye Ins. Co.* 65 Iowa, 468.

There is nothing in the sickness of the insured and his family to excuse his delay. In fact, none even of the statutory exceptions are applicable to a limitation by contract and the time runs on in spite of them. *O'Laughlin* v. *Union Cent. L. Ins. Co. supra; Williams* v. *Vermont Ins. Co.* 20 Vt. 222; *Suggs* v. *Travelers Ins. Co.* 1 L R. A. 847, 71 Tex. 579; *Wilkinson* v. *First Nat. F. Ins. Co. of Worcester*, 72 N. Y. 500; *Riddlesbarger* v. *Hartford F. Ins. Co. supra.*

No question is made as to the validity of the limitation clause in the policy. Such provisions are valid in the absence of a statute. This is settled law. Our Statute relates to such provisions (Comp. Laws, § 3582), but it is conceded that the Statute has no application to the facts of this case, because the contract was a Minnesota contract, insuring property there, made there and to be performed there. The limitation was valid in that State, and it in terms extinguished the right, and did not merely bar the remedy. May, Ins. §432; *Williams* v. *Vermont Ins. Co.* and *Suggs* v. *Travelers Ins. Co. supra.*

As the plaintiff may be able on a new trial to show that the limitation was waived, we will not direct judgment against him, but *reverse the judgment of the District Court, and order a new trial.*

All concur.

Wallin, *J.*, having been of counsel, did not sit in the above case, **Templeton,** *J.*, of the First Judicial District, taking his place.

KANSAS SUPREME COURT.

W. E. SWIFT, *Piff. in Err.*,
v.
CITY OF TOPEKA.

(...... Kan.......)

*1. **A person who rides on his bicycle** across that part of the Kansas River Bridge that is used for the passage of street-cars, carriages and other vehicles does not violate section 17 of the City Ordinance No. 861 of the City of Topeka, that reads as follows: "It shall be unlawful for any person to ride on any bicycle or velocipede upon any sidewalk in the City of Topeka, or across the Kansas River Bridge. Any person violating this section shall, upon conviction thereof, be fined in a sum not less than $1, nor more than $10, for each offense."

2. **Whenever a city ordinance can be so construed** and applied as to give it force and validity, this will be done by the courts, although the construction so put upon it may not be the most obvious and natural one, or the literal one.

(May 10, 1890.)

ERROR to the District Court for Shawnee County to review a judgment convicting defendant of, and fining him for, a violation of a city ordinance regulating the use of bicycles. *Reversed.*

The facts sufficiently appear in the opinion.

*Head notes by SIMPSON, C.

NOTE.—*Bicycle a vehicle.*

A bicycle is a carriage or vehicle, and the rider has the same right upon the highway as a carriage drawn by horses. Holland v. Bartch, 120 Ind. 46; Mercer v. Corbin, 3 L. R. A. 221, 117 Ind. 450.

When meeting any other person traveling with any carriage or other vehicle on a highway or bridge the bicycle rider must pass to the right of the center of the traveled roadway. State v. Collins, 8 L. R. A. 394, 16 R. I. —

A statute forbidding the use of bicycles on a certain highway, unless by permission of the road superintendents, is not unconstitutional as depriving wheelmen of the use of their property. State v. Yopp, 97 N. C. 477, 2 Am. St. Rep. 305.

The use of a sidewalk by a person on a bicycle is unlawful, as the sidewalk is intended for the use of pedestrians. Mercer v. Corbin, *supra.*

Messrs. **Johnson, Martin & Keeler,** for plaintiff in error:

A common street in a city or town, being common to all the people, is a public highway.

3 Kent, Com. 432.

Highways are public streets which every citizen has a right to use by such modes of conveyance as each individual may choose to use.

Angell, Highways, p. 3, § 2; 3 Kent, Com. 32; *Sutcliffe* v. *Greenwood*, 8 Price, 535; *Peck* v. *Smith*, 1 Conn. 103; *Stackpole* v. *Healy*, 16 Mass. 33.

A bridge is a part of the public highway and those principles of the common law which relate to highways in general are alike applicable to public bridges.

Angell, Highways, 3d ed. § 40; Thompson, Highways, p. 11.

A bicycle or velocipede is a carriage.

Taylor v. *Goodwin*, 48 L. J. N. S. Q. B. 427; *Holland* v. *Bartch*, 120 Ind. 46; *Mercer* v. *Corbin*, 3 L. R. A. 221, 117 Ind. 450; *State* v. *Collins*, 3 L. R. A. 394, 16 R. I. —.

The right to travel in the highways and streets is one of those "privileges and immunities which are in their nature fundamental."

U. S. Const. art. 4, § 2; *Corfield* v. *Coryell*, 4 Wash. C. C. 380.

Municipal legislation may control the conduct of persons using the highway in such matters as the rate of speed, the manner of passing each other, whether going in the same or in opposite directions. But the right to such use can never be taken away under the guise of police regulation.

Cooley, Const. Lim. 734, 741; *Com.* v. *Temple*, 14 Gray, 74; 4 Abbott, N. Y. Dig. 555, and cases cited.

A street is made for the passage of persons and property, and the law cannot define what exclusive means of transportation and passage shall be used.

Moses v. *Pittsburgh, Ft. W. & C. R. Co.* 21 Ill. 522; *Langley* v. *Gallipolis*, 2 Ohio St. 110.

Mr. **S. B. Isenhart,** for defendant in error:

The regulation imposed was to protect the people traveling over the bridge from accidents which might happen from horses becoming frightened at bicycles passing by them on this bridge. The Legislature of the State could impose a regulation such as the one in question, and when, as in this State, the power has been delegated to the municipality, it can exercise such power to the same extent as the Legislature.

State v. *Yopp*, 97 N. C. 477.

The commissioners of Central Park, New York, adopted an ordinance providing that no bicycles or tricycles be allowed in the central or city parks; and in *Re Wright*, 29 Hun, 357, this ordinance was held valid, and a proper and reasonable exercise of the police power.

See Horr & Bemis, Mun. Pol. Ord. §§ 246, 247, and authorities cited.

Simpson, *C.*, filed the following opinion:

W. E. Swift was convicted in the Police Court of the City of Topeka of violating section 17 of the Ordinance of said City, No. 361, and fined the sum of $1 and costs. From this conviction he appealed to the District Court of Shawnee County, where a jury was waived, and a trial had by the court that resulted in his conviction, and a fine of $1 and costs imposed. He brings the case here for review, and alleges the invalidity of the ordinance as a cause for reversal. Section 17 of the ordinance in question reads as follows: "It shall be unlawful for any person to ride on any bicycle or velocipede upon any sidewalk in the City of Topeka, or across the Kansas River Bridge. Any person violating this section shall, upon conviction thereof, be fined in a sum not less than $1, nor more than $10, for each offense." It was admitted at the trial that the defendant, W. E. Swift, on the 21st day of June, 1839, was riding upon a bicycle across the Kansas River Bridge, situated on Kansas Avenue, within the corporate limits of the City of Topeka; that he was engaged in riding his bicycle across the said bridge when he was arrested, which bridge is 900 feet long, and spans the Kansas River between North and South Topeka; that the main part of said bridge is constructed wide enough for teams to pass each other, going in opposite directions, being about seventeen feet in the clear; that on each side of the wagon road there is a passageway for foot passengers, and that the defendant was riding his bicycle, at the time named in the complaint, on that part of the bridge used for wagons, carriages and other vehicles; that the bridge just described is the only bridge on the Kansas River between North and South Topeka, and is the only means of communication between those points; that it is used and occupied with a double track by the Topeka City Railway Company, that continually runs its street-cars between the two points named; that there is a large travel across said bridge, between the two parts of the City of Topeka, by vehicles drawn by horses and otherwise, and that teams and other vehicles are constantly passing over said bridge each way. It is further shown by the evidence that a bicycle can be driven at the rate of from two to twenty miles per hour; that the ordinary and usual rate of speed is eight miles per hour; that they can be stopped within from ten to twenty feet, when being driven at the rate of ten miles per hour, the limit within which they can be stopped depending somewhat on the kind of bicycle and the experience of the rider; that bicycles have been in use in this City for several years, and at the time of this arrest that there were more than one hundred in constant use in the City. These are the substantial and material facts that are shown by the record.

It will be seen, by an ordinary inspection of the record, that the ordinance only prohibits the use of a bicycle or velocipede upon any sidewalk in the City of Topeka, or across the Kansas River Bridge. It does not, either in express terms or by fair implication, forbid riding upon a bicycle on the roadway, or that part of any of the public streets that is devoted to the use of carriages, wagons and other vehicles, and, while the ordinance is subject to the construction that it was only along or across the foot passageway or sidewalk of the Kansas River Bridge that persons were forbidden to ride on bicycles, yet for the present we shall adopt the construction necessarily adhered to by the trial court, that the ordinance intended to forbid all riding upon bicycles across any part of the Kansas River Bridge. It is an admitted fact in this case that at the time of the arrest Swift was riding his bicycle on that part of the bridge used for wagons, carriages and other vehicles. A "bicycle" is defined by lexicographers, and by the courts of England and of this country, to be a carriage. Webster, Dict.; *Taylor* v. *Goodwin*, 40 L. T. N. S. 458; *Mercer* v. *Corbin*, 117 Ind. 450, 3 L. R. A. 221; 2 Am. & Eng. Cyclop. Law, 191; *State* v. *Collins*, 16 R. I. ——, 3 L. R. A. 394 (decided by Supreme Court of Rhode Island in December, 1888).

A bridge in the City of Topeka is a part of the public street. *Eudora* v. *Miller*, 30 Kan. 494.

The exact question then is, Have the authorities of the City of Topeka, by an ordinance, the power to forbid Swift riding upon his carriage on that part of a public street of the City devoted to the use of vehicles? This statement of the question necessarily assumes that the power of the City could be exercised to prevent the use of bicyles along the sidewalks of the public streets (and these sidewalks will include the footways across the bridge) to the same extent as the use of all other kind of vehicles, no matter how propelled, could be prevented. Public streets are highways, and every citizen has a right to use them. Both the sidewalks and roadways must remain unobstructed, so that people can walk along one without interruption or danger, or drive along the other without delay or apprehension.

One of the most imperative duties of city governments in this country is to keep their public streets in such a condition that citizens can travel along them with safety, and without any unnecessary delay. Each citizen has the absolute right to choose for himself the mode of conveyance he desires, whether it be by wagon or carriage, by horse, motor or electric car, or by bicycle, or astride of a horse, subject to the sole condition that he will observe all those requirements that are known as the "law of the road." This right of the people to the use of the public streets of a city is so well established and so universally recognized in this country that it has become a part of the alphabet of fundamental rights of the citizen. While the tyranny of the American system of government very largely consists in the action of the municipal authorities, this right has not yet been questioned or attempted to be abridged. There can be no question, then, but what a citizen riding on a bicycle in that part of the street devoted to the passage of vehicles is but exercising his legal right to its use, and a city ordinance that attempted to forbid such use of that part of a public street would be held void, as against common right.

It may be said of bicycles with greater force, as was said of the first use by railroads of public streets, that they are not an obstruction to, or an unreasonable use of, the public streets of a city, but rather a new and improved method of using the same, and germane to their principal object as a passageway. Mills, Em. Dom. 2d ed. § 201; *Briggs* v. *Lewiston & A. H. R. Co.* 79 Me. 363; *Slatten* v. *Des Moines Valley R. Co.* 29 Iowa, 149.

So that, if the construction necessarily given to this ordinance of the City of Topeka should prevail, we would be compelled to say that the part of the ordinance that forbids a citizen riding across any part of the Kansas River Bridge was of no validity. But, if a statute or a city ordinance is susceptible of two different constructions, that one must prevail that will preserve the validity of the ordinance in preference to a construction that will render it invalid; and this must be done, although the construction adopted may not be the most obvious or natural one, or the literal one. *Newland* v. *Marsh*, 19 Ill. 376; *Iowa Homestead Co.* v. *Webster Co.* 21 Iowa, 221; *Roosevelt* v. *Godard*, 52 Barb. 533; *Colwell* v. *May's Landing Water Power Co.* 19 N. J. Eq. 245; *Bigelow* v. *West Wisconsin R. Co.* 27 Wis. 478; *Dow* v. *Norris*, 4 N. H. 17; Cooley, Const. Lim. 184; *Inkster* v. *Carver*, 16 Mich. 484.

Hence we say that the true intent and meaning of section 17 of the city ordinance in question is that all persons are forbidden to ride on bicycles upon any sidewalk in the City, or the sidewalks or footways of the Kansas River Bridge. Sidewalks are intended and constructed to be used solely by pedestrians, and not for the use of vehicles. It is presumably true that every organized town or city in this country forbids the use of its sidewalks to vehicles of every description. A bicycle, being a carriage, can properly be excluded from the use of sidewalks, and persons riding on them should be forbidden to occupy the sidewalks and footways of the public streets, at least longitudinally along such sidewalks or footways. They should be permitted to go across them at such public places as other vehicles are permitted. With this construction of the ordinance, it is plain that Swift has not violated its provisions, and his conviction was wrongful.

The judgment of the District Court is reversed, and the cause remanded, with instructions to dismiss the prosecution and discharge the appellant.

Per Curiam:

It is so ordered, all the Justices concurring.

STATE OF KANSAS

v.

James SMITH *et al.*, *Plffs. in Err.*

(....Kan.....)

***Discharge of jury in defendants' absence.** At the trial of a criminal action, after the evidence both for the State and the defendants had been given, the jury were permitted to separate, and go to their homes. During this recess, it was reported to the court that one of the jurors was sick, and unable to attend. The determination of the fact of sickness on the part of the absent juror must be by judicial methods, and these include the presence of the defendants while that fact was being investigated, their right to produce witnesses, and of cross-examination; and it is error in the trial court to pro-

*Head note by SIMPSON, C.

NOTE.—Constitutional rights of person charged with crime; right to be present during the trial. See *notes* to Gore v. State (Ark.) 5 L. R. A. 834; King v. State (Tenn.) 8 L. R. A. 211.

ceed to investigate and determine the fact of sickness of the absent juror, and for that cause to discharge the jury from any further consideration of the case, in the absence of the defendants from the court-room, they being charged with a felony.

(June 7, 1890.)

ERROR to the District Court for Rice County to review a judgment convicting defendants of the crime of larceny. *Reversed.*

The facts are fully stated in the opinion.

Messrs. **C. F. Foley** and **W. E. Borah,** for plaintiffs in error:

When on the 10th day of January, 1890, the jury was empanelled and sworn to try defendants under the information in this cause, jeopardy attached and could be subsequently removed only by legal discharge of the jury.

Dobbins v. *State*, 14 Ohio St. 493; *Mitchell* v. *State*, 42 Ohio St. 393; *People* v. *Webb*, 38 Cal. 477; *People* v. *Cage*, 48 Cal. 324; 1 Bishop, Crim. Law, § 1014; 1 Bishop, Crim. Proc. § 961; *Maden* v. *Emmons*, 83 Ind. 331; *Hilands* v. *Com.* 111 Pa. 1; *Com.* v. *Cook*, 6 Serg. & R. 578; *Com.* v. *Clue*, 3 Rawle, 498; *Peiffer* v. *Com.* 15 Pa. 468; *McFadden* v. *Com.* 23 Pa. 12; *Alexander* v. *Com.* 105 Pa. 2; *State* v. *Jennings*, 24 Kan. 655.

There was never any legal and competent evidence introduced to the court, tending to establish the juror Kelly's sickness. There was no evidence which the court could legally receive and consider.

Rulo v. *State*, 19 Ind. 298; *People* v. *Cage*, *supra; Conklin* v. *State*, 25 Neb. 784.

Assuming that the evidence was such as the court could legally receive and consider, it did not establish a case of necessity for the discharge of the jury, such as the law contemplates and requires.

Rulo v. *State*, *supra; Wright* v. *State*, 5 Ind. 290, 7 Ind. 324; *Maden* v. *Emmons*, 83 Ind. 334; *Hines* v. *Ohio*, 24 Ohio St. 134; *Com.* v. *Fitzpatrick*, 1 L. R. A. 451, 121 Pa. 109; *State* v. *Shuchardt*, 18 Neb. 454; *Hilands* v. *Com. supra; Poage* v. *Ohio*, 8 Ohio St. 229.

Assuming that the evidence was sufficient, nevertheless it could not legally be received, entertained and considered by the court during the enforced absence of the defendants, nor could the jury be legally discharged upon such evidence.

State v. *Myrick*, 38 Kan. 238; *Maurer* v. *People*, 43 N. Y. 1; *Jones* v. *State*, 26 Ohio St. 208; *State* v. *Wilson*, 50 Ind. 487; *Nolan* v. *State*, 55 Ga. 521; *Roberts* v. *State*, 6 Bush, 563; *Smith* v. *People*, 8 Colo. 457; Bishop, Crim. Proc. §§ 272, 278; *Green* v. *People*, 3 Colo. 68; *Rose* v. *State*, 20 Ohio, 32; *O'Brian* v. *Com.* 6 Bush, 563.

Messrs. **L. B. Kellogg,** *Atty-Gen.*, and **J. W. Brinckerhoff,** *Pros. Atty.*, for defendant in error:

The court had a right to discharge the jury on account of the sickness of one of the twelve.

1 Bishop, Crim. Law, §§ 1032, 1041; 1 Bishop, Crim. Proc. § 949; *Bates* v. *State*, 19 Tex. 122; *Vanderkarr* v. *State*, 51 Ind. 91.

The defendants were not prejudiced and the discharge was immaterial error not affecting the substantial rights of the defendants, which this court will disregard on appeal.

Gen. Stat. 1889; Crim. Proc. § 293; *State* v. *Skinner*, 34 Kan. 268; *State* v. *Baldwin*, 36 Kan. 1; *State* v. *Winner*, 17 Kan. 298; *Montgomery* v. *State*, 3 Kan. 275; *State* v. *Baxter*, 41 Kan. 518; *State* v. *White*, 19 Kan. 445; *United States* v. *Perez*, 22 U. S. 9 Wheat. 579 (6 L. ed. 165); *State* v. *Vaughan*, 29 Iowa, 286.

In the case at bar a new trial was granted, a speedy trial as guaranteed by the Constitution at the same term of court. It would be error in such a case to grant a discharge.

State v. *Hays*, 2 Lea, 156.

Simpson, *C.*, filed the following opinion:

At the regular January Term, 1890, of the District Court of Rice County, the appellants, James Smith, John Smith and Martin Smith, were placed upon their trial, charged with burglary and larceny. They waived arraignment, entered a plea of not guilty, a jury was sworn, and the State and defendants both submitted their evidence. All this transpired on the 10th day of January. When the court met on the morning of the 11th of January, counsel for appellants asked permission to introduce further evidence in their behalf. The jurors were called, and all were present, and took their seats in the jury-box, and thereupon Frank Fry, a juror, stated to the court that he was unable to sit as a juror on that day, on account of sickness; and upon this statement the court adjourned the hearing of the case until the 13th day of January. When the court met on the 13th, and the jury were called, all were present except two jurors,—John Johnson and John Kelly. The court was informed that these two jurymen were sick, and an adjournment was ordered until the mornin g of the 14th of January. On that morning all the jurors were present and ready for duty, except John Kelly. The jury were permitted to separate until 5 o'clock P. M. of that day, the 14th of January. At 5 o'clock P. M. the jury were again called; and, it appearing that the juror Kelly was still absent, and reported sick, the trial court discharged the jury from any further consideration of the case. During all this day, except during a short time in the morning, the defendants were absent from the court-room, being confined in the Rice County Jail. They were not present at the time the jury was discharged, but their attorneys were in attendance, and objected to the discharge of the jury. The trial court entered on the journal the following order discharging the jury: "Afterwards, to wit, on the 14th day of January, 1890, and just before adjourning for supper, court being duly convened, the said jury was by the clerk called, and all responded to their names except John Kelly, who was then absent from court, and, upon inquiry being made regarding the absence of said juror, Kelly, the sheriff informed the court that a messenger had been sent for the said juror, John Kelly, and that said messenger stated that said Kelly reported himself too sick to be present in court; that said Kelly did not know when he would be able to be present in court; that he might not be able to come into court for a week; and that said Kelly stated he would come into court as soon as he was able. And the court being satisfied from the report of said sheriff, and also from a letter received from said juror by said court purporting to be written by said juror, Kelly, that said juror, John Kelly, was seriously sick, and unable to attend court, thereupon discharged said eleven jurors from the further consideration of said case. Whereupon, and at the same time, the defendants being then absent from the court-room, and confined in the county jail of Rice County, Kan., the court discharged the said jury from the further consideration of this cause; to all of which action of the court the defendants, by their counsel, then and there duly excepted, which exception was by the court allowed. That, at the time of the discharge of said eleven jurors, neither of defendants' counsel, Messrs. Borah and Foley, who were present and defendants' said counsel, objected to the discharge of said eleven jurors from said case, on the ground that their said clients, James, John and Martin Smith, defendants herein, were not present in court. During all the proceedings had in this cause on the 14th day of January, 1890, except upon convening of court in the morning, at which time no proceedings in this cause were had except to adjourn the further hearing of the same till the afternoon of the same day, in order to hear from juror, for whom a messenger was sent, the defendants, and each of them, were absent from the court-room, and were confined in the county jail of Rice County, Kan. Before the said eleven jurymen in attendance upon the trial of said cause were by the court discharged, the court duly inquired of said Foley and Borah if they were willing to proceed with the trial of the cause with the eleven jurors who were able to be and were present, and they replied that they were not willing so to do, but would require a full panel. That the continuance from the 13th to the 14th day of January was made by the court at its own instance, the defendants, by their counsel, objecting to such continuance."

On the 20th day of January, 1890, the appellants were arraigned upon the same information upon which they had previously been put upon trial, and objected to being required to plead to the information on the ground that a jury had once been sworn to try them, and that said jury had been discharged without their consent, in their absence, and while they were confined in the jail, and that they had once been put in jeopardy upon the offenses charged against them in the information. This was overruled. The appellants then filed their plea in abatement, setting up the same facts, and this was overruled. The appellants then pleaded not guilty, and pleaded these same facts in bar. The trial proceeded, and the appellants were convicted of the larceny of goods of the value of $50.93. A motion for a new trial and a motion in arrest of judgment, in which all these facts were again set forth, were both overruled. The appellants had all proper exceptions noted and saved on all these various rulings. At least, they have done enough to fairly present the questions they discuss here for review. Their contention is embraced in these two propositions: that there was no evidence of the sickness of the juror Kelly that authorized the court to discharge the jury, and that such discharge was not legal without the presence of the appellants.

Section 281 of the Civil Code provides: "The jury may be discharged by the court on account of the sickness of a juror, or other action or calamity requiring their discharge, or by consent of both parties, or after they have been kept together until it satisfactorily appears that there is no probability of their agreeing." Section 208 of the Criminal Code provides: "The proceedings prescribed by law in civil cases in respect to the impaneling of jurors, the keeping of them together and the manner of rendering their verdict, shall be had upon trials on indictments and informations for criminal offenses, except in cases otherwise provided by statute." The court had the right to discharge the jury on account of the sickness of one of the members thereof. *State* v. *White*, 19 Kan. 445.

It is insisted upon one side that the determination of the existence of such a sickness rests largely, and almost exclusively, in the discretion of the court, while the appellants contend that its existence must be established as a fact in accordance with the rules of evidence, and that a trial court cannot of its own motion, or from mere reports, unverified by affidavits or unsupported by oaths administered in open court, determine that there exists such an unavoidable necessity that the remaining jurors should be discharged, and, by such an arbitrary exercise, deprive the appellants of the plea of once in jeopardy. The power to so discharge a jury is not to be arbitrarily exercised. One of the constitutional rights of a party charged with crime is that he is not to be twice put in jeopardy for the same offense, and the power of a court to discharge a jury that has been sworn to pass upon the question of his guilt and innocence must be exercised with a view to preserve inviolate his constitutional right in this respect. The sickness of a juror is one of those unavoidable necessities that arise beyond the power of the court or the prosecution to foresee. It seems clear on principle, as well as in view of the constitutional privileges of the prisoner, that this authority cannot be arbitrarily exercised; for, in the language of the Supreme Court of the State of Pennsylvania in the case of *Com.* v. *Clue*, 3 Rawle, 498: "Why it should be thought that the citizen has no other assurance than the arbitrary discretion of the magistrate for the enforcement of the constitutional principle which protects him from being twice put in jeopardy of life or member for the same offense, I am at a loss to imagine. If discretion is to be called in, there can be no remedy for the most palpable abuse of it but an interposition of the power to pardon, which is obnoxious to the very same objection. Surely, every right secured by the Constitution is guarded by sanctions more imperative. But, in those States where the principle has no higher sanction than what is derived from the common law, it is nevertheless the birthright of the citizen, and consequently demandable as such. But a right which depends upon the will of the magistrate is essentially no right at all, and for this reason the common law abhors the exercise of a discretion in matters that may be subjected to fixed and definite rules." This was said in a capital case, but the language of the section of the Bill of Rights in our State Constitution is broad enough to include all felonies. It seems, however, to be the rule in all grades of felony that the only justification for the exercise of the power of a trial court to discharge a jury which has heard the evidence in a criminal case is the existence of an absolute necessity for the discharge. Some unforeseen fact must intervene, beyond the power of the court to control, before such a power can be legally exerted. The existence of this unforeseen fact that operates to stop the deliberation of the jury, and prevents a verdict, must be judicially ascertained and determined. That is to say, if the sickness of the juror does not occur in the immediate presence of the court, but commences during a recess, and is reported, the fact of sickness must be established as any other fact is established in a court of justice, in accordance with the rules of evidence governing such matters. When an order is made by a trial court discharging a jury without verdict, to whom has been committed the question of the guilt or innocence of a prisoner charged with a crime, the record ought to show affirmatively the existence of the fact that induced such order and justified the exercise of such extraordinary power. This much seems demanded in order to preserve to the prisoner the full benefit of the constitutional requirement in his behalf.

The case of *Conklin* v. *State*, decided by the Supreme Court of Nebraska in February, 1889, and reported in 25 Neb. 784, illustrates this view. Section 485 of the Criminal Code of that State provides that "in case a jury shall be discharged on account of sickness of a juror, or other accident or calamity requiring their discharge, or after they have been kept so long together that there is no probability of agreeing, the court shall, upon directing their discharge, order that the reasons for such discharge shall be entered on the journal, and such discharge shall be without prejudice to the prosecution." The journal showed this order: "Come also the jury, . . . and report in open court their inability to agree upon a verdict in this cause; and it appearing to the satisfaction of the court, upon examination of M. L. Brown, one of the jurors in said case, that, by reason of his sickness, he was unable to further perform his duties as a juror, and upon further examination of each and every juror in said case, the court finds that there is no probability of the jurors agreeing upon a verdict, and that they had been out twenty-one hours without sleep, or a suitable place to sleep or rest, said jury is therefore discharged without day, without prejudice to the prosecution." Commenting on this journal entry, the court says: "The sickness of a juror is one of the causes recognized by the Statute above quoted for the discharge of a jury, but it is submitted that such sickness is classed with 'other accident or calamity requiring their discharge;' and it appears to me that such sickness must be of a sudden and calamitous character, and of such a nature as to render his further detention in the jury-room manifestly improper. It does not appear here that the jury reported the sickness of one of their number, or that the juror himself claimed to be sick or incapacitated on account of sickness from further service on the jury, nor in what the examination of the juror by the court consisted, nor whether the advice and services of a physician were had to ascertain and advise the court of the condition of the juror. Again, it does not appear that the jury were discharged solely on account of the sickness of this juror; but, on the contrary, I think that, taking the whole journal entry together, it fairly appears that the sickness of the juror was not such that the court would have discharged the jury for that cause alone. If the sickness of this juror was such that his further service on the jury was impossible, what was the necessity, or even the propriety, of further examining each and every juror as to the probability of their agreeing upon a verdict, the length of time they had been out without sleep or a suitable place to sleep or rest?" The logic of this case seems to require that there should in effect be a finding of fact as to the incapacity of the juror, by reason of sickness, to properly discharge his duty.

In the case of *State* v. *Shuchardt*, 18 Neb. 454, *Judge* Maxwell says: "It was never intended to permit a court arbitrarily to discharge a jury for disagreement until a sufficient time had elapsed to preclude all reasonable expectation that they will ever agree."

In the case of *Dobbins* v. *State*, 14 Ohio St. 493, the court, commenting on the power to discharge juries in criminal cases, says "that this power does not rest upon the arbitrary or uncontrollable discretion of the judge presiding at the trial, but is a legal discretion to be exercised in conformity with known and established rules; and, finally, unless the facts stated in the record clearly establish a case of necessity, the discharge will operate as an acquittal of the accused and preclude his further prosecution."

This court, in the case of *State* v. *White*, 19 Kan. 445, by the chief justice, says that where the jury have deliberated so long, without finding a verdict, as to preclude a reasonable expectation that they will agree, they may be discharged if the record shows a necessity for such action, without the consent of the defendant, and the prisoner be tried by another jury. All these authorities require that there must be a legal showing made and entered on the record of the necessity for the discharge, and of the existence of the facts that authorize the exercise of the extraordinary power of the court.

Now, the record in this case shows that one of the causes for which the trial court is authorized to discharge a jury in a criminal case, by the Statute of this State, happened on this trial, to wit: the sickness of a juror. This sickness did not happen in the immediate presence of the court. The juror took sick at home during a recess of the court, and the fact of sickness had to be established in accordance with the rules that govern in all cases when a fact is to be judicially established and made a finding upon which to base a legal conclusion or judicial action. Then, in accordance with these authorities quoted, and in view of the constitutional rights of the appellants and the requirements of section 207 of the Code of Criminal Procedure, these appellants ought to have been present in person during the investigation and determination of the existence of the fact of sickness.

This case is not like that of *State* v. *White*,

supra, where the jury were discharged because there was no reasonable probability of their agreement. In such cases a consulting jury is in legal contemplation always in the presence of the court. All their reports, of every kind and character, are made directly to the court, and the court alone has the sole right to question them as to the probabilities of an agreement. In the very nature of things, as no one is allowed to be present at their deliberations, a determination by the court as to whether or not there is a reasonable probability of their agreement must be made on the report of the jury. So the language of the court in the case of *State* v. *White*, as to the absence of the defendant at the time of the discharge of the jury, cannot be fairly applied in a case like this, when the fact alleged as justifying a discharge of this jury happened out of the presence of the court and while the jury were temporarily discharged from attendance in court. In one case the court acts on an official report made by the jury, which the defendant has no right to question. In the other, an inquiry as to the existence of a fact alleged to have occurred away from the presence and observation of the court is to be made by judicial methods; and these include the presence of the parties interested, their right to introduce evidence and cross-examine witnesses. We think that error was committed in determining the sickness of a juror as a cause for the discharge of the jury in the absence of the appellants. It is evident from the record that error was also committed on the trial of the issue of fact made by the plea in abatement filed by the appellants and the replication filed by the county attorney. This issue of fact was the sickness of the juror Kelly; and, to maintain the issue on the part of the State, the county attorney was permitted, over the objection of the appellants, to read in evidence a letter purporting to have been written by the juror Kelly to the trial judge, without any preliminary proof whatever of its genuineness. For these errors there must be a reversal; and for the reasons suggested by the court in the case of *Conklin* v. *State*, 25 Neb. 784, we prefer this course rather than to pass upon the other question until all the facts are fully and fairly presented. This accords, too, with the case of *State* v. *Myrick*, 38 Kan. 238.

We recommend that the judgment of the District Court of Rice County be reversed, and the cause remanded, with instructions to grant the appellants a new trial.

Per Curiam:

It is so ordered; all the Justices concurring.

IOWA SUPREME COURT.

Mary C. McCONNELL, *Appt.*,
v.
CITY OF OSAGE.

(....Iowa....)

1. **An order limiting the number of witnesses** on each side on a certain point, when made at or near the beginning of a trial without objection by either party, cannot be complained of afterwards.

2. **Opinions as to length of time** a certain kind of lumber will last in sidewalks may be given by competent witnesses on the question of negligence in permitting a sidewalk to become rotten.

3. **The defective condition of a sidewalk** for its entire length may be proved in order to show notice in a suit for injuries resulting from a board in such sidewalk being loose.

4. **Evidence of plaintiff's statements as to her health,** made many years before the injury for which suit was brought, is not too remote to be used against her where she has herself testified as to her robust health for a period nearly as remote.

5. **The privilege against a disclosure of confidential communications** made to a physician is not waived by the fact that the one claiming it gives testimony in her own behalf, which is alleged to be false and which the physician's testimony is needed to contradict, concerning her general health and vigor during a certain period of time when she says he was her attending physician.

6. **A party cannot be asked** as a witness whether he is willing to waive his privilege as to confidential communications with a physician.

(May 27, 1890.)

APPEAL by plaintiff from a judgment o the District Court for Mitchell County in favor of defendant in an action brought to recover damages for personal injuries sustained by falling on a sidewalk in defendant City. *Reversed.*

The case sufficiently appears in the opinion.

Messrs. **F. F. Coffin, G. E. Marsh** and **Cummins & Wright** for appellant.

Messrs. **W. L. Eaton** and **L. M. Ryce,** for appellee:

The record discloses a waiver of the statute privilege or bar by appellant. She broke the seal of secrecy—the functional ban—with her own lips. She removed the reason of the law conferring the privilege, and "*cessante ratione legis cessat ipsa lex*" applies.

The patient cannot use this privilege both as a sword and a shield, to waive when it inures to her advantage and wield when it does not.

McKinney v. *Grand Street P. P. & F. R. Co.* 6 Cent. Rep. 496, 104 N. Y. 352.

Having assumed to state what her physical condition had been for several years immediately preceding her injury, having assumed to narrate and describe all the ailments and disabilities that had affected her during that period, and named her attending physician, if her testimony therein was simulated and false, she could not plead the statute privilege, when the defendant offered to impeach her therein by producing her said physician, Dr. Chase, or any other physician in attendance with him as assistant.

Campau v. *North*, 39 Mich. 606, 33 Am. Rep. 433; *Edington* v. *Ætna L. Ins. Co.* 77 N.Y. 564; *People* v. *Barker*, 60 Mich. 277; *McKinney* v. *Grand Street P. P. & F. R. Co. supra; Brown*

v. *Metropolitan L. Ins. Co.* 8 West. Rep. 775, 65 Mich. 306; *Dotton* v. *Albion*, 57 Mich. 575.

The words used in our Code are "any confidential communication properly intrusted and which is necessary," etc., and they should receive a strict construction to prevent the obvious mischiefs, frauds and abuses that, under a construction more latitudinarian, would creep in.

Renihan v. *Dennin*, 5 Cent. Rep. 416, 103 N. Y. 573; *McKinney* v. *Grand Street P. P. & F. R. Co. supra.*

Granger, *J.*, delivered the opinion of the court:

1. The trial court limited the number of witnesses for each side to six on the question of the general condition of the walk where the plaintiff was injured, and appellant complains of such action of the court. So far as we can judge, the order was made near the commencement of the trial, and without objection by either party. Later plaintiff desired to introduce additional witnesses, which the court refused. From the state of the record, it does not appear that the question is properly before us for review, for we find no exceptions taken to the action of the court. If the order was made without objection, we must assume that the parties assented thereto; and of such action they could not afterwards complain.

2. The testimony tends to show that the sidewalk on which the injury occurred was in a rotted condition, so that the sills would not retain the nails by which the boards were fastened to them. The sidewalk was built in 1872, and the accident happened in 1884. The walk was built by the defendant City. The law requires it to use reasonable diligence in keeping its walks in suitable repair.

As bearing on the question of defendant's negligence, the plaintiff offered certain witnesses, whose competency is not questioned, to testify to the length of time the kind of lumber of which the walk was constructed would last. Under the objections of the defendant, it was excluded, and, as we understand, on the theory that it was not a proper subject for expert testimony. We think the testimony should have been admitted. As was said in *Ferguson* v. *Davis County*, 57 Iowa, 601, we may say in this case: "Conceding that the knowledge is such as may be acquired by observation, yet the matter is one which all persons do not have the inclination nor the opportunity to observe;" and, while the judgments of persons generally might not differ to any great extent on such a subject, we believe that persons who have not given the matter particular thought or observation would in their judgments make years of difference. Much would depend on their business, and their opportunities for such observation. The business of many men would operate to almost entirely exclude them from such observations, and there would be nothing to particularly call their attention to the subject. The case of *Muldowney* v. *Illinois Cent. R. Co.*, 36 Iowa, 462, cited by appellee, is by no means against this view. It is there said: "It is often very difficult to determine in regard to what particular matters and points witnesses may give testimony by way of opinion. It is doubtful whether all the cases can be harmonized, or brought within any general rule or principle." It seems to us quite clear that the judgment of men whose business and observations give them accurate information on the question of durability of material in bridges or walks would be of great value to a jury in properly determining such a question. No question as to the competency of the witnesses, or the materiality of the testimony offered, is made in the case. Our holding is that the jury in such cases may be aided by the testimony of competent witnesses. It is doubtful if for this error alone we should have reversed the case, there being so much other evidence as to the condition of the walk.

3. The plaintiff was injured by tripping on a loose board in the walk; and, with a view to show that the City did or should have known of the condition of the walk where the injury occurred, she offered to prove a defective condition of the walk the entire length of the block. The offer was refused. In this the court erred. The point is clearly controlled by the case of *Armstrong* v. *Ackley*, 71 Iowa, 76.

Appellee thinks the point should be controlled by *Ruggles* v. *Nevada*, 63 Iowa, 185. The offer in this case was to prove a continuous condition of the walk from the place of injury. In the *Ruggles Case* the inquiry was not as to the continuous condition of the walk, but it was as to another place "near there" or "in that locality." The accident in that case was also caused by a loose board, and a defect at some other place, near there, would not be as likely to show the particular defect complained of as would the fact that the defect complained of was a part of one continuous defect; and that is a distinguishing feature of the cases.

4. There was testimony tending to show that, because of plaintiff's injuries, her spine and nervous system were affected; and it was claimed that her injuries were permanent. One Dr. Russell, who had attended her, after testifying as to her condition, was asked this question: "Where there is an injury to the nervous system, in shock or strain to the spinal column, of such a character that it continues for a period of two and a half years, occasioned by a fall, what are the probabilities or chances, in your opinion, as to the recovery of a person, or not?" An objection to the question was sustained, and, on appeal, appellee does not question the admissibility of such proof; but its contention is that the doctor had before given the answer sought by the question, and, inferentially, that there could have been no prejudicial error in the ruling. In this we think appellee is correct, and we have only given the point this notice to avoid a misapprehension on another trial.

5. Several lady witnesses were, against the objections of the plaintiff, permitted to testify as to statements made to them by plaintiff, many years before the accident, as to her health. It is urged that such statements, if made, are too remote, and hence incompetent. The plaintiff, as affecting the question of the damage she had sustained from the injury, had given testimony as to her health and ability to perform labor at least as far back as 1870, showing that she was a strong, robust woman. In view of this fact, we think the proof of statements made by her not earlier than 1866

or 1867, and later, were not too remote to be considered as affecting the truth of her statements.

6. Dr. S. B. Chase, being a witness for the defendant, testified that he treated the plaintiff professionally in the years 1866, 1867 and 1871. In doing so, against the objections of the plaintiff, he related confidential communications made to him, and necessary for her proper treatment.

Code, § 3643, provides: "No practicing attorney, counselor, physician, surgeon, minister of the gospel or priest of any denomination shall be allowed, in giving testimony, to disclose any confidential communication properly intrusted to him in his professional capacity, and necessary and proper to enable him to discharge the functions of his office according to the usual course of practice or discipline. Such prohibition shall not apply to cases where the party in whose favor the same are made waives the rights conferred."

The only theory upon which the action of the court is sought to be sustained is that the plaintiff waived the provisions of the Statute in her favor. It will be observed, from the closing sentence of the section, that the party in whose favor the prohibition is may waive it. The facts urged as constituting the waiver are as follows: The plaintiff was a witness in her own behalf, and testified that she had worked on the farm, and traveled and sold books and sewing machines; that, since the birth of her children, her health had been good; that she had done heavy work indoors and outdoors, and that she had been sick but little. It may be said that her testimony, if true, showed her to be a remarkably robust and vigorous woman. She also stated that Dr. Chase had been her attending physician at times. Counsel for appellee states his proposition in support of a waiver as follows: "Having assumed to state what her physical condition had been for several years immediately preceding her injury, having assumed to narrate and describe all the ailments and disabilities that had affected her during that period, and named her attending physician, if her testimony therein was simulated and false, she could not plead the statute privilege when the defendant offered to impeach her therein by producing her said physician, Dr. Chase, or any other physician in attendance with him as assistant." It will be observed that the ground on which the waiver is based is that the plaintiff had given false testimony. It may be well to briefly inquire how such a rule would operate in practice. If the waiver is only because the testimony given is false, that fact must appear before the testimony can properly be admitted. Will the court, when such testimony is offered, assume, as a basis for its admission, that the statements made by the plaintiff are untrue? If so, it must be because the law justifies the assumption; and, if it does, why not at once declare them false, and not attempt to prove what must be assumed as a basis for the proof? If "the statute privilege" is claimed it must be when the testimony is offered; and, if false testimony is the basis of its admission, the fact must then appear. If it appears, there is no necessity for proof to show it. The ruling must be the same as if the cause was tried to the court without a jury. It is not difficult to see that the rule could not obtain in practice. If a waiver can be claimed because of the testimony of the plaintiff, it must be alone because the opposite party desires to contradict the plaintiff by testimony of the physician, and leave the falsity of her statements for determination by the jury. All that can be said at the time of admission is that a party claims her statements to be false. If at the conclusion, with the testimony admitted, her statements are found to be true as against those of the physician, what is the situation? The testimony has been used to defeat the truth, and the Statute as to prohibiting such testimony violated. It is not enough to say that in some cases it may operate to defeat the designs of falsehood. Such a rule would practically annul the provisions of the Statute. It could not be questioned that greater freedom as to such testimony would in some cases work good results, and in others bad. It is a proper matter for legislative regulation; and, after considering the reasons for and against the rule, it has placed the obligation of secrecy on the lips of the physician unless it is removed by the party in whose interest it was so placed. The Statute should be looked at practically to know the legislative intent. It does not provide for such secrecy, except in cases where testimony as to such communications is necessary to contradict or prove that the party has testified falsely, but the secrecy remains unless waived. We think the rule on reason is against the position of appellee.

Let us look to the authorities, briefly. Several cases are cited by appellee, some of which we notice. *McKinney* v. *Grand Street P. P. & F. R. Co.*, 104 N. Y. 352, 6 Cent. Rep. 496, is one wherein the party entitled to the prohibition put the physician on the stand as a witness, and the facts were there stated. In another trial of the same case the other party called the physician to show the same facts; and the court held that, she herself having used the physician, and by him made public the confidential matter,—having herself "removed the seal from the lips of the witness,"—the evidence could be received. How different the cases! In that case the lips of the physician were sealed in the plaintiff's interest. She removed the seal to allow him to speak. The holding was that she could not in that case replace it. In this case, Dr. Chase was allowed to speak against the objections of the plaintiff, not by her permission, unless that permission is to be implied from the fact of her giving testimony. The case cited does not go to that extent, and is not an authority for such a rule. The case of *Brown* v. *Metropolitan L. Ins. Co.*, 8 West. Rep. 775, 65 Mich. 306, is a Michigan case, and the holding is that, the plaintiff having stated in her application for life insurance that Dr. H. had treated her for typhoid fever, he could be allowed, against her objection, to testify whether he had so treated her or not. The court says: "The fact as to treatment or nontreatment for this disease was not, under the circumstances of this case, a matter of privilege upon which the plaintiff could insist." The same question is not in this case, nor is it an authority for our guidance. We are not holding that, if plaintiff had testified that Dr. Chase treated her for a particular disease, he might not have stated, against her objection, whether he did or not. Such a question would not necessarily have involved a "confidential communication."

In *Dotton* v. *Albion*, 57 Mich. 575, also a Michigan case, we think counsel misapprehended the import of the ruling. It seems to be in support of our view, so far as it is an authority in the case. It is a case in which one of two attending physicians was made a witness for plaintiff, and testified as to the effect of her injuries, and also as to her previous good health. The defense endeavored to show that she was before afflicted with chronic ailments, and for that purpose called other attending physicians; but the court excluded their testimony. On appeal it was urged that the court erred in so doing, "because the plaintiff waived her privilege to have the seal of professional confidence preserved unbroken when she put her own physician on the stand to testify to her condition." To this the court said, no: that, as to the witness she used, she doubtless did to the extent she examined him, but not as to others. The case has no reference to a waiver being implied because of false statements by the plaintiff as to conditions known to a physician. This case cites in its support that of *Campau* v. *North*, 39 Mich. 606, on which counsel for appellee seems to place much reliance. In that case the question of a waiver is not presented or referred to. The plaintiff claimed to have been injured by the violence of the defendant while in his employ, and she gave testimony as to her being ruptured by his violence. The trial involved an inquiry as to her condition before the injury, she having testified that she was previously in good health. On cross-examination she denied that she had admitted to her attending physician that she was ruptured before the injury. The physician being called to contradict her, his testimony was admitted. But the court does not put its rulings on the ground that she, by her testimony, had waived the provisions of the Statute in her favor, but, as we understand, she had never brought herself within its provision. The particular ground of the holding is: "It does not appear in the record, from the doctor's testimony or in any way, that, in case she made the admission as to the pre-existence of the rupture, and as to its being caused by the plaintiff in error, it was information necessary to enable the doctor to prescribe for her as a physician, or to do any act for her as a surgeon. And yet this is one of the fundamental conditions for exclusion which the Statute specifies."

It is not urged in this case but that the plaintiff, under the facts, was entitled to protection unless she had waived it; and the case does not hold that the giving of false testimony, which it might be desirable to contradict, would constitute a waiver. We need not notice other errors of the same character.

7. While plaintiff was on the witness stand, and being cross-examined, she was asked this question: "Q. Are you willing that the physicians who have treated you for the past ten or fifteen years may disclose to this jury any conversation you made to them, at times they treated you, in reference to your condition?" Objections to the question being overruled, the plaintiff answered that she was not. The ruling is assigned as error, and we think it was manifestly so. Counsel for appellee does not in argument attempt to vindicate the ruling, and it would seem that an attempt must result in failure. The Statute gives the prohibition. It is a legal right, and a party should no more be required to state under oath that he did not want to surrender it than any other legal right he possessed. We think a fair trial requires that such a matter should not even be referred to; that a jury should not be impressed with a belief that there is even reluctance to giving such assent. The subject matter of such a waiver has no place for reference in the taking of testimony except by the party permitted to make it. That prejudice resulted from the ruling in question is more than probable. After making oath that she would not consent to the testimony, the jury was left to assume something,—we know not what. It would naturally believe that, if assent had been given, testimony unfavorable to the plaintiff would have been the result. However, we need not speculate as to the probable consequences. It was clearly error.

8. Some errors are assigned as to instructions which we think it unnecessary to consider, as the same objections will not likely arise on another trial. We call attention to the definition of the word "negligence" in the fifth instruction, with the suggestion that its correctness is seriously questioned, and may be doubted.

Because of the errors pointed out in this opinion, ***the judgment of the District Court is reversed.***

WISCONSIN SUPREME COURT.

Horace J. HOFFMAN *et al.*, *Respts.*,
v.
CHIPPEWA COUNTY, *Appt.*

(.... Wis.....)

1. An offer to print a delinquent tax list for less than the statutory rate, and the tender of a bond for the faithful performance of the work, in accordance with which a contract is entered into with the county clerk, who has no power to make such contract, will not prevent recovery of the full statutory rate.

2. The doctrine of waiver or estoppel has no application to a contract made by a public officer without authority for the performance of work at less than the rates fixed therefor by statute, and such doctrine cannot be invoked as a defense to a suit for the full statutory rate.

(June 21, 1890.)

APPEAL by defendant from an order of the Circuit Court for Chippewa County sustaining a demurrer to the answer in an action brought to recover the statutory fees for printing a delinquent tax list, which answer set up a special contract to do the printing at a lower rate. *Affirmed.*

The case sufficiently appears in the opinion.

Mr. **T. J. Connor**, for appellant:

Within the thirty-cent limit fixed by section 1174, the county clerk, by necessary implication, has the right, if he shall choose to exercise it, of making a contract with the publisher of the list as to compensation.

State v. *Dixon County Supers.* 24 Neb. 106.

Messrs. **Dickinson & Buchanan**, for respondents:

An officer has no authority to vary or change in any respect, without express statutory warrant, the compensation fixed by the law for services to be performed by another officer; and there is no good reason why a different rule should apply to private individuals.

Goldsborough v. *United States*, Taney, C. C. Dec. 80; *Brady* v. *New York*, 20 N. Y. 312.

The clerk had no authority to bind us to an illegal contract by which our compensation was reduced below the rate fixed by the Statute.

People v. *Board of Police*, 75 N. Y. 38; *People* v. *French*, 91 N. Y. 265; *Kehn* v. *State*, 93 N. Y. 291; *Riley* v. *New York*, 96 N. Y. 331; *Edmondson* v. *Jersey City*, 2 Cent. Rep. 718, 48 N. J. L. 121; *State* v. *Nashville*, 15 Lea, 697, 54 Am. Rep. 427.

Cole, *Ch. J.*, delivered the opinion of the court:

The learned circuit court sustained the demurrer to the answer of the defendant on the ground that as the Statute provides, when the number of descriptions in the list was less than 3,000, the printer publishing it should receive thirty cents for each lot or tract in the list, that this was controlling. The language of the Statute is certainly clear and explicit on the subject. It is even mandatory in form, and says that "the printer who shall publish the list and notice of the time when the redemption of lands sold for the nonpayment of taxes will expire shall receive thirty cents for each lot or tract of land in such list, for all the insertions." Rev. Stat. § 1174.

Thus the Statutes expressly prescribe the fees which the printer shall receive, and the county clerk had no authority to make a contract which changed them. The Statute, indeed, does not give the clerk any power to contract for the publication of the list where the number of descriptions in the list does not exceed 3,000. He is required to cause the list to be published as the Statute prescribes (§ 1170),—that is, he can select or designate the paper, but the compensation for the service has been fixed by the Legislature. But, where the number of descriptions in the advertised list exceed 3,000, there the county clerk is required to let by contract the publication to the lowest bidder, in the same manner, and with like conditions and limitations, as the county treasurer is authorized to contract for the publication of lists of lands for delinquent taxes for sale. Section 1173.

In the case at bar, it is insisted that the contract which the clerk attempted to make with the plaintiffs amounted to nothing more than the designation of the paper in which the list should be published, but did not bind or compel the plaintiffs to do the work for less than the fees fixed by law. The principle of law relied on is that, when the compensation of a party performing services for the State is fixed by Statute, it cannot be reduced by the officer or person by whom he is employed; and, since here the Statute expressly declares that the printer shall receive thirty cents for each lot or tract of land in the advertised list, the compensation could not be diminished by any arrangement or contract which the county clerk might make in respect thereto. This contention of counsel is sustained by a number of well-considered decisions. *Goldsborough* v. *United States*, Taney, C. C. Dec. 80; *People* v. *Board of Police*, 75 N. Y. 38; *People* v. *French*, 91 N. Y. 265; *Kehn* v. *State*, 93 N. Y. 291; *Riley* v. *New York*, 96 N. Y. 331.

The following cases have likewise a bearing on the question we are considering: *Beal* v. *St. Croix Co. Supers.* 13 Wis. 501; *State* v. *Purdy*, 36 Wis. 213; *State* v. *Nashville*, 15 Lea, 697, 54 Am. Rep. 427; *Edmondson* v. *Jersey City*, 48 N. J. L. 121, 2 Cent. Rep. 718.

We have already stated that the clerk had no power to enter into any contract for the publication in this case. He was only authorized to select the paper in which the publication should be made.

The only doubt I have had in the case grows out of this fact: The answer shows that the plaintiffs filed with the county clerk an offer, in writing, to print the delinquent list in their paper for three cents for each description, and tendered a bond for the faithful performance of the work. On the good faith of this offer or proposition, the clerk doubtless entered into the contract which he made with them. While it is clear that he had no authority in law to make such a contract, still I have had some doubt whether they were not bound to stand by the proposition which they made. It is true this was for much less than the rate of compensation fixed by the Statute. But could they not waive a provision for their benefit? And, having voluntarily done so, is not the offer or proposition binding upon them? But to this view it is answered that the doctrine of waiver or estoppel has no application to the case, and cannot be invoked to aid the defendant County; that the law does not sanction the principle that an officer shall make a contract to reduce the compensation fixed by statute for services. In some of the cases above cited the facts showing waiver were quite as strong as in this case, but the courts gave no effect to them.

In *People* v. *Board of Police* it is said: "There is no principle upon which an individual appointed or elected to an official position can be compelled to take less than the salary fixed by law. The acceptance and discharge of the duties of the office after appointment are not a waiver of the statutory provision fixing the salary thereof, and do not establish a binding contract to perform the duties . . . for the sum named. The law does not recognize the principle that a board of officers can reduce the amount fixed by law for a salaried officer, and procure officials to act at a less sum than the Statute provides, or that such officials can make a binding contract to that effect. The doctrine of waiver has no application to any such case, and cannot be invoked to aid the respondent." The same principle is recognized and enforced in *Kehn* v. *State* and *Riley* v. *New York, supra*, and the reason for the rule applies in full force here. For reasons satisfactory to the Legislature, it saw fit to prescribe the amount of compensation which the printer should receive for the service. Whether it was thought that this compensation would secure better service, or greater faithfulness in the execution of the work, we cannot tell. It is sufficient to say that the law is so enacted, and the courts must conform to it. It follows from these views that *the order of the Circuit Court must be affirmed*, and the cause be remanded for further proceedings according to law.

MISSOURI SUPREME COURT.

B. KELLNY, *Respt.*,
v.
MISSOURI PACIFIC R. CO., *Appt.*

(....Mo.....)

1. A recovery, by one who has been guilty of contributory negligence, of damages for injuries which have resulted in part from the negligence of another, is permitted, where the latter, before the injury, discovered, or by the exercise of ordinary care might have discovered, the former's peril, and neglected to use the means at his command to prevent the injury, upon the ground that the latter's recklessness, willfulness or wantonness prevents his taking advantage of the negligence of the former.

2. The negligence of defendant in such case, in failing to discover plaintiff's peril and to use the means at his command to prevent the injury, need not be set out as a separate and independent cause of action to warrant a recovery.

3. Failure to look for a train before turning upon a railroad track along a public street, on which one has a perfect right to travel, subject to the duty simply to make way for a train, will not prevent recovery for injuries sustained when struck by a train coming at an unlawful speed, if by looking he would not have discovered that it was imprudent to drive on the track.

4. Where one rightfully drives along and upon a railroad track laid in a public street and is injured by a train running at an unlawful speed, in an action to recover damages for such injury the instructions should submit to the jury the question of plaintiff's contributory negligence in failing to look out for the train, if such defense is alleged, and also the question whether or not, if plaintiff was negligent, the railroad employés could, by the exercise of reasonable care, have discovered his situation and thereafter have stopped the train in time to have prevented the accident.

(May 19, 1890.)

APPEAL by defendant from a judgment of the Circuit Court for the City of St. Louis in favor of plaintiff in an action brought to re-

---

NOTE.—*Contributory negligence; when not a defense.*

A person to whom contributory negligence may be imputed cannot recover for damages caused by a railroad train at a crossing, unless there was such reckless negligence on the part of the railroad company that the question of contributory negligence cannot arise. Freeman v. Duluth, S. S. & A. R. Co. 3 L. R. A. 594, 74 Mich. 86; Richmond & D. R. Co. v. Howard, 79 Ga. 44; Atchison, T. & S. F. R. Co. v. Townsend, 39 Kan. 115.

The contributory negligence of a person walking upon a railroad track, and failing to keep out of the way of a passing train, will not constitute a defense where an engineer of a train, having noticed such person, fails to stop his engine, or acts willfully or recklessly. Bouwmeester v. Grand Rapids & I. R. Co. 6 West. Rep. 364, 63 Mich. 557.

In an action for damages for injury caused by a railroad company through negligence of its employés, if the injury could not have been sustained if the plaintiff had not been careless and neglectful in providing for his own safety, there can be no recovery in the action. But if it is apparent, from the evidence, that the plaintiff, although negligent, would have suffered no injury had proper care and caution been observed by defendant, it must be held liable for damages. Baltimore & O. R. Co. v. Kean, 3 Cent. Rep. 716, 65 Md. 394; Louisville & N. R. Co. v. Ynicstra, 21 Fla. 701.

It is the duty of an engineer, under Mill. & V. (Tenn.) Code, § 1298, subsec. 4, on discovering any person, animal or other obstruction upon the track, not only to use every possible means to stop the train, but also every means to prevent the accident by sounding the alarm whistle and otherwise. Memphis & C. R. Co. v. Scott, 87 Tenn. 494.

The precautions prescribed by Mill. & V. (Tenn.) Code, § 1298, to prevent an accident, where an engineer sees a person, animal or other obstruction on the track, are not required to be observed in the exact order in which they are named in the Statute, but in the order best calculated and most effectual to prevent the accident, under all the circumstances. *Ibid.*

If two men are seen on a track in front of a train, and one risks his safety in signaling the foremost man, the engineer, seeing the signal, is guilty of willful wrong in not using ordinary care to stop the train. Palmer v. Chicago, St. L. & P. R. Co. 11 West. Rep. 676, 112 Ind. 250.

Where a collision at a railroad crossing would not have occurred if the train had not been run at an excessive rate of speed, the company is liable. Gulf, C. & S. F. R. Co. v. Breitling (Tex.) Jan. 10, 1890.

Where a man attempted to cross a railroad, in the exercise of due caution, with a team of horses, a traction engine, a tank and separator and a stacker, all attached together, which were seen by the engineer more than 700 yards away, whose train was running at 35 miles an hour, and who reduced it to 20 miles, and could have stopped it before reaching the crossing, but who, thinking there was time for the balance of the threshing train to cross, released the air-brake and increased the speed, in consequence of which he struck the latter part of it, which became uncoupled before it had cleared the track and when it was too late to avoid the collision,—the accident is due to the negligence of the engineer. Atchison, T. & S. F. R. Co. v. Walz, 40 Kan. 433.

Duty of engineer when person seen crossing railroad track. See *notes* to Parsons v. New York Cent. & H. R. R. Co. (N. Y.) 3 L. R. A. 683; Erickson v. St. Paul & D. R. Co. (Minn.) 5 L. R. A. 786.

See also 10 L. R. A. 674.

cover damages for personal injuries alleged to have resulted from the negligence of defendant's servants. *Reversed.*

The facts are fully stated in the opinion.

Messrs. **T. J. Portis** and **Henry G. Herbel** for appellant.

Messrs. **William C. Jones** and **James C. Jones** for respondent.

Brace, *J.*, delivered the opinion of the court:

Action for damages for personal injuries. Verdict and judgment for plaintiff for $5,000. Defendant appeals.

The petition charged negligence in defendant's employés in managing and operating the train which caused the injury, specifying failure to ring the bell and running at a greater rate of speed than six miles an hour, in violation of city ordinance. On the first act of alleged negligence no evidence was given; the answer was a general denial, and a plea of contributory negligence. The accident happened in the City of St. Louis, on the levee between Christy Avenue and Morgan Street. The evidence for the plaintiff tended to prove that the plaintiff was a rag-peddler; that in the course of his business he was pursuing his way in a one-horse wagon along the levee, in the City of St. Louis, which lies in a general direction north and south, and on which the defendant's track was laid, and on which it was operating its train. He was going north on the levee, near the corner of Christy Avenue and the levee. He found the space on each side of the track for a distance of about fifty feet occupied by standing wagons, leaving an open way between them occupied by defendant's track as the only way for him to pursue his journey unobstructed. He entered this gangway between the wagons, drove along it, the east wheels of his wagon on the inside of the west rail of the track, and his west wheels on the outside, a distance of about forty or fifty feet, when the hind wheel of his wagon was struck by the defendant's engine drawing a train of freight cars, going north on its tracks. The plaintiff was thrown out of his wagon, onto the west rail of the track, in front of or under the engine, which passed over him, crushing his left arm and elbow so that his arm had to be amputated, bruising one of his legs, inflicting a cut over one of his eyes, and several contusions on his back. That at the time of the collision the train was going at the rate of about fifteen miles an hour. That it did not stop, but passed on at the same rate of speed. That a train of fifteen loaded cars going north on this grade, at fifteen miles an hour, could not be stopped within less than 900 feet, and going at the rate of six miles could not be stopped within sixty feet, and that a train of eight loaded cars, going four or five miles an hour, could be stopped within thirty feet, and going at the rate of fifteen miles an hour within from 400 to 450 feet. That at the time plaintiff's wheel passed inside the track he did not look back south, in the direction from which the train was coming, nor afterwards, before he was struck.

The defendant, to sustain the issues on its part, introduced the evidence of the employés engaged upon the train, the leading witness of whom, John A. Cook, testified as follows: "I was a switchman and brakeman on the Missouri Pacific Railway on the 9th day of July last. Remember of an accident occurring on the afternoon of that day, between 4:30 and 5:30 o'clock, on the levee, between Morgan Street and Christy Avenue. I was on the rear end of the rear car of a train going north on the levee at that time and place. I saw a one-horse wagon, with three persons in it, standing near the curbstone. As the train was passing it, the horse began to back, and backed the wagon up against the last, or next to the last, car of the train. I was on the top of the rear box car at the time, about thirty feet from the wagon, and looking at it. I did not know whether plaintiff was in the wagon or not. I did not know him at that time. When we came back, I went in to see how seriously he was injured, but could not learn anything from him, as he couldn't talk, and would not tell us anything. The wagon did not tilt up. The rear wheels backed into the car, and the horse started up again. Don't know whether Kellny fell or jumped out of the wagon. Our train went up to Biddle Street, and came back again in five or six minutes. There were ten or eleven cars in the train,—box cars. The train was not moving faster than five or six miles an hour at that time. The rear wheels of the wagon struck the car. The cars were loaded."

Tatley, the brakeman, testified that he was standing on the front of the engine from the time it left Poplar Street, and did not notice any team on the track as the engine passed along between Christy Avenue and Morgan Street; that he was in a position to see one, if there had been one on the track, and that the train was running between four and six miles an hour: that he saw the plaintiff's wagon on the west side as he passed. The fireman and engineer also testified that they were at their posts, observing the track, and they did not see plaintiff's wagon on the track, and that it was not struck by the engine. On cross-examination, the engineer, Lunderberg, testified that he "saw no obstruction between Christy Avenue and Morgan Street as we went north on the levee. Saw none from the bridge to Biddle Street. The way was perfectly clear, and if Kellny had been on the track I would have seen him."

The evidence of Donderville, the fireman, was to the same general purport as the others. In addition, he testified that the train was loaded with ice and beer, and upon this grade could be stopped to prevent an accident, when going at the rate of four or five miles an hour, within sixty feet, and going at the rate of fifteen miles an hour, "within five car lengths or less,—say eighty feet."

It seems to be undisputed that the distance from the bridge to the place of the accident was about 450 feet; that there was nothing to prevent the defendant's employés from seeing the plaintiff's wagon on the track (if it was on the track) during the whole time the train was passing from the bridge to the place where the collision took place.

Upon this state of facts the court, upon its own motion, gave the following instruction on the main question: "(1) Under the pleadings and evidence in this case, the court instructs you that, at and just before the alleged injury, the plaintiff was not exercising ordinary or proper care to avoid injury or danger; and therefore your verdict should be for defendant, unless you further find the facts to be as mentioned in instruction 2. (2) If you find from the evidence that in the early part of July, 1886, the plaintiff's wagon was struck by an engine of a train operated at the time by defendant on the levee between Christy Avenue and Morgan Street; that, in consequence thereof, plaintiff was run over by said engine and injured; that said wagon was so struck by reason of the fact that said train was then running at a rate of speed greater than six miles an hour, and that, if said train had not been running at a rate greater than six miles an hour, the train could have been stopped in time to have averted the said collision with plaintiff's wagon, after defendant's employés in charge of said train had discovered (or by the exercise of ordinary care could have discovered) that plaintiff or his wagon was in danger of being so struck; and if you so find the facts to be, your verdict should be for the plaintiff."

The second was the only instruction given presenting a theory upon which the jury were authorized to find for the plaintiff, and it seems to us that it cuts the throat of the first. In the first the jury are told, as matter of law, that the plaintiff was guilty of an act of negligence that contributed to his injury; therefore he cannot recover. Nevertheless they were told in the second that, if they find that the defendant committed an act of negligence which also contributed to his injury, but which would not have done so if it had not been committed, then they will find for the plaintiff. The whole theory of plaintiff's case was that he was injured by the negligence of defendant in running its train at a greater rate of speed than six miles an hour; that this act was the sole direct cause of his injury. Now, while to find the fact that, if the defendant had not been running its train at a greater rate of speed than six miles an hour, the injury would not have occurred, is to find a fact tending to prove that the running of the train at a greater rate of speed than six miles an hour was a cause of plaintiff's injury, how can it make such excessive running any more than a contributory cause, when plaintiff's act was also there and then present at the same time, contributing to the injury? The instruction presents this strange anomaly, that, if the jury find that the wagon was struck by reason of the fact that said train was then running at a rate of speed greater than six miles an hour, and by reason of the fact that the plaintiff was negligently on the track, the plaintiff cannot recover, on the ground that defendant's negligence was the sole cause of the injury, because of plaintiff's contributory negligence; but, if they find that if the train had not been running at a greater rate of speed than six miles an hour, the plaintiff would not have been struck, then the plaintiff can recover, although the injury was the joint product of plaintiff's act of negligence and this very negligent act of defendant. How can the fact that the injury would not have resulted if the defendant had not committed the act of negligence change the character of the injury which actually did occur as the joint product of plaintiff's and defendant's contributive acts of negligence, as assumed in the instructions?

We know of but one exception to the rule that, where the injury is the product of the joint concurring acts of negligence of both plaintiff and defendant, the plaintiff cannot recover, and that is an exception made, on grounds of public policy and in the interest of humanity, to prevent and restrain, as far as may be, a willful, reckless or wanton disregard of human life or limb or property, under any circumstances, and that is when the injury was produced by the concurrent negligent acts of both plaintiff and defendant, yet if the defendant, before the injury, discovered, or by the exercise of ordinary care might have discovered, the perilous situation in which the plaintiff was placed, by the concurring negligence of both parties, and neglected to use the means at his command to prevent the injury, then his plea of plaintiff's contributory negligence shall not avail him. This exception proceeds, not upon the theory that the defendant has been guilty of another and independent act of negligence, which is the sole cause of the injury, and which must be charged as a separate and independent cause of action, but upon the ground that the negligence he was then in the very act of perpetrating was characterized by such recklessness, willfulness or wantonness as that he shall not be heard to say that the plaintiff was also guilty of contributory negligence. In this case, it is contended by counsel for the defendant that, conceding plaintiff's theory of the facts to be true, the evidence tends to show that defendant's employés, if they had been in the exercise of ordinary care, could have discovered the plaintiff's wagon on the track in time to have prevented the accident, and that it could have been prevented if they with promptness, after such discovery, had used the means at their command to stop the train. Therefore the sole cause of the injury was the negligence of the defendant in failing to discover the perilous situation of the plaintiff, and thereafter failing to use the means at their command to prevent the injury, and, as the plaintiff's petition did not contain a count charging this negligence as a separate and independent cause of action, the plaintiff cannot recover. This view seems, on the trial, to have been acquiesced in by counsel for the plaintiff, and adopted by the court, and perhaps led to the anomalous instructions in the case, and was, we think, a misapprehension of the principle upon which a recovery is permitted for an injury resulting from concurrent acts of negligence of plaintiff and defendant, but which might have been avoided if, after the consequences of such negligence became apparent to the defendant, or ought to have been known to him, he failed to use the means at his command to prevent it. What has been said is upon the theory that the first instruction ought to have been given.

But, on the facts in the case, could the court, as matter of law, declare that the plaintiff was guilty of such contributory negligence as to prevent his recovery? The plaintiff was no trespasser. He was where he had a right to be,—as much right as the defendant. He was pursuing his way along one of the most crowded public streets of the city, along which the defendant's track was laid. He came to a point in the street where it was blocked by wagons for a short distance on both sides. The only way open to him was the space occupied by the defendant's track, and a narrow margin between the wagons and the track. In order to get over this space to the open street beyond, a distance, say, of about 50 feet, he turns his team a little to the right, which causes the right wheels to pass within one rail of the track a short distance, and, in less time probably than a minute, he reaches the open street again, turns to the left, his fore wheel passes out over the rail, the hind wheel is caught by the engine before it gets entirely clear of the passway of the train, is "tilted up," and he is thrown under the wheels, the train running at the time at the rate of 15 miles an hour. This was the case that the plaintiff's evidence tended to make. If it be true that the train was g ing at the rate of 15 miles an hour, confessedly he would have gotten clear of the track without injury if the train had only been going 6 miles an hour.

Now, what act of negligence had he been guilty of that warranted the court in declaring, as matter of law, that he could not recover? That just before and while making his brief passage he did not look behind him for an approaching train. When can one be said to be guilty of negligence that will *per se* prevent a recovery because he does not look behind him for a train approaching him from the rear, before turning upon a railroad track along a public street on which he had a perfect right to travel, and whose duty it is simply to make way for such train? We should say when by so looking he would have discovered that the train was approaching him at such a distance that probably he could not, if he got upon the track, move out of its way in time for it to pass him without striking him. He would be guilty of negligence if, upon looking, he had discovered that the train was so near that, at the rate of speed he might expect it was traveling, it would be hazardous for him to turn upon the track; and he is negligent in not looking only because by looking he would have discovered that, taking into consideration the speed he was traveling at, the distance he had to go on the track, the distance he was from the train, the rate of speed he had a right to believe the train was traveling, it would appear to a reasonably prudent man to be dangerous for him to drive on the track. These are all questions of fact to be passed upon by the jury, in the light of the established law "that the violation of municipal ordinances which regulate the speed of trains is negligence *per se*," and that every person on a public street in a municipality has the right to presume that the railroad will obey such ordinances. *Schlereth* v. *Missouri Pac. R. Co.* 96 Mo. 509; *Erwin* v. *St. Louis, I. M. & S. R. Co.* Id. 290.

It must be remembered that the plaintiff was no trespasser. He was not crossing a railroad track at a point where the train might be run at an unlimited rate of speed. He had but about 50 feet to go. He had a right to rely upon the fact that no train would be run on that track at a greater rate of speed than six miles an hour; that it was as much the duty of the railroad employés to look out for him on the track as it was for him to look out for the train. *Erwin* v. *St. Louis, I. M. & S. R. Co. supra.*

The evidence in this record does not show at what gait he was traveling, nor how far the train was behind him, when he turned his wheel inside the rail. He may have acted imprudently in attempting to make the passage in the manner and at the time he did, but we think the question whether he did or not should have been passed upon by the jury, in the light of all the facts and circumstances in the case. There are risks which the most prudent man may take, and the plaintiff is not to be barred of recovery if he adopted a course that the most prudent man would have taken under the circumstances. *Kelly* v. *Hannibal & St. J. R. Co.* 70 Mo. 604; *Smith* v. *Union R. Co.* 61 Mo. 588; *Meyer* v. *Pacific R. Co.* 40 Mo. 151.

Paraphrasing the language of this court in the last case, it may be said that the proposition is monstrous that, because a man does not "look," although that is not the proximate cause of the injury, he is placed beyond the pale of legal protection. He can be placed beyond the pale of such protection not simply because he did not look, but because if he had looked he would have discovered such a condition of affairs as that it would have been imprudent for him to pursue the course which he did pursue, and in which he met with the injury. If by looking he would not have discovered such a state of affairs, his failure to look cannot be the proximate cause of his injury. This was evidently a difficult case to try. The plaintiff and his witnesses were Poles, some of whom could not speak the English language, and the others but imperfectly. From the record here, it is difficult to clearly understand the actual situation at the time the accident happened, but we do not think it was tried on the correct theory; and, if we have been able to properly appreciate the force of the evidence as it appears in this record, an instruction ought to have been given submitting to the jury the question of plaintiff's alleged contributory negligence, and one submitting the question whether the defendant's employés could, by the exercise of reasonable care, have discovered his situation, and thereafter have stopped the train in time to have prevented the accident. The instructions upon the defendant's theory of the case, as well as the other instructions, are unobjectionable.

For error in the instructions quoted the judgment will be reversed, and the cause remanded for new trial, with the concurrence of **Ray**, *Ch. J.*, and **Black**, *J.*; **Sherwood**, *J.*, concurring in the result; **Barclay**, *J.*, not sitting.

GEORGIA SUPREME COURT.

Lucy PEEL, *Pff. in Err.*,
v.
CITY OF ATLANTA.

(......Ga.......)

1. **Private property is not "damaged** for public purposes" by a public improvement within a constitutional provision requiring compensation for such damages, where no invasion is made of any right or use of such property.

2. **The test of damage requiring compensation** caused to private property by public improvement is whether a cause of action would arise if the injury was caused by a private person without authority of statute.

3. **Opening a public street adjacent to one's property,** thus bounding it by streets on three sides, rendering it ungainly and unsightly to the public, and destroying its privacy and thus diminishing its value, does not give the owner a right to compensation under a constitution declaring that private property shall not be taken or damaged without just and adequate compensation.

(April 14, 1890.)

ERROR to the Superior Court for Fulton County to review a judgment dismissing the declaration in an action brought to recover damages for injuries to plaintiff's property alleged to have resulted from the opening of a street by defendant City. *Affirmed.*

The facts sufficiently appear in the opinion.

Mr. **George S. Thomas,** for plaintiff in error:

The Constitution and laws of Georgia guard with vigilance and jealousy the private rights and property of the citizen, and the courts of this State have ever extended their aid and assistance in the same direction.

Butler v. *Thomasville*, 74 Ga. 575.

Private property shall not be taken or damaged for public purposes without just compensation.

Ga. Const. art. 1, § 3, pt. 1; Ga. Code, §§ 2225, 5024.

While the damages must be real and not speculative, the article of the Constitution does not define whether the damage shall be immediate and direct or consequential. Any damage to private property for public use must receive its compensation.

Atlanta v. *Green*, 67 Ga. 386; *Atkinson* v. *Atlanta*, 81 Ga. 625; *Campbell* v. *Metropolitan St. R. Co.* 82 Ga. 320.

Plaintiff also alleges as a ground of injury and damages to her said property the filling up of a well of good water upon the premises, converted by the defendant into a part of its public street, and the servitude of an easement upon said premises in favor of the plaintiff and her tenants to the free use of said well. The doctrine of *damnum absque injuria* does not apply to cases where there has been a violation of any right of a party complaining, or a breach of any duty to him.

Taylor v. *Dyches*, 69 Ga. 455; *Imboden* v. *Etowah & B. B. H. M. Co.* 70 Ga. 87; *Augusta Nat. Exch. Bank* v. *Sibley*, 71 Ga. 726; *Martin* v. *Gainesville, J. & S. R. R.* 78 Ga. 308.

The maxim "*sic utere tuo ut alienum non lædas*" applies to rights of defendant in error and to its grantor Nix alike. Nix would have had no right to sell, or dedicate her property to the City, to be used as a street and to the injury and damage of the plaintiff without making herself liable to the plaintiff for damages, and the Constitution and laws of Georgia would not allow the City to damage a citizen indirectly when it would not allow the same damage to be done directly without just compensation.

Atlanta v. *Green*, 67 Ga. 386.

Messrs. **J. B. Goodwin** and **J. A. Anderson** for defendant in error.

Blandford, *J.*, delivered the opinion of the court:

This was an action brought by Lucy Peel against the City of Atlanta to recover damages for alleged injury to certain property of hers. Her declaration alleged that she was the owner of a certain tract of land in the City of Atlanta; that she sold a portion thereof lying on Harris Street to one Nix, who sold the same to the City of Atlanta, and, after the City bought the said lot, it opened a public street on said lot adjoining the balance of her land, thereby making the remaining portion of her land to be bounded on three sides by three public streets of the City, rendering it ungainly and unsightly to the public, and depriving it of all privacy; that the City had filled up a well on the portion that was sold, which her tenants had the right to use; and that she had reason to fear assessments upon all three sides of her lot for

---

NOTE.—Damnum absque injuria.

Where depreciation in the value of property of one proprietor by reason of the careful erection of a public improvement is caused by the lawful use of adjacent or neighboring property of another proprietor, it is *damnum absque injuria.* Montgomery City Council v. Townsend, 80 Ala. 489.

Where depreciation in the value of the property of one proprietor is caused by the lawful use of property by an adjacent proprietor, it is *damnum absque injuria. Ibid.*; Hot Springs R. Co. v. Williamson, 45 Ark. 429; Reardon v. San Francisco, 66 Cal. 492; Denver v. Bayer, 7 Colo. 113; Atkinson v. Atlanta, 81 Ga. 625; Atlanta v. Green, 67 Ga. 386; Rigney v. Chicago, 102 Ill. 64; Chicago & W. I. R. Co. v. Ayres, 106 Ill. 511; Green & B. R. Nav. Co. v. Chesapeake, O. & S. W. R. Co. 2 L. R. A. 540, 10 Ky. L. Rep. 625; Gottschalk v. Chicago, B. & Q. R. Co. 14 Neb. 550; Gulf, C. & S. F. R. Co. v. Fuller, 63 Tex. 467; Johnson v. Parkersburg, 16 W. Va. 402; Davenport v. Richmond City, 81 Pa. 636; Clark v. Lincoln County (Wash. Terr.) Jan. 29, 1889; Deobold v. Oppermann, 2 L. R. A. 644, 111 N. Y. 531; Metropolitan Board of Works v. McCarthy, L. R. 7 H. L. 243; Caledonian R. Co. v. Walker, L. R. 7 App. Cas. 259; Central Trust Co. of N. Y. v. Wabash, St. L. & P. R. Co. 32 Fed. Rep. 566; Bell v. Norfolk S. R. Co. 101 N. C. 21; Fulmer v. Williams (Pa.) 1 L. R. A. 603, 22 W. N. C. 269; Delaware & H. Canal Co. v. Goldstein, 125 Pa. 246. See *note* to Kinnaird v. Standard Oil Co. (Ky.) 7 L. R. A. 451.

improvements in the way of sidewalks and streets. It is not alleged in the declaration that the defendant invaded her property in any way, or any right or use of hers therein, but she alleges that it was diminished in value by reason of public improvements made in the vicinity.

Under demurrer to this declaration, the court held that it set forth no cause of action, and dismissed the same; and this is the case presented for our consideration. We think the true rule is that where property is taken, or where it is damaged, for the public use, by an invasion of the right of the property holder as to its use or enjoyment, and the property thereby becomes diminished in value, an action may be maintained by the owner of such property to recover for the damages thus incurred. But we are inclined to think that where there has been no invasion of any right or use of private property by the public, by the erection or laying out or building of any sewers, public highways, streets or pavements, no action can be maintained by the owner of adjacent land to recover for any damages that may be suffered in consequence thereof. If this highway or street had been opened or dedicated by Nix to the use of the public upon the land which she sold to the City, and such act on the part of a private owner was no invasion of any right, use or enjoyment in the property of an adjacent owner, no action would result to the latter thereby; and in this respect the City occupies as high a position as a private person, where it puts an improvement upon its own land.

The Constitution of this State (Code, § 5024) declares: "Private property shall not be taken or damaged for public purposes without just and adequate compensation being first paid." The same provision is in the Constitutions of Illinois and Missouri, and of other States. Lewis, Em. Dom. § 221.

The English Statute, which has the same purpose as these constitutional provisions, uses the term "injuriously affected." Some statutes on the same subject use the word "injured." All these terms are believed to be equivalent in meaning and extent. Id. § 222.

The effect of such provisions is not to authorize compensation in all cases where property may be injured by public works, but only where the enjoyment of some right of the plaintiff in reference to his property is interfered with, and the property thereby rendered less valuable. The test is, Would the injury, if caused by a private person without authority of statute, give the plaintiff a cause of action against such person? If so, then he is entitled to compensation notwithstanding the Statute which legalizes the damaging work. The constitutional or statutory provision simply prevents the defendant from shielding himself under legislative authority against liability for damages consequent upon the work. Hence, if no part of the plaintiff's land is taken, and no other right of his is disturbed, he cannot have compensation. Lewis, Em. Dom. §§ 235, 236; *Reg.* v. *Metropolitan Board of Works*, 3 Best & S. 710; *Ricket* v. *Metropolitan R. Co.* L. R. 2 H. L. 175; *Rude* v. *St. Louis*, 93 Mo. 408, 12 West. Rep. 238; *Chamberlain* v. *West End & C. P. R. Co.* 31 L. J. N. S. Q. B. 201; *Rigney* v. *Chicago*, 102 Ill. 64.

Where no land of the plaintiff is taken, and no other right infringed, he is not entitled to compensation on the ground that the privacy of his residence is destroyed. *Re Penny*, 26 L. J. N. S. Q. B. 225.

The fear of being assessed is a mere apprehension not yet realized, and cannot sustain a claim for damages. Besides, it seems that one who is delinquent, as this plaintiff promises to be, in the payment of assessments, cannot save his or her property from sale to get payment for the improvements put there by the City under the constitutional provision invoked by this declaration. That provision refers to the exercise of the right of eminent domain, and not to the enforcement of lawful assessments. *White* v. *People*, 94 Ill. 604.

It follows that the court did not err in sustaining the demurrer to the declaration.

Judgment affirmed.

COLORADO SUPREME COURT.

FIRST NATIONAL BANK of Central City, *Pltf. in Err.*,
v.
HUMMEL *et al.*

(....Colo.....)

1. **Money received by one as agent,** who dies before paying it over, although it has been mingled with his own so that it cannot be distinguished, constitutes a trust fund, which can be recovered from his personal representative.

2. **A claim for a trust fund included in the assets of a decedent's estate,** as to which the relation of debtor and creditor never existed between the parties, is not a "debt" or "demand" within the meaning of the Statutes relating to the order of payment of demands against such an estate.

3. **The beneficial owner of a claim,** who was also a party to the contract upon which the

---

NOTE.—*Commingling trust funds.*

If a trustee or agent mixes and confuses the property which he holds in a fiduciary character, with his own property, so that they cannot be separated with perfect accuracy, he is liable for the whole. 2 Pom. Eq. 655; Utica Ins. Co. v. Lynch, 11 Paige, 520, 5 N. Y. Ch. L. ed. 219; Mumford v. Murray, 6 Johns. Ch. 1, 2 N. Y. Ch. L. ed. 85; Kip v. Bank of N. Y. 10 Johns. 63; Com. v. McAlister, 28 Pa. 486; Gunter v. Janes, 9 Cal. 643, 660-662; Livingston v. Wells, 8 S. C. 347; Case v. Abeel, 1 Paige, 393, 2 N. Y. Ch. L. ed. 689.

Trust funds are to be kept separate from the private funds of the trustee; and if mingled with his own, he may be charged with such funds, as being himself the borrower. Seawell v. Greenway, 22 Tex. 691; *Re* Stafford, 11 Barb. 353; Kellett v. Rathbun, 4 Paige, 102, 3 N. Y. Ch. L. ed. 361; Freeman v. Fairlie, 3 Meriv. 29.

See also 29 L. R. A. 664; 40 L. R. A. 552.

action is based, and which is brought by one holding the legal title to it as the "real party in interest," is properly joined as defendant, when he refuses to unite with the plaintiff.

4. **There is no misjoinder of causes of action,** where there is but one cause of action stated, merely by stating that one of the defendants, who was the beneficial owner of the claim, was made defendant because he refused to unite with the plaintiff, and asking that he be required to pay the costs and expenses.

(February 28, 1890.)

ERROR to the District Court for Arapahoe County to review a judgment sustaining a demurrer to the complaint in an action brought to recover from a personal representative money alleged to have been received by the decedent in trust for plaintiff. *Reversed.*

Commissioner's opinion.

The facts sufficiently appear in the opinion.

Messrs. **Hugh Butler** and **A. B. McKinley** for plaintiff in error.

Mr. **A. H. De France** for defendants in error.

Pattison, *C.*, delivered the following opinion:

In this case, plaintiff in error seeks to review a judgment sustaining a demurrer to the complaint. It is alleged, in substance, that June 28, 1884, Risdon borrowed from one Heatly, then a resident of Golden, the sum of $1,200, for which he gave his note secured by a trust deed; that the money was not paid by Heatly to Risdon at the time, but an arrangement for the payment thereof was entered into between Heatly and Risdon and one Everett; that, by the terms of the arrangement, it was provided

---

Where a trustee loaned the fund of the trust on note and mortgage executed to himself, it was a commingling of the trust funds with his own, and a destruction of their identification; and he is liable for their loss. De Jarnette v. De Jarnette, 41 Ala. 710; Kellett v. Rathbun, 4 Paige, 102, 3 N. Y. Ch. L. ed. 361; Hart v. Ten Eyck, 2 Johns. Ch. 108, 1 N. Y. Ch. L. ed. 312; Diffenderffer v. Winder, 3 Gill & J. 342; Jameson v. Shelby, 2 Humph. 198; *Re* Stafford, *supra;* West Branch Bank v. Fulmer, 3 Pa. 399; Com. v. McAlister, 28 Pa. 480; McAllister v. Com. 30 Pa. 536; Royer's App. 11 Pa. 36; Stanley's App. 8 Pa. 431; Matthews v. Brise, 6 Beav. 239; Macdonnell v. Harding, 7 Sim. 178; Freeman v. Fairlie, 3 Meriv. 28; Wren v. Kirton, 11 Ves. Jr. 377; Massey v. Banner, 4 Madd. 418; Fletcher v. Walker, 3 Madd. 73; Rowth v. Howell, 3 Ves. Jr. 565; Verner's Estate, 6 Watts, 260.

Confusion of property does not destroy the equity to follow misapplied property, but converts it into a charge upon the entire mass, giving to the party injured by the unlawful diversion a priority of right over the other creditors of the possessor. Peters v. Bain, 133 U. S. 670 (33 L. ed. 696).

It is the equitable right of a person whose property has been wrongfully converted to trace and retake his own, and, where its identity is lost by mixture with other property or funds, then to retake its equivalent from the fund so enriched, and to the extent of the enrichment. Francis v. Evans, 69 Wis. 115; Cavin v. Gleason, 7 Cent. Rep. 285, 105 N. Y. 256.

To follow trust money into land and impress the land with a trust, the money must be distinctly traced and clearly proved to have been invested in the land; and it is not sufficient to show the possession of moneys of a decedent's estate by the executor or administrator, and the purchase of lands by him. Phillips v. Overfield (Mo.) May 19, 1890.

So it has been held, in recent cases, that where a bank acting as collecting agent receives certificates of deposit issued by it instead of cash, for a deed of land intrusted to it for delivery and receipt of the consideration, its assets in the hands of its assignee are impressed with a trust in favor of the maker of the deed who has a paramount right to be first paid out of the assets. Francis v. Evans, 69 Wis. 115; McLeod v. Evans, 66 Wis. 401; Third Nat. Bank v. Stillwater Gas Co. 36 Minn. 75; Bowers v. Evans, 71 Wis. 133.

So long as trust property can be traced and distinguished it may be claimed by the *cestui que trust.* Gilchrist v. Stevenson, 9 Barb. 16; Shepherd v. M'Evers, 4 Johns. Ch. 137, 1 N. Y. Ch. L. ed. 791. See *note* to Philadelphia Nat. Bank v. Dowd (N. C.) 2 L. R. A. 480.

If a person having charge of the property of another so mingles and confounds it with his own that it cannot be distinguished, he must bear all the inconvenience of the confusion. Brackenridge v. Holland, 2 Blackf. 383; Jewett v Dringer, 30 N. J. Eq. 308; Brakeley v. Tuttle, 3 W. Va. 126.

It is for him to distinguish his own property, or lose it. Jewett v. Dringer, 30 N. J. Eq. 308; Railroad Co. v. Hutchins, 37 Ohio St. 298; Kreuzer v. Cooney, 45 Md. 592; Wotherbee v. Green, 22 Mich. 318; Moore v. Bowman, 47 N. H. 501; United States v. Thompson, 93 U. S. 586 (23 L. ed. 982); Diversey v. Johnson, 93 Ill. 569.

If a man mixes trust funds with his, the whole will be treated as trust property, except so far as he may be able to distinguish what is his. Central Nat. Bank of Baltimore v. Connecticut Mut. L. Ins. Co. 104 U. S. 54 (26 L. ed. 693).

The trustee is liable for trust money lost while mingled with his own, or while being used in his own business, no matter how or from what cause the loss occurs; for if a trustee or agent mixes and confuses the property which he holds in a fiduciary character with his own property, so that it cannot be separated with perfect accuracy, he is liable for the whole. Torry v. Frazer, 2 Redf. 486; De Jarnette v. De Jarnette, 41 Ala. 710; Davis v. Harman, 21 Gratt. 200. See Malone v. Kelley, 54 Ala. 532; Davis v. Coburn, 128 Mass. 377; Gunter v. Janes, 9 Cal. 660; Kip v. Bank of N. Y. 10 Johns. 63; Com. v. McAlister, 28 Pa. 480; Livingston v. Wells, 8 S. C. 347; Marine Bank of Chicago v. Fulton Bank of N. Y. 69 U. S. 2 Wall. 252 (17 L. ed. 785); Case v. Abeel, 1 Paige, 393, 2 N. Y. Ch. L. ed. 689; Utica Ins. Co. v. Lynch, 11 Paige, 520, 5 N. Y. Ch. L. ed. 219; Mumford v. Murray, 6 Johns. Ch. 1, 2 N. Y. Ch. L. ed. 35.

Following trust property. See *notes* to Philadelphia Nat. Bank v. Dowd (N. C.) 2 L. R. A. 480; Little v. Chadwick (Mass.) 7 L. R. A. 570.

Property held in trust, not assets of decedent's estate.

Property held in trust does not pass to the representatives of the trustee; but as long as it can be traced and distinguished it inures to the benefit of the *cestui que trust. Re* Van Duzer, 51 How. Pr. 411; Kip v. Bank of N. Y. 10 Johns. 63.

Where the executor took the estate under the sale as trustee, subject to the conditions under which it was held by the testator, the fund is not assets. Dias v. Brunell, 24 Wend. 13.

So, a mortgage is not assets in the hands of the executor; he holds it merely as his testator held it, as trustee. Allen v. Roll, 25 N. J. Eq. 164; Kip v. Bank of N. Y. *supra;* Dias v. Brunell, 24 Wend. 9; Trecothick v. Austin, 4 Mason, 16; De Valengin v. Duffy, 39 U. S. 14 Pet. 282 (10 L. ed. 457); Banks v. Wilkes, 3 Sandf. Ch. 90, 7 N. Y. Ch. L. ed. 785; Moses v. Murgatroyd, 1 Johns. Ch. 119, 1 N. Y. Ch. L. ed. 82.

An interest in a contract for the purchase of land is real estate, and descends to the heirs of the purchaser. Griffith v. Beecher, 10 Barb. 434.

that Risdon should draw his draft at sight on Everett, at Golden, for said sum of $1,200; that, upon the receipt of the draft, Heatly should provide the money to pay it, and that thereupon Everett should transmit the sum received from Heatly to Risdon, or make such other disposition of it as Risdon should direct; that on July 15, 1884, pursuant to the arrangement, Risdon made his draft upon Everett, "in and by which draft he directed the said F. E. Everett to pay said sum of $1,200 to this plaintiff, and said Risdon then and there delivered said draft to this plaintiff, whereby the plaintiff became entitled to receive of and from the said Everett said sum of $1,200 upon presentation and delivery of said draft;" that on the 16th day of July, 1884, the plaintiff sent the draft by mail to Everett, accompanied by a letter instructing him to remit the said sum of $1,200 to the German National Bank, at Denver, Colo., for the benefit of the plaintiff; that on July 17, 1884, the draft and the letter were received at the banking office of Everett, in Golden, and at or about the same time the said Heatly paid into said banking office the sum of $1,200, being the money called for and mentioned in the draft and the letter of plaintiff, and the draft was then stamped and canceled as paid; that the said sum of $1,200 was received by said Everett, or someone in his employ for him, as the money mentioned in the draft and letter, and was paid by Heatly, in pursuance of the arrangement mentioned; and that, under said arrangement, it was the duty and obligation of Everett to at once remit the said sum to the German National Bank of Denver for the credit of the plaintiff. It is then alleged that, within a short time after the money was received, Everett suddenly died, and the Bank was immediately closed, and no further business transacted therein, and that when Everett died, and when said Bank was closed, the said sum of $1,200 remained in the Bank, and had not been remitted to the German National Bank at Denver, as directed; that the Bank was not opened thereafter. It is further alleged that on November 12, 1884, the defendant Hummel took possession of the said banking office and its contents, and kept possession of the same; that, among other effects therein, he took possession, and has since had possession, of said sum of $1,200; that thereafter, and on November 20, 1884, plaintiff demanded of Hummel the payment and delivery of said sum of $1,200, but that he refused to pay the same. It is then alleged, in effect, that, by the terms of the contract between plaintiff and Risdon, the plaintiff was to collect the draft, and, in case it was paid, and the amount thereof deposited in the German National Bank of Denver to the credit of the plaintiff, then plaintiff was to give Risdon credit for the sum of $1,200; that on August 12, 1884, plaintiff informed Risdon that the draft had been paid by Heatly, but that its proceeds had not been remitted to the German National Bank of Denver, as requested; that the money was in the possession of the person in charge of Everett's property; and plaintiff then notified and requested Risdon to take early and proper steps for the recovery of the same; that Risdon refused to take such steps, and notified plaintiff that he should look to plaintiff only for said sum of money; that plaintiff requested Risdon to join as co-plaintiff in the suit; that he refused, and for that reason he was made a party defendant. Judgment is demanded "that said Hummel deliver and pay over to the plaintiff said sum of $1,200, together with interest thereon at the rate of 10 per cent per annum from said 20th day of November, 1884, and costs."

There is also an additional prayer, in the following language: "And demands judgment against John S. Risdon that he pay plaintiff a reasonable sum of money, sufficient to reimburse plaintiff for all costs and expenses paid and incurred in the prosecution and maintenance of this suit, and for the recovery of said money; that he be adjudged the owner of said sum of $1,200, less the expense of collection so found as aforesaid; and that plaintiff be released from any and all liability to said John S. Risdon by reason of making presentation and payment of said draft as aforesaid, and of all the other facts hereinbefore set forth."

To this complaint the defendant in error demurred upon the grounds: *first*, that the complaint did not state facts sufficient to constitute a cause of action; *second*, that there is misjoinder of parties defendant, etc.; *third*, that several causes of action have been improperly united, etc.; *fourth*, that the causes of action so improperly united are not separately stated. The demurrer was sustained. Plaintiff in error "elected to abide by said complaint," and thereupon the judgment was rendered now sought to be reviewed. The causes of demurrer will be considered in the order in which they have been stated.

First, then, are the facts alleged sufficient to constitute a cause of action against the defendant in error? In other words, upon the facts stated, is plaintiff entitled to the judgment demanded, or to any judgment or relief in the premises whatever? In the discussion of this question, it will be necessary, first, to define the relation of the several parties to the fund in question. That relation must be determined from the facts as alleged in the complaint. The facts, then, are that on June 28, 1884, Heatly agreed to loan to Risdon $1,200. On that day Risdon made his note, and delivered the same to Heatly. The money to be loaned was not paid over by Heatly to Risdon. It was arranged that, on July 15 following, Risdon should be paid by Heatly. To accomplish this, it was agreed between Heatly, Everett and Risdon that, on the day named, Risdon should draw a draft on Everett which Everett should pay if Heatly provided the funds for payment. Pursuant to the arrangement, Risdon drew his draft upon Everett, and delivered it to the plaintiff. It is a fair inference from the allegations of the complaint that the draft was payable to the order of the plaintiff. The plaintiff sent the draft to Everett with instructions that, when Heatly paid the money to him, he (Everett) should transmit the money received from Heatly to the German National Bank for the credit of the plaintiff. Upon this state of facts, the relation between the several parties is clear and well defined. Risdon made the plaintiff in error his agent to obtain the fund in question. The plaintiff made Everett its agent to receive the fund from Heatly.

When he received the fund, it was his duty to transmit the identical money received to the German National Bank for the credit of the plaintiff. When the money was paid by Heatly to Everett, therefore, the title to the fund was vested in the plaintiff. The beneficial ownership was vested in Risdon; Everett had no title or interest in the money, or any part of it. His failure, therefore, to transmit the money received from Heatly to the German National Bank was a violation of the duty he owed the plaintiff and Risdon. When he received the money, it became the money of the plaintiff and Risdon. When he died, the fund was their property, and was their property when received by defendant in error. The question presented upon these facts is whether this sum of $1,200 can be recovered. The action is brought against the defendant in error individually. It will be assumed, however, that the fund was taken by him as the personal representative of the decedent. The case will first be considered without reference to the Statute of this State relating to the administration of estates of deceased persons. It was conceded by counsel for defendant in error, upon the oral argument, that, if the specific sum of $1,200 could be identified in any way, then the action could be maintained. But it was insisted, if the fund when received was mingled with other funds belonging to decedent so that its identity was lost, then, and in that event, no action could be maintained to recover it. This proposition was predicated upon the principle that money, as such, cannot be recovered, because, in the language of the books, it has no "earmark" by which it can be distinguished. If this principle can be successfully invoked in this case, then a fund to which decedent had no title, and in which he had no beneficial interest whatever, became a part of the body of his estate to be distributed among the general creditors. If the estate of Everett is insolvent, such a result would not only be inequitable and unjust, but a reproach to the law.

It is undoubtedly true that the principle contended for was at one time so well settled as to be elementary. It is clearly stated in Schouler, Exrs., § 205. Attention is only called to two clauses of this section: "Only those things in which the decedent had a beneficial interest at his death are assets, and not those which he holds in trust, or as the bailee or factor of another. In order, however, that the third party or new fiduciary may claim his specific thing as separable from assets, its identity should have been preserved; and the rule is that, if the deceased held money or other property in his hands belonging to others, whether in trust or otherwise, and it has no ear-mark, and is not distinguishable from the mass of his own property, it falls within the description of 'assets,' in which case the other party must come in as a general creditor."

In support of the proposition last quoted the author cites two cases: *Trecothick* v. *Austin*, 4 Mason, 29; *Johnson* v. *Ames*, 11 Pick. 173. The first case was decided in 1825; the second, in 1831. It is needless to trace the development of the law which has resulted in a radical change in the principle stated since these decisions were made. At this time the owner of money which has been received by another as trustee, or in any fiduciary capacity, can undoubtedly recover the money or its equivalent whenever the same can be followed, no matter what form it may take.

The departure from the rigid doctrine of "ear-mark" or identification of money, to entitle the owner to recover, seems to have been first initiated in England. As the English cases cited have been very generally followed by the courts of this country, attention will be first called to them.

The case of *Pennell* v. *Duffell*, 4 De G. M. & G. 372, was a controversy between creditors and the administratrix of one George Green, who in his lifetime was one of the official assignees of the court of bankruptcy. It is only necessary to say that, in the course of the administration of his office, the deceased was accustomed to mingle trust funds with his own, and to deposit the same in bank. In the discussion of the proposition in question, *Lord Justice* Knight Bruce uses the following hypothesis: "Thus, let me suppose that the several sums for which, as I have said, Mr. Green was accountable at the time of his death, had been (that is to say, that the very coins and the very notes received by him on account of the trusts, respectively, had been) placed by him together in a particular repository, such as a chest, mixed confusedly together as among themselves, but in a state of clear and distinct separation from everything else, and had so remained at his death. It is, I apprehend, certain that after his death the coins and notes thus circumstanced would not have formed part of his general assets,—would not have been permitted so to be used,—but would have been specifically applicable to the purposes of the trusts on account of which he had received them. Suppose the case that I have just suggested to be varied only by the fact that, in the same chest with these coins and notes, Mr. Green had placed money of his own—in every sense his own—of a known amount, had never taken it out again, but had so mixed and blended it with the rest of the contents of the chest that the particular coins or notes of which this money of his own consisted could not be pointed out,—could not be identified. What difference would that make? None, as I apprehend, except, if it is an exception, that his executors would possibly be entitled to receive from the contents of the repository an amount equal to the ascertained amount of the money in every sense his own so mixed by himself with the other money. But not in either case, as I conceive, would the blending together of the trust moneys, however confusedly, be of any moment as between the various *cestuis que trustent* on the one hand, and the executors, as representing the general creditors, on the other." In the same case, *Lord Justice* Turner said: "It is, I apprehend, an undoubted principle of this court that as between *cestui que trust* and trustee, and all parties claiming under the trustee, otherwise than by purchase for valuable consideration, without notice, all property belonging to a trust, however much it may be changed or altered in its nature or character, and all the fruit of such property, whether in its original or in its altered state, continues to be subjected to or affected by the trust."

Again, in *Knatchbull* v. *Hallett*, 13 Ch. Div.

696, a most exhaustive discussion of this question is found. At page 710, Jessel, *M. R.*, said: "Now, that being the established doctrine of equity on this point, I will take the case of the pure bailee. If the bailee sells the goods bailed, the bailor can in equity follow the proceeds, and can follow the proceeds wherever they can be distinguished, either by being actually kept separate, or being mixed up with other moneys. I have only to advert to one other point, and that is this: Supposing, instead of being invested in the purchase of land or goods, the moneys were simply mixed with other moneys of the trustee, using the term again in its full sense, as including every person in a fiduciary relation, does it make any difference, according to the modern doctrine of equity? I say, none." At page 723, Thesiger, *L. J.*, said: "There is no doubt that there are to be found, here and there in the books, dicta, principally of common-law judges, which would appear to militate against the generality of that proposition, and which would appear to show that, in the minds of those judges, there was the view that, while chattels might be followed, or money so long as it could be looked upon as a specific chattel, as moneys numbered and placed in a bag, yet, when those moneys had been mixed with other moneys, that there was no ear-mark, and neither at law nor in equity could they be followed. With reference, however, to those dicta, it appears to me there are two observations to be made: in the first place, I cannot find any decision which has followed out those dicta to their consequence, assuming that those dicta are to be treated as having the generality which at first sight attaches to them; and, in the second place, it appears to me that in many cases those dicta, looking to the facts of the particular case, may be restrained to those facts, and possibly may have a more limited meaning than that which has been attached to them by *Mr. Justice* Fry in the case of *Ex parte Dale*, L. R. 11 Ch. Div. 772, or by the master of the rolls in his judgment in the present case. As far as I can judge, the only exception to the general proposition which I have stated is not a real exception, but an apparent exception: for all cases where it has been held that moneys mixed and confounded, but still existing, in a mass, cannot be followed, may, I think, be resolved into cases where, although there may have been a trust with reference to the disposition of the particular chattel which those moneys subsequently represented, there was no trust, no duty, in reference to the moneys themselves, beyond the ordinary duty of a man to pay his debts. In other words, that they were cases in which the relationship of debtor and creditor had been constituted, instead of the relation either of trustee and *cestui que trust*, or principal and agent." At page 718 the master of the rolls says: "Now, let us see, therefore, what *Whitecomb* v. *Jacob*, 1 Salk. 161, decides. It decides that the equity as to following the proceeds attaches to the case of a factor as well as to the case of *cestui que trust* and trustee. That is what it decides; but it decides, secondly, that you could not follow money, because it had no ear-mark. The first part is good law at the present day; the second is not. Whether it was good law or not at the time of Salkeld, it is immaterial to consider. It is very doubtful whether equity had got quite so far at that date as since, and therefore I will not say it was not; but it is not so now."

This case is cited with approval in *Central Nat. Bank of Baltimore* v. *Connecticut Mut. L. Ins. Co.*, 104 U. S. 54 [26 L. ed. 693], in which this and many of the English cases are reviewed. In the syllabus of the case last cited the rule is stated as follows: "As long as trust property can be traced and followed, the property into which it has been converted remains subject to the trust; and, if a man mixes trust funds with his, the whole will be treated as trust property, except so far as he may be able to distinguish what is his. This doctrine applies in every case of a trust relation, and as well to moneys deposited in bank, and to the debt thereby created, as to every other description of property." *Van Alen* v. *Am. Nat. Bank*, 52 N. Y. 1.

Again, in *Farmers & M. Nat. Bank* v. *King*, 57 Pa. 202, it is held: "Equity will follow a fund through any number of transmutations, and preserve it for the owners, so long as it can be identified, no matter in whose name the legal right stands." Strong, *J.*, says: "But it is insisted there was no ear-mark to the money. What of that, if the money can be followed, or if it can be traced into a substitute? This is often done through the aid of an ear-mark. But that is only an index enabling a beneficial owner to follow his property. It is no evidence of ownership. An ear-mark is not indispensable to enable a real owner to assert his right to property, or to its product or substitute. Evidence of substantial identity may be attached to the thing itself, or it may be extraneous. It is freely admitted that, if a trustee or agent receive money of a *cestui que trust* or principal, and mingle it with his own so that it cannot be followed, the *cestui que trust* or principal cannot recover it specifically. This is not because the ownership is changed, but because a court cannot lay hold of the property as that of the owner. But, in regard to money, substantial identity is not oneness of pieces of coin, or of bank-bills. If an agent to collect money puts the money collected into a chest where he has money of his own, he does not thereby make it all his own, and convert himself into a mere debtor to his principal. The principal may, by the law, claim out of the chest the sums which belonged to him before the admixture. *Pennell* v. *Deffell*, *supra*."

In *Peak* v. *Ellicott*, 30 Kan. 156, Horton, *Ch. J.*, says: "Counsel suggest: 'If there was a trust created, there must have been a *cestui que trust*, and that if anyone is entitled to follow and reclaim the money, it must be the owner and holder of the note of plaintiff.' It does not make any difference that, instead of trustee and *cestui que trust*, the case is one of fiduciary relationship. If a wrong arises out of such relationship, the same remedy exists against the wrong-doer on behalf of the principal as exists against a trustee on behalf of the *cestui que trust*. Wherever a fiduciary relationship exists, and money coming from the trust lies in the hands of the person standing in that relationship, it can be followed by the principal, and separated from any money of the wrong-doer."

In *McLeod* v. *Evans*, 66 Wis. 401, the rule

contended for by counsel for defendant in error was, after a careful discussion by Cole, *Ch. J.*, practically repudiated. The proposition decided is thus stated in the syllabus: "M. left with H., a banker, for collection, a draft upon a New York bank. H. sent the draft to a bank in Chicago, received credit for the amount, and afterwards made drafts upon such bank, which were cashed. Before payment to M., H. made an assignment for the benefit of creditors. At that time nothing was due him from the Chicago bank. Held, that the proceeds of the draft were a trust fund in the hands of H., and that, as against other creditors, M. might enforce full payment from the assets in the hands of the assignee, although the trust fund could not be traced to any specific property." *People* v. *City Bank of Rochester*, 96 N.Y. 32.

No one of the cases cited differs in principle from the case at bar. Suppose the money in question had been placed by Everett in his own pocket, with a mass of other funds belonging to himself, and that he had then died. Suppose that immediately upon his death the mass of currency had been taken into the possession of the defendant in error. If demand had then been made by the plaintiff for the money, could defendant in error have required the plaintiff in error to designate the particular bills which were claimed as a condition of the right to recover them? Certainly not. How does the case supposed differ from the case at bar? It is alleged that the money was paid to Everett, received and retained by him; that it was in his possession at the time of his death; that the same sum came to the possession of the defendant in error. Is it not clear that Everett received the fund in a fiduciary capacity? Does it not follow that the instant it passed into his hands a trust arose, by operation of law, in favor of plaintiff in error? Did not the trust follow the fund when it passed to the hands of defendant in error? If it was mingled with the assets of the decedent, is not the estate impressed with the same trust? Can it be possible that the fact of death increases a man's estate, by adding thereto all property which may be in his hands? Can a man, by an abuse of trust or violation of his fiduciary relations, acquire moneys for distribution among his general creditors at his decease? Whatever may have been the law applicable to these questions in the past, it is clear that at the present time the estate of no man can be increased by a wrong committed by him under the circumstances set forth in the complaint in this case.

Is the conclusion reached in any wise affected by sections 126 and 136 of the Statute of this State relating to wills and administration of estates? It will be observed in this connection that the question at issue is one of title. The conclusion already reached is that at the time of the death of Everett the title to the fund in controversy was in the plaintiff in error; that Everett had no beneficial interest therein whatever. The fund therefore constituted no part of his estate. Schouler, Exrs. § 205.

It is contended by defendant in error, however, that the sections of the Statute cited have the effect, in law, to convert the fund in question into assets by their operation in the classification of claims, and the order of their payment. The 3d subdivision of section 126 provides that, "where any executor, administrator or guardian has received money as such, his executor or administrator shall pay out of his estate the amount thus received and not accounted for, which shall compose the third class." The 4th subdivision provides that "all other debts and demands, of whatsoever kind, without regard to quality or dignity, which shall be exhibited within one year from the granting of letters as aforesaid, shall compose the fourth class." Section 136 relates to the order of payment, and requires that claims be paid according to the classification contained in section 126.

It is claimed, first, that the fund in question does not belong to the third class, because debts of the third class are limited to moneys which have been received by the decedent as executor, administrator or guardian. This is undoubtedly true. As a natural sequence, it is argued that the demand in issue in this suit is a debt, and belongs to the fourth class. If the plaintiff in error was proceeding against the defendant in error as a general creditor, then, as a matter of course, the position of defendant in error would be correct. Such, however, is not the case. The relation of debtor and creditor, as between plaintiff in error and Everett, never existed. The Statute, therefore, has no application. The ultimate fact upon which the right of action in the case at bar is predicated is that the funds in question were never the property of Everett at all; that neither the legal title nor the beneficiary interest vested in him; that the identical fund was in his possession at the time of his death, and that the same fund came to the defendant.

Prior to 1872 the provision of the Statute of Illinois classifying claims against the estate of a deceased person was identical in language with that of this State. In the year last mentioned the Legislature of Illinois amended that provision so that it read as follows: "(6) Where the decedent has received money in trust for any purpose, his executor or administrator shall pay out of his estate the amount thus received and not accounted for."

In the case of *Wilson* v. *Kirby*, 88 Ill. 566, it was held that "the clause of the Statute relating to the classification of claims against estates of deceased persons, and which gives a preference in cases where the deceased has 'received money in trust for any purpose,' does not necessarily extend to and embrace every kind of trust. It does not embrace trusts implied by the law." The same case was before the Supreme Court of Illinois a second time, and is reported in 98 Ill. 240. It was there held that "where a person sells the cattle of another as his agent, under a contract, and receives and retains the purchase money until his death, it becomes the money of the owner of the cattle, as the substitute or representative of the cattle; and the fact that the widow of the person so selling, during his illness or after his death, takes such funds, and deposits the same in bank in her own name, and afterwards gives her check for the same to her husband's executor, will nor destroy the identity of the fund, and make it subject to the general creditors of the testator, but the owner of the cattle so sold will have a preference over the other general creditors of the estate. In such case, it is not necessary that the identical bills received by the testator should have come into the hands of his executor." Upon examination of this case, it will be discovered that the decision is based upon the sole fact that the money in controversy was the money of the owners of the cattle, and that the section of the Statute cited is without application, for the reason that, as was said by the court (*Wilson v. Kirby, supra*), the Statute does not embrace trusts implied by the law. In the decisions of this case, therefore, the provisions of our Statute which have been cited should be disregarded, and the conclusion predicated upon the legal and equitable principles which have been discussed. In the light of these principles, it is clear that the complaint states a cause of action.

The next question presented is whether John S. Risdon was improperly joined as a defendant. It is claimed that, if plaintiff in error was the real party in interest, Risdon could not be properly joined either as plaintiff or defendant. The relation of the parties to each other was as follows: (1) Risdon was one of the original parties to the contract or arrangement upon which the action was predicated, to wit, the payment of $1,200 by Heatly to Everett for him. (2) The plaintiff was the agent of Risdon for the purpose of collecting the money to be paid by Heatly to Everett, and had the legal title to the draft which was drawn, and the right in the first instance to receive the money; but Risdon was the beneficial owner of the fund. This being the relation of the parties, the question of parties plaintiff does not seem to be difficult.

Section 8 of the Code, which was in force when this action was brought, provides that "every action shall be prosecuted in the name of the real party in interest, except as otherwise provided."

Section 5 provides that the trustee of an express trust may bring an action without joining beneficiaries, and that a trustee of an express trust includes a person in whose name a contract is made for the benefit of another.

Section 10 declares that "all persons having an interest in the subject of the action, and in obtaining the relief demanded, may be joined as plaintiffs."

Section 12 provides that, "of the parties to the action, those who are united in interest shall be joined as plaintiffs or defendants; but, if the consent of anyone who should have been joined as plaintiff cannot be obtained, he may be made a defendant, the reason thereof being stated in the complaint."

The meaning of the language of the first section cited has been frequently construed by the courts. The "real party in interest" is held to mean the person in whom the legal title to the claim in suit is vested. *Bassett v. Inman*, 7 Colo. 270, and cases cited.

The suit, therefore, was properly brought in the name of the plaintiff. But, inasmuch as Risdon was a party to the contract upon which the action was predicated, and was in fact the beneficial owner of the claim, he must be deemed to be interested in the subject of the action, within the meaning of section 10, above cited, and therefore a proper party plaintiff in the suit. In commenting upon the section last mentioned, Pomeroy, in his work on Remedies and Remedial Rights, at section 199, says: "The extent of the interest is not the criterion, nor its source, nor origin. If the persons have any interest,—whether complete or partial, whether absolute or contingent, whether resulting from a common share in the proceeds of the suit, or arising from the stipulations of the agreement,—the language applies, without any limitation or exception, and without any distinction suggested between actions which are equitable and those which are legal."

All persons standing in the relation to the subject matter of the action, as above defined, may be properly joined as plaintiffs. In this particular case, Risdon refused to unite with plaintiff, and was properly joined as defendant.

It is also contended that different causes of action are improperly united. This position cannot be sustained for the simple reason that no cause of action is stated against Risdon. As a part of the prayer for relief, the court is asked to allow the plaintiff a reasonable sum for its costs and expenses, and to require this amount to be paid to plaintiff by Risdon. No attempt is made to state a cause of action against him. The only allegations are those which are made in compliance with section 12 of the Code, as the reason for making Risdon a party defendant. Two causes of action, therefore, are not improperly united, there being but one cause of action stated.

The judgment is reversed.

Richmond and **Reed**, *CC.*, concur.

Elliott, *J.*:

Having heard and determined this case in the court below, I have given the foregoing opinion careful consideration. At *nisi prius* I must have overlooked some of the averments of the complaint showing that Everett was, by the previous arrangement of the parties, constituted as trustee of the particular fund paid to him by Heatly, for the express purpose of being immediately paid over to Risdon or his order.

Per Curiam:

For the reasons expressed in the opinion of *Mr. Commissioner* **Pattison**, *the judgment of the District Court is reversed, with leave to defendants below to answer the complaint.*

INDIANA SUPREME COURT.

John W. JOHNSON *et al.*, *Appts.*,
v.
Joseph JOUCHERT *et al.*, Exrs.

(....Ind.....)

1. **The wife's conveyance of her separate real estate** directly to her husband is void, unless the transaction can be sustained upon the principles of equity.

2. **A mortgage on the separate estate of a married woman** to secure a loan to her husband may be upheld to the extent that the proceeds are invested in property purchased for her in her name.

3. **Remote grantees of a married woman** cannot set up a plea of coverture in their own behalf against a mortgage executed by her unless it appears that they are entitled to do so in equity and good conscience for the protection of a consideration actually paid her without notice of the invalid incumbrance, or with the mutual intention and agreement that they should be permitted to set up its invalidity.

(May 27, 1890.)

APPEAL by plaintiffs from a judgment of the Circuit Court of Gibson County in favor of defendants in an action brought to quiet title to a certain piece of real estate, and to have a mortgage executed thereon by a married woman and her husband canceled for the reason that, the property having been hers when it was executed, it was void. *Affirmed.*

The facts are fully stated in the opinion.

Messrs. **Thomas R. Paxton** and **Lucius C. Embree** for appellants.

Mr. **C. A. Buskirk** for appellees.

Mitchell, *J.*, delivered the opinion of the court:

The questions for decision arise out of the following facts: In January, 1884, Mrs. Grubbs, wife of Thomas J. Grubbs, was the owner of forty acres of land in Gibson County, which she inherited from her father. She attempted to convey the land directly to her husband by a deed containing covenants of warranty, her purpose in making the conveyance being to enable her husband to mortgage it as security for a loan of $400 which he had nego-

NOTE.—*Deed by married woman of her separate property to her husband.*

The common-law disability incident to the relation of husband and wife with regard to conveyances of real property still exists, except in so far as it has been swept away by express legislative enactments. Dean v. Metropolitan E. R. Co. 119 N. Y. 540.

Gifts by a wife to her husband are to be closely inspected on account of the danger of improper influence; but if they appear to be fairly made, and to be free from coercion and undue influence, they ought to be sustained. Farmer v. Farmer, 39 N. J. Eq. 216.

The evidence to establish a gift by a wife of her property to her husband must be clear and unequivocal, and the intention free from doubt. Brooks v. Fowler, 82 Ga. 329.

A married woman, being able to convey her separate estate, in Alabama, only by an instrument jointly executed by herself and husband, etc., cannot make a valid deed to him of such property. Trawick v. Davis, 85 Ala. 342.

A deed by a married woman, without her husband joining, is void. Mantoursville v. Fairfield, 2 Cent. Rep. 593, 112 Pa. 99.

If signed by her alone without her husband, it is absolutely void. Franklin v. Pollard Mill Co. 88 Ala. 318.

An assignment by a married woman of her separate estate as collateral security to pay a note in which she has joined with her husband for his debt is void. Livingston v. Shingler, 30 S. C. 159.

In Connecticut the only limitation upon the wife's power of alienation of her real estate is her husband's consent; and a conditional sale or mortgage evidenced by her husband joining in the deed is valid, when made to secure his debt. Stafford Sav. Bank v. Underwood, 3 New Eng. Rep. 125, 54 Conn. 2.

Mortgage to secure husband's debts; rule in various States.

In Alabama a wife cannot mortgage a statutory separate estate for the husband's benefit, and such mortgage is void. Such a mortgage is a nullity. Lippincott v. Mitchell, 94 U. S. 767 (24 L. ed. 315); Bergen v. Jeffries, 80 Ala. 349; Steed v. Knowles, 79 Ala. 446.

When a bill seeks to foreclose a mortgage of the wife's land, executed by her and her husband jointly, it must clearly show the character of her estate, and her capacity to mortgage it. Houston v. Williamson, 81 Ala. 482.

In the District of Columbia, a wife by uniting with her husband in a deed of trust can charge her property with the payment of a debt. Kaiser v. Stickney, 102 U. S. (26 L. ed. 176).

She may incumber her individual property to secure her husband's debts, by an instrument in writing, by which she expressly charges her separate property for the payment of such debts. Stephen v. Beall, 89 U. S. 22 Wall. 329 (22 L. ed. 786).

The Code of Georgia, which provides that a wife cannot bind her separate estate by any assumption of the debts of her husband, cannot be extended to destroy a power expressly bestowed, and render property inalienable which the donor granted upon condition that it might be conveyed as specified. Brodnax v. Ætna Ins. Co. 128 U. S. 236 (32 L. ed. 445).

In Indiana a mortgage by a married woman on her separate property, in which her lawful husband does not join, is void, under 1 Rev. Stat. 1876, p. 550 (Rev. Stat. 1881, § 5117), although he has been absent fifteen years, and she, believing him to be dead, is living with another man whom she believes to be her lawful husband, and who joins with her in executing the instrument. As to the effect of the Indiana Statute of 1881 touching estoppels *in pais* affecting married women, on such an instrument, if made after the passage of that Act—*quære*. Cook v. Walling, 2 L. R. A. 769, 117 Ind. 9.

To render a mortgage of a wife's real estate, in which her husband joined, invalid, prior to Ind. Act of 1881, it must appear that her property came to her within the restrictive terms of the Act of 1879. Noland v. State, 115 Ind. 529.

In such a case a mortgage executed by her, in which her husband joined, is enforceable to the extent that the funds it secures were used in discharging valid prior incumbrances on her land. *Ibid.*

Since Rev. Stat. 1881, § 5119, a married woman cannot mortgage her separate real estate to secure

tiated from the agent of Jouchert. The money was loaned; and the note of Grubbs, secured by a mortgage on the land, in which both husband and wife joined, was taken as evidence of the debt. The husband expended $287 of the money borrowed in the purchase of real estate, the title to which was taken in the name of his wife, and in making improvements on the land purchased for her. Afterwards, Grubbs and wife conveyed the land mortgaged by warranty deed to Smith, who subsequently conveyed by like deed to the appellants, John W. and George W. Johnson. The latter brought this suit for the purpose of having their title quieted, and the mortgage executed by Grubbs and wife canceled. The conclusions stated by the court were to the effect that the mortgage was void as to the wife, but that the plaintiffs below, as subsequent purchasers of the land, under the ruling in *Bennett* v. *Mattingly*, 110 Ind. 197, 9 West. Rep. 282, could not avail themselves of her coverture for the purpose of avoiding the mortgage.

The conveyance from Mrs. Grubbs to her husband was a nullity. A married woman has no power or capacity to convey or incumber her separate real estate except by deed in which her husband shall join. Rev. Stat. 1888, § 5117. Any conveyance executed by her, in which her husband has not joined, is absolutely void because of the want of capacity on her part to convey or incumber her real estate by such an instrument. *Cook* v. *Walling*, 117 Ind. 9, 2 L. R. A. 769.

Besides, the common-law rule respecting the unity of husband and wife prevails to such an extent in this State as to render nugatory any attempt by a married woman to convey her separate real estate directly to her husband, unless the transaction can be sustained upon the principles of equity. *Barnett* v. *Harshbarger*, 105 Ind. 410, 3 West. Rep. 750; *Harrell* v. *Harrell*, 117 Ind. 94; *Preston* v. *Fryer*, 38 Md. 221; *Gebb* v. *Rose*, 40 Md. 387; 9 Am. & Eng. Cyclop. Law, 789–791; *Jenne* v. *Marble*, 37 Mich. 319.

The conveyance from Mrs. Grubbs to her husband is therefore to be eliminated from the case, and the facts are to be considered as though she joined in a mortgage on her separate real estate to secure a loan of money negotiated by and made to her husband, who employed $287 of it in purchasing and improving other real estate for her, and the residue for his own personal benefit. To the extent that the money borrowed was invested in property, the title to which was taken in the name

---

her husband's debt. Engler v. Acker, 3 West. Rep. 673, 106 Ind. 223; Brown v. Will, 1 West. Rep. 130, 103 Ind. 71.

Under the provisions of that section a mortgage executed by husband and wife on land held by them as tenants by entireties, to secure the individual debt of the husband, is invalid as to the wife; it is a suretyship. Brown v. Will, *supra*.

A mortgage executed by a married woman and her husband, of land held by the wife in virtue of her previous marriage, there being children alive of such previous marriage, is void, under Rev. Stat. 1881, § 2484. The mortgagee cannot be subrogated to the lien of the State for taxes and assessments voluntarily paid. Ætna L. Ins. Co. v. Buck, 6 West. Rep. 419, 108 Ind. 174.

A wife joining in a mortgage with her husband to secure his debt has a right to have his two-thirds interest in the land first sold to pay the debt. Hoppes v. Hoppes (Ind.) April 24, 1890.

In Missouri where a wife is a surety for her husband and others, proceedings characterized by illegalities and fraud, the fraud being especially directed against her property, justify the wife in invoking equitable interposition, notwithstanding her principals are in no position to demand a like relief. Henry v. Sneed, 99 Mo. 407.

A married woman of New Hampshire may bind herself by a note and mortgage of real estate, given by her as principal debtor to obtain money for her husband to pay his debts. Wells v. Foster, 6 New Eng. Rep. 909, 64 N. H. 585.

She may bind herself as principal by a note given to the holder of a mortgage upon personalty bought by her husband, to discharge the lien. Jones v. Holt, 6 New Eng. Rep. 908, 64 N. H. 546.

In New Jersey where husband and wife unite in a mortgage of land, part of which belongs to him, and the rest to her as her separate estate, and the mortgagee (at husband's request and without consideration, and for his accommodation, and without the wife's knowledge and consent) releases part of his land, the debt must, as between the mortgagee or his assignee and the wife, be held to be paid to the extent of the value of the land released. McFillin v. Hoffman, 5 Cent. Rep. 837, 42 N. J. Eq. 144.

A wife joining with her husband in a mortgage of her own property to secure his debt is his surety merely, and entitled to all the rights and privileges of a surety. *Ibid.*

In Pennsylvania a married woman may bind her real estate by mortgage duly executed by herself and her husband, to secure the payment of a debt of a stranger. Hagenbuch v. Phillips, 3 Cent. Rep. 154, 112 Pa. 284.

A married woman joined with her husband in executing a mortgage on her real estate, and afterwards conveyed to another, who conveyed to her husband. On a *scire facias* to foreclose the mortgage, the wife was joined as a co-defendant with the husband. It was held that, as to her, the action was *in rem*, and that she was not interested in the result of the suit so as to set up the defense of the payment of usurious interest by the husband. Broomell v. Anderson (Pa.) 6 Cent. Rep. 723.

In South Carolina a note and mortgage given by a married woman to secure a sum of money borrowed to pay off debts of her husband and for the purchase of family supplies are absolutely void where the lender knew the purposes for which the money was borrowed. Goodjoin v. Vaughn (S. C.) April 14, 1890.

Where a mortgage by a married woman shows on its face that it was given solely for the purpose of securing the debt of third persons, and therefore that under the law it was invalid, there is no room for an estoppel against her. Tribble v. Poore, 30 S. C. 97.

In the absence of evidence that the mortgagee knew or had reason to suspect that the money was for the use of the husband, the fact that he afterwards applied it to his own use will not relieve the wife from liability. Chambers v. Bookman (S. C.) April 9, 1890.

Where a married woman, under the pretext of borrowing money for the purpose of relieving her separate estate from a lien previously fixed upon it, at the same time borrows and gives a mortgage for a sum in excess of the amount necessary for that purpose, with a view to let her husband have the benefit of such excess, the lender having knowledge of the excess, but not of her purpose in borrowing it, she will be held liable for the full amount. Erwin v. Lowry (S. C.) July 12, 1889.

of Mrs. Grubbs, for her separate use and benefit, the mortgage constituted a valid security. A mortgage properly executed by a married woman upon her separate real estate is a valid and binding security, unless it constitutes a contract of suretyship, within the meaning of section 5119, Rev. Stat. 1881. Strictly speaking, a contract of suretyship is an engagement whereby one person undertakes to answer for the debt, default or miscarriage of another; but the relation of surety may arise out of arrangements or equities between the parties to a contract, without any regard to its form. One whose relation to a contract or transaction is such as to entitle him to be indemnified in case he is compelled to pay a debt or perform an obligation for which he is bound with another, in order to relieve himself from personal liability, or discharge his property from an incumbrance, may be said to stand in the relation of surety. *Sefton* v. *Hargett*, 113 Ind. 592, 13 West. Rep. 42; *Smith* v. *Shelden*, 35 Mich. 42; *Wendlandt* v. *Sohre*, 37 Minn. 162.

One who has received and who retains the consideration or benefit of a contract cannot, in equity, occupy the attitude of a surety. Accordingly, it has been held again and again that, where money was borrowed by a wife, or by a husband and wife, or by either of them, for the purpose of discharging liens on the wife's separate property, or for a purpose which inures to the benefit of her estate, a mortgage properly executed on her separate property to secure the repayment of money so borrowed may be enforced. *Noland* v. *State*, 115 Ind. 529, and cases cited.

"With respect to contracts for her own benefit or for the benefit of her estate, the power of a married woman is plenary." *Jouchert* v. *Johnson*, 108 Ind. 436, 6 West. Rep. 880.

To the extent that the consideration of a contract or security inures to the benefit of a married woman, she occupies the attitude of a principal; for the plain reason that she would have no equitable right to be indemnified by someone else in case the contract or security should be enforced against her. *Vogel* v. *Leichner*, 102 Ind. 55.

A married woman, by force of section 5119, is protected as at common law in all transactions which do not relate to or benefit her separate estate or business, or which are not to her personal benefit; but such as relate to or benefit her separate estate, or her lawful business transactions, will be binding upon her. *Haydock Carriage Co.* v. *Pier*, 74 Wis. 582.

Although the facts found are not very definite upon the point, it may fairly be assumed that all the parties to the transaction knew of the purpose for which the money was borrowed. The creditor who took a mortgage on the separate estate of a married woman as security for a loan made, ostensibly, to her husband, was bound at his peril to inquire; and, since Mrs. Grubbs received, and, so far as appears, retains, the title to property purchased and paid for out of the money borrowed, it will be presumed that she had knowledge, and that she executed the mortgage upon the consideration that the principal part of the money was to be used in augmenting her separate estate. In respect to the money borrowed and thus applied she would have no standing in a court of equity to enforce indemnity against her husband in case she is compelled to pay the debt. The conclusion follows that to the extent of $287, with the interest accumulated thereon, the mortgage was not a contract of suretyship, but a valid incumbrance on the land when it was conveyed to the appellants. In respect to the residue, since the loan which the mortgage was given to secure was made to her husband, and applied to his personal use, she occupied the relation of surety, and the mortgage was invalid.

The inquiry remains, Can the appellants, who are remote grantees of Mrs. Grubbs, avail themselves of the invalidity of the mortgage? The court below was of the opinion that, although the mortgage was void *in toto*, the appellants, as subsequent grantees, were not in a situation to avail themselves of its invalidity. A parallel is supposed to exist between the civil acts, contracts and deeds of married women and those of infants; and it has been said that coverture, like infancy, is a personal defense, and hence one which cannot be made by a third party for his own benefit. *Bennett* v. *Mattingly*, 110 Ind. 197, 9 West. Rep. 282; *Ætna Ins. Co. of Hartford* v. *Baker*, 71 Ind. 102; *Crooks* v. *Kennett*, 111 Ind. 347, 10 West. Rep. 256.

This statement is true in a limited and qualified sense. The contracts of infants, according to modern classification, are either valid or voidable, while those of married women are, as a rule, either valid or void. The contracts of infants, which are voidable at the election of the infant, are distinguishable from those of married women, which, owing to the disability of coverture, are void at common law, and, when constituting contracts of suretyship, are expressly so declared, as to her, by statute. *Kent* v. *Rand*, 64 N. H. 45, 2 New Eng. Rep. 858; *Musick* v. *Dodson*, 76 Mo. 624, 22 Am. L. Reg. 522.

In respect to voidable contracts, the established rule is that only the person whose disability renders the contract voidable, or those in privity of blood or in representation, can avoid it. Such a contract cannot be avoided by privies in estate without the co-operation of those whose personal privilege it is to disaffirm or avoid it, unless that which is equivalent to a disaffirmance or avoidance has already taken place. *Harris* v. *Ross*, 112 Ind. 314, 11 West. Rep. 670; *Schrock* v. *Crowl*, 83 Ind. 243; *Price* v. *Jennings*, 62 Ind. 111; *Breckenridge* v. *Ormsby*, 1 J. J. Marsh. 236.

But where a deed or contract is absolutely void, and to enforce it as though it were valid would operate to the injury of the person who made it, or to the prejudice of a third person who is in privity of estate with the person who made it, the proposition cannot be maintained as universally true that one who is in privity of estate cannot set up the invalidity of the contract or deed. *State* v. *Kennett*, 114 Ind. 160, 13 West. Rep. 818, and cases cited.

For example, by the common law a married woman had no power to convey or incumber her separate real estate, and under the Statute she has no power to do so except by deed in which her husband shall join. The mere fact of coverture, under any and all circumstances, disqualifies her to convey or incumber her real estate except in the manner prescribed, and a conveyance made in disregard of the prescribed manner is an absolute nullity, and cannot operate even by way of estoppel or otherwise. *Cook* v. *Walling, supra; Rogers* v. *Union Cent. L. Ins. Co.* 111 Ind. 343, 9 West. Rep. 878, 27 Am. L. Reg. 48, and *note.*

It would hardly be claimed that a mortgage executed by a married woman, in which her husband had not joined, could nevertheless be enforced against a subsequent purchaser, without notice, who had paid the full purchase price for the land. But we need not pursue the general subject further. While the Statute prohibits a married woman from entering into any contract of suretyship, and declares all such contracts void as to her, it is nevertheless true that the restraint is imposed upon her solely for her benefit.

As is in effect said in *Sutton* v. *Aiken*, 62 Ga. 733, 741, the purpose of the Statute is economical, not moral; and its policy is in favor of a class, and not of the public at large. It is not wicked or immoral for a wife to pay her husband's debts, nor has the public an interest in compelling her to abstain from doing so. *Brodnax* v. *Ætna Ins. Co.* 128 U. S. 236 [32 L. ed. 445].

A married woman may have entered into a contract of suretyship under such circumstances as to be legally and morally estopped from asserting that she should not be held as principal. *Rogers* v. *Union Cent. L. Ins. Co. supra; Lane* v. *Schlemmer*, 114 Ind. 296, 12 West. Rep. 922.

Moreover, she may have elected, for other sufficient reasons, to perform her contract, invalid though it be; and until it appears that her grantee will be injuriously affected by her election, a court of equity will not lend its aid merely to take money from one stranger, and put it into the pocket of another. *Stiger* v. *Bent*, 111 Ill. 328.

While a contract such as that under consideration is declared to be void, yet, in order to make its invalidity available, the coverture of the mortgagor must be set up as a defense. In the absence of any facts or circumstances making it appear that in equity and good conscience the owner of the land should be permitted to set up the invalidity of the mortgage, the mortgagor has the primary right to elect whether she will avail herself of the defense or not. A usurious contract may be void, but the promisor may elect to perform it. If he chooses to do so, and no one else has been injured by it, no one has the right to say that he may not waive the defense of usury. *Union Nat. Bank* v. *International Bank*, 123 Ill. 510, 12 West. Rep. 773.

Those who are in privity of estate with the borrower may set up the defense for their own protection, under certain circumstances. Thus it is laid down that one who has purchased land with the expressed intention on his part, and that of the grantor, to avoid a previous invalid mortgage, may make the defense; or where the purchaser has in no way agreed to pay the mortgage debt, or where it has not been agreed that the debt should be deducted out of the purchase price, he may take advantage of the invalidity of a mortgage, and avoid it. *Newman* v. *Kershaw*, 10 Wis. 333; *Ludington* v. *Harris*, 21 Wis. 240; 1 Jones, Mortg. § 745.

The Statute prohibits a married woman from entering into a contract of suretyship, and declares that "such contract, as to her, shall be void." As was said in *Bennett* v. *Mattingly, supra*, the provision against married women becoming sureties was intended for their protection alone, and the defense of coverture cannot be made solely for the benefit of a third person. A stranger, in other words, cannot interfere between a married woman and the person with whom she contracted, and by pleading her coverture save the money due on an invalid contract, merely to put it in his own pocket. *Studabaker* v. *Marquardt*, 55 Ind. 341.

If one in privity of estate with a married woman should make it appear that the plea of coverture would inure to her benefit, or protect her from liability on the covenants in her deed, or that he paid her the consideration of an invalid incumbrance upon a mutual agreement that he should have the right to avoid it, a different question would be presented, and one which might require further consideration of the questions in *Crooks* v. *Kennett*, 111 Ind. 347, 10 West. Rep. 256.

For all that appears in the present case, the amount of the debt secured by the mortgage sought to be canceled may have been deducted from the purchase price. In that event, Mrs. Grubbs would have paid the debt, and the plea of coverture would be wholly for the benefit of her grantees who have the money in their pockets. The plea of coverture is so far the personal privilege of a married woman, or of those who are privies in blood or in representation with her, that, before any third person can plead it in her behalf, it must affirmatively appear that it is made for her benefit, and with her consent, or that in equity and good conscience the person setting up the defense should be permitted to do so in order to protect a consideration actually paid her without notice of the invalid incumbrance, or with the mutual intention and agreement that he should be permitted to set up its invalidity. These conclusions lead to an affirmance of the judgment.

Judgment affirmed, with costs.

NEW JERSEY SUPREME COURT.

Mary WELLER, *Plff. in Err.*,
v.
Bartholomew McCORMICK.

(....N. J. L....)

*1. **In the absence of any statutory or municipal regulations** to the contrary, a tree planted by a private person on the sidewalk of the street in front of his premises belongs to and is under the control of the owner and occupant of the abutting property.

2. **Under such circumstances the owner and occupant of the property is bound** to use reasonable care to prevent the tree from becoming dangerous to travelers upon the street, and every person specially injured through a

*Head notes by DIXON, J.

breach of that obligation is entitled to a private action against the party in fault to recover compensation for the damages arising therefrom.

3. Under the circumstances stated, the owner and occupant of the abutting premises is chargeable with knowledge of his duty.

(June 9, 1890.)

ERROR to the Circuit Court for Middlesex County to review a judgment of nonsuit in an action brought to recover damages for personal injuries inflicted by a limb falling from a tree in front of defendant's premises. *Reversed.*

The case sufficiently appears in the opinion.

Argued before Beasley, *Ch. J.*, and Reed and Dixon, *JJ.*

Mr. **Charles T. Cowenhoven** for plaintiff in error.

Messrs. **Alan H. Strong** and **Robert Adrain** for defendant in error.

Dixon, *J.*, delivered the opinion of the court:

When the above-entitled cause was before this court at June Term, 1885, on a rule certified by the Middlesex Circuit, the circuit was advised to set aside the verdict for the plaintiff on the ground that nothing had been shown from which it could legally be inferred that there rested on the defendant any duty with regard to the shade tree, by the falling of whose branch the plaintiff was injured. The tree stood near the curb in one of the streets of New Brunswick, and it appeared that since 1863 the city had had power to make ordinances and rules for directing and regulating the planting, rearing, trimming and preserving of ornamental shade trees in the streets, parks and grounds of the city. Whether the tree in question had been planted under this authority was not shown, but the only fact to connect the defendant with it was that it stood in front of his property. Under these circumstances, we decided that the testimony gave no more support to an inference that the tree belonged to the defendant than it did to an inference that it belonged to the city, and that, therefore, the plaintiff had not adduced a preponderance of evidence to establish the liability of the defendant. Upon a retrial at the Middlesex Circuit in December, 1888, proof was made or offered that the tree was planted before 1855 by a former owner of the defendant's premises; that he and his successors in title, down to the defendant, had cared for the tree, and that the same title had passed to the defendant in September, 1881, and remained in him until after the accident, which occurred January 21, 1883; that the City of New Brunswick had adopted no rules or ordinances for the planting, rearing, trimming or preserving of trees in the streets, except an ordinance, passed after 1863, directing the position in which trees might thereafter be set out, and forbidding any person except the owner to cut down, destroy, break or in any manner injure trees or shrubs standing in any public street or highway. Nevertheless the plaintiff was nonsuited, in supposed compliance with the judgment of this court.

The facts presented at the second trial render the case essentially different from its former aspect. It now appears that the tree was planted by a private person upon his own property, and, it is to be assumed, chiefly for his own ends. Although the public had the easements of a highway in this property, yet the planting of the tree was perfectly lawful. By devolution of title from the person who planted the tree, the defendant became its owner, and acquired control of it. His right of control might, indeed, have been regulated by the municipal authorities, by virtue of the power delegated to them in the charter, since the public rights in the highway included the right to assume charge of trees standing therein. But, up to the time of the accident, those authorities had imposed no restriction whatever upon the defendant, their ordinance in terms excepting the owners of trees from its provisions. From the ownership and unlimited right of control thus possessed by the defendant, it must be concluded that he maintained the tree in the street for his private purpose; and hence, as stated in our former opinion in this cause (*Weller* v. *McCormick*, 47 N. J. L. 397, 1 Cent. Rep. 462), he was bound to exercise due care to prevent its becoming dangerous. This obligation is plainly deducible from the relative rights of the public and the abutting owner in the highway. The public right is paramount, and includes the right to have the street safe for travel. That of the abutting owner is subordinate to this public right. He may use the highway in front of his premises, when not restricted by positive enactment, for loading and unloading goods, for vaults and shutes, for awnings, for shade trees, etc., but only on condition that he does not unreasonably interfere with the safety of the highway for public travel. Any such interference arising from want of due care on his part is unreasonable; and, therefore, to occasion such interference by negligence in the exercise of his subordinate private rights is a breach of public duty. This public duty to exercise reasonable care, imposed on every person using the highway for such private ends as will endanger the highway if negligence take place, exists for the benefit of individual travelers; and hence, when an individual sustains peculiar personal injury as the result of such negligence, a private action accrues to him against the person in default; for it is a general principle that where there rests upon any person a public duty either arising at common law or created by statute, and that duty is due to the public, considered as composed of individuals, and for their protection, each person specially injured by a breach of the obligation is entitled to a private action to recover compensation for his damage. *Couch* v. *Steel*, 3 El. & Bl. 402; *Atkinson* v. *Newcastle & G. W. Co.* L. R. 2 Exch. Div. 441; *Hayes* v. *Michigan Cent. R. Co.* 111 U. S. 228 [28 L. ed. 410]; *Van Winkle* v. *American S. B. Ins. Co.* 52 N. J. L. —.

But it is said that there was no evidence of notice to the defendant that the tree had been planted and maintained by his predecessors in title and therefore he was not bound to take care of it, as he would have been had he known it was his property. It appeared, however, that he was in actual occupation as owner of the premises abutting upon the street where the tree stood; and his title and possession presumably extended to the middle of the street, subject only to the public rights. *Winter* v.

Peterson, 24 N. J. L. 524; *Salter* v. *Jonas*, 39 N. J. L. 469.

As he had no notice that the public claimed to own or to exercise any control over the tree, and as in fact no attempt was ever made to set up such a public right, the defendant was chargeable with knowledge of his exclusive proprietorship, and of the duties which it entailed.

Whether the defendant did in fact take proper care of the tree is not now to be decided. The evidence tended to show that the limb that fell, and part of the trunk, were rotten; and two witnesses swore to having observed that the limb was dead some time before the accident. As the defendant had been in possession of the premises through one season of foliage and part of another, this testimony would warrant the submission to the jury of the question of negligence.

The judgment of nonsuit should be set aside.

KENTUCKY COURT OF APPEALS.

Joseph RICHARDSON'S ADMR., *Appt.*,
v.
GERMAN INSURANCE CO. of Freeport, Ill.

(....Ky.....)

The death of the insured does not make a change in the title such as will avoid a policy insuring him, "his executors, administrators and assigns," against loss by fire, which provides that it shall be void in case "any change takes place in the title, use, occupation or possession thereof whatsoever."

(February 20, 1890.)

APPEAL by plaintiff from a judgment of the Circuit Court for Garrard County in favor of defendant in an action brought to recover the amount alleged to be due under a policy of fire insurance. *Reversed.*

The case sufficiently appears in the opinion.

Messrs. **P. B. Thompson, Sr.,** and **H. C. Kauffman** for appellant.

Mr. **D. S. Clay** for appellee.

Lewis, *Ch. J.*, delivered the opinion of the court:

This is an appeal from a judgment dismissing an action instituted by appellant, administrator of the estate of Joseph Richardson, to recover of appellee value of a dwelling-house and furniture destroyed by fire, which was insured by a policy issued to decedent.

As all other conditions necessary to recover appear, from allegations of the petition, to exist, the single question presented is whether the policy became void and of no effect, upon death of the assured, which occurred before destruction of the property. The policy, dated March 17, 1883, contains the following: "The German Insurance Company, by this policy of insurance, in consideration of two notes for $26.50, do insure Joseph Richardson against loss or damage by fire and lightning, to the amount of $——, on . . . dwelling-house and furniture. . . . And the said Company hereby agree to make good unto the said assured, his executors, administrators and assigns, all such immediate loss or damage, not exceeding in amount the sum insured, nor the interest of the assured in the property, nor the cash value of any building or other property at the time of loss, as shall happen by fire or lightning to the property above specified, from the 10th day of March, 1883, at 12 o'clock, noon, to the 10th day of March, 1888, at 12 o'clock noon, except such portion of the above mentioned period of time as this Company shall hold against the insured any promissory note past due and unpaid in whole or part; and during such portion of time the policy shall be null and void, and so continue till such promissory note is fully paid."

Following provisions in regard to amount of loss and damage to be estimated, and right of the Company to repair or rebuild the property destroyed, and others having no application to this case, is this clause in the policy: "If there is, or shall be, other prior, concurrent or subsequent insurance, whether valid or not, on said property, or on any part thereof, without the Company's consent hereon; or if said building . . . now is, or shall become, vacant or unoccupied; or if the hazard shall be increased in any way; or if the property, or any part thereof, shall be sold, conveyed, incumbered by mortgage or otherwise, or any change takes place in the title, use, occupation or possession thereof, whatever; or if foreclosure proceedings shall be commenced; or if the interest of the insured in said property, or any part thereof, now is, or shall become, any other or less than a perfect legal and equitable title and ownership, free from any lien whatever except as stated in writing hereon; or if the building or buildings stand on leased land, of which the assured has not a perfect title; or if this policy shall be assigned without written consent hereon,—then and in every such case this policy shall be void."

The right was in terms given to the Insurance Company to terminate the policy at any time by giving notice to that effect, and refunding unearned premium, and also to the insured, to be, however, exercised only after full payment of premium.

According to the only meaning we think the language used fairly capable of, the property was insured for a specified period of time, which could, after the premium had been fully paid, be adjudged by the Company only upon notice and refunding the unearned part of the premium; and it agreed to make good unto, not merely the insured himself, but his executors, administrators and assigns, the immediate loss or damage that might happen by fire or lightning to the property at any time during that period, whether before or after his death. And therefore to treat that event as *ipso facto* a termination of the policy and liability under it, would be contrary to the express terms of it, render the stipulation for payment to the personal representative of the insured superfluous, and allow the Company to retain the full consideration paid, while being held to only part performance of its agreement. It is true, as urged, the property might have been destroyed before, though the loss not made good until after, his death; but the stipulation of the Company to pay his personal representative was not necessary to meet such contingency, because the amount due could have in that case been collected without. On the other hand, it is both rational and provident for a person obtaining a policy of fire insurance to have provision in it against destruction of the property after his death; and in such case the stipulation mentioned becomes applicable and necessary. It seems to us the force and effect of language so comprehensive and clear should not be neutralized, or to any extend impaired, by a subsequent forfeiting clause of a policy of insurance, unless the words used for that purpose be so definite, explicit and free from ambiguity as to leave no other reasonable alternative; for, while forfeitures are not favored by the law, and provisions in a contract therefor are always to be strictly construed, the terms of a policy of insurance, as said in *Ætna Ins Co.* v. *Jackson*, 16 B. Mon. 242, should be liberally construed for the benefit of the insured, and so as to effectuate, as far as may reasonably be done, the indemnity he justly expected. It is evident the clause referred to was prepared with care, and a purpose to guard every supposed right and interest of the Company; yet, of the seven distinct causes for forfeiting the policy therein enumerated, not one of them, in express terms or by fair implication, relates to or includes the death of the insured, nor is it anywhere mentioned as a condition or cause for forfeiting or terminating the policy. The only part of the clause which can be construed to have any relation at all is expressed as follows: "Or any change takes place in the title, use, occupation or possession thereof, whatsoever;" and that, we think, does not necessarily or properly refer to a change unavoidably resulting from his death, but rather to such as might be caused or suffered by act of the insured while living, which is the case in each one of the other causes or conditions set forth in the forfeit clause, as well those which precede as those following the one quoted. But, be that as it may, each condition of forfeiture mentioned may, without destroying or lessening its proper meaning or effect, be reconciled with a continuation of the policy after such death to the end of the period; and it therefore should be done, rather than defeat what was elsewhere in the policy clearly provided for.

We have been referred to the cases of *Sherwood* v. *Agricultural Ins. Co.*, 73 N. Y. 447, 29 Am. Rep. 180, and *Wyman* v. *Wyman*, 26 N. Y. 253. The first one has no application to this case, because there a change "by operation of law" was in terms made a cause of forfeiture. The latter involves practically the same question as this case, and the conclusion arrived at is different from what we think is the proper one; for according to rules of construction frequently approved by this court, a forfeiting clause in a contract should never defeat a right previously agreed upon, and provided for, unless the language used, strictly interpreted, requires it. We think a cause of action is stated in the petition; and *the judgment must be reversed, and cause remanded*, with directions to overrule the general demurrer, and for further proceedings consistent with this opinion.

Petition for rehearing overruled.

MISSOURI SUPREME COURT.

BELCHER'S SUGAR REFINING CO., *Respt.*,
v.
ST. LOUIS GRAIN ELEVATOR CO., *Appt.*

(....Mo.....)

1. **The maintenance of an elevator on a public wharf** for handling grain thereat is no new or additional servitude. It is simply a new method of using the wharf for the very purpose for which it was condemned.

2. **A lease of the unpaved portion of a public wharf to an elevator company** for the purpose of maintaining thereon a shed or warehouse for the storage and handling of grain or other merchandise in connection with the use of an elevator is not in excess of the authority of a city, at least when it has express power in its charter to set aside and lease a portion of the unpaved wharf for such purposes, where the right to terminate the lease on six months' notice is reserved, and also the right by ordinance to prescribe regulations governing the business of the lessee.

3. **A shed or warehouse in connection with an elevator** for the storage and handling of grain or other merchandise, which is one of the connecting links between the great land and water common carriers, although it is private property and operated for private gain, is for a public use and has a public trust attached to it, and therefore a lease therefor of part of a public wharf is not void on the ground that the property is to be used for private purposes.

4. **A wharf is unpaved,** within the meaning of a charter allowing the lease of the unpaved portions of wharves, where it is not paved in a manner suitable for wharf purposes, although it had once been paved with irregular stones placed on edge and covered with macadam, but the macadam had been washed away and a dirt roadway made over it by the city, which, with accumulated rubbish, covered the remaining stone to the depth of five or six feet.

5. **The limitation to 500 feet** in the charter of a corporation of its right to acquire and hold land fronting on the river free from condemnation does not apply to its right to occupy property on the city wharves by consent of the city authorities under a further clause which provides that it "may also erect one or more grain elevators upon public wharves."

6. **The right of a corporation to occupy city wharves** with a warehouse connecting

with an elevator for any other purpose than to store and handle grain cannot be questioned by the owner of the fee of the wharf property on the ground that the corporation is exceeding its corporate powers.

(June 2, 1890.)

APPEAL by defendant from a judgment of the Circuit Court for the City of St. Louis in favor of plaintiff in an action brought to enjoin the erection of an elevator warehouse on a public wharf in the City of St. Louis. *Reversed.*

The facts are fully stated in the opinion.

Mr. **James O. Broadhead,** for appellant:

The City of St. Louis had authority under its charter to make the lease of January 7, 1885.

See art. 3, § 26, subd. 2, of the City Charter. See also Cooley, Const. Lim. 2d ed. pp. 521-553; *Moses* v. *Pittsburg, Ft. W. & C. R. Co.* 21 Ill. 522; *West* v. *Bancroft,* 32 Vt. 367; *Kelsey* v. *King,* 32 Barb. 410; *Lexington & O. R. Co.* v. *Applegate,* 8 Dana, 289; *Illinois & St. L. R. & C. Co.* v. *St. Louis,* 2 Dill. 70; *Julia Bldg. Asso.* v. *Bell Teleph. Co.* 5 West. Rep. 357, 88 Mo. 269; Charter of St. Louis Grain Elevator Company, Acts Mo. Legislature 1863, Adjourned Sess. p. 223; Gould, Waters, p. 214, § 118; *Munn* v. *Illinois,* 94 U. S. 113-151 (24 L. ed. 77-93); *Broadway & L. Pt. F. Co.* v. *Hankey,* 31 Md. 348; *Keokuk* v. *Keokuk Northern Line Packet Co.* 45 Iowa, 196, 95 U. S. 80 (24 L. ed. 377); *New Orleans, M. & T. R. Co.* v. *Ellerman,* 105 U. S. 166 (26 L. ed. 1015); *Barney* v. *Keokuk,* 4 Dill. 594.

The St. Louis Grain Elevator Company has full authority under its charter to accept the lease from the City of St. Louis.

See Sess. Acts Mo. Legislature 1863, Adjourned Sess. p. 223.

But if such act of acceptance is *ultra vires,* the plaintiff has no right to complain.

See *New Orleans, M. & T. R. Co.* v. *Ellerman,* 105 U. S. 174 (26 L. ed. 1017).

Mr. **Smith P. Galt** for respondent.

Black, *J.,* delivered the opinion of the court:

This is a suit to enjoin the defendant from erecting and maintaining a shed or warehouse for the storage of grain or other merchandise upon the wharf of the City of St. Louis. The circuit court on the first trial dismissed the petition, but the judgment was reversed, and the cause remanded, by this court. 82 Mo. 121. Pending that appeal the defendant erected the warehouse. The second trial resulted in a decree for the plaintiff requiring the defendant to remove the buildings, and restore the ground so that it might be used as a wharf.

The plaintiff is a corporation organized under the laws of this State; and the defendant, the St. Louis Grain Elevator Company, was organized under the special Act of December 18, 1863, the 3d section of which provides:

"The corporation hereby created shall have power to acquire, by purchase or otherwise, any real estate in the City of St. Louis, fronting on the Mississippi River, not exceeding 500 feet frontage on the same in any one locality. The real estate so obtained by this corporation shall not be subject to condemnation for any purpose so long as the same shall be used for grain elevators, and uses connected therewith; and the said corporation may also erect one or more grain elevators upon the public wharves of the City of St. Louis, with the consent and under the direction of the constituted authorities of the same." The elevators are to be so constructed as to give railroads a trackway through the same, and so as "to accommodate the river interests, giving all requisite facilities for the elevating and storing grain in bulk or otherwise, and so as not to interfere with or obstruct the navigation of the river. No provision of this charter shall be construed to interfere with the right of the city to collect wharfage within the city limits." Besides the general powers to establish and regulate public wharves and docks, and to collect wharfage, the Charter of the City of St. Louis of 1876 provides that the mayor and assembly shall have power, by ordinance, "to set aside and lease portions of the unpaved wharf for special purposes, such as the erection of sheds, elevators and warehouses, and for railroad tracks, for quay places for the loading of lumber for mills, for cotton presses, for manufactories, and for any purpose tending to facilitate the trade of the city; but no permit to use any portion of the wharf, or any lease of the same, shall be granted for a term exceeding fifty years."

The city, by an ordinance approved the 6th of August, 1864, established a wharf, "as a public highway for wharf purposes," along the river front from Biddle Street to the northern boundary of the city. The streets passed, going north from Biddle, are Ashley, O'Fallon, Bates, etc. City block 226 lies between Ashley and O'Fallon Streets, and city block 225 lies between O'Fallon and Bates Streets. Both of these blocks are bounded on the west by Lewis Street, and, at the date of the ordinance establishing the wharf, extended east to the river, a distance of about 300 feet. The wharf, as established by the ordinance, was opened under condemnation proceedings instituted by the city in 1867; and by virtue of these proceedings the city comdemned the greater portion of the above-designated blocks, leaving only a strip along Lewis Street having a width of 80 feet. The plaintiff owned a large portion of both of these blocks, the parts owned by it extending from Lewis Street to the river, and received as a compensation for that part which was condemned the sum of $21,643. Before the institution of this suit the plaintiff had acquired additional property in these blocks, so that, at the commencement of the suit, it owned 180 feet front on Lewis Street in block 226, the whole front of that block being 215 feet. On this property, and that owned by plaintiff in block 225, there are coal-sheds, and other buildings used in connection with the refining works. Plaintiff also owns several blocks of ground on the west side of Lewis Street, with large buildings thereon, wherein it carries on its business of refining sugar. The business is extensive, and it is estimated that 75,000 tons of sugar are received annually from boats which are unloaded at the city wharf. The defendant, on and prior to the 18th of August, 1879, owned and operated an elevator which had been built, under its charter, upon the river front, and extended southwardly from the south line of Ashley Street for a distance of 500 feet. On the last-mentioned date the proper city officers, in conformity with an ordinance dated the 8th of August, 1879, leased to defendant 90 by 298 feet of the wharf, extending along the waterline from the south line of Ashley Street northward to O'Fallon, the part thus leased being the entire river landing in front of block 226, and including the foot of Ashley Street extended. This lease was for the term of twenty years, upon an annual rental of $300, and provided that the leased premises should be used by the Elevator Company "for erecting and maintaining thereon a shed or warehouse for storage and handling of grain or other merchandise in connection with the use of the elevator."

On the foregoing state of facts the circuit court dismissed the plaintiff's bill, but that judgment was reversed, and the cause remanded, by this court. Thereafter the city passed an ordinance approved December 10, 1884; and in compliance with and in pursuance to this ordinance the defendant surrendered the prior lease, and the proper city authorities executed to it a new one, covering the same portion of the wharf, for a period of fifteen years, upon the same rental and for the same purpose, save that the new lease contains these additional stipulations: "The City of St. Louis reserves the right to cancel this lease on six months' notice in writing to the lessee, whenever it shall elect to pave and extend the wharf on the premises mentioned aforesaid. The buildings and structures placed on the said premises by the lessee, and the said premises, shall during the term of this lease be used by the lessee for the storage and handling and loading and unloading of grain and merchandise, and the loading and unloading of boats and barges and vessels and railroad cars engaged in carrying the same, and for no other purpose. The City of St. Louis shall retain control over the buildings and structures placed on said grounds by said lessee, and over the use of the same by said lessee, and over the ground covered by this lease, and may at any time, by ordinance, prescribe regulations governing the same, and the business of the said lessee. The defendant, by an amended answer, set up this new lease, and now justifies under it.

1. The plaintiff insists that the last lease is as objectionable as the first one, while the defendant insists that it was made in exact conformity to the rulings of this court on the former hearing. The property in question was condemned for wharf purposes, and it cannot be appropriated to a different and inconsistent use; nor can it, or any part thereof, be disposed of by the city for private purposes. These general propositions were asserted in strong terms when the case was here before. They are again contended for on the one side, and conceded on the other, so that on these points additional observations are unnecessary. The principal and important inquiry presented by this record is twofold: *first*, whether the maintenance of the building upon the wharf to be used, in connection with the defendant's elevator, for storing and handling grain and merchandise, and for loading and unloading boats and railroad cars carrying such freight, is a use incident to a public wharf; *second*, whether the erection and maintenance of the structure in this case is for private purposes only, and an illegal use of the wharf for that reason. In respect of these questions, as this case stood on the old lease, this court said:

"In order to meet the demands of commerce, and the changed methods of handling grain and other produce, the city may license the erection of elevators and warehouses in connection with them, upon the unpaved portion of the wharf, without violating the rights of the owners of the fee; but she has no right to lease any portion of it for a term of years without a reservation of the right to cancel the lease whenever it should become necessary to pave and extend the wharf so leased." And further on it is said: "There is no reservation by the city, in the lease to defendant, of any control whatever of the building or business. The property is conveyed away from the city for twenty years; and if, at any time within that period, it should become necessary to extend the wharf and pave it in front of the block in question, the needed work could not be done. The city has no right, and can acquire none from the Legislature, to make such a disposition of the property condemned for wharf purposes as will prevent her, in the event it becomes necessary to extend and pave the wharf, from doing its duty in that respect." 82 Mo. 126, 127.

In *Illinois & St. L. R. & C. Co.* v. *St. Louis*, 2 Dill. 70, the City of St. Louis had, by ordinance passed and approved in 1872, leased 150 by 600 feet of the wharf to the Pacific Elevator Company for a period of fifty years, with no reserved rights to cancel the same. The ordinance was held to be illegal because it set aside to the exclusive use of the elevator company the leased portion of the wharf for fifty years, and that the city had no right or power to thus tie up its hands in disregard of the future wants of the public. This was the principal ground upon which the ordinance was held to be invalid. The City of St. Louis then had general power to erect, repair and regulate wharves; but it had no express authority, as it now has, to set aside and lease portions of the wharf for elevator and warehouse purposes. The want of such express authority constitutes the substructure of the whole opinion. Though the city had but general powers to establish, repair and regulate wharves, yet *Judge* Dillon makes these pertinent and forcible observations: "The dedication of the property was perpetual, and for the benefit of the public. The extent of the dedication—its scope—remains the same, but the mode of using property dedicated for a wharf may change from time to time as the wants of commerce or the public may require; and this the dedicator is presumed to contemplate when he makes the dedication. . . . A wharf is intended to afford convenience for the landing of vessels, the loading or unloading of their cargoes and to supply a place on which the wares discharged from vessels, or awaiting shipment, may be laid or deposited; and it would seem that structures or appliances of any kind intended, and which have the effect, to facilitate the handling and preservation of merchandise arriving at the wharf, erected upon it under municipal authority, and remaining at all times subject to municipal control, would be lawful, and within the purposes for which the wharf property was acquired or dedicated. . . . And we are clearly of opinion that the erection, under the sanction of the city, of an elevator to be used in handling grain at the wharf, and at all times under the direction and control of the municipal authorities, is such a use of wharf property as does not fall without the scope of dedication; and such a structure would not therefore be a public nuisance."

In *Barney* v. *Keokuk*, 4 Dill. 593, affirmed in 94 U. S. 325 [24 L. ed. 224], a strip of land along the river margin had been dedicated to public use for a street, and the plaintiff owned two lots fronting thereon. The City of Keokuk widened the street in front of plaintiff's lots by filling in stone and earth for a space of about 200 feet. A packet company leased from the city a portion of the street thus widened, for wharf purposes, for ten years, and erected thereon, at the waterline, a building for its own use, for storing merchandise for the convenience of shippers and for its own offices, but was not allowed to make storage charges. There was also a railroad freight depot on that part of the street next to plaintiff's lots. It was held that the railroad freight depot was an unauthorized and improper use of the street, but that the packet-company depot was a necessary and proper use of the landing and wharf.

There is a wide difference between a street and a wharf. Wharves on our rivers are not only ways for traveling, but they are necessarily used for the deposit of merchandise. The products of the soil and of the manufactories find there legitimate place of temporary deposit, whether outgoing or incoming. There can be no doubt but a city, having only a general power to establish and regulate wharves, may erect sheds and warehouses thereon to protect such property from damage and theft, and the wharfage charges may be proportioned to the accommodations afforded. So, too, the maintenance of an elevator on a public wharf for handling grain thereat is no new or additional burden or servitude. It is simply a new method for using the wharf for the very purposes for which it was condemned or dedicated. There is no reason or sound law for holding that the old method of shipping grain in sacks, and covering them up while on the wharf with tarpaulins, must be continued. Elevators not only furnish a cheaper, better and more rapid method of handling grain, but they economize wharf space, and are to be commended, rather than condemned.

This much has been said concerning warehouses and grain elevators because the structure in question, though used in connection with the defendant's elevator, is used for handling grain and other merchandise, and performs the duties of both a warehouse and an elevator. The erection and maintenance of such a structure is a proper and legitimate use of a portion of a public wharf, when used in handling property going to and from the same. The cases cited from 2 and 4 Dillon justify the conclusion that the city may permit such a structure to be erected and used under a general power to erect, repair and regulate wharves, and to collect wharfage, provided the structure and business is at all times under the control of the municipal legislature; and for a much stronger reason may this be done when, as here, the city has express power to set aside and lease portions of the unpaved wharf for such purposes. We do not say that the State has the power to confer upon the city the right to turn the wharf to purely private uses, or to charge it with burdens not contemplated by the condemnation, without additional compensation; but there is a wide field over which the Legislature is supreme. and many structures may be justified under legislative sanction which would otherwise be a nuisance.

The lease considered on the former occasion was for twenty years, without any right on the part of the city to terminate it should the public wants demand such action; and there were no other reserved rights save that of collecting wharfage from boats landing at the leased premises. The city has the right to terminate the lease now in question, on six months' notice, whenever it shall elect to pave and extend the wharf on the leased ground; and it is also provided that the city may by ordinance prescribe regulations governing the business of defendant. It is to be remembered that the city has miles of what is denominated "unimproved wharf;" and it would be a remarkable state of affairs if portions thereof cannot be used for warehouse and elevator purposes, and especially so in view of the fact that they are proper adjuncts to a wharf.

In *Broadway & L. Pt. F. Co.* v. *Hankey*, 31 Md. 347, the Legislature conferred upon the ferry company, not the exclusive right of ferrying across the harbor, but the exclusive right of using a designated end of the wharf. The Act was upheld, and the exclusive right of the company to the particular part of the wharf enforced. The power of the Legislature to set apart portions of these public places for designated purposes is illustrated by the case of *New Orleans, M. & T. R. Co.* v. *Ellerman*, 105 U. S. 166 [26 L. ed. 1015]. The present lease is so framed as to enable the city at all times to keep within its charter powers, and there can be no doubt but the lease on its face is valid, and a proper exercise of the charter powers of the City of St. Louis.

The next question is whether the lease is

void on the ground that the property is to be used for private purposes. According to the plain words of the charter of the Elevator Company, railroads are to have a connection with, and a track through, any elevator erected by it; and the elevator is to be so constructed as to accommodate the river interests, giving all requisite facilities for elevating and storing grain in bulk or otherwise. The elevator, it will be seen, is made one of the connecting links between the great land and water common carriers. The defendant can show no favoritism between railroads, nor as between different vessels. It must treat all alike, and is bound by its charter to afford requisite facilities to all. This is the plain meaning of the charter, and there is no escaping it. As we understand the evidence, there is a railroad track constructed through the building now in question. The powers granted to and duties imposed upon the Elevator Company, of themselves, show that the property of the Company is clothed with, and has attached to it, a public trust. Just like a railroad or a steam-boat, the property is private, and it is operated for private gain; but the use is public. It is true the defendant is entitled to collect compensation for handling grain and other merchandise, and so may a railroad or steam-boat establish rates and collect compensation for transporting persons and property. The wharf itself is not absolutely free; for the city has the right to make reasonable wharf charges, and so may the defendant make reasonable charges when performing wharf duties. But it is said the city has no control over the charges which defendant may make. If this Elevator Company has, as we hold, engaged to execute a public trust, then it is subject to public regulations, and the State may prescribe regulations even as to the charges. *Munn* v. *Illinois*, 94 U. S. 113 [24 L. ed. 77].

Whether the State has delegated the power to the city to regulate charges is a matter of no consequence to the present inquiry. It is enough to know that the combined elevator and warehouse is erected and maintained to aid in carrying on business which has a public trust attached to it, and a business which may be properly conducted at and upon the wharf.

2. The city charter powers in question are "to set aside and lease portions of the unpaved wharf for special purposes, such as the erection of sheds, elevators and warehouses;" but the permit or lease must not exceed the term of fifty years. The contention is that the portion of the wharf leased to the defendant was not an unpaved portion thereof, and for this reason the lease is unauthorized by the charter. There is a diversity of opinion among the witnesses as to what is meant by "paved." Some of them say it means stone cut in parallelograms, and laid in sand; and they call irregular stone set on edge, and then covered with macadam, "riprapping." Others regard the latter as a pavement when laid upon a street or wharf. "Pavement" is a generic term, and includes many species. It may be of wood, brick, stone, iron, or of many other substances. 2 Dill. Mun. Corp. 3d ed. § 796, and *note*.

A pavement is not limited to uniformly arranged masses of solid material, as blocks of wood, brick or stone; but it may be as well formed of pebbles or gravel, or other hard substance, which makes a compact, even, hard way or floor. *Burnham* v. *Chicago*, 24 Ill. 499.

There can be no doubt but macadam is a species of pavement, and may well be called a pavement. But, whether we are considering an agreement or statute, the great object is to get at its true meaning. Here the charter is speaking of a particular wharf, namely, that of the City of St. Louis; and it may well be read in the light of the facts as they existed when it was adopted. We say "adopted," because it was framed and approved by the qualified voters of the City of St. Louis under constitutional authority It seems the wharf from Biddle Street soutn to Chouteau Avenue was and is paved with stone fashioned to parallelograms, and placed so as to form a convenient place for loading and unloading cargoes, and so as to resist the pressure of heavily-loaded vehicles. Other portions were in a state of nature. In 1871 or 1872 the city graded that portion now in question from the railroad tracks to the water, and paved it with irregular stone, placed on edge, covered with macadam. It was used by a stone company for unloading their barges in 1873, but the high water washed away the macadam, and in 1874 the city built a scavenger dump thereon; and it was used for that purpose until 1879, the date of the first lease to the defendant. A dirt roadway to the dump, made by the city and accumulated rubbish, covered the remaining stone to a depth of five or six feet. The plaintiff never received any sugar or other freight at this place, and the evidence is that it was always too steep and narrow for a boat landing. Paved portions of the wharf cannot be set aside and leased for warehouse and elevator purposes, but the exemption applies to that part which is paved in a manner suitable for wharf purposes,—for landing and receiving passengers, or for loading and unloading freight. It is perfectly plain that the part of the wharf in question was in no such a condition. For all purposes of a wharf, it was unpaved, and could, under the provisions of the charter, be leased for warehouse or elevator purposes.

3. The defendant at the date of the lease held and occupied 500 feet south from the south line of Ashley Street, and the lease in question covers a strip 298 feet long adjoining and to the north thereof; and the contention is that by defendant's charter it can only occupy 500 feet at any one place. The 3d section of defendant's charter has been set out in the statement of this case. This charter was enacted before the city extended its wharves by condemnation, and the design of the Legislature seems to have been to allow the defendant to own 500 feet exempt from condemnation. After giving the defendant the right to acquire and hold 500 feet fronting on the river free from condem-

nation for any purpose, the section goes on to say: "The said corporation may also erect one or more grain elevators upon the public wharves of the City of St. Louis," with the consent of the city authorities. The limitation is as to the amount of river front which the Company may hold exempt from condemnation, but it does not apply to any property which it may occupy on the city wharves by consent of the city authorities. This, we are convinced, is the true meaning of that limitation.

4. The defendant's charter gives to it the right to handle and store grain in bulk or in any other way, and the lease in question contemplates that the structure will be used, not only for such purposes, but for the purpose of handling and storing merchandise; and the latter, it is urged, is beyond the defendant's charter powers. For all the purposes of the present inquiry, it will be assumed, but not decided, that the defendant's charter does not authorize it to store and handle property other than grain. We have seen that the city, under its charter, has a perfect right to set apart and lease to natural persons this portion of the wharf for the very purposes for which it has been leased to the defendant. The plaintiff, though the owner of the fee, has no right to complain because the property is used for a warehouse and elevator. No rights of the plaintiff have been invaded, and the complaint is simply this: that the defendant corporation is acting *ultra vires*. The defendant's stockholders and the State may complain, but the plaintiff cannot base a cause of action alone on any such ground. He must show that some duty owing to him is being violated before he can maintain this suit because the defendant is exceeding its charter powers. The case of *New Orleans, M. & T. R. Co.* v. *Ellerman*, 105 U. S. 166 [26 L. ed. 1015], is to the point, and disposes of this question.

The ultimate question in this case is whether the lease in question is valid,—whether the city authorities had the right, under the charter, to make the contract in the lease expressed. The question is one of vast importance to the commercial interests of the City of St. Louis, and it has been most thoroughly presented on both sides; and it is our opinion that the lease is valid, and that plaintiff has no just ground of complaint. The property is being used for the very purpose for which it was condemned, and full compensation paid.

The judgment is reversed, and the cause remanded, with directions to the Circuit Court to dismiss the bill. Costs of this appeal, and costs accruing since the filing of the amended answer setting up the second lease, should be taxed to plaintiff, the prior costs to defendant.

Brace, *J.*, absent. The other Judges concur.

WISCONSIN SUPREME COURT.

Christian HORSCH, *Respt.*,
v.
DWELLING HOUSE INSURANCE CO.
Appt.

(....Wis.....)

A man has an insurable interest in buildings on land purchased and paid for by him though conveyed to his wife, where he has in fact possession and the entire beneficial use of the premises and is the owner of all the personal property thereon, managing the place on his own account and using the proceeds to support the family, while there is an understanding between him and his wife that she will convey the land to him at his request.

(May 20, 1890.)

APPEAL by defendant from a judgment of the Circuit Court for Brown County in favor of plaintiff in an action brought to recover the amount alleged to be due under a policy of fire insurance. *Affirmed.*

The facts are sufficiently stated in the opinion.

Messrs. **Vroman & Sole,** for appellant:

The plaintiff had no insurable interest in the buildings. They were erected with the intent that they should be permanent improvements upon the land; this made them fixtures.

Huebschmann v. *McHenry*, 29 Wis. 655; *Taylor* v. *Collins*, 51 Wis. 123.

The land belongs to plaintiff's wife. Her ownership of it is as absolute, and as free from the plaintiff's control, as though she were unmarried.

Wis. Rev. Stat. chap. 108; *Oatman* v. *Goodrich*, 15 Wis. 592; *Beard* v. *Dedolph*, 29 Wis. 141; *McKesson* v. *Stanton*, 50 Wis. 302.

In *Agricultural Ins. Co.* v. *Montague*, 38 Mich. 551, silverware belonging to the wife was covered by a policy to the husband. The court held that he could not recover the loss on the silver, because he had no interest in or control over the wife's property.

An interest in property to be insurable must be definite, fixed and specific, the loss of which will be a direct pecuniary loss to its owner. It must be a legal or equitable interest or such as the courts will recognize and protect in any proper judicial proceeding where it becomes involved.

Grevemeyer v. *Southern Mut. F. Ins. Co.* 62 Pa. 340; *Bayles* v. *Hillsborough Ins. Co.* 27 N. J. L. 163; *Howard* v. *Albany Ins. Co.* 3 Denio, 303; *Baldwin* v. *State Ins. Co.* 60 Iowa, 497; *Murdock* v. *Chenango Co. Mut. Ins. Co.* 2 N. Y. 210.

Messrs. **Hudd, Wigman & Martin,** for respondent:

Plaintiff had an insurable interest. He bought the land, paid for it, built the buildings on it. He was occupying the buildings with his family. He was interested in their preservation. He was damaged by their loss.

Lucena v. *Craufurd*, 2 Bos. & P. N. R. 269; *King* v. *State Mut. F. Ins. Co.* 7 Cush. 10; Ang. & A. Ins. § 56.

Interest does not necessarily imply property.

See also 36 L. R. A. 374.

An insurable interest may be proven in the assured without evidence of any legal or equitable title in the property.

Ang. & A. *supra; Putnam* v. *Mercantile M. Ins. Co.* 5 Met. 386; *Lazarus* v. *Com. Ins. Co.* 19 Pick. 81, 98, 2 Am. Lead. Cas. 80, and *note.*

Injury from its loss or benefit from its preservation to accrue to the assured may be sufficient, and a contingent interest then arising may be made the subject of a policy.

Hooper v. *Robinson*, 98 U. S. 528 (25 L. ed. 219). See *Hancox* v. *Fishing Ins. Co.* 3 Sumn. 132; *Trade Ins. Co.* v. *Barracliff*, 45 N. J. L. 543; *Merrett* v. *Farmers Ins. Co.* 42 Iowa, 13; 1 Phillips, Ins. §§ 175, 342, 346; Flanders, Ins. 342; *Warren* v. *Davenport F. Ins. Co.* 31 Iowa, 464; *Springfield F. & M. Ins. Co.* v. *Allen*, 43 N. Y. 395, 396; *Herkimer* v. *Rice*, 27 N. Y. 163; *Williams* v. *Roger Williams Ins. Co.* 107 Mass. 377–379.

The plaintiff, living on the place and occupying the buildings with his wife and children, who looked to him for their support, had an insurable interest in the buildings.

Wood, Ins. § 288; *Franklin M. & F. Ins. Co.* v. *Drake*, 2 B. Mon. 47; *Mutual F. Ins. Co.* v. *Deale*, 18 Md. 26; *Harris* v. *York Mut. Ins. Co.* 50 Pa. 341; *Trade Ins. Co.* v. *Barracliff*, 45 N. J. L. 543; *Merrett* v. *Farmers Ins. Co.* 42 Iowa, 11.

He had not only an insurable interest; he had also an equitable estate recognized by courts of law and equity.

Kirby v. *Sisson*, 1 Wend. 83; *Tyler* v. *Ætna F. Ins. Co.* 12 Wend. 507; *Lazarus* v. *Com. Ins. Co.* 19 Pick. 81, 2 Am. Lead. Cas. 809; *Redfield* v. *Holland Purchase Ins. Co.* 56 N. Y. 357; *Dreutzer* v. *Lawrence*, 58 Wis. 594; *Brown's App.* 94 Pa. 362, 367; *Love* v. *Watkins*, 40 Cal. 547, 6 Am. Rep. 624; *Spafford* v. *Warren*, 47 Iowa, 47–51; *Baker* v. *Hathaway*, 5 Allen, 103–105; *Kingsley* v. *Gilman*, 15 Minn. 59–61.

Taylor, *J.*, delivered the opinion of the court:

This is an action to recover damages upon a fire insurance policy. The policy insured the plaintiff against loss by fire upon a dwelling-house, several barns, household furniture, wearing apparel, farming implements, grain and hay. The policy was issued June 4, 1888, and a fire occurred August 30, 1888, destroying most of the property insured. On the trial in the circuit court the plaintiff recovered $140 for the loss of personal property insured, and $725 for the loss on the insured buildings. The defendant only appeals from that part of the judgment which gave the plaintiff $725 for loss on the insured buildings. The only ground stated by the appellant for reversing the judgment as to the part appealed from is that it claims the plaintiff had no insurable interest in the buildings destroyed, either at the time the policy was issued, or at the time of the loss.

The evidence on the trial shows that, some years before the policy of insurance was issued to the plaintiff, he bought the land on which the insured buildings were located from one Charles Rogers, and paid for it with his own money, and by his direction Rogers conveyed the land to his wife. The house was on the land at the time he purchased it. Plaintiff built the barns himself, made all the other improvements on the farm at his own expense, took actual possession thereof with his family, and cultivated the land at his own expense and on his own account, and had the entire and sole management of the farm. The proceeds of the farm were used to support the family. This was done with the consent of the wife. There was an understanding between the plaintiff and his wife that she would deed the farm to him at his request. All the stock, farm implements, household furniture and other personal property on the farm were the property of the plaintiff. This was the situation of affairs when the policy was issued, and when the fire occurred. It was also proved that at the time the policy was issued, and delivered to the plaintiff, the agent who issued the same was informed that the title to the land was in the wife.

Upon this state of facts, we think it is very clear that the plaintiff had an insurable interest in the house and barns at the time the policy was issued, as well as at the time of the fire. The actual possession and beneficial use of the farm were in the plaintiff, with the full consent of the wife, at the time the policy was issued as well as at the time of the loss. There can be no doubt, therefore, but that the plaintiff had a pecuniary and valuable interest in the property insured and destroyed, and therefore an insurable interest. The possession and use of the house and barns was of the utmost importance to him in providing a support for himself and family, and their destruction was substantially as disastrous to him in his endeavors to support himself and family as though he had the actual title. He had in fact the possession and the entire beneficial use, of which he was deprived by their destruction. The actual possession and use of property is a valuable right and it is especially valuable when held with the permission of the real owner. It has even been held that a disseisor who is in peaceable possession, after having ousted the real owner, has an insurable interest without regard to the question of actual ownership, especially when the disseisor has acted in good faith, believing he had the right to such possession. See cases hereafter cited.

It seems very clear to us that a person in the actual possession and use of real property for his personal benefit, with the assent of the real owner, stands in a much better position, and has a pecuniary interest much more valuable, than a mere disseisor in possession holding adversely to the real owner. What constitutes an insurable interest, so as to take the case out of the law prohibiting wager policies, is not very clearly defined, and it is difficult to lay down any general rule applicable to all cases. Flanders, in his work on Insurance, says: "But an 'insurable interest' does not rigorously mean that the assured must have an absolute right of property in the thing insured. If he has a special, limited interest, or if he would suffer any disadvantage by the destruction of the premises, or any reasonable expectation of profit would be thereby defeated, he may protect or indemnify himself by insurance. . . . In a word, if the party insured has any interest that would be injured in the event that the peril insured against should happen, the courts will maintain his policy." Flanders, Ins. 377.

Wood, in his work on Insurance, says: "It is not necessary that the assured should have either a legal or equitable interest, or indeed any property interest, in the subject matter insured. It is enough if he holds such a relation to the property that its destruction by the peril insured against involves pecuniary loss to him, or those for whom he acts." 1 Wood, Ins. § 281, p. 645.

May, in his work on Insurance, says: "An insurable interest is *sui generis*, and peculiar in its texture and operation. It sometimes exists when there is not any present property. . . . Yet such a connection must be established between the subject matter insured, and the party in whose behalf the insurance has been effected, as may be sufficient for the purpose of deducing the existence of a loss to him from the occurrence of an injury to it." Again he says: "When a man is so circumstanced with respect to matters exposed to risks or dangers as to have a moral certainty of advantage or benefit but for those risks or dangers, he may be said to be interested in the safety of the thing." Parts of §§ 76, 77.

These statements of what is an insurable interest have been considered, discussed and approved in such an almost endless number of cases that we shall content ourselves with citing a few of them, which were cases based upon facts analogous to the facts in the case at bar: *Redfield* v. *Holland Purchase Ins. Co.* 56 N. Y. 354; *Farmers L. & T. Co.* v. *Harmony F. & M. Ins. Co.* 51 Barb. 33; *Strong* v. *Manufacturers Ins. Co.* 10 Pick. 40; *Putnam* v. *Mercantile M. Ins. Co.* 5 Met. 386; *Springfield F. & M. Ins. Co.* v. *Allen*, 43 N. Y. 389; *Eastern R. Co.* v. *Relief F. Ins. Co.* 98 Mass. 420; *Trade Ins. Co.* v. *Barracliff*, 45 N. J. L. 543; *Harris* v. *New York Mut. Ins. Co.* 50 Pa. 341; *Merrett* v. *Farmers Ins. Co.* 42 Iowa, 11; *American Cent. Ins. Co.* v. *McLanathan*, 11 Kan. 533; *Goulstone* v. *Royal Ins. Co.* 1 Fost. & F. 276; *Williams* v. *Roger Williams Ins. Co.* 107 Mass. 377–379; *Cohn* v. *Virginia F. & M. Ins. Co.* 3 Hughes (U. S.) 272; *Rohrbach* v. *Germania F. Ins. Co.* 62 N. Y. 54; *Travis* v. *Continental Ins. Co.* 32 Mo. App. 198–206; *Amsinck* v. *New England Mut. Ins. Co.* 129 Mass. 185, 186.

The cases above cited are quite sufficient to show that the objection taken by the learned counsel for the appellant, that the evidence in the case at bar does not show that the plaintiff had an insurable interest in the house and barns, is wholly unsupported by principle or authority.

Whether the insurance might be held valid on the ground that the insurer had full knowledge of the state of the title when the policy was issued, and he must therefore be held to have intended to insure the property in the name of the plaintiff for the benefit of the real owner, and that plaintiff may be considered as having insured as the agent of his wife, and for her benefit, as well as for his own, need not be decided in this case. Upon this point, see *Harris* v. *New York Mut. Ins. Co.* and *American Cent. Ins. Co.* v. *McLanathan*, *supra*. The judgment of the circuit court was clearly right.

That part of the judgment appealed from is affirmed.

CITY OF JANESVILLE *et al.*, *Respts.*,
v.
Edwin F. CARPENTER, *Appt.*

(....Wis.....)

1. **An injunction cannot be granted against the erection of a building** upon piles in the bed of a river on defendant's own land which will not damage anyone, merely because others may follow defendant's example and a row of similar buildings may be erected which may give rise to dangers from fire and flood and to the public health.

2. **A complaint for an injunction does not charge facts sufficient** to state any cause of action by an allegation that a building on defendant's premises which is sought to be enjoined will cause the water to set back on complainant's premises "to some extent."

3. **Some special injury or necessity** to protect the rights of some person is necessary as a basis of an injunction.

4. **Wrong without damage** or damage without wrong does not constitute a cause of private action.

5. **That a building will violate an ordinance** will not of itself give cause of action for an injunction.

6. **A statute making it unlawful for the owner of ground** having the right to use it to drive piles into it anywhere within a river for any purpose prevents the lawful use of his property and takes it away from him without compensation or due process of law, and denies him the equal protection of the law.

7. **The enactment of a statute is a usurpation of judicial power** where it adjudicates an act unlawful and presumptively injurious and dangerous which is not and cannot be made to be so without a violation of constitutional rights, and where it imperatively commands the court to enjoin such action without proof that any injury or danger has been or will be caused by it.

8. **A statute violates the essential spirit, purpose and intent of the Constitution,** and is contrary to public justice, where it declares that it shall be unlawful within the limits of a single county to drive piles, etc., in a river which flows through other counties also, and gives only to resident taxpayers and owners or

NOTE.—*Right to use of one's own property.*

A person cannot be restrained from making a reasonable improvement on his own premises, upon the ground that it cannot be made without endangering an edifice erected on the adjacent premises, if the owner of the adjacent premises does not possess any special privileges protecting him from the consequences of such improvement, either by prescription or by grant from the person making the improvement, or from those under whom he claims title. Simmons v. Camden, 26 Ark. 276; Lasala v. Holbrook, 4 Paige, 169, 3 N. Y. Ch. L. ed. 390. See Simmons v. Camden, 26 Ark. 276.

A man may do many things under a lawful authority, or on his own land, which may result in an injury to the property of others, without being answerable for the consequences. Radcliff v. Brooklyn, 4 N. Y. 195.

A person may build a house and make cellars upon his soil, whereby a house in the adjoining soil falls down. Radcliff v. Brooklyn, 4 N. Y. 201, 53 Am. Dec. 361; Auburn & C. Pl. Road Co. v. Douglass, 9 N. Y. 448; Payne v. Western & A. R. Co. 13

lessees of the right to use water of said river for a mill or factory within said county the right to an injunction against the prohibited acts without proof that any injury or danger has been or will be caused thereby.

(June 21, 1890.)

APPEAL by defendant from an order of the Circuit Court for Rock County denying a motion to dissolve an injunction restraining defendant from proceeding to erect a building over Rock River. *Reversed.*

The case is fully stated in the opinion.

Messrs. **Winans & Hyzer**, for appellant:

The plaintiff City of Janesville could not maintain an action for an injunction for a threatened injury to a highway, or for threatened injury to property or buildings in said City.

Milwaukee v. *Milwaukee & B. R. Co.* 7 Wis. 85; *Sheboygan* v. *Sheboygan & F. du L. R. Co.* 21 Wis. 668.

If this be intended to be an action to prevent a public nuisance which would result in private or special injury peculiar to the plaintiffs, the complaint should show that the threatened acts would constitute a public nuisance, and should further show that the plaintiffs are likely to sustain private or special injury peculiar to themselves from such public nuisance.

Walker v. *Shepardson*, 2 Wis. 384, 4 Wis. 486; *Greene* v. *Nunnemacher*, 36 Wis. 50; *Carpenter* v. *Mann*, 17 Wis. 156; *Enos* v. *Hamilton*, 27 Wis. 256; *Barnes* v. *Racine*, 4 Wis. 454; *Newell* v. *Smith*, 23 Wis. 261; *Remington* v. *Foster*, 42 Wis. 608; *Larson* v. *Furlong*, 50 Wis. 681.

Chapter 423 of the Laws of 1887 is void in that:

1. It takes private property without compensation.

See *State* v. *Carpenter*, 68 Wis. 165; *A. C. Conn Co.* v. *Little Suamico Lumber Mfg. Co.* 74 Wis. 652; *Jones* v. *Pettibone*, 2 Wis. 320; *Walker* v. *Shepardson*, 4 Wis. 508; *Diedrich* v. *Northwestern U. R. Co.* 42 Wis. 264; *State* v. *St. Croix Boom Corp.* 60 Wis. 570; *Yates* v. *Milwaukee*, 77 U. S. 10 Wall. 497 (19 L. ed. 984).

Whenever the use of land is restricted in any way, or some incorporeal hereditament is taken away, which was appurtenant thereto, it constitutes as much a taking as if the land itself had been appropriated.

Tiedeman, Pol. Powers, § 121*d*, p. 397; *Pumpelly* v. *Green Bay & M. Canal Co.* 80 U. S. 13 Wall. 166 (20 L. ed. 557); *Wynehamer* v. *People*, 13 N. Y. 378; *People* v. *Otis*, 90 N. Y. 48; *Hutton* v. *Camden*, 39 N. J. L. 122; *Durkee* v. *Janesville*, 28 Wis. 464; *Calder* v. *Bull*, 3 U. S. 3 Dall. 387 (1 L. ed. 648); *Varner* v. *Martin*, 21 W. Va. 548; *Tyler* v. *Wilkinson*, 4 Mason, 397; *A. C. Conn Co.* v. *Little Suamico Lumber Mfg. Co.* 74 Wis. 657; *Stadler* v. *Grieden*, 61 Wis. 500; *Bigelow* v. *Hartford Bridge Co.* 14 Conn. 565.

2. It is not an exercise of the police power.

Tiedeman, Pol. Powers, § 122, p. 423; *Taylor* v. *State*, 35 Wis. 298; *Donnelly* v. *Decker*, 58 Wis. 461; *Re Jacobs*, 98 N. Y. 98; *Yates* v. *Milwaukee*, 77 U. S. 10 Wall. 487 (19 L. ed. 984); *Watertown* v. *Mayo*, 109 Mass. 315; Sedgwick, Stat. and Const. Law, 2d ed. p. 151.

3. It is discriminating and class legislation.

Durkee v. *Janesville*, 28 Wis. 464.

4. It is an attempted infringement of the judicial power.

Ervine's App. 16 Pa. 256.

Messrs. **Joseph B. Doe, Jr.**, and **William Ruger** for respondents.

Orton, *J.*, delivered the opinion of the court:

It is charged in the complaint as follows: Many years since a building known as the "Myers Building" was erected on the southerly side of and adjoining Milwaukee Street Bridge, in the City of Janesville, over the center of Rock River, as the same flowed in its natural state. Said building is 40 feet in width, and is supported by large stone piers resting on the bed of said river, and which have so obstructed its flow as to cause a large sandbar to form in said river, near to and on the down-stream side of the building. Within the period of three years last past, the defendant, Edwin F. Carpenter, erected a building south of and adjoining the southerly side of said bridge at or near its easterly end, 40 feet in width, fronting on said bridge, and extending southerly over said river a distance of 100 feet, and supported by numerous piles driven into the bed of said river, the most westerly of which being in the channel of said river in or near the deepest water in the same, leaving a vacant space about 87 feet in width between the westerly side of said building so erected by

---

Lea, 507, 49 Am. Rep. 676; Mahan v. Brown, 13 Wend. 261.

A man may in general do what he will on his own land, so that he does not affect the adjoining premises of his neighbor in their natural state. Partridge v. Gilbert, 15 N. Y. 612; Radcliff v. Brooklyn, 4 N. Y. 195; Wyatt v. Harrison, 3 Barn. & Ad. 871.

Where the nuisance or damage apprehended is doubtful or contingent equity will not interfere by injunction, but will leave the party to his remedy at law. Morrison v. Latimer, 51 Ga. 522.

Where a person in the exercise of care and skill in making an excavation for the purpose of laying the foundation of a house on his own land, dug so near the foundation of the house on an adjoining lot as to cause it to crack and settle, he was held not liable for the injury. Charless v. Rankin, 22 Mo. 566; Gilmore v. Driscoll, 122 Mass. 199; Panton v. Holland, 17 Johns. 92; Busby v. Holthaus, 46 Mo. 161; McGuire v. Grant, 25 N. J. L. 356.

It is not the duty of a person excavating on his own land to support the buildings of adjoining owners. Aston v. Nolan, 63 Cal. 269; McMillen v. Watt, 27 Ohio St. 306.

A city was held not liable for an injury to property, caused by an excavation of the street, made with a view to its improvement. Humes v. Knoxville, 1 Humph. 403.

So a city was held not liable for injury to a storehouse in consequence of a change of grade in the street, made in a prudent and skillful manner. Creal v. Keokuk, 4 G. Greene, 47.

A party who is about to endanger the building of his neighbor by a reasonable improvement on his land is bound to give his neighbor proper notice thereof, and to use ordinary skill in conducting the same, and it is the duty of the latter to shore or prop up his building so as to render it secure in the meantime. Shafer v. Wilson, 44 Md. 261.

Right to use and improve one's own property. See *note* to Moellering v. Evans (Ind.) 6 L. R. A. 449.

the defendant and the easterly side of said Myers building. The defendant threatens that he will, without the permission of or an order from the common council of said city, drive numerous piles into the bed of said river, and erect thereon a building south of and adjoining the southerly side of said Milwaukee Street Bridge, and extending from said building so heretofore erected by him, to said Myers building, and having a frontage of 80 feet or more on said bridge, and extending over and down said river for a distance of about 100 feet, and commenced the driving of piles in the bed of said river for such purpose. The consequences of permitting the defendant to so erect said building, as affecting the interests of the City of Janesville, will be that others will soon erect buildings fronting on said bridges, and supported in like manner, until the whole space over said river, on both sides of said bridges, is occupied by similar buildings fronting on said bridges, and extending up and down said river a distance of about 100 feet from the sides of said bridges; and by reason thereof the flow of the water in said river will be further permanently obstructed, and the interests of said City and its inhabitants greatly prejudiced and injured by obstruction to the circulation of air, and in respect to the dangers of fire and flood, and to the public health, and as respects equality in the matter of taxation and assessments and the benefits thereof, and that said building will be in violation of an ordinance of said City against erecting any buildings in said river. As affecting the interests of the other plaintiff, the Janesville Cotton-Mills, it is alleged that the erection of said building will cause the waters of said river to set back "to some extent" at the place where the water used by said Janesville Cotton-Mills is discharged into said river.

In the affidavit of Edward Ruger, a civil engineer, in support of the complaint, it is stated that said building would, to some extent, cause the water to set back to such place, and in his affidavit procured by the defendant it is stated that said building would cause the water to set back on the water-wheels of said Janesville Cotton-Mills "to some extent, but to what extent he could not then say, but it would be slight." It is alleged, also, that the Janesville Cotton-Mills is a taxpayer of said City and a corporation, and that Rock River is a public highway, and has been returned as navigable, and has been meandered, and for a great many years a dam across said river, about 70 rods above said bridge, has existed by lawful authority, and that a considerable number of mills and factories have received their water-power therefrom, and among them the Janesville Cotton-Mills. The complaint shows also that, by the foundation of buildings and the building up within the natural margins of the river on the northerly side of the bridge, the width of the river has already been diminished one third, and the waters have been set back as far as the dam, and that said Milwaukee Street Bridge and Court Street Bridge have obstructed the flow of the river to a considerable extent, and that the abutments and piling thereof in the bed of the river, and the filling in of earth and other materials, and placing the foundations, walls and piers for the support of buildings, and the throwing in of ashes and other materials in the bed of the river, have greatly obstructed the river between said bridges and other localities, and that there is danger that other buildings and obstructions will be placed in the river by the example of the defendant.

These are substantially the material allegations of the complaint on which the circuit court granted a temporary injunction against the erection of said building. The defendant, after answering said complaint, moved that the said injunction be dissolved. The motion was heard upon the pleadings and one affidavit presented by the defendant, and seven affidavits presented by the plaintiffs, and denied. From the order denying said motion this appeal is taken. The answer denies all of the speculative and predicted consequences which the complaint alleges will follow the erection of said building, and the setting back of the water to any extent, and the effect as to the public health and danger from fire or flood, and the consequences of his pernicious example, and that the river is navigable in fact, and that the bridges are old and dilapidated, and will soon be replaced by iron ones, and some other immaterial allegations and the other allegations are admitted. The answer then alleges as follows: The Rock River throughout its whole length is crossed and obstructed by dams, bridges and buildings and other structures, and within the City there have been maintained six bridges resting upon piers and piles, four of which were constructed by the City within the space of a mile and a half, and two of them within the space of 40 rods. The lower bridge is known as "Court Street Bridge," and is about 40 rods below the proposed building, and its abutments and approaches are built within the river, and diminish its width so that it is 20 feet narrower at that place than where the defendant's proposed building will be, and three of said bridges are between two dams across the river. The lower dam obstructs the flow of the river so that it is virtually a mill-pond between the dams, and the water is raised upwards of two feet when it sets back to the upper dam, and the proposed building is between these dams. There are numerous buildings and structures along the bank of the river resting upon piles driven in the bed of the river, among which are certain buildings of the plaintiff, the Janesville Cotton-Mills, and of other mill owners, and there is a large sand-bar six feet above the bed of the river, between the Cotton-Mills and the proposed building. The proposed building will be constructed on piles driven into the bed of the river in line with the piles of the said Milwaukee Street Bridge, and the building itself will be above the river. The piles under the said bridge are driven at an angle to the current of the river, and, if piles could obstruct the current (which is denied), such a network of piles would do so. The defendant acquired his title in fee to the bed of the river where he proposes to build from the riparian owner of the lot, one Thomas Lappin. The defendant pleads in abatement that several causes of action are improperly united in the same action.

The affidavits in support of the complaint cannot, of course, go furthur than the complaint in stating the cause of action, and therefore need not be specially referred to. The affiant Edward Ruger made affidavits on behalf of both parties as to the extent to which the waters of the river would be set back below the wheels of the Janesville Cotton-Mills, and he leaves the question with the qualification that it would be slight, and the extent of it he could not state. The learned counsel of the appellant contends that the complaint does not show that the proposed building will injure to any extent either the City of Janesville or the Janesville Cotton-Mills. The condition of the river as to its uses and obstructions, other than by the proposed building, are only material to show that it would be impossible for anyone to state the extent, if any, that the proposed building would contribute, by example or otherwise, to produce the consequences, which, if they exist at all, must have already been produced to their fullest extent by other far more adequate causes. How can it be said that the proposed building, standing on piles driven in the river, could, even by example, affect the general health, cause fires and freshets, obstruct the circulation of the air, affect the equality of taxation and assessments, or the general welfare, when, if any such consequences could be appreciably produced by it, they must have already been overwhelmingly produced by a great many far greater obstructions in the river by dams, bridges, buildings and other constructions. And precisely so as to its injury to the water-power of the Janesville Cotton-Mills, as to which one of the most competent civil engineers of the State was unable to say to what extent it injured it, if at all, and did state that it must be slight. It would seem that if such a comparatively slight cause would produce any effect whatever, such far greater obstructions in the river, which have existed for a long time, must have produced all such consequences to a most astounding and alarming extent, and the City must have suffered in its health, and by polluted atmosphere, by unequal taxation and by fires and floods, to an extent that would have rendered it uninhabitable, and the water-power of the Janesville Cotton-Mills would have been destroyed. These consequences would have been facts susceptible of proof, and yet the complaint fails to show the existence of any such terrible consequences. What effect, if any, this proposed building by its example may have in any such direction, so as to injure any private or public interest, is left to mere prediction and conjecture. The action does not involve any question of obstruction or injury to navigation, or of injury to any public right. Many of the consequences to the City, predicted, would follow as well the erection of said building outside of the river. The complaint does not show that the proposed building would be a private or a public nuisance. The action is based upon the allegations of anticipated injury to the respective plaintiffs, which ought to be prevented by an injunction. It is a private, and not a public, action. I have stated the case more fully, that we may understand what is involved in it and what is not.

In respect to injury to any interest that the City represents, the complaint is very obscure and defective. It is not alleged that the public will suffer by this one building at all, but by a row of buildings which somebody might erect in following the example of the defendant, and so, also, as to danger from fire and flood. That will arise only from "similar buildings, fronting on the bridges, and supported in like manner, and extending up and down the river from the sides of said bridges until the whole space over said river on both sides of said bridges is occupied." It is only when such similar buildings erected by others fill that whole space that it is claimed in the complaint "dangers by fire and flood, and to the public health, and as respects equality in the matter of taxation, and the benefits thereof," will even arise or occur. The only injury to these interests that is alleged is from what somebody else may do in the future, through the influence of the defendant's example, and that is a mere prediction or conjecture. It is not shown how or in what manner such injury could occur. This is a most remarkable case, and there has never been anything like it. It is not charged that the proposed building will in itself do any harm in any respect whatever, or that the defendant has not the right to build it where he proposes to build it, but that it may possibly be followed as an example by others in building buildings which may possibly do harm. It would be a new case where one had actually done something in itself right and harmless, and he should be sued, because others had done something wrong and injurious by following his example, and it would be a strange case to enjoin one from doing something right and harmless in itself, because others may possibly do something wrong and injurious by following his example; and yet the latter is the present case. A mere example is not actionable. Such is the action in favor of the City.

That in favor of the Janesville Cotton-Mills is not based on any real injury to its water-power. The charge is "that the erection of such proposed buildings by the said defendant at the place and in the manner aforesaid would cause the water of said river to rise and set back to some extent at the place where the water used by the said Janesville Cotton-Mills, to operate its said mill, is discharged into the river." It would cause the water to set back at that place to some extent. What harm will it do? Will it retard the action of the water-wheel? Will it lessen the head or fall of the water-power? If it would do either, it would have been easy to say so. It depends upon how high or low the wheels are set. It is not even inferentially stated that it would be any injury at all to the Janesville Cotton-Mills. How much will it raise or set back the water at that place? "To some extent." The very least extent possible is some extent. The millionth part of an inch is some extent. The very smallest extent susceptible of measurement is some extent. It seems probable that this expression in the complaint was furnished by Edward Ruger, the civil engineer who made the affidavit in its support, and used the same language, and who in another affidavit qualified it by saying, "to what extent he could not state, but it would be slight." The word "slight," according to Webster, means "inconsiderable, unimportant." If any injury to the water-power could be inferred from this allegation, it would be too slight for legal cognizance.

The complaint states no cause of action against the defendant in favor of the Janesville Cotton-Mills. Should a court of chancery enjoin the defendant from erecting his building on his own land, on such an allegation as this? We think the learned counsel of the appellant is right in claiming that the complaint does not charge facts sufficient to state any cause of action known to the general laws of the land and the practice of courts in favor of either plaintiffs. But, even if the complaint sufficiently charged that the consequences predicted would be produced by the proposed building, the City of Janesville has no such corporate interest in them as would authorize it to maintain such an action. *Milwaukee* v. *Milwaukee & B. R. Co.* 7 Wis. 85; *Sheboygan* v. *Sheboygan & F. du L. R. Co.* 21 Wis. 668.

But it is sufficient that no wrong, injury or damage is charged. By the extended jurisdiction of the court in equity, by chapter 190 of the Laws of 1882 amending section 3180, Rev. Stat., there must be some special injury or necessity to protect the rights of some person, to grant an injunction. As a private nuisance or a public nuisance, by which some private person has suffered some special and peculiar injury, there must be material annoyance, inconvenience, discomfort or hurt, and the violation of another's rights in an essential degree. Wood, Nuis. 1-4.

The law gives protection only against substantial injury, and the injury must be tangible, or the comfort, enjoyment or use must be materially impaired. *Stadler* v. *Grieben*, 61 Wis. 500; *Pennoyer* v. *Allen*, 56 Wis. 502, and many other cases in this court.

It is a maxim of the law that wrong without damage or damage without wrong does not constitute a cause of private action. It is charged that this building will be in violation of an ordinance of said City. That would not give a cause of action for an injunction, even if the ordinance so provided. *Waupon* v. *Moore*, 34 Wis. 450.

The argument of the learned counsel of the respondents, and the authorities cited on the question whether the proposed building will obstruct the navigation of the river, are impertinent to the case. There is nothing in the case that involves any such question in the remotest degree. Within any grounds or reasons known to the well-settled principles and practice of equity jurisprudence, the complaint states no case for an injunction, or for any other purpose. The action is not based on any statute which gives a right of action in such a case. But the learned counsel of the respondent cites chapter 423, Laws 1887, in support of the action. This Statute is, if possible, more marvelous than the complaint. The enactment of the Statute was obviously obtained to create just such a right of action, and it is a little singular that it is not referred to in the complaint as the foundation of this action, as the action can stand on nothing else, and this Statute most clearly sanctions it, excepting as to the City of Janesville as plaintiff. The first section is as follows: "It shall be unlawful and *presumptively* injurious and dangerous to persons and property to drive piles, build piers, cribs or or other structures, . . . in Rock River, *within the limits of the County of Rock;* and the doing of any such act *shall be enjoined* at the suit of any *resident tax-payer without proof* that *any injury or danger has been or will be* caused by reason of such act." (The italics are not in the Act, and are used to save comment.) Section 2 is especially appropriate to this action, and is as follows: "The doing of any *such act shall also be enjoined* at the suit of any owner or lessee of the right to use water of said river to operate any mill or factory *within said county*, without proof of any further fact than that such act will cause the water of said river to rise or set back, *to some extent*, at the place where the water used to operate such mill or factory is discharged into said river." The complaint copies this last part as the only grievance of the plaintiff, the Janesville Cotton-Mills. The last section is unimportant. It excepts the building of railway and highway bridges, and the repair and reconstruction of mill-dams across the river, and a pending suit of the Janesville Cotton-Mills and others against Edwin F. Carpenter, probably of subject matter the same as or similar to that of this action.

The learned counsel of the appellant contends that this Act is unconstitutional, and therefore void. The Legislature would have saved time and expense if it had issued the injunction in the case for which the Act was made. This is the first time that any legislature of any enlightened country ever attempted to create an action without any cause of action; to authorize a complaint to be made to a court when there is nothing to complain of; to compel the courts to enjoin the lawful use and enjoyment of one's own property "without proof that any injury or danger has been or will be caused by reason of such act;" to create a cause of action without wrong, injury or damage; to authorize an action to be brought by a person without any interest in the subject matter, or privity with the defendant, of contract, estate, duty, obligation or liability, if he is only a resident tax-payer, and to exclude all others who have any interest or privity in the subject matter, and are presumptively injured in person or property; to make that act unlawful and actionable in one county and as to one river that is lawful in all other counties and as to all other rivers, under precisely the same circumstances, or to adjudicate and decide the case, and then order and compel the court to execute its judgment by issuing an injunction. These are some of the strange and novel provisions of this Statute. That Thomas Lappin, the owner in fee of this ground, has the right to use and enjoy it to the center of the river in any manner not injurious to others and subject to the public right of navigation, has been too often decided by this court and other courts to be questioned. As a riparian owner of the land adjacent to the water, he owns the bed of the river *usque ad filum aquæ*, subject to the public easement, if it be navigable in fact, and with due regard to the rights of other riparian proprietors. He may construct docks, landing places, piers and wharves out to navigable waters, if the river is navigable in fact, and if it is not so navigable he may construct anything he pleases to the thread of the stream, unless it injures some other riparian proprietor, or those having the superior right to use the waters for hydraulic purposes. *Jones* v. *Pet-*

tibone, 2 Wis. 308; *Arnold* v. *Elmore*, 16 Wis. 510; *Yates* v. *Judd*, 18 Wis. 119; *Walker* v. *Shepardson*, 4 Wis. 486; *Wisconsin R. Imp. Co.* v. *Lyons*, 30 Wis. 61; *Delaplaine* v. *Chicago & N. W. R. Co.* 42 Wis. 214; *Cohn* v. *Wausau Boom Co.* 47 Wis. 314; *Stevens Point Boom Co.* v. *Reilly*, 46 Wis. 237; *Hazeltine* v. *Case*, 46 Wis. 391.

Subject to these restrictions, he has the right to use his land under water the same as above water. It is his private property under the protection of the Constitution, and it cannot be taken, or its value lessened or impaired, even for public use, "without compensation" or "without due process of law," and it cannot be taken at all for anyone's private use.

1. This Statute makes it unlawful for the defendant who owns this ground, and has the right to use it under said Lappin, to drive piles into it anywhere within the river for any purpose. It prevents the lawful use of his property. It takes it away from him without compensation or due process of law, and denies the defendant "the equal protection of the laws." It is therefore in direct violation of articles 5 and 14 of the Amendments of the Constitution of the United States, and of section 13 of article 1 of the State Constitution, and is therefore void. It takes his property away from him, and leaves him no remedy whatever by which he can regain it or obtain redress. It is therefore in conflict with section 9 of article 1 of the State Constitution, which "entitles him to a certain remedy in the laws for all injuries or wrongs which he may receive in his person, property or character." Any restriction or interruption of the common and necessary use of property that destroys its value, or strips it of its attributes, or to say that the owner shall not use his property as he pleases, takes it in violation of the Constitution. *Pumpelly* v. *Green Bay & M. Canal Co.* 80 U. S. 13 Wall. 166 [20 L. ed. 557]; *Wynehamer* v. *People*, 13 N. Y. 378; *People* v. *Otis*, 90 N. Y. 48; *Hutton* v. *Camden*, 39 N. J. L. 122.

2. The Legislature usurped the judicial power of the courts by the enactment of this Statute. It adjudicates an act unlawful and presumptively injurious and dangerous, which is not and cannot be made to be so without a violation of the constitutional rights of the defendant, and imperatively commands the court to enjoin it without proof that any injury or danger has been or will be caused by it. It reverses very many decisions of this court, on the very questions involved in it, and which have the effect of a judicial determination of the defendant's rights of property. It violates section 2 of article 7 of the State Constitution, which provides that the judicial power of the State, both as to matters of law and equity, shall be vested in the various courts. It takes away the jurisdiction of the courts to inquire into the facts and determine the necessity and propriety of granting or refusing an injunction in such a case, according to the established rules of a court of equity. *Ervine's App.* 16 Pa. 256.

It is said in that case "that is not legislation which adjudicates in a particular case, prescribes the rule, contrary to the general law, and orders it to be enforced. Such power assimilates itself more closely to despotic rule than to any other attribute of government."

3. This Statute is discriminating and class legislation, in violation of the spirit of our Constitution, and contrary to the principles of civil liberty and natural justice. It gives to a certain class of citizens privileges and advantages which are denied to all others in the State under like circumstances, and subjects one class to losses, damages, suits or actions from which all others, under like circumstances, are exempted. *Holden* v. *James*, 11 Mass. 396.

Its operation is restricted and partial to that part of Rock River within the County of Rock, while said river elsewhere and all other rivers are excluded. It gives the right of action to the resident taxpayers of said county while all others are excluded from the exercise of such right, whatever interest they may have in the subject matter of the action. It gives the right of action to the owners or lessees of the right to use the water of said river to operate any mill or factory within said county, and excludes all other owners or lessees of such water-powers, by means of said river, elsewhere. It gives to such favored classes the stupendous advantage and exceptional privilege of maintaining such actions without proof that any injury or danger has been or will be caused by reason of such act. It would be difficult, if not impossible, to crowd into so short a statute any more or greater violations of that principle, so essential to a free government, of "equal, general and standing laws." For these reasons this Statute is unconstitutional and void. It is not, perhaps, a violation of any special clause of the Constitution in these respects, but it is a violation of its essential spirit, purpose and intent, and contrary to public justice. *Bull* v. *Conroe*, 13 Wis. 234; *Durkee* v. *Janesville*, 28 Wis. 464, and cases cited in the opinion.

In this connection I cannot forbear quoting the language of *Mr. Justice* Chase in *Calder* v. *Bull*, 3 U. S. 3 Dall. 387, 388 [1 L. ed. 648, 649]: "I cannot subscribe to the omnipotence of a State Legislature, or that it is absolute and without control, although its authority should not be expressly restrained by the Constitution or fundamental law of the State. . . . The nature and ends of the legislative power will limit the exercise of it. . . . There are certain vital principles in our free republican government which will determine and overrule an apparent and flagrant abuse of legislative power,—as to authorize manifest injustice by positive law, or to take away that security of personal liberty or private property for the protection whereof the government was established. An Act of the Legislature (for I cannot call it a law), contrary to the great first principles of the social compact, cannot be considered a rightful exercise of legislative authority."

This language is quoted in the above case of *Durkee* v. *Janesville*, but it will bear repeating here, as more apt and appropriate than in that case. It has been suggested that this Statute was procured for this case and perhaps like cases in the City of Janesville, as if, when the courts deny an injunction, the Legislature is made to intervene and enact that an injunction shall be granted, and that, too, without proof of injury or danger. It is hard to believe that anyone would procure the passage of such an Act or any Act of the Legislature to circumvent and overrule the courts in cases which have failed for want of any proof of injury. This Act is sought to be sustained as a proper exercise of the police power of the State. The Act itself makes no such claim, and has not the remotest reference to any such object or purpose. It is sufficient to say that such an objectionable statute cannot be sustained by the exercise of any power inherent in or conferred upon the Legislature. The complaint states no cause of action, and therefore the circuit court ought to have sustained the motion to dissolve the injunction.

The order of the Circuit Court is reversed, and the cause remanded, with direction to dissolve the injunction, and for further proceedings.

Mary V. DUDLEY, *Respt.*,
v.
Elizabeth H. DUDLEY, *Appt.*

(....Wis....)

1. **A widow's homestead right** in property of her deceased husband prevents the seisin of an heir, and therefore excludes any dower right of his widow therein upon his death during the continuance of the homestead right.

2. **A conveyance made just before marriage** in fraud of the wife's rights can be set aside by her only to the extent of her dower.

3. **The mere failure** of a grantor to inform his intended wife of a conveyance by him just before marriage is not of itself sufficient to make it fraudulent as to her.

4. **A conveyance to the grantor's mother,** to whom he was largely indebted, to carry out the wishes of his deceased father, and in the belief that she needed the property much more than he did, although it was not made in payment of the debt, but on a nominal consideration and without the knowledge of his intended wife whom he soon after married, is not fraudulent as to her.

(April 29, 1890.)

APPEAL by defendant from a judgment of the Circuit Court for Dane County in favor of plaintiff in an action brought to set aside a conveyance of certain real estate alleged to have been made in fraud of plaintiff's rights. *Reversed.*

The facts are fully stated in the opinion.

Messrs. **Pinney & Sanborn,** with *Messrs.* **LaFollette, Siebecker & Harper,** for appellant:

The plaintiff never acquired by right of marriage any right of dower, either inchoate or otherwise, in or to the homestead. The estate which descended to the widow was a life estate, a freehold estate which gave her the seisin.

4 Kent, Com. *26; 1 Washb. Real Prop. 87, 88, and *note* 5, 846, 349, 850; Co. Litt. *42a;* 1 Greenl. Cruise, *102, 103, pl. 2, 3, 7; *Roseboom* v. *Van Vechten*, 5 Denio, 415; *Holbrook* v. *Wightman*, 31 Minn. 168; *Abbott* v. *Abbott*, 97 Mass. 138; *Kerley* v. *Kerley*, 13 Allen, 286; *Browning* v. *Harris*, 99 Ill. 456.

Charles L. Dudley having "never been seised of an estate of inheritance" in the homestead, his widow, the plaintiff, could not have any claim for dower in it.

4 Kent, Com. *39, and *notes;* 1 Bishop, Married Women, §§ 273-277; 1 Scribner, Dower, 217, 308; *Durando* v. *Durando*, 23 N. Y. 331; *Blood* v. *Blood*, 23 Pick. 80; *Eldredge* v. *Forrestal*, 7 Mass. 253; *Fisk* v. *Eastman*, 5 N. H. 240, 479; *Arnold* v. *Arnold*, 8 B. Mon. 204; *Gardner* v. *Greene*, 5 R. I. 104; *Cocke* v. *Philips*, 12 Leigh, 248.

A conveyance can be set aside only for causes affecting it when made, as for fraud then committed, or for the protection of rights then existing.

Chandler v. *Hollingsworth*, 3 Del. Ch. 99.

Chandler v. *Hollingsworth*, *supra*, utterly overthrows the pretense that the plaintiff, Charles' widow, may maintain this bill on the

---

NOTE.—*Antenuptial fraud of husband or wife; relief in equity.*

A husband in contemplation of marriage may commit frauds upon the rights which on the marriage would accrue to the intended wife, from which after marriage a court of equity will relieve her, as it would relieve the husband from the antenuptial fraud of the wife. Swaine v. Perine, 5 Johns. Ch. 482, 1 N. Y. Ch. L. ed. 1148; Kelly v. McGrath, 70 Ala. 75. See, however, Baker v. Chase, 6 Hill, 483.

A conveyance upon the eve of marriage, to be regarded in equity as a fraud upon the legal rights of the intended wife, and consequently not binding upon her, must be made without her consent or knowledge. Murray v. Murray, 8 L. R. A. 95, 11 Ky. L. Rep. 815; Leach v. Duvall, 8 Bush, 201.

Voluntary conveyances made by one about to enter into marital relations with another may be set aside in a court of equity. Pomeroy v. Pomeroy, 54 How. Pr. 228.

It is as much a fraud for the husband to place his property out of his hands for the purpose of avoiding the dower right of his wife as it is for a debtor to voluntarily dispose of his property to defeat the claims of future creditors. Youngs v. Carter, 10 Hun, 199.

So a deed given to a daughter upon the eve of her father's marriage, and kept secret from the intended wife until after his marriage, is fraudulent against her claim to dower. Thayer v. Thayer 14 Vt. 107; Youngs v. Carter, 50 How. Pr. 411; Pomeroy v. Pomeroy, *supra.*

So where a few days before his marriage he conveyed lands to one of his children by a former marriage by way of advancement it was a fraud upon his wife's claim to dower. Klein v. Wolfsohn, 1 Abb. N.C. 137, *note.* See Petty v. Petty, 4 B. Mon. 215.

A voluntary conveyance by either party to a marriage contract of his or her entire property, made without the knowledge of the other and just prior to the marriage, is a fraud upon marital rights. Butler v. Butler, 21 Kan. 521; Smith v. Smith, 6 N. J. Eq. 515; Leach v. Duvall, 8 Bush, 201; Duncan's App. 43 Pa. 67; Kline v. Kline, 57 Pa. 120; Logan v. Simmons, 3 Ired. Eq. 487.

When such a gift is made with and for the purpose of defrauding his wife, it will be set aside to the extent that it may affect her rights as widow. Hays v. Henry, 1 Md. Ch. 337; Dunnock v. Dunnock, 3 Md. Ch. 140; Dearmond v. Dearmond, 10 Ind. 194; Davis v. Davis, 5 Mo. 183; Stone v. Stone, 18 Mo. 389; Tucker v. Tucker, 29 Mo. 350; Smith v. Smith, 6 N. J. Eq. 521; Thayer v. Thayer, 14 Vt. 122. See Fennessey v. Fennessey, 84 Ky. 519; Manikee v. Beard, 85 Ky. 20.

See also 41 L. R. A. 258.

theory of the very remote expectation that she might be her husband's heir-at-law, there being no issue.

See also 3 Washb. Real Prop. p. 359; 2 Bishop, Married Women, § 353; *Robinson* v. *Buck*, 71 Pa. 386.

No deceptive, cunning or treacherous art or practice is a fraud in its legal or equitable sense, unless it results in loss or damage to another.

Ableman v. *Roth*, 12 Wis. 90; 1 Story, Eq. § 187; Bispham, Eq. § 217; *Clarke* v. *White*, 37 U. S. 12 Pet. 178, 196 (9 L. ed. 1046, 1054); *Marr's App.* 78 Pa. 67, 69; *Rogers* v. *Higgins*, 57 Ill. 245, 249.

The extent to which relief may be granted in this case is confined to the question of dower.

Youngs v. *Carter*, 10 Hun, 194; *Green* v. *Green*, 41 Kan. 472; *Butler* v. *Butler*, 21 Kan. 521; *Hafer* v. *Hafer*, 33 Kan. 449; *Busenbark* v. *Busenbark*, Id. 572; *Jones* v. *Jones*, 64 Wis. 301, 71 Wis. 513.

The deed will be set aside only so far as it is void.

Norton v. *Simmes*, Hobart, *14; *Maleverer* v. *Redshaw*, 1 Mod. 35; *Mackie* v. *Cairns*, 5 Cow. 554; *Beverly* v. *Gatacre*, 2 Rolle, 305, cited in *White* v. *Drake*, 3 Keb. 6; *Mosely* v. *Mosely*, 15 N. Y. 334; *Darling* v. *Rogers*, 22 Wend. 483; *Hait* v. *Houle*, 19 Wis. 473; *Pickering* v. *Ilfracombe R. Co.* L. R. 3 C. P. 250; *Ex parte Browning*, L. R. 9 Ch. App. 583; *Milwaukee & M. R. Co.* v. *Soutter*, 80 U. S. 13 Wall. 517 (20 L. ed. 543); *Barnes* v. *Chicago, M. & St. P. R. Co.* 122 U. S. 1 (30 L. ed. 1128).

In cases of this character a settlement which has been merely concealed may be vindicated on the ground that it was dictated by equitable or meritorious considerations in respect to the character of the objects provided for.

England v. *Downs*, 2 Beav. 522; *Hunt* v. *Matthews*, 1 Vern. 408; *King* v. *Cotton*, 2 P. Wms. 675.

The property conveyed may be so inconsiderable in amount as not to bring the conveyance within the condemnation of the rule. Each case must depend upon its own circumstances.

St. George v. *Wake*, 1 Myl. & K. 610; *Duncan's App.* 43 Pa. 67; *Robinson* v. *Buck*, 71 Pa. 386.

All plaintiff has a right to ask is that the instrument in question shall not be allowed to operate to the detriment of her rights, if any, as dowress of the estate of which Charles L. Dudley was seised during his lifetime.

Swaine v. *Perine*, 5 Johns. Ch. 482, 1 N. Y. Ch. L. ed. 1148; *Petty* v. *Petty*, 4 B. Mon. 215; *Cranson* v. *Cranson*, 4 Mich. 230; *Smith* v. *Smith*, 6 N. J. Eq. 515.

It is for the court to determine, in each case, whether, having regard to the condition of the parties and the attendant circumstances, a transaction complained of as a fraud on marital rights should be held fraudulent.

Adams, Eq. § 406; Bigelow, Fraud, 51; *Jones* v. *Jones*, 64 Wis. 307, 308; *Fennessey* v. *Fennessey*, 84 Ky. 527; *Hamilton* v. *Smith*, 57 Iowa, 15; 1 Scribner, Dower, 591, 595; *Champlin* v. *Champlin*, 6 New Eng. Rep. 707, 16 R. I. —; 1 White & T. Lead. Eq. Cas. (Bl. ed.) 605, 618, 623; 2 Kent, Com. 175; *King* v. *Cotton*, 2 P. Wms. 674; *Jones* v. *Cole*, 2 Bailey, L. 330; 2 Bishop, Married Women, § 347, and cases cited in *note 3*; *Saunders* v. *Harris*, 1 Head, 185; *Jordan* v. *Black*, Meigs, 142; *Logan* v. *Simmons*, 3 Ired. Eq. 487; *Ramsay* v. *Joyce*, McMull. Eq. 236, 242; *De Manneville* v. *Crompton*, 1 Ves. & B. 354; 2 Vaizey, Marriage Settlements, 1581, 1583, 1584; *Maber* v. *Hobbs*, 2 Younge & C. 317; *Loader* v. *Clarke*, 2 Mac. & G. 382.

Mr. **William Ruger** for respondent.

Orton, *J.*, delivered the opinion of the court:

The facts of this case are substantially as follows: William H. Dudley died on the 2d day of July, 1879, seised of lots 7 and 8, and the east 25 feet of lots 6 and 9, in block 7, in the City of Madison. On lot 8 and the east 25 feet of lot 9 there was a dwelling-house, where he lived and died. He left also a personal estate, which, after the payment of all debts and expenses, amounted to the sum of over $26,000, one half of which was assigned to the defendant as his widow, and the other half to his son, Charles L. Dudley, on the 12th day of February, 1880, the whole of which remained, however, in the hands of said Charles as administrator, and only a small portion of the defendant's share has ever been paid to her, but was retained by him until his death. All of the above real estate was also assigned to said Charles, subject to his mother's homestead right and right of dower. The homestead embraced the whole of lot 8 and the east 25 feet of lot 9. Lot 7 and the east 25 feet of lot 6 was vacant property, and was worth the sum of $1,300, and the homestead property was worth $7,000, at the time of William H. Dudley's death. In May, 1879, the said Charles L. Dudley and the plaintiff entered into an agreement of marriage to be consummated thereafter upon request, and this agreement was known to both the father and mother of Charles; and in the summer of 1880 the day of the marriage was fixed to take place on the 7th day of October following, which was also known to his mother, the defendant, and on said day the marriage took place. On the 27th of September, 1880, the said Charles gave to the defendant, his mother, a quitclaim deed of said real property for the nominal consideration of one dollar, and caused the same to be recorded on the same day. At that time the said Charles owed the defendant a large amount of money, which he had appropriated to his own use, of the moneys of said estate,—at least the sum of $5,000; and it has never yet been paid. Charles L. Dudley, for some time before executing said quitclaim deed, took counsel of several of his friends, among whom were two former clerks and partners of his father, a neighboring lady, an old friend of the family, and Mr. Seibecker, an attorney at law and now the judge of this circuit, and who had been his legal partner in this city,—all persons of the very highest respectability and integrity, —as to what he ought to do about conveying to his mother the fee or vested remainder in the homestead property and the title of the vacant lots. After having stated to them the circumstances, and the fact that his father had intended to leave said property to his mother, but was unable to do so in his last sickness, to which time he had deferred it, and that his mother would need it, and that, if he conveyed it to her, it would come back to him again in time, and that he felt it his duty to his mother to so convey it, they advised him that he ought to do so. The said Charles at the time had control of all the moneys of the estate, and was supposed to be worth much more in pecuniary means than the value of said real property; and he told his friends that he would not need it, and that his mother would, and that he thought it but justice and right to his mother to deed the property to her.

The plaintiff, as the widow and sole heir at law of the said Charles L. Dudley, who died on the 2d day of November, 1883, in the City of Chicago, Ill., brings this suit, and, after stating the main facts in her complaint, prays that said deed be adjudged fraudulent and void as to her, and be set aside and canceled, and that she be adjudged to be seised in fee of the title to said premises, and entitled to the possession thereof, subject only to the defendant's right of dower and homestead, and for other relief. The ground upon which this relief is asked is stated in the complaint as follows: "That the defendant well knew, and had for a long time prior thereto known, of said contract of marriage, and knew that said Charles L. Dudley and plaintiff were then intending shortly thereafter to be married, and knew that said Charles L. Dudley was then arranging and preparing for the celebration of such marriage, . . . and then having such knowledge, wrongfully and fraudulently persuaded and induced the said Charles L. Dudley to convey to defendant all and singular his right, title and interest in and to the lands and premises hereinbefore described. The plaintiff had no knowledge or information respecting said deed until after the death of said Charles L. Dudley, . . . and that plaintiff has never assented to or ratified it. That said deed was procured, and was executed and delivered, for the wrongful and fraudulent purpose of preventing the plaintiff from acquiring, by marriage with said Charles L. Dudley, any interest in the lands and premises hereinbefore described, and that said deed is fraudulent as to the plaintiff, in that it was executed and delivered without consideration, and in that it was fraudulently intended that it should, and that it fraudulently and wrongfully did, prevent the descent of the premises hereinbefore described, and of any interest in the same, to the plaintiff." It will be observed that the gravamen of the complaint is the actual fraud of the defendant in inducing and persuading the said Charles to make the conveyance. There is no charge of intended secrecy on the part of the said Charles, but only that the deed was made without the plaintiff's knowledge or information. There is no charge or proof that the said Charles L. Dudley ever informed the plaintiff before the deed was made that he owned the said property, or had any interest in it. He may have informed others of it, and they may have informed the plaintiff, and she no doubt knew something of the situation of the property, but, as to whether she knew what other property or means he had, or his financial or pecuniary circumstances, the record is silent. The defendant has continued in the possession of said premises since her husband's death, and her dower therein has never been assigned, and she has continued to occupy the homestead thereon. A part of the time the said Charles and the plaintiff occupied the house with the defendant, but left and abandoned it some time before his death, and moved to the City of Chicago, where they resided at the time of his death.

The circuit court, besides other facts, found that the defendant persuaded and induced the said Charles to make the deed, and that the deed was fraudulent as to the plaintiff. We are unable to assent to either of these findings. The facts above stated are sustained by a clear preponderance of the testimony. We do not think the evidence shows that the defendant persuaded or induced the said Charles to make the deed. Those are strong terms, even when unaccompanied by the qualifying word "fraudulently." Mrs. Dudley, the defendant, may have assented to the making of the deed, or she may have expressed the wish to have it done; and that is scarcely proved. The evidence shows most clearly that Charles L. Dudley, in making that deed to his mother, acted from his own sense of right and duty. The testimony of Judge Seibecker, Mrs. Burgess and Messrs. Baker and Tehnter, shows this beyond a doubt. He had been reckless, and used a large portion of her money in his hands as administrator, and he was indebted to her many thousands of dollars. Perhaps that money could not properly be called the consideration of the deed, for it is not named as such; but it was no doubt a consideration that in part induced him to make it. The wish of his father that his mother should have the real property, and which from his last sickness he was unable to carry into effect, we may well suppose, weighed heavily on his mind, for he frequently spoke of it to others, and was an almost irresistible motive to repair the omission of his father, and do justice to his mother. He had nearly all of the estate besides this, and thought his mother needed it much more than he did. He had entered upon the business of his profession with Judge Seibecker, with excellent prospects, and he spoke of this as one reason why she needed it more than he did. These were the inducements that caused him to make the deed. It is hard to believe that he had a single thought of preventing his intended wife from the enjoyment of the property, or to defeat her expectations of it. It probably never entered his mind that she had a thought or cared anything about it, or felt any concern about his property, or ability to support a family. If Charles L. Dudley had informed the plaintiff at the time that he intended to deed this property to his mother, and had told her his reasons for so doing, as above, can we think for a moment that she would have objected to it, or would not have approved it? There was no fraud in this, in fact or in law, actual or constructive. The learned counsel of the respondent admitted on the trial that Charles Dudley had no intention to defraud his wife in making the deed, and only claimed that the transaction was fraudulent in law because of its concealment from the plaintiff. But there was no concealment in fact. The deed was placed on record the same day; and, if the plaintiff wished to be sure of what property he owned before the marriage should take place, she or her friends could have consulted the record. But the learned counsel contends that non-information was concealment.

1. What expectations did the plaintiff have of estate in this property that were cut off or defeated by this deed? The defendant held her dower interest in the property, and a life estate by homestead in the south half or improved portion of it. She was seised of that life estate, and therefore Charles Dudley did not die seised of it, and the plaintiff could have no dower in it. We shall see hereafter that the only expectation she could have was of dower. For this object alone could the deed be declared fraudulent and void, under any circumstances. Charles Dudley had the same right to convey the fee before as after the marriage. It must be the expectation of present possession and enjoyment that is defeated. Her dower in the homestead was not defeated by the deed, for she could have none in it. The defendant had dower in the unimproved portion of the property. That would leave to the plaintiff only one third dower interest in two thirds of that. The whole value of that portion of the lots was $1,300. That is a very small interest, at most, hardly sufficient as the basis of expectation. The homestead descended to the defendant as a freehold estate for life, and on the death of William Dudley she became seised of it in fact and in law. Rev. Stat. § 2271; 4 Kent, Com. *26; 1 Washb. Real Prop. 87, 88, and *note* on 346–350; *Holbrook* v. *Wightman*, 31 Minn. 168.

This homestead estate of the defendant excludes the possibility of the plaintiff's dower in those lots. Rev. Stat. § 2159. It is an estate in possession and actual occupancy in one alone for life, inconsistent with dower in another person. *Browning* v. *Harris*, 99 Ill. 456; *Hafer* v. *Hafer*, 33 Kan. 449, and other cases in appellant's brief.

When the deed was made, she could have had no expectation of the enjoyment of the remainder vested in her husband, because that would depend upon too many contingencies. Her husband could have conveyed the fee after marriage as well as before, and have defeated any right she might have had in it, except her dower. Charles L. Dudley is dead, and now the plaintiff would claim that, if the fee as a remainder had not been conveyed by him to the defendant, she would be entitled to inherit it as his sole heir at law. But this she did not know, and none of the parties knew, when that deed was made. At that time she had no reason to expect but that Charles Dudley would live, and peradventure convey the fee of the homestead or of the other lots. It is her dower right only that she lost by this antenuptial deed, and that is all she could recover in this case, under any circumstances.

The leading case in this country on this question is that of *Chandler* v. *Hollingsworth*, 3 Del. Ch. 99. In that case the chancellor says "that such a conveyance will be set aside . . . when it is in fraud of some legal right, and one existing at the time. . . . Its validity cannot be held in suspense, to be determined by future contingencies. This would subject titles to distressing uncertainty. . . . He [the husband] could after marriage have effectually disposed of his whole personal estate, and of the inheritance of his real estate, by just such a deed." The chancellor shows conclusively, both on principle and by authority, that the deed in such a case can be set aside only as to the intended wife's right of dower. There is a note appended to this case, of approvals of many legal publications and text-book authors, and the decision has never been disapproved. 3 Washb. Real Prop. 359; 2 Bishop, Married Women, § 353; *Youngs* v. *Carter*, 10 Hun, 194.

Nothing, therefore, can be recovered in such a case except the plaintiff's right of dower, and no relief except to set aside the deed only to save that right. The deed is not wholly void. It is void only in respect to the plaintiff's right of dower. *Chandler* v. *Hollingsworth*, *supra*, and other cases cited in appellant's brief.

Nearly all the cases cited by the learned counsel of the respondent are to set aside the deed to save the wife's right of dower, or the husband's curtesy. Such being the law, the interest the plaintiff had in the property conveyed is comparatively very small. It is really a life interest of dower in only two thirds of the vacant lots. This is all she could possibly obtain by setting aside the deed. The plaintiff is only interested in the conveyance as far as she is injured by it. Is there enough of this case to support the arbitrary theory of defeated expectations by concealment, which makes such a conveyance a constructive fraud?

2. The only remaining question of law is whether the mere non-communication of the fact of the making of the deed establishes the transaction as a legal fraud which cannot be questioned or repelled under any circumstances. It must be admitted that there is a class of cases which hold that nothing can be shown against it except notice or information given to the intended wife, and that non-communication is conclusive evidence of fraud. But all such cases must be understood to have been decided upon their own facts, where there was nothing to repel the presumption of fraud. But in most if not all the recent cases, and in some not so recent, it is held that concealment or the non-existence of communication to the intended wife or husband is not always a constructive fraud, but that it will depend upon the circumstances of each case, as in *England* v. *Downs*, 2 Beav. 522. There is a very full discussion of this question, also, in *Chandler* v. *Hollingsworth*, *supra*.

In *St. George* v. *Wake*, 1 Myl. & K. 610, it is held that "the court will take into consideration the meritorious object of such conveyance, and the situation of the intended husband in point of pecuniary means." *Lord* Brougham examines the cases very fully and holds that the principle depended very much on the dicta of courts, but that "the cases would even seem to authorize us in taking all the circumstances of the parties into consideration."

The case oftenest referred to as laying down this principle is *Strathmore* v. *Bowes*, 2 Cox, 28. *Mr. Justice* Buller strongly intimated that circumstances might be considered against holding the settlement void *per se*.

In *Gregory* v. *Winston*, 23 Gratt. 102, it is said: "The courts will consider the nature of the provision, the situation of the husband . . . and other facts which tend to show that no fraud was intended."

In *Taylor* v. *Pugh*, 1 Hare, 608 the same doctrine is held. Bigelow, Fraud, 605.

The case of *Champlin* v. *Champlin*, 16 R. I. —, 6 New Eng. Rep. 707, is closely in point: "A widow is not entitled to dower in lands conveyed by her deceased husband a few hours before his marriage, without her knowledge, to his son by a former wife, where it appears that he had long before promised the land to the son upon consideration of his working it," and he made improvements on the land, etc. It was held that the circumstances rebutted the inference of fraud. *Firestone* v. *Firestone*, 2 Ohio St. 415, is much like the above case.

In *Hamilton* v. *Smith*, 57 Iowa, 15, it is held that the secrecy of the conveyance did not necessarily show fraud.

In *Cowman* v. *Hall*, 3 Gill & J. 398, the husband had promised a conveyance to his mother after having received more than his share of his father's estate, and conveyed just before his marriage. It was held that his widow had no dower in the lands conveyed. 1 Scribner, Dower, 592.

In *Butler* v. *Butler*, 21 Kan. 521, the facts were held to rebut the presumption of fraud in such a case. It would be useless to incumber this opinion with more cases. Many others can be found in appellant's brief. In one of the above cases the placing the deed on record at the time was held to rebut the secrecy of the transaction. The reasonable doctrine seems now to be well established that the deed is not necessarily fraudulent if not disclosed to the intended wife, but that the facts and circumstances may be taken into consideration as to whether a fraud was actually intended. The old doctrine was utterly unreasonable. Suppose the intended husband was worth millions in city property and owned hundreds of lots, and should convey on the eve of his marriage one or a few of such lots, and not disclose it. Would the deed be *ipso facto* void? Yes, by the doctrine of some cases. We conclude, therefore, that the facts and circumstances of this case may be considered in determining whether the giving of that deed was fraudulent. We have sufficiently stated such facts and circumstances, and we cannot believe that Charles L. Dudley had any thought of defrauding the plaintiff as his intended wife. The defendant, Mrs. Dudley, already held by far the most valuable interest in the property, and the present loss to the plaintiff was not great. The learned judge of the court below most probably applied the arbitrary principle that the concealment established the fraud. We cannot think that he meant to hold that any fraud was intended, or that the conveyance was not honest, just and right.

The judgment of the Circuit Court is reversed, and the cause remanded, with direction to dismiss the complaint on the merits.

Lyon, *J.*, took no part.

NEW YORK COURT OF APPEALS (2d Div.)

George H. BRENNAN, *Appt.*,
v.
Read GORDON, Jr., *et al.*

(118 N. Y. 489.)

1. A master, who commits the running of his elevator to an employe who is ignorant in regard to such service, is bound to furnish him for a reasonable length of time with a competent instructor, and will be liable to the employé for any injury resulting from the incompetence or negligence of the instructor furnished.

2. An instruction in an action by a servant to recover from his master damages for injuries alleged to have resulted from the negligence of one

NOTE.—*Vice-principals and agents.*

It is not the rank of an employé, or his authority over other employés, but the nature of the duty or service he performs, which determines whether he is a vice-principal or a fellow servant. Lindvall v. Woods, 4 L. R. A. 793, 41 Minn. 212.

To the extent of the discharge of his specific duty the agent of the master stands in the place of the master. *Ibid.*

The master is chargeable for any act of negligence by a servant in so far as the servant is charged with the performance of the master's duty to other servants. Anderson v. Barnett, 16 Or. 515.

The master is liable for the neglect of a duty which he has impliedly contracted to perform, no matter what the rank or grade may be of the person designated to perform it. Galveston, H. & S. A. R. Co. v. Smith, 76 Tex. 611.

The fact that there is an intermediate party in whose general employment the person whose acts are in question is engaged does not prevent the principal from being held liable for the negligent conduct of his sub-agent or under-servant, unless the intermediate party had exclusive control and direction. Southern Exp. Co. v. Brown (Miss.) Feb. 17, 1890.

An employer impliedly engages to make the service of the employé a reasonably safe one. When acting through agents, he undertakes that his agent shall be a capable person for the position he holds. Stewart v. Philadelphia, W. & B. R. Co. (Del.) May 24, 1889.

An employer must use ordinary care and reasonable skill to make safe a place where he requires his employés to work; and he cannot delegate this duty to another so as to relieve himself from responsibility. Louisville, N. A. & C. R. Co. v. Graham (Ind.) May 27, 1890.

Ordinary risks are such as remain after the employer has used all reasonable means to prevent them; and the employer is liable for injuries resulting to the employé from risks coming to him alone from the employer's negligence. Seley v. Southern Pac. R. Co. (Utah) March 4, 1890.

The neglect of the superintendent of a railroad in respect to giving such information and orders to the company's servants in charge of its trains as will enable them to avoid collisions is the neglect of the company, making it liable for an injury thereby occasioned to a section hand. Galveston, H. & S. A. R. Co. v. Smith, *supra.*

As to liability of master for negligence of vice-principal, see *note* to Muhlman v. Union Pac. R. Co. (Colo.) 2 L. R. A. 198.

Duty of master to instruct servant in use of dangerous machinery.

It is the duty of the master to supervise, direct and control the operation and management of his

See also 12 L. R. A. 232; 16 L. R. A. 519; 17 L. R. A. 190, 636, 811.

furnished by the master to instruct the servant as to how to run an elevator is erroneous if it gives the jury to understand that the master's whole duty was performed if he furnished an instructor as competent as he himself was.

(February 25, 1890.)

APPEAL by plaintiff from a judgment of the General Term of the Court of Common Pleas for the City and County of New York, affirming a judgment of the Trial Term in favor of defendants in an action brought to recover damages for personal injuries alleged to have resulted from the negligence of defendant's servant. *Reversed.*

Statement by **Potter**, *J.*:

Appeal from a judgment of the General Term of the Court of Common Pleas of the City of New York, affirming a judgment in favor of the defendants entered upon a verdict of a jury. The action was brought by the plaintiff, who was a servant of the defendants, against them to recover damages for personal injuries occasioned by the fall of an elevator which the defendants had just put into their store and business, and which was being put to use for the first time. The case has been twice tried. On the first trial the complaint was dismissed. This was reversed by the general term, and a new trial was ordered. Reported in 13 Daly, 208.

On the second trial the jury rendered a verdict for the defendants, and this appeal is to review such judgment. The defendants were a firm doing business in manufacturing preserves, in the City of New York. The plaintiff had been in defendants' employment in such business, as one of the porters, for a long time prior to March 1, 1881, when this accident occurred. In the month of February, 1881, the defendants caused to be erected and put into their building an elevator to be operated by steam, and to be used in carrying persons and goods to the various floors and lofts in the building in which they were doing business. Henry Dillworth (who was a brother of the defendant William H. Dillworth) had been in the defendants' employment, as general superintendent of defendants' establishment, for some time, and exercised the functions of hiring and discharging employés in that business. It is claimed by plaintiff, and the trial proceeded in the main upon that theory, that the defendants selected the plaintiff, among their numerous employés, to run and manage this elevator; that the plaintiff had no previous experience or knowledge in running an elevator, and the defendants undertook to instruct him in that respect, and for the purpose assigned as such instructor said Henry Dillworth. Previous to this time his duty in the defendants' service was that of porter, moving boxes, unloading trucks, wrapping bottles, washing and capping them, etc. The defendants knew that the plaintiff had no acquaintance or skill in running said elevator, and had never before

business, so that no injury shall ensue to his employés through his own carelessness or negligence in carrying it on, or else to furnish some person who will do so, for whom he must stand sponsor. Hunn v. Michigan Cent. R. Co. (Mich.) 7 L. R. A. 500.

If the master intrusts the performance of his duty to an agent, the agent's negligence is that of the master. Kreuger v. Louisville, N. A. & C. R. Co. 9 West. Rep. 247, 111 Ind. 51; authorities cited in Pennsylvania Co. v. Whitcomb, 9 West. Rep. 825, 111 Ind. 212.

A duty devolves upon a master of a servant hitherto serving in the capacity of a common hand laborer, before such laborer is put in charge of dangerous machinery with which he is not acquainted, to instruct and qualify him for such new duty. Brennan v. Gordon, 118 N. Y. 489.

A master who selects a co-servant to instruct and qualify a servant for a new and more dangerous service is bound to provide for a reasonable length of time an instructor competent to teach the art of managing the dangerous machinery and appliances, regardless of the competency of the master. *Ibid.*

It is the duty of the master to give such instructions to a youthful and inexperienced employé as would enable him, with the exercise of ordinary care, to perform the duties of his employment with safety to himself. Whitelaw v. Memphis & C. R. Co. 16 Lea, 391.

If an employé of immature years (here a female of fourteen years) has had no instructions as to the danger of a machine at which she is set at work, and has never worked at any machinery before, and is injured by such machine within a short time of her employment, because of her unfamiliarity with, and lack of appreciation of, the dangers attendant upon the working of the machine, the employer will be liable. Ruger, *Ch. J.*, and Danforth, J., dissent. Hickey v. Taaffe, 7 Cent. Rep. 72, 105 N. Y. 26.

If a girl thirteen years of age, not properly instructed as to the management of a machine which she was tending, believed that she had given a motion to a wheel which would cause only a partial revolution, but, from lack of instructions as to the peculiar mode of giving such motion, caused it to revolve much farther, she is not barred from recovery because she attempted to pick off a piece of waste from a spoke while thus in motion. Glover v. Dwight Mfg. Co. 148 Mass. 22.

Where an employé is inexperienced and wholly ignorant as to the particular nature of the attendant dangers of his employment, it is the duty of the employer to instruct him as to such attendant dangers, and put him on his guard against them (Nadau v. White River Lumber Co. (Wis.) Dec. 3, 1889); and the employer will be liable for an injury to such servant if the latter is not guilty of any contributory negligence. Roth v. Northern P. L. Co. (Or.) Dec. 3, 1889.

A master who carries on an imminently dangerous undertaking—such as the generation and distribution of electricity—is bound to know the character and extent of the danger, and to notify the same to the servant specially and unequivocally, so as to be clearly understood by him. Myhan v. Louisiana E. L. & P. Co. (La.) 7 L. R. A. 172.

As to the duty of the master to inform his servant of risks to which the latter is subjected in the course of his employment, see *notes* to Brazil Block Coal Co. v. Gaffney (Ind.) 4 L. R. A. 850; Hinckley v. Horazdowski (Ill.) 8 L. R. A. 491.

Instances.

Where an ignorant boy apprentice in a machine shop was directed by the foreman to obey the directions of another employé, who was an unskilled mechanic, and was engaged upon work which required a skillful mechanic to safely undertake; and the boy was killed in following out the instructions of the latter employé, it was held that the boy and such employé were not fellow servants; and that the negligence of the latter was the negligence

performed, or attempted to perform, such a service. In accordance with these purposes, the defendants informed the plaintiff that they had selected him to run and operate the elevator, and that said Henry C. Dillworth, who had knowledge and experience in that service, would instruct and qualify him to perform such service. The elevator was built and furnished to the defendants by the firm of Reedy & Co., who were doing a large business in that line. One Mulcahy and Sanders, employés of Reedy & Co., who had constructed the elevator, placed the elevator and apparatus in position, and prepared it for use. It is claimed by the defendants that Mulcahy, foreman of Reedy & Co., gave instruction to the plaintiff, at least in part; and there is some evidence tending to show that at times, when the elevator was in operation, carrying things from below to the floors above, and with which Mulcahy was engaged in respect to another elevator, or in making some changes in connection with another elevator, had given the plaintiff, when he was with him in the car or elevator, some instruction in regard to running it; and it is sought thereby, on the part of the defendants, to relieve themselves from the consequences of any incompetency or failure to impart instruction sufficiently to the plaintiff by the said Henry Dillworth.

The elevator had been used more or less on Monday, the 28th day of February, 1881, and was in use on the Tuesday succeeding; and at about 5 o'clock on this latter day, while the elevator was carrying three beams to the upper floor of the building, and had proceeded up with the beams to be used to strengthen some shafting used in connection with other apparatus on the top floor, and at a time when the plaintiff, with another of the employés of the defendants, was in the elevator, and just after two of the beams had been taken out of the elevator at the third floor, and with the third and longer beam, with its lower end resting on the floor of the elevator, and its upper end protruding beyond the top of the elevator, the elevator was started, with this third beam, towards the floor above. The elevator was stopped between the third and fourth floors, in order to take out the third beam before the upper end of it should come against the roof, and, while taking or preparing to take out this third beam, the elevator was started by somebody, and the evidence leaves it in some doubt who that person was, or started without anyone's interference from some inherent defect in the machinery, as it is claimed; and, while thus moving up, the upper end of the third beam came in collision with the roof, which caused the cogs of the wheel upon the apparatus, one or more of them, to break, and thereby the elevator fell to the bottom, with the plaintiff

---

of the employer. Missouri Pac. R. Co. v. Peregoy, 36 Kan. 424.

Where a servant is directed by a foreman to warm a quantity of dynamite, and the substance explodes and injures him, such servant not having been employed to perform that particular service, or warned of the danger accompanying it, which was unknown to him, the employer is liable for the act of the former. Lofrano v. New York & Mt. V. Water Co. 55 Hun, 452.

An employé is entitled to recover for an injury sustained while attempting, in the use of due care, to obey the command of the superintendent ordering him to perform a dangerous service not within the purview of his employment, where the superintendent did not use due care. Galveston Oil Co. v. Thompson, 76 Tex. 235.

A foreman in a mine is presumed to know the condition of the roof, and his negligence in directing an employé to work under a dangerous portion of the roof will render the master liable for an injury to the latter, who was ignorant of such danger. Consolidated Coal Co. v. Wombacher (Ill.) April 22, 1890.

A pit boss in a mine having authority to command the workmen in respect to what work they shall do, and when they shall discontinue, is a vice-principal. *Ibid.*

Late cases of accidents in use of elevators.

An employer knowing, or whose duty it is to know, that an elevator which an employé is obliged to use on occasions has been undergoing repairs which are not completed, and that the elevator is out of order, and who neglects to inform the employé, who is ignorant of that fact, on a day when, with the employer's knowledge, the employé will have occasion to use the elevator, is liable to the latter for resulting injuries. Dervin v. Herrman, 31 N. Y. S. R. 179.

The employé does not assume the risk of the elevator being in a dangerous condition on a day when, without his knowledge, it was undergoing repairs. *Ibid.*

Where it appears that a scrubbing girl was obliged in her work to use a hotel freight elevator, which was a movable platform with iron guards on the sides which did not reach to the floor, but left space enough for a foot to pass under them, and at the time of the accident it had swayed to one side and tilted over, and she was thrown down and her foot passed under the guard, and she was injured, the defendant is liable, the elevator being unfitted for the safe transportation of human beings. McKinnie v. Kilgallon (Pa). 10 Cent. Rep. 347.

An employé who has been for some time engaged in the use of an elevator which runs only from the first to the second floor is guilty of contributory negligence, where, on pushing up the rod by which the car was lowered, and repeating this act, without starting the car, he put his head into the well to see what was the matter, knowing the bottom of the car was only six feet above, and was struck by the car and injured, when he could have examined the matter safely by simply going upstairs. Murphy v. Webster (Mass.) Feb. 26, 1890.

An employé who, having ridden in a freight elevator to the highest floor in the building, and, after getting off, stood upon the floor or landing endeavoring to remove a car containing grain from the elevator, his hands having hold of the car and his body being over the elevator, cannot recover against his employer for injuries received, due to the carelessness of the engineer in starting the elevator in the wrong direction, whereby the whole force of the engine drew the elevator against a solid beam above, causing the rope to break and the elevator to fall, taking the employé with it. The negligence of the engineer being that of a fellow servant, the employer is not liable therefor. Stringham v. Stewart, 1 L. R. A. 483, 111 N. Y. 188.

In an action to recover for injuries from falling into an elevator well not properly guarded, the evidence showing that plaintiff was not in the exercise of proper care, the fact that all the other floors of the factory were provided with self-closing hatches is immaterial. Taylor v. Carew Mfg. Co. 3 New Eng. Rep. 875, 143 Mass. 470.

in the car, and by means of which the plaintiff was seriously injured. This action is brought to recover damages of the defendants for such injuries, upon the theory that the plaintiff being inexperienced in the running of an elevator, and that to the knowledge of the defendants, and that having been assigned by the defendants to perform this duty, the defendants were bound to qualify him for such service, and that in doing so the machinery was found to be defective, or Henry Dillworth, who was assigned as instructor for the plaintiff, was incompetent to perform this duty, or was negligent in his manner of performing it, and by reason of the premises the defendants are liable to pay plaintiff the damages he has sustained.

Mr. **Edward C. James,** for appellant:

Defendants are liable in this case, because Henry C. Dillworth was the plaintiff's instructor in the operation of the elevator, and *pro hac vice* represented them.

Loughlin v. *State*, 7 Cent. Rep. 70, 105 N. Y. 159; *Crispin* v. *Babbitt*, 81 N. Y. 516; *Brennan* v. *Gordon*, 13 Daly, 208; *Scott* v. *London Dock Co.* 3 H. & C. 597; *Lyons* v. *Rosenthal*, 11 Hun, 46; *Roberts* v. *Johnson*, 58 N. Y. 613; *Seybolt* v. *New York, L. E. & W. R. Co.* 95 N. Y. 562; *Mullen* v. *St. John*, 57 N. Y. 567; *Hill* v. *Ninth Ave. R. Co.* 11 Cent. Rep. 921, 109 N. Y. 239; *Erlach* v. *Edelmeyer*, 15 Jones & S. 292, 88 N. Y. 645.

To order an unskilled servant to do anything requiring skill, in respect to dangerous machinery, of the use of which he is ignorant, without first instructing him in its use, is negligence on the part of a master, rendering him liable to the servant for an injury incurred in attempting to obey his order.

Lalor v. *Chicago, B. & Q. R. Co.* 52 Ill. 401; *Union Pac. R. Co.* v. *Fort*, 84 U. S. 17 Wall. 554 (21 L. ed. 739); *Siegel* v. *Schantz*, 2 Thomp. & C. 353; *Connolly* v. *Poillon*, 41 Barb. 366; *Grizzle* v. *Frost*, 3 Fost. & F. 622; Wood, Mast. and Serv. §§ 349, 350, 444.

Mr. **E. H. Benn,** with *Mr.* **Charles Kitchell,** for respondents:

If the accident was caused by what Harry Dillworth did in the business of taking up and unloading the beams, the defendants cannot be held liable, as in doing that work Harry Dillworth and the plaintiff were co-servants.

Hussey v. *Coger*, 112 N. Y. 614; *Loughlin* v. *State*, 7 Cent. Rep. 70, 105 N. Y. 159; *Crispin* v. *Babbitt*, 81 N. Y. 516.

Potter, *J.*, delivered the opinion of the court:

The principles of law involved in this action are well defined, and are not seriously controverted by the counsel upon this appeal. Those principles are that a duty devolved upon the master of a servant hitherto in the capacity of a common hand laborer, before such laborer should be put in charge of dangerous machinery with which he is not acquainted, to instruct and qualify him for such new duty. *Connolly* v. *Poillon*, 41 Barb. 366, 369; *Ryan* v. *Fowler*, 24 N. Y. 410; *Noyes* v. *Smith*, 28 Vt. 59; *Union Pac. R. Co.* v. *Fort*, 84 U. S. 17 Wall. 552 [21 L. ed. 739].

That, if the master selects a co-servant in his employment to instruct and qualify the servant for the new and more dangerous service, the master must select a competent instructor, or be liable for his incompetency or his negligence while performing the duty of instructor, or for discontinuance of his instruction until it is completed, by which the promoted servant is injured, and, if such is the case, the master will be liable for the injury, and it will be no defense that the injury was caused by one servant to his co-servant; for the servant whose negligence caused the injury stands for the master, and the latter is liable in such case, the same as if the injury was caused by the personal negligence of the master. *Mann* v. *Delaware & H. Canal Co.* 91 N. Y. 500; Wood, Mast. and Serv. §§ 349, 350, 444; *Brennan* v. *Gordon*, 13 Daly, 208, 219 (this case on former appeal); *Loughlin* v. *State*, 105 N. Y. 159, 162, 163, 7 Cent. Rep. 90; *Union Pac. R. Co.* v. *Fort*, *supra*.

The questions in dispute in this case, therefore, are whether the person giving the instructions for the defendants, to qualify the plaintiff to run and manage the elevator, properly performed that duty, or was himself guilty of negligence in starting the elevator, or in leaving it in plaintiff's charge before he was qualified, or whether the machinery was imperfect in any respect, and the defendants were negligent in selecting and putting it in use. If any of these conditions exist upon proper and sufficient evidence to support it, the defendants would be liable to plaintiff for the injuries he sustained. It does not strike me that it can be reasonably claimed that the machinery was defective in starting up at the time the accident occurred, from inherent defect, and without somebody's interference. It was not intended to do so, and never had been known to do so, unless the rope was applied to start it. The testimony in this case is abundant to show that somebody applied the rope to start the elevator up. The difficulty just here is that the evidence is too abundant, so much so that it is difficult, from its superabundance, to decide just who it was that applied the rope to move the elevator up. The case seems to have been tried upon the true theory, to determine whether or not the defendants are liable; and, if any mistrial has taken place, it is owing to errors in the charge of the learned trial judge, or in receiving or rejecting testimony, or in rulings in conducting the trial. It is very evident from a perusal of the case, and the exceptions to the rulings upon the evidence, and the requests to charge, and the exceptions thereto, that the trial was very closely contested; and it would be somewhat remarkable if a trial court, in the hurry and confusion incident to a trial conducted in this manner, should have avoided the commission of some error. In order to properly dispose of these exceptions, it is necessary to have a just understanding of the questions upon trial. They are whether Henry Dillworth was designated by the defendants as the instructor of the plaintiff, to run and manage the elevator, and, if so, whether he properly and sufficiently performed the duty thus devolved upon him by the defendants. I think there was error in the charge of the court, made at the request of the defendants: "If the jury find, as a matter of fact, that the plaintiff was put under instruction of a competent instructor, and that he [instructor] was as well acquainted as defendants with the nature and character of the service which he undertook to perform, he cannot recover." The jury could not otherwise understand this instruction than to mean that the defendants' whole duty to the plaintiff was performed when they assigned as competent an instructor to plaintiff as the defendants were. This was erroneous in two respects. The degree of the instructor's competency was guaged by the competency of the defendants. The plaintiff was entitled to have, and the defendants were bound to provide him with, an instructor competent to teach the art of managing an elevator, regardless of the competency of the defendants in that regard, and of which there was no proof whatever in the case. But the defendants were not only bound to furnish the plaintiff with an instructor absolutely competent to manage an elevator, but the defendants were also bound to provide such an instructor for a reasonable length of time, to teach the plaintiff how to manage the elevator, and that the instructor should be guilty of no negligence, to the injury of the plaintiff, while he was being instructed. These relations spring from the fact that during this period the instructor is doing the work and standing in the place of the defendants, the masters. There are other questions in the case deserving consideration upon this appeal, but I do not deem it necessary or worth the while to discuss them, having reached the conclusion that a new trial must be granted on account of the ruling already considered.

The judgment should be reversed, and a new trial granted, with costs to abide the event.

All concur, except **Haight** and **Parker**, *JJ.*, not sitting.

MICHIGAN SUPREME COURT.

Ariston J. COOK, *Appt.*,
v.
Landan WINCHESTER *et al.*

(......Mich.......)

1. **The words "in presence of the testator,"** in the Statute relating to the execution of wills, do not necessarily mean that the testator and the witnesses must be in the same room, or that he must have actual sight or inspection of the process of signing.

2. **The fact that testatrix could not see the witnesses write their names** or the scrivener write her own, because they signed at a table in an adjoining room about twelve feet from her bed, and out of the line of her vision, although the door was open, unless she moved,

---

NOTE.—*Formal execution of will; what law governs.*

So far as regards the mere formal execution of the testament, it is sufficient if it conforms to the law of the country where the will is made. *Re* Alexander, Tuck. 115; *Re* Roberts' Will, 8 Paige, 519, 4 N. Y. Ch. L. ed. 527, 8 Paige, 446, 4 N. Y. Ch. L. ed. 497.

Title and transfer of, by will and devise, are governed by *lex loci rei sitæ.* Clark v. Graham, 19 U. S. 6 Wheat. 578 (5 L. ed. 335); Elmendorf v. Taylor, 23 U. S. 10 Wheat. 152 (6 L. ed. 289); Darby v. Mayer, 23 U. S. 10 Wheat. 465 (6 L. ed. 367); St. John v. Chew, 25 U. S. 12 Wheat. 153 (6 L. ed. 583).

When a will conveys real estate, it must be executed and attested in accordance with the law of the place where the property is situated, and the testamentary capacity of the testator must be determined by the same law, while the testamentary disposition of personal property is governed by the law of the testator's domicil. Dickey v. Vann, 81 Ala. 425; Hunt v. Mootrie, 3 Bradf. 351.

The general rule is that the law of a testator's domicil at the time of his death controls the testamentary disposition of his personal property, and of all his real property situated within the jurisdiction of the State of his domicil. Bonati v. Welsch, 24 N. Y. 164; Stanley v. Bernes, 3 Hagg. Eccl. 373; Price v. Dewhurst, 4 Myl. & C. 76; *Re* Roberts' Will, 8 Paige, 446, 4 N. Y. Ch. L. ed. 497; Thornton v. Curling, 8 Sim. 310; Ferraris v. Hertford, 7 Jur. 262; Descebats v. Berquier, 1 Binn. 336; *Re* Easton's Will, 6 Paige, 183, 3 N. Y. Ch. L. ed. 948; Chamberlain v. Chamberlain, 43 N. Y. 435; Moultrie v. Hunt, 23 N. Y. 409.

Requisites to due execution of will.

Four things, at least, are requisite for the due execution of a will, which may be succinctly stated as follows: the testator's subscription at the end of the will, done in presence of each of the attesting witnesses, or acknowledging such subscription to them; publication, or declaring to them at the time of making or acknowledging subscription that it is his last will and testament, and attestation by at least two witnesses, who sign their names as such at the end of the will, at his request. Butler v. Benson, 1 Barb. 530; Rutherford v. Rutherford, 1 Denio, 33; Chaffee v. Baptist Missionary Conv. 10 Paige, 85, 4 N. Y. Ch. L. ed. 896; Brinckerhoff v. Remsen, 8 Paige, 488, 4 N. Y. Ch. L. ed. 514.

The Legislature has power to prescribe the formalities to be observed in the execution of a will; and by so doing it does not interfere with the natural right of an individual to dispose of his property as he sees fit. *Re* McCabe, 68 Cal. 519.

If the intended disposition of property be of a testamentary character, not to take effect in the testator's lifetime, such disposition is inoperative unless in writing in conformity to the Statute relating to wills. Comer v. Comer, 8 West. Rep. 675, 120 Ill. 420.

It is not necessary that the presentation of a will be manual or more formally made than by an affirmative answer to the question by the testator whether the paper contains his last will. Pfarr v. Belmont, 39 La. Ann. 294.

The Civil Code of Louisiana employs the word "testaments" in its generic sense, and it was intended to convey the idea that the several formalities required in the confection of different testaments must be observed therein "respectively" and not "collectively." Murray's Succession (La.) Dec. 16, 1889.

Wills of personal property, except nuncupative wills of a certain character, must be executed in writing. *Ex parte* Turner, 24 S. C. 211.

See also 12 L. R. A. 452; 15 L. R. A. 606; 16 L. R. A. 367; 18 L. R. A. 458.

which she was unable to do, will not invalidate the execution of the will under a statute requiring her signature if made by another, as well as those of the witnesses, to be subscribed in "her presence," where the will was read to her both before and after signing and the names of the witnesses shown to her and they told her in answer to her question that they had signed it and she made her mark in their presence.

(July 2, 1890.)

APPEAL by proponent from a judgment of the Circuit Court for Kent County affirming a judgment of the Probate Court refusing to admit to probate the alleged will of Alzina Page, deceased. *Reversed.*

The facts are fully stated in the opinion.

Messrs. **Maher & Felker** for appellant.

Messrs. **Butterfield & Keeney** and **Thompson & Temple** for appellees.

Morse, *J.*, delivered the opinion of the court:

This controversy involves the validity of a will, the sole question being whether or not it was duly executed, or rather witnessed, under the laws of this State. There is no question of fraud or undue influence in the case, nor did the testatrix lack mental capacity to execute a will. It must be conceded from all the testimony in the case that the will was drawn by an honest, disinterested and trustworthy man; that he was the chosen instrument of Mrs. Page to draft it; that she had frequently consulted and advised with him before as to the disposition of her property, and had told him how she intended to bequeath it; that the will as made was just as she wanted it, and as she had long intended to make it; that it was read to her before she signed it and after she signed, at both of which times she expressed herself as fully satisfied with it; that she signed it in the presence of the persons who witnessed it, and that she requested them to witness it; that she asked them after it was executed if they had witnessed it, and received an affirmative answer, and was then shown their signatures, and their names were read over to her. If the will is not sustained, the property will certainly go, under the law, where she did not wish it to go. It is therefore the duty of the courts to uphold it if possible. It is claimed that the requirements of our Statute were not complied with in the witnessing of this will. The Statute provides (How. Stat. § 5789) that three things are requisite to the validity of a will: (1) that it shall be in writing; (2) that it shall be signed by the testator, or by some person in his presence, and by his express direction; (3) that it shall be attested and subscribed in the presence of the testator, by two or more competent witnesses.

The will was drawn by James Toland, supervisor of the Township of Byron, Kent County, who lived only a few rods from Mrs. Page, and with whom she had frequently talked about making her will, and how she wished it drawn. On the 30th of June, 1888, she sent for him. Mrs. Page had been an invalid for many years, and at this time was confined to her bed, and unable to leave it without help. Toland found her in a bedroom adjoin-

Requisites of statute to be complied with.

In the execution of the instrument the Statute does not require any particular form of words to be used by the testator either in the admission of his signature, in the publication of the instrument or in the communication to the witnesses of his desire that they subscribe their names to the will as attesting witnesses. It is sufficient if the formalities required by the Statute are complied with. Lyman v. Phillips, 3 Dem. 475.

It is sufficient if the requisitions of the Statute are complied with in substance. Brown v. De Selding, 4 Sandf. 16, 8 N. Y. Legal Obs. 228; Remsen v. Brinckerhoff, 26 Wend. 332.

The substance of the testator's intention, if manifested by such acts as the law recognizes, is to govern in preference to any formal or literal following of the words of the Statute. Simmons v. Simmons, 26 Barb. 77.

The *onus* of satisfying the court that they have all been complied with lies upon the party seeking to establish the will. Baskin v. Baskin, 36 N. Y. 421, 424; Lewis v. Lewis, 11 N. Y. 224.

Subscription to will.

No one of the requisites of the Statute as to subscription of a will can be dispensed with, and, without a substantial compliance with them all, the will cannot be admitted to probate. Haton v. Sigman, 1 Dem. 529; Lewis v. Lewis, 13 Barb. 22; Baskin v. Baskin, 36 N. Y. 421, 424; Seymour v. Van Wyck, 6 N. Y. 120; Mitchell v. Mitchell, 16 Hun, 97; Jackson v. Jackson, 39 N. Y. 153.

Where a Statute provides that a will must be "subscribed by the testator," etc., it is held that where another person, in the presence and at the request of the testator, signs his name to the will, it is a good execution under the Statute. Scott v. Seaver, 59 Wis. 134; Barnard v. Heydrick, 49 Barb. 66, 2 Abb. Pr. N. S. 51, 32 How. Pr. 101; *Re* McElwaine, 18 N. J. Eq. 502.

It is sufficient that it be either made, or acknowledged, in the presence of those who attest it. If it be unsigned, it is no will; and in that case publication and attestation are alike unavailing. Baskin v. Baskin, 36 N. Y. 419, 2 Trans. App. 17.

The law allows the will to be subscribed by the testator making his mark, or his name may be written by another person at his request. Simpson's Will, 2 Redf. 32. See *note* to Knox's App. (Pa.) 6 L. R. A. 353.

The attesting witnesses should see the testator or someone for him sign the instrument, or the testator should either say or do something in their presence and hearing, indicating that he intends to recognize such instrument as one which has been signed by him as a valid will. Gardiner v. Raines, 3 Dem. 108; Lyman v. Phillips, 3 Dem. 474.

Where testatrix subscribed the will by making her mark, but not in the presence of the attesting witnesses, and afterwards in their presence placed her finger on her name and said, "I acknowledge this to be my last will and testament," the will was not well executed. *Re* Shaffer, 2 How. Pr. N. S. 496; Willis v. Mott, 36 N. Y. 486, 2 Trans. App. 67; Porteus v. Holm, 4 Dem. 18; Lewis v. Lewis, 11 N. Y. 225; Larabee v. Ballard, 1 Dem. 497; Buckhout v. Fisher, 4 Dem. 233.

The subscription, by a witness to a will, of the name of the testatrix, made under her direction, in her presence and at her request, is a sufficient execution of the will, although the person signing her name omits to write his own name near by as a witness to her signature. *Re* Langan, 74 Cal. 353.

The first name only may be a sufficient signature to a will, where it is clearly intended as a complete execution of the instrument. Knox's App. 6 L. R. A. 353, 131 Pa. 220.

See also 11 L. R. A. 796.

ing, and opening by a door into the kitchen,—a kitchen bedroom,—which communicated with no other room. He asked Mrs. Page, who said that she was ready to make her will, and wished him to draw it, if she wanted it drawn in the same manner as she had before told him to draw it. She said, "Yes," and he proceeded. There was no table in the room where Mrs. Page was, and he drew the will on a table in the kitchen. This table was near the bedroom door, but when the door was open it was impossible for anyone lying squarely on the bed to see the table or anyone sitting at it. Mrs. Page could not move in bed, and was not able to see the table. Toland drew the will, and took it into the bedroom, and read it to Mrs. Page. She was satisfied with the will. Not being able to handle a pen very well, she requested Toland to write her name. He went to the kitchen table and wrote it. He then came in, and she made her mark. Three ladies were present in the room, Mrs. Weaver, Mrs. McConnell and Mrs. Miller. Mrs. Page requested Mrs. Weaver and Mrs. McConnell to witness the will. Mrs. Weaver did not wish to sign it for some reason, and Mrs. Page then signified that she wished Mrs. Miller to witness it. Mrs. Miller and Mrs. McConnell then stepped into the kitchen and signed the will as witnesses. Mr. Toland and the witnesses then went into the room again, and Toland read the will over to her again, and asked her if it suited her. She said it was all right,—just as she intended it should be. Toland showed the names of the witnesses to her, and also read them to her. He testified that previous to his showing it to her she asked the witnesses if they had signed it, and they told her they had. The door was open between the kitchen and bedroom when the witnessing was done. Mrs. Miller's testimony agrees with Toland, except she says that she stood in the door when the will was being read over after the witnesses had signed it, and did not hear Mrs. Page ask her or Mrs. McConnell if they had signed as witnesses, but heard Toland tell her that they had witnessed the will, and read their names to her. Mrs. McConnell (now Mrs. Merritt) states that when they went back into the bedroom after witnessing the will, and Toland read it all over to Mrs. Page again, she said it was all right, and just as she wanted it,—the witnesses and everything were all right. "She asked me if we had signed it, and I told her we had. Mrs. Miller and Mr. Toland were there."

The room in which Mrs. Page was lying was eight feet square. The kitchen was about fifteen feet square. The distance from where the witnesses sat while signing the will to the bed of Mrs. Page was about twelve feet. The will was denied probate by the judge of probate of Kent County, and on appeal to the circuit court his action was affirmed.

It is claimed that the will was not executed—witnessed—in the presence of the testatrix. It is true that it was physically impossible for her to see the witnesses when they were in the act of signing it without moving herself upon the edge of the bed, which she was unable to do. And it is argued by counsel for the contestants that there are no cases to be found in the books, except possibly two, which can be claimed as

---

Acknowledgment of signature.

The testator must declare the instrument to be his last will and testament to each of the subscribing witnesses. Abbey v. Christy, 49 Barb. 279; Nelson v. McGiffert, 3 Barb. Ch. 158, 5 N. Y. Ch. L. ed. 855; Orser v. Orser, 24 N. Y. 51; Auburn Theological Seminary v. Calhoun, 25 N. Y. 422; Thompson v. Seastedt, 6 Thomp. & C. 78; Tarrant v. Ware, *note* to 25 N. Y. 425; Peck v. Cary, 27 N. Y. 10.

A declaration by a testator to the witness, that the instrument is his will, or even a request by him to the witness to attest his will, or other varied form of expression implying that the same had been signed by the testator, are either of them quite sufficient. Willis v. Mott, 36 N. Y. 497, 2 Trans. App. 72; Ela v. Edwards, 16 Gray, 91.

Where the testator produces the will, with the signature visibly apparent on the face of it, to the witnesses, and requests them to subscribe it, it is a sufficient acknowledgment of his signature. *Re* Harder, Tuck. 430; Rash v. Purnel, 2 Harr. (Del.) 448; Dewey v. Dewey, 1 Met. 349; Hogan v. Grosvenor, 10 Met. 54.

Where one of the witnesses in the presence of the other asked the testator if the name at the end of the instrument was his, and the testator replied that it was, it was a sufficient subscription. If he held the instrument open in his hand and said to one of the witnesses "I want you to witness my will," and then to the other "I want you to witness it too," it was sufficient as a publication. Van Hooser v. Van Hooser, 1 Redf. 368.

If the testator knew the nature of the instrument he executed, and that the witnesses were informed at the time that it was his will, either by himself or by any person acting for him in his presence, this was sufficient. Auburn Theological Seminary v. Calhoun, 38 Barb. 160; Seguine v. Seguine, 2 Barb. 385; Nipper v. Groesbeck, 22 Barb. 670; Coffin v. Coffin, 23 N. Y. 9.

Where testatrix took the will drawn by one of the witnesses, read it and pronounced it all right, and said, in the presence and hearing of all, that the one she had brought in would be a witness to it, and requested him to sign it, which he did, and the other witness was told in her presence that he was needed to sign as a witness, which he did, this was a substantial compliance with the Statute. Thompson v. Stevens, 62 N. Y. 635; Gilbert v. Knox, 52 N. Y. 125; Peck v. Cary, 27 N. Y. 9.

No formal declaration of a paper executed as a last will and testament is necessary; it is only required that the witnesses should be given to understand by words or acts of decedent that the proposed paper was intended as a will. Jones v. Jones, 42 Hun, 563.

Under the Code, it is not necessary that there should be particular words or a set form of speech to constitute a declaration that the instrument is the testator's will. Bourke v. Wilson, 38 La. Ann. 320.

Any act which indicates the same thing with unmistakable certainty is sufficient. Allison v. Allison, 46 Ill. 63; Nickerson v. Buck, 12 Cush. 332.

It is sufficient that enough is said or done in the presence and with the knowledge of the testator to make the witnesses understand distinctly that he desires them to know that the paper is his will, and that they are to witness it. Elkinton v. Brick, 1 L. R. A. 161, 44 N. J. Eq. 154; *Re* Hunt, 110 N. Y. 278.

Where the only declaration made by testator in the presence of the witnesses was his reply to the question whether it was his last will and testament, to which he answered "Yes,"—it was a sufficient acknowledgment of the genuineness of his signature. *Re* Austin, 45 Hun, 1.

authority for the admission of the will to probate. That the Statute has been uniformly held to require that "the condition and position of the testator when his will is attested, and in reference to the act of signing by the witnesses, and their locality when signing, must be such that he has knowledge of what is going forward, and is mentally observant of the specific act in progress, and, unless he is blind, the signing by the witnesses must occur where the testator, as he is circumstanced, may see them sign if he chooses to do so. If in this state of things some change in the testator's posture is requisite to bring the action of the witnesses within the scope of his vision, and such movement is not prevented by his physical infirmity, but is caused by an indisposition or indifference on his part to take visual notice of the proceedings, the act of witnessing is to be considered as done in his presence. If, however, the testator's ability to see the witnesses subscribe is dependent upon his ability to make the requisite movement, then if his ailment so operates upon him as to prevent this movement, and on account of this he does not see the witnesses subscribe, the will is not witnessed in his presence." See opinion of *Justice* Graves in *Aikin* v. *Weckerly*, 19 Mich. 504.

A large number of cases are cited in support of the counsel's claim, to wit: *Mandeville* v. *Parker*, 31 N. J. Eq. 242; *Doe* v. *Manifold*, 1 Maule & S. 294; *Reynolds* v. *Reynolds*, 1 Speers, L. 253; *Robinson* v. *King*, 6 Ga. 539; *Brooks* v. *Duffell*, 23 Ga. 441; *Reed* v. *Roberts*, 26 Ga. 294; *Jones* v. *Tuck*, 3 Jones, L. 202; *Eccleston* v. *Petty*, Carth. 79; *Broderick* v. *Broderick*, 1 P. Wms. 239; *Lamb* v. *Girtman*, 33 Ga. 289; *Neil* v. *Neil*, 1 Leigh, 6; *Orndorff* v. *Hummer*, 12 B. Mon. 626; *Re Downie*, 42 Wis. 66; *Duffie* v. *Corridon*, 40 Ga. 122; *Edelen* v. *Hardey*, 7 Har. & J. 61; *Russell* v. *Falls*, 3 Har. & McH. 457; *Graham* v. *Graham*, 10 Ired. L. 219; *Re Cox's Will*, 1 Jones, L. 321; *Ragland* v. *Huntingdon*, 1 Ired. L. 561; *Chase* v. *Kittredge*, 11 Allen, 49; *Compton* v. *Mitton*, 12 N. J. L. 71; *Combs* v. *Jolly*, 3 N. J. Eq. 625; *Den* v. *Matlack*, 17 N. J. L. 86; *Hindmarsh* v. *Carlton*, 8 H. L. Cas. 160.

It must be conceded that these cases all fully support the contention that the will must be witnessed in the same room with the testator, or, if out of the room, where he can see them sign if he desires to do so,—he must be in a position where it is possible to see them. The fact that the will, after being witnessed out of the testator's sight, is brought to the view of the testator, and he looks upon the signatures of the witnesses, and they then acknowledge the witnessing of it before him, will not cure this defect in its execution, according to the authority of some of these cases. See *Chase* v. *Kittredge*, 11 Allen, 61; *Re Cox's Will*, *Graham* v. *Graham*, *Russell* v. *Falls*, *Lamb* v. *Girtman* and *Re Downie*, *supra*.

The extreme rule laid down in some of these cases cited by counsel for contestants, notably *Graham* v. *Graham*, *supra*, a North Carolina case, was criticised, and I think justly so, by *Justice* Champlin in *Maynard* v. *Vinton*, 59 Mich. 148, 149, but for the purposes of that case the doctrine of *Aikin* v. *Weckerley* was adhered to.

But where the name of the testator was not signed to the will in the presence of either of the attesting witnesses, and testator did not acknowledge the signature to be his to either of such witnesses, his answer "Yes," to a question of one of the subscribing witnesses when she inquired on entering, referring to the testator and his wife, whether they were making their wills, is not a compliance with the requirement of the Statute. *Re* Simmons, 30 N. Y. S. R. 446.

His acknowledgment that the seal and signature are his, with a request to the witnesses to attest the instrument, is sufficient. Osborn v. Cook, 11 Cush. 532.

In the absence of a subscription in the presence of the witnesses, there must be substantially an acknowledgment; and the law will not deem sufficient proof of subscription that which does not come up to this. Sisters of Charity v. Kelly, 67 N. Y. 413.

It is not sufficient acknowledgment by the testator that he has signed the will, unless the witnesses see the signature. *Re* Mackay, 44 Hun, 571.

The law requires that the testator shall communicate to the witnesses that it is his will and he desires them to attest it. An unlimited latitude of expression may be used if it conveys the proper meaning. *Re* Harder, Tuck. 429.

Publication of will.

No particular form of words is required or necessary to effect publication. Lane v. Lane, 95 N. Y. 494; *Re* Beckett, 4 Cent. Rep. 381, 103 N. Y. 167.

Publication of will may be made in any form of communication by testator to witnesses, whereby he makes known to them that he intends the instrument to take effect as his will. See Coffin v. Coffin, 23 N. Y. 9, 80 Am. Dec. 235, and *note*.

If signed before being presented to them, the exhibition of the paper with his acknowledgment that it was his last will and testament was a sufficient acknowledgment of the signature and publication of the will, within the rule laid down by this court in *Re* Phillips, 98 N. Y. 267.

If signed by another than the testator, and the signature be purposely concealed from his view and that of the attesting witnesses, the mere publication of the instrument as his last will and testament cannot fairly be deemed an acknowledgment that the unseen subscription was made by his direction. Baskin v. Baskin, 36 N. Y. 419, 2 Trans. App. 17; Rutherford v. Rutherford, 1 Denio, 33.

The signing of a will by the testatrix and witnesses in the presence of each other is a sufficient publication of it, where the person who drew it announced that it was her will. Denny v. Pinney, 5 New Eng. Rep. 639, 60 Vt. 524.

If the will was signed before its attestation, the exhibition of the will, and of the testator's signature attached thereto, and his declaration that it was his last will and testament, and a request to the witnesses to attest the same, is a sufficient acknowledgment of the signature and publication. *Re* Hunt, 42 Hun, 434.

It has been doubted whether, as to a will of real estate, publication, in the sense required by the Statute of this State, was ever necessary since the enactment of 29 Car. II., chap. 3. *Re* Simpson, 56 How. Pr. 135.

There is a difference between our former Statute of Wills and the present one, which shows the necessity of the publication of the instrument by declaring it to be the last will and testament of the testator. Proctor v. Clarke, 3 Redf. 448.

Attesting witnesses.

Under the Statute of Wisconsin, the witnesses to a will need not know the nature of the instrument to which they attach their names as witnesses to

In *Maynard* v. *Vinton* the testatrix was in a position where she might have seen the witnesses sign, as they were within the range of her vision if she saw fit to look, as was also the case with the testator in *Aikin* v. *Weckerley*.

The precise question raised by the record in this case has never been presented to this court, and neither of the two cases above mentioned seems to stand in the way of a just and liberal construction of the Statute in this case in favor of the validity of the execution of this will of Alzina Page. I agree with *Judge* Champlin that "presence," as used in the Statute, has been too narrowly construed by many of the courts as meaning that the witnesses must be under the eye of the testator. I find two cases referred to on the argument where the facts are almost identical with those found by the circuit judge in this case, and in both of which the will was sustained.

In the first (*Sturdivant* v. *Birchitt*, 10 Gratt. 67), the will was attested by the witnesses subscribing their names as such in a different room from that in which the testator was lying at the time of such signing. The testator could not see the witnesses in the act of signing, either from the bed on which he lay or from any other place within the room. The testator signed the will in the presence of the witnesses, and requested them to attest it. They went together into another room for that purpose, it being inconvenient to do so in the room where the testator was lying. When they subscribed their names no other person was in the room, and they immediately returned to the room where the testator was. They were gone from that room not over two minutes. They took the will to the testator, who was lying in bed, and, both of the witnesses being together, one of them said to him, "Mr. Sturdivant, here is your will witnessed," at the same time pointing with his finger to the names of the witnesses, and holding the will open before him, the names of said witnesses being on the same page, and close to that of the testator. He took the will in his hands, and looked at it as if he was examining it. He then closed or folded it. On being told that he was ill, and had better give the will to someone to keep for him, he asked whether if he got well he could take it back from the person to whom he might give it. Being answered in the affirmative, he said: "It is my will, and I wish it to stand, but I may hereafter, on getting well, wish to make some slight alteration in it." He then handed the will to a friend.

In the other case of *Riggs* v. *Riggs*, 135 Mass. 238 (decided June 21, 1883), the witnesses to

---

the signature of the person who has subscribed the same. Allen v. Griffin, 69 Wis. 529.

There shall be at least two attesting witnesses, each of whom shall sign his name as a witness at the end of the will at the request of the testator. *Re* Lewis, 9 N. Y. Legal Obs. 152; Doe v. Roe, 2 Barb. 200.

In Pennsylvania two witnesses are indispensable to the probate of every will. Lewis v. Maris, 1 U. S. 1 Dall. 278 (1 L. ed. 136). But see, *contra*, Hight v. Wilson, 1 U. S. 1 Dall. 94 (1 L. ed. 51).

The requirement of the Statute that a will shall be attested by "at least two credible witnesses" means that it shall be attested by such persons as are not disqualified by mental imbecility, interest or crime from giving testimony in a court of justice. It was therefore error in this case to require the jury to find that the witnesses to the will in contest were credible persons, in order to sustain the will; but as there was no testimony even tending to show that the witnesses to the will were not credible, the instruction was not prejudicial. Fuller v. Fuller, 83 Ky. 345.

A deaf person is disqualified to witness a will. Dauterive's Succession, 39 La. Ann. 1092.

The want of knowledge by a witness of the language in which the will is drawn up and the testator expresses himself cannot be supplied by translating the language to such witness while the will is being drawn. *Ibid.*

Courts in many cases have authoritatively declared it is a sufficient compliance with those requirements where the will was subscribed in the presence of one witness and the signature thereafter acknowledged to the other. Gardiner v. Raines, 3 Dem. 107.

In Kentucky, although more than one witness is required to subscribe a will disposing of lands, the evidence of one may be sufficient to prove it. Davis v. Mason, 26 U. S. 1 Pet. 503 (7 L. ed. 239).

A person may become an attesting witness to a will by making his mark, although the person who writes his name fails to sign his own name as a witness of that fact. Davis v. Semmes, 51 Ark. 48.

It is not an insuperable objection that one of the subscribing witnesses makes his mark instead of writing his name; it is still a signing within the meaning of the Statute. Morris v. Kniffin, 37 Barb. 340; Keeney v. Whitmarsh, 16 Barb. 141; Meehan v. Rourke, 2 Bradf. 385.

Witnesses must sign in presence of testator.

The attesting witnesses must sign in the presence of the testator. Pawtucket v. Ballou, 1 New Eng. Rep. 131, 15 R. I. 58; Moore v. Spier, 80 Ala. 129; Welch v. Adams, 1 New Eng. Rep. 59, 63 N. H. 344.

An attestation made in the same room in which the testator is, is prima facie made in his presence. Ayres v. Ayres, 11 Cent. Rep. 230, 43 N. J. Eq. 565.

Where a will was subscribed to in an adjoining room, the communicating door being open, and testator could have seen the witnesses signing if he desired, it is subscribed in his presence. Will of Meurer, 44 Wis. 396.

By the Mississippi statutes, a will of realty must be written and signed by the testator, or by someone in his presence by his direction, and must be attested by witnesses in his presence, if not wholly written or subscribed by him. Everhart v. Everhart, 34 Fed. Rep. 82.

Proof that witnesses to a will were present and saw testator sign, that he was sitting in a chair at the time, and that they subscribed in his presence, with nothing to show that he did not see them subscribe, or that he was in a position where he could not see them,—is sufficient to prove the execution of the will. Spratt v. Spratt (Mich.) Oct. 11, 1889.

If the testator presents the will already subscribed by him to the witness, acknowledges that he has executed it as such will, that the same is his will, and requests him to sign the same as a witness, and he signs it in the presence of the testator, it is sufficient. Willis v. Mott, 36 N. Y. 492.

A Mexican will is not null because it does not appear on the face of the will that the witnesses were present during the whole time of the execution of the will, and heard and understood the dispositions it contained. Adams v. Norris, 64 U. S. 23 How. 353 (16 L. ed. 539).

In Pennsylvania a will devising real estate need not be sealed or subscribed by the witnesses. Hight v. Wilson, 1 U. S. 1 Dall. 94 (1 L. ed. 51).

In Rhode Island the witnesses to a will must subscribe their names in the presence of the testator.

the will saw the testator sign it, and were in the room with him at the time. They signed it as witnesses in a room adjoining the one testator was in, and at a distance of about nine feet from him, the door being open. The testator was in bed, and in such a position that if he had been able to turn his head around he might, by so turning it, have seen the witnesses when they signed their names, and also the will itself, unless during a part of the time when their bodies obstructed the view; but from the effect of an injury which he had received he could not in point of fact turn his head sufficiently to see them and the will at the time when they were signing their names as witnesses. After the witnesses had signed the will it was handed to the testator as he was lying upon the bed, and he read their names as signed, and said he was glad that it was done.

These cases differ from the one at bar only in the fact that the will was taken, after witnessing, into the hands of the testator, who in one case looked at it, and in the other read the names, while in Mrs. Page's case the names were shown her while the will was in the hands of the scrivener, and read to her, as well as the names of the witnesses to it. The difference is unimportant. In all three of the cases the maker of the will knew what he or she was doing, and what was being done, being conscious of all that took place, and no claim of fraud is made or entertainable in any of them. The majority of the Virginia Supreme Court (three out of five judges) sustained the will in the first case, and held that the Statute was substantially complied with, in a very able and exhaustive opinion by *Justice* Lee. In his opinion the learned justice shows conclusively from the authorities that the words "in presence of" do not necessarily imply that the testator and the witnesses must be in the same room, nor that actual sight or inspection of the process of signing is peremptorily required, because it is well settled that a blind man may make a will. He holds that the recognition by the witnesses of their signatures to the will made within the immediate sight and presence of the testator, immediately after they have signed it in an adjoining room, furnishes as complete a security against the frauds and impositions sought to be guarded against by the Statute as the actual manual operation of writing their names by the witnesses under his eye. The identity of the witnesses is also equally assured in both modes. In the Massachusetts case the court was unanimous in sustaining the will. In referring to the holding by some of the courts that an attestation was insufficient when the testator did not and could not see the

---

Acknowledgment by a witness, in the presence of the testator, of the witness's signature affixed in the testator's absence, is a nullity. Pawtucket v. Ballou, 1 New Eng. Rep. 181, 15 R. I. 58.

It is not necessary to the legal execution of a will that it be signed or sealed in the presence of the subscribing witnesses, nor that the witnesses sign in the presence of each other. Welch v. Adams, 1 New Eng. Rep. 59, 63 N. H. 344; Gen. Laws, chap. 193, § 6.

It is unnecessary, under the Indiana Statute, that witnesses should simultaneously subscribe. Johnson v. Johnson, 4 West. Rep. 517, 106 Ind. 475.

It is not necessary that testator and subscribing witnesses sign in the presence of each other. Welch v. Adams, 1 New Eng. Rep. 59, 63 N. H. 344.

It was the common law, until the change made by express statute in 1837, that it was not necessary that the subscribing witnesses should attest the will at the same time, or in each other's presence. Johnson v. Johnson, 4 West. Rep. 518, 106 Ind. 475, 55 Am. Rep. 762; Hoysradt v. Kingman, 22 N. Y. 375; Wright v. Wright, 7 Bing. 457; Moore v. Spier, 80 Ala. 129.

It suffices that each witness subscribe in the presence and at the request of the testator, although it is severally and apart as respects each other. Hoysradt v. Kingman, 22 N. Y. 375.

Signing at request of testator.

The witnesses must attest and subscribe the will at the request of the testator. Bundy v. McKnight, 48 Ind. 502; Coffin v. Coffin, 23 N. Y. 9; Reed v. Watson, 27 Ind. 443; Watson v. Pipes, 32 Miss. 454; Dean v. Dean, 27 Vt. 746; Sechrest v. Edwards, 4 Met. (Ky.) 163; Hogan v. Grosvenor, 10 Met. 54; Pollock v. Glassell, 2 Gratt. 439; Morris v. Kniffin, 37 Barb. 340.

If the attesting witnesses sign the will in the testator's presence, without objection on his part, he knowing that they are signing as such witnesses, that is sufficient, without any special request by him that they sign it. Will of Meurer, 44 Wis. 401.

That the witnesses signed and attested in the presence and at the request of the testator leads to the conclusion that the will was duly executed in all the particulars required by law. Morris v. Kniffin, *supra;* Torry v. Bowen, 15 Barb. 304.

The fact that the will was signed, sealed and witnessed as such in the presence of the testator and subscribing witnesses was evidence from which the jury might find that the will was attested by the subscribing witnesses at the request of the testator. Welch v. Adams, 1 New Eng. Rep. 59, 63 N. H. 344.

Not only the witnesses, but the testator himself, must have understood that they were witnessing the execution of the will, in conformity with his desire and wish, although he may not have said in terms, "I request you, and each of you, to subscribe your names to this my will." Mairs v. Freeman, 3 Redf. 196; Bundy v. McKnight, 48 Ind. 508; *Re* Smith, 40 How. Pr. 126.

A request to a witness to subscribe a will may be made by a third person, provided testator hears and understands it, and does not dissent. Cheatham v. Hatcher, 30 Gratt. 56.

Where the draftsman who was attending to the execution of the will called upon third persons within hearing to come forward and witness the will, they should be held to have signed at the request of the testatrix. Cheatham v. Hatcher, 30 Gratt. 61.

No precise form of words, addressed to each of the witnesses, at the very time of the attestation, is required. Peck v. Cary, 28 N. Y. 27.

Where a friend of testatrix entered the room with two witnesses, saying, "These gentlemen have come to witness the will," to which she bowed her head in assent; whereupon the will was read to her by her friend in an audible voice, and, being asked if she understood it, she signified her assent as before, and then signed it in a legible manner, her arm being held to steady the pen, but the pen not being touched; after which she was laid back in a recumbent position, and the witnesses subscribed the will at a table near the foot of the bed while she was so lying that she was obliged to see them unless she shut her eyes or turned her head away,—it was held that the will was duly executed in her presence. Baldwin v. Baldwin, 81 Va. 405.

witnesses subscribe their names, *Chief Justice* Morton, speaking for the court, says: "We are of opinion that so nice and narrow a construction is not required by the letter, and would defeat the spirit, of our Statute." He further says: "The Statute does not make the test of the validity of a will to be that the testator must see the witnesses subscribe their names. They must subscribe 'in his presence,' but in cases where he has lost or cannot use his sense of sight, if his mind and hearing are not affected, if he is sensible of what is being done, if the witnesses subscribe in the same room, or in such close proximity as to be within the line of vision of one in his position who could see, and within his hearing, they subscribe in his presence. . . . In a case like the one before us, there is much less liability to deception or imposition than there would be in the case of a blind man, because the testator, by holding the will before his eyes, could determine by sight that the will subscribed by the witnesses was the same will executed by him. . . . The door was open, and the table was within the line of vision of the testator, if he had been able to look, and the witnesses were within his hearing. The testator could hear all that was said, and knew and understood all that was done; and, after the witnesses had signed it, . . . it was handed to the testator, and he read their names as signed, and said he was glad it was done. For the reasons before stated, we are of opinion that this was an attestation in his presence, and was sufficient."

So, in this case, the witnesses were in the line of the testatrix's vision if she could have moved to one side of the bed, which she could not do, as in the Massachusetts case the witnesses were in the range of the testator's vision if he could have turned his head, but he could not. I am better satisfied with the liberal construction of the Statute and the reasoning of these two cases than I am with the authorities cited to the opposite, and sustaining the "nice and narrow" interpretation of the Statute; and in the case at bar such holding, as it will in most cases, reaches the justice and equity of the case, which adds to my satisfaction. No fraud was perpetrated, and none well could have been, under the circumstances of the execution of this will. But, in holding the will invalid, a fraud is committed upon the testatrix, as well as her chosen beneficiary, by the law, and her property is disposed of contrary to her wish and intention, to those from whom she sought to keep it away. It is not the purpose or province of the law to do this when it can be avoided. In the definition of the phrase "in the presence of" due regard must be had to the circumstances of each particular case, as it is well settled by all the authorities that the Statute does not require absolutely that the witnessing must be done in the actual sight of the testator, nor yet within the same room with him. If, as before shown, they sign within his hearing, knowledge and understanding, and so near as not to be substantially away from him, they are considered to be in his presence. But we hold that the execution of this will was valid expressly upon the ground that not only was the act of signing by the witnesses within the hearing, knowledge and understanding of the testatrix, but after such signing the witnesses came back into the room where she was with the will, which was on one sheet of paper; that the will was then again all read over to her by the scrivener, and the names of the witnesses read to her and their signatures shown to her, and she informed by the witnesses, or one of them in the presence of the other, that the will had been signed by them; and that she then said it was all right, "just as she wanted it; witnesses and everything was all right." This seems to us to have been a substantial compliance with the Statute, and a witnessing in the presence of the testatrix. The circuit judge returns in his findings of fact that his decision was based entirely on the ground that the will was not properly witnessed under the Statute; that, the will not being admitted in evidence for this reason, the case proceeded no further, the proponent taking an exception, and resting. The contestants announced that they were prepared to show that the testatrix was incompetent to make a will.

The judgment of the Circuit Court will be reversed, and a new trial granted.

The other Justices concurred.

MAINE SUPREME JUDICIAL COURT.

INHABITANTS OF CHARLOTTE
v.
PEMBROKE IRON WORKS.

(....Me.....)

1. **The right of parties upon public ways** and streets is a public right in which the whole community have an equal interest with an equa right to complain of any infringement upon any such right.

2. **Encroachments upon the right to pass** along a public highway, which amount to public nuisances, may be prosecuted in behalf of the public.

NOTE.—*Use of streets in cities and towns.*

Subject to such rights as are vested in the owners, a city may give direction in the use of the public streets, and the authorities can properly allow them to be used for pleasure traveling, either by vehicles drawn by horses or sleds drawn by children. Arther v. Cohoes, 56 Hun, 36.

The occupancy, for drainage purposes, of an alley dedicated by parol without any restrictions as to its use, by putting under it connections with city sewers, is a proper use of it. McElhone's App. 11 Cent. Rep. 392, 118 Pa. 618.

The entire street is for the use of the public; and an unauthorized use of part of it for a market is a public nuisance. McDonald v. Newark, 5 Cent. Rep. 649, 42 N. J. Eq. 136.

A sidewalk is intended for the use of pedestrians, and a person on a bicycle makes an unlawful use of it when he rides or drives his bicycle along it

See also 10 L. R. A. 188; 12 L. R. A. 259; 26 L. R. A. 410.

3. No length of time, unless there be a limit by statute, will legalize a public nuisance.

4. Rev. Stat., chap. 18, § 95, in relation to adverse possession of ways and streets by buildings and fences fronting thereon, has no application where the act complained of consists in maintaining a dam, whereby water is caused to overflow a highway and injure the same.

5. The maintenance of a dam in such a manner as to cause water to overflow a highway and wash gullies therein constitutes a public nuisance; and if the town which is bound to maintain such highway suffers special damage from such nuisance, it may recover the same against the party maintaining it.

(February 21, 1890.)

REPORT from the Supreme Judicial Court for Washington County, for the opinion of the full court of questions arising upon exceptions to the report of the referee in favor of plaintiffs in an action brought to recover damages for the maintenance of a public nuisance. *Affirmed.*

The case sufficiently appears in the opinion.

Messrs. **Rounds & McKusick** for plaintiffs.

Mr. **A. McNichol** for defendant.

Foster, J., delivered the opinion of the court:

The defendants and their grantors had maintained a dam on the Pemaquam River, in the Town of Charlotte, on account of which the waters in the outlet of Round Pond were raised so that during portions of the year they overflowed the highway passing near the foot of the pond, and washed out, gullied and otherwise injured the same, thereby causing the Town to incur expenses from year to year in repairing the same. The water had overflowed the road in the same manner and to the same extent as during the time covered by the plaintiffs' declaration, for more than twenty years prior to the time embraced in this suit.

The only question presented in this case is whether the defendants have acquired a prescriptive right thus to overflow and injure the highway which the Town was bound by law to

longitudinally. Mercer v. Corbin, 3 L. R. A. 221, 117 Ind. 450. See *note* to Swift v. Topeka City, *ante*, 772.

Where teamsters spend their idle time, with their horses and wagons, in a public street in front of a private dwelling, to such an extent that noxious odors are created which are carried into the dwelling, it is an unlawful use of the street and will be enjoined; and complainant's motives cannot be inquired into. Lippincott v. Lasher, 12 Cent. Rep. 238, 44 N. J. Eq. 120.

The highway may be a convenient place for the owner of carriages to keep them in, but the law, looking to the convenience of the greater number, prohibits any such use of the public streets. The old cases said the king's highway is not to be used as a stable yard, and a party cannot eke out the inconvenience of his own premises by taking in the public highway. These general statements are familiar and borne out by the cases. Cohen v. New York, 4 L. R. A. 406, 113 N. Y. 533; Rex v. Russell, 6 East, 427; Rex v. Cross, 3 Camp. 224; Rex v. Jones, 3 Camp. 230; People v. Cunningham, 1 Denio, 524; Davis v. New York, 14 N. Y. 524; Callanan v. Gilman, 9 Cent. Rep. 900, 107 N. Y. 360.

Where a dangerous piece of machinery is placed in an alley by the owner of abutting lots, and is allowed to remain for years, both the individual and the corporation are guilty of negligence, and both are liable for injuries sustained by a child under nine years who was hurt upon such machinery. Osage City v. Larkins, 2 L. R. A. 56, 40 Kan. 206.

The driver of a fire-engine has a right to cross the neutral ground in the street of a city at points between crossings, for the purpose of arriving speedily at a fire. Wilson v. Great Southern Teleph. & Teleg. Co. 41 La. Ann.—, Nov. 18, 1889.

Length of time will not legalize encroachment on highway.

Encroachment on a highway cannot be legalized by lapse of time. The public right to its use cannot be lost by negligence of public officers. Tainter v. Morristown, 19 N. J. Eq. 46; Cross v. Morristown, 18 N. J. Eq. 305; State v. Troth, 34 N. J. L. 379; State v. Trenton, 36 N. J. L. 201; Hoboken L. & I. Co. v. Hoboken, Id. 549; Humphreys v. Woodstown, 7 Cent. Rep. 114, 48 N. J. L. 588.

The doctrine is embodied in the maxim "*nullum tempus occurrit regi.*" Cross v. Morristown, 18 N.J. Eq. 311; Stoughton v. Baker, 4 Mass. 522; Com. v. Upton, 6 Gray, 476; Jac. Law Dict. title *King.*

No length of time will legitimate a nuisance or enable a party to prescribe for its continuance. People v. Cunningham, 1 Denio, 536; Mills v. Hall, 9 Wend. 315; Dygert v. Schenck, 23 Wend. 448.

Buildings on highways acquire no right from time or expenditure. Com. v. Moorehead, 10 Cent. Rep. 611, 118 Pa. 344.

A decree directing that the walls of a building encroaching on public streets be torn down was reversed, it appearing that the building had projected over the line of the street four and one half inches for more than twenty-five years. Big Rapids v. Comstock, 8 West. Rep. 136, 65 Mich. 78.

One who encroaches upon a street and contends that there is no street at that place, or that he has acquired title by adverse possession, makes himself willfully guilty of such encroachment. Childs v. Nelson, 69 Wis. 125.

Permitting street obstruction for building purposes.

The Legislature has expressly enacted that the city shall have no power to authorize the placing or continuing of any encroachments or obstructions upon any street or sidewalk, except the temporary occupation thereof during the erection or repair of a building on a lot opposite the highway. Cohen v. New York, 113 N. Y. 537; Consolidation Act, § 86, subd. 4, pp. 25, 26; People v. New York, 59 How. Pr. 277; Ely v. Campbell, 59 How. Pr. 333; Lavery v. Hannigan, 20 Jones & S. 463. See *note* to McCoull v. Manchester (Va.) 2 L. R. A. 691.

The general charter powers of a corporation, and the right to exercise special powers at any time and in any reasonable manner, are impliedly reserved in every grant of property to private individuals, and in every license to use or obstruct the streets. Winter v. Montgomery, 83 Ala. 589.

A license by legislative Act, legalizing obstructions in the streets of a municipality which otherwise would be nuisances, is dependent on the legislative will, and may be withdrawn. *Ibid.*

The fact that a city has given to the land owner a license to use a street for the deposit of building material does not suspend the duty of the city to exercise reasonable care to keep it in safe condition. Grant v. Stillwater, 35 Minn. 242.

Scaffolding suspended from the eaves of a house is not necessarily a nuisance. It is not prohibited by an ordinance prohibiting hanging goods, etc., in front of a building. Hexamer v. Webb, 2 Cent. Rep. 489, 101 N. Y. 377.

Materials for building may be placed in the

maintain and keep in a condition safe and convenient for public use.

We are satisfied that, as against the Town or the public, the defendants have acquired no prescriptive right which, from mere lapse of time, could render the acts complained of legal, and thus authorize their continuance.

The cases are exceptional which hold that the rights of the municipality or of the public may be lost either by nonuser, or by adverse possession, where no statutory enactment intervenes to govern the common law as understood and applied with reference to public rights. The doctrine that to the sovereign power the maxim, "*nullum tempus occurrit regi*," applies, has long been understood. It is a maxim of the common law which we have inherited from our English ancestors, substituting the public or State for the king. Towns and other municipalities are regarded as public agencies, exercising, in behalf of the State, public duties in the administration of civil government, and as such are but the auxiliaries of the sovereign power.

The highways and streets, where there is no special restriction when acquired, are for the public use, and not alone for the people of the town or municipality in which they are located. The use is none the less for the general public because they are situated within such municipality, and because the Legislature may have given the supervision and control of them to the local authorities. The whole community have an equal interest and right to all the privileges and advantages of the public ways, and have an equal right to complain of any infringement upon such privileges and advantages.

The rights which the public have are of an easement, merely, or the right of passing upon such ways. Although the easement is a public one, and the Town in the distribution of the public burdens, and as incident to its recognized duties in connection with the government of the State, is bound to preserve and maintain such easement, yet it cannot be considered, in any legal point of view, as the easement or property of the Town. The Town is but the trustee for the public in reference to such easements. "To the Commonwealth

---

street, provided it be done in the most convenient manner. Chicago v. Robins, 67 U. S. 2 Black, 418 (17 L. ed. 298.)

Permitting use for business purposes.

The lease of a street for private uses is void. Marine Ins. Co. v. St. Louis, I. M. & S. R. Co. 41 Fed. Rep. 643.

When a city, without the pretense of authority and in direct violation of a statute, assumes to grant to a private individual the right to obstruct the public highway while in the transaction of his private business, and, for such privilege, takes compensation, it must be regarded as itself maintaining a nuisance so long as the obstruction is continued by reason of and under such license; and it must be liable for all damages which may naturally result to a third party who is injured in his person or his property by reason or in consequence of the placing of such obstruction in the highway. Cohen v. New York, 4 L. R. A. 406, 113 N. Y. 532.

One doing business on a street in a populous city has a right to obstruct the sidewalk temporarily for the necessities of his business if exercised in a reasonable manner and so as not to unnecessarily obstruct and incumber it, and he is under no obligation to furnish pedestrians a safe passage around the obstruction. See *notes* to Welsh v. Wilson, 2 Cent. Rep. 749, 101 N. Y. 254; Jochem v. Robinson (Wis.) 1 L. R. A. 178.

He becomes liable only for his negligence in the use of the privilege. Kelly v. Doody, 116 N. Y. 575.

Where a merchant obstructs a sidewalk for an hour or more at a time, amounting in all to four or five hours a day, by a bridge made of skids, from his building, to convey goods to and from his trucks, it constitutes a public nuisance. Callanan v. Gilman, 9 Cent. Rep. 900, 107 N. Y. 360.

The use of a bridge made of skids to load or unload a single truck, by placing it from the stoop of the building across the sidewalk to such truck, not obstructing the street for any considerable time, is not a nuisance. *Ibid.*

One doing business on a city street may obstruct the sidewalk temporarily for the necessities of business, as by using skids to load merchandise. Welsh v. Wilson, 2 Cent. Rep. 749, 101 N. Y. 254.

The necessity required to justify the use of a sidewalk by placing skids thereover in front of a store, for the purpose of unloading heavy barrels from a wagon, need only be reasonable. Jochem v. Robinson, 1 L. R. A. 178, 66 Wis. 638.

Public nuisances on highways.

A common nuisance seems to be an offense against the public, either by doing a thing which tends to the annoyance of all the king's subjects or by neglecting to do a thing which the common good requires. State v. Godwinsville & P. M. R. Co. 9 Cent. Rep. 128, 49 N. J. L. 266.

A public nuisance can only be redressed by a public prosecution, unless the party complaining suffers some peculiar damages differing in kind from those sustained by the public at large. School District No. 1 v. Neil, 36 Kan. 617.

A railroad constructed across a street in a city by a private person or corporation, pursuant to an unlawful authority given by the city authorities, is a public nuisance. Glaessner v. Anheuser-Busch Brew. Asso. (Mo.) May 19, 1890.

The use of steam as a motive power for the movement of cars on a highway, at a place where there is no authority for such use, in consequence of which the property of an abutting owner was depreciated in value, constitutes a nuisance. Hussner v. Brooklyn City R. Co. 114 N. Y. 433.

An unguarded area not within the limits of, but so near to, an alley as to endanger persons passing along the alley, is a public nuisance. Bond v. Smith, 44 Hun, 219.

The use of parts of certain streets and sidewalks in front of complainant's dwelling-house, by hucksters as a market place, by permission of the city officers on payment of a license fee, constitutes not only a public nuisance, but, as to complainant and others similarly affected a private nuisance, entitling complainant to an injunction against the city as the wrong-doer. McDonald v. Newark, 5 Cent. Rep. 647, 42 N. J. Eq. 136.

If defendant, being the owner of the soil, laid out a street on his land between high and low water mark, the right to use it became appurtenant to the lands of the adjoiners; and anything which obstructs such right is a nuisance. Richardson v. Boston, 60 U. S. 19 How. 263 (15 L. ed. 639).

A gate and shed erected on an alley after a grant of land to which it was made appurtenant, without the grantee's consent, are properly assumed nuisances *per se*, in case of their continuance after a former verdict on the case for their erection; and the grantee may recover damages for their continuance after the former recovery, although they do not materially interfere with his use of the alley. Ellis v. American Academy of Music, 120 Pa. 608

here," says *Chief Justice* Gibson in *O'Connor* v. *Pittsburgh*, 18 Pa. 187, "as to the King in England, belongs the franchise of every highway as a trustee for the public." Unauthorized obstructions or erections which encroach upon these rights are deemed public nuisances, and may be prosecuted in behalf of the public. No length of time, unless there be a limit by statute, will legalize a public nuisance; and, in the absence of a grant from competent authority, no presumption from mere lapse of time can be made to support a nuisance which is an encroachment upon the public right.

Principles analogous to the question now before us have been decided by the courts, and whenever they have arisen the current of authority is in one direction.

Thus, in the very early case of *Arundel* v. *M'Culloch*, 10 Mass. 70, which was for trespass in removing a bridge built across a navigable stream, where it had remained for fifty years, the court held that "public rights cannot be destroyed by long continued encroachments. At least the party who claims the exercise of any right inconsistent with the free enjoyment of a public easement or privilege must put himself upon the ground of prescription, unless he has a grant, or some valid authority, from the government; and a right by prescription does not exist in the present case."

In Pennsylvania several cases have arisen involving the principle under discussion; and in *Com.* v. *Alburger*, 1 Whart. 469, 488, the Supreme Court of that State thus gives expression upon this subject: "These principles, indeed, pervade the laws of the most enlightened nations, as well as our own Code, and are essential to the protection of public rights which would be gradually frittered away if the want of complaint or prosecution gave the party a right. Individuals may reasonably be held to a limited period to enforce their right against adverse occupants, because they have interest sufficient to make them vigilant. But, in public rights of property, each individual feels but a slight interest, and rather tolerates even a manifest encroachment than seeks a dispute to set it right."

The same doctrine is discussed and affirmed in *Barter* v. *Com.*, 3 Penr. & W. 253, where the

---

Sliding in a street, accompanied by boisterous conduct liable to frighten horses traveling therein, may be a public nuisance; but one damaged thereby must show that it was the proximate cause of his damage, to enable him to recover from one creating it. Jackson v. Castle, 5 New Eng. Rep. 857, 80 Me. 119.

In the case of a public nuisance, it does not follow that suit cannot be brought by a private person, because the State, at the relation of the law officer, can bring suit. Personal wrongs may be both public and private; in which case the individual injured has his action. Cummings v. St. Louis, 7 West. Rep. 274, 90 Mo. 259; McDonald v. Newark, 5 Cent. Rep. 649, 42 N. J. Eq. 136.

Public nuisances; abatement of.

Where the town authorities suffered a fence to remain across a street until there seemed to them a need for its public use, the fence should be removed; all erections put upon the street were mere encroachments made by parties at their peril, and may be removed by the town authorities. Lake View v. Le Bahn, 6 West. Rep. 786, 120 Ill. 92.

Under the Mississippi statutes the board of mayor and aldermen of the town has jurisdiction to order the removal of a fence across a street. Nixon v. Biloxi (Miss.) Feb. 25, 1889.

If timber standing upon a roadway obstructs or impairs the use of the road by the public, it is the duty of the overseer of the road to have it removed; and the overseer's authority is sufficient to protect another whom the overseer permitted to cut the timber, against all criminal liability. Cooper v. Langway, 76 Tex. 121.

An action to abate a nuisance caused by obstructing the highway, under the Political Code, as amended, is properly brought in the name of the overseer of the road district wherein the obstruction exists. Bailey v. Dale, 71 Cal. 34.

Abatement of nuisance under police power of States. See *note* to Pine City v. Munch (Minn.) 6 L. R. A. 763.

Injunction to restrain nuisances in streets.

A municipality, having the control and supervision of the public highways within its territorial limits, may maintain a suit in equity to prevent any alteration of the streets, or injury to them, which will deprive the public of their use. Jersey City v. Central R. Co. 4 Cent. Rep. 327, 40 N. J. Eq. 417.

The mayor and common council are proper persons to file a bill to prevent obstruction or destruction of streets. Newark v. Delaware, L. & W. R. Co. 5 Cent. Rep. 629, 42 N. J. Eq. 196.

For an obstruction to a public highway an injunction is not a favored remedy, whether sought by the public or an individual. To justify its issue at the suit of an individual, the injury must be special, pressing and otherwise irremediable; and, as a condition to the issue of permanent injunction, the right must either not be in controversy or have been settled at law. Irwin v. Dixion, 50 U. S. 9 How. 10 (13 L. ed. 25).

Even in the case of an obstruction to a public street, amounting to a public nuisance, the court of chancery is loath to act by injunction. Pavonia Land Asso. v. Feenfer (N. J.) 5 Cent. Rep. 640.

The real injury is to the public, if there be any injury; the plaintiffs cannot sustain their suit unless they show clearly a special and peculiar damage distinct from that suffered by the public at large. Wheeler v. Bedford, 2 New Eng. Rep. 831, 54 Conn. 246; O'Brien v. Norwich & W. R. Co. 17 Conn. 375; Frink v. Lawrence, 20 Conn. 120; Clark v. Saybrook, 21 Conn. 313, 327; Lexington & O. R. Co. v. Applegate, 8 Dana, 299; McKeon v. See, 4 Robt. 466; Gilbert v. Mickle, 4 Sandf. Ch. 357, 7 N. Y. Ch. L. ed. 1132.

The official action of corporate officers should not be interfered with or restrained unless it be injurious and wrongful in its nature, especially where the parties aggrieved have an adequate remedy at law and the pecuniary responsibility of the defendants is unquestioned. Davis v. Am. Society for Prev. Cruelty to Animals, 6 Daly, 85, 16 Abb. Pr. N. S. 73; Sterman v. Konnedy, 15 Abb. Pr. 201; Moore v. Pilot Comrs. 32 How. Pr. 184; Prendorill v. Kennedy, 34 How. Pr. 416.

If the right of the public to the use of a highway is clear, and a special injury is threatened by an obstruction of the highway, and this special injury is serious, reaching the very substance and value of the plaintiff's estate, and is permanent in its character, a court of equity by an injunction ought to prevent such a nuisance. Keystone Bridge Co. v. Summers, 13 W. Va. 485; Mohawk Bridge Co. v. Utica & S. R. Co. 6 Paige, 563, 3 N. Y. Ch. L. ed. 1103; Jerome v. Ross, 7 Johns. Ch. 322, 2 N. Y. Ch. L. ed. 308.

The injury to him must not be trivial, or such as may be compensated in damages, but must be seri-

Watts, 23, claims of ownership in a public square; *Penny Pot Landing Case*, 16 Pa. 79; *Philadelphia* v. *Philadelphia & R. R. Co.* 58 Pa. 253. In New Jersey, in *Jersey City* v. *Morris Canal & Bkg. Co.*, 12 N. J. Eq. 547, where the doctrine of prescriptive right as against the public was rejected and characterized as eminently disastrous to the public interests; *Smith* v. *State*, 23 N. J. L. 712. In Rhode Island, in *Simmons* v. *Cornell*, 1 R. I. 519. In New York, in *St. Vincent Orphan Asylum* v. *Troy*, 76 N. Y. 108; *Mills* v. *Hall*, 9 Wend. 315, wherein the court held that "there is no such thing as a prescriptive right, or any right, to maintain a public nuisance;" *Milhau* v. *Sharp*, 27 N. Y. 611. In Massachusetts, see *Stoughton* v. *Baker*, 4 Mass. 522; *Com.* v. *Blaisdell*, 107 Mass. 234,235. And see *Franklin Wharf* v. *Portland*, 67 Me. 46, 55; *Dwinel* v. *Barnard*, 28 Me. 554, 570; *Knox* v. *Chaloner*, 42 Me. 150, where it was said that a public nuisance can never be legitimated by lapse of time.

claim of right, give title by prescription to the land so inclosed and occupied, as against the public. Such are the cases of *Knight* v. *Heaton*, 22 Vt. 480; *Beardslee* v. *French*, 7 Conn. 125; *Rowan* v. *Portland*, 8 B. Mon. 232; *Webber* v. *Chapman*, 42 N. H. 326, and others to which we have no occasion to allude, as they have no application to the decision of this case.

In *Cutter* v. *Cambridge*, 6 Allen, 20, where it was held that such occupation or inclosure under a claim of right gave the owner an absolute right as against the public, the decision of the court was based upon the statute provision of that Commonwealth, which was held to be an innovation upon the common law. The language of that Statute, the court says, recognizes as an existing rule of law that fences maintained under a claim of right for forty years, within the limits of the highway, gave the owner an absolute right to continue them there as against the public.

A similar statute exists in our own State (Rev. Stat. chap. 18, § 95), in which it is pro-

---

ous, affecting the substance and value of the plaintiff's estate. Talbott v. King (W. Va.) Jan. 29, 1889.

He must show some special injury over and above the general injury to the general public. Glaessner v. Anheuser-Busch Brew. Asso. (Mo.) May 19, 1890.

One having right of possession of property may sue for nuisance resulting from unlawful use of a public street upon which it abuts (Hopkins v. Baltimore & P. R. Co. 12 Cent. Rep. 398, 6 Mackey, 311), as for the unlawful occupation of the street by a railroad. Pennsylvania R. Co. v. Mish, 4 Cent. Rep. 276, 115 Pa. 514.

Where a private person or corporation, under an unlawful authority conferred by municipal officers, constructs railroad tracks across a street, thereby diverting travel and decreasing the value of the property of a lot owner and taking away trade, such owner suffers such an injury as entitles him to maintain an injunction to restrain the construction and operation of the tracks as a public nuisance. Glaessner v. Anheuser-Busch Brew. Asso. *supra*.

Where water pipes had, without consent of the owner of the soil, been laid in the soil of a highway, an injunction to restrain the continuance of the nuisance was granted. Broome v. New York & N. J. Teleph. Co. 5 Cent. Rep. 816, 42 N. J. Eq. 141.

But an injunction to compel the removal of a building erected upon land designated upon a plat as a street, but which did not appear to have been accepted by the public or used as a highway, was refused. Pavonia Land Asso. v. Feenfer (N. J.) 5 Cent. Rep. 640.

Private right of action.

A special and peculiar injury irreparable in its nature, and different in kind from that sustained by the general public, is necessary to give a private right of action for a public nuisance. Fogg v. Nevada C. O. R. Co. (Nev.) Jan. 31, 1890.

One whose only means of ingress to and egress from buildings on his lands is by a public alley or highway has such a special interest in the way, not common to the public generally, as entitles him to maintain a private action for damages for the obstruction of the highway. Fassion v. Landrey (Ind.) April 5, 1890.

The fact that adjoining owners have more occasion to use the street in front of them than most others have, and that the inconvenience and annoyance to them from a nuisance created by a railroad in the street is greater in degree than it is to other citizens, does not authorize a private right of action. Fogg v. Nevada C. O. R. Co. *supra*.

An adjacent owner is not entitled to any damages for the obstruction of a highway on the ground merely of inconvenience in passing along the way. McDonnell v. Cambridge R. Co. (Mass.) Feb. 26, 1890

Where a wall to prevent the earthwork of a street from encroaching upon adjoining premises is a part of the plan approved by the common council for the improvement of a street, and no error of the judgment or discretion of the council in approving it is shown, or any defect in the construction, no recovery can be had on account of the inconvenience occasioned by it. Watson v. Kingston, 114 N. Y. 88.

In trespass for encroachment upon a highway, where defendant gives notice that he will prove location of the fence to be upon his own soil, title to the soil is in issue. Osburn v. Longsduff, 14 West. Rep. 212, 70 Mich. 127.

Until service upon him of an order locating the encroachment, defendant need not serve a notice denying existence of the highway. *Ibid.*

A petition in trespass against a railway company, for heaping up earth on land outside its right of way, need not aver negligence. McCord v. Doniphan B. R. Co. 3 West. Rep. 395, 21 Mo. App. 92.

As against the owner of the soil over which a street passes, a trespasser cannot set up as a defense the existence of an easement which the public or a third person may have in the premises. Hurley v. Mississippi & R. R. Boom Co. 34 Minn. 143.

If one does or authorizes the doing of an act creating a public nuisance, by obstructing a highway, he is answerable in damages to those suffering injuries thereby. Carlin v. Driscoll, 10 Cent. Rep. 178, 50 N. J. L. 28.

One who, in violation of an express statutory duty, obstructs a public highway, cannot be heard to say that he did not anticipate an injury which was the direct result of his unlawful act, where the person injured was without fault. Evansville & T. H. R. Co. v. Carvener, 12 West. Rep. 204, 113 Ind. 1. See *note* to Collins v. Chartiers Valley Gas Co. (Pa.) 6 L. R. A. 280.

vided that, where the limits of ways, streets or land appropriated to public use can be ascertained by records or monuments, a period of at least forty years must elapse to give any adverse right of possession, and "buildings or fences" fronting upon such land are the only erections mentioned in the Statute which will be deemed the true boundaries, even to give an adverse right of possession, as against records or monuments, and that no adverse rights can be acquired, as against the public, in such ways or lands, where the boundaries thereof cannot be made certain by records or monuments, without such erections existing for a period of at least twenty years.

"This Statute," remarks the court in *Stetson* v. *Bangor*, 73 Me. 357, 359, "is the only one in this State which in this respect limits the common-law force of the maxim, *nullum tempus occurrit regi*."

In the case before us there was no such occupancy of the way by any fences or buildings as would give the defendants any rights under the Statute. The acts of the defendants in flowing the highway constituted a public nuisance; and, as we have said, the maintaining of a public nuisance for twenty years does not afford any prescriptive right to maintain it.

In *New Salem* v. *Eagle Mill Co.*, 138 Mass. 8, the plaintiffs complain of a public nuisance by reason of which they have suffered special damages, as in *Calais* v. *Dyer*, 7 Me. 155; *Andover* v. *Sutton*, 12 Met. 182, and *Freedom* v. *Weed*, 40 Me. 383.

The referee, by his report, has awarded such damages as in his judgment the plaintiffs had sustained.

It may be proper to state that, although this action was brought in 1881, the long delay in determining the rights of the parties should not be attributed to the court; for, though entered in the law court in 1884, it was not submitted to the court until June, 1889.

Judgment of the referee affirmed.

Peters, *Ch. J.*, and **Virgin, Libbey** and **Emery**, *JJ.*, concurred.

DOE
v.
ROE.

(82 Me. 503.)

An action for debauching and carnally knowing her husband, thereby alienating his affections, cannot be maintained by a wife against another woman.

(March 27, 1890.)

EXCEPTIONS by plaintiff to a judgment of the Supreme Judicial Court for York County sustaining a demurrer to the declaration in an action brought to recover damages from defendant for debauching and carnally knowing plaintiff's husband and for alienating his affection from plaintiff. *Overruled.*

The case sufficiently appears in the opinion.

Mr. **James A. Edgerly** for plaintiff.

Messrs. **W. L. Putnam** and **W. S. Pierce** for defendant.

Walton, *J.*, delivered the opinion of the court:

This is an action by a married woman against another woman. The plaintiff has alleged in her declaration that the defendant debauched and carnally knew her husband, thereby alienating his affection, and depriving her of his comfort, society and support.

The question is whether such an action is maintainable. For such a wrong the law does not leave the injured wife without redress. She may obtain a divorce and a restoration of all her property, real and personal, and, in addition thereto, alimony, or an allowance out of her husband's estate, and the law will punish the guilty parties criminally. But does the law, in addition to these remedies, secure to her a right of action to recover a pecuniary compensation from her husband's paramour? We think not. We have been referred to no reliable authority for the existence of such a right, and we can find none.

It is true that a husband may maintain an action for the seduction of his wife. But such an action has grounds on which to rest that cannot be invoked in support of a similar action in favor of the wife. A wife's infidelity may impose upon her husband the support of another man's child, and, what is still worse, it may throw suspicion upon the legitimacy of his own children. A husband's infidelity can inflict no such consequences upon his wife. If she remains virtuous, no suspicion can attach to the legitimacy of her children. And an action in favor of the husband for the seduction of his wife has been regarded as of doubtful expediency. It has been abolished in England (Bouvier, L. Dict., title, *Crim. Con.*), and the trials we have had in this country of such actions are not very encouraging. They seem to be better calculated to inflict pain upon the innocent members of the families of the parties than to secure redress to the persons injured, and we fear such would be the result if such actions were maintainable by wives. Such a power would furnish them with the means of inflicting untold misery upon others, with little hope of redress for themselves. At any rate, we are satisfied that the law never has, and does not now, secure to wives such a power; and, if it is deemed wise that they should have it, the Legislature, and not the court, must give it to them.

Exceptions overruled. Demurrer sustained. Declaration adjudged bad.

Peters, *Ch. J.*, and **Virgin, Emery, Foster** and **Haskell**, *JJ.*, concurred.

NOTE.—*Personal rights of married woman.*

A married woman can maintain an action for enticing away her husband and depriving her of his comfort and protection and society. Bennett v. Bennett, 6 L. R. A. 553, 116 N. Y. 584.

She may maintain an action against another woman for alienating his affections. Foot v. Card, 6 L. R. A. 829, 58 Conn. 1.

But see, *contra*, Duffies v. Duffies (Wis.) 8 L. R. A. 420.

See also 10 L. R. A. 468; 14 L. R. A. 545; 26 L. R. A. 412; 27 L. R. A. 120, 686; 32 L. R. A. 623; 38 L. R. A. 242; 40 L. R. A. 549; 43 L. R. A. 114; 47 L. R. A.

G. H. LOOMIS, *Appt.*,
v.
ROCKFORD INSURANCE CO., of Rockford, Ill., *Respt.*

(....Wis.....)

A contract of insurance on houses several miles apart, which insures each house for a specified amount, is divisible, although the premium is stated as a gross sum, where there is nothing to show any difference between the houses in class or rates. A transfer of one without the consent of the insurer, avoiding the policy as to that, does not make it void as to the other.

(May 20, 1890.)

APPEAL by plaintiff from a judgment of the Circuit Court for Dane County in favor of defendant in an action brought to recover the amount alleged to be due under a policy of fire insurance. *Reversed.*

Statement by **Lyon**, *J.*:

This is an action upon a policy of insurance to recover for a loss by fire of a portion of the insured property. The first paragraph of the policy is as follows: "The Rockford Insurance Company of Rockford, Illinois, in consideration of a note for $16.50, due July 1, 1886, does insure G. H. Loomis and his legal representatives against loss or damage by fire or lightning to the amount of $1,100, as follows: $300 on 1½-story frame dwelling-house No. 1, and additions thereto, including foundation and cellar walls, occupied by —— as a private family residence; $200 on house No. 2; $300 on tobacco shed; $300 on tobacco, fodder, hay or grain on sections 1, 2 and 11, situate except as otherwise provided, on sections 1, 2 and 11, Townships of Burke and Westport, Dane County, in State of Wisconsin,—from the 18th day of January, 1886, at 12 o'clock noon, to the 18th day of January, 1891, at 12 o'clock noon." The note above mentioned was paid at maturity. It is stipulated in the policy that, if any change takes place in the title to the property insured without the consent of the secretary of the defendant Company, the policy shall be null and void. A breach of this stipulation by the insured as to a part of the insured property is relied upon to defeat a recovery in the action. The testimony introduced on the trial shows, or tends to show, that, when the policy was issued, plaintiff owned three farms in Dane County,—one in the Town of Burke, on section 11, on which is located dwelling-house No. 1, mentioned in the policy; another on section 2, in the Town of Westport, several miles distant from the Burke farm, on which house No. 2, therein mentioned, is located; and the other on section 1, in Westport, on which stood the insured tobacco shed,—and that the tobacco shed and a quantity of tobacco and hay on section 1 were destroyed by fire August 21, 1888; also, that after the policy was issued, and before the fire, plaintiff sold and conveyed his farm in Burke, including dwelling-house No. 1, without the

NOTE.—*Fire insurance; entire and severable contracts.*

Where the amount of insurance is apportioned to distinct items, but the premium paid is gross, the contract is entire. McQueeney v. Phœnix Ins. Co. (Ark.) 5 L. R. A. 744; Herman v. Adriatic F. Ins. Co. 18 Jones & S. 402; May, Ins. §§ 189, 277; 1 Wood, Ins. 384; Day v. Charter Oak F. & M. Ins. Co. 51 Me. 91; Lovejoy v. Augusta Mut. F. Ins. Co. 45 Me. 472; Richardson v. Maine Ins. Co. 46 Me. 394; Associated F. Ins. Co. v. Assum, 5 Md. 165; Bowman v. Franklin F. Ins. Co. 40 Md. 620; Friesmuth v. Agawam Mut. F. Ins. Co. 10 Cush. 587; Kimball v. Howard F. Ins. Co. 8 Gray, 33; Lee v. Howard F. Ins. Co. 3 Gray, 583; Ætna Ins. Co. v. Resh, 44 Mich. 55; Plath v. Minnesota F. M. F. Ins. Asso. 23 Minn. 479; Baldwin v. Hartford F. Ins. Co. 60 N. H. 422; Gottsman v. Pennsylvania Ins. Co. 56 Pa. 210; McGowan v. People's Mut. F. Ins. Co. 54 Vt. 211; Moore v. Virginia F. & M. Ins. Co. 28 Gratt. 508; Bryan v. Peabody Ins. Co. 8 W. Va. 605.

Opposed to this view are Peoria M. & F. Ins. Co. v. Anapow, 51 Ill. 283; Phœnix Ins. Co. v. Lawrence, 4 Met. (Ky.) 9; Koontz v. Hannibal Sav. & Ins. Co. 42 Mo. 126; Lochner v. Home Mut. Ins. Co. 19 Mo. 628; State Ins. Co. v. Schreck (Neb.) 6 L. R. A. 524; Merrill v. Agricultural Ins. Co. 73 N. Y. 452; Quarrier v. Peabody Ins. Co. 10 W. Va. 530.

Where property covered by one policy appears to be so situated as to constitute substantially one risk, even though separate amounts of insurance be apportioned to the building and to the furniture, if the considerations for the risk are indivisible, the contract must be treated as entire. Havens v. Home Ins. Co. 9 West. Rep. 635, 111 Ind. 90.

Where the premium is a gross sum, though the amount of the insurance on the different items of property is fixed in the policy, contract is not divisible; and where it is vitiated as to one item of the property it is vitiated as to all. Garver v. Hawkeye Ins. Co. 69 Iowa, 202.

One policy providing for payment of one premium, covering several distinct pieces of property, is a severable contract, such that a breach of condition affecting one property will not affect another, it not appearing that the assuming the one risk was in consideration of taking the other risk. Schuster v. Dutchess County Mut. Ins. Co. 3 Cent. Rep. 133, 102 N. Y. 260.

A policy in the amount of $3,000 on property of the aggregate value of $90,000, which is insured in twenty-one separate items, providing that it insures one thirtieth part of each of such items, and that it shall make the company liable for no greater proportion of any loss than the sum insured by that policy bears to the whole sum insured—makes the company liable on a loss of a portion of the property, not merely for one thirtieth of the loss, but for such proportion of the loss as $3,000 bears to the whole amount of the insurance on those items of the property on which the loss was sustained. Illinois Mut. Ins. Co. v. Hoffman (Ill.) April 22, 1890.

When property is valued at a certain amount, and an insurance effected on one thirty-sixth of that amount, and there is a total loss, the company is responsible for the amount insured upon which it received a premium, and the policy cannot be construed as rendering the insurer liable for only one thirty-sixth of the loss. Westinghouse Electric Co. v. Western Assur. Co. (La.) Jan. 6, 1890.

Insurance policy; rule of construction. See *note* to Kratzenstein v. Western Assur. Co. (N. Y.) 5 L. R. A. 799.

See also 16 L. R. A. 174.

consent of the secretary of the defendant Company. There was some testimony which, it is claimed, proves a waiver by the Insurance Company of the alleged breach of the contract. This feature of the case is not considered in the opinion, and it is therefore unnecessary to state such testimony. The circuit court held that the contract of insurance is entire and indivisible, and that such conveyance of the Burke farm, on which stood one of the insured buildings, vitiated the whole contract. Whereupon the court nonsuited the plaintiff. The plaintiff appeals from the judgment of nonsuit.

Messrs. **Rogers & Hall**, for appellant:

Whether a contract of insurance is an entire or divisible one should be determined by facts other than the entirety of the consideration. Whether or not the risk is distributed and the divisibility of the risk is evident are the controlling facts from which the court must determine whether the insurance contract is entire. In this case the policy, on its face, shows that the risk was distributed, and the evidence proves beyond question that the risk was divisible.

See *Phenix Ins. Co.* v. *Pickel*, 119 Ind. 155; also *Pickel* v. *Phenix Ins. Co.* 119 Ind. 291; *Merrill* v. *Agricultural Ins. Co.* 73 N. Y. 452; *Quarrier* v. *Peabody Ins. Co.* 10 W. Va. 507.

The court to prevent a forfeiture "is bound to construe such contract as strongly against the insurer, and as favorably for the insured, as its terms will reasonably permit," and hence the rule is pretty well settled that in order to work such forfeiture a substantial breach must be established.

Kircher v. *Milwaukee Mechanics Mut. Ins. Co.* 74 Wis. 470; *State Ins. Co.* v. *Schreck* (Neb.) 6 L. R. A. 524; *City P. & S. Mills Co.* v. *Merchants, Mfrs. & C. Mut. F. Ins. Co.* 72 Mich. 654; *Hoffman* v. *Ætna Ins. Co.* 32 N. Y. 413; *White* v. *Hoyt*, 73 N. Y. 505; *Hitchcock* v. *North Western Ins. Co.* 26 N. Y. 68; *Dilleber* v. *Home L. Ins. Co.* 69 N. Y. 256; *Coyne* v. *Weaver*, 84 N. Y. 386.

Mr. **H. W. Chynoweth** for respondent.

Lyon, *J.*, delivered the opinion of the court:

If, as the learned circuit judge held, the contract of insurance is entire and indivisible, the conveyance by the plaintiff of the Burke farm, on which stood dwelling house No. 1, without the consent of the secretary of the defendant Company, before certain other of the insured property was burned, renders the whole policy null and void, and the nonsuit was properly ordered; otherwise not.

In the cases of *Hinman* v. *Hartford F. Ins. Co.*, 36 Wis. 159, and *Schumitsch* v. *American Ins. Co.*, 48 Wis. 26, the contracts of insurance there in question were held indivisible. In those cases the property insured consisted of buildings, and personal property contained therein, and in the application for the policies there were misrepresentations by the assured of their title to the realty. In each case the risk was distributed to the different items of property insured. These cases will be adhered to, and the question is whether they rule the present case.

There is some apparent conflict of authority as to the rules by which it is to be determined whether the contract in a given case, which insures several items of property, is an entire contract, or whether it is divisible. An examination of the cases will show, we think, that, as to a large majority of them, the conflict is apparent, rather than real. All the cases seem to agree that, although the insurance is distributed to the different items of insured property, the contract is indivisible if the breach of the contract as to an item of the property affects, or may reasonably be supposed to affect, the other items, by increasing the risk thereon.

In *Fire Asso. of Phila.* v. *Williamson*, 26 Pa. 196, the insurance was upon three adjoining buildings,— a specified sum on each,—and the breach of the contract alleged was the keeping of gunpowder in one of the buildings, which caused the burning of them all. The contract was held indivisible.

In *Gottsman* v. *Pennsylvania Ins. Co.*, 56 Pa. 210, the insurance was distributed upon a barn and certain property in an hotel standing within about sixty feet of the barn. As in the cases in this court, above cited, the assured misrepresented his title to the real property, which misrepresentation, by the terms of the policy, invalidated the whole insurance. The property in the hotel was burned. The contract was held indivisible, and the whole insurance forfeited. Several Massachusetts cases are cited in the opinion, among which are *Friesmuth* v. *Agawam Mut. F. Ins. Co.*, 10 Cush. 590; *Brown* v. *People's Mut. Ins. Co.*, 11 Cush. 280, and *Kimball* v. *Howard F. Ins. Co.*, 8 Gray, 33. These cases, in their essential facts, are in principle like the above cases in this court, except that in the case last cited there was no misrepresentation, but the assured obtained additional insurance upon a portion of the insured property, contrary to the conditions of the policy.

Lee v. *Howard F. Ins. Co.*, 3 Gray, 583, is also cited. In that case the contract of insurance was held indivisible, because, by the terms of the policy, "the property was insured as one risk, and was in fact closely connected together."

In *Kelly* v. *Humboldt F. Ins. Co.* (Pa.), 6 Atl. Rep. 740, the insurance was for a specified sum on each of two connected buildings, and a house situated in the rear of them. The contract was held indivisible on the authority of the cases in that State above cited.

In *Bowman* v. *Franklin F. Ins. Co.*, 40 Md. 620, the insurance was distributed upon a distillery and machinery therein, and there was a breach of the condition as to the real estate which worked a forfeiture of the policy, by its terms.

Lovejoy v. *Augusta Mut. F. Ins. Co.*, 45 Me. 472, and *Dole* v. *Merchants Mut. M. Ins. Co.*, 51 Me. 91, are also similar in principle to the two cases in this court first above cited. The property insured in each was a building and its contents, and there was a misrepresentation by assured of his title to the realty. None of the above cases seem to have been decided upon the proposition that the contract was entire merely because the premium was not also distributed to the several items of insured property, yet there are expressions in some of the opinions which seem to give weight to that circumstance.

But in *Plath* v. *Minnesota F. M. F. Ins. Asso.*, 23 Minn. 479, and *Garver* v. *Hawkeye Ins. Co.*, 69 Iowa, 202, the contracts seem to have been held indivisible mainly upon the ground that the premiums were not so distributed.

The foregoing cases have been referred to at some length because they are chiefly relied upon by the learned counsel for the defendant Company to establish the invalidity of the contract of insurance in the present case, and because they are believed fairly to represent nearly all the cases in which such contracts have been held indivisible.

The same counsel also cited and relied upon *McGowan* v. *People's Mut. F. Ins. Co.*, 54 Vt. 211. The facts of that case are not very fully stated, but it may be gathered from the report that the insurance was upon a dwelling-house and personal property in it, and the assured mortgaged the realty contrary to a condition in his policy. It was there claimed that the contract was divisible, and that the assured should recover the insurance upon the personal property which had been burned, although the policy had become void as to the dwelling-house. The court negatived this claim, and held the contract indivisible. The decision is placed upon the ground that by the terms of the policy the insurer had a lien upon the insured buildings for the payment of assessments upon the premium note, and the cause which rendered the policy void as to the buildings affected such security. The court might well have held, also, that the contract was entire because of the fact that the personal property insured was located in such buildings, and any breach of the contract in respect to the buildings must necessarily affect the risk upon the property therein, to the injury of the insurer. In that case the court laid down general rules for determining whether such a contract is divisible or not. These rules are so reasonable and satisfactory that we feel justified in quoting somewhat at length from the opinion. The court says: "This is a question of great practical importance, as a large proportion of insurance contracts embrace more than one item of property insured. The decisions are apparently conflicting, but, we think, are easily reconciled by referring to the plain principles which should govern them. The general rule, 'void in part, void *in toto*,' should apply to all cases where the contract is affected by some all-pervading vice, such as fraud or some unlawful act, condemned by public policy or the common law; cases where the contract is entire, and not divisible, and all those cases where the matter that renders the policy void in part, and the result of its being so rendered void affects the risk of the insurer upon the other items in the contract. Keeping these rules in mind, the leading cases upon this subject can all be reconciled. A recovery should be had in all those cases where the contract is divisible, the different properties insured for separate sums and the risk upon the property, which is claimed to be valid, unaffected by the cause that renders the policy void in part. Such are the cases of *Howard F. & M. Ins. Co.* v. *Cornick*, 24 Ill. 455; *Hartford F. Ins. Co.* v. *Walsh*, 54 Ill. 164; *Clark* v. *New England Mut. F. Ins. Co.* 6 Cush. 342; *Date* v. *Gore Dist. M. F. Ins. Co.* 14 U. C. C. P. 548; *Phœnix Ins. Co.* v. *Lawrence*, 4 Met. (Ky.) 9; *Loehner* v. *Home Mut. Ins. Co.* 17 Mo. 247; *Koontz* v. *Hannibal Sav. & Ins. Co.* 42 Mo. 126; *Cucullu* v. *Orleans Ins. Co.* 6 Mart. (N. S.) 11."

It is believed that the rules thus laid down by the Vermont court do not conflict with any of the cases above referred to, except possibly the two cases in Minnesota and Iowa. The proposition determined in those two cases does not commend itself to our judgments as sound. While the fact that the premium is stated in the policy at a gross sum, and is not distributed to the different items of insured property, is a circumstance to be considered in interpreting the contract, we do not think it is controlling. If two houses, located one mile apart, are insured in the same policy for $1,000 each, and there is nothing to show that they do not belong to the same class of risks, we cannot believe that, merely because the premium is stated in the policy to be $20 on both houses, instead of $10 on each, the contract thereby becomes indivisible, when it would undoubtedly have been divisible had the latter formula been adopted.

In the present case the aggregate of the insurance is $1,100, and the premium is stated in gross at $16.50, which is 1½ per cent on the amount of the insurance. There is nothing in the policy or testimony to show that the insured property belonged in different classes, upon which are charged respectively different rates of insurance, or that the percentage of premium is an average between higher and lower rates, which the parties understood were charged and paid upon different items of the insured property. The presumption is therefore that each item was insured at 1½ per cent premium, and the contract should be construed as though it was so expressed in the policy. Had it been so expressed therein, there can be no doubt the contract would be divisible, and so the learned counsel for the defendant Company frankly admitted during the argument of the cause.

The views above indicated are fully sustained by the cases of *Clark* v. *New England Mut. F. Ins. Co.*, 6 Cush. 342; *Havens* v. *Home Ins. Co.*, 111 Ind. 90, 9 West. Rep. 635; *Phenix Ins. Co.* v. *Pickel*, 119 Ind. 155; *Merrill* v. *Agricultural Ins. Co.*, 73 N. Y. 452; *Schuster* v. *Dutchess County Ins. Co.*, 102 N. Y. 260, 3 Cent. Rep. 183; *Loehner* v. *Home Mut. Ins. Co.* 17 Mo. 247; *Quarrier* v. *Peabody Ins. Co.*, 10 W. Va. 507. Indeed, many of the above cases go much further than this court has gone in asserting the divisibility of such contracts.

It is not denied that the policy in suit was valid when issued. No misrepresentation or breach of warranty on the part of the assured is claimed. But after the policy was issued the assured violated one of its material conditions by conveying to another one of the insured houses without consent of the insurer, which certainly invalidated the policy as to that house. But it is quite impossible to say from the record before us that the risk upon the insured property destroyed by fire, which property was located five miles distant from the house so conveyed, was increased, or in the slightest degree affected, by such conveyance. We are constrained to hold, therefore, that the contract is divisible, and hence that it was error to nonsuit the plaintiff.

The judgment of the Circuit Court is reversed, and the cause will be remanded for a new trial.

ILLINOIS SUPREME C(

John HRONEK, *Piff. in Err.*,

v.

PEOPLE OF the State of ILLINOIS.

(....Ill.....)

1. An Act does not embrace more than one subject because, with regulations as to the manufacture, transportation, use and sale of explosives, it also prescribes a punishment for violation of such regulations.

2. A statute does not involve more than one subject of legislation because, with provisions regulating the manufacture, etc., of explosives for legitimate purposes, it prohibits their manufacture or procurement for the unlawful destruction of life or property.

3. A statute is sufficiently definite to authorize imprisonment in the penitentiary for violation of its provisions, although not stating that the imprisonment shall be in the penitentiary, where the violation is declared a felony, punishable by imprisonment for not less than five nor more than twenty-five years, and the Criminal Code of the State declares that a felony is punishable by death or confinement in the penitentiary.

4. A verdict finding "the defendant" guilty, without specifying any person by name, is not void for uncertainty, where but one person was put upon trial, although several others were indicted with him.

5. An accessory before the fact being punishable as a principal, under § 1 of Stat. June 16, 1887, regulating the use, etc., of explosives, an instruction that any person abetting or assisting in the offense mentioned in that section is to be punished as provided in said section is not erroneous.

6. An instruction that the evidence of private detectives and of the police should be received with a large degree of caution does not contain a correct proposition of law.

7. Religious opinion or belief, or want of the same, is not a test or qualification of the competency of citizens to testify as witnesses in courts of justice, under Const. 1870, art. 2, § 3, which provides that "no person shall be denied any civil or political right, privilege or capacity on account of his religious opinions."

8. A presumption arises that a person found in possession of explosives which are not called for or required in his business procured them for an unlawful purpose, where he has avowed an intention of using them for such purpose.

9. The corpus delicti of the making, procuring, etc., of dynamite with intent to use the same for the unlawful destruction of the lives of certain persons is sufficiently proved by the facts that defendant had such explosives in his possession, and kept them concealed, and on different occasions threatened to take the lives of such per-

sons, and wherever

ERROR County defendant ing dynam the lives of

The case ion.

Mr. **Jul** error:

The Statu defined sub facture, sal for legitim manufactur purposes.

State v.]

The pena uncertainty.

Horner v.

In all cri in order, th authorities, has actually

Starkie, E

No presun to that pivo lish it.

Hale, P. Hagg. C. R Ev. 733.

In a case proof of the ing he had h killed the vi criminal.

3 Greenl. Gratt. 819;

In a case o of any theft for a proof similar testin sustained.

Tyner v. *St*

Without ot a crime even defendant is i tion.

See Bishop, *note 2; Bergen People*, 18 N.

A person wi trine of punis lation of the d essarily incom

NOTE.—*Criminal procedure; verdict of guilty.*

A verdict of guilty of unlawful shooting as charged in the indictment may be sustained by aid of its reference to the indictment, although it does not name the person shot. Price v. Com. 77 Va. 393; Hoback v. Com. 28 Gratt. 922.

The name given in the verdict of the party found guilty need not correspond with that in the indictment if the accused is as well known by the one name as the othe 529.

In Nebraska th accused. Willia v. State, 54 Ga. 24

A statute must shall be expresse ville Iron Works A. 362; Astor v. N L. R. A. 789; Evan

Starkie, Ev. p. 30; Taylor, Ev. p. 1177; 1 Greenl. Ev. § 368; *Jackson* v. *Gridley*, 18 Johns. 103; *Central M. T. R. Co.* v. *Rockafellow*, 17 Ill. 553, 554.

Our Statute does not provide that every felony shall be punished by death or penitentiary imprisonment. The wording of the Statute is: "A felony is an offense punishable by death or imprisonment in the penitentiary." The term "punishable" as used in this Act does not mean "must be punished," but "liable to be punished by."

United States v. *Watkinds*, 7 Sawy. 94; *State* v. *Neuner*, 49 Conn. 233; *Miller* v. *State*, 58 Ga. 200; *Com.* v. *Pemberton*, 118 Mass. 42.

Under our Criminal Code, the word "felonious," although occasionally used, expresses a signification no less vague and indefinite than the word "criminal."

Matthews v. *State*, 4 Ohio St. 542; *State* v. *Felch*, 58 N. H. 2.

Tested by the common law, this term has no meaning.

United States v. *Coppersmith*, 2 Flipp. 551.

"Felony," as a term, is incapable of any definition, and is descriptive of no offense.

Lynch v. *Com.* 88 Pa. 192.

It will thus be apparent that the term "felony" does not affix any peculiar distinguishing mark to the crime that might guide us in determining the punishment merely from such denomination.

Brugier v. *United States*, 1 Dak. 7.

In all our penal legislation, when the word "imprisonment," only, is used it is understood to mean imprisonment in a county jail or local prison, and whenever the Legislature has intended imprisonment in the penitentiary it has been so expressed.

Cheaney v. *State*, 36 Ark. 80; *State* v. *Hyland*, 36 La. Ann. 710.

Mr. **George Hunt**, *Atty-Gen.*, for the People:

It is only the general subject of the Act that is required to be expressed in the title.

Mix v. *Illinois Cent. R. Co.* 8 West. Rep. 486, 116 Ill. 502; *Abington* v. *Cabeen*, 106 Ill. 200; *People* v. *Hazelwood*, 8 West. Rep. 538, 116 Ill. 319; *Montclair Twp.* v. *Ramsdell*, 107 U. S. 147 (27 L. ed. 431); *People* v. *Brislin*, 80 Ill. 423; *Timm* v. *Harrison*, 109 Ill. 593; *Burke* v. *Monroe County*, 77 Ill. 610; *Plummer* v. *People*, 74 Ill. 361.

The general purpose of the constitutional provision is accomplished when a law has but one general object which is fairly indicated by its title.

Cooley, Const. Lim. 1st ed. 144; *People* v. *Mahaney*, 13 Mich. 495; *Sun Mut. Ins. Co.* v. *New York*, 8 N. Y. 253. See also *Billings* v. *New York*, 68 N. Y. 413; *People* v. *Commissioner of Taxes*, 47 N. Y. 501; *Neuendorff* v. *Duryea*, 69 N. Y. 557; *Fuller* v. *People*, 92 Ill. 182.

It is not necessary that the title shall express results expected to flow from the Act, but if it does it will not render the Act void.

Plummer v. *People*, 74 Ill. 361; See *Magner* v. *People*, 97 Ill. 320; *Cole* v. *Hall*, 103 Ill. 30; *Prescott* v. *Chicago*, 60 Ill. 121; *Potwin* v. *Johnson*, 108 Ill. 71; *O'Leary* v. *Cook County*, 28 Ill. 534; *Neifing* v. *Pontiac*, 56 Ill. 172; *Johnson* v. *People*, 83 Ill. 431; *Timm* v. *Harrison*, 109 Ill. 593; *Hawthorn* v. *People*, 109 Ill. 302; *People* v. *Wright*, 70 Ill. 389; *Fuller* v. *People*, 92 Ill. 182; *Blake* v. *People*, 109 Ill. 504; *Larned* v. *Tiernan*, 110 Ill. 173; *Abington* v. *Cabeen*, 106 Ill. 200; *Virden* v. *Allen*, 107 Ill. 505.

Baker, *J.*, delivered the opinion of the court:

The plaintiff in error, John Hronek, was indicted with Frank Chapek, Frank Chleboun and Rudolph Sevic for violation of an Act of the Legislature of this State entitled "An Act to Regulate the Manufacture, Transportation, Use and Sale of Explosives, and to Punish an Improper Use of the Same," approved June 16, 1887, and in force July 1, 1887. Rev. Stat. 1889, chap. 38, §§ 54*h*–54*n*.

The first count charged the defendants with unlawfully making dynamite with the unlawful intention of destroying the lives of certain persons therein named; and in the five remaining counts the defendants were charged successively in such several counts with manufacturing, compounding, buying, selling and procuring dynamite, with the same unlawful purpose and intent. The defendant Hronek was alone put upon trial, and that trial resulted in a verdict of guilty, and fixing his punishment at twelve years' imprisonment in the penitentiary. Motions for a new trial and in arrest of judgment were severally overruled, and the said defendant was sentenced on the verdict. Numerous grounds are urged for reversal, which we shall consider substantially in the order they are made.

It is insisted that the Statute upon which the prosecution is based is unconstitutional in that it is obnoxious to section 13 of article 4 of the Constitution of the State, which provides "that no Act hereafter passed shall embrace more than one subject, and that shall be expressed in the title." The specific objection is made that two distinct subjects are expressed in the title. That objection is without merit. The Act is entitled "An Act to Regulate the Manufacture, Transportation, Use and Sale of Explosives, and to Punish an Improper Use of the Same." The regulation of the use necessarily implies the right to punish an improper use. To "regulate" means to adjust by rule or regulation; and any attempt to fix rules for the manufacture, transportation, use and sale of explosives that did not also prescribe punishment for violation of such rules and regulations would necessarily be imperfect. Two different subjects are not included or expressed in or by the title; for the punishment of an improper use flows necessarily and legitimately from the main or substantive object as stated in the title, *i. e.*, to regulate the use, etc., of explosives. It is not necessary that the title shall express all of the minor divisions of the general subject to which the Act relates; and it is sufficient if it express the general subject of the Act, and all the minor subdivisions germane to the general subject will be held to be included in it. But, if the title expresses such minor subdivisions, which without such expressions would be held to be included within the general subject, such expression will not render the title obnoxious to the constitutional provision. *Plummer* v. *People*, 74 Ill. 361; *Fuller* v. *People*, 92 Ill. 182; *Magner* v. *People*, 97 Ill. 320; *Cole* v. *Hall*, 103 Ill. 30; *Prescott* v. *Chicago*, 60 Ill. 121; *Potwin* v. *Johnson*, 108 Ill. 71; *Timm* v. *Harrison*, 109 Ill. 593; *Hawthorn* v. *People*, Id. 302; *People* v. *Wright*, 70 Ill. 389; *Virden* v. *Allan*, 107 Ill. 505.

The contention that the Statute itself treats of two separate and well-defined subjects is not tenable. It is said that the first three sections of the Act relate to the "manufacture and use of explosives for illegal purposes," while the four remaining sections relate to the "manufacture, sale and transportation of explosives for legitimate purposes." It is therefore claimed that the former sections should properly be found in the Criminal Code, and that they are not germane to the other sections of the Act, which are mere police regulations. The general subject of the Statute is the manufacture, transportation, use and sale of explosives; and it cannot be said that because one section provides for a license or permit to be obtained for their manufacture, and another prohibits the storing of explosives within a certain distance of inhabited dwellings, and another punishes fraudulent acts to procure the transportation of explosives in public conveyances, that still another section, or other sections, making it unlawful to manufacture or procure such explosives with the intent to use the same for unlawful destruction of life or property, and affixing a penalty therefor, would not be within the same general subject of legislation. It can no more be said that the prohibition, under a penalty, against storing explosives in dangerous proximity to a dwelling, is a police regulation, than that a like prohibition against manufacturing or procuring the same for an unlawful use or purpose is a police regulation. All of the provisions of the Act are within the subject expressed in the title, and are germane to each other, and to the general scope and purpose of the Act.

It is next claimed that the section of the Statute under which this indictment was prosecuted is not sufficiently definite to authorize imprisonment in the penitentiary. Section 1 of the Act provides that whoever shall be guilty of the acts therein denounced "shall be deemed guilty of felony, and upon conviction thereof shall be punished by imprisonment for a term of not less than five years, nor more than twenty-five years." It is urged that as it is not stated the imprisonment shall be in the penitentiary, and the Statute is highly penal, and requires strict construction, a sentence thereunder to the penitentiary cannot be sustained. We are not prepared to adopt this view. The offense is by the Act declared to be a felony. A felony is by the Criminal Code of the State declared to be an offense punishable by death or confinement in the penitentiary. Rev. Stat. 1889, chap. 38, § 277.

While the Legislature undoubtedly may provide for the punishment of misdemeanors by imprisonment in the penitentiary, and undoubtedly might, if they saw proper, punish felonies otherwise than by imprisonment in the penitentiary, yet there is nothing in these sections of the Act which indicates an intention to do the latter. Applying the well-known rule that a criminal statute is to be strictly construed, and that nothing is to be taken by intendment or implication against the accused beyond the literal and obvious meaning of the Statute, it is nevertheless clear, we think, when this Statute is considered in connection with the General Criminal Code, which it must be presumed the Legislature had in contemplation when passing it, the punishment to be inflicted for violation of said sections of the Act is by imprisonment in the penitentiary.

It is insisted that the verdict is void for uncertainty, in that it simply finds "the defendant" guilty, without specifying the plaintiff in error by name. Before plaintiff in error was put upon trial a separate trial had been awarded to the defendants Chapek and Sevic. The defendant Chleboun was not put upon trial, but was used as a witness on behalf of the People. The record shows that on the 26th day of November, 1888, at the term of the criminal court then being held, the following proceedings were had and entered of record, to wit; "*The People of the State of Illinois* v. *John Hronek, Impleaded*," etc. "This day come the said People by Joel M. Longnecker, state's attorney, and the said defendant, as well in his own proper person as by his counsel, also comes. And now, issue being joined, it is ordered that a jury come," etc. Then follows the impaneling of a jury. It is manifest from the foregoing that no one was put upon trial other than the defendant Hronek, and the verdict finding "the defendant" guilty could not refer to any other defendant. There was no uncertainty in the verdict.

Complaint is made of the second instruction given on behalf of the People. That instruction told the jury that any person abetting or assisting in the perpetration of the offense mentioned in section 1 of the Act was upon conviction to be punished as provided in said first section. This was not error. The Statute provides that any person abetting or in any way assisting in making, manufacturing, buying, procuring, etc., such explosives, etc., knowing or having reason to believe that the same are intended to be used by any person or persons in any way for the unlawful injury to or destruction of life or property, shall be deemed a principal, and upon conviction shall be subject to the same punishment as provided in section 1 of the Act. Under this Statute a defendant, if guilty as an accessory before the fact, is to be indicted and punished as a principal. In view of the evidence tending to show the connection of plaintiff in error with the other defendants in the perpetration of the offense, the instruction was entirely proper.

It is objected that the court erred in refusing an instruction that the evidence of private detectives and of the police "should be received with a large degree of caution."

to affect his credibility or bias his judgment, are competent to be shown to and considered by the jury in determining the weight and credit to be given to his testimony. In view of the facts and circumstances thus shown, it is for the jury to determine its weight as matter of fact.

It is urged that the court erred in modifying an instruction asked by the defendant. The instruction as asked was as follows: "The jury are instructed that, to constitute the crime charged against the defendant in the indictment, two things are necessary, namely: *First*, the making, manufacturing, compounding, buying, selling or disposing of the dynamite, or some portion thereof, described in the indictment, on or subsequent to the 1st day of July, A. D. 1887." To this the court added the following: "Therefore the jury must disregard any evidence as to the making or compounding or procuring of any dynamite at Chapek's house or elsewhere prior to said date." The instruction then proceeds: "*Second*," etc. Hronek's defense in part consisted in accounting for the dynamite found in his possession by testifying that it was left in his house in the fall of 1886 by one Karafiat; and it became important for the jury to consider testimony tending to show that he was in possession of dynamite in the spring of 1887 prior to the law under which he was prosecuted going into effect, on the 1st day of July of that year. It is insisted that the effect of the modification was to take from the consideration of the jury this evidence offered by the defendant of prior possession of the explosives. It is conceded that such was not the purpose, and it is clear to us that such was not the effect, of the modification. The instruction related solely to the elements necessary to constitute the crime charged. The jury were told that, to constitute the crime, it was necessary that the making, etc., of the dynamite must have been on or subsequent to the 1st day of July, 1887, and that therefore the jury must disregard the making or procuring, etc., prior to that date. It must be presumed that the jury were men of reasonable intelligence and would understand that what followed the introductory part of the instruction related to what was necessary to constitute the crime, and not to the defense set up, that the dynamite was in the possession of the defendant prior to the date fixed by the instruction. Moreover the jury, by a lengthy series of instructions, were fairly instructed as to the law of the case,—fully as favorably to the defendant as he could rightfully ask. They were told that they must consider all the facts and circumstances proven, and determine therefrom whether the defendant procured, etc., the explosives in question after the law went into force, and that his possession prior thereto would raise no presumption of guilt. It is, we think, impossible that the jury could have been misled to the prejudice of the plaintiff in error by the modification. It is not contended that the instruction, when considered as defining what would constitute guilt a substantially accurate statement of the law. As the jury were not misled by the modification to the prejudice of the plaintiff in error, he has no cause of complaint.

Objection is made to the competency of Frank Chleboun, a witness for the People, who was permitted to testify over the objection of the defendant. He was examined upon his *voir dire*, and avowed his belief in the existence of God, and "a hereafter;" that he believed, if he swore falsely, he would be punished under the criminal laws of the State; that he had never thought seriously of whether God would punish him either in this world or the next, and had never considered the question whether he would be punished for false swearing in any other way than by that inflicted by the law. He had, it seems, no religious belief or conviction of his accountability to the Supreme Being, either in this world or in any after life. The test of the competency of a witness in respect to religious belief, as generally held, is, Does the witness believe in God, and that he will punish him if he swears falsely?

It is stated by Rapalje in his Law of Witnesses (§ 11). that "the great weight of authority in this country now is that it is immaterial whether the witness believes God's vengeance will overtake him before or after death." This doctrine was approved in *Central M. T. R. Co.* v. *Rockafellow*, 17 Ill. 541, where, after a consideration of the authorities, it was held that all persons are competent to be sworn as witnesses who believe there is a God and that he will punish them, either in this world or the next, if they swear falsely, and that a want of such belief rendered them incompetent to take an oath as witnesses. This case seemingly overruled the doctrine of the earlier case of *Noble* v. *People*, 1 Ill. 29.

Without pausing here to determine whether the court erred in subjecting the witness to an examination touching his religious belief (Rapalje Witnesses, § 12, and cases cited), it may be said that the better practice, and that which now prevails, forbids the examination of the witness in respect thereof on his *voir dire*. If there was error in this regard, it was committed at the instance of the defendant, and in his interest; and he cannot complain.

Returning to the question of the competency of the witness, the rule seems to be as above stated, unless changed by constitutional provision or legislative enactment. The tendency of modern times by the courts and in legislation is towards liberalizing the rule, and in many jurisdictions incompetency for the want of religious belief has been abolished. See Rapalje, Witnesses, § 13, and Wharton, Ev. § 395.

Has the rule announced by this court in *Central M. T. R. Co.* v. *Rockafellow* been changed in this State? By section 3 of article 2 of the Constitution of 1870, it would seem that a radical change was effected in respect to the matter under consideration. This section guarantees non-interference of the State with the religious faith of its citizens.

In *Chase* v. *Cheney*, 58 Ill. 509, it was said: "The only exception to uncontrolled liberty is that acts of licentiousness shall not be excused, and practices inconsistent with the peace and safety of the State shall not be justified." The section provides: "No person shall be denied any civil or political right, privilege or capacity on account of his religious opinions; but the liberty of conscience hereby secured shall not be construed to dispense with oaths or affirmations, excuse acts of licentiousness, or justify practices inconsistent with the peace or safety of the State." No religious belief is required to qualify a citizen to take an oath, and no citizen can be excused from taking an oath or affirmation because of his religious belief. The liberty of conscience secured by the Constitution is not to be construed as dispensing with oaths or affirmations in cases where the same are required by law. No man, because of his religious belief, is to be excused from taking the prescribed oath of office before entering upon the discharge of the public duty; nor can he be permitted to testify because of such religous belief or opinion except upon taking the oath, or making the affirmation, required by law. Now, as before the adoption of this provision, oaths are to be taken and affirmations made, whenever required by law; but the right to take such oath or make such affirmation, if such right be a civil right, privilege or capacity, cannot be denied to any citizen. It is said that one who holds proscribed religious opinions is incompetent—that is, has not the legal capacity—to testify. The incapacity, if it exists, grows out of, and is based upon, his failure to hold certain religious beliefs and opinions in accord with the prevailing religious opinions of the people; and the contention is that he should not, by reason of such incapacity, be permitted to testify, however great and important the interest at stake to himself, his family, his neighbor or the State. It is clear from the authorities that the rule contended for does not apply when the witness is testifying in his own behalf; but if the life, liberty, reputation or property of his family or neighbor be involved, or his testimony be necessary to the protection of society, he is, under such rule, to be excluded from the privilege of testifying in courts of justice because of such incapacity. If it exists at all, the incapacity is created by law, and it is therefore a civil incapacity. The Constitution provides that no person shall be denied any civil or political right, privilege or capacity on account of his religious opinions. In Bouvier's Law Dictionary capacity is defined to be "ability, power, qualification or competency of persons, natural or artificial, for the performance of civil acts depending on their state or condition as defined or fixed by law." It is also defined as follows: "Power; competency; qualification; ability, power or qualification to do certain acts." 2 Am. & Eng. Cyclop. Law, 722.

The obvious meaning of the provision in the Constitution is that whatever civil rights, privileges or capacities belong to or are enjoyed by citizens generally shall not be taken from or denied to any person on ac-

count of i
the Supre
ing a sin
of that St
"It is a d
which is v
is held to
in a court
a certain o
another cla
ity becaus
scribed bel
Legislature
in rewards
pose any ot
the judgme
inant belie
requisite sa
In *Perry*
conclusion
constitution
be free to p
tain, their c
and the same
ish or enlarg
are of the op
stitutional p
which obtain
Constitution
longer any te
religious opi
same, which
to testify as w
follows that
the witness t
The only
deem it nec
that the evid
conviction.
proof of the
of the offens
the making,
with intent t
destruction c
in the indict
of plaintiff
dynamite, a
ent make a
possession.
indicating h
Grinnell an
throw the b
made to the
was reduced
duced in ev
he went wit
dine Square
nell's resid
companions,
find Grinne
talking of k
that he poin
house, or w
It is also sh
he threatene
persons nar
that he wou
the court-ro
he might m
tioned that
intent of p
lives of sai
plosives, if

the dynamite with the unlawful intent indicated from the fact that such dynamite was found in his possession. Where a party is found in possession of explosives, and has the avowed intention of using them for a particular purpose, the presumption would arise that he procured the same for such unlawful use. It is to be remarked that there was nothing in the business or vocation of Hronek that would call for or require the use or possession of explosives. Moreover, it was shown by the witness Chleboun that he was at Hronek's house the last Sunday in May, 1888, when Hronek showed him some unfilled bombs, and Hronek then said that he would get dynamite with which to load them. He at that time spoke of an opportunity he had to kill Bonfield; that he did not do it because he didn't have the necessary weapon, but that he regretted it very much. The witness saw no dynamite that day. In June following the witness again saw Hronek at his request, and Hronek had a number of bombs which were charged. Some of them had fuses attached, and others had fulminating caps. Can it be questioned that, if no explanation had been offered by Hronek as to when and how he came into the possession of the dynamite, the fact of its being in his possession in the month of June with the avowed intent of using it in the particular unlawful way charged, coupled with his declaration in May that he would procure dynamite for the accomplishment of such unlawful purpose, would be sufficient to maintain a conviction for unlawfully procuring the explosive with the intent to use the same? In other words, would not the jury be justified in finding therefrom that the *corpus delicti* had been proved? The fact that he procured the explosive is shown by his having it in his possession. The unlawful intent is manifested by the character of the substance itself, his concealment of it and his contemporaneous declarations of his intent. A jury, from the necessity of the case, must be allowed to draw conclusions from the facts proved; and intent can ordinarily be shown only by inferences drawn from the acts actual possession of the dynamite in June, 1888, and subsequently, by unquestioned evidence; and the fact of his intention is shown by his declarations and acts. If from the facts proved, the conclusion is irresistible, if the testimony is believed, that the offense was committed, then the *corpus delicti* is established.

Some question is made in respect of the evidence of the date when the dynamite was procured by Hronek. He testified that one Karafiat left it at his house in the fall of 1886, and had never called for it. Without entering into a discussion of the evidence it must be said there was much in his own testimony, as there was also in the testimony of the witness Chleboun, that tended to discredit his evidence. The question was fully and fairly submitted to the jury as to whether or not he procured the dynamite with the unlawful intent charged, after the 1st day of July, 1887, when the Statute went into effect. They were told in numerous instructions that unless they believed from the evidence, beyond a reasonable doubt, that he procured the same, with the specific intent charged, on or subsequent to that date, they must acquit.

Without extending this opinion—already too long—by an analysis of the evidence, it must suffice for us to say that we have carefully considered the record, and the facts and circumstances proved, and are unable to say that the jury were palpably wrong in the conclusion reached by them. It is not enough that we, sitting as a jury, might have found differently. They saw the witnesses,—had means of determining their credibility which we do not possess, and, before we would be justified in setting aside their verdict for error in finding of fact, the error must be palpable.

Other minor objections are urged, which we have carefully considered, and there is no reversible error in them; and no good purpose would be served, either to the defendant or the profession, by their discussion.

We find no error in this record for which the judgment of the court below should be reversed, and it is accordingly affirmed.

NEW JERSEY SUPREME COURT.

Cora NEWMAN, by Ella Newman, Her Next Friend,

v.

PHILLIPSBURGH HORSE CAR R. CO.

(....N. J. L....)

*1. **An infant of tender years** is not to be charged with the negligence of the person having it in charge.

2. **The plaintiff, about two years of age, being under the care of her adult sister,** wandered onto the track of the horse railroad, and was there run over by the carelessness of the driver of the car. *Held*, that plaintiff's right of action was not lost even if the sister's carelessness of supervision, in part, was cause of her injury.

(June 5, 1890.)

*Head notes by Beasley, *Ch. J.*

CASE certified from the Circuit Court for Warren County for the advisory opinion

Note.—*Care to be exercised toward children to avoid injuries.*

A higher degree of care should be exercised toward a child incapable of using discretion commensurate with the perils of his situation than towards one of mature age and capacity. Harriman v. Pittsburgh, C. & St. L. R. Co. 9 West. Rep. 443, 444, 46 Ohio St. 11; Frost v. Eastern R. 4 New Eng. Rep. 529, 64 N. H. 220; Isabel v. Hannibal & St. J. R. Co. 60 Mo. 475; Bannon v. Baltimore & O. R.

See also 38 L. R. A. 633.

of this court after verdict for plaintiff in an action brought to recover damages for personal injuries inflicted on plaintiff, an infant, through the alleged negligence of defendant. *Judgment on the verdict advised.*

Statement by **Beasley**, *Ch. J.:*

The plaintiff was a child two years of age. She was in the custody of her sister, who was twenty-two. The former, being left by herself for a few minutes, got upon the railroad track of the defendant, and was hurt by the car. The occurrence took place in a public street of the Village of Phillipsburgh. The carelessness of the defendant was manifest, as at the time of the accident there was no one in charge of the horse drawing the car, the driver being in the car collecting fares. The circuit judge submitted the three following propositions to this court for its advisory opinion, viz.: "first, whether the negligence of the persons in charge of the plaintiff, an infant minor, should be imputed to the said plaintiff; second, whether the conduct of the persons in charge of the plaintiff at the time of the injury complained of was not so demonstrably negligent that the said circuit court should have nonsuited the plaintiff, or that the court should have directed the jury to find for the defendant; third, whether a new trial ought not to be granted on the ground that the damages awarded are excessive."

Mr. **J. G. Shipman**, for plaintiff:

The negligence of the sister cannot be imputed to the child, and the doctrine of contributory negligence does not enter into the case at all.

Pollock, Torts, 1886, *388; *Robinson* v. *Cone*,

22 Vt. 218
L. ed. 652
546; *Wait*
El. 727; *I*
S. 30; *M'*
Prendegast
58 N. Y. C
par. 41, p.
Mr. **Geo**
tiff:
Hartfield
very much
cases, and
the authori
reasoning i
gence, p. 1
See also *B*
908, 64 N. E
Schuster, 4
lor v. *Delawa*
113 Pa. 162;
Welch, 6 We
v. *South Bos*
142 Mass. 30
777; *Central*
R. Co. 81 Fe
Vt. 218; *Mul*
Mr. **Willi**
Negligence
who permits
Lygo v. *Ne*
Macfie and *Ab*
Waite v. *Nort*
719, 5 Jur. N.
When anot
of tender yea
having such
Mangan v.
Hartfield v.
v. *Brooklyn*

Co. 24 Md. 108; Chicago, B. & Q. R. Co. v. Dewey, 26 Ill. 255; Walters v. Chicago, R. I. & P. R. Co. 41 Iowa, 71; O'Mara v. Hudson R. R. Co. 38 N. Y. 445; Philadelphia & R. R. Co. v. Spearen, 47 Pa. 300; Smith v. O'Connor, 48 Pa. 218; Pennsylvania R. Co. v. Morgan, 82 Pa. 134.

A child of tender years is not required to exercise the same degree of care as an adult. Cooper v. Lake Shore & M. S. R. Co. 10 West. Rep. 184, 66 Mich. 261.

But such child is to be held only to the degree of care expected of ordinarily careful children of its years. Moebus v. Herrmann, 11 Cent. Rep. 90, 108 N. Y. 349; Baker v. Flint & P. M. R. Co. 12 West. Rep. 485, 68 Mich. 90.

Due care according to age and capacity is all that the law exacts of a child of tender years. Ordinary care—which is that of every prudent man—is not the standard for a child. Western & A. R. Co. v. Young (Ga.) Oct. 21, 1889.

A minor four or five years old is not, as a matter of law, to be charged with contributory negligence in not exercising reasonable care to avoid a personal injury. Westbrook v. Mobile & O. R. Co. 66 Miss. 560.

It cannot be inferred as matter of law that an infant of six years can be guilty of contributory negligence. Mackey v. Vicksburg, 64 Miss. 777.

A boy fourteen years of age cannot be held to the same degree of care, in determining his contributory negligence, that an adult should be. Wright v. Detroit, G. H. & M. R. Co. (Mich.) Oct. 25, 1889.

In the application of the doctrine of contributory negligence to children, in actions by them or in their behalf, for injuries occasioned by the negli-

gence of other
by the same ru
while it is thei
avoid the injur
care for them
of the same ag
accustomed to
ces. Clevelan
A. 385, 46 Ohio
L. R. A. 418, 12
As to the ru
mining whet
chargeable wi
the degree of
wards them,
Co. 1 New E
Whittier Mac
337; Nolan v.
Rep. 826, 53 C
Eng. Rep. 759,
R. Co. 2 New
South Boston
note, 142 Mass
Eng. Rep. 362
Mfg. Co. 3 Ne
delphia, W. &
112 Pa. 414; S
168, 112 Pa. 43
R. Co. 3 Cent.
Iron & Steel
troleum Brid
Pa. 321; Erie
Rep. 919, 113
gan (Pa.) 5 C
City R. R. Co

Forty second St. & G. St. F. R. Co. 47 N. Y. 320-323; *Fallon* v. *Central Park, N. & E. R. Co.* 64 N. Y. 13; *McGarry* v. *Loomis*, 63 N. Y. 107; *Cosgrove* v. *Ogden*, 49 N. Y. 258; *Birkett* v. *Knickerbocker Ice Co.* 110 N. Y. 506; *Holly* v. *Boston Gas Light Co.* 8 Gray, 123-132; *Wright* v. *Malden & M. R. Co.* 4 Allen, 283, 289; *Callahan* v. *Bean*, 9 Allen, 401; *Lynch* v. *Smith*, 104 Mass. 58; *Collins* v. *South Boston R. Co.* 2 New Eng. Rep. 649, 142 Mass. 313.

There is no evidence justifying actual damages to the amount of $2,500.

Beasley, *Ch. J.*, delivered the opinion of the court:

There is but a single question presented by this case, and that question plainly stands among the vexed questions of the law. The problem is whether an infant of tender years can be vicariously negligent, so as to deprive itself of a remedy that it would otherwise be entitled to. In some of the American States this question has been answered by the courts in the affirmative, and in others in the negative. To the former of these classes belongs the decision in *Hartfield* v. *Roper*, reported in 21 Wend. 615. This case appears to have been one of first impression on this subject; and it is to be regarded not only as the precursor, but as the parent, of all the cases of the same strain that have since appeared. The inquiry with respect to the effect of the negligence of the custodian of the infant, too young to be intelligent of situations and circumstances, was directly presented for decision in the primary case thus referred to; for the facts were these, viz.: The plaintiff, a child of about two years of age, was standing or sitting in the snow in a public road, and in that situation was run over by a sleigh driven by the defendants. The opinion of the court was that, as the child was permitted by its custodian to wander into a position of such danger, it was without remedy for the hurts thus received unless they were voluntarily inflicted, or were the product of gross carelessness on the part of the defendants. It is obvious that the judicial theory was that the infant was, through the medium of its custodian, the doer, in part, of its own misfortune, and that consequently, by force of the well-known rule under such conditions, he had no right to an action. This, of course, was visiting the child for the neglect of the custodian; and such infliction is justified in the case cited in this wise: "An infant," says the court, "is not *sui juris*. He belongs to another, to whom discretion in the care of his person is exclusively confided. That person is keeper and agent for this purpose, and, in respect to third persons, his act must be deemed that of the infant; his neglect, the infant's neglect."

It will be observed that the entire context of this quotation is the statement of a single fact, and a deduction from it,—the premise being that the child must be in the care and charge of an adult, and the inference being that for that reason the neglects of the adult are the neglects of the infant. But surely this is conspicuously a *non sequitur*. How does the custody of the infant justify or lead to the imputation of another's fault to him? The law, natural and civil, puts the infant

delphia, W. & B. R. Co. v. Gunther, 6 Cent. Rep. 480, 66 Md. 501; Kunz v. Troy, 6 Cent. Rep. 498, 104 N. Y. 344; Miller v. Pennsylvania R. Co. (Pa.) 6 Cent. Rep. 607; St. Clair Street R. Co. v. Eadie, 1 West. Rep. 88, 43 Ohio St. 91; Chicago v. Keefe, 1 West. Rep. 353, 114 Ill. 222; Stafford v. Rubens, 1 West. Rep. 640, 115 Ill. 196; Saare v. Union R. Co. 2 West. Rep. 538, 20 Mo. App. 211; Duffy v. Missouri Pac. R. Co. 2 West. Rep. 198, 19 Mo. App. 380; Indianapolis, P. & C. R. Co. v. Pitzer, 4 West. Rep. 250, and *note*, 258, 7 West. Rep. 396, 109 Ind. 179; Whitehead v. St. Louis, I. M. & S. R. Co. 5 West. Rep. 84, 22 Mo. App. 60; Dowling v. Allen, 5 West. Rep. 370, 88 Mo. 293; Indianapolis v. Emmelman, 6 West. Rep. 566, 108 Ind. 530; Muehlhausen v. St. Louis R. Co. 6 West. Rep. 857, 91 Mo. 332; Chicago, St. L. & P. R. Co. v. Welsh, 6 West. Rep. 540, 118 Ill. 572; Schmidt v. Kansas City Distilling Co. 7 West. Rep. 124, 90 Mo. 284; Ecliff v. Wabash, St. L. & P. R. Co. 7 West. Rep. 464, 64 Mich. 196; Battishill v. Humphrey, 7 West. Rep. 806, 64 Mich. 494; Hughes v. Detroit, G. H. & M. R. Co. 8 West. Rep. 100, 65 Mich. 10; Rafferty v. Missouri Pac. R. Co. 8 West. Rep. 255, 91 Mo. 33; Chrystal v. Troy & B. R. Co. 7 Cent. Rep. 245, *note*, 105 N. Y. 164.

Negligence of another cannot be imputed to a child.

A parent's negligence, while it may bar an action for his own benefit for injuries to the child, cannot be imputed to the child when the latter sues, or when suit is brought for his benefit. Westbrook v. Mobile & O. R. Co. 66 Miss. 560.

In an action for an injury to a child while getting off from a street car, the question whether the child's mother was exercising due care for the safety of the child is immaterial, where the child himself was using all the care which the occasion required. Chicago City R. Co. v. Robinson, 4 L. R. A. 126, 127 Ill. 9.

Where a child of seven years and three months was injured by a switch engine pushing coal cars on a street, the only question which can arise on the trial is whether defendant had been guilty of negligence. The doctrine of comparative negligence does not apply. Chicago, St. L. & P. R. Co. v. Welsh, 6 West. Rep. 540, 118 Ill. 572. See *note* to Nisbet v. Garner (Iowa) 1 L. R. A. 152.

One negligent person cannot escape liability for his negligence because the negligence of another concurred in producing the injury. Louisville, N. A. & C. R. Co. v. Lucas, 6 L. R. A. 193, 119 Ind. 583.

That a defendant is liable for injury to children of tender years when such injury is caused by his want of due care, and the doctrine of imputed negligence does not apply, see Bay Shore R. Co. v. Harris, 67 Ala. 6; Bronson v. Southbury, 37 Conn. 199; Donahoe v. Wabash, St. L. & P. R. Co. 83 Mo. 543; Huff v. Ames, 16 Neb. 139; St. Clair Street R. Co. v. Eadie, 1 West. Rep. 88, 43 Ohio St. 91; North Pa. R. Co. v. Mahoney, 57 Pa. 187; Philadelphia & R. R. Co. v. Long, 75 Pa. 257; Birkett v. Knickerbocker Ice Co. 110 N. Y. 507; Murphy v. Orr, 96 N. Y. 14; Moebus v. Herrmann, 11 Cent. Rep. 90, 108 N. Y. 349; Whirley v. Whiteman, 1 Head, 610; Galveston, H. & H. R. Co. v. Moore, 59 Tex. 64; Texas M. R. Co. v. Herbeck, 60 Tex. 602; Robinson v. Cone, 22 Vt. 212; Norfolk & P. R. Co. v. Ormsby, 27 Gratt. 455.

The negligence of one person cannot be imputed to another. See *note* to Dean v. Pennsylvania R. Co. (Pa.) 6 L. R. A. 143.

The doctrine of negligence of parent or guardian imputed to child, discussed in *notes* to Wymore v. Mahaska Co. (Iowa) 6 L. R. A. 545; Chicago City R. Co. v. Robinson (Ill.) 4 L. R. A. 126; Cleveland Rolling Mill Co. v. Corrigan (Ohio St.) 3 L. R. A. 385.

Infant not chargeable with contributory negligence. See *note* to Winter v. Kansas City Cable R. Co. (Mo.) 6 L. R. A. 536.

under the care of the adult; but how can this right to care for and protect be construed into a right to waive or forfeit any of the legal rights of the infant? The capacity to make such waiver or forfeiture is not a necessary or even convenient incident of this office of the adult, but on the contrary is quite inconsistent with it; for the power to protect is the opposite of the power to harm, either by act or omission.

In this case, in 21 Wend. 615, it is evident that the rule of law enunciated by it is founded in the theory that the custodian of the infant is the agent of the infant. But this is a mere assumption, without legal basis; for such custodian is the agent, not of the infant, but of the law. If such supposed agency existed, it would embrace many interests of the infant, and could not be confined to the single instance when an injury is inflicted by the co-operative tort of the guardian. And yet it seems certain that such custodian cannot surrender or impair a single right of any kind that is vested in the child, nor impose any legal burden upon it. If a mother traveling with her child in her arms should agree with a railway company that, in case of an accident to such infant by reason of the joint negligence of herself and the company, the latter should not be liable to a suit by the child, such an engagement would be plainly invalid on two grounds: *first*, the contract would be *contra bonos mores;* and, *second*, because the mother was not the agent of the child authorized to enter into the agreement. Nevertheless the position has been deemed defensible that the same evil consequences to the infant will follow from the negligence of the mother, in the absence of such supposed contract, as would have resulted if such contract should have been made, and should have been held valid.

In fact, this doctrine of the imputability of the misfeasance of the keeper of a child to the child itself is deemed to be a pure interpolation into the law; for, until the case under criticism, it was absolutely unknown, nor is it sustained by legal analogies. Infants have always been the particular objects of the favor and protection of the law. In the language of an ancient authority, this doctrine is thus expressed: "The common principle is that an infant, in all things which sound in his benefit, shall have favor and preferment in law as well as another man, but shall not be prejudiced by anything to his disadvantage." 9 Vin. Abr. 374.

And it would appear to be plain that nothing could be more to the prejudice of an infant than to convert, by construction of law, the connection between himself and his custodian into an agency to which the harsh rule of *respondeat superior* should be applicable. The answerableness of the principal for the authorized acts of his agent is not so much the dictate of natural justice as of public policy, and has arisen, with some propriety, from the circumstances that the creation of the agency is a voluntary act, and that it can be controlled and ended at the will of its creator. But in the relationship between the infant and its keeper all these decisive characteristics are wholly wanting. The law imposes the keeper upon the child, who of course can neither control nor remove him; and the injustice, therefore, of making the latter responsible in any measure whatever for the torts of the former would seem to be quite evident. Such, subjectively, would be hostile in every respect to the natural rights of the infant, and consequently cannot with any show of reason be introduced into that provision which both necessity and law establish for his protection. Nor can it be said that its existence is necessary to give just enforcement to the rights of others. When it happens that both the infant and its custodian have been injured by the co-operative negligence of such custodian and a third party, it seems reasonable, at least in some degree, that the latter should be enabled to say to the custodian: "You and I, by our common carelessness, have done this wrong, and therefore neither can look to the other for redress." But when such wrong-doer says to the infant: "Your guardian and I, by our joint misconduct, have brought this loss upon you; consequently, you have no right of action against me, but you must look for indemnification to your guardian alone,"—a proposition is stated that appears to be without any basis either in good sense or law. The conversion of the infant, who is entirely free from fault, into a wrong-doer, by imputation, is a logical contrivance uncongenial with the spirit of jurisprudence. The sensible and legal doctrine is this: An infant of tender years cannot be charged with negligence, nor can he be so charged with the commission of such fault by substitution, for he is incapable of appointing an agent; the consequence being that he can in no case be considered to be the blameable cause, either in whole or in part, of his own injury. There is no injustice nor hardship in requiring all wrong-doers to be answerable to a person who is incapable either of self-protection, or of being a participator in their misfeasance. Nor is it to be overlooked that the theory here repudiated, if it should be adopted, would go the length of making an infant in its nurse's arms answerable for all the negligences of such nurse while thus employed in its service. Every person so damaged by the careless custodian would be entitled to his action against the infant. If the neglect of the guardian is to be regarded as the neglect of the infant, as was asserted in the New York decision, it would, from logical necessity, follow that the infant must indemnify those who should be harmed by such neglect. That such a doctrine has never prevailed is conclusively shown by the fact that in the reports there is no indication that such a suit has ever been brought.

It has already been observed that judicial opinions touching the subject just discussed are in a state of direct antagonism, and it would therefore serve no useful purpose to refer to any of them. It is sufficient to say that the leading text-writers have concluded that the weight of such authority is adverse to the doctrine that an infant can become in any wise a tort-feasor by imputation. 1 Shearm. & Redf. Neg. 75; Wharton, Neg. § 311; 2 Wood, Railway Law, 1284. In our

scale.

It remains to add that we do not think the damages so excessive as to place the verdict be advised to render *judgment on the finding of the jury.*

MARYLAND COURT OF APPEALS.

TOLCHESTER BEACH IMPROVEMENT CO., of Kent County, *Appt.*,
v.
Daniel STEINMEIER.

(....Md.....)

1. A corporation cannot be held liable for an arrest ordered by the superintendent of its property at a certain place whose office is not mentioned or described in its charter, unless it is shown that he had express precedent authority for giving the order, or that it was ratified and adopted by the corporation.

2. A policeman appointed on the application of a corporation which is required by law to pay his salary, is an officer of the State, and the corporation is not responsible for his acts as such officer in making an arrest, especially if it is not done on the premises of the corporation.

3. A corporation cannot be held to have ratified the act of a special policeman whose salary it is required to pay, in making an arrest, as he does not act in the matter as its agent, but as an officer of the State.

(June 18, 1890.)

APPEAL by defendant from a judgment of the Circuit Court for Talbot County in favor of plaintiff in an action brought to recover damages for an assault and false imprisonment, for which defendant was alleged to be responsible. *Reversed.*

The facts sufficiently appear in the opinion.

Argued before Alvey, *Ch. J.*, and Bryan, McSherry, Fowler, Briscoe and Irving, *JJ.*

Messrs. **H. H. Barroll, H. V. D. Johns, Albert Constable** and **C. S. Carrington** for appellant.

Messrs. **James A. Pearce** and **Harrison W. Vickers**, for appellee:

The Company controls the appointment of the officer in every respect, and the officer is amenable to the Company alone. If the officer is in any measure subject to the direction or control of the corporation, and acts in obedience to its instructions, the relation of master and servant exists, and the principle of *respondeat superior* applies.

Wood, Mast. and Serv. § 459; *Singer Mfg. Co.* v. *Rahn*, 132 U. S. 523 (33 L. ed. 442).

The right of selection lies at the foundation of the responsibility of a master or principal, for the act of his servant or agent.

Kelly v. *New York*, 11 N. Y. 436; *Blake* v. *Ferris*, 5 N. Y. 48; *Oliver* v. *Worcester*, 102 Mass. 489; *Maxmilian* v. *New York*, 62 N. Y. 165; *Scott* v. *Manchester*, 2 Hurlst. & N. 205; *Walcott* v. *Swampscott*, 1 Allen, 101.

If it was an act done, in doing that which the master employed the servant to do, though done contrary to the master's will, against his instructions, and without his knowledge, although unnecessary to accomplish the work, ill-advised, malicious or wanton, he is liable, because he has set in motion the agency that produces the wrong.

Wood, Mast. and Serv. § 303, p. 571; *Limpus* v. *London Gen. Omnibus Co.* 1 Hurlst. & C. 526; *Ramsden* v. *Boston & A. R. Co.* 104 Mass. 117; *Howe* v. *Newmarch*, 12 Allen, 49.

If the servant is authorized to use force against another, when executing his master's order, the master commits it to him to decide what degree of force he shall use, and if, through misjudgment or violence of temper, he goes beyond the necessity of the occasion, and gives a right of action to another, he cannot as to third persons be said to have been acting without the line of his duty, or to have departed from his master's business.

Rounds v. *Delaware, L. & W. R. Co.* 64 N. Y. 129. See *Chicago City R. Co.* v. *McMahon*, 103 Ill. 485; *Carter* v. *Howe Mach. Co.* 51 Md. 296; *Evansville & T. H. R. Co.* v. *McKee*, 99 Ind. 519; *Goff* v. *Great Northern R. Co.* 30 L. J. Q. B. 152.

It is not necessary that authority should have been expressly conferred; it is only necessary that the act was such as was incident to the performance of the duties intrusted to the agents by the master, even though in opposition to his express orders.

Wood, Mast. and Serv. § 307; *Wheeler & Wilson Mfg. Co.* v. *Boyce*, 36 Kan. 350; *Goddard* v. *Grand Trunk R. Co. of Canada*, 57 Me. 202; *Fenton* v. *Wilson Sewing Mach. Co.* 9 Phila. 189; *Boogher* v. *Life Asso. of America*, 75 Mo. 319; *Cumberland Valley R. Co.* v. *Baab*, 9 Watts, 458.

The test of liability is whether the servant's purpose was to serve his employer's interest by the act, provided it is within the course of his employment.

Limpus v. *London Gen. Omnibus Co. supra; Seymour* v. *Greenwood*, 6 Hurlst. & N. 355; *Shea* v. *Sixth Ave. R. Co.* 62 N. Y. 180; *Birmingham Water Works Co.* v. *Hubbard*, 85 Ala. 179; Cooley, Torts, 538.

Retention of servants long after full knowledge of their conduct is strong evidence of ratification.

Goddard v. *Grand Trunk R. Co. of Canada, supra.*

NOTE.—*Special policeman.*

Under N. Y. Laws 1884, chap. 180, § 269, relating to special patrolmen, one on whose premises a special patrolman is appointed for duty, and by whom his salary is paid, is not liable for his official acts. Hershey v. O'Neill, 36 Fed. Rep. 168.

Arrest by peace officer. See exhaustive note to State v. Hunter (N. C.) *ante*, 529.

No action by directors is necessary to show ratification.

Bank of New South Wales v. *Owston,* L. R. 4 App. Cas. 286, 288; *Mackay* v. *Commercial Bank,* L. R. 5 P. C. 416; *Brickner* v. *New York Cent. R. Co.* 49 N. Y. 672; Wood, Mast. and Serv. § 451.

If, in furtherance of the particular business of the Company, it is necessary to arrest a person, the servants of the Company have an implied authority to do it.

Edwards v. *London & N. W. R. Co.* L. R. 5 C. P. 445.

No express authority was needed.

Bayley v. *Manchester, S. & L. R. Co.* L. R. 7 C. P. 419; *Bank of New South Wales* v. *Owston,* L. R. 4 App. Cas. 270; *Barwick* v. *English Joint Stock Bank,* L. R. 2 Exch. 265; *Goff* v. *Great Northern R. Co.* and *Mackay* v. *Commercial Bank, supra.*

Irving, *J.,* delivered the opinion of the court:

This is a suit for assault and false imprisonment. The appellant is a corporation known as "The Tolchester Beach Improvement Company of Kent County," and carries on an excursion business by steamboats, bringing passengers from Baltimore and elsewhere to Tolchester Beach in Kent County, where the Company has a wharf, hotel, baths, small boats for hire, etc. The plaintiff carried on a business on the shore in hiring small boats and fishing tackle, and got his customers mainly from persons who were appellant's excursionists, and out of this rivalry in trade grew ill feeling and controversy which culminated in the quarrel which gave rise to this suit. A public county road ran through the appellant's grounds to the water, where there was a public landing adjoining the appellant's premises and wharf, and on this public landing this controversy had its origin.

Upon application to the governor of the State, the appellant had secured the appointment of Thomas J. Fletcher as a policeman "for the protection of the property of the corporation, and for the preservation of peace and good order on their premises." This officer was appointed on the nomination of the appellant and was duly commissioned as a state officer, under the seal of the State, under the Act of 1880, chap. 460, which gives sections 288, 289, 290, 291, 292 and 293 to the present Code, article 23. Oliver H. Paxton was appellant's superintendent at the beach, and he was, on the occasion of this disturbance, engaged in booming and securing certain drift logs which had come down the bay and floated around the appellant's wharf and the public landing. He was upon the public landing, and securing them there. The plaintiff (appellee here) and his partner came with their boat and found their access to the landing obstructed. The appellee came ashore by stepping on the logs, obtained a rope to throw to his partner in the boat, in order to draw the boat around the logs and make it fast. His contention is that he stepped on a log upon which Paxton was standing, and in throwing the line the log turned in the water and cast him and Paxton both into the water, whereupon the appellee contends and testified that Paxton at once or-

dered Fl
you see h
Paxton
fully took
the water
It make
particular
cision are
arrest the
pistol and
being con
around to
under leas
out warra
and havin
took him t
til, after t
quitted an
The app
that it is n
prisonment
its employé
of an order
to order a
that Fletch
the Compa
ble, and he
Paxton w
Company;
does not fol
an arrest an
quences of i
Company at
tioned and d
the duties a
ent were the
the appellan
restricted ch
authority to
was to be bo
the arrest, it
intendent," o
such authorit
swerable for
have been don
authority. I
inference, fro
name, that th
the Company.
State which w
the corporatio
act, the court
51 Md. 298, "
was expressly
corporation."
not, in the nat
of the ordinar
intrusted with
and before the
for such an act
there was expr
ing the act o
adopted by the
tainly no expre
ton to set in n
State, and we sl
no ratification a
lant.

The question
court right in h
ble for the act of
officer of the Co
powers of arres

for his arrest, maltreatment and imprisonment of Steinmeier? For the purposes of this decision and in support of our view of it, it is not necessary for us to be told that Fletcher was in no sense an officer of that Company, and that, if called on to enforce regulations and by-laws of the Company, and he did so purely because of his relation to the Company, the Company would not be answerable for what was wrongfully done in pursuance of that authority, but within the scope of his employment. But primarily Fletcher was a State's officer, appointed by the governor under the law, and commissioned accordingly. It is true he was appointed upon the nomination or designation of the appellant, and by the law was to receive his compensation from the appellant. He was removable at the pleasure of the governor, by the express provision of § 289, art. 23, of the Code; and if the Company wanted such a policeman, still, in such case, it would have to nominate another man. It is true that under section 298, when the services of such policeman were no longer required, "the Company could file a notice to that effect in the office where his oath was recorded," and then he would be discharged. But it is to be noted that this power on the part of the Company existed only when the Company no longer needed such an officer. If such officer was still needed, but the incumbent was inefficient or unsatisfactory, resort to the governor for relief under his power of removal at pleasure would seem necessary. He took the oath taken by all other police officers. He was responsible to the State for the proper discharge of his duty, and not to the Company. He was not amenable to the Company, but the State, and would be indicted for malfeasance as any other state officer. His duty was the same as any other policeman or constable. His authority was coextensive with the limits of Kent County and the City of Baltimore, and for the protection of the property of said company corporation and the preservation "of peace and good order on its premises" the law authorized the corporation to command his presence on their boats and premises on the condition of paying his whole compensation, and that no part of his compensation was to be chargeable against the State or county. §§ 290-292.

It was for the privilege of commanding at all times when needed an officer with constabulary powers for the protection of their property and preserving the peace on their boats and premises where in their peculiar business a need for such person, or clothed with such authority, so often arose, that the law required such corporation to pay his salary.

In *Sinclair* v. *Baltimore*, 59 Md. 592, this court decided that the City of Baltimore was not responsible for wanton acts of its policemen in their discharge of duty, notwithstanding their compensation was paid by the city. It would seem, therefore, that this Company was not bound for Fletcher's acts simply because appointed by the governor at its designation, nomination or request, and because it paid his salary. He was undoubtedly a state officer, and whenever he attempted to enforce the criminal laws of the State he did it in virtue of his oath as a state officer, and in the exercise of his common-law powers as such officer; and the Company had no quasi judicial power to order him to arrest anyone, and certainly none to restrain him in the exercise of his office when his sworn duty required him to do anything of the kind. The Company needed such officer at command because neither it nor its officers had the power with which the law clothed him.

In addition to all these reasons why Fletcher's act cannot be regarded as the act of the appellant, it is to be noted especially that, so far as the appellant is concerned, his duty to it, so far as the exercise of his peace powers were concerned, is, by the language of the Statute and his commission, restricted to the premises of the Company. Whatever was done was not done on the premises of the Company; nor was the order of Paxton given on the premises of the Company. The occasion for such order arose on the public highway; and the arrest was in fact actually made on the plaintiff's own premises. It cannot be contended that it was done in the preservation of the property of the Company; for assuming that, in collecting the drift logs, the superintendent was acting for the Company [which its president denies], still it is not contended that the plaintiff was interfering to prevent their collection and being secured. The testimony only shows that Paxton complained of the plaintiff assaulting him and casting him into the water, and for that ordered the arrest. What Fletcher did was in the execution of the criminal law upon his own view of the affair, without warrant and in discharge of what he supposed was his duty at common law. It is worthy of note also that by plaintiff's own testimony Paxton told Fletcher to "get a warrant," which was not done.

Unless the trespass was to the use or benefit of the defendant, he cannot be held to have effectually adopted it, after it was done. Ewell's Evans on Agency, 2d Eng. ed. 84.

There is not the slightest ground for appellee's contention in that respect. The act of Fletcher in no way inured to the benefit of the appellant. It is useless to discuss this contention on the part of the appellee, for by the sixth prayer of the appellant, granted by the court below and not excepted to or appealed from, it became the law of this case that there was no evidence of liability arising in that way. The contention is based wholly on declarations of Eliason, the president of the Company, and Paxton, the superintendent, made after Steinmeier's trial, acquittal and discharge. Those declarations the circuit court decided did not tend to prove any liability of the Company. If this was not the law of this case by an unappealed ruling of the court below, we could not support the contention in this case, because the act to be ratified must be held to be the act of an agent of the Company authorized to commit it, whereas it was the act of a state officer in the exercise of his common-law powers and not executing the orders of the appellees. The view we have taken of the case renders it unnecessary for us to review the prayers *seriatim*, to the granting of which exception was taken. Their theory was baseless and the case should have been withdrawn from the jury. For the failure to so rule the judgment must be reversed without awarding a new trial.

Judgment reversed without remand for new trial.

John G. PENDERGAST, *Appt.*,
v.
George B. YANDES, Receiver of the Broad Ripple Natural Gas Co.

(......Ind.......)

A "superintendent" of a natural gas company, who is not a general manager, or a general agent or an officer of the company, but whose principal duties are to superintend the construction of trenches and the laying of gas pipes, is a laborer within the meaning of that term as used in Elliott's Supp., § 1605, giving a preference to laborers' claims for wages against corporations.

(May 29, 1890.)

APPEAL by plaintiff from a judgment of the Superior Court for Marion County refusing to declare his claim against the Broad Ripple Natural Gas Company for wages a preferred claim. *Reversed.*

The facts sufficiently appear in the opinion.

Messrs. **McMaster & Boice,** for appellant:

The Statute in question is remedial legislation, and should have a fair and liberal construction.

Bass v. *Doerman*, 112 Ind. 390; *Warren* v. *Sohn*, Id. 213.

Under the decisions appellant was a laborer within the meaning of the Statute.

Conlee Lumber Co. v. *Ripon Lumber & Mfg. Co.* 66 Wis. 481; *Flagstaff Silver Min. Co. of Utah* v. *Cullins*, 104 U. S. 176 (26 L. ed. 704); *Capron* v. *Strout*, 11 Nev. 304; *Stryker* v. *Cassidy*, 76 N. Y. 50; *Mulligan* v. *Mulligan*, 18 La. Ann. 20; *Knight* v. *Norris*, 13 Minn. 473; *Bank of Pennsylvania* v. *Gries*, 35 Pa. 423; *Caraker* v. *Mathews*, 25 Ga. 571; *Gurney* v. *Atlantic & G. W. R. Co.* 58 N. Y. 358.

A number of cases have arisen under Stockholders' Liability Statutes, in which the character of services rendered the corporation was quite similar to the character of services rendered in this case, and in which it has been uniformly held that the stockholders were liable.

Sleeper v. *Goodwin*, 67 Wis. 577; *Harris* v. *Norvell*, 1 Abb. N. C. 127; *Williamson* v. *Wadsworth*, 49 Barb. 294; *Hovey* v. *Ten Broeck*, 3 Robt. (N. Y.) 316; *Vincent* v. *Bamford*, 42 How. Pr. 109; *Short* v. *Medberry*, 29 Hun, 39; *Conant* v. *Van Schaick*, 24 Barb. 87.

By any fair construction, appellant's services must be rated as physical labor; but if not, he must be at least an "employé" within the Statute, if that term is to have anything like its ordinary and accepted meaning.

Gurney v. *Atlantic & G. W. R. Co.* 58 N. Y. 371. See also *Stone* v. *United States*, 3 Ct. Cl. 260; Marshall's decision as to term "employé," *United States* v. *Belew*, 2 Brock. 280.

Messrs. **Duncan & Smith** for appellee.

Coffey, *J.*, delivered the opinion of the court:

The appellee was duly appointed and qualified as Receiver of the Broad Ripple Natural

Gas Comp
purpose of
gas. Afte
the claim
the same
claim. Tl
made a spe
and stated
appears fr
Broad Ripp
poration o
State for the
natural gas.
it employed
for the purp
tion of its
lis and Mari
so employed
tendent, he
of gas trenc
the testing o
with the pi
many emplo
them at his
over said en
from one hu
He was hims
pany, and h
except the p
duty was al
tending the e
discharge of
a great deal
and, when te
for him to h
for a few min
charge of his
for him to do
other than suc
superintenden
such work, al
his own voliti
there was scar
labor in the h
work incident
His salary or
month. His d
the men who w
of laying the p
herein specifie
done properly,
skill; and, as th
into different g
to travel back a
other. There i
sociation or by-l
such an office a
receiver was ap
April, 1889. T
its assets are no
against it in full
pellant for servi
superintendent t
accrued within s
ment of the Re
court rendered a
pellant for the su
clare it a preferre
Section 1605, E
lows: "Hereafte

ral or other business or employment, or in the construction of any work or building, shall be seized upon any mesne or final process of any court of this State, or where their business shall be suspended by the action of creditors, or put into the hands of any assignee, receiver or trustee, then in all such cases the debts owing to laborers or employés, which have accrued by reason of their labor or employment, to an amount not exceeding $50 to each employé, for work and labor performed within six months next preceding the seizure of such property, shall be considered and treated as preferred debts, and such laborers or employés shall be preferred creditors, and shall be first paid in full; and, if there be not sufficient to pay them in full, then the same shall be paid to them *pro rata* after paying costs."

The sole question presented for our consideration and decision is the one involving the construction of this Statute. It is contended by the appellant that his claim falls within the letter as well as the spirit of the Statute, while, on the other hand, it is contended by the appellee that the Statute was intended to cover and secure such employés only as perform physical or manual labor. The argument of the appellee is that the word "or" is used as a disjunctive conjunction, and the words between which it stands are simply used as synonymous, and both expressing the same idea, and that the word "employé" is altogether synonymous with the word "laborer." It is contended on the other hand, by the appellant, that the words "laborer" and "employé" are not used in this Statute as synonymous terms, but that the word "employé" was intended to have, and should receive, a much broader interpretation than the word "laborer." In view of the conclusion we have reached in this case, we deem it unnecessary to inquire whether the words "laborer" and "employé," as used in this Statute, are to be regarded as synonymous or otherwise, as in our opinion, under the facts found by the court, the appellant was a laborer, within the meaning of the Statute.

In the case of *Conlee Lumber Co.* v. *Ripon Lumber & Mfg. Co.*, 66 Wis. 481, it was held, however, that the words "laborer" and "employé," as used in a statute similar to the one now under consideration, were not synonymous.

There is much confusion and some apparent conflict in the authorities upon the subject now under consideration. As to how this confusion and conflict arose, it would perhaps be unprofitable to inquire in this case, as the authorities all agree that statutes of this kind are to be liberally construed.

In the case of *Capron* v. *Strout*, 11 Nev. 304, Stewart was employed as foreman of a mine at $8 per day, payable monthly. His duties were to act as guard foreman, to "boss" the men who were at work in the mine, keep their time and give them orders for their pay at the end of each month. He sought to enforce his claim for wages as a lien against the mining property. In answer to the argument that he was not a laborer, within the meaning of the law, the court said: "It is said that he performed no work or labor in or upon the mine, upon the mine with their hands; that to give it a wider construction, one that will make it include the wages of a foreman like Stewart, will make it cover the case of a general superintendent, and other officers of a corporation, and thereby impair the remedy of those who are the special objects of the legislative care. We do not admit that no distinction could be made in this respect between a foreman of miners and the superintendent of a company; but whether there could or not, we have no doubt that respondent's claim comes within the spirit as well as the letter of the law. According to the findings, he certainly did work in the mine, though not with his hands, and it is clear that the direct tendency of his work was to develop the property. We think the foreman of work in the mine is as fully secured by the law as the miners who work under his direction."

In the case of *Stryker* v. *Cassidy*, 76 N. Y. 50, the claimant was an architect. He sought to enforce a statutory lien for his labor as such architect, and the court, in commenting upon his right to such lien, said: "The architect who superintends the construction of a building performs labor as truly as the carpenter who frames it, or the mason who lays the walls, and labor of a most important character. It is not any less labor, within the general meaning of the word, that it is done by a person who is fitted by special training and skill for its performance. The language quoted makes no distinction between skilled and unskilled labor, or between mere manual labor, and the one who supervises, directs and applies the labor of others."

The case of *Flagstaff Silver Min. Co. of Utah* v. *Cullins*, 104 U. S. 176 [26 L. ed. 704], is strongly in point here. In that case the claimant was employed for an indefinite time to direct the work in the mine, with authority to employ and discharge and procure miners, and procure and purchase supplies for working the mine. It was his duty to oversee and direct the work in said mine, direct the shipping of ore, and generally to control and direct the actual working and development of the mine. Under a statute giving a lien for work and labor, he sought to enforce a lien for his wages. The court, in answer to the claim that he was not a laborer, within the meaning of the Statute, said: "Statutes giving liens to laborers and mechanics for their work and labor are to be liberally construed. The finding of the district court makes clear the character of the services rendered by the defendant in error. He was not the general agent of the mining business of the plaintiff in error. . . . He was not a contractor. The services rendered by him were not of a professional character, such as those of a mining engineer. He was the overseer and foreman of the body of miners who performed the manual labor upon the mine. He planned and personally superintended and directed the work, with a view to develop the mine, and make it a successful venture. . . . Such duties are very different from those which belong to the general superintendent of a railroad, or the contractor for erecting a house. Their performance may well be called work and labor. They require the personal attention and supervision of the foreman, and occasionally—in an emergency, or for an example—it becomes necessary for him to assist with his own hands. Such duties cannot be performed without much physical exertion, which, while not so severe as that demanded of the workmen under the control of the foreman, is nevertheless as really work and labor. Bodily toil, as well as some skill and knowledge in directing the work, is required for their successful performance. We think that the discharge of such duties may well be called 'work and labor,' and that the district court rightfully declared the person who performed them entitled to a lien under the law of the Territory."

See also *Mulligan* v. *Mulligan*, 18 La. Ann. 20; *Knight* v. *Norris*, 13 Minn. 473 (Gil. 438); *Caraker* v. *Mathews*, 25 Ga. 571; *Gurney* v. *Atlantic & G. W. R. Co.* 58 N. Y. 358; *Bass* v. *Doerman*, 112 Ind. 390.

In the case last cited it was held by this court that the Statute now under consideration should receive a liberal construction.

While the appellant in this case was called "superintendent," it is shown that he was not an officer of the Company, nor was he general manager or a general agent. His principal duties were to superintend the construction of trenches, and the laying of gas-pipes. Within the authorities above cited, he was to all intents and purposes a laborer. Under the liberal construction to be given to the Statute before us, he was a laborer, within that term as used in the Statute, and his claim for wages should be declared a preferred claim, and paid before a distribution of the assets among the general creditors. It follows that the Marion Superior Court erred in refusing to declare the claim in controversy preferred, for which reason the judgment must be reversed in so far as it adjudges said claim to be paid as a general debt.

The judgment of the Marion Superior Court, in so far as it adjudges the claim in suit to be a general debt to be paid out of the assets in the hands of the receiver, is reversed, with direction to enter the proper order declaring the same a preferred claim.

MICHIGAN SUPREME COURT.

VILLAGE OF CEDAR SPRINGS

v.

Bartholomew SCHLICH, Impleaded with the Toledo, Saginaw & Muskegon R. Co., *Appt.*

(......Mich.......)

A village will be denied relief in equity against bonds issued under an Act of the Legislature authorizing bonds for public improvements in the village and used in aid of a railroad, for which purpose they could not be legally authorized, where the Act was obtained by the people of the village by falsely representing to the Legislature that the power to issue bonds was desired for the purpose of making public improvements in the village. The people must be left to such defense as they may be found entitled to in a court of law.

(June 13, 1890.)

APPEAL by defendant, Schlich, from a decree of the Circuit Court for Kent County in favor of complainant on a suit brought to have certain bonds declared to be null and void and to enjoin defendant from disposing of them. *Reversed.*

The facts fully appear in the opinion.

Messrs. **Smiley & Earle**, for appellant:

The recitals in the bonds that they were issued for the purpose of public improvements in pursuance of an Act of the Legislature, and also in pursuance of a vote of the electors, are conclusive against the Village, while the bonds are in the hands of a bona fide purchaser, and all such purchaser need to look at is the authority conferred by the Legislature and the recitals in the bonds that the legislative authority has been complied with.

See *Walnut* v. *Wade*, 103 U. S. 683 (26 L. ed. 526); 1 Dillon, Mun. Corp. § 512; 2 Daniel, Neg. Inst. § 1537.

It is no defense that the village officer issued the bonds contrary to conditions imposed or contrary to orders, or that the village authorities or their agents have been guilty of fraud in the issue of the bonds, or that the Village received no consideration for the bonds.

See *Brooklyn* v. *Ætna L. Ins. Co.* 99 U. S. 362, 370 (25 L. ed. 416, 418); *East Lincoln* v. *Davenport*, 94 U. S. 801 (24 L. ed. 322), and other cases cited; 2 Daniel, Neg. Inst. § 1537.

"He that hath committed iniquity shall not have equity." The complainant comes into a court of equity and says, "I have been guilty of a breach of faith and a violation of law by means of which I have become involved in difficulty, and I come into this court for relief." Equity will not grant it.

1 Pom. Eq. Jur. § 397; *Jackson* v. *Detroit*, 10 Mich. 248; *Motz* v. *Detroit*, 18 Mich. 495; *Sexsmith* v. *Smith*, 32 Wis. 299; Story, Eq. Jur. § 64, *note E.*

A purchaser of municipal bonds which purport to have been issued for a lawful purpose may rely upon the recital and is not bound to inquire whether there has been a diversion from that purpose though it be shown by the municipal records.

Portland Sav. Bank v. *Evansville*, 25 Fed. Rep. 389; *Rogers* v. *Burlington*, 70 U. S. 3 Wall. 654 (18 L. ed. 79).

The fact that the bonds were found in circulation is evidence of their issue, and their recitals show that they were issued in pursuance of the legislative Act, and these recitals are conclusive in the hands of a bona fide purchaser.

Fulton v. *Riverton* (Minn.) Jan. 23, 1890; *Society for Savings* v. *New London*, 29 Conn. 189; *State* v. *Kiowa County*, 39 Kan. 657; *Kerr* v. *Corry*, 105 Pa. 282; *Walnut* v. *Wade*, 103 U. S. 695 (26 L. ed. 530); *Coloma* v. *Eaves*, 92 U. S. 484 (23 L. ed. 579); *Knox County* v. *Nichols*, 14 Ohio St. 260; *Knox County* v. *Aspinwall*, 62

Messrs. **William Alden Smith** and **Frederick W. Stevens,** for appellee:

Bonds issued by a municipal corporation for railroad aid are illegal and void.

People v. *Salem*, 20 Mich. 452; *People* v. *State Treasurer*, 23 Mich. 499; *Thomas* v. *Port Huron*, 27 Mich. 320; *Pierson Twp.* v. *Reynolds*, 49 Mich. 225.

The validity of municipal bonds depends upon acts of the common council of the municipality. Its acts are manifested and preserved by records. Those records are public and are open to the inspection of all interested persons.

Lippincott v. *Pana*, 92 Ill. 24; *People* v. *Cornell*, 47 Barb. 329; *State* v. *Williams*, 41 N. J. L. 332; Dillon, Mun. Corp. §§ 240, 584, 585; Ang. & A. Corp. § 707; 1 Greenl. Ev. §§ 471, 478; *Silver* v. *People*, 45 Ill. 225; *State* v. *Meadows*, 1 Kan. 90; *Hawes* v. *White*, 66 Me. 305.

A purchaser of such bonds may therefore have knowledge of every matter appearing from the records.

Cooley, Taxn. p. 328; *Worley* v. *Cicero*, 9 West. Rep. 50, 110 Ind. 208.

Because of the existence of records the following cases have held that a purchaser at a tax sale comes strictly within the rule *caveat emptor:*

People v. *Auditor-General*, 30 Mich. 12; *Hamilton* v. *Valiant*, 30 Md. 139; *Jenks* v. *Wright*, 61 Pa. 410.

Mere recitals by the officers of a municipal corporation in bonds issued in aid of a railroad corporation do not preclude an inquiry, even where the rights of a bona fide holder are involved, as to the existence of a legislative authority to issue them.

Northern Bank of Toledo v. *Porter Twp.* 110 U. S. 608 (28 L. ed. 258); *Lake County* v. *Graham*, 130 U. S. 674 (32 L. ed. 1065); Bigelow, Estop. ed. 1886, p. 530.

A municipal corporation is not estopped by its contract made in violation of its charter powers.

Syracuse Water Co. v. *Syracuse*, 5 L. R. A. 546, 116 N. Y. 167.

Purchasers of municipal bonds are charged with notice of the laws of the State granting power to make the bonds they find on the market. The question of legislative authority in a municipal corporation to issue bonds in aid of a railway company cannot be concluded by mere recitals.

Anthony v. *Jasper County*, 101 U. S. 693 (25 L. ed. 1005); *Hayes* v. *Holly Springs*, 114 U. S. 120 (29 L. ed. 81); *Aspinwall* v. *Daviess County*, 63 U. S. 22 How. 364 (16 L. ed. 296); *Marsh* v. *Fulton County*, 77 U. S. 10 Wall. 676 (19 L. ed. 1040); *St. Joseph Twp.* v. *Rogers*, 83 U. S. 16 Wall. 644 (21 L. ed. 328); *Citizens S. & L. Asso. of Cleveland* v. *Topeka*, 87 U. S. 20 Wall. 655 (22 L. ed. 455); *Schuyler County* v. *Farwell*, 25 Ill. 182; *Force* v. *Batavia*, 61 Ill. 100; *Williams* v. *Roberts*, 88 Ill. 13; *Lippincott* v. *Pana*, 92 Ill. 24; *Sykes* v. *Columbus*, 65 Miss. 115; *Williamson* v. *Keokuk*, 44 Iowa, 88; *McPherson* v. *Foster*, 43 Iowa, 48; Herman, Estop. ed. 1886, § 1232; Bigelow, Estop. p. 365; *Boyce* v. *Towsontown Station of M. E. Church*, 46 Md. 359; *Bogart* v. *Lamotte Twp.*

Unless the specific power was granted, all subscriptions and donations, as well as the corporate bonds issued for their payment, are absolutely void, even as against bona fide holders of the bonds.

Ottawa v. *Carey*, 108 U. S. 123 (27 L. ed. 675); *Thompson* v. *Lee County*, 70 U. S. 3 Wall. 327 (18 L. ed. 177); *Marsh* v. *Fulton County*, 77 U. S. 10 Wall. 676 (19 L. ed. 1040); *St. Joseph Twp.* v. *Rogers*, 83 U. S. 16 Wall. 644 (21 L. ed. 328); *McClure* v. *Oxford Twp.* 94 U. S. 429 (24 L. ed. 129); *Wells* v. *Pontotoc County*, 102 U. S. 625 (26 L. ed. 122); *Allen* v. *Louisiana*, 103 U. S. 80 (26 L. ed. 318); *Lewis* v. *Shreveport*, 108 U. S. 286 (27 L. ed. 729); *Kelley* v. *Milan*, 127 U. S. 150 (32 L. ed. 82); *Daviess County* v. *Dickinson*, 117 U. S. 657 (29 L. ed. 1026); *Norton* v. *Dyersburg*, 127 U. S. 160 (32 L. ed. 85); *Concord* v. *Robinson*, 121 U. S. 165 (30 L. ed. 885); *Claiborne County* v. *Brooks*, 111 U. S. 406 (28 L. ed. 472).

The purchasers of the bonds in question were bound to see that the bonds were put into circulation by order of the council.

McClure v. *Oxford Twp. supra.*

The objection that complainant does not come with clean hands is not a good one. The illegal acts set up in the bill were committed by one common council. At the next charter election after the commission of the illegal acts, a new council was elected which repudiated the illegal acts of its predecessor. By the aid of the writ of injunction, it prevents the bonds passing to others who might be less informed, and, in the same suit, asks that the whole matter be disposed of, under that principle that when equity once acquires jurisdiction of a matter for any purpose, it will settle it in all its features.

See *McPherson* v. *Foster*, 43 Iowa, 48; *Lippincott* v. *Pana*, 92 Ill. 24.

Grant, J., delivered the opinion of the court:

On February 18, 1887, a petition was presented by some of the inhabitants of the Village of Cedar Springs to the common council, requesting it to take action to obtain from the Legislature a special Act enabling the Village to issue special improvement bonds in the sum of $5,000, the proceeds thereof to be used in inducing the Railroad Company to construct its road through the Village. The prayer of the petition was granted. The council appointed an agent to proceed to Lansing for the purpose of procuring such action from the Legislature; and on February 22, the Act in question was passed, entitled "An Act to Authorize the Village of Cedar Springs, in the County of Kent, to Borrow Money to Make Public Improvements in Said Village." The bill was introduced in the Legislature, and passed both Houses on the same day. The Act authorized the common council to borrow the money, and issue bonds therefor, upon a vote of the majority of the qualified electors of said Village, and provided that the money arising therefrom should be expended in making public improvements within said Village. Pursuant to the provisions of this Act, the common council, on the 28th of February, made due provision for submitting the question to the electors at the coming charter election in March. The vote stood 189 for and 6 against the issue of the bonds. On March 19 the council adopted a resolution reciting the Act of the Legislature, the vote of the electors, and provided for the issue of the bonds, to be deposited with the treasurer to await the further orders of the council. Thereupon five bonds of $1,000 each were issued, and recited that they were issued in pursuance of the above Act of the Legislature and of a vote of the electors, and for the purpose of public improvements in said Village. On April 1 the common council adopted the following resolution: "Whereas, the Toledo, Saginaw & Muskegon Railroad Company propose running their road from Greenville to Muskegon, and should they do so, and make Cedar Springs a station on said road, it is the judgment of this council that it would be a public benefit and improvement to the Village of Cedar Springs; therefore, be it resolved by the common council of the Village of Cedar Springs that the bonds of such Village, lately issued thereby, and numbering from one to five, inclusive, for the sum of $1,000 each, be disposed of, the proceeds of which shall be expended in ditching the land along the side of said roadbed, and in making the roadbed through said Village of Cedar Springs, and in making a suitable depot therein, and in fixing the watercourse on the old Field and Nickerson land, should the road run there; that said bonds be deposited with B. Middleton, of Greenville, Michigan, to be delivered to David Robinson, Jr., president of the said Railroad Company, for the purposes aforesaid, upon said Robinson depositing with said Middleton first-mortgage bonds of said Railroad Company, on said railroad, for the sum of $5,000, and the note of said Company for the sum of $5,000, as security that the proceeds of said bonds shall be expended as aforesaid, and said railroad be completed and ready for cars on or before January 1, 1888, from Greenville to Muskegon, Michigan, or the bonds or proceeds returned to the Village of Cedar Springs within said time; and the treasurer of the Village of Cedar Springs is hereby instructed to forthwith deposit said bonds with B. Middleton as herein directed."

These bonds were negotiated in Toledo, and were purchased by Spitzer & Co., of that city, about September 12, 1887, for the sum of $4,000. Prior to this purchase, there were submitted to Spitzer & Co. the following documents, duly certified: (1) a statement from the president of the Village, dated April 9, 1887, made for the purpose of selling the bonds, and giving the number of inhabitants, the assessed valuation of the Village, the amount of money then in the treasury, and stating that the Village had no indebtedness except that represented by these bonds; (2) the resolution of submission to the vote of the electors; (3) the election notice, and the result of the election; (4) the resolution of the common council of March 19, above stated; (5) a certified copy of the Act of the Legislature. The resolution of April 1, above given in full, was not submitted to Spitzer & Co. Subsequently, and about January 11, 1888, Spitzer & Co. sold these bonds, through Mr. Verdier, cashier of the Kent County Savings Bank,

Grand R
for $4,63
common
to pay th
these bon
in this ca
be declare
tion to pr
the same.
under oat
chaser for
Courts
to those
good faith
where, un
an adequa
not be suc
taking adv
and willf
the citizen
and the de
into the di
defeat the
as interpre
deavored t
forms of la
be accompl
they had n
an Act of
Act, if pass
real object
in the title
fore falsely
they desired
for the purp
if fearing an
jection on th
ant sent an
the Legislat
fore us the c
accomplishm
therefore en
imposed, bu
who promot
transaction
from its ow
The maxim,
shall not ha
lar force to
in this case.
complainants
the defendan
they have de
fense as a cou
titled to.

If the defen
chaser witho
which these b
bound to pay
that can be in
cover upon t
void in the ha
tory of the t
which they w
design of the
agents, and c
Company, to
whom they de
must have kno
negotiated if t
whether or not
should be dete
the result of de

should be that these bonds may be transferred by the defendant Schlich to some other person who may be bona fide holder, it is only a result of the complainant's own wrong-doing, and it is entitled to no relief in this court.

The decree of the court below must be reversed, with the costs of both courts, and a decree entered here dismissing the bill.

SOUTH CAROLINA SUPREME COURT.

Town Council of SUMMERVILLE, *Respt.*,
v.
Benjamin C. PRESSLEY, *Appt.*

(....S. C.....)

1. **A town council which has power** to pass all such ordinances as shall appear necessary and requisite for the health, welfare, etc. of the town, has the exclusive right to judge what is "necessary and requisite" to preserve the health of the town.

2. **An ordinance prohibiting the cultivation** for agricultural purposes of more than one eighth of an acre by any family or household within the corporate limits, except for flower gardens or grapes, or trees, and except for planting oats, rye or barley, between November 1st and February 15th, is a valid exercise of police power, under a charter giving full power to make ordinances which shall appear to the council "necessary and requisite" for the welfare, convenience and health of the town.

3. **Police laws and regulations** are not unconstitutional, although they prevent the enjoyment of individual rights in property without providing compensation therefor.

4. **An ordinance is not "unequal and unjust"** on the ground that it permits the owner of a small parcel of ground to cultivate a larger proportion of his ground than the owner of a larger tract can do, where the same maximum limit is fixed for all persons.

5. **An ordinance does not violate the constitutional law** of "equality" because it applies to one village of the State only.

(May 19, 1890.)

APPEAL by defendant from a judgment of the Court of General Sessions for Berkeley County, dismissing an appeal from an order of the Town Council of Summerville, imposing upon him a fine for the violation of a municipal ordinance. *Affirmed.*

The facts are fully stated in the opinion.

Messrs. **Inglesby & Miller** and **Lord & Hyde,** for appellant:

In all the crowded towns and villages of this State, and of every other State, there are within their corporate limits gardens, market farms and cotton plantations. If, then, this use of land be universal, and that use be forbidden by law for the promotion of the public health, that is plainly the taking of such land for public purposes.

Strasburg v. *Bachman* (Pa.) 21 W.N. C. 462.

Private property cannot be taken for public use without just compensation.

S. C. Const. art. 1, § 23; U. S. Const. art. 5.

Municipal corporations cannot, under any general grant of authority, adopt by-laws which infringe the spirit or are repugnant to the policy of the State as settled by its general legislation.

Dillon, Mun. Corp. § 329; Cooley, Const. Lim. p. 199.

NOTE.—*Private interests subservient to public interests.*

Private interests must be made subservient to the general interest of the community. Slaughter-House Cases, 83 U. S. 16 Wall. 62 (21 L. ed. 404); Com. v. Alger, 7 Cush. 84; Taunton v. Taylor, 116 Mass. 254; Watertown v. Mayo, 109 Mass. 315.

Every citizen holds his land subservient to such police regulation as the Legislature in its wisdom may enact for the general welfare. Brown v. Keener, 74 N. C. 714; Pool v. Trexler, 76 N. C. 297.

Police power extends to the protection of the lives, limbs, health, comfort, morals and quiet of all persons, and the protection of property. Munn v. Illinois, 94 U. S. 147 (24 L. ed. 91); Toledo, W. & W. R. Co. v. Jacksonville, 67 Ill. 37; *Ex parte* Shrader, 33 Cal. 279; Davis v. Central R. & Bkg. Co. 17 Ga. 323; Philadelphia, W. & B. R. Co. v. Bowers, 4 Houst. (Del.) 506; Bartemeyer v. Iowa, 85 U. S. 18 Wall. 138 (21 L. ed. 932).

The Legislature may authorize cities and towns to prohibit the erection of wooden buildings for protection of persons and property against fire (Salem v. Maynes, 123 Mass. 372); or it may authorize an ordinance regulating the transportation of heavy merchandise in a city. People v. James, 16 Hun, 426.

The line between the valid exercise of the police power and the invasion of private rights, as enunciated in *Re* Jacobs, 98 N. Y. 98, was approved in Powell v. Com., 5 Cent. Rep. 893, 114 Pa. 265.

The Legislature is largely the judge of its own powers with reference to matters of police regulation. If it can be seen that the rights of property are invaded under the pretense of a police regulation, it would be the duty of the court to interfere to protect them. Com. v. Bearse, 132 Mass. 542.

The point of contact between the power of the Legislature and that of the courts with respect to the exercise of the police power may be illustrated by the decisions relating to the power of taxation, which power, when exercised in the mode prescribed by the Constitution, is practically unlimited; yet the courts will determine whether a so-styled taxing Act is in reality such, and if it be not, it will be declared unconstitutional and void; but, if the Act is within the scope of legislative authority, it must stand. Pennsylvania R. Co. v. Riblet, 66 Pa. 164.

Another illustration is furnished by cases relating to the exercise by the Legislature of the power of eminent domain. While the Legislature may condemn private property for public use, and its exercise of that power, though within constitutional restriction, is practically unlimited, it is not beyond the reach of judicial inquiry, as to whether or not the proposed use is a public use, and if it is not, no legislative fiat can make it so. Palairet's App. 67 Pa. 488; Powell v. Com. 5 Cent. Rep. 893, 114 Pa. 265.

Police power of State. See *note* to State v. Marshall (N. H.) 1 L. R. A. 51; W. U. Teleg. Co. v. New York (N. Y.) 3 L. R. A. 449, 2 Inters. Com. Rep. 583. And see *note* to State v. Goodwill (W. Va.) 6 L. R. A. 621.

Mr. **Charles Boyle,** for respondent:

Under its police power the State can pass any law which does not conflict with the Constitution of the State, and which does no violence to any contract or vested rights of the citizens.

Acts cannot be declared null and void because they invade the natural rights of the citizen.

Eastman v. *State,* 7 West. Rep. 418, 109 Ind. 278; Cooley, Const. Lim. 5th ed. p. 197; *Powell* v. *Com.* 5 Cent. Rep. 800, 114 Pa. 265; *Slaughter-House Cases,* 83 U. S. 16 Wall. 36 (21 L. ed. 394).

The right to cultivate the soil for agricultural purposes is a natural right, which the State, in the exercise of its police power, has the authority to restrict; and if in so doing, property of an individual is rendered less useful or less valuable because he is restricted in using it in that particular way, it is only a sacrifice that each individual is alike called upon to make, to promote the welfare of the community at large.

Lumb v. *Pinckney,* 21 S. C. 476; *State* v. *Gaillard,* 11 S. C. 309.

The Town Council being invested with the authority to pass the ordinance, it is not within the province of the court to inquire into the propriety or expediency of enacting such a law; that is entirely within the discretion of the Council.

Charleston City Council v. *Wentworth St. Baptist Church,* 4 Strobh. L. 310; *Copes* v. *Charleston,* 10 Rich. L. 502.

McGowan, *J.,* delivered the opinion of the court:

The Village of Summerville was originally chartered in 1847, and the corporate authorities were "invested with all the powers and privileges conferred, and subject to the same restrictions and penalties imposed, on the Village of Newberry, by an Act passed on December 17, 1841," of which Act section 5 provides as follows: "And the intendant and wardens shall have full power, under their corporate seal, to make and establish all such rules, by-laws and ordinances respecting roads, streets, markets, public spring and police of said village as shall appear to them necessary and requisite for the security, welfare and convenience of the said village, or for preserving the health, peace, order and good government within the same," etc. The charter of Summerville was amended in 1885, enlarging the boundaries, adding two wardens and changing the name to that of the "Town of Summerville," but without changing the powers and privileges conferred by the charter of 1847, adopting those given in the charter of Newberry. In 1883 the Town Council passed an ordinance "to limit the culture of the soil, and more effectually to prevent the destruction of trees in the Town of Summerville." The preamble recited: "Whereas, it is necessary, for the protection of the public health of Summerville, that the soil should not be cultivated beyond a limited extent, and that the injury and destruction of trees should be more effectually prevented;" the ordinance prohibited entirely the culture of rice, and then provided as follows: "That from and after the date herein the maximum quantity of land which it shall be lawful for any family or household, or the immediate servants or employés of such family or household, to fertilize, plant or cultivate for agricultural purposes within the corporate limits shall be one eighth (⅛) of one acre, which shall be on the lot or premises of such family or household, regardless of the quantity or extent of the lot or tract of land owned or occupied by such family or household, or its immediate servants, or which may form part of the premises of said family residence or tract of land. But this section shall not be construed so as to abolish or prohibit the planting of oats, rye or barley between the 1st day of November and February 15, or the planting or proper cultivation of flower gardens, or of the grape, or fruit trees, or any other kind of trees whatsoever," etc.

It seems that under this ordinance the Town Council imposed upon the defendant, a citizen of the Town, a fine of $20 for violating the ordinance in cultivating his lands for agricultural purposes without regard to the limit imposed. He admitted that he had violated the ordinance, but denied the authority of the Town Council to pass such an ordinance. Upon appeal *Judge* Witherspoon held that the duty of the court was limited to the inquiry whether or not the power existed, and, if so, whether or not its exercise violated any constitutional provision. Concluding that the ordinance was valid at the time the fine was imposed on the appellant, he ordered that the appeal be dismissed, and the judgment of the Town Council in imposing the fine be affirmed. From this decision the defendant now appeals to this court, upon the following grounds: "(1) because his [defendant's] garden has been continuously cultivated in excess of said town ordinance for more than thirty years, and there is no allegation, claim or proof that such cultivation was negligent, or in any manner so conducted as to create a nuisance; (2) because, in the absence of such allegation and proof, the Legislature has not conferred, and could not confer, on the Town Council, any authority to prevent the usual, proper use of cleared land by the owner without full compensation to him; (3) because the ordinance of said Town Council is unequal and unjust, in that it permits the owner of one fourth or one half of an acre of land to cultivate one fourth or one half of his possessions, and denies to the owner of six acres the right to cultivate more than one forty-ninth part of his land; (4) because his honor omitted to decide one important point argued by the defendant before him, to wit: the power of town council, reversed in section 3 of said ordinance, whereby it may give permission to anyone to cut down trees in the town, violates the 14th Amendment of the United States Constitution," etc.

There must be some misprint in the last ground of appeal, especially in reference to the word "reversed." But as there is no question before this court arising under the third clause of the ordinance, which allows permission to be given to some persons, and not to all, to cut down trees, etc., within the corporate limits, it it will not be necessary to consider now whether it violates the 14th Amendment of the Constitution of the United States.

The first exception complains that a citizen of the corporation who owned cleared land in excess of the limit imposed by the ordinance at the time of its passage was not bound to conform to the restriction as to the amount to be cultivated for general agricultural purposes, without allegation and proof that such cultivation was negligent, or of such a character as to create a nuisance. As it seems to us, this view ignores entirely the existence of the ordinance. Undoubtedly, as a rule, every man may cultivate his own land in his own way, but even in that case he may use his land in such a manner as to amount to a "nuisance" indictable at common law. That, however, does not touch the question under the ordinance passed by virtue of the powers conferred upon the corporate authorities by the Legislature "for preserving the health, peace, order and good government of the town." The ordinance, by its declared purpose, was a police regulation for preserving the health of Summerville, a small town in the pines about twenty miles out of Charleston, which affords a convenient summer resort for health. Assuming for the present that the Town Council had the power to pass the ordinance, no question can be made whether "a nuisance" had been created, nor whether the restrictions complained of were necessary to accomplish the purpose in view. It was their exclusive right to judge what was "necessary and requisite" to preserve the health of the Town. 1 Dillon, Mun. Corp. § 144, and authorites in *note*.

The second exception makes the objection that the Legislature has not conferred, and could not confer, on the Town Council, any authority to prevent the usual, proper use of cleared lands by the owner without full compensation paid to him. The State, through the law-making body, certainly possesses the police power, which from its very nature has no well-defined limits, but must be as extensive as the necessities which call for its exercise. *Judge* Dillon describes it thus: "Every citizen holds his property subject to the proper exercise of this [police] power, either by the State Legislature directly, or by public corporations to which the Legislature may delegate it. Laws and ordinances relating to the comfort, health, convenience, good order and general welfare of the inhabitants are comprehensively styled 'police laws or regulations;' and it is well settled that laws and regulations of this character, though they may disturb the enjoyment of individual rights, are not unconstitutional, though no provision is made for compensation for such disturbances. They do not appropriate private property for public use, but simply regulate its use and enjoyment by the owner. If he suffers injury, it is either *damnum absque injuria*, or, in the theory of the law, he is compensated for it by sharing in the general benefits which the regulations are intended and calculated to secure. The citizen owns his property absolutely, it is true; it cannot be taken from him for any private use whatever without his consent, nor for any public use without compensation. Still he owns it subject to this restriction, namely, that it must be so used as not to injure others, and that the sovereign authority may, by police regulations, so direct the use of it that it shall not prove pernicious to his neighbors, or the citizens generally. These regulations rest upon the maxim, *salus populi suprema est lex*. This power to restrain a private injurious use of property is very different from the right of eminent domain. It is not a taking of private property for public use," etc. 1 Dillon, Mun. Corp. 3d ed. § 141.

In the great leading case upon the subject, of *Com.* v. *Alger*, 7 Cush. 85, *Chief Justice* Shaw said: "Rights of property, like all other social and conventional rights, are subject to such reasonable limitations in their enjoyment as shall prevent them from being injurious, and to such reasonable restraints and regulations established by law as the Legislature, under the governing and controlling power vested in them by the Constitution, may think necessary and expedient. This is very different from the right of eminent domain,—the right of a government to take and appropriate private property to public use whenever the public exigency requires it,—which can be done only on condition of providing a reasonable compensation therefor. The power we allude to is rather the public power,—the power vested in the Legislature by the Constitution to make, ordain and establish all manner of wholesome and reasonable laws, statutes and ordinances, either with penalties or without, not repugnant to the Constitution, as they shall judge to be for the good and welfare of the Commonwealth, and of the subjects of the same. It is much easier to perceive and realize the existence and sources of this power than to mark its boundaries, or to prescribe limits to its exercise," etc. It would seem that these authorities are conclusive of the right of the State, in the exercise of the police power, to make the restriction complained of. If the Legislature itself had passed the Summerville ordinance just as it stands, it could not, as we think, be doubted that it was a constitutional exercise of the police power. It is said, however, that it was a mistake to suppose that the cultivation of the soil in certain crops was dangerous to health, and therefore the restriction was not a "proper" one. We suppose that the cultivation inhibited must have been considered dangerous to health in the locality of Summerville. But, be that as it may, it was a question for the law-making body. "The judiciary can only arrest the execution of a statute when it conflicts with the Constitution. It cannot run a race of opinions upon points of right, reason and expediency with the law-making power." Cooley, Const. Lim. 201.

Assuming that the Legislature had the power to pass the Summerville ordinance, there can be no doubt that it had the right to delegate that power to the municipal authorities of Summerville as the governmental agent of the State within the corporate limits of the Town. "The preservation of the public health and safety is often made a matter of municipal duty; and it is competent for the Legislature to delegate to municipalities the power to regulate, restrain, and even suppress, particular branches of business, if deemed necessary for the public good." See 1 Dillon, Mun. Corp. 3d ed. § 144; *Harrison* v. *Baltimore*, 1 Gill, 264.

The charter of the Town of Summerville has

the following: "Sec. 5. And the said intendant and wardens shall have full power, under their corporate seal, to make all such rules, by-laws and ordinances respecting the roads, streets, markets, public spring and police of said Village as shall appear to them necessary and requisite for the security, welfare and convenience of said Village, or for preserving health, peace, order and good government within the same," etc.

This provision was adopted from the charter of the Town of Newberry, and seems to be as full and comprehensive as municipal charters generally are. We think that the Legislature intended to give to the City Council of Summerville all the police powers it possessed, to be exercised within the corporate limits of the Town. As was said by the court in the case of *Harrison* v. *Baltimore, supra:* By its charter the City of Baltimore was vested with full power and authority to make all ordinances " 'necessary to preserve the health of the city.' . . . The transfer of this salutary and essential power is given in terms as explicit and comprehensive as could have been used for such a purpose. To accomplish within the specified territorial limits the objects enumerated, the corporate authorities were clothed with all the legislative powers which the General Assembly could have exerted. Of the degree of necessity for such municipal legislation the mayor and city council of Baltimore were the exclusive judges. To their sound discretion was committed the selection of the means and manner contributory to the end of exercising the powers which they might deem requisite to the accomplishment of the objects of which they were made the guardians," etc. 1 Dillon, Mun. Corp. § 144; *Charleston City Council* v. *Wentworth St. Baptist Church*, 4 Strobh. L. 310; *Copes* v. *Charleston*, 10 Rich. L. 502.

The third exception complains that the ordinance is "unequal and unjust in that it permits the owner of one fourth or one half of one acre of land to cultivate one fourth or one half of his possessions, and denies the owner of six acres the right to cultivate more than one forty-ninth of his lands." The second clause of the ordinance declares what shall be the maximum quantity of land it shall be lawful for any family to cultivate in ordinary agricultural crops. Section 12, art. 1, of our Constitution declares that "no person . . . shall be subjected in law to any other restraints or disqualifications in regard to any personal rights than such as are laid upon others under like circumstances." And the 14th Amendment to the Constitution of the United States provides, among other things, that "no State shall . . . deny to any person within its jurisdiction the equal protection of the laws," etc. Under these provisions, one or both, it is contended that the section of the ordinance which fixes a maximum of soil to be cultivated is unconstitutional —being, as alleged, "unequal and unjust"—in that the maximum allowed is the same for all citizens, without regard to their "possessions," respectively. The intent of the ordinance was to limit to a certain point the cultivation of certain crops; and, as it seems to us, the question of "equality" should be determined, not by the number of acres a citizen may happen to own, but by the limit imposed, which, it is admitted, is precisely the same upon all. It is manifest that the object was, not to impose a burden on the citizens in the nature of a tax, which, of course, would have to be levied in proportion to property, but to limit the cultivation of the soil with a view to the preservation of the health of the Town. A restriction only according to the quantity of land owned, as suggested, would certainly have failed in accomplishing the purpose in view, and possibly might have been obnoxious to the very objection made here, as creating a distinction among citizens dependent upon the amount of lands owned by them, respectively. Although the citizens may own lands within the corporate limits in different amounts, some more and some less, yet in that regard we are obliged to consider that they are all "under like circumstances;" and, the amount of soil allowed to be cultivated in particular crops being the same to all, we cannot hold that this section of the ordinance is unconstitutional on the ground of "inequality" in its provisions.

It is further contended in the argument that the ordinance was unconstitutional for another reason, to wit, that it violated the constitutional law of "equality" by prohibiting the cultivation of dry land in one village of the State without including in the Act all its towns and villages like situated, and under like circumstances. A nuisance in one place must be a nuisance in every other place, in like circumstances. As we have endeavored to show, there is no question of actual nuisance in the case. The Town Council, which alone had the right to judge, deemed the ordinance necessary to preserve the health of the Town, and we have no right to review that judgment. In reference to the local character of the ordinance, it can hardly be necessary to say more than repeat what was said in *Utsey* v. *Hiott*, 30 S. C. 365: "The local character of the Act does not make it necessarily unconstitutional. While there must be some just objections to local laws in general, it is well established that 'the authority that legislates for the State at large must determine whether particular rules shall extend to the whole State and all its citizens, or, on the other hand, to a subdivision of the State, or a single class of its citizens only. The circumstances of a particular locality, or the prevailing sentiment in that section of the State, may require or make acceptable different police regulations from those demanded in another.' . . . As *Mr. Justice* McIver said in the case of *State* v. *Berlin*, 21 S. C. 296: 'The whole matter is well summed up in a *note* to 1 Cooley, on Constitutional Limitations, 2d ed. 390, in the following words: "To make a statute a public law of general obligation, it is not necessary that it should be equally applicable to all parts of the State. All that is required is that it shall apply equally to all persons within the territorial limits described in the Act;" ' " and authorities.

The judgment of this court is that *the judgment of the Circuit Court be affirmed.*

Simpson, *Ch. J.*, and **McIver**, *J.*, concur.

Henrietta SNELL *et al.*, *Appts.*,
v.
CITY OF CHICAGO *et al.*

(....Ill....)

1. **Sections of an Act providing for a plank road** from Chicago to the north line of Cook County are invalid, under Const. 1848, which provides that "no private or local law . . . shall embrace more than one subject, and that shall be expressed in the title," where the title of the Act mentions only a plank road from Oswego in Kendall County to the Indiana line.

2. **The legalization of unauthorized acts** cannot be regarded as germane to the subject expressed in the title of an Act, which is "an Act to incorporate" a certain company

3. **The illegality of corporate acts** of a plank-road company in acquiring a highway for its road, because of the invalidity of the Act of incorporation, is cured by a statute which recognizes the corporate existence of the company by amending its charter, and also recognizes its right to substitute stone or gravel for plank upon a road already constructed.

4. **A company is dissolved** upon the consummation of a sale of its corporate property, and the execution of a deed therefor, under a statute which states that the object of the sale is to dissolve the company.

5. **The privilege of collecting tolls** and maintaining toll-gates, acquired by a purchaser of "the franchises, the property and immunities" of a plank-road company, expires upon his death, although he had the right to organize as a corporation, if he did not do so, and the statute authorizing the sale did not state that his heirs and assigns might enjoy such privileges, but merely that the purchaser should enjoy them.

6. **The location of toll-gates and toll-houses** having become established, the discretion as to such location is exhausted and they cannot be moved, especially after toll has been collected for several years.

7. **The sale of part of a plank road,** with the franchise of using the same and collecting tolls thereon, is invalid, where a statute under which it is made contemplated the sale of the whole road.

8. **A provision that "a plank-road company may collect** the same tolls and enjoy

---

NOTE.—*Corporation; dissolution of.*

A corporation may cease to do business, sell or assign its property for the payment of its debts, etc., and yet not cease to be a corporation. DeCamp v. Alward, 52 Ind. 473; Wilde v. Jenkins, 4 Paige, 481, 3 N. Y. Ch. L. ed. 524; Dana v. Bank of U. S. 5 Watts & S. 223; Ward v. Sea Ins. Co. 7 Paige, 294, 4 N. Y. Ch. L. ed. 162.

Where a corporation has remained insolvent or suspended its ordinary business for a year, it shall be deemed to have surrendered its franchises, and shall be adjudged to be dissolved; which adjudication might be at the suit either of the attorney-general or of any creditor or stockholder. Folger v. Columbian Ins. Co. 99 Mass. 275; Mickles v. Rochester City Bank, 11 Paige, 118, 5 N. Y. Ch. L. ed. 77.

But where a corporation kept up its organization, and its officers continued to discharge their duties, and prosecuted and defended actions to which it was a party, it cannot be said to have suspended business. Kelsey v. Pfaudler Process F. Co. 45 Hun, 14, 19 Abb. N. C. 427.

Corporations are deemed to continue their existence after dissolution, for the purpose of suing and being sued, in order to wind up the business. N. J. Rev. p. 187, § 59; Camp v. Taylor (N. J.) May 19, 1890.

An insolvent corporation, which continues to transact business, and against which a suit is pending and judgment obtained, is not dissolved within Mo. Rev. Stat., § 744, providing that the directors of a dissolved corporation shall be trustees to settle its affairs. Adams v. Kehlor Milling Co. 35 Fed. Rep. 433.

In case of trading corporations it is competent for a majority of the stockholders to dissolve the company and bring its business to a close. Skinner v. Smith Moquette Loom Co. 56 Hun, 437.

An Act providing that a company shall proceed to wind up its affairs and pay and discharge its debts, whereupon it shall be dissolved, is an order that the company "be wound up," within the meaning of an Act providing as to the distribution of its property when it is ordered to be wound up. *Re* Uxbridge & R. R. Co. L. R. 43 Ch. Div. 536.

An entire dissolution, being the consequence of permanent incapacity to restore the deficient part, never happens where the legitimate existence of the part is not indispensable to a valid election, or other means of reproduction. Lehigh Bridge Co. v. Lehigh Coal & Nav. Co. 4 Rawle, 9, 26 Am. Dec. 112; Slee v. Bloom, 5 Johns. Ch. 366, 1 N. Y. Ch. L. ed. 1111; Fisk v. Keeneville Woolen & Cotton Mfg. Co. 10 Paige, 592, 4 N. Y. Ch. L. ed. 1108.

Dissolution of corporation. See *note* to Chicago Mut. L. Indemnity Asso. v. Hunt (Ill.) 2 L. R. A. 549.

Statute construction; title to Act.

Where the subject of a statute is the effective prohibition of the right to exercise the franchise of collecting tolls by corporations which disregard the law, and there is no want of unity in the subject, the methods directed to the attainment of the one general purpose only being diverse, the statute embraces but a single subject, and is constitutional. Crawfordville & S. W. Turnp. Co. v. Fletcher, 1 West. Rep. 247, 104 Ind. 97. See *notes* to Titusville Iron Works v. Keystone Oil Co. (Pa.) 1 L. R. A. 362; People v. McElroy (Mich.) 2 L. R. A. 609; Evansville v. State (Ind.) 4 L. R. A. 93.

Special and local legislation inhibited. See *note* to Ayars' App. (Pa.) 2 L. R. A. 577.

Plank-road companies; late decisions.

A right to exact tolls on a plank road cannot be established by user. Pontiac & L. Pl. Road Co. v. Hilton, 13 West. Rep. 578, 69 Mich. 115.

A charter to construct a plank road from one city to another does not authorize the erection of a toll-gate upon one of the thoroughfares of either city. *Ibid.*

In an action by a plank-road company to recover a penalty, under the statute, for passing a toll-gate without payment, the defendant's offer to show an agreement between the plaintiff and the city that, in consideration of the enlargement of franchises, the plaintiff would cease to collect toll, was properly excluded because the contract was not made with the defendant, where it was not pretended that the company ever surrendered its right to toll within the city. Detroit & S. Pl. Road Co. v. Mahoney, 12 West. Rep. 549, 68 Mich. 265.

That the defendant thought the gate illegal is no defense, where he intentionally passed it without paying toll. *Ibid.*

See also 11 L. R. A. 355; 12 L. R. A. 328.

the same privileges granted to plank-road companies by the General Plank-Road Law" does not fix the rights of the company according to the General Law as it then exists, but makes them coincide with those of other companies under the General Law, whether it remains the same or is changed afterwards.

9. It is not a violation of a contract with a plank-road company, created by its Act of incorporation, to enact that no toll-gate can be kept, or toll demanded, within the corporate limits of a city, where such corporation had accepted the provisions of a statute amending its charter which makes the privileges of the company the same as those of other companies under the General Law.

10. A statute authorizing the construction of a plank road "from the City of Chicago" gives no authority to construct any part of the road within the city, where it is completely silent as to streets, but provides for the use of highways under permission of the county and property owners.

11. Tolls cannot be exacted for the use of a toll-road after it is included within the boundaries of a city, where the charter of the toll-road company was accepted under a State Constitution which gives the corporate authorities of a city exclusive authority over highways therein, and the exclusive right to assess and collect taxes therein.

(May 14, 1890.)

APPEAL by complainants from a decree of the Superior Court for Cook County dismissing the bill in a suit brought to enjoin the removal of a certain toll-gate. *Affirmed.*

The facts are fully stated in the opinion.

Messrs. **Frank J. Crawford** and **Sidney Smith** for appellants.

Mr. **Edward Roby**, with *Messrs.* **Jonas Hutchinson** and **M. W. Robinson**, for appellees.

Magruder, *J.*, delivered the opinion of the court:

Under recent Acts of the Legislature, a large area of new territory has been annexed to the City of Chicago, so as greatly to extend its boundaries. A portion of the highway known as the "Milwaukee Road," upon which the toll-gate and toll-house in question are located, was outside of the city limits prior to such annexation, but thereafter, and by reason of the enlargement of the City, the portion in question was taken into the City and is now a part of the street called "Milwaukee Avenue." The effect of this change upon the rights of the plank-road company or its successors, is the subject presented for consideration. Section 12 of the Act of March 25, 1874, "To Revise the Law in Relation to Toll-roads" (Rev. Stat. chap. 138), provides that "no toll-gate shall be erected or kept or toll demanded, within the corporate limits of any incorporated city, or within one hundred and sixty rods of such limits." Can this section be enforced against the appellants, so as to compel them to desist from keeping a toll-gate and demanding toll at the intersection of Milwaukee and Fullerton Avenues, in the City of Chicago? Is there a contract existing between the State and appellants which relieves them from the duty of obeying this requirement? Unquestionably, sections 21 and 22 of the Act of February 12, 1849, were uncon-

stitutional
They pr
"Northw
struct a p
to Oak R
and to th
were inser
was "An .
Oswego, i
Line, by t
was a clea
of article
provides t
embrace m
be express

It must
Lockport v
of the Act
The title o
Incorporat
Company.'
that the co
and procee
the road u
1849, attem
acts done i
legalization
regarded as
in the title.
1 and 2 of
copies of se
ruary 12, 1
sections are
in their c
conferred b
future.

It appear
the bill, tha
organizatio
the County
County, and
consenting
known as "
called "Milw
of the Act
company to
construction
The bill doe
were done,
were taken,
1854, but pr
were legalize
Owing to th
they were no
of February
amend the c
Road Compa
corporate ex
recognized t
tute stone or
the road as
without obta
missioners' c
corporate act
garded as ha
1865. 1 Mor
Grand Trunk
rich v. *Reyno*

It is averr
which the tol
a public high
commissioner
priation of th

petition of three fourths of the adjoining property owners, merely vested in said corporation "the right to use said highway for the purposes of said plank road." The public has only an easement in a highway, while the fee remains in the owners of the land. The highway continues to be such after it becomes a toll-road. *Craig* v. *People*, 47 Ill. 487.

The public still has the right to use the road, but such use is subject to the payment of tolls. The right of the plank-road company, under the acts already referred to, was the right to exact of the public a charge for the use of a mere easement or right of way over land. How long could the company, under its charter, continue to exercise the privilege of exacting tolls and maintaining toll-houses?

Section 1 of the Act of 1854 provides that Gray, Filkins, Richmond and their associates are "constituted a body corporate and politic under the name and style of the Northwestern Plank-Road Company, and by that name shall have perpetual succession, and the right to sue and be sued, together with all other rights and ordinary powers of a corporate body." This grant of perpetual succession was an incorporation of the company for an unlimited period of time. 1 Morawetz, Priv. Corp. § 411, *note 3*.

No limit was fixed by its charter for the duration of its corporate existence, and, so long as its existence as a corporation lasted, it could continue to exercise the powers conferred upon it. But by proceedings under the provisions of the Act of 1865, the plank-road company was dissolved in 1870. The Act of 1865 was not only an Act to amend the charter of the company, but also an Act "to authorize the sale of the franchise." Section 8 of this Act provides that "the president, by the advice and direction of a majority of the stockholders, may sell to the County of Cook the franchise, the property and immunities, of said company, or to any other party or parties, and thus dissolve said company, and divide the avails among the stockholders."

It is quite clear that the intention of the Legislature in authorizing the sale thus provided for was to dissolve the corporation, and put an end to its existence. Section 5 provides that "the deed of the president of said company to the said County of Cook, or to any other party purchasing, shall be a good and lawful title to the same: provided always, that all the debts and liabilities of said company shall be paid," etc.

The bill alleges that the company accepted the amendment of its charter as made by the Act of 1865. It also appears from the recitals in the deed from the president of the company to Amos J. Snell, as set forth in the bill, that at a meeting of the stockholders held in Chicago on January 5, 1866, where all but 80 of the 5,120 shares of the stock were represented, a resolution was passed, authorizing the president "to sell the plank road, toll-houses and other property belonging to the company, with the franchise, and all its rights and privileges, and give a deed of the same to the purchaser," etc. It is there averred that a sale was afterwards made to Snell, and a deed dated August 5, 1870, was executed to him by the president of the company. The deed recites that the company is entirely free from debt. Section 4 of the Act of 1865 provides that the supervisors of Cook County may purchase said franchise, property and immunities; "and should said county fail to purchase the same, any person or persons may purchase the same, and thereby make the same private property." Evidently, the design of the Act was to give the county the right in the first place to obtain a surrender to itself of the privileges granted to the company. The right of other parties to purchase would seem to have been conditioned upon the failure of the county to do so. There is, however, no allegation in the bill that the county authorities were ever informed of the resolution of January 5, 1866, or were ever given an opportunity of making the purchase referred to in section 4.

The only averment upon that subject is that the county did not purchase; but the county supervisors certainly could not be said to have failed to purchase until they were in some way made aware of the action of the stockholders, because such action was a necessary prerequisite to the right of the corporation to sell. But if it be admitted that the company had the authority to make the sale which it did make to Snell, the question arises, What effect did such sale have upon the company itself, and what rights did it confer upon the purchaser? As the debts were all paid, and there were no creditors or third person whose rights demanded that the existence of the corporation should be continued, the company became dissolved upon the consummation of the sale and the execution of the deed. This is so, because section 3 states that the object of selling is to dissolve the company. It is also a general rule that, where the charter of a corporation or its franchise to be a corporation is transferred or sold, there is a surrender or abandonment of the old charter by the corporators. In the case of such sale or transfer, the effect is the same as though the old corporation was dissolved, and its franchise surrendered to the State. *State* v. *Sherman*, 22 Ohio St. 411; *Memphis & L. R. R. Co.* v. *Berry*, 112 U. S. 609 [28 L. ed. 837].

What rights are acquired by the transferees or purchasers? It has been said that the essence of a corporation consists in a capacity (1) to have perpetual succession under a special name, and in an artifical form; (2) to take and grant property, contract obligations, sue and be sued, by its corporate name as an individual; and (3) to receive and enjoy in common grants of privileges and immunities. *Thomas* v. *Dakin*, 22 Wend. 71.

The first two describe the franchises which belong to the corporators, the last, those which belong to the corporation. "A corporation is itself a franchise belonging to the members of the corporation; and a corporation, being itself a franchise, may hold other franchises as rights and franchises of the corporation." *Pierce* v. *Emery*, 32 N. H. 484.

By the Act of 1854, Gray, Filkins, Richmond and their associates became a corporate body, with the right to perpetual succession, etc. This was the franchise of the corporators. By the same Act the corporate body received the right to construct and maintain a toll road, and to build toll-houses and collect tolls. These were the franchises of the corporation. The former franchise—that is to say, the franchise-to be a corporation—cannot be transferred without express provision of law pointing out the mode in which the transfer is to be made. *Coe* v. *Columbus, P. & I. R. Co.* 10 Ohio St. 372; *Memphis & L. R. R. Co.* v. *Berry, supra.*

The Act of 1865 authorizes the sale of "the franchise, the property and immunities" of the plank road company, and specifies that such transfer is to be made by deed of the president. If the word "franchise," as here used, is broad enough to include the franchise to be a corporation, with the power of perpetual succession, even then Snell was not thereby made a corporation under the old charter; he was merely vested with the "right to organize as a corporation." *Memphis & L. R. R. Co.* v. *Berry, supra.*

But such organization never took place. Neither he nor his heirs or representatives are claiming as the corporate successors of the plank-road company. The appellants are claiming as the heirs of Snell, the individual. "The franchise of becoming and being a corporation, in its nature, is incommunicable by the act of the parties, and incapable of passing by assignment." *Memphis & L. R. R. Co.* v. *Berry, supra.*

If Snell in his lifetime was the owner of such franchise by express legislative grant, he could not assign it, and it could not descend to his heirs. He failed to use it for the purpose of effecting any corporate organization, and it died with him. Even if this were not so, his failure to effect said organization within ten days after the Constitution of 1870 went into effect rendered it impossible, under section 2 of article 11 of that Constitution, to give any validity to an organization made after the lapse of such period of ten days. If the franchises designated as those which belong to the corporation, as distinguished from the corporators, passed to Snell by the transfer, and if he had the right to maintain the toll-houses transferred to him, and to collect the tolls therefrom, did such franchises and right pass to the appellants at his death? The second proviso of section 5 of the Act of 1865 is as follows: "Provided, further, that the purchaser or purchasers of said franchise and road shall be bound by all the obligations said 'Northwestern Plank-Road Company' is by its charter, and shall enjoy all the rights and privileges enjoyed by said company, and no more." This provision is to be strictly construed in favor of the public, and against the grantee of the privileges in question. Ang. & D. Highw. § 357; 1 Morawetz, Priv. Corp. § 323; *Stormfeltz* v. *Manor Turnp. Co.* 13 Pa. 555.

The person who is to "enjoy all the rights and privileges enjoyed by said company," is stated to be the purchaser of the franchise and road. It is not stated that the purchaser and his heirs and assigns shall enjoy such rights and privileges. If it had been the intention of the Legislature that the heirs of the purchaser should succeed to the privilege of collecting tolls and maintaining toll-gates it would have been so specified.

The dissolution of the corporation did away with the right of perpetual succession, which attached to the corporate body. By neglecting to organize a corporation with such privilege of perpetual succession, if the power to do so passed to him, Snell failed to preserve the ele-

ment of p
tolls and n
heirs, and
ble by the
a continua
been abrog
ration. It
president (
to him, "I
and assign
language o
lature auth

In *St. Cl*
[24 L. ed. 6
ed States h
to the char
gave to the
using a bri
gate on the
was express
lege, and no
suming or r
and *Mr. Ju*
be presume
petual gran
a limited pe
a grant to a
inheritance,
of the grant
longer than
of franchise
to be constr
nee, and in
cided in *Ko*
thirteenth se
no applicatio
the privilege
upon an ease
road certainl
erty" in such
company co
same way, an
vate property
sition of the
cided in *Crai*
of such a roa
vent the publ

The deed to
of said compa
its amendme
way, the gradi
and drainage
implements of
from the old
mile post, toge
and chattels
nature or desc
in connection
conveys the in
made to Snell
quired to be b
not yet been c
posed upon th
was "to constr
of Chicago to
Wheeling and
The considera
State was that
from the City
the county. T
State ever relea
to build and m
not sufficient t

from persons using so much of the road as may be completed; but the privilege of collecting tolls before completion did not excuse the company from the obligation of finally building the whole road.

It clearly appears from the statements in the bill that the original route of the road included the portion thereof that was sold to Snell, and that what he bought did not cover the whole extent of the original route. If it be true that the road was not yet finished when the sale was made, then Snell was bound to finish it, if all the franchises of the company passed to him. The Act of 1865 provides that "the purchaser of said franchise and road shall be bound by all the obligations said Northwestern Plank-Road Company is by its charter." But it is not alleged in the bill that he ever finished the balance of the road, nor is it pretended that he or his representatives have ever claimed or exercised any control over any part of the road except that named in the deed. Upon the assumption that the road was unfinished in 1870, and that, as purchaser of the franchise, he could have proceeded with the construction, it cannot be said that, if he had the right to erect and maintain such toll-houses and toll-gates as he might deem suitable to his interests, such right could have been exercised upon any other part of the road than that constructed by himself. It is distinctly averred in the bill that the Northwestern Plank-Road Company had built that part of the road described in the deed to Snell, and had erected thereon toll-gates and toll-houses which it deemed suitable to its interests, and had maintained the toll-road, toll-gates and toll-houses, and collected "toll therefor and thereat," long before the sale to Snell. This being so, the location of the toll-gates and toll-houses had become established, and the company had no power to move them or change their location. Tolls can only be collected at the legally established gates; and the public are interested in the permanency of the location of the gates, and entitled to the right of paying tolls at the established gates, especially when such payments have been made there for a number of years. By section 7 of the Act of February 12, 1849, the company was authorized "to erect and maintain such toll-houses, toll-gates and other buildings for the accommodation and management of the said road, and the travel and transport thereon, as the said corporation may deem suitable to its interests." But when the company had once exercised its discretion by locating the gates, then its power was exhausted. *Griffen* v. *House,* 18 Johns. 397; *State* v. *Norwalk & D. Turnp. Co.* 10 Conn. 157; *Hartford, N. L. W. & T. Turnp. Society* v. *Hosmer,* 12 Conn. 361; *Hartford & D. Turnp. Corp.* v. *Baker,* 17 Pick. 432; *People* v. *Louisville & N. R. Co.* 120 Ill. 48, 8 West. Rep. 90; Ang. & D. Highw. § 360.

When, therefore, the sale was made to Snell, he took the road from the City to the nine-mile post, with such toll-gates and toll-houses as were already established thereon. He had no more power to change their location than the company had at the time of his purchase. He could only enjoy the rights and privileges en- at the established gates, and not elsewhere. He was bound by the obligations which had been imposed upon the company by its charter. One of those obligations was to refrain from changing the location of the toll-houses, or removing them, or building others at other points than those originally selected.

It is alleged in the bill that the toll-gate at the intersection of Milwaukee Avenue with Fullerton Avenue was erected by Snell himself "several years prior to his death," which did not occur until February 8, 1888. The intersection of the two avenues was upon that part of the toll-road named in the deed. He had no right to locate the toll gate at the place thus selected. The toll-gates already established had not only been in use for the collection of tolls for years before his purchase, but for years thereafter. His use of the gates already existing for so long a period of time before the erection of the one in controversy amounted to an acceptance of what had been done by his predecessor, even if he himself had originally any discretion in the matter of their relocation.

But let it be admitted that the whole road was constructed by the plank-road company along the route named in the charter. If this was so, then the charter contemplated the erection of toll-gates and the collection of tolls along the line of the road from the old city limits to the north line of the county. The franchise was one and indivisible. *People* v. *Kankakee River Imp. Co.* 103 Ill. 491.

The Act of 1865 contemplated the sale of the whole franchise and the whole road. It is manifest that Snell only bought a part of the plank road, nine miles in length, and the franchise of using the same and collecting the tolls thereon. What became of the balance of the road? Was it abandoned or was it sold to some other purchaser? In either case there was a division of the franchise authorized to be sold as a whole by the Act of 1865. It was not the design of the original charter or of the Act of 1865 that there should be more than one ownership of the whole road and all its franchises. The contract between the State and the plank-road company was that the company, and no one else, should construct and keep in repair the whole road, and in consideration thereof should collect tolls. The contract between the State and the purchaser named in the Act of 1865 was that such purchaser should finish, or, if finished, should maintain and keep in repair, the whole road, in consideration of collecting tolls thereon. There was no contract between the State and Snell, or anybody else, that only a part of the road should be built or kept in repair, or that one part should be kept in repair by the county and the other part by some other owner, or that different owners should maintain and operate different parts of the road. Therefore, upon the assumption that the whole road had been completed and was in operation on August 5, 1870, it must follow that the sale made to Snell and the deed executed to him were not in pursuance of the Act of 1865, and cannot be regarded as binding upon the State.

The Act of 1865 evidently intended to put

the Northwestern Plank-Road Company upon the same footing with plank roads organized under the General Law of the State. Said road, if stone or gravel was substituted for plank, was to be "constructed so as to pass the examination of the inspectors of plank roads" in Cook County. It was to "collect the same tolls and enjoy the same privileges granted to plank-road companies by the General Plank-Road Law." *Turney* v. *Wilton*, 36 Ill. 393.

It might collect the same penalties, fines and damages authorized by the General Law, and be subject to the same penalties imposed by that law. Words of permission, if tending to promote the public benefit, are obligatory. Boone, Corp. § 36; *Rex* v. *Hastings*, 1 Dowl. & R. 148.

It was promotive of the public benefit that this particular plank-road company should not enjoy any greater privileges than other plank-road companies. It accepted the provisions of the Act of 1865, and made sale of its property under the last three sections of that Act. The words "may enjoy the same privileges" will be construed to mean "shall enjoy the same privileges."

There is nothing in the language of sections 1 and 2 of the Act of 1865 which limits the provisions of those sections to the General Plank-Road Law as it existed on February 15, 1865. The inspection was to be such as the General Law might provide for in the future. The company might collect the same tolls allowed by the General Law as it then was, and as it might become by amendment, and could enjoy the same privileges granted to plank-road companies by the General Plank-Road Law, whether such law should remain the same or be afterwards changed. *Kugler's App.* 55 Pa. 123; *McKnight* v. *Grinnion*, 22 Mo. 559.

By accepting the Act of 1865, the Northwestern Plank-Road Company consented that thereafter its privileges should be no more nor less than those which the Legislature should award to other plank-road companies by General Law. It consented thereby to accept the same restriction or enlargement which the General Law might make in the privileges of other plank-road companies. When Snell made his purchase, he was to enjoy the rights and privileges enjoyed by the company, and no more; therefore, he also was only to have such privileges as should be granted by the General Law. *Cairo & F. R. Co.* v. *Hecht*, 95 U. S. 168 [24 L. ed. 423].

The Act of March 25, 1874, already referred to, was a general Act relating to turnpikes, and plank, gravel, macadamized and other toll-roads. We have already seen that by section 12 of this General Law no toll-gate can be kept or toll demanded within the corporate limits of any city. The toll-gate at the intersection of Milwaukee and Fullerton Avenues is within the limits of a city. Appellants have no right to keep it there, or to demand toll there. Even if the interest of Snell became invested in them as his heirs, they took such interest subject to the same conditions under which their ancestor held it. He only enjoyed the same privilege as to the collection of tolls which other companies could enjoy under the General Law, and the privilege of such other companies was that of collecting tolls outside of the city limits, and not within such limits, nor within 160 rods thereof. Section 12, as applied to the Northwestern Plank-Road Company, or the purchaser therefrom, cannot be regarded as a violation of its or his contract with the State, in view of the acceptance of the provisions of the Act of 1865. The right to maintain the toll-gate in question is negatived by all the implications from the Acts of 1849, 1854 and 1865, and by the general law and policy of this State in regard to the character and powers of incorporated cities.

The road was to be constructed "from the City of Chicago," and although this language has sometimes been construed to mean "from a point within the City," yet such cannot be its construction in the present case. The bill does not so claim, but alleges that the road was begun at the northern limit of the City, as it existed from 1849 to 1854; that is to say, from North Avenue. The charter of the City of Chicago at that time placed its streets entirely under the control of the city authorities. The Act of February 12, 1849, authorizes the plank-road company to use state roads, and to acquire property from individuals, companies and corporations for the construction of the road; and the Act of March 1, 1854, provides for the use, for such purpose, of highways, with the permission of the county and the property owners. But nowhere in any of the Acts is any provision made for locating or constructing the road through any incorporated city or town. An Act passed in February, 1851, amending the General Plank Road Law of 1849, provided that no street of a city should be used for a plank road without the consent of the city authorities. An Act approved February 21, 1859, providing "for constructing, maintaining and keeping in repair plank, gravel or macadamized roads or pikes by a general law" (Laws 1859, p. 154), which Act was in force when the Act of February 15, 1865, was passed, required an agreement with the corporate authorities of a city before any plank road could be located upon any street of such city. The entire absence of any of these provisions from the Acts which constitute the charter now under consideration, together with the mention of only highways, state roads and private property in such charter, and the complete silence therein as to streets, leads to the conclusion that the contemplated road was intended to be one that should lie entirely outside of the limits of any city. *Reg.* v. *Cottle*, 3 Eng. L. & Eq. 474; *Stormfeltz* v. *Manor Turnp. Co. supra*; *Salem & H. Turnp. Co.* v. *Lyme*, 18 Conn. 451; *Charles River Bridge* v. *Warren Bridge*, 36 U. S. 11 Pet. 420 [9 L. ed. 773]; *Snell* v. *Buresh*, 123 Ill. 151, 11 West. Rep. 696; *Northwestern Fertilizing Co.* v. *Hyde Park*, 97 U. S. 659 [24 L. ed. 1036]; *Ohio & M. R. Co.* v. *McClelland*, 25 Ill. 140.

The policy of this State has always been to give the control of the streets, both as to repairs and general management, to the corporate authorities of the city through which such streets run. The fee of the streets is vested in the city for the use of the public, and their free and untrammeled use belongs to the public. Cities are bodies politic and corporate, established by law, not only to regulate and administer their own local affairs, but to assist in the

It can hardly be supposed that the Legislature intended to barter away the right of the State to carry on the government through the organization and extension of cities by making contracts with toll-road companies for the perpetual control of the public highways. By the natural growth of the country, many of such highways must become, in part, at least, streets of cities; and when they are so absorbed by the increase of population they must be subject to the control of the municipal authorities. Any other result would lead to inextricable confusion. One street cannot be under the management of two distinct governing powers. The Constitutions of 1848 and of 1870 have both been interpreted by this court to mean that the Legislature has no power to grant to any other than the corporate authorities of a city the right to assess and collect taxes, and that such taxation must be for corporate purposes; and that "the corporate authorities" are those who are either directly elected by the people of the municipality, or appointed to some mode to which they have given their consent. *Wetherell* v. *Devine*, 116 Ill. 631, 3 West. Rep. 519.

Whatever may be the rule in other States, it is the settled doctrine of this State, and was the doctrine of the State when the Act of 1865 was accepted by the plank-road company, that a statute, conferring upon the commissioners of highways the authority to maintain roads within their towns, will not be so construed as to authorize the exercise of such authority over highways within the limits of a city, and a tax levied by such commissioners for the repair or improvement of a public road or street lying within the limits of a city is illegal. *Ottawa* v. *Walker*, 21 Ill. 605; *Lancaster Highway Comrs.* v. *Baumgarten*, 41 Ill. 254; *People* v. *La Salle County Supre.* 111 Ill. 527; *People* v. *Chicago & N. W. R. Co.* 118 Ill. 520, 6 West. Rep. 342.

The same principle was applicable when the highways were under control of the counties, as when they were under the control of towns. Counties, under the Constitution of 1848, had no more right than towns to maintain a road within the limits of a city, or to levy taxes up on the people of a city for the maintenance of a road or street therein. When a toll-road was established, the town or county surrendered to the toll-road company the duty of maintaining the highway and keeping it in repair. The toll company was substituted for that purpose, and to that extent, for the authorities of the town or county. Whereas, theretofore the county or town levied a tax upon the people, payable either in money or labor, to keep the highway in repair, thereafter the toll road company required the people to pay tolls for the just the same as had been the case when the town or county exacted money or labor. Now, it will not be contended, when a city is enlarged so as to include within its boundaries a part of a highway, and so as to make such part of the highway a part of the street, with a fee-simple title thereto in the city, that the authority of the town or county over the portion of the road thus taken into the city will continue to exist any longer. It will be admitted that thereafter the city will have entire control. Why does not the same result follow when the part of the highway so added to the city has been under the management of a toll-road company? Such company is not a corporate authority of the city, selected by the people thereof. It levies upon the people an exaction in the nature of a tax, to which they have never given their consent. It imposes a charge upon them without their consent, for the purpose of keeping in repair one of their own streets, intrusted by the law to the management of their own officials. Any statute whose application leads to such a result as is thus indicated contravenes the spirit, if not the letter, of section 5 of article 9 of the Constitution of 1848, and of section 9 of article 9 of the Constitution of 1870, as those sections have been interpreted by this court. The Legislature had no power in 1849 or 1854 or 1865 to pass a special charter which could be so used or applied, under a given state of facts, as to violate the fundamental law of the State. The State could not be bound by a contract whose enforcement under new conditions would be forbidden by the Constitution. It follows that the plank-road company and its vendee must be held to have accepted the charter granted to them, upon the implied condition, and under the implied understanding, that the right to use the highway for a toll-road should give way as to such part thereof as should become subjected, by the growth of the State and its increase in population, to the control and government of an incorporated city. The State had authorized the company to use the highway by permission of the county, upon petition of three fourths of the adjoining property owners; but, under the requirements of the Organic Law, that use could not continue after the authority of an incorporated city had become substituted for that of the county, and the title of the adjoining property owners to the land subject to the easement of the highway had become vested in the incorporated municipality of a city.

We are therefore of the opinion that the Common Council of the City of Chicago had the right to direct its superintendent of public works to remove the toll-gate in question.

The decree of the Superior Court is affirmed.

END OF CASES IN BOOK VIII.

RÉSUMÉ OF THE DECISIONS PUBLI

SUBJECTS Discussed and Points Decided During
Year, Beginning with Oct., 1889, Clas

I. Governmental and Politic
II. Contractual Relations.
III. Commercial Relations.
IV. Fiduciary Relations.
V. Domestic Relations.
VI. Property Rights and Reme
VII. Damages for Torts.
VIII. Criminal Law and Practic

I. Governmental and Political

Taxes and assessments. Taxes imposed by the county court for road purposes are to be included with other taxes levied by that court in determining whether the limit of taxation will be exceeded. (W. Va.) 304. Rolling stock of a nonresident railroad company, used in interstate commerce, is not subject to taxation in a State where it is operating a leased railroad. (N. C.) 299. A provision for taxation *"ad valorem"* is violated by an ordinance taxing different classes of property at different rates per cent. (Ga.) 270. A local assessment for pavements, to be apportioned according to benefit, is not a tax within the provision requiring taxes to be in proportion to the value of property, and limiting the amount to be levied or collected. (Ala.) 369. Mere taxation of an unlawful business does not legalize it. (Tenn.) 280.

County taxes for bridge purposes. A county cannot impose taxes except for county purposes, and building a bridge within the corporate limits of a municipality for the sole benefit and advantage of the municipality is not a county purpose. (Fla.) 55. Where a bill for an injunction to prevent appropriation of county revenue alleges that the bridge is on a city street and not a county road or highway, and it is for the sole benefit and advantage of the city, a demurrer thereto will be sustained. *Id.* But where a bridge is for the use and benefit of the county at large, and intended as well for those outside as for those inside the city, the authority of the county to build is not annulled by the local city statute. *Id.* The circumstances in each case must determine the line of authority, and in case of conflict between municipal and county officials the county should give way in deference to the general policy against a clashing of jurisdiction. *Id.* If a county may build a bridge within a municipality it may also aid the municipality in building one under like circumstances, even though it is to be constructed by contract with, and under control of, the municipality. *Id.*

United States revenue. Under the Revenue Laws of the United States anyone, upon payment of the government dues, is in law entitled

to the poss
Hence a lice
call the go
purposes of
ceipts, does
pening of th

Condemna
Private prop
poses where
or use. (G
quiring com
action would
a private per
bounding on
sides and th
give the own
Depreciation
construction
right to com
(Ill.) 330. D
in the value
construction
limited to th
to the dimini
on the actual
are. (N. Y.)
graph compa
county road d
right to comp
in violation of
construction o
tion, when th
in its nature an
it is left free,
abutting own
transportation
county road w
owner of the f
will not be gr
pipes where he
to proceed und
missioner and
quired rights
completion of t
pensation can l
action. *Id.*
a reservoir site
all available us

time of its appropriation. (Tenn.) 128. The possibility of unskillful and improper construction of a reservoir cannot be considered in estimating damages to adjacent property. It must be assumed that the work will be skillfully and properly done. *Id.* The burden of proof as to the right to take property and to show that the particular property is necessary is on the corporation, and the concession by the owner of the right to condemn land, and limitation of the contest to the question of damages only, do not relieve from this burden of proof, or give the owner the right to open and close the argument. *Id.*

Statute construction. A bill published as a law cannot be shown by journals of the Legislature or by other evidence to be different from the statute actually enacted or to be invalid for failure to comply with formalities required by the Constitution. (Tex.) 326. A statute is not presumed to have extraterritorial force, where such intention would make it void. (Mo.) 549. A proviso in a statute should always be construed with reference to the immediately preceding part of the clause or section to which it is attached. (Md.) 680. A common error has the force of law only where it is shown that a considerable number of persons have relied upon or sought to fix their rights upon it. (Mont.) 629. The existence and effect of an alleged common error are for the court and not for the jury. *Id.* Where the rights of parties depend upon the law of a sister State, like a foreign law, to have effect it must be proved as a fact. (Mo.) 147. The burden of proof rests with the party claiming rights under it, as the court, in the absence of proof, may presume that the same law exists in the other State as exists here. *Id.* The Statute which authorizes a suit against the Commonwealth to recover "all claims" does not include an action for damages caused by the neglect of the servant of the Commonwealth in the performance of his duties. (Mass.) 399.

Game laws; possession of wild animals. Possession of animals reclaimed from a wild state is prima facie evidence of title. (Me.) 448. Liberating an animal captured during close time in violation of statute interferes with no legal right or title of the person illegally holding it captive, and gives him no right of action. *Id.* Following a moose in a forest until it becomes snow-bound and then capturing it during close time is a violation of Rev. Stat., chap. 30, § 9, prohibiting hunting, killing or destroying a moose during that time. *Id.*

Easement; right of way. The creation of a public road through private land gives the public merely a right of way. (Va.) 429. The erection of a telegraph line upon a highway is an additional servitude for which compensation must be made to the owner of the soil. *Id.* An easement of a right of way is not presumed to be personal, where it can fairly be construed to be appurtenant to some other estate, and a right of way across a lot given by conveyance of another lot is a right appurtenant to the lot conveyed. (Wis.) 617. A reservation in a conveyance of a lot which has a right of way appurtenant, of such right of way to the grantor, is ineffectual. He cannot enlarge the right, or retain any interest in the right of way as separate and distinct from the lot to which it belongs. *Id.* Building another railroad on a portion of the unused right of way of a company having an easement only in the land creates an additional servitude requiring the consent of the owner to be first made and compensation to be paid. (Tex.) 180.

Highways and streets. The right of the public upon highways and streets is a public right, the whole community having an equal interest and an equal right to complain of its infringement. (Me.) 828. Encroachments upon the right to pass along a highway may be prosecuted in behalf of the public as a nuisance which no length of time, unless there be a limit by statute, will legalize. *Id.* A statute in relation to adverse possession of ways and streets by buildings and fences has no application to a dam whereby water is caused to overflow and injure the same. *Id.* A dam so maintained as to overflow a highway and injure it constitutes a public nuisance, and the town may recover special damages against the party maintaining it. *Id.* Condemnation of land for a private way cannot be authorized. (Ind.) 58. The circuit court has jurisdiction of the proceedings to establish a way of necessity. *Id.* A grantee of land across which a prior grantee has a right of way takes it subject to such right. *Id.*

Plank and toll road corporations. Sections of an Act providing for a plank road from Chicago to the north line of Cook County are invalid, where the title of the Act mentions only a plank road from Oswego in Kendall County to the Indiana line. (Ill.) 858. This Act gives no authority to construct any part of the road within the city, where it is completely silent as to streets, but provides for the use of highways under permission of the county and property owners; and tolls cannot be exacted within the boundaries of the city under a Constitution which gives the city exclusive authority over highways therein, and the exclusive right to assess and collect taxes therein. *Id.* The legalization of unauthorized acts is not germane to the subject expressed in the title of an Act. *Id.* The illegality of corporate acts of a plank-road company in acquiring a highway for its road, because of the invalidity of the Act of incorporation, is cured by a statute which recognizes the corporate existence of the company by amending its charter, and also recognizes its right to substitute stone or gravel for plank upon a road already constructed. *Id.* A company is dissolved upon a sale of its corporate property, under a statute which states that the object of the sale is to dissolve the company. *Id.* The privilege of collecting tolls and maintaining toll-gates, acquired by a purchaser of "the franchises, the property and immunities" of a plank-road company, expires upon his death, although he had the right to organize as a corporation, if he did not do so, and the statute authorizing the sale did not state that his heirs and assigns might enjoy such privileges, but merely that the purchaser should enjoy them. *Id.* The location of toll-gates and toll-houses having become established, the discretion as to such location is exhausted, and they cannot be moved, especially after toll has been collected for several years. *Id.* The sale of part of a plank road, with the franchise of using the same and collecting tolls thereon, is invalid, where a statute under which it is made contemplated the sale of the whole road. *Id.* A provision that "a plank road company may collect the same tolls and enjoy the same privileges granted to plank-road companies by the General Plank-Road Law" does not fix the rights of the company according to the General Law as it then exists, but makes them coincide with those of other companies under the General Law, whether it remains the same or is afterwards changed. *Id.* It is not a violation of a contract with a plank-road company to enact that no toll-gate can be kept, or toll demanded, within the corporate limits of a city, where such corporation has accepted the provisions of a statute amending its charter which makes the privileges of the company the same as those of other companies under the General Law. *Id.*

Wharves and elevators. The maintenance of an elevator on a public wharf for handling grain thereat is no new or additional servitude. It is simply a new method of using the wharf for the very purpose for which it was condemned. (Mo.) 801. A lease of the unpaved portion of a public wharf to an elevator company is not in excess of the authority of the city where the right to terminate the lease on six months' notice is reserved, and also the right by ordinance to prescribe regulations governing the business of the lessee. *Id.* A shed or warehouse in connection with an elevator, for the storage and handling of grain or other merchandise, is for a public use and attached to it, and therefore a lease therefor of part of a public wharf is not void on the ground that the property is to be used for private purposes. *Id.* A wharf is unpaved where it is not paved in a manner suitable for wharf purposes. *Id.* The limitation in the charter of a corporation of the right to acquire river frontage does not apply to the right to occupy property on the city wharves by consent of the city, under a further clause in the charter. *Id.* The right of a corporation to occupy city wharves with a warehouse connecting with an elevator for any other purpose than to store and handle grain cannot be questioned by the owner of the fee of the wharf property. *Id.*

Office and officers. Parol evidence may be given of what was said and done in the presence of the court acting in a ministerial capacity, as in approving official bonds. (Mo.) 735. No appropriation is necessary where a State Constitution plainly declares what amount of compensation an officer shall receive. (Mont.) 403. A territorial governor cannot be compelled by mandamus to sign a warrant on the treasurer for funds for the insane asylum. (Ariz.) 188. The incumbent is not a necessary party to a peremptory mandamus to compel a corporation to restore relator to office. (N. J.) 697. When an office is full *de facto* under a color of right, the proper remedy to test the claim and title is *quo warranto* and not mandamus. *Id.* An office is deemed full *de facto* when a person elected is admitted to it, though the election upon legal grounds turns out to be invalid but consistent with an honest misapprehension of the law. *Id.* When a relator in

office
one wl
manda
remed
superi
be inq
institut
is no n
cluded
months
may b
that ye
whose
title the
from s
case of
he has
228. N
office in
surrend
title on
ment un
exercise,
son deri
the Legi
governo
acts are
a title to
mission.

Courts
confined
wherein
and can
determini
of law or
of indivic
lations.
jurisdictio
at law, nor
and irrep
barrassed
cotted by
of others
with or w
to the pers
union or t
adjudicati
to the vali
injunction
sociation c
be punishe
less it woul
and he has
Where the
ishment pr
right to inj
the remedy
a person ma
to pay fine
shown, is no
against his
laws. *Id.*
with jurisdi
graph comp
of messages.
lation of a p
nor in part f
189. A jud
diction of th
Legislative f
nicipal corpo
dicial court.
a foreign co

udice and local influence the circuit court will not inquire into the proof of the affidavit, if made by a proper person upon his own knowledge. (U. S. C. C. N. D. Ga.) 866. When a state court yields to and adopts the opinion of the United States Supreme Court on a given subject which has been acquiesced in for many years it will not be departed from without strong reason. (Mass.) 644.

Contempt of court. Only such acts and omissions can be deemed contempts of court as are specified as such in section 650 of the Civil Code of Oregon and in other sections thereof, and they can be punished only in the mode therein prescribed. (Or.) 584. An article published in a newspaper is not a contempt unless it reflects upon the conduct of the court in reference to a pending proceeding and tends to influence its decision or impede or embarrass its proceedings. *Id.* Acts not committed in the immediate view and presence of the court, unless the facts constituting the contempt are presented by affidavit, cannot be proceeded against. *Id.* Suspension of the execution of a judgment for contempt in violating an injunction during the pleasure of the court is void (Iowa) 767.

Police and police power. Government has an inherent right to impose restraints and provide regulations in regard to the pursuits of life. (Md.) 551. A town council which has power to pass all such ordinances as shall appear necessary and requisite for the health, welfare, etc, of the town has the exclusive right to judge what is "necessary and requisite" to preserve the health of the town. (S. C.) 854. An ordinance prohibiting the cultivation for agricultural purposes of more than one eighth of an acre by any family or household within the corporate limits, except for flower gardens or grapes, or trees, and except for planting oats, rye or barley, is a valid exercise of police power. *Id.* Police laws and regulations are not unconstitutional, although they prevent the enjoyment of individual rights in property without providing compensation therefor. *Id.* An ordinance is not "unequal and unjust" on the ground that its permits the owner of a small parcel of ground to cultivate a larger proportion of his ground than the owner of a larger tract can do, where the same maximum limit is fixed for all persons. Nor does an ordinance violate the constitutional law because it applies to one village of the State only. *Id.* Prohibiting any but registered plumbers to engage in the business is the ordinary exercise of the police power. (Md.) 551. The general law of the State does not authorize conferring the degree of M. D. by literary and scientific institutions. (Vt.) 112. A diploma not authorized by law does not authorize the issue of a license to a physician. *Id.* Removal of a church will not affect that portion of a statute prohibiting the sale of intoxicating liquor within three miles of it. (N. C.) 259. A corporation cannot be held liable for an arrest ordered by the superintendent of his property unless it is shown that he had express precedent authority for giving the order or that it was ratified by the corporation. (Md.) 846. A policeman appointed on application of a corporation required by law to pay his salary is an officer of the State and the corporation is not responsible for his acts as such officer and it cannot be held to have ratified the act where the officer does not act as its agent but as an officer of the State. *Id.* Insanity which leads the person afflicted with it to make indecent exposure of his person in public renders him dangerous to community within the meaning of the Statute which provides for the restraint of such persons at public expense and the reimbursement of the public treasury out of their estates. (Ind.) 461. Person arrested in a sister State without being extradited is unlawfully deprived of his liberty and is entitled to be discharged on habeas corpus. (Neb.) 398.

Police regulation. Merely standing still on a sidewalk and refusing to move at the command of a policeman does not make one guilty of a nuisance, and if all disperse except one, upon request of an officer, that one is not subject to arrest for obstructing the free passage of the street. (N. C.) 529.. An ordinance providing that a person may be arrested without warrant or hearing, because he refuses to "move on," and, in the opinion of an officer, "unreasonably persists in remaining so as to incommode others passing," violates a constitutional provision that "no person should be taken, imprisoned . . . or in any manner deprived of his life, liberty or property, but by the law of the land." *Id.* An officer must determine at his peril whether an offense has been committed, before making an arrest without a warrant. *Id.* The mere fact that a person is drunk on the streets will not authorize his arrest, under an ordinance permitting arrest for being "found drunk in the streets, hallooing or making an unusual noise." *Id.* Riding in a carriage on Sunday for exercise is not a violation of the Sunday Law in Maine. (Me.) 427.

Poor and poor laws. Where it is necessary that a girl of weak mind should remain under the control of her parents she takes the settlement of her father and he is bound to furnish her with support. The promise of aid by the overseer of the poor to such father is without consideration and unenforceable. (Vt.) 708.

Hawkers and peddlers. Only the person who itinerates for trading purposes is a peddler. He is one who goes from place to place, exhibits a sample and procures orders, which his employer afterwards fills by delivery of the article. But though a peddler, if he be a nonresident he is protected by the Federal Constitution against the provisions of a State Code requiring a license to peddle. (Ga.) 273. Canvassers for books are not hawkers or peddlers within the meaning of the Statute which gives municipal corporations power to compel hawkers and peddlers to obtain a license. (Ill.) 328.

Lotteries, suppression of. Bonds of foreign governments with conditions and stipulations which change their character to a species of lottery tickets are within the condemnation of statutes against lotteries. (Md.) 671. Any device whereby money or other thing is to be paid on the happening of any event is in the nature of a lottery. *Id.* The fact that there are no blanks to be drawn does not prevent a distribution of prizes by lot or chance from being a lottery; and that the scheme provides for a return of the entire investment with interest, if such return depends upon the revolution of a wheel, with a possibility of getting a bonus, will not prevent its being condemned as a lottery. *Id.* Gaming devices seized by the sheriff on arrest of their owner are as properly subject to the order of the court trying the offender as if they had been seized by authority of a search warrant. (Ind.) 488. Property seized for violation of law cannot be summarily destroyed without affording the owner an opportunity to be heard upon the subject of its value for some lawful purpose. *Id.* An order of court is necessary to justify destruction of gaming apparatus seized by the sheriff upon conviction of the person offending, when the sheriff shall forthwith cause to be destroyed the apparatus used for unlawful purposes. *Id.* Selling pools on a horse race run outside of the State is not licensed by placing a tax on the business of selling pools in this or any other State. (Tenn.) 280.

Public charities. County commissioners are not authorized to contract for care and support of persons in asylums organized solely for public charity, as for care and support furnished for an insane person. (Ind.) 461. The law raises no implied obligation on the part of one received into a charitable institution to pay therefor; such relief is referred to motives of charity unless the charter of the institution provide otherwise. *Id.*

Municipal corporations. Taxpayers may sue out injunction in behalf of themselves and others to prevent illegal acts of municipal authorities. (S. C.) 291. An amended city charter providing that the city may borrow money by issuing bonds gives authority to issue bonds subsequent to the date of the charter although a bonded indebtedness already existed. *Id.* A city may own an electric-light plant for lighting streets where it is given power to own property. *Id.* The purchase of an electric plant is beyond its implied authority so far as it is intended to furnish light for residences and places of business of private individuals. *Id.* The furnishing and distribution of gas and electricity for public use may be conferred on cities and towns together with power to raise money by taxation for construction of necessary works. Such power may be lawfully conferred to enable cities and towns to produce gas and electricity to be sold to their own citizens for the lighting of their private property. (Mass.) 488. A city is estopped to claim land dedicated to public use where it has permitted a person to occupy and has collected city taxes thereon, as his property. (Iowa) 633. The purchase of land including a spring will not justify diverting the water flowing therefrom from its natural channel to supply a city with water. (Pa.) 202.

Municipal ordinances. It will be presumed that an ordinance was properly signed where the journal recites that the signature of the speaker was affixed in open session and no objection is noted on the journal. (Mo.) 110. The adjournment of the house of delegates on the day bills are presented to the mayor for his approval will not prevent them from becoming valid ordinances if duly filed by the mayor with his approval in the city register's office. *Id.* That the work of street paving prescribed by an ordinance is covered by letters-patent held exclusively by one company will not prevent let-

ting a c
providi
lowest
rides hi
used fo
the city
bicycles
(Kan.) 7
strued a
ity. *Id.*
pany to
not an e
penal or
is void,
health o
Munic
granted
ment to t
eys colle
the purp
any adju
equitable
bonds m
and acqu
taxpayers
poration
no power
ing whet
cause of l
limitation
lent to
shall be
denial of
Failure fo
dealing w
affirmative
investmen
their canc
the issue
to purchas
tional, be
"necessary
In ordinar
restrain lo
tion for th
courts. *Id*
of bonds
injunction
the statute
law. *Id.*
issue of v
was obtaine
resentation
the people
may be fou
(Mich.) 851.
Municipa
liable for re
from which
752. A city
negligence c
workhouse
duty in the
although so
city from th
where its offi
an independ
is not liable f
occurring on
pants of a s
frightening c
ance of two
neighboring

condition at the time and having been habitually traveled for years without accident. (W. Va.) 82. In the absence of statutory or municipal regulations to the contrary a tree planted by a private person on the sidewalk is under control of the owner and occupant of the abutting property, and he is bound to use reasonable care to prevent it from becoming dangerous to travelers; and those specially injured through a breach of that obligation may recover for damages arising therefrom, and the occupant of the abutting premises is chargeable with knowledge of his duty. (N. J.) 798.

Street railways. When two rival companies have each received permission to construct a railway system in the streets of a city, the one which first begins work has the better right to the use of that portion of the street which its tracks will cover and this right continues so long as the work is diligently prosecuted. (Ind.) 539. A municipality may prescribe the motive power to be used in propelling street cars, and when prescribed no other can be used. *Id.* A street railway having authority to use a cable for motive power acquires no right to the exclusive use of the street upon which it intends to use a different motive power. *Id.* It may, to defeat the rights which its rival claims on a street in which both companies have equal rights, show that prior occupation was not in conformity with such rival's charter power, the intention being to use a motive power different from that permitted by the charter. *Id.* A grant or permission with which to use a certain motive power will not relate back to the time of construction of the tracks so as to cut off intervening rights. *Id.* A company having power to own and operate a street railway may use the tracks, cars and property purchased from another company previously chartered with like power although the latter had no power to transfer its franchise. *Id.*

Private corporations. Officers of a corporation who sign and issue certificates of its stock in the usual form thereby represent that the stock is not spurious nor invalid because of their known acts or omissions, and that everything has been done necessary to make the stock rightfully exempt from further assessment, and if such representations are false they will be liable in damages to one who takes them in good faith for value relying upon the representations. (Mass.) 750. A premature and void contract made by a corporation to promote the purposes of the incorporation, carried out, after it became enabled to make it valid, does not release a subscription for corporate stock. (Conn.) 637. Shares of stock in a sporting club having power to own property cannot be sold on execution where the club is not compelled to issue any shares of stock, although it has done so. (Mich.) 358. Permission to purchase the capital stock of other corporations will authorize its recipient to purchase shares of such stock although a distinction may exist between "capital stock" and "shares of stock." (Ill.) 497. The provisions of the General Incorporation Act enter into and form a part of the charter of a corporation. *Id.* Merely naming a power in the statement filed with the secretary of state does not warrant its exercise if it is not essential to the accomplishment of the corporate object, and is not expressly permitted by the Act. The law must determine what incidental powers can be exercised. *Id.* Power to purchase, hold and sell stock in other gas companies cannot be exercised under the General Incorporation Act for the creation of gas companies. *Id.* An allegation of liability to pay without alleging payment or actual loss sufficiently shows damage to a corporation for acts of its directors in issuing promissory notes in its name which have come into the hands of bona fide purchasers for value. (N. Y.) 258. Directors incur a personal liability to the corporation by voting for a resolution, which they have no power expressed or implied to pass, to negotiate its notes, which are in effect void. *Id.* One who fraudulently places in circulation negotiable instruments of another is guilty of a tort and presumptively liable to the injured party for the face value thereof. *Id.*

Creation of monopolies. The purpose of purchasing and holding all the shares of the capital stock of companies in the business of a public character is not a lawful purpose as it tends to the creation of a monopoly. (Ill.) 497. Though the determination of questions of public policy is ordinarily a legislative function, yet the judiciary may refuse to sustain that which is against the public policy of the State. *Id.* The business of manufacturing and distributing illuminating gas is of a public character, and unreasonable restraint upon performance of this duty by companies engaged therein is in contravention of public policy. *Id.*

Social clubs. The members of a social club may regulate through their by-laws the causes for and mode of expulsion of its members. (Pa.) 196. Such by-laws are not unreasonable, arbitrary or oppressive, nor do they violate any principle of natural justice. Failure to designate or define specific acts which will be deemed disorderly does not render a by-law illegal. *Id.* A minor offense may justify expulsion if the club acts in good faith under powers conferred by its charter. *Id.* On trial of a charge against a member the club acts as a judicial tribunal and its judgment will preclude the reexamination of the case on its merits by a judicial court. *Id.* A return will be sufficient to warrant a denial of a writ of mandamus to reinstate a person in a social club where it appears therefrom that the expulsion was regular and in good faith, and the whole proceeding is stated with substantial accuracy. *Id.* The enforcement of the provisions of the charter and by-laws of a social club can deprive a member of no legal or constitutional right. *Id.*

Benevolent associations. A Young Men's Christian Association is not a corporation formed for purposes of religious worship so as to preclude it from acquiring more than ten acres of land. The association contemplates benevolent and missionary work rather than religious worship. (Ill.) 556. A corporation having power to hold real estate for some purposes can be questioned as to such power only by the State. *Id.*

II. CONTRACTUAL RELATIONS.

Contracts in general. Whatever is necessary to be done to accomplish work specially contracted to be performed is parcel of the contract, though not specified. (Conn.) 118. Whatever may fairly be implied from the terms or nature of an instrument is, in judgment of law, contained in it. *Id.* The certificate of architects must be obtained before an action can be maintained on the contract if they have not been guilty of fraud or collusion. (Mich.) 207. Recovery upon *quantum meruit* cannot be based on a contract which makes such certificate a condition precedent to a right of action. *Id.* Remedying the defects pointed out by architects, but without obtaining from them the certificate, made a condition precedent, cannot give a cause of action; their own assertion or the opinion of the jury cannot be substituted for the decision of the architects. *Id.* Taking possession of real estate after the contractor has left the premises does not constitute an unequivocal acceptance of the work. *Id.* Issuing five cards each good for twenty crossings is a substantial compliance by a bridge company with a contract to sell one hundred tickets for $1. (Ky.) 484. In case one fails to deliver furniture sold for a hotel until long after the appointed time he is liable for the loss occasioned by reason of such failure. (Ind.) 65.

Specific performance. Specific performance of a contract will not be decreed where the injury can be redressed by damages in an action at law. (S. C.) 625. A provision in a contract for sale of real property that the title is to be passed upon by purchaser's conveyancer does not make his decision a condition precedent to vendor's right to enforce the contract. (N. Y.) 591. A stipulation that title shall be first-class means that it shall be marketable. *Id.* Absence of a party from home for upwards of twenty-four years is not sufficiently strong presumption of death to make marketable a title to real estate which depends on his death. *Id.*

Contracts, validity of. Parol negotiations on Sunday have no effect on the validity of a contract within the Statute of Frauds which is actually executed in writing and delivered on a secular day. (Conn.) 657. A parol promise to leave real and personal property to a child in consideration of taking the family name and becoming a member of the family is void, under the Statute of Frauds. (Ill.) 414. Becoming a member of a man's family and taking his name is not such part performance as to make it amount to a fraud to refuse performance of the promise. *Id.* The entire contract if void as to real estate is void also as to the personalty. *Id.* Exclusive right to use a railroad platform for receiving and discharging passengers cannot be granted to one hack owner. (Mont.) 753. A contract not to teach a foreign language is unreasonable where the restraint extends beyond any apparently necessary protection to the other party. (R. I.) 469. A contract restraining the exercise of one's calling for a certain time is not void as against public policy merely because it extends throughout the State. *Id.* A contract giving an exclusive agency for the sale of a brand of cigars in a certain Territory is not void as in restraint of trade. (Mont.) 440. The rule which prohibits the granting of monopolies applies only to such things as are of common right. It is never applied to things which are monopolies in their nature; hence it will not prevent the granting for a reasonable and fixed period of the exclusive right to operate a railway line in certain streets. (Ind.) 589. A mere agreement by a municipal corporation not to grant rights and privileges which will impair those already conferred by ordinance will not prevent like permission to others. *Id.* Where a contract was entered into with a county clerk, who has no power to make it, to print a delinquent tax list for less than the statutory rate, the full statutory rate can be recovered. (Wis.) 781. Waiver or estoppel has no application to a contract made by an officer without authority. *Id.* An executed parol agreement modifying a contract under seal will be upheld. (N. Y.) 257.

Usury. The law of the State in which a note for a loan is given governs on the question of usury, although the note is expressly made payable in another State. (Ga.) 170. A transaction cannot be devested of the taint of usury by the fact that the party subsequently sells the securities taken in his own name, if he was in fact the actual lender. (Ill.) 724.

Suretyship and guaranty. A surety who merely gives his note to a co-surety who has paid the debt acquires no right of action against his principal, at least where any cause of action against the latter in favor of the co-surety was barred. (Cal.) 425. After a cause of action against the principal is barred a surety cannot acquire any right of action against the principal by payment of the demand. *Id.* A surety is not liable on a bond signed by him alone purporting to be signed by the principal also, where he did not consent to its delivery, and the burden of proof to show his consent is on the obligee. (Mass.) 486. Erasing the name of a surety and substituting another before approval of an official bond, without knowledge or consent of the other sureties, discharges them. (Mo.) 735. Signing as surety and leaving the bond with a principal to procure other signatures for acceptance and approval does not authorize the principal to discharge a person who might thereafter become a party to the instrument. *Id.* A surety who signs in ignorance that the other sureties have been released by the erasure of a name cannot be held liable on the bond. *Id.* The doctrine of spoliation has nothing to do with the effect of erasing of the name of a surety, before approval of the bond, upon the liability of other sureties. *Id.* An estoppel cannot arise to prevent sureties from insisting upon relief from liability from the fact that they permitted the principal while ignorant of the alteration to perform his official duty without objection. *Id.* The withdrawal of a claim against the estate of a principal debtor does not discharge a guarantor from liability under an unconditional guaranty. (Conn.) 657. A guaranty, in consideration of forbearing collection of notes for two years, of the come due, cannot be limited to interest before maturity of the notes, especially where the first note was already overdue when the guaranty was made. *Id.* A demand upon the principal is not a condition precedent to the maintenance of an action against the guarantor upon a guaranty which is absolute in its terms. *Id.* A guaranty that cattle of another person will sell for a certain price and an agreement by the other person to pay any excess above that price is a gambling contract. (Iowa) 275. A separate guaranty written at the foot of the bond of another person is a separate sealed instrument and the signer may be sued as principal obligor and the action may be brought at any time within ten years under the Code. (N. C.) 380.

Mutual benefit associations. An agreement by an association to pay a death assessment, with a further provision that the death claim shall be payable within sixty days, imports a promise by the association to make or cause to be made the necessary assessment. (Conn.) 113. Individual members of an unincorporated association are liable for contracts made in the name of the association even if the other party was ignorant of their name. *Id.* An action lies for breach of a contract of a mutual benefit society to make an assessment. The measure of damages for such breach is prima facie the sum received from the death assessment. *Id.* A complaint alleging a state of facts from which an agreement to make an assessment upon members of an insurance organization can be implied, and claiming damages for failure to make the assessment, is not insufficient because it does not state in terms an agreement to make the assessment. *Id.*

Fire insurance. A binding slip in a contract of insurance is a contract for temporary insurance subject to conditions contained in the ordinary policy. (N. Y.) 719. A notice to brokers is a good notice of a cancellation of insurance obtained by them. *Id.* Cancellation of a policy which may be terminated on notice is effected *eo instanti* if no premium has been paid. *Id.* A man has an insurable interest in buildings on land purchased and paid for by him, though conveyed to his wife, where there was an understanding between him and his wife that she would convey the land to him at his request. (Wis.) 806. A contract of insurance on scattered houses, each insured for a specific amount, is divisible. A transfer of one, avoiding the policy as to it, does not make it void as to others. (Wis.) 834. The death of the insured does not make a change in the title such as will avoid a policy against loss by fire under a provision against any change in the title, use or occupation of the premises. (Ky.) 800. The time for bringing suit on an insurance policy does not elapse with the expiration of the twelve months after the fire where it also provides that a claim on the policy shall be payable sixty days after full completion of certain requirements of the policy. (Cal.) 48. Where a policy provides that action for loss must be brought within a specified time the limitation runs from the date of the fire. (N. D.) 769. A mortgagee to whom mortgagor's policy is made payable may sue alone where no privity between the original insured and the re-insurer; but, where the loss or risk is expressly assumed by another company, the original insured may sue upon such contract as having been made for his benefit. *Id.* Machinery and apparatus used in manufacturing, being the only property covered by a policy of insurance, do not constitute a mill, or the standing still thereof create a forfeiture under the provision in a policy against vacancy or unoccupancy or a mill or manufactory standing idle. (N. Y.) 79. Where proofs of loss are duly authorized and taken by the adjuster the insured has the right to assume, until notified to the contrary, that no other or different proof will be required. (Kan.) 70. In an application for insurance, where correct answers are given to a general agent respecting incumbrances, who fails to mention them in the written application, the company will not be relieved from liability on account of misrepresentations therein, although it was stipulated that it should be considered a part of the policy and a warranty of the truth of the statements. *Id.* A general agent can modify the contract or waive the condition of a written policy by parol; so a provision respecting incumbrances may be waived notwithstanding a printed stipulation that no person other than the president or secretary shall have authority to waive the terms or conditions. *Id.*

Life insurance. Corporations organized under the Revised Statutes of Ohio, which do not comply with the laws regulating mutual life insurance companies, cannot issue policies for a fixed amount to be paid at the death of the member, except upon the assessment plan; and those which do comply with such laws may issue endowment policies payable to members during life. When such corporations are not permitted to do business in other States upon substantially the same basis and limitations, corporations organized on the assessment plan in other States are not entitled to do business in this State. (Ohio) 129. The business which corporations of other States organized under the assessment plan are permitted to do in this State does not include the business of insuring lives of their members for the benefit of others than their families and heirs, nor those organized without other limitation than that the policy holder shall have an insurable interest in the life of the member. *Id.* Corporations of other States, organized for the purpose of insuring lives of members for the benefit of others than their families and heirs are not entitled to transact business in this State, until they procure a certificate of authority to do so; nor can an agent act for them until a license to do so is procured from the superintendent of insurance, which license continues in force until the 1st day of April next after its date. *Id.* Where a foreign corporation exercises its franchise in contravention of the laws of this State it may be ousted by proceedings in *quo warranto.* *Id.* The word "heirs" in a certificate of life insurance, without context to explain it, means those who would, under the Statute of Distribution, be entitled to the personal estate. (Ark.) 732. A widow is not an heir of her deceased husband so as to be entitled to share in the proceeds of an insurance policy under the Arkansas Statute. *Id.* No one except the insurer by a benefit certificate can object to brothers and sisters of the person insured taking the proceeds of his certificate, the constitution limiting the right to take benefits to members of the family of the insured or those dependent on him. *Id.* A slight blow on the throat while fencing does not constitute "any wound, hurt or serious bodily injury" within the meaning of a question in an application for life insurance. (N. Y.) 68. The words "hurt" and "wound" mean an injury to the body causing an impairment of health or strength or rendering one more liable to disease or less able to resist it. *Id.*

III. COMMERCIAL RELATIONS.

Commercial paper. Certainty in a negotiable instrument as to the payor and payee, the amount to be paid and the terms of payment, is essential, and that certainty must continue until the obligation is discharged. (S. D.) 893. Blanks in the body of a note will not render it non-negotiable if the amount is expressed in figures at the head of the note. (Ind.) 865. The owner and indorser of drafts in blank placed with the bank for collection may have the benefit of a restrictive indorsement placed thereon by the bank for the purpose of collection. (Mass.) 42. Legal title to commercial paper indorsed "For collection" passes only so far as to enable indorsee to demand, receive and sue for the moneys to be paid; while the owner may control his paper until paid, and may intercept the proceeds in the hands of an intermediate agent. *Id.* A bank's indorsement directing payment "for account of itself" does not imply ownership of the paper where the indorsement of the bank from which its title was derived was of the same kind. *Id.* Where a note was surreptitiously taken from the owner by its nominal payee and sold, he may recover it from the purchaser although the latter paid value for it, without notice of defect in the title. (Ind.) 61. If an innocent party has been defrauded into giving notes he is not obliged to contest them in the hands of a stranger unless on certain information that he is not a bona fide holder. (Mich.) 476. Knowledge of a warranty, where a note was given for the purchase price, will not affect the rights of the bona fide purchaser of the note if he had no knowledge of the breach of warranty. (Mich.) 428.

Commercial agency. A written contract creating a commercial agency for one year having been renewed expressly for the next year and the agency in fact continued for several years, it was a tacit renewal from year to year and the principal could not by notice, pending the last year's services, terminate the contract before the expiration of that year. (Ga.) 410.

Common carriers. A common carrier cannot exempt itself by contract from liability for losses resulting from its gross negligence or willful misconduct. (Ill.) 508. An amount named in a bill of lading as the limit of liability will not restrict recovery for a loss due to gross negligence. *Id.* Delay in transportation, caused solely by a mob, will not render the carrier liable for losses by a decline in their market price or for their deterioration in quality. (Tex.) 823. Owners of gunpowder consigned for sale on commission are not liable for an explosion of the powder in the hands of the consignee. (N. M.) 878. "Shipment," in a contract providing for marine insurance by the buyers, means delivery on some vessel and not a clearance of the vessel. A shipment which does not constitute a full cargo is made by placing the goods on board a vessel bound for the intended port. (N. Y.) 245. A statute compelling railroad companies to furnish double-deck cars for sheep is void as an attempted regulation of commerce when applied to interstate shipments. (Mo.) 549.

Foreign companies. Where a policy of insurance is issued on property in one State by a company in another State, and it does not appear where the contract was made, it may be inferred that the contract was made in either State. (Iowa) 236. A statutory prohibition against insurance by foreign corporations without compliance with certain requirements, under a certain penalty, does not make a policy issued without such compliance void as to the insured. *Id.* Evidence that notice and proofs of loss were sent to a firm through which the policy was procured, and that they forwarded the papers by mail to the insurer, is admissible as tending to show that the insurer received them. *Id.* Proof of the mailing addressed to an insurer and properly stamped, opposed by testimony of the insurer's officers and clerks that the documents were never received, presents a question for the jury as to whether the documents were received or not. *Id.* A special finding by a jury that they were received within sixty days, the time limited by the policy, is sufficiently definite without stating the exact day. *Id.* Instructions that notice of loss must have been given within a reasonable time, while the policy requires it to be given "forthwith," are not prejudicial, as the terms are so nearly synonymous. *Id.*

IV. FIDUCIARY RELATIONS.

Trust and trustees. Money received by one as agent, who dies before paying it over, although mingled with his own, constitutes a trust fund recoverable from his personal representatives. (Colo.) 788. A claim for a trust fund as to which the relation of debtor and creditor never existed is not a debt or demand within the Statute relating to the payment of demands against decedents' estates. *Id.* The beneficial owner of a claim, a party to the contract in suit brought by a holder of the legal title, is properly joined as defendant when he refuses to unite with the plaintiff. *Id.* Where there is but one cause of action stated, merely by stating that one of the defendants, a beneficial owner of the claim, was made defendant for refusing to unite with plaintiff, and seeking to charge him with costs and expenses, there is no misjoinder of causes. *Id.* A disclaimer by a person sued as trustee, and who has never executed a bond as such, relates back to the time of his appointment. (Tenn.) 480. An action against *cestuis que trustent* lies without having any trustee as a party, where there is a vacancy in the trusteeship. *Id.* Distribution of property to trustees in trust under a will giving a life estate does not authorize a person dealing with the property to regard the distributee as sole beneficiary. (Conn.) 666. Property purchased from a fund including moneys held under different trusts is chargeable with the same trusts that attached originally to the fund as against those knowing it to be trust property. *Id.* A trustee is under obligation to keep property safely which it is his duty to hold in trust during the life of a person. *Id.* No notice of the resignation of a trustee and appointment of his successor is required to be given to the heirs who are entitled to the property absolutely. *Id.* One who knowingly sells trust securities for unauthorized purposes, although he makes the sale simply as agent, is liable for breach of the trust. *Id.* Knowledge that property is held in trust puts one dealing in it as agent upon inquiry and charges him with all knowledge that inquiry would bring. *Id.* Brokers who sell stock which they know belongs to the trust fund, its proceeds to be used in stock speculations, are liable to account to the other *cestuis que trustent* for their share of the proceeds. *Id.* The bar of the Statute of Limitations against *cestuis que trustent* is not saved by the pendency of a suit until within one year preceding against the woman and her husband and a person as trustee who was no longer such, on the dismissal of the suit for failure to make the children, remaindermen, parties to the proceeding. (Tenn.) 480. A suit to charge payment of an equitable claim upon a trust estate is subject to the Statute of Limitations. *Id.* A remedy at law on the bond of a trustee having proved inadequate by reason of insolvency of the sureties, a remedy in equity to reach property not subject to execution is barred when the bond and also the decree thereon are barred. *Id.* Express continuing trusts are excepted from the operation of the Statute of Limitations, while implied trusts are subject thereto. (Conn.) 647. Leaving corporate stock in possession and name of the seller creates an implied trust in the seller which is enforceable at law and subject to the Statute of Limitations. *Id.* There is no legal presumption of the death of a person who has not been heard from until after the expiration of seven years. *Id.*

Innkeepers and guests. Guests, travelers and others entering a hotel with the bona fide intent of becoming guests cannot be prevented from entering the hotel or be put out by force after entrance without a cause if they are able to pay the charges and tender the money necessary for that purpose. (N. C.) 516. Where objectionable persons enter for their pleasure or profit, they are there merely under implied license which may be revoked at any time, and those violating reasonable regulations may be expelled. *Id.* The innkeeper has a right to make regulations for the conduct of his inn, and may request one not a guest to depart, and may expel him if he refuses. Even if one enters at the request of a guest, if he engages in "drumming" for his employer after notice to desist, he may be expelled. *Id.* The innkeeper may establish a livery stable or may contract with a livery stable keeper to secure the patronage of his hotel for a percentage of the proceeds and expel others who seek to interfere with the business. *Id.* The responsibility of an innkeeper for goods and moneys of his guest extends to moneys stolen by a servant or companion of the guest. (Pa.) 97. Intoxication of a guest at an inn is no excuse for his negligence which contributes to the loss of his property by theft. *Id.* Whether a guest should be treated as having notice of the existence of a safe is a question for the jury, where he frequently stopped at the inn and there is evidence that on some visits his attention had been called to the safe by the landlord. *Id.* Whether carrying money to his room instead of placing in the safe is negligence on the part of the guest is a question for the jury. *Id.*

Banking. A bank receiving commercial paper for collection cannot dispute the right of the owner to stop payment although it has made credits or advances on account of the paper, if the same were made before collection; nor can such advances be recovered as money paid for the owner's use. (Mass.) 42.

Foreign receiver. The right of a foreign receiver to wind up an insolvent partnership will not be recognized as against the claims of nonresident creditors who have attached such moneys under domestic laws before such receiver obtained actual possession of the money or an enforceable lien thereon even under a general assignment. (Ind.) 62.

Partnership. The renewal of a limited partnership operates merely as an extention of the partnership and in practical effect is the same as if such time had been embraced within the terms of the original formation. (N. Y.) 712. Impairment of the capital furnished to a limited partnership without fault of the special partner does not prevent renewal of the partnership, and a false statement in the certificate of renewal does not render him liable as a general partner to one not induced thereby to give credit to the firm. *Id.* A partnership is created by an agreement under which one person advances money for investment on joint account. (Conn.) 657. A person is liable as a partner on a note given in the name of another as part of the purchase price of land although he authorized the other only to procure options, where he afterwards accepted the benefits of the purchase and continued to furnish money to effectuate the common object. *Id.* Prima facie liability of partners may be rebutted by evidence that credit was given to the individual partner alone. *Id.* An election to give exclusive credit to one partner is established only by full knowledge of the relation of the parties between whom the choice is to be made. *Id.* A partnership formed for executing the street contract and to borrow money and execute notes therefor has no implied authority except in case of actual necessity or usage for the exercise of such power. (Md.) 677.

V. DOMESTIC RELATIONS.

Husband and wife. A marriage declared void by the Code by reason of the minority of the husband may nevertheless be ratified and confirmed by continuing the relation after coming of legal age. (Ga.) 362. A conveyance on the eve of marriage, to be in equity a fraud upon the intended wife, must be made without her consent or knowledge. (Ky.) 95. Where without her knowledge he gives all or the greater portion of his property to his children by a former marriage, it is a fraud on the wife's natural rights. *Id.* A deed to a woman and her husband, and "the survivor of them, in his or her own right," gives each a life estate, with a fee to the survivor. (Ill.) 655. The fact that land was purchased with pension money and conveyed to the wife does not exempt it from liability for the husband's debts. (Ky.) 552. The wife's conveyance of her separate real estate directly to her husband is void, unless the transaction can be sustained upon the principles of equity. (Ind.) 795. Where a wife executes articles of separation from her husband under menace, she is entitled to rescind and set the same aside. (S. D.) 562. A wife may by the misconduct of her husband be justified in living separate from him, and may maintain an independent action against him for her support, without regard to the question of divorce, and if she is destitute an allowance for attorney's fees may be made as for necessaries in the action. *Id.* Enticing a husband away from his wife and depriving her of his society and support give her no right of action. (Wis.) 420. Proof of the conduct of husband and wife toward each other, as to non-access, may be admitted on the question of legitimacy of a child. (Ky.) 102. The presumption of legitimacy from birth in wedlock may be overcome by clear proof to the contrary, as that either was incompetent to have sexual intercourse. *Id.* The mother is a competent witness on the question of the legitimacy of her child. *Id.*

Adultery of wife. A woman who, during abandonment of her husband, admits men to her periodically, is living in adultery within the meaning of the Kentucky Statutes. (Ky.) 102.

Rights of married women. The statutory defense which makes suretyship an exception to the general power conferred on married women to contract must be affirmatively proved in a suit on a promissory note which bears on its face evidence of coverture or suretyship. (Ind.) 406. Conveyance to a third person of land purchased by a married woman according to her direction does not violate any right of the husband. (Ill.) 511. A mortgage on the separate estate of a married woman to secure a loan to her husband may be upheld to the extent that the proceeds are invested in property purchased for her in her name. (Ind.) 795. Her remote grantees cannot set up the plea of coverture against such mortgage unless entitled to do so in equity and good conscience, or through mutual intention or agreement. *Id.* The proviso in the Code making the wife liable for debts in her separate business, and authorizing suits against her, does not extend to an action for injury to her person. (Md.) 680. A married woman is not estopped by covenants of warranty in a deed in which she joined with her husband, although she is given by statute power to contract as if unmarried. Such estoppel will not prevent her from relying upon a title so acquired to enable her to redeem from foreclosure sale. (Ill.) 724.

Dower right. The inchoate right of the wife to dower has a present value as property, and when she incumbers it by joining in a mortgage of her husband's land to secure his debt, she becomes his surety. (N. C.) 443. Where a wife joins her husband in a mortgage of his property to secure his debt, and he afterwards executes a second mortgage including the same and other property, the fund arising upon the sale of the personal property should be paid upon the debt secured by the first mortgage in exoneration of the wife's inchoate dower interest. *Id.* A widow's homestead right prevents the seisin of an heir and therefore excludes the dower right of his widow during continuance of the homestead right. (Wis.) 814. A conveyance just before marriage in fraud of the wife's right can be set aside by her only to the extent of her dower. *Id.* The mere failure of a grantor to inform his intended wife of a conveyance made by him just before marriage is not sufficient to make it fraudulent as to her. *Id.* A conveyance to his mother, to whom he was largely indebted, to carry out the wishes of his deceased father, is not fraudulent as to his wife. *Id.*

VI. PROPERTY RIGHTS AND REMEDIES.

Title to land. A title to land is not marketable if one link in the chain consists of a deed the execution and delivery of which can be established only by parol evidence. (N. Y.) 620. The title of one in possession of real estate under a valid unrecorded deed must prevail over that of a subsequent mortgagee from the same grantor. (N. Y.) 211. The rule that actual possession of real estate is sufficient notice to a mortgagee and to all the world of any right which the person in possession is able to establish is not changed by the fact that the property is occupied by numerous tenants. *Id.* Persons *in pari delicto* are without remedy against each other. (Ill.) 511. A deed given to defraud creditors will not support an action of ejectment against the grantor. *Id.* A common source of title will not prevent a subsequent grantee in possession of property from claiming adversely to a prior one, where, although he claims under a deed from the same person, each insists that the deed of the other is invalid and passes no title. (Iowa) 633.

Riparian and littoral rights. A non-navigable inland lake is the subject of private ownership, and where so owned neither the public nor the adjacent owner whose title extends to the margin has a right to boat upon or take fish from its waters. (Ohio) 578. Such riparian proprietor, however, is entitled to the use of its water for domestic and agricultural purposes. *Id.* Where one who owns land that surrounds and underlies such a lake, whose length is greater than its breadth, conveys a parcel that borders on the lake, the title of the purchaser extends to the center. *Id.* But if the call in the description be to and thence along the margin of the lake the title of the purchaser will extend to low-water mark only, or if the description be by metes and bounds, no reference being made to the lake, then only the land included within the lines as fixed by the terms used in the deed will pass. *Id.* A drain made by adjoining proprietors across their land to conduct waters drained by a swale cannot be stopped up or its course changed by the lower proprietor without consent after it has been acquiesced in by all parties. (Iowa) 277. The assent of the lower proprietor to the construction of a ditch on his land to connect with another on land of an upper proprietor is in the nature of a license which, having been accepted and acted on, cannot be set aside or disregarded. *Id.* Title to lands covered by navigable rivers is in the State, whether the tide ebbs and flows in them or not; hence the holder of the patent for land bordering on such river cannot recover damages for the removal of gravel from its bed. (Ark.) 559. The dividing line between proprietors of such lands and the State is the high-water mark. *Id.* A gravel bar covered by the ordinary state of high water, when steamers pass over it safely, but which is bare at low water and not covered by soil, is the property of the State. *Id.* The State holds title to the soil in navigable waters to low-water mark in trust for the people and chiefly for protection of the right of navigation. (Minn.) 89. Riparian owners may fill in and improve land under shallow water in front of their land to the line of navigability. These rights pertain to the use and occupancy of the soil below low-water mark. *Id.* The establishment of a dock or harbor line under legislative authority gives to the owners of the upland the privilege of filling in and building out to such line. *Id.* Where it is doubtful from the terms of the grant whether the mill or machinery for furnishing water indicates its quantity and measures the extent of power conveyed, or is referred to as a limit of the use of the mill or machinery, the former construction will be favored. (Me.) 446. A grant of a certain water privilege for the purpose of propelling a factory will be construed to measure the quantity of water and will not limit the use to machinery in the main building if some of it is in an annex and requires no additional power to propel it. *Id.* Where there is no limitation in the grant, parties can run their factory as many hours a day as they deem proper. *Id.* Owners of uplands bordering upon a bay after establishment of the dock lines may not only occupy and improve the same in connection with the dry land, but may stipulate in deeds to their grantee and obligate each and all to use and improve their land in conformity with the general plan within the dock line, and a court of equity will not, in favor of a grantee of the upland, set aside prior deeds of sites in submerged land. (Minn.) 89.

Conveyances. A deed-poll, when accepted by the grantee, becomes the mutual act of the parties, and the grantee is as much bound by its covenants as the grantor is. (Ind.) 604. Its acceptance by grantee gives it the effect of a written contract in respect to the obligations assumed by him, and it will be so regarded in determining the bar of the Statute of Limitations. *Id.*

Vendor's lien. The right to enforce a vendor's lien is not a right to rescind the contract, but to detain the goods until the time for payment and to sell and apply their proceeds to liquidation of the indebtedness. (Mo.) 147. It is an additional security for payment, and is not waived by resorting to any other security not itself a waiver of the lien. *Id.* Where facts are numerous, whether there has been such a delivery as devests the vendor's lien is a question for the jury. *Id.* Inferences of fact fairly within the scope of the evidence are not reviewable on appeal. *Id.* As between vendor and vendee, the lien is not devested by any species of constructive delivery so long as the vendor retains the actual custody of the goods, either by himself or his agent. *Id.* When the goods at the time the contract of sale is made, though in the legal custody and control, are not in the actual possession, of the vendee, but are so situated that he cannot obtain actual possession until a specific act is done by the vendor, if the vendee becomes insolvent before this act has been done, and the actual possession of the goods has not been changed, the vendor may detain the goods as security for the payment of the contract price. *Id.* When the contract stipulated for the doing of certain things by the vendor before delivery should be complete, presumptively there has been no actual delivery until the last of them has been performed. *Id.* The lien of the vendor is not destroyed by invoicing the goods to the purchaser, or by marking the packages with the purchaser's name, or by agreement that the goods shall remain with the vendor subject to storage, to be paid by vendee. *Id.* The lien for distilled spirits is not destroyed by putting them in a government warehouse. *Id.* The lien is not self-executing, and if not asserted in time it is lost. *Id.*

Mechanic's lien. The general phrase in the Act, "any other structure,"—following, as it does, a specific enumeration of works declared to be subject to a lien for labor and materials furnished for their construction, such as a "building," "ditch," "flume" and "tunnel,"—includes a railway. (Or.) 700. A person entitled to a lien on a railway for materials furnished for its construction may in his notice of lien confine his claim to that portion or section of the road in the construction of which his material was used. *Id.* Giant powder furnished by the manufacturer to a contractor is "material" within the Lien Law, for the value of which he is entitled to a lien. *Id.*

Leasehold estate. Each room in a building occupied by a separate tenant is a house, and a removal of property of a tenant, with the landlord's consent, from one room to another, taken under a new contract, defeats the landlord's lien. (N. M.) 691. A mere general creditor, although made party defendant in a suit to foreclose a chattel mortgage and to determine the existence of a lien claimed by

him, cannot question the validity of the mortgage. *Id.* Where a lease for years contains the clause of forfeiture for breach of its covenant, but no clause of re entry for such forfeiture, demand and re-entry is not the only mode by which the landlord may enforce the forfeiture. (W. Va.) 759. The execution of a second lease is a sufficient declaration of forfeiture without demand and re-entry, and the second lessee may maintain a lawful detainer against the first lessee in possession. *Id.* Going into possession under a parol lease, void because for longer than one year, does not create a yearly tenancy, although payment of an aliquot part of the annual rent is the evidence of such tenancy. A mere tenancy at will would be thereby created. (N. Y.) 221.

Mortgage estates. The legal or equitable effect of a mortgage and its contents are unaffected by statutes regulating a mode of signing, sealing and acknowledging them. The rights of parties are determined by the general rules of law and equity. (Ohio) 614. A mortgagor who while in possession verbally leased the premises cannot recover from the lessee for use of the premises preceding the mortgagee's entry and the lessee's attornment to him, where the mortgagee before expiration of the current quarter entered and took possession for conditions broken, and the tenant agreed to and at the expiration of the quarter actually paid him the rent for the whole quarter. (Me.) 566. It is not necessary in all cases to clothe the creditor with the legal title; if the intent to pledge as a security clearly appears and the instrument is duly executed and recorded, it is sufficient. (Ohio) 614. A mortgage to a partnership in its firm name, duly executed and recorded, is a valid lien upon the property as a security for indebtedness to it. *Id.* A grantee who assumes payment, as part of the purchase price, of a mortgage on the land given by his grantor, thereby undertakes to discharge the lien and not simply to cancel the mortgage debt, and his failure to do so will render him liable for at least nominal damages. (Mass.) 315. If several mortgages are assumed and the property is sold for the payment of the first one due, the grantee will be liable in damages to his grantor for the loss of security of the latter up to the amount of debt secured by them, though they are not yet due. *Id.* Set-off cannot be allowed in an action to recover unliquidated damages for breach of contract of a claim which is of the same kind as that which the action is brought to recover. *Id.* Where two or more persons are interested in mortgaged property, and one pays the mortgage for his own protection, he is entitled simply to succeed to the lien of the mortgage to the extent of his claim for indemnity by way of subrogation. (R. I.) 553. One who pays a mortgage is not entitled to an assignment thereof on the ground that it covers other property than his own, where the divided ownership and complication have arisen after the mortgage was given. *Id.* The title of a bona fide purchaser for value without notice at a mortgage sale is not affected by the fact that a tender was prevented by refusing to accept payment except on conditions. *Id.* A sale under a power in a mortgage will not be enjoined or set aside where the mortgagee is act-

ing with
perversi
sion is n
tage ma
ment of
of a mo
thereby
transferr
(Ill.) 724.
in gross c
voidable
50.

Forecle
gage, an
property
judgment
tion whet
charged
his right
to the m
mortgage
the sale o
the debt s
must appl
gage for
ble, in ex
C.) 443.
a railroad
granting
porated, a
an agreem
is bound t
liability to
quent gran
nant, alth
the deed
604.

Pledge.
possession
fice to cons
not be cre
house rece
hold the go
a contract
tion, evider
not be appe
But it may
terms by a
Where pers
actual deli
of parcels
in creation
requiring a
other custo
Id.

Estates o
appeal in p
delay on t
payment c
of other d
against de
within the
Disability
to present
to ownersh
under a wil
an action
Id. Admi
tee paymen
to take up
indorser an
thorizing t
on behalf o

a decedent's estate is saved from insolvency by parties who were infants at the time voluntarily sacrificing their own private funds they are entitled to have the whole estate and not merely their shares of it bear the burden. *Id.* Where decedent's assets are not sufficient to pay creditors in full a dividend in favor of a mortgage creditor can be computed only on the balance of the mortgage debt, where he accepted the proceeds on sale of the premises to pay debts as part payment of his claim. (S. C.) 875. Infant heirs are not liable to a contribution at law for the amount of liability voluntarily incurred by other heirs in saving the estate from insolvency. (Conn.) 119. A case will not be remanded for a more specific finding of facts where the facts necessary are stated in effect, and have been assumed by both parties, and the case heard on its merits without objection. *Id.* The superior court has jurisdiction of a suit to compel an intestate's estate, which has been saved from insolvency by the voluntary act of all the heirs of legal age, to refund the expense incurred thereby before distribution. *Id.*

Transfer by will. The words "in the presence of testator" in the Statute relating to wills do not mean that testator and the witnesses must be in the same room or in actual sight or inspection of the signing. (Mich.) 822. That the testatrix could not see the witnesses write their names or the scrivener write her own because done at a table in an adjoining room will not invalidate the execution of the will. *Id.* Where a word erased from a will is not so obliterated as to be illegible the interlineation and erasure are not a revocation but an alteration, and if as altered the instrument is not executed as required by statute the will remains intact as before. (N. H.) 383. The presumption in favor of the revocation of the will by canceling is repelled when the cancellation is made with a view to a new disposition of the property which fails to be carried into effect. In such case the will will stand as originally framed. *Id.* An adjudication that a person was not in such mental condition as to be incapable of taking care of himself, by the denial of an application to appoint a guardian for him, does not estop the applicant from claiming that such person is incompetent to make a will. (Vt.) 707. A verbal will reduced to writing and subscribed by two witnesses, of whom one is legatee and the other is his wife, is invalid, the husband not being a competent witness. (Ohio) 39. The two witnesses to a verbal will must be disinterested at the time of their attestation and their disqualification cannot be removed by subsequent renunciation. *Id.* The Statute as to the effect of a witness being a devisee or legatee is not applicable to verbal wills. *Id.* Meaning of words in a will is to be arrived at by considering them not only in their relation to the clause immediately in question but to the whole will. (Mass.) 740. Mere grammatical or ordinary sense of words used is not adhered to if repugnant or inconsistent with the rest of the instrument. *Id.* Where an intention to dispose of the whole estate appears a partial intestacy would not be recognized unless deficiencies of expression compel it. *Id.* The court, in order to carry into effect as far as possible the manifest intent of the testator as expressed by the whole will, will supply a defect by implication and so mould the language as to carry out such intent. *Id.* If he divides his estate into a number of parcels equal to the number of children living and deceased, and manifests a purpose to have each branch of his family have one portion, only providing for a devise over in case a particular branch becomes extinct, and in disposing of the portion of a deceased child provides that the income of it shall be divided among her three children during their lives, and in case one dies leaving issue one third of the principal shall be given to them absolutely, but in case there is no issue his share of the income shall be divided between the survivors, but does not dispose of the principal in such event, in case two die without issue and the other afterwards dies leaving issue the principal will all be divided between such issue, and no part of it will be given to the heirs and next of kin of the testator. *Id.* A clause declaring that testator "desires" is merely precatory and will not prevent the wife as devisee from taking the fee-simple title of the land and the absolute property in the subject of the bequest. (Iowa) 696.

Limitation of action. When a person is a nonresident and is absent from the State when a cause of action accrues against him, and during the period of the limitation occasionally comes into the State, such presence will not set the Statute of Limitations to running although plaintiff might at such time have commenced an action against him. (Ohio) 833. Under the Statute presence of the defendant in the State for the full period of the time limited, either continuously or in the aggregate, is necessary to constitute a bar of the action. *Id.* The period of six years from the discovery of fraud, within which an action to set aside a fraudulent conveyance must be brought, under the Code, does not apply where a judgment creditor brings an action to recover possession after death of a widow having a superior claim of dower, to whom he temporarily surrenders possession. (S. C.) 687. One who has made out a prima facie case for the recovery of land is not prevented from attacking as fraudulent a deed set up in defense because the time for bringing an action to set aside the conveyance has expired. *Id.*

Process and procedure. The words "process in an action" include an execution. (Ky.) 552. A coroner cannot execute process directed to the sheriff. Where he is authorized to act the process must be directed to him. *Id.* A citizen may be restrained from proceeding in another State to seize by garnishment the wages of a fellow citizen in evasion of the laws of their own State. (Tex.) 722. A return to writ of attachment without stating that the officer went upon the land is insufficient to sustain the attachment even after judgment as against the intervening rights of others. (Miss.) 727. The judgment in an attachment suit cannot create a lien operating retroactively so as to cut out intervening rights. *Id.* A cross-bill in a suit to remove a cloud from title will not be dismissed where the denial of title is qualified and explained by showing a conveyance canceled was the foundation of the denial. *Id.* A garnishee is not bound to set up an Exemption Law in favor of the principal defendant, who fails to make a defense. (Tenn.) 412. An Exemption Law of one State has no effect in an action in another State. *Id.* Failure of a garnishee to state facts which show an exemption of the principal will deprive him of the protection of a judgment against him, as against the principal defendant the latter has not been cited to appear in the garnishment proceedings. (Tex.) 321. Where an employé of a foreign railway company sues to recover his wages the fact that the company has been garnished in the State of its creation by a creditor of such employé, service of summons being obtained only by publication, is no defense to such suit. (Kan.) 385.

Equitable relief. A reconveyance by a natural daughter to her father, given by her without time for reflection or advice while deeply moved by his distress and urged thereto by the family lawyer, will be set aside. (Va.) 261. Relief will not be denied on a cross-bill in a suit to remove a cloud on title because defendant shows a perfect title on which he might maintain ejectment. (Miss.) 727. A party will not be enjoined from erecting a building on his own land, on piles in a river, merely because others may follow his example and build such structures on their own lands and thereby give rise to dangers from fire, and to the public health. (Wis.) 808. Some special injury or necessity to protect the rights of someone is necessary as a basis for injunction; as wrong without damage, or damage without wrong, does not constitute a cause of private action. That a building will violate an ordinance will not of itself give cause of action. *Id.* A statute which makes it unlawful for the owner of ground having the lawful right to use it by driving piles within a river, and imperatively commands the court to enjoin such use, is a usurpation of judicial power and unconstitutional. *Id.* If a party having no knowledge of the Bohemian oat scheme relies entirely upon the statement of another as to the corporation and its business he is not precluded from maintaining an action for fraud against those who induced him to give his note in pursuance of such scheme although fraudulent. (Mich.) 476. If a man knows that a scheme is fraudulent and goes into it solely for the purpose of making money, though he may not be equally in fault with the promoter, a court on the ground of public policy will deny him any relief against the other party. *Id.*

Partition. Purchasers in good faith of land in a portion of which their grantors have in fact only a life estate, who make valuable improvements before learning of the defect in their title, should be allowed, on a sale in partition, the value of the improvements before division of the proceeds. (Iowa) 289. Such allowance should be made instead of compelling claimant to bring an action at law under the Occupying Claimant Act. *Id.* A court of equity, having acquired jurisdiction of the case, has power to afford the proper equitable relief. *Id.*

Debtor and creditor. A creditor of an insolvent has the right to prove and have dividends upon his entire claim, irrespective of collateral securities held by him. (N. Y.) 459. Transferring a just debt to an attorney, and causing attachment and garnishment to issue and be prosecuted in an adjoining State to evade the laws of this State exempting wages from such process, constitutes no cause of action in favor of the debtor against the creditor. (Ga.) 514. If an equitable attachment is prohibited the property cannot be reached in equity merely by a change in form of proceedings. (Mass.) 623. A suit to reach and apply property to the payment of a debt cannot be maintained, either under general equity jurisdiction or under a statute, where the property is in its nature attachable by trustee process, but not in the particular case because of a statute prohibition against collecting that kind of a debt by attachment by trustee process or otherwise. *Id.* One of several judgment debtors, who holds the judgment out to the world as valid and procures a sale of his own land on execution, becoming himself purchaser in another's name, is estopped from claiming that the judgment was paid before the sale in order to prevent the exercise of the right of redemption by another judgment creditor. (Ill.) 566. An execution cannot be said to be issued so as to preserve the lien of a judgment until it is delivered to an officer to execute. *Id.* A discharge of a judgment debtor in bankruptcy although the judgment has ceased to be a lien does not render it unavailing for the redemption of the debtor's land from paying under a prior judgment. *Id.* A gift may be made of the balance of a debt after payment of part only, although payment of such part cannot constitute an accord and satisfaction. A receipt in full may be evidence of the gift. (N. Y.) 257. A discharge under Insolvency Laws will not release existing debts due to nonresident creditors who do not come in and prove their claim in the insolvency proceedings. (Mass.) 644. There is no intent in the Insolvency Law to refuse foreign creditors access to local courts to enforce their claims after their discharge. *Id.* Letters-patent may be sold and transferred by a court of equity through its master for the benefit of creditors, although the owner is a nonresident of the State, if the court has acquired jurisdiction to bind him with a personal judgment. (Mass.) 309.

Redemption from execution sale. No exception can be made from the right allowed by statute, of redemption from sale under execution decree, etc., in the case of a sale on a creditor's bill of the property of an insolvent mining company. (Ill.) 598. A court, by requiring conveyance to its receiver in a creditor's suit of real property which might have been seized and sold on an execution at law, cannot thereby take it out of the operation of the Statute in relation to redemption. *Id.*

Trade-marks and labels. A label cannot be treated as a trade-mark which does not indicate the maker of the article but only that he was a member of an association and as such had the right to use the mark, its rightful use belonging to many not connected in business and unknown to each other. (Mass.) 640. To entitle one to restrain an invasion of his right of property in a trade-mark he must show ownership thereof by reason of some business to which it is incident, not merely that it was a personal privilege which he possesses as member of an association embracing varied interests. *Id.* The fraudulent use of marks and labels will not be enjoined at the instance of officers and members of an association which has adopted a label to indicate articles manufactured by its members. *Id.* Labels and trade-marks may be sold or transferred by a proprietor of a business so as to prevent him from afterward using them to the detriment of his vendee. (Me.) 570. The breach of a stipulation in the sale of a plant, label and trade-mark of a business to employ the seller to manage the business will not forfeit the buyer's exclusive right to use the label and trade-mark. *Id.* The purchaser of the right to their exclusive use cannot have an injunction on accounting if he has exercised his right so as to mislead the public and in no way indicated that he had succeeded the original producer and originator of the mark. *Id.* A corrected label may be protected in favor of mortgagees in possession the improper use having been made by mortgagors before they lost possession. *Id.* Purchasers of labels and trade-marks will be restrained from using them so as to lead the public to suppose the goods were packed by the vendors. *Id.* A suit will not lie in favor of one corporation to enjoin the use of a name by another corporation, nor will suit lie to protect the first name as a trade-name, when taken subject to whatever interference might be permitted by the Statute. (Mass.) 320.

VII. DAMAGES FOR TORTS.

Damages for personal injuries. Suffering in mind as well as in body is ground for damages in a personal injury. (Ill.) 765. No allegation of special damage in a suit for personal injury is necessary in order to permit recovery for mental suffering which was inseparable from bodily injuries. *Id.* An averment that plaintiff suffered great pain and agony is sufficient to cover any effect upon the mind that resulted from the injury. *Id.* Instructions which virtually tell the jury that certain facts constitute negligence are properly refused. *Id.* A defect in a petition setting up a claim for damages which is special to plaintiff is not reached by a general demurrer. (Tex.) 180. The words "all persons" in the Statute, requiring notice of blasting operations to give persons and teams time to retire to a distance, do not apply to workmen in quarries. (Me.) 450.

Carriers' negligence; injury to passengers. Passenger carriers are bound to exercise the utmost care, skill and diligence consistent with the nature of their business in the matter of access to their trains and of departure from them; but if a passenger is injured while attempting to alight at a regular station, the carrier, to relieve itself of liability, must show that it used that degree of care which the law imposed. (Md.) 673. The existence of negligence cannot be determined as a matter of law unless the inference from the fact is certain and incontrovertible. *Id.* Whether or not a passenger was negligent in attempting to alight from the car in the night when his station was called is a question for the jury. *Id.* He cannot be held guilty of contributory negligence as a matter of law because he failed before leaving the car to look out for an approaching train by which he was injured. *Id.* A passenger on the railroad train during the time required to repair a defect in the road is entitled to all the rights of a passenger upon a moving train including protection from willful misconduct of the company's servants. (N. Y.) 224. The porter of a railroad car under contract with its owner, who sells separate tickets for privileges and furnishes his own servants, is the servant of the railroad company, for whose acts it is responsible, notwithstanding any contract between the company and the owner of the car. *Id.* As to whether a sleeping-car porter was a servant of the railroad company at the time he assaulted a passenger is a question for the jury, where an accident rendered it necessary to transfer the passenger to another train. *Id.* A carrier is liable for an unlawful and improper act of its servant towards its passenger while engaged in a duty which the carrier owes to a passenger, whatever motive may incite its commission. *Id.* It is no defense to a suit against a carrier by a passenger for assault committed by its servant that at the time of the assault the servant had finished the temporary service he had undertaken to render the passenger, if the duty still rested on the carrier to protect the passenger. *Id.*

Infants, negligence not imputed to. An infant is not to be charged with the negligence of the person having it in charge. (N. J.) 842. The right of action of a child of tender years for damages for injuries caused by negligence is not lost by reason of the carelessness of a sister's supervision, which was in part the cause of the injury. *Id.* Omission of duty by a parent is not to be imputed to a child in a suit by it for damages caused by negligence of a third person. (Ill.) 494. Whether a child six years of age is guilty of negligence is a question for the jury. *Id.*

Master and servant. Instructions to an employé when sent on an errand not to break the law, knowing that the errand is likely to excite resistance, will not relieve the employer from liability for a wrongful assault made by the employé while engaged in the business of his employer. (Pa.) 204. The law requires those who use dangerous agencies in their business to observe the greatest care in their custody and use, and this duty cannot be shifted by a master to his servant. Their proper custody and use become part of the servant's employment and his negligence is imputable to the master, and it is immaterial as to what use may have been made of it by the servant. (Ohio) 464. A master who commits running his elevator to an employé ignorant of the service is bound to furnish him with an instructor and will be liable to him for injury resulting from negligence or incompetence of such instructor. (N. Y.) 818. An instruction is erroneous which gives the jury to understand that the master's whole duty was performed if he furnish an instructor as competent as he was himself. *Id.* Fellow servants owe to each other the duty to exercise ordinary care in the prosecution of their work. (Me.) 450. A master is not liable for injuries to one servant resulting from the negligence of his fellow servant where he used due diligence and care in selecting them. (Ill.) 490. It is not conclusive against the right of a child to recover against his employer for negligence in giving him dangerous work that he had done it for some time before he was injured. *Id.* The rule that a common master is not liable for negligence of a fellow servant does not apply where the injured servant is a child incapable of comprehending the risk. *Id.* A boy twelve years old, who is injured while attempting under orders of the foreman to do a service disconnected from that for which he was employed, may recover damages from his employer. *Id.* An averment that plaintiff had no knowledge of the danger of continuing in the service of his employer, which existed because of the latter's failure to provide suitable machinery and competent workmen, is necessary to warrant a recovery for injuries resulting from such failure. An allegation of freedom from fault is not sufficient. (Ind.) 636.

Negligent collision at railroad crossing. Where a railroad company to show that a train sounded a whistle on approaching the road crossing gives evidence that there were other road crossings in the vicinity, witnesses living near other crossings may testify that no whistle was sounded near them. (Ind.) 594. A person present when others started out upon a drive may be permitted to testify as to where they were going. *Id.* In order to entitle a person injured by a collision with a railway train at a crossing to recover damages he must show that both he and his driver vigilantly used their eyes and ears to ascertain if a train was approaching, and the fact that no whistle was sounded cannot be considered in determining his negligence. *Id.* A person injured in crossing a railroad track must show affirmatively that his fault or negligence did not contribute to the injury. This is done, however, where all facts illustrating his conduct are shown and inference of proper care and caution on his part arises therefrom. *Id.* The fact that a train is running faster than its usual speed does not excuse one from exercising all the care and caution required when attempting to cross the track. *Id.* Obstructions to sight or hearing in the direction of an approaching train require increased care in proportion to the increase of danger that may come from the use of the highway. *Id.* A recovery by one guilty of contributory negligence for injuries resulting in part from the negligence of another is permitted where the latter before the injury discovered, or might have discovered, the peril of the former, and neglected to use the means at his command to prevent the injury. (Mo.) 783. Negligence of defendant in such cases in failing to discover the peril and to use means at his command to prevent injury need not be set out as a separate independent cause of action. *Id.* Failure to look for a train before turning upon a railroad track upon a street will not prevent recovery for injuries by a train coming at a lawful speed if by looking he would not have discovered that it was imprudent to drive on the track. *Id.* The plaintiff's contributory negligence in failing to look out for the train if such defense is alleged, and the question whether or not if he was negligent the railroad employés could with reasonable care have discovered his situation and have stopped the train in time to prevent the accident, were properly submitted to the jury. *Id.*

Negligent injury to cattle by railroad. Pro-

vision of
fence its
live stock
(Or.) 135.
requiring
the inclos
where th
some exce
to go at
track and
not liable
agement c
on the oth
allowing h
of omissio
are injure
unless it ex
vent that
tributed to
ting his stc
cause of tl
law it is
Where a p
which mad
and which
able with it
liable for c
being out of
Telegraph
telegraph c
reason of no
will not, un
an action fo
Libel and
no libel in a
the court m
is admitted,
and admit of
publication a
had become
constitutes a
no crime, for
him in his b
as a teller.
defamatory n
or inadverte
with an hones
ing that a tea
is using the
without autl
Written word
fession or calli
an innuendo is
set upon the w
have that mea
plaintiff. *Id.*
is not necessa
profession or
clergyman to
be given to th
was made in
person slander
tionable *per se.*
damage may
spoken were ac
necessary alleg
been insufficie
been waived.
ter suit comme
ted upon the qu
the evidence su
ation an instru
cover by reason

fused. *Id.* The jury may find that words spoken by a clergyman were spoken maliciously and for the purpose of injuring a physician in his business. *Id.* A declaration in a suit for slander claiming special damages for loss of trade will not be held to be insufficient for failing to set out the names of those who seek to employ plaintiff after proceeding to trial without noticing such failure. The objection by a request for instruction comes too late. *Id.* An action will lie for a false imputation although not actually defamatory if made with a purpose of injuring plaintiff in his profession and such injury follows as the natural result of the speaking of the words. *Id.*

Conversion of property. Where several attaching creditors conduct proceedings simultaneously, they are joint actors, and, where the suits were consolidated and proceeded together, either is guilty of a conversion in case any levies are tortious. (Mo.) 147. Trover and replevin are concurrent remedies. A party may claim as exempt a judgment for the conversion of property, which he could have replevied as exempt. (Wis.) 467. The tort in conversion of goods may be waived, and an action brought against the wrong-doer upon an implied contract of sale, although he still retains possession of the property. (N. Y.) 216. The title to property converted passes to the wrong-doer when the owner elects to treat the transaction as a sale, and brings an action *ex contractu* against him for the price. *Id.* An election to bring an action *ex contractu* against one who has converted property, upon the implied contract of sale, precludes a subsequent action for conversion of the same property against other persons who participated in the same acts which have already been treated as constituting a sale of the property. *Id.* A judgment roll in a former suit by the same plaintiff against other defendants is admissible to show that he had elected to treat as a sale acts which he now claims to constitute conversion of property. *Id.*

Malicious prosecution. An action for malicious prosecution will not lie where the party accused of a criminal offense was not apprehended and process for his arrest was not issued. (N. Y.) 47. Although an action for libel or slander may in such case be maintained, yet an action brought for malicious prosecution cannot be retained if the defamatory words are not set out in the complaint. *Id.*

Nuisance. A fence erected maliciously, and with no other purpose than to shut out the light and air from a neighbor's window, is a nuisance. (Mich.) 183. A concealed well under a house, from which noxious vapors arise, constitutes a nuisance for which the owner is liable for damages sustained by a tenant who had no knowledge of it. (Mich.) 682. Overflow from the river may be kept off from land by a barrier or embankment if the owners of land nearer the river will co-operate in erecting a levee on the bank to protect the lands from overflow. (Cal.) 575.

Trespass on real property. A person has no right from mere caprice or express malice to drive upon and destroy a strip of grass growing on the sides of a highway, in the wrought or traveled part of the road, of which another person owns the fee. (Mich.) 472. A defense in an action of trespass that plaintiff is a married woman, and has proved no title, where the husband testifies that the land belongs to her, cannot avail. (Pa.) 202. Even the owner of real estate has no right to make a forcible entry upon the actual possession of another who is not a recent trespasser or intruder. (N. C.) 537. In addition to the damages for a forcible entry, he can recover for any injury inflicted upon his person or personal property, and exemplary damages may be recovered if the act is done in a wanton and reckless manner. *Id.* Occupation of a parsonage by a minister after his suspension does not render him a trespasser or permit his forcible ejection by church officers, at least where he is appointed by an annual conference. (N. Y.) 710. Where numerous acts are committed and their continuance threatened under a claim of right by a person on the land of another, which acts constitute trespass, the owner of the property injured may resort in the first instance to a court of equity for appropriate relief. (Ohio) 578.

VIII. CRIMINAL LAW AND PRACTICE.

Crimes and their punishment. Merely pushing the horses of another from grass growing on the right of way of a railroad, the fee remaining in the owner of the land appropriated, and defending against the attack of the owner of the trespassing horses, does not make one guilty of assault and battery. (Mich.) 472. The *corpus delicti* of making dynamite for the unlawful destruction of the lives of persons is sufficiently proved by having such explosives in possession, keeping them concealed and on different occasions threatening to take the lives of certain persons. (Ill.) 837. An Act does not embrace more than one subject because it prescribes regulation as to manufacture, transportation, use and sale of explosives and prescribes a punishment for their violation or prohibits their manufacture or procurement for the unlawful destruction of life or property. *Id.* There is a sufficient criminal intent to sustain conviction where one compels another through fear of death to make an actual attempt to commit a crime, although the latter acts solely under compulsion. (N. C.) 297. So, a husband is guilty of an assault with intent to commit rape upon his wife, where by threats of death he compels another man to attempt to ravish her. *Id.* An accessory before the fact being punishable as a principal any person abetting or assisting in the offense is to be punished as provided in the section relating to an accessory. (Ill.) 837. Where the violation of a statute is declared a felony and the Criminal Code of the State declares that a felony is punishable by death or confinement in the penitentiary, a statute is sufficiently definite to authorize imprisonment in the penitentiary although not stating so expressly in terms. (Ill.) 837. A minimum punishment of three years except in cases of the first offense, with a maximum of fifteen years, is not cruel or unusual punishment. (Mich.) 685. Where the statute makes premeditation an essential element the fact that the accused was drunk at the time when he committed the crime may be considered for the purpose of determining whether or not there was premeditation. (Ind.) 83. Intoxication of a person cannot be proved by the intoxication of a companion who had taken the same number of drinks. (Pa.) 801.

Practice and procedure. In a criminal trial it is error in the court to determine the fact of the sickness of an absent juror and to discharge the jury from further consideration of the case in the absence of defendants from the court room, they being charged with felony. (Kan.) 774. Plea of guilty to an information charging larceny in one count and horse stealing in another applies to both counts and authorizes a sentence for horse stealing. (Mich.) 685. Religious opinion or belief or want of the same is not a test or qualification of the competency of citizens to testify in courts of justice under a constitutional provision for the protection of religious liberty. (Ill.) 837. A presumption arises that a person found in possession of explosives not required in his business procured them for an unlawful purpose where the intention for using them for such purpose was avowed. *Id.* It is not a correct principle of law that evidence of police and private detectives should be received with a large degree of caution. *Id.* A party cannot in general demand the exclusion of evidence called out in fair response to questions asked without objection. (Mo.) 608. Objection to the admission of testimony must state opportunely the reasons therefor in order to preserve the rulings for review. *Id.* Where no objection is taken at the hearing the fact that a witness testified for the State without being first sworn is not ground for error. *Id.* The benefit of good character of a person charged with crime is not limited to cases where there is a reasonable doubt; evidence of good character may of itself create the doubt. (Pa.) 801. Instructions designed to cast discredit or suspicion upon a defense which an accused person is making in apparent good faith are not regarded with favor. (Ind.) 83. A statute permitting a verdict during voluntary absence of defendant does not violate his constitutional right to be present at the trial. (Mo.) 608. A verdict finding the defendant guilty without specifying any person by name is not void for uncertainty where but one person was put on trial although others were indicted with him. (Ill.) 837. An arrest of judgment is granted for a defect appearing upon the face of the record. Knowledge derived from the evidence cannot be considered. (N. C.) 259.

INDEX TO NOTES.

(The General Index follows this.)

GENERAL I

TO

OPINIONS, NOTES A

(Separate Index to Notes pre

the name of a surety before the approval of a bond, upon the liability of other sureties. *State* v. *McGonigle* (Mo.) 735

ANIMALS. See also EVIDENCE, 35.

1. Liberating an animal captured during close time in violation of statute interferes with no legal right or title of the person illegally holding it captive, and gives him no right of action. *James* v. *Wood* (Me.) 448

2. Following a moose in a forest until it becomes snowbound, and then capturing it during close time, is a violation of Me. Rev. Stat. chap. 30, § 9, prohibiting hunting, killing, or destroying a moose during that time. *Id.*

3. The common-law rule requiring an owner to keep his stock within his own enclosure is not in force in Oregon. *Moses* v. *Southern P. R. Co.* (Or.) 135

NOTES AND BRIEFS.

Feræ naturæ, property in; game laws of various States. 448

APPEAL AND ERROR.

1. An attack upon one of several paragraphs of a complaint, made for the first time in the assignment of errors, will be unavailing, even although the paragraph assailed is radically defective. *Louisville, N. A. & C. R. Co.* v. *Corps* (Ind.) 636

2. Objections to the admission of testimony in criminal as well as in civil cases must state opportunely the reasons therefor, in order to preserve rulings for a review. *State* v. *Hope* (Mo.) 608

3. An objection to the admission of evidence in answer to a question propounded to a witness, on the ground that it is "improper and incompetent," or that it is "irrelevant and immaterial and does not rebut anything," is too general to raise any question for the consideration of the appellate court. *Cincinnati, I. St. L. & C. R. Co.* v. *Howard* (Ind.) 593

4. The exclusion of a question designed only to show the bias of a witness already effectually impeached by record evidence is not prejudicial error. *Tyler* v. *Waddingham* (Conn.) 657

5. The fact that a witness testified on behalf of the State in a criminal case without having first been sworn is not ground for error, where no objection was made at the hearing before he was fully cross-examined. *State* v. *Hope* (Mo.) 608

6. An order limiting the number of witnesses on each side on a certain point, when made at or near the beginning of a trial without objection by either party, cannot be complained of afterwards. *McConnell* v. *Osage* (Iowa) 778

7. Erroneous instructions are not cured by others contradicting them. *Chicago City R. Co.* v. *Wilcox* (Ill.) 494

8. A case cannot be affirmed on other grounds, where erroneous instructions on one count have been given to the jury. *Amaker* v. *New* (S. C.) 687

9. In an action at law, the inferences of fact made by the trial court are not reviewable on appeal, provided they are fairly within the scope of the evidence. *Conrad* v. *Fisher* (Mo. App.) 147

10. A case will not be remanded for a more specific finding where the facts necessary are stated in effect and have been assumed by both parties, and the case heard on its merits without objection. *Benedict* v. *Chase* (Conn.) 120

11. Where a defendant was totally deprived of his defense by the action of the court in first sustaining a demurrer to his answer, which set up a contract for the sole agency of the goods purchased by him, and a breach thereof by plaintiffs, and then, on his amended answer setting up the invalidity of the contract as an absolute defense, making a ruling, after the case was submitted on the pleadings, to the effect that the contract was valid, although the latter ruling was correct the judgment will be reversed. *Newell* v. *Meyendorff* (Mont.) 440

12. Costs on motion are regarded on appeal as in the discretion of the court below. *Below* v. *Robbins* (Wis.) 467

NOTES AND BRIEFS.

Exception to rulings; necessity of, in court below; must be specific and definite; must state grounds; what bill of exceptions must show; what record must show. 608

APPROPRIATIONS.

An appropriation is "made by law" for the salary of an officer by a State Constitution which plainly declares what the amount of his compensation shall be; and no legislative appropriation is necessary in that case to authorize payment. *State, Rotwitt,* v. *Hickman* (Mont.) 403

ARBITRATION. See also EVIDENCE, 25.

1. The certificate of architects which is, by a contract, made a condition precedent to a right of action, must be obtained before an action can be maintained on the contract, if the architects have not been guilty of fraud or collusion. *Hanley* v. *Walker* (Mich.) 207

2. Recovery upon a *quantum meruit* cannot be based on a contract which makes a certificate of architects a condition precedent to a right of action, where the certificate has not been obtained. *Id.*

3. Remedying the defects pointed out by architects, but not in the ways suggested by them, and without obtaining from them the certificate made by the contract a condition precedent to a right of action, cannot give a cause of action. Plaintiffs cannot substitute their own assertion, or the opinion of the jury, for the decision of the architects. *Id.*

ARREST.

1. The mere fact that a person is drunk on the streets will not authorize his arrest, under an ordinance for being "found drunk in the streets, hallooing or making an unusual noise." *State* v. *Hunter* (N. C.) 529

2. An officer must determine at his peril whether an offense has been committed, before making an arrest without a warrant, where his power to arrest without warrant is expressly

confined to cases where he sees an offense committed, or where he knows it has been committed, and has reasonable ground to apprehend an escape. *Id.*

3. An ordinance providing that a person may be arrested and taken, without warrant or hearing, to the station-house because he refuses to "move on," and, in the opinion of an officer, "unreasonably persists in remaining so as to incommode others passing," violates a constitutional provision that "no person shall be taken, imprisoned . . . or in any manner deprived of his life, liberty, or property, but by the law of the land." *Id.*

4. If all except one of those who are obstructing a sidewalk disperse upon request of an officer, the one remaining is not subject to arrest for obstructing the free passage of the street "and failing to disperse upon notice." *Id.*

NOTES AND BRIEFS.

Constitutional protection; with and without warrant; for crime committed within view; for breach of the peace; for misdemeanors; right of private person to arrest; how made; notice to person arrested; right to use necessary means; authority to break in doors; calling for assistance; right to kill in making arrest; right to resist. 529

ASSAULT AND BATTERY.

1. Merely pushing off the horses of another from grass which one is entitled to cut in a highway, where the other is wantonly endeavoring to spoil the grass, and then defending against the latter's attack, does not make one guilty of assault and battery. *People* v. *Foss* (Mich.) 472

2. An innkeeper may be justified, on a prosecution for assault and battery, in removing from his hotel a person who was not there as a guest or on business with guests, if he did not use excessive force, and first requested him to depart. *State* v. *Steele* (N. C.) 516

NOTES AND BRIEFS.

Defending rights in land. 472

ASSESSMENT. See also PUBLIC IMPROVEMENTS.

NOTES AND BRIEFS.

For special benefit; power to make; districts; for paving streets; for repaving; cost of grading; rule of apportionment; front-foot rule. 369

ASSIGNMENT.

NOTES AND BRIEFS.

Of open account. 63

ASSOCIATIONS. See also INJUNCTION, 13.

1. Individual members of an unincorporated association are liable for contracts made in the name of the association, without regard to the question whether they so intended, or so understood the law, and even if the other party contracted in form with the association, and was ignorant of the names of the individual members composing it. *Lawler* v. *Murphy* (Conn.) 113

2. The members of a social club may regulate through their by-laws the causes for the expulsion of members and the manner of effecting the same, when such power has been expressly conferred upon them by the Legislature. *Com. Burt,* v. *Union League* (Pa.) 195

3. The enforcement of the provisions of the charter and by-laws of a social club, which provide for the expulsion of members, in the case of a person who became a member after their adoption, can deprive him of no legal constitutional right on the ground that his personal franchise and property-rights are subject to the action of a majority of the members. *Id.*

4. By-laws of a social club providing for the expulsion of members guilty of acts or conduct which the board of directors shall deem disorderly or injurious to the interests or hostile to the objects of the club are not unreasonable, arbitrary, or oppressive, nor do they violate any principle of natural justice. *Id.*

5. Failure of a by-law to designate and define the various and specific acts which will be deemed disorderly within the rule subjecting members of a social club to expulsion therefor, the determination of which question is left to the board of directors, does not render the by-law illegal. *Id.*

6. A minor offense is sufficient to justify the expulsion of a member from a social club, if the club acts in good faith and exercises only the powers conferred by its charter. *Id.*

7. A social club, in the trial of a charge against one of its members, conviction of which will, under its charter and by-laws, subject him to expulsion, acts as a judicial tribunal, and its judgment therein renders the case *res judicata*, and will preclude its re-examination on its merits by a judicial court. *Id.*

NOTES AND BRIEFS.

By-laws conclusive on members. 175

Conclusiveness of expulsion from. 194

ASSUMPSIT. See ACTION OR SUIT, 4.

ATTACHMENT. See also LEVY AND SEIZURE, 5.

The judgment of a court in an attachment case cannot create a lien operating retroactively, so as to cut out intervening rights of others. *West* v. *People's Bank* (Miss.) 727

NOTES AND BRIEFS.

Validity of; how law construed; sufficiency of levy to create lien. 728

For what garnishee held liable. 63

BANKRUPTCY.

The discharge of a judgment debtor in bankruptcy, although the judgment has ceased to be a lien, does not render it unavailing for the purpose of redeeming the debtor's lands from sale under a prior judgment. *Pease* v. *Ritchie* (Ill.) 566

BANKS AND BANKING.

1. The owner of drafts, who indorses them in blank and places them with a bank for collection, may avail himself of the benefit of a restrictive indorsement placed thereon by such bank when it transmitted them to its correspondent for the purpose of effecting such collection. *Freeman's Nat. Bank* v. *National Tube Works Co.* (Mass.) 42

2. The legal title to commercial paper indorsed "For collection" passes only so far as to enable the indorsee to demand, receive, and sue for the money to be paid. Upon such indorsement the owner may control his paper until it is paid, and may intercept the proceeds thereof in the hands of an intermediate agent. *Id.*

3. A bank's indorsement of commercial paper directing payment "for account of itself" does not imply that it is the owner of the paper, where the indorsement of the bank from which its title was derived was of the same kind. *Id.*

4. A bank to which commercial paper has been transmitted for collection will not be permitted to dispute the right of the owner to stop payment thereof, although it has made credits or advances to an intermediate collecting agent on account of the paper, if the same were made before the paper had been collected; nor can such advances be recovered from the owner as money paid for his use. *Id.*

BICYCLE. See also HIGHWAYS, 5, 6.

BILL OF SALE. See HORSE RACING.

BILLS AND NOTES. See also BANKS AND BANKING; REPLEVIN.

1. Certainty as to the payor and payee, the amount to be paid, and the terms of payment, is the essential quality of a negotiable promissory note; and that certainty must continue until the obligation is discharged. *Hegeler* v. *Comstock* (S. D.) 393

2. A note promising to pay a certain sum, "with interest from date until paid, at the rate of 10 per cent per annum, 8 per cent if paid when due,"—is not negotiable because of uncertainty in the amount to be paid. *Id.*

3. Blanks in the body of a note where the amount and place of payment should be named will not render the note non-negotiable, if the amount is expressed in figures at the head of the note,—especially under a statute making negotiable any written promise to pay money which is signed by the promisor. *Witty* v. *Michigan Mut. L. Ins. Co.* (Ind.) 365

4. Knowledge of a warranty on a sale in which a note was given will not affect the rights of a bona fide purchaser of the note for value before maturity, if he had no knowledge of a breach of the warranty. *Miller* v. *Ottaway* (Mich.) 428

5. A person who fraudulently places in circulation the negotiable instrument of another, whether made by him or by his apparent authority, and thereby renders him liable to pay the sum to a bona fide purchaser, is guilty of a tort, and, in the absence of special circumstances diminishing its value, is presumptively liable to the injured party for the face value thereof. *Metropolitan Elev. R. Co.* v. *Kneeland* (N. Y.) 253

6. If an innocent party has been defrauded into giving notes, he is not obliged to contest them in the hands of a stranger on any information short of a certainty that the latter is not a bona fide holder, before bringing an action against the party defrauding him. *Knight* v. *Linzey* (Mich.) 476

BLASTING.

The words "all persons," in Me. Rev. Stat. chap. 17, §§ 23, 24, requiring notice by those engaged in blasting before an explosion, so that "all persons" or teams shall have time to retire to a safe distance, do not apply to the workmen in the quarries. *Hare* v. *McIntyre* (Me.) 450

BOHEMIAN OATS. See CONTRACTS, 21.

BONDS. See also CONTRACTS, 19.

1. The issue of county bonds to be paid by tax, for the purpose of procuring seed grain for needy farmers, is for a public purpose; and a statute authorizing counties to take such action is not unconstitutional. Such tax is for the necessary support of the poor. *State, Goodwin,* v. *Nelson County* (N. D.) 283

2. An amended city charter providing that the city may borrow money by issuing bonds not to exceed the sum of $100,000, omitting the words of the former charter, "but never in any form to make the city liable for exceeding that amount in the aggregate," gives authority to issue bonds subsequent to the date of the charter to the extent of $100,000, although a bonded indebtedness already existed. *Mauldin* v. *Greenville* (S. C.) 291

3. A surety is not liable on a bond signed by him alone, but purporting to be signed by the principal also, where he did not consent to a delivery of the bond without the principal's signature. *Goodyear Dental Vulcanite Co.* v. *Bacon* (Mass.) 486

4. A surety who signs a bond in ignorance of the fact that the other sureties thereon have been released by erasing the name of a surety

cannot be held liable on the bond, as he did not intend to become the sole surety. *State* v. *McGonigle* (Mo.) 785

5. Erasing the name of a surety at his request, and the substitution of another before the approval of an official bond, and without the consent or knowledge of the other sureties, discharges them, when the approval of the bond by the court was made with knowledge of the substitution and of the fact that the other sureties had no knowledge thereof. *Id.*

NOTES AND BRIEFS.

What essential to bind surety. 486

Of officer; liability of surety; erasures; estoppel. 786

Municipal; action to cancel; when maintainable. 249

Conclusiveness of recitals; right of municipality to dispute; protection of bona fide purchaser. 851

BOOK-AGENTS. See PEDDLERS.

BOUNDARIES.

1. If a description be by metes and bounds, no reference being made therein to a lake by which the land lies, then only the land included within the lines as fixed by the terms used by the parties to the deed will pass to the grantee. *Lembeck* v. *Nye* (Ohio) 578

2. If the call in the description of land lying by an inland non-navigable lake be to and thence along the margin of the lake, the title of the purchaser will extend to low-water mark only. *Id.*

3. Where one who owns a tract of land that surrounds and underlies a non-navigable lake, the length of which is distinguishably greater than its breadth, conveys a parcel thereof that borders on the lake, by a description that makes the lake one of its boundaries, the presumption is that the parties do not intend that the grantor should retain the title to the land between the edge of the water and the centre of the lake; and the title of the purchaser, therefore, will extend to the centre thereof. *Id.*

BRIDGES. See also CONTRACTS, 7; COUNTIES, 1; HIGHWAYS, 2, NOTES AND BRIEFS.

A statute authorizing a city to build bridges within its limits does not necessarily revoke authority given to the county by general statute, without restriction as to locality, to build a bridge within those limits. As there may be bridges serving only a city purpose, so there may be others demanded in the same territory for county purposes; and where the circumstances create this demand, and the bridge is for the use and benefit of the people of the county at large or of some considerable portion of them, and intended and needed as well for those outside as for those inside the city, the authority of the county to build it is not annulled by the local city statute. *Skinner* v. *Henderson* (Fla.) 55

BURDEN OF PROOF. See EVIDENCE, II.

BY-LAW. See ASSOCIATIONS, 2, 4, 5.

CANCELLATION. See LIMITATION OF ACTIONS, 13, 14.

CANVASSERS. See PEDDLERS.

CARRIERS. See also TRIAL, 16.

1. Passenger carriers are bound to exercise the utmost degree of care, skill, and diligence consistent with the nature of their business, in providing safe and convenient modes of access to their trains and of departure from them. *Philadelphia, W. & B. R. Co.* v. *Anderson* (Md.) 673

2. A passenger is justified in assuming that no train will be permitted to pass a station at which a passenger train has stopped for the discharge and receipt of passengers, in such manner as to interfere with them. Hence he cannot be held guilty of contributory negligence as matter of law because he failed, before leaving the car on which he was traveling, to look out for an approaching train by which he was injured. *Id.*

3. Where a passenger was injured while attempting to alight from a train at a regular station, by another train belonging to the same carrier and in charge of its servants, which ran past the station platform while the passengers of the former train are being received and discharged, the carrier, to relieve itself from liability for damages, must show that it used the degree of care which the law imposes upon it. *Id.*

4. A carrier is liable for an unlawful and improper act, and for the natural and legitimate consequences thereof, which is committed by its servant towards its passenger while such servant is engaged in performing a duty which the carrier owes to the passenger, no matter what the motive is which incites the commission of the act. *Dwinelle* v. *New York C. & H. R. R. Co.* (N. Y.) 224

5. If the performance of a railroad company's contract to transport a passenger is temporarily suspended by a defect in the roadbed, he is entitled, during the time required to overcome the defect, to all the rights of a passenger upon a moving train, including that of protection from the willful misconduct of the company's servants. *Id.*

6. The porter of a sleeping or drawing-room car which forms a part of the train of a railroad company under a contract with its owner, who sells separate tickets for privileges upon such cars, and who furnishes his own servants to collect tickets and assist passengers, is the servant of the railroad company, for whose acts done in the performance of a contract to carry a passenger it is responsible, notwithstanding an agreement which may be made upon the subject between the company and the owner of the car. *Id.*

7. It is no defense to a suit against a carrier to recover damages for an assault committed by its servant upon a passenger, that at the time the assault was committed the servant had finished the temporary and particular service which he had undertaken to render to the passenger, if the contract of carriage was not yet performed and the duty still rested on the car-

rier to protect the passenger from the violence of its servants. *Dwinelle* v. *New York C. & H. R. R. Co.* (N. Y.) 224

8. A common carrier cannot, even by express contract, exempt itself from liability for gross negligence or willful misconduct. *Chicago & N. W. R. Co.* v. *Chapman* (Ill.) 508

9. An amount named in a bill of lading as the limit of liability will not restrict recovery for a loss due to gross negligence, where the amount was inserted by the carrier's agent without asking any questions as to the value of the property, and without notice to the shipper of any difference in rates in case of such limitation. *Id.*

10. Delay in the transportation of goods, which is caused solely by a mob, will not render the carrier liable at common law to make good losses arising from a decline in the market price, or from the deterioration in their quality on account of their perishable nature, during time of transit. *Gulf, C. & S. F. R. Co.* v. *Levi* (Tex.) 323

11. The exclusive right to use the platform of a railway company for receiving and discharging passengers cannot be granted by the company to one hack-owner. *Montana U. R. Co.* v. *Langlois* (Mont.) 753

NOTES AND BRIEFS.

Care for passengers; contributory negligence. 678

Regulations for use of depot and grounds. 753

CASE. See ANIMALS, 1; GARNISHMENT, 5.

CHARACTER. See EVIDENCE, 38.

CHARITABLE INSTITUTIONS. See CONTRACTS, 1.

CITIZENS.

NOTES AND BRIEFS.

Political rights of. 337

CLAIMS.

An action to recover damages for injuries resulting from the negligence of a servant of the Commonwealth in the performance of his duties is not a claim, within the meaning of Mass. Acts 1887, chap. 246, which authorizes the maintenance of a suit against the Commonwealth to recover "all claims" against it, whether at law or in equity. *Murdock Parlor Grate Co.* v. *Com.* (Mass.) 399

CLOUD ON TITLE.

1. A cross-bill in a suit to remove a cloud from title will not be dismissed because defendant denies the title to have been in the person under whom both parties claim, at the time of the levy of a writ of attachment under which plaintiff claims, where this denial is qualified and explained by allegations showing that a conveyance canceled at suit of defendant was the foundation of the denial. *West* v. *People's Bank* (Miss.) 727

2. Relief will not be denied on a cross-bill in a suit to remove a cloud on title, because defendant shows a perfect title on which he might maintain ejectment. *Id.*

NOTES AND BRIEFS.

Removal; jurisdiction; possession; prevention by injunction. 727

CLUBS. See ASSOCIATIONS, 2–7; LEVY AND SEIZURE, 4; MANDAMUS, NOTES AND BRIEFS.

COLLEGES.

No power to confer the degree of M. D., or any other degree, is given to a corporation by the general law of a State authorizing incorporation for the purpose of maintaining a literary and scientific institution. *Townshend* v. *Gray* (Vt.) 112

COMMERCE. See also TAXES, 8.

1. A state statute requiring a license from every peddler or itinerant trader by sample or otherwise, unless he is a disabled soldier of the State, is unconstitutional as a regulation of commerce. *Wrought Iron Range Co.* v. *Johnson* (Ga.) 273

2. A state statute compelling railroad companies to furnish double-decked cars for sheep, under a penalty for failure to do so, and limiting the price per carload, is void as an attempted regulation of commerce, when applied to interstate shipments. *Stanley* v. *Wabash, St. L. & P. R. Co.* (Mo.) 549

NOTES AND BRIEFS.

Extraterritorial effect of state statutes affecting. 550

COMMON ERROR. See also CUSTOM AND USAGE; TRIAL, 5.

NOTES AND BRIEFS.

May pass for right. 629

CONFLICT OF LAWS. See also RECEIVERS.

1. The law of the State in which a note for money loaned is given, governs on the question of usury, where it is secured by a deed of land located in the State, and part of the money, representing the usury, was deducted from the loan, and never paid over to the borrower, although the note is expressly made payable in another State. *Martin* v. *Johnson* (Ga.) 170

2. An exemption law of one State has no effect in an action brought in another State. *Carson* v. *Memphis & C. R. Co.* (Tenn.) 412

3. A discharge under state insolvency laws will not release existing debts due to nonresident creditors who do not come in and prove their claims in the insolvency proceedings. *Phœnix Nat. Bank* v. *Batcheller* (Mass.) 644

4. Where a policy of insurance is issued on property in one State by a company in another State, and it does not appear where it was delivered or payable, or where the contract was made or the premium paid, it may be inferred that the contract was made in either

State, as readily as in the other. *Pennypacker v. Capital Ins. Co.* (Iowa) 236

NOTES AND BRIEFS.

What law governs execution of will. 822

As to contracts; under Usury Laws. 170

CONSTITUTIONAL LAW. See also APPROPRIATIONS; HIGHWAYS, 5; MASTER AND SERVANT, 3; STREET RAILWAYS, 6.

1. A statute authorizing the creation of a municipal corporation by a judicial court, upon petition of a majority of the inhabitants of the territory to be incorporated, is unconstitutional as delegating legislative functions to the court. *Territory, Kelly, v. Stewart* (Wash.) 106

2. The enactment of a statute is a usurpation of judicial power where it adjudicates an act unlawful and presumptively injurious and dangerous which is not and cannot be made to be so without a violation of constitutional rights, and where it imperatively commands the court to enjoin such action without proof that any injury or danger has been or will be caused by it. *Janesville v. Carpenter* (Wis.) 808

3. An ordinance does not violate the constitutional law of "equality" because it applies to one village of the State only. *Summerville v. Pressley* (S. C.) 854

4. A statute violates the essential spirit, purpose, and intent of the Constitution and is contrary to public justice, where it declares that it shall be unlawful within the limits of a single county to drive piles, etc., in a river which flows through other counties also, and gives only to resident taxpayers and owners or lessees of the right to use water of said river for a mill or factory within said county the right to an injunction against the prohibited acts, without proof that any injury or danger has been or will be caused thereby. *Janesville v. Carpenter* (Wis.) 808

5. A statute making it unlawful for the owner of ground having the right to use it, to drive piles into it anywhere within a river, for any purpose, prevents the lawful use of his property, and takes it away from him without compensation or due process of law, and denies him the equal protection of the law. *Id.*

6. Unless articles seized because used for violating law are of such a character that the law will not recognize them as property entitled as such to its protection under any circumstances, they cannot be summarily destroyed without affording the owner an opportunity to be heard upon the subject of their lawful use, and to show whether or not they are intrinsically useful or valuable for some lawful purpose. *State v. Robbins* (Ind.) 438

7. An ordinance is not "unequal and unjust" on the ground that it permits the owner of a small parcel of ground to cultivate a larger proportion of his ground than the owner of a larger tract can do, where the same maximum limit is fixed for all persons. *Summerville v. Pressley* (S. C.) 854

8. A government has an inherent right to impose such restraint and to provide such regulations in regard to the pursuits of life as the public w (Md.)

9. Prol ers who l tency fro business ercise of does not dividuals.

Title of

CONTE

1. A c against a p not comm ence of th the conter sented to t

2. The paper is no the conduc ing suit or ner to influ pede, inter of the cou

3. Acts tempts of laws of Ore fied as such the Civil C and can be described.

4. A co tempt of a sale of into tion of this ing the plea void. *State*

In presenc mary punisl ceedings; dis injunction.

CONTRAC

I. REQUISI

II. PERFOR MENT.

III. VALIDIT

IV. RELIEF

NOTES A

See also ARBI 2; PRIN PERFORM

I. REQ

1. The law the part of one tution for sup for, in the abs referred to mo ter or by-laws compensation *Montgomery Co*

2. An offer t less than the s

a bond for the faithful performance of the work, on which a contract is entered into with the county clerk, who has no power to make such contract, will not prevent recovery for the full statutory rate. *Hoffman* v. *Chippewa County* (Wis.) 781

3. Whatever may fairly be implied from the terms or nature of an instrument is, in judgment of law, contained in it. *Lawler* v. *Murphy* (Conn.) 113

4. Whatever is necessary to be done in order to accomplish work specially contracted to be performed is parcel of the contract, though not specified. *Id.*

5. The word "shipment," in a contract purchasing 1,000 tons of sugar "for shipment within thirty days, by sail or steam, seller's option," and providing for marine insurance by the buyers, means the delivery, within the time required, on some vessel destined to the proper port, which the seller has reason to suppose will sail within a reasonable time after shipment, and does not mean a clearance of the vessel as well as putting the goods on board, where there is nothing to indicate that the seller was expected to exercise any control over the clearance of the vessel or her subsequent management. *Mora y Ledon* v. *Havemeyer* (N. Y.) 245

6. A guaranty that cattle of another person will sell in market for 4 cents per pound, made in consideration of the payment of $30 and an agreement by the other party to pay the guarantor any excess in the selling price above 4 cents per pound, is a gambling contract. *Creston First Nat. Bank* v. *Carroll* (Iowa) 275

II. Performance; Violation; Enforcement.

7. Issuing 5 cards, each good for 20 crossings, is a substantial compliance by a bridge company with a contract to sell 100 tickets for $1. *Newport* v. *Newport & C. Bridge Co.* (Ky.) 484

8. Shipment of goods which do not constitute a full cargo is sufficiently made by placing them on board the vessel bound for the intended port and engaged in an honest effort to obtain a cargo for such port. *Mora y Ledon* v. *Havemeyer* (N. Y.) 245

9. Taking possession of real estate, after work in constructing buildings has been done thereon and the contractor has left the premises, and appropriating to the owner's use and benefit the labor or materials of the contractor, does not constitute an unequivocal acceptance of the work, although it may be taken into consideration in determining that matter. *Hanley* v. *Walker* (Mich.) 207

10. It is not a violation of a contract with a plank-road company, created by its Act of incorporation, to enact that no toll gate can be kept or toll demanded within the corporate limits of a city, where such corporation had accepted the provisions of a statute amending its charter, which made the privileges of the company the same as those of other companies under the general law. *Snell* v. *Chicago* (Ill.) 858

11. Becoming a member of a man's family, and taking his name, and living with him as his child until his death, under a parol promise by him to leave all his property, real, personal, and mixed, to such child, is not such a part performance of the contract as to make it amount to a fraud to refuse performance of the promise on the ground that it is within the Statute of Frauds. *Pond* v. *Sheean* (Ill.) 414

III. Validity.

12. An executed parol agreement modifying a contract under seal will be upheld. *McKenzie* v. *Harrison* (N. Y.) 257

13. An entire contract relating to personal as well as real estate, if void as to the real estate, under the Statute of Frauds, is void as to the personal property also. *Pond* v. *Sheean* (Ill.) 414

14. A parol promise by a person to leave all his property, real, personal, and mixed, to a child in consideration of her becoming a member of his family and taking his name, is void under the Statute of Frauds. *Id.*

15. A contract restraining the exercise of one's calling for a certain time is not necessarily void upon grounds of public policy, simply because the restraint extends throughout an entire State. *Herreshoff* v. *Boutineau* (R. I.) 469

16. A contract not to teach the French or German language, or aid or advertise to teach them, or be connected in any way with any person, persons, or institutions that teach them, in the State of Rhode Island, during the year after the end of a term of employment as teacher, is unreasonable because the restraint extends beyond any apparently necessary protection to the other party, unless it is shown that the latter would be seriously injured by such teaching in any part of the State. *Id.*

17. A contract giving a person an exclusive agency for the sale of a brand of cigars in a certain Territory is not void as in restraint of trade. *Newell* v. *Meyendorff* (Mont.) 440

IV. Relief from; Pari Delicto.

18. A reconveyance by a natural daughter to her father will be set aside where he had deliberately conveyed the property to her as a gift, and, after becoming feeble in body and mind, was, although unwilling, driven by other members of his family to ask her for a reconveyance, and she gave it without time for reflection, consultation, or advice, while deeply moved by his distress and urged by the family lawyer, who had been sent with him and who told her that it would be best for her to do so, although he knew that her father's latest will had omitted all provisions for her which former wills contained. *Davis* v. *Strange* (Va.) 261

19. A village will be denied relief in equity against bonds issued under an Act of the Legislature authorizing bonds for public improvements in the village and used in aid of a railroad, for which purpose they could not be legally authorized, where the Act was obtained by the people of the village by falsely representing to the Legislature that the power to issue bonds was desired for the purpose of making public improvements in the village. The people must be left to such defense as they

may be found entitled to in a court of law. *Cedar Springs* v. *Schlick* (Mich.) 851

20. Parties concerned in illegal agreements are to be left without remedy against each other. *Kirkpatrick* v. *Clark* (Ill.) 511

21. If a person having no knowledge of the scheme of the Bohemian-oat business, or of the corporate existence of the pretended company, or of want of integrity of its purpose and the honesty of its business, relies entirely upon and believes the statements of another that there is such a corporation and that its business is honest, he is not precluded, on the ground of guilty participation, from maintaining an action for fraud against the person who induced him to give his notes in pursuance of such scheme, although fraudulent. *Knight* v. *Linzey* (Mich.) 476

22. If a man, knowing that a scheme is fraudulent and that the natural outcome of it will be to defraud some innocent person, goes into it solely for the purpose of making money out of it, though he may not be equally in fault with another who is the moving party in the fraud and influences him by his persuasions and representations, a court will, on the ground of public policy, deny him any relief against the other party. *Id.*

NOTES AND BRIEFS.

CONTRIBUTION.

Infant heirs are not liable to contribution at law for the amount of liability voluntarily incurred by other heirs in saving the estate from insolvency. *Benedict* v. *Chase* (Conn.) 120

CONVERSION. See TROVER.

CORONER. See WRIT AND PROCESS.

CORPORATIONS.

I. RIGHT TO EXIST.
II. POWERS; USURPATION; REMEDY.
III. STOCKHOLDERS; OFFICERS; DIRECTORS.
IV. SUITS; DISSOLUTION.
NOTES AND BRIEFS.

See also CONTRACTS, 10; FALSE IMPRISONMENT, INSURANCE, 14; TOLL ROADS, 3, 4, 5.

I. RIGHT TO EXIST.

1. Where a corporation is organized under a general statute, a provision in the declaration of its corporate purpose, the necessary effect of which is the creation of a monopoly, is void as against public policy. *People, Peabody,* v. *Chicago Gas Trust Co.* (Ill.) 497

2. A corporation organized with the object of purchasing and holding all the shares of the capital stock of any gas company in the city or State is not a corporation organized for a lawful purpose, within the meaning of the Illinois General Incorporation Act (Ill. Rev. Stat. chap 32, § 1), providing that corporations may be formed for any lawful purpose with the exception stated therein. *Id.*

3. The word "unlawful," as applied to the purposes for which corporations are formed, is not used exclusively in the sense of *malum in se* or *malum prohibitum*, but is also used to designate such acts, powers, and contracts as are *ultra vires*. *Id.*

4. Inasmuch as Michigan statutes allow policies of life insurance to be issued only when they specify the sum payable at a fixed amount, and do not permit endowment policies by assessment companies, while assessment companies in Ohio are not allowed to guarantee any fixed sum further than what might be realized from assessments, unless they have complied with the statutes relating to regular mutual life insurance companies, and in that case are allowed to issue endowment policies at a fixed sum, Ohio companies are not permitted to do business in Michigan on substantially the same basis and limitations as they are in Ohio, and therefore, under the proviso of Ohio Rev. Stat. § 3630 *E*, Michigan insurance corporations are not entitled to a license to do business in Ohio. *State, Attorney-General,* v. *Western U. Mut. L. & Acc. Soc.* (Ohio) 129

II. POWERS; USURPATION; REMEDY.

5. When a corporation is formed, under the Illinois General Incorporation Act, for the purpose of carrying on a lawful business, the law, and not the statement or license or certificate, must determine what powers can be exercised as incidents of such business. *People, Peabody,* v. *Chicago Gas Trust Co.* (Ill.) 497

6. A corporation formed, under the Illinois General Incorporation Act, for a purpose other than that of dealing in stocks, cannot exercise the power of purchasing and holding stock in other corporations, where such power cannot be necessarily implied from the nature of the power specifically granted, and is not necessary to carry the latter into effect. *Id.*

7. A gas company formed for the purpose of erecting or operating gas works and manufacturing and selling gas has no power to purchase and hold or sell shares of stock in other gas companies as an incident to such purpose of its formation, even though such power is specified in its articles of incorporation. *Id.*

8. The illegality of corporate acts because of the invalidity of the Act of incorporation is

cured by a statute which recognizes the corporate existence of the company by amending its charter, and also recognizes its right to substitute stone or gravel for plank upon a road already constructed. *Snell* v. *Chicago* (Ill.) 858

9. When a foreign corporation doing business in Ohio is exercising its franchises in contravention of the laws thereof, it may be ousted therefrom by proceedings in *quo warranto*. *State, Attorney-General*, v. *Western U. Mut. L. & Acc. Soc.* (Ohio) 120

10. The right of a corporation to occupy city wharves with a warehouse connected with an elevator, for any other purpose than to store and handle grain, cannot be questioned by the owner of the fee of the wharf property on the ground that the corporation is exceeding its corporate powers. *Belchers Sugar Ref. Co.* v. *St. Louis Grain Elev. Co.* (Mo.) 801

11. The power of a corporation to acquire and hold title to real estate cannot be questioned by any party except the State, where it has power to hold real estate for some purposes. *Hamsher* v. *Hamsher* (Ill.) 556

III. STOCKHOLDERS; OFFICERS; DIRECTORS.

12. A premature and void contract made by a corporation before there had been paid in the amount of capital stock required by statute to be paid in before corporate powers could be exercised, the contract being to promote the purposes of the corporation, and being carried out after the corporation became enabled to make it valid,—does not release a subscription for corporate stock. *Naugatuck Water Co.* v. *Nichols* (Conn.) 637

13. A "superintendent" of a natural gas company, who is not a general manager, or a general agent, or an officer of the company, but whose principal duties are to superintend the construction of trenches and the laying of gas pipes, is a laborer within the meaning of that term as used in Elliott's (Ind.) Supp. § 605, giving a preference to laborer's claims for wages against corporations. *Pendergast* v. *Yandes* (Ind.) 849

14. Directors of a corporation incur a personal liability to it by voting for a resolution which they have no power, express or implied, to pass, authorizing the issue and negotiation of notes of the corporation, which are in effect void, where such notes are issued and come into the hands of bona fide purchasers for value. *Metropolitan Elev. R. Co.* v. *Kneeland* (N.Y.) 253

15. Officers of a corporation who sign and issue certificates of its stock in the usual form, stating upon their faces that the corporation is incorporated according to the laws of a particular State, and that the stock is nonassessable, thereby represent that the stock is not spurious or invalid because of their known acts or omissions, and also that everything has been done which is necessary to make the stock rightfully exempt from further assessment; and if such representations are false, the officers will be liable in damages to one who has taken the certificates in good faith and for value, relying upon the representations. *Windram* v. *French* (Mass.) 750

IV. SUITS; DISSOLUTION.

16. No suit will lie in favor of one corporation, organized under Mass. Act 1888, chap. 429, to enjoin either the organization of another corporation with a name so similar to the first as to be within the apparent prohibition of § 2 of that Act, or the use of such name, since § 7 makes it the duty of the commissioner of insurance to determine whether the names conflict, before the certificate, which is made conclusive evidence of the existence of the corporation, is issued; nor will the suit lie to protect the first name as a trade-name, since it was taken subject to whatever interference might be permitted by the statute. *American Order of Scottish Clans* v. *Merrill* (Mass.) 320

17. A company is dissolved upon the consummation of a sale of its corporate property and the execution of a deed therefor, under a statute which states that the object of the sale is to dissolve the company. *Snell* v. *Chicago* (Ill.) 858

NOTES AND BRIEFS.

Foreign; law of comity. 236

Liability of directors for unauthorized acts. 253

Contracts by; against public policy; franchise as public grant; forfeiture and dissolution for misuse of franchise; formation of trusts by; illegal combination; monopolies. 497

Power to purchase stock of other corporations. 498

Subscription to capital stock; premature contracts. 638

Illegal issue of stock; liability of directors; pleading. 750

Privilege of claims for laborers' wages; superintendent. 849

Dissolution of. 858

COUNTIES. See also BRIDGES.

1. Under the Constitution and laws of Florida, a county cannot impose taxes except for county purposes; and the building of a bridge in a county, within the corporate limits of a municipality, in which the county outside of those limits is in nowise interested, the same being for the sole benefit and advantage of the municipality, is not a county purpose. *Skinner* v. *Henderson* (Fla.) 55

2. If a county may build a bridge within the limits of a municipality when the circumstances suit, it may also aid the municipality in building one under like circumstances, even though it is to be constructed under a contract with the municipality, and is to be under its control. *Id.*

COURTS. See also ACTION OR SUIT, 8; JUDGMENT, 5.

1. The superior court in Connecticut has jurisdiction of a suit to compel an intestate's estate which has been saved from insolvency by the voluntary act of all the heirs of legal age, to refund the expense incurred thereby, before distribution. *Benedict* v. *Chase* (Conn.) 120

2. The circuit court in Indiana has jurisdiction of a proceeding to establish a way of necessity over the land of another, since the Act of March 9, 1889, which attempted to confer jurisdiction of such proceedings upon the board of county commissioners, is unconstitutional. *Logan* v. *Stogdale* (Ind.) 58

3. A statute authorizing a county to issue bonds to procure seed grain for needy farmers is a matter of local concern, and the Supreme Court of North Dakota has not original jurisdiction to issue an injunction in such matter. *State, Goodwin,* v. *Nelson County* (N. D.) 283

4. When a state court has yielded its opinion and adopted that of the United States Supreme Court upon a given subject, and such decision has been acquiesced in for many years, it will not be departed from unless the court is very sure it is wrong, and also that the United States court either will not regard the state decision as subject to review by it, or will change its own decision. *Phœnix Nat. Bank* v. *Batcheller* (Mass.) 644

5. A citizen may be restrained from proceeding in another State by garnishment to seize the wages of a fellow citizen, in evasion of the laws of their own State, by which such wages are exempt. *Moton* v. *Hull* (Tex.) 722

NOTES AND BRIEFS.

Concurrent jurisdiction; which prevails. 63
First acquired, conclusive. 885

COVENANT. See also DEED; REAL PROPERTY, NOTES AND BRIEFS; WATERS AND WATERCOURSES, 7.

Covenants in a deed of submerged land between low-water mark and an established dock line are binding on subsequent grantees of the upland from the same grantor. *Miller* v. *Mendenhall* (Minn.) 89

CREDITORS' BILL. See also EXECUTION, 3, 4.

1. If an equitable attachment of a debtor's property is prohibited by statute, the property cannot be reached in equity and the statute avoided merely by a change in the form of proceedings. *Venable* v. *Rickenberg* (Mass.) 623

2. A suit in equity to reach and apply property to the payment of a debt cannot be maintained, either under the general equity jurisdiction, or under a statute which permits such suit in case the property "cannot be come at to be attached or taken on execution in a suit at law," where the property is in its nature attachable by trustee process, but cannot be attached in the particular case because of a statute prohibiting the collecting of that particular kind of debt attachment, "either by trustee process or otherwise." *Id.*

3. Letters-patent may be sold and transferred by a court of equity through its master for the benefit of creditors of their owner, under Mass. Stat. 1884, chap. 285, even although he is a nonresident of the State, if the court has acquired jurisdiction which will enable it to bind him with a personal judgment. *Wilson* v. *Martin-Wilson Automatic Fire Alarm Co.* (Mass.) 309

What
To re
nonresid

CRIM

1. On
being d
erate or
which th
sential el
commit t
so intoxic
charged
first deg
sential el
drunk at
be consid
whether
man v. *S*

2. Ther
sustain a
other thro
attempt to
ter acts
Dowell (N.

3. A mi
for horse
offense, wl
a maximu
unusual pu
must be gr
for homicid

4. A pl
charging h
one count,
plies to bo
for horse

5. A stat
fendant is
not violate
at the trial.

6. An arr
a defect app
On motion
the evidence
Eaves (N. C.

Voluntary
crime.
Good chara
Proof of
defined.

CURTESY

Conveyance
a purchase by
her directions
husband. *K*

CUSTOM A

A common
law is not sho
of the mining
territory durin
of verification
fatally defectiv
reason of omitt

cation, where it does not show that any considerable number of persons have relied upon, or sought to fix their rights upon, the alleged common error, or that large property interests depend upon upholding such notice. *O'Donnell* v. *Glenn* (Mont.) 629

DAMAGES. See also CARRIERS, 9; INSURANCE, 22.

1. The possibility of unskillful and improper construction of a reservoir which is not yet completed cannot be considered in estimating damages to adjacent property in proceedings by eminent domain. It must be assumed that the work will be done in a skillful and proper manner. *Alloway* v. *Nashville* (Tenn.) 123

2. The value, for a reservoir site, of property taken for that purpose, cannot be taken as the measure of damages for the taking, but must be considered as one of the elements that make up its market value. The market value, in view of all available uses, is the measure of compensation. *Id.*

3. Damages for the permanent diminution in the value of lots, caused by an elevated railway in front of them, cannot be recovered in an action for damages after construction of the road, but the damages must be limited to the time preceding the action. *Tallman* v. *Metropolitan Elev. R. Co.* (N. Y.) 173

4. Damages to lots by construction of an elevated railroad in front of them, without compensation to the owner, where he subsequently sues for the damages sustained, are limited to diminished or usable value during the time prior to the suit, and must be based on the actual condition of the lots just as they are. What the effect on their value would have been if buildings had been erected thereon, which in fact were not, is immaterial. *Id.*

5. Suffering in mind as well as in body is ground for damages for a personal injury. *Chicago* v. *McLean* (Ill.) 765

6. In case one who has sold furniture for a hotel and contracted with the proprietor to deliver it by or on a certain date, knowing the purpose for which it is to be used and that it is necessary for the operation of the hotel, fails to deliver it until long after the appointed time, thereby preventing the renting of the rooms to guests, he is liable for the loss sustained by reason of such failure; and such loss may be determined by finding the difference between the value, for the purpose for which they were intended, of the rooms furnished and unfurnished during the time they could not be used for such purpose. *Berkey & G. Furniture Co.* v. *Hascall* (Ind.) 65

7. Exemplary damages for forcible entry may be recovered if the unlawful act is done in a wanton and reckless manner. *Mosseller* v. *Deaver* (N. C.) 537

8. In addition to nominal damages for a forcible entry upon the peaceable possession of plaintiff, even by the owner, he can recover for any injury inflicted upon his person or personal property *Id.*

NOTES AND BRIEFS.

For property condemned. 123
For land condemned. 330
Recoverable for malicious abuse of process. 515
For libel. 525
For personal injuries; mental anguish. 765

DEDICATION. See also ESTOPPEL, 8.

NOTES AND BRIEFS.

Cannot be recalled. 633

DEED.

A purchaser, at a foreclosure sale, of a railroad company's interest under a deed granting it a right of way over certain lands, in which is incorporated, as part of the consideration therefor, an agreement by the company to build a fence, is bound to carry out the agreement; and its liability to do so may be enforced by a subsequent grantee of the fee in an action of covenant, although the company merely accepted the deed without acknowledging it. *Midland R. Co.* v. *Fisher* (Ind.) 604

DEFENSE. See INSURANCE, 4.

DEFINITIONS. See also CONTRACTS, 5; INSURANCE, 8; LICENSE, 2; WHARFAGE AND WHARVES, 4; WILLS, 1.

The words "process in an action" include an execution. *Johnson* v. *Elkins* (Ky.) 552

NOTES AND BRIEFS.

See also HEIRS.
Meaning of "shipment." 245

DEMAND. See GUARANTY, 2.

DEPOSITIONS.

A party who has answered interrogatories propounded before trial, under Ind. Rev. Stat. 1881, § 359, cannot object to introduction of the answers in evidence at the trial, upon the ground that they are irrelevant. *Cincinnati, I. St. L. & C. R. Co.* v. *Howard* (Ind.) 593

DISCLAIMER. See TRUSTS, 1.

DOWER.

1. The inchoate right of the wife to dower in her husband's land, under N. C. Code, chap. 53, has a present value as property, depending on the ages, health, and habits of both, and other circumstances competent to show the probabilities as to the length of life of each; and when she incumbers it by joining in a mortgage of his land to secure his debts, she becomes his surety. *Gore* v. *Townsend* (N.C.) 443

2. A widow's homestead right in certain premises prevents the seisin of an heir, and therefore excludes any dower right of his widow therein upon his death during the continuance of the homestead right. *Dudley* v. *Dudley* (Wis.) 814

3. A conveyance made just before marriage, in fraud of the wife's rights, can be set aside by her only to the extent of her dower. *Id.*

4. A woman who, during her abandonment of her husband, admits any man or men to her periodically or whenever it is convenient or opportunity is afforded, is living in adultery, within the meaning of the Kentucky statutes which forfeit her dower or distributable share in her husband's property when she voluntarily leaves him and lives in adultery. *Goss* v. *Froman* (Ky.) 102

NOTES AND BRIEFS.

Right of wife protected. 443

DRAINS AND SEWERS. See WATERS AND WATERCOURSES, 13, 14.

DRUNKENNESS. See ARREST, 1; CRIMINAL LAW; EVIDENCE, NOTES AND BRIEFS.

EASEMENTS. See also COURTS, 2; WATERS AND WATERCOURSES, 12.

1. An easement of a right of way is not presumed to be personal, where it can fairly be construed to be appurtenant to some other estate. *Reise* v. *Enos* (Wis.) 617

2. A right of way across a lot, given by a conveyance of an adjoining lot, to be used in common with the grantors and the owners and occupants of the former lot, is a right appurtenant to the lot conveyed; and the grantee, after he has conveyed the lot, cannot claim to be still entitled to use the right of way in connection with any other lot subsequently acquired. *Id.*

3. A reservation, in a conveyance of a lot which has a right of way appurtenant, of such right of way to the grantor, is ineffectual. He cannot enlarge the right, or retain any interest in the right of way, as separate and distinct from the lot to which it belongs. *Id.*

4. A grantee of land across which a prior grantee from the same grantor has the right to a way by necessity takes it subject to such right, although it had been neither exercised nor claimed before his title was acquired. *Logan* v. *Stogdale* (Ind.) 58

NOTES AND BRIEFS.

See also WATERS AND WATERCOURSES.

Way of necessity. 58

Defined; how created; rights of parties. 617

EJECTMENT.

A deed given to defraud the grantor's creditors will not support an action of ejectment against him. *Kirkpatrick* v. *Clark* (Ill.) 511

ELECTION.

An election to give exclusive credit to one partner is not established in the absence of full knowledge of the relation of the parties between whom the choice is to be made; and the knowledge must be actual in contradistinction to that which is constructive. *Tyler* v. *Waddingham* (Conn.) 657

ELECTRIC LIGHT. See also MUNICIPAL CORPORATIONS, 8, 9.

1. A city may own an electric light plant and manufacture electricity for lighting the streets, where it is expressly given power to own property and also has an implied right to light the streets. *Mauldin* v. *Greenville* (S. C.) 291

2. The purchase of an electric-light plant is beyond the authority of a city so far as it is intended to furnish lights for the residences and places of business of private individuals, either with or without compensation. *Id.*

ELECTRIC RAILWAYS.

NOTES AND BRIEFS.

When allowed in streets. 539

ELEVATED RAILWAYS. See also DAMAGES, 3, 4.

NOTES AND BRIEFS.

Construction; appropriation of right of way; damages for personal injuries. 178

EMINENT DOMAIN. See also DAMAGES, 1, 2; INTEREST.

1. The condemnation of land for a private way cannot be authorized by the Legislature. Hence the Indiana Act of March 9, 1889, which attempts to do so, is void. *Logan* v. *Stogdale* (Ind.) 58

2. The test of damage requiring compensation caused to private property by public improvement is whether a cause of action would arise if the injury was caused by a private person without authority of statute. *Peel* v. *Atlanta* (Ga.) 787

3. Private property is not "damaged for public purposes" by a public improvement, within a constitutional provision requiring compensation for such damages, where no invasion is made of any right or use of such property. *Id.*

4. Building another railroad on a portion of the unused right of way of a company which has acquired an easement only therein creates an additional servitude; and the consent of the owner of the land must first be obtained and compensation made to him for the damage. *Fort Worth & R. G. R. Co.* v. *Jennings* (Tex.) 180

5. The construction and operation of a surface railroad along and upon a city street, substantially upon the same grade therewith, under authority from the Legislature and by permission of the city, is not a taking of any property of an abutting landowner who has no title to any portion of the street, which will entitle him to compensation either for interference with any of his easements in the street or for consequential damages to his adjoining property necessarily resulting from a reasonable operation of the road, where the use of the street is not exclusive in its nature and the passage through and across it is left free and unobstructed for the public. *Fobes* v. *Rome, W. & O. R. Co.* (N. Y.) 453

6. The depreciation in the value of land

lying along the highway, due to the construction of a railway next to the highway on the opposite side thereof, gives the owner a right to compensation, under a constitutional provision that private property shall not be taken "or damaged" without just compensation. *Lake Erie & W. R. Co.* v. *Scott* (Ill.) 330

7. The maintenance of an elevator on a public wharf, for handling grain thereat, is no new or additional servitude. It is simply a new method of using the wharf for the very purpose for which it was condemned. *Belchers Sugar Ref. Co.* v. *St. Louis Grain Elev. Co.* (Mo.) 801

8. Pipes for the transportation of natural gas cannot be laid in a country road without making compensation to the owner of the fee, although the right to do so has been granted by the board of county commissioners. *Kincaid* v. *Indianapolis Natural Gas Co.* (Ind.) 602

9. Opening a public street adjacent to one's property, thus bounding it by streets on three sides, rendering it ungainly and unsightly to the public, and destroying its privacy, and thus diminishing its value, does not give the owner a right to compensation under a constitution declaring that private property shall not be taken without just and adequate compensation. *Peel* v. *Atlanta* (Ga.) 787

10. The Virginia Act of Feb. 10, 1880, authorizing a telegraph company to construct a line along county roads, provided the ordinary use of the road is not obstructed, does not give any right to build such line without compensation to the owner of the fee. If the Act is intended to give such right, it is in violation of the constitutional provision against taking private property without just compensation. *Western U. Teleg. Co.* v. *Williams* (Va.) 429

11. The erection of a telegraph line upon a highway is an additional servitude for which compensation must be made to the owner of the soil. *Id.*

NOTES AND BRIEFS.

See also DAMAGES.

Right of. 58
By municipal corporation; compensation. 128
Nature of title acquired. 180
Damnum absque injuria. 787
Damages. 787

EQUITY. See also HUSBAND AND WIFE, 14.

1. Equity will not entertain jurisdiction of cases where there is an adequate remedy at law, or grant relief, unless for the purpose of preventing serious and irreparable injury. *Thomas* v. *Musical Mut. Prot. Union* (N. Y.) 175

2. A court of equity, having acquired jurisdiction of the case, has power to afford the proper equitable relief which is demanded. *Killmer* v. *Wuchner* (Iowa) 289

NOTES AND BRIEFS.

Not interfere with discretionary power. 175
Power to set aside instruments. 815

ESTOPPEL. See also COVENANT.

1. The doctrine of waiver or estoppel has no application to a contract made by a public officer, without authority for the performance of work at less than the rates fixed therefor by statute, and such doctrine cannot be invoked as a defense to a suit for the full statutory rate. *Hoffman* v. *Chippewa County* (Wis.) 781

2. An estoppel by failure to object to the erasure of the name of a cosurety cannot arise to prevent denial of liability as surety on account of such erasure, where the sureties had no knowledge of the erasing. *State* v. *McGonigle* (Mo.) 735

3. A city is estopped to set up any claim to land dedicated to public use, but never used by the public, where it has permitted a person to occupy it, and has levied and collected city taxes thereon, as his private property. *Smith* v. *Osage* (Iowa) 633

4. A married woman is not estopped by covenants of warranty in a deed in which she joined with her husband merely for the purpose of releasing her dower right, so as to make the title subsequently acquired by her inure to the grantee's benefit, although she is given by statute power to contract as if unmarried. *Sanford* v. *Kane* (Ill.) 724

5. Where one of several judgment debtors, for whom the judgment has been secretly purchased in another's name, holds the judgment out to the world as valid, and procures a sale of his own land on execution under it, becoming the purchaser himself in another's name, he is estopped from claiming that the judgment was paid before the sale, in order to prevent the exercise of a right of redemption by another judgment creditor. *Pease* v. *Ritchie* (Ill.) 566

NOTES AND BRIEFS.

Of married woman. 406

EVIDENCE.

I. JUDICIAL NOTICE.
II. PRESUMPTIONS AND BURDEN OF PROOF.
III. RELEVANCY; MATERIALITY.
IV. RECORDS, ETC.
V. PAROL, CONCERNING WRITINGS.
VI. OPINIONS; DECLARATIONS; PRIVILEGE.
VII. WEIGHT AND SUFFICIENCY.
NOTES AND BRIEFS.

I. JUDICIAL NOTICE.

1. The law of a sister State of the American Union is a foreign law in the sense that it is not judicially noticed, but must, in order to have effect, be proved as a fact. *Conrad* v. *Fisher* (Mo. App) 147

II. PRESUMPTIONS AND BURDEN OF PROOF.

2. A presumption arises that a person found in possession of explosives which are not called for or required in his business procured them for an unlawful purpose. *Hronek* v. *People* (Ill.) 837

3. Notice and proofs of loss mailed to an insurer will be presumed to have been duly re-

ceived, in the absence of evidence to the contrary. *Pennypacker* v. *Capital Ins. Co.* (Iowa) 236

4. The presumption that a child born in wedlock is legitimate, where the husband and wife had opportunities of access, is not conclusive, but may be overcome by clear proof of the contrary, which may consist of proof that the husband was incompetent to have sexual intercourse with his wife or she with him. *Goss* v. *Froman* (Ky.) 102

5. It will be presumed that an ordinance was properly signed by the speaker of the House of Delegates, where the journal recites that his signature was affixed in open session, and no objection is noted on the journal, although it does not expressly recite that all the matters of detail were complied with, and the charter of the city provides that it shall be signed in open session, and that before the officer's signature is affixed "he shall suspend all other business, declaring that such bill will now be read." *Barber Asphalt Paving Co.* v. *Hunt* (Mo.) 110

6. There is no legal presumption of the death of a person who has left home and has not since been heard from, until after the expiration of seven years. *Cone* v. *Dunham* (Conn.) 647

7. When a person crossing a railroad track is injured by collision with a train, the fault is prima facie his own; and he must show affirmatively that his fault or negligence did not contribute to the injury, before he can recover therefor. This is done, however, if all the facts and circumstances illustrating his conduct at the time of the accident are shown, and the inference that he exercised proper caution arises therefrom. *Cincinnati, I. St. L. & C. R. Co.* v. *Howard* (Ind.) 593

8. The defense arising under Ind. Rev. Stat. 1881, § 5119, which makes contracts of suretyship exceptions to the general power conferred by § 5115 upon married women to enter into contracts, must be affirmatively proved when interposed to a suit upon a promissory note which bears on its face no evidence of coverture or suretyship, and no attempt is made to negative the existence of those facts in the complaint. *Miller* v. *Shields* (Ind.) 406

9. The burden of proof to show that a surety consented to the delivery of a bond purporting to be signed by the principal, without the latter's signature, is on the obligee. *Goodyear Dental Vulcanite Co.* v. *Bacon* (Mass.) 486

10. The burden of proof as to the right of a corporation to take property in the exercise of the right of eminent domain, and to show that the particular property is necessary for its corporate use, is on the corporation. *Alloway* v. *Nashville* (Tenn.) 123

11. The burden of proving the law of another State rests upon the party claiming rights under it; and in the absence of such proof, the trial court is authorized to presume that the same rule of law which obtains there obtains in the other State, it being founded in the principles of the common law, and not the necessary outgrowth of a local and peculiar statute. *Conrad* v. *Fisher* (Mo. App.) 147

I

12. A
of eject
owner o
(Ill.)

13. E
given in
words sp
admissib
special d
if defen
v. *Broch*

14. Pr
wife tow
sions of
their sta
together
to nonacc
cess, on t
child 6

15. Pro
tent on t
child, to
was not c
or that h
with his w

16. Evi
were sent
was procu
surer, and
mail to th
show that
packer v.

17. It is
cation of a
one who w
same num

18. A p
whether he
to confide
cian. *McC*

19. Evid
her health,
for which
to be used
testified as
nearly as r

20. The c
its entire len
notice, in a
loose board

21. Whe
pose of show
when it ap
an accident
were other
the whistle
near such ot
testify that
Cincinnati,
(Ind.)

22. A pers
started out
came into co
a railroad cr
permitted to
ing, such tes

IV. RECORDS, ETC.

23. Records of the official acts of the governor, which are kept in a public office, are competent evidence upon the question of the title of a person to an office which he claims under the governor's commission. *State, Worrel*, v. *Peelle* (Ind.) 228

24. A judgment roll in a former suit by the same plaintiff against other defendants is admissible to show that he had elected to treat as a sale acts which he now claims to constitute conversion of property. *Terry* v. *Munger* (N. Y.) 216

25. An award made upon a submission to arbitrators, by executors, of a question as to the ownership of certain corporate stock which was in the possession of testator, and had been distributed under his will before the agreement to arbitrate was made, is not admissible in evidence against the distributees, in an action to recover possession of the stock. *Cone* v. *Dunham* (Conn.) 647

26. The record of a deed cannot be read in evidence if such deed was acknowledged and proved by a subscribing witness whose place of residence does not appear from any part of the deed, acknowledgment, or notarial certificate. *Irving* v. *Campbell* (N. Y.) 620

V. PAROL, CONCERNING WRITINGS.

27. It is competent to show that parties in their dealings under a written contract varied its terms by a subsequent parol agreement. *Conrad* v. *Fisher* (Mo. App.) 147

28. Where a contract is in writing and is so distinctly drawn as to leave no ambiguities for parol explanation, evidence of a prior course of dealing between the parties to it—and especially of a prior course of dealing between one of the parties to it and the predecessors of the other party—cannot be appealed to, to supply an interpretation of it. *Id.*

29. A conversation relative to the construction of a written contract is properly excluded, if the contract is unambiguous in its terms. *Tyler* v. *Waddingham* (Conn.) 657

30. Parol evidence may be given to show what was said and done in the presence of the court acting in a ministerial capacity,—as, in the matter of approving an official bond,—in order to show notice. *State* v. *McGonigle* (Mo.) 735

VI. OPINIONS; DECLARATIONS; PRIVILEGE.

31. Opinions as to length of time a certain kind of lumber will last in sidewalks may be given by competent witnesses on the question of negligence in permitting a sidewalk to become rotten. *McConnell* v. *Osage* (Iowa) 778

32. Defendant's declarations made after the commencement of a suit against him for slander may be admitted in evidence upon the question of malice. *Morasse* v. *Brochu* (Mass.) 524

33. The privilege of a plaintiff against a disclosure of confidential communications to a physician is not waived by her own testimony concerning her ailments and disabilities, which is alleged to be false and which the physician's testimony is needed to contradict. *McConnell* v. *Osage* (Iowa) 778

VII. WEIGHT AND SUFFICIENCY.

34. A prima facie case of fraud on a wife's marital rights in her husband's estate exists where, without her knowledge, he gives, either before or after marriage, all or the greater portion of his property to his children by a former marriage. *Murray* v. *Murray* (Ky.) 95

35. Possession of animals reclaimed from a wild state is prima facie evidence of title. *James* v. *Wood* (Me.) 448

36. The *corpus delicti* of the making, procuring, etc., of dynamite, with intent to use the same for the unlawful destruction of the lives of certain persons, is sufficiently proved by the fact that defendant had such explosives in his possession and kept them concealed, and on different occasions threatened to take the lives of such persons, and said he would throw bombs at them wherever he might meet them. *Hronek* v. *People* (Ill.) 837

37. Facts admitted by a demurrer to one count are not admitted for the purposes of evidence at all, and can have no bearing upon questions arising on the trial under other counts. *Tyler* v. *Waddingham* (Conn.) 657

38. The benefit of the good character of a person charged with crime is not limited to cases where there is a reasonable doubt of his guilt, but evidence of his good character may itself create the reasonable doubt which will entitle him to acquittal. *Com.* v. *Cleary* (Pa.) 301

39. It is not conclusive against the right of a child to recover against his employer for negligence in giving him dangerous work, that he had done it for some time before he was injured. *Hinckley* v. *Horazdowski* (Ill.) 490

NOTES AND BRIEFS.

EXECUTION. See also DEFINITIONS; LEVY AND SEIZURE, 1, 2.

1. An execution cannot be said to be issued, within the meaning of the statute requiring it to be issued within one year in order to preserve the lien of a judgment, until it is delivered to an officer to execute. *Pease* v. *Ritchie* (Ill.) 566

2. The right to pay a debt to the sheriff, if he has an execution against the creditor for the amount due, under Wis. Rev. Stat. § 3028, does not extend to a judgment which is exempt because rendered for the value of exempt property. *Below* v. *Robbins* (Wis.) 467

3. No exception can be made from the right, under Ill. Rev. Stat. chap. 77, § 16, of redemption from sale under execution, decree, etc., in case of the sale, on a creditors' bill, of both the real and personal property of an insolvent mining corporation; at least where the

severance of the personal property from the real estate will not materially impair its value or usefulness, although the property is more available and valuable when in combination, and although a large expense will be necessary to keep the mines from deterioration during the period of redemption, when no one can be permitted to operate them. *Lacey Coal Mines v. Chicago, W. & V. Coal Co.* (Ill.) 598

4. A court, by requiring conveyance to its receiver in a creditors' bill of real property which might have been seized and sold on an execution at law, cannot thereby take it out of the operation of the statute in relation to redemption. *Id.*

NOTES AND BRIEFS.

Shares in joint-stock company subject to. 358

Satisfaction of; exempt debt cannot be applied to. 468

Sale of entire property. 599

EXECUTORS AND ADMINISTRATORS. See also CONTRIBUTION; COURTS, 1.

1. Money received by one as agent, who dies before paying it over, although it has been mingled with his own so that it cannot be distinguished, constitutes a trust fund which can be recovered from his personal representative. *Central City First Nat. Bank v. Hummel* (Colo.) 788

2. A claim against a deceased person's estate is forever barred if it is not exhibited within the time limited by the court of probate for the presentation of such claims. Disability of claimants is no excuse for failure to present a claim. *Cone v. Dunham* (Conn.) 647

3. The pendency of an appeal from an order admitting a will to probate will not excuse a delay of over two years on the part of the executors who have qualified thereunder to present for payment claims of testator against the estates of other deceased persons. *Id.*

4. Where a decedent's estate is saved from insolvency by the act of all the parties interested who were of age and legally capable of acting, in guaranteeing, to a certain extent, with the approval of the administrator, the bonds of a corporation, for which the intestate was liable as indorser, the amount which they were compelled to pay on such guaranty should be refunded to them before distribution, although objection is made by the other interested parties, who were infants at the time, and although no claim against the estate was presented within the time limited therefor by law. Having voluntarily sacrificed their own private funds to save the estate, and having in fact saved it, they are equitably entitled to have the whole estate, and not merely their shares of it, bear the burden. *Benedict v. Chase* (Conn.) 120

5. A claim for a trust fund included in the assets of a decedent's estate, as to which the relation of debtor and creditor never existed between the parties, is not a "debt" or "demand," within the meaning of the Colorado statutes relating to the order of payment of demands

agains
Nat.
6.
which
can
credit
debt,
mortg
land f

Liab
Divi
on; eff
Trus

EXEI

EXPI

Regu
penaltie

EXTR

Whe
and for
extradit
trial fo
his libe
habeas

FALSI

1. A
of a cor
salary, u
cer of th
sponsibl
an arres
premises
Imp. Co.
2. A c
arrest or
pany at
mention
it is sho
thority f
fied and
3. A c
fied the
it is requ
he does
as an off

FENCI
Nor

FORC
ER

Even
right to
possessio
passer o

As to
pleading

FRAUD AND FRAUDULENT CONVEYANCES. See also BILLS AND NOTES, 5, 6; CONTRACTS, 22; CORPORATIONS, 15; DOWER, 8; HUSBAND AND WIFE, 8.

NOTES AND BRIEFS.

Voluntary conveyance pending a marriage contract. 95

GAME LAWS.

NOTES AND BRIEFS.

Of various States. 448

GAMING.

1. Gaming devices seized by the sheriff while executing a warrant for the arrest of their owner upon the charge of unlawfully keeping such devices for the purpose of gain are as properly subject to the order of the court trying the offender as if they had been seized by authority of a search warrant. *State v. Robbins* (Ind.) 438

2. An order by the court, which must be passed before or at the time of the final sentence of a person convicted of unlawfully keeping gaming devices for gain, is necessary to justify a destruction of such person's gaming apparatus which has been seized by the sheriff, under the statute which provides that, "upon conviction of the person offending, the sheriff shall forthwith destroy or cause to be destroyed the apparatus used for unlawful purposes. *Id.*

GARNISHMENT.

1. An exemption law of one State has no effect in an action brought in another State. *Carson v. Memphis & C. R. Co.* (Tenn.) 412

2. A garnishee is not bound to set up an exemption law in favor of the principal defendant, who, with actual knowledge of the proceedings, fails to make a defense. *Id.*

3. Garnishment, in another State, of a corporation for wages, which are exempt in both States, of an employé who is served only by publication, is no defense to a subsequent action by him in the State where he resides, against the corporation, to recover such wages. *Missouri P. R. Co. v. Sharitt* (Kan.) 385

4. Failure of a garnishee to state in his answer the facts which show an exemption of the principal defendant, under a statute providing that "no current wages for personal services shall be subject to garnishment," will deprive him of the protection of a judgment against him as against the principal defendant, if the latter has not appeared or been formally cited to appear in the garnishment proceedings, although he made default in the principal suit. *Missouri P. R. Co. v. Whipker* (Tex.) 321

5. That a creditor transferred to his attorney a just debt, and caused attachment and garnishment to issue and be prosecuted in an adjoining State, thus coercing payment, though both parties were citizens of Georgia, and though the motive for proceeding elsewhere was to evade the laws of Georgia exempting the debtor's wages from garnishment,—constitutes no cause of action in favor of the debtor against the creditor. *Harwell v. Sharp* (Ga.) 514

NOTES AND BRIEFS.

Duty to set up exemption of principal debtor. 412

GAS. See EMINENT DOMAIN, 8; INJUNCTION, 10; MUNICIPAL CORPORATIONS, 8, 9.

GAS COMPANIES. See also CORPORATIONS, 2, 7.

The business of manufacturing and distributing illuminating gas by means of pipes laid in the streets of a city is a business of a public character; and any unreasonable restraint upon the performance of their duty to the public by companies engaged therein is prejudicial to the public interest and in contravention of public policy. *People, Peabody, v. Chicago Gas Trust Co.* (Ill.) 497

NOTES AND BRIEFS.

Franchise of; right to lay pipes in streets. 487

GIFT.

A gift may be made of the balance of a debt after payment of part only, although payment of such part cannot constitute an accord and satisfaction. A receipt in full may be evidence of the gift. *McKenzie v. Harrison* (N. Y.) 257

GRAVEL. See WATERS AND WATERCOURSES, 2, 8.

GUARANTY.

1. The words, "I guarantee payment of the foregoing bond," with signature and seal, written at the foot of the bond of another person under seal, constitute a separate sealed instrument, the signer of which can be sued as a principal obligor, and not merely as surety to the preceding bond; and such action, therefore, is not barred in three years by the North Carolina Statute of Limitations applicable to sureties, but may be brought at any time within ten years, under N. C. Code, § 152, ¶ 2, relating to actions against principal obligors on sealed instruments. *Coleman v. Fuller* (N. C.) 380

2. The withdrawal of a claim against the estate of a principal debtor does not discharge a guarantor from liability under an unconditional guaranty. *Tyler v. Waddingham* (Conn.) 657

3. A demand is not a condition precedent to the maintenance of an action against the guarantor upon a guaranty which is absolute in its terms. *Id.*

4. A guaranty, in consideration of forbearing collection of a note for two years, of "the punctual payment of each and every installment of interest on said note as they shall become due, and also of each and every installment of interest that shall become due," on a certain other note, cannot be limited to interest before maturity of the notes, especially where the first note was already overdue when the guaranty was made. *Id.*

NOTES AND BRIEFS.

Contract of; continuing; severable. 380
Extent of obligation to guarantor. 659
Validity of contract of. 678

GUNPOWDER. See NUISANCES, 5.

HABEAS CORPUS. See EXTRADITION.

HAWKERS. See PEDDLERS, NOTES AND BRIEFS.

HEIRS.

NOTES AND BRIEFS.

Meaning of the word. 732, 747

HIGHWAYS. See also EMINENT DOMAIN, 5, 8; PUBLIC IMPROVEMENTS; TOLL ROADS, 6.

1. Towns and other municipalities have the supervision and control of public ways and streets within their borders, and are to preserve and maintain the rights of the public therein. *Charlotte* v. *Pembroke Iron Works* (Me.) 828

2. A party who built a dam on the line of a highway where it crossed a ravine, making a safe and suitable crossing by a causeway composed of logs, brush, stone and earth, which was used by the public and for a time maintained and repaired by the highway officers, is not chargeable with its maintenance and repair, or liable for injuries occasioned by its being out of repair. *Wallace* v. *Evans* (Kan.) 52

3. The failure of city authorities to clean out a gutter which has become improperly obstructed, or to remove snow between the sidewalk and the curb of a street, within a reasonable time after due notice that the melting of the snow permitted the formation of ice from day to day on the sidewalk, renders the city liable for injuries occasioned by slipping on ice which had thus formed upon the walk. *Gaylord* v. *New Britain* (Conn.) 752

4. The right of parties upon public ways and streets is a public right in which the whole community have an equal interest, with an equal right to complain of any infringement upon any such rights. *Charlotte* v. *Pembroke Iron Works* (Me.) 808

5. An ordinance forbidding the use of bicycles on that part of a public street devoted to the use of vehicles is void as against common right. *Swift* v. *Topeka* (Kan.) 772

6. An ordinance making it unlawful to ride upon any bicycle or velocipede upon any sidewalk within the city of Topeka, Kansas, or across the Kansas River bridge, will not be construed to forbid riding on that part of the bridge used for other vehicles, as such a construction would render the ordinance void. *Id.*

7. The creation of a public road through land of a private owner does not devest him of the fee, but gives the public merely a right of way. *Western U. Teleg. Co.* v. *Williams* (Va.) 429

8. A strip of grass left to grow in a rural or country road on the side of the beaten track belongs to the owner of the fee, and he has the right to harvest it. *People* v. *Foss* (Mich.) 472

9. A person has no right, from mere caprice or express malice, to drive upon and destroy a strip of grass growing between the two ditches on the sides of a highway, in the space usually known as the wrought or traveled part of the road, but of a portion of which another person owns the fee. *Id.*

10. The owner of premises must use reasonable care to prevent a tree on a sidewalk in front of them, which is under his control, from becoming dangerous to travelers upon the street, and for failure to do so is liable to a private action in favor of one thereby injured. *Weller* v. *McCormick* (N. J.) 798

11. A tree planted by a private person on a sidewalk in front of his premises is under his control, in the absence of statutory or municipal regulations to the contrary. *Id.*

12. In the absence of notice that the public claims to own, or exercise any control over, a tree on a sidewalk, the owner of the premises, who is in the actual occupation of them, is chargeable with knowledge of his exclusive proprietorship, and the duties which it entails, although the tree was there when he bought the premises. *Id.*

13. The frightening of a horse which was ordinarily gentle, by a yoke of calves coming suddenly out from bushes beside the highway, causing the horse to back the wagon over a steep river bank, and seriously injuring the occupants, is the proximate cause of the injury, where the road was in good condition for the width of 12 or 18 feet, although the driver could have managed the horse if the road had been wider. *Smith* v. *Kanawha County* (W. Va.) 82

NOTES AND BRIEFS.

See also ASSESSMENTS.

Injuries to, by means of dam. 53
Liability for damages resulting from defect in; contributory negligence; duty to keep in repair; care required in using. 83
Taxes for. 304
Rights of owner of fee. 429
Rights of owner of soil. 472
Right of abutter to crops growing in. 473
Adverse possession of; payment of taxes upon, estoppel of municipality; title by. 634
Right to use; bridges a part of; regulation of use of. 773
Use of streets in cities and towns; encroachment not legalized by time; use for business purposes; nuisance on; abatement; injunction against, private right of action. 828

HOMICIDE.

NOTES AND BRIEFS

Murder in first degree; what constitutes; premeditation. 84

HORSE-RACING.

Selling pools on a horse race run outside of the State is not licensed by the Tennessee Act of 1889 placing a tax on the business of selling pools upon any such race "in this or any other State." That Act does not repeal

Tenn. Code, § 4870, which makes betting a misdemeanor; nor does it enlarge the exemption therefrom, made by § 4871, of bets upon a horse race run upon a licensed track within the State. *Palmer* v. *State* (Tenn.) 280

HUSBAND AND WIFE. See also CURTESY; DOWER, 1; ESTOPPEL, 4; EVIDENCE, 4, 8, 14, 15; PAYMENT; RAPE.

1. The marriage of a boy in his sixteenth year, although declared by the Georgia Code to be void in the sense of being absolutely void, may nevertheless be ratified and confirmed by continuing, after arriving at the age of seventeen years, to cohabit with his wife as such. *Smith* v. *Smith* (Ga.) 362

2. A deed to a woman and her husband, and "the survivor of them, in his or her own right," gives each a life estate, with a fee to the survivor. *Mittel* v. *Karl* (Ill.) 655

3. The wife's conveyance of her separate real estate directly to her husband is void in Indiana, unless the transaction can be sustained upon the principles of equity. *Johnson* v. *Jouchert* (Ind.) 795

4. The provision that a married woman may sue "upon any cause of action in her own name," in the proviso to Md. Code, art. 45, § 7, which makes a wife liable for debts contracted in her separate business, and authorizes her to be sued for such debts as a *feme sole*, must be restricted by the preceding part of the section, and does not extend to an action for injury to her person. *Wolf* v. *Bauereis* (Md.) 680

5. A married woman may sue for injuries to her person without joining her husband, where, without her fault, he has deserted her, and left the State without intention of returning. *Id.*

6. A mortgage on the separate estate of a married woman, to secure a loan to her husband, may be upheld to the extent that the proceeds are invested in property purchased for her in her name. *Johnson* v. *Jouchert* (Ind.) 795

7. Remote grantees of a married woman cannot set up a plea of coverture in their own behalf against a mortgage executed by her, unless it appears that they are entitled to do so in equity and good conscience for the protection of a consideration actually paid her without notice of the invalid incumbrance, or with the mutual intention or agreement that they should be permitted to set up its invalidity. *Id.*

8. The mere failure of a grantor to inform his intended wife of a conveyance by him just before marriage is not of itself sufficient to make it fraudulent as to her. *Dudley* v. *Dudley* (Wis.) 814

9. A conveyance to the grantor's mother, to whom he was largely indebted, to carry out the wishes of his deceased father, and in the belief that she needed it much more than he did, although it was not made in payment of the debt, but on a nominal consideration and without the knowledge of his intended wife, whom he soon after married, is not fraudulent as to her. *Id.*

10. The fact that a conveyance made by a man with the consent of his intended wife reserved a life estate in himself is not a matter of which she can complain. *Murray* v. *Murray* (Ky.) 95

11. A conveyance upon the eve of marriage, to be regarded in equity as a fraud upon the legal rights of the intended wife, and consequently not binding upon her, must be made without her consent or knowledge. *Id.*

12. In South Dakota a wife justified by her husband's misconduct in living separate from him, may maintain an independent action against him for her support without regard to the question of divorce. *Bueter* v. *Bueter* (S. D.) 562

13. In an independent action for her support by a wife justified by her husband's misconduct in living separate from him, if the wife is destitute the court has power to include in its judgment an allowance of attorneys' fees as necessaries for her. *Id.*

14. A wife who executed articles of separation between herself and her husband under menace is entitled to have them rescinded, and to a judgment annulling and setting them aside. *Id.*

15. Enticing a husband away from his wife and depriving her of his society and support give her no right of action. *Duffies* v. *Duffies* (Wis.) 420

16. An action for debauching and carnally knowing her husband, thereby alienating his affections, cannot be maintained by a wife against another woman. *Doe* v. *Roe* (Me.) 833

NOTES AND BRIEFS.

Suretyship of married woman; foreclosure of wife's mortgage; defense of coverture; estoppel. 406

Action by wife for personal injuries. 680

Deed of separate property to husband; mortgage to secure his debts. 795

Ante-nuptial fraud; relief in equity. 814

Dower in life estate. 814

IMPROVEMENTS. See also PARTITION, NOTES AND BRIEFS.

Purchasers in good faith of land in which their grantors have in fact only a life estate, who make valuable improvements while in possession, before learning of the defect in their title, should be allowed, on a sale in partition, the value of the improvements before division of the proceeds. *Killmer* v. *Wuchner* (Iowa) 289

INFANTS. See NEGLIGENCE, 3, 4.

INJUNCTION. See also CORPORATIONS, 16; COURTS, 3, 5.

1. Some special injury, or necessity to protect the rights of some person, is necessary as the basis of an injunction. *Janesville* v. *Carpenter* (Wis.) 808

2. That a building will violate an ordinance will not of itself give cause of action for an injunction. *Id.*

3. An injunction cannot be granted against the erection of a building upon piles in the bed of a river on defendant's own land, which will not damage anyone, merely because others may

follow his example and a row of similar buildings may be erected which may give rise to dangers by fire and flood and to the public health. *Id.*

4. The fraudulent use of marks and labels for the purpose of deceiving the public will not be enjoined at the instance of one who does not show that he is himself a manufacturer or owner of or dealer in the articles which are fraudulently represented by the counterfeited labels to be his. Hence the fact that persons are officers or members of an association which has adopted a label to show that the articles bearing it were manufactured by its members does not, without more, entitle them to maintain a bill to enjoin the fraudulent use of such label. *Weener* v. *Brayton* (Mass.) 640

5. To entitle one to an injunction to restrain an alleged invasion of his right of property in a trade-mark, he must show that he is in some way the owner thereof by reason of some business which he is transacting and to which its use is incident, and that its use is not merely a personal privilege which he possesses as a member of a particular association of wide extent and embracing many members of varied interests. *Id.*

6. Where numerous acts are being committed and their continuance threatened under a claim of right by one person on the land of another, which acts constitute a trespass, and the injury resulting from each act is, or would be, trifling in amount as compared with the expense of prosecuting actions at law to recover damages therefor, the owner may resort, in the first instance, to a court of equity for appropriate relief. *Lembeck* v. *Nye* (Ohio) 578

7. Taxpayers may maintain a suit for an injunction, in behalf of themselves and other taxpayers, to prevent illegal acts of municipal authorities which will increase the burden of taxation. *Mauldin* v. *Greenville* (S. C.) 291

8. An injunction will not be granted in favor of taxpayers to restrain payment, to the holders of void town bonds, of moneys which have been collected without hindrance or protest for the special purpose of paying such bonds. *Calhoun* v. *Delhi & M. R. Co.* (N. Y.) 248

9. Where an injunction is sought against a county to prevent the appropriation of its revenues to aid in the building of a bridge in a city, and the allegations of the bill are that the bridge is on a city street, and not a county road or highway, and that the county outside of the city is nowise interested in it, and that it is for the sole benefit and advantage of the city, it is error to sustain a demurrer to the bill. *Skinner* v. *Henderson* (Fla.) 55

10. An injunction will not be granted to restrain the use of pipes laid in a highway for the transportation of natural gas, at the instance of the owner of the fee, who has received no compensation, where he knowingly permitted the work to proceed under a license from the board of county commissioners until large sums of money had been expended, and it would be ruinous to the company to stop it, and where many citizens have acquired rights on the faith of the successful completion of the work,—especially where compensation can be recovered by the landowner in an appropriate action for that purpose. *Kincaid* v. *Indianapolis Natural Gas Co.* (Ind.) 602

11. The possibility that a person may be expelled from an incorporated association in case of his neglect to pay fines if they should be imposed upon him, where no intention to expel him is shown, is not sufficient to warrant an injunction against proceeding to try him for alleged violation of the by-laws making him liable to fines. *Thomas* v. *Musical Mut. Prot. Union* (N. Y.) 175

12. Where the imposition of fines, payment of which the corporation has no means of enforcing except through the courts, is the only punishment provided for violation of by-laws, a party cited for trial under such by-laws has no right to an injunction restraining such action, since his remedy at law is sufficient. *Id.*

13. An adjudication cannot be obtained in advance as to the validity of the by-laws of an incorporated association, on an application for injunction by a member who has been cited to show cause why he should not be punished for violating such by-laws, unless such punishment would subject him to irreparable injury, and other adequate means of redress are not open to him. *Id.*

NOTES AND BRIEFS.

To restrain collection of debt in foreign State. 515

To protect trade mark. 640

To restrain citizen from bringing suit in courts of another State. 723

To prevent cloud on title. 727

INNKEEPERS. See also ASSAULT AND BATTERY, 2.

1. The intoxication of a guest at an inn is no excuse for his negligence which contributes to the loss of his property by theft. *Shultz* v. *Wall* (Pa.) 97

2. The responsibility of an innkeeper for goods and moneys of his guest extends to moneys stolen from the guest, unless they were stolen by a servant or companion of the guest. *Id.*

3. When persons unobjectionable on account of character and race enter a hotel, not as guests, but intent on pleasure or profit to be derived from intercourse with its inmates, they are there not of right, but under an implied license that the landlord may revoke at any time. *State* v. *Steele* (N. C.) 516

4. The proprietor of a public house has a right to request a person who visits it, not as a guest or on business with guests, to depart; and if he refuses, the innkeeper may expel him without using excessive force. *Id.*

5. If a person who has previously violated the rules of a hotel by soliciting business there is found on the premises, he may be ejected forcibly if he does not go when requested or explain his purpose, although he entered for a proper purpose. *Id.*

6. One who goes into a hotel at the request of a guest, to confer with him on business, may

be expelled if while there he engages in "drumming" for his business, against rules of the hotel, after notice to desist. *State* v. *Steele* (N. C.) 516

7. Regulations of a hotel providing that "no liveryman, or agent of any transportation or baggage company, no washerwoman or sewing woman not connected with the house, or loafers, or loungers, or objectionable persons, will be allowed in the hotel," are reasonable; and any person violating them may be expelled after notice to desist from violating them, if it be done without using excessive force. *Id.*

8. Guests of a hotel, and travelers or other persons entering it with the bona fide intent of becoming guests, cannot be lawfully prevented from going in, or put out by force after entrance, provided they are able to pay the charges and tender the money necessary for that purpose, if requested by the landlord, unless they be persons of bad or suspicious character or of vulgar habits, or so objectionable to the patrons of the house on account of the race to which they belong that it would injure the business of the house to admit them, or unless they undertake to take advantage of the freedom of the hotel to injure the landlord's chances of profit derived either from his inn or any business incidental to or connected with its management, constituting a part of the provisions for the wants and pleasure of his patrons. *Id.*

9. The mere failure to order or put out one liveryman, who has been notified not to solicit business in a hotel, does not make it unlawful to expel another who is violating a rule against such business. *Id.*

10. An innkeeper can make a valid contract to give another the exclusive privilege of remaining in the house and soliciting patronage from the guests in any business that grows out of providing for their comfort and pleasure. *Id.*

11. A contract by an innkeeper for a percentum of the amount realized by another person from the exercise of the exclusive privilege of doing a livery business with his guests is not invalid; and rivals in the livery business may be properly excluded from soliciting business in the house. *Id.*

NOTES AND BRIEFS.

Responsibility of; liability as insurer; as bailee. 97

INSANE PERSONS.

1. Insanity which leads the person afflicted with it to make indecent exposure of his person in public renders him dangerous to community, within the meaning of Ind. Rev. Stat. 1881, §§ 5142–5150, which provide for the restraint of such persons at public expense and the reimbursement of the public treasury out of their estates. *Montgomery County* v. *Ristine* (Ind.) 461

2. County commissioners are not authorized to enter into contracts for the care and support of persons in the county asylums for the poor, which are organized solely for the purpose of public charity and benevolence. Hence no recovery can be had by them upon a contract to pay for care and support furnished to an insane person. *Id.*

NOTES AND BRIEFS.

Insanity as a defense. 84

INSOLVENCY AND ASSIGNMENT FOR CREDITORS.

See also CONFLICT OF LAWS, 3.

1. A creditor of an insolvent has the right to prove and have dividends upon his entire estate, irrespective of collateral securities. *People* v. *Remington & Sons* (N. Y.) 458

2. There is nothing in the Massachusetts Insolvency Law indicating an intent to refuse foreign creditors access to the local courts to enforce their claims after a discharge, as a merely local rule of procedure, or otherwise than as a consequence of the substantive right having been barred by the discharge. Hence, since the right cannot be barred, the action may be maintained. *Phœnix Nat. Bank* v. *Batcheller* (Mass.) 644

NOTES AND BRIEFS.

Insolvency; rule of distribution of estate. 458

No extraterritorial efficacy to statutes concerning. 644

INSURANCE.

See also ACTION OR SUIT, 6, 8; TRIAL, 28.

1. A man has an insurable interest in buildings on land purchased and paid for by him, though conveyed to his wife, where he has in fact possession and the entire beneficial use of the premises, and is the owner of all the personal property thereon, managing the place on his own account and using the proceeds to support the family, while there is an understanding between him and his wife that she will convey the land to him at his request. *Horsch* v. *Dwelling-House Ins. Co.* (Wis.) 806

2. A contract of insurance on houses several miles apart, which insures each house for a specified sum, is divisible, although the premium is stated as a gross sum, where there is nothing to show any difference between the houses in class or rates. A transfer of one without the consent of the insurer, avoiding the policy as to that, does not make it void as to the other. *Loomis* v. *Rockford Ins. Co.* (Wis.) 834

3. A binding slip containing a memorandum to identify the parties to a contract of insurance, the subject matter, and the principal terms, "to be binding until policy is delivered," is a contract for temporary insurance subject to the conditions contained in the ordinary policy in use by the company. *Lipman* v. *Niagara F. Ins. Co.* (N. Y.) 719

4. The word "heirs," in a certificate of life insurance, where there is no context to explain it, means those who would, under the Statute of Distributions, be entitled to the personal estate of the insured. *Johnson* v. *Supreme Lodge Knights of Honor* (Ark.) 732

5. A widow is not one of the heirs of her deceased husband, within the meaning of an insurance policy, so as to be entitled to share in the proceeds, under Arkansas statutes, which

give her half of the husband's personal estate as dower, absolutely and independently of creditors, and provide for distribution subject to debts and the widow's dower. *Id.*

6. No one except the insurer by a benefit certificate can object to the right of brothers and sisters of a person insured to take the proceeds of his certificate, on the ground that the constitution of the insurer limits the right to take the benefits to members of the family of the insured. *Id.*

7. An applicant for insurance, who gives correct answers to a general agent respecting incumbrances, is not prejudiced by the agent's failure to mention them in the written application which the applicant signs, although the policy stipulates that the application shall be considered a part of the policy and a warranty of the statements therein contained. *German Ins. Co.* v. *Gray* (Kan.) 70

8. The words "hurt" and "wound," in a question asked of an applicant for life insurance, as to any "wound, hurt, or serious bodily injury" received by him, mean an injury to the body causing an impairment of health or strength, or rendering the person more liable to contract disease, or less able to resist its effects. *Bancroft* v. *Home Ben. Asso.* (N. Y.) 68

9. A slight blow on the throat while engaged in fencing, which causes a person to raise a little blood, in consequence of which he is confined to his bed and attended by a physician for the greater part of three days, with no further hemorrhage from the day he was struck to the date of his death, a year and a half thereafter, does not constitute "any wound, hurt, or serious bodily injury," within the meaning of a question in an application for life insurance. *Id.*

10. Machinery and apparatus used in the business of manufacturing leather and morocco, including boiler, engine, etc., being the only property covered by a policy of insurance, do not constitute a mill, and the standing still thereof does not create a forfeiture, under a policy which provides that "if a building covered by this policy shall become vacant or unoccupied, or if a mill or manufactory shall stand idle, . . . all liability hereunder shall thereupon cease," where a further provision of the policy as to the falling of a building expressly declares that the policy shall cease as to property therein as well as to the building. *Halpin* v. *Ins. Co. of North America* (N. Y.) 79

11. The death of the insured does not make a change in the title such as will void a policy insuring him, "his executors, administrators, and assigns," which provides that it shall be void in case "any change takes place in the title, use, occupation, or possession thereof whatsoever." *Richardson* v. *German Ins. Co.* (Ky.) 800

12. A notice to brokers is a good notice of a cancellation of insurance obtained by them, where it is subject to a condition that it may be terminated by notice to the "person who procured the insurance." *Lipman* v. *Niagara F. Ins. Co.* (N. Y.) 719

13. The cancellation of an insurance policy which provides that it may be terminated on notice is effected *eo instanti* on notice given in good faith by the insurer, if no premium has been paid. *Id.*

14. A statutory prohibition against insurance by foreign corporations without compliance with certain requirements, under a certain penalty, does not make a policy issued without such compliance void as to the insured. *Pennypacker* v. *Capital Ins. Co.* (Iowa) 236

15. An agreement to pay a sum received from a death assessment, not exceeding $1,000, with a further provision that the death claim shall be payable within sixty days after proof, giving the form of notice and process for collecting death assessments, and containing a promise by insured to pay assessments,—imports a promise by the insurance association to make, or cause to be made, the necessary assessment. *Lawler* v. *Murphy* (Conn.) 113

16. A general agent of an insurance company can modify the insurance contract or waive a condition of a written policy by parol. *German Ins. Co.* v. *Gray* (Kan.) 70

17. A provision in an insurance policy that no agent, other than the president or secretary, shall have authority to waive any terms or conditions of the policy, is ineffectual to prevent such waiver by a general agent. *Id.*

18. The failure of an insurance company to object, within a reasonable time, to proofs of loss taken by its duly authorized adjuster, who has expressed satisfaction with the same and promised payment of the loss, precludes it from thereafter objecting that they are insufficient. *Id.*

19. An action at law can be sustained for breach of the contract of an insurance organization to make an assessment. *Lawler* v. *Murphy* (Conn.) 113

20. When a policy of fire insurance provides that action thereon must be brought within a specified time after the loss occurs, the limitation runs from the date of the fire, although, under other provisions of the policy, the cause of action does not accrue until some time after the fire. *Travelers Ins. Co.* v. *California Ins. Co.* (N. D.) 769

21. The time for bringing suit on a policy which provides that no suit or action shall be commenced unless within twelve months next after the fire, and also provides that a claim on the policy shall be due and payable sixty days after full completion by the assured of certain requirements of the policy, is not lost by the expiration of the twelve months after the fire, where a cause of action has not then accrued by completion of such requirements, if the company has insisted on these requirements and the insured has complied as rapidly as he was able. *Case* v. *Sun Ins. Co.* (Cal.) 48

22. The measure of damages for breach of an agreement by an insurance organization to make an assessment, and to pay the proceeds thereof, not exceeding $1,000, where each member contracts to pay an assessment of whatever the officials deem necessary upon the death of any member, is prima facie the sum of $1,000. *Lawler* v. *Murphy* (Conn.) 113

NOTES AND BRIEFS.

INSURANCE COMPANIES.

A corporation of another State, authorized to issue policies on the lives of members, upon the assessment plan, for the benefit of any person who has an insurable interest, is not entitled to carry on business in Ohio, under Ohio Rev Stat. §§ 3630, 3630 *E*, which allow assessment companies to insure lives of members only for the benefit of their families and heirs. *State, Attorney-General,* v. *Western U. Mut. L. & Acc. Soc.* (Ohio) 129

NOTES AND BRIEFS.

INTEREST.

Interest should be allowed on the value of property condemned for public use, from the time of its appropriation. *Alloway* v. *Nashville* (Tenn.) 123

INTOXICATING LIQUORS.

The removal of a certain church will not affect the portion of a statute prohibiting the sale of intoxicating liquor within 3 miles of such church, where the statute does not show that its object was to protect the church alone. *State* v. *Eaves* (N. C.) 259

INTOXICATION. See CRIMINAL LAW, NOTES AND BRIEFS.

JUDGMENT. See also ASSOCIATIONS, 7; BANKRUPTCY; CONTEMPT, 4; GARNISHMENT, 8.

1. A foreign judgment cannot be reviewed for any reasons other than for fraud or want of jurisdiction, where it was rendered by a court of competent jurisdiction, after due service of process or entry of appearance, and a hearing upon the issues. *McMullen* v. *Richie* (C. C. N. D. Ohio) 268

2. Defendant's absence, and his ignorance of the fact that judgment was entered against him, give him no right to impeach it, where he had appeared in the case by counsel. *Id.*

3. An adjudication that a person is not in such mental condition as to be incapable of taking care of himself, by denial of an application to appoint a guardian for him, is not necessarily an adjudication that he is not insane at all, and does not estop the applicant from claiming that such person is incompetent to make a will. *Manley* v. *Staples* (Vt.) 707

4. A judgment of a court having no jurisdiction of the subject-matter is not a bar to another suit. *Western U. Teleg. Co.* v. *Taylor* (Ga.) 189

5. A decision in a suit which is practically carried on by one party, who pays all the expenses of both sides, will not be held conclusive of the question involved when presented in another suit. *Calhoun* v. *Delhi & M. R. Co.* (N. Y.) 248

NOTES AND BRIEFS.

JUDICIAL NOTICE. See EVIDENCE, I.

LABORERS. See CORPORATIONS, 13.

LACHES. See LIMITATION OF ACTIONS, 14.

LAKES. See WATERS AND WATERCOURSES, NOTES AND BRIEFS.

LANDLORD AND TENANT.

1. The mere fact that a person goes into possession under a parol lease which is void because for a longer time than one year does not create a yearly tenancy, although payment of an aliquot part of the annual rent would be evidence of a yearly tenancy. *Talamo* v. *Spitzmiller* (N. Y.) 221

2. A mere tenancy at will, subject to the payment of the stipulated rate of rent as for use and occupation, is created by going into possession under an oral lease for more than one year. *Id.*

3. A second lessee may maintain unlawful detainer against the first lessee in possession, after all his rights are absolutely forfeited. *Guffey* v. *Hukill* (W. Va.) 759

4. Where a lease for years for drilling for petroleum oil and gas contains a provision that the parties of the second part covenant to commence operations within nine months or to thereafter pay $1.33⅓ per month until work is commenced, and that a failure to comply with either condition shall work an absolute forfeiture of the lease, and there is no covenant for re-entry, if on failure to commence operations or to pay money in lieu thereof, the lessor leases to another person, the first lease is avoided and the second lease is good against it, as the execution thereof is a sufficient declaration of forfeiture without demand and re-entry *Id.*

5. The occupation of a parsonage by a min-

ister of the gospel after his suspension by the church authorities is not that of a servant of the church or trustees, in such sense as to render him a trespasser on his refusal to leave it or permit his eviction by officers. *Bristor* v. *Burr* (N. Y.) 710

6. Each of several rooms in a building occupied by separate tenants is a "house," within the meaning of a statute which gives a lien on the property of a tenant while it remains in the house rented; and a removal of such property, with the landlord's consent, from one room to another in the same building, taken under a new contract, defeats the lien. *Wolcott* v. *Ashenfelter* (N. M.) 691

7. Where a lease for years contains a clause of forfeiture for breach of its covenant to pay rent or other covenant, but no clause of re-entry for such forfeiture, demand and re-entry is not the only mode by which the landlord may enforce the forfeiture. *Guffey* v. *Hukill* (W. Va.) 759

8. A mortgagor who, while in possession, verbally leases the premises at a rent payable quarterly, cannot recover from the lessee for two and one half months' use and occupation preceding the mortgagee's entry and the lessee's attornment to him, where the mortgagee, fifteen days before the expiration of the current quarter, has duly entered and taken possession for condition broken, and the tenant, on his demand, thereupon agrees to, and at the expiration of the quarter does, pay to him the rent for the whole quarter. *Anderson* v. *Robbins* (Me.) 568

9. A concealed well operating as a cesspool under a house, being only partly filled up and containing water, dead vermin, and filth, from which noxious vapors, etc., arise to the injury of the health of the occupants, constitutes a nuisance and renders the owner who erected the house over it liable for damages sustained therefrom by a tenant who had no knowledge of it. *Kern* v. *Myll* (Mich.) 682

NOTES AND BRIEFS.

Tenancy from year to year; termination of; effect of payment of rent. 221

Duty of landlord to repair. 682

Part of house as dwelling. 691

Landlord's lien; house defined. 692

Re-entry on forfeiture; election of remedies. 759

LARCENY. See REPLEVIN.

LAW OF PLACE. See CONFLICT OF LAWS.

LEGISLATURE. See CONSTITUTIONAL LAW, 2.

LEVY AND SEIZURE. See also CONSTITUTIONAL LAW, 6; GAMING, 1.

1. A judgment for conversion of exempt property, including costs, is itself exempt. *Below* v. *Robbins* (Wis.) 467

2. Trover and replevin being concurrent remedies, the fact that a party could have replevied exempt property will not prevent him from clain
conversion

3. The t
pension n
made to th
it from liat
Stat. § 474

4. Share
corporated
which has
property, w
tions so far
sold on exe
§ 7097, pro
"bank, insu
stock comp
pelled to is
has done so
fer, and h
thereof shal
privileges of
a member.

5. A retu
was levied u
personally u
copy, witho
upon the lan
whose posse
there declare
by Miss. Cod
occupied pre
upon,—is ins
the attachme
the interveni
v. *People's Ba*

6. Where
actors, all o
sion in case a
tious. *Contra*

LIBEL A

PLEADIN

1. Any wri
dency to inju
profession, cal
v. *Conway* (P

2. A public
a certain syste
to teach that
authority, the
is libelous.

3. A publica
bank had becor
work, and whi
injurious state
affairs, which
tory in a legal
se, although it
him to no disg
the reason that
a temporal loss
character and e
Francis (N. Y.)

4. It is compe
words spoken b
tion, to the ef
had been excom
longer employe
maliciously and
physician in his
(Mass.)

5. An action will lie to recover damages for the utterance of a false imputation, although not actually defamatory, if it was made with the express purpose of injuring plaintiff in his profession, and such injury actually follows as the probable and natural result of the speaking of the words, just as was intended by defendant. *Morasse* v. *Brochu* (Mass.) 524

6. It is not a legal excuse that defamatory matter was published accidentally or inadvertently, or with good motives, and with an honest belief in its truth. *Moore* v. *Francis* (N. Y.) 214

7. Although an action for libel or slander may be maintained, if a criminal accusation was made with no bona fide intention of prosecuting it, yet an action brought for malicious prosecution cannot be retained and treated as one for libel and slander, if the defamatory words are not set out in the complaint. *Cooper* v. *Armour* (C. C. N. D. N. Y.) 47

NOTES AND BRIEFS.

See also TRIAL.

Words tending to injure person in office, or professional persons, or person in calling or trade. 193

Stating that one is insane; necessity of malice. 214

Office of innuendo; words actionable *per se;* measure of damages; averment of damages. 526

LICENSE. See also CONSTITUTIONAL LAW, 9; HORSE RACING; INNKEEPERS, 3; PEDDLERS, NOTES AND BRIEFS; WATERS AND WATERCOURSES, 13.

1. Mere taxation of an unlawful business does not legalize it. *Palmer* v. *State* (Tenn.) 280

2. One whose vocation is to go from place to place with a sample stove carried upon a wagon, exhibiting the sample and procuring orders to be filled by his employers through their agents, is a peddler, within the meaning of Ga. Code, § 1631, requiring a license of "every peddler or itinerant trader by sample or otherwise." *Wrought Iron Range Co.* v. *Johnson* (Ga.) 273

3. Only the person who itinerates for trading purposes is a peddler. His employer, though the owner of the goods, team, and vehicle, is not required to obtain a license, or subject to any forfeiture for failure to do so. *Id.*

LIENS. See also LANDLORD AND TENANT, 6.

1. A person entitled to a lien on a railway for materials furnished for its construction may in his notice of lien confine his claim to that portion or section of the road in the construction of which his material was used. *Giant Powder Co.* v. *Oregon P. R. Co.* (Or.) 700

2. Giant powder furnished by the manufacturer to a contractor for the construction of a railway, and used by the latter in the progress of such work, is "material," within the purview of the Oregon Lien Law of 1885, for the value of which such manufacturer is entitled to a lien on the railway, or such portion thereof as the powder was used in the construction of. *Id.*

3. The general phrase in the Oregon Act of 1885, "any other structure," following, as it does, a specific enumeration of works declared to be subject to a lien for labor and materials furnished for their construction,—such as a "building," "ditch," "flume," and "tunnel,"—must be held to include a railway. *Id.*

NOTES AND BRIEFS.

Mechanics'; on railroads; decisions of different States. 700

LIMITATION OF ACTIONS. See also GUARANTY, 1; INSURANCE, 20, 21.

1. After a cause of action against a principal debtor is barred, a surety as to whom the statute has not run because he has been absent from the State cannot acquire any right of action against the principal by payment of the demand. *Stone* v. *Hammell* (Cal.) 425

2. One who has made out a prima facie case for the recovery of land is not prevented from attacking as fraudulent a deed set up in defense, because the time for bringing an action to set aside the conveyance as fraudulent has expired. *Amaker* v. *New* (S. C.) 687

3. The period of six years from the discovery of the fraud, within which an action to set aside a fraudulent conveyance must be brought, under S. C. Code, § 112, does not apply where a judgment creditor, who has purchased the land on execution sale made in disregard of the fraudulent deed, brings an action to recover possession after the death of a widow having a superior claim of dower, to whom he had been obliged temporarily to surrender possession. *Id.*

4. Express continuing trusts are excluded from the operation of Statutes of Limitation, while implied trusts are subject thereto. *Cone* v. *Dunham* (Conn.) 647

5. Leaving corporate stock in the possession and name of the seller, the sale being evidenced only by a declaration thereof in a receipt given for the money paid, and there being no agreement as to the future disposition of the stock or the dividends thereon, creates an implied trust in the seller which is enforceable at law and subject to the operation of the Statute of Limitations. *Id.*

6. The bar of the Statute of Limitations against a suit brought against a woman and her children, all being *cestuis que trust*, there being no trustee, is not saved, under Tenn. Code, § 2755, by a suit brought within one year preceding against the woman and her husband and a person as trustee who was no longer such, which suit was dismissed because of the failure to make the children, who were remaindermen, as well as *cestuis que trust*, parties to the case. *Hughes* v. *Brown* (Tenn.) 480

7. The amendment of a declaration does not extend the running of the Statute of Limitations, if it is not founded upon a new cause of action. *Wolf* v. *Bauereis* (Md.) 680

8. If a nonresident is absent from the State when a cause of action accrues against him, the statute will not commence running against

him because he occasionally comes into the State, although an action at such times could be commenced against him by the exercise of ordinary diligence. *Stanley* v. *Stanley* (Ohio) 833

9. The presence of the defendant in the State for the full period of the time limited for bringing an action, either continuously or in the aggregate, is necessary to constitute a bar of the action, under Ohio Rev. Stat. § 4989. *Id.*

10. A remedy at law on the bond of a trustee having proved inadequate by reason of the insolvency of the sureties, a remedy in equity to reach property not subject to execution is barred when delayed until the bond, and also the decree thereon, is barred. *Hughes* v. *Brown* (Tenn.) 480

11. A bill to charge the payment of an equitable claim upon a trust estate, although purely equitable, is subject to the Statute of Limitations. *Id.*

12. A statutory period of limitation of equitable actions is not, where a purely equitable remedy is invoked, equivalent to a direction that no shorter period shall be a bar to relief in any case, and does not preclude a denial of relief for unreasonable delay, in accordance with equitable principles. *Calhoun* v. *Delhi & M. R. Co.* (N. Y.) 248

13. The failure, for nearly ten years, of a town and its taxpayers to give warning or protest against dealing with or taking its void bonds, with affirmative acts of recognition encouraging investment therein as safe and valid securities, is sufficient to defeat an equitable action for their cancellation. *Id.*

14. The equitable remedy for the cancellation of town bonds may be refused by reason of long delay and acquiescence on the part of the town and its taxpayers, accompanied by frequent acts recognizing the validity of the bonds, although the delay is not continued for the statutory period of limitation of equitable actions. *Id.*

15. The inability of a municipal corporation to make valid by acquiescence or recognition, obligations which it had no power to create, will not prevent consideration of such matters in determining whether it shall be denied a remedy because of laches. *Id.*

NOTES AND BRIEFS.

Rule as to laches. 248

Against persons absent from State. 833

Absence from State, effect of. 425

Application to trusts and equitable actions. 480

As to trusts; effect of repudiation; in cases of concurrent jurisdiction in law and equity; on claim against estates. 647

In case of concealed fraud. 687

LIS PENDENS.

Notice of the pendency of a bill is not notice to a purchaser of lands of matters set up by a subsequent amendment to the bill. *Holland* v. *Citizens Sav. Bank* (R. I.) 553

Notice

LOTTI

1. Any thing is ing of a of a lotte land as *lock* v. *St*

2. The drawn, b or ticket prevent a from bein

3. Bon with cond their char for the pa a species c demnation subject to

Schemes

MALICI

An acti not lie in f tion has charging a prehended issued. *C*

Damages

MANDA

1. The g compelled b the trustees who hold hi public dutie on the trea *Territorial I*

2. The fa of schools w cannot be rel of a mandate commissione if, upon his votes, a certi to him, and upon the disc His right to b into except b for that pur *County Comrs*

3. A return denial of a w person in a so expelled, if th expulsion, wh proceedings o ducted in goo accorded a fu proper judgme the whole proc accuracy, altho

racy of statement is lacking, and it does not appear that the accused was found guilty *in totidem verbis* of the acts for which the by-laws permit expulsion. *Com. Burt,* v. *Union League* (Pa.) 195

4. Mandamus, and not *quo warranto,* is the proper remedy when a relator in office *de jure et de facto* is interfered with by one whose lack of title *de jure* is *res judicata. State, Leeds,* v. *Atlantic City* (N. J.) 697

5. The proper remedy to test the claimant's title to an office occupied *de facto* by a person claiming it under color of right is *quo warranto,* and not mandamus. *Id.*

6. Where a mandamus is applied for to compel a municipal corporation to restore relator to an office to which he is prima facie entitled, the incumbent is not a necessary party to the allowance of a peremptory mandamus. *Id.*

NOTES AND BRIEFS.

Power of, to control governor of Territory. 188

To obtain reinstatement in social organization or club. 195

Answer to writ; how facts must be pleaded. 197

MARRIAGE. See FRAUD AND FRAUDULENT CONVEYANCES, NOTES AND BRIEFS; HUSBAND AND WIFE.

MARRIED WOMAN. See HUSBAND AND WIFE.

MARSHALING ASSETS. See EXECUTORS AND ADMINISTRATORS, 1, 5.

MASTER AND SERVANT. See also CARRIERS, 4, 6, 7; TRIAL, 16.

1. A boy twelve years old employed to take lumber away from a flooring machine and load it on a wagon, who is injured in attempting, under orders of the foreman of the mill, to oil dangerous machinery while in motion, which was disconnected with the service for which he was employed, may recover damages from his employer. *Hinckley* v. *Horazdowski* (Ill.) 490

2. The rule that the common master is not liable for an injury caused by the negligence of a fellow servant does not apply where the injured servant is a child incapable of comprehending the risk of the employment arising from the possibility of such negligence. *Id.*

3. A statute making railway companies liable to employés for negligence of fellow servants must, to avoid the imputation of class legislation, be construed to apply only to the peculiar hazards incident to the use and occupation of railroads, and injuries resulting from such dangers. *Johnson* v. *St. Paul & D. R. Co.* (Minn.) 419

4. Injuries to one of a crew of men engaged in repairing a bridge, caused by the negligence of a fellow servant in leaving the draw unfastened, are not the result of dangers peculiar to the use and operation of railroads, and do not give him a right of action against the company, under a statute making railroad companies liable to employés for injuries caused by negligence of a fellow servant. *Id.*

5. Fellow servants owe to each other the duty to exercise ordinary care and prudence in the prosecution of their work, and for failure to do so are liable at common law to each other for resulting personal injury. *Hare* v. *McIntyre* (Me.) 450

6. A master, who commits the running of his elevator to an employé who is ignorant in regard to such service is bound to furnish him for a reasonable length of time with a competent instructor, and will be liable to the employé for any injury resulting from the incompetency or negligence of the instructor furnished. *Brennan* v. *Gordon* (N. Y.) 818

7. An instruction in an action by a servant to recover from his master damages for injuries alleged to have resulted from the negligence of one furnished by the master to instruct the servant as to how to run an elevator, is erroneous if it gives the jury to understand that the master's whole duty was performed if he furnished an instructor as competent as he himself was. *Id.*

8. If a torpedo is placed on a railroad track by an employé of the company, although through mere caprice and contrary to the rules of the company, and negligently left there where he knows children are accustomed to pass, and is picked up by children, and injures them by an explosion, the company is liable. *Pittsburgh, C. & St. L. R. Co.* v. *Shields* (Ohio) 464

9. The duty of observing the greatest care in the custody and use of dangerous agencies cannot be shifted by a master to his servants, so as to exonerate him from the negligence of a servant in the use and custody of them. *Id.*

10. It is immaterial, so far as the liability of the master is concerned, what use may have been made of a dangerous instrument, where injury results from negligence in the custody of it. *Id.*

11. Instructions by a master to an employé not to commit an assault and battery on any person and not to break the law, when sending him to get an organ which is in the possession of another person, knowing that the errand is likely to excite indignation and resistance, will not relieve him from liability for a wrongful assault made by his employé while engaged in the business of seizing and carrying away the organ. *McClung* v. *Dearborne* (Pa.) 204

NOTES AND BRIEFS.

Liability for torts of servant. 204, 225, 846

Liability for servant's negligence. 464

Duty as to minor employés; assumption of risks by minors; contributory negligence. 490

Liability for defective and dangerous appliances; burden of proof. 636

Vice-principals and agents; duty to instruct servant in use of dangerous machinery; accidents in use of elevators. 818

MAXIMS. See also ACTION OR SUIT, 1.

1. A communi observantia non est recedendum. *O'Donnell* v. *Glenn* (Mont.) 629

2. Communis error facit jus. *Id.*

3. Ex dolo malo non oritur actio. *Kirkpatrick* v. *Clark* (Ill.) 511

4. Ex turpi causa non oritur actio. *Id.*

5. In pari delicto, potior est conditio defendentis et possidentis. *Id.*

6. Minime mutanda sunt quæ certam interpretationem habuerunt. *O'Donnell* v. *Glenn* (Mont.) 629

7. Necessitas inducit privilegium. *State* v. *Dowell* (N. C.) 297

8. Non dormientibus sed vigilantibus, leges subveniunt. *Friesleben* v. *Shallcross* (Del.) 337

9. Nullum tempus occurrit regi. *Charlotte* v. *Pembroke Iron Works* (Me.) 828

10. Qui facit per alium facit per se. *McClung* v. *Dearborne* (Pa.) 204

11. Res judicata pro veritate habetur. *O'Donnell* v. *Glenn* (Mont.) 629

12. Respondeat superior. *Abrahams* v. *California Powder Works* (N. M.) 878

13. Volenti non fit injuria. *Shultz* v. *Wall* (Pa.) 97

MONOPOLY. See also CARRIERS, 11; CORPORATIONS, 1, 2, 7.

The rule which prohibits the granting of monopolies applies only to such things as are of common right, and is never applied to things which are monopolies in their nature. Hence it will not prevent the granting, for a reasonable and fixed period, of the exclusive right to operate a railway line in certain streets. *Indianapolis Cable Street R. Co.* v. *Citizens Street R. Co.* (Ind.) 539

MORTGAGE. See also DEED; EXECUTORS AND ADMINISTRATORS, 6; PLEDGE AND COLLATERAL SECURITY, 6.

1. A mortgage upon real estate, made by the owner to a partnership in its firm name, to secure an indebtedness to it, duly executed and recorded as required by the statute, constitutes a valid lien upon the property in favor of the firm as a security for the indebtedness to it. *New Vienna Bank* v. *Johnson* (Ohio) 614

2. In order to mortgage land as security for a debt, it is not necessary, in all cases, to clothe the creditor with the legal title; it is sufficient if the intent to pledge the land as a security clearly appears from the instrument, and the instrument is duly executed and recorded as required by statute. *Id.*

3. The statutes of Ohio regulating the mode of signing, sealing, acknowledging, and recording mortgages, are limited in their application to these particulars; the legal or equitable effect of the instrument and its contents are unaffected thereby; and the rights of the parties and of third persons subsequently dealing with the land are to be determined by the general rules of law and equity applicable to the subject in analogous cases. *Id.*

4. The assignee of a mortgage cannot execute a power of sale thereby given, unless the debt secured has been transferred to him so as to pass the legal title thereto. *Sanford* v. *Kane* (Ill.) 724

5. A sale under a power in a mortgage, in gross as one parcel, of several separate and distinct tracts of land, is not void, but only voidable for good cause shown,—as, that it was the result of fraud, or that prejudice resulted to the mortgagor or owner of the equity of redemption. *Willard* v. *Finnegan* (Minn.) 50

6. A sale under a power in a mortgage will not be enjoined and set aside on the ground of a perversion of the power to improper purposes, where the mortgagee is acting within the letter of his power, unless the perversion is very clearly shown. *Holland* v. *Citizens Sav. Bank* (R. I.) 553

7. Perversion of the power to sell land under a mortgage is not shown by the fact that some advantage may accrue to the mortgagee besides the payment of the debt, or an advantage may accidently accrue thereby to others. *Id.*

8. The title of a bona fide purchaser for value without notice on a mortgage sale is not affected by the fact that the holder of the mortgage had prevented a tender by refusing to accept payment except on conditions which he had no right to make. *Id.*

9. Where two or more persons are interested in property subject to a mortgage, and one of them pays the mortgage debt for his own protection, he is entitled, not to have the mortgage assigned to him, but simply to succeed to the lien of the mortgage against the others in equity to the extent of his claim against them for indemnity, by way of subrogation. *Id.*

10. One who pays a mortgage is not entitled to an assignment thereof on the ground that it covers other property than her own, and because complications have arisen in the settlement of the mortgagor's estate making it important for her to have an assignment, where the divided ownership and the complications have arisen after the mortgage was given. *Id.*

11. A mere general creditor without any specific lien, although made a party defendant in a suit to foreclose a mortgage on the debtor's chattels, for the determination of a lien claimed by him, cannot question the validity of the mortgage. *Wolcott* v. *Ashenfelter* (N. M.) 691

12. A grantee who assumes and agrees to pay, as part of the purchase price of land, a mortgage which his grantor has given thereon, thereby undertakes to discharge the mortgagee's lien upon the land, and not simply to cancel the mortgage debt so far as it is a claim against individuals; and his failure to do so will render him liable to at least nominal damages. *Rice* v. *Sanders* (Mass.) 315

13. If several mortgages are assumed, and the grantee fails to pay the one first due, and permits it to be foreclosed and the property sold for its payment, he will be liable in damages to his grantor for the latter's loss of security against liability upon subsequent mortgages up to the amount of debts secured by them, even though they are not yet due. *Id.*

14. A redemption by a judgment creditor from a mortgage which is good on its face, and at most is merely voidable at the election of the purchaser at the mortgage sale, cannot be attacked in a suit between him and a ven-

dee of the mortgagor, whose rights have been cut off by the foreclosure. *Willard* v. *Finnegan* (Minn.) 50

NOTES AND BRIEFS.

Power of sale in; requisites to validity of sale. 50

Conveyance subject to; liability of county. 815

Attornment of tenant to mortgagee in possession. 568

Formalities as to execution. 614

Chattel; renewal of. 691

Assignee's power of sale. 724

MUNICIPAL CORPORATIONS. See also BONDS, 2; CONSTITUTIONAL LAW, 1, 3, 7; ELECTRIC LIGHTS; EVIDENCE, 5.

1. A town council which has power to pass all such ordinances as shall appear necessary and requisite for the health, welfare, etc., of the town, has the exclusive right to judge what is "necessary and requisite" to preserve the health of the town. *Summerville* v. *Pressley* (S. C.) 854

2. A penal ordinance to enforce a contract with a city is void where it does not relate to the morals, health, or safety of the people. *Newport* v. *Newport & C. Bridge Co.* (Ky.) 484

3. Whenever a city ordinance can be so construed and applied as to give it force and validity this will be done by the courts, although the construction so put upon it may not be the most obvious and natural one, or the literal one. *Swift* v. *Topeka* (Kan.) 772

4. An ordinance prohibiting the cultivation for agricultural purposes of more than one eighth of an acre by any family or household within the corporate limits, except for flower gardens, or grapes, or trees, and except for planting oats, rye, or barley, between November 1 and February 15, is a valid exercise of police power, under a charter giving full power to make ordinances which shall appear to the council "necessary and requisite" for the welfare, convenience, and health of the town. *Summerville* v. *Pressley* (S. C.) 851

5. The adjournment of the House of Delegates on the day bills are presented to the mayor for his approval will not prevent them from becoming valid ordinances, if duly filed by the mayor, with his approval, in the city register's office, although the charter of the city provides that every bill shall be "returned within ten days to the House in which the same originated." *Barber Asphalt Paving Co.* v. *Hunt* (Mo.) 110

6. An ordinance to compel a bridge company to sell 100 tickets for $1 according to its contract with a city is not an exercise of police power, but relates merely to a contract in respect to a financial matter. *Newport* v. *Newport & C. Bridge Co.* (Ky.) 484

7. The fact that the work of street paving prescribed by an ordinance is covered by letters patent under which the exclusive right is held by one company, and that therefore no competition for the work is possible, will not prevent letting a contract for the work, under a charter providing that such contracts shall be let to the lowest responsible bidder. *Barber Asphalt Paving Co.* v. *Hunt* (Mo.) 110

8. Power to manufacture and distribute gas and electricity for public use in lighting streets and public buildings may lawfully be conferred by the Legislature on cities and towns, together with the power to raise money by taxation for the construction and maintenance of the necessary works, as such service is a public one. *Opinion of Justices* (Mass.) 487

9. Power may be lawfully conferred to enable cities and towns to produce gas and electricity to be sold to their own citizens for the lighting of their private property, if the Legislature is of opinion that the common convenience and welfare of such citizens will be promoted thereby, at least where all inhabitants of a city or town are given the same or similar rights to be supplied so far as is reasonably practicable, and are compelled to pay therefor a sum sufficient to reimburse to the cities and towns the reasonable cost of what is furnished. *Id.*

10. A city is not liable for injuries resulting from the negligence of officers engaged in the management of a workhouse which has been established purely for the public service, and to assist in the performance of its public duty of supporting paupers and criminals, and who also conduct the work incidental to the maintenance of the institution and to the employment of its inmates, although the establishment was voluntarily erected and maintained under legislative permission; and the fact that some revenue is derived by the city from the labor of the inmates is immaterial if the institution is not conducted with a view to pecuniary profit, and none is in fact obtained. This is especially true where such officers are appointed and directed by an independent board which is in no way the agent of the city. *Curran* v. *Boston* (Mass.) 243

NOTES AND BRIEFS.

Creation of; right of Legislature to delegate power. 106

Right to use patented pavement on streets. 111

Condemnation of property for public uses. 123

Authority to light streets; power to enjoin. 292

Authority to lay streets. 487

Duty to keep sidewalks free from ice. 752

Private interests subservient to public interests. 854

Right to prohibit cultivation of ground within limits. 855

NAME. See CORPORATIONS, 16.

NEGLIGENCE. See also MASTER AND SERVANT, 5; TRIAL, 9.

1. The law requires those who use dangerous agencies in the prosecution of their business to observe the greatest care in the custody and use of them. *Pittsburgh, C. & St. L. R. Co.* v. *Shields* (Ohio) 464

at law under the Occupying Claimant Act. *Killmer* v. *Wuchner* (Iowa) 289

NOTES AND BRIEFS.

Jurisdiction in equity; allowance for improvements. 289

PARTNERSHIP. See also ELECTION, 2; MORTGAGE, 1.

1. A partnership is created by an agreement under which one person advances money to another for investment in land on their joint accounts the profits to be shared between them in a certain proportion. *Tyler* v. *Waddingham* (Conn.) 657

2. The renewal or continuance of a limited partnership operates merely as an extension for the designated period of the partnership originally formed, and in practical effect is the same as if such time had been embraced within the term of the original formation. *Fifth Ave. Bank* v. *Colgate* (N.Y.) 712

3. The impairment of the capital furnished to a limited partnership by a special partner, without his fault, does not prevent the renewal or continuance of the partnership; and a statement in the certificate or affidavit of renewal, that the capital is unimpaired, is mere surplusage, which, although it may be false, does not render him liable as a general partner to one who has not been induced thereby to give credit to the firm. *Id.*

4. Prima facie liability of partners for a debt contracted by one partner may be rebutted by evidence that credit was given to the individual partner alone. *Tyler* v. *Waddingham* (Conn.) 657

5. A person is liable as partner on a note given in the name of another as part of the purchase price of land purchased in pursuance of a scheme for profits to be shared between them, although he authorized the other only to procure options, and not to complete any purchase of land, where, after he knew of the facts, he accepted the benefits of the purchase, continued to furnish money to effectuate the common object, and was active in schemes for the development of the property. *Id.*

6. There is no implied authority in members of a partnership formed for taking and executing paving and curbing contracts, to borrow money and execute promissory notes therefor to bind the firm, unless there be proof to show actual necessity, or usage, for the exercise of such power by the individual members of the firm in conducting the work. *Harris* v. *Baltimore* (Md.) 677

NOTES AND BRIEFS.

What constitutes, in real estate speculation. 657

Distinction between trading and nontrading; dealing with nontrading; rights of parties. 677

Limited; renewal certificates; validity; liability of special partner. 712

PATENTS. See CREDITORS' BILL, 3.

PAYMENT. See also EXECUTION, 2; GIFT.

Where a wife joined her husband in a mortgage of both real and personal property belonging to him, to secure his debts, and he subsequently gave a second mortgage covering the same and other personal property, to secure a second note, the proceeds of a part of the personal property sold by the mortgagee, as to the application of which no directions were given, must be applied by the mortgagee on the first mortgage, in exoneration of the wife's inchoate dower interest. *Gore* v. *Townsend* (N. C.) 443

NOTES AND BRIEFS.

Satisfaction of debt by less than amount due. 257

Acceptance of note as. 426

PEDDLERS. See also COMMERCE, 1; LICENSE, 2, 3.

Canvassers for books are not hawkers or peddlers, within the meaning of a statute which gives municipal corporations power to compel hawkers and peddlers to obtain a license. *Emmons* v. *Lewistown* (Ill.) 328

NOTES AND BRIEFS.

Defined; license. 273

PENSION. See LEVY AND SEIZURE, 3.

PHYSICIAN AND SURGEON. See also COLLEGES.

A diploma from an institution having no power to give it is not sufficient to entitle a person to demand a license as physician from the censors of a medical society, under Vt. R. L. § 3911. *Townshend* v. *Gray* (Vt.) 112

PLANK ROADS. See also TOLL ROADS, 4, 5.

NOTES AND BRIEFS.

Plank roads. 858

PLEADING.

1. In pleading, plaintiff must state all the facts essential to a cause of action. If any material fact is lacking, the complaint will go down before a demurrer. *Louisville, N. A & C. R. Co.* v. *Corps* (Ind.) 636

2. A complaint alleging a state of facts from which an agreement to make an assessment upon members of an insurance organization may be implied, and claiming damages for failure to make the assessment, is not insufficient because it does not state in terms an agreement to make the assessment. *Lawler* v. *Murphy* (Conn.) 113

3. An allegation of liability to pay, without allegation either of payment or of actual loss, sufficiently shows damage to a corporation for acts of its directors in issuing promissory notes in its name, which have come into the hands of bona fide purchasers for value. *Metropolitan Elev. R. Co.* v. *Kneeland* (N. Y.) 253

4. An averment of special damage is not necessary in an action for libel, where the words are spoken of plaintiff in his or her profession or trade. *Price* v. *Conway* (Pa.) 193

5. The office of an innuendo is to define the defamatory meaning which the plaintiff in a

libel suit sets upon the words, to show how they came to have that meaning, and how they relate to the plaintiff. *Id.*

6. A declaration in a suit for slander, which claims special damages because of loss of trade, will not be held insufficient for failing to set out the names of persons who ceased or refused to employ plaintiff, after defendant has proceeded to trial without noticing such failure. An objection raised for the first time by a request for instructions comes too late. *Morasse* v. *Brochu* (Mass.) 524

7. An averment that plaintiff had no knowledge of the danger of continuing in the service of his employer, which existed because of the latter's failure to provide suitable machinery and competent workmen, is necessary to warrant a recovery for injuries alleged to have resulted from such failure. Otherwise it will be assumed that the danger was known to and assumed by the employé. An allegation of freedom from fault is not sufficient for this purpose. *Louisville, N. A. & C. R. Co.* v. *Corps* (Ind.) 636

8. A declaration which, taken as a whole, was apparently intended to present a certain case, will not be pronounced bad for want of technical accuracy of allegation, unless the specific defect is unmistakably pointed out. Hence an allegation that plaintiff took certain stock, relying on its validity, may be taken to mean that he relied upon representations made in the certificate, which it appears he had seen. *Windram* v. *French* (Mass.) 750

9. An averment that plaintiff suffered "great pain and agony" is sufficient to cover any effect upon the mind that resulted from an injury to the body. *Chicago* v. *McLean* (Ill.) 765

10. No allegation of special damage, in a suit for a personal injury, is necessary in order to permit a recovery for mental suffering which was inseparable from the bodily injury. *Id.*

11. A complaint for an injunction does not charge facts sufficient to state any cause of action by an allegation that a building on defendant's premises which is sought to be enjoined will cause the water to set back on complainant's premises "to some extent." *Janesville* v. *Carpenter* (Wis.) 808

12. An allegation that both parties to a suit reside in a certain city and county, "where they now are, and for several years have been residents," and that for many months plaintiff has been engaged in railroad shops at that place, and that a garnishment suit was instituted against him,—sufficiently alleges his residence at that place at the time such suit was commenced. *Moton* v. *Hull* (Tex.) 722

13. A defect in a petition setting up a claim for damages which are too remote to furnish a basis for an action, and an injury which is not special to plaintiff, is not reached by a general demurrer. *Fort Worth & R. G. R. Co.* v. *Jennings* (Tex.) 180

14. Pleas to an information charging a corporation with purchasing and holding a majority of the shares of stock of other corporations, which admit the holding of capital stock, without setting out whether such stock is a

major
are de
Gas T

15.
absenc
the tin
tion to
it alleg
injurie
had de
the Sta
v. *Bau*

16. A
murrer
to has t
debarre
differen
one alre
and ren
court, if
ferent ti
swer to
(Ind.)

Avern

PLED(
CU

1. The
warehous
by issuin
form of a
fesses to
an attem
contrary
1879, §
which req
cording in
Conrad v.

2. The
of a pledg
an attorn
custodian
a delivery
force in th

3. Whe
property is
manual de
of a pledge
delivery,—
and a ware

4. The
garded as t
dee, on the
shows that
vendee has
of the pledg

5. Where
credit rema
under such
vive upon th
vendee, a pl
his creditor,
cedent indel
no new valu
delay, does
chaser for v
a better righ

pledgor and cuts off the lien of the unpaid vendor. *Conrad* v. *Fisher* (Mo. App.) 147

6. The delivery, as collateral security, of a bill of sale, copies of gaugers' returns, and a warehouse receipt, of whiskey held in a United States bonded warehouse, creates a pledge, and not a chattel mortgage. *Id.*

POLICEMEN.

NOTES AND BRIEFS.

POLICE POWER. See MUNICIPAL CORPORATIONS, 4.

POOLS. See HORSE-RACING.

POOR AND POOR-LAWS.

1. A girl of weak mind, incapable of exercising any choice as to the place of her residence and suffering from such mental infirmity as makes it necessary that she should remain under the care and control of her parents, and who has never been emancipated, takes the settlement of her father, though acquired after she reach the age of majority. *Rowell* v. *Vershire* (Vt.) 708

2. The promise of aid by the overseer of the poor to a man who is charged with the duty of supporting his daughter, if he will give her such support, is without consideration and legally nonenforceable. *Id.*

NOTES AND BRIEFS.

PRESUMPTIONS. See EVIDENCE, II.

PRINCIPAL AND AGENT.

A written contract creating a commercial agency for one year at a fixed compensation for services, wharfage, storage, etc., having been renewed expressly for the next year, and the agency continued for several successive years thereafter in conformity to the contract, there is a tacit renewal from year to year, and the agency cannot be revoked so as to deprive the agent of his monthly compensation for an unexpired portion of a year which has been begun. *Standard Oil Co.* v. *Gilbert* (Ga.) 410

NOTES AND BRIEFS.

PRINCIPAL AND SURETY. See also BONDS, 3-5; DOWER, 1; LIMITATION OF ACTIONS, 1.

A surety who merely gives his note for his share of the original debt, to a cosurety who has paid the debt, does not thereby acquire any right of action against his principal; at least where any cause of action against the latter in favor of the cosurety was barred by time. *Stone* v. *Hammell* (Cal.) 425

NOTES AND BRIEFS.

PRIVATE ROADS.

NOTES AND BRIEFS.

PROCESS. See DEFINITIONS.

PROXIMATE CAUSE. See HIGHWAYS, 13.

PUBLIC IMPROVEMENTS. See ASSESSMENTS, NOTES AND BRIEFS.

A local assessment against property, to pay for pavements constructed along its front, to be apportioned with reference to the benefits which are assumed to accrue to the owners of the property, is not a tax, within the meaning of a constitutional provision requiring that "all taxes levied on property in this State shall be assessed in exact proportion to the value of the property." *Birmingham* v. *Klein* (Ala.) 369

PUBLIC PRINTING. See CONTRACTS, 2.

QUO WARRANTO. See CORPORATIONS, 9; MANDAMUS, 4, 5.

RAILROADS. See also EVIDENCE, 7; LIENS; MASTER AND SERVANT, 3.

1. A railroad company is liable in damages for injury to stock through its negligence, where the owner contributed to the injury only by permitting his stock to run at large. *Moses* v. *Southern P. R. Co.* (Or.) 135

2. The liability of a railroad company for negligence in killing stock which the owner has permitted to run at large depends on the question whether the law of the place requires owners to keep their stock within their own enclosure. *Id.*

3. The Oregon statute requiring a railroad to fence its road against livestock does not apply to depot grounds, and the company is not liable for stock killed thereon, in the absence of negligence. *Id.*

4. In order to entitle a person injured by a collision with a railway train at a highway crossing to recover damages for such injuries from the company, he must show by a preponderance of evidence that both he and his driver vigilantly used their eyes and ears to ascertain if a train was approaching. He has no right to assume that no train is approaching, if his view is obstructed, from the fact that no whistle is sounded; and such fact cannot be considered in determining the question of his negligence. *Cincinnati, I. St. L. & C. R. Co.* v. *Howard* (Ind.) 593

5. The fact that a train is behind time and is running faster than its usual speed does not excuse one attempting to cross the track from exercising all the care and caution required of him when the train is on time and running at its usual rate of speed. *Id.*

6. Obstructions to sight or hearing in the direction of an approaching train as a traveler upon a highway nears a railroad crossing require increased care on his part, the care required being in proportion to the increase of

danger that may come from the use of the highway at such place. *Id.*

7. Failure to look before turning upon a railroad track along a public street, on which one has a perfect right to travel, and subject to the duty simply to make way for a train, will not prevent recovery for injuries sustained when struck by a train coming at an unlawful speed, if by looking he would not have discovered that it was imprudent to drive on the track. *Kelny* v. *Missouri P. R. Co.* (Mo.) 788

NOTES AND BRIEFS.

See also CARRIERS.

Liability for failure to fence track; rules in other States. 135

Effect of failure to give statutory signals at highway crossing. 595

RAPE.

A husband may be guilty of an assault with intent to commit rape upon his wife, where by threats of death he compels another man to attempt to ravish her. *State* v. *Dowell* (N. C.) 297

NOTES AND BRIEFS.

Defined; aiders and abettors as principals. 297

RATIFICATION. See PARTNERSHIP, 5.

REAL PROPERTY. See also EVIDENCE, 26; HUSBAND AND WIFE, 2.

The title of one in possession of real estate under a valid unrecorded deed must prevail over that of a subsequent mortgagee from the same grantor, although the latter took his mortgage without notice of the prior title, and the building upon the premises had been erected for tenement purposes and contained a large number of apartments which were occupied by many lessees, and the grantee in the unrecorded deed had occupied a store and living apartment in the building as a tenant before receiving the grant, and made no visible material change in his occupation of the building afterwards, except that he then leased apartments and collected rents. *Phelan* v. *Brady* (N. Y.) 211

NOTES AND BRIEFS.

Covenants, upon whom operated; when run with the land. 90

Charging remainderman for improvements. 290

Grant to two persons and the survivor of them; construction of. 655

Right to use one's own property. 808

RECEIVERS.

The right of a receiver appointed by a foreign tribunal to wind up an insolvent partnership situated within its jurisdiction, to take possession of money due to such partnership from domestic debtors, will not be recognized as against the claims of nonresident creditors of the insolvent partnership who have attached such money under the domestic laws after the appointment of the receiver, but before he obtained actual possession of the money or an

enforceal
received
ship prop
Co. (Ind.,

Foreign

RECOR

Proof o

RECOR

REDEM

RELIGI
LAND

A Youn
exercising
members,
for them,
for failure
poration
i. e., for pu
to be forbic
of 1872 to
The associ
missionary
ship. *Ham*

Power to

Right of

REMOVA

The circ
the truth of
moval, wher
in the cause,
companied b
son, stating
from prejudi
will not be
courts. *Coo*
N. D. Ga.)

Affidavit;

REPLEVI

The owner
maturity, su
knowledge or
its nominal
may recover
the latter paid
the defect in
v. *Springer* (I

RÉSUMÉ C

Subjects dis

SALE.

1. The right
respect of goo
right to rescin
right to detain
ness for the pu

before the expiration of the credit, and, if not so discharged, to sell them and apply the proceeds of their sale to the liquidation of the indebtedness. *Conrad* v. *Fisher* (Mo. App.) 147

2. As between vendor and vendee, and in cases where the rights of subsequent purchasers of the vendee are not concerned, a vendor's lien is not devested by any species of constructive delivery, so long as the vendor retains the actual custody of the goods, either by himself or by his agent or servant. This lien is not destroyed by invoicing the goods to the purchaser, or by marking the packages with the purchaser's name, or by an agreement between the vendor and vendee that the goods shall remain in the warehouse of the vendor subject to the payment of storage by the vendee. *Id.*

3. The fact that by the agreement between the vendor and vendee something remains to be done to the goods by the vendor is not conclusive that there has not been such a delivery as cuts off the vendor's lien, but creates a prima facie presumption to that effect, which may be rebutted by circumstances. *Id.*

4. When goods at the time the contract of sale is made, though in the legal custody and control, are not in the actual possession, of the vendee, but are so situated that he cannot obtain actual possession until a specific act is done by the vendor, if the vendee becomes insolvent before this act has been done, and the actual possession of the goods has not been changed, the vendor may detain the goods as security for the payment of the contract price. *Id.*

5. The lien of an unpaid vendor for distilled spirits is not destroyed by placing them in a government warehouse in charge of a government storekeeper. *Id.*

6. The lien of an unpaid vendor of goods is not self-executing. It is a right which he may or may not assert, and which, if not asserted in time, is lost. If, therefore, the vendor, retaining the goods, under a contract with the vendee, in the vendor's distillery warehouse, allows the vendee to call the warehouse his own for the purposes of his trade, and to issue warehouse receipts in respect of the goods, the license thus given to the vendee to issue warehouse receipts does not, *ipso facto*, expire upon the happening of the vendee's insolvency. *Id.*

NOTES AND BRIEFS.

When title passes. 245

SCHOOLS. See MANDAMUS, 2.

SET-OFF AND COUNTERCLAIM.

A set-off cannot be allowed, under Mass. Pub. Stat. chap. 168, §§ 3-7, in an action brought to recover unliquidated damages for a breach of contract, of a claim which is of the same kind as that to recover which the action is brought. *Rice* v. *Sanders* (Mass.) 315

SETTING ASIDE INSTRUMENT. See HUSBAND AND WIFE, 14.

SHIPMENT. See CONTRACTS, 5, 8; DEFINITIONS, NOTES AND BRIEFS.

SOCIAL CLUB. See ASSOCIATIONS, 2.

SPECIFIC PERFORMANCE. See also CONTRACTS, 11.

Specific performance will not be granted of a contract to clear out the channel of a creek so as to allow running water to flow freely, and to make a ditch of sufficient size to drain the lands of another party, and to keep such ditch open and unobstructed forever. The case is one in which the injury can be redressed by damages in an action at law. *McCarter* v. *Armstrong* (S. C.) 625

NOTES AND BRIEFS.

Discretion as to granting remedy at law. 625

STATE.

NOTES AND BRIEFS.

Suit against. 399

STATUTE OF LIMITATIONS. See LIMITATION OF ACTIONS.

STATUTES. See also CORPORATIONS, 8; HORSE-RACING; LICENSE, 1.

1. A proviso in a statute should always be construed with reference to the immediately preceding part of the clause or section to which it is attached. *Wolf* v. *Bauereis* (Md.) 680

2. A statute will not be presumed to have been intended by the Legislature to have any extraterritorial force, where such intention would make it unconstitutional. *Stanley* v. *Wabash, St. L. & P. R. Co.* (Mo.) 549

3. A statute is sufficiently definite to authorize imprisonment in the penitentiary for violation of its provisions, although not stating that the imprisonment shall be in the penitentiary, where the violation is declared a felony, punishable by imprisonment for not less than five nor more than twenty-five years, and the Criminal Code of the State declares that a felony is punishable by death or confinement in the penitentiary. *Hronek* v. *People* (Ill.) 837

4. A bill published as a law after it has been deposited in the office of the secretary of state, signed by the president of the Senate, speaker of the House of Representatives, and the governor, cannot be shown by journals of the Legislature, or any other evidence, to be different from the statute actually enacted, or invalid for failure of any formalities required by the Constitution. *Re Tipton* (Tex. App.) 326

5. An Act does not embrace more than one subject because, with regulations as to the manufacture, transportation, use, and sale of explosives, it also prescribes a punishment for violation of such regulations. *Hronek* v. *People* (Ill.) 837

6. A statute does not involve more than one subject of legislation because, with provisions regulating the manufacture, etc., of explosives for legitimate purposes, it prohibits their manufacture or procurement for the unlawful destruction of life or property. *Id.*

7. Sections of an Act providing for a plank road from Chicago to the north line of Cook County are invalid, under the Illinois Consti-

tution of 1848, which provides that no private or local law . . . shall embrace more than one subject, and that shall be expressed in the title, where the title of the Act mentions only a plank road from Oswego, in Kendall County, to the Indiana line. *Snell* v. *Chicago* (Ill.) 858

8. The legalization of unauthorized acts cannot be regarded as germane to the subject expressed in the title of an Act, which is "An Act to Incorporate" a certain company. *Id.*

NOTES AND BRIEFS.

Steps necessary to pass. 111
Passage of. 826
Title to. 858

STREET RAILWAYS. See also MONOPOLY.

1. A company having power to own and operate a street railway in a particular city may use the tracks, cars, and other property which it purchases from another company previously chartered with like power, although the latter had no power to sell and transfer its franchise. *Indianapolis Cable Street R. Co.* v. *Citizens Street R. Co.* (Ind.) 539

2. A municipality having control over its streets may prescribe the motive power to be used in propelling street cars thereon; and when it prescribes one kind of power no other can be used. *Id.*

3. A street-railway company having authority to use a cable for motive power acquires no right to the exclusive use of a street by entering thereon and laying tracks upon which it intends to use a different motive power. *Id.*

4. A grant of permission to use a certain motive power upon street-railway tracks wrongfully constructed with the intention of using such power, when another was prescribed by the company's charter, will not relate back to the time of the construction of the tracks, so as to cut off intervening rights. *Id.*

5. Where two rival companies have each received permission to construct a railway system in the streets of a city, the one which first begins work on a line involving a certain street, in good faith and acting within the terms of its grant, has the better right to the use of that portion of the street which its tracks will cover; and this right will continue so long as money is expended and the work diligently prosecuted with a view to its completion. *Id.*

6. A mere agreement by a municipal corporation not to grant any rights or privileges which will impair or destroy those conferred by its ordinance giving a certain corporation permission to operate a street-railway system in its streets will not prevent it from granting like permission to others. *Id.*

7. A street railway, for the purpose of defeating the rights which its rival claims to have acquired by reason of prior occupation of a street in which both companies have equal rights, may allege and prove that such occupation was not in conformity to such rival's charter powers, in that the tracks were laid with the intention of using motive power different from that permitted by the charter. *Id.*

Right
structior
Right
Conclu
effect of
build as

SUBR

SUNDA

1. Ridi
for no ot
Maine st
walking
Maine C.

2. Paro
effect on
Statute of
in writin
Tyler v.

TAXES.
LICEN

1. A co
shall be "
be taxed" i
a tax of 2½
on bank st
al property

2. Taxes
road purpo
1881, chap.
taxes assess
the meanin
are to be ir
the county
limit of tax
Brannon v

3. Rolling
company us
subject to t
rating a leas
D. R. Co. (N

Ad valoren
Limitation
On railroa
For highw
Constitutio
Fees for pr

TELEGRA
EMINEN

Payment
penses incurr
nondelivery o
for a penalty,
or by way of
U. Teleg. Co.

TENDER
COURT

N

Tender; effe

TOLL ROADS. See also CONTRACTS, 10.

1. Tolls cannot be exacted for the use of a toll road after it is included within the boundaries of a city, where the charter of the toll-road company was accepted under a State Constitution which gives the corporate authorities of a city exclusive authority over highways therein and the exclusive right to assess and collect taxes therein. *Snell* v. *Chicago* (Ill.) 858

2. The privilege of collecting tolls and maintaining toll gates, acquired by a purchaser of "the franchises, the property and immunities" of a plank-road company expires upon his death, although he had the right to organize as a corporation, if he did not do so, and the statute authorizing the sale did not state that his heirs and assigns might enjoy such privileges, but merely that the purchaser should enjoy them. *Id.*

3. The location of toll gates and toll houses having become established, the discretion as to such location is exhausted and they cannot be moved, especially after toll has been collected for several years. *Id.*

4. The sale of part of a plank road, with the franchise of using the same and collecting tolls thereon, is invalid where a statute under which it is made contemplated the sale of the whole road. *Id.*

5. A provision that "a plank-road company may collect the same tolls and enjoy the same privileges granted to plank-road companies by the general plank-road law" does not fix the rights of the company according to the general law as it then exists, but makes them coincide with those of other companies under the general law, whether it remains the same or is changed afterwards. *Id.*

6. A statute authorizing the construction of a plank road "from the city of Chicago" gives no authority to construct any part of the road within the city, where it is completely silent as to streets, but provides for the use of highways under permission of the county, and property owners. *Id.*

TOWN.

A town suffering special damage from a public nuisance in relation to a highway which it is bound to maintain may sustain an action for the recovery of such damages against the party maintaining such nuisance. *Charlotte* v. *Pembroke Iron Works* (Me.) 808

TRADE. See CONTRACTS, NOTES AND BRIEFS.

TRADE-MARK. See also INJUNCTION, 4, 5.

1. The owner of an established business, in which he uses certain peculiar labels and trade-marks, may make a valid conveyance of them, although they consist largely of his name, initials of his name, or residence, in connection with a conveyance of the plant and good will of the business. *Symonds* v. *Jones* (Me.) 570

2. Purchasers of trade marks and labels which consist largely of the name, residence, etc., of the former owner, should not use them without change, if they indicate that the articles to which they are applied are made by the vendor. Words must be added to show that the vendor has retired and the goods were made by his successors. *Id.*

3. A label cannot be treated as a trade-mark where it does not indicate by what person the articles upon which it is used were made, but only that he was a member of a certain association, which membership confers the right to use the mark, and of which there is no exclusive use, its rightful use not being connected with any business, but belonging to many persons not connected in business and unknown to each other. *Weener* v. *Brayton* (Mass.) 640

NOTES AND BRIEFS.

Generic names cannot be appropriated; forfeited by fraud and deception; transfer of. 570

Title and right to exclusive use; right to protection; labels protected; injunction to protect. 640

Trade-marks and trade-names; protection of; when equity will interfere. 820

TREES. See HIGHWAYS, 10–12.

TRESPASS. See also ACTION OR SUIT NOTES AND BRIEFS; INJUNCTION, 6.

A defense in an action of trespass, that plaintiff is a married woman, and has proved no title, and has no possession except as the wife of her husband, cannot avail where he testifies that the land belongs to her, and is estopped from claiming damages in another suit. *Lord* v. *Meadville Water Co.* (Pa.) 202

TRIAL.

I. CONDUCT OF TRIAL.
II. QUESTIONS OF LAW AND FACT
III. INSTRUCTIONS.
IV. FINDINGS.

NOTES AND BRIEFS.

See also CRIMINAL LAW, 5; MASTER AND SERVANT, 7.

I. CONDUCT OF TRIAL.

1. Concession by the owner of petitioner's right to condemn land, and limitation of the contest to the question of damages only, do not relieve the petitioner of the burden of proof or give the landowner the right to open and close the argument. *Alloway* v. *Nashville* (Tenn.) 123

2. A court does not abuse its discretion in interfering to prevent questions to be asked of counsel as a witness for his client, in such form as to call out certain facts and exclude others connected with the same transaction. *Tyler* v. *Waddingham* (Conn.) 657

3. A party cannot in general demand the exclusion of evidence called out in fair response to questions asked without objection. *State* v. *Hope* (Mo.) 608

4. The fact of sickness of an absent juror, which is one ground under the statute for discharging the jury, cannot be determined on

trial for a felony in the absence of defendant from the court-room. *State* v. *Smith* (Kan.) 774

II. Questions of Law and Fact.

5. The existence and effect of an alleged common error is for the court and not for the jury. *O'Donnell* v. *Glenn* (Mont.) 629

6. The question of libel or no libel, in a civil action, is one of law which the court must decide, where the publication is admitted and the words are unambiguous and admit of but one sense. *Moore* v. *Francis* (N.Y.) 214

7. A statement by a clergyman to his congregation, in effect that a certain physician was excommunicated by reason of his marriage, that he should be debarred from being employed as a physician in the parish, and patients who employed him could not in their sickness have the ministrations of the clergyman,—may properly be given to the jury to determine whether or not it was made of the physician in respect to his profession so as to render it actionable *per se*. *Morasse* v. *Brochu* (Mass.) 524

8. The existence of negligence cannot be determined as a matter of law unless the inference of it from the facts is certain and incontrovertible. *Philadelphia, W. & B. R. Co.* v. *Anderson* (Md.) 673

9. Instructions that a child six years of age cannot be guilty of negligence are erroneous. That is a question for the jury. *Chicago City R. Co.* v. *Wilcox* (Ill.) 494

10. The question of negligence of railroad employés in failing to discover a person driving on the track in a public street and to stop the train, and his alleged contributory negligence, are questions for the jury. *Kellny* v. *Missouri P. R. Co.* (Mo.) 783

11. Whether or not a passenger was guilty of negligence, who, in the night, after the name of his station had been called and the train had stopped, attempted to alight from the car, is a question for the jury, although the car had stopped before reaching the platform, which fact he might have discovered by looking for the station lights, and after a momentary pause had begun to move again slowly before he made the attempt,—at least if there is nothing to show that he knew the purpose of the renewed movement of the train. *Philadelphia, W. & B. R. Co.* v. *Anderson* (Md.) 673

12. Where the facts are numerous and equivocal, susceptible of different inferences in respect of the question, What was the real intent of the parties?—the question whether there has been such a delivery as devests the vendor's lien is a question of fact for the jury. *Conrad* v. *Fisher* (Mo. App.) 147

13. Whether carrying a certain amount of money to his room, instead of placing it in the hotel safe, is negligence on the part of the guest, is a question for the jury. *Shultz* v. *Wall* (Pa.) 97

14. Whether a guest at a hotel should be treated as having notice of the existence of a safe is a question for the jury where he has frequently stopped there, and there is evidence that on some visit his attention has been called to the safe by the landlord. *Id.*

15. On a hotel w of his roo in the mo folded an money wh outer doo while his showing some ext question o jury, cons mystery o

16. The sleeping-c his duties the time h senger, so his act, mu the eviden it necessar from the ti another tra surrendere person wh sleeping ca that the pa ticket, or charge of t ceive sleepi thereupon *Dwinelle* v (N. Y.)

17. Proof of loss add stamped, or officers and never receiv as to wheth *Pennypacke*

18. An in to the evider although it law in the ab *R. Co.* v. *Ho*

19. Where ports the dec tiff cannot r properly refu

20. An acc special instru finding of an raise any pres is conveyed b *Assman* v. *St*

21. An ins sponsibility o the guilt of a concurring i given if sea

22. Instruct are designed upon a defens as legitimate, making in app with favor, ev of insanity.

23. Instruct

without looking, into a dangerous place, or failed to observe the condition of the sidewalk on which she was walking, she cannot recover for injuries received, are properly refused as virtually telling the jury that certain facts constitute negligence. *Chicago* v. *McLean* (Ill.) 765

24. An instruction that a master is not liable for injuries to one servant resulting from the negligence of his fellow servant is properly refused if it is not limited to cases in which the master used due care in selecting him. *Hinckley* v. *Horazdowski* (Ill.) 490

25. A statement by the court to the jury, made in open court without objection by either party, that certain facts stated are admitted, is not in any sense an instruction to the jury; and therefore the fact that it was not made in writing, as instructions are required to be, is not error, especially where it was immaterial in the case. *Id.*

26. An accessory before the fact being punishable as a principal, under Ill. Stat. June 16, 1887, § 1, regulating the use, etc., of explosives, an instruction that any person doing or assisting in the offense mentioned in that section is to be punished as provided in said section is not erroneous. *Hronek* v. *People* (Ill.) 837

27. An instruction that the evidence of private detectives and of the police should be received with a large degree of caution does not contain a correct proposition of law. *Id.*

28. Instructions that notice of loss must have been given within a reasonable time, while the policy requires it to be given "forthwith," are not prejudicial, as the terms are so nearly synonymous. *Pennypacker* v. *Capital Ins. Co.* (Iowa) 236

IV. FINDINGS.

29. A special finding by a jury that notice and proofs of loss sent by mail were received within sixty days, the time limited by the policy, is sufficiently definite without stating the exact day. *Id.*

30. A finding at the conclusion of a special finding of facts which says, "And upon said finding I further find," etc.,—is not a finding of fact on independent evidence, but is only an application of the special facts previously stated. *Tyler* v. *Waddingham* (Conn.) 657

31. A verdict finding "the defendant" guilty, without specifying any person by name, is not void for uncertainty where but one person was put upon trial, although several others were indicted with him. *Hronek* v. *People* (Ill.) 837

NOTES AND BRIEFS.

Jury to be convinced beyond reasonable doubt. 34

Question of law or fact in libel and slander. 214

When jeopardy attaches; dismissing jury for sickness. 775

Party not allowed to take inconsistent positions; inconsistent ruling. 440

Sufficiency of verdict of guilty. 837

TROVER.

The title to property converted passes the wrongdoer when the owner elects to treat the transaction as a sale and brings an action *ex contractu* against him. *Terry* v. *Munger* (N. Y.) 216

NOTES AND BRIEFS.

Remedy for conversion; following property. 216

TRUSTS. See also ACTION OR SUIT, 10; LIMITATION OF ACTIONS, 5, 11.

1. A disclaimer by a person sued as trustee long after his appointment, although he has never executed a bond as such, relates back to the time of appointment. *Hughes* v. *Brown* (Tenn.) 480

2. Property purchased with a fund which includes moneys held under different trusts, the title being taken as under one of the trusts only, is chargeable with the same trusts that attached to the fund, as against those who deal in it knowing it to be trust property. *Leake* v. *Watson* (Conn.) 666

3. One who sells trust securities, knowing that the sale is for unauthorized purposes, in violation of the trust, although he makes the sale simply as an agent, is liable to the beneficiaries for the breach of the trust. *Id.*

4. Distribution by the probate court of property to trustees in trust for a certain person, under a will giving her a life interest only, does not authorize persons dealing with the property to regard her as sole beneficiary. *Id.*

5. No notice of the resignation of a trustee is required to be given to the heirs of one for whom, during her life, the trust is held, and whose heirs on her death are entitled to the property absolutely, since she has no heirs until after her death. *Id.*

6. The right of a trustee to sue for property which it is his duty to hold in trust for a certain person during her life, and which will then go to her heirs, does not depend on her interest in the property. He is under obligation to keep it safely until her death. *Id.*

NOTES AND BRIEFS.

Person taking property subject to; liability of; sale of trust property as agent. 668

Mingling trust funds. 788

UNDUE INFLUENCE.

NOTES AND BRIEF

What is; effect of. 261

UNLAWFUL ENTRY AND DETAINER. See ACTION OR SUIT, NOTES AND BRIEFS; LANDLORD AND TENANT, 3.

USURY. See also CONFLICT OF LAWS, 1, NOTES AND BRIEFS.

A transaction cannot be devested of the taint of usury caused by the lender's acceptance of a sum which he calls a commission, by the fact that he subsequently sells the securities taken in his own name, if he was in fact the actual lender. *Sanford* v. *Kane* (Ill.) 724

VENDOR AND PURCHASER. See also MORTGAGE, 12, 18; REAL PROPERTY.

1. A provision in a contract for the sale of real property, that the title is to be passed upon by the purchaser's lawyer or conveyancer, does not make his decision that the title is good a condition precedent to the vendor's right to enforce the performance of the contract. *Vought* v. *Williams* (N. Y.) 591

2. A stipulation that the title to real estate shall be "first class" means nothing more than it shall be marketable. *Id.*

3. The presumption of death of one who left home for causes unknown, and has not been seen or heard of by his family or friends for upwards of twenty-four years, and who, when last seen, was about twenty-three years old, unmarried, dissipated, in feeble health, and in destitute condition, being in want of clothing,—is not sufficiently strong to make marketable a title to real estate which depends on his death. *Id.*

4. A title to land is not marketable if one link in the chain consists of a deed, the execution and delivery of which can be established only by parol evidence. *Irving* v. *Campbell* (N. Y.) 620

VERDICT. See TRIAL, 81.

VOTERS AND ELECTIONS.

1. There is no natural right to vote. Contributing to the support of the government may be made a condition of the privilege. *Friesleben* v. *Shallcross* (Del.) 337

2. The exclusion of a person from the assessment list for twelve months on failure to pay his county poll tax, in consequence of which he may be precluded from being qualified to vote during that year, is not a violation of Del. Const. art. 4, § 1, which provides that a citizen otherwise qualified, who has "within two years next before the election paid a county tax which shall have been assessed at least six months before the election, shall enjoy the right of an elector," or of art. 1, § 3, which provides that "all elections shall be free and equal." *Id.*

NOTES AND BRIEFS.

Qualification of voters; Registration Law 337

WAREHOUSEMEN. See PLEDGE AND COLLATERAL SECURITY, 1, 2.

WATERS AND WATERCOURSES. See also BOUNDARIES.

1. The State holds the title to the soil in navigable waters to low-water mark in trust for the people, and chiefly for the protection of the right of navigation. *Miller* v. *Mendenhall* (Minn.) 89

2. The title to lands covered by rivers which are navigable in fact is in the State, whether the tide ebbs and flows in them or not. Hence the holder under a United States patent

of land b
tain an a
moval of
his land
I. M. & E

3. A g
covered a
which tin
which is
vegetation
soil, is the
riparian p

4. High
between t
a navigabl
beyond w
are so com
in all ordi
a characte
respect to
the soil its

5. The
line in pur
be constru
upland the
out to such

6. A rip
and make
front of his
his rights t
by the Sta

7. Where
tablishment
and plan of
pation, to
abreast of t
the right to
rights whic
and bind th
upland by a
ference wit
thus transfe

8. Overfl
kept off fro
by a barrier
set it back o
er of the lat
behind him
protect all t
Daniel v. *C*

9. A non-
ject of priva
owned, nei
jacent lands
margin ther
take fish fr
(Ohio)

10. A ripa
navigable la
the water th
purposes co
on which he
tivating.

11. The p
will not jus
channel to s
Meadville Wa

12. An ea
face water

given by Cal. Code Civ. Proc. § 801. That section is a mere definition of easements appurtenant, and does not prescribe or regulate the manner of acquiring them. *McDaniel* v. *Cummings* (Cal.) 575

13. The assent of the lower proprietor to the construction of a ditch on his land to connect with another on the land of the upper proprietor, for the purpose of carrying off the drainage of a natural swale having the same general course, is in the nature of a license, which, having been accepted, and the rights conferred, assumed and exercised, cannot be set aside or disregarded. *Vannest* v. *Fleming* (Iowa) 277

14. A drain made by adjoining proprietors across their lands, to conduct the waters that were naturally drained by a swale running in the same direction, cannot be stopped up or its course changed by the lower proprietor without the consent of the other, after it has been acquiesced in by all parties. *Id.*

15. Parties have the right to run their factory as many hours a day as they consider proper, where they have a grant of water for the purposes of their factory, with no limitation therein upon the number of hours per day in which they can run the factory. *Carleton Mills Co.* v. *Silver* (Me.) 446

16. If it is doubtful from the terms of a grant whether the kind of mill or particular machinery mentioned therein, for which water is to be furnished, indicates the quantity of water and measures the extent of the power intended to be conveyed, or is referred to as a limit of the use to the particular kind of mill or specified machinery, the former construction will be favored. *Id.*

17. A grant of a certain water privilege for the purpose of propelling a factory and its machinery and appurtenances, the building to be of a certain size, with necessary appurtenances and machinery, will be construed to measure the quantity of water, and will not limit the use of water to carry only such machinery as may be in the main building, if some of the machinery is in an annex and no more power is required to propel it than if it were in the main building. *Id.*

NOTES AND BRIEFS.

Backing up water with a dam; liability for; damages to highway. 53

Title to soil below ordinary high-water mark; littoral owner; right to soil to low-water mark; right to construct piers, wharves, etc.; alienation of right. 89

Easement as to flow; prescriptive right. 277

Conveyance of water privilege. 446

Title of riparian owner bordering on navigable stream. 559

Easement and servitude as to flowage water. 575

Right of landowner to protect himself against flowage of. 576

Property in non-navigable lake; conveyance of land bordering on. 578

WHARFAGE AND WHARVES. See also CORPORATIONS, 10; EMINENT DOMAIN, 7.

1. A shed or warehouse in connection with an elevator for the storage and handling of grain or other merchandise, which is one of the connecting links between the great land and water common carriers, although it is private property and operated for private gain, is for a public use and has a public trust attached to it; and therefore a lease therefor of part of a public wharf is not void on the ground that the property is to be used for private purposes. *Belchers Sugar Ref. Co.* v. *St. Louis Grain Elev. Co.* (Mo.) 801

2. The limitation of 500 feet, in the charter of a corporation, of its right to acquire and hold land fronting on the river free from condemnation, does not apply to its right to occupy property on the city wharves by consent of the city authorities, under a further clause which provides that it "may also erect one or more grain elevators upon public wharves." *Id.*

3. A lease of the unpaved portion of a public wharf to an elevator company, for the purpose of maintaining thereon a shed or warehouse for the storage and handling of grain or other merchandise in connection with the use of an elevator, is not in excess of the authority of a city,—at least when it has express power in its charter to set aside and lease a portion of the unpaved wharf for such purposes,—where the right to terminate the lease on six months' notice is reserved, and also the right by ordinance to prescribe regulations governing the business of the lessee. *Id.*

4. A wharf is unpaved, within the meaning of a charter allowing the lease of the unpaved portions of wharves, where it is not paved in a manner suitable for wharf purposes, although it had once been paved with irregular stones placed on edge and covered with macadam, but the macadam had been washed away and a dirt roadway made over it by the city, which, with accumulated rubbish, covered the remaining stone to the depth of 5 or 6 feet. *Id.*

NOTES AND BRIEFS.

Right to lease. 803

WILLS. See also JUDGMENT, 3.

1. The words, "in presence of the testator," in the statute relating to the execution of wills, do not necessarily mean that the testator and the witnesses must be in the same room, or that he must have actual sight or inspection of the process of signing. *Cook* v. *Winchester* (Mich.) 822

2. The fact that testatrix could not see the witnesses write their names or the scrivener write her own because they signed at a table in an adjoining room, about 12 feet from her bed and out of the line of her vision, although the door was open, unless she moved, which she was unable to do, will not invalidate the execution of the will under a statute requiring her signature, if made by another, as well as those of the witnesses, to be subscribed in "her presence," where the will was read to her both before and after signing and the names of the

witnesses shown to her, and they told her, in answer to her question, that they had signed it, and she made her mark in their presence. *Id.*

3. Section 5925 of the Ohio Revised Statutes, as to the effect of a witness being a devisee or legatee under the will, is not applicable to verbal wills. *Vrooman* v. *Powers* (Ohio) 89

4. The two witnesses to a verbal will must be competent, disinterested witnesses at the time of their attestation, and their disqualification as witnesses, by reason of interest under the will, cannot be removed by a renunciation of such interest at the time the will is admitted to probate, or at the trial of an issue to contest the validity of the will. *Id.*

5. Where a verbal will is reduced to writing, and subscribed by two witnesses, one of whom is a legatee thereunder, and the other is his wife, the husband is not a competent, disinterested witness, within the meaning of section 5991 of the Revised Statutes, and the will is invalid. *Id.*

6. The true meaning of words used in a will is to be arrived at by considering them, not only in their relation to the clause immediately in question, but to the whole will. *Boston Safe Deposit & T. Co.* v. *Coffin* (Mass.) 740

7. The mere grammatical or ordinary sense of words used in a will is not to be adhered to if it would be repugnant to or inconsistent with the remainder of the instrument. *Id.*

8. Where an intention to dispose of the whole of an estate appears in a will, a partial intestacy should not be recognized unless the deficiencies of expression are such as will compel it. *Id.*

9. When a conviction that a testator must necessarily have intended an interest to be given which is not bequeathed by express and formal words is produced by a reading of the whole will, the court will supply the defect by implication, and so mould the language of the testator as to carry into effect, as far as possible, the intention it is of opinion that he has on the whole sufficiently declared. *Id.*

10. A clause in a will declaring that testator "desires" that a certain disposition should be made of all that remains on his wife's death of the real and personal property given her by previous clauses of the will is merely precatory, and will not prevent her from taking the fee-simple title of the land and the absolute property in the subject of the bequest. *Bills* v. *Bills* (Iowa) 696

11. If a testator divides his estate into a number of parcels equal to the number of his children, living and deceased, and manifests a purpose to have each branch of his family have one portion, only providing for a devise over in case a particular branch becomes extinct; and in disposing of the portion of a deceased child provides that the income of it shall be divided among her three children during their lives, and in case one dies leaving issue, one third of the principal shall be given to them absolutely; but in case there is no issue, his share of the income shall be divided between

the su
cipal i
issue,
issue,
such i
the hei
ton Sa
12.
tatrix,
the wo
illegibl
and if t
as requ
codicil,
remains
iner (N.
13. T
cation o
pelled w
view to
which f
tial inte
In such
framed.

Forma
sites; sul
ture; pul
in preser
Undue
Interli
Compe
of guard
Constr
Constr
and part
whole w
language
"childre

WITN

Religi
same, is
petency
courts o
§ 8, wh
denied a
capacity
Hronek

Comn
ilege.
Comp

WRIT

A cor
to the s
Where
process
Elkins (

YOUN
CI.
No

L. R. A. CASES AS AU

CASES IN 8 L. R.

8 L. R. A. 33, ASZMAN v. STATE, 123 Ind. 347, 24 N

Intent as element of crime.

Cited in Perugi v. State, 104 Wis. 243, 76 Am. St holding homicide perpetrated after deliberation, howev der in first degree.

Cited in note (11 L. R. A. 810) on ignorance of fac

— Effect of intoxication.

Cited in Booher v. State, 156 Ind. 440, 54 L. R. A. evidence of intoxication admissible in prosecution fo intent; Northwestern Benev. Soc. v. Dudley, 27 Ind. recognizing that intoxication may prevent formation liams, 122 Iowa, 123, 97 N. W. 992, holding failure to should be considered as bearing on degree of murder, err 10 Wyo. 323, 68 Pac. 1006, holding that intoxication m mining whether defendant is guilty of murder in first

Cited in footnote to State v. O'Neil, 24 L. R. A. 55 intoxication no excuse for crime.

Cited in note (36 L. R. A. 465) on what intoxicatio

Improper instructions by court.

Cited in Davidson v. State, 135 Ind. 266, 34 N. E. 97 should be given attempting to discredit evidence; McI 259, 51 N. E. 354, holding improper instruction on "rea other instructions stating law clearly.

Instruction as to innocence or reasonable doubt.

Cited in Farley v. State, 127 Ind. 421, 26 N. E. 898, h to charge that presumption of innocence prevails thro State, 136 Ind. 293, 35 N. E. 1105, holding it error to ref accused is entitled to benefit of reasonable doubt.

Special instructions.

Cited in Barker v. State, 40 Fla. 183, 24 So. 69, h special charge on question of reasonable doubt not e charged before.

8 L. R. A. 39, VROMAN v. POWERS, 47 Ohio St. 191, 24 N. E. 267.

Competency of witnesses.

Approved in Fisher v. Spence, 150 Ill. 258, 41 Am. St. Rep. 360, 37 N. E. 314, holding that attesting witnesses to will must be competent at time of execution.

Construction of wills.

Cited in footnote to Ferris v. Neville, 54 L. R. A. 464, which holds sufficient, paper executed as will, stating that it is good to specified person for specified amount from writer's estate.

Cited in note (10 L. R. A. 93) as to wills.

8 L. R. A. 42, FREEMAN'S NAT. BANK v. NATIONAL TUBE WORKS CO. 151 Mass. 413, 21 Am. St. Rep. 461, 24 N. E. 779.

Bank collections.

Approved in Haskell v. Avery, 181 Mass. 108, 92 Am. St. Rep. 401, 63 N. E. 15, holding that bank receiving note bearing indorsement disclosing trust may pass legal title, subject thereto, to one making collection; Citizens' Nat. Bank v. City Nat. Bank, 111 Iowa, 215, 82 N. W. 464, holding bank paying forged check which it indorses for collection to drawee bank liable to latter; People's Bank v. Jefferson County Sav. Bank, 106 Ala. 534, 54 Am. St. Rep. 59, 17 So. 728, holding collecting bank receiving draft from correspondent receiving it for collection cannot apply proceeds to indebtedness from forwarding bank; Commercial Nat. Bank v. Armstrong, 148 U. S. 57, 37 L. ed. 367, 13 Sup. Ct. Rep. 533, holding collections in correspondent bank's subagent's hands at time of insolvency not relieved from trust obligation; National Exch. Bank v. Beal, 50 Fed. 359, refusing to adjudicate right to set off collection where collecting bank not a party; National Bank of Commerce v. Johnson, 6 N. D. 185, 69 N. W. 49, holding indorsement for collection and for credit creates relation of creditor and debtor after collection.

Cited in footnotes to Armstrong v. Boyertown Nat. Bank, 9 L. R. A. 553, which denies right of receiver or creditors of bank crediting owner with draft received for collection to demand proceeds from collecting bank; State Bank v. Byrne, 21 L. R. A. 753, which holds drawee's acceptance of draft presented by collecting bank not payment; Tyson v. Western Nat. Bank, 23 L. R. A. 161, which holds that title does not pass by "indorsing for collection;" Beal v. Somerville, 17 L. R. A. 291, which holds that no title to check passes by depositing for collection; St. Nicholas Bank v. State Nat. Bank, 13 L. R. A. 241, which holds collecting bank's duty not fulfilled by delivering correspondent's draft on third person to itself; Northwestern Nat. Bank v. Bank of Commerce, 15 L. R. A. 102, which holds signature of drawer not guaranteed by indorsing draft "for collection."

Cited in notes (15 L. R. A. 498; 7 L. R. A. 853) as to bank collections; (32 L. R. A. 721) as to trust in proceeds of collection made by bank when insolvent.

— Collections for account.

Approved in Branch v. United States Nat. Bank, 50 Neb. 474, 70 N. W. 34, holding mere credits to remitting bank by correspondent making collection for remitter's account, no defense to action by owner of paper for proceeds; United States Nat. Bank v. Geer, 55 Neb. 465, 41 L. R. A. 444, 70 Am. St. Rep. 390,

75 N. W. 1088, holding indorsement "for account'
paper in indorsee.

8 L. R. A. 47, COOPER v. ARMOUR, 42 Fed. 21

Action for malicious prosecution.

Cited in Wade v. National Bank of Commerce,
maintainable for injuries to reputation and busine
civil action in which complaint containing false an

8 L. R. A. 48, CASE v. SUN INS. CO. 83 Cal. 473,

Limitation of action for insurance.

Approved in Sample v. London & L. F. Ins. Co. 4
57 Am. St. Rep. 701, 24 S. E. 334, and German In
59 N. W. 698, holding that limitation on action
accrual of action, not from fire.

Cited in notes (8 L. R. A. 769) on limitatio
(47 L. R. A. 703) as to whom stipulation limitin
policy begins to run.

Distinguished in Harrigan v. Home L. Ins. Co.
holding, under covenant to pay within sixty days
death, demand must be made within period of limi

8 L. R. A. 50, WILLARD v. FINNEGAN, 42 Minn.

When mortgage foreclosure sale voidable.

Cited in Clark v. Kraker, 51 Minn. 448, 53 N. W
44 Minn. 354, 46 N. W. 559, holding foreclosure sal
tract not void, but voidable only; Middlesex Bkg.
64 N. W. 168, holding foreclosure sale in parcels, i
be set aside on motion of mortgagee bidding at sale a
Northwestern Mortg. Trust Co. v. Bradley, 9 S. D.
foreclosure sale by advertisement *en masse*, instead
not void; Phelps v. Western Realty Co. 89 Minn. 3
mortgage sale as one parcel, of separate tracts, inc
only for good cause.

8 L. R. A. 52, WALLACE v. EVANS, 43 Kan. 509,

Liability to public for building dam.

Cited in note (59 L. R. A. 848) on liability for dam

8 L. R. A. 55, SKINNER v. HENDERSON, 26 Fla. 12

Taxation for county purposes.

Approved in Duval County v. Jacksonville, 36 Fla.
So. 339, holding appropriation of special road tax to
for other than county purposes.

Cited in State *ex rel.* Milton v. Dickenson, 44 Fla. 6
514 (dissenting opinion), majority holding act requ
state militia company to provide armory, unconstitut

8 L. R. A. 58, LOGAN v. STOGDALE, 123 Ind. 372, 24 N. E. 135.

Way of necessity; private roads.

Cited in Ritchey v. Welsh, 149 Ind. 217, 40 L. R. A. 107, 48 N. E. 1031, holding right of way of necessity does not exist over land of another when the lands have not been inherited from common ancestor; Ellis v. Bassett, 128 Ind. 120, 25 Am. St. Rep. 421, 27 N. E. 344, holding way of necessity exists in partition, where it is necessary to reach highway, is open and visible, and has been used continuously for many years.

Cited in footnotes to Lebus v. Boston, 47 L. R. A. 79, which holds parol evidence that grantor agreed he should have no passway over land conveyed admissible to rebut implied reservation of way of necessity; Ritchey v. Welsh, 40 L. R. A. 105, as to how way of necessity created, and who entitled to locate same; Kingsley v. Gouldsboro Land Improv. Co. 25 L. R. A. 502, which holds access by water sufficient to prevent right to way of necessity by land.

Cited in notes (16 L. R. A. 81, 82) on constitutionality of condemnation proceedings to establish private road; (8 L. R. A. 618) on how easement created.

Right of eminent domain.

Cited in Gifford Drainage Dist. v. Shroer, 145 Ind. 574, 44 N. E. 636, holding that owner cannot compel others to pay for draining lands unless public benefited; Great Western Natural Gas & Oil Co. v. Hawkins, 30 Ind. App. 566, 66 N. E. 765, holding legislative declaration that use is public not conclusive.

Cited in note (13 L. R. A. 431) on right of eminent domain.

8 L. R. A. 61, MERRELL v. SPRINGER, 123 Ind. 485, 24 N. E. 258.

Replevin for chattels wrongfully detained.

Cited in Pritchard v. Norwood, 155 Mass. 542, 30 N. E. 80, holding replevin will lie for promissory note.

Cited in footnote to Sinnott v. Feiock, 53 L. R. A. 565, which holds replevin not maintainable for goods obtained by fraud, of which defendant has lost possession.

Cited in note (46 L. R. A. 775) on rights of holder of negotiable paper transferred after maturity.

8 L. R. A. 62, CATLIN v. WILCOX SILVER PLATE CO. 123 Ind. 477, 18 Am. St. Rep. 338, 24 N. E. 250.

Extraterritorial power of receiver or assignee for creditors.

Cited in Burr v. Smith, 113 Fed. 863, upholding right of receiver to enforce in foreign jurisdiction liability of stockholders of insolvent corporation, when right of resident creditors not violated; Rogers v. Haines, 96 Ala. 590, 11 So. 651, and Security Trust Co. v. Dodd, 173 U. S. 620, 43 L. ed. 838, 19 Sup. Ct. Rep. 545, holding general rule that state insolvent laws operate upon property within jurisdiction and in foreign states, subject to rights of creditors; Security Sav. & L. Asso. v. Moore, 151 Ind. 177, 50 N. E. 869, holding authority of receiver coextensive with court appointing him.

Priority of resident creditors as to funds of nonresident.

Cited in Ward v. Connecticut Pipe Mfg. Co. 71 Conn. 356, 42 L. R. A. 710, 71 Am. St. Rep. 207, 41 Atl. 1057, holding attachment, in foreign jurisdiction, of property of insolvent corporation ineffectual against receiver to whom it has voluntarily conveyed its property; Schroder v. Tompkins, 58 Fed. 675, holding voluntary assignment executed in Ohio conveys property of debtors in Indiana; Lackmann v. Supreme Council, O. C. F. 142 Cal. 26, 75 Pac. 583, and Gray v. Covert, 25 Ind. App. 564, 81 Am. St. Rep. 117, 58 N. E. 731, sustaining attachment of resident creditor against receiver of foreign insolvent corporation; Frowert v. Blank, 205 Pa. 302, 54 Atl. 1000, holding holders of matured certificates of foreign benefit association entitled to payment out of fund before transmission to foreign receiver; Clark v. Chandler, 13 C. C. A. 637, 29 U. S. App. 447, 66 Fed. 567, holding vessel sent by receiver out of jurisdiction subject to lien for supplies furnished; Small v. Smith, 14 S. D. 625, 86 Am. St. Rep. 807, 86 N. W. 649 (dissenting opinion), majority holding receiver appointed by foreign court may sue in South Dakota, rights of resident creditors not intervening.

Cited in footnote to Boulware v. Davis, 9 L. R. A. 601, which holds that courts may recognize foreign receiver, if no injustice done to citizens.

Cited in notes (20 L. R. A. 392) on exclusiveness of jurisdiction by appointment of receiver; (23 L. R. A. 53) on rights of receivers beyond jurisdiction; (23 L. R. A. 37, 40) on assignment for benefit of creditors.

Distinguished in Bloomingdale v. Weil, 29 Wash. 625, 70 Pac. 94, holding foreign voluntary assignee of foreign debtor entitled to realty as against foreign attaching creditor.

Criticized in Weil v. Bank of Burr Oak, 76 Mo. App. 39, denying distinction between rights in foreign state of receiver of voluntary and involuntary assignor.

— Rights of foreign creditors.

Approved in Pitman v. Marquardt & Sons, 20 Ind. App. 444, 50 N. E. 894, holding that attaching creditor cannot question legality of assignment made in Kentucky of property in Indiana.

Cited in Michigan Trust Co. v. Probasco, 29 Ind. App. 114, 63 N. E. 255, holding action maintainable by nonresident to determine ownership of stock certificate and enjoin payment; Corn Exch. Bank v. Rockwell, 58 Ill. App. 515, holding foreign creditor obtaining judgment in Ohio afforded same remedies as resident creditor; Nathan v. Lee, 152 Ind. 243, 43 L. R. A. 826, 52 N. E. 987, sustaining right of foreign corporation to mortgage land in Indiana to secure preferred creditor, when not prohibited by foreign statute.

8 L. R. A. 65, BERKEY & G. FURNITURE CO. v. HASCALL, 123 Ind. 502, 24 N. E. 336.

Damages for breach of contract.

Cited in Sinker, D. & Co. v. Kidder, 123 Ind. 531, 24 N. E. 341, holding rental value of mill while idle from explosion of steam boiler, proper element of damage for breach of warranty; Acme Cycle Co. v. Clarke, 157 Ind. 277, 61 N. E. 561, holding estimated profits from sale of bicycles that could have been manufactured with aid of improved hub plant contracted for, not recoverable for failure to furnish plant at time agreed upon; Elwood Planing Mills Co. v. Harting, 21 Ind. App. 411, 52 N. E. 621, holding, when inferior quality of lumber furnished for house not known until after house completed, measure of damage is difference in value of house as it is and what it would have been with lumber contracted for; Western U. Teleg. Co. v. Henley, 23 Ind. App. 25, 54 N. E. 775, holding damages for mental distress and nervous prostration not recoverable for failure to deliver telegraph message.

Objections made first on appeal.

Cited in Chicago & C. Terminal R. Co. v. Eggers, 147 Ind. 303, 45 N. E. 786; Hawks v. Mayor, 144 Ind. 349, 43 N. E. 304; Indiana Racing Asso. v. Allen, 140 Ind. 438, 39 N. E. 669; Allen v. Berndt, 133 Ind. 357, 32 N. E. 1127,—holding only mode by which party can present on appeal question as to form of decree is by motion to modify; Heal v. Niagara Oil Co. 150 Ind. 483, 50 N. E. 482; Midland R. Co. v. Dickason, 130 Ind. 166, 29 N. E. 775, holding judgment cannot be assailed on appeal on account of objections not made in court below.

8 L. R. A. 68, BANCROFT v. HOME BEN. ASSO. 120 N. Y. 14, 23 N. E. 997.

Statements as to health of insured.

Cited in Providence Life Assur. Soc. v. Reutlinger, 58 Ark. 535, 25 S. W. 835, holding questions asked applicant for insurance refer only to illness or injuries affecting risk assumed; Peterson v. Des Moines Life Asso. 115 Iowa, 673, 87 N. W. 397, holding question as to spitting or coughing blood refers to such spitting or coughing as would indicate physical condition affecting the risk; Black v. Travellers' Ins. Co. 61 L. R. A. 501, footnote, p. 500, 58 C. C. A. 15, 121 Fed. 733, holding injury or infirmity, to constitute breach of warranty, must affect health or condition of insured.

8 L. R. A. 70, GERMAN INS. CO. v. GRAY, 43 Kan. 497, 19 Am. St. Rep. 150, 23 Pac. 637.

Imputation of agent's knowledge to company.

Approved in Capitol Ins. Co. v. Bank of Pleasanton, 50 Kan. 451, 31 Pac. 1069, holding knowledge of general agent concerning title to be knowledge of company; Kahn v. Traders Ins. Co. 4 Wyo. 455, 62 Am. St. Rep. 47, 34 Pac. 1059, holding company bound by knowledge of general agent as to additional insurance; Rockford Ins. Co. v. Farmers' State Bank, 50 Kan. 432, 31 Pac. 1063, holding defense that insured was not owner in fee not available when he made no representation, and agent had knowledge of the fact.

Cited in McElroy v. British America Assur. Co. 36 C. C. A. 622, 94 Fed. 998, holding parol testimony of agent's knowledge of encumbrance and additional insurance admissible.

Cited in footnote to Follett v. United States Mut. Acci. Asso. 15 L. R. A. 668, which holds agent's knowledge of deafness of applicant for insurance imputable to company.

Distinguished in Reed v. Equitable F. & M. Ins. Co. 17 R. I. 788, 18 L. R. A. 497, 24 Atl. 833, holding knowledge of prior insurance by agent authorized only to receive applications not binding on company.

Estoppel by agent's knowledge or fraud.

Approved in Phenix Ins. Co. v. Weeks, 45 Kan. 758, 26 Pac. 410, holding inaccurate statements in application filled out by agent, who has knowledge of facts, do not render policy void; Standard Life & Acci. Ins. Co. v. Davis, 59 Kan. 527, 53 Pac. 856, holding policy not rendered void by fact known to agent, who failed to state it in application; Kansas Farmers' F. Ins. Co. v. Saindon, 52 Kan. 493, 39 Am. St. Rep. 356, 35 Pac. 15, holding policy not rendered void by false answers filled in by agent without knowledge of insured.

Agent's powers to waive provisions in poli

Approved in Union Trust Co. v. Provident Sav 365, holding general agent may waive forfeiture; 4 Kan. App. 24, 45 Pac. 789, holding general agen iting additional insurance; Manufacturers & M. I 476, 34 N. E. 553, holding agent may waive conditio ing appliances be provided within sixty days; Bur Mo. App. 635; Burnham v. Greenwich Ins. Co. 63 tion for bidding agent to waive conditions of polic Ins. Co. 4 Wyo. 464, 62 Am. St. Rep. 47, 34 Pac. 1 iting agent to waive or alter conditions of policy Co. v. Johnson, 4 Kan. App. 10, 45 Pac. 722, holdin although policy contains general limitation upon a v. Provident Sav. Life Assur. Soc. 132 N. C. 929, agent may waive provision for increase of rate ir clause forbidding such waiver: German Ins. Co. v. S 93 N. W. 972, holding agent may orally waive pro mium, though policy provides for waiver only by v. Mutual Ben. L. Ins. Co. 10 Kan. App. 9, 61 Pa may waive forfeiture of policy by nonpayment of p its agent's power.

Cited in Long Island Ins. Co. v. Great Western Pac. 738, as questioning rule that company is not b ing limited powers, where policy states waiver canno

Cited in footnotes to Hall v. Union Cent. L. Ins. holds admissions by insurance agent after death o paid, binding on company; Cole v. Union Cent. L. In holds credit for part of first premium, extended b company.

Cited in notes (9 L. R. A. 318) on waiver of con icy; (11 L. R. A. 599) on waiver of conditions by re A. 610) on responsibility of insurance company for R. A. 344) on acts and agreements of agent binding

Proofs of loss.

Cited in Dwelling-House Ins. Co. v. Osborn, 1 Ka holding denial of liability by adjuster waives proof Munger, 49 Kan. 194, 33 Am. St. Rep. 360, 30 Pac. tract cannot be modified by custom of other compa pensing with proofs of loss.

Cited in footnote to Paltrovitch v. Phoenix Ins. (holds further certificate of notary as to loss waived b out giving name or address of nearer notary.

Cited in note (18 L. R. A. 85) on forfeiture of insu proofs of loss.

Authority of manager.

Cited in Kansas City v. Cullinan, 65 Kan. 78, 68 manager of town site company authorized to sign pav

8 L. R. A. 79, HALPIN v. INSURANCE CO. OF N. A. 120 N. Y. 73, 23 N. E. 989.

Construction of forfeiture clause.

Approved in McFadden v. Bloch, 50 App. Div. 421, 64 N. Y. Supp. 101, construing limitation of term so as not to defeat rights reserved to vendor; Robertson v. Ongley Electric Co. 146 N. Y. 24, 40 N. E. 390, holding provision of chattel mortgage not to permit attachment "against property," not applicable to property unmortgaged; Gillet v. Bank of America, 160 N. Y. 556, 55 N. E. 292, holding pledge of collateral for payment of note or any other liability contracted or existing, not inclusive of note to third party not paid by payee or charged by it to customer's account; Wright v. Reusens, 133 N. Y. 305, 31 N. E. 215, holding instalments on building contract, each of specified amount, and to be paid upon performance of work, due when such proportion performed as particular instalment bears to whole contract.

— In insurance policy.

Approved in Phenix Ins. Co. v. Holcombe, 57 Neb. 630, 73 Am. St. Rep. 532, 78 N. W. 300, holding merchandise and machinery used in manufacturing not manufacturing establishment within insurance forfeiture clause; Caraher v. Royal Ins. Co. 63 Hun, 93, 17 N Y. Supp. 858, holding "occupancy" of church by purchaser, question of fact where services discontinued, but resumable; Huber v. Manchester F. Assur. Co. 92 Hun, 230, 36 N. Y. Supp. 873, holding, under policy covering house and contents, insurance on personalty lapsed when house unoccupied, thereby working forfeiture of "entire policy;" Limburg v. German F. Ins. Co. 90 Iowa, 712, 23 L. R. A. 100, footnote, p. 99, 48 Am. St. Rep. 468, 57 N. W. 626, holding that storage use does not constitute occupancy within insurance policy on store and factory building; St. Paul F. & M. Ins. Co. v. Kidd, 5 C. C. A. 90, 14 U. S. App. 201, 55 Fed. 239, holding that where insurance is "as per form attached," which covers special risks to which many conditions in policy do not attach, inconsistent terms in body of policy are superseded.

Cited in footnotes to Louck v. Orient Ins. Co. 33 L. R. A. 712, which holds policy on idle distillery not void because not in operation: Stone v. Howard Ins. Co. 11 L. R. A. 771, which holds custom to cease operations in shoe factory in dull season does not render nugatory provision avoiding policy if operations cease; Henderson Trust Co. v. Stuart, 48 L. R. A. 49, which holds executor liable for loss of insurance from failure to apply for extension of vacancy permit; Moody v. Amazon Ins. Co. 26 L. R. A. 313, which holds nonoccupancy, without increase of risk or fraud, insufficient to avoid policy; Hampton v. Hartford F. Ins. Co. 52 L. R. A. 344, which holds church in which services held. and with windows boarded up, not unoccupied at matter of law; Home Ins. Co. v. Hancock, 52 L. R. A. 665, which holds house not vacant because custodian has access to only one room; German Ins. Co. v. Russell, 58 L. R. A. 234, which holds policy absolutely forfeited by premises allowed to remain vacant time specified in policy.

Cited in note (9 L. R. A. 82) as condition against vacancy and nonoccupancy in fire insurance.

Distinguished in Couch v. Farmers' F. Ins. Co. 64 App. Div. 370, 72 N. Y. Supp. 95, holding policy upon house and contents, void if vacant or unoccupied for ten days, void where house not entered for five months.

Approved in Carrico v. West Virginia C. & P. R. Co. 35 W. Va. 394, 14 S. E.

Exclusion of evidence.

Approval in Carrico v. West Virginia C. & P. R. Co. 35 W. Va. 394, 14 S. E. 12, holding evidence cannot be excluded as insufficient to sustain issue after movant's evidence introduced; Ketterman v. Dry Fork R. Co. 48 W. Va. 611, 37 S. E. 683, holding that case should not be withdrawn from jury on defendant's motion, where verdict for plaintiff would have to be set aside.

Proximate cause.

Approved in Hungerman v. Wheeling, 46 W. Va. 768, 34 S. E. 778, holding city not liable for absence of embankment rail, where prudent driver may make proper effort to regain control of frightened horse.

Cited in footnotes to Western R. Co. v. Mutch, 21 L. R. A. 316, which holds excessive speed not proximate cause of death of boy attempting to catch on train; Missouri P. R. Co. v. Columbia, 58 L. R. A. 399, which holds placing on platform heavy doors, blown on track by severe gale, not proximate cause of derailment of engine; Chicago, St. P. M. & O. R. Co. v. Elliott, 20 L. R. A. 582, as to proximate cause of injury to shipper while stepping from stock car to caboose; Schumaker v. St. Paul & D. R. Co. 12 L. R. A. 257, which holds master's neglect to furnish transportation proximate cause of injury in walking to find shelter; McClain v. Garden Grove, 12 L. R. A. 482, which holds narrowness of bridge and insufficiency of railings not proximate cause of injury from horse falling from disease or choking; Gibney v. State, 19 L. R. A. 365, which holds unsafe bridge cause of drowning father, trying to save child falling into water through defect; Wood v. Pennsylvania R. Co. 35 L. R. A. 199, which holds failure to give warning approach of train not proximate cause of injury to one struck by body of other person hit by train; Kieffer v. Hummelstown, 17 L. R. A. 217, which holds borough not liable for injury to one thrown on stone pile on roadside by fall of horse, due to struggles of other horse frightened by shooting; Herr v. Lebanon, 16 L. R. A. 106, which holds want of barrier not proximate cause of omnibus going over wall while horse attempting to rise; Vallo v. United States Exp. Co. 14 L. R. A. 743, which holds throwing trunk from delivery wagon in highway proximate cause of traveler falling over another trunk; Southwestern Teleg. & Teleph. Co. v. Robinson, 16 L. R. A. 545, which holds telephone company liable for injury by electricity generated by thunder storm in low hanging telephone wire; Southern R. Co. v. Webb, 59 L. R. A. 109, which holds negligent jolting of train, hurling passenger through door on track, insensible, cause of death by train of other company; McKenna v. Baessler, 17 L. R. A. 310 which holds original fire cause of destruction of property by back fire; Jacksonville, T. & K. W. R. Co. v. Peninsular Land, Transp. & Mfg. Co. 17 L. R. A. 38, which holds fire escaping from locomotive proximate cause of loss of buildings set on fire by other buildings first set on fire; Mueller v. Milwaukee Street R. Co. 21 L. R. A. 721, which holds sudden stopping of street car in front of funeral procession cause of injury to first carriage by pole of second; Daniels v. New York, N. H. & H. R. Co. 62 L. R. A. 751, holding person whose negligence caused injury not liable for suicide of person thereby rendered insane.

Cited in notes (7 L. R. A. 843) as to party placed in dilemma by another's fault; (12 L. R. A. 282) on concurrent or co-operating causes of injury; (12 L. R. A. 283) on causal connection broken by intervening agency; (13 L. R. A. 193) as to responsibility for proximate or direct consequences of negligence; (13 L. R. A. 733) as to proximate and remote cause of damage.

Distinguished in Rohrbough v. County Court, 39 W. Va. 473. 45 Am. St. Rep. 925, 20 S. E. 565, holding county liable for absence of guard rail from bridge approach, where horse was frightened and accident occurred simultaneously.

Action for death or injury.

Cited in note (12 L. R. A. 339) on action for damages for personal injuries or death.

8 L. R. A. 89, MILLER v. MENDENHALL, 43 Minn. 95. 19 Am. St. Rep. 219, 44 N. W. 1141.

State ownership of waters and land under same.

Approved in Farm Invest. Co. v. Carpenter, 9 Wyo. 139, 50 L. R. A. 757, 87 Am. St. Rep. 918, 61 Pac. 258, holding that state ownership of navigable waters is for benefit of public.

Cited in Willow River Club v. Wade. 100 Wis. 115, 42 L. R. A. 329, 76 N. W. 273 (concurring opinion) to point that state may part with its title to bed of navigable waters so far as public interest is not interfered with.

Cited in footnotes to St. Louis, I. M. & S. R. Co. v. Ramsey, 8 L. R. A. 559, which holds title to land under navigable river in state; St. Paul v. Chicago, M. & St. P. R. Co. 34 L. R. A. 184, which denies power of legislature to give any part of levee as permanent site for freight warehouse.

Cited in note (12 L. R. A. 677) on title to soil under navigable waters.

Riparian owner's right subordinate to interests of public.

Approved in Mills v. United States, 12 L. R. A. 679, 46 Fed. 743, holding right of riparian owner in tidal lands subordinate to interests of navigation; Sage v. New York, 154 N. Y. 78, 38 L. R. A. 613, footnote, p. 606, 61 Am. St. Rep. 592, 47 N. E. 1096, holding city may improve tidal water front for benefit of navigation without interference from riparian owner.

Cited in footnotes to Allen v. Allen, 30 L. R. A. 497, which holds public right of fishery paramount to riparian right to cut grass or sedge; Slingerland v. International Contracting Co. 56 L. R. A. 494, which holds riparian owner has no right of action for interference by government, in improving navigation, with right to fish in and take ice from the water; Farist Steel Co. v. Bridgeport, 13 L. R. A. 590, which requires compensation to riparian owner on appropriation of land by city in establishing harbor lines.

Cited in note (12 L. R. A. 636) on extent of right and title of littoral proprietors.

Reclaiming submerged land.

Cited in Gilbert v. Eldridge, 47 Minn. 213, 13 L. R. A. 413, footnote, p. 411, 49 N. W. 679, holding right to reclaim submerged land does not attach to land which becomes a shore line by encroachment of the water.

Rights of riparian owners below high-water mark.

Cited in footnotes to McBurney v. Young, 29 L. R. A. 539, which defines low-water mark as ordinary low-water mark; Webb v. Demopolis, 21 L. R. A. 62, which holds riparian owner's title extends to low-water mark on navigable river; Carr v. Carpenter, 53 L. R. A. 333, which sustains upland owner's right to take seaweed stranded on beach.

Cited in notes (16 L. R. A. 354) on ownership of
(12 L. R. A. 617) on right of riparian owners to
(45 L. R. A. 240) on title to land between high an

Establishment of dock and harbor lines.

Cited in notes (12 L. R. A. 635) on establishme
(14 L. R. A. 498) on effect of establishing dock line

Right to build wharves.

Cited in footnotes to Prior v. Swartz, 18 L. R.
right to build wharves not destroyed by designati
Lewis v. Portland, 22 L. R. A. 736, which upholds r
wharves.

Cited in note (40 L. R. A. 647) on right to erect

Separation and transfer of riparian rights.

Approved in Hanford v. St. Paul & D. R. Co. 43
N. W. 1144; Gilbert v. Eldridge, 47 Minn. 214, 13
Bradshaw v. Duluth Imperial Mills Co. 52 Minn.
riparian right to reclaim submerged land may be
transferred.

Cited in note (40 L. R. A. 394) on separation of r

Ejectment against occupant of wharf.

Cited in Turner v. Mobile, 135 Ala. 129, 33 So. 13
occupant of wharf will not be enjoined where he ha
able at law.

8 L. R. A. 95, MURRAY v. MURRAY, 90 Ky. 1, 13 S

Transfers in fraud of wife.

Cited in Arnegaard v. Arnegaard, 7 N. D. 493, 41
holding secret transfer by father to child by forme
stead cut off, fraudulent and void as to prospective b
112 Ky. 766, 66 S. W. 745, holding widow entitled to
husband to son for purpose of defeating her right.

Cited in footnotes to Walker v. Walker, 27 L. R.
lent, transfer of corporate stock to defeat wife's di
Smith, 34 L. R. A. 49, which holds delivery by hus
deed of all realty, made years before, fraudulent as
L. R. A. 858, which holds second wife's right to dower
antenuptial conveyance to sons by former marriage.

Cited in note (8 L. R. A. 814) on relief in equity
husband or wife.

8 L. R. A. 97, SHULTZ v. WALL, 134 Pa. 262, 19 Am

Liability of innkeepers.

Cited in Turner v. Stafford, 9 Pa. Super. Ct. 88, 43
keepers' common-law liability as insurer not changed
keeping of valuable property by landlords.

Cited in footnotes to Fay v. Pacific Improv. Co. 16 L
unnecessary to deposit with innkeeper jewelry worn

Maxwell House Co. 64 L. R. A. 471, which holds watch within statute relieving hotel keeper from liability for jewels not deposited in safe.

Cited in note (12 L. R. A. 382) on responsibility of innkeeper as bailee.

8 L. R. A. 102, GOSS v. FROMAN, 89 Ky. 318, 12 S. W. 387.

Presumption of adulterous living.

Cited in footnote to Cox v. State, 41 L. R. A. 760, which holds bigamous cohabitation continues so long as parties live together ostensibly as husband and wife.

Cited in note (11 L. R. A. 791) as to abandonment of marriage obligations.

Presumption of legitimacy.

Cited in footnote to *Re* Pickens, 25 L. R. A. 477, which holds presumption of legitimacy very strong after lapse of ninety years from birth.

Cited in notes (10 L. R. A. 662) on the presumption of legitimacy of child born in wedlock; (18 L. R. A. 377) antenuptial pregnancy or inchastity as a ground of divorce or annulment of marriage.

Limited in Sergent v. North Cumberland Mfg. Co. 112 Ky. 892, 66 S. W. 1036, holding person asserting illegitimacy must show husband could not possibly have been father of child.

Right of dower.

Cited in footnotes to Land v. Shipp, 50 L. R. A. 560, which holds wife's right of dower not affected by release made directly to husband in deed of separation; Price v. Price, 12 L. R. A. 359, which holds wife not entitled to dower on annulment of marriage because husband had former wife living.

8 L. R. A. 106, TERRITORY *ex rel.* KELLY v. STEWART, 1 Wash. 98, 23 Pac. 405.

Constitutionality of incorporation act.

Approved in Pullman v. Hungate, 8 Wash. 520, 36 Pac. 483; State *ex rel.* Traders' Nat. Bank v. Winter, 15 Wash. 408, 46 Pac. 644; Ballard v. West Coast Improv. Co. 15 Wash. 574, 46 Pac. 1055; State *ex rel.* Hemen v. Ballard, 16 Wash. 419, 47 Pac. 970; Lewis County v. Gordon, 20 Wash. 88, 54 Pac. 779,— holding incorporation act of 1888 unconstitutional; State *ex rel.* Cole v. New Whatcom, 3 Wash. 9, 27 Pac. 1021; Denver v. Spokane Falls, 7 Wash. 230, 34 Pac. 927; Ferguson v. Snohomish, 8 Wash. 669, 24 L. R. A. 797, 36 Pac. 970, — holding attempted incorporation under act of 1888 void; Abernethy v. Medical Lake, 9 Wash. 112, 37 Pac. 306, holding contracts for street improvements by town illegally incorporated under void act made binding on it by act for its reincorporation and declaring legal all contracts made under the void law.

Delegation of legislative power.

Approved in *Re* North Milwaukee, 93 Wis. 624, 33 L. R. A. 641, footnote, p. 638, 67 N. W. 1033, holding statute giving court power to enlarge or diminish boundaries of municipalities unconstitutional delegation of legislative power.

Disapproved in Young v. Salt Lake City, 24 Utah. 333, 67 Pac. 1066, statute authorizing court, on petition, to disconnect land bordering on city, not a delegation of legislative power.

8 L. R. A. 110, BARBER ASPHALT PAVING CO.
St. Rep. 530, 13 S. W. 98.

Validity of ordinances.

Approved in Aurora Water Co. v. Aurora, 129 M provision for three readings before final passage d not read three times; Verdin v. St. Louis, 131 Mo paving ordinance not invalid because of material sp ing invalidity extends merely to method of letting.

Municipal contracts for patented or monopol

Approved in State *ex rel.* Dawes v. Shawnee Coun holding patents upon proposed bridge do not necessa in bidding; Rhodes v. Public Works, 10 Colo. App. 1 petitive bids not to be excluded because material sp monopolized.

Cited in Field v. Barber Asphalt Paving Co. 194 Sup. Ct. Rep. 784, holding ordinance specifying Trin an interference with interstate commerce; Shoenberg 68 S. W. 945, raising, without deciding, power of patented or monopolized material where public lettin Verdin v. St. Louis, 131 Mo. 100, 33 S. W. 480, hol for purchase of monopolized pavement.

Cited in note (18 L. R. A. 46) as to municipal co which embody patented invention.

Distinguished in State *ex rel.* Irondale Chert Pa Orleans, 48 La. Ann. 650, 19 So. 690, holding council contract for paving with material selected by propert

8 L. R. A. 112, TOWNSHEND v. GRAY, 62 Vt. 373, 1

Regulation of practice of medicine.

Approved in State *ex rel.* Burroughs v. Webster, 15 50 N. E. 750, sustaining requirement that licensed n new license under later act.

8 L. R. A. 113, LAWLER v. MURPHY, 58 Conn. 294,

Liability of incorporators for corporate debts.

Cited in Wechselberg v. Flour City Nat. Bank, 26 L 24 U. S. App. 308, 64 Fed. 94, holding signers of arti was not perfected liable for debts of concern until re

Incidents necessary to carrying out contract.

Cited in Godkin v. Monahan, 27 C. C. A. 415, 53 U. holding banking of logs, being necessary to the complet a term in contract for delivery.

Construction of written instruments.

Cited in New Blue Springs Mill. Co. v. De Witt, 65 K ing whatever may be fairly implied from indorsement therein.

Benefit certificates.

Cited in footnote to Thuenen v. Iowa Mut. Ben. Asso. 37 L. R. A. 587, which sustains provision in benefit certificate for specified amount that payment of full assessment on members shall be payment in full.

Cited in notes (9 L. R. A. 189) on forfeiture of benefit certificate for nonpayment of assessment; (13 L. R. A. 625) on binding effect of judiciary decisions on mutual benefit associations; (12 L. R. A. 210) on distinction between benefit certificate and life insurance policy.

8 L. R. A. 120, BENEDICT v. CHASE, 58 Conn. 196, 20 Atl. 448.

8 L. R. A. 123, ALLOWAY v. NASHVILLE, 88 Tenn. 510, 13 S. W. 123.

Damages in condemnation proceedings.

Cited in San Diego Land & Town Co. v. Neale, 88 Cal. 56, 11 L. R. A. 607, 25 Pac. 977, and Spring Valley Waterworks v. Drinkhouse, 92 Cal. 539, 28 Pac. 681, holding evidence of value of land for reservoir purposes admissible in condemnation proceedings; *Re* Gilroy, 85 Hun, 427, 32 N. Y. Supp. 891, holding availability of property for use in connection with city's water supply element of market value; Seattle & M. R. Co. v. Roeder, 30 Wash. 265, 94 Am. St. Rep. 864, 70 Pac. 498, holding value of land as stone quarry, but not possible profits, may be considered on condemnation; Allison v. Cocke, 112 Ky. 228, 65 S. W. 342, holding evidence of existence of unusual demand for suburban property at time of breach of land contract admissible on question of value; *Re* Brookfield, 78 App. Div. 526, 81 N. Y. Supp. 10 (dissenting opinion), majority holding value as reservoir cannot be considered in determining value of bed of pond.

Cited in footnotes to Philadelphia Ball Club v. Philadelphia, 46 L. R. A. 724, which requires damages from taking of property in eminent domain to be estimated as of the time when injury was done, without considering future profits of business or subsequent change of circumstances; Martin v. Tyler, 25 L. R. A. 838, which holds order on drainage fund not sufficient payment for land taken for public use.

Cited in notes (13 L. R. A. 431) on compensation for taking by eminent domain; (58 L. R. A. 255) on measure of damages for taking by eminent domain in acquiring water supply; (11 L. R. A. 604) on market price as element of damages in condemnation proceedings; (61 L. R. A. 44) on establishment and regulation of municipal water supply.

Right to open and close.

Cited in McBee v. Bowman, 89 Tenn. 135, 14 S. W. 481, holding assumption of burden of proving revocation by execution of later will does not destroy proponent's right to open and close; Woodward v. Iowa L. Ins. Co. 104 Tenn. 52, 56 S. W. 1020, holding admission of plaintiff's *prima facie* right by defendant pleading avoidance gives no right to open and close; Seattle & M. R. Co. v. Murphine, 4 Wash. 453, 30 Pac. 720, holding petitioner in condemnation proceedings has right to open and close.

Power of appellate court to correct judgment.

Cited in Nighbert v. Hornsby, 100 Tenn. 88, 66 Am. St. Rep. 736, 42 S. W. 1060, holding supreme court has power to correct judgment.

Cited in notes (47 L. R. A. 52) on increase of inadequate damages by court; (43

L. R. A. 38) on inadequacy of damages as ground 1 tions with relation to property.

8 L. R. A. 129, STATE *ex rel.* ATTY. GEN. v. ACCI. SOC. 47 Ohio St. 167, 24 N. E. 392.

Assessment plan.

Cited in State *ex rel.* National Life Asso. v. Matt A. 423, 49 N. E. 1034, holding company exacting fi payable in advance, at stated periods, not conducte facturers' Fire Asso. v. Lynchburg Drug Mills, 8 (obligation of insurance association is limited to ass meet losses.

Amenability of foreign corporation to local

Approved in State *ex rel.* Atty. Gen. v. Fidelity & 16 L. R. A. 612, 34 Am. St. Rep. 573, 31 N. E. 658 illegally exercising franchises may be ousted therefro 61 Neb. 33, 87 Am. St. Rep. 449, 84 N. W. 413, hol may be prevented by injunction or quo warranto fr trary to law; Wright v. Lee, 4 S. D. 248, 55 N. W. be brought to annul existence within state of foreign

Cited in footnote to Fort v. State, 23 L. R. A. 86, agents to assist Accident Lloyds in transacting busin

Cited in notes (13 L. R. A. 585) on amenability of law; (24 L. R. A. 295) on remedy against for franchises.

Law of comity.

Cited in note (8 L. R. A. 236) on law of comity tions.

Retaliatory statutes.

Cited in footnote to State *ex rel.* Atty. Gen. v. Fidel 611, which requires retaliatory legislation to be con its letter.

Cited in note (24 L. R. A. 305) on retaliatory statu

8 L. R. A. 135, MOSES v. SOUTHERN P. R. CO. 18 Or

Liability for injury to animals on track.

Cited in note (11 L. R. A. 461) on duty of railroad stock on track.

—Lack of proper fence.

Approved in Sullivan v. Oregon R. & Nav. Co. 19 Currie v. Southern P. Co. 21 Or. 572, 28 Pac. 886, hol liable, in absence of negligence, for stock killed at plac fence; State *ex rel.* Hardy v. Gleason, 19 Or. 163, 23 company not required to fence its depot; Eaton v. M 875, holding railroad company not liable where stock grounds which company not required to fence.

Cited in footnotes to St. Louis, I. M. & S. R. Co. v.

which holds railroad company not liable for injury by barbed-wire fence to colt frightened from track by train whistle; Johnson v. Oregon Short Line R. Co. 53 L. R. A. 744, which holds railroad company liable for horses killed on unfenced track.

Cited in note (12 L. R. A. 181) on duty of railroad company to fence its tracks.

Contributory negligence.

Approved in Keeney v. Oregon R. & Nav. Co. 19 Or. 292, 24 Pac. 234, holding owner of stock killed on railroad track not guilty of contributory negligence in letting them run at large; Keeney v. Oregon R. & Nav. Co. 19 Or. 294, 24 Pac. 233, holding that contributory negligence of herder, in leaving sheep unguarded by track, bars recovery.

Cited in Hamerlynck v. Banfield, 36 Or. 441, 59 Pac. 712, holding one driving on bridge at invitation of workman, and injured by falling in aperture which became uncovered, not chargeable with contributory negligence.

Cited in note (55 L. R. A. 458) on doctrine of last clear chance.

8 L. R. A. 147, CONRAD v. FISHER, 37 Mo. App. 352.

Transfer of commercial paper.

Cited in Wells v. Jones, 41 Mo. App. 11, holding mere transfer of note as collateral security for antecedent indebtedness does not make transferer holder for value.

Presumption as to payment as condition precedent.

Cited in Burke v. Dunn, 117 Mich. 432, 75 N. W. 931, holding, unless otherwise specified, payment is presumed to be condition precedent to delivery on sale.

Estoppel in pais.

Cited in Wind v. Fifth Nat. Bank, 39 Mo. App. 87, holding depositor not estopped from recovery by negligent failure to notify bank of payment of paper on forged indorsement, unless bank is thereby prejudiced.

Delivery of personal property.

Cited in Kaes v. St. Louis Lime Co. 71 Mo. App. 108, holding where wood was placed on defendant's premises, but not all measured, question of acceptance was for jury; Wachtel v. Ewing, 82 Mo. App. 597, holding immediate turning over to vendee by officer in possession of whiskey in bond on vendor's order, sufficient change of possession; Citizens Bkg. Co. v. Peacock, 103 Ga. 180, 29 S. E. 752, holding delivery of warehouse receipts for cotton in pledge, constructive delivery of cotton itself.

Cited in footnote to Geilfuss v. Corrigan, 37 L. R. A. 166, which holds indorsement and delivery of storage warrants not constructive delivery sustaining pledge of pig iron.

Parol evidence as to writing.

Cited in footnote to Anderson v. Portland Flouring Mills Co. 50 L. R. A. 235, which holds parol evidence of contract under which grain was delivered admissible though negotiable warehouse receipts were given therefor.

Pledge to secure debt.

Cited in Storts v. Mills, 93 Mo. App. 208, holding attempt to pledge notes not in possession of pledgor or pledgee, invalid; Chitwood v. Lanyon Zinc Co. 93 Mo.

App. 230, holding attempt to pledge ore without
Howell v. Caryl, 50 Mo. App. 449, holding eviden
law or statutory mortgage does not show valid con

Owner's receipt upon goods in his own warel

Cited in Franklin Nat. Bank v. Whitehead, 149
Am. St. Rep. 302, 49 N. E. 592, holding that one
cannot give a valid warehouse receipt, upon his g
secure his own debt.

Incidents of vendor's lien.

Cited in Eads v. Kessler, 121 Cal. 246, 53 Pac.
passed to vendee to support vendor's lien; Vogelsa
S. W. 13, holding acceptance of notes of vendee b
vendor's lien.

Unrecorded liens and secret equities.

Cited in Napa Valley Wine Co. v. Rinehart, 42 M
grantee to be protected from prior encumbrances mu
consideration before notice.

Presumption as to law.

Cited in note (21 L. R. A. 472) on presumption a

8 L. R. A. 170, MARTIN v. JOHNSON, 84 Ga. 481,

Conflict of laws.

Distinguished in Hager v. National German-Ameri
E. 141, holding contract by *feme covert* void at place
law of place of performance.

— As to loans and usury.

Cited in National Mut. Bldg. & L. Asso. v. Braha
794, 31 So. 840, and Shannon v. Georgia State Bldg.
L. R. A. 802, 84 Am. St. Rep. 657, 30 So. 51, holding
through established local agents governed by local usu
in foreign state; British American Mortg. Co. v. Bate
holding loan by foreign corporation governed by loca
gage executed locally though payable in foreign state;
L. Asso. 104 Ga. 322, 31 S. E. 215, holding loan gove
of borrower, where note, mortgage, etc., executed the
Loan Asso. v. Burch, 124 Mich. 64, 83 Am. St. Re
Meroney v. Atlanta Bldg. & L. Asso. 116 N. C. 888, 47
924, holding loan by foreign corporation through loca
made, governed by local law; Bigelow v. Burnham, 83
294, 49 N. W. 104, holding loan contract presumptiv
which stipulated interest lawful; Building & L. Asso.
W. 656, holding loan by foreign corporation through loc
usury law though payable in foreign state; Washington
Asso. v. Stanley, 38 Or. 342, 58 L. R. A. 824, 84 Am.
holding stipulation in loan contract for its construct
payable, not controlling where actually local.

Cited in footnote to Dugan v. Lewis, 12 L. R. A. 9
rate of interest of either state, on contract between cit

Cited in notes (55 L. R. A. 934, 940) as to whether *lex rei sitæ* with respect to interest and usury necessarily controls in action to foreclose mortgage on real estate; (62 L. R. A. 63) on conflict of laws as to interest and usury.

What constitutes usury.

Cited in Kilcrease v. Johnson, 85 Ga. 602, 11 S. E. 870, holding reservation of $69 by payee of note for $300 usury.

Distinguished in Burns v. Equitable Bldg. & L. Asso. 108 Ga. 181, 33 S. E. 856, holding misapplication by officers of building association of payments on valid loan, does not render contract usurious.

8 L. R. A. 173, TALLMAN v. METROPOLITAN ELEV. R. CO. 121 N. Y. 119, 23 N. E. 1134.

Time to which damages recoverable.

Approved in Mitchell v. White Plains, 91 Hun, 192, 36 N. Y. Supp. 204, holding that no action lies to recover prospective damages to real estate; Kenyon v. New York C. & H. R. R. Co. 29 App. Div. 82, 51 N. Y. Supp. 386, holding that damages to real estate cannot be recovered to date of entry of judgment; Rumsey v. New York & N. E. R. Co. 63 Hun. 206, 17 N. Y. Supp. 672, holding riparian owner can only recover damages to time of commencing suit, for intercepting access; Hollenbeck v. Marion, 116 Iowa, 80, 89 N. W. 210, holding instruction in action for past damages that pollution destroying potability of water constitutes nuisance, erroneous in absence of evidence of such use.

Measure of damages.

Approved in Reisert v. New York, 174 N. Y. 207, 66 N. E. 731, Reversing 69 App. Div. 310, 74 N. Y. Supp. 673, holding rental value measure for continuing injury by removal of appurtenant waters; Rosenheimer v. Standard Gaslight Co. 36 App. Div. 11, 55 N. Y. Supp. 192, holding gas manufacturer liable for diminution of rental value of adjoining premises in owner's occupancy; Rumsey v. New York & N. E. R. Co. 133 N. Y. 84, 15 L. R. A. 620, 28 Am. St. Rep. 600, 30 N. E. 654; same case on subsequent appeal in 136 N. Y. 545, 32 N. E. 979, holding damage from loss of access to river, to be diminished rental value while in same general condition; Rummel v. New York, L. & W. R. Co. 30 N. Y. S. R. 239, 9 N. Y. Supp. 404 (concurring opinion) to point that measure of damages for authorized obstruction of street by railroad embankment is depreciation in rental value; Randall v. United States Leather Co. 72 App. Div. 320, 76 N. Y. Supp. 82, holding damages from nuisance not usable value as including business profits.

— Elevated street railroads.

Cited in American Bank Note Co. v. New York Elev. R. Co. 27 Jones & S. 185, 13 N. Y. Supp. 626, holding elevated street railway, which did not acquire right in street liable to abutter for diminished rental value though buildings erected after road constructed; Mortimer v. Manhattan R. Co. 129 N. Y. 85, 29 N. E. 5, and Hine v. New York Elev. R. Co. 37 N. Y. S. R. 608, 13 N. Y. Supp. 510, holding abutter entitled to damages for depreciation in rental value while premises in possession of tenants, for elevated railroad built without acquiring easements; Kernochan v. New York Elev. R. Co. 128 N. Y. 567, 29 N. E. 65, holding lessor in lease subsequent to construction of elevated railroad without obtaining easement, has action for subsequent loss of rents; Martin v. Manhattan R. Co. 63 Hun. 351, 18 N. Y. Supp. 238, holding rental damages while old building being pulled down and new one erected, not allowable for elevated

railway; Woolsey v. New York Elev. R. Co. 134 N.
N. E. 891, holding abutter entitled to damages fr
to the diminished rental or usable value.

Distinguished in Pappenheim v. Metropolitan Ele
R. A. 407, 26 Am. St. Rep. 486, 28 N. E. 518, hol
abutting on street occupied by elevated railroad b
parent easements conveys all grantor's rights and r

Right to damages for construction of elevate

Cited in Paret v. New York Elev. R. Co. 40 N. Y.
holding alleged loss upon sale of realty, from elevat
able in action for money only.

Cited in footnotes to Aldrich v. Metropolitan We
A. 237, which denies right to recover for injury to a
road crossing highway 19 feet away; De Geofroy v.
R. Co. 64 L. R. A. 959, which holds abutting owner
construction of elevated railroad in street.

Injunction against continuing trespass or nu

Approved in United States Freehold Land & Emig
C. A. 475, 61 U. S. App. 13, 89 Fed. 773, holding tha
uing trespass upon real estate to the damage of ow
N. Y. Supp. 954, holding injunction remedy for int
pier in mill race without owner's consent; Carmichae
holding that equity has jurisdiction to restrain conti
of stream with sewage; Dimick v. Shaw, 36 C. C. A
that equity may restrain trespasser from working a
to belong to complainant; Coombs v. Salt Lake & Ft.
248, holding injunction against operation of railroa
not lost by mere silence and inactivity; Galway v. M
N. Y. 144, 13 L. R. A. 792, 28 N. E. 479, holding rem
ance of trespasses upon real estate, not barred and
of ten years from original trespass; Bly v. Edison El
N. Y. 23, 58 L. R. A. 508, 64 N. E. 745 (dissenting
that renewal of lease after creation of nuisance does n
to abate and for damages.

8 L. R. A. 175, THOMAS v. MUSICAL MUT. PROTE
45, 24 N. E. 24.

Adjudication of speculative questions.

Cited in The Minnehaha, 114 Fed. 674, denying right
test action where no injury suffered.

Equitable relief; when granted.

Cited in Whitney v. Whitney, 63 Hun, 73, 18 N. Y.
relief when remedy at law adequate; Wormser v. Brow
524, denying injunction against construction of bay w
not resulting; Kinnan v. Sullivan County Club, 26 App
95, denying injunction restraining assessments on stock
law for collection: Thomas v. Grand View Beach R. C
Supp. 201, denying equitable relief when ejectment p

Cement Co. v. Consolidated Rosendale Cement Co. 178 N. Y. 187, 70 N. E. 451 (dissenting opinion) majority holding equity will enjoin owner of canal from imposing illegal tolls; Niagara Falls v. New York C. & H. R. R. Co. 168 N. Y. 617, 61 N. E. 185, by O'Brien, J., dissenting, who denies right to use of land for road bed preventing use for street, where title involved.

Cited in note (11 L. R. A. 68) on equitable jurisdiction where remedy at law exists.

Injury as essential to equitable remedy.

Approved in Sullivan v. Venner, 45 N. Y. S. R. 688, 18 N. Y. Supp. 398, denying injunction when evils anticipated indefinite and imaginary.

Cited in Brown v. Duane, 60 Hun, 101, 14 N. Y. Supp. 450, denying mandamus when anticipated wrong not yet inflicted; McWilliams v. Jewett, 14 Misc. 496, 36 N. Y. Supp. 620, denying injunction against publication of notice for public meeting where injury uncertain; McSorley v. Gomprecht, 30 Abb. N. C. 416, 26 N. Y. Supp. 917, denying mandatory injunction requiring removal of wall, irreparable injury not resulting from erection.

Legal interference with affairs of societies.

Approved in Whiteside v. Noyac Cottage Asso. 142 N. Y. 589, 60 N. Y. S. R. 305, 37 N. E. 624, Affirming 68 Hun, 567, 23 N. Y. Supp. 63, denying legal interference till remedies afforded by association invoked; Johansen v. Blume, 53 App. Div. 529, 65 N. Y. Supp. 987, holding that courts will not interfere with association until all remedies provided in regulations are exhausted; People *ex rel.* Wilson v. Medical Society, 84 Hun, 450, 32 N. Y. Supp. 415, holding member expelled from county society should appeal to state society before resorting to law.

Distinguished in Brown v. Supreme Court, I. O. F. 34 Misc. 561, 70 N. Y. Supp. 397, holding right to reinstatement without exhausting association remedies, when question one of law.

Conclusiveness of by-laws.

Cited in footnotes to American Live Stock Commission Co. v. Chicago Live Stock Exchange, 18 L. R. A. 191, which holds illegality of stock exchange by-laws not ground for compelling their disobedience; Northport Wesleyan Grove Camp Meeting Asso. v. Perkins, 48 L. R. A. 272, which denies right of camp-meeting association to impose revenue tax on persons soliciting orders for provisions, etc., from lessees; Industrial Trust Co. v. Green, 17 L. R. A. 202, which holds illegal deposition of president not ground for subsequent dissolution of benevolent association.

8 L. R. A. 180, FT. WORTH & R. G. R. CO. v. JENNINGS, 76 Tex. 373, 13 S. W. 270.

Additional servitude upon right of way.

Approved in Blakely v. Chicago, K. & N. R. Co. 34 Neb. 287, 51 N. W. 767, holding second railway additional burden.

Cited in Rische v. Texas Transp. Co. 27 Tex. Civ. App. 37, 66 S. W. 324, holding abutter entitled to compensation for construction of street railway for transporting freight.

Cited in footnotes to Miller v. Green Bay, W. & St. P. R. Co. 26 L. R. A. 443, which holds additional burden on street not made by allowing other companies to use tracks; Gurney v. Minneapolis Union Elevator Co. 30 L. R. A. 534, which holds erection of public warehouse on railroad land not abandonment of easement.

Distinguished in Stevens v. St. Louis Merchan Mo. 219, 53 S. W. 1066, holding second railway j depot purposes not additional servitude; Gray v. Depot Co. 13 Tex. Civ. App. 166, 36 S. W. 352, h involved in action based purely upon equitable re

8 L. R. A. 183, FLAHERTY v. MORAN, 81 Mich. W. 381.

Malice in use of one's own property.

Followed in Kirkwood v. Finegan, 95 Mich. 544, tenance of fence erected between neighbors on acc 110 Mich. 53, 67 N. W. 1080, holding board fence out light and rendering house damp is a nuisance.

Cited in Horan v. Byrnes, 72 N. H. 97, 62 L. R. . statute declaring fence unnecessary exceeding 5 fe a nuisance.

Cited in footnote to Hague v. Wheeler, 22 L. R. to adjoining owner for permitting escape of gas fro

Cited in notes (40 L. R. A. 180) on liability fo (62 L. R. A. 676, 686) on effect of bad motive to otherwise not be.

Distinguished in Kuzniak v. Kozminski, 107 Mi 67 N. W. 275, holding darkening of windows by er ble although inspired by malicious motive.

8 L. R. A. 188, TERRITORIAL INSANE ASYLU 22 Pac. 383.

When mandamus lies.

Cited in notes (11 L. R. A. 763) on mandamus to (58 L. R. A. 867) on original jurisdiction of court case.

8 L. R. A. 189, WESTERN U. TELEG. CO. v. TAY

Jurisdiction of courts of special powers.

Cited in Western U. Teleg. Co. v. Bright, 90 V circuit court without jurisdiction to decree on m deliver telegram.

Judgment of court without jurisdiction.

Cited in Freer v. Davis. 52 W. Va. 12, 59 L. R. A S. E. 164, holding plaintiff not estopped to deny on tion of subject-matter.

Liability for nondelivery of telegram.

Cited in Conyers v. Postal Teleg. Cable Co. 92 Ga. S. E. 253, holding right to recover penalty for dela on statute not contract; Woodburn v. Western U. T 116, holding penalty for failure to deliver telegran not damages for breach of contract; Chapman v. V

776, 17 L. R. A. 434, 30 Am. St. Rep. 183, 15 S. E. 901, holding delay in sending message gives no action for mental pain, but for penalty; Mathis v. Western U. Teleg. Co. 94 Ga. 340, 47 Am. St. Rep. 167, 21 S. E. 564, holding right to penalty, being based on public policy, not contract, company cannot defeat it by regulations; Western U. Teleg. Co. v. Nunnally, 86 Ga. 503, 12 S. E. 578, holding lapse of year bars action for penalty for violation of statute.

Cited in footnote to Western U. Teleg. Co. v. Short, 9 L. R. A. 744, which holds company prima facie liable for failure to deliver telegram.

Refunding charges as bar to action for penalty.

Followed in Western U. Teleg. Co. v. Brightwell, 94 Ga. 434, 21 S. E. 518, holding right to penalty not abrogated by company's refunding message charges.

Cited in Western U. Teleg. Co. v. Moss, 93 Ga. 497, 21 S. E. 63, holding repayment of charges no bar to penalty for failure to transmit message.

8 L. R. A. 193, PRICE v. CONWAY, 134 Pa. 340, 19 Am. St. Rep. 704, 19 Atl. 687.

Office of innuendoes.

Cited in Goebeler v. Wilhelm, 17 Pa. Super. Ct. 440, holding court must instruct jury whether publication is libelous, supposing innuendoes to be true: Naulty v. Bulletin Co. 206 Pa. 134, 55 Atl. 862; Walter v. Erdman, 4 Pa. Super. Ct. 355; Leitz v. Hohman, 18 Lanc. L. Rev. 220, 16 Pa. Super. Ct. 282—holding court must decide whether alleged words are capable of meaning ascribed in innuendo, jury whether it was truly ascribed to them.

What constitutes libel.

Cited in notes (16 L. R. A. 625) on libel by filing lien; (9 L. R. A. 623) on what constitutes libel of tradesmen and business men; (13 L. R. A. 98) on fair criticism of public men allowable.

Special damages.

Cited in Dun v. Weintraub, 111 Ga. 419, 50 L. R. A. 673, 36 S. E. 808, and St. James Military Academy v. Gaiser, 125 Mo. 525, 28 L. R. A. 674, 46 Am. St. Rep. 502, 28 S. W. 851, holding false publication injurious to one in his profession, trade, or business actionable without proof of special damages; McIntyre v. Weinert, 195 Pa. 57, 45 Atl. 666, holding special damage need not be averred in action for publishing merchant as delinquent debtor; Moore v. Rolin, 89 Va. 111, 16 L. R. A. 627, 15 S. E. 520, holding malicious premature filing of mechanic's lien actionable if special damages result.

8 L. R. A. 195, COM. *ex rel.* BURT v. UNION LEAGUE, 135 Pa. 301, 20 Am. St. Rep. 870, 19 Atl. 1030.

When mandamus lies.

Cited in note (32 L. R. A. 575) on mandamus to enforce provision of corporate by-laws.

Assent to constitution and by-laws of organization.

Cited in Myers v. Fritchman, 6 Pa. Super. Ct. 582, and Brubaker v. Denlinger, 17 Lanc. L. Rev. 222, holding person becoming member of an incorporated beneficial association accepts and is bound by its rules; People *ex rel.* Elwell v. Manhattan Chess Club, 23 Misc. 502, 52 N. Y. Supp. 726, upholding legality of expulsion of member by club by regular proceeding, wi participate; Evans v. Chamber of Commerce, 86 Mi right of business association to expel member foi arbitration in violation of by-laws.

Right to hearing.

Cited in Miles v. Stevenson, 80 Md. 366, 30 Atl. removable except for causes specified in statute a Farmer v. Board of Trade, 78 Mo. App. 564, holdin violate its own rules and expel member without noti

Formality of proceedings to expel member.

Cited in United States *ex rel.* De Yturbide v. M C. 196, upholding judgment of expulsion expressed Brandenburger v. Jefferson Club Asso. 88 Mo. App. expulsion are not required to be technically regular; Louis Medical Soc. 91 Mo. App. 83, holding it suff compliance with constitution and by-laws, and notic nounced with proper motives and in good faith.

Offenses sufficient for expulsion.

Cited in Brandenburger v. Jefferson Club Asso. 88 pulsion of member of political club for publishing st its members.

Conclusiveness of regular trial in organizatio

Cited in Brandenburger v. Jefferson Club Asso. 88 powerless where expulsion is regular for offense fo pelled; Miller v. Wolf, 18 Lanc. L. Rev. 109, holding ber cannot recover claim after regular adverse decis opportunity of full hearing; Harman v. Raub, 18 L Ct. 102, holding claimant of unincorporated benefit s denied a hearing in society may resort to courts.

Cited in note (49 L. R. A. 359, 360, 362, 368) o of tribunals of associations or corporations.

8 L. R. A. 202, LORD v. MEADVILLE WATER CO. 864, 19 Atl. 1007.

Rights of lower riparian owners to flow of

Cited in Standard Plate Glass Co. v. Butler Wate W. N. C. 197, and Clark v. Pennsylvania R. Co. 14 Am. St. Rep. 710, 22 Atl. 989, holding upper ripari for purposes not relating to his land to injury o Sinking Spring Water Co. 7 Pa. Super. Ct. 67, and Water Co. 8 Kulp, 314, holding that spring owne stream running therefrom to injury of lower prop Pa. Co. Ct. 631, holding that no riparian propriet of another, as a general rule; Philadelphia & R. 182 Pa. 426, 38 Atl. 404, Affirming 18 Pa. Co. Ct. cannot divert and sell running waters to strangers & Nav. Co. v. Scranton Gas & Water Co. 6 Pa. Di riparian ownership does not justify upper propriet

riparian land for consumption; Craig v. Shippensburg, 7 Pa. Super. Ct. 520, holding that borough cannot, without compensation, divert stream for water supply, to injury of lower owners; Filbert v. Dechert, 22 Pa. Super. Ct. 366, holding insane asylum may take water of stream for domestic use, to injury of lower riparian owner; Salem Mills Co. v. Lord, 42 Or. 98, 69 Pac. 1033, holding riparian ownership does not entitle state to water for necessary purposes of penitentiary, farm, and insane asylum; Standard Plate Glass Co. v. Butler Water Co. 5 Pa. Super. Ct. 577, 28 Pittsb. L. J. N. S. 166, denying right of water company as upper riparian proprietor to use water to supply inhabitants of borough; Rudolph v. Pennsylvania & S. Valley R. Co. 186 Pa. 551, 47 L. R. A. 786, 42 W. N. C. 380, 40 Atl. 1083, holding riparian owner entitled to compensation for pollution of stream by railroad appropriating right of way through land; Com. v. Yost, 197 Pa. 174, 46 Atl. 845, holding pollution of stream in which riparian owners alone have an interest is a private wrong; Irving v. Media, 7 Del. Co. Rep. 381, 10 Pa. Super. Ct. 145, 44 W. N. C. 134, holding riparian proprietors have property right in stream which cannot be appropriated without compensation.

Cited in note (41 L. R. A. 740) on correlative rights of upper and lower proprietors as to use and flow of water in stream.

Extent of watercourse.

Cited in Lehigh Coal & Nav. Co. v. Pocono Spring Water Ice Co. 7 Northampton Co. Rep. 358, holding water begins where water comes to surface and continues to flow in a channel to the sea.

Eminent domain.

Cited in Irving v. Media, 7 Del. Co. Rep. 385, 10 Pa. Super. Ct. 148, holding appropriation of water without exercise of right of eminent domain a tort; *Re* Centre Street, 8 Kulp, 22, holding involuntary proceedings to take private property for public use must strictly conform to statute; Shippensburg Water Case, 21 Pa. Co. Ct. 89, holding under statutes borough may condemn small mountain stream not amounting to river or creek.

Cited in footnote to Brosnan v. Harris, 54 L. R. A. 628, which sustains right under statute to appropriate water of spring without natural outlet.

8 L. R. A. 204, McCLUNG v. DEARBORNE, 134 Pa. 396, 19 Am. St. Rep. 708, 19 Atl. 698.

Liability for torts of servant or agent.

Approved in Hower v. Ulrich, 156 Pa. 413, 33 W. N. C. 22, 27 Atl. 37, holding parent liable for independent tort of child who converted corn of another, of which parent made use.

Cited in Ahern v. Melvin, 21 Pa. Super. Ct. 467, holding master liable for act of servant while discharging duties in manner contrary to instructions.

Cited in notes (14 L. R. A. 737) on liability of master for assault by servant; (27 L. R. A. 194) on master's liability for malicious act of servant.

Distinguished in Ellis v. Lamb, 24 Pa. Co. Ct. 151, 9 Pa. Dist. R. 492, 31 Pittsb. L. J. N. S. 44, holding landlord not liable for unauthorized assault on tenant by constable while executing distress warrant.

8 L. R. A. 207, HANLEY v. WALKER, 79 Micl

Performance of contract; certificate as cond

Approved in Guthat v. Gow, 95 Mich. 531, 55 N performance and extra work not for jury when biter; Boots v. Steinberg, 100 Mich. 139, 58 N. tractor cannot recover for work to be performed owner's dissatisfaction not captious; Brown v. Kr 51, holding evidence admissible in action on bui general issue, to show its noncompletion; White 65 N. E. 1061, holding principal claiming right expense must show architect's certificate agreed Weggner v. Greenstine, 114 Mich. 315, 72 N. W. on building contract where condition unperforme tions and specifications must be determined by arcl v. North Yakima, 12 Wash. 128, 40 Pac. 790, holc requisite to recovery where payment conditioned schmidt, 12 Mont. 320, 30 Pac. 280, holding that formance of extra work only under architect's w extra work at owner's request; Vanderhoof v. Sh holding provision for architect's certificate waived owner agreed to accept building, excepting certai Wormser, 28 Mont. 180, 72 Pac. 428, holding compl chanic's lien must allege giving of necessary arch why not given.

Cited in footnote to Arnold v. Bournique, 20 L. tractor entitled to payment on delivery of archit without presentation to owner.

Cited in note (9 L. R. A. 53) as to "substantia contract.

Distinguished in Moran v. Schmitt, 109 Mich. 280 tractor entitled to maintain action for extras wher to act; National Home Bldg. & L. Asso. v. Dwellii 238, 64 N. W. 21, sustaining action without awar of amount when appraisers demanded, where no ap months after fire.

Recovery on quantum meruit where certificat

Cited in Eaton v. Gladwell, 121 Mich. 449, 80 N. possession of building not conforming to plans and *tum meruit.*

Distinguished in United States use of Croll v. Ja 1049, holding material man may recover on *quantu* contractor's creditors notwithstanding condition o proval.

8 L. R. A. 211, PHELAN v. BRADY, 119 N. Y. 587,

Possession as constructive notice of title.

Cited in Welsh v. Schoen, 59 Hun, 358, 13 N. Y. of grantee under unrecorded deed notice of his rig

Chapman v. Chapman, 91 Va. 402, 50 Am. St. Rep. 846, 21 S. E. 813. and Sanders v. Riedinger. 30 App. Div. 284, 51 N. Y. Supp. 937. holding occupation under unrecorded deed notice to subsequent grantee; Titcomb v. Fonda. J. & G. R. Co. 38 Misc. 632, 78 N. Y. Supp. 226, holding possession of vendee under land contract notice of his rights to foreclosing mortgagee; Dumois v. New York, 37 Misc. 618, 76 N. Y. Supp. 161, holding open possession under unrecorded lease notice of lessor's rights; Ward v. Metropolitan R. Co. 152 N. Y. 43, 46 N. E. 319, Affirming 82 Hun, 547, 31 N. Y. Supp. 527, holding elevated railroad's operation of road notice to subsequent purchaser of abutting owner's release of easements; Smith v. Reid, 19 N. Y. Civ. Proc. Rep. 366, 34 N. Y. S. R. 491, 11 N. Y. Supp. 739, holding possession of grantee of purchaser under execution notice to subsequent grantee of one claiming under fraudulent conveyance; Holland v. Brown, 140 N. Y. 347, 35 N. E. 577, holding possession of uplands may constitute notice of title to water front designated by visible monuments at or near shore; Cornell v. Maltby, 165 N. Y. 560, 59 N. E. 291, holding mortgagee relying upon record title, not chargeable with notice of fraud of which possessor was then ignorant.

Cited in footnotes to Gray v. H. M. Loud & Sons Lumber Co. 54 L. R. A. 731, which denies priority of one having unrecorded contract for part of tract of land, as to subsequent mortgage on entire tract, over subsequent purchasers of remainder; Rock Island & P. R. Co. v. Dimick, 19 L. R. A. 105, which holds open and exclusive possession of passageway through railroad embankment notice of rights to purchaser of railroad.

Cited in note (11 L. R. A. 661) on possession as notice of title, sufficient to put purchaser on inquiry.

Distinguished in Baker v. Thomas, 61 Hun, 22, 15 N. Y. Supp. 359, holding fencing of pasture not possession constituting notice of purchaser's rights; Shneider v. Mahl, 84 App. Div. 5, 82 N. Y. Supp. 27, holding mortgagee not chargeable with knowledge of rights of equitable mortgagee in possession as tenant.

— When occupancy shared by others.

Cited in Kirby v. Tallmadge, 160 U. S. 388, 40 L. ed. 467, 16 Sup. Ct. Rep. 349, holding joint occupation by husband and wife notice of wife's title to purchaser from holder of record title; Marden v. Dorthy, 160 N. Y. 52, 46 L. R. A. 699, 54 N. E. 726, Affirming 12 App. Div. 198, 42 N. Y. Supp. 827, holding possession by one from whom record title has been obtained by trickery, although obscured by grantee's residence, notice to mortgagee.

8 L. R. A. 214, MOORE v. FRANCIS, 121 N. Y. 199, 18 Am. St. Rep. 810, 23 N. E. 1127.

Libel and slander defined.

Cited in Woodruff v. Woodruff, 36 Misc. 16, 72 N. Y. Supp. 39, defining libel as written defamatory declarations; Spurlock v. Lombard Invest. Co. 59 Mo. App. 230, defining libel *per se* as malicious publication tending to injure business and blacken reputation; Cady v. Brooklyn Union Pub. Co. 23 Misc. 410, 51 N. Y. Supp. 198; Le Massena v. Storm, 62 App. Div. 153, 70 N. Y. Supp. 882; Green v. Meyer, 78 N. Y. S. R. 82, 44 N. Y. Supp. 81; Gates v. New York Recorder Co. 155 N. Y. 234, 49 N. E. 769,—adopting classification of slanderous words actionable *per se*.

Question of law and fact as to libel or slan

Cited in Schuyler v. Busbey, 68 Hun. 478, 23 : tion of libel one of law when publication is admi ous; Mattice v. Wilcox, 71 Hun. 487, 24 N. Y. S nal Co. 26 Misc. 593. 57 N. Y. Supp. 905; Turton 319, 22 N. Y. Supp. 766,—holding article capable question of law; Urban v. Helmick, 15 Wash. 158, Pub. Co. 60 App. Div. 539, 69 N. Y. Supp. 895; Ku Div. 617, 80 N. Y. Supp. 1050,—holding duty of words when article unambiguous; Jesper v. Press Supp. 619, holding refusal to charge publication li possible, error; Shanks v. Stumpf, 23 Misc. 267, 51 ticle characterizing conduct "utterly indefensible belous *per se* as matter of law; Clark v. Anderson, Supp. 729, holding language susceptible of innoc jury; Gallagher v. Bryant, 44 App. Div. 529, 60 N. susceptible of interpretation imputing moral turp

Words actionable per se.

Cited in Hussey v. New York Recorder Co. 89 H holding that complaint states libel; Weston v. Westc Supp. 351, holding words, not slanderous when sp published; Martin v. Press Pub. Co. 93 App. Div. 5 ing newspaper article on poverty-stricken conditio libelous *per se*; Cassavoy v. Pattison, 93 App. Di holding charge of dishonesty not slanderous *per se* occupation.

— Touching vocation.

Followed in Sawyer v. Bennett, 49 N. Y. S. R. 7 ing article in paper stating failure caused by reck tionable *per se*.

Cited in Bornmann v. Star Co. 174 N. Y. 219, characterizing doctor "brute graduated to care for s v. Dwyer, 87 Hun, 249, 33 N. Y. Supp. 754, hold turf tends to injure party in business; Cady v. Misc. 412, 51 N. Y. Supp. 198, holding publicatio libelous *per se*; Chiatovich v. Hanchett, 88 Fed. 87 to refrain from associating and dealing with merc v. Sun Printing & Pub. Asso. 71 App. Div. 569, 76 lication reporting removal of attorney for inefficien tice; Davey v. Davey, 22 Misc. 670, 50 N. Y. Sup paper characterizing one as unscrupulous grocer damages; Woodruff v. Woodruff, 36 Misc. 17, 72 N tending to injure business actionable *per se*; East 48 N. Y. Supp. 158, and Potter v. New York Evening 98, 74 N. Y. Supp. 317, sustaining rule holding in business; Daily v. De Young, 127 Fed. 492; D Journal, 94 App. Div. 321, 88 N. Y. Supp. 6, hol extravagant management of manager of mining c v. Burger & H. Brewing Co. 37 N. Y. S. R. 289, 1

right to damages for words destroying business; Mattice v. Wilcox, 147 N. Y. 632, 42 N. E. 270, holding publication charging attorney with incapacity to perform ordinary duties libelous *per se;* Ratzel v. New York News Pub. Co. 35 Misc. 489, 71 N. Y. Supp. 1069, upholding right of recovery without proof of special damage for words tending to injure trade; Morey v. Morning Journal Asso. 123 N. Y. 210, 9 L. R. A. 624, 20 Am. St. Rep. 730, 25 N. E. 161, holding publication tending to disgrace and ruin business libelous *per se;* Stokes v. Stokes, 76 Hun, 317, 28 N. Y. Supp. 165, upholding right to damages for words tending to diminish respectability and injure business; Labouisse v. Evening Post Pub. Co. 10 App. Div. 31, 41 N. Y. Supp. 688, holding publication charging one with attempt to "corner" cotton not actionable *per se.*

Cited in note (9 L. R. A. 623) on libel and slander affecting reputation of tradesmen and business men.

Distinguished in Keene v. Tribune Asso. 76 Hun, 490, 27 N. Y. Supp. 1045, denying liability where publication produces no injury.

—Charging moral turpitude.

Approved in Stafford v. Morning Journal Asso. 68 Hun, 471, 22 N. Y. Supp. 1008, holding publication defaming reputation libelous *per se.*

Cited in Charwat v. Vopelak, 19 Misc. 502, 44 N. Y. Supp. 26, holding statements that one failed yet has money actionable *per se;* Lehmann v. Tribune Asso. 37 Misc. 509, 75 N. Y. Supp. 1034, holding article charging attempt to smuggle libelous; Butterfield v. Bennett, 18 N. Y. Supp. 432, holding imputing inchastity to woman libelous *per se;* Hollingsworth v. Spectator Co. 49 App. Div. 19, 63 N. Y. Supp. 2, holding article libelous *per se* charging insurance examiner as not properly commissioned; Johnson v. Synett, 89 Hun, 193, 35 N. Y. Supp. 79, holding publication of arrest of minister as too much of family man libelous *per se;* Hartman v. Morning Journal Asso. 46 N. Y. S. R. 182, 19 N. Y. Supp. 401, holding writings imputing connection with insurance swindle libelous *per se;* Gillan v. State Journal Printing Co. 96 Wis. 465, 71 N. W. 892, denying that words not charging moral turpitude or touching vocation are actionable *per se;* Gallup v. Belmont, 41 N. Y. S. R. 234, 16 N. Y. Supp. 483, holding publication reporting discharge of club member not libelous.

Defense in action for libel or slander.

Approved in Schuyler v. Busbey, 68 Hun, 477, 23 N. Y. Supp. 102, holding publication in good faith no excuse.

Cited in Cady v. Brooklyn Union Pub. Co. 23 Misc. 410, 51 N. Y. Supp. 198, upholding right to damages for actionable statements made with good motive.

Damages for failure to verify statements.

Cited in footnote to Press Pub. Co. v. McDonald, 26 L. R. A. 531, which authorizes punitive damages for failure of effort to verify truth of libelous despatch before printing in newspaper.

8 L. R. A. 216, TERRY v. MUNGER, 121 N. Y. 161, 18 Am. St. Rep. 803, 24 N. E. 272.

Right to waive tort.

Cited in Central Gas & Electric Fixture Co. v. Sheridan, 1 Misc. 387, 22 N. Y. Supp. 76, upholding right to waive conversion of gas fixtures and sue on implied contract; Anderson v. First Nat. Bank, 5 N. D. 88, 64 N. W. 114, upholding right to waive conversion of proceeds from sale of notes, and sue in assumpsit; Phelps v. Church of Our Lady Help of Christians, 40 C. C. A. 74, 99 Fed. 684, upholding right to waive action for conversion of store and sue in assumpsit; Braithwaite v. Akin, 3 N. D. 371, 56 N. W. 133, holding that owner of property may waive tort and sue for benefits received by wrongdoer; Sage v. Shepard & M. Lumber Co. 4 App. Div. 297, 39 N. Y. Supp. 449, sustaining liability upon implied contract for lumber tortiously acquired; Doherty v. Shields, 86 Hun, 308, 33 N. Y. Supp. 497, holding that conversion may be waived, where property is still with wrongdoer, and recovery had for goods sold and delivered; Carey v. Flack, 20 Misc. 296, 45 N. Y. Supp. 759, upholding right to waive conversion and sue on implied assumpsit; Moore v. Richardson, 68 N. J. L. 309, 53 Atl. 1032, holding value of converted property at time of conversion, recoverable in assumpsit.

Effect of election on title.

Cited in Schoeneman v. Chamberlin, 55 App. Div. 356, 67 N. Y. Supp. 284, holding title passes to wrongdoer when tort waived and transaction treated as sale; Disbrow v. Westchester Hardwood Co. 164 N. Y. 424, 58 N. E. 519, holding recovery in assumpsit for timber tortiously cut precludes enjoining removal; Deitz v. Field, 10 App. Div. 427, note, 41 N. Y. Supp. 1087, Affirming 17 Misc. 27, 39 N. Y. Supp. 257, holding action for conversion of bonds precludes claim for their recovery; Merritt v. American Steel-Barge Co. 24 C. C. A. 537, 49 U. S. App. 85, 79 Fed. 234, holding action in assumpsit for value of stock, election to abandon title thereto; Lytle v. Bank of Dothan, 121 Ala. 221, 26 So. 6, holding action for purchase price of cotton on election to treat transaction as a sale; Campbell v. Kauffman Mill Co. 42 Fla. 343, 29 So. 435, holding principal taking judgment against agent for proceeds of sales cannot claim uncollected accounts.

Cited in footnote to Crompton v. Beach, 18 L. R. A. 187, which holds that conditional vendor's exercise of option to enforce payment of note for purchase price, defeats right to retake property.

Election of remedies.

Cited in Sweetser v. Davis, 26 App. Div. 398, 49 N. Y. Supp. 874, holding that creditors waive fraudulent assignment and ratify same by motion to remove assignee, substituting another; O'Bryan Bros. v. Glenn Bros. 91 Tenn. 110, 30 Am. St. Rep. 862, 17 S. W. 1030, holding election to repudiate assignment precludes benefits thereunder.

Cited in footnote to Walden Nat. Bank v. Birch, 14 L. R. A. 211, which holds recovery of judgment against bank cashier on note secured by bank stock not bar to action on bond for misappropriating stock.

Cited in notes (13 L. R. A. 92, 473) on election of remedy.

Distinguished in Woodworth v. Gorsline, 30 Colo. 190, 58 L. R. A. 424, 69 Pac. 705, holding unaccepted tender of property in replevin no bar to action on indemnity bond of sheriff.

— Action ex delicto.

Cited in Lee v. Burnham, 82 Wis. 212, 52 N. W. 255, holding that action on contract brought by agent without authority when discontinued does not preclude replevin; Emerald & P. Brewing Co. v. Leonard, 22 Misc. 122, 48 N. Y. Supp. 706, holding that action by bailor for goods sold and delivered precludes suit for conversion; Rochester Distilling Co. v. Devendorf, 72 Hun, 431, 25 N. Y.

Supp. 200, holding recovery on contract without knowledge of fraud no bar to replevin action after its discovery; Johnson-Brinkman Commision Co. v. Missouri P. R. Co. 126 Mo. 351, 26 L. R. A. 842, footnote, p. 840, 47 Am. St. Rep. 675, 28 S. W. 870, Reversing 52 Mo. App. 415, holding suit in attachment afterwards dismissed no bar to replevin, no rights intervening; A. C. Nellis Co. v. Nellis, 62 Hun, 68, 16 N. Y. Supp. 545, holding sale of collaterals no ratification of unauthorized loan, estopping suit for conversion; Russell v. McCall, 141 N. Y. 449, 38 Am. St. Rep. 807, 36 N. E. 498, holding action against partner for misappropriation no bar to suit against rest as trustees *de son tort;* Weaver v. Lawyers' Surety Co. 36 Misc. 637, 74 N. Y. Supp. 462, holding replevin barred by assignment of action on contract by one having action *ex contractu* or *ex delicto;* Seeman v. Bandler, 26 Misc. 373, 56 N. Y. Supp. 210, holding replevin against transferee of fraudulent vendee bars action *ex contractu* against vendee; Kearney Mill. & Elevator Co. v. Union P. R. Co. 97 Iowa, 724, 59 Am. St. Rep. 434, 66 N. W. 1059, upholding right of stoppage *in transitu*, buyer obtaining goods by fraud; National Commercial Bank v. Lackawanna Transp. Co. 59 App. Div. 274, 69 N. Y. Supp. 396, holding one bringing suit for conversion cannot recover on different cause of action.

Cited in footnote to Miller v. Hyde, 25 L. R. A. 42, which holds replevin of horse not defeated by prior attachment suit for trover.

Cited in notes (58 L. R. A. 430) on effect of judgment against one tort feasor upon other in proceedings before entry; (13 L. R. A. 92, 473) on election of remedy.

— Action ex contractu.

Cited in Droege v. Ahrens & O. Mfg. Co. 163 N. Y. 470, 57 N. E. 747, holding filing proof of claim with assignee affirms sale and precludes action to rescind for fraud; *Re* Hildebrant, 120 Fed. 996, holding vendor of goods fraudulently purchased cannot file claims for goods sold and also for return of goods in bankrupt's possession; Starr Cash Car Co. v. Reinhart, 2 Misc. 119, 20 N. Y. Supp. 874, holding counterclaim for conversion proper in action *ex contractu* when tort waived; Crook v. First Nat. Bank, 83 Wis. 43, 35 Am. St. Rep. 17, 52 N. W. 1131, holding action *ex contractu* ratifies unauthorized payment made by bank; Ladew v. Hart, 8 App. Div. 154, 40 N. Y. Supp. 509, sustaining right of action *ex contractu* against sheriff for wrongful levy, where property is undisposed of; Hess v. Smith, 16 Misc. 55, 37 N. Y. Supp. 635, holding recovery *ex contractu* bar to subsequent action *ex delicto;* Johnson-Brinkman Commission Co. v. Missouri P. R. Co. 126 Mo. 351, 26 L. R. A. 842, footnote, p. 840, 47 Am. St. Rep. 675, 28 S. W. 870, holding suit for purchase price of wheat precludes subsequent action in replevin; Birdsell Mfg. Co. v. Oglevee, 187 Ill. 152, 58 N. E. 231, holding election to treat unauthorized disposition of machinery as sale waives action for conversion; McNutt v. Hilkins, 80 Hun, 238, 29 N. Y. Supp. 1047, holding party unsuccessful in action *ex delicto* not precluded from suit *ex contractu* upon same facts; Crown Cycle Co. v. Brown, 39 Or. 289, 64 Pac. 451, holding that vendor, induced to part with goods by fraud on time payment, may sue in assumpsit at once, waiving tort; Schoeneman v. Chamberlin, 55 App. Div. 354, 67 N. Y. Supp. 284, holding vendor may replevin part of goods from fraudulent vendee's assignee and waiving fraud sue vendee on contract for remainder; Crossman v. Universal Rubber Co. 127 N. Y. 37, 13 L. R. A. 94, 27 N. E. 400, holding former unsuccessful proceedings *in rem* no bar to collection of purchase-money notes; Brady v. Cassidy, 9 Misc. 114, 29 N. complete delivery waived by vendee using part of nondelivery of balance; Roberge v. Winne, 144 N. action compelling performance of contract maintai election; Houston v. Curran, 101 Ill. App. 207, clause in mortgage by accepting payments, while pr National Granite Bank v. Tyndale, 179 Mass. 394, tinuance of suit against indorser of void note no bar money loaned; Maders v. Whallon, 46 N. Y. S. R. 21 ing that judgment cannot be granted in foreclosur gated; Washburn v. Benedict, 46 App. Div. 490, 6 assailing assignments of mortgage election to ratify gage; *Re* Linforth, 87 Fed. 390, holding mortgage barred by foreclosure in state court subsequently dis 79 Hun, 60, 29 N. Y. Supp. 644, denying that claim ing amount due for board is election to relinquish gage; Henderson v. Bartlett, 32 App. Div. 440, 53 N. suit against firm upon obligation precludes action ag tion substituted therefor; Cook v. Adams, 32 App. Di holding right to foreclose mortgage consistent with to pay taxes; Genet v. Delaware & H. Canal Co. 170 dissenting opinion (same case on former appeal in 2 Supp. 377) to point that party to contract waives ri receiving royalties and bringing suits thereunder.

Cited in footnote to Barchard v. Kohn, 29 L. R. A ment of chattel mortgage on exempt property not defe attempted levy on exempt property.

Cited in notes (13 L. R. A. 92, 473) on election of

Record in former suit as evidence.

Cited in Carroll v. Fethers, 102 Wis. 443, 78 N. W. *ex contractu* admissible to show tort waived; Davis v. C. 238, 43 S. E. 650, holding defense to action to dis insolvent bank, that action has been brought for proc

Distinguished in Mandeville v. Avery, 44 N. Y. S. holding judgment in replevin establishing title under sible against claim to surplus money.

8 L. R. A. 221, TALAMO v. SPITZMILLER, 120 N. 23 N. E. 980.

Tenancy from year to year; how created.

Cited in Phelan v. Anderson, 118 Cal. 506, 50 Pac. nual rent under void lease creates presumption of ye ley, 52 W. Va. 482, 61 L. R. A. 959, footnote p. 957 entering under void lease, paying annual rent in mont year to year; Earle v. McGoldrick, 15 Misc. 136, 3 tenant occupying premises for nearly year under void Gilfoyle v. Cahill, 18 Misc. 70, 41 N. Y. Supp. 29, h and mode of payment may determine nature of tenanc Cohoes, 127 N. Y. 181, 28 N. E. 25, holding parol le

no yearly tenancy created unless occupied so long; Johnson v. Albertson, 51 Minn. 335, 53 N. W. 642, holding monthly payments under void lease not alone sufficient to prove yearly tenancy; Hellams v. Patton, 44 S. C. 459, 22 S. E. 608, holding acts of tenant under void lease may convert tenancy at will into yearly tenancy: Wilder v. Stace, 61 Hun, 235, 15 N. Y. Supp. 870, holding void lease makes new contract necessary to create yearly tenancy, and payment to "bind bargain" ineffectual; Matthews v. Hipp, 66 S. C. 170, 44 S. E. 577, holding tenant holding over after termination of oral lease for a year may be tenant at will or tenant from year to year.

Occupation under void lease.

Cited in Lawrence v. Hasbrouck, 21 Misc. 40, 46 N. Y. Supp. 868, holding tenant under unexecuted lease for thirteen months liable for use from month to month; Borderre v. Den, 106 Cal. 600, 39 Pac. 946, holding lease exceeding one year executed by agent, not authorized in writing, void.

Cited in note (26 L. R. A. 800) on rent for use of premises under invalid lease.

Agreement as to reducing rent.

Cited in footnote to Goldsbrough v. Gable, 15 L. R. A. 294, which holds agreement to reduce rent of tenant holding over, without consideration.

8 L. R. A. 224, DWINELLE v. NEW YORK C. & H. R. R. CO. 120 N. Y. 117, 17 Am. St. Rep. 611, 24 N. E. 319.

Liability of carrier for act of other carrier.

Cited in Murray v. Lehigh Valley R. Co. 66 Conn. 518, 32 L. R. A. 539, 34 Atl. 506, holding carrier operating train on road of another answerable to one jumping to avoid collision with latter's train; Barron S. S. Co. v. Kane, 31 C. C. A. 454, 59 U. S. App. 574, 88 Fed. 199, holding steamship company answerable for assault upon passenger by subordinate carrier.

Questions for jury.

Cited in McLeod v. New York, C. & St. L. R. Co. 72 App. Div. 120, 76 N. Y. Supp. 347, holding question for jury whether arrest and removal of passenger by detective and conductor violated contract of carriage; P. Cox Mfg. Co. v. Gorsline, 63 App. Div. 520, 71 N. Y. Supp. 619, holding it for jury to determine responsibility of master for removal of plug from pipe by laborers repairing sewer; Wright v. Glens Falls, S. H. & Ft. E. Street R. Co. 24 App. Div. 619, 48 N. Y. Supp. 1026; Guinney v. Hand, 153 Pa. 410, 32 W. N. C. 29, 26 Atl. 20; Tinker v. New York, O. & W. R. Co. 71 Hun, 433, 24 N. Y. Supp. 977—holding existence of relation of master and servant question for jury.

Distinguished in Collins v. Butler, 83 App. Div. 18, 81 N. Y. Supp. 1074, holding storekeeper liable, as matter of law, for clerk's assault on customer.

Respondeat superior.

Cited in notes (21 L. R. A. 297) on liabilities as to passengers on sleeping cars; (37 L. R. A. 83) on constructive service predicated from duties of railroad companies as carriers.

— For ejecting passenger.

Cited in Lyons v. Broadway & S. Ave. R. Co. 32 N. Y. S. R. 233, 10 N. Y. Supp. 237, holding company answerable for driver wilfully throwing passenger from platform; Monnier v. New York C. & H. R. R. Co. 70 App. Div. 408, 75 N. Y.

Supp. 521, holding company answerable for ejection of passenger refusing to pay extra for lack of ticket; Wright v. Glens Falls, S. E. & Ft. E. Street R. Co. 24 App. Div. 619, 48 N. Y. Supp. 1026, sustaining responsibility of carrier for tortious ejection of passenger refusing to pay higher fare; Hines v. Dry Dock, E. B. & B. R. Co. 75 App. Div. 392, 78 N. Y. Supp. 170, holding carrier answerable for breach of contract by refusal of conductor to accept fare, followed by ejection; Miller v. Manhattan R. Co. 73 Hun, 513, 26 N. Y. Supp. 162, upholding liability of carrier for injuries inflicted by guard pushing passenger from platform.

— For unlawful detention.

Followed in Woodhull v. New York, 76 Hun, 396, 28 N. Y. Supp. 120, holding carrier responsible for unlawful arrest and injury of passenger.

Cited in Gillingham v. Ohio River R. Co. 35 W. Va. 92, 14 L. R. A. 800, 29 Am. St. Rep. 827, 14 S. E. 243, holding carrier liable for arrest of passenger by mistake; Atchison, T. & S. F. R. Co. v. Henry, 55 Kan. 723, 29 L. R. A. 467, 41 Pac. 952, holding carrier answerable for unlawful arrest and assault upon passenger by servants; Palmeri v. Manhattan R. Co. 133 N. Y. 266, 16 L. R. A. 137, 28 Am. St. Rep. 632, 30 N. E. 1001, Affirming 39 N. Y. S. R. 23, 14 N. Y. Supp. 468, upholding liability of company for act of agent in detaining passenger regardless of motive; Mulligan v. New York & R. B. R. Co. 129 N. Y. 515, 14 L. R. A. 797, 26 Am. St. Rep. 539, 29 N. E. 952 (dissenting opinion), majority denying liability of company for arrest of passenger by agent for passing counterfeit bill.

— For acts beyond scope of employment.

Cited in Flinn v. World's Dispensary Medical Asso. 64 App. Div. 493, 72 N. Y. Supp. 243, denying liability of master for injury caused by starting printing press by one repairing rheostat; Birmingham R. & Electric Co. v. Baird, 130 Ala. 345, 54 L. R. A. 753, 89 Am. St. Rep. 43, 30 So. 456, and Haver v. Central R. Co. 62 N. J. L. 285, 43 L. R. A. 85, 72 Am. St. Rep. 648, 41 Atl. 916, holding carrier liable for malicious assault by employee on passenger; Johnson v. Detroit R. Co. 130 Mich. 455, 90 N. W. 274, holding railroad liable for assault by conductor on passenger, even when outside of scope of employment; Willis v. Metropolitan Street R. Co. 76 App. Div. 345, 78 N. Y. Supp. 478, holding street car company liable for conductor's assault on one boarding car contrary to his directions; Gillespie v. Brooklyn Heights R. Co. 178 N. Y. 358, 70 N. E. 857, holding street railroad liable for abusive language used by conductor to passenger; Gabrielson v. Waydell, 36 N. Y. S. R. 675, 14 N. Y. Supp. 125, holding owners liable for assault of captain upon member of crew, unless unconnected with command; Wyllie v. Palmer, 137 N. Y. 257, 19 L. R. A. 288, 33 N. E. 381, holding relation of master and servant necessary to charge master for tort; Donivan v. Manhattan R. Co. 1 Misc. 369, 21 N. Y. Supp. 457, holding master not answerable in punitive damage for tort of servant unless authorized; Kennedy v. White, 91 App. Div. 478, 86 N. Y. Supp. 852, denying master's liability for injury inflicted on passerby by janitor chasing away noisy boys; Cain v. Syracuse, B. & N. Y. R. Co. 20 Misc. 461, 45 N. Y. Supp. 538, denying liability of master not selecting servant; Daniel v. Petersburg R. Co. 117 N. C. 608, 23 S. E. 327 (concurring opinion), majority denying liability of carrier for violent conduct of servant outside line of duty.

Cited in footnotes to Farber v. Missouri P. R. Co. 20 L. R. A. 350, which holds driving of trespasser from freight train by brakeman not to be within scope of employment; Guille v. Campbell, 55 L. R. A. 111, which denies master's liability for injury to bystander by slipping of hook from servants hand while pretending to throw at boys playing on cotton bales.

Cited in notes (14 L. R. A. 740, 37 L. R. A. 83) on liability of master for assaults by servants.

Distinguished in Jones v. St. Louis S. W. R. Co. 125 Mo. 674, 26 L. R. A. 720, 46 Am. St. Rep. 514, 28 S. W. 883, denying liability of railroad company for injury to Pullman porter by negligence of engineer; New York, N. H. & H. R. Co. v. Baker, 50 L. R. A. 203, 39 C. C. A. 240, 98 Fed. 697, denying liability of carrier for injury to passenger by swinging of derrick controlled by municipal board.

Directions for guidance of passengers.

Cited in Appleby v. St. Paul City R. Co. 54 Minn. 171, 40 Am. St. Rep. 308, 55 N. W. 1117, holding carrier liable for failure to furnish directions thereby causing injury to passenger by ejection; Jackson v. Grand Ave. R. Co. 118 Mo. 227, 24 S. W. 192, holding duty of passengers to read directions adopted by carrier.

8 L. R. A. 228, STATE *ex rel.* WORREL v. PEELLE, 124 Ind. 515, 24 N. E. 440.

Writ of mandate against state auditor to compel payment of salary alleged to be due, in State *ex rel.* Worrell v. Carr, 129 Ind. 49, 13 L. R. A. 179, 28 Am. St. Rep. 163, 28 N. E. 88.

Eligibility to office.

Cited in footnotes to Steusoff v. State, 12 L. R. A. 364, which holds citizen of state not eligible to office in county of residence into which he had removed so recently as not to be entitled to vote; State *ex rel.* Taylor v. Sullivan, 11 L. R. A. 272, which holds alien not entitled to hold office, notwithstanding declaration of intention to become citizen after election.

Officers de facto.

Cited in footnote to State *ex rel.* Van Amringe v. Taylor, 12 L. R. A. 202, which holds mere intruder not officer *de facto.*

Cited in notes (11 L. R. A. 105) on officers *de facto;* (13 L. R. A. 178) on officers *de facto* and *de jure* distinguished; (13 L. R. A. 670) on tenure of public office; incompatibility of offices.

Removal from and abandonment of office.

Cited in Maddox v. York, 21 Tex. Civ. App. 625, 54 S. W. 24, holding that sheriff voluntarily surrendering office to appointed successor, abandons office; Cameron v. Parker, 2 Okla. 342, 38 Pac. 14, upholding power of governor to remove officer for cause without trial in court of law.

Inconsistent defenses.

Cited in note (48 L. R. A. 203) on right to plead inconsistent defenses.

8 L. R. A. 236, PENNYPACKER v. CAPITAL INS. CO. 80 Iowa, 56, 20 Am. St. Rep. 395, 45 N. W. 408.

What law governs insurance contracts.

Cited in footnote to Union Cent. L. Ins. Co. v. Pollard, 36 L. R. A. 271, as to law governing effect of answers in application for policy and their use in evidence.

Cited in note (63 L. R. A. 835) on conflict of laws as to contracts of insurance.

Want of authority to do business.

Approved in Vermont Loan & T. Co. v. Hoffmai 95 Am. St. Rep. 186, 49 Pac. 314, holding tha loaned although he had not procured license prescr

— Foreign corporations.

Cited in Lumberman's Mut. Ins. Co. v. Kansa Mo. 178, 50 S. W. 281, sustaining suit by foreig business within state upon foreign contract; Sea 367, 59 N. W. 290, raising without determining unenforceable because of insurer's incapacity to tr

Cited in notes (8 L. R. A. 129) on foreign in imposed by statute; (12 L. R. A. 366) on foreig (20 L. R. A. 406) as to effect on insurance whe business of foreign insurance companies has not l

Evidence as to proofs of loss.

Approved in Ruthven Bros. v. American F. Ins. (holding proof that agent mailed notice of loss t bind company.

Presumption of receipt of mail.

Cited in Watson v. Richardson, 110 Iowa, 677, letter handed to mail agent will be presumed to h no showing to contrary.

Cited in footnote to Ross v. Hawkeye Ins. Co. notice by registered letter completed by due registra

Distinguished in Bostain v. De Laval Separator holding time of reasonable notice runs from recei letter, where time of transit not shown.

8 L. R. A. 243, CURRAN v. BOSTON, 151 Mass. N. E. 781.

Nonliability of state, municipality, etc., for

Cited in Murdock Parlor Grate Co. v. Com. 152 N. E. 854, holding state not liable for negligence o leased apartment.

— Counties.

Cited in Hughes v. Monroe County, 147 N. Y. 58, Affirming 79 Hun, 126, 29 N. Y. Supp. 495, holdin insane deriving incidental revenue from paying pa in asylum for negligence; McAndrews v. Hamilto S. W. 483, holding county not liable for negligence rection voluntarily maintained, regardless of incom

— Cities and villages.

Cited in Mahoney v. Boston, 171 Mass. 431, 50 N incidental revenue from subway not liable to empl Taggart v. Fall River, 170 Mass. 327, 49 N. E. 6 dental advantage from increased value of farm b liable to injured employee; McCann v. Waltham, holding city incidentally benefited by repair of street not liable to employee for negligence of superintendent under independent board; Russell v. Tacoma, 8 Wash. 159, 40 Am. St. Rep. 893, 35 Pac. 605, holding city not liable for negligence of officers engaged in improving public park; Ulrich v. St. Louis, 112 Mo. 146, 34 Am. St. Rep. 372, 20 S. W. 466, holding city not liable to prisoner in workhouse for superintendent's negligence; Howard v. Worcester, 153 Mass. 428, 12 L. R. A. 161, 25 Am. St. Rep. 651, 27 N. E. 11, holding city constructing public schoolhouse not liable for servant's negligence; Royce v. Salt Lake City, 15 Utah, 407, 49 Pac. 290, holding city not liable for injury to prisoner wrongfully required to work by chief of police; Doty v. Port Jervis, 23 Misc. 315, 52 N. Y. Supp. 57, holding village not liable for death of one killed by incompetent special policeman.

Cited in notes (44 L. R. A. 796, 800, 801) on liability of municipal corporations for false imprisonment and unlawful arrest.

Distinguished in Coan v. Marlborough, 164 Mass. 208, 41 N. E. 238, and Norton v. New Bedford, 166 Mass. 51, 43 N. E. 1034, holding city responsible for negligence of servants in work of constructing sewer.

When city agency of state.

Cited in Mt. Hope Cemetery v. Boston, 158 Mass. 513, 35 Am. St. Rep. 515, 33 N. E. 695, holding city not agency of state in ownership of cemetery, hence title not subject to legislative control.

8 L. R. A. 245, MORA LEDON v. HAVEMEYER, 121 N. Y. 179, 24 N. E. 297.

Construction of word "shipment."

Approved in Clark v. Lindsay, 19 Mont. 4, 61 Am. St. Rep. 479, 47 Pac. 102, holding "shipment" means delivery to carrier but not commencement of transportation; Browne v. Paterson, 165 N. Y. 466, 59 N. E. 296, Reversing 36 App. Div. 172, 55 N. Y. Supp. 404, holding words "bought to be a March or April shipment" not a warranty or condition precedent that shipment was to be made in those months; Schwann v. Clark, 9 Misc. 120, 29 N. Y. Supp. 289, Affirming 7 Misc. 243, 27 N. Y. Supp. 262, holding delivery of goods on board vessel during month constituted "shipment within the month."

Burden of proof.

Approved in Eppens, S. & W. Co. v. Littlejohn, 27 App. Div. 25, 50 N. Y. Supp. 251, holding that plaintiff must prove performance of executory contract for sale and delivery of merchandise.

8 L. R. A. 248, CALHOUN v. DELHI & M. R. CO. 121 N. Y. 69, 24 N. E. 27.

Conditional signing of petition for issuance of bonds.

Cited in Andes v. Ely, 158 U. S. 317, 39 L. ed. 1000, 15 Sup. Ct. Rep. 954, holding petition for issuance of railroad aid bonds by town not void because conditional as to some of signers.

Cancelation of bonds or stock.

Approved in Cherry Creek v. Becker, 123 N. Y. 172, 25 N. E. 369, holding that equity will not cancel town bonds when not questioned until after interest had been paid thereon many years.

Cited in Reno Oil Co. v. Culver, 33 Misc. 719, 68 N. Y. Supp. 303, upholding right to cancelation of spurious stock collusively issued but valid on face.

Laches.

Approved in Belden v. Burke, 147 N. Y. 539, 4 acquiescence will defeat review of transactions b of which purchaser had knowledge; Galway v. N. Y. 157, 13 L. R. A. 796, 28 N. E. 479, hold stances and is addressed to discretion of court; 55 L. R. A. 664, footnote p. 658, 66 Pac. 552, h upon lapse of definite time, but upon want of due stances; Woodbridge v. Bockes, 59 App. Div. 521 beneficiary approving breach of trust and deriving twenty-five years compel trustee to restore pri Hockemeyer, 46 N. Y. S. R. 331, 19 N. Y. Supp. not prevent maintenance of stable contrary to cove years; Wolf v. Great Falls Water Power & Town 115, holding suit for specific performance of contr years; Kennedy v. Montgomery County, 98 Tenn. collection of taxes will not be enjoined where comp year and until greater part of tax was collected.

Cited in Syracuse Solar Salt Co. v. Rome, W. N. Y. Supp. 321, holding laches limited to equitable equity court called on to sustain legal right; Merel W. Va. 33, 56 Am. St. Rep. 828, 23 S. E. 681, hol paid for invalid county order accrues at once an order is due; Kessler Co. v. Ensley Co. 123 Fed. 56 to set aside corporation's conveyances for fraud, ba limitations.

Cited in note (10 L. R. A. 127) as to when doc voked.

Distinguished in Simpkins v. Taylor, 81 Hun, 471, that obligee's failure to notice for several years tha tion instead of payment as agreed, due to failure c kind of guaranty, does not deprive him of right to v. Raymond, 40 Misc. 609, 83 N. Y. Supp. 15, holdin transfer procured by fraud, barred only by running time of discovery.

Estoppel.

Approved in Andes v. Ely, 158 U. S. 321, 39 L. e holding town estopped to deny as against bona fid that necessary steps were taken; Oswego County S Div. 336, 72 N. Y. Supp. 786, holding town cannot b of void bonds or estop itself from questioning their

Injunctive relief.

Approved in Hughes v. Bingham, 135 N. Y. 352, R. 391, 32 N. E. 78, holding injunctive relief to re of invalid deed discretionary; Hygeia Water Ice Co 140 N. Y. 97, 35 N. E. 417, refusing to enjoin use corporation never engaged in business and witho chises; Meyers v. Pennsylvania Steel Co. 77 App.

denying injunction against further execution of public contract containing provisions required by law subsequently declared unconstitutional.

Res judicata.

Cited in Wells v. Salina, 71 Hun, 572, 25 N. Y. Supp. 134, holding judgment at law for money advanced not a bar to action as equitable assignee for money expended and services rendered.

Defect of parties.

Cited in Herkimer County Light & P. Co. v. Johnson, 37 App. Div. 265, 55 N. Y. Supp. 924, by Follett, J., dissenting, who holds judgment should not be rendered on submission when it appears there are interested parties not before the court.

8 L. R. A. 253, METROPOLITAN ELEV. R. CO. v. KNEELAND, 120 N. Y. 134, 17 Am. St. Rep. 619, 24 N. E. 381.

Liability for fraud.

Cited in Conley v. Blinebry, 29 Misc. 373, 60 N. Y. Supp. 531, holding mortgagee may recover from mortgagor before maturing of mortgage bond, where before mortgage was recorded, mortgagor's grantee records deed.

— Issuance of negotiable paper.

Cited in Nashville Lumber Co. v. Fourth Nat. Bank, 94 Tenn. 378, 27 L. R. A. 522, 45 Am. St. Rep. 727, 29 S. W. 368, holding party transferring negotiable note after notice of *ultra vires* of corporate accommodation indorsement, liable to corporation before maturity; Ontario v. Union Bank, 21 Misc. 777, 47 N. Y. Supp. 927, holding town official transferring apparently valid municipal bonds to bank as collateral, liable to town where issued by him in excess of authority; Petrie v. Williams, 68 Hun, 595, 23 N. Y. Supp. 237, holding attorney and third party procuring negotiation and retaining portion of proceeds of notes given to infant, guilty of conversion; Jones v. Crawford, 107 Ga. 322, 45 L. R. A. 107, 33 S. E. 51, holding payee liable to party induced to sign negotiable note as coprincipal by assurance of nonliability; Davison v. Farr, 18 Misc. 126, 41 N. Y. Supp. 170, holding party fraudulently induced to indorse, may before maturity pay bona fide holder, and sue maker.

Cited in note (27 L. R. A. 520) on liability for transferring negotiable note to bona fide holder so as to cut off defenses.

Who is a bona fide holder.

Cited in Wilson v. Metropolitan Elev. R. Co. 120 N. Y. 150, 17 Am. St. Rep. 625, 24 N. E. 384, holding party receiving corporate note in discharge of director's personal debt, bona fide holder, where issue authorized by resolution; Wile & B. Co. v. Rochester & K. F. Land Co. 4 Misc. 574, 25 N. Y. Supp. 794, holding party purchasing corporate notes payable to director, after inquiring of secretary as to authorization, bona fide holder.

Liability of directors for unauthorized acts.

Cited in Bassett v. Fairchild, 132 Cal. 653, 52 L. R. A. 619, 64 Pac. 1082 (dissenting opinion) majority holding directors not liable for unauthorized bona fide compensation to party performing active services as director and vice president.

Cited in notes (9 L. R. A. 653) on liability of corporate directors; (55 L. R. A. 772) on liability of directors to corporation; (12 L. R. A. 366) on individual liability on contracts by corporations.

Stockholders' interest as property.

Cited in *Re* Fitch, 160 N. Y. 95, 54 N. E. 701, ration left by nonresident dying out of state taxal ty where corporate property is located.

8 L. R. A. 257, McKENZIE v. HARRISON, 120 1 24 N. E. 458.

Modification of written agreement by par

Cited in Romaine v. Beacon Lithographic Co. 13 holding acceptance of less salary under parol agree Hurley v. Sehring, 43 N. Y. S. R. 242, 17 N. Y. Su der of premises terminates tenancy though lease pı Donohue, 27 Misc. 517, 58 N. Y. Supp. 319, holding of tenant's surrender and abandonment of defense Hotel Co. v. Brennan, 64 Hun, 611, 19 N. Y. Supp. reduction of rent in ten-year lease, where supporte payments at such rate accepted; Bowman v. Wrigh holding amount of parol reduction cannot be rec duced rent; Butler v. Mail & Exp. Pub. Co. 54 App. holding executed contract to pay for judgment by ing although not supported by consideration.

Distinguished in Voege v. Ronalds, 83 Hun, 116, lease for term not modified by unexecuted oral a Howie v. Kasnowitz, 83 App. Div. 297, 82 N. Y. Su seal cannot be modified by parol unexecuted agre Misc. 544, 38 N. Y. Supp. 104, holding acceptance mortgagee under parol agreement does not preven in future; Hayne v. Sealy, 71 App. Div. 419, 75 cuted parol agreement not to take interest on fund ing only to time of repudiation; Munson v. Mage Supp. 942, holding obligor in contract released b third party liable thereon.

Gift.

Cited in Merritt v. Youmans, 21 App. Div. 258, that mortgagee cannot recover of intermediate g remitted to subsequent grantee by receipt therefor.

Cited in note (11 L. R. A. 711) on payment c without new consideration.

Distinguished in *Re* Gregg, 11 Misc. 156, 32 N or rent under lease not shown by oral statements c

Payment.

Cited in Serat v. Smith, 61 Hun, 45, 15 N. Y. statement of account and draft for balance due t draft indorsed.

8 L. R. A. 259, STATE v. EAVES, 106 N. C. 752, 1

Selling liquor within prescribed area.

Cited in State v. Barringer, 110 N. C. 527, 14 S.

power to restrict sale of liquor within prescribed area though already carried on there; Jones v. Moore County, 106 N. C. 438, 11 S. E. 514, holding liquors cannot be sold within statutory limit of building recognized as church when act passed.

Cited in note (21 L. R. A. 580) on discretion in granting of liquor licenses.

Statutory construction.

Cited in Randall v. Richmond & D. R. Co. 107 N. C. 755, 11 L. R. A. 462, 12 S. E. 605, holding spirit of act must be gathered from statute itself; Randall v. Richmond & D. R. Co. 107 N. C. 752, 11 L. R. A. 462, 12 S. E. 605, holding language cannot be interpolated into a plain, unambiguous statute to obtain a meaning not disclosed by it; Sherrill v. Conner, 107 N. C. 545, 12 S. E. 588, holding "may" cannot be construed as "shall" in statute amended by substituting former word for latter; State *ex rel.* Harris v. Scarborough, 110 N. C. 236, 14 S. E. 737, holding that every presumption is in favor of validity of statute and of good faith of legislature in enacting it.

Regularity of indictment.

Cited in State v. Downs, 116 N. C. 1066, 21 S. E. 689, holding word added to title of church in indictment for selling liquor harmless.

8 L. R. A. 261, DAVIS v. STRANGE, 86 Va. 793, 11 S. E. 406.

Undue influence.

Approved in Thomas v. Turner, 87 Va. 15, 12 S. E. 149, holding transactions between persons occupying confidential relations must be fair, voluntary, and well understood.

Cited in Jones v. McGruder, 87 Va. 378, 12 S. E. 792, setting aside conveyance without consideration by drunkard to trusted friends made about three months before grantor's death; Sims v. Sims, 101 Mo. App. 418, 74 S. W. 449, holding woman constrained by husband and father-in-law to execute deed of trust to father-in-law for greater amount than advanced, entitled to equitable relief.

Cited in footnote to *Re* Shell, 53 L. R. A. 387, which holds undue influence in procuring will not inferable from motive and opportunity alone.

Distinguished in Coleman's Estate, 193 Pa. 612, 44 Atl. 1085, sustaining deed from spendthrift son to mother in consideration of large annual income to himself.

8 L. R. A. 268, McMULLEN v. RITCHIE, 41 Fed. 502.

Effect of foreign judgment on merits.

Affirmed in 159 U. S. 235, 40 L. ed. 133, 16 Sup. Ct. Rep. 171.

Cited in MacDonald v. Grand Trunk R. Co. 71 N. H. 455, 59 L. R. A. 454, 93 Am. St. Rep. 550, 52 Atl. 982, sustaining foreign judgment on merits when it resulted from failure to prove law of state where cause of action arose; Ritchie v. Burke, 109 Fed. 17, holding Federal court not ousted of jurisdiction between citizens of different states based on judgment between one of the parties and other parties all of same state; Fisher v. Fielding, 67 Conn. 137, 32 L. R. A. 250, 52 Am. St. Rep. 270, 34 Atl. 714, holding English judgment when jurisdiction obtained by service of process in England conclusive on merits between parties; American Mut. L. Ins. Co. v. Mason, 159 Ind. 18, 64 N. E. 525, holding judgment of courts of another state having jurisdiction of parties and subject-matter, conclusive on merits.

Cited in note (20 L. R. A. 675, 676) on conclu in foreign country.

8 L. R. A. 270, SAVANNAH v. WEED, 84 Ga. 683

Uniform taxation.

Cited in Weaver v. State, 89 Ga. 642, 15 S. E. 8 or occupation not tax upon property within *ad valo* Constitution; Singer Mfg. Co. v. Wright, 97 Ga. 1 249, upholding power of legislature to classify su Savannah, 181 U. S. 546, 45 L. ed. 994, 21 Sup. Ct 400, 13 S. E. 442, holding purchaser properly taxed to real estate sold as security; Georgia State Bldg. Ga. 67, 35 S. E. 67, holding proviso in taxing act tha to be in lieu of all other taxes, void; Mutual Reserve 109 Ga. 70, 35 S. E. 71, holding tax on nonresident i companies being exempted, void; Indianapolis v. B 857, holding provision in ordinance to license brewer bottlers, void; State v. Bixman, 162 Mo. 70, 62 S. V majority holding that legislature may put exporte separate classes in assessing fees for sale of beer.

Cited in note (60 L. R. A. 349) on constitutional e in relation to corporate taxation.

8 L. R. A. 273, WROUGHT IRON RANGE CO. v. Inters. Com. Rep. 146, 11 S. E. 233.

Followed without comment in McClelland v. Mariet

Meaning of term "peddler."

Cited in Kimmel v. Americus, 105 Ga. 695, 31 S. E. ipal ordinance to license peddlers.

Cited in footnotes to Emmons v. Lewistown, 8 L. canvassers not peddlers; Stuart v. Cunningham, 20 I delivering goods previously sold not a peddler; Hew R. A. 736, which holds agent delivering from wagon taking other orders not a peddler; State v. Wells, 48 soliciting orders for goods and carrying goods to fill

Who must obtain license.

Cited in Troy v. Harris, 102 Mo. App. 60, 76 S. W. for nonpayment of ad valorem tax on merchants' license issues; Racine Iron Co. v. McCommons, 111 S. E. 866, holding property of foreign principal not execution against agent for nonpayment of license Iron Range Co. 111 Ga. 860, 36 S. E. 907, holdin against corporation for peddler's license tax.

Cited in footnotes to Brownback v. North Wales, valid as to residents, ordinance requiring license for soliciting orders from house to house; Rosenbloom v sustains license tax on peddlers, though vendors of t

Interference with interstate commerce.

Cited in McLaughlin v. South Bend, 126 Ind. 472, 10 L. R. A. 358, footnote p. 357, 26 N. E. 185, holding peddler's licensing ordinance unenforceable against one negotiating for sale of property situated without state; *Re* Tinsman, 95 Fed. 651, and Overton v. Vicksburg, 70 Miss. 560, 13 So. 226, holding peddler's licensing ordinance void as to nonresident travelers selling goods of foreign corporation by sample; Miller v. Goodman, 91 Tex. 43, 40 S. W. 718, holding foreign corporation not required to file articles of incorporation in state and receive permit before selling goods manufactured elsewhere as such selling is interstate commerce.

Cited in notes (7 L. R. A. 667) on hawkers and peddlers subject to state license; (11 L. R. A. 219) on state authority to impose licenses; (12 L. R. A. 624) on supreme power of Congress to regulate interstate commerce; (14 L. R. A. 98) on peddlers and drummers as relating to interstate commerce; (60 L. R. A. 690) on corporate taxation and the commerce clause.

Distinguished in Price Co. v. Atlanta, 105 Ga. 365, 31 S. E. 619, upholding tax where goods were shipped to warehouse within state and from there distributed; Racine Iron Co. v. McCommons, 111 Ga. 547, 51 L. R. A. 139, 36 S. E. 866, upholding peddlers' tax where traveling agents for foreign principals received goods in bulk and broke original packages for distribution.

8 L. R. A. 275, FIRST NAT. BANK v. CARROLL, 80 Iowa, 11, 45 N. W. 304.

Gaming contracts.

Cited in People's Sav. Bank v. Gifford, 108 Iowa, 279, 79 N. W. 63, holding note given in settlement of balance growing out of dealings in options, void.

8 L. R. A. 277, VANNEST v. FLEMING, 79 Iowa, 638, 18 Am. St. Rep. 387, 44 N. W. 906.

Discharging water upon adjoining land.

Cited in Collins v. Keokuk, 91 Iowa, 295, 59 N. W. 202, refusing to enjoin discharge of water on adjoining land coming from tile 10 feet from said land; Williamson v. Oleson, 91 Iowa, 291, 59 N. W. 267, refusing to enjoin flow of water upon adjoining proprietor's land through drain tile; Stinson v. Fishel, 93 Iowa, 661, 61 N. W. 1063, holding that owner cannot dig ditches to gather water in one channel so as to increase natural flow over adjoining land; Holmes v. Calhoun County, 97 Iowa, 364, 66 N. W. 145, holding discharge of water upon another's land except in the natural course of drainage, actionable; Wharton v. Stevens, 84 Iowa, 110, 15 L. R. A. 633, 35 Am. St. Rep. 296, 50 N. W. 562, upholding adjoining proprietor's right to drain into natural drainage way flowing over another's land.

Cited in notes (8 L. R. A. 575) on element of servitude in flowage of water; (10 L. R. A. 484) on right by prescription to use of lands ot another; (10 L. R. A. 487) on right to use of flowing water.

License to flow.

Cited in Hansen v. Farmers Co-Operative Creamery, 106 Iowa, 170, 76 N. W. 652, holding license on part of lessee to use other land, of lessor for flowage during lease-hold period, exists where money and labor have been expended with lessors consent; Spink v. Corning, 61 App. Div. 91, 70 N. Y. Supp. 143, holding improved watercourse cannot be closed after acquiescence for long period merely because artificially deepened and enlarged.

Cited in note (49 L. R. A. 513) on revocability on land after licensee has incurred expense and cr

8 L. R. A. 280, PALMER v. STATE, 88 Tenn. 553,

Effect of licensing unlawful business.

Cited in Blaufield v. State, 103 Tenn. 598, 53 S of privilege tax does not authorize unlawful sale 95 Tenn. 476, 32 S. W. 391, holding unauthorized ticipator in unlawful gaming.

Cited in note (14 L. R. A. 846) on implied sanct lations.

Gambling, what is.

Cited in Guarantee Co. v. Mechanics' Sav. Bank ed. 261, 22 Sup. Ct. Rep. 124, holding dealing in nessee laws.

Cited in footnotes to People *ex rel.* Lawrence v. F holds test of speed or endurance of horses for prize State *ex rel.* Matthews v. Forsyth, 33 L. R. A. 221 meetings on neighboring tracks with same horses, j regulating duration and frequency.

8 L. R. A. 283, STATE *ex rel.* GOODWIN v. NELS Am. St. Rep. 609, 45 N. W. 33.

Taxation for relief and charitable purposes.

Cited in Yeatman v. King, 2 N. D. 426, 33 Am. holding obligation of person supplied with grain t mere debt, and not a tax; Lund v. Chippewa Coun 136, 67 N. W. 927, upholding constitutionality of a home for feeble minded.

Cited in note (14 L. R. A. 475) on public purpo appropriated, or raised by taxation.

Distinguished in *Re* Relief Bills, 21 Colo. 65, 39 to enable settlers in certain district to obtain seed William Deering & Co. v. Peterson. 75 Minn. 124, grain loan act unconstitutional.

Original jurisdiction of supreme court.

Cited in State *ex rel.* Moore v. Archibald, 5 N. I ing original jurisdiction of supreme court in mand removal of superintendent of state hospital; State D. 462, 83 N. W. 914, upholding original jurisdic county auditor to receive certificates of nominatio D. 482, 52 L. R. A. 135, footnote p. 134, 83 N. W. writ must be procured on information filed by stat thority in name of state.

Cited in notes (51 L. R. A. 63, 107) on superinte jurisdiction of the superior over the inferior or su A. 864) on original jurisdiction of court of last re

8 L. R. A. 289, KILLMER v. WUCHNER, 79 Iowa, 722, 18 Am. St. Rep. 392, 45 N. W. 299.

Allowance for improvements.

Cited in Bergman v. Kammlade, 109 Iowa, 308, 80 N. W. 418, denying tenant in possession allowance for improvements on partition where rent withheld by him exceeded their value; Leake v. Hayes, 13 Wash. 222, 52 Am. St. Rep. 34, 43 Pac. 48, holding tenant in common making estate productive by improvements entitled on partition to all the profits without deducting increase of value.

8 L. R. A. 291, MAULDIN v. GREENVILLE, 33 S. C. 1, 11 S. E. 434.

Taxpayers' action.

Cited in Butler v. Ellerbe, 44 S. C. 259, 22 S. E. 425, holding state not indispensable party to action by taxpayer to restrain comptroller general from drawing warrants.

Power to maintain public-service plants.

Cited in Mayo v. Washington, 122 N. C. 9, 40 L. R. A. 165, 29 S. E. 343, holding debt for purchase of electric light plant not necessary expense of town which does not need sanction of voters; Fawcett v. Mt. Airy, 134 N. C. 129, 63 L. R. A. 872, 45 S. E. 1029, holding expenditure for water and lighting plants within town's power to incur necessary expenses; Wadsworth v. Concord, 133 N. C. 593, 45 S. E. 948, by Clark, C. J., concurring in result, who holds furnishing light for streets "a necessary purpose;" Crawfordsville v. Broden, 130 Ind. 159, 14 L. R. A. 272, 30 Am. St. Rep. 214, 28 N. E. 849, holding that city may establish electric light plant for private as well as public use; Ellinwood v. Reedsburg, 91 Wis. 134, 64 N. W. 885, holding that city can build waterworks and electric lighting plant under police power; Christensen v. Fremont, 45 Neb. 164, 63 N. W. 364, holding that city may use general fund to pay for electric light system to be used for lighting streets; Jacksonville Electric Light Co. v. Jacksonville, 36 Fla. 265, 30 L. R. A. 543, 51 Am. St. Rep. 24, 18 So. 677, holding that city under its charter can maintain electric plant to furnish light to citizens; Jones v. Camden, 44 S. C. 322, 51 Am. St. Rep. 819, 23 S. E. 141, holding validity of bonds for which building erected not affected by fact that small portions of building used for other than public purposes.

Cited in notes (64 L. R. A. 41) on definitions of manufacturing; (64 L. R. A. 60) on taxation of electric plants as manufacturing corporations.

Power of state to engage in trade.

Cited in McCullough v. Brown, 41 S. C. 252, 23 L. R. A. 423, 19 S. E. 458, holding dispensary act whereby state attempts monopoly of liquor traffic invalid.

Distinguished in State *ex rel.* George v. Aiken, 42 S. C. 247, 26 L. R. A. 357, 20 S. E 221, holding dispensary act giving state monopoly of liquor traffic valid as a police measure.

Construction of municipal charters.

Cited in Holmes v. Weinheimer, 66 S. C. 21, 44 S. E. 82, refusing to construe municipal charter as impliedly giving purchaser at municipal tax sale rights superior to purchaser at state tax sale.

8 L. R. A. 297, STATE v. DOWELL, 106 N. C. 722, 19 Am. St. Rep. 568, 11 S. E. 525.

8 L. R. A. 299, BAIN v. RICHMOND & D. R. CO. 105 N. C. 363, 3 Inters. Com. Rep. 149, 18 Am. St. Rep. 912, 11 S. E. 311.

Right of state treasurer to sue for unpaid taxes.

Cited in Worth v. Wright, 122 N. C. 337, 29 S. E. 361, upholding right of state treasurer to sue to recover unpaid license tax.

Tax on foreign carriers.

Cited in footnotes to Union Refrigerator Transit Co. v. Lynch, 48 L. R. A. 790, which authorizes taxation of cars within state under lease from foreign corporation; Cumberland & P. R. Co. v. State, 52 L. R. A. 764, which sustains state tax on proportionate part of gross receipts of interstate railroad; Hall v. American Refrigerator Transit Co. 56 L. R. A. 89, which sustains tax on average number of refrigerator cars coming into state in course of interstate business; Grigsby Constr. Co. v. Freeman, 58 L. R. A. 349, which holds contractor's outfit brought into state for use several months in constructing railroad taxable in state.

Cited in note (60 L. R. A. 656) on corporate taxation and the commerce clause.

Disapproved in Union Refrigerator Transit Co. v. Lynch, 18 Utah, 392, 48 L. R. A. 793, 55 Pac. 639, upholding tax on leased cars of foreign corporation, passing through or within state.

8 L. R. A. 301, COM. v. CLEARY, 135 Pa. 64, 19 Atl. 1017.

Report of later appeal in 148 Pa. 26, 23 Atl. 1110.

Good character as defense in criminal action.

Cited in State v. Porter, 32 Or. 159, 49 Pac. 964; Com. v. Gibbons, 3 Pa. Super. Ct. 413, 39 W. N. C. 568, holding evidence of good reputation of defendant in criminal action admissible; Seymour v. State, 102 Ga. 806, 30 S. E. 263, holding evidence of good character to be considered on question of defendant's guilt; Com. v. Sayars, 21 Pa. Super. Ct. 79, holding instruction that "good character should be considered in doubtful case," erroneous; State v. Van Kuran, 25 Utah, 16, 69 Pac. 60, holding instruction limiting consideration of evidence as to defendant's good character to determination of truth of evidence for prosecution, erroneous.

Reasonable doubt.

Cited in Com. v. Yost, 11 Pa. Super. Ct. 344, holding reasonable doubt as to guilt must arise out of evidence.

Cited in note (20 L. R. A. 617) on evidence of character creating doubt.

Comments of prosecuting counsel.

Cited in note (12 L. R. A. 449) on criminal practice, comments of prosecuting counsel on absence of witnesses, and testimony.

8 L. R. A. 304, BRANNON v. COUNTY COURT, 33 W. Va. 789, 11 S. E. 34.

Delegation of taxing power.

Cited in Neale v. County Court, 43 W. Va. 96, 27 S. E. 370, holding power of levying taxes limited to states, counties, school districts, and municipal corporations.

County taxes for road purposes.

Cited in footnotes to Gilson v. Rush County, 11 L. R. A. 835, which holds personal property liable to taxation for price of toll road, purchased to make it a free road; Duval County v. Jacksonville, 29 L. R. A. 416, which upholds statute requiring half of funds raised for county roads and bridges to be turned over to city authorities for city streets.

Constitutional limitations upon county taxation.

Cited in Spilman v. Parkersburg, 35 W. Va. 613, 14 S. E. 279; Davis v. County Court, 38 W. Va. 107, 18 S. E. 373, holding county court prohibited by constitution from incurring indebtedness other than for current fiscal year, unless authorized by three-fifths vote of people; Neale v. County Court, 43 W. Va. 100, 27 S. E. 370, holding magisterial district subscription to work of internal improvement regarded as county indebtedness in determining whether constitutional limit reached.

8 L. R. A. 309, WILSON v. MARTIN-WILSON AUTOMATIC FIRE ALARM CO. 151 Mass. 515, 24 N. E. 784.

Letters patent; how reached by creditors.

Cited in Vail v. Hammond, 60 Conn. 383, 25 Am. St. Rep. 330, 22 Atl. 954, holding that letters patent may be reached in equitable proceeding for payment of debts.

Distinguished in effect in Wolf v. Bonta Plate Glass Co. 5 Lack. L. News, 54, 6 Northampton Co. Rep. 399, holding that patent right cannot be sold *fi. fa.*

Creditor's bills; what may be reached by.

Cited in Wemyss v. White, 159 Mass. 486, 34 N. E. 718, holding beneficiary's interest, where trustees have discretionary power to discontinue payments, cannot be reached by creditor's bill.

Cited in footnote to Harper v. Clayton, 35 L. R. A. 211, which denies power to reach unassigned right of dower by creditor's bill.

Right of equity to transfer title.

Cited in Wilson v. Welch, 157 Mass. 80, 31 N. E. 712, holding that equity cannot, unless authorized by statute, transfer title by decree.

Distinguished in Russell v. Burke, 180 Mass. 544, 62 N. E. 963, holding that decree in equity should order conveyance by resident defendant upon master's sale.

8 L. R. A. 315, RICE v. SANDERS, 152 Mass. 108, 23 Am. St. Rep. 804, 24 N. E. 1079.

Covenant to assume mortgage; effect of.

Cited in Wamesit Power Co. v. Sterling Mills, 158 Mass. 444, 33 N. E. 503, holding duty of grantee assuming mortgage subsequently assigned to him to discharge it; Stites v. Thompson, 98 Wis. 331, 73 N. W. 774, holding purchaser assuming mortgage debt liable thereon as principal.

— Recovery of damages for breach.

Cited in Baldwin v. Emery, 89 Me. 499, 36 Atl. 994, and Walton v. Ruggles, 180 Mass. 26, 61 N. E. 267, holding right to recover for grantee's breach of covenant to pay mortgage not affected by plaintiff's nonpayment; Paro v. St. Martin, 180 Mass. 31, 61 N. E. 268, holding grantor in consideration of annuity entitled to recover value thereof upon foreclosure of mortgage assumed by

grantee; Pearson v. Bailey, 180 Mass. 232, 62 N. 1
ties assuming mortgage not damnified by failure
nants to look wholly to land; Bray v. Booker, 8 N.
damages recoverable for grantee's promise to pay

8 L. R. A. 320, AMERICAN ORDER OF S. C. v.
N. E. 918.

Right to use name similar to one already in

Cited in Armington v. Palmer, 21 R. I. 112,
95, 79 Am. St. Rep. 786, 42 Atl. 308, holding wron
name enjoinable, in absence of contrary statute.

Cited in footnotes to International Committee,
Women's Christian Asso. 56 L. R. A. 888, which s
C. A. to enjoin deceptive use of similar name by
corporated; Peck Bros. & Co. v. Peck, Bros. Co. 6
purchasers of name and goodwill of corporation ma
by purchasers of branch thereof; Illinois Watch Cas
429, which holds license to form corporation unde
other corporation calling meeting to vote on chang
Lodge K. of P. v. Improved Order, K. of P. 38 L.
seceding Knights of Pythias to use name "Improved

Distinguished in effect in Paulino v. Portuguese
20 L. R. A. 273, 26 Atl. 36, holding use of corporate
charter not enjoinable by association having same

Name of patented article; when open to gener

Cited in Dover Stamping Co. v. Fellows, 163 Ma
Am. St. Rep. 448, 40 N. E. 105, holding name of pat
use upon expiration of patent.

8 L. R. A. 321, MISSOURI P. R. CO. v. WHIPK
Rep. 734, 13 S. W. 639.

Garnishment; defense of principal defendant.

Cited in Ball v. Bennett, 21 Tex. Civ. App. 399, 52
debtor entitled to intervene in garnishment proceedi
to question sufficiency of proceeding; Laurel v. T
965, holding garnishee failing to plead exemption
garnished remains liable to him therefor.

Cited in notes (8 L. R. A. 413, 19 L. R. A. 580)
up exemption of principal debtor.

8 L. R. A. 323, GULF, C. & S. F. R. CO. v. LEVI,
45, 13 S. W. 191.

Liability for delay in delivery of freight.

Cited in Gulf, C. & S. F. R. Co. v. Gatewood,
14 S. W. 913, holding strike of railway employees
good defense to action on special contract; Internati
3 Tex. Civ. App. 21, 21 S. W. 622, holding carrier n
of goods resulting from causes beyond its control,

their preservation of property; Empire Transp. Co. v. Philadelphia, & R. Coal & I. Co. 35 L. R. A. 632, 23 C. C. A. 571, 40 U. S. App. 157, 77 Fed. 926, holding under charter party without stipulation for time of unloading, reasonable time therefor to be determined from existing circumstances; Burnham v. Alabama & V. R. Co. 81 Miss. 54, 32 So. 912, denying railroad's liability for deterioration of perishable goods, delayed in transportation by unprecedented flood.

Cited in notes (9 L. R. A. 836) on excuse of carrier for delay in transportation; (35 L. R. A. 627, 628) on effect of violence and intimidation upon liability for delay in transportation; (35 L. R. A. 624) on delay in transportation in general.

8 L. R. A. 326, *Re* TIPTON, 28 Tex. App. 438, 13 S. W. 610.

Statutes; regularity of passage.

Cited in Williams v. Taylor, 83 Tex. 674, 19 S. W. 156, holding legislative journals will not be examined to determine whether procedure prescribed by Constitution has been followed; McLane v. Paschal, 8 Tex. Civ. App. 401, 28 S. W. 711, holding court will not look beyond enrolled bill, signed by proper officers, for purpose of determining whether statute duly enacted; Narregang v. Brown County, 14 S. D. 365, 85 N. W. 602, holding properly authenticated enrolled bill not subject to impeachment by entries in legislative journals; State *ex rel.* Reed v. Jones, 6 Wash. 476, 23 L. R. A. 353, 34 Pac. 201, holding enrolled bill, if fair on its face, and signed by proper officers, is conclusive evidence of regularity of legislative procedure; *Re* Duncan, 139 U. S. 459, 35 L. ed. 224, 11 Sup. Ct. Rep. 573, holding judgment of state court in favor of validity of adoption of state statute not reviewable in Federal court.

Cited in notes (23 L. R. A. 345) on admissibility of evidence to contradict enrolled bill; (11 L. R. A. 491, 492) on passage of bills through legislature in general.

Violation of unconstitutional statute.

Cited in note (39 L. R. A. 456) on conviction for violating unconstitutional statute.

8 L. R. A. 328, EMMONS v. LEWISTOWN 132 Ill. 380, 22 Am. St. Rep. 540, 24 N. E. 58.

Who are hawkers or peddlers.

Cited in Kennedy v. People, 9 Colo. App. 493, 49 Pac. 373; State v. Hoffman, 50 Mo. App. 588; Cerro Gordo v. Rawlings, 135 Ill. 40, 25 N. E. 1006,— holding traveling salesman selling goods by sample, for future delivery, not peddler; Olney v. Todd, 47 Ill. App. 440, holding neither traveling salesman taking orders for goods from sample, nor person subsequently making deliveries and collecting money therefor, are peddlers; Twining v. Elgin, 38 Ill. App. 350, holding person going from place to place, and soliciting orders for enlargement and framing of pictures not itinerant merchant nor transient vender of merchandise; Hewson v. Englewood Twp. 55 N. J. L. 524, 21 L. R. A. 737, 27 Atl. 904, holding person soliciting orders for groceries, for future delivery, not "hawker, peddler, or itinerant vendor."

Cited in footnote to State v. Wells, 48 L. R. A. 99, which holds one soliciting orders for goods and carrying goods to fill previous sales, not a peddler.

Municipal corporations; powers strictly cons

Cited in Cairo v. Coleman, 53 Ill. App. 688, and App. 478, holding any doubt as to power of muni solved against corporation; Savanna v. Robinson, 8. to regulate inspection and weighing of coal not weighmasters, and to require that all coal sold Kennedy v. People, 9 Colo. App. 493, 49 Pac. 373, license of "peddlers," city cannot enlarge term to within such description; Delisle v. Danville, 36 ordinance requiring license of peddlers, and providin place and selling goods by sample for future deliver peddler, in excess of power.

Distinguished in Laugel v. Bushnell, 197 Ill. 27, 58 holding under power to declare what shall be deeme municipal corporation that thing of doubtful charact

Statutes; construction of things enumerated.

Cited in Gundling v. Chicago, 176 Ill. 346, 48 L. R ing general words following enumeration of particul things as are of same kind as those enumerated.

8 L. R. A. 330, LAKE ERIE & W. R. CO. v. SCOTT

Cited without discussion in Louisville, E. & St. I App. 341.

Damage to adjoining property by railroad.

Cited in Metropolitan West Side Elevated R. Co. and Illinois C. R. Co. v. Kuehle, 95 Ill. App. 186, h taken away because act authorized by law, where i such as would, in absence of legislative authority, con Chicago, M. & St. P. R. Co. v. Darke, 148 Ill. 234, 35 tion in value of land by reason of noise of trains is Calumet & C. Canal & Dock Co. v. Morawetz, 195 Ill injury from noise, soot, and cinders proper element sary incidents to operation of railway; Illinois C. 678, 62 N. E. 798, and Illinois C. R. Co. v. Schmidg inconveniences occasioned by operation of railroad, an ably probable to ensue, may be considered in detern of property; Wisconsin C. R. Co. v. Wieczorek, 51 and vibration of ground causing ceilings and walls to crack, and consequent depreciation in value of r damage; Chicago, P. & St. L. R. Co. v. Leah, 152 Il special disadvantages and annoyances, which interi property, resulting from construction of railway on sidered in estimating damage; Davenport R. I. & N. App. 81, holding depreciation in market value resu operation of railroad, measure of adjoining owner's d Davis, 71 Ill. App. 102, holding railroad relocatin owner of fee or by authority of ordinance of city, ages to private property; Metropolitan West Side

App. 336, holding that recovery can be had for injury from public use of railroad, as distinguished from such private use as railroad may lawfully make of its own land.

Damage distinct from that of public.

Cited in Chicago v. Spoor, 190 Ill. 348, 60 N. E. 540, holding recovery for erection of public improvement in street must be based upon special damage, in excess of that to public, from direct physical disturbance to right connected with property; Pennsylvania Co. v. Chicago, 181 Ill. 303, 53 L. R. A. 228, 54 N. E. 825, holding remedy of abutting-property owner for injury from use of street for hack stand is distinct from that of public for which he may have compensation in damages.

When damage accrues.

Cited in Eachus v. Los Angeles Consol. Electric R. Co. 103 Cal. 622, 42 Am. Rep. 149, 37 Pac. 750, holding in action for damages from change of grade, plaintiff entitled to recover entire damage done to lot by permanent change in street; Chicago, P. & St. L. R. Co. v. Leah, 41 Ill. App. 588, holding recovery for depreciation in value of property from construction of railway in highway covers all damages that may accrue from future maintenance and operation of railroad in proper manner.

Condemnation of land for railroad purposes.

Cited in footnotes to Jacksonville, T. & K. W. R. Co. v. Adams, 14 L. R. A. 533, which authorizes condemnation of land irregularly entered upon; Becker v. Philadelphia & R. Terminal R. Co. 35 L. R. A. 583, which holds diminution in profits and value of merchandise by removal of business from condemnation of land not element of damages.

Cited in note (9 L. R. A. 299) on elements of damage from condemnation of land for railroad purposes.

8 L. R. A. 333, STANLEY v. STANLEY, 47 Ohio St. 225, 21 Am. St. Rep. 806, 24 N. E. 493.

Statute of limitations; interruption by absence from state.

Cited in Lindsay v. Maxwell, 4 Ohio N. P. 354, holding debtor's temporary absence from state for several months does not suspend running of statute; Webster v. Citizens Bank, 2 Herdman (Neb.) 358, 96 N. W. 118, holding statute continues to run in favor of nonresident coming into state each business day.

Cited in footnotes to George v. Butler, 57 L. R. A. 396, which sustains right of grantee of mortgaged premises to plead limitations against foreclosure, though debt not barred as to mortgagor because of absence from state; Hogg v. Hartley, 54 L. R. A. 215, which holds personal judgment against one previously leaving state not excused by absence from statute of limitations.

8 L. R. A. 337, FRIESZLEBEN v. SHALLCROSS, 9 Houst. (Del.) 1, 19 Atl. 576.

Power of taxation; extent of.

Cited in English v. Wilmington, 2 Marv. (Del.) 85, 37 Atl. 158, holding front-foot assessment for sewer constitutional.

Right to vote.

Cited in footnotes to Morris v. Powell, 9 L. R. A. 326, which holds law requir-

ing registration of only part of voters, void; Brew
845, which holds statute requiring notice of claim
residing less than six months in county, void.

Cited in notes (14 L. R. A. 580) on constitutio
munities, and protection; (25 L. R. A. 482) on h
tax or property qualification; (29 L. R. A. 414)
qualification of electors.

8 L. R. A. 358, LYON v. DENISON, 80 Mich. 371, 4

Property not subject to execution.

Cited in footnotes to Lowenberg v. Greenebaum,
levy on and sale of stock exchange seat ineffectual
Bank v. Morrow, 38 L. R. A. 758, which holds per
in consideration of donation, not property subject t

8 L. R. A. 362, SMITH v. SMITH, 84 Ga. 440, 11 S.

Marriage; conflict of laws.

Cited in note (57 L. R. A. 173) on conflict of laws

Grounds for divorce.

Cited in Ring v. Ring (Ga.) 62 L. R. A. 879, 44
habit will not justify divorce on ground of cruelty.

8 L. R. A. 365, WITTY v. MICHIGAN MUT. L. IN
St. Rep. 327, 24 N. E. 141.

Promissory note; what constitutes.

Cited in Kraft v. Thomas, 123 Ind. 515, 18 Am.
holding following instrument promissory note; "For
man three hundred dollars in full, with use or beare
praisement laws. Paid when kald for. Edward K

8 L. R. A. 366, COOPER v. RICHMOND & D. R. C

Removal of action to Federal court for prejudi

Followed in Brodhead, v. Shoemaker, 11 L. R. A
petition for removal, accompanied by affidavit by a
his own knowledge existence of prejudice and local i

Cited in Walcott v. Watson, 46 Fed. 531, raising,
whether cause may be removed for prejudice and l
and affidavit; Reeves v. Corning, 51 Fed. 778, hol
prejudice or local influence may be made *ex parte;*
488, holding motion to remove for prejudice or loc
upon notice.

Cited in notes (11 L. R. A. 568) on removal of
influence; (9 L. R. A. 232, 11 L. R. A. 571) on remo
local influence; sufficiency of petition and affidavit.

Disapproved in Niblock v. Alexander, 44 Fed. 306,
ant's attorney, averring knowledge of prejudice or
for removal of cause.

8 L. R. A. 369, BIRMINGHAM v. KLEIN, 89 Ala. 461, 7 So. 386.

Cited in Bacon v. Savannah, 86 Ga. 305, 12 S. E. 580, without special discussion.

Taxation; constitutional restriction of rate.

Cited in Elyton Land Co. v. Birmingham, 89 Ala. 481, 7 So. 901, holding amount of state assessment for preceding year, not enhanced value of property, basis for ascertaining limit of taxation; State v. Southern R. Co. 115 Ala. 257, 22 So. 589, holding state cannot collect school tax not leviable by municipality directly because exceeding constitutional limit.

Constitutional requirement that tax be according to value.

Distinguished in Smith v. County Court, 117 Ala. 198, 23 So. 141, holding special vehicle tax for improvement of roads, unconstitutional.

Taxation for local improvements.

Approved in Birmingham v. Lewis, 92 Ala. 356, 9 So. 243, holding lack of funds no defense to city for injury by uncovered ditch crossing sidewalk where corporate powers for raising funds are not exhausted; Montgomery v. Birdsong, 126 Ala. 651, 28 So. 522, upholding enforcement of paving tax against abutting owner for one quarter of the cost of the improvement; Austin v. Seattle, 2 Wash. 669, 27 Pac. 557, sustaining assessment for street improvement upon lands benefitted, according to frontage.

Cited in Atlanta v. First Presby. Church, 86 Ga. 737, 12 L. R. A. 854, 13 S. E. 252, holding church exemption from general taxation does not include assessments for local improvements.

Cited in footnotes to Gilson v. Rush County, 11 L. R. A. 835, which holds personal property liable to taxation for price of toll road purchased to make it a free road; *Re* Orkney Street, 48 L. R. A. 274, which denies right to assess property abutting on *cul-de-sac* for extension converting same into open street.

Cited in notes (28 L. R. A. 499) on charging expense of grading for sidewalk upon abutting owner; (12 L. R. A. 852) on nonexemption of church property from special assessment.

Legislative power limited only by constitutional restriction.

Cited in Southern R. Co. v. St. Clair County, 124 Ala. 494, 27 So. 23, holding legislation not prohibited by Constitution, valid; Nicrosi v. Phillipi, 91 Ala. 307, 8 So. 561, holding constitutional provision as to rights of resident foreigners limitation, not grant, of legislative power.

8 L. R. A. 375, WHEAT v. DINGLE, 32 S. C. 473, 11 S. E. 394.

Insolvent estates; dividends on secured claims.

Cited in Jamison v. Adler-Goldman Commission Co. 59 Ark. 557, 28 S. W. 35, and Erle v. Lane, 22 Colo. 278, 44 Pac. 591, holding dividend should be computed on balance after crediting security; *Ex parte* Felder, 61 S. C. 537, 39 S. E. 737 (dissenting opinion), to point that dividend should not be computed on balance after applying proceeds of foreclosure.

Distinguished in Ragsdale v. Winnsboro Bank, 45 S. C. 582, 23 S. E. 947, holding secured creditors entitled to dividend from sureties' estates upon face of claim, regardless of amount received from principal's estate; Chemical Nat. Bank v. Armstrong, 28 L. R. A. 235, 8 C. C. A. 160, 16 U. S. App. 465, 59 Fed. 377, holding that claims of creditors of insolvent nation credit for collections from collaterals after bank's i Bank, 173 U. S. 169, 43 L. ed. 654, 19 Sup. Ct. R majority holding secured creditor of insolvent natio upon face of claim without crediting security.

Assignment; acceptance by secured creditor.

Distinguished in Atlantic Phosphate Co. v. Law, holding creditor does not waive security by acceptin

8 L. R. A. 378, ABRAHAMS v. CALIFORNIA POW 23 Pac. 785.

Negligence as to explosives.

Cited in note (29 L. R. A. 727) on negligence in

8 L. R. A. 380, COLEMAN v. FULLER, 105 N. C. 32

Guaranty.

Cited in footnotes to Staver v. Locke, 17 L. R. A. (notes taken by agent for goods sold, not covered by g of agent's engagements; Blyth v. Pinkerton, 57 L. R anty of detective's salary and expenses in working up viction of suspect and settlement of bill.

8 L. R. A. 383, GARDINER v. GARDINER, 65 N. H

Revocation of wills; by subsequent additions o

Cited in Barnewall v. Murrell, 108 Ala. 389, 18 Sc made as required by statute do not affect validity of

Cited footnotes to Billington v. Jones, 56 L. R. A voked by writing on it statement that it is void, s filing it away; Miles's Appeal, 36 L. R. A. 176, wh legacy from will not revocation of legacy; Cutler v. C holds will revoked by adopting mutilations by vermi

8 L. R. A. 385, MISSOURI P. R. CO. v. SHARITT, 4 143, 23 Pac. 430.

Garnishment in another state as defense.

Followed, in Chicago, R. I. & P. R. Co. v. Sturn, 5 holding judgment for wages against employer as ga are not exempt, no bar to action for wages in stat

Cited in Chicago, R. I. & P. R. Co. v. Campbell, 5 holding garnishment proceedings pending in anot exempt no defense to employee's action; National (Del.) 60, 44 L. R. A. 121, 69 Am. St. Rep. 99, 42 of debt in another state without personal jurisdicti action; Willard v. Sturm, 96 Iowa, 556, 65 N. W. 84 ings against employer for wages due employee not suit for wages in other state against former, and rec

Cited in footnote to O'Connor v. Walter, 23 L. R.

ment of wages in other state by assignee of claim against employee not conclusive as between assignor and employee.

Disapproved in Chicago, R. I. & P. R. Co. v. Sturm, 174 U. S. 713, 43 L. ed. 1145, 19 Sup. Ct. Rep. 797, holding garnishment proceedings pending in another state defense to employee's action for wages; Harvey v. Great Northern R. Co. 50 Minn. 408, 17 L. R. A. 89, 52 N. W. 905, holding prior attachment in another state bars action on debt.

Successive garnishments.

Cited in footnotes to Siever v. Union P. R. Co. 61 L. R. A. 319, which sustains right to injunction against prosecuting multiplicity of garnishment proceedings for exempt wages; Rustad v. Bishop, 50 L. R. A. 168, which denies right to hold back successive exempt wages by successive garnishments, and reach same by new garnishment after exemption period expires.

Situs of debts.

Cited in Central Trust Co. v. Chattanooga, R. & C. R. Co. 68 Fed. 689, holding situs of debt follows creditor's domicil; Gibbins v. Adamson, 5 Kan. App. 93, 48 Pac. 871, holding situs of mortgage for purposes of taxation is owner's residence; Illinois C. R. Co. v. Smith, 70 Miss. 347, 19 L. R. A. 580, 35 Am. St. Rep. 651, 12 So. 461, holding domicil of debtor and creditor, where debt is payable, situs of debt.

— For purposes of garnishment.

Cited in Louisville & N. R. Co. v. Nash, 118 Ala. 487, 41 L. R. A. 333, 72 Am. St. Rep. 181, 23 So. 825, holding debt garnishable only at creditor's domicil; Atchinson, T. & S. F. R. Co. v. Maggard, 6 Colo. App. 96, 39 Pac. 985, holding wages can be garnished only in state where employee resides and renders services; Everett v. Connecticut Mut. L. Ins. Co. 4 Colo. App. 514, 36 Pac. 616, holding debt owing nonresident creditor cannot be garnished by service of process on agent of nonresident debtor; Reimers v. Seatco Mfg. Co. 30 L. R. A. 367, 17 C. C. A. 231, 37 U. S. App. 426, 70 Fed. 577, holding debt cannot be garnished in state where plaintiff, defendant, and garnishee nonresidents, by service on garnishee's agent; National Bank v. Furtick, 2 Marv. (Del.) 53, 44 L. R. A. 118, 69 Am. St. Rep. 99, 42 Atl. 479, holding debt due nonresident for loss of property insured in another state, from foreign insurance company, not garnishable.

Cited in footnotes to Strause Bros. v. Aetna Ins. Co. 48 L. R. A. 452, which holds debt of insurance company for loss in other state without situs for garnishment purposes in third state where company has agent; Lancashire Ins. Co. v. Corbetts, 36 L. R. A. 640, which authorizes garnishment of foreign corporation for debt due nonresident; Tootle v. Coleman, 57 L. R. A. 120, which holds right to garnish debtor not limited to situs of chose in action; Louisville & N. R. Co. v. Nash, 41 L. R. A. 331, which holds garnishment of debt due nonresident not personally served in state, invalid.

Distinguished in McBee v. Purcell Nat. Bank, 1 Ind. Terr. 292, 37 S. W. 55, holding deposit in bank garnishable there regardless of depostior's residence; Pennsylvania R. Co. v. Rogers, 52 W. Va. 459, 62 L. R. A. 184, 44 S. E. 300, holding debt owing by foreign railroad corporation having agency, but operating no line, within state, not garnishable.

Disapproved in Tootle v. Coleman, 57 L. R. A. 123, 46 C. C. A. 135, 107 Fed. 43, holding debt due nonresident creditor from resident debtor may be attached.

Conclusiveness of judgments of other states.

Cited in Wyeth Hardware & Mfg. Co. v. Lang, 54 tutional requirement that faith and credit be givei states does not preclude inquiry into jurisdiction.

Statutes of other states.

Cited in Baltimore & O. S. W. R. Co. v. McDon statutes of another state will not be judicially noti

8 L. R. A. 393, HEGELER v. COMSTOCK, 1 S. D.

Negotiability of note.

Cited in National Bank of Commerce v. Feeney, 76 Am. St. Rep. 594, 80 N. W. 186, Reversing 9 S. W. 874, holding stipulation on margin of note foi turity destroys negotiability; Randolph v. Hudson holding provision for interest at certain rate from renders note non-negotiable; Second Nat. Bank v. U. S. App. 541, 65 Fed. 61, holding stipulation to collection" destroys negotiability; Stadler v. First Am. St. Rep. 582, 56 Pac. 111, and Stebbins v. La 847, holding note including promise to pay attorne suit non-negotiable; Brooke v. Struthers, 110 Mich. 272. holding provision in mortgage accompanying become due on failure to pay taxes, destroys negoti

Cited in footnotes to Gordon v. Anderson, 12 L. payable to certain person "*et al.*, or order," non-r delphia Ball Club, 11 L. R. A. 860, which holds nego ing no seal not affected by purported seal.

Distinguished in Merrill v. Hurley, 6 S. D. 598, 5 958, holding negotiability of note not affected by pr after maturity; Chandler v. Kennedy, 8 S. D. 64, 6 stipulation for attorney's fee does not destroy negoti

Non-negotiable notes; rights of assignee.

Cited in Searles v. Seipp, 6 S. D. 477, 61 N. W. negotiable note takes subject to equities between o

8 L. R. A. 398, *Re* ROBINSON, 29 Neb. 135, 26 Am

Liability of extradited persons to civil or cri

Distinguished in State *ex rel.* Petry v. Leidigh, holding extradited person may be prosecuted for ot Walker, 61 Neb. 814, 86 N. W. 510, holding one ext titled to reasonable time to return before service o

8 L. R. A. 399, MURDOCK PARLOR GRATE CO. E. 854.

Liability of state or governmental agency to

Cited in Nash v. Com. 174 Mass. 338, 54 N. E. 865 be party to action to subject moneys due to contra ment of material man; Locke v. State, 140 N. Y. 482

cannot be sued in case where it has not consented to liability; Moody v. State Prison, 128 N. C. 14, 53 L. R. A. 855, 38 S. E. 131, holding act establishing liability of state to suit does not extend to actions for negligence; Houston v. State, 98 Wis. 487, 42 L. R. A. 50, 74 N. W. 111, holding statute permitting action against state does not extend to action for wrongful destruction of supposedly diseased cattle.

Cited in footnote to Gross v. Kentucky Board of Managers, 43 L. R. A. 703, which sustains right to sue state board of managers of World's Fair Exposition without consent of state.

Cited in notes (11 L. R. A. 370) on state immunity from suit in its own courts (42 L. R. A. 35); on what claims constitute valid demands against state.

— Governmental agency.

Cited in Sargent v. Gilford, 66 N. H. 543, 27 Atl. 306, holding towns not liable for defective highways in absence of statutory provision.

8 L. R. A. 403, STATE *ex rel.* ROTWITT v. HICKMAN, 9 Mont. 370, 23 Pac. 740.

Appropriations; necessity and sufficiency.

Cited in State *ex rel.* Wade v. Kenney, 10 Mont. 486, 26 Pac. 197, holding statute providing definite salary for definite service sufficient appropriation to authorize payment; State *ex rel.* Buck v. Hickman, 10 Mont. 499, 26 Pac. 387, holding constitutional provision for judge's salary sufficient appropriation of same; Weston v. Herdman, 64 Neb. 29, 89 N. W. 384, holding legislative appropriation unnecessary where Constitution provides officer's salary "shall be fixed by law, not to exceed" certain sum; State *ex rel.* Hawes v. Mason, 153 Mo. 59, 54 S. W. 524, holding appropriation by municipal council not necessary where statute provides for police salary and its auditing; State *ex rel.* Henderson v. Burdick, 4 Wyo. 280, 24 L. R. A. 268, footnote p. 266, 33 Pac. 125, holding special appropriation to meet state examiner's salary provided for by statute creating office, unnecessary; Carr v. State, 127 Ind. 210, 11 L. R. A. 372, 22 Am. St. Rep. 624, 26 N. E. 778, holding sinking fund created expressly for payment of state indebtedness sufficient appropriation of designated funds.

Cited in note (13 L. R. A. 222) on preliminaries necessary to withdrawal of public funds.

Distinguished in State *ex rel.* Journal Pub. Co. v. Kenney, 9 Mont. 394, 24 Pac. 97, holding public printer not entitled to mandamus to compel state auditor to draw warrant, in absence of legislative appropriation for payment; Shattuck v. Kincaid, 31 Or. 388, 49 Pac. 758, holding statutory determination of amount and time of payment of salary not continuing appropriation obviating necessity of renewal; Pickle v. Finley, 91 Tex. 486, 44 S. W. 480, holding statute fixing salary indefinitely not valid as appropriation for more than constitutional period of two years.

8 L. R. A. 406, MILLER v. SHIELDS, 124 Ind. 166, 24 N. E. 670.

Rights and disabilities of married women.

Cited in Haynes v. Nowlin, 129 Ind. 585, 14 L. R. A. 790, 28 Am. St. Rep. 213, 29 N. E. 389, holding that wife may maintain action for alienation of husband's affections.

Cited in footnote to Hunt v. Reilly, 59 L. R. A. 206, which holds that wife's

failure to notify purchaser of rights after lean
husband's deed does not estop her to claim dowe

— As to contracts.

Cited in Dailey v. Dailey, 26 Ind. App. 18, 58 N
tract to join in conveyance of husband's separa
promise to pay her portion of proceeds: Crisma
N. E. 1101, holding liability of wife on lease and
that she did not occupy premises; Young v. McFad
holding wife bound on note executed jointly with h
in defense of husband; Kedy v. Kramer, 129 Ind. 4
liable on purchase-money notes for land, executec
she acquires beneficial interest; Magel v. Milligan,
382, 50 N. E. 564, holding husband and wife pre
note secured by property held as tenants by entiret
Ind. 22, 27 N. E. 173, holding secret agreement l
of loan secured by wife by mortgage of separate pr
bility; Lackey v. Boruff, 152 Ind. 374, 53 N. E. 4
defense on suretyship contracts, not available to th
wife's mortgage; Morningstar v. Hardwick, 3 Ind.
ing wife's note in payment for transcript on appeal
surety contract, where benefit accrues to her by re
Ind. 56, 38 N. E. 406, holding married woman not
against payee aware of application of proceeds; V
275, 16 L. R. A. 48, 31 N. E. 70 (dissenting opinio
woman not liable to innocent purchaser in due co
suretyship on face.

Cited in footnotes to National Granite Bank v. T
authorizes action at law against estate of married
on her credit, though notes given by her void; Ki
914, which holds married woman liable on her gu
and payable to her order.

Burden of proving and pleading exception.

Cited in Potter v. Sheets, 5 Ind. App. 510, 32
plaintiff to prove that wife is principal in note e
where answer shows marital relation; Field v. N
841, holding exception sufficiently pleaded by stat
of note for husband's debt, and nonreceipt of proce
529, 65 N. E. 186, holding burden on wife to pro
note and mortgage on land held by entireties, as
Ind. 165, 64 N. E. 603, holding complaint showing
ed by married woman alone or with husband, no
principalship, sufficient; Jackson County v. State
holding nonexistence of exception under statute
building need not be pleaded, being matter of de
compliance.

8 L. R. A. 410, STANDARD OIL CO. v. GILBERT

8 L. R. A. 412, CARSON v. MEMPHIS & C. R. CO. 88 Tenn. 646, 17 Am. St. Rep. 921, 13 S. W. 588.

Duty of garnishee to plead exemption.

Cited in footnote to Missouri P. R. Co. v. Whipker, 8 L. R. A. 321, which holds garnishee unprotected who does not set out facts showing exemption.

Cited in note (19 L. R. A. 580) on duty of garnishee to set up exemption of principal debtor.

Extraterritorial effect of exemption laws.

Cited in Chicago, R. I. & P. R. Co. v. Sturm, 174 U. S. 718, 43 L. ed. 1147, 19 Sup. Ct. Rep. 797, holding exemption laws do not follow debt into another jurisdiction; Central Trust Co. v. Chattanooga, R. & C. R. Co. 68 Fed. 697, raising, without deciding, whether exemption laws of one state have effect in another; Graham v. Stull, 92 Tenn. 680, 21 L. R. A. 247, 22 S. W. 738, holding nonresident's widow not entitled to year's support out of estate.

8 L. R. A. 414, POND v. SHEEAN, 132 Ill. 312, 23 N. E. 1018.

Statute of frauds.

Cited in Dicken v. McKinley, 163 Ill. 322, 54 Am. St. Rep. 471, 45 N. E. 134, holding oral promise to devise land to adopted child, based upon consent of child and parents, not binding as against other devisees, in absence of possession by child.

Cited in notes (14 L. R. A. 862) on effect of statute of frauds; (9 L. R. A. 129) on promises not to be performed within one year.

Distinguished in Quinn v. Quinn, 5 S. D. 333, 49 Am. St. Rep. 875, 58 N. W. 808, holding oral contract with another that child should inherit adopting parent's property, enforceable against fraudulent donees and devisees thereof; Whiton v. Whiton, 76 Ill. App. 568, holding parol agreement not to disinherit, based upon payment of money, binding against donee, where gift operates only as testamentary disposal.

— Entire contracts.

Cited in Swash v. Sharpstein, 14 Wash. 436, 32 L. R. A. 799, 44 Pac. 862, holding parol agreement to devise portion of estate, including both personalty and realty, void as to both where void as to realty; Hamilton v. Thirston, 93 Md. 218, 48 Atl. 709, holding performance by plaintiff does not take parol entire contract to devise share of both real and personal estate out of statute; Grant v. Grant, 63 Conn. 538, 38 Am. St. Rep. 379, 29 Atl. 15, refusing specific performance of oral contract to devise estate, both real and personal, where void as to realty, although promisee's obligation performed; Michigan City v. Leeds, 24 Ind. App. 275, 55 N. E. 799, holding written lease altered orally as to premises occupied, though in other respect unchanged, void where term exceeds length of valid parol lease.

— Effect of part performance of oral contract.

Cited in Swash v. Sharpstein, 14 Wash. 436, 32 L. R. A. 799, 44 Pac. 862, holding transfer of possession essential to validity of oral contract to convey realty; Wright v. Raftree, 181 Ill. 473, 54 N. E. 998, holding oral contract for transfer of land taken out of statute only by payment of purchase money, possession, and valuable improvements; Koenig v. Dohm, 209 Ill. 479, 70 N. E. 1061, holding part payment of purchase money will no out of statute.

Cited in note (14 L. R. A. 863) on effect of pa

Proof of oral contract.

Cited in Wright v. Raftree, 181 Ill. 470, 54 N to enforce, has burden of establishing contract cl

8 L. R. A. 419, JOHNSON v. ST. PAUL & D. R. (

Statutory liability of railroads to employee gence.

Cited in Schus v. Powers-Simpson Co. 85 Mi owner of private logging railroad liable to empl gence; Helms v. Northern P. R. Co. 120 Fed. 39 bility is wholly statutory, joint action for negl employee against it and coemployee; Sams v. St Mo. 78, 61 L. R. A. 482, 73 S. W. 686, holding to employees for fellow servants' negligence inappl

— Hazards peculiar to railroading.

Cited in Akeson v. Chicago, B. & Q. R. Co. 106 railroad liable to employee engaged in filling tende negligence; Steffenson v. Chicago, M. & St. P. R. 272, 47 N. W. 1068, holding railroad liable to fellow servant in operating hand car; Missouri, Kan. 155, 55 Pac. 875, holding railroad not liable around depot for fellow servant's negligence; O' 80 Minn. 31, 51 L. R. A. 539, 82 N. W. 1086, section hand engaged in tearing down bridge, fo Weisel v. Eastern R. Co. 79 Minn. 249, 82 N. W. to employee in gravel pit, injured by coal fallin Pearson v. Chicago, M. & St. P. R. Co. 47 Minn. road not liable for negligence of plaintiff's fellow

Distinguished in Smith v. St. Paul & D. R. Co holding railroad liable to section hand working on

Disapproved in effect in Callahan v. St. Louis M Co. 170 Mo. 490, 60 L. R. A. 254, 94 Am. St. Re railroad liable for negligence of fellow section han

Class and special legislation.

Cited in State *ex rel.* Courthouse & City Hall C 58 N. W. 150, holding act authorizing bonds to courthouse in Minneapolis not special; State *ex re* County, 48 Minn. 239, 31 Am. St. Rep. 650, 51 N claring emission of dense smoke in city of St. P nuisance, unconstitutional; State v. Garbroski, 11 82 Am. St. Rep. 524, 82 N. W. 959, holding act exempting Union soldiers, unconstitutional; Low 142, 24 L. R. A. 708, 43 Am. St. Rep. 670, 59 N. W excepting from its operation farm and domestic la Dawson County v. Farmers & M. Irrig. Co. 59 Neb exempting irrigation companies from operation of law requiring maintenance of bridges over ditches crossing highways, invalid.

Cited in footnote to Ballard v. Mississippi Cotton Oil Co. 62 L. R. A. 407, which holds statute making corporations, but not individuals, liable for defective appliances of which employees knew, unconstitutional.

8 L. R. A. 420, DUFFIES v. DUFFIES, 76 Wis. 374, 20 Am. St. Rep. 79, 45 N. W. 522.

Action for alienating affections.

Cited in note (11 L. R. A. 549) on inducements to violate obligations, not actionable.

— Of wife.

Cited in footnote to Sanborn v. Gale, 26 L. R. A. 864, which holds running of limitation against action for alienation of wife's affections not prevented by agreement of parties to adultery; known to husband, to deny same.

— Of husband.

Discussed at length and reaffirmed in Lonstorf v. Lonstorf, 118 Wis. 160, 95 N. W. 961, denying wife's right of action for alienation of husband's affections.

Cited in footnotes to Doe v. Roe, 8 L. R. A. 833, which holds action for alienating husband's affections by debauching and carnally knowing him, not maintainable; Houghton v. Rice, 47 L. R. A. 311, which denies right of action against other woman for alienating husband's affections, unaccompanied by adultery; Hodgkinson v. Hodgkinson, 27 L. R. A. 120, which holds one bringing about husband's desertion liable to suit by wife; Dietzman v. Mullin, 50 L. R. A. 808, and Betser v. Betser, 52 L. R. A. 630, which sustain wife's right of action for alienating her husband's affections.

Cited in notes (10 L. R. A. 468) on liability for interrupting marital relations; (32 L. R. A. 623) on right of wife to maintain action.

Disapproved in Warren v. Warren, 89 Mich. 125, 14 L. R. A. 546, footnote p. 545, 50 N. W. 842; Humphrey v. Pope, 122 Cal. 257, 54 Pac. 847; Wolf v. Frank, 92 Md. 140, 52 L. R. A. 104, footnote p. 102, 48 Atl. 132,— holding that wife may maintain action for alienation of husband's affections; Smith v. Smith, 98 Tenn. 107, 60 Am. St. Rep. 838, 38 S. W. 439, holding that wife cannot, without enabling statute, enforce right of action for alienating husband's affections; Price v. Price, 91 Iowa, 696, 29 L. R. A. 151, 51 Am. St. Rep. 360, 60 N. W. 202; Gernerd v. Gernerd, 185 Pa. 237, 40 L. R. A. 550, 42 W. N. C. 51, 64 Am. St. Rep. 646, 39 Atl. 884; Haynes v. Nowlin, 129 Ind. 586, 14 L. R. A. 790, 28 Am. St. Rep. 213, 29 N. E. 389; Clow v. Chapman, 125 Mo. 103, 26 L. R. A. 413, footnote p. 412, 46 Am. St. Rep. 468, 28 S. W. 328; Beach v. Brown, 20 Wash. 267, 43 L. R. A. 115, 72 Am. St. Rep. 98, 55 Pac. 46,— holding under enabling acts wife may sue for alienation of husband's affections.

Wife's action for crim. con.

Cited in Kroessin v. Keller, 60 Minn. 375, 27 L. R. A. 686, 51 Am. St. Rep. 533, 62 N. W. 438, holding wife cannot maintain action for *crim. con.* against another woman.

Loss of consortium as element of husband's damages.

Cited in Selleck v. Janesville, 104 Wis. 577, 47 L. R. A. 694, 76 Am. St. Rep.

892, 80 N. W. 946, holding husband may recove assistance, as well as money value of wife's ser

Actions for damage to person; what are.

Cited in Murray v. Buell, 76 Wis. 662, 20 . holding cause of action for conspiracy not assi person."

Damages for mental suffering.

Cited in Rueping v. Chicago & N. W. R. Co. 1013, 93 N. W. 843, holding compensatory dama arising from wilful act.

8 L. R. A. 425, STONE v. HAMMELL, 83 Ca Pac. 703.

Surety's right of action against principal.

Approved in Yule v. Bishop, 133 Cal. 579, 65 surety paying obligation has action for money p of payment; Barth v. Graf, 101 Wis. 38, 76 N. W action upon principal's implied promise to inden ment.

Limitation of action as to surety.

Approved in Northwestern Nat. Bank v. Great 7, 57 Pac. 440, holding surety's statutory action not "ordinary action" barred by lapse of three Ohio St. 35, 71 Am. St. Rep. 707, 53 N. E. 447, subrogated to mortgage paid for principal, barre

8 L. R. A. 427, SULLIVAN v. MAINE C. R. C

Violation of Sunday laws.

Cited in Donovan v. McCarty, 155 Mass. 547, ment of property in trust, by severely injured wo day.

Cited in footnote to Com. v. Waldman, 11 L. barber shop open on Sunday not work of necessit

Cited in note (11 L. R. A. 63) on legality of cc

— As defense to negligence action.

Cited in Cleveland v. Bangor, 87 Me. 266, 47 holding driving for air and exercise no violation 89 Me. 573, 36 Atl. 1048, holding riding bicycle to v. Portsmouth Bridge, 68 N. H. 383, 73 Am. St. traveling for pleasure on Sunday violation of stat

Cited in footnote to Gloss v. Miller, 26 L. R. Sunday law by hunting no defense to action for

8 L. R. A. 428, MILLER v. OTTAWAY, 81 Mic N. W. 665.

Rights of bona fide holders.

Approved in Rublee v. Davis, 33 Neb. 784, 2

135. holding bona fide purchaser before maturity of note given for purchase price of jack not affected by breach of warranty of which he did not know.

Cited in Jennings v. Todd, 118 Mo. 305, 40 Am. St. Rep. 373, 24 S. W. 148; United States Nat. Bank v. Floss, 38 Or. 72, 84 Am. St. Rep. 752, 62 Pac. 751; Kinkel v. Harper, 7 Colo. App. 54, 42 Pac. 173,— holding knowledge of existence of executory agreement for which note given does not defeat bona fide transferee's right to recover.

Presumption of indorsee's good faith.

Cited in Voorhees v. Fisher, 9 Utah, 308, 34 Pac. 64, holding possession of note before maturity presumptively lawful and bona fide.

8 L. R. A. 429, WESTERN U. TELEG. CO. v. WILLIAMS, 86 Va. 696, 19 Am. St. Rep. 908, 11 S. E. 106.

Ownership of fee in highway.

Cited in Page v. Belvin, 88 Va. 989, 14 S. E. 843, and Hodges v. Seaboard & R. R. Co. 88 Va. 654, 14 S. E. 380, holding fee of highway remains in abutting owner.

What is additional servitude.

Cited in Jaynes v. Omaha Street R. Co. 53 Neb. 649, 39 L. R. A. 757, 74 N. W. 67, holding poles and wires of electric railway additional servitude; Reid Bros. v. Norfolk City R. Co. 94 Va. 121, 36 L. R. A. 275, 64 Am. St. Rep. 708, 26 S. E. 428, holding conversion of single track horse-car railway into double track electric not additional servitude; Meyer v. Richmond, 172 U. S. 95, 43 L. ed. 379, 19 Sup. Ct. Rep. 106, holding obstruction of street under municipal ordinance by railroad not in front of plaintiff's property, not additional taking; Home Bldg. & Conveyance Co. v. Roanoke, 91 Va. 61, 27 L. R. A. 554, 20 S. E. 895, holding approach to bridge over tracks in city street not additional servitude.

— Telegraph and telephone lines.

Approved in Krueger v. Wisconsin Teleph. Co. 106 Wis. 108, 50 L. R. A. 304, 81 N. W. 1041; Donovan v. Allert (N. D.) 58 L. R. A. 779, 91 N. W. 441; Chesapeake & P. Teleph. Co. v. Mackenzie, 74 Md. 47, 28 Am. St. Rep. 219, 21 Atl. 690; East Tennessee Teleph. Co. v. Russellville, 106 Ky. 670, 51 S. W. 308; Bronson v. Albion Teleph. Co. (Neb.) 60 L. R. A. 428, 93 N. W. 201,— holding telephone poles and wires additional servitude; Hodges v. Western U. Teleg. Co. 133 N. C. 235, 45 S. E. 572, holding telegraph line on railroad's right of way, additional servitude; Cater v. Northwestern Teleph. Exch. Co. 60 Minn. 550, 28 L. R. A. 315, 51 Am. St. Rep. 543, 63 N. W. 111 (dissenting opinion), majority holding telephone poles and wires not additional servitude.

Cited in notes (17 L. R. A. 480, 24 L. R. A. 721) on telegraph and telephone lines as additional burden on highway.

Distinguished in Magee v. Overshiner, 150 Ind. 139, 40 L. R. A. 374, 65 Am. St. Rep. 358, 49 N. E. 951, holding reasonable use of city streets for telephone system not additional servitude.

8 L. R. A. 438, STATE v. ROBBINS, 124 Ind. 308, 24 N. E. 978.

Right to seize articles connected with criminal act.

Cited in Newman v. People, 23 Colo. 311, 47 Pac. 278, holding it sheriff's duty, independent of statute, to seize gambling devices, and Mutual Commission

& Stock Co. v. Moore, 13 App. D. C. 86, holdin guilt may be seized by officer making arrest.

Due process in seizure or destruction of p

Cited in Newman v. People, 23 Colo. 307, 47 deciding, question whether act providing for dest out notice to owner constitutional; Loesch v. Ko 683, 41 N. E. 326, holding statute permitting k jured, abandoned, or diseased animals without n

Cited in footnotes to Police Comrs. v. Wagne police officers may be empowered to seize propert Gee, 24 L. R. A. 355, which upholds act authorizi lands without notice for highway repairs.

Disapproved in Lawton v. Steele, 152 U. S. 143, 499, upholding act authorizing summary destructi

8 L. R. A. 440, NEWELL v. MEYENDORFF, 9 1 23 Pac. 333.

Formulation of record.

Approved in Becker v. Yellowstone County, 10 to consider record where material in disordered Mont. 60, 24 Pac. 699, refusing to consider staten script of stenographer's notes by question and an Co. 16 Mont. 116, 40 Pac. 182, holding stateme orderly and chronological order.

Contracts in restraint of trade.

Distinguished in State *ex rel.* Robert Mitchell F 35, 55 L. R. A. 649, 91 Am. St. Rep. 386, 66 Pa made after advertisement limiting right to bid to

Estoppel — By obtaining ruling.

Approved in State v. Lucey, 24 Mont. 304, 61 complain of instructions submitted by counsel;] 43 Pac. 706, holding party unable to complain Reynolds v. Fitzpatrick, 28 Mont. 177, 72 Pac. 510 decision obtained upon his prior appeal; State *ex* Dist. Court, 10 Mont. 460, 26 Pac. 183, holdin cannot decline to pay costs and offer to proceed w

Distinguished in Fisher v. Briscoe, 10 Mont. 1 upon motion to strike not conclusive on court, pleadings after amendment.

— By pleading.

Approved in Maul v. Schultz, 19 Mont. 341, suing for reasonable value who proves written le proof of modification of lease; Newell v. Nichols holding plaintiff in action for entire purchase] sold by defendants; Gettings v. Buchanan, 17 M original complaint *functus officio* by filing amende

Distinguished in State *ex rel.* Leech v. Choteau

879, holding canvassing board in answer to mandate to canvass, not confined to reasons in official record.

New trial for change in ruling.

Cited in Porter v. Industrial Printing Co. 26 Mont. 180, 66 Pac. 839, holding change in ruling of court, before and after trial, as to sufficiency of pleading of counterclaims, ground for new trial.

8 L. R. A. 443, GORE v. TOWNSEND, 105 N. C. 228, 11 S. E. 160.

Inchoate dower as property.

Cited in Crosby v. Farmers' Bank, 107 Mo. 444, 17 S. W. 1004, holding wife's inchoate dower entitles her to have mortgaged land sold in parcels; Lackett v. Rumbaugh, 45 Fed. 36, holding wife's inchoate dower right valuable consideration for transfer; Southern Loan & T. Co. v. Benbow, 135 N. C. 312, 47 S. E. 435, holding wife's joining in mortgage of husband's lands valuable consideration for his note to her.

Cited in note (13 L. R. A. 442) on dower; bar of inchoate right.

Wife as husband's surety.

Cited in Hedrick v. Byerly, 119 N. C. 421, 25 S. E. 1020, holding wife joining in conveyance of separate property to secure husband's debt, becomes surety; Smith v. Old Dominion Bldg. & L. Asso. 119 N. C. 259, 26 S. E. 40, holding tender releases wife's property mortgaged as security for husband's debt; Shew v. Call, 119 N. C. 455, 56 Am. St. Rep. 678, 26 S. E. 33, holding husband's land should be sold first under mortgage of lands of husband and wife to secure his debt; Hinton v. Greenleaf, 113 N. C. 7, 18 S. E. 56, holding agreement to postpone sale of husband's security discharges property of wife mortgaged to secure husband's debt.

8 L. R. A. 446, CARLETON MILLS CO. v. SILVER, 82 Me. 215, 19 Atl. 154.

Grant of water power.

Cited in Hall v. Sterling Iron & R. Co. 148 N. Y. 440, 42 N. E. 1056, construing grant of water power sufficient to operate designated establishment, where intention doubtful, as indicating quantity, not restricting use.

Cited in note (9 L. R. A. 195) on franchises of water companies.

8 L. R. A. 448, JAMES v. WOOD, 82 Me. 173, 19 Atl. 160.

Property in animals feræ naturæ.

Cited in State v. Parker, 89 Me. 85, 35 L. R. A. 280, footnote p. 279, 35 Atl. 1021, holding deer in park not "possessed" within exception of statute prohibiting killing during close season; Smith v. State, 155 Ind. 623, 51 L. R. A. 409, 58 N. E. 1044 (dissenting opinion), majority holding possession during close season, though commenced in open, unlawful.

Trover.

Cited in Stevens v. Gordon, 87 Me. 567, 33 Atl. 27, holding mere possession of land sufficient to support trover for grass cut therefrom.

Trespass.

Cited in Corthell v. Holmes, 88 Me. 380, 34 Atl. 173, holding act done in removal of obstruction to public way, not invasion of property right.

:8 L. R. A. 450, HARE v. McINTYRE, 82 Me. 240,

Fellow servant's liability for negligence.

Cited in note (28 L. R. A. 440) on liability
negligence.

Correspondence between pleading and pro

Cited in Glover v. Jones, 95 Me. 307, 49 Atl.
not alleged will not justify decree.

Assumption of risk.

Cited in Adolff v. Columbia Pretzel & Baking
321' holding assumption of risk by employee orde
for which hired, question for jury; Tucker v. No
68 Pac. 426, holding employee's assumption of ri
ness need not be averred.

:8 L. R. A. 453, FOBES v. ROME, W. & O. R. CC

Actionable invasion of abutter's right.

Approved in Mangam v. Sing Sing, 11 App.
holding abutter's right to recover abandoned hi
other public purposes; Brown v. San Francisco, 12
mere inconvenience to abutter upon street diminish
not damage to be compensated.

Cited in Garrett v. Lake Roland Elev. R. Co.
20 Atl. 830, holding construction of stone abutme
interfering with light and air, no taking of abutt
Island R. Co. 89 App. Div. 385, 85 N. Y. Supp. 93
fee in highway, cannot recover damages for constr
railroad; Reining v. New York, L. & W. R. Co. 35
238, holding abutter to be compensated for loss
constituting change of grade; Castle v. Bell Tele
N. Y. Supp. 482 (dissenting opinion), majority
accommodate wires on poles therein, not additional

Distinguished in Palmer v. Larchmont Electric
Supp. 522; Eels v. American Teleph. & Teleg. Co.
38 N. E. 202, holding electric wire line upon c
abutter's rights.

— Railway in street.

Approved in Case v. Cayuga County, 88 Hun, 61,
v. Coney Island & B. R. Co. 5 App. Div. 468, 39 N.
of highway for surface railroad not infringement o
to street; Syracuse Solar Salt Co. v. Rome, W. &
N. Y. Supp. 590, holding abutter bounded by exteri
for consequential damages from reasonable use of
v. Mineola, H. & F. Traction Co. 178 N. Y. 515, 71
Div. 492, 78 N. Y. Supp. 937, holding abutter not
enjoin construction of street railroad; Peck v. Sch
63 N. E. 357, holding electric surface railroad
Taylor v. New York & H. R. Co. 27 App. Div. 202
railway liable for use of temporary structure outsid

by city; Fries v. New York & H. R. Co. 169 N. Y. 285, 62 N. E. 358, holding abutter not damaged by change for public convenience of grade of railway rightfully in street; Peck v. Schenectady R. Co. 67 App. Div. 360, 73 N. Y. Supp. 794, sustaining right of abutter with fee in street, to injunction against street railway; Syracuse Solar Salt Co. v. Rome, W. & O. R. Co. 43 App. Div. 206, 60 N. Y. Supp. 40, holding abutter with title in street to be compensated for damage to business from dirt and dust from railway in street; Lamm v. Chicago, St. P. M. & O. R. Co. 45 Minn. 78, 10 L. R. A. 271, 47 N. W. 455, holding that abutter has easements of access, light, and air in whole width of street irrespective of ownership of fee; Conabeer v. New York C. & H. R. R. Co. 156 N. Y. 487, 51 N. E. 402, holding that deed conveying right to operate and maintain railway in street includes consequential damages from operation; McCruden v. Rochester R. Co. 5 Misc. 61, 25 N. Y. Supp. 114, holding right to lay tracks without compensation to owner of fee, not within common council's authorization; Bucholz v. New York, L. E. & W. R. Co. 66 Hun, 380, 21 N. Y. Supp. 503, holding railway not liable for cutting off travel upon premises by authorized change of crossing; Detroit Citizens' Street R. Co. v. Detroit, 26 L. R. A. 675, 12 C. C. A. 373, 22 U. S. App. 570, 64 Fed. 637, raising without deciding question whether general power to regulate use of streets authorizes consent to use for street railway purposes for term or in perpetuity; Kane v. New York Elev. R. Co. 125 N. Y. 176, 11 L. R. A. 642, 26 N. E. 278; Duyckinck v. New York Elev. R. Co. 3 Silv. Ct. App. 319, 26 N. E. 278, holding abutter on street belonging to other individuals, entitled to compensation from elevated railway; De Geofroy v. Merchants Bridge Terminal R. Co. 179 Mo. 718, 64 L. R. A. 967, 79 S. W. 386, holding elevated street railroad an additional servitude; Sperb v. Metropolitan Elev. R. Co. 61 Hun, 541, 16 N. Y. Supp. 392, holding elevated railway acquiring right to maintain structure not bound to compensate for injuries incidental to operation; Hindley v. Metropolitan Elev. R. Co. 42 Misc. 63, 85 N. Y. Supp. 561, holding elevated railroad does not acquire easement in certain premises by prescription where recognizing right of other abutting owners to compensation; Sun Printing & Pub. Asso. v. New York, 8 App. Div. 285, 40 N. Y. Supp. 607 (dissenting opinion), majority holding construction of rapid transit railroad within city, legitimate city purpose.

Cited in note (14 L. R. A. 382) in note on injury to abutter's easements by railroad in street.

Distinguished in Abendroth v. Manhattan R. Co. 122 N. Y. 17, 11 L. R. A. 640, 19 Am. St. Rep. 461, 25 N. E. 496, holding elevated railroad liable for obstructing lights and for smoke and cinders, to abutter without interest in street; Sperb v. Metropolitan Elev. R. Co. 137 N. Y. 158, 20 L. R. A. 756, 32 N. E. 1050, holding future damages to abutter's easements to be included in alternative damages given in lieu of injunction; Egerer v. New York C. & H. R. R. Co. 130 N. Y. 116, 14 L. R. A. 385, 29 N. E. 95, holding railroad liable for embankment cutting off access to abutting premises and damaging light and air, although street had been abandoned where no compensation had been made; Reining v. New York, L. & W. R. Co. 128 N. Y. 162, 14 L. R. A. 135, 28 N. E. 640, holding abutter without fee in street entitled to compensation for authorized railway embankment substantially stopping ordinary street usage; Merriman v. Utica Belt Line Street R. Co. 18 Misc. 275, 41 N. Y. Supp. 1049, holding abutter without fee in street may restrain construction of trolley railroad without requisite

consents; Emigrant Mission Committee v. Brook
598, 47 N Y. Supp. 344, holding elevated railroad
ground without specific legislative authority, li
to adjoining property; Jeaume v. New York, L. &
13 N. Y. Supp. 249, holding railroad constructing
formal change of grade, liable for deprivation of
York & H. R. Co. 74 App. Div. 435, 77 Am. St. Re
liability to abutter under statute requiring surfa
does not cover special damages from maintenance o

8 L. R. A. 458, PEOPLE v. E. REMINGTON & S
793.

Action for interest on withheld dividends in Pe
59 Hun, 308, 12 N. Y. Supp. 829.

Obligation of creditor to resort primarily to

Cited in Benecke v. Haebler, 38 App. Div. 348, 58
need not sell collateral before proceeding against
Bristow, 51 App. Div. 304, 64 N. Y. Supp. 892, ho
not bound to resort to collateral given by payee,
maker; Jenkins v. Smith, 21 Misc. 752, 48 N. Y.
need not enforce remedies against indorser of mor
lateral stock before foreclosing, though thereby in
chanic's lien.

Secured creditor's right to share in insolven

Cited in Ragsdale v. Winnsboro Bank, 45 S. C. 5
31 Misc. 304, 64 N. Y. Supp. 360; Williams v. Ov
E. 226,—holding creditor entitled to share *pro rata*
ing on credit assigned as collateral; Third Nat. Ba
L. R. A. 330, 47 N. W. 33, holding mortgagee entitle
on equality with unsecured creditors; Winston v. B
316, holding creditor entitled to share in proportion
realizing on mortgage collateral; *Re* Levin Bros. 13
ing firm creditor secured by mortgage on partner's h
on entire claim; *Re* Simpson, 36 App. Div. 564, 55 N
gagee entitled to prove entire claim against mort
spite of subsequent foreclosure of mortgage; Peopl
Asso. 41 App. Div. 265, 58 N. Y. Supp. 510, holding
insolvent corporation need not prove against speci
ing against general assets; *Re* Snyder, 29 Misc. 6,
creditor entitled to share *pro rata* on face of claim
fund; *Re* Meyer, 78 Wis. 622, 11 L. R. A. 842, foot
435, 48 N. W. 55, holding due-course holder of no
for face of note in assets of both maker and indor
75 N. Y. Supp. 312, holding stock-exchange credi
claim against general assets, in addition to sharing
exchange seat; Davidson v. John Good Cordage &
71 N. Y. Supp. 565, holding court has no power to e
by creditor pending sequestration proceedings; Pe
dent Asso. 161 N. Y. 496, 55 N. E. 1053, upholding

foreign receiver of foreign insolvent, against discrimination against domestic creditors by reason of domestic trust fund transmitted; *Re* Binghamton General Electric Co. 143 N. Y. 264, 38 N. E. 297, refusing to enjoin sale of corporate bonds by creditors on voluntary dissolution of corporation; Chemical Nat. Bank v. Armstrong, 28 L. R. A. 235, 8 C. C. A. 161, 16 U. S. App. 465, 59 Fed. 378, Reversing 50 Fed. 805, holding amount realized in collaterals after insolvency, but before proof of claim, need not be deducted from face of claim; New York Security & T. Co. v. Lombard Invest. Co. 73 Fed. 554, holding realization on collateral since appointment of receiver, does not deprive creditor of right to dividend on face of claim; Tod v. Kentucky Union Land Co. 57 Fed. 64, holding creditor entitled to share in proportion to face of claim where amount realized on collateral does not cover debt; Wheeler v. Walton & W. Co. 72 Fed. 968, holding creditor entitled to share in dividends without surrendering or realizing on collateral; Merrill v. National Bank, 173 U. S. 141, 43 L. ed. 644, 19 Sup. Ct. Rep. 360 (Distinguished in dissenting opinion, Merrill v. National Bank, 173 U. S. 170, 43 L. ed. 654, 19 Sup. Ct. Rep. 375) holding creditor of insolvent national bank may receive dividends on face of claim without deducting realizations on collateral; High v. Fifth Nat. Bank, 97 Mich. 507, 21 L. R. A. 825, 56 N. W. 927 (distinguished in dissenting opinion) holding trustee in certain mortgages for creditors entitled to share in debtor's assets to full-face value of claims.

Cited in footnote to High v. American Wheel Co. 21 L. R. A. 822, which holds secured creditor entitled to dividend on full claim.

Cited in note (11 L. R. A. 328) on creditor's right to dividends.

Distinguished in *Re* Atwood, 3 App. Div. 581, 38 N. Y. Supp. 338, holding consignee cannot prove full amount of claim at time of consignor's assignment where goods held and sales made subsequently; Doolittle v. Smith, 104 Iowa, 406, 73 N. W. 867, and Sullivan v. Erle, 8 Colo. App. 6, 44 Pac. 948, holding creditor realizing on collateral after allowance of full claim against insolvent's assets, may share in final settlement, only on basis of balance; Levy v. Chicago Nat. Bank, 158 Ill. 96, 30 L. R. A. 382, 42 N. E. 129, Reversing 57 Ill. App. 149, holding creditor may share only in proportion to amount of claim at time of proof as reduced by realization on collateral after insolvency; Jamison v. Adler-Goldman Commission Co. 59 Ark. 556, 28 S. W. 35, holding amount realized on collateral by secured creditors should be deducted before ratable distribution of insolvent decedent's estate; *Re* Waddell-Entz Co. 67 Conn. 337, 35 Atl. 257, holding creditor entitled under statute to share only in proportion to amount of claim, less value of security not surrendered.

Disapproved in *Re* Frasch, 5 Wash. 346, 31 Pac. 755, and Philadelphia Warehouse Co. v. Anniston Pipe Works, 106 Ala. 362, 18 So. 43, holding creditor entitled to dividend only in proportion to amount of claim as reduced by collateral realized on.

8 L. R. A. 461, MONTGOMERY COUNTY v. RISTINE, 124 Ind. 242, 24 N. E. 990.

Right of county to reimbursement for charitable expenditures.

Cited in Marshall County v. Burkey, 1 Ind. App. 571, 27 N. E. 1108, holding county cannot recover from husband's estate for wife's clothing and expense of inquest of insanity.

Disapproved in McNairy County v. McCoin, 101 Tenn. 81, 41 L. R. A. 864. 45

S. W. 1070, holding county providing for lunatic indemnity out of estate.

8 L. R. A. 464, PITTSBURGH, C. & ST. L. R. CO. 21 Am. St. Rep. 840, 24 N. E. 658.

Care as to dangerous agencies.

Approved in Alsever v. Minneapolis & St. L. R. 751, 88 N. W. 841, holding employer liable for act off cock to frighten children; Rush v. Spokane Fa 63 Pac. 500, holding railway required to exercise h gence in custody of dynamite; Euting v. Chicago 60 L. R. A. 160, 96 Am. St. Rep. 936, 92 N. W. 3 injury to bystander from torpedo exploded by engin land Terminal & Valley R. Co. v. Marsh, 63 Ohio N. E. 821 (dissenting opinion) majority holding r on right of way where not open to public travel.

Cited in footnotes to St. Louis, A. & T. R. Co. which holds master's duty to protect repair track sufficient if faithfully observed by employees; Nel 793, which holds storing dynamite in partially b quented by children, negligence.

Cited in notes (14 L. R. A. 675) as to negligence i dangerous agencies; (27 L. R. A. 163, 200) as to for the wrongful or negligent act of his servant or claim upon the master by reason of a contract in

8 L. R. A. 467, BELOW v. ROBBINS, 76 Wis. 600, 416.

Exemption laws, what covered by.

Cited in Cleveland v. McCanna, 7 N. D. 459, 41 670, 75 N. W. 908, holding mutual judgments can exemption laws; Wabash R. Co. v. Bowring, 103 holding judgment for exempt property is exempt; 494, 28 N. E. 726, holding debtor may recover fro nished in another state; Puget Sound Dressed Be Wash. 473, 27 L. R. A. 811, 48 Am. St. Rep. 885, 39 property attaches to proceeds of insurance thereon Wis. 355, 91 N. W. 990, holding landlord cannot by asserting claim for rent; Millington v. Laurer, 385, 56 N. W. 533, holding exemption of debtor' assignee.

Cited in note (19 L. R. A. 34) on setting off jud erty.

8 L. R. A. 469, HERRESHOFF v. BOUTINEAU, 1 19 Atl. 712.

Contracts in restraint of trade.

Approved in Oakdale Mfg. Co. v. Garst, 18 R. I. p. 639, 49 Am. St. Rep. 784, 28 Atl. 973, holding oleomargarine will not again engage in business for five years, not unreasonable: Swigert v. Tilden, 121 Iowa, 656, 63 L. R. A. 611, 100 Am. St. Rep. 374, 97 N. W. 82, holding contract of custom-shirt maker, not to compete within state for ten years with purchaser of business, valid; Cowan v. Fairbrother, 118 N. C. 412, 32 L. R. A. 835, 54 Am. St. Rep. 733, 24 S. E. 212, holding agreement not to do newspaper work in county in which is published a newspaper goodwill of which is transferred, not void; Harrison v. Glucose Sugar Ref. Co. 58 L. R. A. 919, 53 C. C. A. 489, 116 Fed. 309, holding employee's contract not to become interested in rival concern within 1,500 miles of plant, not unreasonable; Tillinghast v. Boothby, 20 R. I. 60, 37 Atl. 344, holding stipulation by contract not to practise in county after termination of contract, not unreasonable: Mallinckrodt Chemical Works v. Nemnich, 83 Mo. App. 24 (dissenting opinion) majority holding stipulation not to engage in business sold, for ten years in United States, unreasonable.

Cited in footnotes to Texas Standard Cotton Oil Co. v. Adoue, 15 L. R. A. 598, which holds combination to fix prices of cotton seed and seed cotton void; State v. Phipps, 18 L. R. A. 658, which holds combination by foreign companies to increase rates of insurance unlawful; Nester v. Continental Brewing Co. 24 L. R. A. 247, which holds combination of brewers to stifle competition within specified place void; Chaplin v. Brown, 12 L. R. A. 428, which holds grocer's agreement not to buy butter from maker's for two years if firm opens butter store, void; Kramer v. Old, 34 L. R. A. 389, which sustains contract restricting seller from engaging in milling business in vicinity of certain city; Clark v. Needham, 51 L. R. A. 785, which holds void, lease of manufacturing machinery with agreement against lessor engaging in business for five years; Drown v. Forrest, 14 L. R. A. 80, which holds contract not to re-engage in same business in same town not discharged by forming partnership with purchaser; Dills v. Doebler, 20 L. R. A. 432, which denies injunction to prevent resumption of dentistry practice without paying sum agreed on; Wilkinson v. Colley, 26 L. R. A. 114, which holds injunction against violating agreement not to practise medicine in certain district, not prevented by naming penalty.

Cited in notes (11 L. R. A. 504) on contracts in restraint of trade; (13 L. R. A. 771) on nature of monopolies; price fixed by illegal combination is void.

Distinguished in United States v. Addyston Pipe & Steel Co. 46 L. R. A. 131, 29 C. C. A. 151, 54 U. S. App. 723, 85 Fed. 282, holding contract solely to restrain competition and enhance or maintain process, void; Gamewell Fire Alarm Teleg. Co. v. Crane, 160 Mass. 57, 22 L. R. A. 677, 39 Am. St. Rep. 458, 35 N. E. 98, holding manufacturer's stipulation not to engage in manufacturing or selling of apparatus nor compete with purchaser for ten years, void.

8 L. R. A. 472, PEOPLE v. FOSS, 80 Mich. 559, 20 Am. St. Rep. 532, 45 N. W. 480.

Rights of abutting owner in highway.

Cited in Huffman v. State, 21 Ind. App. 453, 69 Am. St. Rep. 371, 52 N. E. 713, holding pipe-line company unlawfully upon highway liable in trespass to abutting owner; Stretch v. Cassopolis, 125 Mich. 168, 51 L. R. A. 346, 84 Am. St. Rep. 567, 84 N. W. 51, holding village liable to abutting owner for cutting trees within highway.

Defending right in highway.

Cited in People v. Sayers, 105 Mich. 716, 63 N. W. 1002 (dissenting opinion) majority holding one unjustified in committing assault, evidence failing to show it necessary to prevent removal of drain.

Acts constituting assault.

Cited in footnote to People v. Lee Kong, 17 L. R. A. 626, which holds firing pistol at hole in roof where policeman believed to be watching, an assault.

8 L. R. A. 476, KNIGHT v. LINZEY, 80 Mich. 396, 45 N. W. 337.

Transfer of negotiable paper to cut off defenses.

Cited in Leland v. Goodfellow, 84 Mich. 362, 47 N. W. 591, holding person procuring Bohemian oats note through fraudulent representations as to character of transaction, liable in damages to maker compelled to pay same to innocent purchaser.

Cited in note (27 L. R. A. 520, 521) on liability for transferring note to bona fide holder so as to cut off defenses.

Who are bona fide purchasers.

Cited in footnote to Griffith v. Shipley, 14 L. R. A. 405, which holds purchaser of note known to have been given for "hulless oats" not a bona fide purchaser.

Relief of parties to illegal contract.

Distinguished in Wright v. Stewart, 130 Fed. 926, holding money lent to stakeholder to make showing recoverable by one induced to bet money furnished by conspirators on fake race.

Cited in footnote to Wassermann v. Sloss, 38 L. R. A. 176, which holds illegality of transfer of stock to president for corrupting government officials will not prevent recovery where taken by president for own use instead.

8 L. R. A. 480, HUGHES v. BROWN, 88 Tenn. 578, 13 S. W. 286.

Statute of limitations.

Cited in Ballard v. Scruggs, 90 Tenn. 589, 25 Am. St. Rep. 703, 18 S. W. 259 holding ten-year statute bars suit to enforce lien of levy on land; Poindexter v. Rawlings, 106 Tenn. 101, 82 Am. St. Rep. 869, 59 S. W. 766, holding renewal of purchase-money note or new promise saves vendor's lien from bar of statute; Cooper v. Hill, 36 C. C. A. 410, 94 Fed. 590, holding nonoperation of limitations during coverture does not disqualify married woman from suing, joining husband as nominal plaintiff.

—— Against person in fiduciary relation.

Cited in Wallace v. Lincoln Sav. Bank, 89 Tenn. 650, 24 Am. St. Rep. 625, 15 S. W. 448, holding statute of limitations applicable to action against directors for loss to corporation caused by negligence; Eames v. Manly, 54 C. C. A. 564, 117 Fed. 390, holding relief against allowance in excess of claims fraudulently procured by confidential adviser, barred by twelve years delay after discovering fraud; Boyd v. Mutual Fire Asso. 116 Wis. 181, 61 L. R. A. 929, 96 Am. St. Rep. 948, 94 N. W. 171, holding statute of limitations runs against director's liability for misfeasance or malfeasance in office; Fink v. Campbell, 17 C. C. A. 329,

37 U. S. App. 402, 70 Fed. 668, holding laches bars bill to set aside sale for fraud and abuse of confidence.

Liability of sureties on representative's bond.

Cited in footnote to Abshire v. Salyer, 56 L. R. A. 936, which holds sureties on guardian's bond given to obtain silence from future liabilities of surety on prior bond, liable for past defalcations.

8 L. R. A. 484, NEWPORT v. NEWPORT & C. BRIDGE CO. 90 Ky. 193, 13 S. W. 720.

Injunction against enforcing ordinance.

Cited in South Covington & C. Street R. Co. v. Berry, 93 Ky. 46, 15 L. R. A. 604, 40 Am. St. Rep. 161, 18 S. W. 1026, holding injunction lies to prevent multiplicity of prosecutions under void ordinance.

Cited in note (21 L. R. A. 88) on injunction against prosecutions under city ordinances affecting property or franchises.

8 L. R. A. 486, GOODYEAR DENTAL VULCANITE CO. v. BACON, 151 Mass. 460, 24 N. E. 404.

Effect of principal's failure to sign bond or note.

Cited in State v. Hill, 47 Neb. 498, 66 N. W. 541, and Novak v. Pittick, 120 Iowa, 291, 98 Am. St. Rep. 360, 94 N. W. 916, holding bond unsigned by principal invalid; Gay v. Murphy, 134 Mo. 104, 56 Am. St. Rep. 496, 34 S. W. 1091, holding principal's failure to sign joint and several bond, excuses sureties; Dole Bros. Co. v. Cosmopolitan Preserving Co. 167 Mass. 482, 57 Am. St. Rep. 477, 46 N. E. 105, holding agent's want of authority to sign bond for principal unless known, releases sureties; Fuller v. Dupont, 183 Mass. 598, 67 N. E. 662, holding surety signing on representation that certain person would be other surety liable on bond.

Cited in footnotes to Hurt v. Ford, 41 L. R. A. 823, which denies right to make subsequent signature of another person essential to validity of note delivered to payee or his agent; Belden v. Hurlbut, 37 L. R. A. 853, which holds delivery of probate bond without getting other sureties as promised no defense to surety.

8 L. R. A. 487, OPINION OF JUSTICES, 150 Mass. 592, 24 N. E. 1084.

What constitutes a taking.

Cited in Gulf Coast Ice & Mfg. Co. v. Bowers, 80 Miss. 582, 32 So. 113, holding erection of poles and wires for lighting street not a taking requiring additional compensation.

Public enterprises by municipality — Furnishing electricity or gas to citizens.

Approved in Jacksonville Electric Light Co. v. Jacksonville, 36 Fla. 229, 30 L. R. A. 544, 51 Am. St. Rep. 24, 18 So. 677, and Citizens' Gaslight Co. v. Wakefield, 161 Mass. 439, 31 L. R. A. 461, 37 N. E. 444, sustaining power of legislature to authorize town to purchase and maintain gas or electric plant to furnish light to inhabitants.

Cited in Mealey v. Hagerstown, 92 Md. 754, 48 Atl. 746, holding legislature may authorize municipality owning plant for street lighting to supply light to citizens; Mitchell v. Negaunee, 113 Mich. 366, 38 468, 71 N. W. 646, holding municipalities may lighting plants and furnish light to citizens; Sta 48 Ohio, St. 137, 11 L. R. A. 738, 26 N. E. 1061, hc municipality to acquire natural-gas supply for pul 153 Mass. 130, 10 L. R. A. 398, 26 N. E. 421, hol gas or electric works to light streets not to be in tain street lamps; Wadsworth v. Concord, 133 N. C. J. concurring in result, who holds furnishing l purpose."

Cited in note (14 L. R. A. 268) on power of r and operate electric light plants.

— Furnishing water or fuel.

Cited in Watson v. Needham, 161 Mass. 410, 24 holding municipality may legally contract to supp greenhouse; Sutherland-Innes Co. v. Evart, 30 C. C. Fed. 603, holding legislature cannot authorize contr tain hydrants to encourage establishment of priva the Justices, 155 Mass. 601, 15 L. R. A. 810, 30 N. fuel by city or town and resale to inhabitants cannot

Transportation of gas.

Cited in footnotes to Indianapolis v. Consumers' G which holds gas company's right to repair pipes laid subsequent ordinance against digging in street wi Indianapolis Natural Gas Co. 8 L. R. A. 602, whicl of fee before laying gas pipes in highway.

Cited in notes (10 L. R. A. 194) on power of ga L. R. A. 193) on supplying natural gas as business

Electric plants.

Cited in Rockingham County Light & P. Co. v. Hc sustaining right of electric light and power compan

Cited in note (64 L. R. A. 41) on definitions of (64 L. R. A. 60) on taxation of manufacturing corp

8 L. R. A. 490, HINCKLEY v. HORAZDOWSKI, 618, 24 N. E. 421.

Master's liability to young employee.

Cited in Morris v. Stanfield, 81 Ill. App. 273, ho gree of care required of master in employing young Chicago, B. & Q. R. Co. v. Eggman, 59 Ill. App. 682 injury to sixteen-year-old boy going under cars, ienced and fully aware of character of service; Ne 59 Ill. App. 633, holding master liable for loss of on pulley close to revolving saws at master's di Reardon, 56 Ill. App. 544, holding jury should cons squeezed between car and lumber on another car Forge & Foundry Co. v. Van Dam, 149 Ill. 342, 36

consider age and discretion of boy continuing to work with defective tools upon promise to furnish better, on question of contributory negligence.

Duty to warn employee.

Cited in National Enameling & Stamping Co. v. Brady, 93 Md. 650, 49 Atl. 845, holding master must instruct young employee of hazard of machine especially when contract of employment required that he shall not be employed on machines.

Cited in notes (8 L. R. A. 819) on master's duty to instruct servant in use of dangerous machinery; (44 L. R. A. 47, 63, 72) on master's duty to instruct and warn servants as to perils of employment.

Assumption of risk by employee.

Cited in footnotes to Cudahy Packing Co. v. Marcam, 54 L. R. A. 258, which holds risk of block on which minor employee works slipping on greasy floor assumed; Stager v. Troy Laundry Co. 53 L. R. A. 459, which holds risk of hand passing under guard rails into rollers not assumed as matter of law by servant operating mangle in laundry; Marino v. Lehmaier, 61 L. R. A. 812, which holds risk of employment not assumed *per se*, by child whose employment is illegal because of immature age.

Instructions.

Cited in Corcoran v. Lehigh & F. Coal Co. 37 Ill. App. 579, holding party cannot insist on appeal that court erred in instructing that admission had been made if no objection was made at the time; Bradley v. Sattler, 54 Ill. App. 505. refusing to consider complaints to instructions which do not recognize difference between adults and children engaged in dangerous service; Chicago Anderson Pressed Brick Co. v. Reinneiger, 140 Ill. 337, 33 Am. St. Rep. 249, 29 N. E. 1106, holding instruction proper that boy of proper age and discretion with information of danger of service cannot recover for injury resulting from ordinary peril and danger of employment.

8 L. R. A. 494, CHICAGO CITY R. CO. v. WILCOX (Ill.) 24 N. E. 419.

Imputing negligence.

Cited in notes (17 L. R. A. 79) on imputing parent's negligence to child; (10 L. R. A. 654) on imputing negligence of another to child; (9 L. R. A. 157) on imputing driver's negligence to passenger.

Distinguished in Bamberger v. Citizens' Street R. Co. 95 Tenn. 28, 28 L. R. A. 490, 49 Am. St. Rep. 909, 31 S. W. 163, holding negligence of custodian of three-year-old child defeats administrator's action for benefit of next of kin.

Contributory negligence of minor.

Cited in footnote to Gleason v. Smith, 55 L. R. A. 622, which denies liability for injury by collision with team, to twelve-year-old boy using street as playground.

Cited in note (12 L. R. A. 217) on contributory negligence of infant of tender age.

8 L. R. A. 497, PEOPLE *ex rel.* PEABODY v. CHICAGO GAS TRUST CO. 130 Ill. 268, 17 Am. St. Rep. 319, 22 N. E. 798.

Corporate ownership of stocks.

Cited in Knowles v. Sandercock, 107 Cal. 643, 40 Pac. 1047, holding that furniture manufacturing company cannot own stock in hotel company; Peshtigo Co. v. Great Western Teleg. Co. 50 Ill. App. 625, holding lumber company cannot be assessed for shares in telegraph company to which it subscribed; People *ex rel.* Moloney v. Pullman's Palace Car Co. 175 Ill. 159, 64 L. R. A. 374, 51 N. E. 664, holding manufacturing corporation has no implied power to hold stock in another corporation; Martin v. Ohio Stove Co. 78 Ill. App. 108, holding corporation cannot acquire stock of other companies through the medium of third persons; Northern Securities Co. v. United States, 193 U. S. 341, 48 L. ed. 701, 24 Sup. Ct. Rep. 436, Affirming 120 Fed. 726, holding corporation formed to hold stock of competing railroads, obtained in exchange for its own, an unlawful combination; Robotham v. Prudential Ins. Co. 64 N. J. Eq. 696, 53 Atl. 842, holding corporations may be formed to purchase and deal in stocks of others; Marshall & B. Co. v. Nashville, 109 Tenn. 510, 71 S. W. 815, holding ordinance requiring union label on city printing invalid; John D. Park & Sons Co. v. National Wholesale Druggists' Asso. 175 N. Y. 36, 62 L. R. A. 647, 96 Am. St. Rep. 578, 67 N. E. 136 (dissenting opinion) majority holding plan of druggists' association, adopted by manufacturers, for rebate to concerns maintaining selling price, valid.

Distinguished in Whalen v. Stephens, 193 Ill. 141, 61 N. E. 921, Affirming, 92 Ill. App. 254, holding that donation of corporate stock can be made to other corporation; Chicago Union Traction Co. v. Chicago, 199 Ill. 637, 65 N. E. 470, holding corporation cannot obtain control of another corporation by having latter's stock turned over to trust company for its benefit; McCoy v. World's Columbian Exposition, 186 Ill. 360, 78 Am. St. Rep. 288, 57 N. E. 1043, Affirming 87 Ill. App. 607, holding subscriber to stock cannot defend against assessments because other subscribers are corporations unless their obligations have not been fulfilled; De La Vergne Refrigerating Mach. Co. v. German Sav. Inst. 175 U. S. 55, 44 L. ed. 70, 20 Sup. Ct. Rep. 20, holding statute permitting manufacturing companies to purchase other property necessary for their business does not authorize purchase of stock of other corporations; Parsons v. Tacoma Smelting & Ref. Co. 25 Wash. 508, 65 Pac. 765, holding corporation cannot acquire stock of another corporation by expression of such power in its articles of incorporation; Tourtelot v. Whithed, 9 N. D. 478, 84 N. W. 8, holding bank can receive stock of milling company in payment of debt, believing it can more quickly realize; Willoughby v. Chicago Junction R. & United Stock-Yards Co. 50 N. J. Eq. 676, 25 Atl. 277, holding questions relating to invalidity of corporation controlling stock of another company should be presented by attorney general in behalf of state.

Liability on subscription to stock.

Cited in Bent v. Underdown, 156 Ind. 519, 60 N. E. 307, holding stockholder cannot be compelled to pay more of subscription than he agreed to in articles of incorporation; Loverin v. McLaughlin, 161 Ill. 432, 44 N. E. 99, holding articles of incorporation not conclusive evidence that all subscriptions are bona fide.

Power of corporations to combine.

Cited in United States v. Addyston, Pipe & Steel Co. 46 L. R. A. 136, 29 C. C. A. 160, 54 U. S. App. 723, 85 Fed. 291, holding ruinous competition threatening business suicide no excuse for combination in restraint of trade under United States statute; Levin v. Chicago Gaslight & Coke Co. 64 Ill. App. 397, holding stockholder in illegal trust, who has taken stock in successor corporation, cannot tear down that corporation; Bishop v. American Preservers' Co. 157 Ill. 310, 48 Am. St. Rep. 317, 41 N. E. 765, holding company formed to purchase preserving companies, illegal combination; Distilling & Cattle Feeding Co. v. People, 156 Ill. 489, 47 Am. St. Rep. 200, 41 N. E. 188, holding combination to control manufacture and sale of distillery products, illegal; Holmes & G. Mfg. Co. v. Holmes & W. Metal Co. 127 N. Y. 257, 21 Am. St. Rep. 448, 27 N. E. 831, holding purely private corporation may sell its plant and retire from business with consent of all stockholders; Brunswick Gaslight Co. v. United Gas, Fuel & Light Co. 85 Me. 539, 35 Am. St. Rep. 385, 27 Atl. 525, holding gas company cannot sell, lease, or assign its corporate rights to another gas company; National Lead Co. v. S. E. Grote Paint Store Co. 80 Mo. App. 270, holding combination illegal under antitrust law cannot be operated as corporation by its constituent members; Queen Ins. Co. v. State, 86 Tex. 266, 22 L. R. A. 492, 24 S. W. 397, holding combination of insurance companies fixing rates not unreasonable restraint of trade aimed at by statute; McCutcheon v. Merz Capsule Co. 31 L. R. A. 419, 19 C. C. A. 113, 37 U. S. App. 586, 71 Fed. 792, holding corporation cannot sell its entire plant to another corporation to be organized to carry on same business; Chevra Bnai Israel v. Chevra Bikur Cholim, 24 Misc. 190, 52 N. Y. Supp. 712, holding a benevolent and a religious corporation cannot consolidate without legislative sanction; Stockton v. Central R. Co. 50 N. J. Eq. 76, 17 L. R. A. 107, 24 Atl. 964, holding railroad cannot be leased to foreign corporation by device of a nominal lessee; State v. Nebraska Distilling Co. 29 Neb. 715, 46 N. W. 155, annulling franchise of a distilling company which has sold to trust all of its property and rights; State *ex rel.* Snyder v. Portland Natural Gas & Oil Co. 153 Ind. 488. 53 L. R. A. 415, 74 Am. St. Rep. 314, 53 N. E. 1089, holding gas company owed duty to public and may be deprived of franchise for combining with rival company to fix prices; Harding v. American Glucose Co. 182 Ill. 617, 64 L. R. A. 764, 74 Am. St. Rep. 189, 55 N. E. 577, holding glucose company, formed to take all properties of competing companies, a trust; South Chicago City R. Co. v. Calumet Electric Street R. Co. 171 Ill. 397, 49 N. E. 576, holding contract by competing street car lines virtually agreeing not to cross each other's tracks illegal; United States v. E. C. Knight Co. 156 U. S. 29, 39 L. ed. 335, 15 Sup. Ct. Rep. 249 (dissenting opinion) majority holding combination of sugar refineries cannot be suppressed under act to protect trade and commerce against monopolies.

Cited in footnotes to San Diego Water Co. v. San Diego Flume Co. 29 L. R. A. 839, which upholds, appointment of other corporation to act as sole agent for sale of water within city by plants of both corporations; Gloucester Isinglass & Glue Co. v. Russia Cement Co. 12 L. R. A. 563, which holds agreement to prevent competition between corporations in manufacture of glue under patent, valid.

Cited in note (52 L. R. A. 380, 381, 391) on right of corporations to consolidate.

What included in implied and incidental powers.

Cited in Fritze v. Equitable Bldg. & L. Soc. 186 Ill. 196, 57 N. E. 873, holding building and loan society cannot adopt amendment to by-laws; National Home Bldg. & L. Asso. v. Home Sav. Bank, 181 Ill. 42, 64 L. R. A. 402, 72 Am. St. Rep. 245, 54 N. E. 619, holding building association not liable for deficiency in foreclosure of mortgage it had assumed to pay outside of its powers; Chicago v. Wilkie, 88 Ill. App. 321, holding requirement that plumbers must be licensed within implied power of city; People *ex rel.* Moloney v. Pullman's Palace Car

Co. 175 Ill. 137, 64 L. R. A. 374, 51 N. E. 664, hol
has implied power to build office building sufficie
own whole city; Bath Gaslight Co. v. Claffy, 151]
E. 390, holding corporation has not implied pow
quarter of century; State *ex rel.* Jackson v. New
St. Rep. 476, 25 So. 408, holding incidental powei
and immediately appropriate to specific power
176 Ill. 347, 48 L. R. A. 232, 52 N. E. 44, holdin
cigarettes to minors under sixteen valid as impli
Ind. 261, 64 N. E. 880, holding manufacture of elec
to purpose of electric light and. power company.

Cited in footnote to Newell v. Meyendorff, 8 L.
contract giving exclusive agency in certain territor

How charter affected by statute of incorpora

Cited in Carlyle v. Carlyle Water, Light & P.
city must take water from company with whic
period of years and at reasonable price until subs
State, 69 Ark. 530, 65 S. W. 465, holding state
powers of corporation if not deprived of property
ville v. Danville Water Co. 178 Ill. 306, 69 Am.
holding provisions of general act were incorporate
pany and subject to alteration by legislature; N
600, holding act under which benefit association
tract between corporation and member; Bixler v.
N. E. 849, holding charter of corporation include
Chicago Union Traction Co. v. Chicago, 199 Ill. 5
451, holding provisions of general incorporation a
of traction company formed to lease and operate
Ross v. Anderson, 31 Ind. App. 44, 67 N. E. 207,
of incorporation, in contravention of statute pro
officers, void.

Contracts against public policy.

Cited in Jay County v. Taylor, 123 Ind. 153,
holding contract by county board to employ couns
against public policy; Visalia Gas & Electric Li
43 Am. St. Rep. 105, 37 Pac. 1042, holding lease
its whole plant is against public policy; People
Ill. App. 362, holding public policy did not req
affecting elevated railroad to be tested; Wittenbe
83 N. W. 842, holding right to run hotel not a fr
no duty to public except as his guests; Consume
Ind. 568, 51 Am. St. Rep. 193, 41 N. E. 1048, ho
or gasoline anywhere in state outside of one cit
straint of trade; Hannah v. People, 198 Ill. 96,
change public policy based on Constitution does n
Fishburn v. Chicago, 171 Ill. 340, 39 L. R. A. 482
532, holding contract under ordinance requiring
kind controlled by monopoly, void; Wakefield
L. R. A. 515, 95 Am. St. Rep. 207, 63 N. E. 8

against grain elevators, not against public policy; Robson v. Hamilton, 41 Or. 245, 69 Pac. 651, setting aside transfer of property in fraud of creditor whose judgment was for price of land sold to take husband and son out of state to avoid prosecution.

Cited in note (13 L. R. A. 384) on power of municipality to create monopoly.

Quasi-public corporations.

Cited in Westfield Gas & Mill. Co. v. Mendenhall, 142 Ind. 545, 41 N. E. 1033, holding gas company owes duty to public and cannot charge consumer more than maximum rate; Woodberry v. McClurg, 78 Miss. 836, 29 So. 514, refusing to grant charter to company with power to dig gravel pits, own mills, electric light plants, hotels, and stock of other corporations.

Cited in footnote to People v. Buffalo Stone & Cement Co. 15 L. R. A. 240, which requires dissolution of corporation on failure to pay in capital stock within two years.

Cited in note (13 L. R. A. 384) on power of municipality to create monopoly.

8 L. R. A. 508, CHICAGO & N. W. R. CO. v. CHAPMAN, 133 Ill. 96, 23 Am. St. Rep. 587, 24 N. E. 417.

Power to limit liability by express contract.

Cited in Springer v. Ford, 88 Ill. App. 541, holding carrier only freed from liability for ordinary negligence by express contract; Chicago & N. W. R. Co. v. Calumet Stock Farm, 194 Ill. 13, 88 Am. St. Rep. 68, 61 N. E. 1095, holding question of assent to bill of lading stipulation limiting liability, for jury; Baltimore & O. S. W. R. Co. v. Ross, 105 Ill. App. 60, holding contract limiting time for presenting claim to carrier for damages, binding on shipper; Chicago & A. R. Co. v. Davis, 159 Ill. 59, 50 Am. St. Rep. 143, 42 N. E. 382, holding carrier not released by mere bill of lading stipulation from liability for furnishing defective refrigerator cars; Chicago & N. W. R. Co. v. Simon, 160 Ill. 652, 43 N. E. 596, Affirming 57 Ill. App. 504, holding carrier not exempted by mere statement in receipt or bill, from common-law liability; United States Exp. Co. v. Council, 84 Ill. App. 497, holding carrier not exempted by special contract from liability for negligently causing death of live stock; Chicago & N. W. R. Co. v. Calumet Stock Farm, 96 Ill. App. 340, holding carrier not exempt from liability for carelessly injuring live stock by making "flying switch;" Georgia R. & Bkg. Co. v. Keener, 93 Ga. 810, 53 L. R. A. 722, 44 Am. St. Rep. 197, 21 S. E. 287, holding contract limiting liability on household goods, for reduced rate, inoperative in case of carrier's negligence; Ullman v. Chicago & N. W. R. Co. 112 Wis. 167, 56 L. R. A. 249, 88 Am. St. Rep. 949, 88 N. W. 41, holding doubtful whether carrier could obtain exemption from liability for negligence; Brockway v. American Exp. Co. 168 Mass. 258, 47 S. E. 87, holding contract exempting carrier's liability, invalid where made, not enforceable in Massachusetts; Wabash R. Co. v. Harris, 55 Ill. App. 162, holding mere acceptance without objection of bill of lading, limiting liability, not conclusive of assent thereto.

Cited in notes (10 L. R. A. 419) on restriction of carrier's power to limit liability by contract; (14 L. R. A. 434) on carrier's power to limit amount of liability in cases of negligence.

Distinguished in Chicago, B. & Q. R. Co. v. Gardiner, 51 Neb. 75, 70 N. W. 508, refusing to enforce contract limiting liability of carrier, admitting it to be valid in state where made; Blank v. Illinois C. R. Co. 80 Ill. App. 484, upholding express messenger's contract relieving carrier from liability for injury, for license to ride in cars.

Liability for gross negligence.

Cited in Chicago & N. W. R. Co. v. Calumet Stock Farm, 194 Ill. 13, 88 Am. St. Rep. 68, 61 N. E. 1095, holding question whether injury was caused by defendant's gross negligence for jury; Wabash R. Co. v. Brown, 51 Ill. App. 658, holding exemption from liability for accident, not applicable to accident caused by gross negligence of carrier's servants; Illinois C. R. Co. v. Leiner, 202 Ill. 628, 95 Am. St. Rep. 266, 67 N. E. 398, holding railroad liable for death of person wrongfully on train, resulting from gross negligence.

Fixing value of goods shipped.

Cited in Pacific Exp. Co. v. Foley, 46 Kan. 474, 12 L. R. A. 806, 26 Am. St. Rep. 107, 26 Pac. 665 (dissenting opinion), majority upholding contract limiting amount of liability in case of ordinary negligence, value of goods not being stated on shipment; Central R. Co. v. Murphey, 113 Ga. 517, 53 L. R. A. 722, 38 S. E. 970, holding general stipulation as to value of fruit shipments per car not an agreement as to value of particular car load of grapes; Ullman v. Chicago & N. W. R. Co. 112 Wis. 159, 56 L. R. A. 249, 88 Am. St. Rep. 949, 88 N. W. 41, holding limitation of amount of liability in bill of lading not an agreement as to value of property shipped; Chicago, B. & Q. R. Co. v. Miller, 79 Ill. App. 477, holding shipper bound by value he himself placed upon his goods.

Goods shipped at reduced freight rate.

Cited in Wabash R. Co. v. Brown, 152 Ill. 490, 39 N. E. 273, holding limitation of amount of liability for reduced rate, without due notice to shipper, not enforceable.

Distinguished in Jennings v. Smith, 99 Fed. 190, holding shipper bound by limitation stipulation, knowingly accepting lower rate in consideration therefor.

Construction of term "accident."

Cited in Ullman v. Chicago & N. W. R. Co. 112 Miss. 168, 56 L. R. A. 249, 88 Am. St. Rep. 949, 88 N. W. 41, construing stipulation as to "accident" in bill of lading to include negligence.

8 L. R. A. 511, KIRKPATRICK v. CLARK, 132 Ill. 342, 22 Am. St. Rep. 531, 24 N. E. 71.

Remedies between parties in pari delicto.

Cited in Bishop v. American Preservers' Co. 157 Ill. 315, 48 Am. St. Rep. 317, 41 N. E. 765, holding trust agreement to monopolize certain trade admissible by *particeps criminis* as defense in replevin by another; Ellwood v. Walter, 103 Ill. App. 221, holding mortgagor may prove mortgage given to defraud creditors in action to foreclose it; Brady v. Huber, 197 Ill. 296, 90 Am. St. Rep. 161, 64 N. E. 264, holding deed by father to daughter to defraud creditors will not be canceled at his request; Drinkall v. Movins State Bank, 57 L. R. A. 346, holding payee of cashier's check which he indorsed to another for gambling debt can enforce payment against drawer; Halloran v. Halloran, 137 Ill. 110, 27 N. E. 82, holding mortgagor in fraudulent mortgage may have same canceled as cloud upon title after its payment.

Cited in footnotes to Chateau v. Singla, 33 L. R. A. 750, which denies relief.

to either party for settlement of partnership to carry on unlawful business; Rock v. Mathews, 14 L. R. A. 508, which refuses to cancel obligations given under agreement to compound felony.

Cited in note (12 L. R. A. 122) on parties *in pari delicto.*

Distinguished in Cook County Brick Co. v. Labahn Brick Co. 92 Ill. App. 535, holding injunction lies by one *in pari delicto* to restrain enforcement of illegal agreement to raise price of brick.

Admissibility of evidence of ownership.

Cited in Glos v. Randolph, 138 Ill. 271, 27 N. E. 941, holding plaintiff's solicitor's testimony not objected to, that his client owned land, with documentary evidence sufficient prima facie evidence of ownership against void tax deed; Lavery v. Brooke, 37 Ill. App. 53, holding legal title to land not provable by parol.

Jurisdiction of court of law over cases of fraud.

Cited in Supreme Council C. K. & L. v. Beggs, 110 Ill. App. 147, holding defense of fraud admissible in action at law on benefit certificate.

8 L. R. A. 514, HARWELL v. SHARP, 85 Ga. 124, 21 Am. St. Rep. 149, 11 S. E. 561.

Conflict of laws.

Cited in Cross v. Brown, 19 R. I. 228, 33 Atl. 147, upholding garnishment attachment over foreign insolvency proceeding transferring foreign debtor's property to trustee; Chicago, R. I. & P. R. Co. v. Sturm, 174 U. S. 717, 43 L. ed. 1146, 19 Sup. Ct. Rep. 797, holding continuance in action for wages in one state should be granted pending garnishment proceedings against debtor for same wages in another state.

Cited in note (19 L. R. A. 580) on protection of nonresident creditor against garnishment.

Abuse of process.

Cited in Leeman v. McGrath, 116 Wis. 51, 92 N. W. 425, holding assignment of account for collection by garnishment in another state, to evade exemption laws, not actionable.

Cited in note (36 L. R. A. 582) on debtor's right of action against creditor for collecting debt in another jurisdiction in evasion of exemption laws of domicil.

8 L. R. A. 516, STATE v. STEELE, 106 N. C. 766, 19 Am. St. Rep. 573, 11 S. E. 478.

Right to exclude certain persons from hotel, school, etc.

Approved in Hutchins v. Durham, 118 N. C. 471, 32 L. R. A. 707, 24 S. E. 723, sustaining expulsion from stall in market of licensee refusing to vacate after revocation of license and notice to leave; McMillan v. District No. 4, 107 N. C. 614, 10 L. R. A. 825, 12 S. E. 330, upholding legislative provision for separate schools for Indians, and excluding negroes therefrom; Hedding v. Gallagher, 72 N. H. 389, 64 L. R. A. 819, 57 Atl. 225, holding railroad may give teamster exclusive right to solicit baggage on depot grounds.

8 L. R. A. 524, MORASSE v. BROCHU, 151 .
25 N. E. 74.

Sufficiency of declaration.

Cited in May v. Wood, 172 Mass. 13, 51 N. E
false and malicious statements, such statements
Doyle v. Kirby, 184 Mass. 411, 68 N. E. 843,
averring plaintiff was injured in candidacy for
special damage.

Injury to person's profession, business, or

Cited in Hanchett v. Chiatovich, 41 C. C. A
Military Academy v. Gaiser, 125 Mo. 525, 28
502, 28 S. W. 851; Lovejoy v. Whitcomb, 174 M
false and disparaging statement, about person in
able *per se;* Chiatovich v. Hanchett, 96 Fed. 6
actionable in themselves may become so when s
occupation of a person; Passaic Print Works v
L. R. A. 697, 44 C. C. A. 433, 105 Fed. 171 (dis
ing intentional injury to business by undersel
Dunphy, 177 Mass. 487, 52 L. R. A. 116, 83 A
holding maliciously inducing employer to dischar
Vegelahn v. Guntner, 167 Mass. 105, 35 L. R. A
N. E. 1077, holding damage by combined persuasi
by falsehood and fraud; McLoughlin v. American
89. 125 Fed. 205, holding special damage result
facturer of letter to agent charging use of electr
insurers, actionable.

Cited in notes (28 L. R. A. 675) on libel or sl
comments without misstating facts; (62 L. R. A.
make actionable what would otherwise not be.

Publications libelous upon proof of specia

Cited in Hollenbeck v. Ristine, 105 Iowa, 491,
355, holding publication of any untrue, malicious
resulting therefrom.

8 L. R. A. 529, STATE v. HUNTER, 106 N. C. 79

Invalid ordinances.

Cited in State v. Tenant, 110 N. C. 614, 15 L. R
14 S. E. 387, holding ordinance making right to
arbitrary decision, void.

Cited in footnote to *Re* Stegenga, 61 L. R. A.
thority to provide for punishment of loiterers in s

Distinguished in State v. Earnhardt, 107 N. C
ordinance providing for arrest and fine of violato
as to fine.

Violation of unlawful ordinance.

Cited in State v. Webber, 107 N. C. 967, 22 An
holding violation of unauthorized ordinance not cr

Arrest without warrant.

Cited in North v. People, 139 Ill. 105, 28 N. E. 966, holding officer may arrest without warrant person carrying concealed weapons in his presence; State v. McAfee, 107 N. C. 816, 10 L. R. A. 609, footnote p. 607, 12 S. E. 435, holding commission of assault in officer's presence justifies arrest without warrant.

Cited in footnotes to Cabell v. Arnold, 22 L. R. A. 87, which holds deputy marshal not justified in making arrest on warrant in marshal's hands; Burroughs v. Eastman, 24 L. R. A. 859, which upholds legislative power to authorize arrest without warrant for misdemeanors; State v. Lewis, 19 L. R. A. 449, which denies officer's right to arrest for breach of peace not committed in his presence; McCullough v. Greenfield, 62 L. R. A. 906, which holds arrest under telephonic direction of officer holding warrant, unlawful; Baltimore & O. R. Co. v. Cain, 28 L. R. A. 688, which holds officer's arrest of disorderly passenger without warrant in response to telegram by conductor, who pointed out person to be arrested, not unlawful.

Illegal arrest.

Cited in State v. Rollins, 113 N. C. 733, 18 S. E. 394, holding good faith does not validate illegal arrest.

Killing by officer making arrest.

Cited in footnotes to Thomas v. Kinkead, 15 L. R. A. 558, which denies officer's right to kill one charged with misdemeanor to prevent escape from arrest; Petrie v. Cartwright, 59 L. R. A. 720, which denies right of peace officer without warrant to kill fleeing person guilty of misdemeanor but suspected of felony.

Killing of officer making arrest.

Cited in footnotes to Roberson v. State, 52 L. R. A. 751, which holds malicious and premeditated killing of officer not reduced to manslaughter because he was making arrest without warrant; Montgomery v. State, 55 L. R. A. 866, which sustains right to resist with whatever force necessary officer attempting to make arrest without warrant, for carrying arms, without disclosing authority.

Liability for arrest.

Cited in footnotes to Tolchester Beach Improv. Co. v. Steinmeier, 8 L. R. A. 846, which holds corporation not liable for arrest by policeman appointed on its application and paid by it; Boutte v. Emmer, 15 L. R. A. 63, which holds mayor not liable for brief imprisonment unless action arbitrary.

Right to bail.

Cited in note (10 L. R. A. 847) on constitutional right to admission to bail on arrest for crime.

Breach of the peace.

Cited in note (13 L. R. A. 165) on breach of the peace.

8 L. R. A. 537, MOSSELLER v. DEAVER, 106 N. C. 494, 19 Am. St. Rep. 540, 11 S. E. 529.

Forcible entry.

Approved in State v. Howell, 107 N. C. 840, 12 S. E. 569, holding one breaking open building with knowledge that his former landlord had taken possession, indictable for wilful injury.

Cited in footnote to State v. Davis, 14 L. R. A. 206, which holds breaking open door of leased blacksmith shop a forcible entry, though lessee not in shop.

8 L. R. A. 539, INDIANAPOLIS CABLE STREET R. CO. v. CITIZENS STREET R. CO. 127 Ind. 369, 24 N. E. 1054, 26 N. E. 893.

Granting of exclusive privileges.

Cited in Crowder v. Sullivan, 128 Ind. 489, 13 L. R. A. 648, 28 N. E. 94, holding permission to one company to use streets, to supply light and water, does not necessarily exclude others.

Cited in note (11 L. R. A. 437) on validity of contracts to regulate competition in trade.

Construction of franchises.

Cited in Muncie Natural Gas Co. v. Muncie, 160 Ind. 112, 60 L. R. A. 830, 66 N. E. 436, construing gas franchise fixing maximum charges in favor of public.

Acceptance of franchise offered by municipality.

Cited in Africa v. Knoxville, 70 Fed. 734, holding valid franchise accepted by corporation becomes a contract irrevocable by municipality.

Distinguished in Vincennes v. Citizens' Gaslight Co. 132 Ind. 121, 16 L. R. A. 488, 31 N. E. 573, holding ordinance granting right to lay pipes and offering to take gas, when accepted, becomes contract binding on city.

Rights of rival companies under franchise.

Cited in Africa v. Knoxville, 70 Fed. 741, holding as between rival companies contending for right of way under franchises, prior occupancy determines prior right; Hamilton G. & C. Traction Co. v. Hamilton & L. Electric Transit Co. 69 Ohio St. 411, 69 N. E. 991, denying right of street railroad to construct track along right of way occupied by another; Indiana Power Co. v. St. Joseph & E. Power Co. 159 Ind. 48, 63 N. E. 304, holding power company may condemn land acquired by another power company by purchase without filing appropriation proceedings.

Cited in note (12 L. R. A. 221) on location of railroad; what sufficient to exclude appropriation of land by rival road.

Municipal authority over streets.

Cited in Williams v. Citizens' R. Co. 130 Ind. 73, 15 L. R. A. 67, 30 Am. St. Rep. 201, 29 N. E. 408, holding jurisdiction of cities over streets does not oust courts of jurisdiction over questions of personal or property rights.

Consent for railways in streets.

Cited in Chicago & C. Terminal R. Co. v. Whiting, H. & E. C. Street R. Co. 139 Ind. 303, 26 L. R. A. 339, 47 Am. St. Rep. 264, 38 N. E. 604, holding that street railway cannot be laid upon streets without license or franchise from legislature or municipality.

Who may question corporation's right to engage in business.

Cited in Seattle Gas & Electric Co. v. Citizens' Light & P. Co. 123 Fed. 596, holding gas company may question power of rival paralleling its mains to take franchise.

Motive power for street railroad.

Cited in footnotes to *Re* Third Ave. R. Co. 9 L. R. A. 124, which holds valid statute giving street car company right to adopt new motive power; Hooper v. Baltimore City Pass. R. Co. 38 L. R. A. 509, which authorizes use of trolley system for street railway without sanction of municipal authorities; Chicago General R. Co. v. Chicago City R. Co. 50 L. R. A. 734, which denies liability for collision with cars of other company because of running cable cars under authority to use animal power only.

Cited in note (10 L. R. A. 176) on regulation as to motive power of street railroads.

8 L. R. A. 549, STANLEY v. WABASH, ST. L. & P. R. CO. 100 Mo. 435, 3 Inters. Com. Rep. 176, 13 S. W. 709.

Presumption as to extraterritorial force of statute.

Approved in Gibson v. Connecticut F. Ins. Co. 77 Fed. 564, holding statute respecting insurance on real property will be presumed to have been intended to operate only on property within state.

Regulation of commerce.

Approved in State v. Rankin, 11 S. D. 149, 76 N. W. 299, holding state cannot burden interstate commerce by imposing license tax on solicitors.

Reversal for error.

Cited in Boggess v. Metropolitan Street R. Co. 118 Mo. 334, 23 S. W. 159, holding judgment will not be reversed for error not affecting merits of the action.

8 L. R. A. 551, SINGER v. STATE, 72 Md. 464, 19 Atl. 1044.

Government regulation of occupations.

Approved in Ford v. State, 85 Md. 475, 41 L. R. A. 552, 60 Am. St. Rep. 337, 37 Atl. 172, sustaining statute making possession of prohibited articles an offense; State *ex rel.* Burroughs v. Webster, 150 Ind. 618, 41 L. R. A. 217, 50 N. E. 750, holding requirement that all physicians shall obtain new certificate and license upon proper showing, valid; State v. Randolph, 23 Or. 82, 17 L. R. A. 472, 37 Am. St. Rep. 655, 31 Pac. 201, holding exemption of practitioners at time of passage of medical-practice act, valid; Scholle v. State, 90 Md. 740, 50 L. R. A. 413, 46 Atl. 326, holding exemption from medical-practice act of surgeons of United States Army, Navy, or marine hospital service, those in consultation from other states, and those temporarily under preceptors, not unreasonable; State v. Knowles, 90 Md. 657, 49 L. R. A. 698, 45 Atl. 877, holding statute requiring dentists to obtain certificate of proficiency from state board, valid; State v. Gardner, 58 Ohio St. 609, 41 L. R. A. 691, 65 Am. St. Rep. 785, 51 N. E. 136, and State *ex rel.* Winkler v. Benzenberg, 101 Wis. 177, 76 N. W. 345, sustaining statute regulating business of plumbing; State v. Heinemann, 80 Wis. 257, 27 Am. St. Rep. 34, 49 N. W. 818, sustaining statute requiring retailing, compounding, or dispensing medicines by registered pharmacist; State v. Zeno, 79 Minn. 84, 48 L. R. A. 90, 79 Am. St. Rep. 422, 81 N. W. 748, holding statute restricting occupation of barber to registered barbers, valid; *Ex parte* Lucas, 160 Mo. 233, 61 S. W. 218, holding statute regulating occupation of barbers in towns of over 50,000 inhabitants, valid.

Cited in note (21 L. R. A. 791) as to constitutionality of statutes restricting contracts and business.

Distinguished in Long v. State, 74 Md. 572, 12 L. R. A. 427, 28 Am. St. Rep.

268, 22 Atl. 4, holding statutory prohibition of gift enterprise without element of chance, invalid.

8 L. R. A. 552, JOHNSON v. ELKINS, 90 Ky. 163, 13 S. W. 448.

Exemptions.

Approved in Dickinson v. Johnson, 110 Ky. 247, 54 L. R. A. 575, 96 Am. St. Rep. 434, 61 S. W. 267, holding salaries of public officers under $5,000 per year, not to be ordered set apart in part for payment of debts.

Cited in Curtis v. Helton, 109 Ky. 496, 95 Am. St. Rep. 388, 59 S. W. 745, holding land purchased with pension check, not exempt.

Cited in footnote to Crow v. Brown, 11 L. R. A. 110, which holds exempt, property purchased with pension money.

Cited in note (19 L. R. A. 35) as to how far proceeds of exempt property retain exempt character.

Distinguished in Falkenburg v. Johnson, 102 Ky. 548, 80 Am. St. Rep. 369, 44 S. W. 80, holding transfer of pension check to pensioner's wife as separate estate no fraud against creditors.

Disapproved in Reiff v. Mack, 160 Pa. 269, 40 Am. St. Rep. 720, 28 Atl. 699, holding bank deposit of proceeds of collected pension check, not subject to attachment execution.

8 L. R. A. 553, HOLLAND v. CITIZENS' SAV. BANK, 16 R. I. 734, 19 Atl. 654.

Compelling assignment of mortgage.

Approved in McCulla v. Beadleston, 17 R. I. 23, 20 Atl. 11, holding mortgagor not entitled to compel assignee of mortgage to receive payment from, and assign mortgage to, third person.

Subrogation to mortgagee's rights.

Cited in footnote to Meeker v. Larson, 57 L. R. A. 901, which denies right of one furnishing money to discharge mortgage, to be subrogated to mortgagee's rights.

Lis pendens.

Cited in footnote to Taylor v. Carroll, 44 L. R. A. 479, which holds purchaser of property relieved from effect of *lis pendens* as notice by over twenty years' delay in proceeding with foreclosure.

Rights of subsequent purchaser.

Cited in Blackmar v. Sharp, 23 R. I. 426, 50 Atl. 852, upholding validity of mortgages not showing they were given for future advances, against one acquiring lien intermediate recording and advances.

8 L. R. A. 556, HAMSHER v. HAMSHER, 132 Ill. 273. 23 N. E. 1123.

What is a religious corporation formed for religious purpose.

Cited in *Re* Fay, 37 Misc. 535, 76 N. Y. Supp. 62, holding Young Men's Christian Association not religious corporation within meaning of transfer tax law; *Re* Walker, 200 Ill. 571, 66 N. E. 144, holding building devoted in part to uses of Sunday school and in part to promiscuous gatherings of religious society, not within exemption from taxation of property "exclusively used for public worship."

Power to take and hold property.

Cited in Alden v. St. Peter's Parish, 158 Ill. 641, 30 L. R. A. 236, 42 N. E. 392, holding prohibition against incorporated religious societies receiving more than 10 acres of land not applicable to unincorporated society; Wunderle v. Wunderle, 144 Ill. 64, 19 L. R. A. 89, 33 N. E. 195, holding under statute making nonresident alien incapable of acquiring title to real estate, alien cannot hold defeasible title subject to forfeiture to state.

Cited in footnote to Thompson v. West, 49 L. R. A. 337, which denies right of religious corporation to buy real estate for speculation.

Right to question acts ultra vires of corporation.

Cited in Hagerstown Mfg. Min. & Land Improv. Co. v. Keedy, 91 Md. 438, 46 Atl. 965, holding where corporation has limited power to hold real estate, its right to hold particular lands can be questioned only by state; Farrington v. Putnam, 90 Me. 431, 38 L. R. A. 340, 37 Atl. 652, holding devise to charitable association of property exceeding in value limitation in its charter will not be declared void at instance of heirs; Brigham v. Peter Bent Brigham Hospital, 126 Fed. 801, holding next of kin cannot question power of corporation to take devise increasing property beyond charter limit; Chicago General R. Co. v. Chicago City R. Co. 87 Ill. App. 26, holding fact that tort committed by corporation result of act *ultra vires*, not available to plaintiff, if act is not prohibited, and does not constitute nuisance; Texarkana & Ft. S. R. Co. v. Texas & N. O. R. Co. 28 Tex. Civ. App. 554, 67 S. W. 525, holding railroad cannot justify trespass on another's track by denying right to build such track; Hill v. Gruell, 42 Ill. App. 419, holding stockholders of dissolved corporation receiving proportionate share of assets are trustees for creditors of corporation.

Cited in note (32 L. R. A. 294) on right of private persons to contest power of corporation to take or hold property.

8 L. R. A. 559, ST. LOUIS, I. M. & S. R. CO. v. RAMSEY, 53 Ark. 314, 22 Am. St. Rep. 195, 13 S. W. 931.

Riparian ownership.

Approved in Ft. Smith & V. B. Bridge Co. v. Hawkins, 54 Ark. 517, 12 L. R. A. 491, 16 S. W. 565, holding boundary of incorporated town on navigable river extends to high-water mark although county bounded by channel; Peuker v. Canter, 62 Kan. 372, 63 Pac. 617, sustaining riparian ownership of accretion within original boundaries of intervening lots; Wallace v. Driver, 61 Ark. 435, 31 L. R. A. 319, 33 S. W. 641, holding island formed in navigable river where land formerly existed not appurtenant to upland unless formed by accretion; Crawford Co. v. Hall (Neb.) 60 L. R. A. 901, 93 N. W. 781, holding rights of owner in boundary stream not navigable in fact inferior to public right to appropriate for irrigation.

Cited in footnote to Webb v. Demopolis, 21 L. R. A. 62, which holds riparian owner's title extends to low-water mark on navigable river.

Cited in notes (42 L. R. A. 171) as to title to land under water; (12 L. R. A. 635, 677) on navigable waters; title to land below high-water line; (42 L. R. A. 171) as to title to land under water.

Test of navigability.

Cited in note (42 L. R. A. 318) as to what waters are navigable.

8 L. R. A. 562, BUETER v. BUETER, 1 S. D. 94, 45 N. W. 208.

Jurisdiction of suit for support.

Approved in Edgerton v. Edgerton, 12 Mont. 139, 16 L. R. A. 99, 33 Am. St. Rep. 557, 29 Pac. 966, holding suit to compel husband if able to support his deserted and destitute wife, within jurisdiction of equity.

Allowance of attorney's fees in divorce suit.

Cited in note (9 L. R. A. 698) concerning divorce for desertion.

8 L. R. A. 566, PEASE v. RITCHIE, 132 Ill. 638, 24 N. E. 433.

Appeal dismissed in 140 U. S. 693, 35 L. ed. 594, 11 Sup. Ct. Rep. 1026.

Who may redeem from mortgage sale.

Cited in Paddack v. Staley, 13 Colo. App. 370, 58 Pac. 363, holding judgment creditor may redeem before his judgment becomes a lien.

Validity of execution.

Cited in McDonald v. Fuller, 11 S. D. 360, 74 Am. St. Rep. 815, 77 N. W. 581, holding execution to other county valid though issued before transcript of judgment filed in county where judgment rendered.

Title of purchaser at judicial sale.

Cited in Pease v. Hale, 37 Ill. App. 273, holding purchaser on execution sale has interest of mortgagor subject to mortgage; Smith v. Mace, 137 Ill. 73, 26 N. E. 1092, holding homestead passes to junior judgment creditor redeeming from purchaser at mortgage sale.

Effect of discharge in bankruptcy.

Cited in Mallin v. Wenham, 209 Ill. 258, 65 L. R. A. 606, 70 N. E. 564, Affirming 103 Ill. App. 612, holding discharge in bankruptcy does not invalidate assignment of future wages as security.

Cited in footnote to Colwell v. Tinker, 58 L. R. A. 765, which holds judgment for criminal conversation not released by discharge in bankruptcy.

8 L. R. A. 568, ANDERSON v. ROBBINS, 82 Me. 422, 19 Atl. 910.

8 L. R. A. 570, SYMONDS v. JONES, 82 Me. 302, 17 Am. St. Rep. 485, 19 Atl. 820.

Assignment of trademark.

Cited in Geo. T. Stagg Co. v. Taylor, 95 Ky. 669, 27 S. W. 247, holding that manufacturer's autograph cannot be used on label by vendee of plant; Alaska Packers' Asso. v. Alaska Improv. Co. 60 Fed. 104, holding trademark used as mark of special qualities imparted by originator, not property of assignee; Wilmer v. Thomas, 74 Md. 490, 13 L. R. A. 382, 22 Atl. 403, holding good will and trademarks not personal in character, pass to purchaser under assignment of all property in old mills.

8 L. R. A. 575, McDANIEL v. CUMMINGS, 83 Cal. 515, 23 Pac. 795.

Surface water.

Approved in Cushing v. Pires, 124 Cal. 665, 57 Pac. 572, holding that landowner cannot protect his own land by turning surface water on another's land to his injury.

Cited in Sanguinetti v. Pock, 136 Cal. 472, 89 Am. St. Rep. 160, 69 Pac. 98, holding lower owner may protect from overflow of natural stream although to injury of higher land.

Cited in notes (25 L. R. A. 530) as to what is surface water; (21 L. R. A. 594, 599) on rights as to flow of surface water; (10 L. R. A. 487) as to right to use of flowing water.

8 L. R. A. 578, LEMBECK v. NYE, 47 Ohio St. 336, 21 Am. St. Rep. 828, 24 N. E. 686.

Boundaries — By highway.

Cited in Paine v. Consumers' Forwarding & Storage Co. 19 C. C. A. 102, 37 U. S. App. 539, 71 Fed. 629, holding description bounding by monument having width, presumed to carry fee to center rather than edge; Avery v. United States, 44 C. C. A. 164, 104 Fed. 713, assuming without deciding that grantee of property bounded by side line of street takes only to such line.

— By water.

Cited in Hardin v. Jordan, 140 U. S. 393, 35 L. ed. 437, 11 Sup. Ct. Rep. 808, holding freshwater lakes and ponds belong to owners of adjacent soil; Gouverneur v. National Ice Co. 134 N. Y. 363, 18 L. R. A. 700, 30 Am. St. Rep. 669, 31 N. E. 865, holding land under small inland lakes and ponds presumed to belong with uplands; Lamprey v. State, 52 Minn. 194, 18 L. R. A. 676, 38 Am. St. Rep. 541, 53 N. W. 1139, holding patent for bed of meandered lake void where lands bordering thereon previously granted without reservation; Poynter v. Chipman, 8 Utah, 450, 32 Pac. 690, holding grantee to meander line entitled to dry land made by gradual recession of water; Fuller v. Shedd, 161 Ill. 488, 33 L. R. A. 159, 52 Am. St. Rep. 380, 44 N. E. 286, holding grant bounded on meandered lake does not include land under water; Boardman v. Scott, 102 Ga. 414, 51 L. R. A. 184, 30 S. E. 982, holding that deed of land bounded by permanent artificial pond conveys to low-water mark at date of execution; Concord Mfg. Co. v. Robertson, 66 N. H. 28, 18 L. R. A. 694, 25 Atl. 718, holding diversion of waters of great pond unlawful where to damage of riparian owner on outlet.

Cited in notes (18 L. R. A. 697) as to ownership of bed of lakes and ponds; (40 L. R. A. 394) on separation of riparian rights from upland.

Limited in Lake Shore & M. S. R. Co. v. Platt, 53 Ohio St. 208, 29 L. R. A. 55, 41 N. E. 243, holding conveyance of riparian lands bounded by line of navigation conveys to thread of stream; Head v. Chesbrough, 4 Ohio N. P. 76, holding conveyance of platted lots upon bank of navigable stream conveys grantor's rights to thread of stream where bed not platted.

Right to injunction.

Distinguished in Snyder v. Union Depot Co. 19 Ohio C. C. 371, refusing injunction on cross-petition where plaintiffs are not shown to be insolvent.

— Against continuing trespasses.

Approved in Strawberry Valley Cattle Co. v. Chipman, 13 Utah, 471, 45 Pac. 348, and Roddy v. Dickson, 25 Pa. Co. Ct. 93, holding restraining order proper against continuing trespass; Nashville, C. & St. L. R. Co. v. McConnell, 82 Fed. 70, and Boston & M. R. Co. v. Sullivan, 177 Mass. 233, 83 Am. St. Rep. 275, 58 N. E. 689, sustaining injunction suit where only remedy at law is by large number of suits for damages without substantial results; Great Southern Fire Proof

Hotel Co. v. McClain, 3 Ohio N. P. 253, granting temporary injunction against threatened acts constituting repeated trespasses.

Fishery rights.

Cited in note (60 L. R. A. 497, 513, 522) on the right to fish.

8 L. R. A. 584, STATE v. KAISER, 20 Or. 50, 23 Pac. 964.

Affidavit in contempt proceedings.

Approved in State *ex rel.* Hammer v. Downing, 40 Or. 325, 66 Pac. 917, holding facts constituting contempt not committed in presence of court must be shown by affidavit; State *ex rel.* Jones v. Conn, 37 Or. 598, 62 Pac. 289, to point that affidavit for constructive contempt is essential to jurisdiction of court.

Cited in State v. Lavery, 31 Or. 84, 49 Pac. 852, holding amendment to relator's affidavit charging contempt must be sworn to; State *ex rel.* Victor Boom Co. v. Peterson, 29 Wash. 579, 70 Pac. 71, holding court cannot punish for disobedience of injunction order one whom affidavit does not show in privity with nominal parties.

Publication constituting contempt.

Approved in State v. Tugwell, 19 Wash. 249, 43 L. R. A. 722, 52 Pac. 1056, holding publication tending to embarrass or influence the court in a pending case a contempt; Field v. Thornell, 106 Iowa, 16, 68 Am. St. Rep. 281, 75 N. W. 685, holding publication of scurrilous article concerning pending trial and handing copy of paper to jurors during adjournment, a contempt of court.

Cited in footnotes to Telegram Newspaper Co. v. Com. 44 L. R. A. 159, which holds corporation guilty of contempt in publishing article calculated to prejudice jury and prevent fair trial; State v. Bee Pub. Co. 50 L. R. A. 195, which sustains punishment for contempt of newspaper publishing articles threatening judges with public odium if they decide pending cause in certain way.

Statute as declaratory of common law.

Cited in State v. Tugwell, 19 Wash. 252, 43 L. R. A. 723, 52 Pac. 1056, to point that Washington statute on contempt is declaratory of common law.

Enforcing answer by imprisonment.

Cited in footnote to *Re* Clark, 28 L. R. A. 242, which upholds right to summarily enforce answer by imprisoning witness.

8 L. R. A. 591, VOUGHT v. WILLIAMS, 120 N. Y. 253, 17 Am. St. Rep. 634, 24 N. E. 195.

Right to marketable title.

Cited in McGuire Bros. v. Blanchard, 107 Iowa, 493, 78 N. W. 231, holding vendee entitled to marketable title under contract binding vendor to "carry out abstract . . . and show title vested in him."

What is a marketable title.

Cited in Stevenson v. Fox, 40 App. Div. 358, 57 N. Y. Supp. 1094, holding that encroachment of buildings and foundations upon adjoining lots renders title unmarketable; McPherson v. Schade, 149 N. Y. 21, 43 N. E. 527, holding encroachment of building upon adjoining common alley way renders title unmarketable; Smithers v. Steiner, 13 Misc. 518, 34 N. Y. Supp. 678, holding title rendered unmarketable by latent encroachment of front wall 3 inches on street; Heller v.

Cohen, 154 N. Y. 306,48 N. E. 527, Affirming 15 Misc. 384, 36 N. Y. Supp. 668, holding defective description of premises renders sale unenforceable; Egelhoff v. Simpson, 50 App. Div. 601, 64 N. Y. Supp. 336, holding error in description due to widening of street, renders title unmarketable; Reynolds v. Cleary, 61 Hun, 594, 16 N. N. Supp. 421, holding restrictive covenant running with land, and improperly foreclosed mortgage, render title unmarketable; Kerrigan v. Backus, 69 App. Div. 331, 74 N. Y. Supp. 906, holding title unmarketable where subject to unimproved streets platted on map by which other conveyances made; Bullard v. Bicknell, 26 App. Div. 321, 49 N. Y. Supp. 666, holding title not marketable where land possessed adversely to vendor; Hamershlag v. Duryea, 38 App. Div. 132, 56 N. Y. Supp. 615, holding title unmarketable where adverse possession against tenant in common not established; Simis v. McElroy, 12 App. Div. 436, 42 N. Y. Supp. 290, holding contract for good-record title not satisfied by offer of title by adverse possession unsupported by proof; Darrow v. Cornell, 30 App. Div. 119, 51 N. Y. Supp. 828, holding title not marketable where deeds essential to clear record not filed; Irving v. Campbell, 121 N. Y. 358, 8 L. R. A. 621, 24 N. E. 821, holding vendor's title unmarketable where grantor's deed defectively acknowledged and not entitled to record; Paolillo v. Faber, 56 App. Div. 244, 67 N. Y. Supp. 638, holding title not marketable where acquired under power of attorney defectively acknowledged; Hatt v. Hagaman, 12 Misc. 173, 33 N. Y. Supp. 5, holding sale of property held by trustee under power to acquire but not to sell, not specifically enforceable; Horne v. Rodgers, 113 Ga. 227, 38 S. E. 768, holding title unmarketable where based upon invalid sale "on the premises," out of city, by ordinary; Stuyvesant v. Weil, 41 App. Div. 559, 58 N. Y. Supp. 697, holding vendee entitled to recover part payments where vendor's title dependent upon judicial proceeding in which owner erroneously named in summons and complaint; Schenck v. Wicks, 23 Utah, 582, 65 Pac. 732, holding outstanding trust deed in favor of grantor renders title unmarketable; Haffey v. Lynch, 143 N. Y. 247, 38 N. E. 298, holding *lis pendens* filed subsequent to sale contract renders title unmarketable; Brokaw v. Duffy, 165 N. Y. 399, 59 N. E. 196, Affirming 36 App. Div. 150, 55 N. Y. Supp. 469, holding title unmarketable where lunacy proceedings are pending against vendor's grantor; Marks v. Halligan, 61 App. Div. 183, 70 N. Y. Supp. 444, holding title unmarketable where interest under unconstrued will uncertain; Reynolds v. Strong, 82 Hun, 214, 31 N. Y. Supp. 329, holding title unmarketable where election of widow to accept will, adverse to her ownership, uncertain; Dworsky v. Arndstein, 29 App. Div. 278, 51 N. Y. Supp. 597, holding title not marketable where probate proceedings are irregular for failure to cite testator's brother, and there is an outstanding disputable dower interest; Emens v. St. John, 79 Hun, 102, 29 N. Y. Supp. 655, holding title under grant by less than all of devisees unmarketable where executor has power of sale; Griffith v. Maxfield, 63 Ark. 551, 39 S. W. 852, holding title unmarketable where purchased for benefit of administrator at administrator's sale, and outstanding unbarred dower interest exists; Casey v. Casey, 19 App. Div. 223, 79 N. Y. S. R. 879, 45 N. Y. Supp. 877 (concurring opinion) holding purchaser in partition proceedings not bound to complete sale where record does not show death without issue of heirs not joined; Fowler v. Manheimer, 70 App. Div. 58, 75 N. Y. Supp. 17, holding title unmarketable where record fails to show decease of heirs unmarried and without issue; Stephens v. Flammer, 40 Misc. 281, 81 N. Y. Supp. 1064, holding purchaser on foreclosure not required to take title validity of which depends on disputable fact; Ormsby v. Graham, 123 Iowa, 210, 98 N. W. 724, holding owner of contract for sale of land has no marketable title; Barger v. Gery, 64 N. J. Eq. 270, 53 Atl. 483, holding title not rendered unmarketable by break in chain of recorded assignments of mortgage theretofore foreclosed.

Distinguished in Neil v. Radley, 31 App. Div. 29, 52 N. Y. Supp. 398, holding title by adverse possession sufficient where record not clear through scrivener's error in description; Moot v. Business Men's Invest. Asso. 157 N. Y. 211, 45 L. R. A. 670, 52 N. E. 1, holding record of title corrected before tender though defective at time of contract, marketable; Sloane v. Martin, 77 Hun, 252, 24 N. Y. Supp. 663, holding title marketable where defective record of service on infants cured by judgment; Corbin v. Baker, 56 App. Div. 37, 67 N. Y. Supp. 249, holding title of party to partition proceedings purchasing at sale, marketable where court order permits same, and purchase confirmed; Kullman v. Cox, 167 N. Y. 420, 53 L. R. A. 887, 60 N. E. 738 (dissenting opinion) majority holding title marketable where acquired in good faith by husband of mortgagor from mortgagee buying in on foreclosure.

Provision for approval of title by third party.

Cited as *obiter* in Flanagan v. Fox, 6 Misc. 136, 26 N. Y. Supp. 48, Reversing 3 Misc. 370, 23 N. Y. Supp. 344, holding approval by title company condition precedent on sale subject thereto.

Distinguished in Allen v. Pockwitz, 103 Cal. 88, 42 Am. St. Rep. 99, 36 Pac. 1039, holding purchaser's deposit recoverable where attorney's adverse opinion on sufficient examination, honestly formed; Trowbridge v. New York City, 24 Misc. 521, 53 N. Y. Supp. 616, refusing to restrain issue of stock to unconditioned bidder in preference to higher bidder, "subject to opinion of counsel" as to validity.

Presumption of death.

Cited in Johnson v. Johnson, 170 Mo. 56, 59 L. R. A. 755, 70 S. W. 241, holding testimony of sister that missing heir ran away twenty years ago when eighteen, and not heard from since, insufficient; Dunn v. Travis, 56 App. Div. 321, 67 N. Y. Supp. 743, refusing to distribute share of runaway beneficiary in absence of proof of death without issue; McNulty v. Mitchell, 41 Misc. 294, 84 N. Y. Supp. 89, holding death of man disappearing when thirty presumed after forty-three years.

8 L. R. A. 593, CINCINNATI, I. ST. L. & C. R. CO. v. HOWARD, 124 Ind. 280, 19 Am. St. Rep. 96, 24 N. E. 892.

Contributory negligence.

Cited in Lake Erie & W. R. Co. v. Pence, 24 Ind. App. 21, 55 N. E. 1036, holding party attempting to cross ahead of train cannot recover, though speed thereof unlawful; Bush v. Union P. R. Co. 62 Kan. 715, 64 Pac. 624, holding defendant's violation of regulation as to time between following trains, no excuse for plaintiff's lack of care; Pennsylvania Co. v. Meyers, 136 Ind. 250, 36 N. E. 32, holding duty of track walker to be upon railway does not absolve him from obligation to use due care as to approaching trains; Miller v. Louisville, N. A. & C. R. Co. 128 Ind. 101, 25 Am. St. Rep. 416, 27 N. E. 339, holding wife guilty of contributory negligence where she failed to warn husband, driving, of apparent danger; Silcock v. Rio Grande Western R. Co. 22 Utah, 189, 61 Pac. 565, denying right to recover for injuries received in stopping team, carelessly left untied near railway track.

Cited in footnote to Howe v. Minneapolis, St. P. & S. M. R. Co. 30 L. R. A. 684, which holds negligence of one riding with another when injured at railroad crossing a question for jury.

Cited in note (9 L. R. A. 164) on contributory negligence of passenger approaching crossing.

Distinguished in Louisville & N. R. Co. v. Williams, 20 Ind. App. 585, 51 N. E. 128, upholding instruction to jury to consider defendant's failure to ring bell or blow whistle in determining plaintiff's contributory negligence; Scofield v. Myers, 27 Ind. App. 376, 60 N. E. 1005, holding failure to look and listen for approaching runaway team in rear does not constitute contributory negligence; Chicago, St. L. & P. R. Co. v. Butler, 10 Ind. App. 273, 38 N. E. 1 (dissenting opinion) majority holding guest riding in wagon may recover where possibility of train approaching duly apprehended.

Imputing negligence.

Cited in Lake Shore & M. S. R. Co. v. Boyts, 16 Ind. App. 648, 45 N. E. 812, holding guest riding in carriage must prove his own diligence and freedom from negligence; Abbitt v. Lake Erie & W. R. Co. 150 Ind. 514, 50 N. E. 729, holding contributory negligence of coemployee acting as agent, imputable so as to defeat recovery by employee injured.

Cited in footnote to Illinois C. R. Co. v. McLeod, 52 L. R. A. 954, which holds hirer of team bound to check driver's attempt to cross track without stopping or listening for train.

Presumption of negligence from injury.

Cited in Evansville & T. H. R. Co. v. Marohn, 6 Ind. App. 651, 34 N. E. 27, holding presumption rebutted where evidence shows use of all reasonable care under circumstances; Cincinnati, I. & St. L. & C. R. Co. v. Grames, 8 Ind. App. 143, 34 N. E. 613, holding presumption rebutted by proof that, before driving over crossing, plaintiff stopped and listened, view being obstructed; Lamport v. Lake Shore & M. S. R. Co. 142 Ind. 275, 41 N. E. 586, holding where no affirmative proof in rebuttal, presumption not overcome by proof of defendant's negligence.

Cited in footnote to Phillips v. Milwaukee & N. R. Co. 9 L. R. A. 521, which holds person killed on sidewalk by railroad car presumed to have been making ordinary use of walk.

Doubted in Pittsburgh, C. & St. L. R. Co. v. Bennett, 9 Ind. App. 110, 35 N. E. 1033, holding presumption of contributory negligence of person injured by collision at crossing rebutted by slight evidence.

Necessity of alleging and proving freedom from contributory negligence.

Cited in Sale v. Aurora & L. Turnp. Co. 147 Ind. 330, 46 N. E. 669, holding complaint not stating facts from which freedom from negligence can be inferred, nor expressly asserting same, demurrable; Indianapolis, D. & W. R. Co. v. Wilson, 134 Ind. 99, 33 N. E. 793, holding complaint excusing failure to look and listen only on ground of want of time, demurrable; Oleson v. Lake Shore & M. S. R. Co. 143 Ind. 410, 32 L. R. A. 151, 42 N. E. 736, and Sutherland v. Cleveland, C. C. & St. L. R. Co. 148 Ind. 310, 47 N. E. 624, holding averment and proof of freedom from negligence, essential to plaintiff's recovery; Evansville Street R. Co. v. Gentry, 147 Ind. 416, 37 L. R. A. 381, 62 Am. St. Rep. 421.

44 N. E. 311, and Kauffman v. Cleveland, C. C. & St. L. R. Co. 144 Ind. 457, 43 N. E. 446, holding verdict properly directed where no affirmative proof of freedom from contributory negligence; Lake Shore & M. S. R. Co. v. Boyts, 16 Ind. App. 648, 45 N. E. 812, holding burden on plaintiff to prove both negligence of defendant and also his own freedom therefrom; Louisville, N. A. & C. R. Co. v. Stommel, 126 Ind. 39, 25 N. E. 863, holding owner of team must allege and prove want of negligence on part of servant in charge at time of accident; Pittsburgh, C. & St. L. R. Co. v. Bennett, 9 Ind. App. 103, 35 N. E. 1033, holding proof of excessive speed and failure to give signals does not dispense with proof of freedom from contributory negligence.

Duty to look and listen at crossing.

Cited in Blackburn v. Southern P. Co. 34 Or. 223, 55 Pac. 225; Carter v. Central Vermont R. Co. 72 Vt. 200, 47 Atl. 797; Cincinnati, H. & I. R. Co. v. Duncan, 143 Ind. 526, 42 N. E. 37, — holding one failing to stop, look, and listen where view obstructed, cannot recover; Malott v. Hawkins, 159 Ind. 134, 63 N. E. 308, holding person approaching railroad crossing must look, listen, and, under exceptional circumstances, stop; Miller v. Terre Haute & I. R. Co. 144 Ind. 326, 43 N. E. 257, and Louisville, N. A. & C. R. Co. v. Stommel, 126 Ind. 41, 25 N. E. 863, holding defendant's violation of statutory requirement as to signals does not excuse failure to stop, look, and listen; Baltimore & O. & C. R. Co. v. Walborn, 127 Ind. 148, 26 N. E. 207, holding negligence for jury where facts reasonably permit of more than one inference; Baltimore & O. R. Co. v. Talmage, 15 Ind. App. 214, 43 N. E. 1019 (concurring opinion) holding party failing to look and listen, negligent though engine had passed crossing within minute.

Cited in footnotes to Woehrle v. Minnesota Transfer R. Co. 52 L. R. A. 349, which holds traveler's failure to look and listen when watchman absent not negligence *per se;* Western & A. R. Co. v. Ferguson, 54 L. R. A. 802, which holds failure to look within 30 feet of track does not prevent recovery; Keenan v. Union Traction Co. 58 L. R. A. 217, which holds failure to look for train within 35 feet of track, negligence; Oleson v. Lake Shore & M. S. R. Co. 32 L. R. A. 149, which holds it negligent to attempt to cross track immediately after passage of train whose smoke obstructs view; Lorenz v. Burlington, C. R. & N. R. Co. 56 L. R. A. 753, which holds negligence of one pursuing cow in not looking and listening before crossing railroad track, for jury; Van Auken v. Chicago & W. M. R. Co. 22 L. R. A. 33, which holds that failure to look and listen on dark night does not prevent recovery for injury by engine running backward.

Cited in notes (9 L. R. A. 162) on duty of traveler approaching railroad crossing; (11 L. R. A. 388) on negligence in crossing railroad track.

Distinguished in Marchal v. Indianapolis Street R. Co. 28 Ind. App. 141, 62 N. E. 286, holding contributory negligence for jury where plaintiff drove on street railway crossing without looking, immediately after passage of car.

Effect of general verdict.

Cited in Diamond Plate Glass Co. v. De Hority, 143 Ind. 385, 40 N. E. 681, and Shirk v. Wabash R. Co. 14 Ind. App. 137, 42 N. E. 656, holding general verdict of freedom from contributory negligence controlled by special findings showing contrary; Bedford v. Neal, 143 Ind. 430, 41 N. E. 1029, setting aside verdict of freedom from contributory negligence where evidence fails to show exercise of care proportioned to known danger.

Distinguished in Indianapolis Union R. Co. v. Neubacher, 16 Ind. App. 46, 44

N. E. 669, holding verdict conclusive where evidence is not in record, and answers to interrogatories do not absolutely antagonize same.

Time to take exceptions.

Cited in Combs v. Union Trust Co. 146 Ind. 693, 46 N. E. 16, holding party failing to make motion to reject interrogatories at time offered in evidence, waives objection.

Form of exceptions and objections.

Cited in Musser v. State, 157 Ind. 431, 61 N. E. 1, holding objection that interrogatory "incompetent, immaterial, and too remote" presents no question; Musser v. State, 157 Ind. 428, 431, 61 N. E. 1, holding objection that evidence "hearsay, and wholly immaterial and irrelevant," not sufficiently specific; Stratton v. Lockhart, 1 Ind. App. 383, 27 N. E. 715, holding objection to judgment on ground of alteration insufficient where changes not specified.

Cited in note (8 L. R. A. 609) on consideration of general exceptions on appeal.

8 L. R. A. 598, LOCEY COAL MINES v. CHICAGO, W. & V. COAL CO. 131 Ill. 9, 22 N. E. 503.

Redemption.

Approved in Bruschke v. Wright, 166 Ill. 198, 57 Am. St. Rep. 125, 46 N. E. 813, holding resale of property on foreclosure by officer of court should be made subject to redemption.

Distinguished in Blair v. Illinois Steel Co. 159 Ill. 362, 31 L. R. A. 274, 42 N. E. 895, holding receiver on sale of corporate property under winding-up statute may sell without redemption.

Separate ownership of surface and minerals.

Cited in Ames v. Ames, 160 Ill. 601, 43 N. E. 592, holding ownership of surface and of under-lying minerals may be separated in partition suit; Catlin Coal Co. v. Lloyd, 176 Ill. 283, 52 N. E. 144, holding owner of minerals, title to which has been severed from the surface, may invoke in respect thereto the statute of limitations.

Corporate ownership of buildings.

Cited in People *ex rel.* Moloney v. Pullman's Palace Car Co. 175 Ill. 174, 64 L. R. A. 388, 51 N. E. 664 (dissenting opinion) majority holding manufacturing corporation authorized to hold land for transaction of its business cannot erect and rent dwellings, stores, schools, and churches.

8 L. R. A. 602, KINCAID v. INDIANAPOLIS NATURAL GAS CO. 124 Ind. 577, 19 Am. St. Rep. 113, 24 N. E. 1066.

Right to compensation for additional burden in highway.

Cited in Huffman v. State, 21 Ind. App. 454, 69 Am. St. Rep. 368, 52 N. E. 713, and Consumers' Gas Trust Co. v. Huntsinger, 14 Ind. App. 164, 39 N. E. 423, holding compensation must be made to fee owner for construction of pipe line along highway; Egbert v. Lake Shore & M. S. R. Co. 6 Ind. App. 354, 33 N. E. 659, holding railroad liable to owners abutting on highway for damages caused by graded approach to crossing; Haslett v. New Albany Belt & Terminal R. Co. 7 Ind. App. 607, 34 N. E. 845, holding municipal permission to construct railroad along street does not impair abutting owner's right to compensation.

Cited in note (17 L. R. A. 480) on what use of street or highway constitutes additional burden.

Extent of abutting owner's rights in highways.

Cited in Magee v. Overshiner, 150 Ind. 133, 40 L. R. A. 372, 65 Am. St. Rep. 358, 49 N. E. 951, holding public easement greater in urban than in suburban highways; Lostutter v. Aurora, 126 Ind. 438, 12 L. R. A. 260, 26 N. E. 184, recognizing city's right to maintain well and pump in street; Lake Erie & W. R. Co. v. Lee, 14 Ind. App. 330, 14 N. E. 1058, upholding recovery for obstruction of private crossing under railroad upon public highway; Huffman v. State, 21 Ind. App. 459, 69 Am. St. Rep. 368, 52 N. E. 713, holding refusal of one unlawfully upon highway to depart at command of abutting owner renders him liable for criminal trespass; Hamilton County v. Indianapolis Natural Gas Co. 134 Ind. 212, 33 N. E. 972, holding county cannot enjoin laying gas pipes by company under permit of county officers and grant of abutting owners.

Distinguished in Huffman v. State, 21 Ind. App. 456, 69 Am. St. Rep. 368, 52 N. E. 713, holding abutting owner not estopped from maintaining trespass for removal of pipe line in highway without his knowledge.

Public rights as affecting character of remedy.

Cited in Whitlock v. Consumers Gas Trust Co. 127 Ind. 65, 26 N. E. 570, denying injunction against laying gas-pipe line; Midland R. Co. v. Smith, 135 Ind. 350, 35 N. E. 284, denying injunction against railroad's use of right of way, public rights having attached; Morgan v. Lake Shore & M. S. R. Co. 130 Ind. 104, 28 N. E. 548, denying ejectment to recover land occupied by railroad after public rights have intervened.

Distinguished in Adams v. Ohio Falls Car Co. 131 Ind. 380, 31 N. E. 57, holding wrongful use of public wharf by private company under permission from common council enjoinable.

Public use.

Cited in Rushville v. Rushville Natural Gas Co. 132 Ind. 584, 15 L. R. A. 325, 28 N. E. 853, holding business of supplying natural gas subject to public regulation.

Right to damages for land taken.

Cited in Evansville & R. R. Co. v. Charlton, 6 Ind. App. 59, 33 N. E. 129, holding that consent to appropriation of land by railroad does not estop claim for damages.

8 L. R. A. 604, MIDLAND R. CO. v. FISHER, 125 Ind. 19, 21 Am. St. Rep. 189, 24 N. E. 756.

Covenants running with land.

Cited in Scott v. Stetler, 128 Ind. 388, 27 N. E. 721, holding covenant in deed "together with mill and all privileges thereto belonging," runs with land; Branson v. Studabaker, 133 Ind. 164, 33 N. E. 98, holding deed granting mill race, etc. conveys land forming essential part thereof; Hamilton v. Shelbyville, 6 Ind. App. 541, 33 N. E. 1007, denying power of municipality to enter into contract running with fee to drain private property.

— By railway companies.

Approved in Kelly v. Nypano R. Co. 23 Pa. Co. Ct. 187, holding covenant in deed of right of way to erect fence runs with land; Lake Erie & W. R. Co. v. Priest, 131 Ind. 416, 31 N. E. 77, holding covenant to maintain crossing, cattle-guards, etc., binds purchaser under mortgage foreclosure.

Cited in Cambria Iron Co. v. Union Trust Co. 154 Ind. 306, 48 L. R. A. 48, 55 N. E. 745, holding condition in franchise requiring pavement between tracks carried into mortgage covering property; Doty v. Chattanooga Union R. Co. 103 Tenn. 572, 48 L. R. A. 164, 53 S. W. 944, holding covenant in deed of right of way that certain trains shall run, as chief consideration, follows fee; Lake Erie & W. R. Co. v. Griffin, 25 Ind. App. 142, 53 N. E. 1042, holding covenant to maintain fence attaches to fee; Toledo, St. L. & K. C. R. Co. v. Burgan, 9 Ind. App. 610, 37 N. E. 31; Toledo, St. L. & K. C. R. Co. v. Cosand, 6 Ind. App. 224, 33 N. E. 251; Lake Erie & W. R. Co. v. Lee, 14 Ind. App. 330, 41 N. E. 1058, — holding agreement in deed to construct crossings and build fences imposes duty running with land.

Acceptance of unexecuted instruments.

Approved in Doty v. Chattanooga Union R. Co. 103 Tenn. 575, 48 L. R. A. 165, 53 S. W. 944, and Harlan v. Logansport Natural Gas Co. 133 Ind. 328, 32 N. E. 930, holding grant of right of way signed by grantor, accepted by grantee, binds both; Reagan v. First Nat. Bank, 157 Ind. 661, 61 N. E. 575, holding accepting provisions of mortgage for benefit of creditors constitutes contract as if signed by all.

Cited in Thiebaud v. Union Furniture Co. 143 Ind. 344, 42 N. E. 741, holding acceptance of deed containing contract to pump water for grantor and acting thereunder equivalent to signature; McPherson v. Fargo, 10 S. D. 616, 66 Am. St. Rep. 723, 74 N. W. 1057, and Indianapolis Natural Gas Co. v. Kibbey, 135 Ind. 361, 35 N. E. 392, holding acceptance of lease signed by lessor alone, and recording same, makes instrument contract; Doxey v. Service, 30 Ind. App. 178, 65 N. E. 757, holding lease accepted by lessees not signing, binding upon them; Terre Haute & I. R. Co. v. State, 159 Ind. 475, 65 N. E. 401, holding state charter, under which railroad was built, written contract, action on which not barred by six-year statute.

8 L. R. A. 607, STATE *ex rel.* TAYLOR v. WARRICK COUNTY, 124 Ind. 554, 25 N. E. 10.

Mandamus to compel performance of ministerial duty.

Cited in State *ex rel.* Butler v. Callahan, 4 N. D. 489, 61 N. W. 1025, holding mandamus will lie in favor of candidate holding certificate of election against incumbent holding over; State *ex rel.* Dunkleberg v. Porter, 134 Ind. 67, 32 N. E. 1021, holding action maintainable to compel issuance of certificate of exemption from highway duty, right thereto admitted; Coats v. State, 133 Ind. 38, 32 N. E. 737, holding mandamus proper remedy for refusal of justice of the peace to accept and approve sufficient bond.

8 L. R. A. 608, STATE v. HOPE, 100 Mo. 347, 13 S. W. 490.

Necessity of objecting and excepting to rulings.

Cited in State v. Taylor, 132 Mo. 287, 33 S. W. 1145, holding failure to object to order for change of venue at time thereof bars exception on appeal; Matson v. Frazer, 48 Mo. App. 309, and State v. Goddard, 162 Mo. 226, 62 S. W. 697, holding that errors of trial court will not be reviewed on appeal if no exceptions are saved.

— As to evidence.

Cited in Boggs v. Pacific Steam Laundry Co. 86 Mo. App. 624, holding waiver of incompetent evidence by neglect to object and except; Adair v. Mette, 156 Mo. 507, 57 S. W. 551, holding failure to object to improper evidence on trial bars exclusion on appeal; State v. McCollum, 119 Mo. 474, 24 S. W. 1021, holding failure to except to improper evidence prevents review on appeal; State v. Marcks, 140 Mo. 669, 41 S. W. 973, holding no error in refusing to exclude evidence, no objection and exception being made till close of testimony; State v. Higgins, 124 Mo. 648, 28 S. W. 178, denying duty of court to exclude improper evidence without objection and exception; Hickman v. Green, 123 Mo. 173, 29 L. R. A. 43, 22 S. W. 455, holding motion to exclude incompetent testimony too late after evidence received without objection; State v. Lehman, 175 Mo. 625, 75 S. W. 139, holding testimony cannot be excluded after cross-examination, on ground disclosed by direct examination; State v. Foley, 144 Mo. 618, 46 S. W. 733, holding omission to object to question no bar to exclusion when it appears incompetent.

Sufficiency of objections.

Cited in State v. Moore, 117 Mo. 401, 22 S. W. 1086, holding general objection to admission of evidence not sufficient for review; Burlington Ins. Co. v. Miller, 8 C. C. A. 614, 19 U. S. App. 588, 60 Fed. 257, holding objection to evidence as "incompetent, irrelevant, immaterial" too general to show grounds.

Waiver of rights.

Cited in Moore v. State, 96 Tenn. 220, 33 S. W. 1046, holding failure to swear witness waived by cross-examination with knowledge of omission; State v. Gamble, 119 Mo. 431, 24 S. W. 1030, holding that error in removing cause to wrong county may be waived.

Statute construed.

Cited in State v. Terry, 109 Mo. 624, 19 S. W. 206, holding courts refuse to declare statute unconstitutional unless invalid beyond doubt; State *ex rel.* Macklin v. Rombauer, 104 Mo. 631, 15 S. W. 850, and Bowers v. Smith, 111 Mo. 56, 16 L. R. A. 759, 33 Am. St. Rep. 491, 20 S. W. 101, holding consideration of effect of proposed construction of statute necessary to ascertain intent.

8 L. R. A. 614, NEW VIENNA BANK v. JOHNSON, 47 Ohio St. 306, 24 N. E. 503.

Estate conveyed by mortgage.

Cited in Stambach v. Fox, 16 Ohio C. C. 431, expressing opinion that mortgage omitting word "heir" passes fee, language showing such intention.

Enforcement of partner's lien.

Cited in Ervin v. Masterman, 16 Ohio C. C. 74, holding partner's lien attaches to property acquired with partnership funds, though individual has title.

8 L. R. A. 617, REISE v. ENOS, 76 Wis. 634, 45 N. W. 414.

Severance of easement from land.

Cited in footnote to Flickinger v. Shaw, 11 L. R. A. 134, holding construction of ditch under agreement across another's land to be used in common gives builder vested right which injunction will protect.

Cited in notes (10 L. R. A. 484) on right by prescription to use another's land; (14 L. R. A. 300) on effect of attempt to sever appurtenant easement from premises for benefit of which it exists.

Distinguished in Macy v. Metropolitan Elev. R. Co. 59 Hun, 367, 12 N. Y. Supp. 804, holding release by tenant of demised interest does not sever easement from land, but reinvests fee.

8 L. R. A. 620, IRVING v. CAMPBELL, 121 N. Y. 353, 24 N. E. 821.

Sufficiency of acknowledgment or verification.

Cited in Lemmer v. Morison, 89 Hun, 279, 35 N. Y. Supp. 623, holding recording of deed ineffectual where acknowledgment insufficient; Freedman v. Oppenheim, 80 App. Div. 488, 81 N. Y. Supp. 110, and Paolillo v. Faber, 56 App. Div. 243, 67 N. Y. Supp. 638, holding acknowledgment defective where not stating notary's knowledge that the maker is the individual described in, and who executed, conveyance; Albany County Sav. Bank v. McCarty, 149 N. Y. 80, 43 N. E. 427, holding prima facie case of conveyance made by certificate of acknowledgment; Cream City Furniture Co. v. Squier, 2 Misc. 440, 21 N. Y. Supp. 972, holding notice of mechanic's lien, verified before foreign commissioner but without certificate of secretary of state, insufficient to create lien.

Right to marketable title.

Cited in Tupy v. Kocourek, 66 Ark. 436, 51 S. W. 69, holding vendee under executory sale of two tracts of land for lump sum may rescind contract if title to one fails; Hatt v. Hagaman, 12 Misc. 173, 33 N. Y. Supp. 5, holding specific performance cannot be decreed upon contract to purchase realty, where ability to convey good, marketable title doubtful.

What is a marketable title.

Approved in Miner v. Hilton, 15 App. Div. 59, 44 N. Y. Supp. 155, holding tender of lot with building which encroached 2¼ inches beyond, not of marketable title; Snow v. Monk, 81 App. Div. 210, 80 N. Y. Supp. 719, holding 2-inch encroachment of building renders title thereto unmarketable; Harrass v. Edwards, 94 Wis. 464, 69 N. W. 69, holding title dependent upon record of deed attested by but one of several grantors not marketable; Lahey v. Kortright, 132 N. Y. 455, 30 N. E. 989, holding substituted trustees can convey marketable title where power of sale applicable to subject of trust was created; Simis v. McElroy, 12 App. Div. 436, 42 N. Y. Supp. 290, holding title not marketable when involving the rights of one not party to suit; Kountze v. Helmuth, 67 Hun, 347, 22 N. Y. Supp. 204, holding title not marketable where property is encumbered with agreements as to its use; Marshall v. Wenninger, 20 Misc. 530, 46 N. Y. Supp. 670, holding mere nonuser and inclosure for more than twenty years of land laid down on map as street, not such abandonment of easement as will make title marketable.

Distinguished in Holly v. Hirsch, 135 N. Y. 598, 49 N. Y. S. R. 19, 32 N. E. 709, holding vendor has marketable title where only question is one of law, which is determined; Freedman v. Oppenheim, 80 App. Div. 492, 81 N. Y. Supp. 110, holding proof of twenty years' undisturbed possession under deed does not establish marketable title; Kullman v. Cox, 26 App. Div. 163, 49 N. Y. Supp. 908 (dissenting opinion), majority holding title marketable where obtained in good faith through purchase at mortgage foreclosure, for default upon lands which owner formerly held in trust; Jay v. Wilson, 91 Hun, 394, 36 N. Y. Supp. 186, holding title marketable although, subsequent to record of deed of bona fide purchaser, previous deed from his grantor appears on record.

— Facts resting in parol.

Cited in Darrow v. Cornell, 30 App. Div. 119, 51 N. Y. Supp. 828, holding tender not effectual where vendor's title depends upon unrecorded deeds; McPherson v. Schade, 149 N. Y. 21, 43 N. E. 527, denying specific performance where title depends upon facts resting in parol; Moot v. Business Men's Invest. Asso. 157 N. Y. 212, 45 L. R. A. 670, 52 N. E. 1, holding title not unmarketable for incorrect record, not demanding resort to parol evidence: Egelhoff v. Simpson, 50 App. Div. 602, 64 N. Y. Supp. 336, denying specific performance because title unmarketable, where record title contains defect which can be supplied only by parol evidence; Huber v. Case, 93 App. Div. 483, 87 N. Y. Supp. 663, holding title depending on declaration that property belonged to partnership not marketable; Heller v. Cohen, 154 N. Y. 306, 48 N. E. 527, Affirming 15 Misc. 384, 36 N. Y. Supp. 668, holding title not marketable where descriptions in essential instruments vary and no record title appears; Nelson v. Jacobs, 99 Wis. 561, 75 N. W. 406, holding adverse possession creates marketable title under statute of limitations; Ruess v. Ewen, 34 App. Div. 487, 54 N. Y. Supp. 357, holding title originating in tax lease, since expired, not marketable unless title by adverse possession reasonably established; Simis v. McElroy, 160 N. Y. 162, 73 Am. St. Rep. 673, 54 N. E. 674, holding fee simple not assured where title rests in adverse possession proved by parol.

8 L. R. A. 623, VENABLE v. RICKENBERG, 152 Mass. 64, 24 N. E. 1083.

Creditor's bill.

Cited in Geist v. St. Louis, 156 Mo. 649, 79 Am. St. Rep. 545, 57 S. W. 766, holding that salary of municipal officer not garnishable in law cannot be reached by creditor's bill.

Cited in footnote to Harper v. Clayton, 35 L. R. A. 211, which denies power to reach unassigned right of dower by creditor's bill.

Cited in note (63 L. R. A. 694) on equitable remedy to subject choses in action to judgment after return of no property found.

Distinguished in Haman v. Brennan, 170 Mass. 407, 49 N. E. 655, holding nonresident creditor may maintain bill in equity on domestic judgment to reach discharged insolvent's interest in partnership property.

8 L. R. A. 625, McCARTER v. ARMSTRONG, 32 S. C. 203, 10 S. E. 953.

Petition for rehearing denied in 32 S. C. 601, 11 S. E. 634.

Specific performance of contract.

Cited in footnote to Atchison, T. & S. F. R. Co. v. Chicago & W. I. R. Co. 35 L. R. A. 167, which refuses to require payment of interest not provided for as condition of specific performance of contract.

Cited in notes (11 L. R. A. 143) on specific performance; (59 L. R. A. 883) on equitable remedy for damming back water of stream.

Distinguished in Murray v. Northwestern R. Co. 64 S. C. 536, 42 S. E. 617, holding equity will decree specific performance of railroad's covenant to establish depot on lands granted.

Disapproved in Blair v. St. Louis, K. & N. W. R. Co. 92 Mo. App. 557, granting specific performance of agreement to construct and maintain pass-ways for cattle under railroad, water gate, and *cul-de-sac* to low-water mark of river.

8 L. R. A. 629, O'DONNELL v. GLENN, 9 Mont. 452, 23 Pac. 1018.

Verification of location notice.

Approved in Davidson v. Bordeaux, 15 Mont. 251, 38 Pac. 1070; Brownfield v. Bier, 15 Mont. 410, 39 Pac. 465; McCowan v. Maclay, 16 Mont. 236, 40 Pac. 602,— holding declaratory statement of location of mining claim must be under oath: Preston v. Hunter, 15 C. C. A. 151, 29 U. S. App. 621, 67 Fed. 999, holding want of verification of location notice does not invalidate claim, where no adverse rights attach before record is perfected.

Common error.

Cited in Baker v. Butte City Water Co. 24 Mont. 116, 60 Pac. 817, as discussing and applying the maxim *Communis error facit jus.*

8 L. R. A. 633, SMITH v. OSAGE, 80 Iowa, 84, 45 N. W. 404.

Estoppel by taxation.

Cited in Davenport v. Boyd, 109 Iowa, 250, 77 Am. St. Rep. 536, 80 N. W. 314, holding city estopped from claiming land held adversely, where taxes and special assessments levied for thirty years; Corey v. Ft. Dodge, 118 Iowa, 749, 92 N. W. 704, holding city estopped to deny title of one occupying for many years and improving part of street; Weber v. Iowa City, 119 Iowa, 640, 93 N. W. 637, holding public right in unused street extinguished by long-continued, actual, adverse possession.

Distinguished in Hanger v. Des Moines, 109 Iowa, 483, 80 N. W. 549, denying that collection of taxes for ten years on property occupied by public estops claiming it as street.

8 L. R. A. 636, LOUISVILLE, N. A. & C. R. CO. v. CORPS, 124 Ind. 427, 24 N. E. 1046.

Review of questions not raised below.

Cited in Taggart v. Tevanny, 1 Ind. App. 349, 27 N. E. 511, as to question of right to raise on appeal objections to sufficiency of complaint not made in lower court; Diggs v. Way, 22 Ind. App. 623, 54 N. E. 412 (dissenting opinion), majority holding that case tried on theory of insufficient paragraph of complaint will be so treated on appeal, although another count good.

Duty of employer.

Cited in Chicago & E. R. Co. v. Lee, 17 Ind. App. 219, 46 N. E. 543, and Matchett v. Cincinnati, W. & M. R. Co. 132 Ind. 342, 31 N. E. 792, holding employer must use reasonable care to provide safe working place and appliances; Rogers v. Leyden, 127 Ind. 51, 26 N. E. 210, holding employer required to use ordinary care and skill to make and keep place of work in reasonably safe condition: Evansville & T. H. R. Co. v. Duel, 134 Ind. 158, 33 N. E. 355, holding reasonable care required to provide reasonably safe place to work and appliances, and competent persons for service; Rogers v. Leyden, 127 Ind. 57, 26 N. E. 210, holding whether there has been breach of duty to keep place of work safe, and whether dangers of service increased thereby, questions for jury; Evansville & R. R. Co. v. Doan, 3 Ind. App. 455, 29 N. E. 940, holding assumption of risk by employee does not relieve master from duty to exercise reasonable care as to place of work and appliances; Baltimore & O. S. W. R. Co. v. Spaulding, 21 Ind. App. 328, 52 N. E. 410, holding it duty of employer to keep in safe condition scrap-iron bin, to which employees of blacksmith shop required to go, even if inspection necessary for that purpose.

Presumption or proof of master's negligence.

Cited in footnote to Duntley v. Inman, P. & Co. 59 L. R. A. 785, which holds want of care not shown by breaking of piece of machinery, causing servant's death.

Employee's assumption of risk.

Cited in notes (13 L. R. A. 375) on when servant assumes risk; (49 L. R. A. 52) on assumption of risk as conclusive defense; (13 L. R. A. 375) on question of assumption of risk by servant.

— Ordinary hazard.

Cited in Hoosier Stone Co. v. McCain, 133 Ind. 242, 31 N. E. 956, holding employee assumes risk of perils incident to service; Louisville & N. R. Co. v. Kemper, 147 Ind. 567, 47 N. E. 214, and Peerless Stone Co. v. Wray, 143 Ind. 577, 42 N. E. 927, holding employee assumes defects or damages open to view, or which could be known by exercise of ordinary care; O'Neal v. Chicago & I. Coal R. Co. 132 Ind. 113, 31 N. E. 669, holding employee must use reasonable care to ascertain ordinary perils of service, and knowledge of such as are open and obvious presumed.

— Increased hazard.

Cited in Peirce v. Oliver, 18 Ind. App. 94, 47 N. E. 485; Lynch v. Chicago, St. L. & P. R. Co. 8 Ind. App. 519, 36 N. E. 44; Indianapolis Union R. Co. v. Ott, 11 Ind. App. 580, 38 N. E. 842, — holding employee continuing service after knowledge of defects assumes increased risk; Kentucky & I. Bridge Co. v. Eastman, 7 Ind. App. 516, 34 N. E. 835, holding, though master negligent, employee voluntarily remaining in service after knowledge of defects cannot recover for injury therefrom; Chicago & E. I. R. Co. v. Richards, 28 Ind. App. 55, 61 N. E. 18, holding knowledge of defect alone not sufficient to charge employee with assumption of risk, if without knowledge of danger; Southern Kansas R. Co. v. Drake, 53 Kan. 8, 35 Pac. 825, and Romona Oolitic Stone Co. v. Johnson, 6 Ind. App. 556, 33 N. E. 1000, holding employee continuing service without knowledge of danger from known defect, or after promise of employer to repair, does not assume risk.

Distinction between assumption of risk and contributory negligence.

Cited in Wortman v. Minich, 28 Ind. App. 36, 62 N. E. 85, holding assumption of risks, whether obvious or incidental, depends on contract, and has no relation to contributory negligence; Bowles v. Indiana R. Co. 27 Ind. App. 676, 87 Am. St. Rep. 279, 62 N. E. 94, holding statute making contributory negligence matter of defense does not relieve employee from obligation to negative knowledge of defect in complaint; Carver v. Minneapolis & St. L. R. Co. 120 Iowa, 350, 94 N. W. 862, as to distinction between assumption of risk and contributory negligence.

Cited in note (49 L. R. A. 52) on relation between assumption of risk and contributory negligence.

Sufficiency of complaint in action by servant for personal injury.

Cited in Evansville & T. H. R. Co. v. Duel, 134 Ind. 158, 33 N. E. 355; Ohio & M. R. Co. v. Levy, 134 Ind. 344, 32 N. E. 815; Ames v. Lake Shore & M. S. R. Co. 135 Ind. 365, 35 N. E. 117; Peerless Stove Co. v. Wray, 143 Ind. 576, 42 N. E. 927; Salem-Bedford Stone Co. v. Hobbs, 144 Ind. 153, 42 N. E. 1022; Parke County Coal Co. v. Barth, 5 Ind. App. 163, 31 N. E. 585; Cole Bros. v. Wood, 11 Ind. App. 71, 36 N. E. 1074; Chicago & E. I. R. Co. v. Beatty, 13 Ind. App. 622, 42 N. E. 284; Wabash & W. R. Co. v. Morgan, 132 Ind. 446, 32 N. E. 85, — holding that complaint for injury from defect adding to perils of service must allege defects were unknown to employee; American Rolling Mill Co. v. Hallinger, 161 Ind. 686, 69 N. E. 460, holding complaint under employers' liability act must state facts showing nonassumption of risk; Gaar, S. & Co. v. Wilson, 21 Ind. App. 97, 51 N. E. 502, and Pennsylvania Co. v. Witte, 15 Ind. App. 586, 43 N. E. 319, holding knowledge operating as assumption of risk is independent element in right of action for injury, which must be specifically denied; Brunell v. Southern P. Co. 34 Or. 260, 56 Pac. 129, holding complaint must allege employer knew, or ought to have known, of defect, and that employee was ignorant of danger; Cleveland, C. C. & St. L. R. Co. v. Parker, 154 Ind. 154, 56 N. E. 86, holding complaint in action for causing death through negligent construction of side track, causing engine to overturn, must negative knowledge of defect by deceased; South Florida Teleg. Co. v. Maloney, 34 Fla. 342, 16 So. 280, holding, where complaint based on omission of particular duty, complaint must state specifically nature of duty omitted; Eureka Block Coal Co. v. Wells, 29 Ind. App. 6, 94 Am. St. Rep. 259, 61 N. E. 236, holding complaint in negligence action against employer, showing employee had no knowledge of danger, sufficient.

Distinguished in Indiana Natural Gas & Oil Co. v. O'Brien, 160 Ind. 271, 65 N. E. 918, holding plaintiff injured by breaking of defective bridge need not negative previous knowledge of unsafe condition.

8 L. R. A. 637, NAUGATUCK WATER CO. v. NICHOLS, 58 Conn. 403, 20 Atl. 315.

Release from subscription to stock.

Approved in Barrows v. Natchaug Silk Co. 72 Conn. 664, 45 Atl. 951, holding failure to file certificate of increase of stock does not exempt subscriber who has acted as stockholder from paying for stock.

8 L. R. A. 640. WEENER v. BRAYTON, 152 Mass. 101, 25 N. E. 46.

Protection of trade-mark or label.

Approved in State v. Bishop, 128 Mo. 381, 29 L. R. A. 205, 49 Am. St. Rep. 569, 31 S. W. 9, holding state, by appropriate legislation, may protect labor unions in use of labels to designate articles manufactured by its members.

Cited in Tracy v. Banker, 170 Mass. 270, 39 L. R. A. 509, 49 N. E. 308, holding unincorporated trade union protected from use of counterfeit label by Mass. Stat. 1895, chap. 462.

Cited in footnotes to McVey v. Brendel, 13 L. R. A. 377, which holds equity will not protect labor union in use of nontrade-mark label; Cohn v. People, 23

L. R. A. 821, which holds statute giving right t
Fuller v. Huff, 51 L. R. A. 332, which susta
"health food" for foods previously known as
Sanders, 9 L. R. A. 576, which denies right to
as trade-mark; Scott v. Standard Oil Co. 31 l
"fire proof oil" cannot be claimed as trade-mar

Cited in notes (17 L. R. A. 130) on right
(29 L. R. A. 200) on protection of trade unio

Questioned in State v. Hagen, 6 Ind. App.
equity will protect trade union label against fr

Disapproved in Schmalz v. Wooley, 57 N.
Am. St. Rep. 637, 41 Atl. 939, holding workme
right in trade-mark designed to distinguish tl
Hetterman Bros. v. Powers, 102 Ky. 140, 39
348, 43 S. W. 180, holding unincorporated labo
tion of label, although not owner of goods to w

— Deceptive trade-marks.

Approved in American Washboard Co. v. Sag
43 C. C. A. 237, 103 Fed. 285, holding false de
minum will not be enjoined where defendant does
of complainant; Messer v. The Fadettes, 168 Ma
St. Rep. 371, 46 N. E. 407, holding purchaser of
members have left cannot enjoin use of name l
lead to public deception; Schmalz v. Wooley,
holding label adopted by association of journeym
where they do not trade in hats or caps to which

Cited in note (19 L. R. A. 56) on invalidity o

8 L. R. A. 644, PHŒNIX NAT. BANK v. BA
N. E. 917.

Effect of discharge in insolvency on forei

Cited in Olivieri v. Atkinson, 168 Mass. 32, 4
66 N. H. 404, 49 Am. St. Rep. 623, 22 Atl. 451; F
156 Mass. 12, 30 N. E. 176, — holding discharge
by foreign creditor; Chase v. Henry, 166 Mass.
E. 988, holding discharge in insolvency not a l
always having been a citizen and resident of an
84 Me. 131, 30 Am. St. Rep. 340, 24 Atl. 795, l
barred, even though citizen of insolvent's state
ner & E. Brewing Co. v. Dreyfus, 172 Mass. 1
E. 531, holding foreign corporation not barred b
having place of business and license in state o
mond Beef & Provision Co. v. Best, 91 Me. 437
holding foreign corporation not bound by insol
dent agent was duly served with process; Secon
97 Wis. 273, 39 L. R. A. 578, 73 N. W. 39 (di
discharge in insolvency does not relieve from de
not present their claims.

Cited in footnotes to Lowenberg v. Levine, 16 I

judgment not released by discharge in insolvency proceedings; Pattee v. Paige, 163 Mass. 353, 28 L. R. A. 451, 47 Am. St. Rep. 459, 40 N. E. 108, which holds nonresident's waiver of exemption from discharge of one firm not extend to claim against other firm composed in part of same members.

Cited in note (17 L. R. A. 84) on supremacy of state or nation over devolution of property.

Distinguished in Columbia Falls Brick Co. v. Glidden, 157 Mass. 177, 31 N. E. 801, holding right of action by foreign creditor lost by proving claim against insolvent's estate.

— Garnishee proceedings.

Cited in Louisville & N. R. Co. v. Nash, 118 Ala. 486, 41 L. R. A. 332, 72 Am. St. Rep. 181, 23 So. 825, holding payment by garnishee of judgment void for want of jurisdiction, no defense to action by nonresident creditor.

8 L. R. A. 647, CONE v. DUNHAM, 59 Conn. 145, 20 Atl. 311.

Presentation of claim.

Approved in Gay's Appeal, 61 Conn. 450, 23 Atl. 829, holding time within which claim must be exhibited does not begin to run until administrator is appointed; Winchell v. Sanger, 73 Conn. 405, 47 Atl. 706, and Connecticut Trust & S. D. Co. v. Security Co. 67 Conn. 443, 35 Atl. 342, holding statute of nonclaim does not apply to express trust, which does not lose its character by commingling of trust funds with other's funds.

Cited in Frisbie v. Preston, 67 Conn. 454, 35 Atl. 278, to point that failure to present claim within time limited bars it.

8 L. R. A. 655, MITTEL v. KARL, 133 Ill. 65, 24 N. E. 553.

Estates in land; right of survivorship.

Cited in Mette v. Feltgen, 148 Ill. 371, 36 N. E. 81, holding parties not prevented by statute from conveying estates, with right of survivorship, when clearly intending to do so; Slater v. Gruger, 165 Ill. 332, 46 N. E. 235, holding deed to grantees "and the survivor of them," expressly declared to be in joint tenancy, creates such estate.

Cited in footnotes to *Re* Albrecht, 18 L. R. A. 329, which denies tenancy by entirety in bond and mortgage to husband and wife; Thornburg v. Wiggins, 22 L. R. A. 42, which holds tenancy by entirety not created by conveyance to husband and wife "in joint tenancy."

Cited in note (30 L. R. A. 324) on tenancy by entireties.

Intent of parties to written instruments.

Cited in Peoria & P. Union R. Co. v. Tamplin, 156 Ill. 294, 40 N. E. 960, holding that in construing written instruments effect must be given to each clause, word, or term employed.

Passing of title.

Cited in Fletcher v. Shepherd, 174 Ill. 270, 51 N. E. 212, holding grantor delivering quitclaim deed to daughter, and taking one in return on same premises but not recording it, does not hold title in trust for daughter.

8 L. R. A. 657, TYLER v. WADDINGHAM, 58 Conn. 375, 20 Atl. 335.

Review of conclusion.

Approved in Nolan v. New York, N. H. & H. R. Co. 70 Conn. 175, 43 L. R.

A. 325, 39 Atl. 115, holding findings that railro sufficiently provide for the safe operation of t of law.

How partnership created.

Approved in Norwalk *ex rel.* Fawcett v. Irela holding one running millinery store not partne kept in store but not commingled, and who on sa

Cited in footnotes to Flower v. Barnekoff, 11 L. ners persons jointly agreeing to secure option o and sharing profits; Dutcher v. Buck, 20 L. R. ship created between land owner and one cutti equal division of profits; Webster v. Clark, 27 partnership with community of interest in capi called lease; Shrum v. Simpson, 49 L. R. A. 79 created by contract for working farm and dividi

Distinguished in Hughes v. Ewing, 162 Mo. 300, plated participation of profits between purchase broker, does not make them partners.

Interest of partners in real estate.

Cited in footnote to *Re* Oliver, 9 L. R. A. 421, ber of firm organized to deal in land, personal e

Cited in note (27 L. R. A. 481) on partnershi

Responsibility of partners.

Cited in note (12 L. R. A. 223) on responsibi credit.

Absolute guaranty.

Approved in Garland v. Gaines, 73 Conn. 666, 19, holding guarantor of payment of rent and per for full term, in consideration of letting premises,

Cited in Beardsley v. Hawes, 71 Conn. 43, 40 A note "for security for payment" which he guaran antor.

Cited in note (20 L. R. A. 262) on guaranty of

Validity of Sunday contract.

Cited in footnote to First M. E. Church v. Don sustains subscription to church indebtedness made

8 L. R. A. 666, LEAKE v. WATSON, 58 Conn. 3 Atl. 343.

Report of subsequent appeal in 60 Conn. 501,

Following trust funds.

Approved in Randolph v. East Birmingham Lan St. Rep. 64, 16 So. 126, holding purchasers with lands conveyed to assignor in violation of a trust ac ciary.

Cited in *Re* Mitchell, 74 Vt. 194, 52 Atl. 523, 1

fund derived from sale of property devised to certain persons for life, remainder to their heirs.

Cited in footnotes to Indiana, I. & I. R. Co. v. Swannell, 30 L. R. A. 290, which holds that property purchased by trustee for bondholders may be followed by latter into hands of purchaser with notice; Central Stock & Grain Exchange v. Bendinger, 56 L. R. A. 875, which holds broker liable to refund to principal, money illegally taken from agent as margins on gambling transaction.

8 L. R. A. 671, BALLOCK v. STATE, 73 Md. 1, 25 Am. St. Rep. 559, 20 Atl. 184.

Lottery.

Approved in United States v. Fulkerson, 74 Fed. 629, condemning as lottery, scheme for raising fund for purpose of redistribution by chance.

Cited in footnotes to State *ex rel.* Prout v. Nebraska Home Co. 60 L. R. A. 448, which holds scheme by which common fund distributed among contributors, a valuable preference in distribution depending on chance, a lottery; Thornhill v. O'Rear, 31 L. R. A. 792, which holds agreement by one person to take all chances of raffle not unlawful; Lynch v. Rosenthal, 31 L. R. A. 835, which holds sale of lots to be drawn by lot with one prize lot to be given to one of purchasers as result of chance void; State *ex rel.* Sheets v. Interstate Sav. Invest. Co. 52 L. R. A. 531, which holds contracts of investment security, which by chance might be called in and redeemed before reserve credit would regularly accumulate, unlawful.

Distinguished in Equitable Loan & Security Co. v. Waring (Ga.), 62 L. R. A. 124, footnote, p. 93, 44 S. E. 320, holding determination by chance of time of redeeming investment certificates entitling holders to sum paid in, with interest, and share of accumulations from earnings and lapses, does not make scheme a lottery.

Validity of legislation against lotteries.

Cited in Ford v. State, 85 Md. 475, 41 L. R. A. 552, 60 Am. St. Rep. 337, 37 Atl. 172, holding deprivation of liberty under statute against possession of record of lottery drawings not without due process; Otis v. Parker, 187 U. S. 609, 47 L. ed. 327, 23 Sup. Ct. Rep. 168, holding state constitutional provision declaring void stock-margin contracts not in conflict with Federal Constitution; Lottery Case (Champion v. Ames), 188 U. S. 370, 47 L. ed. 507, 23 Sup. Ct. Rep. 321 (dissenting opinion), majority holding act prohibiting carriage of lottery tickets from one state to another, within power of Congress to regulate interstate commerce.

8 L. R. A. 673, PHILADELPHIA, W. & B. R. CO. v. ANDERSON, 72 Md. 519, 20 Am. St. Rep. 483, 20 Atl. 2.

Degree of care required of carrier of passengers.

Cited in Baltimore City Pass. R. Co. v. Baer, 90 Md. 108, 44 Atl. 992, upholding action by person injured by being thrown to ground while boarding trolley car, by sudden starting of car; Wanzer v. Chippewa Valley Electric R. Co. 108 Wis. 329, 84 N. W. 423, holding instructions requiring of carrier highest degree of care and skill which a careful and vigilant man would observe in like circumstance erroneous; Illinois C. R. Co. v. Kuhn, 107 Tenn. 111, 64 S. W. 202, holding carrier of passengers to highest, greatest, or utmost care, skill, and foresight as

to motive power, appliances, and servants, they w
tection; Burke v. Chicago & N. W. R. Co. 108
liable for injury to drunken passenger deposited c

Cited in notes (11 L. R. A. 367) on duty of c
sengers; (11 L. R. A. 720) on duty of railroad
passengers; (20 L. R. A. 521) on measure of care
keep its platforms and approaches safe.

Contributory negligence of passenger.

Cited in People's Bank v. Morgolofski, 75 Md. 4
1027, holding it question for jury whether it was
through open door into dark elevator shaft.

Cited in note (11 L. R. A. 130) on contributo
feating recovery of damages for injuries.

— At station or while alighting.

Cited in Chesapeake & O. R. Co. v. King, 49 L.
Fed. 255, and Atlantic City R. Co. v. Goodin, 62
72 Am. St. Rep. 652, 42 Atl. 333, holding questio
failing to look for trains when crossing track in
for jury; Pennsylvania Co. v. McCaffrey, 173 Ill.
senger has right to assume carrier will not expose
ing from trains at stations; St. Louis & S. W. R
26 S. W. 593, holding failure to look and liste
alighting upon implied invitation, not contributory
Warner v. Baltimore & O. R. Co. 168 U. S. 347, 4
68, holding question whether injured person was gu
in crossing tracks at station improperly taken fro
O. R. Co. 21 D. C. 358, holding jumping from tr
not contributory negligence, as matter of law; Uni
bridge, 97 Md. 637, 55 Atl. 444, holding passenge
matter of law, in alighting from street car stoppi
street; United R. & Electric Co. v. Beidelman, 95
plaintiff with rheumatism only bound to use ordina
of defendant's negligence.

Cited in footnote to Chesapeake & Ohio R. Co. v.
sustains right of passengers alighting to presume
of trains.

Distinguished in Warner v. Baltimore & O. R.
passenger in absence of special inducement has n
track without stopping and looking.

Res ipsa loquitur.

Cited in United R. & Electric Co. v. Beidelman, 95
proof of occurrence of injury to passenger prima
United R. & Electric Co. v. Woodbridge. 97 Md. 63
of injury to passenger getting off street car prim
negligence; Houston v. Brush, 66 Vt. 345, 29 Atl.
tackle block from want of derrick prima facie evide
Wheeling Electrical Co. 43 W. Va. 669, 39 L. R. A. 5
E. 733, holding mere falling of wire charged with h

surface of street, killing man, makes prima facie case of negligence; Horowitz v. Hamburg-American Packet Co. 18 Misc. 26, 41 N. Y. Supp. 54, holding fall of pile of baggage without apparent cause prima facie evidence of negligence: Richmond R. & Electric Co. v. Hudgins, 100 Va. 416, 41 S. E. 736, holding negligence presumed where horse was frightened by short circuiting of current while passing electric car.

8 L. R. A. 677, HARRIS v. BALTIMORE, 73 Md. 22, 25 Am. St. Rep. 565, 17 Atl. 1046, 20 Atl. 111, 985.

Limited authority of partners of nontrading partnership.

Cited in Presbrey v. Thomas, 1 App. D. C. 178, holding partners in nontrading partnership have no implied authority to bind firm by indorsement of commercial paper; Snively v. Matheson, 12 Wash. 95, 50 Am. St. Rep. 877, 40 Pac. 628, holding that member of general contracting and building partnership cannot, in absence of authority, usage, or necessity, bind firm by note and mortgage; Schellenbeck v. Studebaker, 13 Ind. App. 440, 55 Am. St. Rep. 240, 41 N. E. 845, holding partner in nontrading partnership without implied authority to execute firm note, in absence of necessity or custom.

Part assignment of claim.

Cited in Bruns v. Spalding, 90 Md. 360, 45 Atl. 194, upholding in equity assignment of a definite portion of partnership profit.

8 L. R. A. 680, WOLF v. BAUEREIS, 72 Md. 481, 19 Atl. 1045.

Right of married woman to sue in own name for personal wrongs.

Cited in Dashiell v. Griffith, 84 Md. 379, 35 Atl. 1094, holding action for tort to wife properly brought in name of husband and wife; Samarzevosky v. Baltimore City Pass. R. Co. 88 Md. 480, 42 Atl. 206, holding that prior to October, 1892, husband and wife were required to join in action for personal injuries to wife; Wolf v. Frank, 92 Md. 143, 52 L. R. A. 105, 48 Atl. 132, upholding action by married woman in own name for alienation of husband's affections under statute; Capital Traction Co. v. Rockwell, 17 App. D. C. 380, holding that married woman may maintain action for negligence in own name under "married woman's act" of 1896.

Proviso or exception in statute or Constitution.

Cited in Leader Printing Co. v. Nicholas, 6 Okla. 309, 50 Pac. 1001, holding proviso or exception relates to paragraph or distinct portion of the enactment immediately preceding it, unless intent is contrary; State *ex rel.* Riter v. Quayle, 26 Utah, 30, 71 Pac. 1060, holding that proviso in Constitution should be confined to paragraph next preceding, unless contrary intention appears.

Interruption of running of limitations; amendment.

Cited in footnote to Love v. Southern R. Co. 55 L. R. A. 471, which sustains right to file new declaration after limitation period has elapsed, naming statutory beneficiaries in action for death.

8 L. R. A. 682, KERN v. MYLL, 80 Mich. 525, 45 N. W. 587.

Landlord's liability for condition of premises.

Approved in Willcox v. Hines, 100 Tenn. 550, 41 L. R. A. 281, 66 Am. St. Rep.

778, 46 S. W. 297, holding landlord liable to ten of lease; Sunasack v. Morey, 196 Ill. 573, 63 N. for injury resulting from failure to inform te Borggard v. Gale, 205 Ill. 514, 68 N. E. 1063. landlord's liability for latent defect in premises,

Cited in notes (34 L. R. A. 828) on liability o ment of defects; (33 L. R. A. 454) on implied co other than furnished houses.

Distinguished in second appeal in 94 Mich. 47 not chargeable with negligent ignorance of existe edge, when well had been filled ten years and nc Works v. Fraser, 110 Ill. App. 129, holding false leak not invalidate lease.

8 L. R. A. 685, PEOPLE v. MORRIS, 80 Mich. 6

Policy of law as affecting court.

Cited in *Re* McDonald, 4 Wyo. 161, 33 Pac. is within province of legislature rather than co

Cruel or unusual punishment.

Approved in State v. Becker, 3 S. D. 41, 51 more than $500 and imprisonment for not more unusual punishment for maintaining common liquor; Territory v. Ketchum (N. M.) 55 L. R. A penalty for assault upon train with intent to c not cruel or unusual punishment.

Cited in footnote to Com. v. Murphy, 30 L. R. imposing imprisonment for life for criminal intim

Cited in note (35 L. R. A. 564, 573) on cruel a

8 L. R. A. 687, AMAKER v. NEW, 33 S. C. 28, 11

Statute of limitation for fraud.

Cited in Goforth v. Goforth, 47 S. C. 133, 25 S. tion does not run from discovery of fraud, if par under deed assailed; Jackson v. Plyler, 38 S. C. S. E. 255, holding statutory limitation for beginn of fraud does not apply to simple case of forec Jones, 34 S. C. 153, 13 S. E. 326, holding statute o right of action exists.

Cited in footnotes to Sanborn v. Gale, 26 L. R. limitation against action for alienation of wife' agreement of parties to adultery, known to husl Blachley, 53 L. R. A. 849, which holds running recover back money not prevented by fraud, unl affirmative efforts; Mereness v. First Nat. Bank, running of limitations on demand certificate of de misrepresentations in denial of liability.

Instructions to jury.

Cited in Parr v. Lindler, 40 S. C. 201, 18 S. E. 636, holding correctness of instruction to jury could not be considered in this case.

Joinder of causes of action.

Cited in Ferst's Sons v. Powers, 58 S. C. 403, 36 S. E. 744, holding action on account for goods sold and delivered may be joined with one to set aside for fraud of creditors, and attachment may issue; Miller v. Hughes, 33 S. C. 542, 12 S. E. 419, holding demand for money due and for relief from fraud may be sought in same action.

Admissibility of evidence on question of fraud.

Cited in Archer v. Long, 38 S. C. 277, 16 S. E. 998, holding evidence admissible to show claim to property void without alleging fraud; Williams v. Griffin, 58 S. C. 372, 36 S. E. 665, holding evidence admissible to show that bill of sale to defendant was intended as mortgage, and its payment.

8 L. R. A. 691, WOLCOTT v. ASHENFELTER, 5 N. M. 442, 23 Pac. 780.

8 L. R. A. 696, BILLS v. BILLS, 80 Iowa, 269, 20 Am. St. Rep. 418, 45 N. W. 748.

Precatory words in wills.

Approved in *Re* Marti, 132 Cal. 671, 61 Pac. 964, holding word "desire" not import a trust or charge.

Cited in McDuffie v. Montgomery, 128 Fed. 110, holding request as to disposal of property at devisee's death accompanying absolute devise creates no trust.

Cited in footnotes to Jewell v. Louisville Trust Co. 53 L. R. A. 377, which denies creation of precatory trust by will of merchant expressing desire for retention, on liberal terms, of specified person in employ of firm of which testator a partner; Williams v. Baptist Church, 54 L. R. A. 427, which holds absolute gift, not trust, created by bequest to church and "suggesting" as to its application.

Cited in note (13 L. R. A. 563) on effect of precatory words in will.

Limitation of devise by subsequent or repugnant conditions.

Followed in Hambel v. Hambel, 109 Iowa, 463, 80 N. W. 528, holding absolute devise to widow not limited by subsequent directions to divide property among children on her death or remarriage.

Approved in Meacham v. Graham, 98 Tenn. 206, 39 S. W. 12, holding absolute estate not limited by subsequent provision unless clear, certain, and unmistakable; Meyer v. Weiler, 121 Iowa, 54, 95 N. W. 254, and Mulvane v. Rude, 146 Ind. 483, 45 N. E. 659, holding after absolute devise a gift over of property undisposed of by first taker at his death void for repugnancy; Channell v. Aldinger, 121 Iowa, 299, 96 N. W. 781, holding provision for further disposition of property in case of devisee's death intestate and without issue repugnant to absolute devise.

Cited in Jordan v. Woodin, 93 Iowa, 463, 61 N. W. 948, holding bequest to widow and son limited by provision that if both die before son attains majority, estate should go to testator's heirs; Stivers v. Gardner, 88 Iowa, 311, 55 N. W. 516, holding devise limited by subsequent provision that on husband's death or remarriage land should go to testatrix's son and daughter.

Cited in footnote to Roth v. Rauschenbusch, 61 L. R. A. 455, which holds fee simple by devise to one absolutely and forever not cut down by subsequent words as to disposition of any remainder on devisee's death.

Distinguished in Iimas v. Neidt, 101 Iowa, 35
to daughter limited by charge in favor of other chi
of shares of children dying before majority.

Estate passing under will.

Cited in footnote to Cornwell v. Wulff, 45 L.
power of disposition in instrument conveying la
itself.

Distinguished in *Re* Proctor, 95 Iowa, 173, 63 N
for life with power to sell property to pay debts ar
absolute estate in her; Wilhelm v. Calder, 102 Io
devise to children did not vest on testator's deat
by executor until widow's death or until youngest
divided between those living; Shaw v. Shaw, 115 I
widow does not take absolute title under devise
testator's widow, with gift over to heirs on her r

8 L. R. A. 697, STATE, LEEDS, PROSECUTOR, v.
332, 19 Atl. 780.

Mode of testing title to office — By certiora

Approved in State, Roberts, Prosecutor, v. Shafe
holding, in testing the validity of laws or regulati
questions involving the legality of an election to o

— By mandamus.

Approved in Fort v. Howell, 58 N. J. L. 543, 3
improper remedy to test title of incumbent holdin
ex rel. Bennett v. Trenton, 55 N. J. L. 74, 25 Atl.
proceeding where contest is not over right to pos
office; Morton v. Broderick, 118 Cal. 482, 50 Pac.
compel entry of tax levy, although title to office inc

Cited in *Re* Delgado, 140 U. S. 592, 35 L. ed. 581,
mandamus may issue to compel recognition of *de*
of the board; Kimball v. Olmsted, 20 Wash. 636, 56
majority holding mandamus not proper remedy o
office, when legality of removal depends upon statute

Cited in footnote to People *ex rel.* Daley v. Ric
thorizes mandamus to compel canvassing board to d

— By quo warranto.

Distinguished in State, Roberson, Prosecutor, v.
Atl. 734, holding quo warranto exclusive remedy to

8 L. R. A. 700, GIANT POWDER CO. v. OREGON
Fed. 470.

What is a "structure" within lien law.

Approved in Ban v. Columbia Southern R. Co. 5
holding term "other structure" in lien law includes ra
Dock Co. 68 App. Div. 584, 73 N. Y. Supp. 908, hol
struction in ship yard a "structure," within law a
scaffolds about structures.

Distinguished in Pennsylvania Steel Co. v. J. E. Potts Salt & Lumber Co. 11 C. C. A. 14, 22 U. S. App. 537, 63 Fed. 14, holding statutory lien given one who builds structure does not give lien for material used in constructing railroad.

Filing lien on part of road.

Approved in Ban v. Columbia Southern R. Co. 54 C. C. A. 417, 117 Fed. 37, holding subcontractor building extension need not file lien on entire road.

Lien for giant powder.

Approved in Rapauno Chemical Co. v. Greenfield & N. R. Co. 59 Mo. App. 10, holding giant powder a lienable article.

Lien on railroads or against corporation.

Cited in New England Engineering Co. v. Oakwood Street R. Co. 75 Fed. 165, holding lien given for work done on any railroad includes street railways; Choctaw & M. R. Co. v. Speer Hardware Co. 71 Ark. 132, 71 S. W. 267, denying right of person furnishing provisions and supplies to employees of subcontractor to lien on railroad.

Cited in footnote to Steger v. Arctic Refrigerating Co. 11 L. R. A. 580, which holds lien for laying pipes on land of strangers for refrigerating company enforceable against entire plant of company.

Cited as changed by statute in Ban v. Columbia Southern R. Co. 109 Fed. 500, holding that amount of liens of subcontractors, etc., against railroad cannot exceed amount actually due to original contractor.

8 L. R. A. 707, MANLEY v. STAPLES, 62 Vt. 153, 19 Atl. 983.

8 L. R. A. 708, ROWELL v. VERSHIRE, 62 Vt. 405, 19 Atl. 990.

Liability for support of child or parent.

Approved in Parkhurst v. Krellinger, 69 Vt. 379, 38 Atl. 67, holding parent liable for support of emancipated daughter, furnished at his request and in mutual expectation of payment.

Cited in footnote to McCook County v. Kammoss, 31 L. R. A. 461, which holds children liable under statute to county furnishing support to poor parents.

Distinguished in Brandon v. Jackson, 74 Vt. 79, 52 Atl. 114, holding town may recover on promise of person legally liable to pay for pauper's support.

Insane person.

Approved in Vershire v. Hyde Park, 64 Vt. 641, 25 Atl. 431, holding unemancipated insane daughter takes settlement of father and is not transient pauper.

Cited in footnote to Bon Homme County v. Berndt, 50 L. R. A. 351, which sustains statute making estates of insane persons, without heirs in United States dependent thereon for support, chargeable with expense of maintenance in hospital.

Town's liability for aid to poor person.

Reaffirmed on second appeal in 63 Vt. 512, 22 Atl. 604, which denies right of parent to recover from town for support of his insane pauper child under overseer's agreement to pay for same, though he is poor and has large family .

Cited in footnote to Patrick v. Baldwin, 53 L. R. A. 613, which denies liability of town to private person furnishing relief to poor person.

8 L. R. A. 710, BRISTOR v. BURR, 120 N. Y. 4

Recovery of real property; right of posses

Cited in Ofschlager v. Surbeck, 22 Misc. 597, upon premises as place of abode, and occupanc sion; Jennings v. McCarthy, 40 N. Y. S. R. 680, session of premises by servant, after terminati verted into tenancy at will, if continued until it

Cited in footnote to Bowman v. Bradley, 17 hand's right to occupy house ceases on terminati

Distinguished in School Dist. No. 11 v. Bats 578, 64 N. W. 196, holding when occupancy of e form service for employer, and no rent is rese ployer.

Right to maintain ejectment.

Cited in Danihee v. Hyatt, 151 N. Y. 496, 45 N not lie against husband assisting wife in mainta

Forcible ejection of tenant.

Cited in Johnson v. Maxwell, 19 Misc. 707, Supp. 1156, holding landlord using only such fo ant, after his refusal to vacate on request, not li Federgreen, 80 Hun, 245, 29 N. Y. Supp. 1039, h titiously barring tenant's access to premises, ac entitles him to forcibly resist tenant's efforts to e 96, 88 N. W. 426, holding landlord not entitled, in his favor in forcible entry and detainer, to eject

8 L. R. A. 712, FIFTH AVE. BANK v. COLGAT

Limited partnerships.

Cited in footnotes to State, Tide Water Pipe Co. 27 L. R. A. 684, which holds limited partnershi taxation; Edwards v. Warren Linoline & Gasoline holds partnership association organized under la partnership instead of corporation in Massachuset

— Rights and liabilities of special partner.

Cited in Van Voorhis v. Webster, 85 Hun, 594, for purpose of compelling accounting, special pa eral partner; White v. Eiseman, 134 N. Y. 103, exempting limited partner from common-law li liberally construed; Spencer Optical Mfg. Co. v. J 392, holding special partner liable as general partn contributed to be specified in certificate not comp

— Renewal of partnership agreement.

Cited in Hardt v. Levy, 72 Hun, 234, 25 N. Y. mality required in certificate of renewal or conti as in original formation; Hardt v. Levy, 72 Hun, ing certificate reciting capital originally contrib not state it remains unimpaired.

Distinguished in Durgin v. Colburn, 176 Mass. 112, 57 N. E. 213, holding special partner liable as general, if capital at time of renewal not equal in amount to that originally contributed, as required by statute.

Disapproved in Fourth Street Nat. Bank v. Haines, 15 Pa. Co. Ct. 38, 3 Pa. Dist. R. 439, 35 W. N. C. 355, holding special partner liable as general partner if at time of renewal capital contributed by him has been impaired.

Construction of statutes.

Cited in *Re* Manning, 71 Hun, 249, 24 N. Y. Supp. 1039, holding language used in statute must be given its natural and obvious meaning; Coughlin v. New York, 35 Misc. 449, 71 N. Y. Supp. 91, holding interpretation which gives significance to all words of statute preferred; *Re* Clark, 61 App. Div. 340, 70 N. Y. Supp. 353, holding court cannot correct errors or cure supposed defects in statute to meet exigencies of particular case.

8 L. R. A. 719, LIPMAN v. NIAGARA F. INS. CO. 121 N. Y. 454, 24 N. E. 699.

Insurance; legal effect of binding slip.

Cited in Belt v. American Cent. Ins. Co. 29 App. Div. 551, 53 N. Y. Supp. 316, holding "binding slip" and agreement as to premium constitute present contract of insurance; J. C. Smith & W. Co. v. Prussian Nat. Ins. Co. 68 N. J. L. 676, 54 Atl. 458, holding delivery of binding slip effects valid temporary insurance, though rate undetermined; Hicks v. British America Assur. Co. 162 N. Y. 288, 48 L. R. A. 426, 56 N. E. 743, holding oral contract to insure property, subject to provisions of standard policy, conditions of which must be complied with; Van Tassel v. Greenwich Ins. Co. 28 App. Div. 166, 51 N. Y. Supp. 79, and Underwood v. Greenwich Ins. Co. 161 N. Y. 420, 55 N. E. 936, holding binding slip subject to conditions of original policy, when renewal, and subject to terms of usual policy of insurer, if independent agreement; Van Tassel v. Greenwich Ins. Co. 72 Hun, 145, 25 N. Y. Supp. 301, holding that binding slip issued for purposes of renewal continues original policy, subject to stipulations contained therein; Springer v. Anglo-Nevado Assur. Corp. 33 N. Y. S. R. 544, 11 N. Y. Supp. 533, holding agreement to continue insurance valid, and that recovery may be had thereon before issuance of policy or payment of premium; Sproul v. Western Assur. Co. 33 Or. 107, 54 Pac. 180, holding, when kind of policy not stipulated in preliminary agreement, law presumes usual and ordinary policy of company contemplated.

Distinguished in Imperial Shale Brick Co. v. Jewett, 169 N. Y. 150, 62 N. E. 167, holding liability of individual underwriters upon certificate of agents of unincorporated association subject to conditions of open policy, which certificate stated was issued by association.

Parol evidence as to usage under binding slip.

Cited in Underwood v. Greenwich Ins. Co. 54 App. Div. 390, 66 N. Y. Supp. 651, holding it admissible to show usage as to temporary nature of binding slip and method of terminating liability.

Cancelation of policy.

Cited in Karelsen v. Sun Fire Office, 122 N. Y. 549, 25 N. E. 921, holding notice sufficient if served on agents of assured, when such notice sufficient under terms of usual policy.

Cited in notes (10 L. R. A. 145) on cancelation of insurance policies; (20 L. R. A. 285) on notice of cancelation.

8 L. R. A. 722, MOTON v. HULL, 77 Tex. 80, 13 S. W. 849.

Injunction against maintenance of action in another state.

Cited in note (21 L. R. A. 75) on injunction against maintenance of attachment proceeding in foreign jurisdiction.

8 L. R. A. 724, SANFORD v. KANE, 133 Ill. 199, 23 Am. St. Rep. 602, 24 N. E. 414.

Rights of assignee.

Approved in Romberg v. McCormick, 194 Ill. 210, 62 N. E. 537, holding security of mortgage passes as equitable incident to assignee of note secured thereby, but that right is subject to defenses.

Cited in footnote to Taylor v. Carroll, 44 L. R. A. 479, which holds special title acquired by assignee of mortgage for foreclosure will not vest in his administrator.

Cited in note (13 L. R. A. 294) on form and sufficiency of assignment of mortgage.

Execution of power of sale.

Approved in Stevens v. Shannahan, 160 Ill. 344, 43 N. E. 350, holding administratrix may execute power of sale granted to mortgagee or legal representatives, although his heirs, representatives, administrators, or assigns are authorized to make deed.

Usury.

Approved in Fowler v. Equitable Trust Co. 141 U. S. 400, 35 L. ed. 791, 12 Sup. Ct. Rep. 1, holding loan usurious where, besides interest, lender's agent, in pursuance of agreement with lender, exacts commission for procuring loan.

Husband's or wife's liability on covenants.

Approved in Center v. Elgin City Bkg. Co. 185 Ill. 537, 57 N. E. 439, holding husband joining in deed to release his dower not liable on covenants in deed; Granath v. Johnson, 90 Ill. App. 311, holding wife joining in deed to release her dower not liable on covenants; Western Springs v. Collins, 40 C. C. A. 34, 98 Fed. 934, holding married woman not liable on covenants in deed of husband's lands under statute authorizing married woman to contract as if unmarried.

Cited in Granath v. Johnson, 90 Ill. App. 310, to point that at common law married woman not bound by covenant in trust deed to pay indebtedness of husband.

Cited in note (22 L. R. A. 780) on estoppel by covenant from acquiring superior title.

Construction of deed.

Approved in Elgin City Bkg. Co. v. Center, 83 Ill. App. 413, holding, in construing deed, court will not only look at its words but to the circumstances and condition of the parties; Granath v. Johnson, 90 Ill. App. 313, holding equity will construe deeds according to true intent and meaning, as understood by the parties.

8 L. R. A. 727, WEST v. PEOPLE'S BANK, 67 Miss. 729, 7 So. 513.

Title in suit to remove cloud.

Cited in Wilkinson v. Hiller, 71 Miss. 679, 14 So. 442, holding complainant seeking to cancel title must show good legal or equitable title in himself.

Cited in footnote to Oppenheimer v. Levi, 60 L. R. A. 729, which holds possession unnecessary to enable reversioner to sue, for removal of cloud, tenant acquiring tax title after agreeing to pay taxes.

8 L. R. A. 732, JOHNSON v. SUPREME LODGE, K. OF H. 53 Ark. 255, 13 S. W. 794.

Who are heirs.

Cited in footnotes to Conger v. Lowe, 9 L. R. A. 168, which holds word "heirs" in will will be construed as word of limitation; Hindry v. Holt, 39 L. R. A. 351, which holds right of action for death limited to lineal descendants by words "heirs or heirs" in statute.

Cited in notes (13 L. R. A. 48) as to who are heirs; (30 L. R. A. 593) as to meaning of word "heirs" in life insurance policy.

Widow as heir at law.

Cited in Lyons v. Yerex, 100 Mich. 217, 43 Am. St. Rep. 452, 58 N. W. 1112, holding widow entitled to share in proceeds of life insurance policy payable to heirs at law.

Cited in footnote to Mullen v. Reed, 24 L. R. A. 664, which holds widow not an heir at law.

Cited in note (30 L. R A. 596) on widow as "heir" within meaning of insurance policy.

Widow as trustee.

Distinguished in McDonald v. Humphries, 56 Ark. 66, 19 S. W. 234, holding widow has interest only as trustee in policy made payable to her for the purpose of better securing repayment of assessments advanced by third person.

Who may object to beneficiary.

Approved in Nye v. Grand Lodge, A. O. U. W. 9 Ind. App. 154, 36 N. E. 429, holding that contestant for insurance cannot take advantage of rules of association or corporation as to who may be beneficiary, waived by it.

Cited in Maynard v. Life Ins. Co. 132 N. C. 712, 44 S. E. 405, holding administrator of insured debtor cannot contest validity of creditor's insurance or its assignment.

Insurance contract as affected by pecuniary interest.

Cited in Ingersoll v. Knights of Golden Rule. 47 Fed. 274, holding beneficiary's absence of pecuniary interest in life insured does not render contract void as against public policy.

8 L. R. A. 735, STATE v. McGONIGLE, 101 Mo. 353, 20 Am. St. Rep. 609, 13 S. W. 758.

Courts as ministerial agents.

Cited in Sears v. Stone County, 105 Mo. 242, 24 Am. St. Rep. 378, 16 S. W. 878, holding that judges act in administrative capacity in auditing claims against county.

Alteration of instruments — Bonds.

Followed in State *ex rel.* Howell County v. Findley, 101 Mo. 372, 14 S. W. 111, holding material alteration of contract releases surety *in toto*.

Cited in Schuster v. Weiss, 114 Mo. 166, 19 L. R. A. 185, 21 S. W. 438, holding

change in appeal bond without consent releases
Mo. App. 425, holding surety discharged wher
consent; State v. Allen, 69 Miss. 525, 30 Am. S
erasure without authority of surety after execu
Fred Heim Brewing Co. v. Hazen, 55 Mo. App.
by change of contract into bond after execution.

— Notes.

Cited in McMurtrey v. Sparks, 71 Mo. App.
in note by payee bars recovery on original contr

Effect of forging other signatures or relea

Followed in State *ex rel.* Howell County v. Fin
holding subsequent sureties on county collectors's
signature of solvent surety, without their conser

Cited in Sullivan v. Williams, 43 S. C. 510, 2
topped, by intrusting bond to one of the principal
principal's name.

Cited in footnote to Hurt v. Ford, 41 L. R.
make subsequent signature of another person es
livered to payee or his agent.

Cited in note (45 L. R. A. 331) on condition
parol agreement that it shall not take effect unti

Effect of spoliation.

Cited in State *ex rel.* Pemiscot County v. Scott,
ing mutilation of bond after execution, delivery,

Ratification of alteration.

Followed in State *ex rel.* Howell County v. Find
holding waiver of alteration necessary to estop re

Liability for acts of agent.

Cited in Fogg v. School District, 75 Mo. App.
ble on original bonds fraudulently resold before n
by agent intrusted to redeem such bonds with pro

8 L. R. A. 740, BOSTON SAFE DEPOSIT & T. (
25 N. E. 30.

Construction to avoid partial intestacy.

Approved in Carney v. Kain, 40 W. Va. 820, 2
be construed to prevent intestacy if intent to disp
pears.

Cited in footnote to Balch v. Pickering, 14 L.
construction of will, resulting in intestacy, against

Implication to effectuate intent.

Approved in Allen's Succession, 48 La. Ann. 1
So. 193, and Seaver v. Griffing, 176 Mass. 62, 57
words may be supplied to effectuate testator's obvi

Cited in note (10 L. R. A. 818) on supplying om
tor's intent into effect.

Bequest to survivor.

Approved in Bailey v. Brown, 19 R. I. 682, 36 Atl. 581, holding bequest to survivor means those who outlive or live after testator.

Heirs.

Cited in footnotes to Hindry v. Holt, 39 L. R. A. 351, which holds word "heirs" in statute giving right of action for death limits right to lineal descendants; Gannon v. Peterson, 55 L. R. A. 701, which holds use of words "heirs," "issue," or "children" indiscriminately by testator warrants court in reading them interchangeably.

Cited in note (12 L. R. A. 723) on meaning of heirs at law.

Comity.

Cited in note (10 L. R. A. 767) on recognition of foreign laws.

8 L. R. A. 750, WINDRAM v. FRENCH, 151 Mass. 547, 24 N. E. 914.

Fraudulent representations.

Cited in Burns v. Dockray, 156 Mass. 137, 30 N. E. 551, holding positive statement that title is good when it is not, by person in position to know, fraudulent; Nash v. Minnesota Title Ins. & T. Co. 159 Mass. 442, 34 N. E. 625, holding false representations in a letter to one person, intended and used to defraud others relying upon it, actionable; Light v. Jacobs, 183 Mass. 211, 66 N. E. 799, holding conspirators liable for fraud of one, though ignorant of manner of its perpetration.

Cited in footnote to Hindman v. First Nat. Bank, 57 L. R. A. 108, which holds bank falsely certifying that all of authorized capital of insurance company is on deposit liable to one purchasing stock in reliance on same.

Extent of reliance upon representations and promises.

Cited in Roberts v. French, 153 Mass. 62, 10 L. R. A. 657, 25 Am. St. Rep. 611, 26 N. E. 416, holding false representations, relied on, need not have furnished only motive for buying, to be actionable; Light v. Jacobs, 183 Mass. 210, 66 N. E. 799, holding fraudulent representations as to security ground for rescinding contract, though plaintiff also made separate inquiries; Martin v. Meles, 179 Mass. 117, 60 N. E. 397, upholding action to recover contribution promised toward fund to defend lawsuit.

Rules as to technical objections to pleadings.

Cited in Billings v. Mann, 156 Mass. 205, 30 N. E. 1136, holding clerical error must be pointed out distinctly in the demurrer, to allow amendment; Stratton v. Seaverns, 163 Mass. 77, 39 N. E. 779, holding court will not for first time on appeal "go into nice verbal criticism" of bill in equity; Emmons v. Alvord, 177 Mass. 469, 59 N. E. 120, holding attention should be specifically called in the demurrer to minute verbal criticism of declaration; Steffe v. Old Colony R. Co. 156 Mass. 263, 30 N. E. 1137, holding mere defects or omissions in form of statement relied on must be pointed out in demurrer; Soper v. Manning, 158 Mass. 384, 33 N. E. 516, holding that general request to rule petition to vacate judgment insufficient in form must point out defect; May v. Wood, 172 Mass. 16, 51 N. E. 191 (dissenting opinion), majority holding false and malicious statements relied upon to support action should be substantially alleged.

Conclusions of law and facts.

Cited in Com. v. Clancy, 154 Mass. 132, 27 N. E. 1001, holding, after allegations of city, county, and state, charging defendant with committing offense within judicial district of court, sufficient; Haskell v. Merrill, 179 Mass. 123, 60 N. E. 485, holding words "loan," "security," and "delivery" in findings not conclusions of law; Mulhall v. Fallon, 176 Mass. 267, 54 L. R. A. 938, 79 Am. St. Rep. 309, 57 N. E. 386, holding testimony that woman was almost entirely dependent upon son for support not inadmissible as conclusion.

Right to recover back payments.

Cited in Alton v. First Nat. Bank, 157 Mass. 343, 18 L. R. A. 145, 34 Am. St. Rep. 285, 32 N. E. 228, holding money paid to bank by indorser of discounted instrument, supposed negotiable by both, cannot be recovered back.

8 L. R. A. 752, GAYLORD v. NEW BRITAIN, 58 Conn. 398, 20 Atl. 365.

Municipal liability for accumulation of ice.

Approved in Magaha v. Hagerstown, 95 Md. 74, 51 Atl. 832, holding municipality may be liable for accumulation of ice resulting from its own negligence.

Cited in notes (21 L. R. A. 271, 272) on liability of city for ice on street; (58 L. R. A. 326) on liability for ice on walk from temporary causes.

Distinguished in Stanke v. St. Paul, 71 Minn. 53, 73 N. W. 629, holding city not liable for negligent failure to keep gutter open, whereby ice formed on walk, unless notified that ice usually formed there.

Question for jury.

Cited in Scoville v. Salt Lake City, 11 Utah, 65, 39 Pac. 481, holding question whether existence of defect constituted sufficient notice, for jury.

8 L. R. A. 753, MONTANA UNION R. CO. v. LANGLOIS, 9 Mont. 419, 18 Am. St. Rep. 745, 24 Pac. 209.

Rights of solicitors of patronage at depots, etc.

Approved in McConnell v. Pedigo, 92 Ky. 471, 18 S. W. 15, denying right of railroad company to give exclusive platform rights to one carrier.

Cited in Kalamazoo Hack & Bus Co. v. Sootsma, 84 Mich. 200, 10 L. R. A. 821, 22 Am. St. Rep. 693, 47 N. W. 667; Pennsylvania Co. v. Chicago, 181 Ill. 300, 53 L. R. A. 227, 54 N. E. 825; State v. Reed, 76 Miss. 222, 43 L. R. A. 136, 71 Am. St. Rep. 528, 24 So. 308, — denying right to grant to one hackman exclusive right to solicit patronage; Hedding v. Gallagher, 69 N. H. 663, 76 Am. St. Rep. 204, 45 Atl. 96, and Kates v. Atlanta Baggage & Cab Co. 107 Ga. 649, 46 L. R. A. 437, 34 S. E. 372, denying right of carrier to enter into contract allowing baggage company exclusive privilege of entering depot; Lindsay v. Anniston, 104 Ala. 262, 27 L. R. A. 437, 53 Am. St. Rep. 44, 16 So. 545, holding ordinance against soliciting patronage at depot not void as violating contract giving exclusive right to transfer company; Colorado Springs v. Smith, 19 Colo. 558, 36 Pac. 540, holding ordinance providing that hotel runners, etc., must occupy allotted portion of platform not construed as allowing carrier to grant exclusive privileges; Lucas v. Herbert, 148 Ind. 66, 37 L. R. A. 377, 47 N. E. 146, not deciding right of railroad company to grant exclusive privilege to hackman; Godbout v. St. Paul Union Depot Co. 79 Minn. 196, 47 L. R. A. 535, 81 N. W. 835, upholding right of railroad company to grant exclusive privileges to hackmen to solicit business, if regulations are reasonable.

Cited in notes (13 L. R. A. 848) on rights of solicitors of patronage at depots, etc. (16 L. R. A. 449) on regulations as to admission of passengers to depot.

Distinguished in Hedding v. Gallagher, 72 N. H. 390, 64 L. R. A. 819, 57 Atl. 225, sustaining railroad's right to grant exclusive privilege of soliciting baggage at depot, where service adequate and rates reasonable.

Disapproved in effect in Brown v. New York C. & H. R. R. Co. 75 Hun, 362, 27 N. Y. Supp. 69, upholding right of common carrier to grant exclusive privilege to coach company to enter trains and depot; Donovan v. Pennsylvania Co. 61 L. R. A. 143, 57 C. C. A. 363, 120 Fed. 216, holding railroad may give hackman exclusive right to solicit within station.

8 L. R. A. 759, GUFFEY v. HUKILL, 34 W. Va. 49, 26 Am. St. Rep. 901, 11 S. E. 754.

Enforcing forfeiture clause in lease.

Sustained in Hukill v. Guffey, 37 W. Va. 429, 16 S. E. 544, holding execution of second lease works forfeiture of first lease for breach of condition, without re-entry.

Approved in Island Coal Co. v. Combs, 152 Ind. 390, 53 N. E. 452, holding failure of lessee to comply with condition *ipso facto* terminates lease.

Cited in Eclipse Oil Co. v. South Penn Oil Co. 47 W. Va. 87, 34 S. E. 923, holding lease to other party and possession thereunder invalidates prior executory lease; Island Coal Co. v. Combs, 152 Ind. 391, 53 N. E. 452, holding possession of premises sufficient re-entry by lessor; Martin v. Ohio River R. Co. 37 W. Va. 354, 16 S. E. 589, holding re-entry unnecessary under statute to work forfeiture of conditional estate; Duffield v. Michaels, 97 Fed. 833, holding right to terminate lease not waived by accepting payments, previous rentals unpaid; Reese v. Zinn, 103 Fed. 98, upholding lessor's right to cancel lease, when premises abandoned by lessee; Huggins v. Daley, 48 L. R. A. 325, 40 C. C. A. 20, 99 Fed. 614, holding requirement in lease of completion of well within fixed time condition precedent to vesting estate in lessee; Elk Fork Oil & Gas Co. v. Jennings, 84 Fed. 851, holding acquiescence in delays in completing wells waives breach of forfeiture clause in lease; Gadbury v. Ohio & I. Consol. Natural & Illuminating Gas Co. (Ind.) 62 L. R. A. 899, 67 N. E. 259, holding condition subsequent to develop property implied in oil and gas lease; Gadbury v. Ohio & I. Consol. Natural & Illuminating Gas Co. (Ind.) 62 L. R. A. 899, 67 N. E. 259, holding forfeiture of gas lease sufficiently evidenced by long-continued failure to develop property, where lessor continued in possession.

Cited in footnote to Kneeland v. Schmidt, 11 L. R. A. 498, holding exclusive possession by landlord acceptance terminating lease.

Cited in notes (12 L. R. A. 290) on leases of oil lands; (31 L. R. A. 673) on manner of enforcing forfeiture clause.

Distinguished in Thomas v. Hukill, 34 W. Va. 397, 12 S. E. 522, holding unequivocal declaration necessary to terminate lease conveying conditional estate; Friend v. Mallory, 52 W. Va. 60, 43 S. E. 114, holding oil lease not terminated by execution of another during term for which rent was paid.

Remedy against unlawful possession under oil lease.

Cited in Haskell v. Sutton, 53 W. Va. 225, 44 S. E. 533 (dissenting opinion), majority holding that drilling wells and taking oil under void lease may be enjoined.

8 L. R. A. 765, CHICAGO v. McLEAN, 133 Ill. 148, 24 N. E. 527.

Followed without special discussion in Chicago v. Moore, 40 Ill. App. 335.

Damages for mental and bodily suffering.

Approved in Pittsburg, C. C. & St. L. R. Co. v. Story, 63 Ill. App. 244; South Chicago City R. Co. v. Walters, 70 Ill. App. 272; West Chicago Street R. Co. v Lups, 74 Ill. App. 426; Kellyville Coal Co. v. Yehnka, 94 Ill. App. 82; Central R. Co. v. Serfass, 153 Ill. 384, 39 N. E. 119; Norfolk & W. R. Co. v. Marpole, 97 Va. 600, 34 S. E. 462, — holding mental and bodily suffering resulting from injury ground of damage; Chicago City R. Co. v. Canevin, 72 Ill. App. 90, holding mental pain resulting from or accompanying physical pain element of damages; Chicago v. Davies, 110 Ill. App. 429, holding damages allowable for mental suffering resulting from bodily injuries; North Chicago Street R. Co. v. Duebner, 85 Ill. App. 604, holding mental pain not element of damage unless directly connected with physical pain; Chicago City R. Co. v. Taylor, 170 Ill. 57, 48 N. E. 831, holding mental suffering due to injury and part of it, ground of damage, otherwise as to injured feelings not part of attendant pain; Mueller v. Kuhn, 59 Ill. App. 356, holding pain and suffering of body and mind subjects of compensatory, not punitive, damages; Central R. Co. v. Serfass, 53 Ill. App. 452, holding instruction authorizing recovery for pain and suffering, both mental and physical, not misleading so as to allow recovery for vexation of mind arising from reflection, where plaintiff was child three years old; Braun v. Craven, 175 Ill. 408, 42 L. R. A. 202, 51 N. E. 657, holding fright or terror superinducing nervous shock not ground of liability; Western U. Teleg. Co. v. Wood, 21 L. R. A. 712, 6 C. C. A. 452, 13 U. S. App. 317, 57 Fed. 478, holding damages not recoverable for mental suffering due to delay in delivering telegram; Butner v. Western U. Teleg. Co. 2 Okla. 241, 4 Inters. Com. Rep. 772, 37 Pac. 1087, holding mental pain or anguish resulting from nondelivery of telegram not independent basis of damage.

Cited in footnotes to Chapman v. Western U. Teleg. Co. 17 L. R. A. 430, which holds pain and suffering due to delay in delivering message not recoverable; Wilcox v. Richmond & D. R. Co. 17 L. R. A. 804, which denies recovery f. r mental anguish from nonperformance of contract.

Cited in notes (11 L. R. A. 45) on pain and suffering as elements of damages; (12 L. R. A. 699) on mental suffering as an element of damages; (13 L. R. A. 860) on damages for mental anguish alone not recoverable; (17 L. R. A. 72) on recovery for pain and suffering.

Allegation of damage.

Approved in West Chicago Street R. Co. v. McCallum, 169 Ill. 243, 48 N. E. 424, holding permanency of injury need not be pleaded; Chicago City R. Co. v. Taylor, 170 Ill. 57, 48 N. E. 831, holding mental suffering may be shown under general allegations of declaration; Baltimore & O. S. W. R. Co. v. Slanker, 180 Ill. 358, 54 N. E. 309, holding all particulars of injury need not be enumerated in order to prove them; Denver & R. G. R. Co. v. Roller, 49 L. R. A. 90, 41 C. C. A. 42, 100 Fed. 758, holding allegation of bodily injury in railroad collision admits proof of fright and shock to system; Western Brewery Co. v. Meredith, 166 Ill. 310, 46 N. E. 720, permitting recovery for mental and bodily suffering, although special damages for mental suffering not alleged; Croco v. Oregon Short Line R. Co. 18 Utah, 319, 44 L. R. A. 288, 54 Pac. 985, holding plaintiff need not

specially aver all the physical injuries sustained, resulting from or aggravated by the negligent act complained of.

Question for jury.

Approved in Vandalia v. Ropp, 39 Ill. App. 349, and William Graver Tank Works v. McGee, 58 Ill. App. 254, holding question whether facts show want of ordinary care, for jury; Chicago v. Moore, 139 Ill. 209, 28 N. E. 1071, holding negligence question of fact for jury under circumstances disclosed; North Chicago Street R. Co. v. Williams, 140 Ill. 281, 29 N. E. 672, holding exercise of due care while getting on street car question for jury; Lake Shore & M. S. R. Co. v. Hundt, 140 Ill. 530, 30 N. E. 458, holding question whether putting car in motion without brakeman on it is negligence, for jury; Pullman Palace Car Co. v. Connell, 74 Ill. App. 452, holding question whether failure to look where one steps constitutes negligence, for jury; Tucker v. Champaign County Agri. Board, 52 Ill. App. 325, holding question whether one who stepped into hole in floor, exercised ordinary care, for jury; Chicago v. McCrudden, 92 Ill. App. 259, holding question whether child, injured while walking backwards and talking to playmates, was negligent, for jury; Columbus v. Strassner, 124 Ind. 486, 25 N. E. 65, holding question whether plaintiff injured on defective walk was, under the circumstances, guilty of contributory negligence, for jury; McLeansboro v. Trammel, 109 Ill. App. 526, holding question whether failure to look at pathway constitutes negligence, for jury; Upper Alton v. Green, 112 Ill. App. 443, holding failure to keep constant watch of sidewalk for defects not negligence *per se*.

8 L. R. A. 767, STATE v. VOSS, 80 Iowa, 467, 45 N. W. 898.

Effect of postponement of execution of sentence.

Cited in Miller v. Evans, 115 Iowa, 102, 56 L. R. A. 102, footnote, p. 101, 91 Am. St. Rep. 143, 88 N. W. 198, denying right to relief suspending mittimus, under sentence of imprisonment on failure to pay fine; *Re* Strickler, 51 Kan. 702, 33 Pac. 620, holding sentence of imprisonment, to begin at indefinite future time, illegal; *Re* Markuson, 5 N. D. 185, 64 N. W. 939, holding court orders postponing imprisonment void; Neal v. State, 104 Ga. 512, 42 L. R. A. 191, footnote, p. 190, 69 Am. St. Rep. 175, 30 S. E. 858, which holds void, attempt to suspend execution of sentence after pronouncing it.

Cited in footnotes to Weber v. State, 41 L. R. A. 472, which sustains power of court to suspend sentence and set aside suspension at any time during term; Miller v. State, 40 L. R. A. 109, which upholds statute for indiscriminate sentence of criminals; People *ex rel.* Forsyth v. Monroe County Ct. of Sessions, 23 L. R. A. 856, which holds valid, act authorizing court to suspend sentence; State v. Crook, 29 L. R. A. 260, which holds power of court over accused after suspension of sentence not lost by committing him for refusal to pay costs as ordered.

8 L. R. A. 769, TRAVELERS INS. CO. v. CALIFORNIA INS. CO. 1 N. D. 151, 45 N. W. 703.

Limitation of action on insurance policy.

Cited in Egan v. Oakland Ins. Co. 29 Or. 406, 54 Am. St. Rep. 798, 42 Pac. 990, holding right of action on policy computed from date of loss; State Ins. Co. v. Meesman, 2 Wash. 464, 26 Am. St. Rep. 870, 27 Pac. 77, and Hart v. Citizens'

Ins. Co. 86 Wis. 70, 21 L. R. A. 745, footnote
N. W. 332, which requires time for suing on
of fire; Farmer's Co-op. Creamery Co. v. Iowa
N. W. 904, holding that failure to sue on p
extinguishes right; Provident Fund Soc. v. Ho
McFarland v. Railway Officials & E. Acci. Asso
note, p. 48, 63 Am. St. Rep. 29, 38 Pac. 347.
for action on policy begins from time of dea

Cited in footnote to Cooper v. United States
which holds limitation period for death ind
instead of accident.

Cited in note (47 L. R. A. 697) on literal
on policy for fixed period after loss; (63 L. R.
contracts of insurance.

Disapproved in effect in Read v. State Ins. C
180, 72 N. W. 665, holding right to sue on poli
of proof of loss; Sample v. London & L. F. Ins.
57 Am. St. Rep. 701, 24 S. E. 334, holding limi
begins at accrual of right.

Who may sue on policy.

Cited in Palmer Sav. Bank v. Insurance Co. o
617, 55 Am. St. Rep. 387, 44 N. E. 211, holdi
policy issued to mortgagor; Brown v. Commerc
holding mortgagee to whom loss is made paya
maintain action on policy.

Cited in note (25 L. R. A. 306) on who may
insurance.

8 L. R. A. 772, SWIFT v. TOPEKA, 43 Kan.

Rights of bicyclists.

Approved in Laredo Electric & R. Co. v. H
56 S. W. 998, holding bicyclist may recover for
Geiger v. Perkiomen & R. Turnp. Road, 4 Pa. Di
use turnpike as traveling public; North Chicago
614, 68 N. E. 88, holding bicyclist must use sa
other vehicles.

Cited in notes (8 L. R. A. 829) as to use
(19 L. R. A. 632) as to regulation of bicycle ri
bicycle law.

8 L. R. A. 774, STATE v. SMITH, 44 Kan. 75,

Discharge of jury.

Approved in Upchurch v. State, 36 Tex. Crim.
note, p. 695, 38 S. W. 206, upholding right of a
sity for discharge of jury before verdict is inve

Cited in State v. Reed, 53 Kan. 770, 42 Am.
State v. Allen, 59 Kan. 761, 54 Pac. 1060, holding
operates as acquittal unless record discloses su

8 L. R. A. 778, McCONNELL v. OSAGE, 80 Iowa, 293, 45 N. W. 550.

Order limiting number of witnesses.

Approved in Preston v. Cedar Rapids, 95 Iowa, 74, 63 N. W. 577, sustaining right of trial court to limit number of witnesses on given point; Larson v. Eau Claire, 92 Wis. 90, 65 N. W. 731, sustaining limitation of number of witnesses upon single question where made after reasonable number examined; Meier v. Morgan, 82 Wis. 294, 33 Am. St. Rep. 39, 52 N. W. 174, holding that ruling limiting witnesses on particular fact must be objected to when made.

Expert evidence.

Approved in Morgan v. Fremont County, 92 Iowa, 646, 61 N. W. 231, holding testimony of bridge builder as to life of timbers like those used in bridge admissible; Anderson v. Illinois C. R. Co. 109 Iowa, 528, 80 N. W. 561, holding testimony of man familiar with methods of work incompetent to show implements commonly used for moving timbers.

Cited in note (10 L. R. A. 739) on evidence as to defendant's negligence.

Evidence of general defective condition.

Approved in Munger v. Waterloo, 83 Iowa, 561, 49 N. W. 1028; Smith v. Des Moines, 84 Iowa, 687, 51 N. W. 77; Bailey v. Centerville, 108 Iowa, 23, 78 N. W. 831; Ledgerwood v. Webster City, 93 Iowa, 729, 61 N. W. 1089; Wilberding v. Dubuque, 111 Iowa, 488, 82 N. W. 957,—holding evidence of general defective condition of walk admissible to prove notice of particular defect; Kircher v. Larchwood, 120 Iowa, 582, 95 N. W. 184, holding evidence of general condition of walk competent as bearing upon defendant's knowledge of condition at place of accident; Lorig v. Davenport, 99 Iowa, 482, 68 N. W. 717, holding evidence that walk was old and in bad condition admissible as showing notice; Faulk v. Iowa County, 103 Iowa, 447, 72 N. W. 757, holding testimony of absence of cap rail from bridge for some time before accident admissible on question of notice; Harrison v. Ayrshire, 123 Iowa, 532, 99 N. W. 132, holding evidence of condition of stringer in walk competent in action for injury caused by board breaking; Frohs v. Dubuque, 109 Iowa, 221, 80 N. W. 341, holding evidence of construction of walk from old material admissible to show notice of defect; Smith v. Sioux City, 119 Iowa, 33, 93 N. W. 81, holding city chargeable with notice of defects in walk notoriously decayed; Smith v. Pella, 86 Iowa, 240, 53 N. W. 226, holding ordinance prescribing manner of constructing sidewalks admissible upon question of proper construction of walk claimed defective.

Cited in note (10 L. R. A. 740) on necessity of evidence of notice of defect.

Privileged communications.

Approved in Prader v. National Masonic Acci. Asso. 95 Iowa, 157, 63 N. W. 601, holding incompetency of confidential communications to physicians extends to knowledge acquired by personal examination; Briesenmeister v. Supreme Lodge K. of P. 81 Mich. 536, 45 N. W. 977, holding privilege of confidential communication to physician waived if not claimed before testimony admitted; Burgess v. Sims Drug. Co. 114 Iowa, 280, 54 L. R. A. 366, footnote p. 364, 89 Am. St. Rep. 359, 86 N. W. 307, which holds waiver of patient's privilege as to communication to physician confined to trial in which made.

Distinguished in Crago v. Cedar Rapids, 123 Iowa, 50, 98 N. W. 354, holding testimony of attending physician, based on hypothetical questions, not incompetent as disclosing confidential communications; State v. Booth, 121 Iowa, 713,

97 N. W. 74, holding mere offer of attending physician as witness, no ground for reversal.

8 L. R. A. 781, HOFFMAN v. CHIPPEWA COUNTY, 77 Wis. 214, 45 N. W. 1083.

Alteration of compensation fixed by law.

Cited in Endion Improv. Co. v. Evening Telegram Co. 104 Wis. 439, 80 N. W. 734, holding county cannot compromise claim for publishing notices at rate fixed by law; Rettinghouse v. Ashland, 106 Wis. 597, 82 N. W. 556, holding public officer's agreement to accept less than legal compensation void.

Powers of counties.

Cited in Frederick v. Douglas County, 96 Wis. 417, 71 N. W. 798, holding county quasi corporation only, without power to employ attorney.

Estoppel of counties.

Cited in Gilbert v. Pier, 102 Wis. 336, 78 N. W. 566, holding county not estopped from claiming title to lands by misstatement of officer making tax sale as to county's interest.

8 L. R. A. 783, KELLNY v. MISSOURI P. R. CO. 101 Mo. 67, 13 S. W. 806.

Contributory negligence.

Approved in Jennings v. St. Louis, I. M. & S. R. Co. 112 Mo. 276, 20 S. W. 490. holding one who stops within 20 feet of track without seeing or hearing indication of danger not guilty of contributory negligence in going on track without looking again; Baker v. Kansas City, Ft. S. & M. R. Co. 147 Mo. 166, 48 S. W. 838, holding one driving on track after freight train passes, and struck by cars that had got loose. not negligent where view was obstructed; Dahlstrom v. St. Louis, I. M. & S. R. Co. 108 Mo. 540, 18 S. W. 919, holding plaintiff's failure, before stopping on track, to look in direction of car that struck him does not prevent recovery unless he would have discovered immediate danger.

Cited in Indianapolis Union R. Co. v. Neubacher, 16 Ind. App. 41, 43 N. E. 576, holding contributory negligence of one injured in crossing large number of parallel tracks usually question for jury; Moore v. Lindell R. Co. 176 Mo. 545, 75 S. W. 672, denying street railroad's liability for killing woman stepping on track directly in front of car.

Cited in footnote to Neal v. Carolina C. R. Co. 49 L. R. A. 684, which denies liability for death of person on track by train running at excessive speed without ringing bell.

— Proximate cause.

Approved in Hogan v. Citizens' R. Co. 150 Mo. 55, 51 S. W. 473, holding plaintiff's direct contributory negligence will bar recovery; Oates v. Metropolitan Street R. Co. 168 Mo. 548, 58 L. R. A. 451, 68 S. W. 906, holding negligence or contributory negligence must be direct and proximate cause of injury; Corcoran v. St. Louis, I. M. & S. R. Co. 105 Mo. 406, 24 Am. St. Rep. 394, 16 S. W. 411, holding concurring negligence of plaintiff which defendant did not or was not required to know at time of injury, bars recovery; Klockenbrink v. St. Louis & M. River R. Co. 81 Mo. App. 357, holding negligence of party having last opportunity of avoiding accident sole proximate cause of injury.

Cited in note (12 L. R. A. 283) that proximate cause of injury fixes liability.

— Defendant's failure to use reasonable care.

Approved in Hutchinson v. St. Louis & M. River R. Co. 88 Mo. App. 382; Hanlon v. Missouri P. R. Co. 104 Mo. 389, 16 S. W. 233; Dlauhi v. St. Louis, I. M. & S. R. Co. 139 Mo. 297, 40 S. W. 890, — holding plaintiff may recover notwithstanding contributory negligence, if defendant by reasonable care could have prevented accident; Schlereth v. Missouri P. R. Co. 115 Mo. 101, 21 S. W. 1110, holding contributory negligence no defense if engineer could have avoided injury after danger became apparent; Edwards v. Chicago & A. R. Co. 94 Mo. App. 41, 67 S. W. 950, holding engineer's failure to take measures to stop train after discovering plaintiff's peril, actionable; Burnstein v. Cass Ave. & Fair Grounds R. Co. 56 Mo. App. 53, holding duty to stop car arises on first appearance of danger and should be in time to prevent injury; Jett v. Central Electric R. Co. 178 Mo. 673, 77 S. W. 738, holding street railroad's liability for killing children playing on track, question for jury, where evidence shows motorman might have seen them in time to stop; Klockenbrink v. St. Louis & M. River R. Co. 172 Mo. 688, 72 S. W. 900, sustaining instruction that street car company would be liable for collision with person negligently driving along track, if avoidable by ordinary care; Parks v. St. Louis & Suburban R. Co. 178 Mo. 117, 77 S. W. 70, holding street car company's liability for injury to passenger crushed between cars passing on curve, while riding on step, with knowledge of motorman and conductor, question for jury; Zumault v. Kansas City Suburban Belt R. Co. 175 Mo. 315, 74 S. W. 1015, denying railroad's liability for striking man sitting dangerously near track, where engineer was not guilty of wanton recklessness; Carrier v. Missouri P. R. Co. 175 Mo. 482, 74 S. W. 1002, denying railroad's liability for killing pedestrian on track, by engineer not showing wilful disregard of human life.

Cited in footnote to Cincinnati, H. & D. R. Co. v. Kassen, 16 L. R. A. 674, which authorizes recovery for injury to negligent person by one not using care after discovering danger.

Distinguished in Koons v. Kansas City Suburban Belt R. Co. 178 Mo. 608, 77 S. W. 755, denying railroad's liability for avoidable killing of flagman who also might have avoided accident; McGauley v. St. Louis Transit Co. 179 Mo. 592, 79 S. W. 461, holding contributory negligence bars recovery for collision by street car, in absence of evidence showing accident avoidable by ordinary care of motorman; Guyer v. Missouri P. R. Co. 174 Mo. 351, 73 S. W. 584, denying railroad's liability for crossing accident where evidence does not show engine might have been stopped in time.

— Traveler's presumption that railway will obey law.

Approved in Jennings v. St. Louis, I. M. & S. R. Co. 112 Mo. 276, 20 S. W. 490; Sullivan v. Missouri P. R. Co. 117 Mo. 222, 23 S. W. 149; Weller v. Chicago, M. & St. P. R. Co. 120 Mo. 652, 23 S. W. 1061, — holding traveler may presume company will obey state and municipal laws in running train.

— Wanton or wilful injuries.

Approved in Holwerson v. St. Louis & Suburban R. Co. 157 Mo. 236, 50 L. R. A. 856, 57 S. W. 770; Morgan v. Wabash R. Co. 159 Mo. 276, 60 S. W. 195; Sharp v. Missouri P. R. Co. 161 Mo. 236, 61 S. W. 829; Tanner v. Missouri P. R. Co. 161 Mo. 511, 61 S. W. 826, — holding contributory negligence no defense to injury wantonly or wilfully inflicted.

Distinguished in Feeback v. Missouri P. R. Co. 167 Mo. 217, 66 S. W. 965, holding company owes trespasser no duty except to avoid wanton injury.

Violation of ordinance.

Approved in Dahlstrom v. St. Louis, I. M. & S. R. Co. 108 Mo. 538, 18 S. W. 919; Gratiot v. Missouri P. R. Co. 116 Mo. 463, 16 L. R. A. 191, 21 S. W. 1094; Jackson v. Kansas City, Ft. S. & M. R. Co. 157 Mo. 641, 80 Am. St. Rep. 650, 58 S. W. 32; Hutchinson v. Missouri P. R. Co. 161 Mo. 253, 84 Am. St. Rep. 710, 61 S. W. 635, — holding running train in violation of ordinance negligence *per se.*

Cited in Baker v. Kansas City, Ft. S. & M. R. Co. 147 Mo. 166, 48 S. W. 838, holding contributory negligence must be clearly made out where violation of law results in injury.

Sufficiency of pleading.

Approved in Shaw v. Missouri P. R. Co. 104 Mo. 656, 16 S. W. 832, holding petition alleging negligent management of train whereby deceased was fatally injured states cause of action.

Admissibility of evidence.

Approved in Hanlon v. Missouri P. R. Co. 104 Mo. 391, 16 S. W. 233, holding proof of negligence of railway company after its employees saw plaintiff's peril admissible under allegation of negligent management of train.

8 L. R. A. 787, PEEL v. ATLANTA, 85 Ga. 138, 11 S. E. 582.

Damages in eminent domain.

Cited in Austin v. Augusta Terminal R. Co. 108 Ga. 679, 47 L. R. A. 753, 34 S. E. 852, holding "damages to property taken for public purpose" refers to land; O'Connell v. East Tenessee, V. & G. R. Co. 87 Ga. 261, 13 L. R. A. 401, 27 Am. St. Rep. 246, 13 S. E. 489, holding damages recoverable for injury due to overflow of river, caused by erection of embankment; Metropolitan West Side Elev. R. Co. v. Goll, 100 Ill. App. 335, denying liability of railroad company for depreciation in value of adjoining property.

Cited in notes (11 L. R. A. 548) on action on case based on contract; (12 L. R. A. 675) on right of eminent domain.

Distinguished in Austin v. Augusta Terminal R. Co. 108 Ga. 732, 47 L. R. A. 779, 34 S. E. 852 (dissenting opinion), majority holding railroad company not liable for depreciation in value of property, due to smoke and noise in absence of physical interference with property.

Test of damages.

Cited in Austin v. Augusta Terminal R. Co. 108 Ga. 676, 47 L. R. A. 759, 34 S. E. 852, holding railroad company liable to same extent as individual at common law for "private property damaged for public purpose."

8 L. R. A. 788, FIRST NAT. BANK v. HUMMEL, 14 Colo. 259, 20 Am. St. Rep. 257, 23 Pac. 986.

Reaffirmed on later appeal in 2 Colo. App. 571, 32 Pac. 72.

What constitutes trust fund.

Cited in Myers v. Board of Education, 51 Kan. 102, 37 Am. St. Rep. 263, 32 Pac. 658, holding entire assets of insolvent bank subject to lien for public moneys wrongfully deposited therein; State v. Thum, 6 Idaho, 330, 55 Pac. 858, holding trust, and not debt, created by unauthorized deposit of public money in bank; Lincoln v. Morrison, 64 Neb. 826, 57 L. R. A. 887, 90 N. W. 905, holding municipality entitled to preference over general creditors in fund enriched by trust moneys; Cady v. South Omaha Nat. Bank, 49 Neb. 120, 68 N. W. 358, holding money deposited in bank without notice by commission merchant, trust fund for principal; Peters Shoe Co. v. Murray, 31 Tex. Civ. App. 261, 71 S. W. 977; Meldrum v. Henderson, 7 Colo. App. 258, 43 Pac. 148; Foster v. Rincker, 4 Wyo. 493, 35 Pac. 470, — holding money collected by bank on negotiable instrument, trust fund recoverable as such by payee on bank's insolvency; Capital Nat. Bank v. Coldwater Nat. Bank, 49 Neb. 789, 59 Am. St. Rep. 572, 69 N. W. 115, holding money subject to call in payment of due and canceled note constitutes trust fund taking precedence in insolvent's estate; McClure v. La Plata County, 19 Colo. 125, 34 Pac. 763, holding public moneys embezzled by county treasurer collectible out of estate, only if latter enriched thereby; Bramell v. Adams, 146 Mo. 86, 47 S. W. 931, holding equitable proceeding against administrator to recover proceeds of trust property not barred by limitation applicable to claim; *Re* Belt, 29 Wash. 543, 92 Am. St. Rep. 916, 70 Pac. 74, holding probate court may determine whether property in dispute should be included in inventory of estate.

Cited in footnotes to Ferchen v. Arndt, 29 L. R. A. 664, which denies power of consignors to impress, with trust lien, funds of consignees in hands of receiver; Bohle v. Hasselbroch, 61 L. R. A. 323, which holds *cestuis que trust* entitled to lien upon land purchased in part with trust funds, or to land itself, subject to charge for amount paid in excess of trust funds.

Distinguished in Holden v. Piper, 5 Colo. App. 73, 37 Pac. 34, holding administrator *de bonis non* of insolvent trustee not entitled to preference where assignment does not disclose that trust fund included; Pearson v. Haydel, 90 Mo. App. 261, holding creditor's claims not enforceable against estate where not shown that estate enriched by embezzled trust funds; Kimmel v. Bean (Kan.) 64 L. R. A. 788, 75 Pac. 1118, denying bank's liability to principal for deposit applied in good faith on agent's overdraft.

Party in interest.

Cited in Moulton v. McLean, 5 Colo. App. 464, 39 Pac. 78, holding county treasurer, and not county, proper party to action against bank on personal bond to secure deposit of county moneys; Stewart v. Price, 64 Kan. 207, 64 L. R. A. 601, 67 Pac. 553 (dissenting opinion), majority holding assignee of account for purpose of collection not real party in interest.

Cited in note (64 L. R. A. 585) on who is real party in interest within meaning of statutes defining parties by whom action must be brought.

8 L. R. A. 795, JOHNSON v. JOUCHERT, 124 Ind. 105, 24 N. E. 580.

Wife's separate estate.

Cited in Cochran v. Benton, 126 Ind. 62, 25 N. E. 870, holding mortgage securing money borrowed to discharge prior lien thereon, valid; Till v. Collier, 27 Ind. App. 340, 61 N. E. 203, holding mortgage securing loan to pay off prima facie valid prior lien enforceable though prior lien voidable; Goff v. Hankins, 11 Ind. App. 458, 39 N. E. 294, holding pledge of personalty for husband's debt void, though no agreement signed or personal liability incurred; Herbert v. Rupertus,

31 Ind. App. 555, 68 N. E. 598, holding husband
first applicable to mortgage securing loan for l
31 Ind. App. 251, 67 N. E. 542, holding marri
voidable at her election.

Cited in note (20 L. R. A. 702) on validity c

Distinguished in Heal v. Niagara Oil Co. 15
lease to gas and oil well company not encumb

Defense of coverture.

Cited in McCoy v. Barns, 136 Ind. 381, 36 N.
band and wife to secure purchase money for h
binding, since wife not surety; Taylor v. Hea
holding wife estopped as against mortgagee to
loan made to her on representation that it is fo

— Parties entitled to.

Cited in Lackey v. Boruff, 152 Ind. 378, 53 N
itors of husband cannot set aside wife's suret
Storey, 131 Ind. 51, 30 N. E. 886, holding lienor
to secure her liability upon husband's notes as
Nussbaum, 131 Ind. 270, 16 L. R. A. 47, 31 N. 1
to defense of nonliability on her suretyship note
for value in due course.

Distinguished in Columbian Oil Co. v. Blake,
holding defense available to defendant in action
able by her at her election.

Necessity of pleading coverture.

Cited in Dickey v. Kalfsbeck, 20 Ind. App. 29
not available unless pleaded, even though compla

Common-law disabilities generally.

Cited in Postlewaite v. Postlewaite, 1 Ind. App.
for alienation of husband's affections maintainab
v. Patton, 5 Ind. App. 275, 31 N. E. 1130, holdin
property to wife in consideration of her joining
valid in equity.

8 L. R. A. 798, WELLER v. McCORMICK, 52 N.

Trees in highway.

Cited in Western U. Teleg. Co. v. Krueger, 30 I
ing proprietor of fee of highway may maintain ac

Cited in note (15 L. R. A. 554) on ownership

Rights and liabilities as to use of highway

Cited in Halsey v. Rapid Transit Street R. Co.
denying abutting owner's right to enjoin erectio
Sutphen v. Hedden, 67 N. J. L. 327, 51 Atl. 72
injury to passerby by blowing down of fence erect
building in street; Ivins v. Trenton, 68 N. J. I
ordinance prohibiting erection of signs or statior
Fielders v. North Jersey Street R. Co. 68 N. J. I

St. Rep. 552, 53 Atl. 404, holding person injured by defect in paving between car tracks cannot maintain action against company charged by ordinance with repair.

Cited in note (12 L. R. A. 190) on liability of abutting owners for injuries caused by material falling into street.

8 L. R. A. 800, RICHARDSON v. GERMAN INS. CO. 89 Ky. 571, 13 S. W. 1.

Change of title as affecting insurance policy.

Cited in Gerling v. Agricultural Ins. Co. 39 W. Va. 700, 20 S. E. 691, holding invalid deed not such transfer of title as to forfeit policy; Planters' Mut. Ins. Asso. v. Dewberry, 69 Ark. 300, 86 Am. St. Rep. 195, 62 S. W. 1047, and Forest City Ins. Co. v. Hardesty, 182 Ill. 49, 74 Am. St. Rep. 161, 55 N. E. 139, Affirming 77 Ill. App. 421, holding change of title by death of insured works no forfeiture of policy.

8 L. R. A. 801, BELCHER'S SUGAR REF. CO. v. ST. LOUIS GRAIN ELEVATOR CO. 101 Mo. 192, 13 S. W. 822.

Public use.

Approved in Knapp, S. & Co. v. St. Louis Transfer R. Co. 126 Mo. 34, 28 S. W. 627, holding property used as stock yards for convenience of public devoted to public use; Chicago, S. F. & C. R. Co. v. McGrew, 104 Mo. 299, 15 S. W. 931, holding land appropriated to public use cannot be transferred unconditionally to private use; Reighard v. Flinn, 194 Pa. 356, 44 Atl. 1080, Affirming 26 Pittsb. L. J. N. S. 340, holding city may maintain wharf to facilitate use of public landing; State *ex rel.* Citizens Electric Lighting & P. Co. v. Longfellow, 169 Mo. 129, 69 S. W. 374, holding city cannot, without violation of public trust, permit riparian owner on navigable river to erect building beyond low-water mark.

— Of streets for wires or poles.

Approved in State *ex rel.* National Subway Co. v. St. Louis, 145 Mo. 573, 42 L. R. A. 122, 46 S. W. 981, holding city in its proprietary capacity may permit telegraph and telephone companies to lay wires and construct conduits in the street; St. Louis v. Western U. Teleg. Co. 149 U. S. 471, 37 L. ed. 814, 13 Sup. Ct. Rep. 990, holding use of streets for telegraph poles not a private use, and city may charge rental therefor.

Equity jurisdiction.

Cited in Bridgens v. Dollar Sav. Bank, 66 Fed. 14, holding equity may inquire into alleged fraudulent transactions conducted between insolvent bank and another bank of which it was an adjunct, by managing agent of both.

8 L. R. A. 806, HORSCH v. DWELLING HOUSE INS. CO. 77 Wis. 4, 45 N. W. 945.

Insurable interest.

Cited in Davis v. Phœnix Ins. Co. 111 Cal. 414, 43 Pac. 1115, and Gettelman v. Commercial Union Assur. Co. 97 Wis. 241, 72 N. W. 627, holding person in possession of real estate under contract of purchase, upon which substantial payment has been made, has insurable interest; Edwards v. Agricultural Ins. Co. 88 Wis. 452, 60 N. W. 782, holding mechanic's-lien claimant has insurable interest in building subject to lien.

Cited in footnote to Home Ins. Co. v. Mendenhall, 36 L. R. A. 374, which holds expectant heir, placed in possession by his father with assurance that property has been devised to him by will, has insurable interest.

8 L. R. A. 808, JANESVILLE v. CARPENTER, 77 Wis. 288, 20 Am. St. Rep. 123, 46 N. W. 128.

Unjust discrimination.

Cited in State *ex rel.* Zillmer v. Kreutzberg, 114 Wis. 534, 58 L. R. A. 751, 91 Am. St. Rep. 934, 90 N. W. 1098, holding penal statute forbidding discharge of employee because member of labor union invalid.

Equitable remedy for nuisance.

Approved in Madison v. Mayers, 97 Wis. 415, 40 L. R. A. 651, 65 Am. St. Rep. 127, 73 N. W. 48, holding suit to enjoin filling of lake outside of street not within city's power to make general police regulations and provide for abatement of nuisance; McCann v. Strang, 97 Wis. 553, 72 N. W. 1118, holding electric light plant, under circumstances of case, not abatable as nuisance; Ryan v. Schwartz, 94 Wis. 409, 69 N. W. 178, holding abutter has action to abate building partly in highway.

Cited in note (51 L. R. A. 659) as to right of municipality to maintain suit to enjoin or abate public nuisance.

Distinguished in North Bloomfield Gravel Min. Co. v. United States, 32 C. C. A. 96, 59 U. S. App. 377, 88 Fed. 676, holding injunction will lie against hydraulic mining not conducted as required by statute.

Rights of riparian owners.

Approved in Hall v. Alford, 114 Mich. 167, 38 L. R. A. 207, 72 N. W. 138, holding fowling in marsh, trespass as to riparian owner; Green Bay & M. Canal Co. v. Kaukauna Water Power Co. 90 Wis. 390, 28 L. R. A. 446, 48 Am. St. Rep. 937, 61 N. W. 1121, holding rights of lower riparian owners in stream can be taken by state only for public use, and then upon compensation; Willow River Club v. Wade, 100 Wis. 95, 42 L. R. A. 314, 76 N. W. 273, holding fishing in navigable river with hook and line from rowboat not trespass against riparian owner; Jones v. Seaboard Air Line R. Co. 67 S. C. 194, 45 S. E. 188, holding riparian owner on navigable river may maintain action for damages against railroad obstructing flow of freshet waters by negligently constructed bridge piers; Grand Rapids v. Powers, 89 Mich. 115, 14 L. R. A. 507, 28 Am. St. Rep. 276, 50 N. W. 661, holding legislature cannot fix building line upon non-navigable river subject to riparian proprietorship; St. Louis v. Hill, 116 Mo. 536, 21 L. R. A. 228, 22 S. W. 861, holding establishment of building line without notice to lot owners unlawful taking; Kaukauna Water Power Co. v. Green Bay & M. Canal Co. 142 U. S. 271, 35 L. ed. 1010, 12 Sup. Ct. Rep. 173, holding ownership of riparian proprietors extends to center of stream subject to right of public to use it as highway if it is navigable; St. Anthony Falls Water Power Co. v. St. Paul Water Comrs. 168 U. S. 364, 42 L. ed. 503, 18 Sup. Ct. Rep. 157, holding rights of riparion proprietorship to be measured by decisions of state courts; Priewe v. Wisconsin State Land v. Improv. Co. 93 Wis. 547, 33 L. R. A. 650, 67 N. W. 918, holding legislature cannot take rights of riparian owner for sole benefit of private parties.

Cited in note (40 L. R. A. 637) as to right to erect wharves.

Equal protection and privileges.

Approved in Opinion of the Justices, 66 N. H. 664, 33 Atl. 1076, holding taking for public use of property of particular railroad for less than its value. not justified; Anderton v. Milwaukee, 82 Wis. 284, 15 L. R. A. 832, 52 N. W. 95, holding statute invalid which discriminates between owners of lots similarly situated as to compensation for change of street grade; State *ex rel.* Kellogg v. Currens, 111 Wis. 435, 56 L. R. A. 255, 87 N. W. 561. sustaining requirement of examination of graduates of foreign schools before receiving license to practise medicine. from which local graduates excepted; Gulf, C. & S. F. R. Co. v. Ellis, 165 U. S. 164, 41 L. ed. 671, 17 Sup. Ct. Rep. 255, holding statute imposing attorney's fee upon railway corporations omitting to pay certain claims as specified, invalid; Atchison, T. & S. F. R. Co. v. Matthews, 175 U. S. 120. 43 L. ed. 918, 19 Sup. Ct. Rep. 609 (dissenting opinion), majority holding valid, statute making proof that fire was caused by operation of railroad, and of damages, prima facie evidence of negligence.

8 L. R. A. 814, DUDLEY v. DUDLEY, 76 Wis. 567, 45 N. W. 602.

Conveyances in fraud of wife.

Cited in Arnegaard v. Arnegaard, 7 N. D. 494, 41 L. R. A. 265, footnote, p. 258, 75 N. W. 797, holding secret deed to son just before marriage to prevent wife's right from vesting on marriage. void as to her homestead right, when building of home thereon was inducement to marriage.

Cited in footnotes to Ward v. Ward. 51 L. R. A. 858, which holds second wife's right to dower not defeated by fraudulent antenuptial conveyance to sons by former marriage; Arnegaard v. Arnegaard, 41 L. R. A. 258, which holds secret unrecorded deed to son on eve of grantor's marriage fraudulent as to wife.

Cited in note (18 L. R. A. 79) on power of husband to defeat dower.

Distinguished in Murray v. Murray, 115 Cal. 272, 37 L. R. A. 628, 56 Am. St. Rep. 97, 47 Pac. 37, sustaining action by deserted wife for setting aside of husband's deed given for purpose of depriving her of her right to maintenance.

8 L. R. A. 818, BRENNAN v. GORDON, 118 N. Y. 489, 16 Am. St. Rep. 775, 23 N. E. 810.

Master's duty to instruct employee.

Cited in Felton v. Girardy, 43 C. C. A. 442, 104 Fed. 130, and Louisville & N. R. Co. v. Miller, 43 C. C. A. 438, 104 Fed. 126, holding master having notice of dangers, and of inexperience of employee. must use reasonable care in cautioning and instructing him how best to discharge duty; Ferguson v. Smith, 15 Misc. 253, 36 N. Y. Supp. 415, holding superficial instructions to boy set to work cutting wedges on buzz saw do not relieve master from liability for injury due to saw binding in wet and knotty lumber; Corbett v. St. Vincent's Industrial School. 79 App. Div. 339, 79 N. Y. Supp. 369, holding question whether master negligent in putting inexperienced boy to work on laundry mangle, without proper instructions, for jury; Koehler v. Syracuse Specialty Mfg. Co. 12 App. Div. 59, 42 N. Y. Supp. 1105 (concurring opinion), majority holding inexperienced employee assumes risk of perils incident to use of machinery, when apparent to person of ordinary observation.

Cited in footnotes to Holland v. Tennessee Coal, Iron & R. Co. 12 L. R. A. 232, which holds it master's duty to warn servant of danger of flying iron when boil of iron punctured; Fisher v. Oregon Short Lin holding it section foreman's duty to notify c snowslide.

Cited in notes (8 L. R. A. 819) on duty of of dangerous machinery; (44 L. R. A. 88) on reference to doctrine of common employment; from servant's transfer to new duties.

Distinguished in Gaertner v. Schmitt, 21 Ap holding negligence cannot be predicated on omi perienced employee as to dangers of machinery,

Master's responsibility for due perform another.

Cited in Louisville & N. R. Co. v. Miller, 43 C duty of qualifying inexperienced servant for safe ous duty is personal to master; Strauss v. Hat 48 N. Y. Supp. 425, holding foreman altering such way as to increase risk, without instructin master; Lebbering v. Struthers, 157 Pa. 323, 33 master responsible for incompetency or negligen of instructing inexperienced employee as to opera

Cited in footnote to Spees v. Boggs, 52 L. R. bound to explain cause of elevator injuring empl

Cited in notes (12 L. R. A. 97) on when maste ant acting under authority; (54 L. R. A. 97) o for negligence of servants who transmit orders; (superiors.

Who are fellow servants.

Cited in footnotes to Baltimore & O. R. Co. v. holds conductor and engineer fellow servants of v. Pennsylvania Co. 17 L. R. A. 811, which hold member of another gang fellow servants; Palmer A. 637, which holds assistant roadmaster not fello ing under him; Fisher v. Oregon, Short Line & U. holds section foreman and conductor not fellow se

8 L. R. A. 822, COOK v. WINCHESTER, 81 Mich.

Wills; execution.

Cited in Raymond v. Wagner, 178 Mass. 318, 59 in room adjoining that where testatrix was in bed to her, sufficient; Cunningham v. Cunningham, 80 Am. St. Rep. 256, 83 N. W. 58, holding attestatior testator was, after which paper was returned to hi "all right," sufficient.

Cited in footnotes to *Re* Booth, 12 L. R. A. 452 containing maker's name at beginning only, insufi 11 L. R. A. 796, which holds reference, before sign on back, insufficient.

Conflict of laws.

Cited in footnotes to Cross v. United States Trust Co. 15 L. R. A. 606, which upholds bequest valid by law of testator's domicil; Cotting v. DeSartiges, 16 L. R. A. 367, which holds question whether will of donee constitutes execution of power of appointment given by will, to be governed by law of donor's domicil; Hope v. Brewer, 18 L. R. A. 458, which holds valid, gift to charity in foreign country, if valid by law thereof.

8 L. R. A. 828, CHARLOTTE v. PEMBROKE IRON WORKS, 82 Me. 391, 19 Atl. 902.

Municipal powers over obstructions affecting highway.

Cited in Com. v. Fitzgerald, 164 Mass. 589, 42 N. E. 119, holding county has special property in bridge used as highway sufficient to sustain indictment for burning.

Cited in footnotes to Lostutter v. Aurora, 12 L. R. A. 259, which authorizes city to fit up abandoned well in street without abutting owner's consent; Fitch v. New York, P. & B. R. Co. 10 L. R. A. 188, which holds temporary use of street by railroad company while building approach to bridge not a trespass.

Cited in notes (39 L. R. A. 653, 656, 683) on power of municipality over nuisances affecting highways and waters in general; (16 L. R. A. 474) on liability of municipality for permitting street obstruction.

Abatement of nuisance by action.

Cited in footnotes to O'Brien v. Central Iron & Steel Co. 57 L. R. A. 508, which authorizes private action for permanent obstruction of street within 200 feet of abutter; Jacksonville, T. & K. W. R. Co. v. Thompson, 26 L. R. A. 410, which denies right to maintain private action for inconvenience from obstruction of highway in common with others.

Cited in note (9 L. R. A. 716, 717) on remedy for nuisance by action.

Right to maintain nuisance.

Cited in notes (53 L. R. A. 891, 899) on prescriptive right to maintain obstructions and encroachments in general; (59 L. R. A. 847) on rights in general as against public to dam stream.

8 L. R. A. 833, DOE v. ROE, 82 Me. 503, 17 Am. St. Rep. 499, 20 Atl. 83.

Liability for interrupting marital relations.

Approved in Lonstorf v. Lonstorf, 118 Wis. 161, 95 N. W. 961, and Morgan v. Martin, 92 Me. 192, 42 Atl. 354, denying right of wife to damages for alienation of husband's affections by another woman; Smith v. Smith, 98 Tenn. 107, 60 Am. St. Rep. 838, 38 S. W. 439, holding wife's right to damages for alienation of husband's affections unenforceable without enabling statute, until coverture terminated.

Cited in Kroessin v. Keller, 60 Minn. 375, 27 L. R. A. 686, 51 Am. St. Rep. 533, 62 N. W. 438, denying right of wife to maintain action in nature of criminal conversation against another woman.

Cited in footnotes to Tucker v. Tucker, 32 L. R. A. 623, which holds parent not liable for advising son to separate from wife; Houghton v. Rice, 47 L. R. A. 311, which denies right of action against another woman for alienation of husband's affections unaccompanied by adultery; Hodgkinson v. Hodgkinson, 27 L. R. A.

120, which holds one bringing about husband's desertion liable to suit by wife; Wolf v. Frank, 52 L. R. A. 102; Betser v. Betser, 52 L. R. A. 630; Clow v. Chapman, 26 L. R. A. 412; Dietzman v. Mullin, 50 L. R. A. 808; Warren v. Warren, 14 L. R. A. 545, which authorizes action for alienating husband's affections.

Cited in notes (10 L. R. A. 468; 11 L. R. A. 549) on liability for destroying marital relations.

Disapproved in effect in Gernerd v. Gernerd, 185 Pa. 237, 40 L. R. A. 550, 64 Am. St. Rep. 646, 39 Atl. 884, upholding right of wife to recover for alienation of husband's affections by father; Wolf v. Frank, 92 Md. 140, 52 L. R. A. 104, 48 Atl. 132, upholding statutory right of wife to recover for alienation of husband's affections; Gernerd v. Gernerd, 42 W. N. C. 51; Knapp v. Wing, 72 Vt. 337, 47 Atl. 1075; Price v. Price, 91 Iowa, 696, 29 L. R. A. 151, 51 Am. St. Rep. 360, 60 N. W. 202; Humphrey v. Pope, 122 Cal. 257, 54 Pac. 847; Warren v. Warren, 89 Mich. 125, 14 L. R. A. 546, 50 N. W. 842,—sustaining right of wife to recover damages for alienation of husband's affections and loss of support.

Effect on limitations of agreement to deny cause of action.

Cited in footnote to Sanborn v. Gale, 26 L. R. A. 864, which holds running of limitation against action for alienation of wife's affections not prevented by agreement of parties to adultery, known to husband, to deny same.

8 L. R. A. 834, LOOMIS v. ROCKFORD INS. CO. 77 Wis. 87, 20 Am. St. Rep. 96, 45 N. W. 813.

Indivisible contracts of insurance.

Followed and explained on subsequent appeal in 81 Wis. 366, 51 N. W. 564, which holds evidence that property insured belongs to different classes, insurable at different rates, does not sufficiently establish indivisibility of contract.

Approved in Taylor v. Anchor Mut. F. Ins. Co. 116 Iowa, 630, 57 L. R. A. 331, 93 Am. St. Rep. 261, 88 N. W. 807, holding entirety of premium in policy upon dwelling and live stock will not prevent recovery for loss of former, although liability for latter avoided by encumbrance; Stevens v. Queen Ins. Co. 81 Wis. 338, 29 Am. St. Rep. 905, 51 N. W. 555, holding policy covering buildings and personalty contained therein, entire contract, although risk distributed; Dohlantry v. Blue Mounds Fire & Lightning Ins. Co. 83 Wis. 187, 53 N. W. 448, holding policy indivisible which distributes risk between house and other farm buildings and contents; Burr v. German Ins. Co. 84 Wis. 78, 36 Am. St. Rep. 905, 54 N. W. 22, holding policy indivisible where upon personalty in warehouse, risk being distributed to several items, but premium paid in gross; Worechek v. New Denmark Mut. Home F. Ins. Co. 102 Wis. 90, 78 N. W. 411, holding false swearing as to loss forfeits entire policy covering building and contents; Kahler v. Iowa State Ins. Co. 106 Iowa, 385, 76 N. W. 734, holding entire policy which covers house and contents avoided by change of title in former; Liverpool & L. & G. Ins. Co. v. Tillis, 110 Ala. 210, 17 So. 672, raising, without deciding, question whether breach of "iron safe clause" defense to liability for loss of building.

Cited in footnote to Coleman v. New Orleans Ins. Co. 16 L. R. A. 174, which holds policy for separate amounts on storehouse and goods severable.

Cited in notes (19 L. R. A. 212; 20 L. R. A. 271) as to severability of insurance in same policy.

8 L. R. A. 837, HRONEK v. PEOPLE, 134 Ill. 139, 23 Am. St. Rep. 652, 24 N. E. 861.

Single subject expressed in act.

Cited in Feek v. Bloomingdale 82 Mich. 416 10 L. R. A. 77, 47 N. W. 37, holding local option law, as a whole, has but a single object,—prohibition; State *ex rel.* Dunn v. Humboldt County, 21 Nev. 238, 29 Pac. 974, holding matters connected with subject of act need not be mentioned in title; State v. Haas, 2 N. D. 204, 50 N. W. 254, holding but one subject embraced in act regulating sale of liquor and excepting pharmacists.

Credibility of witnesses.

Cited in Cicero & P. Street R. Co. v. Priest, 89 Ill. App. 308, holding witness may be asked if he is not gambler, to affect his credibility.

Religious test for witnesses.

Cited in McAmore v. Wiley, 49 Ill. App. 618, holding no religious test required to qualify person to be a witness.

Cited in note (42 L. R. A. 554, 558) on religious belief as qualification of witness.

Punishment of accessory to crime.

Cited in State v. Kent, 4 N. D. 582, 27 L. R. A. 688, 62 N. W. 631, holding accessory before the fact may be convicted of murder.

8 L. R. A. 842, NEWMAN v. PHILLIPSBURGH HORSE CAR R. CO. 52 N. J. L. 446, 19 Atl. 1102.

Imputing negligence of parent or guardian to child.

Cited in Evansville v. Senhenn, 151 Ind. 53, 41 L. R. A. 732, 68 Am. St. Rep. 218, 47 N. E. 634; Jeffersonville v. McHenry, 22 Ind. App. 15, 53 N. E. 183; Berry v. Lake Erie & W. R. Co. 70 Fed. 683; Chicago & G. W. R. Co. v. Kowalski, 34 C. C. A. 4, 92 Fed. 312,—holding, in suit by infant in its own right for personal injury, parent's negligence cannot be imputed to it; Markey v. Consolidated Traction Co. 65 N. J. L. 84, 46 Atl. 573, holding child who is *non sui juris* cannot be charged with negligence of person having it in custody; Bottoms v. Seaboard & R. R. Co. 114 N. C. 711, 25 L. R. A. 792, 41 Am. St. Rep. 799, 19 S. E. 730, holding negligence of parent allowing child twenty-two months old to go on railroad track cannot be imputed to child in action in its behalf for injury; South Covington & C. Street R. Co. v. Herrklotz, 104 Ky. 415, 47 S. W. 265, holding child under four years of age cannot be guilty of contributory negligence; Bergen County Traction Co. v. Heitman, 61 N. J. L. 683, 40 Atl. 651, holding traction company not relieved from liability for death of child under three years old, by fact that child was permitted to roam streets unattended; Profit v. Chicago G. W. R. Co. 91 Mo. App. 375, holding injury inflicted upon infant by wrongdoer not excused by negligence of third party having child in custody, though parent; Warren v. Manchester Street R. Co. 70 N. H. 359, 47 Atl. 735, holding negligence of parent in exposing infant to danger not imputable to child in action by administrator for causing death; Atlanta & C. Air-Line R. Co. v. Gravitt 93 Ga. 379, 26 L. R. A. 557, 44 Am. St. Rep. 145, 20 S. E. 550, holding negligence of parent not imputable to child, but such negligence is good defense to action by parent for death of child.

Cited in note (21 L. R. A. 77, 81) on contributory negligence of parent or custodian as bar to child's action for personal injury.

Contributory negligence of children.

Cited in footnotes to Gleason v. Smith, 55 L. R. A. 622, which denies liability for injury by collision with team, to twelve year old boy using street as playground; Graney v. St. Louis, I. M. & S. R. Co. 38 L. R. A. 633, which denies negligence *per se* of twelve year old boy in standing so near passing train as to be drawn under by current of air.

8 L. R. A. 846, TOLCHESTER BEACH IMPROV. CO. v. STEINMEIER, 72 Md. 313, 20 Atl. 188.

Special officer acting in public and private capacity.

Cited in Wells v. Washington Market Co. 8 Mackey, 394, holding unsalaried officer of police force, employed by market company to collect rents, etc., when making arrests acts in capacity of police officer; Tyson v. Joseph H. Bauland Co. 68 App. Div. 314, 74 N. Y. Supp. 59, holding jury might properly find arrest by special officer in department store was pursuant to his private employment therein; Brill v. Eddy, 115 Mo. 605, 22 S. W. 488, holding presumption that special officer in employ of private corporation acted in his public capacity may be rebutted by proof to contrary; Sharp v. Erie R. Co. 90 App. Div. 507, 85 N. Y. Supp. 553, denying railroad's liability for shooting, in attempt to arrest person stealing ride, by policeman employed as railroad detective.

Cited in note (37 L. R. A. 40) on test of existence of relation of master and servant.

Ratification of illegal act.

Cited in Central R. Co. v. Brewer, 78 Md. 403, 27 L. R. A. 65, 28 Atl. 615, holding ratification of superintendent's arrest of passenger for putting counterfeit coin in box for fare, not shown by fact that officers and servants of company testified against person arrested.

Unauthorized act of servant in making or causing arrest.

Cited in Barabasz v. Kabat, 86 Md. 36, 37 Atl. 720, holding master not liable for servant's unauthorized act in causing an unlawful arrest; Baltimore & Y. Turnp. Road v. Green, 86 Md. 167, 37 Atl. 642, holding turnpike company, without ratification, not liable for unauthorized arrest and prosecution of person for nonpayment of tolls; Markley v. Snow, 207 Pa. 453, 64 L. R. A. 687, 56 Atl. 999, denying partnership's liability for arrest at instance of superintendent, on charge of burning its building; Carter v. Worchester County, 94 Md. 626, 51 Atl. 830, holding county commissioners not liable for unauthorized and unratified act of road supervisor in causing an illegal arrest.

Distinguished in St. Louis, I. M. & S. R. Co. v. Hackett, 58 Ark. 388, 41 Am. St. Rep. 105, 24 S. W. 881, holding railroad company liable for act of night watchman, also a deputy sheriff, for wrongfully shooting another in course of employment.

8 L. R. A. 849, PENDERGAST v. YANDES, 124 Ind. 159, 24 N. E. 724.

Liberal construction of lien statutes.

Cited in Aurora Nat. Bank v. Black, 129 Ind. 598, 29 N. E. 396, holding contract for delivery of iron, "property" within employees' lien law; Jenckes v.

Jenckes, 145 Ind. 633, 44 N. E. 632, holding mechanics' liens take priority over mortgage not recorded until rights to liens had been created; Heckman v. Tammen, 84 Ill. App. 550, and Bell v. Hiner, 16 Ind. App. 186, 44 N. E. 576, holding laborer's lien for wages superior to prior chattel mortgage; Heckman v. Tammen, 84 Ill. App. 545, construing terms "labor," etc., as used in labor claim statute, to include all service involving physical labor.

Cited in note (18 L. R. A. 307) on who are laborers, employees, or servants within the meaning of statutes giving them preferences.

Distinguished in Raynes v. Kokomo Ladder & Furniture Co. 153 Ind. 318, 54 N. E. 1061, holding general manager of concern not entitled to protection of laborers' lien statute.

8 L. R. A. 851, CEDAR SPRINGS v. SCHLICH, 81 Mich. 405, 45 N. W. 994.

Bona fide holder of bonds.

Cited in Schmid v. Frankfort, 131 Mich. 200, 91 N. W. 131, and Thompson v. Mecosta, 127 Mich. 528, 86 N. W. 1044, holding bond reciting its issue for public improvement good in hands of bona fide purchaser, although issued for private improvement; Grant Twp. v. Reno Twp. 107 Mich. 414, 65 N. W. 376, to point that invalid bonds showing prima facie authority are good in hands of bona fide purchaser without notice; Risley v. Howell, 12 C. C. A. 221, 22 U. S. App. 635, 64 Fed. 455, holding that bona fide purchaser may recover on bonds, although ordinance, misappropriating them to unlawful use, is mentioned in them by date.

Aid of private enterprise.

Approved in Cheboygan County v. Mentor Twp. 94 Mich. 388, 54 N. W. 169, denying mandamus to compel imposition of tax ostensibly to buy a county farm, but really to aid a private enterprise; Dodge v. Van Buren Circuit Judge, 118 Mich. 193, 76 N. W. 315, holding act invalid which attempts to authorize issue of bonds in aid of railroad enterprise in violation of Constitution.

Injunctive relief as to ultra vires contract.

Cited in Detroit v. Detroit City R. Co. 60 Fed. 163, holding equity will not refuse injunctive relief to parties to *ultra vires* contract made in good faith and under mistake of law.

8 L. R. A. 854, SUMMERVILLE v. PRESSLEY, 33 S. C. 56, 26 Am. St. Rep. 659, 11 S. E. 545.

Right to judge of what necessary for health.

Cited in Darlington v. Ward, 48 S. C. 573, 38 L. R. A. 336, 26 S. E. 906, holding town council has exclusive right to judge what necessary and requisite for health in passing ordinance prohibiting keeping of hogs within town limits; Darlington v. Ward, 48 S. C. 578, 38 L. R. A. 337, 26 S. E. 906, holding ordinance regulating health, comfort, and convenience may disturb enjoyment of individual rights and yet be valid; State *ex rel.* George v. Aiken, 42 S. C. 236, 26 L. R. A. 353, 20 S. E. 221, holding dispensary act by which state assumes entire control of liquor traffic valid; Charleston v. Werner, 38 S. C. 495, 37 Am. St. Rep. 776, 17 S. E. 33, holding act amending charter of city to authorize the filling up of low lots and grounds valid; Feek v. Bloomingdale, 82 Mich. 416, 10 L. R. A. 77, 47 N. W. 37, holding local option act valid.

Cited in notes (11 L. R. A. 286) on constitutional protection of property rights; (14 L. R. A. 583) on constitutional e and protection; (36 L. R. A. 602) on power o prevent, and abate nuisances.

Jurisdiction of local offense.

Cited in Sullivan v. Haug, 82 Mich. 559, 10 L criminal subject to jurisdiction of court in wh mode of procedure.

8 L. R. A. 858, SNELL v. CHICAGO, 133 Ill.

Followed without discussion in Chicago & A. N. E. 1029.

In whom powers of taxation reside.

Cited in Givins v. Chicago, 188 Ill. 351, 58 improvement not constitute corporate authoriti taxation for local improvements.

Cited in notes (33 L. R. A. 181, 189) on leg or prices; (15 L. R. A. 651) on right to take t

Power of county or city over highways.

Cited in Trotier v. St. Louis, B. & S. R. Co. ing county board, and not highway commissione of electric railway on highway in which is turn

Distinguished in Ft. Wayne Land & Improv. (Co. 132 Ind. 82, 15 L. R. A. 651, 30 N. E. 88(municipality not take from private turnpike co

Legalization of corporate acts.

Cited in State *ex rel.* Crow v. Lincoln Trust holding mere recognition by legislature of pow corporation not create them; Lindsay v. United 175, 42 L. R. A. 789, 24 So. 171, holding act re ciations void to the extent of attempt to legaliz fraud; Shields v. Ross, 158 Ill. 221, 41 N. E. 98 ers cannot lay out any part of highway within

Cited in footnote to Republic L. Ins. Co. v. S holds corporation in suit to wind it up entitled t for unpaid stock subscriptions.

Cited in notes (33 L. R. A. 576) on period of e (9 L. R. A. 275) on dissolution of corporation.

Subject expressed in title.

Cited in Culver v. People, 161 Ill. 98, 43 N. E. special assessments, which only adopted article quent amendments to that act; Hogan v. Akin, 18 title of act "to regulate assignment of" chattel mortgages generally were not intended to be reg

Cited in footnote to State v. Snow, 11 L. R. of article intended for use as lard, containing othe within title.

Lightning Source UK Ltd.
Milton Keynes UK
UKHW010742011218
333024UK00013B/2099/P